SAN AUGUSTINE PUBLIC LIBRARY
The Confederate soldier in the C
REF 973.7 CON
111069
P9-CMK-364
10562
SAN AUGUSTINE PUBLIC LIBRARY
10562
TO RENEW THIS BOOK
CALL 275-5367

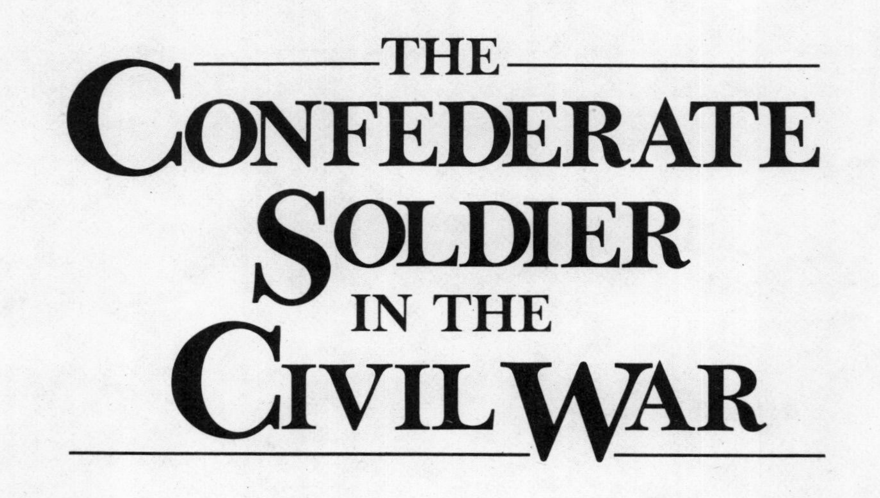
THE
CONFEDERATE
SOLDIER
IN THE
CIVIL WAR

THE CONFEDERATE SOLDIER IN THE CIVIL WAR

THE CAMPAIGNS, BATTLES, SIEGES, CHARGES AND SKIRMISHES

Described by ROBERT E. LEE, ALBERT S. JOHNSTON, JOSEPH E. JOHNSTON, PIERRE G. T. BEAUREGARD, BRAXTON BRAGG, E. KIRBY SMITH, JOHN B. HOOD, JAMES LONGSTREET, THOMAS J. JACKSON, A. P. HILL, LEONIDAS POLK, D. H. HILL, WILLIAM J. HARDEE, RICHARD S. EWELL, J. E. B. STUART *and other military leaders.*

THE FOUNDATION AND FORMATION OF THE CONFEDERACY

Described by JEFFERSON DAVIS, ALEXANDER H. STEPHENS, JUDAH P. BENJAMIN *and others.*

THE CONFEDERATE STATES NAVY

Described by FRANKLIN BUCHANAN, RAPHAEL SEMMES *and other naval leaders.*

Eulogy by FITZHUGH LEE

The Fairfax Press

LIBRARY OF CONGRESS CATALOG CARD NUMBER: 77-21259

THIS EDITION IS PUBLISHED BY THE FAIRFAX PRESS
A DIVISION OF IMPRINT SOCIETY, INC., DISTRIBUTED BY
CROWN PUBLISHERS, INC.

a b c d e f g h

FLAGS OF THE CONFEDERATE STATES OF AMERICA.

NO. 1. The "Stars and Bars" was the first flag of the Confederate States, and was adopted by the Confederate Congress, in session at Montgomery, Ala., and was elevated to the summit of the staff on the Capitol at Montgomery, Ala., on March 4, 1861, by Miss L. C. Tyler, of Virginia, granddaughter of John Tyler, ex-President of the United States.

NO. 2. The "Battle Flag" was designed by General Beauregard, adopted by General Joseph E. Johnston, after the first battle of Manassas (Bull Run), and afterward adopted by the Confederate Congress. The reason for its adoption was, that in the smoke and dust of battle the "Stars and Bars" was frequently mistaken for the "Stars and Stripes." The "Battle Flag" was conceived on the field of battle, lived on the field of battle, and was proudly borne on every field from Manassas to Appomattox.

NO. 3. Adopted May 1, 1863, as the "National Flag" of the Confederate States by the Confederate Congress.

NO. 4. Adopted March 4, 1865, as the "National Flag" of the Confederate States by the Confederate Congress, for the reason that when the flag adopted May 1, 1863, fell limp around the staff it resembled a flag of truce.

CONFEDERATE GENERALS.

KEY TO PORTRAITS.

1. John P. Preston, of S. C.
2. A. P. Hill.
3. E. F. Paxton.
4. H. H. Sibley.
5. R. Semmes, C. S. N.
6. J. Z. York.
7. J. J. Archer.
8. James A. Walker.
9. R. B. Garnett.
10. George E. Pickett.
11. J. L. Rosser.
12. P. M. B. Young.
13. A. J. Dobbins.
14. Joseph Lewis.
15. Joseph Davis.
16. Harry Heth.
17. Samuel Jones.
18. L. O'B. Branch.
19. Bradley T. Johnson.
20. Phil Cook.
21. M. L. Smith.
22. J. D. Johnston.
23. T. F. Drayton.
24. Henry A. Wise.
25. John S. Mosby.
26. W. R. Peck.
27. L. Baker.
28. M. C. Butler.
29. Fitzhugh Lee.
30. Robert H. Anderson.
31. J. L. Kemper.
32. P. T. Moore.
33. R. F. Hoke.
34. Dick Taylor.
35. T. N. Waul.
36. G. B. Cosby.
37. Wm. Smith, Virginia.
38. R. E. Colston.
39. M. Jenkins.
40. M. W. Gary.
41. Harry T. Hays.
42. L. McLaws.
43. R. D. Lilly.
44. M. D. Corse.
45. G. H. Stewart.
46. J. C. Breckinridge, Secretary of War.
47. J. B. Gordon, Georgia.
48. H. B. Lyon.
49. E. C. Thomas.
50. John H. Morgan.
51. Arnold Elzey.
52. J. M. Jones.
53. R. F. Pinkney, C. S. N.
54. B. F. Cheatham.
55. N. H. Harris.
56. Samuel Cooper, Adjutant and Inspector General.
57. W. H. F. Lee.
58. J. Williams.
59. A. R. Lawton, Q. M. G.
60. Mansfield Lovell.
61. James Longstreet.
62. John Echols.
63. G. T. Beauregard.
64. J. H. McNeill.
65. G. T. Anderson.
66. Gideon J. Pillow.
67. John B. Hood.
68. J. D. Imboden.
69. Alexander H. Stephens, Vice-President.
70. Ed Johnson.
71. J. S. Hollins, C. S. N.
72. M. L. Bonham.
73. J. B. Kershaw.
74. L. L. Lomax.
75. John Bratton.
76. R. H. Chilton.
77. James H. Lane.
78. C. M. Wilcox.
79. Albert Sidney Johnston.
80. R. E. Rodes.
81. Ben McCulloch.
82. Sterling Price.
83. Wade Hampton.
84. S. M. Barton.
85. J. E. B. Stuart.
86. E. Kirby Smith.
87. J. C. Pemberton.
88. R. S. Ewell.
89. William B. Taliaferro.
90. W. D. Pender.
91. Bushrod Johnson.
92. Jefferson Davis, Pres't.
93. Joseph E. Johnston.
94. Jubal A. Early.
95. T. J. (Stonewall) Jackson.
96. Braxton Bragg.
97. Robert E. Lee, General-in-Chief.

The Confederate Soldier in the Civil War

BY

MAJOR-GENERAL FITZHUGH LEE.

AN IMPARTIAL study of the early history of the American Republic from the period a band of patriots, following the wave of Washington's sword, transferred power from king to people, will demonstrate that when Colonies were transformed into States, the latter delegated, in a written Constitution, the powers to be conferred on the United States, but all powers not so delegated were reserved to the States themselves, because they had never parted from them. Hence, sovereign power belonged to a State, while only derivative, and not primitive, power was possessed by the general Government.

The States did not confer upon the Government they were then forming a right to coerce one of their number for any purpose, for it is not natural that the creator should create either executive, judicial or legislative authority anywhere which should be potent to destroy its life or diminish or alter the power it had reserved for its own purposes. A State speaks through its representative bodies, and the majority of delegates in a convention directs its course.

The people of the original thirteen States believed in State sovereignty, and Pennsylvania and the New England States are upon record as primarily holding such opinions. The Southern people were educated in the belief that the allegiance of the citizen was first due to his State, and that in any conflict between his Commonwealth and the United States, or other country, his place was at her side—at her feet he should kneel and at her foe his gun should be pointed.

This is the only explanation of the great and enthusiastic response by the masses of the people to the action of their State Conventions, when they decided their States should no longer be members of the Federal Union, but, resuming their original independence, be free afterward to make such other alliances as they might deem best to protect their rights and promote their growth and glory.

The Southern masses were the private soldiers of the armies; they may not have understood all the public questions involved, or the gravity of secession, or the importance of pending issues, as thoroughly as the statesman of the period, but they must have been thoroughly impressed in a conscious manner with the right of secession and with a fidelity and loyalty to the commands of their respective States.

It has been said that man is under no circumstances so independent as he is when the next step is for life or death. The men who were to be enrolled as the soldiers of a new Confederacy of States, to battle for its existence, knew they were taking a step which might bring to them a hostile bullet and a soldier's grave.

The existence of the slightest doubt as to the justice of the course of their States, or the presence of the smallest suspicion that their bayonets would glisten with treason, would have surely brought that independence of action spoken of, against which the pleading eloquence of their leaders would recoil as the waters are dashed back from a great rock.

No earthly mandate can compel men to leave their firesides, families and friends, and embrace death with rapture, unless their God-given consciences stamp with approval the motives which control their conduct.

Major-General Fitzhugh Lee.

With a free, fair and honest ballot, undisturbed by extraneous influences, and untouched by the modern methods of bribery and corruption, the masses of the people, from which came unbroken ranks of gallant men, voted with practical unanimity to ratify the decision of their State Conventions. The movement to change the map of North America and make two republics grow where only one grew before, was enthusiastically received by the great body of the Southern people. Men rushed to arms, companies were rapidly enrolled in every locality—grew into regiments, and regiments into brigades. Orders were joyfully received which carried local troops to the places where armies were forming, and the preparations for the impending battle were eagerly hailed by men whose previous footsteps had only fallen upon the paths of peace.

The private soldier of the Confederacy had no hope of conspicuous honors, no opportunity to lay up riches, while meager rations and scant clothing banished any prospect he may have cherished for a reasonable amount of the pleasures of army life. The separation from his home, in many instances, marked the period when domestic sorrow replaced domestic happiness, and absolute want followed a fair competence.

The producer was taken away, the consumers remained; while added to the infelicity of the wife, the grief of the mother, and the sister's sadness, was the ever tormenting thought that he, whose heart held the concentrated love of the household, might never again enter his doors alive, or even his dead body find a resting place in the little family burying ground, where loving hands could guard it from desecration.

It was a terrible ordeal for those left behind, and it was a torturing thought for the soldier, that he might fall, bequeathing to those he cared most for a life of destitution and sorrow. To the usual hardships and dangers which accompany a soldier's career everywhere, must be added these peculiar conditions which surrounded the service of the Southerners in the late war, because so many of the rank and file had homes, and some property, and being for the most part from the rural districts, their absence in the army immeasurably increased the discomforts of their families, and was a source of never ceasing care and concern to them. It is true, however, that men of means, influence and position were also to be found in the ranks.

At the outbreak of the war all wanted to fight, but all could not hold commissions. Out of 604 students at the University of Virginia when the war broke out, largely over one-half joined the Confederate army at the first trumpet sound of war, and more than 2,000 graduates of that University were in the Confederate service from 1861 to 1865, and more than 400 fell and were buried in soldiers' graves; while from Harvard, the great Northern University, but 1,040 men served in the armies and navies of the United States during the four years of war, and only 155 of these lost their lives.

Beauregard, after the first battle of Manassas, in visiting one of his generals, whose tent was pitched not far from his headquarters, ordered one of his couriers, a private soldier, to accompany him. Upon dismounting he threw the bridle-rein to the soldier to hold his horse while he paid his visit, but seeing he was a neat, trim-looking cavalryman, remarked,

"I suppose holding horses is a new business to you!" "Yes," said the soldier, who was a wealthy planter, "when I am in Mississippi I have a hundred negroes to hold my horse." General Lee's son was a private soldier in the artilery, and there were numerous similar instances, but the bulk of the fighting material of the South were men who could not well afford to leave their little farms or moderate business for any purpose, as the daily bread of so many others depended on their daily labor.

Many were intelligent and thinking men, and in instruction and training were far above the average soldiers of the world. It has been well said that, "had the need arisen, as in the case of the Theban army in Thessaly, more than one Epaminondas might have been found serving as a private in the Confederate ranks." An army composed, large part, of brave, thoughtful, sensible soldiers, must write a grand record on the pages of history.

With the component parts of a great engine working true, its work is most satisfactorily performed; so the more faithful, sensible and courageous the soldiers who make up the army, the more they can be wielded to the greatest advantage by a master of war.

The difficulties and embarrassments which confronted the Confederate soldier were overcome; and when the numbers of those who opposed him, their munitions of war, the efficiency of their well-stored quartermaster, commissary and ordnance departments are contrasted with the great deficiency in the South of everything that mobilizes armies and contributes to their strength, the world wonders at what was accomplished.

When "I see the battle-scarred soldiers and sailors of the Confederacy, with uncovered head and profoundest reverence I bow before those dauntless heroes, feeling that if the greatest suffering with the least hope of reward is worthy of the highest honor, these deserve to stand shoulder to shoulder with their greatest army commanders in the brotherhood of glory."

When McDowell, at first Manassas, succeeded in turning Beauregard's left flank, and was driving the fragmentary forces which first encountered his huge turning column, it was the heroic stand taken by the soldiers, almost without command, on a line of battle perpendicular to the original line along Bull Run, which checked his impetuous onset, christened Thomas Jonathan Jackson "Stonewall," and gave to Johnston and Beauregard the victory; and from that period to 1865 it was the resistless charge of gallant troops in offensive battle, or their determined and courageous stand in defensive conflict, which so greatly contributed to promote the glory of their own deeds and the fame of their great generals.

It was a wonderful exhibition of courage, constancy and suffering, which no disaster could diminish, no defeat darken. The soldiers went to battle from a sense of duty, and were not lured into the ranks by bounties or kept there by the hope of pension. The records show 600,000 Southern men were enlisted during the whole war, while 2,700,000 represent the total enlistments of their opponents during the same period.

"It would be difficult to convince the world," General Lee would often say, "of the numerical superiority of our opponents." And yet, for four years success trembled in the balance, and though fate denied the Confederate soldiers the final victory, it "clothed them with glorious immortality."

It was a grand struggle on the part of the South, and illustrated in the highest degree the splendid fighting qualities of sons whose movements upon the field of battle were directed by the tactical genius of their great leaders.

There was no "passion-swept mob rising in mad rebellion against constituted authority," but armies whose ranks were filled by men whose convictions were honest, and whose loyalty to the Southern cause was without fear and without reproach—men who remained faithful to military duty in the conflict between fidelity to the Confederate banners or adherence to the trust assumed in the marriage vow, who resisted the pressure of letters from home, and whose heart-strings were breaking from the sad tale of starvation and despair in the family homestead. As the hostile invasion swept over more territory the more frequent the appeals came, marked by the pathos and power which agony inspires, until at last the long silence told the soldier his home was within his enemies' lines, and the fate of his family was concealed from his view.

Under such conditions the private soldier of the South promptly fell into line. If saved from the dangers of the contest, his reward was the commendation of his immediate commanding officers and the conscientiousness of duty faithfully performed. If drowned amid the hail of shot and shell, his hastily buried body filled a nameless grave, without military honors and without religious ceremonies. No pages of history recounted in lofty language his courage on the field or his devotion to his country, or described how, like a soldier, he fell in the fore-front of battle. His battle picture, ever near the flashing of the guns, should be framed in the memory of all who admire true heroism, whether found at the cannon's mouth, or in the blade of the cavalry, or along the blazing barrels of the infantry. There he stood, with the old, torn slouch hat, the bright eye, the cheek colored by exposure and painted by excitement, the face stained with powder, with jacket rent, trousers torn and the blanket in shreds, printing in the dust of battle the tracks of his shoeless feet. No monument can be built high enough to commemorate the memory of a typical representative private soldier of the South.

Very truly yours
Fitzhugh Lee

JEFFERSON DAVIS,

PRESIDENT OF THE CONFEDERATE STATES.

BORN IN TODD, CHRISTIAN COUNTY, KENTUCKY, JUNE 3, 1808. DIED, DECEMBER 6, 1889.

[From a photograph taken in 1861.]

THE FOUNDATION AND FORMATION OF THE CONFEDERACY

AND

ORDINANCES OF SECESSION OF THE SOUTHERN STATES.

ON the 5th day of November, 1860, the Legislature of South Carolina convened in extra session at Columbia in compliance with the proclamation of Governor Gist. This extra session was called ostensibly for the purpose of appointing electors of President and Vice-President, in conformity with the Act of Congress, which fixed the time when these electors were to be appointed on a day when the Legislature of the State was not in session. In his message to this Legislature, Governor Gist uses the following language:

> Under ordinary circumstances, your duty could be soon discharged by the election of electors representing the choice of the people of the State; but in view of the threatening aspect of affairs, and the strong probability of the election to the presidency of a sectional candidate by a party committed to the support of measures which, if carried out, will inevitably destroy our equality in the Union, and ultimately reduce the Southern States to mere provinces of consolidated despotism, to be governed by a fixed majority in Congress hostile to our institutions, and fatally bent upon our ruin, I would respectfully suggest that the Legislature remain in session and take such action as will prepare the State for any emergency that may arise. That an expression of the will of the people may be obtained on a question involving such momentous consequences, I would earnestly recommend that in the event of the election of Abraham Lincoln to the presidency, a convention of the people of this State be immediately called to consider and determine the "mode and measure of redress."

The success of Mr. Lincoln in being elected to the presidency having been announced, resolutions were introduced in the House, and also in the Senate, declaring it to be the duty of South Carolina to at once withdraw from the Federal Union, and that for this purpose a convention of the people should be called to assemble at an early day.

In compliance with the provisions of these resolutions, delegates from the several districts and parishes of the State were elected, who assembled in convention at Columbia, on the 17th day of December, 1860.

Upon the organization of the convention Hon. David F. Jamison was chosen president. Without delay such committees were appointed by him as were necessary to formulate the work of the convention. Most important among these was the committee to which was intrusted the duty of drafting an ordinance of secession of South Carolina from the Federal Union. The committee was composed of the following: John A. Inglis, R. B. Rhett, James Chestnut, Jr., James L. Orr, Maxcy Gregg, B. F. Dunkin and W. H. Hutson. They drafted an ordinance and submitted it to the convention, which adopted it unanimously, as below, under the head of ordinances of secession (South Carolina).

SOUTH CAROLINA.

DECEMBER 20, 1860.

Vote of Convention—Unanimous.

*GOVERNOR FRANCIS W. PICKENS.

At a convention of the people of the State of South Carolina, begun and holden at Columbia on the 17th day of December, in the year of our Lord one thousand eight hundred and sixty, and thence continued by adjournment to Charleston, and there, by divers adjournments, to the 20th of December in the same year:

An Ordinance to dissolve the Union between the State of South Carolina and other States united with her under the Compact entitled the Constitution of the United States of America.

We, the people of the State of South Carolina, in convention assembled, do declare and ordain, and it is hereby declared and ordained, that the ordinance adopted by us in convention on the 23d day of May, in the year of our Lord one thousand seven hundred and eighty-eight, whereby the Constitution of the United States of America was ratified, and also all acts and parts of acts of the General Assembly of this State ratifying amendments of said Constitution, are hereby repealed; and that the Union now subsisting between South Carolina and other States, under the name of The United States of America, is hereby dissolved.

Done at Charleston, the 20th day of December, in the year of our Lord one thousand eight hundred and sixty.

D. F. JAMISON,
Delegate from Barnwell and President of the Convention, and others.

Attest: BENJAMIN F. ARTHUR, *Clerk of the Convention.*

The secession of South Carolina was followed in rapid succession by other States in the following order:

MISSISSIPPI.

JANUARY 9, 1861.

Vote of Convention—84–15.

*GOVERNOR JOHN J. PETTUS.

The people of Mississippi, in convention assembled, do ordain and declare, and it is hereby ordained and declared, as follows, to-wit:

That all the laws and ordinances by which the said State of Mississippi became a member of the Federal Union of the United States of America be, and the same are hereby, repealed; and that all obligations on the part of said State, or the people thereof, to observe the same, be withdrawn; and that the said State shall hereby resume the rights, functions and powers which by any of said laws and ordinances were conveyed to the Government of the said United States, and is dissolved from all the obligations, restraints and duties incurred to the said Federal Union, and shall henceforth be a free, sovereign and independent State.

FLORIDA.

JANUARY 11, 1861.

Vote of Convention—62–7.

*GOVERNOR M. S. PERRY.

An Ordinance to dissolve the Union now existing between the State of Florida and other States united with her under the Compact of Government, entitled the Constitution of the United States.

WHEREAS, All hope of preserving the Union upon terms consistent with the safety and honor of the Slaveholding States has been finally dissipated by the recent indications of the strength of the anti-slavery sentiment of the Free States; therefore,

Be it resolved by the people of Florida, in convention assembled, That it is undoubtedly the right of the several States of the Union, at such time, and for such cause as in the opinion of the people of such State, acting in their sovereign capacity, may be just and proper; and, in the opinion of this convention, the existing causes are such as to compel Florida to proceed to exercise that right.

We, the people of the State of Florida, in convention assembled, do solemnly ordain, publish and declare that the State of Florida hereby withdraws herself from the Confederacy of States existing under the name of the United States of America, and from the existing Government of the said States; and that all political connection between her and the Government of said States ought to be, and the same is hereby, totally annulled, and said Union of States dissolved; and the State of Florida is hereby declared a sovereign and independent nation; and that all ordinances heretofore adopted, in so far as they create or recognize said Union, are rescinded; and all laws, or parts of laws, in force in this State, in so far as they recognize or assent to said Union, be, and they are hereby, repealed.

ALABAMA.

JANUARY 11, 1861.

Vote of Convention—61–39.

*GOVERNOR ANDREW D. MOORE.

An Ordinance to dissolve the Union between the State of Alabama and other States united under the Compact and style of the United States of America.

WHEREAS, The election of Abraham Lincoln and Hannibal Hamlin to the offices of President and Vice-President of the United States of America, by a sectional party, avowedly hostile to the domestic institutions and the peace and security of the people of the State of Alabama, following upon the heels of many and dangerous infractions of the Constitution of the United States by many of the States and people of the Northern section, is a political wrong of so insulting and menacing a character as to justify the people of the State of Alabama in the adoption of prompt and decided measures for their future peace and security.

Therefore, be it declared and ordained by the people of the State of Alabama, in convention assembled, that the State of Alabama now withdraws from the Union known as the United States of America, and henceforth ceases to be one of the said United States, and is, and of right ought to be, a sovereign independent State.

SECTION 2. And be it further declared and ordained by the people of the State of Alabama, in convention assembled, that all powers over the territories of said State and over the people thereof, heretofore delegated to the Government of the United States of America, be, and they are hereby, withdrawn from the said Government, and are hereby resumed and vested in the people of the State of Alabama.

And as it is the desire and purpose of the people of Alabama to meet the Slaveholding States of the South who approve of such a purpose, in order to frame a provisional or a permanent government, upon the principles of the Government of the United States, be it also

Resolved by the people of Alabama, in convention assembled, that the people of the States of Delaware, Maryland, Virginia, North Carolina, South Carolina, Florida, Georgia, Mississippi, Louisiana, Texas, Arkansas, Tennessee, Kentucky and Missouri be, and they are hereby, invited to meet the people of the State of Alabama, by their delegates, in convention, on the 4th day of February next, in Montgomery, in the State of Alabama, for the purpose of consultation with each other as to the most effectual mode of securing concerted, harmonious action in whatever measures may be deemed most desirable for the common peace and security. And be it

Further Resolved, That the president of this convention be, and he is hereby, instructed to transmit forthwith a copy of the foregoing preamble, ordinance and resolutions to the Governors of the several States named in the said resolutions.

Done by the people of Alabama, in convention assembled, at Montgomery, this 11th day of January, 1861.

GEORGIA.

JANUARY 19, 1861.

Vote of Convention—208–29.

*GOVERNOR JOSEPH E. BROWN.

An Ordinance to dissolve the Union between the State of Georgia and other States united with her under the Compact of Government entitled the Constitution of the United States.

We, the people of the State of Georgia, in convention assembled, do declare and ordain, and it is hereby declared and ordained, that the ordinances adopted by the people of the State of Georgia in convention in 1788, whereby the Constitution of the United States was assented to, ratified and adopted, and also all acts and parts of acts of the General Assembly ratifying and adopting amendments to the said Constitution, are hereby repealed, rescinded and abrogated.

And we do further declare and ordain that the Union now subsisting between the State of Georgia and other States, under the name of the United States, is hereby dissolved, and that the State of Georgia is in full possession and exercise of all those rights of sovereignty which belong and appertain to a free and independent State.

* In office at the time ordinance of secession was passed.

LOUISIANA.

JANUARY 26, 1861.

Vote of Convention—113-17.

*GOVERNOR THOMAS OVERTON MOORE.

An ordinance to dissolve the Union between the State of Louisiana and the other States united with her under the Compact entitled the Constitution of the United States of America.

We, the people of the State of Louisiana, in convention assembled, do declare and ordain, and it is hereby declared and ordained, that the ordinance passed by the State of Louisiana, on the 22d day of November, 1807, whereby the Constitution of the United States of America and the amendments of said Constitution were adopted, and all the laws and ordinances by which Louisana became a member of the Federal Union, be, and the same are hereby, repealed and abrogated, and the Union now subsisting between Louisiana and the other States, under the name of the United States of America, is hereby dissolved.

We further declare and ordain that the State of Louisiana hereby resumes the rights and powers heretofore delegated to the Government of the United States of America, and its citizens are absolved from allegiance to the said Government, and she is in full possession of all the rights and sovereignty that appertain to a free and independent State.

We further declare and ordain that all rights acquired and vested under the Constitution of the United States, or any act of Congress or treaty, or under laws of this State, not incompatible with this ordinance, shall remain in force and have the same effect as though this ordinance had not passed.

We, the people of Louisiana, recognize the right of free navigation of the Mississippi River and tributaries by all friendly States bordering thereon: we also recognize the right of the ingress and egress of the mouths of the Mississippi by all friendly States and powers, and hereby declare our willingness to enter into stipulations to guarantee the exercise of those rights.

TEXAS.

FEBRUARY 1, 1861.

Vote of Convention—166-7.

*GOVERNOR EDWARD CLARK.

An Ordinance to dissolve the Union between the State of Texas and the other States under the Compact styled the Constitution of the United States of America.

WHEREAS, The Federal Government has failed to accomplish the purposes of the compact of union between these States, in giving protection either to the persons of our people upon an exposed frontier, or to the property of our citizens, and

WHEREAS, The action of the Northern States is violative of the compact between the States and the guarantees of the Constitution; and,

WHEREAS, The recent developments in Federal affairs make it evident that the power of the Federal Government is sought to be made a weapon with which to strike down the interests and property of the people of Texas, and her sister Slaveholding States, instead of permitting it to be, as was intended, our shield against outrage and aggression,

Therefore, We, the people of the State of Texas, by delegates in convention assembled, do declare and ordain that the ordinance adopted by our convention of delegates on the fourth (4th) day of July, A. D. 1845, and afterward ratified by us, under which the Republic of Texas was admitted into the Union with other States, and became a party to the compact styled "The Constitution of the United States of America," be, and is hereby, repealed and annulled.

That all the powers which, by the said compact, were delegated by Texas to the Federal Government are resumed. That Texas is of right absolved from all restraints and obligations incurred by said compact, and is a separate sovereign State, and that her citizens and people are absolved from all allegiance to the United States or the government thereof.

SECTION 2. The ordinance shall be submitted to the people of Texas for their ratification or rejection, by the qualified voters, on the 23d day of February, 1861, and unless rejected by a majority of the votes cast, shall take effect and be in force on and after the 2d day of March, A. D. 1861; *Provided*, That in the Representative District of El Paso said election may be held on the 18th day of February, 1861.

Done by the people of the State of Texas, in convention assembled, at Austin, the 1st day of February, A. D. 1861.

VIRGINIA.

APRIL 17, 1861.

*GOVERNOR JOHN LETCHER.

An Ordinance to repeal the Ratification of the Constitution of the United States of America by the State of Virginia, and to resume all the rights and powers granted under said Constitution.

The people of Virginia, in their Ratification of the Constitution of the United States of America, adopted by them in convention on the 25th day of June, in the year of our Lord one thousand seven hundred and eighty-eight, having declared that the powers granted under said Constitution were derived from the people of the United States, and might be resumed whensoever the same should be perverted to their injury and oppression, and the Federal Government having perverted said powers, not only to the injury of the people of Virginia, but to the oppression of the Southern Slaveholding States:

Now, therefore, we, the people of Virginia, do declare and ordain that the ordinance adopted by the people of this State in convention, on the 25th day of June, one thousand seven hundred and eighty-eight, whereby the Constitution of the United States of America was ratified, and all acts of the General Assembly of this State ratifying or adopting amendments to said Constitution, are hereby repealed and abrogated; that the union between the State of Virginia and the other States under the Constitution aforesaid is hereby dissolved, and that the State of Virginia is in the full possession and exercise of all the rights of sovereignty which belong and appertain to a free and independent State. And they do further declare that the said Constitution of the United States of America is no longer binding on any of the citizens of this State.

This ordinance shall take effect and be an act of this day when ratified by a majority of the votes of the people of this State, cast at a poll to be taken thereon on the fourth Thursday in May next, in pursuance of a schedule to be hereafter enacted.

Done in convention, in the city of Richmond, on the 17th day of April, in the year of our Lord one thousand eight hundred and sixty-one, and in the eighty-fifth year of the Commonwealth of Virginia.

JOHN L. EUBANK,
Secretary of Convention.

An Ordinance for the Adoption of the Constitution of the Provisional Government of the Confederate States of America.

We, the delegates of the people of Virginia, in convention assembled, solemnly impressed by the perils which surround the Commonwealth, and appealing to the Searcher of Hearts for the rectitude of our intentions in assuming the great responsibility of this act, do, by this ordinance, adopt and ratify the Constitution of the Provisional Government of the Confederate States of America ordained and established at Montgomery, Alabama, on the 8th day of February, eighteen hundred and sixty-one; provided, that this ordinance shall cease to have any legal operation or effect, if the people of this Commonwealth, upon the vote directed to be taken on the ordinance of secession passed by this convention on the 17th day of April, eighteen hundred and sixty-one, shall reject the same.

A True Copy. JOHN L. EUBANK,
Secretary.

ARKANSAS.

MAY 6, 1861.

Vote of Convention—69-1.

*GOVERNOR HENRY M. RECTOR.

An Ordinance to dissolve the Union now existing between the State of Arkansas and the other States united with her under the Compact entitled the Constitution of the United States of America.

WHEREAS, In addition to the well-founded cause of complaint set forth by this convention in resolutions adopted on the 11th of March, A. D. 1861, against the sectional party now in power at Washington City, headed by Abraham Lincoln, he has, in the face of the resolutions passed by this convention, pledging the State of Arkansas to resist to the last extremity any attempt on the part of such power to coerce any State that seceded from the old Union, proclaimed to the world that war should be waged against such States until they should be compelled to submit to their rule, and large forces to accomplish this have by the same power been called out, and are now being marshaled to carry out this inhuman design, and longer to submit to such rule or remain in the old Union of the United States would be disgraceful and ruinous to the State of Arkansas:

Therefore, We, the people of the State of Arkansas, in convention assembled, do hereby declare and ordain, and it is hereby declared and ordained, that the "ordinance and acceptance of compact," passed and approved by the General Assembly of the State of Arkansas on the 18th of October, A. D. 1836, whereby it was by said General Assembly ordained that, by virtue of the authority vested in said General Assembly, by the provisions of the ordinance adopted by the convention of delegates assembled at Little Rock, for the purpose of forming a constitution and system of government for said State, the propositions set forth in "an act supplementary to an act entitled an act for the admission of the State of Arkansas into the Union, and to provide for the due execution of the laws of the United States within the same, and for other purposes, were freely accepted, ratified and irrevocably confirmed articles of compact and union between the State of Arkansas and the United States," and all other laws, and every other law and ordinance, whereby the State of Arkansas became a member of the Federal Union, be, and the same are hereby, in all respects, and for every purpose herewith consistent, repealed, abrogated and fully set aside; and the Union now subsisting between the State of Arkansas and the other States under the name of the United States of America is hereby forever dissolved.

And we do further declare and ordain that the State of Arkansas hereby resumes to herself all rights and powers heretofore delegated to the Government of the United States of America; that her citizens are absolved from all allegiance to said Government of the United States, and that she is in full possession and exercise of all the rights and sovereignty which appertain to a free and independent State.

We do further ordain and declare that all rights acquired and vested under the Constitution of the United States of America, or of any act or acts of Congress, or treaty, or under any law of this State, and not incompatible with this ordinance, shall remain in full force and effect, in nowise altered or impaired, and have the same effect as if this ordinance had not been passed.

Adopted and passed in open convention on the 6th day of May, Anno Domini 1861.

ELIAS C. BOUDINOT,
Secretary of the Arkansas State Convention.

NORTH CAROLINA.

MAY 20, 1861.

*GOVERNOR JOHN W. ELLIS.

We, the people of the State of North Carolina, in convention assembled, do declare and ordain, and it is hereby declared and ordained, that the ordinance adopted by the State of North Carolina, in the convention of 1789, whereby the Constitution of the United States was ratified and adopted, and also all acts and parts of acts of the General Assembly ratifying and adopting amendments to the said Constitution, are hereby repealed, rescinded and abrogated.

We do further declare and ordain that the Union now subsisting between the State of North Carolina and the other States, under the title of the United States of America, is hereby dissolved, and that the State of North Carolina is in the full possession and exercise of all those rights of sovereignty which belong and appertain to a free and independent State.

Done at Raleigh, the 20th day of May, in the year of our Lord 1861.

We, the people of North Carolina, in convention assembled, do declare and ordain, and it is hereby declared and ordained, that the State of North Carolina does hereby assent to and ratify the "Constitution for the Provisional Government of the Confederate States of America," adopted at Montgomery, in the State of Alabama, on the 8th of February, 1861, by the Convention of Delegates from the States of South Carolina, Georgia, Florida, Alabama, Mississippi and Louisiana, and that North Carolina will enter into the Federal Association of States upon the terms therein proposed, when admitted by the Congress or any competent authority of the Confederate States.

Done at Raleigh, the 20th day of May, in the year of our Lord 1861.

TENNESSEE.

ORDINANCE OF SEPARATION AND REPRESENTATION AND MILITARY LEAGUE WITH THE CONFEDERATE STATES.

JUNE 24, 1861.

*GOVERNOR ISHAM G. HARRIS.

JOINT RESOLUTION.

To appoint Commissioners from the State of Tennessee to confer with the authorities of the Confederate States in regard to entering into a Military League.

Resolved, By the General Assembly of the State of Tennessee, that the Governor be, and he is hereby, authorized and requested to appoint three Commissioners on the part of Tennessee to enter into a Military League with the authorities of the Confederate States, and with the authorities of such other Slaveholding States as may wish to enter into it, having in view the protection and defense of the entire South against the war that is now being carried on against it.

Adopted May 1, 1861. W. C. WHITTHORNE
Speaker of the House of Representatives.
B. L. STOVALL,
Speaker of the Senate.

*In office at the time ordinance of secession was passed.

STATE OF TENNESSEE.

I, J. E. R. Ray, Secretary of State, hereby certify that the foregoing is a true copy of the original resolution now on file in my office.

In testimony whereof, I have hereunto set my hand, and, with the warrant of the Governor, affixed the great seal of the State, at the Department in Nashville, on this 8th day of May, A. D. 1861. J. E. R. RAY, *Secretary*.

To the Congress of the Confederate States of America:

I lay before Congress for their consideration and action in relation thereto, copies of a convention between the Confederate States and the State of Tennessee, which was concluded and signed by the Commissioners of both parties, at the city of Nashville, on the 7th day of May, A. D. 1861, and of the ratification and confirmation of the same by the General Assembly of the State of Tennessee.

Montgomery, May 13, 1861. JEFFERSON DAVIS.

A resolution to ratify the agreement and convention entered into between the Commonwealth of Tennessee and the Confederate States of America.

Resolved by the Congress of the Confederate States of America, two-thirds of the Congress concurring therein, that the Congress advise and consent to the ratification of the convention and agreement entered into on the 7th day of May, eighteen hundred and sixty-one, at Nashville, Tennessee, between the Commonwealth of Tennessee, by her Commissioners, and the Confederate States of America, by their Commissioner, the Hon. Henry W. Hilliard.

CONGRESS, May 15, 1861.

I, Johnson J. Hooper, Secretary of Congress of the Confederate States of America, do hereby certify that the foregoing is a true and correct copy of a resolution which was unanimously adopted by the Congress, in executive session, this 15th day of May, eighteen hundred and sixty-one.

Given under my hand, the day above written, at the Capitol in the city of Montgomery. JOHNSON J. HOOPER,
Secretary of the Congress.

Convention between the State of Tennessee and the Confederate States of America.

The State of Tennessee, looking to a speedy admission into the Confederacy established by the Confederate States of America, in accordance with the Constitution for the Provisional Government of said States, enters into the following temporary convention, agreement and military league with the Confederate States, for the purpose of meeting pressing exigencies affecting the common rights, interests and safety of said States and said Confederacy:

1. Until the said State shall become a member of said Confederacy, according to the Constitutions of both powers, the whole military force and military operations, offensive and defensive, of said State, in the impending conflict with the United States, shall be under the chief control and direction of the President of the Confederate States, upon the same basis, principles and footing as if said State were now, and during the interval, a member of said Confederacy, said force, together with that of the Confederate States, to be employed for the common defense.

2. The State of Tennessee will, upon becoming a member of said Confederacy, under the permanent Constitution of said Confederate States, if the same shall occur, turn over to said Confederate States all the public property, naval stores and munitions of war, of which she may then be in possession acquired from the United States, on the same terms and in the same manner as the other States of said Confederacy have done in like cases.

3. Whatever expenditures of money, if any, the said State of Tennessee shall make before she becomes a member of said Confederacy, shall be met and provided for by the said Confederate States.

This convention entered into and agreed on in the city of Nashville, Tennessee, on the 7th day of May, A. D. 1861, by Henry W. Hilliard, the duly authorized Commissioner to act in the matter for the Confederate States, and Gustavus A. Henry, Archibald W. O. Totten and Washington Barrow, Commissioners duly authorized to act in like manner for the State of Tennessee, the whole subject to the approval and ratification of the proper authorities of both Governments respectively.

In testimony whereof the parties aforesaid have hereunto set their hands and seals, the day and year aforesaid, in duplicate originals.

HENRY W. HILLIARD,
Commissioner for the Confederate States of America.
GUSTAVUS A. HENRY,
A. W. O. TOTTEN,
WASHINGTON BARROW,
Commissioners on the part of Tennessee.

JOINT RESOLUTION.

Ratifying and confirming a military league with the Confederate States.

WHEREAS, A military league, offensive and defensive, was formed on this the 7th day of May, 1861, by and between A. W. O. Totten, Gustavus A. Henry and Washington Barrow, Commissioners on the part of the State of Tennessee, and H. W. Hilliard, Commissioner on the part of the Confederate States of America, subject to the confirmation of the two Governments. Be it therefore

Resolved, by the General Assembly of the State of Tennessee, that said league be in all respects ratified and confirmed, and the said General Assembly hereby pledges the faith and honor of the State of Tennessee, to a faithful observance of the terms and conditions of said League.

Adopted May 7, 1861. W. C. WHITTHORNE,
Speaker of the House of Representatives.
B. L. STOVALL,
Speaker of the Senate.

STATE OF TENNESSEE.

I, J. E. R. Ray, Secretary of State, hereby certify that the foregoing is a true copy of the original resolution on file in my office.

In testimony whereof, I have hereunto set my hand, and, with the warrant of the Governor, affixed the great seal of the State, at the Department in Nashville, on this 8th day of May, A. D. 1861.

J. E. R. RAY, *Secretary.*

RICHMOND, July 1, 1861.

HON. JEFFERSON DAVIS,
President of the Confederate States.

Sir: I have the honor herewith, by direction of Isham G. Harris, Governor of the State of Tennessee, to transmit to your excellency authentic copies of his late Proclamation, of the Ordinance of Separation, and of the official returns of the election by which, on the 8th of June last, the people of Tennessee, in their original and sovereign capacity, resumed the powers delegated to the Federal Government, dissolved forever all connection with the United States, and adopted for their government the Provisional Constitution of the Confederate States of America.

I am, respectfully, your obedient servant,
LANDON C. HAYNES.

PROCLAMATION

BY ISHAM G. HARRIS, GOVERNOR OF THE STATE OF TENNESSEE.

To all [to] whom these Presents shall come, greeting:

WHEREAS, by an Act of the General Assembly of the State of Tennessee, passed May 6, 1861, an election was held on the 8th day of June, 1861, in the several counties of the State, in accordance therewith, upon the Ordinance of "Separation" and "Representation," and also

WHEREAS, it appears from the official returns of said election (hereto appended) that the people of the State of Tennessee have in their sovereign will and capacity, by an overwhelming majority, cast their votes for separation, dissolving all political connection with the late United States Government and adopted the Provisional Government of the Confederate States of America; now,

Therefore, I, Isham G. Harris, Governor as aforesaid, do "make it known and declare all connection by the State of Tennessee with the Federal Union dissolved and that Tennessee is a free, independent government, free from all obligation to, or connection with, the Federal Government" of the United States of America.

In testimony whereof, I have hereunto set my hand and caused the great seal of the State to be affixed, at the Department in Nashville, on this the 24th day of June, A. D. 1861.

By the Governor. ISHAM G. HARRIS.
J. E. R. RAY, *Secretary of State.*

MISSOURI.

*GOVERNOR CLAIBORNE F. JACKSON.

Admitted August 20, 1861, as a member of the Confederate States of America, by an act of the Provisional Congress, third session.

PREAMBLE.

WHEREAS, The people of the State of Missouri have been prevented, by the unconstitutional interference of the Government of the United States, from expressing their will, through their legally constituted authorities, in regard to a union with the Confederate States of America, and are now engaged in repelling a lawless invasion of their territory by armed forces; and,

WHEREAS, It is the right and duty of the Confederate States to aid the people and government of the said State in resisting such invasion, and in securing the means and the opportunity of expressing their will upon all questions affecting their rights and liberties; now,

Therefore, The Congress of the Confederate States of America do enact that the President of the Confederate States of America be, and he is hereby, authorized to co-operate, through the military power of this Government, with the authorities and the people of the State of Missouri in defending that State against a lawless invasion by the United States, and in maintaining the liberty and independence of her people; and that he be authorized and empowered, at his discretion, to receive and muster into the service of the Confederate States, in the State of Missouri, such troops of that State as may volunteer to serve in the army of the Confederate States, subject to the rules and regulations of said army, and in accordance with the laws of Congress; and said troops may be received into service by companies, battalions or regiments, with their officers elected by the troops, and the officers so elected shall be commissioned by the President, and when mustered into service said companies, battalions, or regiments may be attached to such brigades or divisions as the President may determine; and the President shall have power to appoint field officers for all battalions and regiments organized out of separate companies mustered into service, and to add to battalions a sufficient number of separate companies to complete their organization into regiments, and to appoint the additional field officers necessary for the complete organization of the regiments so formed; and all vacancies that may occur among the commissioned officers, of troops mustered into service under this act, shall be filled in the manner provided in the act entitled "An act for the establishment and organization of the army of the Confederate States of America," approved the 6th day of March, eighteen hundred and sixty-one.

SECTION 2. That the State of Missouri shall be admitted a member of the Confederate States of America upon an equal footing with the other States, under the constitution for the Provisional Government of the same, upon the condition that the said constitution for the Provisional Government of the Confederate States shall be adopted and ratified by the properly and legally constituted authorities of said State, and the Governor of said State shall transmit to the President of the Confederate States an authentic copy of the proceedings touching said adoption and ratification by said State of said Provisional Constitution; upon the receipt whereof, the President, by proclamation, shall announce the fact; whereupon, and without any further proceedings upon the part of Congress, the admission of said State of Missouri into this Confederacy, under said constitution for the Provisional Government of the Confederate States, shall be considered as complete, and the laws of this Confederacy shall be thereby extended over said State of Missouri as fully and completely as over other States now composing the same.

SECTION 3. That the Congress of the Confederate States recognize the government of which Claiborne F. Jackson is the chief magistrate, to be the legally elected and regularly constituted government of the people and State of Missouri, and that the President of the Confederate States be, and he is hereby, empowered, at his discretion, at any time prior to the admission of the said State as a member of this Confederacy, to perfect and proclaim an alliance, offensive and defensive, with the said Government, limited to the period of the existing war between this Confederacy and the United States, the said treaty or alliance to be in force from the date thereof, and until the same shall be disaffirmed or rejected by this Congress.

Approved August 20, 1861.

KENTUCKY.

*GOVERNOR GEORGE W. JOHNSON.

Admitted December 10, 1861, into the Confederate States by an act passed by the Provisional Congress, fifth session, held at Richmond, Va., as follows:

The Congress of the Confederate States of America do enact, that the State of Kentucky be, and is hereby, admitted a member of the Confederate States of America, on an equal footing with the other States of this Confederacy.

Approved December 10, 1861.

* In office at the time ordinance of secession was passed.

SOVEREIGNTY FLAG OF SOUTH CAROLINA.

INAUGURATION OF HON. JEFFERSON DAVIS, AS PRESIDENT OF THE CONFEDERATE STATES, AT MONTGOMERY, ALA., FEBRUARY 18, 1861. TAKING THE OATH OF OFFICE.

[From a Sketch Made at the Time.]

THE ELECTION AND INAUGURATION OF HON. JEFFERSON DAVIS, OF MISSISSIPPI, AND HON. ALEXANDER H. STEPHENS, OF GEORGIA, PRESIDENT AND VICE-PRESIDENT OF THE CONFEDERACY.

SOUTH CAROLINA in her ordinance of secession invited all her Southern sister States who might secede, to join her in sending delegates to a Congress to be assembled in Montgomery on the 4th day of February, 1861. The States of Florida, Alabama, Georgia, Louisiana, Texas and South Carolina had passed ordinances of secession, and all had sent delegates equal in number to their senators and representatives in the Congress of the United States.

The Congress was temporarily organized by the selection of the Hon. Robert Barnwell, of South Carolina, as chairman, and Mr. Albert R. Lamar, of Georgia, as secretary. Subsequently a permanent organization was effected by the election of the Hon. Howell Cobb, of Georgia (who had filled the Speaker's chair in the Thirty-first (U. S.) Congress with such rare ability), as the presiding officer, and J. J. Hooper, of Alabama, Secretary.

THE ELECTION OF PRESIDENT AND VICE-PRESIDENT.

After the formation of a temporary Provisional Government, the election of the executive officers of that Government was in order, and on the 9th of February, 1862, the electoral vote for President and Vice-President of the Confederate States was formally counted in Joint Convention of the Provisional Senate and House of Representatives of said States, with the following result:

Total number of States voting	11
Total number of Electoral votes cast	109
Of which number Jefferson Davis, of Mississippi, received for the office of President of the Confederate States	109
Alexander H. Stephens, of Georgia, received for the office of Vice-President of the Confederate States	109

The number of Electoral votes cast by the several States:

Alabama	11
Arkansas	6
Florida	4
Georgia	12
Louisiana	8
Mississippi	9
North Carolina	12
South Carolina	8
Tennessee	15
Texas	6
Virginia	18
Total	109

The result was announced by Hon. R. M. T. Hunter, President of the Senate, who then said it was his duty to declare that Jefferson Davis had been duly elected President of the Confederate States, and that Alexander H. Stephens had been duly elected Vice-President of the Confederate States.

THE INAUGURATION.

Mr. Davis was at his home, Brierfield, Miss., when his election was announced to him, and he set out for Montgomery, Ala., to take the oath of office. At every principal station along the route he was met by thousands of his enthusiastic fellow-countrymen. During the trip he delivered about twenty-five short speeches, and his reception at Montgomery was a grand ovation. Eight miles from the capitol he was met by a large body of distinguished citizens, and amid the huzzas of thousands and the booming of cannon he entered the city.

RESIDENCE OF PRESIDENT JEFFERSON DAVIS AT MONTGOMERY, ALA., CALLED "THE WHITE HOUSE."

Notice that the inaugural ceremonies would take place on Monday, the 18th of February, had been sent by telegram, printed and posted everywhere throughout the country—North as well as South. As early as Friday before the time fixed, the streets evidenced the growth of the crowd that, from adjoining States, far and near, had come to witness the natal day of the new Government. Promptly at 10 o'clock Colonel H. P. Watson, of Montgomery, as chief marshal, appeared in front of the Exchange Hotel, accompanied by the following aids, appointed by the convention to represent the several States: Florida, Hamilton Wright; Georgia, Daniel S. Printup; South Carolina, Henry D. Capers; Louisiana, Robert C. Wood; Mississippi, Joseph P. Billups; Texas, Preston H. Roberts.

As the hour of noon approached an immense procession was formed, and to the music of fife, drum and artillery it moved toward the capitol building. On the platform, awaiting the arrival of Mr. Davis, were the members of Congress, the president of that body, the Governor of Alabama and committees, and a number of other distinguished persons. Round after round of cheers greeted Mr. Davis' arrival. After being seated on the platform, the Rev. Dr. Manley arose and offered a deeply impressive prayer. President Davis then arose and read his inaugural address; then turning, he placed one hand upon the Bible, and, with the other uplifted, listened to the oath. His face was upturned and reverential in expression. At the conclusion of the oath, in solemn, earnest voice, he exclaimed: "So help me God!" He lowered his head in tears, and hundreds wept as they viewed the solemn scene. Thus was officially launched upon a tempestuous political sea the Confederate Ship of State.

THE PROCESSION.

In order to insure the preservation of details of so important an event in the transactions of human affairs, the order of procession, which formed on Montgomery street and marched to the capitol building, is here given:

Music.

Military escort, under command of Captain Semmes, of Columbus, Ga., consisting of Montgomery German Fusileers, Captain Schenssler; Montgomery Rifles, Captain Farriss; Eufala Rifles, Captain Alf. Baker; Columbus (Ga.) Guard, Lieutenant Ellis commanding.

The President-elect, with Vice-President Stephens and Chaplain Dr. Basil Manley, in open carriage drawn by six horses.

Congressional Committee on Ceremonies of the Inauguration.

Committee on part of the State of Alabama. Committee on part of the authorities of the city of Montgomery.

Commissioners to the Government from States other than the States of the Confederacy.

Governors of the several Confederate States. Judges of the Supreme Courts of the several States of the Confederacy.

Ministers of the Gospel.

The above in carriages.

Citizens generally, in carriages.

Citizens generally, on foot.

The whole under command of Colonel H. P. Watson, Marshal of the Day.

MEMBERS OF

PRESIDENT JEFFERSON DAVIS' CABINET.

1. JOHN C. BRECKINRIDGE, of Kentucky, Secretary of War from February 6, 1865, to close of war.
2. STEPHEN R. MALLORY, of Florida, Secretary of Navy from March 4, 1861, to close of war.
3. JUDAH P. BENJAMIN, of Louisiana, Attorney-General from February 25 to September 17, 1861; Secretary of War from September 17, 1861, to March 23, 1862; Secretary of State from March 18, 1862, to close of war.
4. GEORGE W. RANDOLPH, of Virginia, Secretary of War from March 18 to November 17, 1862.
5. ROBERT TOOMBS, of Georgia, Secretary of State from February 21 to July 25, 1861.
6. CHRISTOPHER G. MEMMINGER, of South Carolina, Secretary of Treasury from February 21, 1861, to July 18, 1864.
7. JOHN H. REAGAN, of Texas, Postmaster-General from March 6, 1861, to close of war.
8. LEROY POPE WALKER, of Alabama, Secretary of War from February 21 to September 17, 1861.
9. R. M. T. HUNTER, of Virginia, Secretary of State from July 25, 1861, to March 18, 1862.
10. JAMES A. SEDDON, of Virginia, Secretary of War from November 21, 1862, to February 6, 1865.
11. THOMAS H. WATTS, of Alabama, Attorney-General from March 18, 1862, to January 1, 1864.

THE EXECUTIVE OFFICERS OF THE CONFEDERATE STATES, 1861-1865.

PRESIDENT AND COMMANDER-IN-CHIEF OF THE ARMY AND NAVY,
JEFFERSON DAVIS, OF MISSISSIPPI.

VICE-PRESIDENT AND PRESIDING OFFICER OF THE SENATE,
ALEXANDER H. STEPHENS, OF GEORGIA.

[NOTE.—The President and Vice-President were inaugurated at Montgomery, Alabama, February 18, 1861, and again at Richmond, Virginia, February 22, 1862.]

CABINET OFFICERS AND HEADS OF DEPARTMENTS.

DEPARTMENT OF STATE.

ROBERT TOOMBS, Georgia, February 21, 1861, first Secretary of State; subsequently entered the Confederate army, with the rank of Brigadier-General; also a delegate to the Provisional Congress.

R. M. T. HUNTER, Virginia, July 25, 1861, to March 18, 1862, succeeded General Toombs as Secretary of State; delegate to Provisional Congress, and Senator from Virginia.

JUDAH P. BENJAMIN, Louisiana, March 18, 1862, to close of war, succeeded Mr. Hunter as Secretary of State; had been Attorney-General and Secretary of War.

WM. M. BROWNE, Assistant Secretary of State.

L. T. WASHINGTON, Chief Clerk.

DEPARTMENT OF JUSTICE.

JUDAH P. BENJAMIN, Louisiana, first Attorney-General, February 25 to September 17, 1861.

THOMAS BRAGG, North Carolina, second Attorney-General, November 21, 1861, to March 18, 1862.

T. H. WATTS, Alabama, third Attorney-General, March 18, 1862, to January 1, 1864; subsequently elected Governor of Alabama.

GEORGE DAVIS, North Carolina, January 2, 1864, to close of war, fourth Attorney-General; delegate to Provisional Congress; Senator from North Carolina.

WADE KEYS, Assistant Attorney-General.

JULES ST. MARTIN, Chief Clerk.

TREASURY DEPARTMENT.

CHRISTOPHER G. MEMMINGER, South Carolina, February 21, 1861, to July 18, 1864, first Secretary of the Treasury.

GEORGE A. TRENHOLM, South Carolina, July 18, 1864, to close of war, second Secretary of the Treasury, succeeding Mr. Memminger.

PHILIP CLAYTON, Georgia, Assistant Secretary of the Treasury.

E. C. ELMORE, Alabama, Treasurer.

H. D. CAPERS, South Carolina, Chief Clerk and Disbursing Officer.

LEWIS CRUGER, South Carolina, Comptroller and Solicitor.

BOLLING BAKER, Georgia, first Auditor.

A. C. CLITHERALL, Registrar.

WAR DEPARTMENT.

LE ROY POPE WALKER, Alabama, first Secretary of War, from February 21, 1861, to September 17, 1861; appointed Brigadier-General September 17, 1861.

JUDAH P. BENJAMIN, Louisiana, second Secretary of War, from September 17, 1861, to March 17, 1862; Acting Secretary of War, March 18 to 23, 1862; also Secretary of State and Attorney-General.

GEORGE W. RANDOLPH, Virginia (appointed Brigadier-General February 13, 1862), third Secretary of War; confirmed March 18, 1862, and assumed duties March 24, 1862, to November 17, 1862.

GENERAL GUSTAVUS W. SMITH, Kentucky, Acting Secretary of War, from November 17, 1862, to November 21, 1862; Brigadier-General and Major-General in Confederate service.

JAMES A. SEDDON, Virginia, fourth Secretary of War, from November 21, 1862, to February 6, 1865.

JOHN C. BRECKINRIDGE, Kentucky, fifth Secretary of War, from February 6, 1865, to close of war. (Summoned from the field, where he was serving with the rank and command of a Major-General, to discharge the duties of the office.)

A. T. BLEDSOE, Virginia, Assistant Secretary of War.

JOHN A. CAMPBELL, Louisiana, Assistant Secretary of War.

GENERAL SAMUEL COOPER, Virginia, Adjutant-General.

COLONEL A. C. MYERS, Quartermaster-General.

GENERAL A. R. LAWTON, Quartermaster-General.

COLONEL L. B. NORTHROP, South Carolina, Commissary-General.

GENERAL ISAAC M. ST. JOHN, Commissary-General.

GENERAL JOSIAH GORGAS, Chief of Ordnance.

COLONEL THOMAS S. RHETT, Chief of Ordnance Bureau.

COLONEL J. F. GILMER, South Carolina, Chief of Engineers.

GENERAL S. P. MOORE, South Carolina, Surgeon-General.

GENERAL JOHN S. PRESTON, South Carolina, Chief of Conscript Bureau.

COLONEL T. P. AUGUST, Virginia, Superintendent of Bureau of Conscription.

GENERAL JOHN H. WINDER, Maryland, Provost Marshal-General, and Commanding Prison Camps.

COLONEL ROBERT OULD, Virginia, Chief of Bureau of Exchange.

COLONEL RICHARD MORTON, Chief of Niter and Mining Bureau.

COLONEL R. G. H. KEAN, Chief of Bureau of War.

LIEUTENANT-COLONEL I. H. CARRINGTON, Assistant Provost Marshal-General.

COLONEL THOMAS S. BAYNE, Louisiana, Chief of Bureau of Foreign Supplies.

NAVY DEPARTMENT.

STEPHEN R. MALLORY, Florida, Secretary of the Navy, March 1, 1861.

E. M. TIDBALL, Chief Clerk, Office of Order and Detail.

CAPTAIN FRENCH FORREST, Chief of Bureau, January, 1863.

COMMANDER JOHN K. MITCHELL, Chief of Bureau, January, 1864.

COMMANDER JOHN M. BROOKE, Florida, Chief of Bureau of Ordnance and Hydrography.

CAPTAIN A. SINCLAIR, Assistant Chief of Bureau, January, 1864.

CAPTAIN S. S. LEE, Acting Chief of Bureau, from May 24 to June 15, 1864.

JAMES A. JONES, Chief Clerk.

OFFICE OF ORDNANCE AND HYDROGRAPHY.

CAPTAIN GEORGE MINOR, Chief of Bureau, March, 1861.

CAPTAIN J. M. BROOKE, Assistant Chief of Bureau, January, 1863.

J. P. MCCORKLE, Chief Clerk.

A. B. UPSHUR, Chief Clerk.

OFFICE OF PROVISION AND CLOTHING.

JOHN DE BREE, Chief of Bureau, January, 1863.

T. C. DE LEON, Chief Clerk, January, 1863.

OFFICE OF MEDICINE AND SURGERY.

W. A. W. SPOTSWOOD, Chief of Bureau, January, 1863.

C. N. FENNELL, Chief Clerk, January, 1863.

REGISTER OF THE NAVY.

JAMES S. JONES, Register of Navy Department, July, 1864.

ADMIRAL.

FRANKLIN BUCHANAN, August 26, 1862.

POST-OFFICE DEPARTMENT.

HENRY T. ELLET, Mississippi, first Postmaster-General, February 25, 1861, to March 5, 1861.

JOHN H. REAGAN, Texas, second Postmaster General, March 6, 1861, to close of war; delegate from Texas to the Provisional Congress.

H. ST. GEORGE OFFUTT, Missouri, Chief of Contract Bureau.

B. N. CLEMENTS, Tennessee, Chief of Bureau of Appointment.

J. S. HARRELL, Alabama, Chief of Finance Bureau.

PATENT OFFICER.

RUFUS R. RHODES, Mississippi, Commissioner of Patents.

PRESIDENT DAVIS' MILITARY FAMILY.

NAMES OF OFFICERS ON HIS STAFF.

COLONEL JOSEPH R. DAVIS, Mississippi, A. D. C., with rank of Colonel of Cavalry; in 1863 entered the field as Brigadier-General.

COLONEL G. W. CUSTIS LEE, Virginia, A. D. C., with rank of Colonel of Cavalry; subsequently entered the field and rose to the grade of Major-General.

COLONEL JOSEPH C. IVES, A. D. C., with rank of Colonel of Cavalry.

COLONEL WILLIAM PRESTON JOHNSTON, Kentucky, A. D. C., with rank of Colonel of Cavalry.

COLONEL WILLIAM M. BROWNE, Georgia, A. D. C., with rank of Colonel of Cavalry; subsequently entered the field and rose to the grade of Brigadier-General.

COLONEL JOHN TAYLOR WOOD, Louisiana, A. D. C., with rank of Colonel of Cavalry.

COLONEL JAMES CHESTNUT, JR., South Carolina, A. D. C., with rank of Colonel of Cavalry; subsequently entered the field and rose to the grade of Brigadier-General.

COLONEL FRANCIS R. LUBBOCK, Texas, A. D. C., with rank of Colonel of Cavalry; also a Confederate Governor of Texas.

ROBERT JOSSELYN, Mississippi, Private Secretary to the President during the Provisional Government.

BURTON N. HARRISON, Mississippi, Private Secretary to the President during the Permanent Government.

COLONEL JOHN M. HUGER, A. D. C., with rank of Colonel of Cavalry.

COLONEL JOHN B. SALE, Military Secretary, with rank of Colonel of Cavalry, to General Braxton Bragg, who was assigned to duty at the Seat of Government at Richmond, and, under the direction of the President, was charged with the conduct of military operations in the armies of the Confederacy. Colonel Sale was thus brought into intimate relationship with the President's military family.

A GROUP OF SIGNERS OF THE CONFEDERATE CONSTITUTION.

No. 1.

HON. DR. THOMAS FEARN, OF ALABAMA.

HON. WILLIAM S. BARRY, OF MISSISSIPPI.

JUDGE R. W. WALKER, OF ALABAMA.

HON. JOHN HEMPHILL, OF TEXAS

HON. JEFFERSON DAVIS, OF MISSISSIPPI,
President of the Confederate States, 1861-1865.
(Not a Signer.)

JUDGE THOMAS J. WITHERS, OF SOUTH CAROLINA.

BRIG.-GEN. THOMAS R. R. COBB, OF GEORGIA.

BRIG.-GEN. JAMES CHESTNUT, JR., OF SOUTH CAROLINA.

BRIG.-GEN. R. BARNWELL RHETT, OF SOUTH CAROLINA.

[Reproduced from old and original photographs, daguerreotypes, tin types, etc., taken in 1859-60-61.]

PERMANENT CONSTITUTION

OF

THE CONFEDERATE STATES OF AMERICA.

WE, the people of the Confederate States, each State acting in its sovereign and independent character, in order to form a Permanent Federal Government, establish justice, insure domestic tranquillity and secure the blessings of liberty to ourselves and our posterity, invoking the favor and guidance of Almighty God, do ordain and establish this Constitution for the Confederate States of America.

ARTICLE I.

SECTION I.—All legislative powers herein delegated shall be vested in a Congress of the Confederate States, which shall consist of a Senate and House of Representatives.

MISSISSIPPI STATE CAPITOL AT JACKSON.

SEC. II.—1. The House of Representatives shall be composed of members chosen every second year by the people of the several States; and the electors in each State shall be citizens of the Confederate States, and have the qualifications requisite for electors of the most numerous branch of the State Legislature; but no person of foreign birth, not a citizen of the Confederate States, shall be allowed to vote for any officer, civil or political, State or Federal.

2. No person shall be a Representative who shall not have attained the age of twenty-five years, and be a citizen of the Confederate States, and who shall not, when elected, be an inhabitant of that State in which he shall be chosen.

3. Representatives and direct taxes shall be apportioned among the several States which may be included within this Confederacy according to their respective numbers, which shall be determined by adding to the whole number of free persons, including those bound to service for a term of years, and, excluding Indians not taxed, three-fifths of all slaves. The actual enumeration shall be made within three years after the first meeting of the Congress of the Confederate States, and within every subsequent term of ten years, in such manner as they shall by law direct. The number of Representatives shall not exceed one for every fifty thousand, but each State shall have at least one Representative; and until such enumeration shall be made, the State of South Carolina shall be entitled to choose six; the State of Georgia, ten; the State of Alabama, nine; the State of Florida, two; the State of Mississippi, seven; the State of Louisiana, six, and the State of Texas, six.

4. When vacancies happen in the representation from any State the executive authority thereof shall issue writs of election to fill such vacancies.

5. The House of Representatives shall choose their Speaker and other officers; and shall have the sole power of impeachment; except that any judicial or other Federal officer, resident and acting solely within the limits of any State, may be impeached by a vote of two-thirds of both branches of the Legislature thereof.

SEC. III.—1. The Senate of the Confederate States shall be composed of two Senators from each State, chosen for six years by the Legislature thereof, at the regular session next immediately preceding the commencement of the term of service; and each Senator shall have one vote.

2. Immediately after they shall be assembled, in consequence of the first election, they shall be divided as equally as may be into three classes. The seats of the Senators of the first class shall be vacated at the expiration of the second year; of the second class, at the expiration of the fourth year; and of the third class, at the expiration of the sixth year; so that one-third may be chosen every second year; and if vacancies happen by resignation or otherwise, during the recess of the Legislature of any State, the Executive thereof may make temporary appointments until the next meeting of the Legislature, which shall then fill such vacancies.

3. No person shall be a Senator who shall not have attained the age of thirty years, and be a citizen of the Confederate States; and who shall not, when elected, be an inhabitant of the State for which he shall be chosen.

4. The Vice-President of the Confederate States shall be President of the Senate, but shall have no vote, unless they be equally divided. The Senate shall choose their other officers; and also a President *pro tempore* in the absence of the Vice-President, or when he shall exercise the office of President of the Confederate States.

5. The Senate shall have the sole power to try all impeachments. When sitting for that purpose they shall be on oath or affirmation. When the President of the Confederate States is tried the Chief Justice shall preside; and no person shall be convicted without the concurrence of two-thirds of the members present.

6. Judgment in cases of impeachment shall not extend further than to removal from office, and disqualification to hold and enjoy any office of honor, trust or profit under the Confederate States; but the party convicted shall, nevertheless, be liable and subject to indictment, trial, judgment and punishment according to law.

SEC. IV.—1. The times, places and manner of holding elections for Senators and Representatives shall be prescribed in each State by the Legislature thereof, subject to the provisions of this Constitution; but the Congress may, at any time, by law, make or alter such regulations, except as to the times and places of choosing Senators.

2. The Congress shall assemble at least once in every year; and such meeting shall be on the first Monday in December, unless they shall, by law, appoint a different day.

SEC. V.—1. Each House shall be the judge of the elections, returns and qualifications of its own members, and a majority of each shall constitute a quorum to do business, but a smaller number may adjourn from day to day, and may be authorized to compel the attendance of absent members, in such manner and under such penalties as each House may provide.

2. Each House may determine the rules of its proceedings, punish its members for disorderly behavior, and, with the concurrence of two-thirds of the whole number, expel a member.

3. Each House shall keep a journal of its proceedings, and from time to time publish the same, excepting such parts as may in their judgment require secrecy; and the yeas and nays of the members of either House, on any question, shall, at the desire of one-fifth of those present, be entered on the journal.

4. Neither House, during the session of Congress, shall, without the consent of the other, adjourn for more than three days, nor to any other place than that in which the two Houses shall be sitting.

SEC. VI.—1. The Senators and Representatives shall receive a compensation for their services, to be ascertained by law, and paid out of the treasury of the Confederate States. They shall, in all cases, except treason, felony and breach of the peace, be privileged from arrest during their attendance at the session of their respective Houses, and in going to and returning from the same; and for any speech or debate in either House they shall not be questioned in any other place.

2. No Senator or Representative shall, during the time for which he was elected, be appointed to any civil office under the authority of the Confederate States which shall have been created, or the emoluments whereof shall have been increased, during such time; and no person holding any office under the Confederate States shall be a member of either House during his continuance in office. But Congress may, by law, grant to the principal officer in each of the Executive Departments a seat upon the floor of either House, with the privilege of discussing any measures appertaining to his department.

SEC. VII.—1. All bills for raising the revenue shall originate in the House of Representatives, but the Senate may propose or concur with amendments, as on other bills.

2. Every bill which shall have passed both Houses shall, before it becomes a law, be presented to the President of the Confederate States; if he approve, he shall sign it, but if not, he shall return it, with his objections, to that House in which it shall have originated, who shall enter the objections at large on their journal, and proceed to reconsider it. If, after such reconsideration, two-thirds of that House shall agree to pass the bill, it shall be sent, together with the objections, to the other House, by which it shall likewise be reconsidered, and if approved by two-thirds of that House, it shall become a law. But in all such cases the votes of both Houses shall be determined by yeas and nays, and the names of the persons voting for and against the bill shall be entered on the journal of each House respectively. If any bill shall not be returned by the President within ten days (Sundays excepted) after it shall have been presented to him, the same shall be a law in like manner as if he had signed it, unless the Congress, by their adjournment, prevent its return, in which case it shall not be a law. The President may approve any appropriation and disapprove any other appropriation in the same bill. In such case he shall, in signing the bill, designate the appropriations disapproved, and shall return a copy of such appropriations, with his objections, to the House in which the bill shall have originated, and the same proceedings shall then be had as in the case of other bills disapproved by the President.

FLORIDA STATE CAPITOL AT TALLAHASSEE.

3. Every order, resolution or vote to which the concurrence of both Houses may be necessary (except on a question of adjournment), shall be presented to the President of the Confederate States, and before the same shall take effect shall be approved by him, or being disapproved, shall be repassed by two-thirds of both Houses, according to the rules and limitations prescribed in case of a bill.

SEC. VIII.—The Congress shall have power—

1. To lay and collect taxes, duties, imposts and excises, for revenue necessary to pay the debts, provide for the common defense, and carry on the Government of the Confederate States, but no bounties shall be granted from the treasury, nor shall any duties or taxes on importations from foreign nations be laid to promote or foster any branch of industry, and all duties, imposts and excises shall be uniform throughout the Confederate States:

2. To borrow money on the credit of the Confederate States:

3. To regulate commerce with foreign nations, and among the several States and with the Indian tribes; but neither this nor any other clause contained in the Constitution shall ever be construed to delegate the power to Congress to appropriate money for any internal improvement intended to facilitate commerce, except for the pur-

pose of furnishing lights, beacons and buoys, and other aid to navigation upon the coasts, and the improvement of harbors and the removing of obstructions in river navigation, in all which cases such duties shall be laid on the navigation facilitated thereby as may be necessary to pay the costs and expenses thereof:

4. To establish uniform laws of naturalization, and uniform laws on the subject of bankruptcies, throughout the Confederate States; but no law of Congress shall discharge any debt contracted before the passage of the same:

5. To coin money, regulate the value thereof, and of foreign coin, and fix the standard of weights and measures:

6. To provide for the punishment of counterfeiting the securities and current coin of the Confederate States:

7. To establish post-offices and post-routes; but the expenses of the Post-Office Department, after the first day of March in the year of our Lord eighteen hundred and sixty-three, shall be paid out of its own revenues:

8. To promote the progress of science and useful arts by securing, for limited times, to authors and inventors the exclusive right to their respective writings and discoveries:

9. To constitute tribunals inferior to the Supreme Court:

10. To define and punish piracies and felonies committed on the high seas, and offenses against the law of nations:

11. To declare war, grant letters of marque and reprisal and make rules concerning captures on land and on water:

12. To raise and support armies; but no appropriation of money to that use shall be for a longer term than two years:

13. To provide and maintain a navy:

14. To make rules for the government and regulation of the land and naval forces:

15. To provide for calling forth the militia to execute the laws of the Confederate States, suppress insurrections and repel invasions:

16. To provide for organizing, arming and discipling the militia, and for governing such part of them as may be employed in the service of the Confederate States, reserving to the States, respectively, the appointment of the officers and the authority of training the militia according to the discipline prescribed by Congress:

17. To exercise exclusive legislation, in all cases whatsoever, over such district (not exceeding ten miles square) as may, by cession of one or more States and the acceptance of Congress, become the seat of the Government of the Confederate States, and to exercise like authority over places purchased by the consent of the Legislature of the State in which the same shall be, for the erection of forts, magazines, arsenals, dockyards, and other needful buildings, and

ALABAMA STATE CAPITOL AT MONTGOMERY, ALSO FIRST CAPITOL OF THE CONFEDERACY.

18. To make all laws which shall be necessary and proper for carrying into execution the foregoing powers, and all other powers vested by this Constitution in the Government of the Confederate States, or in any department or officer thereof.

SEC. IX.—1. The importation of negroes of the African race from any foreign country other than the slave-holding States or Territories of the United States of America is hereby forbidden, and Congress is required to pass such laws as shall effectually prevent the same.

2. Congress shall also have power to prohibit the introduction of slaves from any State not a member of, or Territory not belonging to, this Confederacy.

3. The privilege of the writ of habeas corpus shall not be suspended unless when, in case of rebellion or invasion, the public safety may require it.

4. No bill of attainder, *ex post facto* law, or law denying or impairing the right of property in negro slaves, shall be passed.

5. No capitation or other direct tax shall be laid, unless in proportion to the census or enumeration hereinbefore directed to be taken.

6. No tax or duty shall be laid on articles exported from any State except by a vote of two-thirds of both Houses.

7. No preference shall be given by any regulation of commerce or revenue to the ports of one State over those of another.

8. No money shall be drawn from the treasury but in consequence of appropriations made by law, and a regular statement and account of the receipts and expenditures of all public money shall be published from time to time.

9. Congress shall appropriate no money from the treasury except by a vote of two-thirds of both Houses, taken by yeas and nays, unless it be asked and estimated for by some one of the heads of departments, and submitted to Congress by the President; or for the purpose of paying its own expenses and contingencies; or for the payment of claims against the Confederate States, the justice of which shall have been judicially declared by a tribunal for the investigation of claims against the government, which it is hereby made the duty of Congress to establish.

LOUISIANA STATE CAPITOL AT BATON ROUGE.

10. All bills appropriating money shall specify in Federal currency the exact amount of each appropriation and the purposes for which it is made; and Congress shall grant no extra compensation to any public contractor, officer, agent or servant, after such contract shall have been made or such service rendered.

11. No title of nobility shall be granted by the Confederate States, and no person holding any office of profit or trust under them shall, without the consent of the Congress, accept of any present, emolument, office or title of any kind whatever from any king, prince or foreign state.

12. Congress shall make no law respecting an establishment of religion, or prohibiting the free exercise thereof; or abridging the freedom of speech or of the press; or the right of the people peaceably to assemble and petition the government for a redress of grievances.

13. A well-regulated militia being necessary to the security of a free State, the right of the people to keep and bear arms shall not be infringed.

14. No soldier shall, in time of peace, be quartered in any house without the consent of the owner; nor in time of war but in a manner to be prescribed by law.

15. The right of the people to be secure in their persons, houses, papers and effects against unreasonable searches and seizures shall not be violated; and no warrants shall issue but upon probable cause, supported by oath or affirmation, and particularly describing the place to be searched and the persons or things to be seized.

16. No person shall be held to answer for a capital or otherwise infamous crime unless on a presentment or indictment of a Grand Jury, except in cases arising in the land or naval forces, or in the militia, when in actual service in time of war or public danger; nor shall any person be subject for the same offense to be put twice in jeopardy of life or limb; nor be compelled in any criminal case to be a witness against himself; nor be deprived of life, liberty or property without due process of law; nor shall private property be taken for public use without just compensation.

17. In all criminal prosecutions the accused shall enjoy the right to a speedy and public trial, by an impartial jury of the State and district wherein the crime shall have been committed, which district shall have been previously ascertained by law, and to be informed of the nature and cause of the accusation; to be confronted with the witnesses against him; to have compulsory process for obtaining witnesses in his favor, and to have the assistance of counsel for his defense.

18. In suits at common law, where the value in controversy shall exceed twenty dollars, the right of trial by jury shall be preserved, and no fact so tried by a jury shall be otherwise re-examined in any court of the Confederacy than according to the rules of the common law.

19. Excessive bail shall not be required, nor excessive fines imposed, nor cruel and unusual punishment inflicted.

20. Every law, or resolution having the force of law, shall relate to but one subject, and that shall be expressed in the title.

SEC. X.—1. No State shall enter into any treaty, alliance or confederation; grant letters of marque and reprisal; coin money; make anything but gold and silver coin a tender in payment of debts; pass any bill of attainder or *ex post facto* law, or law impairing the obligation of contracts; or grant any title of nobility.

2. No State shall, without the consent of the Congress, lay any imposts or duties on imports or exports, except what may be absolutely necessary for executing its inspection laws; and the net produce of all duties and imposts, laid by any State on imports or exports, shall be for the use of the treasury of the Confederate States, and all such laws shall be subject to the revision and control of Congress.

3. No State shall, without the consent of Congress, lay any duty on tonnage, except on sea-going vessels, for the improvement of its rivers and harbors navigated by the said vessels; but such duties shall not conflict with any treaties of the Confederate States with foreign nations; and any surplus revenue thus derived shall, after making such improvement, be paid into the common treasury. Nor shall any State keep troops or ships of war in time of peace, enter into any agreement or compact with another State, or with a foreign power, or engage in war unless actually invaded or in such imminent danger as will not admit of delay. But when any river divides or flows through two or more States they may enter into compacts with each other to improve the navigation thereof.

ARTICLE II.

SECTION I.—1. The executive power shall be vested in a President of the Confederate States of America. He and the Vice-President shall hold their offices for the term of six years; but the President shall not be re-eligible. The President and Vice-President shall be elected as follows:

2. Each State shall appoint, in such manner as the Legislature thereof may direct, a number of electors equal to the whole number of Senators and Representatives to which the State may be entitled in the Congress; but no Senator or Representative, or person holding an office of trust or profit under the Confederate States, shall be appointed an elector.

3. The electors shall meet in their respective States and vote by ballot for President and Vice-President, one of whom, at least, shall not be an inhabitant of the same State with themselves; they shall name in their ballots the person voted for as President, and in distinct ballots the person voted for as Vice-President, and they shall make distinct lists of all persons voted for as President, and of all persons voted for as Vice-President, and of the number of votes for each, which lists they shall sign and certify, and transmit, sealed, to the seat of the Government of the Confederate States, directed to the President of the Senate; the President of the Senate shall, in the presence of the Senate and House of Representatives, open all the certificates, and the votes shall then be counted; the person having the greatest number of votes for President shall be the President, if such number be a majority of the whole number of electors appointed; and if no person have such majority, then, from the persons having the highest numbers, not exceeding three, on the list of those voted for as President, the House of Representatives shall choose immediately, by ballot, the President. But in choosing the President the votes shall be

VIRGINIA STATE CAPITOL AT RICHMOND, ALSO SECOND CAPITOL OF THE CONFEDERACY.

taken by States—the representation from each State having one vote. A quorum for this purpose shall consist of a member or members from two-thirds of the States, and a majority of all the States shall be necessary to a choice. And if the House of Representatives shall not choose a President, whenever the right of choice shall devolve upon them, before the fourth day of March next following, then the Vice-President shall act as President, as in case of the death or other constitutional disability of the President.

4. The person having the greatest number of votes as Vice-President, shall be the Vice-President, if such number be a majority of the whole number of electors appointed; and if no person have a majority, then, from the two highest numbers on the list, the Senate shall choose the Vice-President. A quorum for the purpose shall con-

A GROUP OF SIGNERS OF THE CONFEDERATE CONSTITUTION.

No. 2.

BRIG.-GEN. THOMAS N. WAUL, OF TEXAS.

BRIG.-GEN. FRANCIS S. BARTOW, OF GEORGIA.

BRIG.-GEN. J. PATTON ANDERSON, OF FLORIDA.

HON. ALEXANDER H. STEPHENS, OF GEORGIA.
Vice-President of the Confederacy.

A. H. KENAN, OF GEORGIA.

JNO. GREGG, OF TEXAS.

LOUIS T. WIGFALL, OF TEXAS.

[Reproduced from old and original photographs, daguerreotypes, tin types, etc., taken in 1859-60-61.]

sist of two-thirds of the whole number of Senators, and a majority of the whole number shall be necessary to a choice.

5. But no person constitutionally ineligible to the office of President shall be eligible to that of Vice-President of the Confederate States.

6. The Congress may determine the time of choosing the electors, and the day on which they shall give their votes, which day shall be the same throughout the Confederate States.

7. No person except a natural-born citizen of the Confederate States, or a citizen thereof at the time of the adoption of this Constitution, or a citizen thereof born in the United States prior to the 20th of December, 1860, shall be eligible to the office of President; neither shall any person be eligible to that office who shall not have attained the age of thirty-five years and been fourteen years a resident within the limits of the Confederate States as they may exist at the time of his election.

8. In case of the removal of the President from office, or of his death, resignation, or inability to discharge the powers and duties of the said office, the same shall devolve on the Vice-President; and the Congress may, by law, provide for the case of removal, death, resignation or inability both of the President and Vice-President, declaring what officer shall then act as President; and such officer shall act accordingly until the disability be removed or a President shall be elected.

9. The President shall, at stated times, receive for his services a compensation which shall neither be increased nor diminished during the period for which he shall have been elected; and he shall not receive within that period any other emolument from the Confederate States, or any of them.

10. Before he enters on the execution of his office he shall take the following oath or affirmation: "I do solemnly swear (or affirm) that I will faithfully execute the office of President of the Confederate States of America, and will, to the best of my ability, preserve, protect and defend the Constitution thereof."

SEC. II.—1. The President shall be Commander-in-Chief of the Army and Navy of the Confederate States, and of the Militia of the several States, when called into the actual service of the Confederate States; he may require the opinion, in writing, of the principal officer in each of the executive departments upon any subject relating to the duties of their respective offices, and he shall have power to grant reprieves and pardons for offenses against the Confederacy, except in cases of impeachment.

2. He shall have power, by and with the advice and consent of the Senate, to make treaties; *Provided*, two-thirds of the Senators present concur; and he shall nominate, and by and with the advice and consent of the Senate, shall appoint ambassadors, other public ministers and consuls, judges of the Supreme Court, and all other officers of the Confederate States whose appointments are not herein otherwise provided for, and which shall be established by law. But the Congress may, by law, vest the appointment of such inferior officers, as they think proper, in the President alone, in the courts of law, or in the heads of departments.

ARKANSAS STATE CAPITOL AT LITTLE ROCK.

3. The principal officer in each of the executive departments, and all persons connected with the diplomatic service, may be removed from office at the pleasure of the President. All other civil officers of the executive departments may be removed at any time by the President or other appointing power, when their services are unnecessary, or for dishonesty, incapacity, inefficiency, misconduct or neglect of duty; and when so removed, the removal shall be reported to the Senate, together with the reasons thereof.

4. The President shall have power to fill all vacancies that may happen during the recess of the Senate, by granting commissions, which shall expire at the end of their next session; but no person rejected by the Senate shall be reappointed to the same office during their ensuing recess.

SEC. III.—The President shall, from time to time, give to the Congress information of the state of the Confederacy, and recommend to their consideration such measures as he shall judge necessary and expedient; he may, on extraordinary occasions, convene both Houses, or either of them; and in case of disagreement between them with respect to the time of adjournment, he may adjourn them to such time as he shall think proper; he shall receive ambassadors and other public ministers; he shall take care that the laws be faithfully executed, and shall commission all the officers of the Confederate States.

SEC. IV.—The President, Vice-President and all civil officers of the Confederate States shall be removed from office on impeachment for and conviction of treason, bribery, or other high crimes and misdemeanors.

ARTICLE III.

SECTION I.—The judicial power of the Confederate States shall be vested in one Supreme Court, and in such inferior courts as the Congress may from time to time ordain and establish. The judges, both of the Supreme and inferior courts, shall hold their offices during good behavior, and shall at stated times receive for their services a compensation which shall not be diminished during their continuance in office.

NORTH CAROLINA STATE CAPITOL AT RALEIGH.

SEC. II.—1. The judicial power shall extend to all cases arising under this Constitution, the laws of the Confederate States, and treaties made, or which shall be made, under their authority; to all cases affecting ambassadors, other public ministers and consuls; to all cases of admiralty and maritime jurisdiction; to controversies to which the Confederate States shall be a party; to controversies between two or more States; between a State and citizen of another State, where the State is plaintiff; between citizens claiming lands under grants of different States, and between a State or the citizens thereof and foreign States, citizens or subjects; but no State shall be sued by a citizen or subject of any foreign State.

2. In all cases affecting ambassadors, other public ministers and consuls, and those in which a State shall be a party, the Supreme Court shall have original jurisdiction. In all the other cases before mentioned the Supreme Court shall have appellate jurisdiction both as to law and fact, with such exceptions and under such regulations as the Congress shall make.

3. The trial of all crimes, except in cases of impeachment, shall be by jury, and such trial shall be held in the State where the said crimes shall have been committed; but when not committed within any State, the trial shall be at such place or places as the Congress may by law have directed.

SEC. III.—1. Treason against the Confederate States shall consist only in levying war against them, or in adhering to their enemies, giving them aid and comfort. No person shall be convicted of treason unless on the testimony of two witnesses to the same overt act, or on confession in open court.

2. The Congress shall have power to declare the punishment of treason; but no attainder of treason shall work corruption of blood, or forfeiture, except during the life of the person attainted.

ARTICLE IV.

SECTION I.—Full faith and credit shall be given in each State to the public acts, records and judicial proceedings of every other State. And the Congress may, by general laws, prescribe the manner in which such acts, records and proceedings shall be proved, and the effect thereof.

SEC. II.—1. The citizens of each State shall be entitled to all the privileges and immunities of citizens in the several States, and shall have the right of transit and sojourn in any State of this Confederacy, with their slaves and other property; and the right of property in said slaves shall not be thereby impaired.

2. A person charged in any State with treason, felony, or other crime against the laws of such State, who shall flee from justice and be found in another State, shall, on demand of the executive authority of the State from which he fled, be delivered up, to be removed to the State having jurisdiction of the crime.

3. No slave or other person held to service or labor in any State or Territory of the Confederate States under the laws thereof, escaping or lawfully carried into another, shall, in consequence of any law or regulation therein, be discharged from such service or labor, but shall be delivered up on claim of the party to whom such slave belongs, or to whom such service or labor may be due.

SEC. III.—1. Other States may be admitted into this Confederacy by a vote of two-thirds of the whole House of Representatives and two-thirds of the Senate, the Senate voting by States; but no new State shall be formed or erected within the jurisdiction of any other State; nor any State be formed by the junction of two or more States, or parts of States, without the consent of the Legislatures of the States concerned, as well as of the Congress.

2. The Congress shall have power to dispose of and make all needful rules and regulations concerning the property of the Confederate States, including the lands thereof.

3. The Confederate States may acquire new territory; and Congress shall have power to legislate and provide governments for the inhabitants of all territory belonging to the Confederate States lying without the limits of the several States; and may permit them, at such times and in such manner as it may by law provide, to form States to be admitted into the Confederacy. In all such territory the institution of negro slavery, as it now exists in the Confederate States, shall be recognized and protected by Congress and by the Territorial Government; and inhabitants of the several Confederate States and Territories shall have the right to take to such territory any slaves lawfully held by them in any of the States or Territories of the Confederate States.

4. The Confederate States shall guarantee to every State that now is or hereafter may become a member of this Confederacy a republican form of government, and shall protect each of them against invasion; and on application of the Legislature (or of the Executive when the Legislature is not in session), against domestic violence.

ARTICLE V.

SECTION I.—Upon the demand of any three States, legally assembled in their several conventions, the Congress shall summon a convention of all the States, to take into consideration such amendments to the Constitution as the said States shall concur in suggesting at the time when the said demand is made; and should any of the proposed amendments to the Constitution be agreed on by the said convention—voting by States—and the same be ratified by the Legislatures of two-thirds of the several States, or by conventions in two-thirds thereof—as the one or the other mode of ratification may be proposed by the general convention—they shall thenceforward form a part of this Constitution. But no State shall, without its consent, be deprived of its equal representation in the Senate.

ARTICLE VI.

SECTION I.—1. The Government established by this Constitution is the successor of the Provisional Government of the Confederate States of America, and all the laws passed by the latter shall continue in force until the same shall be repealed or modified; and all the officers appointed by the same shall remain in office until their successors are appointed and qualified or the offices abolished.

TENNESSEE STATE CAPITOL AT NASHVILLE.

2. All debts contracted and engagements entered into before the adoption of this Constitution shall be as valid against the Confederate States under this Constitution as under the Provisional Government.

3. This Constitution, and the laws of the Confederate States made in pursuance thereof, and all treaties made or which shall be made under the authority of the Confederate States, shall be the supreme law of the land; and the judges in every State shall be bound thereby, anything in the Constitution or laws of any State to the contrary notwithstanding.

4. The Senators and Representatives before mentioned, and the members of the several State Legislatures, and all executive and judicial officers, both of the Confederate

States and of the several States, shall be bound by oath or affirmation to support this Constitution, but no religious test shall ever be required as a qualification to any office or public trust under the Confederate States.

MISSOURI STATE CAPITOL AT JEFFERSON CITY.

5. The enumeration in the Constitution of certain rights shall not be construed to deny or disparage others retained by the people of the several States.

6. The powers not delegated to the Confederate States by the Constitution, nor prohibited by it to the States, are reserved to the States, respectively, or to the people thereof.

ARTICLE VII.

SECTION I.—1. The ratification of the Conventions of five States shall be sufficient for the establishment of this Constitution between the States so ratifying the same.

2. When five States shall have ratified this Constitution, in the manner before specified, the Congress under the Provisional Constitution shall prescribe the time for holding the election of President and Vice-President, and for the meeting of the Electoral College, and for counting the votes and inaugurating the President. They shall also prescribe the time for holding the first election of members of Congress under this Constitution, and the time for assembling the same. Until the assembling of such Congress the Congress under the Provisional Constitution shall continue to exercise the legislative powers granted them, not extending beyond the time limited by the Constitution of the Provisional Government.

Adopted unanimously by the Congress of the Confederate States of South Carolina, Georgia, Florida, Alabama, Mississippi, Louisiana and Texas, sitting in convention at the Capitol, in the city of Montgomery, Alabama, on the 11th day of March, in the year eighteen hundred and sixty-one.

HOWELL COBB,
President of the Congress.

SOUTH CAROLINA.—R. Barnwell Rhett, C. G. Memminger, Wm. Porcher Miles, James Chesnut, Jr., R. W. Barnwell, William W. Boyce, Lawrence M. Keitt, T. J. Withers.

GEORGIA.—Francis S. Bartow, Martin J. Crawford, Benjamin H. Hill, Thos. R. R. Cobb.

FLORIDA.—Jackson Morton, J. Patton Anderson, James B. Owens.

ALABAMA.—Richard W. Walker, Robert H. Smith, Colin J. McRae, William P. Chilton, Stephen F. Hale, David P. Lewis, Thos. Fearn, John Gill Shorter, J. L. M. Curry.

MISSISSIPPI.—Alex. M. Clayton, James T. Harrison, William S. Barry, W. S. Wilson, Walker Brooke, W. P. Harris, J. A. P. Campbell.

LOUISIANA.—Alex. de Closset, C. M. Conrad, Duncan F. Kenner, Henry Marshall.

TEXAS.—John Hemphill, Thomas N. Waul, John H. Reagan, Williamson S. Oldham, Louis T. Wigfall, John Gregg, William Beck Ochiltree.

[*Extract from the Journal of the Congress.*]

CONGRESS, March 11, 1861.

On the question of the adoption of the Constitution of the Confederate States of America the vote was taken by yeas and nays, and the Constitution was unanimously adopted as follows:

Those who voted in the affirmative being Messrs. Walker, Smith, Curry, Hale, McRae, Shorter and Fearn, of Alabama (Messrs. Chilton and Lewis being absent); Messrs. Morton, Anderson and Owens, of Florida; Messrs. Toombs, Howell, Cobb, Bartow, Nisbet, Hill, Wright, Thomas, R. R. Cobb and Stephens, of Georgia (Messrs. Crawford and Kenan being absent); Messrs. Perkins, de Closset, Conrad, Kenner, Sparrow and Marshall, of Louisiana; Messrs. Harris, Brooke, Wilson, Clayton, Barry and Harrison, of Mississippi (Mr. Campbell being absent); Messrs. Rhett, Barnwell, Keitt, Chesnut, Memminger, Miles, Withers and Boyce, of South Carolina; Messrs. Reagan, Hemphill, Waul, Gregg, Oldham and Ochiltree, of Texas (Mr. Wigfall being absent).

A True Copy. J. J. HOOPER,
Secretary of the Congress.

KENTUCKY STATE CAPITOL AT FRANKFORT.

CONGRESS, March 11, 1861.

I do hereby certify that the foregoing are, respectively, true and correct copies of "The Constitution of the Confederate States of America," unanimously adopted this day, and of the yeas and nays on the question of the adoption thereof. HOWELL COBB,
President of the Congress

GOVERNORS OF SOUTHERN STATES, 1861-1865.

ALABAMA.

ANDREW B. MOORE, December 1, 1860, to December 1, 1861.

JOHN GILL SHORTER, December, 1861, to December, 1, 1863; delegate to Provisional Congress at Montgomery.

THOMAS HILL WATTS, December, 1863, to December, 1865; had been Attorney-General of the Confederate States.

ARKANSAS.

HENRY M. RECTOR, November, 15, 1860, to November, 15, 1862.

THOMAS FLETCHER (acting), November 4 to 15, 1862.

HARRIS FLANAGAN, November, 1862, to April, 1864.

ISAAC MURPHY, April, 1864, to 1868.

FLORIDA.

M. S. PERRY, November, 1859, to November, 1861.

JOHN MILTON, November, 1861, to April, 1865; died before term expired.

A. K. ALLISON (acting), April 1, 1865.

GEORGIA.

JOSEPH E. BROWN, 1861 to 1865; sole Governor of Georgia during the war.

KENTUCKY.

GEORGE W. JOHNSON, 1861 to 1862; killed at the battle of Shiloh.

RICHARD HAWES, 1862 to 1865. The Confederate States Government of Kentucky was only provisional; no terms of office were prescribed. Governor Johnson was elected by the Russellville Convention on the 20th of November, 1861, and served as Provisional Governor until he was killed at the battle of Shiloh, April 7, 1862, while bravely fighting without rank or command. Governor Hawes was elected by the Provisional Council as his successor, and he served in the capacity of Provisional Governor of Kentucky until the close of the war.

LOUISIANA.

THOMAS OVERTON MOORE, January, 1860, to January, 1864.

HENRY WATKINS ALLEN, January 1, 1864, to close of war; had served in the Confederate army with the rank of Brigadier-General and Major-General.

MISSISSIPPI.

JOHN J. PETTUS, January, 1860, to January, 1863.

JAMES WHITFIELD, January, 1863, to January, 1864.

CHARLES CLARK, January, 1864 and 1865; had served in the Confederate army with rank of Brigadier-General.

MISSOURI.

CLAIBORNE F. JACKSON, January, 1860, to July, 1861; he was deposed in July, 1861, by the Legislature; he entered the Confederate army with the rank of Brigadier-General.

NORTH CAROLINA.

JOHN W. ELLIS, January to July, 1861.

HENRY T. CLARK (President of Senate), July, 1861, to January 1, 1863.

ZEBULON B. VANCE, January 1, 1863, to close of war; previously in active service as Colonel in Confederate army.

SOUTH CAROLINA.

FRANCIS W. PICKENS, December, 1860, to December, 1862.

MILLEDGE L. BONHAM, December, 1862, to 1864; also Brigadier-General Confederate army.

A. G. MAGRATH, December, 1864, to the close of war; ousted by the U. S. military authorities; had been judge of the Confederate court for the District of South Carolina.

TENNESSEE.

ISHAM G. HARRIS, from 1857 to close of war; served in the army during his term.

ROBERT L. CARUTHERS, elected Governor in August, 1863. Isham G. Harris was Governor when the war commenced. He was re-elected in August, 1861; this constituted his third term. Being ineligible to a fourth term, Robert L. Caruthers was elected as his successor in 1863. Nashville and a large portion of Tennessee being then occupied by the Federal army, Mr. Caruthers was never inaugurated, and Governor Harris held over, under the law until the close of the war. Mr. Caruthers had been a member of the Provisional Congress of the Confederate States.

TEXAS.

EDWARD CLARK, March to November, 1861, succeeding Samuel Houston, who was ousted by Confederate Convention.

F. R. LUBBOCH, November, 1861, to November, 1863; entered the Confederate army as Lieutenant-Colonel in 1864; was appointed on the staff of President Davis with the rank of Colonel; was with Mr. Davis when he was captured, and was confined in Fort Delaware till December, 1865.

PENDLETON MURRAH, November, 1863, to close of war.

VIRGINIA.

JOHN LETCHER, January, 1860, to January, 1864.

WILLIAM SMITH, January, 1864, to close of war; previous to election, had served in Confederate army as Colonel, Brigadier-General, and Major-General.

A GROUP OF WAR GOVERNORS OF THE SOUTHERN STATES.

GOVERNOR EDWARD CLARK, OF TEXAS.

GOVERNOR JOSEPH E. BROWN, OF GEORGIA.

GOVERNOR JOHN LETCHER, OF VIRGINIA.

GOVERNOR JOHN W ELLIS, OF NORTH CAROLINA.

GOVERNOR FRANCIS W. PICKENS, OF SOUTH CAROLINA.

GOVERNOR ANDREW B. MOORE, OF ALABAMA

GOVERNOR CLAIBORNE F. JACKSON, OF MISSOURI.

GOVERNOR THOMAS OVERTON MOORE, OF LOUISIANA.

GOVERNOR GEORGE W. JOHNSON, OF KENTUCKY.

[Reproduced from old and original photographs, daguerreotypes, tin types, etc., taken at the time the Governors were in office.]

CONFEDERATE CONGRESSES.

PROVISIONAL, FIRST AND SECOND.

[COMPILED FROM OFFICIAL CONFEDERATE RECORDS.]

PROVISIONAL CONGRESS.

FIRST SESSION.

At Montgomery, Ala., February 4, 1861. Adjourned March 16, 1861, to meet second Monday in May.

SECOND SESSION (*Called*).

At Montgomery, Ala., April 29, 1861. Adjourned May 21, 1861.

THIRD SESSION.

At Richmond, Va., July 20, 1861. Adjourned August 31, 1861.

FOURTH SESSION (*Called*).

At Richmond, Va., September 3, 1861. Adjourned same day.

FIFTH SESSION.

At Richmond, Va., November 18, 1861. Adjourned February 17, 1862.

FIRST CONGRESS.

FIRST SESSION.

At Richmond, Va., February 18, 1862. Adjourned April 21, 1862.

SECOND SESSION.

At Richmond, Va., August 18, 1862. Adjourned October 13, 1862.

THIRD SESSION.

At Richmond, Va., January 12, 1863. Adjourned May 1, 1863.

FOURTH SESSION.

At Richmond, Va., December 7, 1863. Adjourned February 17, 1864.

SECOND CONGRESS.

FIRST SESSION.

At Richmond, Va., May 2, 1864. Adjourned June 14, 1864.

SECOND SESSION.

At Richmond, Va., November 7, 1864. Adjourned March 18, 1865.

DEPUTIES TO THE PROVISIONAL CONGRESS.

ASSEMBLED AT MONTGOMERY, ALA., FEBRUARY 4, 1861.

PRESIDENT OF PROVISIONAL CONGRESS,
HON. HOWELL COBB, of Georgia.
Afterward Brigadier-General and Major-General C. S. Army.

SECRETARY,
HON. J. J. HOOPER, of Alabama.

ALABAMA.

Hon. J. J. Hooper, Secretary of Provisional Congress.
Hon. W. P. Chilton, afterward member of First and Second Congresses.
Hon. Jabez L. M. Curry, afterward member of First Congress and Lieutenant-Colonel of Cavalry.
Hon. Stephen L. Hale.
Hon. David P. Lewis.
Hon. Colin J. McRae, afterward Special Agent to London and Paris.
Hon. John Gill Shorter, afterward Governor of Alabama.
Hon. Thomas M. Fearn.
Hon. Robert H. Smith, afterward Colonel in Confederate Army.
Hon. Richard W. Walker, afterward Confederate Senator.

FLORIDA.

Hon. J. Patton Anderson, afterward Brigadier-General and Major-General Confederate Army.
Hon. Jackson Morton.
Hon. James B. Owens.

GEORGIA.

Hon. Frank S. Bartow, afterward Brigadier-General Confederate States Army.
Hon. Howell Cobb, afterward Brigadier-General and Major-General Confederate States Army.

HON. HOWELL COBB, Georgia,
President of Provisional Congress Confederate States, afterward Brigadier and Major-General C. S. A.

Hon. Thomas R. R. Cobb, afterward Brigadier-General Confederate States Army.
Hon. Martin Crawford, afterward delegate to United States.
Hon. Benjamin H. Hill, afterward Confederate Senator.
Hon. Augustus H. Kenan, afterward member of First Congress.
Hon. Eugene A. Nisbet.
Hon. Alexander H. Stephens, elected Vice-President of the Confederate States.
*Hon. Robert Toombs, afterward Secretary of State, Brigadier-General Confederate States Army, etc.
Hon. Augustus R. Wright, afterward member of First Congress.

LOUISIANA.

Hon. Alexander de Clouet.
Hon. Charles M. Conrad, afterward member of First and Second Congresses.
Hon. Duncan F. Kenner, afterward member of First and Second Congresses.
Hon. Henry Marshall, afterward member of First and Second Congresses.
Hon. John Perkins, Jr., afterward member of First and Second Congresses.
Hon. Edward Sparrow, afterward Confederate Senator.

MISSISSIPPI.

Hon. William S. Barry, afterward Brigadier-General Confederate States Army.
Hon. Walker Brooke.
Hon. J. A. P. Campbell.
Hon. Alexander M. Clayton.
Hon. W. P. Harris.
Hon. James T. Harrison.
Hon. W. S. Wilson.

* Declined Senatorship.

SOUTH CAROLINA.

Hon. Robert W. Barnwell, afterward Confederate Senator from South Carolina.
Hon. William W. Boyce, afterward member of First and Second Congresses.
Hon. James Chestnut, Jr., afterward A. D. C. to the President, with rank of Colonel, and subsequently Brigadier-General.
Hon. Lawrence M. Keitt, afterward Colonel Confederate States Army.
Hon. Charles G. Memminger, afterward Secretary of the Treasury.
Hon. William Porcher Miles, afterward member of First and Second Congresses.
Hon. R. Barnwell Rhett.
Hon. Thomas J. Withers.

TEXAS.

Hon. John Gregg, afterward Brigadier-General.
Hon. John Hemphill.
Hon. W. B. Ochiltree.
Hon. Williamson S. Oldham, afterward Confederate Senator.
Hon. John H. Reagan, afterward Postmaster-General.
Hon. Thomas N. Waul, afterward Brigadier-General.
Hon. Louis T. Wigfall, afterward Brigadier-General in the Confederate Army and Confederate Senator.

ADDITIONAL DELEGATES TO THE PROVISIONAL CONGRESS

UPON ITS ASSEMBLING IN RICHMOND, VIRGINIA, JULY 20, 1861.

NORTH CAROLINA.

Hon. William W. Avery.
Hon. Burton Craige.
Hon. Andrew T. Davidson, afterward member of First Congress.
Hon. George Davis, afterward Confederate Senator and Attorney-General.
Hon. Thomas D. McDowell, afterward member of First Congress.
Hon. Thomas Morehead.
Hon. Robert C. Puryear.
Hon. Thomas Ruffin.
Hon. Wm. N. H. Smith, afterward member of First Congress.
Hon. Abraham W. Venable.

TENNESSEE.

Hon. John D. C. Atkins, afterward member of First and Second Congresses.
Hon. Robert L. Caruthers, elected Governor of Tennessee, 1863, but never inaugurated.
Hon. David M. Currin, afterward member of First Congress.
Hon. W. H. DeWitt.
Hon. John F. House.
Hon. James H. Thomas.
Hon. George W. Jones, afterward member First Congress.

VIRGINIA.

Hon. Thomas S. Bocock, afterward member of First and Second Congresses and Speaker of House.
Hon. J. W. Brockenborough.
Hon. R. M. T. Hunter, afterward Confederate Senator, Secretary of State, etc.
Hon. Robert Johnson, afterward member First and Second Congresses.
Hon. Wm. McFarland.
Hon. James Mason, afterward Commissioner to Europe.

Hon. Walter Preston, afterward member First Congress.

Hon. Wm. Ballard Preston, afterward Confederate Senator.

Hon. Roger A. Pryor, afterward member First Congress, Brigadier-General C. S. Army, etc.

Hon. Wm. C. Rives, afterward member Second Congress.

Hon. Charles W. Russell, afterward member First and Second Congresses.

Hon. Robert E. Scott.

Hon. James A. Seddon, afterward Secretary of War.

Hon. Waller R. Staples, afterward member First and Second Congresses.

Hon. John Tyler, afterward member First Congress.

MEMBERS OF THE FIRST AND SECOND CONGRESSES.

First Congress from February 22, 1862, to February 22, 1864.

Second Congress from February 22, 1864, to overthrow of the Confederacy.

CONFEDERATE SENATE IN SESSION AT MONTGOMERY, ALA. [From an old drawing.]

OFFICERS OF THE SENATE.

PRESIDENT.

HON. ALEXANDER H. STEPHENS, of Georgia, Vice-President of the Confederate States.

PRESIDENT PRO TEMPORE.

HON. R. M. T. HUNTER, of Virginia.

Secretary, James H. Nash, South Carolina.
Assistant Secretary, Edward H. Stevens, Virginia.
Journal Clerk, C. T. Bruen, Virginia.
Recording Clerk, J. W. Anderson, Alabama.
Sergeant-at-Arms, L. H. Fitzhugh, Kentucky.
Doorkeeper, James Page, North Carolina.
Assistant Doorkeeper, John Wadsworth, Georgia.

SENATORS.

ALABAMA.

Hon. Clement C. Clay, Jr., First Congress.

Hon. Wm. L. Yancey, First Congress, afterward Commissioner to Europe.

Hon. Robert Jemison, Jr., Second Congress.

Hon. Richard W. Walker, Second Congress.

ARKANSAS.

Hon. Robert W. Johnson, First and Second Congresses.

Hon. Charles B. Mitchell, First Congress.

†Hon. Augustus H. Garland, Second Congress.

†Presented credentials as successor of Senator Mitchell, November 8, 1864.

FLORIDA.

Hon. James M. Baker, First and Second Congresses.

Hon. Augustus E. Maxwell, First and Second Congresses.

GEORGIA.

Hon. Benjamin H. Hill, First and Second Congresses.

Hon. John W. Lewis, First and Second Congresses.

Hon. Herschel V. Johnson, Second Congress.

KENTUCKY.

Hon. Henry C. Burnett, First and Second Congresses.

Hon. William E. Simms, First and Second Congresses.

LOUISIANA.

Hon. Thomas J. Semmes, First and Second Congresses.

Hon. Edward Sparrow, First and Second Congresses.

MISSISSIPPI.

Hon. Albert G. Brown, First and Second Congresses.

Hon. James Phelan, First Congress.

Hon. J. W. C. Watson, Second Congress.

MISSOURI.

Hon. John B. Clark, First Congress.

Hon. R. L. Y. Peyton, First Congress.

Hon. Waldo P. Johnson, Second Congress.

Hon. L. M. Louis, Second Congress.

NORTH CAROLINA.

Hon. Wm. T. Dortch, First and Second Congresses.

Hon. George Davis, First Congress, afterward Attorney-General.

Hon. Wm. A. Graham, Second Congress.

Hon. E. G. Reade, Second Congress.

SOUTH CAROLINA.

Hon. Robert W. Barnwell, First and Second Congresses.

Hon. James L. Orr, First and Second Congresses.

TENNESSEE.

Hon. Gustavus A. Henry, First and Second Congresses.

Hon. Landon C. Haynes, First and Second Congresses.

TEXAS.

Hon. Louis T. Wigfall, First and Second Congresses, had been Brigadier-General C. S. Army.

Hon. Williamson S. Oldham, First and Second Congresses.

VIRGINIA.

Hon. R. M. T. Hunter, First and Second Congresses, President pro tempore of Senate, had been Secretary of State.

Hon. Wm. Ballard Preston, First Congress.

Hon. Allen T. Caperton, Second Congress.

HOUSE OF REPRESENTATIVES.

OFFICERS.

SPEAKER (both Congresses).

HON. THOMAS S. BOCOCK, of Virginia.

Clerk, Robert E. Dixon, of Georgia, First Congress.
Clerk, Albert R. Lamar, of Georgia, Second Congress, and Assistant Clerk First Congress.
Assistant Clerk, De Louis Dalton.
Assistant Clerk, Henry C. Loving.
Doorkeeper, Robert H. Wynne.
Assistant Doorkeeper, John A. Crawford.
Assistant Doorkeeper, James A. Patterson.
Assistant Doorkeeper, James T. Jackson.
Assistant Doorkeeper, George W. Jackson.

MEMBERS OF THE HOUSE.

ALABAMA.

Hon. Wm. P. Chilton, First and Second Congresses.

Hon. David Clopton, First and Second Congresses.

Hon. Williamson R. W. Cobb, Second Congress.

Hon. M. H. Cruikshank, Second Congress.

Hon. Jabez L. M. Curry, First Congress.

Hon. Edward S. Dargan, First Congress.

Hon. J. S. Dickinson, Second Congress.

Hon. Thomas J. Foster, First and Second Congresses.

Hon. Francis S. Lyon, First and Second Congresses.

Hon. James L. Pugh, First and Second Congresses.

Hon. John P. Ralls, First Congress.

Hon. Wm. R. Smith, First and Second Congresses.

ARKANSAS.

Hon. Felix J. Batson, First and Second Congresses.

Hon. Augustus H. Garland, First Congress.

Hon. Rufus K. Garland, First and Second Congresses.

Hon. Thomas B. Hanley, First and Second Congresses.

Hon. Grandison B. Royston, First Congress.

FLORIDA.

Hon. James B. Dawkins, First Congress.

Hon. Robert B. Hilton, First and Second Congresses.

Hon. John M. Martin, First and Second Congresses.

Hon. St. George Rogers, First and Second Congresses.

Hon. J. P. Sanderson, First and Second Congresses.

Hon. George T. Ward, Second Congress, had been Colonel in Confederate service.

GEORGIA.

Hon. Warren Akin, Second Congress.

Hon. Clifford Anderson, First and Second Congresses.

Hon. H. P. Bell, First and Second Congresses.

Hon. Mark H. Blanford, First and Second Congresses.

Hon. William W. Clark, First Congress.

Hon. Joseph H. Echols, Second Congress.

Hon. Lucius J. Gartrell, First Congress, afterward Brigadier-General in Confederate service.
Hon. Julian Hartridge, First and Second Congresses.
Hon. Hines Holt, First Congress.
Hon. Augustus H. Kenan, First Congress.
Hon. David W. Lewis, First Congress.
Hon. Charles J. Munnerlyn, First Congress.
Hon. John T. Shewmake, Second Congress.
Hon. James M. Smith, Second Congress, had been Colonel in Confederate service.
Hon. William E. Smith, Second Congress.
Hon. Hardy Strickland, First Congress.
Hon. Robert P. Trippe, First Congress.
Hon. Augustus R. Wright, First Congress.

KENTUCKY.

Hon. Benjamin F. Bradley, Second Congress.
Hon. R. J. Breckinridge, Jr., First and Second Congresses.
Hon. Eli M. Bruce, First and Second Congresses.
Hon. H. W. Bruce, First and Second Congresses.
Hon. Theodore L. Burnett, First and Second Congresses.
Hon. James S. Chrisman, First and Second Congresses.
Hon. John W. Crockett, First and Second Congresses.
Hon. John M. Elliott, First and Second Congresses.
Hon George W. Ewing, First and Second Congresses.
Hon. George B. Hodge, First Congress, afterward Brigadier-General in Confederate service.
Hon. James W. Moore, First and Second Congresses.
Hon. Henry E Reed, First and Second Congresses.
Hon. George W. Triplett, Second Congress.

LOUISIANA.

Hon. Charles M. Conrad, First and Second Congresses.
Hon. Lucius J. Dupre, First and Second Congresses.
Hon. Duncan F. Kenner, First and Second Congresses.
Hon. Henry Marshall, First Congress.
Hon. John Perkins, Jr., First and Second Congresses.
Hon. Charles J. Villiere, First and Second Congresses.

MISSISSIPPI.

Hon. Ethel Barksdale, First and Second Congresses.
Hon. Henry C. Chambers, First and Second Congresses.
Hon. J. W. Clapp, First Congress.
Hon. Reuben Davis, First Congress.
Hon. W. D. Holder, Second Congress.
Hon. J. T. Lampkin, Second Congress.
Hon. John J. McRae, First Congress.
Hon. John A. Orr, Second Congress.
Hon. Otho R. Singleton, First and Second Congresses.
Hon. Israel Welch, First and Second Congresses.

MISSOURI.

Hon. Casper W. Bell, First Congress.
Hon. John B. Clarke, Second Congress; Brigadier-General in Confederate service.
Hon. A. H. Conrow, First and Second Congresses.
Hon. Wm. M. Cooke, First Congress.
Hon. Thomas W. Freeman, First Congress.
Hon. Thomas A. Harris, First Congress; Brigadier-General in Confederate service.
Hon. R. A. Hatcher, Second Congress.
Hon. N. L. Norton, Second Congress.
Hon. Thomas L. Snead, Second Congress.
Hon. George G. Vest, First and Second Congresses.
Hon. Peter D. Wilkes, Second Congress.

NORTH CAROLINA.

Hon. Archibald H. Arrington, First Congress.
Hon. Thomas S. Ashe, First Congress.
Hon. Robert R. Bridgers, First Congress.
Hon. A. T. Davidson, First Congress.
Hon. Thomas C. Fuller, Second Congress.
Hon. B. S. Gaither, First and Second Congresses.
Hon. John A. Gilmer, Second Congress.
Hon. Owen R. Kenan, First Congress.
Hon. William Lander, First Congress.
Hon. James M. Leach, Second Congress.
Hon. J. T. Leach, Second Congress.
Hon. George W. Logan, Second Congress.
Hon. T. D. McDowell, First Congress.
Hon. J. R. McLean, First Congress.
Hon. James G. Ramsay, Second Congress.
Hon. W. H. N. Smith, First Congress.
Hon. Josiah Turner, Jr., Second Congress.

SOUTH CAROLINA.

Hon. Lewis M. Ayer, First and Second Congresses.
Hon. M. L. Bonham, First and Second Congresses, Brigadier-General in Confederate service, Governor of South Carolina, etc.
Hon. William W. Boyce, First and Second Congresses.
Hon. James Farrow, First and Second Congresses.
Hon. John McQueen, First Congress.
Hon. Wm. Porcher Miles, First and Second Congresses.
Hon. Wm. D. Simpson, First and Second Congresses.
Hon. James M. Witherspoon, Second Congress.

TENNESSEE.

Hon. John D. C. Atkins, First and Second Congresses.
Hon. Michael W. Cluskey, Second Congress.
Hon. A. S. Colyar, Second Congress.
Hon. David M. Currin, First Congress.
Hon. Henry S. Foote, First and Second Congresses.
Hon. E. L. Gardenhier, First Congress.
Hon. Meredith P. Gentry, First Congress.
Hon. James B. Heiskell, First and Second Congresses.
Hon. George W. Jones, First Congress.
Hon. E. A. Keeble, Second Congress.
Hon. James McCallum, Second Congress.
Hon Thomas Menees, First and Second Congresses.
Hon. John P. Murray, Second Congress.
Hon. W. G. Swan, First and Second Congresses.
Hon. W. H. Tibbs, First Congress.
Hon. John V. Wright, First and Second Congresses.

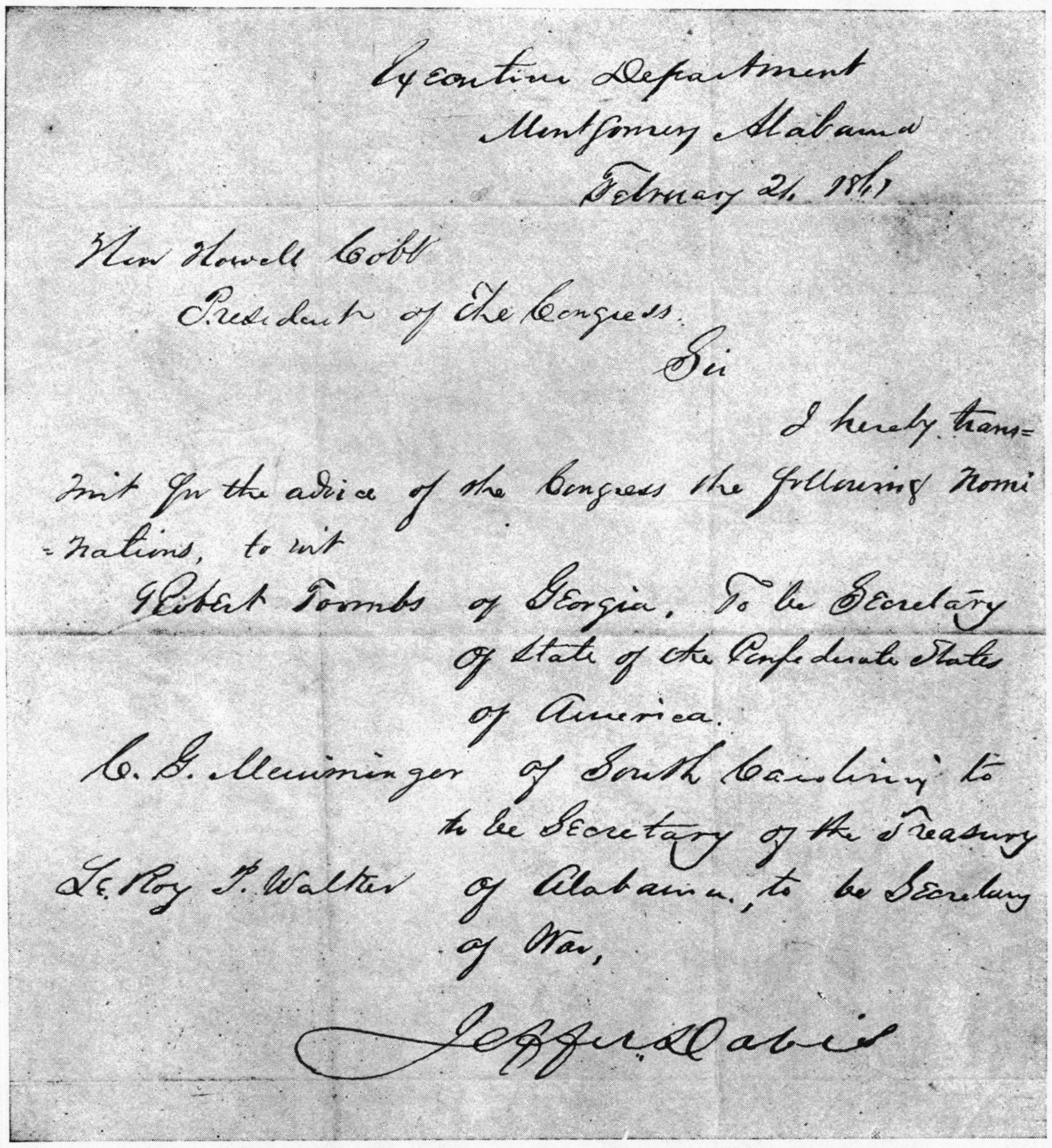

TEXAS.

Hon. J. R. Baylor, Second Congress.
Hon. A. M. Branch, Second Congress.
Hon. Stephen H. Darden, Second Congress.
Hon. B. H. Epperson, First Congress.
Hon. M. D. Graham, First Congress.
Hon. P. W. Gray, First Congress.
Hon. C. C. Herbert, First and Second Congresses.
Hon. S. H. Morgan, Second Congress.
Hon. Frank B. Senton, First and Second Congresses.
Hon. John R. Wilcox, First Congress.
Hon. Wm. B. Wright, First Congress.

VIRGINIA.

Hon. John B. Baldwin, First and Second Congresses.
Hon. Thomas S. Bocock, First and Second Congresses, and Speaker.

Executive Department
Montgomery Alabama
February 21. 1861
Hon Howell Cobb
President of the Congress.
Sir
I hereby transmit for the advice of the Congress the following nominations, to wit
Robert Toombs of Georgia, To be Secretary of State of the Confederate States of America.
C. G. Memminger of South Carolina to be Secretary of the Treasury
LeRoy P. Walker of Alabama, to be Secretary of War,
Jeffer. Davis

THE FIRST MESSAGE TO THE CONFEDERATE CONGRESS BY PRESIDENT DAVIS. [From the original.]

Hon. Alexander R. Boteler, First Congress.

Hon. John B. Chambliss, First Congress; Brigadier-General in Confederate service.

Hon. R. C. De Jarnette, First and Second Congresses.

Hon. David Funsten, Second Congress.

Hon. M. R. H. Garnett, First Congress.

Hon. Thomas S. Gholson, Second Congress.

Hon. John Goode, Jr., First and Second Congresses.

Hon. James P. Holcombe, First Congress, afterward Special Agent to Canada.

Hon. F. W. M. Holliday, Second Congress.

Hon. Albert G. Jenkins, First Congress; Brigadier-General in Confederate service.

Hon. Robert Johnson, First and Second Congresses.

Hon. Fayette McMullin, Second Congress.

Hon. Samuel A. Miller, Second Congress.

Hon. Robert L. Montague, Second Congress.

Hon. Walter Preston, First Congress.

Hon. Roger A. Pryor, First Congress, afterward Brigadier-General in Confederate service.

Hon. William C. Rives, Second Congress.

Hon. Charles W. Russell, First and Second Congresses.

Hon. William Smith, First Congress, afterward Brigadier-General and Major-General in Confederate service, and Governor of Virginia.

Hon. Waller R. Staples, First and Second Congresses.

Hon. John Tyler, First Congress.

Hon. Robert H. Whitfield, Second Congress.

Hon. Wm. C. Wickham, Second Congress; Brigadier-General in Confederate service.

TERRITORIAL DELEGATES TO FIRST AND SECOND CONGRESSES.

ARIZONA.—Hon. M. H. McWillie and Hon. G. H. Owry.

CHEROKEE NATION.—Hon. E. C. Boudinot.

CREEK AND SEMINOLE NATION.—Hon. S. B. Callahan.

CHOCTAW NATION.—Hon. Robert M. Jones.

ORGANIZATION OF THE TERRITORY OF ARIZONA.

PROCLAMATION BY THE PRESIDENT OF THE CONFEDERATE STATES OF AMERICA.

WHEREAS, An act of the Congress of the Confederate States of America, entitled, "An Act to Organize the Territory of Arizona," was approved by me on the 18th day of January, A. D. 1862;

AND, WHEREAS, It is therein declared that the provisions of the act are suspended until the President of the Confederate States shall issue his proclamation declaring the act to be in full force and operation, and shall proceed to appoint the officers therein provided to be appointed in and for said Territory.

Now, therefore, I, Jefferson Davis, President of the Confederate States of America, do issue this, my proclamation, declaring said "Act to Organize the Territory of Arizona" to be in full force and operation, and that I have proceeded to appoint the officers therein provided to be appointed in and for said Territory.

Given under my hand and the seal of the Confederate States of America, at Richmond, this fourteenth day of February, A. D. 1862.

[SEAL.] JEFFERSON DAVIS.

By the President,
R. M. T. HUNTER, *Secretary of War.*

THE TERRITORY OF ARIZONA.

OFFICERS APPOINTED BY COLONEL BAYLOR, THE MILITARY GOVERNOR, AND PRESIDENT JEFFERSON DAVIS.

On the 1st of March, 1861, at Mesilla, Arizona, the seat of government, John R. Baylor, Lieutenant-Colonel commanding the Confederate army in the Territory of Arizona, issued a proclamation taking possession of the Territory in the name and on behalf of the Confederate States of America, the Territory to comprise all that portion of New Mexico lying south of the 34th parallel of north latitude, and declaring said Territory temporarily organized as a military government until such times as Congress might otherwise provide.

In accordance with a provision of the proclamation the following appointments were declared: John R. Baylor, Governor; James A. Lucas, Secretary; M. H. McWillie, Attorney-General; E. Augorstein, Treasurer; George M. Frazier, Marshal; Frank Higgins, Probate Judge, First Judicial District; L.W. Greek, Justice of Peace, Dona Ana county; M. A. Verimendi, Justice of Peace, Mesilla; Henry L. Dexter, Justice of Peace, Mesilla; Theodore J. Miller, Justice of Peace, La Mesa; M. M. Steinthal, Justice of Peace, Pinos Altos; C. Lanches, Justice of Peace, San Tomas.

The officers appointed by President Davis for the Territory of Arizona, as per his proclamation organizing the Territory, dated February 14, 1862, are as follows: John R. Baylor, Arizona, Governor; Robert Josselyn, Mississippi, Secretary; Alexander M. Jackson, New Mexico, Chief Justice; Columbus Upson, Texas, Associate Justice, Russell Howard, Arizona, Attorney-General; Samuel J. Jones, Arizona, Marshal; Delegate to Confederate Congress, M. H. McWillie.

THE GREAT SEAL OF THE CONFEDERACY.

GENERAL ROBERT E. LEE.

BORN IN WESTMORELAND COUNTY, VA., JANUARY 19, 1807. DIED IN LEXINGTON, VA., OCTOBER 12, 1870.

[From a photograph taken in 1864.]

CAMPAIGNS, BATTLES, SIEGES, CHARGES, SKIRMISHES, ETC.

FORTS AND DEFENSES IN CHARLESTON HARBOR, 1860.

CHARLESTON and Charleston harbor were, before the war, defended by three fortifications. Castle Pinckney, a small, old-fashioned work on the main land; Fort Moultrie, near the entrance to the harbor, on Sullivan's Island; and Fort Sumter, a splendid work, on an artificial island toward the mouth of the harbor.

Fort Moultrie was situated on Sullivan's Island, north side of Charleston harbor, nearly opposite Fort Sumter, and distant from it about one and one-eighth miles. Correctly speaking, it was a huge water battery, without any guns under cover. Its armament consisted of eleven guns of heavy caliber and several mortars.

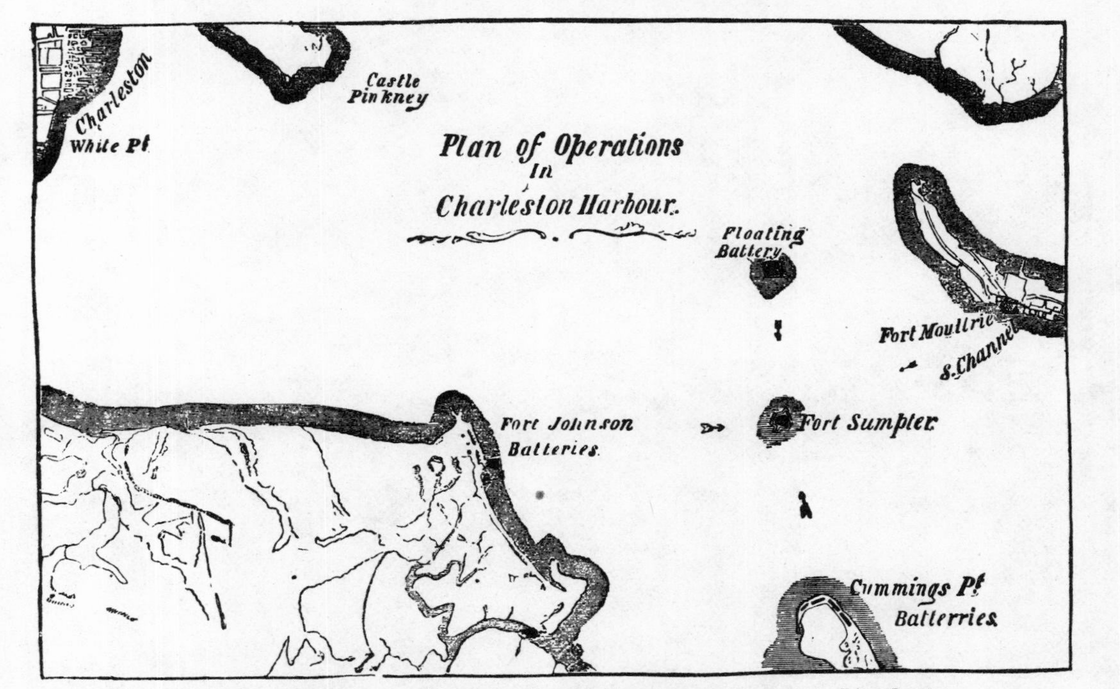

PLAN OF THE SIEGE OPERATIONS IN CHARLESTON HARBOR, SHOWING THE POSITION OF FORT SUMTER IN RELATION TO THE ATTACKING BATTERIES.

The outer and the inner walls were of brick, capped with stones and filled with earth, making a solid wall fifteen or sixteen feet in thickness. After its abandonment by Major Anderson, and before the attack on Fort Sumter, it was much strengthened, sand-bag coverts having been built between the guns, so that the latter were protected from a transverse or raking fire. Fort Moultrie occupied the site of the old palmetto fort of the same name, where was fought one of the most brilliant battles of the Revolution, when a few hundred men, who had never before fired a gun, beat off and nearly destroyed a formidable British fleet, with a greater slaughter, in proportion to the number engaged, than that of the bloody fights of Trafalgar and the Nile.

Upon the plan of Charleston harbor the relative positions of Fort Sumter, Fort Moultrie and Castle Pinckney, the batteries on Morris Island, and the city of Charleston, are shown. The position taken by the floating battery, on the day preceding the attack on Fort Sumter, is also indicated on the plan. These illustrations present at a glance the operations against the Federal force in Fort Sumter, the immediate effect of which was so profound on the country at large.

THE Orderly Sergeant was calling the roll. "Jehoshaphat Jenkins!" "Here," promptly responded Jehoshaphat. "George Squib!" "Here," in a firm voice responded the heroic Squib. "Ebenezer Mead!" No answer. "Ebenezer Mead, what do you mean by standing there staring me in the face and not answering when your name is called?" said the Sergeant, impatiently. "You didn't call my name," gruffly answered the private. "Isn't your name Ebenezer Mead?" "Nary time." "What is it, then?" "Eben Mead." "What's the difference?" "A heap." "I can't see any." "Now, Sergeant, your name is Peter Wright, isn't it?" "Yes." "Well, would you answer to the name of Peternezer Wright?" "Of course not." A laugh from the company, and after roll-call a mutual smile between Eben and Peter, at the latter's expense, settled the matter in a manner satisfactory to all concerned.

BOMBARDMENT OF FORT SUMTER, APRIL 12-13, 1861.

BY

GENERAL G. T. BEAUREGARD.

HEADQUARTERS PROVISIONAL ARMY,
CHARLESTON, S. C., April 27, 1861.

HAVING completed my channel defenses and batteries in Charleston harbor necessary for the reduction of Fort Sumter, I dispatched two of my aids at 2:20 P. M. on Thursday, the 11th of April, with a communication to Major Anderson, in command of the fortification, demanding its evacuation. I offered to transport himself and command to any port in the United States he might elect; to allow him to move out of the fort with company arms and property and all private property, and to salute his flag in lowering it. He refused to accede to my demand. As my aids were about leaving, Major Anderson remarked that if we did not batter him to pieces he would be starved out in a few days, or words to that effect. This being reported to me by my aids on their return with his refusal, at 5:10 P. M., I deemed it proper to telegraph the purport of his remark to the Secretary of War. In reply I received by telegraph the following instructions at 9:10 P. M.: "Do not desire needlessly to bombard Fort Sumter. If Major Anderson will state the time at which, as indicated by him, he will evacuate, and agree in the meantime he will not use his guns against us unless ours should be employed against Fort Sumter, you are authorized thus to avoid effusion of blood. If this, or its equivalent, be refused, reduce the fort as your judgment decides to be most practicable."

At 11 P. M. I sent my aids with a communication to Major Anderson, based on the foregoing instructions. It was placed in his hands at 12:45 A. M., 12th inst. He expressed his willingness to evacuate the fort on Monday at noon, if provided with the necessary means of transportation, and if he should not receive contradictory instructions from his government, or additional supplies, but he declined to agree not to open his guns upon us in the event of any hostile demonstrations on our part against the flag. This reply, which was opened and shown to my aids, plainly indicated that if instructions should be received contrary to his purpose to evacuate, or if he should receive his supplies, or if the Confederate troops should fire on hostile troops of the United States, or upon transports bearing the United States flag, containing men, munitions and supplies designed for hostile operations against us, he would still feel himself bound to fire on us and to hold possession of the fort. As, in consequence of a communication from the President of the United States to the Governor of South Carolina, we were in momentary expectation of an attempt to reinforce Fort Sumter, or of a descent upon our coast to that end from the United States fleet then lying at the entrance of the harbor, it was manifestly an imperative necessity to reduce the fort as speedily as possible and not to wait until the ships and the fort should unite in a combined attack on us. Accordingly my aids, carrying out my instructions, promptly refused to accede to the terms proposed by Major Anderson and notified him in writing that our batteries would open upon Fort Sumter in one hour. This notification was given at 3:20 A. M. of Friday, the 12th instant. The signal shell was fired from Fort Johnson at 4:30 A. M. At about five o'clock the fire from our batteries became general. Fort Sumter did not open fire until seven o'clock, when it commenced with a vigorous fire upon the Cummings Point iron battery. The enemy next directed his fire upon the enfilade battery on Sullivan's Island, constructed to sweep the parapet of Fort Sumter, to prevent the working of the barbette guns and to dismount them. This was also the aim of the floating battery, the Dahlgren battery, and the gun batteries at Cummings Point. The enemy next opened on Fort Moultrie, between which and Fort Sumter a steady and almost constant fire was kept up throughout the day. These three points—Forts Moultrie, Cummings Point and the end of Sullivan's Island, where the floating battery, Dahlgren battery and the enfilade battery were placed—were the points to which the enemy seemed almost to confine his attention, although he fired a number of shots at Captain Butler's mortar battery, situated to the east of Fort Moultrie, and a few at Captain James' mortar batteries at Fort Johnson.

During the day (12th instant) the fire of my batteries was kept up most spiritedly, the guns and mortars being worked in the coolest manner, preserving the prescribed intervals of firing. Toward evening it became evident that our firing was very effective, as the enemy was driven from his barbette guns, which he attempted to fire in the morning, and his fire was confined to his casemated guns, but in a less active manner than in the morning, and it was observed that several of his guns *en barbette* were disabled.

During the whole of Friday night our mortar batteries continued to throw shells, but, in obedience to orders, at longer intervals. The night was rainy and dark, and as it was almost confidently expected that the United States fleet would attempt to land troops upon the islands, or to throw men into Fort Sumter by means of boats, the greatest vigilance was observed at all our channel batteries and by our troops on both Morris and Sullivan's Islands.

THE FLOATING BATTERY ENGAGING FORT SUMTER.

Early on Saturday morning all our batteries reopened upon Fort Sumter, which responded vigorously for a time, directing its fire specially against Fort Moultrie. About 8 o'clock A. M. smoke was seen issuing from the quarters of Fort Sumter. Upon this the fire of our batteries was increased, as a matter of course, for the purpose of bringing the enemy to terms as speedily as possible, inasmuch as his flag was still floating defiantly above him.

Fort Sumter continued to fire from time to time, but at long and irregular intervals, amid the dense smoke, flying shot and bursting shells. Our brave troops, carried away by their natural generous impulses, mounted the different batteries and at every discharge from the fort cheered the garrison for its pluck and gallantry and hooted the fleet lying inactive just outside the bar.

About 1:30 P. M., it being reported to me that the flag was down (it afterward appeared that the flagstaff had been shot away) and the conflagration, from the large volume of smoke, being apparently on the increase, I sent three of my aids with a message to Major Anderson to the parties. Meanwhile, before these circumstances were reported to me, and, in fact, soon after the aids whom I had dispatched with the offer of assistance had set out on their mission, hearing that a white flag was flying over the fort, I sent Major Jones, the chief of my staff, and some other aids with substantially the same propositions I had submitted to Major Anderson on the 11th instant, with the exception of the privilege of saluting his flag. The Major (Anderson) replied: "It would be exceedingly gratifying to him, as well as to his command, to be permitted to salute their flag, having so gallantly defended the fort under such trying circumstances, and hoped that General Beauregard would not refuse it, as such privilege was not unusual." He further said he "would not urge the point, but would prefer to refer the matter again to me." The point was therefore left open until the matter was submitted to me.

Previous to the return of Major Jones I sent a fire engine under Mr. M. H. Nathan, Chief of the Fire Department, and Surgeon-General Gibbes, of South Carolina, with several of my aids, to offer further assistance to the garrison at Fort Sumter, which was declined. I very cheerfully agreed to allow the salute as an honorable testimony to the gallantry and fortitude with which Major Anderson and his command had defended their post, and I informed Major Anderson of my decision about 7:30 o'clock, through Major Jones, my chief of staff.

SHOT AND SHELL FIRED AT FORT SUMTER.

Return of shot and shell fired from the batteries of Fort Moultrie, Sullivan's Island and Mount Pleasant, commanded by Lieutenant-Colonel R. P. Ripley, artillery, South Carolina army, during the cannonade and bombardment of Fort Sumter, April 12 and 13, 1861:

	Shell.			Shot.				Hot Shot.
	10-inch.	9-inch.	8-inch.	64 pounds.	42 pounds.	32 pounds.	24 pounds.	32 pounds.
Fort Moultrie	..	..	6	248	..	305	105	41
Enfilade Battery	..	..	..	..	..	300	300	..
Point Battery	..	61	..	..	..	..	..	..
Floating Battery	..	..	..	..	247	223	..	..
Mortar Battery No. 1	185	..	..	..	..	..	..	..
Mortar Battery No. 2	88	..	..	..	..	..	..	..
Mount Pleasant Mortar Battery	81	..	..	..	..	..	..	..
Total	354	61	6	248	247	828	405	41

Scene on the Floating Battery in Charleston Harbor During the Bombardment of Fort Sumter. [From an old drawing.]

effect that seeing his flag no longer flying, his quarters in flames and supposing him to be in distress, I desired to offer him any assistance he might stand in need of. Before my aids reached the fort the United States flag was displayed on the parapet, but remained there only a short time, when it was hauled down and a white flag substituted in its place. When the United States flag first disappeared the firing from the batteries almost entirely ceased but reopened with increased vigor when it reappeared on the parapet and was continued until the white flag was raised, when it ceased entirely. Upon the arrival of my aids at Fort Sumter they delivered their message to Major Anderson, who replied that he thanked me for my offer but desired no assistance.

Just previous to their arrival Colonel Wigfall, one of my aids, who had been detached for special duty on Morris Island, had, by order of Brigadier-General Simons, crossed over to Fort Sumter from Cummings Point in an open boat, with private G. Young, amidst a heavy fire of shot and shell, for the purpose of ascertaining from Major Anderson whether his intention was to surrender, his flag being down and his quarters in flames.

On reaching the fort the Colonel had an interview with Major Anderson, the result of which was that Major Anderson understood him as offering the same conditions on the part of General Beauregard as had been tendered him on the 11th instant, while Colonel Wigfall's impression was that Major Anderson unconditionally surrendered, trusting to the generosity of General Beauregard to offer such terms as would be honorable and acceptable to both

The arrangements being completed, Major Anderson embarked with his command on the transport prepared to carry him to the United States fleet lying outside the bar and our troops immediately garrisoned the fort and before sunset the flag of the Confederate States floated over the ramparts of Fort Sumter.

* * * * * *

G. T. BEAUREGARD,
Brigadier-General Commanding.

JEFFERSON DAVIS and Abraham Lincoln were born in Kentucky, in 1808 and 1809, respectively; both left their native State in childhood's days; one emigrated North, the other South; both served in the Indian wars of the West; both commenced their political life about the same time, being Presidential electors in the election of 1844, Davis for Polk and Lincoln for Clay; both were elected to Congress about the same time (1845 or 1846), and were in the same year, and almost the same day, elected to preside over their respective governments—one as President of the United States, the other as President of the Confederate States of America.

THE FIRST ORDER CONCERNING PRISONERS ISSUED DURING THE WAR.

ORDER FROM GOVERNOR LETCHER TO CARRY CAPTAIN RODGERS, OF THE UNITED STATES NAVY, AND CAPTAIN WRIGHT, OF THE UNITED STATES ARMY, TO WASHINGTON AS PRISONERS.

EXECUTIVE DEPARTMENT,
RICHMOND, VA., April 24, 1861.

Lieutenant Sims, of the navy, and Colonel I. B. Cocke, of the volunteers, are specially charged with the duty of accompanying Captain Wright, of the United States army, and Captain Rodgers, of the United States navy, from this city to Washington; and they will see that these gentlemen are protected from insult or annoyance. The citizens of Virginia are earnestly requested to abstain from all demonstrations of passion and violence, and are requested to observe the laws of the Commonwealth. They have been released, by the action of the Executive, upon the recommendation of the Council of State, and the Military Committee of the Convention now in session.

Given under my hand, as Governor of the Commonwealth of Virginia, this 24th day of April, 1861.

[*Signed*] JOHN LETCHER.

INTERIOR VIEWS OF FORTS MOULTRIE AND SUMTER, APRIL 15-16, 1861.

BARRACKS ON NORTH FACE OF PARADE, FORT MOULTRIE, APRIL 16, 1861.

VIEW OF TERRE-PLEIN AND PARAPET OF EASTERN FLANK OF FORT SUMTER.
Also showing traverse constructed to counteract enfilading fire.

PARADE OF FORT MOULTRIE, SHOWING SOUTHWESTERN PORTION OF BARRACKS, ETC., APRIL 16, 1861.

WESTERN BARRACKS, FORT MOULTRIE, SEEN FROM PARAPETS, SHOWING THE BACK OF THE BUILDINGS, APRIL 16, 1861.

CHANNEL FACE AND SOUTHWESTERN ANGLE OF THE RAMPARTS OF FORT MOULTRIE, APRIL 16, 1861.

OFFICERS' QUARTERS, EASTERN PORTION OF PARADE, FORT MOULTRIE, APRIL 16, 1861.

NORTHWESTERN ANGLE OF FORT MOULTRIE.
Interior of ramparts back of western barracks, Western side of citadel, brick traverse for protection of magazine, sand bags covering magazine, April 16, 1861.

VIEW OF TERRE-PLEIN OF THE GORGE OF FORT SUMTER. SHOWING GUNS ON BARBETTE, APRIL 15, 1861.

[The above are from old and original photographs.]

INAUGURAL ADDRESS
OF
PRESIDENT JEFFERSON DAVIS
AT
MONTGOMERY, ALA., FEB. 18, 1861.

Gentlemen of Congress of the Confederate States of America:

CALLED to the difficult and responsible station of Executive Chief of the Provisional Government which you have instituted, I approach the discharge of the duties assigned me with an humble distrust of my abilities, but with a sustaining confidence in the wisdom of those who are to aid and guide me in the administration of public affairs, and an abiding faith in the patriotism and virtue of the people. Looking forward to the speedy establishment of a provisional government to take the place of the present one, and which, by its great moral and physical powers, will be better able to contend with the difficulties which arise from the conflicting incidents of separate nations, I enter upon the duties of the office for which I have been chosen with the hope that the beginning of our career as a Confederacy may not be obstructed by hostile opposition to the enjoyment of that separate and independent existence which we have asserted, and which, with the blessing of Providence, we intend to maintain.

INTERIOR OF FORT SUMTER AFTER THE BOMBARDMENT. [From an old drawing.]

Our present position has been achieved in a manner unprecedented in the history of nations. It illustrates the American idea that government rests upon the consent of the governed, and that it is the right of the people to alter or abolish a government whenever it becomes destructive of the ends for which it was established. The declared purposes of the compact of Union from which we have withdrawn were to establish justice, insure domestic tranquillity, to provide for the common defense, to promote the general welfare, and to secure the blessings of liberty for ourselves and our posterity; and when in the judgment of the sovereign States now comprising this Confederacy it had been perverted from the purposes for which it was ordained, and had ceased to answer the ends for which it was established, an appeal to the ballot-box declared that so far as they were concerned the government created by that compact should cease to exist. In this they merely asserted a right which the Declaration of Independence of 1776 defined to be inalienable. Of the time and occasion for its exercise, they, as sovereign, were the final judges each for itself. The impartial and enlightened verdict of mankind will vindicate the rectitude of our conduct, and He who knows the hearts of men will judge the sincerity with which we have labored to preserve the government of our fathers, in its spirit and in those rights inherent in it, which were solemnly proclaimed at the birth of the States, and which have been affirmed and re-affirmed in the Bills of Rights of the several States. When they entered into the Union of 1789, it was with the undeniable recognition of the power of the people to resume the authority delegated for the purposes of that government, whenever, in their opinion, its functions were perverted and its ends defeated. By virtue of this authority, the time and occasion requiring them to exercise it having arrived, the sovereign States here represented have seceded from that Union, and it is a gross abuse of language to denominate the act rebellion or revolution. They have formed a new alliance, but in each State its government has remained as before. The rights of person and property have not been disturbed. The agency through which they have communicated with foreign powers has been changed, but this does not necessarily interrupt their international relations.

Sustained by a consciousness that our transition from the former Union to the present Confederacy has not proceeded from any disregard on our part of our just obligations, or any failure to perform every constitutional duty—moved by no intention or design to invade the rights of others—anxious to cultivate peace and commerce with all nations—if we may not hope to avoid war, we may at least expect that posterity will acquit us of having needlessly engaged in it. We are doubly justified by the absence of wrong on our part, and by wanton aggression on the part of others. There can be no cause to doubt that the courage and patriotism of the people of the Confederate States will be found equal to any measure of defense which may be required for their security. Devoted to agricultural pursuits, there chief interest is the export of a commodity required in every manufacturing country. Our policy is peace, and the freest trade our necessities will permit. It is alike our interest and that of all those to whom we would sell and from whom we would buy, that there should be the fewest practicable restrictions upon interchange of commodities. There can be but little rivalry between us and any manufacturing or navigating community, such as the Northwestern States of the American Union.

It must follow, therefore, that mutual interest would invite good will and kindness between them and us. If, however, passion or lust of dominion should cloud the judgment and inflame the ambition of these States, we must prepare to meet the emergency, and maintain, by the final arbitrament of the sword, the position we have assumed among the nations of the earth. We have now entered upon our career of independence, and it must be inflexibly pursued.

Through many years of controversy with our late associates, the Northern States, we have vainly endeavored to secure tranquillity and obtain respect for the rights to which we were entitled. As a necessity, not a choice, we have resorted to separation, and henceforth our energies must be devoted to the conducting of our own affairs, and perpetuating the Confederacy we have formed. If a just perception of mutual interest shall permit us peaceably to pursue our separate political career, my most earnest desire will have been fulfilled. But if this be denied us, and the integrity and jurisdiction of our territory be assailed, it will but remain for us with a firm resolve to appeal to arms and invoke the blessings of Providence upon a just cause.

As a consequence of our new constitution, and with a view to meet our anticipated wants, it will be necessary to provide a speedy and efficient organization of the several branches of the executive departments having special charge of our foreign intercourse, financial and military affairs, and postal service. For purposes of defense, the Confederate States may, under ordinary circumstances, rely mainly upon their militia; but it is deemed advisable, in the present condition of affairs, that there should be a well instructed, disciplined army, more numerous than would be usually required for a peace establishment.

I also suggest that for the protection of our harbors and commerce on the high seas, a navy adapted to those objects be built up. These necessities have doubtless engaged the attention of Congress.

With a constitution differing only in form from that of our forefathers, in so far as it is explanatory of their well known intents, freed from sectional conflicts, which have so much interfered with the pursuits of the general welfare, it is not unreasonable to expect that the States from which we have parted may seek to unite their fortunes with ours under the government we have instituted. For this your constitution has made adequate provision, but beyond this, if I mistake not the judgment and will of the people, our reunion with the States from which we have separated is neither practicable nor desirable. To increase power, develop the resources, and promote the happiness of this Confederacy, it is necessary that there should be so much homogeniety as that the welfare of every portion be the aim of the whole. When this homogeniety does not exist, antagonisms are engendered which must and should result in separation.

Actuated solely by a desire to protect and preserve our own rights and promote our own welfare, the secession of the Confederate States has been marked by no aggression upon others, and followed by no domestic convulsion. Our industrial pursuits have received no check; the cultivation of our fields has progressed as heretofore; and even should we be involved in war, there would be no considerable diminution in the production of the great staple which constitutes our exports, and in which the commercial world has an interest scarcely less than our own. This common interest of producer and consumer can only be interrupted by external force, which would obstruct shipments to foreign markets—a course of conduct which would be detrimental to manufacturing and commercial interests abroad. Should reason guide the action of the government from which we have separated, a policy so injurious to the civilized world, the Northern States included, could not be dictated even by the strongest desire to inflict injury upon us; but if otherwise, a terrible responsibility will rest upon it, and the suffering of millions will bear testimony to the folly and wickedness of our aggressors. In the meantime there will remain to us, besides the ordinary remedies before suggested, the well known resources for retaliation upon the commerce of our enemy.

Experience in public stations of subordinate grade to this which your kindness has conferred on me, has taught me that care and toil and disappointments are the price of official elevation. You will have many errors to forgive, many deficiencies to tolerate, but you will not find in me either a want of zeal or fidelity to a cause that has my highest hopes and most enduring affection. Your generosity has bestowed upon me an undeserved distinction—one which I neither sought nor desired. Upon the continuance of that sentiment, and upon your wisdom and patriotism, I rely to direct and support me in the performance of the duties required at my hands. We have changed the constituent parts, not the system, of our government. The constitution formed by our fathers is the constitution of the "Confederate States." In *their* exposition of it, and in the judicial constructions it has received, it has a light that reveals its true meaning. Thus instructed as to the just interpretations of that instrument,

FORT PICKENS, ON SANTA ROSA ISLAND, PENSACOLA BAY, 1861. [Reproduced from an old sketch.]

and ever remembering that all public offices are but trusts, held for the benefit of the people, and that delegated powers are to be strictly construed, I will hope that by due diligence in the discharge of my duties, though I may disappoint your expectations, yet to retain, when retiring, something of the good will and confidence which welcome my entrance into office. It is joyous in perilous times to look around upon a people united in heart, who are animated and actuated by one and the same purpose and high resolve, with whom the sacrifices to be made are not weighed in the balance against honor, right, liberty and equality. Obstacles may retard, but can not prevent their progressive movements. Sanctified by justice and sustained by a virtuous people, let me reverently invoke the God of our fathers to guide and protect us in our efforts to perpetuate the principles which by HIS blessing they were able to vindicate, establish and transmit to their posterity, and with the continuance of HIS favor, ever to be gratefully acknowledged, let us look hopefully forward to success, to peace and to prosperity.

SINKING OF THE STONE FLEET AT THE ENTRANCE OF CHARLESTON HARBOR.

The United States Government, in order to blockade the Southern harbors without the presence of a large force of armed vessels, determined to purchase a fleet of old vessels of large tonnage, load them with stones, sail them to the mouths of the harbors of Charleston and Savannah, and then sink them in the channels. They would thus seal the cities to future commerce.

On the 20th of November, 1861, there sailed from the harbor of New Bedford, Mass., a fleet of twenty-five vessels for this purpose, averaging 335 tons each. They cost the United States Government $50,000. The following are the names of the vessels purchased:

1861.	NAME.	PORT.	TONS.
October 16	Ship Ceres	New London	356
"	Bark Tenedos	New London	245
"	Ship Lewis	New London	308
"	Bark Fortune	New London	292
"	Ship Robin Hood	Mystic	395
October 17	Ship Archer	New Bedford	322
"	Bark Cossack	New Bedford	354
"	Bark Amazon	Fairhaven	318
"	Bark Frs. Henrietta	New Bedford	407
October 18	Bark Garland	New Bedford	243
October 21	Bark Harvest	Fairhaven	314
"	Bark America	Edgartown	329
"	Ship Timor	Sag Harbor	289
"	Ship Meteor	Mystic	324
October 22	Ship Rebecca Sims	Fairhaven	400
October 23	Ship L. C. Richmond	New Bedford	341
"	Ship Courier	New Bedford	381
"	Ship Maria Theresa	New Bedford	330
"	Ship Kensington	New Bedford	357
"	Ship Herald	New Bedford	274
October 28	Ship Potomac	Nantucket	356
"	Bark Peter Demill	New York	300
"	Ship Phœnix	New London	400
November 1	Bark Leonidas	New Bedford	231
"	Bark South America	New Bedford	606
Twenty-five vessels		Total tons	8,376
Average tonnage			335

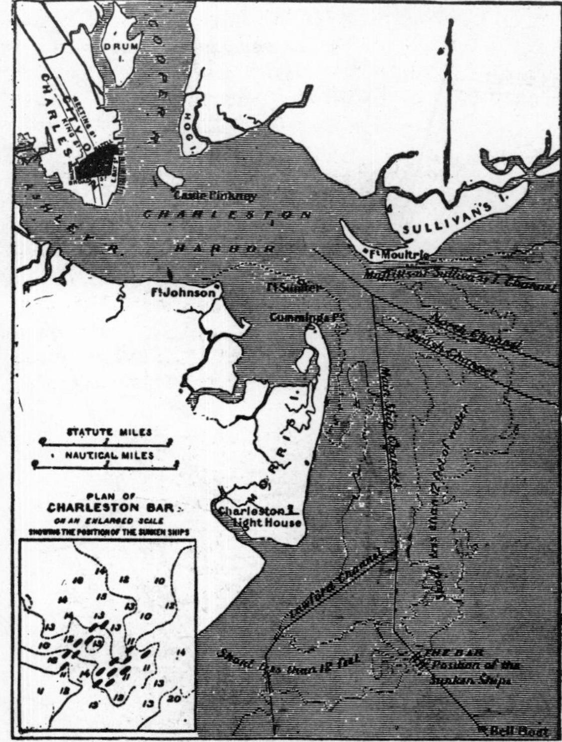

Plan of Charleston Harbor, showing position of Forts, Sunken Ships, etc.

The fleet arrived off Charleston early in December, and sixteen of the vessels were got into position as indicated on the map, the plugs previously prepared knocked out, and the ships, with sails set and flags flying, gradually sank out of sight, leaving but the upper rigging to view.

PENSACOLA HARBOR, 1861.

PENSACOLA BAY possesses rare properties as a harbor. It is accessible to large vessels; the bar is near the coast, and the channel across it short and easily passed. The harbor is perfectly land-locked and the roadstead very capacious. There are excellent positions within for repairing, building and launching vessels, and for docks and dockyards.

The supply of good water was abundant. The advantage in connection with the position of the harbor as regards the coast induced the United States Government to select it as a naval station and a place of rendezvous and repair.

Pensacola Bay, fortified as it was, with all its ordnance in position and properly garrisoned, was deemed impregnable, except by a long and hazardous siege by an overwhelming and well-appointed land force, and, it was said by an enthusiastic writer of the time, "could defy all the navies of the world combined till it filled the harbor's mouth with the carcasses of sunken ships."

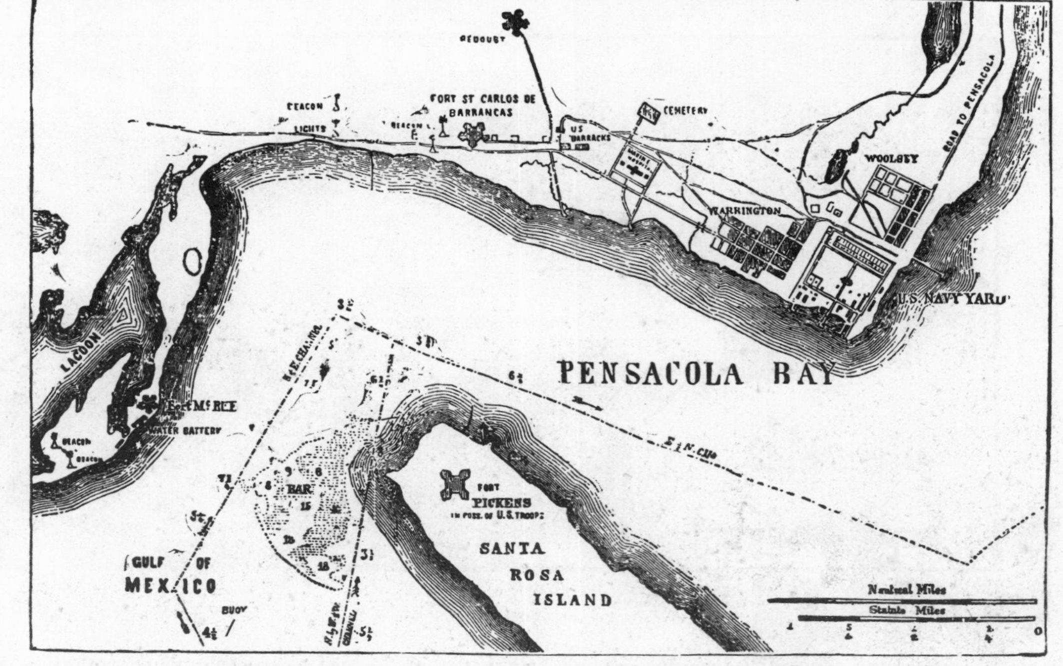

NAVY YARD AT PENSACOLA, FLA., SANTA ROSA ISLAND, GULF AND BAY FORTS, 1861.

Fort Pickens is situated on Santa Rosa Island, the west of which is at the mouth of Pensacola Bay, and completely shuts out Pensacola from the sea.

The fort was a first-class pentagonal bastioned work, built of stone, brick and bitumen, with covert ways, dry ditch, glacis and outworks complete. Its walls were forty feet in height by twelve feet in thickness, and were embrasured for two tiers of guns in bomb-proof and one tier of guns *en barbette*. The guns from this point radiated to every point of the horizon, with flank and enfilading fire in the ditches and at every angle of approach.

The work was begun in 1838 and finished in 1853. When on a war footing its garrison consisted of 1,260 soldiers. Its armament in January, 1861, consisted of: In bastion, twenty 24-pound howitzers; casemate, two 42-pounders, sixty-four 32-pounders, fifty-nine 24-pounders; in barbette, twenty-four 8-inch howitzers, six 18-pounders, twelve 12-pounders, one 10-inch columbiad, mounted, and four 10-inch mortars in bad order.

The possession of this work by the Confederates was, of course, of the first importance, for unless they could occupy it it would secure to the United States troops a base of operations along the whole Gulf coast, and keep open a road into the heart of the South, which could not be obstructed by any fixed fortifications. An enemy holding Fort Pickens could rendezvous a naval force there, and keep up a blockade of all ports of the Gulf unless it could be met on the sea.

The fort was only approachable by land on one side, and, owing to the openness of the country, which was but a barren bed of sand, a party attacking from that quarter would be very much exposed.

Fort Barrancas was built as a powerful defense of the entrance of the harbor, but neither its construction nor position was adapted to resist a strong land attack. It stood upon the same shore with Fort McRee, a mile and a quarter further up the bay.

The navy yard is situated upon the same shore of the bay with Forts McRee and Barrancas, about a mile and a half above the latter; at the outbreak of the war it was under the command of Commodore James Armstrong, the next officer in rank at the yard being Commander Ebenezer Farrand, who afterward resigned and entered the Confederate States Navy. The disposable force at the yard consisted of seventy sailors, or "ordinary men," as they are termed, and forty-eight marines, commanded by Captain Joseph Watson. There were at the yard, subject to the command of Commodore Armstrong, the United States storeship Supply, with two 30-pounders and thirty-eight men, and the steamer Wyandotte, with six 32's and eighty men.

THE FIRST DAY OF REAL WAR IN THE SOUTH.

The rapidly moving events preliminary to the actual opening of the greatest drama of modern times had keyed the proud and enthusiastic people of Charleston to a high pitch of excitement. That they would triumph in the end no one doubted. That their cause was just none disputed. Looking back and reflecting upon that splendid gallantry which, on the same theater nearly a hundred years before, had immortalized their ancestors, they felt no doubt of the ultimate issue in defense of what they conceived to be the right. The negotiations between General Beauregard and Major Anderson were known and discussed by all shortly after the accomplishment of each step taken, and when word was received of the determination of President Lincoln to provision Fort Sumter it was readily perceived that a conflict was inevitable. The die had been cast, the gage of battle tendered, and it was not declined. And when the sun set on the evening of that memorable 11th of April the hearts of the people beat with apprehensive solicitude as to what the morrow might bring. All the preparations for a struggle had been completed at the batteries and in the forts whose guns pointed toward Sumter. The people of Charleston slept lightly, many of them not closing their eyes at all, so wrought up were they by the fast-crowding events of the past few days.

They were startled from their slumbers when, at the hour of 4 o'clock in the morning, the guns of Fort Johnson opened on Sumter. The dread reveille, booming across the bay and rolling far into the back country, was the signal for a great rush of the population to the water front, where they might view the sublime spectacle of a bombardment. With tearful eyes, beating hearts and many prayers for their safety the mothers, wives, daughters and sweethearts of Charleston had sent their loved ones forth to the field of combat, adjuring them, even as the women of Sparta did, to be brave and true. They felt no doubt of the fact that they would prove themselves worthy and brave sons of a noble people, but with this pride and confidence was mixed that natural solicitude and fear for the safety of loved ones.

Hope and enthusiasm at once gave place to fear and depression, and the booming of the guns and mortars of Moultrie, Fort Johnson and Cummings Point stirred every heart with the keenest sense of martial ardor. Under this intense strain they forgot the cravings of hunger, and all day long they watched the progress of the fight. The shades of evening brought a lull in the conflict, which was now only kept up during the night by an occasional gun. The intense strain and excitement of the previous twenty-four hours had exhausted nature, and the people of Charleston slept soundly. They knew that the morrow would likely bring forth yet greater events, but they were getting accustomed to exciting scenes and began to view them with more philosophic composure. There was no division in sentiment. Every heart was in accord, every thought attuned to the one idea of success. Their gallant ones at the batteries, with smoke-begrimmed faces but undiminished ardor, were to them heroes indeed, worthy of and entitled to their deepest love and adoration.

BATTLE OF BIG BETHEL,

JUNE 10, 1861.

BY

COLONEL (AFTERWARD LIEUTENANT-GENERAL) D. H. HILL.

FIRST NORTH CAROLINA INFANTRY,
YORKTOWN, June 12, 1861.

IN obedience to orders from the colonel commmanding, I marched on the 6th inst., with my regiment and four pieces of Major Randolph's battery, from Yorktown, on the Hampton road, to Bethel church, nine miles from Hampton. We reached there after dark on a wet night and slept without tents. Early on the morning of the 7th I made a reconnoissance of the ground, preparatory to fortifying.

I found a branch of Back River on our front and encircling our right flank. On our left was a dense and almost impassable wood, except about one hundred and fifty yards of old field. The breadth of the road, a thick wood and narrow, cultivated field covered our rear. The nature of the ground determined me to make an inclosed work, and I had the invaluable aid of Lieutenant-Colonel Lee, of my regiment, in its plan and construction. Our position had the inherent defect of being commanded by an immense field immediately in front of it, upon which the masses of the enemy might be readily deployed. Presuming that an attempt would be made to carry the bridge across the stream, a battery was made for its especial protection, and Major Randolph placed his guns so as sweep all the approaches to it.

The occupation of two commanding eminences beyond the creek and on our right would have greatly strengthened our position, but our force was too weak to admit of the occupation of more than one of them. A battery was laid out on it for one of Randolph's howitzers. We had only twenty-five spades, six axes and three picks, but these were busily plied all day and night of the 7th and all day on the 8th. On the afternoon of the 8th I learned that a marauding party of the enemy was within a few miles of us. I called for a party of thirty-four men to drive them back. Lieutenant Roberts, of Company F of my regiment, promptly responded, and in five minutes his command was en route.

I detached Major Randolph with one howitzer to join them, and Lieutenant-Colonel Lee, First Regiment North Carolina Volunteers, requested and was granted permission to take command of the whole. After a march of five miles they came across the marauders, busy over the spoils of a plundered house. A shell soon put the plunderers to flight, and they were chased over New Market bridge, where our little force was halted, in consequence of the presence of a considerable body situate on the other side.

Lieutenant-Colonel Lee brought in one prisoner. How many of the enemy were killed and wounded is not known. None of our command was hurt. Soon after Lieutenant-Colonel Lee left a citizen came dashing in with the information that seventy-five marauders were on the Back River road.

I called for Captain McDowell's company (E), of the First Regiment of North Carolina Volunteers, and in three minutes it was in hot pursuit. Lieutenant West, of the Howitzer Battalion, with one piece, was detached to join them, and Major Lane, of my regiment, volunteered, dispersed and chased the wretches over the New Market bridge, this being the second race on the same day over the New Market course, in both of which the Yankees reached the goal first. Major Lane brought in one prisoner. Reliable citizens reported that two cart loads and one buggy load of wounded were taken into Hampton.

We had not a single man killed or wounded. Colonel Magruder came up that evening and assumed command.

On Sunday, the 9th, a fresh supply of tools enabled us to put more men to work, and when not engaged in religious duties the men worked vigorously on the intrenchments. We were aroused at 3 o'clock on Monday morning for a general advance upon the enemy, and marched three and a half miles, when we learned that the foe, in large force, was within a few hundred yards of us. We fell back hastily upon our intrenchments and awaited the arrival of our invaders. Lieutenant-Colonel Stuart, of the Third Virginia Regiment, having come with some one hundred and eighty men, was stationed on the hill on the extreme right, beyond the creek, and Company G of my regiment was also thrown over the stream to protect the howitzer under Captain Brown.

Captain Bridgers, of Company A, First North Carolina Regiment, took post in the dense woods beyond and to the left of the road. Major Montague, with three companies of his battalion, was ordered up from the rear and took post on our right, beginning at the church and extending along the entire front on that side.

This fine body of men and the gallant command of Lieutenant-Colonel Stuart worked with great rapidity, and in an hour had constructed temporary shelters against the enemy's fire.

Just at 9 o'clock A. M. the heavy columns of the enemy were seen approaching rapidly and in good order, but when Randolph opened upon them at 9:15 their organization was completely broken up. The enemy promptly replied with his artillery, firing briskly but wildly. He made an attempt at deployment on our right of the road under cover of some houses and paling. He was, however, very promptly driven back by our artillery, a Virginia company—the Life Guards—and Companies B and G of my regiment. The enemy attempted no deployment within musketry range during the day, except under cover of woods, fences or paling.

Under cover of the trees he moved a strong column to an old ford some three-quarters of a mile below, where I had placed a picket of some forty men. Colonel Magruder sent Captain Worth's company, of Montague's command, with one howitzer, under Sergeant Crane, to drive back this column, which was done by a single shot from the howitzer.

Before this a priming wire had been broken in the vent of the howitzer commanded by Captain Brown, which rendered it useless.

A force estimated at 1,500 was now attempting to outflank us and get in the rear of Lieutenant-Colonel Stuart's small command. He was accordingly directed to fall back, and the whole of our advanced troops were withdrawn. At this critical moment I directed Lieutenant-Colonel Lee to call Captain Bridgers out of the swamp, and ordered him to reoccupy the nearest advanced work, and I ordered Captain Ross, Company C, First Regiment North Carolina Volunteers, to the support of Lieutenant-Colonel Stuart.

These two captains, with their companies, crossed over to Randolph's battery under a very heavy fire in a most gallant manner. As Lieutenant-Colonel Stuart had withdrawn, Captain Ross was detained at the church, near Randolph's battery. Captain Bridgers, however, crossed over and drove the zouaves out of the advanced howitzer battery and reoccupied it.

It is impossible to overestimate this service. It decided the action in our favor.

In obedience to orders from Colonel Magruder, Lieutenant-Colonel Stuart marched back, and in spite of the presence of a foe ten times his superior in number resumed in the most heroic manner possession of his intrenchments.

A fresh howitzer was carried across and placed in the

Fort Pickens. Fort McRee. Navy Yard.

PANORAMIC VIEW OF PENSACOLA BAY.—THE NAVY YARD AND FORTS, 1861. [From an old sketch.]

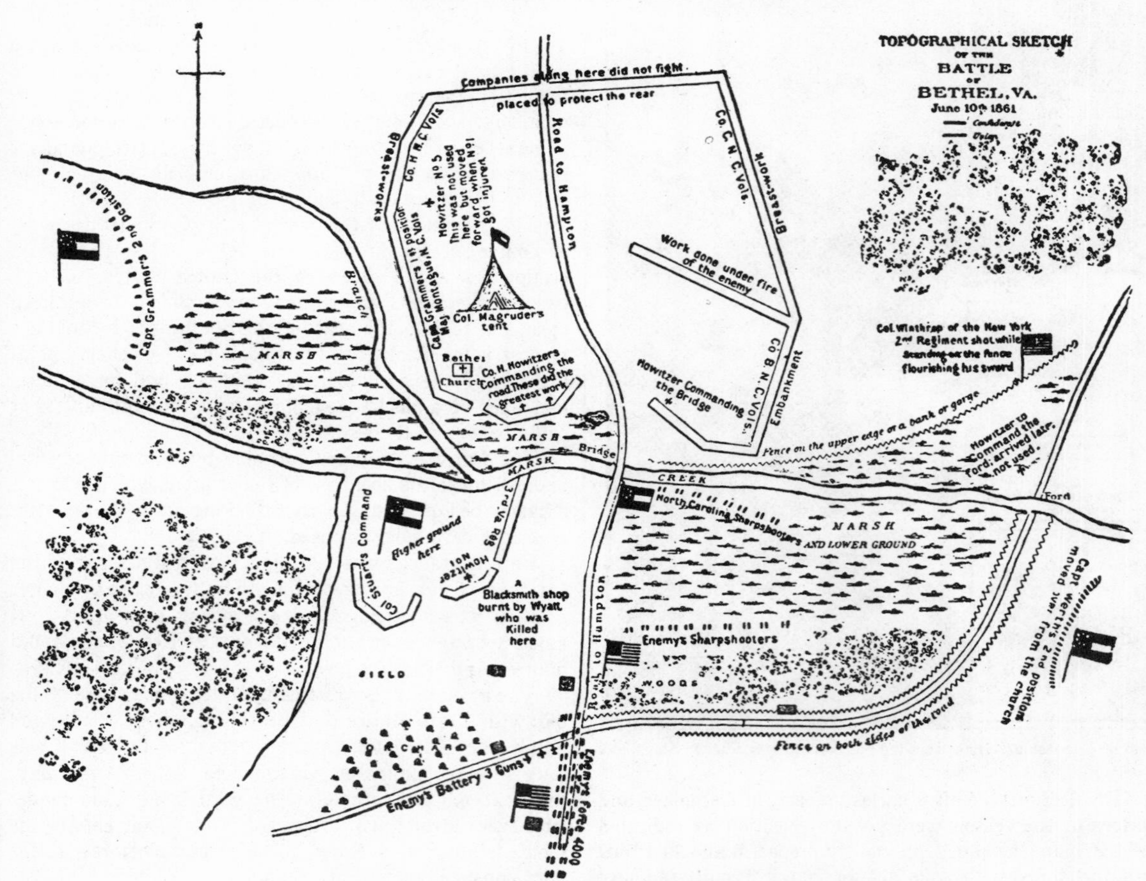

MAP OF THE BATTLE FIELD OF BIG BETHEL, JUNE 10, 1861.

battery, and Captain Avery, of Company G, was directed to defend it at all hazards. We were now as secure as at the beginning of the fight, and as yet had no man killed. The enemy, finding himself foiled on our right flank, next made his final demonstration on our left. A strong column, supposed to consist of volunteers from different regiments, and under command of Captain Winthrop, aid-de-camp to General Butler, crossed over the creek and appeared at the angle on our left. Those in advance had put on our distinctive badge of a white band around the cap, and they cried out repeatedly, "Don't fire." This ruse was practiced to enable the whole column to get over the creek and form in good order. They now began to cheer most lustily, thinking that our work was open at the gorge, and that they could get in by a sudden rush. Companies B and C, however, dispelled the illusion by a cool, deliberate and well-directed fire. Colonel Magruder sent over portions of Companies G, C and H of my regiment to our support; and now began as cool firing on our side as was ever witnessed.

The three field officers of the regiment were present, and but few shots were fired without their permission, the men repeatedly saying, "May I fire?" "I think I can bring him." They were all in high glee, and seemed to enjoy it as much as boys do rabbit shooting. Captain Winthrop, while most gallantly urging on his men, was shot through the heart, when all rushed back with the utmost precipitation.

So far as my observation extended, he was the only one of the enemy who exhibited even an approximation to courage during the whole day.

The fight at the angle lasted but twenty minutes. It completely discouraged the enemy, and he made no further effort at assault. The house in front, which had served as a hiding place for the enemy, was now fired by a shell from a howitzer, and the outhouses and palings were soon in a blaze. As all shelter was now taken from him, the enemy called in his troops and started back for Hampton. As he had left sharpshooters behind him in the woods on our left, the dragoons could not advance until Captain Hoke, of Company K, First North Carolina Volunteers, had thoroughly explored them.

As soon as he gave the assurance of the road being clear, Captain Douthatt, with some one hundred dragoons, in compliance with Colonel Magruder's orders, pursued. The enemy in his haste threw away hundreds of canteens, haversacks, overcoats, etc.; even the dead were thrown out of the wagons. The pursuit soon became a chase, and for the third time the enemy won the race over the New Market course.

The bridge was torn up behind him, and our dragoons returned to camp. There were not quite 800 of my regiment engaged in the fight, and not one-half of these drew trigger during the day.

All remained manfully at the post assigned them, and not a man in the regiment behaved badly. The companies not engaged were as much exposed, and rendered equal service with those participating in the fight. They deserve equally the thanks of the country. In fact, it is the most trying ordeal to which soldiers can be subjected, to receive a fire which their orders forbid them to return. Had a single company left its post our works would have been exposed, and the constancy and discipline of the unengaged companies can not be too highly commended.

A detachment of fifteen cadets from the North Carolina Military Institute defended the howitzer under Lieutenant Hudnall, and acted with great coolness and determination.

The Confederates had in all 1,200 men in the action.

The enemy had the regiments of Colonel Duryee (zouaves), Colonel Carr, Colonel Allen, Colonel Bendix and Colonel Wardrop (Massachusetts), from Old Point Comfort, and five companies of Phelps' regiment from Newport News. We had never more than 300 actively engaged at any one time.

The Confederate loss was eleven wounded—of these, one mortally. The enemy must have lost some 300. I could not, without great disparagement of their courage, place their loss at a lower figure.

* * * * * *

D. H. HILL,
Colonel First Regiment North Carolina Volunteers.

CITY POINT, on the James River, was the landing for transports with soldiers released from Northern prisons on parole. One day a most woe-begone and emaciated "Johnny" sat swinging his shoeless feet from a barrel, awaiting his turn, when a pompous Federal major remarked, to no one in particular: "It isn't far to Richmond?" "Reck'n et's near onto three thousin' mile," drawled Johnny, weakly. "Nonsense! you must be crazy!" replied the officer, staring. "Wal, I ent a-recknin' edzact," was the slow reply. "Jest thought so, kinder." "Oh, you did! And why, pray?" "'Cause it took'n youens nigh onto foore years to git thar from Washington," was the settled retort.

BATTLE OF MANASSAS (BULL RUN)

JULY 21, 1861.

BY

GENERAL G. T. BEAUREGARD,
Commanding Army of the Potomac (afterward First Corps).

HEADQUARTERS FIRST CORPS, ARMY OF THE POTOMAC,
MANASSAS, Oct. 14, 1861.

BEFORE entering upon a narrative of the general military operations in the presence of the enemy on the 21st of July I propose, I hope not unseasonably, first to recite certain events which belong to the strategy of the campaign, and consequently form an essential part of the history of the battle.

BRIG.-GEN. BARNARD E. BEE, OF SOUTH CAROLINA.
Killed at the Battle of First Manassas, July 21, 1861.

Having become satisfied that the advance of the enemy, with a decidedly superior force, both in numbers and war equipage, to attack or turn my position in this quarter, was immediately impending, I dispatched, July 13th, one of my staff, Colonel Chestnut, of South Carolina, to submit for the consideration of the President a plan of operations as follows: I proposed that General Johnston should unite the bulk of the Army of the Shenandoah with that of the Potomac, then under my command, leaving sufficient forces to garrison his strong works at Winchester and to guard the fine defensive passes of the Blue Ridge, and thus hold General Patterson in check. At the same time Brigadier-General Holmes was to march hither with all of his command not essential for the defense of the position of Acquia Creek. These junctions having been effected at Manassas, an immediate impetuous attack of our combined armies upon General McDowell was to follow as soon as he approached my advanced positions at and around Fairfax Courthouse, with the inevitable result, as I submitted, of his complete defeat and the destruction or capture of his army. This accomplished, the Army of the Shenandoah, under General Johnston, increased with a part of my forces and rejoined, as he returned, by the detachments left to hold the mountain passes, was to march back rapidly into the valley, fall upon and crush Patterson with a superior force wheresoever he might be found. This I confidently estimated could be achieved within fifteen days after General Johnston should march from Winchester to Manassas. Meanwhile I was to occupy the enemy's works on this side of the Potomac, if, as I anticipated, he had been so routed as to enable me to enter them with him; or, if not, to retire again for a time within the lines of Bull Run with my main force. Patterson having been virtually destroyed, then General Johnston would re-enforce General Garnett sufficiently to make him superior to his opponent, General McClellan, and able to defeat that officer. This done, General Garnett was to form an immediate junction with General Johnston, who was forthwith to cross the Potomac into Maryland with his whole force, arouse the people as he advanced to the recovery of their political rights and the defense of their homes and families from an offensive invader, and then march to the investment of Washington in the rear, while I resumed the offensive in front. This plan of operations, you are aware, was not accepted at the time, from considerations which appeared so weighty as to more than counterbalance its proposed advantages.

Informed of these views, and of the decision of the War Department, I then made my preparations for the stoutest practicable defense of the line of Bull Run, the enemy having now developed his purposes by the advance on and occupation of Fairfax Courthouse, from which my advance brigade had been withdrawn.

The War Department having been informed by me by telegraph, on the 17th of July, of the movement of General McDowell, General Johnston was immediately ordered to form a junction of his army corps with mine, should the movement in his judgment be deemed advisable. General Holmes was also directed to push forward with two regiments, a battery and one company of cavalry.

In view of these propositions, approaching re-enforcements modifying my plan of operations so far as to deter mine on attacking the enemy at Centreville as soon as I should hear of the near approach of the two re-enforcing columns, I sent one of my aids, Colonel Chisolm, of South Carolina, to meet and communicate my plans to General Johnston, and my wish that one portion of his forces should march by the way of Aldie, and take the enemy on his right flank and in reverse at Centreville. Difficulties, however, of an insuperable character, in connection with means of transportation and the marching condition of his troops, made this impracticable, and it was determined our forces should be united within the lines of Bull Run, and thence advance to the attack of the enemy.

General Johnston arrived here about noon on the 20th of July, and being my senior in rank, he necessarily assumed command of all the forces of the Confederate States then concentrating at this point. Made acquainted with my plan of operations and dispositions to meet the enemy, he gave them his entire approval, and generously directed their execution under my command.

In consequence of the untoward detention, however, of

A PORTION OF THE CONFEDERATE WORKS ON MUNSON'S HILL.

some 5,000 of General Johnston's army corps, resulting from the inadequate and imperfect means of transportation for so many troops at the disposition of the Manassas Gap Railroad, it became necessary, on the morning of the 21st, before daylight, to modify the plan accepted to suit the contingency of an immediate attack on our lines by the main force of the enemy, then plainly at hand.

The enemy's forces, reported by their best-informed journals to be 55,000 strong, I had learned from reliable sources, on the night of the 20th, were being concentrated in and around Centreville and along the Warrenton Turnpike road to Bull Run, near which our respective pickets were in immediate proximity. This fact, with the conviction that, after his signal discomfiture on the 18th of July before Blackburn's Ford—the center of my lines—he would not renew the attack in that quarter, induced me at once to look for an attempt on my left flank, resting on the Stone Bridge, which was but weakly guarded by men, as well as but slightly provided with artillery.

In view of these palpable military conditions, by 4:30 A. M. on the 21st of July I had prepared and dispatched orders directing the whole of the Confederate forces within the lines of Bull Run, including the brigades and regiments of General Johnston, which had arrived at that time, two companies of the Eleventh Mississippi, Lieutenant-Colonel Liddell; the Second Mississippi, Colonel Falkner, and Fourth Alabama, with Seventh and Eighth Georgia regiments, Colonel Gartrell and Lieutenant-Colonel Gardner—in all 2,732 bayonets. Bonham's brigade, as before, held Mitchell's Ford, its right near Longstreet's left, its left extending in the direction of Cocke's right. It was organized as at the end of the 18th of July, with Jackson's brigade, as before said, as a support.

Cocke's brigade, increased by seven companies of the Eighth (Hunton's), three companies of the Forty-ninth (Smith's) Virginia regiments, two companies of cavalry, and a battery under Rogers of four 6-pounders, occupied the line in front and rear of Bull Run, extending from the direction of Bonham's left, and guarding Island, Ball's and Lewis' Fords, to the right of Evans' demi-brigade, near the Stone Bridge, and its left covered a farm ford about one mile above the bridge.

Stuart's cavalry, some 300 men, of the Army of the Shenandoah, guarded the level ground extending in rear from Bonham's left to Cocke's right.

Two companies of Radford's cavalry were held in reserve a short distance in rear of Mitchell's Ford, his left extending in the direction of Stuart's right. Colonel Pendleton's reserve battery of eight pieces was temporarily placed in rear of Bonham's extreme left. Major Walton's reserve battery of five guns was in position on McLean's farm, in a piece of woods in rear of Bee's right.

Hampton's Legion of six companies of infantry, 600 strong, having arrived that morning by the cars from Richmond, was subsequently, as soon as it arrived, ordered forward to a position in the immediate vicinity of the Lewis house as a support for any troops engaged in that quarter.

The effective force of all arms of the Army of the Potomac on that eventful morning, including the garrison at Camp Pickens, did not exceed 21,833 and twenty-nine guns. The Army of the Shenandoah, ready for action on the field, may be set at 6,000 men and twenty guns. (That is, when the battle began. Smith's brigade and Fisher's North Carolina came up later, and made total of Army of the Shenandoah engaged, of all arms, 8,334. Hill's Virginia regiment, 550 men, also arrived, but was posted as reserve to right flank.) The brigade of General Holmes mustered about 1,265 bayonets, six guns, and a company of cavalry about ninety strong.

Informed at 5:30 A. M. by Colonel Evans that the enemy had deployed some 1,200 men (these were what Colonel Evans saw of General Schenck's brigade of General Tyler's division and two other heavy brigades, in all over 9,000 men and thirteen pieces of artillery—Carlisle's and Ayres' batteries; that is, 900 men and two 6-pounders confronted by 9,000 men and thirteen pieces of artillery, mostly rifled) with several pieces of artillery in his immediate front, I at once ordered him, as also General Cocke, if attacked, to maintain their position to the last extremity.

In my opinion the most effective method of relieving that flank was by a rapid, determined attack with my right wing and center on the enemy's flank and rear at Centreville, with due precautions against the advance of his reserves from the direction of Washington. By such a movement I confidently expected to achieve a complete victory for my country by 12 M.

These new dispositions were submitted to General Johnston, who fully approved them, and the orders for their immediate execution were at once issued.

Brigadier-General Ewell was directed to begin the movement, to be followed and supported successively by Generals D. R. Jones, Longstreet and Bonham, respectively, supported by their several appointed reserves. The cavalry, under Stuart and Radford, were to be held in hand, subject to future orders and ready for employment, as might be required by the exigencies of battle.

About 8:30 A. M. General Johnston and myself transferred our headquarters to a central position, about half a mile in rear of Mitchell's Ford, whence we might watch the course of events. Previously, as early as 5:30, the Federalists in front of Evans' position (Stone Bridge) had opened with a large 30-pounder Parrott rifled gun, and thirty minutes later with a moderate, apparently tentative, fire from a battery of rifled pieces, directed first in front of Evans and then in the direction of Cocke's position, but without drawing a return fire and discovery of our positions, chiefly because in that quarter we had nothing but eight 6-pounder pieces, which could not reach the distant enemy.

Humorous Side of War. The Stampede at the Battle of Manassas (Bull Run). [Sketched by an English artist at the time.]

to be held in readiness to march at a moment's notice. At that hour the following was the disposition of our forces: Ewell's brigade, constituted as on the 18th of July, remained in position at Union Mills Ford, its left extending along Bull Run in the direction of McLean's Ford, and supported by Holmes' brigade, Second Tennessee and First Arkansas regiments, a short distance to the rear—that is, at and near Camp Wigfall. D. R. Jones' brigade, from Ewell's left, in front of McLean's Ford and along the stream to Longstreet's position. It was unchanged in organization and was supported by Early's brigade, also unchanged, placed behind a thicket of young pines a short distance in the rear of McLean's Ford. Longstreet's brigade held its former ground at Blackburn's Ford, from Jones' left to Bonham's right at Mitchell's Ford, and was supported by Jackson's brigade, consisting of Colonels James F. Preston's Fourth, Harper's Fifth, Allen's Second, the Twenty-seventh, Lieutenant-Colonel Echols, and the Thirty-third (Cummings') Virginia regiments, 2,611 strong, which were posted behind the skirting of pines to the rear of Blackburn's and Mitchell's Fords; and in rear of this support was also Barksdale's Thirteenth Regiment Mississippi Volunteers, which had lately arrived from Lynchburg. Along the edge of a pine thicket, in rear of, and equidistant from, McLean's and Blackburn's Fords, ready to support either position, I had also placed all of Bee's and Bartow's brigades that had arrived, namely:

As the Federalists had advanced with an extended line of skirmishers in front of Evans, that officer promptly threw forward the two flank companies of the Fourth South Carolina Regiment and one company of Wheat's Louisiana Battalion, deployed as skirmishers to cover his small front. An occasional scattering fire resulted, and thus the two armies in that quarter remained for more than an hour, while the main body of the enemy was marching his devious way through the Big Forest to take our forces in the flank and rear.

By 8:30 A. M. Colonel Evans, having become satisfied of the counterfeit character of the movement on his front, and persuaded of an attempt to turn his left flank, decided to change his position to meet the enemy, and for this purpose immediately put in motion to his left and rear six companies of Sloan's Fourth South Carolina Regiment,

Wheat's Louisiana battalion's five companies, and two 6-pounders of Latham's battery, leaving four companies of Sloan's regiment under cover as the sole immediate defense of the Stone Bridge, but giving information to General Cocke of his change of position and the reasons that impelled it.

Following a road leading by the old Pittsylvania (Carter) mansion, Colonel Evans formed in line of battle some four hundred yards in rear, as he advanced, of that house, his guns to the front and in position, properly supported, to its immediate right. Finding, however, that the enemy did not appear on that road, which was a branch of one leading by Sudley Springs Ford to Brentsville and Dumfries, he turned abruptly to the left, and marching across the fields for three-quarters of a mile, about 9:30 A. M. took a position in line of battle, his left, Sloan's companies, resting on the main Brentsville Road in a shallow ravine, the Louisiana Battalion to the right, in advance some two hundred yards, a rectangular copse of wood separating them, one piece of his artillery planted on an eminence some seven hundred yards to the rear of Wheat's battalion and the other on a ridge near and in the rear of Sloan's position, commanding a reach of the road just in front of the line of battle. In this order he awaited the coming of the masses of the enemy, now drawing near.

In the meantime, about 7 o'clock A. M., Jackson's brigade, with Imboden's and five pieces of Walton's battery, had been sent to take up a position along Bull Run, to guard the interval between Cocke's right and Bonham's left, with orders to support either in case of need, the character and topographical features of the ground having been shown to General Jackson by Captain D. B. Harris, of the Virginia Engineers, of this army corps. So much of Bee's and Bartow's brigades, now united, as had arrived, some 2,800 muskets, had also been sent forward to the support of the position of the Stone Bridge.

The enemy, beginning his detour from the turnpike at a point nearly halfway between Stone Bridge and Centreville, had pursued a tortuous, narrow trace of a rarely used road through a dense wood the greater part of his way until near the Sudley Road. A division under Colonel Hunter, of the Federal regular army, of two strong brigades, was in the advance, followed immediately by another division, under Colonel Heintzelman, of three brigades and seven companies of regular cavalry and twenty-four pieces of artillery, eighteen of which were rifled guns. This column as it crossed Bull Run numbered over 16,000 men of all arms by their own accounts.

Burnside's brigade, which here, as at Fairfax Courthouse, led the advance, at 9:45 A. M. debouched from a wood in sight of Evan's position some five hundred yards distant from Wheat's battalion. He immediately threw forward his skirmishers in force and they became engaged with Wheat's command and the 6-pounder gun under Lieutenant Leftwitch. The Federalists at once advanced — as they reported officially — the Second Rhode Island Regiment Volunteers with its vaunted battery of six 13-pounder rifled guns. Sloan's companies were then brought into action, having been pushed forward through the woods. The enemy, soon galled and staggered by the fire and pressed by the determined valor with which Wheat handled his battalion until he was desperately wounded, hastened up three other regiments of the brigade and two Dahlgren howitzers, making in all quite 3,500 bayonets and eight pieces of artillery opposed to less than 800 men and two 6-pounder guns. Despite the odds this intrepid command of but eleven weak companies maintained its front to the enemy for quite an hour and until General Bee came to their aid with his command. The heroic Bee, with a soldier's eye and recognition of the situation, had previously disposed his command with skill. Imboden's battery having been admirably placed between the two brigades, under shelter, behind the undulations of a hill about one hundred and fifty yards north of the now famous Henry house and very near where he subsequently fell mortally wounded, to the great misfortune of his country, but after deeds of deliberate and ever-memorable courage. Meanwhile the enemy had pushed forward a battalion of eight companies of regular infantry and one of their best batteries of six pieces (four rifled), supported by four companies of marines, to increase the desperate odds against which Evans and his men had maintained their stand with an almost matchless tenacity. General Bee, now finding Evans sorely pressed under the crushing weight of the masses of the enemy, at the call of Colonel Evans threw forward his whole force to his aid across a small stream (Young's Branch and Valley), and engaged the Federalists with impetuosity, Imboden's battery at the time playing from his well-chosen position with brilliant effect with spherical case, the enemy having first opened on him from a rifled battery (probably Griffin s) with elongated cylindrical shells which flew a few feet over the heads of our men and exploded in the crest of the hill immediately in rear.

As Bee advanced under a severe fire he placed the Seventh and Eighth Georgia regiments, under the chivalrous Bartow, at about 11 A. M., in a wood of second-growth pines, to the right and front of, and nearly perpendicular to, Evan's line of battle; the Fourth Alabama to the left of them along a fence, connecting the position of the Georgia regiments with the rectangular copse in which Sloan's South Carolina companies were engaged and into which he also threw the Second Mississippi. A fierce and destructive conflict now ensued. The fire was withering on both sides, while the enemy swept our short thin lines with their numerous artillery, which, according to their official reports, at this time consisted of at least ten rifled guns and four howitzers. For an hour did these stout-hearted men of the blended commands of Bee, Evans and Bartow breast an unintermitting battle storm, animated surely by something more than ordinary courage of even the bravest men under fire. It must have been indeed the inspiration of the cause and consciousness of the great stake at issue which thus nerved and animated one and all to stand unawed and unshrinking in such extremity.

Two Federal brigades of Heintzelman's division were now brought into action, led by Rickett's superb light battery of six 10-pounder rifled guns, which, posted on an eminence to the right of the Sudley Road, opened fire on Imboden's battery—about this time increased by two rifled pieces of the Washington Artillery under Lieutenant Richardson, and already the mark of two batteries, which divided their fire with Imboden and two guns under Lieutenants Davidson and Leftwitch, of Latham's battery, posted as before mentioned. At this time confronting the enemy we had still but Evans' eleven companies and two guns, Bee's and Bartow's four regiments, the two companies, Eleventh Mississippi, under Lieutenant-Colonel Liddell, and the six pieces under Imboden and Richardson. The enemy had two divisions of four strong brigades, including seventeen companies of regular infantry, cavalry and artillery, four companies of marines and twenty pieces of artillery. Against this odds, scarcely credible, our advance position was still for awhile maintained and the enemy's ranks constantly broken and shattered under the scorching fire of our men; but fresh regiments of the Federalists came upon the field. Sherman's and Keyes' brigades of Tyler's division, as is stated in their reports, numbering over 6,000 bayonets, which had found a passage across the run about 800 yards above the Stone Bridge, threatened our right.

CONFEDERATE TROOPS PASSING ARLINGTON MILL ON ITS WAY TO MUNSON'S HILL.

Heavy losses had now been sustained on our side, both in numbers and in the personal worth of the slain. The Eighth Georgia Regiment had suffered heavily, being exposed, as it took and maintained its position, to a fire from the enemy, already posted within a hundred yards of their front and right, sheltered by fences and other cover. It was at this time that Lieutenant-Colonel Gardner was severely wounded, as also several other valuable officers. The adjutant of the regiment, Lieutenant Branch, was killed, and the horse of the regretted Bartow was shot under him. The Fourth Alabama also suffered severely from the deadly fire of the thousands of muskets which they so dauntlessly confronted under the immediate leadership of Bee himself. Its brave colonel (E. J. Jones) was dangerously wounded and many gallant officers fell, slain or *hors de combat*.

Now, however, with the surging mass of over 14,000 Federal infantry pressing on their front, and under the incessant fire of at least twenty pieces of artillery, with the fresh brigades of Sherman and Keyes approaching, the latter already in musket range, our lines gave back, but under orders from General Bee. The enemy, maintaining their fire, pressed their swelling masses onward as our shattered battalions retired. The slaughter for the moment was deplorable, and has filled many a Southern home with lifelong sorrow. Under this inexorable stress the retreat continued until arrested by the energy and resolution of General Bee, supported by Bartow and Evans, just in rear of the Robinson house, and Hampton's Legion, which had been already advanced and was in position near it. Imboden's battery, which had been handled with marked skill, but whose men were almost exhausted, and the two pieces of Walton's battery, under Lieutenant Richardson, being threatened by the enemy's infantry on the left and front, were also obliged to fall back. Imboden, leaving a disabled piece on the ground, retired until he met Jackson's brigade, while Richardson joined the main body of his battery near the Lewis house.

As our infantry retired from the extreme front the two 6-pounders of Latham's battery before mentioned fell back with excellent judgment to suitable positions in the rear, where an effective fire was maintained upon the still advancing lines of the Federalists, with damaging effect, until their ammunition was nearly exhausted, when they, too, were withdrawn in the near presence of the enemy and rejoined their captain.

From the point, previously indicated, where General Johnston and myself had established our headquarters, we heard the continuous roll of musketry and the sustained din of the artillery, which announced the serious outburst of the battle on our left flank, and we anxiously but confidently awaited similar sounds of conflict from our front at Centreville, resulting from the prescribed attack in that quarter by our right wing.

At 10:30 A. M., however, this expectation was dissipated, from Brigadier-General Ewell informing me, to my profound disappointment, that my orders for his advance had miscarried, but, in consequence of a communication from General D. R. Jones, he had just thrown his brigade across the stream at Union Mills. But, in my judgment, it was now too late for the effective execution of the contemplated movement, which must have required quite three hours for the troops to get into position for the attack. Therefore it became immediately necessary to depend on new combinations and other dispositions suited to the now pressing exigency. The movement of the right and center, already begun by Jones and Longstreet, was at once countermanded, with the sanction of General Johnston, and we arranged to meet the enemy on the field upon which he had chosen to give us battle.

Under these circumstances our reserves not already in movement were immediately ordered up to support our left flank, namely, Holmes' two regiments and battery of artillery, under Captain Lindsey Walker, of six guns, and Early's brigade. Two regiments from Bonham's brigade, with Kemper's four 6-pounders, were also called for, and with the sanction of General Johnston, Generals Ewell, Jones (D. R.), Longstreet and Bonham were directed to make a demonstration to their several fronts, to retain and engross the enemy's reserves, and any forces on their flank and at and around Centreville. Previously our respective chiefs of staff, Major Rhett and Colonel Jordan, had been left at my headquarters to hasten up and give directions to any troops that might arrive at Manassas.

These orders having been duly dispatched by staff officers, at 11 A. M. General Johnston and myself set out for the immediate field of action, which we reached in the rear of the Robinson and Widow Henry's houses at about 12 M., and just as the commands of Bee, Bartow and Evans had taken shelter in a wooded ravine behind the former, stoutly held at the time by Hampton with his legion, which had made a stand there after having previously been as far forward as the turnpike, where Lieutenant-Colonel Johnson, an officer of brilliant promise, was killed, and other severe losses were sustained.

Before our arrival upon the scene General Jackson had moved forward with his brigade of five Virginia regiments from his position in reserve and had judiciously taken post below the brim of the plateau, nearly east of the Henry house, and to the left of the ravine and woods occupied by the mingled remnants of Bee's, Bartow's and Evans' commands, with Imboden's battery and two of Stanard's pieces placed so as to play upon the oncoming enemy, supported in the immediate rear by Colonel J. F. Preston's and Lieutenant-Colonel Echol's regiments, on the right by Harper's and on the left by Allen's and Cummings' regiments.

As soon as General Johnston and myself reached the field we were occupied with the reorganization of the heroic troops, whose previous stand, with scarce a parallel, has nothing more valiant in all the pages of history, and whose losses fitly tell why at length their ranks had lost their cohesion.

It was now that General Johnston impressively and gallantly charged to the front with the colors of the Fourth Alabama Regiment by his side, all the field officers of the regiment having been previously disabled. Shortly afterward I placed S. R. Gist, Adjutant and Inspector-General of South Carolina, a volunteer aid of General Bee, in command of this regiment, and who led it again to the front as became its previous behavior.

As soon as we had thus rallied and disposed our forces I urged General Johnston to leave the immediate conduct of the field to me, while he, repairing to Portici, the Lewis house, should urge re-enforcements forward. At first he was unwilling; but reminded that one of us must do so, and that properly it was his place, he reluctantly, but fortunately, complied; fortunately, because from that position, by his energy and sagacity, his keen perception and anticipation of my needs, he so directed as to insure the success of the day.

As General Johnston departed for Portici Colonel Bartow reported to me with the remains of the Seventh Georgia Volunteers, Gartrell's, which I ordered him to post on the left of Jackson's line in the edge of the belt of pines bordering the southeastern rim of the plateau, on which the battle was now to rage so long and so fiercely.

Colonel William Smith's battalion of the Forty-ninth Virginia Volunteers having also come up by my orders, I placed it on the left of Gartrell's, as my extreme left at the time. Repairing then to the right, I placed Hampton's Legion, which had suffered greatly, on that flank, somewhat to the rear of Harper's regiment, and also the seven companies of the Eighth (Hunton's) Virginia Regiment, which, detached from Cocke's brigade by my orders and those of General Johnston, had opportunely reached the ground. These with Harper's regiment constituted a reserve to protect our right flank from an advance of the enemy from the quarter of the Stone Bridge, and served as a support for the line of battle which was formed on the right by Bee's and Evan's commands, in the center by four regiments of Jackson's brigade, with Imboden's four 6-pounders, Walton's five guns (two rifled), two guns (one piece rifled) of Stanard's and two 6-pounders of Roger's battery, the latter under Lieutenant Heaton, and on the left by Gartrell's reduced ranks and Colonel Smith's battalion, subsequently re-enforced, Falkner's Second Mississippi Regiment, and by another regiment of the Army of the Shenandoah, just arrived upon the field—the Sixth (Fisher's) North Carolina. Confronting the enemy at this time, my forces numbered at most not more than 6,500 infantry and artillerists, with but thirteen pieces of artillery and two companies (Carter's and Hoge's) of Stuart's cavalry.

The enemy's force now bearing hotly and confidently down on our position, regiment after regiment of the best equipped men that ever took the field according to their own official history of the day, was formed of Colonels Hunter's and Heintzelman's divisions, Colonels Sherman's and Keyes' brigades of Tyler's division, and of the formidable batteries of Ricketts, Griffin and Arnold (regulars) and Second Rhode Island and two Dahlgren howitzers—a force of over 20,000 infantry, seven companies of regular cavalry and twenty-four pieces of improved artillery. At the same time perilous heavy reserves of infantry and artillery hung in the distance around the Stone Bridge, Mitchell's, Blackburn's and Union Mills Fords, visibly ready to fall upon us, and I was also assured of the existence of other heavy corps at and around Centreville and elsewhere within convenient supporting distances.

Fully conscious of this portentous disparity of force, as I posted the lines for the encounter, I sought to infuse into the hearts of my officers and men the confidence and determined spirit of resistance to this wicked invasion of the homes of a free people which I felt. I informed them that re-enforcements would rapidly come to their support and that we must at all hazards hold our posts until re-enforced. I reminded them that we fought for our homes, our firesides and for the independence of our country. I urged them to the resolution of victory or death on that field. These sentiments were loudly cheered wheresoever proclaimed, and I then felt reassured of the unconquerable spirit of that army, which would enable us to wrench victory from the host then threatening us with destruction.

Oh, my country! I would readily have sacrificed my life and those of all the brave men around me to save your honor and to maintain your independence from the degrading yoke which those ruthless invaders had come to impose and render perpetual; and the day's issue has assured me that such emotions must have animated all under my command.

In the meantime the enemy had seized upon the plateau on which Robinson's and the Henry houses are situated—the position first occupied in the morning by General Bee before advancing to the support of Evans. Rickett's battery of six rifled guns, the pride of the Federalists, the object of their unstinted expenditure in outfit, and the equally powerful regular light battery of Griffin, were brought forward and placed in immediate action after having, conjointly with the batteries already mentioned, played from former positions with destructive effect upon our forward battalions.

The topographical features of the plateau, now become the stage of the contending armies, must be described in outline. A glance at the map* will show that it is inclosed on three sides by small water courses which empty into Bull Run within a few yards of each other a half-mile to the south of the Stone Bridge. Rising to an elevation of quite one hundred feet above the level of Bull Run at the bridge it falls off on three sides to the level of the inclosing streams in gentle slopes, but which are furrowed by ravines of irregular direction and length and studded with clumps and patches of young pines and oaks. The general direction of the crest of the plateau is oblique to the course of Bull Run in that quarter and to the Brentsville and Turnpike Roads, which intersect each other at right angles. Immediately surrounding the two houses before mentioned are small open fields of irregular outline not exceeding one hundred and fifty acres in extent. The houses, occupied at the time, the one by the Widow Henry and the other by the free negro Robinson, are small wooden buildings, the latter densely embowered in trees and environed by a double row of fences on two sides. Around the eastern and southern brow of the plateau an almost unbroken fringe of second-growth pines gave excellent shelter for our marksmen, who availed themselves of it with the most satisfactory skill. To the west, adjoining the fields, a broad belt of oaks extends directly across the crest on both sides of the Sudley Road, in which during the battle regiments of both armies met and contended for the mastery. From the open ground of this plateau the view embraces a wide expanse of woods and gently undulating open country of broad grass and grain fields in all directions, including the scene of Evans' and Bee's recent encounter with the enemy, some twelve hundred yards to the northward.

In reply to the play of the enemy's batteries our own artillery had not been either idle or unskillful. The ground occupied by our guns, on a level with that held by the batteries of the enemy, was an open space of limited extent behind a low undulation just at the eastern verge of the plateau, some five or six hundred yards from the Henry house. Here, as before said, thirteen pieces, mostly 6-pounders, were maintained in action; the several batteries of Imboden, Stanard, Pendleton (Rockbridge Artillery) and Alburtis, of the Army of the Shenandoah, and five guns of Walton's and Heaton's section of Rogers' battery, of the Army of the Potomac, alternating to some extent with each other and taking part as needed, all from the outset displaying that marvelous capacity of our people as artillerists which has made them, it would appear, at once the terror and admiration of the enemy. As was soon apparent the Federalists had suffered severely from our artillery and from the fire of our musketry on the right and especially from the left flank, placed under cover, within whose galling range they had been advanced; and we are told in their official reports how regiment after regiment thrown forward to dislodge us was broken, never to recover its entire organization on that field.

In the meantime, also, two companies of Stuart's cavalry (Carter's and Hoge's) made a dashing charge down the Centreville and Sudley Road upon the Fire Zouaves, then the enemy's right on the plateau, which added to their disorder wrought by our musketry on that flank. But still the press of the enemy was heavy in that quarter of the field, as fresh troops were thrown forward to outflank us, and some three guns of a battery, in an attempt to obtain a position, apparently to enfilade our batteries, were thrown so close to the Thirty-third Regiment, Jackson's brigade, that that regiment springing forward seized them, but with severe loss, and was subsequently driven back by an overpowering force of Federal musketry.

Now, full 2 o'clock P. M., I gave the order for the right of my line, except my reserves, to advance to recover the plateau. It was done with uncommon resolution and vigor, and at the same time Jackson's brigade pierced the enemy's center with the determination of veterans and the spirit of men who fought for a sacred cause; but it suffered seriously. With equal spirit the other parts of the line made the onset and the Federal lines were broken and swept back at all points from the open ground of the plateau. Rallying soon, however, as they were strongly re-enforced by fresh regiments, the Federalists returned, and by weight of numbers pressed our lines back, recovered their ground and guns and renewed the offensive.

By this time, between 2:30 and 3 o'clock P. M., our re-enforcements pushed forward, and directed by General Johnston to the required quarter, were at hand just as I had ordered forward, to a second effort for the recovery of the disputed plateau, the whole line, including my reserve, which at this crisis of the battle I felt called upon to lead in person. This attack was general, and was shared in by every regiment then in the field, including the Sixth (Fisher's) North Carolina Regiment, which had just come up and taken position on the immediate left of the Forty-ninth Virginia Regiment. The whole open ground was again swept clear of the enemy, and the plateau around the Henry and Robertson houses remained finally in our possession, with the greater part of Ricketts' and Griffin's batteries, and a flag of the First Michigan Regiment, captured by the Twenty-seventh Virginia Regiment, Lieutenant-Colonel Echols, of Jackson's brigade.

This part of the day was rich with the deeds of individual coolness and dauntless conduct, as well as well-directed embodied resolution and bravery, but fraught with the loss to the service of the country of lives of inestimable preciousness at this juncture. The brave Bee was mortally wounded at the head of the Fourth Alabama and some Mississippians. In the open field near the Henry house, a few yards distant, the promising life of Bartow, while leading the Seventh Georgia Regiment, was quenched in blood. Colonel F. J. Thomas, acting chief of ordnance, of General Johnston's staff, after gallant conduct and most efficient service, was also slain. Colonel Fisher, Sixth North Carolina, likewise fell, after soldierly behavior at the head of his regiment, with ranks greatly thinned.

Withers' Eighteenth Regiment, of Cocke's brigade, had come up in time to follow this charge, and, in conjunction with Hampton's Legion, captured several rifled pieces, which may have fallen previously in possession of some of our troops, but if so had been recovered by the enemy. These pieces were immediately turned and effectively served on distant masses of the enemy by the hands of some of our officers.

While the enemy had thus been driven back on our right entirely across the turnpike and beyond Young's Branch on our left, the woods yet swarmed with them, when re-enforcements opportunely arrived in quick succession and took position in that portion of the field. Kershaw's Second and Cash's Eighth South Carolina regiments, which had arrived soon after Withers', were led through the oaks just east of the Sudley-Brentsville Road, brushing some of the enemy before them, and taking an advantageous position along and west of that road, opened with much skill and effect on bodies of the enemy that had been rallied under cover of a strong Federal brigade posted on a plateau in the southwest angle formed by intersection of the turnpike with the Sudley-Brentsville Road. Among the troops thus engaged were the Federal regular infantry.

At the same time Kemper's battery, passing northward by the Sudley-Brentsville Road, took position on the open space, under orders of Colonel Kershaw, near where an enemy's battery had been captured, and was opened with effective results upon the Federal right, then the mark also of Kershaw's and Cash's regiments. Preston's Twenty-eighth Regiment, of Cocke's brigade, had by that time entered the same body of oaks, and encountered some Michigan troops, capturing their brigade commander, Colonel Wilcox.

Another important accession to our forces had also occurred about the same time, 3 o'clock P. M. Brigadier-General E. K. Smith, with some 1,700 infantry of Elzey's brigade, of the Army of the Shenandoah, and Beckham's battery, came upon the field from Camp Pickens, Manassas, where they had arrived by railroad at noon. Directed in person by General Johnston to the left, then so much endangered, on reaching a position in rear of the oak woods south of the Henry house and immediately east of the Sudley Road, General Smith was disabled by a severe wound, and his valuable services were lost at that critical juncture; but the command devolved upon a meritorious officer of experience, Colonel Elzey, who led his infantry at once somewhat further to the left, in the direction of the Chinn house, across the road, through the oaks skirting the west side of the road, and around which he sent the battery under Lieutenant Beckham. This officer took up a most favorable position near that house, whence with a clear view of the Federal right and center, filling the open fields to the west of the Brentsville-Sudley Road, and gently sloping southward, he opened fire with his battery upon them with deadly and damaging effect.

Colonel Early, who by some mischance did not receive orders until 2 o'clock which had been sent him at noon, came on the ground immediately after Elzey, with Kemper's Seventh Virginia, Hays' Seventh Louisiana and Barksdale's Thirteenth Mississippi regiments. This brigade, by the personal direction of General Johnston, was marched by the Holkam house across the fields to the left, entirely around the woods through which Elzey had

* Map not found.

From an original painting, copyrighted by Kurz & Allison, Chicago, Ill.

BATTLE OF MANASSAS (BULL RUN), JULY 21, 1861.

passed, and, under a severe fire, into a position in line of battle near Chinn's house, outflanking the enemy's right.

At this time, about 3:30 P. M., the enemy, driven back on their left and center, and brushed from the woods bordering the Sudley Road, south and west of the Henry house, had formed a line of battle of truly formidable proportions, of crescent outline, reaching on their left from vicinity of Pittsylvania (the old Carter mansion), by Mathews' and in rear of Dogan's, across the turnpike near to Chinn's house. The woods and fields were filled with their masses of infantry and their carefully preserved cavalry. It was a truly magnificent, though redoubtable spectacle as they threw forward in fine style, on the broad, gentle slopes of the ridge occupied by their main lines, a cloud of skirmishers, preparatory for another attack.

But as Early formed his line and Beckham's pieces played upon the right of the enemy, Elzey's brigade, Gibbon's Tenth Virginia, Lieutenant-Colonel Stewart's First Maryland, and Vaughn's Third Tennessee regiments, Cash's Eighth and Kershaw's Second South Carolina, Wither's Eighteenth and Preston's Twenty-eighth Virginia advanced in an irregular line, almost simultaneously, with great spirit, from their several positions upon the front and flanks of the enemy in their quarter of the field. At the same time, too, Early resolutely assailed their right flank and rear. Under this combined attack the enemy was soon forced, first, over the narrow plateau in the southern angle, made by the two roads so often mentioned, into a patch of woods on its western slope, thence back over Young's Branch and the turnpike into the fields of the Dogan farm and rearward, in extreme disorder, in all available directions toward Bull Run. The rout had now become general and complete.

About the time that Elzey and Early were entering into action a column of the enemy (Keyes' brigade of Tyler's division) made its way across the turnpike between Bull Run and the Robinson house, under cover of a wood and brow of the ridges, apparently to turn my right, but was easily repulsed by a few shots from Latham's battery, now united and placed in position by Captain D. B. Harris, of Virginia Engineers, whose services during the day became his character as an able, cool and skillful officer, and from Alburtis' battery, opportunely ordered by General Jackson to a position to the right of Latham, on a hill commanding the line of approach of the enemy, and supported by portions of regiments collected together by the staff officers of General Johnston and myself.

Early's brigade, meanwhile, joined by the Nineteenth Virginia Regiment, Lieutenant-Colonel Strange, of Cocke's brigade, pursued the now panic-stricken, fugitive enemy. Stuart, with his cavalry, and Beckham, had also taken up the pursuit along the road by which the enemy had come upon the field that morning, but soon, cumbered by prisoners who thronged his way, the former was unable to attack the mass of the fast-fleeing, frantic Federalists. Withers', R. T. Preston's, Cash's and Kershaw's regiments, Hampton's Legion and Kemper's battery also pursued along the Warrenton Road by the Stone Bridge, the enemy having opportunely opened a way for them through the heavy abatis which my troops had made on the west side of the bridge several days before; but this pursuit was soon recalled, in consequence of a false report which unfortunately reached us that the enemy's reserves, known to be fresh and of considerable strength, were threatening the position of Union Mills Ford.

Colonel Radford, with six companies of Virginia cavalry, was also ordered by General Johnston to cross Bull Run and attack the enemy from the direction of Lewis' house. Conducted by one of my aids, Colonel Chisolm, by the Lewis Ford to the immediate vicinity of the Suspension Bridge, he charged a battery with great gallantry, took Colonel Corcoran, of the Sixty-ninth Regiment of New York Volunteers, a prisoner, and captured the Federal colors of that regiment, as well as a number of the enemy. He lost, however, a promising officer of his regiment, Captain Winston Radford.

Lieutenant-Colonel Munford also led some companies of cavalry in hot pursuit, and rendered material service in the capture of prisoners, and of cannon, horses, ammunition, etc., abandoned by the enemy in their flight. Captain Lay's company of the Powhattan Troops and Utterback's Rangers, Virginia Volunteers, attached to my person, did material service under Captain Lay in rallying troops broken for the time by the onset of the enemy's masses.

During the period of the momentous events, fraught with the weal of our country, which were passing on the blood-stained plateau along the Sudley and Warrenton Roads, other portions of the line of Bull Run had not been void of action of moment and of influence on the general result.

While Colonel Evans and his sturdy band were holding at bay the Federal advance beyond the turnpike the enemy made repeated demonstrations with artillery and infantry upon the line of Cocke's brigade, with the serious intention of forcing the position, as General Schenck admits in his report. They were driven back with severe loss by Latham's (a section) and Roger's four 6-pounders, and were so impressed with the strength of that line as to be held in check and inactive, even after it had been stripped of all its troops but one company of the Nineteenth Virginia Regiment, under Captain Duke, a meritorious officer; and it is worthy of notice that in this encounter of our 6-pounder guns, handled by our volunteer artillerists, they had worsted such a notorious adversary as the Ayre's (formerly Sherman's) battery, which quit the contest under the illusion that it had weightier metal than its own to contend with.

The center brigades, Bonham's and Longstreet's, of the line of Bull Run, if not closely engaged, were, nevertheless, exposed for much of the day to an annoying, almost incessant fire of artillery of long range; but by a steady, veteran-like maintenance of their positions they held virtually paralyzed all day two strong brigades of the enemy, with their batteries (four) of rifled guns.

As before said, two regiments of Bonham's brigade—Second and Eighth South Carolina Volunteers—and Kemper's battery took a distinguished part in the battle. The remainder—Third (Williams') and Seventh (Bacon's) South Carolina Volunteers, the Eleventh (Kirkland's) North Carolina Regiment, six companies of the Eighth Louisiana Volunteers, Shields' battery, and one section of Walton's battery, under Lieutenant Garnett—whether in holding their post or taking up the pursuit, officers and men, discharged their duty with credit and promise.

Longstreet's brigade, pursuant to orders prescribing his part of the operations of the center and right wing, was thrown across Bull Run early in the morning, and under a severe fire of artillery was skillfully disposed for an assault of the enemy's batteries in that quarter, but was withdrawn subsequently, in consequence of the change of plan already mentioned and explained. The troops of this brigade were, First (Major Skinner), Eleventh (Garland's), Twenty-fourth (Lieutenant-Colonel Hairston), Seventeenth (Corse's), Virginia regiments; Fifth North Carolina (Lieutenant-Colonel Jones), and Whitehead's company of Virginia cavalry. Throughout the day these troops evinced the most soldierly spirit.

After the rout, having been ordered by General Johnston in the direction of Centreville in pursuit, these brigades advanced nearly to that place when, darkness intervening, General Bonham thought it proper to direct his own brigade and that of General Longstreet back to Bull Run.

General D. R. Jones early in the day crossing Bull Run with his brigade, pursuant to orders indicating his part of the projected attack by our right wing and center on the enemy at Centreville, took up a position on the Union Mills and Centreville Road, more than a mile in advance of the run. Ordered back, in consequence of the miscarriage of the orders to General Ewell, the retrograde movement was necessarily made under a sharp fire of artillery.

At noon this brigade, in obedience to new instructions, was again thrown across Bull Run to make demonstration. Unsupported by other troops, the advance was gallantly made until within musket range of the enemy's force—Colonel Davies' brigade, in position near Rocky Run—and under the concentrated fire of their artillery. In this affair the Fifth (Jenkins') South Carolina and Captain Fontaine's company of the Eighteenth Mississippi Regiment are mentioned by General Jones as having shown conspicuous gallantry, coolness and discipline under a combined fire of infantry and artillery. Not only did the return fire of the brigade drive to cover the enemy's infantry, but the movement unquestionably spread through the enemy's ranks a sense of insecurity and danger from an attack by that route on their rear at Centreville, which served to augment the extraordinary panic which we know disbanded the entire Federal army for the time.

This is evident from the fact that Colonel Davies, the immediate adversary's commander, in his official report, was induced to magnify one small company of our cavalry which accompanied the brigade into a force of 2,000 men; and Colonel Miles, the commander of the Federal reserves at Centreville, says the movement caused painful apprehensions for the left flank of their army.

General Ewell, occupying for the time the right of the line of Bull Run, at Union Mills Ford, after the miscarriage of my orders for his advance upon Centreville, in the afternoon was ordered by General Johnston to bring up his brigade into battle, then raging on the left flank. Promptly executed as this movement was, the brigade, after a severe march, reached the field too late to share the glories as they had the labors of the day. As the important position at the Union Mills had been left with but a slender guard, General Ewell was at once ordered to retrace his steps and resume his position, to prevent the possibility of its seizure by any force of the enemy in that quarter. Brigadier-General Holmes, left with his brigade as a support to the same position in the original plan of battle, had also been called to the left, whither he marched with the utmost speed, but not in time to join actively in the battle. Walker's rifled guns of the brigade, however, came up in time to be fired with precision and decided execution at the retreating enemy, and Scott's cavalry, joining in the pursuit, assisted in the capture of prisoners and war munitions.

This victory, the details of which I have thus sought to chronicle as fully as were fitting an official report, it remains to record, was dearly won by the death of many officers, and men of inestimable value, belonging to all grades of our society. In the death of General Bernard E. Bee the Confederacy sustained an irreparable loss, for, with great personal bravery and coolness, he possessed the qualities of an accomplished soldier and an able, reliable commander. Colonels Bartow and Fisher, and Lieutenant-Colonel Johnson, of Hampton's Legion, in the fearless command of their men, gave earnest of great usefulness to the service had they been spared to complete a career so brilliantly begun. Besides the field officers already mentioned as having been wounded while in the gallant discharge of their duties, many others also received severe wounds, after equally honorable and distinguished conduct, whether in leading their men forward or in rallying them when overpowered or temporarily shattered by the largely superior force to which we were generally opposed.

The conduct of General Jackson also requires mention as eminently that of an able, fearless soldier and sagacious commander—one fit to lead his efficient brigade. His prompt, timely arrival before the plateau of the Henry house, and his judicious disposition of his troops, contributed much to the success of the day. Although painfully wounded in the hand, he remained on the field to the end of the battle, rendering invaluable assistance.

Colonel William Smith was as efficient as self-possessed and brave. The influence of his example and his words of encouragement were not confined to his immediate command, the good conduct of which is especially noticeable, inasmuch as it had been embodied but a day or two before the battle.

Colonels Harper, Hunton and Hampton, commanding the reserve, attracted my notice by their soldierly ability, as with their gallant commands they restored the fortunes of the day at a time when the enemy, by a last desperate onset with heavy odds, had driven our forces from the fiercely contested ground around the Henry and Robinson houses. Veterans could not have behaved better than these well-led regiments. High praise must also be given to Colonels Cocke, Early and Elzey, brigade commanders; also to Colonel Kershaw, commanding for the time the Second and Eighth South Carolina regiments. Under the instructions of General Johnston these officers reached the field at an opportune, critical moment, and disposed, handled and fought their respective commands with sagacity, decision and successful results, which have been described in detail.

Colonel J. E. B. Stewart likewise deserves mention for his enterprise and ability as a cavalry commander. Through his judicious reconnoissance of the country on our flank he acquired information, both of topographical features and the positions of the enemy, of the utmost importance in the subsequent and closing movements of the day on that flank, and his services in the pursuit were highly effective.

Captain E. P. Alexander, Confederate States Engineer, gave me seasonable and material assistance early in the day with his system of signals.

It must be permitted me here to record my profound sense of my obligations to General Johnston for his generous permission to carry out my plans, with such modifications as circumstances had required. From his services on the field as we entered it together, already mentioned, and his subsequent watchful management of the re-enforcements as they reached the vicinity of the field, our countrymen may draw the most auspicious auguries.

While glorious for our people, and of crushing effect upon the *morale* of our hitherto confident and overweening adversary, as were the events of the battle of Manassas, the field was won only by stout fighting, and, as before reported, with much loss.

The actual loss of the enemy will never be known; it may now only be conjectured. Their abandoned dead, as they were buried by our people where they fell, unfortunately were not enumerated; but many parts of the field were thick with their corpses as but few battlefields have ever been. The official reports of the enemy are studiously silent on this point, but still afford us data for an approximate estimate. Left almost in the dark in respect to the losses of Hunter's and Heintzelman's divisions, first, longest and most hotly engaged, we are informed that Sherman's brigade, Tyler's division, suffered in killed, wounded and missing 609; that is about eighteen per cent of the brigade. A regiment of Franklin's brigade (Gorman's) lost twenty-one per cent; Griffin's (battery) loss was thirty per cent; and that of Keyes' brigade, which was so handled by its commander as to be exposed only to occasional volleys from our troops, was at least ten per cent. To these facts add the repeated references in the reports of the more reticent commanders to the "murderous" fire to which they were habitually exposed, the "pistol range" volleys and galling musketry of which they speak as scourging their ranks, and we are warranted in placing the entire loss of the Federalists at over 4,500 in killed, wounded and prisoners. To this may be legitimately added as a casualty of the battle the thousands of fugitives from the field who have never rejoined their regiments, and who are as much lost to the enemy's service as if slain or disabled by wounds. These may not be included under the head of missing, because in every instance of such report we took as many prisoners of those brigades or regiments as are reported missing.

A list appended exhibits some 1,460 of their wounded and others who fell into our hands and were sent to Richmond: namely, three colonels, one major, thirteen captains, thirty-six lieutenants, two quartermasters, five surgeons, seven assistant surgeons, two chaplains, fifteen citizens, and 1,376 enlisted men. Some were sent to other points, so that the number of prisoners, including wounded who did not die, may be set down as not less than 1,600.

twenty miles of their base of operations, has been converted into one virtually besieged and exclusively occupied for months in the construction of a stupendous series of fortifications for the protection of its own capitol.

In conclusion it is proper, and doubtless expected, that through this report my countrymen should be made acquainted with some of the sufficient causes that prevented the advance of our forces and prolonged vigorous pursuit of the enemy to and beyond the Potomac. The War Department has been fully advised long since of all those causes, some of which are only proper to be here communicated. An army which had fought as ours on that day, against uncommon odds, under a July sun, most of the time without water, and without food except a hastily snatched, scanty meal at dawn, was not in condition for the toil of an eager, effective pursuit of an enemy immediately after battle.

On the following day an unusually heavy, unintermitting fall of rain intervened to obstruct our advance with

SECOND BRIGADE.

BRIGADIER-GENERAL R. S. EWELL.

Fifth Alabama; Sixth Alabama; Sixth Louisiana.

THIRD BRIGADE.

BRIGADIER-GENERAL D. R. JONES.

Seventeenth Mississippi; Eighteenth Mississippi; Fifth South Carolina.

FOURTH BRIGADE.

BRIGADIER-GENERAL J. LONGSTREET.

Fifth North Carolina; First Virginia; Eleventh Virginia; Seventeenth Virginia.

FIFTH BRIGADE.

COLONEL P. ST. GEORGE COCKE.

First Louisiana battalion; Eighth Virginia, seven companies; Eighteenth Virginia; Nineteenth Virginia; Twenty-eighth Virginia; Forty-ninth Virginia, three companies.

GENERAL THOMAS J. ("STONEWALL") JACKSON AT THE BATTLE OF BULL RUN (FIRST MANASSAS) JULY 21, 1861. [Produced from a Photograph of an Oil Painting.]

Besides these, a considerable number who could not be removed from the field died at several farmhouses and field-hospitals within ten days following the battle.

To serve the future historian of this war, I will note the fact that among the captured Federalists are officers and men of forty-seven regiments of volunteers, besides from some nine different regiments of regular troops, detachments of which were engaged. From their official reports we learn of a regiment of volunteers engaged, six regiments of Miles' division and five regiments of Runyon's brigade from which we have neither sound nor wounded prisoners. Making all allowances for mistakes, we are warranted in saying that the Federal army consisted of at least fifty-five regiments of volunteers, eight companies of regular infantry, four of marines, nine of regular cavalry, and twelve batteries of forty-nine guns. These regiments at one time numbered in the aggregate 54,140, and average 964 each. From an order of the enemy's commander, however, dated July 13th, we learn that one hundred men from each regiment were directed to remain in charge of their respective camps. Some allowance must further be made for the sick and details, which would reduce the average to 800 men.

Added to these results may rightly be noticed here that by this battle an invading army, superbly equipped, within

reasonable prospect of fruitful results. Added to this, the want of a cavalry force of sufficient numbers made an efficient pursuit a military impossibility.

G. T. BEAUREGARD.

CONFEDERATE FORCES AT THE BATTLE OF MANASSAS (BULL RUN).

Organization at the dates indicated of the Confederate forces, combined at the battle of Manassas, under the command of Brigadier-General Johnston, C. S. A.

ARMY OF THE POTOMAC (AFTERWARD FIRST CORPS), JULY 21, 1861.*

BRIGADIER-GENERAL G. T. BEAUREGARD.

FIRST BRIGADE.

BRIGADIER-GENERAL M. L. BONHAM.

Eleventh North Carolina; Second South Carolina; Third South Carolina; Seventh South Carolina; Eighth South Carolina.

SIXTH BRIGADE.

COLONEL J. A. EARLY.

Thirteenth Mississippi; Fourth South Carolina; Seventh Virginia; Twenty-fourth Virginia.

TROOPS NOT BRIGADED.

Seventh Louisiana; Eighth Louisiana; Hampton Legion (S. C.); Thirtieth Virginia cavalry; Harrison's battalion, cavalry; independent companies (ten), cavalry; Washington (La.) battalion, artillery.

ARTILLERY.

Kemper's batttery; Latham's battery; Loudoun battery; Shields' battery; Camp Pickens companies.

"ARMY OF THE SHENANDOAH" (JOHNSTON'S DIVISION), JUNE 30, 1861.†

BRIGADIER-GENERAL JOSEPH E. JOHNSTON.

FIRST BRIGADE.

COLONEL T. J. JACKSON.

Second Virginia; Fourth Virginia; Fifth Virginia; Twenty-seventh Virginia; Pendleton's battery.

* From a field return of that date, but dated September 25, 1861. † From return of that date.

SECOND BRIGADE.

COLONEL F. S. BARTOW.

Seventh Georgia; Eighth Georgia; Ninth Georgia; Duncan's Kentucky battalion; Pope's Kentucky battalion; Alburtis' battery.

THIRD BRIGADE.

BRIGADIER-GENERAL B. E. BEE.

Fourth Alabama; Second Mississippi; Eleventh Mississippi; First Tennessee; Imboden's battery.

FOURTH BRIGADE.

COLONEL A. ELZEY.

First Maryland (battalion); Third Tennessee; Tenth Virginia; Thirteenth Virginia; Grove's battery.

NOT BRIGADED.

First Virginia Cavalry; Thirty-third Virginia.

TROOPS OF THE SHENANDOAH ARMY ENGAGED IN THE BATTLE OF MANASSAS.

HEADQUARTERS, ARMY OF THE POTOMAC,
August 25, 1861.

Colonel: In accordance with your request I send you a list of the regiments actually in the battle of the 21st of July, 1861:

JACKSON'S BRIGADE — Second Virginia Regiment, Colonel J. H. Allen commanding; Fourth Virginia Regiment, Colonel James F. Preston commanding; Fifth Virginia Regiment, Colonel Kenton Harper commanding; Twenty-seventh Virginia Regiment, Lieutenant-Colonel Echols commanding, Colonel Gordon absent; Thirty-third Virginia Regiment, Colonel A. C. Cummings commanding.

UNDER GENERAL BEE, consisting of a part of his own and a part of Colonel Bartow's brigade—Seventh and Eighth Georgia regiments, Bartow's; Second Mississippi Regiment, Fourth Alabama Regiment, Sixth North Carolina Regiment, and two companies Eleventh Mississippi Regiment, Bee's.

E. K. SMITH'S BRIGADE—Colonel Elzey's Tenth Virginia Regiment, Third Tennessee Regiment, and First Maryland Regiment.

BATTERIES IN ACTION—Colonel Pendleton's, four pieces; Captain Imboden's, four pieces; Captain Alburtis', four pieces; Captain Stanard's, four pieces, and Lieutenant Beckham's, four pieces.

CAVALRY—Colonel J. E. B. Stuart's, with twelve companies.

I can not furnish the strength of the regiments, companies, etc. Respectfully, your obedient servant,

THOMAS G. RHETT,
Assistant Adjutant-General.

COLONEL THOMAS JORDAN,
Assistant Adjutant-General,
First Corps, Army of the Potomac.

CASUALTIES IN THE ARMY OF THE POTOMAC (CONFEDERATE), JULY 21, 1861.*

FIRST CORPS. COMMAND.	Killed. Officers	Killed. Enlisted Men	Wo'nded Officers	Wo'nded Enlisted Men	Missing. Officers	Missing. Enlisted Men	Aggregate
First Louisiana Battalion		8	5	33	.	2	48
Seventh Louisiana	. .	3	.	23	. .	. .	26
Thirteenth Mississippi	. .	. .	. .	6	. .	. .	6
Seventeenth Mississippi	. .	2	. .	9	. .	. .	11
Eighteenth Mississippi	2	6	2	28	. .	. .	38
Fifth North Carolina	. .	1	. .	3	. .	. .	4
Second South Carolina	. .	5	6	37	. .	. .	48
Fourth South Carolina	1	10	9	70	. .	6	96
Fifth South Carolina	. .	3	. .	23	.	. .	26
Eighth South Carolina	. .	5	3	20	. .	. .	28
Hampton Legion	. .	19	. .	100	. .	2	121
First Virginia	. .	. .	.	6	. .	. .	6
Seventh Virginia	. .	9	1	37	. .	. .	47
Eighth Virginia	. .	6	. .	23	. .	1	30
Seventeenth Virginia	. .	1	. .	3	. .	. .	4
Eighteenth Virginia	. .	6	1	12	. .	. .	19
Nineteenth Virginia	. .	1	. .	4	. .	1	6
Twenty-eighth Virginia	. .	. .	. .	9	. .	.	9
Forty-ninth Virginia	1	9	1	29	. .	. .	40
Artillery.							
Alexandria Light Artillery	. .	1	. .	2	. .	. .	3
Latham's	. .	. .	. .	1	. .	. .	1
Loudoun	. .	. .	. .	3	. .	. .	3
Washington (La.)	. .	1	. .	2	. .	.	3
Cavalry.							
Thirtieth Virginia	2	3		4	. .	. .	9
Hanover	. .	. .	1	3	. .	. .	4
Total	6	99	29	490	. .	12	636

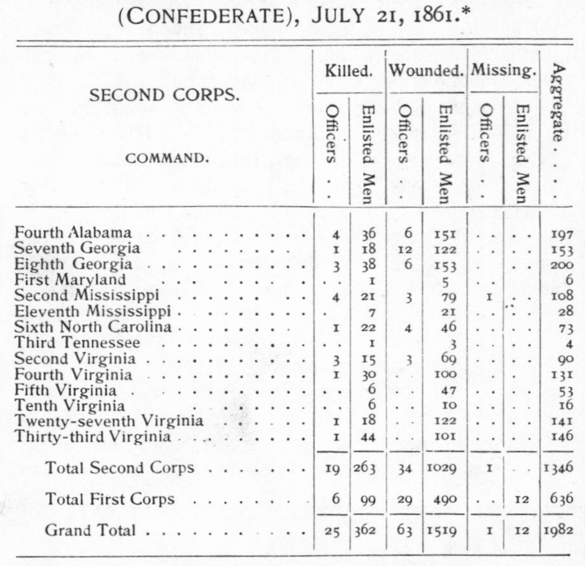

CASUALTIES IN THE ARMY OF THE POTOMAC (CONFEDERATE), JULY 21, 1861.*

SECOND CORPS. COMMAND.	Killed. Officers	Killed. Enlisted Men	Wounded. Officers	Wounded. Enlisted Men	Missing. Officers	Missing. Enlisted Men	Aggregate
Fourth Alabama	4	36	6	151	. .	. .	197
Seventh Georgia	1	18	12	122	. .	. .	153
Eighth Georgia	3	38	6	153	.	. .	200
First Maryland	. .	1		5	. .		6
Second Mississippi	4	21	3	79	1	. .	108
Eleventh Mississippi	.	7		21	. .	. .	28
Sixth North Carolina	1	22	4	46	. .	. .	73
Third Tennessee	. .	1		3	. .	. .	4
Second Virginia	3	15	3	69	. .	. .	90
Fourth Virginia	1	30	. .	100	. .	.	131
Fifth Virginia	. .	6	. .	47	. .	. .	53
Tenth Virginia	. .	6	. .	10	. .	. .	16
Twenty-seventh Virginia	1	18	. .	122	. .	. .	141
Thirty-third Virginia	1	44	. .	101	. .	. .	146
Total Second Corps	19	263	34	1029	1	. .	1346
Total First Corps	6	99	29	490	. .	12	636
Grand Total	25	362	63	1519	1	12	1982

* Compiled from the several reports and returns. The First Corps was known as the Army of the Potomac; the Second, as the Army of the Shenandoah.

STRENGTH OF THE UNION ARMY AT BATTLE OF MANASSAS (BULL RUN), JULY 21, 1861.

(As reported by Confederate authority.)

Command	Strength
Burnside's brigade	4,272
Porter's brigade	4,453
Wilcox's brigade	3,810
Franklin's brigade	2,115
Howard's brigade	4,030
Sherman's brigade	4,452
Keyes' brigade	3,230
Schenck's brigade	3,060
Richardson's brigade	3,920
Davies' brigade	4,129
Blenker's brigade	3,922
Runyon's division	6,392
Unattached infantry	6,085
Unattached artillery	270
Total	54,140

THOMAS JORDAN, *Ass't Adjutant General.*

A PROCLAMATION BY GOVERNOR LETCHER OF VIRGINIA.

RICHMOND, May 3, 1861.

The sovereignty of the Commonwealth of Virginia having been denied, her territorial rights assailed, her soil threatened with invasion by the authorities at Washington, and every artifice employed which could inflame the people of the Northern States and misrepresent our purpose and wishes, it becomes the solemn duty of every citizen of this State to prepare for the impending conflict. These misrepresentations have been carried to such an extent that foreigners and naturalized citizens, who but a few years ago were denounced by the North and deprived of essential rights, have now been induced to enlist into regiments for the purpose of invading this State, which then vindicated those rights and effectually resisted encroachments which threatened their destruction. Against such a policy, and against a force which the Government at Washington, relying upon its numerical strength, is now rapidly concentrating, it becomes the State of Virginia to prepare proper safeguards. To this end, for these purposes, and with a determination to repel invasion, I, John Letcher, Governor of the Commonwealth of Virginia, by authority of the Convention, do hereby authorize the commanding general of the military forces of this State to call out and cause to be mustered into the service of Virginia, from time to time, as the public exigencies may require, such additional number of volunteers as he may deem necessary.

To facilitate this call the annexed schedule will indicate the places of rendezvous, at which the companies called for will assemble upon receiving orders for service. Given under my hand as Governor, and under the seal of the Commonwealth, at Richmond, this 3d day of May, 1861, and in the eighty-fifth year of the Commonwealth.

JOHN LETCHER.

By the Governor.

GEORGE W. MUNFORD,
Secretary of the Commonwealth.

ABSTRACT FROM FIELD RETURN, FIRST CORPS ARMY OF THE POTOMAC (CONFEDERATE), JULY 21, 1861.

[DATED SEPTEMBER 25, 1861.]

COMMANDS.	General and Staff Officers	Infantry. Officers	Infantry. Men	Cavalry. Officers	Cavalry. Men	Artillery. Officers	Artillery. Men	REMARKS.
First Brigade	4	211	4,070					
Second Brigade	4	133	2,307					
Third Brigade	4	128	1,989					
Fourth Brigade	4	160	2,364					
Fifth Brigade	3	208	3,065					
Sixth Brigade	3	261	2,356					
Seventh Louisiana		44	773					
Eighth Louisiana		43	803					
Hampton Legion		27	627					This table shows the actual strength of Confederate forces on the battlefield of Manassas.
Thirtieth Virginia				34	642			
Harrison's Battalion, three companies				13	196			
Troops (ten) of cavalry				38	545			
Washington (La.) Artillery						19	201	
Kemper's Battery						4	76	
Latham's Battery						4	86	
Loudoun's Battery						3	55	
Shields' Battery						3	82	
Camp Pickens (heavy artillery)						18	275	
Total	22	1,215	18,354	85	1,383	51	775	

AGGREGATES.

Infantry	19,569
Cavalry	1,468
Artillery	826
Total	21,863

ABSTRACT FROM FIELD RETURN OF THE TROOPS (OF FIRST CORPS, CONFEDERATE) ENGAGED AT THE BATTLE OF MANASSAS.

[DATED SEPTEMBER 25, 1861.]

COMMANDS.	General Staff	Infantry. Officers	Infantry. Men	Cavalry. Officers	Cavalry. Men	Artillery. Officers	Artillery. Men	Guns	REMARKS.*
First Brigade		83	1,444						Second and Eighth South Carolina regiments.
Fifth Brigade	3	208	3,065						First Special Louisiana Battalion, seven companies; Eighth Virginia, three companies; Forty-ninth Virginia, and the Eighteenth, Nineteenth and Twenty-Eighth Virginia regiments.
Sixth Brigade	3	117	1,655						Thirteenth Mississippi, Fourth South Carolina and Seventh Virginia regiments.
Seventh Louisiana		54	773						
Eighth Louisiana, six companies		27	481						
Hampton Legion, six companies		27	600						
Thirtieth Virginia, ten companies				34	642				Not more than 500 of the Cavalry engaged on the 21st.
Cavalry, eight troops				29	444				
Washington Artillery, one company						4	56	5	6-pounders—two rifled, three smooth-bore.
Kemper's Battery						4	76	4	6-pounders, smooth-bore.
Latham's Battery						4	86	4	
Loudoun's Battery						3	55	4	
Total	6	516	8,018	63	1,086	15	273	17	Aggregate, 9,994.

* The returns of Casualties show losses in organizations not embraced in this return.

BATTLE OF MANASSAS (BULL RUN)

JULY 21, 1861.

BY

GENERAL JOSEPH E. JOHNSTON,

Commanding Confederate Armies of the Shenandoah and Potomac.

HEADQUARTERS ARMY OF THE POTOMAC,
FAIRFAX COURTHOUSE, October 14, 1861.

I ASSUMED command at Harper's Ferry on the 23d of May. The force at that point then consisted of nine regiments and two battalions of infantry, four companies of artillery, with sixteen pieces without caissons, harness or horses, and about three hundred cavalry. They were, of course, undisciplined, several regiments without accouterments, and with an entirely inadequate supply of ammunition.

I lost no time in making a complete reconnoissance of the place and its environs, in which the chief engineer, Major (now Brigadier-General) Whiting, ably assisted. The result confirmed my preconceived ideas. The position is untenable by any force not strong enough to take the field against an invading army and to hold both sides of the Potomac.

It is a triangle, two sides being formed by the Potomac and the Shenandoah, and the third by Furnace Ridge itself, the only defensible position; which, however, required, for its adequate occupation, double our numbers and was exposed to enfilade and reverse fires of artillery from heights on the Maryland side of the river. Within that line the ground was more favorable to an attacking than to a defending force. The Potomac can be easily crossed at many points above and below, so that it is easily turned. It is twenty miles from the great route into the Valley of Virginia from Pennsylvania and Maryland by which General Patterson's approach was expected. Its garrison was thus out of position to defend that valley or to prevent General McClellan's junction with General Patterson. These were the obvious and important objects to be kept in view. Besides being in position for them, it was necessary to be able on emergency to join General Beauregard.

I was employed until the 15th of June in continuing what had been begun by my predecessor, Colonel (now Major-General) Jackson—the organization, instruction and equipment of the troops, and providing means of transportation and artillery horses. The river was observed from the Point of Rocks to the western part of the county of Berkeley, the most distant portions by the indefatigable Stuart with his cavalry. General Patterson's troops were within a few hours of Williamsport, and General McClellan's, in Western Virginia, was supposed to be approaching to effect a junction with Patterson, whose force was reported by well-informed persons to be 18,000 men.

On the morning of the 16th intelligence was received that General Patterson's army had crossed the Potomac at Williamsport; also that the United States force at Romney had fallen back. A courier from Richmond brought a dispatch authorizing me to evacuate Harper's Ferry at my discretion. The army was ordered to gain the Martinsburg turnpike by a flank movement to Bunker Hill, in order to place itself between Winchester and the expected advance of Patterson. On hearing of this the enemy recrossed the river precipitately.

Intelligence from Maryland indicating another movement by Patterson, Colonel Jackson with his brigade was sent to the neighborhood of Martinsburg to support Colonel Stuart. The latter officer had been placed in observation on the line of the Potomac with his cavalry, his unceasing vigilance and activity relied on to repress the small incursions of the enemy, to give intelligence of invasions by them, and to watch, harass and circumscribe their every movement. Colonel Jackson was instructed to destroy such of the rolling stock of the Baltimore and Ohio Railroad as could not be brought off, and to have as much of it as could be made available to our service brought to Winchester.

Major Whiting was ordered to plan defensive works, to have some heavy guns and navy carriages mounted. About 2,500 militia, under Brigadier-General Carson, were called out from Frederick and the neighboring counties to man them.

On the 2d of July General Patterson again crossed the Potomac. Colonel Jackson, pursuant to instructions, fell back before him. In retiring he gave him a severe lesson in the affair at Falling Waters. With a battalion of the Fifth Virginia Regiment (Harper's) and Pendleton's battery of field artillery he engaged the enemy's advance. Skillfully taking a position where the smallness of his force was concealed, he engaged them for a considerable time, inflicted a heavy loss, and retired when about to be outflanked, scarcely losing a man, but bringing off forty-five prisoners.

Upon this intelligence the army, strengthened by the arrival of General Bee, and Colonel Elzey, and the Ninth Georgia Regiment, was ordered forward to the support of Jackson. It met him at Darkesville, six miles from Martinsburg, where it took up a position for action, as General Patterson, it was supposed, was closely following Colonel Jackson. We waited for him in this position four days, hoping to be attacked by an adversary at least double our numbers, but unwilling to attack him in a town so defensible as Martinsburg, with its solid buildings and inclosures of masonry. Convinced at last that he would not approach us, I returned to Winchester, much to the disappointment of our troops, who were eager for battle with the invaders. Colonel Stuart, with his cavalry, as usual remained near the enemy.

Before the 15th of July the enemy's force, according to the best intelligence to be obtained, amounted to about 32,000. Ours had been increased by eight Southern regiments. On the 15th of July Colonel Stuart reported the advance of General Patterson from Martinsburg. He halted, however, at Bunker Hill, nine miles from Winchester, where he remained on the 16th. On the 17th he moved to his left to Smithfield. This created the impression that he intended to attack us on the south, or was merely holding us in check while General Beauregard should be attacked at Manassas by General Scott. About one o'clock on the morning of July 18th I received from the government a telegraphic dispatch informing me that the Northern army was advancing upon Manassas, then held by General Beauregard, and directing me, if practicable, to go to that officer's assistance, after* sending my sick to Culpeper Courthouse. In the exercise of the discretion conferred by the terms of the order, I at once determined to march to join General Beauregard. The best service which the Army of the Shenandoah could render was to prevent the defeat of that of the Potomac. To be able to do this it was necessary, in the first instance, to defeat General Patterson or to elude him. The latter course was the most speedy and certain, and was, therefore, adopted. Our sick, nearly 1,700 in number, were provided for in Winchester. For the defense of that place the militia of Generals Carson and Meem seemed ample, for I thought it certain that General Patterson would follow my movement as soon as he discovered it. Evading him by the disposition made of the advance guard, under Colonel Stuart, the army moved through Ashby's Gap to Piedmont, a station of the Manassas Gap Railroad. Hence the infantry were to be transported by the railway, while the cavalry and artillery were ordered to continue their march.

GENERAL JOSEPH E. JOHNSTON.

I reached Manassas about noon on the 20th, preceded by the Seventh and Eighth Georgia regiments and by Jackson's brigade, consisting of the Second, Fourth, Fifth, Twenty-seventh and Thirty-third Virginia regiments. I was accompanied by General Bee, with the Fourth Alabama, the Second and two companies of the Eleventh Mississippi. The president of the railroad company had assured me that the remaining troops should arrive during the day. I found General Beauregard's position too extensive, and the ground too densely wooded and intricate, to be learned in the brief time at my disposal, and therefore determined to rely upon his knowledge of it and of the enemy's positions. This I did readily from full confidence in his capacity.

His troops were divided into eight brigades, occupying the defensive line of Bull Run. Brigadier-General Ewell's was posted at the Union Mills Ford; Brigadier-General D. R. Jones' at McLean's Ford; Brigadier-General Longstreet's at Blackburn's Ford; Brigadier-General Bonham's at Mitchell's Ford; Colonel Cocke's at Ball's Ford, some three miles above, and Colonel Evans, with a regiment and battalion, formed the extreme left at the Stone Bridge. The brigades of Brigadier-General Holmes and Colonel Early were in reserve in rear of the right. I regarded the arrival of the remainder of the Army of the Shenandoah during the night as certain, and Patterson's junction with the Grand Army on the 22d as probable.

During the evening it was determined, instead of remaining in the defensive positions then occupied, to assume the offensive and attack the enemy before such a junction. General Beauregard proposed a plan of battle, which I approved without hesitation. He drew up the necessary order during the night, which was approved formally by me at half-past four o'clock on the morning of the 21st. The early movements of the enemy on that morning and the non-arrival of the expected troops prevented its execution. General Beauregard afterward proposed a modification of the abandoned plan—to attack with our right while the left stood on the defensive. This, too, became impracticable, and a battle ensued different in place and circumstances from any previous plan on our side.

Soon after sunrise on the morning of the 21st a light cannonade was opened upon Colonel Evans' position. A similar demonstration was made against the center soon after, and strong forces were observed in front of it and of the right. About eight o'clock General Beauregard and I placed ourselves on a commanding hill in rear of General Bonham's left. Near nine o'clock the signal officer, Captain Alexander, reported that a large body of troops was crossing the Valley of Bull Run some two miles above the bridge. General Bee, who had been placed near Colonel Cocke's position, Colonel Hampton, with his legion, and Colonel Jackson, from a point near General Bonham's left, were ordered to hasten to the left flank. The signal officer soon called our attention to a heavy cloud of dust to the northwest and about ten miles off, such as the march of an army would raise. This excited apprehensions of General Patterson's approach.

The enemy, under cover of a strong demonstration on our right, made a long detour through the woods on his right, crossed Bull Run two miles above our left, and threw himself upon the flank and rear of our position. This movement was fortunately discovered by us in time to check its progress, and ultimately to form a new line of battle nearly at right angles with the defensive line of Bull Run.

On discovering that the enemy had crossed the stream above him, Colonel Evans moved to the left with eleven companies and two field-pieces to oppose his advance, and disposed his little force under cover of the wood near the intersection of the Warrenton Turnpike and the Sudley Road. Here he was attacked by the enemy in immensely superior numbers, against which he maintained himself with skill and unshrinking courage. General Bee, moving toward the enemy, guided by the firing, had, with a soldier's eye, selected the position near the Henry house, and formed his troops upon it. They were the Seventh and Eighth Georgia, Fourth Alabama, Second Mississippi, and two companies of the Eleventh Mississippi, with Imboden's battery. Being compelled, however to sustain Colonel Evans, he crossed the valley and formed on the right, and somewhat in advance of his position. Here the joint force, little exceeding five regiments with six field-pieces, held the ground against about fifteen thousand United States troops for an hour, until, finding themselves outflanked by the continually arriving troops of the enemy, they fell back to General Bee's first position, upon the line of which Jackson, just arriving, formed his brigade and Stanard's battery. Colonel Hampton, who had by this time advanced with his legion as far as the turnpike, rendered efficient service in maintaining the orderly character of the retreat

* This word erased from some official copies of the report. See Mr. Davis' indorsment accompanying this account of battle.

from that point; and here fell the gallant Lieutenant-Colonel Johnson, his second in command.

In the meantime I waited with General Beauregard, near the center, for the full development of the enemy's designs. About 11 o'clock the violence of the firing on the left indicated a battle, and the march of a large body of troops from the enemy's center toward the conflict was shown by clouds of dust. I was thus convinced that his great effort was to be made with his right. I stated that conviction to General Beauregard, and the absolute necessity of immediately strengthening our left as much as possible. Orders were accordingly at once sent to General Holmes and Colonel Early to move with all speed to the sound of the firing, and to General Bonham to send up two of his regiments and a battery. General Beauregard and I then hurried at a rapid gallop to the scene of action, about four miles off. On the way I directed my chief of artillery, Colonel Pendleton, to follow with his own and Alburtis' batteries.

We came not a moment too soon. The long contest against five-fold odds, and heavy losses, especially of field officers, had greatly discouraged the troops of General Bee and Colonel Evans. Our presence with them under fire and some example had the happiest effect on the spirit of the troops. Order was soon restored and the battle re-established, to which the firmness of Jackson's brigade greatly contributed. Then, in a brief and rapid conference, General Beauregard was assigned to the command of the left, which, as the younger officer, he claimed, while I returned to that of the whole field. The aspect of affairs was critical, but I had full confidence in the skill and indomitable courage of General Beauregard, the high soldierly qualities of Generals Bee and Jackson and Colonel Evans, and the devoted patriotism of their troops.

Orders were first dispatched to hasten the march of General Holmes', Colonel Early's and General Bonham's regiments. General Ewell was also directed to follow with all speed. Many of the broken troops, fragments of companies and individual stragglers, were reformed and brought into action with the aid of my staff and a portion of General Beauregard's. Colonel (late Governor) Smith with his battalion, and Colonel Hunton with his regiment, were ordered up to re-enforce the right. Colonel Smith's cheerful courage had a fine influence not only upon the spirit of his own men, but upon the stragglers of the troops engaged. The largest body of these, equal to about four companies, having no competent field officer, I placed under the command of one of my staff, Colonel F. J. Thomas, who fell while gallantly leading it against the enemy. These re-enforcements were all sent to the right to re-establish more perfectly that part of our line. Having attended to these pressing duties at the immediate scene of conflict, my eye was next directed to Colonel Cocke's brigade, the nearest at hand. Hastening to his position, I desired him to lead his troops into action. He informed me, however, that a large body of the enemy's troops beyond the stream and below the bridge threatened us from that quarter. He was, therefore, left in his position.

My headquarters were now established near the Lewis house. From this commanding elevation my view embraced the position of the enemy beyond the stream and the approaches to the Stone Bridge, a point of especial importance. I could also see the advances of our troops far down the valley in the direction of Manassas, and observe the progress of the action and the maneuvers of the enemy.

We had now sixteen guns and two hundred and sixty cavalry, and a little above nine regiments of the army of the Shenandoah and six guns, and less than the strength of three regiments of that of the Potomac, engaged with about 35,000 United States troops, among whom were fully 3,000 of the old Regular Army. Yet this admirable artillery and brave infantry and cavalry lost no foot of ground. For nearly three hours they maintained their position, repelling five successive assaults by the heavy masses of the enemy, whose numbers enabled him continually to bring up fresh troops as their preceding columns were driven back. Colonel Stuart contributed to one of these repulses by a well-timed and vigorous charge on the enemy's right flank with two companies of his cavalry.

The efficiency of our infantry and cavalry might have been expected from a patriotic people accustomed like ours to the management of arms and horses, but that of the artillery was little less than wonderful. They were opposed to batteries far superior in the number, range and equipment of their guns, with educated officers and thoroughly instructed soldiers. We had but one educated artillerist, Colonel Pendleton, that model of a Christian soldier, yet they exhibited as much superiority to the enemy in skill as in courage. Their fire was superior both in rapidity and precision.

About 2 o'clock an officer of General Beauregard's Adjutant-General's office galloped from Manassas to report to me that a United States army had reached the line of the Manassas Gap Railroad, was marching toward us, and then but three or four miles from our left flank. The expected re-enforcements appeared soon after. Colonel Cocke was then desired to lead his brigade into action to support the right of the troops engaged, which he did with alacrity and effect. Within a half hour the two regiments of General Bonham's brigade (Cash's and Kershaw's) came up, and were directed against the enemy's right, which he seemed to be strengthening. Fisher's North Carolina Regiment was soon after sent in the same direction. About 3 o'clock, while the enemy seemed to be striving to outflank and drive back our left, and thus separate us from Manassas, General E. K. Smith arrived with three regiments of Elzey's brigade. He was instructed to attack the right flank of the enemy, now exposed to us. Before the movement was completed he fell severely wounded. Colonel Elzey, at once taking command, executed it with great promptitude and vigor. General Beauregard rapidly seized the opportunity thus afforded him, and threw forward his whole line. The enemy was driven back from the long-contested hill, and victory was no longer doubtful.

HARPER'S FERRY, 1861.

He made yet another attempt to retrieve the day. He again extended his right with a still wider sweep to turn our left. Just as he reformed to renew the battle Colonel Early's three regiments came upon the field. The enemy's new formation exposed his right flank more even than the previous one. Colonel Early was, therefore, ordered to throw himself directly upon it, supported by Colonel Stuart's cavalry and Beckham's battery. He executed this attack bravely and well, while a simultaneous charge was made by General Beauregard in front. The enemy was broken by this combined attack. He lost all the artillery which he advanced to the scene of the conflict. He had no more fresh troops to rally on, and a general rout ensued.

Instructions were instantly sent to General Bonham to march by the quickest route to the turnpike to intercept the fugitives, and to General Longstreet to follow as closely as possible upon the right. Their progress was checked by the enemy's reserve and by night at Centreville. Schenck's brigade made a slight demonstration toward Lewis' Ford, which was quickly checked by Holmes' brigade, which had just arrived from the right. His artillery, under Captain Walker, was used with great skill. Colonel Stuart pressed the pursuit on the enemy's principal line of retreat, the Sudley Road. Four companies of cavalry, under Colonel Radford and Lieutenant-Colonel Munford, which I had held in reserve, were ordered to cross the stream at Ball's Ford to reach the turnpike, the line of retreat of the enemy's left. Our cavalry found the roads encumbered with dead and wounded (many of whom seemed to have been thrown from wagons), arms, accouterments and clothing.

A report came to me from the right that a strong body of United States troops was advancing upon Manassas. General Holmes, who had just reached the field, and General Ewell, on his way to it, were ordered to meet this unexpected attack. They found no foe, however.

Our victory was as complete as one gained by infantry and artillery can be. An adequate force of cavalry would have made it decisive. It is due, under Almighty God, to the skill and resolution of General Beauregard, the admirable conduct of Generals Bee, E. K. Smith and Jackson, and of Colonels (commanding brigades) Evans, Cocke, Early and Elzey, and the courage and unyielding firmness of our patriotic volunteers. The admirable character of our troops is incontestably proved by the result of the battle, especially when it is remembered that little more than 6,000 men of the Army of the Shenandoah with sixteen guns, and less than 2,000 of that of the Potomac with six guns, for full five hours successfully resisted 35,000 United States troops with a powerful artillery and a superior force of regular cavalry. . . . The brunt of this hard-fought engagement fell upon the troops who held their ground so long with such heroic resolution. The unfading honor which they won was dearly bought with the blood of many of our best and bravest. Their loss was far heavier in proportion than that of the troops coming later into action.

Every regiment and battery engaged performed its part well. The loss of the Army of the Potomac was 108 killed, 510 wounded and twelve missing. That of the Army of the Shenandoah was 270 killed, 979 wounded and eighteen missing. Total killed, 378; wounded, 1,489; missing, thirty. That of the enemy could not be ascertained. It must have been four or five thousand.

Twenty-eight pieces of artillery, about 5,000 muskets, and nearly 500,000 cartridges, a garrison flag and ten colors were captured on the field or in the pursuit. Besides these, we captured sixty-four artillery horses with their harness, twenty-six wagons, and much camp equipage, clothing and other property abandoned in their flight.

It will be remarked that the three Brigadier-Generals of the Army of the Shenandoah were all wounded. I have already mentioned the wound of General Smith. General Jackson, though painfully wounded early in the day, commanded his brigade until the close of the action. General Bee, after great exposure at the commencement of the engagement, was mortally wounded just as our re-enforcements were coming up.

The apparent firmness of the United States troops at Centreville, who had not been engaged, which checked our pursuit; the strong forces occupying the works near Georgetown, Arlington and Alexandria; the certainty, too, that General Patterson, if needed, would reach Washington with his army of thirty thousand men sooner than we could, and the condition and inadequate means of the army in ammunition, provisions and transportation, prevented any serious thoughts of advancing against the capital. It is certain that the fresh troops within the works were in number quite sufficient for their defense. If not, General Patterson's army would certainly re-enforce them soon enough. . . . .

J. E. JOHNSTON, *General.*

(INDORSEMENT.)

The telegram referred to by General Johnston in this report as received by him "about one o'clock on the morning of the 18th of July" is inaccurately reported. The following is a copy:

RICHMOND, July 17, 1861.

General J. E. Johnston, Winchester, Va.:

General Beauregard is attacked. To strike the enemy a decisive blow, a junction of all your effective force will be needed. If practicable make the movement, sending your sick and baggage to Culpeper Courthouse, either by railroad or by Warrenton. In all arrangements exercise your discretion.

S. COOPER,
Adjutant and Inspector General.

The word "after" is not found in the dispatch before the words "sending your sick," as is stated in the report, so that the argument based on it requires no comment. The order to move "if practicable" had reference to General Johnston's letters of 12th and 15th July, representing the relative strength and positions of the enemy under Patterson and of his own forces to be such as to make it doubtful whether General Johnston had the power to effect the movement.

JEFFERSON DAVIS.

ORIGIN OF THE CONFEDERATE BATTLE FLAG.

(SEE FLAG NO. 2, PAGE 5.)

[The facts concerning the origin of the battle flag contained in this article are derived from a speech by General Beauregard before a special meeting of Louisiana Division, Army of Northern Virginia Association, December 6, 1878.—EDITOR.]

This banner, the witness and inspiration of many victories, which was proudly borne on every field from Manassas to Appomattox, was conceived on the field of battle—lived on the field of battle—and on the last fatal field ceased to have place or meaning in the world.

FAIRFAX COURTHOUSE. HEADQUARTERS OF GENERAL BEAUREGARD.

But the men who followed it, and the world which watched its proud advance or defiant stand, see in it still the unstained banner of a true and generous people, whose deeds have outlived their country, and whose final defeat but added luster to their grandest victories.

It was not the flag of the Confederacy, but simply the banner—the battle flag—of the Confederate soldier. As such it should not share in the condemnation which our *cause* received, or suffer from its downfall. The whole world can unite in a chorus of praise to the gallantry of the men who followed where this banner led.

It was at the battle of Manassas, about 4 o'clock of the afternoon of the 21st of July, 1861, when the fate of the Confederacy seemed trembling in the balance, that General Beauregard, looking across the valley between the position of the Confederates and the elevations beyond occupied by the Federal line, saw a body of troops moving toward his left, and the Federal right. He was greatly concerned to know, but could not decide, what troops they were—whether Federal or Confederate. The similarity of uniform and of the colors carried by the opposing armies, and the clouds of dust, made it almost impossible to decide.

Shortly before this time General Beauregard had received from the signal officer, Captain Alexander, a dispatch saying that from the signal station in the rear he had sighted the colors of this column, drooping and covered with the dust of journeyings, but could not tell whether they were the stars and stripes or the stars and bars. He thought, however, that they were probably Patterson's troops arriving on the field and re-enforcing the enemy. General Beauregard was momentarily expecting help from the right, and the uncertainty and anxiety of this hour amounted to anguish.

Still the column pressed on. Calling a staff officer, General Beauregard instructed him to go at once to General Johnston, at the Lewis house, and say that the enemy were receiving heavy re-enforcements, that the troops on the plateau were very much scattered, and that he would be compelled to retire to the Lewis house and there reform—hoping that the troops ordered up from the right would arrive in time to enable him to establish and hold the new line.

Meanwhile, the unknown troops were pressing on. The day was sultry, and only at long intervals was there the slightest breeze. The colors of the mysterious column hung drooping on the staff. General Beauregard tried again and again to decide what colors they carried. He used his glass repeatedly, and handing it to others begged them to look, hoping that their eyes might be keener than his.

General Beauregard was in a state of great anxiety, but finally determined to hold his ground, relying on the promised help from the right, knowing that if it arrived in time victory might be secured, but feeling also that if the mysterious column should be Federal troops the day was lost.

Suddenly a puff of wind spread the colors to the breeze. It was the Confederate flag—the stars and bars! It was Early with the Twenty-fourth Virginia, the Seventh Louisiana, and the Thirteenth Mississippi. The column had by this time reached the extreme right of the Federal lines. The moment the flag was recognized Beauregard turned to his staff right and left, saying, "See that the day is ours!" and ordered an immediate advance. In the meantime Early's brigade deployed into line and charged the enemy's right—Elzey, also, dashed upon the field—and in one hour not an enemy was to be seen south of Bull Run.

While on this field and suffering this terrible anxiety, General Beauregard determined that the Confederate soldier must have a flag so distinct from that of the enemy that no doubt should ever again endanger his cause on the field of battle.

Soon after the battle he entered into correspondence with Colonel William Porcher Miles, who had served on his staff during this day, with a view to securing his aid in the matter, and proposing a blue field, red bars, crossed, and gold stars.

They discussed the matter at length. Colonel Miles thought it was contrary to the law of heraldry that the ground should be blue, the bars red, and the stars gold. He proposed that the ground should be red, the bars blue, and the stars white.

General Beauregard approved the change, and discussed the matter freely with General Johnston. Meanwhile it became known that the design for a flag was under discussion, and many designs were sent in. One came from Mississippi; one from J. B. Walton and E. C. Hancock, which coincided with the design of Colonel Miles. The matter was freely discussed at headquarters, till, finally, when he arrived at Fairfax Courthouse, General Beauregard caused his draughtsman (a German) to make drawings of all the various designs which had been submitted. With these designs before them the officers at headquarters agreed on the famous old banner—the red field, the blue cross, and the white stars. The flag was then submitted to the War Department, and was approved.

The first three flags received were made from "ladies' dresses" by the Misses Carey, of Baltimore and Alexandria, at their residences and the residences of friends, as soon as they could get a description of the design adopted. One of the Misses Carey sent the flag she made to General Beauregard. Her sister sent hers to General Van Dorn, who was then at Fairfax Courthouse. Miss Constance Carey, of Alexandria, sent hers to General Joseph E. Johnston.

General Beauregard sent the flag he received at once to New Orleans for safe keeping. After the fall of New Orleans, Mrs. Beauregard sent the flag by a Spanish man-of-war, then lying in the river opposite New Orleans, to Cuba, where it remained till the close of the war, when it was returned to General Beauregard, who presented it for safe-keeping to the Washington Artillery at New Orleans.

CARLTON McCARTHY.

ARMY OPERATIONS IN MISSOURI

FROM JULY 25 TO AUGUST 11, 1861,

INCLUDING

THE BATTLE OF WILSON'S CREEK

(OAK HILLS, OR SPRINGFIELD),

AUGUST 10, 1861.

BY

MAJOR-GENERAL STERLING PRICE,
Commanding Missouri State Guards.

HEADQUARTERS MISSOURI STATE GUARD,
SPRINGFIELD, MO., August 12, 1861.

I SUBMIT the following report of the operations of the army under my command at and immediately preceding the battle at Springfield.* I began to move my command from its encampment on Cowskin Prairie, in McDonald county, on July 25th, toward Cassville, in Barry county, at which place it had been agreed upon between Generals McCulloch, Pearce and myself that our respective forces, together with those of Brigadier-General McBride, should be concentrated, preparatory to a forward movement.

We reached Cassville on Sunday, July 28th, and on the next day effected a junction with the armies of Generals McCulloch and Pearce. The combined armies were then put under marching orders, and the first division, General McCulloch commanding, left Cassville on August 1st, upon the road to this city. The second division, under General Pearce, of Arkansas, left on August 1st; and the third division, Brigadier-General Steele, of this State, commanding, left on August 2d. I went forward with the second division, which embraced the greater portion of my infantry, and encamped with it some twelve miles northwest of Cassville.

The next morning a messenger from General McCulloch informed me that he had reason to believe that the enemy was in force on the road to Springfield, and that he should remain at his then encampment on Crane Creek until the second and third divisions of the army had come up. The second division consequently moved forward to Crane Creek, and I ordered the third division to a position within three miles of the same place. An advance guard of the army, consisting of six companies of mounted Missourians, under command of Brigadier-General Rains, was at this time (Friday, August 2d), encamped on the Springfield road, about five miles beyond Crane Creek. About 9 A. M. of that day General Rains' pickets reported to him that they had been driven in by the enemy's advance guard, and that officer immediately led forward his whole force, amounting to nearly 400 men, until he found the enemy in position some three miles on the road. He sent back at once to General McCulloch for re-enforcements, and Colonel McIntosh, C. S. A., was sent forward with 150 men; but a reconnoissance of the ground having satisfied the latter that the enemy did not have more than 150 men on the ground, he withdrew his own and returned to Crane Creek. General Rains soon discovered, however, that he was in presence of the main body of the enemy, numbering, according to his estimate, more than 5,000 men, with eight pieces of artillery, and supported by a considerable body of cavalry. A severe skirmish ensued, which lasted several hours, until the enemy opened their batteries on us and compelled our troops to retire. In this engagement the greater portion of General Rains' command, and especially that part which acted as infantry, behaved with great gallantry, as the result demonstrates, for our loss was only one killed (Lieutenant Northcut) and five wounded, while five of the enemy's dead were buried on the field, and a large number are known to have been wounded.

Our whole forces were concentrated the next day near Crane Creek, and during the same night the Texas regiment, under Colonel Greer, came up within a few miles of the same place. Reasons which will be hereafter assigned induced me, on Sunday, the 4th inst., to put the Missouri forces under the direction, for the time being, of General McCulloch, who accordingly assumed the command-in-chief of the combined armies. A little after midnight we took up the line of march, leaving our baggage trains, and expected to find the enemy near the scene of the late skirmish; but we found as we advanced that he was retreating rapidly toward Springfield. We followed him hastily about seventeen miles to a place known as Moody's Spring, where we were compelled to halt our forces, who were already nearly exhausted by the intense heat of the weather and the dustiness of the roads.

Early the next morning we moved forward to Wilson's Creek, ten miles southwest of Springfield, where we encamped. Our forces were here put in readiness to meet the enemy, who was posted at Springfield to the number of about 10,000. It was finally decided to march against him in four separate columns at 9 o'clock that night, so as to surround the city and begin a simultaneous attack at daybreak. The darkness of the night and a threatened storm caused General McCulloch, just as the army was about to march, to countermand this order and to direct that the troops should hold themselves in readiness to move whenever ordered. Our men were consequently kept under arms till toward daybreak, expecting momentarily an order to march.

The morning of Saturday, August 10th, found them still encamped at Wilson's Creek, fatigued by a night's watching and loss of rest.

About 6 o'clock I received a messenger [message] from General Rains that the enemy was advancing in great force from the direction of Springfield, and was already within two or three hundred yards of the position where he was encamped with the second brigade of his division, consisting of about 1,200 mounted men, under Colonel Cawthorn. A second messenger came immediately afterward from General Rains to announce that the main body of the enemy was upon him, but that he would endeavor to hold him in check until he could receive re-enforcements. General McCulloch was with me when these messengers came, and left at once for his own headquarters to make the necessary disposition of our forces. I rode forward instantly toward General Rains' position, at the same time ordering Generals Slack, McBride, Clark and Parsons to move their infantry and artillery rapidly forward. I had ridden but a few hundred yards when I came suddenly upon the main body of the enemy, commanded by General Lyon in person. The infantry and artillery, which I had ordered to follow me, came up immediately, to the number of 2,036 men, and engaged the enemy.

A severe and bloody conflict ensued, my officers and

MAJ.-GEN. STERLING PRICE, OF MISSOURI.

men behaving with the greatest bravery, and with the assistance of a portion of the Confederate forces successfully holding the enemy in check. Meanwhile, and almost simultaneously with the opening of the enemy's batteries in this quarter, a heavy cannonading was opened upon the rear of our position, where a large body of the enemy, under Colonel Sigel, had taken position in close proximity to Colonel Churchill's regiment, Colonel Greer's Texan Rangers and 679 mounted Missourians, under command of Colonel Brown and Lieutenant-Colonel Major. The action now became general, and was conducted with the greatest gallantry and vigor on both sides for more than five hours, when the enemy retreated in great confusion, leaving their commander-in-chief, General Lyon, dead upon the battlefield, over 500 killed, and a great number wounded.

The forces under my command have possession of three 12-pounder howitzers, two brass 6-pounders and a great quantity of small arms and ammunition, taken from the enemy; also the standard of Sigel's regiment, captured by Captain Staples. They have also a large number of prisoners.

The brilliant victory thus achieved upon this hard-fought field was won only by the most determined bravery and distinguished gallantry of the combined armies, which fought nobly side by side, in defense of their common rights and liberties, with as much courage and constancy as were ever exhibited upon any battlefield.

Where all behaved so well it is invidious to make any distinction, but I can not refrain from expressing my sense of the splendid services rendered under my own eyes by the Arkansas infantry, under General Pearce, the Louisiana regiment of Colonel Hebert, and Colonel Churchill's regiment of mounted riflemen. These gallant officers and their brave soldiers won upon that day the lasting gratitude of every true Missourian.

This great victory was dearly bought by the blood of many a skillful officer and brave men of my army.

Among those who fell mortally wounded upon the battlefield none deserve a dearer place in the memory of Missourians than Richard Hanson Weightman, colonel commanding the first brigade of the second division of the army. Taking up arms at the very beginning of this unhappy contest, he had already done distinguished services at the battle of Rock Creek, of the lamented Holloway (*sic*), and at Carthage, where he won unfading laurels by the display of extraordinary coolness, courage and skill. He fell at the head of his brigade, wounded in three places, and died just as the victorious shout of our army began to rise upon the air. Here, too, died in the discharge of his duty Colonel Benjamin Brown, of Ray county, President of the Senate, a good man and true. Brigadier-General Slack's division suffered severely. He himself fell dangerously wounded at the head of his column.

Of his regiment of infantry, under Colonel John T. Hughes, consisting of about 650 men, thirty-six were killed, seventy-six wounded, many of them mortally, and thirty are missing. Among the killed were C. F. Bennett, adjutant of the regiment, Captain Blackburn and Lieutenant Hughes.

Colonel Rives' squadron of cavalry, dismounted, some 234 men, lost four killed and eight wounded. Among the former were Lieutenant-Colonel Austin and Captain Engart.

Brigadier-General Clark was also wounded. His infantry, 200 men, lost and killed seventeen, and wounded seventy-one. Colonel Burbridge was severely wounded; Captains Farris and Halleck and Lieutenant Haskins were killed.

General Clark's cavalry, together with the Windsor Guards, were under the command of Lieutenant-Colonel Major, who did good service. They lost six killed and five wounded.

Brigadier-General McBride's division, 605 men, lost, twenty-two killed, sixty-seven severly wounded and fifty-seven slightly wounded. Colonel Foster and Captains Nichols, Dougherty, Armstrong and Mings were wounded while gallantly leading their respective commands.

General Parsons' brigade, 256 infantry and artillery, under command, respectively, of Colonel Kelly and Captain Guibor, and 406 cavalry, under Colonel Brown, lost, the artillery, three killed and seven wounded; the infantry, nine killed and thirty-eight wounded; and the cavalry, three killed and two wounded. Colonel Kelly was wounded in the hand. Captain Coleman was mortally wounded, and has since died.

General Rains' division was composed of two brigades. The first, under Colonel Weightman, embracing infantry and artillery, 1,306 strong, lost not only their commander, but thirty-four others killed and one hundred and eleven wounded. The second brigade, mounted men, Colonel Cawthorn commanding, about 1,200 strong, lost twenty-one killed and seventy-five wounded. Colonel Cawthorn was himself wounded, and Major Charles Rodgers, of St. Louis, adjutant of the brigade, was mortally wounded, and died the day after the battle. He was a gallant officer, and at all times vigilant and attentive to his duties, and fearless upon the field of battle.

Your excellency will perceive that our State forces consisted only of 5,221 officers and men; that of those no less than one hundred and fifty-six died upon the field, while five hundred and seventeen were wounded. These facts attest more powerfully than words can the severity of the conflict and the dauntless courage of our brave soldiers.

It is also my painful duty to announce the death of one of my aids, Lieutenant-Colonel George W. Allen, of Saline county. He was shot down while communicating an order, and we left him buried on the field. I have appointed to the position thus sadly vacated Captain James T. Cearnel, in recognition of his gallant conduct and valuable services throughout the battle as a volunteer aid. Another of my staff, Colonel Horace H. Brand, was made prisoner by the enemy, but has since been released.

* * * * * *

STERLING PRICE,
Major-General, Commanding Missouri State Guards.

DR. J. L. BURROWS was everywhere, in the hospitals, in camp or on the march, cheering the living, comforting the dying or exhorting the sinner, and no man was dearer to the Confederate soldier than Dr. Burrows. On one occasion he preached on the subject that the victory was not always with the strong, and took for illustration the story of David and Goliath, but the war soon after demonstrated that victory was with the side having the most men and cannon. The plowshare and pruning-hook epoch succeeded the siege of cannon and sword, and the reverened doctor was one day accosted by a citizen whose halting step proclaimed that he had been a soldier. After introducing himself the ex-soldier, with a merry twinkle of the eye, asked the doctor this question, over which he still unsatisfactorily broods: "Say, doctor, what about that David and Goliath story?"

* This report is printed from official copy, and it has been impossble to verify the names of individuals or organizations.

BATTLE OF WILSON'S CREEK, MO.

(OAK HILLS, OR SPRINGFIELD),

AUGUST 10, 1861.

BY

BRIGADIER-GENERAL BEN McCULLOCH.

HEADQUARTERS McCULLOCH'S BRIGADE,
CAMP WEIGHTMAN,
NEAR SPRINGFIELD, MO., August 12, 1861.

HAVING taken position about ten miles from Springfield, I endeavored to gain the necessary information of the strength and position of the enemy stationed in and about the town. The information was very conflicting and unsatisfactory. I, however, made up my mind to attack the enemy in their position, and issued orders on the 9th instant to my force to start at 9 o'clock at night to attack at four different points at daylight. A few days before General Price, in command of the Missouri force, turned over his troops to me, and I assumed command of the entire force, comprising my own brigade, the brigade of Arkansas State forces under General Pearce, and General Price's Missourians.

My effective force was 5,300 infantry, fifteen pieces of artillery, and 6,000 horsemen, armed with flintlock muskets, rifles and shotguns. There were other horsemen with the army who were entirely unarmed, and instead of being a help were continually in the way. When the time arrived for the night march, it commenced to rain slightly, and fearing, from the want of cartridge boxes, that my ammunition would be ruined, I ordered the movement to be stopped, hoping to move the next morning. Many of my men had but twenty rounds of ammunition, and there was no more to be had.

While still hesitating in the morning the enemy were reported advancing, and I made arrangements to meet him. The attack was made simultaneously at 5:30 A. M., on our right and left flanks, and the enemy had gained the positions they desired. General Lyon attacked us on our left, and General Sigel on our right and rear. From these points batteries opened upon us. My command was soon ready. The Missourians, under Generals Slack, Clark, McBride, Parsons and Rains, were nearest the position taken by General Lyon with his main force. They were instantly turned to the left, and opened the battle with an incessant fire of small arms.

Woodruff opposed his battery to that of the enemy under Captain Totten, and a constant cannonading was kept up between these batteries during the battle. Hebert's regiment of Louisiana volunteers and McIntosh's regiment of Arkansas mounted riflemen were ordered to the front, and after passing the battery turned to the left, and soon engaged the enemy with regiments deployed. Colonel McIntosh dismounted his regiment, and the two marched up abreast to a fence around a large cornfield, when they met the left of the enemy already posted.

A terrible conflict of small arms took place here. The opposing force was a body of regular United States infantry, commanded by Captains Plummer and Gilbert. Notwithstanding the galling fire poured upon these two regiments, they leaped over the fence, and, gallantly led by their colonels, drove the enemy before them back upon the main body. During this time the Missourians, under General Price, were nobly attempting to sustain themselves in the center, and were hotly engaged on the sides of the height upon which the enemy were posted. Far on the right Sigel had opened his battery upon Churchill's and Greer's regiments, and gradually made his way to the Springfield road, upon each side of which the enemy was encamped, and in a prominent position had established his battery. I at once took two companies of the Louisiana regiment, which were nearest me, and marched them rapidly from the front and right to the rear, with orders to Colonel McIntosh to bring up the rest.

When we arrived near the enemy's battery we found that Reid's battery had opened upon it, and it was already in confusion. Advantage was taken of it, and soon the Louisianians were gallantly charging among the guns, and swept the cannoneers away. Five guns were here taken, and Sigel's command, completely routed, were in rapid retreat with a single gun, followed by some companies of the Texas regiment and a portion of Colonel Major's Missouri regiment of cavalry. In the pursuit many of the enemy were killed and taken prisoners, and their last gun captured.

Having cleared our right and rear, it was necessary to turn all our attention to the center, under General Lyon, who was pressing upon the Missourians, having driven them back. To this point McIntosh's regiment, under Lieutenant-Colonel Embry, and Churchill's regiment on foot, Gratiot's regiment and McRea's battalion were sent to their aid.

A terrible fire of musketry was now kept up along the whole side and top of the hill upon which the enemy were posted. Masses of infantry fell back and again rushed forward. The summit of the hill was covered with the dead and wounded. Both sides were fighting with desperation for the day. Carroll's and Greer's regiments, led gallantly by Captain Bradfute, charged the battery (Totten's), but the whole strength of the enemy were immediately in rear, and a deadly fire was opened upon them.

At this critical moment, when the fortunes of the day seemed to be at the turning point, two regiments of General Pearce's brigade were ordered to march from their position (as reserves) to support the center. The order was obeyed with alacrity, and General Pearce gallantly marched with his brigade to the rescue. Reid's battery was also ordered to move forward, and the Louisiana regiment was again called into action on the left of it. The battle then became general, and probably no two opposing forces ever fought with greater desperation. Inch by inch the enemy gave way, and were driven from their position. Totten's battery fell back; Missourians, Arkansans, Louisianians and Texans pushed forward. The incessant roll of musketry was deafening, and the balls fell thick as hailstones, but still our gallant Southerners pushed onward, and with one wild yell broke upon the enemy, pushing them back and strewing the ground with their dead. Nothing could withstand the impetuosity of our final charge. The enemy fled and could not again be rallied, and they were seen at 12 M. fast retreating among the hills in the distance.

Thus ended the battle. It lasted six hours and a half. The force of the enemy, between nine and ten thousand,

BRIG.-GEN. BEN McCULLOCH, OF TEXAS.
Killed at the Battle of Pea Ridge, Ark., March 7, 1862.
[From a photo taken in 1861.]

was composed of well-disciplined troops, well armed, and a large part of them belonging to the old army of the United States. With every advantage on their side they have met with a signal repulse. The loss of the enemy is 800 killed, 1,000 wounded and 300 prisoners. We captured six pieces of artillery, several hundred stand of small arms and a number of their standards.

Major-General Lyon, chief in command, was killed, and many of their officers high in rank wounded.

Our loss was also severe, and we mourn the death of many a gallant officer and soldier. Our killed amounts to 265, and 800 wounded; also thirty missing. Colonel Weightman fell at the head of his brigade of Missourians while gallantly charging upon the enemy. His place will not easily be filled. Generals Slack and Clark, of Missouri, were severely wounded; General Price, slightly. Captain Hinson, of the Louisiana regiment; Captain McAlexander, of Churchill's regiment; Captains Bell and Brown, of Pearce's brigade, Lieutenants Walton and Weaver, all fell while nobly and gallantly doing their duty. Colonel McIntosh was slightly wounded by a grapeshot while charging with the Louisiana regiment. Lieutenant-Colonel Neal, Major F. Ward, Captains King, Pearson, Gibbs, Ramsaur, Porter, Lieutenants Dawson, Chambers, Johnson, King, Adams, Hardesty, McIvor, and Saddler were wounded while at the head of their companies.

* * * * * * *

BEN McCULLOCH,
Brigadier-General Commanding.

SAID a hungry Confederate to the lady who met him at the door, when out foraging one day, "Madam, will you please give me something to eat? I haven't had a mouthful for three days—to-day, to-morrow and next day."

MANASSAS.

(First Battle of Bull Run, July 21, 1861.)

BY CATHERINE M. WARFIELD.

They have met at last—as storm clouds
Meet in Heaven!
And their thunders have been stilled,
And their leaders crushed or killed,
And their ranks, with terror thrilled,
Rent and riven!

Like the leaves of Vallombrosa
They are lying,
In the moonlight, in the midnight,
Dead and dying;
Like those leaves before the gale
Swept their legions, wild and pale;
While the host that made them quail
Stood defying.

When aloft in morning sunlight
Flags were flaunted,
And "swift vengeance on the rebel"
Proudly vaunted,
Little did they think that night
Should close upon their shameful flight,
And rebels, victors in the fight,
Stand undaunted.

But peace to those who perished
In our passes!
Light be the earth above them;
Green the grasses!
Long shall Northmen rue the day
When they met our stern array,
And shrunk from battle's wild affray,
At Manassas!

ORGANIZATION OF THE TROOPS IN THE DEPARTMENT OF THE PENINSULA,

COMMANDED BY

MAJ.-GEN. J. BANKHEAD MAGRUDER, C. S. A.,

JANUARY 31, 1862.

YORKTOWN, VICINITY AND SHIP POINT.

FIRST DIVISION.

BRIG.-GEN. G. J. RAINS COMMANDING.

Thirteenth Alabama; Second Florida; Sixth Georgia; Twenty-third Georgia; Fourteenth Louisiana; Louisiana Zouave Battalion; Second Mississippi; Fifteenth North Carolina; Thirty-second Virginia, two companies; Fifty-third Virginia, eight companies; One Hundred and Fifteenth Virginia militia; Maurin's Louisiana battery; Nelson's Louisiana battery; First Virginia artillery, three companies. Serving as heavy artillery—Barton's independent company; De Gourney's independent company; Duke's independent company; Elletot's independent company; Peyton's independent company; Preston's independent company.

MULBERRY POINT BATTERY, LAND'S END, ETC.

SECOND DIVISION.

BRIG.-GEN. LAFAYETTE McLAWS COMMANDING.

Eighth Alabama; Cobb's Legion; Tenth Georgia; Sixteenth Georgia; Greenville Guards; Second Louisiana; Fifth Louisiana; Tenth Louisiana; Fourteenth Virginia; Fifteenth Virginia; Thirty-second Virginia, two companies; Fifty-third Virginia, one company; Third Virginia (four companies) cavalry; First Virginia (five companies) artillery.

GLOUCESTER POINT.

COLONEL C. A. CRUMP, COMMANDING.

Twenty-sixth Virginia; Ninth Virginia Militia; Twenty-first Virginia Militia; Eighty-seventh Virginia militia; Third Virginia (one company) cavalry; First Virginia (one company) artillery. Serving as heavy artillery—Bagley's company Virginia volunteers; Jordan's company Virginia volunteers; Montague's company Virginia volunteers; Otey's company Virginia volunteers.

WILLIAMSBURG AND SPRATLEY'S.

COLONEL B. S. EWELL COMMANDING.

First Louisiana battery; Thirty-second Virginia, two companies; Fifty-third Virginia, one company.

MATTHEWS COUNTY.

COLONEL J. G. BOHANNAN COMMANDING.

Sixty-first Virginia militia; Captain Todd's company Virginia cavalry.

LEBANON CHURCH AND CAVALRY CAMPS.

(Near Yorktown.)

COLOLEL R. JOHNSTON COMMANDING.

Third Virginia (six companies) cavalry.

JAMESTOWN ISLAND.

COLONEL HILL CARTER COMMANDING.

Fifty-second Virginia militia; First Virginia (one company) artillery; Jordan's independent company Virginia artillery; Rambaut's independent company Virginia artillery.

SIEGE OF LEXINGTON, MISSOURI.

OPERATIONS

FROM SEPTEMBER 10-20, 1861.

BY

MAJOR-GENERAL STERLING PRICE,
Commanding Missouri State Guard.

HEADQUARTERS MISSOURI STATE GUARD,
CAMP WALLACE,
LEXINGTON, MO., September 21, 1861.

I SUBMIT the following report of the action which terminated on the 20th instant with the surrender of the United States forces and property at this place to the army under my command:

After chastising the marauding armies of Lane and Montgomery and driving them out of the State, and after compelling them to abandon Fort Scott, as detailed in my last report, I continued my march toward this point with an army increasing hourly in numbers and enthusiasm.

On the 10th instant, just as we were about to encamp for the day a mile or two west of Rose Hill, I learned that a detachment of Federal troops and home guards were marching from Lexington to Warrensburg, to rob the bank in that place and plunder and arrest the citizens of Johnson county, in accordance with General Fremont's proclamation and instructions. Although my men were greatly fatigued by a number of days' continuous and rapid marching, I determined to press forward in order to surprise the enemy, if possible, at Warrensburg. Therefore, after resting a few hours, we resumed the march at sunset, and marched without intermission until 2 o'clock in the morning, when it became evident that the infantry, very few of whom had eaten a mouthful in twenty-two hours, could march no further. I then halted them, and went forward with the largest part of my mounted men until we came, about daybreak, within view of Warrensburg, where I ascertained that the enemy had hastily fled about midnight, burning the bridges behind them.

The rain began to fall about the same time. This circumstance, coupled with the fact that my men had been fasting for more than twenty-four hours, constrained me to abandon the idea of pursuing the enemy that day. My infantry and artillery having come up, we encamped at Warrensburg, whose citizens vied with each other in feeding my almost famished soldiers. An unusually violent storm delayed our march the next morning (September 12th) until about 10 o'clock. We then pushed forward rapidly, still hoping to overtake the enemy. Finding it impossible to do this with my infantry, I again ordered a detachment to move forward, and placing myself at their head continued the pursuit to within two and a half miles of Lexington, when, having learned that the enemy were already within town, and it being late and my men fatigued and utterly without provisions, I halted for the night.

About daybreak the next morning (September 13th) a sharp skirmish took place between our pickets and the enemy's outposts. This threatened to become general. Being unwilling, however, to risk a doubtful engagement when a short delay would make success certain, I fell back two or three miles and awaited the arrival of my infantry and artillery. These having come up, we advanced upon the town, driving the enemy's pickets until we came within a short distance of the city itself. Here the enemy attempted to make a stand, but they were speedily driven from every position and forced to take shelter within their intrenchments. We then took position within easy range of the college, which building they had strongly fortified, and opened upon them a brisk fire from Bledsoe's battery, which, in the absence of Captain Bledsoe, who had been wounded at Big Dry Wood, was gallantly commanded by Captain Emmett MacDonald, and by Parson's battery, under the skillful command of Captain Guibor.

Finding, after sunset, that our ammunition, the most of which had been left behind on the march from Springfield, was nearly exhausted, and that my men, thousands of whom had not eaten a particle in thirty-six hours, required rest and food, I withdrew to the fair-ground and encamped there. My ammunition wagons having been at last brought up, and large re-enforcements having been received, I again moved into town on Wednesday, the 18th instant, and began the final attack on the enemy's works.

Brigadier-General Rains' division occupied a strong position on the east and northeast of the fortifications, from which an effective cannonading was kept up on the enemy by Bledsoe's battery, under command, except on the last day, of Captain Emmett MacDonald, and another battery under command of Captain Churchill Clark, of St. Louis. Both these gentlemen, and the men and officers under their command, are deservedly commended in accompanying report of Brigadier-General Rains. General Parsons took a position southwest of the works, whence his battery, under command of Captain Guibor, poured a steady fire into the enemy. Skirmishers and sharpshooters were also sent forward from both of these divisions to harass the enemy, as well as to cut them off from the water on the north, east and south of the college, and they did inestimable service in the accomplishment of these purposes.

Colonel Congreve Jackson's division and a part of General Steele's were posted near Generals Rains and Parsons as a reserve, but no occasion occurred to call them into action. They were, however, at all times vigilant and ready to rush upon the enemy.

Shortly after entering the city on the 18th, Colonel Rives, who commanded the Fourth Division in the absence of General Slack, led his regiment and Colonel Hughes' along the river bank to a point immediately beneath and west of the fortifications, General McBride's command and a portion of Colonel (General) Harris' having been ordered to re-enforce him. Colonel Rives, in order to cut off the enemy's means of escape, proceeded down the bank of the river to capture a steamboat which was lying just under their guns. At this moment a very heavy fire was opened upon him from Colonel Anderson's large dwelling-house on the summit of the bluffs, which the enemy were occupying as a hospital, and upon which a white flag was flying. Several companies of General Harris' command, and the gallant soldiers of the Fourth Division, who have won upon so many battlefields the proud distinction of always being among the bravest of the brave, immediately rushed upon and took the place. The important positions thus secured was within one hundred and twenty-five yards of the enemy's entrenchments. A company from Colonel Hughes' regiment then took possession of the boats, one of which was freighted with valuable stores.

General McBride's and General Harris' divisions meanwhile gallantly stormed and occupied the bluffs immediately north of Anderson's house. The possession of these heights enabled our men to harass the enemy so greatly that, resolving to regain them, they made upon the house a successful assault, and one which would have been honorable to them had it not been accompanied by an act of savage barbarity—the cold-blooded and cowardly murder of three defenseless men who had laid down their arms and surrendered themselves as prisoners.

The position thus retaken by the enemy was soon regained by the brave men who had been driven from it, and was thenceforward held by them to the very end of the contest. The heights to the left of Anderson's house, which had been taken, as before stated, by Generals McBride and Harris, and by part of Steele's command, under Colonel Boyd and Major Winston, were rudely fortified by our soldiers, who threw up breastworks as well as they could with their slender means.

On the morning of the 20th instant I caused a number of hemp bales to be transported to the river heights, where movable breastworks were speedily constructed out of them by Generals Harris and McBride, Colonel Rives and Major Winston, and their respective commands. Captain Kelly's battery (attached to General Steele's division) was ordered at the same time to the position occupied by General Harris' force, and quickly opened a very effective fire, under the direction of its gallant captain, upon the enemy.

These demonstrations, and particularly the continued advance of the hempen breastworks, which were as efficient as the cotton bales at New Orleans, quickly attracted the attention and excited the alarm of the enemy, who made many daring attempts to drive us back. They were, however, repulsed in every instance by the unflinching courage and fixed determination of our men.

In these desperate encounters the veterans of McBride's and Slack's divisions fully sustained their proud reputation, while Colonel Martin Green and his command, and Colonel Boyd and Major Winston and their commands, proved themselves worthy to fight by the side of the men who had by their courage and valor won imperishable honor in the bloody battle of Springfield.

After 2 o'clock in the afternoon of the 20th, and after fifty-two hours of continuous firing, a white flag was displayed by the enemy on that part of the works nearest to Colonel Green's position, and soon after another was displayed opposite to Colonel Rives'. I immediately ordered a cessation of all firing on our part, and sent forward one of my staff officers to ascertain the object of the flag and to open negotiations with the enemy, if such should be their desire.

It was finally, after some delay, agreed by Colonel Marshall and the officers associated with him for that purpose by Colonel Mulligan, that the United States forces should lay down their arms and surrender themselves as prisoners of war to this army. These terms having been made known, were ratified by me and immediately carried into effect.

Our entire loss in this series of engagements amounts to twenty-five killed and seventy-two wounded. The enemy's loss was much greater.

The visible fruits of this almost bloodless victory are great—about 3,500 prisoners, among whom are Colonels Mulligan, Marshall, Peabody, White and Grover; Major Van Horn, and 118 other commissioned officers; five pieces of artillery and two mortars, over 3,000 stands of infantry arms, a large number of sabers, about 750 horses, many sets of cavalry equipments, wagons, teams and ammunition, more than $100,000 worth of commissary stores, and a large amount of other property. In addition to all this, I obtained the restoration of the great seal of the State and the public records, which had been stolen from their proper custodian, and about $900,000 in money of which the bank at this place had been robbed, and which I have caused to be returned to it.

This victory has demonstrated the fitness of our citizen soldiers for the tedious operations of a siege as well as for a dashing charge. They lay for fifty-two hours in the open air without tents or covering, regardless of the sun and rain, and in the very presence of a watchful and desperate foe, manfully repelling every assault, and patiently awaiting any orders to storm the fortifications. No general ever commanded a braver or better army. It is composed of the best blood and the bravest men of Missouri.

Where nearly every one, officers and men, behaved so well, as is known to your Excellency, who was present with the army during the whole period embraced in this report, it is impossible to make special mention of individuals without seemingly making invidious distinctions; but I may be permitted to express my personal obligations to my volunteer aids, as well as my staff, for their efficient services and prompt attention to all my orders.

* * * * * *

STERLING PRICE,
Major-General Commanding.

PAY OF OFFICERS, ENLISTED MEN, ETC., CONFEDERATE STATES ARMY.

General	Per Month,	$500 00
Lieutenant-General	"	450 00
Major-General	"	350 00
Brigadier-General	"	301 00

General commanding army, $100 per month additional. A Lieutenant-General, Major-General and a Brigadier-General while serving in the field, $50 per month additional.

ENGINEER CORPS.

Colonel	Per Month,	$210 00
Major	"	162 00
Captain	"	140 00
First Lieutenant	"	100 00
Second Lieutenant*	"	90 00

ARTILLERY.

Colonel	Per Month,	$210 00
Lieutenant-Colonel	"	185 00
Major	"	150 00
Captain	"	130 00
First Lieutenant	"	90 00
Second Lieutenant*	"	80 00

INFANTRY.

Colonel	Per Month,	$195 00
Lieutenant-Colonel	"	170 00
Major	"	150 00
Captain	"	130 00
First Lieutenant	"	90 00
Second Lieutenant*	"	80 00

CAVALRY.

Colonel	Per Month,	$210 00
Lieutenant-Colonel	"	185 00
Major	"	162 00
Captain	"	140 00
First Lieutenant	"	100 00
Second Lieutenant*	"	90 00

* Lieutenants when serving as Adjutants, $10 per month in addition to regular pay.

OFFICERS OF GENERAL STAFF.

The pay of the officers of the general staff, except those of the medical department, shall be the same as that of the officers of cavalry of the same grade.

ENLISTED MEN.—ENGINEER CORPS.

Sergeant, Major or Master-Workman	Per Month,	$34 00
Quartermaster-Sergeant	"	34 00
Sergeants	"	34 00
Corporals or Overseer	"	20 00
Privates—of the first class or Artificers,	"	17 00
Privates—second class or laborers	"	13 00
Musicians	"	13 00

CAVALRY.

Sergeant-Major	Per Month,	$21 00
First Sergeants	"	20 00
Sergeants	"	17 00
Corporals, Farriers and Blacksmiths	"	13 00
Musicians	"	13 00
Privates	"	12 00

INFANTRY AND ARTILLERY.

Sergeant-Major	Per Month,	$21 00
First Sergeants	"	20 00
Sergeants	"	17 00
Corporals and Artificers	"	13 00
Musicians	"	12 00
Privates	"	11 00

Master Armorer, Master Carriage-maker, Master Blacksmith, $34 per month; armorers, carriage-makers and blacksmiths, $20 per month; artificers $17, and laborers $13 per month.

SIEGE OF LEXINGTON, MO., SEPTEMBER 13–20, 1861, RESULTING IN THE SURRENDER OF THE FEDERAL FORCES TO MAJOR-GENERAL STERLING PRICE, COMMANDING THE MISSOURI STATE GUARD.

THE BATTLE
OF
LEESBURG, BALL'S BLUFF AND EDWARD'S FERRY,

OCTOBER 21-22, 1861.

BY

BRIGADIER-GENERAL N. S. EVANS, C. S. A.

HEADQUARTERS OF THE SEVENTH BRIGADE,
LEESBURG, VA., October 31, 1861.

I SUBMIT the following report of the action of the Seventh Brigade in the battle of the 21st and 22d instant with the enemy at Leesburg, Va. On Saturday night, the 19th instant, about 7 o'clock P. M., the enemy commenced a heavy cannonading from three batteries, one playing on my intrenchment (known as Fort Evans), one on the Leesburg Turnpike and one on Edward's Ferry. Heavy firing was also heard in the direction of Dranesville.

At 12 o'clock at night I ordered my entire brigade to the Burnt Bridge, on the turnpike. The enemy had been reported as approaching from Dranesville in large forces. Taking a strong position on the north side of Goose Creek, I awaited his approach. Reconnoitering the turnpike on Sunday morning, the courier of General McCall was captured, bearing dispatches to General Meade to examine the roads leading to Leesburg. From this prisoner I learned the position of the enemy near Dranesville. During Sunday the enemy kept up a deliberate fire without any effect.

Early on Monday morning, the 21st instant, I heard the firing of my pickets at Big Spring, who had discovered that at an unguarded point the enemy had effected a crossing in force of five companies, and were advancing on Leesburg. Captain [W. L.] Duff, of the Seventeenth Regiment, immediately attacked him, driving him back, with several killed and wounded.

On observing the movements of the enemy from Fort Evans at 6 o'clock A. M., I found he had effected a crossing both at Edward's Ferry and Ball's Bluff, and I made preparations to meet him in both positions, and immediately ordered four companies of infantry (two of the Eighteenth, one of the Seventeenth and one of the Thirtieth) and a cavalry force to relieve Captain Duff; the whole force under the immediate command of Lieutenant-Colonel W. H. Jenifer, who was directed to hold the position till the enemy made further demonstration of the design of his attack. This force soon became warmly engaged with the enemy, and drove them back for some distance in the woods.

At about 10 o'clock I became convinced that the main point of attack would be at Ball's Bluff, and ordered Colonel Hunton with his regiment, the Eighth Virginia Volunteers, to repair immediately to the support of Colonel Jenifer. I directed Colonel Hunton to form line of battle immediately in the rear of Colonel Jenifer's command, and to drive the enemy to the river; that I would support his right with artillery. About 12:20 o'clock P. M. Colonel Hunton united his command with that of Colonel Jenifer, and both commands soon became hotly engaged with the enemy in their strong position in the woods.

Watching carefully the action, I saw the enemy was constantly being re-enforced, and at 2:30 o'clock P. M. I ordered Colonel Burt to march his regiment, the Eighteenth Mississippi Volunteers, and attack the left flank of the enemy, while Colonels Hunton and Jenifer attacked him in front. On arriving at his position, Colonel Burt was received with a tremendous fire from the enemy concealed in a ravine, and was compelled to divide his regiment to stop the flank movement of the enemy. At this time, about 3 o'clock, finding the enemy was in large force, I ordered Colonel Featherston with his regiment, the Seventeenth Mississippi, to repair at double-quick to the support of Colonel Burt, where he arrived in twenty minutes, and the action became general along my whole line, and was very hot and brisk for more than two hours, the enemy keeping up a constant fire with his batteries on both sides of the river. At about 6 o'clock P. M. I saw that my command had driven the enemy near the banks of the Potomac. I ordered my entire force to charge and to drive him into the river. The charge was immediately made by the whole command, and the forces of the enemy were completely routed, and cried out for quarter along his whole line.

In this charge the enemy was driven back at the point of the bayonet, and many killed and wounded by this formidable weapon. In the precipitate retreat of the enemy on the bluffs of the river many of his troops rushed into the water and were drowned, while many others in overloading the boats sunk them and shared the same fate. The rout now, about 7 o'clock, became complete, and the enemy commenced throwing his arms into the river. During this action I held Colonel W. Barksdale, with nine companies of his regiment, the Thirteenth Mississippi, and six pieces of artillery, as a reserve, as well as to keep up a demonstration against the force of the enemy at Edward's Ferry.

At 8 o'clock P. M. the enemy surrendered his forces at Ball's Bluff, and the prisoners were marched to Leesburg. I then ordered my brigade (with the exception of the Thirteenth Mississippi Regiment, which remained in front of Edward's Ferry) to retire to the town of Leesburg and rest for the night.

On Tuesday morning I was informed by Colonel Barksdale that the enemy was still in considerable force at Edward's Ferry. I directed him to make a thorough reconnoissance of the position and strength of the enemy and attack him. At 2 o'clock P. M. he gallantly attacked a much superior force in their intrenchments, driving them to the bank of the river, killing thirty or forty and wounding a considerable number. About sundown, the enemy being strongly re-enforced and stationed in rifle-pits, Colonel Barksdale wisely retired with his regiment to Fort Evans, leaving a guard of two companies to watch the movements of the enemy, who, evidently expecting a renewed attack, retired during the night and recrossed the river at Edward's Ferry.

On Wednesday morning, finding my brigade very much exhausted, I left Colonel Barksdale, with his regiment, with two pieces of artillery and a cavalry force, as a grand guard, and I ordered the other three regiments to fall back toward Carter's Mill to rest and to be collected in order. Colonel Hunton, with his regiment and two pieces of artillery, were halted at a strong position on the south bank of the Sycolin, about three miles south of Leesburg.

BATTLE OF BALL'S BLUFF, VIRGINIA. RETREAT OF THE FEDERALS.

I would here state that in an interview on Monday night with the commissioned officers of the Federal army taken prisoners, I was convinced that they expected to be recaptured either during the night or the next day, and as the captured officers refused their parol not to take up arms against the Southern Confederacy till duly exchanged, I ordered the whole number to be immediately marched to Manassas. This parol was only offered to give them the liberty of the town, as I did not wish to confine them with privates.

The force of the enemy, as far as I have been able to ascertain, was five regiments and three pieces of artillery at Ball's Bluff, and four regiments, two batteries and a squadron of cavalry at Edward's Ferry, numbering in all about 8,000 troops. In addition to this force, three batteries of long-range were constantly firing on my troops from the Maryland side of the river.

The loss of the enemy, so far as known, is as follows: 1,300 killed, wounded and drowned; captured, 710 prisoners, 1,500 stand of arms, three pieces of cannon, one stand of colors, a large number of cartridge boxes, bayonet scabbards and a quantity of camp furniture. Among the killed of the enemy was General Baker, formerly Senator from Oregon, and several other commissioned officers. Among the prisoners taken were twenty-two commissioned officers. General C. P. Stone commanded the Federal forces until 3 o'clock on the morning of the 22d, when he was superseded by Major-General N. P. Banks.

The engagement on our side was fought entirely with the musket. The artillery was in position to do effective service should the enemy have advanced from their cover. The enemy were armed with the minie musket, the Belgian gun and Springfield musket; a telescopic target rifle was also among the arms found. In closing my report I would call the attention of the general commanding to the heroism and gallantry displayed by the officers and men of the Seventh Brigade in the actions of the 21st and 22d of October. The promptness with which every commander obeyed, and the spirit with which their men executed, my orders to attack the enemy—in much superior force and in a position where he had great advantages—entitles them to the thanks of the Southern Confederacy. Without food or rest for more than twelve hours previous to the commencement of the battle, they drove an enemy four times their number from the soil of Virginia, killing and taking prisoners a greater number than our whole force engaged. To witness the patience, enthusiasm and devotion of the troops to our cause during an action of thirteen hours excited my warmest admiration.

As my entire brigade exceeded my most sanguine expectations in their intrepidity and endurance, I am unable to individualize any particular command, as the tenacity with which each regiment held their positions was equaled only by their undaunted courage and firm determination to conquer.

To my general staff I am much indebted. Major John D. Rogers, brigade quartermaster, was directed to conduct the baggage train beyond Goose Creek, which difficult duty was performed in the night with great regularity. Captain Orr, brigade commissary, was actively engaged in securing commissary stores and in providing cooked rations for the brigade. To my acting aid-de-camp, Lieutenant Charles B. Wildman, of the Seventeenth Regiment Virginia Volunteers, and my volunteer aid, Mr. William H. Rogers, I am particularly indebted for services on the field of battle. Lieutenant Wildman conducted the Eighteenth Regiment and Mr. Rogers the Seventeenth Regiment of Mississippi Volunteers to their respective positions in the action, and both repeatedly bore my orders under heavy fire. Captain A. L. Evans, assistant adjutant-general, though detained by other duty till 2 o clock P. M., rendered valuable service. The medical staff, both brigade and regimental, were actively engaged during the day in removing the dead and wounded, and in patriotically administering relief to the dying on the field. I am pained to report the fall of the gallant Colonel E. R. Burt, of the Eighteenth Regiment Mississippi Volunteers. He was mortally wounded about 4 o'clock P. M., while gallantly leading his regiment under a tremendous fire. His loss is truly severe to his regiment and to our common cause.

At about 2 o'clock P. M. on the 21st I sent a message to General R. L. Wright to bring his militia force to my assistance at Fort Evans. He reported to me in person that he was unable to get his men to turn out, though there were a great number in town and arms and ammunition were offered them.

The prisoners taken were sent to Manassas, under charge of Captain O. R. Singleton, Eighteenth Regiment Mississippi Volunteers, with his company, and Captain W. A. P. Jones, of the Seventeenth Regiment Mississippi Volunteers, and a detachment of cavalry, the whole under the command of Captain Singleton, who conducted 529 prisoners nearly twenty-five miles after the great fatigue of the battle.

* * * * * * *

N. G. EVANS,

Brigadier-General, Commanding Seventh Brigade.

CASUALTIES.

Return of casualties in the Seventh Brigade, First Corps, Army of the Potomac, at the battle of Leesburg (Ball's Bluff), Va., October 21 and 22, 1861:

COMMAND.	Killed.		Woun'd.		Missing.		Aggregate
	Officers	Enlisted Men	Officers	Enlisted Men	Officers	Enlisted Men	
Thirteenth Mississippi	1	3	..	2	..	1	7
Seventeenth Mississippi	2	..	1	8	..	..	11
Eighteenth Mississippi *	..	22	7	56	.	..	85
Eighth Virginia †	..	8	4	39	1	..	52
Total	3	33	12	105	1	1	155

* Colonel Burt, since dead.

† Three privates, since dead; one lieutenant captured.

BOMBARDMENT

OF

FORTS WALKER AND BEAUREGARD,

NOVEMBER 7, 1861.

BY

BRIG.-GEN. THOMAS F. DRAYTON, C. S. A.

HEADQUARTERS OF PROVISIONAL FORCES,
THIRD MILITARY DISTRICT, DEPARTMENT OF SOUTH CAROLINA.
CAMP LEE, HARDEEVILLE, November 24, 1861.

I HAVE the honor of presenting my official report of the engagement on the 7th instant between the Federal fleet, numbering fifteen war steamers and gunboats, and Forts Walker and Beauregard, upon Hilton Head and Bay Point, at the entrance of Port Royal Sound. The Fleet was commanded by Captain S. F. Dupont, flag officer of the South Atlantic Blockading Squadron, and the troops on board the transports by Brigadier-General [T. W.] Sherman. The distance between the forts is by Coast Survey two and five-eighth miles.

The enemy's fleet had been collecting in our waters since the morning of the 4th instant, and had increased in the afternoon to thirty-two war steamers and transports. On receiving a dispatch to this effect from Colonel William C. Heyward, commanding the troops at Camp Walker, I left my headquarters in Beaufort and repaired by steamer to Bay Point, which I reached at 6 P. M., passing on the way the ever-watchful little fleet of Flag Officer [Josiah] Tatnall, C. S. N.

BRIG.-GEN. THOMAS F. DRAYTON, OF SOUTH CAROLINA.

After remaining in consultation until 1:30 A. M. with Colonel R. G. M. Dunovant, commandant of the post, I took my departure, leaving him such general instructions as the uncertain mode and direction from which an attack might be expected would permit. I then visited Commodore Tatnall, and after an interchange of views took leave, crossed to Hilton Head Island, landed there at daylight on the 5th, and immediately dispatched a courier to Braddock's Point, south end of the island, ordering Captain Stuart's company, of Ninth Regiment, to march on Fort Walker, and embark thence to strengthen Captain Elliott's gunners in Fort Beauregard. This company did not leave on the 6th, as proposed, as Captain Sapord of the steamer Edith failed to comply with his orders to carry it across early in the morning. They were dispatched, however, by the first steamer at my disposal on the 7th, and before they had reached half-way across the bay they were cut off from Bay Point by the advancing fleet of the enemy, and obliged to seek shelter in Skull Creek, where Captain Stuart disembarked his whole command in safety.

On inspecting Fort Walker, shortly after my arrival, I found twenty guns, of various caliber, mounted upon the ramparts, thirteen of which were on the channel battery, viz., one 10-inch columbiad in the center, flanked to the right by five 32-pounders and one 9-inch Dahlgren rifled cannon, and to the left by six other cannon in the following order: one 32-pounder, one 8-inch columbiad, three 42-pounders and one rifled 24-pounder; north bastion, one 32-pounder; south bastion, one 32-pounder, one 8-inch howitzer and one long 12-pounder; south flank of bastion, one navy 32-pounder; demi-lune, two 24-pounders; redan, one navy 8-inch howitzer. Of these eight guns, one in the north bastion and two in the south flank could occasionally be used against the ships of war. The rest were for the land defense.

To man the guns within the fort, and for an infantry reserve outside, we had, until re-enforcements came from Savannah on the afternoon of the 6th, two companies of Colonel Wagener's First Regiment Artillery, South Carolina Militia, numbering 152 men; three companies of Colonel Heyward's Ninth [Eleventh] Regiment, South Carolina Volunteers, 210 men; four companies of Colonel R. G. M. Dunovant's Twelfth Regiment, South Carolina Volunteers, under Major Jones, 260 men. Total, 622 men.

There were stationed on the beach at Camp Lookout, six miles off, Captain I. H. Screven's Mounted Guerrillas, numbering sixty-five, who acted as scouts and couriers.

About 9 o'clock A. M. of the 5th, Commodore Tatnall, who had boldly attacked the enemy's gunboats on the previous day, again gallantly steamed out to exchange shots with them, but he was met by too large a force, and therefore retired slowly behind our forts. The enemy followed and engaged both batteries for about forty-five minutes, with no other injury than three men slightly burned in Fort Beauregard from the explosion of a caisson struck by a rifle shell.

On the 6th instant the fleet and transports, which had increased to about forty-five sail, would probably have attacked us had not the weather been very boisterous. In the afternoon, about 4 o'clock, we received our first re-enforcements from Georgia, 450 infantry, under command of Captain Berry, C. S. A., and Captain Read's battery of two 12-pounder howitzers and fifty men.

I had reason for supposing that this assistance would have arrived sooner, for General A. R. Lawton, commanding provisional forces in Georgia, wrote from Savannah to Colonel W. C. Heyward, on the 4th instant, 8:30 P. M., as follows: "From a dispatch received to-day from General Ripley, I infer that you (Colonel W. C. Heyward) have been sufficiently re-enforced from his command until the plans of the enemy shall be more fully developed."

Two hours after the gallant Georgians came to the rescue, I received the welcome intelligence that Colonel De Saussure's Fifteenth Regiment, South Carolina Volunteers, 650 strong, had landed at Seabrook's Wharf, upon Skull Creek, and were close at hand. At last the memorable 7th dawned upon us bright and serene, not a ripple upon the broad expanse of water to disturb the accuracy of fire from the broad decks of that magnificent armada about advancing in battle array to vomit forth its iron hail with all the spiteful energy of long-suppressed rage and conscious strength. At 9:25 A. M. one 9-inch Dahlgren gun opened fire upon the steamship Wabash, flagship of Captain S. F. Dupont, which led the van, closely succeeded by fourteen other large steamers and gunboats. The shell from the Dahlgren exploded near the muzzle and was harmless. Other shots followed from both forts, and soon the fire became general on land and water. In spite of our fire, directed with deliberation and coolness, the fleet soon passed both batteries apparently unharmed, and then returning delivered in their changing rounds a terrific shower of shot and shell in flank and front.

Besides this moving battery, the fort was enfiladed by two gunboats anchored to the north of the mouth of Fish Hall Creek, and another at a point on the edge of the shoals to the south. This enfilading fire on so still a sea annoyed and damaged us excessively, particularly as we had no gun on either flank of the bastion to reply with, for the 32-pounder on the right flank was shattered very early by a round shot, and on the north flank, for want of a carriage, no gun had been mounted.

After the fourth fire the 10-inch columbiad bounded over the limber and became useless. The 24-pounder rifled cannon was choked while ramming down a shell, and lay idle during nearly the whole engagement. The shells for the 9-inch Dahlgren were also too large. The fourth shell attempted to be rammed home could not be driven below the trunnions, and was then at great risk discharged. Thus far the fire of the enemy had been endured and replied to with the unruffled courage of veterans. At 10:30 our gunners became so fatigued that I left the fort, accompanied by one of my volunteer aids, Captain H. Rose, and went back to Captain Read's battery (one and three-quarter miles in the rear of the fort) and brought the greater part of his men back to take the places of our exhausted men inside the fort. It was while thus engaged with Captain Read's company that Colonel W. H. Stiles rode up and reported his regiment about two miles off. I instantly directed my aid, Lieutenant Drayton, to accompany Colonel Stiles to the road along which his regiment was advancing, and to station it in position by the side of the other Georgia troops. On entering the fort with Captain Read's company they were cordially greeted by both officers and men.

The vigorous attack from the fleet continued unabated, with still no decided damage to any of their ships. About 12:30 P. M. I again went out of the fort with my assistant adjutant-general, Captain Young, for the purpose of mustering together the infantry and reserves, and have them in readiness for any eventuality. Before leaving, however, I turned over the command to Colonel Heyward, with directions to hold out as long as any effective fire could be returned.

Having mounted our horses, we rejoined the troops

near Hospital No. 2. I received information through one of the vedettes that a steamer and small boats were sounding close to the beach. I detached Captain Berry, with three companies of his battalion, under the guidance of Captain Ephraim Barnard, volunteer aid, to watch the enemy, beat them back if they attempted to land, and give notice if he wanted support. I then, with some of my staff, rode to collect together the other troops, who, through ignorance of our island roads, had lost their way and had not yet come up. On the road leading to the wharf on Skull Creek, about one and one-fourth miles from Fort Walker, I unexpectedly met General Ripley and staff. Saluting him, I inquired if he visited the island to assume command, and whether he wished to go back with me into the fort. He said no, but that he would return to Coosawhatchie to collect and bring back two or three regiments to my support. We then moved from under the fire of the ships to the shelter of some myrtles, where we could not be seen. I then stated to him the incidents of the morning; how the men had fought; that the day was going against us, and I was then collecting my forces for any emergency that might arise; and, if compelled to defend the island, it should be retained to the last extremity. We then parted, he taking the road toward the ferry, and I in pursuit of the purposes which brought me out of the fort.

On reaching my reserves at Hospital No. 2 I learned that the enemy had ceased making soundings, and had gone back to sea, whereupon I dispatched Captain Read to order Captain Berry to return from the beach.

Two o'clock had now arrived when I noticed our men coming out of the fort, which they had bravely defended for four and a half hours against fearful odds, and then only retiring when all but three of the guns on the water-front had been disabled, and only five hundred pounds of powder in the magazine, commencing the action with 220 men inside the fort, afterward increased to 255 by the accession from Read's battery. These heroic men retired slowly and sadly from their well-fought guns, which to have defended longer would have exhibited the energy of despair rather than the manly pluck of the true soldier.

The defense of this post involved a twofold preparation, first, to repel the attack from the fleet, and secondly, an assault by the beach from the troops upon the transports. By the beach we had to provide against an attack from the north under cover of the bluff south of Fish Hall Creek, and from the south by the beach under cover of the woods, between where a picket of twenty-five men were posted, under Captain Paul H. Seabrook; and lastly, by the road leading from the beach to the second hospital. To guard against surprise either by Fish Hall Creek or by the beach, when I was returning to the fort with a portion of Captain Read's company, I at the same time led up Colonel De Saussure's regiment to the hollow west of the road and directed them to lie down. They were perfectly masked from the fire of the fort, but not from that of the fleet, for the watchmen at the mastheads gave notice of their position, compelling Colonel De Saussure after a short time to fall back under a heavy fire to a less dangerous locality.

Had the intrenched camp, with storehouses and magazines, been made in time several lives and large quantities of public property might have been saved; but it was impossible to have made this within the short time and with the diminutive force at my disposal, for on my arrival at headquarters in Beaufort on the night of the 17th of October the number of troops at Camp Walker was but 362, afterward increased on the 24th to 622 by the accession of four companies under Major Jones of the Twelfth Regiment South Carolina Volunteers. To this may be added the engineer force of some sixty men, who, with the soldiers, worked incessantly day and night. As for evidence of what they accomplished: The 8-inch columbiad on the water-front was only mounted on the 1st of November; one 8-inch howitzer, in the salient of the south bastion, mounted on the 4th; one 32-pounder, on the right flank of bastion, mounted on the 5th; one 8-inch howitzer, mounted on a ship carriage; embrasure cut through parapet of demi-lune on the night of the 5th; covered way and hot-shot furnace for 42-pounders, constructed of earth and dry masonry, on the morning of the 6th, together with wads of moss and hay for same; splinter proof, occupying only one-half terre-plein behind the principal traverse, was finished on the morning of the engagement (7th instant), the material not having arrived before the 4th instant. The retreat was commenced about 3 P. M. toward Ferry Point, about six miles off, Colonel De Saussure's regiment and Captain I. Read's company of artillery bringing up the rear. At 1:30 A. M., by the aid of Commodore Tatnall's fleet, the steamers St. Johns and Edisto, and three large flats, capable of holding 150 men each, the troops were all safely embarked, without provisions, no ammunition but what was contained in the cartridge boxes (the 100,000 cartridges I had made requisition for, and been anxiously expecting, not having reached us until after the battle), and fearing that our retreat would be cut off by the enemy's gunboats at Skull Creek, no other alternative was left but to leave the island and concentrate upon the mainland, where we would be enabled to fight the enemy on more equal terms should he venture beyond the protection of his fleet and attack us there. The muskets captured by the enemy, with the exception of some ten or fifteen, were those left in the fort, shattered by shot and shell; others left in camp belonging to men on sick leave, or to those engaged in heating hot-shot furnaces two days before the fight, and some boxes of arms which had been left on the wharf the night before the battle, belonging to the sick men of Colonel De Saussure's regiment, who had been left behind at Lightwood Knot, and which could have been saved, with a box of swords, if the captains of the steamers Edisto and St. Johns had not refused to take them on board when directed to do so.

To Captain Tatnall, Flag Officer, C. S. N., and the officers and men of his little fleet, I can not too highly express my admiration of their intrepidity and hardihood in attacking the enemy's gunboats on the 4th and 5th instants. These encounters, by interrupting their soundings and the location of their buoys, no doubt prevented our being attacked on Tuesday, the 5th instant, before our re-enforcements reached us. I must acknowledge the assistance extended to us by the gallant Commodore with his boats on the night of our retreat from the island.

Plan of Fort Walker.

FORT BEAUREGARD.

The attack upon the fort, though not so concentrated and heavy as that upon Walker, was, nevertheless, very severe. Its armament was nineteen guns, of which the following, viz., one 8-inch Rodman, bored to 24-pounder and rifled; two 42-pounders; one 10-inch columbiad; two 42-pounders, reamed to eight inches, and one 32-pounder in hot-shot battery, were the only guns capable of being used against the fleet.

The force on Bay Point was 640 men, commanded by Colonel R. G. M. Dunovant, Twelfth Regiment South Carolina Volunteers. Of the above 149 garrisoned Fort Beauregard, under the immediate command of Captain Stephen Elliott, Jr., Beaufort Volunteer Artillery, Company A, Ninth Regiment, South Carolina Volunteers. The infantry force of Colonel Dunovant's regiment was intrusted with the protection of the eastern part of the island, and of the defense of the bastion line at the Island Narrows, where an attack was expected from the enemy.

Knowing how small a force Captain Elliott had to command his batteries, I ordered, as soon as I reached Hilton Head, on the 5th instant, Captain Stuart's company (Hamilton Guards), Ninth [Company E, Eleventh] Regiment, South Carolina Volunteers, to march upon Fort Walker from Braddock's Point, and take thence the steamer Edith for Bay Point; but the unfortunate failure of Captain Sapord of the Edith to fulfill his appointment at the hour designated prevented me from rendering support to Captain Elliott as I desired. But on Thursday morning, 7th instant, having obtained the steamer Emma, I dispatched Captain Stuart's company on her to Fort Beauregard. The rapid advance of the enemy's fleet, however, to the attack on the batteries cut off and compelled her, at the risk of being intercepted, to turn back and seek shelter in Skull Creek, on the shores of which Captain Stuart's company safely disembarked and joined me in the afternoon; and here again was exhibited another act of heroism on the part of our veteran commodore, who, in order to save the Emma, interposed his own frail flag steamer between her and the advancing flagship of Commodore Dupont, drawing upon himself her entire broadside, and thus diverting the huge leviathan temporarily from her course, secured the safety of the Emma at the peril of his own vessel. The non-arrival of any re-enforcements at Camp Walker until the night of the 6th instant also prevented me from sending the four companies of the Twelfth Regiment, South Carolina Volunteers, under Major Jones, to the support of the other six companies of the regiment at Bay Point.

The delays and dangers incident to the manner in which troops and supplies of all kinds were landed at the forts of Port Royal, and the absence of all means of retreat in case of disaster, had attracted my most serious attention immediately after I assumed command at Beaufort, on the evening of the 7th instant. I immediately took steps for remedying the first and providing for the last.

With the double object of landing supplies in all weather at Bay Point, and at the same time of furnishing the means of retreat beyond the range of the enemy's guns, I directed one of my volunteer aids, Captain T. R. S. Elliott, to make an examination of the adjacent creeks to the north of the fort. He reported that about three miles from the mouth of Moss Creek there was a depth of water sufficient for steamers drawing seven feet at low water, and that from thence a causeway of 300 yards over the marsh might easily be made, and furnish a sure means of transportation, and thus avoid the losses and delays which had previously occurred in landing from the steamers into flats upon the beach.

From the point above indicated in Moss Creek flats were to have been provided and stationed to convey the soldiers in case of emergency across the creek, thence by land to Station Creek, where other flats were to be placed for the same object as at Moss Creek. Landing at St. Helena, the transit to White Hall Ferry, opposite Beaufort, was comparatively safe.

On Hilton Head I also commenced repairing the wharf at Seabrook's Landing, on Skull Creek, with a view of transporting stores to Fort Walker when the weather was too boisterous to land them in the surf. The completion of the wharf was prevented, however, by the unexpected attack of the enemy, though in its incomplete state it had already been put to successful use. I succeeded, however, in obtaining from Charleston two flats and two troop boats, and from Savannah three large flats, capable of containing 150 men each, which reached Jenkins' Island Ferry in time to assist in embarking our troops on the night of the retreat. Three other smaller ones were sent at the same time to White Hall Ferry, which assisted in performing the same good offices for Colonel Dunovant's command. The rest of the scheme, for want of time and flats, could not be carried out in the manner I intended.

For the purpose of sending messages between Forts Walker and Beauregard, and thence to my headquarters at Beaufort, I had prepared, by the assistance of Captain Lynah, another of my aids, a number of signal flags, the designs of which had already been prepared and painted, and only needed a few more days to have been put into operation.

In alluding as I have to these matters I do not mean to reflect upon any person, or to say these pressing wants could have been supplied anterior to the period when I entered upon my new duties. My design has been to exhibit the condition in which I found my command, and to show that I have left no effort untried to improve it.

CASUALTIES.

The following is a correct list of killed, wounded, missing and prisoners:

COMMAND.	Killed	Wounded	Captured	Missing	Aggregate
Fort Walker	10	20	..	..	30
Fort Beauregard	..	13	..	..	13
Fifteenth South Carolina	1	15	..	..	16
Sick in Hospital	..	..	3	..	3
Command not Stated	..	..	..	4	4
Total	11	48	3	4	66

The heads of the quartermaster's and commissary's departments, Major E. Willis and Captain C. D. Owens, discharged their several duties with economy and fidelity. These officers and their assistants were unwearied, and earnest were their efforts to save the public property left at the headquarters in Beaufort. I must likewise make honorable mention of Colonel W. C. Heyward, Ninth [Eleventh] Regiment, South Carolina Volunteers, who commanded in Fort Walker and its vicinity, and who during the battle made the best use of the means at his disposal. Colonel John A. Wagener, First Regiment Artillery, South Carolina Militia, supported by Major Arthur M. Huger, of the same regiment, was placed in the immediate command of all the batteries, nine of which, upon the water-front, were manned by the German Artillery, Companies A and B, Captains H. Harms and D. Werner, First Regiment Artillery, South Carolina Militia, all of whom fought under the flag of their adopted country with an enthusiasm which could not have been surpassed had they been fighting in defense of their own fatherland.

The remaining four batteries on the left flank of the water-front were under direction of Captain Josiah Bedon's, Canady's and White's companies, Ninth [Eleventh] Regiment, South Carolina Volunteers. Major F. D. Lee, South Carolina Engineers and constructing engineer of Fort Walker, not only fought gallantly at the batteries, but afforded valuable assistance at other points in the work during the contest. Captain Joseph A. Yates, Battalion South Carolina Artillery, and acting ordnance officer, was zealous in the execution of all the duties assigned to him. Toward the close of the fight he was severely wounded. Dr. Ogier and his able assistants, Drs. W. C. Ravenel and William Elliott, a volunteer from Savannah, Ga., were present and rendered efficient service in the hospitals. I can not but regret the painful wound which has been the cause of the resignation of Dr. Ogier as medical director in my military district.

In conclusion, I can not but express my high appreciation of the gallant behavior of my aids, Captain Henry E. Young and Lieutenant J. E. Drayton, as also that of the gentlemen comprising my volunteer staff, Captains L. Cheves, H. Rose, E. Lynah, J. E. Eddings, J. I. Middleton, Jr., and Joseph A. Huger.

* * * * * * *

THOMAS F. DRAYTON,
Brigadier-General Commanding.

"DON'T be uneasy," said an anxious mother to the conscript officer. "Sir, I'd rather see my son in his coffin than to see him go into the army." "Don't give yourself any uneasiness on that subject," said the officer; "I assure you that he will *soon* be there."

BATTLE OF MANASSAS.

HISTORICAL CORRESPONDENCE.

REPORTS OF GENERAL IRWIN McDOWELL, COMMANDING UNITED STATES FORCES.

CENTREVILLE, July 21, 1861—5:45 P. M.

We passed Bull Run. Engaged the enemy, who, it seems had just been re-enforced by General Johnston. We drove them for several hours, and finally routed them. They rallied and repulsed us, but only to give us again the victory, which seemed complete. But our men, exhausted with the fatigue and thirst, and confused by firing into each other, were attacked by the enemy's reserves, and driven from the position we had gained, overlooking Manassas. After this the men could not be rallied, but slowly left the field. In the meantime the enemy outflanked Richardson at Blackburn's Ford, and we have now to hold Centreville till our men can get behind it.

* * * * * * *

IRWIN McDOWELL,
Brigadier-General Commanding.

LIEUTENANT-COLONEL TOWNSEND.

FAIRFAX COURTHOUSE, July 21, 1861.

The men have thrown away their haversacks in the battle and left them behind; they are without food; have eaten nothing since breakfast. We are without artillery ammunition. The larger part of the men are a confused mob—entirely demoralized. It was the opinion of all the commanders that no stand could be made this side of the Potomac. We will, however, make the attempt at Fairfax Courthouse. From a prisoner we learn that 20,000 from Johnston joined last night, and they march on us to-night.

IRWIN McDOWELL.

COLONEL TOWNSEND.

FAIRFAX COURTHOUSE, July 22, 1861.

Many of the volunteers did not wait for authority to proceed to the Potomac, but left on their own decision. They are now pouring through this place in a state of utter disorganization. They could not be prepared for action by to-morrow morning even were they willing. I learn from prisoners that we are to be pressed here to-night and to-morrow morning, as the enemy's force is very large and they are elated. I think we heard cannon on our rear guards. I think now, as all my commanders thought at Centreville, there is no alternative but to fall back to the Potomac, and I shall proceed to do so with as much regularity as possible.

IRWIN McDOWELL.

COLONEL TOWNSEND.

BATTLE OF MANASSAS.

RETURN OF CAPTURES AND ABSTRACT OF FEDERAL PRISONERS TAKEN.

HEADQUARTERS, FIRST CORPS,
FAIRFAX COURTHOUSE, October 12, 1861.

Return of captured ordnance and ordnance stores turned in to Ordnance Department, Army of Potomac, up to August 16, 1861: One 30-pounder Parrott gun with three hundred rounds of ammunition; nine 10-pounder Parrott guns, with one hundred rounds of ammunition each; three 6-pounder brass guns, with one hundred rounds of ammunition each; three 12-pounder brass howitzers, with one hundred rounds of ammunition each; two 12-pounder boat howitzers, with one hundred rounds of ammunition each; nine James rifled field-pieces, with one hundred rounds of ammunition each; thirty-seven caissons, six traveling forges, four battery wagons, splendidly equipped; sixty-four artillery horses, with harness; 500,000 rounds small-arm ammunition, 4,500 sets accouterments, cartridge boxes, etc.; 4,000 muskets.

No accurate return of drums, swords, pistols, knapsacks, canteens, bridles, etc., can be obtained. One 6-pounder gun and one 12-pounder howitzer were found spiked, but they were easily withdrawn. One of the enemy's caissons exploded in the field, in addition to those captured.

Hospital equipments turned in up to August 16, 1861: five medicine chests, partially filled; six cases surgical instruments, two sets of panniers, seven ambulances.

Returns of litters, instruments, supplies, etc., are all very incomplete, so much having been appropriated by surgeons of regiments, etc., besides the loss from plundering by privates and citizens.

Quartermaster's stores turned in up to August 16, 1861: 870 axes, spades and intrenching tools, two sets carpenter's and blacksmith's tools, twelve sets harness, twenty-three extra traces for artillery, seven platform and other scales, 1,650 camp cooking utensils, 2,700 camp mess utensils, 302 pairs pantaloons, drawers and socks; 700 blankets, twenty-two tents and flies, twenty-one wagons, thirty-three horses, twenty-five trunks and carpet-bags, one coil rope.

SAID a Federal soldier the other day: "A Johnny Reb got away with me entirely one day after we captured him at Resaca. He said to me that they had found out how to fight us without getting fired at in return. They simply stood a negro upon the breastworks and fired at us from behind him. The result was that we did not fire back, for fear of killing the negro."

BOMBARDMENT OF FORT WALKER, S. C., NOVEMBER 7, 1861. INTERIOR VIEW OF THE FORT. [From an old sketch, the property of Mrs. Frank Leslie.]

BATTLE OF DRANESVILLE, VA.,

DECEMBER 20, 1861.

BY

BRIGADIER-GENERAL J. E. B. STUART, C. S. A.

HEADQUARTERS OUTPOSTS ARMY OF THE POTOMAC,
December 23, 1861.

ON the 20th instant I was placed in command of four regiments of infantry, 150 cavalry and a battery of four pieces of artillery, viz.: Eleventh Virginia, Colonel S. Garland, Jr.; Sixth South Carolina, Lieutenant-Colonel Secrest; Tenth Alabama, Colonel J. H. Forney, and First Kentucky, Colonel Thomas H. Taylor; making an aggregate force of 1,600 infantry; Sumter Flying Artillery (four pieces), Captain A. S. Cutts; One Hundredth [V.] North Carolina Cavalry, Major Gordon, and Fifty-second [V.] Virginia Cavalry, Captain Pitzer, for the purpose of covering an expedition of all the wagons of our army that could be spared (after hay) to the left of Dranesville.

I proceeded at once by the nearest route, at daylight, toward Dranesville.

Knowing the situation of the enemy's advance posts, I sent the cavalry forward far in advance of the infantry, to take possession of the two turnpikes to the right of Dranesville, leading directly to the enemy's advanced posts, so as to prevent any communication of our movements reaching them, and with the main body I followed on to take a position with two regiments and a section of artillery on each turnpike, also to the right of Dranesville, and close enough to their intersection to form a continuous line.

Such a position I knew I could hold against almost any odds, but as my cavalry came in sight of the turnpike Captain Pitzer discovered the enemy on the ridge and sent me word immediately. I galloped forward at once, and, reconnoitering for myself, found that a portion of the enemy was in possession of the ridge, and I could hear distinctly artillery carriages passing up the Georgetown turnpike in considerable numbers, and presently saw the cannons, mounted on limber boxes, passing up toward Dranesville. I knew, too, that the enemy's infantry were in advance, and I at once suspected that he was either marching upon Leesburg or had received intelligence through a spy of our intended forage expedition and was marching upon it. In either case our wagons would have fallen an easy prey to him, and I saw at once that my only way to save them was to make a vigorous attack upon his rear and left flank, and to compel him to desist from such a purpose.

I sent back for the infantry to hurry forward, and sent Captain Pitzer with his detachment of cavalry to gain the roads toward Leesburg, give notice to our wagons to return at once to camp and keep between them and the enemy, threatening his front and flank; and I will state here, parenthetically, that this duty was performed by Captain Pitzer and his gallant little detachment in the most creditable manner, all our wagons reaching camp safely.

In the meantime the enemy's skirmishers took possession of the dense pine in our front, and as our infantry was met by my messenger three-fourths of a mile back, it was some time coming up. Colonel Garland's regiment, leading, was directed to deploy two companies on each side of the road to clear the ground of the enemy's skirmishers. One of these companies, having mistaken its direction, went too far to the right, and Colonel Garland had to replace it with another. The pines were cleared at double-quick, and the battery was ordered in position and fired very effectively during the whole of the engagement to the front.

The infantry were placed in position as follows: Garland's regiment on the right of the road, a little in advance of the artillery; Secrest's (South Carolina) on the left of the road. Forney's regiment, arriving later, replaced Garland's, which moved by the flank to the right; and the First Kentucky, Colonel Taylor, at first intended as a reserve, was ordered to take position on the Sixth South Carolina.

As our infantry was well secured from the enemy's view, their artillery fire, which opened about fifteen minutes after ours began, had little effect upon the infantry, but played with telling effect along the road, as from its position and the straightness of the road in our rear, it raked the latter with shell and round shot completely. Their caissons and limbers were behind in a brick house, completely protected from our shot, while our limbers and caissons were necessarily crowded and exposed. There was no outlet to right or left for a mile back by which the artillery could change its position. When our forces took their position the fire of the artillery caused great commotion in the enemy's lines, and a part evidently took to their heels. The right wing was ordered forward, and the Tenth Alabama rushed with a shout in a shower of bullets, under the gallant lead of their colonel (Forney) and Lieutenant-Colonel Martin, the latter falling in the charge. A part of this regiment crossed the road and took position along a fence, from which the enemy felt the trueness of their aim at short range. The colonel was here severely wounded, and had to retire. In his absence the command devolved upon Major Woodward.

The Eleventh Virginia, holding position on the right of the Tenth Alabama, were not so much exposed to the fire of the enemy, and consequently suffered less. The Sixth South Carolina gradually gained ground also to the front, and being, together with the Tenth Alabama, exposed to the fire of the enemy's sharpshooters from a two-story brick house, suffered most. My orders to Colonel Taylor, First Kentucky, were given through Colonel Forney, and I soon knew by the commotion on my left that it was in place. The thicket where the Sixth South Carolina and First Kentucky operated was so dense that it was impossible to see either their exact position or their progress in the fight, and I regret to say that the First Kentucky and the Sixth South Carolina mistook each other for the enemy, and a few casualties occurred in consequence; but with that exception the whole force acted with admirable unison, and advanced upon the enemy with the steadiness of veterans, driving him several times from his position with heavy loss. When the action had lasted about two hours I found that the enemy, being already in force larger than my own, was recovering from his disorder and receiving heavy re-enforcements. I could not, with my small number, being beyond the reach of re-enforcements, force his position without fearful sacrifice, and seeing that his artillery, superior to ours in numbers and position only, was pouring a very destructive fire into Cutt's battery, I decided to withdraw the latter at once, preparatory to retiring from the field, judging, too, that I had given our wagons sufficient time to get beyond the reach of the enemy.

MAJOR-GENERAL J. E. B. STUART, OF VIRGINIA.

The battery suffered greatly. Its position was necessarily such that it could fire only to the front, and the caissons and limbers had no cover whatever from such a fire. Three or four cannoneers had been shot at their posts and several wounded, and every shot of the enemy was dealing destruction on either man, limber or horse.

The conduct of the brave, true and heroic Cutts attracted my admiration frequently during the action—now acting No. 1 and now as gunner, and still directing and disposing the whole with perfect self-command and a devotion to his duty that was, I believe, scarcely ever equaled. He executed my orders to withdraw his battery under a ricochet fire of great accuracy.

One piece I found it necessary to detail some infantry (Eleventh Virginia) to assist in conducting to the rear, which was done by them under great personal exposure.

Having secured the artillery, I sent orders to the four regimental commanders to disengage themselves from the enemy and retire slowly and in perfect order to the railroad, where a stand would be made. This delicate duty was performed admirably, and our troops marched back leisurely, bringing with them all the wounded that could be found.

The men gathered up their blankets as they passed the points where they had been deposited before the fight. I regret to say, however, that one of the regiments reached the road this side of their blankets and knapsacks, thus missing them entirely, a circumstance which the enemy will construe into precipitate flight. The enemy was evidently too much crippled to follow in pursuit, and after a short halt at the railroad I proceeded to Fryingpan Church, where the wounded were cared for.

Early next morning, with the two fresh regiments furnished me (the Ninth Georgia and Eighteenth Virginia) and a detachment of cavalry under Lieutenant-Colonel Baker, I proceeded toward the scene of action of the previous day, the cavalry being sent in advance. Learning that the enemy had evacuated Dranesville and had left some of our wounded there, I pushed on to that place to recover them and to take care of the dead. I found our dead on the field, and proceeded at once to remove them all to Centreville for interment. The wounded (about ten) were left by the enemy at a house at Dranesville, who intended to send for them the next day. They had been cared for with the utmost devotion by several of the ladies of the place. They were also removed to Centreville, except two, who were not able to survive the removal, and so, at their own desire and on the surgeon's advice, were left in charge of the ladies.

As to the strength of the enemy, if the concurrent statements of the citizens residing along his route of march can be credited, he had fifteen regiments of infantry, several batteries and seven companies of cavalry. The latter had started in the direction of our wagons just before the action began, but were then recalled.

Our wounded, who were for the time prisoners, say that the enemy's loss was acknowledged by them to be very heavy, and among the officers killed or mortally wounded was Colonel Kane, of Utah notoriety, and citizens living below declared that they carried off twenty wagon loads of killed and wounded, besides many dead before them on their horses, and that as soon as their dead and wounded were removed they left the field precipitately, leaving behind much of the material which we left on the field, but which we recovered next day.

I can not speak in too high terms of Colonel Forney, that gallant son of Alabama, whose conspicuous bravery, leading his men in a galling fire, was the admiration of all; nor of his lieutenant-colonel (Martin), who, with the battle cry of "Forward!" on his lips, fell, bravely encouraging his men. Nor can I do more than simple justice to the officers and men of that regiment, who seemed determined to follow their colonel wherever he would lead.

Colonel Garland and Major Langhorne, of the Eleventh Virginia, behaved with great coolness under fire, and the men of that regiment, though deprived by locality from sharing as much of the danger of the engagement as the Tenth Alabama Regiment, yet acquitted themselves to my entire satisfaction.

The Sixth South Carolina and First Kentucky were, I regret to say, too much screened from my view to afford me the privilege of bearing witness by personal observation of individual prowess; but that the Sixth South Carolina, under the feerless Secrest, did its whole duty, let the list of killed and wounded and her battle flag, bathed in blood, with its staff shivered in the hand of the bearer, be silent but eloquent witnesses. Their major (Woodward) was painfully wounded, but bore himself heroically notwithstanding. From the sounds that I could distinctly hear from the left I felt assured that the First Kentucky, under the gallant Taylor, the intrepid Major Crossland and daring Desha, was all right.

Our batteries' loss in killed and wounded was great, and the men deserve great credit for their devotion to their pieces under such perilous circumstances. The detachment of North Carolina Cavalry, under Major Gordon, was of great service in watching the approaches to our flanks, though the ground was extremely unfavorable for cavalry.

Had we effected the safety of our wagons—constituting the greater part of the available means of transportation of this army—with great loss to ourselves, without inflicting much on the enemy, alone would have been a triumph of which the brave men of the four regiments under my command could be proud; but when it is considered what overwhelming odds were against us, notwithstanding which we saved the transportation, inflicted upon the enemy a loss severer than our own, rendering him unequal to the task of pursuit, retired in perfect order and bringing with us nearly all our wounded, we may rightly call it a glorious success. Our entire loss is as follows:

COMMANDS.	Killed	Wounded	Missing
Eleventh Virginia Volunteers	6	15	..
Sixth South Carolina Volunteers	18	45	..
Tenth Alabama Volunteers	15	45	6
First Kentucky Volunteers	1	23	2
Cutts' Battery	3	15	..
Cavalry	..	..	..
Total	43	143	8

The list of killed has been materially increased by deaths which have occurred since the battle, as the number found dead on the field was only twenty-seven.

J. E. B. STUART,
Brigadier-General Commanding.

BOMBARDMENT OF FORT HENRY,

FEBRUARY 6, 1862.

BY

BRIG.-GEN. LLOYD TILGHMAN, C. S. A.,
Commanding Fort Henry.

RICHMOND, VA., August 9, 1862.

ON Monday, February 3d, in company with Major Gilmer, of the engineers, I completed the inspection of the main work as well as outworks at Fort Heiman, south of Tennessee River, as far as I had been able to perfect them, and also the main work, intrenched camp and exterior line of rifle-pits at Fort Henry. At 10 A. M. on that morning (the pickets on both sides of the Tennessee river extended well in our front, having reported no appearance of the enemy), I left, in company with Major Gilmer, for Fort Donelson, for the purpose of inspecting with him the defenses of that place. Tuesday, the 4th instant, was spent in making a thorough examination of all the defenses at Fort Donelson. At noon I heard heavy firing at Fort Henry for half an hour. At 4 P. M. a courier reached me from Colonel Heiman, at Fort Henry, informing me that the enemy was landing in strong force at Bailey's Ferry, three miles below, and on the east bank of the river.

BRIG.-GEN. LLOYD TILGHMAN, OF KENTUCKY.
[Killed at Champion's Hill, Mississippi, May 16, 1863.]

Delaying no longer than was necessary to give all proper orders for the arrangement of matters at Fort Donelson, I left with an escort of Tennessee cavalry, under command of Lieutenant-Colonel Gantt, for Fort Henry, accompanied by Major Gilmer, reaching that place at 11:30 P. M. I soon became satisfied that the enemy was really in strong force at Bailey's Ferry, with every indication of re-enforcements arriving constantly. Colonel Heiman, of the Tenth Tennessee, commanding, with most commendable alacrity and good judgment, had thrown forward to the outworks covering the Dover Road two pieces of light artillery, supported by a detachment from the Fourth Mississippi Regiment, under the command of Captain W. C. Red. Scouting parties of cavalry, operating on both sides of the river, had been pushed forward to within a very short distance of the enemy's lines. Without a moment's delay after reaching the fort I proceeded to arrange the available force to meet whatever contingency might arise.

The First Brigade, under Colonel Heiman, was composed of the Tenth Tennessee, Lieutenant-Colonel MacGavock commanding; the Twenty-seventh Alabama, under Colonel Hughes; the Forty-eighth Tennessee, under Colonel Voorhies; light battery of four pieces, commanded by Captain Culbertson, and the Tennessee battalion of cavalry, under Lieutenant-Colonel Gantt. Total, officers and men, 1,444. The Second Brigade, Colonel Joseph Drake (Fourth Mississippi Regiment) commanding, was composed of the Fourth Mississippi, under Major Adaire; the Fifteenth Arkansas, Colonel Gee; the Fifty-first Tennessee, Colonel Browder; the Alabama Battalion, Major Garvin; a light battery of three pieces, under Captain Crain; the Alabama battalion of cavalry; Captain Milner's company of cavalry, with Captain Padgett's spy company, and a detachment of rangers, under Acting Captain Milton. Total, officers and men, 1,215. The heavy artillery, under the command of Captain Taylor, numbering seventy-five men, were placed at the guns in Fort Henry.

As indicated some time since to the general commanding the department, I found it impossible to hold the commanding ground south of the Tennessee River with the small force of badly armed men at my command, and, notwithstanding the fact that all my defenses were commanded by the high ground on which I had commenced the construction of Fort Heiman, I deemed it proper to trust to the fact that the extremely bad roads leading to that point would prevent the movement of heavy guns by the enemy, by which I might be annoyed, and, leaving the Alabama battalion of cavalry and Captain Padgett's spy company on the western bank of the river, transferred the force encamped on that side to the opposite bank. At the time of receiving the first intimation of the approach of the enemy the Forty-eighth and Fifty-first Tennessee regiments, having only just reported, were encamped at Danville and at the mouth of Sandy River, and had to be moved from five to twenty miles in order to reach Fort Henry. This movement, together with the transfer of the Twenty-seventh Alabama and Fifteenth Arkansas regiments from Fort Heiman across the river, was all perfected by 5 A. M. on the morning of the 5th.

Early on the morning of the 5th the enemy was plainly to be seen at Bailey's Ferry, three miles below. The large number of heavy transports reported by our scouts gave evidence of the fact that the enemy was there in force, even at that time, and the arrival every hour of additional boats showed conclusively that I should be engaged with a heavy force by land, while the presence of seven gunboats and fifty-four guns indicated plainly that a joint attack was contemplated by land and water.

On leaving Fort Donelson I ordered Colonel Head to hold his own and Colonel Sugg's regiments, Tennessee Volunteers, with two pieces of artillery, ready to move at a moment's warning, with three days' cooked rations, and without camp equipage or wagon train of any kind, except enough to carry the surplus ammunition.

On the morning of the 5th I ordered him, in case nothing more had been heard from the country below, on the Cumberland, at the time of the arrival of my messenger, indicating an intention on the part of the enemy to invest Fort Donelson, to move out with the two regiments and the two pieces of artillery and take position at the Furnace, half way on the Dover Road to Fort Henry. The force embraced in this order was about 750 men, to act as circumstances might dictate.

Thus matters stood at 9 A. M. on the morning of the 5th. The wretched military position of Fort Henry and the small force at my disposal did not permit me to avail myself of the advantages to be derived from the system of outworks built with the hope of being re-enforced in time, and compelled me to determine to concentrate my efforts by land within the rifle-pits surrounding the camp of the Tenth Tennessee and Fourth Mississippi regiments in case I deemed it possible to do more than operate solely against the attack by the river. Accordingly, my entire command was paraded and placed in the rifle-pits around the above camps, and minute instructions given, not only to brigades, but to regiments and companies, as to the exact ground each was to occupy. Seconded by the able assistance of Major Gilmer, of the engineers, of whose valuable service I thus early take pleasure in speaking, and by Colonels Heiman and Drake, everything was arranged to make a formidable resistance against anything like fair odds.

It was known to me on the day before that the enemy had reconnoitered the roads leading to Fort Donelson from Bailey's Ferry by way of Iron Mountain Furnace, and at 10 A. M. on the 5th I sent forward from Fort Henry a strong reconnoitering party of cavalry. They had not advanced more than one and a half miles in the direction of the enemy when they encountered their reconnoitering party. Our cavalry charged them in gallant style, upon which the enemy's cavalry fell back, with a loss of only one man on each side. Very soon the main body of the Federal advance guard, composed of a regiment of infantry and a large force of cavalry, was met, upon which our cavalry retreated.

On receipt of this news I moved out in person with five companies of the Tenth Tennessee, five companies of the Fourth Mississippi and fifty cavalry, ordering at the same time two additional companies of infantry to support Captain Red at the outworks. Upon advancing well to the front I found that the enemy had retired. I returned to camp at 5 P. M., leaving Captain Red re-enforced at the outworks. The enemy was again re-enforced by the arrival of a number of large transports.

At night the pickets from the west bank reported the landing of troops on that side (opposite Bailey's Ferry), their advance picket having been met one and a half miles from the river. I at once ordered Captain Hubbard, of the Alabama cavalry, to take fifty men, and, if possible, surprise them. The inclemency of the weather, the rain having commenced to fall in torrents, prevented anything being accomplished. Early on the morning of the 6th Captain Padgett reported the arrival of five additional transports over night, and the landing of a large force on the west bank of the river at the point indicated above. From that time up to 9 o'clock it appeared as though the force on the east bank was again re-enforced, which was subsequently proven to be true.

The movements of the fleet of gunboats at an early hour prevented any communication, except by a light barge, with the western bank, and by 10 A. M. it was plain that the boats intended to engage the fort with their entire force, aided by an attack on our right and left flanks from the two land forces in overwhelming numbers. To understand properly the difficulties of my position it is right that I should explain fully the unfortunate location of Fort Henry in reference to resistance by a small force against an attack by land co-operating with the gunboats, as well as its disadvantages in even an engagement with boats alone. The entire fort, together with the intrenched camp spoken of, is enfiladed from three or four points on the opposite shore, while three points on the eastern bank completely command them both, all at easy cannon range. At the same time the intrenched camp, arranged as it was in the best possible manner to meet the case, was two-thirds of it completely under the control of the fire of the gunboats. The history of military engineering records no parallel to this case. Points within a few miles of it, possessing great advantages and few disadvantages, were totally neglected, and a location fixed upon without one redeeming feature, or filling one of the many requirements of a site for a work such as Fort Henry. The work itself was well built; it was completed long before I took command, but strengthened greatly by myself in building embrasures and epaulements of sand bags. An enemy had but to use their most common sense in obtaining the advantage in high water, as was the case, to have complete and entire control of this position.

I am guilty of no act of injustice in this frank avowal of the opinions entertained by myself, as well as by all other officers who have become familiar with the location of Fort Henry; nor do I desire the defects of location to have an undue influence in directing public opinion in relation to the battle of the 6th instant. The fort was built when I took charge, and I had no time to build anew. With this seeming digression, rendered necessary, as I believe, to a correct understanding of the whole affair, I will proceed with the details of the subsequent movements of the troops under my command.

By 10 A. M. on the 6th the movements of the gunboats and land force indicated an immediate engagement, and in such force as gave me no room to change my previously conceived opinions as to what, under such circumstances, should be my course. The case stood thus: I had at my command a grand total of 2,610 men, only one-third of whom had been at all disciplined or well armed. The high water in the river filling the sloughs gave me but one route by which to retire, if necessary, and that route for some distance in a direction at right angles to the line of approach of the enemy, and over roads well-nigh impassable for artillery, cavalry or infantry. The enemy had seven gunboats, with an armament of fifty-four guns, to engage the eleven guns at Fort Henry. General Grant was moving up the east bank of the river from his landing, three miles below, with a force of 12,000 men, verified afterward by his own statement; while General Smith, with 6,000 men, was moving up the west bank, to take a position within four or five hundred yards, which would enable him to enfilade my entire works.

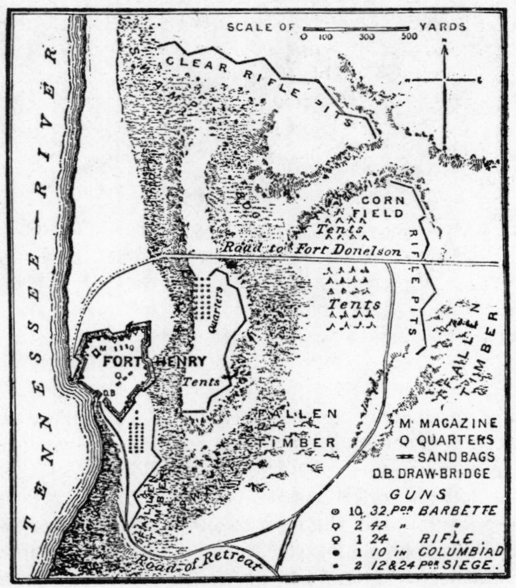

MAP OF FORT HENRY.

The hopes (founded on a knowledge of the fact that the enemy had reconnoitered on the two previous days thoroughly the several roads leading to Fort Donelson) that a portion only of the land force would co-operate with the gunboats in an attack on the fort were dispelled, and but little time left me to meet this change in the circumstances which surrounded me. I argued thus: Fort Donelson might possibly be held, if properly re-enforced, even though Fort Henry should fall; but the reverse of this proposition was not true. The force at Fort Henry was necessary to aid Fort Donelson, either in making a successful defense, or in holding it long enough to answer the purpose of a new disposition of the entire army from Bowling Green to Columbus, which would necessarily follow the breaking of our center, resting on Forts Donelson and Henry. The latter alternative was all that I deemed possible. I knew that re-enforcements were difficult to be had, and that unless sent in such force as to make the defense certain, which I did not believe practicable, the fate of our right wing at Bowling Green depended upon a concentration of my entire division on Fort Donelson and the holding of that place as long as possible, trusting that the delay by an action at Fort Henry would give time for such re-enforcements as might reasonably be expected to reach a point sufficiently near Fort Donelson to co-operate with my division, by getting to the rear and right flank of the enemy, and in such a position as to control the roads over which a safe retreat might be effected. I hesitated not a moment. My infantry, artillery and cavalry, removed of necessity, to avoid the fire of the gunboats, to the outworks, could not meet the enemy there; my only chance was to delay the enemy every moment possible, and retire the command, now outside the main work, toward Fort Donelson, resolving to suffer as little loss as possible. I retained only the heavy artillery company to fight the guns, and gave the order to commence the movement at once.

At 10:15 o'clock Lieutenant-Colonel MacGavock sent a messenger to me, stating that our pickets reported General Grant approaching rapidly and within half a mile of the advance work, and movements on the west bank indicated that General Smith was fast approaching also. The enemy, ignorant of any movement of my main body, but knowing that they could not engage them behind our intrenched camp until after the fort was reduced or the gunboats retired, without being themselves exposed to the fire of the latter, took a position north of the forks of the River Road, in a dense wood (my order being to retreat by way of the Stewart Road), to await the result.

At 11 A. M. the flotilla assumed their line of battle. I had no hope of being able successfully to defend the fort against such overwhelming odds, both in point of numbers and in caliber of guns. My object was to save the main body by delaying matters as long as possible, and to this end I bent every effort. At precisely 11:45 A. M. the enemy opened from their gunboats on the fort. I waited a few moments until the effects of the first shots of the enemy were fully appreciated. I then gave the order to return the fire, which was gallantly responded to by the brave little band under my command. The enemy, with great deliberation, steadily closed upon the fort, firing very wild until within 1,200 yards. The cool deliberation of our men told from the first shot, fired with tremendous effect. At 12:35 P. M. the bursting of our 24-pounder rifled gun disabled every man at the piece. This great loss was to us in a degree made up by our disabling entirely the Essex gunboat, which at once floated downstream. Immediately after the loss of this valuable gun we sustained another loss, still greater, in the closing up of the vent of the 10-inch columbiad, rendering that gun perfectly useless and defying all efforts to reopen it. The fire on both sides was now perfectly terrific. The enemy's entire force was engaged, doing us but little harm, while our shot fell with unerring certainty upon them, and with stunning effect. At this time a question presented itself to me with no inconsiderable degree of embarrassment. The moment had arrived when I should join the main body of troops retiring toward Fort Donelson, the safety of which depended upon a protracted defense of the fort. It was equally plain that the gallant men working the batteries, for the first time under fire, with all their heroism, needed my presence. Colonel Heiman, the next in command, had returned to the fort for instructions. The men working the heavy guns were becoming exhausted with the rapid firing. Another gun became useless by an accident, and yet another by the explosion of a shell immediately after, striking the muzzle, involving the death of two men and disabling several others. The effect of my absence at such a critical moment would have been disastrous. At the earnest solicitation of many of my officers and men I determined to remain, and ordered Colonel Heiman to join his command and keep up the retreat in good order, while I should fight the guns as long as one man was left, and sacrifice myself to save the main body of my troops.

No sooner was this decision made known than new energy was infused. The enemy closed upon the fort to within 600 yards, improving very much in their fire, which now began to tell with great effect upon the parapets, while the fire from our guns (now reduced to seven) was returned with such deliberation and judgment that we scarcely missed a shot. A second one of the gunboats retired, but I believe was brought into action again.

At 1:10 P. M. so completely broken down were the men that but for the fact that four only of our guns were then really serviceable I could not well have worked a greater number. The fire was still continued with great energy and tremendous effect upon the enemy's boats.

At 1:30 P. M. I took charge of one of the 32-pounders, to relieve the chief of that piece, who had worked with great effect from the beginning of the action. I gave the flagship Cincinnati two shots, which had the effect to check a movement intended to enfilade the only guns now left me. It was very plain to be seen that the enemy were breaching the fort directly in front of our guns, and that I could not much longer sustain their fire without an unjustifiable exposure of the valuable lives of the men who had so nobly seconded me in this unequal struggle.

Several of my officers, Major Gilmer among the number, now suggested to me the propriety of taking the subject of a surrender into consideration. Every moment I knew was of vast importance to those retreating on Fort Donelson, and I declined, hoping to find men enough at hand to continue awhile longer the fire now so destructive to the enemy. In this I was disappointed. My next effort was to try the experiment of a flag of truce, which I waved from the parapets myself. This was precisely at 1:50 P. M. The flag was not noticed, I presume from the dense smoke that enveloped it, and leaping again into the fort, I continued the fire for five minutes, when, with the advice of my brother officers, I ordered the flag to be lowered, and, after an engagement of two hours and ten minutes with such an unequal force, the surrender was made to Flag Officer Foote, represented by Captain Stembel, commanding the gunboat Cincinnati, and was qualified by the single condition that all officers should retain their side arms, and both officers and men should be treated with the highest consideration due prisoners of war, which was promptly and gracefully acceded to by Commodore Foote.

FORT HENRY. BURSTING OF A TWENTY-FOUR-POUND GUN DURING THE BOMBARDMENT, FEBRUARY 6, 1862.

The retreat of the main body was effected in good order, though involving the loss of about twenty prisoners, who from sickness and other causes were unable to encounter the heavy roads. The rear of the army was overtaken at a distance of some three miles from Fort Henry by a body of the enemy's cavalry, but, on being engaged by a small body of our men, under Major Garvin, were repulsed and retired.

This fact alone shows the necessity of the policy pursued by me in protracting the defense of the fort as long as possible, which only could have been done by my consenting to stand by the brave little band. No loss was sustained by our troops in this affair with the enemy.

I have understood from the prisoners that several pieces of artillery also were lost, it being impossible to move them over four or five miles with the indifferent teams attached to them.

The entire absence of transportation rendered any attempt to move the camp equipage of the regiments impossible. This may be regarded as fortunate, as the roads were utterly impassable, not only from the rains, but the back water of the Tennessee River. A small amount of quartermaster's and commissary stores, and what was left of the ordnance stores, were lost to us also.

The tents of the Alabama regiment were left on the west bank of the river, the gunboats preventing an opportunity to cross them over.

Our casualties may be reported strictly as follows: Killed by the enemy, two; wounded severely by the enemy (one since dead), three; wounded slightly by the enemy, two; killed by premature explosion, two; wounded seriously by premature explosion, one; slightly wounded, one; temporarily disabled by explosion of rifle gun, five. Making total killed, five; seriously wounded, three; slightly wounded, three; disabled, five; missing, five. Total casualties, twenty-one. The total casualties of the enemy were stated in my presence on the following morning to be seventy-three, including one officer of the Essex killed, and Captain Porter, commanding the Essex, badly scalded. The enemy report the number of shots that struck their vessels to have been seventy-four, twenty-eight of which struck the flagship Cincinnati, so disabling her as to compel her to return to Cairo. The Essex received twenty-two shots, one of which passed, we know, entirely through the ship, opening one of her boilers and taking off the head of Captain Porter's aid-de-camp. Several shots passed entirely through the Cincinnati, while her outer works were completely riddled. The weak points in all their vessels were known to us, and the cool precision of our firing developed them, showing conclusively that this class of boats, though formidable, can not stand the test of even the 32-pounders, much less the 24-caliber rifled shot or that of the 10-inch columbiad. It should be remembered that these results were principally from no heavier metal than the ordinary 32-pounders, using solid shot, being fired at point-blank, giving the vessels all the advantages of their peculiar structure, with planes meeting this fire at angles of forty-five degrees. The immense area forming what may be called the roof is in every respect vulnerable to either a plunging fire from even 32-pounders or a curved line of fire from heavy guns. In the latter case shell should be used in preference to shot.

Confident of having performed my whole duty to my government in the defense of Fort Henry with the totally inadequate means at my disposal, I have but little to add in support of the views before expressed. The reasons for the line of policy pursued by me are to my mind convincing.

Against such overwhelming odds as 16,000 well-armed men (exclusive of the force on the gunboats) to 2,610 badly armed, in the field, and fifty-four heavy guns against eleven medium ones in the fort, no tactics or bravery could avail.

The rapid movements of the enemy, with every facility at their command, rendered the defense from the beginning a hopeless one.

I succeeded in doing even more than was to be hoped for at first. I not only saved my entire command outside of the fort, but damaged materially the flotilla of the enemy, demonstrating thoroughly a problem of infinite value to us in the future.

Had I been re-enforced, so as to have justified my meeting the enemy at the advanced works, I might have made good the land defense on the east bank. I make no inquiry as to why I was not, for I have entire confidence in the judgment of my commanding-general. The elements even were against us, and had the enemy delayed their attack a few days, with the river rising, one-third of the entire fortifications (already affected by it) would have been washed away, while the remaining portion of the works would have been untenable by reason of the depth of water over the whole interior portion.

The number of officers surrendered was twelve; the number of non-commissioned officers and privates in the fort at the time of the surrender was sixty-six, while the number in the hospital boat, Patton, was sixteen. I take great pleasure in making honorable mention of all the officers and men under my command. To Captain Taylor, of the artillery, and the officers of his corps, Lieutenant Watts and Weller; to Captain G. R. G. Jones, in command of the right battery; to Captains Miller and Hayden, of the engineers; to Acting Assistant Adjutant-General McConnico; to Captain H. L. Jones, brigade quartermaster; to Captain McLaughlin, quartermaster of the Tenth Tennessee, and to Surgeons Voorhies and Horton, of the Tenth Tennessee, the thanks of the whole country are due for their consummate devotion to our high and holy cause. To Sergeants John Jones, Hallam, Dubine and Silcurk; to Corporals Copass, Cavin and Renfro, in charge of the guns, as well as to all the men, I feel that a large debt is due for their bravery and efficiency in working the heavy guns so long and so efficiently.

Officers and men alike seemed actuated but by one spirit—that of devotion to a cause in which was involved life, liberty and the pursuit of happiness. Every blow struck was aimed by cool heads, supported by strong arms and honest hearts.

I feel that it is a duty I owe to Colonel A. Heiman, commanding the Tenth Tennessee Regiment (Irish), to give this testimony of my high appreciation of him as a soldier and a man, due to his gallant regiment, both officers and men. I place them second to no regiment I have seen in the army.

To Captain Dixon, of the engineers, I owe (as does the whole country) my special acknowledgments of his ability and unceasing energies. Under his immediate eye were all the works proposed by myself at Fort Donelson and Heiman executed, while his fruitfulness in resources to meet the many disadvantages of position alone enabled us to combat its difficulties successfully.

To Lieutenant Watts, of the heavy artillery, as acting ordnance officer at Fort Henry, I owe this special notice of the admirable condition of the ordnance department at that post.

I take pleasure in acknowledging the marked courtesy and consideration of Flag Officer Foote, of the Federal Navy; of Captain Stembel and the other naval officers, to myself, officers and men. Their gallant bearing during the action gave evidence of a brave and therefore generous foe.

* * * * * *

LLOYD TILGHMAN,
Brigadier-General Commanding.

TO GENERAL SAMUEL COOPER,
Adjutant-General.

BATTLE BETWEEN FORT HENRY AND THE UNITED STATES GUNBOATS, FEBRUARY 6, 1862.
[From a sketch by Rear Admiral Walke.]

ORGANIZATION OF THE CONFEDERATE POST-OFFICE DEPARTMENT.

[The following article was taken from the columns of the *Register*, published at Mobile, Ala., April, 1861.]

"Immediately after accepting his appointment to the reputation-tearing office of the Postmaster-Generalship Judge Reagan sedulously applied himself to 'set his house in order' and be ready for any emergency which daily deepening events might thrust upon him. War had not then taken its gory grasp of the land, and hopes were entertained that a pacific adjustment of the difficulty was possible. Whether the new Postmaster-General participated or not in this pleasant delusion we know not; but he proceeded to work as if it was wiser not to entertain any such expectation. The mail machinery of the South was still worked by the lever at Washington. To be ready for the withdrawal of this lever Judge Reagan promptly and patiently went on with the construction of a new one. His first office was his room at the Exchange Hotel, in Montgomery, and his first assistants—indeed, his only office staff for some time—were Mr. J. L. C. Danner, who was subsequently promoted to the chief clerkship of the Patent Office; Mr. J. C. Bach, still an efficient officer in the department and son of one of the most esteemed citizens of New Orleans, and Mr. W. W. Lester, since promoted to a principal clerkship in the Treasury Department. These constituted the department at its start. The first difficulty its chief had to contend with was one of much delicacy and demanding the utmost discrimination—the choice of assistants thoroughly fit to aid him in building up a new department under the deterring circumstances described in our last article. The act organizing the department provided for a chief of the contract, a chief of the appointment, a chief of the finance bureau, and a chief clerk, with such a number of clerks as was needed to perform all the duties assigned to the several divisions thus made. The chiefs of the three bureaus correspond with the first, second and third Assistant Postmaster-Generals of the old Government. How to fill these important posts in the organization of the department did not long puzzle Judge Reagan. He decided on choosing as many of them and their assistants as he could from the most experienced men of Southern birth who had resigned office at Washington because of the accession of Lincoln. Thus determined, he selected the chief of the contract bureau in the person of H. St. George Offutt, of Missouri, who had just resigned an office which enabled him to bring to his duty a most valuable amount of the very thing the new Postmaster-General needed most in his first officers—official experience. The same motive induced him to invite B. N. Clements, of Tennessee, who had just quitted the chief clerkship of the old department, to come, and, as chief of the appointment bureau in the new, give its start the benefit of all the knowledge his former position necessarily enabled him to acquire. The control of the finance bureau he then handed to J. L. Harrell, of Alabama, reputed to be one of the best financiers in the South; and to the chief clerkship he called W. D. Miller, of Texas, a gentleman of high attainments and just that class of experience which eminently fitted him for this post. The organization was thus far complete before the end of March, and these were the men chosen to 'work up into life and move on' the postal machinery of the South. Of them now a little that is personal.

"Mr. Offutt, who was born in Hampshire County, Va., has all the appearance of the sleek, steady, clear-headed worker. He is now forty years of age, but looks younger. Unlike his chief, he takes pains to bear himself sprucely, as becometh one trained in metropolitan society. Having resided some time in Missouri, he 'hails' from that State. He commenced official life in 1845, as a clerk in the Auditor's Office for the Postoffice Department, at a salary of $1,000 a year, but promotions duly followed, and at last, in 1856, they placed Mr. Offutt in the chief clerkship of the office, where he remained at a salary of $2,000 a year until he resigned in March last, and took the post he now fills with marked benefit to the postal service of the South. He is said to be industrious, methodical and prescient. In manners he is easy and affable and somewhat sprightly.

"Mr. Clements was born in Lincoln County, Tennessee. He is a bachelor, and Swift says 'after twenty-five they have no age.' His father is known in the South as General Clements, of 'the Volunteer State,' and is the marshal of our government there. Although the county of Mr. C.'s birth has such an ominous name, it is the 'banner county' of the State, and was eager to secede from the State if she delayed very long in flinging off the old Union yoke. Mr. Clements was in the Mexican War in 1846, and is said to have gallantly distinguished himself. On his return he was appointed deputy marshal of Middle Tennessee. His first connection with the Postoffice Department was under Postmaster-General Brown, from whom he received a clerkship in 1857. He was promoted in another year to the chief clerkship of the whole department, at a salary of $2,200, ample evidence of his capacity. This he retained until he resigned on the accession of Lincoln. Then Judge Reagan tendered him the important bureau he now holds, and in administering its multifarious duties all the experience, coolness and discrimination he possesses are of the utmost need. Mr. Clements is, physically and in manners, a fine specimen of the Tennessee gentleman, and in appearance shows signs of the bachelor. As an officer he works deliberately and perseveringly.

"Mr. Harrell was born twenty-eight years ago, in Greensborough County, Alabama. Having received an excellent education at the Howard College, in Marion, he went to Mobile and took charge of the financial business of the cotton factory of E. K. Carlisle. In 1855 he became connected as a partner and cashier with the banking firm of John Henley & Co., of Montgomery, Alabama. He remained there until a little before the time that Judge Reagan called him to take charge of the finance division of the department. Mr. Harrell is what Dickens styles a 'neat, dapper little gentleman.' He is retiring and agreeable in manner, painstaking and prompt in business, as precise and wary as the intricate and delicate nature of his duties requires. To his family honor we should add that he is a son-in-law of the noble Senator Yancey.

"We have thus briefly sketched the three heads of the bureaus in the Postoffice Department to give the reader an idea of the 'manner of men' whom Judge Reagan has selected to aid him in constructing and pushing the department ahead and producing the great results which we propose to show as the first fruits of his toils and the truest index to our present strength and proximate greatness."

CAPTURE OF FORT DONELSON,

FEBRUARY 16, 1862.

BY

BRIG.-GEN. GIDEON J. PILLOW, C. S. A.

COLUMBIA, TENN., February 18, 1862.

ON the 9th inst. General A. S. Johnston ordered me to proceed to Fort Donelson and take command of that post. On the 10th inst. I arrived at that place. In detailing the operations of the forces under my command at Fort Donelson it is proper to state the condition of that work and of the forces constituting its garrison. When I arrived I found the work on the river battery unfinished and wholly too weak to resist the force of heavy artillery. I found a 10-inch columbiad and a 32-pounder rifled gun which had not been mounted. Deep gloom was hanging over the command, and the troops were greatly depressed and demoralized by the circumstances attending the surrender of Fort Henry, and the manner of retiring from that place. My first attention was given to the necessity of strengthening this work, mounting the two heavy guns, and to the construction of defensive works to protect the rear of the river battery. I imparted to the work all the energy which it was possible to do, working day and night with the whole command. The battery was without a competent number of artillerists, and those that were there were not well instructed in the use of their guns.

BRIG.-GEN. GIDEON J. PILLOW, OF TENNESSEE.

To provide for this want I placed the artillery companies under active course of instruction in the use of their guns. I detailed Captain Ross, with his company of light artillerists, to the command of one of the river batteries. These heavy guns being mounted, and provisions made for working them, and a proper supply of ammunition having been procured by my orders from Nashville, I felt myself prepared to test the effect of the fire of heavy metal against the enemy's gunboats, though the work stood much in need of more heavy pieces.

The armament of the batteries consisted of eight 32-pounders, three 32-pounder carronades, one 10-inch columbiad and one rifled gun of 32-pound caliber.

The selection of the site for the fort was an unfortunate one. While its command of the river was favorable, the site was commanded by the heights above and below on the river, and by a continuous range of hills all around the works to its rear. A field-work of very contracted dimensions had been constructed by the garrison to protect the battery; but the field-work was commanded by the hills already referred to, and lay open to a fire of artillery from every direction except from the hills below.

To guard against the effects of fire of artillery from these heights a line of defensive works, consisting of rifle pits and abatis for infantry, detached on our right but continuous on our left, with defenses for our light artillery, were laid off by Major Gilmer, engineer of General A. S. Johnston's staff (but on duty with me at the post), around the rear of the battery and on the heights from which artillery could reach our battery and inner field-work, enveloping the inner work and the town of Dover, where our principal supplies of commissary and quartermaster's stores were in depot.

These works, pushed with the utmost possible energy, were not quite completed, nor were my troops all in position, though nearly so, when Brigadier-General Floyd, my senior officer, reached that station. The works were laid off with great judgment and skill by Major Gilmer, and were well executed and designed for the defense of the rear of the work, the only objection being to the length of the line, which, however, was unavoidable from the surroundings. The length of the line and the inadequacy of the force for its defense proved a source of embarrassment throughout the struggle which subsequently ensued in the defense of the position.

I had placed Brigadier-General Buckner in command of the right wing, and Brigadier-General B. R. Johnson in command of the left. By extraordinary efforts we had barely got these works in defensible condition when the enemy made an advance in force around and against the entire line of outer works.

THE BATTLE OF THE TRENCHES.

The assault was commenced by the enemy's artillery against the center of our left wing, which was promptly responded to by Captain Green's battery of field artillery. After several hours of firing between the artillery of the two armies the enemy's infantry advanced to the conflict all along the line, which was kept up and increased in volume from one end of the line to the other for several hours, when at last the enemy made a vigorous assault against the right of our left wing, the position assaulted being a height commanded by Colonel A. Heiman and defended by his brigade, consisting of the Tenth Tennessee, under command of Lieutenant-Colonel R. W. MacGavoch, Colonel W. M. Voorhies', Colonel A. A. Hughes'* and Colonel (J. W.) Head's regiments of Tennessee volunteers, and defended by Captain (Frank) Maney's field battery.

The assault was vigorously made and the position as vigorously defended, and resulted in the repulse of the enemy here and everywhere around the line. The result of the day's work pretty well tested the strength of our defensive line, and established beyond question the gallantry of the entire command, all of which fought gallantly their portion of the line.

The loss sustained by our forces in this engagement was not large, our men being mostly under shelter in the rifle pits; but we, nevertheless, had quite a number killed and wounded; yet, owing to the continued fighting which followed, it was impossible to get any official report of the casualties of the day.

On the same day our battery on the river was engaged with one of the enemy's gunboats, which occasioned quite a lively cannonading for more than an hour, in which the gallant Captain Joseph Dixon, of the engineer corps, was killed instantly at the battery. This officer had been on duty for some months at the post, and had shown great energy and professional skill, and by his gallant bearing on that day, while directing the operations, under my orders, had justly earned for himself high distinction. His death was a serious loss to the service, and was a source of no little embarrassment in our after operations.

On the 12th (13th) we had quiet, but we saw the smoke of a large number of gunboats and steamboats a short distance below. We also received reliable information of the arrival of a large number of new troops, greatly increasing the strength of the enemy's forces, already said to be from 20,000 to 30,000 strong.

BATTLE WITH THE GUNBOATS.

On the 13th (14th) these re-enforcements were seen advancing to their position in the line of investment, and while this was being done six of the enemy's iron-cased gunboats were seen advancing up the river, five of which were abreast and in line of battle, and the sixth some distance to the rear. When these gunboats arrived within a mile and a half of our battery they opened fire on it.

My orders to the officers (Captain Shuster and Standewitz (Stankiewitz or Starkovitch) † who commanded the lower battery of eight guns, and Captain Ross, who commanded the upper battery of four guns) were to hold their fire until the enemy's boats should come within point-blank range of their guns. This they did, though the ordeal of holding their fire while the enemy's shot and shell fell thick around their position was a severe restraint to their patriotic impulses; but, nevertheless, our batteries made no response until the enemy's gunboats got within range of their guns. Our entire line of batteries then opened fire. The guns of both parties were well served, the enemy constantly advancing, delivering direct fire against our batteries from his line of five gunboats, while the sixth boat, moving up in rear of the line, kept the air filled with shells, which fell thick and close around the position of our batteries.

The fight continued, the enemy steadily advancing slowly up the river, the shot and shell from fifteen heavy rifled guns tearing our parapets, and plunging deep into the earth around and over our batteries for nearly two hours, until his boats had reached within the distance of one hundred and fifty yards of our batteries. Having come in such close conflict, I could distinctly see the effects of our shot upon his iron-cased boats. We had given two or three well-directed shots from the heavy guns to one of his boats, when she instantly shrank back and drifted helpless below the line. Several shot struck another boat, tearing her iron case and splintering her timbers, and making them crack as if by a stroke of lightning, when she, too, fell back. Then a third received several severe shots, making her metal ring and her timbers crack, when the whole line gave way and fell rapidly back from our fire until they passed out of range.

Thus ended the first severe and close conflict of our

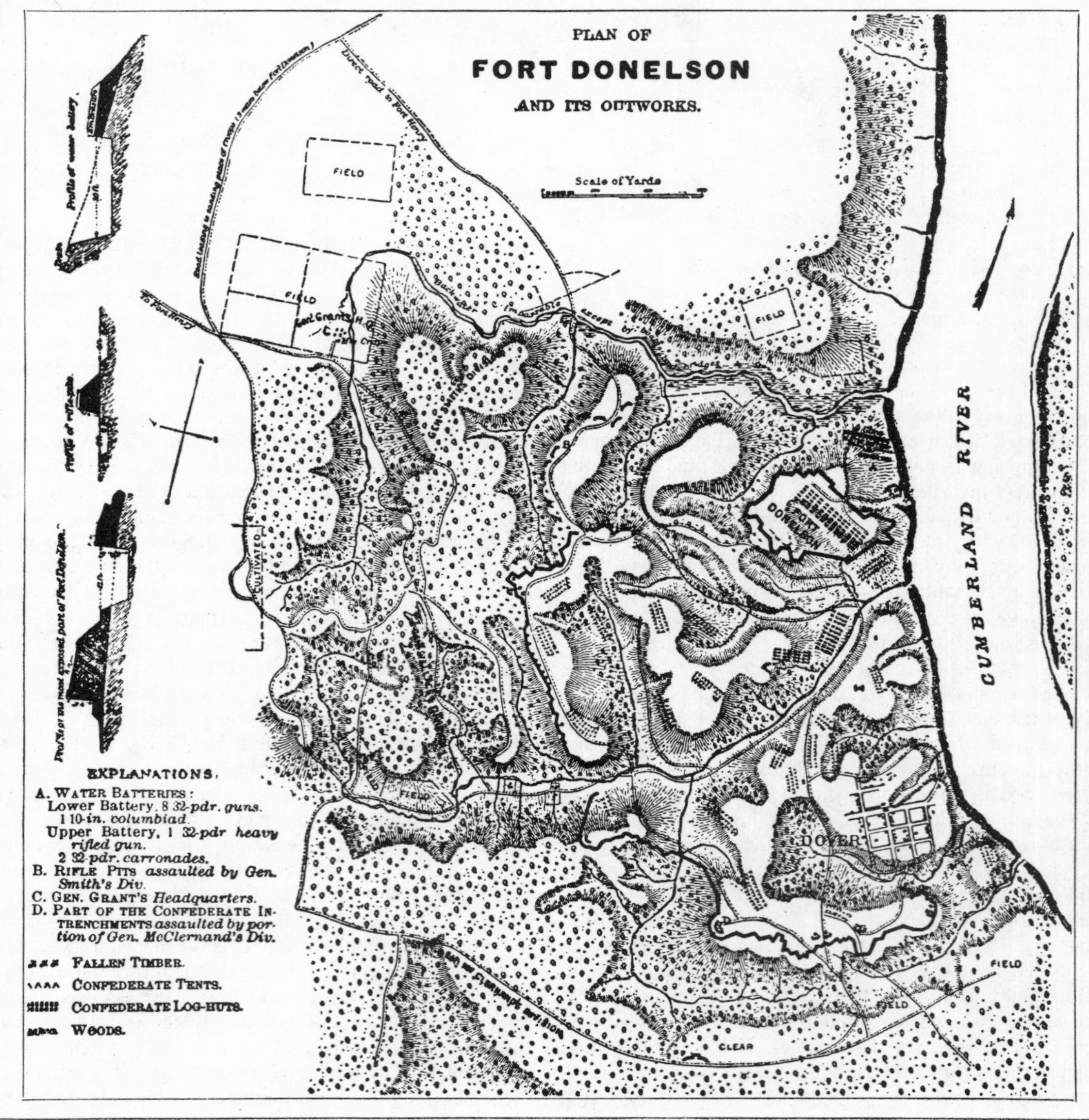

* Hughes' regiment was the Twenty-seventh Alabama.

† Probably Stanklewriz.

heavy guns with the enemy's gunboats, testing their strength and the power of our heavy guns to resist them. The shot from our 32-pounder guns produced but little effect. They struck and rebounded, apparently doing but little damage; but I am satisfied, by close observation, that the timbers of the frame-work did not and could not withstand the shock of the 10-inch columbiad or 32-pounder rifled guns.

These gunboats never renewed the attack. I learned from citizens living on the river below that one of the injured boats sank, and that the others had to be towed to Cairo. This information may or may not be true, but it is certain that all of the boats were repulsed and driven back after a most vigorous and determined attack, and that two of the boats were badly damaged and a third more or less injured.

It is difficult to overestimate the gallant bearing and heroic conduct of the officers and men of our batteries,

Brigadier-General John B. Floyd, of Virginia.
[From an old photograph.]

who so well and so persistently fought our guns until the enemy's determined advance brought his boats and guns into such close and desperate conflict. Where all did their duty so well it is almost impossible to discriminate. The captains already named and their lieutenants (whose names, for want of official reports, I can not give) all deserve the highest commendation. Lieutenant George S. Martin, whose company is at Columbus, Ky., but who was ordered to that post by Major-General Polk, commanding one of the guns, particularly attracted my attention by his energy and the judgment with which he fought his gun. The wadding of his gun having given out, he pulled off his coat and rammed it down his gun as wadding, and thus kept up the fire until the enemy were finally repulsed.

On the evening of this day we received information of the arrival of additional re-enforcements of infantry, cavalry and light artillery by steamboat, all of which were disembarked a short distance below our position.

BATTLE OF DOVER.

On the 14th inst. the enemy were busy throwing his forces of every arm around us, extending his line of investment and completely enveloping us.

On the evening of this day we ascertained that the enemy had received by steamboat additional re-enforcements. We were now surrounded by an immense force, said by prisoners, whom we had taken, to amount to fifty-two regiments, and every road and possible avenue of departure cut off, with the certainty that our sources of supply by river could soon be cut off by the enemy's batteries placed upon the river above us.

At a meeting of general officers, called by General Floyd, it was determined unanimously to give the enemy battle next day at daylight, so as to cut open a route of exit for our troops to the interior of the country, and thus save our army. We had knowledge that the principal portion of the enemy's forces were massed in encampment in front of the extreme left of our position, commanding the two roads leading to the interior, one of which we must take in retiring from our position.

We knew he had massed in encampment another large force on the Wynn's Ferry Road, opposite the center of our left wing, while still another was massed nearly in front of the left of our right wing, his fresh arrival of troops being encamped on the bank of the river two miles and a half below us, from which latter encampment a stream of fresh troops were constantly pouring around us on his line of investment, and strengthening his general encampment on the extreme right. At each of his encampments and on each road he had in position a battery of field artillery and 24-pounder iron guns on siege carriages. Between these encampments on the roads was a thick undergrowth of brush and blackjack, making it impossible to advance or maneuver any considerable body of troops.

The plan of attack agreed upon and directed by General Floyd to be executed was, that with the main body of the forces defending our left wing, I should attack the right wing of the enemy, occupying and resting on the heights reaching to the bank of the river, accompanied by Colonel Forrest's brigade of cavalry; that General Buckner, with the forces under his command, and defending the right of our line, should strike the enemy's encampment and forces on the Wynn's Ferry Road; that the forces under Colonel Heiman should hold his position, and that each command should leave in the trenches troops to hold the same. In this order of battle it was easy to be seen that if my attack was successful and the enemy was routed his retreat would be along his line of investment, toward the Wynn's Ferry encampment, and thence toward his reserve, at the gunboats below. In other words, my success would roll the enemy's force in retreat over upon General Buckner, when by his attack in flank and rear we could cut up the enemy and put him completely to rout.

Accordingly dispositions were made to attack the enemy. At five o'clock on the morning of the 15th I moved out of my position to engage the enemy. In less than one-half hour our forces were engaged. The enemy was prepared to receive me in advance of his encampment, and he did receive me before I had assumed a line of battle and while I was moving against him without any formation for the engagement. For the first half hour of the engagement I was much embarrassed in getting the command in position properly to engage the enemy. Having extricated myself from the position and fairly engaged the enemy, we fought him for nearly two hours before I made any decided advance upon him. He contested the field most stubbornly.

The loss of both armies on this portion of the field was heavy—the enemy's particularly so, as I discovered by riding over the field after the battle. The enemy, having been forced to yield this portion of the field, retired slowly toward the Wynn's Ferry Road—Buckner's point of attack.

The fight was hotly contested and stubborn on both sides, and consumed the day till 12 o'clock to drive the enemy as far back as the center, where General Buckner's command was to flank him. While my command was slowly advancing and driving back the enemy I was anxiously expecting to hear General Buckner's command open fire in his rear, which not taking place, I was apprehensive of some misapprehension of orders, and came from the field of battle within the work to ascertain what was the matter. I there found the command of General Buckner, massed behind the ridge within the work, taking shelter from the enemy's artillery on the Wynn's Ferry Road, it having been forced to retire before the battery, as I learned from him. My force was still slowly advancing, driving the enemy toward the battery. I directed General Buckner immediately to move his command around to the rear of the battery, turning its left, keeping in the hollow, and attack and carry it. Before the movement was executed my forces, forming the attacking party on the right, with Colonel Forrest's regiment of cavalry, had reached the position of the battery. Colonel Forrest's cavalry gallantly charged a large body of infantry supporting the battery, driving it and forcing the battery to retire, and taking six pieces of artillery—four brass pieces and two 24-pounder iron pieces.

In pursuing the enemy, falling back from this position, General Buckner's forces became united with mine, and engaged the enemy in a hot contest of nearly an hour, with large forces of fresh troops that had now met us. This position of the enemy being carried by our joint forces, I called off the further pursuit, after seven and a half hours of continuous and bloody conflict. After the troops were called off from the pursuit, orders were immediately given to the different commands to form and retire to their original intrenchments.

The operations of the day had forced the entire command of the enemy around to our right and in front of General Buckner's position in the intrenchments, and when he reached his position he found the enemy advancing rapidly to take possession of his portion of our works. He had a stubborn conflict, lasting one and a half hours, to regain his position, and the enemy actually got possession of the extreme right of his works, and held them so firmly that he could not dislodge him. The position thus gained by the enemy was a most important and commanding one, being immediately in rear of our river battery and field-work for its protection. From it he could readily turn the intrenched work occupied by General Buckner and attack him in reverse, or he could advance, under cover of an intervening ridge, directly upon our battery and field-work. While the enemy held the position it was manifest we could not hold the main work or battery. Such was the condition of the two armies at nightfall, after nine hours of conflict, on the 15th instant, in which our loss was severe, and leaving not less than 1,000 of the enemy dead upon the field. We left upon the field nearly all of his wounded, because we could not remove them. We left his dead unburied, because we could not bury them. Such carnage and conflict have perhaps never before occurred on this continent. We took about 300 prisoners and a large number of arms.

We had fought the battle to open the way for our army and to relieve us from an investment, which would necessarily reduce us and the position we occupied by famine. We had accomplished our object, but it occupied the whole day, and before we could prepare to leave, after taking in the wounded and dead, the enemy had thrown around us again in the night an immense force of fresh troops and reoccupied his original position in the line of investment, thus again cutting off our retreat. We had only about 13,000 troops all told; of these we had lost a large proportion in the three battles. The command had been in the trenches night and day for five days, exposed to the snow, sleet, mud and ice-water, without shelter, without adequate covering and without sleep. In this condition the general officers held a consultation, to determine what we should do. General Buckner gave it as his decided opinion that he could not hold his position a half-hour against an assault of the enemy, and said he was satisfied the enemy would attack him at daylight the next morning. The proposition was then made by the undersigned to again fight our way through the enemy's line and cut our way out. General Buckner said his command was so worn out, cut to pieces and demoralized that he could not make another fight; that it would cost the command three-fourths its present numbers to cut its way out; that it was wrong to sacrifice three-fourths of a command to save one-fourth, and that no officer had a right to cause such a sacrifice. General Floyd and Major Gilmer I understood to concur in this opinion. I then expressed the opinion that we could hold out another day, and in that time we could get steamboats and set the command over the river, and probable save a large portion of it. To this General Buckner replied that the enemy would certainly attack him in the morning, and that he could not hold his position a half-hour.

The alternative of these propositions was a surrender of the position and command. General Floyd said he would not surrender the command, nor would he surrender himself a prisoner. I had taken the same position. General Buckner said he was satisfied nothing else could be done, and that therefore he would surrender the command, if placed in authority. General Floyd said he would turn over the command to him if he could be allowed to withdraw his troops. To this General Buckner consented. Thereupon the command was turned over to me, I passing it instantly to General Buckner, saying I would neither surrender the command nor myself. I directed Colonel Forrest to cut his way out.

Under these circumstances General Buckner accepted the command, and sent a flag of truce to the enemy for an armistice of six hours, to negotiate for terms of capitulation. Before this flag and communication were delivered I retired from the garrison.

Before closing my report of the operations of the army at Fort Donelson I must, in justice to the brave officers

The "Water Battery" at Fort Donelson.

and men under my immediate command, say that harder fighting or more gallant conduct in officers and men I have never witnessed. In the absence of official reports of brigade and regimental commanders, of which I am deprived by the circumstances detailed in this report, I may not be able to do justice to the different corps. I will say, however, that the forces under my immediate command during the action bore themselves most gallantly throughout the long and bloody conflict. I speak with especial commendation of the brigades commanded by Colonels (William E.) Baldwin, (G. C.) Wharton, (John) McCausland, (J. M.) Simonton and (Joseph) Drake, and of Captains Maney and Green, who fought their guns under the constant and annoying fire of the enemy's sharpshooters, and of the concentrated fire from his field batteries, from which both commands suffered severely. Captain Maney was himself wounded, and had several lieutenants killed and wounded, and many of his company killed and wounded; so did Captains Porter and Graves.

Our total force in the field did not exceed 10,000 men, while from what I saw of the enemy's force, and from information derived from many prisoners of the enemy, we are sure he had between 30,000 and 40,000 men in the field.

Colonel Baldwin's brigade constituted the front of the attacking force, sustained immediately by Colonel Wharton's brigade. These two brigades deserve especial commendation for the manner in which they sustained the first shock of battle, and, under circumstances of great embarrassment, threw themselves into position and followed up the conflict throughout the day. Being mostly with these two brigades, I can speak from personal knowledge of the gallant conduct and bearing of the two brigade commanders, Colonels Baldwin and Wharton. I must also acknowledge my obligation to Brigadier-General B. R. Johnson, who assisted me in the command of the forces with which I attacked the enemy, and who bore himself gallantly throughout the conflict; but having received no official report from him, I can not give the detailed operations of his command.

* * * * * *

GID. J. PILLOW,
Brigadier-General, C. S. A.

THE APPROXIMATE AGGREGATE STRENGTH OF THE VARIOUS REGIMENTS AT FORT DONELSON WAS AS FOLLOWS:

ORGANIZATIONS.	Totals	Aggregate
Third Tennessee	750	
Eighteenth Tennessee	625	
Thirty-second Tennessee	400	
Fourteenth Mississippi	650	
Forty-first Tennessee	400	
Second Kentucky	600	
Aggregate strength of Buckner's Division, under his own command, exclusive of two batteries of artillery	...	3,425
Twenty-sixth Tennessee	401	
Twenty-sixth Mississippi	443	
Aggregate detached under General Pillow	...	844
Aggregate infantry of Buckner's Division under him and General Pillow	...	4,269

AT FORT DONELSON, SUMMARY OF KILLED AND WOUNDED IN THE SECOND DIVISION, CENTRAL ARMY OF KENTUCKY.

ORGANIZATIONS.	Killed	Wounded	Aggregate
In the Third Brigade, Colonel John C. Brown commanding	38	246	284
Second Kentucky Regiment (about)	...	...	80
Issaquena Battery (about)	...	...	3
Porter's Battery (about)	...	...	25
	38	246	392
In the two regiments of the Second Brigade, Colonel Baldwin, detached and under the command of General Pillow:			
Twenty-sixth Tennessee	11	78	
Twenty-sixth Mississippi	11	68	
Staff and other officers	2	15	
Aggregate	24	161	185
Total	...	...	577

ESTIMATES OF KILLED AND WOUNDED IN PORTIONS OF GENERAL PILLOW'S COMMAND, REPORTING THROUGH GENERAL BUCKNER.

ORGANIZATIONS.	Killed	Wounded
Colonel Heiman's brigade	10	30
Colodel Gregg's regiment	20	34
Major Brown's regiment	18	55
Aggregate	48	119
Total	...	167

SUMMARY REPORT OF THE LOSSES OF EACH CONFEDERATE STATE ON THE BATTLEFIELD OF FORT DONELSON, FEBRUARY 15, 1862.

	Engaged	Killed	Wounded	Total Killed and Wounded.
Tennessee	5,461	45	287	332
Kentucky	918	32	117	149
Texas	296	21	32	53
Arkansas	270	7	17	24
Alabama	376	3	9	12
Mississippi	2,875	78	336	414
Virginia	1,275	45	171	216
Artillery	756	14	39	53
Cavalry	1,112	8	16	24
Total amount	13,339	253	1,024	1,277

CAPTURE OF FORT DONELSON,

FEBRUARY 16, 1862.

BY

BRIG.-GEN. SIMON B. BUCKNER, C. S. A.,
Commanding Division.

RICHMOND, VA., August 11, 1862.

I HAVE the honor to make the following report of the operations of that portion of the Second Division of the Central Army of Kentucky which was detached from Bowling Green and Russellville, Ky., to aid in the defense of Fort Donelson and the village of Dover, on the Cumberland River, Tenn.

By the courtesy of Brigadier-General Grant, U. S. A., I was permitted to transmit to Clarksville, Tenn., a brief report of the surrender of Fort Donelson; but as I now learn it never reached the headquarters of General A. S. Johnston, I transmit herewith a copy.

I have been prevented from making an early report by the refusal of the Federal authorities during my imprisonment either to permit me to make a report or to receive the report of subordinate commanders. Such, indeed, was the discourtesy of the Federal War Department, that, though kept in solitary confinement during my imprisonment, and prevented from holding communication with any of my fellow-prisoners, a request on my part to be informed of the cause of a proceeding so unusual among nations pretending to follow the rules of civilized warfare, failed to elicit a response.

LIEUT.-GEN. SIMON B. BUCKNER, OF KENTUCKY.
[From a photo taken in 1862.]

On February 11th ultimo Brigadier-General Floyd had resolved to concentrate his division and my own at Cumberland City, with a view of operating from some point on the railway west of that position in the direction of Fort Donelson or Fort Henry, thus maintaining his communications with Nashville by the way of Charlotte.

I reached Fort Donelson on the night of February 11th, with orders from General Floyd to direct General Pillow to send back at once to Cumberland City the troops which had been designated.

Before leaving Clarksville I had, by authority of General Floyd, ordered Scott's regiment of Louisiana cavalry to operate on the north side of the Cumberland River, in the direction of Fort Donelson, with a view to prevent the establishment of any of the enemy's field-batteries which might interfere with our transports. General Pillow declined to execute the order of which I was the bearer until he should have a personal interview with General Floyd.

Accordingly, on the morning of the 12th he left me temporarily in command, and proceeded himself in a steamer to Cumberland City. Before leaving he informed me that he had directed a reconnoissance to be made by Colonel Forrest's cavalry, with instructions in no event to bring on an engagement should the enemy approach in force.

General Pillow left me under the impression that he did not expect an immediate advance of the enemy, and regarded their approach from the direction of Fort Henry as impracticable. During the morning Forrest reported the enemy advancing in force, with the view of enveloping our line of defense, and for a time he was engaged with his usual gallantry in heavy skirmishing with them, at one time driving one of their battalions back on their artillery. About noon General Pillow returned and resumed command, it having been determined to re-enforce the garrison with the remaining troops from Cumberland City and Clarksville.

The defenses were in a very imperfect condition. The space to be defended by the army was quadrangular in shape, being limited on the north by the Cumberland River, on the east and west by small streams now converted into deep sloughs by the high water, and on the south by our line of defense. The river line exceeded a mile in length. The line of defense was about two miles and a half long, and its distance from the river varied from one-fourth to three-fourths of a mile. The line of intrenchments consisted of a few logs rolled together, and but slightly covered with earth, forming an insufficient protection even against field artillery.

Not more than one-third of the line was completed on the morning of the 12th. It had been located, under direction of that able engineer officer Major Gilmer, near the crests of a series of ridges, which sloped backward to the river and were again commanded in places by other ridges at a still greater distance from the river. This chain of heights was intersected by deep valleys and ravines, which materially interfered with communications between different parts of the line. Between the village of Dover and the water batteries a broad and deep valley, extending directly back from the river and flooded by the high water, intersected the quadrangular area occupied by the army, and almost completely isolated the right wing. That part of the line which covered the land approach to the water batteries and constituted our right wing was assigned to me, with a portion of my division, consisting of the Third, or Colonel John C. Brown's Brigade, which was composed of the Third Tennessee Volunteers (which was Colonel Brown's regiment); Eighteenth Tennessee Regiment, Colonel Joseph B. Palmer; Thirty-second Tennessee Regiment, Colonel (E. C.) Cook; half of Colonel Baldwin's Second Brigade (temporarily attached to Colonel Brown's); Second Regiment Kentucky Volunteers, Colonel R. W. Hanson; Fourteenth Mississippi Volunteers, Major (W. L.) Doss; Forty-first Tennessee Volunteers, Colonel (Robert) Farquharson; Porter's battery of six field-pieces, and Graves' battery of six field-pieces.

The remaining regiments of Baldwin's brigade, the Twenty-sixth Tennessee Volunteers, Colonel (John M.) Lillard, and the Twenty-sixth Mississippi Volunteers, Colonel (A. E.) Reynolds, together with the brigade commander, were detached from my command by Brigadier-General Pillow, and assigned a position on the left of the line of intrenchments.

The work on my lines was prosecuted with energy, and was urged forward as rapidly as the limited number of tools would permit, so that by the morning of the 13th my position was in a respectable state of defense.

My disposition of the troops was as follows: Hanson's regiment on the extreme right; Palmer's regiment, with its reserve, in position to re-enforce Hanson; Porter's battery occupying the advanced salient, sweeping the road which led to the front, and flanking the intrenchments both to the right and to the left. The reserve of the Fourteenth Mississippi was held as its support; Brown's, Cook's and Farquharson's regiments were on the left. Graves' battery occupied a position near the extreme left of the intrenchments on the declivity of the hill, whence it swept the valley with its fire and flanked the position of Colonel Heiman to the east of the valley.

From three to five companies of each regiment were deployed as skirmishers in the rifle pits. The other companies of each regiment were massed in columns, sheltered from the enemy's fire behind the irregularities of the ground, and held in convenient positions to re-enforce any portion of the line that might be seriously threatened.

No serious demonstration was made on our lines on the 12th.

Early on the morning of the 13th a column of the enemy's infantry, which was apparently forming to move down the valley between my left and Heiman's right, was driven back by a few well-directed shots from Graves' battery.

About 10 o'clock in the morning the enemy made a vigorous attack upon Hanson's position, but was repulsed with heavy loss. The attack was subsequently renewed by three heavy regiments, but was again repulsed by the Second Kentucky Regiment, aided by a part of the Eighteenth Tennessee. In both these affairs, and also in a third repulse of the enemy from the same position, Porter's battery played a conspicuous part.

About 11 o'clock a strong attack was made on Colonel Heiman's position beyond my left. A well-directed fire from Graves' battery upon the flank of the assaulting column materially contributed to repulse the enemy with heavy loss.

The fire of the enemy's artillery and riflemen was incessant throughout the day, but was responded to by a well-directed fire from the intrenchments, which inflicted upon the assailant considerable loss, and almost silenced his fire late in the afternoon.

On the preceding night General Floyd had arrived and

assumed command of all the troops, and during the morning visited and inspected my lines. My loss during the day was thirty-nine in killed and wounded.

The enemy were comparatively quiet in front of my position during the 14th. On the morning of that day I was summoned to a council of general officers, in which it was decided unanimously, in view of the arrival of heavy re-enforcements of the enemy below, to make an immediate attack upon their right, in order to open our communications with Charlotte, in the direction of Nashville. It was urged that this attack should be made at once, before the disembarkation of the enemy's re-enforcements, supposed to be about 15,000 men. I proposed with my division to cover the retreat of the army should the sortie prove successful. I made the necessary dispositions preparatory to executing the movement; but early in the afternoon the order was countermanded by General Floyd, at the instance, as I afterward learned, of General Pillow, who, after drawing out his troops for the attack, thought it too late for the attempt.

On the night of the 14th it was unanimously decided, in a council of general officers and regimental commanders, to attack the enemy's right at daylight. The object of the attack was to force our way through his lines, recover our communications and effect our retreat upon Nashville by way of Charlotte, Tenn. This movement had become imperatively necessary in consequence of the vastly superior and constantly increasing force of the enemy, who had already completely enveloped our position. The general plan was for General Pillow to attack his extreme right, and for that portion of my division remaining under my command, after being relieved in the rifle pits by Colonel Head's regiment, to make an attack upon the right of the enemy's center, and if successful, to take up a position in advance of our works on the Wynn's Ferry Road, to cover the retreat of the whole army, after which my division was to act as the rear guard.

On Saturday morning, the 15th, a considerable portion of my division was delayed by the non-arrival of Head's regiment at the appointed time, and by the slippery condition of the icy road, which forbade a rapid march. My advance regiment, however (the Third Tennessee), reached its position by daylight, in rear of a portion of the intrenchments which had been occupied by General Pillow's troops. As no guards had been left in this portion of the line, and even a battery was left in position without a cannoneer, I deployed the Third Tennessee in the rifle pits, to cover the formation of my division as it arrived. The regiments were formed partly in line and partly in column, and covered from the enemy's artillery fire by a slight acclivity in front. In the meantime the attack on the enemy's right was made in the most gallant and determined manner by the division of General Pillow. For the progress of that action I refer to the reports of Colonel Baldwin, Colonel Gregg and their subordinate commanders, which have been transmitted to me as the senior officer left with the army.

In front of my position the enemy had a heavy battery posted on the Wynn's Ferry Road, with another battery opposite my left—both sustained by a heavy infantry force. Major Davidson, acting chief of my artillery, established Graves' battery to the left of the Wynn's Ferry Road, and opened upon the enemy's batteries a destructive fire. I also directed a portion of the artillery to open upon the flank and left rear of the enemy's infantry, who were contesting the advance of General Pillow's division. In view of the heavy duty which I expected my division to undergo in covering the retreat of the army, I thought it unadvisable to attempt an assault at this time in my front until the enemy's batteries were, to some extent, crippled and their supports shaken by the fire of my artillery.

About 9 o'clock General Pillow urged an advance to relieve his forces. I accordingly sent forward the Fourteenth Mississippi, Major Doss, deployed as skirmishers. At the request of its commander I assigned the direction of its movements to Major Alexander Casseday, of my staff. The line of skirmishers was sustained by the Third and Eighteenth Tennessee. Their line of march unfortunately masked the fire of my artillery upon the Wynn's Ferry Road, but it continued to play with effect upon the force which was opposing General Pillow's advance. The combined attack compelled the enemy to retire, not, however, without inflicting upon my troops considerable loss. Under a misapprehension of instructions, at a time when my artillery was directed, over the heads of the advanced troops, upon the enemy's battery, these regiments withdrew without panic, but in some confusion, to the trenches, after the enemy's infantry had been driven a considerable distance from their position. As the enemy's line of retreat was along the Wynn's Ferry Road, I now organized an attack further to my right, up a deep valley, which led from Heiman's left, in rear of the position occupied by the enemy's batteries.

In order to cover the advance of the infantry column I directed Captain Porter, with his artillerists, to serve Green's battery, which was already in position, and at the same time sent a request to Colonel Heiman to direct Maney's battery to open its fire, while he should deploy a line of skirmishers in advance of his position to cover the right of the valley. General Pillow was at this time, as I afterward learned, on the heights to my right, occupied by Heiman. Maney's, Porter's and Graves' batteries now opened a cross fire upon the enemy's battery and position, soon crippling some of his guns and driving their supports, while the Third, Eighteenth and Thirty-second Tennessee regiments, under their brigade commander, Colonel John C. Brown, moved steadily up the valley, preceded by their skirmishers, who soon became engaged with those of the enemy. This movement, combined with the brisk fire of three batteries, induced a rapid retreat of the enemy, who abandoned a section of his artillery. At the same time my infantry were thus penetrating the enemy's line of retreat Forrest, with a portion of his cavalry, charged upon their right, while General Pillow's division, under the orders of General B. R. Johnson and Colonel Baldwin, were pressing their extreme right about half a mile to the left of this position.

In this latter movement a section of Graves' battery participated, playing with destructive effect upon the enemy's left, while about the same time the Second Kentucky, under Colonel Hanson, charged in quick time, as if upon parade, through an open field and under a destructive fire, without firing a gun, upon a superior force of the enemy, who broke and fled in all directions. A large portion of the enemy's right dispersed through the woods, and made their way, as was afterward learned, to Fort Henry.

Upper Battery. Water Battery. The opposing armies engaged, in the distance. Federal Gunboats.
BATTLE OF FORT DONELSON. [From an old India-ink sketch by Admiral Walke.]

While this movement was going on I conducted one piece of artillery, under Captain Graves, along the Wynn's Ferry Road, supported by the Fourteenth Mississippi, and sent orders to the residue of Graves' battery, Porter's and Jackson's batteries and Farquharson's Tennessee Regiment to follow the movement with rapidity. I also sent to direct Hanson's regiment to rejoin me. The enemy, in his retreat, had now taken up a strong position on the road beyond the point where it crosses the valley. I directed the position to be attacked by the Third, Eighteenth and Thirty-second Tennessee Regiments, the first on the left, the others on the right of the road, while Graves' piece took position in the road within two hundred and fifty or three hundred yards of the enemy's guns. These regiments, under the immediate command of Colonel Brown, advanced gallantly to the attack, while Graves' piece responded with effect to the enemy's artillery. Notwithstanding their vast superiority in numbers, the enemy were driven, with very heavy loss, from their position, and retreated to the right of Wynn's Ferry Road, leaving it entirely open. In this position I waited the arrival of my artillery and reserves, either to continue the pursuit of the enemy or to defend the position I now held, in order that the army might pass out on the Forge Road, which was now completely covered by the position occupied by my division. But General Pillow had prevented my artillery from leaving the intrenchments, and had ordered Farquharson not to join me, and also sent me reiterated orders to return to my intrenchments on the extreme right.

I was in the act of returning to the lines when I met General Floyd, who seemed surprised at the order. At his request to know my opinion of the movement I replied that nothing had occurred to change my views of the necessity of the evacuation of the post, that the road was open, that the first part of our purpose was fully accomplished, and I thought we should at once avail ourselves of the existing opportunity to regain our communications. These seemed to be his own views; for he directed me to halt my troops and remain in position until he should have conversed with General Pillow, who was now within the intrenchments.

After that consultation he sent me an order to retire within the lines, and to repair as rapidly as possible to my former position on the extreme right, which was in danger of attack. The enemy made no attempt at pursuit. I secured the section of artillery which had been captured, and covered my retrograde movement by Hanson's and Farquharson's regiments. My troops were already much exhausted, but returned as rapidly as possible, a distance of two miles, to their positions. But a small portion of my division had reached their position when a division of the enemy, under command of General C. F. Smith, assaulted the extreme right of my position, falling upon Hanson's regiment before it had reached its rifle pits. This gallant regiment was necessarily thrown back in confusion upon the position of the Eighteenth Tennessee. At this period I reached that position, and, aided by a number of officers, I succeeded in hastily forming a line behind the crest of the hill which overlooked the detached works which had been seized by the enemy before Hanson had been able to throw his regiment into them. The enemy advanced gallantly upon this new position, but was repulsed with heavy loss. I re-enforced this position by other regiments as they successively arrived, and by a section of Graves' battery, while a section of Porter's battery was placed in its former position. During a contest of more than two hours the enemy threatened my left with a heavy column and made repeated attempts to storm my line on the right, but the well-directed fire of Porter's and Graves' artillery and the musketry fire of the infantry, repelled the attempts, and finally drove him to seek shelter behind the works he had taken and amid the irregularities of the ground.

There was probably no period of the action when his force was not from three to five times the strength of mine. Toward the close of the action I was re-enforced by the regiments of Colonels Quarles, Sugg and Bailey. Generals Floyd and Pillow also visited the position about the close of the action.

In a council of general and field officers, held after night, it was unanimously resolved that if the enemy had not re-occupied in strength the position in front of General Pillow the army should effect its retreat, and orders to assemble the regiments for that purpose were given by General Floyd; but as the enemy had late in the afternoon appeared in considerable force on the battlefield of the morning, a reconnoissance was ordered, I think, by General Pillow, under the instructions of General Floyd. The report of this reconnoissance, made by Colonel Forrest, has been fully stated by Generals Floyd and Pillow, and, from what I have been able to learn since, I am satisfied the information reported was correct.

Among other incidents showing that the enemy had not only re-occupied their former ground, but extended their lines still further to our left, is the fact that Overton's cavalry, following after Forrest's, was cut off from retreat by an infantry force of the enemy at the point where Forrest had crossed the stream on the river road. When the information of our re-investment was reported, General Floyd, General Pillow and myself were the only members of the council present. Both of these officers have stated the views of the council, but my recollection of some of the incidents narrated differ so materially from that of General Pillow, that, without intending any reflection upon either of those gentlemen, I feel called upon to notice some of the differences of opinion between us.

Both officers have correctly stated that I regarded the position of the army as desperate, and that an attempt to extricate it by another battle, in the suffering and exhausted condition of the troops, was almost hopeless. The troops had been worn down with watching, with labor, with fighting. Many of them were frosted by the intensity of the cold; all of them were suffering and exhausted by their incessant labors. There had been no regular issue of rations for a number of days, and scarcely any means of cooking. Their ammunition was nearly expended. We were completely invested by a force fully four times the strength of our own. In their exhausted condition they could not have made a march. An attempt to make a sortie would have been resisted by a superior force of fresh troops, and that attempt would have been the signal for the fall of the water batteries and the presence of the enemy's gunboats sweeping with the fire at close range the positions of our troops, who would thus have been assailed on their front, rear and right flank at the same instant. The result would have been a virtual massacre of the troops, more disheartening in its effects than a surrender.

In this opinion General Floyd coincided, and I am certain that both he and I were convinced that General Pillow agreed with us in opinion. General Pillow then asked our opinion as to the practicability of holding our position another day. I replied that my right was already turned, a portion of my intrenchments in the enemy's possession—they were in position to successfully assail my position and the water batteries—and that with my weakened and exhausted force, I could not successfully resist the assault which would be made at daylight by a vastly superior force. I further remarked that I understood the principal object of the defense of Donelson to be to cover the movement of General A. S. Johnston's army from Bowling Green to Nashville, and that if that movement was not completed it was my opinion that we should attempt a further defense, even at the risk of destruction of our entire force, as the delay of only a few hours might gain the safety of General Johnston's force. General Floyd remarked that General Johnston's army had already reached Nashville. I then expressed the opinion that it would be wrong to subject the army to a virtual massacre when no good could result from the sacrifice, and that the general officers owed it to their men, when further resistance was unavailing, to obtain the best terms of capitulation possible for them.

General Floyd expressed himself in similar terms, and in his opinion I understood General Pillow to acquiesce. General Floyd then announced his purpose to leave, with such portions of his division as could be transported in two small steamers, which were expected about daylight.

General Pillow, addressing General Floyd, then remarked that he thought there were no two persons in the Confederacy whom the Yankees would prefer to capture than himself and General Floyd, and asked the latter's opinion as to the propriety of his accompanying General Floyd. To this inquiry the latter replied that it was a question for every man to decide for himself. General Pillow then addressed the inquiry to me, to which I remarked that I could only reply as General Floyd had done, that it was a question for every officer to decide for himself, and that in my own case I regarded it as my duty to remain with my men and share their fate, whatever it might be. General Pillow, however, announced his purpose to leave, when General Floyd directed me to consider myself in command. I remarked that a capitulation would be as bitter to me as it could be to any one, but I regarded it as a necessity of our position, and I could not reconcile it with my sense of duty to separate my fortunes from those of my command. It is due to General Pillow to state that some time after the command had been transferred to me, and while preparations were making for his departure, he returned to the room, and said to General Floyd and myself that he wished it understood that he had thought it would have been better to have held the fort another day, in order to await the arrival of steamers to transport the troops across the river. I again recapitulated my reasons for thinking it impossible to hold our position; and whatever may have been General Pillow's opinion, he certainly impressed me with the belief that he again acquiesced in the necessity of a surrender.

It was now near daylight of Sunday morning, the 16th. I ordered the troops back to their positions in intrenchments, and addressed a note, a copy of which is inclosed, to the Federal commander, Brigadier-General U. S. Grant. His reply is also transmitted. When it was received but a small portion of the troops had returned to their lines. A portion of my field-guns had been spiked when the troops had been withdrawn under General Floyd's order. The gunners had not yet returned to the water batteries. A degree of confusion, amounting almost to a state of disorganization, resulting from the knowledge of our position, pervaded a considerable portion of the troops. A corps of not less than 15,000 of the enemy, with fifteen pieces of artillery, were in position to assault the extreme right of the line, which was effectually turned, and the water batteries exposed to assault without the power of resisting the attack. At the point most strongly threatened I could not have opposed at the time a thousand men. Every road leading from the lines was effectually closed. Even the river road, by which the cavalry had left, and which was impassable by infantry, was closed by a force of the enemy within fifteen minutes after Forrest had passed and Overton's cavalry was forced to return to the lines. The troops were broken down by unusual privations. Most of them had labored or fought almost incessantly for a week. From Thursday morning until Saturday night they had been almost constantly under fire. From Thursday evening until Sunday morning they had suffered intensely in a heavy snowstorm and from intense cold, almost without shelter, with insufficient food, and almost without sleep. They had behaved with a gallantry unsurpassed until the power of further endurance was exhausted. The supply of ammunition was very small.

The aggregate of the army, never greater than 12,000, was now reduced to less than 9,000 men after the departure of General Floyd's brigade. The investing force of the enemy was about 50,000 strong, and considerably exceeded that force by the following morning. Under these circumstances no alternative was left me but to accept the terms demanded by our ungenerous enemy. A copy of the order of General Grant, fixing the terms of surrender, is herewith inclosed.

I do not seek to avoid any responsibility which, in the judgment of the President, may attach to my action, which was guided in every instance by a feeling of duty. My chief wish is that he will find it consistent with the public interest to permit me still to unite my fortunes in the contest for independence with those of the brave men whose gallantry I have witnessed, whose dangers and hardships I have shared and in common with whom I have endured the privations of imprisonment among a vindictive and tyrannical foe.

FORT DONELSON, AS SEEN FROM THE BANKS OF THE RIVER.

I can not close this report without calling special attention to the gallant and able conduct of my brigade commanders, Colonel John C. Brown, of the Third Tennessee; William E. Baldwin, of the Fourteenth Mississippi; and R. W. Hanson, commanding the Second Kentucky, detached from Breckinridge's Kentucky brigade.

My aggregate force at the beginning of the contest, which was constantly diminishing, did not exceed 3,025 infantry and two batteries of artillery. Two of my regiments, in addition (844 men), were constantly under the command of General Pillow. The length of my lines exceeded three-fourths of a mile.

* * * * * *

S. B. BUCKNER,
Brigadier-General, C. S. A.

Commanding Second Division, Central Army of Kentucky.

AN OFFICER'S WIT.—A gallant soldier and distinguished politician, who commanded one of the regiments, perpetrated an "Irish bull" one day which the other regiments of the brigade never suffered his men to hear the last of. Having halted on the march, and the men not falling in with sufficient rapidity when the order to move was given, the gallant colonel exclaimed: "Fall in there, men! Fall in quickly! If you don't fall in I'll march the regiment off and leave every man of you!" At the battle of Winchester, in June, 1863, this same officer (now a brigadier-general) was very deliberately forming his line of battle when the division commander grew inpatient and sent an aid, who came galloping up to the old hero to say: "General, General —— wants to know if you are proposing to have dress parade down here?" The instant retort was, "Go back and tell him yes; we are going to dress on the enemy." "Dress on the enemy" at once became a slang phrase among the men.

THE BATTLE OF PEA RIDGE, OR ELKHORN TAVERN,

MARCH 6, 1862.

BY

BRIGADIER-GENERAL ALBERT PIKE, C. S. A.
Commanding Department of Indian Territory.

DWIGHT MISSION, CHEROKEE NATION, I. T.,
March 14, 1862.

ON February 25th I reached Cantonment Davis, near Fort Gibson, with Colonel Cooper's Choctaw and Chickasaw battalion, which had been encamped near the mouth of the Canadian. The same evening Colonel D. N. McIntosh's regiment of Creeks arrived at the same point. I had in charge a large amount of coin and other moneys for the different Indian tribes, and found delegations of the Osages, Comanches and Reserve Indians awaiting me, and the disposition of the moneys left unexpectedly in my hands, together with the dealings with the Indian tribes, detained me there three days.

The Choctaws, Chickasaws and Creeks refused to march until they were paid off, and as by their treaties with us they could not be taken out of the Indian country without their consent, I had no alternative but to submit. The payment of the Choctaws and Chickasaws occupied three days.

On the morning of the third day I left them behind at Fort Gibson, except O. G. Welch's squadron of Texans, part of the First Choctaw and Chickasaw regiment, with which, and the Creek regiment, whom I persuaded to move by the promise that they should be paid at the Illinois River, I marched to Park Hill, near that river, remained there one day, and not being overtaken, as I expected to be, by the Choctaw and Chickasaw troops, moved the next day, Monday, March 3d, toward Evansville, and the next day to Cincinnati, on the Cherokee line, where I overtook Colonel Stand Watie's regiment of Cherokees.

The next day, Wednesday, with Colonel Watie's regiment and Captain Welch's squadron, I reached Freschlag's Mill, and on Thursday overtook Colonel Drew's regiment of Cherokees at Smith's Mill, and came up with the rear of General McCulloch's division late that afternoon. That night I encamped within two miles of Camp Stephens, and at 9:30 o'clock received General Van Dorn's order, to the effect that the army would move at 8 o'clock, and that I would follow General McCulloch's division. I sent to General McCulloch to ascertain at what hour the road would be clear for me to move, and received his reply that it would be clear at 12 o'clock, and that his train would not move until daylight. At 12 o'clock I marched with my command, overtook and passed General McCulloch's train, which was in motion, and had to wait until sunrise, a little south of Sugar Creek, until his infantry had passed it on a little bridge of rails. We followed closely in his rear until the head of my command had passed the houses on what is called Pea Vine Ridge, where we were halted, and Colonel Sims' Texas regiment, countermarching, passed us to the rear, an officer informing me that I was to countermarch and follow the other troops. I did so, and we were then marched off the Bentonville Road to the south through the woods. Soon after Captain Lomax, of General McCulloch's staff, informed me that the enemy had fortified a little place called Leetown, about four miles and a half to the south, which we were marching to attack, and that General McCulloch's orders were that my command, on reaching the spot, should form in line in rear of General McIntosh's brigade, which would itself be in rear of a line of infantry, and that when the firing should begin all were to dismount and charge together.

We had marched from the road in a southeasterly direction about a mile from the point where we left it, and were passing along a narrow road, between a piece of woods on our left and a fenced field on our right, when we discovered in front of us, at the distance of about three hundred yards, a battery of three guns, protected by five companies of regular cavalry. A fence ran from east to west through the woods, and behind this we formed in line, with Colonel Sims' regiment on the right, the squadron of Captain Welch next to him, and the regiments of Colonels Watie and Drew in continuation of the line on the left. The enemy was in a small prairie, about two hundred and fifty yards across, on the right of which was the fenced

From an original painting, owned and copyrighted by Kurz & Allison, Chicago, Ill.

BATTLE OF PEA RIDGE, OR ELKHORN TAVERN, ARK., MARCH 6, 1862.

field, and on our left it extended to a large prairie field, bounded on the east by a ridge. In rear of the battery was a thicket of underbrush, and on its right, a little to the rear, a body of timber.

General McIntosh's cavalry had passed on into the large prairie field to our left, and the infantry were quite across it, close to the ridge, about six hundred yards from us. My whole command consisted of about 1,000 men, all Indians except one squadron.

The enemy opened fire into the woods where we were, the fence in front of us was thrown down, and the Indians (Watie's regiment on foot and Drew's on horseback), with part of Sims' regiment, gallantly led by Lieutenant-Colonel Quayle, charged full in front through the woods and into the open ground with loud yells, routed the cavalry, took the battery, fired upon and pursued the enemy, retreating

Brigadier-General Albert Pike, of Arkansas.

through the fenced field on our right, and held the battery, which I afterward had drawn by the Cherokees into the woods. Four of the horses of the battery alone remained on the ground, the others running off with the caissons, and for want of horses and harness we were unable to send the guns to the rear.

The officers of my staff, Captains Schwarzman and Hewitt and Lieutenant Pike, with Captain Lee of Acting Brigadier-General Cooper's staff, rode with us in the charge. Our loss was two of Colonel Drew's men killed and one wounded. Colonel Sims had one man killed and one wounded. Of the enemy, between thirty and forty were killed in the field and around the guns. The charge was made just at noon.

We remained at the battery for some twenty minutes, when Colonel Watie informed me that another battery was in our front, beyond the skirt of underbrush, protected by a heavy force of infantry. General McIntosh's force was not near us, nor do I know where it then was. The infantry were still in their position near the ridge, across the large field on the left, and did not approach us; indeed, at one time it moved further off along the ridge. Colonel Drew's regiment was in the field on our right, and around the taken battery was a mass of Indians and others in the utmost confusion; all talking, riding this way and that, and listening to no orders from any one. I directed Captain Roswell W. Lee, of Acting Brigadier-General Cooper's staff, always conspicuous for gallantry and coolness, to have the guns which had been taken faced to our front, that they might be used against the battery just discovered, but he could not induce a single man to assist in doing so.

At this moment the enemy sent two shells into the field, and the Indians retreated hurriedly into the woods out of which they had made the charge. Well aware that they would not face shells in the open ground, I directed them to dismount, take their horses to the rear, and each take to a tree, and this was done by both regiments, the men thus awaiting patiently and coolly the expected advance of the enemy, who now and for two hours and a half afterward, until perhaps twenty minutes before the action ended, continued to fire shot and shell into the woods where the Indians were, from their battery in front, but never advanced. This battery also was thus, with its supporting force, by the presence of the Indians, rendered useless to the enemy during the action.

In the meantime our artillery had come into action some distance to our left and front, beyond a large field, extending from the woods in which we were to a line of woods beyond it, which hid the conflict from our view. Leaving the Indians in the woods, I passed beyond them to the left into the open ground nearer the conflict, and remained some time.

About 1:30 o'clock there was a very heavy fire of musketry for about ten minutes, and soon after about two regiments of our cavalry came into the field on our left front and formed in line, facing the woods upon that side. Colonel Drew then came to me with his regiment, about 500 strong, and I sent him across the field, directing him to form in rear of the line of cavalry, and if they advanced through the woods to follow them, dismount his men nearer the other edge, and let them join in the fight in their own fashion. They crossed the field and took the position indicated.

It was just after this that I directed Sergeant-Major West, of Colonel Watie's regiment, to take some of the Cherokees and drag the captured guns into the woods, which was done, the enemy still firing over them into the woods, where he placed a guard of Cherokees over the cannon.

Soon after the cavalry force crossed to our side of the field and formed in line in front of the woods in which the Indians were, and remained there until the enemy threw a shot in that direction, when they also took shelter in the woods. During all this time I received no orders whatever, nor any message from any one. About 3 o'clock I rode toward the fenced field. I saw nothing of our cavalry, but found a body of our infantry halted on the road running along the fence by which we had originally come. It consisted of the regiments of Colonels Churchill, Hill and Rector, and Major Whitfield's battalion. Major Whitfield informed me that Generals McCulloch and McIntosh were both killed, and that 7,000 of the enemy's infantry were marching to gain our left, one body of which, at least 3,000 strong, he had himself seen. Totally ignorant of the country and the roads, not knowing the number of the enemy, nor whether the whole or what portion of General McCulloch's command had been detached from the main body for this action, I assumed command, and prepared to repel the supposed movement of the enemy.

To our left, beyond the field where our infantry had first been seen by me in the forenoon, was a wooded ridge of no great height, with a fence running along the foot of it on the west and northwest; between it and the Bentonville Road was open and level ground. I marched the infantry—Welch's squadron and Watie's regiment—across the field, dismounted the horsemen, directed all to be posted behind the fences, and sent Major Boudinot, of Watie's regiment, to inform General Van Dorn that I would try to hold the position; but upon riding up and along the ridge to the rear I found the position not tenable, as the enemy could cross it and descend upon our rear by an open road that ran over it.

At this time the firing on the field had ceased, and I saw coming into the road at the farm-house a large body of cavalry and Good's battery. It was evident enough that the field was left to the enemy, and as we were not in sufficient numbers to resist them, and the ground afforded no defensive position, I determined to withdraw the troops and lead them to General Van Dorn. Indeed, the officers assured me that the men were in such condition that it would be worse than useless to bring them into action again that day.

I accordingly sent orders to the artillery and cavalry to join me. What had become of the other troops engaged no one could inform me. I concluded they had retreated toward Camp Stephens, gaining the road by which we had come in the morning. Colonel Stone and Captain Good came to me, and I informed them of my purpose. Placing the squadron of Captain Welch in front, the infantry marching next, followed by Good's battery, with the Cherokees on the flanks, and, as I supposed, Colonel Stones's regiment in the rear, we gained the Bentonville Road, and marched on it in perfect order to the Telegraph Road.

The order sent to the Cherokees to join us had not, by some accident, reached Colonel Drew, and his regiment remained in the woods, and after a time retreated toward Camp Stephens, where, he informed me, he found Colonel Stone's regiment arrived before him. This regiment, understanding, I have learned, that part of the enemy's force was marching to attack the train, took that direction.

The infantry had, in three days, marched sixty miles, had been on foot all the preceding night, and fought that day without water, and Colonel Churchill begged me to leave them where they could procure it. When we reached the Telegraph Road I was about to conduct them to headquarters; but unable to learn the position of the two armies, or how the road came upon the field, and learning that where our forces were there was no water and that there was a running stream on the Pineville Road, about a mile and a half from the point where the Bentonville Road descends into the valley, I led them to and on the Pineville Road, intending to halt at the water, and letting the men have that, at least, as they had nothing to eat, to join the main army early in the morning. Orders from General Van Dorn caused us to retrace our steps and march to his headquarters, which we reached long after dark.

On Saturday morning I was directed by General Van Dorn to post part of Colonel Watie's men—who were my whole command, except Captain Welch's squadron—on the high ridge to our right, and the residue on another ridge on the left, to observe the enemy and give him information if any attempt was made by them in force to turn his left flank. I accompanied those sent on the ridge to the right, and sent Captain Fayette Hewitt, of my staff, to post the others. To Captain Welch I gave permission to join any Texan regiment he chose, and he joined that of Colonel Greer, and remained with it until the action ended.

After remaining for some two hours near the foot of the ridge, on the south side, observing the enemy's infantry, heavy columns of which were in the fields beyond, and the fire of their batteries in full view of me, and seeing no movement of the infantry to the left, I recrossed the ridge, descended it and went toward General Van Dorn's headquarters. Being told that he and General Price were in the field to the left of his headquarters, I took the road that led there and halted on the first hill below headquarters, where a battery was posted, facing the Telegraph Road, and which, I was told, had been sent to the rear for ammunition. Here I heard that orders had been given for the army to fall back and take a new position. Another battery came up and the captain asked me for orders. I told him he had better place his battery in position, in line with the others, to play upon the road, and then send to General Van Dorn for orders. In the meantime I sent two officers to the general to deliver him a message, and myself remained with the batteries.

We now heard long-continued cheering in front. Bodies of our troops had come across the ridge on the right and down the Hospital Hollow, in good order apparently, and I supposed they were marching to the left to repel, perhaps, the attempt upon our left flank apprehended by General Van Dorn in the morning. Seeing no fugitives on the Telegraph Road, we supposed the cheering to proceed from our own troops and that the day was ours, when an officer rode down and informed me that the field was occupied by Federal troops, and soon after another came and told me that no one had seen either General Van Dorn or General Price for some time, and it was supposed they were captured, as the field where they were last seen was full of Federals, and he remarked to me: "You are not safe here, for the enemy's cavalry are within one hundred and fifty yards of you."

The troops that had come across the ridge and down the Hospital Hollow were now below us, on the Telegraph Road. Colonel Watie had sent to me for orders. I had sent to him to bring his men from the ridge down into the valley and there halt for orders, and I supposed he had done so; but he did not receive the order, and remained on the mountain, from which he went direct to Camp Stephens.

Just at this moment the two batteries close to me commenced to wheel, and hurried down the hill into the road.

Brigadier-General William Y. Slack, of Missouri.
[Killed at the Battle of Pea Ridge.]

I do not know that any one gave them any order to fall back. The captain of one battery said that some one ordered it, but I think that the information of the capture of our generals was overheard, and that no order was given. No one was there to give an order. The batteries rattled down the steep hill and along the Telegraph Road, and as I rode by the side of them I heard an officer cry out: "Close up—close up, or you will all be cut to pieces!"

On reaching the road I rode past the batteries to reach a point at which to make a stand, for, having passed the road but once, and then in the night, it was all an unknown land to me. When we reached the first open level ground I halted the leading gun, directed the captain of the company in front to come into battery, facing to the rear, on the right of the plain going northward—the battery in the rear I knew had no ammunition—saw the first gun so placed in position; rode back to the second battery and directed the only officer I could find to do the same on the left of the plain, and when I turned around to go to the front found that the gun faced to the rear had been again turned into the road, and that the whole concern was again going up the road northward. I rode again to the front and halted the leading battery at the foot of the next level, ordered it into line, facing to the rear, gave the necessary commands myself and had three guns brought into position. Two regiments of infantry were standing there in lines ranging up and down the valley, the flank of each to the enemy. I directed them to form in the rear of the batteries; but at this moment a shell was sent by the enemy up the road from the point of the hill around which we had just passed. The cry of "The cavalry are coming!" was raised, and everything became confusion.

It was impossible to bring the other guns into battery. Those already faced turned again into the road, and supposing that, of course, they would take the Bentonville Road—which, at leaving the other, ascends a steep hill—and thinking I could certainly halt them, after a slow ascent, on its summit, I galloped through the bottom and up the ravine on the left of the hill, dismounted and climbed the hill on foot, remounted at the summit, rode to the brow of the hill, looked down into the road, and found that our retreating troops, batteries and all, had passed by on the Telegraph Road, the enemy's cavalry pursuing, en route for Springfield, Mo.

Captain Hewitt and my aid-de-camp, Lieutenant W. L. Pike, had followed me, and, except half a dozen stragglers, we were alone. We waited a few moments on the brow of the hill, uncertain what course to pursue, when, on our right, as we faced the valley, and at a distance of about one hundred yards, a gun of the enemy sent a shot into the valley, and another on the other side, further off, replied with another.

We then turned and rode up the road toward Bentonville, and after riding about a mile found that the enemy's cavalry were pursuing at full speed. Leaving them in the rear by rapid riding, we turned into the woods on the right, passed around the farmhouse on the Pea Vine Ridge and rode westward between the Pineville and Bentonville roads.

We had been informed by my brigade commissary, who had come up from Camp Stephens about 10 o'clock, that our whole train had been turned back and was encamped at Pea Vine Ridge.

Three miles from the Telegraph Road we saw a small body of our retreating horsemen fired upon by the enemy's infantry, and concluded, as they had evidently anticipated our retreat, and made every arrangement necessary in view of it to destroy our retreating forces, that General Sigel, returning by the route up Sugar Creek, by which he

Brigadier-General James M. McIntosh, of Florida.
[Killed at the Battle of Pea Ridge, March 7, 1862.]

had retreated, was in front of our train and it was lost. Owing to the circuit which we were constrained to make and to the fatigued condition of our starved horses, we were unable to gain the front of our retreating forces until after they had left Elm Springs, and learning that the Indian troops had marched from that point to Cincinnati, we joined them at that place.

The enemy, I learn, had been encamped at Pea Vine Ridge for three weeks, and Sigel's advance was but a ruse to induce our forces to march northward and give them battle in position selected by themselves.

I may add that in their pursuit of our retreating train they followed no further than Bentonville and returned from that point. I was within five miles of that place on Monday morning and was misled by information that they had taken it that morning; but they did not enter it until the afternoon.

I did not know until I reached Cincinnati what had become of the main body of our forces. I there met Captain Schwarzman and Major Lanigan, who informed me of their retreat, and that Generals Van Dorn and Price were marching from Huntsville to Van Buren, and also heard of the order to burn all the wagons on the Cove Creek Road that could not cross Boston Mountains.

Just before night, Saturday afternoon, I had met Colonel Rector in the hills, who told me he had about 500 men with him; that they were in such condition that they could not go more than six or eight miles a day, and that he thought he would take them into the mountains, hide their arms in a secure place, and, as he could not keep them together and feed them, let them disperse. He asked my opinion as to this, and I told him that no one knew where the rest of the army was; that Generals Van Dorn and Price were supposed to be captured and the train taken; that if his men dispersed with their arms they would throw them away, and that I thought the course he proposed was the wisest one under the circumstances. The enemy was pursuing on all the roads, and as it was almost impossible for even a dozen men in a body to procure food, I still do not see what better he could have done.

General Cooper, with his regiment and battalion of Choctaws and Chickasaws, and Colonel McIntosh, with two hundred men of his regiment of Creeks, came up with our retreating train at Camp Stephens, where they found Colonel Drew's regiment, and remained with General Green, protecting the train until it reached Elm Springs, where they were all ordered to march with their own train to Cincinnati.

* * * * * * *

ALBERT PIKE,
Brigadier-General.
Commanding Department of Indian Territory.

BATTLE OF NEWBERN, N. C.,

March 14, 1862.

by

BRIGADIER-GENERAL L. O'B. BRANCH.

Headquarters of the First Division,
In the Field, March 26, 1862.

The defensive works were located and constructed before I assumed command. The troops under my command had performed a large amount of work, but it was mainly on the river defenses, which were not assailed by the enemy. They had been originally planned for a force much larger than any ever placed at my disposal, and I was for six weeks engaged in making the necessary changes to contract them, but the failure of all my efforts to obtain implements and tools with which the troops could carry on the work prevented me from making satisfactory progress. I had circulated handbills over the State, calling on the citizens generally to assist me, and received from two counties a small party of free negroes without implements. I then inserted in the newspaper an advertisement calling on the slaveowners to hire their slaves, with implements, for a few days, and I got but a single negro.

During all this time I continued the troops at work, and when the enemy came into the river five hundred per day were being detailed to construct breastworks, with less than half that number of worn and broken shovels and axes, without pick or grubbing hoes. If the fate of Newbern shall prevent a similar supineness on the part of citizens, and especially slaveowners, elsewhere, it will be fortunate for the country.

Ten miles below Newbern, on the south side of the Neuse, is the mouth of Otter Creek. From this creek, one mile above its mouth, the Croatan breastwork runs across to an impracticable swamp about three-fourths of a mile. This is a well-planned and well-constructed work, which two thousand men and two field batteries could hold against a very large force. But from the mouth of Otter Creek to Fort Thompson, the lowest of the river batteries, is a distance of six miles of river shore, on any part of which the enemy could land and take the Croatan work in reverse. It is obvious that the breastwork was useless if I had not sufficient force to hold it and at the same time guard six miles of river shore. I had at no time been able to place four thousand men in the field at Newbern, and at the time of the battle had been seriously weakened by the re-enlistment furloughs.

Coming up the river from the Croatan work, you reach the Fort Thompson breastwork. This had been constructed from Fort Thompson to the railroad, about one mile, before I assumed command. Finding that, from inadequate force, the Croatan work might be of no avail to me, I determined to extend the Fort Thompson work about one mile and a fourth, and rest its right on a swamp. This is the work I was engaged on when the enemy appeared. In order to make the line as short as possibie and to avail of a small branch by throwing it in front the line was thrown back about one hundred and fifty yards on the railroad and thence a series of small breastworks, conforming to the features of the ground, ran off in the direction of the swamp, making an obtuse angle with the older portion of the line on the other side of the railroad. To guard this gap I directed that the old brick-kiln on the railroad should be loopholed, and the evening before the battle had ordered two 24-pounder guns to be brought from Newbern and placed in battery there. The enemy's skirmishers drove the laborers from the battery, when an hour more would have enabled them to get the guns in position. Of course I lost all the benefit I expected from it. The line of small breastworks from the railroad to the swamp was partially finished for about half the distance.

Running parallel to the river and to each other, and

Brig.-Gen. L. O'B. Branch, of North Carolina.
[Killed at the Battle of Antietam or Sharpsburg.]

crossing the line at right angles are, first, after leaving the river, the old Beaufort Road, and then the railroad; still further on and near the swamp, the Weathersby Road. The railroad and the Beaufort Road intersect about two miles behind the breastwork, the former crossing the river on a bridge 1,840 feet long at the town of Newbern, and the latter at an indifferent private bridge about one mile and a half above Newbern. Both these bridges are accessible to gunboats, so that when we stood at the Fort Thompson breastwork, fronting the enemy, we had Neuse River on our left, Bryce Creek (an impassable stream) on our right, and the Neuse and Trent in our rear, the only possible mode of escape in case of defeat being across the two bridges I have described, five miles in our rear.

I hope this description, with the aid of the map inclosed, will put you in possession of our situation at the opening of the battle.

I omitted to state that the timber had been felled in front of the breastwork for about three hundred and fifty yards, and the space was swept by ten field-pieces, besides three navy 32-pounders, discharging grape and canister from the rear face of Fort Thompson.

It is useless to describe the river defenses, on which the largest amount of labor had been bestowed, as the enemy prudently refrained from attacking the batteries in front, and the gunboats did not come within range of their guns until they had been silenced from the rear.

I now proceed to detail the incidents of the battle.

On Wednesday, the 12th, at 4 P. M., the approach of the enemy's fleet was reported to me, and at dark I learned that twelve vessels had anchored below the mouth of Otter Creek, and about forty-five were ascending the river in their rear.

Orders were issued to Colonel Sinclair, of the Thirty-fifth Regiment, to proceed immediately with his regiment to Fisher's Landing, which is just above the mouth of Otter Creek, and to resist any attempt of the enemy to land there. Colonel Avery, Thirty-third Regiment, and Lieutenant-Colonel Haywood, Seventh Regiment, constituting the reserve, were ordered to proceed across the river, so as to be in position at the intersection of the Beaufort Road and the railroad at daybreak in the morning. Colonel R. P. Campbell, commanding my right wing, was instructed to guard the river shore from the mouth of Otter Creek to Fort Thompson, while Colonel C. C. Lee, who commanded my left wing, was to guard the remainder of the shore, support the river batteries and re-enforce Colonel Campbell in case he should be hard pressed. Colonel Campbell was instructed to establish his headquarters at the intersection of the Beaufort Road and the breastwork, and to collect his troops around him by daybreak. Both commanders were instructed that, in case it should be necessary to fall back from the river shore to the breastwork, Colonel Campbell should hold that part to the right of the Beaufort Road, and Colonel Lee that part to the left of it.

These orders having been dispatched by 9 P. M., the night was spent by the troops in getting into position, and other preparations for the contest.

Having given all the necessary directions to staff officers and all others before 3 o'clock Thursday morning, and seen all the men and material forwarded from the camp and depot in Newbern, I proceeded to Colonel Campbell's headquarters. On the road I met dispatches from Colonel Sinclair and Captain P. G. Evans, commanding the pickets, informing me that the enemy were landing troops below the mouth of Otter Creek, and Colonel Vance was directed to send his regiment to the Croatan breastwork to occupy it. Railroad trains were on the spot to carry down re-enforcements or to draw off Colonels Vance's and Sinclair's regiments and Brem's battery, as the case might require.

Intelligence was soon brought to me that the enemy's gunboats, having driven Colonel Sinclair's regiment from Fisher's Landing, were rapidly landing troops at that place, and that Colonel Campbell, seeing that the Croatan breastwork was turned, had ordered Vance, Sinclair and Brem to fall back to the Fort Thompson breastwork.

My force was wholly inadequate to guard the six miles of river shore between the mouth of Otter Creek and Fort Thompson. The result was, therefore, not wholly unexpected, but I had hoped that a line of rifle pits I had caused to be made for a mile along the bluffs at and on both sides of Fisher's Landing would have enabled me to hold the enemy in check, and to inflict on him serious loss at the first moment of his placing his foot on our soil. I was, therefore, surprised when the position was yielded with a loss of only one killed and two wounded, all three of which casualties occurred in the retreat. After the abandonment of Fisher's Landing to the enemy the prompt withdrawal of Vance and Brem could alone save them from being cut off, and the enemy thus come into possession of my strongest work without having received a single shot from us.

The Fort Thompson breastwork now became my sole reliance for resisting his advance, and throughout the remainder of the day and night of Thursday the most active efforts were made to strengthen that unfinished work. Both officers and men executed my orders with unflagging energy.

In the afternoon the gunboats shelled the breastwork heavily from a position they had taken out of reach of the guns of our batteries. The composure with which all classes of my troops received this attack from an unseen foe strengthened the confidence I felt in their standing under fire.

No damage was inflicted on us by the shells, but the accuracy with which they were thrown over a thick, intervening woodland convinced me of the necessity of driving traitors and enemies in disguise from all towns and neighborhoods of which we desire to hold military possession.

During the day on Thursday the troops were posted behind the intrenchments, and it was painfully apparent that my force was not sufficient to man them even with a thin line for the finished portions of them. I was compelled to withdraw Lieutenant-Colonel Haywood, of the Seventh Regiment, from the reserve and place him on the line. The regiments were posted as follows, commencing on the left: Lieutenant-Colonel Barbour, Thirty-seventh Regiment, and Major Gilmer, Twenty-seventh Regiment, between Fort Thompson and the Beaufort country road. Lieutenant Colonel Haywood, Seventh; Colonel Sinclair, Thirty-fifth, and Colonel Clark (militia), between the Beaufort Road and the railroad. Colonel Vance, Twenty-sixth Regiment, to the right of the railroad. A few unattached companies were placed between the regiments. My headquarters were about two hundred yards in rear of the intrenchments at the railroad, and the reserve was about two hundred yards in my rear; the cavalry regiment about half a mile to the rear. In this order the troops slept on their arms.

At 11 o'clock Thursday night Colonel Lee brought me intelligence that signal rockets had just been seen on our extreme right, from which I inferred that the enemy, having found the Weathersby Road, were in front of that portion of my line.

Orders were sent to Colonel Vance to extend his regiment so that its right might rest on the Weathersby Road, and in an hour a section of Brem's battery was moving by a circuitous route to a position on that road.

On taking my position Friday morning the center appeared so weak that I dispatched my aid-de-camp to Colonel Campbell to say to him that it must be re-enforced, if possible.

At about 7:30 o'clock on Friday morning the fire opened along the line from the railroad to the river. I soon received a message from Colonel Lee that the enemy were attempting to turn our left. This proved to be a feint, as I replied to him that I thought it would. The next incident of the battle was the appearance of the enemy's skirmishers in front of Vance, and consequently on the prolongation of the line held by the militia. It was to drive the enemy from that position that I had directed the 24-pounder battery to be placed there; and supposing it was ready for service, I sent Captain Rodman, with his company, to man it, but they found the guns not mounted, and were ordered into position to act as infantry. The shirmishers of the enemy, finding themselves on the flank of the militia, fired at them a few shots from their flank files, which caused a portion of them to flee in great disorder.

I instantly ordered Colonel Avery to send five companies to dislodge them. He sent them instantly, under Lieutenant-Colonel Hoke; but before Colonel Hoke had fully got into position, though he moved with the greatest promptness and celerity, I received a message from Colonel Clark, of the militia, informing me that the enemy were in line of battle in great force on his right. I instantly ordered up the remaining five companies of Colonel Avery's regiment, and the whole ten opened a terrific fire from their Enfield rifles. The militia, however, had now abandoned their positions, and the utmost exertions of myself and my staff could not rally them. Colonel Sinclair's regiment very quickly followed their example, retreating in the utmost disorder.

NEWBERN, N. C., VIEW OF, FROM THE OPPOSITE BANK OF THE NEUSE RIVER.

This laid open Haywood's right, and a large portion of the breastwork was left vacant. I had not a man with whom to re-occupy it, and the enemy soon poured in a column along the railroad and through a portion of the cut-down ground in front, which marched up behind the breastwork to attack what remained of Campbell's command.

The brave Seventh met them with the bayonet and drove them headlong over the parapet, inflicting heavy loss upon them as they fled; but soon returning with heavy re-enforcements, not less than five or six regiments, the Seventh was obliged to yield, falling back slowly and in order. Seeing the enemy behind the breastwork, without a single man to place in the gap through which he was entering, and finding the day lost, my next care was to secure the retreat. This was a critical operation, as the enemy, having pierced our center, had possession of the two shortest roads to the bridges, and, besides, could approach them at pleasure with their gunboats.

Having dispatched two couriers to Colonel Avery and two to Colonel Vance with orders for them to fall back to the bridges, I moved to the intersection of the Beaufort Road and railroad to rally the troops and cover the retreat across the bridges. Here I found a train of cars with the Twenty-eighth Regiment, Lieutenant-Colonel Lowe, who had arrived too late to reach the battlefield, and formed them to hold the enemy in check until all should pass. Colonel Lee was directed to proceed to Newbern and form all the men he could collect in the upper part of the town. The Seventh Regiment, arriving in two different parties, was directed to proceed to the Trent Bridge and hold it, while I remained with Lieutenant-Colonel Lowe at the intersection to hold the enemy in check and cover the retreat.

Remaining until there were no more stragglers in sight on either road, I directed Colonel Lowe to fall back to the Trent Bridge, which he did, the enemy showing themselves on the road as his rear guard moved off. Proceeding to the Trent Bridge I placed Colonel Campbell in command of all the forces there, with instructions to hold the bridge as long as possible for the passage of Avery and Vance, and then to move up the Trent Road or join me in town, as I might direct after reaching there, leaving with him, to conduct him, that gallant gentleman and soldier Captain Peter G. Evans, whom I had not allowed to leave my person for two days, except to obey orders. The railroad bridge was in flames before I left the intersection.

Arriving in town I found it in flames in many places and evacuated. Orders written in the street under the lurid glare of the flames were dispatched in every direction through the town to search for Colonel Lee. At Railroad Street I learned that a gunboat had already landed at one of the lower wharves. Going up Railroad Street to see whether Colonel Lee was at the Fair Grounds, I found, on reaching the depot, that the gunboats were already there, and the enemy in the Fair Grounds. Colonel Lee, finding himself in no condition to make resistance, had properly drawn off and marched up the Kinston Road. Following on, and directing all the officers I could overtake to conduct their men to Tuscarora, the nearest railroad depot, I proceeded to that place, and, having made arrangements for the transportation of the troops to Kinston by railroad, and seen most of them off, reached that place myself at 11 o'clock on Saturday.

My loss was 64 killed, 101 wounded and 413 missing; about 200 are prisoners and the remainder at home.

The horses of Latham's battery and those of four pieces of Brem's battery were killed, and we lost in consequence ten pieces of field artillery. There were other pieces at the breastwork, but they were condemned guns from Fort Macon, belonging to no company.

The ammunition and ordnance stores at Newbern were saved, and the camp equipage and baggage of the regiments would have been saved, but we had not the field transportation with which to haul it to the railroad.

In five days after the battle I had my brigade in camp, in advance of Kinston, ready for action and but little demoralized.

I had, at an early day, placed Colonels R. P. Campbell, Seventh Regiment, and C. C. Lee, Thirty-seventh Regiment, in command of the two wings of my brigade. All the troops, except the Thirty-third Regiment and the cavalry regiment, which were in reserve, fought under their immediate command. I could have taken no better security against any errors and oversights I might commit than I did in placing those two trained and experienced officers in immediate command of the troops.

As the Thirty-third Regiment was under my own command, it is proper for me to say that its conduct was all I could desire. It moved into action with as much promptness and steadiness as I ever saw in its ranks on dress parade, and its fire was terrific. It was engaged within one hundred yards of my position, and Colonel Avery, Lieutenant-Colonel Hoke and Major Lewis did their duty fully against an overwhelming force. Its gallant colonel was captured at his post; two different couriers, whom I sent to him with orders to withdraw, having failed to reach him.

The panic alluded to occurred after the troops had left Newbern. It was in advance of me and I did not witness it, but the names of officers who contributed to it or participated in it will be reported to you if they can be discovered. It was soon counteracted by the steadiness of Colonel Lee and some other officers.

Yours very respectfully,

L. O'B. BRANCH,

Brigadier-General Commanding.

A FEW days before the battle of Gettysburg one of General Lee's soldiers questioned him as to his plans. "Are you a soldier?" asked the general. "Yes." "Then, sir, be one," said the general, as he walked away.

SIEGE OF FORT MACON,

MARCH 23 TO APRIL 28, 1862.

BY

COLONEL MOSES J. WHITE, C. S. A.

GOLDSBOROUGH, N. C., May 4, 1862.

A DEMAND was made for the surrender of Fort Macon on March 23d last by Brigadier-General Parke, United States Army, which demand was refused. General Parke then, having collected a large force at Carolina City, took possession of Beaufort and Shackelford Banks, thus cutting us off from any communication without the range of our guns. Having established his camp eight miles from the fort, on Bogue Banks, the enemy drove in our pickets on April 10th and established themselves just without the range of our guns and their pickets within one mile of the fort. In retiring before them our pickets showed great coolness, and forced the enemy to advance with caution, although flanked by a fire from the sea. The enemy, after fully establishing themselves, commenced their advance on the fort by means of ditches, using the sand hills as a covering for their working parties. With their larger force (being well protected by the sand hills) they were able, by April 22d, to establish their batteries within fourteen hundred yards of Fort Macon.

Only one sortie was made during their advance, which consisted of an attempt made with two companies to drive in their working parties and pickets on April 11th, but, they being largely re-enforced from their camp, our companies were forced to retire. Occasional firing took place between our pickets and those of the enemy at night, but without any casualties on our side. We could only annoy the enemy by the fire of our artillery, which, fired horizontally, could do them no damage and only force them to keep behind the sand hills.

Not having a mortar in the fort, we mounted six old 32-pounder carronades which had been placed in the fort for defending the ditch, with 40° elevation, and used them for throwing shell behind the enemy's coverings. Two 10-inch guns were also used for the same purpose. They were, however, so completely concealed that we could seldom ascertain the position of their working parties, and when driven from them we could not see when they returned, and from scarcity of shell could not keep up a continued fire. Had the fort been built and armed for defense from a land attack the siege might have lasted longer; but as neither was the case, the enemy were able to complete their batteries, completely masked, in a shorter time than I had hoped for. During the siege some discontent arose among the garrison, which ended in several desertions. The men complained of their fare, although furnished with full rations, and seemed to be dissatisfied with being shut up in such a small place, so near their relatives and friends, but unable to communicate with them. I am sorry to say that the officers did not act in a proper manner to suppress the difficulty. The health of the troops did not seem to be good, although we lost but one man by sickness. Nearly one-third were generally on the sick list.

On April 22d General Burnside arrived with several boats and anchored about four miles down the sound, but was forced by the fire of a rifled gun to retire and take up a position near Harker's Island.

On the 23d a demand was made by General Burnside for the surrender of Fort Macon, which being refused, a request was made that I should meet him in person the next day on Shackelford Banks upon very important business.

At 8 A. M. on the 24th I met General Burnside, as he requested. He then attempted by persuasion to produce a change in my determination, but was told that the fort would be defended as long as possible.

At 6 A. M. on the 25th the enemy's land batteries opened upon the fort, and at 6:30 A. M. their warships, consisting of three war steamers and one sailing vessel, commenced a cross fire with rifles and 11-inch shell. The fire from both directions was immediately returned, and at 7 A. M. the ships retired, one disabled and two others in a damaged condition. The attack from land was kept up with great vigor, the enemy having immense advantage from their superior force, being able to relieve their men at the guns, while our morning reports showed only two hundred and sixty three men for duty. Our guns were well managed, but being able to do little damage to water batteries and siege guns; firing through very narrow embrasures. The enemy kept up a very vigorous and accurate fire from both rifles and mortars, dismounting guns, disabling men and tearing the parade, parapet and walls of the fort.

INTERIOR OF FORT MACON AFTER THE BOMBARDMENT, APRIL 26, 1862.

At 6:30 P. M., finding that our loss had been very great, and from the fatigue of our men being unable to keep up the fire with but two guns, a proposition was made to General Parke for the surrender of Fort Macon. General Parke demanded an unconditional surrender, which was refused, and the general informed that the firing would be renewed immediately. He then requested that the firing should cease until the next morning, in order that he might consult with General Burnside, and that the general should meet me the next morning at Shackelford Banks. This proposition was accepted.

On the 26th, at 7 A. M., I met General Burnside, as proposed, and a surrender was agreed to. The Southern flag was hauled down at 12 M., and the men left the fort as soon as means could be furnished. A portion crossed to Beaufort. Captain Guion's company started for Newbern on the 27th, and on the same day one hundred and fifty men, consisting of parts of several companies, started for Wilmington on the United States gunboat Chippewa, arriving at Fort Caswell at 7 P. M. on the 28th.

Our loss during the fight was seven killed and eighteen wounded, two dangerously. Privates Langston and Jewell I was forced to leave in the fort. All others of the wounded were brought off. A nurse was left with the two men. The fort was very much damaged and fifteen guns disabled.

M. J. WHITE, *Colonel. C. S A.*

JUST before the battle of the Wilderness, Sergeant Billy Bass received a letter from his wife. She said she heard that there was to be a big battle, and she did so wish to see him before it was fought! When Billy read it he said he would like also to see her before the battle, but he would a great sight rather see her after it was over.

TWO ADDRESSES OF PRESIDENT JEFFERSON DAVIS TO THE SOLDIERS OF THE CONFEDERACY.

[These ringing appeals of our Chief Magistrate to our soldiers were issued, the first in August, 1863, and the second in February, 1864. They are worth preserving as indicating "the situation" at those important periods of our history.]

Soldiers of the Confederate States:

After more than two years of a warfare scarcely equaled in the number, magnitude and fearful carnage of its battles; a warfare in which your courage and fortitude have illustrated your country, and attracted not only gratitude at home, but admiration abroad, your enemies continue a struggle in which our final triumph must be inevitable. Unduly elated with their recent successes, they imagine that temporary reverses can quell your spirit or shake your determination, and they are now gathering heavy masses for a general invasion, in the vain hope that by a desperate effort success may at length be reached.

You know too well, my countrymen, what they mean by success. Their malignant rage aims at nothing less than the extermination of yourselves, your wives and children. They seek to destroy what they can not plunder. They propose, as the spoils of victory, that your homes shall be partitioned among the wretches whose atrocious cruelties have stamped infamy on their government. They design to incite servile insurrection and light the fires of incendiarism whenever they can reach your homes, and they debauch the inferior race, hitherto docile and contented, by promising indulgence of the vilest passions as the price of treachery. Conscious of their inability to prevail by legitimate warfare, not daring to make peace lest they should be hurled from their seats of power, the men who now rule in Washington refuse even to confer on the subject of putting an end to outrages which disgrace our age, or to listen to a suggestion for conducting the war according to the usages of civilization.

Fellow citizens, no alternative is left you but victory, or subjugation, slavery and the utter ruin of yourselves, your families and your country. The victory is within your reach. You need but stretch forth your hands to grasp it. For this and all that is necessary is that those who are called to the field by every motive that can move the human heart, should promptly repair to the post of duty, should stand by their comrades now in front of the foe, and thus so strengthen the armies of the Confederacy as to insure success. The men now absent from their posts would, if present in the field, suffice to create numerical equality between our force and that of the invaders—and when, with any approach to such equality, have we failed to be victorious? I believe that but few of those absent are actuated by unwillingness to serve their country; but that many have found it difficult to resist the temptation of a visit to their homes and the loved ones from whom they have been so long separated; that others have left for temporary attention to their affairs, with the intention of returning, and then have shrunk from the consequences of their violation of duty; that others, again, have left their posts from mere restlessness and desire of change—each quieting the upbraidings of his conscience by persuading himself that his individual services could have no influence on the general result.

These and other causes (although far less disgraceful than the desire to avoid danger, or to escape from the sacrifices required by patriotism) are, nevertheless, grievous faults, and place the cause of our beloved country, and of everything we hold dear, in imminent peril. I repeat,

FORT PULASKI, COMMANDING ENTRANCE TO THE SAVANNAH RIVER, LEADING UP TO THE CITY OF SAVANNAH, GA.

that the men who now owe duty to their country, who have been called out and have not yet reported for duty, or who have absented themselves from their posts, are sufficient in number to secure us victory in the struggle now impending.

I call on you, then, my countrymen, to hasten to your camps, in obedience to the dictates of honor and duty, and summon those who have absented themselves without leave, or who have remained absent beyond the period allowed by their furloughs, to repair without delay to their respective commands; and I do hereby declare that I grant a general pardon and amnesty to all officers and men within the Confederacy, now absent without leave, who shall with the least possible delay, return to their proper posts of duty, but no excuse will be received for any delay beyond twenty days after the first publication of this proclamation in the State in which the absentee may be at the date of the publication. This amnesty and pardon shall extend to all who have been accused, or who have been convicted and are undergoing sentence for absence without leave, or desertion, excepting only those who have been twice convicted of desertion.

Finally, I conjure my countrywomen—the wives, mothers, sisters and daughters of the Confederacy—to use their all-powerful influence in aid of this call, to add one crowning sacrifice to those which their patriotism has so freely and constantly offered on their country's altar, and to take care that none who owe service in the field shall be sheltered at home from the disgrace of having deserted their duty to their families, to their country, and to their God.

[SEAL] Given under my hand and the seal of the Confederate States, at Richmond, the 1st day of August, in the year of our Lord one thousand eight hundred and sixty-three.

JEFFERSON DAVIS.

By the President:

J. P. BENJAMIN, *Secretary of State.*

Soldiers of the Armies of the Confederate States:

In the long and bloody war in which your country is engaged you have achieved many noble triumphs. You have won glorious victories over vastly more numerous hosts. You have cheerfully borne privations and toil to which you were unused. You have readily submitted to restraints upon your individual will, that the citizen might better perform his duty to the State as a soldier. To all these you have lately added another triumph, the noblest of human conquests—a victory over yourselves.

As the time drew near when you who first entered the service might well have been expected to claim relief from your arduous labors and restoration to the endearments of home, you have heeded only the call of your suffering country. Again you come to tender your service for the public defense--a free offering, which only such patriotism as yours could make—a triumph worthy of you and the cause to which you are devoted.

I would in vain attempt adequately to express the emotions with which I received the testimonials of confidence and regard which you have recently addressed to me. To some of those first received, separate acknowledgments were returned. But it is now apparent that a like generous enthusiasm pervades the whole army, and that the only exception to such magnanimous tender will be of those who, having originally entered for the war, can not display anew their zeal in the public service. It is, therefore, deemed appropriate, and, it is hoped, will be equally acceptable, to make a general acknowledgment, instead of successive special responses. Would that it were possible to render my thanks to you in person, and in the name of our common country, as well as in my own, while pressing the hand of each war-worn veteran, to recognize his title to our love, gratitude and admiration.

Soldiers! By your will (for you and the people are but one) I have been placed in a position which debars me from sharing your dangers, your sufferings and your privations in the field. With pride and affection my heart has accompanied you in every march; with solicitude it has sought to minister to your every want; with exultation it has marked your every heroic achievement. Yet, never in the toilsome march, nor in the weary watch, nor in the desperate assault, have you rendered a service so decisive in results as in this last display of the highest qualities of devotion and self-sacrifice which can adorn the character of the warrior-patriot.

Already the pulse of the whole people beats in unison with yours. Already they compare your spontaneous and unanimous offer of your lives, for the defense of your country, with the halting and reluctant service of the mercenaries who are purchased by the enemy at the price of higher bounties than have hitherto been known in war. Animated by this contrast, they exhibit cheerful confidence and more resolute bearing. Even the murmurs of the weak and timid, who shrink from the trial which make stronger and firmer your noble natures, are shamed into silence by the spectacle which you present. Your brave battle-cry will ring loud and clear through the land of the enemy, as well as our own; will silence the vain-glorious boastings of their corrupt partisans and their pensioned press, and will do justice to the calumny by which they seek to persuade a deluded people that you are ready to purchase dishonorable safety by degrading submission.

Soldiers! The coming spring campaign will open under auspices well calculated to sustain your hopes. Your resolution needed nothing to fortify it. With ranks replenished under the influence of your example, and by the aid of your representatives, who give earnest of their purpose to add, by legislation, largely to your strength, you may become the invader with a confidence justified by the memory of past victories. On the other hand, debt, taxation, repetition of heavy drafts, dissensions, occasioned by the strife for power, by the pursuit of the spoils of office, by the thirst for the plunder of the public treasury, and, above all, the consciousness of a bad cause, must tell with fearful force upon the over-strained energies of the enemy. His campaign in 1864 must, from the exhaustion of his resources, both in men and money, be far less formidable than those of the last two years, when unimpaired means were used with boundless prodigality, and with results which are suggested by the mention of the glorious names of Shiloh and Perryville, and Murfreesboro and Chickamauga, and the Chickahominy and Manassas, and Fredericksburg and Chancellorsville.

Soldiers! Assured success awaits us in our holy struggle for liberty and independence, and for the preservation of all that renders life desirable to honorable men. When that success shall be reached, to you, your country's hope and pride, under Divine Providence, will it be due. The fruits of that success will not be reaped by you alone, but your children and your children's children, in long generations to come, will enjoy blessings derived from you that will preserve your memory ever-living in their hearts.

Citizen defenders of the homes, the liberties, and the altars of the Confederacy! that the God whom we all humbly worship may shield you with his fatherly care and preserve you for safe return to the peaceful enjoyment of your friends and the association of those you most love, is the earnest prayer of your commander-in-chief.

JEFFERSON DAVIS.

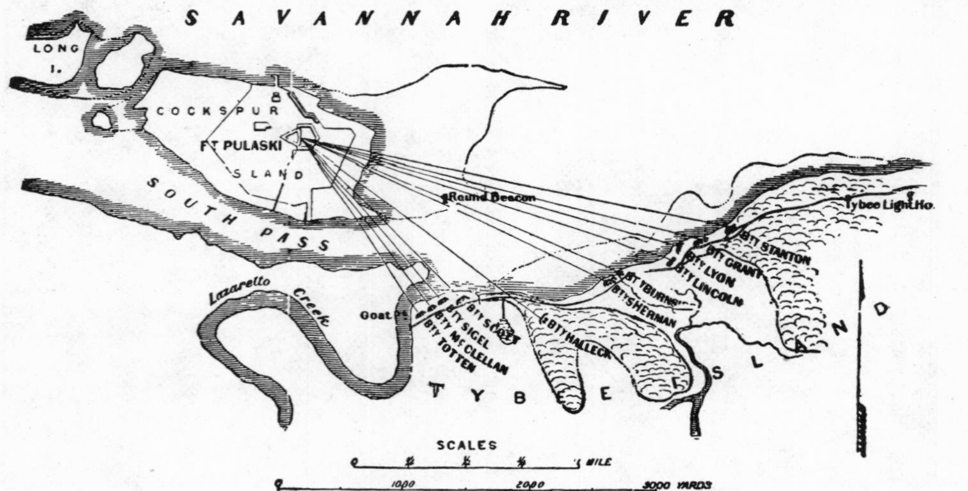

MAP OF FORT PULASKI AND THE POSITIONS OF THE FEDERAL BATTERIES ON TYBEE ISLAND.

THE LAST OFFICIAL APPOINTMENTS BY PRESIDENT DAVIS.

The last two appointments bearing the official signature of President Jefferson Davis was made at Washington, Ga., May 4, 1865, viz.:

John H. Reagan, Acting Secretary of Treasury.

Mr. H. Clark, Acting Treasurer, C. S. A.

BOMBARDMENT OF FORT PULASKI,

APRIL 10-11, 1862.

BY

BRIG.-GEN. ALEX. R. LAWTON, C. S. A.

HEADQUARTERS DEPT. (DISTRICT) GEORGIA,
SAVANNAH, GA., April 14, 1862.

I HAVE the honor to report that the enemy opened fire on Fort Pulaski early on the morning of the 10th instant, as was evident from the rapid and continuous firing and bursting of shells, which could be seen from the city of Savannah and other accessible points of observation. As communication with the fort was cut off, my knowledge of what occurred during the first day's bombardment was derived exclusively from distant views and the sound of guns. The firing continued during the entire day, and at intervals during the night.

On the night of the 10th I attempted to communicate

BRIG.-GEN. ALEXANDER R. LAWTON, OF GEORGIA.

with the fort by a small boat, for the purpose of conveying to it a man detailed on signal service, who had recently arrived, under orders, from Richmond. He was carried there by Corporal Law, of the Phœnix Riflemen, stationed at Thunderbolt, who had successfully communicated with the fort more than once before since the steamers had been cut off.

It was observed that the fire on both sides ceased about 2 P. M. on the 11th, and these two men returned to the battery at Thunderbolt about 8 o'clock that evening. The only detailed information I have is derived from the verbal statements of these two men. They represent that they reached the fort about 6 o'clock on the morning of the 11th, in the midst of a heavy fire, both from the fort and the enemy; that soon after their arrival a breach was made in the wall at the southeast angle, nearest Tybee Island, and that before the fort surrendered this breach was wide enough to drive a four-horse team through; that the wall, which embraced seven casemates in succession, was nearly all knocked down, and that all the barbette guns which could play on their batteries at Tybee Island had been disabled; that several shots had been fired into the magazine. They further state that the ships were not engaged at all, but that all the firing was from batteries on Tybee Island, chiefly from a battery of Parrott guns at King's Landing, the nearest point of Tybee Island to the fort. As these men constituted no part of the garrison, they were advised by Colonel Olmstead to make their escape, if possible.

In reporting the statements of these two men I must express my belief that they gave an exaggerated account of the injury done to the fort, owing, perhaps, to the very exciting circumstances under which they must have entered and left it. It is truly painful to be left without any more definite or reliable details, but it is quite certain that Pulaski has fallen, as the enemy's flag has been distinctly seen flying above the ramparts, and I consider it my duty to give you these statements as they were made to me. As there have been no returns received from Fort Pulaski for some time, I can not give you the precise strength of the garrison. It consisted, however, of five companies, numbering a little over 400 men, and commanded by Colonel C. H. Olmstead. The armament consisted of five 10-inch columbiads, nine 8-inch columbiads, three 42-pounders, three 10-inch mortars, one 12-inch mortar, one 24-pounder howitzer, two 12-pounder howitzers, twenty 32-pounders and two 4½-inch (Blakely) rifle guns, with 130 rounds of ammunition per gun.

A. R. LAWTON,
Brigadier-General Commanding.

BOMBARDMENT OF

FORTS JACKSON AND ST. PHILIP,

APRIL 16 to 24, 1862.

BY

BRIG.-GEN. JOHNSON K. DUNCAN, C. S. A.,
Commanding Coast Defenses.

NEW ORLEANS, LA., April 30, 1862.

ABOUT March 27th I was informed by Lieutenant-Colonel E. Higgins, commanding Forts Jackson and St. Philip, composing a part of the coast defenses under my command, that the enemy's fleet was crossing the bars and entering the Mississippi River in force. In consequence I repaired at once to that post, to assume the general command during the threatened attack upon New Orleans, which I had always anticipated would be made from that quarter.

Upon my arrival I found that Fort Jackson was suffering severely from transpiration and backwater, occasioned by the excessive rise in the river and the continued prevalence of strong easterly winds. Notwithstanding every effort which could be made, the water kept daily increasing upon us, partly owing to the sinking of the entire site and to the natural lowness of the country around it, until the parade and casemates were submerged to a depth of from three to eighteen inches. It was with the utmost difficulty, and only then by isolating the magazines and by pumping day and night, that the water could be kept out of them. As the officers and men were all obliged to live in these open and submerged casemates, they were greatly exposed to discomfort and sickness, as their clothing and feet were always wet. The most of their clothing and blankets, besides, were lost by the fire hereinafter mentioned. Fort St. Philip, from the same causes, was in a similar condition, but to a lesser extent. No attention having been previously paid to the repeated requisitions for guns of heavy caliber for these forts, it became necessary, in their present condition, to bring in and mount, and to build the platforms for, the three 10-inch and three 8-inch columbiads, the rifled 42-pounder and the five 10-inch seacoast mortars recently obtained from Pensacola on the evacuation of that place, together with the two rifled 7-inch guns temporarily borrowed from the naval authorities in New Orleans. It was also found necessary to prepare the old water battery to the rear of and below Fort Jackson, which had never been completed, for the reception of a portion of these guns, as well as to construct mortar-proof magazines and shell-rooms within the same.

In consequence also of the character of the expected attack by heavy mortars, it was deemed advisable to cover all the main magazines at both forts with sand-bags, to a considerable depth, to protect them against a vertical fire.

After great exertions, cheerfully made by both officers and men, and by working the garrisons by reliefs night and day, this work was all accomplished by April 13th. No sooner had the two rifled 7-inch navy guns been placed in position, however, than orders arrived to dismount one of them immediately, and to send the same to the city at once, to be placed on board of the iron-clad steamer Louisiana. I strongly remonstrated against this removal by telegraph, but was informed, in reply, that the orders were imperative, and that the gun must be sent without fail. It was accordingly sent, but with great difficulty, owing to the overflow and the other causes stated.

The garrisons of both forts were greatly fatigued and worn out by these labors, performed as they were under pressure and within sight of the enemy, and owing to the many discomforts and disadvantages we were laboring under in consequence of high water.

In the meantime I had called upon the general commanding the department for two regiments, to be stationed at the Quarantine buildings, six miles above the forts, to act as a reserve force and to co-operate with the forts in case of a combined land and water attack. I also asked for Captain W. G. Mullen's company of scouts and sharpshooters, to be stationed in the woods below Fort Jackson, on the right bank of the river, for the purpose of picking off the officers and men from the enemy's vessels when assuming their several positions of attack.

Captain Mullen's company, of about one hundred and twenty-five men, was sent down as requested, and stationed in part in the point of woods below Fort Jackson, and the remainder on the Fort St. Philip side, opposite the raft obstructing the river.

The Chalmette regiment, consisting of about five hundred men, Colonel Szymanski commanding, was sent to the Quarantine. A part of it was stationed there and company detachments were placed at the heads of the several canals leading from the river into the bays back of the same, to guard against a land force being thrown in launches above us.

Four steamers of the river fleet, protected and to a certain extent made shot-proof with cotton bulkheads, and prepared with iron prows to act as rams, viz.: the Warrior, Stonewall Jackson, Defiance and Resolute, commanded by Captains Stephenson, Philips, McCoy and Hooper, respectively, were sent down to report to and co-operate with me. The steamers Governor Moore and General Quitman, prepared as those before mentioned, and commanded by Captains B. Kennon and A. Grant, were sent down in a like manner, to co-operate with the forts, and ram such vessels of the enemy as might succeed in passing.

The naval authorities also sent down the Confederate States steam ram Manassas, Captain [A. F.] Warley, C. S. N., commanding. She was stationed a short distance above Fort Jackson, with her steam up constantly, to act against the enemy as the occasion might offer.

Subsequently, also, Captain F. B. Renshaw, C. S. N., arrived, in command of the Confederate States steamer Jackson.

The raft of logs and chains which had been formerly placed across the river having proven a failure upon the rise in the stream and consequent increase of the velocity of the drift-bearing current, a new obstruction had been placed across the river, opposite Fort Jackson, by Lieutenant-Colonel E. Higgins, prior to his assumption of the command of the forts. This consisted of a line of schooners anchored at intervals, with bows up stream, and thoroughly chained together amidships, as well as stem and stern. The rigging, ratlines and cables were left to trail astern of these schooners, as an additional impediment, to tangle in the propeller wheels of the enemy.

The schooner raft was seriously damaged by the windstorm on April 10th and 11th, which parted the chains, scattered the schooners and materially affected its character and effectiveness as an obstruction. In addition to the wind, the raft was also much damaged by allowing some of the fire-barges to get loose and drift against it, through the carelessness of those having them in charge. A large number of these fire-barges were tied to the banks above both forts, ready at all times to be towed into the current and against the enemy, for the double purpose of firing his ships and to light up the river by night to insure the accuracy of our fire.

My instructions to the river fleet, under Captain Stephenson, were to lie in stream above the raft, with such boats as had stern guns, in order to assist the forts with their fire in case the enemy should attempt the passage, as well as to turn in and ram at all hazards all such vessels as might succeed in getting above the raft. He was also required to take entire control of the fire-barges, to reconnoiter the enemy above the Head of the Passes, and to keep a watch-boat below every night, near the point of woods, to signal the approach of the enemy. The accompanying diagram will illustrate all the points referred to in this report.

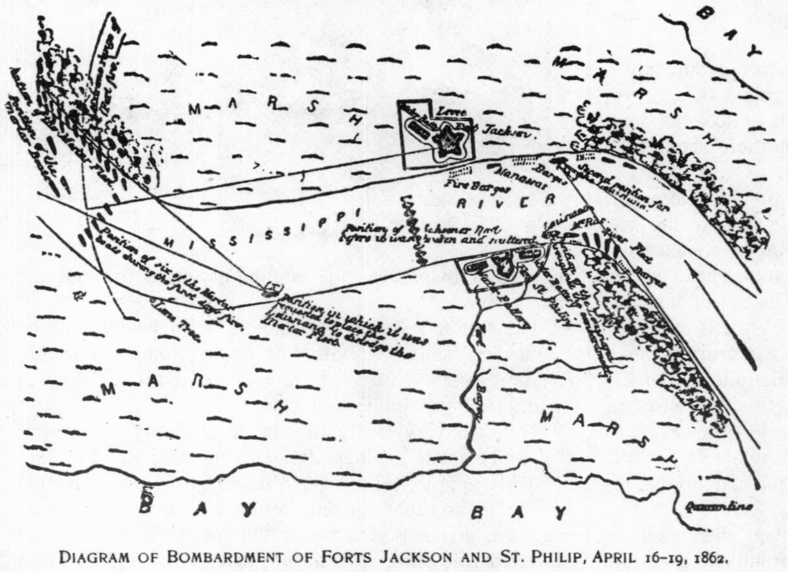

DIAGRAM OF BOMBARDMENT OF FORTS JACKSON AND ST. PHILIP, APRIL 16-19, 1862.

The same instructions were given to Captains Kennon and Grant, and upon his arrival Captain Renshaw was duly informed of the arrangements made, in which he promised heartily to co-operate.

While the enemy remained at the Head of the Passes, twenty-two and a half miles below the forts, and later, when he came up to the Jump, or Wilder's Bayou, the boats of the river fleet took turns in running down and watching him. For a few nights, also, at this time one of them was kept below as a guard boat. We had telegraphic communication, besides, down to within half a mile of the Jump, nine miles below the forts, which, together with scouts operating in the bays to the east and west of the river in skiffs and pirogues, kept us duly posted meanwhile of the enemy's movements below as far down as the Southwest Pass.

The enemy was not idle in the interim. His larger vessels were worked over the Southwest Bar after failing to make an entrance at Pass à l'Outre, and the mortar fleet was brought up as far as the Southwest Point Station, where the mortars were scaled and afterward tested. From seven to thirteen steam sloops of war and gunboats were constantly kept at the Head of the Passes or at the Jump, to cover his operations below and to prevent our observing his movements by way of the river. By gradual and regular approaches he carefully closed upon the forts day by day, and opened the attack as hereinafter detailed.

APRIL 9th.—One of our reconnoitering steamers was chased and followed up by two of the enemy's gunboats as far as the point of woods below Fort Jackson, but was soon forced to retire by a few shots from our batteries. This was his first reconnoissance, and our fire was not returned.

APRIL 13th.—Several of the hostile gunboats again came up to make observations. They would occasionally show themselves, singly or in pairs, above the point of woods and exchange a few shots with the forts and then retire again behind the point. Our sharpshooters obtained a few shots on this occasion, but with very partial success, owing to the lowness of the country and the extreme rise in the river. Many of the men were up to their waists in water, and, in consequence, sickness prevailed among them and unfitted them for duty. The enemy spent the principal part of the day in firing grape and canister and in shelling the woods to drive them out. This was repeated the following day, the enemy not coming within range or sight of the forts, but confining himself to shelling the woods below. The sharpshooters were all driven out by this second day's firing. Our telegraphic communication below was also broken up, as the wires were removed and many of the posts cut and torn down by the enemy.

FORT JACKSON OPENING FIRE ON THE FEDERAL FLEET.

There being no other point above or below where the sharpshooters could profitably act in that capacity, and as many of them were unfit for duty from exposure, I deemed it advisable to dispense with their services and send them to the city, which was accordingly done.

It being of the highest importance, however, to keep up the telegraphic connection below, Lieutenant T. J. Royster, company of sappers and miners, Twenty-second Regiment, Louisiana Volunteers, volunteered his services, with fifteen men of his company, to act as sharpshooters in pirogues, and cover the operator in repairing the line and re-establishing the connection with the forts above, as well as to annoy the enemy. This also failed, from the great difficulty of managing the pirogues effectively in the dense undergrowth of the swampy woods below, and the telegraph and the sharpshooters had to be abandoned in consequence.

APRIL 15th.—The enemy brought up his whole fleet, extending the same from the Head of the Passes to the point of woods below the forts. Orders were repeatedly given to Captain Stephenson, of the river fleet, to cause the fire-barges to be sent down nightly upon the enemy; but every attempt seemed to prove a perfect abortion, the barges being cut adrift too soon, so that they drifted against the banks directly under the forts, firing our wharves and lighting us up, but obscuring the position of the enemy. In consequence, I turned the control of them, as well as the boats employed to tow them into the stream, over to Captain Renshaw, the senior naval officer present. I also directed Captains Kennon and Grant to report to him for orders, as I found great difficulty in communicating with or controlling the vessels afloat, and directed Captain Stephenson, with his four boats, to co-operate with Captain Renshaw in every possible way. These boats of the river fleet, it seemed, could not be turned over directly to the immediate command of naval officers, owing to certain conditions imposed by the Navy Department.

APRIL 16th.—From 7:30 A. M. the enemy's gunboats came around the point repeatedly for observation, but were invariably forced to retire by our fire. In the meantime, he was locating the position of the mortar flotilla, composed of twenty-one schooners, each mounting one 13-inch mortar and other guns, close against the bank on the Fort Jackson side and behind the point of woods.

At 4:15 P. M. the enemy ran out a gunboat and fired upon the fort, under the cover of which two of the mortar boats were brought out into the stream.

These boats opened fire upon Fort Jackson at 5 P. M., which was continued for an hour and a half, the enemy, under our fire, retiring behind the point of woods.

APRIL 17th.—One fire-barge sent down successfully against the enemy at 4 A. M., which drifted in among his vessels and was fired upon by them, creating considerable movement and perturbation.

During the day Captains Renshaw, Beverly Kennon, Grant, Stephenson and Hooper passed in turns with their

THE LOUISIANA.

boats below the raft, now very much disconnected and scattered, and exchanged a few shots with the hostile gunboats and mortar boats.

Two more abortive attempts were made to send down fire-barges against the enemy during the night.

APRIL 18th.—At 9 A. M. the enemy opened upon Fort Jackson with his entire mortar fleet of twenty-one vessels and with rifled guns from his gunboats. Fifteen of them were concealed behind the point of woods and the other six hauled out in stream at an angle with them (see diagram), just at the extreme range of our heaviest guns. Our fire disabled one gunboat and one mortar boat, causing those in the stream to retire behind the cover of the woods. Generally our shots fell short, for lack of elevation and in consequence of the inferiority of our powder compared to that of the enemy. Even our nearest gun, a 10-inch seacoast mortar, would not reach his boats with the heaviest charges.

The enemy ceased firing at 7 P. M., having fired this day 2,997 mortar shells.

The quarters in the bastions were fired and burned down early in the day, as well as all the quarters immediately without the fort. The citadel was set on fire and extinguished several times during the first part of the day, but later it became impossible to put out the flames, so that when the enemy ceased firing it was one burning mass, greatly endangering the magazines, which at one time were reported to be on fire. Many of the men and most of the officers lost their bedding and clothing by these fires, which greatly added to the discomforts of the overflow. The mortar fire was accurate and terrible, many of the shells falling everywhere within the fort and disabling some of our best guns.

I endeavored to get the naval forces to carry down fire-barges against the enemy so as to disperse them, but they were all let go above the raft, and with such a lack of judgment that they only lodged under the forts and did not reach the enemy.

None of the boats acted as a guard-boat below the raft at night, so that, in consequence, the enemy sent up two launches to examine the character of the raft obstructing the river.

APRIL 19th.—The mortar fleet again opened at 6 A. M. and the fire was constantly kept up throughout the day. Gunboats constantly came above the point during the day to engage the forts, but were as constantly driven back by our fire. One of them we crippled, which was towed behind the point of woods. The enemy's fire was excellent, a large proportion of his shells falling within Fort Jackson. The terre-plein, parade plain, parapets and platforms were very much cut up, as well as much damage done to the casemates. The magazines were considerably threatened, and one shell passed through into the casemate containing fixed ammunition.

One 10-inch and one 8-inch columbiad, one 32-pounder, one 24-pounder and one 10-inch siege mortar were disabled in the main work; also two rifled 32-pounders in the water battery. Bombardment continued very regularly and accurately all night. Failures again were made in sending down fire-barges.

APRIL 20th.—Some rain in the morning. Bombardment constant throughout the day, with occasional shots from the gunboats around the point. Wind very high. No fire-barges sent down to light up the river or distract the attention of the enemy at night. In consequence, between 11 and 12 P. M., under cover of the heaviest shelling during the bombardment thus far, one of the enemy's gunboats came up in the darkness and attempted to cut the chains of the raft and drag off the schooners. A heavy fire was opened upon her, which caused her to retire, but not until she had partially accomplished her purpose. The raft, after this, could not be regarded as an obstruction. The fire continued uninterruptedly all night.

APRIL 21st.—Firing continued all day and night without interruption. Several guns were disabled. Disabled guns were repaired as far as practicable as often as accidents happened to them or their platforms. Fort Jackson by this time was in need of extensive repairs almost everywhere, and it was with extreme pleasure that we learned of the arrival during the night of the ironclad steamer Louisiana, under the cover of whose heavy guns we expected to make the necessary repairs.

APRIL 22d.—By the direction of the major-general commanding the department, everything afloat, including the towboats and the entire control of the fire barges, was turned over to Captain John K. Mitchell, C. S. N., commanding the Confederate States naval forces in the lower Mississippi River. I also gave Captain Mitchell one hundred and fifty of our best men from Forts Jackson and St. Philip, under Lieutenants Dixon and Gandy and Captain Ryan, to serve a portion of the guns of the Louisiana and to act as sharpshooters on the same vessel.

In an interview with Captain Mitchell, on the morning of this date, I learned that the motive power of the Louisiana was not likely to be completed within any reasonable time, and that in consequence it was not within the range of probabilities that she could be regarded as an aggressive steamer, or that she could be brought into the pending action in that character. As an ironclad invulnerable floating battery, with sixteen guns of the heaviest caliber, however, she was then as complete as she would ever be.

Fort Jackson had already undergone, and was still subjected to, a terrible fire of 13-inch mortar shells, which it was necessary to relieve at once to prevent the disabling of all the best guns at that fort, and, although Fort St. Philip partially opened out the point of woods concealing the enemy and gallantly attempted to dislodge him or draw his fire, he nevertheless doggedly persisted in his one main object of battering Fort Jackson. Under these circumstances I considered that the Louisiana could only be

THE MANASSAS.

regarded as a battery, and that her best possible position would be below the raft, close in on the Fort St. Philip shore, where her fire could dislodge the mortar boats from behind the point of woods and give sufficient respite to Fort Jackson to repair *in extenso*. This position (X on the accompanying diagram) would give us three direct cross fires upon the enemy's approaches and at the same time insure the Louisiana from a direct assault, as she would be immediately under the guns of both forts. Accordingly, I earnestly and strongly urged these views upon Captain Mitchell in a letter of this date (copy lost), but without avail.

Being so deeply impressed myself with the importance of this position for the Louisiana, and of the necessity of prompt action in order to insure the success of the impending struggle, I again urged this subject upon Captain Mitchell, during the latter part of the same day, as absolutely indispensable and imperative to the safety of New Orleans and to the control of the lower Mississippi. My efforts were ineffectual to get him to move the boat from her original position above the forts.

I also addressed him two other notes through the day—one in regard to sending fire-barges against the enemy, and the other relative to keeping a vigilant lookout from all his vessels, and asking for co-operation should the enemy attempt to pass during the night.

Bombardment continued throughout the day and night, being at times very heavy. During the day our fire was principally confined to shelling the point of woods from both forts, and apparently with good results, as the mortar fire was slackened toward evening. The casemates were very much cut up by the enemy's fire, which was increased at night. There was little or no success in sending down fire-barges as usual, owing, in part, to the condition of the towboats Mosher, Music and Belle Algerine, in charge of the same. This does not excuse the neglect, however, as there were six boats of the river fleet available for this service, independent of those alluded to, and fire-barges were plentiful.

APRIL 23d.—The day broke warm, clear and cloudless. No immediate relief being looked for from our fleet, the entire command was turned out to repair damages, under a very heavy fire of the enemy.

The bombardment continued without an intermission throughout the day, but slackened off about 12 M., at which hour there was every indication of an exhaustion on the part of the mortar flotilla; hence it became evident that the tactics of the enemy would necessarily be changed into an attack with broadsides by his larger vessels. In consequence, these views were laid before Captain Mitchell, and he was again urged to place the Louisiana at the point before mentioned, below the raft and near the Fort St. Philip bank of the river, to meet the emergency. Captain Mitchell positively declined again to assume the only position which offered us every possible chance of success. and Captains (Chas. F.) McIntosh, (Thomas B.) Huger and Warley sustained Captain Mitchell in his views of the case.

Just before sundown, under a very heavy mortar fire. the enemy sent up a small boat, and a series of white flags were planted on the Fort St. Philip bank of the river, commencing about three hundred and fifty yards above the lone tree upon that shore. (See Diagram.)

This confirmed my previous views of an early and different attack from the usual mortar bombardment, especially as I presumed that these flags indicated the positions to be taken up by the several vessels in their new line of operations. As nothing was to be expected from the Louisiana, after the correspondence during the day, I could only inform Captain Mitchell of this new movement of the enemy, and particularly impress upon him the necessity of keeping the river well lit up with fire-barges, to act as an impediment to the enemy, and assist the accuracy of our fire in a night attack.

Lieutenant (Geo. S.) Shryock, C. S. N. (Captain Mitchell's aid), came on shore about 9 P. M., to inform me that the Louisiana would be ready for service by the next evening—the evening of the 24th. I informed him that time was everything to us, and that to-morrow would in all probability prove too late. Lieutenant-Colonel Higgins warmly seconded my opinion, and warned Lieutenant Shryock that the final battle was imminent within a few hours.

In regard to lighting the river, Lieutenant Shryock stated that fire-barges would be regularly sent down throughout the night every two hours, and as none had been sent up to that hour (9:30 P. M.), he left, informing me that this matter would be attended to as soon as he arrived on board. To my utter surprise, not one single fire-barge was sent down the river, notwithstanding, at any hour of this night. It was impossible for us to send them down, as everything afloat had been turned over to Captain Mitchell, by order of the major-general commanding, and the fire-barges and the boats to tow them into the stream were exclusively under his control. In consequence of this criminal neglect the river remained in complete darkness throughout the entire night. The bombardment continued all night and grew furious toward morning.

APRIL 24th.—At 3:30 A. M. the larger vessels of the enemy were observed in motion, and, as we presumed, to take up the positions indicated by the small flags planted by them on the previous evening. I then made my last and final appeal to Captain Mitchell.

The Louisiana was still in her old position above Fort St. Philip, surrounded by her tenders, on board of which was the majority of her cannoneers and crew, and the other boats of the fleet were generally at anchor above her, excepting the Jackson, Captain Renshaw, C. S. N. commanding, which had been sent the day before at my

THE C. S. STEAMER GOVERNOR MOORE.

suggestion to prevent the landing of forces through the canals above.

The McRae lay near and above the Louisiana, and the steam-ram Manassas, with her tender, remained in her constant position above Fort Jackson, both with steam up and ready for immediate action.

The enemy evidently anticipated a strong demonstration to be made against him with fire-barges. Finding, upon his approach, however, that no such demonstration was made, and that the only resistance offered to his passage was the expected fire of the forts (the broken and scattered raft being then no obstacle), I am satisfied that he was suddenly inspired, for the first time, to run the gauntlet at all hazards, although not a part of his original design. Be this as it may, a rapid rush was made by him in column of twos *en échelon*, so as not to interfere with each other's broadsides.

The mortar fire upon Fort Jackson was furiously increased, and in dashing by each vessel delivered broadside after broadside of shot, shell, grape, canister and spherical case to drive the men from our guns. Both the officers and men stood up manfully under this galling and fearful hail, and the batteries of both forts were promptly opened at their longest range with shot, shell, hot-shot and a little grape, and most gallantly and rapidly fought until the enemy succeeded in getting above and beyond our range.

The absence of light on the river, together with the smoke of the guns, made the obscurity so intense that scarcely a vessel was visible, and, in consequence, the gunners were obliged to govern their firing entirely by the flashes of the enemy's guns.

I am fully satisfied that the enemy's dash was successful mainly owing to the cover of darkness, as a frigate and several gunboats were forced to retire as day was breaking. Similar results had attended every previous attempt made by the enemy to pass or to reconnoiter when we had sufficient light to fire with accuracy and effect. The passage by was of short duration, having been accomplished between 3:30 A. M. and daylight, under a very rapid and heavy pressure of steam.

Of the part taken in this action by the Louisiana, Manassas and other vessels comprising the co-operative naval forces, I can not speak with any degree of certainty, excepting that the Louisiana is reported to have fired only twelve shots during the engagement; but to the heroic and gallant manner in which Captain Huger handled and fought the McRae we can all bear evidence. The Defiance, Captain McCoy commanding, was the only vessel saved out of the river fleet.

Shortly after daylight the Manassas was observed drifting down by the forts. She had been abandoned and fired, and was evidently in a sinking condition.

The McRae was considerably cut up in this action by shot and grape. The Resolute was run on shore about a mile above the forts, where she hoisted a white flag, but by the prompt action of the McRea she was prevented from falling into the hands of the enemy. She was subsequently wrecked and burned. The Warrior was run ashore and fired on the point just above Fort St. Philip.

Nothing was known by us of the movements of the Stonewall Jackson, the Governor Moore or the General Quitman.

The steamers Mosher, Music and Belle Algerine, in charge of the fire-barges, were all destroyed. So also was the Star.

The heroic courage displayed by the officers and men at both forts was deserving of a better success, especially after the fortitude which they constantly exhibited through the long tedium of a protracted bombardment, unsurpassed for its terrible accuracy, constancy and fury.

Thirteen of the enemy's vessels out of twenty-three succeeded in getting by, viz., the Hartford, Pensacola, Richmond, Brooklyn, Mississippi, Oneida, Iroquois, Cayuga, Wissahickon, Sciota, Kineo, Katahdin and Pinola.

In addition to the foregoing and to the Varuna and such other vessels as were sunk, there were six gunboats and one frigate engaged in this action, besides the mortar flotilla. Heavy chains were flaked along the sides of most of these vessels as an iron-proof protection.

The extent of the damage which was done to the enemy we had no means of ascertaining.

The vessels which passed all came to an anchor at or below the Quarantine, six miles above the forts, where they remained until about 10 A. M., when they all passed slowly up the river, with the exception of two gunboats, left at the Quarantine as a guard.

Shortly after the fleet above got under way a gunboat from below made her appearance with a flag of truce, and verbally demanded the surrender of the forts in the name of Commander D. D. Porter, U. S. N., commanding the mortar flotilla, under the penalty of re-opening the bombardment (which had ceased shortly after the passage) in case of refusal.

The demand was rejected, and the bombardment was re-opened about 12 M. It continued until near sundown, when it ceased altogether. The entire mortar fleet, and all the other vessels except six gunboats, then got under way and passed down the river and out of sight under full steam and sail. A vigilant lookout was kept up above and below during the night, but all remained quiet. So long as the mortar fleet remained below, the position wherein the Louisiana could render the greatest assistance to the forts was the one below Fort St. Philip, hereinbefore mentioned, where the fire of her batteries could dislodge the enemy from behind the point of woods.

After the mortar fleet had left, however, and when the enemy had got in force above the forts, the question was materially changed, in consequence of the fact that all of our heavy guns at both forts had been mounted to bear upon the lower approaches and not on those above. The most effective position which the Louisiana could then take as a battery was in the fight above Fort Jackson, where her guns could protect our rear and sweep the long reach of river above toward the Quarantine. This would still insure her safety, as she would be under the guns of both forts. This is evident by a reference to the point (X X) on the diagram.

In several personal interviews and by correspondence with Captain Mitchell, on this date, I requested him during the morning of the 24th, while the mortar fleet was below, to place the Louisiana below the raft and dislodge it, and later in the day, when the mortar fire was nearly exhausted, to place her in the position (X X) above Fort Jackson, to assist in repelling an attack from the vessels above.

During the day she was in an unfit condition to assume either position, for the reasons given by Captain Mitchell in his letters to me.

BATTLE BETWEEN FORTS JACKSON AND ST. PHILIP AND FEDERAL GUNBOATS. THE LOUISIANA EXPLODING.
[From an old India-ink sketch by Admiral Walke.]

The intoxicated volunteers referred to were none of my men, nor did they get their liquor at the forts, as there was none on hand during the bombardment, excepting the small supplies of hospital stores in the medical department.

APRIL 25th.—No attack attempted during the day by the enemy either from above or below. The gunboats from the Quarantine above and from the point of woods below occasionally showed themselves for observation, but without firing.

During the day all the principal guns that would admit of it at both forts were prepared at once so as to traverse in a full circle and bear above or below, as necessity might require. Some of the 24-pounder barbette guns at Fort Jackson were also replaced by guns of heavier caliber to bear on the river above.

Permission was granted by the enemy to the Confederate States steamer McRae to proceed to New Orleans under a flag of truce with the wounded. Availing ourselves of the offer of Captain Mitchell, the seriously wounded of both forts were sent on board of her. As it was late when the wounded were all gotten on board, the McRae did not get off until the next morning.

Still failed during the day in getting Captain Mitchell to place the Louisiana in the bight above Fort Jackson where she could act against the enemy from above.

One of the raft-schooners was burned during the night to light the river, and all remained quiet.

APRIL 26th.—A gunboat, with a white flag, dropped down from the Quarantine to escort the McRae on her mission. The McRae did not return again to the forts. Four of the enemy's steamers were in sight at the Quarantine at dawn. A gunboat occasionally showed herself below to reconnoiter.

In the direction of Bird Island, and back of the salt works, a large steam frigate and an ordinary river steamer appeared in sight, the latter working her way up the bay behind Fort St. Philip, apparently toward the Quarantine.

During the day Captain Mitchell communicated with the enemy above under a flag of truce, and learned that the city had surrendered, and that the Confederate States steam-ram Mississippi had been burned by our authorities. The wreck of the floating dock or battery drifted by the forts about 4 P. M.

The Louisiana was not placed in the position required of her during the day, Captain Mitchell promising to put her there the next day, the 27th. Another raft-schooner burned for light, and all quiet during the night. No shots exchanged during the day.

APRIL 27th.—At daylight the steamer which had been observed the day before working her way up in the back bay was in view, immediately in the rear of Fort St. Philip, and near the mouth of Fort Bayou. A frigate and five other vessels were also in sight toward Bird Island, one of which was seen working her way up the bay. From ten to thirteen launches were visible near the boat back of Fort St. Philip, by means of which troops were being landed at the Quarantine above us.

About 12 M. one of the enemy's gunboats from below made her appearance under a flag of truce, bearing a written demand for the surrender of the forts, signed by Commander David D. Porter, U. S. N., commanding mortar flotilla. The forts refused to surrender.

About 4 P. M. the French man-of-war Milan, Captain Clouet commanding, passed up to the city, after asking and obtaining permission of the forts to do so. The position of the Louisiana still remained unchanged.

So far, throughout the entire bombardment and final action, the spirit of the troops was cheerful, confident and courageous. They were mostly foreign enlistments without any great interest at stake in the ultimate success of the revolution. A reaction set in among them during the lull of the 25th, 26th and 27th, when there was no other excitement to arouse them than the fatigue duty of repairing our damages, and when the rumor was current that the city had surrendered and was then in the hands of the enemy. No reply had been received from the city to my dispatches sent by couriers on the 24th and 25th, by means of which I could reassure them. They were still obedient, but not buoyant and cheerful. In consequence, I endeavored to revive their courage and patriotism by publishing an order to both garrisons.

I regret to say that it did not produce the desired effect. Everything remained quiet, however, until midnight, when the garrison at Fort Jackson revolted in mass, seized upon the guard and posterns, reversed the field-pieces commanding the gates, and commenced to spike the guns, while many of the men were leaving the fort in the meantime under arms. All this occurred as suddenly as it was unexpected. The men were mostly drawn up under arms, and positively refused to fight any longer, besides endeavoring by force to bring over the St. Mary's cannoneers and such other few men as remained true to their cause and country.

The mutineers stated that the officers intended to hold out as long as possible, or while the provisions lasted, and then blow up the forts and everything in them; that the city had surrendered, and that there was no further use in fighting; that the enemy were about to attack by land and water on three sides at once, and that a longer defense would only prove a butchery. Every endeavor was made by the officers to repress the revolt and to bring the men to reason and order, but without avail. Officers upon the ramparts were fired upon by the mutineers in attempting to put a stop to the spiking of the guns.

I am greatly indebted to the Rev. Father Nachon for his efforts to quell the mutineers, through some of whom he learned that the revolt had been discussed among them for two days, and yet there was no one man among them true enough to communicate the fact to his officers.

Signals also were said to have been passed between the forts during the night, and while the mutiny was at its height. Being so general among the men, the officers were helpless and powerless to act. Under these circumstances there was but one course left, viz., to let those men go who wished to leave the fort, in order to see the number left and to ascertain what reliance could be placed upon them. About one-half of the garrison left immediately, including men from every company excepting the St. Mary's cannoneers, volunteers and regulars, non-commissioned officers and privates, and among them many of the very men who had stood last and best to their guns throughout the protracted bombardment and the final action when the enemy passed. It was soon evident that there was no further fight in the men remaining behind; that they were completely demoralized, and that no faith or reliance could be placed in the broken detachments of companies left in the forts.

In the meantime we were totally ignorant of the condition of affairs at Fort St. Philip, and as all our small boats had been carried away by the mutineers we could not communicate with that fort until the next morning. As the next attack upon the forts was likely to be a combined operation by land and water, and as Fort St. Philip was the point most threatened, from the nature of the country around it and from the character of the work itself, with narrow and shallow ditches, and but little relief to the main work, it was self-evident that no reduction could be made in its garrison to strengthen that of Fort Jackson, even if all the men there remained true. In fact, two additional regiments had been asked for at the Quarantine in anticipation of such an attack, to act as a reserve to strengthen the garrisons of both forts.

With the enemy above and below us, it will be apparent at once to any one at all familiar with the surrounding country that there was no chance of destroying the public property, blowing up the forts and escaping with the remaining troops. Under all these humiliating circumstances there seemed to be but one course open to us, viz., to await the approach of daylight, communicate then with the gunboats of the mortar flotilla below under a flag of truce, and negotiate for a surrender under the terms offered us by Commander Porter, and which had previously been declined.

APRIL 28th.—A small boat was procured, and Lieutenant Morse, post adjutant, sent over to convey the condition of affairs at Fort St. Philip, as well as to Captain Mitchell on the Louisiana. Captain Mitchell and Lieutenant Shryock, C. S. N., came on shore and discussed the whole question, after which they left, remarking that they would go on board and endeavor to attack the enemy above, at the Quarantine, notwithstanding that reasons had been given from time to time for not moving this vessel into her proper position, only a few hundred yards distant.

Captains Squires and Bond, Louisiana artillery, and Lieutenant Dixon, commanding the company of Confederate States regular recruits, came on shore shortly afterward from Fort St. Philip, and concurred with us that, under the circumstances, we could do nothing else than surrender, as they were not at all confident of the garrison there after the unlooked-for revolt at Fort Jackson, although none of their men had left or openly revolted. For these reasons a flag of truce was sent down to communicate with the enemy below and to carry a written offer of surrender under the terms offered on the 27th inst.

This communication brought up the Harriet Lane and three other gunboats opposite the forts, with white flags at the fore, white flags being displayed from the yards of the flag-masts at both forts, while the Confederate flags waved at the mastheads.

While negotiations were pending on the Harriet Lane it was reported that the steamer Louisiana, with her guns protruding, and on fire, was drifting down the river toward the fleet. As the wreck in descending kept close into the Fort St. Philip shore, the chances were taken by the enemy without changing the position of his boats. The guns of the Louisiana were discharged at random as she floated down, and the boat finally blew up near Fort St. Philip, scattering its fragments everywhere within and around the fort, killing one of our men and wounding three or four others.

Captain McIntosh, C. S. N., who had been severely wounded in the discharge of his duty on the night of the enemy's passage, and who was then lying in a tent at that fort, was nearly killed also.

As far as I could learn, however, the Louisiana was fired prior to the time that the enemy's boats with white flags came to an anchor abreast of the forts to negotiate. She was fired in her first and original position without a change of any kind since her arrival at the forts.

The officers of Fort Jackson and the St. Mary's cannoneers left about 4 P. M. for the city, on board of the United States gunboat Kennebec, and arrived on the morning of the 29th in New Orleans.

The officers of Fort St. Philip were sent up the next day, and all the men subsequently within a few days, as transportation could be furnished, excepting the men who revolted on the night of the 27th, many of whom enlisted with the enemy.

Upon my arrival in the city I found that the enemy's vessels were lying off the town, and that no flag, excepting that of the State of Louisiana on the City Hall, was visible upon the shore. I also learned that Flag Officer Farragut had directed it to be hauled down, and the United States flag hoisted in its stead, upon the penalty of shelling the city within forty-eight hours if the demand was not complied with, and that he had warned the city authorities to remove the women and children within the time specified. I therefore deemed it my duty to call at once upon the mayor at the City Hall and inform him of the fate of the forts below, which I did accordingly.

Fort St. Philip. Mortar Boats in the Distance Shelling Forts. Fort Jackson.

THE ENGAGEMENT BETWEEN FORTS JACKSON AND ST. PHILIP, CONFEDERATE VESSELS, AND THE FEDERAL GUNBOATS.
[From an old and original painting.]

Learning there from one of his aids that the major-general commanding the department was still in the city, I called upon him in person and verbally reported the main incidents of the bombardment, the passage of the enemy and the capitulation of the forts.

All the officers distinguished themselves by cool courage, skill and patriotism throughout the entire bombardment, and by the patient fortitude with which they performed their duties throughout the bombardment and up to the sad night when the men took the rash and disgraceful step of rising against their officers, breaking through all discipline, and leading to such disastrous and fatal consequences. I can charitably account for it only on the grounds of great reaction after the intense physical strain of many weary days and nights of terrible fire, through which they were necessarily subjected to every privation from circumstances beyond our control, but which they had not the moral courage to share and sustain with their officers, all of whom were subjected to the same hardships in every particular.

To Lieutenant-Colonel E. Higgins, commanding the forts, my thanks are especially due for his indefatigable labors in preparing his heavy batteries preparatory to the attack, almost in the face of the enemy, and for the quiet, skillful and judicious manner in which he caused them to be fought. He was present everywhere and did his whole duty well and thoroughly.

Captain M. T. Squires, Louisiana regiment of artillery, as senior officer in charge of Fort St. Philip, under the orders of Lieutenant-Colonel Higgins, commanding, fully sustained every anticipation entertained of his gallantry, skill and efficiency.

During the first day's bombardment, when Captain Anderson was wounded, my aid-de-camp (Lieutenant William M. Bridges, Louisiana artillery) volunteered to command the two 10-inch columbiads on the main work, and I return him my thanks for the gallant and efficient manner in which he fought them during the rest of the action.

I take great pleasure in making personal mention of my volunteer aids, Captains William J. Seymour and J. R. Smith, for the valuable assistance which they rendered me at all times.

My thanks are also due to Doctors Bradbury and Foster, who volunteered their services to assist Assistant Surgeons S. Burke and C. D. Lewis at Forts Jackson and St. Philip, respectively; and most efficiently did they aid in this department. Doctor Bradbury remained at Fort Jackson until its fall and was paroled. Doctor Foster, at my request, accompanied the wounded soldiers to the city on the Confederate States steamer McRae.

Messrs. Fulda and Stickney and Sergeant J. R. Poindexter, Fourth Mississippi volunteers, telegraph operators, rendered the most valuable services in keeping open our communications above and below, under the most dangerous and difficult circumstances.

Although we have failed in our mission of keeping the enemy's fleet from passing the forts, and have been subjected to the deep humiliation of surrendering the charge intrusted to our keeping to the enemies of our country, I must nevertheless state, in common justice to myself and those under my command, that to the very best of our ability, with the means at our disposal, our whole duty was performed faithfully, honestly and fearlessly. If all had to be gone through with again, under similar events and circumstances, I know that we should be forced to the same results and consequences. Great as the disaster is, it is but the sheer result of that lack of cheerful and hearty co-operation from the defenses afloat which we had every right to expect, and to the criminal negligence of not lighting up the river at night when the danger was imminent and the movements of the enemy absolutely known almost to the hour of the final attack. Except for the cover afforded by the obscurity of the darkness, I shall always remain satisfied that the enemy would never have succeeded in passing Forts Jackson and St. Philip.

* * * * * * *

J. K. DUNCAN,
Brigadier-General, late Commanding Coast Defenses.

THE FALL OF NEW ORLEANS,

APRIL 18 TO MAY 1, 1862.

BY

MAJOR-GENERAL MANSFIELD LOVELL,
Commanding at New Orleans.

VICKSBURG, MISS., May 22, 1862.

THE department is fully aware, from my official correspondence and telegraphic dispatches, of the exact nature of the defenses erected for the protection of the city of New Orleans, consisting, in general terms, of an exterior line of forts and earthworks, intended to prevent the entrance of the armed vessels of the enemy, and an interior line in the immediate vicinity of the city, which was constructed almost entirely with reference to repelling any attack made by land with infantry. Where this line crossed the river below the city it was intended to have a battery of twelve 32-pounders and ten 42-pounders, which it was considered would enable us to drive back any small number of ships that might succeed in passing the obstructions at the forts under the fire of their guns; but whether sufficient or not, no more were to be had, and subsequently, at the earnest request of the naval authorities, I transferred the 42-pounders to the steamers Carondelet and Bienville for service on Lake Pontchartrain in connection with Forts Pike and Macomb.

Immediately after I assumed command of the department, finding that there were no guns of the heaviest caliber, I applied to Richmond, Pensacola and other points for some 10-inch columbiads and seacoast mortars, which I considered necessary to the defense of the lower river; but none could be spared, the general impression being that New Orleans would not be attacked by the river, and I was therefore compelled to make the best possible defense with the guns at my disposal. Twelve 42-pounders were sent to Forts Jackson and St. Philip, together with a large additional quantity of powder; and being convinced that with the guns of inferior caliber mounted there we could not hinder steamers from passing unless they could be detained for some time under the fire of the works, I pushed forward rapidly the construction of a raft which offered a complete obstruction to the passage of vessels up the river, except through a small opening, and then only one at a time. The forts had seventy-five or eighty guns that could be brought successively to bear upon the river, were manned by garrisons of well-trained artillerists, affording a double relief to each gun, and commanded by officers who had no superiors in any service.

Under these circumstances, although I feared that the high water in the spring, with the accompanying drift, would carry away the raft, yet every confidence was felt that the river would remain closed until such time as the ironclad steamers Mississippi and Louisiana could be finished, which I was confidently informed would not be later than February 1st. The first raft constructed was not carried away by the high water and drift until the latter part of February; but with funds placed at my disposal by the citizens of New Orleans another was placed in position in March by the energetic labors of Colonel Higgins and others, and the position was again temporarily secure. No heavy guns had yet been received, although strenuous applications were made by me to get some from Pensacola when that place was abandoned. The general impression of all those to whom I applied was that the largest guns should be placed above New Orleans, not below (although I had notified the department on March 22d that, in my judgment, the fleet only awaited the arrival of the mortar vessels to attempt to pass up the river from below). By means, however, of an energetic and persevering officer, Major W. P. Duncan, commissary of subsistence, three 10-inch columbiads and five mortars were finally procured and brought over just in time to be put up as the firing commenced.

Thinking that the enemy's troops at Isle Breton were intending to land at Quarantine and act in the rear of Fort St. Philip, I ordered Colonel Szymanski's regiment of ninety-day men, armed with shotguns, to that point as a protection. I had likewise organized two companies of sharpshooters and swamp hunters, under Captains Mullen and Lartigue, which were sent down for operation upon the enemy's vessels from the banks of the river; but the high water, keeping the men day and night nearly waist-deep in the water, soon compelled them to abandon their positions.

I will here state that every Confederate soldier in New Orleans, with the exception of one company, had been ordered to Corinth, to join General Beauregard, in March, and the city was garrisoned by only about three thousand ninety-day troops, called out by the governor at my request, of whom about twelve hundred had muskets and the remainder shotguns of an indifferent description.

The river rose rapidly in April and soon drove out Szymanski's regiment, which was removed to the west bank, about six miles above Fort Jackson. The whole country became one vast sheet of water, which rose in the forts and covered places heretofore safe from its encroachments.

Under the tremendous pressure of this current and a storm of wind and rain the second raft was broken away on the night of Friday, April 11th, two days before the enemy first opened fire. The fourteen vessels of Montgomery's River Defense Expedition had been ordered by the department, when completed, to be sent up to Memphis and Fort Pillow; but, believing the danger of attack to be greater from below, I detained six of them at New Orleans, of which change the department was fully advised.

At my suggestion Governor Moore had also fitted up two steamers, which were sent to the forts below the city. A large number of fire-rafts were also constructed and towed down; and two smaller steamers were employed for the special purpose of towing these rafts into position where they could be most effective so as to leave the armed vessels free to operate against the enemy.

I telegraphed General Beauregard to send down the ironclad ram Manassas, and when the Secretary of the Navy ordered the steamer Louisiana to be sent also up the river I protested through the War Department, being satisfied that we required more heavy guns below. She was eventually permitted to go down the river on Sunday, April 20th, but not in a condition to use her motive power with effect It was hoped that, notwithstanding this, she would be able to assume a position below Fort St. Philip, discovering the location of the mortar boats, and, being herself proof against direct fire, dislodge the enemy with her guns, which were of very heavy caliber. Knowing, also, that the incessant bombardment kept General Duncan closely confined to Fort Jackson, so that he could give no orders to the river-defense steamers, I placed the whole under the control of Captain Mitchell—the armed steamers, as well as the tugs intended to tow down the fire-rafts.

I will here state that the river-defense fleet proved a failure for the very reasons set forth in my letter to the department on April 15th. Unable to govern themselves, and unwilling to be governed by others, their almost total want of system, vigilance and discipline rendered them nearly useless and helpless when the enemy finally dashed upon them suddenly on a dark night. I regret very much that the department did not think it advisable to grant my request to place some competent head in charge of these steamers.

Learning subsequently that the Louisiana was anchored above the forts and that the fire-rafts were not sent down, I telegraphed Captain Mitchell, requesting him to attend to it, and afterward called upon Commodore Whittle and entreated him to order the steamer to take the desired position below the forts. This he declined to do, but telegraphed Captain Mitchell, telling him to "strain a point to place the vessel there, if, in his judgment, it was advisable." No change, however, was made, and on the night of April 23d I went down myself in a steamboat, to urge Captain Mitchell to have the Louisiana anchored in the position indicated, and also to ascertain why the fire-rafts were not sent down. A few moments after I arrived the attack commenced, and the enemy succeeded in passing with fourteen ships, as described in General Duncan's report, and the battle of New Orleans, as against ships of war, was over.

I returned at once to the city, narrowly escaping capture, and giving orders to General Smith, in command of the interior lines, to prepare to make all possible resistance to the enemy's fleet at the earthwork batteries below the city, instructed Colonel Lovell to have several steamers ready to remove, as far as possible, the commissary and ordnance stores, being satisfied that the low developments at Chalmette could offer no protracted resistance to a powerful fleet whose guns, owing to the high water, looked down upon the surface of the country and could sweep away any number of infantry by an enfilading fire. These lines, as before remarked, were intended mainly to repel a land attack, but in a high stage of water were utterly untenable by infantry against guns afloat. It having been reported to me that a sufficient number of desperately bold men could easily be got together to board the enemy's vessels and carry them by assault, I authorized Major James to seize such steamers as might be necessary for his purpose and to attempt it. He called for one thousand men, by

Major-General Mansfield Lovell, of Maryland.

public advertisement, but being able to find but about one hundred who would undertake it, he abandoned the project.

On the morning of the 25th the enemy's fleet advanced upon the batteries and opened fire, which was returned with spirit by the troops as long as their powder lasted, but with little apparent effect upon the enemy. The powder intended for this battery of 32-pounders had been transferred by me to the steamer Louisiana a few days before, under the supposition that it would render much better service from her heavy rifles and shell guns than with a battery of light 32-pounders. For the operations at these works you are respectfully referred to General Smith's report.

The greater portion of the ordnance stores, provisions, and quartermaster's property were sent from the city by rail or steamer, and a portion of the volunteers also took the cars for Camp Moore, seventy-eight miles distant, on the Jackson Railroad. The greater part of the ninety-day troops disbanded and returned to their homes. There were two or three regiments and smaller bodies of men raised for Confederate service in the city at the time, but being entirely without arms of any kind, they could be of no service, and were also ordered to Camp Moore.

I adopted this course, recognizing the perfect absurdity of confronting more than one hundred guns afloat, of the largest caliber, well manned and served, and looking down upon the city, with less than three thousand militia, mostly armed with indifferent shotguns. It would, in my judgment, have been a wanton and criminal waste of the blood of women and children, without the most remote possibility of any good result, for the enemy had only to anchor one of his ships at Kenner to command the Jackson Railroad, and he could have reduced the city to ashes at his leisure, without our being able to make any resistance whatever; or, without firing a shot, he could have starved the city into a surrender in less than three weeks, as there was not more than eighteen days' food on hand for the population, from which my troops were almost entirely drawn. Why he did not occupy Kenner, and cut off all exit from the city immediately, I do not understand. Presuming that he would do so, as a matter of course, I had requested Captains Poindexter and Gwathmey, of the navy, to have all steamers ready in Lake Pontchartrain to carry the troops over to Madisonville, whence they could march to Camp Moore. A portion of them were taken over by this route.

Knowing that the enemy would at once seize the Opelousas Railroad, and thus cut off the troops occupying the works on the coast of West Louisiana, I sent orders to the different commanding officers at Forts Livingston, Guion, Quitman, Berwick and Chene to destroy their guns, and taking their small arms, provisions and ammunition, join me at Camp Moore.

Major Ivey brought away the troops at the two latter forts in a very creditable manner, but those at the other works became demoralized, disbanded and returned to New Orleans. I gave verbal instructions to Colonel Fuller to have the garrisons of Forts Pike and Macomb and Batteries Bienvenue and Lower Dupre ready to move at a moment's notice, as their posts were dependent on the city for provisions and often for water. It was understood that the naval steamers, in connection with other vessels in the lake, should bring away these garrisons when called upon to do so; and after my arrival at Camp Moore orders were given, on the 26th, to go for them, as I had been informed that Forts Jackson and St. Philip had been surrendered.

Finding that this report was untrue, I immediately countermanded the orders, giving instructions that they should be held until further notice; but before either order could reach Madisonville it was reported to me that the whole command was already at Covington. I advised Captain Poindexter to make his way to Mobile with his armed steamers, but he concluded to destroy them. We, however, procured from them some of the guns and ordnance stores, which I ordered immediately to Vicksburg, to be put in position there.

On the 25th Captain Bailey, of the Federal Navy, demanded the surrender of the city, and that the flags should be taken down, and the United States flag be put up over the Mint, Customhouse and other public buildings.

To this demand I returned an unqualified refusal, declaring that I would not surrender the city or any portion of my command, but added that, feeling unwilling to subject the city to bombardment, and recognizing the utter impossibility of removing the women and children, I should withdraw my troops and turn it over to the civil authorities. This I did in compliance with the openly expressed opinion of all prominent citizens around me that it would be a useless waste of blood, without being productive of any beneficial results to the cause for the troops to remain.

Captain Bailey then returned to his ship, under escort through the city (at his own request) of two officers of my staff, Colonel Lovell and Major James, and I then advised the Mayor not to surrender the city, nor to allow the flags to be taken down by any of our people, but to leave it to the enemy to take them down himself.

This advice was followed by the civil authorities; but the idea being held out, in their subsequent correspondence with the Federal officers, that they were placed in a defenseless condition by the withdrawal of the troops, but for which a different course might be pursued, I promptly telegraphed to Major James, of my staff, then in the city, offering to return at once with my command, if the citizens felt disposed to resist to the last extremity, and remain with them to the end.

I had deliberately made up my mind that, although such a step would be entirely indefensible in a military point of view, yet, if the people of New Orleans were desirous of signalizing their patriotism and devotion to the cause by the bombardment and burning of their city, I would return with my troops, and not leave as long as one brick remained upon another. The only palliation for such an act would be that it would give unmistakable evidence to the world that our people were in deadly earnest.

This determination, plainly expressed in my dispatches to Major James, was read by him to the Mayor, and also to the City Council, in the presence of one or more prominent citizens. The opinion was generally and freely expressed by the Mayor and others that the troops ought not to return.

I went to the city myself, however, on the night of April 28th, and, in order that there might be no mistake, made the same proposition in person to the Mayor. He said he did not think it advisable for the troops to return; that such a step would only be followed by a useless sacrifice of life without any corresponding benefit, and urged decidedly that it be not done.

I, however, addressed the Mayor a letter declaring my willingness to return and share a bombardment with them, and waited until the night of the 29th for an answer; but, receiving none in writing, returned to Camp Moore. The same proposition was made by me in the course of the day to several prominent citizens, but was invariably discountenanced by them.

For a week after the withdrawal of the troops, I had a number of officers in the city, and kept trains running regularly, which brought out a large amount of government property and stores, as well as those of the State of Louisiana. Nearly everything was brought away except the heavy guns and some property which persons in their flight had destroyed, and everything might have been saved had not persons refused to work for my officers, fearing that they might be subjected to punishment by the enemy. Many also refused to work for Confederate money, which occasioned some delay and difficulty in the removal of stores.

I feel gratified, however, in being able to state that we brought away all the troops that would leave, and, including the property of the State, a greater amount in value than belonged to the government. What we failed to bring was from inability to get transportation.

In this duty I was mainly assisted by Colonel Lovell, Majors James and Bell, Captain Venable and Lieutenant McDonald, to whom the government is greatly indebted for the safety of much valuable property. It was a source of great distress to me to see the result of months of toil and labor swept away in a few hours; but it was, in my opinion, mainly attributable to the following causes, which I could not, by any possibility, control:

1. The want of a sufficient number of guns of heavy caliber, which every exertion was made to procure without success.

2. The unprecedented high water, which swept away the obstructions upon which I mainly relied, in connection with the forts, to prevent the passage of a steam fleet up the river; and—

3. The failure, through inefficiency and want of energy, of those who had charge of the construction of the ironclad steamers Louisiana and Mississippi to have them completed in the time specified, so as to supply the place of obstructions; and finally, the declension of the officers in charge of the Louisiana to allow her, though not entirely ready, to be placed as a battery in the position indicated by General Duncan and myself. On these last points I could only advise and suggest, as they appertained to a separate and independent department, over which I had no control whatever.

Opened fire on April 13th, which was kept up at intervals for five days, when the mortars opened, and from that time, with but a single intermission of a few hours, a bombardment was kept up for seven days and nights, which, for great rapidity and wonderful accuracy of range, has no parallel. More than 25,000 shells were thrown, of which not less than one-third fell within the limits of Fort Jackson; yet the garrisons held out, although wet, without change of clothing, and exhausted for want of rest and regular food, with a heroic endurance which is beyond all praise. That the enemy succeeded in passing a large portion of his fleet by the flats on a dark night, under a heavy fire, is due to no fault of the garrisons of the forts. They did their whole duty nobly and heroically, and had they been seconded, as they should have been, by the defenses afloat, we should not have had to record the fall of New Orleans.

To the officers of my staff, who underwent months of severe and arduous labor collecting supplies, creating resources with the most limited means, and preparing all sorts of materials and munitions of war by ingenious makeshifts, I return my warmest thanks. Left in the city with a small force of badly-armed militia, all opportunity for distinction or glory was cut off, yet they never flagged in their zeal and devotion to the cause. When the country knows all that was done, and in what disadvantage it was accomplished, I feel confident that its verdict will do ample justice to those who shared equally in the labors of preparation, while they were denied the glory of taking part in the defense.

The battle for the defense of New Orleans was fought and lost at Forts Jackson and St. Philip. The extraordinary and remarkable conduct of the garrisons of these forts in breaking out in open mutiny after covering themselves with glory by their heroic defense is one of those strange anomalies for which I do not pretend to account. The facts are recorded and speak for themselves. The causes will probably never be known in full.

I had frequent occasion to regret that it was found impossible to give me control of the defenses afloat as well as ashore. A single controlling head might have made all the resources more available and efficient in working out the desired results.

For a detailed description of the bombardment of Forts Jackson and St. Philip I refer to the report of General Duncan.

* * * * * *

M. LOVELL,
Major-General Commanding.

ORDERS FOR BATTLE
AT
SHILOH, OR PITTSBURG LANDING,

APRIL 6 AND 7, 1862.

HEADQUARTERS ARMY OF THE MISSISSIPPI,
CORINTH, MISS., April 3, 1862.
SPECIAL ORDERS, NO. 8.

IN the impending movement the corps of this army will march, assemble and take order of battle in the following manner, it being assumed that the enemy is in position about a mile in advance of Shiloh Church, with his right resting on Owl Creek and his left on Lick Creek.

I. The Third Corps, under Major-General Hardee, will advance as soon as practicable on the Ridge Road, from Corinth to what is known as the Bark Road, passing about half a mile northward of the workhouse. The head of this column will bivouac, if possible, to-night at Mickey's house, at the intersection of the road from Monterey to Savannah. The cavalry, thrown well forward during the march, to reconnoiter and prevent surprise, will halt in front of the Mickey house, on the Bark Road.

GENERAL G. T. BEAUREGARD, OF LOUISIANA.

2. Major Waddell, aid-de-camp to General Beauregard, with two good guides, will report for service to Major-General Hardee.

3. At 3 o'clock A. M. to-morrow the Third Corps, with the left in front, will continue to advance by the Bark Road until within sight of the enemy's outposts or advanced positions, when it will be deployed in line of battle, according to the nature of the ground, its left resting on Owl Creek, its right toward Lick Creek, supported on that flank by one-half of its cavalry, the left flank being supported by the other half. The interval between the extreme right of this corps and Lick Creek will be filled by a brigade or division, according to the extent of the ground, from the Second Corps. These troops during the battle will also be under the command of Major-General Hardee. He will make the proper disposition of the artillery along the line of battle, remembering that the rifled guns are of long ranges and should be placed on any commanding position in rear of the infantry, to fire mainly on the reserves and second line of the enemy, but will occasionally be directed on his batteries and heads of columns.

II. The Second Corps, under Major-General Braxton Bragg, will assemble on Monterey, and move thence as early as practicable, the right wing, with left in front, by the road from Monterey to Savannah, the head of column to reach the vicinity of Mickey's house, at the intersection of the Bark Road, before sunset. The cavalry with this wing will take position on the road to Savannah, beyond Mickey's as far as Owl Creek, having advanced guards and pickets well to the front. The left wing of this corps will advance at the same time, also left in front, by the road from Monterey to Purdy, the head of the column to reach, by night, the intersection of that road with the Bark Road.

This wing will continue the movement in the morning as soon as the rear of the Third Corps shall have passed the Purdy Road, which it will then follow.

The Second Corps will then form the second line of battle about one thousand yards in rear of the first line. It will be formed, if practicable, with regiments in double columns at half distance, disposed as advantageously as the nature of the ground will admit, and with a view to facility of deployment, the artillery placed as may seem best to Major-General Bragg.

III. The First Corps, under Major-General Polk, with the exception of the detached division at Bethel, will take up its line of march by the Ridge Road, hence to Pittsburg, half an hour after the rear of the Third Corps shall have passed Corinth, and will bivouac to-night in rear of that corps, and on to-morrow will follow the movements of said corps with the same interval of time as to-day. When its head of column shall reach the vicinity of the Mickey house it will be halted in column or massed on the line of the Bark Road, as a reserve.

Meantime one regiment of its cavalry will be placed in observation on the road from Johnston's house to Stantonville, with advance guards and pickets thrown out well in advance toward Stantonville. Another regiment or battalion of cavalry will be posted in the same manner in the road from Monterey to Purdy, with its rear resting on or about the intersection of that road with the Bark Road, having advanced guards and pickets in the direction of Purdy.

The forces at Bethel and Purdy will defend their positions, as already instructed, if attacked; otherwise they will assemble on Purdy, and thence advance with advanced guards, flankers, and all other prescribed military precautions, by the road thence to Monterey, forming a junction with the next of the First Corps at the intersection of that road with the Bark Road leading from Corinth.

IV. The reserve of the forces will be concentrated by the shortest and best routes at Monterey as soon as the rear of the Second Corps shall have moved out of that place. Its commander will take up the best position whence to advance, as required, either in direction of Mickey's or of Pratt's house, on the direct road to Pittsburg, if that road is found practicable, or in direction of the Ridge Road to Hamburg, throwing all its cavalry on the latter road as far as its intersection with the one to Pittsburg, passing through Guersford, on Lick Creek. This cavalry will throw well forward advanced guards and vedettes toward Guersford and in the direction of Hamburg, and during the impending battle, when called to the field of combat, will move by the Guersford Road. A regiment of the infantry reserve will be thrown forward to the intersection of the Gravel Hill Road with the Ridge Road to Hamburg, as a support to the cavalry.

The reserve will be formed of Breckinridge's, Bowen's and Statham's brigades as now organized, the whole under command of Brigadier-General Breckinridge.

V. General Bragg will detach the Fifty-first and Fifty-second regiments Tennessee volunteers, Blount's Alabama and Desha's Arkansas battalion, and Bain's battery from his corps, which, with two of Carroll's regiments, now en route for these headquarters, will form a garrison for the post and depot of Corinth.

VI. Strong guards will be left at the railroad bridges between Iuka and Corinth, to be furnished in due proportion from the commands at Iuka, Burnsville and Corinth.

VII. Proper guards will be left at the camps of the several regiments of the forces in the field. Corps commanders will determine the strength of these guards.

VIII. Wharton's regiment of Texas cavalry will be ordered forward at once to scout on the road from Monterey to Savannah, between Mickey's and its intersection with the Pittsburg-Purdy Road; it will annoy and harass any force of the enemy moving by the latter way to assail Cheatham's division at Purdy.

IX. The chief engineer of the forces will take all due measures and precautions and give all requisite orders for the repair of the bridges, causeways and roads on which our troops may move in the execution of these orders.

X. The troops, individually so intelligent, and with such great interests involved in the issue, are urgently enjoined to be observant of the orders of their superiors in the hour of battle. Their officers must constantly endeavor to hold them in hand and prevent the waste of ammunition by heedless, aimless firing. The fire should be slow, always at a distinct mark. It is expected that much and effective work will be done with the bayonet.

By command of
GENERAL A. S. JOHNSTON.
THOMAS JORDAN, *Assistant Adjutant-General.*

BATTLE OF SHILOH, OR PITTSBURG LANDING,

APRIL 6 AND 7, 1862.

BY

GENERAL G. T. BEAUREGARD,
General Commanding.

HEADQUARTERS ARMY OF THE MISSISSIPPI,
CORINTH, MISS., April 11, 1862.

On the 2d ultimo, having ascertained conclusively, from the movements of the enemy on the Tennessee River and from reliable sources of information, that his aim would be to cut off my communications in West Tennessee with the Eastern and Southern States, by operating from the Tennessee River, between Crump's Landing and Eastport, as a base, I determined to foil his designs by concentrating all my available forces at and around Corinth.

Meanwhile, having called on the Governors of the States of Tennessee, Mississippi, Alabama and Louisiana to furnish additional troops, some of them (chiefly regiments from Louisiana) soon reached this vicinity, and with two divisions of General Polk's command from Columbus, and a fine corps of troops from Mobile and Pensacola, under Major-General Bragg, constituted the army of the Mississippi. At the same time General Johnston, being at Murfreesborough, on the march to form a junction of his forces with mine, was called on to send at least a brigade by railroad, so that we might fall on and crush the enemy, should he attempt an advance from under his gunboats.

The call on General Johnston was promptly complied with. His entire force was also hastened in this direction, and by April 1st our united forces were concentrated along the Mobile & Ohio Railroad from Bethel to Corinth, and on the Memphis & Charleston Railroad from Corinth to Iuka.

It was then determined to assume the offensive and strike a sudden blow at the enemy, in position under General Grant on the west bank of the Tennessee, at Pittsburg and in the direction of Savannah, before he was re-enforced by the army under General Buell, then known to be advancing for that purpose by rapid marches from Nashville via Columbia. About the same time General

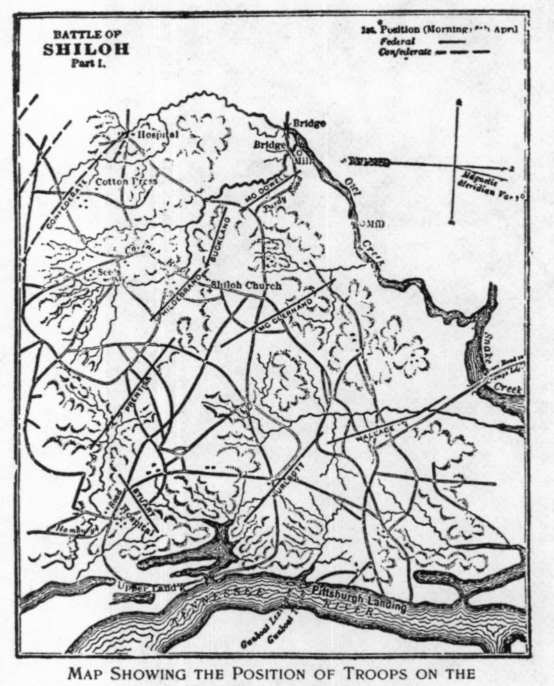

MAP SHOWING THE POSITION OF TROOPS ON THE MORNING OF THE 6TH.

Johnston was advised that such an operation conformed to the expectations of the President.

By a rapid and vigorous attack on General Grant it was expected he would be beaten back into his transports and the river, or captured, in time to enable us to profit by the victory, and remove to the rear all the stores and munitions that would fall into our hands in such an event before the arrival of General Buell's army on the scene. It was never contemplated, however, to retain the position thus gained and abandon Corinth, the strategic point of the campaign.

Want of general officers needful for the proper organization of divisions and brigades of an army brought thus suddenly together, and other difficulties in the way of an effective organization, delayed the movement until the night of the 2d instant, when it was heard from a reliable quarter, that the junction of the enemy's armies was near at hand. It was then, at a late hour, determined that the attack should be attempted at once, incomplete and imperfect as were our preparations for such a grave and momentous adventure. Accordingly, that night at 1 A. M., the preliminary orders to the commanders of corps were issued for the movement.

On the following morning the detailed orders of movements were issued, and the movement, after some delay, commenced, the troops being in admirable spirits. It was expected we should be able to reach the enemy's lines in time to attack him early on the 5th instant. The men, however, for the most part, were unused to marching, and the roads, narrow and traversing a densely wooded country, became almost impassable after a severe rainstorm on the night of the 4th, which drenched the troops in bivouac; hence our forces did not reach the intersection of the roads

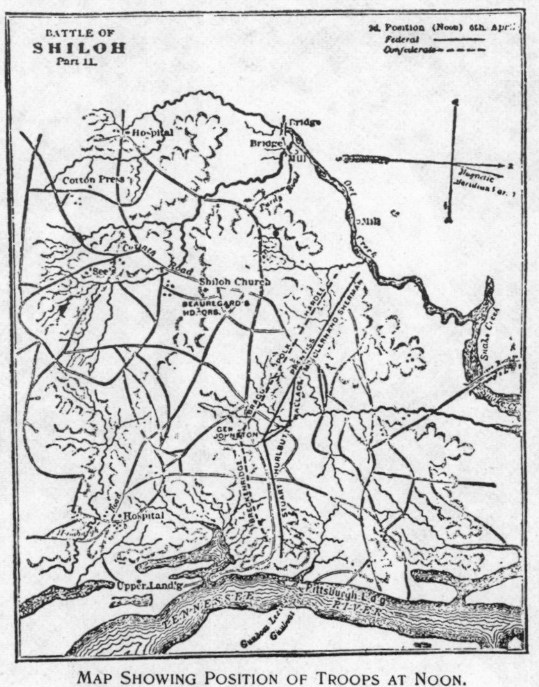

MAP SHOWING POSITION OF TROOPS AT NOON.

from Pittsburg and Hamburg, in the immediate vicinity of the enemy, until late Saturday afternoon.

It was then decided that the attack should be made on the next morning, at the earliest hour practicable, in accordance with the orders of movement; that is, in three lines of battle, the first and second extending from Owl Creek, on the left, to Lick Creek, on the right, a distance of about three miles, and supported by the third and the reserve. The first line, under Major-General Hardee, was constituted of his corps, augmented on the right by Gladden's brigade, of Major-General Bragg's corps, deployed in line of battle, with their respective artillery following immediately by the main road to Pittsburg and the cavalry in rear of the wings. The second line, composed of the other troops of Bragg's corps, followed the first at a distance of five hundred yards in the same order as the first. The army corps under General Polk followed the second line, at a distance of about eight hundred yards, in lines of brigades deployed, with their batteries in rear of each brigade, moving by the Pittsburg Road, the left wing supported by cavalry. The reserve, under Brigadier-General Breckinridge, followed closely the third line in the same order, its right wing supported by cavalry.

These two corps constituted the reserve, and were to support the front lines of battle, by being deployed, when required, on the right and left of the Pittsburg Road, or otherwise act according to the exigencies of the battle.

At 5 A. M. on the 6th instant a reconnoitering party of the enemy having become engaged with our advance pickets, the commander of the forces gave orders to begin the movement and attack as determined upon, except that Trabue's brigade, of Breckinridge's division, was detached and advanced to support the left of Bragg's corps and line of battle when menaced by the enemy, and the other two brigades were directed to advance by the road to Hamburg to support Bragg's right; and at the same time Maney's regiment, of Polk's corps, was advanced by the same road to re-enforce the regiment of cavalry and battery of four pieces, already thrown forward to watch and guard Greer's, Tanner's and Borland's fords, on Lick Creek.

At 5:30 A. M. our lines and columns were in motion, all animated, evidently, by a promising spirit. The front line was engaged at once, but advanced steadily, followed, in due order, with equal resolution and steadiness, by the other lines, which were brought successively into action with rare skill, judgment and gallantry by the several corps commanders, as the enemy made a stand with his masses rallied for the struggle for his encampments. Like an Alpine avalanche our troops moved forward, despite the determined resistance of the enemy, until after 6 P. M., when we were in possession of all his encampments between Owl and Lick creeks but one; nearly all of his field artillery; about thirty flags, colors and standards; over three thousand prisoners, including a division commander (General Prentiss), and several brigade commanders; thousands of small arms, an immense supply of subsistence, forage and munitions of war, and a large amount of means of transportation—all the substantial fruits of a complete victory, such, indeed, as rarely have followed the most successful battles; for never was an army so well provided as that of our enemy.

The remnant of his army had been driven in utter disorder to the immediate vicinity of Pittsburg under the shelter of heavy guns of his ironclad gunboats, and we remained undisputed masters of his well-selected, admirably provided cantonments, after over twelve hours of obstinate conflict with his forces, who had been beaten from them and the contiguous covert, but only by a sustained onset of all the men we could bring into action.

Our loss was heavy. Our commander in chief, General A. S. Johnston, fell mortally wounded, and died on the field at 2:30 P. M., after having shown the highest qualities of the commander and a personal intrepidity that inspired all around him, and gave resistless impulsion to his columns at critical moments.

The chief command then devolved upon me, though at the time I was greatly prostrated and suffering from the prolonged sickness with which I had been afflicted since early in February. The responsibility was one which in my physical condition I would have gladly avoided, though cast upon me when our forces were successfully pushing the enemy back upon the Tennessee River, and though supported on the immediate field by such corps commanders as Major-Generals Polk, Bragg and Hardee, and Brigadier-General Breckinridge, commanding the reserve.

It was after 6 P. M., as before said, when the enemy's last position was carried, and his forces finally broke and sought refuge behind a commanding eminence covering the Pittsburg Landing, not more than half a mile distant, and under the guns of the gunboats, which opened on our eager columns a fierce and annoying fire with shot and shell of the heaviest description.

Darkness was close at hand; officers and men were exhausted by a combat of over twelve hours without food, and jaded by the march of the preceding day through mud and water. It was, therefore, impossible to collect the rich and opportune spoils of war scattered broadcast on the field left in our possession, and impracticable to make any effective dispositions for their removal to the rear.

I accordingly established my headquarters at the Church of Shiloh, in the enemy's encampments, with Major-General Bragg, and directed our troops to sleep on their arms in such positions, in advance and rear, as corps commanders should determine, hoping from news received by a special dispatch, that delays had been encountered by General Buell in his march from Columbia, and that his main force, therefore, could not reach the field of battle in time to save General Grant's shattered fugitive forces from capture or destruction on the following day.

During the night the rain fell in torrents, adding to the discomforts and harassed condition of the men. The enemy, moreover, had broken their rest by a discharge at measured intervals of heavy shells thrown from the gunboats; therefore, on the following morning, the troops under my command were not in a condition to cope with an equal force of fresh troops, armed and equipped like our adversary, in the immediate possession of his depots and sheltered by such an auxiliary as the enemy's gunboats.

About 6 o'clock on the morning of April 7th, however, a hot fire of musketry and artillery, opened from the enemy's quarter on our advanced line, assured me of the junction of his forces, and soon the battle raged with a fury which satisfied me I was attacked by a largely superior force. But from the outset our troops, notwithstanding their fatigue and losses from the battle of the day before, exhibited the most cheering, veteranlike steadiness. On the right and center the enemy was repulsed in every

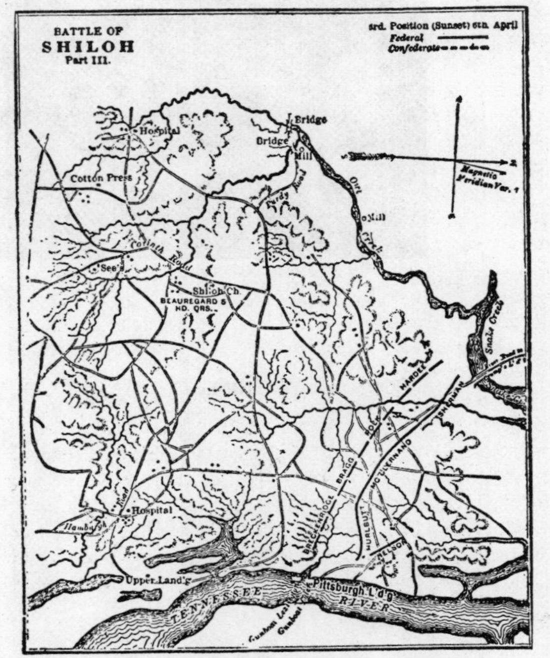

MAP SHOWING POSITION OF TROOPS AT SUNSET.

GENERAL ALBERT SIDNEY JOHNSTON.

BORN AT WASHINGTON, MASON COUNTY, KY., FEBRUARY 2, 1802. KILLED AT THE BATTLE OF SHILOH, TENN., APRIL 6, 1862.

attempt he made with his heavy columns in that quarter of the field. On the left, however, and nearest to the point of arrival of his re-enforcements, he drove forward line after line of his fresh troops, which were met with a resolution and courage of which our country may be proudly hopeful. Again and again our troops were brought to the charge, invariably to win the position in issue; invariably to drive back their foe. But hour by hour, thus opposed to an enemy constantly re-enforced, our ranks were perceptibly thinned under the unceasing, withering fire of the enemy, and by 12 M. eighteen hours of hard fighting had sensibly exhausted a large number. My last reserves had necessarily been disposed of, and the enemy was evidently receiving fresh re-enforcements after each repulse; accordingly about 1 P. M. I determined to withdraw from so unequal a conflict, securing such results of the victory of the day before as was then practicable.

Beauregard. Polk. Breckinridge. Johnston. Bragg. Hardee.

A Council of War. The Night Before the Battle of Shiloh.

Officers of my staff were immediately dispatched with the necessary orders to make the best dispositions for a deliberate, orderly withdrawal from the field, and to collect and post a reserve to meet the enemy, should he attempt to push after us.

In this connection I will mention particularly my adjutant-general, Colonel Jordan, who was of much assistance to me on this occasion, as he had already been on the field of battle on that and the preceding day.

About 2 P. M. the lines in advance, which had repulsed the enemy in their last fierce assault on our left and center, received the orders to retire. This was done with uncommon steadiness, and the enemy made no attempt to follow.

The line of troops established to cover this movement had been disposed on a favorable ridge commanding the ground of Shiloh Church. From this position our artillery played upon the woods beyond for awhile, but upon no visible enemy and without reply. Soon satisfied that no serious pursuit would be attempted, this last line was withdrawn; and never did troops leave a battlefield in better order. Even the stragglers fell into the ranks and marched off with those who had stood more steadily by their colors.

A second strong position was taken up about a mile in rear, where the approach of the enemy was awaited for nearly an hour; but no effort to follow was made, and only a small detachment of horsemen could be seen at a distance from this last position, warily observing our movements.

Arranging through my staff officers for the completion of the movements thus begun, Brigadier-General Breckinridge was left with his command as a rear guard to hold the ground we had occupied the night preceding the first battle, just in front of the intersection of the Pittsburg and Hamburg roads, about four miles from the former place, while the rest of the army passed to the rear in excellent order.

On the following day General Breckinridge fell back about three miles, to Mickey's, which position we continued to hold, with our cavalry thrown considerably forward in immediate proximity to the battlefield.

Unfortunately, toward night of the 7th instant it began to rain heavily. This continued throughout the night; the roads became almost impassable in many places, and much hardship and suffering now ensued before all the regiments reached their encampments; but despite the heavy casualties of the two eventful days of April 6th and 7th, this army is more confident of ultimate success than before its encounter with the enemy.

To Major-Generals Polk, Bragg and Hardee, commanding corps, and to Brigadier-General Breckinridge, commanding the reserve, the country is greatly indebted for the zeal, intelligence and energy with which all orders were executed, for the foresight and military ability they displayed in the absence of instructions in the many exigencies of the battle on a field so densely wooded and broken, and for their fearless deportment as they repeatedly led their commands personally to the onset upon their powerful adversary. It was under these circumstances that General Bragg had two horses shot under him; that Major-General Hardee was slightly wounded, his coat rent by balls and his horse disabled, and that Brigadier-General Breckinridge was twice struck by spent balls.

For the services of their gallant subordinate commanders and of other officers, as well as for the details of the battlefield, I must refer to the reports of corps, division and brigade commanders, which will be forwarded as soon as received.

To give more in detail the operations of the two battles resulting from the movement on Pittsburg than now attempted must have delayed this report for weeks and interfered materially with the important duties of my position. But I may be permitted to say that not only did the obstinate conflict for twelve hours on Sunday leave the Confederate army masters of the battlefield and our adversary beaten, but we left that field on the next day only after eight hours' incessant battle with a superior army of fresh troops, whom we had repulsed in every attack on our lines—so repulsed and crippled, indeed, as to leave it unable to take the field for the campaign for which it was collected and equipped at such enormous expense and with such profusion of all the appliances of war.

These successful results were not achieved, however, as before said, without severe loss—a loss not to be measured by the number of the slain or wounded, but by the high social and personal worth of so large a number of those who were killed or disabled, including the commander of the forces, whose high qualities will be greatly missed in the momentous campaign impending. I deeply regret to record also the death of the Hon. George W. Johnson, Provisional Governor of Kentucky, who went into action with the Kentucky troops, and continually inspired them by his words and example. Having his horse shot under him on Sunday, he entered the ranks of a Kentucky regiment on Monday, and fell mortally wounded toward the close of the day. Not his State alone, but the whole Confederacy, has sustained a great loss in the death of this brave, upright and able man.

Another gallant and able soldier and captain was lost to the service of the country when Brigadier-General Gladden, commanding the First Brigade, Withers' division, Second Army Corps, died from a severe wound received on the 6th instant, after having been conspicuous to his whole corps and the army for courage and capacity.

Major-General Cheatham, commanding the First Division, First Corps, was slightly wounded and had three horses shot under him.

Brigadier-General Clark, commanding Second Division of the First Corps, received a severe wound also on the first day, which will deprive the army of his valuable services for some time.

Brigadier-General Hindman, engaged in the outset of the battle, was conspicuous for a cool courage, efficiently employed in leading his men ever in the thickest of the fray, until his horse was shot under him and he was unfortunately so severely injured by the fall that the army was deprived on the following day of his chivalrous example.

Brigadier-Generals B. R. Johnson and Bowen, most meritorious officers, were also severely wounded in the first combat, but it is hoped will soon be able to return to duty with their brigades.

To mention the many field officers who died or were wounded while gallantly leading their commands into action, and the many brilliant instances of individual courage displayed by officers and men in the twenty hours of battle, is impossible at this time, but their names will be duly made known to their countrymen.

The immediate staff of the lamented commander in chief, who accompanied him to the field, rendered efficient service, and, either by his side or in carrying his orders, shared his exposure to the casualties of the well-contested battlefield. I beg to commend their names to the notice of the War Department, namely: Captains H. P. Brewster and N. Wickliffe, of the adjutant and inspector-generals' department; Captain Theodore O'Hara, acting inspector-general; Lieutenants George Baylor and Thomas M. Jack, aids-de-camp; Volunteer Aids-de-camp Colonel William Preston, Major D. M. Hayden, E. W. Munford and Calhoun Benham, Major Albert J. Smith and Captain Wickham, of the quartermaster's department.

To these gentlemen was assigned the last sad duty of accompanying the remains of their lamented chief from the field, except Captains Brewster and Wickliffe, who remained and rendered valuable services as staff officers on April 7th.

Governor Isham G. Harris, of Tennessee, went upon the field with General Johnston, was by his side when he was shot, aided him from his horse, and received him in his arms when he died. Subsequently the Governor joined my staff and remained with me throughout the next day, except when carrying orders or employed in encouraging the troops of his own State, to whom he gave a conspicuous example of coolness, zeal and intrepidity.

I am also under many obligations to my own general, personal and volunteer staff, many of whom have been so long associated with me. I append a list of those present on the field on both days, and whose duties carried them constantly under fire, namely: Colonel Thomas Jordan,

Log Chapel where the Battle of Shiloh Commenced.

Captain Clifton H. Smith and Lieutenant John M. Otey, adjutant-general's department; Major George W. Brent, acting inspector-general; Colonel R. B. Lee, chief of subsistence, whose horse was wounded; Lieutenant-Colonel S. W. Ferguson and Lieutenant A. R. Chisolm, aids-de-camp; Volunteer Aids-de-camp Colonel Jacob Thompson, Majors Numa Augustin and H. E. Peyton, and Captains Albert Ferry and B. B. Waddell. Captain W. W. Porter, of Major-General Crittenden's staff, also reported for duty and shared the duties of my volunteer staff on Monday. Brigadier-General Trudeau, of Louisiana Volunteers, also for a part of the first day's conflict was with me as a volunteer aid. Captain E. H. Cummins, signal officer, also was actively employed as staff officer on both days.

Nor must I fail to mention that Private W. E. Goolsby, Eleventh Regiment Virginia Volunteers, orderly to my headquarters since last June, repeatedly employed to carry my verbal orders to the field, discharged the duty with great zeal and intelligence.

Other members of my staff were necessarily absent from the immediate field of battle, intrusted with responsible duties at these headquarters, namely: Captain F. H. Jordan, assistant adjutant-general, in charge of general headquarters; Major Eugene E. McLean, chief quartermaster, and Captain E. Deslonde, quartermaster's department.

Lieutenant Colonel Ferguson, aid-de-camp, early on Monday was assigned to command and directed the movements of a brigade of the Second Corps. Lieutenant-Colonel Gilmer, chief engineer, after having performed the important and various duties of his place with distinction to himself and materal benefit to the country, was wounded late on Monday. I trust, however, I shall not long be deprived of his essential services.

Captain Lockett, Engineer Corps, chief assistant to Colonel Gilmer, after having been employed in the duties of his corps on Sunday, was placed by me on Monday in command of a battalion without field officers.

Captain Fremaux, provisional engineers, and Lieutenants Steele and Helm, also rendered material and even dangerous service in the line of their duty.

Major-General (now General) Braxton Bragg, in addition to his duties of chief of staff, as has been before stated, commanded his corps—much the largest in the field—on both days with signal capacity and soldiership.

Surgeons Foard, medical director, R. L. Brodie and S. Choppin, medical inspectors, and D. W. Yandell, medical director of the Western Department, with General Johnston, were present in the discharge of their arduous and high duties, which they performed with honor to their profession.

Captain Tom Saunders, Messrs. Scales and Metcalf, and Mr. Tully, of New Orleans, were of material aid on both days, ready to give news of the enemy's positions and movements regardless of exposure.

While thus partially making mention of some of those who rendered brilliant, gallant or meritorious service on the field, I have aimed merely to notice those whose positions would most probably exclude the record of their services from the reports of corps or subordinate commanders.

From this agreeable duty I turn to one in the highest degree unpleasant; one due, however, to the brave men under me as a contrast to the behavior of most of the army who fought so heroically. I allude to the fact that some officers, non-commissioned officers and men abandoned their colors early on the first day to pillage the captured encampments; others retired shamefully from the field on both days while the thunder of cannon and the roar and rattle of musketry told them that their brothers were being slaughtered by the fresh legions of the enemy. I have ordered the names of the most conspicuous on this roll of laggards and cowards to be published in orders.

It remains to state that our loss on the two days, in killed outright, was 1,728; wounded, 8,012, and missing, 959; making an aggregate of casualties, 10,699. This sad list tells in simple language of the stout fight made by our countrymen in front of the rude log chapel of Shiloh, especially when it is known that on Monday, from exhaustion and other causes, not 20,000 men on our side could be brought into action.

Of the losses of the enemy I have no exact knowledge. Their newspapers report it as very heavy. Unquestionably it was greater even in proportion than our own on both days, for it was apparent to all that their dead left on the field outnumbered ours two to one. Their casualties, therefore, can not have fallen many short of 20,000 in killed, wounded, prisoners and missing. Through information derived from many sources, including the newspapers of the enemy, we engaged on Sunday the divisions of Generals Prentiss, Sherman, Hurlbut, McClernand and Smith, of 9,000 men each, or at least 45,000 men. This force was re-enforced Sunday night by the divisions of Generals Nelson, McCook, Crittenden and Thomas, of Major-General Buell's army, some 25,000 strong, including all arms; also General L. Wallace's division, of General Grant's army, making at least 33,000 fresh troops, which, added to the remnant of General Grant's forces—on Monday morning amounting to over 20,000—made an aggregate force of some 53,000 men, at least, arrayed against us on that day.

In connection with the results of the battle I should state that most of our men who had inferior arms exchanged them for the improved arms of the enemy; also that most of the property, public and personal, in the camps from which the enemy was driven on Sunday was rendered useless or greatly damaged, except some of the tents.

With this is transmitted certain papers, to-wit: order of movement, a list of the killed and wounded, a list of the captured flags and a map of the battlefield, etc., all of which are respectfully submitted.

* * * * * *

G. T. BEAUREGARD,
General Commanding.

General Prentiss' (Federal) Headquarters, Captured by the Confederates.

BATTLE OF SHILOH, OR PITTSBURG LANDING,

APRIL 6 AND 7, 1862.

BY

LIEUTENANT-GENERAL WILLIAM J. HARDEE,
Commanding Third Corps.

HEADQUARTERS HARDEE'S CORPS,
ARMY OF THE TENNESSEE,
TULLAHOMA, TENN., February 7, 1863.

AFTER the fall of Fort Donelson the commanding general, Albert Sidney Johnson, having successfully made his retreat through Tennessee amid many difficulties, rapidly concentrated all his remaining forces at Corinth, for the purpose of inflicting a decisive blow upon the enemy. The position was important from being the center of the railroad communications passing southwardly from the Ohio River through Western Tennessee to the Gulf of Mexico, and from the Mississippi River eastwardly to the Atlantic. Marshes and muddy streams in its vicinity rendered it difficult to approach, and made it strong and defensible.

The enemy, flushed with their recent success, moved forward to conquer the territory on the left of the Mississippi. Large forces were transported on steamers, conveyed by iron-clad gunboats, under the command of General Grant, to Pittsburg, while an army under General Buell, commanding the remaining forces of the United States in the west, moved from Nashville through Columbia, by land, to effect a junction with General Grant. General Johnston, having received information of these movements, resolved at once to defeat or dislodge General Grant before the arrival of the forces under General Buell. On Thursday, April 3d, the Army of the Mississippi was ordered to advance from Corinth toward Shiloh, a little country church near Pittsburg, around which the forces of General Grant were encamped.

The Third Corps, then under my command, marched in advance by the Bark Road toward Shiloh, and reached Mickey's house, about sixteen miles from Corinth and eight from Pittsburg, on the morning of April 4th. A portion of Brigadier-General Cleburne's command in the afternoon engaged the cavalry of the enemy and repulsed it promptly. We took some prisoners, and bivouacked for the night.

It was the purpose of the general to continue the movement at 3 A. M. the succeeding morning, but torrents of rain having fallen, a night march over the swollen streams and flooded ravines became impracticable. The advance was suspended until dawn, when my command again marched forward.

About 10 o'clock on Saturday morning, April 5th, my corps reached the outposts and developed the lines of the enemy. It was immediately deployed in line of battle about a mile and a half east of Shiloh Church, where Lick Creek and Owl Creek approach most nearly. The right was extended toward Lick Creek, and the left rested near Owl Creek, which streams at that point are rather more than three miles apart.

The Tennessee River runs nearly due north from above Lick Creek to the mouth of Owl Creek, which creeks, after flowing nearly parallel to each other, empty into the river about four miles apart. Pittsburg is situated near the foot of the hills, and nearly midway between the mouths of the two creeks, on the left bank of the river. This bank of the Tennessee is a range of bold, wooded hills, bordering the stream closely, which, as they recede from the river, gradually diminish, the slopes falling away from a ridge on the south toward Lick Creek, and on the north toward Owl Creek. From Mickey's, eight miles west from Pittsburg, rolling uplands, partially cultivated, interspersed with copses, thickets and forests, with small fields cultivated or abandoned, characterize the country from that point to the river.

The storm of the preceding night rendered the roads so miry that the different commands were not collected at Shiloh until 4 or 5 o'clock in the afternoon. This rendered it necessary to postpone the attack until the next day. Some of the troops having failed to provide themselves with provisions, or having improvidently consumed or lost them, the propriety of returning to Corinth without attacking the enemy was urged and considered; but the commanding general determined, regardless of all objections, to force a battle the succeeding morning. By the order of battle our troops were arranged in two parallel lines; the first, under my command, being composed of my corps, consisting of the brigades of Brigadier-Generals Hindman, Wood and Cleburne, numbering six thousand seven hundred and eighty-nine effective men, and the brigade of Brigadier-General Gladden, which was attached to my command to fill the interval between my right and Lick Creek. The second was composed of five brigades, under Major-General Bragg, one thousand yards in rear of mine; while four brigades, under Major-General Polk, supported the left, and three under Brigadier-General Breckinridge supported the right of the lines. The order was given to advance at daylight on Sunday, April 6th. The morning was bright and bracing. At early dawn the enemy attacked the skirmishers in front of my line, commanded by Major (now Colonel) Hardcastle, which was handsomely resisted by that promising young officer. My command advanced, and in half an hour the battle became fierce.

Hindman's brigade engaged the enemy with great vigor in the edge of a wood and drove him rapidly back over the field toward Pittsburg, while Gladden's brigade, on the right, about 8 o'clock, dashed upon the encampments of a division under the command of General Prentiss. At the same time Cleburne's brigade, with the Fifteenth Arkansas, deployed as skirmishers, and the Second Tennessee, *en échelon* on the left, moved quickly through the fields, and though far outflanked by the enemy on our left, rushed forward under a terrific fire from the serried ranks drawn up in front of the camp. A morass covered his front, and being difficult to pass, caused a break in the brigade. Deadly volleys were poured upon the men as they advanced, from behind bales of hay, logs and other defenses, and after a series of desperate charges the brigade was compelled to fall back.

In this charge the Sixth Mississippi, under Colonel Thornton, lost more than three hundred killed and wounded out of an effective force of four hundred and twenty-five men. It was at this point also that Colonel (now Brigadier-General) Bates fell severely wounded while bravely leading his regiment.

Supported by the arrival of the second line, Cleburne, with the remainder of his troops, again advanced and entered the enemy's encampments, which had been forced on the center and right by the dashing charges of Gladden's, Wood's and Hindman's brigades. The brave Gladden had fallen by a cannon shot about 8 o'clock, at the instant the camp was carried, and the command devolved upon Colonel D. W. Adams, who continued the attack with signal courage.

About 2:30 o'clock Colonel Adams was wounded severely in the head, and the command devolved upon Colonel Z. C. Deas.

In the attack of the left center of my line Brigadier-General Wood charged an enemy's battery on a gentle acclivity, and captured six guns, with the Second and Twenty-seventh Tennessee and Sixteenth Alabama regiments.

In this attack Colonel Christopher H. Williams, of the Twenty-seventh Tennessee, was killed. The army and the Confederacy sustained a severe loss in the death of this gallant officer. General Wood, about the same time, was thrown from his horse and temporarily disabled. The command devolved upon Colonel Patterson, of the Eighth Arkansas, who led the brigade with courage and ability until about 2:30 o'clock, when General Wood returned to the field and resumed command. A portion of the brigade was afterward detached, with prisoners, to the rear, and the remainder, joining General Ruggles, drove back the enemy, capturing Lieutenant-Colonel Miller, of the Sixteenth Missouri, with some three hundred prisoners.

This brigade was by my order moved forward late in the afternoon in the direction of the heavy cannonade in front, but about sunset was ordered to withdraw by a staff officer from General Beauregard.

In the arrangement of my line of battle two brigades were intrusted to Brigadier-General Hindman; his own, under the immediate command of Colonel Shaver, who conducted his command to my satisfaction, and the other under command of Brigadier-General Wood.

The conduct of General Hindman on the field was marked by a courage which animated his soldiers and a skill which won their confidence. He was disabled in the action on Sunday. He has never transmitted his report, and I am not able to do justice to his brave command; but I can not omit to mention the death of Lieutenant-Colonel Dean, commanding the Seventh Arkansas, who fell in the fight on Sunday. He was a brave and deserving officer.

Nothing could be more brilliant than the attack. The fierce volleys of one hundred thousand muskets and the boom of two hundred cannon, receding steadily toward the river, marked, hour by hour, from dawn until night, our slow but ceaseless advance. The captured camps, rich in the spoils of war—in arms, horses, stores, munitions and baggage—with throngs of prisoners moving to the rear, showed the headlong fury with which our men had crushed the heavy columns of the foe.

General Johnston, about 11 o'clock, brought up the reserve under Breckinridge. Deploying it *en échelon* of brigades with admirable skill and rapidity, he turned the enemy's left, and conducting the division in person, swept down the river toward Pittsburg, cheering and animating the men and driving the enemy in wild disorder to the shelter of their gunboats.

At this moment of supreme interest it was our misfortune to lose the commanding general, who fell mortally wounded at 2:30 o'clock, and expired in a few minutes in a ravine near the spot where Breckinridge's division had charged under his eye.

This disaster caused a lull in the attack on the right, and precious hours were wasted. It is, in my opinion, the candid belief of intelligent men that but for this calamity we would have achieved before sunset a triumph signal not only in the annals of this war, but memorable in future history.

At the commencement of the battle my position was near the center of my command, but finding Brigadier-General Hindman conducting operations at that point to my satisfaction, I passed to the extreme right. Here General Johnston in person was directing the battle. A heavy cannonade soon attracted me to the left.

On my arrival in that quarter our forces were found hotly engaged with the lines of the enemy in front. Rapidly collecting four regiments under cover of a ravine, screening them from the view and fire of the enemy, I placed them in a position which outflanked their line. Availing myself of a critical moment when the enemy in front was much shaken, I ordered these regiments from the ravine, and hurled them against the right flank of their line, and it gave away in tumultuous rout.

At this juncture General Beauregard ordered me to push forward the cavalry, and I ordered Colonel Wharton to charge their fleeing battalions. The command was obeyed with promptitude, but in the ardor of the charge the cavalry fell into an ambuscade and was repulsed with some loss. The gallant Wharton himself was wounded. Simultaneously Morgan dashed forward with his usual daring on their left, and drove the scattered remnants of their regiments from the field.

Upon the death of General Johnston, the command having devolved upon General Beauregard, the conflict was continued until near sunset, and the advance divisions were within a few hundred yards of Pittsburg, where the enemy were huddled in confusion, when the order to withdraw was received. The troops were ordered to bivouac on the field of battle. Exhausted by fasting and the toils of the day, scattered and disordered by a continued combat of twelve hours, many straggled to find food amid the profuse stores of the enemy or shelter in the forest.

General Buell, hearing the cannonade, hurried heavy re-enforcements up the river in steamers to the succor of the beaten troops of Grant, and our wearied men found before them a fresh army to encounter.

On Monday, about 6 o'clock, portions of my command were formed upon an alignment with other troops on the left to resist the enemy, who soon opened a hot fire on our advanced lines. The battle reanimated our men, and the strong columns of the enemy were repulsed again and again by our tired and disordered, but brave and steadfast, troops.

LIEUTENANT-GENERAL WILLIAM J. HARDEE, OF GEORGIA.

The enemy brought up fresh re-enforcements, pouring them continually upon us. At times our lines recoiled as it were before the overwhelming physical weight of the enemy's forces; but the men rallied readily and fought with unconquerable spirit. Many of our best regiments, signalized in the battle of Sunday by their steady valor, reeled under the sanguinary struggle on the succeeding day. In one instance, that of the Second Texas Regiment, commanded by Colonel Moore, the men seemed appalled, fled from the field without apparent cause, and were so dismayed that my efforts to rally them were unavailing.

This fierce and indecisive struggle continued till about 1 o'clock, when General Beauregard determined to withdraw to Corinth. Lines of troops to cover the movement were deployed near Shiloh Church, but the enemy slackened in the attack and were unable to follow. Our artillery shelled the woods, but evoked no reply, while disordered regiments and stragglers, assembling, withdrew slowly, without pursuit or molestation, to the rear. Other positions further to the rear were successively taken to cover our columns; but no serious effort was made to follow, and we withdrew toward Corinth. Thus ended the battle of Shiloh.

My thanks are due to the officers and men for the courage and devotion they displayed in the battle. I refer to the reports of subordinate officers, which are transmitted, for a detailed account of operations and for the many signal instances of individual daring and disciplined valor which they commemorate.

It would, however, be unjust to my brave and enduring soldiers, who stood by their colors to the end, if I did not mention that many straggled from their ranks or fell back without orders. Some, allured by the rich plunder, halted in the conquered camps, and a few, terrified by the bloody scenes, fled toward Corinth. From these causes and the casualties of the battle we could not, on Monday, form in line of battle more than twenty thousand men.

During the action Brigadier-General Cleburne conducted his command with persevering valor. No repulse discouraged him; but after many bloody struggles he assembled the remnant of his brigade and was conspicuous for his gallantry to the end of the battle.

Brigadier-General Wood, though suffering from a fall from his horse, which compelled him to withdraw temporarily, returned to the field and bravely led his men.

The loss sustained by my corps (not including that suffered by Gladden's brigade) amounted to:

Killed	404
Wounded	1,936
Missing	141
Total	2,481

W. J. HARDEE,
Lieutenant-General.

BATTLE OF SHILOH, OR PITTSBURG LANDING,

APRIL 6 AND 7, 1862.

BY

MAJOR-GENERAL LEONIDAS POLK,
Commanding First Corps.

HEADQUARTERS, RIGHT WING,
ARMY OF THE MISSISSIPPI, Sept. 9, 1862.

I BEG to submit the following account of the part taken by the troops comprising my corps in the battle of Shiloh:

It was resolved by our commander-in-chief, General Johnston, to attack the enemy in his position on the Tennessee River if possible at daybreak on April 5th.

My corps consisted of two divisions, of two brigades each, commanded, respectively, by Major-General Cheatham and Brigadier-General Clark, and, with the exception of three regiments—one from Louisiana, Mississippi and Arkansas, respectively—was composed of Tennesseeans.

Major-General Cheatham's division was on outpost duty at and near Bethel, on the Mobile & Ohio Railroad, and was ordered to proceed to a point near Pittsburg Landing, on the river, for the purpose of joining in the contemplated attack.

On April 3d I was directed to march so much of my corps as was still at Corinth toward the same point. The route to be taken was that pursued by the corps of General Hardee over the Ridge and Bark roads, and I was ordered to march so as to allow an interval of half an hour between the two corps.

This order I was directed to observe until I reached Mickey's. On reaching Mickey's, my instructions were to halt, to allow the corps of General Bragg—whose route fell into ours at that point—to fall in and follow in the immediate rear of General Hardee. The plan of battle was that the corps of General Hardee should form the front line; that of General Bragg, the second; my corps and that of General Breckinridge to constitute the third, or reserve.

I maintained the interval ordered between General Hardee's and my corps during the night of the 3d and during the following day, and halted the head of my column at the crossroads at Mickey's about dark on the 4th, according to instructions, my column being well up.

At Mickey's we were about two miles and a half from the place at which our line of battle was to be formed, and here the head of General Bragg's corps also bivouacked on the same night.

At 3 o'clock on the following morning (Saturday, the 5th) the whole of my command was under arms in waiting on the road, which it could not take, as it was occupied by the troops of General Bragg, which were filing into the rear of those of General Hardee. It was now manifest that the attack at daybreak could not be made; that the troops could not reach their position in time, and that the failure was owing to the condition of the roads, which were exceedingly bad in consequence of the heavy rains which had fallen.

I took a position early in the morning near the forks of the road to wait for the troops of General Bragg to pass. While there in waiting, at 10 A. M., Generals A. S. Johnston and Beauregard, with their staffs, rode up from the rear, and halting opposite me, gave me orders to move promptly in rear of General Bragg so that I might give the road to General Breckinridge, who was to follow me, coming in from General Bragg's route. I was also ordered to halt my column one mile and a half in rear of the place at which General Bragg's line of battle crossed the road, and to deploy my corps to the left on a line parallel to that of General Bragg, General Breckinridge having been ordered to halt at the same point and deploy his corps to the right, with his left resting on my right.

It was near 2 o'clock before the whole of General Bragg's corps had passed. I then put my column in motion and rode to the front. Proceeding half a mile, I sent Lieutenant Richmond, my aid-de-camp, forward to ascertain the point at which General Bragg's line would cross the road, and to measure back for the place at which I was to halt and deploy. This he did, and on reaching the place Lieutenant Richmond informed me that the road I was pursuing ran into that across which General Bragg was forming at an obtuse angle. It became necessary, then, before I could form, to ascertain the general direction of the line in front of me. To effect this I sent forward my Inspector-General (Blake), and leaving a staff officer to halt my column at the proper place, I proceeded myself to aid in the reconnoissance. I had not advanced far before I came upon General Ruggles, who commanded General Bragg's left, deploying his troops. Having ascertained the direction of the line, I did not wait for him to complete it, but returned to the head of my column to give the necessary orders.

By this time it was near 4 o'clock, and on arriving I was informed that General Beauregard desired to see me immediately. I rode forward to his headquarters at once, where I found General Bragg and himself in conversation. He said, with some feeling, "I am very much disappointed at the delay which has occurred in getting the troops into position." I replied, "So am I, sir; but so far as I am concerned my orders are to form on another line, and that line must first be established before I can form upon it." I continued, "I reached Mickey's at nightfall yesterday, from whence I could not move, because of the troops which were before me, until 2 P. M. to-day. I then promptly followed the column in front of me, and have been in position to form upon it so soon as its line was established." He said he regretted the delay exceedingly, as it would make it necessary to forego the attack altogether; that our success depended upon our surprising the enemy; that this now was impossible, and we must fall back to Corinth.

Here General Johnston came up and asked what was the matter. General Beauregard repeated what he said to me. General Johnston remarked that this would never do, and proceeded to assign reasons for that opinion. He then asked what I thought of it. I replied that my troops were in as good condition as they had ever been, that they were eager for the battle; that to retire now would operate injuriously upon them, and I thought we ought to attack.

General Breckinridge, whose troops were in the rear, and by this time had arrived upon the ground, here joined us, and after some discussion it was decided to postpone further movement until the following day, and to make the attack at daybreak. I then proceeded to dispose of my divisions — Cheatham having arrived — according to an alteration in the programme, and we bivouacked for the night.

At the appointed hour on the morning of the 6th my troops were moved forward, and as soon as they were freed from an obstruction, formed by a thicket of underbrush, they were formed in column of brigades, and pressed onward to the support of the second line.

General Clark's division was in front. We had not proceeded far before the first line, under General Hardee, was under fire throughout its length, and the second, under General Bragg, was also engaged.

The first order received by me was from General Johnston, who had ridden to the front to watch the opening operations, and who, as commander-in-chief, seemed deeply impressed with the responsibilities of his position. It was observed that he entered upon his work with the ardor and energy of the true soldier, and the vigor with which he pressed forward his troops gave assurance that his persistent determination would close the day with a glorious victory.

The order was to send him a brigade to the right for the support of General Bragg's line, then hotly engaged. The brigade of General Stewart, of General Clark's division, was immediately dispatched to him, and was led by him in person to the point requiring support. I was then ordered by General Beauregard to send one of the brigades of my rear division to the support of General Bragg's left, which was pressed by the enemy. Orders were given to that effect to General Cheatham, who took charge of the brigade in person, and executed the movement promptly. My two remaining brigades were held in hand until I received orders to move them directly to the front, to the support of General Bragg's center. These were Colonel Russell's, of General Clark's division, which was directed by that officer, and General Bushrod R. Johnson's, of General Cheatham's division. They moved forward at once, and were both very soon warmly engaged with the enemy. The resistance at this point was as stubborn as at any other on the field.

The forces of the enemy to which we were opposed were understood to be those of General Sherman, supported by the command of General McClernand, and fought with determined courage and contested every inch of ground. Here it was that the gallant Blythe, colonel of the Mississippi regiment bearing his own name, fell under my eye, pierced through the heart, while charging a battery. It was here that Brigadier-General Johnson, while leading his brigade, fell also, it was feared, mortally wounded; and General Clark, too, while cheering his command amid a shower of shot and shell, was struck down and so severely wounded in the shoulder as to disable him from further service, and compel him to turn over a command he had taken into the fight with such distinguished gallantry; and here also fell many officers of lesser grade, among them the gallant Captain Marshal T. Polk, of Polk's battery (who lost a leg), as well as a large number of privates, who sealed their devotion to our cause with their blood.

We, nevertheless, drove the enemy before us, dislodged him from his strong positions, and captured two of his batteries; one of them was taken by the Thirteenth Regiment of Tennessee Volunteers, commanded by Colonel Vaughan; the other by the One Hundred and Fifty-fourth (senior) Regiment, Tennessee Volunteers, commanded by Colonel Preston Smith; the former of Colonel Russell's and the latter of General Johnson's brigade.

Death of General Albert Sidney Johnston.

After these successes the enemy retired in the direction of the river, and while they were being pressed I sought out General Bragg, to whose support I had been ordered, and asked him where he would have my command. He replied, "If you will take care of the center, I will go to the right." It was understood that General Hardee was attending to the left. I accepted the arrangement, and took charge of the operations in that part of the general line for the rest of the day. It was fought by three of my brigades only—General Stewart's, General Johnson's (afterward Colonel Preston Smith's) and Colonel Russell's. My fourth brigade, that of Colonel Maney, under the command of General Cheatham, was on the right, with Generals Bragg and Breckinridge. These three brigades, with occasionally a regiment of some other corps, which became detached, were fully employed in the field assigned me. They fought over the same ground three times, as the fortunes of the day varied, always with steadiness (a single instance only excepted, and that only for a moment), and with occasional instances of brilliant courage. Such was the case of the Thirty-third Regiment, Tennessee Volunteers, under Colonel A. W. Campbell, and the Fifth Tennessee, under Lieutenant-Colonel C. D. Venable, both for the moment under command of Colonel Campbell.

Shortly after they were first brought forward as a supporting force they found themselves ordered to support two regiments of the line before them, which were lying down and engaging the enemy irregularly. On advancing they drew the enemy's fire over the heads of the regiments in their front. It was of so fierce a character that they must either advance or fall back. Campbell called to the regiments before him to charge. This they declined to do. He then gave orders to his own regiments to charge, and led them in gallant style over the heads of the regiments lying in advance of him, sweeping the enemy before him and putting them completely to rout.

In this charge Colonel Campbell was severely wounded, but still retained his command.

Such, also, was the charge made by the Fourth Tennessee, Lieutenant-Colonel Strahl. This was against a battery of heavy guns, which was making sad havoc in our ranks, and was well supported by a large infantry force.

In reply to an inquiry by their cool and determined brigade commander, General Stewart, "Can you take that battery?" their colonel said, "We will try;" and at the order Forward, they moved at a double-quick to within thirty paces of the enemy's guns, halted, delivered one round, and with a yell charged the battery, and captured several prisoners and every gun. These prisoners reported their battery was supported by four Ohio and three Illinois regiments.

It was a brilliant achievement, but an expensive one. In making the charge the regiment lost thirty-one killed on the spot and one hundred and fifty wounded; yet it illustrated and sustained the reputation for heroism of the gallant State of which it was a representative.

About 3 o'clock intelligence reached me that the commander-in-chief (General Johnston) had fallen. He fell in the discharge of his duty, leading and directing his troops. His loss was deeply felt. It was an event which deprived the army of his clear, practical judgment and determined character, and himself of an opportunity which he had coveted for vindicating his claims to the confidence of his countrymen against the inconsiderate and unjust reproaches which had been heaped upon him. The moral influence of his presence had, nevertheless, been already impressed upon the army, and an impulse given to its action, which the news of his death increased instead of abated. The operations of the day had now become so far developed as to foreshadow the result with a good degree of certainty, and it was a melancholy fate to be cut off when victory seemed hastening to perch upon his standard. He was a true soldier, high-toned, eminently honorable and just, considerate of the rights and feelings of others, magnanimous and brave. His military capacity was also of a high order, and his devotion to the cause of the South unsurpassed by that of any of her many noble sons who have offered up their lives on her altar. I knew him well from boyhood—none knew him better—and I take pleasure in laying on his tomb, as a parting offering, this testimonial of my appreciation of his character as a soldier, a patriot and a man.

The enemy in our front was gradually and successively driven from his positions and forced from the field back on the river bank.

About 5 P. M. my line attacked the enemy's troops—the last that were left upon the field—in an encampment on my right. The attack was made in front and flank. The resistance was sharp, but short. The enemy, perceiving he was flanked and his position completely turned, hoisted the white flag and surrendered. It proved to be the commands of Generals Prentiss and William H. L. Wallace; the latter, who commanded the left of their line, was killed by the troops of General Bragg, who was pressing him at the same time from that quarter. The former yielded to the attack of my troops on their right, and delivered his sword with his command to Colonel Russell, one of my brigade commanders, who turned him over to me. The prisoners turned over were about two thousand. They were placed in charge of Lieutenant Richmond, my aid-de-camp, and, with a detachment of cavalry, sent to the rear. I take pleasure in saying that in this part of the operations of my troops they were aided by the Crescent regiment of Louisiana, Colonel M. L. Smith.

This command was composed chiefly of young men from the city of New Orleans, and belonged to General Bragg's corps. It had been posted on the left wing in the early part of the day, to hold an important position, where it was detained, and did not reach the field until a late hour. On arriving it came to the point at which I was commanding and reported to me for orders. The conduct of this regiment during the whole afternoon was distinguished for its gallantry both before and after the capture of the command of General Prentiss, in which it actively participated.

Immediately after the surrender I ordered Colonel

Lindsay, in command of one of the regiments of cavalry belonging to my corps, to take command of all the cavalry at hand and pursue such of the enemy as were fleeing. He detached Lieutenant-Colonel Miller, of his own regiment, on that service immediately, while he proceeded to collect and take charge of other commands. Colonel Miller dashed forward and intercepted a battery within one hundred and fifty yards of the river—the Second Michigan—and captured it before it could unlimber and open fire. It was a six-gun battery, complete in all its equipments, and was captured—men, horses and guns. A portion of this cavalry rode to the river and watered their horses.

By this time the troops under my command were joined by those of Generals Bragg and Breckinridge, and my fourth brigade, under General Cheatham, from the right. The field was clear; the rest of the forces of the enemy were driven to the river and under its banks. We had one hour or more of daylight still left; were within from one hundred and fifty to four hundred yards of the enemy's position, and nothing seemed wanting to complete the most brilliant victory of the war but to press forward and make a vigorous assault on the demoralized remnant of his forces.

At this juncture his gunboats dropped down the river, near the landing, where his troops were collected, and opened a tremendous cannonade of shot and shell over the bank in the direction from where our forces were approaching. The height of the plain on which we were, above the level of the water, was about one hundred feet, so that it was necessary to give great elevation to his guns to enable him to fire over the bank. The consequence was that shot could take effect only at points remote from the river's edge. They were comparatively harmless to our troops nearest the bank, and became increasingly so as we drew near the enemy and placed him between us and his boats.

Here the impression arose that our forces were waging an unequal contest; that they were exhausted and suffering from a murderous fire; and by an order from the commanding general they were withdrawn from the field.

One of my divisions (that of General Clark), consisting of Stewart's and Russell's brigades, now under the command of General Stewart, bivouacked on the ground with the rest of the troops, and were among the first to engage the enemy on the following morning. They were actively engaged during the day, and sustained the reputation they had won the day before.

The other division, under General Cheatham—a brigade of which was separated from me at an early hour on the 6th, and was fought throughout the day with a skill and courage which always distinguishes that gallant officer—was moved by him to his camp of the night before. They were taken there to obtain rations and to prepare for the work of the following day. Hearing they had gone thither, I informed General Beauregard I should follow them, to insure their being on the ground at an early hour in the morning. This I did, and gave orders that night in person to General Cheatham to be ready to move at daylight. Before day I dispatched my aid-de-camp (Lieutenant Richmond) to put them in motion.

Their march was stopped for some time, to arrest a stampede which came from the front. They then moved, under the command of General Cheatham, to the field. I sent forward a staff officer to General Beauregard to inform him of their approach, and was directed to post them in the rear of Shiloh Church and hold them until further ordered. This was about 8 A. M.

It was not long before an order from the commanding general was received to move these troops to the support of the line in my front. They were formed in line of battle and moved forward half a mile to the position held by General Breckinridge. Finding he was able to hold his position without assistance, they were moved by the left flank past Shiloh Church to form on left of our line. Here they were formed, under the supervision of General Cheatham, immediately in front of a very large force of the enemy, now pressing vigorously to turn our left flank. They engaged the enemy so soon as they were formed, and fought him for four hours one of the most desperately contested conflicts of the battle. The enemy was driven gradually from his position, and, though re-enforced several times during the engagement, he could make no impression on that part of our line.

During this engagement the command of General Cheatham was re-enforced by a Louisiana brigade under Colonel Gibson, the Thirty-third Tennessee, under Colonel Campbell, and the Twenty-seventh Tennessee under Major Love, all of whom did admirable service, and the last fell mortally wounded. Colonel Preston Smith, commanding a brigade, was at the same time severely wounded, but retained his command.

This force maintained the position it had held for so many hours up to 2:30 o'clock, the time at which orders were received from the general commanding to withdraw the troops from the field. I gave orders accordingly, and the command was retired slowly and in good order in the direction of our camp, the enemy making no advance whatever. In the operations of this morning, as well as the day before, those of my troops who acted under the immediate orders of Major-General Cheatham bore themselves with conspicuous gallantry. One charge particularly was made under the eye of the commander in chief and his staff, and drew forth expressions of the most unqualified applause.

The conduct of the troops of my corps, both officers and men, was of the most gratifying character; many of them had never been under fire before, and one company of artillery—that of Captain Stanford—from the scarcity of ammunition, had never before heard the report of their own guns. Yet, from that facility which distinguishes our Southern people, under the inspiration of the cause which animates them, they fought with the steadiness and gallantry of well-trained troops. The fact that the corps lost within a fraction of one-third of its number in killed and wounded attests the nature of the service in which it was engaged.

Battle of Shiloh. A Section of the Field.

To my division commanders, Major-General Cheatham and Brigadier-General Clark, I feel greatly indebted for their cordial co-operation and efficient support; also to Brigadier-Generals Stewart and Johnson, and Colonels Russell, Maney, Stephens and Preston Smith, commanders of brigades.

My obligations are due to my personal and general staff; to Major George Williamson, my adjutant-general, who had his horse shot under him and was himself wounded; to my inspector-general, Lieutenant-Colonel Blake; to my chief of artillery, Major Bankhead; to Captain Champneys, my chief of ordnance, to whom I am indebted for taking off from the field thirteen of the fourteen guns reported by the general commanding to have been secured by the army from the enemy; also to my aids-de-camp, Lieutenants W. B. Richmond and A. H. Polk; also to Lieutenants Spence, Lanier Rawle and W. M. Porter, who acted on my staff during the battle.

Above all, I feel I am indebted to Almighty God for the courage with which He inspired our troops, and for the protection and defense with which He covered our heads in the day of battle. L. POLK, *Major-General,*

Commanding First Corps, Army of the Mississippi.

ORGANIZATION OF THE ARMY OF THE MISSISSIPPI, APRIL 6 AND 7, 1862, AT THE BATTLE OF SHILOH.

K.—Killed. *M. W.*—Mortally Wounded. *W.*—Wounded.

FIRST CORPS.*

Major-General Leonidas Polk.

FIRST DIVISION.

Brigadier-General Charles Clark (*w*).

FIRST BRIGADE.

Colonel R. M. Russell.

Eleventh Louisiana—(1) Colonel S. F. Marks (*w*); (2) Lieutenant-Colonel R. H. Barrow.
Twelfth Tennessee—Lieutenant-Colonel T. H. Bell.
Thirteenth Tennessee — Lieutenant - Colonel A. J. Vaughan, Jr.
Twenty-second Tennessee—(1) Colonel T. J. Freeman (*w*); (2) Lieutenant-Colonel Stewart (*w*).
Bankhead's battery—Captain S. B. Bankhead.

SECOND BRIGADE.

Brigadier-General A. P. Stewart.

Thirteenth Arkansas—(1) Lieutenant-Colonel A. D. Grayson (*k*); (2) Major J. A. McNeely (*w*); (3) Colonel J. C. Tappan.
Fourth Tennessee—(1) Colonel Rufus P. Neely; (2) Lieutenant-Colonel O. F. Stiahl.
Fifth Tennessee—Lieutenant-Colonel C. D. Venable.
Thirty-third Tennessee—Colonel A. W. Campbell.
Stanford's battery—Captain T. T. Stanford.

SECOND DIVISION.

Brigadier-General B. F. Cheatham.

FIRST BRIGADE.

(1) Brigadier-General B. R. Johnson (*w*); (2) Colonel Preston Smith (*w*).
Mississippi Battalion—(1) Colonel A. K. Blythe (*k*); (2) Lieutenant-Colonel D. Herron (*k*); (3) Major Moore.
Second Tennessee—Colonel J. Knox Walker.
Fifteenth Tennessee—(1) Lieutenant-Colonel R. C. Tyler (*w*); (2) Major Hearn.
One hundred and Fifty-fourth Tennessee (senior)—(1) Colonel Preston Smith (*w*); (2) Lieutenant-Colonel Marcus J. Wright.
Polk's battery—Captain W. T. Polk (*w*).

SECOND BRIGADE.

(1) Colonel W. H. Stephens; (2) Colonel Geo. Maney.
Seventh Kentucky—Colonel Chas. Wickliffe (*m w*).
First Tennessee—Colonel Geo. Maney.
Sixth Tennessee—(1) Lieutenant-Colonel T. P. Jones; (2) Colonel W. H. Stephens.
Ninth Tennessee—Colonel Henry L. Douglass.
Smith's battery—Captain M. Smith.

SECOND CORPS.

Major-General Braxton Bragg.

FIRST DIVISION.

Brigadier-General Daniel Ruggles.

FIRST BRIGADE.

Colonel R. L. Gibson.

First Arkansas—Colonel James F. Fagan.
Fourth Louisiana—Colonel H. W. Allen (*w*).
Thirteenth Louisiana—(1) Major A. P. Avegno (*m w*); (2) Captain E. M. Dubroca.
Ninteenth Louisiana—Colonel B. L. Hodge.
Bain's battery—Captain M. Bain.

SECOND BRIGADE.

Brigadier-General Patton Anderson.

First Florida (battalion)—(1) Major T. A. McDonell (*w*); (2) Captain W. G. Poole; (3) Captain W. C. Bird.
Seventeenth Louisiana—(1) Lieutenant-Colonel Charles Jones (*w*); (2) Colonel S. S. Heard.
Twentieth Louisiana—Colonel August Richard.
Ninth Texas—Colonel W. A. Stanley.
Confederate Guards Response Battalion (two companies)—Major F. H. Clack.
Hodgson's battery—Captain W. I. Hodgson

THIRD BRIGADE.†

Colonel Preston Pond, Jr.

Sixteenth Louisiana—Major Daniel Gober (*w*).
Eighteenth Louisiana—Colonel Alfred Mouton (*w*).
Thirty-eighth Tennessee—Colonel A. F. Looney.
Crescent (Louisiana) Regiment—Colonel Marshall J. Smith.
Ketchum's battery—Captain W. H. Ketchum.

SECOND DIVISION.

Brigadier-General Jones M. Withers.

FIRST BRIGADE.

(1) Brigadier-General A. H. Gladden (*k*); (2) Colonel D. W. Adams (*w*); (3) Colonel Z. C. Deas (*w*); (4) Colonel J. Q. Loomis.

Twenty-first Alabama — Lieutenant - Colonel S. W. Cayce.
Twenty-second Alabama—(1) Colonel Z. C. Deas (*w*); (2) Lieutenant-Colonel J. Q. Marrast.
Twenty-fifth Alabama—(1) Colonel J. Q. Loomis; (2) Major J. D. Johnston.
Twenty-sixth Alabama—(1) Colonel Coltart (*w*); (2) Lieutenant-Colonel W. D. Chadick.
First Louisiana—(1) Colonel D. W. Adams (*w*); (2) Major F. H. Farrar.
Battery—Captain Robertson.

SECOND BRIGADE.

Brigadier-General James R. Chalmers.

Fifth Mississippi—Colonel A. E. Fant.
Seventh Mississippi—Colonel H. Mayson.
Ninth Mississippi — Lieutenant-Colonel W. A. Rankin (*k*).
Tenth Mississippi—Colonel R. A. Smith.
Fifty-second Tennessee—Colonel B. J. Lea.
Battery—Captain Gage.

THIRD BRIGADE.*

Brigadier-General J. K. Jackson.

Seventeenth Alabama—Lieutenant-Colonel Robert C. Farris.
Eighteenth Alabama—Colonel Eli D. Shorter.
Nineteenth Alabama—Colonel Joseph Wheeler.
Alabama Battalion.
Arkansas Battalion.
Second Texas—Colonel John C. Moore.
Girardeys' battery—Captain J. P. Girardeys.

THIRD CORPS.

Major-General W. J. Hardee.

FIRST BRIGADE.

(1) Brigadier-General T. C. Hindman; (2) Colonel R. G. Shaver.

Second Arkansas—(1) Colonel Govan; (2) Major R. T. Harvey; (3) Lieutenant-Colonel Patterson (*w*).
Sixth Arkansas—Colonel A. T. Hawthorn.
Seventh Arkansas—(1) Lieutenant-Colonel John M. Dean (*k*); (2) Major James T. Martin.
Third Confederate—Colonel John S. Marmaduke.
Miller's battery.
Swett's battery.

SECOND BRIGADE.†

Brigadier-General P. R. Cleburne.

Fifteenth Arkansas—(1) Lieutenant-Colonel A. K. Patton (*k*); (2) Major J. T. Harris (*k*).
Sixth Mississippi—(1) Colonel J. J. Thornton (*w*); (2) Major Lowry.
Fifth (Thirty-fifth) Tennessee—Colonel B. J. Hill.
Twenty-third Tennessee—(1) Lieutenant-Colonel James F. Neill (*w*); (2) Lieutenant-Colonel R. Cantrell.
Twenty-fourth Tennessee—Lieutenant-Colonel Thos. H. Peebles.
Shoup's artillery battalion.‡
Watson's battery.

THIRD BRIGADE.§

Brigadier-General S. A. M. Wood.

Seventh Alabama.
Sixteenth Alabama — Lieutenant-Colonel John W. Harris.
Eighth Arkansas—Colonel W. K. Patterson.
Ninth Arkansas (battalion)—Major John H. Kelly.
Third Mississippi—Major A. B. Hardcastle.
Twenty-seventh Tennessee — (1) Lieutenant-Colonel Brown (*w*); (2) Colonel C. H. Williams (*k*); (3) Major Love (*w*).
Forty-fourth Tennessee—Colonel C. A. McDaniel (*w*).
Fifty-fifth Tennessee—Colonel McKoin.
Harper's battery (Captain Harper)—four guns.

RESERVE CORPS.

Brigadier-General J. C. Breckinridge.

FIRST BRIGADE.

Colonel R. P. Trabue.

Fourth Alabama (battalion)—Major J. M. Clifton.
Thirty-first Alabama—Lieutenant-Colonel Galbraith.
Third Kentucky—Lieutenant-Colonel Ben Anderson.
Fourth Kentucky—(1) Lieutenant-Colonel A. R. Hines (*w*), (2) Major Thomas B. Monroe (*k*).
Fifth Kentucky—Colonel Thomas H. Hunt.
Sixth Kentucky—Colonel Joseph H. Lewis.
Ninth Kentucky.
Tennessee Battalion (Crews).
Byrne's battery—Captain E. P. Byrne.
Lyon's battery—Captain Cobb.

SECOND BRIGADE.

(1) Brigadier-General J. S. Bowen (*w*); (2) Colonel John D. Martin.

Ninth Arkansas—Colonel Isaac L. Dunlop.
Tenth Arkansas—Colonel T. D. Merrick.
Second Confederate—(1) Colonel John D. Martin; (2) Major Mangum.
First Missouri—Lieutenant-Colonel Amos C. Riley.
Hudson's battery.

THIRD BRIGADE.

Colonel W. S. Statham.

Fifteenth Mississippi—Colonel W. S. Statham.
Twenty-second Mississippi.
Nineteenth Tennessee—Colonel D. Cummings.
Twentieth Tennessee.
Twenty-eighth Tennessee.
Forty-fifth Tennessee.
Rutledge's battery.

CAVALRY.

——— Regiment—Colonel N. B. Forrest (*w*).
Mississippi Regiment—Colonel A. J. Lindsay.
Alabama Regiment—Colonel Clanton.
Texas Regiment—Colonel John A. Wharton (*w*).
——— Squadron—Lieutenant-Colonel R. A. Brewer.
Kentucky Squadron (three companies)—Major John H. Morgan.
Kentucky Company—Captain Phil Thompson.
Four Companies—Captains Jenkins, Tomlinson, Cox and Robins.

NOTE—Wharton's Texas Rangers, Clanton's regiment and McClung's battery, not accounted for above, are accounted for in the reports.

* The First Mississippi Cavalry, Brewer's Battalion and Cox's, Jenkins', Lindsay's, Robins' and Tomlinson's cavalry, not accounted for in this table, appear from the reports to have belonged to Polk's corps.

† The Orleans Guard Battalion also belonged to this brigade.

* The Forty-seventh Tennessee, Colonel Hill, arrived on the field on the 7th; the Alabama and Arkansas battalions of the Third Brigade, Wither's division, not in the battle.

† The Second Tennessee, Colonel Bate, was also in this brigade; the other "Second Tennessee" was in the First Corps.

‡ Calvert's and Trigg's batteries, according to Cleburne's report, and Hubbard's battery, according to Thrall's statement.

§ A company of Georgia dragoons, Captain Isaac W. Avery, also in this brigade.

LIST OF FLAGS CAPTURED AT THE BATTLE OF SHILOH.

HEADQUARTERS ARMY OF THE MISSISSIPPI,
CORINTH, MISS., April 23, 1862.

5 Blue silk Regimental colors.
20 Federal flags.
1 Garrison flag.
2 Guidons.

THOMAS JORDAN,
Acting Assistant Adjutant-General.

LIST OF KILLED AND WOUNDED AT THE BATTLE OF SHILOH, APRIL 6 AND 7, 1862.

COMMAND.	Killed.	Wounded.	Missing.
FIRST CORPS. MAJOR-GENERAL LEONIDAS POLK.			
FIRST DIVISION. Brigadier-General Charles Clark.			
First Brigade—Colonel R. M. Russell	97	512	..
Second Brigade—Brigadier-General A. P. Stewart	93	421	3
SECOND DIVISION. Major-General B. F. Cheatham.			
First Brigade—Brigadier-General B. R. Johnson	120	607	13
Second Brigade—Colonel W. H. Stephens	75	413	3
Total, First Corps	385	1,953	19
SECOND CORPS. MAJOR-GENERAL BRAXTON BRAGG.			
FIRST DIVISION. Brigadier-General Daniel Ruggles			
First Brigade—Colonel R. L. Gibson	97	488	97
Second Brigade—Brigadier-General Patton Anderson	69	313	52
Third Brigade—Colonel Preston Pond	89	336	169
SECOND DIVISION. Brigadier-General J. M. Withers.			
First Brigade—Brigadier-General A. H. Gladden	129	597	103
Second Brigade—Brigadier-General J. R. Chalmers	83	343	19
Third Brigade—Brigadier-General J. K. Jackson	86	364	194
Total, Second Corps	553	2,441	634

LIST OF KILLED AND WOUNDED AT THE BATTLE OF SHILOH, APRIL 6 AND 7, 1862.—Continued.

COMMAND.	Killed.	Wounded.	Missing.
THIRD CORPS. MAJOR-GENERAL W. J. HARDEE.			
First Brigade—Brigadier-General T. C. Hindman	109	546	38
Second Brigade—Brigadier-General P. R. Cleburne	188	790	65
Third Brigade—Brigadier-General S. A. M. Wood	107	600	38
Total, Third Corps	404	1,936	141
RESERVE CORPS. BRIGADIER-GENERAL J. C. BRECKINRIDGE.			
First (Kentucky) Brigade—Colonel R. P. Trabue	151	557	92
Second Brigade—Brigadier-General J. S. Bowen	98	498	28
Third Brigade—Colonel W. S. Statham	137	627	45
Total, Reserve Corps	386	1,682	165
Grand Total	1,728	8,012	959

THOMAS JORDAN, *Assistant Adjutant-General.*

ONE of the quiet boroughs of Pennsylvania was suddenly thrown into a state of excitement by a report, afterward ascertained to be false, that Stuart's cavalry were within a few miles of town. During this excitement the burgess, a very ignorant and illiterate man, issued a proclamation, of which the following is a copy: "Fellow cidens, I order yous to take up armes to defend our borow, so I order yous to take up armes amedly, and so do not delay. By order of the Burgess, Peter Van Brunt, Burgess."

A COMPANY of Confederate soldiers, bound for Chattanooga, on the cars, were indulging in some Munchausen stories of the war. One had seen a man shot through the head, and *he lived;* another had seen a soldier whose arms and legs had been carried away, and *he lived;* a third had known a man to be shot in the side and through the head, and *he lived;* and the fourth had seen a man shot clean through the body by a ten-pound cannon ball, and — "He lived?" asked his listening comrades. "No," quietly responded the narrator, "*he died.*"

[F]

FIELD RETURN OF THE CONFEDERATE FORCES THAT MARCHED FROM CORINTH TO THE TENNESSEE RIVER, APRIL 3, 1862.

COMMAND.	PRESENT.											ABSENT.								Present and Absent.	
	For Duty.		Sick.		Extra Duty.		In Arrest.		Effective Total	Total	Aggregate	Detached Duty.		With Leave.		Without Leave.		Sick.			
	Officers	Enlisted Men	Officers	Enlisted Men	Officers	Enlisted Men	Officers	Enlisted Men				Officers	Enlisted Men	Officers	Enlisted Men	Officers	Enlisted Men	Officers	Enlisted Men	Total	Aggregate
INFANTRY.																					
First Corps	561	8,440	148	1,343	18	548	5	36	9,024	10,367	10,999	26	152	73	922	30	408	9	60	11,909	12,679
Second Corps	1,000	14,590	41	3,569	23	624	3	42	14,868	18,435	19,564	48	432	111	2 288	9	481	3	85	22,071	23,371
Third Corps	339	4,108	41	811	8	439	5	4	4,545	5,365	5,750	13	159	22	81	1	255	46	942	6,988	7,462
Reserve Corps	479	6,132	64	1,000	11	151	2	7	6,290	7,290	7,846	10	137	60	653	5	153	71	887	9,120	9,822
Total Infantry	2,379	33,270	294	6,723	60	1,762	15	89	34,727	41,457	44,159	97	880	266	4,144	45	1,297	129	1,974	50,088	53,334
ARTILLERY.																					
First Corps	20	331		34	..	10	..	5	398	432	452	..	3	2	37	1	5	..	..	480	501
Second Corps	28	661	1	109	..	..	..	..	661	770	779	..	..	4	99	..	..	..	..	869	902
Third Corps	16	284	1	28	2	23	..	3	310	338	457	1	1	..	1	..	5	1	37	380	405
Reserve Corps	19	581	2	39	1	18	..	5	604	643	665	1	7	..	10	..	11	3	81	752	778
Total Artillery	83	1,857	4	210	3	51	..	13	1,973	2,183	2,353	2	11	6	147	1	21	4	118	2,481	2,586
Cavalry	125	1,884	13	712	8	187	1	2	2,073	2,785	2,932	14	359	1	57	..	16	19	466	3,683	3,854
Grand Total	2,587	37,011	311	7,645	71	2,000	16	104	38,773	46,425	49,444	113	1,250	273	4,348	46	1,334	152	2,558	56,252	59,774

NOTE.—Colonel Hill's regiment (Tennessee) came upon the field during the engagement on Monday.

Respectfully submitted and forwarded,

June 30, 1862.

BRAXTON BRAGG, *General Commanding.*

[G]

FIELD RETURN OF THE ARMY OF THE MISSISSIPPI AFTER THE BATTLE OF SHILOH, APRIL 10, 1862.

COMMAND.	PRESENT.											ABSENT.								Present and Absent.	
	For Duty.		Sick.		Extra Duty.		In Arrest.		Effective Total	Total	Aggregate	Detached Duty.		With Leave.		Without Leave.		Sick.			
	Officers	Enlisted Men	Officers	Enlisted Men	Officers	Enlisted Men	Officers	Enlisted Men				Officers	Enlisted Men	Officers	Enlisted Men	Officers	Enlisted Men	Officers	Enlisted Men	Total	Aggregate
INFANTRY.																					
First Corps	461	7,198	93	1,828	2	378	4	10	7,582	9,414	9,974	34	274	122	1,224	18	544	86	1,426	12,855	13,671
Second Corps	590	8,453	277	4,748	23	628	5	35	9,118	13,866	14,761	46	455	80	1,440	9	370	67	1,065	17,196	18,293
Third Corps	425	4,305	144	2,301	9	559	2	1	4,865	7,166	7,746	27	227	56	959	5	820	47	1,303	10,475	11,190
Reserve Corps	379	4,334	94	1,475	10	491	2	7	5,232	6,707	7,192	26	238	90	1,455	5	702	110	1,887	10,989	11,705
Total Infantry	1,855	24,290	608	10,352	44	2,056	13	53	26,797	37,153	39,673	133	1,194	348	5,078	37	2,436	310	5,681	51,515	54,859
ARTILLERY.																					
First Corps	18	386	1	99	..	..	..	..	390	489	504	6	2	2	39	..	20	5	58	608	636
Second Corps	19	487	4	210	1	15	..	1	504	714	738	1	5	..	13	..	3	2	70	805	832
Third Corps	8	272	3	60	..	12	1	..	284	344	356	..	1	1	7	..	..	5	47	399	417
Reserve Corps	25	489	1	44	..	15			504	548	574	1	10	1	34	..	46	3	65	703	734
Total Artillery	70	1,634	9	413	1	42	1	1	1,682	2,095	2,172	8	18	4	93	..	69	15	240	2,515	2,619
Cavalry	259	3,584	42	1,507	5	248	2	1	3,833	5,340	5,648	33	527	48	691	3	155	17	228	6,931	7,022
Grand Total	2,184	29,508	659	12,272	50	2,346	16	55	32,312	44,588	47,493	174	1,739	400	5,862	40	2,660	342	6,149	60,961	64,500

NOTE.—The difference in aggregates and totals between this and the preceding return is accounted for thus: First, by killed, wounded and missing in battle, and the arrival of Carroll's brigade and a portion of the cavalry heretofore detached.

Respectfully submitted and forwarded,

June 30, 1862.

BRAXTON BRAGG, *General Commanding.*

[E]

FIELD RETURN OF THE ARMY OF THE MISSISSIPPI BEFORE AND AFTER THE BATTLE OF SHILOH.

COMMAND.	COMMANDER.	Effective Total Before Battle.*	Effective Total After Battle.*	REMARKS.
First Army Corps	Major-General L. Polk	9,136	6,779	Casualties in the battle of Shiloh: Killed, 1,728; Wounded, 8,012; Missing, 959.
Second Army Corps	Major-General Braxton Bragg	13,589	9,961	
Third Army Corps	Major-General W. J. Hardee	6,789	4,609	
Reserve	Brig.-Gen. J. C. Breckinridge	6,439	4,206	
Total infantry and artillery		35,953	25,555	
Cavalry	Brigadier-General F. Gardner	4,382	4,081	The battlefield was so thickly wooded that the cavalry was useless and could not operate.
Grand total		40,335	29,636	

* These columns do not agree with the effective totals in Reports F and G.

OPERATIONS IN THE SHENANDOAH VALLEY,

MAY 15 TO JUNE 1, 1862,

INCLUDING BATTLES OF

FRONT ROYAL AND WINCHESTER, VA.

BY

LIEUTENANT-GENERAL T. J. JACKSON.

HEADQUARTERS OF SECOND CORPS,
ARMY OF NORTHERN VIRGINIA,
April 10, 1863.

I RETURNED to McDowell on May 14, 1862, from the pursuit of Generals Milroy and Schenck toward Franklin. On the following day I crossed the Shenandoah Mountain, and encamped that night near the Lebanon White Sulphur Springs. Here the troops were halted for a short rest after their fatiguing marches, to enable them to attend divine service and to observe the fast recommended by the proclamation of the President of the Confederate States.

On the 17th the march was resumed toward Harrisonburg. In the meantime, while the pursuit of the Federal troops west of the Shenandoah Mountain was in progress, General Banks had fallen back to Strasburg, which position, it was understood, he was fortifying. We moved from Harrisonburg down the Valley Turnpike to New Market, in the vicinity of which a junction was effected with Ewell's division, which had marched from Elk Run Valley. Leaving the Valley Turnpike at New Market, we moved via Luray toward Front Royal, with the hope of being able to capture or disperse the garrison at the latter place and get in the rear of Banks or compel him to abandon his fortifications at Strasburg.

To conceal my movements as far as possible from the enemy, Brigadier-General Ashby, who had remained in front of Banks during the march against Milroy, was directed to continue to hold that position until the following day, when he was to join the main body, leaving, however, a covering force sufficient to prevent information of our movements crossing our lines. My command at this time embraced Ashby's cavalry; the First Brigade, under General Winder; the Second Brigade, Colonel Campbell commanding; the Third Brigade, Colonel Fulkerson commanding; the troops recently under command of Brigadier-General Edward Johnson; the division of General Ewell, comprising the brigades of Generals Elzey, Taylor, Trimble; and the Maryland Line, consisting of the First Maryland Regiment and Brockenbrough's battery, under Brigadier-General George H. Stewart; and the Second and Sixth Virginia cavalry, under Colonel Flournoy. On Thursday, the 22d, my entire command moved down the road leading from Luray to Front Royal, the advance (under General Ewell) bivouacking about ten miles from the last-named place.

Moving at dawn on Friday, the 23d, and diverging to the right, so as to fall into the Gooney Manor Road, we encountered no opposition until we came within one and a half miles of Front Royal, when, about 2 P. M., the enemy's pickets were driven in by our advance, which was ordered to follow rapidly. The First Maryland Regiment, supported by Wheat's battalion of Louisiana Volunteers, and the remainder of Taylor's brigade, acting as a reserve, pushed forward in gallant style, charging the Federals, who made a spirited resistance, driving them through the town and taking some prisoners.

The main force of the enemy now retired a short distance beyond Front Royal, and took position on a commanding height, to the right of the turnpike. From this point they opened rifled artillery upon our troops as they advanced beyond the town.

Colonel Crutchfield, chief of artillery, placed some rifled guns in position to dislodge them, and the Sixth Louisiana Regiment was moved to the left, through the woods, to flank their battery; but in the meantime Wheat's battalion, Major Wheat, and the First Maryland Regiment, Colonel Bradley T. Johnson, advancing more directly, and driving in their skirmishers, the Federals retreated across both forks of the Shenandoah, attempting in their retreat to burn the bridge over the North Fork; but before they could fully accomplish their purpose our troops were upon them and extinguished the flames, crossed the river, the enemy in full retreat toward Winchester, and our artillery and infantry in pursuit.

The cavalry, under General Ashby and Colonel Thomas S. Flournoy, had crossed the South Fork of the Shenandoah at McCoy's Ford, above the enemy's position, for the purpose of destroying the railroad and telegraphic communication between Front Royal and Strasburg, and also to check the advance of any re-enforcements from Strasburg or the retreat of any portion of the enemy in that direction from Front Royal. Colonel Flournoy kept a short distance west of that river, and, having executed his orders, was now in readiness to join in pursuit of the retreating Federals. Delayed by difficulties at the bridge over the North Fork, which the Federals had made an effort to burn, Colonel Flourney pushed on with Companies A, B, E and K of the Sixth Virginia cavalry, and came up with a body of the enemy near Cedarville, about five miles from Front Royal. This Federal force consisted of two companies of cavalry, two pieces of artillery, the First (Federal) Regiment Maryland Infantry, and two companies of Pennsylvania infantry, which had been posted there to check our pursuit.

Dashing into the midst of them, Captain Grimsley, of Company B, in the advance, these four companies drove the Federals from their position, who soon, however, re-formed in an orchard on the right of the turnpike, when a second gallant and decisive charge being made upon them, the enemy's cavalry was put to flight, the artillery abandoned, and the infantry, now thrown into great confusion, surrendered themselves prisoners of war.

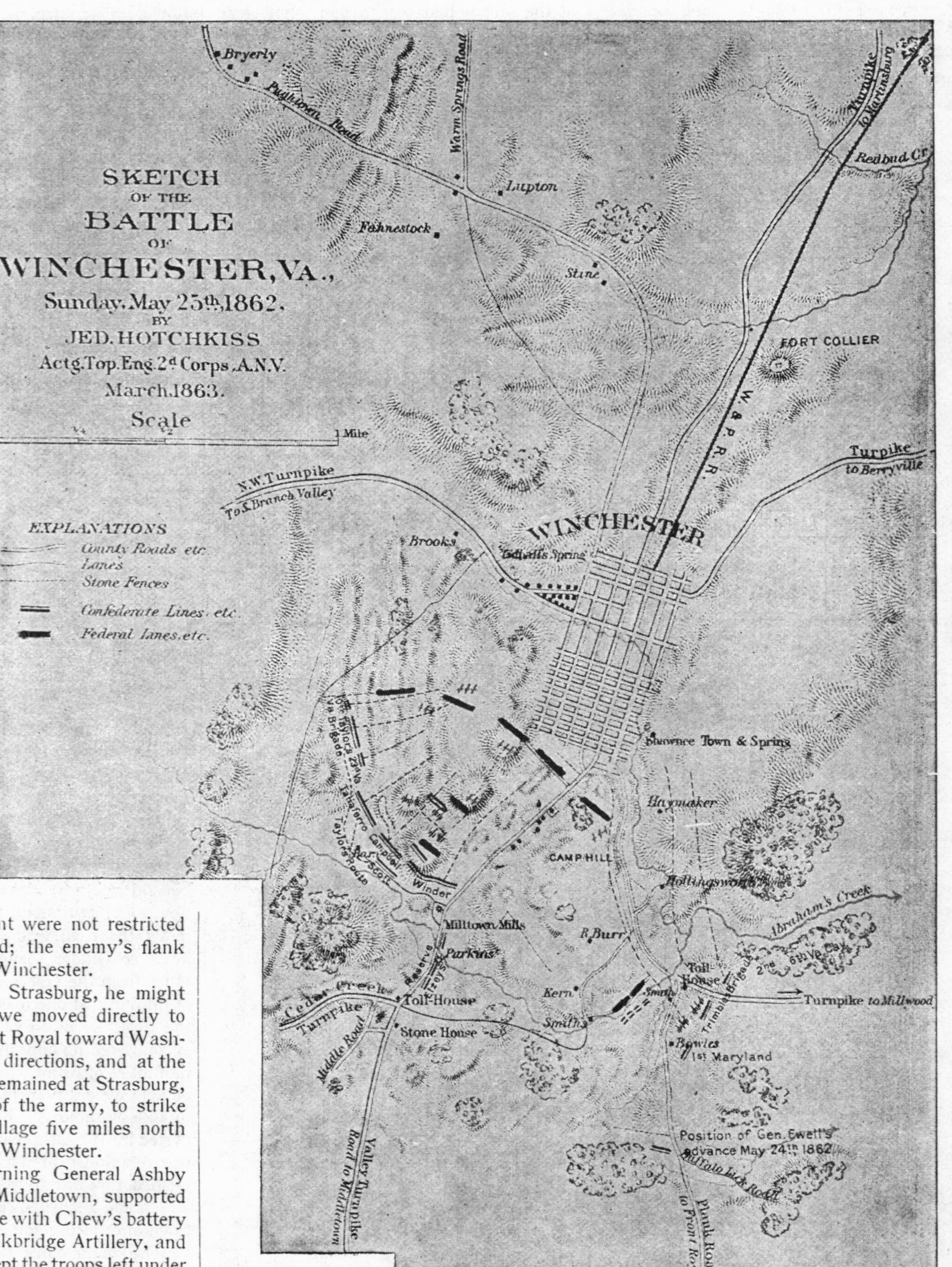

In this successful pursuit our loss was twenty-six killed and wounded. Among the killed was Captain Baxter, of Company K, while gallantly leading his men in the charge.

While these occurrences were in progress General Ashby, who, after crossing at McCoy's Ford, had moved with his command further to the west, so as to skirt the base of the Mossanutten Mountain, met with a body of the enemy posted as a guard at Buckton in a strong position, protected by the railroad embankment. Ashby drove back and dispersed the enemy, but with the loss of some of the most valuable of his followers, among them Captains Sheetz and Fletcher. The infantry and artillery pursued but a short distance before darkness rendered it necessary to go into camp.

The results of this first day's operations were the capture of about seven hundred prisoners, among them about twenty officers, a complete section of rifled artillery (10-pounder Parrotts), and a very large amount of quartermaster and commissary stores. The fruits of this movement were not restricted to the stores and prisoners captured; the enemy's flank was turned and the road opened to Winchester.

In the event of Banks leaving Strasburg, he might escape toward the Potomac, or, if we moved directly to Winchester, he might move via Front Royal toward Washington city. In order to watch both directions, and at the same time advance upon him if he remained at Strasburg, I determined, with the main body of the army, to strike the turnpike near Middletown, a village five miles north of Strasburg, and thirteen south of Winchester.

Accordingly, the following morning General Ashby advanced from Cedarville toward Middletown, supported by skirmisher's from Taylor's brigade with Chew's battery and two Parrott guns from the Rockbridge Artillery, and followed by the whole command, except the troops left under command of General Ewell near Cedarville. General Ewell, with Trimble's brigade, the First Maryland Regiment and the batteries of Brockenbrough and Courtney, had instructions to move toward Winchester. Ashby was directed to keep scouts on his left to prevent Banks from passing unobserved by Front Royal. Brigadier-General George H. Stewart, who was now temporarily in command of the Second and Sixth Virginia cavalry, had been previously dispatched to Newtown, a point further north, and nine miles from Winchester, with instructions to observe the movements of the enemy at that point. He there succeeded in capturing some prisoners and several wagons and ambulances, with arms and medical stores. He also advised me of movements which indicated that Banks was preparing to leave Strasburg. I accompanied the movement of the main body of the army to Middletown. Upon arriving there we found the Valley Turnpike crowded with the retreating Federal cavalry, upon which the batteries of Poague and Chew, with Taylor's infantry, promptly opened, and in a few moments the turnpike, which had just before teemed with life, presented a most appalling spectacle of carnage and destruction. The road was literally obstructed with the mingled and confused mass of struggling and dying horses and riders. The Federal column was pierced, but what proportion of its strength had passed north toward Winchester I had then no means of knowing. Among the surviving cavalry the wildest confusion ensued, and they scattered in disorder in various directions, leaving, however, some two hundred prisoners, with their equipments, in our hands. A train of wagons was seen disappearing in the distance toward Winchester, and Ashby, with his cavalry, some artillery and a supporting infantry force from Taylor's brigade, was sent in pursuit.

But a few moments elapsed before the Federal artillery, which had been cut off with the rear of the column, opened upon us with the evident intention of cutting its way through to Winchester. Our batteries were soon placed in position to return the fire, and General Taylor was ordered with his command to the attack. After a spirited resistance this fragment of the Federal army retreated to Strasburg, and from thence made its escape through the mountains across the Potomac. A large amount of baggage fell into our hands at this point. Entire regiments, apparently in line of battle, had laid down their knapsacks and abandoned them.

Having become satisfied that the main body of Banks' army had already passed this point on its way to Winchester, our troops, which had been halted, moved on in pursuit in that direction. The large number of wagons loaded with stores and abandoned by the enemy between Middletown and Newtown plainly indicated his hurried retreat. From the attack upon Front Royal up to the present moment every opposition had been borne down, and there was reason to believe, if Banks reached Winchester, it would be without a train, if not without an army; but in the midst of these hopes I was pained to see, as I am now to record the fact, that so many of Ashby's command, both cavalry and infantry, forgetful of their high trust as the advance of a pursuing army, deserted their colors and abandoned themselves to pillage to such an extent as to make it necessary for that gallant officer to discontinue further pursuit. The artillery, which had pushed on with energy to the vicinity of Newtown, found itself, from this discreditable conduct, without a proper support from either infantry or cavalry. This relaxation in the pursuit was unfortunate, as the enemy was encouraged by it to bring up, about two hours later, four pieces of artillery, which were planted on the northern skirt of Newtown and opened upon our batteries. The fire was replied to by Captain Poague's two rifled guns with skill and accuracy.

When I overtook the advance it was thus held in check by the enemy's artillery. We were retarded until near dark, when the Federals retreated and the pursuit was renewed. As we advanced beyond Newtown the same profusion of abandoned Federal wagons loaded with stores met the eye; but we derived no benefit from this property, as the time lost during the disorder and pillage, before referred to, and the consequent delay of our advance at Newtown, enabled the enemy to make arrangements for burning them. Shortly after leaving Newtown the advance was fired upon by a body of the concealed enemy; but they were soon driven off by the Thirty-third Virginia Regiment (Colonel Neff) and the march resumed.

On reaching Bartonsville another ambuscade from the right, left and front was encountered, and heavy firing kept up for some time. In repelling this, the Twenty-seventh (Colonel Grigsby), Second (Colonel Allen) and Fifth Virginia regiments (Colonel Baylor) acquitted themselves with credit. Skirmishing continued during the night, the enemy ambuscading from point to point. So important did I deem it to occupy before dawn the heights overlooking Winchester, that the advance continued to move forward until morning, notwithstanding the darkness and other obstacles to its progress. The other troops were permitted to halt for about an hour during the night.

In the meantime Major-General Ewell, with Trimble's brigade, the First Maryland Regiment, and Stewart's cavalry, which had now joined him from Newtown, and Brockenbrough's and Courtney's batteries, was advancing to Winchester by the turnpike from Front Royal to that place, and had occupied a position about three miles from the town as early as 10 o'clock in the night, and thrown forward his picket about a mile in advance of his position.

As we approached Winchester soon after dawn the enemy's skirmishers were occupying the hill to the southwest overlooking the town. An order was given to General Winder to seize that height as speedily as possible. The Fifth Virginia Regiment (Colonel Baylor) was accordingly thrown out in advance as skirmishers, and the Second, Fourth, Twenty-seventh and Thirty-third Virginia regiments being placed in order of battle, the whole line was ordered to advance, which was done in handsome style, and the position on the crest secured, although the enemy made a resolute but unsuccessful effort to dislodge our troops from so commanding a position. Two Parrott guns from the Rockbridge artillery and the batteries of Carpenter and Cutshaw were promptly posted on the height to dislodge a battery of the enemy which was playing from the front with great animation and effect upon the hill.

At this moment a body of the enemy's sharpshooters was seen crossing the ridge to our left, between us and a battery, which soon opened an enfilade fire upon our batteries. Poague's guns were promptly turned to the left, which compelled the infantry to seek shelter behind a stone fence, from which their fire upon the cannoneers and horses was for a while very destructive. By the well-directed guns of Carpenter and Cutshaw the Federal battery in front had now become silenced, but the battery upon the left still kept up a brisk and damaging fire.

Withdrawing his battery to the left and rear, so as to

avoid the exposure under which he was severely suffering, Poague opened his guns upon the enfilading battery of the enemy. He was also directed by General Winder to throw some solid shot against the stone wall, under the shelter of which their sharpshooters were pouring a fatal fire into our ranks.

During these operations valuable officers and privates suffered; among the number, Colonel J. A. Campbell, commanding the Second Brigade, was wounded.

While the enemy's artillery was playing upon our position his infantry moved to the left, as if designing to get possession of that portion of the hill immediately to the north of us. General Taylor was ordered to advance his brigade to the left and check the movement. Promptly leaving the turnpike, he passed under cover of the hill in the rear of Winder and formed his line of battle in the face of a heavy fire of artillery and musketry from the sharpshooters, the Tenth Virginia infantry taking position upon the left and the Twenty-third Virginia on the right of his line.

Steadily and in fine order mounting the hill and there fronting the enemy, where he stood in greatest strength, the whole line magnificently swept down the declivity and across the field, driving back the Federal troops and bearing down all opposition before it. In this gallant advance all the troops of General Winder joined, except those left as supports to the batteries. This successful charge being followed by the giving way of the whole Federal army, General Elzey, who had been in reserve on the Valley Turnpike, was now ordered to pursue, and eagerly uniting in the general advance, soon entered Winchester with the other troops.

On the right the attack under General Ewell was executed with skill and spirit. The Twenty-first North Carolina and the Twenty-first Georgia gallantly drove back the advance post of the enemy. The Twenty-first North Carolina soon became exposed to a destructive fire from a Federal regiment posted behind a stone wall, and after suffering severely in both officers and men was forced to fall back. The Twenty-first Georgia, having succeeded in driving the regiment from its shelter, re-enforced its brigade.

With the First Maryland on his left and Trimble's brigade on his right, General Ewell now moved toward the eastern outskirts of the town. That advance was made about the time that Taylor's brigade was so gallantly crossing the hill and charging toward the western side of the town. This simultaneous movement on both his flanks, by which his retreat might soon have been cut off, may account for the suddenness with which the entire army gave way and for the slight resistance which it made while passing through the town. The Federal forces were now in full retreat.

As our troops, now in rapid pursuit, passed through the town, they were received with the most enthusiastic demonstrations of joy by its loyal people, who for more than two months had been suffering under the hateful surveillance and rigors of military despotism.

Notwithstanding the fatiguing marches and almost sleepless nights to which the mass of our troops had been subjected, they continued to press forward with alacrity. The Federal forces, upon falling back into the town, preserved their organization remarkably well. In passing through its streets they were thrown into confusion, and shortly after, debouching into the plain and turnpike to Martinsburg and after being fired upon by our artillery, they presented the aspect of a mass of disordered fugitives. Never have I seen an opportunity when it was in the power of cavalry to reap a richer harvest of the fruits of victory. Hoping that the cavalry would soon come up, the artillery, followed by infantry, was pressed forward for about two hours, for the purpose of preventing, by artillery fire, a reforming of the enemy; but as nothing was heard of the cavalry, and as but little or nothing could be accomplished without it in the exhausted condition of our infantry, between which and the enemy the distance was continually increasing, I ordered a halt and issued orders for going into camp and refreshing the men.

I had seen but some fifty of Ashby's cavalry since prior to the pillaging scenes of the previous evening, and none since an early hour of the past night. The Second and Sixth Virginia regiments of cavalry were under the command of Brigadier-General George H. Stewart, of Ewell's command.

About an hour after the halt of the main body had been ordered Brigadier-General George H. Stewart, with his cavalry, came up, and, renewing the pursuit, pushed forward in a highly creditable manner and succeeded in capturing a number of prisoners; but the main body of Bank's army was now beyond the reach of successful pursuit and effected its escape across the Potomac.

Before reaching Bunker Hill General Stewart was joined by General Ashby with a small portion of his cavalry. Upon my inquiring of General Ashby why he was not where I desired him at the close of the engagement, he stated that he had moved to the enemy's left for the purpose of cutting off a portion of his force. General Stewart pushed on to Martinsburg, where he captured a large amount of army stores. There is good reason for believing that, had the cavalry played its part in this pursuit as well as the four companies had done under Colonel Flournoy two days before in the pursuit from Front Royal, but a small portion of Banks' army would have made its escape to the Potomac.

On the following day (26th) divine service was held for the purpose of rendering thanks to God for the success with which He had blessed our arms and to implore His continued favor.

In order to make a demonstration toward the Potomac, General Winder, early on the morning of the 28th, left his encampment near Winchester with the Fourth, Fifth, Twenty-seventh and Thirty-second Virginia regiments and Carpenter's and Poague's batteries, and took up the line of march for Charlestown by Summit Point. When about five miles from Charlestown he received information that the enemy was in possession of that place in heavy force. Upon being advised of this I ordered General Ewell, with re-enforcements, to his support. Notwithstanding the report of the large number of the enemy and the expectation of re-enforcements in the course of the day, General Winder moved forward cautiously toward Charlestown, and, as he emerged from the woods less than a mile distant from the town, he discovered the enemy in line of battle about fifteen hundred strong, and decided to attack them. Upon the appearance of our troops they were fired upon by two pieces of artillery. Carpenter's battery was immediately placed in position, the Thirty-third Virginia Regiment to support it. This battery was so admirably served that in twenty minutes the enemy retired in great disorder, throwing away arms, blankets, haversacks, etc. The pursuit was continued rapidly with artillery and infantry to Halltown. A short distance beyond that point, observing the enemy in position on Bolivar Heights, General Winder returned to the vicinity of Charlestown.

On the following day the main body of the army took position near Halltown, and the Second Regiment, Virginia Infantry, was sent to the Loudoun Heights, with the hope of being able to drive the enemy from Harper's Ferry across the Potomac.

In the meantime Shields was moving from Fredericksburg on my right, and Fremont from the South Branch on my left, with a view to concentrating a heavy force in my rear and cutting off my retreat up the valley. To avoid such a result orders were issued for all the troops, except Winder's brigade and the cavalry, to return to Winchester on the 30th. Directions were given to General Winder to recall the Second Regiment from Loudoun Heights, and as soon as it should return to its brigade to move with its command, including the cavalry, and rejoin the main body of the army.

Before I reached Winchester the enemy's cavalry had appeared at Front Royal, and Colonel Conner, who held that town with the Twelfth Georgia and a section of Rice's battery, hastily and improvidently abandoned the place, permitting not only Federal prisoners then in our possession, but some of his own men, to fall into the hands of the enemy. Quartermaster and commissary stores which we had previously captured at that place, and which Major Harman in his report estimates at the value of $300,000, were, before they could be recaptured by the enemy, through the energy and vigilance of Captain Cole, assistant quartermaster Thirty-seventh Virginia Regiment, fired, with the depot and buildings in which they were stored, and destroyed.

Early on the morning of the 31st the Twenty-first Virginia Regiment (Colonel Cunningham commanding) left Winchester in charge of some twenty-three hundred Federal prisoners and moved up the valley toward Staunton. It was followed by the other troops then near Winchester, which at that time embraced all my command except that part which had been left with Winder. The command encamped that night near Strasburg.

On the following morning General Fremont, who was approaching by way of Wardensville, attacked my outpost in that direction. As it was necessary for me to maintain my position at Strasburg until Winder should arrive with his command, General Ewell was ordered, with his division, to hold Fremont in check. Other troops were subsequently sent to his support, and after a spirited resistance the enemy's advance fell back a short distance.

FRONT ROYAL, VA.

Toward evening Winder arrived, part of his brigade (the Second Virginia Regiment) having in one day marched thirty-six miles. The command being again united, the retreat was resumed toward Harrisonburg.

The public property captured in this expedition at Front Royal, Winchester, Martinsburg and Charlestown was of great value, and so large in quantity that much of it had to be abandoned for want of necessary means of transportation. Major Harman, my chief quartermaster, had but one week within which to remove it, and although his efforts were characterized by his usual energy, promptitude and judgment, all the conveyances that within that short period could be hired or impressed were inadequate to the work. The medical stores, which filled one of the largest storehouses in Winchester, were fortunately saved. Most of the instruments and some of the medicines, urgently needed at that time by the command, were issued to the surgeons; the residue was sent to Charlottesville and turned over to a medical purveyor. Two large and well furnished hospitals, capable of accommodating some seven hundred patients, were found in the town and left undisturbed, with all their stores, for the use of the sick and wounded of the enemy.

Commissary supplies, consisting of upward of one hundred head of cattle, thirty-four thousand pounds of bacon, flour, salt, sugar, coffee, hard bread and cheese, were turned over to the proper officers, besides large amounts taken by the troops and not accounted for. Sutler's stores valued at $25,000, and for want of transportation abandoned to the troops, were captured. Quartermaster's stores to the value of $125,185 were secured, besides an immense amount destroyed. Many horses were taken by the cavalry. Among the ordnance stores taken and removed in safety were nine thousand three hundred and fifty-four small arms and two pieces of artillery and their caissons.

The official reports of the casualties of my command during the expedition, including the engagements at Front Royal and Winchester, show a list of sixty-eight killed and three hundred and twenty-nine wounded, with three missing, making a total loss of four hundred.

In addition to the prisoners in Colonel Cunningham's charge there were found in the hospitals at Winchester about seven hundred sick and wounded of the enemy, and at Strasburg some fifty, making the total number who fell into our hands about three thousand and fifty. Those left in the hospitals were paroled. Eight Federal surgeons attending the sick and wounded at Winchester were at first held as prisoners of war, though paroled, and the next day unconditionally released.

While I have had to speak of some of our troops in disparaging terms, yet it is my gratifying privilege to say of the main body of the army that its officers and men acted in a manner worthy of the great cause for which they were contending, and to add that, so far as my knowledge extends, the battle at Winchester was on our part a battle without a straggler.

* * * * * *

T. J. JACKSON,
Lieutenant-General.

BATTLE OF FAIR OAKS, OR SEVEN PINES,

MAY 31 AND JUNE 1, 1862.

BY

GENERAL JOSEPH E. JOHNSTON,
Commanding Army of Northern Virginia.

RICHMOND, VA., June 24, 1862.

BEFORE the 30th of May I had ascertained from trusty scouts that Keyes' corps was encamped on this side of the Chickahominy, near the Williamsburg Road. On that day Major-General D. H. Hill reported a strong body immediately in his front. On receiving this report I determined to attack them next morning, hoping to be able to defeat Keyes' corps completely in its more advanced position before it could be re-enforced. Written orders were dispatched to Major-Generals Hill, Huger and G. W. Smith. General Longstreet, being near my headquarters, received verbal instructions. The receipt of the orders was acknowledged. General Hill, supported by the division of General Longstreet (who had the direction of the operations on the right), was to advance by the Williamsburg Road to attack the enemy in front. General Huger, with his division, was to move down the Charles City Road, in order to attack in flank the troops who might be engaged with Hill and Longstreet, unless he found in his front force enough to occupy his division. General Smith was to march to the junction of the New Bridge Road and Nine Mile Road, to be in readiness either to fall on Keyes' right flank or to cover Longstreet's left. They were to move at daybreak. Heavy and protracted rains during the afternoon and night, by swelling the stream of the Chickahominy, increased the probability of our having to deal with no other troops than those of Keyes. The same cause prevented the prompt and punctual movement of the troops. Those of Smith, Hill and Longstreet were in position early enough, however, to be ready to commence operations by 8 A. M.

Major-General Longstreet, unwilling to make a partial attack instead of the combined movement which had been planned, waited from hour to hour for General Huger's division. At length, at 2 P. M., he determined to attack without those troops. He accordingly commenced his advance at that hour, opening the engagement with artillery and skirmishers. By 3 o'clock it became close and heavy.

In the meantime I had placed myself on the left of the force employed in this attack with the division of General Smith, that I might be on a part of the field where I could observe and be ready to meet any counter movements which the enemy's general might make against our center or left. Owing to some peculiar condition of the atmosphere the sound of the musketry did not reach us. I consequently deferred giving the signal for General Smith's advance until about 4 o'clock, at which time Major Jasper S. Whiting, of General Smith's staff, whom I had sent to learn the state of affairs with General Longstreet's column, returned, reporting that it was pressing on with vigor. Smith's troops were at once moved forward. The principal attack was made by Major-General Longstreet, with his own and Major-General D. H. Hill's division, the latter mostly in advance. Hill's brave troops, admirably commanded and most gallantly led, forced their way through the abatis which formed the enemy's external defenses, and stormed their intrenchments by a determined and irresistible rush. Such was the manner in which the enemy's first line was carried. The operation was repeated with the same gallantry and success as our troops pursued their victorious career through the enemy's successive camps and intrenchments. At each new position they encountered fresh troops belonging to it and re-enforcements brought on from the rear. Thus they had to repel repeated efforts to retake works which they had carried, but their advance was never successfully resisted. Their onward movement was only staid by the coming of night. By nightfall they had forced their way to the Seven Pines, having driven the enemy back more than two miles through their own camps and from a series of intrenchments, and repelled every attempt to recapture them with great slaughter.

The skill, vigor and decision with which these operations were conducted by General Longstreet are worthy of the highest praise. He was worthily seconded by Major-General Hill, of whose conduct and courage he speaks in the highest terms.

Major-General Smith's division moved forward at 4 o'clock, Whiting's three brigade's leading. Their progress was impeded by the enemy's skirmishers, which, with their supports, were driven back to the railroad. At this point Whiting's own and Pettigrew's brigade engaged a superior force of the enemy. Hood's, by my order, moved on to co-operate with Longstreet. General Smith was desired to hasten up with all the troops within reach. He brought up Hampton's and Hatton's brigades in a few minutes. The strength of the enemy's position, however, enabled him to hold it until dark.

About sunset, being struck from my horse and severely wounded by the fragment of a shell, I was carried from the field, and Major-General G. W. Smith succeeded to the command. He was prevented from renewing his attack on the enemy's position next morning by the discovery of strong intrenchments not seen on the previous evening. His division bivouacked on the night of the 31st within musket shot of the intrenchments which they were attacking when darkness staid the conflict. The skill, energy and resolution with which Major-General Smith directed his attack would have secured success if it could have been made an hour earlier. The troops of Longstreet and Hill passed the night of the 31st on the ground which they had won. The enemy was strongly re-enforced from the north side of the Chickahominy on the evening and night of the 31st. The troops engaged by General Smith were undoubtedly from the other side of the river.

On the morning of June 1st the enemy attacked the brigade of General Pickett, which was supported by that of General Pryor. The attack was vigorously repelled by those two brigades, the brunt of the action falling on General Pickett. This was the last demonstration made by the enemy. Our troops employed the residue in securing and bearing off the captured artillery, small arms and other property, and in the evening quietly returned to their own camps.

We took ten pieces of artillery, six thousand muskets, one garrison flag and four regimental colors, besides a large quantity of tents and camp equipage. Major-General Longstreet reports the loss in his command as being about 3,000. Major-General G. W. Smith reports his loss at 1,283. Total, 4,283.

Had Major-General Huger been in position, ready for action when Smith, Longstreet and Hill moved, I am satisfied that Keyes' corps would have been destroyed instead of being merely defeated. Had he gone into action even at 4 o'clock the victory would have been much more complete.

Major-Generals Smith and Longstreet speak in high terms of the conduct of their superior and staff officers. I beg leave to ask attention of the government especially to the manner in which Brigadier-Generals Whiting and R. H. Anderson, and Colonels Jenkins, Kemper and Hampton, exercising commands above their grades, and Brigadier-General Rodes, are mentioned.

* * * * * *

J. E. JOHNSTON, *General.*

CONFEDERATE ARMY ON ITS WAY TO FAIR OAKS, VA.

BATTLE OF FAIR OAKS, OR SEVEN PINES,

MAY 31 AND JUNE 1, 1862.

BY

MAJOR-GENERAL JAMES LONGSTREET,
Commanding Right Wing.

HEADQUARTERS RIGHT WING, June 10, 1862.

AGREEABLY to verbal instructions from the commanding general, the division of Major-General D. H. Hill was, on the morning of the 31st ultimo, formed at an early hour on the Williamsburg Road as the column of attack upon the enemy's front on that road. A brigade was placed on each side of the road to advance to the attack, and each was supported by one of the other brigades of the same division. In advance of each of the columns of attack a regiment as skirmishers

BRIG.-GEN. ROBERT HATTON, OF TENNESSEE.
Killed at the Battle of Fair Oaks.
[From an old Daguerreotype.]

was deployed. The plan for the forward movement was that the fields should be passed by a flank movement of the regiment of skirmishers, and the woods in front once in our possession, the brigades were to advance rapidly, occupy them and move rapidly forward. Abatis and intrenched positions were ordered to be taken by a flank movement of the brigades or brigade in front of them, the skirmishers engaging the sharpshooters and the supporting brigade occupying the position of the brigades during the flank movement.

The division of Major-General Huger was intended to make a strong flank movement around the left of the enemy's position and attack him in rear of that flank. This division did not get into position, however, in time for any such attack, and I was obliged to send three of my small brigades on the Charles City Road to support the one of Major-General Huger's, which had been ordered to protect my right flank.

After waiting some six hours for these troops to get into position I determined to move forward without regard to them, and gave orders to that effect to Major-General D. H. Hill. The forward movement began about 2 o'clock, and our skirmishers soon became engaged with those of the enemy. The entire division of General Hill became engaged about 3 o'clock, and drove the enemy steadily back, gaining possession of his abatis and a part of his intrenched camp, General Rodes, by a movement to the right, driving in the enemy's left.

The only re-enforcements on the field in hand were my own brigades, of which Anderson's, Wilcox's and Kemper's were put in by the front, on the Williamsburg Road, and Colston's and Pryor's by my right flank; Colston's just in time to turn the enemy's flank. At the same time the decided and gallant attack made by the other brigades gained entire possession of the enemy's position, with his artillery, camp equipage, etc. Anderson's brigade, under Colonel Jenkins, pressing forward rapidly, continued to drive the enemy until nightfall.

The severest part of the work was done by Major-General D. H. Hill's division; but the attack of the two brigades under General R. H. Anderson—one commanded by Colonel Kemper (now brigadier-general), the other by Colonel M. Jenkins—was made with such spirit and regularity as to have driven back the most determined foe. This decided the day in our favor.

General Pickett's brigade was held in reserve. General Pryor's did not succeed in getting upon the field of Saturday in time to take part in the action of the 31st. Both, however, shared in repulsing a serious attack upon our position on Sunday, the 1st instant, Pickett's brigade bearing the brunt of the attack and repulsing it. Some of the brigades of Major-General Huger's division took part in defending our position on Sunday, but, being fresh at the work, did not show the same steadiness and determination as the troops of Hill's division and my own.

I have reason to believe that the affair would have been a complete success had the troops upon the right been put in position within eight hours of the proper time. The want of promptness on that part of the field and the consequent severe struggle in my front so greatly reduced my supply of ammunition that at the late hour of the move on the left I was unable to make the rush necessary to relieve that attack.

SLEEPING ON THE BATTLE FIELD

Besides the good effect produced by driving back such heavy masses of the enemy, we have made superior soldiers of several brigades that were entirely fresh and unreliable. There can scarcely be a doubt about our ability to overcome the enemy upon any fair field. The conduct of the attack was left entirely to Major-General Hill. The entire success of the affair is sufficient evidence of his ability, courage and skill. I refer you to his report for particular mention of the conduct of his officers and soldiers. I will mention Brigadier-General Rodes, of that division, as distinguished for coolness, ability and determination. He made one of the most important and decisive movements on the field, and held his command some hours after receiving a severe wound.

My own troops have been so often tried and distinguished on other fields that they need no praise from my lips. A truer, better body of men never marched upon a battlefield. I will mention, however, as distinguished for their usual gallantry and ability, Generals R. H. Anderson, C. M. Wilcox, George E. Pickett, R. E. Colston and Roger A. Pryor, and Colonels Kemper and Jenkins (commanding brigades), Corse, Winston, Funston and Sydendam Moore, the latter twice shot and once severely wounded.

I desire also to mention the conspicuous courage and energy of Captain James Dearing, of the Lynchburg artillery, and his officers and men. His pieces were served under the severest fire, as his serious loss will attest. Captain Carter, of General Hill's division, also displayed great gallantry and skill in the management of his battery.

Brigadier-General J. E. B. Stuart, in the absence of any opportunity to use his cavalry, was of material service by his presence with me on the field.

My personal staff—Majors G. M. Sorrel, J.W. Fairfax, P. T. Manning and Captains Thomas Gorse, Thomas Walton, and my young aid, Lieutenant Blackwell—have my kind thanks for their activity, zeal and intelligence in carrying orders and the proper discharge of their duties. Captain Walton was slightly wounded.

I am also indebted to General Wigfall and Colonel P. T. Moore, volunteer aids, for assistance in rallying troops and conveying orders during the battle of the 31st ultimo and 1st instant.

Captain Ochiltree, of the adjutant-general's department, joined me on the 1st instant and kindly aided in carrying orders during the several assaults made by the enemy on that day. I am also indebted to Colonel R. H. Chilton for material aid.

Dr. J. S. D. Cullen, surgeon-in-chief, and the officers of his department, kindly and untiringly devoted themselves to the wounded. They have none of the chances of distinction of other officers, but discharge the most important duties. I refer to his report for the conduct of the officers of his department.

Our loss in valuable officers and men has been severe. Colonels Giles (Fifth South Carolina), Jones (Twelfth Alabama) and Lomax (Third Alabama) fell at the head of their commands, gallantly leading them to victory.

Three hundred and forty-seven prisoners, ten pieces of artillery, 5,000 small arms, one garrison and several regimental standards were taken. A rough estimate of the loss on this part of the field may be put at 3,000 killed and wounded. The loss on the part of the enemy may be put at a much higher figure, inasmuch as he was driven from his positions, and some half-dozen attempts to recover them were successfully repulsed.

* * * * * *

JAMES LONGSTREET,
Major-General Commanding.

List of killed, wounded and missing [in General Longstreet's command] May 31 and June 1, 1862:

	Officers	Enlisted Men	Aggregate
Killed	61	755	816
Wounded	209	3,530	3,739
Missing	3	293	296
Total	273	4,578	4,851

BATTLE OF FAIR OAKS, OR SEVEN PINES,

MAY 31 AND JUNE 1, 1862.

BY

MAJOR-GENERAL DANIEL H. HILL, C. S. A.,
Commanding Division.

HEADQUARTERS DIVISION, June 5, 1862.

I HAVE the honor to report the part taken by my division in the battle of Seven Pines, on May 31st and June 1st.

Two of my brigades (that of Garland and that of Rodes) were sent out on picket duty a few days before the battle. Garland guarded the Williamsburg Road, while Rodes defended the Charles City Road. Both of these officers made armed reconnoissances by my order and under my personal supervision. These reconnoissances satisfied me that the enemy was not in force on the Charles City Road, but was on the Williamsburg Road, and that he had fortified himself about the Seven Pines. The fact was further established that the whole of Keyes' corps had crossed the Chickahominy.

These facts I communicated to General Johnston about noon on Friday, May 30th. I received a prompt answer from him, saying that, being satisfied by my report of the presence of the enemy in force in my immediate front, he had resolved to attack him, and directed me to serve with Major-General Longstreet and under his orders. I was directed by General Longstreet to move with my whole division at dawn on the Williamsburg Road and to lead the attack on the Yankees. I was, however, directed not to move until relieved by Huger's division.

The relieving force not having reached me at 1 o'clock, the signal guns were fired and my division moved off in fine style, Rodes' brigade on the right of the road, supported by Raines' brigade; Garland on the left, supported by G. B. Anderson. Each wing was preceded by a regiment deployed as skirmishers. Having been long delayed in waiting for the relieving force, the right wing did not advance for a quarter of an hour after the left. This exposed Garland and Anderson to the whole Yankee force. The right wing was hurried forward and came up handsomely, preserving the line, although wading through the mud and water, in places two or three feet deep. I now detached General Raines to make a wide flank movement to take the Yankee works in reserve, while Rodes moved steadily to the front. Before he (Rodes) reached the Yankee abatis Garland and Anderson had captured a two-gun battery enfilading the road. A heavy column of re-enforcements was now coming up to the assistance of the Yankee general (Casey) commanding at Seven Pines.

Having previously put the battery of Bondurant in position, I now brought up that of Carter, which opened just at the critical moment. The Yankee column was almost in musket range of the gallant Colonel William Smith, Forty-ninth Virginia, and his noble regiment. The Yankees came up as on a parade day, until Carter's shot and shell began to play among them, when they broke and sought shelter in the woods.

An animated artillery duel now began between Carter's four guns and six Yankee guns. General Raines had now gained the rear of the Yankee redoubt and opened fire on the infantry posted in the woods. I now noticed commotion in the camps and redoubts and indications of evacuating the position. Rodes took skillful advantage of this commotion and moved up his brigade in beautiful order and took possession of the redoubts and rifle-pits. So rapid was the advance that six pieces were abandoned by the Yankees. These Rodes had turned upon the retreating column with effect. Carter galloped with his pieces, and these, with the captured guns, successfully repulsed an attempt of fresh Yankee troops to recapture the works.

We had now captured eight pieces of artillery, the camp, tents and stores of a brigade, and had successfully driven the Yankees back one and a half miles, forcing them to abandon a wide skirt of abatis, rifle-pits and redoubts. My division had beaten Casey's division and all the re-enforcements brought him, and had driven him and his supports into the woods and swamps. It was desirable, however, to press the Yankees as closely as possible. I therefore sent back to General Longstreet and asked for another brigade. In a few minutes the magnificent brigade of R. H. Anderson came to my support. A portion of this force, under Colonel Jenkins, consisting of the Palmetto Sharpshooters and the Sixth South Carolina was sent on the extreme left to scour along the railroad and Nine Mile Road, and thus get in rear of the enemy, while a portion, under General Anderson in person, was sent on the immediate left of the redoubt into the woods, where the Yankees had hid after being repulsed by the fire of Carter's battery and the captured guns under the direction of General Rodes. The Yankees permitted General R. H. Anderson to get within a few yards of them, when they opened a murderous fire upon him from their cover in the woods. His heroes replied with interest, and some guns, which were brought to enfilade the Yankee lines, added to their confusion, and they were soon in full retreat. They were hotly pursued, and R. H. Anderson and Jenkins, assisted by portions of G. B. Anderson's brigade, of my division, swept on the left of the road, driving brigade after brigade of the Yankees before them, capturing two more cannon, several camps, with their commissary and quartermaster's stores, and finally, after dark, halting more than a mile beyond the main works of the Yankees at Seven Pines.

MARCHING THROUGH SWAMP.

While this was going on Dearing's battery had been sent up by General Longstreet, and rendered important service during the day, the officers and men behaving most heroically. I now resolved to drive the Yankees out of the woods on the right of the road, where they were still in strong force. General Raines was near them, and a written order was carried him by my adjutant to move further to the right. I regret that that gallant and meritorious officer did not advance further in that direction. He would have taken the Yankees in flank, and the direct attack of Rodes in front would have been less bloody. The magnificent brigade of Rodes moved over the open ground to assault the Yankees strongly posted in the woods. He met a most galling fire, and his advance was checked. A portion of his command met with a disastrous repulse.

Kemper's brigade was now sent me by General Longstreet, and directed by me to move directly to the support

LIEUT.-GEN. DANIEL H HILL, OF NORTH CAROLINA.

of Rodes. This brigade, however, did not engage the Yankees, and Rodes' men were badly cut up. By nightfall, nevertheless, the Yankees were driven out of the woods, and we held undisputed possession of all the ground a mile around and in advance of the redoubt, which had been the object of the struggle. The remaining brigades of General Longstreet—Pickett's, Wilcox's, Pryor's and Colston's—reported to me for orders that night.

The tents and commissariat of the Yankee general (Casey) were found to be in excellent condition, and we all fared well that night. The result of the day had been most cheering. My division, weakened by one brigade and numbering less than nine thousand men, had driven the Yankees one and a half miles and captured their stronghold, and when it had been strengthened by two more brigades the Yankees were driven a mile further in, and prisoners were taken from three divisions. We had, therefore, fought with the odds against us of two to one in numbers, and this disparity rendered more formidable by abatis and earthworks.

At daylight next morning I learned that heavy re-enforcements had come up to the support of Keyes. Longstreet's, Huger's and my own divisions had opposed to us three Yankee corps—Keyes', Sumner's and Heintzelman's. We also learned that General G. W. Smith had been checked upon the Nine Mile Road, and that no help could be expected in that direction. I therefore resolved to concentrate my troops around the captured works, in the hope that the Yankees would attempt to retake them. Orders were accordingly given to the advance brigades, commanded by Pickett, Pryor and Wilcox, to draw in their extended lines and form near the late headquarters of General Casey.

Before these orders were received a furious attack was made upon Generals Armistead, Mahone, Pickett, Pryor and Wilcox and their brigades, on the left of the road. Armistead's men fled early in the action, with the exception of a few heroic companies, with which that gallant officer maintained his ground against an entire brigade. Mahone withdrew his brigade without any orders. I sent up Colston's to replace him, but he did not engage the Yankees as I had expected him to do. Pickett, Pryor and Wilcox received their orders to fall back after the firing began, and wisely resolved not to do so until the assault was repulsed. As soon as that was done Wilcox and Pryor withdrew, but Pickett held his ground against the odds of ten to one for several hours longer, and only retired when the Yankees had ceased to annoy him. The Yankees were too prudent to attack us in position, and contented themselves for the balance of the day in a desultory fire of artillery, which hurt no one and was only attended with the gratifying result of stampeding the amateur fighters and the camp plunderers from Richmond.

The batteries of Maurin, Stribling and Watson had been added to those of the preceding day by General Longstreet, and an occasional shot was fired in response to the Yankee artillery. The day was spent in removing 6,700 muskets and rifles in fine condition, ordnance, commissary and medical stores. Ten captured guns had been removed the night before. As the Yankees occupied the ground in our rear, on the Nine Mile Road, General Longstreet sent me an order after dark to withdraw my whole command.

The thirteen brigades were not got together until near midnight, and the delicate operation of withdrawing thirty thousand men in the presence of a superior force of the enemy had to be performed before daylight. The artillery and wagons had to pass through slush and mud holes over their axles, and the whole road was almost impassable for infantry. Nevertheless, we regained our own intrenchments by sunrise without leaving behind a gun, caisson, wagon, or even a straggling soldier.

The officers and men of other divisions who especially distinguished themselves will be appropriately noticed by their own commanders. It will only be expected of me to call attention to gallantry and good conduct among my own men.

Generals Garland, G. B. Anderson and Rodes, of my division, who led the attack in front, did all that brave and skillful officers could possibly do.

The flank attack of General Raines was most opportune and important. General Garland, when his brigade was not actually engaged, reported to me with his aids and adjutants to serve on my staff. In that capacity he rendered the most valuable services, and was much exposed. His adjutant, Meem, was killed, and his aid, Halsey, severely wounded near me. I had frequent occasion to notice the gallant bearing of these two officers.

All the regimental commanders acquitted themselves with great credit. Colonel Jones, of the Twelfth Alabama, left a sick bed to find a bloody grave on the battlefield. He was one of the very best officers and purest men in the army. The company, as well as the regimental officers, deserve the highest praise, and the rank and file fought with a gallantry never surpassed. It is seldom that even veteran troops will endure a greater loss than one-fourth, but these noble fellows marched steadily on after one-third of their number had been struck down. The heroism shown at Seven Pines has had a most wonderful influence upon the subsequent battles around Richmond. After this decisive victory, under such disadvantageous circumstances, not a brigade in the ranks seemed to entertain the remotest doubt of our ultimate success over the besieging army of Yankees.

It is due to my gallant division to say that the great majority of the men had never before been in battle, and yet they infused a spirit into the whole army which told with powerful effect in all the subsequent engagements, ending in the total rout of McClellan.

My thanks are especially due to all of my staff, who were active, brave and efficient. Majors Ratchford, assistant adjutant-general, and Pierson, chief of artillery; Captain Taylor, inspector-general, and Lieutenant West, aide-de-camp; Lee, engineer officer, and Moore and Fitzhugh, volunteer aids, were in all parts of the field, and, more or less, all had personal marks of exposure. Lieutenant West had two horses killed under him and a third wounded. Several of the others had their clothes perforated by balls.

Sergeant Harmilin and his detachment of couriers were active and faithful. Courier Braden and the two Chamblins were specially distinguished. The sergeant had his horse killed under him and was himself wounded.

Two of my batteries, under Hardaway and Nelson, were left behind in our intrenchments. These gallant officers would have been worthy compeers on the field of Carter and Bondurant.

From the list of killed and wounded it appears that of the less than nine thousand taken into action nearly three thousand were struck down. The loss was principally in the three brigades which made the front attack. Raines' brigade, which executed the flank movement, suffered but little in comparison.

The gallant charge of my division demoralized the Yankees, and our re-enforcements were not hotly engaged, the succor brought to Casey not fighting so well as his own men. This accounts for the fact that more than half of the entire loss in the two days' fight fell upon my division.

* * * * * * *

D. H. HILL, *Major-General.*

STUART.

BY MRS. HENRY J. VOSE.

Oh, mother of States and of men,
Bend low thy queenly head!
On his shield is borne to thy arms again
Thy youngest, fairest dead!
Drop tears like rain for that strong heart stilled,
For that dauntless spirit fled!

Sleep well, O stainless knight,
'Neath the folds of the starry cross!
For the day now breaks o'er the long, long night
Of our anguish, peril and loss.
But alas for the eyes that smiled on death,
And the life that held life dross!

They say thine ancestral line
Swayed the scepter and wore the crown;
But none girded a nobler sword than thine,
Nor more stainless life laid down,
And we ask no gleam from the grand old past
To brighten thy young renown.

On the field thy life was given,
Where our best blood has been poured;
At the feet of our country's God, in heaven,
Thou hast laid another sword,
When Jackson's head was so lately bowed,
The tired soldier of the Lord.

Oh, swords of the South! like flame
Leap forth for this lifeblood shed!
Strike the foe till he flies from the field in shame!
Sheathe not till the hilt is red!
And redeem the land that enshrines in her heart
The graves of her glorious dead!

STUART'S RAID,

JUNE 12 TO 15, 1862.

BY

BRIG.-GEN. J. E. B. STUART, C. S. A.,
Commanding Cavalry Brigade.

HEADQUARTERS CAVALRY BRIGADE,
DEPARTMENT OF NORTHERN VIRGINIA,
June 17, 1862.

I UNDERTOOK an expedition to the vicinity of the enemy's lines on the Pamunkey, with about 1,200 cavalry and a section of the Stuart Horse Artillery. The cavalry was composed of portions of the First, Fourth and Ninth Virginia cavalry. The second-named, having no field officers present, was, for the time being, divided between the First and last mentioned, commanded respectively by Colonel Fitz Lee and Colonel W. H. Fitzhugh Lee; also two squadrons of the Jeff. Davis Legion, commanded by First Lieutenant James Breathed. Although the expedition was prosecuted further than was contemplated in your instructions, I feel assured that the considerations which actuated me will convince you that I did not depart from their spirit, and that the boldness developed in the subsequent direction of the march was the quintessence of prudence.

The destination of the expedition was kept a profound secret (so essential to success), and was known to my command only as the actual march developed it. The force was quietly concentrated beyond the Chickahominy, near Kilby's Station, on the Richmond, Fredricksburg & Potomac Railroad, and moved thence parallel to and to the left of that road. Scouts were kept far to the right, to ascertain the enemy's whereabouts, and advanced guard, flankers and rear guard, to secure our column against surprise. I purposely directed my first day's march toward Louisa, so as to favor the idea of re-enforcing Jackson, and encamped just opposite Hanover Courthouse, near South Anna Bridge, twenty-two miles from Richmond.

Our noiseless bivouac was broken early next morning, and without flag or bugle sound we resumed our march, none but one knew whither. I, however, immediately took occasion to make known my instructions and plans

BURNING DEAD HORSES ON THE BATTLEFIELD OF FAIR OAKS, VA.

confidentially to the regimental commanders, so as to secure an intelligent action and co-operation in whatever might occur. Scouts had returned, indicating no serious obstacles to my march from that to Old Church, directly in rear end of and on the overland avenue of communication to New Bridge and vicinity.

I proceeded, therefore, via Hanover Courthouse. I found it in possession of the enemy. But very little could be ascertained about the strength and nature of his force. I therefore sent Colonel Fitz Lee's regiment (First Virginia Cavalry) to make a detour to the right and reach the enemy's route behind him, to ascertain his force here and crush it, if possible; but the enemy, proving afterward to be one hundred and fifty cavalry, did not tarry long, but left, my column following slowly down, expecting every moment to hurl him upon Lee; but, owing to a bad marsh, Colonel Lee did not reach the intersection of the roads in time, and the cavalry (the Regular Sixth) passed on in the direction of Mechanicsville. This course deviating too much from our direction, after the capture of a sergeant, they were allowed to proceed without interruption on their way.

Our march led thence to Taliaferro's mill and Erron Church to Hawes' shop; here we encountered the first pickets, surprised and caught several vedettes, and pushed boldly forward, keeping advance guard well to the front.

after a hotly-contested, hand-to-hand conflict put him to flight, but not until the gallant captain had sealed his devotion to his native soil with his blood. The enemy's rout (two squadrons by one of ours) was complete; they dispersed in terror and confusion, leaving many dead on the field and blood in quantities in their tracks. Their commander, Captain Royall, was reported mortally wounded, several officers and a number of privates were taken in the conflict, and a number of horses, arms and equipments, together with five guidons. The woods and fields were full of the scattered and disorganized foe straggling to and fro, and but for the delay and the great encumbrance which they would have been to our march many more would have been captured.

Colonel Fitz Lee, burning with impatience to cross sabers with his old regiment, galloped to the front at this point and begged to be allowed to participate with his regiment (the First Virginia Cavalry) in the discomfiture of his old comrades—a request I readily granted; and his leading squadron charged without resistance into the enemy's camp (five companies), and took possession of a number of horses, a quantity of arms and stores of every kind, several officers and privates. The stores as well as the tents, in which everything had been left, were speedily burned, and the march resumed.

but while none accorded a full assent, all assured me a hearty support in whatever I did.

With an abiding trust in God, and with such guarantees of success as the two Lees and Martin, and their devoted followers, this enterprise I regarded as most promising. Taking care, therefore, more particularly after this resolve, to inquire of the citizens the distance and the route to Hanover Courthouse, I kept my horse's head steadily toward Tunstall's Station.

There was something of the sublime in the implicit confidence and unquestioning trust of the rank and file in a leader guiding them straight, apparently, into the very jaws of the enemy, every step appearing to them to diminish the faintest hope of extrication. Reports of the enemy's strength at Garlick's and Tunstall's were conflicting, but generally indicated a small number. Prisoners were captured at everv step, including officers, soldiers and negroes.

The rear now became of as much importance as the front, but the duties of rear guard devolving on the Jeff. Davis Legion, with the howitzer attached, its conduct was intrusted to its commander, Lieutenant-Colonel Martin, in whose judgment and skill I had much confidence. He was not attacked, but at one time the enemy appeared in his rear bearing a flag of truce, and the party, twenty-five

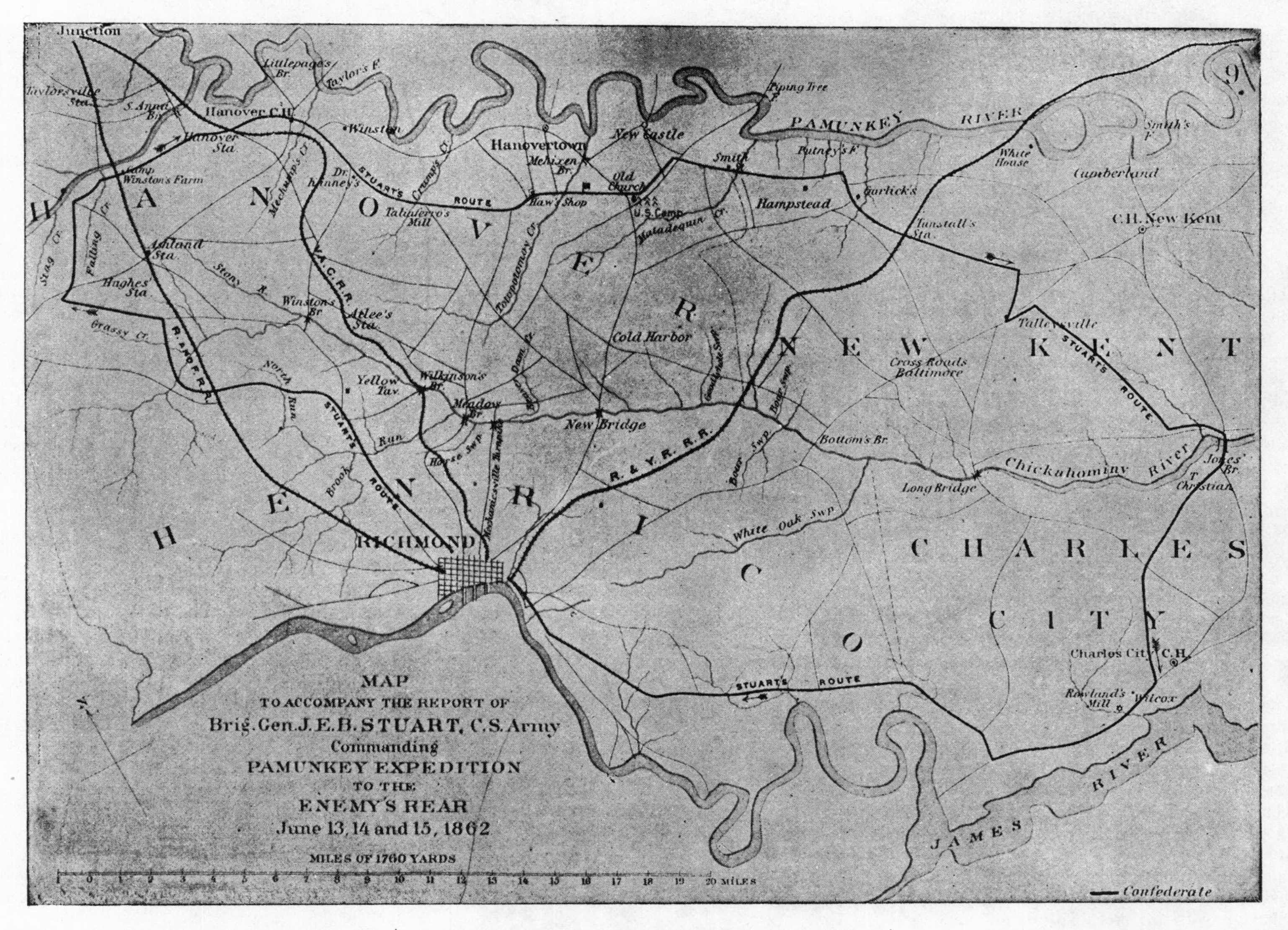

The regiment in front was the Ninth Virginia Cavalry (Colonel W. H. F. Lee), whose advance guard, intrusted to the command of the adjutant (Lieutenant Robins), did admirable service, Lieutenant Robins handling it in the most skillful manner, managing to clear the way for the march with little delay, and infusing by a sudden dash at a picket such a wholesome terror that it never paused to take a second look.

Between Hawes' shop and Old Church the advance guard in front came up with the enemy; it proved to be the Fifth Regular U. S. Cavalry (formerly the Second). The leading squadron was ordered forward at a brisk gait, the main body following closely, and gave chase to the enemy for a mile or two, but not coming up with him.

We crossed the Totopotomoy, a strong position of defense which the enemy failed to hold, confessing a weakness. In such places half a squadron was deployed afoot as skirmishers till the extreme point of danger was passed.

On, on dashed Robins, here skirting a field, there leaping a fence or ditch, and clearing the woods beyond, when, not far from Old Church, the enemy made a stand, having been re-enforced.

The only mode of attack being in column of fours along the road, I still preferred to oppose the enemy with one squadron at a time, remembering that he who brings on the field the last cavalry reserve wins the day. The next squadron therefore moved to the front under the lamented Captain Latane, making a brilliant and most successful charge with drawn sabers upon the picketed ground, and

Here was the turning point of the expedition. Two routes were before me — the one, to return by Hanover Courthouse; the other, to pass around through New Kent, taking the chances of having to swim the Chickahominy, and make a bold effort to cut the enemy's lines of communication. The Chickahominy was believed by my guide to be fordable near Forge Bridge. I was fourteen miles from Hanover Courthouse, which I would have to pass. If I returned the enemy had a much shorter distance to pass to intercept me there; besides, the South Anna was impassable, which still further narrowed the chances of escape in that direction; the enemy, too, would naturally expect me to take that route. These circumstances led me to look with more favor to my favorite scheme, disclosed to you before starting, of passing around. It was only nine miles to Tunstall's Station, on the York River Railroad, and that point once passed I felt little apprehension beyond. The route was one of all others which I felt sure the enemy would never expect me to take. On that side of the Chickahominy infantry could not reach me before crossing, and I felt able to whip any cavalry force that could be brought against me. Once on the Charles City side, I knew you would, when aware of my position, if necessary, order a diversion in my favor on the Charles City Road, to prevent a move to intercept me from the direction of White Oak Swamp. Besides this, the hope of striking a serious blow at a boastful and insolent foe, which would make him tremble in his shoes, made more agreeable the alternative I chose. In a brief and frank interview with some of my officers I disclosed my views,

in number, bearing it actually surrendered to his rear guard, so great was the consternation produced by our march. An assistant surgeon was also taken. He was *en route*, and not in charge of sick.

Upon arriving opposite Garlick's I ordered a squadron from the Ninth Virginia Cavalry to destroy whatever could be found at the landing on the Pamunkey. Two transports loaded with stores and a large number of wagons were here burned, and the squadron rejoined the column with a large number of prisoners, horses and mules. A squadron of the First Virginia Cavalry (Hammond's) assisted in this destruction.

A few picked men, including my aids Burke, Farley and Mosby, were pushed forward rapidly to Tunstall's to cut the wires and secure the depot. Five companies of cavalry, escorting large wagon trains, were in sight, and seemed at first disposed to dispute our progress; but the sight of our column, led by Lee, of the Ninth, boldly advancing to the combat, was enough. Content with a distant view, they fled, leaving their train in our hands. The party that reached the railroad at Tunstall's, surprised the guard at the depot (fifteen or twenty infantry), captured them without the firing of a gun, and set about obstructing the railroad; but before it could be thoroughly done, and just as the head of our column reached it, a train of cars came thundering down from the grand army. It had troops on board, and we prepared to attack it. The train swept off the obstructions without being thrown from the track; but our fire, delivered at only a few rods' distance, either killed or caused to feign death everyone on board, the engineer being one of the first victims from the unerring fire of Captain Farley. It is fair to presume that a serious collision took place on its arrival at White House, for it made extraordinary speed in that direction. The railroad bridge over Black Creek was fired, under the direction of Lieutenant Burke, and it being now dark, the burning of the immense wagon train and the extrication of the teams involved much labor and delay, and illuminated the country for miles.

The roads at this point were far worse than ours, and the artillery had much difficulty in passing. Our march was finally continued by bright moonlight to Talleysville, where we halted three and a half hours for the column to close up. At this point we passed a large hospital of one hundred and fifty patients. I deemed it proper not to molest the surgeons and attendants in charge.

At 12 o'clock at night the march was continued without incident, under the most favorable auspices, to Forge Bridge (eight miles), over the Chickahominy, where we arrived just at daylight. Lee, of the Ninth, by personal experiment having found the stream not fordable, axes were sent for, and every means taken to overcome the difficulties by improvised bridges and swimming. I immediately dispatched to you information of my situation, and asked for the diversion already referred to. The progress in crossing was very slow at the point chosen, just above Forge Bridge, and learning that at the bridge proper, enough of the old debris remained to facilitate the construction of another, material for which was afforded by a large warehouse adjacent, I moved to that point at once. Lieutenant Redmond Burke, who in every sphere has rendered most valuable service, and deserves the highest consideration at the hands of the government, set to work with a party to construct the bridge. A footbridge was soon improvised, and the horses were crossed over as rapidly as possible by swimming. Burke's work proceeded like magic; in three hours it was ready to bear artillery and cavalry; and as half the latter had not yet crossed, the bridge enabled the whole to reach the other bank by 1 P. M. Another branch of the Chickahominy still further on was with some difficulty forded, and the march was continued without interruption toward Richmond. Having passed the point of danger, I left the column with Colonel Lee, of the First. I rode on to report to you in person, reaching your headquarters at daylight next morning.

Returning to my command soon after, the prisoners, one hundred and sixty-five in number, were transferred to the proper authority; two hundred and sixty horses and mules captured, with more or less harness, were transferred to the quartermaster's departments of the different regiments, and the commands were sent to their respective camps. The number of captured arms has not been as yet accurately ascertained. A pole was broken, which obliged us to abandon a limber this side of the Chickahominy.

The success attending this expedition will no doubt cause 10,000 or 15,000 men to be detached from the enemy's main body to guard his communications, besides accomplishing the destruction of millions' worth of property, and the interruption for a time of his railroad communication.

The three commanders (the two Lees and Martin) exhibited the characteristics of skilled leaders, keeping their commands well in hand, and managing them with skill and good judgment, which proved them worthy of higher trust. Their brave men behaved with coolness and intrepidity in danger, unswerving resolution before difficulties, and stood unparalleled before the rushing torrent of the Chickahominy with the probability of an enemy at their heels, armed with the fury of a tigress robbed of her whelps. The perfect order and systematic disposition for crossing maintained throughout the passage insured its success and rendered it the crowning feature of a successful expedition.

I hope, general, your sense of delicacy, so manifest on former occasions, will prompt you to award the two Lees (your son and nephew) not less than their full measure of praise. Embalmed in the hearts and affections of their regiments; tried on many occasions requiring coolness, decision and bravery; everywhere present to animate, direct and control, they held their regiments in their grasp, and proved themselves brilliant cavalry leaders.

The discipline maintained by Lieutenant-Colonel Martin in his command is especially worthy of notice, as also the energy displayed by First Lieutenant James Breathed, of the Stuart Horse Artillery.

I am also indebted to First Lieutenant D. A. Timberlake, Corporal Turner Doswell, and Private J. A. Timberlake, Fourth Virginia Cavalry; Second Lieutenant Jones R. Christian and Private R. E. Frazier, Third Virginia Cavalry, who were ever in advance, and without whose thorough knowledge of the country and valuable assistance rendered I could have effected nothing.

Assistant Surgeon J. B. Fontaine, Fourth Virginia Cavalry (the enemy giving him little to do in his profession), was bold and indefatigable in reconnoissance, and was particularly active in his effort to complete the bridge. Captain Heros von Borche, a Prussian cavalry officer, who lately ran the blockade, assigned me by the Honorable Secretary of War, joined in the charge of the first squadron in gallant style, and subsequently, by his energy, skill and activity, won the praise and admiration of all.

To my staff present my thanks are especially due for the diligent performance of the duties assigned them. They were as follows: First Lieutenant John Esten Cooke, ordnance officer—my principal staff officer for the occasion; First Lieutenant C. Dabney, aid-de-camp.

Rev. Mr. Landstreet, Captains Farley, Towles, Fitzhugh and Mosby rendered conspicuous and gallant service during the whole expedition.

My escort, under Corporal Hogan, are entitled individually to my thanks for their zeal and devotion to duty; particularly Privates Carson of the Jeff. Davis Legion and Pierson of the Fourth Virginia Cavalry.

* * * * * *

J. E. B. STUART,
Brigadier-General, Commanding Cavalry.

THE SEVEN DAYS' BATTLES

BEFORE RICHMOND, VA.,

EMBRACING

THE BATTLES OF MECHANICSVILLE, GAINES' MILL (OR COLD HARBOR) AND SAVAGE STATION; ENGAGEMENT AT WHITE OAK SWAMP BRIDGE; AND BATTLES OF FRAZIER'S FARM AND MALVERN HILL,

JUNE 25 TO JULY 1, 1862.

BY

GENERAL ROBERT E. LEE,
Commanding the Army of Northern Virginia.

HEADQUARTERS ARMY OF NORTHERN VIRGINIA,
March 6, 1863.

AFTER the battle of Seven Pines the Federal army, under General McClellan, preparatory to an advance upon Richmond, proceeded to fortify its position on the Chickahominy, and to perfect the communications with its base of supplies near the head of

MAJ.-GEN. BENJAMIN HUGER, OF SOUTH CAROLINA.

York River Its left was established south of the Chickahominy, between White Oak Swamp and New Bridge, defended by a line of strong works, access to which, except by a few narrow roads, was obstructed by felling the dense forests in front. These roads were commanded for a great distance by the heavy guns in the fortifications. The right wing lay north of the Chickahominy, extending beyond Mechanicsville, and the approaches from the south side were strongly defended by intrenchments. Our army was around Richmond, the divisions of Huger and Magruder, supported by those of Longstreet and D. H. Hill, in front of the enemy's left, and that of A. P. Hill extending from Magruder's left beyond Meadow Bridge.

The command of General Jackson, including Ewell's division, operating in the Shenandoah Valley, had succeeded in diverting the army of McDowell, at Fredericksburg, from uniting with that of McClellan. To render this diversion more decided, and effectually mask his withdrawal from the valley at the proper time, Jackson, after the defeat of Fremont and Shields, was re-enforced by Whiting's division, composed of Hood's Texas brigade and his own, under Colonel Law, from Richmond, and that of Lawton, from the South.

The intention of the enemy seemed to be to attack Richmond by regular approaches. The strength of his left wing rendered a direct assault injudicious, if not impracticable. It was, therefore, determined to construct defensive lines, so as to enable part of the army to defend the city, and leave the other part free to cross the Chickahominy and operate on the north bank. By sweeping down the river on that side and threatening his communications with York River, it was thought that the enemy would be compelled to retreat or give battle out of his intrenchments. The plan was submitted to His Excellency the President, who was repeatedly on the field in the course of its execution.

While preparations were in progress a cavalry expedition, under General Stuart, was made around the rear of the Federal army to ascertain its position and movements. This was executed with great address and daring by that accomplished officer. As soon as the defensive works were sufficiently advanced General Jackson was directed to move rapidly and secretly from the valley, so as to arrive in the vicinity of Ashland by June 24th.

The enemy appeared to be unaware of our purpose, and on the 25th attacked General Huger on the Williamsburg Road, with the intention, as appeared by a dispatch from General McClellan, of securing his advance toward Richmond. The effort was successfully resisted and our line maintained.

BATTLE OF MECHANICSVILLE.

According to the general order of battle, General Jackson was to march from Ashland on the 25th in the direction of Slash Church, encamping for the night west of the Central Railroad, and to advance at 3 A. M. on the 26th and turn Beaver Dam. A. P. Hill was to cross the Chickahominy at Meadow Bridge, when Jackson's advance beyond that point should be known, and move directly upon Mechanicsville. As soon as the Mechanicsville Bridge should be uncovered Longstreet and D. H. Hill were to cross, the latter to proceed to the support of Jackson, and the former to that of A. P. Hill. The four commands were directed to sweep down the north side of the Chickahominy toward the York River Railroad, Jackson on the left and in advance, Longstreet nearest the river and in the rear. Huger and Magruder were ordered to hold their positions against any assault of the enemy, to observe his movements, and follow him closely should he retreat. General Stuart, with the cavalry, was thrown out on Jackson's left to guard his flank and give notice of the enemy's movements.

Brigadier-General Pendleton was directed to employ the reserve artillery so as to resist any approach of the enemy toward Richmond, to superintend that portion of it posted to aid in the operations of the north bank, and hold the remainder ready for use when it might be required. In consequence of unavoidable delays the whole of General Jackson's command did not arrive at Ashland in time to enable him to reach the point designated on the 25th.

His march on the 26th was consequently longer than had been anticipated, and his progress being also retarded by the enemy, A. P. Hill did not begin his movement until 3 P. M., when he crossed the river and advanced upon Mechanicsville. After a sharp conflict he drove the enemy from his intrenchments and forced him to take refuge in his works on the left bank of Beaver Dam, about one mile distant. This position was a strong one, the banks of the creek in front being high and almost perpendicular, and the approach to it over open fields, commanded by the fire of artillery and infantry intrenched on the opposite side. The difficulty of crossing the stream had been increased by felling the woods on its banks and destroying the bridges.

Jackson being expected to pass Beaver Dam above and turn the enemy's right, a direct attack was not made by General Hill. One of his regiments on the left of his line crossed the creek to communicate with Jackson, and remained until after dark, when it was withdrawn. Longstreet and D. H. Hill crossed the Mechanicsville Bridge as soon as it was uncovered and could be repaired, but it was late before they reached the north bank of the Chickahominy. D. H. Hill's leading brigade, under Ripley, advanced to the support of the troops engaged, and at a late hour united with Pender's brigade, of A. P. Hill's division, in an effort to turn the enemy's left; but the troops were unable, in the growing darkness, to overcome the obstructions, and, after sustaining a destructive fire of musketry and artillery at short range, were withdrawn. The fire was continued until about 9 P. M., when the engagement ceased. Our troops retained the ground on the right bank, from which the enemy had been driven.

Ripley was relieved at 3 A. M. on the 27th by two of Longstreet's brigades, which were subsequently re-enforced. In expectation of Jackson's arrival on the enemy's right, the battle was renewed at dawn and continued with animation for about two hours, during which the passage of the creek was attempted and our troops forced their way to its banks, where their progress was arrested by the nature of the stream. They maintained their position while preparations were being made to cross at another point nearer the Chickahominy. Before they were completed Jackson crossed Beaver Dam above, and the enemy abandoned his intrenchments and retired rapidly down the river, destroying a great deal of property, but leaving much in his deserted camps.

BATTLE OF THE CHICKAHOMINY (GAINES' MILL, OR COLD HARBOR).

After repairing the bridges over Beaver Dam the several columns resumed their march as nearly as possible as prescribed in the order; Jackson, with whom D. H. Hill had united, bore to the left in order to cut off re-enforcements to the enemy or intercept his retreat in that direction. Longstreet and A. P. Hill moved nearer the Chickahominy. Many prisoners were taken in their progress, and the conflagration of wagons and stores marked the way of the retreating army. Longstreet and Hill reached the vicinity of New Bridge about noon. It was ascertained that the enemy had taken a position behind Powhite Creek, prepared to dispute our progress. He occupied a range of hills, with his right resting in the vicinity of McGehee's house, and his left near that of Dr. Gaines', on a wooded bluff which rose abruptly from a deep ravine. The ravine was filled with sharpshooters, to whom its banks gave protection. A second line of infantry was stationed on the side of the hill behind a breastwork of trees above the first; a third occupied the crest, strengthened with rifled trenches and crowned with artillery. The approach to this position was over an open plain, about a quarter of a mile wide, commanded by this triple line of fire and swept by the heavy batteries south of the Chickahominy. In front of his center and right the ground was generally open, bounded on the side of one approach by a wood, with dense and tangled undergrowth, and traversed by a sluggish stream which converted the soil into a deep morass. The woods on the further side of the swamp were occupied by sharpshooters, and trees had been felled to increase the difficulty of its passage and detain our advancing columns under the fire of infantry massed on the slopes of the opposite hills and of the batteries on their crests. Pressing on toward the York River Railroad, A. P. Hill, who was in advance, reached the vicinity of New Cold Harbor about 2 P. M., where he encountered the enemy. He immediately formed his line nearly parallel to the road leading from that place toward McGehee's house, and soon became hotly engaged. The arrival of Jackson on our left was momentarily expected, and it was supposed his approach would cause the extension of the enemy's line in that direction. Under this impression Longstreet was held back until this movement should commence. The principal part of the Federal army was now on the north side of the Chickahominy. Hill's single division met this large force with the impetuous courage for which that officer and his troops are distinguished. They drove the enemy back and assailed him in his strong position on the ridge. The battle raged fiercely and with varying fortune for more than two hours. Three regiments pierced the enemy's line and forced their way to the crest of the hill on his left, but were compelled to fall back before overwhelming numbers. The superior force of the enemy assisted by the fire of his batteries south of the Chickahominy, which played incessantly on our columns as they pressed through the difficulties that obstructed their way, caused them to recoil. Though most of the men had never been under fire until the day before, they were rallied, and in turn repelled the advance of the enemy. Some brigades were broken, others stubbornly maintained their positions, but it became apparent that the enemy was gradually gaining ground.

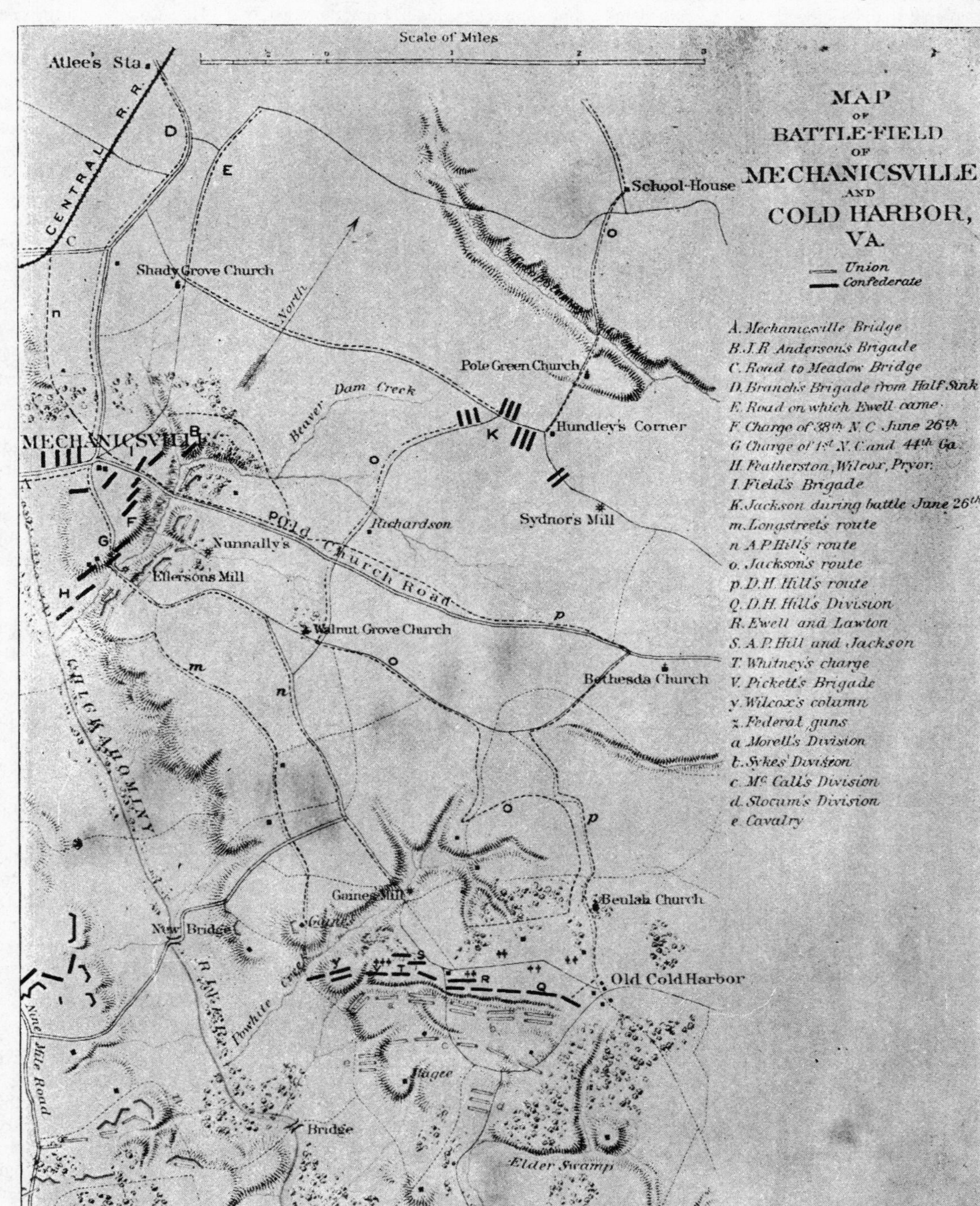

From original in the possession of the Southern Historical Society.

The attack on our left being delayed by the length of Jackson's march and the obstacles he encountered, Longstreet was ordered to make a diversion in Hill's favor by a feint on the enemy's left. In making this demonstration the great strength of the position already described was discovered, and General Longstreet perceived that to render the diversion effectual the feint must be converted into an attack. He resolved, with characteristic promptness, to carry the heights by assault. His column was quickly formed near the open ground, and as his preparations were completed Jackson arrived, and his right division, that of Whiting, took position on the left of Longstreet. At the same time D. H. Hill formed on our extreme left, and after a short but bloody conflict forced his way throug the morass and obstructions and drove the enemy from the woods on the opposite side. Ewell advanced on Hill's right and engaged the enemy furiously. The First and Fourth brigades of Jackson's own division filled the interval between Ewell and A. P. Hill. The Second and Third were sent to the right. The arrival of these fresh troops enabled A. P. Hill to withdraw some of his brigades, wearied and reduced by their long and arduous conflict. The line being now complete, a general advance from right to left was ordered. On the right the troops moved forward with steadiness, unchecked by the terrible fire from the triple lines of infantry on the hill and the cannon on both sides of the river, which burst upon them as they emerged upon the plain. The dead and wounded marked the way of their intrepid advance, the brave Texans leading, closely followed by their no less daring comrades. The enemy was driven from the ravine to the first line of breastworks, over which our impetuous column dashed up to the intrenchments on the crest. These were quickly stormed, fourteen pieces of artillery captured, and the enemy driven into the field beyond. Fresh troops came to his support, and he endeavored repeatedly to rally, but in vain. He was forced back with great slaughter until he reached the woods on the banks of the Chickahominy, and night put an end to the pursuit. Long lines of dead and wounded marked each stand made by the enemy in his stubborn resistance, and the field over which he retreated was strewn with the slain.

On the left the attack was no less vigorous and successful. D. H. Hill charged across the open ground in his front, one of his regiments having first bravely carried a battery whose fire enfiladed his advance. Gallantly supported by the troops on his right, who pressed forward with unfaltering resolution, he reached the crest of the ridge, and after a sanguinary struggle broke the enemy's line, captured several of his batteries, and drove him in confusion toward the Chickahominy until darkness rendered further pursuit impossible. Our troops remained in undisturbed possession of the field, covered with the Federal dead and wounded, and their broken forces fled to the river or wandered through the woods.

Owing to the nature of the country the cavalry was unable to participate in the general engagement. It rendered valuable service in guarding Jackson's flank, and took a large number of prisoners. On the morning of the 28th it was ascertained that none of the enemy remained in our front north of the Chickahominy. As he might yet intend to give battle to preserve his communications, the Ninth Virginia Cavalry, supported by Ewell's division, was ordered to seize the York River Railroad, and General Stuart, with his main body, to co-operate. When the cavalry reached Dispatch Station the enemy retreated to the south bank of the river, and burned the railroad bridge. Ewell, coming up shortly afterward, destroyed a portion of the track.

During the forenoon columns of dust south of the Chickahominy showed that the Federal army was in motion. The abandonment of the railroad and destruction of the bridge proved that no further attempt would be made to hold that line; but from the position it occupied the roads which led toward James River would also enable it to reach the lower bridges over the Chickahominy and retreat down the peninsula. In the latter event it was necessary that our troops should continue on the north bank of the river, and until the intention of General McClellan was discovered it was deemed injudicious to change their disposition. Ewell was therefore ordered to proceed to Bottom's Bridge to guard that point, and the cavalry to watch the bridges below. No certain indications of a retreat to James River were discovered by our forces on the south side of the Chickahominy, and late in the afternoon the enemy's works were reported to be fully manned. The strength of these fortifications prevented Generals Huger and Magruder from discovering what was passing in their front. Below the enemy's works the country was densely wooded and intersected by impassable swamps, at once concealing his movements and precluding reconnoissances except by the regular roads, all of which were strongly guarded. The bridges over the Chickahominy in rear of the enemy were destroyed, and their reconstruction impracticable in the presence of his whole army and powerful batteries. We were therefore compelled to wait until his purpose should be developed. Generals Huger and Magruder were again directed to use the utmost vigilance and pursue the enemy vigorously should they discover that he was retreating. During the afternoon and night of the 28th the signs of a general movement were apparent, and no indications of his approach to the lower bridges of the Chickahominy having been discovered by the pickets in observation at those points, it became manifest that General McClellan was retreating to the James River.

BATTLE OF SAVAGE STATION.

Early on the 29th Longstreet and A. P. Hill were ordered to recross the Chickahominy at New Bridge, and move by the Darbytown to the Long Bridge Road.

Major R. K. Meade and Lieutenant S. R. Johnston, of the engineers, attached to General Longstreet's division, who had been sent to reconnoiter, found, about sunrise, the work on the upper extremity of the enemy's line of intrenchments abandoned. Generals Huger and Magruder were immediately ordered in pursuit, the former by the Charles City Road, so as to take the Federal army in flank, and the latter by the Williamsburg Road, to attack its rear. Jackson was directed to cross at Grapevine Bridge and move down the south side of the Chickahominy. Magruder and Huger found the whole line of works deserted and large quantities of military stores of every description abandoned or destroyed.

The former reached the vicinity of Savage Station about noon, where he came upon the rear guard of the retreating army. Being informed that the enemy was advancing, he halted and sent for re-enforcements. Two brigades of Huger's division were ordered to his support, but subsequently withdrawn, it being apparent that the force in Magruder's front was covering the retreat of the main body. Jackson's route led to the flank and rear of Savage Station, but he was delayed by the necessity of reconstructing Grapevine Bridge.

Late in the afternoon Magruder attacked the enemy with one of his divisions and two regiments of another. A severe action ensued and continued about two hours, when it was terminated by night. The troops displayed great gallantry, and inflicted heavy loss upon the enemy; but, owing to the lateness of the hour and small force employed, the result was not decisive, and the enemy continued his retreat under cover of darkness, leaving several hundred prisoners, with his dead and wounded, in our hands.

At Savage Station were found about two thousand five hundred men in hospital and a large amount of property. Stores of much value had been destroyed, including the necessary medical supplies for the sick and wounded. But the time gained enabled the retreating column to cross White Oak Swamp without interruption and destroy the bridge.

BATTLE OF FRAZIER'S FARM.*

Jackson reached Savage Station early on the 30th. He was directed to pursue the enemy on the road he had taken, and Magruder to follow Longstreet by the Darbytown Road. As Jackson advanced he captured such numbers of prisoners and collected so many arms that two regiments had to be detached for their security. His progress was arrested at White Oak Swamp. The enemy occupied the opposite side, and obstinately resisted the reconstruction of the bridge.

Longstreet and A. P. Hill, continuing their advance on the 30th, soon came upon the enemy strongly posted across the Long Bridge Road, about one mile from its intersection with the Charles City Road. Huger's route led to the right of this position, Jackson's to the rear, and the arrival of their commands was awaited to begin the attack.

On the 29th General Holmes had crossed from the south side of James River with part of his division.

On the 30th, re-enforced by General Wise with a detachment of his brigade, he moved down the river road and came upon the line of the retreating army near Malvern Hill. Perceiving indications of confusion, General Holmes was ordered to open upon the column with artillery. He soon discovered that a number of batteries, advantageously posted, supported by an infantry force superior to his own, and assisted by the fire of the gunboats in the James River, guarded this part of the line.

Magruder, who had reached the Darbytown Road, was ordered to re-enforce Holmes, but being at a greater distance than had been supposed, he did not reach the position of the latter in time for an attack.

Huger reported that his progress was obstructed, but about 4 P. M. firing was heard in the direction of the Charles City Road, which was supposed to indicate his approach. Longstreet immediately opened with one of his batteries to give notice of his presence. This brought on the engagement; but Huger not coming up, and Jackson having been unable to force the passage of White Oak Swamp, Longstreet and Hill were without the expected support.

The battle raged furiously until 9 P. M. By that time the enemy had been driven with great slaughter from every position but one, which he maintained until he was enabled to withdraw under cover of darkness.

At the close of the struggle nearly the entire field remained in our possession, covered with the enemy's dead and wounded. Many prisoners, including a general of division, were captured, and several batteries, with some thousands of small arms, taken. Could the other commands have co-operated in the action the result would have proved most disastrous to the enemy.

After the engagement Magruder was recalled to relieve the troops of Longstreet and Hill. His men, much fatigued by their long, hot march, arrived during the night.

BATTLE OF MALVERN HILL.

Early on July 1st Jackson reached the battlefield of the previous day, having succeeded in crossing White Oak Swamp, where he captured a part of the enemy's artillery and a number of prisoners. He was directed to continue the pursuit down the Willis Church Road, and soon found the enemy occupying a high range, extending obliquely across the road, in front of Malvern Hill. On this position of great natural strength he had concentrated his powerful artillery, supported by masses of infantry, partially protected by earthworks. His left rested near Crew's house and his right near Beriford's. Immediately in his front the ground was open, varying in width from a quarter to half a mile, and sloping gradually from the crest, was completely swept by the fire of his infantry and artillery. To reach this open ground our troops had to advance through a broken and thickly wooded country, traversed nearly throughout its whole extent by a swamp passable at but few places, and difficult at those. The whole was within range of the batteries on the heights and the gunboats in the river, under whose incessant fire our movements had to be executed. Jackson formed his line with Whiting's division on his left and D. H. Hill's on his right, one of Ewell's brigades occupying the interval. The rest of Ewell's and Jackson's own divisions were held in reserve. Magruder was directed to take position on Jackson's right, but before his arrival two of Huger's brigades came up and were placed next to Hill. Magruder subsequently formed on the right of these brigades, which, with a third of Huger's, were placed under his command. Longstreet and A. P. Hill were held in reserve and took no part in the engagement. Owing to ignorance of the country, the dense forests impeding necessary communication, and the extreme difficulty of the ground, the whole line was not formed until a late hour in the afternoon. The obstacles presented by the woods and swamp made it impracticable to bring up a sufficient amount of artillery to oppose successfully the extraordinary force of that arm employed by the enemy, while the field itself afforded us few positions favorable for its use, and none for its proper concentration. Orders were issued for a general advance at a given signal, but the causes referred to prevented a proper concert of action among the troops.

A SCENE AFTER THE BATTLE OF SAVAGE STATION.

D. H. Hill pressed forward across the open field and engaged the enemy gallantly, breaking and driving back his first line; but a simultaneous advance of the other troops not taking place, he found himself unable to maintain the ground he had gained against the overwhelming numbers and numerous batteries of the enemy. Jackson sent to his support his own division and that part of Ewell's which was in reserve, but owing to the increasing darkness and intricacy of the forest and swamp they did not arrive in time to render the desired assistance. Hill was therefore compelled to abandon part of the ground he had gained after suffering severe loss and inflicting heavy damage upon the enemy.

On the right the attack was gallantly made by Huger's and Magruder's commands. Two brigades of the former commenced the action; the other two were subsequently sent to the support of Magruder and Hill. Several determined efforts were made to storm the hill at Crew's house. The brigades advanced bravely across the open field, raked by the fire of a hundred cannon and the musketry of large bodies of infantry. Some were broken and gave way, others approached close to the guns, driving back the infantry, compelling the advanced batteries to retire to escape capture, and mingling their dead with those of the enemy. For want of concert among the attacking columns their assaults were too weak to break the Federal line, and after struggling gallantly, sustaining and inflicting great loss, they were compelled successively to retire. Night was approaching when the attack began, and it soon became difficult to distinguish friend from foe. The firing continued until after 9 P. M., but no decided result was gained. Part of the troops were withdrawn to their original positions, others remained on the open field, and some rested within a hundred yards of the batteries that had been so bravely but vainly assailed. The general conduct of the troops was excellent—in some instances heroic. The lateness of the hour at which the attack necessarily began gave the enemy the full advantage of his superior position and augmented the natural difficulties of our own.

After seizing the York River Railroad on June 28th and driving the enemy across the Chickahominy, as already narrated, the cavalry under General Stuart proceeded down the railroad to ascertain if there was any movement of the enemy in that direction.

He encountered little opposition, and reached the vicinity of the White House on the 29th. At his approach the enemy destroyed the greater part of the immense stores accumulated at that depot and retreated toward Fort Monroe. With one gun and some dismounted men General Stuart drove off a gunboat which lay near the White House, and rescued a large amount of property, including more than ten thousand stands of small arms, partially burned. Leaving one squadron at the White House, in compliance with his orders, he returned to guard the lower bridges of the Chickahominy.

On the 30th he was directed to recross and co-operate with General Jackson. After a long march he reached the rear of the enemy at Malvern Hill, on the night of July 1st, at the close of the engagement. On July 2d it was discovered that the enemy had withdrawn during the night, leaving the ground covered with his dead and wounded, and his route exhibiting abundant evidence of precipitate retreat. The pursuit was commenced—General Stuart with his cavalry in the advance—but a violent storm which prevailed throughout the day greatly retarded our progress. The enemy, harassed and closely followed by the cavalry, succeeded in gaining Westover, on James River, and the protection of his gunboats. He immediately began to fortify his position, which was one of great natural strength, flanked on each side by a creek, and the approach to his front commanded by the heavy guns of his shipping, in addition to those mounted in his intrenchments. It was deemed inexpedient to attack him, and in view of the condition of our troops, who had been marching and fighting almost incessantly for seven days under the most trying circumstances, it was determined to withdraw, in order to afford them the repose of which they stood so much in need.

Several days were spent in collecting arms and other property abandoned by the enemy, and in the meantime some artillery and cavalry were sent below Westover to annoy his transports. On July 8th the army returned to the vicinity of Richmond.

Under ordinary circumstances the Federal army should have been destroyed. Its escape was due to the causes stated. Prominent among these was the want of correct and timely information; this fact, attributable chiefly to the character of the country, enabled General McClellan skillfully to conceal his retreat and to add much to the obstructions with which nature had beset the way of our pursuing columns; but regret that more was not accomplished gives way to gratitude to the Sovereign Ruler of the Universe for the results achieved. The siege of Richmond was raised, and the object of a campaign which had been prosecuted after months of preparation, at an enormous expenditure of men and money, completely frustrated. More than ten thousand prisoners, including officers of rank, fifty-two pieces of artillery and upward of thirty-five thousand stands of small arms were captured. The stores and supplies of every description which fell into our hands were great in amount and value, but small in comparison with those destroyed by the enemy. His losses in battle exceeded our own, as attested by the thousands of dead and wounded left on every field, while his subsequent inaction shows in what condition the survivors reached the protection to which they fled.

Among the dead will be found many whose names will ever be associated with the great events in which they all bore so honorable a part. I can not forbear expressing my admiration of the noble qualities displayed by officers and men under circumstances which demanded the exercise of every soldierly virtue. To the officers commanding divisions and brigades belongs the credit for the management of their troops in action. The extent of the fields of battle, the nature of the ground and the denseness of the forest rendered more than general directions impracticable.

* * * * * * *

R. E. LEE, *General.*

* Called also Glendale, or Nelson's Farm, and Charles City Road.

THE SEVEN DAYS' BATTLES

BEFORE RICHMOND, VA.,

INCLUDING

KING'S SCHOOLHOUSE, MECHANICSVILLE, OAK GROVE, GAINES' MILL, WHITE OAK SWAMP BRIDGE, MALVERN HILL, ETC.,

JUNE 25 TO JULY 1, 1862.

BY

MAJOR-GENERAL D. H. HILL.

HEADQUARTERS DIVISION, August —, 1862.

I SUBMIT my report of the part taken by my division in the engagements around Richmond which resulted in lifting the young Napoleon from his intrenchments around that city and setting him down on the banks of the James, twenty-five miles further off, with a loss of

MAJ.-GEN. JOHN B. MAGRUDER, OF VIRGINIA.
[From an old photo, taken in 1861.]

fifty-one pieces of artillery, 27,000 stand of arms and 10,000 prisoners.

On June 25th my division constituted the supporting force to a portion of the brigades of Generals Wright and Ransom, which were engaged with the Yankees near King's Schoolhouse, on the Williamsburg Road. We were exposed all day to an artillery fire, but with little loss.

We marched that night through the mud to the vicinity of the Mechanicsville Bridge, and there awaited the advance of Major-Generals Jackson and A. P. Hill. The plan of operations was for the former officer to come down by the way of Hanover Junction and get in rear of Mechanicsville, while the latter should cross at Meadow Bridge and move directly upon Mechanicsville, so as to unmask the bridge opposite it, and enable my division to cross over, followed by that of Major-General Longstreet. To the four divisions of Generals Longstreet, Jackson, A. P. Hill and myself was intrusted the task of turning the right flank of the Yankee army.

About 3 o'clock on the afternoon of June 26th, the firing began at Meadow Bridge, and was followed by the rapid running of the Yankees toward Mechanicsville. My division was put in motion, and crossed the Chickahominy after a little delay in repairing the bridge. General A. P. Hill was then hotly engaged about the town, and my leading brigade (Ripley's) was pushed forward to his support. The Yankees were beginning to retreat across the creek (Beaver Dam) toward Ellison's mill, but their artillery was still on the plain on this side. The three batteries of Jones' battalion, of my division, and Hardaway's battery and Bondurant's, were brought into action, and drove the Yankee artillery off the field.

In the meantime I had received several messages from General Lee, and one from the President of the Confederate States, to send forward a brigade. In advancing with this brigade I met Brigadier-General Pender, whose brigade had just been roughly handled, who told me that with the assistance of two regiments of Ripley's brigade he could turn the position at Ellison's mill by the right, while two regiments should advance in front. Brigadier-General Ripley was directed to co-operate with General Pender, and the attack was made about dark. The enemy had intrenchments of great strength and development on the other side of Beaver Dam, and had the banks lined with his magnificent artillery. The approach was over an open plain, exposed to a murderous fire of all arms, and an almost impassable stream was to be crossed. The result, as might have been anticipated, was a disastrous and bloody repulse. Nearly every field officer in the brigade was killed or wounded, and a large number of officers of all grades were equally unfortunate.

Those hero martyrs, Colonel [M. S.] Stokes, of the First North Carolina Regiment, and Colonel Robert A. Smith, Forty-fourth Georgia, deserve more than a passing notice. The former had served with credit in the Mexican War, and was widely and favorably known in his own State. The latter, though in feeble health and scarcely able to walk, insisted upon being at the head of his regiment, and attracted my particular attention by his gallantry.

Lieutenant-Colonel [John B.] Estes, of the Forty-fourth, was severely wounded, and two captains, ten lieutenants and three hundred and twenty-one privates were killed and wounded in this regiment. Of the First North Carolina Regiment, Colonel Stokes and Major T. L. Skinner, six captains and the adjutant were killed, and one hundred and thirty-three privates were killed and wounded. These two regiments (never before under fire) were badly demoralized, and scarcely preserved their organization in the subsequent operations. Captain H. A. Brown, of the First North Carolina Regiment, and Captains [J. W.] Beck and [S. P.] Lumpkin, of the Forty-fourth Georgia, rallied the fragments of their commands, and are handsomely spoken of by Brigadier-General Ripley.

The Third North Carolina Regiment and the Forty-eighth Georgia were less exposed than the other two regiments of Ripley's brigade, and in consequence suffered less severely; but Major [Edward] Savage, of the Third North Carolina, fell badly wounded.

The batteries of Captain Rhett and Captain Hardaway were particularly distinguished in this engagement.

The division slept on the field that night. About 9 P. M. I received an order from General Lee to co-operate with Major-General Jackson on the Cold Harbor Road, going by way of Bethesda Church. The route we had to take was found at daylight to be held by the enemy in force, with strong intrenchments mounted with artillery. I sent the brigades of Garland and Anderson to the left to turn the position, while my other three brigades and all the division artillery were kept on the main road, ready to advance when the rear of the works was gained. The Yankees abandoned their earthworks when Garland and Anderson gained their rear, and the whole division moved onward.

The shorter road, upon which Major-General Jackson marched, being obstructed, he was compelled to turn off and follow in my rear. We therefore reached Cold Harbor first, capturing a few wagons, ambulances and prisoners. The division moved up cautiously to the edge of Powhite Swamp, where the Yankees were found to be strongly posted, with ten pieces of artillery commanding the only road upon which our guns could be moved. Captain Bondurant's battery was brought into action, but in less than half an hour was withdrawn, badly crippled. By the order of Major-General Jackson the division was moved back to the edge of the woods parallel to the road, to cut off the retreat of the enemy from the attack of Major-Generals Longstreet and A. P. Hill.

It soon became apparent, however, that the fire on our right was receding and that the Yankees were gaining ground. Jackson's division and mine were then ordered forward to the support of Longstreet and A. P. Hill, who had been hotly engaged for several hours. My division occupied the extreme left of the whole Confederate line. The order of advance of the division was: Garland on the left, next Anderson, next Rodes, next Colquitt; Ripley being on the extreme right. In advancing we had a dense swamp to cross, with tangled undergrowth, and the radius of the wheeling circle had to be shortened. These combined causes produced much confusion, and a lapping of brigades and the separation of regiments from their proper places. Several regiments of my division were thrown into the rear and did not engage the enemy. The Forty-eighth Georgia and the fragments of the Forty-fourth Georgia (Ripley's brigade) were thus thrown into the rear. The Sixth and Twenty-seventh Georgia (Colquitt's brigade) were the only regiments of their brigade which drew trigger. The other three regiments of this brigade—Twenty-third Georgia, Twenty-eighth Georgia and Thirteenth Alabama—preserved their positions in rear, but did not engage the Yankees. The Fifth and Twenty-sixth Alabama (Rodes' brigade) encountered a battery in their front, which they charged and captured. Colonel C. C. Pegues, the noble Christian commander of the Fifth Alabama, fell mortally wounded in this charge.

Anderson's brigade, on the left, met the Yankees on the edge of the swamp, and was first engaged. The contest was short but bloody, and the woods were entirely cleared of the Yankees, who fell back behind a fence and ditch and the brow of a hill.

My division now occupied the edge of the wooded swamp, separated from the Yankees by an open field some four hundred yards wide. Confederate troops upon our right, subsequently discovered to be Winder's and Lawton's brigades, were advancing across the plain to attack them. I found Generals Anderson and Garland discussing, with great enthusiasm, the propriety of attacking the Yankees in flank with their two brigades while Lawton and Winder attacked in front. The only objection to the movement was that a Yankee battery on our extreme left could enfilade our line on its advance. Garland observed: "I don't think it can do much harm, and I am willing to risk it." Anderson responded in the same spirit, and I ordered an advance of the whole division. To prevent the destruction of life from the battery I resolved to make an attempt to capture it.

Two regiments of Elzey's brigade (I think) were found separated from their command, and these I ordered, under my volunteer aid, Mr. Sydnor, perfectly acquainted with the ground, to get in rear of the battery, while the Twentieth North Carolina, Colonel Alfred Iverson, the Third North Carolina, Colonel Gaston Meares, and the First North Carolina, commanded by Captain H. A. Brown, were ordered to make a direct advance. Unfortunately Colonel Iverson alone carried out his orders fully.

Says General Garland: "Colonel Iverson was seriously wounded at an early period while gallantly leading up his regiment to take the battery. The regiment, after he was wounded, was led by Lieut.-Col. Franklin J. Faison. It advanced gallantly and took the battery, which it held for ten minutes. The gallant Faison received a mortal wound in the very act of turning a captured piece upon the fleeing foe. He was greatly beloved, and his memory will be cherished with veneration and pride. The enemy soon returned to the battery, and the regiment, having sustained a loss of seventy killed and two hundred and two wounded, and being without support, retired, by order of Major [William H.] Toon."

Heavy as was this loss, no doubt a greater loss was saved to the division in its advance by this gallant attack. The temporary silence of the battery enabled the division to move up in fine style, and turn the tide of battle in our favor.

"The effect of our appearance," says General Garland, "at this opportune moment upon the enemy's flank, cheering and charging, decided the fate of the day. The enemy broke and retreated, made a second stand, which induced my immediate command to halt under cover of the roadside and return their fire, when, charging forward again, we broke and scattered them in every direction." The statements of the Yankees themselves and of the French princes on McClellan's staff fully concur with General Garland that it was this final charge upon their right flank

BRIG.-GEN. ROBERT H. CHILTON, OF VIRGINIA,
Assistant Adjutant-General, Army of Northern Virginia.
[From an old Daguerreotype taken in 1862.]

which decided the fortunes of the day. The Yankees made no further resistance, but fled in great confusion to Grapevine Bridge.

It was now fairly dark, and, hearing loud cheers from the Yankees in our immediate front, some two hundred yards distant, I ordered our whole advance to halt and wait an expected attack of the enemy. Brigadier-General Winder, occupying the road to Grapevine Bridge, immediately halted, and the whole advance columns were halted also. The cheering, as we afterward learned, was caused by the appearance of the Irish Brigade to cover the retreat. A vigorous attack upon it might have resulted in the total rout of the Yankee army and the capture of thousands of prisoners, but I was unwilling to leave the elevated plateau around McGehee's house to advance in the dark along an unknown road, skirted by dense woods in the possession of Yankee troops.

The night was spent in caring for the wounded and making preparations for the morning. I drew back the advanced troops several hundred yards to McGehee's house, and sent across the swamp for my division artillery. This, however, did not come up until sunrise next morning. All of the advanced troops of General Jackson reported to me for orders, and with my own were intrusted with guarding the road to Grapevine Bridge. Soon after daylight it was discovered that the Yankees had retreated across the Chickahominy, destroying all the bridges. The Yankee general, John F. Reynolds, with his aid, was discovered in the woods by my pickets and brought to me. Major-General Jackson came up after sunrise and assumed command of his own and my division.

My thanks are especially due to Brigadier-Generals Garland and Anderson for their skill in discovering the weak point of the Yankees and their boldness in attacking it. Their brigades, being more exposed than the others of my command, suffered more severely. Brigadier-General Rodes was on the field, and displayed his usual coolness and judgment, though very feeble from the unhealed wound received at Seven Pines. The brigade of Brigadier-General Ripley was not engaged, owing to that officer not keeping it in hand and not pressing vigorously to the front. Colonel Colquitt, commanding brigade, in like manner did not keep his brigade in hand, and three of his regiments did not draw trigger. The Sixth and Twenty-seventh Georgia, of this brigade, commanded by those pure, brave, noble Christian soldiers, Lieutenant-Colonel J. M. Newton and Colonel Levi B. Smith, behaved most heroically, and maintained their ground when half their number had been struck down.

My seven division batteries, under Captains Carter, Hardaway, Bondurant, Rhett, Clark, Peyton and Nelson, were all engaged at one time or another at Mechanicsville, and all in like manner at Cold Harbor. Bondurant had three men killed, ten wounded, and twenty-eight horses killed or disabled at the latter place. The other six batteries suffered but little. Under the immediate supervision of Major-General Jackson they opened across the swamp upon the Yankee batteries just before our final charge.

On June 28th Major-General Ewell was sent with his division to Dispatch Station, on the York River Railroad, while General Stuart went down to the White House, the terminus of this road. Both expeditions were completely successful, and the Yankee line of communications being thus cut, McClellan was compelled to change his base. He spent two days in destroying vast military and medical stores south of the Chickahominy, and attempted to hold the crossings over that stream. Scouts from Hood's brigade and the Third Alabama (Rodes' brigade) succeeded in crossing, and my pioneer corps, under Captain Smith, of the engineers, repaired Grapevine Bridge on the 29th, and we crossed over at 3 o'clock that night. McLaws' division had a bloody fight at Savage Station on the afternoon of the 29th instant. That night the Yankees continued their retreat, leaving 1,100 sick and wounded in our hands.

Scene on the Battlefield After a Charge.

Jackson's command, my division leading, passed Savage Station early in the morning of the 30th instant, and followed the line of the Yankee retreat toward White Oak Creek. We picked up about one thousand prisoners, and so many arms that I detached the Fourth and Fifth North Carolina regiments to take charge of both. At White Oak Creek we found the bridge destroyed and the Yankee forces drawn up on the other side. Twenty-six guns from my division and five from Whiting's division opened a sudden and unexpected fire upon the Yankee batteries and infantry. A feeble response was attempted, but silenced in a few minutes. Munford's cavalry and my skirmishers crossed over, but the Yankees got some guns under cover of a wood which commanded the bridge, and the cavalry was compelled to turn back. The skirmishers staid over all day and night. We attempted no further crossing that day. The hospitals and a large number of sick and wounded at White Oak Creek fell into our hands. Major-Generals Longstreet and A. P. Hill attacked the Yankees in flank at Frazier's farm, some two miles in advance of us that day, and a corresponding vigorous attack by Major-General Huger on their rear must have resulted most disastrously to them. The obstacles he met which prevented his advance may have been of a character not to be overcome. I do not know and can not judge of them. The bridge being repaired, Jackson's command crossed over, Brigadier-General Whiting's division leading, and effected a junction with General Lee near a church a few miles from Malvern Hill. Whiting's division was turned off the road to the left at the foot of this hill, and mine to the right. We had to advance across an open field and ford a creek before getting under cover of the woods. We were in full view while effecting these objects, and suffered heavily from the Yankee artillery. Brigadier-General Anderson, on the extreme left, had become engaged, his brigade being roughly handled and himself wounded and carried off the field before the other brigades had crossed the creek. By the order of Major-General Jackson the division was halted in the woods and an examination made of the ground. The Yankees were found to be strongly posted on a commanding hill, all the approaches to which could be swept by his artillery, and were guarded by swarms of infantry securely sheltered by fences, ditches and ravines. Tier after tier of batteries were grimly visible on the plateau, rising in the form of an amphitheater. One flank was protected by Turkey Creek and the other by gunboats. We could only reach the first line of batteries by traversing an open space of from three to four hundred yards, exposed to a murderous fire of grape and canister from the artillery and musketry from the infantry. If that first line were carried another and another still more difficult remained in the rear. I had expressed my disapprobation of a further pursuit of the Yankees to the commanding general and to Major-Generals Jackson and Longstreet even before I knew of the strength of their position. A close examination now satisfied me that an attack could not but be hazardous to our arms.

About 2 o'clock, I think, I received a note from General Jackson, inclosing one from Colonel R. H. Chilton, chief of General Lee's staff, saying that positions were selected from which our artillery could silence the Yankee artillery, and as soon as that was done Brigadier-General Armistead would advance with a shout and carry the battery immediately in his front. This shout was to be the signal for a general advance, and all the troops were then to rush forward with fixed bayonets. I sent for all my brigade commanders and showed them the note. Brigadier-General Rodes being absent sick, the gallant Gordon was put in command of his brigade. That accomplished gentleman and soldier, Colonel C. C. Tew, Second North Carolina Regiment, took command of Anderson's brigade. Garland, Ripley and Colquitt, and these two colonels, were present at the interview. Instead of ordering up one or two hundred pieces of artillery to play on the Yankees, a single battery (Moorman's) was ordered up, and knocked to pieces in a few minutes. One or two others shared the same fate of being beat in detail. Not knowing how to act under these circumstances, I wrote to General Jackson that the firing from our batteries was of the most farcical character. He repeated the order for a general advance at the signal of the shouting from General Armistead. As well as I could learn the position of our troops, the division of Brigadier-General Whiting was on my left, Major-Generals Magruder and Huger on my right, and Major-General Holmes some miles in our rear.

While conversing with my brigade commanders shouting was heard on our right, followed by the roar of musketry. We all agreed that this was the signal agreed upon, and I ordered my division to advance. This, as near as I could judge, was about an hour and a half before sundown. We advanced alone; neither Whiting on the left, nor Magruder and Huger, on the right, moved forward an inch. The division fought heroicly and well, but fought in vain. Garland, in my immediate front, showed all his wonted courage and enthusiasm, but he needed and asked for re-enforcements. I sent Lieutenant-Colonel Newton, Sixth Georgia, to his support, and observing a brigade by a fence in our rear, I galloped back to it and found it to be that of Brigadier-General Toombs. I ordered it forward to support Garland, and accompanied it. The brigade advanced handsomely to the brow of the hill, but soon retreated in disorder. Gordon, commanding Rodes' brigade, pushed gallantly forward and gained considerable ground, but was forced back. The gallant and accomplished Meares, Third North Carolina Regiment, Ripley's brigade, had fallen at the head of his regiment, and that brigade was streaming to the rear. Colquitt's and Anderson's brigades had also fallen back. Ransom's brigade had come up to my support from Major-General Huger. A portion of it came, but without its brigadier. It moved too far to the left, and became mixed up with the mass of troops near the Parsonage on the Quaker Road, suffering heavily and effecting little. Brigadier-General Winder was sent up by Major-General Jackson, but he came too late, and also went to the same belt of woods near the Parsonage, already overcrowded with troops. Finally Major-General Ewell came up, but it was after dark and nothing could be accomplished. I advised him to hold the ground he had gained and not to attempt a forward movement.

Battle of Malvern Hill.

The battle of Malvern Hill might have been a complete and glorious success had not our artillery and infantry been fought in detail. My division batteries having been three times engaged, had exhausted all their ammunition and had been sent back for a fresh supply. If I had had them with me, with a good supply of ammunition, I feel confident that we could have beaten the force immediately in front of us. Again, the want of concert with the infantry divisions was most painful. Whiting's division did not engage at all; neither did Holmes'. My division fought an hour or more the whole Yankee force without assistance from a single Confederate soldier.

The front line of the Yankees was twice broken and in full retreat, when fresh troops came to its support. At such critical junctures the general advance of the divisions on my right and left must have been decisive. Some half an hour after my division had ceased to struggle against odds of more than ten to one and had fallen back, McLaws' division advanced, but to share a similar fate.

So far as I can learn none of our troops drew trigger except McLaw's division, mine and a portion of Huger's. Notwithstanding the tremendous odds against us and the blundering management of the battle we inflicted heavy loss upon the Yankees. They retreated in the night, leaving their dead unburied, their wounded on the ground, three pieces of artillery abandoned and thousands of superior rifles thrown away. None of their previous retreats exhibited such unmistakable signs of rout and demoralization. The wheat-fields about Shirley were all trampled down by the frightened herd, too impatient to follow the road. Arms, accouterments, knapsacks, overcoats and clothing of every description were wildly strewn on the roadside, in the woods and in the field. Numerous wagons and ambulances were found stuck in the mud, typical of Yankee progress in war.

The actual loss in battle was, in my opinion, greater on our side than on that of the Yankees, though most persons differ with me. The advantage in position, range, caliber and number of guns was with them. The prestige of victory and the enthusiasm inspired by it were with us. Their masses, too, were so compact that shot, shell and ball could hardly fail to accomplish a noble work.

My division was employed during the week after the battle in gathering up arms and accouterments, burying our own and the Yankee dead, and removing the wounded of both armies. We then returned to our old camp near Richmond, with much cause for gratitude to the Author of all good for raising the siege of that city and crowning our arms with glorious success. The following list of killed and wounded will show that we lost four thousand out of a little less than ten thousand taken into the field. Among these we have to mourn those gallant spirits, Colonel Robert A. Smith, Forty-fourth Georgia; Colonel M. S. Stokes and Major T. L. Skinner, First North Carolina; Colonel Gaston Mears, Third North Carolina; Colonel T. J. Warthen, Twenty-eighth Georgia; Lieutenant-Colonel [Franklin J.] Faison, Twentieth North Carolina; and Captain Thomas M. Blount, quartermaster of the Fourth North Carolina Regiment, who fell while gallantly carrying on horseback the colors of the Thirtieth North Carolina Regiment.

LIST OF CASUALTIES.

COMMANDS.	Killed	Wounded	Missing
Ripley's Brigade	164	731	30
Garland's Brigade	192	637	12
Rodes' Brigade	122	440	. .
Anderson's Brigade	159	704	. .
Colquitt's Brigade	72	633	6
Jones' Artillery	5	22	. .
Hardaway's Battery	1	25	. .
Nelson's Battery (no report)	. .	. .	. .
Total	715	3,192	48
Aggregate	. . .	. . .	3,955

This embraces the entire loss in the division with the exception of one battery, from which no report has been received.

* * * * * *

D. H. HILL, *Major-General.*

THE SEVEN DAYS' BATTLES

BEFORE RICHMOND, VA.,

INCLUDING

HUNDLEY'S CORNER, GAINES' MILL, MALVERN HILL AND WESTOVER,

JUNE 25 TO JULY 1, 1862.

AS DESCRIBED BY

MAJOR-GENERAL R. S. EWELL,

Commanding Third Division.

HEADQUARTERS THIRD DIVISION,
NEAR SOMERSET, VA.,
August 4, 1862.

THE march from Ashland and the movements preliminary to the fight at Gaines' mill were all made under the immediate direction of the major-general commanding. I need only mention that in the skirmish at Hundley's Corner, on Thursday evening, the First Maryland and Thirteenth Virginia, and in that on the next day the Thirteenth Virginia and Sixth Louisiana, were the regiments engaged.

On Friday, having formed line along the edge of a wood, I was ordered to throw skirmishers across a field on my right into a wood some four hundred yards distant, in which the enemy was understood to be posted, and to follow them with my main body.

The skirmishers passed through the wood without becoming engaged, but before the division reached it orders came to turn more to the left, as heavy firing was heard in that direction. Before arriving at the field of battle I was met by Colonel Taylor, of General Lee's staff, sent to bring up re-enforcements, and received directions for the march of my division.

On nearing the battle ground I ordered the Fourth Brigade, General Elzey, into the woods, on the left of the road passing from Gaines' house toward McGehee's; and as my other two brigades were not yet up, I took advantage of the interval to report to General Lee, who ordered me to hurry up my division as rapidly as possible, indicating where it was to take part in the action. I accordingly ordered the Seventh Brigade, General Trimble, and the Eighth Brigade, Colonel Seymour, into the woods on the right of the road, and, by General Lee's instructions, sent back Captain G. Campbell Brown, assistant adjutant-general, to bring up the divisions of Generals Jackson and Whiting and Lawton's brigade. Having crossed the branch and commenced the ascent of the hill, my division soon became warmly engaged with the enemy. The density of the woods and the nature of the ground were such as to prevent any extended view; and this fact, together with the importance of holding the position occupied by the Louisiana brigade, and that portion of Trimble's which was on its left, now severely pressed by the enemy, made it necessary to confine my exertions mainly to that locality. These troops were attacked in front and flank by superior numbers, and were for hours without re-enforcements. The Louisiana brigade having sustained a very severe loss in field officers, besides suffering in rank and file, was driven off the field, but the line was held by part of Trimble's brigade, consisting of a portion of the Fifteenth Alabama Regiment, under Lieutenant-Colonel Trentlen (Colonel Cantey with the balance having accidentally become separated from the regiment), and the Twenty-first Georgia Regiment, under Major Hooper. I can not speak too highly of the conduct of these troops, which were immediately under my observation. They were opposed to constantly renewed forces of the enemy, and held their ground against vastly superior numbers, advantageously posted, after the troops immediately to their right had fallen back, gaining ground slowly against large odds.

Lieutenant-Colonel Trentlen, of the Fifteenth Alabama, displayed the most indomitable bravery, encouraging and keeping his men in place when in many instances their ammunition was exhausted and their pieces had become too hot to load, and at a time when there were no troops in supporting distance and the abandonment of this position might have been attended with the most disastrous results. I was also particularly struck by the gallantry of Private Frank Champion, Company F, Fifteenth Alabama Regiment, who, on horseback, was very conspicuous in rallying and encouraging the troops, those he was ordering taking him for an officer of rank.

Among many officers who attracted attention by their gallant bearing I would enumerate Major A. A. Lowther, Captain Feagin, of Company B; Second Lieutenant Brear, Company G; Brevet Second Lieutenant Bethune, Company K, Fifteenth Alabama Regiment.

General Trimble also furnishes the names of the following officers as having shown conspicuous bravery: Major T. W. Hooper (wounded); Captain J. B. Akridge, Company K; Captain James C. Nisbet, Company H; First Lieutenant W. J. Warren, Company I; First Lieutenant M. T. Castleberry, Company C; Second Lieutenant J. W. Patrick, Company K, Twenty-first Georgia Regiment; and Captains P. V. Guerry, Company C, Fifteenth Alabama, and James Brown, Company A, Sixteenth Mississippi, who were shot dead while leading their companies in a charge.

During the late campaign in the valley Captain Brown's company was detached as scouts, and he rendered very effective service in this capacity, giving much valuable information and proving himself a most capable and brave officer. Colonel James Cantey, Fifteenth Alabama Regiment, accidentally separated from his regiment in the confusion, succeeded, with the assistance of Captain G. Campbell Brown, assistant adjutant-general, just returned from carrying orders, in rallying a number of the fugitives, whom he led again into the action.

The Fifth Texas, of Hood's brigade, and a portion of the Hampton Legion first came to my assistance, and rendered valuable service in keeping back the enemy until the arrival of General Lawton enabled our forces to take the initiative. General Lawton, after assisting in clearing the front, wheeled part of his brigade to the right, attacking the enemy in flank, thus opening the way to the remainder of General Trimble's brigade, which was on my right, and which advanced to the field beyond the woods.

The small body of troops with me had held their ground for two hours or more alone, when the re-enforcements already mentioned came up; and they having exhausted all their own ammunition, and in many cases that of the dead and wounded, and having been closely engaged for more than four hours, the most of them were withdrawn from the field about dusk.

I remained on the ground myself until after dark, in order that the troops which came up later in the day might profit by what I had learned of the ground and the position of the enemy. I found the Thirteenth Georgia Regiment, Colonel Douglas, temporarily separated from the rest of Lawton's brigade on its left, but, instead of waiting for orders, gallantly and successfully advancing against the enemy (though he was strongly posted) until assurances that those in front were friends caused doubts in the minds or the men, and made it advisable to halt them under cover until the movement of the Fifth Texas and the balance of Lawton's brigade was certain to dislodge the enemy.

On Saturday, under orders from Major-General Jackson, I advanced, preceded by a cavalry force, down the north bank of the Chickahominy to Dispatch Station, and destroyed a portion of the railroad track. The station and stores had unfortunately been burned by the cavalry advance guard before my arrival.

About noon on Sunday I was ordered to prevent the enemy from crossing Bottom's Bridge, and took position accordingly until about 6 P. M., when I received directions to return to Grapevine Bridge and follow General Jackson's division.

ABANDONED POSITIONS ON THE BATTLEFIELD.

Tuesday morning, on the march, I was joined by General Early, ordered to my division, who took command of the Fourth Brigade, General Elzey having been dangerously wounded at Cold Harbor. At this time General Early was so disabled from the effects of a wound received at Williamsburg as to be unable to mount his horse without assistance.

At Malvern Hill my division was in reserve. General Trimble being posted in rear of General Whiting's left; Colonel Stafford, with the Louisiana brigade, on the right of General Whiting's line, and General Early in rear of Colonel Stafford.

About dark General Early was ordered to the right to support General D. H. Hill, and was exposed on the march and after his arrival to a heavy artillery fire. When morning came his troops were the only ones on that part of the field.

Colonel Stafford's brigade was detached from my command, and consequently I can give no account of his movements.

At Westover, on the Friday following, my division was placed in front, and advanced until our skirmishers became engaged with those of the enemy, when we were ordered to halt.

My staff at Gaines' Mill (or Cold Harbor) consisted of Lieutenant-Colonel J. M. Jones, Major James Barbour, Captain G. Campbell Brown and Lieutenant Hugh M. Nelson. At Malvern Hill the same, with the addition of Lieutenant T. T. Turner and Major B. H. Green.

* * * * * *

R. S. EWELL, *Major-General.*

THE SEVEN DAYS' BATTLES

BEFORE RICHMOND, VA.,

EMBRACING

THE BATTLES OF MECHANICSVILLE, GAINES' MILL (COLD HARBOR), WHITE OAK SWAMP, FRAZIER'S FARM, MALVERN HILL, ETC.,

JUNE 25 TO JULY 1, 1862.

BY

GEN. THOMAS J. (STONEWALL) JACKSON,
Commanding Second Corps.

HEADQUARTERS OF SECOND CORPS,
ARMY OF NORTHERN VIRGINIA,
February 20, 1863.

I HEREWITH submit a report of the operations of my corps in the battle of Cold Harbor and other engagements before Richmond.

On June 17th last, leaving the cavalry and Chew's battery under Brigadier-General Robertson near Harrisonburg, Whiting's division, then near Staunton, and Ewell's and Jackson's, near Weyer's Cave, Augusta County, Va., moved toward Richmond. Lawton's brigade, subsequently of Jackson's division, being part at Staunton and part near Weyer's Cave, moved with the troops nearest their positions. Subsequently Colonel Munford, with his cavalry, marched in the same direction.

On June 25th we reached the vicinity of Ashland, on the Richmond, Fredricksburg & Potomac Railroad, about twelve miles from Richmond.

The division of Brigadier-General Whiting embraced the Texas Brigade, General Hood, and the Third Brigade, Colonel Law commanding, with the batteries of Reilly and Balthis.

The division of Major-General Ewell, the Fourth Brigade, General A. Elzey; the Seventh Brigade, General Trimble; the Eighth Brigade, Colonel I. G. Seymour, and the Maryland Line, Colonel Bradley T. Johnson, with the batteries of Brockenbrough, Carrington and Courtney.

Jackson's division, the First Brigade, General Charles S. Winder; the Second Brigade, Lieutenant-Colonel R. H. Cunningham commanding; the Third Brigade, Colonel S. V. Fulkerson commanding, and the Fourth Brigade, General A. R. Lawton, with the batteries of Poague, Carpenter and Wooding.

On the morning of the 26th, in pursuance of instructions from the commanding general, I took up the line of march for Cold Harbor, Whiting's division in front.

Pursuing the Ashcake Road, we crossed the Central Railroad about 10 A. M. Approaching the Totopotomoy Creek, the Federal pickets crossed to the south side of the stream and partially destroyed the bridge, and, by felling trees across the road further on, attempted to delay our advance. After the Texas skirmishers had gallantly crossed over, and Reilly shelled the woods for the purpose of driving the enemy from it, in order that we might safely effect a lodgment beyond the creek, Whiting rapidly repaired the bridge, and the march was resumed.

That night the three divisions bivouacked near Hundley's Corner. While there some skirmishing took place with detachments of the enemy, in which Brockenbrough's battery, the First Maryland, Thirteenth Virginia and Sixth Louisiana regiments participated.

We were now approaching the ground occupied by that portion of the grand army of McClellan which was posted north of the Chickahominy. His right was then resting upon Mechanicsville, from which point his lines extended some miles down the river. As our route that day inclined toward the south, and brought us in the direction, but to the left, of Mechanicsville, we distinctly heard the rapid and continued discharges of cannon, announcing the engagement of General A. P. Hill with the extreme right of the enemy.

Early the next morning (27th) the three divisions resumed the march, General Ewell in the lead. After crossing Beaver Dam we halted to dislodge a force of the enemy observed on our right near the intersection of the road then occupied by us with the road leading from Mechanicsville to Bethesda Church. But the Federals observing the division of General D. H. Hill, then coming into view, and which was advancing from Mechanicsville toward the point of intersection, and at the same time seeing General Ewell moving down from my command, they promptly abandoned their position and fell back. The enemy seen by us, as before stated, on our right, having fallen back, and the road being open for pressing further along his rear, the march was resumed toward Walnut Grove Church, where I again halted until General A. P. Hill came up. Continuing to carry out the plan of the commanding-general, I inclined to the left and advanced on Cold Harbor, while General A. P. Hill moved toward the same point by a different road to the right. The enemy having obstructed the road which I had taken, and adopted the additional precaution to delay my march by defending the obstructions with sharpshooters, it became necessary, for the purpose of saving time, to take a road still further to the left. The time consumed in this delay threw me in rear of General D. H. Hill, who had moved by Bethesda Church. Upon reaching and passing Cold Harbor about half a mile his division was opened upon by a heavy fire from a position on his right, and also from artillery in his front.

Soon after General A. P. Hill became engaged, and being unacquainted with the ground, and apprehensive, from what appeared to me to be the respective positions of the Confederate and Federal forces engaged, that if I then pressed forward our troops would be mistaken for the enemy and be fired into, and hoping that Generals A. P. Hill and Longstreet would soon drive the Federals toward me, I directed General D. H. Hill to move his division to the left of the road, so as to leave between him and the wood on the right of the road an open space across which I hoped the enemy would be driven. Thus arranged, it was in our power to distinguish friend from foe in case the enemy should be driven as expected. Major-General Stuart, who had been covering my left with his cavalry, was also posted so as to charge should the Federals attempt to retreat to the Pamunkey by Cold Harbor; but it soon becoming apparent, from the direction and sound of the firing, that General A. P. Hill was hard pressed, I ordered a general advance of my entire corps, which commenced with General D. H. Hill upon the left, and extending to the right through Ewell's, Jackson's and Whiting's divisions, posted from left to right in the order named.

The Federal commander had withdrawn his troops from their positions west of the Powhite, a small tributary of the Chickahominy, and had concentrated them in strong positions near Cold Harbor and east of that creek. The ground which had been selected to receive our attack had natural advantages for defense, and was strengthened by artificial works. His forces were posted upon an elevated ridge running nearly parallel to the Chickahominy, his right resting near McGehee's house, and his left upon an abrupt bluff, surmounted by artillery and protected by a deep ravine and a double line of breastworks for infantry. This position on the ridge was further favored on his right by points still more elevated rising in his rear, well adapted for batteries, from which a destructive fire could be maintained against an advancing line over the heads of his own infantry. In his front was a wood of deep and tangled undergrowth, through which a sluggish stream passed, converting into swamp or marsh the adjacent soil. This natural obstruction was further increased by felled timber, designed to retard the advance of our troops and to keep them as long as possible exposed to fire.

In advancing to the attack General D. H. Hill had to cross this swamp, densely covered with tangled undergrowth and young timber. This caused some confusion and a separation of the regiments. On the further edge of the swamp he encountered the enemy. The conflict was fierce and bloody. The Federals fell back from the wood under the protection of a fence, ditch and hill. Separated now from them by an open field some four hundred yards wide, he promptly determined to press forward. Before doing so, however, it was necessary to capture a battery on his left, which could enfilade his line upon its advance. To effect this he sent two regiments of Elzey's brigade, which had become separated from their command, to go in rear of the battery, and ordered Colonel [Alfred] Iverson, with the Twentieth North Carolina and the First and Third North Carolina regiments to make the attack in front. The order was promptly and gallantly obeyed and carried into execution by Colonel Iverson with the Twentieth North Carolina. He was severely wounded in the advance. The battery was captured with severe loss and held for a short time—sufficiently long, however, to enable the division to move on free from its terrific fire, when it was retaken by the enemy. Again pressing forward, the Federals again fell back, but only to select a position for a more obstinate defense, when at dark—under the pressure of our batteries, which had then begun to play with marked effect upon the left, of the other concurring events of the field, and of the bold and dashing charge of General Hill's infantry, in which the troops of General C. S. Winder joined—the enemy yielded the field and fled in disorder.

In the meantime General Ewell, on General D. H. Hill's right, had moved the Fourth Brigade, General Elzey, to the left of the road passing from Gaines' house to McGehee's, and a portion of the Seventh, General Trimble, and the Eighth Brigade into the wood on the right of that road. Having crossed the swamp and commenced the ascent of the hill, his division became warmly engaged with the enemy. For two hours, assailed in front and flank by superior numbers, without re-enforcements, Colonel Seymour, then commanding, having fallen, the Eighth Brigade was drawn from the field, but the line was still held by a portion of General Trimble's. The Fifth Texas and a part of the Hampton Legion now came to his support, and rendered important service in holding the enemy in check until the arrival of General Lawton, of Jackson's division, enabled him to assume the offensive. Lawton, after aiding in clearing the front, wheeled a part of his brigade to the right, attacked the enemy in flank, and opened the way for the remainder of Trimble's brigade, which advanced to the field beyond the woods. General Ewell's troops having now exhausted their own ammunition, and in many cases such as they could gather from the dead and wounded, and having been engaged for more than four hours, the most of them withdrew from the field about dusk.

The four brigades of Jackson's division did not act together during the engagement, but were called to separate fields of service. In pursuance of the order to charge the enemy's front, the First Virginia Brigade, commanded by General C. S. Winder, moved forward through the swamp, and upon emerging into the open field its ranks,

BATTLE OF FRAZIER'S FARM, JUNE 30, 1862.

broken by the obstacles encountered, were re-formed. Meeting at that point with the Hampton Legion, First Maryland, Twelfth Alabama, Fifty-second Virginia and Thirty-eighth Georgia, they were formed upon his line. Thus formed they moved forward under the lead of that gallant officer, whose conduct here was marked by the coolness and courage which distinguished him on the battlefields of the Valley. The enemy met this advance with spirit and firmness. His well-directed artillery and heavy musketry played with destructive effect upon our advancing line. Nothing daunted by the fall of officers and men, thinning their ranks at every step, these brave men moved steadily forward, driving the enemy from point to point, until he was finally driven from his last position, some three hundred yards beyond McGehee's house, when night prevented further pursuit. In the charge near McGehee's house Colonel [J. W.] Allen, of the Second Virginia Infantry, fell at the head of his regiment. Five guns, numerous small arms and many prisoners were among the fruits of this rapid and resistless advance. General Reynolds and an officer of his staff, who lingered on this side of the river after the Federal troops had crossed over, were among the number of prisoners.

The Second Brigade, by request of General Wilcox, was removed to a point of woods about half a mile from the river. When it reached there the enemy had already been repulsed at that point by a flank movement of Brigadier-General R. H. Anderson.

The Third Brigade was sent to support General Whiting's attack upon the enemy's left, but reached there only in time to witness the evidences of a bloody triumph and the guns of the enemy in possession of the gallant Texas Brigade. Colonel S. V. Fulkerson, commanding the brigade, fell mortally wounded shortly after his arrival on the spot. General Lawton, of the Fourth Brigade, after rendering timely and important support, before described, to General Ewell's command, pressed to the brow of the hill, driving the enemy before him, and co-operating in that general charge late in the evening that closed the labors of the day.

On my extreme right General Whiting advanced his division through the same dense forest and swamp, emerging from the wood into the field near the public road and at the head of the deep ravine which covered the enemy's left. Advancing thence through a number of retreating and disordered regiments, he came within range of the enemy's fire, who, concealed in an open wood and protected by breastworks, poured a destructive fire for a quarter of a mile into his advancing line, under which many brave officers and men fell. Dashing on with unfaltering step in the face of those murderous discharges of canister and musketry, General Hood and Colonel Law, at the heads of their respective brigades, rushed to the charge with a yell. Moving down a precipitous ravine, leaping ditch and stream, clambering up a difficult ascent, while exposed to an incessant and deadly fire from the intrenchments, these brave and determined men pressed forward, driving the enemy from his well-selected and fortified position.

In this charge, in which upward of one thousand men fell killed and wounded before the fire of the enemy, and in which fourteen pieces of artillery and nearly a regiment were captured, the Fourth Texas, under the lead of General Hood, was the first to pierce these strongholds and seize the guns. Although swept from their defenses by this rapid and almost matchless display of daring and valor, the well-disciplined Federals continued in retreat to fight with stubborn resistance.

Apprehensive, from their superior numbers and sullen obstinacy, that the enemy might again rally, General Whiting called upon General Longstreet for re-enforcements. He promptly sent forward General R. H. Anderson's brigade, which came in gallant style to his support, and the enemy was driven to the lower part of the plateau. The shouts of triumph which rose from our brave men as they, unaided by artillery, had stormed this citadel of their strength, were promptly carried from line to line, and the triumphant issue of this assault, with the well-directed fire of the batteries and successful charges of Hill and Winder upon the enemy's right, determined the fortunes of the day. The Federals, routed at every point and aided by the darkness of the night, escaped across the Chickahominy.

During the earlier part of the action the artillery could not be effectively used. At an advanced stage of it Major John Pelham, of Stuart's Horse Artillery, bravely dashed forward and opened on the Federal batteries posted on the left of our infantry. Re-enforced by the guns of Brockenbrough, Carrington and Courtney, of my command, our artillery now numbered about thirty pieces. Their fire was well-directed and effective, and contributed to the successful issue of the engagement.

On the following day, the 28th, General Ewell, preceded by a cavalry force, advanced down the north side of the Chickahominy to Dispatch Station and destroyed a portion of the railroad track.

On the 29th he moved his division to the vicinity of Bottom's Bridge, to prevent the enemy crossing at that point, but on the following day was ordered to return to co-operate with the movements of the corps.

The 28th and 29th were occupied in disposing of the dead and wounded and repairing Grapevine Bridge, over the Chickahominy, which McClellan's forces had used in their retreat and destroyed in their rear.

During the night of the 29th we commenced crossing the Chickahominy, and on the following morning arrived at Savage Station, on the Richmond & York River Railroad, where a summer hospital, remarkable for the extent and convenience of its accommodations, fell into our possession. In it were about twenty-five hundred sick and wounded, besides some five hundred persons having charge of the patients.

Many other evidences of the hurried and disordered flight of the enemy were now visible—blankets, clothing and other supplies had been recklessly abandoned. D. H. Hill, who had the advance, gathered up probably one thousand stragglers and so many small arms that it became necessary to detach two regiments to take charge of them and to see to the security of the prisoners.

A Bayonet Fight, Frazier's Farm.

About noon we reached White Oak Swamp, and here the enemy made a determined effort to retard our advance and thereby to prevent an immediate junction between General Longstreet and myself.

We found the bridge destroyed and the ordinary place of crossing commanded by their batteries on the opposite side, and all approach to it barred by detachments of sharpshooters, concealed in a dense wood close by.

A battery of twenty-eight guns from Hill's and Whiting's artillery was placed by Colonel S. Crutchfield in a favorable position for driving off or silencing the opposing artillery. About 2 P. M. it opened suddenly upon the enemy. He fired a few shots in reply, then withdrew from that position, abandoning part of his artillery. Captain Wooding was immediately ordered near the bridge to shell the sharpshooters from the woods, which was accomplished, and Munford's cavalry crossed the creek, but was soon compelled to retire. It was now seen that the enemy occupied such a position beyond a thick intervening wood on the right of the road as enabled him to command the crossing.

Captain Wooding's battery was consequently recalled and our batteries turned in the new direction. The fire so opened on both sides was kept up until dark. We bivouacked that night near the swamp.

A heavy cannonading in front announced the engagement of General Longstreet at Frazier's farm and made me eager to press forward; but the marshy character of the soil, the destruction of the bridge over the marsh and creek and the strong position of the enemy for defending the passage prevented my advancing until the following morning. During the night the Federals retired. The bridge was rapidly repaired by Whiting's division, which soon after crossed over and continued the pursuit, in which it was followed by the remainder of my corps.

At White Oak we captured a portion of the enemy's artillery, and also found another hospital with about three hundred and fifty sick and wounded, which fell into our hands.

Upon reaching Frazier's farm I found General Longstreet's advance near the road. The commanding general soon after arrived, and in pursuance of his instructions I continued to press forward. The head of my advancing column was soon fired upon by the enemy, who nevertheless continued to fall back until he reached Malvern Hill, which strong position he held in force. General Whiting was directed to move to the left and take position on the Poindexter farm; General D. H. Hill to take position further to the right; Taylor's brigade, of General Ewell's division, to move forward between the divisions of Hill and Whiting; the remainder of Ewell's division to remain in rear of the first line. Jackson's division was halted near Willis' Church, in the wood, and held in reserve.

General D. H. Hill pursued the route indicated, crossing an open field and creek. His troops were then brought in full range of the enemy's artillery and suffered severely. Brigadier-General Anderson was wounded and carried from the field. The division was halted under cover of a wood, which afforded an opportunity for a more particular examination of the ground in front. The enemy in large force were found strongly posted on a commanding hill, all the approaches to which in the direction of my position could be swept by his artillery and were guarded by infantry. The nearest batteries could only be approached by traversing an open space of three or four hundred yards, exposed to the murderous fire of artillery and infantry.

The commanding general had issued an order that at a given signal there should be a general advance of the whole line. General D. H. Hill, hearing what he believed to be the signal, with great gallantry pressed forward and engaged the enemy. Not supported by a general advance, as he had anticipated, he soon saw that it was impossible without support to sustain himself long against such overwhelming numbers. He accordingly sent to me for re-enforcements. I ordered that portion of General Ewell's division held in reserve and Jackson's division to his relief; but from the darkness of the night and the obstructions caused by the swamp and undergrowth, through which they had to march, none reached him in time to afford him the desired support.

General Hill, after suffering a heavy loss and inflicting a severe one upon the enemy, withdrew from the open field. In the meantime, the re-enforcements ordered—after struggling with the difficulties of their route, and exposed to the shelling of the enemy, which was continued until about 10 P. M.—came up too late to participate in the engagement that evening.

On my left General Whiting moved his division, as directed, to a field on the Poindexter farm. Batteries were ordered up. The position of the enemy, as already shown, naturally commanding, was materially strengthened by the judicious distribution of his artillery. The first battery placed in position, finding itself exposed to the superior cross fire of the enemy, was compelled to retire with loss. Balthis', Poague's and Carpenter's batteries held their positions and fought well. The position occupied by the artillery rendering infantry support necessary, Whiting formed his line accordingly, and, supported by Trimble's brigade on his left and by the Third Brigade of Jackson's division as a reserve, was directed to remain there until further orders. Some of these batteries were well served and effectually drove back at one time an advance of the enemy upon my center.

Toward night Whiting received orders to send General Trimble's brigade to the support of General D. H. Hill, on the right, which order was promptly executed, but the brigade did not reach its destination until after Hill had withdrawn his division to the woods.

Our troops slept in front of the Federal army during the night, expecting a renewal of the action; but early the next morning the enemy had withdrawn from the field, abandoning his dead and leaving behind some artillery and a number of small arms.

I herewith forward to you official reports of the casualties of this corps, from which it will be seen, as far as I have been able to ascertain, that in the battle of Cold Harbor, on June 27th, there were 589 killed, 2,671 wounded and 24 missing; and in the engagement at Malvern Hill, on July 1st, 377 killed, 1,746 wounded and 39 missing.

I regret that I have not before me the data by which to ascertain with absolute precision the loss sustained, respectively, at Cold Harbor and Malvern Hill, or of distinguishing throughout the entire corps the number of officers killed and wounded from the enlisted men. But Brigadier-Generals Garland and Anderson, both since killed, having omitted in their reports to state the separate losses of their brigades in those two actions, and Brigadier-Generals Rodes, Colquitt and Ripley having omitted to classify their losses as between officers and men, I have, so far as it relates to the two first-named brigades, apportioned the aggregate of the reported losses between Cold Harbor and Malvern Hill according to a probable estimate of the fact, and omitted any statements of the loss of officers as distinguished from men in that division. In the three remaining divisions—Ewell's, Whiting's and Jackson's—the returns show a loss at Cold Harbor of thirty officers killed and ninety-nine wounded; of enlisted men, 305 killed and 1,420 wounded; and at Malvern Hill, three officers killed and nineteen wounded; of enlisted men, thirty-eight killed and 354 wounded. The principal loss sustained by my command at Malvern Hill fell upon the division of Major-General D. H. Hill.

On July 2d, by order of the commanding-general, my corps, with the exception of Major-General D. H. Hill's division, which remained near Malvern Hill, was moved in the direction of Harrison's Landing, to which point the Federals had retreated, under the shelter of their gunboats in the James River. On the morning of the 3d my command arrived near the landing and drove in the enemy's skirmishers, and continued in front of the enemy until the 8th, when I was directed to withdraw my troops and march to the vicinity of Richmond.

The conduct of officers and men was worthy of the great cause for which they were contending.

* * * * * * *

T. J. JACKSON, *Major-General.*

ORGANIZATION OF THE CONFEDERATE FORCES AROUND RICHMOND, VA.,*

INCLUDING BATTLES OF

MECHANICSVILLE, GAINES' MILL (COLD HARBOR), WHITE OAK SWAMP, FRAZIER'S FARM, MALVERN HILL, OAK GROVE, BOTTOM'S BRIDGE, MALVERN CLIFF, GLENDALE, WHITE HOUSE, ETC.,

JUNE 20 TO JULY 1, 1862,

JACKSON'S CORPS.

Major-General Thomas J. Jackson.

WHITING'S DIVISION.

Brigadier-General William H. C. Whiting.

FIRST (OR TEXAS) BRIGADE.
Brigadier-General John B. Hood.

Eighteenth Georgia; First Texas; Fourth Texas; Fifth Texas; Hampton Legion.

THIRD BRIGADE.
Colonel E. M. Law.

Fourth Alabama; Second Mississippi; Eleventh Mississippi; Sixth North Carolina.

ARTILLERY.

Balthis' Battery, Staunton (Va.) Artillery; Reilly's battery, Rowan (N. C.) Artillery.

JACKSON'S DIVISION.

FIRST BRIGADE.†
Brigadier-General Charles S. Winder.

Second Virginia; Fourth Virginia; Fifth Virginia; Twenty-seventh Virginia; Thirty-third Virginia; Carpenter's (Va.) battery; Poague's battery, Rockbridge (Va.) Artillery.

MAJ.-GEN. W. H. C. WHITING, OF MISSISSIPPI.

SECOND BRIGADE.†
Lieutenant-Colonel R. H. Cunningham, Jr.; Brigadier-General J. R. Jones.

Twenty-first Virginia; Forty-second Virginia; Forty-eighth Virginia; First Virginia battalion (Irish); Caskie's battery, Hampden (Va.) Artillery.

THIRD BRIGADE.†
Colonel S. V. Fulkerson; Colonel E. T. H. Warren; Brigadier-General Wade Hampton.

Tenth Virginia; Twenty-third Virginia; Thirty-seventh Virginia; Wooding's battery, Danville (Va.) Artillery.

* Compiled from the reports.
† These brigades are numbered as of the Valley District.

FOURTH BRIGADE.*
Brigadier-General A. R. Lawton.

Thirteenth Georgia; Twenty-sixth Georgia; Thirty-first Georgia; Thirty-eighth Georgia; Sixtieth Georgia (or Fourth Battalion); Sixty-first Georgia.

EWELL'S DIVISION.

Major-General Richard S. Ewell.

FOURTH BRIGADE.*
Brigadier-General Arnold Elzey; Colonel James A. Walker; Brigadier-General Jubal A. Early.

Twelfth Georgia; Thirteenth Virginia; Twenty-fifth Virginia; Thirty-first Virginia; Forty-fourth Virginia; Fifty-second Virginia; Fifty-eighth Virginia.

SEVENTH BRIGADE.*
Brigadier-General I. R. Trimble.

Fifteenth Alabama; Twenty-first Georgia; Sixteenth Mississippi; Twenty-first North Carolina; First North Carolina Battalion; Courtney's (Va.) battery.

EIGHTH BRIGADE.*
Brigadier-General Richard Taylor; Colonel I. G. Seymour; Colonel L. A. Stafford.

Sixth Louisiana; Seventh Louisiana; Eighth Louisiana; Ninth Louisiana; First Louisiana Special Battalion, Carrington's battery, Charlottesville (Va.) Artillery.

MARYLAND LINE.
Colonel Bradley T. Johnson.

First Maryland; Brockenbrough's battery, Baltimore (Md.) Artillery.

HILL'S DIVISION.†

Major-General Daniel H. Hill.

FIRST BRIGADE.
Brigadier-General R. E. Rodes.

Third Alabama; Fifth Alabama; Sixth Alabama; Twelfth Alabama; Twenty-sixth Alabama.

SECOND BRIGADE.
Brigadier-General George B. Anderson.

Second North Carolina; Fourth North Carolina; Fourteenth North Carolina; Thirtieth North Carolina.

THIRD BRIGADE.
Brigadier-General Samuel Garland.

Fifth North Carolina; Twelfth North Carolina; Thirteenth North Carolina; Twentieth North Carolina; Twenty-third North Carolina.

FOURTH BRIGADE.
Colonel A. H. Colquitt.

Thirteenth Alabama; Sixth Georgia; Twenty-third Georgia; Twenty-seventh Georgia; Twenty-eighth Georgia.

FIFTH BRIGADE.
Brigadier-General Roswell S. Ripley.

Forty-fourth Georgia; Forty-eighth Georgia; First North Carolina; Third North Carolina.

ARTILLERY.‡

Bondurant's battery, Jeff. Davis (Ala.) Artillery; Carter's battery, King William (Va.) Artillery; Clark's (Va.) battery; Hardaway's (Ala.) battery; Nelson's battery, Hanover (Va.) Artillery; Peyton's battery, Orange (Va.) Artillery; Rhett's (S. C.) battery.

MAGRUDER'S CORPS.

Major-General John B. Magruder.

FIRST DIVISION.

Brigadier-General David R. Jones.

FIRST BRIGADE.
Brigadier-General Robert Toombs.

Second Georgia; Fifteenth Georgia; Seventeenth Georgia; Twentieth Georgia.

THIRD BRIGADE.
Colonel George T. Anderson.

First Georgia (regulars); Seventh Georgia; Eighth Georgia; Ninth Georgia; Eleventh Georgia.

ARTILLERY.
Major John J. Garnett.

Brown's battery, Wise (Va.) Artillery; Hart's battery, Washington (S. C.) Artillery; Lane's (Ga.) battery; § Moody's (La.) battery; Woolfolk's battery, Ashland (Va.) Artillery. ‖

MCLAW'S DIVISION.

Major-General Lafayette McLaws.

FIRST BRIGADE.
Brigadier-General Paul J. Semmes.

Tenth Georgia; Fifty-third Georgia; Fifth Louisiana, Tenth Louisiana; Fifteenth Virginia; Thirty-Second Virginia; Manley's (N. C.) battery.

* These brigades are numbered as of the Valley District.
† Temporarily attached to Jackson's command.
‡ Bondurant's, Carter's, Hardaway's and Nelson's batteries belonged to the division. Those of Clark, Peyton and Rhett (Jones' battalion) were temporarily assigned.
§ Of Cutt's battalion, temporarily attached.
‖ Of Richardson's battalion.

FOURTH BRIGADE.
Brigadier-General J. B. Kershaw.

Second South Carolina; Third South Carolina; Seventh South Carolina; Eighth South Carolina; Kemper's battery, Alexandria (Va.) Artillery.

MAGRUDER'S DIVISION.

SECOND BRIGADE.
Brigadier-General Howell Cobb.

Sixteenth Georgia; Twenty-fourth Georgia; Cobb (Ga.) Legion; Second Louisiana; Fifteenth North Carolina; Troup (Ga.) Artillery.

THIRD BRIGADE.
Brigadier-General R. Griffith; Colonel Wm. Barksdale.

Thirteenth Mississippi; Seventeenth Mississippi; Eighteenth Mississippi; Twenty-first Mississippi; McCarthy's (Va.) battery.

ARTILLERY.
Colonel S. D. Lee.

Kirkpatrick's battery,* Amherst (Va.) Artillery; Page's battery, Magruder (Va.) Artillery; Read's battery, Pulaski (Ga.) Artillery; Richardson's battery.

MAJ.-GEN. ISAAC R. TRIMBLE, OF MARYLAND.

LONGSTREET'S DIVISION.

Major-General James Longstreet.

FIRST BRIGADE.
Brigadier-General James L. Kemper.

First Virginia; Seventh Virginia; Eleventh Virginia; Seventeenth Virginia; Twenty-fourth Virginia; Rogers' (Va.) battery.

SECOND BRIGADE.
Brigadier-General R. H. Anderson; Colonel M. Jenkins.

Second South Carolina Rifles; Fourth South Carolina; Fifth South Carolina; Sixth South Carolina; Palmetto (S. C.) Sharpshooters.

THIRD BRIGADE.
Brigadier-General George E. Pickett; Colonel Eppa Hunton; Colonel J. B. Strange.

Eighth Virginia; Eighteenth Virginia; Nineteenth Virginia; Twenty-eighth Virginia; Fifty-sixth Virginia.

FOURTH BRIGADE.
Brigadier-General Cadmus M. Wilcox.

Eighth Alabama; Ninth Alabama; Tenth Alabama; Eleventh Alabama; Anderson's battery, Thomas (Va.) Artillery.

FIFTH BRIGADE.
Brigadier-General Roger A. Pryor.

Fourteenth Alabama; Second Florida; Fourteenth Louisiana; First Louisiana Battalion; Third Virginia; Maurin's battery, Donaldsonville (La.) Artillery.

SIXTH BRIGADE.
Brigadier-General W. S. Featherston.

Twelfth Mississippi; Nineteenth Mississippi; Second Mississippi Battalion; Smith's battery, Third Richmond Howitzers.

ARTILLERY.

Washington (La.) Battalion.

HUGER'S DIVISION.†

Major-General Benjamin Huger.

SECOND BRIGADE.
Brigadier-General William Mahone.

Sixth Virginia; Twelfth Virginia; Sixteenth Virginia; Forty-first Virginia; Forty-ninth Virginia; Grimes' (Va.) battery; Moorman's (Va.) battery.

* Of Nelson's battalion, temporarily attached.
† Ransom's and Walker's brigades, of the Department of North Carolina, were temporarily attached to Huger's division.

THIRD BRIGADE.
Brigadier-General A. R. Wright.

Forty-fourth Alabama; Third Georgia; Fourth Georgia; Twenty-second Georgia; First Louisiana; Huger's (Va.) battery; Ross' (Ga.) battery.*

FOURTH BRIGADE.
Brigadier-General Lewis A. Armistead.

Ninth Virginia; Fourteenth Virginia; Thirty-eighth Virginia; Fifty-third Virginia; Fifty-seventh Virginia; Fifth Virginia Battalion; Stribling's battery, Fauquier (Va.) Artillery; Turner's (Va.) battery.

HILL'S (LIGHT) DIVISION.
Major-General Ambrose P. Hill.

FIRST BRIGADE.
Brigadier-General Charles W. Field.

Fortieth Virginia; Forty-seventh Virginia; Fifty-fifth Virginia; Sixtieth Virginia.

MAJ.-GEN. ARNOLD ELZEY, OF MARYLAND.

SECOND BRIGADE.
Brigadier-General Maxcy Gregg.

First South Carolina; First South Carolina Rifles; Twelfth South Carolina; Thirteenth South Carolina; Fourteenth South Carolina.

THIRD BRIGADE.
Brigadier-General Joseph R. Anderson; Colonel Edward L. Thomas.

Fourteenth Georgia; Thirty-fifth Georgia; Forty-fifth Georgia; Forty-ninth Georgia; Third Louisiana Battalion.

FOURTH BRIGADE.
Brigadier-General L. O'B. Branch.

Seventh North Carolina; Eighteenth North Carolina; Twenty-eighth North Carolina; Thirty-third North Carolina; Thirty-seventh North Carolina.

FIFTH BRIGADE.
Brigadier-General James J. Archer.

Fifth Alabama Battalion; Nineteenth Georgia; First Tennessee; Seventh Tennessee; Fourteenth Tennessee.

SIXTH BRIGADE.
Brigadier-General William D. Pender.

Second Arkansas Battalion; Sixteenth North Carolina; Twenty-second North Carolina; Thirty-fourth North Carolina; Thirty-eighth North Carolina; Twenty-second Virginia Battalion.

ARTILLERY.
Lieutenant-Colonel Lewis M. Coleman.

Andrews' (Md.) battery; Bachman's (S. C.) battery; Braxton's battery, Fredericksburg (Va.) Artillery; Crenshaw's (Va.) battery; Davidson's battery, Letcher (Va.) Artillery;† Johnson's (Va.) battery; Masters' (Va.) battery; McIntosh' battery, Pee Dee (S. C.) Artillery; Pegram's (Va.) battery.

DEPARTMENT OF NORTH CAROLINA.
Major-General Theophilus H. Holmes.

SECOND BRIGADE.‡
Brigadier-General Robert Ransom, Jr.

Twenty-fourth North Carolina; Twenty-fifth North Carolina; Twenty-sixth North Carolina; Thirty-fifth North Carolina; Forty-eighth North Carolina; Forty-ninth North Carolina.

THIRD BRIGADE.
Brigadier-General Junius Daniel.

Forty-third North Carolina; Forty-fifth North Carolina; Fiftieth North Carolina; Burrough's Battalion Cavalry.

* Of Cutt's battalion, temporarily attached.
† With the Reserve Artillery, Richardson's battalion.
‡ Temporarily attached to Huger's division.

FOURTH BRIGADE.*
Brigadier-General J. G. Walker; Colonel Van H. Manning.

Third Arkansas; Second Georgia Battalion; Twenty-seventh North Carolina; Forty-sixth North Carolina; Thirtieth Virginia; Fifty-seventh Virginia; Goodwyn's Cavalry.

ARTILLERY.
Colonel James Deshler.

Branch's (Va.) battery; Brem's (N. C.) battery; French's (Va.) battery; Graham's (Va.) battery; Grandy's (Va.) battery; Lloyd's (N. C.) battery.

WISE'S COMMAND.
Brigadier-General Henry A. Wise.

Twenty-sixth Virginia; Forty-sixth Virginia; Fourth Virginia Heavy Artillery; Tenth Virginia Cavalry; † Andrews' (Va.) battery; Armistead's (Va.) battery; French's (Va.) battery; Rives' (Va.) battery.

RESERVE ARTILLERY.
Brigadier-General W. N. Pendleton.

FIRST VIRGINIA ARTILLERY. ‡
Colonel J. T. Brown.

Coke's battery; Macon's battery; Richardson's battery; Smith's battery; Watson's battery.

RICHARDSON'S BATTALION.
Major Charles Richardson.

Ancell's (Va.) battery; Milledge's (Ga.) battery; Woolfolk's battery, Ashland (Va.) Artillery.

JONES' BATTALION.
Major H. P. Jones.

Clark's (Va.) battery; Peyton's (Va.) battery; Rhett's (S. C.) battery.

NELSON'S BATTALION.
Major William Nelson.

Huchstep's (Va.) battery; Kirkpatrick's (Va.) battery; R. C. M. Page's battery.

SUMTER (GEORGIA) BATTALION.
Lieutenant-Colonel A. S. Cutts.

Blackshear's battery; Lane's battery; Price's battery; Ross' battery.

MISCELLANEOUS. §

Chapman's battery, Dixie (Va.) Artillery; Dabney's (Va.) battery; Dearing's battery; Grimes' (Va.) battery; Hamilton's battery.

CAVALRY.
Brigadier-General James E. B. Stuart.

First North Carolina; First Virginia; Third Virginia; Fourth Virginia; Fifth Virginia; Ninth Virginia; Tenth Virginia; Cobb (Ga.) Legion; Critcher's (Va.) battalion; Hampton (S. C.) Legion; Jeff. Davis Legion; Stuart Horse Artillery.

* Served also in Armistead's brigade.
† Serving with Stuart.
‡ Only the batteries mentioned in the reports are here given.
§ Including all batteries mentioned in the reports and not otherwise accounted for.

GENERAL MORGAN'S FIRST KENTUCKY RAID,

JULY 4 TO 30, 1862.

BY

BRIG.-GEN. JOHN H. MORGAN, C. S. A.

BRIGADE HEADQUARTERS,
TOMPKINSVILLE, KY., July 9, 1862.

I HAVE the honor to report that I arrived with my command at the Cumberland River, and passed the ford at about 2 P. M., yesterday, 8th instant. My forces consisted of Colonel Hunt's Georgia regiment cavalry, my own regiment, and a squadron of Texas Rangers; we were joined at the river by two companies under Captains Hamilton and McMillan. I received information that the enemy had passed the Cumberland River at Salma the day of my arrival with about one hundred and eighty men, but did not deem it right to attack that force, as I was aware that a considerable body of cavalry, about three hundred and eighty or four hundred strong, were stationed at this town, and I thought by a rapid night march I might succeed in surprising them. I left the river at 10 P. M. on the 8th instant, and at 5 A. M. this day I surprised the enemy, and having surrounded them, threw four shells into their camp, and then carried it by a dashing charge. The enemy fled, leaving about twenty-two dead and thirty or forty wounded in our hands. We have thirty prisoners, and my Texas squadron are still in pursuit of the fugitives. Among the prisoners is Major Jordan, their commander, and two lieutenants. The tents, stores and camp equipage I have destroyed, but a valuable baggage train, consisting of some twenty wagons and fifty mules, is in my possession; also some forty cavalry horses, and supplies of sugar, coffe, etc. I did not lose a single man in killed, but have to regret that Colonel Hunt, while leading a brilliant charge, received a severe wound in the leg, which prevents his going on with the command. I also had three members of the Texas squadron wounded, but not seriously.

JOHN H. MORGAN, *Colonel Commanding.*

MAJOR-GENERAL E. KIRBY SMITH,
Commanding, Knoxville, Tenn.

HEADQUARTERS OF MORGAN'S COMMAND,
KNOXVILLE, TENN., July 30, 1862.

I have the honor to report that upon the day of the engagements at Tompkinsville, a full report of which I have already sent you, I moved my command (consisting of my own regiment, the Georgia regiment of Partisan Rangers, commanded by Colonel A. A. Hunt, and Major Gano's Texas squadron, to which were attached two companies of Tennessee cavalry) in the direction of Glasgow, which place I reached at 12 o'clock that night.

There were but few troops in the town, who fled at our approach. The commissary stores, clothing, etc., together with a large supply of medical stores, were burned, and the guns were distributed among my command, about two hundred of which were unarmed when I left Knoxville.

From Glasgow I proceeded along the main Lexington Road to Barren River, halting for a short time at a point near Cave City, my object being to induce the belief that I intended destroying the railroad bridge between Bowling Green and Woodsonville. I caused wires connecting with the portable battery that I carried with me to be attached to the telegraph line near Horse Cave, and intercepted a number of dispatches.

At Barren River I detached three companies, under Captain Jack Allen, to move forward rapidly and destroy the Salt River Bridge, that the troops along the line of railroad might be prevented from returning to Louisville.

On the following morning I moved on toward Lebanon, distant thirty-five miles from Barren River. At 11 o'clock at night I reached the bridge over Rolling Fork, six miles from Lebanon. The enemy had received information of my approach from their spies, and my advance guard was fired upon at the bridge. After a short fight the force at the bridge was dispersed, and the planks which had been torn up having been replaced, the command moved on to Lebanon. About two miles from the town a skirmish commenced between two companies I caused to dismount and deploy and a force of the enemy posted upon the road, which was soon ended by its dispersion and capture. Lieutenant-Colonel A. Y. Johnson, commanding the troops in the town, surrendered, and I entered the place. The prisoners taken, in number about sixty-five, were paroled. I took immediate possession of the telegraph, and intercepted a dispatch to Colonel Johnson, informing him that Colonel Owen, with the Sixtieth Indiana Regiment, had been ordered to his assistance, so I at once dispatched a company of Texas Rangers, under Major Gano, to destroy the railroad bridge on the Lebanon Branch, which he successfully accomplished in time to prevent the arrival of the troops. I burned two long buildings which were filled with commissary stores, consisting of upward of five hundred sacks of coffee and a large amount of all other supplies in bulk, marked for the enemy at Cumberland Gap. I also destroyed a very large amount of clothing, boots, etc. I burned the hospital buildings, which appeared

MAJOR-GENERAL JOHN H. MORGAN, OF KENTUCKY,
Killed at Greenville, Tenn., September 4, 1864.
[From an oil portrait.]

to have been recently erected and fitted up, together with about thirty-five wagons and fifty-three new ambulances. I found in the place a large store of medicines, five thousand stand of arms, with accouterments, about two thousand sabers, and an immense quantity of shell, etc. I distributed the best arms among my command, and loaded one wagon with them to be given to recruits that I expected to join me; I also loaded a wagon with ammunition; the remainder of the arms, ammunition and the hospital and medical stores I destroyed.

While in Lebanon I ascertained from telegraph dispatches that I intercepted that the force which had been started from Lebanon Junction to re-enforce Lieutenant-Colonel Johnson had met and driven back the force under Captain Jack Allen, killing one of the men, and preventing him from accomplishing the purpose for which he had been detached.

Brig.-Gen. John H. Morgan's Raiders Capturing the Licking Bridge and Entering Cynthiana, Ky., July 17, 1862.

I proceeded from Lebanon on the following day through Springfield to Mackville, at which point I was attacked by Home Guards. Two of my men were taken prisoners and one severely wounded. I remained at Mackville that night to recover the prisoners, which I did the next morning. I then left for Harrodsburg, capturing a Federal captain and lieutenant on the road; reached Harrodsburg at 12:30 o'clock. Found that the Home Guards of all that portion of country had fled to Lexington; a force was also stationed on the bridge where the Lexington Road crossed the Kentucky River.

My reception at this place was very encouraging. The whole population appeared to turn out and vie with each other as to who should show us most attention. I left Harrodsburg at six o'clock the same evening, and moved to Lawrenceburg, twenty miles distant, threatening Frankfort, in order to draw off the troops from Georgetown. Remained there until the return of my courier from Frankfort, who brought the information that there was a force in Frankfort of two or three thousand men, consisting of Home Guards collected from the adjacent counties, and a few regular troops. From Lawrenceburg I proceeded to Shryock Ferry, on the Kentucky River, raised the boat which had been sunk, and crossed that evening, reaching Versailles at 7 o'clock. I found this place abandoned by its defenders, who had fled to Lexington; remained there that night, and on the next morning marched toward Georgetown.

While at Versailles I took about three hundred government horses and mules. I passed through Midway on the way to Georgetown, and was informed, just before reaching the place, that a train from Frankfort was nearly due with two regiments of Federals. I tore up the track and posted the howitzers to command it, and formed my command along the line of the road; but the train was warned of our presence, and returned to Frankfort. Having taken possession of the telegraph office, I intercepted a dispatch asking if the road was clear, and if it would be safe to start the train from Lexington. I replied to send the train, and made preparations to receive it, but it was also turned back and escaped. I reached Georgetown, twelve miles from Lexington, that evening. Just before entering the town I was informed that a small force of Home Guards had mustered to oppose us. I sent them word to surrender their arms and they should not be molested; but they fled.

The people of Georgetown also welcomed us with gladness, and provided my troops with everything that they needed. I remained at Georgetown two days, during which time I sent out a company under Captain McMillin to destroy the track between Midway and Lexington and Midway and Frankfort, and to blow up the stone bridge on that road, which he successfully accomplished. Hearing that a company of Home Guards were encamped at Stamping Grounds, thirteen miles distant, I dispatched a company under Captain Hamilton to break up their encampment, burn the tents and stores, and destroy the guns. This was also accomplished, Captain Hamilton taking fifteen prisoners and all their guns, and destroying a large amount of medical and commissary stores. I also, while at Georgetown, sent Captain Castleman with his company to destroy the railroad bridges between Paris and Lexington, and report to me at Winchester. This was done.

Determining to move on Paris with a view of returning, and hearing that the place was being rapidly re-enforced from Cincinnati, I deemed it of great importance to cut off the communication from that place while I drew off the troops that were already there by a feint on Lexington. I therefore dispatched a portion of two companies toward Lexington, with instructions to drive the pickets to the very entrance of the city, while I moved the command toward Cynthiana. When I arrived within three miles of this place I learned that it was defended by a considerable force of infantry, cavalry and artillery. I dispatched the Texas squadron, under Major Gano, to enter the town on the right, and the Georgia regiment to cross the river and get in the rear, while I moved my own regiment, with the artillery under the command of Lieutenant J. E. Harris, down the Georgetown Pike. A severe engagement took place, which lasted about an hour and a half before the enemy were driven into the town and compelled to surrender. I took four hundred and twenty prisoners, including about seventy Home Guards.

I regret to have to mention the loss of eight of my men in killed and twenty-nine wounded. The enemy's loss was one hundred and ninety-four in killed and wounded, according to their own account. Their excess in killed and wounded is remarkable, as they fought us from behind stone fences and fired at us from buildings as we charged through the town. We captured a very fine 12-pounder brass piece of artillery, together with a large number of small arms, and about three hundred government horses. I found a very large supply of commissary and medical stores, tents, guns and ammunition at this place, which I destroyed. The paroled prisoners were sent under an escort to Falmouth, where they took the train for Cincinnati.

I proceeded the next morning toward Paris, and was met on the road by the bearer of a flag of truce, offering the unconditional surrender of the place. I reached Paris at 4 o'clock; remained there that night, and started toward Winchester the next morning. As my command was filing out of Paris in the Winchester Pike I discovered a large force of Federals coming toward the town from the direction of Lexington. They immediately countermarched, supposing, no doubt, that my intention was to get in their rear. This enabled me to bring off my entire command without molestation, with the exception of two of my pickets, who probably were surprised; reached Winchester that day at 12 o'clock, remained until 4 o'clock, when I proceeded toward Richmond. At Winchester I found a number of arms, which were destroyed.

I arrived at Richmond at 12 o'clock that night, and remained until the next afternoon, when I proceeded to Crab Orchard. I had determined to make a stand at Richmond and await re-enforcements, as the whole people appeared ready to rise and join me; but I received information that large bodies of cavalry, under General Clay Smith and Colonels Wolford, Metcalfe, Munday and Wynkoop, were endeavoring to surround me at this place, so I moved on to Crab Orchard. There I attached my portable battery to the telegraph leading from Stanford to Louisville, and learned the exact position of the enemy's forces, and directed my movements accordingly.

Leaving Crab Orchard at 11 o'clock, I arrived at Somerset, distant twenty-eight miles, at sundown. I took possession of the telegraph, and countermanded all the previous orders that had been given by General Boyle to pursue me, and remained here in perfect security all night. I found a very large supply of commissary stores, clothing, blankets, shoes, hats, etc., at this place, which were destroyed. I also found the arms that had been taken from General Zollicoffer, together with large quantities of shell and ammunition, all of which were destroyed. I also burned at this place and Crab Orchard about one hundred and twenty government wagons. From Somerset I proceeded to Monticello, and from thence to a point between Livingston and Sparta, where my command is now encamped.

I left Knoxville upon the 4th day of this month, with about nine hundred men, and returned to Livingston on the 28th instant with nearly twelve hundred, having been absent just twenty-four days, during which time I traveled over one thousand miles, captured seventeen towns, destroyed all the government supplies and arms in them, dispersed about fifteen hundred Home Guards, and paroled nearly twelve hundred regular troops. I lost in killed, wounded and missing, of the number that I carried into Kentucky, about ninety.

Brig.-Gen. John H. Morgan and His Command Bivouacking in Courthouse Square, Paris, Ky.

I take great pleasure in testifying to the gallant bravery and efficiency of my whole command. There were individual instances of daring so conspicuous that I must beg the privilege of referring to them. Private Moore, of Louisiana, a member of Company A of my regiment, particularly distinguished himself by leading a charge which had an important effect in winning the battle. I feel indebted to all my aids for the promptness with which my orders were executed, and particularly to Colonel St. Leger Grenfell for the assistance which his experience afforded me.

* * * * * * *

JOHN H. MORGAN,
Acting Brigadier-General, C. S. A.

MORGAN'S WAR SONG.

BY GENERAL BASIL DUKE, OF KENTUCKY.

Air—A combination of the "Marseillaise" and the "Old Granite State."

YE sons of the South, take your weapons in hand,
For the foot of the foe hath insulted your land.
Sound! sound the loud alarm!
Arise! arise and arm!
Let the hand of each freeman grasp the sword to maintain
Those rights which, once lost, he can never regain.

Chorus.—Gather fast 'neath our flag,
For 'tis God's own decree
That its folds shall still float
O'er a land that is free!

See ye not those dark clouds which now threaten the sky?
Hear ye not that stern thunder now bursting so nigh?
Shout! shout your battle cry!
Win! win this fight or die!
What our fathers achieved our own valor can keep,
And we'll save our fair land, or we'll sleep our last sleep.

On our hearts and our arms and our God we rely,
And a nation shall rise or a people shall die.
Form! form the serried line!
Advance! advance our proud ensign!
To your country devote every life that she gave,
Let the land they invade give their army its grave.

Though their plunder-paid hordes come to ravage our land,
Give our fields to the spoiler, our homes to the brand,
Our souls are all aglow
To face the hireling foe,
Give the robbers to know that we never will yield
While the arm of one Southron a weapon can wield.

From our far Southern shore now arises a prayer,
While the cry of our women fills with anguish the air.
Oh! list that pleading voice;
Each youth now make his choice;
Now tamely submit like a coward or slave,
Or rise and resist like the free and the brave.

Kentucky! Kentucky! can you suffer the sight
Of your sisters insulted, your friends in the fight?
Awake! be free again!
Oh! break the tyrant's chain!
Let each hand seize the sword it drew for the right,
From the homes of your fathers drive the dastard in flight.

BATTLE OF CEDAR RUN, OR CEDAR MOUNTAIN,

AUGUST 9, 1862.

BY

LIEUT.-GEN. THOMAS J. JACKSON.

HEADQUARTERS OF SECOND CORPS,
ARMY OF NORTHERN VIRGINIA, April 4, 1863.

I HAVE the honor herewith to submit a report of the operations of my command in the battle of Cedar Run, on August 9, 1862: Intelligence having reached the commanding general that Gordonsville was endangered by the approach of the enemy, I was ordered to move in that direction with Ewell's and Jackson's divisions from my position on the Mechanicsville Turnpike near Richmond. I arrived near Gordonsville on July 19th. From information received respecting the strength of the opposing Federal army, under General Pope, I requested the commanding general to re-enforce me. He accordingly sent forward Major-General A. P. Hill, with his division.

On August 2d, while Colonel (now Brigadier-General) W. E. Jones, by direction of Brigadier-General Robertson, was moving with the Seventh Virginia Cavalry to take charge of picket posts on the Rapidan, he received intelligence before he reached Orange Courthouse that the enemy was in possession of the town. Finding the main street filled with Federal cavalry, Colonel Jones boldly charged the head of the Federal column, while his flank was attacked by another portion of the regiment, under Major Marshall. Both attacks were successful, and the enemy was hastily driven from the town; but as our cavalry was vastly outnumbered it was soon after forced to fall back, in consequence of the enemy's greatly superior force in front and the fire from his flanking parties. Upon Colonel Jones' subsequent show of resistance, near where the engagement commenced, the enemy retired a short distance, and about an hour afterward retreated. While Colonel Jones was gallantly leading his men in the charge

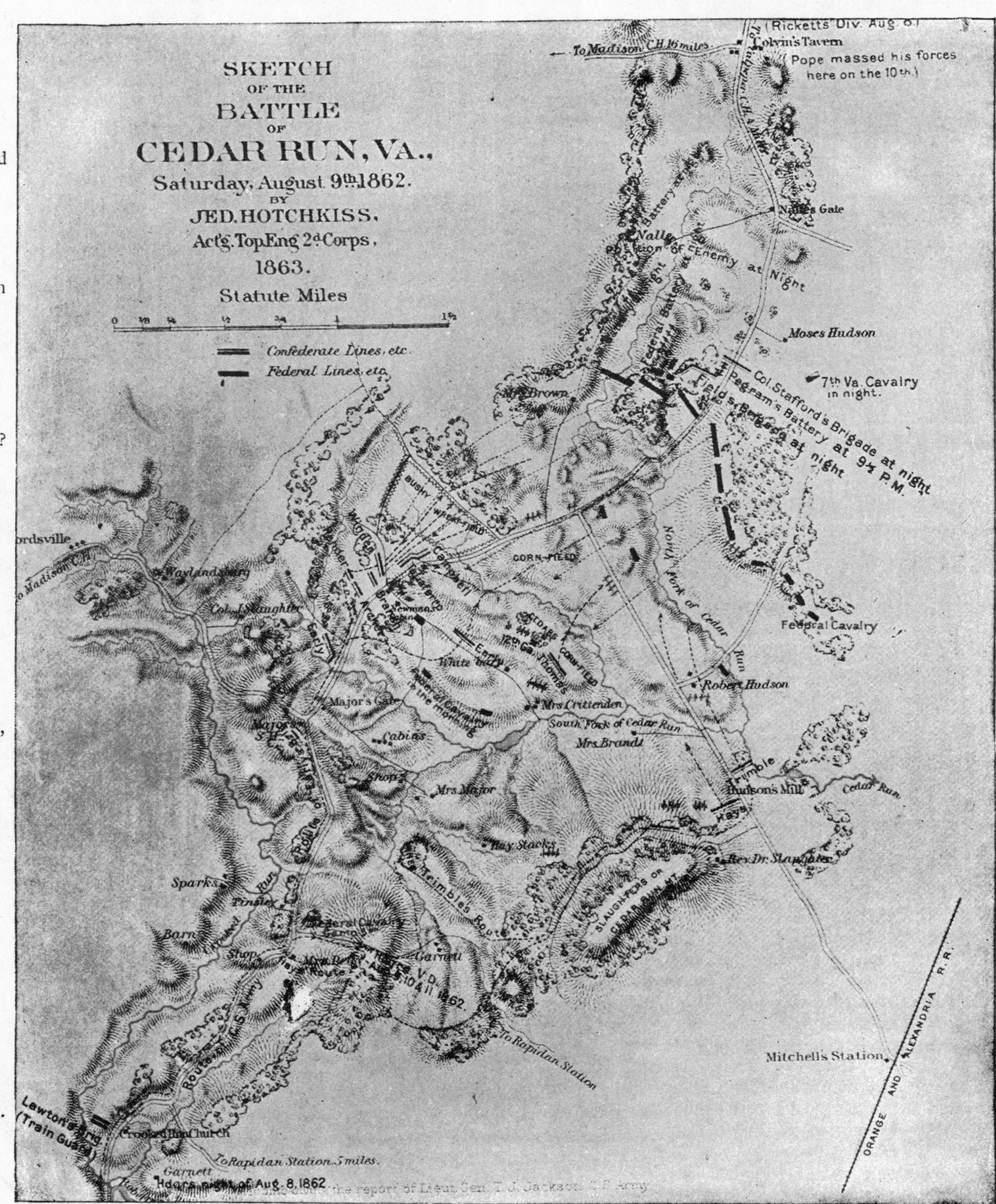

he received a saber wound. I regret to say that during the engagement Major Marshall was captured.

Having received information that only part of General Pope's army was at Culpeper Courthouse, and hoping, through the blessing of Providence, to be able to defeat it before re-enforcements should arrive there, Ewell's, Hill's and Jackson's divisions were moved on the 7th in the direction of the enemy from their respective encampments near Gordonsville. On the morning of the 8th the enemy's cavalry north of the Rapidan was driven back by ours, under Brigadier-General Robertson. Our cavalry pursued the enemy's on the direct road from Barnett's Ford to Culpeper Courthouse, and was followed by the other troops, Ewell's division leading. As the Federal cavalry subsequently displayed unusual activity, and, from reports received by me, was seriously endangering the train of Jackson's division, I directed General Lawton to guard it with his brigade. He was thus thrown in the rear of the division and prevented from taking part in the battle of the following day.

On the 9th, as we arrived within about eight miles of Culpeper Courthouse, we found the enemy in our front, near Cedar Run, and a short distance west and north of Slaughter Mountain. When first seen his cavalry in large force occupied a ridge to the right of the road. A battery under Lieutenant Terry opened upon the cavalry, which soon forced it to retire. Our fire was responded to by some guns beyond the ridge from which the Federal advance had just been driven. Soon after this the enemy's cavalry returned to the position where it was first seen. General Early was ordered forward, keeping near the Culpeper Road, while General Ewell, with his two remaining brigades—Trimble's and Hay's, the latter commanded by Colonel Forno—diverged from the road to the right, advancing along the western slope of Slaughter Mountain. General Early, forming his brigade in line of battle, moved into the open field, and passing a short distance to the right of the road, but parallel to it, pushed forward, driving the Federal cavalry before him to the crest of a hill which overlooked the ground between his troops and the opposite hill, along which the enemy's batteries were posted. In his front the country was for some distance open and broken. A corn-field, and to the left of it a wheat-field, upon which the shocks were yet standing, extended to the opposite hill, which was covered with timber. So soon as Early reached the eminence described the Federal batteries were opened upon him. Large bodies of cavalry were seen in the wheat-field to the left. General Early having retired his troops under the protection of the hill, Captain Brown, with one piece, and Captain Dement, with three pieces of artillery, planted their guns in advance of his right and opened a rapid and well-directed fire upon the Federal batteries. By this time General Winder, with Jackson's division, had arrived, and after having disposed Campbell's brigade, Lieutenant-Colonel Garnett commanding, to the left, under cover of the wood, near the wheat-field; Taliaferro's brigade parallel to the road, in rear of the batteries of Poague, Carpenter and Caskie, then being placed near the road, under the direction of Major Andrews, chief of artillery of the division, and Winder's brigade, Colonel Ronald commanding, as a reserve, he was proceeding to direct, with his usual skill and coolness, the movements of these batteries, when he was struck by a shell, from which he expired in a few hours.

It is difficult within the proper reserve of an official report to do justice to the merits of this accomplished officer. Urged by the medical director to take no part in the movements of the day because of the then enfeebled state of his health, his ardent patriotism and millitary pride could bear no such restraint. Richly endowed with those qualities of mind and person which fit an officer for command, and which attract the admiration and excite the enthusiasm of troops, he was rapidly rising to the front rank of his profession. His loss has been severely felt.

The command of Jackson's division now devolved upon Brigadier-General William B. Taliaferro, whose brigade during the remainder of the action was commanded by Colonel A. G. Taliaferro.

In the meantime General Ewell, with the brigades of Trimble and Hays, reached the northwest termination of Slaughter Mountain, and upon an elevated spot about two hundred feet above the valley below, had planted Latimer's guns, which opened with marked effect upon the enemy's batteries. For some two hours a rapid and continuous fire of artillery was kept up on both sides. Our batteries were well served, and damaged the enemy seriously. Especial credit is due to Major Andrews for the success and gallantry with which his guns were directed, until he was severely wounded and taken from the field. About 5 o'clock the enemy threw forward his skirmishers through the corn-field and advanced his infantry, until then concealed in the woods, to the rear and left of his batteries. Another body of infantry, apparently debouching from one of those valleys hid from the view by the undulating character of the country, moved upon Early's right, which rested near a clump of cedars, where the guns of Brown and Dement were posted. The infantry fight soon extended to the left and center. Early became warmly engaged with the enemy on his right and front. He had previously called for re-enforcements. As General Hill had arrived with his division, one of his brigades (General Thomas') was sent to Early, and joined him in time to render efficient service. While the attack upon Early was in progress the main body of the Federal infantry moved down from the wood through the corn and wheat fields, and fell with great vigor upon our extreme left, and by the force of superior numbers, bearing down all opposition, turned it and poured a destructive fire into its rear. Campbell's brigade fell back in disorder. The enemy pushing forward, and the left flank of Taliaferro's brigade being by these movements exposed to a flank fire, fell back, as did also the left of Early's line, the remainder of his command holding its position with great firmness. During the advance of the enemy, the rear of the guns of Jackson's division becoming exposed, they were withdrawn. At this critical moment Branch's brigade, of Hill's division, with Winder's brigade, further to the left, met the Federal forces, flushed with their temporary triumph, and drove them back with terrible slaughter through the wood. The fight was still maintained with obstinacy between the enemy and the two brigades just named, when, Archer and Pender coming up, a general charge was make, which drove the enemy across the field into the opposite wood, strewing the narrow valley with their dead. In this charge Archer's brigade was subjected to a heavy fire. At this time the Federal cavalry charged upon Taliaferro's brigade with impetuous valor, but were met with such determined resistance by Taliaferro's brigade in its front, and by so galling a fire from Branch's brigade in flank, that it was forced rapidly from the field with loss and disorder.

In the meantime General Ewell, on the right, found himself kept back from advancing by the incessant fire from our batteries in the valley, which swept his only approach to the enemy's left. This difficulty no longer existing, he moved with his two brigades (Trimble in the advance) and pressed forward under a heavy fire from the enemy's artillery, the front covered by skirmishers from the Fifteenth Alabama, and the brigades advancing in echelon of regiments. Thus repulsed from our left and center, and now pressed by our right center and left, the Federal force fell back at every point of their line and commenced retreating, leaving their dead and wounded on the field of battle.

Though late, I was so desirous of reaching Culpeper Courthouse before morning as to induce me to pursue. The advance was accordingly ordered. General Hill, with his division, leading; but owing to the darkness of the night it was necessary to move cautiously. Stafford's brigade, which was in front, captured some prisoners. Before we had advanced more than one and a half miles, Farrow, my most reliable scout, reported to me that the enemy was but a few hundred yards from our advance. Pegram's battery, supported by Field's brigade, soon took position just beyond the wood through which we had passed, and opened fire upon the enemy. This well-directed and unexpected fire produced much disorder and confusion among that portion of the Federal troops. Three batteries were, however, soon opened in reply, and a heavy cannonade was continued for some time, causing Captain Pegram severe loss and silencing him.

FLYING ARTILLERY COMING INTO ACTION AT THE BATTLE OF CEDAR RUN, AUGUST 9, 1862.

In the meantime Colonel Jones, with the Seventh Virginia Cavalry, had passed to our right and front. He succeeded in capturing some prisoners, one of whom reported that Federal re-enforcements had arrived. Believing it imprudent to continue to move forward during the darkness, I ordered a halt for the night. On the following morning (10th), having reason to believe that the Federal army had been so largely re-enforced as to render it imprudent for me to attempt to advance further, directions were given for sending the wounded to the rear, for burying the dead and collecting arms from the battle-field. In the course of the same morning General J. E. B. Stuart arrived on a tour of inspection. At my request he took command of the cavalry, and made a reconnoissance for the purpose of gaining information respecting the numbers and movements of the enemy. From his report, as well as from other sources of information, I was confirmed in my opinion that the heavy forces concentrated in front rendered it unwise on my part to renew the action. The main body of my troops were, however, so posted as to receive the attack if the enemy decided to advance. On the 11th a flag of truce was received from the enemy, who requested permission until 2 o'clock to remove and bury his dead not already interred by our troops. This was granted, and the time subsequently extended, by request of the enemy, to 5 o'clock in the evening.

We captured some four hundred prisoners, and among them Brigadier-General Prince; five thousand three hundred and two small arms; one 12-pounder Napoleon and its caisson, with two other caissons and a limber, and three colors by Winder's brigade, one being from the Fifth Connecticut and another from the Twenty-eighth New York.

The official reports of the casualties of my command in this battle show a loss of nineteen officers killed and one hundred and fourteen wounded; of non-commissioned officers and privates, two hundred and four killed and nine hundred and forty-six wounded, with thirty-one missing, making two hundred and twenty-three killed and one thousand and sixty wounded; total loss of killed, wounded and missing, one thousand three hundred and fourteen. This loss was probably about one-half that sustained by the enemy.

I remained in position until the night of the 11th, when I returned to the vicinity of Gordonsville, in order to avoid being attacked by the vastly superior force in front of me, and with the hope that, by thus falling back, General Pope would be induced to follow me until I should be re-enforced.

The conduct of officers and men during the battle merits great praise. My chief of artillery, Colonel S. Crutchfield, ably discharged his duties. In the prompt transmission of orders great assistance was received from Major E. F. Paxton, acting assistant adjutant-general; Captain A. S. Pendleton, assistant adjutant-general; First Lieutenant J. K. Boswell, chief engineer; First Lieutenant J.G. Morrison, aid-de-camp; First Lieutenant H. K. Douglas, acting inspector-general; First Lieutenant Thomas T. L. Snead, of the engineer corps, and Colonels William L. Jackson and A. R. Boteler, volunteer aids-de-camp. The wounded received special attention from my medical director, Dr. Hunter McGuire.

The quartermasters' and commissary departments were well managed during the expedition by their respective chiefs, Majors J. A. Harman and W. J. Hawks.

In order to render thanks to God for the victory at Cedar Run and other past victories, and to implore His continued favor in the future, divine service was held in the army on August 14th.

* * * * * *

T. J. JACKSON,
Lieutenant-General.

ENGAGEMENT AT BATON ROUGE,

AUGUST 5, 1862,

AND THE

OCCUPATION OF PORT HUDSON.

BY

MAJ.-GEN. JOHN C. BRECKINRIDGE.

HEADQUARTERS BRECKINRIDGE'S DIVISION,
September 30, 1862.

I HAVE the honor to report the operations of a portion of my division recently ordered from Vicksburg to Camp Moore and Baton Rouge, La., by Major-General Van Dorn.

I left Vicksburg on July 27th, with somewhat less than four thousand men, and arrived at Camp Moore the evening of the 28th. The major-general commanding the district having received intelligence that the enemy was threatening Camp Moore in force, the movement was made suddenly and rapidly by railroad, and having but few cars, nothing could be transported except the troops, with their arms and ammunition. Brigadier-General Charles Clark, who had reported for duty a few days before our departure from Vicksburg, promptly and kindly consented to accompany the expedition. Brigadier-General Ruggles was already at Camp Moore, in command of a small force, with which he had kept the enemy in check. The troops were immediately organized in two divisions, General Clark taking command of the First, and General Ruggles of the Second Division. The rumor of an advance of the enemy in force upon Camp Moore proved to be unfounded. On July 30th, in obedience to a dispatch of the 29th from the major-general commanding the district, the troops were put in motion for Baton Rouge. During the march I received information that the effective force of the enemy was not less than five thousand men, and that the ground was commanded by their gunboats lying in the river. My own troops, having suffered severely from the effects of exposure at Vicksburg, from heavy rains, without shelter, and from the extreme heat, did not now number more than three thousand four hundred men. Under these circumstances I determined not to make the attack unless we could be relieved from the fire of the fleet. Accordingly I telegraphed to the major-general commanding the condition and number of the troops and the reported strength of the enemy, but said I would undertake to capture the garrison if the Arkansas could be sent down to clear the river or divert the fire of the gunboats. He promptly answered that the Arkansas would be ready to co-operate at daylight on Tuesday, August 5th. On the afternoon of Monday, the 4th, the command having reached the Comite River, ten miles from Baton Rouge, and learning by an express messenger that the Arkansas had passed Bayou Sara in time to arrive at the proper moment, preparations were made to advance that night. The sickness had been appalling. The morning report of the 4th showing but three thousand effectives, and deducting those taken sick during the day and the number that fell out from weakness on the night march, I did not carry into the action more than two thousand six hundred men. This estimate does not include some two hundred Partisan Rangers, who had performed efficient service in picketing the different roads, but who, from the nature of the ground, took no part in the action, nor about the same number of militia hastily collected by Colonel D. C. Hard e in the neighborhood of Clinton, who, though making every effort, could not arrive in time to participate.

BRIG.-GEN. DANIEL RUGGLES, OF VIRGINIA.

The command left the Comite at 11 P. M. and reached the vicinity of Baton Rouge a little before daybreak on the morning of the 5th. Some hours before the main body moved, a small force of infantry, with a section of Semmes' battery, under Lieutenant T. K. Fauntleroy, the whole commanded by Lieutenant-Colonel Shields, of the Thirtieth Louisiana, was sent by a circuitous route to the road leading from Clinton to Baton Rouge, with orders to drive in any pickets of the enemy, and attack his left as soon as the action should begin in front. This service was well performed, but for details, reference is made to the report of Brigadier-General Ruggles, from whose command the force was detached. While waiting for daylight, to make the attack, an accident occurred which deprived us of several excellent officers and enlisted men and two pieces of artillery. The Partisan Rangers were placed in rear of the artillery and infantry, yet during the darkness a few of them leaked through, and riding forward encountered the enemy, causing exchange of shots between the pickets. Galloping back, they produced some confusion which led to rapid firing for a few moments, during which Brigadier-General Helm was dangerously injured by the fall of his horse; Lieutenant A. H. Todd, his aid-de-camp, killed; Captain Roberts, of the Fourth Kentucky, severely wounded; several enlisted men killed and wounded, and two of Captain Cobb's three guns rendered for the time, wholly useless. After General Helm was disabled, Colonel Thomas H. Hunt assumed command of his brigade. Order was soon restored, and the force placed in position on the right and left of the Greenwell Springs Road. I was obliged to content myself with a single line of battle and a small regiment of infantry, with one piece of artillery, to each division as a reserve. The enemy (expecting the attack) was drawn up in two lines, or rather in one line, with strong reserves distributed at intervals. At the moment there was light enough our troops moved rapidly forward. General Ruggles, commanding the left, brought on the engagement with four pieces of Semmes' battery, the Fourth and Thirtieth Louisiana, and Boyd's Louisiana battalion, under the command of Colonel Allen, of the Fourth Louisiana, and the Third, Sixth and Seventh Kentucky and the Thirty-fifth Alabama, under the command of Colonel Thompson, of the Third Kentucky. These troops moved forward with great impetuosity, driving the enemy before them, while their ringing cheers inspired all our little command. The Louisiana troops charged a battery and captured two pieces. At this point Colonel Allen, commanding the brigade, while pressing forward with the colors in his hands had both legs shattered, and Lieutenant-Colonel Boyd received a severe wound. This produced confusion, and the enemy at the same moment throwing forward a strong re-enforcement, the brigade was forced back in some disorder. It was rallied by the efforts of Colonel Breaux, Lieutenant-Colonel Hunter, and other officers, and, although it did not further participate in the assault, it maintained its position under a fire from the gunboats and land batteries of the enemy. During this time Thompson's brigade, which composed the right of Ruggles' division, was behaving with great gallantry, often driving back superior forces, and toward the close of the action took part in the final struggle from a position immediately on the left of the First Division, Colonel Thompson being severely wounded in a charge, the command devolved on Colonel Robertson, of the Thirty-fifth Alabama, whose conduct fully justified the confidence of his troops.

The Louisiana [?] battery, Captain Semmes, was admirably handled throughout. The First Division, under General Clark, being the Second Brigade, composed of the Fourth and Fifth Kentucky, Thirty-first Mississippi, Thirty-first and Fourth Alabama, commanded by Colonel Hunt, of the Fifth Kentucky, and the Fourth Brigade, composed of the Fifteenth and Twenty-second Mississippi; and the Nineteenth, Twentieth, Twenty-eighth and Forty-fifth Tennessee, consolidated into one battalion, commanded by Colonel Smith, of the Twentieth Tennessee, together with the Hudson battery and one piece of Cobb's battery, advanced to the right of the Greenwell Springs Road. On the right, as on the left, the enemy was constantly pressed back, until, after several hours of fighting, he was driven to his last encampment—in a large grove just in rear of the penitentiary. Here the contest was hot and obstinate, and it was here the First Division suffered the greatest loss. Colonel Hunt was shot down, and in the fall of that excellent officer, at the suggestion of General Clark and with the consent of the officers concerned, I placed Captain John A. Buckner, assistant adjutant-general on my staff, in command of the Second Brigade. In the management of his command he displayed so high a degree of skill and courage that I commend him especially to the notice of the government.

General Clark pressed the attack at this point with great vigor until he received a wound which was supposed to be mortal, when, through some misapprehension, the Second Brigade began to fall back down the slope, but without confusion.

Captain Buckner, learning upon inquiry from me that I did not desire a retrograde movement, immediately, aided by Major Wickliffe, of the Fifth Kentucky Regiment, Lieutenant-Colonel Caldwell, who was injured by the accident of the preceding night (having been obliged to retire), and other regimental officers, faced the brigade about and renewed the attack. At the same time Colonel Smith, commanding Fourth Brigade, composed of the consolidated Tennessee regiments and the Twenty-second Mississippi, Captain F. Hughes, was ordered forward and moved against the enemy in fine style. In a few moments Captain Hughes received a mortal wound at the head of his regiment.

Observing some troops on the left partially sheltered by a shallow cut in the road (who proved to be the remnant of Thompson's brigade, and out of ammunition), I ordered them to advance to the support of the First Division with the bayonet. The order was promptly obeyed, and in executing it I happened to observe as distinguished for alacrity Colonel Crossland, of the Seventh Kentucky; Lieutenant-Colonel Goodwin, of the Thirty-fifth Alabama, and Lieutenant Terry, of the Eighth Kentucky, on duty with sharpshooters. At this critical moment, Major Brown, chief commissary, and Captain Richards, one of my aids, were conspicuous in urging on the troops. In this assault we suffered considerably from the fire of the fleet, until the opposing lines approached each other so closely that a regard for their own friends obliged them to suspend. The contest at and around this last encampment was bloody, but at the end of it the enemy was completely routed, some of our men pursuing and firing at them for some distance down the street running in front of the arsenal and barracks. They did not reappear during the day.

It was now 10 o'clock. We had listened in vain for the guns of the Arkansas. I saw around me not more than one thousand exhausted men, who had been unable to procure water since we left the Comite River. The enemy had several batteries commanding the approaches to the arsenal and barracks, and the gunboats had already reopened upon us with a direct fire. Under these circumstances, although the troops showed the utmost indifference to danger and death, and were even reluctant to retire, I did not deem it prudent to pursue the victory further. Having scarcely any transportation, I ordered all the camps and stores of the enemy to be destroyed, and directing Captain Buckner to place one section of Semmes' battery, supported by the Seventh Kentucky, in a certain position on the field, withdrew the rest of the troops about one mile, to Wood's Creek, with the hope of obtaining water, but finding none there fit for man or beast, I moved the command back to the field of battle, and procured a very imperfect supply from some cisterns in the suburbs of the town. This position we occupied for the rest of the day.

The citizens of the surrounding and thinly settled country exhibited the warmest patriotism, and with their assistance conveyances enough were procured to carry off all our wounded who could bear removal. A few, armed with shot-guns and other weapons, had been able to reach the field in time to join in the attack. Having neither

BATON ROUGE, LA.

picks nor shovels, we were unable to dig graves for the burial of the dead.

I still hoped for the co-operation of the Arkansas, and in that event intended to renew the attack. But late in the afternoon I learned by express that before daylight, and within four miles of Baton Rouge, her machinery had become disabled and she lay helpless on the right bank of the river. Upon receiving this intelligence, I returned with my command to the Comite River, leaving a force of observation near the suburbs of the town.

The Hudson battery, Lieutenant Sweaney, and Cobb's one piece, in charge of Sergeant Frank Peak, played their parts well.

I am unable to give the exact force of the enemy, but by comparing all my information with the number and

PORT HUDSON, AS SEEN FROM BELOW.

size of their camps, and the extent and weight of their fire, I do not think they brought into action less than four thousand five hundred men. We had eleven pieces of field artillery; they brought to bear on us not less than eighteen pieces, exclusive of the guns of the fleet. In one respect the contrast between the opposing forces was very striking. The enemy were well clothed, and their encampments showed the presence of every comfort and even luxury. Our men had little transportation, indifferent food, and no shelter. Half of them had no coats, and hundreds were without either shoes or socks; yet no troops ever behaved with greater gallantry and even reckless audacity. What can make this difference, unless it be the sublime courage inspired by a just cause?

The wound of Brigadier-General Charles Clark being thought mortal, and the least motion causing great agony, he was left on the field at his own request, his aid, Lieutenant Yerger, remaining with him. The next morning they gave themselves up to the enemy.

I can not speak in terms too strong of the skill, coolness and courage of General Clark. He played the part of a perfect soldier. Brigadier-General Ruggles conducted the attack on the left with uncommon rapidity and precision, and exhibited throughout the qualities of a brave and experienced officer.

In addition to the officers of my staff already mentioned, I desire to express my acknowledgment of the zeal and gallantry of Major Wilson, chief of artillery; Major Hope, inspector-general, whose horse was shot under him; Captain James Nocquet, chief of engineers; Lieutenant Breckinridge, aid-de-camp, and Doctor Pendleton, medical director, assisted by Doctor Weatherly, on temporary service.

A few days after the engagement, knowing the desire of the major-general commanding to secure a strong position on the Mississippi below the mouth of Red River, I occupied Port Hudson with a portion of the troops under the command of Brigadier-General Ruggles. The next day I received orders to remove all the troops to that point. Brigadier-General Bowen, who had just arrived, was left with his command on the Comite River to observe Baton Rouge from that quarter, to protect our hospitals, and to cover the line of communication between Clinton and Camp Moore. I directed General Ruggles to select eligible positions at Port Hudson for heavy batteries, and ordered Captain Nocquet, chief engineer, to report to him temporarily for this duty.

Upon my arrival there I found that rapid progress had been made, and some of the works under charge of Captain Nocquet were ready to receive the guns, which the major-general commanding wrote me were on the way. Port Hudson is one of the strongest points on the Mississippi (which Baton Rouge is not) and batteries there will command the river more completely than at Vicksburg.

On August 19th, in obedience to orders from the headquarters of the department, I moved from Port Hudson to Jackson, Miss., with a portion of the force, leaving Brigadier-General Ruggles in command.

In concluding this report I have to express my obligations for the prompt and cordial support which I received at all times from the major-general commmading the department.

* * * * * * *

JOHN C. BRECKINRIDGE,
Major-General.

P. S.—I omitted to mention that the Fifteenth Mississippi, Major Binford, was not brought into action. This admirable regiment, much reduced by long and gallant service, was held as a reserve.

ROBERT E. LEE.

TRIBUTE OF A DISTINGUISHED ENGLISHMAN.

The following beautiful lines were written by Philip Stanhope Wormsley, of Oxford University, England, in the dedication of his translation of Homer's Iliad to General Robert E. Lee: "The most stainless of earthly commanders, and, except in fortune, the greatest":

The grand old bard that never dies,
Receive him in our English tongue;
I send thee, but with weeping eyes,
The story that he sung.

Thy Troy is fallen, thy dear land
Is marred beneath the spoiler's heel;
I can not trust my trembling hand
To write the things I feel.

Ah, realm of tombs! but let her bear
This blazon to the end of time.
No nation rose so white and fair,
None fell so pure of crime.

The widows' mourn, the orphans' wail
Come round thee—but in truth be strong—
Eternal right, though all else fail,
Can never be made wrong.

An angel's heart, an angel's mouth,
Not Homer's, could alone for me
Hymn well the great Confederate South,
Virginia first and Lee!

CAMPAIGN IN NORTHERN VIRGINIA

AUGUST 13 TO SEPTEMBER 2, 1862,

INCLUDING THE BATTLE OF

SECOND MANASSAS, OR BULL RUN,

AUGUST 30, 1862.

BY

GENERAL ROBERT E. LEE.

HEADQUARTERS ARMY OF NORTHERN VIRGINIA,
June 8, 1863.

THE victory at Cedar Run effectually checked the progress of the enemy for the time, but it soon became apparent that his army was being largely increased. The corps of Major-General Burnside from North Carolina, which had reached Fredericksburg, was reported to have moved up the Rappahannock a few days after the battle to unite with General Pope, and a part of General McClellan's army was believed to have left Westover for the same purpose. It therefore seemed that active operations on the James were no longer contemplated, and that the most effectual way to relieve Richmond from any danger of attack from that quarter would be to re-enforce General Jackson and advance upon General Pope. Accordingly, on August 13th, Major-General Longstreet, with his division and the two brigades under General Hood, were ordered to proceed to Gordonsville. At the same time General Stuart was directed to move with the main body of his cavalry to that point, leaving a sufficient force to observe the enemy still remaining in Fredericksburg and to guard the railroad. General R. H. Anderson was also directed to leave his position on James River and follow Longstreet.

On the 16th the troops began to move from the vicinity of Gordonsville toward the Rapidan, on the north side of which, extending along the Orange & Alexandria Railroad in the direction of Culpeper Courthouse, the Federal army lay in great force. It was determined with the cavalry to destroy the railroad bridge over the Rappahannock in rear of the enemy, while Longstreet and Jackson crossed the Rapidan and attacked his left flank. The movement was appointed for August 18th; but the necessary preparations not having been completed, its execution was postponed to the 20th. In the interval, the enemy being apprised of our design, hastily retired beyond the Rappahannock. General Longstreet crossed the Rapidan at Raccoon Ford, and, preceded by Fitzhugh Lee's cavalry brigade, arrived early in the afternoon near Kelly's Ford, on the Rappahannock, where Lee had a sharp and successful skirmish with the rear guard of the enemy, who held the north side of the river in strong force. Jackson passed the Rapidan at Somerville Ford, and moved toward Brandy Station. Robertson's brigade of cavalry was encountered, which was gallantly attacked and driven across the Rappahannock by Robertson's command.

General Jackson halted for the night near Stevensburg, and on the morning of the 21st moved upon Beverly Ford, on the Rappahannock. The Fifth Virginia Cavalry, under Colonel Rosser, was sent forward by General Stuart to seize the north bank of the river at this point, and gallantly accomplished the object, capturing a number of prisoners and arms. General Stuart subsequently arrived, and being furnished by General Jackson with a section of artillery, maintained his position for several hours, skirmishing warmly with the enemy. General Robertson, who had crossed the river above Beverly Ford, reported that the enemy was advancing in large force upon the position held by General Stuart, and as it had been determined in the meantime not to attempt the passage of the river at that point with the army, that officer withdrew to the south side. The enemy soon afterward appeared in great strength upon the opposite bank, and an animated fire was kept up during the rest of the day between his artillery and the batteries attached to Jackson's leading division, under Brigadier-General Taliaferro.

As our positions on the south bank of the Rappahannock were commanded by those of the enemy, who guarded all the fords, it was determined to seek a more favorable place to cross higher up the river, and thus gain the enemy's right. Accordingly, General Longstreet was directed to leave Kelly's Ford on the 21st and take the position in front of the enemy in the vicinity of Beverly Ford and the Orange & Alexandria Railroad Bridge, then held by Jackson, in order to mask the movement of the latter, who was instructed to ascend the river. On the 22d Jackson crossed Hazel River at Welford's mill and proceeded up the Rappahannock, leaving Trimble's brigade near Freeman's Ford to protect his trains. In the afternoon Longstreet sent General Hood, with his own and Whiting's brigade, under Colonel Law, to relieve Trimble. Hood had just reached the position when he and Trimble were attacked by a considerable force, which had crossed at Freeman's Ford. After a short but spirited engagement

BURNING OF DEPOT AND COMMISSARY STORES AT MANASSAS JUNCTION.

the enemy was driven precipitately over the river with heavy loss. General Jackson arrived at the Warrenton Springs Ford in the afternoon, and immediately began to cross his troops to the north side, occupying the springs and the adjacent heights. He was interrupted by a heavy rain, which caused the river to rise so rapidly that the ford soon became impassable for infantry and artillery. Under these circumstances it was deemed advisable to withdraw the troops who had reached the opposite side, and they recrossed during the night of the 23d on a temporary bridge constructed for the purpose. General Stuart, who had been directed to cut the railroad in rear of General Pope's army, crossed the Rappahannock on the morning of the 22d about six miles above the springs, with parts of Lee's and Robertson's brigades. Passing through Warrenton, he reached Catlett's Station at night, but was prevented from destroying the railroad bridge at that point by the same storm that had arrested Jackson's movements. He captured more than three hundred prisoners, including a number of officers. Becoming apprehensive of the effect of the rain upon the streams which separated him from the main body of the army, he retired after firing the enemy's camp, and recrossed the Rappahannock at Warrenton Springs.

On the 23d General Longstreet directed Colonel Walton, with part of the Washington Artillery and other batteries of his command, to drive back a force of the enemy that had crossed to the south bank of the Rappahannock near the railroad bridge upon the withdrawal of General Jackson on the previous day. Fire was opened about sunrise and continued with great vigor for several hours, the enemy being compelled to withdraw with loss. Some of the batteries of Colonel S. D. Lee's battalion were ordered to aid those of Colonel Walton, and under their united fire the enemy was forced to abandon his position on the north side of the river, burning in his retreat the railroad bridge and the neighboring dwellings. The rise of the river rendering the lower fords impassable enabled the enemy to concentrate his main body opposite General Jackson, and on the 24th Longstreet was ordered to proceed to his support. Although retarded by the swollen condition of Hazel River and other tributaries of the Rappahannock, he reached Jeffersonton in the afternoon. General Jackson's command lay between that place and the [Warrenton] Springs Ford, and a warm cannonade was progressing between the batteries of General A. P. Hill's division and those of the enemy. The enemy was massed between Warrenton and the Springs, and guarded the fords of the Rappahannock as far above as Waterloo. The army of General McClellan had left Westover. Part of [it] had already marched to join General Pope, and it was reported that the rest would soon follow. The captured correspondence of General Pope confirmed this information, and also disclosed the fact that the greater part of the army of General Cox had been withdrawn from the Kanawha Valley for the same purpose. Two brigades of D. H. Hill's division, under General Ripley, had already been ordered from Richmond, and the remainder, under General D. H. Hill in person, with the division of General McLaws, two brigades under General Walker, and Hampton's cavalry brigade, were now directed to join this army, and were approaching. In pursuance of the plan of operations determined upon, Jackson was directed on the 25th to cross above Waterloo and move around the enemy's right, so as to strike the Orange & Alexandria Railroad in his rear. Longstreet in the meantime was to divert his attention by threatening him in front, and to follow Jackson as soon as the latter should be sufficiently advanced.

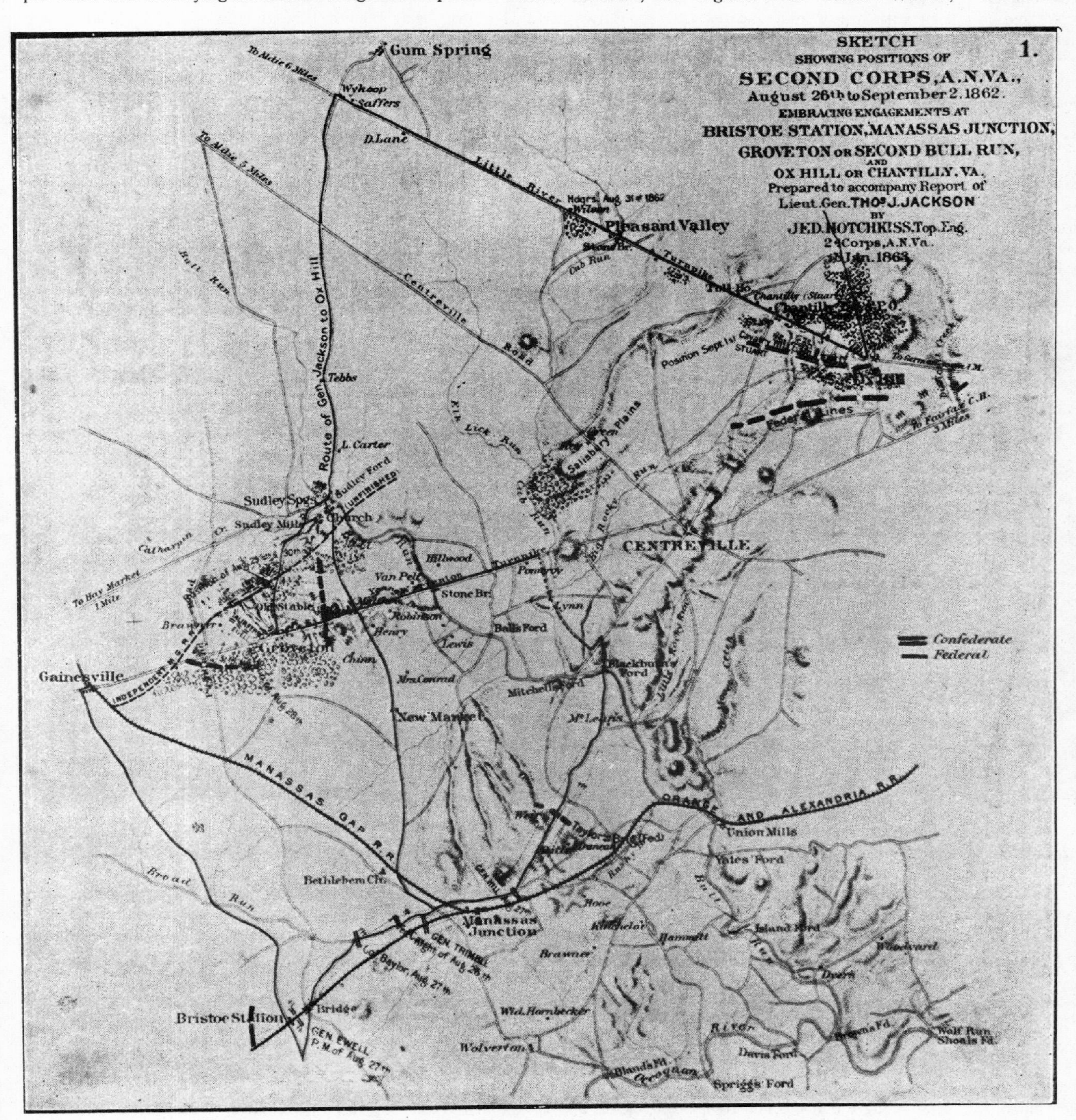

BATTLE OF MANASSAS.

General Jackson crossed the Rappahannock at Hinson's mill, about four miles above Waterloo, and passing through Orleans, encamped on the night of the 25th near Salem, after a long and fatiguing march. The next morning, continuing his route with his accustomed vigor and celerity, he passed the Bull Run Mountains at Thoroughfare Gap, and proceeding by way of Gainesville, reached the railroad at Bristoe Station after sunset. At Gainesville he was joined by General Stuart with the brigades of Robertson and Fitzhugh Lee, who continued with him during the rest of his operations, vigilantly and effectually guarding both his flanks. General Jackson was now between the large army of General Pope and the Federal capital. Thus far no considerable force of the enemy had been encountered, and he did not appear to be aware of his situation. Upon arriving at Bristoe the greater part of the guard at that point fled. Two trains of cars coming from the direction of Warrenton were captured and a few prisoners were taken. Notwithstanding the darkness of the night and the long and arduous march of the day, General Jackson determined to lose no time in capturing the depot of the enemy at Manassas Junction, about seven miles distant on the road to Alexandria. General Trimble volunteered to proceed at once to that place with the Twenty-first North Carolina and the Twenty-first Georgia regiments. The offer was accepted, and to render success more certain General Jackson directed General Stuart to accompany the expedition with part of his cavalry, and as ranking officer to assume the command. Upon arriving near the Junction General Stuart sent Colonel Wickham, with his regiment, the Fourth Virginia Cavalry, to get in rear of the enemy, who opened with musketry and artillery upon our men as they approached. The darkness of the night and ignorance of the enemy's numbers and position made it necessary to move cautiously, but about midnight the place was taken with little difficulty, those that defended it being captured or dispersed. Eight pieces of artillery, with their horses, ammunition and equipments, were taken. More than three hundred prisoners, one hundred and seventy-five horses besides those belonging to the artillery, two hundred new tents and immense quantities of commissary and quartermaster's stores fell into our hands. General Jackson left Ewell's division, with the Fifth Virginia Cavalry, under Colonel Rosser, at Bristoe Station, and with the rest of his command proceeded to the Junction, where he arrived early in the morning. Soon afterward a considerable force of the enemy, under Brigadier-General Taylor, approached from the direction of Alexandria, and pushed forward boldly to recapture the stores that had been lost. After a sharp engagement the enemy was routed and driven back, leaving his killed and wounded on the field, General Taylor himself being mortally wounded during the pursuit. The troops remained at Manassas Junction during the rest of the day, supplying themselves with everything they required from the captured stores. In the afternoon the enemy advanced upon General Ewell at Bristoe from the direction of Warrenton Junction. They were attacked by three regiments and the batteries of Ewell's division, and two columns of not less than a brigade each were broken and repulsed. Their places were soon supplied by fresh troops, and it was apparent that the Federal commander had now become aware of the situation of affairs, and had turned upon General Jackson with his whole force. In pursuance of instructions to that effect, General Ewell, upon perceiving the strength of the enemy, withdrew his command, part of which was at the time engaged, and rejoined General Jackson at Manassas Junction, having first destroyed the railroad bridge over Broad Run. The enemy halted at Bristoe. General Jackson's force being much inferior to that of General Pope, it became necessary for him to withdraw from Manassas and take a position west of the Turnpike Road from Warrenton to Alexandria, where he could more readily unite with the approaching column of Longstreet. Having fully supplied the wants of his troops, he was compelled, for want of transportation, to destroy the rest of the captured property. This was done during the night of the 27th, and 50,000 pounds of bacon, 1,000 barrels of corned beef, 2,000 barrels of salt pork, and 2,000 barrels of flour, besides other property of great value, were burned. Taliaferro's division moved during the night by the road to Sudley, and crossing the turnpike near Groveton, halted on the west side, near the battlefield of July 21, 1861, where it was joined on the 28th by the divisions of Hill and Ewell. Perceiving during the afternoon that the enemy, approaching from the direction of Warrenton, was moving down the turnpike toward Alexandria, thus exposing his left flank, General Jackson advanced to attack him. A fierce and sanguinary conflict ensued, which continued until about 9 P. M., when the enemy slowly fell back and left us in possession of the field. The loss on both sides was heavy, and among our wounded were Major-General Ewell and Brigadier-General Taliaferro, the former severely. The next morning, the 29th, the enemy had taken a position to interpose his army between General Jackson and Alexandria, and about 10 A. M. opened with artillery upon the right of Jackson's line. The troops of the latter were disposed in rear of Groveton along the line of the unfinished branch of the Manassas Gap Railroad, and extended from a point a short distance west of the turnpike toward Sudley mill, Jackson's division, under Brigadier-General Starke, being on the right; Ewell's, under General Lawton, in the center, and A. P. Hill's on the left. The Federal army was evidently concentrating upon Jackson with the design of overwhelming him before the arrival of Longstreet. The latter officer left his position opposite Warrenton Springs on the 26th, being relieved by General R. H. Anderson's division, and marched to join Jackson. He crossed at Hinson's mill in the afternoon and encamped near Orleans that night. The next day he reached the White Plains, his march being retarded by the want of cavalry to ascertain the meaning of certain movements of the enemy from the direction of Warrenton, which seemed to menace the right flank of his column.

On the 28th, arriving at Thoroughfare Gap, he found the enemy prepared to dispute his progress. General D. R. Jones' division, being ordered to force the passage of the mountain, quickly dislodged the enemy's sharpshooters from the trees and rocks and advanced into the gorge. The enemy held the eastern extremity of the pass in large force, and directed a heavy fire of artillery upon the road leading through it and upon the sides of the mountain. The ground occupied by Jones afforded no opportunity for the employment of artillery. Hood, with two brigades, and Wilcox, with three, were ordered to turn the enemy's right, the former moving over the mountain by a narrow path to the left of the pass, and the latter further to the north by Hopewell Gap. Before these troops reached their destinations the enemy advanced and attacked Jones' left, under Brigadier-General G. T. Anderson. Being vigorously repulsed, he withdrew to his position at the eastern end of the gap, from which he kept up an active fire of artillery until dark, and then retreated.

Generals Jones and Wilcox bivouacked that night east of the mountain, and on the morning of the 29th the whole command resumed the march, the sound of cannon at Manassas announcing that Jackson was already engaged. Longstreet entered the turnpike near Gainesville, and moving down toward Groveton, the head of his column came upon the field in rear of the enemy's left, which had already opened with artillery upon Jackson's right, as previously described. He immediately placed some of his batteries in position, but before he could complete his dispositions to attack the enemy withdrew, not, however, without loss from our artillery. Longstreet took position on the right of Jackson, Hood's two brigades, supported by Evans, being deployed across the turnpike and at right angles to it. These troops were supported on the left by three brigades under General Wilcox, and by a like force on the right under General Kemper. D. R. Jones' division formed the extreme right of the line, resting on the Manassas Gap Railroad. The cavalry guarded our right and left flanks, that on the right being under General Stuart in person. After the arrival of Longstreet the enemy changed his position and began to concentrate opposite Jackson's left, opening a brisk artillery fire, which was responded to with effect by some of General A. P. Hill's batteries. Colonel Walton placed a part of his artillery upon a commanding position between the lines of Generals Jackson and Longstreet by order of the latter, and engaged the enemy vigorously for several hours. Soon afterward General Stuart reported the approach of a large force from the direction of Bristoe Station, threatening Longstreet's right. The brigades under General Wilcox were sent to re-enforce General Jones, but no serious attack was made, and after firing a few shots the enemy withdrew. While this demonstration was being made on our right a large force advanced to assail the left of Jackson's position, occupied by the division of General A. P. Hill. The attack was received by his troops with their accustomed steadiness, and the battle raged with great fury. The enemy was repeatedly repulsed, but again pressed on to attack with fresh troops. Once he succeeded in penetrating an interval between General Gregg's brigade, on the extreme left, and that of General Thomas, but was quickly driven back with great slaughter by the Fourteenth South Carolina Regiment, then in reserve, and the Forty-ninth Georgia, of Thomas' brigade. The contest was close and obstinate, the combatants sometimes delivering their fire at ten paces. General Gregg, who was most exposed, was re-enforced by Hay's brigade, under Colonel Forno, and successfully and gallantly resisted the attacks of the enemy until, the ammunition of his brigade being exhausted and all his field officers but two killed or wounded, it was relieved, after several hours of severe fighting, by Early's brigade and the Eighth Louisiana Regiment. General Early drove the enemy back with heavy loss, and pursued about two hundred yards beyond the line of battle, when he was recalled to the position on the railroad where Thomas, Pender and Archer had firmly held their ground against every attack. While the battle was raging on Jackson's left General Longstreet ordered Hood and Evans to advance, but before the order could be obeyed Hood was himself attacked, and his command at once became warmly engaged. General Wilcox was recalled from the right and ordered to advance on Hood's left, and one of Kemper's brigades, under Colonel Hunton, moved forward on his right. The enemy was repulsed by Hood after a severe contest, and fell back, closely followed by our troops.

The battle continued until 9 P. M., the enemy retreating until he reached a strong position, which he held with a large force. The darkness of the night put a stop to the engagement, and our troops remained in their advanced position until early next morning, when they were withdrawn to their first line. One piece of artillery, several stands of colors and a number of prisoners were captured.

Our loss was severe in this engagement. Brigadier-Generals Field and Trimble, and Colonel Forno, commanding Hay's brigade, were severely wounded, and several other valuable officers killed or disabled. On the morning of the 30th the enemy again advanced, and skirmishing began along the line. The troops of Jackson and Longstreet maintained their positions of the previous day. Fitzhugh Lee, with three regiments of his cavalry, was posted on Jackson's left, and R. H. Anderson's division, which arrived during the forenoon, was held in reserve near the turnpike. The batteries of Colonel S. D. Lee took the position occupied the day before by Colonel Walton, and engaged the enemy actively until noon, when firing ceased and all was quiet for several hours. About 3 P. M. the enemy, having massed his troops in front of General Jackson, advanced against his position in strong force. His front line pushed forward until engaged at close quarters by Jackson's troops, when its progress was checked and a fierce and bloody struggle ensued. A second and third line of great strength moved up to support the first, but in doing so came within easy range of a position a little in advance of General Longstreet's left. He immediately ordered up two batteries, and two others being thrown forward about the same time by Colonel S. D. Lee, under their well-directed and destructive fire the supporting lines were broken and fell back in great confusion. Their repeated efforts to rally were unavailing, and Jackson's troops, being thus relieved from the pressure of overwhelming numbers, began to press steadily forward, driving the enemy before them. He retreated in confusion, suffering severely from our artillery, which advanced as he retired. General Longstreet, anticipating the order for a general advance, now threw his whole command against the Federal center and left. Hood's two brigades, closely followed by Evans, led the attack. R. H. Anderson's division came gallantly to the support of Hood, while the three brigades under Wilcox moved forward on his left, and those of Kemper on his right. D. R. Jones advanced on the extreme right, and the whole line swept steadily on, driving the enemy with great carnage from each successive position until 10 P. M., when darkness put an end to the battle and the pursuit. During the latter part of the engagement General Wilcox, with his own brigade, was ordered to the right, where the resistance of the enemy was most obstinate, and rendered efficient assistance to the troops engaged on that part of the line. His other two brigades, maintaining their position in line, acted with General Jackson's command. The obscurity of night and the uncertainty of the fords of Bull Run rendered it necessary to suspend operations until morning, when the cavalry, being pushed forward, discovered that the enemy had escaped to the strong position of Centreville, about four miles beyond Bull Run. The prevalence of a heavy rain, which began during the night, threatened to render Bull Run impassable, and impeded our movements. Longstreet remained on the battlefield to engage the attention of the enemy and cover the burial of the dead and the removal of the wounded, while Jackson proceeded by Sudley Ford to the Little River Turnpike to turn the enemy's right and intercept his retreat to Washington. Jackson's progress was retarded by the inclemency of the weather and the fatigue of his troops, who, in addition to their arduous marches, had fought three severe engagements in as many days. He reached Little River Turnpike in the evening, and the next day, September 1st, advanced by that road toward Fairfax Courthouse.

Last Stand Made by the Federals at Manassas.

The enemy in the meantime was falling back rapidly toward Washington, and had thrown out a strong force to Germantown, on the Little River Turnpike, to cover his line of retreat from Centreville. The advance of Jackson's column encountered the enemy at Ox Hill, near Germantown, about 5 P. M. Line of battle was at once formed, and two brigades of A. P. Hill's division (those of Branch and Field, under Colonel Brockenbrough) were thrown forward to attack the enemy and ascertain his strength and position. A cold and drenching rainstorm drove in the faces of our troops as they advanced and gallantly engaged the enemy. They were subsequently supported by the brigades of Gregg, Thomas and Pender; also of Hill's division, which, with part of Ewell's, became engaged. The conflict was obstinately maintained by the enemy until dark, when he retreated, having lost two general officers, one of whom, Major-General Kearny, was left dead on the field.

Longstreet's command arrived after the action was over, and the next morning it was found that the enemy had conducted his retreat so rapidly that the attempt to intercept him was abandoned. The proximity of the fortifications around Alexandria and Washington rendered further pursuit useless, and our army rested during the 2d near Chantilly, the enemy being followed only by the cavalry, who continued to harass him until he reached the shelter of his intrenchments.

In the series of engagements on the plains of Manassas more than 7,000 prisoners were taken, in addition to about 2,000 wounded left in our hands. Thirty pieces of artillery, upward of 20,000 stand of small arms, numerous colors and a large amount of stores, besides those taken by General Jackson at Manassas Junction, were captured. The history of the achievements of the army from the time it advanced from Gordonsville leaves nothing to be said in commendation of the courage, fortitude and good conduct of both officers and men. During all these operations the cavalry under General Stuart, consisting of the brigades of Generals Robertson and Fitzhugh Lee, rendered most important and valuable service. It guarded the flanks of the army, protected its trains, and gave information of the enemy's movements. Besides engaging the cavalry of the enemy on several occasions with uniform success, a detachment under the gallant and lamented Major Patrick, assisted by the Stuart Horse Artillery, under Major Pelham, effectually protected General Jackson's trains against a body of the enemy, who penetrated to his rear on the 29th before the arrival of General Longstreet. Toward the close of the action on the 30th General Robertson, with the Second Virginia Regiment, under Colonel Munford, supported by the Seventh and Twelfth, made a brilliant charge upon a brigade of the enemy's cavalry, Colonel Munford leading with great gallantry, and completely routed it. Many of the enemy were killed and wounded, more than three hundred prisoners were captured, and the remainder pursued beyond Bull Run.

* * * * * *

R. E. LEE, *General.*

CAMPAIGN IN NORTHERN VIRGINIA

AUGUST 15 TO SEPTEMBER 3, 1862,

INCLUDING BATTLES OF

MANASSAS JUNCTION, OX HILL, BRISTOE STATION AND SECOND MANASSAS, OR BULL RUN

BY

LIEUT.-GEN. THOMAS J. JACKSON,
Commanding Second Corps.

HEADQUARTERS SECOND CORPS, ARMY OF NORTHERN VIRGINIA,
April 27, 1863.

I HAVE the honor herewith to submit to you a report of the operations of my command from August 15 to September 5, 1862, embracing the several engagements of Manassas Junction, Bristoe Station, Ox Hill, and so much of the battles of Groveton (on August 28th, 29th and 30th) as was fought by the troops under my command.

On August 15th, in obedience to instructions from the commanding general, I left my encampment, near Gordonsville, and, passing Orange Courthouse, encamped in the evening near Mount Piszah Church, where I remained until the 20th, when, in accordance with my instructions, while General Longstreet was crossing the Rapidan at Raccoon Ford, I crossed the same river at Somerville Ford. The command encamped for the night near Stevensburg.

My command at this time comprised Ewell's, A. P. Hill's and Jackson's divisions. Ewell's was composed of the brigades of Generals Lawton, Early, Hays (Colonel Forno commanding) and Trimble, with the batteries of William D. Brown, [W. F.] Dement, [J. W.] Latimer, [W. L.] Balthis and [L. E.] D'Aquin. A. P. Hill's division was composed of the brigades of Generals Branch, Gregg, Field, Pender, Archer and Colonel Thomas, with the batteries of [C. M.] Braxton, [H. G.] Latham, [W. G.] Crenshaw, [D. G.] McIntosh, [Greenlee] Davidson and [W. J.] Pegram. Jackson's division, commanded by Brigadier-General William B. Taliaferro, was composed of Winder's brigade, Colonel Baylor commanding; Colonel Campbell's brigade, Major John Seddon commanding; Brigadier-General William B. Taliaferro's brigade, Colonel A. G. Taliaferro commanding, and Starke's brigade, with the batteries of Brockenbrough, [George W.] Wooding, [W. T.] Poague, [Joseph] Carpenter, [W. H.] Cashie and [Charles I.] Raine. Major-General Stuart, with his cavalry, co-operated during the expedition, and I shall more than once have to acknowledge my obligations for the valuable and efficient aid which he rendered.

Early on the morning of the 21st the command left its encampment and moved in the direction of Beverly Ford, on the Rappahannock, General Taliaferro's command in the lead. On approaching the ford the enemy was seen on the opposite bank. Batteries of that division, under the direction of Major Shumaker, chief of artillery, were placed in position, which, after a short resistance (as reported by General Taliaferro), silenced the enemy's guns and dispersed his infantry. Major-General Stuart had crossed with a portion of his cavalry supported by some pieces of artillery, and after skirmishing with the enemy a few hours, taking some prisoners and arms, returned with the information that the Federal forces were moving in strength upon his position and were close at hand. The enemy soon appeared on the opposite bank, and an animated firing was opened and, to a considerable extent, kept up across the river for the rest of the day between the Federal artillery and the batteries of Taliaferro's command.

On the following morning (22d) the three divisions continued their march up the bank of the Rappahannock, General Ewell in the advance, and crossed Hazel River, one of its tributaries, at Wellford's mill, near which General Trimble was left with his brigade to protect the flank of our wagon-train from the enemy, who was moving up the north side of the Rappahannock simultaneously with the advance of our troops on the south side.

About 12 M. a small party surprised part of the train and captured some ambulances and mules, which were, however, soon recovered and some prisoners taken, who gave information that a more considerable Federal force had crossed the river.

About 4 P. M. General Trimble, supported by General Hood (who was the advance of Longstreet's command), had a sharp engagement with his force, in which, after gallantly charging and taking a number of prisoners, they drove the residue, with severe loss, across the river under the protection of the guns of the main body of the Federal army on the opposite side. In the meantime the command passed Freeman's Ford, which it found strongly guarded, and moved on to a point opposite the Fauquier White Sulphur Springs, where we found the bridge destroyed and other evidence that the enemy was in close proximity.

In the afternoon of the 22d the Thirteenth Georgia (Colonel [M.] Douglass), Brown's and Dement's batteries of four guns each, and Early's brigade crossing over, took possession of the springs and adjacent heights,

VIEW OF "STONEWALL" JACKSON'S POSITION NORTH OF WARRENTON PIKE, NEAR GROVETON (SECOND MANASSAS BATTLE.)

and taking some prisoners and incurring some risk from the rain and sudden rise of the water, which for a few hours cut off communication with the main body. In this critical situation the skill and presence of mind of General Early was favorably displayed. It was deemed advisable not to attempt a passage at that point, but to proceed higher up the river. By dawn on the morning of the 24th General Early, by means of a temporary bridge, which had been constructed for his relief, had his troops and artillery safely on the southern side.

On the 24th there was a fierce cannonade between General Hill's artillery and that of the enemy across the river. In the meantime General Stuart, who had preceded me, crossed the Rappahannock, striking the enemy in his rear, making his brilliant night attack upon his camp at Catlett's Station, capturing many prisoners, personal baggage of General Pope, and his dispatch book, containing information of value to us in this expedition. In the evening we moved near Jeffersonton.

Pursuing the instructions of the commanding general, I left Jeffersonton on the morning of the 25th, to throw my command between Washington City and the army of General Pope, and to break up his railroad communication with the Federal capital. Taking the route by Amissville, crossing Hedgeman River (one of the tributaries of the Rappahannock) at Hensen's mill, and moving via Orleans, we reached the vicinity of Salem after a seven days' march, and bivouacked there for the night.

On the next day (26th) the march was continued, diverging to the right at Salem, crossing the Bull Run Mountain through Thoroughfare Gap, and passing Gainesville, reached Bristoe Station, on the Orange & Alexander Railroad, after sunset. At Gainesville I was joined by General Stuart, who, after leaving the vicinity of Waterloo Bridge about 2 A. M., had by a rapid march come up in time to render all needful assistance. He kept upon my right flank during the residue of the day. My command was now in rear of General Pope's army, separating it from the Federal capital and its base of supply. As we approached Bristoe Station the sound of cars coming from the direction of Warrenton Junction was heard, and General Ewell divided his force so as to take simultaneous possession of two points of the railroad. Colonel [T. T.] Munford, with his Second Virginia Cavalry, co-operated in this movement. Two trains of cars and some prisoners were captured, the largest portion of the small Federal force at that point making its escape.

Learning that the enemy had collected at Manassas Junction, a station about seven miles distant, stores of great value, I deemed it important that no time should be lost in securing them. Notwithstanding the darkness of the night and the fatiguing march, which would, since

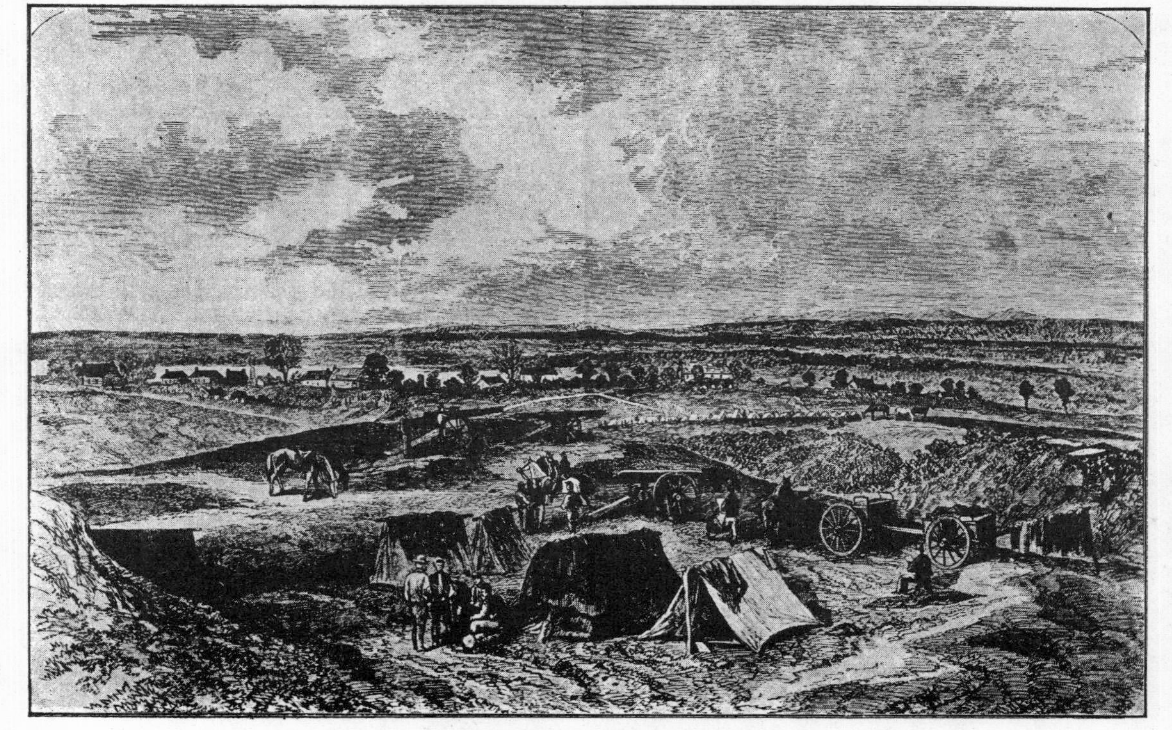

BATTLEFIELD OF SECOND MANASSAS.

dawn, be over thirty miles before reaching the junction. Brigadier-General Trimble volunteered to proceed there forthwith with the Twenty-first North Carolina, Lieutenant-Colonel [R.] Fulton commanding, and the Twenty-first Georgia, Major [T. C.] Glover commanding, in all about five hundred men, and capture the place. I accepted the gallant offer, and gave him orders to move without delay. In order to increase the prospect of success, Major-General Stuart, with a portion of his cavalry, was subsequently directed to move forward, and, as the ranking officer, to take command of the expedition. The duty was cheerfully undertaken by all who were assigned to it and most promptly and successfully executed. Notwithstanding the Federal fire of musketry and artillery, our infantry dispersed the troops placed there for the defense of the place, and captured eight guns, with seventy-two horses, equipments, and ammunition complete, immense supplies of commissary and quartermaster's stores, upward of two-hundred new tents; and General Trimble also reports the capture of over three hundred prisoners and one hundred and seventy-five horses, exclusive of those belonging to the artillery, besides recovering over two hundred negroes.

Longstreet's Position South of the Warrenton Pike.

The next morning the divisions under command of Generals Hill and Taliaferro moved to Manassas Junction, the division of General Ewell remaining at Bristoe Station. About a mile before reaching the Junction, Colonel [W. S. H.] Baylor encountered and dispersed a regiment of Federal cavalry. Soon after the advance of the troops from Bristoe Station reached the Junction, they were fired upon by a distant battery of the enemy posted in the direction of the battlefield of Manassas. This artillery was soon driven off, and retreated in the direction of Centreville. Soon after a considerable body of Federal infantry, under Brigadier-General Taylor, of New Jersey, came in sight, having, it is believed, that morning left Alexandria, in the cars, and boldly pushed forward to recover the position and stores which had been lost the previous night. The advance was made with great spirit and determination, and under a leader worthy of a better cause. Assailed by the batteries of Poague and Carpenter and some of General Hill's division, and apparently seeing that there was no danger of its retreat being cut off by retreating, and being subjected to a heavy fire from our batteries, was soon routed, leaving its killed and wounded upon the field. Several brigades of General Hill's division pressed forward in pursuit. In this conflict the Federal commander, General Taylor, was mortally wounded. Our loss was small. In the afternoon of the same day heavy columns of the enemy were seen approaching Bristoe Station from the direction of Warrenton Junction and on the right of the railroad. General Ewell promptly made his dispositions to meet them. So soon as the enemy came within range the batteries of his division opened upon them from their several positions, as did also the Sixth and Eighth Louisiana and Sixtieth Georgia regiments. By this combined fire two columns of the enemy, of not less than a brigade each, were driven back; but fresh columns soon supplied their places, and it was obvious that the enemy was advancing in heavy force. General Ewell's instructions were, if hard pressed, to fall back and join the main command at Manassas Junction, and orders were accordingly given for the withdrawal of his forces north of Broad Run. At the moment of issuing this order a portion of the troops were actively engaged and the enemy advancing, and yet the withdrawal of the infantry and artillery were conducted with perfect order, General Early closing up the rear. The Federals halted near Bristoe Station, and General Ewell moved without further molestation, Colonel Munford, of the Second, and Colonel [T. L.] Rosser, of the Fifth Virginia Cavalry bringing up his rear to Manassas. The destruction of the railroad bridge across Broad Run was intrusted to Lieutenant (now Captain) [J. K.] Boswell, of the Engineer Corps, under whose superintendence the duty was promptly and efficiently executed. Orders were given to supply the troops with rations and other articles which they could properly make subservient to their use from the captured property. It was vast in quantity and of great value, comprising 50,000 pounds of bacon, 1,000 barrels of corned beef, 2,000 barrels of salt pork, 2,000 barrels of flour, quartermaster's, ordnance, and sutler's stores deposited in buildings and filling two trains of cars. Having appropriated all that we could use, and unwilling that the residue should again fall into the hands of the enemy, who took possession of the place the next day, orders were given to destroy all that remained after supplying the immediate wants of the army. This was done during the night. General Taliaferro moved his division that night across to the Warrenton and Alexandria turnpike, pursuing the road to Sudley's mill, and crossing the turnpike in the vicinity of Groveton, halted near the battlefield of July 21, 1861. Ewell's and Hill's divisions joined Jackson's on the 28th.

My command had hardly concentrated north of the turnpike before the enemy's advance reached the vicinity of Groveton from the direction of Warrenton. General Stuart kept me advised of the general movements of the enemy, while Colonel Rosser, of the cavalry, with his command, and Colonel Bradley T. Johnson, commanding Campbell's brigade, remained in front of the Federals and operated against their advance. Dispositions were promptly made to attack the enemy, based upon the idea that he would continue to press forward upon the turnpike toward Alexandria; but as he did not appear to advance in force, and there was reason to believe that his main body was leaving the road and inclining toward Manassas Junction, my command was advanced through the woods, leaving Groveton on the left, until it reached a commanding position near Bronner's house. By this time it was sunset; but as his column appeared to be moving by with its flank exposed, I determined to attack at once, which was vigorously done by the divisions of Taliaferro and Ewell. The batteries of Wooding, Poague and Carpenter were placed in position in front of Starke's brigade and above the village of Groveton, and, firing over the heads of our skirmishers, poured a heavy fire of shot and shell upon the enemy. This was responded to by a very heavy fire from the enemy, forcing our batteries to select another position. By this time Taliaferro's command, with Lawton's and Trimble's brigades on his left, was advanced from the woods to the open field, and was now moving in gallant style until it reached an orchard on the right of our line, and was less than one hundred yards from a large force of the enemy. The conflict here was fierce and sanguinary. Although largely re-enforced, the Federals did not attempt to advance, but maintained their ground with obstinate determination.

Both lines stood exposed to the discharge of musketry and artillery until about 9 o'clock, when the enemy slowly fell back, yielding the field to our troops.

The loss on both sides was heavy, and among our wounded were Major-General Ewell and Brigadier-General Taliaferro. The latter, after a few months, was able to resume his duties; the former, I regret to say, is still disabled by his wound, and the army thus deprived of his valuable services.

This obstinate resistance of the enemy appears to have been for the purpose of protecting the flank of his column until it should pass the position occupied by our troops. Owing to the difficulty of getting artillery through the woods I did not have as much of that arm as I desired at the opening of the engagement; but this want was met by Major Pelham, with the Stuart Horse Artillery, who dashed forward on my right and opened upon the enemy at a moment when his services were much needed.

Although the enemy moved off under cover of the night and left us in quiet possession of the field, he did not long permit us to remain inactive or in doubt as to his intentions to renew the conflict.

The next morning (29th) I found that he had abandoned the ground occupied as the battlefield the evening before and had moved further to the east and to my left, placing himself between my command and the Federal capital. My troops on this day were distributed along and in the vicinity of the cut of an unfinished railroad (intended as a part of the track to connect the Manassas road directly with Alexandria), stretching from the Warrenton Turnpike in the direction of Sudley's mill. It was mainly along the excavation of this unfinished road that my line of battle was formed on the 29th. Jackson's division, under Brigadier-General Lawton, in the center, and Hill's division the left

In the morning, about 10 o'clock, the Federal artillery opened with spirit and animation upon our right, which was soon replied to by the batteries of Poague, Carpenter, Dement, Brockenbrough, and Latimer, under Major [L. M.] Shumaker. This lasted for some time, when the enemy moved around more to our left, to another point of attack. His next effort was directed against our left. This was vigorously repulsed by the batteries of Braxton, Crenshaw and Pegram.

About 2 P. M. the Federal infantry, in large force, advanced to the attack of our left, occupied by the division of General Hill. It pressed forward, in defiance of our fatal and destructive fire, with great determination, a portion of it crossing a deep cut in the railroad track and penetrating in heavy force an interval of nearly one hundred and seventy-five yards, which separated the right of Gregg's from the left of Thomas' brigade. For a short time Gregg's brigade, on the extreme left, was isolated from the main body of the command, but the Fourteenth South Carolina Regiment, then in reserve, with the Forty-ninth Georgia, left of Colonel Thomas, attacked the exultant enemy with vigor, and drove them back across the railroad track with great slaughter. General McGowan reports that the opposing forces at one time delivered their volleys into each other at the distance of ten paces. Assault after assault was made on the left, exhibiting on the part of the enemy great pertinacity and determination, but every advance was most successfully and gallantly driven back. General Hill reports that six separate and

Scene of the Last Fighting (Second Manassas).

distinct assaults were thus met and repulsed by his division, assisted by Hay's brigade, Colonel Forno commanding.

By this time the brigade of General Gregg, which from its position on the extreme left was most exposed to the enemy's attack, had nearly expended its ammunition. It had suffered severely in its men, and all its field officers except two were killed or wounded. About 4 o'clock it had been assisted by Hays' brigade (Colonel Forno.) It was now retired to the rear to take some repose, after seven hours of severe service, and General Early's brigade, of Ewell's division, with the Eighth Louisiana Regiment, took its place. On reaching his position General Early found that the enemy had obtained possession of the railroad and a piece of wood in front—there being at this point a deep cut—with great slaughter, and followed in pursuit some two hundred yards; the Thirteenth Georgia at the same time advanced to the railroad and crossed with Early's brigade. As it was not desirable to bring on a general engagement that evening General Early was recalled to the railroad, where Thomas, Pender and Archer had firmly maintained their positions during the day. Early kept his position there until the following morning. Brigadier-General Field and Colonel Forno (commanding Hays' brigade) were severely wounded. Brigadier-General Trimble was also seriously wounded.

During the day a force of the enemy penetrated the wood in my rear, endangering the safety of my ambulances and train. Upon being advised of this by General Stuart, I sent a body of infantry to drive them from the wood; but in the meantime the vigilant Pelham had unlimbered his battery and dispersed that portion of them which had reached the wood. At a later period Major [William] Patrick of the cavalry, who was by General Stuart intrusted with guarding the train, was attacked, and although it was promptly and effectually repulsed, it was not without the loss of that intrepid officer, who fell in the attack while setting an example of gallantry to his men well worthy of imitation. During the day the commanding general arrived, and also General Longstreet with his command.

On the following day (30th) my command reoccupied the ground, and the divisions the same relative position to each other and to the field which they held the day before, forming the left wing of the army, General Longstreet's command forming the right wing. A large quantity of artillery was posted upon a commanding eminence in the center. After some desultory skirmishing and heavy cannonading during the day the Federal infantry, about 4 o'clock in the evening, moved from under cover of the wood and advanced in several lines, first engaging the right, but soon extending its attack to the center and left. In a few moments our entire line was engaged in a fierce and sanguinary struggle with the enemy. As one line was repulsed another took its place and pressed forward as if determined by force of numbers and fury of assault to drive us from our positions. So impetuous and so well sustained were these onsets as to induce me to send to the commanding general for re-enforcements, but the timely and gallant advance of General Longstreet on the right relieved my troops from the pressure of overwhelming numbers and gave to those brave men the chances of a more equal conflict. As Longstreet pressed upon the right the Federal advance was checked, and soon a general advance of my whole line was ordered. Eagerly and fiercely did each brigade press forward, exhibiting in parts of the field scenes of close encounter and murderous strife not witnessed often in the turmoil of battle. The Federals gave way before our troops, fell back in disorder, and fled precipitately, leaving their dead and wounded on the field. During their retreat the artillery opened with destructive power upon the fugitive masses. The infantry followed until darkness put an end to the pursuit.

Our loss was heavy; that of the enemy, as shown by the battlefield, of which we were in possession, much heavier. Among the losses was Colonel Baylor, commanding Winder's brigade, who fell in front of his brigade while nobly leading and cheering it on to the charge.

We captured eight pieces of artillery with their caissons, and six thousand five hundred and twenty small arms were collected from the battlefield.

It being ascertained next morning that the Federal army had retreated in the direction of Centreville, I was ordered by the commanding general to turn that position, crossing Bull Run at Sudley Ford, thence pursuing a country road until we reached the Little River Turnpike, which we followed in the direction of Fairfax Courthouse until the troops halted for the night.

Sudley Springs (Second Manassas).

Early the next morning (September 1st) we moved forward, and late in the evening, after reaching Ox Hill, came in contact with the enemy, who were in position on our right and front, covering his line of retreat from Centreville to Fairfax Courthouse. Our line of battle was formed, General Hill's division on the right, Ewell's division, General Lawton commanding, in the center, and Jackson's division, General Starke commanding, on the left; all on the right of the turnpike road. Artillery was posted on an eminence to the left of the road. The brigades of Branch and Field, Colonel [J. M.] Brockenbrough commanding the latter, were sent forward to feel and engage the enemy. A cold and drenching thunder-shower swept over the field at this time, striking directly into the faces of our troops. These two brigades gallantly engaged the enemy; but so severe was the fire in front and flank of Branch's brigade as to produce in it some disorder and falling back. The brigades of Gregg, Thomas and Pender were then thrown into the fight. Soon a portion of Ewell's division became engaged. The conflict now raged with great fury; the enemy obstinately and desperately contesting the grounds until their generals (Kearny and Stevens) fell in front of Thomas' brigade, after which they retired from the field. By the following morning the Federal army had entirely disappeared from our view, and it soon appeared, by a report from General Stuart, that it had passed Fairfax Courthouse and had moved in the direction of Washington City.

On September 3d we left Ox Hill, taking the road by Dranesville and Leesburg, and on the 4th bivouacked near the Big Spring, between Leesburg and the Potomac.

The official reports of the casualties of my command, in its operations from the Rappahannock to the Potomac, will show a loss of 75 officers killed and 273 wounded; 730 non-commissioned officers and privates killed; 3,274 wounded and 35 missing, making a total loss of 4,387.

Colonel S. Crutchfield, chief of artillery, discharged his duties well. The conduct of officers and men during the serious engagements described were such as to entitle them to great praise. The wounded were skillfully cared for by Medical Director Dr. Hunter McGuire.

In the transmission of orders I was greatly assisted during the expedition by the following members of my staff: Colonel A. Smead, Assistant Inspector-General; Major E. F. Paxton, Acting Assistant Adjutant-General; Captain R. E. Wilbourn, Chief Signal Officer; First Lieutenant H. K. Douglas, Assistant Inspector-General; First Lieutenant J. G. Morrison, Aid-de-camp, and Colonel William L. Jackson, Volunteer Aid-de-camp. Captain Wilbourn was so severely wounded at the battle of Groveton as to be unable to go further with the army. The ordnance, quartermaster's and commissary departments were well managed by their respective chiefs, Majors G. H. Bier, J. A. Harman and W. J. Hawks.

For further information respecting the detailed movements of troops, and the conduct of individuals, I would respectfully refer you to the accompanying reports. For these great and signal victories our sincere and humble thanks are due unto Almighty God. We should in all things acknowledge the hand of Him who reigns in heaven and rules among the armies of men. In view of the arduous labors and great privations the troops were called to endure and the isolated and perilous position which the command occupied while engaged with greatly superior numbers of the enemy, we can but express the grateful conviction of our mind that God was with us and gave to us the victory; and unto His holy name be the praise.

T. J. JACKSON, *Lieutenant-General.*

ORGANIZATION OF THE ARMY OF NORTHERN VIRGINIA,

DURING THE BATTLES OF

AUGUST 28 TO SEPTEMBER 1, 1862.

INCLUDING THE BATTLES OF

SECOND MANASSAS (BULL RUN OR GROVETON HEIGHTS), THOROUGHFARE GAP, GAINESVILLE, LEWIS' FORD, CHANTILLY, OR OX HILL, ETC.

RIGHT WING, OR LONGSTREET'S CORPS.

Major-General James Longstreet.

ANDERSON'S DIVISION.

Major-General R. H. Anderson.

ARMISTEAD'S BRIGADE.

Brigadier-General L. A. Armistead.

Ninth Virginia; Fourteenth Virginia; Thirty-eighth Virginia; Fifty-third Virginia; Fifty-seventh Virginia; Fifth Virginia Battalion.

MAHONE'S BRIGADE.

Brigadier-General W. Mahone.

Sixth Virginia; Twelfth Virginia; Sixteenth Virginia; Forty-first Virginia; Forty-ninth Virginia.

WRIGHT'S BRIGADE.

Brigadier-General A. R. Wright.

Third Georgia; Twenty-second Georgia; Forty-fourth Georgia; Forty-eighth Georgia.

JONES' DIVISION.

Brigadier-General D. R. Jones.

TOOMBS' BRIGADE.

Colonel H. L. Benning; Brigadier-General R. Toombs.

Second Georgia; Fifteenth Georgia; Seventeenth Georgia; Twentieth Georgia.

DRAYTON'S BRIGADE.

Brigadier-General T. F. Drayton.

Fiftieth Georgia; Fifty-first Georgia; Fifteenth South Carolina; Phillips' Legion.

JONES' BRIGADE.

Colonel George T. Anderson.

First Georgia (Regulars); Seventh Georgia; Eighth Georgia; Ninth Georgia; Eleventh Georgia.

Stone House, Warrenton Pike.

WILCOX'S DIVISION.
Brigadier-General C. M. Wilcox.

WILCOX'S BRIGADE.
Brigadier-General C. M. Wilcox.

Eighth Alabama; Ninth Alabama; Tenth Alabama; Eleventh Alabama; Anderson's battery, Thomas (Va.) Artillery.

PRYOR'S BRIGADE.
Brigadier-General R. A. Pryor.

Fourteenth Alabama; Fifth Florida; Eighth Florida; Third Virginia.

FEATHERSTON'S BRIGADE.
Brigadier-General W. S. Featherston; Colonel Carnot Posey.

Twelfth Mississippi; Sixteenth Mississippi; Nineteenth Mississippi; Second Mississippi Battalion; Chapman's battery, Dixie (Va.) Artillery.

HOOD'S DIVISION.
Brigadier-General John B. Hood.

HOOD'S BRIGADE.
Brigadier-General John B. Hood.

Eighteenth Georgia; Hampton (S. C.) Legion; First Texas; Fourth Texas; Fifth Texas.

WHITING'S BRIGADE.
Colonel E. M. Law.

Fourth Alabama; Second Mississippi; Eleventh Mississippi; Sixth North Carolina.

ARTILLERY.
Major B. W. Frobel.

Bachman's battery, German (S. C.) Artillery; Garden's battery, Palmetto (S.C.) Artillery; Reilly's battery, Rowan (N. C.) Artillery.

LIEUT.-GEN. RICHARD H. ANDERSON, OF SOUTH CAROLINA.

KEMPER'S DIVISION.
Brigadier-General James L. Kemper.

KEMPER'S BRIGADE.
Colonel M. D. Corse.

First Virginia; Seventh Virginia; Eleventh Virginia; Seventeenth Virginia; Twenty-fourth Virginia.

JENKINS' BRIGADE.
Brigadier-General M. Jenkins; Colonel Joseph Walker.

First South Carolina (Volunteers); Second South Carolina Rifles; Fifth South Carolina; Sixth South Carolina; Fourth South Carolina Battalion; Palmetto (S. C.) Sharpshooters.

PICKETT'S BRIGADE.
Colonel Eppa Hunton.

Eighth Virginia; Eighteenth Virginia; Nineteenth Virginia; Twenty-eighth Virginia; Fifty-sixth Virginia.

EVANS' BRIGADE.
Brigadier-General N. G. Evans; Colonel P. F. Stevens.

Seventeenth South Carolina; Eighteenth South Carolina; Twenty-second South Carolina; Twenty-third South Carolina; Holcombe (S. C.) Legion; Boyce's battery, Macbeth (S. C.) Artillery.

ARTILLERY OF THE RIGHT WING.

WASHINGTON (LA.) ARTILLERY.
Colonel J. B. Walton.

Eshleman's (Fourth) company; Miller's (Third) company; Richardson's (Second) company; Squires' (First) company.

LEE'S BATTALION.
Colonel S. D. Lee.

Eubank's (Va.) battery; Grimes' (Va.) battery; Jordan's battery, Bedford (Va.) Artillery; Parker's (Va.) battery; Rhett's (S. C.) battery; Taylor's (Va.) battery.

MISCELLANEOUS BATTERIES.

Huger's (Va.) battery; Leake's (Va.) battery; Maurin's battery, Donaldsonville (La.) Artillery; Moorman's (Va.) battery; Rogers' battery, Loudoun (Va.) Artillery; Stribling's battery, Fauquier (Va.) Artillery.

BURYING THE DEAD, ANTIETAM.

LEFT WING, OR JACKSON'S CORPS.
Major-General T. J. Jackson.

JACKSON'S DIVISION.
Brigadier-General William B. Taliaferro; Brigadier-General William E. Starke.

FIRST BRIGADE.
Colonel W. S. H. Baylor; Colonel A. J. Grigsby.

Second Virginia; Fourth Virginia; Fifth Virginia; Twenty-seventh Virginia; Thirty-third Virginia.

SECOND BRIGADE.
Colonel Bradley T. Johnson.

Twenty-first Virginia; Forty-second Virginia; Forty-eighth Virginia; First Virginia Battalion.

THIRD BRIGADE.
Colonel A. G. Taliaferro.

Forty-seventh Alabama; Forty-eighth Alabama; Tenth Virginia; Twenty-third Virginia; Thirty-seventh Virginia.

FOURTH BRIGADE.
Brigadier-General W. E. Starke; Colonel Leroy A. Stafford.

First Louisiana; Second Louisiana; Ninth Louisiana; Tenth Louisiana; Fifteenth Louisiana; Coppen's (La.) battalion.

ARTILLERY.
Major L. M. Shumaker.

Brockenbrough's (Md.) battery; Carpenter's (Va.) battery; Caskie's battery, Hampden (Va.) Artillery; Cutshaw's (Va.) battery; Poague's battery, Rockbridge (Va.) Artillery; Raines' battery, Lee (Va.) Artillery; Rice's (Va.) battery; Wooding's battery, Danville (Va.) Artillery.

HILL'S (LIGHT) DIVISION.
Major-General Ambrose P. Hill.

BRANCH'S BRIGADE.
Brigadier-General L. O'B. Branch; Brigadier-General J. H. Lane.

Seventh North Carolina; Eighteenth North Carolina; Twenty-eighth North Carolina; Thirty-third North Carolina; Thirty-seventh North Carolina.

SCENE AT THE FENCE, ANTIETAM.

PENDER'S BRIGADE.
Brigadier-General W. D. Pender.

Sixteenth North Carolina; Twenty-second North Carolina; Thirty-fourth North Carolina; Thirty-eighth North Carolina.

ARCHER'S BRIGADE.
Brigadier-General J. J. Archer.

Fifth Alabama Battalion; Nineteenth Georgia; First Tennessee (Provisional Army); Seventh Tennessee; Fourteenth Tennessee.

FIELD'S BRIGADE.
Brigadier-General C. W. Field; Colonel J. M. Brockenbrough.

Fortieth Virginia; Forty-seventh Virginia; Fifty-fifth Virginia; Twenty-second Virginia Battalion.

GREGG'S BRIGADE.
Brigadier-General Maxcy Gregg.

First South Carolina; First South Carolina Rifles; Twelfth South Carolina; Thirteenth South Carolina; Fourteenth South Carolina.

THOMAS' BRIGADE.
Brigadier-General E. L. Thomas.

Fourteenth Georgia; Thirty-fifth Georgia; Forty-fifth Georgia; Forty-ninth Georgia.

ARTILLERY.
Lieutenant-Colonel R. L. Walker.

Braxton's battery, Fredericksburg (Va.) Artillery; Crenshaw's (Va.) battery; Davidson's battery, Letcher (Va.) Artillery; Fleet's battery, Middlesex (Va.) Artillery; Latham's battery, Branch (N. C.) Artillery; McIntosh's battery, Pee Dee (S. C.) Artillery; Pegram's battery, Purcell (Va.) Artillery.

EWELL'S DIVISION.
Major-General R. S. Ewell; Brigadier-General A. R. Lawton.

LAWTON'S BRIGADE.
Brigadier-General A. R. Lawton; Colonel M. Douglass.

Thirteenth Georgia; Twenty-sixth Georgia; Thirty-first Georgia; Thirty-eighth Georgia; Sixtieth Georgia; Sixty-first Georgia.

HENRY HOUSE, ANTIETAM BATTLEFIELD.

TRIMBLE'S BRIGADE.
Brigadier-General I. R. Trimble; Captain W. F. Brown.

Fifteenth Alabama; Twelfth Georgia; Twenty-first Georgia; Twenty-first North Carolina; First North Carolina Battalion.

EARLY'S BRIGADE.
Brigadier-General J. A. Early.

Thirteenth Virginia; Twenty-fifth Virginia; Thirty-first Virginia; Forty-fourth Virginia; Forty-ninth Virginia; Fifty-second Virginia; Fifty-eighth Virginia.

HAYS' BRIGADE.
Brigadier-General Harry T. Hays; Colonel Henry Forno; Colonel H. B. Strong.

Fifth Louisiana; Sixth Louisiana; Seventh Louisiana; Eighth Louisiana; Fourteenth Louisiana.

ARTILLERY.

Balthis' battery, Staunton (Va.) Artillery; Brown's battery, Chesapeake (Md.) Artillery; D'Aquin's battery, Louisiana Guard Artillery; Dement's (Md.) battery; John R. Johnson's (Va.) battery; Latimer's battery, Courtney (Va.) Artillery.

CAVALRY.
Major-General J. E. B. Stuart.

HAMPTON'S BRIGADE.
Brigadier-General Wade Hampton.

First North Carolina; Second South Carolina; Tenth Virginia; Cobb (Ga.) Legion; Jeff. Davis Legion.

ROBERTSON'S BRIGADE.
Brigadier-General B. H. Robertson.

Second Virginia; Sixth Virginia; Seventh Virginia; Twelfth Virginia; Seventeenth Virginia Battalion.

LEE'S BRIGADE.
Brigadier-General Fitzhugh Lee.

First Virginia; Third Virginia; Fourth Virginia; Fifth Virginia; Ninth Virginia.

ARTILLERY.

Hart's (S. C.) battery; Pelham's (Va.) battery.

MY MARYLAND.

BY JAMES R. RANDALL.

[Written at Point Coupée, La., April 26, 1861. First published in the New Orleans *Delta*.]

The despot's heel is on thy shore,
Maryland!
His torch is at thy temple door,
Maryland!
Avenge the patriotic gore
That flecked the streets of Baltimore,
And be the battle queen of yore,
Maryland! my Maryland!

Hark to an exiled son's appeal,
Maryland!
My mother State, to thee I kneel,
Maryland!
For life or death, for woe and weal,
Thy peerless chivalry reveal,
And gird thy beauteous limbs with steel,
Maryland! my Maryland.

Thou wilt not cower in the dust,
Maryland!
Thy beaming sword shall never rust,
Maryland!
Remember Carroll's secret trust,
Remember Howard's warlike thrust,
And all thy slumberers with the just,
Maryland! my Maryland!

Come! 'tis the red dawn of the day,
Maryland!
Come! with thy panoplied array,
Maryland!
With Ringgold's spirit for the fray,
With Watson's blood at Monterey,
With fearless Low and dashing May,
Maryland! my Maryland!

Come! for thy shield is bright and strong,
Maryland!
Come! for thy dalliance does thee wrong,
Maryland!
Come to thine own heroic throng,
That stalks with Liberty along,
And ring thy dauntless slogan song,
Maryland! my Maryland!

Dear mother! burst the tyrant's chain,
Maryland!
Virginia should not call in vain,
Maryland!
She meets her sisters on the plain—
"*Sic semper!*" 'tis the proud refrain
That baffles minions back amain,
Maryland!
Arise in majesty again,
Maryland! my Maryland!

THE MARYLAND CAMPAIGN,

SEPTEMBER 3 TO 20, 1862,

INCLUDING THE BATTLES OF

SOUTH MOUNTAIN, CRAMPTON'S GAP AND ANTIETAM, OR SHARPSBURG.

BY

GENERAL ROBERT E. LEE,

Commanding the Army of Northern Virginia.

HEADQUARTERS, October —, 1862.

THE enemy having retired to the protection of the fortifications around Washington and Alexandria, the army marched on September 3d toward Leesburg. The armies of Generals McClellan and Pope had now been brought back to the point from which they set out on the campaigns of the spring and summer. The objects of those campaigns had been frustrated and the designs of the enemy on the coast of North Carolina and in Western Virginia thwarted by the withdrawal of the main body of his forces from those regions. Northeastern Virginia was freed from the presence of Federal soldiers up to the intrenchments of Washington, and soon after the arrival of the army at Leesburg information was received that the troops which had occupied Winchester had retired to Harpers Ferry and Martinsburg. The war was thus transferred from the interior to the frontier, and the supplies of rich and productive districts made accessible to our army. To prolong a state of affairs in every way desirable, and not to permit the season for active operations to pass without endeavoring to inflict further injury upon the enemy, the best course appeared to be the transfer of the army into Maryland. Although not properly equipped for invasion, lacking much of the material of war, and feeble in transportation, the troops poorly provided with clothing, and thousands of them destitute of shoes, it was yet believed to be strong enough to detain the enemy upon the northern frontier until the approach of winter should render his advance into Virginia difficult, if not impracticable. The condition of Maryland encouraged the belief that the presence of our army, however inferior to that of the enemy, would induce the Washington Government to retain all its available force to provide against contingencies, which its course toward the people of that State gave it reason to apprehend. At the same time it was hoped that military success might afford us an opportunity to aid the citizens of Maryland in any efforts they might be disposed to make to recover their liberties. The difficulties that surrounded them were fully appreciated, and we expected to derive more assistance in the attainment of our object from the just fears of the Washington Government than from any active demonstration on the part of the people, unless success should enable us to give them assurance of continued protection. Influenced by these considerations, the army was put in motion, D. H. Hill's division, which had joined us on the 2d, being in advance, and between September 4th and 7th crossed the Potomac at the fords near Leesburg, and encamped in the vicinity of Fredericktown.

It was decided to cross the Potomac east of the Blue Ridge, in order, by threatening Washington and Baltimore, to cause the enemy to withdraw from the south bank, where his presence endangered our communications and the safety of those engaged in the removal of our wounded and the captured property from the late battlefields. Having accomplished this result, it was proposed to move the army into Western Maryland, establish our communications with Richmond through the valley of the Shenandoah, and, by threatening Pennsylvania, induce the enemy to follow, and thus draw him from his base of supplies.

It had been supposed that the advance upon Fredericktown would lead to the evacuation of Martinsburg and Harpers Ferry, thus opening the line of communications through the valley. This not having occurred, it became necessary to dislodge the enemy from those positions before concentrating the army west of the mountains. To accomplish this with the least delay, General Jackson was directed to proceed with his command to Martinsburg, and, after driving the enemy from that place, to move down the south side of the Potomac upon Harpers Ferry. General McLaws, with his own and R. H. Anderson's division, was ordered to seize Maryland Heights, on the north side of the Potomac, opposite Harpers Ferry, and Brigadier-General Walker to take possession of Loudoun Heights, on the east side of the Shenandoah, where it unites with the Potomac. These several commands were directed, after reducing Harpers Ferry and clearing the valley of the enemy, to join the rest of the army at Boonsborough or Hagerstown.

The march of these troops began on the 10th, and at the same time the remainder of Longstreet's command and the division of D. H. Hill crossed the South Mountain and moved toward Boonsborough. General Stuart, with the cavalry, remained east of the mountains to observe the enemy and retard his advance.

A report having been received that a Federal force was approaching Hagerstown from the direction of Chambersburg, Longstreet continued his march to the former place, in order to secure the road leading thence to Williamsport, and also to prevent the removal of stores which were said to be in Hagerstown. He arrived at that place on the 11th; General Hill halting near Boonsborough to prevent the enemy at Harpers Ferry from escaping through Pleasant Valley, and at the same time to support the cavalry. The advance of the Federal army was so slow at the time we left Fredericktown as to justify the belief that the reduction of Harpers Ferry would be accomplished and our troops concentrated before they would be called upon to meet it. In that event, it had not been intended to oppose its passage through the South Mountains, as it was desired to engage it as far as possible from its base.

General Jackson marched very rapidly, and, crossing the Potomac near Williamsport on the 11th, sent A. P. Hill's division directly to Martinsburg, and disposed the rest of his command to cut off the retreat of the enemy westward. On his approach, the Federal troops evacuated Martinsburg, retiring to Harpers Ferry on the night of the 11th, and Jackson entered the former place on the 12th, capturing some prisoners and abandoned stores.

In the forenoon of the following day his leading division, under General A. P. Hill, came in sight of the enemy strongly intrenched on Bolivar Heights, in rear of Harpers Ferry. Before beginning the attack, General Jackson proceeded to put himself in communication with the cooperating forces under Generals McLaws and Walker, from the former of whom he was separated by the Potomac, and from the latter by the Shenandoah. General Walker took possession of Loudoun Heights on the 13th, and the next day was in readiness to open upon Harpers Ferry. General McLaws encountered more opposition. He entered Pleasant Valley on the 11th. On the 12th he directed General Kershaw, with his own and Barksdale's brigade, to ascend the ridge, whose southern extremity is known as Maryland Heights, and attack the enemy, who occupied that position with infantry and artillery, protected by intrenchments. He disposed the rest of his command to hold the roads leading from Harpers Ferry eastward through Weverton and northward from Sandy Hook, guarding the pass in his rear, through which he had entered Pleasant Valley, with the brigades of Semmes and Mahone. Owing to the rugged nature of the ground on which Kershaw had to operate, and the want of roads, he was compelled to use infantry alone. Driving in the advance parties of the enemy on the summit of the ridge on the 12th, he assailed the works the next day. After a spirited contest they were carried, the troops engaged in their defense spiking their heavy guns and retreating to Harpers Ferry. By 4:30 P. M. Kershaw was in possession of Maryland Heights.

On the 14th a road for artillery was cut along the ridge, and at 2 P. M. four guns opened upon the enemy on the opposite side of the river, and the investment of Harpers Ferry was complete.

In the meantime events transpired in another quarter which threatened to interfere with the reduction of the place. A copy of the order directing the movement of the army from Fredericktown had fallen into the hands of General McClellan, and disclosed to him the disposition of our forces. He immediately began to push forward rapidly, and on the afternoon of the 13th was reported approaching the pass in South Mountain, on the Boonsborough and Fredericktown Road. The cavalry under General Stuart fell back before him, materially impeding his progress by its gallant resistance, and gaining time for preparations to oppose his advance. By penetrating the mountains at this point he would reach the rear of McLaws and be enabled to relieve the garrison at Harpers Ferry. To prevent this, General D. H. Hill was directed to guard

AFTER THE BATTLE OF ANTIETAM.

The above is reproduced from the celebrated painting (copyrighted) by Captain James Hope, who made a sketch of the scene on the evening of September 17, 1862.

No spot on the battlefield of Antietam presented a more ghastly spectacle than did the "Sunken Road" or "Bloody Lane." This position was occupied by the Confederates, who had formed a breastwork of the low but steep banks through which the road was cut. The scene is one never to be forgotten; the lane was bankful of dead and dying, while the slopes and approaches were literally covered by the bodies of those who fell under the withering fire from the enemy's guns.

the Boonsborough Gap, and Longstreet ordered to march from Hagerstown to his support.

On the 13th General Hill sent back the brigades of Garland and Colquitt to hold the pass, but subsequently ascertaining that the enemy was near in heavy force, he ordered up the rest of his division.

Early on the 14th a large body of the enemy attempted to force its way to the rear of the position held by Hill, by a road south of the Boonsborough and Fredericktown Turnpike. The attack was repulsed by Garland's brigade, after a severe conflict, in which that brave and accomplished young officer was killed. The remainder of the division arriving shortly afterward, Colquitt's brigade was disposed across the turnpike road; that of G. P. Anderson, supported by Ripley, was placed on the right, and Rodes occupied an important position on the left. Garland's brigade, which had suffered heavily in the first attack, was withdrawn, and the defense of the road occupied by it intrusted to Colonel Rosser, of the Fifth Virginia Cavalry, who reported to General Hill with his regiment and some artillery. The small command of General Hill repelled the repeated assaults of the Federal army, and held it in check for five hours. Several attacks on the center were gallantly repulsed by Colquitt's brigade, and Rodes maintained his position against heavy odds with the utmost tenacity. Longstreet, leaving one brigade at Hagerstown, had hurried to the assistance of Hill, and reached the scene of action between 3 and 4 P. M. His troops, much exhausted by a long, rapid march and the heat of the day, were disposed on both sides of the turnpike. General D. R. Jones, with three of his brigades—those of Pickett (under General Garnett), Kemper and Jenkins (under Colonel Walker)—together with Evans' brigade, was posted along the mountain on the left; General Hood, with his own and Whiting's brigade (under Colonel Law), Drayton's and D. R. Jones' (under Colonel G. T. Anderson), on the right. Batteries had been placed by General Hill in such positions as could be found, but the ground was unfavorable for the use of artillery. The battle continued with great animation until night. On the south of the turnpike the enemy was driven back some distance, and his attack on the center repulsed with loss. His great superiority of numbers enabled him to extend beyond both of our flanks.

By this means he succeeded in reaching the summit of the mountain beyond our left, and, pressing upon us heavily from that direction, gradually forced our troops back after an obstinate resistance. Darkness put an end to the contest.

The effort to force the passage of the mountains had failed, but it was manifest that without re-enforcements we could not hazard a renewal of the engagement, as the enemy could easily turn either flank. Information was also received that another large body of Federal troops had, during the afternoon, forced their way through Crampton's Gap, only five miles in rear of McLaws. Under these circumstances it was determined to retire to Sharpsburg, where we would be upon the flank and rear of the enemy should he move against McLaws, and where we could more readily unite with the rest of the army. This movement was efficiently and skillfully covered by the cavalry brigade of General Fitzhugh Lee, and was accomplished without interruption by the enemy, who did not appear on the west side of the pass at Boonsborough until about 8 A. M., on the following morning. The resistance that had been offered to the enemy at Boonsborough secured sufficient time to enable General Jackson to complete the reduction of Harpers Ferry.

On the afternoon of the 14th, when he found that the troops of Walker and McLaws were in position to co-operate in the attack, he ordered General A. P. Hill to turn the enemy's left flank and enter Harpers Ferry. Ewell's division (under General Lawton) was ordered to support Hill, while Winder's brigade, of Jackson's division (under Colonel Grigsby), with a battery of artillery, made a demonstration on the enemy's right near the Potomac. The rest of the division was held in reserve. The cavalry, under Major Massie, was placed on the extreme left, to prevent the escape of the enemy. Colonel Grigsby succeeded in getting possession of an eminence on the left, upon which two batteries were advantageously posted. General A. P. Hill, observing a hill on the enemy's extreme left occupied by infantry without artillery, and protected only by an abatis of felled timber, directed General Pender, with his own brigade and those of [General] Archer and Colonel Brockenbrough, to seize the crest, which was done with slight resistance. At the same time he ordered Generals Branch and Gregg to march along the Shenandoah, and, taking advantage of the ravines intersecting its steep banks, to establish themselves on the plain to the left and rear of the enemy's works. This was accomplished during the night. Lieutenant-Colonel Walker, chief of artillery of A. P. Hill's division, placed several batteries on the eminence taken by General Pender, and, under the directions of Colonel Crutchfield, General Jackson's chief of artillery, ten guns belonging to Ewell's division were posted on the east side of the Shenandoah, so as to enfilade the enemy's entrenchments on Bolivar Heights, and take his nearest and most formidable works in reverse. General McLaws, in the meantime, made his preparations to prevent the force which had penetrated at Crampton's Gap from coming to the relief of the garrison. This pass had been defended by the brigade of General Cobb, supported by Semmes and Mahone; but, unable to oppose successfully the superior numbers brought against them, they had been compelled to retire with loss. The enemy halted at the gap, and during the night General McLaws formed his command in line of battle across Pleasant Valley, about one and a half miles below Crampton's [Gap], leaving one regiment to support the artillery on Maryland Heights, and two brigades on each of the roads from Harpers Ferry.

The attack on the garrison began at dawn. A rapid and vigorous fire was opened from the batteries of General Jackson and those on Maryland and Loudoun Heights. In about two hours the garrison, consisting of more than eleven thousand men, surrendered. Seventy-three pieces of artillery, about thirteen thousand small arms, and a large quantity of military stores fell into our hands. Leaving General A. P. Hill to receive the surrender of the Federal troops and secure the captured property, General Jackson, with his two other divisions, set out at once for Sharpsburg, ordering Generals McLaws and Walker to follow without delay. Official information of the fall of Harpers Ferry and the approach of General Jackson was received soon after the commands of Longstreet and D. H. Hill reached Sharpsburg, on the morning of the 15th, and reanimated the courage of the troops. General Jackson arrived early on the 16th, and General Walker came up in the afternoon. The presence of the enemy at Crampton's Gap embarrassed the movements of General McLaws. He retained the position taken during the night of the 14th to oppose an advance toward Harpers Ferry until the capitulation of that place, when, finding the enemy indisposed to attack, he gradually withdrew his command toward the Potomac. Deeming the roads to Sharpsburg on the north side of the river impracticable, he resolved to cross at Harpers Ferry, and marched by way of Shepherdstown. Owing to the condition of his troops and other circumstances, his progress was slow, and he did not reach the battlefield at Sharpsburg until some time after the engagement of the 17th began. The commands of Longstreet and D. H. Hill, on their arrival at Sharpsburg, were placed in position along the range of hills between the town and the Antietam, nearly parallel to the course of that stream, Longstreet on the right of the road to Boonsborough and Hill on the left. The advance of the enemy was delayed by the brave opposition he encountered from Fitzhugh Lee's cavalry, and he did not appear on the opposite side of the Antietam until about 2 P. M. During the afternoon the batteries on each side were slightly engaged.

On the 16th the artillery fire became warmer, and continued throughout the day. The enemy crossed the Antietam beyond the reach of our batteries and menaced our left. In anticipation of this movement, Hood's two brigades had been transferred from the right and posted between D. H. Hill and the Hagerstown Road. General Jackson was now directed to take position on Hood's left, and formed his line with his right resting upon the Hagerstown Road and his left extending toward the Potomac, protected by General Stuart with the cavalry and horse artillery. General Walker, with his two brigades, was stationed on Longstreet's right. As evening approached, the enemy opened more vigorously with his artillery and bore down heavily with his infantry upon Hood, but the attack was gallantly repulsed. At 10 P. M. Hood's troops were relieved by the brigades of Lawton and Trimble, of Ewell's division, commanded by General Lawton. Jackson's own division, under General J. R. Jones, was on Lawton's left, supported by the remaining brigades of Ewell.

At early dawn on the 17th the enemy's artillery opened vigorously from both sides of the Antietam, the heaviest fire being directed against our left. Under cover of this fire a large force of infantry attacked General Jackson. They were met by his troops with the utmost resolution, and for several hours the conflict raged with great fury and alternate success. General J. R. Jones was compelled to leave the field, and the command of Jackson's division devolved on General Starke. The troops advanced with great spirit and the enemy's lines were repeatedly broken and forced to retire. Fresh troops, how-

Williamsport. Battery Magazine. Ford Where Army Crossed.

FORD OF THE POTOMAC, NEAR WILLIAMSPORT, MD., WHERE A LARGE PORTION OF GENERAL LEE'S ARMY CROSSED AFTER THE BATTLE OF ANTIETAM (SHARPSBURG), MD.
[From an old sketch.]

DUNKER CHURCH, ANTIETAM BATTLEFIELD (1880).

From an original painting, owned and copyrighted by Kurz & Allison, Chicago, Ill.

BATTLE OF ANTIETAM (OR SHARPSBURG), MD., SEPTEMBER 16 AND 17, 1862. THE FIGHT AT THE BRIDGE.

ever, soon replaced those that were beaten, and Jackson's men were in turn compelled to fall back. The brave General Starke was killed, General Lawton was wounded, and nearly all the field officers, with a large proportion of the men, killed or disabled. Our troops slowly yielded to overwhelming numbers, and fell back, obstinately disputing the progress of the enemy. Hood returned to the field and relieved the brigades of Trimble, Lawton and Hays, which had suffered severely. General Early, who succeeded General Lawton in the command of Ewell's division, was ordered by General Jackson to move with his brigade to take the place of Jackson's division, most of which was withdrawn, its ammunition being nearly exhausted and its numbers much reduced. A small part of the division, under Colonels Grigsby and Stafford, united with Early's brigade, as did portions of the brigades of Trimble, Lawton, and Hays. The battle now raged with great violence, the small commands under Hood and Early holding their ground against many times their own numbers of the enemy, and under a tremendous fire of artillery. Hood was re-enforced by the brigades of Ripley, Colquitt and Garland (under Colonel McRae), of D. H. Hill's division, and afterward by D. R. Jones' brigade, under Colonel G. T. Anderson. The enemy's lines were broken and forced back, but fresh numbers advanced to their support, and they began to gain ground. The desperate resistance they encountered, however, delayed their progress until the troops of General McLaws arrived, and those of General Walker could be brought from the right. Hood's brigade, greatly diminished in numbers, withdrew to replenish their ammunition, their supply being entirely exhausted. They were relieved by Walker's command, who immediately attacked the enemy vigorously, driving him back with great slaughter. Colonel Manning, commanding Walker's brigade, pursued until he was stopped by a strong fence, behind which was posted a large force of infantry with several batteries. The gallant colonel was severely wounded, and his brigade retired to the line on which the rest of Walker's command had halted.

View of the Shenandoah River from Camp Hill, near Harpers Ferry.

Upon the arrival of the re-enforcements under General McLaws, General Early attacked with great resolution the large force opposed to him. McLaws advanced at the same time, and the enemy were driven back in confusion, closely followed by our troops beyond the position occupied at the beginning of the engagement. The enemy renewed the assault on our left several times, but was repulsed with loss. He finally ceased to advance his infantry, and for several hours kept up a furious fire from his numerous batteries, under which our troops held their position with great coolness and courage. The attack on our left was speedily followed by one in heavy force on the center. This was met by part of Walker's division and the brigades of G. B. Anderson and Rodes, of D. H. Hill's command, assisted by a few pieces of artillery. The enemy was repulsed, and retired behind the crest of a hill, from which they kept up a desultory fire. General R. H. Anderson's division came to Hill's support, and formed in rear of his line. At this time, by a mistake of orders, General Rodes' brigade was withdrawn from its position during the temporary absence of that officer at another part of the field. The enemy immediately pressed through the gap thus created, and G. B. Anderson's brigade was broken and retired, General Anderson himself being mortally wounded. Major-General R. H. Anderson and Brigadier-General Wright were also wounded and borne from the field.

The heavy masses of the enemy again moved forward, being opposed only by four pieces of artillery, supported by a few hundred men belonging to different brigades, rallied by General D. H. Hill and other officers, and parts of Walker's and R. H. Anderson's commands, Colonel Cooke, with the Twenty-seventh North Corolina Regiment, of Walker's brigade, standing boldly in line without a cart-ridge. The firm front presented by this small force and the well-directed fire of the artillery, under Captain Miller, of the Washington Artillery, and Captain Boyce's South Carolina battery, checked the progress of the enemy, and in about an hour and a half he retired. Another attack was made soon afterward, a little further to the right, but was repulsed by Miller's guns, which continued to hold the ground until the close of the engagement, supported by a part of R. H. Anderson's troops.

While the attack on the center and left was in progress, the enemy made repeated efforts to force the passage of the bridge over the Antietam, opposite the right wing of General Longstreet, commanded by Brigadier-General D. R. Jones. This bridge was defended by General Toombs, with two regiments of his brigade (the Second and Twentieth Georgia) and the batteries of General Jones. General Toombs' small command repulsed five different assaults, made by greatly superior force, and maintained its position with distinguished gallantry.

In the afternoon the enemy began to extend his lines as if to cross the Antietam below the bridge, and at 4 P. M. Toomb's regiments retired from the position they had so bravely held. The enemy immediately crossed the bridge in large numbers and advanced against General Jones, who held the crest with less than two thousand men. After a determined and brave resistance he was forced to give way, and the enemy gained the summit.

General A. P. Hill had arrived from Harpers Ferry, having left that place at 7:30 A. M. He was now ordered to re-enforce General Jones, and moved to his support with the brigades of Archer, Branch, Gregg and Pender, the last of whom was placed on the right of the line, and the other three advanced and attacked the enemy, now flushed with success. Hill's batteries were thrown forward and united their fire with those of General Jones, and one of General D. H. Hill's also opened with good effect from the left of the Boonsborough road. The progress of the enemy was immediately arrested and his lines began to waver. At this moment General Jones ordered Toombs to charge the flank, while Archer, supported by Branch and Gregg, moved upon the front of the Federal line. The enemy made a brief resistance, then broke and retreated in confusion toward the Antietam, pursued by the troops of Hill and Jones, until he reached the protection of his batteries on the opposite side of the river. In this attack the brave and lamented Brigadier-General L. O'B. Branch was killed while gallantly leading his brigade.

It was now nearly dark, and the enemy had massed a number of batteries to sweep the approaches to the Antietam, on the opposite side of which the corps of General Porter, which had not been engaged, now appeared to dispute our advance. Our troops were much exhausted and greatly reduced in numbers by fatigue and the casualties of battle. Under these circumstances it was deemed injudicious to push our advantage further in the face of fresh troops of the enemy, much exceeding the number of our own. They were accordingly recalled and formed on the line originally held by General Jones. While the attack on our center was progressing, General Jackson had been directed to endeavor to turn the enemy's right, but found it extending nearly to the Potomac, and so strongly defended with artillery that the attempt had to be abandoned. The repulse on the right ended the engagement, and, after a protracted and sanguinary conflict, every effort of the enemy to dislodge us from our position had been defeated with severe loss.

The arduous service in which our troops had been engaged, their great privations of rest and food, and the long marches without shoes over mountain roads, had greatly reduced our ranks before the action began. These causes had compelled thousands of brave men to absent themselves, and many more had done so from unworthy motives. This great battle was fought by less than forty thousand men on our side, all of whom had undergone the greatest labors and hardships in the field and on the march. Nothing could surpass the determined valor with which they met the large army of the enemy, fully supplied and equipped, and the result reflects the highest credit on the officers and men engaged. Our artillery, though much inferior to that of the enemy in the number of guns and weight of metal, rendered most efficient and gallant service throughout the day, and contributed greatly to the repulse of the attacks on every part of the line. General Stuart, with the cavalry and horse artillery, performed the duty intrusted to him of guarding our left wing with great energy and courage, and rendered valuable assistance in defeating the attack on that part of our line.

On the 18th we occupied the position of the preceding day, except in the center, where our line was drawn in about two hundred yards. Our ranks were increased by the arrival of a number of troops, who had not been engaged the day before; and, though still too weak to assume the offensive, we awaited without apprehension the renewal of the attack. The day passed without any demonstration on the part of the enemy, who, from the reports received, was expecting the arrival of re-enforcements. As we could not look for a material increase in strength, and the enemy's force could be largely and rapidly augmented, it was not thought prudent to wait until he should be ready again to offer battle. During the night of the 18th the army was accordingly withdrawn to the south side of the Potomac, crossing near Shepherdstown, without loss or molestation.

The enemy advanced the next morning, but was held in check by General Fitzhugh Lee with his cavalry, who covered our movement with boldness and success. General Stuart, with the main body, crossed the Potomac above Shepherdstown and moved up the river. The next day he recrossed at Williamsport, and took position to operate upon the right and rear of the enemy should he attempt to follow us. After the army had safely reached

Maryland Heights, Commanding Harpers Ferry.

the Virginia shore with such of the wounded as could be removed and all its trains, General Porter's corps, with a number of batteries and some cavalry, appeared on the opposite side. General Pendleton was left to guard the ford with the reserve artillery and about six hundred infantry. That night the enemy crossed the river above General Pendleton's position, and his infantry support giving way, four of his guns were taken. A considerable force took position on the right bank, under cover of their artillery on the commanding hills on the opposite side. The next morning General A. P. Hill was ordered to return with his division and dislodge them. Advancing under a heavy fire of artillery, the three brigades of Gregg, Pender and Archer attacked the enemy vigorously, and drove him over the river with heavy loss.

The condition of our troops now demanded repose, and the army marched to Opequon, near Martinsburg, where it remained several days, and then moved to the vicinity of Bunker Hill and Winchester. The enemy seemed to be concentrating in and near Harpers Ferry, but made no forward movement. During this time the Baltimore & Ohio Railroad was destroyed for several miles, and that from Winchester to Harpers Ferry broken up to within a short distance of the latter place, in order to render the occupation of the valley by the enemy after our withdrawal, more difficult. On October 8th General Stuart was ordered to cross the Potomac above Williamsport with twelve or fifteen hundred cavalry, and endeavor to ascertain the position and designs of the enemy. He was directed if practicable, to enter Pennsylvania, and do all in his power to impede and embarrass the military operations of the enemy. This order was executed with skill, address and courage. General Stuart passed through Maryland, occupied Chambersburg, and destroyed a large amount of public property, making the entire circuit of General McClellan's army. He recrossed the Potomac below Harpers Ferry without loss. The enemy soon after crossed the Potomac east of the Blue Ridge, and advanced southward, seizing the passes of the mountains as he progressed. General Jackson's corps was ordered to take position on the road between Berryville and Charleston, to be prepared to oppose an advance from Harpers Ferry or a movement into the Shenandoah Valley from the east side of the mountains, while at the same time he would threaten the flank of the enemy should he continue his march along the eastern base of the Blue Ridge. One division of Longstreet's corps was sent to the vicinity of Upperville to observe the enemy's movements in front.

About the last of October the Federal army began to incline eastwardly from the mountains, moving in the direction of Warrenton. As soon as this intention developed itself, Longstreet's corps was moved across the Blue Ridge, and about November 3d, took position at Culpeper Courthouse, while Jackson advanced one of his divisions to the east side of the Blue Ridge. The enemy gradually concentrated about Warrenton, his cavalry being thrown forward beyond the Rappahannock in the direction of Culpeper Courthouse. This situation of affairs continued without material change until about the middle of November, when the movements began which resulted in the winter campaign on the Lower Rappahannock.

* * * * * * *

R. E. LEE, *General.*

FAMOUS DUNKER CHURCH ON THE ANTIETAM BATTLEFIELD.
[From a sketch made after the battle.]

ORGANIZATION OF THE ARMY OF NORTHERN VIRGINIA,

GENERAL ROBERT E. LEE,
Commanding during the Maryland Campaign,*

SEPTEMBER 3 TO 20, 1862.

LONGSTREET'S CORPS.

Major-General James Longstreet.

McLAWS' DIVISION.

Major-General Lafayette McLaws.

KERSHAWS' BRIGADE.
Brigadier-General J. B. Kershaw.

Second South Carolina—Colonel John D. Kennedy.
Third South Carolina—Colonel James D. Nance.
Seventh South Carolina—Colonel D. Wyatt Aiken and Captain John S. Hard.
Eighth South Carolina—Lieutenant-Colonel A. J. Hoole.

COBB'S BRIGADE.
Brigadier-General Howell Cobb; Lieutenant-Colonel C. C. Sanders; Lieutenant-Colonel Wm. McRae.

Sixteenth Georgia; Twenty-fourth Georgia; Cobb's (Ga.) Legion; Fifteenth North Carolina.

SEMMES' BRIGADE.
Brigadier-General Paul J. Semmes.

Tenth Georgia—Captain P. H. Loud.
Fifty-third Georgia—Lieutenant-Colonel Thos. Sloan and Captain S. W. Marshborne.

Fifteenth Virginia—Captains E. M. Morrison and E. J. Willis.
Thirty-second Virginia—Colonel E. B. Montague.

BARKSDALE'S BRIGADE.
Brigadier-General Wm. Barksdale.

Thirteenth Mississippi—Lieutenant-Colonel Kennon McElroy.
Seventeenth Mississippi—Lieutenant-Colonel John C. Fiser.
Eighteenth Mississippi—Major J. C. Campbell and Lieutenant-Colonel Wm. H. Luse.
Twenty-first Mississippi—Captain John Sims and Colonel Benj. G. Humphreys.

ARTILLERY.
Major S. P. Hamilton. Colonel H. C. Cabell.

Manly's (N. C.) battery—Captain B. C. Manly.
Pulaski (Ga.) Artillery—Captain J. P. W. Read.
Richmond (Fayette) Artillery—Captain M. C. Macon.
Richmond Howitzers (first company)—Captain E. S. McCarthy.
Troup (Ga.) Artillery—Captain H. H. Carlton.

ANDERSON'S DIVISION.

Major-General Richard H. Anderson.

WILCOX'S BRIGADE.
Colonel Alfred Cumming.

Eighth Alabama; Ninth Alabama; Tenth Alabama; Eleventh Alabama.

MAHONE'S BRIGADE.
Colonel Wm. A. Parham.

Sixth Virginia; Twelfth Virginia; Sixteenth Virginia; Forty-first Virginia; Sixty-first Virginia.

ARMISTEAD'S BRIGADE.
Brigadier-General Lewis A. Armistead; Colonel J. G. Hodges.

Ninth Virginia; Fourteenth Virginia; Thirty-eighth Virginia; Fifty-third Virginia; Fifty-Seventh Virginia.

PRYOR'S BRIGADE.
Brigadier-General Roger A. Pryor.

Fourteenth Alabama; Second Florida; Eighth Florida; Third Virginia.

FEATHERSTON'S BRIGADE.
Brigadier-General Winfield S. Featherston; Colonel Carnot Posey.

Twelfth Mississippi; Sixteenth Mississippi (Captain A. M. Feltus); Nineteenth Mississippi; Second Mississippi Battalion.

WRIGHT'S BRIGADE.
Brigadier-General A. R. Wright.

Forty-fourth Alabama; Third Georgia; Twenty-second Georgia; Forty-eighth Georgia.

ARTILLERY.
Major John S. Saunders.

Donaldsonville (La.) Artillery (Maurin's battery); Huger's (Va.) battery; Moorman's (Va.) battery; Thompson's (Grimes') (Va.) battery.

* Compiled from the reports.

GENERAL LONGSTREET'S CORPS CROSSING THE BLUE RIDGE MOUNTAINS FROM THE SHENANDOAH TO THE RAPPAHANNOCK RIVER, VA., TO HOLD IN CHECK THE FEDERAL FORCES.

JONES' DIVISION.

Brigadier-General David R. Jones.

TOOMBS' BRIGADE.

Brigadier-General Robert Toombs; Colonel Henry L. Benning.

Second Georgia—Lieutenant-Colonel Wm. R. Holmes and Major Skidmore Harris.
Fifteenth Georgia—Colonel W. T. Millican.
Seventeenth Georgia—Captain J. A. McGregor.
Twentieth Georgia—Colonel J. B. Cumming.

DRAYTON'S BRIGADE.

Brigadier-General Thomas F. Drayton.

Fiftieth Georgia—Lieutenant-Colonel F. Kearse.
Fifty-first Georgia.
Fifteenth South Carolina—Colonel W. D. De Saussure.

PICKETT'S BRIGADE.

Colonel Eppa Hunton; Brigadier-General R. B. Garnett.

Eighth Virginia—Colonel Eppa Hunton.
Eighteenth Virginia—Major George C. Cabell.
Nineteenth Virginia—Colonel J. B. Strange; Lieutenant W. N. Wood and Captain J. L. Cochran.
Twenty-eighth Virginia—Captain Wingfield.
Fifty-sixth Virginia—Colonel William D. Stuart and Captain McPhail.

KEMPER'S BRIGADE.

Brigadier-General J. L. Kemper.

First Virginia; Seventh Virginia; Eleventh Virginia; Seventeenth Virginia; Twenty-fourth Virginia.

RANSOM'S BRIGADE.

Brigadier-General Robert Ransom, Jr.

Twenty-fourth North Carolina—Lieutenant-Colonel John L. Harris.
Twenty-fifth North Carolina—Colonel H. M. Rutledge.
Thirty-fifth North Carolina—Colonel M. W. Ransom.
Forty-ninth North Carolina—Lieutenant-Colonel Lee M. McAfee.
Branch's Field Artillery (Va.)—Captain Branch.

HOOD'S DIVISION.

Brigadier-General John B. Hood.

HOOD'S BRIGADE.

Colonel W. T. Woffird.

Eighteenth Georgia—Lieutenant-Colonel S. Z. Ruff.
Hampton (S. C.) Legion—Lieutenant-Colonel M. W. Gary.
First Texas—Lieutenant-Colonel P. A. Work.
Fourth Texas—Lieutenant-Colonel B. F. Carter.
Fifth Texas—Captain I. N. M. Turner.

LAW'S BRIGADE.

Colonel E. M. Law.

Fourth Alabama—Lieutenant-Colonel O. K. McLemore.
Second Mississippi—Colonel J. M. Stone.
Eleventh Mississippi—Colonel P. F. Liddell.
Sixth North Carolina—Major Robert F. Webb.

THE CORNFIELD AT ANTIETAM.

JENKINS' BRIGADE.

Colonel Joseph Walker.

First South Carolina (Volunteers)—Lieutenant-Colonel D. Livingston.
Second South Carolina Rifles.
Fifth South Carolina—Captain T. C. Beckham.
Sixth South Carolina—Lieutenant-Colonel J. M. Steedman and E. B. Cantey.
Fourth South Carolina Battalion.
Palmetto (S. C.) Sharpshooters.

ANDERSON'S BRIGADE.

Colonel George T. Anderson.

First Georgia (Regulars), Colonel W. J. Magill; Seventh Georgia; Eighth Georgia; Ninth Georgia; Eleventh Georgia, Major F. H. Little.

ARTILLERY.

Fauquier (Va.) Artillery (Stribling's battery);* Loudoun (Va.) Artillery (Rogers' battery);* Turner (Va.) Artillery (Leake's battery);* Wise (Va.) Artillery (J. S. Brown's battery).

WALKER'S DIVISION.

Brigadier-General John G. Walker.

WALKER'S BRIGADE.

Colonel Van H. Manning; Colonel E. D. Hall.

Third Arkansas—Captain John W. Reedy.
Twenty-seventh North Carolina—Colonel J. R. Cooke.
Forty-sixth North Carolina—Colonel E. D. Hall.
Forty-eighth North Carolina—Colonel R. C. Hill.
Thirtieth Virginia.
French's (Va.) battery—Captain Thomas B. French.

* Left at Leesburg.

ARTILLERY.

Major B. W. Frobel.

German Artillery (S. C.)—Captain W. K. Bachman.
Palmetto Artillery (S. C.)—Captain H. R. Garden.
Rowan Artillery (N. C.)—Captain James Reilly.

EVANS' BRIGADE.

Brigadier-General Nathan G. Evans; Colonel P. F. Stevens.*

Seventeenth South Carolina—Colonel F. W. McMaster.
Eighteenth South Carolina—Colonel W. H. Wallace.
Twenty-second South Carolina—Lieutenant-Colonel T. C. Watkins and Major M. Hilton.
Twenty-third (S. C.)—Captain S. A. Durham and Lieutenant E. R. White.
Holcombe (S. C.) Legion—Colonel P. F. Stevens.
Macbeth (S. C.) Artillery—Captain R. Boyce.

ARTILLERY.

Washington (La.) Artillery—Colonel J. B. Walton.
First Company—Captain C. W. Squires.
Second Company—Captain J. B. Richardson.
Third Company—Captain M. B. Miller.
Fourth Company—Captain B. F. Eshleman.

LEE'S BATTALION.

Colonel S. D. Lee.

Ashland (Va.) Artillery—Captain P. Woolfolk, Jr.
Bedford (Va.) Artillery—Captain T. C. Jordan.
Brooks (S. C.) Artillery—Lieutenant W. Elliott.
Eubank's (Va.) battery—Captain J. L. Eubank.
Madison (La.) Light Artillery—Captain G. V. Moody.
Parker's (Va.) battery—Captain W. W. Parker.

* Commanding brigade while General Evans commanded provisional division.

BRIG.-GEN. WILLIAM E. STARKE, OF LOUISIANA.
Killed at Antietam (Sharpsburg), Md., September 17, 1862.

JACKSON'S CORPS.

Major-General Thomas J. Jackson.

EWELL'S DIVISION.

Brigadier-General A. R. Lawton; Brigadier-General Jubal A. Early.

LAWTON'S BRIGADE.

Colonel M. Douglass; Major J. H. Lowe; Colonel John H. Lamar.

Thirteenth Georgia; Twenty-sixth Georgia; Thirty-first Georgia, Lieutenant-Colonel J. T. Crowder; Thirty-eighth Georgia; Sixtieth Georgia; Sixty-first Georgia.

EARLY'S BRIGADE.

Brigadier-General Jubal A. Early; Colonel William Smith.

Thirteenth Virginia, Captain F. V. Winston; Twenty-fifth Virginia; Thirty-first Virginia; Forty-fourth Virginia; Forty-ninth Virginia, Colonel William Smith; Fifty-second, Colonel M. G. Harman; Fifty-eighth Virginia.

TRIMBLE'S BRIGADE.

Colonel James A. Walker.

Fifteenth Alabama—Captain I. B. Feagin.
Twelfth Georgia—Captain Rodgers.
Twenty-first Georgia—Major Thomas C. Glover.
Twenty-first North Carolina—Captain Miller.
First North Carolina Battalion.*

HAYS' BRIGADE.

Brigadier-General Harry T. Hays.

Fifth Louisiana; Sixth Louisiana, Colonel H. B. Strong; Seventh Louisiana; Eighth Louisiana; Fourteenth Louisiana.

ARTILLERY.†

Major A. R. Courtney.

Charlottesville (Va.) Artillery (Carrington's battery); Chesapeake (Md.) Artillery (Brown's battery); Courtney (Va.) Artillery (Latimer's battery); Johnson's (Va.) battery; Louisiana Guard Artillery (D'Aquin's battery); First Maryland Battery (Dement's battery); Staunton (Va.) Artillery (Balthis' battery).

*Attached to Twenty-first North Carolina Regiment.

†The Charlottesville Artillery, left at Richmond in August, did not rejoin the army till after the battle of Sharpsburg. John R. Johnson's and D'Aquin's batteries were the only ones present with this division at Sharpsburg, the others having been left at Harpers Ferry and Shepherdstown.

BRIGADIER-GENERAL GEORGE B. ANDERSON, OF NORTH CAROLINA.
Killed at Antietam (Sharpsburg), Md., September 17, 1862.

HILL'S LIGHT DIVISION.

Major-General Ambrose P. Hill.

BRANCH'S BRIGADE.

Brigadier-General L. O'B. Branch; Colonel James H. Lane.

Seventh North Carolina; Eighteenth North Carolina, Lieutenant-Colonel Purdie; Twenty-Eighth North Carolina; Thirty-Third North Carolina; Thirty-seventh North Carolina.

BRIG.-GEN. J. J. ARCHER, OF VIRGINIA.

GREGG'S BRIGADE.

Brigadier-General Maxcy Gregg.

First South Carolina (Provisional Army)—Major E. McCrady, Jr.; Colonel D. H. Hamilton.
First South Carolina Rifles—Lieutenant-Colonel James M. Perrin.
Twelfth South Carolina—Colonel Dixon Barnes, Lieutenant-Colonel C. Jones, and Major W. H. McCorkle.
Thirteenth South Carolina—Colonel O. E. Edwards.
Fourteenth South Carolina—Lieutenant-Colonel W. D. Simpson.

FIELD'S BRIGADE.

Colonel John M. Brockenbrough.

Fortieth Virginia; Forty-seventh Virginia; Fifty-fifth Virginia; Twenty-second Virginia Battalion.

ARCHER'S BRIGADE.

Brigadier-General J. J. Archer; Colonel Peter Turney.

Fifth Alabama Battalion—Captain Hooper.
Nineteenth Georgia—Major J. H. Neal and Captain F. M. Johnston.
First Tennessee (Provisional Army)—Colonel Peter Turney.
Seventh Tennessee—Major S. G. Shepard and Lieutenant G. A. Howard.
Fourteenth Tennessee—Lieutenant-Colonel J. W. Lockert.

PENDER'S BRIGADE.

Brigadier-General William D. Pender; Colonel R. H. Brewer.

Sixteenth North Carolina, Lieutenant-Colonel Stowe; Twenty-second North Carolina, Major C. C. Cole; Thirty-fourth North Carolina; Thirty-eighth North Carolina.

THOMAS' BRIGADE.

Colonel Edward L. Thomas.

Fourteenth Georgia, Colonel R. W. Folsom; Thirty-fifth Georgia; Forty-fifth Georgia, Major W. L. Grice; Forty-ninth Georgia, Lieutenant-Colonel S. M. Manning.

ARTILLERY.*

Major R. L. Walker.

Branch (N. C.) Artillery (A. C. Latham's battery); Crenshaw's (Va.) battery; Fredericksburg (Va.) Artillery (Braxton's battery); Letcher (Va.) Artillery (Davidson's battery); Middlesex (Va.) Artillery (Fleet's battery); Pee Dee (S. C.) Artillery (McIntosh's battery); Purcell (Va.) Artillery (Pegram's battery).

* Braxton's, Crenshaw's, McIntosh's and Pegram's batteries, engaged at Sharpsburg; Davidson's battery had been left at Harpers Ferry, and Fleet's and Latham's batteries at Leesburg.

JACKSON'S DIVISION.

Brigadier-General John R. Jones; Brigadier-General W. E. Starke; Colonel A. J. Grigsby.

WINDER'S BRIGADE.

Colonel A. J. Grigsby; Lieutenant-Colonel R. D. Gardner (Fourth Va.); Major H. J. Williams.

Second Virginia—Captain R. T. Colston.
Fourth Virginia—Lieutenant-Colonel R. D. Gardner.
Fifth Virginia—Major H. J. Williams.
Twenty-seventh Virginia—Captain F. C. Wilson.
Thirty-third Virginia—Captain Golladay and Lieutenant Walton.

TALIAFERRO'S BRIGADE.

Colonel E. T. H. Warren; Colonel J. W. Jackson; Colonel J. L. Sheffield.

Forty-seventh Alabama; Forty-eighth Alabama; Tenth Virginia; Twenty-third Virginia; Thirty-seventh Virginia.

JONES' BRIGADE.

Colonel B. T. Johnson; Brigadier-General J. R. Jones; Captain J. E. Penn; Captain A. C. Page; Captain R. W. Withers.

Twenty-first Virginia—Captain A. C. Page.
Forty-second Virgina—Captain R. W. Withers.
Forty-eighth Virginia—Captain Candler.
First Virginia Battalion—Lieutenant C. A. Davidson.

STARKE'S BRIGADE.

Brigadier-General William E. Starke; Colonel L. A. Stafford; Colonel E. Pendleton.

First Louisiana—Lieutenant-Colonel M. Nolan.
Second Louisiana—Colonel J. M. Williams.
Ninth Louisiana.
Tenth Louisiana.
Fifteenth Louisiana—Captain H. D. Monier.
Coppens' (La.) Battalion.

BRIG.-GEN. PAUL J. SEMMES, OF GEORGIA.
Killed at Antietam (Sharpsburg), Md., September 17, 1862.

ARTILLERY.

Major L. M. Shumaker.

Alleghany (Va.) Artillery (Carpenter's battery); Brockenbrough's (Md.) battery; Danville (Va.) Artillery (Wooding's battery); Hampden (Va.) Artillery (Caskie's battery); Lee (Va.) battery (Raine's battery); Rockbridge (Va.) Artillery (Poague's battery).

HILL'S DIVISION.*

Major-General Daniel H. Hill.

RIPLEY'S BRIGADE.

Brigadier-General Roswell S. Ripley; Colonel George Doles.

Fourth Georgia—Colonel George Doles.
Forty-fourth Georgia—Captain Key.
First North Carolina—Lieutenant-Colonel H. A. Brown.
Third North Carolina—Colonel Wm. L. De Rosset.

RODES' BRIGADE.

Brigadier-General R. E. Rodes.

Third Alabama—Colonel C. A. Battle.
Fifth Alabama—Major E. L. Hobson.
Sixth Alabama—Colonel J. B. Gordon.
Twelfth Alabama—Colonel B. B. Gayle and Lieutenant-Colonel S. B. Pickens.
Twenty-sixth Alabama—Colonel E. A. O'Neal.

* On "field return," Army of Northern Virginia, for September 22d, this division appears as of Jackson's Corps.

GARLAND'S BRIGADE.

Brigadier-General Samuel Garland, Jr.; Colonel D. K. McRae.

Fifth North Carolina—Colonel D. K. McRae and Captain T. M. Garrett.
Twelfth North Carolina—Captain S. Snow.
Thirteenth North Carolina—Lieutenant-Colonel Thos. Ruffin, Jr.
Twentieth North Carolina—Colonel Alfred Iverson.
Twenty-third North Carolina—Colonel D. H. Christie.

ANDERSON'S BRIGADE.

Brigadier-General George B. Anderson; Colonel R. T. Bennett.

Second North Carolina—Colonel C. C. Tew and Captain G. M. Roberts.
Fourth North Carolina—Colonel Ryan Grimes and Captains W. T. Marsh and D. P. Latham.
Fourteenth North Carolina—Colonel R. T. Bennett.
Thirtieth North Carolina—Colonel F. M. Parker and Major W. W. Sillers.

COLQUITT'S BRIGADE.

Colonel A. H. Colquitt.

Thirteenth Alabama—Colonel B. D. Fry.
Sixth Georgia—Lieutenant-Colonel J. M. Newton.
Twenty-third Georgia—Colonel W. P. Barclay.
Twenth-seventh Georgia—Colonel L. B. Smith.
Twenty-eighth Georgia—Major T. Graybill and Captain N. J. Garrison.

ARTILLERY.*

Major Pierson.

Hardaway's (Ala.) battery—Captain R. A. Hardaway.
Jeff. Davis (Ala.) Artillery—Captain J. W. Bondurant.
Jones' (Va.) battery—Captain Wm. B. Jones.
King William (Va.) Artillery—Captain T. H. Carter.

RESERVE ARTILLERY.†

Brigadier-General William N. Pendleton.

BROWN'S BATTALION.‡

Colonel J. Thompson Brown.

Powhattan Artillery (Dance's battery.); Richmond Howitzers, second company (Watson's battery); Richmond Howitzers, third company (Smith's battery); Salem Artillery, Hupp's battery; Williamsburg Artillery (Coke's battery).

CUTTS' BATTALION.§

Lieutenant-Colonel A. S. Cutts.

Blackshear's (Ga.) battery; Irwin (Ga.) Artillery (Lane's battery); Lloyd's (N. C.) battery; Patterson's (Ga.) battery; Ross' (Ga.) battery.

JONES' BATTALION.§

Major H. P. Jones.

Morris' (Va.) Artillery (R. C. M. Page's battery); Orange (Va.) Artillery (Peyton's battery); Turner's (Va.) battery; Wimbish's (Va.) battery.

NELSON'S BATTALION.

Major William Nelson.

Amherst (Va.) Artillery (Kirkpatrick's battery); Fluvonna (Va.) Artillery (Ancell's battery); Huchstep's (Va.) battery; Johnson's (Va.) battery;‖ Milledge (Ga.) Artillery (Milledge's battery).

* Cutts' and Jones' battalions also under D. H. Hill's command at Sharpsburg.
† Including all batteries mentioned in the reports, or in the reorganization of October 4th, and not elsewhere accounted for. Brooks', Deering's and Nelson's Virginia batteries joined after the campaign had terminated.
‡ First Virginia Artillery.
§ With D. H. Hill's division at Sharpsburg.
‖ Marmaduke Johnson's battery.

BRIG.-GEN. SAMUEL GARLAND, JR., OF VIRGINIA.
Killed at the Battle of South Mountain, September 14, 1862.

MISCELLANEOUS.

Cutshaw's (Va.) battery; Dixie (Va.) Artillery (Chapman's battery); Magruder (Va.) Artillery (T. J. Page, Jr., battery); Rice (Va.) battery, Captain W. H. Rice;* Thomas (Va.) Artillery (E. J. Anderson's battery).†

CAVALRY.

Major-General James E. B. Stuart.

HAMPTON'S BRIGADE.

Brigadier-General Wade Hampton.

First North Carolina—Colonel L. S. Baker.
Second South Carolina—Colonel M. C. Butler.
Tenth Virginia.
Cobb's (Ga.) Legion—Lieutenant-Colonel P. M. B. Young.
Jeff. Davis Legion—Lieutenant-Colonel N. T. Martin.

LEE'S BRIGADE.

Brigadier-General Fitzhugh Lee.

First Virginia—Lieutenant-Colonel L. Tiernan Brien.
Third Virginia—Lieutenant Colonel John T. Thornton.
Fourth Virginia—Colonel Wm. C. Wickham.
Fifth Virginia—Colonel T. L. Rosser.
Ninth Virginia.

ROBERTSON'S BRIGADE.

Brigadier-General B. H. Robertson; Colonel Thomas T. Munford.

Second Virginia—Colonel T. T. Munford and Lieutenant-Colonel Burks.
Sixth Virginia.
Seventh Virginia—Captain S. B. Myers.
Twelfth Virginia—Colonel A. W. Harman.
Seventeenth Virginia Battalion.

HORSE ARTILLERY.

Captain John Pelham.

Chew's (Va.) battery; Hart's (S. C.) battery; Pelham's (Va.) battery.

* Not mentioned between September 1st and 22d, but probably with the army, in reserve.
† Left at Leesburg.

BATTLE OF MUNFORDVILLE, KY.,

SEPTEMBER 14 TO 16, 1862.

BY

BRIGADIER-GENERAL JAMES R. CHALMERS.

HEADQUARTERS SECOND BRIGADE, RESERVE DIVISION, RIGHT WING ARMY OF THE MISSISSIPPI, FORT CRAIG, NEAR MUNFORDVILLE, KY.,
September 19, 1862.

IN obedience to orders from Major-General Withers, received on the afternoon of the 12th, while passing through Glasgow, Ky., I halted my brigade at Beaver Creek, about three miles from that place, on the Louisville Turnpike, to cook rations, and then moved forward at 8 P. M., leaving all my wagons except the ordnance train in camp at Cave City. I sent forward a small detachment of cavalry which had been furnished to me by General Withers, under the command of my aid-de-camp, Lieutenant G. T. Banks, with orders to enter the town without giving any alarm, if possible, to take possession of the telegraph and post offices, and to place guards on all the avenues of approach, so as to prevent all passing, and I followed them as rapidly as possible with the infantry and artillery.

After a march of eleven miles, which was made in excellent order, we reached Cave City at 11:30 P. M. The town was completely taken by surprise, and possession was immediately and quietly taken of the telegraph and post offices and of the railroad depot. It being expected that one or more trains of the enemy's troops would pass up the road from Bowling Green toward Louisville, the track was torn up and other preparations were made to capture it, but the train did not make its appearance.

The brigade was encamped near the town, and strong pickets were thrown out on all the roads leading to it. By the aid of Sergeant Bradford, First Regiment, Louisiana Infantry, who had been detailed to accompany me for that purpose, I established telegraphic communication with Louisville and intercepted a few messages passing to and from the enemy at that place, the most of which, together with those found on file in the office, I forwarded to you. Unfortunately, the wires had been cut by our troops south of Cave City, and the operator at Louisville soon began to suspect that something was wrong; otherwise I might have obtained more valuable information.

On the morning of the 13th I made a reconnoissance of the country in the direction of Munfordville, and finding a mill near Horse Cave containing a considerable quantity of wheat, I ordered the Tenth Mississippi Regiment (commanded by Lieutenant-Colonel James Moore) up to take possession of it, with the view of having the wheat ground for the use of the troops. During the day I learned from intercepted dispatches that the advance of our army to Glasgow had thrown the enemy into consternation along the whole line from Louisville to Bowling Green, and that they were under the impression that the force occupying Cave City was seven thousand strong, and was advancing on Munfordville, where they had a camp of instruction, from which place they were asking for re-enforcements and provisions.

Late in the afternoon I intercepted a dispatch from General Gilbert, commanding at Louisville, ordering transportation to be ready at 7 P. M. to convey Colonel Dunham's regiment, five hundred strong, and five days' rations for three thousand men, to Munfordville. About 9 P. M. I received a message from Colonel Scott, commanding brigade of cavalry, through one of his officers, to the effect that the force of the enemy at Munfordville was not more than eighteen hundred men, entirely raw troops, and that they were fortifying their position, but that the railroad and telegraph had been destroyed in the rear, cutting them off completely from all communication and re-enforcements. He also informed me that he intended to attack them at daylight on the following morning, and desired that I would co-operate with him with a part of my force.

Relying upon the information thus received and that gleaned from the intercepted dispatches, I determined to support him with my whole brigade, leaving only a sufficient force behind to protect Cave City and its approaches, and accordingly moved out of the town at 10 P. M., and after a march of twelve miles I reached the enemy's lines in front of Munfordville at daylight on the 14th instant.

The enemy's works, as I afterward found, consisted of three distinct parts. On their right was a range of rifle-pits sufficient to contain three thousand men, semicircular in form, and terminating on the extreme right in a strong stockade, which stood upon the brink of the lofty bluff overlooking Green River. About one hundred yards to the left of this was another rifle-pit, capable of holding at least one regiment; and still further to the left and upon higher ground stood their principal work, a regular bastion earthwork, in and about which were stationed about three hundred men. The passages between these works were almost entirely protected from our fire by the nature of the ground. The whole work protected the railroad bridge over Green River, and was connected with the opposite bank by a pontoon bridge. While on the march I had learned from citizens who had been in the works that they were much stronger than I had at first been led to believe; but I was unable to obtain any definite or clear description of them, and the foggy nature of the morning prevented me from making any satisfactory reconnoissance. I learned, however, that the right of their works could be shelled from an eminence known as Mrs. Lewis' hill, and my original intention was to open a fire upon them from that point for some time before making an assault. With this view the battalion of sharpshooters was ordered forward to drive in the enemy's pickets, who were stationed in the woods on the left of the turnpike.

BRIG.-GEN. JAMES R. CHALMERS, OF MISSISSIPPI.

The firing commenced at 5 A. M. by the sharpshooters driving the enemy's pickets from the hill across an open field to their supporting line, which was supposed to be two regiments of infantry. Major W. C. Richards, commanding battalion of sharpshooters, was severely wounded at the first fire, and Captain West, who succeeded to the command, having sent back information of the force by which he was opposed, the Ninth and Twenty-ninth Mississippi regiments were ordered up to his support, but the enemy were driven into their intrenchments by the sharpshooters before they could be brought into action. At the same time the battery (Ketchum's, under the command of Lieutenant James Garrity) was ordered to take position on Mrs. Lewis' hill and to open fire on the intrenchments, and the Tenth Mississippi Regiment was ordered to support it.

A heavy volume of flame and smoke which arose at this time near the enemy's works was supposed to proceed from the railroad bridge, and this, coupled with the fact that they had retired so rapidly before our advance and had refused almost altogether to reply to the fire of our artillery, led me to the belief that they were preparing to evacuate their position. I therefore determined to press forward at once against the works, and moved one section of the artillery, under the immediate command of Lieutenant Garrity, with the Seventh Mississippi (Colonel W. H. Bishop), the Ninth Mississippi (Colonel T. W. White), and the Twenty-ninth Mississippi regiments (Colonel E. C. Walthall) to the Knob, an eminence in front of the bastion fort, from which I opened a fire on it. Blythe's regiment was left to guard the ordnance train, and the sharpshooters were pressed forward to keep the enemy within their works. The section of the battery left on Lewis' hill, under the command of Lieutenant Bond, was ordered to move further down the hill and nearer to the rifle-pits on our left, and Colonel Smith was instructed to move with the Tenth Mississippi Regiment to the banks of the river and to advance up it toward the fort as near as possible, and if he saw a favorable opportunity to storm them.

The artillery on the Knob opened a rapid fire on the bastion fort, but, owing to the light caliber of the guns and the very defective character of the ammunition, with but little effect. From this point I discovered a house surrounded with woods on the right of the fort and within range of it, and I at once ordered the Ninth and Twenty-ninth regiments to move forward and occupy the woods opposite the fort, with instructions to keep the men under cover, to approach the works as closely as possible, and to storm them if they could do so successfully. The Seventh Regiment was ordered to follow them within supporting distance. This was accomplished with small loss, the enemy stationed in the woods falling back at once before our advance. Our regiments attained a position under cover within range of the fort, and the sharpshooters, who were deployed in front as skirmishers, kept the enemy closely within their walls. I immediately ordered up the artillery from the Knob and planted it near the house, not more than two hundred yards from the fort, and in a position where it was protected in some measure from the fire of the enemy by a depression in the ground and by the timber. This position completely flanked the enemy's rifle-pits and stockade on the center and left of their works, and if my guns had been of longer range I could have rendered them untenable. The distance was, however, too great for my guns, which could only reach the bastion and the rifle-pits in the center, from the latter of which their fire drew every man. The fire of my artillery was maintained from this point during the continuance of hostilities.

When making this movement I notified Colonel Smith of it, and repeated my previous instructions to him. In attempting to carry out these instructions, being entirely ignorant of the ground to be passed over, he came within range of the enemy's guns from the right of their work and in front of the abatis of fallen trees, in a position where it was equally dangerous to advance or retreat, and immediately advanced against the works. Hearing the firing, I ordered Blythe's regiment to support the Tenth, and that regiment was soon engaged with the enemy in endeavoring, under a very heavy fire, to force its way through the abatis. In this attack Colonel Smith, of the Tenth Mississippi Regiment, was dangerously wounded; Lieutenant-Colonel Bullard, of the same regiment, was killed; Lieutenant-Colonel Moore, commanding Blythe's Mississippi regiment, was mortally wounded, with a large number of their officers and men. By the fall of these officers the command of Blythe's regiment devolved upon Major [J. C.] Thompson, and that of the Tenth upon Captain [J. M.] Walker, both of whom discharged that duty during the remainder of the engagement in a highly satisfactory manner. As soon as I was informed of the loss of these officers I instructed Major [James] Barr [Jr.], of the Tenth Mississippi Regiment, who was acting on my staff as inspector-general of the brigade, to assume command of his regiment, but before he could reach it the firing had ceased.

Before I knew the disastrous nature of this attack, believing that the bastion fort could be carried by a combined attack by my whole force, I sent orders to Colonel Smith to move to the right and join me with the two regiments under his command; but he was wounded before the order reached him, and his regiment was so engaged that it would have been impossible to withdraw it without great loss. Perceiving, however, after the order was sent, that a furious struggle was going on upon the enemy's right, I thought it a favorable opportunity to move against them upon the left, and I at once ordered the three regiments under my immediate command to advance from their cover, the Seventh on the right, the Ninth on the left, and the Twenty-ninth in the center, and to storm the fort. This movement was made in fine style. The regiments moved in a perfect line across the road and up the hill upon which the fort stood to a point where they were in some measure protected by a depression in the ground and by the ruins of a church which the enemy had burned early in the morning, and which we had supposed to be the railroad bridge. Here they halted, and poured in so deadly a fire that the enemy were compelled to seek shelter behind their walls, and only ventured to return the fire from their artillery or by holding their guns at arm's length over the walls without exposing their persons.

Seeing that the Ninth Mississippi Regiment was more exposed than the others, I ordered it to move by the right flank in the rear of the others, intending to form it on the right of the Seventh, and to advance it against the fort from the direction of the river. The order to advance was repeated, and the foremost files were within twenty-five yards of the ditch and pressing rapidly forward toward it, when a fire from artillery was unexpectedly opened from a hill in our rear, the shells falling among our ranks. Supposing that the enemy must have established a battery in our rear, I ordered the Seventh and Ninth regiments to about face and charge it. This order was promptly obeyed, and these regiments were already within a short distance of the battery, which fell back before them, when I was informed that it was attached to Colonel Scott's cavalry brigade, and had come up to our relief. I immediately halted the two regiments, intending to lead them again upon the fort, but unfortunately the other regiment, not understanding, in the confusion, the object of the movement which had been made, and supposing that a retreat had been ordered, had fallen back. It being impossible to renew the attack at once under the circumstances, the whole force was withdrawn, in good order, to a position in the woods near that from which they had made the attack. It was then 9:30 A. M.

A careful examination of the ground since the engagement has satisfied me that had we not been surprised and disconcerted by the unexpected fire from Colonel Scott's artillery in our rear this attack would have been successful. The enemy had in that work, as I have since learned, only about three hundred men, who had been driven by our fire to hide themselves, while I had before it not less than seven hundred men, who were pressing forward toward it in the most gallant and determined manner. A few steps further would have carried them into the ditch, and once in close contest the issue could not be doubted. That work once taken, and the rest lay at our mercy. Its guns could have been turned to rake the other works, and the remainder of the enemy's force would have had no choice but to surrender or be slaughtered.

Soon after regaining our position I had an interview with Colonel Scott, who said he had made repeated efforts to inform me of his presence and of his intention to plant his battery upon the hill from which it fired. Unfortunately none of them had reached me. He also stated that he was inclined to believe that the enemy would surrender if a demand was made upon them, from the fact that, when he had approached the place on the afternoon of the day before from the opposite side of the river and demanded its surrender, Colonel Wilder, the officer in command, had replied that he could not surrender to a cavalry force, leaving it to be inferred that he would surrender if attacked by infantry and artillery; and he repeated what his messenger had told me on the night before in reference to the destruction of the railroad and telegraph in their rear and the impossibility of their receiving any re-enforcements. At his suggestion I addressed a note to Colonel Wilder by Major [J. B.] Morgan, of the Twenty-ninth Mississippi Regiment, under a flag of truce, stating my strength and renewing the demand for a surrender; to which Colonel Wilder replied, saying that he had also been re-enforced since the engagement began and refusing to surrender, but proposing a truce to enable both parties to remove their dead and wounded. I acceded to his proposition, stating in my reply that I would take as much time as might be necessary and would notify him of its conclusion.

Fatigue parties were immediately sent out to remove the dead and wounded, but as tools for burying the former had to be obtained from the enemy, from whom I could get only a few, and as the latter had to be removed more than a mile in order to put them in comfortable quarters, this work was not accomplished until 5 P. M. In accordance with the terms of the truce, I then notified Colonel Wilder that it was at an end, when, much to my surprise, Colonel Dunham, who had assumed command of the fort in the meantime, requested that it might be prolonged in order to enable them to complete burying their dead. Major Morgan, who bore my message, promised that I would make no offensive movement, and afterward Colonels White and Walthall, whom I sent to communicate with Colonel Dunham as soon as I heard of his request, agreed that this might continue for one hour.

After my interview with Colonel Scott in the morning I determined that I would not renew my attack upon the works. My previous attempt had satisfied me that I had been deceived as to the strength of the enemy's works, as well as their numbers and disposition and the possibility of their being re-enforced. They had at the commencement of the engagement, as I have since learned from their officers, about twenty-three hundred men, and were re-enforced by Colonel Dunham with five hundred men from the north side of the river during its continuation. Their works were mounted with ten guns, of which there were two 12-pounder Napoleon guns, one 3¼-inch Parrott gun, and the others 6-pounders, mostly rifled. My own force, owing to the heavy details left as pickets at Cave City, numbered only one thousand six hundred and thirteen officers and men, including Ketchum's battery of two 6-pounders and two 12-pounder howitzers. The force with which Colonel Scott joined me was three hundred cavalry, with two small mountain howitzers, and he reported that there were two regiments of cavalry belonging to his brigade on the opposite side of the river. I felt assured that with this force, disproportioned as it was to that of the enemy, I might, by a determined assault, have taken the fort, but the heavy loss which I had already sustained, especially on my left, and the certainty that it would be greatly increased by a renewal of the attack, coupled with the conviction that the place could be easily and speedily taken by a larger force without loss of life, determined me not to make another attempt upon it. As soon, therefore, as notice had been given to the enemy of the termination of the truce I withdrew my troops under cover of the woods to the turnpike. While on the march I was informed of the request of Colonel Dunham that the truce might be prolonged, and immediately sent Colonels White and Walthall to communicate with him, as I have before stated. I halted the brigade on the turnpike, just beyond the bridge crossing the railroad, and remained there until the expiration of the hour agreed on, when I resumed the march and proceeded without molestation to Cave City, which I reached about midnight.

My loss in this affair was three officers and thirty-two men killed, and twenty-eight officers and two hundred and twenty-five wounded, of whom some have since died. Of these the greater part in proportion to the numbers engaged fell in the attack on the right of the enemy's works. The wounded were first removed from the field to the depot and other buildings at Rowlett's Station, where their wounds were dressed, and afterward those who could bear transportation were conveyed in ambulances and wagons to Cave City, where they were placed in the hotel and depot, and every possible arrangement made for their comfort. Those whom it was not thought proper to remove were left at Rowlett's Station, under the charge of surgeons and with the assurance from Colonel Wilder that they should not be molested, which assurance, I am glad to say, was fully carried out.

On the following day, 15th instant, having taken the pledge of the telegraphic operator captured at Cave City not to give any information to the enemy, I sent him into their lines under the charge of Captain [R. A.] Bell, of the Tenth Mississippi Regiment, with a flag of truce. I at the same time sent by Captain Bell a note to Colonel Dunham, requesting permission to remove such of my wounded from the hospital as might be able to bear it, and also the bodies of such as had died, which he granted at once, and in his reply stated that I could have access to my wounded at Rowlett's Station at any time.

At 5 o'clock on the morning of the 16th instant, in obedience to orders from Headquarters Right Wing, Army of the Mississippi, this brigade moved from its camp at Cave City, in advance of the main body, toward Munfordville. About 8 A. M., when within two and a half miles of the fort, my cavalry scouts encountered those of the enemy and fired upon them, killing one horse. A detachment from the battalion of sharpshooters was immediately ordered forward as skirmishers, and soon after the whole battalion, under the command of Captain West, was ordered to advance and drive back the enemy's skirmishers, who began to show themselves in considerable numbers in the woods on the crest of Mrs. Lewis' hill.

At this time Brigadier-General Duncan came up with his brigade, and I at once resigned the command to him. A section of my battery (Ketchum's) was ordered forward to shell the woods in which the enemy's skirmishers were concealed, but after a few shots they were compelled to cease firing, as their shells were endangering our own men, who were driving the enemy before them. The Seventh Mississippi Regiment was then ordered forward to support the sharpshooters, but before it could be brought into action the enemy had fallen back, and did not make another stand until they had reached their works. The sharpshooters continued to annoy the enemy until 6 P. M., when they rejoined the main body of the brigade. The remainder of the brigade was ordered to move to the left of the turnpike, and was halted behind a spur of Mrs. Lewis' hill, and afterward, by order from General Bragg, it moved further to the left and took position with its left resting on the river and right extending toward the turnpike, where it was entirely protected from the fire of the fort by a hill. Here we remained until the next morning (the 17th), when we were ordered up to witness the surrender of the garrison of the fort, and afterward, by order of General Bragg, in compliment, as he stated, to our gallant attack upon the place, we took possession of the works.

Battle of Munfordville, Ky.

The Tenth Mississippi, commanded by Colonel R. A. Smith, charging through the abatis of fallen trees in front of the Federal fortifications near Green River.

The only loss sustained in this movement was by the battalion of sharpshooters, who had three men severely wounded while engaged with the enemy's skirmishers.

In the attack on the 14th instant I took two prisoners, who have since been turned over to the proper officers to be paroled with the others. At Cave City we captured three boarding-cars, one box-car, two hand-cars, one telegraphic machine and battery, two boxes new clothing (uniforms), six boxes worn clothing (uniforms), one box boots and one barrel salt; and at Woodsonville I captured and brought off to Cave City one hand-car and three barrels salt. The cars were left on the track at Cave City when our forces moved out of that place. The telegraphic machine and battery were sent to Major-General Polk. The salt was turned over to the commissary department, and the clothing and boots were turned over to the quartermasters of this brigade and issued to the men, who were greatly in need of them.

I can not close this report without expressing my admiration of the conduct of the officers and men under my command. The cheerfulness with which they endured the hardships of the march from Chattanooga; the alacrity with which, after a march of ordinary length during the day, they made the night march from Glasgow to Cave City, and then on the following night from that place to Woodsonville; the courage with which they drove the enemy into his works and then attacked him in them, and which drew encomiums even from their foes; the endurance with which they fought for four hours against heavy odds, without an opportunity for rest and with but little food or water, and the orderly manner in which, after a day of such toils, they retraced their steps to Cave City, entitled them to the highest praise that I can give. Nor can I omit the opportunity to express my regret at the loss of the many brave officers and men who were killed or wounded. Most prominent among these—not more by their rank than by their soldierly qualities—were Colonel Smith, of the Tenth Mississippi Regiment, who fell severely wounded in advance of his regiment and within a few yards of the enemy's works, while leading a charge against them; Lieutenant-Colonel Bullard, of the same regiment, who was killed; Lieutenant-Colonel Moore, commanding Blythe's Mississippi Regiment, who was mortally wounded in the same attack, and Major W. C. Richards, commanding battalion of sharpshooters, who was severely wounded early in the action. They fell where they would have but liked to have fallen—in the very face of the enemy, and while leading their men against them; but their loss will be severely felt in this brigade, and their places can not easily be supplied.

* * * * * *

JAMES R. CHALMERS,
Brigadier-General.

BATTLE OF CORINTH, MISS.,

AND

OTHER OPERATIONS OF THE ARMY,

SEPTEMBER 27 TO OCTOBER 5, 1862.

BY

MAJOR-GENERAL STERLING PRICE, C. S. A.

HEADQUARTERS ARMY OF THE WEST,
HOLLY SPRINGS, MISS.,
October 20, 1862.

I HAVE the honor to submit the following report of the operations of this army connected with the several engagements at Corinth and Davis' Bridge of the 3d, 4th and 5th instant. Having arranged with Major-General Van Dorn to unite my forces with his for active operations, I joined him at Ripley on the 27th ultimo. My force at this time consisted of 10,498 effective infantry, 2,437 effective cavalry, 928 effective artillerymen and 44 guns, including two 24-pounder howitzers and four rifled pieces of 3⅝ caliber. The infantry was divided into two divisions, commanded by Brigadier-Generals Maury and Hebert. Maury's division consisted of three brigades, commanded by Brigadier-General Moore and Acting Brigadier-Generals Cabell and Phifer. Hebert's

CORONA FEMALE COLLEGE AT CORINTH, MISS.
[From a sketch made before the battle.]

division consisted of four brigades, commanded by Brigadier-General Green and Colonels Martin, Gates and Colbert. The cavalry, except such companies as were on detached service, was under command of Acting Brigadier-General Armstrong. The artillery was apportioned as follows: With Maury's division, Hoxton's battery (Lieutenant Tobin commanding), Bledsoe's battery, McNally's battery (Lieutenant Moore commanding), Bryan's battery, Lucas' battery and Sengstak's battery. Hoxton's and Sengstak's batteries were held as reserves, under command of Lieutenant Burnet, acting chief of artillery of the division. With Hebert's division were Wade's, Landis', Guibor's, Dawson's and King's. The cavalry force under General Armstrong reported to the major-general commanding the combined forces and afterward acted under orders direct from him.

On the morning of the 30th ultimo we took up the line of march in the direction of Pocahontas, which place we reached on the 1st instant, and from which we moved upon the enemy at Corinth, bivouacking on the night of the 2d instant at a point nearly opposite to Chewalla, having left one regiment of infantry and a section of artillery with the wagon train as a guard.

At 4 o'clock on the morning of the 3d instant we resumed the march, my command moving on the main Pocahontas and Corinth Road in rear of General Lovell's. At a point about one and a half miles from the enemy's outer line of fortifications my command made a detour to the left, with instructions to occupy the ground between the Memphis & Charleston and Mobile & Ohio Railroads. This done, my line—Maury occupying the right and Hebert the left, with Cabell's and Colbert's brigades in reserve—fronted the enemy's works in a southeasterly direction, the right resting upon the Memphis & Charleston Railroad. While these dispositions were making General Lovell engaged the enemy upon our right.

All being now ready for the attack my line was ordered forward about 10 A. M. Almost simultaneously with the movement the opposed armies became engaged in desperate conflict along the whole extent of my line. My command had scarcely cleared the position of its first formation when, entering an abatis of more than three hundred yards, it became unmasked before a position naturally exceedingly formidable, and rendered trebly so by the extent of felled timber through which it must be approached and the most approved and scientifically constructed intrenchments, bristling with artillery of large caliber and supported by heavy lines of infantry. My troops charged the enemy's position with the most determined courage, exposed to a murderous fire of musketry and artillery. Without faltering they pressed forward over every obstacle, and with shouts and cheers carried, in less than twenty minutes, the entire line of works, the enemy having fled, leaving in our hands many prisoners and two pieces of artillery, one a 4-inch Parrott gun, the other a 24-pounder howitzer.

Our loss in this attack was comparatively small. This is attributable to the impetuosity with which the charge was made and the works carried.

It becomes my painful duty in this connection to revert to the distinguished services of two gallant officers who fell in this engagement—Colonel John D. Martin, commanding a brigade of Mississippians, and Lieutenant Samuel Farrington, of Wade's (Mo.) battery. Colonel Martin fell mortally wounded while leading the charge against an angle in the enemy's works exposed to the fire of enfilading batteries. The gallant bearing of this officer upon more than one bloody field had won for him a place in the hearts of every Mississippian and the admiration and confidence of his superior officers. Lieutenant Farrington was struck and instantly killed by a shot from a rifled gun while bringing one of the guns of his battery into position. This gallant soldier and courteous and chivalric gentleman, forgetful of personal interest and mindful of the necessities of the service only, resigned a lieutenant-colonelcy in the service of his State for a lieutenancy in the Confederate service, and gave up his life a glorious sacrifice upon the altar of his country's honor in the seventh of the battles in which he had been conspicuous for cool, determined and effective bravery. Though young, his country mourns no more valiant defender, his command no abler commander, his friends no worthier recipient of their affection.

The outer works being in our possession, my troops moved forward in pursuit of the retreating enemy until within about one mile of Corinth, where the foe was encountered in position and in force. The necessary disposition being made, my whole line again moved forward to the attack at about 3 P. M. Here the fighting was of unparalleled fierceness along the whole extent of my line. The position of the enemy along the entire length of his lines was covered by fencing, heavy timber or thick underbrush, while portions of my troops advanced through open fields, exposed to a deadly fire of batteries operating over the enemy's line of infantry. After continuous and most desperate fighting along the whole extent of my line of nearly two hours' duration, the enemy, notwithstanding his lines had been trebled by re-enforcements, was driven from his positions and forced to take refuge in his innermost works in and around the town. The troops of my command, having nearly exhausted their ammunition in the heavy fighting through the day, were withheld from immediate pursuit, and the delay in procuring the necessary supplies of ammunition forced us to close the fight for the day. My troops were withdrawn for cover, and lay on their arms during the night in the position from which the enemy had been driven.

About 4 o'clock on the morning of the 4th three batteries of my command were placed in position, and opened fire upon the town, under the immediate orders of the major-general commanding. About daylight orders were received to advance my whole line. In the execution of this order a delay was occasioned by the illness of Brigadier-General Hebert, commanding a division. He was necessarily relieved from duty. The command devolved upon Brigadier-General Green, who moved forward as soon as he could make the necessary disposition of his troops.

It was after 9 o'clock when my line became generally and furiously engaged with the enemy in his innermost and most formidable works, from which his infantry and artillery could jointly operate against my troops. Here, as in the previous actions, my artillery could not be effectively brought into action, and but few of the guns were engaged. The fighting by my command was almost entirely confined to the infantry. My men pressed forward upon the enemy, and with heavy loss succeeded in getting

SCENE IN THE INTRENCHMENTS IN FRONT OF CORINTH.

into his works, having driven him from them, capturing more than forty pieces of artillery, and forcing him to take refuge in the houses of the town and in every place that would afford protection from our galling fire. He was followed from house to house with great slaughter. In the town were batteries in mask, supported by heavy reserves, behind which the retreating enemy took shelter, and which opened upon our troops a most destructive fire at short range. My men held their positions most gallantly, returning the fire of the enemy with great spirit until portions of them exhausted their ammunition and were compelled to retire. This necessitated the withdrawal of the whole line, which was done under a withering fire. The attack was not resumed, and we fell back to our supply train, the men being almost exhausted from exertion and want of food and water. General Villepigue's brigade moved over to our assistance, but did not become engaged, as the enemy was too badly cut up to follow us. We fell back, in order to obtain water, some six miles from Corinth, where we bivouacked for the night, bringing off all of our artillery and arms save one rifled piece, which had been inadvertently driven into the enemy's line while going into battery before daylight in the morning and had been left. We brought off also the two guns captured at the outer line of fortifications on the 3d.

It is impossible for me to do justice to the courage of my troops in these engagements, nor can I discriminate between officers or commands where all behaved so nobly. This is the less necessary, as the operations of my command were under the immediate observation of the major-general commanding.

For minute details of the actions, and particularly of the artillery, of the 3d and 4th instant, as well as for instances of personal and distinguished gallantry, I beg leave to refer the major-general commanding to the reports of the commanding officers, herewith inclosed.

On the morning of the 5th instant we resumed the march in the direction of Pocahontas, my command moving by divisions, Maury's in front, each in rear of its ordnance and supply train, except Moore's brigade, which constituted the advance guard. After crossing the Tuscumbia Moore's brigade was hurried forward to protect Davis' Bridge across the Hatchie, which was threatened by an advance of the enemy. It being found that the enemy was in force, the remainder of Maury's division was ordered forward, and finally I was ordered to move up the whole of my command. Moore's brigade, with a section of the St. Louis battery and Sengstak's battery, were thrown across the Hatchie, but the enemy having possession of the heights commanding the crossing, as well as the position in which these troops were placed, and it being found that he was in very heavy force, it was deemed advisable to cross the Hatchie by another road, and these troops were withdrawn, after serious loss, to the east side of the Hatchie, where, being joined by Cabell's and Phifer's brigades, and assisted by the batteries of McNally, Hogg, Landis and Tobin, they effectually checked the advance of the enemy. Green's division, which had been delayed by passing the wagon train that had been parked near the Tuscumbia, arriving on the ground, was formed in line of battle, but the enemy making no further effort to advance, the whole of my command was moved off by another route, General Lovell's command being in our rear. This was our last engagement with the enemy. In this engagement we lost four guns, occasioned by the killing of horses. Our whole wagon train came off without molestation or loss, except a few wagons that were broken down and had to be abandoned.

The history of this war contains no bloodier page, perhaps, than that which will record this fiercely contested battle. The strongest expressions fall short of my admiration of the gallant conduct of the officers and men under my command. Words can not add luster to the fame they have acquird through deeds of noble daring which, living through future time, will shed about every man, officer and soldier who stood to his arms through this struggle a halo of glory as imperishable as it is brilliant.

The bloodiest record of this battle is to come. The long list of the gallant dead upon this field will carry sorrow to the hearthstone of many a noble champion of our cause, as it does to the hearts of those who are to avenge them. A nation mourns their loss, while it cherishes the story of their glorious death, pointing out to their associate officers in this mighty struggle for liberty the pathway to victory and honor. They will live ever in the hearts of the admiring people of the government, for the establishment of which they have given their lives.

Of the field officers killed were Colonels Rogers, Second Texas Infantry, who fell in the heart of the town, of eleven wounds; Johnson, Twentieth Arkansas, and Daly, of the Eighteenth Arkansas; Lieutenant-Colonels Maupin, First Missouri Cavalry (dismounted), and Leigh, Forty-third Mississippi; Majors Vaughn, Sixth Missouri Infantry; Dowdell, Twenty-first Arkansas, and McDonald, Fortieth Mississippi.

Many of my ablest and most gallant field officers are wounded, several mortally. Of this number are Colonels Erwin, Sixth Missouri Infantry; McFarlane, Fourth Missouri Infantry; Pritchard, Third Missouri Infantry; Moore, Forty-third Mississippi, and McLain, Thirty-seventh Mississippi; Lieutenant-Colonels Pixlee, Sixteenth Arkansas; Hedgpeth, Sixth Missouri Infantry; Terral, Seventh Mississippi Battalion; Lanier, Forty-second Alabama; Hobson, Third Arkansas Cavalry; Matheny, Twenty-first Arkansas; Campbell, Fortieth Mississippi, and Boone, Fifteenth Arkansas Infantry; Majors Senteny, Second Missouri Infantry; Keirn, Thirty-eighth Mississippi; Slaton, Thirty-seventh Alabama; Timmins, Second Texas; Jones, Twenty-first Arkansas; Russell, Third Louisiana; Yates, Thirty-sixth Mississippi, and McQuiddy, Third Missouri Cavalry.

* * * * * *

STERLING PRICE, *Major-General.*

BATTLE OF CORINTH, MISS.,

OCTOBER 3 TO 5, 1862.

BY

MAJOR-GENERAL EARL VAN DORN.

HOLLY SPRINGS, MISS., October 7, 1862.

Hon. Secretary of War:

Dispatch received at Pocahontas, near Corinth. Attacked Corinth. Took all the outer works by storm, and got within the town. Enemy received fresh re-enforcements, and we could not complete the work. Retired. The Bolivar force came down on my line of retreat and prevented crossing of Hatchie. Moved south. Crossed six miles below, and now at Ripley with all baggage and as many of the wounded as could carry. Bloody affair. Enemy still threaten. Will fight him at all points. There are about forty thousand men still in West Tennessee. Will have hard fighting.

EARL VAN DORN,
Major-General.

[INDORSEMENT.]

Respectfully submitted to the President.

G. W. RANDOLPH, *Secretary of War.*

HEADQUARTERS ARMY OF WEST TENNESSEE,
HOLLY SPRINGS, MISSISSIPPI.
October 20, 1862.

I HAVE the honor to make the following report of the battle of Corinth:

Having established batteries at Port Hudson, secured the mouth of Red River and the navigation of the Mississippi River to Vicksburg, I turned my special attention to affairs in the northern portion of my district.

On August 30th I received a dispatch from General Bragg informing me that he was about to march into Kentucky, and would leave to General Price and myself the enemy in West Tennessee.

On September 4th I received a communication from General Price, in which was inclosed a copy of the dispatch from General Bragg, above-named, making an offer to co-operate with me. At this time General Breckinridge was operating on the Mississippi River between Baton Rouge and Port Hudson with all the available force I had for the field; therefore I could not accept General Price's proposition. Upon the return, however, of General Breckinridge I immediately addressed General Price, giving him my views in full in regard to the campaign in West Tennessee, and stating that I was then ready to join him with all my troops.

In the meantime orders were received by him from General Bragg to follow Rosecrans across the Tennessee River into Middle Tennessee, whither it was then supposed he had gone. Upon the receipt of this intelligence I felt at once that all my hopes of accomplishing anything in West Tennessee with my small force were marred. I nevertheless moved up to Davis' mill, a few miles from Grand Junction, Tenn., with the intention of defending my district to the best of my ability, and to make a demonstration in favor of General Price, to which latter end also I marched my whole command, on September 20th, to within seven miles of Bolivar, driving three brigades of the enemy back to that place and forcing the return to Corinth of one division (Ross') which had been sent there to strengthen Grant's army.

CORINTH, MISS., AFTER ITS EVACUATION. BURNING OF RAILWAY STATIONS, WAREHOUSES AND SUPPLIES.
[From a sketch by Henry Lovie, owned by Mrs. Frank Leslie.]

General Price, in obedience to his orders, marched in the direction of Iuka to cross the Tennessee, but was not long in discovering that Rosecrans had not crossed that stream. This officer, in connection with Grant, attacked him on September 19th, and compelled him to fall back toward Baldwyn, on the Mobile & Ohio Railroad.

On the 25th day of the same month I received a dispatch by courier from General Price, stating that he was at Baldwyn, and was then ready to join me with his forces in an attack on Corinth, as had been previously suggested by me.

We met at Ripley on September 28th, according to agreement, and marched the next morning toward Pocahontas, which place we reached on October 1st.

From all the information I could obtain the following was the situation of the Federal army at that time: Sherman at Memphis with about 6,000 men; Hurlbut (afterward Ord) at Bolivar with about 8,000; Grant's headquarters at Jackson with about 3,000; Rosecrans at Corinth with about 15,000, together with the following outposts, viz., Rienzi, 2,500; Burnsville, Jacinto, Iuka, about 6,000; at important brigades and on garrison duty about 2,000 or 3,000; making in the aggregate about 42,000 men in West Tennessee.

Memphis, Jackson, Bolivar and Corinth were fortified, the works mounting siege guns; the outposts slightly fortified, having field-pieces. Memphis, Bolivar and Corinth are on the arc of a circle, the chord of which from Memphis to Corinth makes an angle with the due east line of about fifteen degrees south. Bolivar is about equidistant from Memphis and Corinth, somewhat nearer the latter, and is at the intersection of the Hatchie River and the Mississippi Central & Ohio Railroad. Corinth is the strongest but the most salient point.

Surveying the whole field of operations before me calmly and dispassionately, the conclusion forced itself irresistibly upon my mind that the taking of Corinth was a condition precedent to the accomplishment of anything of importance in West Tennessee. To take Memphis would be to destroy an immense amount of property without any adequate military advantage, even admitting that it could be held without heavy guns against the enemy's gun and mortar boats.

The line of fortifications around Bolivar is intersected by the Hatchie River, rendering it impossible to take the place by quick assault, and re-enforcements could be thrown in from Jackson by railroad; and, situated as it is in the re-entrant angle of the three fortified places, an advance upon it would expose both my flanks and rear to an attack from the forces at Memphis and Corinth. It was clear to my mind that if a successful attack could be made upon Corinth from the west and northwest, the forces there driven back on the Tennessee and cut off, Bolivar and Jackson would easily fall, and then, upon the arrival of the exchanged prisoners of war, West Tennessee would soon be in our possession and communication with General Bragg effected through Middle Tennessee. The attack on Corinth was a military necessity, requiring prompt and vigorous action. It was being strengthened daily under that astute soldier General Rosecrans.

Convalescents were returning to fill his ranks, new levies were arriving to increase his brigades, and fortifications were being constructed at new points, and it was very evident that unless a sudden and vigorous blow could be struck there at once no hope could be entertained of driving the enemy from a base of operations so convenient that in the event of misfortune to Bragg in Kentucky the whole Valley of the Misisssippi would be lost to us before winter. To have waited for the arrival, arming, clothing and organization of the exchanged prisoners would have been to wait for the enemy to strengthen themselves more than we could possibly do.

With these reflections, and after mature deliberation, I determined to attack Corinth. I had a reasonable hope of success. Field returns at Ripley showed my strength to be about twenty-two thousand men. Rosecrans at Corinth had about fifteen thousand, with about eight thousand additional men at outposts from twelve to fifteen miles distant. I might surprise him and carry the place before these troops could be brought in. I therefore marched toward Pocahontas, threatening Bolivar; then turned suddenly across the Hatchie and Tuscumbia, and attacked Corinth without hesitation, and did surprise that place before the outpost garrisons were called in. It was necessary that this blow should be sudden and decisive, and, if unsuccessful, that I should withdraw rapidly from the position between the two armies of Ord and Rosecrans.

The troops were in fine spirits, and the whole Army of West Tennessee seemed eager to emulate the Armies of the Potomac and of Kentucky. No army ever marched to battle with prouder steps, more hopeful countenances or with more courage than marched the Army of West Tennessee out of Ripley on the morning of September 29th on its way to Corinth.

Fully alive to the responsibility of my position as commander of the army, and after mature and deliberate reflection, the march was ordered. The ground was well known to me, and required no study to determine where to make the attack. The bridge over the Hatchie was soon reconstructed, and the army crossed at 4 A. M. on October 2d. Adams' brigade of cavalry was left here to guard this approach to our rear and to protect the train, which was parked between the Hatchie and Tuscumbia. Colonel Hawkins' regiment of infantry and Captain Dawson's battery of artillery were also left on the Boneyard Road, in easy supporting distance of the bridge. The army bivouacked at Chewalla, after the driving in of some pickets from that vicinity by Armstrong's and Jackson's cavalry. This point is about ten miles from Corinth.

At daybreak on the 3d the march was resumed, the precaution having been taken to cut the railroad between Corinth and Jackson, which was done by a squadron of Armstrong's cavalry. Lovell's division in front kept the road on the south side of the Memphis & Charleston Railroad. Price, after marching on the same road about five miles, turned to the left, crossing the railroad, and formed line of battle in front of the outer line of intrenchments and about three miles from Corinth. Lovell formed line of battle, after some heavy skirmishing—having to construct a passage across the dry bed of Indian Creek for his artillery under fire—on the right and in front of the same line of intrenchments.

The following was the first order of battle: The three brigades of Lovell's division—Villepigue's, Bowen's and

Rust's—in line, with reserves in rear of each; Jackson's cavalry brigade on the right in echelon, the left flank of the division on the Charleston Railroad; Price's corps on the left, with the right flank resting on the same road; Maury's division on the right, with Moore's and Phifer's brigades in line, Cabell's in reserve; Hebert's division on the left, with Gate's and Martin's brigades in line, Colbert's in reserve; Armstrong's cavalry brigade on the extreme left, somewhat detached and out of view. Hebert's left was masked behind a timbered ridge, with orders not to bring it into action until the last moment. This was done in hopes of inducing the enemy to weaken his right by re-enforcing his center and left—where the attack was first to be made—that his right might be forced.

At 10 o'clock all skirmishers were driven into the intrenchments, and the two armies were in line of battle, confronting each other in force. A belt of fallen timber or abatis, about four hundred yards in width, extended along the whole line of intrenchments. This was to be crossed.

The attack was commenced on the right by Lovell's division, and extended gradually to the left, and by 1:30 o clock the whole line of outer works was carried, several pieces of artillery being taken. The enemy made several ineffectual efforts to hold their ground, forming line of battle at advantageous points, and resisting obstinately our advance to the second line of detached works.

I had been in hopes that one day's operations would end the contest and decide who should be the victors on this bloody field, but a ten miles' march over a parched country, on dusty roads, without water, getting into line of battle in forests with undergrowth, and the more than equal activity and determined courage displayed by the enemy, commanded by one of the ablest generals of the United States Army, who threw all possible obstacles in our way that an active mind could suggest, prolonged the battle until I saw, with regret, the sun sink behind the horizon as the last shot of our sharpshooters followed the retreating foe into their innermost lines. One hour more of daylight and victory would have soothed our grief for the loss of the gallant dead who sleep on that lost but not dishonored field. The army slept on their arms within six hundred yards of Corinth, victorious so far.

During the night three batteries were ordered to take position on the ridge overlooking the town from the west, just where the hills dip into the flat extending into the railroad depot, with instructions to open on the town at 4 A. M. Hebert on the left, was ordered to mask part of his division on his left; to put Cabell's brigade in echelon on the left also, Cabell's brigade being detached from Maury's division for this purpose; to move Armstrong's cavalry brigade across the Mobile & Ohio Railroad, and, if possible, to get some of his artillery in position across the road. In this order of battle he was directed to attack at daybreak with his whole force, swinging his left flank in toward Corinth, and advance down the Purdy Ridge. Lovell—on the extreme right, with two of his brigades in line of battle, and one in reserve, with Jackson's cavalry on the extreme right on College Hill, his left flank resting

MAJ.-GEN. EARL VAN DORN, OF MISSISSIPPI.
Died in Spring Hill, Tenn., May 8, 1863.
[From a photo taken in 1861.]

on the Memphis & Charleston Railroad—was ordered to await in this order, or to feel his way along slowly with his sharpshooters until Hebert was heavily engaged with the enemy on the left. He was then to move rapidly to the assault and force his right inward across the low grounds southwest of the town. The center, under Maury, was to move at the same time quickly to the front and directly at Corinth. Jackson was directed to burn the railroad bridge over the Tuscumbia during the night.

Daylight came, and there was no attack on the left. A staff officer was sent to Hebert to inquire the cause. That officer could not be found. Another messenger was sent, and a third, and about 7 o'clock General Hebert came to my headquarters and reported sick. General Price then put Brigadier-General Green in command of the left wing, and it was 8 o'clock before the proper dispositions of the attack at this point were made. In the meantime the troops of Maury's left became engaged with the enemy's sharpshooters, and the battle was brought on and extended along the whole center and left wing, and I regretted to observe that my whole plan of attack was, by this unfortunate delay, disarranged. One brigade after another went gallantly into the action, and pushing forward through direct and cross fire over every obstacle, reached Corinth and planted their colors on the last stronghold of the enemy. A hand-to-hand contest was being enacted in the very yard of General Rosecrans' headquarters and in the streets of the town. The heavy guns were silenced, and all seemed about to be ended, when a heavy fire from fresh troops from Iuka, Burnsville and Rienzi, that had succeeded in reaching Corinth in time, poured into our thinned ranks. Exhausted from loss of sleep, wearied from hard marching and fighting, companies and regiments without officers, our troops—let no one censure them—gave way. The day was lost.

BATTLE NEAR CORINTH.

Lovell's division was at this time advancing, pursuant to orders, and was on the point of assaulting the works when he received my orders to throw one of his brigades (Villepigue's) rapidly to the center to cover the broken ranks thrown back from Corinth and prevent a sortie. He then moved his whole division to the left, and was soon afterward ordered to move slowly back and take position on Indian Creek and prevent the enemy from turning our flank. The center and left were withdrawn on the same road on which they approached, and being somewhat in confusion on account of the loss of officers, fatigue, thirst, want of sleep, thinned ranks and the nature of the ground, Villepigue's brigade was brought in opportunely and covered the rear to Chewalla. Lovell came in rear of the whole army, and all bivouacked again at Chewalla. No enemy disturbed the sleep of the weary troops.

During the night I had a bridge constructed over the Tuscumbia, and sent Armstrong's and Jackson's cavalry with a battery of artillery to seize and hold Rienzi until the army came up, intending to march to and hold that point; but after consultation with General Price, who represented his troops to be somewhat disorganized, it was deemed advisable to return by the same route we came, and fall back toward Ripley and Oxford.

Anticipating that the Bolivar force would move out and dispute my passage across the Hatchie Bridge, I pushed rapidly on to that point in hopes of reaching and securing the bridge before their arrival, but I soon learned by couriers from Colonel Wirt Adams that I would be too late. I nevertheless pushed on with the intention of engaging the enemy until I could get my train and reserve artillery unparked and on the Boneyard Road to the crossing at Crum's mill. This road branches off south from the State Line Road about two and a half miles west of Tuscumbia Bridge, running south or up the Hatchie. No contest of long duration could be made here, as it was evident that the army of Corinth would soon make its appearance on our right flank and rear.

The trains and reserve artillery were therefore immediately ordered on the Boneyard Road, and orders were sent to Armstrong and Jackson to change their direction and cover the front and flank of the trains until they crossed the Hatchie, and then to cover them in front until they were on the Ripley Road. The enemy were then engaged beyond the Hatchie Bridge by small fragments of Maury's division as they could be hastened up, and were kept in check sufficiently long to get everything off. General Ord commanded the forces of the enemy, and succeeded in getting into position before any number of our travel-worn troops could get into line of battle. It is not surprising, therefore, that they were driven back across the bridge, but they maintained their positions on the hill overlooking it, under their gallant leader, General Price, until orders were sent to fall back and take up their line of march on the Boneyard Road in rear of the whole train.

At one time, fearing that the enemy, superior in numbers to the whole force I had in advance of the train, would drive us back, I ordered General Lovell to leave one brigade to guard the rear at the Tuscumbia Bridge and to push forward with the other two to the front. This order was quickly executed, and very soon the splendid brigades of Rust and Villepigue made their appearance close at hand. The army corps of General Price was withdrawn, and Villepigue filed in and took position as a rear guard to the army against Ord's forces. Rust was ordered forward to report to General Price, who was directed to cross the Hatchie at Crum's mill and take position to cover the crossing of the trains and artillery. Bowen was left at Tuscumbia Bridge as rear guard against the advance of Rosecrans from Corinth, with orders to defend the bridge until the trains were unparked and on the road, then to cross the bridge and burn it and to join Villepigue at the junction of the roads. In the execution of this order, and while in position near the bridge, the head of the Corinth army made its appearance and engaged him, but was repulsed with heavy loss and in a manner that reflected great credit on General Bowen and his brigade. The army was not again molested in its retreat to Ripley, nor on its march to this place.

The following was found to be our loss in the several conflicts with the enemy and on the march to and from Corinth, viz.: killed, 594; wounded, 2,162; prisoners and missing, 2,102. One piece of artillery was driven in the night by mistake into the enemy's lines and captured. Four pieces were taken at the Hatchie Bridge, the horses being shot. Nine wagons were upset and abandoned by teamsters on the night march to Crum's mill. Some baggage was thrown out of the wagons, not amounting to any serious loss. Two pieces of artillery were captured from the enemy at Corinth by General Lovell's division, one of which was brought off. Five pieces were also taken by General Price's corps, two of which were brought off, thus making a loss to us of only two pieces.

The enemy's loss in killed and wounded, by their own accounts, was over three thousand. We took over three hundred prisoners. Most of the prisonere taken from us were stragglers from the army on the retreat.

The retreat from Corinth was not a rout, as it has been industriously represented to be by the enemy and by the cowardly deserters from the army. The division of General Lovell formed line of battle facing the rear on several occasions when it was reported the enemy was near, but not a gun was fired after the army retired from the Hatchie and Tuscumbia Bridges, nor did the enemy follow, except at a respectful distance.

Although many officers and soldiers who distinguished themselves in the battle of Corinth and in the affair at Hatchie Bridge came under my personal observation, I will not mention them to the exclusion of others who may have been equally deserving, but who did not fall under my own eye. I have deemed it best to call on the different commanders to furnish me a special report and a list of the names of the officers and soldiers of their respective commands who deserve special mention. These lists and special reports I will take pleasure in forwarding, together with one of my own, when completed, and I respectfully request that they may be appended as part of my report.

I can not refrain, however, from mentioning here the conspicuous gallantry of a noble Texan, whose deeds at Corinth are the constant theme of both friends and foes. As long as courage, manliness, fortitude, patriotism and honor exist the name of Rodgers will be revered and honored among men. He fell in the front of battle, and died beneath the colors of his regiment, in the very center of the enemy's stronghold. He sleeps, and glory is his sentinel.

The attempt at Corinth has failed, and in consequence I am condemned and have been superseded in my command. In my zeal for my country I may have ventured too far with inadequate means, and I bow to the opinion of the people whom I serve. Yet I feel that if the spirits of the gallant dead who now lie beneath the batteries of Corinth see and judge the motives of men, they do not rebuke me. for there is no sting in my conscience, nor does retrospection admonish me of error or of a reckless disregard of their valued lives.

EARL VAN DORN, *Major-General.*

BATTLE OF PERRYVILLE, KY.,

OCTOBER 6, 7 AND 8, 1862.

BY

MAJOR-GENERAL LEONIDAS POLK,
Commanding Army of the Mississippi.

HEADQUARTERS ARMY OF THE MISSISSIPPI,
KNOXVILLE, TENN.,
November 16, 1862.

I HAVE the honor to submit the following as my official report of the battle of Perryville, Ky.:

At Bardstown, on September 28th, the Army of the Mississippi, by order from General Bragg, was placed under my command. Up to that time I had command of the right wing only, General Hardee having command of the left. My orders from the general commanding, who was called on public duty to the capital at Frankfort, were to press in the enemy's pickets upon Louisville and to maintain my position. If the enemy advanced upon me in moderate force, to attack him; if in large force, I was to fall back upon Harrodsburg, marching in two columns by the way of Perryville and Mackville, respectively. The enemy having made a general advance, I moved upon Harrodsburg, and in consequence of the state of the roads marched the whole column by the Springfield and Perryville Pike. The object of this movement was to form a junction with the Army of the Kentucky, under General Kirby Smith, who was to move for that purpose upon Harrodsburg, also from the north side of the Kentucky River. Another object was to cover our base, which, after the evacuation of Cumberland Gap by the enemy, was established at Camp Dick Robinson, in the forks of the Dick and Kentucky Rivers. On arriving at Perryville I communicated with the general commanding the forces then at Harrodsburg, informing him that the right wing, under command of General Cheatham, had been ordered forward to take a position on the further side of that town, and as there was a scarcity of water, I had ordered General Hardee to halt Buckner's division near Perryville and to post Anderson's on Salt River, between the two towns. These dispositions were carried into effect, and I reported to the general commanding in person.

The enemy had been held in check along the whole line of march, from in front of Louisville up to our present position, by those gallant cavalry commanders Colonels Wharton and Wheeler, and we were constantly advised of his position and movements. He left Louisville in five columns on as many different routes, extending from the road to Elizabethtown around to that to Shelbyville, and we had reason to believe that much the larger portion of this force was concentrated upon Bardstown and followed our retiring army in the march to Perryville. The rest of his force pursued a route further north to threaten General Kirby Smith.

Information having been received through General Hardee that the enemy was pressing with heavy force upon his position, it was resolved by the general commanding the forces to attack him at that point. He accordingly directed me, on the evening of October 7th, to order Anderson's division, of Hardee's wing, to return to Perryville, and also to order General Cheatham, with Donelson's division of this wing, to follow it immediately, and to return myself to that place, to take charge of the forces and attack the enemy the next morning. I urged the strong expediency of concentrating all our forces upon the point to be attacked, and at all events the necessity of having the remaining division of the Army of the Mississippi (Withers') placed at my disposal. To this the general objected, upon the ground that General Kirby Smith had informed him that the enemy was in force in his front, and that his troops could not be spared from that part of the field, nor could the division of Withers be spared, as he thought the force in front of Smith made it necessary for him to be re-enforced. He therefore proposed to order Withers to the support of Smith, and to take charge of those combined forces himself in person. Generals Anderson and Cheatham proceeded to Perryville and reported to General Hardee as ordered, and on arriving were posted by that officer in a line of battle which he had selected. I followed as soon as practicable, arrived during the night, and reconnoitered the line of battle early on the following morning.

At a meeting of the general officers, held about daylight, it was resolved, in view of the great disparity of our forces, to adopt the defensive-offensive—to await the movements of the enemy, and to be guided by events as they were developed. The line of battle selected was that indicated by the course of Chaplin Fork of Salt River, on the banks of which our troops were posted. The division of General Buckner, of the left wing, occupied the extreme right; that of General Anderson, the center; that of General Donelson of the right wing, under General Cheatham, the left. General Wharton's brigade of cavalry covered the right wing, General Wheeler the left. General McCown, who reached the field by a forced march with a cavalry force at an early hour, was directed by order of General Bragg to turn over his command to Colonel Wheeler, and to report to him for orders. The whole of our force, including all arms, did not exceed fifteen thousand. We have good reason to believe that the force of General Buell immediately in front of us, consisting of the corps of Generals McCook and Gilbert, each about eighteen thousand strong, and that of General Crittenden, with a corps of about the same number, was within eight miles of the field at the opening of the attack. General Liddell's brigade of General Buckner's division was thrown forward in observation about one mile in front of Perryville, between the Springfield and Mackville Roads. Light skirmishing opened the operation of the morning, which grew heavier as the day advanced.

About 10 o'clock Liddell became hotly engaged, and it became evident that the enemy was disposed to press upon our right. I directed General Buckner to retire Liddell's brigade and let it fall back upon our general line, and ordered General Cheatham to move the whole of his command from the left to the right of our line. These orders were promptly executed, and Cheatham's command was held in column of brigades.

It was now near 1 o'clock, and the movements of the enemy were not continued. It was then determined by General Bragg, commander of the forces, who had arrived on the field some hours before, to assume the offensive, and by his direction orders were given for a general movement throughout our whole line. General Cheatham's column of brigades was deployed into line and ordered, with Wharton's cavalry still upon its right, to attack. At this juncture I was informed by Colonel Wharton that a column of the enemy's infantry was seen approaching by the Mackville Road in a direction to support the enemy's left. This column, I discovered, was still quite distant, but concluding that our chances of success were greater against the line in my front, even when re-enforced, than it would be by attacking it as it stood and exposing my flank to the approaching force, I awaited until the re-enforcements got into position. The attack was then ordered.

MAJ.-GEN. BENJAMIN F. CHEATHAM, OF TENNESSEE.

Wharton charged the enemy's extreme left with great fury, passing on over stone walls and ravines, and driving back the enemy's infantry several hundred yards. This movement placed in our possession a skirt of woods and an eminence of great importance to our success, on our right. It was quickly followed by the brigades of General Cheatham, under Brigadier-Generals Donelson, Stewart and Maney. These mounted the steep and difficult cliffs of Chaplin River in gallant style, and moved forward upon the enemy's position with a most determined courage. Their approach was met by a storm of shot, shell and musketry from several batteries strongly posted, and supported by heavy masses of infantry. Their progress was, nevertheless, steadily onward; and although mowed down by well-directed volleys of musketry and well-served artillery, the gaps thus produced in our lines were promptly filled, and our troops pressed forward with resistless energy, driving the enemy before them, and capturing three of his batteries. In this movement the enemy's left was forced back about a mile, until his three lines were pressed into one. Here, being heavily re-enforced, he recovered one of his batteries, but did not attempt to regain any of the ground he had lost. This charge of these brigades was one of the most heroic and brilliant movements of the war. Considering the disparity of the numbers of the troops engaged, the strength of the enemy's position, the murderous character of the fire under which they had to advance, the steadiness with which they endured the havoc which was being made in their ranks, their knowledge that they were without any supporting force, the firmness with which they moved upon the enemy's masses of infantry and artillery, it will compare favorably with the most brilliant achievements of historic valor. In this charge General James S. Jackson, who commanded a division of the enemy, was killed amid the guns of one of the batteries that was taken.

While directing the operations in this part of the field I received a message from General Bragg informing me that the right center, occupied by a portion of the troops of General Hardee, was hard pressed, and suggesting the sending re-enforcements to its relief. This was done at the earliest moment, the brigades of Generals Stewart and Donelson being detached for that purpose. These generals advanced their brigades in gallant style on the right of that of General Cleburne, and, in conjunction with that efficient officer, drove the enemy with great slaughter from his successive positions a full mile and a half.

As the enemy was yielding toward the close of the day, the brigade of Brigadier-General Liddell approached

PERRYVILLE, KENTUCKY.

from my left and rear, and halted on the crest of a hill to determine a point at which to offer its support. It was directed to the place where it was most wanted, and moved upon it with deafening cheers. Here, owing to the fading twilight, it was for a few moments difficult to determine whether the firing in our front was from our men or the enemy's troops. This difficulty, however, was speedily removed; it was the enemy, and, in obedience to orders, that veteran brigade, under its gallant commander, closed the operations of the day in that part of the field with a succession of the most deadly volleys I have witnessed. The enemy's command in their immediate front was well-nigh annihilated.

At this point a number of prisoners were taken, and among them several corps, division and brigade staff officers, and, darkness closing in, I ordered the troops to cease firing and to bivouac for the night.

The operations of the left wing, which were under the immediate superintendence of Major-General Hardee, were not less satisfactory or successful. His combinations for the attack were judiciously made, and immediately after the onset of the right wing, under Major-General Cheatham, had been fully developed, he ordered General Buckner to move forward his division and unite in the assault. This order was executed with promptness and vigor. The position assailed—one of great strength and the key of that part of the field—was carried, and, by a combined movement with two of the brigades of General Anderson's division and a skillful handling of his artillery, the whole of the enemy's line, reaching to Cheatham's left, was driven in confusion near a mile to the rear, and night put an end to further pursuit. The gallantry of these troops and of their able and skillful commanders in that desperate struggle was in keeping with that of their comrades of the right wing, and the part they bore in the bloody conflict of the field of Perryville entitles them to a distinguished place in the records of that eventful day.

I desire to return thanks to Almighty God for the persistent energy, determination and courage with which He has inspired the hearts of our troops in the prosecution of this unrighteous war, and for shielding our heads in the day of battle.

* * * * * * *

L. POLK, *Major-General Commanding.*

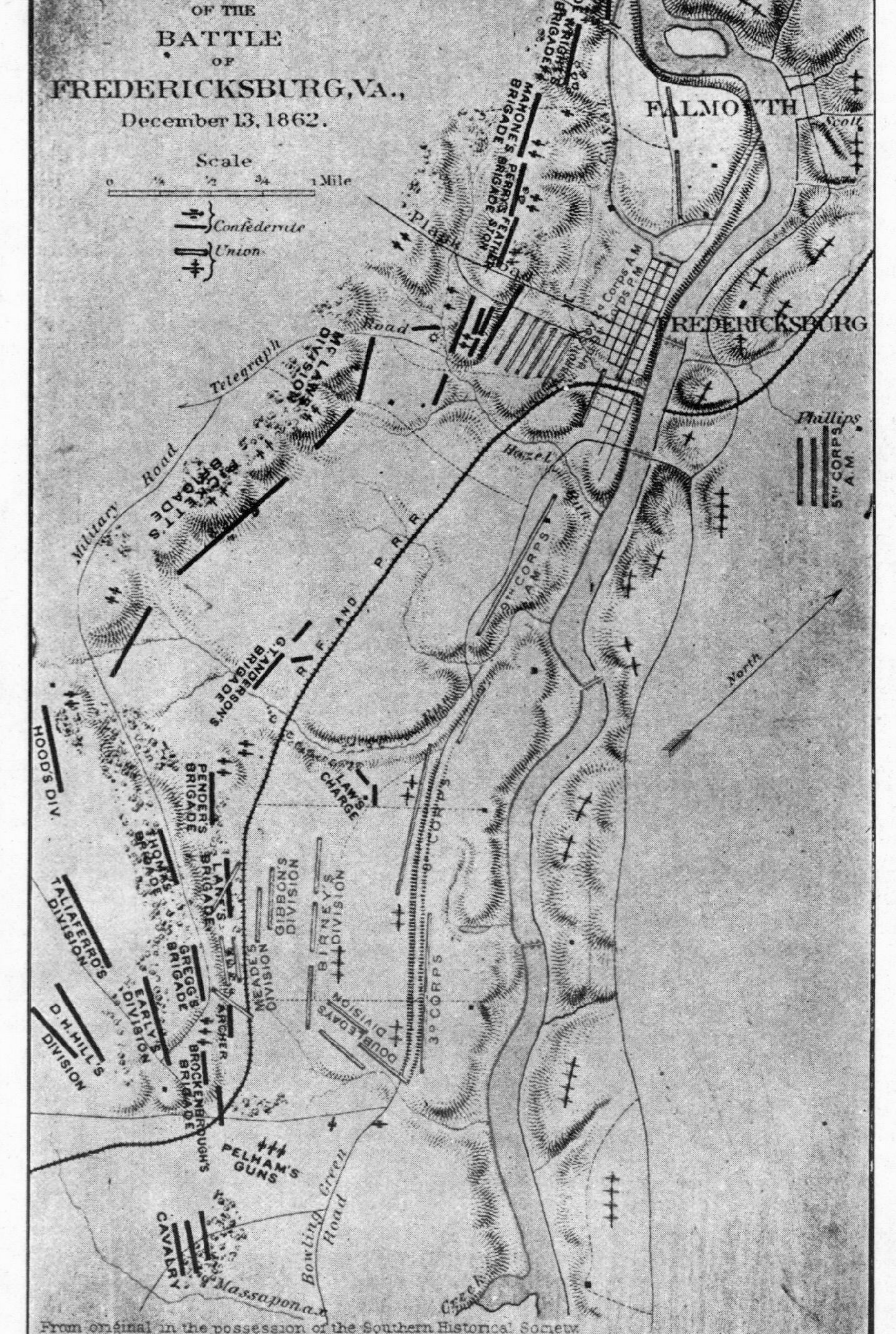

From original in the possession of the Southern Historical Society.

BATTLE OF FREDERICKSBURG, VA.,

DECEMBER 11 TO 15, 1862.

BY

GENERAL R. E. LEE.

HEADQUARTERS ARMY OF NORTHERN VIRGINIA,
April 10, 1863.

ON November 15 [1862], it was known that the enemy was in motion toward the Orange & Alexandria Railroad, and one regiment of infantry, with a battery of light artillery, was sent to re-enforce the garrison at Fredericksburg.

On the 17th it was ascertained that Sumner's corps had marched from Catletts Station in the direction of Falmouth; and information was also received that on the 15th some Federal gunboats and transports had entered Aquia Creek. This looked as if Fredericksburg was again to be occupied, and McLaws' and Ransom's divisions, accompanied by W. H. F. Lee's brigade of cavalry and Lane's battery, were ordered to proceed to that city. To ascertain more fully the movements of the enemy, General Stuart was directed to cross the Rappahannock.

On the morning of the 18th he forced a passage at Warrenton Springs, in the face of a regiment of cavalry and three pieces of artillery, guarding the ford, and reached Warrenton soon after the last of the enemy's column had left. The information he obtained confirmed the previous reports, and it was clear that the whole Federal army, under Major-General Burnside, was moving toward Fredericksburg.

On the morning of the 19th, therefore, the remainder of Longstreet's corps was put in motion for that point.

The advance of General Sumner reached Falmouth on the afternoon of the 17th, and attempted to cross the Rappahannock, but was driven back by Colonel [William B.] Ball, with the Fifteenth Virginia Cavalry, four companies of Mississippi infantry and [Captain J. W.] Lewis' light battery.

On the 21st it became apparent that General Burnside was concentrating his whole army on the north side of the Rappahannock.

On the same day General Sumner summoned the corporate authorities of Fredericksburg to surrender the place by 5 P. M., and threatened, in case of refusal, to bombard the city at 9 o'clock next morning. The weather had been tempestuous for two days, and a storm was raging at the time of the summons. It was impossible to prevent the execution of the threat to shell the city, as it was completely exposed to the batteries on the Stafford Hills, which were beyond our reach. The city authorities were informed that, while our forces would not use the place for military purposes, its occupation by the enemy would be resisted, and directions were given for the removal of the women and children as rapidly as possible. The threatened bombardment did not take place, but, in view of the imminence of a collision between the two armies, the inhabitants were advised to leave the city, and almost the entire population, without a murmur, abandoned their homes. History presents no instance of a people exhibiting a purer and more unselfish patriotism, or a higher spirit of fortitude and courage than was evinced by the citizens of Fredericksburg. They cheerfully incurred great hardships and privations, and surrendered their homes and property to destruction rather than yield them into the hands of the enemies of their country.

General Burnside now commenced his preparations to force the passage of the Rappahannock and advance upon Richmond. When his army first began to move toward Fredericksburg, General Jackson, in pursuance of instructions, crossed the Blue Ridge, and placed his corps in the vicinity of Orange Courthouse, to enable him more promptly to co-operate with Longstreet.

About November 26th he was directed to advance toward Fredericksburg, and as some Federal gunboats had appeared in the river at Port Royal, and it was possible that an attempt might be made to cross in that vicinity, D. H. Hill's division was stationed near that place, and the rest of Jackson's corps so disposed as to support Hill or Longstreet, as occasion might require. The fords of the Rappahannock above Fredericksburg were closely guarded by our cavalry, and the brigade of General W. H. F. Lee was stationed near Port Royal, to watch the river above and below.

On the 28th General Hampton, guarding the Upper Rappahannock, crossed to make a reconnoissance on the enemy's right, and, proceeding as far as Dumfries and Occoquan, encountered and dispersed his cavalry, capturing two squadrons and a number of wagons. About the same time some dismounted men of Beale's regiment, Lee's brigade, crossed in boats below Port Royal, to observe the enemy's left, and took a number of prisoners.

On December 5th General D. H. Hill, with some of his field-guns, assisted by Major Pelham, of Stuart's Horse Artillery, attacked the gunboats at Port Royal and caused them to retire.

With these exceptions, no important movement took place, but it became evident that the advance of the enemy would not be long delayed. The interval was employed in strengthening our lines, extending from the river about one and a half miles above Fredericksburg along the range of hills in the rear of the city to the Richmond Railroad. As these hills were commanded by the opposite heights in possession of the enemy, earthworks were constructed upon their crest at the most eligible positions for artillery. These positions were judiciously chosen and fortified, under the direction of Brigadier-General Pendleton, chief of artillery; Colonel Cabell, of McLaws' division; Colonel E. P. Alexander and Captain S. R. Johnston, of the engineers. To prevent gunboats from ascending the river, a battery, protected by intrenchments, was placed on the bank, about four miles below the city, in an excellent position selected by my aid-de-camp Major [T. M. R.] Talcott. The plain of Fredericksburg is so completely commanded by the Stafford Heights that no effectual opposition could be made to the construction of bridges or the passage of the river without exposing our troops to the destructive fire of the numerous batteries of the enemy. At the same time the narrowness of the Rappahannock, its winding course and deep bed, presented opportunities for laying down bridges at points secure from the fire of our artillery. Our position was, therefore, selected with a view to resist the enemy's advance after crossing, and the river was guarded only by a force sufficient to impede his movements until the army could be concentrated.

Before dawn, on December 11th, our signal guns announced that the enemy was in motion. About 2 A. M. he commenced preparations to throw two bridges over the Rappahannock, opposite Fredericksburg, and one about one and a quarter miles below, near the mouth of Deep Run. Two regiments of Barksdale's brigade, McLaws' division (the Seventeenth and Eighteenth Mississippi), guarded these points; the former, assisted by the Eighth Florida, of Anderson's division, being at the upper. The rest of the brigade, with the Third Georgia Regiment, also of Anderson's division, was held in reserve in the city. From daybreak until 4 P. M. the troops, sheltered behind the houses on the river bank, repelled the repeated efforts of the enemy to lay his bridges opposite the town, driving back his working parties and their supports with great slaughter. At the lower point, where there was no such protection, the enemy was successfully resisted until nearly noon, when, being greatly exposed to the fire of the batteries on the opposite heights and a superior force of infantry on the river bank, our troops were withdrawn, and about 1 P. M. the bridge was completed.

Soon afterward one hundred and fifty pieces of artillery opened a furious fire upon the city, causing our troops to retire from the river bank about 4 P. M. The enemy then crossed in boats and proceeded rapidly to lay down the bridges. His advance into the town was bravely resisted until dark, when our troops were recalled, the necessary time for concentration having been gained.

During the night and the succeeding day the enemy crossed in large numbers at and below the town, secured from material interruption by a dense fog. Our artillery could only be used with effect when the occasional clearing of the mist rendered his columns visible. His batteries on the Stafford Heights fired at intervals upon our position. Longstreet's corps constituted our left, with Anderson's division resting upon the river, and those of McLaws, Pickett and Hood extending to the right in the order named. Ransom's division supported the batteries on Marye's and Willis' hills, at the foot of which Cobb's brigade, of McLaws' division, and the Twenty-fourth North Carolina, of Ransom's brigade, were stationed, protected by a stone wall. The immediate care of this point was committed to General Ransom. The Washington Artillery, under Colonel Walton, occupied the redoubts on the crest of Marye's Hill, and those on the heights to the right and left were held by part of the reserve artillery, Colonel E. P. Alexander's battalion, and the division batteries of Anderson, Ransom and McLaws. A. P. Hill, of Jackson's corps, was posted between Hood's right and Hamilton's Crossing on the railroad. His front line, consisting of the brigades of Pender, Lane and Archer, occupied the edge of a wood. Lieutenant-Colonel Walker, with fourteen pieces of artillery, was posted near the right, supported by the Fortieth and Fifty-fifth Virginia regiments, of Fields' brigade, commanded by Colonel Brockenbrough. Lane's brigade, thrown forward in advance of the general line, held the woods, which here projected into the open ground. Thomas' brigade was stationed behind the interval between Lane and Pender; Gregg's in rear of that, between Lane and Archer. These two brigades with the Forty-seventh Virginia Regiment and Twenty-second Virginia Battalion, of Field's brigade, constituted General Hill's reserve. Early's and Taliaferro's divisions composed Jackson's second line; D. H. Hill's division his reserve. His artillery was distributed along his line in the most eligible positions, so as to command the open ground in front. General Stuart, with two brigades of cavalry and his horse artillery, occupied the plain on Jackson's right, extending to Massaponax Creek.

MARYE'S HEIGHTS, FREDERICKSBURG, VA.

On the morning of the 13th the plain on which the Federal army lay was still enveloped in fog, making it impossible to discern its operations. At an early hour the batteries on the Heights of Stafford began to play upon Longstreet's position. Shortly after 9 A. M. the partial rising of the mist disclosed a large force moving in line of battle against Jackson. Dense masses appeared in front of A. P. Hill, stretching far up the river in the direction of Fredericksburg. As they advanced, Major Pelham, of Stuart's Horse Artillery, who was stationed near the Port Royal road with one section, opened a rapid and well-directed enfilade fire, which arrested their progress. Four batteries immediately turned upon him, but he sustained their heavy fire with the unflinching courage that ever distinguished him. Upon his withdrawal the enemy extended his left down the Port Royal Road, and his numerous batteries opened with vigor upon Jackson's line. Eliciting no response his infantry moved forward to seize the position occupied by Lieutenant-Colonel Walker. The latter, reserving his fire until their line had approached within less than eight hundred yards, opened upon it with such destructive effect as to cause it to waver and soon to retreat in confusion.

About 1 P. M. the main attack on our right began by a furious cannonade, under cover of which three compact lines of infantry advanced against Hill's front. They were received, as before, by our batteries, by whose fire they were momentarily checked, but, soon recovering, they pressed forward until, coming within range of our infantry, the contest became fierce and bloody. Archer and Lane repulsed those portions of the line immediately in front of them, but before the interval between these commands could be closed the enemy pressed through in overwhelming numbers and turned the left of Archer and the right of Lane. Attacked in front and flank, two regiments of the former and the brigade of the latter, after a brave and obstinate resistance, gave way. Archer held his line with the First Tennessee, and, with the Fifth Alabama Battalion, assisted by the Forty-seventh Virginia Regiment and the Twenty-second Virginia Battalion, continued the struggle until the arrival of re-enforcements. Thomas came gallantly to the relief of Lane, and, joined by the Seventh and part of the Eighteenth North Carolina, of that brigade, repulsed the column that had broken Lane's line and drove it back to the railroad.

In the meantime a large force had penetrated the wood as far as Hill's reserve, and encountered Gregg's brigade. The attack was so sudden and unexpected that Orr's Rifles, mistaking the enemy for our own troops retiring, were thrown into confusion. While in the act of rallying them that brave soldier and true patriot, Brigadier-General Maxcy Gregg, fell mortally wounded. Colonel Hamilton, upon whom the command devolved, with the four remaining regiments of the brigade and one company of the Rifles, met the enemy firmly and checked his further progress. The second line was advancing to the support of the first. Lawton's brigade, of Early's division, under Colonel Atkinson, first encountered the enemy, quickly followed on the right and left by the brigades of Trimble (under Colonel Hoke) and Early (under Colonel Walker). Taliaferro's division moved forward at the same time on Early's left, and his right regiment (the Second Virginia, belonging to Paxton's brigade) joined in the attack. The contest in the woods was short and decisive. The enemy was quickly routed and driven out with loss, and though largely re-enforced, he was forced back and pursued to the shelter of the railroad embankment. Here he was gallantly charged by the brigades of Hoke and Atkinson, and driven across the plain to his batteries. Atkinson continuing the pursuit too far, his flank became exposed and at the same time a heavy fire of musketry and artillery was directed against his front. Its ammunition becoming exhausted, and Colonel Atkinson being severely, and Captain E. P. Lawton, [assistant] adjutant-general, mortally, wounded, the brigade was compelled to fall back to the main body, now occupying our original line of battle, with detachments thrown forward to the railroad.

The attack on Hill's left was repulsed by the artillery on that part of the line, against which the enemy directed a hot fire from twenty-four guns. One brigade advanced up Deep Run, sheltered by its banks from our batteries, but was charged and put to flight by the Sixteenth North Carolina, of Pender's brigade, assisted by the Fifty-fourth and Fifty-seventh North Carolina, of Law's brigade, Hood's division.

The repulse of the enemy on our right was decisive, and the attack was not renewed, but his batteries kept up an active fire at intervals, and sharpshooters skirmished along the front during the rest of the afternoon.

While these events were transpiring on our right, the enemy, in formidable numbers, made repeated and desperate assaults upon the left of our line.

About 11 A. M., having massed his troops under cover of the houses of Fredericksburg, he moved forward in strong columns to seize Marye's and Willis' hills. General Ransom advanced Cooke's brigade to the top of the hill, and placed his own, with the exception of the Twenty-fourth North Carolina, a short distance in the rear. All the batteries on the Stafford Heights directed their fire upon the positions occupied by our artillery, with a view to silence it, and cover the movement of the infantry. Without replying to this furious cannonade, our batteries poured a rapid and destructive fire into the dense lines of the enemy as they advanced to the attack, frequently breaking their ranks and forcing them to retreat to the shelter of the houses. Six times did the enemy, notwithstanding the havoc caused by our batteries, press on with great determination to within one hundred yards of the foot of the hill, but here encountering the deadly fire of our infantry, his columns were broken and fled in confusion to the town.

In the third assault, the brave and lamented Brigadier-General Thomas R. R. Cobb fell, at the head of his gallant troops, and, almost at the same moment, Brigadier-General Cooke was borne from the field severely wounded. Fearing that Cobb's brigade might exhaust its ammunition, General Longstreet had directed General Kershaw to take two regiments to its support. Arriving after the fall of General Cobb, he assumed command, his troops taking position on the crest and at the foot of the hill, to which point General Ransom also advanced three other regiments. The Washington Artillery, which had sustained the heavy fire of artillery and infantry with unshaken steadiness and having contributed much to the repulse of the enemy, having exhausted its ammunition, was relieved about 4 P. M. by Colonel Alexander's battalion. The latter occupied the position during the rest of the engagement, and, by its well-directed fire, rendered great assistance in repelling the assaults made in the afternoon, the last of which occurred shortly before dark. This effort met the fate of those that preceded it, and, when night closed in, the shattered masses of the enemy had disappeared in the town, leaving the field covered with dead and wounded. Anderson's division supported the batteries on Longstreet's left, and, though not engaged, was exposed throughout the day to a hot artillery fire, which it sustained with steady courage.

During the night our lines were strengthened by the construction of earthworks at exposed points, and preparations made to receive the enemy next day.

The 14th, however, passed without a renewal of the attack. The enemy's batteries on both sides of the river played upon our lines at intervals, our own firing but little. The sharpshooters on each side skirmished occasionally along the front.

On the 15th the enemy still retained his position, apparently ready for battle, but the day passed as the preceding.

The attack on the 13th had been so easily repulsed, and by so small a part of our army, that it was not supposed the enemy would limit his efforts to an attempt, which, in view of the magnitude of his preparations and the extent

HAMILTON'S CROSSING, NEAR FREDERICKSBURG, VA.

of his force, seemed to be comparatively insignificant. Believing, therefore, that he would attack us, it was not deemed expedient to lose the advantages of our position and expose the troops to the fire of his inaccessible batteries beyond the river, by advancing against him, but we were necessarily ignorant of the extent to which he had suffered, and only became aware of it when, on the morning of the 16th, it was discovered that he had availed himself of the darkness of night and the prevalence of a violent storm of wind and rain, to recross the river. The town was immediately reoccupied and our position on the river bank resumed.

In the engagement more than nine hundred prisoners and nine thousand stands of arms were taken. A large quantity of ammunition was found at Fredericksburg.

The extent of our casualties will appear from the accompanying report of the medical director. We have again to deplore the loss of valuable lives. In Brigadier-Generals Gregg and Cobb the Confederacy has lost two of its noblest citizens and the army two of its bravest and most distinguished officers. The country consents to the sacrifice of such men as these, and the gallant soldiers who fell with them, only to secure the inestimable blessing they died to obtain.

The troops displayed at Fredericksburg in a high degree the spirit and courage that distinguished them throughout the campaign, while the calmness and steadiness with which orders were obeyed and maneuvers executed in the midst of battle evinced the discipline of a veteran army.

The artillery rendered efficient service on every part of the field, and greatly assisted in the defeat of the enemy. The batteries were exposed to an unusually heavy fire of artillery and infantry, which officers and men sustained with a coolness and courage worthy of the highest praise. Those on our right, being without defensive works, suffered more severely. Among those who fell was Lieutenant-Colonel [Lewis M.] Coleman, First Regiment Virginia Artillery, who was mortally wounded while bravely discharging his duty.

To the vigilance, boldness and energy of General Stuart and his cavalry is chiefly due the early and valuable information of the movements of the enemy. His reconnoissances frequently extended within the Federal lines, resulting in skirmishes and engagements, in which the cavalry was greatly distinguished. In the battle of Fredericksburg the cavalry effectually guarded our right, annoying the enemy and embarrassing his movements by hanging on his flank, and attacking when opportunity occurred. The nature of the ground and the relative positions of the armies prevented them from doing more.

To Generals Longstreet and Jackson great praise is due for the disposition and management of their respective corps. Their quick perception enabled them to discover the projected assaults upon their positions, and their ready skill to devise the best means to resist them. Besides their services in the field—which every battle of the campaign, from Richmond to Fredericksburg, has served to illustrate—I am also indebted to them for valuable counsel, both as regards the general operations of the army and the execution of the particular measures adopted.

To division and brigade commanders I must also express my thanks for the prompt, intelligent and determined manner in which they executed their several parts.

To the officers of the general staff—Brigadier-General R. H. Chilton, adjutant and inspector-general, assisted by Major [Henry E.] Peyton; Lieutenant-Colonel [James L.] Corley, chief quartermaster; Lieutenant-Colonel [Robert G.] Cole, chief commissary; Surgeon Guild, medical director, and Lieutenant-Colonel B. G. Baldwin, chief of ordnance—were committed the care of their respective departments, and the charge of supplying the demands upon each. They were always in the field anticipating, as far as possible, the wants of the troops.

* * * * * * *

R. E. LEE, *General.*

BATTLE OF FREDERICKSBURG,

DECEMBER 11 TO 15, 1862.

BY

LIEUTENANT-GENERAL THOMAS J. JACKSON,

Commanding Second Corps.

HEADQUARTERS SECOND CORPS, ARMY OF NORTHERN VIRGINIA,

January 31, 1863.

I HAVE the honor herewith to submit to you a report of the operations of my corps on Saturday, December 13, 1862.

In pursuance to orders, Major-General A. P. Hill moved his division at dawn on the morning of the 12th from his encampment near Yerby's, and relieved Major-General Hood, then posted near Hamilton's Crossing. At the same time Brigadier-General [William B.] Taliaferro, then in command of Jackson's division, moved from his encampment above Guiney's Depot, and took position in rear of Major-General A. P. Hill.

Early on the morning of the 13th Ewell's division, under command of Brigadier-General J. A. Early, and Major-General D. H. Hill, with his division, arrived, after a severe night's march, from their respective encampments in the vicinity of Buckner's Neck and Port Royal, the troops of Major-General D. H. Hill being fifteen to eighteen miles distant from the point to which they were ordered.

On the morning of that day the troops were arranged as follows: Major-General A. P. Hill occupied the front line, formed of two regiments of Field's brigade, commanded by Colonel [J. M.] Brockenbrough, and the brigades of Archer, Lane and Pender (posted from right to left in the order named), his right resting on the road leading from Hamilton's Crossing to the Port Royal Road, and his left extending to within a short distance of Deep Run. These troops were partially concealed by the wood, near the edge of which they were posted. The remainder of Brockenbrough's command, consisting of the Fortieth and Fifty-fifth Virginia, was immediately in rear of Walker's batteries, and acting as a support to them. Of the other two brigades, Gregg's and Thomas', of the same division, the first was in rear of the interval between Archer and Lane, and the second in rear of the interval between Archer and Pender. The divisions under Generals Early and Taliaferro formed the second line, Early being on the right. The divisions of Major-General D. H. Hill, which were further in rear, constituted the reserve. Upon the eminence immediately to the right Lieutenant-Colonel [R. L.] Walker (Major-General A. P. Hill's chief of artillery) had in position fourteen guns, composed of the batteries of Pegram and McIntosh, with sections from the batteries of Crenshaw, Latham and Johnson, commanded respectively by Lieutenants [J.] Ellett, [J. R.] Potts and [Valentine J.] Clutter. On the left of the line, and near the Bernard cabin, were posted twenty-one guns, of the batteries of Captains Davidson, Raine, Caskie and Braxton, all under the immediate direction of Captain Davidson. To the right, and some two hundred yards in front of these, and beyond the railroad, were posted twelve guns from the batteries of Captains Carpenter, Wooding and Braxton, under the direction of Captain Brockenbrough, General Taliaferro's chief of artillery; Carpenter's battery commanded by Lieutenant [George] McKendree, and Braxton's by Lieutenant [Edward A.] Marye. On my left was Major-General [John B.] Hood, of Longstreet's corps, and on my right and front the cavalry, under command of Major-General [J. E. B.] Stuart, with a battery near the Port Royal Road, under the direction of Major [John] Pelham, of the Stuart Horse Artillery, aided in the course of the day by sections from the batteries of Captain [William T.] Poague, Lieutenant [Archibald] Graham commanding; Captains David Watson, B. H. Smith, Jr., [A.W.] Garber, [Willis J.] Dance, and the Louisiana Guards, of my corps, thrown into position so as to cross their fire with the guns of Lieutenant-Colonel Walker, and designed to check the advance of the enemy in that direction.

About 10 o'clock, as the fog disappeared, the lines of the enemy, arranged in order of battle, were distinctly visible in the plain between us and the river, covering my front and extending far to the left toward Fredericksburg. The force in front of me I supposed to number about fifty-five thousand.

Pelham, with part of the Stuart Horse Artillery, was soon engaged with the artillery of the enemy, and a brisk and animated contest was kept up for about an hour. Soon after Pelham, in obedience to orders, had withdrawn from his position on the Port Royal Road, the enemy directed his artillery on the heights, held by Lieutenant-Colonel Walker, and upon the wood generally occupied by our troops, evidently with a view of causing us to disclose whatever troops or artillery were there. Not eliciting any response, the enemy was seemingly satisfied that he would experience but little resistance to an effort to obtain possession of this hill. Accordingly, about 11 o'clock, he advanced by the flank parallel to the Port Royal Road nearly to the road running from thence to Hamilton's Crossing, now unimpeded in his march, as Pelham was withdrawn. Facing to the front, he advanced in line of battle across the plain straight upon the position occupied by Walker. His batteries reserved their fire until the enemy's lines came within less than eight hundred yards, when the fourteen guns opened, pouring such a storm of shot and shell into his ranks as to cause him first to halt, then to waver, and at last to seek shelter by flight.

About 1 o'clock the main attack was made by heavy and rapid discharges of artillery. Under the protection of this warm and well-directed fire his infantry, in heavy force, advanced, seeking the partial protection of a piece of wood extending beyond the railroad. The batteries on the right played on their ranks with destructive effect. The advancing force was visibly staggered by our rapid and well-directed artillery, but soon recovering from the shock, the Federal troops, consisting of the main body of Franklin's grand division, supported by a portion of Hooker's grand division, continued to press forward. Advancing within point-blank range of our infantry, and thus exposed to the murderous fire of musketry and artillery, the struggle became fierce and sanguinary. They continued, however, still to press forward, and before General A. P. Hill closed the interval which he had left between Archer and Lane it was penetrated, and the enemy, pressing forward in overwhelming numbers through that interval, turned Lane's right and Archer's left. Thus attacked in front and rear, the Fourteenth Tennessee and Nineteenth Georgia, of Archer's brigade, and the entire brigade of Lane fell back, but not until after a brave and obstinate resistance. Notwithstanding the perilous situation in which Archer's brigade was placed, his right, changing front, continued to struggle with undaunted firmness, materially checking the advance of the enemy until re-enforcements came to its support. The brigade of General Thomas, posted as before stated, moved gallantly forward, and, joined by the Seventh and part of the Eighteenth North Carolina, of Lane's brigade, gallantly drove back a Federal column which had broken through Lane's line.

In the meantime a large force of the enemy penetrated the wood in rear of the position occupied by the brigades of Lane and Archer, and came in contact with Gregg's brigade. Taken by surprise, Orr's Rifles were thrown into confusion. It was in the act of rallying this regiment that Brigadier-General Maxcy Gregg fell in front of the rifles, mortally wounded. General Gregg was a brave and accomplished officer, full of heroic sentiment and chivalrous honor. He had rendered valuable service in this great struggle for our freedom, and the country has much

POSITION OF THE CONFEDERATE AND FEDERAL PICKETS ON THE RAPPAHANNOCK AT FREDERICKSBURG, DECEMBER 4, 1862.

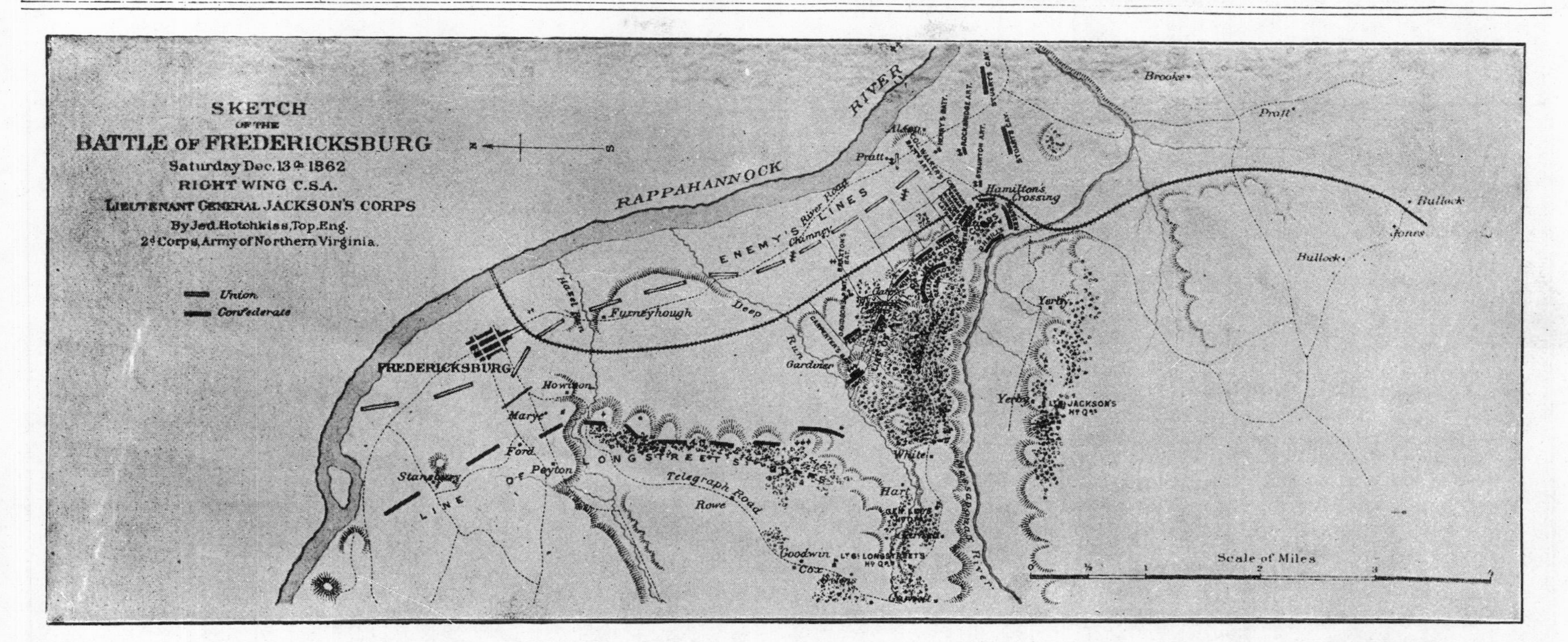

reason to deplore the loss sustained by his premature death.

Colonel Hamilton, upon whom the command of that brigade now devolved, hastened to meet the emergencies of his position, and with the four remaining regiments and one company of the Orr Rifles (Lieutenant [J. D.] Charles) gave the enemy a warm reception. The enemy was not long permitted to hold the advantage which he had thus gained. The second line came promptly to the support of the first. Lawton's brigade, commanded by Colonel [E. N.] Atkinson, subsequently by Colonel [C. A.] Evans; Trimble's brigade, commanded by Colonel R. F. Hoke, and Early's brigade, commanded by Colonel [J. A.] Walker (all under the command of Brigadier-General Early), and the Twenty-second and Forty-seventh Virginia regiments, of Colonel Brockenbrough's command, were already rushing with impetuous valor to the support of the first line. In Taliaferro's command his right regiment—the Second Virginia, of Paxton's brigade—became engaged with part of the enemy, which, after a slight resistance, retreated. The combat in the wood was brief and decisive. The further advance of the enemy was checked. He was driven with great slaughter from the wood to the railroad, the two regiments of Brockenbrough's command, Archer with the first Tennessee and Fifth Alabama Battalion, and the three brigades commanded by Colonels Hoke, Walker and Atkinson, pursuing the retreating Federals to the railroad, where they made a brief stand, when Hoke and Atkinson charged upon them with impetuosity, destroying many in the charge and taking a large number of prisoners. Nor did they stop there, but impelled by an ardor which reflects the highest credit on their courage and patriotism, this comparatively small force pressed the discomfited foe in hot pursuit until they appeared so far within range of his artillery and the fire of a large force of his infantry as to make further pursuit an act of rashness.

In this gallant charge Colonel Atkinson was severely wounded, and fell into the hands of the enemy. Captain E. P. Lawton, assistant adjutant-general of the brigade, though injured during the advance by the fall of his horse, continued to press forward on foot, heroically encouraging the brigade, until he fell, mortally wounded.

During the day some of the guns under Lieutenant-Colonel Walker, becoming short of men and ammunition, and otherwise disabled from further service, were relieved by Captain Poague's battery with two 20-pounder Parrotts. These two pieces actively engaged the enemys' artillery, and afterward opened on the infantry. The exact range of the hill having been accurately obtained by much previous firing, the loss at this point was heavy. It is due to Captain Poague here to state that when, late on the evening previous, he received orders to move his battery, he was distant some sixteen miles from the battlefield, and the promptitude with which he responded to the order by a fatiguing night's march is worthy of notice. Some guns of Major-General D. H. Hill's division were put in at this time on our right, under the direction of his chief of artillery, Major T. H. Carter, which were all well served.

Later in the evening Lieutenant-Colonel [L. M.] Coleman brought up two howitzers from Captain [Willis J.] Dance's battery and placed them on the left of Captain Poague's guns. About this time Lieutenant-Colonel Coleman was severely wounded. On the extreme right, beyond the Massaponax, was a Whitworth gun under the command of Captain Hardaway, of Major-General D. H. Hill's division, which was well served.

On the extreme left the day did not pass without some incidents worthy of notice. Early in the day the enemy opened upon the left with sixteen guns, afterward increased to twenty-four. The officers in command obeyed their orders, and, reserving their fire, the enemy advanced his skirmishers in heavy line upon the points occupied by the commands of Captains Davidson and Brockenbrough. They were soon driven off by canister; but the position of these batteries being thus disclosed to the enemy, a heavy artillery fire was directed upon them, which was replied to with animation and spirit. The ammunition of Captain [C. I.] Raine's battery proving defective, it was withdrawn, and Captain [J. W.] Latimer, acting chief of artillery of Ewell's division, was ordered to take a position still further to the front and left. These last pieces were admirably served, and, though suffering severely from skirmishers and sharpshooters, drove them back, and by the accuracy and rapidity of their fire inflicted a severe loss upon the enemy. As the Federal infantry pressed forward upon our front it was deemed advisable to withdraw the batteries of Captain Brockenbrough, placed in advance of the railroad, before the enemy should seize the point of woods to their right and rear, which they a short time afterward penetrated, the withdrawal of the batteries being covered by Lieutenant-Colonel [J. L.] Hill, of the Seventh North Carolina. The brigade of General Pender was immediately in rear of the batteries of Captains Davidson and Latimer, and was without any protection from the enemy's artillery; and thus, notwithstanding the efficacy of the batteries, acting in conjunction with Major [Chris. C.] Cole, of the Twenty-second North Carolina, in dispersing the cloud of skirmishers and sharpshooters that hung all day upon that part of the line, that brigade received much of the fire that was directed at these guns, and suffered severely. General Pender was himself wounded. The Sixteenth North Carolina, Colonel [John S.] McElroy, which had been thrown out as a support to Latimer's battery, became warmly engaged with a brigade of the enemy, which had advanced up Deep Run under cover, and, acting with two other North Carolina regiments (the Fifty-fourth and Fifty-seventh) of Law's brigade, Hood's division, drove them back.

Repulsed on the right, left and center, the enemy soon after reformed his lines and gave some indications of a purpose to renew the attack. I waited some time to receive it; but he making no forward movement, I determined, if prudent, to do so myself. The artillery of the enemy was so judiciously posted as to make an advance of our troops across the plain very hazardous; yet it was so promising of good results, if successfully executed, as to induce me to make preparations for the attempt. In order to guard

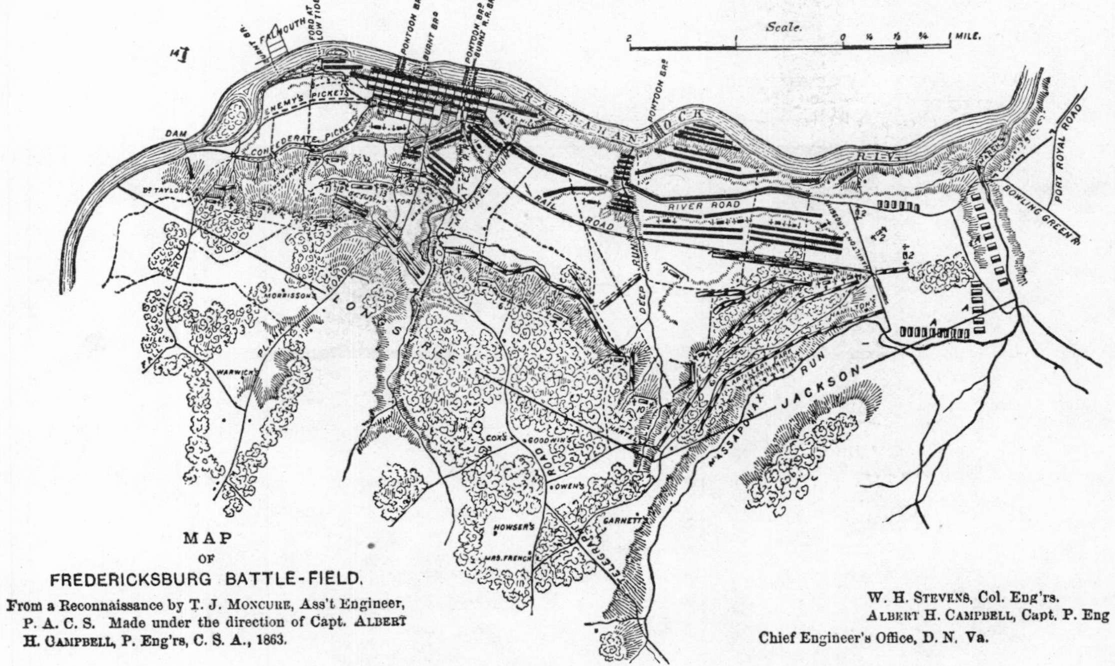

MAP OF FREDERICKSBURG BATTLE-FIELD.

From a Reconnaissance by T. J. Moncure, Ass't Engineer, P. A. C. S. Made under the direction of Capt. Albert H. Campbell, P. Eng'rs, C. S. A., 1863.

W. H. Stevens, Col. Eng'rs.
Albert H. Campbell, Capt. P. Eng
Chief Engineer's Office, D. N. Va.

EXPLANATION OF MAP.

Redoubts represented
Rifle-pits represented
Roads represented
Houses represented
Mills represented
Forests represented
Artillery:
Confederate batteries
Union batteries
Park
Infantry:
Confederate
Union
Confederate cavalry represented
Pontoon bridges
Burned bridges
Railroads

A. Stuart's cavalry, not engaged; Stuart commanded the field artillery on the right flank; Jackson's corps extended from Hamilton's Crossing to Deep Run, and formed connection with Longstreet's Corps.

1. Walker's regiment, composed of Latham's, Letcher's, Braxton's, Pegram's, Crenshaw's, Johnson's and McIntosh's batteries.
2. Pelham's Horse Artillery.
3. Washington Artillery.
4. Read's artillery; 30-pounder Parrott gun on right. General Lee's headquarters during battle.
5. Macon's artillery.
6. Carlton's artillery; 30-pounder Parrott gun on right. Longstreet's corps occupied the left wing in the following order: Anderson on extreme left; Ransom next, McLaws next, Pickett next, Hood next, forming Longstreet's right flank, and resting on Deep Run, to which Jackson's left flank reached. Cobb occupied Marye's Hill and the stone wall below where the fight was thickest. Was reenforced by Cook and Kershaw.
7. McCarthy's battery.
8. Lane's battery; Whitworth gun on right. All of the redoubts were occupied by batteries.
9. Huger's battery.
11. Lewis' battery.
12. Granby's battery.
13. Moran's battery, of Alexander's battalion.
14. Enemy's battery, enfilading stone wall. Anderson's division extends from Dr. Taylor's to plank road; Ransom's and McLaws' divisions extend from plank road crossing Marye's Hill to Telegraph road; Pickett's division extends from Telegraph road along foot to below Battery No. 7; thence, crossing field, to Deep Run. Hood's division, from foot of hill below No. 7, up to battery No. 10. A. P. Hill's division, from Battery No. 10 to Hamilton's Crossing. D. H. Hill in reserve in rear of A. P. Hill. Early in reserve, but had a portion of his troops engaged.

View of Fredericksburg, Va., 1863.

Fredericksburg, Va. The Federal Army on the Heights in the Distance Bombarding the City.

against disaster the infantry was to be preceded by artillery, and the movement postponed until later in the evening, so that, if compelled to retire, it would be under cover of night. Owing to unexpected delays, the movement could not be gotten ready until late in the evening. The first gun had hardly moved forward from the wood one hundred yards when the enemy's artillery reopened, and so completely swept our front as to satisfy me that the proposed movement should be abandoned.

The next day (14th) the divisions under the command of Brigadier-Generals Early and Taliaferro formed the first line, that of Major-General D. H. Hill the second, and the division of Major-General A. P. Hill the reserve. The enemy continued in our front all day, apparently awaiting an attack from us. During the night our lines were again changed, so as to place the division of Major-General D. H. Hill in the front line, Major-General A. P. Hill in the second, and the divisions commanded by Brigadier-Generals Early and Taliaferro the reserve.

On the 15th the enemy still remained in our front, and in the evening of that day sent in a flag of truce requesting a cessation of hostilities between his left and our right wing for the purpose of removing his wounded from the field, which, under previous instructions from the commanding general, was granted.

Our troops patiently remained in position on that, as they had done the previous, day, eagerly awaiting another attack from the enemy, and such was the desire to occupy the front line when such an attack should be made that the division of Major-General D. H. Hill sent in a written request to be permitted to remain in the front line until next day. But our brave troops were disappointed in the expectation of another attack, for while they patiently waited during the night of the 15th, in the hope of another encounter on the following day, and of visiting upon the invaders of their sacred homes and firesides a just retribution for the outrages of this most unprovoked and unchristian war, the enemy hurriedly and silently during that night made good his retreat by recrossing the river.

I herewith forward to you a list of the casualties of this corps on December 13th, from which it will appear that twenty-six officers were killed and five hundred and eight enlisted men missing, making a total loss in this corps of three thousand four hundred and fifteen. Nearly all who are reported as missing were taken prisoners in the fight.

By the official report of Major Bridgford, provost marshal of the corps, it appears that we captured five hundred and twenty-one prisoners, of whom eleven were officers. The report of Major Bridgford exhibits a gratifying statement of the small number who straggled from the ranks during the last action, and affords further evidence of the improving discipline and spirit of the army.

The report of Major Bier, my chief of ordnance, shows that we captured four thousand four hundred and forty-six small arms.

During the action I received valuable assistance in transmitting orders and discharging other duties from the following members of my staff: Colonel S. Crutchfield, chief of artillery; Colonel A. Smead, inspector-general; Captain A. S. Pendleton, assistant adjutant-general; Captain J. K. Boswell, chief engineer; First-Lieutenants J. G. Morrison and J. P. Smith, aids-de-camp, and Second-Lieutenant W. G. Williamson, engineer department.

* * * * * *

T. J. JACKSON, *Lieutenant-General.*

FREDERICKSBURG, VA. REPULSE OF THE FEDERALS IN THEIR ASSAULT ON MARYE'S HILL AND THE BATTERY OF THE WASHINGTON ARTILLERY.

BATTLE OF FREDERICKSBURG.

DECEMBER 11 TO 15, 1862.

BY

LIEUTENANT-GENERAL JAMES LONGSTREET,
Commanding the First Army Corps.

HEADQUARTERS OF THE FIRST ARMY CORPS, DEPARTMENT OF NORTHERN VIRGINIA, NEAR FREDERICKSBURG, VA.

December 20, 1862.

UPON my arrival at Fredericksburg on November 19th the troops of this command were assigned to positions as follows, viz.: McLaws' division upon the heights immediately behind the city and south of the Telegraph Road; Anderson's division on McLaws' left and occupying the heights as far as Taylor's Hill, on the Rappahannock; Pickett's division on McLaws' right, and extending to the rear along the margin of the wood which skirts Deep Run Valley; Hood's division near Hamilton's Crossing of the railroad; Ransom's division in reserve near my headquarters. Our batteries were assigned positions along the heights by General Pendleton, Colonels Cabell and Alexander and Captain [S. R.] Johnston, Colonel Walton being absent sick. Pits were made for the protection of the batteries under the supervision of these officers. A portion of General Pendleton's reserve artillery was assigned to the heights with Major-General McLaws' division. Colonel Walton's Washington Artillery occupied the heights at Marye's Hill, and a portion of Colonel Alexander's reserve occupied the other portion of Anderson's front, extending to the Taylor House, on our left. The brigade batteries that were not assigned to positions on the heights were held in readiness to co-operate with their commands, or for any other service that might be required of them. Our picket line was established along the river bank, extending from Banks' Ford to Talcott Battery, the most important portion of it under the immediate orders of Major-General McLaws.

Upon the approach of General Jackson's army Hood's division was closed in upon the right of General Pickett and put in position upon the heights on the opposite side of Deep Run Valley. In addition to the natural strength of the position, ditches, stone fences and road cuts were found along different portions of the line, and parts of General McLaws' line were further strengthened by rifle trenches and abatis.

The enemy held quiet possession of the Stafford Heights until 3 o'clock on the morning of the 11th, when our signal guns gave notice of his approach. The troops, being at their different camp grounds, were formed immediately and marched to their positions along the line. Ransom's division was ordered to take a sheltered position in easy supporting distance of the batteries on the Marye Hill. Before the troops got to their positions McLaws' pickets (Barksdale's brigade) engaged the enemy at the river, and from time to time drove back different working parties engaged in laying the bridges. The enemy was compelled eventually to abandon his plan of laying his bridges, and began to throw his troops across the river in boats, under cover of the fire of his sharpshooters and one hundred and fifty odd pieces of artillery. At many points along the river bank our troops could get no protection from the artillery fire. This was particularly the case at the mouth of Deep Run, where the enemy succeeded in completing his bridge early in the afternoon. Later in the afternoon he succeeded in throwing large bodies of troops across at the city by using his boats. Barksdale, however, engaged him fiercely at every point, and with remarkable success. Soon after dark General McLaws ordered Barksdale's brigade to retire. The general was so confident of his position that a second order was sent him before he would yield the field. His brigade was then relieved by that of Brigadier-General T. R. R. Cobb, which was placed by General McLaws along the Telegraph Road, in front of the Marye House. A stone fence and cut along this road gave good protection against infantry. When Cobb's brigade got into position Ransom's division was withdrawn and placed in reserve. During the night the enemy finished his bridges and began to throw his troops across.

His movements early on the 12th seemed to be directly against our right, but when the fog lifted columns were seen opposite Fredericksburg, the head of them then crossing at the bridges opposite the city. Ransom's division

MARYE HOUSE, NEAR THE FAMOUS STONE WALL, FREDERICKSBURG, VA.

was moved back to the Marye Hill. Featherston's brigade, of Anderson's division (previously occupying this hill), was closed in upon the other brigades of Anderson. The entire day was occupied by the enemy in throwing his forces across the river and in deploying his columns. Our batteries were opened upon the masses of infantry whenever they were in certain range. Our fire invariably drew that of the enemy's batteries on the opposite heights, and they generally kept up the fire long after our batteries had ceased.

Early on the morning of the 13th I rode to the right of my position (Hood's division). The dense fog in the early twilight concealed the enemy from view, but his commands, "Forward, guide center, march!" were distinctly heard at different points near my right. From the direction of the sound and the position of his troops the day before, I concluded his attack would be upon General Jackson at some point beyond my right. I therefore rode back to a point near the center of my forces, giving notice to General Hood that the enemy would attack General Jackson beyond his right; that he should watch carefully the movements, and when an opportunity offered he should move forward and attack the enemy's flank. Similar instructions were given to General Pickett, with orders to co-operate with General Hood. The attack was made as had been anticipated. It did not appear to have all the force of a real attack, however, and General Hood did not feel authorized to make more than a partial advance. When he did move out he drove the enemy back in handsome style. About 11 A. M. I sent orders for the batteries to play upon the streets and bridges beyond the city, by way of diversion in favor of our right. The batteries had hardly opened when the enemy's infantry began to move out toward my line. Our pickets in front of the Marye House were soon driven in, and the enemy began to deploy his forces in front of that point. Our artillery, being in position, opened fire as soon as the masses became dense enough to warrant it. This fire was very destructive and demoralizing in its effects, and frequently made gaps in the enemy's ranks that could be seen at the distance of a mile. The enemy continued his advance and made his attack at the Marye Hill in handsome style. He did not meet the fire of our infantry with any heart, however, and was therefore readily repulsed. Another effort was speedily made, but with little more success. The attack was again renewed and again repulsed. Other forces were seen preparing for another attack, when I suggested to General McLaws the propriety of re-enforcing his advanced line by a brigade. He had previously re-enforced it with part of General Kershaw's brigade, and ordered forward the balance.

About this time Brigadier-General T. R. R. Cobb fell, mortally wounded, and almost simultaneously Brigadier-General J. R. Cooke was severely wounded. General Kershaw dashed to the front to take command.

General Ransom, on the Marye Hill, was charged with the immediate care of the point attacked, with orders to send forward additional re-enforcements if it should become necessary, and to use Featherston's brigade, Anderson's division, if he should require it.

The attack upon our right seemed to subside about 2 o'clock, when I directed Major-General Pickett to send me two of his brigades. One (Kemper's) was sent to General Ransom, to be placed in some secure position, to be ready in case it should be wanted. The other (Jenkins') was ordered to General McLaws, to replace that of Kershaw in his line. The enemy soon completed his arrangements for a renewed attack, and moved forward with much determination. He met with no better success than he had on the previous occasions. These efforts were repeated and continued, from time to time, until after night, when he left, the field literally strewn with his dead and wounded. Colonel Walton's ammunition was exhausted about sunset, and his batteries were relieved by Colonel Alexander's. Orders were given for fresh supplies of ammunition, and for everything to be prepared for a renewal of the battle at daylight.

On the 14th there was little firing between the sharpshooters. The enemy, screening his forces under a slight descent in the ground, held a position about four hundred yards in front of us. In the afternoon I sent Captain [Osman] Latrobe, of my staff, to the left, to place artillery in position to play along the enemy's line, with instructions to Colonel Alexander to use such artillery there as he might think proper. The point was selected, and pits made by light the following morning. General Ransom was also ordered to strengthen his position on the Marye Hill by rifle-trenches. Similar instructions were sent along the entire line. These preparations were made to meet the grand attack of the enemy, confidently expected on Monday morning. As the attack was not made, this artillery and General Ransom's sharpshooters opened upon the enemy and drove him back to cover in the city.

During the night the enemy recrossed the river. His retreat was not discovered until he had crossed the river and cut his bridges at this end. Our sharpshooters were moved forward and our old positions resumed. Four hundred prisoners, 5,500 stand of small arms, and 250,000 rounds of small-arms ammunition were taken.

Federal Forces Burying Their Dead on the Battlefield in Front of "Stonewall" Jackson's Batteries at Fredericksburg.

Our loss, for the number engaged, was quite heavy. Brigadier-General T. R. R. Cobb fell mortally wounded in the heat of battle on the 13th. He defended his position with great gallantry and ability. In him we have lost one of our most promising officers and statesmen.

Much credit is due Major-General McLaws for his untiring zeal and ability in preparing his troops and his position for a successful resistance, and the ability with which he handled his troops after the attack.

I would also mention as particularly distinguished in the engagement of the 13th Brigadier-Generals Ransom, Kershaw and Cooke (severely wounded), and Colonel McMillan, who succeeded to the command of Cobb's brigade, and Colonel Walton (Washington Artillery), and Lieutenant-Colonel Alexander (reserve artillery).

Brigadier-General Barksdale, with his brigade, held the enemy's entire army at the river bank for sixteen hours, giving us abundance of time to complete our arrangements for battle. A more gallant and worthy service is rarely accomplished by so small a force.

Major-Generals Anderson, Pickett and Hood, with their gallant divisions, were deprived of their opportunity by the unexpected and hasty retreat of the enemy. A portion of General Anderson's command was engaged in defending the passage of the river, a portion of General Hood's in driving back the attack against our right, and a portion of General Pickett's did important service near the Marye Hill.

Major [John J.] Garnett held three batteries in reserve in the valley between the positions of Generals Pickett and Hood, and was much disappointed not to have the opportunity to use them.

My staff officers, Major [G. M.] Sorrel, Lieutenant-Colonel [P. T.] Manning, Major [J. W.] Fairfax, Captains [Osman] Latrobe and [Thomas J.] Goree and Lieutenant [R. W.] Blackwell gave me their usual intelligent, willing aid. Major [John C.] Haskell and Captains H. E. Young and Rodgers volunteered their assistance and rendered important services.

My thanks are also due to Surgeon [J. S. D.] Cullen, chief surgeon; Major [S. P.] Mitchell, chief quartermaster;

Scene at Fredericksburg, Va., after the Bombardment.

Major [R. J.] Moses, chief of the subsistence department, and Captain [J. H.] Manning, signal officer, for the valuable services in their respective departments.

JAMES LONGSTREET,
Lieutenant-General Commanding.

ORGANIZATION OF THE ARMY OF NORTHERN VIRGINIA, AT THE BATTLE OF FREDERICKSBURG,

DECEMBER 11 TO 15, 1862.

GENERAL ROBERT E. LEE,
Commanding.

FIRST CORPS.

Lieutenant-General James Longstreet.

McLaws' Division.

Major-General Lafayette McLaws.

KERSHAW'S BRIGADE.

Brigadier-General Joseph B. Kershaw.

Second South Carolina—Colonel John D. Kennedy.

Third South Carolina—Colonel James D. Nance, Lieutenant-Colonel William D. Rutherford, Major Robert C. Maffett, Captain William W. Hance, Captain John C. Sumner, Captain John K. G. Nance.

Seventh South Carolina—Lieutenant-Colonel Elbert Bland.

BARKSDALE'S BRIGADE.

Brigadier-General William Barksdale.

Thirteenth Mississippi—Colonel J. W. Carter.

Seventeenth Mississippi—Colonel John C. Fiser.

Eighteenth Mississippi—Lieutenant-Colonel W. H. Luse

After the Battle. A Section of the Stone Wall.

Twenty-first Mississippi—Colonel Benjamin G. Humphreys.

Eighth South Carolina—Captain E. T. Stackhouse.

Fifteenth South Carolina*—Colonel W. D. De Saussure.

Third South Carolina Battalion—Lieutenant-Colonel W. G. Rice.

* Transferred from Drayton's brigade November 26, 1862.

COBB'S BRIGADE.

Brigadier-General T. R. R. Cobb; Colonel Robert McMillan.

Sixteenth Georgia—Colonel Goode Bryan.
Eighteenth Georgia—Lieutenant-Colonel S. Z. Ruff.
Twenty-fourth Georgia*—Colonel Robert McMillan.
Cobb Legion.
Phillips Legion – Colonel B. F. Cooke.

SEMMES' BRIGADE.

Brigadier-General Paul J. Semmes.

Tenth Georgia; Fiftieth Georgia;† Fifty-first Georgia;† Fifty-third Georgia.

ARTILLERY.

Colonel H. C. Cabell.‡

Manly's (N. C.) battery; Read's (Ga.) battery; Richmond Howitzers (First), McCarthy's battery; Troup (Ga.) Artillery (Carlton's battery).

BRIGADIER-GENERAL MAXCY GREGG, OF SOUTH CAROLINA.
Killed at Fredericksburg, Va., December 13, 1862.
[From an old photo taken in 1861.]

ANDERSON'S DIVISION.

Major-General Richard H. Anderson.

WILCOX'S BRIGADE.

Brigadier-General Cadmus M. Wilcox.

Eighth Alabama; Ninth Alabama; Tenth Alabama; Eleventh Alabama; Fourteenth Alabama.§

MAHONE'S BRIGADE.

Brigadier-General William Mahone.

Sixth Virginia; Twelfth Virginia; Sixteenth Virginia; Forty-first Virginia; Sixty-first Virginia.

FEATHERSTON'S BRIGADE.

Brigadier-General W. S. Featherston.

Twelfth Mississippi; Sixteenth Mississippi; Nineteenth Mississippi; Forty-eighth Mississippi (five companies).

WRIGHT'S BRIGADE.

Brigadier-General A. R. Wright.

Third Georgia—Colonel Edward J. Walker.
Twenty-second Georgia.
Forty-eighth Georgia—Captain M. R. Hall.
Second Georgia Battalion‖—Captain C. J. Moffett.

PERRY'S BRIGADE.

Brigadier-General E. A. Perry.¶

Second Florida; Fifth Florida; Eighth Florida, Captain David Lang, Captain Thomas R. Love.

ARTILLERY.

Donaldsonville (La.) Artillery—Captain V. Maurin.
Huger's (Va.) battery**—Captain John W. Lewis.
Norfolk (Va.) Light Artillery Blues – Lieutenant William T. Peet.

PICKETT'S DIVISION.

Major-General George E. Pickett.

GARNETT'S BRIGADE.

Brigadier-General Richard B. Garnett.††

Eighth Virginia; Eighteenth Virginia; Nineteenth Virginia; Twenty-eighth Virginia; Fifty-sixth Virginia.

* Transferred from Robertson's brigade November 26, 1862.
† Transferred from Drayton's brigade, November 26, 1862.
‡ Cabell also commanded Nelson's battalion and Branch's, Cooper's, Dearing's, Ells', Eubank's, Lane's, Macon's and Ross' batteries.
§ Transferred from Pryor's brigade November 10, 1862.
‖ Transferred from Cooke's brigade November 26, 1862.
¶ Assigned November 10, 1862.
** Assigned December 1, 1862.
†† Assigned November 26, 1862. Corse was assigned November 6th, *vice* Pickett promoted, and was succeeded by Garnett.

ARMISTEAD'S BRIGADE.

Brigadier-General Lewis A. Armistead.

Ninth Virginia; Fourteenth Virginia; Thirty-eighth Virginia; Fifty-third Virginia; Fifty-seventh Virginia.

KEMPER'S BRIGADE.

Brigadier-General James L. Kemper.

First Virginia; Third Virginia;* Seventh Virginia; Eleventh Virginia; Twenty-fourth Virginia.

JENKINS' BRIGADE.

Brigadier-General M. Jenkins.

First South Carolina (Hagood's); Second South Carolina (Rifles); Fifth South Carolina; Sixth South Carolina; Hampton Legion; Palmetto Sharpshooters.

CORSE'S BRIGADE.†

Brigadier-General Montgomery D. Corse.

Fifteenth Virginia; Seventeenth Virginia; Thirtieth Virginia; Thirty-second Virginia.

ARTILLERY.‡

Dearing's (Va.) battery; Fauquier (Va.) Artillery (Stribling's battery); Richmond (Fayette) Artillery (Macon's battery).§

HOOD'S DIVISION.

Major-General John B. Hood.

LAW'S BRIGADE.

Brigadier-General E. M. Law.

Fourth Alabama; Forty-fourth Alabama;‖ Sixth North Carolina; Fifty-fourth North Carolina, Colonel J. C. S. McDowell; Fifty-seventh North Carolina, Colonel A. C. Godwin.

ANDERSON'S BRIGADE.

Brigadier-General George T. Anderson.

First Georgia (Regulars); Seventh Georgia; Eighth Georgia; Ninth Georgia; Eleventh Georgia.

ROBERTSON'S BRIGADE.

Brigadier-General J. B. Robertson.

Third Arkansas;¶ First Texas; Fourth Texas; Fifth Texas.

TOOMBS' BRIGADE.

Colonel H. L. Benning.

Second Georgia; Fifteenth Georgia; Seventeenth Georgia; Twentieth Georgia.

ARTILLERY.

German (S. C.) Artillery (Bachman's battery); Palmetto (S. C.) Light Artillery (Gorden's battery); Rowan (N. C.) Artillery (Reilly's battery).

RANSOM'S DIVISION.

Brigadier-General Robert Ransom, Jr.

RANSOM'S BRIGADE.

Brigadier-General Robert Ransom, Jr.

Twenty-fourth North Carolina; Twenty-fifth North Carolina, Lieutenant-Colonel S. C. Bryson; Thirty-fifth North Carolina; Forty-ninth North Carolina; Branch's (Va.) battery.

COOKE'S BRIGADE.

Brigadier-General J. R. Cooke; Colonel E. D. Hall.

Fifteenth North Carolina. **
Twenty-seventh North Carolina—Colonel John A. Gilmer, Jr.
Forty-sixth North Carolina—Colonel E. D. Hall.
Forty-eighth North Carolina—Lieutenant-Colonel S. H. Walkup.
Cooper's (Va.) battery.

FIRST CORPS ARTILLERY.††

Washington (La.) Artillery—Colonel J. B. Walton.
First Company—Captain C. W. Squires.
Second Company—Captain J. D. Richardson.
Third Company—Captain M. B. Miller.
Fourth Company—Captain B. F. Eshleman.

ALEXANDER'S BATTALION.

Lieutenant-Colonel E. P. Alexander.

Bidford (Va.) Artillery—Captain Tyler C. Jordan.
Eubank's (Va.) battery—Captain J. L. Eubank.
Madison (La.) Light Artillery—Captain George V. Moody.
Parker's (Va.) battery—Captain William W. Parker.
Rhett's (S. C.) battery—Captain A. B. Rhett.
Woolfolk's (Va.) battery—Captain P. Woolfolk, Jr.

* Transferred from Pryor's brigade November 10, 1862.
† Brigade organized and Corse assigned November 26, 1862.
‡ Other batteries of this division are probably noted as "Miscellaneous," their assignments not being clearly indicated by the reports. Stribling's battery was assigned on December 1, 1862, "for service with the brigade to which it has long been attached."
§ Transferred from McLaws' division December 8, 1862.
‖ Transferred from Wright's brigade November 26, 1862.
¶ Transferred from Cooke's brigade, November 26, 1862.
** Transferred from Cobb's brigade, November 26, 1862.
†† Not assigned to divisions.

SECOND CORPS.

Lieutenant-General Thomas J. Jackson.

D. H. HILL'S DIVISION.

Major-General Daniel H. Hill.

FIRST BRIGADE.

Brigadier-General R. E. Rodes.

Third Alabama; Fifth Alabama; Sixth Alabama; Twelfth Alabama; Twenty-sixth Alabama.

SECOND (RIPLEY'S) BRIGADE.

Brigadier-General George Doles.

Fourth Georgia; Forty-fourth Georgia, Colonel John B. Estes; First North Carolina; Third North Carolina.

THIRD BRIGADE.

Brigadier-General A. H. Colquitt.

Thirteeenth Alabama; Sixth Georgia; Twenty-third Georgia; Twenty-seventh Georgia; Twenty-eighth Georgia.

FOURTH BRIGADE.

Brigadier-General Alfred Iverson.

Fifth North Carolina; Twelfth North Carolina; Twentieth North Carolina; Twenty-third North Carolina.

FIFTH (RAMSEUR'S) BRIGADE.

Colonel Bryan Grimes.

Second North Carolina; Fourth North Carolina; Fourteenth North Carolina; Thirtieth North Carolina.

ARTILLERY.

Major H. P. Jones.

Hardaway's (Ala.) battery; Jeff. Davis (Ala.) Artillery (Bondurant's battery); King William (Va.) Artillery (Carter's battery); Morris (Va.) Artillery (Page's battery); Orange (Va.) Artillery (Fry's battery).

A. P. HILL'S DIVISION.

Major-General Ambrose P. Hill.

FIRST (FIELD'S) BRIGADE.

Colonel J. M. Brockenbrough.

Fortieth Virginia; Forty-seventh Virginia, Colonel Robert M. Mayo; Fifty-fifth Virginia; Twenty-second Virginia Battalion, Lieutenant-Colonel E. P. Taylor.

SECOND BRIGADE.

Brigadier-General Maxcy Gregg; Colonel D. H. Hamilton.

First South Carolina (Provisional Army), Colonel D. H. Hamilton; First South Carolina Rifles; Twelfth South Carolina; Thirteenth South Carolina; Fourteenth South Carolina, Colonel Samuel McGowen.

THIRD BRIGADE.

Brigadier-General E. L. Thomas.

Fourteenth Georgia; Thirty-fifth Georgia; Forty-fifth Georgia; Forty-ninth Georgia.

BRIGADIER-GENERAL THOMAS R. R. COBB, OF GEORGIA.
Killed at Fredericksburg, Va., December 13, 1862.
[From an oil portrait.]

FOURTH BRIGADE.

Brigadier-General J. H. Lane.

Seventh North Carolina—Lieutenant-Colonel J. L. Hill.
Eighteenth North Carolina—Colonel Thomas J. Purdie.
Twenty-eighth North Carolina—Colonel S. D. Lowe.
Thirty-third North Carolina—Colonel Clark M. Avery.
Thirty-seventh North Carolina—Colonel W. M. Barbour.

FIFTH BRIGADE.
Brigadier-General J. J. Archer.

Fifth Alabama Battalion—Major A. S. Van De Graaff, Captain S. D. Stuart.
Nineteenth Georgia—Lieutenant-Colonel A. J. Hutchins.
First Tennessee (Provisional Army)—Colonel Peter Turney, Lieutenant-Colonel N. J. George, Captain M. Turney, Captain H. J. Hawkins.
Seventh Tennessee—Colonel John F. Gardner.
Fourteenth Tennessee—Lieutenant-Colonel J. W. Lockert.

SIXTH BRIGADE.
Brigadier-General William D. Pender; Colonel A. M. Scales.

Thirteenth North Carolina—Colonel A. M. Scales.
Sixteenth North Carolina—Colonel John S. McElroy.
Twenty-second North Carolina—Major Christopher C. Cole.
Thirty-fourth North Carolina.
Thirty-eighth North Carolina.

ARTILLERY.
Lieutenant-Colonel R. L. Walker.

Branch (N. C.) Artillery—Lieutenant J. R. Potts.
Crenshaw's (Va.) battery—Lieutenant J. Ellett.
Fredericksburg (Va.) Artillery—Lieutenant E. A. Marye.
Johnson's (Va.) battery—Lieutenant V. J. Clutter.
Letcher (Va.) Artillery—Captain G. Davidson.
Pee Dee (S. C.) Artillery—Captain D. G. McIntosh.
Purcell (Va.) Artillery—Captain W. J. Pegram.

EWELL'S DIVISION.*
Brigadier-General Jubal A. Early.

LAWTON'S BRIGADE.
Colonel E. N. Atkinson; Colonel C. A. Evans.

Thirteenth Georgia—Colonel J. M. Smith.
Twenty-sixth Georgia—Captain B. F. Grace.
Thirty-first Georgia—Colonel C. A. Evans.
Thirty-eighth Georgia—Captain W. L. McLeod.
Sixtieth Georgia—Colonel W. H. Stiles.
Sixty-first Georgia—Colonel J. H. Lamar and Major C. W. McArthur.

TRIMBLE'S BRIGADE.
Colonel R. F. Hoke.

Fifteenth Alabama; Twelfth Georgia; Twenty-first Georgia, Lieutenant-Colonel Thomas W. Hooper; Twenty-first North Carolina; First North Carolina Battalion.

EARLY'S BRIGADE.
Colonel J. A. Walker.

Thirteenth Virginia, Lieutenant-Colonel J. B. Terrill; Twenty-fifth Virginia; Thirty-first Virginia; Forty-fourth Virginia; Forty-ninth Virginia; Fifty-second Virginia; Fifty-eighth Virginia.

HAYS' (FIRST LOUISIANA) BRIGADE.
Brigadier-General Harry T. Hays.

Fifth Louisiana; Sixth Louisiana; Seventh Louisiana; Eighth Louisiana; Ninth Louisiana.

FORGE DAM ON THE RAPPAHANNOCK RIVER, NEAR FREDERICKSBURG, VA.

ARTILLERY.
Captain J. W. Latimer.

Charlottesville (Va.) Artillery—Captain J. McD. Carrington.
Chesapeake (Md.) Artillery—Lieutenant John E. Plater.
Courtney (Va.) Artillery—Lieutenant W. A. Tanner.
First Maryland Battery—Captain William F. Dement.
Louisiana Guard Artillery—Captain Louis E. D'Aquin.
Staunton (Va.) Artillery—Lieutenant Asher W. Garver.

JACKSON'S DIVISION.
Brigadier-General William B. Taliaferro.

FIRST BRIGADE.
Brigadier-General E. F. Paxton.

Second Virginia—Captain J. Q. A. Nadenbousch.
Fourth Virginia—Lieutenant-Colonel R. D. Gardner; Major William Terry.

* From division returns for December 10, 1862, and Early's report.

Fifth Virginia—Lieutenant-Colonel H. J. Williams.
Twenty-seventh Virginia—Lieutenant-Colonel J. K. Edmondson.
Thirty-third Virginia—Colonel Edwin G. Lee.

SECOND BRIGADE.
Brigadier-General J. R. Jones.

Twenty-first Virginia; Forty-second Virginia; Forty-eighth Virginia; First Virginia Battalion.

THIRD (TALIAFERRO'S) BRIGADE.
Colonel E. T. H. Warren.

Forty-seventh Alabama—Captain James M. Campbell.
Forty-eighth Alabama—Captain C. B. St. John.
Tenth Virginia—Captain W. B. Yancey.
Twenty-third Virginia—Captain A. J. Richardson.
Thirty-seventh Virginia—Colonel T. V. Williams.

FOURTH (STARKE'S) BRIGADE.
Colonel Edmund Pendleton.

First Louisiana (Volunteers)—Lieutenant-Colonel M. Nolan.
Second Louisiana—Major M. A. Grogan.
Tenth Louisiana—Major John M. Legett.
Fourteenth Louisiana—Captain H. M. Verlander.
Fifteenth Louisiana—Lieutenant-Colonel McG. Goodwyn.
Coppen's (La.) Battalion.

ARTILLERY.
Captain J. B. Brockenbrough.

Carpenter's (Va.) battery—Lieutenant George McKendree.
Danville (Va.) Artillery—Captain G. W. Wooding.
Hampden (Va.) Artillery—Captain W. H. Caskie.
Lee (Va.) Artillery—Lieutenant C. W. Statham.
Lusk's (Va.) battery.

RESERVE ARTILLERY.*
Brigadier-General W. N. Pendleton.

BROWN'S BATTALION.
Colonel J. Thompson Brown.

Brook's (Va.) battery; Dance's battery, Powhatan Artillery;† Hupp's battery, Salem Artillery;† Poague's (Va.) battery, Rockbridge Artillery; Smith's battery, Third Howitzers;† Watson's battery, Second Howitzers.†

CUTTS' (GA.) BATTALION.

Lane's battery; Patterson's battery; Ross' battery, Captain H. M. Ross.

NELSON'S BATTALION.
Major William Nelson.

Kirkpatrick's (Va.) battery, Amherst Artillery; Massie's (Va.) battery, Fluvanna Artillery; Milledge's (Ga.) battery.

MISCELLANEOUS BATTERIES.‡

Ell's (Ga.) battery.
Nelson's (Va.) battery, Hanover Artillery—Captain G. W. Nelson.

CAVALRY.§
Major-General James E. B. Stuart.

FIRST BRIGADE.‖
Brigadier-General Wade Hampton.

First North Carolina—Colonel L. S. Baker.
First South Carolina—Colonel J. L. Black.
Second South Carolina—Colonel M. C. Butler.
Cobb (Ga.) Legion—Lieutenant-Colonel P. M. B. Young.
Phillips (Ga.) Legion—Lieutenant-Colonel William W. Rich.

SECOND BRIGADE.
Brigadier-General Fitzhugh Lee.

First Virginia—Colonel James H. Drake.
Second Virginia—Colonel Thomas T. Munford.
Third Virginia—Colonel T. H. Owen.
Fourth Virginia—Colonel W. C. Wickham.
Fifth Virginia.¶

THIRD BRIGADE.
Brigadier-General W. H. F. Lee.

Second North Carolina—Colonel S. Williams.
Ninth Virginia—Colonel R. L. T. Beale.
Tenth Virginia—Colonel J. Lucius Davis.
Thirteenth Virginia—Colonel J. R. Chambliss, Jr.
Fifteenth Virginia—Colonel W. B. Ball.

* Majors Garnett, Hamilton and T. J. Page, Jr., are mentioned in the reports as commanding artillery battalions, but their composition is not stated.
† Of the First Virginia Light Artillery.
‡ Mentioned in the reports, but assignments not indicated.
§ Organization of brigades as established November 10, 1862. On roster for December 16, 1862. Hart's, Breathed's, Moorman's and Chew's batteries appear as attached, respectively, to the First, Second, Third and Fourth Brigades. Commanders are given as reported December 16, 1862.
‖ Detachment on raid to Dumfries.
¶ Transferred from Third Brigade between November 10th and December 31st.

FOURTH BRIGADE.*
Brigadier-General W. E. Jones.

Sixth Virginia—Colonel John S. Green.
Seventh Virginia—Colonel R. H. Dulanoy.
Twelfth Virginia—Colonel A. W. Harman.
Seventeenth Virginia Battalion—Lieutenant-Colonel O. R. Funsten.
White's (Va.) Battalion—Major E. V. White.

HAULING PONTOONS.

ARTILLERY.
Major John Pelham.

Breathed's (Va.) Battery—Captain J. Breathed.
Chew's (Va.) Battery—Captain R. P. Chew.
Hart's (S. C.) Battery—Captain J. F. Hart.
Henry's (Va.) Battery—Captain M. W. Henry.
Moorman's (Va.) Battery—Captain M. M. Moorman.

* In the Shenandoah Valley.

THE STONE'S RIVER CAMPAIGN,

DECEMBER 31, 1862, TO JANUARY 3, 1863,

INCLUDING BATTLES OF

STONE'S RIVER AND MURFREESBORO.

BY

GENERAL BRAXTON BRAGG.
Commanding Army of Tennessee.

HEADQUARTERS ARMY OF TENNESSEE,
TULLAHOMA, TENN., February 23, 1863.

On December 26th last, the enemy advanced in force from Nashville to attack us at Murfreesboro. It had been well ascertained that his strength was over sixty thousand effective men. Before night on that day the object of the movement was developed by our dispositions in front, and orders were given for the necessary concentration of our forces, then distributed as follows: Polk's corps and three brigades of Breckinridge's division, Hardee's corps, at Murfreesboro; the balance of Hardee's corps near Eagleville, about twenty miles west of Murfreesboro; McCown's division (which, with Stevenson's division removed, constituted Smith's corps) at Readyville, twelve miles east of Murfreesboro, the three cavalry brigades of Wheeler, Wharton and Pegram occupying the entire front of our infantry and covering all approaches to within ten miles of Nashville; Buford's small cavalry brigade of about six hundred, at McMinnville. The brigades of Forrest and Morgan (about five thousand effective cavalry) were absent on special service in West Tennessee and Northern Kentucky, as will be more fully noticed hereafter. Jackson's small infantry brigade was in rear, guarding the railroad from Bridgeport, Ala., to the mountains.

On Sunday, the 28th, our main force of infantry and artillery was concentrated in front of Murfreesboro, while the cavalry, supported by three brigades of infantry and three batteries of artillery, impeded the advance of the enemy by constant skirmishing and sudden and unexpected attacks. To the skillful manner in which the cavalry, thus ably supported, was handled, and to the exceeding gallantry of its officers and men, must be attributed the four days' time consumed by the enemy in reaching the battlefield, a distance of only twenty miles from his encampments, over fine macadamized roads.

Fully aware of the greatly superior numbers of the enemy, it was our policy to await attack. The position was selected and line developed with this intention. Owing to the convergence upon our depot at Murfreesboro of so many fine roads by which the enemy could approach, as will appear by the map, we were confined in our selection to a line near enough the point of juncture to enable us to successfully cover them all until the real point of attack should be developed.

On Monday, the 29th, it was reported that heavy columns moved on both the direct road from La Vergne and on the one leading into the Lebanon road by way of Jefferson, but on Tuesday, the 30th, it was ascertained that the Jefferson Pike was abandoned by a countermarch and the whole forces of the enemy were concentrated on and near the direct road on the west of Stone's River. The dispositions of troops made for the unequal contest were all

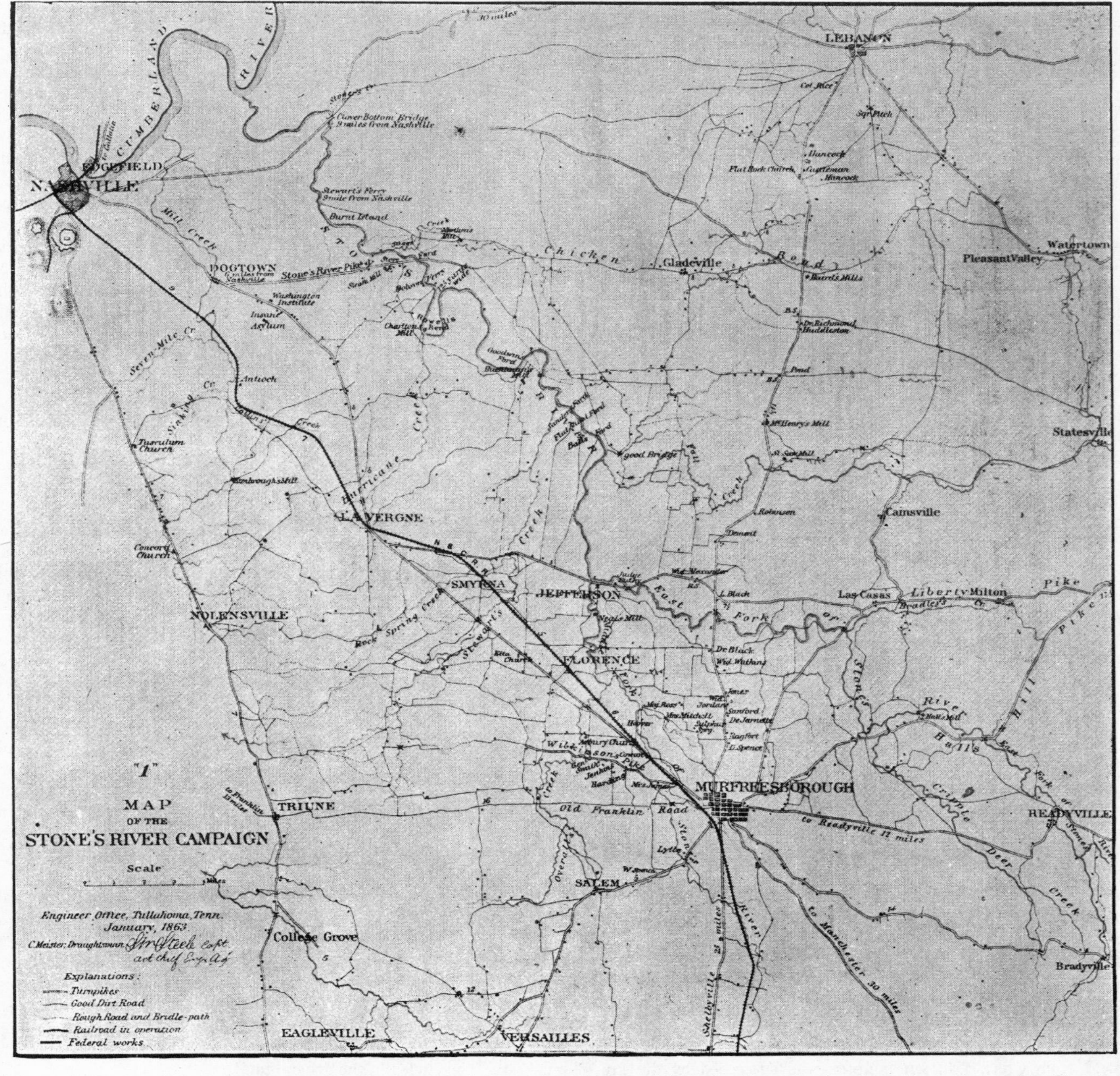

completed before the enemy crossed Stewart's Creek, nine miles out, and the infantry brigades were at once called in and the cavalry was ordered to fall back more rapidly, having most gallantly discharged its duty and fully accomplished the object desired.

Late on Monday it became apparent the enemy was extending his right, so as to flank us on the left. McCown's division, in reserve, was promptly thrown to that flank and added to the command of Lieutenant-General Polk. The enemy not meeting our expectations of making an attack on Tuesday, which was consumed in artillery firing and heavy skirmishing, with the exception of a dash late in the evening on the left of Withers' division, which was repulsed and severely punished, it was determined to assail him on Wednesday morning, the 31st. For this purpose Cleburne's division, Hardee's corps, was moved from the second line on the right to the corresponding position on the left, and Lieutenant-General Hardee was ordered to that point and assigned to the command of that and McCown's division. This disposition, the result of necessity, left me no reserve, but Breckinridge's command on the right, now not threatened, was regarded as a source of supply for any re-enforcements absolutely necessary to other parts of the field. Stone's River, at its then stage, was fordable at almost any point for infantry, and at short intervals perfectly practicable for artillery.

These dispositions completed, Lieutenant-General Hardee was ordered to assail the enemy at daylight on Wednesday, the 31st, the attack to be taken up by Lieutenant-General Polk's command in succession to the right flank, the move to be made by a constant wheel to the right, on Polk's right flank as a pivot, the object being to force the enemy back on Stone's River, and, if practicable, by the aid of the cavalry, cut him off from his base of operations and supplies by the Nashville pike. The lines were now bivouacked at a distance in places of not more than five hundred yards, the camp-fires of the two being within distinct view. Wharton's cavalry brigade had been held on our left to watch and check the movements of the enemy in that direction and to prevent his cavalry from gaining the railroad in our rear, the preservation of which was of vital importance. In this he was aided by Brigadier-General A. Buford, who had a small command of about six hundred new cavalry. The duty was most ably, gallantly and successfully performed.

On Monday night Brigadier-General Wheeler proceeded with his cavalry brigade and one regiment from Pegram's, as ordered, to gain the enemy's rear. By Tuesday morning, moving on the Jefferson pike around the enemy's left flank, he had gained the rear of their whole army, and soon attacked the trains, their guards and the numerous stragglers. He succeeded in capturing several hundred prisoners and destroying hundreds of wagons loaded with supplies and baggage. After clearing the road he made his way entirely around and joined the cavalry on our left.

The failure of Major-General McCown to execute during the night an order for a slight change in the line of his division, and which had to be done the next morning, caused some delay in the general and vigorous assault by Lieutenant-General Hardee. But about 7 o'clock the rattle of musketry and roar of artillery announced the beginning of the conflict. The enemy was taken completely by surprise. General and staff officers were not mounted, artillery horses not hitched and infantry not formed. A hot and inviting breakfast of coffee and other luxuries, to which our gallant and hardy men had long been strangers, was found upon the fire unserved, and was left while we pushed on to the enjoyment of a more inviting feast—that of captured artillery, fleeing battalions and hosts of craven prisoners begging for the lives they had forfeited by their acts of brutality and atrocity.

While thus routing and pushing the enemy in his front, Lieutenant-General [W. J.] Hardee announced to me by a messenger that the movement was not being as promptly executed by Major-General Cheatham's command on his right (the left of Lieutenant-General Polk's corps) as he expected, and that his line was, consequently, exposed to an enfilade fire from the enemy's artillery in that front. The necessary instructions for prompt movement at that point were immediately dispatched, and in a short time our whole line, except Breckinridge's command, was warmly engaged. From this time we continued to drive the enemy more or less rapidly until his line was thrown entirely back at right angles to his first position, and occupied the cut of the railroad, along which he had massed his reserve and posted very strong batteries.

The enemy's loss was very heavy in killed and wounded, far exceeding our own, as appeared from a critical examination of the field, now almost entirely in our possession. Of artillery alone we had secured more than twenty-five pieces.

While the infantry and artillery were occupied in this successful work, Brigadier-General Wharton, with his cavalry command, was most actively and gallantly engaged on the enemy's right and rear, where he inflicted a heavy loss in killed and wounded, captured a full battery of artillery endeavoring to escape, and secured and sent in near two thousand prisoners. These important successes and results had not been achieved without heavy sacrifices on our part, as the resistance of the enemy after the first surprise was most gallant and obstinate. Numbering at least two to our one, he was enabled to bring fresh troops at every point to resist our progress, and he did so with a skill and judgment which have ever characterized his able commander. Finding Lieutenant-General Hardee so formidably opposed by the movement of the enemy to his front, re-enforcements for him were ordered from Major-General Breckinridge, but the orders were countermanded, as will hereafter appear, and Polk's corps was pressed forward with vigor, hoping to draw the enemy back, or rout him on the right, as he already had been on the left. We succeeded in driving him from every position except the strong one held by his extreme left flank, resting on Stone's River, and covered by a concentration of artillery of superior range and caliber, which seemed to bid us defiance. The difficulties of our general advance had been greatly enhanced by the topography of the country. All parts of our line had to pass, in their progress, over ground of the roughest character, covered with huge stones and studded with the densest growth of cedar, the branches reaching to the ground, and forming an almost impassable brake. Our artillery could rarely be used, while the enemy, holding defensive lines, had selected formidable positions for his batteries and this dense cover for his infantry, from both of which he had to be dislodged by our infantry alone. The determined and unvarying gallantry of our troops and the uninterrupted success which attended their repeated charges against these strongholds, defended by double their numbers, fully justified the unbounded confidence I had ever reposed in them and had so often expressed. To meet our successful advance and retrieve his losses in the front of our left, the enemy early transferred a portion of his reserves from his left to that flank, and by 2 o'clock had succeeded in concentrating such a force in Lieutenant-General Hardee's front as to check his further progress. Our two lines had by this time become almost blended, so much weakened were they by losses, exhaustion and extension to cover the enemy's whole front.

As early as 10 A. M. Major-General Breckinridge was called on for one brigade, and soon after for a second, to re-enforce, or act as a reserve to, Lieutenant-General Hardee. His reply to the first call represented the enemy crossing Stone's River in heavy force in his immediate front, and in receiving the second order he informed me they had already crossed in heavy force and were advancing on him in two lines. He was immediately ordered not to await attack, but to advance and meet them. About this same time a report reached me that a heavy force of the enemy's infantry was advancing on the Lebanon Road, about five miles in Breckinridge's front. Brigadier-General Pegram, who had been sent to that road to cover the flank of the infantry with his cavalry brigade (save two regiments detached with Wheeler and Wharton), was ordered forward immediately to develop any such movement. The orders for the two brigades from Breckinridge were countermanded, while dispositions were made, at his request, to re-enforce him. Before they could be carried out the movements ordered disclosed the facts that no force had crossed Stone's River; that the only enemy in our immediate front there was a small body of sharpshooters, and that there was no advance on the Lebanon Road. These unfortunate misapprehensions on that part of the field (which, with proper precautions, could not have existed) withheld from active operations three fine brigades until the enemy had succeeded in checking our progress, had re-established his lines and had collected many of his broken battalions. Having now settled the question that no movement was being made against our right, and none even to be apprehended, Breckinridge was ordered to leave two brigades to support the battery at A, on his side of Stone's River, and with the balance of the force to cross to the left and report to Lieutenant-General Polk. By the time this could be accomplished it was too late to send this force to Lieutenant-General Hardee's support, who was unable to make further progress, and he was directed to maintain his position. Lieutenant-General Polk was directed with these re-enforcements to throw all the force he could collect upon the enemy's extreme left, and thereby either carry that strong point, which had so far resisted us successfully, or, failing in that, at least to draw off from Hardee's front the formidable opposition there concentrated. The three brigades of Jackson, Preston and Adams were successively reported for this work. How gallantly they moved to their task, and how much they suffered in the determined effort to accomplish it, will best appear from reports of subordinate commanders and the statement of losses herewith. Upon this flank, their strongest defensive position, resting on the river bank, the enemy had concentrated not less than twenty pieces of his heaviest artillery, masked almost entirely from view, but covering an open space in front of several hundred yards. Supported right, left and rear by heavy masses of infantry, this position proved impracticable, and after two unsuccessful efforts the attempt to carry it by infantry was abandoned. Our heaviest batteries of artillery and rifled guns of long range were now concentrated in front of, and their fire opened on, this position.

After a cannonade of some time the enemy's fire slackened, and finally ceased near nightfall. Lieutenant-General Hardee had slightly retired his line from the furthest point he had attained for better position and cover without molestation from the enemy. Lieutenant-General Polk's infantry, including the three re-enforcing brigades, uniting their left with Hardee's right and extending to our extreme right flank, formed a continuous line very nearly perpendicular to the original line of battle, thus leaving nearly the whole field with all its trophies—the enemy's dead and many of his wounded, his hospitals and stores—in our full possession. The body of Brigadier-General Sill, one of their division commanders, was found where he had fallen, and was sent to town and decently interred, though he had forfeited all claim to such consideration by the acts of cruelty, barbarity and atrocity but a few days before committed under his authority on the women, children and old men living near the road on which he had made a reconnoissance.

During the afternoon, Brigadier-General Pegram, discovering a hospital and large numbers of stragglers in rear of the enemy's line and across Stone's River, charged them with his cavalry and captured about one hundred and seventy prisoners.

Both armies, exhausted by a conflict of fully ten hours' duration, rarely surpassed for its continued intensity and the heavy losses sustained, sank to rest with the sun, and perfect quiet prevailed for the night.

At dawn on Thursday morning, January 1st, orders were sent to the several commanders to press forward their skirmishers, feel the enemy, and report any change in his position. Major-General Breckinridge had been transferred to the right of Stone's River, to resume the command of that position, now held by two of his brigades. It was soon reported that no change had occurred, except the withdrawal of the enemy from the advanced position occupied by his left flank. Finding, upon further examination, that this was the case, the right flank of Lieutenant-General Polk's corps was thrown forward to occupy the ground for which we had so obstinately contended the evening before. This shortened our line considerably, and gave us possession of the entire battlefield, from which we gleaned the spoils and trophies throughout the day and transferred them rapidly to the rear. A careful reconnoissance of the enemy's position was ordered and most of the cavalry was put in motion for the roads in his rear, to cut off his trains and develop any movement. It was soon ascertained that he was still in very heavy force all along our front, occupying a position strong by nature and improved by such work as could be done at night and by his reserves.

In a short time reports from the cavalry informed me heavy trains were moving toward Nashville, some of the wagons loaded and all the ambulances filled with wounded. These were attacked at different places; many wagons were destroyed and hundreds of prisoners paroled. No doubt this induced the enemy to send large escorts of artillery, infantry and cavalry with later trains, and thus the impression was made on our ablest cavalry commanders that a retrograde movement was going on. Our forces, greatly wearied and much reduced by heavy losses, were held ready to avail themselves of any change in the enemy's position, but it was deemed unadvisable to assail him as then established. The whole day, after these dispositions, was passed without an important movement on either side, and was consumed by us in gleaning the battlefield, burying the dead and replenishing ammunition.

At daylight on Friday, the 2d, the orders to feel the enemy and ascertain his position were repeated, with the same results. The cavalry brigades of Wheeler and Wharton had returned during the night greatly exhausted from long-continued service with but little rest or food to either men or horses. Both commanders reported the indications from the enemy's movements the same. Allowing them only a few hours to feed and rest, and sending the two detached regiments back to Pegram's brigade, Wharton was ordered to the right flank across Stone's River, to assume command in that quarter and keep me advised of any change. Wheeler with his brigade was ordered to gain the enemy's rear again, and remain until he could definitely report whether any retrograde movement was being made. Before Wharton had taken his position, observation excited my suspicions in regard to a movement having been made by the enemy across Stone's River immediately in Breckinridge's front. Reconnoissances by several staff officers soon developed the fact that a division had quietly crossed unopposed and established themselves on and under cover of an eminence, from which Lieutenant-General Polk's line was both commanded and enfiladed. The dislodgment of this force or the withdrawal of Polk's line was an evident necessity. The latter involved consequences not to be entertained. Orders were accordingly given for the concentration of the whole of Major-General Breckinridge's division in front of the position to be taken, the addition to his command of ten 12-pounder Napoleon guns, under Captain F. H. Robertson, an able and accomplished artillery officer, and for the cavalry forces of Wharton and

General Braxton Bragg, of Louisiana.

Pegram, about two thousand men, to join in the attack on his right. Major-General Breckinridge was sent for and advised of the movement and its objects, the securing and holding of the position which protected Polk's flank and gave us command of the enemy's by which to enfilade him. He was informed of the forces placed at his disposal, and instructed to drive the enemy back, crown the hill, intrench his artillery, and hold the position. To distract their attention from our real object, a heavy artillery fire was ordered to be opened from Polk's front at the exact hour at which the movement was to begin. At other points throughout both lines all was quiet. General Breckinridge, at 3:30 P. M., reported he would advance at 4 o'clock. Polk's batteries promptly opened fire and were soon answered by the enemy. A heavy cannonade of some fifteen minutes was succeeded by the fire of musketry, which soon became general. The contest was short and severe; the enemy was driven back and the eminence gained, but the movement as a whole was a failure, and the position was again yielded. Our forces were moved, unfortunately, so far to the banks as to throw a portion of them into and over Stone's River, where they encountered heavy masses of the enemy, while those against whom they were intended to operate on our side of the river had a destructive enfilade on our whole line. Our second line was so close to the front as to receive the enemy's fire, and, returning it, took their friends in rear. The cavalry force was left entirely out of the action. Learning from my own staff officers, sent to the scene, of the disorderly retreat being made by General Breckinridge's division, Brigadier-General Patton Anderson's fine brigade of Mississippians (the nearest body of troops) was promptly ordered to his relief.

On reaching the field and moving forward, Anderson found himself in front of Breckinridge's infantry, and soon encountered the enemy's light troops close upon our artillery, which had been left without support. This noble brigade, under its cool and gallant chief, drove the enemy back and saved all the guns not captured before its arrival. Captain F. H. Robertson, after the disabling wound received by Major [R. E.] Graves (General Breckinridge's gallant and efficient chief of artillery), took the entire charge of all the artillery of the division, in addition to his own. To his gallantry, energy and fearlessness is due the smallness of our loss sustained before the arrival of support—only three guns. Before the end of the whole movement it was quite dark. Anderson's command held a position next the enemy, corresponding nearly with our original line, while Breckinridge's brigade commanders collected their scattered men, as far as practicable in the darkness, and took irregular positions on Anderson's left and rear. At daylight in the morning they were moved to the front, and the whole line re-established without opposition. During the night Major-General Cleburne's division was re-transferred to its original position on the right, and Lieutenant-General Hardee directed to resume his command there and restore our line.

On Saturday morning, the 3d, our forces had been in line of battle for five days and nights, with but little rest, having no reserves; their baggage and tents had been loaded, and the wagons were four miles off; their provisions, if cooked at all, were most imperfectly prepared with scanty means; the weather had been severe from cold and almost constant rain, and we had no change of clothing, and in many places could not have fires. The necessary consequence was great exhaustion of officers and men, many having to be sent to the hospitals in the rear, and more still were beginning to straggle from their commands an evil from which we had so far suffered but little. During the whole of this day the rain continued to fall with little intermission, and the rapid rise in Stone's River indicated that it would soon be unfordable. Late on Friday night I had received the captured papers of Major-General [A. McD.] McCook, commanding one corps d'armee of the enemy, showing their effective strength to have been very near, if not quite, seventy thousand men. Before noon reports from Brigadier-General Wheeler satisfied me the enemy, instead of retiring, was receiving re-enforcements Common prudence and the safety of my army, upon which even the safety of our cause depended, left no doubt on my mind as to the necessity of my withdrawal from so unequal a contest. My orders were accordingly given about noon for the movement of the trains, and for the necessary preparation of the troops.

Under the efficient management of the different staff departments, everything had been secured and transferred to the rear, including prisoners, captured artillery, small arms, subsistence, means of transportation, and nearly all our wounded able to bear moving. No movement of any kind was made by the troops on either side during this most inclement day, until just at night, when a sharp skirmish occurred between Polk's right and the enemy's left flank, resulting in nothing decisive. The only question with us was, whether the movement should be made at once, or delayed for twenty-four hours, to save a few more of our wounded. As it was probable we should lose by exhaustion as many as we should remove of the wounded, my inclination to remain was yielded. The whole force, except the cavalry, was put in motion at 11 P. M., and the army retired in perfect order to its present position behind Duck River, without receiving or giving a shot. Our cavalry held the position before Murfreesboro until Monday morning, the 5th, when it quietly retired, as ordered, to cover our front.

We left about twelve hundred badly wounded, one-half of whom we learn have since died from the severity of their injuries; about three hundred sick, too feeble to bear transportation, and about two hundred well men and medical officers as their attendants. In addition to this, the enemy had captured about eight hundred prisoners from us. As the twelve hundred wounded are counted once under that head among our losses, they should be excluded in the general total.

As an offset to this loss, we had secured considerably over six thousand prisoners; had captured over thirty pieces of artillery, six thousand stand of small-arms, a number of wagons, ambulances, mules and harness, with a large amount of other valuable property, all of which was secured and appropriated to proper uses. Besides all this secured, we had destroyed not less than eight hundred wagons, mostly loaded with various articles, such as arms, ammunition, provisions, baggage, clothing, medicines and hospital stores. We had lost three pieces of artillery only —all in Breckinridge's repulse.

A number of stand of colors (nine of which are forwarded with this report) was also captured on the field. Others known to have been taken have not been sent in. A tabular statement of our forces shows the number of fighting men we had on the field on the morning of December 31st to have been less than thirty-five thousand, of which about thirty thousand were infantry and artillery. Our losses are also reported in this same comprehensive table, so as to show how much each corps, division and brigade suffered, and, in case of Breckinridge's division, the losses are reported separately for Wednesday and Friday. These reports are minute and suggestive, showing the severity of the conflict, as well as when, where and by whom it was sustained.

Among the gallant dead the nation is called to mourn, none could have fallen more honored or regretted than

Brigadier-Generals James E. Rains and R. W. Hanson.

Brigadier-Generals James R. Chalmers and D. W. Adams received disabling wounds on Wednesday.

During the time the operations at Murfreesboro were being conducted, important expeditions, under Brigadier-Generals Forrest and Morgan, were absent in West Tennessee and Northern Kentucky.

* * * * * *

BRAXTON BRAGG,
General Commanding.

BATTLE OF MURFREESBORO,

DECEMBER 31, 1862, TO JANUARY 2, 1863.

BY

GENERAL J. C. BRECKINRIDGE.

HEADQUARTERS BRECKINRIDGE'S DIVISION,
January —, 1863.

ON the morning of Sunday, the 28th of December, the brigades moved from their encampments and took up line of battle about one and a half miles from Murfreesboro in the following order: Adams' brigade on the right, with its right resting on the Lebanon Road and its left extending toward the ford over Stone's River a short distance below the destroyed bridge on the Nashville Turnpike; Preston on the left of Adams; Palmer on the left of Preston, and Hanson forming the left of the line, with his left resting on the right bank of the river near the ford. The right of Major-General Withers, of Lieutenant-General Polk's corps, resting near the left bank of the river and slightly in advance of Hanson's left.

Brigadier-General Jackson, having reported to me with his command, was placed, by the direction of the lieutenant-general commanding, upon the east side of the Lebanon Road, on commanding ground, a little in advance of the right of Brigadier-General Adams.

My division formed the front line of the right wing of the army. Major-General Cleburne's division, drawn up some six hundred yards in rear, formed the second line of the same wing, while the division of Major-General McCown, under the immediate direction of the general commanding, composed the reserve. My line extended from left to right along the edge of a forest, save an open space of four hundred yards, which was occupied by Wright's battery of Preston's brigade, with the Twentieth Tennessee in reserve to support it. An open field eight hundred yards in width extended along nearly the whole front of the line, and was bounded on the opposite side by a line of forest similar to that occupied by us. In the opinion of the lieutenant-general commanding (who had twice ridden carefully over the ground with me) and the general commanding, who had personally inspected the lines, it was the strongest position the nature of the ground would allow.

About six hundred yards in front of Hanson's center was an eminence which it was deemed important to hold. It commanded the ground sloping toward the river in its front and on its left, and also the plain on the west bank occupied by the right of Withers' line. Colonel Hunt, with the Forty-first Alabama, the Sixth and Ninth Kentucky, and Cobb's battery, all of Hanson's brigade, was ordered to take and hold this hill, which he did, repulsing several brisk attacks of the enemy, and losing some excellent officers and men. A few hundred yards to the left and rear of this position a small earthwork, thrown up under the direction of Major Graves, my chief of artillery, was held during a part of the operations by Semple's battery of Napoleon guns.

In the afternoon of Tuesday, the 30th, I received intelligence from Lieutenant-General Hardee that the divisions of Cleburne and McCown were to be transferred to the extreme left, and soon after an order came to me from the general commanding to hold the hill at all hazards. I immediately moved the remainder of Hanson's brigade to the hill and strengthened Cobb's battery with a section from Lumsden's battery and a section from Slocomb's Washington Artillery. At the same time Adams' brigade was moved from the right and formed on the ground originally occupied by Hanson's brigade. Jackson was moved to the west side of the Lebanon Road to connect with the general line of battle.

All the ground east of Stone's River was now to be held by one division, which in a single line did not extend from the ford to the Lebanon Road. I did not change my general line, since a position in advance, besides being less favorable in other respects, would have widened considerably the interval between my right and the Lebanon Road. The enemy did not again attack the hill with infantry, but our troops there continued to suffer during all the operations from heavy shelling. Our artillery at that position often did good service in diverting the enemy's fire from our attacking lines of infantry, and especially, on Wednesday, the 31st, succeeded in breaking several of their formations on the west bank of the river.

On the morning of Wednesday, the 31st, the battle opened on our left. From my front information came to me from Pegram's cavalry force in advance that the enemy, having crossed at the fords below, were moving on my position in line of battle. This proved to be incorrect. . .

About 10:30 o'clock A. M., I received through Colonel J. Stoddard Johnston a suggestion from the general commanding to move against the enemy, instead of awaiting his attack. (I find that Colonel Johnston regarded it as an order, but as I moved at once it is not material.) I preferred to fight on the ground I then occupied, but supposing that the object of the general was to create a diversion in favor of our left, my line, except Hanson's brigade, was put in motion in the direction from which the enemy was supposed to be advancing. We had marched about half a mile when I received through Colonel Johnston an order from the general commanding to send at least one brigade to the support of Lieutenant-General Polk, who was hard pressed, and, as I recollect, two, if I could spare them. I immediately sent Adams and Jackson, and at the same time suspended my movement, and sent forward Captain Blackburne with several of my escort, and Captain Coleman and Lieutenant Darragh of my staff, with orders to find and report with certainty the position and movements of the enemy. Soon after an order came from the general commanding to continue the movement. The line again advanced, but had not proceeded far when I received an order from the general commanding through Colonel Johnston, repeated by Colonel Greenfell, to leave Hanson in position on the hill, and with the remainder of my command to report at once to Lieutenant-General Polk. The brigades of Preston and Palmer were immediately moved by the flank toward the ford before referred to, and the order of the general executed with great rapidity. In the meantime, riding forward to the position occupied by the general commanding and Lieutenant-General Polk, near the west bank of the river and a little below the ford, I arrived in time to see at a distance the brigades of Jackson and Adams recoiling from a very hot fire of the enemy. I was directed by Lieutenant-General Polk to form my line with its right resting on the river and its left extending across the open field, crossing the Nashville Turnpike almost at a right angle. While my troops were crossing the river and getting into line, I rode forward with a portion of my staff, assisted by gentlemen of the staffs of Generals Bragg and Polk, to rally and form Adams' brigade, which was falling back chiefly between the turnpike and the river. Jackson, much cut up, had retired further toward our left.

BRIG.-GEN. EVANDER MCNAIR, OF ARKANSAS.

The brigade of Brigadier-General Adams was rallied and placed in line across the field behind a low and very imperfect breastwork of earth and rails. These brigades did not again enter the action that day (which, indeed, closed soon after with the charge of Preston and Palmer). They had suffered severely in an attack upon superior numbers, very strongly posted and sustained by numerous and powerful batteries, which had repulsed all preceding assaults. The list of casualties shows the courage and determination of these troops.

General Adams having received a wound while gallantly leading his brigade, the command devolved upon Colonel R. L. Gibson, who discharged its duties throughout with marked courage and skill.

Preston and Palmer being now in line—Preston on the right—Lieutenant-General Polk directed me to advance across the plain until I encountered the enemy. The right of my line rested on the river (and from the course of the stream would, in advancing, rest on or very near it), while the left touched a skirt of woods from which the enemy had been driven during the day. At the opposite extremity of the plain a cedar brake extended in front of Palmer's whole line and two-thirds of Preston's line, the remaining space to the right being comparatively open, with commanding swells, and through this ran the railroad and turnpike nearly side by side. It was supposed that the enemy's line was parallel to ours, but the result showed that in advancing our right and his left the point of contact would form an acute angle.

These two brigades, passing over the troops lying behind the rails, moved across the plain in very fine order under the fire of the enemy's artillery. We had advanced but a short distance when Colonel O'Hara (my acting Adjutant-General) called my attention to a new battery in the act of taking position in front of our right between the turnpike and the river. I immediately sent him back to find some artillery to engage the enemy's battery. He found and placed in position the Washington artillery. About the same time Captain E. P. Byrne reported his battery to me, and received an order to take the best position he could find and engage the enemy. He succeeded in opening on them after our line had passed forward.

A number of officers and men were killed along the whole line; but in this charge the chief loss fell upon Preston's right and center. His casualties amounted to one hundred and fifty-five. The Twentieth Tenneesee, after driving the enemy on the right of the turnpike and taking twenty-five prisoners, was compelled to fall back before a very heavy artillery and musketry fire, Colonel Smith, commanding, being severely wounded; but it kept the prisoners and soon rejoined the command. The Fourth Florida and Sixtieth North Carolina encountered serious difficulty at a burnt house (Cowan's) on the left of the turnpike from fences and other obstacles, and was for a little while thrown into some confusion. Here for several minutes they were exposed to a destructive and partially enfilading fire at short range of artillery and infantry. But they were soon rallied by their gallant brigade commander, and rushing with cheers across the intervening space entered the cedar glade. The enemy had retired from the cedars and was in position in a field to the front and right.

By changing the front of the command slightly forward to the right my line was brought parallel to that of the enemy and was formed near the edge of the cedars. About this time, meeting Lieutenant-General Hardee, we went together to the edge of the field to examine the position of the enemy, and found him strongly posted in two lines of battle supported by numerous batteries. One of his lines had the protection of the railroad cut, forming an excellent breastwork. We had no artillery, the nature of the ground forbidding its use.

It was deemed reckless to attack with the force present. Night was now approaching. Presently the remainder of Lieutenant-General Hardee's corps came up on the left, and with McCown's command and a part of Cheatham's prolonged the line of battle in that direction. Adams' brigade also appeared and formed on the right of Preston. The troops bivouacked in position.

The commanding general, expecting an attack upon his right the next morning, ordered me during the night to recross the river with Palmer's brigade. Before daylight Thursday morning Palmer was in position on the right of Hanson. No general engagement occurred on this day, the troops generally being employed in replenishing the ammunition, cooking rations, and obtaining some repose.

On Friday, the 2d of January, being desirous to ascertain if the enemy was establishing himself on the east bank of the river, Lieutenant-Colonel Buckner and Major Graves, with Captain Byrne's battery and a portion of the Washington artillery, under Lieutenant D. C. Vaught, went forward to our line of skirmishers toward the right and engaged those of the enemy, who had advanced perhaps a thousand yards from the east bank of the river. They soon revealed a strong line of skirmishers, which was driven back a considerable distance by our sharpshooters and artillery—the latter firing several houses in the fields in which the enemy had taken shelter. At the same time, accompanied by Major Pickett, of Lieutenant-General Hardee's staff, and Major Wilson, Colonel O'Hara and Lieutenant Breckinridge of my own, I proceeded toward the left of our line of skirmishers, which passed through a thick wood about five hundred yards in front of Hanson's position and extended to the river. Directing Captain Bosche, of the Ninth, and Captain Steele, of the Fourth Kentucky, to drive back the enemy's skirmishers, we were enabled to see that he was occupying with infantry and artillery the crest of a gentle slope on the east bank of the river. The course of the crest formed a little less than a right angle with Hanson's line, from which the center of the position I was afterward ordered to attack was distant about one thousand six hundred yards. It extended along ground part open and part woodland.

While we were endeavoring to ascertain the force of the

enemy, and the relation of the ground on the east bank to that on the west bank of the river, I received an order from the commanding general to report to him in person. I found him on the west bank near the ford below the bridge, and received from him an order to form my division in two lines and take the crest I have just described with the infantry. After doing this, I was to bring up the artillery and establish it on the crest, so as at once to hold it and enfilade the enemy's lines on the other side of the river. Pegram and Wharton, who, with some cavalry and a battery, were beyond a point where my right would rest when the new line of battle should be formed, were directed, as the general informed me, to protect my right and co-operate in the attack. Captain Robertson was ordered to report to me with his own and Semple's batteries of Napoleon guns. Captain Wright, who, with his battery, had been detached some days before, was ordered to join his brigade (Preston's). The brigades of Adams and Preston, which were left on the west side of the river Wednesday night, had been ordered to rejoin me. At the moment of my advance our artillery in the center and on the left was to open on the enemy. One gun from the center was the signal for the attack. The commanding general desired that the movement should be made with the least possible delay.

It was now 2:30 o'clock P. M. Two of the brigades had to march about two miles, the other two about one mile. Brigadier-General Pillow, having reported for duty, was assigned by the commanding general to Palmer's brigade, and that fine officer resumed command of his regiment, and was three times wounded in the ensuing engagement. The Ninth Kentucky and Cobb's battery, under command of Colonel Hunt, were left to hold the hill so often referred to.

The division, after deducting the losses of Wednesday, the troops left on the hill and companies on special service, consisted of some four thousand five hundred men. It was drawn up in two lines, the first in a narrow skirt of woods, the second two hundred yards in rear. Pillow and Hanson formed the first line, Pillow on the right. Preston supported Pillow, and Adams' brigade (under Colonel Gibson) supported Hanson. The artillery was placed in rear of the second line under orders to move with it and occupy the summit of the slope as soon as the infantry should rout the enemy. Feeling anxious about my right, I sent two staff officers in succession to communicate with Pegram and Wharton, but received no intelligence up to the moment of assault. The interval between my left and the troops on the hill was already too great, but I had a battery to watch it with a small infantry support.

There was nothing to prevent the enemy from observing nearly all our movements and preparations. To reach him it was necessary to cross an open space six or seven hundred yards in width with a gentle ascent. The river was several hundred yards in rear of his position, but departed from it considerably as it flowed toward his left.

I had informed the commanding general that we

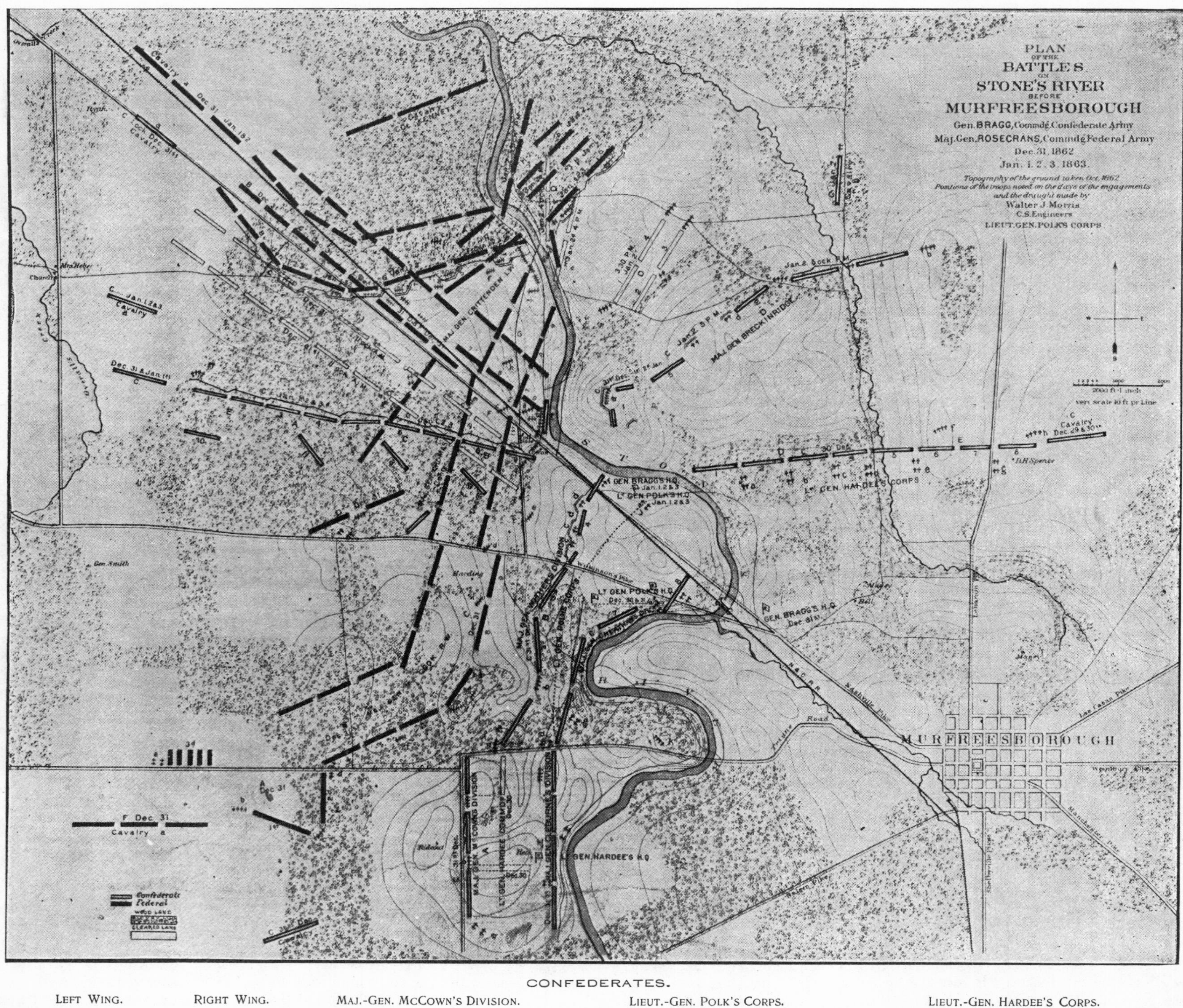

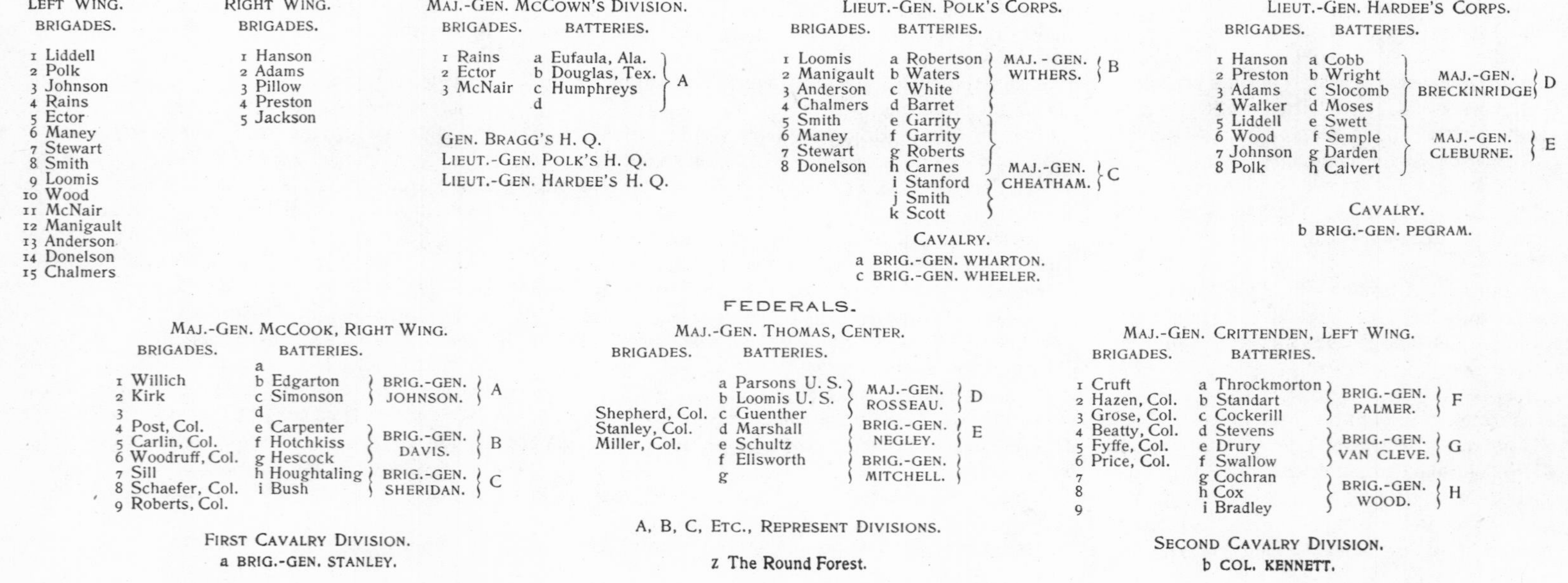

CONFEDERATES.

LEFT WING. BRIGADES.

1 Liddell
2 Polk
3 Johnson
4 Rains
5 Ector
6 Maney
7 Stewart
8 Smith
9 Loomis
10 Wood
11 McNair
12 Manigault
13 Anderson
14 Donelson
15 Chalmers

RIGHT WING. BRIGADES.

1 Hanson
2 Adams
3 Pillow
4 Preston
5 Jackson

MAJ.-GEN. MCCOWN'S DIVISION.

BRIGADES.	BATTERIES.	
1 Rains	a Eufaula, Ala.	A
2 Ector	b Douglas, Tex.	
3 McNair	c Humphreys	
	d	

GEN. BRAGG'S H. Q.
LIEUT.-GEN. POLK'S H. Q.
LIEUT.-GEN. HARDEE'S H. Q.

LIEUT.-GEN. POLK'S CORPS.

BRIGADES.	BATTERIES.		
1 Loomis	a Robertson	MAJ.-GEN. WITHERS.	B
2 Manigault	b Waters		
3 Anderson	c White		
4 Chalmers	d Barret		
5 Smith	e Garrity	MAJ.-GEN. CHEATHAM.	C
6 Maney	f Garrity		
7 Stewart	g Roberts		
8 Donelson	h Carnes		
	i Stanford		
	j Smith		
	k Scott		

CAVALRY.
a BRIG.-GEN. WHARTON.
c BRIG.-GEN. WHEELER.

LIEUT.-GEN. HARDEE'S CORPS.

BRIGADES.	BATTERIES.		
1 Hanson	a Cobb	MAJ.-GEN. BRECKINRIDGE	D
2 Preston	b Wright		
3 Adams	c Slocomb		
4 Walker	d Moses		
5 Liddell	e Swett	MAJ.-GEN. CLEBURNE.	E
6 Wood	f Semple		
7 Johnson	g Darden		
8 Polk	h Calvert		

CAVALRY.
b BRIG.-GEN. PEGRAM.

FEDERALS.

MAJ.-GEN. MCCOOK, RIGHT WING.

BRIGADES.	BATTERIES.		
	a		
1 Willich	b Edgarton	BRIG.-GEN. JOHNSON.	A
2 Kirk	c Simonson		
3	d		
4 Post, Col.	e Carpenter	BRIG.-GEN. DAVIS.	B
5 Carlin, Col.	f Hotchkiss		
6 Woodruff, Col.	g Hescock		
7 Sill	h Houghtaling	BRIG.-GEN. SHERIDAN.	C
8 Schaefer, Col.	i Bush		
9 Roberts, Col.			

FIRST CAVALRY DIVISION.
a BRIG.-GEN. STANLEY.

MAJ.-GEN. THOMAS, CENTER.

BRIGADES.	BATTERIES.		
	a Parsons U. S.	MAJ.-GEN. ROSSEAU.	D
	b Loomis U. S.		
Shepherd, Col.	c Guenther		
Stanley, Col.	d Marshall	BRIG.-GEN. NEGLEY.	E
Miller, Col.	e Schultz		
	f Ellsworth	BRIG.-GEN. MITCHELL.	
	g		

A, B, C, ETC., REPRESENT DIVISIONS.

z The Round Forest.

MAJ.-GEN. CRITTENDEN, LEFT WING.

BRIGADES.	BATTERIES.		
1 Cruft	a Throckmorton	BRIG.-GEN. PALMER.	F
2 Hazen, Col.	b Standart		
3 Grose, Col.	c Cockerill		
4 Beatty, Col.	d Stevens	BRIG.-GEN. VAN CLEVE.	G
5 Fyffe, Col.	e Drury		
6 Price, Col.	f Swallow		
7	g Cochran	BRIG.-GEN. WOOD.	H
8	h Cox		
9	i Bradley		

SECOND CAVALRY DIVISION.
b COL. KENNETT.

would be ready to advance at 4 o'clock, and precisely at that hour the signal gun was heard from our center. Instantly the troops moved forward at a quickstep and in admirable order. The front line had bayonets fixed, with orders to deliver one volley and then use the bayonet.

The fire of the enemy's artillery on both sides of the river commenced as soon as the troops entered the open ground. When less than half the distance across the field, the quick eye of Colonel O'Hara discovered a force extending considerably beyond our right. I immediately directed Major Graves to move a battery to our right and open on them. He at once advanced Wright's battery and effectually checked their movements.

Before our line reached the enemy's position his artillery fire had become heavy, accurate and destructive. Many officers and men fell before we closed with their infantry; yet our brave fellows rushed forward with the utmost determination, and after a brief but bloody conflict routed both the opposing lines, took four hundred prisoners and several flags, and drove their artillery and the great body of their infantry across the river. Many were killed at the water's edge. Their artillery took time by the forelock in crossing the stream. A few of our men, in their ardor, actually crossed over before they could be prevented, most of whom, subsequently moving up under the west bank, recrossed at a ford three quarters of a mile above.

The second line had halted when the first engaged the enemy's infantry and laid down under orders; but very soon the casualties in the first line, the fact that the artillery on the opposite bank was more fatal to the second line than the first, and the eagerness of the troops, impelled them forward, and at the decisive moment, when the opposing infantry was routed, the two lines had mingled into one—the only practical inconvenience of which was that at several points the ranks were deeper than is allowed by a proper military formation.

A strong force of the enemy beyond our extreme right yet remained on the east side of the river. Presently a new line of battle appeared on the west bank directly opposite our troops and opened fire, while at the same time large masses crossed in front of our right and advanced to the attack. We were compelled to fall back.

As soon as our infantry had won the ridge Major Graves advanced the artillery of the division and opened fire. At the same time Captain Robertson threw forward Semple's battery toward our right, which did excellent service. He did not advance his own battery (which was to have taken position on the left), supposing that that part of the field had not been cleared of the enemy's infantry. Although mistaken in this, since the enemy had been driven across the river, yet I regard it as fortunate that the battery was not brought forward. It would have been a vain contest.

It now appeared that the ground we had won was commanded by the enemy's batteries within easy range on better ground upon the other side of the river. I know not how many guns he had. He had enough to sweep the whole position from the front, the left, and the right, and to render it wholly untenable by our force present of artillery and infantry. The infantry, after passing the crest and descending the slope toward the river, were in some measure protected, and suffered less at this period of the action than the artillery. We lost three guns, nearly all the horses being killed, and not having the time or men to draw them off by hand. One was lost because there was but one boy left (Private Wright of Wright's battery) to limber the piece, and his strength was unequal to it.

The command fell back in some disorder, but without the slightest appearance of panic, and reformed behind Robertson's battery, in the narrow skirt of timber from which we emerged to the assault. The enemy did not advance beyond the position in which he received our attack. My skirmishers continued to occupy a part of the field over which we advanced until the army retired from Murfreesboro. The action lasted about one hour and twenty minutes. As our lines advanced to the attack several rounds of artillery were heard from our center, apparently directed against the enemy on the west bank of the river.

About twilight Brigadier-General Anderson reported to me with his brigade, and remained in position with me until the army retired. I took up line of battle for the night a little in rear of the field over which we advanced to the assault, and Captain Robertson at my request disposed the artillery in the positions indicated for it.

Many of the reports do not discriminate between the losses of Wednesday and Friday. The total loss in my division, exclusive of Jackson's command, is two thousand one hundred and forty, of which, I think, seventeen hundred occurred on Friday. The loss of the enemy on this day was, I think, greater than our own, since he suffered immense slaughter between the ridge and the river.

I can not forbear to express my admiration for the courage and constancy of the troops, exhibited even after it became apparent that the main object could not be accomplished. Beyond the general good conduct, a number of enlisted men displayed at different periods of the action the most heroic bravery. I respectfully suggest that authority be given to select a certain number of the most distinguished in each brigade to be recommended to the President for promotion.

I can not enumerate all the brave officers who fell, nor the living who nobly did their duty; yet I may be permitted to lament, in common with the army, the premature death of Brigadier-General Hanson, who received a mortal wound at the moment the enemy began to give way. Endeared to his friends by his private virtues, and to his command by the vigilance with which he guarded its interest and honor, he was, by the universal testimony of his military associates, one of the finest officers that adorned the service of the Confederate States. Upon his fall the command devolved upon Colonel Trabue, who in another organization had long and ably commanded most of the regiments composing the brigade.

I can not close without expressing my obligations to the gentlemen of my staff. This is no formal acknowledgment. I can never forget that during all the operations they were ever prompt and cheerful by night and day in conveying orders, conducting to their positions regiments and brigades, rallying troops on the field, and, indeed, in the discharge of every duty.

It gives me pleasure to name Lieutenant-Colonel Buckner, Assistant Adjutant-General, who was absent on leave, but returned upon the first rumor of battle; Colonel O'Hara, Acting Adjutant-General; Lieutenant Breckinridge, Aid-de-Camp; Major Graves, Chief of Artillery (twice wounded, and his horse shot under him); Major Wilson, Assistant Inspector-General (horse shot); Captain Semple, ordnance officer; Lieutenant Darragh, severely wounded. Captains Martin and Coleman, of my volunteer staff, were active and efficient. The former had his horse killed under him.

Drs. Heustis and Pendleton, chief surgeon and medical inspector, were unremitting in attention to the wounded. Dr. Stanhope Breckinridge, assistant surgeon, accompanied my headquarters, and pursued his duties through the fire of Wednesday. Mr. Buckner and Mr. Zantzinger, of Kentucky, attached themselves to me for the occasion, and were active and zealous.

Captain Blackburn, commanding my escort, ever cool and vigilant, rendered essential service, and made several bold reconnoissances.

Charles Choutard, of the escort, acting as my orderly on Wednesday, displayed much gallantry and intelligence.

The army retired before daybreak on the morning of the 4th of January. My division, moving on the Manchester Road, was the rear of Hardee's corps. The Ninth Kentucky, Forty-first Alabama and Cobb's battery, all under the command of Colonel Hunt, formed a special rear-guard. The enemy did not follow us.

My acknowledgments are due to Colonel J. Stoddard Johnston, Lieutenant-Colonel Brent and Lieutenant-Colonel Garner, of General Bragg's staff, and to Major Pickett, of Lieutenant-General Hardee's staff, for services on Friday, the 2d of January.

JOHN C. BRECKINRIDGE,
Major-General C. S. A.

MURFREESBORO, TENNESSEE.

ORGANIZATION OF THE ARMY OF TENNESSEE*

DURING THE

STONE'S RIVER CAMPAIGN,

DECEMBER 26, 1862, TO JANUARY 5, 1863.

GENERAL BRAXTON BRAGG,
Commanding.

POLK'S CORPS.

Lieutenant-General Leonidas Polk.

FIRST DIVISION.

Major-General B. F. Cheatham.

FIRST BRIGADE.

Brigadier-General Daniel S. Donelson.

Eighth Tennessee—Colonel W. L. Moore; Lieutenant-Colonel J. H. Anderson.
Sixteenth Tennessee—Colonel John H. Savage.
Thirty-eighth Tennessee—Colonel John C. Carter.
Fifty-first Tennessee—Colonel John Chester.
Eighty-fourth Tennessee—Colonel S. S. Stanton.
Carnes' (Tennessee) battery—Lieutenant L. G. Marshall.

SECOND BRIGADE.

Brigadier-General Alexander P. Stewart.

Fourth Tennessee, Fifth Tennessee—Colonel O. F. Strahl.
Nineteenth Tennessee—Colonel F. M. Walker.
Twenty-fourth Tennessee—Colonel H. W. L. Bratton; Major S. E. Shannon.
Thirty-first Tennessee, Thirty-third Tennessee—Colonel E. E. Tansil.
Mississippi battery—Captain T. J. Stanford.

THIRD BRIGADE.

Brigadier-General George Maney.

First Tennessee, Twenty-seventh Tennessee—Colonel H. R. Field.
Fourth Tennessee (Provisional Army)—Colonel J. A. McMurry.
Sixth Tennessee, Ninth Tennessee—Colonel C. S. Hurt; Major J. L. Harris.
Tennessee Sharpshooters—Captain Frank Maney.
Smith's (Mississippi) battery—Lieutenant William B. Turner.

* Compiled from the reports. Other officers than those named may have also been in actual command of the organizations indicated.

FOURTH (PRESTON SMITH'S) BRIGADE.
Colonel A. J. Vaughan, Jr.

Twelfth Tennessee—Major J. N. Wyatt.
Thirteenth Tennessee—Lieutenant-Colonel W. E. Morgan; Captain R. F. Lanier.
Twenty-ninth Tennessee—Major J. B. Johnson.
Forty-seventh Tennessee—Captain W. M. Watkins.
One Hundred and Fifty-fourth Tennessee—Lieutenant-Colonel M. Magevney, Jr.
Ninth Texas—Colonel W. H. Young.
Allin's (Tennessee) Sharpshooters—Lieutenant J. R. J. Creighton; Lieutenant T. F. Pattison.
Tennessee battery—Captain W. L. Scott.

BRIGADIER-GENERAL ROGER W. HANSON, OF KENTUCKY.
Killed at Murfreesboro, Tenn., December 31, 1862.

SECOND DIVISION.
Major-General Jones M. Withers.

FIRST (DEAS') BRIGADE.
Colonel J. Q. Loomis; Colonel J. G. Coltart.

Nineteenth Alabama; Twenty-second Alabama; Twenty-fifth Alabama; Twenty-sixth Alabama; Thirty-ninth Alabama; Seventeenth Alabama Battalion (Sharpshooters), Captain B. C. Yancey; First Louisiana (Regulars), Lieutenant-Colonel F. H. Farrar, Jr.; Robertson's battery, Captain F. H. Robertson.

SECOND BRIGADE.
Brigadier-General James R. Chalmers; Colonel T. W. White.

Seventh Mississippi; Ninth Mississippi, Colonel T. W. White; Tenth Mississippi; Forty-first Mississippi; Ninth Mississippi Battalion (Sharpshooters), Captain O. F. West; Blythe's (Miss.) Regiment; Garrity's (Ala.) battery.

THIRD (WALTHALL'S) BRIGADE.
Brigadier-General J. Patton Anderson.

Forty-fifth Alabama—Colonel James G. Gilchrist.
Twenty-fourth Mississippi—Lieutenant-Colonel R. P. McKelvaine.
Twenty-seventh Mississippi—Colonel T. M. Jones; Lieutenant-Colonel J. L. Autry; Captain E. R. Neilson.
Twenty-ninth Mississippi—Colonel W. F. Brantly; Lieutenant-Colonel J. B. Morgan.
Thirtieth Mississippi—Lieutenant-Colonel J. I. Scales.
Thirty-ninth North Carolina—Captain A. W. Bell.
Missouri Battery—Captain O. W. Barret.

FOURTH (ANDERSON'S) BRIGADE.
Colonel A. M. Manigault.

Twenty-fourth Alabama; Twenty-eighth Alabama; Thirty-fourth Alabama; Tenth South Carolina and Nineteenth South Carolina, Colonel A. J. Lythgoe; Alabama Battery, Captain D. D. Waters.

HARDEE'S CORPS.
Lieutenant-General William J. Hardee.

FIRST DIVISION.
Major-General John C. Breckinridge.

FIRST BRIGADE.
Brigadier-General Daniel W. Adams; Colonel Randall L. Gibson.

Thirty-second Alabama—Lieutenant-Colonel Henry Maury; Colonel Alexander McKinstry.
Thirteenth Louisiana, Twentieth Louisiana—Colonel R. L. Gibson, Major Chas. Guillet.
Sixteenth Louisiana, Twenty-fifth Louisiana—Colonel S. W. Fisk, Major F. C. Zacharie.
Fourteenth Louisiana Battalion—Major J. E. Austin.
Washington Artillery (Fifth Battery)—Lieutenant W. C. D. Vaught.

SECOND BRIGADE.
Colonel J. B. Palmer; Brigadier-General Gideon J. Pillow.

Eighteenth Tennessee—Colonel J. B. Palmer; Lieutenant-Colonel W. R. Butler.
Twenty-sixth Tennessee—Colonel J. M. Lilliard.
Twenty-eighth Tennessee—Colonel P. D. Cunningham.
Thirty-second Tennessee—Colonel Ed. C. Cook.
Forty-fifth Tennessee—Colonel A. Searcy.
Moses' (Ga.) battery—Lieutenant R. W. Anderson.

THIRD BRIGADE.
Brigadier-General William Preston.

First Florida, Third Florida—Colonel Wm. Miller.
Fourth Florida—Colonel J. A. McDowell.
Twentieth Tennessee—Colonel T. B. Smith; Lieutenant-Colonel F. M. Lavender; Major F. Claybrooke.
Tennessee Battery—Captain E. E. Wright; Lieutenant J. W. Mebane.

FOURTH BRIGADE.
Brigadier-General R. W. Hanson; Colonel R. P. Trabue.

Forty-first Alabama—Colonel H. Talbird; Lieutenant-Colonel M. L. Stansel.
Second Kentucky—Major James W. Hewitt.
Fourth Kentucky—Colonel R. P. Trabue; Captain T. W. Thompson.
Sixth Kentucky—Colonel Joseph H. Lewis.
Ninth Kentucky—Colonel T. H. Hunt.
Kentucky Battery—Captain R. Cobb.

JACKSON'S BRIGADE.*
Brigadier-General John K. Jackson.

Fifth Georgia—Colonel W. T. Black; Major C. P. Daniel.
Second Georgia Battalion Sharpshooters—Major J. J. Cox.
Fifth Mississippi—Lieutenant-Colonel W. L. Sykes.
Eighth Mississippi—Colonel J. C. Wilkinson; Lieutenant-Colonel A. McNeill.
Pritchard's (Ga.) battery—Lieutenant H. H. Cribbs.

SECOND DIVISION.
Major-General P. R. Cleburne.

FIRST BRIGADE.
Brigadier-General L. E. Polk.

First Arkansas—Colonel John M. Colquitt.
Thirteenth Arkansas.
Fifteenth Arkansas.
Fifth Confederate—Colonel J. A. Smith.
Second Tennessee—Colonel W. D. Robinson.
Fifth Tennessee—Colonel B. J. Hill.
Helena (Ark.) Artillery—Lieutenant T. J. Key.

SECOND BRIGADE.
Brigadier-General St. John R. Liddell.

Second Arkansas—Colonel D. C. Govan.
Fifth Arkansas—Lieutenant-Colonel John E. Murray.
Sixth Arkansas, Seventh Arkansas—Colonel S. G. Smith. Lieut.-Colonel F. J. Cameron. Major W. F. Douglass.
Eighth Arkansas—Colonel John H. Kelly; Lieutenant-Colonel G. F. Baucum.
Swett's (Miss.) battery—Lieutenant H. Shannon.

THIRD BRIGADE.
Brigadier-General Bushrod R. Johnson.

Seventeenth Tennessee—Colonel A. S. Marks; Lieutenant-Colonel W. W. Floyd.
Twenty-third Tennessee—Lieutenant-Colonel R. H. Keeble.
Twenty-fifth Tennessee—Colonel J. M. Hughs; Lieutenant-Colonel Samuel Davis.
Thirty-seventh Tennessee—Colonel M. White; Major J. T. McReynolds; Captain C. G. Jarnagin.
Forty-fourth Tennessee—Colonel John S. Fulton.
Jefferson's (Miss.) Artillery—Captain Put. Darden.

FOURTH BRIGADE.
Brigadier-General S. A. M. Wood.

Sixteenth Alabama—Colonel W. B. Wood.
Thirty-third Alabama—Colonel Samuel Adams.
Third Confederate—Major J. F. Cameron.
Forty-fifth Mississippi—Lieutenant-Colonel R. Charlton.
Fifteenth Mississippi Battalion Sharpshooters—Captain A. T. Hawkins.
Alabama Battery—Captain Henry C. Semple.

MCCOWN'S DIVISION.†
Major-General J. P. McCown.

FIRST BRIGADE.‡
Brigadier-General M. D. Ector.

Tenth Texas Cavalry—Colonel M. F. Locke.
Eleventh Texas Cavalry—Colonel J. C. Burks; Lieutenant-Colonel J. M. Bounds.
Fourteenth Texas Cavalry—Colonel J. L. Camp.
Fifteenth Texas Cavalry—Colonel J. A. Andrews.
Texas Battery—Captain J. P. Douglas.

* Temporarily assigned to Breckinridge's Division.
† Of Smith's corps, serving with Hardee.
‡ The regiments of this brigade serving as infantry.

SECOND BRIGADE.
Brigadier-General James E. Rains; Colonel R. B. Vance.

Third Georgia Battalion—Lieutenant-Colonel M. A. Stovall.
Ninth Georgia Battalion—Major Joseph T. Smith.
Twenty-ninth North Carolina—Colonel R. B. Vance.
Eleventh Tennessee—Colonel G. W. Gordon; Lieutenant-Colonel Wm. Thedford.
Eufaula (Ala.) Light Artillery—Lieutenant W. A. McDuffie.

THIRD BRIGADE.
Brigadier-General Evander McNair; Colonel R. W. Harper.

First Arkansas (Mounted Rifles)*—Colonel R. W. Harper; Major L. M. Ramsaur.
Second Arkansas (Mounted Rifles)*—Lieutenant-Colonel J. A. Williamson.
Fourth Arkansas—Colonel H. G. Bunn.
Thirtieth Arkansas—Major J. J. Franklin; Captain W. A. Cotter.
Fourth Arkansas Battalion—Major J. A. Ross.
Arkansas Battery—Captain J. T. Humphreys.

CAVALRY.
Brigadier-General Joseph Wheeler.

WHEELER'S BRIGADE.
Brigadier-General Joseph Wheeler.

First Alabama—Colonel W. W. Allen.
Third Alabama—Major F. Y. Gaines; Captain T. H. Mauldin.
Fifty-first Alabama—Colonel John T. Morgan; Lieutenant-Colonel J. D. Webb.
Eighth Confederate—Colonel W. B. Wade.
First Tennessee—Colonel James E. Carter.
Tennessee Battalion—DeWitt C. Douglass.
Tennessee Battalion—Major D. W. Holman.
Arkansas Battery—Captain J. H. Wiggins.

PEGRAM'S BRIGADE.
Brigadier-General John Pegram.

First Georgia; First Louisiana.

WHARTON'S BRIGADE.
Brigadier-General John A. Wharton.

Fourteenth Alabama Battalion—Lieutenant-Colonel James C. Malone.
First Confederate—Colonel John T. Cox.
Third Confederate—Lieutenant-Colonel Wm. N. Estes.
Second Georgia—Lieutenant-Colonel J. E. Dunlap; Major F. M. Isom.
Third Georgia (detachment)—Major R. Thompson.
Second Tennessee—Colonel H. M. Ashby.

BRIGADIER-GENERAL JAMES E. RAINS, OF TENNESSEE.
Killed at Murfreesboro, Tenn., December 31, 1862.
[From a photo taken in 1862.]

Fourth Tennessee—Colonel Baxter Smith.
Tennessee Battalion—Major John R. Davis.
Eighth Texas—Colonel Thomas Harrison.
Murray's (Tenn.) Regiment—Major W. S. Bledsoe.
Escort Company—Captain Paul F. Anderson.
McCown's Escort Company—Captain L. T. Hardy.
White's (Tenn.) battery—Captain B. F. White, Jr.

ARTILLERY.

Baxter's (Tenn.) battery; Byrne's (Ky.) battery; Gibson's (Ga.) battery.

* Serving as infantry.

VICKSBURG SONG.

BY CAPTAIN J. W. A. WRIGHT.

Air—"A Life on the Ocean Wave."

A life on the Vicksburg bluff,
A home in the trenches deep,
Where we dodge "Yank" shells enough,
And our old "pea bread" won't keep.
On "Old Logan's" beef I pine,
For there's fat on his bones no more.
Oh! give me some pork in brine
And "truck" from a sutler's store.

Chorus—A life on the Vicksburg bluff,
A home in the trenches deep,
Where we dodge "Yank" shells enough,
And our old "pea bread" won't keep—
Pea bread, pea bread, pea bread,
And our old pea bread won't keep.

Old Grant is starving us out,
Our grub is fast wasting away,
Pemb don't know what he's about,
And he hasn't for many a day.
So we'll bury "Old Logan" to-night—
From tough beef we'll be set free;
We'll put him far out of sight—
No more of his meat for me.

Texas "steers" are no longer in view,
Mule steaks are now "done up brown,"
While "pea bread," mule roast and mule stew
Are our fare in old Vicksburg town;
And the song of our hearts shall be,
While the "Yanks" and their gunboats rave,
A life in "bomb-proofs" for me,
And a tear o'er "Old Logan's" grave.

THE SIEGE OF VICKSBURG, MISS.,

MAY 19 TO JULY 4, 1863.

BY

MAJOR-GENERAL MARTIN L. SMITH,
Commanding Division.

MOBILE, ALA., August 9, 1863.

THE line of defense surrounding the city was divided into three commands, corresponding with the army division, one of which was assigned to me and constituted the left of the line. The left of my division rested on the river above the city and extended to the right about one and one-quarter miles, where it touched Major-General Forney's command. The division consisted of three brigades, General Shoup, commanding the Twenty-sixth, Twenty-seventh and Twenty-eighth [Twenty-ninth] Louisiana, on the right; General Baldwin, commanding the Seventeenth and Thirty-first Louisiana, the Fourth and Forty-sixth Mississippi, occupying the center; General Vaughn, commanding the Sixtieth, Sixty-first, Sixty-second Tennessee, and Mississippi State troops under Brigadier-General Harris, together with a detachment of Loring's command, on the left.

The works occupied by me, and which may be termed my front, were along a narrow ridge, and consisted of a line of rifle trenches with points prepared for field artillery. This point was rather strong, although parallel with it, and some six hundred yards distant, ran another ridge of the same elevation, and in every respect similar, which was occupied by the enemy and afforded excellent positions for their batteries as well as sharpshooters, and, when prepared with field-works looking in our direction, became itself as difficult to assail as our own line. Many advantages would have resulted from occupying this parallel ridge, and it was included in the system of defense; but, increasing as it did the length of the entire line of defense, was abandoned for want of sufficient force to occupy it.

The enemy made his appearance before the works on my right early in the afternoon of May 18th, and immediately attacked the position with artillery and infantry. They were first met by the Twenty-seventh Louisiana, subsequently by the Seventeenth and Thirty-first Louisiana and Forty-sixth Mississippi in advance of the line, and held at bay until dark terminated the attack. During the night of the 18th my troops and artillery were all withdrawn within the main lines, and placed in positions from which they were never for an instant dislodged during the entire siege.

On the 19th, the enemy's main forces arrived and proceeded at once to make a direct assault on my right. The first effort was directed against the center of Shoup's brigade; but being exposed to a heavy and well-directed fire, the enemy broke and fled. Reforming again, a second advance was attempted against my extreme right, and a bold effort made to rush over and into the works. The assaulting column seemed to consist of six or seven regiments, and was formed behind an elevation, concealing it from sight. After coming into view it moved confidently and determinedly forward. The Twenty-sixth and Twenty-seventh Louisiana, supported by the First Missouri, in reserve, received the charge with a withering fire, and after the second volley the enemy fled in confusion, leaving five colors on the field and the ground strewn with the dead and wounded. One or two feeble attempts to rally were easily repulsed, and the day closed with the artillery and sharpshooters keeping up a continuous and heavy fire.

The 20th and 21st were spent by the enemy in erecting new batteries, and keeping up from daylight till dark the heaviest possible firing, both of musketry and artillery.

The 22d passed in the same manner until about 2 P. M., when a column was discovered advancing against the right of Shoup's brigade. It was immediately driven back. Another then approached on the right of the center. This was dispersed without great effort and with considerable loss. Again the enemy appeared in increased force on my right and Forney's left. He was promptly repulsed with heavy loss. This terminated the day's operations, with the exception of the same heavy fire of musketry and artillery kept up until dark along my entire front. After these several decided repulses the enemy seemed to have abandoned the idea of taking by assault, and went vigorously at work to thoroughly invest and attack by regular approaches; and the history of one day is pretty much the history of all.

For the more particular description of operations you are respectfully referred to the daily reports of operations handed in during the siege. While the opposing force was running new parallels, establishing new works for heavy guns and gradually nearing our lines, we were strengthening our positions, protecting the men with traverses and bomb-proofs from the terrific fire of shot and shell constantly poured in upon them, and which only ceased at times when the enemy seemed to have temporarily exhausted their supplies of ammunition. The fire of the enemy was only occasionally replied to, except when there were indications of an assault, or it became necessary to retard or stop operations on some particular work. The limited amount of ammunition on hand rendered this course necessary, though I am inclined to think caution in this respect was pushed rather to an extreme, and that a little more firing would have proved beneficial.

MAJ.-GEN. M. L. SMITH, OF FLORIDA.

Toward the close of the siege the attack was mainly carried on by mining. Along my front the enemy exploded no mines on us. On the contrary, counter ones were prepared, and, when their galleries approached within proper distance, were charged and fired, and it is believed with all the desired effect.

The good conduct of both officers and men during the forty-seven days in the trenches is worthy of special praise. Neither one nor the other could have behaved better; and all credit is to be accorded the brigadier-generals and their staffs for their vigilance, activity and heroic example set to their soldiers.

Brigadier-General Baldwin received a severe wound early in the siege, but reported for duty before its close, and, together with General Shoup, receives my special acknowledgments for gallant services. The heaviest and most dangerous attack was on the extreme right, and nobly did the Twenty-sixth, Twenty-seventh, Twenty-eighth [Twenty-ninth] and Thirty-first Louisiana repel and endure it. The casualties among the officers of these regiments indicate the nature of the defense required. In the Twenty-sixth Louisiana, Major [W. W.] Martin, one captain and two lieutenants killed; Colonel W. Hall severely wounded. In the Twenty-seventh Louisiana, Lieutenant-Colonel [L. L.] McLaurin, one captain and one lieutenant killed; Colonel L. D. Marks dangerously wounded. To the brave Colonel Marks and his gallant regiment (Twenty-seventh Louisiana) belong the distinction of taking the first colors, prisoners and arms lost by the enemy during the siege. The conduct of the entire division was most exemplary, and its courage and cheerfulness increased, if possible, from day to day under the hardships and privations of the siege.

* * * * * * *

M. L. SMITH,
Major-General C. S. A.

THE SIEGE OF VICKSBURG, MISS.,

MAY 19 TO JULY 4, 1863.

BY

MAJOR-GENERAL JOHN H. FORNEY.

HEADQUARTERS FORNEY'S DIVISION,
May 19, 1863.

ON the morning of May 17th, while the main body of the army was falling back to the intrenchments around Vicksburg, I assumed command of my division proper, and, in pursuance of instructions from the lieutenant-general commanding, directed General Hebert to prepare to evacuate the post of Snyder's mill, and to hurry into Vicksburg all commissary stores possible. For this purpose all available wagons were sent to him. In the afternoon of the same day, I was directed to place my division in the trenches. Accordingly, General Moore's brigade was brought at once from its position near Warrenton and placed in the intrenchments on either side of the Baldwins Ferry Road. General Hebert was directed to march his troops to Vicksburg, bringing with him all ordnance and ordnance stores he could; to send up the Yazoo all boats at Haynes' Bluff, with orders that they should be fired rather than allowed to fall into the hands of the enemy; to send mounted men to watch the approaches from Bridgeport and the railroad bridge, and to leave behind, at Snyder's, a few companies to keep up a show of occupation, with orders to destroy the heavy guns and other public property (previously prepared for destruction) whenever it should become evident the place would fall into the possession of the enemy, and then to make the best of their way to Vicksburg, or endeavor to escape across the Yazoo. A report of the proceedings of this detachment has, I presume, been made to the lieutenant-general commanding by Colonel I. W. Patton, who was by him sent back to attend to the matter.

The detachment rejoined its command in Vicksburg on the morning of the 18th. General Hebert arrived in Vicksburg, with his command, before daylight on the morning of the 18th, having succeeded in bringing with him, from Snyder's, besides all the light pieces, two 20-pounder Parrotts and a Whitworth gun. His troops were soon in the intrenchments on either side of the Jackson Road. In bringing my troops from their former position I directed them to drive inside of the fortifications all the beef-cattle, hogs and sheep that had been collected from the surrounding country, and squads of mounted men had previously been sent out for this purpose.

On May 18th, at about 1 P. M., Brigadier-General Shoup, of General Smith's division, reported the enemy advancing on his position, and, by direction of the lieutenant-general, two of General Hebert's regiments were sent from his right to re-enforce his left. The whole of the division (the effective strength of which was about four thousand seven hundred) was now in the trenches, from the railroad, on the right, to Graveyard Road, on the left, a distance of about two miles (Moore on the right, Hebert on the left). On this line there were twenty-seven pieces of artillery, most of which were field pieces. This number was afterward increased by three or four siege guns placed in rear of my right. Besides my own troops, Colonel Waul's Texas Legion was also assigned to me and held in reserve behind Moore's brigade. Brigadier-General Lee's brigade, of Major-General Stevenson's division, was on my immediate right; Brigadier-General Shoup's brigade, of Major-General Smith's division, on my immediate left. On the 19th, the enemy made his first assault on my extreme left, and extending along Smith's division. He was several times repulsed and finally fell back. By this time my entire division's front was completely and closely invested. My skirmishers were withdrawn, and skirmishing prohibited (by order) in order to husband ammunition. During the next day the enemy kept up his sharpshooting and artillery fire, but made no assault.

On May 22d, he assaulted three points on my line as follows: Three times on my extreme left and extending to General Smith's front, twice on the Jackson road, and twice on Baldwins Ferry Road, at 11 A. M. and 5 P. M. These assaults were made by larger bodies, and apparently with greater determination than those of May 19th. Colonel Waul's Legion had previously been sent to General Stevenson; but Green's brigade, of Bowen's division, was in reserve behind my right, and assisted in repelling the attack at that point. There were also on this day two Louisiana regiments, of Smith's division, in reserve behind my division.

The enemy was repulsed in each of his attempts, though he succeeded in getting a few men into our exterior ditches at each point of attack, from which they were, however, driven before night. Hand-grenades were used at each point with good effect. A color-bearer and two stand of colors were captured by the Second Texas Regiment, of Moore's brigade.

On this day the casualties in my division were forty-two killed and ninety-five wounded. The loss of the enemy must have reached two thousand.

From this time to the close of the siege the enemy kept up an incessant fire of sharpshooting and cannonading, in the meantime planting batteries and continuing his approaches, the main points being the work on the Baldwins Ferry Road, the one on the Jackson Road and a point midway between the Graveyard and Jackson Roads.

Approaches were also made on my extreme left, but this point was, properly speaking, under the supervision of Major-General Smith.

On or about June 2d my line was contracted by closing in to the right, in consequence of its close investment and the reduction of its numbers by casualties, my left now resting midway between the Graveyard and Jackson Roads. The approaches at all the above-mentioned points were brought to within easy hand-grenade distance, and mines were pushed forward under the works. The enemy made strenuous efforts to possess himself of the main work on the Jackson Road, defended by the Third Louisiana Regiment, the occupation of which by him would necessitate the abandonment of our trenches for a considerable distance to the right and left, as it would give him an enfilade fire either way. Opposite this point he planted a number of heavy siege guns, with which he made a serious breach in the parapet of the redan. The fire of these guns was, however, in a great measure, diverted by the fire of a 10-inch mortar, which we had planted close in the rear of our lines. We were only permitted to retain this mortar a few days, when it was again removed to the right and its place supplied by a 9-inch Dahlgren gun, which the enemy disabled the second day after it opened fire.

On June 25th, at about 5 P. M., the enemy sprung his first mine under the parapet of this work. The explosion effected a breach, through which the enemy immediately attempted to charge, but was promptly and gallantly repulsed. The Sixth Missouri Regiment, which had been held in reserve, was on the spot immediately after the explosion, and its commander, Colonel Eugene Erwin, was instantly killed while attempting to lead a charge over the works. Six men of the Forty-third Mississippi Regiment, who were in a shaft countermining at the time of the explosion, were buried and lost. At dark the enemy had possessed himself of the ditch and slope of the parapet, and our forces retired to an interior line a few feet back. This point was now re-enforced by a part of Colonel [F. M.] Cockrell's brigade, of Bowen's division, and work was resumed by the enemy and by us, they mining and we countermining, until July 1st, at about 1 P. M., when the enemy sprung his second mine, which was much heavier than the first. The result was the entire demolition of the redan, leaving only an immense chasm where it stood. The greater portion of the earth was thrown toward the enemy, the line of least resistance being in that direction. Our interior line was much injured. Nine men who were countermining were necessarily lost, and a large number of those manning the works were killed and wounded. The enemy, however, made no attempt to charge, seeming satisfied with having materially weakened the position. I understand that the amount of powder used by the enemy in this explosion was one ton.

While this was taking place on the Jackson Road the enemy was by no means idle at other points. At the work on the Baldwins Ferry Road his sappers had nearly reached the ditch. At this place we sprung a countermine, which was unfortunately a little premature.

The artillery, though well served, was of but little advantage to us during the siege. The enemy concentrated a heavy fire, dismounting or disabling gun after gun. To this fire we could make but a feeble response. Ammunition was scarce, and orders forbade its use except against advancing columns of infantry or batteries being planted. The proportionate loss of officers and men of the artillery was unusually great.

On July 1st I received a confidential note from the lieutenant-general commanding, informing me that unless the siege of Vicksburg was raised or supplies thrown in it would be necessary very shortly to evacuate the place; that he saw no prospect of the former, and that very great, if not insuperable, obstacles were in the way of the latter, and calling for a report as to the condition of my troops and their ability to make the marches and undergo the fatigues necessary to accomplish a successful evacuation. I laid the matter clearly before my brigade commanders, and they in turn before their regimental and battalion commanders. It was their unanimous opinion, in which I concurred, that although the spirit of the men was good, their physical condition and health were so much impaired by their long confinement in narrow trenches, without exercise and without relief, being constantly under fire and necessarily on the alert, and living upon greatly reduced rations, that they could not make the marches they would have to make and fight the battles they would have to fight against the greatly superior numbers that would be brought against them in making the attempt to break through the enemy's lines. I therefore favored a capitulation rather than make this attempt, attended, as I thought, with such little hope of success.

Finally, on July 4th, at 10 A. M., in accordance with the terms of the capitulation, my troops were marched by regiments over the intrenchments, their arms stacked and left in possession of the enemy, while they returned to bivouac in rear of the trenches.

The siege of Vicksburg was a contest which tried more the endurance and resolution of the men and their company and regimental commanders than the skill of their generals.

My men during the siege did their duty, and their whole duty, to the entire satisfaction of their general and, I trust, of their country. The patience with which my troops submitted to the many privations and hardships to which they were subjected, and the unabated courage and cheerfulness which they sustained throughout, are worthy of all praise and merited a better fortune.

The casualties in my division during the siege were as follows:

Hebert's brigade—killed, 203; wounded, 480.
Moore's brigade—killed, 72; wounded, 385.
Total—killed, 275; wounded, 865.

* * * * * * *

JOHN. H. FORNEY, *Major-General.*

VICKSBURG, MISS. ENGAGEMENT BETWEEN THE CONFEDERATE BATTERIES AND THE UNITED STATES GUNBOATS ON THE NIGHT OF APRIL 15, 1863.

THE SIEGE OF VICKSBURG, MISS.,

MAY 19 TO JULY 4, 1863.

BY

MAJOR-GENERAL CARTER L. STEVENSON.

HEADQUARTERS STEVENSON'S DIVISION,
DEMOPOLIS, ALA.,
July 29, 1863.

I SUBMIT the following report of the operations of my division from its advance from Vicksburg to the capitulation of the city:

At about 10 A. M. (May 17th) I received orders to take command of the army, and conduct its retreat to the fortifications around Vicksburg. The brigade of Brigadier-General Baldwin, of Smith's division, was assigned to the duty of bringing up the rear. Just before getting into the works I was joined by the brigade of Colonel Reynolds, to whom, as I before stated, had been intrusted the charge of the trains of the whole army. He had crossed the Big Black, after much difficulty and delay, occasioned by the absence of any facilities for so doing, at Bridgeport.

By a mistake in the transmission of the order, the regiment of Colonel Beck (Lee's brigade) remained at the river, resisted the attempts of the enemy to cross until 11 o'clock that night, and only withdrew upon the receipt of a peremptory order.

The retreat was conducted in a leisurely and orderly manner, and the troops entered the line of fortifications at about 3 P. M.

On the morning of May 18th the positions to be held by each of the different divisions were assigned by the lieutenant-general himself. The portion of the line of defense which was assigned to my division included the river front and the works south of the city from the river to the railroad, a line of about five miles in length. Barton occupied the river front and the fortifications on the right; Reynolds those on the right center to the Halls Ferry Road; Cumming the left center, and Lee, re-enforced by Waul's Texas Legion, the extreme left. Several sections and companies of artillery not properly belonging to my division were posted on my line. Captain [J. W.] Johnston, Botetourt Artillery Company, was assigned to duty as inspector-general of light artillery on my staff, and the artillery on the right of the Halls Ferry Road placed under the command of Captain J. B. Grayson, First Louisiana Heavy Artillery, and that on the left under that of Captain J. F. Waddell, of my division.

On the evening of the 18th, the enemy made his appearance in front of our lines and immediately began to push forward his sharpshooters. The number of guns, superiority of range and metal, and exhaustless supply of ammunition, enabled them in a very short time to plant many batteries in such commanding positions as to damage our works materially and inflict a very considerable loss among the men.

On the morning of May 22d many indications showed that they contemplated an assault upon the line of General [S. D.] Lee. A tremendous artillery fire was opened and kept up for about two hours, while the fire of their large force of sharpshooters was heavy and incessant.

At about 1 P. M. a heavy force moved out to the assault, making a gallant charge. They were allowed to approach unmolested to within good musket range, when every available gun was opened upon them with grape and canister, and the men, rising in the trenches, poured into their ranks volley after volley with so deadly an effect that, leaving the ground literally covered in some places with their dead and wounded, they precipitately retreated. An angle of one of our redoubts had been breached by their artillery before the assault and rendered untenable. Toward this point, at the time of the repulse of the main body, a party of about sixty of the enemy, under the command of a lieutenant-colonel, made a rush and succeeded in effecting a lodgment in the ditch at the foot of the redoubt and planting two flags on the edge of the parapet. The work was constructed in such a manner that this ditch was commanded by no part of the line, and the only means by which they could be dislodged was to retake the angle by a desperate charge and either kill or compel the surrender of the whole party by the use of hand-grenades. A call for volunteers for this purpose was made and promptly responded to by Lieutenant-Colonel E. W. Pettus, Twentieth Alabama Regiment, and about forty men of Waul's Texas Legion. A more gallant feat than this charge has not illustrated our arms during the war.

The preparations were quietly and quickly made, but the enemy seemed at once to divine our intention and opened upon the angle a terrible fire of shot, shell and musketry. Undaunted, this little band, its chivalrous commander at its head, rushed upon the work, and in less time than it requires to describe it, it and the flags were in our possession.

Preparations were then quickly made for the use of hand-grenades, when the enemy in the ditch, being informed of our purpose, immediately surrendered.

From this time forward, although on several occasions their demonstrations seemed to indicate other intentions, the enemy relinquished all idea of assaulting us and confined himself to the more cautious policy of a system of gradual approaches and mining.

The weakness of our garrison prevented anything like a system of sallies, but from time to time, as opportunities offered and the enemy effected lodgments too close to our works, they were made with spirit and success. Among them I may particularize a night sally made under the command of Lieutenant-Colonel [C. S.] Guyton, of the Fifty-seventh Georgia Regiment, with a portion of that regiment and of the Forty-third Tennessee—the former of Cummings', the latter of Reynolds' brigades. The enemy had intrenched themselves at three different points on and to the left of the Halls Ferry Road. The command sallied out, charged their works with admirable gallantry and took them, with considerable loss to the enemy, who were in greatly superior force.

On the lines occupied by General Barton and Colonel Reynolds, the configuration of the ground favoring it, the enemy were prevented from making any close lodgments by a judicious system of picketing and a series of attacks; and although they sometimes succeeded by force of numbers in gaining favorable positions, they were invariably dispossessed by the daring sallies of the garrison. A reconnoissance made of the Warrenton Road, under Colonel Curtiss, Forty-first Georgia, resulted in the capture of one hundred and seven of the enemy's pickets. The reconnoissance was conducted in a manner which reflects credit on that able officer.

I can not find words sufficiently strong to express the pride and gratification afforded me by the dauntless spirit with which officers and men encountered all the dangers, and by the unmurmuring endurance with which they bore up, for forty-seven sleepless nights and days, under all the hardships incident to their position. Confined, without a moment's relief, from the very day of their entrance into the fortifications to that of the capitulation of the city, to the narrow trenches; exposed without shelter to the broiling sun and drenching rain; subsisting on rations barely sufficient for the support of life; engaged from the earliest dawn till dark and often during the night in one ceaseless conflict with the enemy, they neither faltered nor complained, but, ever looking forward with confidence to relief, bore up bravely under every privation—saw their ranks decimated by disease and the missiles of the enemy—with the fortitude that adorns the soldier and the spirit that becomes the patriot who battles in a holy cause.

Inhabitants of Vicksburg Encamping in the Woods near the City during the Siege.

It was thus that the true soldier and gifted patriot, Colonel [Isham W.] Garrott, of the Twentieth Alabama, died, as did the brave Captain [F. O.] Claiborne, of the artillery, and many others whose names I can not mention without extending this report to too great a length. The regiment of Colonel Garrott was fortunate in having for his successor Lieutenant-Colonel [E. W.] Pettus, an officer who deserves and is competent to fill a higher position.

On July 1st, I received the accompanying confidential communication, marked A, from the lieutenant-general commanding. I immediately addressed a circular to my brigade commanders requiring their opinions on the points suggested in the note of the commanding general. Having received their opinions in writing (copies of which are appended, marked B, C, D, E), I submitted the following reply to the lieutenant-general:

HEADQUARTERS STEVENSON'S DIVISION,
VICKSBURG, July 2, 1863.

GENERAL: Your confidential note of yesterday, requesting me to inform you as to the condition of my troops and their ability to make the marches and undergo the fatigues necessary to accomplish a successful evacuation of this city, was duly received, and I have the honor to state, in reply thereto, that my men are very cheerful, but from long confinement in the trenches and short rations are necessarily much enfeebled, and a considerable number would be unable to make the march and undergo the fatigues which would probably be necessary in a successful evacuation of this city. If pressed by the enemy, and it should be necessary to place the Big Black in our rear in one march, the chances are that a considerable number of those now in the trenches could not succeed. I believe, however, that most of them, rather than be captured, would exert themselves to the utmost to accomplish it.

I respectfully transmit herewith the opinions of my brigade commanders on these points.

I am, general, respectfully your obedient servant,
C. L. STEVENSON, *Major-General.*

A council was then called on the 3d instant by the lieutenant-general, in which he stated that, from information received from General Johnston, all hope of raising the siege of Vicksburg must be abandoned, and that it was only possible to save the garrison. The opinions of those present were then asked as to the best manner of accomplishing it, and it was their unanimous opinion that, rather than surrender, the garrison would attempt to cut its way out under all circumstances, but that if an honorable capitulation could be effected it would be the best and wisest course, considering the condition of the men, as stated at that time by their commanders, and it was suggested that a communication should be addressed to Major-General Grant, commanding United States forces, asking him to appoint commissioners to meet a like number of ours to agree upon terms. It was consented to by the lieutenant-general, reluctantly, I think, and a communication was addressed to General Grant, which resulted in the capitulation. The correspondence between the two commanders has already been made public. A strong argument with me in favor of the capitulation was that we would march the army out intact; that they would be exchanged in a very short time, and again be equipped for service.

In conclusion, I desire to return my thanks to the officers and men of my command.

I have to thank my brigade commanders, Brigadier-Generals Barton, Cumming, Lee, and Colonel Reynolds, as also Colonel [T. N.] Waul, of the Texas Legion, to whose efficient co-operation I am greatly indebted for the successful defense of my line at Vicksburg, for the untiring energy which they displayed in the management of their brigades, and for examples of devotion, intrepidity and coolness under every danger, by which they inspired their men.

Major G. L. Gillespie, chief of subsistence, is deserving of especial commendation. To his energy, zeal and judicious exertions we were indebted, in my opinion, for the supplies which enabled us to make so protracted a defense of Vicksburg. Captain J. W. Johnston, inspector-general of light artillery, and Captains [James F.] Waddell and Grayson, commanding artillery on the left and right of the Halls Ferry Road, respectively, were always at their posts, and by the intelligence with which they discharged their duties contributed very materially to the defense.

Captain [Powhatan] Robinson, engineer officer in charge of my lines, performed his duties promptly and efficiently.

Major [J. E.] McElrath, acting quartermaster of my division during the siege, has placed me under many obligations by his ready anticipation of the wants of the command, and his untiring energy in supplying them.

Lieutenant G. D. Wise, ordnance officer of Cumming's brigade, has already been especially mentioned. During the siege he was selected to carry important dispatches through the lines of the enemy, and the duty was successfully performed. I commend him to the notice of the lieutenant-general as a bold and intelligent officer, and one who deserves a higher position.

Accompanying, please find a tabular statement of the casualties of my division in the different actions, etc., in which it participated up to June 16th.

The absence of subordinate officers renders it impossible for me to give my whole loss during the siege of Vicksburg.

C. L. STEVENSON,
Major-General.

Abstract from monthly report of the troops in the Department of Mississippi and East Louisiana, Lieutenant-General John C. Pemberton, C. S. A., commanding, for month of March, 1863.*

COMMAND.	Present for Duty.		Aggregate Present	Aggregate Present and Absent
	Officers	Men		
Third Military District, Major-General Frank Gardner commanding, headquarters Port Hudson:				
General and staff	10	. . .	12	17
Beall's brigade	277	2,917	3,782	5,063
Buford's brigade	230	2,505	3,458	4,396
Grigg's brigade	226	2,519	3,323	4,130
Maxey's brigade	297	2,470	3,608	4,536
Rust's brigade	187	2,750	3,401	4,685
Troops not brigaded	139	1,760	2,804	3,901
Total	1,366	14,921	20,388	26,728

* Embraces only so much of original return as relates to the Third Military District.

ORGANIZATION OF TROOPS
IN THE
THIRD MILITARY DISTRICT,
DEPARTMENT OF
MISSISSIPPI AND EAST LOUISIANA,
MAJ.-GEN. FRANKLIN GARDNER,
Commanding,
MARCH 31, 1863.

MAXEY'S BRIGADE.
Brigadier-General Samuel B. Maxey.

Fourth Louisiana—Colonel S. E. Hunter.
Thirtieth Louisiana—Major C. J. Beall.
Forty-second Tennessee—Lieutenant-Colonel Isaac N. Hulme.
Forty-sixth Tennessee—Colonel A. J. Brown.
Fifty-fifth Tennessee—Colonel A. J. Brown.
Forty-eighth Tennessee—Colonel W. M. Voorhies.
Forty-ninth Tennessee—Colonel J. E. Bailey.
Fifty-third Tennessee—Captain H. H. Aymett.
Texas Battalion Sharpshooters—Major James Burnet.
Louisiana Battery—Captain C. E. Fenner.
Mississippi Battery—Captain Calvit Roberts.

BEALL'S BRIGADE.
Brigadier-General W. N. R. Beall.

Eleventh Arkansas—Colonel John L. Logan.
Seventeenth Arkansas—Colonel John L. Logan.
Twelfth Arkansas—Colonel T. J. Reid.
Fourteenth Arkansas—Colonel O. P. Lyles.
Eighteenth Arkansas—Colonel O. P. Lyles.
Twenty-third Arkansas—Colonel O. P. Lyles.
Fifteenth Arkansas—Colonel B. W. Johnson.
Sixteenth Arkansas—Colonel B. W. Johnson.
Eighth Arkansas Battalion—Colonel B. W. Johnson.
First Mississippi—Colonel J. M. Simonton.
Thirty-ninth Mississippi—Colonel W. B. Shelby.
First Mississippi Light Artillery, Battery B—Captain A. J. Herod.
First Mississippi Light Artillery, Battery F—Captain J. L. Bradford.
First Mississippi Light Artillery, Battery K—Captain George F. Abbay.

GRIGG'S BRIGADE.
Brigadier-General John Grigg.

Ninth Louisiana Battalion—Captain T. B. R. Chinn.
Third Tennessee—Colonel R. W. MacGavock.
Tenth Tennessee—Colonel R. W. MacGavock.
Thirtieth Tennessee—Colonel R. W. MacGavock.
Forty-first Tennessee—Lieut.-Col. T. W. Beaumont.
Fiftieth Tennessee—Lieut.-Col. T. W. Beaumont.
Fifty-first Tennessee—Lieut.-Col. T. W. Beaumont.
First Tennessee Battalion—Lieut.-Col. T. W. Beaumont.
Seventh Texas—Major K. M. Van Zandt.
Brookhaven (Miss.) Artillery—Captain J. A. Hoskins.
Missouri Battery—Captain H. M. Bledsoe.

RUST'S BRIGADE.
Brigadier-General Albert Rust.

Thirty-fifth Alabama—Lieutenant-Colonel Ed. Goodwin.
Ninth Arkansas—Colonel Isaac L. Dunlap.
First Confederate Battalion—Major G. H. Forney.
Twelfth Louisiana—Colonel T. M. Scott.
Sixth Mississippi—Colonel Robert Lowry.
Fifteenth Mississippi—Lieutenant-Colonel J. R. Binford.
Hudson's battery—Lieutenant J. R. Sweaney.
Pointe Coupee, Battery A—Lieutenant C. L. Ilsley.
Pointe Coupee, Battery C—Captain A. Chust.

BUFORD'S BRIGADE.
Brigadier-General A. Buford.

Twenty-seventh Alabama—Colonel James Jackson.
Forty-ninth Alabama—Colonel Jeptha Edwards.
Fourth Alabama Battalion*—Lieutenant-Colonel John Snodgrass.
Sixth Alabama Battalion—Lieutenant-Colonel John Snodgrass.
Tenth Arkansas—Colonel A. R. Witt.
Third Kentucky—Colonel A. P. Thompson.
Seventh Kentucky—Colonel Ed. Crossland.
Miles Louisiana Legion.†
Boones Battery.†
Watson Louisiana Battery—Lieutenant E. A. Toledano.
First Alabama Heavy Artillery—Colonel I. G. W. Steedman.
Twelfth Louisiana Battalion Heavy Artillery—Lieutenant-Colonel P. F. De Gournay.
First Tennessee Battalion Heavy Artillery—Lieutenant-Colonel P. F. De Gournay.
Mississippi Battery—Captain R. T. English.

CAVALRY.

Ninth Louisiana Battalion—Colonel J. H. Wingfield.
Mississippi Battalion ‡—Major W. H. Garland.
Herren's company§—Lieutenant-Colonel Miller.
Lester's company§—Lieutenant-Colonel Miller.
Lewis' infantry company.†
Norman's company.§
Stuart's company.§

MAJ.-GEN. JOHN H. FORNEY, OF ALABAMA.

Ninth Tennessee Battalion—Lieut.-Col. George Gantt.
Bryan's company—Lieut.-Colonel George Gantt.
Cage's company—Lieut.-Colonel George Gantt.
Daigre's company—Lieut.-Col. George Gantt.
Stockdale's company—Lieut.-Col. George Gantt.
Terrell's company—Lieut.-Col. George Gantt.
Wilbourn's (Miss.) battalion—Lieut.-Col. George Gantt.

* Known also as the Sixteenth Battalion.
† Omitted from one of the two returns on file and commanders not indicated on the other.
‡ Captain T. C. Rhodes' Mississippi company attached.
§ On one of the returns Herren's and Lester's under Miller's command; on the other Norman's and Stuart's companies, no battalion commander being indicated.

Abstract from return of the District of Texas, New Mexico and Arizona, commanded by Major-General J. B. Magruder, for March, 1863.

[Headquarters Houston, Tex.]

COMMANDING OFFICER.	TROOPS.	Present for Duty.		Pieces of Artillery.			Aggregate Present	Aggregate Present and Absent
		Officers	Men	Heavy	Field	Mountain		
Brig.-Gen. H. P. Bee	Western Sub-Dist. of Texas	181	2,350	9	17	1	3,041	4,693
Brig.-Gen. W. R. Scurry	Eastern Sub-Dist. of Texas	234	3,717	. .	. .	. .	4,769	7,200
Grand total	. . . .	415	6,067	9	17	1	7,810	11,893

OFFICERS REPORTED KILLED.

CUMMING'S BRIGADE—Thirty-ninth Georgia, Lieutenant J. R. Redmond.

LEE'S BRIGADE—Twentieth Alabama, Colonel Isham W. Garrott; Forty-sixth Alabama, Lieutenants J. K. P. Cotton and J. T. House.

REYNOLDS' BRIGADE—Third Tennessee, Major J. C. Boyd, Captain B. F. Goddis and Lieutenant J. H. Cody; Forty-third Tennessee, Captain Sterling T. Turner, Lieutenant Wilson Clepper and Assistant Surgeon W. B. Johnson; Third Maryland Battery, Captain F. O. Claiborne.

WAUL'S TEXAS LEGION—Major Allen Cameron and Captains Samuel Carter and J. A. Ledbetter.

HEBERT'S BRIGADE—Staff, Colonel Charles H. Herrick; Third Louisiana, Captains J. E. Johnson and John Kinney, and Lieutenant A. S. Randolph; Twenty-first Louisiana, Captain J. Ryan and Lieutenant G. H. Mann; Twenty-second Louisiana, Captain F. Gomez and Lieutenant R. E. Lehman; Thirty-sixth Mississippi, Major Alexander Yates and Captain J. S. Tatom (Captain T. J. Chrisman and Lieutenant A. T. Murrell died of wounds); Thirty-seventh Mississippi, Lieutenant J. F. H. Trussell; Thirty-eighth Mississippi, Captain L. M. Graves and Lieutenant H. Lanehart (Captain W. A. Selph died of wounds); Forty-third Mississippi, Lieutenant M. D. L. Hods; Seventh Mississippi Battalion, Captain S. C. Pearson and Lieutenant J. C. C. Welburn (Captain W. T. Baylis died of wounds); Appeal Battery, Captain W. N. Hogg and Lieutenant R. S. Walker; Emanuel's battery, Captain T. K. Emanuel; Pointe Coupee Artillery, Lieutenant O. D'Antigue.

MOORE'S BRIGADE—Forty-second Alabama, Lieutenant Capers W. Bodie; Thirty-fifth Mississippi, Captains S. R. Coopwood and H. M. Walsh, and Lieutenant G. Moody; Fortieth Mississippi, Major R. B. Campbell; Second Texas, Captain A. F. Gommell and Lieutenant Robert S. Henry (Lieutenant William F. Kirk died of wounds).

BALDWIN'S BRIGADE—Thirty-first Louisiana, Colonel S. H. Griffin; Fourth Mississippi, Captain William H. Adaire.

VAUGHN'S BRIGADE—(No report).

SHOUP'S BRIGADE—Staff, Captains Louis Florence and J. F. Spencer; Twenty-sixth Louisiana, Major W. W. Martin, Captain Felix G. Winder and Lieutenants M. Arnaux and Peter Feriner; Twenty-seventh Louisiana, Lieutenant-Colonel L. L. McLaurin and Lieutenant George Harris (Colonel L. D. Marks mortally wounded); Twenty-eighth [Twenty-ninth] Louisiana, Captain F. Newman and Lieutenants B. F. Millet and J. G. Sims.

COCKRELL'S BRIGADE—Second Missouri, Lieutenant-Colonel P. S. Senteny; Sixth Missouri, Colonel Eugene Erwin and Lieutenants John T. Crenshaw and John Roseberry.

DOCKERY'S BRIGADE—Brigadier-General Martin E. Green.

SUMMARY OF THE CASUALTIES IN THE CONFEDERATE FORCES DURING THE SIEGE OF VICKSBURG. MAY 19 TO JULY 4, 1863.

[Compiled from the reports, and incomplete.]

COMMAND.	Killed.			Wounded.			Missing.			Aggregate	REMARKS.
	Officers	Enlisted Men	Total	Officers	Enlisted Men	Total	Officers	Enlisted Men	Total		
Stevenson's Division.											
Barton's brigade	. .	6	6	. .	20	20	. .	5	5	31	Stevenson's report.
Cumming's brigade	1	21	22	4	70	74	. .	. .	. .	96	Stevenson's report.
Lee's brigade	3	67	70	10	137	147	1	6	7	224	Stevenson's report.
A.W. Reynolds' brigade	4	10	14	. .	25	25	1	13	14	53	Stevenson's report.
Waddell's battery	.	9	9	2	28	30	. .	. .	. .	39	Stevenson's report.
Texas Legion	10	37	47	37	153	190	1	7	8	245	Waul's report.
Total	18	150	168	53	433	486	3	31	34	688	
Forney's Division.											
Hebert's brigade	25	194	219	39	416	455	. .	21	21	635	Nominal list.
Moore's brigade	8	113	121	20	284	304	. .	. .	. .	485	Nominal list.
Total	33	307	340	59	700	759	. .	21	21	1,120	
Smith's Division.											
Baldwin's brigade	. .	. .	. .	. .	.	. .	. .	. .	. .	. .	Not reported.
Vaughn's brigade	. .	. .	. .	. .	. .	. .	. .	. .	. .	. .	Not reported.
Shoup's brigade	12	95	107	11	188	199	. .	. .	. .	306	Shoup's report.
Total	12	95	107	11	188	199	. .	. .	. .	306	

ORGANIZATION OF THE CONFEDERATE ARMY OF VICKSBURG,

LIEUT.-GEN. JOHN C. PEMBERTON,
Commanding,

JULY 4, 1863.*
(The Date of Surrender.)

STEVENSON'S DIVISION.
Major-General C. L. Stevenson.

FIRST BRIGADE.
Brigadier-General S. M. Barton.

Fortieth Georgia—Lieutenant-Colonel R. M. Young.
Forty-first Georgia—Colonel Wm. E. Curtiss.
Forty-second Georgia—Colonel R. J. Henderson.
Forty-third Georgia—Captain M. M. Grantham.
Fifty-second Georgia—Major John Jay Moore.
Henderson's (Miss.) battery—Lieutenant Milton H. Trantham.
Pointe Coupee (La.) Artillery, Company A (section)—Lieutenant John Yoist.
Pointe Coupee (La.) Artillery, Company C—Captain Alexander Chust.

SECOND BRIGADE.
Brigadier-General Alfred Cumming.

Thirty-fourth Georgia—Colonel James A. Johnson.
Thirty-sixth Georgia—Major Charles E. Broyles.
Thirty-ninth Georgia—Lieutenant-Colonel J. F. B. Jackson.
Fifty-sixth Georgia—Lieutenant-Colonel J. T. Slaughter.
Fifty-seventh Georgia—Colonel William M. Barkuloo.
Cherokee (Ga.) Artillery—Captain M. Van Den Corput.

THIRD BRIGADE.
Brigadier-General S. D. Lee.

Twentieth Alabama—Colonel Edmund W. Pettus.
Twenty-third Alabama—Colonel F. K. Beck.
Thirtieth Alabama—Captain John C. Francis.
Thirty-first Alabama—Lieutenant-Colonel T. M. Arrington.
Forty-sixth Alabama—Captain George E. Brewer.
Alabama Battery—Captain J. F. Waddell.

FOURTH BRIGADE.
Colonel A. W. Reynolds.

Third Tennessee (Provisional Army)—Colonel N. J. Lillard.
Thirty-ninth Tennessee†—Colonel Wm. M. Bradford.
Forty-third Tennessee—Colonel James W. Gillespie.
Fifty-ninth Tennessee—Colonel William L. Eakin.
Third Maryland Battery—Captain John B. Rowan.

WAUL'S TEXAS LEGION.
Colonel T. N. Waul.

First Battalion (infantry)—Major Eugene S. Bolling.
Second Battalion (infantry)—Lieutenant-Colonel James Wrigley.
Cavalry battalion—Lieutenant Thomas J. Cleveland.
Artillery company—Captain J. Q. Wall.

* The commanders are given as indicated by the paroles.
† Paroled as the Thirty-first Regiment, and so known prior to June, 1863.

LIEUT.-GEN. JOHN C. PEMBERTON, OF VIRGINIA.

ATTACHED.

First Tennessee Cavalry (Carter's regiment), Company C—Captain R. S. Vandyke.
Botetourt (Va.) Artillery*—Lieutenant James P. Wright.
Signal Corps—Lieutenant C. H. Barrot.

"WHISTLING DICK," THE FAMOUS CONFEDERATE GUN ON THE HEIGHTS OVERLOOKING THE RIVER AT VICKSBURG, MISS.

FORNEY'S DIVISION.
Major-General John H. Forney.

HEBERT'S BRIGADE.
Brigadier-General Louis Hebert.

Third Louisiana—Major David Pierson.
Twenty-first Louisiana—Lieutenant-Colonel J. T. Plattsmier.
Thirty-sixth Mississippi—Colonel W. W. Witherspoon.
Thirty-seventh Mississippi—Colonel O. S. Holland.
Thirty-eighth Mississippi—Captain D. B. Seal.
Forty-third Mississippi—Colonel Richard Harrison.
Seventh Alabama (battalion)—Captain A. M. Dozier.
Second Alabama (artillery battalion), Company C—Lieutenant John R. Sclater.
Appeal (Ark.) battery—Lieutenant R. N. Cotter.

MOORE'S BRIGADE.
Brigadier-General John C. Moore.

Thirty-seventh Alabama—Colonel J. T. Dowdell.
Fortieth Alabama—Colonel John H. Higley.
Forty-second Alabama—Colonel John W. Portis.
First Mississippi Light Artillery†—Colonel William T. Withers.
Thirty-fifth Mississippi—Lieutenant-Colonel C. R. Jordan.
Fortieth Mississippi—Colonel W. B. Colbert.
Second Texas—Colonel Ashbel Smith.
Alabama Battery—Captain H. H. Sengstak.
Pointe Coupee (La.) Artillery, Company B—Captain William A. Davidson.

SMITH'S DIVISION.
Major-General M. L. Smith.

BALDWIN'S BRIGADE.

Seventeenth Louisiana—Colonel Robert Richardson.
Thirty-first Louisiana—Lieutenant-Colonel James W. Draughon.
Fourth Mississippi—Captain Thomas P. Nelson.
Forty-sixth Mississippi—Colonel C. W. Sears.
Tennessee Battery—Captain Thomas F. Tobin.

VAUGHN'S BRIGADE.
Brigadier-General J. C. Vaughn.

Sixtieth Tennessee—Captain J. W. Bachman.
Sixty-first Tennessee—Lieutenant-Colonel James G. Rose.
Sixty-second Tennessee—Colonel John A. Rowan.

SHOUP'S BRIGADE.
Brigadier-General Francis A. Shoup.

Twenty-sixth Louisiana—Lieutenant-Colonel William C. Crow.
Twenty-seventh Louisiana—Captain Joseph T. Hatch.
Twenty-eighth (Twenty-ninth) Louisiana—Colonel Allen Thomas.
McNally's (Ark.) battery—Captain Joseph T. Hatch.

MISSISSIPPI STATE TROOPS.‡
Brigadier-General John V. Harris.

Fifth Regiment—Colonel H. C. Robinson.
Third Battalion—Lieutenant-Colonel Thomas A. Burgin.

ATTACHED.

Fourteenth Mississippi Light Artillery Batteries—Major M. S. Ward.
Mississippi Partisan Rangers—Captain J. S. Smyth.
Signal Corps—Captain Max T. Davidson.

* Assignment uncertain.
† Batteries A, C, D, E, G and I. Battery L (Vaiden artillery) reported in Higgins' command, and batteries B, F and K at Port Hudson, La.
‡ Under Vaughn's command.

BOWEN'S DIVISION.
Major-General John S. Bowen.

FIRST (MISSOURI) BRIGADE.
Colonel Francis M. Cockrell.

First Missouri—Colonel A. C. Riley.
Second Missouri—Major Thomas M. Carter.
Third Missouri—Major J. K. McDowell.
Fifth Missouri—Colonel James McCown.
Sixth Missouri—Major S. Cooper.
Ginter's (Mo.) battery—Lieutenant Cornelius Heffernan.
Landis' (Mo.) battery—Lieutenant John M. Langan.
Wade's (Mo.) battery—Lieutenant R. C. Walsh.

SECOND BRIGADE.
Colonel T. P. Dockery.

Fifteenth Arkansas—Captain Caleb Davis.
Nineteenth Arkansas—Captain James K. Norwood.
Twentieth Arkansas—Colonel D. W. Jones.
Twenty-first Arkansas—Captain A. Tyler.
First Arkansas Cavalry Battalion—Captain John J. Clark.
Twelfth Arkansas Battalion (sharpshooters)—Lieutenant John S. Bell.
First Missouri Cavalry—Major William C. Parker.
Third Missouri Cavalry—Captain Felix Lotspeich.
Third Missouri Battery—Captain William E. Dawson.
Lowe's (Mo.) battery—Lieutenant Thomas B. Catron.

RIVER BATTERIES.*
Colonel Ed. Higgins.

First Louisiana Artillery†—Lieutenant-Colonel D. Beltzhoover.
Eighth Louisiana Heavy Artillery Battalion‡—Major T. N. Ogden.
Twenty-second Louisiana§—Captain Samuel Jones.
First Tennessee Heavy Artillery—Colonel A. Jackson, Jr.
Tennessee battery—Captain J. B. Caruthers.
Tennessee battery—Captain T. N. Johnston.
Tennessee battery—Captain J. P. Lynch.
Vaiden (Miss.) battery—Captain S. C. Bains.

BRIG.-GEN. ALFRED CUMMING, OF GEORGIA.

MISCELLANEOUS.

Fifty-fourth Alabama (detachment)—Lieutenant Joel P. Abney.
City Guards—Captain E. B. Martin.
Signal Corps—Captain C. A. King.

* The troops in this command paroled as of Moore's brigade.
† Bond's, Bruce's, Butler's, Capers', Grayson's, Haynes', Lamon's and Robertson's companies.
‡ Borrow's, Grandpre's and McCrory's companies.
§ P. A. Gomez, Mark's.

MOTHER, IS THE BATTLE OVER?

Mother, is the battle over? Thousands have been killed, they say—
Is my father coming?—tell me, have the Southerners gained the day?
Is he well? or is he wounded? Mother, do you think he's slain?
If you know, I pray you, tell me—will my father come again?
Mother, dear, you're always sighing since you last the paper read—
Tell me why you are crying—why that cap is on your head?
Ah! I see you can not tell me—father's one among the slain!
Altho' he lov'd us very dearly, he will never come again.

THE SURRENDER OF VICKSBURG.

A DEFENSE OF GENERAL PEMBERTON.

BY

MAJOR R. W. MEMMINGER,

A. A. G. and Chief of Staff, Department of Mississippi and East Louisiana.

September ——, 1863.

IN passing judgment upon Lieutenant-General Pemberton the people seem to have considered, not what he *has* done, but what he has *not* done. They say, "Why did he not provision Vicksburg," and not "Did he do everything that could be done toward that object?" The army of Lieutenant-General Pemberton numbering some forty thousand effectives, had to contend against the armies of Grant and Banks, the smaller of which nearly equaled his entire force; the other was vastly superior—and these armies operating three hundred miles apart. In the campaign in North Mississippi Grant was completely out maneuvered, and forced to retire to Memphis, from whence he had set out; the advance of the enemy on Vicksburg via Chickasaw Bayou met with disastrous defeat, and the combined naval and land attack on Fort Pemberton, Tallahatchie River, was signally repulsed—all these successes are overlooked.

In October, 1862, Lieutenant-General Pemberton was assigned to the Department of Mississippi and East Louisiana, and, upon assuming command, he at once perceived the magnitude of the undertaking. The army of North Mississippi, but lately defeated at Corinth, and considerably demoralized required a thorough reorganization. Confusion reigned equally in the quartermaster, commissary, engineer and ordnance departments. No system of any kind prevailed, and the whole department was one chaos.

From this disorganization, order began gradually to arise; chiefs of the various departments were appointed, and, through their untiring exertion, aided and directed by the lieutenant-general commanding, the department was reorganized, remodeled and supplied. Any officer or soldier who served in the army of Mississippi and East Louisiana can vouch for the truth of this speedy revolution. The duties of the department were arduous and extended, and were met with vigor and energy. Holly Springs, Port Hudson, Vicksburg, points separated by hundreds of miles, were continually visited and the works at the latter two places were pushed forward to speedy completion. At the same time the administration of the department was by no means neglected; and frequently the nights, which might have been given to rest, were devoted to the labors of the office.

CONFEDERATE SCOUTS PASSING THROUGH FEDERAL PICKET LINES WITH SUPPLIES OF PERCUSSION CAPS.

When the winter season had closed in, and the enemy had begun to threaten Vicksburg and Port Hudson, the army which had hitherto served in North Mississippi was withdrawn to these points. The cavalry—five thousand strong—which had belonged to that army, was separated and sent to General Bragg. To the withdrawal of this, almost the entire cavalry force of the department, much of the subsequent disaster is to be attributed. This proceeding was contrary to the wishes and judgment of the lieutenant-general commanding, and against his protest. General Pemberton is known to have professed himself totally unable to keep his railroad communications open, and to protect the country from inroads without the aid of a strong force of cavalry.

Grierson's raid, which occurred in April, and closely preceded Grant's advance upon Vicksburg, was evidently concerted for the purpose of cutting all railroad communications and so embarrassing the transportation of supplies. It succeeded in this object, which success is wholly attributable to the absence of a sufficient force of cavalry. To supply this deficiency, under the exigency, General Pemberton was compelled to resort to the impressment of private horses, and to mount infantry, which could illy be spared.

On the night of the 16th of April the enemy's fleet attempted to pass the batteries at Vicksburg. Some six or seven gunboats and transports succeeded; one boat was burned, another sunk and the remainder were forced to put back. With the number of guns and weight of metal, it was impossible to effect more damage. Vicksburg, the grand key to the Mississippi, had only twenty-eight guns, of which two were smooth-bore 32-pounders, two 24-pounders, one 30-pound Parrott, one Whitworth, and one 10-inch mortar. Compare this with the armament of Charleston Harbor; Fort Pemberton alone, on Stono River, can compete with the entire batteries of Vicksburg. Every possible exertion was made to procure more ordnance, and even guns intended for the navy were diverted for army use. But, probably, owing to a scarcity of guns and the time required to transport them, no further supply could be procured, and Vicksburg repelled every assault of the vaunted ironclads, and stood a siege of forty-eight days, with an armament of *twenty-eight guns*.

After the passage of the boats alluded to, the character of the defense of Vicksburg, as expressed by General Pemberton, was changed. The enemy could operate from below. He now made a demonstration on our left flank, landing a force at Chickasaw Bayou; also a naval attack on Haines' Bluff, Yazoo River, and at the same time threw a heavy column across the Mississippi River, on the right flank at Brunisburg, below Port Gibson. To meet this column, Brigadier-General Bowen was ordered to move out from Grand Gulf, which he did, holding the enemy for some time in check near Bayou Pierre. Re-enforcements were at the same time hurried forward, Major-General Loring in command. General Bowen, however, being pressed by vastly superior numbers, was forced to fall back, crossing the Big Black River, after having destroyed the works at Grand Gulf.

It was now General Pemberton's intention to concentrate his troops behind the Big Black, the question of subsistence, proximity to base, and necessity of supporting Vicksburg, being the determining causes. At the same time the arrival of re-enforcements was anxiously awaited.

In the meantime the enemy was heavily re-enforcing and apparently moving on Jackson.

On the 14th of May General Pemberton received instructions to move and attack the enemy toward Clinton, Miss. A council of war was called of the general officers and the matter laid before them for their deliberation and opinions. The majority of those present expressed themselves in favor of the movement. The minority (among whom was General Pemberton) expressed themselves averse, regarding it as too hazardous, preferring a movement by which it might be endeavored to cut off the enemy's supplies from the Mississippi, and not to move the army from its base—Vicksburg. Subsequent developments show that this policy would probably have defeated the objects of Grant's campaign. His army was furnished with only five days' rations, and, as expressed by their own officers, was in almost a starving condition; and the transportation from the Mississippi, a distance of forty miles, open to constant interruption from our forces, was precarious and almost impracticable. It was therefore essential that he should obtain a new base, which could be established only by the opening of the Yazoo River; and his policy was to bring about a battle as the means of obtaining this end. Certainly, under these circumstances, and with our known inferiority of numbers, our policy would have been to have avoided an engagement. Pursuant to instructions, however, General Pemberton moved out of Vicksburg with seventeen thousand five hundred men, and met and engaged the enemy at Baker's Creek, near Raymond. The enemy was at first repulsed; but continuing to receive heavy re-enforcements, General Pemberton was overwhelmed by numbers and forced to fall back to the intrenchments on the Big Black. The enemy pushed on rapidly and again encountered our forces behind these intrenchments, which, however, we failed to defend, and retired in rather a disorderly manner to the inner line of works around Vicksburg. The abandonment of the intrenchments on Big Black necessitated the evacuation of Haines' Bluff, the left flank of that line, thus opening the Yazoo River to the enemy's fleet and rendering his transportation easy.

Although considerably demoralized by the defeats at Baker's Creek and Big Black, the army was now posted within the trenches around Vicksburg. At this juncture instructions were received by General Pemberton to evacuate Vicksburg and bring out his army. A council of war of the general officers was immediately called, in which the opinion was unanimously expressed that it was impossible to withdraw the army from its position with such *morale* and *materiel* as to be of further service to the Confederacy. While the council of war was assembled, the guns of the enemy opened on our works and Vicksburg was besieged. General Pemberton determined to hold the place, hoping that he would receive assistance in maintaining this obstruction to the enemy's free navigation of the Mississippi River.

At the time of the investment, the garrison of Vicksburg was eighteen thousand strong—scarcely sufficient to man the trenches, and affording no force for reserve. The amount of provisions on hand was estimated at forty days' rations, the full ration, however, being considerably reduced. General Pemberton has been censured for not provisioning Vicksburg for a *protracted* siege; and to this cause is attributed, as we think erroneously, the *fall* of that city.

Vicksburg *did* stand a protracted siege of forty-eight days. It was not provisioned for an *indefinite* siege nor could be. It has been stated that General Pemberton assumed command of this department in October, 1862; it has further been shown against what difficulties he had to contend in the organization of his department. Some time must necessarily elapse between such organization and the time when its effects could be felt, before contracts could be made and supplies begin to come in.

The sources from which Vicksburg could be supplied were from the country west of the Mississippi via Red River and Big Black; from Yazoo River via Haines' Bluff (the supplies in this case consisting almost exclusively of corn and being drawn from the section of country on Sunflower and Tallahatchie Rivers, Deer Creek, etc.), and lastly, from the interior of the State of Mississippi—in which case they must be transported over long lines of railroad. Port Hudson could be supplied only from the Mississippi River, being distant sixty miles from the nearest depot on the New Orleans & Jackson railroad.

Large standing garrisons were to be supplied at each of these points, at the one varying from ten to twenty thousand and at the other from eight to fifteen thousand. To accumulate at these points was evidently a difficult undertaking, considering the daily consumption to be met and the small number of boats at government disposal. As soon as the wet season set in and navigation became practicable, supplies of beef cattle, bacon, corn and salt were forwarded by government agents purchasing in the Trans-Mississippi Department. But in the midst of this occupation, early in February, the enemy's gunboats, Queen of the West and Indianola, succeeded in passing the Vicksburg batteries, and thus prevented the safe navigation of the Mississippi. The route was reopened by the capture of the Indianola and Queen of the West, but almost immediately reclosed by a movement of the enemy's fleet. Commodore Farragut attacked our batteries at Port Hudson; two of his vessels, the Hartford and Monongahela, succeeded in passing; the frigate Mississippi was burned; the Richmond disabled and forced to put back. Farragut immediately proceeded to blockade the mouth of Red River, as also that of Big Black. Thus ended all hopes of drawing supplies from the Trans-Mississippi Department. Some few boats subsequently succeeded in running the blockade, but such mode of supply was precarious in the extreme, and was finally destroyed by the passage of the enemy's fleet by Vicksburg.

As a source of supply, the country on Sunflower River, Deer Creek, etc., was not neglected. These streams were not navigable until later in the winter season, and operations could not be commenced so soon. Light draft boats from those above the raft at Haines' Bluff were fitted up and sent after corn; but the great difficulty was to obtain the corn on the banks of the river. The planters generally expressed their inability to haul to such points, being without any means of transportation. Hence very little of the grain in those fertile sections was available to the army. Any one acquainted with the Mississippi bottom lands can vouch for the difficulty—almost impracticability—of transportation during the winter season. But even these operations were frustrated by the passage of the enemy through Yazoo Pass, their descent upon Fort Pemberton, Tallahatchie River, and their naval raids through the numerous bayous which ramify this portion of Mississippi. Previous to this interruption, the grain intended for Vicksburg was unloaded at Haines' Bluff, eleven miles distant, this being rendered necessary by the raft at that point, which was intended to obstruct the passage of the enemy's fleet by our batteries Furthermore, the mouth of the Yazoo River was closely blockaded by the enemy's fleet, and here again the difficulty of transportation over impracticable roads presented itself. The transportation of a single eight or ten inch Columbiad from Vicksburg to Haines' Bluff—eleven miles—was a matter of two weeks. Nevertheless corn, and a considerable supply, was hauled over this road.

Lastly, as to drawing supplies from the interior of the State, every means was taken to accomplish this object. All exportation of supplies from the department was prohibited. Depots were established and agents dispatched in all directions. Supplies were forwarded to Vicksburg, and even Port Hudson, as rapidly as they could be accumulated. The necessity for constantly moving troops to various parts of the department, as they might be threatened, was a serious inconvenience and impeded the transportation of supplies. That portion of the Southern Railroad between Jackson and Vicksburg was in a miserable and even dangerous condition. Accidents occurred almost daily, engines being broken up, and there being a lamentable scarcity of any species of cars. This, the great thoroughfare to Vicksburg, was entirely out of repair and almost impassable. The obstruction offered to transportation by such a thoroughfare can easily be imagined. Notwithstanding all these difficulties, Vicksburg was sufficiently provisioned to hold out for forty days, and Port Hudson sustained a siege of seven weeks.

As above stated, the effective garrison of Vicksburg numbered eighteen thousand. This small force, directed by the untiring vigilance of the lieutenant-general commanding, and defended by his engineering skill, were enabled to repel the repeated assaults of an enemy flushed with success and numbering, at the lowest estimate, some sixty thousand men. All confess that the defense of Vicksburg was resolute and gallant. Soon after the investment Grant attempted to carry the place by two general assaults, apparently bringing his whole army to the attack. His columns, hurled upon the resolute garrison, were as often hurled back with heavy loss, and leaving five stands of colors in our hands and the field for miles strewn with his dead, he was compelled to fall back and sit down to a formal investment of the place.

During the siege the engineering skill of the commander and his fertility and expedients were conspicuously displayed. Works, which under the unceasing and concentrated fire of hundreds of guns were demolished, reappeared in improved forms which could be suggested only by consummate ingenuity. Works built to withstand guns used in ordinary warfare were found wholly inadequate to resist the heavy metal of the enemy, and subjected to incessant and galling fire of musketry, the artillery could with difficulty be worked. Here it was particularly that the ingenuity of the commanding general was exhibited. The position of the pieces was constantly changing; embankments disappeared under the fire of the enemy's guns, but the artillery would still be found in position, and stronger than before. No difficulty could occur for which an expedient was not at hand.

But energy and ingenuity, although tending to postpone, could not prevent the fall of Vicksburg. At the beginning of the siege, it was understood and confidently expected that a force from without would relieve the garrison; and this hope sustained the soldiery and the commanding general during the protracted struggle. But this hope, continually deferred and finally abandoned, resolved the matter into a question of time and honor. Honor was considered to have been sufficiently vindicated. The time it was considered had come. The soldiers who, for forty-eight days and nights, vigilant and undaunted, had watched and fought in the trenches, were worn out. A general assault of the besieging army was confidently anticipated on the 4th of July, and it was improbable that the garrison, exhausted by fatigues and diminished to fifteen thousand, would be able to withstand this overwhelming assault. The lines of the enemy at some points were within a few yards of our own; their mines sapped our works at numerous points, and were supposed to be only awaiting springing. Attempts to countermine were made, but of course not always successfully, and in one of these endeavors the enemy sprung a mine loaded with a ton of powder, blowing up eighty of our men, some of whom were then engaged in the work. Believing themselves to be undermined, the men were becoming restive in the trenches. Provisions also were at a low ebb; it would have been impossible under any circumstances to hold out much longer; and should the place be carried by assault, no terms could be expected and all the horrors of a sacked city were to be anticipated. The only alternative was to cut through the enemy's lines or to capitulate. There being no hope of relief, a council of war of the general officers was called, and this alternative presented. It was the opinion of the majority that it was physically impossible for the men to cut through the enemy's lines and carry the works obstructing their exit—works known to be as formidable as our own. The minority (among whom was the lieutenant-general commanding) were of a contrary opinion, and advocated an attempt to cut their way out. The opinion of the majority prevailed, the commanding general yielding to their discretion, and preparations for the negotiation of terms were entered upon—with what success is before the public.

After the surrender the lieutenant-general commanding remained with his army attending to their wants, and shared with them the hardships of the march to Enterprise, where the army of Vicksburg was dissolved on parole.

Such, in the humble opinion of the undersigned, is a brief synopsis of the events preceding and attending the fall of Vicksburg.

* * * * * *

R. W. MEMMINGER,
Assistant Adjutant-General and Chief of Staff.

SHARPSHOOTERS PROTECTING FEDERAL TROOPS WHILE ENGAGED IN DIGGING AN ENTRANCE INTO THE FORT.

WHY THE PICKETS CEASED FIRING AT EACH OTHER.—The pickets on the left at Sharpsburg, in front of Jackson's corps, were in the habit of shooting at each other until a rebel shouted to a Federal and asked him to agree *not* to shoot, to which the Yankee assented; but in a short time Johnny cried out: "Say, Yank, tell the man on your left not to shoot; would just as lief be shot by *you* as by *him*." So the word passed from man to man till not a gun was fired on the picket line.

FORREST'S EXPEDITION INTO WEST TENNESSEE,

DECEMBER 11, 1862, TO JANUARY 3, 1863.

BY

BRIG.-GEN. NATHAN B. FORREST, C. S. A.,
Commanding Expedition.

BRIGADE HEADQUARTERS,
NEAR UNION CITY, TENN., December 24, 1862.

IN accordance with your order I moved with my command from Columbia on the 11th instant; reached the river at Clifton on Sunday, the 13th, and after much difficulty, working night and day, finished crossing on the 15th, encamping that night eight miles west of the river.

On the 16th [18th] we met the pickets of the enemy near Lexington and attacked their forces at Lexington, consisting of one section of artillery and eight hundred cavalry. We routed them completely, capturing the two guns and one hundred and forty-eight prisoners, including Colonel [R. G.] Ingersoll and Major [L. H.] Kerr, of the Eleventh Illinois Cavalry. We also captured about seventy horses, which were badly needed and immediately put in service in our batteries. The balance of the Federal cavalry fled in the direction of Trenton and Jackson. We pushed on rapidly to Jackson and, on the evening of the 18th, drove in their pickets on all the roads leading out of Jackson. On the same night I sent Colonel [G. G.] Dibrell on the right of Jackson to tear up the railroad track and destroy the telegraph wires. He captured at Webb's Station one hundred and one Federals, destroying their stockade, and tore up the road, switch, etc., at the turn out. At the same time that Dibrell was sent on the right Colonel [A. A.] Russell [Fourth Alabama Cavalry] and Major [N. N.] Cox [Second Battalion Tennessee Cavalry], with their commands, were sent out on the left to destroy bridges and culverts on the railroads from Jackson to Corinth and Bolivar.

The next morning [December 19th] I advanced on Jackson with Colonel [T. G.] Woodward's two companies and Colonel [J. B.] Biffle's battalion of about four hundred men, with two pieces of artillery from Freeman's battery. About four miles from Jackson skirmishing began with the skirmishers, and the enemy was reported advancing with two regiments of infantry and a battalion of cavalry. We opened on them with the guns, and after a running fight of about an hour, drove them into their fortifications. The enemy had heavily re-enforced at Jackson from Corinth, Bolivar and La Grange, and numbered, from the best information I could obtain, about nine thousand men. I withdrew my forces that evening and moved rapidly on Trenton and Humboldt. Colonel Dibrell's command was sent to destroy the bridge over the Forked Deer River between Humboldt and Jackson. Colonel [J. W.] Starnes was sent to attack Humboldt, Colonel Biffle was sent so as to get in the rear of Trenton, while with Major Cox's command and my body-guard, commanded by Captain [M.] Little and [S. L.] Freeman's [Tennessee] battery, I dashed into the town [Trenton], attacking the enemy. They were fortified at the depot, but were without artillery. After a short engagement between their sharpshooters and our cavalry our battery opened on them, and on the third fire from the battery they surrendered.

We lost two men killed and seven wounded; the enemy two killed and over seven hundred prisoners, with a large quantity of stores, arms, ammunition and provisions, which, for want of transportation, we were compelled to destroy. We captured several hundred horses, but few of them were of any value; those that were of service we took, and the balance I handed over to the citizens, from whom many of them had been pressed or stolen. Colonel Russell, who was protecting our rear at Spring Creek, found the enemy advancing and following us with three thousand infantry, two batteries and several hundred cavalry. He skirmished with them during the evening, and the next morning before daylight dismounted half of his command and succeeded in getting within sixty yards of their encampment. They discovered him, and formed in line of battle. He delivered a volley as soon as their line was formed, and the balance of the regiment charged on horseback. The enemy became panic-stricken and retreated hastily across Spring Creek, burning the bridge after them. We have heard nothing from them since in that direction.

Colonel [James W.] Starnes took Humboldt, capturing over one hundred prisoners. He destroyed the stockade, railroad depot, and burned up a trestle bridge near that point.

Colonel Dibrell's command failed to destroy the bridge over the Forked Deer River, as the enemy were strongly fortified and protected by two creeks on one side of the railroad, and a wide, swampy bottom on the other, which rendered the approach of cavalry impossible. He dismounted his men, and while approaching their fort a train arrived from Jackson with a regiment of infantry. Lieutenant [John W., Jr.,] Morton with two guns opened on the train, when it retired, the troops on it gaining the stockade. Owing to the situation of the stockade, and the density of the timber and the wet, miry condition of the bottom, the guns could not be brought to bear on it. Night coming on Colonel Dibrell withdrew and rejoined my command.

We remained in Trenton during the night of the 20th, paroling all the prisoners, and selecting from the stores at the depot such as were needed by the command.

On the morning of the 21st I fired the depot, burning up the remaining supplies, with about six hundred bales of cotton, two hundred barrels of pork, and a large lot of tobacco in hogsheads, used by the enemy for breastworks. After seeing everything destroyed I moved on in the direction of Union City, capturing at Rutherford Station two companies of Federals, and destroying the railroad from Trenton to Kenton Station, at which place we captured Colonel [Thomas J.] Kinney of the One Hundred and Twenty-second [One Hundred and Nineteenth] Illinois Regiment, and twenty-two men left sick in the hospital. I took a portion of the command and pushed ahead to Union City, capturing one hundred and six Federals without firing a gun. I destroyed the railroad bridge over the bayou near Moscow, and am completing the destruction of the bridges over the North and South fork of Obion River, with nearly four miles of trestling in the bottom between them. We have made a clean sweep of the Federals and roads north of Jackson, and know of no Federals except at Fort Heiman, Paducah and Columbus, north of Jackson and west of the Tennessee River. Reports that are reliable show that the Federals are rapidly sending up troops from Memphis. One hundred and twenty-five transports passed down a few days ago within ten hours, and daily they are passing up loaded with troops. General Grant must either be in very critical condition, or else affairs in Kentucky require the movement.

Our loss so far is eight killed, twelve wounded and two missing. The enemy's killed and wounded, over one hundred men; prisoners, over twelve hundred, including four colonels, four majors, ten captains and twenty-three lieutenants.

I left Middleburg on the 25th, proceeding via the Northwestern Railroad to McKenzie's Station, destroying all the bridges and trestles on that road from Union City to McKenzie's Station. From McKenzie's Station we were compelled to move southward in the direction of Lexington, as the enemy in force occupied Trenton, Humboldt, Huntingdon and Lexington. After my command left Trenton they commenced re-enforcing and moving to the points named, with a view of cutting off my command and prevent us recrossing the Tennessee. Understanding a force was moving on me from Trenton in the direction of Dresden, I sent Colonel [J. B.] Biffle [Nineteenth Tennessee Cavalry] in that direction to protect our movements toward Lexington, intending if possible to avoid the enemy and go on and attack the enemy at Bethel Station, on the Mobile & Ohio Road, south of Jackson. We left McKenzie's Station on the morning of December 28th, but in crossing the bottom had great difficulty in crossing our artillery and wagons; the bridges proved to be much decayed, and gave way, forcing us to drag our artillery and wagons through the bottom and the creeks. It was with great difficulty we got through by working the entire night; and our men and horses were so much fatigued, that I was compelled to encamp at Flake's Store about sixteen miles north of Lexington, when, under ordinary circumstances and good roads, we ought to have reached Lexington that night, which place had been evacuated by the enemy, believing that I would either cross the Tennessee at Huntingdon or else that I would move northward.

On the morning of the 31st we moved off in the direction of Lexington, but had not gone more than four miles before we met the skirmishers of the enemy. We engaged and fought six regiments for five hours, driving them back until 3 o'clock in the evening, [when] they took shelter in a grove of timber of about sixty acres, inclosed by a fence and surrounded by open fields. I had sent four companies to Clarksburg to protect and advise me of any advance from Huntingdon, and finding that we were able to whip the enemy, dismounted a portion of my cavalry to support my artillery and attack in front, while I could flank them on each side and get Colonel [A. A.] Russell's regiment [Fourth Alabama Cavalry] in their rear. We drove them through the woods with great slaughter, and several white flags were raised in various portions of the woods, and the killed and wounded were strewn over the ground. Thirty minutes more would have given us the day, when to my surprise and astonishment a fire was opened on us in our rear, and the enemy in heavy force under General [J. C.] Sullivan advanced on us. Knowing that I had four companies at Clarksburg, seven miles from us on the Huntingdon road, I could not believe that they were Federals until I rode up myself into their lines. The heavy fire of their infantry, unexpected and unlooked for by all, caused a stampede of horses belonging to my dismounted men, who were following up and driving the enemy before them. They also killed and crippled many of the horses attached to our caissons and reserved guns.

LIEUTENANT-GENERAL NATHAN BEDFORD FORREST, OF TENNESSEE.

I had sent back two miles for more ammunition. My men had been fighting for five hours, and both artillery and small-arm ammunition were well nigh exhausted. We occupied the battlefield, were in possession of the enemy's dead and wounded and their three pieces of artillery, and had demanded a surrender of the brigade, which would doubtless have been forced or accepted in half an hour, the colonel commanding proposing to leave the field entirely and withdraw his force, provided we would allow him to bury his dead; but, believing I could force—and that in a short time—the demand, the fighting continued, the Federals scattering in every direction. The stampede of horses and horse-holders announced that help was at hand; and, finding my command now exposed to fire from both front and rear, I was compelled to withdraw, which I did in good order, leaving behind our dead and wounded. We were able to bring off six pieces of artillery and two caissons; the balance, with the three guns we captured, we were compelled to leave, as most of the horses were killed or crippled and the drivers in the same condition, which rendered it impossible to get them out under the heavy fire of the enemy from both front and rear. Our loss in artillery is three guns and eight caissons and one piece which burst during the action.

The enemy's loss was very heavy in killed and wounded, and, as we had the field and saw them piled up and around the fences, had a good opportunity of judging their loss. We gave them grape and canister from our guns at three hundred yards, and as they fell back through the timber their loss was terrible. The prisoners say that at least one-third of the command was killed or wounded. From all I could see and learn from my aids and officers, they must have lost in killed and wounded from eight hundred to one thousand men. The fire of our artillery, for accuracy and rapidity, was scarcely, if ever, excelled, and their position in the fence-corners proved to the enemy, instead of a protection, a source of great loss, as our shot and shell scattered them to the winds, and many were killed by rails that were untouched by balls. Captain Freeman and Lieutenant [J. W.] Morton, of our batteries, with all of their men, deserve special mention, keeping up, as they did, a constant fire from their pieces, notwithstanding the enemy made every effort at silencing them by shooting down the artillerists at the guns. The whole command fought well. We had about eighteen hundred men in the engagement, and fought six regiments of infantry, with three pieces of artillery, which we charged and took, but were compelled to leave them, as the horses were all killed or crippled. We brought off eighty-three prisoners, and they report their respective regiments as badly cut off. They lost three colonels and many company officers.

We have, on our side, to deplore the death of Colonel [T.] Alonzo Napier [Tenth Tennessee Cavalry], who was killed while leading his men in a charge on foot. He was a gallant officer, and after he fell his command continued to drive the enemy from their position on the right bank, strewing their path with dead and wounded Federals.

I can not speak in too high terms of all my commanding officers; and the men, considering they were mostly raw recruits, fought well. I have not been able, as yet, to ascertain our exact loss, but am of the opinion that sixty killed and wounded and one hundred captured or missing will cover it. I saved all my wagons except my ammunition wagons, which, by a mistake of orders, were driven right into the enemy's line. This is seriously to be regretted, as we had captured six wagon loads of it; and when I ordered up one wagon of ammunition and two ambulances, the wagon-master and ordnance officer, not knowing exactly what kind was wanted, or misunderstanding the order, brought off all the ammunition; and by the time he reached the point with them where the battle began, that portion of the ground was in possession of the enemy, and the guards, etc., were forced to abandon them.

We have always been short of shot-gun caps, and, as we captured nothing but musket caps, all the men using shot-guns were out, or nearly so, of caps after the action was over. Considering our want of ammunition for small arms and artillery and the worn-down condition of our men and horses, I determined at once to recross the Tennessee River and fit up for a return. Had we been entirely successful in the battle of the 31st I should have attacked Bethel Station on the 2d instant; had already sent a company to cut wires and bridges, and had forage prepared twelve miles south of Lexington for my entire command; but after the fight, and knowing we were followed by Federals in heavy force from Trenton and Huntingdon, and that a force would also move on us from Jackson as soon as they learned I had pushed south of Lexington, I deemed it advisable to cross the Tennessee, which I accomplished yesterday and last night in safety.

Colonel Biffle, who I before mentioned as having been sent to Trenton, or in that direction, returned in time to take part in the battle at Parker's Crossroads. He captured and paroled one hundred and fifty Federals within six miles of Trenton.

The captains of the four companies sent to Clarksburg have not yet reached here with their commands. Had they done their duty by advising me of the approach of the enemy I could have terminated the fight by making it short and decisive, when without such advice I was whipping them badly with my artillery, and unless absolutely necessary was not pressing them with my cavalry. I had them entirely surrounded and was driving them before me, and was taking it leisurely and trying as much as possible to save my men. The four companies, on the approach of the enemy, left for Tennessee River and have not yet reported here.

I do not design this, general, as a regular report, but will make one as soon as I can do so. We crossed the river at three points and the brigade is not yet together, or reports from the different commands have not come in. We have worked, rode and fought hard, and I hope accomplished, to a considerable extent, if not entirely, the object of our campaign, as we drew from Corinth, Grand Junction and La Grange about twenty thousand Federals.

N. B. FORREST,
Brigadier-General Commanding Brigade.

GENERAL FORREST DRIVING THE FEDERALS OUT OF TRENTON, TENN. GENERAL FORREST IN THE FOREGROUND GIVING ORDERS.

THE CHANCELLORSVILLE CAMPAIGN,

APRIL 27 TO MAY 6, 1863.

BY

GENERAL ROBERT E. LEE,
Commanding Army of Northern Virginia.

HEADQUARTERS ARMY OF NORTHERN VIRGINIA,
September 21, 1863.

AFTER the battle of Fredericksburg the army remained encamped on the south side of the Rappahannock until the latter part of April. The Federal army occupied the north side of the river opposite Fredericksburg, extending to the Potomac. Two brigades of [R. H.] Anderson's division—those of Generals [William] Mahone and [Carnot] Posey—were stationed near the United States Mine (or Bark mill) Ford, and a third, under General [C. M.] Wilcox, guarded Banks Ford. The cavalry was distributed on both flanks, Fitzhugh Lee's brigade picketing the Rappahannock above the mouth of the Rapidan and W. H. F. Lee's near Port Royal. Hampton's brigade had been sent into the interior to recruit. General [James] Longstreet, with two divisions of his corps, was detached for service south of James River in February, and did not rejoin the army until after the battle of Chancellorsville.

With the exception of the engagement between Fitzhugh Lee's brigade and the enemy's cavalry near Kellys Ford on March 17th, nothing of interest transpired during this period of inactivity.

On April 14th intelligence was received that the enemy's cavalry was concentrating on the Upper Rappahannock. Their efforts to establish themselves on the south side of the river were successfully resisted by Fitzhugh Lee's brigade and two regiments of W. H. F. Lee's, the whole under the immediate command of General Stuart.

About the 21st small bodies of infantry appeared at Kellys Ford and the Rappahannock Bridge, and almost at the same time a demonstration was made opposite Port Royal, where a party of infantry crossed the river about the 23d. These movements were evidently intended to conceal the designs of the enemy, but, taken in connection with the reports of scouts, indicated that the Federal army, now commanded by Major-General Hooker, was about to resume active operations.

At 5:30 A. M. on April 28th the enemy crossed the Rappahannock in boats near Fredericksburg, and, driving off the pickets on the river, proceeded to lay down a pontoon bridge a short distance below the mouth of Deep Run. Later in the forenoon another bridge was constructed about a mile below the first. A considerable force crossed on these bridges during the day and was massed out of view under the high banks of the river. The bridges, as well as the troops, were effectually protected from our artillery by the depth of the river-bed and the narrowness of the stream, while the batteries on the opposite heights completely commanded the wide plain between our lines and the river. As in the first battle of Fredericksburg, it was thought best to select positions with a view to resist the advance of the enemy rather than incur the heavy loss that would attend any attempt to prevent his crossing. Our dispositions were accordingly made as on the former occasion.

No demonstration was made opposite any other part of our lines at Fredericksburg, and the strength of the force that had crossed and its apparent indisposition to attack indicated that the principal effort of the enemy would be made in some other quarter. This impression was confirmed by intelligence received from General Stuart that a large body of infantry and artillery was passing up the river. During the forenoon of the 29th, that officer reported that the enemy had crossed in force near Kellys Ford on the preceding evening. Later in the day he announced that a heavy column was moving from Kellys toward Germanna Ford, on the Rapidan, and another toward Elys Ford, on that river. The routes they were pursuing after crossing the Rapidan converge near Chancellorsville, whence several roads lead to the rear of our position at Fredericksburg.

On the night of the 29th, General Anderson was directed to proceed toward Chancellorsville and dispose Wright's brigade and the troops from the Bark Mill Ford to cover these roads. Arriving at Chancellorsville about midnight, he found the commands of Generals Mahone and Posey already there, having been withdrawn from the Bark Mill Ford, with the exception of a small guard.

Learning that the enemy had crossed the Rapidan and were approaching in strong force, General Anderson retired early on the morning of the 30th to the intersection of the Mine and Plank roads, near Tabernacle Church, and began to intrench himself. The enemy's cavalry skirmished with his rear guard as he left Chancellorsville, but being vigorously repulsed by Mahone's brigade, offered no further opposition to his march. Mahone was placed on the old turnpike, Wright and Posey on the Plank Road.

In the meantime General Stuart had been directed to endeavor to impede the progress of the column marching by way of Germanna Ford. Detaching W. H. F. Lee with his two regiments (the Ninth and Thirteenth Virginia) to oppose the main body of the enemy's cavalry, General Stuart crossed the Rapidan at Raccoon Ford with Fitzhugh Lee's brigade on the night of the 29th. Halting to give his men a few hours' repose, he ordered Colonel [Thomas H.] Owen, with the Third Virginia Cavalry, to throw himself in front of the enemy, while the rest of the brigade attached his right flank at the Wilderness Tavern, between Germanna Ford and Chancellorsville. By this means the march of this column was delayed until 12 M., when, learning that the one from Elys Ford had already reached Chancellorsville, General Stuart marched by Todd's Tavern toward Spottsylvania Courthouse, to put himself in communication with the main body of the army, and Colonel Owen fell back upon General Anderson.

The enemy in our front near Fredericksburg continued inactive, and it was now apparent that the main attack would be made upon our flank and rear. It was therefore determined to leave sufficient troops to hold our lines, and with the main body of the army, to give battle to the approaching column. Early's division, of Jackson's corps, and Barksdale's brigade, of McLaws' division, with part of the reserve artillery, under General [W. N.] Pendleton, were intrusted with the defense of our position at Fredericksburg, and, at midnight on the 30th, General McLaws marched with the rest of his command toward Chancellorsville. General Jackson followed at dawn next morning with the remaining divisions of his corps. He reached the position occupied by General Anderson at 8 A. M., and immediately began preparations to advance. At 11 A. M. the troops moved forward upon the Plank and old Turnpike roads, Anderson, with the brigades of Wright and Posey, leading on the former; McLaws, with his three brigades, preceded by Mahone's, on the latter. Generals Wilcox and Perry, of Anderson's division, co-operated with McLaws. Jackson's troops followed Anderson on the Plank Road. Colonel Alexander's battalion of artillery accompanied the advance. The enemy was soon encountered on both roads, and heavy skirmishing with infantry and artillery ensued, our troops pressing steadily forward. A strong attack upon General McLaws was repulsed with spirit by Semmes' brigade; and General Wright, by direction of General Anderson, diverging to the left of the Plank Road, marched by way of the unfinished railroad from Fredericksburg to Gordonsville, and turned the enemy's right. His whole line thereupon retreated rapidly, vigorously pursued by our troops until they arrived within about one mile of Chancellorsville. Here the enemy had assumed a position of great natural strength, surrounded on all sides by a dense forest filled with a tangled undergrowth, in the midst of which breastworks of logs had been constructed, with trees felled in front, so as to form an almost impenetrable abatis. His artillery swept the few narrow roads by which his position could be approached from the front, and commanded the adjacent woods. The left of his line extended from Chancellorsville toward the Rappahannock, covering the Bark Mill Ford, where he communicated with the north bank of the river by a pontoon bridge. His right stretched westward along the Germanna Ford Road more than two miles. Darkness was approaching before the strength and extent of his line could be ascertained, and as the nature of the country rendered it hazardous to attack by night, our troops were halted and formed in line of battle in front of Chancellorsville, at right angles to the Plank Road, extending on the right to the Mine Road and to the left in the direction of the Catharine Furnace. Colonel [William C.] Wickham, with the Fourth Virginia Cavalry and Colonel Owen's regiment, was stationed between the Mine Road and the Rappahannock. The rest of the cavalry was upon our left flank.

It was evident that a direct attack upon the enemy would be attended with great difficulty and loss, in view of the strength of his position and his superiority of numbers. It was, therefore, resolved to endeavor to turn his right flank and gain his rear, leaving a force in front to hold him in check and conceal the movement. The execution of this plan was intrusted to Lieutenant-General Jackson, with his three divisions. The commands of Generals McLaws and Anderson, with the exception of Wilcox's brigade, which, during the night, had been ordered back to Banks Ford, remained in front of the enemy.

Early on the morning of the 2d, General Jackson marched by the Furnace and Buck roads, his movement being effectually covered by Fitzhugh Lee's cavalry, under General Stuart in person. As the rear of the train was passing the furnace a large force of the enemy advanced from Chancellorsville and attempted its capture. General Jackson had left the Twenty-third Georgia Regiment, under Colonel [E. F.] Best, at this point to guard his flank, and upon the approach of the enemy Lieutenant-Colonel [J. T.] Brown, whose artillery was passing at the time, placed a battery in position to aid in checking his advance. A small number of men who were marching to join their commands, including Captain [W. S.] Moore, with two companies of the Fourteenth Tennessee, regiments of Archer's brigade, reported to Colonel Brown and supported his guns. The enemy was kept back by this small force until the train had passed, but his superior numbers enabled him subsequently to surround and capture the greater part of the Twenty-third Georgia Regiment. General Anderson was directed to send a brigade to resist the further progress of this column, and detached General Posey for that purpose. General Posey became warmly engaged with a superior force, but being re-enforced by General [A. R.] Wright, the enemy's advance was arrested. After a long and fatiguing march, General Jackson's leading division, under General Rodes, reached the old turnpike, about three miles in rear of Chancellorsville, at 4 P. M. As the different divisions arrived they were formed at right angles to the road—Rodes' in front, Trimble's division, under Brigadier-General [R. E.] Colston, in the second, and A. P. Hill's in the third line.

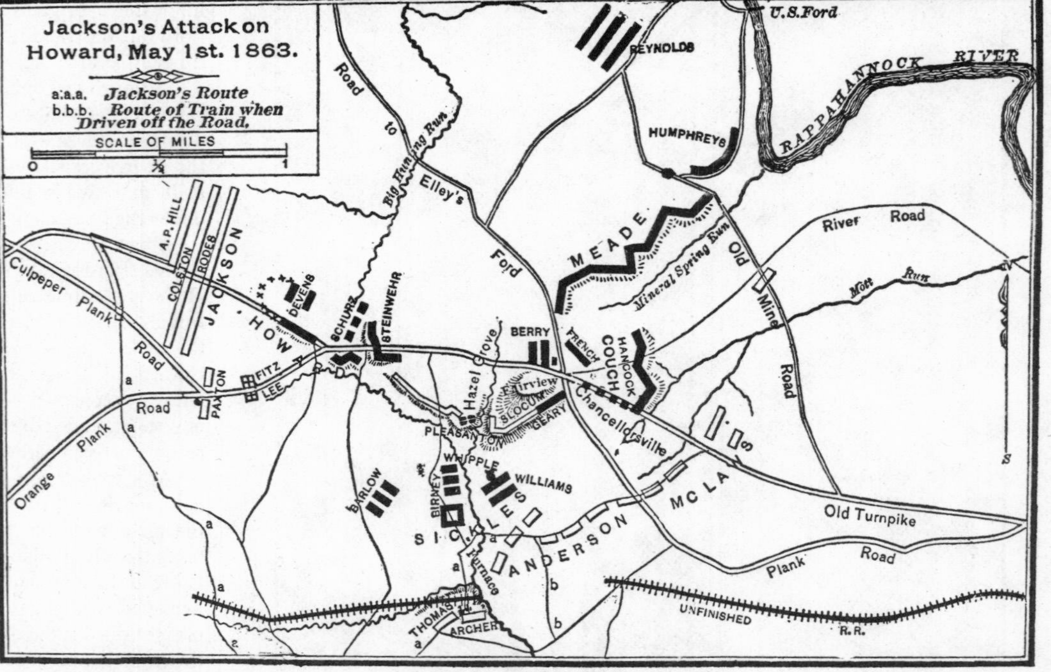

At 6 P. M. the advance was ordered. The enemy were taken by surprise and fled after a brief resistance. General Rodes' men pushed forward with great vigor and enthusiasm, followed closely by the second and third lines. Position after position was carried, the guns captured, and every effort of the enemy to rally defeated by the impetuous rush of our troops. In the ardor of pursuit through the thick and tangled woods the first and second lines at last became mingled and moved on together as one. The enemy made a stand at a line of breastworks across the road, at the house of Melzie Chancellor, but the troops of Rodes and Colston dashed over the intrenchments together, and the flight and pursuit were resumed and continued until our advance was arrested by the abatis in front of the line of works near the central position at Chancellorsville. It was now dark, and General Jackson ordered the third line, under General [A. P.] Hill, to advance to the front and relieve the troops of Rodes and Colston, who were completely blinded and in such disorder from their rapid advance through intricate woods and over broken ground that it was necessary to reform them. As Hill's men moved forward General Jackson, with his staff and escort, returning from the extreme front, met his skirmishers advancing, and in the obscurity of the night were mistaken for the enemy and fired upon. Captain [J. K.] Boswell, chief engineer of the corps, and several others were killed and a number wounded. General Jackson himself received a severe injury and was borne from the field. The command devolved upon Major-General Hill, whose division, under General Heth, was advanced to the line of intrenchments which had been reached by Rodes and Colston. A furious fire of artillery was opened upon them by the enemy, under cover of which his infantry advanced to the attack. They were handsomely repulsed by the Fifty-fifth Virginia Regiment, under Colonel [Francis] Mallory, who was killed while bravely leading his men. General Hill was soon afterward disabled, and Major-General Stuart, who had been directed by General Jackson to seize the road to Elys Ford, in rear of the enemy, was sent for to take command. At this time the right of Hill's division was attacked by the column of the enemy already mentioned as having penetrated to the furnace, which had been recalled to Chancellorsville to avoid being cut off by the advance of Jackson. This attack was gallantly met and repulsed by the Eighteenth and Twenty-eighth and a portion of the Thirty-third North Carolina regiments, Lane's brigade.

Upon General Stuart's arrival, soon afterward, the command was turned over to him by General Hill. He immediately proceeded to reconnoiter the ground and make himself acquainted with the disposition of the troops. The darkness of the night and the difficulty of moving through the woods and undergrowth rendered it advisable to defer further operations until morning, and the troops rested on their arms in line of battle. Colonel [P.] Crutchfield, chief of artillery of the corps, was severely wounded, and Colonel [E. P.] Alexander, senior artillery officer present, was engaged during the entire night in selecting positions for our batteries.

As soon as the sound of cannon gave notice of Jackson's attack on the enemy's right, our troops in front of Chancellorsville were ordered to press him strongly on the left, to prevent re-enforcements being sent to the point assailed. They were directed not to attack in force unless a favorable opportunity should present itself, and, while continuing to cover the roads leading from their respective positions toward Chancellorsville, to incline to the left so as to connect with Jackson's right as he closed in upon the center. These orders were well executed by our troops advancing up to the enemy's intrenchments, while several batteries played with good effect upon his lines until prevented by the increasing darkness.

Early on the morning of the 3d, General Stuart renewed the attack upon the enemy, who had strengthened his right during the night with additional breastworks, while a large number of guns, protected by intrenchments, were posted so as to sweep the woods through which our troops had to advance. Hill's division was in front, with Colston in the second line and Rodes in the third. The second and third lines soon advanced to the support of the first, and the whole became hotly engaged. The breastworks at which the attack was suspended the preceding evening were carried by assault under a terrible fire of musketry and artillery. In rear of these breastworks was a barricade, from which the enemy was quickly driven. The troops on the left of the Plank Road, pressing through the woods, attacked and broke the next line, while those on the right bravely assailed the extensive earthworks, behind which the enemy's artillery was posted. Three times were these works carried, and as often were the brave assailants compelled to abandon them—twice by the retirement of the troops on their left, who fell back after a gallant struggle with superior numbers, and once by a movement of the enemy on their right, caused by the advance of General Anderson. The left being re-enforced finally succeeded in driving back the enemy, and the artillery under Lieutenant-Colonels [T. H.] Carter and [H. P.] Jones being thrown forward to occupy favorable positions secured by the advance of the infantry, began to play with great precision and effect. Anderson, in the meantime, pressed gallantly forward directly upon Chancellorsville, his right resting upon the Plank Road and his left extending around toward the furnace, while McLaws made a strong demonstration to the right of the road. As the troops advancing upon the enemy's front and right converged upon his central position, Anderson effected a junction with Jackson's corps, and the whole line pressed irresistibly on. The enemy was driven from all his fortified positions, with heavy loss in killed, wounded and prisoners, and retreated toward the Rappahannock. By 10 A. M. we were in full possession of the field.

The troops having become somewhat scattered by the difficulties of the ground and the ardor of the contest were immediately reformed preparatory to renewing the attack. The enemy had withdrawn to a strong position nearer to the Rappahannock, which he had previously fortified. His superiority of numbers, the unfavorable nature of the ground, which was densely wooded, and the condition of our troops after the arduous and sanguinary conflict in which they had been engaged, rendered great caution

From an original crayon lithograph, published by Kurz & Allison, Chicago, Ill.

LIEUTENANT-GENERAL THOMAS J. JACKSON.

BORN AT CLARKSBURG, VA. (NOW W. VA.), JANUARY 21, 1824.

DIED AT GUINEYS STATION, VA., MAY 10, 1863, FROM WOUNDS RECEIVED AT THE BATTLE OF CHANCELLORSVILLE, VA.

necessary. Our preparations were just completed when further operations were arrested by intelligence received from Fredericksburg.

General Early had been instructed, in the event of the enemy withdrawing from his front and moving up the river, to join the main body of the army with so much of his command as could be spared from the defense of his lines. This order was repeated on the 2d, but by a misapprehension on the part of the officer conveying it, General Early was directed to move unconditionally. Leaving Hays' brigade and one regiment of Barksdale's at Fredericksburg, and directing a part of General Pendleton's artillery to be sent to the rear, in compliance with the order delivered to him, General Early moved with the rest of his command toward Chancellorsville. As soon as his withdrawal was perceived the enemy began to give evidence of an intention to advance, but the mistake in the transmission of the order being corrected, General Early returned to his original position. The line to be defended by Barksdale's brigade extended from the Rappahannock above Fredericksburg to the rear of Howison's house. Seven companies of the Twenty-first Mississippi Regiment were posted by General Barksdale between the Marye house and the Plank Road, the Eighteenth and the three other companies of the Twenty-first occupied the Telegraph Road at the foot of Marye's Hill, the two remaining regiments of the brigade being further to the right on the hills near Howison's house. The enemy made a demonstration against the extreme right, which was easily repulsed by General Early. Soon afterward a column moved from Fredericksburg along the river bank as if to gain the heights on the extreme left, which commanded those immediately in rear of the town. This attempt was foiled by General Hays and the arrival of General Wilcox from Banks Ford, who deployed a few skirmishers on the hill near Taylor's house, and opened on the enemy with a section of artillery. Very soon the enemy advanced in large force against Marye's and the hills to the right and left of it. Two assaults were gallantly repulsed by Barksdale's men and the artillery. After the second, a flag of truce was sent from the town to obtain permission to provide for the wounded.

Battle of Chancellorsville. Flight of the Federal Baggage Train.

Then heavy lines advanced immediately upon the return of the flag and renewed the attack. They were bravely repulsed on the right and left, but the small force at the foot of Marye's Hill, overpowered by more than ten times their numbers, was captured after a heroic resistance, and the hill carried. Eight pieces of artillery were taken on Marye's and the adjacent heights. The remainder of Barksdale's brigade, together with that of General Hays and the artillery on the right, retired down the Telegraph Road. The success of the enemy enabled him to threaten our communications by moving down the Telegraph Road, or to come upon our rear at Chancellorsville by the Plank Road. He at first advanced on the former, but was checked by General Early, who had halted the commands of Barksdale and Hays, with the artillery, about two miles from Marye's Hill, and re-enforced them with three regiments of Gordon's Brigade. The enemy then began to advance up the Plank Road, his progress being gallantly disputed by the brigade of General Wilcox, who had moved from Banks Ford as rapidly as possible to the assistance of General Barksdale, but arrived too late to take part in the action. General Wilcox fell back slowly until he reached Salem Church, on the Plank Road, about five miles from Fredericksburg.

Information of the state of affairs in our rear having reached Chancellorsville, as already stated, General McLaws, with his three brigades and one of General Anderson's, was ordered to re-enforce General Wilcox. He arrived at Salem Church early in the afternoon, where he found General Wilcox in line of battle, with a large force of the enemy—consisting, as was reported, of one army corps and part of another, under Major-General Sedgwick—in his front. The brigades of Kershaw and Wofford were placed on the right of Wilcox, those of Semmes and Mahone on his left. The enemy's artillery played vigorously upon our position for some time, when his infantry advanced in three strong lines, the attack being directed mainly against General Wilcox, but partially involving the brigades on his left. The assault was met with the utmost firmness, and after a fierce struggle the first line was repulsed with great slaughter. The second then came forward, but immediately broke under the close and deadly fire which it encountered, and the whole mass fled in confusion to the rear. They were pursued by the brigades of Wilcox and Semmes, which advanced nearly a mile, when they were halted to reform in the presence of the enemy's reserve, which now appeared in large force. It being quite dark, General Wilcox deemed it imprudent to push the attack with his small numbers, and retired to his original position, the enemy making no attempt to follow.

The next morning General Early advanced along the Telegraph Road and recaptured Marye's and the adjacent hills without difficulty, thus gaining the rear of the enemy's left. He then proposed to General McLaws that a simultaneous attack should be made by their respective commands, but the latter officer not deeming his force adequate to assail the enemy in front, the proposition was not carried into effect.

In the meantime the enemy had so strengthened his position near Chancellorsville that it was deemed inexpedient to assail it with less than our whole force, which could not be concentrated until we were relieved from the danger that menaced our rear. It was accordingly resolved still further to re-enforce the troops in front of General Sedgwick, in order, if possible, to drive him across the Rappahannock.

Accordingly, on the 4th, General Anderson was directed to proceed with his remaining three brigades to join General McLaws, the three divisions of Jackson's corps holding our position at Chancellorsville. Anderson reached Salem Church about noon and was directed to gain the left flank of the enemy and effect a junction with Early. McLaws' troops were disposed as on the previous day, with orders to hold the enemy in front and to push forward his right brigades as soon as the advance of Anderson and Early should be perceived, so as to connect with them and complete the continuity of our line. Some delay occurred in getting the troops into position, owing to the broken and irregular nature of the ground and the difficulty of ascertaining the disposition of the enemy's forces. The attack did not begin until 6 P. M., when Anderson and Early moved forward and drove General Sedgwick's troops rapidly before them across the Plank Road in the direction of the Rappahannock. The speedy approach of darkness prevented General McLaws from perceiving the success of the attack until the enemy began to recross the river a short distance below Banks Ford, where he had laid one of his pontoon bridges. His right brigades, under Kershaw and Wofford, advanced through the woods in the direction of the firing, but the retreat was so rapid that they could only join in the pursuit. A dense fog settled over the field, increasing the obscurity and rendering great caution necessary to avoid collision between our own troops. Their movements were consequently slow. General Wilcox, with Kershaw's brigade and two regiments of his own, accompanied by a battery, proceeded nearly to the river, capturing a number of prisoners and inflicting great damage upon the enemy. General McLaws also directed Colonel [E. P.] Alexander's artillery to fire upon the locality of the enemy's bridge, which was done with good effect.

The next morning it was found that General Sedgwick had made good his escape and removed his bridges. Fredericksburg was also evacuated and our rear no longer threatened; but as General Sedgwick had it in his power to recross, it was deemed best to leave General Early, with his division and Barksdale's brigade, to hold our lines as before, McLaws and Anderson being directed to return to Chancellorsville. They reached their destination during the afternoon in the midst of a violent storm which continued throughout the night and most of the following day.

Preparations were made to assail the enemy's works at daylight on the 6th, but, on advancing our skirmishers, it was found that, under cover of the storm and darkness of the night, he had retreated over the river.

A detachment was left to guard the battlefield while the wounded were being removed and the captured property collected. The rest of the army returned to its former position.

The conduct of the troops can not be too highly praised. Attacking largely superior numbers in strongly intrenched positions, their heroic courage overcame every obstacle of nature and art, and achieved a triumph most honorable to our arms.

I commend the brave officers and men for extraordinary daring and merit, whose names I am unable to enumerate here. Among them will be found some who have passed, by a glorious death, beyond the reach of praise, but the memory of whose virtues and devoted patriotism will ever be cherished by their grateful countrymen. Many valuable officers and men were killed or wounded in the faithful discharge of duty. Among the former, Brigadier-General Paxton fell while leading his brigade with conspicuous courage in the assault on the enemy's works at Chancellorsville.

The gallant Brigadier-General Nicholls lost a leg.

Brigadier-General McGowan was severely, and Brigadier-Generals Heth and Pender were slightly, wounded in the same engagement. The latter officer led his brigade to the attack under a destructive fire, bearing the colors of a regiment in his own hands up to and over the intrenchments with the most distinguished gallantry.

General Hoke received a painful wound in the action near Fredericksburg.

The movement by which the enemy's position was turned and the fortune of the day decided was conducted by the lamented Lieutenant-General Jackson, who, as has already been stated, was severely wounded near the close of the engagement on Saturday evening. I do not propose here to speak of the character of this illustrious man, since removed from the scene of his eminent usefulness by the hand of an inscrutable but all-wise Providence. I, nevertheless, desire to pay the tribute of my admiration to the matchless energy and skill that marked this last act of his life, forming, as it did, a worthy conclusion of that long series of splendid achievements which won for him the lasting love and gratitude of his country.

Major-General A. P. Hill was disabled soon after assuming command, but did not leave the field until the arrival of Major-General Stuart. The latter officer ably discharged the difficult and responsible duties which he was thus unexpectedly called to perform. Assuming the command late in the night, at the close of a fierce engagement and in the immediate presence of the enemy, necessarily ignorant, in a great measure, of the disposition of the troops and of the plans of those who had preceded him, General Stuart exhibited great energy, promptness and intelligence. During the continuance of the engage-

Dowdall's Tavern (Melzie Chancellor's House), Chancellorsville, Va.

ment the next day, he conducted the operations on the left with distinguished capacity and vigor, stimulating and cheering the troops by the example of his own coolness and daring.

While it is impossible to mention all who were conspicuous in the several engagements, it will not be considered an invidious distinction to say that General Jackson, after he was wounded, in expressing the satisfaction he derived from the conduct of his whole command, commended to my particular attention the services of Brigadier-General (now Major-General) Rodes and his gallant division. Major-General Early performed the important and responsible duty intrusted to him in a manner which reflected credit upon himself and his command. Major-General R. H. Anderson was also distinguished for the promptness, courage and skill with which he and his division executed every order, and Brigadier-General (now Major-General) Wilcox is entitled to especial praise for the judgment and bravery displayed in impeding the advance of General Sedgwick toward Chancellorsville, and for the gallant and successful stand at Salem Church.

To the skillful and efficient management of the artillery the successful issue of the contest is in great measure due. The ground was not favorable for its employment, but every suitable position was taken with alacrity, and the operations of the infantry supported and assisted with a spirit and courage not second to their own. It bore a prominent part in the final assault which ended in driving the enemy from the field at Chancellorsville, silencing his batteries, and by a destructive enfilade fire upon his works opened the way for the advance of our troops.

Colonels Crutchfield, Alexander and [R. L.] Walker, and Lieutenant-Colonels [J. T.] Brown, [T. H.] Carter and [R. S.] Andrews, with the officers and men of their commands, are mentioned as deserving especial commendation. The batteries under General Pendleton also acted with great gallantry.

The cavalry of the army at the time of these operations was much reduced. To its vigilance and energy we were indebted for timely information of the enemy's movements before the battle, and for impeding his march to Chancellorsville. It guarded both flanks of the army during the battle at that place, and a portion of it, as has been already stated, rendered valuable service in covering the march of Jackson to the enemy's rear.

The horse artillery accompanied the infantry and participated with credit to itself in the engagement. The nature of the country rendered it impossible for the cavalry to do more.

When the enemy's infantry passed the Rappahannock at Kellys Ford, his cavalry, under General Stoneman, also crossed in large force, and proceeded through Culpeper County toward Gordonsville, for the purpose of cutting the railroads to Richmond. General Stuart had nothing to oppose this movement but two regiments of Brigadier-General W. H. F. Lee's brigade (the Ninth and Thirteenth Virginia Cavalry). General Lee fell back before the overwhelming numbers of the enemy, and, after holding the railroad bridge over the Rapidan during May 1st, burned the bridge, and retired to Gordonsville at night. The enemy avoided Gordonsville and reached Louisa Courthouse, on the Central Railroad, which he proceeded to break up. Dividing his force, a part of it also cut the Richmond & Fredericksburg Railroad, and a part proceeded to Columbia, on the James River and Kanawha Canal, with a design of destroying the aqueduct at that place. The small command of General Lee exerted itself vigorously to defeat this purpose. The damage done to the railroad was small and soon repaired, and the canal was saved from injury.

The loss of the enemy in the battle of Chancellorsville and the other engagements was severe. His dead, and a large number of wounded, were left on the field. About five thousand prisoners, exclusive of the wounded, were taken, and thirteen pieces of artillery, nineteen thousand five hundred stand of arms, seventeen colors and a large quantity of ammunition fell into our hands.

To the members of my staff I am greatly indebted for assistance in observing the movements of the enemy, posting troops and conveying orders. On so extended and varied a field all were called into requisition, and all evinced the greatest energy and zeal.

The medical director of the army, Surgeon [L.] Guild, and the officers of his department, were untiring in their attention to the wounded.

Lieutenant-Colonel [J. L.] Corley, chief quartermaster, took charge of the disposition and safety of the trains of the army.

Lieutenant-Colonel [Robert G.] Cole, chief commissary of subsistence, and Lieutenant-Colonel [Briscoe G.] Baldwin, chief of ordnance, were everywhere on the field attending to the wants of their departments.

General Chilton, chief of staff, Lieutenant-Colonel [E.] Murray, Major [Henry E.] Peyton, and Captain [H. E.] Young, of the adjutant and inspector-general's department, were active in seeing to the execution of orders; Lieutenant-Colonel [William P.] Smith and Captain [Samuel R.] Johnston, of the engineers, in reconnoitering the enemy and constructing batteries; Colonel [Armistead L.] Long in posting troops and artillery.

Majors [Walter H.] Taylor, [T. M. R.] Talcott, [Charles] Marshall and [Charles S.] Venable were engaged, night and day, in watching the operations, carrying orders, etc.

R. E. LEE, *General.*

SALEM CHURCH, NEAR CHANCELLORSVILLE, VA.

THE CHANCELLORSVILLE CAMPAIGN,

APRIL 27 TO MAY 6, 1863.

BY

MAJOR-GENERAL LAFAYETTE McLAWS,

Commanding Division First Corps.

HEADQUARTERS DIVISION, May 10, 1863.

ON May 1st, instant, at 12:30 o'clock at night, the brigades of Generals Kershaw, Semmes and Wofford were put in march up the Plank Road by orders from your headquarters, the brigade of General Barksdale remaining in Fredericksburg and vicinity, and by 6 o'clock in the morning were in position behind the rifle-pits about Smith's Hill and extending to the right and left, joining General Anderson's command on the left, to defend the approaches from the United States Ford and from the direction of Chancellorsville.

About 11 A. M., General Jackson, who had arrived with his forces and assumed command, directed me to advance along the Turnpike Road, having Mahone's brigade, of Anderson's division, in advance. I collected my own division as rapidly as possible from the rifle-pits, each brigade as it was relieved falling in rear of the others as they advanced in the march. After proceeding but a short distance the skirmishers became engaged. The main column, advancing slowly until the enemy appeared in force, was deployed, and the line of battle formed across the Turnpike Road, Semmes' brigade on the left and those of Mahone, Wofford and Perry, of Anderson's division, in the order here named, to the right, extending so as to cover the Mine Road, [Tyler C.] Jordan's battery on the main turnpike. Our skirmishers were driven in. Fire was opened on our lines from a battery four or five hundred yards in front, and, after skirmishing to the right and left, the main assault was made on the left (Semmes) by Sykes' Regulars, but they were repulsed at every attempt. Before the first assault I sent word to General Jackson by my aid-de-camp that the enemy were in force in my immediate front and were advancing, and that a large force could be seen along the heights about one mile or more to the rear, and that the country was favorable for a flank attack from his side. After the first assault I received answer from General Jackson to hold my position and that he would advance, or was advancing, his artillery, and if that did not answer he would endeavor to gain the rear of the enemy. General Kershaw coming up, his brigade was placed in support of General Semmes, extending beyond his left.

The cavalry reporting that the enemy were advancing along the Mine Road, General Wilcox's brigade was ordered and took position (guided by Captain [S. R.] Johnston, of General Lee's staff) to protect my right, taking artillery with him. General Jackson's artillery and his advance, in conjunction with the failure of the attack on my front, forced the enemy to retire, when, by General Jackson's order, my whole line advanced in the same order as they had been displayed as above stated. The order to advance was received at 4 P. M. My line halted at dark, and bivouacked along the heights just beyond the point where the Mine Run crosses the turnpike.

The next morning (the 2d) my line of battle was reformed along the heights in the same order as before, excepting that General Wilcox had been ordered, during the night previous, to return to Banks Ford and hold that position, it having been reported that the enemy were moving down the River Road, and, besides, were making demonstrations to cross the river at that ford. Two batteries were placed on the heights between Generals Semmes and Wofford. A strong line of skirmishers was advanced, and was constantly engaged with those of the enemy, General Kershaw's brigade held in reserve. I received orders from General Lee to hold my position, as General Jackson would operate to the left and rear. Not long after I was directed to replace General Posey's brigade, on my left, by one from my command, and General Kershaw's moved to that position on the left of General Semmes. Following this order I was directed to send the brigades of Generals Mahone and Perry to the left, and close in my command so as to connect with General Anderson's right, holding my right at the turnpike, but constantly pressing to the left, so as to be in communication with General Anderson; to do which, as the country was broken and densely wooded, and the direction constantly changing, I ordered the two brigades on the left (Kershaw's and Semmes') to advance by battalion from the left, so as to form a broken line, but still covering the front and forming the connection.

The batteries opened whenever the masses of the enemy on the hills in my front offered an opportunity, and with marked results.

My orders were to hold my position; not to engage seriously, but to press strongly so soon as it was discovered that General Jackson had attacked. It was not until late in the evening that it was known General Jackson had commenced his assault, when I ordered an advance along the whole line to engage with the skirmishers, which were largely re-enforced, and to threaten, but not to attack seriously; in doing which General Wofford became so seriously engaged that I directed him to withdraw, which was done in good order, his men in good spirits, after driving the enemy to their intrenchments.

As General Jackson advanced the enemy massed in front of the batteries on my line, which opened on them in excellent effect. This continued until darkness prevented any further efforts in my front. Generals Kershaw and Semmes had been pressing to the left and

FEDERAL ARMY RECROSSING THE RAPPAHANNOCK AFTER THE BATTLE OF CHANCELLORSVILLE, VA.

front and engaging the enemy with their skirmishers, which had left an open space, so far as the main body was concerned, between my right and center of considerable distance, but the skirmishers of General Semmes, composed of the entire Tenth Georgia Regiment, were perfectly reliable and kept the enemy to their intrenchments, so there was nothing to be apprehended from an advance in this direction.

May 3d. Nothing occurred during the night save the magnificent display caused by the night attack of General Jackson. My skirmishers, well to the front and strong in numbers, engaged the enemy as day advanced. The batteries were run forward and played upon the masses of the enemy, in good range, producing much confusion. Finally, the repeated attacks of the forces on my left forced the enemy to give way from Chancellorsville, and our troops could be seen advancing across the plains.

General Wofford threw a portion of his command across the valley between him and the Chancellorsville Heights, and thus prevented the escape of a considerable body of the enemy which had been opposed to his brigade and to his left and front during the morning. I directed a flag of truce to be sent them, and they surrendered. I think that General Wofford is entitled to the most credit for their capture, although the Tenth Georgia, General Semmes, and General Wright, of Anderson's division, claimed their share equally.

THE FEDERAL HEADQUARTERS AT CHANCELLORSVILLE, VA.

Kershaw and Semmes, bearing to the left to co-operate with General Anderson to unite with the two wings of the army, had now swept around to the plains of Chancellorsville, and I directed them to march down the Plank Road and unite with General Wofford's left. As this was in the act of accomplishment information was received that the enemy had carried the heights about Fredericksburg and were advancing up the Plank Road. General Lee here rode up and ordered that the brigades of Generals Mahone and Kershaw should march at once toward Fredericksburg with [B. C.] Manly's battery to meet the enemy, and after their brigades were in march and had advanced some distance he directed me to proceed in the same direction with the remainder of my division, which was done so soon as the brigades could be formed.

On reaching the rifle-pits just beyond the junction of the Turnpike and Mine roads I formed General Mahone's brigade along the rifle-pits; General Kershaw's halted along the road; General Wilcox's brigade was marching to the front. I ordered them all forward, but as I was here informed that the enemy in considerable force were going down the Telegraph Road, and as I thought that it was perhaps their intention to march forward by the Plank and Mine roads, which came together just beyond the junction of the Plank and Turnpike roads, now in my rear, I halted General Wofford, with directions to watch the Mine Road on his right. I then rode on and found General Wilcox with his brigade in line across the Plank Road at Salem Church, General Kershaw forming on his right and General Mahone on the left. I directed General Mahone still more to his left, as he was acquainted with the country, and placed General Semmes to the immediate left of General Wilcox. General Wofford was ordered forward and placed on the right of General Kershaw.

The batteries which I had brought with me had been engaged all the morning, and had but little ammunition left. They had been ordered back in such haste that there was no time for them to replenish their chests, but they engaged the enemy until their supplies were nearly exhausted, and then withdrew, and were posted in the rear to command the ground on the flanks and front. The batteries of the enemy were admirably served and played over the whole ground.

Before my command was well in position, the enemy advanced, driving in our skirmishers, and, coming forward with loud shouts, endeavored to force the center (Wilcox) and left center (General Semmes), extending the attack somewhat to Mahone's brigade. One of Wilcox's regiments gave way, and with the skirmishers running back, created a little confusion. But General Wilcox himself soon corrected this, and reforming his men, charged the enemy in conjunction with two regiments of Semmes' brigade, led by General Semmes, and drove them back for a considerable distance. I now strengthened the left of Mahone's, which was strongly threatened, with two regiments from Wofford's brigade, on the right, and closed General Kershaw to the left, strengthening the center, supposing that the attack would be renewed; but no other assault was attempted, and as night drew on, the firing ceased on both sides, and my command bivouacked in line of battle.

In this engagement three or four hundred prisoners were taken, and about the same number of the enemy were killed and wounded.

Just previous to the assault I sent my inspecting officer, Major [E. L.] Costin, to try and communicate with General Early, and to bring back information as to his position and designs and the whereabouts of the enemy in that direction. A courier, late in the night, brought me a note from General Early, informing me that he would concentrate his forces in the morning and drive the enemy from the heights, Marye's Hill included. I sent his note to General Lee, who approving it, I forwarded to General Early, who, on the next morning, carried the heights with but little opposition. After this General Early sent me word by his staff officer that if I would attack in front he would advance two brigades and strike at the flank and rear of the enemy. I agreed to advance provided he would first attack, and did advance my right (Kershaw and Wofford) to co-operate with him; but finding my force was insufficient for a front attack, I withdrew to my line of the evening previous, General Early not attacking, as I could hear. In the meanwhile I had informed General Lee of the plan proposed, and asking for an additional force I was informed, in reply, that the remainder of General Anderson's division had been ordered forward. I then directed that no attack should be made until General Anderson arrived. General Lee came in person to superintend the movement, arriving about the same time with General Anderson's head of column. General Anderson was ordered to the right with his three brigades. My understanding was that the troops of my own division and the brigades of Wilcox and Mahone were to continue in line facing the enemy, and those of General Early and three brigades of General Anderson were to attack their right and rear. Orders were given that my troops on the right, Kershaw and Wofford, should advance after it was known that the attack on the right had commenced, which would be indicated by the firing in that direction. I was on the right of my line, straightening it and extending to the right, when notice was given that the attack would shortly be made by Generals Early and Anderson, and that Colonel [E. P.] Alexander, who had established a strong battery on a prominent hill, which commanded one of nearly equal force on the other side, which would take my line in reserve and in a measure enfilade it, should open fire. The orders were given at once. Alexander opened his batteries and Generals Kershaw and Wofford advanced to the front through a dense woods. Distant firing in the direction of Fredericksburg was heard, indicating that the attack had commenced on the extreme right. Night now came rapidly on and nothing could be observed of our operations.

It being reported to me from Mahone's position that the noise of crossing on the pontoon bridge at Banks Ford could be heard, I sent to Colonel Alexander, requesting him to throw shells so as to drop them as near as possible about the crossing, which was promptly done.

Shortly afterward General Kershaw's arrival on the Plank Road was reported to me, and I requested General Wilcox to assume the direction of it, and, with such portion of his own brigade as he thought necessary, proceed down the Banks Ford Road, taking a battery with him, to press the enemy, seize the redoubts suitable for shelling the crossing, and open fire with the battery; all of which was done in the most prompt manner, General Wilcox being acquainted with the localities of which I knew nothing except by report. I was as yet ignorant whether or not the attack upon the right had been a success, but the noise of their passage over the pontoon bridges convincing me that the enemy were in full retreat, I thought it best to press on in pursuit.

After these orders had been given and were in execution, I received a communication from General Lee, dated 10 P. M., from Downman's house, informing me of the success of the attack on the right, and his desire that the enemy should be pushed over the river that night. Wofford's brigade advanced as far as the River Road, engaging the enemy as he went, and driving them before him. He halted for the night beyond the River Road, extending his pickets. Wilcox and Kershaw pushed on, driving the enemy before them, and occupied the redoubts commanding the ford and its approaches, and opened fire with artillery in that direction. As my troops advanced I sent to Alexander, requesting him to fire on the approaches from the other side only, as I did not wish to risk his shells dropping among our troops. He did as requested, and the fire from all the batteries is reported by citizens about the ford as producing great confusion and as being very destructive. The enemy, throwing away their arms and breaking ranks, fled across the river in the greatest disorder. The darkness of the night, ignorance of the country and of the events transpiring on the other end of the line, prevented that co-operation which would have led to a more complete success; but I believe that all was gained that could have been expected under the circumstances. The enemy had several batteries (sixteen guns) in front of the left of my line, sweeping every approach from my left. I am not informed when they were withdrawn, but I suppose they were immediately after dark.

By the next morning the enemy had retired from this side of the river, and my command was employed in burying the dead, attending to the wounded and collecting arms and accouterments. I received orders during the morning to assemble my division, send General Anderson's brigade to rejoin him, and to send an intelligent officer to the position of General Heth, at or near the junction of the River and Mine roads, to inform himself of the points to be occupied, and, if General Heth had left, to replace him by the brigade of General Mahone and another of my own; but afterward, in conversation with General Lee, he directed me to move one of my brigades (General Kershaw's) to relieve General Heth. The brigade was already in motion, and I joined with it and went to General Heth's position. The march was not delayed for a moment, as the brigade did not halt even once, and it arrived at its destination before the storm. General Heth's main command was posted in rear of the rifle-pits, which had been constructed two or three hundred yards on the Plank Road side of the junction of the River and Mine roads, with smaller bodies more to the front. His men and officers had their shelter and other tents pitched, and there were no indications of his moving on my arrival. I think he received orders after my arrival to move when I arrived. General Kershaw had relieved him, and was in position before the storm commenced. General Heth informed me that the strength of the three brigades under his command was about nineteen hundred aggregate, which was not so numerous as the single brigade of General Kershaw. Colonel [Williams C.] Wickham offered his services to point out the different crossings on the river, and I rode down the River Road with him. A terrible storm of wind and rain delayed my return to my headquarters until between 8 and 9 o'clock at night, when I learned that General Semmes had been ordered to join General Kershaw.

The next morning early I rode to the position of Generals Kershaw and Semmes, and, advancing the skirmishers and scouts, discovered that the enemy had gone over the river. Shortly after I received orders to retire to my former position in front of Fredericksburg, leaving a brigade (Wofford's) at Banks Ford.

MAJ.-GEN. LAFAYETTE MCLAWS, OF GEORGIA.

The number of killed, wounded and missing in my division [is as follows]: Kershaw's brigade, 104, of which 2 are missing; Barksdale's brigade, 592, of which 341 are missing, besides 14 officers; Semmes' brigade, 603, of which 26 are missing; Wofford's brigade, 562, of which 9 are missing; artillery, 28, of which 2 are missing. Total, 1,889.

My inspector-general reports over 1,200 prisoners taken.

L. MCLAWS,
Major-General.

Orderly. Servant. Lieut.-Gen. A. P. Hill. Lieut.-Gen. Stonewall Jackson. Lieut.-Gen. R. S. Ewell. Lieut.-Col. A. J. Pendleton. Maj. H. K. Douglas, A. D. C. & A. I. G. Dr. Hunter McGuire, Med. Div. Lieut.-Col. Wm. Allen, Capt. of Ordnance. Capt. J. Smith, Aid. Wm. J. Hawks, Major.

PRAYER IN "STONEWALL" JACKSON'S CAMP.

BATTLE OF CHANCELLORSVILLE, VA.,

CAMPAIGN APRIL 27 TO MAY 6, 1863.

LIST OF THE KILLED AND WOUNDED.

COMMAND.	Killed . . .	Wounded . . .	Total . . .
FIRST CORPS.			
McLAWS' DIVISION.			
WOFFORD'S BRIGADE.			
Eighteenth Georgia	14	72	86
Twenty-fourth Georgia	14	73	87
Sixteenth Georgia	18	115	133
Cobb's Legion	22	135	157
Phillips' Legion	3	19	22
Field and staff	1	. . .	1
KERSHAW'S BRIGADE.			
Fifteenth South Carolina	9	45	54
Seventh South Carolina	. .	14	14
Second South Carolina	. .	11	11
James' [Third South Carolina] Battalion	1	8	9
Third South Carolina	1	11	12
BARKSDALE'S BRIGADE.			
Thirteenth Mississippi	7	43	50
Seventeenth Mississippi	10	70	80
Eighteenth Mississippi	25	43	68
Twenty-first Mississippi	3	25	28
SEMMES' BRIGADE.			
Fifty-first Georgia	30	119	149
Tenth Georgia	23	105	128
Fifty-third Georgia	15	105	120
Fiftieth Georgia	17	153	170
ANDERSON'S DIVISION.			
MAHONE'S BRIGADE.			
Twelfth Virginia	5	27	32
Sixteenth Virginia	1	17	18
Forty-first Virginia	5	23	28
Sixty-first Virginia	4	28	32
Sixth Virginia	5	34	39
Grandy's Battery	1	3	4
PERRY'S BRIGADE.			
Eighth Florida	11	36	47
Second Florida	3	29	32
Fifth Florida	6	22	28
WILCOX'S BRIGADE.			
Eighth Alabama	5	45	50
Ninth Alabama	21	90	111
Tenth Alabama	12	61	73
Eleventh Alabama	10	72	82
Fourteenth Alabama	7	116	123
Lewis' Battery	. . .	5	5
POSEY'S BRIGADE.			
Sixteenth Mississippi	17	59	76
Twelfth Mississippi	3	33	36
Nineteenth Mississippi	6	40	46
Forty-eighth Mississippi	10	44	54
WRIGHT'S BRIGADE.			
Second Georgia Battalion	2	26	28
Twenty-second Georgia	5	70	75
Third Georgia	11	111	122
Forty-eighth Georgia	7	41	48
ARTILLERY.			
Cabell's Artillery	4	12	16
Washington Artillery	4	8	12
Alexander's Artillery	5	35	40
CAVALRY.			
Lee's cavalry brigade, Stuart's division	4	7	11
SECOND CORPS.			
Lieutenant-General Thomas J. Jackson	. . .	1	1
Captain J. K. Boswell, Engineer Department	1	. . .	1
Signal Corps	1	. .	1
General's Escort	. . .	2	2
A. P. HILL'S DIVISION.			
Major-General A. P. Hill	. . .	1	1
Captain [James F.] Forbes	1	. . .	1
General's Escort	1	1	2
HETH'S BRIGADE.			
Brigadier-General H. Heth	. . .	1	1
Forty-seventh Virginia	4	48	52
Fifty-fifth Virginia	20	90	110
Twenty-second Virginia Battalion	6	23	29
Fortieth Virginia	14	73	87
M'GOWAN'S BRIGADE.			
Brigadier-General McGowan	. . .	1	1
Captain [A. C.] Haskell, Assistant Adjutant-General	. . .	1	1
First South Carolina (Provisional Army)	12	80	92
Orr's Rifles	19	92	111
Twelfth South Carolina	. .	2	2
Thirteenth South Carolina	6	60	66
Fourteenth South Carolina	9	87	96
THOMAS' BRIGADE.			
Fourteenth Georgia	8	67	75
Thirty-fifth Georgia	6	27	33
Forty-fifth Georgia	4	29	33
Forty-ninth Georgia	3	33	36
LANE'S BRIGADE.			
Seventh North Carolina	37	127	164
Eighteenth North Carolina	30	96	126
Twenty-eighth North Carolina	12	77	89
Thirty-third North Carolina	28	105	133
Thirty-seventh North Carolina	34	193	227
ARCHER'S BRIGADE.			
First Tennessee Provisional Army	8	50	58
Seventh Tennessee	11	45	56
Fourteenth Tennessee	7	28	35
Fifth Alabama Battalion	3	30	33
Thirteenth Alabama	13	127	140
PENDER'S BRIGADE.			
Thirteenth North Carolina	31	178	209
Sixteenth North Carolina	17	73	90
Twenty-second North Carolina	30	139	169
Thirty-fourth North Carolina	18	110	128
Thirty-eighth North Carolina	20	77	97
D. H. HILL'S DIVISION.			
RODES' BRIGADE.			
Twelfth Alabama	14	77	91
Twenty-sixth Alabama	13	85	98
Fifth Alabama	24	130	154
Sixth Alabama	24	125	149
Third Alabama	17	121	138

BATTLE OF CHANCELLORSVILLE, VA.—Continued.

COMMAND.	Killed . . .	Wounded . . .	Total . . .
DOLE'S BRIGADE.			
Fourth Georgia	29	121	150
Twelfth Georgia	11	46	57
Twenty-first Georgia	13	72	85
Forty-fourth Georgia	11	100	111
COLQUITT'S BRIGADE.			
Sixth Georgia	2	39	41
Twenty-third Georgia	. . .	4	4
Twenty-seventh Georgia	2	39	41
Twenty-eighth Georgia	2	31	33
Nineteenth Georgia	2	35	37
IVERSON'S BRIGADE.			
Fifth North Carolina	4	37	41
Twelfth North Carolina	12	95	107
Twentieth North Carolina	13	64	77
Twenty-third North Carolina	32	113	145
RAMSEUR'S BRIGADE.			
Thirtieth North Carolina	25	98	123
Fourth North Carolina	45	110	155
Fourteenth North Carolina	15	116	131
Second North Carolina	47	167	214
EARLY'S DIVISION.			
GORDON'S BRIGADE.			
Captain J. H. Mitchell, Assistant Adjutant-General	. . .	1	1
Thirteenth Georgia	3	27	30
Twenty-sixth Georgia	3	21	24
Thirty-first Georgia	3	20	23
Thirty-eighth Georgia	2	18	20
Sixtieth Georgia	5	30	35
Sixty-first Georgia	. . .	28	28
SMITH'S BRIGADE.			
Thirteenth Virginia	5	31	36
Forty-ninth Virginia	. . .	10	10
Fifty-second Virginia	4	8	12
Fifty-eighth Virginia	2	26	28
HOKE'S BRIGADE.			
Brigadier-General R. F. Hoke	. . .	1	1
Sixth North Carolina	8	21	29
Twenty-first North Carolina	15	63	78
Fifty-fourth North Carolina	3	38	41
Thirty-seventh North Carolina	9	61	70
First North Carolina Battalion	. .	11	11
HAYS' BRIGADE.			
Fifth Louisiana	9	44	53
Sixth Louisiana	16	65	81
Seventh Louisiana	5	75	80
Eighth Louisiana	12	71	83
Ninth Louisiana	21	51	72
TRIMBLE'S BRIGADE.			
General Trimble's Staff	1	2	3
Pioneer Corps	. . .	3	3
PAXTON'S BRIGADE.			
Brigadier-General E. F. Paxton	1	. . .	1
Second Virginia	8	58	66
Fourth Virginia	14	149	163
Fifth Virginia	7	113	120
Twenty-seventh Virginia	9	62	71
Thirty-third Virginia	10	56	66
[J. R.] JONES' BRIGADE.			
General Jones' Staff	. . .	1	1
Twenty-first Virginia	4	40	44
Forty-second Virginia	15	120	135
Forty-fourth Virginia	13	58	71
Forty-eighth Virginia	12	91	103
Fiftieth Virginia	8	110	118
COLSTON'S BRIGADE.			
Tenth Virginia	23	101	124
Twenty-third Virginia	9	53	62
Thirty-seventh Virginia	19	89	108
First North Carolina	34	83	117
Third North Carolina	38	141	179
NICHOLLS' BRIGADE.			
Brigadier-General Nicholls	. . .	1	1
First Louisiana	8	27	35
Second Louisiana	15	90	105
Tenth Louisiana	15	51	66
Fourteenth Louisiana	4	60	64
Fifteenth Louisiana	5	37	42
Artillery Corps, Second Army Corps	26	124	150
Grand Total	1,583	8,700	10,281

ORGANIZATION OF THE ARMY OF NORTHERN VIRGINIA, IN THE CHANCELLORSVILLE CAMPAIGN,

APRIL 27 TO MAY 6, 1863.*

FIRST CORPS.†

McLAWS' DIVISION.

Major-General Lafayette McLaws.

WOFFORD'S BRIGADE.

Brigadier-General W. T. Wofford.

Sixteenth Georgia; Eighteenth Georgia; Twenty-fourth Georgia; Cobb's Georgia Legion; Phillips' Georgia Legion.

SEMMES' BRIGADE.

Brigadier-General Paul J. Semmes.

Tenth Georgia—Lieutenant-Colonel W. C. Holt.

Fiftieth Georgia—Lieutenant-Colonel F. Kearse.

Fifty-first Georgia—Colonel W. M. Slaughter; Lieutenant-Colonel Edward Ball.

Fifty-third Georgia—Colonel James P. Simms.

* Actual commanders indicated as far as possible.

† Lieutenant-General Longstreet, with Hood's and Pickett's divisions and Dearing's and Henry's artillery battalions, in Southeastern Virginia.

KERSHAW'S BRIGADE.

Second South Carolina—Colonel John D. Kennedy.

Third South Carolina—Major R. C. Maffett.

Seventh South Carolina—Colonel Elbert Bland.

Eighth South Carolina—Colonel John W. Henagan.

Fifteenth South Carolina—Lieutenant-Colonel Joseph F. Gist.

Third South Carolina Battalion—Lieutenant-Colonel W. G. Rice.

BARKSDALE'S BRIGADE.

Brigadier-General William Barksdale.

Thirteenth Mississippi—Colonel J. W. Carter.

Seventeenth Mississippi—Colonel W. D. Holder.

Eighteenth Mississippi—Colonel Thomas M. Griffin.

Twenty-first Mississippi—Colonel B. G. Humphreys.

ARTILLERY.

Colonel H. C. Cabell.

Carlton's (Ga.) battery (Troup Artillery); Fraser's (Ga.) battery; McCarthy's (Va.) battery (First Howitzers); Manly's (N. C.) battery.

ANDERSON'S DIVISION.

Major-General Richard H. Anderson.

WILCOX'S BRIGADE.

Brigadier-General C. M. Wilcox.

Eighth Alabama—Colonel Y. L. Royston; Lieutenant-Colonel H. A. Herbert.

Ninth Alabama—Major J. H. J. Williams.

Tenth Alabama—Colonel William H. Forney.

Eleventh Alabama—Colonel J. C. C. Sanders.

Fourteenth Alabama—Colonel L. Pinckard.

WRIGHT'S BRIGADE.

Brigadier-General A. R. Wright.

Third Georgia—Major J. F. Jones; Captain C. H. Andrews.

Twenty-second Georgia—Lieutenant-Colonel J. Wasden.

Forty-eighth Georgia—Lieutenant-Colonel R. W. Carswell.

Second Georgia Battalion—Major George W. Ross.

MAHONE'S BRIGADE.

Brigadier-General William Mahone.

Sixth Virginia—Colonel George T. Rogers.

Twelfth Virginia—Lieutenant-Colonel E. M. Feild.

Sixteenth Virginia—Lieutenant-Colonel R. O. Whitehead.

Forty-first Virginia—Colonel Wm. Allen Parham.

Sixty-first Virginia—Colonel V. D. Groner.

POSEY'S BRIGADE.

Brigadier-General Carnot Posey.

Twelfth Mississippi—Lieutenant-Colonel M. B. Harris; Major S. B. Thomas.

Sixteenth Mississippi—Colonel Samuel E. Baker.

Nineteenth Mississippi—Colonel N. H. Harris.

Forty-eighth Mississippi—Colonel Joseph M. Jayne.

PERRY'S BRIGADE.

Brigadier-General E. A. Perry.

Second Florida; Fifth Florida; Eighth Florida.

ARTILLERY.

Lieutenant-Colonel J. J. Garnett.

Grandy's (Va.) battery; Lewis' (Va.) battery; Maurin's (La.) battery; Moore's [formerly Huger's] (Va.) battery.

ARTILLERY RESERVE.

ALEXANDER'S BATTALION.

Colonel E. P. Alexander.

Eubank's (Va.) battery; Jordan's (Va.) battery; Moody's (La.) battery; Parker's (Va.) battery; Rhett's (S. C.) battery; Woolfolk's (Va.) battery.

WASHINGTON (LA.) ARTILLERY.

Colonel J. B. Walton.

Eshleman's Fourth Company; Miller's Third Company; Richardson's Second Company; Squires' First Company.

SECOND CORPS.

(1) Lieutenant-General Thomas J. Jackson.
(2) Major-General Ambrose P. Hill.
(3) Brigadier-General R. E. Rodes.
(4) Major-General J. E. B. Stuart.

HILL'S DIVISION.

(1) Major-General A. P. Hill.
(2) Brigadier-General Henry Heth.
(3) Brigadier-General W. D. Pender.
(4) Brigadier-General J. J. Archer.

HETH'S BRIGADE.

(1) Brigadier-General Henry Heth.
(2) Colonel J. M. Brockenbrough.

Fortieth Virginia—Colonel J. M. Brockenbrough; Lieutenant-Colonel F. W. Cox; Captain T. E. Betts.

Forty-seventh Virginia—Colonel Robert M. Mayo.

HETH'S BRIGADE—Continued.

Fifty-fifth Virginia—Colonel Francis Mallory; Lieutenant-Colonel William S. Christian; Major A. D. Saunders; Adjutant R. L. Williams; Major Evan Rice.

Twenty-second Virginia Battalion—Lieutenant-Colonel E. P. Taylor.

THOMAS' BRIGADE.

Brigadier-General E. L. Thomas.

Fourteenth Georgia—Colonel R. W. Folsom.
Thirty-fifth Georgia—Captain John Duke.
Forty-fifth Georgia—Lieutenant-Colonel W. L. Grice.
Forty-ninth Georgia—Major S. T. Player.

BRIG.-GEN. E. A. PERRY, OF FLORIDA.

LANE'S (FOURTH) BRIGADE.

Brigadier-General J. H. Lane.

Seventh North Carolina—Colonel E. G. Haywood; Lieutenant-Colonel J. L. Hill; Major William L. Davidson; Captain N. A. Pool.

Eighteenth North Carolina—Colonel Thomas J. Purdie; Lieutenant-Colonel F. George; Major John D. Barry.

Twenty-eighth North Carolina—Colonel S. D. Lowe; Captain Edward F. Lovill.

Thirty-third North Carolina—Colonel Clark M. Avery; Captain Joseph H. Saunders.

Thirty-seventh North Carolina—Colonel W. M. Barbour.

M'GOWAN'S BRIGADE.

(1) Brigadier-General S. McGowan.
(2) Colonel O. E. Edwards.
(3) Colonel A. Perrin.
(4) Colonel D. H. Hamilton.

First South Carolina (Provisional Army)—Colonel D. H. Hamilton; Captain W. P. Shooter.

First South Carolina Rifles—Colonel James M. Perrin; Lieutenant-Colonel F. E. Harrison.

Twelfth South Carolina.

Thirteenth South Carolina—Colonel O. E. Edwards; Lieutenant-Colonel B. T. Brockman.

Fourteenth South Carolina—Colonel A. Perrin.

ARCHER'S (FIFTH) BRIGADE.

(1) Brigadier-General J. J. Archer.
(2) Colonel B. D. Fry.

Thirteenth Alabama—Colonel B. D. Fry.

Fifth Alabama Battalion—Captain S. D. Stewart; Captain A. N. Porter.

First Tennessee (Provisional Army) — Lieutenant-Colonel N. J. George.

Seventh Tennessee—Lieutenant-Colonel John A. Fite.

Fourteenth Tennessee — Captain William McComb; Captain R. C. Wilson.

PENDER'S BRIGADE.

Brigadier-General W. D. Pender.

Thirteenth North Carolina—Colonel A. M. Scales; Lieutenant-Colonel J. H. Hyman.

Sixteenth North Carolina—Colonel John S. McElroy; Lieutenant-Colonel William A. Stowe.

Twenty-second North Carolina—Lieutenant-Colonel Chris. C. Cole.

Thirty-fourth North Carolina.

Thirty-eighth North Carolina — Lieutenant - Colonel John Ashford.

ARTILLERY.

Colonel R. L. Walker.

Brunson's (S. C.) battery; Crenshaw's (Va.) battery; Davidson's (Va.) battery (Letcher's Artillery); McGraw's (Va.) battery; Marye's (Va.) battery.

D. H. HILL'S DIVISION.

(1) Brigadier-General R. E. Rodes.
(2) Brigadier-General S. D. Ramseur.

RODES' BRIGADE.

(1) Brigadier-General R. E. Rodes.
(2) Colonel E. A. O'Neal.
(3) Colonel J. M. Hall.

Third Alabama—Captain M. F. Bonham.

Fifth Alabama—Colonel J. M. Hall; Lieutenant-Colonel E. L. Hobson; Captain W. T. Renfro; Captain T. M. Riley.

Sixth Alabama—Colonel James N. Lightfoot.

Twelfth Alabama—Colonel Samuel B. Pickens.

Twenty-sixth Alabama—Colonel E. A. O'Neal; Lieutenant-Colonel John S. Garvin; Lieutenant M. J. Taylor.

COLQUITT'S BRIGADE.

Brigadier-General A. H. Colquitt.

Sixth Georgia—Colonel John T. Lofton.
Nineteenth Georgia—Colonel A. J. Hutchins.
Twenty-third Georgia—Colonel Emery F. Best.
Twenty-seventh Georgia—Colonel C. T. Zachry.
Twenty-eighth Georgia—Colonel Tully Graybill.

RAMSEUR'S BRIGADE.

(1) Brigadier-General S. D. Ramseur.
(2) Colonel F. M. Parker.

Second North Carolina—Colonel W. R. Cox.
Fourth North Carolina—Colonel Bryan Grimes.
Fourteenth North Carolina—Colonel R. T. Bennett.
Thirtieth North Carolina—Colonel F. M. Parker.

ARTILLERY.

Lieutenant-Colonel T. H. Carter.

Reese's, formerly Bondurant's (Ala.), battery (Jeff Davis Artillery); Carter's (Va.) battery (King William Artillery); Fry's (Va.) battery (Orange Artillery); Page's (Va.) battery (Morris' Artillery).

EARLY'S DIVISION.

Major-General Jubal A. Early.

GORDON'S BRIGADE.

Brigadier-General John B. Gordon.

Thirteenth Georgia; Twenty-sixth Georgia; Thirty-first Georgia; Thirty-eighth Georgia; Sixtieth Georgia; Sixty-first Georgia.

HOKE'S BRIGADE.

Brigadier-General Robert F. Hoke.

Sixth North Carolina; Twenty-first North Carolina; Fifty-fourth North Carolina; Fifty-seventh North Carolina; First North Carolina Battalion.

SMITH'S BRIGADE.

Brigadier-General Wm. Smith.

Thirteenth Virginia; Forty-ninth Virginia; Fifty-second Virginia; Fifty-eighth Virginia, Colonel F. H. Board.

HAYS' BRIGADE.

Fifth Louisiana; Sixth Louisiana; Seventh Louisiana; Eighth Louisiana; Ninth Louisiana.

ARTILLERY.

Lieutenant-Colonel R. S. Andrews.

Brown's (Md.) battery (Chesapeake Artillery); Carpenter's (Va.) battery; Dement's (Md.) battery; Raine's (Va.) battery (Lee Artillery).

TRIMBLE'S DIVISION.

Brigadier-General R. E. Colston.

PAXTON'S (FIRST) BRIGADE.

(1) Brigadier-General E. F. Paxton.
(2) Colonel J. H. S. Funk.

Second Virginia—J. Q. A. Nadenbousch.

Fourth Virginia—Major William Terry.

Fifth Virginia—Colonel J. H. S. Funk; Lieutenant-Colonel H. J. Williams.

Twenty-seventh Virginia—Colonel J. K. Edmonson; Lieutenant-Colonel D. M. Shriver.

Thirty-third Virginia—Colonel A. Spengler.

JONES' (SECOND) BRIGADE.

(1) Brigadier-General J. R. Jones.
(2) Colonel T. S. Garnett.
(3) Colonel A. S. Vandeventer.

Twenty-first Virginia—Captain John B. Moseley.

Forty-second Virginia — Lieutenant - Colonel R. W. Withers.

Forty-fourth Virginia—Major N. Cobb; Captain Thos. R. Buckner.

Forty-eighth Virginia—Colonel T. S. Garnett; Major Oscar White.

Fiftieth Virginia—Colonel A. S. Vandeventer; Major J. L. Perkins; Captain Frank W. Kelly.

COLSTON'S (THIRD) BRIGADE.

(1) Colonel E. T. H. Warren.
(2) Colonel T. V. Williams.
(3) Lieutenant-Colonel S. T. Walker.
(4) Lieutenant-Colonel S. D. Thruston.
(5) Lieutenant-Colonel H. A. Brown.

First North Carolina—Colonel J. A. McDowell.

Third North Carolina—Lieutenant-Colonel S. D. Thruston.

Tenth Virginia—Colonel E. T. H. Warren; Lieutenant-Colonel S. T. Walker; Major Joshua Stover; Captain A. H. Smals.

Twenty-third Virginia—Lieutenant-Colonel Simeon T. Walton.

Thirty-seventh Virginia—Colonel T. V. Williams.

NICHOLLS' (FOURTH) BRIGADE.

(1) Brigadier-General F. T. Nicholls.
(2) Colonel J. M. Williams.

First Louisiana—Captain E. D. Willett.

Second Louisiana—Colonel J. M. Williams; Lieutenant-Colonel R. E. Burke.

Tenth Louisiana—Lieutenant-Colonel John M. Legett.

Fourteenth Louisiana—Lieutenant-Colonel D. Zable.

Fifteenth Louisiana—Captain William C. Michie.

ARTILLERY.

Lieutenant-Colonel H. P. Jones.

Carrington's (Va.) battery (Charlottesville Artillery); Garber's (Va.) battery (Staunton Artillery); Latimer's (Va.) battery (Courtney Artillery); Thompson's battery (Louisiana Guard Artillery).

ARTILLERY RESERVE.

Colonel S. Crutchfield.

BROWN'S BATTALION.

Colonel J. Thompson Brown.

Brook's (Va.) battery (Burke Artillery); Dance's (Va.) battery (Powhatan Artillery); Graham's (Va.) battery (Rockbridge Artillery); Hupp's (Va.) battery (Salem Artillery); Smith's battery (Third Richmond Howitzers); Watson's battery (Second Richmond Howitzers).

McINTOSH'S BATTALION.

Major D. G. McIntosh.

Hunt's (Ala.) battery; Johnson's (Va.) battery; Lusk's (Va.) battery; Wooding's (Va.) battery (Danville Artillery).

BRIG.-GEN. WILLIAM T. WOFFORD, OF GEORGIA.

RESERVE ARTILLERY.

Brigadier-General William N. Pendleton.

SUMTER (GEORGIA) BATTALION.

Lieutenant-Colonel A. S. Cutts.

Patterson's battery (B); Ross' battery (A); Wingfield's battery (C).

NELSON'S BATTALION.

Lieutenant-Colonel W. Nelson.

Kirkpatrick's (Va.) battery (Amherst Artillery); Massie's (Va.) battery (Fluvanna Artillery); Milledge's (Ga.) battery.

CAVALRY.

Major-General James E. B. Stuart.

FIRST BRIGADE.*

Brigadier-General Wade Hampton.

First North Carolina; First South Carolina; Second South Carolina; Cobb's Georgia Legion; Phillip's Georgia Legion.

*"South of James River, recruiting." See Stuart's report.

SECOND BRIGADE.
Brigadier-General Fitzhugh Lee.

First Virginia.
Second Virginia.
Third Virginia—Colonel Thomas H. Owens.
Fourth Virginia—Colonel Williams C. Wickham.

THIRD BRIGADE.*
Brigadier-General W. H. F. Lee.

Second North Carolina—Lieutenant-Colonel W. H. Payne.
Fifth Virginia—Colonel T. L. Rosser.
Ninth Virginia—Colonel R. L. T. Beale.
Tenth Virginia.
Thirteenth Virginia—Colonel John R. Chambliss, Jr.
Fifteenth Virginia.

BRIG.-GEN. E. F. PAXTON, OF VIRGINIA.
Killed at the Battle of Chancellorsville, Va., May 3, 1863.

FOURTH BRIGADE.†
Brigadier-General William E. Jones.

First Maryland Battalion—Major Ridgely Brown.
Sixth Virginia—Lieutenant-Colonel John Shac. Green.
Seventh Virginia—Lieutenant-Colonel Thomas Marshall.
Eleventh Virginia—Colonel L. L. Lomax.
Twelfth Virginia—Colonel A. W. Harman.
Thirty-fourth Virginia Battalion—Lieutenant-Colonel V. A. Witcher.
Thirty-fifth Virginia Battalion — Lieutenant-Colonel Elijah V. White.

HORSE ARTILLERY.
Major R. F. Beckham.

Lynchburg Beauregards—Captain M. N. Maraman.
Stuart Horse Artillery—Captain James Breathed.
Virginia Battery—Captain William M. McGregor.
Washington (S. C.) Artillery—Captain James F. Hart.

* Engaged in resisting "the Stoneman raid." See W. H. F. Lee's report.

† On detached service. See Jones' raid on the Northwestern (Baltimore & Ohio) Railroad.

DO THEY MISS ME IN THE TRENCHES?

A VICKSBURG SONG.

Air—"Do They Miss Me at Home?"

Do they miss me in the trenches, do they miss me,
When the shells fly so thickly around?
Do they know that I've run down the hillside
To hunt for my hole in the ground?
The shell exploded so near me,
It seemed best for me to run;
And although some laughed as I crawfished,
I could not discover the fun.

I often get up in the trenches,
When some Yank is near out of sight,
And fire a round or two at him,
To make the boys think I will fight;
But when the Feds commence shelling
I run to my hole down the hill—
I'll swear my legs never would stay there,
Although all may stay there at will.

I'll save myself through the dread struggle,
And when the great battle is o'er
I'll claim my full rations of laurels,
As always I've done heretofore.
I'll swear that I've fought them as bravely
As the best of my comrades who fell,
And swear to all others around me
That I never had fears of a shell.

DEATH OF STONEWALL JACKSON.

BY

DOCTOR HUNTER McGUIRE,
Medical Director of Jackson's Corps.

SUPPORTED upon either side by his aids—Captain James P. Smith and Joseph Morrison—the general moved slowly and painfully toward the rear. Occasionally resting for a moment to shake off the exhaustion which pain and the loss of blood produced, he at last reached the line of battle, where most of the men were lying down to escape the shell and canister with which the Federals raked the road. General Pender rode up here to the little party and asked who was wounded, and Captain Smith, who had been instructed by General Jackson to tell no one of his injury, simply answered, "A Confederate officer;" but Pender recognized the general, and, springing from his horse, hurriedly expressed his regret, and added that his lines were so much broken he feared it would be necessary to fall back. At this moment the scene was a fearful one. The air seemed to be alive with the shrieks of shells and the whistling of bullets; horses, riderless and mad with fright, dashed in every direction; hundreds left the ranks and fled to the rear, and the groans of the wounded and dying mingled with the wild shouts of others to be led again to the assault. Almost fainting as he was, from loss of blood, fearfully wounded, and as he thought dying, Jackson was undismayed by this terrible scene. The words of Pender seemed to rouse him to life. Pushing aside the men who supported him, he stretched himself to his full height and answered feebly, but distinctly enough to be heard above the din of the battle: "General Pender, you must hold on to the field; you must hold out to the last."

It was Jackson's last order upon the field of battle. Still more exhausted by this effort, he asked to be permitted to lie down for a few moments, but the danger from the fire and capture by the Federal advance was too imminent, and his aids hurried him on. A litter having been obtained, he was placed upon it, and the bearers passed on as rapidly as the thick woods and rough ground permitted. Unfortunately, another one of the bearers was struck down, and the litter, having been supported at each of the four corners by a man, fell and threw the general to the ground. The fall was a serious one, and as he touched the earth he gave, for the first time, expression to his suffering, and groaned piteously.

Captain Smith sprang to his side, and as he raised his head a bright beam of moonlight made its way through the thick foliage and rested upon the pale face of the sufferer. The captain was startled by its great pallor and stillness, and cried out: "Oh! general, are you seriously hurt?" "No," he answered, "don't trouble yourself, my friend, about me;" and presently added something about

LIEUT.-GEN. THOMAS J. ("STONEWALL") JACKSON, OF VIRGINIA.
Mortally Wounded at the Battle of Chancellorsville, Va.

winning the battle first and attending to the wounded afterward. He was placed upon the litter again, and carried a few hundred yards, when I met him with an ambulance. I knelt down by him and said, "I hope you are not badly hurt, general." He replied, very calmly but feebly, "I am badly injured, doctor; I fear I am dying." After a pause he continued, "I am glad you have come. I think the wound in my shoulder is still bleeding." His clothes were saturated with blood, and hemorrhage was still going on from the wound. Compression of the artery with the finger arrested it until, lights being procured from the ambulance, the handkerchief, which had slipped a little, was readjusted.

His calmness amid the dangers which surrounded him, and at the supposed presence of death, and his uniform politeness, which did not forsake him, even under these, the most trying circumstances, were remarkable. His complete control, too, over his mind, enfeebled as it was by loss of blood, pain, etc., was wonderful. His suffering at this time was intense; his hands were cold, his skin clammy, his face pale, and his lips compressed and bloodless; not a groan escaped him—not a sign of suffering except the slight corrugation of his brow, the fixed, rigid face, and the thin lips so tightly compressed that the impression of the teeth could be seen through them. Except these, he controlled by his iron will all evidence of emotion, and,

HOUSE IN WHICH "STONEWALL" JACKSON WAS BORN, CLARKSBURG, VA. (NOW W. VA.), JANUARY 21, 1824.

more difficult than this even, he controlled that disposition to restlessness, which many of us have observed upon the field of battle, attending great loss of blood. Some whisky and morphia were procured from Dr. Straith and administered to him, and placing him in the ambulance it was started for the corps field infirmary at the Wilderness tavern. Colonel Crutchfield, his chief of artillery, was also in the ambulance wagon. He had been wounded very seriously in the leg, and was suffering intensely.

The general expressed, very feelingly, his sympathy for Crutchfield, and once, when the latter groaned aloud, he directed the ambulance to stop, and requested me to see if something could not be done for his relief. Torches had been provided, and every means taken to carry them to the hospital as safely and easily as possible. I sat in the front part of the ambulance, with my finger resting upon the artery above the wound, to arrest bleeding if it should occur. When I was recognized by acquaintances and asked who was wounded, the general would tell me to say, "A Confederate officer." At one time he put his right hand upon my head, and pulling me down to him, asked if Crutchfield was dangerously injured. When answered "No, only painfully hurt," he replied, "I am glad it is no worse." In a few moments after Crutchfield did the same thing, and when he was told that the general was seriously wounded, he groaned and cried out, "Oh, my God!" It was for this that the general directed the ambulance to be halted, and requested that something should be done for Crutchfield's relief.

After reaching the hospital he was placed in bed, covered with blankets, and another drink of whisky and water given him. Two hours and a half elapsed before sufficient reaction took place to warrant an examination. At 2 o'clock Sunday morning, Surgeons Black, Walls and Coleman being present, I informed him that chloroform would be given him and his wounds examined. I told him that amputation would probably be required, and asked, if it was found necessary, whether it should be done at once. He replied promptly: "Yes, certainly. Dr. McGuire, do for me whatever you think best." Chloroform was then administered, and as he began to feel its effects and its relief to the pain he was suffering, he exclaimed: "What an infinite blessing," and continued to repeat the word "blessing" until he became insensible. The round ball (such as is used for the smooth-bore Springfield musket), which had lodged under the skin upon the back of his right hand, was extracted first. It had entered the palm about the middle of the hand, and had fractured two of the bones. The left arm was then amputated about two inches below the shoulder, very rapidly and with slight loss of blood, the ordinary circular operation having been made. There were two wounds in his arm. The first and most serious was about three inches below the shoulder-joint, the ball dividing the main artery and fracturing the bone. The second was several inches in length; a ball having entered the outside of the forearm, an inch below the elbow, came out upon the opposite side just above the wrist. Throughout the whole of the operation, and until all the dressings were applied, he continued insensible. Two or three slight wounds of the skin of his face, received from the branches of trees when his horse dashed through the woods, were dressed simply with isinglass plaster.

About half-past 3 o'clock, Colonel (then Major) Pendleton, the assistant adjutant-general, arrived at the hospital and asked to see the general. He stated that General Hill had been wounded, and that the troops were in great disorder. General Stuart was in command, and had sent him to see the general. At first I declined to permit an interview, but the colonel urged that the safety of the army and success of the cause depended upon his seeing him. When he entered the tent the general said: "Well, major, I am glad to see you. I thought you were killed." Pendleton briefly explained the condition of affairs, gave Stuart's message, and asked what should be done. General Jackson was at once interested, and asked, in his quick, rapid way several questions. When they were answered, he remained silent for a moment, evidently trying to think; he contracted his brow, set his mouth, and for some moments was obviously endeavoring to concentrate his thoughts. For a moment it was believed he had succeeded, for his nostril dilated and his eye flashed its old fire, but it was only for a moment; his face relaxed again, and presently he answered, very feebly and sadly, "I don't know; I can't tell; say to General Stuart he must do what he thinks best." Soon after this he slept for several hours, and seemed to be doing well. The next morning he was free from pain, and expressed himself sanguine of recovery. He sent his aide-de-camp, Morrison, to inform his wife of his injuries, and to bring her at once to see him. The following note from General Lee was read to him that morning by Captain Smith: "I have just received your note, informing me that you were wounded. I can not express my regret at the occurrence. Could I have directed events, I should have chosen, for the good of the country, to have been disabled in your stead. I congratulate you upon the victory, which is due to your skill and energy." He replied: "General Lee should give the praise to God."

About 10 o'clock his right side began to pain him so much that he asked me to examine it. He said he had injured it in falling from the litter the night before, and believed that he had struck it against a stone or the stump of a sapling. No evidence of injury could be discovered by examination. The skin was not broken or bruised, and the lung performed, as far as I could tell, its proper functions. Some simple application was recommended, in the belief that the pain would soon disappear.

At this time the battle was raging fearfully, and the sound of the cannon and musketry could be distinctly heard at the hospital. The general's attention was attracted to it from the first, and when the noise was at its height, and indicated how fiercely the conflict was being carried on, he directed all of his attendants, except Captain Smith, to return to the battlefield and attend to their different duties. By 8 o'clock Sunday night the pain in his side had disappeared, and in all respects he seemed to be doing well. He inquired minutely about the battle and the different troops engaged, and his face would light up with enthusiasm and interest when told how this brigade acted, or that officer displayed conspicuous courage, and his head gave the peculiar shake from side to side, and he uttered his usual "Good, good," with unwonted energy when the gallant behavior of the "Stonewall brigade" was alluded to. He said: "The men of that brigade will be some day proud to say to their children, 'I was one of the Stonewall brigade.'" He disclaimed any right of his own to the name Stonewall. "It belongs to the brigade, and not to me." This night he slept well, and was free from pain.

A message was received from General Lee the next morning directing me to remove the general to Guineys Station as soon as his condition would justify it, as there was some danger of capture by the Federals, who were threatening to cross at Elys Ford. In the meantime, to protect the hospital, some troops were sent to this point. The general objected to being moved, if, in my opinion, it would do him any injury. He said he had no objection to staying in a tent, and would prefer it if his wife, when she came, could find lodging in a neighboring house; "and if the enemy does come," he added, "I am not afraid of them; I have always been kind to their wounded, and I am sure they will be kind to me." General Lee sent word again late that evening that he must be moved if possible, and preparations were made to leave the next morning. I was directed to accompany and remain with him, and my duties with the corps as medical director were turned over to the surgeon next in rank. General Jackson had previously declined to permit me to go with him to Guineys, because complaints had been so frequently made of general officers, when wounded, carrying off with them the surgeons belonging to their commands. When informed of this order of the commanding general he said, "General Lee has always been very kind to me, and I thank him."

PLACE WHERE GENERAL "STONEWALL" JACKSON FELL AT THE BATTLE OF CHANCELLORSVILLE, VA.

Very early Tuesday morning he was placed in an ambulance and started for Guineys Station, and about 8 o'clock that evening he arrived at the Chandler house, where he remained until he died. Captain Hotchkiss, with a party of engineers, was sent in front to clear the road of wood, stone, etc., and to order the wagons out of the track to let the ambulance pass.

The rough teamsters sometimes refused to move their loaded wagons out of the way for an ambulance until told that it contained Jackson, and then, with all possible speed, they gave the way and stood with hats off and weeping as he went by. At Spottsylvania Courthouse and along the whole route men and women rushed to the ambulance, bringing all the poor delicacies they had, and with tearful eyes they blessed him and prayed for his recovery. He bore the journey well, and was cheerful throughout the day. He talked freely about the late battle, and among other things said that he had intended to endeavor to cut the Federals off from United States Ford, and take a position between them and the river, obliging them to attack him; and he added, with a smile: "My men sometimes fail to drive the enemy from a position, but they always fail to drive us away." He spoke of Rodes, and alluded in high terms to his magnificent behavior on the field Saturday evening. He hoped he would be promoted. He thought promotion for gallantry should be made at once, upon the field, and not delayed. Made very early, or upon the field, they would be the greatest incentives to gallantry in others. He spoke of Colonel Willis (subsequently killed in battle), who commanded the skirmishers of Rodes' division, and praised him very highly, and referred to the deaths of Paxton and Boswell very feelingly. He alluded to them as officers of great merit and promise. The day was quite warm, and at one time he suffered from slight nausea. At his suggestion, I placed over his stomach a wet towel, and he expressed great relief from it. After he arrived at Chandler's house he ate some bread and tea with evident relish, and slept well throughout the entire night. Wednesday he was thought to be doing remarkably well. He ate heartily for one in his condition, and was uniformly cheerful.

I found his wounds to be very well to-day. Union by the first intention had taken place to some extent in the stump, and the rest of the surface of the wound exposed was covered with healthy granulations. The wound in his hand gave him little pain, and the discharge was healthy. Simple lint and water dressings were used, both for the stump and hand, and upon the palm of the latter a light, short splint was applied to assist in keeping at rest the fragments of the second and third metacarpal bones. He expressed great satisfaction when told that his wounds were healing, and asked if I could tell from their appearance how long he would probably be kept from the field. Conversing with Captain Smith a few moments afterward, he alluded to his injuries, and said, "Many would regard them as a great misfortune; I regard them as one of the blessings of my life."

Captain Smith replied: "All things work together for good to those that love God."

"Yes," he answered, "that's it, that's it."

At my request Dr. Morrison came to-day and remained with him.

About 1 o'clock Thursday morning, while I was asleep upon a lounge in his room, he directed his servant (Jim) to apply a wet towel to his stomach to relieve an attack of nausea, with which he was again troubled. The servant asked permission to first consult me, but the general, knowing that I had slept none for nearly three nights, refused to allow the servant to disturb me, and demanded the towel. About daylight I was aroused, and found him suffering great pain. An examination disclosed pleuro-pneumonia of the right side. I believed, and the consulting physicians concurred in the opinion, that it was attributable to the fall from the litter the night he was wounded. The general himself referred it to this accident. I think the disease came on too soon after the application of the wet cloths to admit of the supposition, once believed, that it was induced by them. The nausea, for which the cloths were applied that night, may have been the result of inflammation already begun. Contusion of the lung, with extravasation of blood in his chest, was probably produced by the fall referred to, and shock and loss of blood prevented any ill effects until reaction had been well established, and then inflammation ensued. Cups were applied, and mercury, with antimony and opium, administered.

Toward the evening he became better, and hopes were again entertained of his recovery. Mrs. Jackson arrived to-day and nursed him faithfully to the end. She was a devoted wife and earnest Christian, and endeared us all to her by her great kindness and gentleness. The general's joy at the presence of his wife and child was very great, and for him unusually demonstrative. Noticing the sadness of his wife, he said to her tenderly: "I know you would gladly give your life for me, but I am perfectly resigned. Do not be sad. I hope I may yet recover. Pray for me, but always remember in your prayers to use the petition, 'Thy will be done.'"

Friday his wounds were again dressed, and although the quantity of the discharge from them had diminished, the process of healing was still going on. The pain in his side had disappeared, but he breathed with difficulty and complained of a feeling of great exhaustion. When

CHANDLER HOUSE, GUINEYS STATION, VA., IN WHICH "STONEWALL" JACKSON DIED.

Dr. Breckinridge (who, with Dr. Smith, had been sent for in consultation) said he hoped that a blister which had been applied would afford him great relief, he expressed his own confidence in it, and in his final recovery.

Dr. Tucker, from Richmond, arrived on Saturday, and all that human skill could devise was done to stay the hand of death. He suffered no pain to-day, and his breathing was less difficult, but he was evidently hourly growing weaker.

When his child was brought to him to-day he played with it for some time, frequently caressing it and calling it his "little comforter." At one time he raised his wounded hand above his head and, closing his eyes, was for some moments silently engaged in prayer. He said to me: "I see from the number of physicians that you think my condition dangerous, but I thank God, if it His will, that I am ready to go."

About daylight on Sunday morning Mrs. Jackson informed him that his recovery was very doubtful, and that it was better that he should be prepared for the worst. He was silent for a moment, and then said: "It will be infinite gain to be translated to Heaven." He advised his wife, in the event of his death, to return to her father's house, and added: "You have a kind and good father, but there is no one so kind and good as your Heavenly Father." He still expressed a hope of his recovery, but requested her, if he should die, to have him buried in Lexington, in the Valley of Virginia. His exhaustion increased so rapidly that at 11 o'clock Mrs. Jackson knelt by his bed and told him that before the sun went down he would be with his Saviour. He replied, "Oh, no; you are frightened, my child; death is not so near; I may yet get well." She fell over upon the bed, weeping bitterly, and told him again that the physicians said there was no hope. After a moment's pause he asked her to call me. "Doctor, Anna informs me that you have told her that I am to die to-day; is it so?" When he was answered, he turned his eyes toward the ceiling and gazed for a moment or two as if in intense thought, then replied, "Very good, very good, it is all right." He then tried to comfort his almost heart-broken wife, and told her that he had a great deal to say to her, but he was too weak.

THE ROOM IN WHICH "STONEWALL" JACKSON DIED.
[From a photo taken in 1880.]

Colonel Pendleton came into the room about 1 o'clock, and he asked him, "Who was preaching at headquarters to-day?" When told that the whole army was praying for him, he replied: "Thank God, they are very kind." He said: "It is the Lord's Day; my wish is fulfilled. I have always desired to die on Sunday."

His mind now began to fail and wander, and he frequently talked as if in command upon the field, giving orders in his old way; then the scene shifted, and he was at the mess-table, in conversation with members of his staff; now with his wife and child; now at prayers with his military family. Occasional intervals of return of his mind would appear, and during one of them I offered him some brandy and water, but he declined it, saying, "It will only delay my departure, and do no good; I want to preserve my mind, if possible, to the last." About half-past 1 he was told that he had but two hours to live, and he answered again, feebly, but firmly, "Very good, it is all right."

A few moments before he died he cried out in his delirium, "Order A. P. Hill to prepare for action! Pass the infantry to the front rapidly! Tell Major Hawks" —— then stopped, leaving the sentence unfinished. Presently a smile of ineffable sweetness spread itself over his pale face, and he cried quietly and with an expression as if of relief, "Let us cross over the river and rest under the shade of the trees;" and then, without pain or the least struggle, his spirit passed from earth to the God who gave it.

BATTLE OF CHAMPIONS HILL, OR BAKERS CREEK, MISS.,

MAY 16, 1863.

BY

MAJOR-GENERAL W. W. LORING.

HEADQUARTERS CAMP FORREST, MISS.,
August 28, 1863.

ON May 13th Major-General Bowen, in command of his division, having reported the enemy advancing, I was ordered to re-enforce him with my division. General Stevenson soon after coming up with his division, a very strong position was selected about one mile south of Edwards Depot, our left resting on the railroad and the right not far from Bakers Creek.

On the morning of the 14th, General Pemberton ordered a council of war, in which he read a dispatch from General [Joseph E.] Johnston, which stated in substance that the enemy (two or three divisions) was at Clinton, nine miles from Jackson, and (if General Pemberton thought it practicable) advised a movement in connection with him, saying that time was all-important. In the council of war there was great diversity of opinion; two generals were for moving at once upon the road to Clinton; two or three were for remaining or moving back; three were for striking at the communications of the enemy, keeping our own open with the bridge over Big Black River and fighting or not in a position of our own choosing as would seem best. I understood the opinion of the general commanding to be that he did not approve the move proposed by General Johnston, but coincided with those who were for moving to the enemy's rear.

It was determined by the general to move at 8 o'clock in the morning (15th instant), the army intending to cross Bakers Creek at a ford, which was prevented by its swollen condition. It was, however, put in motion about 3 or 4 P. M., crossing the creek upon a bridge a short distance above the ford. A map was furnished marking the road upon which the army was to march, my division being in the advance. After moving four or five miles we were joined by Major [Samuel H.] Lockett, chief engineer, who directed the column to take a cross-road leading to Mrs. Ellison's house, on the middle Raymond Road. At this place the army was to have encamped, it having been discovered that the road which it was intended the entire force should follow was wrongly laid down upon the map furnished.

About dark my division reached Mrs. Ellison's and found a great scarcity of water. This information was at once communicated to General Pemberton, so that he might make some other disposition of the forces which were following. After dark it fortunately happened that the other divisions were still upon the road leading from the bridge and encamped along it in their line of march. It was still more fortunate that my command was upon the middle Raymond Road, which led immediately to the ford at which the army was to have crossed in the morning. Upon this road the enemy was in large force within a few miles of my camp. Being satisfied of this, from prisoners taken and from observations of several of my staff sent in advance, very large picket forces were placed in my front, rear and right flank. Completing my dispositions I soon after met General Pemberton, to whom information of the near proximity of the enemy in large force was given. Additional information was subsequently given him establishing the fact that he was in our immediate front. This was the condition of things until 7 or 8 o'clock next morning (16th), when the general informed us that he had a note from General Johnston advising a junction with him in the direction of Brownsville, his force having fallen back from Jackson. This necessitated a movement toward Edwards Depot. The general then gave an order for the train, which had not come up, to retrace its steps. Pending this it is said the enemy was in line of battle preparing to attack us. Moving rapidly upon my pickets he opened a brisk cannonade. I suggested to General Pemberton that the sooner he formed a line of battle the better, as the enemy would very soon be upon us. He at first directed me to form Tilghman's brigade in a line of battle upon the ground it then occupied, but soon thought it untenable, and ordered it, with Featherston's and Buford's brigades (my whole division), into a line of battle on a ridge about three-quarters of a mile in the rear and across a small creek. This line was almost immediately changed for a ridge still further back, where my artillery was advantageously posted on both sides of the road, the field to the front being entirely open as far as Mrs. Ellison's house. He also directed the division to occupy the road and the country to the right of it, and in orders conveyed to me at different times during the day he instructed me to hold my position, not attacking the enemy unless he attempted to outflank us. Bowen's command was extended so as to join mine on the road. Soon a series of orders came, specifically and with great particularity, for two of my brigades to move to the left, closing the line as often as Bowen moved, and we in this manner followed him.

MAJ.-GEN. W. W. LORING, OF FLORIDA.

During this time I received an order to retire, also one to advance, both of which were countermanded. My whole division, including reserves, was strung out in line of battle, mostly in thick timber. The enemy during these movements remained steadily in front in heavy force, being, apparently, a full corps, occupying a series of ridges, wooded and commanding each other, forming naturally a very strong if not impregnable position, throwing forward a heavy line of skirmishers and showing every indication of an attack in force upon my position, both in front and upon the right flank. General Bowen also informed me that he thought the enemy was moving to the right. While these movements were going on (all of which were brought to the general's attention) desultory firing was heard on the extreme left, and General Bowen was summarily ordered in that direction, without warning either to myself or to General Buford, commanding a brigade of my division next to him. Not long after I was ordered to send a brigade to the left, and General Buford went at double-quick. While passing Bowen two regiments were detached and went into the fight with that command, Buford continuing on to the left. In a half to three-quarters of an hour one brigade was ordered to be left on the road, and the other to be taken by myself to the left. This was most earnestly requested to be done by Colonel [W. T.] Withers, in command of the artillery, who feared the capture of the guns. He tells me that he was gratified in being able to state that my force arrived sooner than he expected, and in time to save his artillery. But for our prompt arrival every piece would have been lost, as the whole sustaining force had, except a few bold skirmishers, been driven back.

Upon the approach of [W. S.] Featherston's brigade,

BRIG.-GEN. W. S. FEATHERSTON, OF MISSISSIPPI.

in rapid march, a considerable force of the retreating army having been rallied behind him, the enemy, who was advancing upon the artillery, fell back in great disorder, Colonel Withers pouring in a most destructive fire upon him. It was here that we witnessed a scene ever to be remembered—when the gallant Withers and his brave men with their fine park of artillery stood unflinchingly amid a shower of shot and shell the approach of an enemy in overwhelming force after his supports had been driven back, and trusting that a succoring command would arrive in time to save his batteries, and displaying a degree of courage and determination that calls for the most unqualified admiration.

Upon my arrival upon this part of the field I found the whole country, on both sides of the road, covered with the fleeing of our army, in many cases in large squads, and as there was no one endeavoring to rally or direct them I at once placed my escort under an efficient officer of my staff, with orders to gather up the stragglers and those in retreat away from the road. This duty was performed with great energy and success. It was also determined that under these circumstances it was necessary, in order to save large numbers of men and guns, as well as to be able, in case the emergency should arise, to retire the army in safety and good order to the ford over Bakers Creek along the only road open to it, that a vigorous and well-directed attack should be made upon the enemy. At this moment I met General [S. D.] Lee and Colonel Withers, and was satisfied, from information obtained from them, that by such an attack upon the enemy's right during the panic which had befallen his center we could overwhelm it,

BELLIGERENT WORK.
Sharpshooters behind fallen trees picking off their exposed enemies.

enemy's center, and about this time the brave Alpheus Baker, of the Fifty-fourth Alabama, was severely wounded in another part of the field.

During this time Tilghman, who had been left with his brigade upon the other road, almost immediately after our parting, met a terrible assault of the enemy, and when we rejoined him was carrying on a deadly and most gallant fight. With less than fifteen hundred effective men he was attacked by from six thousand to eight thousand of the enemy with a fine park of artillery; but being advantageously posted, he not only held him in check, but repulsed him on several occasions, and thus kept open the only line of retreat left to the army. The bold stand of this brigade under the lamented hero saved a large portion of the army.

It is befitting that I should speak of the death of the gallant and accomplished [Lloyd] Tilghman. Quick and bold in the execution of his plans, he fell in the midst of a brigade that loved him well, after repulsing a powerful enemy in deadly fight, struck by a cannon-shot. A brigade wept over the dying hero; alike beautiful as it was touching.

I had some time before this sent an adjutant to General Pemberton and subsequently another to ascertain how his retreating forces were progressing, but having left the field it was impossible to communicate with him. The officer on his return informed me that he had met General Bowen at the ford, who had requested him to say to me, "For God's sake, hold your position until sundown and save the army." He could hold the ford and the bridge was safe. I had scarcely received this message when General Bowen sent me a written communication, stating that the enemy had crossed the bridge and had outflanked him; that he had been compelled precipitately to fall back, and that I must do my best to save my division. I also received a note from Lieutenant-Colonel Jacob Thompson to the same import. We at once made a movement toward the ford, there being no other road of retreat. There being none on my left that I could use, and being wholly unacquainted with the country—my only guide having been taken by General Pemberton to direct him to Big Black Bridge—my first determination was to force my way through by the ford, and rode rapidly to reconnoiter. Arriving there it was found that our troops were gone, some of whom having been driven back upon us. The enemy's skirmishers were advancing and a heavy force occupied the commanding ridge across the creek, his artillery playing upon the crossing. The enemy upon our right flank and rear had been re-enforced, so that we were enveloped upon three sides, leaving no road to move upon. Not far from my place of observation I met Dr. Williamson, a highly respectable gentleman of Edwards Depot, who said he knew the whole country and thought he could take me to a ford on Bakers Creek, three or four miles below.

BATTLE OF CHAMPIONS HILL, MAY 16, 1863.

retrieve the day, certainly cut him off from the bridge on our extreme left (of which it was highly important we should hold possession) and save our scattered forces. Dispositions were at once made for the attack, in which General Lee lent a cordial and able assistance. This fine officer, with General [M. E.] Green and portions of their gallant brigades, we found fighting the enemy when all others, except the brave Withers, had been driven back, and contesting every step of the enemy's advancing columns, Green declaring he never would have been driven back but for the fact that he had not a cartridge left. While thus engaged I received an order for the forces to fall back, and my assistant adjutant-general, who had been dispatched to General Pemberton for orders, returned stating that the general said that the movement must not be made; that I must order a retreat and bring up the rear. Officers were immediately sent to advise those not yet informed to retire, and as rapidly as possible, in the direction of the ford, that being the only road left open. As soon as the enemy realized that we were leaving the field he rallied and moved forward in heavy force.

In the meantime Featherston's brigade was put into position to protect the rear of the retreating forces and to cover the falling back of Buford's brigade. This duty was ably and gallantly executed. This latter brigade (Buford's) about this time met a charge of the enemy (infantry, cavalry and artillery) and repulsed him in splendid style with great slaughter, the heavy fighting being done by the Twelfth Louisiana, a large regiment under the able and daring [T. M.] Scott. This and the gallant [Edward] Goodwin, Thirty-fifth Alabama Regiment, had also distinguished themselves in the charge upon the

A FAMILIAR ARMY SCENE. FORAGERS COOKING A MEAL.

By this time darkness was approaching. I at once decided upon this move. By a well-concerted movement we eluded the enemy upon three sides, and, to his astonishment, made our flank march from between his forces across the fields to a given point in the woods skirting Bakers Creek. The night being dark and the trail a blind one, it was found impossible to get through by following the creek. It was then determined to move across to another road and reach the ford in that direction, my command being compelled to move back upon the ground where the parties were near enough to hear them. The unused plantation roads upon which we moved were in such bad condition as to render it impossible to carry our artillery over them, and we were obliged to destroy that which we had with our commands, bringing the horses and harness with us, the balance having gone with the army into Vicksburg. Soon after striking the timber we discovered Edwards Depot and Withers' gin-house on fire, which convinced us that our forces had passed those points; but, as we were led to believe that we could reach the lower ford in three or four miles, it was hoped that we could pass in between Edwards Depot and Big Black Bridge and rejoin the army. Instead of three or four it was ten or twelve miles before my command reached the lower Raymond Road, which led to the ford, and then it was after midnight. My guide (Dr. Williamson) informed me that it was impossible to guide the division to Big Black Bridge with the enemy in possession of Edwards Depot, which we were convinced he had held for several hours, but referred us to a gentleman by the name of Vaughan, who lived within one mile of the road. I went to his house and brought him to the column to consult with my generals, and proposed that he should take us to Big Black River. He declared that it was impossible, as all the lower fords over Bakers Creek were swimming, and that to Big Black Bridge he could not take us without moving through the enemy's lines at Edwards Depot. He also informed us that a large force of the enemy had that day passed by his house. It was known that the enemy had troops at all ferries over Big Black below the mouth of Bakers Creek, and that the river was a deep and difficult stream to cross. The condition of the command was also taken into consideration, being without artillery, with but few rounds of cartridges; having no implements for immediate construction of a bridge or ferry; our entire train having gone into Vicksburg, and being without supplies of any kind; also, the distance to the river was so great that it would have been impossible to have reached it until late next day, when the enemy was sure to have been posted to prevent crossing. After a full consultation with my brigadiers, all of us were of the opinion that it was impossible to attempt the passage of Big Black at any point, and in doing so the entire division would certainly be lost. Subsequent events have fully shown that we were right in this determination. It was then determined to force the rear of the enemy between Raymond and Utica.

On the evening of the 17th my command, after a hard march, reached Crystal Srprings, a village on the New Orleans & Jackson Railroad, twenty-five miles south of Jackson.

On the 19th, reached Jackson with my entire division, few lingering by the way, and immediately reported to General Johnston, who expressed his gratification that my command had safely arrived.

Of Generals Featherston and Buford and Colonel A. E. Reynolds, commanding brigades, too much can not be said in commendation. The rapidity and skill with which they executed their orders and the boldness with which their gallant commands met and successfully repulsed the powerful attacks of the enemy, delaying the Yankee army and securing a safe retreat to that of ours across the ford, entitles them to the highest praise; and, finally, in lending themselves a sacrifice, enveloped as they were upon three sides (front, right flank and rear), undismayed, with a proud consciousness of having done their whole duty, they withdrew in good order from under fire in face of the enemy, and thus we were enabled to make the dangerous but successful movement to the left.

My staff—Captain Henry Robinson, Assistant Adjutant-General; Captain [A. A.] Bursley, Chief of Artillery; Captain [Belton] Mickle, Assistant Quartermaster; Captain John D. Myrick; Lieutenant [J.] Hanson Thomas, Aid-de-camp; Captain [William] Sykes, Aid-de-camp; Captain Henry de Veuve, Assistant Engineer; Henry Taylor and William McFarland, Volunteer Aids; Captain Russell and Dr. Williamson, Guides—were continually under fire, and themselves, as in other fields, with courage and

W. W. LORING,
Major-General Commanding, etc.

POLK.

BY H. L. FLASH.

A flash from the edge of a hostile trench,
A puff of smoke, a roar,
Whose echo shall roll from Kenesaw Hills
To the furthermost Christian shore,
Proclaim to the world that warrior-priest
Will battle for the right no more.

And that for a cause which is sanctified
By the blood of martyrs unknown—
A cause for which they gave their lives,
And for which he gave his own—
He kneels, a meek ambassador,
At the foot of the Father's throne.

And up to the courts of another world,
That angels alone have trod,
He lives away from the din and strife
Of this blood-besprinkled sod—
Crowned by the amaranthine wreath
That is worn by the blest of God.

THE GETTYSBURG CAMPAIGN,

JUNE 3 TO AUGUST 1, 1863.

BY

GENERAL ROBERT E. LEE,
Commanding Army of Northern Virginia.

HEADQUARTERS ARMY OF NORTHERN VIRGINIA,
June 7, 1864.

I HAVE the honor to submit a detailed report of the operations of this army from the time it left the vicinity of Fredericksburg, early in June, to its occupation of the line of the Rapidan, in August.

Upon the retreat of the Federal army, commanded by Major-General Hooker, from Chancellorsville, it reoccupied the ground north of the Rappahannock, opposite Fredericksburg, where it could not be attacked excepting at a disadvantage. It was determined to draw it from this position, and, if practicable, to transfer the scene of hostilities beyond the Potomac. The execution of this purpose also embraced the expulsion of the force under General Milroy, which had infested the lower Shenandoah Valley during the preceding winter and spring. If unable to attain the valuable results which might be expected to follow a decided advantage gained over the enemy in Maryland or Pennsylvania, it was hoped that we should at least so far disturb his plan for the summer campaign as to prevent its execution during the season of active operations.

GENERAL R. E. LEE'S HEADQUARTERS DURING THE BATTLE OF GETTYSBURG, PA.
[From a photograph.]

The commands of Longstreet and Ewell were put in motion, and encamped around Culpeper Courthouse June 7th. As soon as their march was discovered by the enemy he threw a force across the Rappahannock, about two miles below Fredericksburg, apparently for the purpose of observation. Hill's corps was left to watch these troops, with instructions to follow the movements of the army as soon as they should retire.

The cavalry, under General Stuart, which had been concentrated near Culpeper Courthouse, was attacked on June 9th by a large force of Federal cavalry, supported by infantry, which crossed the Rappahannock at Beverly and Kellys fords. After a severe engagement, which continued from early in the morning until late in the afternoon, the enemy was compelled to recross the river with heavy loss, leaving about five hundred prisoners, three pieces of artillery and several colors in our hands.

General Imboden and General Jenkins had been ordered to co-operate in the projected expedition into the Valley, General Imboden, by moving toward Romney with his command, to prevent the troops guarding the Baltimore & Ohio Railroad from re-enforcing those at Winchester, while General Jenkins advanced directly toward the latter place with his cavalry brigade, supported by a battalion of infantry and a battery of the Maryland Line.

General Ewell left Culpeper Courthouse on June 10th. He crossed the branches of the Shenandoah near Front Royal, and reached Cedarville on the 12th, where he was joined by General Jenkins. Detaching General Rodes with his division and the greater part of Jenkins' brigade to dislodge a force of the enemy stationed at Berryville, General Ewell, with the rest of his command, moved upon Winchester, Johnson's division advancing by the Front Royal Road, Early's by the Valley Turnpike, which it entered at Newtown, where it was joined by the Maryland troops.

BATTLE OF WINCHESTER.

The enemy was driven in on both roads, and our troops halted in line of battle near the town on the evening of the 13th. The same day the force which had occupied Berryville retreated to Winchester on the approach of General Rodes. The following morning General Ewell ordered General Early to carry an intrenched position northwest of Winchester, near the Pughtown Road, which the latter officer, upon examining the ground, discovered would command the principal fortifications.

To cover the movement of General Early, General Johnson took position between the road to Millwood and that to Berryville and advanced his skirmishers toward the town. General Early, leaving a portion of his command to engage the enemy's attention, with the remainder gained a favorable position without being perceived, and, about 5 P. M., twenty pieces of artillery, under Lieutenant-Colonel H. C. Jones, opened suddenly upon the intrenchments. The enemy's guns were soon silenced. Hays' brigade then advanced to the assault, and carried the works by storm, capturing six rifled pieces, two of which were turned upon and dispersed a column which was forming to retake the position. The enemy immediately abandoned the works on the left of those taken by Hays, and retired into his main fortifications which General Early prepared to assail in the morning. The loss of the advanced works, however, rendered the others untenable, and the enemy retreated in the night, abandoning his sick and wounded, together with his artillery, wagons and stores. Anticipating such a movement, as soon as he heard of Early's success, General Ewell directed General Johnson to occupy, with part of his command, a point on the Martinsburg Road, about two and one-half miles from Winchester, where he could either intercept the enemy's retreat or aid in an attack should further resistance be offered in the morning. General Johnson marched with Nicholls' and part of Steuart's brigades, accompanied by Lieutenent-Colonel [R. S.] Andrews with a detachment of his artillery, the Stonewall Brigade being ordered to follow. Finding the road to the place indicated by General Ewell difficult of passage in the darkness, General Johnson pursued that leading by Jordan Springs to Stephensons Depot, where he took a favorable position on the Martinsburg Road about five miles from Winchester. Just as his line was formed, the retreating column, consisting of the main body of General Milroy's army, arrived, and immediately attacked him. The enemy, though in superior force, consisting of both infantry and cavalry, was gallantly repulsed and, finding all efforts to cut his way unavailing, he sent strong flanking parties simultaneously to the right and left, still keeping up a heavy fire in front. The party on the right was driven back and pursued by the Stonewall Brigade, which opportunely arrived. That on the left was broken and dispersed by the Second and Tenth Louisiana regiments, aided by the artillery, and in a short time nearly the whole infantry force, amounting to more than two thousand three hundred men, with eleven stand of colors, surrendered, the cavalry alone escaping. General Milroy, with a small party of fugitives, fled to Harpers Ferry. The number of prisoners taken in this action exceeded the force engaged under General Johnson, who speaks in terms of well-deserved praise ot the conduct of the officers and men of his command.

In the meantime, General Rodes marched from Berryville to Martinsburg, reaching the latter place in the afternoon of the 14th. The enemy made a show of resistance, but soon gave way, the cavalry and artillery retreating toward Williamsport, the infantry toward Shepherdstown, under cover of night. The route taken by the latter was not known until it was too late to follow; but the former were pursued so rapidly, Jenkins' troops leading, that they were forced to abandon five of their six pieces of artillery. About two hundred prisoners were taken, but the enemy destroyed most of his stores.

These operations resulted in the expulsion of the enemy from the Valley; the capture of 4,000 prisoners, with a corresponding number of small-arms; 28 pieces of superior artillery, including those taken by Generals Rodes and Hays; about 300 wagons and as many horses, together with a considerable quantity of ordnance, commissary and quartermaster's stores.

Our entire loss was 47 killed, 219 wounded and 3 missing.

MARCH INTO PENNSYLVANIA.

On the night of Ewell's appearance at Winchester the enemy in front of A. P. Hill, at Fredericksburg, recrossed the Rappahannock, and the whole army of General Hooker withdrew from the north side of the river. In order to mislead him as to our intentions, and at the same time protect Hill's corps in its march up the Rappahannock, Longstreet left Culpeper Courthouse on the 15th, and, advancing along the eastern side of the Blue Ridge, occupied Ashbys and Snickers Gaps. He being joined, while at Culpeper, by General Pickett, with three brigades of cavalry, moved on Longstreet's right, and took position in front of the Gaps. Hampton's and [W. E.] Jones' brigades remained along the Rappahannock and Hazel rivers, in front of Culpeper Courthouse, with

In these engagements the cavalry sustained a loss of five hundred and ten killed, wounded and missing. Among them were several valuable officers. One piece of artillery was disabled and left on the field. The enemy's loss was heavy. About four hundred prisoners were taken and several stand of colors.

The Federal army was apparently guarding the approaches to Washington and manifested no disposition to assume the offensive.

In the meantime the progress of Ewell, who was already in Maryland, with Jenkins' cavalry advanced into Pennsylvania as far as Chambersburg, rendered it necessary that the rest of the army should be within supporting distance, and, Hill having reached the Valley, Longstreet was withdrawn to the west side of the Shenandoah, and the two corps encamped near Berryville.

General Stuart was directed to hold the mountain passes with part of his command as long as the enemy remained south of the Potomac, and with the remainder

important bridges on that route from Martinsburg to Cumberland, besides inflicting serious damage upon the Chesapeake & Ohio Canal. He was at Hancock when Longstreet and Hill reached Chambersburg, and was directed to proceed to the latter place by way of McConnellsburg, collecting supplies for the army on his route. The cavalry force at this time with the army, consisting of Jenkins' brigade and [E. V.] White's battalion, was not greater than was required to accompany the advance of General Ewell and General Early, with whom it performed valuable service, as appears from their reports. It was expected that as soon as the Federal Army should cross the Potomac, General Stuart would give notice of its movements, and nothing having been heard from him since our entrance into Maryland it was inferred that the enemy had not yet left Virginia. Orders were, therefore, issued to move upon Harrisburg. The expedition of General Early to York was designed in part to prepare for this undertaking by breaking the railroad between Baltimore

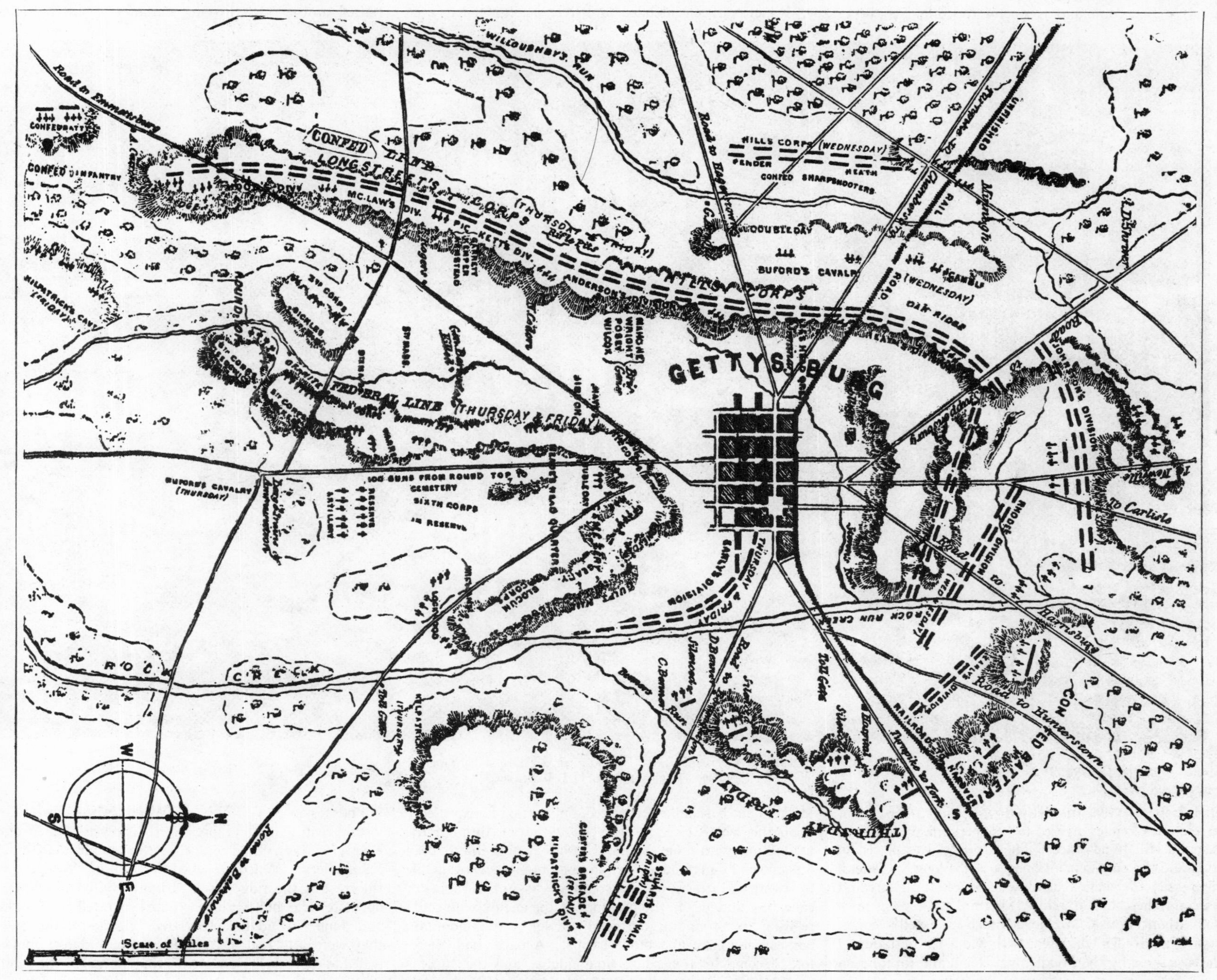

MAP OF THE BATTLEFIELD OF GETTYSBURG, JULY 1, 2 AND 3, 1863.

instructions to follow the main body as soon as Hill's corps had passed that point. On the 17th, Fitz Lee's brigade, under Colonel Munford, which was on the road to Snickers Gap, was attacked near Aldie by the Federal cavalry. The attack was repulsed with loss, and the brigade held its ground until ordered to fall back, its right being threatened by another body, coming from Hopewell toward Middleburg. The latter force was driven from Middleburg and pursued toward Hopewell, by Robertson's brigade, which arrived about dark. Its retreat was intercepted by W. H. F. Lee's brigade, under Colonel Chambliss, Jr., and the greater part of a regiment captured.

During the three succeeding days there was much skirmishing, General Stuart taking a position west of Middleburg, where he awaited the rest of his command.

General Jones arrived on the 19th and General Hampton in the afternoon of the following day, having repulsed, on his march, a cavalry force sent to reconnoiter in the direction of Warrenton.

On the 21st the enemy attacked with infantry and cavalry, and obliged General Stuart, after a brave resistance, to fall back to the gaps of the mountains. The enemy retired the next day, having advanced only a short distance beyond Upperville.

to cross into Maryland and place himself on the right of General Ewell. Upon the suggestion of the former officer that he could damage the enemy and delay his passage of the river by getting in his rear, he was authorized to do so, and it was left to his discretion whether to enter Maryland east or west of the Blue Ridge; but he was instructed to lose no time in placing his command on the right of our column as soon as he should perceive the enemy moving northward.

On the 22d, General Ewell marched into Pennsylvania with Rodes' and Johnson's divisions, preceded by Jenkins' cavalry, taking the road from Hagerstown, through Chambersburg, to Carlisle, where he arrived on the 27th. Early's division, which had occupied Boonsboro moved by a parallel road to Greenwood, and in pursuance of instructions previously given to General Ewell, marched toward York.

On the 24th, Longstreet and Hill were put in motion to follow Ewell, and on the 27th encamped near Chambersburg.

General Imboden, under the orders before referred to, had been operating on Ewell's left while the latter was advancing into Maryland. He drove off the troops guarding the Baltimore & Ohio Railroad and destroyed all the

and Harrisburg and seizing the bridge over the Susquehanna at Wrightsville. General Early succeeded in the first object, destroying a number of bridges above and below York, but on the approach of the troops sent by him to Wrightsville, a body of militia stationed at that place fled across the river and burned the bridge in their retreat. General Early then marched to rejoin his corps.

The advance against Harrisburg was arrested by intelligence received from a scout on the night of the 28th to the effect that the army of General Hooker had crossed the Potomac and was approaching the South Mountain. In the absence of the calvary it was impossible to ascertain his intentions; but, to deter him from advancing further west and intercepting our communication with Virginia, it was determined to concentrate the army east of the mountains.

BATTLE OF GETTYSBURG.

Hill's corps was accordingly ordered to move toward Cashtown on the 29th, and Longstreet to follow the next day, leaving Pickett's division at Chambersburg to guard the rear until relieved by Imboden. General Ewell was recalled from Carlisle and directed to join the army at Cashtown or Gettysburg, as circumstances might require. The advance of the enemy to the latter place was unknown, and the weather being inclement the march was conducted with a view to the comfort of the troops. Heth's division reached Cashtown on the 29th, and the following morning Pettigrew's brigade, sent by General Heth to procure supplies at Gettysburg, found it occupied by the enemy. Being ignorant of the extent of his force, General Pettigrew was unwilling to hazard an attack with his single brigade and returned to Cashtown.

General Hill arrived with Pender's division in the evening, and the following morning (July 1st) advanced with these two divisions, accompanied by Pegram's and McIntosh's battalions of artillery, to ascertain the strengrh of the enemy, whose force was supposed to consist chiefly of cavalry. The leading division, under General Heth, found the enemy's vedettes about three miles west of Gettysburg, and continued to advance until within a mile of the town, when two brigades were sent forward to reconnoiter. They drove in the advance of the enemy very gallantly, but subsequently encountered largely superior numbers and were compelled to retire with loss, Brigadier-General Archer, commanding one of the brigades, being taken prisoner. General Heth then prepared for action, and as soon as Pender arrived to support him, was ordered by General Hill to advance. The artillery was placed in position and the engagement opened with vigor. General Heth pressed the enemy steadily back, breaking his first and second lines, and attacking his third with great resolution. About 2:30 P. M. the advance of Ewell's corps, consisting of Rodes' division, with Carter's battalion of artillery, arrived by the Middletown Road, and forming on Heth's left, nearly at right angles with his line, became warmly engaged with fresh numbers of the enemy. Heth's troops, having suffered heavily in their protracted contest with a superior force, were relieved by Pender's, and Early, coming up by the Heidleburg Road soon afterward, took position on the left of Rodes, when a general advance was made.

The enemy gave way on all sides, and was driven through Gettysburg with great loss. Major-General Reynolds, who was in command, was killed. More than five thousand prisoners, exclusive of a large number of wounded, three pieces of artillery and several colors were captured. Among the prisoners were two brigadier-generals, one of whom was badly wounded. Our own loss was heavy, including a number of officers, among whom were Major-General Heth, slightly, and Brigadier-General Scales, of Pender's division, severely, wounded. The enemy retired to a range of hills south of Gettysburg, where he displayed a strong force of infantry and artillery.

It was ascertained from the prisoners that we had been engaged with two corps of the army, formerly commanded by General Hooker, and that the remainder of that army, under General Meade, was approaching Gettysburg. Without information as to its proximity, the strong position which the enemy had assumed could not be attacked without danger of exposing the four divisions present, already weakened and exhausted by a long and bloody struggle, to overwhelming numbers of fresh troops. General Ewell was, therefore, instructed to carry the hill occupied by the enemy if he found it practicable, but to avoid a general engagement until the arrival of the other divisions of the army, which were ordered to hasten forward. He decided to await Johnson's division, which had marched from Carlisle by the road west of the mountains to guard the trains of his corps, and consequently did not reach Gettysburg until a late hour.

In the meantime the enemy occupied the point which General Ewell designed to seize, but in what force could not be ascertained, owing to the darkness. An intercepted dispatch showed that another corps had halted that afternoon four miles from Gettysburg. Under these circumstances, it was decided not to attack until the arrival of Longstreet, two of whose divisions (those of Hood and McLaws) encamped about four miles in the rear during the night. Anderson's division, of Hill's corps, came up after the engagement.

It had not been intended to deliver a general battle so far from our base unless attacked, but coming unexpectedly upon the whole Federal army, to withdraw through the mountains with our extensive trains would have been difficult and dangerous. At the same time we were unable to await an attack, as the country was unfavorable for collecting supplies in the presence of the enemy, who could restrain our foraging parties by holding tne mountain passes with local and other troops. A battle had, therefore, become in a measure unavoidable, and the success already gained gave hope of a favorable issue.

The enemy occupied a strong position, with his right upon two commanding elevations adjacent to each other, one southeast and the other, known as Cemetery Hill, immediately south of the town, which lay at its base. His line extended thence upon the high ground along the Emmitsburg Road, with a steep ridge in rear, which was also occupied. This ridge was difficult of ascent, particularly the two hills above mentioned as forming its northern extremity, and a third at the other end, on which the enemy's left rested. Numerous stone and rail fences along the slope served to afford protection to his troops and impede our advance. In his front the ground was undulating and generally open for about three-quarters of a mile.

General Ewell's corps constituted our left, Johnson's division being opposite the height adjoining Cemetery Hill, Early's in the center, in front of the north face of the latter, and Rodes upon his right. Hill's corps faced the west side of Cemetery Hill, and extended nearly parallel to the Emmitsburg Road, making an angle with Ewell's. Pender's division formed his left, Anderson's his right, Heth's, under Brigadier-General Pettigrew, being in reserve. His artillery, under Colonel [R. L.] Walker, was posted in eligible positions along his line.

It was determined to make the principal attack upon the enemy's left, and endeavor to gain a position from which it was thought that our artillery could be brought to bear with effect. Longstreet was directed to place the divisions of McLaws and Hood on the right of Hill, partially enveloping the enemy's left, which he was to drive in.

General Hill was ordered to threaten the enemy's center, to prevent re-enforcements being drawn to either wing, and co-operate with his right division in Longstreet's attack. General Ewell was instructed to make a simultaneous demonstration upon the enemy's right, to be converted into a real attack should opportunity offer.

About 4 P. M. Longstreet's batteries opened, and soon afterward Hood's division, on the extreme right, moved to the attack. McLaws followed somewhat later, four of Anderson's brigades, those of Wilcox, Perry, [A. R.] Wright and Posey supporting him on the left, in the order named. The enemy was soon driven from his position on the Emmitsburg Road to the cover of a ravine and a line of stone fences at the foot of the ridge in his rear. He was dislodged from these, after a severe struggle, and retired up the ridge, leaving a number of his batteries in our possession. Wilcox's and Wright's brigades advanced with great gallantry, breaking successive lines of the enemy's infantry and compelling him to abandon much of his artillery. Wilcox reached the foot and Wright gained the crest of the ridge itself, driving the enemy down the opposite side; but having become separated from McLaws and gone beyond the other two brigades of the division they were attacked in front and on both flanks and compelled to retire, being unable to bring off any of the captured artillery. McLaws' left also fell back, and it being now nearly dark General Longstreet determined to await the arrival of General Pickett. He disposed his command to hold the ground gained on the right, withdrawing his left to the first position from which the enemy had been driven.

Four pieces of artillery, several hundred prisoners, and two regimental flags were taken, As soon as the engagement began on our right, General Johnson opened with his artillery, and about two hours later advanced up the hill next to Cemetery Hill with three brigades, the fourth being detained by a demonstration on his left. Soon afterward, General Early attacked Cemetery Hill with two brigades, supported by a third, the fourth having been previously detached. The enemy had greatly increased by earthworks the strength of the positions assailed by Johnson and Early.

The troops of the former moved steadily up the steep and rugged ascent, under a heavy fire, driving the enemy into his intrenchments, part of which was carried by Steuart's brigade, and a number of prisoners taken. The contest was continued to a late hour, but without further advantage. On Cemetery Hill, the attack by Early's leading brigades—those of Hays and Hoke, under Colonel [I. E.] Avery—was made with vigor. Two lines of the enemy's infantry were dislodged from the cover of some stone and board fences on the side of the ascent, and

BATTLE OF GETTYSBURG, PA. CHARGE OF THE LOUISIANA TIGERS.
[From an original painting by F. D. Briscoe.]

From an original painting, owned and copyrighted by Kurz & Allison, Chicago, Ill.

BATTLE OF GETTYSBURG. SCENE AT THE PEACH ORCHARD.

driven back into the works on the crest, into which our troops forced their way, and seized several pieces of artillery.

A heavy force advanced against their right, which was without support, and they were compelled to retire, bringing with them about one hundred prisoners and four stand of colors General Ewell had directed General Rodes to attack in concert with Early, covering his right, and had requested Brigadier-General Lane, then commanding Pender's division, to co-operate on the right of Rodes. When the time to attack arrived, General Rodes, not having his troops in position, was unprepared to co-operate with General Early, and before he could get in readiness the latter had been obliged to retire for want of the expected support on his right. General Lane was prepared to give the assistance required of him, and so informed General Rodes, but the latter deemed it useless to advance after the failure of Early's attack. In this engagement our loss in men and officers was large. Major-Generals Hood and Pender, Brigadier-Generals [J. M.] Jones, Semmes, G. T. Anderson and Barksdale, and Colonel Avery, commanding Hoke's brigade, were wounded, the last two mortally. Generals Pender and Semmes died after their removal to Virginia.

The result of this day's operations induced the belief that, with proper concert of action, and with the increased support that the positions gained on the right would enable the artillery to render the assaulting columns, we should ultimately succeed, and it was accordingly determined to continue the attack. The general plan was unchanged. Longstreet, re-enforced by Pickett's three brigades, which arrived near the battlefield during the afternoon of the 2d, was ordered to attack the next morning, and General Ewell was directed to assail the enemy's right at the same time. The latter during the night re-enforced General Johnson with two brigades from Rodes' and one from Early's division.

General Longstreet's dispositions were not completed as early as was expected, but before notice could be sent to General Ewell, General Johnson had already become engaged, and it was too late to recall him. The enemy attempted to recover the works taken the preceding evening, but was repulsed, and General Johnson attacked in turn.

After a gallant and prolonged struggle, in which the enemy was forced to abandon part of his intrenchments, General Johnson found himself unable to carry the strongly fortified crest of the hill. The projected attack on the enemy's left not having been made, he was enabled to hold his right with a force largely superior to that of General Johnson, and finally to threaten his flank and rear, rendering it necessary for him to retire to his original position about 1 P. M.

General Longstreet was delayed by a force occupying the high, rocky hills on the enemy's extreme left, from which his troops could be attacked in reverse as they advanced. His operations had been embarrassed the day previous by the same cause, and he now deemed it necessary to defend his flank and rear with the divisions of Hood and McLaws. He was, therefore, re-enforced by Heth's division and two brigades of Pender's, to the command of which Major-General Trimble was assigned. General Hill was directed to hold his line with the rest of his command, afford General Longstreet further assistance if required, and avail himself of any success that might be gained.

A careful examination was made of the ground secured by Longstreet, and his batteries placed in positions which, it was believed, would enable them to silence those of the enemy. Hill's artillery and part of Ewell's was ordered to open simultaneously, and the assaulting column to advance under cover of the combined fire of the three. The batteries were directed to be pushed forward as the infantry progressed, protect their flanks and support their attacks closely.

About 1 P. M., at a given signal, a heavy cannonade was opened, and continued for about two hours with marked effect upon the enemy. His batteries replied vigorously at first, but toward the close their fire slackened perceptibly, and General Longstreet ordered forward the column of attack, consisting of Pickett's and Heth's divisions, in two lines, Pickett on the right. Wilcox's brigade marched in rear of Pickett's right, to guard that flank, and Heth's was supported by Lane's and Scales' brigades under General Trimble.

The troops moved steadily on, under a heavy fire of musketry and artillery, the main attack being directed against the enemy's left center.

His batteries reopened as soon as they appeared. Our own having nearly exhausted their ammunition in the protracted cannonade that preceded the advance of the infantry, were unable to reply or render the necessary support to the attacking party. Owing to this fact, which was unknown to me when the assault took place, the enemy was enabled to throw a strong force of infantry against our left, already wavering under a concentrated fire of artillery from the ridge in front, and from Cemetery Hill, on the left. It finally gave way, and the right, after penetrating the enemy's lines, entering his advanced works and capturing some of his artillery, was attacked simultaneously in front and on both flanks and driven back with heavy loss.

The troops were rallied and reformed, but the enemy did not pursue.

A large number of brave officers and men fell or were captured on this occasion. Of Pickett's three brigade commanders, Generals Armistead and [R. B.] Garnett were killed, and General Kemper dangerously wounded.

Major-General Trimble and Brigadier-General Pettigrew were also wounded, the former severely.

The movements of the army preceding the battle of Gettysburg had been much embarrassed by the absence of the cavalry. As soon as it was known that the enemy had crossed into Maryland, orders were sent to the brigades of [B. H.] Robertson and [William E.] Jones, which had been left to guard the passes of the Blue Ridge, to rejoin the army without delay, and it was expected that General Stuart, with the remainder of his command, would soon arrive. In the exercise of the discretion given him when Longstreet and Hill marched into Maryland, General Stuart determined to pass around the rear of the Federal army with three brigades and cross the Potomac between it and Washington, believing that he would be able, by that route, to place himself on our right flank in time to keep us properly advised of the enemy's movements. He marched from Salem on the night of June 24th, intending to pass west of Centreville, but found the enemy's forces so distributed as to render that route impracticable. Adhering to his original plan, he was forced to make a wide detour through Buckland and Brentsville, and crossed the Occoquan at Wolf Run Shoals on the morning of the 27th. Continuing his march through Fairfax Courthouse and Dranesville, he arrived at the Potomac, below the mouth of Seneca Creek, in the evening.

He found the river much swollen by the recent rains, but, after great exertion, gained the Maryland shore before midnight with his whole command. He now ascertained that the Federal army, which he had discovered to be drawing toward the Potomac, had crossed the day before and was moving toward Frederick, thus interposing itself between him and our forces.

Battle of Gettysburg, Pa. Pickett's Charge. Scene at the Angle.
[From an original painting by F. D. Briscoe.]

He accordingly marched northward, through Rockville and Westminster, to Hanover, Pennsylvania, where he arrived on the 30th; but the enemy advanced with equal rapidity on his left, and continued to obstruct communication with our main body.

Supposing, from such information as he could obtain, that part of the army was at Carlisle, he left Hanover that night, and proceeded thither by way of Dover.

He reached Carlisle on July 1st, where he received orders to proceed to Gettysburg. He arrived in the afternoon of the following day, and took position on General Ewell's left. His leading brigade, under General Hampton, encountered and repulsed a body of the enemy's cavalry at Hunterstown, endeavoring to reach our rear.

General Stuart had several skirmishes during his march, and at Hanover quite a severe engagement took place, with a strong force of cavalry, which was finally compelled to withdraw from the town.

The prisoners taken by the cavalry and paroled at various places amounted to about eight hundred, and at Rockville a large train of wagons coming from Washington was intercepted and captured. Many of them were destroyed, but one hundred and twenty-five, with all the animals of the train, were secured.

The ranks of the cavalry were much reduced by its long and arduous march, repeated conflicts and insufficient supplies of food and forage, but the day after its arrival at Gettysburg it engaged the enemy's cavalry with unabated spirit and effectually protected our left.

In this action Brigadier-General Hampton was seriously wounded while acting with his accustomed gallantry.

Robertson's and Jones' brigades arrived on July 3d, and were stationed upon our right flank. The severe loss sustained by the army and the reduction of its ammunition rendered another attempt to dislodge the enemy inadvisable, and it was, therefore, determined to withdraw.

The trains, with such of the wounded as could bear removal, were ordered to Williamsport on July 4th, part moving through Cashtown and Greencastle, escorted by General Imboden, and the remainder by the Fairfield Road.

The army retained its position until dark, when it was put in motion for the Potomac by the last-named route.

A heavy rain continued throughout the night and so much impeded its progress that Ewell's corps, which brought up the rear, did not leave Gettysburg until late in the forenoon of the following day. The enemy offered no serious interruption, and after an arduous march we arrived at Hagerstown in the afternoon of the 6th and morning of July 7th.

The great length of our trains made it difficult to guard them effectually in passing through the mountains and a number of wagons and ambulances were captured. They succeeded in reaching Williamsport on the 6th, but were unable to cross the Potomac on account of the high stage of water. Here they were attacked by a strong force of cavalry and artillery, which was gallantly repulsed by General Imboden, whose command had been strengthened by several batteries and by two regiments of infantry which had been detached at Winchester to guard prisoners and were returning to the army. While the enemy was being held in check General Stuart arrived with the cavalry, which had performed valuable service in guarding the flanks of the army during the retrograde movement, and after a short engagement drove him from the field. The rains that had prevailed almost without intermission since our entrance into Maryland, and greatly interfered with our movements, had made the Potomac unfordable, and the pontoon bridge left at Falling Waters had been partially destroyed by the enemy. The wounded and prisoners were sent over the river as rapidly as possible in a few ferryboats, while the trains awaited the subsiding of the waters and the construction of a new pontoon bridge.

On July 8th, the enemy's cavalry advanced toward Hagerstown, but was repulsed by General Stuart, and pursued as far as Boonsboro. With this exception, nothing but occasional skirmishing occurred until the 12th, when the main body of the enemy arrived. The army then took a position previously selected, covering the Potomac from Williamsport to Falling Waters, where it remained for two days, with the enemy immediately in front, manifesting no disposition to attack, but throwing up intrenchments along his whole line.

By the 13th, the river at Williamsport, though still deep, was fordable, and a good bridge was completed at Falling Waters, new boats being constructed and some of the old recovered. As further delay would enable the enemy to obtain re-enforcements, and as it was found difficult to procure a sufficient supply of flour for the troops, the working of the mills being interrupted by high water, it was determined to await an attack no longer.

Orders were accordingly given to cross the Potomac that night, Ewell's corps by the ford at Williamsport, and those of Longstreet and Hill on the bridge.

The cavalry was directed to relieve the infantry skirmishers, and bring up the rear.

The movement was much retarded by a severe rainstorm and the darkness of the night. Ewell's corps having the advantage of a turnpike road, marched with less difficulty, and crossed the river by 8 o'clock the following morning. The condition of the road to the bridge and the time consumed in the passage of the artillery, ammunition wagons and ambulances, which could not ford the river, so much delayed the progress of Longstreet and Hill, that it was daylight before their troops began to cross. Heth's division was halted about a mile and a half from the bridge, to protect the passage of the column. No interruption was offered by the enemy until about 11 A. M., when his cavalry, supported by artillery, appeared in front of General Heth.

A small number in advance of the main body was mistaken for our own cavalry retiring, no notice having been given of the withdrawal of the latter, and was suffered to approach our lines. They were immediately destroyed or captured, with the exception of two or three, but Brigadier-General Pettigrew, an officer of great merit and promise, was mortally wounded in the encounter. He survived his removal to Virginia only a few days.

The bridge being clear, General Heth began to withdraw. The enemy advanced, but his efforts to break our lines were repulsed and the passage of the river was completed by 1 P. M. Owing to the extent of General Heth's line, some of his men most remote from the bridge were cut off before they could reach it, but the greater part of those taken by the enemy during the movement (supposed to amount in all to about five hundred) consisted of men from various commands who lingered behind, overcome by previous labors and hardships and the fatigue of a most trying night march. There was no loss of material excepting a few broken wagons and two pieces of artillery, which the horses were unable to draw through the deep mud. Other horses were sent back for them, but the rear of the column had passed before their arrival. The army proceeded to the vicinity of Bunker Hill and Darkesville, where it halted to afford the troops repose.

The enemy made no effort to follow, excepting with his cavalry, which crossed the Potomac at Harpers Ferry and advanced toward Martinsburg on July 16th.

They were attacked by General Fitzhugh Lee, with his own and Chambliss' brigades, and driven back with loss.

When the army returned to Virginia it was intended to move into Loudoun, but the Shenandoah was found to be impassable. While waiting for it to subside the enemy crossed the Potomac east of the Blue Ridge and seized the passes we designed to use. As he continued to advance along the eastern slope, apparently with the purpose of cutting us off from the railroad to Richmond, General Longstreet was ordered, on July 19th, to proceed to Culpeper Courthouse, by way of Front Royal. He succeeded in passing part of his command over the Shenandoah in time to prevent the occupation of Manassas and Chester Gaps by the enemy, whose cavalry had already made its appearance.

As soon as a pontoon bridge could be laid down the rest of his corps crossed the river and marched through Chester Gap to Culpeper Courthouse, where it arrived on the 24th. He was followed, without serious opposition, by General A. P. Hill.

General Ewell having been detained in the Valley by an effort to capture a force of the enemy guarding the Baltimore & Ohio Railroad west of Martinsburg, Wright's brigade was left to hold Manassas Gap until his arrival. He reached Front Royal on the 23d, with Johnson's and Rodes' divisions, Early's being near Winchester, and found General Wright skirmishing with the enemy's infantry, which had already appeared in Manassas Gap. General Ewell supported Wright with Rodes' division and some artillery and the enemy was held in check.

Finding that the Federal force greatly exceeded his own, General Ewell marched through Thornton's Gap and ordered Early to move up the Valley by Strasburg and New Market. He encamped near Madison Courthouse on July 29th.

The enemy massed his army in the vicinity of Warrenton, and on the night of July 31st his cavalry, with a large supporting force of infantry, crossed the Rappahannock at Rappahannock Station and Kellys Ford.

The next day they advanced toward Brandy Station, their progress being gallantly resisted by General Stuart with Hampton's brigade, commanded by Colonel [L. S.] Baker, who fell back gradually to our lines about two miles south of Brandy. Our infantry skirmishers advanced and drove the enemy beyond Brandy Station. It was now determined to place the army in a position to enable it more readily to oppose the enemy should he attempt to move southward, that near Culpeper Courthouse being one that he could easily avoid. Longstreet and Hill were put in

BATTLE OF GETTYSBURG, PA. THE PEACH ORCHARD. TERRIFIC FIGHTING AT THE ANGLE.
[From an original painting by F. D. Briscoe.]

motion August 3d, leaving the cavalry at Culpeper. Ewell had been previously ordered from Madison, and by the 4th the army occupied the line of the Rapidan.

The highest praise is due to both officers and men for their conduct during the campaign. The privations and hardships of the march and camps were cheerfully encountered and borne with a fortitude unsurpassed by our ancestors in their struggle for independence, while their courage in battle entitles them to rank with the soldiers of any army and of any time. Their forbearance and discipline under strong provocation to retaliate for the cruelty of the enemy to our own citizens is not their least claim to the respect and admiration of their countrymen and of the world.

A CONFEDERATE SHOT LODGED IN A FEDERAL GUN.

The loss of Major-General Pender is severely felt by the army and the country. He served with this army from the beginning of the war and took a distinguished part in all its engagements.

Brigadier-Generals Armistead, Barksdale, Garnett and Semmes died as they had lived, discharging the highest duty of patriots with devotion that never faltered and courage that shrank from no danger.

The officers of the general staff of the army were unremittingly engaged in the duties of their respective departments. Much depended on their management and exertion. The labors of the quartermaster's, commissary and medical departments were more than usually severe. The inspectors-general were also laboriously occupied in their attention to the troops, both on the march and in camp, and the officers of engineers showed skill and judgment in expediting the passage of rivers and streams, the swollen condition of which, by almost continuous rains, called for extraordinary exertion.

The chief of ordnance and his assistants are entitled to praise for the care and watchfulness given to the ordnance trains and ammunition of the army, which, in a long march and in many conflicts, were always at hand and accessible to the troops.

My thanks are due to my personal staff for their constant aid afforded me at all times, on the march and in the field, and their willing discharge of every duty.

There were captured at Gettysburg nearly seven thousand prisoners, of whom about fifteen hundred were paroled and the remainder brought to Virginia. Seven pieces of artillery were also secured.

R. E. LEE, *General.*

THE GETTYSBURG CAMPAIGN,

JUNE 3 TO AUGUST 1, 1863.

BY

LIEUT.-GEN. JAMES LONGSTREET,
Commanding First Army Corps.

HEADQUARTERS FIRST ARMY CORPS, DEPARTMENT NORTHERN VIRGINIA, NEAR CULPEPER COURT-HOUSE.

July 27, 1863.

IN obedience to orders from the commanding general, my command marched from Fredericksburg on June 3d, for Culpeper Courthouse. On the 15th it moved from Culpeper Courthouse along the eastern slope of the Blue Ridge, and on the 19th McLaws' division was posted in Ashbys Gap, Hood's at Snickers Gap, and Pickett's supporting Hood's and guarding points between the two gaps.

On June 20th I received a dispatch from general headquarters, directing that I should hold myself in readiness to move in the direction of the Potomac, with a view to crossing, etc. As I was ready, and had been expecting an order to execute such purpose, I supposed the intimation meant other preparation, and, knowing of nothing else that I could do to render my preparations complete, I supposed that it was desirable that I should cross the Shenandoah. I therefore passed the river, occupied the banks at the ferries opposite the gaps, and a road at an intermediate ford, which was practicable for cavalry and infantry.

On the following day, the enemy advanced his cavalry in full force against General Stuart, and drove him into and nearly through Ashbys Gap. I succeeded in passing part of McLaws' division across the river in time to occupy the gap before night, and, upon advancing a line of sharpshooters the next morning at daylight, the enemy retired. I believe that he engaged the sharpshooters lightly. General Stuart re-established his cavalry, and McLaws' division was withdrawn to the west bank of the Shenandoah before night.

On the 23d I received orders to march, via Berryville, Martinsburg and Williamsport, into Maryland. The command moved at early dawn on the following day: First, Pickett's division; second, the reserve artillery battalions; third, Hood's division, and, fourth, McLaws' division. Pickett's division and the battalions of reserve artillery crossed the Potomac on the 25th, Hood's and McLaws' divisions on the following day. The command reached Chambersburg, Pa., on the 27th, and a halt of a few days was made for rest.

On the night of the 28th one of my scouts came in with information that the enemy had passed the Potomac and was probably in pursuit of us. The scout was sent to general headquarters, with the suggestion that our army concentrate east of the mountains and bear down to meet the enemy.

I received orders on the following day to move part of my command and to encamp it at Greenwood. The command, excepting Pickett's division, which was left to guard our rear at Chambersburg, moved on the morning of the 30th, and the two divisions and battalions of reserve artillery got into camp at Greenwood about 2 o'clock in the afternoon. General Hood was ordered to put a brigade and a battery on picket at New Guilford. Our march was greatly delayed on this day by Johnson's division, of the Second Corps, which came into the road from Shippensburg, and the long wagon trains that followed him. McLaws' division, however, reached Marsh Creek, four miles from Gettysburg, a little after dark, and Hood's division got within nearly the same distance of the town about 12 o'clock at night. Law's brigade was ordered forward to its division during the day and joined it about noon on the 2d. Previous to his joining I received instructions from the commanding general to move, with the portion of my command that was up, around to gain the Emmitsburg Road on the enemy's left. The enemy, having been driven back by the corps of Lieutenant-Generals Ewell and A. P. Hill the day previous, had taken a strong position extending from the hill at the cemetery along the Emmitsburg Road.

Fearing that my force was too weak to venture to make an attack I delayed until General Law's brigade joined its division. As soon after his arrival as we could make our preparations the movement was begun. Engineers, sent out by the commanding general and myself, guided us by a road which would have completely disclosed the move. Some delay ensued in seeking a more concealed route. McLaws' division got into position opposite the enemy's left about 4 P. M. Hood's division was moved on further to our right and got into position, partially enveloping the enemy's left.

LIEUT.-GEN. JAMES LONGSTREET, OF ALABAMA.

The enemy's first position along the Emmitsburg Road was but little better, in point of strength, than the first position taken by these two divisions. Our batteries were opened upon this position, Hood's division pressing upon his left and McLaws' upon his front. He was soon dislodged and driven back upon a commanding hill, which was so precipitous and rough as to render it difficult of ascent. Numerous stone fences about its base added greatly to its strength. The enemy, taking shelter behind these, held them, one after another, with great pertinacity. He was driven from point to point, however, until nearly night, when a strong force met the brigades of Major-General [R. H.] Anderson's division, which were co-operating upon my left, drove one of them back, and checking the support of the others caused my left to be somewhat exposed and outflanked. Wofford's brigade, of McLaws' division, was driven back at the same time. I thought it prudent not to push further until my other troops came up.

General Hood received a severe wound soon after getting under fire and was obliged to leave the field. This misfortune occasioned some delay in our operations. Brigadier-General G. T. Anderson, of his division, was also severely wounded and obliged to leave the field. In the same attack General McLaws lost two of his brigadiers (Generals Barksdale, mortally wounded, and General Semmes, severely wounded, and since died of his wounds). The command was finally so disposed as to hold the ground gained on the right, with my left withdrawn to the first position of the enemy, resting at the peach orchard.

CONFEDERATE SOLDIERS AND BREASTWORKS.

During the combat of this day four pieces of artillery were captured and secured by the command, and two regimental standards.

On the following morning our arrangements were made for renewing the attack by my right, with a view to passing around the hill, occupied by the enemy on his left, and to gain it by flank and reverse attack. This would have been a slow process, probably, but I think not very difficult. A few moments after my orders for the execution of this plan were given, the commanding general joined me and ordered a column of attack to be formed of Pickett's, Heth's and part of Pender's divisions, the assault to be made directly at the enemy's main position, the Cemetery Hill. The distance to be passed over under the fire of the enemy's batteries and in plain view, seemed too great to insure great results, particularly as two-thirds of the troops to be engaged in the assault had been in a severe battle two days previous, Pickett's division alone being fresh.

Orders were given to Major-General Pickett to form his line under the best cover that he could get from the enemy's batteries, and so that the center of the assaulting column would arrive at the salient of the enemy's position, General Pickett's line to be the guide and to attack the line of the enemy's defenses, and General Pettigrew, in command of Heth's division, moving on the same line as General Pickett, was to assault the salient at the same moment. Pickett's division was arranged, two brigades in the front line, supported by his third brigade, and Wilcox's brigade was ordered to move in rear of his right flank, to protect it from any force that the enemy might attempt to move against it.

Heth's division, under the command of Brigadier-General Pettigrew, was arranged in two lines, and these, supported by part of Major-General Pender's division, under Major-General Trimble, all of the batteries of the First and Third Corps, and some of those of the Second, were put into the best positions for effective fire upon the point of attack and the hill occupied by the enemy's left. Colonel Walton, Chief of Artillery of First Corps, and Colonel Alexander had posted over batteries and agreed with the artillery officer of the other corps upon the signal for the batteries to open. About 2 P. M., General Pickett, who had been charged with the duty of arranging the lines behind our batteries, reported that the troops were in order and on the most sheltered ground. Colonel Walton was ordered to open the batteries. The signal guns were fired, and all the batteries opened very handsomely and apparently with effective fire. The guns on the hill at the enemy's left were soon silenced. Those at the Cemetery Hill combated us, however, very obstinately. Many of them were driven off, but fresh ones were brought up to replace them. Colonel Alexander was ordered to a point where he could best observe the effect of our fire and to give notice of the most opportune moment for our attack.

Some time after our batteries opened fire, I rode to Major [James] Dearing's batteries. It appeared that the enemy put in fresh batteries about as rapidly as others were driven off. I concluded, therefore, that we must attack very soon if we hoped to accomplish anything before night. I gave orders for the batteries to refill their ammunition chests and to be prepared to follow up the advance of the infantry. Upon riding over to Colonel Alexander's position I found that he had advised General Pickett that the time had arrived for the attack, and I gave the order to General Pickett to advance to the assault. I found then that our supply of ammunition was so short that the batteries could not reopen. The order for this attack, which I could not favor under better auspices, would have been revoked had I felt that I had that privilege. The advance was made in very handsome style, all the troops keeping their lines accurately and taking the fire of the batteries with great coolness and deliberation. About halfway between our position and that of the enemy a ravine partially sheltered our troops from the enemy's fire, where a short halt was made for rest. The advance was resumed after a moment's pause, all still in good order. The enemy's batteries soon opened on our lines with canister, and the left seemed to stagger under it, but the advance was resumed, and with some degree of steadiness. Pickett's troops did not appear to be checked by the batteries and only halted to deliver a fire when close under musket range. Major-General Anderson's division was ordered forward to support and assist the wavering columns of Pettigrew and Trimble. Pickett's troops, after delivering fire, advanced to the charge and entered the enemy's lines, capturing some of his batteries and gained his works. About the same moment the troops that had before hesitated broke their ranks and fell back in great disorder, many more falling under the enemy's fire in retiring than while they were attacking. This gave the enemy time to throw his entire force upon Pickett, with a strong prospect of being able to break up his lines or destroy him before Anderson's division could reach him, which would, in its turn, have greatly exposed Anderson. He was, therefore, ordered to halt. In a few moments the enemy, marching against both flanks and the front of Pickett's division, overpowered it and drove it back, capturing about half of those of it who were not killed or wounded. General Wright, of Anderson's division, with all of the officers, was ordered to rally and collect the scattered troops behind Anderson's division, and many of my staff officers were sent to assist in the same service. Expecting an attack from the enemy, I rode to the front of our batteries to reconnoiter and superintend their operations.

The enemy threw forward forces at different times and from different points, but they were only feelers, and retired as soon as our batteries opened upon them. These little advances and checks were kept up till night, when the enemy retired to his stronghold, and my line was withdrawn to the Gettysburg Road on the right, the left uniting with Lieutenant-General A. P. Hill's right. After night, I received orders to make all the needful arrangements for our retreat. The orders for preparation were given and the work was begun before daylight on the 4th.

On the night of the 4th the troops were withdrawn from our line, and my command took up the line o march, following the corps of Lieutenant-General A. P. Hill Our march was much impeded by heavy rains and excessively bad roads. We succeeded, however, in reaching the top of the mountain early in the night of the 5th.

On the 6th my command, passing to the front, marched for Hagerstown. As our exhausted men and animals were not in condition for rapid movement, I thought myself fortunate when I found that I could reach Hagerstown in time to relieve our trains at Williamsport, then seriously threatened. Reaching Hagerstown about 5 P. M., our column moved down the Sharpsburg Turnpike and encamped about two miles from Hagerstown.

The next day the command was put in camp on the best ground that could be found and remained quiet until the 10th, when the enemy was reported to be advancing to meet us. It was supposed at first to be a cavalry force only, but I thought it prudent to move some of the infantry down on the Antietam, at Funkstown. After reaching the Antietam General Stuart asked for infantry supports for his batteries, and two brigades (Semmes', under Colonel [Goode] Bryan, and Anderson's, under Colonel [W. W.] White) were sent across, as he desired. A line of battle was selected, extending from a point on the Potomac near Downsville to the Hagerstown and Williamsport turnpike, my command on the right. The troops were put to work and, in twenty-four hours, our line was comfortably intrenched. A few of the enemy's sharpshooters came up on the Boonsboro Road and to within long-range of our picket-line on the 12th.

On the evening of the same day a light skirmish was brought on by an advance of a line of sharpshooters at the St. James College. That night our bridge was completed and, the day after, I received orders to recross the Potomac after night, and the caissons of the batteries were started back about 5 o'clock in the afternoon. The troops marched as soon as it was dark, my command leading. Having but a single road to travel upon, our trains soon came to a halt. I rode on to the bridge, to hasten the movements as much as possible, and sent my staff officers to different points along the line to keep everything in motion. Details were made to keep up fires to light the road at the worst points, and Captain [J. H.] Manning, with his signal torches, lighted us across the bridge.

The natural difficulties in making such movements were increased by the darkness of the night, a heavy rain storm flooding the road with mud and water, and, finally, by one of our wagons loaded with wounded running off the bridge, breaking it down and throwing our wounded headlong into the river. We were so fortunate, however, as to rescue them in a few moments. They were made somewhat comfortable in other vehicles and sent forward. Major [John J.] Clarke and Captains [Henry T.] Douglas and [S. R.] Johnston, of the corps of engineers, applied themselves diligently to the work of repairing the bridge, and in two hours our line was again in motion.

When the accident occurred at the bridge, I sent back orders for one of my divisions to occupy the redoubts that had been thrown up to protect the bridge, and also directed Colonel Alexander to place his batteries in position on the same line. As soon as the bridge was repaired I rode back to this line, but finding that the enemy was not pursuing, the troops were again put in motion. The rear of my column passed the bridge at 9 o'clock in the morning, and encamped for the night at Hainesville.

On July 19th, at Bunker Hill, I received orders to march with my command for Millwood, in order to obtain possession of Ashbys Gap, with a view of covering our future movements. We marched early on the next day, part of the command reaching Millwood at night. The Shenandoah was found to be past fording, however, and the enemy had driven our cavalry from the Gap, and were in possession down to the river bank. I reported this to the commanding general and continued my march on the following day for Manassas and Chesters gaps. Arriving at the Shenandoah at Front Royal it was found to be past fording, and the work of laying our bridges was hurriedly begun. Brigadier-General Corse, who had been hurried forward with his brigade to secure the Gaps, succeeded in passing the stream with his men and several batteries. Detaching a regiment to Manassas Gap, he marched his main force into Chester Gap, and succeeded in getting possession of the latter some few moments before the enemy appeared. The enemy was in possession of Manassas Gap, but Colonel [Arthur] Herbert, of the Seventeenth Virginia Regiment, secured a strong position with his regiment, from which he held the enemy in check. The rest of Pickett's division was hurried over by crossing the ammunition and arms in a flatboat, the men wading. Re-enforcements were sent to Colonel Herbert, when he drove back the enemy and secured as much of the Gap as was desirable. Re-enforcements were also sent to General Corse, who was engaged in skirmishing with the enemy and was threatened by a strong cavalry force. The cavalry withdrew about the time the re-enforcements reached him. The bridges were completed about 12 o'clock at night, and the passage by our trains commenced.

The next day the enemy appeared in stronger force in

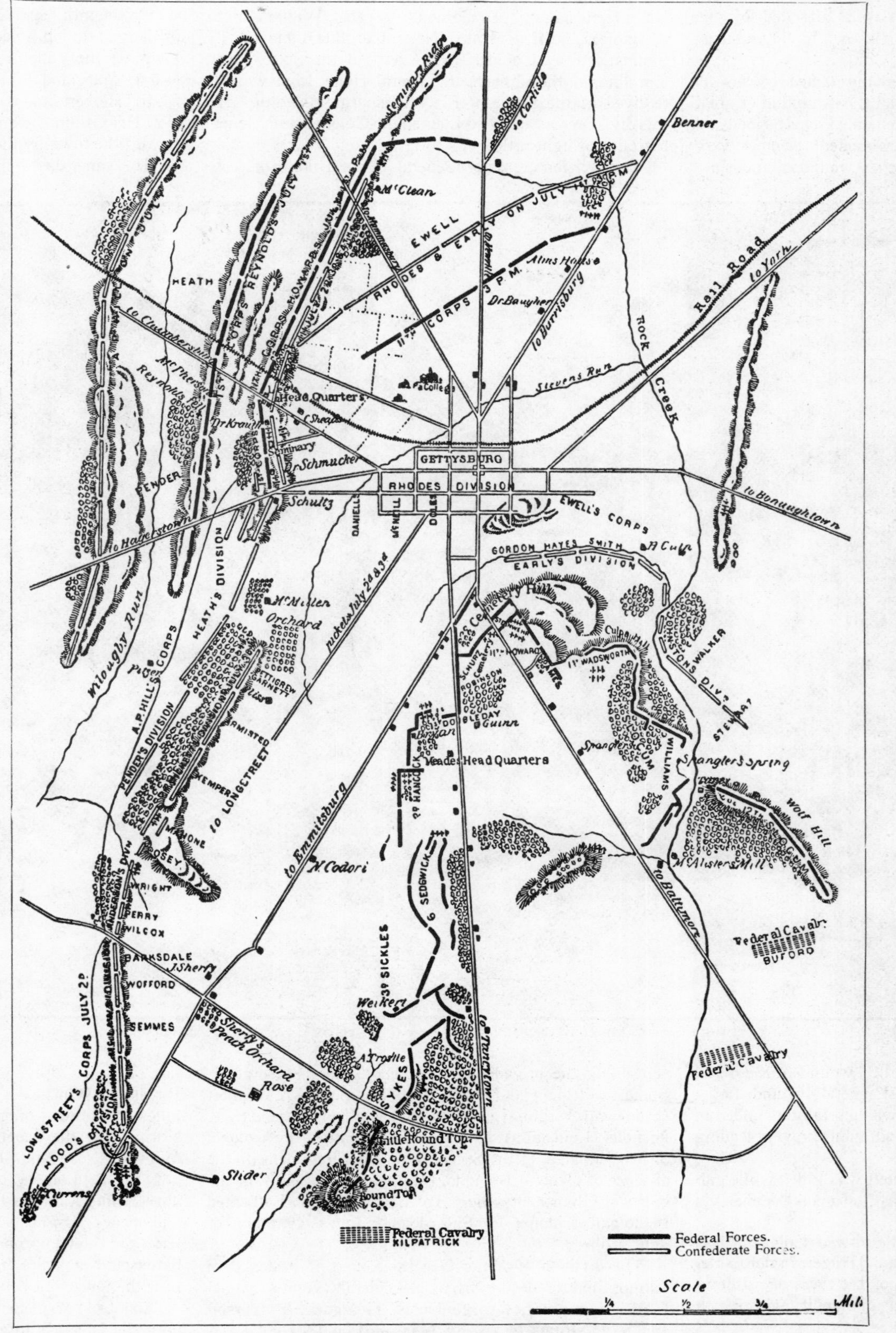

MAP OF THE BATTLEFIELD OF GETTYSBURG.

Manassas Gap, but I had posted Hood's division there, under Brigadier-General E. M. Law, and he gave us but little trouble. He also reappeared at the foot of the mountain, at Chester Gap. As soon as our men finished cooking their rations, General Wofford's brigade, of McLaws' division, was ordered to disperse the cavalry that was at the foot of the mountain, and endeavor to capture his artillery. General Pickett was ordered to send a force down the mountain by a different route, to get in rear of and intercept the cavalry. After a light skirmish with General Wofford, the enemy made a hasty retreat. Our march was continued, arriving at Culpeper Courthouse at noon on the 24th instant.

General Benning's brigade, which had been left on picket at Gaines Crossroads, with the Fourth and Fifteenth Alabama regiments, to await the arrival of Lieutenant-General A. P. Hill's corps, were attacked by the enemy's cavalry while on the march, each having a smart skirmish.

I desire to mention the following-named officers as among those most distinguished for the exhibition of great gallantry and skill, viz.: Major-Generals Pickett, Hood and Trimble, the two latter severely wounded; Kemper, very seriously wounded; Semmes severely wounded, and since died of his wounds; Pettigrew slightly wounded; Kershaw, Law and G. T. Anderson, the last severely wounded.

Brigadier-General Barksdale was mortally wounded in the attack on the evening of the 2d, while bravely leading his brigade in the assault.

Brigadier-General R. B. Garnett was killed while gallantly leading his brigade in the assault upon the enemy's position upon the Cemetery Hill.

Colonel Walton, chief of artillery, and Colonel Alexander, Major Dearing, Major [Frank] Huger, Major Eshleman and Captain [M. B.] Miller, of the corps of artillery, were noted for the courage, zeal and ability with which they discharged their duties.

Major-General Pickett's division merits especial credit for the determined manner in which it assaulted the enemy's strong position upon the Cemetery Hill.

For valuable and meritorious services on the field I desire to express my renewed obligations to the officers of my staff: Lieutenant-Colonel [G. M.] Sorrel, Lieutenant-Colonel [Peyton T.] Manning; Majors [John W.] Fairfax, [O.] Latrobe, [John J.] Clarke and [Thomas] Walton and Captains [Thomas J.] Goree, [John W.] Riely and [H. J.] Rogers; Major [S. P.] Mitchell, Chief Quartermaster; Major [R. J.] Moses, Chief Commissary of Subsistence; Surgeon [J. S. D.] Cullen, Medical Director; Surgeons [Randolph] Barksdale and [Thomas F.] Maury, and Captain Manning, Signal Officer, who discharged the duties of their respective departments with zeal and ability.

* * * * * * *

JAMES LONGSTREET,
Lieutenant-General Commanding.

THE GETTYSBURG CAMPAIGN,

JUNE 3 TO AUGUST 1, 1863.

BY

LIEUT.-GEN. RICHARD S. EWELL,
Commanding Second Army Corps.

HEADQUARTERS SECOND CORPS,
ARMY OF NORTHERN VIRGINIA,
August —, 1863.

THE Second Corps, at the time of leaving Hamilton's Crossing (June 4th), comprised the following troops: The division of Major-General Jubal A. Early, containing the brigades of Brigadier-Generals H. T. Hays (Louisiana), J. B. Gordon (Georgia), William Smith (Virginia), and R. F. Hoke (North Carolina), temporarily commanded by Colonel I. E. Avery, of the Sixth North Carolina, in the absence of General Hoke, from wounds received at the battle of Fredericksburg, May 4th. To this division was attached Lieutenant-Colonel H. P. Jones' battalion of light artillery.

The division of Major-General Edward Johnson, containing the brigades of Brigadier-Generals George H. Steuart (Virginia and North Carolina), James A. Walker (Stonewall, Virginia), John M. Jones (Virginia), and F. T. Nicholls (Louisiana), temporarily commanded by Colonel J. M. Williams, of the Second Louisiana Regiment, in the absence of General Nicholls, from wounds received at the battle of Chancellorsville. To this division was attached Lieutenant-Colonel R. Snowden Andrews' battalion of light artillery.

The division of Major-General Robert E. Rodes, containing the brigades of Brigadier-Generals Junius Daniel (North Carolina), George Doles (Georgia), A. Iverson and S. D. Ramseur (North Carolina), and Rodes' (Alabama) brigade, commanded by Colonel Edward A. O'Neal, of the Twenty-sixth Alabama Regiment. To this division was attached Lieutenant-Colonel Thomas H. Carter's battalion of light artillery.

Lieutenant-Colonel William Nelson's battalion and five batteries of the First Virginia Artillery, under Colonel J. Thompson Brown, acting chief of artillery, in the absence of Colonel S. Crutchfield, from wounds received in the battle of Chancellorsville, May 2d, formed the artillery reserve of the corps.

TO CULPEPER AND WINCHESTER.

Marching via Verdierville and Somerville Ford, the corps reached Culpeper on June 7th.

On the 9th, the enemy being reported to have crossed the Rappahannock in force, I moved my corps, by direction of the general commanding, to General Stuart's support; but, on reaching Brandy Station with General Rodes' division, found the enemy already retiring.

Resuming the march on the 10th, we passed by Gaines Crossroads, Flint Hill and Front Royal, arriving at Cedarville on the 12th. At this point I detached General Rodes' division, together with General Jenkins' cavalry brigade, which here reported to me, to capture, if possible, a force of one thousand eight hundred men under Colonel [A. T.] McReynolds, reported at Berryville, and thence to press on to Martinsburg. With the remaining two divisions and the Sixteenth Virginia Cavalry Battalion [regiment] (Major [James H.] Nounnan), of Jenkins' brigade, I proceeded to attack Winchester. From all the information I could gather, the fortifications of Winchester were only assailable on the west and northwest, from a range of hills which commanded the ridge occupied by their main fortifications. The force there was represented at from six to eight thousand, under General Milroy.

On the 13th I sent Early's division and Colonel Brown's artillery battalion (under Captain [W. J.] Dance) to Newtown, on the Valley Pike, where they were joined by the [First] Maryland Infantry Battalion, Lieutenant-Colonel [J. R.] Herbert, and the Baltimore Light Artillery, Captain [W. H.] Griffin. General Early was directed to advance toward the town by the Valley Pike.

The same day Johnson's division, preceded by Nounnan's cavalry, drove in the enemy's pickets on the Front Royal and Winchester Road, and formed line of battle two miles from town, preparatory to an attack. After some skirmishing the enemy opened from a battery near the Millwood Road and [J. C.] Carpenter's battery, Lieutenant [W. T.] Lambie commanding, was placed by Lieutenant-Colonel Andrews to the left of the Front Royal Road and opened vigorously, soon driving off the opposing battery and blowing up a caisson. This drew upon our battery a heavy fire from twelve or fifteen pieces in and near the town, but beyond the range of our guns.

About 5 P. M. General Early had a pretty sharp skirmish with the enemy's infantry and artillery near Kernstown, Gordon's brigade, supported by Hays', driving them at a run as far as Milltown Mills. Here Early, coming within range of the enemy's fortifications, halted for the night. Before morning the enemy withdrew all their artillery into their fortifications from Bowers Hill and the south and east sides of the town. On examining the enemy's fortifications from General Johnson's position, I found they had put up works on the hills I had intended gaining possession of and were busy strengthening them.

Having reconnoitered with General Early from Bowers Hill (9 A. M. on the 14th), I coincided with his views as to the best point of attack, and directed him to move his main force to the left and carry by assault one of the works above-mentioned—a small, open work on a commanding hill near the Pughtown Road, which overlooked the main fort.

About 11 A. M., finding there was no danger of a sortie, and seeing the enemy fortifying a hill north of their main fort, I directed General Johnson to move to the east of the

THE CONFEDERATE ARMY CROSSING THE POTOMAC RIVER ON ITS WAY TO PENNSYLVANIA.

town and interfere with their work as much as possible, and so divert attention from General Early. He accordingly took up position between the Millwood and Berryville pikes, and threw forward the Fifth Virginia, under Lieutenant-Colonel H. J. Williams, as skirmishers, who annoyed the enemy so as to force them to leave off work and effectually to engross their attention.

General Gordon's brigade and Lieutenant-Colonel Herbert's Maryland Battalion, with two batteries, were left by General Early at Bowers Hill, and pushed their skirmishers into Winchester, who were recalled for fear of drawing the enemy's fire on the town.

By 4 P. M. General Early had attained, undiscovered, a wooded hill (one of the range known as Little North Mountain) near the Pughtown Road, on the south side of which an orchard and on the north a cornfield afforded excellent positions for artillery, in easy range of the work to be attacked—a bastion, front open toward the town. Hays' brigade was designated for the assault, and Smith's for its support, and about 6 o'clock Colonel Jones ran his pieces and those of the First Virginia Artillery, under Captain Dance, forward by hand, into position, and opened simultaneously from twenty guns, completely surprising the enemy, whose entire attention at this point was engrossed by Gordon.

In half an hour their battery was silenced, Jones' artillery firing excellently. General Hays moved quietly to within two hundred yards of their work, when our guns ceased firing, and he charged through an abatis of brushwood, and captured the work, taking six rifled pieces, two of which were at once turned upon and dispersed the columns that the enemy were endeavoring to form to recapture it. Two works to the left of the one taken were immediately abandoned, their defenders retreating to the main fort. It was by this time too late to do more than prepare to improve this important advantage promptly in the morning. This result established the correctness of General Early's views as to the point of attack, and rendered the main fort untenable.

Accordingly anticipating the possibility of the enemy's attempting to retreat during the night, I ordered General Johnson, with the Stonewall, Nicholls', and three regiments of Steuart's brigades, and [W. F.] Dement's battery, with sections of [Charles I.] Raines' and [J. C.] Carpenter's (the whole under Lieutenant-Colonel Andrews), to proceed to a point on the Martinsburg Pike about two and one-half miles from Winchester, so as to intercept any attempt to retreat, or to be ready to attack at daylight if the enemy held their ground.

Finding the road to this point very rough, General Johnson concluded to march, via Jordan Springs, to Stephensons Depot, where the nature of the ground would give him a strong position. Just as the head of his column reached the railroad, two hundred yards from the Martinsburg Road, the enemy were heard retreating down the pike toward Martinsburg. Forming line parallel with the pike behind a stone wall, Steuart on the right and the Louisiana brigade on the left (twelve hundred men in all),

LIEUT.-GEN. RICHARD S. EWELL, OF VIRGINIA.

and posting the artillery favorably, he was immediately attacked by Milroy with all his force of infantry and cavalry, his artillery having been abandoned at the town, the enemy making repeated and desperate efforts to cut their way through. Here was the hardest fighting which took place during the attack, the odds being greatly in favor of the enemy, who were successfully repulsed and scattered by the gallantry of General Johnson and his brave command.

After several front attacks had been steadily met and repulsed, they attempted to turn both flanks simultaneously, but were met on the right by General Walker and his brigade, which had just arrived on the field (having been left behind by a mistake), and on the left by two regiments of Nicholls' brigade, which had been held in reserve. In a few minutes the greater part of them surrendered, twenty-three to twenty-five hundred in number. The rest scattered through the woods and fields, but most of them were subsequently captured by our cavalry. General Milroy, with two hundred and fifty or three hundred cavalry, made his way to Harpers Ferry.

The fruits of this victory were twenty-three pieces of artillery (nearly all rifled), four thousand prisoners, three hundred loaded wagons, more than three hundred horses and quite a large amount of commissary and quartermaster's stores.

My loss was forty-seven killed, two hundred and nineteen wounded and three missing; aggregate, two hundred and sixty-nine. Lieutenant-Colonel Andrews, who handled his artillery with great skill and effect in the engagement of the 15th, was wounded just at the close of the action.

BERRYVILLE AND MARTINSBURG.

General Rodes encamped near Stone Bridge, on the road to Millwood, on the night of June 12th, and moving on next morning toward Berryville his infantry were met by a detachment of Yankee cavalry before reaching Millwood. Finding himself discovered he pushed on rapidly, but before reaching Berryville the enemy's infantry had retreated on the Charlestown Road, holding Jenkins at bay for awhile with their artillery, which was withdrawn as soon as ours came up. Turning off by the road to Summit Point, the enemy retreated to Winchester. After securing the small amount of supplies at Berryville, General Rodes, sending Jenkins in pursuit, followed with his infantry to Summit Point, where he encamped. Jenkins failed from some cause to overtake the enemy.

Late on the 14th General Rodes came to Martinsburg, before reaching which place Jenkins drove the enemy from some barricaded houses at Bunker Hill, capturing seventy-five or a hundred prisoners. At Martinsburg General Rodes found the enemy's infantry and artillery in position before the town. He immediately sent Jenkins' cavalry to the left and rear of the place, and putting some of Carter's artillery in position drove off the opposing battery, which retreated toward Williamsport, so closely pursued by Jenkins' dismounted cavalry and two squadrons mounted that they were forced to abandon five out of their six guns, and many prisoners were taken. The infantry fled by way of Shepherdstown, a fact not known for some hours, which, together with the darkness, will account for their escape. The enemy destroyed many of the stores at Martinsburg, but six thousand bushels of grain and a few quartermaster's and commissary stores fell into our hands.

The results of this expedition were five pieces of artillery, two hundred prisoners and quartermaster's and subsistence stores in some quantity.

General Rodes mentions with commendation the conduct of Major [J. W.] Sweeney, of Jenkins' brigade, wounded in charging the enemy's rear near the Opequon, as they retreated to Winchester from Berryville.

CROSSING POTOMAC—MARCH TO CARLISLE.

I sent notice to General Rodes of Milroy's escape, but he was not in position to intercept him, Jenkins' cavalry being already (10 A. M., 15th) on the Potomac, near Williamsport. The same evening General Rodes crossed at Williamsport with three brigades, sending Jenkins forward to Chambersburg, and on the 19th moved his division by my orders to Hagerstown, where he encamped on the road to Boonsboro, while Johnson crossed to Sharpsburg and Early moved to Shepherdstown, to threaten Harpers Ferry.

In these positions we waited until June 21st for the other two corps to close up, on the afternoon of which day I received orders from the general commanding to take Harrisburg, and next morning (22d) Rodes and Johnson marched toward Greencastle, Pa. Jenkins reoccupied Chambersburg, whence he had fallen back some days before, and Early moved by Boonsboro to Cavetown, where the Seventeenth Virginia Cavalry (Colonel [William H.] French) reported, and remained with him till the battle of Gettysburg.

Continuing our march, we reached Carlisle on the 27th, halting one day at Chambersburg to secure supplies. The marching was as rapid as the weather and the detours made by Major-General Early and Brigadier-General Steuart would admit. Early having marched parallel with us as far as Greenwood, then turned off toward Gettysburg and York. At Carlisle, General George H. Steuart, who had been detached to McConnellsburg from Greencastle, rejoined the corps, bringing some cattle and horses. At Carlisle, Chambersburg and Shippensburg, requisitions were made for supplies and the shops were searched, many valuable stores being secured. At Chambersburg a train was loaded with ordnance and medical stores and sent back. Near three thousand head of cattle were collected and sent back by my corps, and my chief commissary of subsistence, Major [W. J.] Hawks, notified Colonel [R. G.] Cole of the location of five thousand barrels of flour along the route traveled by the command.

From [Carlisle] I sent forward my engineer, Captain [H. B.] Richardson, with General Jenkins' cavalry, to reconnoiter the defenses of Harrisburg, and was starting on the 29th for that place when ordered by the general commanding to join the main body of the army at Cashtown, near Gettysburg. Agreeably to the views of the general commanding, I did not burn Carlisle Barracks.

EXPEDITION TO YORK AND WRIGHTSVILLE.

Colonel E. V. White's cavalry battalion reported to me at Chambersburg, and was sent to General Early, then at Greenwood. Arriving at Cashtown, General Early sent Gordon's brigade, with White's cavalry, direct to Gettysburg, taking the rest of the division on the Mummasburg Road. In front of Gettysburg White charged and routed the Twenty-sixth Regiment Pennsylvania Militia, of whom

MAJ.-GEN. HARRY T. HAYS, OF LOUISIANA.

one hundred and seventy were taken and paroled. From Gettysburg, Gordon, with Tanner's battery and White's battalion, was sent on the direct road to York, and General Early moved in the direction of Dover with the rest of the division.

On approaching York, General Gordon met the mayor and a deputation of citizens, who made a formal surrender of the place.

Pushing on, by order of General Early, to Wrightsville, on the Susquehanna, he found twelve hundred militia strongly intrenched, but without artillery. A few shots drove them across the magnificent railroad bridge, a mile and a quarter long, which they burned as they retreated over it. The little town of Wrightsville caught fire from the bridge, and General Gordon, setting his brigade to work, succeeded in extinguishing the flames. Yet he is accused by the Federal press of having set fire to the town. General Early levied a contribution on the citizens of York, obtaining among other things, $28,600 in United States currency, the greater part of which was turned over to Colonel [J. L.] Corley, chief quartermaster Army of Northern Virginia; 1,000 hats, 1,200 pairs of shoes and 1,000 pairs of socks were also obtained here.

GETTYSBURG.

On the night of June 30th, Rodes' division, which I accompanied, was at Heidlersburg; Early, three miles off, on the road to Berlin, and Johnson, with Colonel Brown's reserve artillery, between Green Village and Scotland. At Heidlersburg, I received orders from the general commanding to proceed to Cashtown or Gettysburg as circumstances might dictate, and a note from General A. P. Hill, saying he was at Cashtown.

Next morning, I moved with Rodes' division toward Cashtown, ordering Early to follow by Hunterstown. Before reaching Middletown, I received notice from General Hill that he was advancing upon Gettysburg, and turned the head of Rodes' column toward that place, by the Middletown Road, sending word to Early to advance directly on the Heidlersburg Road. I notified the general commanding of my movements, and was informed by him that, in case we found the enemy's force very large, he did not want a general engagement brought on till the rest of the army came up.

By the time this message reached me General A. P. Hill had already been warmly engaged with a large body of the enemy in his front, and Carter's artillery battalion, of Rodes' division, had opened with fine effect on the flank of the same body, which was rapidly preparing to attack me, while fresh masses were moving into position in my front. It was too late to avoid an engagement without abandoning the position already taken up, and I determined to push the attack vigorously. General Rodes had drawn up his division, Iverson's brigade on the right, Rodes' (old) brigade (Colonel O'Neal) in the center (these two on the ridge leading to the west of Gettysburg), and Doles on the left in the plain. The Fifth Alabama was retained by General Rodes to guard a wide gap left between O'Neal and Doles. Daniel and Ramseur were in reserve. He at once moved forward and, after advancing for some distance in line, came in sight of the enemy, and O'Neal and Iverson were ordered to attack, Daniel advancing in line two hundred yards in rear of Iverson's right to protect that flank.

At this time only desultory artillery firing was going on on the rest of the field. Carter was warmly engaged. O'Neal's brigade, advancing in some disorder in a direction different from that indicated by Major-General Rodes in person to Colonel O'Neal, and with only three regiments (the Third Alabama being by some mistake left with Daniel's brigade), was soon forced to fall back, notwithstanding the Fifth Alabama was sent to its support. The left of Iverson's brigade was thus exposed, but these gallant troops obstinately stood their ground till the greater part of three regiments had fallen where they stood in line of battle. A few of them, being entirely surrounded, were taken prisoners; a few escaped.

The unfortunate mistake of General Iverson at this critical juncture in sending word to Major-General Rodes that one of his regiments had raised the white flag and gone over to the enemy might have produced the most disastrous consequences. The Twelfth North Carolina, being on the right of his brigade, suffered least. A slight change in the advance of General Iverson had uncovered the whole of Daniel's front, and he found himself opposed to heavy bodies of infantry, whom he attacked and drove before him till he reached a railroad cut extending diagonally across his front and past his right flank, which checked his advance. A battery of the enemy beyond this cut near a barn enfiladed his line, and fresh bodies of infantry poured across the cut a destructive enfilade and reverse fire. Seeing some troops of the Third Corps lying down beyond the railroad, in front of the enemy, who were on his flank, General Daniel sent an officer to get them to advance. As they would not, he was obliged (leaving the Forty-fifth North Carolina and Second North Carolina Battalion to hold his line) to change the front of the rest of his brigade to the rear, and throw part across the railroad beyond the cut, where, having formed line directly in front of the troops of the Third Corps already mentioned, he ordered an advance of his whole brigade and gallantly swept the field, capturing several hundred prisoners in the cut.

About the time of his final charge Ramseur, with his own and Rodes' brigades and remnants of Iverson's, under Captain D. P. Halsey, Assistant Adjutant-General of the brigade, who rallied the brigade and assumed command, had restored the line in the center.

Meantime an attempt by the enemy to push a column into the interval between Doles and O'Neal had been handsomely repulsed by Doles, who, changing front with his two right regiments, took them in flank, driving them in disorder toward the town.

All of General Rodes' troops were now engaged. The enemy were moving large bodies of troops from the town against his left, and affairs were in a very critical condition, when Major-General Early, coming up on the Heidlersburg Road, opened a brisk artillery fire upon large columns moving against Doles' left, and ordered forward Gordon's brigade to the left of Doles', which, after an obstinate contest, broke Barlow's division, captured General [F. C.] Barlow, and drove the whole back on a second line, when they were halted, and General Early ordered up Hays' and Hoke's brigades on Gordon's left, and the three drove the enemy precipitately toward and through the town just as Ramseur broke those in his front.

General Gordon mentions that three hundred of the enemy's dead were left on the ground passed over by his brigade. The enemy had entirely abandoned the north end of the town, and Early entering by the York Railroad at the same time that Rodes came in on the Cashtown Road, they together captured over four thousand prisoners and three pieces of artillery, two of which fell into the hands of Early's division. So far as I can learn no other troops than those of this corps entered the town at all. My loss on this day was less than twenty-nine hundred killed, wounded and missing.

The enemy had fallen back to a commanding position known as Cemetery Hill, south of Gettysburg, and quickly showed a formidable front there. On entering the town, I received a message from the commanding general to attack this hill if I could do so to advantage. I could not bring artillery to bear on it, and all the troops with me were jaded by twelve hours' marching and fighting, and I was notified that General Johnson's division (the only one of my corps that had not been engaged) was close to the town.

Cemetery Hill was not assailable from the town, and I determined, with Johnson's division, to take possession of a wooded hill to my left, on a line with and commanding Cemetery Hill. Before Johnson got up the enemy was reported moving to outflank our extreme left, and I could see what seemed to be his skirmishers in that direction.

Before this report could be investigated by Lieutenant T. T. Turner, aid-de-camp of my staff, and Lieutenant Robert D. Early, sent for that purpose, and Johnson placed in position, the night was far advanced.

Confederate Army Passing Through the Gaps in the Mountains of Virginia.

I received orders soon after dark to draw my corps to the right, in case it could not be used to advantage where it was; that the commanding general thought from the nature of the ground that the position for attack was a good one on that side. I represented to the commanding general that the hill above referred to was unoccupied by the enemy, as reported by Lieutenants Turner and Early, who had gone upon it, and that it commanded their position and made it untenable, so far as I could judge.

He decided to let me remain, and on my return to my headquarters, after 12 o'clock at night, I sent orders to Johnson by Lieutenant T. T. Turner, aid-de-camp, to take possession of this hill, if he had not already done so. General Johnson stated in reply to this order that after forming his line of battle this side of the wooded hill in question, he had sent a reconnoitering party to the hill with orders to report as to the position of the enemy in reference to it. This party, on nearing the summit, was met by a superior force of the enemy which succeeded in capturing a portion of the reconnoitering party, the rest of it making its escape. During this conversation with General Johnson one man arrived bringing a dispatch, dated at 12 midnight, and taken from a Federal courier making his way from General Sykes to General Slocum, in which the former stated that his corps was then halted four miles from Gettysburg, and he would resume his march at 4 A. M. Lieutenant Turner brought this dispatch to my headquarters, and at the same time stated that General Johnson would refrain from attacking the position until I had received notice of the fact that the enemy were in possession of the hill, and had sent him further orders. Day was now breaking and it was too late for any change of place.

Meantime, orders had come from the general commanding for me to delay my attack until I heard General Longstreet's guns open on the right. Lieutenant Turner at once returned to General Johnson and delivered these instructions, directing him to be ready to attack, Early being already in line on the left and Rodes on the right of the main street of the town, Rodes' in line extending out on the Fairfield Road.

Early in the morning I received a communication from the commanding general, the tenor of which was that he intended the main attack to be made by the First Corps, on our right, and wished me, as soon as their guns opened, to make a diversion in their favor to be converted into a real attack if an opportunity offered.

I made the necessary preparations, and about 5 P. M., when General Longstreet's guns opened, General Johnson commenced a heavy cannonade from Andrews' battalion and [Archibald] Graham's battery, the whole under Major [J. W.] Latimer, against the Cemetery Hill.

After an hour's firing, finding that his guns were overpowered by the greater number and superior position of the enemy's batteries, Major Latimer withdrew all but one battery, which he kept to repel any infantry advance. While with this battery this gallant young officer received, from almost the last shell fired, the wound which has since resulted in his death. Colonel Brown says justly of that calamity, "No greater loss could have befallen the artillery of this corps." Major Latimer served with me from March, 1862, to the second battle of Manassas (August 28 to 30, 1862). I was particularly struck at Winchester, May 25, 1862, his first warm engagement, by his coolness, self-possession and bravery under a very heavy artillery fire, showing when most needed the full possession of all his faculties. Though not twenty-one when he fell, his soldierly qualities had impressed me as deeply as those of any officer in my command.

Immediately after the artillery firing ceased, which was just before sundown, General Johnson ordered forward his division to attack the wooded hill in his front, and about dusk the attack was made. The enemy were found strongly intrenched on the side of a very steep mountain, beyond a creek with steep banks, only passable here and there. Brigadier-General J. M. Jones was wounded soon after the attack began, and his brigade, which was on the right with Nicholls' (Louisiana) brigade (under Colonel Williams), was forced back, but Steuart, on the left, took part of the enemy's breastworks and held them till ordered out at noon next day.

As soon as information reached him that Johnson's attack had commenced, General Early, who held the center of my corps, moved Hays' and Hoke's brigades forward against the Cemetery Hill. Charging over a hill into a ravine they broke a line of the enemy's infantry posted behind a stone wall, and advanced up the steep face of another hill, over two lines of breastworks. These brigades captured several batteries of artillery and held them until, finding that no attack was made on the right, and that heavy masses of the enemy were advancing against their front and flank, they reluctantly fell back, bringing away seventy-five to one hundred prisoners and four stand of captured colors. Major-General Rodes did not advance for reasons given in his report.

Before beginning my advance I had sent a staff officer to the division of the Third Corps, on my right, which proved to be General Pender's, to find out what they were to do. He reported the division under command of General Lane, who succeeded Pender, wounded, and who sent word back that the only orders he had received from General Pender were that he was to attack if a favorable opportunity presented. I then wrote to him (it being too late to communicate with the corps commander) that I was about attacking with my corps and requested that he would co-operate. To this I received no answer, nor do I believe that any advance was made. The want of co-operation on the right made it more difficult for Rodes' division to attack, though had it been otherwise, I have every reason to believe, from the eminent success attending the assault of Hays and Avery, that the enemy's lines would have been carried.

I was ordered to renew my attack at daylight Friday morning, and as Johnson's position was the only one affording hopes of doing this to advantage, he was re-enforced by Smith's brigade, of Early's division, and Daniel's and Rodes' (old) brigades, of Rodes' division. Just before the time fixed for General Johnson to advance, the enemy attacked him, to regain the works captured by Steuart the evening before. They were repulsed with very heavy loss, and he attacked in turn, pushing the enemy almost to the top of the mountain, where the precipitous nature of the hill and an abatis of logs and stones, with a very heavy work on the crest of the hill, stopped his further advance.

Half an hour after Johnson attacked, and when too late to recall him, I received notice that Longstreet would not attack until 10 o'clock; but, as it turned out, his attack was delayed till after 2 o'clock. In Johnson's attack, the enemy abandoned a portion of their works in disorder, and, as they ran across an open space to another work, were exposed to the fire of Daniel's brigade at sixty or seventy yards. Our men were at this time under no fire of consequence. Their aim was accurate, and General Daniel thinks that he killed here in half an hour more than in all the rest of his fighting.

Repeated reports from the cavalry on our left that the enemy were moving heavy columns of infantry to turn General Johnson's left, at last caused him, about 1 P. M., to evacuate the works already gained. These reports reached me also, and I sent Captain G. C. Brown, of my staff, with a part of the cavalry, to the left to investigate them, who found them to be without foundation, and General Johnson finally took up a position about three hundred yards in rear of the works he had abandoned, which he held, under a cross-fire of artillery and exposed to the enemy's sharpshooters, until dark. At night my corps fell back, as ordered, to the range of hills west of the town, taken by us on Wednesday, where we remained unmolested during July 4th.

The behavior of my troops throughout this campaign was beyond praise, whether the points considered be their alacrity and willing endurance of the long marches, their orderly and exemplary conduct in the enemy's country, their bravery in action, or their patient endurance of hunger, fatigue and exposure during our retreat.

The lists of killed and wounded, as well as the results gained, will show the desperate character of their fighting. In the infantry, Daniel's brigade, of Rodes' division, and in the artillery, Andrews' battalion, of Johnson's division, suffered most loss. The Second North Carolina Battalion, of Daniel's brigade, lost two hundred or two hundred and forty men, killed and wounded, without yielding an inch of ground at any time.

TELEGRAPH STATION ON THE ROAD.

BACK TO DARKESVILLE.

By order of the commanding general the Third Corps was to move at dark on July 4th, and the First to follow with the prisoners, mine being rear guard. Next day the Third was to take the rear, etc. At 10 A. M. on the 5th, the other corps were not all in the road, and consequently mine did not take up its march till near noon, and only reached Fairfield at 4 P. M. Here the enemy, who had been threatening our rear, and occasionally opening a fire of artillery on the rear guard (Gordon's brigade, of Early's division), showed more boldness in attacking, throwing out a line of skirmishers over a mile in length. They were repulsed, and a battery which was shelling our column driven off.

We encamped for the night on a hill one and a half miles west of Fairfield, and next day, July 6th, the Third Corps, moving by another road, we were still in the rear, Rodes' division acting as rear guard and repelling another attack of the enemy. The Forty-fifth North Carolina, Daniel's brigade, under Captain [James A.] Hopkins, being summoned to surrender, attacked the troops making the summons and drove them out of a wood in which they were posted. The enemy did not follow much beyond Fairfield. The road was again blocked until noon. That night we encamped near Waynesboro and reached Hagerstown about noon of July 7th.

On the 11th we were moved into line between Hagerstown and Williamsport, our right joining the left of the Third Corps, and began fortifying, and in a short time my men were well protected. Their spirit was never better than at this time, and the wish was universal that the enemy would attack.

On the night of the 14th I was ordered with my infantry and artillery to ford at Williamsport, the ammunition-chests going in the ferry-boats. I could find no ferry-boats nor any one in charge; it was dark and raining. The entrance to the river would have been impracticable for artillery in daylight, and, as well as I could ascertain, the exit was worse. Everything was in confusion. Colonel Corley, Chief Quartermaster, Army of Northern Virginia, who had charge of the arrangements, recommended Colonel Brown, my chief of artillery, to cross by the pontoons, and sent to the same point my reserve train of ambulances with wounded, originally intended to cross by the ferry-boats. Just before midnight my advance (Rodes' division) commenced crossing. The men had directions to sling their cartridge-boxes over their shoulders, but many rounds of ammunition were necessarily lost, as the water was up to their armpits the whole way across, sometimes deeper. By 8 o'clock my whole corps was over, all fording except Hays' brigade, which was sent with the artillery to the pontoons.

While in camp near Darkesville, the enemy, under Kelley, were reported between Martinsburg and Hedgesville protecting the Baltimore & Ohio Railroad and occasionally skirmishing with Johnson's division, which was destroying the track.

General Lee, commanding, directed on the 21st an effort to be made to capture this force, said to be six thousand strong, sending Early's division to get in rear through Mill's Gap and down Back Creek, while I joined Rodes to Johnson and marched against their front. Though these movements were made in the night of the 21st, the enemy heard of them through spies, and early on the 22d had retreated out of reach.

The other corps had already marched toward the Blue Ridge, and accordingly we followed and bivouaced near Winchester, and next day, on reaching Manassas Gap, found Wright's brigade, of Anderson's division, deployed to repel a large body of the enemy who were advancing upon it through the Gap. The insignia of two corps could be seen in the Gap, and a third was marching up; over ten thousand men were in sight.

The enemy were so close to Wright's brigade that the line of battle had to be chosen some distance in the rear, and accordingly some two hundred and fifty sharpshooters, of Rodes' division, under Major [Eugene] Blackford, were added to Wright's brigade to hold the enemy in check while the line was formed. Rodes' (old) brigade, Colonel O'Neal, deployed as skirmishers, formed the first, and the remainder of Rodes' division, with Carter's battalion of artillery, the second line. These dispositions were made by General Rodes with his usual promptness, skill and judgment. The enemy were held in check for some time by the line of Wright's brigade and the skirmishers under Major Blackford, which they at last drove back, with considerable loss to themselves, by flanking it. These troops, in full view, showed great gallantry, and though intended merely to make a show, held the enemy back so long and inflicted such loss that they were satisfied not to come within reach of O'Neal, but remained at a safe distance, where they were leisurely shelled by Carter's artillery.

Johnson's division was ordered to take position near the river, to prevent the enemy cutting me off from the ford at Front Royal, and, though not required in action, was promptly in place. Early's division, much jaded, was fifteen miles off, near Winchester, and could not possibly reach me before the afternoon of next day.

I had reason to believe that Meade's whole army was in our front, and, having but two divisions to oppose him, I decided to send Early up the Valley, by Strasburg and New Market, while I marched the other two divisions up the Page Valley to Luray, the route pursued by Jackson, in 1862, in his campaign against Banks. Johnson's and Rodes' divisions moved back two to four miles, and encamped near Front Royal, the rear guard, under Colonel B. T. Johnson, of Johnson's division, leaving Front Royal after 10 o'clock next day, the enemy making only a slight advance, which was driven back by a few rounds of artillery. Rodes' division, the only troops of my corps that I saw during this affair, showed great eagerness and alacrity to meet the enemy, and, had he advanced, would have given him a severe lesson.

In this campaign, the loss of my corps was as follows: At Winchester and in the Valley, 47 killed, 219 wounded, and 3 missing; aggregate, 269. At Gettysburg and in Pennsylvania, 883 killed, 3,857 wounded, 1,347 missing; aggregate, 6,094. For the entire campaign, 930 killed, 4,076 wounded and 1,350 missing; aggregate, 6,356. Before crossing the Potomac, it captured 28 pieces of artillery and about 4,500 prisoners. About 200 prisoners were taken before reaching Gettysburg. At that place over 4,000 prisoners, three pieces of artillery, and four stand of colors, memorable as having been brought off Cemetery Hill, were the spoils gained, making altogether nearly 9,000 prisoners and 31 pieces of artillery.

Iverson' brigade, sent back to guard my wagon train from Fairfield, had a handsome affair with the enemy's cavalry at Hagerstown, in which they are reported by General Iverson as killing, wounding and capturing a number equal to their whole force.

At Winchester, the Maryland battalion was attached to General Steuart's brigade, and the Baltimore Light Artillery to Colonel Brown's battalion, with which they served with their usual gallantry throughout the campaign.

At Gettysburg, July 1st, I was much pleased with the conduct of Captain Carter's battery, which came under my immediate observation.

The conduct of Hays' (Louisiana) and Hoke's (North Carolina) brigades (the latter under Colonel Avery), at Cemetery Hill, Gettysburg, was worthy of the highest praise. In this, and at Winchester, the Louisiana brigade and their gallant commander gave new honor to the name already acquired on the old fields of Winchester and Port Republic, and wherever engaged.

The rapid and skillful advance of Gordon's brigade on June 13th, near Winchester, with great spirit driving the enemy in confusion toward the town, was one of the finest movements I have witnessed during the war, and won for the troops and their gallant commander the highest commendation.

I was fortunate in this campaign in the assistance of three division commanders — Major-Generals Jubal A. Early, Edward Johnson and Robert E. Rodes—whose wise counsel, skillful handling of their commands and prompt obedience to orders are beyond praise — generals whose scars bear witness to the manner in which were won their laurels and rank. Colonel J. T. Brown, commanding artillery of this corps, showed himself competent to his position, and gave me perfect satisfaction. I have to express my thanks to the officers of my staff for their valuable services during the campaign.

* * * * * * *

R. S. EWELL,

Lieutenant-General, Provisional Army C. S. A.

THE GETTYSBURG CAMPAIGN,

JUNE 3 TO AUGUST 1, 1863.

BY

LIEUT.-GEN. AMBROSE P. HILL,

Commanding Third Army Corps.

HEADQUARTERS THIRD ARMY CORPS,
November —, 1863.

I HAVE the honor to submit the following report of the operations of the Third Army Corps during and subsequent to the battle of Gettysburg: On the morning of June 29th the Third Corps, composed of the divisions of Major-Generals Anderson, Heth and Pender, and five battalions of artillery, under command of Colonel R. L. Walker, was encamped on the road from Chambersburg to Gettysburg, near the village of Fayetteville. I was directed to move on this road in the direction of York, and to cross the Susquehanna, menacing the communications of Harrisburg with Philadelphia, and to co-operate with General Ewell, acting as circumstances might require.

Accordingly, on the 29th, I moved General Heth's division to Cashtown, some eight miles from Gettysburg, following on the morning of the 30th with the division of General Pender, and directing General Anderson to move in the same direction on the morning of July 1st. On arriving at Cashtown, General Heth, who had sent forward Pettigrew's brigade to Gettysburg, reported that Pettigrew had encountered the enemy at Gettysburg (principally cavalry), but in what force he could not determine. A courier was then dispatched with this information to the general commanding, and with orders to start Anderson early; also to General Ewell, informing him, and that I intended to advance the next morning and discover what was in my front.

GETTYSBURG. CONFEDERATE DEAD NEAR EMMITSBURG ROAD.
[From a photograph taken after the battle.]

On July 1st, at 5 A. M., Heth took up the line of march with Pegram's battalion of artillery, followed by Pender, with McIntosh's battalion of artillery; Colonel Walker, with the remainder of the artillery, being with General Anderson. About three miles from Gettysburg, Heth's advance brigade (Archer's) encountered the advance of the enemy. Archer and Davis were thrown into line, and, with some pieces of artillery from Pegram, the enemy were steadily driven back to the wooded hills this side of Gettysburg, where their principal force (since ascertained to be the First and Eleventh Corps) were disposed to dispute our further advance.

Heth's whole division was now thrown into line; Davis on the left of the road, Archer, Pettigrew and Brockenbrough on the right, and Pender's formed in his rear; Thomas on the left, and Lane, Scales and Perrin on the right. Pegram's and McIntosh's battalions of artillery were put in position on the crest of a hill overlooking the town of Gettysburg.

Heth's division drove the enemy, encountering a determined resistance. About 2:30 o'clock, the right wing of Ewell's corps made its appearance on the left, and thus formed a right angle with my line. Pender's division was then ordered forward, Thomas' brigade being retained in reserve, and the rout of the enemy was complete, Perrin's brigade taking position after position of the enemy and driving him through the town of Gettysburg. The want of cavalry had been and was again seriously felt.

Under the impression that the enemy were entirely routed, and my own two divisions being exhausted by some six hours' hard fighting, prudence led me to be content with what had been gained, and not push forward troops exhausted and necessarily disordered, probably to encounter fresh troops of the enemy. These two divisions were bivouacked in the positions won, and Anderson, who had just come up, was also bivouacked some two miles in rear of the battle-ground.

The results of this fight were, for the Third Corps, two pieces of artillery and twenty-three hundred prisoners, and the almost total annihilation of the First Corps of the enemy. Major-General Heth was slightly wounded; Brigadier-General Archer was taken prisoner by the enemy; Brigadier-General Scales was also wounded. Pettigrew's brigade, under its gallant leader, fought most admirably, and sustained heavy loss.

On the morning of July 2d, Anderson was ordered to the front, and relieved Heth's division, extending to our right and along a crest of hills which faced the Cemetery Hill at Gettysburg and, continuing to the right, ran nearly parallel to the Emmitsburg Road.

On the 2d, then, my position was this: Pender's division occupying the crest from the theological seminary, extending to the right and joined by Anderson's, who carried on the line, almost entirely covering the whole front occupied by the enemy; Heth's division (now commanded by General Pettigrew) in reserve. Colonel Walker had distributed his artillery along this line in the most eligible positions. The corps of General Longstreet (McLaws' and Hood's divisions) was on my right and in a line very nearly at right angles to mine. General Longstreet was to attack the left flank of the enemy and sweep down his line, and I was ordered to co-operate with him with such of my brigades from the right as could join in with his troops in the attack. On the extreme right Hood commenced the attack about 2 o'clock; McLaws about 5:30 o'clock.

Soon after McLaws moved forward, General Anderson moved forward the brigades of Wilcox, Perry and Wright in echelon. The charge of these three brigades was very gallantly made, and pressed on, until Wilcox's right had become separated from McLaws' left. Wilcox and Wright drove the enemy from their intrenchments, inflicting very heavy loss upon them. Wilcox's brigade succeeded in capturing eight pieces of artillery and Wright's brigade about twenty. The enemy threw forward heavy re-enforcements, and no supports coming to these brigades the ground so hardly won had to be given up, and the brigades occupied their former positions in line of battle. The three brigades lost heavily in this attack. On this day, also, the Confederacy lost the valuable services of Major-General W. D. Pender, wounded by a shell, and since dead. No man fell during this bloody engagement at Gettysburg more regretted than he, nor around whose youthful brow were clustered brighter rays of glory.

On the morning of the 3d the divisions of my corps occupied the same positions as on the 2d. The reserve batteries were all brought up and put in position along the crest of the ridge facing the enemy's line. In addition, the battalion of Colonel Alexander, of Longstreet's corps, was put in position in front of the right wing of Anderson's division, and on the ground won by Wilcox and Wright. I was directed to hold my line with Anderson's division and the half of Pender's (now commanded by General Lane), and to order Heth's division (commanded by Pettigrew) and Lane's and Scales' brigades, of Pender's division, to report to Lieutenant-General Longstreet as a support to his corps in the assault on the enemy's lines. As the troops were filing off to their positions Major-General Trimble reported to me for the command of Pender's division, and took command of the two brigades destined to take part in the assault.

At 1 o'clock our artillery opened, and for two hours rained an incessant storm of missiles upon the enemy's lines. The effect was marked along my front, driving the enemy entirely from his guns.

The assault was then gallantly made, Heth's division and Trimble's two brigades on the left of Pickett. Anderson had been directed to hold his division ready to take advantage of any success which might be gained by the assaulting column, or to support it if necessary. To that end Wilcox and Perry were moved forward to eligible positions. The assault failed, and after almost gaining the enemy's works our troops fell back in disorder. The enemy made no attempt to pursue. Major-General Trimble, Brigadier-General Pettigrew, and Colonel Fry, commanding Archer's brigade, were wounded while most gallantly leading their troops. General Trimble and Colonel Fry were both taken prisoners.

The troops resumed their former positions and remained thus until the night of the 4th, when the march was taken up toward Hagerstown, by Fairfield and Waynesboro.

At Hagerstown we lay in line of battle from the 7th to the night of the 13th, when I moved my corps in the direction of the pontoon bridge at Falling Waters. Being the rear guard of the army, such dispositions as were necessary were made to repel any advance of the enemy. Anderson's division crossed without molestation, and Pender's was in the act of crossing when the enemy made their appearance. A small body of cavalry charged Pettigrew's and Archer's brigades and were annihilated. Only two of ours killed; but, unfortunately for the service, one of them was the gallant and accomplished Pettigrew.

Subsequently the enemy pressed on vigorously, and I directed General Heth to retire his troops and cross the river. In doing this some loss was sustained, principally in stragglers, but not exceeding five hundred, composed of men from the various brigades of the army. Two pieces of artillery were broken down on this night march and abandoned.

Colonel Walker brought off three guns captured on the field of Gettysburg.

On the 21st the march was resumed toward Culpeper Courthouse.

On the 23d Wright's brigade, under Colonel Walker, was left to guard Manassas Gap until relieved by General Ewell. This brigade was attacked while there by an overwhelming force of the enemy, but held its ground stubbornly until relieved by Ewell's corps, when it marched with him to Culpeper. General Ewell speaks in high terms of the admirable conduct of this brigade.

Continuing the march on the morning of the 24th, at Newby's Crossroads a brigade of the enemy's cavalry attempted to arrest our march. Heth's division (his own and Pender's) was leading; General Benning's brigade, of Longstreet's corps, was also along and rendered prompt and valuable assistance. The enemy were soon put to flight in confusion, and no more annoyance occurred on the march to Culpeper Courthouse.

On August 1st Anderson's division was sent out on the road to Brandy [Station], to repel some of the enemy's cavalry, which had driven back our cavalry, and were quite near the Courthouse. This was handsomely done by Mahone's brigade and Perry's, and with but trifling loss.

The total loss of the Third Corps in this campaign: 849 killed, 4,289 wounded, and 3,844 missing. The larger portion of those reported missing were killed or wounded in the fight of July 3d, but the possession of the field by the enemy prevented a true count.

A. P. HILL,
Lieutenant-General, Commanding Third Corps.

ORGANIZATION OF THE ARMY OF NORTHERN VIRGINIA, AT THE BATTLE OF GETTYSBURG,

JULY 1, 2 AND 3, 1863,*

GENERAL ROBERT E. LEE,
Commanding.

STAFF.

Colonel W. H. Taylor, Adjutant-General.
Colonel C. P. Venable, Aid-de-camp.
Colonel Charles Marshall, Aid-de-camp.
Colonel James L Corley, Chief Quartermaster.
Colonel R. S. Cole, Chief Commissary.
Colonel B. G. Baldwin, Chief of Ordnance.
Colonel H. L. Peyton, Assistant Inspector-General.
General W. N. Pendleton, Chief of Artillery.
Dr. L. Guild, Medical Director.
Colonel W. Proctor Smith, Chief Engineer.
Major H. E. Young, Assistant Adjutant-General.
Major G. B. Cook, Assistant Inspector-General.

MAJ.-GEN. GEORGE E. PICKETT, OF VIRGINIA.

FIRST ARMY CORPS.
Lieutenant-General James Longstreet.

MCLAWS' DIVISION.
Major-General Lafayette McLaws.

KERSHAW'S BRIGADE.
Brigadier-General J. B. Kershaw.

Second South Carolina—Colonel J. D. Kennedy; Lieutenant-Colonel F. Gaillard.
Third South Carolina—Major R. C. Maffett; Colonel J. D. Nance.
Seventh South Carolina—Colonel D. Wyatt Aiken.
Eighth South Carolina—Colonel J. W. Henagan.
Fifteenth South Carolina—Colonel W. D. DeSaussure, Major William M. Gist.
Third South Carolina Battalion—Lieutenant-Colonel W. G. Rice.

* The actual commanders are indicated as far as practicable.

BARKSDALE'S BRIGADE.

Brigadier-General William Barksdale; Colonel B. G. Humphreys.

Thirteenth Mississippi—Colonel J. W. Carter.
Seventeenth Mississippi—Colonel W. D. Holder; Lieutenant Colonel John C. Fiser.
Eighteenth Mississippi—Colonel T. M. Griffin; Lieutenant-Colonel W. H. Luse.
Twenty-first Mississippi—Colonel B. G. Humphreys.

SEMMES' BRIGADE.*

Brigadier-General P. J. Semmes; Colonel Goode Bryan.

Tenth Georgia—Colonel John B. Weems.
Fiftieth Georgia—Colonel W. B. Manning.
Fifty-first Georgia—Colonel E. Ball.
Fifty-third Georgia—Colonel James P. Simms.

WOFFORD'S BRIGADE.

Brigadier-General W. T. Wofford.

Sixteenth Georgia—Colonel Goode Bryan.
Eighteenth Georgia—Lieutenant-Colonel S. Z. Ruff.
Twenty-fourth Georgia—Colonel Robert McMillan.
Cobb's (Ga.) Legion—Lieutenant-Colonel Luther J. Glenn.
Phillips' (Ga.) Legion — Lieutenant-Colonel E. S. Barclay.

ARTILLERY.

Colonel H. C. Cabell.

First North Carolina Artillery, Battery A—Captain B. C. Manly.
Pulaski (Ga.) Artillery—Captain J. C. Fraser; Lieutenant W. J. Furlong.
First Richmond Howitzers—Captain E. S. McCarthy.
Troup (Ga.) Artillery—Captain H. H. Carlton; Lieutenant C. W. Motes.

PICKETT'S DIVISION.

Major-General George E. Pickett.

GARNETT'S BRIGADE.

Brigadier-General R. B. Garnett; Major C. S. Peyton.

Eighth Virginia—Colonel Eppa Hunton.
Eighteenth Virginia—Lieutenant-Colonel H. A. Carrington.
Nineteenth Virginia—Colonel Henry Gantt; Lieutenant-Colonel John T. Ellis.
Twenty-eighth Virginia—Colonel R. C. Allen; Lieutenant-Colonel William Watts.
Fifty-sixth Virginia—Colonel W. D. Stuart; Lieutenant-Colonel P. P. Slaughter.

BRIG.-GEN. RICHARD B. GARNETT, OF VIRGINIA, Adjutant and Inspector-General. Killed at the Battle of Gettysburg, July 2, 1863.

KEMPER'S BRIGADE.

Brigadier-General J. L. Kemper; Colonel Joseph Mayo, Jr.

First Virginia—Colonel Lewis B. Williams; Lieutenant-Colonel F. G. Skinner.
Third Virginia—Colonel Joseph Mayo, Jr.; Lieutenant-Colonel A. D. Callcote.
Seventh Virginia—Colonel W. T. Patton; Lieutenant-Colonel C. C. Flowerree.
Eleventh Virginia—Major Kirkwood Otey.
Twenty-fourth Virginia—Colonel William R. Terry.

* No reports on file for this brigade. Bryan was in command July 7th and was probably Semmes' immediate successor. The commanders of the Tenth, Fifty-first and Fifty-third Georgia are given as reported for June 22d and July 31st. Manning reported in command of Fiftieth Georgia June 22d. No commander reported on return for July 31st.

ARMISTEAD BRIGADE.

Brigadier-General L. A. Armistead; Colonel W. R. Aylett.

Ninth Virginia—Major John C. Owens.
Fourteenth Virginia—Colonel James G. Hodges; Lieutenant-Colonel William White.
Thirty-eighth Virginia—Colonel E. C. Edmonds; Lieutenant-Colonel P. B. Whittle.
Fifty-third Virginia—Colonel W. R. Aylett.
Fifty-seventh Virginia—Colonel John Bowie Magruder.

ARTILLERY.

Major James Dearing.

Fauquier (Va.) Artillery—Captain R. M. Stribbling.
Hampden (Va.) Artillery—Captain W. H. Caskie.
Richmond Fayette Artillery—Captain M. C. Macon.
Virginia Battery—Captain Joseph G. Blount.

HOOD'S DIVISION.

Major-General John B. Hood; Brigadier-General E. M. Law.

LAW'S BRIGADE.

Brigadier-General E. M. Law; Colonel James L. Sheffield.

Fourth Alabama—Lieutenant-Colonel L. H. Scruggs.
Fifteenth Alabama—Colonel William C. Oates; Captain B. A. Hill.
Forty-fourth Alabama—Colonel William F. Perry.
Forty-seventh Alabama—Colonel James W. Jackson; Lieutenant-Colonel M. J. Bulger; Major J. M. Campbell.
Forty-eighth Alabama—Colonel James L. Sheffield; Captain T. J. Eubanks.

ROBERTSON'S BRIGADE.

Brigadier-General J. B. Robertson.

Third Arkansas—Colonel Van H. Manning; Lieutenant-Colonel R. S. Taylor.
First Texas—Lieutenant-Colonel P. A. Work.
Fourth Texas—Colonel J. C. G. Key; Major J. P. Bane.
Fifth Texas — Colonel R. M. Powell; Lieutenant-Colonel K. Bryan; Major J. C. Rogers.

ANDERSON'S BRIGADE.

Brigadier-General George T. Anderson; Lieutenant-Colonel William Luffman.

Seventh Georgia—Colonel W. W. White.
Eighth Georgia—Colonel John R. Towers.
Ninth Georgia—Lieutenant-Colonel John C. Mounger; Major W. M. Jones; Captain George Hillyer.
Eleventh Georgia—Colonel F. H. Little; Lieutenant-Colonel William Luffman; Major Henry D. McDaniel; Captain William H. Mitchell.
Fifty-ninth Georgia—Colonel Jack Brown; Captain M. G. Bass.

BENNING'S BRIGADE.

Brigadier-General Henry L. Benning.

Second Georgia—Lieutenant-Colonel William T. Harris; Major W. S. Shepherd.
Fifteenth Georgia—Colonel D. M. Du Bose.
Seventh Georgia—Colonel W. C. Hodges.
Twentieth Georgia—Colonel John A. Jones; Lieutenant-Colonel J. D. Waddell.

ARTILLERY.

Major M. W. Henry.

Branch (N. C.) Artillery—Captain A. C. Latham.
German (S. C.) Artillery—Captain Wm. K. Bachman.
Palmetto (S. C.) Light Artillery—Captain Hugh R. Gorden.
Rowan (N. C.) Artillery—Captain James Reilly.

ARTILLERY RESERVE.

Colonel J. B. Walton.

ALEXANDER'S BATTALION.

Colonel E. P. Alexander.

Ashland (Va.) Artillery—Captain P. Woolfolk, Jr.; Lieutenant James Woolfolk.
Bedford (Va.) Artillery—Captain T. C. Jordan.
Brooks (S. C.) Artillery—Lieutenant S. C. Gibbert.
Madison (La.) Light Artillery—Captain George V. Moody.
Virginia battery—Captain W. W. Parker.
Virginia battery—Captain O. B. Taylor.

WASHINGTON (LOUISIANA) ARTILLERY.

Major B. F. Eshleman.

First Company—Captain C. W. Squires.
Second Company—Captain J. B. Richardson.
Third Company—Captain M. B. Miller.
Fourth Company—Captain Joe Norcom; Lieutenant H. A. Battles.

SECOND ARMY CORPS.

Lieutenant-General Richard S. Ewell.

ESCORT.

Randolph's company Virginia cavalry—Captain Wm. F. Randolph.

EARLY'S DIVISION.

Major-General Jubal A. Early.

HAYS' BRIGADE.

Brigadier-General Harry T. Hays.

Fifth Louisiana—Major Alexander Hart; Captain T. H. Biscoe.
Sixth Louisiana—Lieutenant-Colonel Joseph Hanlon.
Seventh Louisiana—Colonel D. B. Penn.
Eighth Louisiana—Colonel T. D. Lewis; Lieutenant-Colonel A. de Blanc; Major G. A. Lester.
Ninth Louisiana—Colonel Leroy A. Stafford.

SMITH'S BRIGADE.

Brigadier-General Wm. Smith.

Thirty-first Virginia—Colonel John S. Hoffman.
Forty-ninth Virginia—Lieutenant-Colonel J. Catlett Gibson.
Fifty-second Virginia—Lieutenant-Colonel James H. Skinner.

BRIG.-GEN. L. A. ARMISTEAD, OF VIRGINIA. Killed at the Battle of Gettysburg.

HOKE'S BRIGADE.

Colonel Isaac E. Avery; Colonel A. C. Godwin.

Sixth North Carolina—Major S. McD. Tate.
Twenty-first North Carolina—Colonel W. W. Kirkland.
Fifty-seventh North Carolina—Colonel A. C. Godwin.

GORDON'S BRIGADE.

Brigadier-General J. B. Gordon.

Thirteenth Georgia—Colonel James M. Smith.
Twenty-sixth Georgia—Colonel E. N. Atkinson.
Thirty-first Georgia—Colonel Clement A. Evans.
Thirty-eighth Georgia—Captain William L. McLeod.
Sixtieth Georgia—Captain W. B. Jones.
Sixty-first Georgia—Colonel John H. Lamar.

ARTILLERY.

Lieutenant-Colonel H. P. Jones.

Charlottesville (Va.) Artillery—Captain James McD. Carrington.
Courtney (Va.) Artillery—Captain W. A. Tanner.
Louisiana Guard Artillery—Captain C. A. Green.
Staunton (Va.) Artillery—Captain A. W. Garber.

JOHNSON'S DIVISION.

Major-General Edward Johnson.

STEUART'S BRIGADE.

Brigadier-General George H. Steuart.

First Maryland Battalion Infantry—Lieutenant-Colonel J. R. Herbert; Major W. W. Goldsborough; Captain J. P. Crane.
First North Carolina—Lieutenant-Colonel H. A. Brown.
Third North Carolina—Major W. M. Parsley.
Tenth Virginia—Colonel E. T. H. Warren.
Twenty-third Virginia—Lieutenant-Colonel S. T. Walton.
Thirty-seventh Virginia—Major H. C. Wood.

STONEWALL BRIGADE.

Brigadier-General James A. Walker.

Second Virginia—Colonel J. Q. A. Nadenbousch.
Fourth Virginia—Major William Terry.
Fifth Virginia—Colonel J. H. S. Funk.
Twenty-seventh Virginia—Lieutenant-Colonel D. M. Shriver.
Thirty-third Virginia—Captain J. B. Golladay.

NICHOLLS' BRIGADE.*
Colonel J. M. Williams.

First Louisiana—Captain E. D. Willett.
Second Louisiana—Lieutenant-Colonel R. E. Burke.
Tenth Louisiana—Major T. N. Powell.
Fourteenth Louisiana—Lieutenant-Colonel David Zable.
Fifteenth Louisiana—Major Andrew Brady.

JONES' BRIGADE.
Brigadier-General John M. Jones; Lieutenant-Colonel R. H. Dungan.

Twenty-first Virginia—Captain W. P. Moseley.
Twenty-fifth Virginia—Colonel J. C. Higginbotham; Lieutenant-Colonel J. A. Robinson.
Forty-second Virginia—Lieutenant-Colonel R. W. Withers; Captain S. H. Saunders.
Forty-fourth Virginia—Major N. Cobb; Captain T. R. Buckner.
Forty-eighth Virginia—Lieutenant-Colonel R. H. Dungan; Major Oscar White.
Fiftieth Virginia—Lieutenant-Colonel L. H. N. Salyer.

RODES' DIVISION.
Major-General R. E. Rodes.

DANIEL'S BRIGADE.
Brigadier-General Junius Daniel.

Thirty-second North Carolina—Colonel E. C. Brabble.
Forty-third North Carolina—Colonel T. S. Kenan; Lieutenant-Colonel W. G. Lewis.
Forty-fifth North Carolina—Lieutenant-Colonel S. H. Boyd; Major John R. Winston; Captain A. H. Gallaway; Captain J. A. Hopkins.
Fifty-third North Carolina—Colonel W. A. Owens.
Second North Carolina Battalion—Lieutenant-Colonel H. L. Andrews; Captain Van Brown.

DOLES' BRIGADE.
Brigadier-General George Doles.

Fourth Georgia—Lieutenant-Colonel D. R. E. Winn; Major W. H. Willis.
Twelfth Georgia—Colonel Edward Willis.
Twenty-first Georgia—Colonel John T. Mercer.
Forty-fourth Georgia—Colonel S. P. Lumpkin; Major W. H. Peebles.

IVERSON'S BRIGADE.
Brigadier-General Alfred Iverson.

Fifth North Carolina†—Captain Speight B. J. West; Captain Benjamin Robinson.
Twelfth North Carolina—Lieutenant-Colonel W. S. Davis.
Twentieth North Carolina‡—Lieutenant-Colonel Nelson Slough; Captain Lewis T. Hicks.
Twenty-third North Carolina§—Colonel D. H. Christie; Captain William H. Johnson.

RAMSEUR'S BRIGADE.
Brigadier-General S. D. Ramseur.

Second North Carolina—Major D. W. Hurtt; Captain James T. Scales.
Fourth North Carolina—Colonel Bryan Grimes.
Fourteenth North Carolina—Colonel R. Tyler Bennett; Major Joseph H. Lambeth.
Thirtieth North Carolina—Colonel Francis M. Parker; Major W. W. Sillers.

O'NEAL'S BRIGADE.
Colonel E. A. O'Neal.

Third Alabama—Colonel C. A. Battle.
Fifth Alabama—Colonel J. M. Hall.
Sixth Alabama—Colonel J. N. Lightfoot; Captain M. L. Bowie.
Twelfth Alabama—Colonel S. B. Pickens.
Twenty-sixth Alabama—Lieutenant-Colonel John C. Goodgame.

ARTILLERY.
Lieutenant-Colonel Thomas H. Carter.

Jeff. Davis (Ala.) Artillery—Captain W. J. Reese.
King William (Va.) Artillery—Captain W. P. Carter.
Morris (Va.) Artillery—Captain R. C. M. Page.
Orange Virginia Artillery—Captain C. W. Fry.

ARTILLERY RESERVE.
Colonel J. Thompson Brown.

First (Va.) Artillery—Captain Willis J. Dance.
Second Richmond (Va.) Howitzers—Captain David Watson.
Third Richmond (Va.) Howitzers—Captain B. H. Smith, Jr.
Powhatan (Va.) Artillery—Lieutenant John M. Cunningham.

* The regimental commanders are given as reported for June 14th.
† The four Captains present (West, Robinson, James M. Taylor, Thomas N. Jordan), were reported as wounded July 1st; Robinson and Taylor as having rejoined July 2d, but it does not appear who commanded during Robinson's absence.
‡ Lieutenant-Colonel Slough and Major John S. Brooks reported as wounded at 4 P. M., July 1st.
§ Colonel Christie, Lieutenant-Colonel R. D. Johnson, Major C. C. Blacknall, and the senior Captain (Abner D. Peace), reported as wounded early in the fight, July 1st.

Rockbridge (Va.) Artillery—Captain A. Graham.
Salem (Va.) Artillery—Lieutenant C. B. Griffin.

NELSON'S BATTALION.
Lieutenant-Colonel William Nelson.

Amherst (Va.) Artillery—Captain T. J. Kirkpatrick.
Fluvanna (Va.) Artillery—Captain J. L. Massie.
Georgia battery—Captain John Milledge, Jr.

THIRD ARMY CORPS.
Lieutenant-General Ambrose P. Hill.

ANDERSON'S DIVISION.
Major-General R. H. Anderson.

WILCOX'S BRIGADE.
Brigadier-General Cadmus M. Wilcox.

Eighth Alabama—Lieutenant-Colonel Hilary A. Herbert.
Ninth Alabama—Captain J. H. King.
Tenth Alabama—Colonel William H. Forney; Lieutenant-Colonel James E. Shelley.
Eleventh Alabama—Colonel J. C. C. Sanders; Lieutenant-Colonel George E. Taylor.
Fourteenth Alabama—Colonel L. Pinckard; Lieutenant-Colonel James A. Broome.

WRIGHT'S BRIGADE.
Brigadier-General A. R. Wright; Colonel William Gibson. Brigadier-General A. R. Wright.

Third Georgia—Colonel E. J. Walker.
Twenty-second Georgia—Colonel Joseph Warder; Captain B. C. McCurry.
Forty-eighth Georgia—Colonel William Gibson; Captain M. R. Hall; Colonel William Gibson.
Second Georgia Battalion—Major George W. Ross; Captain Charles J. Moffett.

BRIG.-GEN. WILLIAM BARKSDALE, OF MISSISSIPPI.
Killed at the Battle of Gettysburg.

MAHONE'S BRIGADE.
Brigadier-General William Mahone.

Sixth Virginia—Colonel George T. Rogers.
Twelfth Virginia—Colonel D. A. Weisiger.
Sixteenth Virginia—Colonel Joseph H. Ham.
Forty-first Virginia—Colonel William A. Parham.
Sixty-first Virginia—Colonel V. D. Groner.

PERRY'S BRIGADE.
Colonel David Lang.

Second Florida—Major W. R. Moore.
Fifth Florida—Captain R. N. Gardner.
Eighth Florida—Colonel David Lang.

POSEY'S BRIGADE.
Brigadier-General Carnot Posey.

Twelfth Mississippi—Colonel W. H. Taylor.
Sixteenth Mississippi—Colonel Samuel E. Baker.
Nineteenth Mississippi—Colonel N. H. Harris.
Forty-eighth Mississippi—Colonel Joseph M. Jayne.

ARTILLERY (SUMTER BATTALION).
Major John Lane.

Company A—Captain Hugh M. Ross.
Company B—Captain George M. Pattison.
Company C—Captain John T. Wingfield.

HETH'S DIVISION.
Major-General Henry Heth; Brigadier-General J. J. Pettigrew.

FIRST BRIGADE.
Brigadier-General J. J. Pettigrew; Colonel J. K. Marshall.

Eleventh North Carolina—Colonel Collett Leventhorpe.
Sixteenth North Carolina—Colonel Henry K. Burgwyn, Jr.; Captain H. C. Albright.
Forty-seventh North Carolina—Colonel G. H. Faribault.
Fifty-second North Carolina—Colonel J. K. Marshall; Lieutenant-Colonel Marcus A. Parks.

SECOND BRIGADE.
Colonel J. M. Brockenbrough.

Fortieth Virginia—Captain T. E. Betts; Captain R. B. Davis.
Forty-seventh Virginia—Colonel Robert M. Mayo.
Fifty-fifth Virginia—Colonel W. S. Christian.
Twenty-second Virginia Battalion—Major John S. Bowles.

THIRD BRIGADE.
Brigadier-General James J. Archer; Colonel B. D. Fry; Lieutenant-Colonel S. G. Shepard.

Thirteenth Alabama—Colonel B. D. Fry.
Fifth Alabama Battalion—Major A. S. Van de Graaf.
First Tennessee (Provisional Army)—Major Felix G. Buchanan.
Seventh Tennessee—Lieutenant-Colonel S. G. Shepard.
Fourteenth Tennessee—Captain B. L. Phillips.

FOURTH BRIGADE.
Brigadier-General Joseph R. Davis.

Second Mississippi—Colonel J. M. Stone.
Eleventh Mississippi—Colonel F. M. Green.
Forty-second Mississippi—Colonel H. R. Miller.
Fifty-fifth North Carolina—Colonel J. K. Connally.

ARTILLERY.
Lieutenant-Colonel John J. Garnett.

Donaldsonville (La.) Artillery—Captain V. Maurin.
Huger (Va.) Artillery—Captain Joseph D. Moore.
Lewis (Va.) Artillery—Captain John W. Lewis.
Norfolk Light Artillery Blues—Captain C. R. Grandy.

PENDER'S DIVISION.
Major-General Wm. D. Pender; Brigadier-General James H. Lane; Major-General I. R. Trimble.

FIRST BRIGADE.
Colonel Abner Perrin.

First South Carolina (Provisional Army)—Major C. W. McCreary.
First South Carolina Rifles—Captain Wm. M. Hadden.
Twelfth South Carolina—Colonel John L. Miller.
Thirteenth South Carolina—Lieutenant-Colonel B. T. Brockman.
Fourteenth South Carolina—Lieutenant-Colonel Jos. N. Brown.

SECOND BRIGADE.
Brigadier-General James H. Lane; Colonel C. M. Avery.

Seventh North Carolina—Captain J. McLeod Turner; Captain James G. Harris.
Eighteenth North Carolina—Colonel John D. Barry.
Twenty-eighth North Carolina—Colonel S. D. Lowe; Lieutenant-Colonel W. H. A. Speer.
Thirty-third North Carolina—Colonel C. M. Avery.
Thirty-seventh North Carolina—Colonel W. M. Barbour.

THIRD BRIGADE.
Brigadier-General Edward L. Thomas.

Fourteenth Georgia; Thirty-fifth Georgia; Forty-fifth Georgia; Forty-ninth Georgia, Colonel S. T. Player.

FOURTH BRIGADE.
Brigadier-General A. M. Scales; Lieutenant-Colonel G. T. Gordon; Colonel W. Lee J. Lowrance.

Thirteenth North Carolina—Colonel J. H. Hyman; Lieutenant-Colonel H. A. Rogers.
Sixteenth North Carolina—Colonel L. W. Stowe.
Twenty-second North Carolina—Colonel James Connor.
Thirty-fourth North Carolina—Colonel William Lee J. Lowrance; Lieutenant-Colonel G. T. Gordon.
Thirty-eighth North Carolina—Colonel W. J. Hoke; Lieutenant-Colonel John Ashford.

ARTILLERY.
Major William T. Poague.

Albemarle (Va.) Artillery—Captain James W. Wyatt.
Charlotte (N. C.) Artillery—Captain Joseph Graham.
Madison (Miss.) Light Artillery—Captain George Ward.
Virginia battery—Captain J. V. Brooke.

ARTILLERY RESERVE.
Captain R. Lindsay Walker.

McINTOSH'S BATTALION.
Major D. G. McIntosh.

Danville (Va.) Artillery—Captain R. S. Rice.
Hardaway (Ala.) Artillery—Captain W. B. Hurt.
Second Rockbridge (Va.) Artillery—Lieutenant Samuel Wallace.
Virginia battery—Captain M. Johnson.

PEGRAM'S BATTALION.

Major W. J. Pegram; Captain E. B. Brunson.

Crenshaw (Va.) Battery.

Fredericksburg (Va.) Artillery—Captain E. A. Marye.

Letcher (Va.) Artillery—Captain T. A. Brander.

Pee Dee (S. C.) Artillery—Lieutenant W. E. Zimmerman.

Purcell (Va.) Artillery—Captain Joseph McGraw.

CAVALRY.

STUART'S DIVISION.

Major-General J. E. B. Stuart.

HAMPTON'S BRIGADE.

Brigadier-General Wade Hampton; Colonel L. S. Baker.

First North Carolina, Colonel L. S. Baker; First South Carolina; Second South Carolina; Cobb's (Ga.) Legion; Jeff. Davis' Legion; Phillips' (Ga.) Legion.

ROBERTSON'S BRIGADE.

Brigadier-General Beverly H. Robertson.*

Fourth North Carolina—Colonel D. D. Ferebee.

Fifth North Carolina.

FITZHUGH LEE'S BRIGADE.

Brigadier-General Fitzhugh Lee.

First Maryland Battalion † — Major Harry Gilmor; Major Ridgely Brown.

First Virginia—Colonel James H. Drake.

Second Virginia—Colonel T. T. Munford.

Third Virginia—Colonel Thomas H. Owen.

Fourth Virginia—Colonel Williams C. Wickham.

Fifth Virginia—Colonel T. L. Rosser.

JENKINS' BRIGADE.

Brigadier-General A. G. Jenkins; Colonel M. J. Ferguson.

Fourteenth Virginia.

Sixteenth Virginia.

Seventeenth Virginia.

Thirty-fourth Virginia Battalion—Lieutenant-Colonel V. A. Witcher.

Thirty-sixth Virginia Battalion.

Jackson's (Va.) Battery—Captain Thomas E. Jackson.

JONES' BRIGADE.

Brigadier-General William E. Jones.

Sixth Virginia—Major C. E. Flournoy.

Seventh Virginia—Lieutenant-Colonel Thomas Marshall.

Eleventh Virginia—Colonel L. L. Lomax.

W. H. F. LEE'S BRIGADE.

Colonel J. R. Chambliss, Jr.

Second North Carolina.

Ninth Virginia—Colonel R. L. T. Beale.

Tenth Virginia—Colonel J. Lucius Davis.

Thirteenth Virginia.

STUART HORSE ARTILLERY.

Major R. F. Beckham.

Breathed's (Va.) battery—Captain James Breathed.

Chew's (Va.) battery—Captain R. P. Chew.

Griffin's (Md.) battery—Captain W. H. Griffin.

Hart's (S. C.) battery—Captain J. F. Hart.

McGregor's (Va.) battery—Captain W. M. McGregor.

Moorman's (Va.) battery—Captain M. N. Moorman.

IMBODEN'S COMMAND.

Brigadier-General J. D. Imboden.

Eighteenth Virginia Cavalry — Colonel George W. Imboden.

Sixty-second Virginia Infantry ‡—Colonel George H. Smith.

Virginia Partisan Rangers—Captain John H. McNeill.

Virginia Battery—Captain J. H. McClanahan.

ARTILLERY.§

Brigadier-General W. N. Pendleton.

* Commanded his own and W. E. Jones' brigade.
† Serving with Ewell's corps.
‡ Mounted.
§ See the battalions attached to the Army Corps and Stuart's Division.

CAROLINA — 1865.

BY WILLIAM J. CLARKE.

Pale, fainting from the battlefield,
Carolina leaned on dented shield.
Her broken sword and shivered spear
She laid aside to wipe a tear.
Sob-choked, I heard her feebly say,
"My sons, my sons—oh, where are they?"
The evening breeze, soft whisp'ring, sighed,
"On Freedom's battle ground they died;
Fame's loudest trump shall proudly tell,
How bravely fought—how nobly fell."
Loyal, true-hearted men were they;
They sought no portion in the fray;
But Sunny South they could not see
Bow down to Northern tyranny.

BATTLE OF KELLEYSVILLE, VA.,

MARCH 17, 1863.

BY

BRIG.-GEN. FITZHUGH LEE.

HEADQUARTERS LEE'S CAVALRY BRIGADE,
March 23, 1863.

I HAVE the honor to submit the following report of an encounter on the 17th instant between my brigade and a division of the enemy, certainly not less than three thousand men with a battery of artillery. My first intimation of their approach was a telegram received at 11 A. M., on the 16th, from headquarters A. N. V. At 6 P. M. scouts reported them at Morrissville, a little place six miles from Kelleys Ford. At 1 A. M., another report informed me that the enemy had encamped at that place, coming from three different directions.

I that night re-enforced my picket of twenty sharpshooters by forty more. I regret to say that only about eleven or twelve of them got into the rifle-pits in time for the attack of the enemy (owing to an unnecessary delay in carrying their horses to the rear), which commenced about 5 A. M. The force in the pits, under Captain James Breckenridge, of the Second, behaved very gallantly, holding in check a large force of the enemy, mounted and dismounted, for an hour and a half—killing and wounding thirty or forty of them. I also ordered the remaining sharpshooters of the brigade, under that very efficient officer, Major Morgan, First Virginia, to move from their camps by day-

MAJ.-GEN. FITZHUGH LEE, OF VIRGINIA.

break to a point on the railroad where the road turns to Kelleys, half a mile from the railroad bridge, and three and a half from Kelleys, and the rest of the command was ordered to be in readiness to move at the shortest notice. At that time a force was reported to be at Bealeton, supposed to be their advance guard; and it was uncertain whether they would attempt to cross at Kelleys, railroad bridge, or move on toward Warrenton.

The report that the enemy's attack was made at Kelley's never reached me; and the first intimation I received from that point was at 7:30 A. M., to the effect that they had succeeded in crossing, capturing twenty-five of my sharpshooters, who were unable to reach their horses. I moved my command at once down the railroad, taking up a position to await their approach, ordering my baggage-wagons and disabled horses to the rear toward Rapidan Station. Some time elapsing, and they not advancing, I determined to move upon them, and marched immediately for Kelleys. First met the enemy half a mile this side of the ford, and at once charged them. Their position was a very strong one, sheltered by woods and a long, high stone fence, running perpendicular to my advance. My men, unable to cross the fence and ditch in their front, wheeled about, delivering their fire almost in the faces of the enemy, and reformed again, facing about under a heavy fire from their artillery and small arms. The Third, in this charge, was in front, and First Lieutenant Hill Carter was very conspicuous in his behavior. From that time it was a succession of gallant charges by the various regiments, and once by the whole brigade in line, whenever the enemy would show his mounted men; they invariably falling back upon his artillery and sheltered dismounted skirmishers. Their total advance was two miles from the ford. At that time my artillery arrived, and they were driven back, recrossing the river about 7:30 P. M., with us in close pursuit.

My whole command acted nobly. Sabers were frequently crossed, and fences charged up to, the leading men dismounting and pulling them down, under a heavy fire of canister, grape and carbine balls.

Had I my command in the order it arrived in this enervating section of country, and not weakened by the absence of four squadrons on picket guarding a line stretching from Griffinsburg, on the Sperryville Turnpike, to Richards Ford, and by the large numbers of horses unfit for duty by exposure to the severe winter with a very limited supply of forage, I feel confident that the defeat of the enemy would have been changed into a disorderly rout, and the whole brigade be supplied with horses, saddles and bridles.

Commanding officers of the detachments from the various regiments engaged mention in their reports as deserving especial attention:

In the Fifth, Private William J. Haynes, Company F (badly wounded); Private A. R. Harwood, Company E; Private Henry Wooding, Company C (especially commended, seized the colors when the horse of the color-bearer was shot and carried them bravely through the fight); Sergeants Morecocke and Ratliffe, and Private George James, Company H.

In the Fourth, Captains Newton and Old, Lieutenant Hobson and Adjutant Fontaine (seriously wounded). Sergeant Kimbrough, of Company G, deserves particular notice. Wounded early in the day, he refused to leave the field. In the last charge he was the first to spring to the ground to open the fence. Then, dashing on at the head of the column, he was twice sabered over the head, his arm shattered by a bullet, captured and carried over the river, when he escaped and walked back twelve miles to his camp. Lieutenant-Colonel Payne, commanding, also mentions Privates Joseph Gilman, J. R. Gilman, Poindexter, Redd, Sydnor, Terry and N. Priddy.

In the Third, Captain Collins, Company H; Lieutenant Hill Carter and John Lamb, of Company D; Lieutenant Stamper, of Company F; Lieutenant R. T. Hubbard, Company G; and First Lieutenant Hall, of Company C (was twice wounded before he desisted from the charge, and, when retiring, received a third and still more severe wound, and was unable to leave the field). Adjutant H. B. McClellan is also particularly commended for his bravery; Acting Sergeant-Major E. N. Price, Company K; Private Keech, Company I; and Bugler Drilling. Sergeant Betts, of Company C; Privates Young, Company B, Fowler, Company G, and Wilkins, of Company C, died, as became brave men, in the front of the charge at the head of the column.

In the Second, the commanding officer reports, "where so many behaved themselves with so much gallantry, he does not like to discriminate."

In the First, Captain Jordan, Company C, and Lieutenant Cecil, Company K (specially commended for reckless daring without a parallel).

As coming under my own observation, I particularly noticed Colonel T. L. Rosser, of the Fifth, with his habitual coolness and daring, charging at the head of his regiment.

Colonel James Drake, of the First, always ready at the right time and place; Colonel T. H. Owen, of Third, begging to be allowed to charge again and again; Lieutenant-Colonel W. H. Payne, of the Fourth, unmindful of his former dreadful wound, using his saber with effect in hand-to-hand conflict; and the imperturbable, self-possessed Major Breckinridge, of the Second, whose boldness led him so far that he was captured, his horse being shot. Colonel T. L. Munford, of the Second, I regret to say, was president of a court-martial in Culpeper Courthouse, and did not know of the action in time to join his command until the fight was nearly over. I also commend for their behavior, Captain Tebbs, of the Second, and Captain Litchfield and Lieutenant Dorsey, of the First; also Major W. A. Morgan, of the First.

My personal staff, Major Mason, Captains Ferguson and Bowling, Dr. J. B. Fontaine, and Lieutenants Lee, Ryals and Minnegerode, rendered great service by their accurate and quick transmission of orders, and by their conduct under fire. Surgeon Fontaine's horse was killed under him, and my own was also shot, but, through the generosity of Private John H. Owings, Company K, First Virginia Cavalry, attached to my headquarters, was quickly replaced by his.

The conduct of Couriers Owings, Lee, Nightengale and Henry Shackelford, deserves the highest praise.

The enemy's loss was heavy. Besides leaving a number of his dead and wounded on the field, he carried off a large number on horses and in ambulances.

We captured 29 prisoners—a captain, 2 lieutenants and 26 privates. My own loss was 11 killed, 88 wounded, 34 taken prisoners, making aggregate of 133.

In horses, 71 killed, 87 wounded, 12 captured, making aggregate loss of horses, 170.

Among the killed, I deeply regret to report Major Puller, of the Fifth, and Lieutenant Harris, of the Fourth, both gallant and highly efficient officers—a heavy loss to their regiments and country.

In conclusion, I desire especially to state that Major-General J. E. B. Stuart joined me before the fight commenced; was on the field the whole day, assisted immensely by his sagacious counsels, large experience, and by his usual daring and conspicuous example, in turning the fortunes of the day in our favor. We share with him the anguish and deep grief felt at the loss of the noble Pelham of his staff—an officer of the brightest promise for the future.

Major Terrill, of General Stuart's staff, besides being active on the field, assisted the gallant Breathed in the management of the artillery. Captain Gilmer, Twelfth Virginia cavalry, a volunteer for the occasion on the major-general's staff, I also commend for his marked bravery and cool courage.

I append a recapitulation of my loss.

FITZHUGH LEE,
Brigadier-General Commanding.

LOSS OF BRIGADIER-GENERAL FITZHUGH LEE'S CAVALRY BRIGADE, IN THE ENGAGEMENT NEAR KELLEYSVILLE, MARCH 17, 1863.

RECAPITULATION.	Killed.		Wn'd.		Taken Pris's.			Horses.			
	Officers	Enlisted Men	Officers	Enlisted Men	Officers	Enlisted Men	Aggregate Loss	Killed	Wounded	Taken by Enemy	Aggregate Loss
Field and Staff	1	.	.	.	.	.	1	1	1	.	2
First Regiment Virginia Cavalry	.	1	.	7	.	.	8	7	13	1	21
Second Regment Virginia Cavalry	.	1	2	16	1	14	34	6	20	.	26
Third Regiment Virginia Cavalry	.	4	6	31	.	3	44	26	24	1	51
Fourth Regiment Virginia Cavalry	1	1	1	16	.	16	35	15	16	10	41
Fifth Regiment Virginia Cavalry	1	1	2	7	.	.	11	16	13	.	29
Total	3	8	11	77	1	33	133	71	87	12	170

the other at intervals of about three hundred yards, the foremost one moving slowly, and carrying on her prow the "devil," or torpedo-searcher, a description and drawing of which are appended. When within twenty-two hundred yards Fort Moultrie fired the first gun upon her buoy No. 3, then distant about fifteen hundred yards from Fort Sumter, which had previously trained her battery of barbette guns upon the buoy, and opened fire by battery when she reached that position, at three minutes past 3 o'clock.

The first turret opened fire at five minutes past 3, and moved backward, thus developing their maneuver of attack. At this moment the engagement became general. The second turret passed the first, fired and backed, then retired from the action; the other turrets maneuvering in the same relative manner, each time nearing or receding a little from the fort in order not to present a permanent target.

The Ironsides, when at seventeen hundred yards from Moultrie and two thousand yards from Sumter, stopped, discharged a battery at the former, when Sumter concentrated a heavy fire upon her. Numbers of shot were seen to strike her and several to penetrate, three at least, in her wooden stern. Deeming two thousand yards too close quarters she retired out of range, supposed injured, in favor of less prominent and more formidable imps, after an engagement of forty-five minutes. The Keokuk, at five minutes past 4, defiantly turning her prow directly toward Sumter, firing from her forward turret gun, the batteries of Sumter, Moultrie, Bee and Cummings Point were concentrated upon her; her turrets receiving numbers of well-directed shots, several apparently penetrating, showed evidence of considerable damage. When within nine hundred yards she was struck, supposedly by a wrought-iron bolt, one hundred and seventeen pounds, from a seven-inch Brooke rifle in barbette near her bow, penetrating and ripping up a plating about six feet long and two and

these penetrated the wall of the eastern face just below the embrasures in the second tier next to the east pan coupe, not seriously damaging the masonry; one exploding in the casemate set fire to some bedding; the other passed through a window and burst in the center of the fort. Several exploded in contact with the wall, by which the principal craters appear to have been formed. One passed over the parapet into the quarters on the western side, exploded, damaging several walls. Five 11-inch shot struck the faces; one, penetrating near one of the same embrasures pierced by the 15-inch shell, broke through and stuck into the interior wall of the quarters. Only one impression represented any appearance of a rifle projectile. One 15-inch solid shot, one 15-inch hollow shot, several 15-inch shells and 11-inch shot were found in and around the fort. Fragments of 15-inch shells were picked up on the outside. The berme being very narrow and sloping prevented any means of ascertaining by the bodies themselves their kind, all being precipitated into the water after striking. It is reported, also, that several shrapnel were fired over the barbette guns of Sumter. Some of the shells which exploded in contact with the wall may probably have been percussion rifle shells, as some of the turrets are known to carry 8-inch rifles, but no fragments were found, nor do any of the officers report indications of rifle projectiles, by sound or otherwise, with but one exception. The commanding officer of Battery Wagner reports one by sound to have passed over, fired by the Ironsides. Nine shots were fired at Moultrie at distances—of turrets, thirteen hundred yards; of Ironsides, seventeen hundred yards. An 11-inch shot struck down the flag-staff at 3:37, passed through the roof of the quarters, penetrated the wall of the ordnance store-house, about two feet thick, and dropped in the room; another struck the glacis and ricochetted over the fort; a third, a 15-inch shell, burst at the water's edge, a fragment of which was found; the

The French Steam Sloop Milan. Castle Pinckney. The English Gunboat Petrel. Fort Moultrie. Fort Ripley. Fort Sumter. Fort Johnson.

ENTRANCE TO CHARLESTON HARBOR, WITH ITS DEFENSES, JANUARY, 1863.

ENGAGEMENT IN CHARLESTON HARBOR, S. C.,

APRIL 7, 1863.

BY

MAJOR WILLIAM H. ECHOLS,
Confederate States Engineer.

CONFEDERATE STATES ENGINEER'S OFFICE.
CHARLESTON, S. C., April 9, 1863.

I HAVE the honor to make the following report of the engagement between Fort Sumter and the enemy's ironclad fleet on the 7th of April, 1863, at 3 o'clock P. M., lasting two hours and twenty-five minutes.

The incidents which transpired during the engagement are based upon information received from the officers in charge of the works, but more particularly from the observations of Colonel Rhett, commanding Fort Sumter, and Lieutenant S. C. Boyleston, Adjutant First Regiment South Carolina Artillery, who made special observations during the whole action; the remainder from personal inspection afterward.

Forts Sumter, Moultrie, Batteries Bee, Beauregard, Cummings Point and Wagner were engaged. The fleet consisted of the Ironsides, supposed armament sixteen guns; the Keokuk, two stationary turrets carrying one gun each, and seven single revolving turreted vessels carrying, supposed, two guns each, presumed to be the Montauk, Passaic, Weehawken, Patapsco, Nahant, Catskill and Nantucket, which took position from nine to fifteen hundred yards from Fort Sumter.

They steamed up main ship channel toward Fort Moultrie in line of battle as follows: Four single turrets, Ironsides, three single turrets and Keokuk, following one after

one-half wide, which ended her career. She stopped, seemed disabled for a few minutes, then turned to the channel, and proceeded toward the bar at 3:15. She sank off the south end of Morris Island at 8:30 o'clock the following morning. Her smoke-stack and turrets are now visible at low water. From her wreck floated ashore a book, a spy-glass and pieces of furniture, bespattered with blood, and small fragments of iron sticking in them.

The firing of the turrets was timed. They discharged generally at intervals of ten minutes. The engagement lasted two hours and twenty-five minutes. Allowing six of them constantly engaged, they delivered eighty-seven shots; one fired twice and retired; the Keokuk fired three or four times and the Ironsides about seventeen, making the total number fired by the enemy about one hundred and ten, which were principally directed at Sumter. Her walls show the effect of fifty-five missiles—shot, shell and fragments. The carriage of a 10-inch columbiad on western face was completely demolished by a shot coming over the parapet; a 42-pounder rifle on northeast face dismounted by breaking a traverse-wheel; both soon remounted in position; four small holes knocked in the roof of the eastern quarters by grazing shots; an 8-inch columbiad burst on the eastern face, throwing the chassis and half the re-enforce over the parapet, the other half over the quarters in the parade, demolished the carriage, but did no other damage; nearly all the window-panes and some of the sashes in the fort were broken by concussion.

The accompanying table of effects of shot and sketches of the elevations of the faces show the points of impact, the kind of projectile used, so far as could be ascertained by inspection and found; they were principally 15-inch shells and 11-inch shot. The nature of the material against which they were projected crumbling, generally, without retaining an impression, precludes any positive information as to their exact kind or caliber; only a few were evident. To the best of my judgment, according to the effect, eight 15-inch shells struck the faces; two of

others passed over. Five shots were fired at Battery Bee, without effect, at a distance of about two thousand yards; one fell behind the breakwater; another passed along the front of the battery and burst; the others passed over. Six or seven were fired at Battery Beauregard, at a distance of two thousand yards, without effect; two 11-inch shot were found. Two were fired at Cummings Point without effect; one at twelve or thirteen hundred yards, from Ironsides; the other at fourteen to fifteen hundred yards, from a turret. Four were fired at Battery Wagner; one from Ironsides sounded like a rifle shot passing through the air; one grazed top of traverse; another exploded over the battery, sending a fragment into a traverse.

A single turret, which fired her two guns simultaneously, ceased to fire one of them at about 4 o'clock, half of the port being closed the remainder of the action; cause not visible. They were frequently struck upon their decks, and several shot were seen sticking in the hull of one of them, and from another steam issued when struck upon it. A cast-iron bolt rifle 42, struck a leveled plate or guard around the base of a turret, which curved and turned one end up. The projectiles generally broke in pieces, as could be seen by fragments falling in the water or bounded from the vessel. One, after striking, was observed to drop and rest at the foot of the turret. Several of the smoke-stacks were penetrated.

A lookout appeared on top of one of the turrets, apparently observing the effect of the shot; at the flash of a battery from Moultrie he instantly disappeared.

The casualties are slight. At Sumter five men were wounded by fragments of masonry and wood. One of the negroes engaged at work at the fort, who was sitting on the berme of the western face, was wounded by a brick knocked from the parapet and falling upon his head. At Moultrie, one man was killed by the falling of the flag-staff when shot away.

At Battery Wagner an ammunition chest in the angle

of the parapet and traverse in the chamber of the 32-pounder exploded from the blast of the gun, killing three men, mortally wounding one, slightly wounding Lieutenant Steedman, in charge of the gun, and three men; blew them about twenty feet, cracked the traverses, threw the shot from the pile of balls in every direction and slightly damaged the chassis.

I arrived at Fort Sumter about 2 o'clock at night, after the engagement, and found Mr. E. J. White, of the Engineer Department, busily engaged building in the casemates, first and second tiers, behind the damaged walls, with sand-bags; several of these were completed and considerably strengthened. This work was continued all night and the next day by the garrison and the fifty negroes who had been employed at the fort and remained during the engagement. On the following morning the fleet lay inside the bar in the same line of battle in which they approached, the first one about two and one-half miles from Sumter and one and one-half miles from Morris Island. Men were visible all day on the turret of one, hammering, evidently repairing her plating. Wind-sails were set, indicating that their quarters, even at this season of the year, were uncomfortable and badly ventilated. About noon one of the turrets went south, probably to Port Royal for repairs, or for the security of that place against our iron-clads from Savannah.

The Ironsides has kept up a full head of steam since the engagement, as can be seen by her constantly blowing off. Three holes are distinctly seen in her stern; two just above the water line. The "devil" floated ashore on Morris Island; the cables by which it was attached to the turret's bow were cut away. It is probable that the "devil," becoming unmanageable, was the cause of the turret retiring early from the action, it being a massive structure, consisting of two layers of white pine timbers eighteen inches square, strongly bolted together; a re-entering angle twenty feet deep to receive the bow of the vessel, fifty feet long, twenty-seven feet wide, a layer of beveled timbers in the front, forming a bow; seven heavy iron plates, through which passed chains directly down and over the sides through hawser-pipes; to these were attached grappling irons, with double prongs, suspended underneath, at the sides and bow; in the countersinks of the plates were loose iron rollers, apparently to facilitate the drawing of the chains through the holes over them when the grapplings took hold, to drag up to the "devil" whatever he may catch with his hooks.

The colors of the six turrets remaining on the 8th were as follows:

First turret, lead color; stack lead color; top of stack red with black ring.

Second turret and stack, black.

Third turret, black; stack white; top green.

Fourth turret, black; stack black; top stack one-third lead color.

Fifth turret and stack, lead color.

Sixth turret and stack, black.

The hull of the turret in running trim stands about two feet above water level, carrying a whistle, stovepipe and stanchions for swinging a small boat on deck, with a light railing around it. When closed for action she is submerged almost to the water level; the other articles all removed flush with the deck. The issue of steam from the deck several times observed, if not from injury, is probably from the blow-off pipe, taken down flush, as she can not carry it, as other vessels, on her side.

I accompany the report with a sketch of the battle-ground, showing the relative positions of the forts, gun-boats, monitors and other vessels composing the fleet; one of the faces of the fort, showing parts damaged; one of the Keokuk; one of a turret, submerged for action, and one of the "devil."

* * * * * * *

WILLIAM H. ECHOLS,
Major of Engineers.

[INCLOSURE NO. 5.]

TABLE OF EFFECTS OF PROJECTILES ON WALL OF FORT SUMTER.

Number.	Projectile.	Penetration.		Crater.				Remarks.
				Height.		Width.		
		Feet.	Inches.	Feet.	Inches.	Feet.	Inches.	
1			2					Scaled.
2	Fragment of shell		6					Scaled.
3		2	3	4		4		Embrasure A; exterior concrete keystone and interior embrasure arch knocked out; masonry cracked.
4	15-inch		9	3		4		Assisted No. 3; spent.
5	11-inch	1		1		1		Penetrated concrete and new masonry facing.
6	15-inch		33					Ricochet and spent.
7	Fragment of shell							Scaled.
8		1		2		2		Apparently rifle shot; no serious injury.
9	Three shots	2	6	10		8		One 15-inch, other two not known; parapet wall cracked twenty-five feet in length; serious damage, perhaps by exploding shell.
10	15-inch	2	3	6		4		Interior arch of embrasure B dislocated; masonry between piers and embrasure badly shaken and projecting.
11	Fragment of shell							Scaled.
12	15-inch	1	6	3		3		Shook masonry.
13, 14	Fragment of shell							Scaled.
15		1	6	3		3		Interior embrasure C; arch broken; masonry cracked.
16		2	2	3		3		Perhaps exploding shell.
17	15-inch		15					Scaled; spent ball.
18		1	6	3		3		Masonry shaken.
19		3		5		5		Exploding shell on pier; not much injured,
20		1	6	3		3		No serious injury.
21		1	6	4		3		Masonry around embrasure D badly cracked and projecting inside.
22	15-inch	5		4		3		Penetrated, striking head of arch and thrown upward, tearing away a quantity of masonry, not seriously damaging body of masonry; exploded in casemate.
23	11-inch	5		2		2		Same effect as 22; destroyed embrasure E.
24		2	6	3	6	3	6	Not seriously damaging body of masonry.
25	15-inch	5		4		4		Same effect as 22; destroyed embrasure F; exploded in parade.
26	11-inch							Scaled; ricochet and spent.
27		1	4	2	3	2		No serious damage.
28		1						No serious damage.
29		2	4	5		3		Serious damage; wall not much cracked..
30								Scaled.
31	15-inch	1		3		4		Knocked off one foot of angle.
32	11-inch		6	2	6	2		Knocked off six inches of angle.
33			5	3		2		Oblique fire; scaled.
34	Fragment of shell							Scaled.
35		1	6	2	6	2		Shook masonry.
36	15-inch	1	3	3		4		Broke and projected in sole of embrasure G.
37			10	2		3		Very oblique fire; no damage.
38	Fragment of shell		4	2		2		Very oblique fire; no damage.
39			2	4		4		Very oblique fire; no damage.
40		1		2		4		Very oblique fire; no damage.
41		2	1	3		3		Exploding shell.
42			10	1	6	1	6	Oblique; scaled.
43		1	2	2		2		No serious injury.
44								
45	Fragment of shell							Scaled.
46								
47	11-inch							Scaled; very oblique.
48		2	4	5		5		Exploding shell; cracked parapet wall.
49								Knocked out iron embrasure slab one foot wide, six inches thick, three feet long; indented it one and a-half inches and broke it in three pieces; shook masonry
50		1	5	3		3	6	No serious injury.
51	11-inch	2	6	5		7		Brick traverse; east pan coupe.
52	15-inch							Entered western quarters and exploded, damaging wall.
53	11-inch							Entered western quarters and remained in quarters.
54								Demolished ten-inch columbiad carriage and chassis in southwest angle.
55								Struck end stone masonry berme southeast angle; four small holes knocked in brick arch roof of eastern quarters by grazing shots or fragments from traverse.

[INCLOSURE NO. 6.]

TABLE SHOWING THE NUMBER, KIND AND POSITION OF GUNS IN ACTION, AND NUMBER AND KIND OF PROJECTILES USED AGAINST THE IRON-CLAD FLEET BEFORE CHARLESTON, APRIL 7, 1863.

Location.	Number.	Kind of Gun.	Projectile.	Shots.
Fort Sumter; 810 shots east and northeast faces; barbette	2	7-inch Brooke rifles	Wrought-iron bolts	86
	4	10-inch columbiads	Solid shot	120
	4	8-inch columbiads	Solid shot	160
	5	42-pounder rifles	Shot and bolts	138
	2	9-inch Dahlgrens	Shot	54
	3	10-inch sea-coast mortars	Shells filled with melted iron	40
First tier casemate	2	8-inch shell guns (navy)	Shot	60
	2	8-inch guns (navy)	Shot	50
	8	32-pounders	Shot	100
Second tier casemate	1	42-pounder rifle	Shot	2
Fort Moultrie; 868 shots	9	8-inch columbiads	Shot and fire incendiary shells	344
	5	32-pounder rifles	192 bolts; 38 shells	230
	5	32-pounder	Shot	243
	2	10-inch sea-coast mortars	Shells	51
Battery Bee, 283 shots	5	10-inch columbiads	Shot	225
	1	8-inch columbiads	Shot	58
Battery Beauregard; 157 shots		8-inch columbiads	Shot	64
	1	32-pounder rifle	41 bolts (75 pound); 45 shots	
	2		Seven shells	93
Cummings Point; 65 shots	1	10-inch columbiad	Shot	37
	1	9-inch Dahlgren	Shells	28
Battery Wagner; 26 shots	1	32-pounder rifle	Shells	9
	1	24-pounder rifle	Shells	1
	2	32-pounders	Shot	16

Number of Guns, 69. Total number of shots fired, 2,208.

WILLIAM H. ECHOLS, *Major of Engineers.*

CHARLESTON, S. C., AS VIEWED FROM FORT JOHNSON, FEBRUARY, 1863.
[From a sketch made by an artist representing the *London News*.]

CHARLESTON HARBOR.

ASSAULT ON FORT WAGNER; OPERATIONS ON MORRIS ISLAND, ETC.,

JULY 8 TO 22, 1863.

BY

BRIGADIER-GENERAL R. S. RIPLEY,
General Commanding.

HEADQUARTERS FIRST MILITARY DISTRICT,
CHARLESTON, S. C., July 22, 1863.

I HAVE the honor to submit the following report of the daily occurrences of my command, commencing on the 8th instant, on which day the enemy's iron-clad fleet appeared off the bar, and his force of transports at sea and in the Stono River was largely increased, indicating the renewal of the attack on the approaches of the city of Charleston.

With the limited force at my command, such measures as could be taken to guard the salient points of attack (the south end of Morris Island and James Island) were ordered, and directions given for the dispositions of troops ordered by the commanding general for re-enforcements.

On the 9th, the enemy landed a strong force on Battery Island, and unmasked works on Little Folly bearing upon our positions at the south end of Morris. The works at that point were, from various causes, incomplete, and from want of transportation the arrival of re-enforcements was tardy. Endeavors were made to strengthen our position on Morris Island, but, from lack of force, no great improvement was accomplished.

On the morning of the 10th the enemy opened a heavy fire upon our positions from Little Folly with from twenty to thirty long-range guns, which he had placed in battery during the night. Soon after, four monitors took position to the northeast of the position, enfilading it, and taking some of the batteries in reverse.

Our troops defending were composed of the Twenty-first South Carolina Volunteers, under Colonel R. F. Graham; two companies [I and E] of the First South Carolina Artillery, under Captains J. C. Mitchel and J. R. Macbeth, and a detachment of the First South Carolina [Regulars] Infantry [Third Artillery], under Captain Charles T. Haskell, Jr. (in all about seven hundred), with the following artillery placed in position in detached batteries along the shore to command the beach and the crossing from Little Folly, viz.: Three 8-inch navy shell guns, two 8-inch sea-coast howitzers, one rifled 24-pounder, one 30-pounder Parrott, one 12-pounder, Whitworth, and three 10-inch sea-coast mortars—in all, eleven pieces. There were on Morris Island, besides, two companies of artillery under Captains [C. E.] Chichester and [John R.] Mathewes, the garrison of Battery Wagner, and one at Battery Gregg under Captain [Henry R.] Lesesne; all the artillery under Lieutenant-Colonel Joseph A. Yates, First South Carolina Artillery.

After about three hours' furious shelling from the enemy, to which our guns steadily replied, a large number of barges filled with troops came up Little Folly River, and, under cover of their fire, succeeded in effecting a landing on Oyster Point and the main shore of Morris Island. The enemy advanced immediately, driving back our inferior force of infantry, and succeeded in expelling our troops from the south end of Morris Island and capturing the artillery above named, with its munitions. This was not effected without a severe struggle, in which we lost two hundred and ninety-four in killed, wounded and missing, among whom I mention with especial regret the following officers: Captains [Langdon] Cheves and Haskell and Lieutenant [J. S.] Bee, who had rendered important service previous to, and behaved with distinguished gallantry in, the engagement. The first re-enforcements (Nelson's Seventh Battalion, South Carolina Volunteers) arrived at the close of the action and could only assist in covering the retreat, which was made under the flank fire of the monitors, to Battery Wagner, where our troops were formed to resist further advance, and the guns of which opened on the pursuing enemy. Fort Sumter and Battery Gregg also opened fire and put a stop to their proceedings for the day.

In the evening, Battery Wagner was re-enforced by Colonel [C. H.] Olmstead's command of Georgia troops* and the garrison kept on the alert for defending it against an attack. This occurred at dawn on the 11th, when the enemy advanced upon the work in two columns and made a desperate assault, which was gallantly and decidedly repulsed, with a loss to the enemy which may safely be estimated at over eight hundred men. Our burying parties interred over one hundred inside of our lines, and one hundred and thirty were taken prisoners.

Our loss was one officer and five privates killed, and one officer and five privates wounded.

The enemy on land remained comparatively quiet during the day, being engaged burying his dead and strengthening his position. Three monitors and three wooden gunboats engaged and bombarded the fort.

On the 12th Brigadier-General Hagood took command of the positions on James Island. Brigadier-General Taliaferro was assigned [July 13th] to the command of the works on Morris Island. The armament of the fort was increased by four 12-pounder howitzers, under Captain [W. L.] De Pass and Lieutenant [T. D.] Waties, and two 32-pounder carronades on siege-carriages. The enemy's shot took effect on the steam scow Manigault, lying at a partially constructed battery at Vincents Creek, disabling the scow and scattering the workmen. Battery Wagner was shelled by the enemy's fleet continuously during the day. One monitor took a position to the northward, apparently to enfilade the rear of the work. Lieutenant-Colonel Yates ordered Battery Gregg to open rapidly, which it did, driving the monitor off, apparently severely injured, as she transferred her crew at once to one of the gunboats.

On the 13th, under the able supervision of Brigadier-General Taliaferro, continued preparations were made against a renewed attack. The Twenty-first South Carolina Volunteers and two companies of the First South Carolina Artillery were relieved by the Fifty-first North Carolina and a detachment of Georgia artillery, under Captain [James T.] Buckner. The land operations of the enemy consisted in erecting batteries and protections, in which they were interrupted by the fire from Fort Sumter and Battery Gregg. The gunboats and monitors kept up a continued shelling throughout the day with but slight intermission, when they had suffered from the fire of the sea fronts of Wagner and Gregg. In the evening the enemy succeeded in setting fire to the wreck of the steam scow Manigault, in Vincents Creek.

On the 14th two regiments, under Brigadier-General A. H. Colquitt, arrived, which were sent to James Island to re-enforce Brigadier-General Hagood's command. Brigadier-General Clingman's command, consisting of the Eighth, Twenty-first, Fifty-first and Sixty-first North Carolina regiments, had arrived the previous day, and, with the exception of the Fifty-first, were stationed on James Island. The enemy's wooden gunboats shelled Battery Wagner during the day at long range. During the night Brigadier-General Taliaferro threw out a party, one hundred and fifty strong, under Major [James H.] Rion, of the Seventh South Carolina Battalion, which drove in the enemy's pickets from his rifle-pits, extending across the island about three-quarters of a mile from Battery Wagner, back upon his main supports, inflicting a considerable loss, with but small loss upon our part.

On the 15th the enemy landed troops in force on Morris Island, and there were indications of a renewal of the assault on the fort. The frigate Ironsides had crossed the bar on the night of the 14th. During the day the enemy was strengthening his positions, our troops being engaged in repairing damages, replying to the enemy's monitors and gunboats and replying to the enemy's sharpshooters. The Charleston Battalion, under Lieutenant-Colonel P. C. Gaillard, relieved the Seventh Battalion, and three companies of the Twentieth Regiment South Carolina Volunteers, Lieutenant-Colonel J. C. Simpkins, First South Carolina [Regular] Infantry [Third Artillery], relieved Lieutenant-Colonel J. A. Yates in command of the artillery on Morris Island; Captain [Warren] Adams' company of First South Carolina [Regular] Infantry [Company H, Third Artillery] relieving Captain Chichester's company of artillery. Brigadier-General Hagood made a reconnoissance of the enemy in his front on James Island.

ATTACK BY THE FEDERAL IRONCLADS ON THE HARBOR DEFENSES OF CHARLESTON, S. C., AT 3 P. M., APRIL 7, 1863.
[From a sketch made at the time by an artist representing the *London News*.]

On the morning of the 16th, in accordance with instructions, Brigadier-General Hagood advanced against the enemy from his headquarters near Secessionville, James Island, driving in the enemy's pickets on his left, and making an advance against that portion of their force. Two columns made the attack—one led by Brigadier-General A. H. Colquitt, and the other by Brigadier-General Hagood in person. The enemy was protected by the fire of his gunboats in Stono and Little Folly rivers. Brigadier-General Hagood succeeded in driving the enemy (about two thousand in number) from James Island, and inflicting upon him a serious loss in killed and wounded, capturing fourteen negroes belonging to the Fifty-fourth Massachusetts Regiment. Not the least important of these operations was the engagement with the sloop-of-war Pawnee by two sections of Napoleon guns under command of Lieutenant-Colonel Del Kemper, in which the steamer was injured and forced to retire. General Hagood's loss was three killed, twelve wounded and three missing. The enemy withdrew entirely from James Island to Battery Island, where General Hagood advanced his pickets, and the ground has been held to the present date, July 22d. At Battery Wagner and on Morris Island our troops continued their works of repair, subject to a continued shelling from gunboats and monitors at long range.

On the 17th the enemy's vessels all disappeared from the Stono, and his troops were concentrated on Little Folly and Morris Islands. Firing from the enemy's fleet and land batteries was kept up during the day on Battery Wagner, which interfered seriously with the transportation to Cummings Point. This has had ever since to be carried on at night. On the night of the 17th the Thirty-first North Carolina Regiment relieved Colonel Olmstead's command of Georgia troops and Captain [J. A.] Cowan's company of the Twentieth South Carolina Volunteers.

The work of repairs and preparation was proceeded with

* First Volunteers, Georgia, and Twelfth and Eighteenth Georgia Battalions.

during the night, and at daylight on the 18th the enemy's land and sea batteries opened a *feu d'enfer* upon the devoted work. The practice was rapid in the extreme from the Ironsides, from the monitors and from all the wooden gunboats which, without exposing themselves, could get the range. According to Brigadier-General Taliaferro's estimate, over nine thousand shot and shell were thrown; but, as if by the special interposition of Providence, our loss was slight. Indications of an assault at dusk were apparent, and the guns of Sumter and Battery Gregg were in preparation to open fire over Battery Wagner on the columns of the enemy. Brigadier-General Hagood was relieved from the command of James Island, to be in readiness to support or relieve Brigadier-General Taliaferro, and Colonel [George P.] Harrison's [Jr.] Thirty-second Regiment of Georgians proceeded to the re-enforcement and relief of the garrison. While in passage the assault commenced, which was bravely met and repulsed, with terrific slaughter on the part of the enemy, by the heroic garrison and its commander, Brigadier-General Taliaferro, who directed all the operations until the final repulse.

In his report, the details of the assault and its repulse are set forth, and I can not do more or better than to second his commendations of those brave officers and men who stood the tempest of shot and shell, and sent back the columns of the enemy from their works with a loss which may safely be computed at about three thousand in killed, wounded and prisoners. Brigadier-General Hagood, with Colonel Harrison's regiment, assisted in the final repulse of a party who had made a lodgment in the southeastern salient of the battery.

The carnage of the enemy in the confined space in front of Battery Wagner was extreme. The ditch and glacis were encumbered with the slain of all ranks and colors, for the enemy had put the poor negroes, whom they had forced into an unnatural service, in front, to be, as they were, slaughtered indiscriminately. The white colonel who commanded them fell with many officers of the regiment (the Fifty-fourth Massachusetts), and the colors under which they were sent to butchery by hypocrisy and inhumanity, fell, draggled in blood and sand in the ditch, a mournful memorial of the waste of industry.

This result was not accomplished without a loss on our part of brave officers and men; though of those who in this struggle battled for the right, the proportion who fell was far less than that of their enemy. In this engagement our loss in killed, wounded and missing was one hundred and seventy-four. Among the officers whose loss we have to lament and whose position and services entitle them to especial mention, were Lieutenant-Colonel J. C. Simkins, of the First South Carolina [Regular] Infantry; Captain William H. Ryan, Charleston Battalion; Captain W. T. Tatom, First South Carolina [Regular] Infantry, who were killed, and Major David Ramsay, of the Charleston Battalion, who was severely wounded. Other gallant officers and soldiers fell, whose names are mentioned in the reports of their several commanders, and whose memories should be cherished by a grateful country.

While the assault on Battery Wagner was progressing, Battery Gregg, under Captain Lesesne, and the batteries of Fort Sumter, under Colonel Alfred Rhett, kept up a continuous fire upon the ground over which the enemy advanced until Brigadier-General Taliaferro advanced his pickets to the front, when they ceased, and the narrow field of battle was quiet for the night. Brigadier-General Taliaferro, who had been in command and on trench duty for five days, was relieved in the morning by Brigadier-General Hagood.

This report, ending with the second repulse of the enemy from Battery Wagner, will be continued from that time. The operations of the enemy from that date, within the limits of my command, have changed their character.

In closing it I have the honor to express my high appreciation of the distinguished services of Brigadier-General Taliaferro, who commanded the troops in Battery Wagner with great ability and gallantry, and repulsed the memorable assault of the 18th, and of the excellent conduct of Brigadier-Generals Hagood and Colquitt, as evinced in the attack on the enemy's position on the 16th. Besides these, Colonel Graham, Twenty-first South Carolina Volunteers; Colonels Olmstead and Harrison, of the Georgia Volunteers; Lieutenant-Colonel P. C. Gaillard, Charleston Battalion; Lieutenant-Colonel Yates, Captain J. C. Mitchel, Captain Lesesne, First South Carolina Artillery; Captains Chichester, Mathewes, Buckner, [W. J.] Dixon and De Pass; Lieutenant-Colonel [D. B.] Harris, Captains [W. M.] Ramsey and [R. H.] Barnwell, engineers, deserve special consideration for their gallant and valuable services.

The signal corps, under Lieutenant [F.] Markoe, Jr., have been actively employed, and that officer has reported Sergeant J. E. Edgerton and Privates W. S. Lance, E. H. Martin, W. D. DuBarry, A. Grimball and F. K. Huger for their zeal and gallantry in performing their duties under the heavy and continuous fire of the enemy.

During this period of anxiety and activity, the officers serving upon the district staff have performed their duties in such manner as to enable me to rely with confidence upon their further exertions during the continuance of the contest. I feel it proper to refer with special commendation to Captain William F. Nance, assistant adjutant general, whom I have more than once recommended for promotion, and whose services become steadily more valuable as they become more arduous.

FEDERAL IRONCLAD KEOKUK AS SHE APPEARED ON THE MORNING AFTER THE FIGHT, APRIL 8, 1863.

I have also to express my satisfaction with the manner in which their respective and laborious duties have been discharged by Majors Motte A. Pringle and C. H. Suber, quartermasters, and Captain C. C. Pinckney, ordnance officer. Captain B. H. Read, assistant adjutant-general, and Lieutenant [J. M.] Schnierle, acting aid-de-camp, were present and actively engaged in the operations of the 16th. Lieutenants [H. H.] Rogers and [W. H.] Wagner, aids-de-camp, have been continuously employed.

I have to acknowledge the services of Major J. Motte Middleton and Captain Thomas D. Eason, upon my personal staff.

* * * * * *

R. S. RIPLEY,
Brigadier-General Commanding.

HEADQUARTERS FIRST MILITARY DISTRICT,
CHARLESTON, August 1, 1863.

Since my report of the 22d [ultimo], detailing the operations in this command up to the 20th, inclusive, the plan of the enemy, as I then stated, seems to have been changed.

BRIG.-GEN. ROSWELL S. RIPLEY, OF SOUTH CAROLINA.

There has been no attempt at a further assault upon our works upon Morris Island. From the 21st to the 24th there has been occasional firing both from the enemy's fleet and land batteries; but his time has been chiefly occupied in the erection and completion of three new batteries on that portion of the island in his possession, thus advancing his lines as far as could be done with safety.

On the 21st the enemy sent in, by flag of truce, a communication from General Gillmore, with a request that the officer commanding Battery Wagner would give to General [Israel] Vogdes, who accompanied it, a personal interview. While Captain [Carlos] Tracy, the staff officer of General Hagood, then in command, was bearing the message brought by the flag, both the fleet and the land batteries reopened their fire, and General Hagood very properly refused to received any communication until an apology had been made for this violation of the flag. A satisfactory explanation having been offered and accepted, an interview was had between General Hagood and General Vogdes, which terminated in an arrangement to exchange the wounded prisoners on both sides, and 10 o'clock on the following Friday appointed as the hour when the transports from each party should effect the exchange at the point from which the fleet have usually conducted the attack upon Battery Wagner.

On the morning of the 25th, the day upon which the exchange was to be effected, the enemy opened fire about daylight, both from the fleet and land batteries. This fire was vigorously sustained until the arival, about 10 o'clock, of the flag-of-truce boat conveying the prisoners, and for a portion of that time was equal in intensity to the bombardment of the 18th. Upon the arrival of the boat in the neighborhood of the place appointed, the firing ceased and the exchange was regularly effected, we delivering one hundred and five and receiving thirty-nine wounded prisoners. No reference having been made in the agreement to the negro prisoners of the Fifty-fourth Massachusetts Regiment, none of them were included in the exchange, a report of which (by Colonel [E. C.] Anderson and Major [J. M.] Middleton, the officers appointed to conduct it) has already been furnished.

The fire of the enemy on this morning, especially from one of the more advanced land batteries, armed with Parrott guns, did serious damage to Battery Wagner. The remaining 10-inch columbiad was dismounted from the sea face of the battery and the magazines so much exposed that it became necessary to remove the ammunition, and General Taliaferro (who had previously relieved General Hagood in the command), anticipating a renewal of the bombardment upon the completion of the exchange of prisoners, requested, as a matter of prudent precaution, that all necessary arrangements should be made for the transfer of the troops from the island in case of necessity. The exchange of prisoners was completed about 2 o'clock, when the flag-of-truce boat returned. The enemy, however, did not renew his attack, and the time thus allowed was improved to the utmost in repairing the damage which had been done.

The condition of the battery, as reported by General Taliaferro, was submitted to the general commanding, and, after full deliberation, it was determined to hold it, and instructions sent to General Taliaferro not to abandon the works without express orders to that effect.

From that date to the present, the bombardment has never been renewed, although there has been occasional and brief fire upon the battery from the iron-clads. In the meantime, the battery has been thoroughly repaired and placed in a condition even superior to what it was in the beginning. The enemy, meanwhile, are busily at work in improving their present works and erecting new ones, of which our means of observation do not enable me to give a detailed account. On our side, new batteries have been erected, and the work of completing them and mounting the necessary armament actively pressed, and every effort made to annoy the enemy by such batteries as bear upon their working parties and lines, an attempt in which, I have reason to think, we have been to a considerable extent successful. The condition of the new batteries is known to the commanding general and will be mentioned in the succeeding report. The garrisons at Batteries Wagner and Gregg have been relieved as regularly as possible with our means of transportation.

On the 22d Brigadier-General Taliaferro relieved Brigadier-General Hagood. On the 26th [25th] Brigadier-

General Colquitt relieved Brigadier-General Taliaferro. Brigadier-General Colquitt was relieved on the 28th by Brigadier-General Clingman, and the last was relieved on August 1st by Colonel L. M. Keitt.

The fire from the land batteries of the enemy upon Batteries Wagner and Gregg has been annoying, especially upon our communication by steamer between Fort Sumter and Cummings Point.

The casualties which have occurred from July 20th to 31st, inclusive, have been thirteen killed and forty-nine wounded.

* * * * * * *

R. S. RIPLEY,
Brigadier-General Commanding.

BOMBARDMENT OF FORT SUMTER,

AUGUST 12 TO SEPTEMBER 4, 1863.*

BY

COLONEL ALFRED RHETT, S. C. A.,
Commanding Fort Sumter.

AUGUST 12th.—The steamer Hibben was this morning disabled at the wharf by a 200-pounder Parrott shell. Seven negroes were injured, three more or less seriously.

The oven in bakery has been rendered useless, and about one-half bushel of bricks thrown from arch beneath.

Three shells exploded in western barracks, injuring no one.

The commissary stores have been removed to the three casemates on northeast angle.

Mortar firing was kept up during the entire night. The following ammunition was expended: Thirty-eight 10-inch mortar shells. One 8-inch columbiad was dismounted during the night from east face, to be sent to James Island. One 10-inch columbiad was shifted from next to 11-inch Dahlgren to near center of battery on east face.

The center traverse on east face is now being built. The other traverse will be built to-day. Seventeen 200-pounder Parrott shots and shells struck the fort during the entire day, six outside and eleven inside. Two men were wounded—Corporal [James A.] Phillips, Company F, and Private [Patrick] Norton, Company E. They have been sent to the city. One 32-pounder rifle carriage was disabled and gun struck on muzzle; not supposed to be injured. Two traverse circles on western face have been destroyed. A clear breach of three feet has been made in northwest angle by a single 200-pounder shot. One wounded negro died. The wood piles on southern side of fort have been removed to the pits, and curtains will be constructed to protect the men from fragments of bricks.

AUGUST 13th.—The enemy fired three shots, all striking outside, one injuring parapet on gorge face.

The engineer work on the outside of gorge face has to be stopped during the day on account of the enemy's shells.

Mortar firing was kept up during the entire night. The following ammunition was expended: Twenty-eight 10-inch mortar shells. One 8-inch columbiad carriage and chassis is ready for shipment. The 32-pounder rifle gun which was struck was found to be cracked, and was dismounted. The one to the right of it was shifted in its place. Four gunboats came up during the day and threw several shots at this fort. One came in, bursting beneath the platform of one of the mortars, temporarily disabling it. Ten shots struck the fort during the day, injuring no one. The greatest penetration, four feet.

AUGUST 14th.—Two shots struck the fort this morning. A schooner loaded with sand dragged her anchor during the night, and was wrecked near the northeast face of fort. Two men on board were saved. One of the shots this morning carried away the top of flagstaff near southeast angle of fort.

A force of 470 laborers and mechanics has been engaged, in two reliefs, day and night, upon the defenses of the fort. Two sand-bag traverses on east face have been completed and the arches of western magazine covered over. The crib work on east face is being taken away to construct blindages for shelter under gorge wall on interior of fort. During the night 3,000 sand-bags were received, and 2,500 were built up on exterior of gorge.

The fort was struck five times from land batteries and once from shell from gunboats.

AUGUST 15th.—Mortar firing from both mortars in the parade was kept up during the entire night; thirty-seven 10-inch mortar shells were fired. The 10-inch columbiad was mounted during the night on salient. One 10-inch mortar and bed, and one 8-inch columbiad carriage and chassis are ready for shipment.

AUGUST 16th.—Mortar firing was kept up during the entire night from 8 P. M. The following ammunition was expended: Thirty-four 10-inch mortar shells.

Forty-eight shots and shells were fired at this fort during the afternoon; 4 passed over, 4 or 5 fell short, 10 struck inside, and the remainder outside. The pintle of one 24-pounder was loosened by shot striking outside; one shot passed through parapet above terre-plein, and the parapet also received another bulging shot. One man, Company K, slightly wounded.

AUGUST 17th.—The enemy opened fire upon us at 5 A. M. Nine o'clock, 159 shots and shells have struck outside; 68 shots and shells have struck [inside]; 83 shots and shells have passed over or fell short.

One 32-pounder rifle gun has had its trunnion shot away. The upright to carriage of 10-inch columbiad on salient angle has been shot away. The inside of the fort buildings has been much torn. The damage to outside has not yet been ascertained. The firing is still going on.

At 5 A. M. the enemy opened from land batteries on Morris Island with seven guns, five 200-pounder Parrotts and two lighter guns. Fire was opened at the same time upon Battery Wagner and Battery Gregg, the Ironsides and monitors participating in the attack on those batteries at 6 A. M. At 10:45 A. M. the Ironsides and two monitors moved up and commenced fire upon the fort. At 11:15 A. M. we opened upon the iron-clads and continued fire until 1:30 P. M., when the enemy withdrew and our fire was stopped. The following number of rounds were expended, viz.: Sixty-four.

From 5 A. M., August 17th, to 5 A. M., August 18th, 948 shots and shells have been fired; 445 struck outside, 233 inside, and 270 passed over. The firing during the day was very rapid; during the night, one shot in fifteen minutes. The engineer will make report as regards injury done the fort.

Our 32-pounder rifle had trunnion shot away. On northwest face two 10-inch columbiads, one 9-inch Dahlgren, one 8-inch columbiad, and two 42-pounders were disabled. The two 42-pounders were taken from parapet to parade during the night, to be shipped.

All the wounded enlisted men† have been sent to the city.

AUGUST 17th, 11 P. M.—Nine hundred and nineteen shots have been fired; 455 struck outside, 218 inside, and 266 passed over. Casualties: Barringer, Company K,

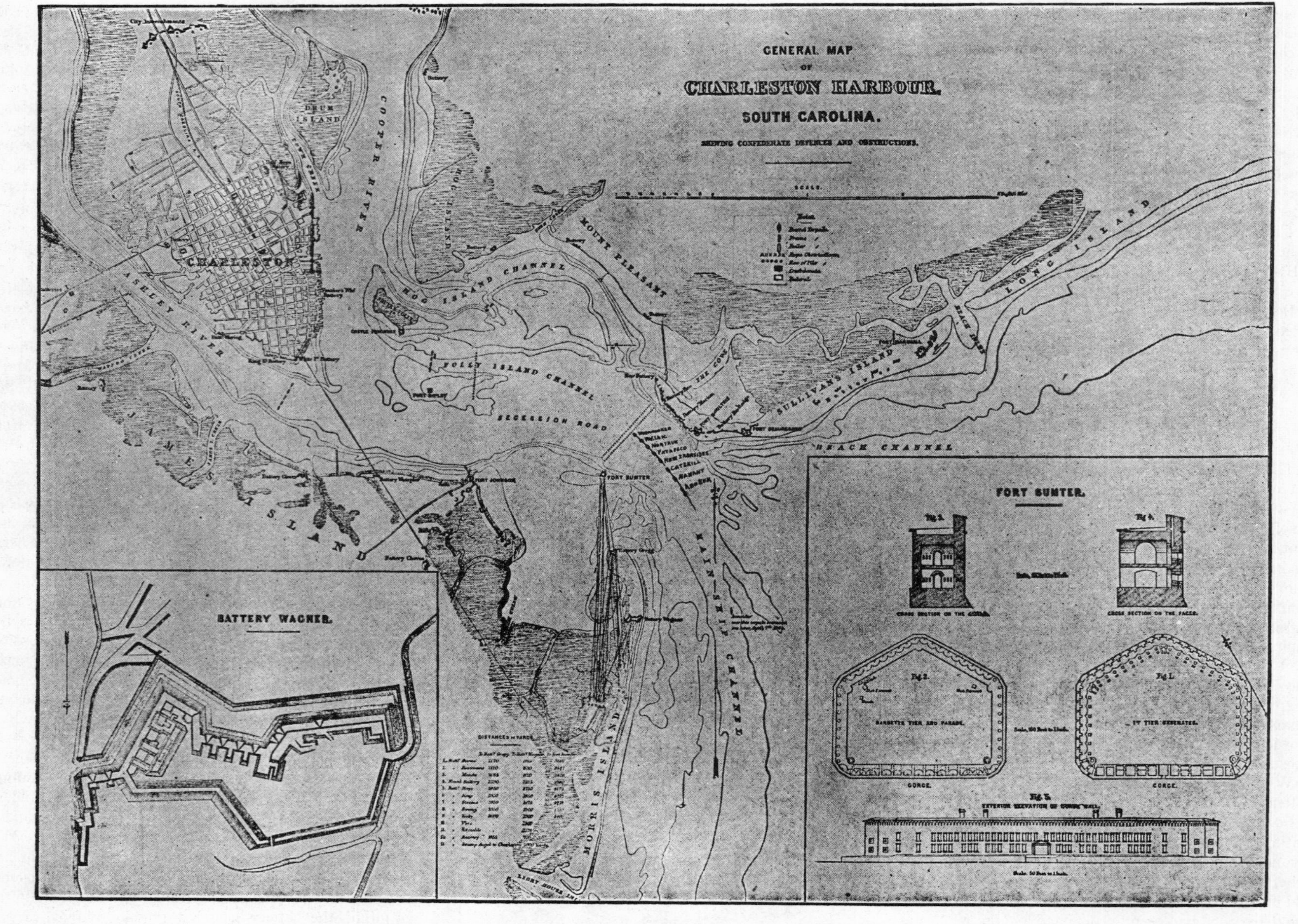

* Being extracts from the daily dispatches from that officer and from the "Journal of the Defense of Fort Sumter," which was kept under Special Orders No. 141, Department Headquarters, of July 17, 1863. The journal is not found among the Confederate archives, but the extracts here given are those forwarded from day to day by the post commandant to district and department headquarters, and thus preserved. The extracts for August 13th and 14th were transmitted by Major Ormsby Blanding, all others by Colonel Rhett.

† Nominal list of casualties reports Private Barringer, Company K, First South Carolina Artillery, killed, and 3 officers and 14 men wounded.

killed; Lieutenants Rhett, John Middleton, and John Johnson, engineer, slightly wounded; Corporal [Patrick] Charles, Company C, severely wounded; Quartermaster Sergeant [William] Nicol, four fingers cut from left hand; and twelve privates slightly wounded. The enemy are still firing once in fifteen minutes to prevent working. All the guns on northwest face have been disabled, excepting one 8-inch columbiad and one 42-pounder, including the big 10-inch columbiad.

AUGUST 18th, 10:15 A. M. (telegram).—It is impossible to get out a gun to-day. The sally-port and the way to it covered with rubbish, and shells continually bursting near. Two 42-pounders were taken off parapet last night, but could not be got out on the wharf.

AUGUST 18th (journal).—No firing took place from this fort. The enemy opened fire with rapidity at 5 A. M. and continued till 7 P. M. Eight hundred and seventy-six shots and shells were fired; 452 struck outside, 244 inside, and 180 passed over. All the guns on gorge face have been disabled but one rifled 32-pounder and one 24-pounder. Both guns on west face disabled. All the guns on northwest face unserviceable. The two 10-inch columbiads, right of flag-staff, disabled. The Brooke gun on southeast angle had its carriage shattered, but was remounted during the night.

The garrison flag was twice cut away. The sand-bag revetment to western magazine was raised two feet higher during the night; three shot-holes higher up were filled; the whole of lower magazine thus defended. Floors of both upper magazines covered with four feet of sand.

AUGUST 19th.—An attempt was made last night to get one of the disabled 10-inch columbiads ready for shipment, but it was found to be impossible.

The enemy opened fire again this morning at 4:30 o'clock, and up to the present time, 9:10 A. M., 245 shots and shells have been fired; 140 struck outside, 77 inside, and 28 passed over.

Casualties: Private [William] Fink, Company K, killed; Private [Jacob] Probst, Company K, severely wounded twice; Private [Z.] Holmes, Company K, slightly wounded; Private [Edward] Hatcher, Company K, slightly wounded; Corporal [C. P.] Barnett, Company C, slightly wounded. All gorge guns useless.

AUGUST 19th, 9:50 A. M. (telegram).—We need all the garrison we have to hold the fort, and are short of officers. The firing this morning is the heaviest yet, and the walls are seriously damaged. One killed and four wounded this morning. All gorge guns useless. Middleton went to town last night.

AUGUST 19th, 10:50.—The first shot has passed through the gorge [wall], coming out of the room on the right of the adjutant's office. The room is known as General Ripley's room (10:20 o'clock). Shot struck close under the arch where there is little sand.

AUGUST 19th, 12:10 P. M. (telegram).—The width of twenty feet of the gorge wall has fallen, and two-thirds will probably be down to-morrow, and light is showing through three or four of the casemates of gorge wall. One mortar dismounted and bed torn and broken. Seven casemates, west face, are shattered; three piers shot away, and three more shattered on second tier. The same for first tier. A good part of terre-plein has fallen in. One killed and four wounded.

Seven hundred and sixty-three shots to-day; 398 struck outside, 236 inside, and 129 over.

AUGUST 19th (journal).—Three fires occurred during the day. These fires were promptly extinguished by the officer of the day, ably and gallantly assisted by Sergeant [Theodore] Schaeffer, Company H, acting provost-sergeant of the garrison, who went among the ruins repeatedly, directly in line of fire from the enemy, and put out the fires.

AUGUST 19th (journal).—The Ironsides moved up, and we opened at long range upon her from a few guns; four shots were fired. The fire of the enemy slackened during the heat of the day, and again increased in rapidity toward the afternoon till 7 o'clock, when the fire for the night was reduced to one shot in thirty minutes. Seven hundred and eighty shots and shells were fired; 408 struck outside, 241 inside, and 131 over.

APPEARANCE OF THE GORGE WALL OF FORT SUMTER, AUGUST 21, 1863.

About one-half of gorge wall has fallen, exposing the arches and sand in rooms, the sand-bag traversing protecting the lower rooms to west of the old sally-ports. A large part of the remaining gorge wall will fall shortly. Three of the casemates were opened through sand.

On northwest face seven casemates in the upper and lower tier are badly shattered, several of them being clean breaches. Almost every one of the piers sustaining the terre-plein are badly shattered. Part of the terre-plein has already fallen in, and more is continually going. The 10-inch mortar in parade is dismounted and bed broken and shattered. Two of the rooms on east side of sally-port on gorge face have been repacked and rammed with sand. The hospital has been traversed and the revetment to western magazine raised higher.

Gorge Wall. APPEARANCE OF FORT SUMTER ON SUNDAY AFTERNOON, AUGUST 23, 1863. Sea Face

AUGUST 20th.—The enemy opened a heavy fire at 5 A. M., and is still keeping it up. Up to this time, 9 A. M., 244 shots have been made; 136 outside, 69 inside, and 39 over. The double-banded rifled 42-pounder, east face, has been disabled.

Twenty-five thousand pounds powder, 275 32-pounder shells, 200 Brooke bolts, 25 11-inch shells, one set of wheels, axles, etc., were shipped during the night, but no guns can be removed. No casualties.

AUGUST 20th (journal).—The enemy kept up a heavy and continuous fire during the whole day, but increasing perceptibly toward the afternoon; 879 shots and shells were fired; 408 struck outside, 296 inside, and 175 passed over. At 12:15 P. M. the flag was shot away. The greater part of the gorge wall has fallen, the debris from the upper revetting in a manner the lower floors. The northwest terre-plein has to a great degree fallen in, and the wall has several clean breaches, one whole casemate being knocked through. One 42-pounder rifle gun, northeast battery, has been disabled.

The enemy ceased firing at 7:15 A. M. Captain Gaillard was slightly wounded, and Captain Fleming struck, though not hurt. Private [James] Connelly, Company K, slightly wounded.

Some large holes opened through northwest Scarp wall by reverse firing to-day. Six upper and three lower embrasures shattered. One opening eight by ten feet. East scarp wall damage very slight. Southeast pan coupe battered under traverse, and one-half parapet in its front fallen. Eastern magazine re-enforce stone work, damage slight; now covered by rubbish from upper part, which is half gone; same way rubbish from upper rooms has covered the lower. Worst effect to-day is demolishing some seven feet of arch and rampart for length of thirty feet along eastern half of gorge. The western magazine is safe as yet.

AUGUST 20th, 12:40 P. M. (telegram)—The fire this morning has been exceedingly heavy, more destructive than it has ever been. Our flag has just been shot away and replaced.

AUGUST 20th, 9:30 P. M. (telegram).—The fire this afternoon was the heaviest that has taken place. Eight hundred and seventy-nine shots were fired to-day; 408 outside, 296 inside, 175 over. The gorge face has been much battered, and the quarter [greater] portion of it has fallen. The lower rooms, however, are in a manner revetted by the debris from the upper. The northwest wall has been breached clearly in seven places, and one casemate second door [floor] is entirely knocked through. Large portions of terre-plein have fallen. The rifled 42-pounder, Captain Fleming's battery, and the left rifled 42-pounder, Captain Harleston's battery, have been disabled. Captain Harleston is slightly wounded, though painfully, by a shell. Captain Fleming was struck, though not hurt, by a shell. Private Connelly, Company K, slightly wounded.

AUGUST 21st.—The enemy opened at 5 A. M. a heavy enfilading fire on east battery.

One heavy 10-inch columbiad, east face, and one rifled 42-pounder, northeast face, disabled.

The flag-staff is disabled, and the flag twice shot away.

A shot came into the adjutant's office, knocking the desks to pieces, but the papers have been saved.

A 75-pounder Whitworth shot has been found in the fort.

The following ordnance stores were shipped: 11-inch shell, 10-inch shell, 10-inch shot, 42-pounder shell, 32-pounder shell, cartridges, bags, sponges and staves, rammers, scoops, worms, scrapers, handspikes and nine hundred pounds of powder.

All the powder in the east magazine taken out, and wall found to be cracked in west corner.

Gorge Wall (northwest face seen above). Sea Face (northeast face seen above).
APPEARANCE OF FORT SUMTER ON TUESDAY AFTERNOON, NOVEMBER 10, 1863.

Commissary stores, one hundred and twenty barrels of pork and seventy-five barrels of flour.

Hospital traverse completed. Strengthened revetment to western magazine. Threw over traverse from gorge wall. Started traverse in rear of three-gun battery. Packed four rooms east of gorge with sand.

AUGUST 21st, 7:40 A. M. (telegram).—The enemy are enfilading our east face this morning. One heavy 10-inch and a rifled 32-pounder, in Harleston's battery, are disabled. I expect both batteries will go to-day.

AUGUST 21st, 10:55 A. M. (telegram).—The fire of the enemy is very heavy on the east battery, and, should the fleet come up, I do not think the men could stay at the guns. Our flag has been twice shot away this morning.

AUGUST 21st, 11:45 A. M. (telegram).—We have now only nine effective guns in barbette, and the probabilities are that this afternoon most of them will be disabled.

AUGUST 21st, 8:45 P. M. (telegram).—The firing ceased at 7 P. M. It has been very heavy all day. Since 5 A. M. 923 shots were fired; 445 struck outside, 259 inside, 219 passed over. The eastern face has been pretty well battered.

northeast face, in good condition· east barracks badly damaged.

At 6:30 P. M. five 11-inch shots were fired at the Ironsides.

Handspikes, elevating bars, sponges, rammers, worms, scrapers, friction-tubes, blocks, set of eccentric axles, etc., for columbiad; eight sets of traversing gear, and 9,700 pounds of powder were shipped; also twelve bags of sugar.

Captain Gaillard's company (K) was sent to Sullivan's Island. Casualties [nominal list omitted]: One man dangerously, four slightly, wounded; two negroes, severely.

AUGUST 22d.—The enemy opened at 6 o'clock. Up to 9 A. M. 266 shots have been fired; 76 struck outside, 85 inside, 105 over. Casualties one man wounded.

AUGUST 22d (journal).—During the entire day 604 shots and shells were fired at this fort; 203 struck outside, 216 inside, 185 missed. All the barbette guns have been disabled, with the exception of the 11-inch Dahlgren and a 10-inch columbiad, east face. The east parapet has been much shattered and undermined; east front much scaled

magazine during the night; 15,000 pounds of powder kept in western magazine and ready for shipment; fifty Brooke bolts, fifty 10-inch solid shots, fifty 10-inch shells, twenty rifle shells, twenty loaded shells, ammunition chests, rammers, sponges, etc., ready for shipment.

The flag-staff was shot away twice. The whole garrison worked all night.

Henry Davis, Company C, died on the way to the city; Henry Osteen, Company D, slightly wounded, head; Lieutenant Boyleston, adjutant, severely wounded, back; Lieutenant Fickling, severely wounded, leg; Lieutenant Scanlan, ordnance officer, slightly wounded, arm; two negroes severely wounded, head; one negro slightly wounded, head.

AUGUST 24th (journal).—The entire day, 150 shots and shells were fired at this post; 112 struck outside, 14 inside, and 24 missed. I consider only one gun, 11-inch Dahlgren, east face, as serviceable in action.

Firing to-day at intervals of half hour, and with some light and one heavy 10-inch Parrott guns. During the night, working parties employed filling with sand-bags

INTERIOR OF FORT SUMTER, DECEMBER 5, 1863, AFTER A CONTINUOUS BOMBARDMENT BY THE FEDERAL BATTERIES ON MORRIS ISLAND.
[From a sketch made on the spot by an artist representing the *London News*.]

One 10-inch columbiad and one 8-inch columbiad, east face, and two rifled 42-pounders, northeast face, were disabled. Seven serviceable guns are now on the parapet.

Private Thos. Powers, Company B, wounded severely; leg amputated above knee; Privates H. Robertson and William Dumphries, Company F, slightly; Corporal [Henry] O'Neil and Private [Thomas] Goggins, Company K, slightly; two negroes—Daniel, slave of Mr. Purvis, and Isaac, slave of Mr. Marmins—dangerously wounded.

Flag-staff shot down four times.

AUGUST 21st (journal).—A heavy and continuous fire was kept up during the entire day. The following number of shots and shells were fired, viz., 943; 465 struck outside, 259 inside, 219 passed over.

One 10-inch columbiad and one 8-inch columbiad, east face, and two 42-pounders, rifled, were disabled. The flag-staff was shattered and the flag was four times shot away. The fire ceased at 7 P. M.

Traverses on east face have been repaired and rebuilt; traverse over 42-pounder rifle gun built up four feet.

East front, scarp wall, deep penetrations on the level of the second tier of casemates; worst displacement under traverses. Upper part of re-enforce to west magazine gone, and one crater in old wall. The demolition of gorge rampart increased. West magazine re-enforce, no increased damage. Northwest scarp wall penetrated at seven upper and five lower casemates; breaches eight by ten and six by eight through two of them. Stairway at salient demolished; only two traverse circles of barbette battery,

by slant fire; large craters under traverses; principal injury at level of arches and terre-plein; magazine safe; one man slightly wounded.

AUGUST 23d, 2:30 P. M. (telegram).—While at dinner-table a shell burst just above our mess-room, parts of the shell coming through on the dinner-table and throwing down brick. Lieutenant Boyleston was seriously bruised; Lieutenant Scanlan, slightly, in the arm; Captain Fleming, bruised; Lieutenant Fickling, slightly hurt; myself, slightly hurt.

AUGUST 23d (journal)—Two hundred 8-inch shell were shipped.

Monitors engaged fort 3:15 A. M. to 5:30 A. M., firing on line east of pan coupe and western magazine; time fuse and rifle shell. One sent particle of shell into ordnance store; one threw sand from below into magazine passage. No material damage done to magazine.

Two 15-inch shells made breaches in east parapet. Number of shots and shells fired by monitors, 27 outside, 15 inside, 17 missed.

Private [Henry] Davis, Company C, severely, two negroes slightly, wounded. The entire day, 633 shots and shells were fired at this post; 282 struck outside, 210 inside, 141 missed.

All the barbette guns have been disabled, with the exception of the 11-inch Dahlgren gun, east face. Scaling effect on east face and southeast pan coupe very great. East parapet very much shattered. All the guns in three-gun battery, second tier of casemates, disabled; east magazine safe. Eleven thousand pounds of powder removed to east

four penetrations at lower embrasure on southeast pan coupe and east scarp; also adding to security of west magazine, and repairing traverses on east barbette. Eleven thousand pounds of powder removed from east to west magazine during the night. During the day, Colonel Gilmer, chief of engineers, and Colonel Harris, chief engineer of the department, visited this post officially, and also General Ripley after dark.

AUGUST 25th (journal).—The entire day, 175 shots and shells were fired at this post; 62 struck outside, 36 inside, 77 missed. The fire to-day more destructive inside than out. East scarp more scaled and cut up, but without any decided breach. Interior damage on northeast casemates, upper and lower; but two of them more or less damaged by fire in reverse, cutting away pieces, chipping arches, and damaging terre-plein.

One shell penetrated gorge ramparts over the east magazine and exploded, sending smoke above this crack in filling of terre-plein, and below this probably cracked arch of passage between inner and outer doors of upper magazine. In magazine proper, no smoke at all was found. The east magazines are without any damage. The stone work of re-enforce is intact. The shock of the 10-inch Parrott shells is very great

Twelve thousand pounds of powder, five boxes portfire, 7,200 priming-tubes, one box paper fuses assorted, fifty Brooke bolts, fifty 10-inch solid shot, fifty 10-inch shells, twenty rifle shells, about fifty damaged muskets, sponges, rammers and iron handspikes shipped on steamer Spaulding.

Companies C and F left this post last night on steamer Spaulding, to proceed to Fort Johnson for duty, with Lieutenant-Colonel Yates. They were replaced by 150 men of the two reserve regiments of Colquitt's brigade, under command of Captain G. W. Warthen.

Nearly the whole garrison at work the entire night. No casualties.

AUGUST 26th (journal).—The entire day, 130 shots and shells were fired at this post; 45 struck outside, 45 inside and 40 missed.

Fire to-day slack and inexact; damage not very perceptible. Most of the holes stopped on the outside last night are undisturbed, and but one or two new ones made on east scarp. Southeast pan coupe and east magazine received most of to-day's outside shots. The upper courses of east solid angle of stone re-enforce to east magazine a little displaced by fire to-day. This angle never yet has been protected by falling rubbish, excepting for two-thirds of its height, some ten feet.

FORT SUMTER. REPULSE OF A NIGHT ATTACK ON THE FORT.
[From an old print.]

Unloaded steamer Etiwan of bags of sand.

A large quantity of 10-inch mortar shells were shipped during the night on steamer Etiwan.

No casualties to-day. Embrasures to casemates in process of being bricked up.

AUGUST 27th (journal).—Only four shots were fired during the day, evidently at the flag; all went over. Consequently no increase of damage to works.

Working parties finished heavy traverse over 42-pounder rifle gun, east barbette battery; repaired others on same. Discharged steamer Etiwan, bringing five hundred bags of sand from Sullivan's Island.

About four hundred 10-inch shots and shells, one parapet gun, one lot sabots, tin straps, brass fuses, blocks, one box bridge sights, six boxes 9-inch Dahlgren shells, one 9-inch Dahlgren gun; one lot of axles, wheels, etc., for columbiad carriage; one lot elevating screws, were shipped at 4:30 A. M. by steamer Etiwan.

The 9-inch Dahlgren gun, mentioned above, and 10-inch columbiads on northwest pan coupe thrown over the parapet during the night, by Mr. J. Fraser Mathewes.

AUGUST 28th (journal).—The entire day 6 shots were fired; 3 struck outside; 3 missed.

No increase of damage to works. Working parties during the night completeted traverse on parade at entrance to magazine and hospital, southwest angle; also repairs and improvement to east barbette battery.

By steamer Etiwan were shipped the following ordnance stores: four hundred 10-inch mortar shells, fifteen hundred paper fuses, one box tops of brass fuses, plugs, three damaged muskets, two elevating screws, six boxes mortar fuses, eighteen 8-inch columbiad incendiary shells, three 9-inch Dahlgren shells prepared, three hundred pounds lead, one 10-inch columbiad gun, one sponge, eight boxes canister, one box of implements, fuse extractors, etc., fragments of gin legs; one box of fuse plugs.

AUGUST 29th (journal).—There was no firing to-day; Company D left for Charleston, and a detachment of the Twenty-seventh Georgia Volunteers, fifty men, under command of Captain [H.] Bussey, arrived here. There are ready for shipment four hundred 10-inch shells (mortar), ammunition chests, wheels, etc. One Brooke gun and one 42-pounder rifle were thrown over the ramparts. Brooke gun shipped last night. Garrison worked all day.

AUGUST 30th.—Firing commenced at 5 A. M., very rapidly.

Casualties: Sergeant Schaeffer, Company H; Private [Hugh] Luguire, Company B, First South Carolina Artillery; Private [S.] Van, Company A, Twenty-seventh Georgia, slightly wounded.

An hour was lost by separating and sending away sixty-one hands; present force, one hundred and ten.

AUGUST 30th (journal).—The entire day, 634 shots and shells were fired at this post; 322 struck outside, 168 inside, 144 missed.

About four hundred 10-inch mortar shells, two hundred 42-pounder rifled bolts, twenty 11-inch shells and shots, a lot of wheels, elevating-screw beds, elevating screws, trunnion plates, one barrel brass, two barrels of lead, twenty-seven pass boxes, one box of sabots, one barrel of tow, two sets of traversing gears and segments, were shipped by steamer Etiwan. Garrison worked a part of the night.

Casualties: Privates A. E. Woolright and F. Ward, Company C, Twenty-eighth Georgia, wounded.

Damage at Fort Sumter most apparent inside. On east barbette battery two 10-inch columbiads, serviceable up to to-day, had carriages broken; one 10-inch columbiad muzzle shot off and dismounted. Parapet all shaky and partially demolished; traverses badly cut up. Three arches, with ramparts, on northeast front, cut away and tumbled in, burying some commissary stores; east scarp, near southeast pan coupe, has large blocks knocked away from face of second-tier casemates arch, exposing segment of arch and displacing sand filling.

Two 10-inch columbiads thrown over ramparts.

[AUGUST 31st.]—At 2:30 A. M. Fort Moultrie opened fire on steamer Sumter, loaded with two regiments relieved from duty at Morris Island, by mistake.

Fort Sumter and navy gunboats sent forth with barges to aid, and saved about six hundred officers and men belonging to the Twentieth Regiment South Carolina Volunteers and Twenty-third Regiment Georgia Volunteers.

Steamer Sumter was disabled and a large hole knocked in her side, and is reported going to pieces.

No report yet of the killed and missing from the steamer Sumter.

AUGUST 31st (journal).—The entire day, 56 shots and shells were fired at this post; 34 struck outside, 5 inside, and 17 missed.

About two hundred and seventy-five rifled bolts, thirty-two 42-pounder and twenty 11-inch shells and shots, one box tallow, one large box brass, one carriage, one pass box, shell implements, one box priming wires, sundries, etc., one hundred and fifty grape, were shipped by steamer Etiwan.

The Twentieth Regiment South Carolina Volunteers, Twenty-third Regiment Georgia Volunteers, and Captain Mathewes' company of artillery, left for Sullivans Island on steamer Chesterfield at 8 P. M. About one hundred incendiary shots were shipped to Sullivans Island.

No casualties.

SEPTEMBER 1st (journal)—The entire day, 382 shots and shells were fired at this post; 166 struck outside, 95 inside, 121 missed.

At 11:40 P. M. six monitors and the Ironsides moved up and commenced shelling the fort; 185 shots were fired till 5 A. M.; 116 struck outside, 35 inside, 34 over.

One box powder-measures and gunners' haversacks, one box locks and covers to 8-inch navy gun, one pass box with dredge boxes, etc., one set of wrenches, ten iron and iron-shod handspikes, one traversing wheel, four budge-barrels, two sets of traversing gear, one 10-inch columbiad bed for screw (one 32-pounder rifled gun, shipped August 31st), two cap-squares, sponges and rammers, one city fire-engine and hose, ammunition chests, ten 7-inch rifled bolts, one hundred and ten 8-inch shots and shells, seventy-five 42-pounder conical shot, fifteen 8-inch columbiad shell, thirty 10-inch columbiad shell, loaded and damaged, were shipped by steamer Etiwan.

One 8-inch gun was thrown over parapet and shipped as monitors came in, and party stopped at 10 P. M., after only one hour's work. Damage very great by day and night fire.

On northeast face the entire terre-plein has fallen in, except east of the two walls next and northeast of the pan coupe. Two shells burst in commissary's store. Scarp in front of three upper casemates at southeast pan coupe shot away; lower scarp somewhat protected by rubbish; east scarp is much cut up, but has not yet fallen in masses large enough to uncover any whole arch or casemate.

Since monitor fire last night, every casemate, upper and lower, has been more or less breached, in most of them exposing sand-bags.

Three shells exploded in immediate proximity to west magazine, two entering into second tier, outer magazine passage, sending blast down stairway into lower outer magazine passage, the outer door being closed at the time. Had the door been open the most serious consequences would have ensued. The third struck and brought up in the sand-bag traverses at parade end of passage into hospital and magazine; it would otherwise have gone into hospital passage used for guard room.

Casualties: Slightly wounded, Privates [R. B.] Foshee, Company 3 (Colonel Rhett's orderly); [William] Brown, Company C, and [F.] Alexander, Company H, Twenty-seventh Georgia Volunteers.

SULLIVANS ISLAND. FORT MOULTRIE, 1864.
[From a photograph owned by the family of the late General G. T. Beauregard.]

SEPTEMBER 2d (journal).—The entire day, 38 shots and shells were fired at this post; 12 struck outside, 9 inside, and 17 missed.

About eleven thousand pounds of powder, two boxes rockets, one box damaged musket cartridges, rammers and sponges were shipped last night by steamer Etiwan.

No material damage was done. It was discovered that one shot had penetrated the scarp-wall, opening daylight into the magazine in southeastern pan coupe.

Lieutenant John Johnson, engineer officer, was relieved from duty at this post, in consequence of the aggravated condition of his wound, and Lieutenant Hall reported for duty as engineer officer in his stead. Mr. William Mathewes was also sent down to assist the latter.

SEPTEMBER 4th.—There is now not a single gun in barbette, and there is but one smooth-bore 32-pounder next the sally-port on western face that can be fired.

Mr. J. F. Mathewes, assisted by an officer and men of the C. S. Navy, have done good service in removing disabled guns from the fort, having dismounted and removed one 10-inch gun and one 9-inch Dahlgren. He has also removed from the berme of the fort the Brooke gun, another 10-inch, an 8-inch and one 32-pounder rifled gun. Lieutenant Rhett, with company B, has dismounted the Brooke gun, two 10-inch, one 8-inch, one 42-pounder rifled, the 11-inch and one 32-pounder rifle gun in the last few nights.

The northeastern and northwestern terre-plein have fallen in. The western wall has a crack in it extending entirely through from parapet to berme. The greater portion of southern wall is down. The upper eastern magazine is penetrated; the lower eastern magazine wall is cracked. The eastern wall is very nearly shot away; a large portion of the wall is down, the ramparts gone, and nearly every casemate breached, and the remaining wall very thin. The casemates, however, on east face are still filled with sand sufficient to protect the garrison from shells.

I consider it impracticable to either mount or use guns on any part of the parapet, and I deem the fort in its present condition unserviceable for offensive purposes. What the engineers may effect by rebuilding or remodeling, I am unable to say.

About forty 32-pounder rifled bolts, twenty 42-pounder rifled bolts, fifty 42-pounder round shots, twenty 10-inch columbiad shots, one lot 32-pounder bolts in boxes, and one lot of sundries, were shipped by steamer Etiwan last night.

Lieutenant Grimball, Company E, assigned to ordnance duty, has rendered efficient service in the collection and shipping of ordnance stores. Captain J. T. Champneys, Engineer Corps, has reported for duty at this post.

Major-General Gilmer and Lieutenant-Colonel Harris visited the fort about 11:30 o'clock last night. Brigadier-General Ripley also came over about 1 o'clock A. M.

The enemy opened fire from battery on Black Island last evening.

SEPTEMBER 4th (journal).—No firing to-day. Seventy-six negroes arrived to-day and finished the traverse and arch of the second tier, and began to fill in the arch.

About 500 shots and shells, viz.: 10-inch columbiad, 8-inch columbiad, 32-pounder rifled bolts, one lot of lead, 8 pieces brass, 5 budge-barrels of powder, cartridge bags, one box friction tubes, two pass boxes implements, were shipped last night by steamer Etiwan.

At 10 P. M. the Charleston Battalion arrived at the fort, under command of Major Elliott, and relieved Colonel Alfred Rhett, commanding, and Captain Fleming, Company B, detachment of First South Carolina Artillery and Twenty-seventh and Twenty-eighth Georgia Volunteers.

SEPTEMBER 5th.—Final report of ordnance at Fort Sumter, South Carolina.*

FORT SUMTER, DECEMBER 9, 1863. VIEW OF ENTRANCE TO THREE-GUN BATTERY.
[From a photograph in the possession of the family of the late General G. T. Beauregard.]

CLASS OF ORDNANCE.	On Hand June 30th	Left Uninjured	Injured	Where Shipped.					
				Charleston	Sullivans Island	James Island	Morris Island	Castle Pinckney	Total
11-inch Dalhgren	1	. .	. .	1	. .	. .	. .	. .	1
10-inch columbiad	10	.	4	. .	3	2	. .	1	6
9-inch Dalhgren	2	. .	1	1	. .	.	. .	. .	1
8-inch columbiad	10	2	. .	1	1	6	. .	. .	8
7-inch rifle	2	. .	. .	1	. .	1	. .	. .	2
42-pounder rifled and banded	9	8	. .	1	. .	.	. .	. .	1
42-inch smooth-bore	4	3	. .	1	. .	. .	. .	. .	1
32-inch rifled and banded	9	3	1	3	. .	1	1	. .	5
32-inch smooth-bore	4	3	. .	1	. .	. .	. .	. .	1
24-inch smooth-bore	4	1	1	2	. .	. .	. .	. .	2
24-pounder howitzer	4	4	. .	. .	. .	. .	. .	. .	. .
8-inch navy gun	5	1	. .	. .		4	. .	. .	4
10-inch sea-coast mortar	4	2	. .	. .	1	. .	1	.	2
Total	68	27	7	12	5	14	2	1	34

REMARKS.—In column "Left Uninjured" are set down all guns that are buried. If some are injured that fact could not be ascertained. It is thought that the majority of guns even in that column are injured. The only gun in working condition is a 32-pounder smooth-bore, situated at the extreme left of northwest casemate battery.

* Made by Lieutenant James S. Heyward, ordnance officer.

BOMBARDMENT OF FORT SUMTER,

SEPTEMBER 5 TO DECEMBER 31, 1863.

BY

LIEUT.-COL. STEPHEN ELLIOTT, JR., C. S. A.,
Commanding Fort Sumter.

SEPTEMBER 6th.—I assumed the command of this post yesterday, pursuant to orders from department headquarters.

There has been no direct fire upon the fort. Two monitors took position after dark and kept up a continuous fire upon the entrance to the harbor during the night, throwing grape and shrapnel. At about 12:15 A. M. heavy firing from the enemy's land batteries and heavy musketry firing induced a belief that an assault was being made upon Battery Gregg. I submit the engineer's report, and would recommend that the timber for bomb-proofs be sawed up in the city, as there are no facilities for doing it here. There are eighteen days' rations for the present garrison. I would also draw your attention to the fact that there is no quartermaster at the post.

SEPTEMBER 7th, 2:40 A. M.—All the garrison of Morris Island who came here have been shipped. Lieutenant Hasker's boat from the Chicora was captured by a Yankee barge. Two of the crew came to Fort Sumter.

SEPTEMBER 7th, 7:20 A. M.—A flag of truce from Commodore [Rear-Admiral] Dahlgren, demanding the surrender of this fort, has been met by Lieutenant [Robert J.] Bowen, of the Palmetto State. I presume I shall refuse.

SEPTEMBER 7th, 7:20 P. M.—The iron-clads still lying off the fort. It is very probable that they will try to move the obstructions with small boats. It would be best if we can throw some lights upon the obstructions from Sullivans Island. They fire an occasional shot at the wharf.

SEPTEMBER 7th.—Up to this time no direct shots have been fired upon this fort. Heavy firing was kept up continuously during yesterday and until 2 o'clock this morning. Two monitors had moved up under cover of the darkness, and, about the time the Morris Island movement commenced, commenced throwing random shots up the harbor approaches, which they continued during the night. The Morris Island movement was accomplished successfully, so far as this post was concerned.

At 8 this morning the Ironsides and five monitors were near this post; one of the latter quite near. There being a fog seaward, the number of vessels inside the bar and at the other points can not be accurately counted, but there is no perceptible change since yesterday.

Two monitors have been employed this morning in sounding along Morris Island. They have taken convenient positions for firing at short range at this fort. I received a communication from Commander [Rear-Admiral] Dahlgren, through Lieutenant Bowen, C. S. Navy, demanding the surrender of this fort. An answer has been sent stating that a definite reply would be returned as soon as I could communicate with the commander of the department. Some valuable time has thus been gained.

SEPTEMBER 8th.—During yesterday the enemy's land batteries were silent. Early in the morning two monitors came up within short range of the fort, the Ironsides and the remaining four monitors taking position near the outer buoy.

About 8 A. M. a flag of truce was sent by the enemy's fleet, which was met by Lieutenant Bowen, C. S. Navy.

FORT SUMTER, DECEMBER 9, 1863. INTERIOR VIEW OF THREE-GUN BATTERY.
[From a photograph in the possession of the family of the late General G. T. Beauregard.]

A reply to the communication received was subsequently sent by a flag of truce from this fort.

At 7 P. M. the Ironsides and six monitors engaged Fort Moultrie, throwing an occasional shot at this post, which did no damage, except tearing away a small portion of the parapet on the west face. During the night the noise of hammering could be distinctly heard from the parapet, indicating that one of the monitors had been injured and was repairing damages. One of the monitors appears to be aground about twelve hundred yards from Sumter. There are thirty-six vessels inside the bar, including the Ironsides and six monitors.

SEPTEMBER 10th.—Everything was very quiet yesterday and last night.

A flag of truce from the enemy's fleet was received at about 9 A. M. in reference to the prisoners.

Another flag was received at 4 P. M., bringing baggage belonging to the captured officers and conveniences for the wounded.

A flag was sent from this post to the fleet at about 6 o'clock, bearing dispatches from General Jordan, and the bodies of their dead. The prisoners, except the wounded, were sent to the city last night.

The Ironsides, four monitors, and twenty-two other vessels inside the bar.

Southern slope of one of Wagner's face directed on this point finished and merlons constructed. No water-boat came last night. Commander of water-boat is an arrant coward, and if the boat is not seized and placed under military control, we will not get our full supply of water.

SEPTEMBER 29th.—I have the honor to report that at 1:45 yesterday land batteries, distant two and one-third miles, opened a slow fire upon this work, directed mainly upon the southwest angle. One hundred shots were thrown, of which 48 struck, 16 fell short, 36 passed over. A negro was killed. The damage to the work is not considerable. A monitor came up apparently to observe the effect of the practice. This morning the fleet retains the position and numbers of yesterday. The usual amount of work appears to have been done on Morris Island. The embrasures of Gregg begin to assume the appearance of an evident development toward the city.

During the bombardment to-day the enemy fired 95 shots, of which 34 struck, without injuring the work materially.

OCTOBER 1st.—The enemy's fire was resumed yesterday at 11:30 A. M. Of 68 shots, 45 struck; the remainder passed over. Some damage was done to the stairway in the southwest angle; one man was wounded in the face by a fragment of brick.

There are two submarine affairs near the Ironsides; there are also several wooden gunboats close in. Look out for some trick to-night.

OCTOBER 6th (to Brigadier-General Jordan).—I have four floating torpedoes in Charleston ready for use. Can you order Sergeant S. E. Barnwell and four men, of the Beaufort Artillery, from Pocotaligo, to operate with them?*

OCTOBER 7th.—The monitor seen off the bar on the 5th instant has taken position inside, and one of those here previously is not to be seen. They are probably going to Port Royal in turn to be overhauled.

Work is going on as usual on Morris Island.

OCTOBER 8th.—Two shots were fired last night by the monitor on advanced post at a schooner containing sand-bags, lying between Sumter and Battery Bee; musketry from the fleet was also heard.

A large Parrott has been mounted in Gregg, in the embrasure directed upon this fort; the breech of the gun, however, lies this way. The Half-Moon Battery in the sand-hills I take to be a mortar battery.

A 42-pounder rifle, banded, was mounted here yesterday, and a 10-inch placed in position ready for mounting. Some necessary alteration in the chassis delayed the operation last night.

OCTOBER 9th.—There is but little change this morning, with the exception of a gradual advance in the completion of the batteries on Morris Island.

FORT SUMTER, DECEMBER 9, 1863. VIEW FROM SOUTHWEST ANGLE.

SEPTEMBER 11th.—Nothing of importance took place yesterday or last night.

The number of vessels inside the bar is exactly the same, and they have not changed their positions during the last twenty-four hours. This morning I noticed that the enemy worked industriously at Battery Gregg, and made several additions to that work.

The wounded prisoners were shipped yesterday in a small boat.

A quantity of shot and shell is lying on the wharf ready for shipment and waiting for transportation.

SEPTEMBER 16th, 12:30 P. M.—Enemy working within four hundred yards southeast of Fort Gregg, perfectly unmolested.

SEPTEMBER 18th.—Apparently no change has taken place in the fleet since my last report.

Yesterday long trains of wagons came down the beach to Gregg, and, after discharging their contents, returned again to the upper end of the island.

The enemy last night displayed a large calcium light at Cummings Point. Its rays were directed on this fort and its approaches.

No shot was fired by the enemy yesterday, and only a few were thrown from our batteries at Sullivans and James Islands.

SEPTEMBER 19th.—The Ironsides, five monitors and twenty-five other vessels are now inside the bar.

The enemy continues to work industriously at Morris Island.

A French steamer is off the bar.

I shipped a large quantity of shot and some shell in the steamer last night which carried up the two guns; also some iron stripped from gun carriages.

SEPTEMBER 28th.—Exchange of companies effected last night; covered way thrown from Gregg to sand-hills.

In the afternoon a long line of men could be observed at Wagner apparently moving a heavy gun.

Two monitors lay in close last night.

Yesterday morning I placed a 42-pounder rifle, banded, in one of the casemates on the northeast face. Last night Mr. Butterfield threw over on the eastern berme a banded 42 and a 10-inch columbiad, with broken trunnions. A portion of the garrison were employed in constructing cushions to receive them.

The enemy's fire was resumed this morning at 8 o'clock.

OCTOBER 2d.—The Ironsides, four monitors, two mortar-boats, and twenty-five other vessels within the bar; elsewhere the status remains the same.

The firing commenced early yesterday; out of 129 shots, 75 struck; the injury was immaterial. Two monitors perform picket duty nightly. All the enemy's movements by land and water show caution and fear of surprise.

OCTOBER 3d.—The firing commenced at 8 A. M. yesterday. Out of 74 shots, 44 struck, two of which penetrated the gorge wall near the officers' old quarters; no other material damage done to the work.

8 A. M.—This morning the enemy's batteries have opened again.

OCTOBER 4th.—Out of 95 shots yesterday, 78 struck the fort. The injury was immaterial, excepting that the top of the breech was knocked off.

Captain [E. W.] Lloyd's company (B), Twenty-fifth South Carolina Volunteers (31 men), relieved Captain [T. E.] Raysor's company (H), Eleventh South Carolina Volunteers (63 men), last night.

OCTOBER 6th.—The enemy have made, and are still making, great improvements on Wagner and Gregg.

Captain Gaillard's company reported last night, numbering fifty men.

A wide embrasure at Gregg directed toward this place is being revetted, as is also the Half-Moon Battery in the sand-hills.

Our fire was effective yesterday; casualties were seen to take place both at Gregg and Wagner.

OCTOBER 11th.—Affairs are not materially changed in the fleet or on shore this morning.

A detachment of five men under the command of Sergeant S. E. Barnwell, of the Beaufort Artillery, sent down four floating torpedoes last night. A heavy explosion took place at the proper time in the fleet, but no results are apparent this morning.

At 8 P. M. the post-boat coming from Fort Johnson overhauled a small boat containing two of the enemy, who surrendered immediately. They were evidently expecting a friendly boat, whether from the city or not is uncertain.

Is it well that this portion of the harbor should be without an armed patrol of some sort? The prisoners were sent up under a guard last night.

A 10-inch was placed upon the wharf last night.

OCTOBER 14th.—The command of the western salient at Gregg is being much increased. A new battery has been commenced to the eastward of and near to the Half-Moon Battery.

OCTOBER 15th.—The Ironsides, four monitors, three mortar-boats and twenty-three other craft within the bar, five blockaders outside, and nineteen vessels in Stono. Judging by the ventilators, an extensive bomb-proof has been built at Gregg. A number of carts may be seen passing behind the covered way. The battery reported yesterday is progressing, and a heavy force is at work on what was the old bomb-proof at Wagner. The detach-

* So ordered, same day.

ment of thirty men from Captain Harleston's company was returned last night by steamer Etiwan, as also some of the iron collected by them at the fort. The presence of a schooner with sand prevented as large a shipment of iron as was advisable.

OCTOBER 18th.—Appearance of the fleet unchanged this morning. The fourth monitor has not been discovered, though she may be concealed by some of the other vessels.

Companies I and K, Eleventh South Carolina Regiment, were relieved last night by the Twelfth Georgia Battalion, Major Hanvey, two hundred and eighteen men. A lot of coal was shipped by the Etiwan last night; the remainder will be sent on Monday night.

OCTOBER 22d.—There are four monitors in the harbor this morning. One of them has a network of wire surrounding and probably covering the forward half of the deck.

The Ironsides has three stout beams projecting obliquely from her bow downward into the water; they are probably braces to some torpedo or anti-torpedo device. One of the mortar-boats has been towed outside, and now lies near the Wabash. In other respects the fleet is as usual. The land batteries are being pushed forward vigorously. Their working parties suffer greatly from the want of being sheltered. The flat was not sent back last night, and a large amount of iron is lying on the wharf ready for shipment.

OCTOBER 24th.—The Ironsides, four monitors, one mortar-boat and twenty other vessels inside; five blockaders and twenty-four craft in Lighthouse Inlet. No new earthworks are being thrown up, but those already in hand are being rapidly pushed forward.

The steamer Randolph, with a raft of logs in tow, allowed herself to be taken by the tide past the fort last night. After some time, being discovered and fired upon by a monitor, she was compelled to cut the logs adrift and return to the wharf. About fifty discharges of small arms from the beach near the Moultrie House were observed at 9 o'clock last night.

OCTOBER 25th.—The state of the fleet is to-day the same in every respect as yesterday, excepting that the number of blockaders is reduced to three, and there are three tugs outside, near the Wabash.

At Gregg portions of three guns can be seen; one bears upon this point, a second upon this point and Fort Johnson, and the third upon Fort Johnson.

At sunset yesterday there was heavy firing from a blockader some ten miles to the northward and eastward.

While the Ironsides was lying in a certain position yesterday, it was apparent that the structure under her bow extended also some distance on her side. This renders it probable that it is a defensive arrangement.

OCTOBER 26th, 4:30.—Enemy has opened upon us from Gregg, Wagner and center battery. We are all right.

OCTOBER 26th.—One hundred and eighty shots from Morris Island; 165 struck, 23 passed over. Ten shots fired from monitors.

OCTOBER 27th.—The enemy's fire was very damaging to the sea face, breaching the traverse in the arches.

The gorge wall was also cut to a thin edge in some places. The land batteries and fleet fired 625 shots.

Lieutenant [Andrew P.] Brown, Georgia Battalion, is dangerously hurt. No other serious casualties.

The number of vessels inside has been reduced by three, while two have been added to the list in Lighthouse Inlet. At 12:30 yesterday, Battery Gregg, the middle battery and Wagner opened upon us, firing 188 shots, of which 165 struck, making some impression upon the gorge wall, upon which their fire is directed. In the afternoon a wooden gunboat steamed up to the two monitors lying at their usual picket station. One of the latter and the gunboat fired nine shots, one of which penetrated the sand-bag traverse above the hospital and wounded a negro.

No other casualties occurred from the fire. There are two guns at Gregg bearing upon us, and embrasures in the curtain for two more. There is a 300-pounder in the middle battery and two smaller guns.

I can not distinctly ascertain the number at Wagner, although there appears to be about five in position for us.

Most of the guns being in embrasures, it is evident from their direction that their intention is to operate regularly against this work.

The powder has been removed from the old magazine, and a part placed in the new magazine near the casemate battery, and the remainder in the bomb-proof near the old sally-port.

Major Pringle took off the flat with iron last night. It is not advisable to send it back at present.

OCTOBER 29th.—Enemy fired 779 shots; 80 missed. The top row of arches on sea face cut down. The whole of that face and the gorge perfectly accessible from the outside. One man killed on post.

OCTOBER 30th.—The haze prevents an accurate report of the fleet this morning. Seven hundred and seventy-nine shots were fired at the fort yesterday; 80 of these passed over. Their effect was to cut away all of the top arches on the sea face, and to make that face and the gorge easy of access throughout their whole extent. Two hundred and sixty shots were fired last night, 80 of which missed. This makes 1,039 of all calibers, from 15-inch mortars and 300-pounder Parrotts downward.

From the present direction of the enemy's fire I am led to conclude that he wishes to avoid injuring the northeast and city faces of the work as much as possible. I think he will try an assault.

Fort Moultrie can sweep our sea face, but there is no enfilade fire for the gorge wall. Unless a gunboat can be placed in position beforehand between this fort and Fort Johnson, her assistance will be useless, as the success of an assault will be determined in a very few minutes.

Private H. C. Castlebury, Company B, Twelfth Georgia Battalion, was killed, while on post yesterday, by the explosion of a 15-inch shell. Private B. W. Griffin, Company A, Twelfth Georgia, slightly wounded in hand; Private Z. Stanford, same company, slightly wounded in leg; Private Augustus Williams, Company A, Twelfth Georgia Battalion, stunned; Private [R. H.] Bearden, same company, wounded in shoulder; Private T. Goggins, Company K, First South Carolina Artillery, slightly, in head; Sergeant A. D. Freeman, Company A, Twelfth Georgia [Battalion], slightly.

Flag-staff shot away after retreat.

I was enabled to keep strong guard on the parapet last night, and the main body within a few yards, in readiness

ASSAULT ON BATTERY WAGNER ON THE NIGHT OF JULY 18, 1863. THE RUSH OF THE GARRISON TO THE PARAPET, REPULSING THE FEDERALS WITH GREAT LOSS. (See page 180.)
[From a sketch made on the spot by an artist representing the *London News*.]

to move immediately. The cutting of the Keokuk angle still continues; the greater portion of the fire this morning is done by mortars.

Three men slightly wounded this morning.

OCTOBER 30th, 6:30.—Number of shots fired at Sumter from sun-up to sun-down to-day, 955, 68 of which missed.

OCTOBER 30th, 10:35 (to General Jordan).—The firing to-day was from two monitors, from two heavy and two light rifled guns at Gregg, from three heavy rifled guns and four 10-inch mortars at the middle battery, and from four medium rifled guns at Wagner; 443 rifled shots were fired, of which 61 missed; 86 shots fired from monitors, all reported as having struck, and 373 mortar shells, of which 120 missed.

OCTOBER 31st.—Sergeant W. C. Owens, Sergeant J. A. Stevens, Privates S. L. Burrows, F. M. Burrows, S. W. Anderson, James Calder, O. J. Burn, W. E. Gibson, J. W. Jones, L. S. Lee and W. N. Patterson, of Washington Light Infantry, Company A, Twenty-fifth Regiment, Private W. Martin, of Twelfth Georgia Battalion, and Mr. Matthewes, an overseer, were buried this morning by the falling in of the barracks on the sea face, where they had severely. The flag-staff was shot away twice and replaced by Sergeant [James] Garahan, Corporal [W. M.] Hitt and Private R. J. Swain, all of Company F, Twelfth Georgia Battalion. The flag-staff was so cut up that it was necessary to raise the battle-flag of the Georgia Battalion in place of the flag.

The following is a list of casualties during yesterday: Private John W. Meyers, Company F, Twelfth Georgia Battalion, killed by mortar shell; Private Milton Gibbs, same company, killed at the same time; Private M. W. Walker, Company D, Twelfth Georgia Battalion, fracture of jaw-bone; Private David J. Hughes, Company F, same corps, wounded severely in back; Private T. A. Honour and Corporal F. H. Honour, Company A, Twenty-fifth South Carolina Volunteers, all wounded by mortar shells.

NOVEMBER 2d.—The fire of the enemy was directed mainly at the southwest angle yesterday, which he succeeded in breaching on the outside, but not to an extent to make the protection within insecure as yet. Monitors opened upon the sea wall, and in reverse upon the city face, doing some damage in the region of the new sallyport. Owing to the difficulty of observing the monitors during their period of action, an accurate estimate of the 135 missed. One man killed by mortar shell. I consider the damage done to the fort, as a defensive position, is, perhaps, less to-day than on any day of the bombardment.

Although the crest of the southwest angle has been much cut, the disjoined masses have assumed a favorable position for the defense of the lower casemates. Besides 15-inch shells, the monitors fire rifled shells, 19 inches long and 6½ inches in diameter, of the pattern styled Wiard. Send us some fresh beef.

NOVEMBER 3d.—The bombardment continued as usual yesterday, the monitors relieving the heavy guns on Morris Island. About noon one hundred and forty 15-inch and 6½-inch rifled shots were fired from the monitors, all of which struck; 250 rifled shots from Morris Island, 55 of which missed, and 345 mortar shells, 135 of which missed.

During the night 87 rifled shots were fired, 36 of which missed, and five mortar shells, which fell in. The upper portion of the scarp on the southwest angle is cut away, but the fragments have assumed the natural slope and contribute to the safety of the lower casemates. Immediately after dark a small boat containing four of the enemy's scouts made a landing at the southeast angle.

BATTERY WAGNER. FIGHT FOR THE RIFLE-PITS IN FRONT OF THE BATTERY. (See page 180.)
[From a sketch made on the spot by an artist representing the *London News*.]

been placed in position for mounting the parapet in case of an assault.

OCTOBER 31st (telegram).—The land batteries and three monitors fired in all, yesterday, 955 shots and shells, 60 of which missed. During the night 68 were fired, 8 of which missed, making an aggregate of 1,020 shots in the twenty-four hours. At 3 o'clock this morning a Parrott shot struck an iron girder in the sea wall, and a moment after the roof fell in crushing thirteen men who were posted there in readiness for an immediate mount to the crest in case of a boat attack. The position was considered comparatively safe, as the roof had resisted the shock of this falling debris.

NOVEMBER 1st.—The fire yesterday proceeded from two monitors, two heavy and two light rifled guns at Gregg, three heavy rifled guns and four 10-inch mortars at the middle battery, and four rifled guns at Wagner; 443 rifled shots were fired from the land batteries, of which 61 missed; 86 shots were fired from the monitors, all of which were reported as having struck, and 373 from mortars, of which 120 missed. The mortar fuses are cut so as to explode the shell a second or two after impact. In fact, during the night 70 rifled shots were fired, mostly with time fuses, of which 10 passed over, and 33 mortar shells, 12 of which did not strike. The fire of the land batteries was directed chiefly at southwest angle, which suffered number of shots from them was not obtained. It bore, however, about the same proportion to the number of shots from the land batteries as on the previous day. The number of their shots, compared with the land guns, was 375, of which 46 missed. The number of mortar shells fired was 308, of which 87 missed. The number last night was 54 rifled shells, of which 7 missed, and 4 mortar shells, of which 2 missed. The number of projectiles of all kinds fired since Monday last is 5,565, of which 817 missed and 4,748 struck. I beg leave to call your attention to the fact that for the second time the movement to relieve a portion of the garrison failed of accomplishment, and to urge that some remedy be applied. Learning that the troops detailed to relieve the companies of the Twenty-fifth South Carolina Volunteers were awaiting transportation at Fort Johnson, I sent over Captain Carson's company in my mail-boat after its arrival from Charleston, making two trips, and bringing over one officer and fourteen men of the relief. The non-fulfillment of official promises is to be regretted, as it shows a want of confidence on the part of the troops. The only casualty yesterday happened to W. Hallett, private, Company D, Twelfth Georgia Battalion, who was wounded slightly on the leg.

NOVEMBER 2d.—One hundred and forty shots from the monitors; all struck; 250 rifled shots from Morris Island, 55 of which missed; 345 mortar shells, of which The darkness having prevented its approach from being observed, and our sentinels not believing that it could be an enemy, hailed and allowed the party to escape, although the officer in command states that several shots struck the boat during its retreat. The delay in firing was due to the fact that there was only one boat, and that it was known that a picket-boat was assigned to this station. The infantry garrison was relieved by a detachment of two officers and forty men from each of the follow regiments: Sixth, Nineteenth, Twenty-third, Twenty-seventh and Twenty-eighth Georgia, and by Companies C and D, Twenty-fifth South Carolina Volunteers, ninety-six men. The different positions of the garrison have been assigned permanently to separate parts of the work, which it is hoped will contribute to the certainty of a repulse. The only casualty yesterday was the death of Private Calvin Giles, Company B, Twelfth Georgia Battalion, by the explosion of a mortar shell.

NOVEMBER 4th.—The following is the number of shots fired to-day: Monitors, 86 shots, all reported hit. Number of rifled shots, 200, 26 of which missed; 136 mortars, 36 of which missed.

The fire from the fleet and batteries continued yesterday. Monitors fired 114 shots, all of which are reported to have struck; Morris Island fired 277 rifled shots, 40 of which missed, and 178 mortar shells, of which 17 missed;

during the night, ninety-two 30-pounder rifled shots with time-fuses were fired, all of which, excepting 15, exploded over and within the fort. The practice with these projectiles is very beautiful, the adjustment of the time being so perfect that the occupants of the gorge wall are secure from the effects of the explosion, which rarely fails to occur during the passage of the shell over the parade. The fire was directed yesterday upon the southwest angle, the upper casemate of which was breached, and in reverse upon the city face, the northern portion of which was somewhat cut and the traverse over the hospital partly knocked down; on the whole, the damage was not great. Captain W. H. Peronneau, Company G, First South Carolina Artillery, forty men, relieved Lieutenant [Edward] Lowndes, Company K, same corps, forty men.

The following is a list of the casualties yesterday from the explosion of a mortar shell, which accidentally found its way into the battery: Privates William B. Eates, Company E; B. F. Morris, Company H; J. A. Smith, Company D; James Chambers, Company E; J. R. Morris, Company E, all of the Twenty-seventh Georgia. Concussion from explosion of shell in battery: Privates I. R. Stephens, Company E. [Apparently incomplete.]

NOVEMBER 5th.—Shots fired to-day as follows: Rifled, 200, of which 43 missed; mortars, fired 213, of which 46 missed; monitors fired, 68, of which 7 missed.

NOVEMBER 6th.—The enemy fired the following number of shots yesterday: Rifled, 200, of which 43 missed; mortars, 213, of which 40 missed; monitors, 98; during the night, 58, of which 21 missed; monitors, 1 struck. The fire of the land batteries was directed on southwest angle, upon which the effect was not very considerable. The fire of the monitors was directed on the eastern pan coupe; the crown of the eastern arch was destroyed; the debris fell in and assisted the work of the engineers.

The flag-staff was shot down to-day, and was replaced by Sergeant N. D. Currie and Corporal S. Montgomery. The following is the number of casualties: Ten men slightly wounded, two severely, and two killed; all of the Twenty-seventh Georgia.

NOVEMBER 7th.—The bombardment continued yesterday to the following extent: Rifled shots fired from land batteries, 153, of which 31 missed; mortar shells, 193, of which 34 missed. Monitors fired 80, of which 14 missed. During the night, 68 light rifled shells were fired from Gregg, 29 of which either failed to explode or exploded after passing over. The fire of the monitors was directed upon the east angle and upon the scarp of the northeast face, to which it did some injury.

The following is a list of the killed and wounded:

Killed: Privates Howell Jones and Robert Vance, Company B, Twenty-eighth Georgia.

Wounded: Private Henry Stoubelfield, Company G, First South Carolina Artillery, slight; Private Aaron Bates, First South Carolina Artillery, hip, severe; Private John Benton, Company G, First South Carolina Artillery, thigh, slight; Private W. T. Butler, Company E, Twenty-eighth Georgia, foot, severe; Private S. C. Lawrence, Company B, Twenty-eighth Georgia, scalp, slight; Private James L. Salter, Company H, Twenty-eighth Georgia, concussion; Privates John Morrell and James A. Lane, Company G, Twenty-eighth Georgia, concussion; Privates James D. Emery, Henry O. Wood and Peter Wood, Company F, Twenty-eighth Georgia, concussion; and H. M. Lawrence, Company B, Twenty-eighth Georgia, side, slight.

Last night Captain [W. H.] Rentfro, with one lieutenant and twenty-four men, from the Twenty-seventh Georgia, Lieutenant [W. P.] Mathews, Sixth Georgia, thirty-four men; Lieutenant [G. W.] Smith, Twenty-eighth Georgia, thirty-three men, relieved detachments of forty and twenty men and three officers, from Twenty-seventh, Sixth and Twenty-eighth Georgia, respectively. The captains of two of these detachments, whose time had expired, were retained for twenty-four hours for the purpose of assisting the new officers, strangers to the works, in the discharge of their duties. Captain John Johnson arrived for the purpose of relieving Captain Champneys.

NOVEMBER 8th.—The enemy's fire continued yesterday with still further abatement. The monitors took no part in the action. Seventy-one rifled shots were fired, 15 of which missed, and 212 mortar shells, of which 46 missed. During the night, 63 time shells were fired, of which 16 missed. The injury done to the work was, perhaps, less marked than on any previous day. The following casualties occurred: First-Lieutenant T. Davis Waties, Company G, First South Carolina Artillery, concussion, slight; Private Thomas H. Watts, Company C, Twenty-eighth Georgia, forearm and hand, severe; Private J. M. Page, Company B, Twenty-ninth Georgia, contusion of side, slight.

NOVEMBER 9th.—The number of the enemy's shots yesterday amounted to, rifled, 93, of which 33 missed; number of shells, 188, of which 45 missed; and monitors, 11, of which 5 missed; during the night, 58 rifled shots were fired, of which 16 missed. The fire of the land batteries during the day was directed chiefly upon the southwest angle, without serious damage; that of the monitors, upon the scarp wall of the northeast face, which was not materially injured.

RECAPITULATION OF THE WEEK:

Rifled, from land batteries:	
Fired	1,803
Missed	411
From mortars:	
Fired	1,467
Missed	359
From monitors:	
Fired	471
Missed	19
Total fired	3,741
Struck	2,952
Missed	789
Total fired during the previous week	5,565
Struck	4,748
Missed	817
Aggregate fired since the opening of the present bombardment	9,306
Struck	7,700
Missed	1,606

NOVEMBER 9th (to General G. T. Beauregard).—On the night of the 4th, 86 rifled shots fired, 60 of which struck; during the day of the 5th, 200 rifled shots fired, 157 of which struck. Mortars fired 213, 173 of which struck. Monitors fired 78, all of which struck. During the night of the 5th, 58 rifled shots fired, 37 of which struck. Mortars fired one shell, which struck. During day of the 8th, 93 rifled shots fired, 60 of which struck; 188 mortar shells fired, 143 of which struck; 11 shots fired by monitors, 6 of which struck; during the night of the 8th, 58 rifled shots fired, 42 of which struck.

NOVEMBER 10th.—The following number of shots were fired yesterday: Rifled, 61, of which 21 missed; monitors, 25, of which 7 missed.

Mortar shelling by night was resorted to for the first time since the commencement of the bombardment. The rifle practice was also more frequent than on previous nights. Number of shots from rifle, 154; missed, 62. From mortars, 182; missed, 50. The heavy guns from the land have ceased their fire to a great extent. The rifle practice is conducted almost exclusively from light pieces. Day firing has in like manner given way to night.

NOVEMBER 11th.—The following number of shots fired yesterday: Rifled, 46, of which 8 missed; mortar shells, 50, of which 25 missed; monitors, 30, of which 9 missed. No casualties occurred.

A detachment of one hundred men and ten officers, under the command of Captain [E. A.] Crawford of the Seventeenth South Carolina Volunteers, relieved a detachment of one hundred men and officers from the Sixth, Nineteenth and Twenty-eighth Georgia Volunteers.

NOVEMBER 12th.—The number of shots fired yesterday was, from rifled guns, 23, of which 13 missed; from mortars, 196, of which 113 missed.

During the night 146 rifled shots were fired, of which 33 missed and — mortar shells, of which 5 missed. First Sergeant Wales S. Langford, Company G, First South Carolina Artillery, was wounded in the head, slightly, by a piece of shell, while with his company on the parapet.

At 8 P. M. a calcium light was displayed at Gregg, for the apparent purpose of illuminating our works and preventing the location of obstruction upon the slopes.

At 11 P. M. Company G, First Regiment South Carolina Artillery, Captain W. H. Peronneau, forty men, was relieved by Company D, First Regiment South Carolina Artillery, Captain Harleston, forty-five men. Owing to the refusal of the captain of the steamer to approach the fort, the final transfer was made on board of small boats, and consumed much time. The flag-staff was shot down and the flag was replaced by Sergeant [G. H.] Mayo, Company B, and Private Robert Autry, Company C, Twenty-eighth Georgia Volunteers.

NOVEMBER 13th.—I submit the following report of the firing yesterday: Rifled shots, 144, of which 34 missed; mortars, 159, of which 92 missed; monitors fired twice, struck both times. One shot passed through the flag. During the night 180 rifled fired, of which 51 passed over; mortars, 282, of which 110 missed.

The following casualties occurred: Private W. J. Hadden, Company I, Twenty-eighth Georgia, killed by a fragment of Parrott shell while on post; Private A. J. Clinton, Company K, Seventeenth South Carolina Volunteers, killed by a mortar shell, while on post; Private E. Johnson, Company C, Twenty-fifth South Carolina Volunteers, wounded severely in face, while on post.

NOVEMBER 14th.—I submit the following report of the shots fired yesterday: Rifled fired 74, of which 9 missed; mortars, 315, of which 128 missed. During the night, rifled, 115, of which 36 missed. To-day there were 21 rifled shots fired, of which 9 missed; mortars fired 225, of which 96 missed. Private J. G. Pound, Company K, Twenty-seventh Georgia, was dangerously wounded in the thigh by a fragment of a mortar shell. A boat was seen lying at the obstructions last night; when hailed, she proved to be our guard boat. Her presence there does not contribute to the safety of this work.

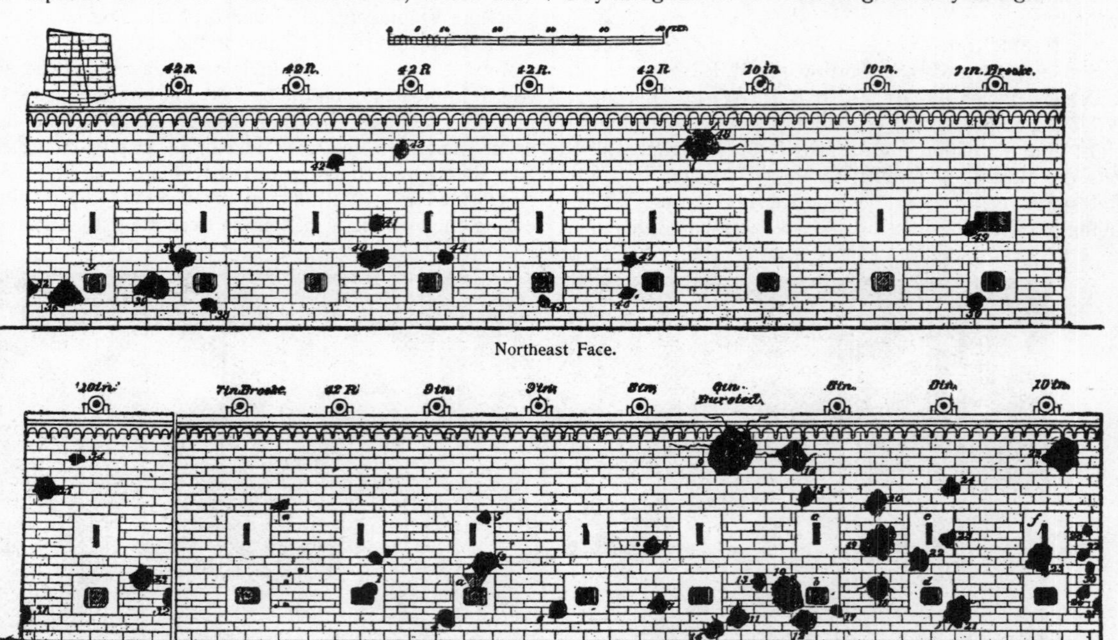

East Pan Coupe. East Face.

ELEVATIONS OF FACES OF FORT SUMTER, SHOWING THE EFFECT OF THE FIRE FROM THE FEDERAL IRONCLAD FLEET, APRIL 7, 1863.
(See Major Echols' description of engagement in Charleston Harbor, page 178.)

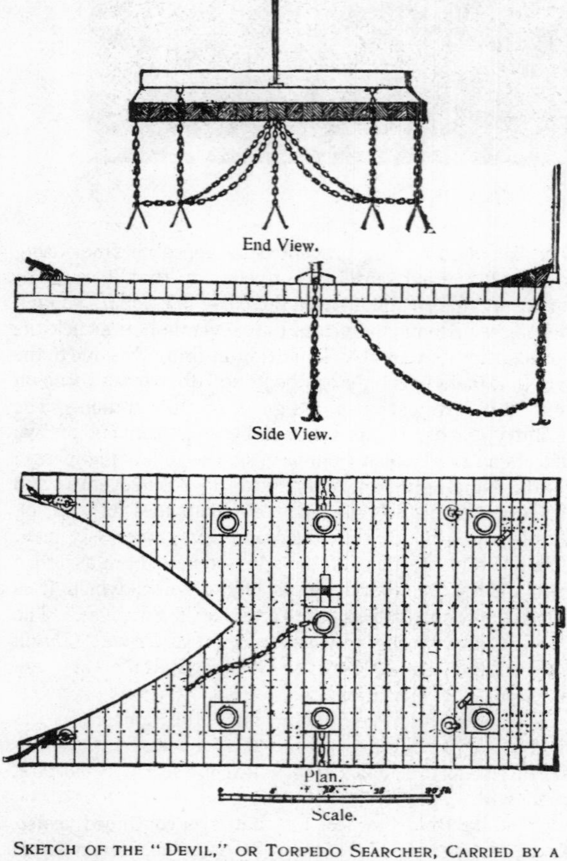

SKETCH OF THE "DEVIL," OR TORPEDO SEARCHER, CARRIED BY A MONITOR IN CHARLESTON HARBOR, APRIL 7, 1863.
(See Major Echol's description of engagement in Charleston Harbor, page 178.)

NOVEMBER 15th.—The shelling continued heavy last night. Ninety-eight rifled shells were fired, of which 39 missed, and 219 mortar shells were thrown, of which 90 missed. Casualties were as follows: Private J. R. Wilson, Company K, Twenty-seventh Georgia, shoulder, slight; . P. Benton, Company A, Twenty-seventh Georgia, scalp, slight; William Ment, Company H, Twenty-seventh Georgia, back, slight. To-day, rifled fired 16, of which 6 missed; mortar shells, 320, of which 115 missed. Casualties to-day: First Sergeant J. C. Grimball, Company D, First Regiment South Carolina Artillery, wounded severely in head, abdomen and knee, by a mortar shell.

NOVEMBER 16th.—The enemy fired last night 184 rifled shots, of which 52 missed, and 12 mortar shells, of which 2 missed. To-day 43 rifled shots were fired, of which 5 missed, and 363 mortar shells, of which 118 missed. Number of shots of all kinds fired during the past week up to this morning, 3,030.

NOVEMBER 17th.—The enemy fired last night as follows: Rifled shots, 156, of which 55 missed; mortar shells, 6, 1 of which missed. To-day 14 rifled shots were fired, of which 5 missed, and 366 mortar shells, of which 117 missed.

Last night Private Edmund Lake, Company D, Twenty-seventh South Carolina Volunteers, acting cockswain of the quartermaster's boat, was killed by a fragment of shell, while approaching the fort. No casualties to-day.

NOVEMBER 18th.—The enemy fired last night as follows: Rifled shots, 133, 11 of which missed. To-day 12 rifled shots were fired, of which 4 missed, and 278 mortar shells; of these 92 missed.

NOVEMBER 19th.—Two hundred and eighty-five rifled shots were fired last night, of which 96 missed, and 3 mortar shells, which struck. To-day 44 rifled shots were fired, of which 9 missed, and 362 mortar shells, of which 113 missed.

No casualties have occurred since the last report. Engineer in charge reports that his working force was engaged during the night repairing large holes over center bomb-proof, also filling ordnance store-room adjoining western magazine, second tier. Completed loop-holes in splinter-proof at east end of center bomb-proof, and continued filling passages inside south angle, and blew up middle kitchen in east barracks.

Captain [R. M.] Mitchell, with three officers and one hundred men, from Sixth, Nineteenth, Twenty-third and Twenty-seventh Georgia regiments, relieved Captain Rentfro, with three officers and one hundred men from the Sixth, Twenty-seventh and Twenty-eighth Georgia.

NOVEMBER 20th.—At 2:30 [A. M.] the moon being down and the weather very favorable for an attack, I aroused and placed the whole garrison under arms. Before visiting Captain Harleston's quarters, I found that he had taken the same precaution.

At 3 o'clock a detachment of the enemy's barges, variously estimated at from four to nine in number, approached within three hundred yards of the fort and opened fire with musketry. Most of the troops got into position very rapidly, but in spite of all instructions, commenced a random fire into the air on the part of many and at the distant boats on the part of others. The troops stationed in the center bomb-proof for the most part refused to ascend the parapet, though encouraged by the example of Lieutenant Mironell and a few other brave men.

I have sent a dispatch to General Taliaferro, asking him to relieve two lieutenants who did not behave well. I have not evidence enough to convict them, but do not want them here longer. I have taken measures which I trust may insure better conduct in the future.

No rockets were sent up, because positive attack was not made. The ricochet practice from Sullivans Island was very handsome. The fire from Johnson was very bad, the balls passing directly over the fort. Private T. Wheeler, Company D, First South Carolina Artillery, was wounded slightly in the head yesterday evening by a brick.

At 9:45 A. M., enemy shelling us more heavily this morning than usual, with mortars. Have fired few rifled shots.

NOVEMBER 21st.—Yesterday the enemy fired 18 rifled shots, of which 8 missed, and 379 mortar shells, of which 146 missed. Last night 124 rifled shots were fired, of which 41 passed over without exploding.

At 9 P. M. Captain [N. A.] Burley, Seventeenth South Carolina Volunteers, and Lieutenant [A. M.] Hutchison, Sixth Georgia, relieved Lieutenants [J. A. F.] Coleman and [J. D.] James, of the same regiments, respectively, who were removed at my request. Thomas J. Hornbuckle, Company C, Twenty-third Georgia, was killed yesterday by the explosion of a mortar shell; wounded, C. Banks, Company K, Seventeenth South Carolina Volunteers, spine, slight; W. P. Brown, private, Mathewes' artillery, shoulder, severe; also Stewart, Company B, Sixth Georgia, scalp, slight. At 5 A. M. the broken arch on the gorge wall was struck by a Parrott shell and fell, killing two negroes and wounding six, and wounding Privates Charles Etheridge, Company H, Sixth Georgia, fractured jaw, and Coote Thayer, Company H, Sixth Georgia, spine, slight. Repeated efforts had been made a few hours before to pull it down, but to no purpose.

NOVEMBER 22d, 10 A. M.—Twenty-three rifled shots were fired yesterday, of which 7 missed, and 238 mortar shells, of which only 99 missed. At night 149 rifled shells were fired; 45 of these exploded after passing the fort.

There have been no casualties, neither has any serious damage been done to the work. At 3 o'clock this morning a blue light was reported at the entrance to Vincents Creek. The parapet was handsomely manned by the garrison. No further indications of the enemy's advance appear.

NOVEMBER 24th.—The enemy fired 7 rifled shells at us yesterday, all of which struck, and 192 mortar shells, of which 81 missed.

During the night, 170 rifled shells were fired, of which 62 exploded after passing, or passed without bursting.

It is my painful duty to report that Captain F. H. Harleston, Company D, First Regiment South Carolina Artillery, was wounded in both thighs and in the arm, by a Parrott shell, at 4:30. He had gone down the slope of the sea face to examine the obstructions, which had been reported as being washed away by the tide. He is mortally hurt. One negro was killed, and another lost his leg by fragments of a Parrott shell.

BATTERY WAGNER. SCENE PRESENTED IN THE DITCH AND ON THE SOUTHERN SLOPE OF THE BATTERY ON THE MORNING AFTER THE ASSAULT OF JULY 18, 1863. (See page 180.)
[From a sketch made on the spot by an artist representing the *London News*.]

NOVEMBER 25th.—During yesterday 2 rifled shells were fired at the fort, both of which missed; also 98 mortar shells were fired, 65 of which struck; 33 missed. Our report for last night is: Rifled, fired 166, of which 115 struck; mortar shells fired, 17, only 6 of which struck.

The casualties last night were Captain Mitchell, Company F, Twenty-third Georgia, slightly wounded; one negro killed, and another severely wounded in shoulder.

NOVEMBER 26th.—Ten rifled shells were thrown yesterday at the fort, of which 3 missed, and 11 mortar shells, of which 3 also missed. During the night, 242 rifled shells were fired, of which 88 missed. There have been no casualties, nor any material injury done to the work since last report.

NOVEMBER 27th.—The enemy fired yesterday 23 rifled shells, of which 5 missed, and 48 mortar shells, of which 18 missed. Last night 169 rifled shells were thrown, of which 92 missed. There have been no casualties during the last twenty-four hours, neither has the injury to the work been serious. Captain [J. A.] Roe, with a detachment of one hundred men from the Nineteenth, Twenty-third,

Twenty-seventh and Twenty-eighth Georgia, were relieved by Captain [W. J.] Jordan, with six officers and one hundred men from the same regiments.

NOVEMBER 28th.—The enemy fired 106 shots yesterday from the land batteries, 53 of which missed, and 105 mortar shells, 40 of which missed. The westernmost of the two heavy guns at Gregg bearing upon this point is ascertained to be a 10-inch columbiad. The shell practice of this gun at southwest angle was very good and rather effective. Fragments of a 13-inch mortar shell were also found yesterday. During the night the usual practice with light Parrotts continued; fired 257, missed 136. Private James Tupper, Jr., shot-marker, Company D, Twenty-seventh South Carolina Volunteers, Charleston Battalion, seeing yesterday morning that the flag had been shot down, walked along the whole extent of the gorge wall, on the parapet, and endeavored to raise it. Finding that the staff was too short, he procured an additional piece of spar and, with the assistance of C. B. Foster, same command, and Corporals W. C. Buckheister and A. J. Bluett, Company B, same corps, succeeded in splicing and planting the staff, under a very heavy fire directed at them. One shot cut the flag from their hands. It was a most distinguished display of gallantry. No casualties have occurred since the last report.

NOVEMBER 29th. — The land guns fired yesterday 97 shots, of which 43 missed; mortars fired 21, of which 6 missed; and a monitor, 22, of which 8 missed. Last night 126 shots were fired, of which 59 missed; 1 mortar shell, which struck. No boats arrived from the city last night. No casualties occurred.

NOVEMBER 30th.—The enemy fired only 8 rifled shots yesterday, 4 of which missed. Last-night 140 rifled shots were fired, 74 of which missed, and 4 mortar shells, all of which fell outside. A negro was killed by a Parrott shell. Last night a good deal of signaling was observed during the night on board the fleet, on Morris Island and on Black Island.

DECEMBER 1st.—The enemy fired yesterday: Rifled, 1, struck; mortar, 22, of which 11 missed. Last night 2 mortar shells were fired; both missed.

DECEMBER 2d, 11:20 A. M.—I have the honor to report the fire on this place as having almost totally ceased. Six mortar shells were thrown yesterday, of which 2 missed. No firing last night.

A detachment of six officers and one hundred men from Nineteenth, Sixth, Twenty-seventh and Twenty-eighth Georgia Volunteers, under Captain [J. M.] Bateman, relieved detachment of three officers and one hundred men under Captain Mitchell, from Nineteenth, Twenty-seventh, Twenty-third and Twenty-eighth Georgia Volunteers.

DECEMBER 3d.—Enemy reopened fire yesterday at 10:30, throwing 72 rifled shots, of which 26 missed; 73 mortar shells, of which 38 missed, and 68 columbiad shots and shells, of which 14 missed.

DECEMBER 4th.—The fire of the enemy commenced yesterday at 10 o'clock at the southwest angle; 27 columbiad shots were thrown, of which 1 missed; and 11 rifled, of which 2 missed; damage inflicted not considerable.

I have made a careful examination of the exterior of the fort this morning. The slope is exceedingly steep and the footing very insecure; nothing like a rush can ever be made up these slopes as long as they retain their present inclination.

DECEMBER 5th.—Forty-two rifled were fired yesterday, of which 11 missed; columbiad, 35, of which 10 missed, and 17 mortar, of which 9 missed. Last night 49 rifled were fired, of which 27 missed; columbiad, 6 fired, of which 2 missed.

Captain Sellers, with three officers and eighty-nine men, relieved Captain Hopkins (six officers and one hundred and seven men).

DECEMBER 9th.—Affairs here continue quiet. The enemy show themselves in considerable numbers at Gregg and Wagner, where the work of cutting, hauling and placing sods continues.

DECEMBER 10th.—The enemy fired 6 light rifled yesterday, 5 of which struck.

Captain [R. A.] Harkey, with six officers and one hundred men from the Sixth, Nineteenth, Twenty-third and Twenty-seventh Georgia, relieved Captain Jordan, six officers and one hundred men, from the Nineteenth, Twenty-third, Twenty-seventh and Twenty-eighth Georgia.

Enemy continue working, but are seriously interrupted by our shelling when it takes place.

DECEMBER 11th—Lieutenant-Colonel Elliott being slightly wounded, and having placed me* temporarily in command of the fort, I would respectfully beg leave to submit the following report of shots fired at the fort to-day: Rifled shots, hit, 125; rifled shots, missed, 18; total rifled fired, 143. Mortar shells, hit, 62; mortar shells, missed, 15. Total shots and shells fired, 220.

The signal corps established communication this evening, but can not to-night.

DECEMBER 12th.—At 9:30 yesterday morning the southwest magazine exploded. Owing to the want of space the ammunition for small arms and howitzers, amounting to about one hundred and fifty pounds of powder, was stored in the inner room. The commissary stores were kept principally in the outer room, which was also used as an issuing office. The materials in these rooms were immediately ignited, their occupants killed, and those stationed in the adjoining passages either killed or burned with greater or less severity.

The passages leading to the lower and upper tiers of casemates, and those casemates themselves, were filled instantly with the most dense smoke, introduced by a blast of great strength, whose flame was visible from the room occupied as headquarters. In total darkness the occupants rushed from the stifling smoke to the open embrasures, leaving their arms and blankets behind. The continuance of the smoke prevented any prolonged attempt to obstruct the progress of the fire.

With great promptness a boat was sent from the navy with a supply of water-buckets. The telegraphic apparatus was removed and located at another position by Mr. W. R. Cathcart, the operator, who behaved remarkably well; but he was compelled to retire from this second position by the advance of the fire.

The signal officers made repeated efforts to attract the attention of Sullivans Island and Fort Johnson, but were unable to succeed until a late hour in the day. The Sullivans Island corps could be seen operating with other points, an inattention, which, when it was known that we were under unusual circumstances and cut off from all communication, seems to me reprehensible in the extreme, and ought, I think, to be looked into.

FORT SUMTER, DECEMBER 9, 1863. VIEW OF SOUTHEAST ANGLE.
[From a photograph in the possession of the family of the late General G. T. Beauregard.]

The effect of the fire was to destroy the roof of the magazine and the southwest stairway, the woodwork in the two tiers of casemates, as far in the lower as the old sally-port.

The damage done will not materially affect the defense of the work. I am deeply indebted to Captain Johnson, of the engineers; he was everywhere, doing everything that man could possibly do.

Lieutenant [L. A.] Harper, Company F, Twenty-fifth South Carolina Volunteers, showed great gallantry in rescuing burning bodies from the smoke and flames. Captain Sellers, of the same company, gave me great assistance in superintending the arrangement last night, at a time when a slight temporary injury prevented me from running about.

Soon after the fire became apparent the enemy opened fire, throwing 143 rifled shots, of which 18 missed, and 77 mortar shells, of which 15 missed. The deficiencies in men, arms, ammunition and commissary stores were most promptly supplied by the authorities.

The following is a list of the casualties:

Killed: Captain Edward D. Frost, Assistant Commissary of Subsistence; Sergeant Hammond, White's Battalion Artillery; Sergeant John King, Thomas McEvoy, Company E; B. Douglas, Company F, of Twenty-fifth South Carolina Volunteers; Sergeant Robert Swanston, P. Cill, A. Surten, all of Company K, First South Carolina Artillery; W. J. Lee, Company I, B. Jones, Company H, Nineteenth Georgia; J. T. Ford, Company G, Twenty-seventh Georgia.

Wounded: Lieutenant-Colonel Elliott, slight, in head and ankle; Captain [N. B.] Mazyck, C. F. Vogler, J. Brennan, Sergeant J. E. Prince, R. Flotwell, T. Callahan, J. H. Hutson and D. H. Clayton, of Company E; C. Fertic, D. J. Avinger, [Edward] Spigner, M. W. Shuler, P. H. Taylor, R. D. Zimmerman, W. C. Zimmerman, H. Shirer and L. W. Dantzler, of Company F, all of Twenty-fifth South Carolina Volunteers; B. Buhn, Company B, N. C. Jones, Company H, J. B. Buckman, Company G, J. M. Huddleston, Company E, N. F. Smith, Company C, W. B. Leatherwood, Company I, H. C. Adair, Company H, and Sergeant Reed, Company K, all of Nineteenth Georgia Volunteers; Elisha Harris, Company E, B. F. Brooks, Company G. H. W. Wells, Company E,

* Captain M. H. Sellers, Twenty-fifth South Carolina.

SULLIVANS ISLAND. BATTERY BEAUREGARD, 1864.
[From a photograph in the possession of the family of the late General G. T. Beauregard.]

J. S. Price, Company C, W. B. Chandler, Company K, J. M. Carney, Company A, and B. F. Watson, Company D, all of Sixth Georgia Volunteers; W. Dunning, Company H, J. Hemphill, Company C, J. Hodge, Company A, W. F. Dannan, Company A, and Sergeant J. C. Calhoun, Company A, all of Twenty-seventh Georgia Volunteers; L. Mashburn, Company K, and J. Leach, Company K, all of First South Carolina Artillery; Percival Elliott, signal corps.

RECAPITULATION.

Killed	11
Wounded	41
	52

FORT MOULTRIE. SCENE DURING THE BOMBARDMENT OF CHARLESTON. THE QUARTERMASTER HOLDING FLAG TO THE BREEZE, UNDER A HEAVY FIRE, UNTIL A JURY MAST WAS ERECTED.

[From a sketch made on the spot by an artist representing the *London News*.]

DECEMBER 14th.—Captain [T. J.] Abercrombie, with six officers and one hundred men from the Sixth, Nineteenth, Twenty-seventh and Twenty-third Georgia regiments, relieved Captain Bateman, six officers, one hundred men, from Sixth, Nineteenth, Twenty-seventh and Twenty-eighth regiments.

The steamer effected a landing last night with a supply of ordnance and commissary stores. Casemates cooling.

DECEMBER 15th, 2 A. M.—A day of extreme quiet yesterday. Details from the garrison were assigned to the engineer for the purpose of assisting in the removal of rubbish. The work of repairs goes on well.

DECEMBER 16th.—Captain [J. D.] Franklin, with six officers and one hundred men from the Sixth, Twenty-third, Twenty-seventh and Twenty-eighth Georgia regiments, relieved Captain Harkey, with six officers and one hundred men from Sixth, Nineteenth, Twenty-third and Twenty-seventh.

Affairs continue quiet. The repair of the damage progressing. Transportation and water were supplied.

DECEMBER 17th.—Captain R. Chisolm, with six officers and one hundred men from the Twenty-seventh South Carolina Volunteers, relieved Captain Sellers, with six officers and eighty-three men, Twenty-fifth South Carolina Volunteers.

DECEMBER 18th.—On my return to my post yesterday evening [from Charleston], I found Captain Johnson, of the engineers, with a high fever, and, as there were no comforts here, recommended his removal to the city until he shall have recovered. Mr. Delisle and Mr. Hall, assistant engineers, are carrying on the work.

I penetrated this morning to the portion of the magazine used as a commissary storehouse. A small amount of burning material is on the floor, but, by the use of buckets, the fire will soon be totally extinguished.

The work of revetting and obstructing the approach to the works on Morris Island is still going forward.

DECEMBER 19th.—We have still been unmolested by the enemy, and the engineer work has progressed as favorably as usual.

DECEMBER 22d.—Last night Captain [W. G. L.] Butt, of the Twenth-third Georgia Regiment, with six officers and one hundred and nine enlisted men of the Nineteenth, Twenty-third, Twenty-seventh and Twenty-eighth Georgia, relieved Captain Abercrombie, of the same regiment, and six officers with one hundred and one enlisted men from the Sixth, Nineteenth, Twenty-third and Twenty-seventh Georgia.

Last night, about 1 o'clock, one of the enemy's barges appeared off the fort and continued sounding for some time. It finally retired toward Morris Island.

The condition of the fort is very much the same as usual, all changes being for the better.

DECEMBER 23d, 11:30 A. M.—The fleet consists of the Ironsides, four monitors, one mortar-boat, three wooden gunboats and fourteen sailing vessels inside; four blockaders outside, and sixteen craft in Lighthouse Inlet. Gregg is undergoing some change, but its nature is not sufficiently developed to report upon.

DECEMBER 24th.—In sight, the Ironsides, four monitors, four gunboats, two mortar-boats, one of which was concealed yesterday; three tugs and fifteen sailing vessels inside; four blockaders, one tug and one schooner outside, and twenty vessels and steamers in Lighthouse Inlet. Discrepancies in morning reports may arise from changes in the grouping of the vessels. In some cases an accurate estimate is very difficult. One and sometimes two monitors come up on picket duty at night within fourteen hundred yards of the fort.

Captain Johnson reported for duty last night.

DECEMBER 25th.—The Ironsides, four monitors, three wooden gunboats, two mortar boats, one tug and fourteen sailing vessels inside this morning. Four blockaders and eighteen vessels in Lighthouse Inlet. Heavy firing at daylight and several hours afterward in direction of Stono.

Detachment of six officers and one hundred men from Sixth, Twenty-third, Twenty-seventh, Twenty-eighth Georgia regiments, under Captain Morse [?], relieved Captain [W. H.] Douglas, six officers and one hundred men from Sixth, Twenty-third, Twenty-seventh, Twenty-eighth Georgia regiments.

The accidental explosion of an old shell wounded Privates Theodore Icault and Joseph Lee, Company K, First South Carolina Artillery, slightly.

DECEMBER 26th.—At 12 yesterday, at the signals of a steam whistle from the fleet and a gun from the direction of Lighthouse Inlet, the enemy raised a flag on the middle battery. It may be a significant fact that at the first attempt the bunting went up union down.

DECEMBER 30th. — The embrasure at the 10-inch columbiad at Gregg is being reopened.

Captain Hammond, six officers and one hundred men from Twenty-fifth South Carolina Volunteers, relieved Captain Chisolm and force from Twenty-seventh South Carolina Volunteers last night.

No. 6.

TABULAR STATEMENTS OF SHOTS FIRED AGAINST FORT SUMTER, AUGUST 12 TO DECEMBER 31, 1863.

AUGUST 12 TO SEPTEMBER 2, 1863, INCLUSIVE.*

DATE.	Outside the Fort	Inside the Fort	Missed	Total
August 12	5	3	4	12
August 13	6	11	....	17
August 14	10	.....	....	10
August 16	30	10	8	48
August 17	445	233	270	948
August 18	452	244	180	876
August 19	408	241	131	780
August 20	408	296	175	879
August 21	445	259	219	923
August 22	203	216	185	604
August 23	282	210	141	633
August 24	112	14	24	150
August 25	62	36	77	175
August 26	45	45	40	130
August 27	....	.....	4	4
August 28	3	3	....	6
August 30	322	168	144	634
August 31	34	5	17	56
September 1	166	95	121	382
September 2	12	9	17	38
Total in twenty days	3,450	2,098	1,757	7,305

* According to revised statement transmitted by Colonel Rhett to department headquarters, October 29, 1863.

SEPTEMBER 28 TO OCTOBER 3, 1863, INCLUSIVE.†

DATE.	Struck	Missed	Total Fired
September 28	48	52	100
September 29	34	60	94
September 30	45	23	68
October 1	75	54	129
October 2	44	30	74
October 3	78	17	95
Total ‡	324	236	560

† Compiled from Elliott's daily reports.

‡ All reported as shots from land batteries.

CHARLESTON HARBOR. CONFEDERATES SINKING TORPEDOES IN THE CHANNEL BY MOONLIGHT.

No. 6.—Continued.

October 26 to November 30, 1863, Inclusive.*

Date.	Struck: Shots from Monitors	Struck: Shots from Land Guns	Struck: Mortar Shells	Struck: Night Shots	Struck: Mortar Shells at Night	Struck: Total	Missed: Shots from Monitors	Missed: Day Shots	Missed: Day Mortar Shells	Missed: Night Shots	Missed: Night Shells	Missed: Total	Total Fired
October 26	9	165				174		23				23	197
October 27	45	487		116		648		93		25		118	766
October 28	72	519		112		703		88		7		95	798
October 29	120	570		180		870		88		80		160	1,030
October 30	127	760		56		943		68		8		76	1,019
October 31	86	382	253	60	21	802		61	120	10	12	203	1,005
November 1	70	259	221	47	2	599		46	87	7	2	142	741
November 2	150	195	210	51	5	611		55	135	36		226	837
November 3	114	237	161	77		589		40	17	15		72	661
November 4	48	212	90	60		410		35	42	26		103	513
November 5	78	157	173	37	1	446		43	40	21		104	550
November 6	66	122	159	39		386	14	31	34	29		108	494
November 7		56	166	47		269		15	46	16		77	346
November 8	6	60	143	42		251	5	33	45	16		99	350
November 9	18	41	20	92	132	303	7	20	5	62	50	144	447
November 10	21	38	25	20		104	9	8	25	11		53	157
November 11		10	83	113	3	209		13	113	33	5	164	373
November 12	2	110	67	129	172	480		34	92	51	110	287	767
November 13		65	187	79		331		9	138	26		173	504
November 14		12	129	59	129	329		9	96	39	90	234	563
November 15		10	205	132	10	357		6	115	52	2	175	532
November 16		38	245	101	5	389		5	118	55	1	179	568
November 17		9	249	122	195	575		5	117	11	75	208	783
November 18		8	186	189	3	386		4	92	96		192	578
November 19		35	249	72		356		9	113	25		147	503
November 20		10	233	83		326		8	146	41		195	521
November 21		16	139	104		259		7	99	45		151	410
November 22		4	80	70		154			63	24		87	241
November 23		7	111	108		226			81	62		143	369
November 24			65	115	6	186		2	33	51	11	97	283
November 25		7	8	154		169		3	3	88		94	263
November 26		18	30	77		125		5	18	92		115	240
November 27		53	65	121		239		53	40	136		229	468
November 28	14	54	15	67	1	151	8	43	6	59		116	267
November 29		4		66		70		4		74	4	82	152
November 30			11			11			11		2	13	24
Total	1,046	4,730	3,978	2,997	685	13,436	43	958	2,090	1,429	364	4,884	18,320

* As corrected by Major Stephen Elliott, Jr., and recorded in Journal of Operations in Charleston Harbor.

December 1 to 31, 1863, Inclusive.†

Date.	Struck: Shots from Monitors	Struck: Shots from Land Guns	Struck: Mortar Shells	Struck: Night Shots	Struck: Mortar Shells at Night	Struck: Total	Missed: Shots from Monitors	Missed: Day Shots	Missed: Day Mortar Shells	Missed: Night Shots	Missed: Night Shells	Missed: Total	Total Fired
December 1			4			4			2			2	6
December 2		140	35			175		40	38			78	253
December 3		35				35		3				3	38
December 4		56	8	26		90		21	9	29		59	149
December 5		4				4		2				2	6
December 9		5				5		1				1	6
December 11		125	62			187		18	15			33	220
December 27								2				2	2
December 31								2				2	2
Total		365	109	26		500		89	64	29		182	682

† According to revised statements of Lieutenant-Colonel Elliott.

RECAPITULATION.

Date.	Missed.	Struck.	Total Fired.
August 12 to September 2	5,548	1,757	7,305
September 28 to October 3	324	236	560
October 26 to November 30	13,436	4,884	18,320
December 1 to 31	500	182	682
Grand Total	19,808	7,059	26,867

Memoranda.—The projectiles from monitors consist of 8-inch rifled shells of the pattern known as Schenkl. The shots from land guns by day consisted at first of 10-inch Parrott bolts and percussion shells and of 100-pounder Parrott percussion shells; latterly the heavier have rarely been used. The mortar shells are exclusively 10-inch. The night shots are 30-pounder Parrotts with time-fuses.

No. 7.

Return of Casualties in the Confederate Forces at Fort Sumter, August 12 to December 11, 1863.

[Compiled from Nominal Lists of Casualties, Returns, etc.]

Date.	Killed: Officers	Killed: Enlisted Men	Killed: Negroes	Wounded: Officers	Wounded: Enlisted Men	Wounded: Negroes	Aggregate
August 12					2	7	9
August 17		1		3	14		18
August 18					3		3
August 19		1			4		5
August 20				1	1		2
August 21					5	2	7
August 23		1		3	1	3	8
August 30					5		5
September 1					3		3
September 28			1				1
September 30					1		1
October 1					1		1
October 26						1	1
October 27				1			1
October 29		1			6		7
October 30					3		3
October 31		15			4		19
November 1					1		1
November 2		1					1
November 3					6		6
November 5					1		1
November 6		3			12		15
November 7				1	2		3
November 8						2	2
November 9					1		1
November 11					1		1
November 12		2			1		3
November 13					1		1
November 14					3		3
November 15					1		1
November 16		1					1
November 19					1		1
November 20		1			3		4
November 21			2		2	6	10
November 23			1	1		1	3
November 24			1	1		1	3
December 2					1		1
December 11	1	10		2	39		52
Total	1	37	5	13	129	23	208

Fort Sumter Resisting the Attack of the Monitor Fleet.

BOMBARDMENT OF CHARLESTON,

August 21 to December 31, 1863.

BY

MAJOR HENRY BRYAN,
Assistant Inspector-General.

Charleston, January 6, 1864.

In compliance with inclosed order, I have the honor to make the following report on the bombardment of Charleston by the Abolition army up to this date.

The general result has been the injury of a large number of dwellings and stores, and many banks, public halls, churches, etc., by the percussion and explosion of the shells thrown; the burning of six buildings and a cotton-press, December 25, 1863, by a fire originating from the explosion of a shell, and the destruction of some medical stores, August 21, 1863, by a shell bursting in the medical purveyor's office and setting fire to it. It has further caused considerable social distress by obliging thousands of persons in the lower part of the city, in order to avoid danger, to leave their homes and close their hotels, and seek refuge in the upper portion of the city or in the interior of the State. This will expose valuable property to theft, and to injury from the elements. The effect upon military operations here has been comparatively unimportant, and has occasioned no loss of material excepting the medical stores, worth about fifteen hundred dollars. As a matter of prudence, all military headquarters, offices and hospitals have been moved out of range to the upper portions of the city, the signal corps remaining at its post, which is out of the line of fire. As equally good buildings have been found in the upper part of the city for these offices, hospitals, etc., their removal can not be considered an injury to the army. The movements of harbor transportation have been much inconvenienced, but not practically impeded, by this bombardment.

The casualties have been remarkably few, and fallen almost entirely upon the civilians who clung to their homes. The whole result has so far been utterly inadequate to the labors and boasts of the besieging forces. That they should attempt to intimidate the people of Charleston into a surrender of their city is not to be wondered at; but having plainly seen that the destruction of property did not shake their determination, it is difficult to imagine what usage of civilization would justify them in continuing it.

Damage to Property.—This will be large, owing to the impracticability of repairs and consequent action of the elements on buildings laid open to it. The immediate damage from the shells can not be considered large in proportion to the area within the enemy's range. From Saint Michaels steeple, which commands a full view, there is but a small appearance of destruction visible. By a rough inspection of the city yesterday, with an intelligent local editor who had already been taking accounts of the effects of the shelling, I learned that one hundred and twenty-six buildings (including kitchens) had been struck by shells, about eighty-five being much injured and forty-one only slightly. I presume that three-fourths of the houses struck can be repaired without pulling down any main wall; but a portion have rafters, joists, or corners very badly shattered—the South Carolina Hall (near Saint Michaels Church) for instance, having been struck three times through the roof.

Damage to Life.—Five deaths have resulted from the bombardment, viz.: Mrs. Hawthorne, No. 70 Church Street, wounded by shell in right side, and died six weeks after; Miss Plane, corner Meeting and Market, left foot crushed by shell and died in six days; Mr. William Knighton, corner Meeting and Market, right leg taken off, and died in four days; Mr. John Dorcher, of German Fire Company, wounded at fire of December 25th, and since died; Rebecca, slave of Mr. Lindsay, No. 5 Beaufair Street, killed instantly by shell. At the fire of December 25th, there were one fireman, one policeman and four soldiers slightly wounded.

Number of Shots.—The number fired at the city from August 21, 1863, to January 5, 1864, as noted by the observer in Saint Michael's, is four hundred and seventy-two. Of these, twenty-seven were thrown on August 21st, 22d and 24th, and three on October 27th. The regular bombardment may be said to have begun on November 17th, from which date to January 5, 1864, four hundred and forty-two are reported. Out of the four hundred and seventy-two shells thrown at the city, twenty-eight are reported to have fallen short, making about four hundred and forty-four which struck in the city; but in my inspection and inquiry, I could only learn of some two hundred and twenty-five, viz.:

Shells striking houses	145
Shells striking yards	19
Shells striking in the streets and on the edge of burned district	61
Total	225

There were certainly a considerable number which had struck in the burned district, and probably in deserted yards, of which I could get no account. I hand with this

BOMBARDMENT OF THE CITY OF CHARLESTON, S. C.

a map* of Charleston (drawn by that skillful artist, Lieutenant [George E.] Walter, C. S. Engineers), in which I have designated roughly by specks of red paint, the locality where each shell fell, the extreme points where shells struck being connected by straight red ink lines.

AVERAGE NUMBER OF SHOTS PER DAY.—During the three shellings in August (21st to 24th), four days, about seven per day. None in September. In October only three shells were thrown, all in one day. From November 17, 1863, to January 5, 1864, fifty days, about nine shells per day.

PROPORTION OF SHELLS WHICH BURST.—The records of this are very imperfect, and the general opinion seems to be that only one-third of the shells thrown at the city have burst. The observer's records for December are 316 shells thrown, of which 20 fell short. Of these 123 are reported as not exploded, equal to about thirty-nine per cent of the number thrown, or forty-two per cent of the number which struck the city.

On January 2, 1864, twelve shells were thrown, of which one-half failed to explode.

WHAT PART OF THE CITY MOST FREQUENTLY STRUCK.—I have indicated this on the accompanying map* by a dotted red ink line. It is nearly bounded north by Market Street from East Bay to Meeting, down Meeting to Horlbecks Alley, and along Horlbecks Alley to Tradd Street, south by Tradd Street from corner of King to Church Street, down Church Street to Longitude Lane, and along that lane to East Bay, and east by East Bay Street. Mr. [T. S.] Hale, the observer at St. Michaels, reports that "the enemy's principal line of fire upon the city has been Saint Michaels Church steeple, radiating to the northeastward as far as Saint Philips Church," and generally limited westwardly in its range to Archdale Street. "Since January 1st the enemy appears to have made Saint Philips Church steeple their line of fire, hence the shells striking higher up in the city." The shells first thrown at the city were 200-pounder Parrotts, but afterward 100-pounder Parrotts.

People are occasionally found living in the lower part of the city apparently indifferent to the danger of the enemy's fire. I think there are a good many west of Meeting Street. The Blakely gun battery appears to be the only one in the line of fire.

HENRY BRYAN,
Major and Assistant Inspector-General.

*Not found.

BOMBARDMENT OF CHARLESTON,

DECEMBER 25, 1863.

BY

COLONEL ALFRED RHETT,
First South Carolina Artillery.

HEADQUARTERS FIFTH MILITARY DISTRICT, DEPARTMENT OF SOUTH CAROLINA, GEORGIA AND FLORIDA.

CHARLESTON, January 1, 1864.

ON the morning of the 25th instant [ultimo], at 12:30 A. M., the enemy commenced to shell the city, firing briskly. This shelling continued up to 1 P. M. of the same date, the enemy having fired 150 shells, 134 of which struck in the city and 16 fell short.

About 1:10 A. M. a fire, supposed to be occasioned by the enemy's shells, broke out in a building on the north side of Broad Street, near Church Street. This house, together with the one adjoining, were consumed. The sparks ignited the house at south corner of Church Street and Saint Michaels Alley. This house, three adjoining, and the cotton-press in Church Street, were consumed. The sparks also ignited a house in Tradd Street, which fire was soon suppressed. The regular members of the fire department were rather tardy in their attendance, owing to some mistake in ringing the bell, but on their appearance rendered good service. I immediately ordered out two hundred men, First Regiment State Troops, who afterward appeared accompanied by Colonel T. B. Roberts. The fire still gaining ground, a detachment from Company A, Lucas' battalion, Captain [E. B.] Colhoun, and Company D, First Regiment South Carolina Artillery, Captain McMillan King, were ordered out. These men promptly appeared and rendered material aid in suppresing the fire. The correct range was gained by one gun of the enemy, which threw several shells in proximity to the engines and the fire.

I beg leave to call your attention to the coolness displayed by the men working the Ætna and Marion fire-engines, especially those on the former. A shell burst very near the engine, but the men continued working and rendered good service.

Casualties occasioned by the enemy's shells: Mr. Knighton, a man eighty-three years old, right leg shot off below the knee by a shell; Miss Plane wounded on foot by shell, both residing in house at the corner Meeting and Market streets; Jerry Murray, a member of Charleston Fire Engine Company, wounded in leg by a brick; Ser-

DEFENSES OF CHARLESTON, S. C., LOOKING SEAWARD FROM FORT JOHNSON, FEBRUARY, 1863.

geant H. P. McClemons, contusion on left arm by a fragment of stone; Thomas R. Brown, private, painfully wounded on right hip and on neck by a fragment of stone; E. Ballinger, private, arm and thigh, flesh wound; W. Meadows, thigh, contusion—all of Company H, First Regiment State Troops.

ALFRED RHETT,
Colonel Commanding.

REPORT OF THE NUMBER OF SHOTS FIRED AT THE CITY FROM THE ENEMY'S BATTERIFS ON MORRIS ISLAND UP TO DATE.

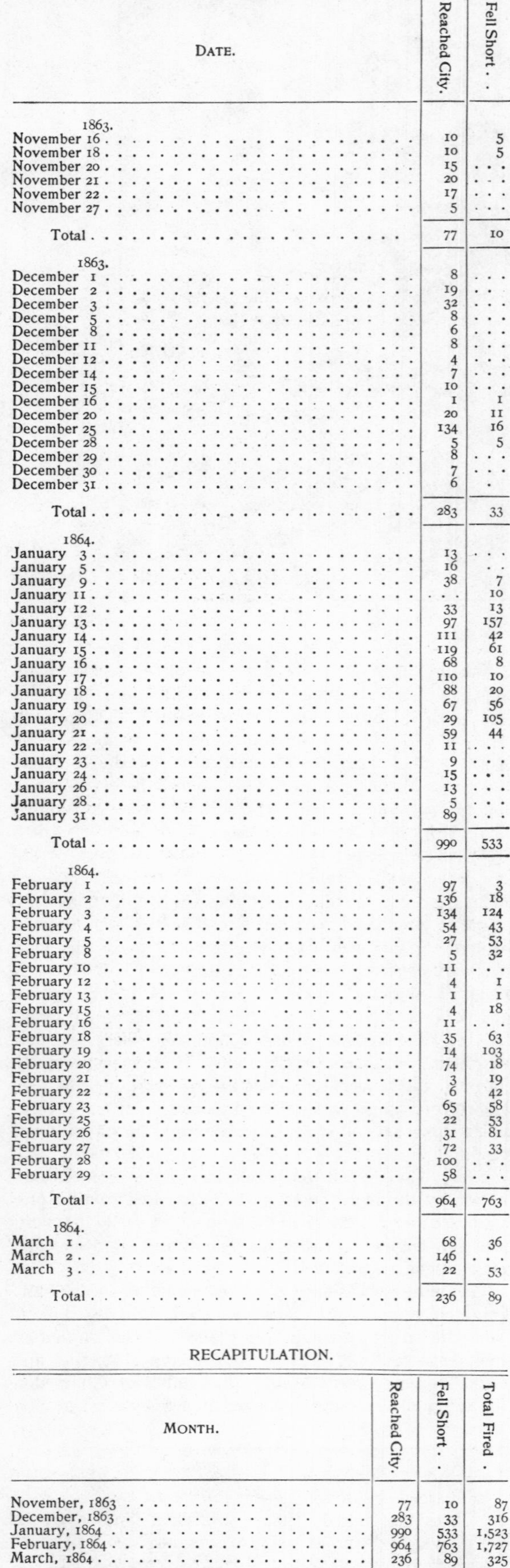

DATE.	Reached City.	Fell Short. .
1863.		
November 16	10	5
November 18	10	5
November 20	15	. . .
November 21	20	. . .
November 22	17	. . .
November 27	5	. . .
Total	77	10
1863.		
December 1	8	. . .
December 2	19	. . .
December 3	32	. . .
December 5	8	. . .
December 8	6	. . .
December 11	8	. . .
December 12	4	. . .
December 14	7	. . .
December 15	10	. . .
December 16	1	1
December 20	20	11
December 25	134	16
December 28	5	5
December 29	8	. . .
December 30	7	. . .
December 31	6	.
Total	283	33
1864.		
January 3	13	. . .
January 5	16	. .
January 9	38	7
January 11	. . .	10
January 12	33	13
January 13	97	157
January 14	111	42
January 15	119	61
January 16	68	8
January 17	110	10
January 18	88	20
January 19	67	56
January 20	29	105
January 21	59	44
January 22	11	. . .
January 23	9	. . .
January 24	15	. . .
January 26	13	. . .
January 28	5	. . .
January 31	89	. . .
Total	990	533
1864.		
February 1	97	3
February 2	136	18
February 3	134	124
February 4	54	43
February 5	27	53
February 8	5	32
February 10	11	. . .
February 12	4	1
February 13	1	1
February 15	4	18
February 16	11	. . .
February 18	35	63
February 19	14	103
February 20	74	18
February 21	3	19
February 22	6	42
February 23	65	58
February 25	22	53
February 26	31	81
February 27	72	33
February 28	100	. . .
February 29	58	. . .
Total	964	763
1864.		
March 1	68	36
March 2	146	. . .
March 3	22	53
Total	236	89

RECAPITULATION.

MONTH.	Reached City.	Fell Short. .	Total Fired.
November, 1863	77	10	87
December, 1863	283	33	316
January, 1864	990	533	1,523
February, 1864	964	763	1,727
March, 1864	236	89	325
Grand total	2,550	1,428	3,978

ALFRED RHETT, *Colonel Commanding.*

CHARLESTON, March 4, 1864.

ADDENDA.

HEADQUARTERS DEPARTMENT OF SOUTH CAROLINA, GEORGIA AND FLORIDA,
CHARLESTON, S. C., January 3, 1864.

Colonel Alfred Rhett, Fifth Military District:

COLONEL: I am directed by the commanding general to request that you address the mayor of the city of Charleston and report to him the efficient manner in which the firemen who worked the engines Ætna and Marion performed their duty, and the coolness displayed by said firemen, while under fire, on the morning of the 25th ultimo.

I am, colonel, very respectfully your obedient servant,

JOHN M. OTEY,
Assistant Adjutant-General.

SIGNAL CORPS
IN THE
CONFEDERATE STATES ARMY.

BY

EDWARD H. CUMMINS,
Late of the Signal Corps, Confederate States Army.

MEMORANDUM of names of officers of the Signal Corps of the Confederate States Provisional Army, appointed under the act of the Confederate Congress, May 29, 1862, providing for the appointment of ten captains and ten sergeants.

CAPTAINS.

1. R. H. T. Adams, November 23, 1863.
2. James H. Alexander, July 7, 1862.
3. William N. Barker, March 30, 1864.
4. Thomas H. Clagett, April 13, 1864.
5. M. T. Davidson, June 9, 1862.
6. Elcan Jones, February 3, 1864.

SIGNAL TOWER.

7. J. H. Manning, June 10, 1862.
8. William Norris (promoted major and chief), July 31, 1862.
9. M. L. Randolph, November 12, 1862.
10. R. E. Wilbourne, July 31, 1862.
11. J. H. Stewart, Mississippi.
12. Richard E. Frazer, Virginia.

SERGEANTS.

(Appointed under Acts of May 29 and September 27, 1862.)

1. J. Bankhead, May 20, 1863.
2. P. D. Bester, April 23, 1863.
3. P. A. H. Brown, September 9, 1864.
4. Mason M. Burrows, November 12, 1862.
5. E. S. Gregory, November 23, 1863.
6. Joseph K. Irving, October 28, 1862.
7. A. W. Pearce, November 21, 1862.
8. Junius L. Powell, November 12, 1862.
9. J. B. Smith, July 4, 1863.
10. H. A. Tutwiler, April 16, 1863.
11. N. J. Watkins, November 12, 1862.

Memorandum of officers of the Signal Corps of the Confederate States Provisional Army, appointed under act of the Confederate Congress of September 27, 1862, providing for the appointment of one major, ten first and ten second lieutenants, and twenty additional sergeants:

MAJOR.

William Norris, October 24, 1862.

FIRST LIEUTENANTS.

1. Edmund Burke, June 19, 1863.
2. James Carey (acting chief of corps), July 4, 1863.
3. H. C. Lindsay (resigned), June 22, 1863.
4. A. L. Lindsay, November 12, 1862.
5. C. G. Memminger, November 29, 1862.
6. W. N. Mercer Otey, November 12, 1862.
7. William C. Schley, November 24, 1862.
8. A. J. Stedman, November 29, 1862.

SECOND LIEUTENANTS.

1. John Bellinger, April 16, 1863.
2. Charles H. Cawood, June 27, 1863.
3. James L. Crittenden, June 26, 1863.
4. J. L. Doggett, March 9, 1863.
5. Eli Duvall, November 24, 1862.
6. George E. Harrison, May 20, 1863.
7. Frank Markoe, Jr., November 12, 1862.
8. E. T. Ruffin, November 12, 1862.
9. George E. Tabb, May 20, 1863.

Memorandum of names of officers of the Independent Signal Corps:

Lieutenant R. A. Forbes, Second Company (see S. O., A. & I. G. O., July 25, 1863.)

The beginnings of the Signal Service in the Confederate Army were about simultaneous in the Peninsular command of General John B. Magruder and in the Army of Northern Virginia under General Beauregard. Captain Norris, a member of General Magruder's staff—a gentleman of scientific education and of some nautical experience—called the attention of the general to the advantages to be derived from a system of signals connecting his outposts and his headquarters with Norfolk. Magruder forthwith gave Captain Norris the necessary authority to establish the service, and appointed him Signal Officer to the command.

The signals used by Captain Norris were similar to the marine signals in use by all maritime nations. Poles were erected on which were displayed flags and balls, the combinations of which indicated various phrases, such as were conceived to be most in demand to express the exigencies likely to arise.

Captain Norris (hereinafter to be spoken of as Major William Norris, Chief of the Signal Corps, Confederate States Army) caused to be made copper stencils, from which colored plates of the combinations were made, and upon the same page of the book which contained the plates were written the meanings of the combinations. The plates were colored by Miss Belle Harrison, of "Brandon," and Miss Jennie Ritchie, of Richmond. The system was from time to time improved by Colonel Norris, and this was one of the beginnings of the signal service in the Confederate States Army.

The other was at Beauregard's headquarters at Manassas Junction, at about the same time—in the summer of 1861. Captain (afterward General) E. P. Alexander, attached to the staff of General Beauregard, was one of the officers who had been detailed by the Secretary of War (United States) to test and report upon the signal system of Dr. (Brigadier-General) Myer, and was consequently completely master of the system. He organized it efficiently, and thoroughly instructed a number of men selected from the ranks for their intelligence and good character. Most of these men afterward became commissioned officers in the Signal Corps.

The service was in full operation at the time of the first conflict at Bull Run, and the third shot from Ayres' battery in front of Stone Bridge went through one of Alexander's signal tents, in front of which the flags were being actively plied.

General Alexander, in reply to a letter asking for information respecting the services rendered by the signal men under his direction, writes as follows: "Perhaps the most important service rendered by the Signal Department in the first year of the war was at the battle of Bull Run, and was in a great measure accidental. Very early in the morning of the 21st, I was on the hill by Wilcox's house, in rear of our right, and watching the flag of our station at the Stone Bridge, when, in the distant edge of the field of view of my glass, a gleam caught my eye. It was the reflection of the sun (which was low in the east behind me) from a polished brass field-piece, one of Ayres' battery, and, observing attentively, I discovered McDowell's columns in the open fields, north of Sudleys Ford, crossing Bull Run and turning our left flank, fully eight miles away, I think—but you can look at the map—from where I was. I signaled Evans at once, 'Look out for your left, your position is turned.' Just as he got my message his pickets made their first report to him of cavalry driving them from Sudleys Ford. At the same time I sent a message of what I had seen to Johnston and Beauregard, who were at Mitchells Ford, on receipt of which, Bee, Hampton and Stonewall Jackson were all hurried in that direction, and the history of the battle tells how they successfully delayed McDowell's progress, till finally the tide was turned by troops arriving in the afternoon.

"The rocket incident referred to I had almost forgotten. It was only that one night, on reports that rockets were seen in the enemy's lines, by our stations, that they were ordered by General Beauregard to send up rockets themselves. It was done simultaneously at many distant points, and in such a manner as to appear to indicate some important and general movement; and, from what appeared afterward in Northern papers, it seemed that McClellan had something on foot which was disconcerted by it, he believing that his plans had been betrayed.

"The Munsons Hill and Washington telegraph was never actually worked, because General Johnston withdrew from the advanced and dangerous position at Munsons Hill Fort before the day fixed for it to open. Bryan was in Washington City, and was selecting a suitable room to rent, not on Pennsylvania Avenue, but in an elevated part of the city, from which Munsons Hill could be seen. He was to take the bearing of the hill by compass from his window, and communicate it to us by an agreed-upon advertisement in a daily paper which we received regularly. This would give us the bearing on which to turn our powerful telescope, loaned for the purpose by a Charleston gentleman, and in position on Munsons Hill. Then we would identify his window by finding a coffee-pot in it, and, by motions of the coffee-pot, and opening and shutting the blinds, etc., he would send his messages, and we would reply, if necessary, by a large flag and by firing guns."

"Bryan," was Captain Pliny Bryan, an ex-member of the Maryland Legislature, who, on the commencement of hostilities, had volunteerd in the Maryland Line, so-called, composed of Maryland volunteers in the service of Virginia, and afterward turned over to the Confederate States. He was detailed for the Signal Service, and went to Washington, accredited to the secret friends of the Confederate States there, and with instructions that may be inferred from General Alexander's letter.

In February, 1862, General Beauregard took command of the Army of the Mississippi, and assigned to duty as chief signal officer Captain E. H. Cummins, of the Engineers Corps, Confederate States Army. This officer advertised for spy-glasses, as there were none to be had by purchase in the department, and repairing to Madrid Bend (then occupied by Major-General J. P. McCown with his forces) with a small squad of men who had been selected and instructed by Captain E. P. Alexander, and a very poor outfit, set up the necessary stations to establish communication between the batteries and intrenchments at New Madrid, Tiptonville and Island No. 10.

The extracts following, from official sources, show that, though under manifold disadvantages, the signal men gave a good account of themselves in the first struggle for the possession of the Mississippi River.

In his report of the attack upon Battery No. 1, by Commodore Foote's fleet, and attempt to destroy it by an overwhelming superiority of fire, March 17, 1862, Brigadier-General Trudeau, commanding the Confederate States Artillery, says:

"At 9 P. M. Captain Cummins, of the Signal Service, went to Battery No. 1 and established there a signal station, which proved of great service during the various engagements."

Further on in his report, the general says: "Besides the officers already mentioned, who were conspicuous for their bravery and coolness under a galling fire, I will mention Signal Officers E. Jones and S. Rose, who never left their posts one minute. While shot and shell were tearing everything to pieces, Signal Officer E. Jones had his flag-staff shot from his hands; he coolly picked up the flag and continued to communicate his message."

Captain (afterward General) Ed. Rucker, commanding the battery, says: "E. Jones and Samuel Rose, of the Signal Corps, were engaged with me the whole day in defense of the redan, and bore themselves with great coolness and gallantry. Signal Officer Jones having the staff of his flag shot away thrice during the engagement, seized the flag in his hand, without looking around to listen to exclamations, and continued his important message to headquarters."

The flag was probably knocked out of Mr. Jones' hands by the mud, tons of which flew in the air every time the heavy projectiles from the fleet struck the parapet. Captain Rucker says: "Many shot and shell fell immediately in rear of our guns, while others passed through the parapet, plowing up the earth and destroying much of the work." This explanation is suggested, because, while it eliminates the marvelous element from the story, it detracts nothing from the credit due Mr. Jones for his gallant conduct. It may seem presumptuous to question the literal truth of reports penned upon the spot by superior officers, and which, by lapse of years, have passed into the domain of history, but it should be remembered that official reports, written immediately after a lively action, are worded under excitement which has not had time to cool, and in great part upon reports of others, for nobody is able at such times to see everything; besides which, the writer of these reflections was himself an eye-witness of the incidents related, through a spy-glass at a safe distance, and held in his hands, after the fight, the identical flag-staff which is said to have been thrice shot away and which was undamaged.

Two more brief extracts are quoted to show that the service of the Signal Corps was not that of carpet knights. Colonel Brown, of the Fifty-fifth Tennessee Volunteers, writes: "The enemy's heavy shot and shell poured an almost incessant volume upon our meager earthwork, riddling the parapet in front of our guns, plowing up the earth in every direction and tearing down immense trees in a manner baffling description. The scene was the most terrific conceivable."

General Trudeau also says: "It," the redan fort, "presented the most appalling picture of ruin and desolation. The parapet was plowed up in every direction and torn to pieces. Trees were hacked down and torn to shreds by the heavy shells and the rifled cannon."

The signal men at Battery No. 1 had no protection whatever—not even that of the parapet behind which the gunners squatted when not firing—for their position was in rear of the guns, where fell, as Captain Rucker says, "many shot and shell."

Upon the capture of New Madrid and Island No. 10 by Admiral Foote and General Pope, the signal party escaped across Reelfoot Lake, taking French leave of the commanding generals and paddling across on a raft of their own construction. They repaired at once, of their own motion and without orders, to Corinth, Miss., then headquarters of the army, and reported for duty. The signal officer is merely mentioned by General Beauregard in his report of the fight at Shiloh Chapel (or Pittsburg Landing) as doing active staff duty. After the battle, seventeen men were detailed to be instructed for duty in the Signal Corps; but as glasses were scarce and all the country between Corinth and the Tennessee River was heavily wooded, the men were mounted and served chiefly as scouts and couriers while their instruction was going on and until sent elsewhere.

Signal Station on Morris Island, S. C.

Among those detailed at this time was Carlo Patti, a private of the One Hundred and Fifty-fourth Tennessee Infantry—Colonel Smith. He quickly learned his duties and was zealous in their performance. When not employed with his flags and spy-glass, he was incessantly playing his violin. He was once sent as lance sergeant in charge of a squad of prisoners to Mobile, and it was amusing to see the care and watchfulness he displayed in authority. It would have broken his heart had one of his prisoners escaped. To finish with Carlo: He remained with the Signal Corps until captured off Havana in a blockade runner in 1864. He was bound for the Rio Grande to join General Slaughter, via Havana and Mexico, but after his capture never returned to the Confederate States. Peace to his ashes; he was not a bad sort of a fellow.

On falling back from Corinth, the signal men being sufficiently instructed to go on duty were dispersed to several points in the command—Clagett with one party going to Mobile, Davidson with another to Vicksburg, and Elcan Jones with another to Kirby Smith across the river. These were three good men meriting the promotion they afterward got. All of them became captains in the Signal Corps, and Elcan Jones, the hero of Battery No. 1, was, at the end of the war, chief signal officer to General Joseph E. Johnston.

Although, as has been shown, the Signal Service was in active and useful operation on several theaters of war—in the East in 1861, and early in 1862 in the West—it was not until April 19, 1862, that the act was approved organizing the Signal Corps as a distinct branch of the Confederate Army, and the Secretary of War was authorized to establish it as a separate corps or to attach it to the Adjutant and Inspector's Department or to the Engineer Corps. The secretary decided to attach it to the Adjutant and Inspector-General's Department, and May 29, 1862, was issued General Orders No. 40, A. & I. G. O., creating the Signal Bureau, with Major Wm. Norris, of General Magruder's staff, as the head of it. No uniform was prescribed for the Signal Corps. The officers wore the uniform of the general staff of the same grade, and the detailed men wore that of the arm of the service to which they belonged, and on the rolls of which they were borne as detailed men. The Signal Corps, as organized, consisted of one major commanding, ten captains, ten first and ten second-class lieutenants and twenty sergeants. There were no privates, as men were detailed from the line of the army whenever wanted, and when their services were no longer required they returned to their respective commands.

The detailed men in all the various branches of the service numbered about fifteen hundred, and it was a remarkable fact that while these men were often employed in independent service and were in possession of important secrets, not one of them ever deserted or betrayed his trust. All the detailed men were instructed in the cipher system and intrusted with the key-word. They were also instructed in the use of the electric telegraph. When occasion required, they became dauntless messengers and agents, going into the enemy's lines and cities, or to lands beyond the sea; communicating with agents and secret friends of the Confederate Government and people; ordering supplies and conveying them to their destination; running the blockade by land and sea; making nightly voyages in bays and rivers; threading the enemy's cordon of pickets and gunboats; following blind trails through swamps and forest, and as much experts with oar and sail, on deck and in the saddle, and with rifle and revolver, as with flags, torches, telegraph and secret cipher.

What were the duties at headquarters in the Adjutant-General's Department at Richmond, is best defined in a letter of Major Norris in answer to an officer, representing the adjutant-general, asking the question. They were: First, management of the entire Signal Corps and Cipher System of Confederate States Army—therein is included also (*a*) manufacture and collection of all signal apparatus and stores; (*b*) manufacture, collection and distribution of all cipher apparatus; second, management and supplying secret lines of communication on the Potomac; third, translation of cipher messages received or sent by the War Department, heads of bureaus, or officers of the army.

The duties of officers and employes on the Potomac are defined as follows: First, to afford transportation from and to Baltimore or Washington for all scouts, agents, etc., who shall present orders for the same from the War Department, heads of bureaus, and generals commanding armies, approved by Chief of Signal Corps; second, to observe and report all movements of the enemy on the Potomac River; third, to secure for Executive Department files of latest Northern papers; fourth, to obtain for heads of bureaus small packages, books, etc.; fifth, to forward letters from War or State departments to agents, commissioners, etc., in foreign countries.

In regard to sources of information and out of what fund paid for, Major Norris says: "Accredited agents constantly in New York, Baltimore and Washington. These agents are gentlemen of high social position, who, without compensation, have voluntarily devoted their time and energies to this work. Among them I mention in confidence the name of the Hon. ———. There is no secret service fund beyond the mere pay, rations and clothing of the officers and detailed men engaged in them. These lines have never cost the Government one farthing since I assumed command.

"When secret information is received, it is transmitted to the Secretary of War, to General Bragg, and the general whose army or department is supposed to be immediately affected thereby; when it comes, as is generally the case, under cover, sealed and directed to a particular general, it is forwarded accordingly. We receive information regularly from the United States on Mondays, Thursdays and Saturdays. For prudential reasons no record of such communications is kept in this office, except in cipher."

To the question, "Do the agents of the Signal Office obtain their information personally or from friendly parties?" Major Norris says: "Two of our agents acquire their information from personal observations, the others from friendly parties within the lines." To the question, "What are the means of testing the credibility of friendly persons living in the enemy's country?" it is answered: "These agents were selected with great care, and with an eye to their intelligence and devotion and energy. Actual experience alone, however, must prove their credibility."

"From the first of April to the last of September," continues Major Norris on another head, "we placed files of Baltimore papers, published one morning, in the hands of the President next evening; New York papers, of course, a day later."

Major Norris gives the history of the secret service branch of the Signal Corps in the following words: "In the fall of 1862, the necessity of having points on the Potomac River, at which Government agents and army scouts might promptly and without delay cross to and from the United States, was so seriously appreciated that the Secretary of War suggested the propriety of establishing one or more camps in King George and Westmoreland counties, with an especial eye to such transportation. The idea was immediately acted upon. In a short time the additional duties were assigned to these stations—first, of observing and reporting all movements of troops, etc., on the Potomac; second, securing complete files of Northern papers for Executive Department; third, upon requisition from heads of bureaus, to obtain from the United States small packages, books, etc. Here our duties, strictly speaking, ended. But as we were forced, in order to perform the other duties, to establish a line of agents from the Potomac to Washington, it was determined, as far as possible, to institute a regular system of espionage. The Government having failed, however, to place at our disposal the necessary means to carry into execution this design, we have been forced to rely almost entirely upon the energy and zeal of a few devoted gentlemen of Maryland for such indications of the enemy's movements as they have been able to acquire from mingling in official circles about Washington, Baltimore and New York."

It was the duty of Major Norris to wait on Mr. Davis every morning with the cipher dispatches from the generals of armies and department commanders. The burden of these dispatches was, toward the close, calamitous and importunate — re-enforcements and supplies were everywhere demanded. All looked to Mr. Davis for relief and support. It was the cry of the king to the prophet: "My father! my father! the chariots of Israel and the horsemen thereof!" Major Norris bears testimony to the unruffled serenity of his chief through all these trying hours — not an impatient or despondent word ever escaped him. If Mr. Davis ever knew when he was whipped he never let any one else know that he knew it.

The secret cipher used by the Confederate States War Department was that known as the court cipher, and has been much used in diplomatic service. A key-word or phrase is agreed upon by the parties who intend to communicate in cipher. The message is written under the key. Suppose, for example, the key to be "In God we trust;" and the message, "Longstreet is marching on Fishers Hill." It will be written thus:

InGodwetrustinGodwetrustinGodwetr
LongstreetismarchingonFishersHill

The alphabet is written out in a square, thus:

A	B	C	D	E	F	G	H	I	J	K	L	M	N	O	P	Q	R	S	T	U	V	W	X	Y	Z
B	C	D	E	F	G	H	I	J	K	L	M	N	O	P	Q	R	S	T	U	V	W	X	Y	Z	A
C	D	E	F	G	H	I	J	K	L	M	N	O	P	Q	R	S	T	U	V	W	X	Y	Z	A	B
D	E	F	G	H	I	J	K	L	M	N	O	P	Q	R	S	T	U	V	W	X	Y	Z	A	B	C
E	F	G	H	I	J	K	L	M	N	O	P	Q	R	S	T	U	V	W	X	Y	Z	A	B	C	D
F	G	H	I	J	K	L	M	N	O	P	Q	R	S	T	U	V	W	X	Y	Z	A	B	C	D	E
G	H	I	J	K	L	M	N	O	P	Q	R	S	T	U	V	W	X	Y	Z	A	B	C	D	E	F
H	I	J	K	L	M	N	O	P	Q	R	S	T	T	V	W	X	Y	Z	A	B	C	D	E	F	G
I	J	K	L	M	N	O	P	Q	R	S	T	U	V	W	X	Y	Z	A	B	C	D	E	F	G	H
J	K	L	M	N	O	P	Q	R	S	T	U	V	W	X	Y	Z	A	B	C	D	E	F	G	H	I
K	L	M	N	O	P	Q	R	S	T	U	V	W	X	Y	Z	A	B	C	D	E	F	G	H	I	J
L	M	N	O	P	Q	R	S	T	U	V	W	X	Y	Z	A	B	C	D	E	F	G	H	I	J	K
M	N	O	P	Q	R	S	T	U	V	W	X	Y	Z	A	B	C	D	E	F	G	H	I	J	K	L
N	O	P	Q	R	S	T	U	V	W	X	Y	Z	A	B	C	D	E	F	G	H	I	J	K	L	M
O	P	Q	R	S	T	U	V	W	X	Y	Z	A	B	C	D	E	F	G	H	I	J	K	L	M	N
P	Q	R	S	T	U	V	W	X	Y	Z	A	B	C	D	E	F	G	H	I	J	K	L	M	N	O
Q	R	S	T	U	V	W	X	Y	Z	A	B	C	D	E	F	G	H	I	J	K	L	M	N	O	P
R	S	T	U	V	W	X	Y	Z	A	B	C	D	E	F	G	H	I	J	K	L	M	N	O	P	Q
S	T	U	V	W	X	Y	Z	A	B	C	D	E	F	G	H	I	J	K	L	M	N	O	P	Q	R
T	U	V	W	X	Y	Z	A	B	C	D	E	F	G	H	I	J	K	L	M	N	O	P	Q	R	S
U	V	W	X	Y	Z	A	B	C	D	E	F	G	H	I	J	K	L	M	N	O	P	Q	R	S	T
V	W	X	Y	Z	A	B	C	D	E	F	G	H	I	J	K	L	M	N	O	P	Q	R	S	T	U
W	X	Y	Z	A	B	C	D	E	F	G	H	I	J	K	L	M	N	O	P	Q	R	S	T	U	V
X	Y	Z	A	B	C	D	E	F	G	H	I	J	K	L	M	N	O	P	Q	R	S	T	U	V	W
Y	Z	A	B	C	D	E	F	G	H	I	J	K	L	M	N	O	P	Q	R	S	T	U	V	W	X
Z	A	B	C	D	E	F	G	H	I	J	K	L	M	N	O	P	Q	R	S	T	U	V	W	X	Y

The first letter in the key is "I," and the letter under it is "L." Take "I" in the top horizontal column and run down the "I" vertical column until it intersects the "L" horizontal column. The letter at the intersection is "T." This is substituted in the message for "L" in Longstreet. The other letters are converted in the same way, and the message will read thus:

Tbturpvxnalunxgklrzfhxbaukfvdmec

Sometimes the small words were run into the contiguous large ones, and sometimes no division into words is made, as in the above example. The last is the best plan. If the words are separated, or if a part of the message is written in plain language, a chance is given to guess at some of the words, of which an expert is not slow to avail himself. How important it is not to give such a clue will be seen hereafter.

To decipher the message, the key was written over it, and the process by which it was put into cipher reversed. To facilitate reading the cipher messages, Captain Wm. N. Barker, of the Signal Corps, invented a simple but convenient apparatus. The alphabetical square was pasted on a cylinder and revolved under a bar, on which was a sliding pointer. Under the pointer and along the bar was pasted the alphabet in a horizontal line. The pointer was brought to the letter in the key on the bar, and the letter in the word to be converted was rolled up under the bar and the pointer rested on the required substitute letter. A model of the Confederate apparatus is preserved among the Confederate records in the War Department at Washington.

The Confederate authorities were sometimes so careless or unskillful in "putting up" their cipher dispatches that some important ones, which fell into the hands of the enemy, were deciphered without much trouble. One from General Beauregard, just after the battle at Shiloh Chapel, giving the number and condition of his forces at Corinth, was put up by merely putting the last half of the alphabet first; that is, substituting "M" for "A," "N" for "B," "O" for "C," etc. This dispatch fell into the hands of the enemy, and first reached Richmond, in a "Yankee" newspaper, translated.

A message from Mr. Davis, at Montgomery, to General E. Kirby Smith, commanding the Trans-Mississippi Department, was partly in plain language and partly in cipher, in which is found the following: "By which you may effect a—t p g g e x y k—above that part—h j o p g k w m c t patrolled by the," etc., etc.

An expert of the United States Military Telegraph Corps guessed that that part of the dispatch was meant to read: "By which you may effect a crossing above that part of the river patrolled by the," etc., etc. The guess was right, and, by applying it, the key-phrase was discovered to be "complete victory," and there was, of course, no trouble in reading what remained of the message in cipher. The author of the history of "The Military Telegraph in the Civil War" says this meaning occurred to him at first sight, and would have occurred to any one familiar with military affairs in that section.

The same writer makes the reflection: "It is a question if the Confederate cipher system was any more difficult to the uninitiated than one of the first examples of secret writing found in history. We refer to the Spartan Scytale cipher. When the general of the army ventured into the enemy's country, or was cut off in his own, he communicated with the Spartan Ephors by the use of a staff called a Scytale, an exact duplicate of which was possessed by the Ephors. The party desiring to write, first wound a slip of parchment around the staff, and then wrote his message lengthwise with the stick. After which, when it was unrolled, only unmeaning letters, wholly unconnected with one another, appeared, but the receiver rewound the ribbon on his Scytale, and all was plain."

The alphabet first used by the Confederate Signal Corps was a modification of that introduced by General Myer into the service of the United States. It became necessary to change it several times during the war, as from observation of messages sent in the field the United States signal men learned to read the Confederate messages, while the Confederates took the same liberty with the messages of the other side.

Early played a ruse on Sheridan in the Valley campaigns. Finding that Sheridan was reading his signals, he caused the following dispatch to be sent to himself by his signal flags:

"*Lieutenant-General Early, Fishers Hill:*

"Be ready to advance on Sheridan as soon as my forces get up, and we can crush him before he finds out I have joined you.

"(Signed) J. LONGSTREET."

SIGNALING FROM THE ROAD.

When this was communicated to Sheridan, as Early intended it to be, Sheridan telegraphed to Washington and Halleck telegraphed to Grant. In time, the answer came to Sheridan that Longstreet was nowhere near Early. This telegram was long a puzzle to the Union general. When Early was asked about it after the war, he simply laughed.

The Signal Corps was nowhere more useful than where the defense and operations were conducted in a field in which water occupied a large place in the topography. Such were Charleston, S. C., and Mobile. The reports of Captain Frank Markoe, signal officer at Charleston, show that during the siege thousands of messages were sent from one post to another, and from outposts to headquarters, most of which could have been sent in no other way, and many were of great importance.

It is hoped that the length of the following extracts from Captain Markoe's reports will be excused by their interest:

"During the month (July, 1863,) my corps has been at work day and night. At Cummings Point (Battery Gregg) Lance Sergeant Edgerton and Privates Du Barry, Lance, Huger, Martin and Grimball have gallantly worked their post with untiring zeal and ability, constantly under heavy fire of the enemy's fleet and land batteries. Fortunately, I have no casualties to report, although their station has suffered from the enemy's fire and is full of holes. As there was no other means of communication with Morris Island, their labors have been very heavy. They have sent over five hundred messages, and at least a third of them under fire. As they are completely exhausted, I have relieved them and sent the men from Sullivans Island to Battery Gregg. I have read nearly every message the enemy has sent. Many of them of great importance. We were forewarned of their attack on the 18th, and were ready for them, with what success is already a part of history. The services rendered by the corps in this respect have been of the utmost importance. But I regret to state that, by the carelessness of staff-officers at headquarters, it has leaked out that we have read the enemy's signals. I have ordered all my men to disclaim any knowledge of them whenever questioned. My men have also been actively employed in guiding the fire of our guns, and have thus rendered valuable service."

In his August report, Captain Markoe says: "At Fort Sumter, H. W. Rice was twice injured by bricks. At Battery Wagner, I. P. Moodie was shot in the thigh by a musket ball; J. D. Creswell was struck in the face by pieces of shell, and I received a slight flesh wound in the side by a piece of shell. These are all the casualties, I am glad to say. The work done has been very large, as the telegraph line has been constantly out of order for days at a time. We have continued to read the enemy's signals, and much valuable information has been obtained. I have temporarily changed the signals, as we intercepted a message from the enemy as follows: 'Send me a copy of Rebel Code immediately, if you have one in your possession.' I make the men, moreover, work out of sight as much as possible, and feel sure that they can make nothing out of our signals."

In his next (September) month's report, Captain Markoe continues: "Morris Island was evacuated by our forces on Sunday night, the 6th of September. I brought off my men and all the signal property on the Island. Lance Sergeant Lawrence and Privates Clark and Legare were stationed at Battery Gregg, and Privates Grimball and Hatch at Battery Wagner from the 1st of September to the day of evacuation. They were exposed to the heaviest fire that the enemy had ever put upon those works, and performed their duties with conspicuous gallantry. Often the enemy's shell, exploding on the fort, would completely envelop the men and flag with smoke and sand for a minute, but as it cleared away the flag would still be waving. I have to report Private Clark badly burned in the left hand, and Lance Sergeant Lawrence struck on the right arm with a piece of shell. From the commencement of the attack on Morris Island to the day of the evacuation my men have transmitted nearly one thousand messages on that island. On the night of the 5th, the enemy made an attack on Battery Gregg, which failed, and was repulsed by the timely notice from Sullivans Island signal station, which intercepted the following dispatch: 'To Admiral Dahlgren—I shall try Cummings Point to-night, and want the sailors again early. Will you please send two or three monitors by dark to open fire on Fort Moultrie as a diversion. The last time they were in they stopped re-enforcements, and may do so to-night. Don't want any fire in the rear. (Signed) General Gillmore.'

"The attack on Fort Sumter, on the night of the 8th, was foiled by a similar notice. The dispatch was: 'General Gillmore—The senior officer will take charge of the assaulting party on Fort Sumter, the whole to be under the command of an experienced naval officer.'

"During the attack on Sumter, Private Frank Huger was placed in charge of the fire-ball party on the parapet, numbering some thirty men, and assisted in giving the enemy a warm reception. Major Elliott, commanding the post, speaks highly of his conduct on that occasion. The enemy have been using a cipher in signaling, which has so far baffled our attempts to read their messages. They have not used it lately, however, and several important dispatches have been read."

Captain Markoe's rolls show the employment of seventy-six men, of which number he lost, through casualties, as large a per cent as any command in the action. Twelve of his men did nothing but read the enemy's papers.

Mr. A. T. Leftwitch, who was stationed in the cupola of the courthouse at Vicksburg, in 1863, contributes the following reminiscence:

"During the siege, a fifteen-inch mortar shell went through the top of the courthouse and exploded on the lower floor, where there were quartered some one hundred or so men. It seemed to me as if the whole earth had exploded, for I was in a room on the second floor—and need scarcely say that the horrible sight of finding fourteen men scattered into fragments and a number of others wounded, was terrible to behold.

"You know, of course, that we emptied every cistern in the town and depended upon the muddy Mississippi water in the hot summer time to quench our thirst; that we ate bread of ground cow-peas, and depended for meat upon dead mules and rats."

An indispensable condition to the prolongation of the war was the running of the blockade of Southern ports by the swift cruisers built and fitted expressly for the purpose. Such were the profits of this business that the owners could well afford to lose vessel and cargo on her third trip if the first two were successful. No life could be more adventurous and exciting than that of a blockade-runner. The Signal Corps played its part here also. Every blockade-runner had its signal officer, furnished with signaling apparatus and the key to the secret cipher. The coast was lined with stations for thirty or forty miles up and down on either side of the blockaded port. The blockade-runners came in close to shore at nightfall and fitfully flashed a light, which was soon answered from the shore station. Advice was then given as to condition o things off the port, the station and movements of the hostile fleet, etc. If the word was "go in," the beacon lights were set and the blockade-runner boldly steamed over the bar and into the port. A naval officer was in charge of the office of orders and details at the several ports, whence proceeded all orders and assignments in relation to pilots and signal officers.

Captain Wilkinson, C. S. N., in his interesting "Narrative of a Blockade-Runner," tells the following incident illustrative of the uses of a signal officer in this line of duty: "The range lights were showing and we crossed the bar without interference and without a suspicion of anything wrong, as it would occasionally happen under particularly favorable circumstances that we would cross the bar without even seeing a blockader. We were under the guns of Fort Fisher, in fact, and close to the fleet of United States vessels, which had crossed the bar after the fall of the fort, when I directed my signal officer to communicate with the shore station. His signal was promptly answered, but, turning to me, he said: 'No Confederate signal officer there, sir; he can not reply to me.' The order to wear around was instantly obeyed; not a moment too soon, for the bow of the Chameleon was scarcely pointed for the bar before two of the light cruisers were plainly visible in pursuit, steaming with all speed to intercept us. Nothing saved us from capture but the twin screws, which enabled our steamer to turn as upon a pivot in the narrow channel between the bar and the ribs. We reached the bar before our pursuers, and were soon lost in the darkness outside."

EDWARD H. CUMMINS.

SIGNAL STATION ON THE JAMES RIVER, VA.

THE CHICKAMAUGA CAMPAIGN,

AUGUST 16 TO SEPTEMBER 22, 1863.

BY

GENERAL BRAXTON BRAGG,
Commanding Army of Tennessee.

WARM SPRINGS, GA., December 28, 1863.

On August 20th, it was ascertained certainly that the Federal army from Middle Tennessee, under General Rosecrans, had crossed the mountains to Stevenson and Bridgeport. His force of effective infantry and artillery amounted to fully seventy thousand, divided into four corps. About the same time General Burnside advanced from Kentucky toward Knoxville, East Tennessee, with a force estimated by the general commanding that department at over twenty-five thousand.

In view of the great superiority of numbers brought against him General Buckner concluded to evacuate Knoxville, and with a force of about five thousand infantry and artillery and his cavalry took position in the vicinity of London. Two brigades of his command (Frazer's, at Cumberland Gap, and Jackson's, in Northeast Tennessee), were thus severed from us.

The enemy having already obtained a lodgment in East Tennessee by another route, the continued occupation of Cumberland Gap became very hazardous to the garrison and comparatively unimportant to us. Its evacuation was accordingly ordered, but on the appeal of its commander, stating his resources and ability for defense, favorably indorsed by Major-General Buckner, the orders were suspended on August 31st. The main body of our army was encamped near Chattanooga, while the cavalry force, much reduced and enfeebled by long service on short rations, was recruiting in the vicinity of Rome, Ga.

Immediately after crossing the mountains to the Tennessee, the enemy threw a corps, by way of Sequatchie Valley, to strike the rear of General Buckner's command, while Burnside occupied him in front. One division already ordered to his assistance proving insufficient to meet the force concentrating on him, Buckner was directed to withdraw to the Hiawassee with his infantry, artillery and supplies, and to hold his cavalry in front to check the enemy's advance. As soon as this change was made the corps threatening his rear was withdrawn, and the enemy commenced a movement in force against our left and rear.

On the last of August it became known that he had crossed his main force over the Tennessee River at and near Capertons Ferry, the most accessible point from Stevenson. By a direct route he was now as near our main depot of supplies as we were, and our whole line of communication was exposed, while his was partially secured by mountains and the river. By the timely arrival of two small divisions from Mississippi, our effective force, exclusive of cavalry, was now a little over thirty-five thousand, with which it was determined to strike on the first favorable opportunity. Closely watched by our cavalry, which had been brought forward, it was soon ascertained that the enemy's general movement was toward our left and rear in the direction of Dalton and Rome, keeping Lookout Mountain between us. The nature of the country and the want of supplies in it, with the presence of Burnside's force on our right, rendered a movement on the enemy's rear with our inferior force extremely hazardous, if not impracticable. It was therefore determined to meet him in front whenever he should emerge from the mountain gorges. To do this and hold Chattanooga was impossible without such a division of our small force as to endanger both parts. Accordingly our troops were put in motion on September 7th and 8th, and took position from Lee and Gordons Mills to La Fayette, on the road leading south from Chattanooga and fronting the east slope of Lookout Mountain. The forces on the Hiawassee and at Chickamauga Station took the route by Ringgold. A small cavalry force was left in observation at Chattanooga, and a brigade of infantry, strongly supported by cavalry, was left at Ringgold to hold the railroad and protect it from raids.

As soon as our movement was known to the enemy, his corps nearest Chattanooga, and which had been threatening Buckner's rear, was thrown into that place, and shortly thereafter commenced to move on our rear by the two roads to La Fayette and Ringgold. Two other corps were now in Wills Valley—one nearly opposite the head of McLemores Cove (a valley formed by Lookout Mountain and a spur of the main range, called Pigeon Mountain), and the other at or near Colonel Winston's opposite Alpine. During the 9th it was ascertained that a column, estimated at from four thousand to eight thousand, had crossed Lookout Mountain into the cove by way of Stevens and Coopers Gaps. Thrown off his guard by our rapid movement, apparently in retreat, when in reality we had concentrated opposite his center, and deceived by the information from deserters and others sent into his lines, the enemy pressed on his columns to intercept us, and thus exposed himself in detail.

Major-General Hindman received verbal instructions on the 9th to prepare his divisions to move against this force, and was informed that another division from Lieutenant-General Hill's command, at La Fayette, would join him. That evening the following written orders were issued to Generals Hindman and Hill:

HEADQUARTERS ARMY OF TENNESSEE,
LEE AND GORDONS MILLS,
September 9, 1863, 11:45 P. M.

Major-General Hindman, Commanding Division.

GENERAL: You will move with your division immediately to Davis Crossroads, on the road from La Fayette to Stevens Gap. At this point you will put yourself in communication with the column of General Hill, ordered to move to the same point, and take command of the joint forces, or report to the officer commanding Hill's column, according to rank. If in command you will move upon the enemy, reported to be four or five thousand strong, encamped at the foot of Lookout Mountain at Stevens Gap. Another column of the enemy is reported to be at Coopers Gap; number not known.

I am, general, etc.,
KINLOCK FALCONER.
Assistant Adjutant-General.

HEADQUARTERS ARMY OF TENNESSEE,
LEE AND GORDONS MILLS,
September 9, 1863, 11:45 P. M.

Lieutenant-General Hill, Commanding Corps.

GENERAL: I inclose orders given to General Hindman. General Bragg directs that you send or take, as your judgment dictates, Cleburne's division to unite with General Hindman at Davis Crossroads, to-morrow morning. Hindman starts at 12 o'clock to-night, and he has thirteen miles to make. The commander of the column thus united will move upon the enemy encamped at the foot of Stevens Gap, said to be four or five thousand. If unforeseen circumstances should prevent your movement, notify Hindman. A cavalry force should accompany your column; Hindman has none. Open communication with Hindman with your cavalry in advance of the junction. He marches on the road from Dr. Anderson's to Davis Crossroads.

I am, general, etc.,
KINLOCK FALCONER,
Assistant Adjutant-General.

On the receipt of his orders, during the night, General Hill replied that the movement required by him was impracticable, as General Cleburne was sick and both the Gaps (Dug and Catletts) had been blocked by falling timber, which would require twenty-four hours for its removal.

Not to lose this favorable opportunity—Hindman, by a prompt movement, being already in position—the following orders were issued at 8 A. M. on the 10th, for Major-General Buckner to move with his two divisions and report to Hindman:

HEADQUARTERS ARMY OF TENNESSEE,
LEE AND GORDONS MILLS,
September 10, 1863, 8 A. M.

Major-General Buckner, Anderson's.

GENERAL: I inclose orders issued last night to Generals Hill and Hindman. General Hill has found it impossible to carry out the part assigned to Cleburne's division. The general commanding desires that you will execute, without delay, the order issued to General Hill. You can move to Davis Crossroads by the direct road from your present position at Anderson's, along which General Hindman has passed. I am, general, etc.,

GEORGE WM. BRENT,
Assistant Adjutant-General.

And both Hindman and Hill were notified. Hindman had halted his division at Morgan's, some three or four miles from Davis Crossroads, in the cove, and at this point Buckner joined him during the afternoon of the 10th.

Reports fully confirming previous information in regard to the position of the enemy's forces were received during the 10th, and it became certain he was running his three columns to form a junction upon us at or near La Fayette. The corps near Colonel Winston's moved on the mountain toward Alpine, a point twenty miles south of us. The one opposite the cove continued its movement and threw forward its advance to Davis Crossroads, and Crittenden moved from Chattanooga on the roads to Ringgold and Lee and Gordons Mills. To strike these isolated commands in succession was our obvious policy. To secure more prompt and decided action in the movement ordered against the enemy's center, my headquarters were removed to La Fayette, where I arrived at about 11:30 P. M. on the 10th, and Lieutenant-General Polk was ordered forward with his remaining division to Anderson's, so as to cover Hindman's rear during the operations in the cove.

At La Fayette, I met Major Nocquet, engineer officer on General Buckner's staff, sent by General Hindman, after a junction of their commands, to confer with me and suggest a change in the plan of operations. After hearing the report of this officer, and obtaining from the active and energetic cavalry commander in front of our position (Brigadier-General Martin) the latest information of the enemy's movements and position, I verbally directed the major to return to General Hindman and say that my plans could not be changed, and that he would carry out his orders. At the same time the following written orders were sent to the general by courier:

HEADQUARTERS ARMY OF TENNESSEE,
LA FAYETTE, GA.,
September 10, 1863, 12 Midnight.

Major-General Hindman, Commanding, etc.

GENERAL: Headquarters are here, and the following is the information: Crittenden's corps is advancing on us from Chattanooga. A large force from the south has advanced to within seven miles of this point. Polk is left at Anderson's to cover your rear. General Bragg orders you to attack and force your way through the enemy to this point at the earliest hour that you can see him in the morning. Cleburne will attack in front the moment your guns are heard.

I am, general, etc.,
GEORGE WM. BRENT,
Assistant Adjutant-General.

Orders were also given for Walker's Reserve corps to move promptly and join Cleburne's division at Dug Gap to unite in the attack. At the same time Cleburne's was directed to remove all obstructions in the road in his front, which was promptly done, and by daylight he was ready to move. The obstructions in Catletts Gap were also ordered to be removed to clear the road in Hindman's rear. Breckinridge's division (Hill's corps) was kept in position south of La Fayette, to check any movement the enemy might make from that direction.

At daylight I proceeded to join Cleburne at Dug Gap, and found him waiting the opening of Hindman's guns to move on the enemy's flank and rear. Most of the day was spent in this position, waiting in great anxiety for the attack by Hindman's column. Several couriers and two staff officers were dispatched at different times urging him to move with promptness and vigor.

About the middle of the afternoon the first gun was heard, when the advance of Cleburne's division discovered the enemy had taken advantage of our delay and retreated to the mountain passes. The enemy now discovered his error and commenced to repair it by withdrawing his corps from the direction of Alpine to unite with the one near McLemore's Cove, while that was gradually extended toward Lee and Gordons Mills. Our movement having thus failed in its justly anticipated results, it was determined to turn upon the Third Corps of the enemy, approaching us from the direction of Chattanooga. The forces were accordingly withdrawn to La Fayette and Polk's and Walker's corps were moved immediately in the direction of Lee and Gordons Mills. The one corps of the enemy in this direction was known to be divided, one division having been sent to Ringgold. Upon learning the disposition of the enemy from our cavalry commander in that direction, on the afternoon of the 12th Lieutenant-General Polk, commanding the advance forces, was directed in the following note to attack at daylight on the 13th:

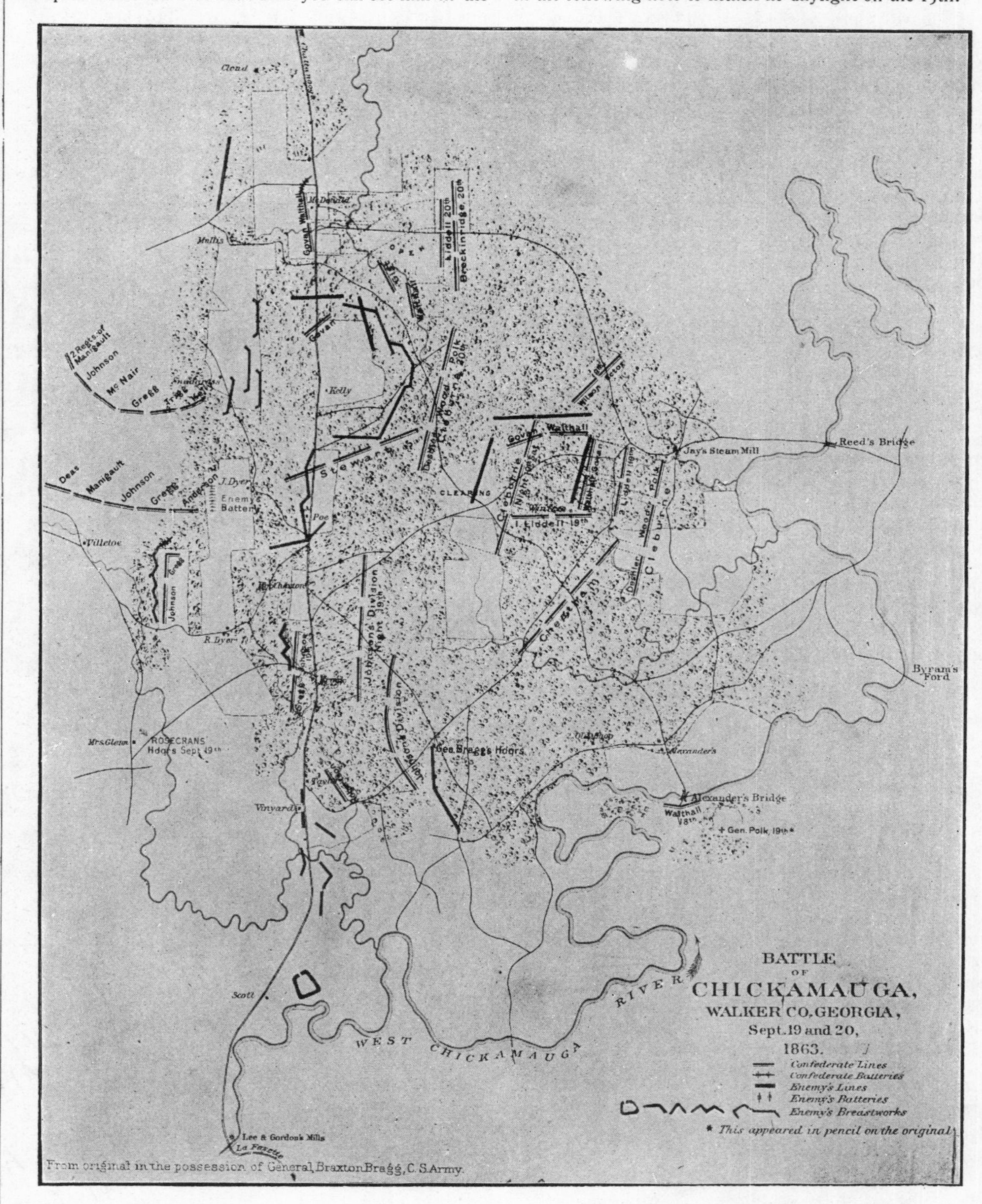

From original in the possession of General Braxton Bragg, C.S. Army.

HEADQUARTERS ARMY OF TENNESSEE,
LA FAYETTE, GA.,
September 12, [1863], 6 P. M.

Lieutenant-General Polk.

GENERAL: I inclose you a dispatch from General Pegram. This presents you a fine opportunity of striking Crittenden in detail, and I hope you will avail yourself of it at daylight to-morrow. This division crushed, and the others are yours. We can then turn again on the force in the cove. Wheeler's cavalry will move on Wilder, so as to cover your right. I shall be delighted to hear of your success.

Very truly yours,
BRAXTON BRAGG.

Upon further information, the order was renewed in two notes at later hours of the same day, as follows:

HEADQUARTERS ARMY OF TENNESSEE,
LA FAYETTE, GA.,
September 12, 1863, 8 P. M.

Lieutenant-General Polk, Commanding Corps.

GENERAL: I inclose you a dispatch, and I now give you the orders of the commanding general, viz., to attack at day-dawn to-morrow. The infantry column reported in

From an original painting, copyrighted by Kurz & Allison, Chicago, Ill.

BATTLE OF CHICKAMAUGA, GA., SEPTEMBER 19 AND 20, 1863.

said dispatch at three-quarters of a mile beyond Pea Vine Church, on the road to Graysville from La Fayette.

I am, general, etc.,

GEORGE WM. BRENT,
Assistant Adjutant-General.

HEADQUARTERS ARMY OF TENNESSEE,
LA FAYETTE, GA.,
September 12, 1863.

Lieutenant-General Polk, Commanding Corps.

GENERAL: The enemy is approaching from the south, and it is highly important that your attack in the morning should be quick and decided. Let no time be lost.

I am, general, etc.,

GEORGE W. BRENT,
Assistant Adjutant-General.

At 11 P. M. a dispatch was received from the general stating that he had taken a strong position for defense, and requesting that he should be heavily re-enforced. He was promptly ordered not to defer his attack—his force being already numerically superior to the enemy—and was reminded that his success depended upon the promptness and rapidity of his movements. He was further informed that Buckner's corps would be moved within supporting distance the next morning.

Early on the 13th, I proceeded to the front, ahead of Buckner's command, to find that no advance had been made on the enemy, and that his forces had formed a junction and recrossed the Chickamauga. Again disappointed, immediate measures were taken to place our trains and limited supplies in safe positions, when all our forces were concentrated along the Chickamauga, threatening the enemy in front. Major-General Wheeler, with two divisions of cavalry, occupied the positions on the extreme left, vacated by Hill's corps, and was directed to press the enemy in McLemores Cove, to divert his attention from our real movement. Brigadier-General Forrest, with his own and Pegram's divisions of cavalry, covered the movement on our front and right. Brigadier-General B. R. Johnson, whose brigade had been at Ringgold holding the railroad, was moved in the direction of Reeds Bridge, which brought him on the extreme right of the line. Walker's corps formed on his left opposite Alexanders Bridge; Buckner's next, near Thedfords Ford; Polk's opposite Lee and Gordons Mills, and Hill's on the extreme left. With Johnson moved two brigades just arrived from Mississippi and three of Longstreet's corps, all without artillery and transportation.

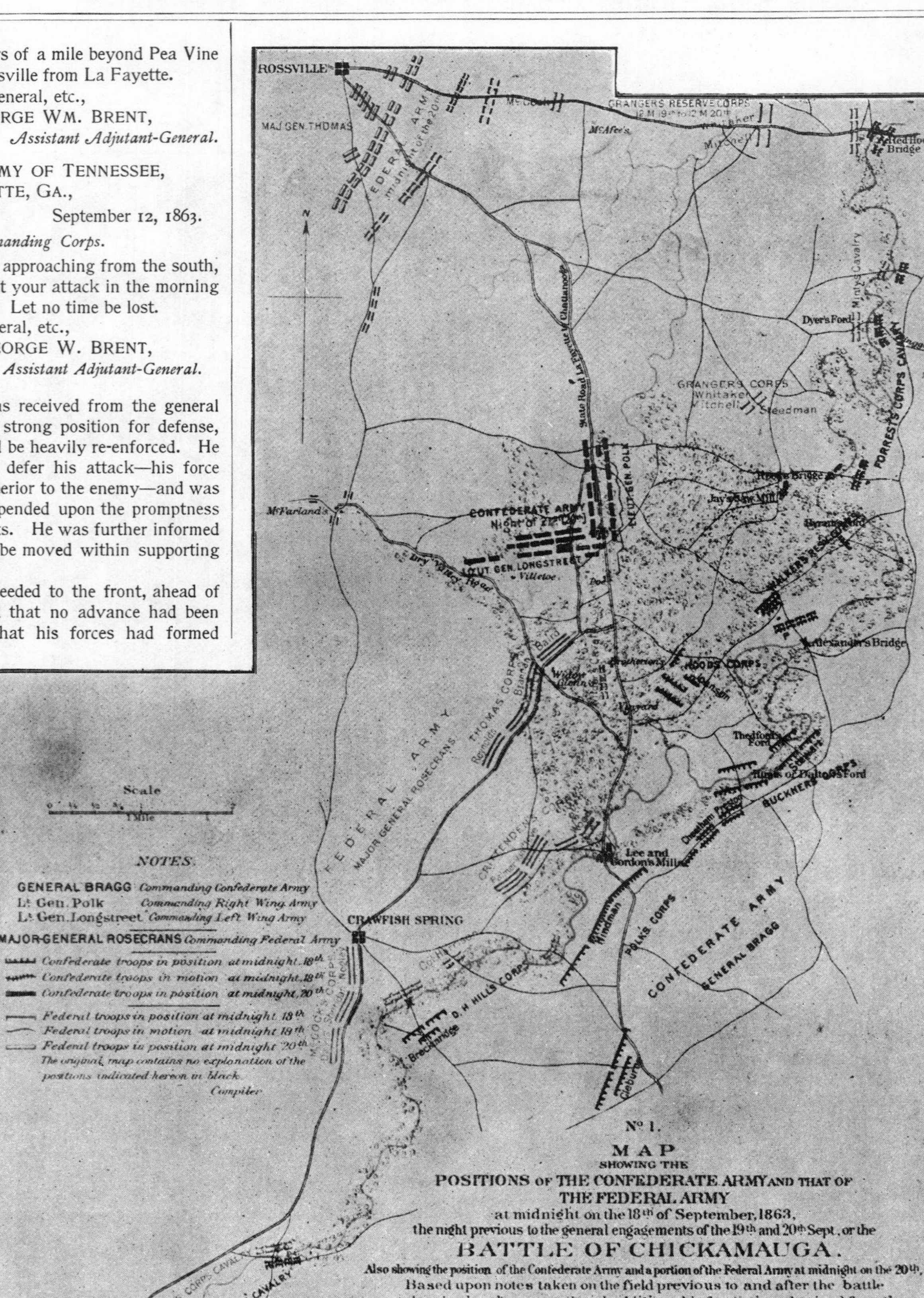

The following orders were issued on the night of the 17th for the forces to cross the Chickamauga, commencing the movement at 6 A. M. on the 18th by the extreme right at Reeds Bridge:

HEADQUARTERS ARMY OF TENNESSEE,
IN THE FIELD, LEET'S TANYARD,
September 18, 1863.

1. Johnson's column (Hood's), on crossing at or near Reeds Bridge, will turn to the left by the most practicable route and sweep up the Chickamauga toward Lee and Gordons Mills.

2. Walker, crossing at Alexanders Bridge, will unite in this move and push vigorously on the enemy's flank and rear in the same direction.

3. Buckner, crossing at Thedfords Ford, will join in the movement to the left and press the enemy up the stream from Polk's front at Lee and Gordons Mills.

4. Polk will press his forces to the front of Lee and Gordons Mills, and if met by too much resistance to cross, will bear to the right and cross at Daltons Ford, or at Thedfords, as may be necessary, and join in the attack wherever the enemy may be.

5. Hill will cover our left flank from an advance of the enemy from the cove, and by pressing the cavalry in his front, ascertain if the enemy is re-enforcing at Lee and Gordons Mills, in which event he will attack them in flank.

6. Wheeler's cavalry will hold the gaps in Pigeon Mountain and cover our rear and left and bring up stragglers.

7. All teams, etc., not with troops, should go toward Ringgold and Dalton, beyond Taylors Ridge. All cooking should be done at the trains. Rations, when cooked, will be forwarded to the troops.

8. The above movements will be executed with the utmost promptness, vigor and persistence.

By command of General Bragg:

GEORGE WM. BRENT,
Assistant Adjutant-General.

The resistance offered by the enemy's cavalry and the difficulties arising from the bad and narrow country roads caused unexpected delays in the execution of these movements. Though the commander of the right column was several times urged to press forward, his crossing was not effected until late in the afternoon. At this time Major-General Hood, of Longstreet's corps, arrived and assumed command of the column, Brigadier-General Johnson resuming his improvised division of three brigades.

Alexanders Bridge was hotly contested and finally broken up by the enemy just as General Walker secured possession. He moved down stream, however, a short distance and crossed, as directed, at Byrams Ford, and thus secured a junction with Hood after night.

The movement was resumed at daylight on the 19th, and Buckner's corps, with Cheatham's division of Polk's, had crossed and formed, when a brisk engagement commenced with our cavalry, under Forrest, on the extreme right about 9 o'clock. A brigade from Walker's was ordered to Forrest's support, and soon after Walker was ordered to attack with his whole force. Our line was now formed, with Buckner's left resting on the Chickamauga about one mile below Lee and Gordons Mills. On his right came Hood with his own and Johnson's divisions, with Walker on the extreme right, Cheatham's division being in reserve, the general direction being a little east of north. The attack ordered by our right was made by General Walker in his usual gallant style, and soon developed a largely superior force opposed. He drove them handsomely, however, and captured several batteries of artillery in most gallant charges. Before Cheatham's division, ordered to his support, could reach him he had been pressed back to his first position by the extended lines of the enemy assailing him on both flanks. The two commands united were soon enabled to force the enemy back again and recover our advantage, though we were yet greatly outnumbered.

These movements on our right were in a direction to leave an opening in our line between Cheatham and Hood. Stewart's division, forming Buckner's second line, was thrown to the right to fill this, and it soon became hotly engaged, as did Hood's whole front.

The enemy, whose left was at Lee and Gordons Mills when our movement commenced, had rapidly transferred forces from his extreme right, changing his entire line, and seemed disposed to dispute with all his ability our effort to gain the main road to Chattanooga, in his rear. Lieutenant-General Polk was ordered to move his remaining division across at the nearest ford, and to assume the command in person on our right. Hill's corps was also ordered to cross below Lee and Gordons Mills and join the line on the right. While these movements were being made our right and center were heavily and almost constantly engaged. Stewart, by a vigorous assault, broke the enemy's center and penetrated far into his lines, but was obliged to retire for want of sufficient force to meet the heavy enfilade fire which he encountered from the right. Hood, later engaged, advanced from the first fire, and continued to drive the forces in his front until night. Cleburne's division, of Hill's corps, which first reached the right, was ordered to attack immediately in conjunction with the force already engaged. This veteran command, under its gallant chief, moved to its work after sunset, taking the enemy completely by surprise, driving him in great disorder for nearly a mile, and inflicting a very heavy loss.

Night found us masters of the ground after a series of very obstinate contests with largely superior numbers. From captured prisoners and others we learned with certainty that we had encountered the enemy's whole force, which had been moving day and night since they first ascertained the direction of our march. Orders had been given for the rapid march to the field of all re-enforcements arriving by railroad, and three additional brigades from this source joined us early next morning. The remaining forces on our extreme left, east of the Chickamauga, had been ordered up early in the afternoon, but reached the field too late to participate in the engagement of that day.

They were ordered into line on their arrival, and disposed for a renewal of the action early next morning. Information was received from Lieutenant-General Longstreet of his arrival at Ringgold and departure for the field. Five small brigades of his corps (about five thousand effective infantry, no artillery) reached us in time to participate in the action, three of them on the 19th and two more on the 20th.

Upon the close of the engagement on the evening of the 19th the proper commanders were summoned to my camp-fire, and there received specific information and instructions touching the dispositions of the troops and for the operations of the next morning. The whole force was divided for the next morning into commands and assigned to the two senior lieutenant-generals, Longstreet and Polk—the former to the left, where all his own troops were stationed—the latter continuing his command of the right. Lieutenant-General Longstreet reached my headquarters about 11 P. M., and immediately received his instructions. After a few hours' rest at my camp-fire he moved at daylight to his line, just in front of my position.

Lieutenant-General Polk was ordered to assail the enemy on our extreme right at day-dawn on the 20th, and to take up the attack in succession rapidly to the left. The left wing was to await the attack by the right, take it up promptly when made, and the whole line was then to be pushed vigorously and persistently against the enemy throughout its extent.

Before the dawn of day myself and staff were ready for the saddle, occupying a position immediately in rear of and accessible to all parts of the line. With increasing anxiety and disappointment I waited until after sunrise without hearing a gun, and at length dispatched a staff officer to Lieutenant-General Polk to ascertain the cause of the delay and urge him to a prompt and speedy movement. This officer, not finding the general with his troops, and learning where he had spent the night, proceeded across Alexanders Bridge to the east side of the Chickamauga and there delivered my message.

Proceeding in person to the right wing, I found the troops not even prepared for the movement. Messengers were immediately dispatched for Lieutenant-General Polk, and he shortly after joined me. My orders were renewed, and the general was urged to their prompt execution, the more important as the ear was saluted throughout the night with the sounds of the ax and falling timber, as the enemy industriously labored to strengthen his position by hastily constructed barricades and breastworks. A reconnoissance made in the front of our extreme right during this delay crossed the main road to Chattanooga and proved the important fact that this greatly desired position was open to our possession.

The reasons assigned for this unfortunate delay by the wing commander appear in part in the reports of his subordinates. It is sufficient to say they are entirely unsatisfactory. It also appears from these reports that when the action was opened on the right, about 10 A. M., the troops were moved to the assault in detail and by detachments, unsupported, until nearly all parts of the right wing were in turn repulsed with heavy losses.

Our troops were led with the greatest gallantry and exhibited great coolness, bravery and heroic devotion. In no instance did they fail when called on to rally and return to the charge. But though invariably driving the enemy with slaughter at the points assailed, they were compelled in turn to yield to the greatly superior numbers constantly brought against them. The attack on the left, promptly made as ordered, met with less resistance, much of the enemy's strength having been transferred to our right, and was successfully and vigorously followed up.

About 2 P. M., passing along the line to our left, I found we had been checked in our progress by encountering a strong position, strengthened by works and obstinately defended. Unable to afford assistance from any other part of the field, written orders were immediately dispatched to Lieutenant-General Polk to again assault the enemy in his front with his whole force, and to persist until he should dislodge him from his position. Directing the operations on our left to be continued, I moved again to the right and soon dispatched a staff officer to General Polk, urging a prompt and vigorous execution of my written orders.

About 4 P. M. this general assault was made, and the attack was continued from right to left until the enemy gave way at different points, and, finally, about dark, yielded us his line. The contest was severe, but the impetuous charge of our troops could not be resisted when they were brought to bear in full force, even where the enemy possessed all the advantage of position and breastworks. The troops were halted by their respective commanders when the darkness of the night and the density of the forest rendered further movements uncertain and dangerous, and the army bivouacked on the ground it had so gallantly won.

Both flanks having advanced more rapidly than the center, they were found confronting each other in lines nearly parallel and within artillery range. Any advance by them, especially at night over ground so thickly wooded, might have resulted in the most serious consequences.

The enemy, though driven from his line, still confronted us, and desultory firing was heard until 8 P. M. Other noises, indicating movements and dispositions for the morrow, continued until a late hour at night.

During the operations by the main forces on the 19th and 20th, the cavalry on the flanks was actively and usefully employed, holding the enemy in observation and threatening or assailing him as occasion offered.

Exhausted by two days' battle, with a very limited supply of provisions and almost destitute of water, some time in daylight was absolutely essential for our troops to supply these necessaries and replenish their ammunition before renewing the contest.

Availing myself of this necessary delay to inspect and readjust my lines, I moved as soon as daylight served on the 21st. On my arrival about sunrise near Lieutenant-General Polk's bivouac, I met the ever vigilant Brigadier-General Liddell, commanding a division in our front line, who was awaiting the general, to report that his picket, this morning, discovered that the enemy had retreated during the night from his immediate front. Instructions were promptly given to push our whole line of skirmishers to the front, and I moved to the left and extended these orders. All the cavalry at hand, including my personal guard, were ordered to the front.

Battle of Chattanooga, Tenn. Hand-to-Hand Bayonet Fight between the Commands of Lieutenant-General Longstreet and Major-General Thomas (Federal).

Members of my staff, in passing through the lines of our left wing with their escort, were warned of danger and told that they were entering on the neutral ground between us and the enemy. But this proved to be an error, and our cavalry soon came upon the enemy's rear guard where the main road passes through Missionary Ridge. He had availed himself of the night to withdraw from our front, and his main body was already in position within his lines at Chattanooga.

Any immediate pursuit by our infantry and artillery would have been fruitless, as it was not deemed practicable with our weak and exhausted force to assail the enemy, now more than double our numbers, behind his intrenchments. Though we had defeated him and driven him from the field with heavy loss in men, arms and artillery, it had only been by heavy sacrifices, in repeated, persistent and most gallant assaults upon superior numbers strongly posted and protected.

The conduct of our troops was excellent throughout the prolonged contest. Often repulsed where success seemed impossible, they never failed to rally and return to the charge until the last combined and determined effort, in which the spirit of every man seemed to conspire for success, was crowned with the reward due to such gallantry in a just cause.

Our loss was in proportion to the prolonged and obstinate struggle. Two-fifths of our gallant troops had fallen, and the number of general and staff officers stricken down will best show how these troops were led.

Major-General Hood, the model soldier and inspiring leader, fell, after contributing largely to our success, and has suffered the irreparable loss of a leg. That his valuable life should be spared to us is, however, a source for thankfulness and gratitude.

Major-General Hindman, highly distinguished for gallantry and good conduct, received a severe contusion, but persisted in keeping the saddle until he witnessed the success in which his command largely participated.

Brigadier-Generals B. H. Helm, Preston Smith and James Deshler died upon the field in the heroic discharge of duty. They were true patriots and gallant soldiers, and worthy of the high reputation they enjoyed.

Brigadier-Generals Adams, Gregg and McNair fell severely wounded while gallantly leading their commands in the thickest of the fight. It is gratifying to know they are convalescing and will be again found at the post of duty and danger.

Judging from appearances on the field, the enemy's losses must have exceeded our own largely, but we have no means of correctly estimating them. We captured over eight thousand prisoners, fifty-one pieces of artillery, fifteen thousand stand of small arms and quantities of ammunition, with wagons, ambulances and teams, medicines, hospital stores, etc., in large quantities.

The officers of my staff, personal and general, served me on this field, and on the arduous marches preceding, with their usual zeal, intelligence and gallantry.

The whole cavalry force having been dispatched to press the enemy and to cut off detachments, orders were given for the army to move to a point near the railroad and convenient to water, still interposing between the enemy and our large number of wounded our trophies and our wounded prisoners whose removal from the field occupied many days.

Our supplies of all kinds were greatly reduced, the railroad having been constantly occupied in transporting troops, prisoners and our wounded, and the bridges having been destroyed to a point two miles south of Ringgold. These supplies were ordered replenished, and as soon as it was seen that we could be subsisted the army was moved forward to seize and hold the only communication the enemy had with his supplies in the rear. His most important road, and the shortest, by half, to his depot at Bridgeport, lay along the south bank of the Tennessee. The holding of this all-important route was confided to Lieutenant-General Longstreet's command, and its possession forced the enemy to a road double the length, over two ranges of mountains, by wagon transportation. At the same time our cavalry, in large force, was thrown across the river to operate on this long and difficult route. These dispositions faithfully sustained insured the enemy's speedy evacuation of Chattanooga for want of food and forage. Possessed of the shortest road to his depot, and the one by which re-enforcements must reach him, we held him at our mercy, and his destruction was only a question of time.

The suggestion of a movement by our right, immediately after the battle, to the north of the Tennessee and thence upon Nashville requires notice only. Such a movement was utterly impossible for want of transportation. Nearly half our army consisted of re-enforcements just before the battle, without a wagon or an artillery horse, and nearly, if not quite, a third of the artillery horses on the field had been lost. The railroad bridges, too, had been destroyed to a point south of Ringgold, and on all the roads from Cleveland to Knoxville. To these insurmountable difficulties were added the entire absence of means to cross the river, except by fording at a few precarious points, too deep for artillery, and the well-known danger of sudden rises, by which all communication would be cut, a contingency which did actually happen a few days after the visionary scheme was proposed. But the most serious objection to the proposition was its entire want of military propriety. It abandoned to the enemy our entire line of communication and laid open to him our depots of supplies, while it placed us, with a greatly inferior force, beyond a difficult and at times impassable river, in a country affording no subsistence to men or animals. It also left open to the enemy at a distance of only ten miles, our battle-field, with thousands of our wounded and his own, and all trophies and supplies we had won. All this was to be risked and given up for what? To gain the enemy's rear and cut him off from his depot of supplies by the route over the mountains, when the very movement abandoned to his unmolested use the better and more practicable route, of half the length, on the south side of the river. It is hardly necessary to say the proposition was not even entertained, whatever may have been the inferences drawn from subsequent movements.

The heroic dead and the survivors of the campaign, who so worthily served their country, will ever be remembered with honor by their countrymen.

* * * * * * *

BRAXTON BRAGG, *General.*

NOTES.

Topographical horizontal lines equal 20 ft. vertical

Confederate troops in motion

Confederate positions and bivouac

Federal troops in motion

Federal positions and bivouac

Confed Artillery — Federal Artillery

No. 2.
MAP OF THE BATTLE OF CHICKAMAUGA
SHOWING THE POSITIONS OF THE CONFEDERATE AND FEDERAL ARMIES
on the 19th September, 1863.
Based upon notes taken by me upon the field to the east of the State Road during the engagement and added to and corrected after the battle and revised and additional information obtained from the official reports of the officers of both Armies
By WALTER J. MORRIS
Captain Engineer Corps and Chief Engineer Officer of Lt. Gen. L. Polk
Comd'g Right Wing Confederate Army

THE CHICKAMAUGA CAMPAIGN,

AUGUST 16 TO SEPTEMBER 22, 1863.

BY

LIEUT.-GEN. JAMES LONGSTREET,
Commanding Left Wing.

HEADQUARTERS, NEAR CHATTANOOGA,
October —, 1863.

OUR train reached Catoosa Platform, near Ringgold, about 2 o'clock in the afternoon of September 19th. As soon as our horses came up (about 4 o'clock), I started with Colonels Sorrel and Manning, of my staff, to find the headquarters of the commanding general. We missed our way and did not report till near 11 o'clock at night. Upon my arrival I was informed that the troops had been engaged during the day in severe skirmishing while endeavoring to get in line for battle. The commanding general gave me a map showing the roads and streams between Lookout Mountain and the Chickamauga River, and a general description of our position, and informed me that the battle was ordered at daylight the next morning, the action to be brought on upon our right and to be taken up successively to the left, the general movement to be a wheel upon my extreme left as a pivot. I was assigned to the command of the left wing, composed of Hood's and Hindman's divisions, an improvised division under Brigadier-General B. R. Johnson, and Buckner's corps, consisting of Stewart's and Preston's divisions. The artillery consisted of the battalions of Majors Williams, Robertson and Legden, together with some other batteries attached to brigades.

As soon as the day of the 20th had dawned I rode to the front to find my troops. The line was arranged from right to left as follows: Stewart's, Johnson's, Hindman's and Preston's divisions. Hood's division (of which only three brigades were up) was somewhat in the rear of Johnson's. Kershaw's and Humphreys' brigades, of McLaws' division, were ordered forward from Ringgold the night before, but were not yet up. General McLaws had not arrived from Richmond. I set to work to have the line adjusted by closing to the right, in order to occupy some vacant ground between the two wings and to make room for Hood in the front line. The divisions were ordered to form with two brigades in the front line, and one supporting where there were but three brigades, and two supporting where there were more than three. General Hood was ordered to take the brigades of Kershaw and Humphreys and use them as supports for his division, thus making his division the main column of attack. Before these arrangements were completed the attack was made by our right wing about 10 o'clock. The battle seemed to rage with considerable fury, but did not progress as had been anticipated. As soon as I was prepared I sent to the commanding general to suggest that I had probably better make my attack. Before the messenger returned I heard that the commanding general had sent orders for the division commanders to move forward and attack. I had no time to find the officer who brought the order, as some of the troops were in motion when I heard of it. Upon this information I at once issued orders to attack, to the troops not already in motion, holding one of Buckner's divisions (Preston's) in reserve. As the battle upon our right was not so successful as had been expected in the plan of attack, I was obliged to reverse the order of battle by retaining my right somewhere near the left of the righ twing. To do this Stewart's division was obliged to halt upon reaching the La Fayette and Chattanooga Road.

Hood's column broke the enemy's line near the Brotherton house and made it wheel to the right. In making this movement Major-General Hood fell, severely, and it was feared mortally, wounded by a minie ball breaking his thigh. He had broken the enemy's line, however, and his own troops and those to his right and left continued to press the enemy with such spirit and force that he could not resist us. Brigadier-General Law succeeded to the command of Hood's division, and Brigadier-General Kershaw to the command of the two brigades of McLaws' division. General Kershaw, having received no definite orders himself (being under the command of General Hood), was not advised of the wheel to the right, and gained more ground to the front than was intended in the movement of his two brigades. Johnson's division followed the movement made by Hood, and gained the Crawfish Spring and Chattanooga Road, having a full share in the conflict. Major-General Hindman, in command of my left division, first met the enemy near the Vineyard house and drove him back upon his strong position near the Widow Glenn's (or burned) house. By a well directed front and flank attack, he gained the position after a severe struggle. The enemy's dead at this point mark well his line of battle. Hindman was then ordered to move by his right flank and re-enforce Johnson near the Vidito house, who was pressing forward against great odds. About 3 o'clock in the afternoon I asked the commanding general for some of the troops of the right wing, but was informed by him that they had been beaten back so badly that they could be of no service to me. I had but one division that had not been engaged, and hesitated to venture to put it in, as our distress upon our right seemed to be almost as great as that of the enemy upon his right. I therefore concluded to hold Preston for the time, and urge on to renewed efforts our brave men, who had already been engaged many hours. The heights extending from the Vidito house across to the Snodgrass house gave the enemy strong ground upon which to rally. Here he gathered most of his broken forces and re-enforced them. After a long and bloody struggle, Johnson and Hindman gained the heights near the Crawfish Spring Road. Kershaw made a most handsome attack upon the heights at the Snodgrass house simultaneously with Johnson and Hindman, but was not strong enough for the work.

It was evident that with this position gained I should be complete master of the field. I therefore ordered General Buckner to move Preston forward. Before this, however, General Buckner had established a battery of twelve guns, raking down the enemy's line which opposed our right wing, and at the same time having fine play upon any force that might attempt to re-enforce the hill that he was about to attack. General Stewart, of his corps, was also ordered to move against any such force in flank. The combination was well-timed and arranged. Preston dashed gallantly at the hill. Stewart flanked a re-enforcing column and captured a large portion of it. At the same time the fire of the battery struck such terror into a heavy force close under it that we took there also a large number of prisoners. Preston's assault, though not a complete success at the onset, taken in connection with the other operations, crippled the enemy so badly that his ranks were badly broken, and by a flank movement and another advance the heights were gained. These re-enforcements were the enemy's last, or reserve corps, and a part also of the line that had been opposing our right wing during the morning. The enemy broke up in great confusion along my front, and about the same time the right wing made a gallant dash and gained the line that had been held so long and obstinately against it. A simultaneous and continuous shout from the two wings announced our success complete.

The enemy had fought every man that he had, and every one had been in turn beaten. As it was almost dark, I ordered my line to remain as it was, ammunition boxes to be refilled, stragglers to be collected, and everything in readiness for the pursuit in the morning.

Early on the 21st, the commanding general stopped at my bivouac and asked my views as to our future movements. I suggested crossing the river above Chattanooga, so as to make ourselves sufficiently felt on the enemy's rear as to force his evacuation of Chattanooga, and, indeed, force him back upon Nashville; and if we should find our transportation inadequate for a continuance of this movement, to follow up the railroad to Knoxville, destroy Burnside, and from there threaten the enemy's railroad communication in rear of Nashville. This I supposed to be the only practicable flank movement, owing to the scarcity of our transportation, and it seemed to keep us very nearly as close to the railroad as we were at the time. At parting I understood the commanding general to agree that such was probably our best move, and that he was about to give the necessary orders for its execution.

Orders came in the afternoon for the march. The rear of the right wing did not move until quite dark. I did not, therefore, put my wing in motion till daylight the following morning.

Wounding of General Hood at the Battle of Chickamauga.

Before moving on the morning of the 22d, McLaws' division was ordered to follow the enemy on to Chattanooga. The remainder of the command marched for the Red House Ford, and halted about noon.

During that night I received orders to march the entire command back to Chattanooga, and moved in pursuance thereof early on the 23d. We reached the Watkins house about 11 A. M., and proceeded to take up a line around the enemy's position at Chattanooga.

I desire to mention the following named officers as distinguished for conduct and ability, viz.: Major-Generals Hood, Buckner, Hindman and Stewart; Brigadier-Generals B. R. Johnson, Preston, Law (respectively in command of divisions), Kershaw, Patton, Anderson, Gracie, McNair (severely wounded), and Colonels Trigg and Kelly, both in command of brigades. Honorable mention should also be made of Brigadier-Generals Humphreys, Benning, Deas, Clayton, Bate, Brown, Robertson and Manigault.

The steady good conduct, throughout the long conflict, of the subordinate officers and men, which the limits of this report will not permit me to particularize, is worthy of the highest praise and admiration.

I am greatly indebted to Lieutenant-Colonel Sorrel, assistant adjutant-general; Lieutenant-Colonel Manning, chief of ordnance; Major Latrobe, assistant adjutant and inspector-general, and Captain Manning, Signal Corps, for their able, untiring and gallant assistance. Colonel Manning received a painful wound. The movement of Stewart's division against the enemy's re-enforcements was made upon the suggestion of Colonel Sorrel and Captain Manning. The result was the beginning of the general break throughout the enemy's line. My other staff officers had not arrived from Virginia.

Major Walton, acting chief of subsistence department, and Major Keiley, acting chief of quartermaster's department, were at the railroad depot in the active discharge of the duties of their departments.

Among the captures made by the left wing during the day were not less than 40 pieces of artillery, over 3,000 prisoners, and 10 regimental standards, besides a few wagons, 17,645 small-arms, and 1,130 sets accouterments, and 393,000 rounds of small-arms ammunition were collected on the field.

The list of casualties shows a loss by the command (without McNair's brigade, from which no report has been received) of 1,089 killed, 6,506 wounded, and 272 missing. Its strength on going into action on the morning of the 20th, was 2,033 officers and 20,849 men.

J. LONGSTREET, *Lieutenant-General.*

IN the first year of the Confederacy State-bank money was at a considerable discount, and at this time the members of a volunteer company, in Richmond for the purpose of equipment, went to the theater to see a play which was of the kind that ends in a happy marriage. The play passed off without interruption until the generous father placed a roll of money in the hands of the blushing bride, when a soldier, who was deeply interested in the heroine of the play and who had some of the depreciated money, yelled out: "Say, miss, you better look at that money and see if 'taint State bank."

First Gun at Chickamauga, September 18, 1863. The Confederates Opening Fire upon the Federal Cavalry, who had begun the Destruction of Reed's Bridge.

THE BATTLE OF CHICKAMAUGA,

SEPTEMBER 19 AND 20, 1863.

BY

BRIG.-GEN. MARCUS J. WRIGHT.

HEADQUARTERS WRIGHT'S BRIGADE, CHEATHAM'S DIVISION, POLK'S CORPS, ARMY OF TENNESSEE, IN THE FIELD,

OCTOBER 9, 1863.

I HAVE the honor to make the following report of the operations of my brigade in the battle of Chickamauga on the 19th and 20th ultimo:

On Saturday, 19th ultimo, at 8:30 A. M., I was ordered by Major-General Cheatham to advance and cross the Chickamauga at a ford known as Hunts Ford, following immediately after Brigadier-General Preston Smith's brigade, and followed by Brigadier-General George Maney's brigade. Immediately after we crossed the ford heavy firing commenced in our front, which was ascertained to be an engagement between the reserve division of Major-General Walker and the enemy, who was in heavy force and was pressing Walker hotly with his largely superior numbers.

My brigade, after crossing, was formed in line of battle in a field in the rear of Brigadier-General Smith. I was ordered to follow immediately upon the rear of Smith when he moved. In an hour Smith moved in the direction of the battlefield, and we followed closely in his rear. After moving into a wood in a direction inclining down the Chickamauga, another halt was made of half an hour, when I received an order from General Cheatham to form in line of battle and move forward in a direction nearly at right angles to the road along which we were posted, with that brave and competent officer, General Preston Smith, still on my right. Maney being in my rear in the line of march, I supposed that he would be ordered up to the left, and, indeed, in the act of executing the forward movement in line of battle, I was informed by General Smith that we were a supporting force to Major-General Walker, who was supposed to be in our front.

My brigade, composed of the following regiments, moved in line from right to left in the order named: Sixteenth Tennessee Regiment, Colonel D. M. Donnell commanding; Eighth Tennessee Regiment, Colonel John H. Anderson commanding; Fifty-first and Fifty-second Tennessee regiments, Lieutenant Colonel John G. Hall commanding; Twenty-eighth Tennessee Regiment, Colonel S. S. Stanton commanding; Thirty-eighth Tennessee Regiment and Murray's (Tennessee) battalion, Colonel John C. Carter commanding, with the battery of light artillery commanded by Captain William W. Carnes.

The men moved up in splendid style, obeying all orders with the alacrity and precision which is their habit on parade. With the information I had received, believing Major-General Walker in our front, I had directed each regiment to throw out skirmishers, and thus guard against the too frequent and often criminal folly of pouring a fire into the rear of our own comrades in arms when engaged against a foe in front. This order I immediately countermanded when it became quite evident that a most galling fire had been opened by the enemy's batteries and infantry upon my right flank and a portion of the center. This fire continued for some minutes before the left flank was engaged, and was the result of my line of battle being advanced obliquely toward the right, instead of being parallel to the enemy's line. It was certainly due, also, somewhat to the fact that the Sixteenth Tennessee and Eighth Tennessee regiments—extending their line into a cornfield in open view of the enemy, whose position was concealed by timber and undergrowth—were compelled to advance into the wood in front, thus finding a better and more secure position and some covering for their men from the murderous fire which they were gallantly sustaining. The center and left, however, soon became earnestly engaged. Having no eligible position for artillery near the center, I was compelled to post Carnes' battery (Steuben Artillery), on the left of the Thirty-eighth Tennessee Regiment, being the extreme left of my position, supposing, too, at that time that I would be supported on the left by the brigades both of Brigadier General Maney and Brigadier-General Strahl. My position was near the foot of a declivity gently rising toward the left, and presenting on that flank the highest ground on our line, and therefore the best position for artillery, while that of the enemy was on an eminence rising from the drain or low ground just in our front, many feet above ours, and protected by works probably thrown up the previous night. Immediately after the enemy's fire was opened I dispatched the order to commence firing to each of the commanding officers of regiments, which was executed promptly and with coolness and precision.

I have reason to believe that the effect of our firing upon the enemy was terrific, from the report of a wounded officer who fell into the hands of the enemy and subsequently escaped, and from a careful survey of the battleground by some of the men after the action.

The enemy opened upon us a cross-fire of two batteries and a concentrated shower of musket shot from a greatly superior force, this line extending the full length of a brigade beyond my unsupported left. Our men met the terrible fire which was hurled upon them with constancy, coolness and undaunted courage, bearing the shock like veterans, and not perceptibly wavering beneath its severity, and returning shot for shot as far as their inferiority of numbers would allow.

After sustaining this fire for three and a half hours (from 12 M. to 3:30 P. M.), seeing that Brigadier-General Smith, immediately on my right, had withdrawn from the field, and learning from some of my officers that their ammunition was nearly exhausted, I determined to order the brigade to retire. Before, however, I could give orders to execute this movement, a courier informed me that the enemy was flanking my position, which, upon moving in that direction, I distinctly discovered, seeing his line moving through the ravine and undergrowth upon the left flank. I then dispatched orders to the colonels and commander of the battery to withdraw to a hill about a quarter of a mile in the rear. Discovering at this opportune moment a supporting brigade approaching in line of battle, and not being able to move rapidly enough to communicate with the general commanding (Brigadier-General Clayton), in consequence of my being dismounted, I requested the colonel commanding the leading regiment to move to my left and protect the men in retiring, which he did promptly and efficiently. At the same time I informed him that the enemy was flanking our position. Each of the regiments was withdrawn slowly and in good order, although all the horses of the battery, except three, were killed, and about one-half of the company shot down, either killed or wounded, thus rendering the battery useless to check the advance of the enemy's flanking force. Captain Carnes, First Lieutenant Marshall, and Second Lieutenant Cockrill, of the artillery, remained with the battery until they received orders to retire, narrowly escaping capture, and gallantly standing at their posts until the last moment. Second Lieutenant Van Vleck gallantly died at his post. After retiring from the field, I at once dispatched a staff officer to Major-General Cheatham, advising him of the position of the brigade, and informing him of the fact that our ammunition was nearly exhausted, which was promptly supplied.

After 5 P. M. the brigade was again ordered to take position about four hundred yards to the right of the ground on which we had fought the enemy. Major-General Cleburne's division and Smith's brigade, of Major-General Cheatham's division, at about 6:30 o'clock, on our immediate right, made a most gallant and successful movement upon the enemy's position, but my brigade was not ordered to participate in the glorious charge, which cost the lives of many brave patriots, and among them the heroic General Preston Smith.

Having bivouacked at this position on Saturday night, on Sunday morning a line of battle was again formed, and held steadily for three hours under a most harassing fire from the enemy's batteries. One man of the Sixteenth Tennessee Regiment was severely wounded by a round shot. About 1 P. M. I was ordered to move the brigade around to the right of our position, following Maney in moving by the right flank. About 6 P. M., Maney being on our left, I was ordered to follow his movements in line of battle. Major-General Walker's division and Brigadier-General Jackson's brigade, of Cheatham's division, were already engaged fiercely in assaulting a fortified position of the enemy, at which a very large force of his artillery had been concentrated. A furious contest was raging with wild and terrible carnage. Though the gallant troops of Walker and Jackson held their position with unsurpassed stubbornness and heroism, yet the enemy, encouraged by the strength, natural and artificial, of his position and his concentrated forces, was making a most stubborn fight. At this critical moment the two brigades (General Maney's and my own) were precipitated with a deafening hurrah and rapid shock to support our gallant comrades, who were contending against unequal odds. The men were in the highest spirits, and moved forward with an animation that I have never seen surpassed. At this time the scene was one of the most animated and exciting that can be imagined. The whole issue of the combat seemed suspended upon a moment's work. The shouts of our gallant patriots presaged success, and every eye was lighted with victory. It came at that propitious moment. The enemy, already daunted by the fierce ordeal through which they had passed from the guns of Walker and Jackson, could no longer bear the trial, when the cheers of our re-enforcing battalion were wafted to them on the evening breeze. They broke in hopeless confusion and rout, precipitately fled before our pursuing columns, leaving their dead and wounded behind them and several pieces of their artillery. Although my brigade did not reach the position in time to fire but a very few guns from the

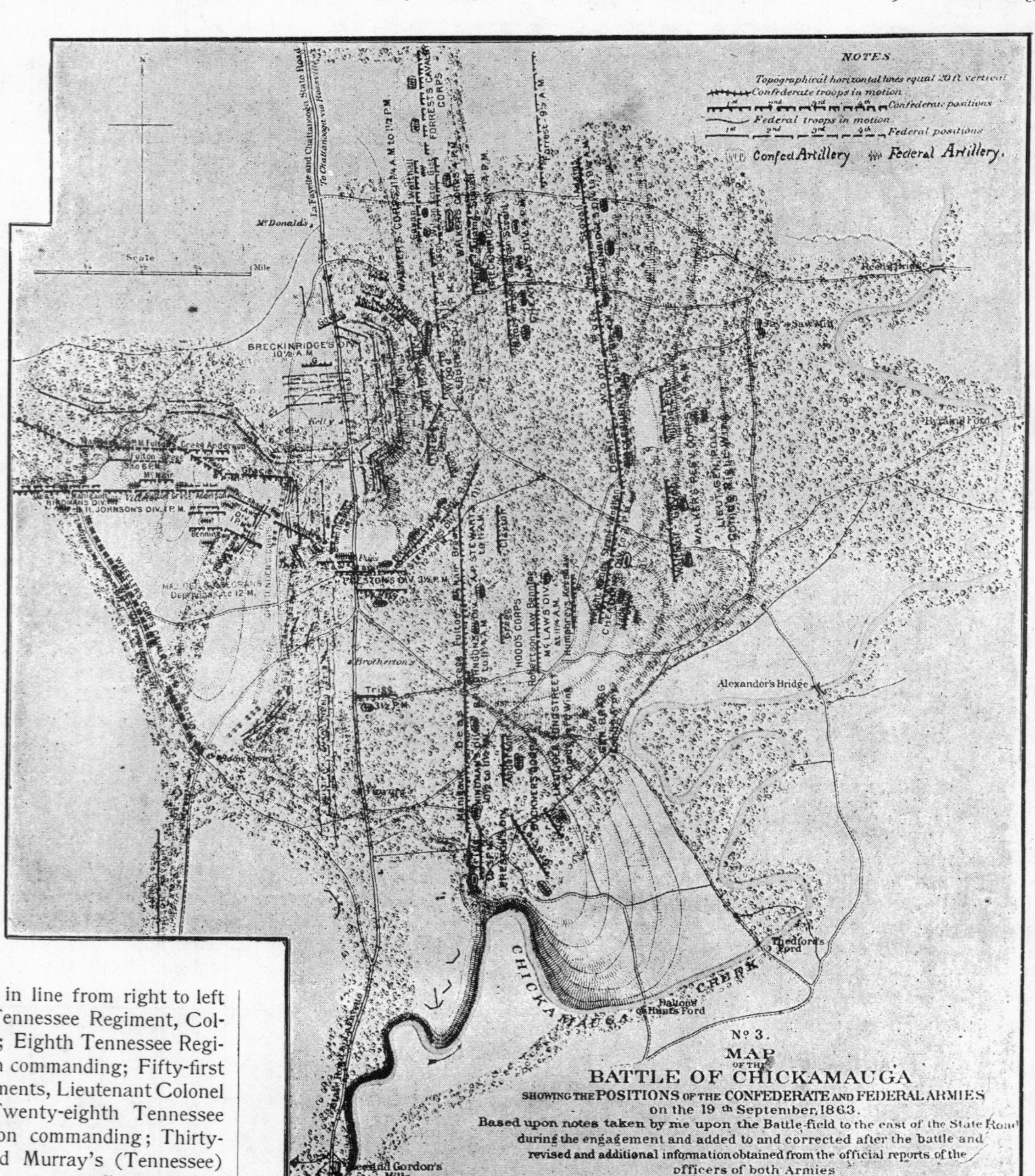

Thirty-eighth Tennessee Regiment, yet it is a source of heartfelt satisfaction that the cheers of the men and their impetuous charge assisted in striking terror into the heart of the foe and in hastening his inglorious flight. In this engagement and that of Saturday the brigade captured seventy-one prisoners, including a captain and two lieutenants. The loss in the brigade was, forty-four killed on the field, forty-three missing (most of whom are known to be and the others are supposed to be in the hands of the enemy), and four hundred wounded.

BRIG.-GEN. MARCUS J. WRIGHT, OF TENNESSEE.

Among the killed I regret to mention Captain Parks, Sixteenth Tennessee Regiment; Lieutenant Harney, Murray's battalion, attached to the Thirty-eighth Tennessee Regiment; Lieutenant Wade, and Color Bearer Bland, of the Fifty-first and Fifty-second Tennessee regiments; Captain Whaley and Lieutenant Craig, of the Twenty-eighth Tennessee Regiment, and Lieutenant Van Vleck, Carnes' battery.

Among the wounded were Colonels John H. Anderson and D. M. Donnell; Lieutenant-Colonel John G. Hall and Major Thomas G. Randle; Captains Puryear, Cullom and Bonds, and Lieutenants Cunningham, Leonard, Flynt and Shaw, Eighth Tennessee Regiment; Lieutenants Potter, Owen, Fisher and Worthington, Sixteenth Tennessee Regiment; Captain McDonald and Lieutenants Apple, Danley and Taylor, Twenty-eighth Tennessee Regiment; Adjutant Caruthers and Lieutenants Banks and Ridout, Thirty-eighth Tennessee Regiment, and Captain Burton, Lieutenants Billings, Chester, White, Haynes, Tilman and Wade, Fifty-first and Fifty-second Tennessee regiments.

All the field officers of the brigade and the officers of the battery acted with such distinguished gallantry that I feel it would be invidious to make a distinction. Company officers and men, with very inconsiderable exceptions that have come to my knowledge, bore themselves with a gallantry and steadiness becoming patriots contending for freedom and all that honorable men hold dear.

I am indebted for valuable assistance during the engagement to my staff officers, Captain Leon Trousdale, assistant adjutant-general; Captain Edward F. Lee, assistant inspector-general; my aids-de-camp, Lieutenant E. T. Harris and Lieutenant Sidney Wormack, and Mr. Charles T. Smith. They each discharged their duties with fidelity and zeal.

One of my couriers, Mr. William S. Hill, won the commendations of all, and my warm thanks, for his gallantry and alacrity in the discharge of his perilous duties. Brigadier-General W. C. Whitthorne, Adjutant-General of Tennessee, volunteered to act as aid-de-camp on the first day's march from Chattanooga, and discharged the various duties that I assigned to him with a promptness, courage and ability which merit and receive my warmest thanks. On the field General Whitthorne conducted himself with conspicuous gallantry. The infirmary corps discharged their duties with such fearlessness and fidelity as to attract my special observation.

The provost guard also, under their worthy and gallant provost-marshal, Lieutenant Richardson, fully fulfilled the standard of their duties. They lost one killed and two wounded in the engagement of Saturday.

I unite with all true patriots of our country in returning thanks to Almighty God, without whose assistance our strength is weakness, for the substantial victory with which he has crowned our efforts.

I herewith transmit the reports of the regimental commanders of the brigade, to which your especial attention is respectfully invoked. I regret I can not accompany this with the report of Captain Carnes, commanding battery, whose absence on business connected with his battery necessarily delays its preparation.

MARCUS J. WRIGHT,
Brigadier-General.

FIELD RETURN OF THE EFFECTIVE STRENGTH OF THE ARMY OF TENNESSEE, AFTER CHICKAMAUGA CAMPAIGN.

INFANTRY:		
Polk's Corps	10,313	
Hill's Corps	10,307	
Longstreet's Corps (includes Buckner's)	15,522	
		36,142
ARTILLERY:		
Polk's Corps	755	
Hill's Corps	922	
Longstreet's Corps	1,027	
		2,704
Total Effective		38,846

The artillery is much crippled by loss of horses.

KINLOCK FALCONER,
Assistant Adjutant-General.

MISSIONARY RIDGE, September 27, 1863.

CASUALTIES OF LEFT WING, ARMY OF TENNESSEE, IN THE ENGAGEMENT OF SEPTEMBER 20, 1863, NEAR CHICKAMAUGA, GA.

COMMAND.	Killed.	Woun'd	Missing	Total.
HOOD'S DIVISION.				
Robertson's brigade	78	457	35	570
Benning's brigade	46	436	6	488
Law's brigade	61	329	...	390
Total	185	1,222	41	1,448
MCLAWS' DIVISION.				
Kershaw's brigade	68	419	1	488
Humphreys' brigade	20	132	...	152
Total	88	551	1	640
HINDMAN'S DIVISION.				
Anderson's brigade	80	464	24	568
Deas' brigade	123	578	28	729
Manigault's brigade	66	426	47	539
Total	269	1,468	99	1,836
JOHNSON'S DIVISION.				
Johnson's brigade	28	271	74	373
Gregg's brigade	113	447	17	577
McNair's brigade	...	...	...	...
Total	141	718	91	950
BUCKNER'S CORPS.				
STEWART'S DIVISION.				
[Headquarters]	...	1	...	1
Brown's brigade	50	426	4	480
Bate's brigade	63	530	11	604
Clayton's brigade	86	518	15	619
Total	199	1,475	30	1,704
PRESTON'S DIVISION.				
Gracie's brigade	90	576	2	668
Trigg's brigade	46	231	4	281
Kelly's brigade	66	241	3	310
Total	202	1,048	9	1,259
Total Infantry	1,084	6,482	271	7,837
Artillery	5	23	1	29
Grand Total	1,089	6,505	272	7,866

THE CONFEDERATE ARMY AT THE BATTLE OF CHICKAMAUGA, GA.,

SEPTEMBER 19 AND 20, 1863.

RIGHT WING.

Lieutenant-General Leonidas Polk, Commanding.

CHEATHAM'S DIVISION.

Major-General B. F. Cheatham.

JACKSON'S BRIGADE.

Brigadier-General J. K. Jackson.

First Confederate Battalion; Fifth Georgia; Second Georgia Battalion; Fifth Mississippi; Eighth Mississippi; Scogin's (Ga.) battery.

MANEY'S BRIGADE.

Brigadier-General George Maney.

First Tennessee; Twenty-seventh Tennessee; Fourth Tennessee; Sixth Tennessee; Ninth Tennessee; Maney's (Tenn.) battalion; Smith's (Miss.) battery.

SMITH'S BRIGADE.

Brigadier-General Preston Smith; Colonel A. J. Vaughan.

Eleventh Tennessee; Twelfth Tennessee; Forty-seventh Tennessee; Thirteenth Tennessee; Twenty-ninth Tennessee; One hundred and fifty-fourth Tennessee; Scott's (Tenn.) battery.

WRIGHT'S BRIGADE.

Brigadier-General M. J. Wright.

Eighth Tennessee; Sixteenth Tennessee; Twenty-eighth Tennessee; Thirty-eighth Tennessee; Fifty-first Tennessee; Fifty-second Tennessee; Carnes' (Tenn.) battery.

STRAHL'S BRIGADE.

Brigadier-General O. F. Strahl.

Fourth Tennessee; Fifth Tennessee; Nineteenth Tennessee; Twenty-fourth Tennessee; Thirty-first Tennessee; Thirty-third Tennessee; Stanford's (Miss.) battery.

HILL'S CORPS.

Lieutenant-General D. H. Hill, Commanding.

CLEBURNE'S DIVISION.

Major-General P. R. Cleburne.

POLK'S BRIGADE.

Brigadier-General L. E. Polk.

First Arkansas; Third Confederate; Fifth Confederate; Second Tennessee; Thirty-fifth Tennessee; Forty-eighth Tennessee; Calvert's (Tenn.) battery.

SHARPSHOOTERS FIRING ON A FEDERAL SUPPLY TRAIN ON THE TENNESSEE RIVER

WOOD'S BRIGADE.
Brigadier-General S. A. M. Wood.

Sixteenth Alabama; Thirty-third Alabama; Forty-fifth Alabama; Thirty-second Mississippi; Forty-fifth Mississippi; Hankin's battalion; Semple's (Ala.) battery.

DESHLER'S BRIGADE.
Brigadier-General James Deshler; Colonel R. Q. Mills.

Nineteenth Arkansas; Twenty-fourth Arkansas; Sixth Texas; Tenth Texas; Fifteenth Texas; Seventeenth Texas; Eighteenth Texas; Twenty-fourth Texas; Twenty-fifth Texas; Douglas' (Tex.) battery.

BRECKINRIDGE'S DIVISION.
Major-General John C. Breckinridge.

HELM'S BRIGADE.
Brigadier-General B. H. Helm; Colonel J. H. Lewis.

Forty-first Alabama; Second Kentucky; Fourth Kentucky; Sixth Kentucky; Ninth Kentucky; Cobb's (Ky.) battery.

ADAMS' BRIGADE.
Brigadier-General Daniel Adams; Colonel R. L. Gibson.

Thirty-second Alabama; Thirteenth Louisiana; Twentieth Louisiana; Sixteenth Louisiana; Twenty-fifth Louisiana; Nineteenth Louisiana; Austin's (La.) battalion; Slocomb's (La.) battery.

STOVALL'S BRIGADE.
Brigadier-General M. A. Stovall.

First Florida; Third Florida; Fourth Florida; Forty-seventh Georgia; Sixtieth North Carolina; Mebane's (Tenn.) battery.

WALKER'S DIVISION.*
(1) Major-General W. H. T. Walker.
(2) Brigadier-General S. R. Gist.

GIST'S BRIGADE.
Brigadier-General S. R. Gist; Colonel P. H. Colquitt.

Forty-sixth Georgia; Eighth Georgia Battalion; Sixteenth South Carolina; Twenty-fourth South Carolina; Ferguson's (S. C.) battery.

ECTOR'S BRIGADE.
Brigadier-General M. D. Ector.

Stone's (Ala.) battery; Pound's (Miss.) battery; Ninth Texas; Tenth Texas Cavalry;† Fourteenth Texas Cavalry;† Thirty-second Texas Cavalry;† Battery.‡

WILSON'S BRIGADE.
Colonel C. C. Wilson.

Twenty-fifth Georgia; Twenty-ninth Georgia; Thirtieth Georgia; First Georgia Battalion; Fourth Louisiana Battalion; Battery.‡

Brig.-Gen. James Deshler, of Georgia.
Killed at the Battle of Chickamauga, Ga., September 20, 1863.
[From an old tintype.]

LIDDELL'S DIVISION.*
Brigadier-General S. J. R. Liddell.

LIDDELL'S BRIGADE.
Colonel D. C. Govan.

Second Arkansas; Fifteenth Arkansas; Fifth Arkansas; Thirteenth Arkansas; Sixth Arkansas; Seventh Arkansas; Eighth Arkansas; First Louisiana; Swett's (Miss.) battalion.

* Walker's and Liddell's divisions constituted a "reserve corps" under Walker's command, Gist commanding Walker's division.
† Dismounted.
‡ General Walker reports five batteries, but those of Ector's and Wilson's brigades are not named in reports.

WALTHALL'S BRIGADE.
Brigadier-General E. C. Walthall.

Twenty-fourth Mississippi; Twenty-seventh Mississippi; Twenty-ninth Mississippi; Thirtieth Mississippi; Thirty-fourth Mississippi; Fowler's (Ala.) battery.

LEFT WING.
Lieutenant-General James Longstreet, Commanding.

MCLAWS' DIVISION.*
(1) Major-General Lafayette McLaws.
(2) Brigadier-General J. B. Kershaw.

KERSHAW'S BRIGADE.
Brigadier-General J. B. Kershaw.

Second South Carolina; Third South Carolina; Seventh South Carolina; Eighth South Carolina; Fifteenth South Carolina; Third South Carolina Battalion.

WOFFORD'S BRIGADE.
Brigadier-General W. T. Wofford.

Sixteenth Georgia; Eighteenth Georgia; Twenty-fourth Georgia; Third Georgia Battalion; Cobb's (Ga.) Legion; Phillips' (Ga.) Legion.

HUMPHREYS' BRIGADE.
Brigadier-General B. G. Humphreys.

Thirteenth Mississippi; Seventeenth Mississippi; Eighteenth Mississippi; Twenty-first Mississippi.

BRYAN'S BRIGADE.†
Brigadier-General Goode Bryan.

Tenth Georgia; Fiftieth Georgia; Fifty-first Georgia; Fifty-third Georgia.

HOOD'S DIVISION.*
(1) Major-General J. B. Hood.
(2) Brigadier-General E. M. Law.

LAW'S BRIGADE.
Brigadier-General E. M. Law; Colonel Sheffield.

Fourth Alabama; Fifteenth Alabama; Forty-fourth Alabama; Forty-seventh Alabama; Forty-eighth Alabama.

ROBERTSON'S BRIGADE.
Brigadier-General J. B. Robertson.

Third Arkansas; Eighteenth Texas; Fourth Texas; Fifth Texas.

ANDERSON'S BRIGADE.
Brigadier-General George T. Anderson.

Seventh Georgia; Eighth Georgia; Ninth Georgia; Eleventh Georgia; Fifty-ninth Georgia.

BENNING'S BRIGADE.
Brigadier-General H. L. Benning.

Second Georgia; Fifteenth Georgia; Seventeenth Georgia; Twentieth Georgia.

ARTILLERY.‡
Major Frank Huger.

Fickling's (Va.) battery; Jordan's (Va.) battery; Moody's (La.) battery; Parker's (Va.) battery; Taylor's (Va.) battery; Woolfolk's (Va.) battery.

HINDMAN'S DIVISION.§
(1) Major-General T. C. Hindman.
(2) Brigadier-General Patton Anderson.

ANDERSON'S BRIGADE.
Brigadier-General Patton Anderson; Colonel J. H. Sharp.

Seventh Mississippi; Ninth Mississippi; Tenth Mississippi; Forty-first Mississippi; Forty-fourth Mississippi; Ninth Mississippi Battalion; Garrity's (Ala.) battery.

DEAS' BRIGADE.
Brigadier-General Z. C. Deas.

Nineteenth Alabama; Twenty-second Alabama; Twenty-fifth Alabama; Thirty-ninth Alabama; Fiftieth Alabama; Seventeenth Alabama Battalion; Dent's (Ala.) battery.

MANIGAULT'S BRIGADE.
Brigadier-General A. M. Manigault.

Twenty-fourth Alabama; Twenty-eighth Alabama; Thirty-fourth Alabama; Tenth South Carolina and Nineteenth South Carolina, consolidated; Water's (Ala.) battery.

BUCKNER'S CORPS.
Major-General S. B. Buckner, Commanding.

STEWART'S DIVISION.
Major-General A. P. Stewart.

JOHNSON'S BRIGADE.||
Brigadier-General B. R. Johnson; Colonel J. S. Fulton.

Seventeenth Tennessee; Twenty-third Tennessee; Twenty-fifth Tennessee; Forty-fourth Tennessee; Ninth Georgia Artillery, Battery E.

* Longstreet's corps organization of these divisions, and of the artillery battalion taken from Return of the Army of Northern Virginia, for August 31, 1863; the artillery is not mentioned in the reports.
† Longstreet's report indicates that these brigades were not engaged.
‡ Served in Johnson's division.
§ Of Polk's corps.
|| See Johnson's division, following.

BROWN'S BRIGADE.
Brigadier-General J. C. Brown.

Eighteenth Tennessee; Twenty-sixth Tennessee; Thirty-second Tennessee; Forty-fifth Tennessee; Newman's (Tenn.) battalion; Dawson's (Ga.) battery.

BATE'S BRIGADE.
Brigadier-General W. B. Bate.

Fifty-eighth Alabama; Thirty-seventh Georgia; Fourth Georgia Battalion; Fifteenth Tennessee; Thirth-seventh Tennessee; Twentieth Tennessee; Oliver's (Ala.) artillery.

CLAYTON'S BRIGADE.
Brigadier-General H. D. Clayton.

Eighteenth Alabama; Thirty-sixth Alabama; Thirty-eighth Alabama; Humphrey's (Ark.) battery.

Brig.-Gen Benj. H. Helm, of Kentucky.
Killed at the Battle of Chickamauga, Ga., September 20, 1863.

PRESTON'S DIVISION.
Brigadier-General William Preston.

GRACIE'S BRIGADE.
Brigadier-General A. Gracie, Jr.

Forty-third Alabama; First Alabama Battalion;* Second Alabama Battalion;* Third Alabama Battalion;* Sixty-third Tennessee Battery.†

TRIGG'S BRIGADE.
Colonel R. C. Trigg.

First Florida Cavalry;‡ Sixth Florida; Seventh Florida; Fifty-fourth Virginia; Peeple's (Ga.) battery.

KELLY'S BRIGADE.
Colonel J. H. Kelly.

Sixty-fifth Georgia; Fifth Kentucky; Fifty-eighth North Carolina; Sixty-third Virginia Battery.†

JOHNSON'S DIVISION.§
Brigadier-General B. R. Johnson.

GREGG'S BRIGADE.
Brigadier-General John Gregg; Colonel C. A. Sugy.

Third Tennessee; Tenth Tennessee; Thirtieth Tennessee; Forty-first Tennessee; Fiftieth Tennessee; First (Twentieth) Tennessee Battalion; Seventh Texas; Bledsoe's (Mo.) battery.

M'NAIR'S BRIGADE.
Brigadier-General E. McNair; Colonel D. Coleman.

First Arkansas Rifles; Second Arkansas Rifles; Fourth Arkansas; Twenty-fifth Arkansas; Thirty-fifth Arkansas; Culpeper's (S. C.) battery.

CAVALRY.
Major-General Joseph Wheeler,|| Commanding.

WHARTON'S DIVISION.
Brigadier-General John A. Wharton.

FIRST BRIGADE.
Colonel C. C. Crews.

Seventh Alabama; Second Georgia; Third Georgia; Fourth Georgia.

SECOND BRIGADE.
Colonel T. Harrison.

Third Confederate; First Kentucky; Fourth Tennessee; Eighth Texas; Eleventh Texas; White's (Ga.) battery.

* Hilliard's Legion.
† It appears that Baxter's (Tenn.) and Jeffress' (Va.) batteries belonged to this division, but their assignment is not clearly indicated.
‡ Dismounted.
§ This was a temporary organization, embracing Benning's, Johnson's, Law's and Robertson's brigades, as well as Gregg's and McNair's.
|| This organization taken from return for August 31, 1863.

MARTIN'S DIVISION.

Brigadier-General W. T. Martin.

FIRST BRIGADE.

Colonel J. T. Morgan.

First Alabama; Third Alabama; Fifty-first Alabama; Eighth Confederate.

SECOND BRIGADE.

Colonel A. A. Russell.

Fourth Alabama;* First Confederate; Wiggin's (Ark.) battery.

RODDEY'S BRIGADE.

Brigadier-General P. D. Roddey.

Fourth Alabama;* Fifth Alabama; Fifty-third Alabama; Forrest's (Tenn.) regiment; Ferrell's (Ga.) battery.

BRIG.-GEN. PRESTON SMITH, OF TENNESSEE.
Killed at the Battle of Chickamauga, Ga., September 20, 1863.

FORREST'S CORPS.

Major-General N. B. Forrest, Commanding.

ARMSTRONG'S DIVISION. †

Brigadier-General F. C. Armstrong.

ARMSTRONG'S BRIGADE.

Third Arkansas; First Tennessee; Second Tennessee; McDonald's battalion.

——— BRIGADE.

Fourth Tennessee; Eighth Tennessee; Ninth Tennessee; Tenth Tennessee; Eleventh Tennessee; Freeman's (Tenn.) battery; Marion's (Tenn.) battery.

PEGRAM'S DIVISION. ‡

Brigadier-General John Pegram.

DAVIDSON'S BRIGADE.

Brigadier-General H. B. Davidson.

First Georgia; Sixth Georgia; Sixty-fifth North Carolina; Rucker's Legion; Huwald's (Tenn.) battery.

SCOTT'S BRIGADE.

Colonel J. L. Scott.

Tenth Confederate; First Louisiana; Fifth Tennessee; Twelfth Tennessee Battalion; Sixteenth Tennessee Battalion; Louisiana Battery (one section).

RESERVE ARTILLERY. §

Barret's (Mo.) battery; Darden's (Miss.) battery; Havis' (Ala.) battery; Le Gardewi's (La.) battery; Lumsden's (Ala.) battery; Massenburg's (Ga.) battery.

* Two regiments of the same designation. Lieutenant-Colonel Johnson commanded that in Roddey's Brigade.
† Taken from return for August 31, 1863, and Forrest's report.
‡ Taken from Pegram's and Scott's reports and assignments, but the composition of this division is uncertain.
§ With exception of Darden's battery taken from return for August, 31, 1863; on that return that battery appears as of Johnson's Brigade.

TRUE COURAGE.

In all ages, courage on the battlefield has been the theme of orators and poets, yet the courage of the warrior is not only a common and a variable quality, but has often been surpassed by that displayed by women. Native valor, too, is sometimes inferior to that which is acquired. Frederic the Great ran like a coward out of his first battle. Flying on the wings of fear, he went a great distance from the field, and, coming to one of his own strongholds, reported that his army was destroyed. What was his surprise and mortification to learn that his men had gained a great victory. He never forgot the lesson taught, and ever afterward was conspicuous for steady courage in action. Many instances might be given of soldiers in the last war who, in their first fight, were "lily-livered," but who afterward faced with dauntless front the gleaming steel; and on the other hand, of some who were lion-hearted till taught by the pain of a wound the perils of a battle, and who then became notable cowards. Bravery in action, though more admired, is really not as great as that displayed in passive suffering. The woman who sticks to her post in the pestilential chamber is far braver than Alexander charging at the head of his cavalry.

BATTLE OF LOOKOUT MOUNTAIN, TENN.,

NOVEMBER 24, 1863.

BY

MAJOR-GENERAL CARTER L. STEVENSON,
Commanding Division and Left Flank, Army of Tennessee.

HEADQUARTERS STEVENSON'S DIVISION, HARDEE'S CORPS, ARMY OF TENNESSEE,
NEAR DALTON, January 2, 1864.

ON November 12th I was directed to move my division from the position near the tunnel on the East Tennessee & Georgia Railroad, which it had occupied since its return from East Tennessee, to the extreme left of our infantry lines—the top of Lookout Mountain—reporting to Lieutenant-General Hardee.

On November 14th the positions of the troops of his command were assigned by the lieutenant-general, Walker's division, commanded by Brigadier-General Gist, to occupy that portion of the line which lay west of the Chattanooga Creek to the Chattanooga Road, at the base of the mountain; Cheatham's division, commanded by Brigadier-General Jackson, that known as the Craven House Slope, extending from the left of Walker's line to Smiths Trail, on the western side of the mountain, and the defense of the mountain was intrusted to my division and a very small and inadequate force of cavalry.

The position assigned to me—the table on top of the mountain—included the pass at Johnsons Crook, distant eighteen miles. The numerous passes along the western crest to Nickajack Pass, a distance of about ten miles, were held by infantry; the rim by the small force of cavalry. The defensive works on the mountain extended from east to west about two and one-half miles from the point. To guard this extended line, to protect these numerous passes, and to complete, with the dispatch so frequently urged upon me by the general commanding, the line of defense, the work upon which was prosecuted, agreeably to his orders, day and night, and the necessity of watching with the utmost vigilance the movements of the heavy force of the enemy threatening my rear at Stevens Gap and Johnsons Crook, demanded and received my constant and undivided attention. By personal inspection and reconnoissance, I familiarized myself with the character of the line intrusted to me, but had neither time nor occasion to make myself acquainted with the dispositions made by the lieutenant-general commanding for the defense of the rest of the line, further than such information as I acquired by personal observation in visiting and adjusting the posts of my pickets and signal stations at and near the point of the mountain, from which place, in favorable weather, both armies could be plainly discerned.

On November 23d, about 1 P. M., my attention was attracted by heavy firing in the valley below. I immediately proceeded to the point of the mountain, from which I could plainly see all the movements of the enemy. I watched them closely until dark, and then hurried off the following dispatch by signal both to Lieutenant-General Hardee and direct to General Bragg:

"I observed closely from the point the movements of the enemy until dark. An object seemed to be to attract our attention. All the troops in sight were formed from center to left. Those on their right moved to center. The troops from Raccoon were in line in full sight. If they intend to attack, my opinion is it will be upon our left. Both of their bridges are gone."

The movements of the enemy and his demonstration against our right center were such that, in my mind, I had not the slightest doubt that his purpose was to attract our attention, induce us to concentrate on our right, thereby weakening our left, and thus render the acquisition of Lookout Mountain practicable for him.

The maneuver had the desired effect, for during that evening Walker's entire division was removed from its position to the extreme right, and the force west of Chattanooga Creek thereby diminished more than one-third. After dark I was informed by Lieutenant-General Hardee that he had been ordered to the extreme right, and I was directed to assume command of the troops west of Chattanooga Creek. To fill, as far as possible, the vacancy caused by the removal of Walker's division, Jackson's brigade, of Cheatham's division, was removed from the Craven House Slope, and Cumming's brigade, of my own division, from the top of the mountain, General Cumming, as senior officer present, being placed in command of the two brigades. I was advised by the lieutenant-general commanding to transfer my headquarters to the Craven house, and subsequently to the camp just vacated by him.

Having thus, without the slightest premonition—not only a large portion of the troops, but even the permanent commander having been removed—been placed in command at night, at a most critical period, over a wing of the army, with whose position and disposition, as I have already stated, I had enjoyed no opportunity of making myself acquainted, I at once used every exertion to gain the necessary information by sending every officer of my staff and devoting the whole night myself to riding over and examining the lines. I found the position at which General Hardee advised me to establish my headquarters to be on the eastern side of Chattanooga Creek, some distance beyond the extreme right of my line, and at least two and one-half miles from the base of the mountain. The distance, and the fact that the situation was most unfavorable for personal observation, determined me to return to the mountain, which afforded me this advantage in the highest degree.

On my way I examined the whole line, and at sunrise reached the Craven house. I found the troops in position as assigned by Lieutenant-General Hardee. Moore's brigade was bivouacked along the eastern side of the mountain near the Craven house, Walthall's on the northwestern slope in front of the Craven house. After examining the ledge I became satisfied that no tenable line could be established on the northwestern slope, so completely was it commanded by batteries which the enemy had erected for the purpose, and that the only feasible plan of defense was for Walthall, in case the enemy should cross the creek and attack him, to fall back fighting upon Moore, on a line near the Craven house, holding them in check until the only movable force that I had could be sent to assist. This would expose the enemy to a flank fire at short range from the crest of the mountain on which I proposed to deploy the remainder of my force not engaged in guarding the passes on the west side, as sharpshooters. Accordingly, after seeing General Moore and conversing with him on the subject of his line and his ability to hold it—of which he spoke with some confidence—being informed that all was quiet on that line, I went to the top of the mountain to make what I conceived to be the proper disposition of the troops there. I directed Brigadier-General Brown, then commanding my division, to hold the larger portion of Pettus' brigade ready to move at a moment's notice to any point to which it should be ordered. I thus provided, as well as the means at my disposal permitted, either for an attack upon Cumming or Jackson.

Immediately upon my arrival upon the mountain I directed the lookouts at the point to keep a close watch and advise me of any movement the enemy might make. About 10 A. M. I received from Brigadier-General Jackson a communication written him by General Walthall, and soon afterward was informed by the men at the point that there was some picket firing on Lookout Creek. I immediately rode to the point to see what was going on. The enemy had by felling trees constructed three temporary bridges over the creek, and in a short time forced a passage. The troops as they crossed formed to cover the passage of the remainder. I immediately sent a staff officer of General Hardee (Major W. D. Picket), who happened to be with me, to General Jackson to inform him of what I had seen, and to direct him at once to place all of his troops in position. He reached General Jackson, I suppose, a little after 10 A. M. I caused the picket at Smiths Trail to be largely increased and a strong force to be posted as sharpshooters along the crest of the mountain. The artillery, with trails raised, opened with spirit and effect, and was used until the enemy advanced so close under the cliff that the guns could not be sufficiently depressed for the shots to take effect.

MAJ.-GEN. CARTER L. STEVENSON, OF VIRGINIA.

General Walthall's pickets and skirmishers extended from the turnpike bridge of Lookout Creek to the railroad bridge, and thence making nearly a right angle across the northwest slope of the mountain to a point near Smiths Trail. The enemy, as Walthall mentions in his report, had threatened to force a passage of the creek on his right, but their real movement was upon his left. A large force had moved up the creek, under cover of the fog, crossed above, and, passing along the western slope, attacked him successfully in flank and rear. Their advance on the flank and from the front was gallantly contested; but though their front line sometimes wavered, they pressed on, Walthall falling back to the line which I have before mentioned, but with very heavy loss in prisoners, owing to the enemy taking him in flank and rear.

Finding that the fog was becoming so dense that the troops on the northern point of the mountain could not see the enemy moving upon Walthall, I gave orders for Pettus, with my own disposable force, to move down and report to Brigadier-General Jackson. He started at 12:30 o'clock and reached the scene of action a little past 1 o'clock, relieving Walthall on the left of Moore's line. This position was held by Moore, Walthall and Pettus until about 8 P. M., when Walthall's and part of Pettus' command were relieved by Clayton's brigade, commanded by Colonel Holtzclaw, which was sent to cover the movement to the right. Moore and Holtzclaw retired from the position about 2 A. M. on the 25th. Brown finding that the enemy could not be seen for the fog, deployed his sharpshooters down the sides of the mountain, who were guided in firing by the reports of the enemy's musketry. At the same time, the men stationed along the crest rolled down rocks in the direction of the Craven house. This, with the shells from the Napoleon guns, doubtless, contributed not a little to checking the advance of the enemy, for soon thereafter his firing materially abated.

About the time the attack was made on Walthall the enemy massed a considerable force upon the Chattanooga Road, in front of Cumming's line, evidently for the purpose of co-operating with and making a diversion in favor order and called both upon Generals Breckinridge and Bragg for them, by a staff officer; I instructed him to say to them that if they would send me re-enforcements I would, when the fog rose, attack the enemy in flank by sharpshooters on the mountain crest, and, descending Smith's Trail, take him in the rear, and, I doubted not, drive him from the slope. This statement I repeated by three other staff officers, sent at intervals of half an hour. After waiting for some time for an answer I received a verbal order from General Bragg to the effect that no re-enforcements could be sent me; that I must withdraw as best I could under cover of the fog, and that a brigade would be sent to the base of the mountain to cover the withdrawal. Subsequently I received the following note:

"2:30 P. M.

"The general commanding instructs me to say that you will withdraw your command from the mountain to this side of Chattanooga Creek, destroying the bridges behind. Fight the enemy as you retire. The thickness of the fog will enable you to retire, it is hoped, without much difficulty."

About five hours after the date of this order I received a note from Major-General Breckinridge, then my corps commander, informing me that he had arrived at the base of the mountain with a brigade (Clayton's) to be used in the retirement, and generously offering to confer with me, and render me any assistance in his power in the withdrawal of the troops. This brigade, as has been heretofore stated, relieved Walthall's and part of Pettus' command about 8 P. M., and was the only force sent to me that day. I was engaged in issuing the necessary orders for the

The withdrawal of Walker's division on the night of the 23d, in my opinion, rendered the position on the left, opposed by so large a force, untenable, and it was beyond the power of the troops there to do more than secure the communication with the top of the mountain and with the main body of the army until General Bragg could decide whether he would re-enforce them sufficiently to hold the line or abandon it. His decision I have already given.

The mountain was held until 2 o'clock the next morning, and the troops, artillery and trains were withdrawn in order to the eastern side of the creek.

C. L. STEVENSON, *Major-General.*

BATTLE OF LOOKOUT MOUNTAIN, TENN.,

NOVEMBER 24, 1863.

BY

BRIGADIER-GENERAL JOHN K. JACKSON,

Commanding Cheatham's Division, Hardee's Corps.

HEADQUARTERS CHEATHAM'S DIVISION,
NEAR DALTON, GA., December 21, 1863.

ON November 9th, in conformity with orders from army headquarters, being temporarily in command of Cheatham's division, I reported to Major-General W. H. T. Walker. A reorganization of the army having just taken place, I had with me to report to General Walker but one brigade of the division, Wright's brigade

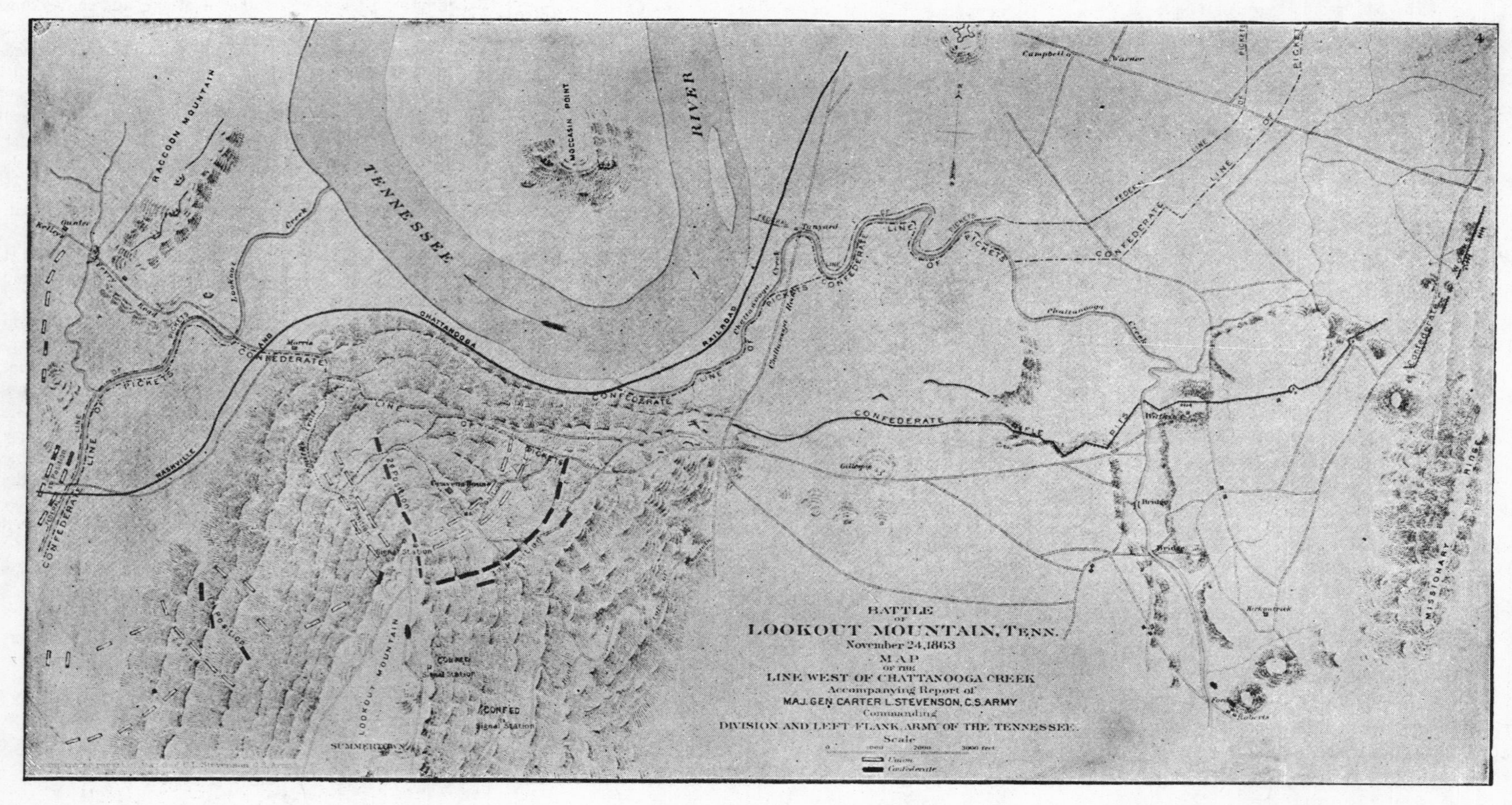

of their assaulting column. The number of his troops massed for this purpose, who had been in plain sight until the view was obscured by the mist; the serious weakness of Cumming's force (there not being a man for yards upon some parts of the line), and the certainty that to re-enforce the command near the Craven house from Cumming's was to give the enemy an opportunity to cut us off from the main body without even a show of resistance, rendered it highly improper to withdraw a man from him. I have already stated that he had but two brigades to hold the line from the Chattanooga Creek to the Chattanooga Road, at the base of the mountain. The force, early that morning, at the Craven House Slope, had consisted of two brigades—Moore's and Walthall's—and were now re-enforced by the larger part of a third (Pettus'), while on the mountain top there were but one small brigade and two regiments of another, the larger portion being between the point and the works, the other picketing and holding a line of about ten miles.

Of my six brigades, it will be perceived from the foregoing account that four were engaged, while the remaining two were threatened by a force which, had it advanced, could soon have driven them from their position and immediately cut us off from the army east of the creek—a position which I had been instructed to hold, even at the expense of the mountain. I had been directed by General Bragg, if I needed re-enforcements, to call for them, and as soon as I saw that the enemy were attacking and would carry the point, I availed myself of the retirement of the troops when Major-General Cheatham arrived. He informed me that he had come to consult with me, but not to assume command. I sent the troops down from the top of the mountain and then proceeded to a point near its base, where General Cheatham and myself had appointed to meet.

Here, as senior officer, he assumed command, and I then gave no further directions with regard to the retirement of the troops, except such as I received from him for those of my own division. Here we met, also, Major-General Breckinridge, who, when Major-General Cheatham took command, returned to his corps. Brown was directed at once to cross Chattanooga Creek (about 11 P. M.), Cumming at 1 o'clock, and Cheatham's division (with which was then serving Pettus' brigade of my own division) afterward—all with directions to await further orders on the eastern side. General Cheatham then left me, as I understood, to get further orders from General Bragg. Except about one hour—from about 10:30 to 11:30 A. M.—the mountain was enveloped in fog during the day.

About 12 M. two staff officers of General Bragg rode up to where I was (General Cumming's quarters) and, stating that they could not find General Cheatham, handed me orders to him from General Bragg to send all the troops that had been west of Chattanooga Creek to the extreme right. This order was immediately given and was executed as quickly as possible. The conduct of the troops was all that could have been desired, and they accomplished all that could have been expected of them.

having been left at Charleston, Tenn., under orders, and Moore's and Walthall's brigades having not then reported to me under the new organization. My headquarters were located on the west side of Chattanooga Creek, at a point advised by General Walker, and my brigade was placed where he directed. On the same day I was invited by General Walker to accompany him and Lieutenant-General Hardee to the Craven house, which I did. The ground in that neighborhood was passed over, viewed and discussed, but no line to fight on was recommended by any one present. Indeed, it was agreed on all hands that the position was one extremely difficult of defense against a strong force of the enemy advancing under cover of a heavy artillery fire. General Walker's opinion was expressed to the effect that at a certain point to which we had walked, which was a narrow pass, artillery should be placed in position extending to the left for a short distance toward the top of the mountain; that this would prevent any surprise by forces approaching in that direction, and at the same time they would answer the guns from the hills on the opposite side of Lookout Creek, also to have artillery near the Craven house to answer the Moccasin battery guns. By the first arrangement, be said, the artillery could have retreated by the road, and the infantry, which was put there to defend the artillery and pass, would have felt strong and been better satisfied and better able to hold their position. He said his experience was that infantry care but little for artillery if they have artillery to respond with, and that they are soon demoralized when they have

From an original painting, copyrighted by Kurz & Allison, Chicago, Ill.

BATTLE OF CHATTANOOGA, TENN. CHARGE NEAR ORCHARD KNOB, NOVEMBER 24, 1863.

quietly to sit and receive artillery fire without having some of their own to reply with. I ventured to express my own opinion to Lieutenant-General Hardee subsequently, and in it I differed somewhat (not without great presumption, but with equal diffidence) from that of so experienced a soldier as General Walker. If we were defeated on the slope, the guns, as I thought, must inevitably be lost, from the impossibility of removing them under fire from their positions. My plan of defense was to place a gun in every available position on Lookout Point, and to sink the wheels or elevate the trails, so as to command the slope of the mountain. In addition to which I respectfully suggested that on the point a sharpshooter should be placed wherever a man could stand, so as to annoy the flank of the enemy. In my judgment there was no place northwest of the Craven house at which our infantry force could be held on the slope of the mountain, and in consequence of this firm conviction I gave orders to Brigadier-General Walthall, which are hereinafter mentioned.

Upon my return to the foot of the mountain, on November 9th, I found Brigadier-General Walthall and his brigade in camp there. Brigadier-General Moore's brigade was then at the Craven house, where it had been for a time—how long I am not informed. General Walker directed that Brigadier-General Gist, commanding his division, and I, with my own and Walthall's brigades of Cheatham's division, should defend the line from Chattanooga Creek to the foot of the mountain, and permitted us to divide the line according to our respective strength as we wished.

After riding along the line with General Gist we made the apportionment of it and gave orders to our respective commands. At that time I had no command over the mountain slope, although one of the brigades (Moore's) of the division was then on duty at or near the Craven house. General Moore was in command of that portion of the line, under General Walker's orders, from November 10th to 14th. The command I found General Walker exercising extended over all the troops west of Chattanooga Creek, under the general supervision of Lieutenant-General Hardee, and upon General Walker's going away on a short leave on November 12th, which he informed me he had some weeks before applied for, and upon the assurance of General Bragg that he would telegraph him when Sherman came up, before which time he anticipated no trouble, this command devolved on me. I at once asked for written instructions from the corps commander as to the mode of defense of the line, but received none. The command was a unit and was doubtless intended to be handled as such. I continued to exercise it, and gave orders, subject to the approval of Lieutenant-General Hardee until his headquarters were removed from the extreme right of the army to a point a little east of Chattanooga Creek. This was about November 14th.

About this time I went to the top of the mountain with Lieutenant-General Hardee. We there met General Bragg, and after a view from Lookout Point, General Bragg indicated a line on the slope of the mountain, which, from that standpoint, he thought ought to be the fighting line. As we descended the mountain I again rode out with Lieutenant-General Hardee to the Craven house and again looked over the ground. The line indicated by General Bragg was found to present quite a different appearance upon a close view from the same as seen from the mountain top. This line, as I understood it, passed from Lookout Point a little in rear of the Craven house and down to a point not far from the junction of the Kelleys Ferry and Craven House roads, and thence to the precipitous rocks near the mouth of Chattanooga Creek. The engineers were put to work under some one's orders — whose I do not know — and fatigue parties furnished to them from my command at their request. On the 14th of November, a new disposition of the command was made. Major-General Stevenson was assigned to the command of the troops and defenses on the top of Lookout Mountain. The ranking officer of Cheatham's division was directed to assume command of all troops and defenses at and near the Craven house. The ranking officer of Walker's division was charged with the line from the base of Lookout Mountain east to Chattanooga Creek, and all the troops not at the points above named. This order emanated from headquarters Hardee's corps, and, in conformity with it, as the ranking officer of Cheatham's division, I assumed command of the troops and defenses at and near the Craven house, and on the following day (November 15th) established my headquarters at the junction of the Summertown Road with the mountain-side road leading to the Craven house, with the approval of Lieutenant-General Hardee. On the same day Brigadier-General Walthall's brigade relieved that of Brigadier-General Pettus, near the Craven house.

BRIG.-GEN. JOHN K. JACKSON, OF GEORGIA.

On the nights of the 16th and 17th, a fatigue party was ordered to report to Lieutenant Steele, of the engineers, to commence work on the new line below the Craven house. By direction of Lieutenant-General Hardee I went out in person to see that the work was progressing; found that there was a misunderstanding as to the place of reporting; walked down the road a considerable distance along the contemplated line, then went to the Craven house and ordered the detail to be reassembled and to report to Lieutenant Steele immediately.

This was at night. The work was directed to be done at night, as the working party would be under the fire of the Moccasin Point batteries. General Walthall's troops being some distance in advance of the proposed line and exposed to the enemy's artillery fire, I ordered him on the 8th, with the approval of Lieutenant-General Hardee, to shorten his picket line, as he proposed, and notice of which I promptly gave to General Stevenson, and to bring back his troops in the rear (south) of the Craven house, leaving his pickets where they were, supported by one regiment. Upon inspection of the ground, General Walthall reported to me that, as General Moore's troops were also in the rear of the Craven house there would not be room enough for his brigade between General Moore's and my headquarters, and said that as he supposed the order I had given him was permissive rather than directory, if I had no objections he would keep his troops where they were. To this I assented, giving him at the same time instructions, if attacked by the enemy in heavy force, to fall back fighting over the rocks. I expected by the time his troops reached the Craven house to be with them and form line of battle with Walthall's left against the cliff and his right at or near the Craven house, and Moore prolonging this line to the right. This was the general line pointed out by General Bragg, although it had not been defined by the engineers, nor had any work been done on it between the cliff and the Craven house. Beyond the Craven house there was no practicable line which was not enfiladed by the enemy's batteries, except the covered way prepared by General Jenkins, and the flank of that was exposed to the infantry attack.

On the afternoon of the 20th (I believe) I visited the works below the Craven house in company with Captain Henry, of the division staff, and spent some time in their inspection. These works, being a mere rifle-pit, would be of no service when the enemy were once in possession of the Craven house, as they would thence be taken in flank —almost in reverse.

On November 22d my own brigade was ordered to report to me, and was moved from the top of the mountain to the slope and placed in the position which I had desired General Walthall to take.

On the 23d it was ordered to the foot of the mountain, out of my command, to take, with Cumming's brigade, the place on the line which had been occupied by Walker's division. My position and that of General Stevenson were thus each weakened by a brigade.

On the same day a brisk fire of artillery and small arms was heard coming from the extreme right. It was supposed to be a struggle for wood.

Late in the afternoon of the 23d General Stevenson was placed in command of the forces west of Chattanooga Creek, Lieutenant-General Hardee having been removed to the extreme right; and on the same night orders were received and distributed to prepare three days' cooked rations and to hold the troops in readiness to move at a moment's notice. In order to avoid anything like a surprise along the line, at about 7:30 P. M. I ordered Captain Henry, of the division staff, to visit the chiefs of pickets and direct them to be unusually vigilant in watching the movements of the enemy and to guard against surprise.

About 9 A. M. of the 24th I received a note from General Walthall to the effect that the enemy were moving in heavy force toward our left; that their tents had nearly all disappeared and their pontoon bridges been cut away. Shortly afterward I received another note from him to the effect that he was mistaken as to the number of tents that had disappeared, but that many of those which could be seen on previous days were not then visible. The originals of both of these notes were immediately dispatched to General Bragg and copies to General Stevenson. I also sent a staff officer to order Generals Moore and Walthall to hold their commands under arms ready for action. I walked out on the road toward the Craven house to a favorable point and distinguished the enemy's troops in the plain in front of Chattanooga—all quiet; no massing, no movements of any kind. From this point I sent another staff officer to the Craven house to report to me immediately anything of interest, and returned myself to my position at the fork of the road. The demonstrations of the enemy did not, down to this time, indicate the point of attack —whether upon my portion of the line or further to the left. General Stevenson inquired of me, about this time, if I needed re-enforcements, to which I replied that I could not tell until there were further developments. I sent orders by a staff officer to Generals Moore and Walthall to place their troops in line as soon

LOOKOUT MOUNTAIN AND STRINGERS RIDGE, TENN., BEFORE THE BATTLE.
[From a sketch by Bill D. Travis.]

as skirmishing commenced, but not unnecessarily to expose them to the fire of the enemy's artillery. I expected, from the rugged nature of the ground, and the fact that the enemy had to ascend the mountain, that the picket fighting would continue for some time before the main body would be engaged. About this time I received information from General Moore that he did not know where the line was. I sent back immediately an order that General Walthall would occupy the left, and that he (General Moore) would form on General Walthall's right, prolonging the line in the earthworks below the Craven house as far as his troops would extend.

About 12 M. I received information from General Moore that the enemy had formed line and commenced skirmishing with our pickets near the railroad bridge crossing Lookout Creek; that he could not then tell their object, and inquiring where he should place his brigade. I sent to General Stevenson to ask for the offered re-enforcements. Information came to me from General Walthall, about the same time that the pickets had commenced firing, and a message from General Stevenson by Major Pickett, that the enemy was making an attack on my line. I now asked in writing for a brigade from General Stevenson to be sent down at once, and ordered Major John Ingram, assistant adjutant-general, to direct General Walthall to fight back the enemy with his pickets and reserves as long as possible, and finally to take position with his left against the cliff, and his right at or in direction of the Craven house, and to direct General Moore to advance and form on the right of General Walthall, and prolong the line in the earthworks below the Craven house. Major Ingram reported to me that he rode rapidly forward to a point some two hundred yards from the Craven house, passing General Moore's brigade moving up to their position, and to support General Walthall's brigade,which was being rapidly driven back by overwhelming numbers. The substance of my order was delivered by Major Ingram to Generals Moore and Walthall. The latter stated that, although the order did not reach him in time, he had carried it out in his efforts to defend the position. General Moore expressing a desire to have a full supply of ammunition, was informed by Major Ingram that Captain Clark, division ordnance officer, had been ordered to furnish him from the division train. Within a few minutes after Major Ingram left as bearer of the above order to Generals Moore and Walthall, I proceeded in person, accompanied by Major Vaulx, of the division staff, to superintend the execution.

Passing a great many stragglers (officers and men) along the road, I was met at some short distance from the Craven house by an officer from General Walthall, who brought the information that his brigade had been driven back in considerable confusion, and that the Craven house was in possession of the enemy. I immediately dispatched a staff officer to speed the re-enforcements and endeavored to rally the mem, who were coming to the rear in large numbers, and form a line where I was, selecting what I considered the most favorable position for a line among rocks, where no regular line was practicable and where the battle could be but a general skirmish. Failing in this, I rode back to the junction of the roads and there met Brigadier-General Pettus, with three regiments of his brigade. He informed me that he had been ordered by General Stevenson to report to me. I directed him to proceed on the road and form line to re-enforce Generals Moore and Walthall. I at the same time sent for a piece of artillery from the battalion of the division, and upon its arrival directed the officer in command to select the most favorable position on the Craven house road and check the enemy. He soon after reported that he could find no position in which he could use his gun to advantage, and for not more than one or two shots at all.

I remained generally at the junction of the two roads, because I considered it most accessible from all points. General Stevenson was communicating with me by the road down the mountain, General Moore by the same road up the mountain, and Generals Pettus and Walthall by the crossroad. General Pettus informed me, by an officer, of the disposition made of his troops, and asked for orders. Having placed his regiments on the left of the crossroads with their left against the cliff and with extended intervals, so as to connect with General Moore on the right of the road, I had no orders to give him except to hold that position against the enemy. His dispositions were satisfactory and I did not wish to change them. I subsequently received a message from him that the enemy was pressing his left and asking for re-enforcements, and about the same time I was informed by one of the division staff that General Walthall had sent the fragments of two regiments to that point, and that there was no danger to be apprehended there. I replied to General Pettus that I had no re-enforcements to send him; that no more could be obtained from General Stevenson and that he must hold his position.

The enemy being held in check, matters so continued not materially changed until quite late in the afternoon, when I received a report by an officer of General Moore's brigade that unless he was re-enforced his right would be turned. Receiving intelligence, also, from officers of pickets who had escaped that way, that the Kelleys Ferry Road was entirely open, I knew that the enemy had only to press forward on it to obtain control of our road from the mountain, and expecting that they certainly would do so, I rode to the top of the mountain to confer with General Stevenson, my immediate superior, upon the subject. We agreed that if the enemy did get possession of the road at or near the base of the mountain, I should withdraw the troops of my command at dark and join him on the top of the mountain, and he so directed. Availing myself of General Stevenson's writing material, I addressed written orders to the division-quartermaster, commissary of subsistence, ordnance officer, and chief of artillery, who were in the plain below, to retire beyond Chattanooga Creek and then look for orders from corps headquarters, as I expected to be cut off from them.

After this short absence I returned to my position on the mountain side, and there remained until near dark, having sent orders to the brigade commanders that if we were cut off or overpowered, we would retire by the top of the mountain, but to hold their positions if possible until dark, and to await further orders. When it was near dark, and when the firing had become rather desultory, I again went to General Stevenson's headquarters for final orders as to withdrawing the troops. I was there informed that General Bragg ordered us to retire down the mountain, the road being still open, and that we must assemble at the Gillespie house to make final arrangements. A guard having been detailed from my command for some subsistence stores on the top of the mountain, I went to relieve them, but found that it had already been done. Proceeding to the Gillespie house, at the base of the mountain, I received orders from General Bragg, through General Cheatham, as to the time and mode of withdrawing the troops, and immediately dispatched them to the brigade commanders by the assistant adjutant-general and the acting inspector-general of the division. In conformity with these orders, the troops retired south of Chattanooga Creek, and the bridge was destroyed.

On November 20th, the date of the report nearest to the day of the battle, Moore's brigade had a total effective of 1,205, and Walthall's brigade, a total effective of 1,489. The casualties in the first were 4 killed, 48 wounded and 199 missing. In the second the casualties were 8 killed, 91 wounded, and 845 captured. In Pettus' brigade there were 9 killed, 38 wounded and 9 missing.

POINT OF LOOKOUT MOUNTAIN, TENN.
[From a photograph taken in 1864, during high water, looking down the river.]

General Moore ventures the opinion that if I had given the proper orders a different result would have been accomplished. I beg leave to differ. The whole effective force at my command at the beginning was twenty-six hundred and ninety-four. Of these, one thousand and forty-four had been captured, some had been wounded, and a few killed. The enemy's force was (as reported) a division and two brigades. They were in possession of the high ground around the Craven house; from which, by General Moore's own statement, his left was completely enfiladed. Under these circumstances I was unwilling to hazard an advance movement with my shattered command, even aided by the three regiments under General Pettus, who was himself pressed by the enemy.

General Moore adds a report of the battle the next day on Missionary Ridge, when he was not under my command, and goes out of his way to say that he did not see me during the engagement. I did not think it necessary for me to show myself to him. If he had desired to see me, he could have found me at all times during the engagement, near the right of my line, which was on the top of the ridge, while the left was down the hill. If General Moore means to reflect upon the conduct of my brigade, I am glad to say that there are other witnesses who bear different testimony.

General Walthall must have misapprehended the remark made to him as I descended the mountain. I expected to receive orders from General Bragg, but not to see him in person. These orders were to come through General Cheatham.

It may be remarked that there were two 6-pounder guns at the Craven house, under the command of Lieutenant Gibson, but they were without horses and could not be moved. In their position they could not be fired without endangering the troops of General Walthall. Lieutenant Gibson's report accompanies this. He never reported to me, although subject to my orders, and his two guns were all the artillery that I could command for the purposes of defense, although I took the responsibility of ordering up a piece from the battalion of Cheatham's division. General Walthall's communication in relation to a piece of artillery to be placed in position was sent by me immediately on its receipt to General Stevenson. Captain Henry, of the division staff, was the bearer of it. The movements of the enemy were very rapid. An impenetrable fog hung around the mountain all day.

JOHN K. JACKSON,
Brigadier-General.

THE following oath was administered to the members of a volunteer company during the war: "You solemnly swear to obey, fight for and maintain the laws of the Confederate Government and Constitution, and support John W. Dean for captain of this company." Upon inquiry it was learned that the reason the last clause was inserted was because he had been quite active in getting up a company before, and when they elected their officers he was left out; so this time he was determined to make it sure.

View of Chattanooga and the Federal Lines as seen from the Confederate Outposts at the Lower Ridge of Lookout Mountain.

View of Chattanooga and the Federal Positions from the Left Center of the Confederate Lines.

BATTLE OF MISSIONARY RIDGE, TENN.,

NOVEMBER 25, 1863.

BY

MAJ.-GEN. PATRICK R. CLEBURNE,

Commanding Division, Breckinridge's Corps.

HEADQUARTERS CLEBURNE'S DIVISION.

ON the morning of the 23d November, 1863, I was with my division at Chickamauga Station, on the Western & Atlantic Railroad, attending to the transportation of Buckner's and my own divisions. I was ordered to report to Lieutenant-General Longstreet, then besieging Knoxville.

I had sent off all of Buckner's division except Reynolds' brigade, when I received the following order from army headquarters, viz.:

"The general commanding desires that you will halt such portions of your command as have not yet left, at Chickamauga; such as may have left halt at Charleston. Do not, however, separate brigades; if parts of brigades have gone, let the remaining portion of the brigade go, but halt at Charleston."

In compliance with the above I sent forward the remainder of Johnson's brigade, but took a portion of Reynolds' brigade off the cars as it was about to start. I also telegraphed to Brigadier-General Bushrod Johnson, commanding Buckner's division, directing him to halt the division at Charleston.

I immediately after received the following dispatch from army headquarters, viz.:

"Order Johnson's troops at Charleston back here. Move up rapidly with your whole force."

I dispatched General Johnson accordingly. In a few minutes after, I received the following, viz.:

"We are heavily engaged. Move up rapidly to these headquarters. "BRAXTON BRAGG."

Instructing Brigadier-General Polk to bring up the division, I galloped forward to headquarters for further instructions. I was ordered to rest for the night immediately behind Missionary Ridge, and placed my division accordingly. Returning to General Bragg's headquarters he informed me that my division would act as reserve for the army and would report directly to him. I ordered Reynolds' brigade, which I brought back with me from Chickamauga, to be reported directly to General Bragg, and had no further control of it.

During the night our line along the western front of Missionary Ridge was abandoned, and at early dawn I commenced to construct a new line of defense along the top of the ridge from the Shallow Ford Road to General Bragg's headquarters. Before this was completed General Bragg informed me that the enemy had crossed the Tennessee River, both above and below the mouth of the Chickamauga, and directed me to send a brigade and battery to the East Tennessee & Georgia Railroad Bridge over the Chickamauga to guard that point. I sent Brigadier-General Polk's command and Semple's battery.

About 2 P. M., on the 24th of November, I received orders to proceed with the remaining three brigades and the batteries of my division to the right of Missionary Ridge, near the point where the tunnel of the East Tennessee & Georgia Railroad passes through Missionary Ridge, where I would find an officer of General Hardee's staff, who would show me my position. At the same time General Bragg informed me that the enemy had already a division in line opposite the position I was intended to occupy; that he was rapidly crossing another, and had nearly completed a pontoon bridge over the Tennessee opposite my position. He also told me I must preserve the railroad bridge in my rear, where Brigadier-General Polk was stationed, at all hazards. Galloping forward ahead of my command I found Major Poole, of General Hardee's staff, at the tunnel, who informed me he had been left by General Hardee to show me my position.

I will attempt here a description of the ground. The right of Missionary Ridge, to which I was ordered, runs nearly north and south, parallel to the Tennessee River, which is about one and a half miles west of it. From the tunnel north along the ridge it is about a mile to the Chickamauga River, which bounds the ridge on that side, flowing thence westwardly into the Tennessee River. To simplify the description, the two rivers and the ridge may be said to form three sides of a square. The Tennessee Valley, between the rivers and the ridge, is mostly level, with a continuation of cleared fields bordering the ridge, but immediately in front of the center of my position, about twelve hundred yards north and six hundred yards west of the railroad tunnel, was a high, detached ridge, which, in a military point of view, dominated over every point within cannon range.

After passing through the tunnel the railroad runs in a northeasterly direction to the Chickamauga, which it crossed on the bridge Brigadier-General Polk was guarding. From the east side of the main ridge there projected two spurs—one on the north boundary, with its precipitous north side washed by the Chickamauga; the other, jutting out just north of the tunnel, did not run directly back, but northeasterly for one thousand yards, forming an acute angle with the parent ridge. Opposite the right of this spur, the main ridge was intersected by a little valley, through which came a road from the Tennessee Valley, where the enemy now was. The highest point on my line, and the point of chief interest in the battle on the right, and which I shall designate in this report as Tunnel Hill, was situated on the main ridge two hundred and fifty yards north of the tunnel. The position pointed out for my command by Major Poole was to occupy, with one brigade, the detached ridge in the Tennessee Valley, and with the remainder of my command to stretch from the top of Tunnel Hill to the right of Walker's division, three-quarters of a mile south of the tunnel. I sent Major Poole to inform General Hardee that I had but three brigades, and could not cover so long a line. The head of my division, Smith's (Texas) brigade, was now at hand, and at the same moment reported to me from the detached ridge. Private Henry Smith, of the signal corps of my division, informed me he was just from that point; that the enemy was advancing on it in line of battle. I ordered Smith to move his brigade rapidly and try to get possession of it before the enemy had gained a foothold, but if he found the enemy in possession to fall back on the main ridge. General Smith moved into the valley, but was fired on from the top of the detached ridge as he approached its

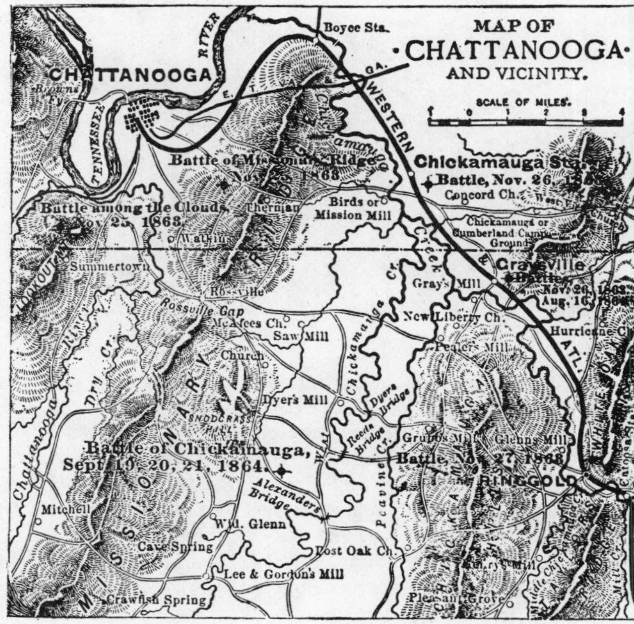

foot. Smith was too late; the enemy had crowned the ridge. He, therefore, marched by his right flank on to the main or Missionary Ridge, and formed on its top, his two left regiments facing the detached ridge, his right regiment thrown back in an easterly direction to protect his flanks. Smith had scarcely thrown out skirmishers before he was briskly attacked by the skirmishers of the enemy. In the meantime, I had placed Lowrey's brigade in position south of the tunnel, and was about placing Govan's brigade on his left, so as to complete my connection with Walker's division, when my attention was attracted to the fighting on my right. It was evident the enemy was endeavoring to turn my right flank and get possession of the main ridge between my right and the Chickamauga. If he succeeded, my connection with Brigadier-General Polk and my line of retreat by the bridge he was guarding was cut off, and the safety of the whole army was endangered. Instead of placing Govan's brigade on the main ridge, I placed him on that spur in rear of it, which jutted out just north of the tunnel and covered the valley and road before described, which led over the main ridge from the direction of the enemy. Govan rapidly threw skirmishers across this road and between it and the Chickamauga.

Lieutenant-General Hardee was soon on the ground in person. He approved my dispositions, directed the destruction of a bridge which crossed the Chickamauga close in rear of my right flank, and ordered two regiments of Lowrey's brigade and some artillery into position in rear of my right flank. Between the left of Smith's brigade and Walker's division, a distance of nearly a mile, there were now but two regiments of Lowrey's brigade, and it so remained all night and until 7 A. M. next day.

It was now dark; the fighting had ceased in front of Smith's; he had maintained his position. Hearing of the disaster at Lookout, I supposed our army would fall back beyond the Chickamauga, and accordingly had sent my ordnance and artillery across that river, with the exception of the two pieces of cannon planted beyond my right flank. I sent Captain Buck, my assistant adjutant-general, to headquarters of the army so as to receive any orders that might be given, as quickly as possible. About midnight he returned with the information that it was determined to await the enemy's attack on Missionary Ridge. I now ordered my artillery and ordnance to join me at daylight, sent to my train for the axes belonging to the division, in order to throw up some defenses, and rode out myself to make a moonlight survey of the ground and line of retreat. I found a hill on the north bank of the Chickamauga, between my right and the railroad bridge guarded by General Polk, which completely commanded my line of retreat.

I ordered Brigadier-General Polk to occupy this hill at once with two regiments of infantry and a section of artillery. Discovering the facility which it afforded for turning me on the extreme right, I determined to immediately throw a line across the other east spur of Missionary Ridge, which jutted out from the north point of the ridge and was washed by the Chickamauga. I placed the two regiments of Lowrey's brigade left near the tunnel, on this line. In the meantime, Smith had thrown up some defenses in his front, but at my suggestion he now abandoned them and took up position as follows, viz.: His left resting on the crest of the main ridge about one hundred and fifty yards north of the tunnel, and running north along the crest for the length of one regiment, the Sixth, Tenth and Fifteenth Texas (consolidated), Colonel R. Q. Mills commanding. The right of this regiment rested close under the crest of Tunnel Hill. On the top of Tunnel Hill a space was left clear of infantry, and Swett's battery of four Napoleon guns, commanded by Lieutenant H. Shannon, was placed on it so as to sweep north in the direction of Smith's old position. Northwest of the detached ridge, or west into the Tennessee Valley as occasion might require, at a point about sixty yards northeast of the right of Mills' regiment, Smith's line recommenced, but instead of continuing north it now ran but slightly north of east down the side of the hill for the length of two regiments, the Seventh Texas, Colonel H. B. Granbury commanding, and the Seventeenth, Eighteenth, Twenty-fourth and Twenty-fifth Dismounted Cavalry (consolidated), Major W. A. Taylor commanding. This formation made the angle on the apex of Tunnel Hill, where Swett's battery was planted, the weak point in Smith's line, but it secured Smith's flank by throwing his extreme right back within two hundred yards of Govan's left, bringing the latter officer's line nearly at right angles to his north front, thus enabling each line to assist the other if attacked. At a favorable point on Govan's line, selected by General Hardee, I placed Douglas' battery, commanded by Lieutenant John H. Bingham, so as to enfilade any line attempting to charge Smith's north front. Lowrey's position, across the spur before mentioned, was in echelon about two hundred paces in front of Govan. I ordered the whole of his brigade to occupy this position, and completed my line from Tunnel Hill to Chickamauga. Lowrey had no artillery, the spur being too steep to admit of its being brought up. Calvert's battery, commanded by Lieutenant Thomas J. Key, I placed directly over the tunnel, and between the tunnel and left of Smith's brigade were placed three regiments of Brown's brigade of Stevenson's division. I was determined to construct a slight work in front of my line. I was prevented for some time by an eclipse of the moon, which rendered the morning very dark, but at length, distributing our few axes, we went to work.

The day broke hazy, so that it was some time before the enemy could discover our operations. As soon as he did, he commenced a heavy fire on General Smith's working party, and prevented us from erecting any work whatever in front of the battery on the top of Tunnel Hill. Up to 10:30 A. M. the enemy contented himself with severe skirmishing and a heavy artillery fire from batteries erected by him during the night on the detached hill. About this hour he drove in Smith's skirmishers and possessed himself of the breastworks which Smith had abandoned that morning. A heavy attack on the tunnel and on Smith's line was now imminent. General Hardee sent me directions to take my position at the tunnel and to take charge of everything in that quarter and to the right of it. The enemy was now in sight, advancing in two long lines of battle, his right stretching far beyond my left, his left stretching beyond Smith's right, where further view of it was prevented by the woods that covered and bordered the detached hill. For the full understanding of the fierce conflict that followed, it would be proper for me in this place to give a statement of the force of the enemy opposite my position, as ascertained at a later hour from prisoners and other sources. It consisted of the divisions of Major-General Jeff. C. Davis, three divisions of the army brought by Sherman from Vicksburg, and Howard's (Eleventh) corps, of the Army of the Potomac, all under the command of Major-General Sherman. At 11 A. M. the first serious fight of the day commenced. It was heavy along Smith's whole line, and extended some distance south of the tunnel. The right of the enemy's line, exposed to the fire of several pieces of artillery planted over the tunnel, and met by a brigade sent by General Hardee to the foot of the ridge, swayed backward and forward for some time, but did not dare to advance nearer than four hundred yards, and finally lay down, contenting itself with sending forward a large body of skirmishers and sending to the rear a much larger number of stragglers. The enemy's left, however, under shelter of Smith's abandoned work of the night before, and protected by the woods on that flank, and by the precipitous, heavily wooded sides of Tunnel Hill, advanced rapidly on Smith's line, and finally made a heavy charge on Swett's battery on the apex of the hill. The artillerymen stood bravely to their guns under a terrible cross-fire, and replied with canister at short range, but still the enemy advanced. When he had reached within fifty steps of the battery Brigadier-General Smith charged him with the right of Mills' Regiment and the left of the Seventh Texas, Smith's north front pouring into him from the breastworks a close volley at the same time. The enemy was routed and driven back to his cover behind the hill-side and abandoned the work.

Part of Missionary Ridge, Tenn.

In this charge Brigadier-General Smith and Colonel Mills were both severely wounded at the head of their men. Colonel H. B. Granbury, Seventh Texas, now assumed command of Smith's brigade. In less than half an hour the enemy made another desperate charge. He was met by the Texas men and artillery in front. Douglas' battery enfiladed him from Govan's Hill, and Lowrey's extreme left regiment got a long-range volley on his flank. He was driven back in confusion as before.

In these attacks Lieutenant H. Shannon, commanding Swett's battery, was wounded. The command devolved on Lieutenant Joseph Ashton; in a few minutes he was mortally wounded. The command then fell on Corporal F. M. Williams. So many non-commissioned officers and men had been killed and disabled in the battery, Colonel Granbury was forced to make a detail from the infantry to work the guns.

There was now a short lull in the battle, during which, at the request of Colonel Granbury, I detailed the Second, Fifteenth and Twenty-fourth Arkansas (consolidated), under Lieutenant-Colonel Warfield, from Govan's left, and posted them immediately in rear of the battery on top of the Tunnel Hill. I sent two of Swett's twelve-pounders to report to Colonel Govan, as Douglas' guns were too light to be effective in their present position. I ordered Key's battery of four light field-pieces to move up and replace the guns sent off, and put Lieutenant Key in command of all the artillery on Tunnel Hill.

About 1 P. M. it was evident that another grand attack was soon to be made on my division. In a few minutes after, it commenced. The enemy again lined Smith's abandoned works, and from them kept up a close, incessant fire on Smith's north front, and particularly on the artillery on top of the hill. Simultaneously a charge was made on the west face of Tunnel Hill. Warfield's regiment was thrown forward outside of the work to the crest of the hill looking into the Tennessee Valley, to meet this charge. Key fired rapidly into the charging line as it crossed the open ground at the west foot of the ridge, but it was soon under shelter. At the steep the enemy's line now seemed to form into a heavy column on the march, and rushed up the hill in the direction of the batteries. Warfield's fire stopped the head of the charging column just under the crest. Here the enemy lay down behind trees, logs and projecting rocks, their first line not twenty-five yards from the guns, and opened fire. Tier after tier of the enemy, to the foot of the hill and in the valley beyond, supplied this fire and concentrated the whole on a space of not more than forty yards, till it seemed like one continuous sheet of hissing, flying lead. This terrific fire prevented Warfield's men from moving sufficiently forward to fire with effect down the hill, but otherwise it only swept over our heads. The cross-fire from Smith's abandoned work was, however, more fatal. It took Warfield in flank, and was constantly disabling men near the top of the hill.

This desperate attack had now lasted more than half an hour. Key was depressing his guns to the utmost and firing shell and canister down the hill in the face of the enemy's fire. Discovering the impossibility of reaching the enemy by a direct fire, the officers of Warfield's regiment were pitching down heavy stones, apparently with effect.

General Hardee, from a hill south of the tunnel, seeing the stubbornness of the fight, had placed some pieces of artillery in position and was endeavoring to dislodge the enemy with a flank fire, but his right flank was protected by an intervening projection of the hill he was on, and this fire was not effective. General Hardee also sent a brigade to move north along the west face of the ridge to strike the enemy in flank, but this brigade returned without accomplishing anything. At this point of the fight Colonel McConnell, commanding a Georgia regiment of Cumming's brigade, came up to the threatened point, and moved his regiment forward to where Warfield's men were fighting. McConnell was shot through the head, and his regiment fell back or was withdrawn. Brigadier-General Cumming, of Stevenson's division, now reported to me with the remainder of his brigade, and was posted in rear of the threatened point. Brigadier-General Maney, of Walker's division, also reported to me with his brigade, and was posted in rear of Smith's line and parallel to it, with instructions to support the Texas brigade behind the works and the artillery at the angle.

The fight had lasted unceasingly for an hour and a half, and the enemy seemed to be constantly re-enforcing. The First and Twenty-seventh Tennessee, of Maney's brigade, Colonel Feild commanding, was moved in front of the work and placed on Warfield's right, the latter officer and his gallant regiment still nobly holding their exposed position, although the regiment was diminished in numbers and almost out of ammunition. It was at this critical period of the day that Lieutenant-Colonel Warfield suggested to me that our men were wasting ammunition and becoming disheartened at the persistency of the enemy, and proposed a charge down upon them with the bayonet. Brigadier-General Cumming gallantly proposed to lead the charge with two of his regiments. I immediately consented, and directed General Cumming to prepare for the charge, and went to the left to see that a simultaneous charge was made on the enemy's right flank. I now ordered the left of Mills' (Texas) regiment, being the extreme left of my division, to make the charge on the enemy's flank the moment that Cumming charged them in front, and I remained at the breastwork myself to see the execution of the order.

In the meantime, General Cumming, having placed the Fifty-sixth Georgia in line for the charge and supported it by placing the Thirty-sixth Georgia ten paces in rear, moved forward to the charge; twice he was checked and had to reform. Warfield's (Arkansas) regiment, with empty guns, and the gallant First and Twenty-seventh Tennessee prepared to share his next effort. At the command the whole rushed forward with a cheer, Lieutenant-Colonel Sanders simultaneously leading the left of Mills' (Texas) regiment on the enemy's flank. The enemy, completely surprised, fled down the foot, the Texas troops on the left pursuing him beyond the foot and nearly across the open ground in front. Our charging columns returned with many prisoners and stand of colors; a fresh force of the enemy attempting to follow us as we returned from this charge, was quickly met and routed by the Fiftieth Tennessee and with troops of my division. Immediately on his last repulse the enemy opened a rapid and revengeful artillery fire on Tunnel Hill from his batteries on the detached hill, and under cover of this fire he went to work felling trees and fortifying his position. It is but justice for me to state that the brunt of this long day's fight was borne by Smith's (Texas) brigade and the Second, Fifteenth and Twenty-fourth Arkansas (consolidated), of Govan's brigade, together with Swett's and Keys' batteries. The remainder of my division was only engaged in heavy skirmishing. The final charge was participated in and successful through the timely appearance and gallant assistance of the regiments of Cumming's and Maney's brigades before mentioned.

Out of the eight stand of colors shown by me to have been captured, four were presented to me by Mills' (Texas) regiment; two were presented by the Fifty-sixth and Thirty-sixth Georgia regiments, of Cumming's brigade; one flag was presented by the First Tennessee, of Maney's brigade, and one by the Second, Fifteenth and Twenty-fourth Arkansas (consolidated), of Govan's brigade; in all, eight colors, six of which I herewith transmit. Among them are the flags of the Twenty-seventh Pennsylvania and Ninety-third Illinois. About five hundred prisoners were captured. At a critical moment of the battle I lost two of the bravest officers of my division — Brigadier-General J. A. Smith, commanding the Texas brigade, and Colonel R. Q. Mills, the same officer who commanded it in the battle of Chickamauga, after General Deshler fell. Besides these gallant officers I lost other noble officers and men, some of whose names are handed down to history in the reports of brigade and regimental commanders.

Part of Missionary Ridge, Tenn.

From an original painting, copyrighted by Kurz & Allison, Chicago, Ill.

BATTLE OF MISSIONARY RIDGE, TENN., NOVEMBER 23 AND 25 1863.

I suffered the following losses in the three brigades of my division engaged, viz.: Forty-two killed, one hundred and seventy-eight wounded and two missing.

Colonel Sugg, of the Fiftieth Tennessee Regiment, Maney's brigade, was dangerously wounded in the last charge. Colonel McConnell, of Cumming's brigade, and other gallant soldiers who fell in front of my works, I can but lament. I did not personally know them, but I saw and can bear witness to their gallant bearing and noble deaths. The enemy must have suffered severely; the hillside and the valley were thickly strewn with his dead, and if we may credit his published reports of casualties in this fight, he lost one major-general, John E. Smith, wounded; three brigadier-generals, Corse, Matthies and Giles Smith, wounded, and one colonel commanding brigade, Colonel Raum, wounded.*

Soon after the final defeat of the enemy in front of Smith's position, I received a dispatch from General Hardee to send to the center all the troops I could spare, as the enemy were pressing us in that quarter. I immediately ordered Generals Cumming and Maney, with their respective brigades, to report accordingly, and went myself to push them forward. Before I had gone far, however, a dispatch from General Hardee reached me with the appalling news that the enemy had pierced our center and were on Missionary Ridge, directing me to take command of my own, Walker's and Stevenson's divisions and form a line across the ridge, so as to meet an attack upon my flank, and take all other necessary measures for the safety of the right wing. I ordered Brigadier-General Gist, commanding Walker's division, to form it across the ridge; ordered all vehicles which could be spared to cross the Chickamauga; sent Brigadier-General Polk orders to dispatch a force to the Shallow Ford Bridge and hold it at all hazards, and sent Govan's brigade to dispute the enemy's advance on the Shallow Ford Road.

Soon after, night was upon us and General Hardee ordered an immediate retreat across the Chickamauga, and that Smith's (Texas) brigade should remain in position and bring up the rear. General Lowrey attacked and drove back the enemy's skirmishers in his front and then retreated. By 9 P. M. everything was across except the dead and a few stragglers lingering here and there under the shadow of the trees for the purpose of being captured, faint-hearted patriots succumbing to the hardships of the war and the imagined hopelessness of the hour.

I now ordered Smith's brigade to move in retreat. Sadly, but not fearfully, this band of heroes left the hill they had held so well and followed the army across the Chickamauga.

P. R. CLEBURNE.

THE CONFEDERATE UNIFORM.—At the outbreak of the war between the States Captain Reynolds raised a company of Mississippians, and in the enthusiasm of the occasion made some rash promises to the parents of the boys. Among these was one to keep his company well uniformed. Years passed, and one of the anxious fathers visiting the Army of Northern Virginia was mortified to see his boy in rags. He upbraided the captain for not keeping his company in uniform. The captain for a moment was stunned, but recovered himself and cried out: "Attention, company! About face!" And as the unconfined rags fluttered like so many banners of poverty from each "Pope's headquarters" Captain R. pointed to the company and said: "They are *uniformed*, sir."

* Neither Smith nor Raum was mortally wounded.

BATTLE OF RINGGOLD GAP,

NOVEMBER 27, 1863,

BY

MAJOR-GENERAL PATRICK R. CLEBURNE.

HEADQUARTERS CLEBURNE'S DIVISION,
TUNNEL HILL, GA., December 9, 1863.

ON the retreat of the Army of Tennessee from Missionary Ridge, Tenn., to Ringgold, Ga., my division covered the retreat of Hardee's corps, arriving safely on the west bank of the East Chickamauga River at 10 o'clock P. M., on the 26th November. At this point the river had to be forded. It was nearly waist deep and the night was freezing cold. I therefore determined to postpone crossing until the morning, and bivouacked on the hills near by.

At 3 oclock A. M., on the 29th, I received the following order, viz.:

"GENERAL: The general desires that you will take strong position in the gorge of the mountain and attempt to check pursuit of enemy. He must be punished until our trains and the rear of our troops get well advanced.

"The reports from the rear are meager, and the general is not thoroughly advised of the state of things there. Will you be good enough to report fully?

"Respectfully,
(Signed), "GEO. W. BRENT,
"*Assistant Adjutant General.*
'MAJOR-GENERAL CLEBURNE."

Leaving staff officers to conduct the troops across the river to the position designated, I went forward myself to examine the ground and form a plan for its defense.

The town of Ringgold, a place of two or three thousand inhabitants, stands on a plain between the East Chickamauga River and the range of hills known as Taylors Ridge. It is on the Western & Atlantic Railroad, about twenty miles southeast of Chattanooga. Taylors Ridge, which rises up immediately back of the town, runs in a northerly and southerly direction. Opposite the town the ridge is intersected by a narrow gap which admits the railroad, a wagon road and a good sized creek, a tributary of the Chickamauga.

The creek hugs the southernmost or left-hand hill as you face Ringgold. The wagon road and railroads run close to the creek.

At its western mouth, next to Ringgold, the gap widens out to a breadth of over one hundred yards, leaving room for a patch of level woodland on each side of the roads. The gap is about half a mile through, but the plain immediately in front of its east or rear mouth is so cut up by the windings of the creek that three bridges, or three fords, have to be crossed in the first half mile of road leading from the gap to Dalton.

It will be perceived at once that this was a dangerous position to be caught in, if the enemy should succeed in turning either flank. The gap and the hills on either hand are thickly wooded, except the base of the right-hand hill, along which, next to the town, a heavy fringe of young timber extends from the gap northward for three or four hundred yards. Behind this fringe of trees I placed two regiments of Smith's Texas brigade, Colonel H. B. Granbury, Seventh Texas, commanding; the Sixth, Tenth and Fifteenth Texas, consolidated, Captain John R. Kennard commanding, on the left; the Seventeenth, Eighteenth, Twenty-fourth and Twenty-fifth Texas dismounted cavalry, consolidated, Major W. A. Taylor commanding, on the right. The remaining regiment of the brigade, the Seventh Texas, Captain C. E. Talley commanding, I sent to the top of the right-hand hill, with instructions to keep out of view, but watch well the right flank of its brigade at the foot. On the precipitous hill at the left of the gap and creek, I placed the Sixteenth Alabama, Major F. A. Ashford commanding, of Lowrey's Alabama and Mississippi brigade, with instructions to conceal itself and guard well the left flank. I also sent on the face of this hill, fronting Ringgold, three companies of the Sixth and Seventh Arkansas, consolidated, of Liddell's Arkansas brigade, under charge of Lieutenant Dulin, of General Liddell's staff.

For the defense of the gap itself I disposed the rest of the Arkansas brigade, under command of Colonel D. C. Govan. The fifth and thirteenth Arkansas, consolidated, Colonel John E. Murray commanding, I placed in a small ravine, running across the mouth of the gap from the right-hand hill to the railroad embankment. The Eighth and Nineteenth Arkansas, consolidated, under command of Lieutenant-Colonel A. S. Hutchinson, fifty paces in rear and parallel to the former regiment. The Sixth and Seventh Arkansas, consolidated, under command of Lieutenant-Colonel Peter Snyder, and the Second, Fifteenth and Twenty-fourth Arkansas regiments, consolidated, under Lieutenant-Colonel E. Warfield, at suitable distances in rear, and covered as well as the nature of the ground would permit, thus giving me four short lines across the gap. From these regiments I sent a body of skirmishers to occupy the patch of woods at the mouth of the gap and left of the railroad, and that portion of the bank of the creek close to the mouth of the gap.

MILITARY BRIDGE OVER THE TENNESSEE RIVER AT CHATTANOOGA, TENN. [From a photograph taken in 1863.]

In front of the mouth of the gap, supported by Govan's foremost regiment in the ravine, I placed a section of Semple's battery—two Napoleon guns—commanded by Lieutenant Goldthwaite. I had screens of withered branches built up in front of these so as to effectually conceal them from view, and made the artillerymen shelter themselves in the ravine close by. The remaining three regiments of Lowrey's brigade, consisting of the Thirty-second and Forty-fifth Mississippi regiments, consolidated, under command of Colonel A. B. Hardcastle; Thirty-third Alabama, under command of Colonel Samuel Adams, and the Forty-fifth Alabama, Lieutenant-Colonel H. D. Lamplay, commanding, I placed in reserve in the center of the gap.

The portion of Polk's Tennessee and Arkansas brigade with me, consisting of the First Arkansas, Colonel J. W. Colquitt, commanding; the Second Tennessee, Colonel W. A. Robinson, commanding, and the Third and Fifth Confederate regiments, consolidated, under Lieutenant-Colonel J. C. Cole, I ordered to take position temporarily near the rear mouth of the gap, with directions to observe my right flank and prevent the enemy from turning me in that quarter.

I had scarcely half an hour to make these dispositions when I was informed the enemy's skirmishers were crossing the Chickamauga, driving our cavalry before them.

Immediately after, the cavalry retreated through the gap at a trot, and the valley in front was clear of our troops, but close in rear of the ridge our immense train was still in full view, struggling through the fords of the creek and the deeply cut-up roads leading to Dalton, and my division, silent, but cool and ready, was the only barrier between it and the flushed and eager advance of the pursuing Federal army.

Shortly after 8 o'clock A. M. the enemy's skirmishers were in view, advancing. They opened fire, and under cover of it his lines of battle were placed and moved with the utmost decision and celerity against the ridge on the right of the gap. So quick and confident was this attack the enemy must have been acting on a concerted plan, and must have had guides who knew well the nature of the country.

As the first line moved toward the ridge its right flank became exposed, at canister range, to my artillery in the mouth of the gap. Five or six rapid discharges broke the right of this line to pieces and caused them to run for shelter under the railroad embankment. Further to his left, however, he continued to advance, and made a heavy attack on the right hand ridge. He continued to advance in the face of a deadly fire from Major Taylor's regiment, with the determination to turn the right flank of the Texas brigade. Major Taylor deployed skirmishers up the hill at right angles to his line of battle, and held him in check while he informed Colonel Granbury of the state of affairs. Colonel Granbury sent two companies of his left regiment to re-enforce his right. With three companies of his own regiment Major Taylor charged down the hill upon the force attempting to turn him, and routed it, capturing between sixty and one hundred prisoners and the colors of the Twenty-ninth Missouri regiment. In the meantime I had ascertained that the enemy was moving another line of battle some distance beyond my present right, with a view of ascending the ridge in that quarter. I instantly notified Brigadier-General Polk, stationed in the rear of the gap, to ascend the ridge and meet this attempt of the enemy.

Luckily General Polk had already heard of this movement from a breathless straggler of our army, who was flying before the enemy, and, anticipating my order, sent the First Arkansas up the hill, and met the enemy's skirmishers within a few yards of the top. With the assistance of the Seventh Texas, after an obstinate fight, the enemy was driven down the hill. By this time large bodies of the enemy had crossed the Chickamauga, and it was evident that the main attack was about to be made upon the right. I ordered General Lowrey to move his command up the hill and assist General Polk in defending that position. Moving rapidly ahead of his command, General Lowrey found the First Arkansas again heavily engaged, but heroically holding its ground against great odds. Assuring the regiment that support was at hand, he brought up the Thirty-second and Forty-fifth Mississippi in double time, and threw them into the fight at the critical moment. The enemy gave way, and went down the ridge in great confusion. Lowrey now brought up the two remaining regiments of his brigade, and Polk the two other regiments of his command. The enemy, constantly re-enforcing, made another powerful effort to crown the ridge still further to the right. A peculiarity of Taylors Ridge is the wavy conformation of its north side. The enemy, moving up in a long line of battle, suddenly concentrated opposite one of the depressions in this wavy surface, and rushed up it in heavy column. General Polk, with the assistance of General Lowrey, as quickly concentrated a double line opposite this point, at the same time placing the Second Tennessee in such a position as to command the flank of any force emerging from it. The attack was again defeated, and the enemy hurled down the hill with the loss of many killed on the spot, several prisoners, and the colors of the Seventy-sixth Ohio Regiment. The colors and most of the prisoners were captured by the First Arkansas. In a fight, where all fought nobly, I feel it my duty to particularly compliment this regiment for its courage and constancy. In the battle the officers fought with pistols and with rocks, and so close was the fight that some of the enemy were knocked down with the latter missiles and captured.

Apprehending another attack, General Polk rapidly threw up some slight defenses in his front.

But I must now return to the extreme left, which the enemy attempted to turn. He sent what appeared to be a brigade of three regiments to the creek upon my left, and crossed over some companies of skirmishers. These were promptly met and stopped by a detachment from the Sixteenth Alabama, posted on the left-hand hill, and the main body was for some time held in check by Dulin's skirmishers on the face of the left-hand hill, and the other skirmishers of Govan's brigade on the creek banks and in the patch of woods to the left of the railroad. He got possession, however, of some houses and barns opposite this point, from which he annoyed me with a constant and well-directed fire of sharpshooters. At length collecting in large numbers behind these houses, he made a charge on Govan's skirmishers on the left of the railroad. Lieutenant Goldthwaite quickly trained round his guns and swept them at quarter-range with a load of canister and a solid shot; they ran back, leaving several dead and a stand of colors on the ground. Lieutenant Goldthwaite then shelled the houses, and greatly relieved us of the firing from that quarter. The stand of colors lay temptingly within sixty yards of my line, and some of the officers wanted to charge and get it, but as it promised no solid advantage—to compensate for the loss of brave soldiers—I would not permit it.

About 12 o'clock M., I received a dispatch from Lieutenant-General Hardee to the effect that the train was now well advanced and I might safely withdraw.

On consultation with Generals Breckinridge and Wheeler, both of whom were present lending me their personal assistance, I determined to withdraw from Taylors Ridge and take up a new position on some wooded hills one mile in rear.

About 1 o'clock P. M. I rebuilt the screen in front of the artillery, which had been partially blown away, and then withdrew both pieces by hand without loss.

By this time the enemy had concentrated a large portion of his army at Ringgold, and was doubtless preparing to throw an overwhelming force on my flanks. He opened a rapid artillery fire down the gap and on the crest of the ridge, but showed no disposition to advance in front. I now simultaneously withdrew the brigades, leaving a few skirmishers to hold the front, which they did without difficulty.

Soon after 2 o'clock P. M. I withdrew my skirmishers, fired the bridges in my rear and proceeded to form a line of battle in my new position. The enemy was visible on the ridge in about half an hour after I had withdrawn my skirmishers.

He saw my new disposition for defense, but showed no further inclination to attack and ceased from all further pursuit of our army. I took into the fight, in Polk's brigade, 545; Lowrey's brigade, 1,330; Smith's Texas brigade, 1,266; Liddell's brigade, 1,016 effective men, making a total of 4,157 bayonets.

My loss was twenty killed, one hundred and ninety wounded, eleven missing. I am confident the enemy's loss was out of all proportion greater than mine. The conduct of officers and men in the fight needs no comment—every man, as far as I know, did his whole duty.

To Brigadier-Generals Polk and Lowrey, and Colonels Govan and Granbury I must return my thanks; four better officers are not in the service of the Confederacy. Lieutenant Goldthwaite, of the artillery, proved himself a brave and skillful officer.

The following officers of my staff have my thanks for the efficient manner in which they discharged their responsible and dangerous duties: Major Calhoun Benham, Assistant Adjutant-General; Major J. K. Dixon, Assistant Adjutant-General; Captain Irving A. Buck, Assistant Adjutant-General; Captain C. S. Hill, Ordnance Officer; Surgeon D. A. Linthicum, Lieutenant L. H. Mangan, S. P. Hauley, Aids-de-camp; Captain C. H. Byrne, Volunteer Aid-de-camp; also Messrs. Henry Smith and W. Rucker, of the Signal Corps, who volunteered their services, and whom I found very efficient and useful.

I forward herewith the reports of brigade, regimental and battery commanders. General Liddell was absent on leave, but, hearing of the fight, returned and rendered me all the assistance in his power. He selected and reformed the new line, after we withdrew from our first position.

P. R. CLEBURNE, *Major-General.*

BATTLE OF RINGGOLD, GA., NOVEMBER 27, 1863, ON THE LINE OF THE WESTERN & ATLANTIC RAILROAD.

ONE of the best companies of the Stonewall brigade was composed of railroad men from Martinsburg, W. Va. In a charge at Manassas, the story goes, the captain offered a barrel of whisky to the man who first reached the guns. When the captain got there one of his men, already astraddle of a cannon, cried out: "Don't forget that barrel, captain!" The next day an admirer of the hero asked him how war compared with railroading. "Well," said he, "the life of a soldier is pretty rough, but it has one advantage over railroading." "What is that?" was asked. "'Tain't near so dangerous," said the man of the rail.

THE ATLANTA CAMPAIGN.

OPERATIONS

DECEMBER 27, 1863, TO JULY 17, 1864,

INCLUDING BATTLES OF

ROCKY FACE RIDGE, RESACA, NEW HOPE CHURCH, DALLAS, KENNESAW MOUNTAIN, PICKETTS MILLS, CASSVILLE, ETC.,
ALSO, THE REMOVAL OF GENERAL JOHNSTON FROM THE COMMAND.

BY

GENERAL JOSEPH E. JOHNSTON,
Commanding Army of the Tennessee.

VINEVILLE, GA., October 20, 1864.

I HAVE the honor to make the following report of operations of the Army of Tennessee while it was under my command. Want of the reports of lieutenant-generals prevents me from being circumstantial.

In obedience to the orders of the President, received by telegraph at Clinton, Miss., December 18, 1863, I assumed command of the Army of Tennessee at Dalton on the 27th of that month.

Letters from the President and Secretary of War, dated, respectively, December 23d and 20th, impressed upon me the importance of soon commencing active operations against the enemy. The relative forces, including the moral effect of the affair of Missionary Ridge, condition of the artillery horses and most of those of the cavalry, and want of field transportation, made it impracticable to effect the wishes of the Executive.

On December 31st the effective total of the infantry and artillery of the army, including two brigades belonging to the Department of Mississippi, was thirty-six thousand eight hundred and twenty-six. The effective total of the cavalry, including Roddey's command at Tuscumbia, was five thousand six hundred and thirteen. The Federal force in our front, exclusive of cavalry and the Ninth and Twenty-third Corps at Knoxville, was estimated at eighty thousand. The winter was mainly employed in improving the discipline and equipment of the army, and bringing back absentees to the ranks. At the end of April more than five thousand had rejoined their regiments.

The horses of the cavalry and artillery had been much reduced in condition by the previous campaign. As full supplies of forage could not be furnished then at Dalton, it was necessary to send about half of each of these arms of service far to the rear, where the country could furnish food. On that account Brigadier-General Roddey was ordered with about three-fourths of his troops from Tuscumbia to Dalton, and arrived at the end of February. On April 2d, however, he was sent back to his former position by the Secretary of War.

On January 15th and 16th Baldwin's and Quarles' brigades returned to the Department of Mississippi and East Louisiana, to which they belonged. His Excellency, Joseph E. Brown, added to the army two regiments of State troops, which were used to guard the railroad bridges between Dalton and Atlanta.

On February 17th the President ordered me by telegraph to detach Lieutenant-General Hardee, with the infantry of his corps, except Stevenson's division, to aid Lieutenant-General Polk against Sherman in Mississippi. This order was obeyed as promptly as our means of transportation permitted. The force detached was probably exaggerated to Major-General Thomas, for on the 23d the Federal army advanced to Ringgold; on the 24th drove in our outposts, and on the 25th skirmished at Mill Creek Gap and in Crows Valley, east of Rocky Face Mountain. We were successful at both places. At the latter, Clayton's brigade, after a sharp action of half an hour, defeated double its number. At night it was reported that a U. S. brigade was occupying Dug Gap, from which it had driven our troops. Granbury's (Texas) brigade, returning from Mississippi, had just arrived. It was ordered to march to the foot of the mountain immediately, and to retake the Gap at sunrise next morning, which was done. In the night of the 26th the enemy retired. On February 27th I suggested to the Executive, by letter, through General Bragg, that all preparations for a forward movement should be made without further delay.

In a letter dated 4th of March General Bragg desired me "to have all things ready at the earliest practicable moment for the movement indicated." In replying, on the 12th, I reminded him that the regulations of the War Department do not leave such preparations to commanders of troops, but to officers who receive their orders from Richmond. On the 18th a letter was received from General Bragg sketching a plan of offensive operations, and enumerating the troops to be used in them under me. I was invited to express my views on the subject. In doing so, both by telegraph and mail, I suggested modifications, and urged that the additional troops named should be sent immediately, to enable us, should the enemy advance, to beat him and then move forward; or should he not advance, do so ourselves. General Bragg replied by telegraph on the 21st:

"Your dispatch of the 19th does not indicate acceptance of plans proposed. Troops can only be drawn from other points for advance. Upon your decision of that point further action must depend."

I replied by telegraph on the 22d:

"In my dispatch of the 19th I expressly accept taking offensive. Only differ with you as to details. I assume that the enemy will be prepared for advance before we will, and will make it, to our advantage. Therefore, I propose, both for offensive and defensive, to assemble our troops here immediately."

BATTLE OF PINE MOUNTAIN, GA. SCENE OF THE DEATH OF LIEUTENANT-GENERAL LEONIDAS POLK.
[From a photograph of a sketch made in 1864.]

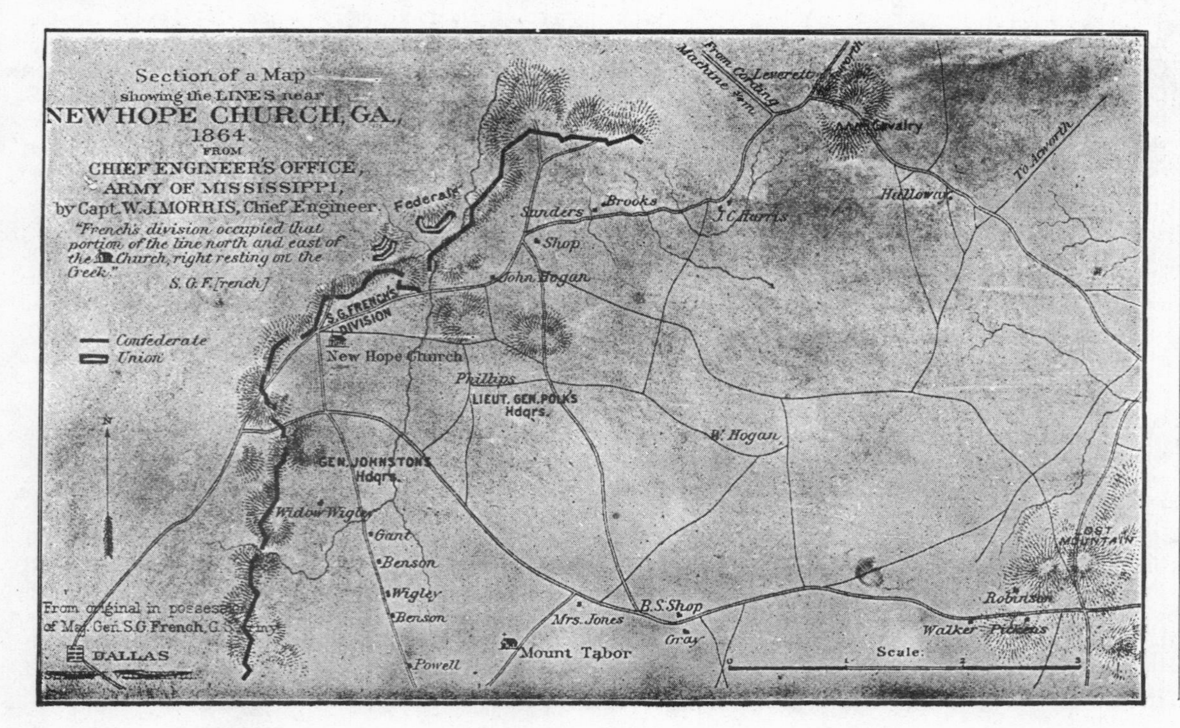

This was not noticed. Therefore, on the 25th I again urged the necessity of re-enforcing the Army of Tennessee, because the enemy was collecting a larger force than that of the last campaign, while ours was less than it had been then.

On the 3d of April Lieutenant-Colonel A. H. Cole arrived at Dalton to direct the procuring of artillery horses and field transportation to enable the army to advance. On the 4th, under orders [No.] 32 of 1864, I applied to the chief of the conscript service for one thousand negro teamsters. None were received. On the 8th of April Colonel B. S. Ewell, assistant adjutant-general, was sent to Richmond to represent to the President my wish to take the offensive, with proper means, and to learn his views. A few days after, Brigadier-General Pendleton arrived from Richmond to explain to me the President's wishes on that subject. I explained to him the modification of the plan communicated by General Bragg (which seemed to me essential), which required that the intended re-enforcements should be sent to Dalton. I urged that this should be done without delay, because our present force was not sufficient even for defense, and to enable us to take the offensive if the enemy did not.

On the 1st of May I reported the enemy about to advance. On the 2d, Brigadier-General Mercer's command arrived—about 1,400 effective infantry. On the 4th I expressed myself satisfied that the enemy was about to attack with his united force, and again urged that a part of Lieutenant-General Polk's troops should be put at my disposal. I was informed by General Bragg that orders to that effect were given. Major-General Martin, whose division of cavalry, coming from East Tennessee, had been halted on the Etowah to recruit its horses, was ordered with it to observe the Oostanaula from Resaca to Rome; and Brigadier-General Kelly was ordered, with his command, from the neighborhood of Resaca, to report to Major-General Wheeler. The effective artillery and infantry of the Army of Tennessee after the arrival of Mercer's brigade amounted to 40,900; the effective cavalry, to about 4,000. Major-General Sherman's army was composed of that of Missionary Ridge (then 80,000) increased by several thousand recruits; 5,000 men under Hovey; the Twenty-third Corps (Schofield's), from Knoxville; and two divisions of the Sixteenth, from North Alabama. Major-General Wheeler estimated the cavalry of that army at 15,000. On the 5th of May this army was in line between Ringgold and Tunnel Hill, and after skirmishing on that and the following day, on the 7th pressed back our advanced troops to Mill Creek Gap. On the same day Brigadier-General Cantey reached Resaca with his brigade, and was halted there. On the 8th, at 4 P. M., a division of Harper's corps assaulted Dug Gap, which was bravely held by two regiments of Reynolds' (Arkansas) brigade and Grigsby's brigade of Kentucky cavalry, fighting on foot, until the arrival of Lieutenant-General Hardee with Granbury's brigade, when the enemy was put to flight. On the 9th five assaults were made on Lieutenant-General Hood's troops on Rocky Face Mountain; all were repulsed. In the afternoon a report was received that Logan's and Dodge's corps were in Snake Creek Gap. These divisions, under Lieutenant-General Hood, were, therefore, sent to Resaca. On the 10th, Lieutenant-General Hood reported the enemy retiring. Skirmishing, to our advantage, continued all day near Dalton. Major-

GENERAL JOSEPH E. JOHNSTON.

BORN IN CHERRY GROVE, NEAR FARMVILLE, VA., FEBRUARY 3, 1807. DIED IN WASHINGTON, D. C., MARCH 21, 1891.

[From a crayon lithograph.]

General Bate repulsed a vigorous attack at night. On the 11th, Brigadier-General Cantey reported that the enemy was again approaching Resaca. Lieutenant-General Polk arrived there in the evening with Loring's division, and was instructed to defend the place with those troops and Cantey's. The usual skirmishing continued near Dalton. Rocky Face Mountain and Snake Creek Gap, at its south end, completely covered for the enemy the operation of turning Dalton. On the 12th, the Federal army, covered by the mountain, moved by Snake Creek Gap toward Resaca. Major-General Wheeler, with twenty-two hundred of ours, attacked and defeated more than double that number of Federal cavalry near Varnell's Station. At night our artillery and infantry marched for Resaca. The cavalry followed on the 13th. On that day the enemy, approaching on the Snake Creek Gap Road, was checked by Loring's troops, which gave time for the formation of Hardee's and Hood's corps, just arriving. the enemy was approaching on the Canton Road, in rear of the right of our original position. He drew back his troops and formed them across that road. When it was discovered that the officer was mistaken, the opportunity had passed by the near approach of the two portions of the Federal army. Expecting to be attacked, I drew up the troops in what seemed to me an excellent position—a bold ridge immediately in rear of Cassville, with an open valley before it. The fire of the enemy's artillery commenced soon after the troops were formed and continued until night. Soon after dark, Lieutenant-Generals Polk and Hood together expressed to me decidedly the opinion, formed upon the observation of the afternoon, that the Federal artillery would render their positions untenable the next day, and urged me to abandon the ground immediately and cross the Etowah. Lieutenant-General Hardee, whose position I thought weakest, was confident that he could hold it. The other two officers were so earnest, position during the night to attack the enemy's left flank at dawn next morning, the rest of the army to join in the action successively from right to left. On the 29th, Lieutenant-General Hood, finding the Federal left covered by a division which had intrenched itself in the night, thought it inexpedient to attack, so reported and asked for instructions. As the resulting delay made the attack inexpedient, even if it had not been so before, by preventing the surprise upon which success in a great degree depended, he was recalled.

Skirmishing continued until the 4th of June, the enemy gradually extending his intrenched line toward the railroad at Acworth. On the morning of the 5th, the army was formed with its left at Lost Mountain, its center near Gilgal Church, and its right near the railroad. On the 7th, the right, covered by Noonday Creek, was extended across the Acworth and Marietta Road. The enemy approached under cover of successive lines of intrenchments.

Buzzard Roost Gap and Rocky Face Ridge, Ga.
[From a photograph in the office of the Chief of Engineers, U. S. A.]

As the army was formed, the left of Polk's corps was on the Oostanaula and the right of Hood's on the Conneasauga. There was brisk skirmishing during the afternoon on Polk's front and Hardee's left. On the 14th, the enemy made several attacks, the most vigorous on Hindman's division (Hood's left). All were handsomely repulsed. At 6 P. M. Hood advanced with Stevenson's and Stewart's divisions, supported by two of Walker's brigades, driving the enemy from his ground before night. He was instructed to be ready to continue the offensive next morning. At 9 P. M. I learned that Lieutenant-General Polk's troops had lost a position commanding our bridges, and receive from Major-General Martin a report that Federal infantry was crossing the Oostanaula, near Calhoun, on a pontoon bridge. The instructions to Lieutenant-General Hood were revoked, and Walker's division sent to the point named by Major-General Martin. On the 15th, there was severe skirmishing on the whole front. Major-General Walker reported no movement near Calhoun. Lieutenant-General Hood was directed to prepare to move forward, his right leading, supported by two brigades from Polk's and Hardee's corps. When he was about to move, information came from Major-General Walker that the Federal right was crossing the river. To meet this movement Lieutenant-General Hood's attack was countermanded. Stewart's division, not receiving the order from corps headquarters in time, attacked unsuccessfully. The army was ordered to cross the Oostanaula that night, destroying the bridges behind it. On the 16th, the enemy crossed the Oostanaula. Lieutenant-General Hardee skirmished with them successfully near Calhoun. The fact that a part of Polk's troops were still in the rear, and the great numerical superiority of the Federal army, made it expedient to risk battle only when position or some blunder on the part of the enemy might give us counterbalancing advantages. I, therefore, determined to fall back slowly until circumstances should put the chances of battle in our favor, keeping so near the U. S. Army as to prevent its sending re-enforcements to Grant, and hoping, by taking advantage of positions and opportunities, to reduce the odds against us by partial engagements. I also expected it to be materially reduced before the end of June by the expiration of the terms of service of many of the regiments which had not re-enlisted. In this way we fell back to Cassville in two marches.

At Adairsville (about midway), on the 17th, Polk's cavalry, under Brigadier-General Jackson, met the army, and Hardee, after severe skirmishing, checked the enemy. At this point, on the 18th, Polk's and Hood's corps took the direct road to Cassville, Hardee's that by Kingston. About half the Federal army took each road. French's division having joined Polk's corps on the 18th, on the morning of the 19th, when half the Federal army was near Kingston, the two corps at Cassville were ordered to advance against the troops that had followed them from Adairsville, Hood's leading on the right.

When this corps had advanced some two miles, one of his staff officers reported to Lieutenant-General Hood that however, and so unwilling to depend on the ability of their corps to defend the ground, that I yielded and the army crossed the Etowah on the 20th, a step which I have regretted ever since. Wheeler's cavalry was placed in observation above and Jackson's below the railroad. On the 22d, Major-General Wheeler was sent with all his troops not required for observation, to the enemy's rear, and on the 24th beat a brigade at Cassville and took or burned two hundred and fifty loaded wagons. In the meantime the enemy was reported by Jackson's troops moving down the Etowah, as if to cross it near Stilesboro, and crossing on the 23d. On the 24th, Polk's and Hardee's corps reached the road from Stilesboro to Atlanta, a few miles south of Dallas, and Hood's four miles from New Hope Church, on the road from Allatoona. On the 25th, the enemy was found to be intrenched near and east of Dallas. Hood's corps was placed with its center at New Hope Church, and Polk's and Hardee's ordered between it and the Atlanta Road, which Hardee's left was to cover. An hour before sunset, Stewart's division, at New Hope Church, was fiercely attacked by Hooker's corps, which it repulsed after a hot engagement of two hours. Skirmishing was kept up on the 26th and 27th. At 5:30 P. M., on the 27th, Howard's corps assailed Cleburne's division and

Lieut.-Gen. Leonidas Polk, of Louisiana.
Killed at the Battle of Pine Mountain, Ga., June 14, 1864.

was driven back about dark with great slaughter. Our loss in each was about four hundred and fifty killed and wounded. On the 27th, the enemy's dead, except those borne off, were counted six hundred. We, therefore, estimated their whole loss at three thousand at least. It was probably greater on the 25th, as we had a larger force engaged then, both of infantry and artillery.

The usual skirmishing was kept up on the 28th. Lieutenant-General Hood was instructed to put his corps in

There was brisk and incessant skirmishing until the 18th. On the 14th, the brave Lieutenant-General Polk, distinguished in every battle in which this army had fought, fell by a cannon shot at an advanced post. Major-General Loring succeeded to the command, which he held until the 7th of July with great efficiency.

On the 4th of June a letter from Governor Brown informed me that he had organized a division of infantry and placed it under my orders. These troops, when ready for service—about the middle of the month, under Major-General G. W. Smith—were employed to defend the crossings of the Chattahoochee to prevent the surprise of Atlanta by the Federal cavalry.

On the 19th, a new line was taken by the army; Hood's corps with its right on the Marietta and Canton Road, Loring's on the Kennesaw Mountain, and Hardee's with its left extending across the Lost Mountain and Marietta Road. The enemy approached as usual under cover of intrenchments. In this position there was incessant fighting and skirmishing until July 3d, the enemy gradually extending his intrenched right toward Atlanta.

On the 20th of June Wheeler, with eleven hundred men, routed Garrard's division of Federal cavalry on our right, On the 21st, Hood's corps was transferred from right to left, Wheeler's cavalry taking charge of the position which it left. On the 22d, Lieutenant-General Hood reported that Hindman's and Stevenson's divisions, of his corps, being attacked, drove back the enemy, taking a line of his breastworks, but were compelled to withdraw by the fire of fortified artillery. On the 24th, Hardee's skirmishers repulsed a line of battle, as did Stevenson's of Hood's corps, on the 25th. On the 27th, after a furious cannonade of several hours, the enemy made a general advance, but was everywhere repulsed with heavy loss. The assaults were most vigorous on Cheatham's and Cleburne's divisions of Hardee's corps, and French's and Featherston's of Loring's. Lieutenant-General Hardee reports that Cheatham's division lost in killed, wounded and missing, 195; the enemy opposed to it, by the statement of a staff officer subsequently captured, 2,000. The loss of Cleburne's division, 11; that of the enemy in his front, 1,000. Major-General Loring reported 236 of his corps killed, wounded and missing, and the loss of the enemy, by their own estimates, at between 2,500 and 3,000, which he thinks very small.

On the 1st of July Major-General Smith's division was ordered to support the cavalry on our left. Their effective total was about fifteen hundred. On the 2d, the enemy's right being nearer to Atlanta by several miles than our left, the army fell back during the night to Smyrna Church. On the 4th, Major-General Smith reported that he should be compelled to withdraw on the morning of the 5th to the line of intrenchments covering the railroad bridge and Turners Ferry. The army was therefore ordered to retire at the same time to that line to secure our bridges. The cavalry crossed the Chattahoochee, Wheeler observing it for some twenty miles above, and Jackson as far below.

The enemy advanced as usual covered by intrenchments. Skirmishing continued until the 9th. Our infantry and artillery were brought to the southeast side of the river that night because two Federal corps had crossed it above Powers Ferry on the 8th and intrenched. Lieutenant-General Stewart took command of his corps on the 7th.

The character of Peach Tree Creek and the numerous fords on the Chattahoochee above its mouth, prevented my attempting to defend that part of the river. The broad and muddy channel of the creek would have separated the two parts of the army. It, and the river below its mouth, were, therefore, taken as our line. A position on the high ground south of the creek was selected for the army from which to attack the enemy while crossing. The engineer officers, with a large force of negroes, were set to work to strengthen the fortifications of Atlanta and mount on them seven heavy rifles borrowed from Major-General Maury. The chief engineer was instructed to devote his attention first to the works between the Decatur and Marietta roads; to put them in such condition that they might be held by the State troops, so that the army might attack the enemy in flank when he approached the town. This, in the event that we should be unsuccessful in attacking the Federal army in its passage of Peach Tree Creek. After the armies were separated by the Chattahoochee, skirmishing became less severe. On the 14th a division of Federal cavalry crossed the river by Moores Bridge, near Newnan, but was driven back by Armstrong's brigade, sent by Brigadier-General Jackson to meet it. On the 15th, Governor Brown informed me orally that he hoped to re-enforce the army before the end of the month with near ten thousand State troops. On the 17th, the main body of the Federal army crossed the Chattahoochee between Roswell and Powers Ferry. At 10 P. M., while I was giving Lieutenant-Colonel Presstman, chief engineer, instructions in regard to his work of the next day on the fortifications of Atlanta, a telegram was received from General Cooper informing me, by direction of the Secretary of War, that as I had failed to arrest the advance of the enemy to the vicinity of Atlanta, and expressed no confidence that I could defeat or repel him, I was relieved from the command of the Army and Department of Tennessee, which would be immediately turned over to General Hood. This was done at once. On the morning of the 18th, the enemy was reported to be advancing, and at General Hood's request I continued to give orders until afternoon, placing the troops in the position selected near Peach Tree Creek.

In transferring the command to General Hood, I explained my plan to him: First to attack the Federal army while crossing Peach Tree Creek. If we were successful, great results might be hoped for, as the enemy would have both the creek and the river to intercept his retreat. Second, if unsuccessful, to keep the enemy by intrenching, to give time for the assembling of the State troops promised by Governor Brown; to garrison Atlanta with those troops, and when the Federal army approached the town attack it on its most exposed flank with all the Confederate troops. These troops, who had been for seventy-four days in the immediate presence of the enemy—laboring and fighting daily, enduring toil, exposure and danger with equal cheerfulness, more confident and high-spirited than when the Federal army presented itself near Dalton—were then inferior to none who ever served the Confederacy.

Under the excellent administration of Brigadier-General Mackall, chief of staff, the troops were well equipped and abundantly supplied. The draft animals of the artillery and quartermaster's department were in better condition on the 18th of July than on the 5th of May. We lost no material in the retreat except the four field-pieces mentioned in the accompanying report of General Hood.

I commenced the campaign with General Bragg's army of Missionary Ridge, with one brigade added (Mercer's), and two taken away (Baldwin's and Quarles'). That opposed to us was Grant's army of Missionary Ridge, then estimated at eighty thousand by our principal officers, increased, as I have stated, by two corps, a division and several thousand recruits—in all at least thirty thousand men. The cavalry of that army was estimated by Major-General Wheeler at fifteen thousand. The re-enforcements which joined our army amounted to fifteen thousand infantry and artillery and four thousand cavalry. Our scouts reported much greater numbers joining the United States Army—garrisons and bridge guards from Tennessee and Kentucky, relieved by one hundred-days' men, and the Seventeenth Corps with two thousand cavalry.

The loss of our infantry and artillery from the 5th of May had been about ten thousand in killed and wounded, and forty-seven hundred from all other causes, mainly slight sickness, produced by heavy, cold rains, which prevailed in the latter half of June. These and the slightly wounded were beginning to rejoin their regiments. For want of reports I am unable to give the loss or the services of the cavalry, which was less under my eye than the rest of the army. Its effective strength was increased by about two thousand during the campaign. The effective force transferred to General Hood was about forty-one thousand infantry and artillery and ten thousand cavalry.

According to the opinions of our most experienced officers, daily reports of prisoners and statements of Northern papers, the enemy's loss in action could not have been less than five times as great as ours. In the cases in which we had the means of estimating it, it ranged from seven to one to ninety-one to one, compared with ours, and averaged thirteen to one. The Federal prisoners concurred in saying that their heaviest loss occurred in the daily attacks made in line of battle upon our skirmishers in their rifle-pits. Whether they succeeded in dislodging our skirmishers or not, their loss was heavy, and ours almost nothing.

At Dalton the great numerical superiority of the enemy made the chances of battle much against us, and even if beaten they had a safe refuge behind the fortified pass of Ringgold and in the fortress of Chattanooga. Our refuge, in case of defeat, was in Atlanta, one hundred miles off, with three rivers intervening. Therefore, victory for us could not have been decisive, while defeat would have been utterly disastrous. Between Dalton and the Chattahoochee we could have given battle only by attacking the enemy intrenched, or so near intrenchments that the only result of success to us would have been his falling back into them, while defeat would have been our ruin. In the course pursued, our troops, always fighting under cover, had very trifling losses compared with those they inflicted, so that the enemy's numerical superiority was reduced daily, and rapidly, and we could reasonably have expected to cope with the Federal army on equal ground by the time the Chattahoochee was passed. Defeat on this side of that river would have been its destruction. We, if beaten, had a place of refuge in Atlanta too strong to be assaulted and too extensive to be invested. I had also hoped that by the breaking of the railroad in its rear the Federal army might be compelled to attack us in a position of our own choosing, or to a retreat easily converted into a rout. After we crossed the Etowah five detachments of cavalry were successively sent with instructions to destroy as much as they could of the railroad between Dalton and the Etowah. All failed because too weak. We could never spare a sufficient body of cavalry for this service, as its assistance was absolutely necessary in the defense of every position we occupied. Captain Harvey, an officer of great courage and sagacity, was detached on this service with one hundred men, on the 11th of June, and remained for several weeks near the railroad, frequently interrupting (although not strong enough to prevent) its use.

Early in the campaign the statements of the strength of the cavalry in the Department of Mississippi and East Louisiana given me by Lieutenant-General Polk, just from the command of that department, and my telegraphic correspondence with his successor, Lieutenant-General S. D. Lee, gave me reason to hope that a competent force could be sent from Mississippi and Alabama to prevent the use of the railroad by the United States Army. I, therefore, suggested it to the President directly on the 13th of June and 16th of July, and through General Bragg on the 3d, 12th, 13th, 16th and 26th of June, and also to Lieutenant-General Lee on the 10th of May, and 3d, 11th and 16th of June. I did so in the belief that this cavalry would serve the Confederacy better by causing the defeat of Major-General Sherman's army than by repelling a raid in Mississippi. Besides the causes of my removal alleged in the telegram announcing it, various other accusations have been made against me; some published in newspapers, in such a manner as to appear to have official authority; and others circulated orally in Georgia and Alabama, and imputed to General Bragg. The principal are: That I persistently disregarded the instructions of the President; that I would not fight the enemy; that I refused to defend Atlanta; that I refused to communicate with General Bragg in relation to the operations of the army; that I disregarded his entreaties to change my course and attack the enemy, and gross exaggerations of the losses of the army. I had not the advantage of receiving the President's instructions in relation to the manner of conducting the campaign, but as the conduct of my predecessor in retreating before odds less than those confronting me had apparently been approved, and as General Lee, in keeping on the defensive and retreating toward Grant's objective point under circumstances like mine, was adding to his great fame, both in the estimation of the administration and people, I supposed that my course would not be censured. I believed then, as I do now, that it was the only one at my command which promised success.

ROSSVILLE GAP, GA.
[From an original photograph in the office of the Chief of Engineers, U. S. A.

I think that the foregoing narrative shows that the Army of Tennessee did fight, and with at least as much effect as it had ever done before. The proofs that I intended to hold Atlanta are: The fact that under my orders the work of strengthening its defenses was going on vigorously; the communication on the subject made by me to General Hood, and the fact that my family was in the town. That the public workshops were removed and no large supplies deposited in the town, as alleged by General Bragg, were measures of common prudence, and no more indicated an intention to abandon the place than the sending the wagons of an army to the rear on a day of battle proves a foregone determination to abandon the field.

While General Bragg was at Atlanta, about the middle of July, we had no other conversation concerning the army there than such as I introduced. He asked me no questions regarding its operations, past or future; made no comments upon them nor suggestions, and had not the slightest reason to suppose that Atlanta would not be defended. He told me that the object of his journey was to confer with Lieutenant-General Lee and communicate with General E. K. Smith in relation to re-enforcements for me. He talked much more of affairs in Virginia than in Georgia, asserting, what I believed, that General Sherman's army outnumbered Grant's, and impressed me with the belief that his visits to me were unofficial.

J. E. JOHNSTON, *General.*

GENERAL HARDEE once came across a straggler and asked him why he did not travel faster and keep up with his command. The soldier wished to know what in the deuce he had to do with it. "Only that I am General Hardee, the commander of this department," was the reply. "Oh, you wrote a book on tactics, did you?" "I did," said the general. "Well," said the private, "I have been taught, according to your rules, how to double column at half distance. Now I wish you would tell me how to double distance on half rations." General Hardee struck spurs to his horse and traveled on.

THE ATLANTA CAMPAIGN.

JOURNAL OF OPERATIONS
OF THE
ARMY OF TENNESSEE

MAY 14 TO JUNE 4, 1864.

[NOTE.—Journal kept at Headquarters Army of Tennessee by Lieutenant T. B. Mackall, aid-de-camp to Brigadier-General W. W. Mackall, chief of staff, and furnished by General J. E. Johnston.]

SATURDAY, MAY 14th.—Several attacks made on our line, beginning on our left and extending toward the right as far as Stevenson's left; only vigorous in front of Hindman. Our loss during the day generally slight, except in officers and artillery horses. At 6 P. M. Stewart and Stevenson, supported by Walker (two or three brigades), swing round, driving the enemy easily. Stevenson's movement particularly "prompt and vigorous;" Stewart not engaged; no enemy in his front.

About 4:20 P. M. I was sent to Geneneral Hardee to tell him to feel if any enemy was in his front, as enemy was attacking Hindman vigorously, so that, if possible, General Hardee might aid General Hood. Found the former behind Bate's line, where fighting was brisk. Just then a staff officer came from Cleburne and said that though not at that time engaged, he could see two lines of battle and he "could hold his position." General Hardee then sent word to General Mackall that so far from being able to aid Hood he could not "weaken Cleburne to aid Bate. He thought two of Walker's brigades had better be brought from south of the river; one to be placed on right of Hood and one on the left —on Bate's right, where he joined Hood, the weakest point. If Walker could not be brought up, Loring's second line could be spared very well." (Walker had already been ordered up, two brigades being in reserve in woods on south bank; Stevens' [brigade] guarding crossing on the Calhoun Road.)

On returning to headquarters General Walker's troops were just coming up the road; delivered message. General Johnston rode off to put Mercer in position behind Stewart; was soon followed by General Mackall. After remaining behind a short time to forward dispatches, etc., joined the general on high hill to the left of point where Dalton Dirt Road and railroad meet. About 6 P. M., Hood driving enemy rapidly. I am sent to tell him that Mr. Wigfall had just taken two brigades of General Walker's division in behind Stewart, that a third brigade of Walker's would soon be up (part of Loring's division; Featherston's brigade also brought up). I was directed to say also that preparations must be made to continue the movement (swinging around our right) at daylight next morning. "Let the troops understand it." Rode up Dalton and Resaca Dirt Road in search of General Hood; inquired but could learn nothing of him; turned back to near the hill where I started from and went up the railroad. There in a cut, where Stewart's line was in the morning, were Generals Johnston, Hood, Walker and Mackall. I reported to latter I had taken wrong road, etc. Presently two prisoners were brought in and questioned by the generals; not communicative. A third brought up said their line of battle ran northeast and southwest; he belonged to Whitaker's brigade, Stanley's division, Fourth Army Corps. They expected to be victorious, had massed their forces near our bridge. About dark Wheeler came up to the cut, and after consulting brought up his cavalry, which went out the railroad. All then rode in to the little house behind Selden's battery, where headquarters are at night.

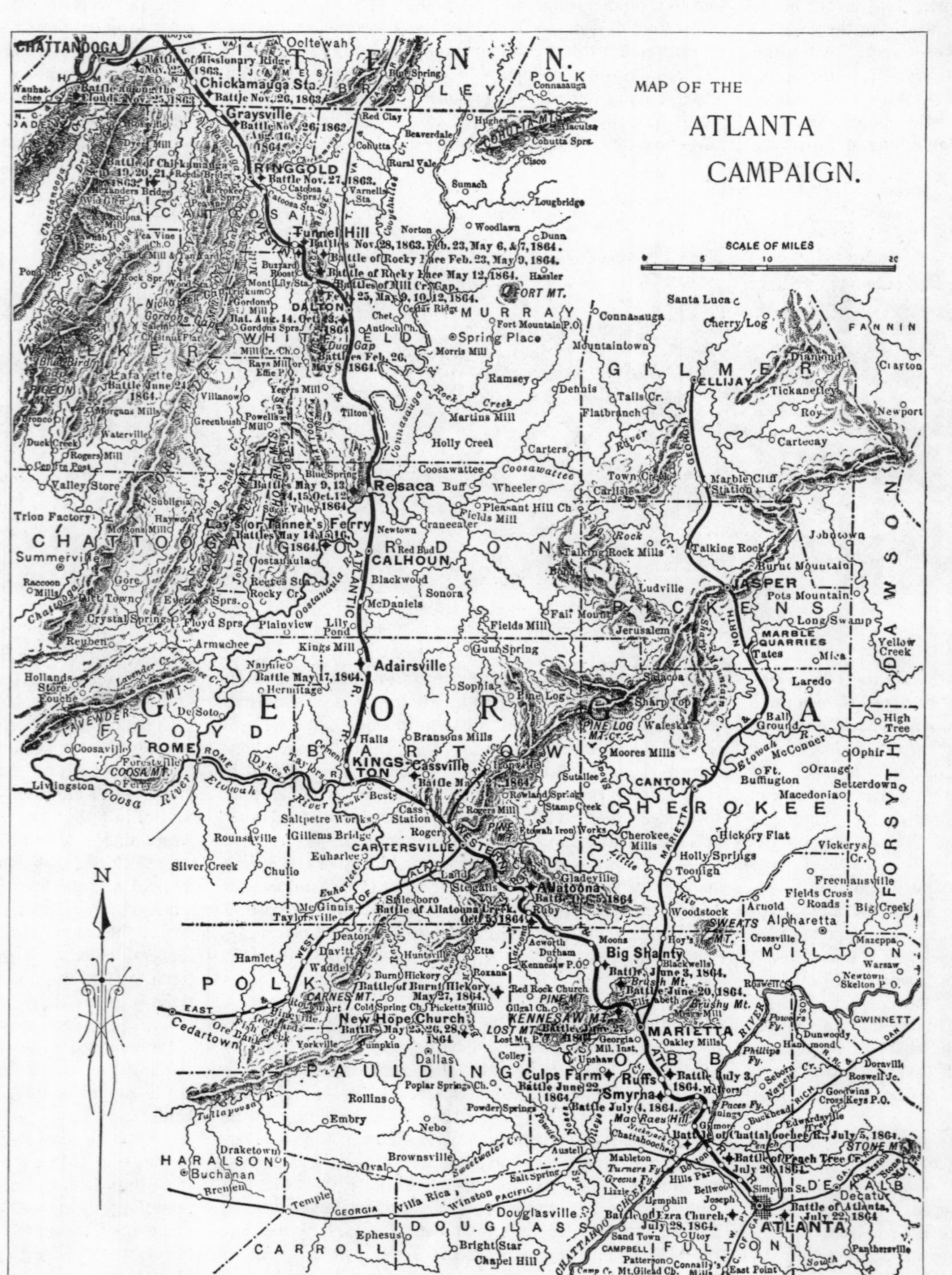

The enemy did not offer much resistance to Hood's right; batteries limbered up and fell back at the approach of our skirmish line. All in good spirits at gaining ground and the railroad, and at the prospect of renewing the attack at daylight and cutting the enemy off from Snake Creek Gap. On the way to headquarters for the night it was found that a severe engagement had taken place on Polk's line. As we attacked on the right, Sherman, supposing our left weakened, promptly assaulted our lines and the battle raged hotly, according to all accounts, for an hour and a half. The firing, strange to say, was not heard where we were. Major Clare says he reported that the enemy had effected a lodgment on the hill opposite to the house where headquarters were established the night of General Johnston's arrival from Dalton.

When we reached the house heavy firing of musketry was going on. Accounts confused. Some said hill was to be retaken; two regiments were ordered to retake it by one of the generals on the line. Hardee at headquarters on General Johnston's arrival. General Hood had accompanied the general. About same time news received from General Martin that the enemy had crossed Oostanaula (two divisions). Featherston, of Loring's command, who had been sent to report to Hood, was ordered to move promptly and occupy trenches south of Selden's battery. Walker and staff sent for. Only six of our guns of thirty on Polk's front are said to have opened to keep back the enemy. Officers of one staff in Polk's corps said the enemy holds the hill gained in evening; others said it had been retaken; others that it was to be. Impossible to learn the truth.

N. B.—In the afternoon, when General Johnston ordered me to tell General Hood to make preparations to "continue the movement" the next day at daylight, following up the success, he directed me to impress upon General Hood his wish that, in executing the plan, he should keep his face toward the mouth of Snake Creek Gap, the mouth of the gap the object to be reached.

T. B. MACKALL,
Aid-de-Camp.

RESACA.

MAY 15, 1864.—Selden's battery, 5:30 A. M., sharp skirmishing on our left. Enemy appears to be preparing for a general attack in the fog. Last night, General Walker crossed to south of Oostanaula; 6:45 A. M., very sharp skirmishing, and an occasional cannon on Hardee's line during last hour. Our skirmishers last night occupied original position on extreme left; enemy not holding the hill commanding railroad and wagon bridge.

Two divisions of enemy reported on south side of river; wagon train has been started; pontoon bridge laid yesterday above exposed bridges; no chance of Cockrell, advance of French, getting up to Rome to-day; 7 A. M., General Johnston has been on the hill where Selden's battery is posted since firing began; is just going to ride to the right, leaving General Mackall here. Skirmishing and artillery still going [on]; 10 A. M., General Johnston returned to Selden's battery an hour ago. Answer sent to cipher of the President received yesterday:

"Sherman can not re-enforce Grant without my [Gen. J.'s] knowledge, and will not, as skirmishing along our entire line. We [are] in presence of whole force of enemy assembled from North Alabama and Tennessee."

Ferguson's brigade of cavalry, also Brigadier-General Jackson, have reached Rome. Wheeler has just gone to repair pontoon bridge, which will not be ready for crossing for fifteen minutes. It is in long range of the 6-gun battery put up last night on the hill which they captured; 11 A. M., very heavy musketry and artillery firing going on, apparently on Hindman's line. Just before it became so rapid General Johnston rode up the Dalton Road, apparently on account of some news brought by Hampton from Hardee; 12 M., about 11:15 battery on our extreme right opened. Firing slackened on Hindman's front. Battery on hill on our left enfilades our trenches; riflemen annoying to our gunners; 12 M., General Johnston has come back to Selden's battery. The firing on extreme right three-quarters of an hour ago caused by enemy's cavalry crossing Connesauga in rear of Hood, capturing Hood's hospital. A brigade of our cavalry after them, supported by a brigade of Stewart's. Captain Porter, who went with General Johnston, came back. Says last reports represent our troops driving enemy's cavalry; 1:30 P. M., heavy musketry and artillery on Hindman's front; began about fifteen minutes ago. Lieutenant Wigfall has just come up to say enemy are making a very determined attack on Hindman. General Johnston preparing to mount to ride to Hood's. Firing continuous; 3:30 P. M., a few minutes after writing above, rode off to General Hood's with General Mackall, who accompanied General Johnston. Found Hood where Dalton Dirt Road and railroad are near each other, and where we now are. Hindman, a few minutes after we arrived, repulsed the enemy, who came up in some places to his breastworks. Our reserves not used. Orders given for Stewart to take enemy in flank; for wagons which were sent back to be brought up to Resaca. Stevenson and Hindman to take up movement of Stewart. Featherston brought from Polk's line, also Maney and —— from Cheatham. These supports came up in very short time. Stevenson, however, sent word that enemy, in three lines, were preparing to attack Stewart's center; 3:40 P. M. (in rear of Stewart's line, near railroad), Stewart directed to receive attack and pursue. But slight skirmishing now; enemy not making attack; 9:30 P. M., at house behind Selden's battery (headquarters at night). Orders given to withdraw from this place; arrangements made and trains moving. This afternoon, about 4:30 P. M., Stewart, in obedience to orders to attack if his position was not assaulted, advanced; soon his line was broken by a terrible fire of Hooker's corps, who were ready to attack. I had been sent to accompany

Major Ratchford to General Featherston (held in reserve), to order him, in the general's name, to take position in support of Stewart's, near Green's house.

MONDAY, MAY 16th.—On Calhoun and Adairsville Road, two miles south of Calhoun. While in field in rear of Stewart's line and near railroad last night, about dark, corps and division commanders assembled, and instructions given to effect withdrawal of army to south bank of Oostanaula. Enemy had crossed force to south bank of river, at Dobbins Ferry; reported two divisions. Walker's was facing them, immediately in our front. He was intrenched, his line extending from Oostanaula River to Tilton, on Connesauga. Stewart had been repulsed in attempting to flank him. What was to prevent him from detaching forty thousand and striking our communications, holding on at same time to their works with a force equal to ours? We could not send a force sufficient to beat the force in our rear and at the same time hold present position. In two hours after Stewart's repulse, Cheatham, Hindman, Cleburne, etc., were assembled around the camp-fires. Hardee had been there all evening. Routes and times fixed; cars to be sent for wounded; wagons and ambulances and most of artillery to cross pontoons above; troops and artillery on Polk's line, on railroad and small trestle bridge; an hour occupied in giving orders, etc., and all dispersed, going to their headquarters. We rode in; wagons not brought over. After writing dispatches to dictation of General Mackall to Polk, Hood and Hardee, telling latter to notify Polk; after troops and skirmishers driven in, lay down (sleeping on porch of house in rear of Selden's battery); waked by noise—firing, confusion, etc.—saddle and mount. General Loring comes up; all ride to

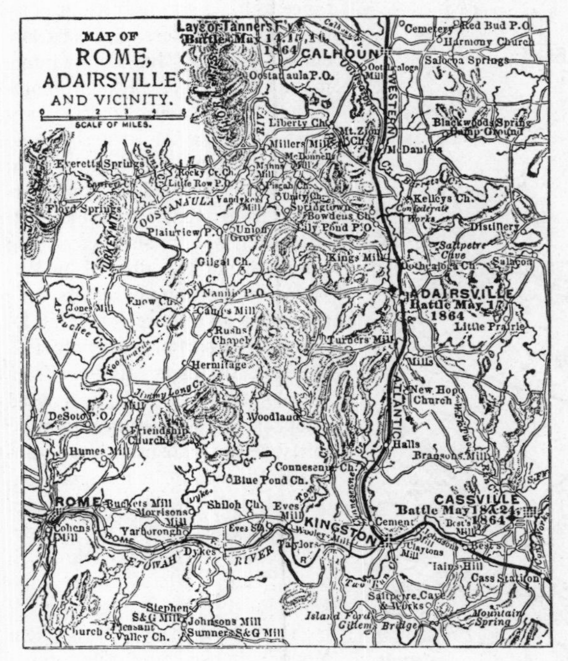

roadside at foot of Selden's battery, passing through Hindman's column going to railroad bridge; Cheatham's pass from his line over small trestle bridge below. Night cloudy. Firing of musketry and small arms on Hood's line, which was rapid and continuous on first waking, decreased. These troops (Cheatham's and Hood's) did not seem at all alarmed, rather noisy and in very good humor. Enemy's line on river remarkably quiet. Matters had been alarming on Hood's front. Enemy learning through [*sic*]. Near Calhoun, 5:30 P. M.—Order given to send wagons back one mile and a half south of Adairsville. 6:30 P. M., our wagons parking; saddling.

TUESDAY, MAY 17, 1864.—We reached Adairsville just before day, a little ahead of troops. Cultivated, rolling country from Resaca to Adairsville. . . . 9:45 P. M., this morning and forenoon guns were heard at intervals at distance; Wheeler skirmishing; 2:30 P. M., dispatch received from Wheeler (2:10) saying enemy pressing rapidly two and a half miles from town, and he would have to fall back. General had ridden out to Hood's line; original sent to him and copies of to H. and H. [Hood and Hardee]. [Hardee] did not receive his until after his infantry informed him. At this time cavalry were coming in. General soon came in. By 5 P. M. Cheatham, who was one mile in advance, was skirmishing. Pack up and saddle. Troops who had not been in line, but massed in bivouac, quickly formed, while firing going on. Sent to Hardee to ask what disposition he had made; found him on his left; Cheatham in advance of all infantry; Walker on his right, Cleburne next, part crossing Oothkaloga Creek; Bate in reserve. Returned soon, all the lieutenant-generals and Wheeler. Enemy reported on west of Oothkaloga Creek. Bate sent over; six thousand cavalry reported six miles of Cartersville. Pontoons at Cassville. Jackson's division cavalry ordered back. One brigade had no corn for three days. (Pontoons ordered to Etowah.) Firing heard at Rome while all this going on. Telegram from Lieutenant-Colonel Steever, Rome, saying enemy in force shelling town. I sent after General Polk about 6 P. M. All in council. Can the army be withdrawn when so many roads into Calhoun? Carry a dispatch in room; General W. W. [Mackall] and J—— looking at map. Latter traces road from here to Cassville; asks how long will it take all to go down one road? [Hood] says can't be done. [Hardee] said we will have to fight. [Hood] has been anxious to get from this place south of Etowah.

BRIG.-GEN. C. H. STEVENS, OF SOUTH CAROLINA.
Killed in action at Atlanta, Ga., July 27, 1864.
[From a photograph taken in 1864.]

7:10 P. M., Roy and Cunningham have just been called for. In waiting. On 16th of May received cipher from General S. D. Lee, Demopolis; not translatable. Repetition received on 17th, at night. Forrest will start on 20th from Corinth to cross Tennessee at Florence with three thousand five hundred picked men and two batteries. Colonel Hill reported on authority of scout that enemy were moving down toward Rome, on Calhoun and Rome Road, Palmer's corps in advance, wagon trains along, and one brigade cavalry. Did not learn whether any other force was behind.

CASSVILLE.

WEDNESDAY, MAY 18th.—Reached creek near Cassville about 7:30 A. M., got into camp 9:30 A. M.; no firing so far (just after breakfast). Left headquarters just beyond Adairsville about 4 A. M. Hardee's corps moved on Adairsville and Kingston Road, Hood's and Polk's on Adairsville and Cassville. Sears' brigade, French's division, reached Adairsville yesterday. French with Cockrell's this A. M., at Kingston; cars gone for Ector's. French had one brigade about starting from Rome to join this army when town was attacked. Cockrell's detained to aid in defense and protect the other brigade. 4 P. M., cipher from S. D. Lee, of 17th, Meridian, received. Forrest's move for 20th suspended on account of demonstrations from Memphis. Colonel Hannon just reports enemy's cavalry in force advancing on Fairmount Road rapidly, and four miles from here. Armstrong ordered to support of Hannon.

Following written Thursday, 19th:

Hood and Hardee and Polk at headquarters discussing over map plans for morning. Prisoner of Hooker's corps brought in; I questioned him. His command was behind Howard's; latter skirmished with Cheatham afternoon of 17th, and all army was assembled close by. Next morning (on 18th) whole command in motion. Howard

BRIG.-GEN. A. J. VAUGHAN, OF TENNESSEE.

moved into Adairsville, halted and cooked dinner. Prisoner got lost among Howard's men and was told Hooker had moved toward our right, and endeavoring to join his regiment was captured by our cavalry; was told that an additional corps was following behind Hooker; knew nothing of other commands. All appear in good spirits. Telegram received in afternoon from Thrasher reporting enemy acknowledge loss of forty-five thousand and thirty-one generals in Virginia. General [Johnston] said Confederacy was as fixed an institution as England or France. Troops very much wearied by night marches; in good spirits and confident; press confident. Anxiety, however, to fight, particularly among officers, certain of whom thought good effect of Virginia and Louisiana news in raising gold in New York to 210 would be impaired by this retreat. Many thought Sherman would not fight; merely wanted to drive us across Etowah and to occupy territory acquired and send re-enforcements to Grant.

THURSDAY, MAY 19th.—Moved out to attack enemy, but column reported advancing on Cartersville Road; line changed; brisk skirmishing. General Ross reports enemy throwing pontoons across Etowah at Wooleys Bridge, and crossed a force—main force.

Following written May 21st, near Allatoona:

Line changed under fire. Brisk skirmishing in afternoon and toward evening to effect the change. New line principally along a ridge running nearly north and south, covering Cassville and Cass Station Road and facing westwardly. The Signal Corps and General Hardee reported in forenoon that enemy in front of Cassville were moving toward Kingston, all advantageous to the designed attack on his left flank. An order was written about 7 or 8 A. M., thanking troops for patience, and telling them they would be led against enemy. General [Johnston] rode over to General Hood's, and then passing by general headquarters

rode out Spring Place Road, north of creek, with Hood and Polk and Hardee, to show former where he was to form his line for attack. General Mackall rode from headquarters east of town to join him; found Generals Johnston, Polk and Hardee returning (Sears' Mississippi brigade formed across road). Riding back, all passed Cockrell's Missouri brigade resting on road, and in town met Hindman's column, advance of Hood's corps, moving to take position on Polk's right. After a few moments in town rode rapidly back out Spring Place Road. General saw Hood and returned to camp-ground and dismounted; Hood's corps passing. Polk's troops shifting. About this time, 10:20 A. M., a few discharges of artillery on Adairsville and Cassville Road, and in ten minutes report of artillery in easterly direction. General Mackall, who had ridden out to Hood with directions "to make quick work," sent word back by courier, who reported to me that, "enemy in heavy force close to Hood on Canton Road." I tell general, who says it can't be. (Armstrong on that road reported none.) Called for map; said if that's so General Hood will have to fall back at once. Presently General Mackall rode up at a rapid rate, spoke with general, who sent him back in haste, riding one of his horses; Mason went off on another; still firing had ceased; confusion in passing backward and forward of Hood's and Polk's troops. At this time could be heard officers all around reading orders to regiments and cheers of troops. Some regiments in field where headquarters were. Polk detains two of Hood's brigades, as Hardee on his left had not closed up a gap. Headquarters wagons sent beyond Cassville. Corps commanders and Wheeler arrive.

Instructions to change line. Generals Johnston and Mackall and Polk ride on high hill overlooking town and back from original line. New line marked out and troops rapidly formed on it and along a ridge. Late in afternoon considerable skirmishing and artillery. Enemy's skirmishers occupied town. At one time confusion; wagons, artillery and cavalry hasten back; noise, dust and heat. Disorder checked; wagons made to halt. Consternation of citizens; many flee, leaving all; some take away few effects, some remain between hostile fires.

General Mackall and I remain several hours on roadside (Cassville and Cartersville Road). Governor Harris brings lunch. General Johnston, about 5 P. M. in afternoon, rides down to Hardee's, leaving General Mackall; I remain. About 6 P. M. General Mackall sets out to find our camp; meets the general, and both go back to a field near road in rear of Polk, as skirmishing brisk. General Johnston tells Governor Harris he will be ready for and happy to receive enemy next day. Wheeler comes up; cavalry falls back behind infantry. Dark ride to camp. By a muddy brook near General Polk's find supper ready and tents pitched. After supper, General Johnston walks over to General Polk. General Mackall and rest turn in. Soon General Johnston sends word by courier to send him two of inspectors-general, mounted; then one of Polk's staff officers brings word that all the staff must report mounted; I was directed to remain.

General Mackall returned to camping-place, where most all staff waited until about 2 A. M., when they rode to Cartersville, passing trains and artillery parked in field; all hurried off without regard to order. Reached Cartersville before day, troops come in after day. General Johnston comes up—all hurried over bridges; great confusion, caused by mixing trains and by trains which crossed first parking at river's edge and others winding around wrong roads; about two thousand wagons crowded on bank.

FRIDAY, MAY 20th (written May 22d).—General Mackall and staff reach Cartersville about 4 A. M., General Johnston later; confusion, hurrying wagons and artillery across Etowah Bridge. Supply train parked on plain on south side, two pontoon bridges, one wagon trestle bridge, one railroad bridge, wagons and artillery blocked up on road; trains mixed. Dust and heat; country rough and hilly; little water near railroad; army in line on north side. Wagons move toward Allatoona on two roads. After great delay trains removed out of range. In afternoon headquarters established near Moore's house (Hardee's headquarters), near a crossing of railroad and lower Allatoona Road, one mile and a half from Allatoona. Etowah Iron Works—most valuable machinery, teams, wagons and negroes, removed by G. W. Smith. Bridges burned in P. M., including railroad bridge by mistake. Troops jaded, artillery and cavalry horses particularly; Georgia troops dropped off; all in pretty good spirits up to falling back from Cassville. Change of line not understood but thought all right, but night retreat after issuing general orders impaired confidence; great alarm in country around. Troops think no stand to be made north of Chattahoochee, where supply train is sent. Dispatch of President of May 18th received; he had read dispatch of —— with disappointment. Governor Brown has ordered all militia to assemble at Atlanta.

SATURDAY, May 21st.—Headquarters still near Moore's house on Etowah and Allatoona Road. Every measure taken to prevent straggling and bring back absentees. Went to Acworth to see General D. Saw Colonel Beard, Inspector-General, who said he could find but few stragglers; many broken down men with sick tickets going to rear. Marietta reported full of stragglers. Over —— thousand barefoot men. Some dissatisfaction, but all will be rectified by rest of few days. Campaign unusually severe, according to officers who have been through those in Virginia. President's dispatch of 18th answered and misstatement of dates in General Johnston's previous dispatch corrected. (Mistake owing to my giving date of leaving Dalton instead of Resaca, which I understood was asked.) About dusk enemy's cavalry appeared near Etowah; our artillery drive them away. In night Brigadier-General Jackson (Walker's division) reports considerable skirmishing near railroad crossing—enemy occupying works on north side.

(Later): Armstrong, commanding Jackson's cavalry, all west of railroad. Jackson (disabled) reports enemy's cavalry crossed at Gillems Bridge (south of Kingston), and infantry and artillery on north side. Colonel Ewell telegraphs to know if service of conscripts will be received; thousands can be had. Newspapers of to-day say nothing of retreat south of Etowah, except battle at Cassville. Supply trains south of Chattahoochee River. Other wagon trains moved south of Allatoona to a more open country. Return called for.

NEAR MOORE'S HOUSE.

SUNDAY, May 22, 1864.—(Memorandum: On 20th asked General Mackall who reported force of enemy on Canton Road on 19th when we were at Cassville. He said General Hood, who said they had a line of battle close to him. General Mackall could see nothing, and didn't believe it.) 9:30 A. M., dispatch this morning, written last night by Allen, of cavalry, gives report of a scout. Enemy fortifying on both sides of river at Gillems Bridge; their cavalry had gone out several miles to Stilesboro; inquired minutely about roads; said that to-day an army one hundred and fifty thousand (?) strong would march out on Cedartown Road to Atlanta; expected but little opposition, thinking this army utterly demoralized. Enemy on short rations. (Memorandum: Left Cleveland and Ringgold with twenty days' rations.) This report sent back to Wheeler, with note advising him not to carry out his expedition without being fully informed of position of enemy. Immediately afterward he was sent for to come to headquarters, where Hood and Hardee are. Copy of said report sent to Armstrong. Wheeler not yet arrived. Jackson's division cavalry picketing river below as far as Rome; Wheeler's above as far as Canton. Wheeler is to cross the river. Wheeler started in afternoon, after considerable delay, crossing near Etowah Bridge. At 3:30 P. M. lieutenant-generals and chief of artillery notified to have everything in readiness to move at moment's notice. Major Moore notified that troops are to carry three days' rations in haversacks. Guides obtained for country south of Etowah and west of railroad. Two bridges being built over Pumpkin Vine Creek, and road made, cutting off considerable distance in moving down river. Country hilly and rocky. Heat oppressive and road dusty. Many disloyal people in this section.

MONDAY, May 23, 1864.—(After sunset, near Moore's house, one mile and a half from Allatoona.) After breakfast, headquarters wagons packed and horses saddled, ready for a move; awaiting information from cavalry. During day Wheeler, who had crossed with escort night before, and was followed by his command in morning, sent back several dispatches giving reports of scouts sent to Cartersville, Cassville, Cass Station, etc. Enemy's infantry (force not known) at Cartersville. Hooker's corps and headquarters at Cassville. (Following written 24th): (Memorandum: Learned about failure at Cassville from ——; mistake about name of road, "Canton.") Wheeler sent word in evening that more than one division at Cartersville. Hooker's headquarters and corps at Cassville. Thomas between Cassville and Kingston. Wheeler ordered off on expedition to cut communications.

Burning of Etowah Iron Works and of town of Cartersville afternoon of 22d, and small force then observed at Cartersville and few cavalry east. Had produced impression on some that entire force of enemy either moved considerably to our left or were falling back. Many rumors of latter kind. Wheeler, after crossing Etowah, said citizens said enemy reported they were falling back. One report that they were going to Knoxville. Jackson's cavalry, under Armstrong, sent unsatisfactory reports, but in afternoon and night reported five thousand cavalry crossed at Milams Bridge, apparently to cover passage of infantry. Heavy columns of dust and of infantry and wagons seen moving on north bank of Etowah toward our left, and Ferguson thought main army on north bank. Ferguson reported infantry having crossed. During day Hardee moved ten miles southwest, and Polk moved on road from Allatoona to Dallas. Hood still watching crossings near railroad. At night orders reiterated for Hardee to move to Dallas and Atlanta Road, and Polk to do same and communicate. General Hardee made mistake; sent word back (date, 10 P. M., received 11:50 P. M.) that unless he received further orders would cross Chattahoochee at Nelsons Ferry; would start his command 2 A. M. Major Mason sent to correct mistake, and note sent by courier telling him he was to take position near intersection of road on which he was with Atlanta and Dallas Road and protect it, supported by General Polk. Armstrong's cavalry, in moving further to left, strangely had fallen back to Burnt Hickory, leaving enemy's cavalry unobserved. Armstrong told of utmost importance to have strong force at position held by Ross and observe enemy closely. Immediate information necessary. Jackson's commanders think main Yankee army west of our position, from Milams Bridge to Rome. Telegram from General B. received. Quarles ordered from Mississippi on 21st. After terrible crisis, sacrificing communications, all well in Virginia. Expect great results here from tone of army reported. S. D. Lee ordered part of Roddey to Talladega: Chalmers' division from Tupelo to ——; Blair passed Paducah on 10th to join Sherman; thirty-seven transports and gunboats. Headquarters wagons unpacked; 3 P. M., go into camp. Wheeler told to observe particularly what force could march directly from Cartersville on Allatoona.

TUESDAY, MAY 24th.—(Near Moore's house, one mile and a half to Allatoona.) All ready to move to Polk's command. (May 25th, yesterday all rode from headquarters near Bartow Furnace (near Moore's) to Powder Mill and Dallas Road, and camped at night on the road, four miles from Dallas. Hood moved his troops by afternoon nearer Dallas from Etowah Bridge, and headquarters where Hardee's had been night before, at Dr. Smith's. Hardee at night camped in supporting distance of Dallas. Polk camped on Marietta and Dallas Road. In afternoon four of enemy's cavalry run into lines of a brigade at Dallas and carry off some of our men; not a gun loaded. Jackson's opinion that main army of enemy approaching Dallas and one corps and twenty-five hundred cavalry going by Villa Rica. This information sent to Hood, who is told to move early in morning, that his advance may reach New Hope Church (on Allatoona and Dallas Road), about four miles and a half from Robinsons, in order to guard against separation. Polk is to move up on Marietta and Dallas Road to Robinson's. Join hands to be ready to fight. Witherspoon, of Quarles' staff, reports brigade coming twenty-eight hundred.

WEDNESDAY, MAY 25, 1864.—(5:30 P. M., at Robinson's house, four miles south of Dallas, near intersection of road from Marietta, Atlanta and Allatoona to Dallas.) Half hour ago few discharges of artillery near New Hope Church, where Hood is, three miles distant. Prisoner says Hooker's corps is in front of him. General Johnston rode there an hour ago. We have been waiting here nearly all day. Few developments of enemy. Reports of their having crossed Pumpkin Vine Creek; citizens think moving around our left. All quiet in front of Dallas. This morning all of Hardee's division in line. Polk got in wrong place. Wheeler reports captured and brought off from near Cassville eighty wagons loaded, and destroyed one hundred and seventy and took one hundred and fifty prisoners. Stewart's division repulsed Hooker's corps.

SATURDAY, MAY 28, 1864.—(11 A. M., Cleburne's intrenched line, where enemy were repulsed last afternoon, Rogers' house.) Few minutes ago started with General Mackall to Wheeler's to see General Hood; met him after going few yards and returned. Brisk cannonading, apparently in front of Loring, and slight skirmishing along line. Blanton, of Hood's staff, came from the right about 9 A. M., after our arrival here (Cleburne's headquarters), with a message from General Hood, who was at Wheeler's headquarters. Captain McFarland, of Cleburne's staff, who came with him, says Hood found enemy's right on Allatoona Road intrenched; could not attack; disappointed in not being able to get in his rear, as he expected last night and this morning. Wrote at sunrise his corps had not crossed; feared he would have some difficulty in crossing Little Pumpkin Vine Creek, where our right last evening rested; when he crossed he would be in enemy's rear. At 11 A. M. fight on French's line; 11:30, generals ride away; follow in fifteen to twenty minutes; when I leave, Cleburne says his skirmishers pressed in. However, no attack on him. All ride to house, where headquarters are established at night. While on Cleburne's line, walk over field; about seven hundred dead left by Howard. Prisoners from Palmer and Schofield, who were supporting but not engaged, captured. Enemy advanced in five to six lines.

MONDAY, MAY 30th.—(8 A. M., Widow Wigley's deserted house on Dallas and Allatoona Road, three-quarters of a mile from New Hope Church.) All very quiet along line except occasional cannon opposite French; hardly a musket fired. Last evening early, on account of reported movement of enemy toward our left, extending from PumpkinVine Creek, from which point forces said to be moving to Dallas, arrangements made to move to Lost Mountain, six miles east. At same time enemy's pickets on their left were contracted, and reports of troops moving to re-enforce Dallas. At 9 o'clock at night some cannonading on French's and Cantey's line; 10 P. M., wagons [at] headquarters packed to move. Some tremendous firing, artillery and musketry, on French's line kept up more than half hour, and renewed two or three times later. About 11 P. M., cannonading heavy on Bate's line for two hours, fortunately Cleburne supporting; various conjectures at the time, and since, about origin. Cantey's line very weak and seventy-five yards from enemy's intrenchments; second line was being made two hundred yards in rear. Was enemy attempting to prevent working? Making genuine attack? False alarm? Latter general impression, confirmed toward morning by officers who reported no enemy seen either in front of Cantey or Bate. Cantey said it was a stampede on part of his men. There we did most of firing. On left it was principally enemy's artillery, great waste of ammunition; reminded some of occurrences at Yorktown; both sides aroused by false alarm. On the heavy firing, movement of the night suspended, all unsaddle; intrenching tools sent to lines. Toward morning scouts reported enemy moving to our left. For several days he has been approaching railroad gradually, intrenching at every point. Yesterday Hood on right, Polk in center, holding Hood's former position, while Hardee on left, his line extending several miles, and for long intervals only skirmishers, principally on the Ellsberry Hills. Bate in front of Dallas, supported by Cleburne, moved up yesterday. In enemy's line a similar gap opposite Cheatham; enemy a mile distant. Stewart on Hood's extreme right across Little Pumpkin Vine Creek; enemy also across creek. Information received now by Hill's, Granbury's and Jackson's and Wheeler's scouts more regular and reliable. One of Longstreet's scouts reports heavy baggage sent back from Chattanooga, and all forage and subsistence sent forward, twenty days, of which ten had been exhausted. Small garrison at Chattanooga. Other day man reported small garrisons at Tullahoma and Huntsville; fifteen hundred at Bridgeport. Many rumors of Forrest having crossed Tennessee River, but nothing from Mississippi to show suspension of order revoked. Forrest would be of more service between Sherman and Chattanooga. Mississippi threatened by raid from Memphis, and other day information that A. J. Smith had landed troops from Red River at Vicksburg. Southwest drained of troops to strengthen this army. Fleet and transports with two thousand infantry off Mobile. No infantry except enough to man batteries. Tennessee over the bar and down the bay; admiral hesitates to attack. 9:30 A. M., Major Preston says firing on right originated by enemy's heavy line of skirmishers advancing on Cantey's line where new fortications being built. Firing there only few minutes taken up by other troops; now new line on ridge further back. Sharpshooters troublesome; artillery lose heavily in men and horses—forty men and forty horses in one battalion; ammunition wasted; only forty rounds allowed to each man.

TUESDAY, MAY 31, 1864.—(Three-quarters of a mile from New Hope Church, at Widow Wigley's; headquarters same for several days.) Prisoner of Fifteenth (Logan's corps), captured night before last in front of Bate, and brought to headquarters yesterday afternoon; says Fifteenth and Sixteenth corps near Dallas, on enemy's right; doesn't think any corps immediately on left; said Seventeenth came up two days before. In night, without drawing in pickets, firing was suddenly commenced by his people; he lay down, and when all was quiet, in endeavoring to escape, got among our skirmishers—so the enemy raised false alarm on Bate's line as Cantey did. Bate reported enemy made several attacks. In the previous affair, when Bate advanced, became hotly engaged, effected lodgment temporarily in enemy's breastworks, and was forced to retire with loss; he says ardor of men could not be restrained; went too far before could be recalled. Lewis, who lost most, and other brigadiers, say orders positive to take works.

Jackson's scouts report enemy's cavalry between Dallas and Draketown moved back during attack of Sunday night; don't know which road they have gone; told [by] citizens, horses starving, forced to go back. (Prisoners say army on half rations for several days, and various confirmations of short supplies; stock suffering). Captain Johnson, of a Georgia regiment, under Wheeler, just from a scout north of Etowah River, says no enemy at Etowah, Cartersville or Cassville; one to two thousand infantry and one regiment cavalry at Cass Station and Kingston; five thousand infantry at Resaca; citizens and soldiers say two supply trains cut off. Forrest captured Chattanooga (no official information received here of his having started). On 29th, S. D. Lee telegraphed that Roddey had been driven back to Jonesboro by ten thousand infantry, artillery and cavalry from Decatur; yesterday, said they had returned—probably a diversion to cover movement of troops to Kingston (probably those landed at Clinton). War Department day or two ago gave notice that nineteen transports with troops had passed Grand Gulf and stopped at Vicksburg, supposed to be Smith's troops, from Red River (on way to Sherman, doubtless). Yesterday afternoon, late, brisk skirmishing and rapid artillery firing on Stewart's line. With this exception, day and night remarkably quiet. Enemy's sharpshooters in trees very annoying. Yesterday colonel and captain of First Missouri killed in trenches. Some supposed one hundred and fifty guns in position would open. Sick and wounded had been moved back, and many thought army would change position. Troops in good spirits. Press in southwest support the general. A victory will confirm all. In one and two weeks enemy will have considerable re-enforcements. Logan's corps go out service in three months. Lincoln calls for four hundred thousand more.

Gap in enemy's line. General believes force (McPherson) in front of Bate is there only to cover roads. Hooker in center, then Howard, Palmer and Schofield. Wheeler's scouts learn from citizens that, from questions [of] enemy's engineers, who examined country and roads to Allatoona, a movement to Allatoona is contemplated.

THURSDAY, JUNE 2.—(Sunset.) Headquarters moved yesterday evening from Widow Wigley's to camp in woods three miles further to our right in rear of Hood on Settlement Road leading into Marietta Road. Yesterday telegram sent to General Bragg (last was on 28th); another to Governor Brown. The quiet of the enemy on Tuesday on the left, sharpshooting only, no reply being made to our batteries, and the small force observed from Ellsberry Mountain, opposite Walker, induced the belief that the force at Dallas was small. Yesterday morning at daylight enemy commenced moving his forces from Dallas to his left. From left of Mercer's brigade on Ellsberry Mountain heavy columns of infantry, well closed up became visible at 7 o'clock and continued in sight until 9 or 10 A. M. Major Lee and others observed them from mountain and reported frequently. About midday the general rides to mountain. In front of Walker the enemy kept their skirmishers close to ours, but no troops at the time to support them in the intrenchments, two lines of which had been erected several days before. We could see a few wagons passing in their front on the Burnt Hickory Road, but in the distance the roads to Burnt Hickory and that from Burnt Hickory to New Hope Church could be seen miles off and wagons three miles off passing continually. The dust marked the progress when the road could not be seen. Wagons were moving to New Hope Church and the dust also showed traveling beyond the cross-roads to Burnt Hickory, in direction of river. Officers observing the movements early in the day said a column moved from left and occupied breastworks in front of Mercer and Cheatham to cover passage of others along road. After-

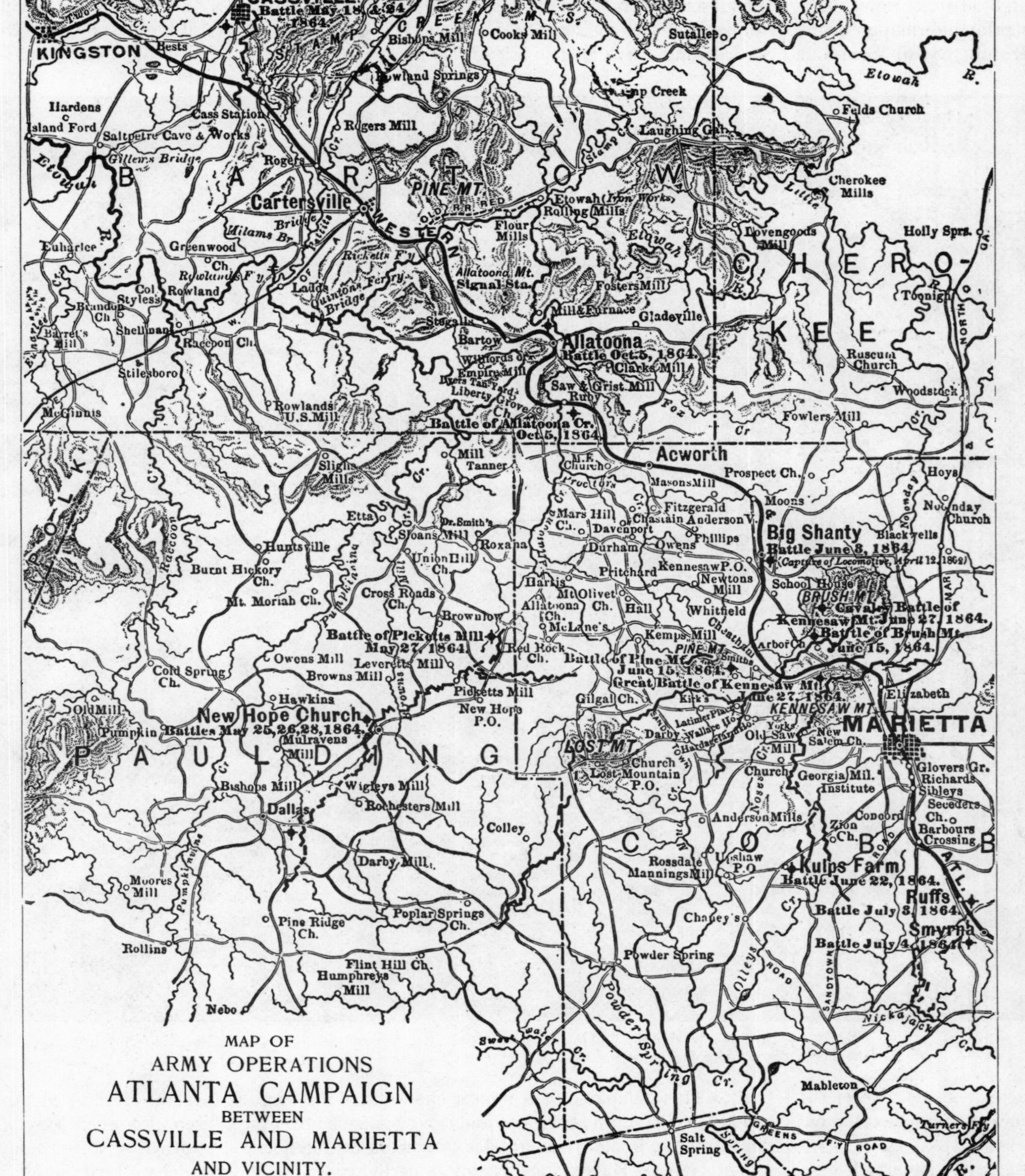

ward line of battle was formed at right angles to fortifications. I saw line of battle when rode first to mountain to see Major Lee and observe with map. Jackson's scouts reported same movement, and about 1 o'clock Armstrong entered Dallas. He reported one-half enemy had taken the Burnt Hickory or Cartersville Road leading toward Donlhardts Bridge (so General Walker was told by residents) and the other corps had taken the Acworth Road leading from Dallas to New Hope Church. No cavalry at Dallas since Sunday. Cleburne was moved from supporting distance of Walker further to right. Last evening heavy columns of cavalry, with artillery, moved from Cartersville and encamped at Allatoona; another cavalry column, reported five thousand, moved last evening up Dallas and Allatoona Road to Allatoona. It seems all their cavalry is on our right. Yesterday confidential circular directing withdrawal at night to Lost Mountain recalled 4 P. M. Last night all quiet; also to-day, except some cannonading on Hood's line. About noon Hood reported enemy double-quicking to his right and attack expected. Bate, Cleburne and Walker sent to right; attack expected in morning, though all quiet now, dusk; all quiet in front of Wheeler. Yesterday information about movements of enemy from Decatur toward Sherman received from S. D. Lee; from Jackson's and Wheeler's scouts, seven or eight thousand moved from Decatur on Somerville Road on 2d.

SATURDAY, June 4, 1864.—(Midday). No attack yesterday by enemy, as Generals Hood and Hardee expected. Headquarters unchanged. Telegram yesterday from General Bragg. Lee in line near Mechanicsville, confronting Grant. Butler gone to join Grant. Beauregard at Richmond. Two more ciphers from Lee yesterday [S. D.]; the last said the Sixteenth Army Corps, with eighteen pieces artillery, was moving toward Okolona rapidly, and that Forrest had been recalled from Russellville, and he would have to withdraw most of his cavalry from Middle Alabama. So, the great results anticipated from a raid of the Mississippi cavalry in Sherman's rear are not to be fulfilled at an early day. This column from Memphis may eventually endeavor to join Sherman. Before receipt of these dispatches, General Johnston had telegraphed Lee that raid between Sherman's army and Chattanooga would do much harm. Telegraphed also to General B. for information of movements of Mississippi cavalry, to which reference was made in B.'s dispatch. Accounts of progress of the column moving toward Rome; from many sources expected at Gadsden on the 1st of June, four days' march from Rome; according to one account, one thousand sent from Huntsville by rail. Chalmers was to move from Montevallo to Blue Mountain a day or two ago. Rumor already places him at Rome. Blair (or Griffin) said to be moving rapidly—fourteen miles per day; made forced marches from Clinton and Pulaski. He hasn't over six to ten thousand; is mounting infantry as fast as [he] can seize horses, desolating the country. One account represented this force from Louisiana; that from Memphis no doubt is. Large detachments were made from Sixteenth and Seventeenth Army Corps and sent, under A. J. Smith, to Red River. Besides these re-enforcements, prisoners and scouts report one hundred-days' men coming down to guard communications. One of Thomas' couriers, recently captured, says nineteen regiments expected soon. Scouts say three thousand of one hundred-days' cavalry at Columbia, Middle Tennessee. Many officers of this army, as well as the people and army in the East, think there is very little disparity in the size of this army and Sherman's, and urge an immediate attack. Sherman has at least sixty thousand effective infantry now, supposing him to have lost twelve to fifteen thousand since leaving Chattanooga. Our effective total infantry about forty-four thousand. Rousseau expected with a division from rear. Since leaving Dalton our entire loss not over six thousand. Many new troops sent to rear foot-sore will come up. Army better fed (one-half pound bacon with meal or hard bread) than ever, whisky or coffee occasionally issued. Troops in fine spirits. Implicit confidence. All baggage wagons south of Chattahoochee. One wagon for cooking utensils of a brigade detached from general train. This campaign of a month shows that the army can get along with no baggage, and can be supplied twenty miles from railroad. General Jackson says captured letters of General Hazen show enemy to be in straits about rations—not paid for three months. (Thomas' orders say men and horses well fed.) Enemy yesterday reported commencing to rebuild Etowah Railroad Bridge; his line moving gradually to right, followed by ours; will not attack, but will fortify on Allatoona Heights and wait for supplies and re-enforcements. No fight for two weeks. Cheatham on extreme left, next Polk, then Hood and Hardee (and their divisions) on right. Colonel Cole, Transportation Quartermaster, here. Feeling in army: One lieutenant-general talks about attack and not giving ground, publicly, and quietly urges retreat.

THE following is given by an eye witness: "On Jones' West Virginia raid, one day there was a fight near a country store. The house was soon abandoned by the occupants, and when the enemy retired precipitately the store was plundered. It was first come, first served. In a twinkling the dry goods were gone; then the mob began on the miscellaneous articles. My most valuable capture was a jar of nutmegs. By the time I had them rolled up in a table-cloth the store was about empty. I saw one poor fellow enter and look around for something to steal. There was nothing left in sight but a pile of grindstones. Uttering a volley of oaths at his bad luck, he shouldered one of these, and marched off triumphantly."

BATTLE OF KENNESAW MOUNTAIN, GA., JUNE 27, 1864.
(On the line of the Western & Atlantic Railroad, near Marietta, Ga.)

BATTLE OF KENNESAW MOUNTAIN,

JUNE 24 TO 27, 1864.

BY

MAJOR-GENERAL S. G. FRENCH.

ON the 14th of June, 1864, the army under General Joseph E. Johnston occupied a line of hastily-constructed works of several miles in length, extending from near Lost Mountain to a point about a mile north of Kennesaw Mountain. The general direction of this line, from our left, was north of east, and it was confronted in its entire length by the Federal army under General W. T. Sherman. Johnston's command numbered forty-eight thousand eight hundred, and that of Sherman, by official reports, one hundred and twelve thousand eight hundred.

The better to explain movements previous to assuming position on Kennesaw Mountain, I will make some extracts from my diary.

JUNE 14, 1864.—This morning, by written orders, General Loring moved to the right; General Cantey from the left to the center, and I extended to the right. Rode over to see General Polk; asked him when General Johnston and he went to the right to come down my line; said they probably would. . . . . At 12 M. heard that General Polk was dead; sent an officer to inquire, and learned the report too true. Went to headquarters at 2:30 P. M., but his remains had just left for Marietta. He had accompanied General Johnston to the left and gone to Pine Mountain, and while there the party was fired on by one of the Federal batteries, and the third shot fired struck the general on the left side and killed him instantly. . . . . .

JUNE 15th.—All quiet at sunrise; soon after, some desultory cannonading along the lines, but chiefly on the right, until 3 P. M., when it became quite heavy, and at the same time opened on my front with a few guns. At 5 P. M. received orders to hold Cockrell's brigade in readiness to move to the right of Loring. Part of Loring's division had their skirmishers driven in to their main works. At 9 P. M. enemy attacked my skirmishers without any result. . . . .

JUNE 16th.—Early this morning the enemy opened on my front with artillery. At 10 A. M. they shelled my front without effect. To-day Cockrell is held in reserve for General Hardee, and thus it always is. I have to hold a reserve for everybody but myself.

JUNE 17th.—To-day the enemy opened on us with artillery. Last night the left wing of the army swung back and took a new line. This has placed my command in a salient of less than ninety degrees, and renders it liable to both an enfilading and reverse fire. In the afternoon cannonading pretty severe.

JUNE 18th.—This morning pickets and skirmishers on my left (Walker's division) gave way and let the enemy in behind Cockrell's skirmishers, and enabled them to gain the Latimer house, four hundred yards distant. Ector's skirmishers also came in. Enemy soon advanced in line of battle, and with batteries opened on the salient an enfilading and reverse fire; and all day long this fire never ceased. They could not carry my lines successfully, and we would not attack them by leaving the trenches; and so the firing went on. My loss was severe, amounting to one hundred and eighty, and as an instance of the severity of the fire on the salient, Captain Guibor had served with his battery throughout the siege of Vicksburg, yet his loss this day of thirteen men is greater than that sustained during the whole siege. Toward evening ordered to withdraw and assume a new line on Kennesaw Mountain.

JUNE 19th.—The enemy made rapid pursuit, and before my line was established on Kennesaw Mountain, skirmishing commenced, and by 12 M. artillery fire from the enemy was rapid. It ranged up and over the spur of the mountain with great fury, and wounded General Cockrell, and put thirty-five of his men *hors du combat*.

The position of our army to-day is: Hood on the right, covering Marietta on the northwest. From his left, Polk's corps (now Loring's) extends over both Big and Little Kennesaw Mountains, with the left on the road from Gilgath Church to Marietta. From this road Hardee extended the line nearly south, covering Marietta on the west; the left of my division was fixed on the Marietta Road; thence it ran up the spur of the mountain called Little Kennesaw, and thence to the top of same and on up to the top of Big Kennesaw, connecting with General Walthall. Featherston was on the right of Walthall and joined General Hood's left; Walker, of Hardee's corps, was on my left; then in order came Bate, Cleburne and Cheatham.

Kennesaw Mountain is about four miles northwest of Marietta. It is over two and a half miles in length and rises abruptly from the plain, solitary and alone, to the height of perhaps six hundred or seven hundred feet. Its western side is rocky and abrupt. Its eastern side can, in a few places, be gained on horseback, and the west of Little Kennesaw, being bald and destitute of timber, affords a commanding view of all the surrounding country as far as the eye can reach, except where the view is interrupted by the higher peak.

JUNE 20th.—Busy this morning in establishing batteries on the road, on the spur of the mountain and on the top of Little Kennesaw. In the afternoon changed the line lower down the mountain side, so as to command the ascent as far as possible. Heavy cannonading on the left of my line. Lost ten horses and a few men.

JUNE 21st.—Went to the top of the mountain this morning, and while there witnessed the artillery duel between the batteries on Hardee's line and those of the enemy in his front. . . . .

JUNE 22d.—The constant rains have ceased; the sky is clear, and the sun, so long hid, now shines out brightly. Skirmishing on my line last night; rode to the top of the mountain quite early, to where I had placed nine guns in position. During the night the enemy had moved a camp close to the base of the mountain. It was headquarters of some general officers. Tent walls were raised, officers sitting around, orderlies coming and going, wagons parked, and soldiers idling about or resting under the shade of the trees; and all this at my very feet. Directed cartridges for the guns to be reduced, so as to drop the shells below, and that the enemy should be left a while in his fancied security, for no doubt they thought we could not place artillery on the height above them, and they were not visible to my infantry on the mountain sides, by reason of the timber.

At length the gunners, impatient of delay, were directed to open fire on them. They were evidently much surprised, and, disregarding rank, stood not on the order of their going, but left quickly, every man for himself; and "their tents were all silent, their banners alone," like Sennacherib's of old.

The enemy appear this morning to be moving permanently to our left, and the firing this afternoon extends further in that direction. Toward dark opened guns again on the enemy, also at 11 P. M.

JUNE 23d.—Yesterday Cockrell had fourteen men wounded. All quiet this morning. During the night the enemy removed their tents, wagons, etc., from their abandoned encampment that was shelled yesterday, and the place looks desolate. At 10 A. M., when all was quiet on the mountain, the enemy commenced a rapid artillery fire from guns put in position during the night, and concentrated it on our guns on the mountain. Yesterday we had it all our own way—to-day they are repaying us, and the cannonade is "fast and furious." Last night there was fighting on our left, but so different are the reports received that I can not get at the truth.

JUNE 24th.—There has been but little fighting during the day.

JUNE 25th.—The everlasting "pop," "pop," on the skirmish line is all that breaks the stillness of the morning. Went early to the left of my line; could not ride in rear of Hoskin's battery, on account of the trees and limbs felled by the shells. From the top of the mountain the vast panorama is ever changing. There are now large trains to the left of Lost Mountain and at Big Shanty, and wagons are moving to and fro everywhere. Encampments of hospitals, quartermasters, commissaries, cavalry and infantry whiten the plain here and there as far as the eye can reach. Our side of the line looks narrow, poor and lifeless, with but little canvas in spots, that contrasts with the green foliage.

The usual flank extension is going on. Troops on both sides move to the left, and now the blue smoke of the musket discloses the line by day trending away, far away south toward the Chattahoochee, and by night it is marked, at times by the red glow of the artillery, amidst the spark-like flash of small arms that looks in the distance like innumerable fire-flies.

At 10 A. M., opened fire on the enemy from the guns on Kennesaw. Enemy replied furiously, and for an hour the firing was incessant. Received an order to hold Ector's brigade in reserve. In the afternoon considerable firing, and all the chests of one of my caissons were blown up by a shell from the enemy, and a shell from one of the chests killed a gunner. They have now about forty guns in my front, and when they concentrate their fire on the mountain at any one place, it is pretty severe, but owing to our height, nearly harmless. Thousands of their parrott-shells pass high over the mountain and, exploding at a great elevation, the after-part of the shell is arrested in its flight and, falling perpendicularly, comes into camp, and they have injured our tents. Last night I heard a peculiar "thud" on my tent, and a rattle of tin pans, and this morning my negro boy cook put his head into my tent and said: "See here, Master Sam, them 'fernal Yanks done shot my pans last night. What am I going to do 'bout it?" A rifle ball coming over the mountain had fallen from a great height, and, perforating the pans, had entered the ground.

BRIGADIER-GENERAL JAMES CANTEY, OF ALABAMA.
[From an old daguerreotype taken in 1863.]

JUNE 26th.—This is Sunday, and all is comparatively still in the lines up to this, 4 P. M., excepting one artillery duel; but now cannon are heard on our extreme left. We have not opened our batteries here, and we have not been annoyed much. Enemy moving to our left. The day has been very warm.

JUNE 27th.—This morning there appeared great activity among staff officers and generals all along my front and up and down the lines. The better to observe what it portended, myself and staff seated ourselves on the brow of the mountain, sheltered by a large rock that rested between our guns and those of the enemy, the infantry being still lower down the side of the mountain.

Artillery firing was common on the line at all times, but now it swelled in volume and extended down to the extreme left, and then from fifty guns burst out in my front, and thence, battery after battery following on the right, disclosed a general attack on our entire lines. Presently, and as if by magic, there sprung from the earth a host of men, and in one long, waving line of blue the infantry advanced and the battle of Kennesaw Mountain began.

I could see no infantry on my immediate front, owing to the woods at the base of the mountain, and, therefore, directed the guns from their elevated position to enfilade Walker's front. In a short time the flank-fire down the line drove them back, and Walker was relieved from the attack.

We sat there, perhaps an hour, enjoying a bird's-eye view of one of the most magnificent sights ever allotted to man—to look down upon an hundred and fifty thousand men arrayed in the strife of battle on the plain below.

As the infantry closed in, the blue smoke of the musket marked out our line for miles, while over it rose in cumuli-like clouds the white smoke of the artillery. Through the rifts of smoke, or, as it was wafted aside by the wind, we could see the assault made on Cheatham; and there the struggle was hard, and there it lasted longest. So many guns were trained on those by our side, and so incessant was the roar of cannon and sharp the explosion of shells, that nought else could be heard. From the fact that I had seen no infantry in my front, and had heard no musketry near, and the elevation of my line on the mountain, I thought I was exempted from the general infantry attack. I was, therefore, surprised and awakened from my dreams when a courier came to me about 9 o'clock and said General Cockrell wanted assistance, that his line had been attacked in force. General Ector was at once directed to send two regiments to report to him. Soon again a second courier came and reported the assault on the left of my line. I went immediately with the remainder of Ector's brigade to Cockrell, but on joining him found the Federal forces had been repulsed. The assaulting column had struck Cockrell's works near the center, recoiled under the fire, swung around into a steep valley where, exposed to the fire of the Missourians in front and right flank and of Sears' men on the left, it seemed to melt away or sink to the earth to rise no more.

The assault on my line repulsed, I returned to the mountain top. The intensity of the fire had slackened, and no movement of troops was visible; and, although the din of arms yet resounded far and near, the battle was virtually ended.

From prisoners, and from papers on their persons shown us, I learned my line had, from its position, been selected for assault by General McPherson, as that of Cheatham's had been by General Thomas.

General McPherson distinguished himself under Grant; was conspicuous at the siege of Vicksburg, and enjoyed the confidence of officers and the affection of his soldiers, and having been directed in orders to make reconnoissances and preparations to assault our line, it would be a reflection on his judgment and skill as a general to infer that he did not, under the eye of his commander, with ample means, make what he deemed adequate preparations for its accomplishment; but, owing to the nature of the ground, and the determined resistance encountered, his men, by an intuitive perception, awakened by action, realized the contest was hopeless, and, where persistence was only death, very properly abandoned the field.

The battle, in its entirety, became a pageantry on a grand scale, and barren of results, because the attacking columns were too small in numbers, considering the character of the troops they knew they would encounter.

General Cheatham's loss was one hundred and ninety-five; mine (French's), one hundred and eighty-six. All other Confederate losses were one hundred and forty-one, being a total of five hundred and twenty-two. What the Federal loss was I do not know. It has been variously estimated from three to eight thousand.

The following orders of General

THE RIFLE-PITS BEFORE KENNESAW, JUNE, 1864.

Sherman will explain the attack clearly, and the telegrams to Generals Schofield and Thomas the result of the attack:

HEADQUARTERS MILITARY DIVISION OF THE MISSISSIPPI, IN THE FIELD, NEAR KENNESAW MOUNTAIN,
June 24, 1864.

The army commanders will make full reconnoissances and preparations to attack the enemy in force on the 27th inst. at 8 o'clock A. M. precisely.

The commanding general will be on Signal Hill, and will have telegraph communication with all the army commanders.

I.—Major-General Thomas will assault the enemy at any point near his center, to be selected by himself, and

BRIG.-GEN. FRANCIS M. COCKRELL, OF MISSOURI.
(From a photograph taken in 1864.)

will make any changes in his troops necessary, by night, so as not to attract the attention of the enemy.

II.—Major-General McPherson will feign by a movement of his cavalry and one division of his infantry on his extreme left, approaching Marietta from the north, and using his artillery freely, but will make his real attack at a point south and west of Kennesaw.

III.—Major-General Schofield will feel to his extreme right, and threaten that flank of the enemy with artillery and display, but attack some one point of the enemy's line as near the Marietta and Powder Spring Road as he can with prospect of success. . . . .

V.—Each attacking column will endeavor to break a single point of the enemy's line, and make a secure lodgment beyond, and be prepared for following it up toward Marietta and the railroad in case of success.

By order of Major-General W. T. Sherman.

L. M. DAYTON, *Aid-de-Camp.*

HEADQUARTERS MILITARY DIVISION OF THE MISSISSIPPI, IN THE FIELD,
June 27, 1864, 11:45 A. M.

GENERAL SCHOFIELD: Neither McPherson nor Thomas have succeeded in breaking through, but each has made substantial progress at some cost. Push your operations on the flank, and keep me advised.

W. T. SHERMAN,
Major-General Commanding.

HEADQUARTERS MILITARY DIVISION OF THE MISSISSIPPI, IN THE FIELD, NEAR KENNESAW,
June 27, 1864, 11:45 A. M.

GENERAL THOMAS: McPherson's column marched near the top of the hill, through very tangled brush, but was repulsed. It is found impossible to deploy, but they hold their ground. I wish you to study well the positions, and, if it be possible, break through the lines to do it; it is easier now than it will be hereafter. I hear Leggett's guns well behind the mountain.

W. T. SHERMAN,
Major-General Commanding.

As nothing decisive was obtained by Sherman's attack, the firing slackened, except on the skirmish line. After dark the enemy withdrew to their main trenches, the roar of guns died gradually away, and the morning of the 28th dawned on both armies in their former positions. The battle of Kennesaw, then, was a display of force and advance of troops by the enemy on the entire length of our line, that opened a furious fire of artillery and musketry, under cover of which two grand attacks were made by assaulting columns—the one on my line and the other on Cheatham's.

S. G. FRENCH, *Major-General.*

ARMY OF TENNESSEE,

APRIL 30, 1864.

GENERAL JOSEPH E. JOHNSTON,
Commanding.

HEADQUARTERS ESCORT.

Guy Dreux's company (A, ——— Louisiana Cavalry), Lieutenant O. De Buys, and Alabama Cavalry (Crocheron Light Dragoons), Captain E. M. Holloway.

HARDEE'S CORPS.

Lieutenant-General William J. Hardee, commanding.

ESCORT.

Mississippi Cavalry—Captain W. C. Raum.

CHEATHAM'S DIVISION.
Major-General B. F. Cheatham.

MANEY'S BRIGADE.*
Colonel George C. Porter.

First and Twenty-seventh Tennessee—Colonel H. R. Feild.
Fourth Tennessee (Confederate)—Lieutenant-Colonel O. A. Bradshaw.
Sixth and Ninth Tennessee—Lieutenant-Colonel J. W. Buford.
Forty-first Tennessee—Lieutenant-Colonel J. D. Tillman.
Fiftieth Tennessee—Colonel Stephen H. Colms.
Twenty-fourth Tennessee Battalion—Lieutenant-Colonel O. A. Bradshaw.

WRIGHT'S BRIGADE.
Colonel John C. Carter.

Eighth Tennessee—Colonel J. H. Anderson.
Sixteenth Tennessee—Captain Ben. Randals.
Twenty-eighth Tennessee—Colonel S. S. Stanton.
Thirty-eighth Tennessee—Lieutenant-Colonel A. D. Gwynne.
Fifty-first and Fifty-second Tennessee—Lieutenant-Colonel John G. Hall.

STRAHL'S BRIGADE.†
Brigadier-General O. F. Strahl.

Fourth and Fifth Tennessee—Colonel J. J. Lamb.
Nineteenth Tennessee—Colonel F. M. Walker.
Twenty-fourth Tennessee—Lieutenant-Colonel S. E. Shannon.
Thirty-first and Thirty-third Tennessee—Lieutenant-Colonel F. E. P. Stafford.

VAUGHAN'S BRIGADE.‡
Brigadier-General A. J. Vaughan.

Eleventh Tennessee—Colonel G. W. Gordon.
Twelfth and Forty-seventh Tennessee—Colonel W. M. Watkins.
Twenty-ninth Tennessee—Colonel Horace Rice.
Thirteenth and One Hundred and Fifty-fourth Tennessee—Colonel M. Magevney, Jr.

ESCORT.

Second Georgia Cavalry, Company G.—Captain T. M. Merritt.

CLEBURNE'S DIVISION.
Major-General P. R. Cleburne.

POLK'S BRIGADE.
Brigadier-General Lucius E. Polk.

First and Fifteenth Arkansas—Lieutenant-Colonel W. H. Martin.
Fifth Confederate—Captain W. A. Brown.
Second Tennessee—Colonel W. D. Robison.
Thirty-fifth Tennessee.§
Forty-eighth Tennessee—Captain H. G. Evans.

LOWREY'S BRIGADE.
Brigadier-General M. P. Lowrey.

Sixteenth Alabama—Lieutenant-Colonel F. A. Ashford.
Thirty-third Alabama—Colonel Sam. Adams.
Forty-fifth Alabama—Colonel H. D. Lampley.
Thirty-second Mississippi—Colonel W. H. H. Tison.
Forty-fifth Mississippi—Colonel A. B. Hardcastle.

GOVAN'S BRIGADE.
Brigadier-General D. C. Govan.

Second and Twenty-fourth Arkansas—Colonel E. Warfield.
Fifth and Thirteenth Arkansas—Colonel J. E. Murray.
Sixth and Seventh Arkansas—Colonel S. G. Smith.
Eighth and Nineteenth Arkansas—Colonel G. F. Baucum.
Third Confederate—Captain M. H. Dixon.

* Formerly of Walker's Division. Transfer reported on return for February 20th.
† Formerly of Stewart's Division. Transfer reported on return for February 20th.
‡ Formerly of Hindman's Division. Transfer reported on return for February 20th.
§ Detached and ordered to report to Colonel Hill, Provost-Marshal General.

GRANBURY'S BRIGADE.*
Brigadier-General H. B. Granbury.

Sixth and Fifteenth Texas—Captain R. Fisher.
Seventh Texas—Captain J. H. Collett.
Tenth Texas—Colonel R. Q. Mills.
Seventeenth and Eighteenth Texas (dismounted cavalry)—Captain G. D. Manion.
Twenty-fourth and Twenty-fifth Texas (dismounted cavalry)—Colonel F. C. Wilkes.

ESCORT.

Tennessee Cavalry (Buckner Guards)—Captain C. F. Sanders.

WALKER'S DIVISION.
Major-General W. H. T. Walker.

JACKSON'S BRIGADE.†
Brigadier-General John K. Jackson.

First Georgia (Confederate)—Colonel G. A. Smith.
Fifth Georgia—Colonel C. P. Daniel.
Forty-seventh Georgia—Colonel A. C. Edwards.
Sixty-fifth Georgia—Captain W. G. Foster.
Fifth Mississippi—Colonel John Weir.
Eighth Mississippi—Colonel J. C. Wilkinson.
Second Georgia Battalion Sharpshooters—Major R. H. Whiteley.

GIST'S BRIGADE.
Brigadier-General S. R. Gist.

Eighth Georgia Battalion—Lieutenant-Colonel Z. L. Watters.
Forty-sixth Georgia—Major S. J. C. Dunlop.
Sixteenth South Carolina—Colonel James McCullough.
Twenty-fourth South Carolina—Colonel E. Capers.

STEVENS' BRIGADE.‡
Brigadier-General C. H. Stevens.

Twenty-fifth Georgia—Colonel W. J. Winn.
Twenty-ninth Georgia—Lieutenant-Colonel W. D. Mitchell.
Thirtieth Georgia—Major H. Hendricks.
Sixty-sixth Georgia—Colonel J. C. Nisbet.
First Georgia Battalion Sharpshooters—Major A. Shaaf.
Twenty-sixth Georgia Battalion—Major J. W. Nisbet.

ESCORT.

Fifty-third Alabama Volunteers, Company G (Partisan Rangers)—Captain P. B. Mastin, Jr.

BATE'S DIVISION.
Major-General William B. Bate.

LEWIS' BRIGADE.§

Second Kentucky—Colonel J. W. Moss.
Fourth Kentucky—Lieutenant-Colonel T. W. Thompson.
Fifth Kentucky—Lieutenant-Colonel H. Hawkins.
Sixth Kentucky—Major G. W. Maxson.
Ninth Kentucky—Colonel J. W. Caldwell.

MAJ.-GEN. WILLIAM B. BATE, OF TENNESSEE.

BATE'S (TYLER'S) BRIGADE.

Thirty-seventh Georgia—Lieutenant-Colonel J. T. Smith.
Tenth Tennessee—Major J. O'Neill.
Fifteenth and Thirty-seventh Tennessee—Major J. M. Wall.
Twentieth Tennessee—Lieutenant-Colonel W. M. Shy.
Thirtieth Tennessee—Lieutenant-Colonel J. J. Turner.
Fourth Georgia Battalion Sharpshooters—Captain W. M. Carter.

* Formerly Smith's.
† Formerly of Cheatham's Division. Transfer reported on return for February 20th.
‡ Formerly Wilson's Brigade.
§ Formerly Breckinridge's Division. Reported on return for February 20th as transferred from Hood's Corps. Actual brigade commander not indicated on original return.

FINLEY'S BRIGADE.*

First and Third Florida—Major G. A. Ball.
First and Fourth Florida—Lieutenant-Colonel E. Badger.
Sixth Florida—Colonel A. D. McLean.
Seventh Florida—Lieutenant-Colonel T. Ingram.

ESCORT.

Mississippi Cavalry—Captain H. L. Foules.

HOOD'S CORPS.†

Lieutenant-General John B. Hood, commanding.

HINDMAN'S DIVISION.

Major-General T. C. Hindman.

DEAS' BRIGADE.

Brigadier-General Z. C. Deas.

Nineteenth Alabama—Colonel S. K. McSpadden.
Twenty-second Alabama—Colonel B. R. Hart.
Twenty-fifth Alabama—Colonel G. D. Johnston.
Thirty-ninth Alabama—Lieutenant-Colonel W. C. Clifton.
Fiftieth Alabama—Colonel J. G. Coltart.
Seventeenth Alabama Battalion Sharpshooters—Captain J. F. Nabers.

MANIGAULT'S BRIGADE.

Brigadier-General A. M. Manigault.

Twenty-fourth Alabama—Colonel N. N. Davis.
Twenty-eighth Alabama—Lieutenant-Colonel W. L. Butler.
Thirty-fourth Alabama—Colonel J. C. B. Mitchell.
Tenth South Carolina—Colonel J. F. Pressley.
Nineteenth South Carolina—Lieutenant-Colonel T. P. Shaw.

TUCKER'S BRIGADE.‡

Brigadier-General W. F. Tucker.

Seventh Mississippi—Lieutenant-Colonel B. F. Johns.
Ninth Mississippi—Captain S. S. Calhoun.
Tenth Mississippi—Captain R. A. Bell.
Forty-first Mississippi—Colonel Byrd Williams.
Forty-fourth Mississippi—Lieutenant-Colonel R. G. Kelsey.
Ninth Mississippi Battalion Sharpshooters—Major W. C. Richards.

WALTHALL'S BRIGADE.§

Brigadier-General E. C. Walthall.

Twenty-fourth and Twenty-seventh Mississippi—Colonel Samuel Benton.
Twenty-eighth, Thirtieth and Thirty-fourth Mississippi—Colonel W. F. Brantly.

ESCORT.

Independent Company Alabama Cavalry—Captain T. M. Lenoir.

MAJ.-GEN. WM. H. T. WALKER, OF GEORGIA.
Killed near Atlanta, Ga., July 22, 1864.

STEVENSON'S DIVISION.*||

Major-General C. L. Stevenson.

BROWN'S BRIGADE.

Brigadier-General John C. Brown.

Third Tennessee—Lieutenant-Colonel C. J. Clack.
Eighteenth Tennessee—Lieutenant-Colonel W. R. Butler.
Twenty-sixth Tennessee—Captain A. F. Boggess.
Thirty-second Tennessee—Major J. P. McGuire.
Forty-fifth Tennessee and Twenty-third Battalion—Colonel A. Searcy.

CUMMING'S BRIGADE.

Brigadier-General Alfred Cumming.

Thirty-fourth Georgia—Major J. M. Jackson.
Thirty-sixth Georgia—Major C. E. Broyles.
Thirty-ninth Georgia—Lieutenant-Colonel J. F. B. Jackson.
Fifty-sixth Georgia—Colonel E. P. Watkins.

REYNOLDS' BRIGADE.

Brigadier-General A. W. Reynolds.

Fifty-eighth North Carolina—Major T. J. Dula.
Sixtieth North Carolina—Lieutenant-Colonel J. T. Weaver.
Fifty-fourth Virginia—Colonel R. C. Trigg.
Sixty-third Virginia—Captain C. H. Lynch.

PETTUS' BRIGADE.

Brigadier-General E. W. Pettus.

Twentieth Alabama—Colonel J. N. Dedman.
Twenty-third Alabama—Lieutenant-Colonel J. B. Bibb.
Thirtieth Alabama—Colonel C. M. Shelley.
Thirty-first Alabama—Colonel D. R. Hundley.
Forty-sixth Alabama—Captain George E. Brewer.

STEWART'S DIVISION.

Major-General Alexander P. Stewart.

STOVALL'S BRIGADE.

Brigadier-General M. A. Stovall.

Fortieth Georgia—Colonel A. Johnson.
Forty-first Georgia—Major M. S. Nall.
Forty-second Georgia—Colonel R. J. Henderson.
Forty-third Georgia—Major W. C. Lester.
Fifty-second Georgia—Captain R. R. Asbury.

CLAYTON'S BRIGADE.

Brigadier-General H. D. Clayton.

Eighteenth Alabama—Colonel J. T. Holtzclaw.
Thirty-second and Fifty-eighth Alabama—Colonel Bushrod Jones.
Thirty-sixth Alabama—Lieutenant-Colonel T. H. Herndon.
Thirty-eighth Alabama—Colonel A. R. Lankford.

GIBSON'S BRIGADE.*

Brigadier-General R. L. Gibson.

First Louisiana—Major S. S. Batchelor.
Thirteenth Louisiana—Lieutenant-Colonel F. L. Campbell.
Sixteenth and Twenty-fifth Louisiana—Colonel J. C. Lewis.
Nineteenth Louisiana—Lieutenant-Colonel H. A. Kennedy.
Twentieth Louisiana—Major S. L. Bishop.
Fourth Louisiana Battalion—Major D. Buie.
Fourteenth Louisiana Battalion Sharpshooters—Major J. E. Austin.

BAKER'S BRIGADE.†

Brigadier-General A. Baker.

Thirty-seventh Alabama—Lieutenant-Colonel A. A. Greene.
Fortieth Alabama—Captain E. D. Willett.
Forty-second Alabama—Lieutenant-Colonel T. C. Lanier.

ESCORT.

Tenth Confederate Cavalry, Company A—Captain J. M. McKleroy.

CAVALRY CORPS.‡

Major-General Joseph Wheeler, commanding.

MARTIN'S DIVISION.

Major-General W. T. Martin.

MORGAN'S BRIGADE.

Brigadier-General John T. Morgan.

First Alabama—Major A. H. Johnson.
Third Alabama—Colonel T. H. Mauldin.
Fourth Alabama—Colonel A. A. Russell.
Seventh Alabama—Colonel James C. Malone.
Fifty-first Alabama—Lieutenant-Colonel M. L. Kirkpatrick.

IVERSON'S BRIGADE.

Brigadier-General A. Iverson.

First and Second Georgia—Colonel C. C. Crews.
Third Georgia—Colonel R. Thompson.
Fourth Georgia—Colonel I. W. Avery.
Sixth Georgia—Colonel John R. Hart.

KELLY'S DIVISION.

Brigadier-General J. H. Kelly.

ALLEN'S BRIGADE.

Brigadier-General W. W. Allen.

Third Confederate—Colonel P. H. Rice.
Eighth Confederate—Lieutenant-Colonel J. S. Prather.
Tenth Confederate—Captain T. G. Holt.
Twelfth Confederate—Captain C. H. Conner.

DIBRELL'S BRIGADE.*

Colonel George G. Dibrell.

Fourth Tennessee—Colonel W. S. McLemore.
Eighth Tennessee—Captain J. Leftwich.
Ninth Tennessee—Colonel J. B. Biffle.
Tenth Tennessee—Colonel W. E. De Moss.
Eleventh Tennessee—Colonel D. W. Holman.

MAJ.-GEN. W. Y. C. HUMES, OF TENNESSEE.
[From a tintype taken in 1863.

HUMES' DIVISION.

Brigadier-General W. Y. C. Humes.

HUMES' BRIGADE.

Colonel J. T. Wheeler.

First Tennessee—Major J. J. Dobbins.
Second Tennessee—Captain J. H. Kuhn.
Fourth Tennessee—Lieutenant-Colonel P. F. Anderson.
Fifth Tennessee—Colonel G. W. McKenzie.
Ninth Tennessee—Major J. H. Akin.

HARRISON'S BRIGADE.*

Colonel Thomas Harrison.

Third Arkansas—Colonel A. W. Hobson.
Eighth Texas—Lieutenant-Colonel G. Cook.
Eleventh Texas—Colonel G. R. Reeves.

GRIGSBY'S BRIGADE.

Colonel J. Warren Grigsby.

First Kentucky—Colonel J. R. Butler.
Second Kentucky—Major T. W. Lewis.
Ninth Kentucky—Lieutenant-Colonel R. G. Stoner.
Allison's Squadron—Captain J. H. Allison.
Dortch's Battalion—Captain J. B. Dortch.
Hamilton's Battalion—Major O. P. Shaw.

HANNON'S BRIGADE.

Colonel M. W. Hannon.

Fifty-third Alabama—Lieutenant-Colonel J. F. Gaines.
Twenty-fourth Alabama Battalion—Major R. B. Snodgrass.

ARTILLERY.

Brigadier-General F. A. Shoup, Chief of Artillery.

HARDEE'S CORPS.†

Colonel Melancthon Smith, Chief.

HOXTON'S BATTALION.

Alabama Battery—Captain John Phelan.
Marion (Fla.) Light Artillery—Lieutenant Thomas J. Perry.
Mississippi Battery—Captain William B. Turner.

HOTCHKISS' BATTALION.

Arkansas Battery—Captain T. J. Key.
Semple's (Ala.) battery—Lieutenant R. W. Goldthwaite.
Warren (Miss.) Light Artillery—Lieutenant H. Shannon.

MARTIN'S BATTALION.

Bledsoe's (Mo.) battery—Lieutenant C. W. Higgins.
Ferguson's (S. C.) battery—Lieutenant R. T. Beauregard.
Howell's (Ga.) battery—Lieutenant W. G. Robson.

COBB'S BATTALION.‡

Cobb's (Ky.) battery—Lieutenant R. B. Matthews.
Johnston (Tenn.) Artillery—Captain J. W. Mebane.
Washington (La.) Light Artillery (Fifth company)—Lieutenant W. C. D. Vaught.

* Formerly Breckinridge's Division. Reported on return for February 20th as transferred from Hood's Corps. Actual brigade commander not indicated on original return.
† Escort not reported.
‡ Formerly Anderson's.
§ Formerly of Cheatham's Division. Transfer reported on return for February 20th
|| Transfer from Hardee's Corps reported on return for February 20th.

* Formerly Adams' Brigade.
† Formerly Moore's. Transfer from Cheatham's Division reported on return for February 20th.
‡ Roddey's Brigade transferred to Department of Alabama, Mississippi and East Louisiana.

* Joined from Department of East Tennessee.
† Actual commanders are not indicated on original return.
‡ Transfer from Hood's Corps reported on return for April 10th.

HOOD'S CORPS.*

Colonel Robert F. Beckham, Chief.

COURTNEY'S BATTALION.

Alabama Battery—Captain James Garrity.
Confederate Battery—Captain S. H. Dent.
Douglas' (Tex.) battery—Lieutenant J. H. Bingham.

ELDRIDGE'S BATTALION.

Eufaula (Ala.) Artillery—Captain McD. Oliver.
Louisiana Battery—Captain Charles E. Fenner.
Mississippi Battery—Captain T. J. Stanford.

JOHNSTON'S BATTALION.†

Cherokee (Ga.) Artillery—Captain Max. Van D. Corput.
Stephens (Ga.) Light Artillery ‡—Captain J. B. Rowan.
Tennessee Battery—Captain L. G. Marshall.

CAVALRY CORPS.

Lieutenant-Colonel Felix H. Robertson, Chief.

FERRELL'S (GEORGIA) BATTERY. §

Huwald's (Tenn.) battery—Lieutenant D. B. Ramsey.
Tennessee Battery—Captain B. F. White.
Wiggins' (Ark.) battery—Lieutenant J. P. Bryant.

ARTILLERY RESERVE.

Lieutenant-Colonel James H. Hallonquist.

PALMER'S BATTALION.

Alabama Battery—Captain C. L. Lumsden.
Georgia Battery—Captain R. W. Anderson.
Georgia Battery—Captain M. W. Havis.

WADDELL'S BATTALION.

Alabama Battery—Captain W. D. Emery.
Bellamy's (Ala.) battery—Lieutenant F. A. O'Neal.
Missouri Battery—Captain O. W. Barret.

WILLIAMS' BATTALION.

Barbour (Ala.) Artillery—Captain R. F. Kolb.
Jefferson (Miss.) Artillery—Captain Put. Darden.
Nottoway (Va.) Artillery—Captain Wm. C. Jeffress.

DETACHMENTS.

CANTEY'S BRIGADE.‖

Brigadier-General James Cantey.

Seventeenth Alabama—Colonel V. S. Murphey.
Twenty-ninth Alabama—Colonel J. F. Conoley.
Thirty-seventh Mississippi.
Battalion Sharpshooters—Major J. S. Moreland.

ENGINEER TROOPS (THIRD REGIMENT).

Major S. W. Presstman.

Company A—Captain R. C. McCalla.
Company B—Captain H. N. Pharr, Cheatham's Division.
Company C—Captain W. Gloster, Stewart's Division.
Company D—Captain E. Winston.
Company F—Captain W. A. Ramsey, Cleburne's Division.
Company G—Lieutenant R. L. Cobb, Hindman's Division.
Sappers and Miners—Captain A. W. Clarkson.

* Actual commanders are not indicated on original return.
† Transfer from Hardee's Corps reported on return for April 10th.
‡ Prior to November, 1863, known as Third Maryland Battery.
§ Only one section present. Remainder transferred, with Roddey's brigade, to Department of Alabama, Mississippi and East Louisiana.
‖ Joined from Department of the Gulf and encamped at Rome, Ga.

LAND OF THE SOUTH.

BY A. F. LEONARD.

Air—"Friend of My Soul."

Land of the South! the fairest land
Beneath Columbia's sky!
Proudly her hills of freedom stand,
Her plains in beauty lie.
Her dotted fields, her traversed streams
Their annual wealth renew;
Land of the South! in brightest dreams
No dearer spot we view.

* * * * * * *

Flag of the South! Ay, fling its folds
Upon the kindred breeze;
Emblem of dread to tyrant holds—
Of freedom on the seas,
Forever may its stars and stripes
In cloudless glory wave;
Red, white and blue—eternal types
Of nations free and brave!

States of the South! the patriot's boast!
Here equal laws have sway;
Nor tyrant lord, nor despot host,
Upon the weak may prey.
Then let them rule from sea to sea,
And crown the queenly isle—
Union of love and liberty,
'Neath Heaven's approving smile.

THE ATLANTA CAMPAIGN.

OPERATIONS

JULY 18, 1864, TO JANUARY 23, 1865,

INCLUDING BATTLES OF

PEACH TREE CREEK, ATLANTA, EZRA CHAPEL, UTOY CREEK, JONESBORO, LOVEJOY STATION, ETC.,

BY

GENERAL JOHN B. HOOD,
Commanding Army of Tennessee.

RICHMOND, VA., February 15, 1865.

I HAVE the honor to submit the following report of the operations of the Army of the Tennessee while commanded by me, from July 18, 1864, to January 23, 1865:

The results of a campaign do not always show how the general in command has discharged his duty. The inquiry should be, not what he has done, but what he should have

accomplished with the means under his control. To appreciate the operations of the Army of Tennessee it is necessary to look at its history during the three months which preceded the day on which I was ordered to its command. To do this it is necessary either to state in this report all the facts which illustrate the entire operations of the Army of Tennessee in the recent campaign, or to write a supplemental or accompanying report. I deem the former more appropriate, and will, therefore, submit in a single paper all the information which seems to me should be communicated to the government.

On the 6th of May, 1864, the army lay at and near Dalton, awaiting the advance of the enemy. Never had so large a Confederate army assembled in the West. Seventy thousand effective men were in the easy direction of a single commander, whose good fortune it was to be able to give successful battle and redeem the losses of the past. Extraordinary efforts had been used to secure easy victory. The South had been denuded of troops to fill the strength of the Army of Tennessee. Mississippi and Alabama were without military support and looked for protection in decisive battle in the mountains of Georgia. The vast forces of the enemy were accumulating in the East, and to retard their advance or confuse their plans, much was

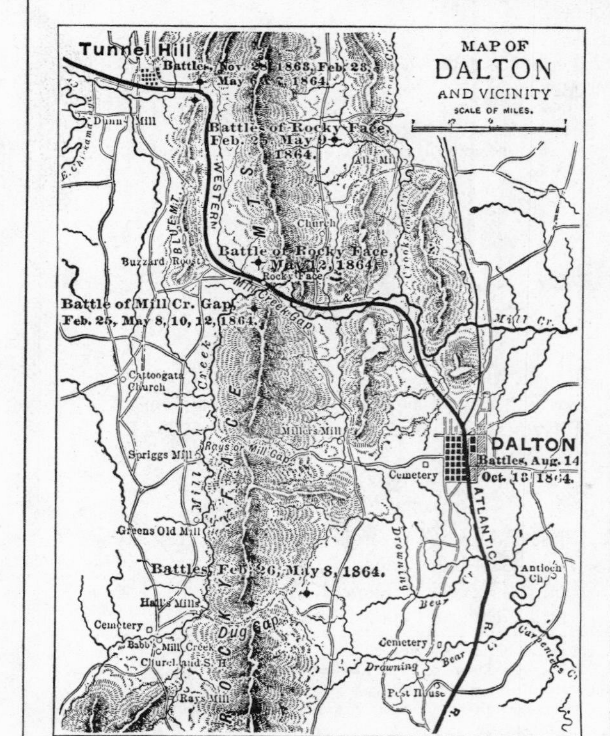

expected by a counter-movement by us in the West. The desires of the government expressed to the Confederate commander in the West were to assume the offensive. Nearly all the men and resources of the West and South were placed at his disposal for the purpose. The men amounted to the number already stated and the resources for their support were equal to the demand. The re-enforcements were within supporting distance. The troops felt strong in their increased numbers, saw the means and arrangements to move forward and recover (not abandon) our own territory, and believed that victory might be achieved. In such condition was that splendid army when the active campaign fairly opened. The enemy—but little superior in numbers, none in organization and discipline, inferior in spirit and confidence—commenced his advance. The Confederate forces, whose faces and hopes were to the North, almost simultaneously commenced to retreat. They soon reached positions favorable for resistance. Great ranges of mountains running across the line of march and deep rivers are stands from which a well-directed army is not easily driven or turned. At each advance of the enemy, the Confederate army, without serious resistance, fell back to the next range or river in the rear. This habit to retreat soon became a routine of the army and was substituted for the hope and confidence with which the campaign opened. The enemy soon perceived this. With perfect security he divided his forces, using one column to menace in front and one to threaten in rear. The usual order to retreat, not strike in detail, was issued and obeyed. These retreats were always at night; the day was consumed in hard labor. Daily temporary works were thrown up, behind which it was never intended to fight. The men became travelers by night and laborers by day. They were ceasing to be soldiers by the disuse of military duty. Thus for seventy-four days and nights that noble army—if ordered to resist, no force that the enemy could assemble could dislodge from a battle-field—continued to abandon their country, to see their strength departing and their flag waving only in retreat or in partial engagements. At the end of that time, after descending from the mountains when the last advantage of position was abandoned, and camping without fortifications on the open plains of Georgia, the army had lost twenty-two thousand seven hundred and fifty of its best soldiers. Nearly one-third was gone, no general battle fought, much of our State abandoned, two others uncovered, and the organization and efficiency of every command, by loss of officers, men and time, seriously diminished. These things were the inevitable result of the strategy adopted. It is impossible for a large army to retreat in the face of a pursuing enemy without such a fate. In a retreat the losses are constant and permanent. Stragglers are overtaken, the fatigued fall by the wayside and are gathered by the advancing enemy. Every position by the rear guard, if taken, yields its wounded to the victors. The soldiers, always awaked from rest at night to continue the retreat, leave many of their comrades asleep in trenches. The losses of a single day are not large. Those of seventy-four days will embrace the strength of an army. If a battle be fought and the field held at the close, however great the slaughter, the loss will be less than to retreat in the face of an enemy. There will be no stragglers. Desertions are in retreat; rarely, if ever, on the field of battle. The wounded are gathered to the rear and soon recover, and in a few weeks the entire loss consists only of the killed and permanently disabled, which is not one-fifth of the apparent loss on the night of the battle. The enemy is checked, his plans deranged, territory saved, the campaign suspended or won. If a retreat still be necessary, it can then be done with no enemy pressing and no loss following. The advancing party loses nothing but its killed and permanently disabled. Neither straggler nor deserter thins its ranks. It reaches the end of its march stronger for battle than when it started. The army commanded by General Sherman and that commanded by General Johnston, not greatly unequal at the commencement of the campaign, illustrate what I have written. General Sherman, in his official report, states that his forces, when they entered Atlanta, were nearly the same in number as when they left Dalton. The Army of Tennessee lost twenty-two thousand seven hundred and fifty men, nearly one-third of its strength. I have nothing to say of the statement of losses made by General Johnston in his official report, except to state that by his own figures he understates his loss some thousands; that he excludes the idea of any prisoners, although his previous official returns show more than seven thousand under the head "absent without leave," and that the returns of the army while he was in command, corrected and increased by the records of the army, which has not been fully reported to the government, and the return signed by me, but made up under him as soon as I assumed command, show the losses of the Army of Tennessee to be what I have stated, and a careful examination of the returns with the army will show the losses to be more than stated.

This statement of the previous conduct of the campaign is necessary so as to show what means I had to

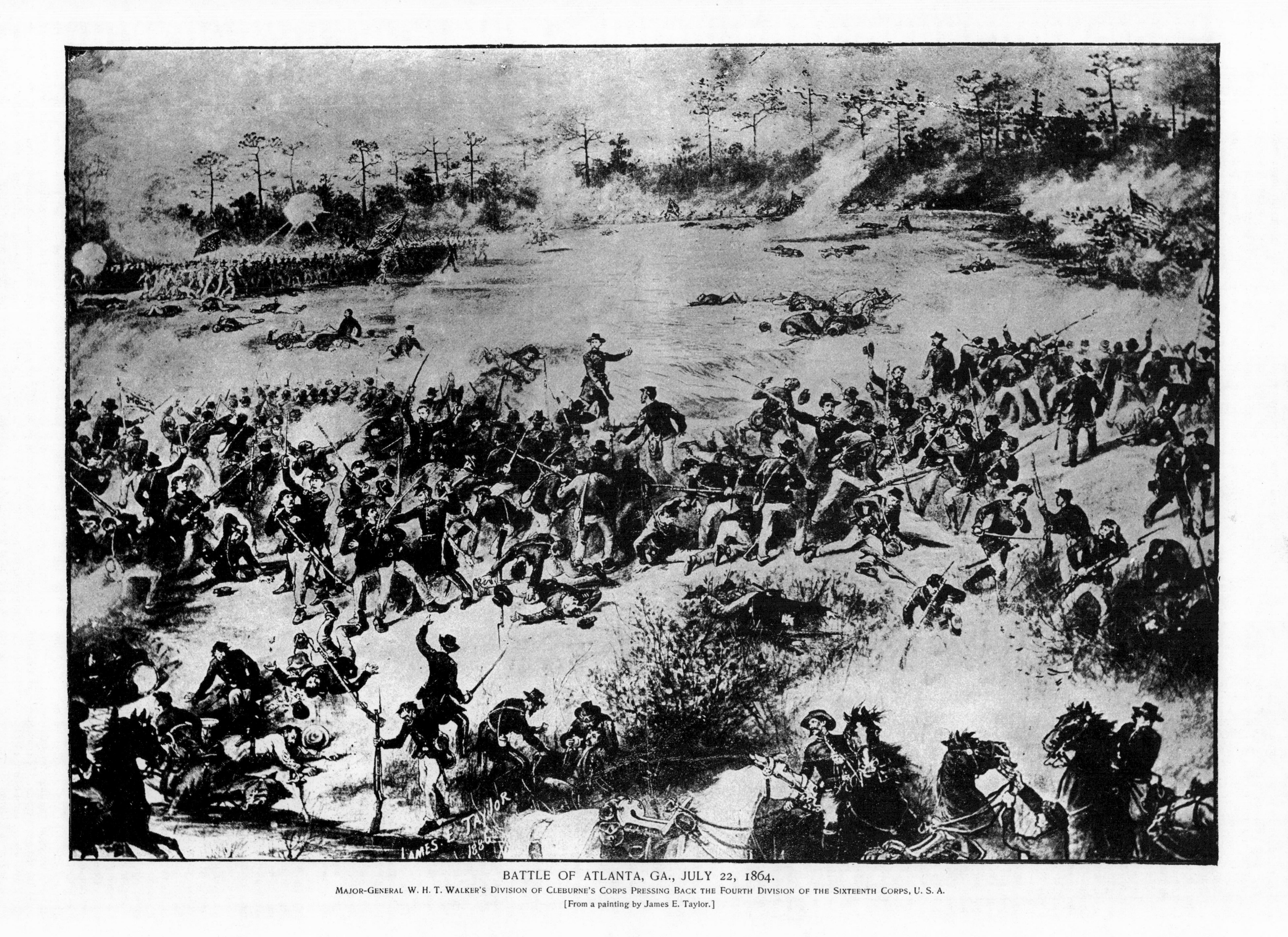

BATTLE OF ATLANTA, GA., JULY 22, 1864.

MAJOR-GENERAL W. H. T. WALKER'S DIVISION OF CLEBURNE'S CORPS PRESSING BACK THE FOURTH DIVISION OF THE SIXTEENTH CORPS, U. S. A.

[From a painting by James E. Taylor.]

retrieve the disasters of the past, and if the results are not such as to bring joy to the country, it is not the first time that the most faithful efforts of duty were unable to repair the injury done by others. If, as is untruly charged, the Army of Tennessee ceased to exist under my command, it is also true that it received its mortal wound when it turned its back in retreat in the mountains of Georgia, and under different management it lingered much longer than it would have done with the same daily loss occurring when it was placed under my direction.

The army was turned over to me, by order of the President, at Atlanta, on the 18th of July, 1864. Its effective strength was: Infantry, 33,750; artillery, 3,500; cavalry, 10,000, with 1,500 Georgia militia, commanded by Major-General G. W. Smith, making a total effective of 48,750. The enemy was in bivouac south of the Chattahoochee River, between Atlanta and that river, and was advancing, the right near Paces Ferry and the left near Roswell. On the evening of the 18th, our cavalry was principally driven across Peach Tree Creek. I caused line of battle to be formed, the left resting near the Paces Ferry Road and the right covering Atlanta.

On the morning of the 19th, the dispositions of the enemy were substantially as follows: The Army of the Cumberland, under Thomas, was in the act of crossing Peach Tree Creek. This creek, forming a considerable obstacle to the passage of an army, runs in a northwesterly direction, emptying into the Chattahoochee River near the railroad crossing. The Army of the Ohio, under Schofield, was also about to cross east of the Buck Head Road. The Army of the Tennessee, under McPherson, was moving on the Georgia Railroad at Decatur. Feeling it impossible to hold Atlanta without giving battle, I determined to strike the enemy while attempting to cross this stream. My troops were disposed as follows: Stewart's corps on the left; Hardee's in the center, and Cheatham's on the right, intrenched. My object was to crush Thomas' army before he could fortify himself, and then turn upon Schofield and McPherson. To do this Cheatham was ordered to hold his left on the creek, in order to separate Thomas' army from the forces on his (Thomas') left. Thus I should be able to throw two corps (Stewart's and Hardee's) against Thomas. Specific orders were carefully given these generals, in the presence of each other, as follows: The attack was to begin at 1 P. M., the movement to be by division in echelon from the right, at the distance of about one hundred and fifty yards, the effort to be to drive the enemy back to the creek, and then toward the river into the narrow space formed by the river and creek, everything on our side of the creek to be taken at all hazards, and to follow up as our success might permit. Each of these generals was to hold a division in reserve. Owing to the demonstrations of the enemy on the right, it became necessary to extend Cheatham a division front to the right. To do this, Hardee and Stewart were each ordered to extend a half division front to close the interval. Foreseeing that some confusion and delay might result, I was careful to call General Hardee's attention to the importance of having a staff officer on his left to see that the left did not take more than half a division front. This, unfortunately, was not attended to, and the line closed to the right, causing Stewart to move two or three times the proper distance. In consequence of this, the attack was delayed until nearly 4 P. M. At this hour the attack began as ordered, Stewart's corps carrying the temporary works in his front. Hardee failed to push the attack, as ordered, and thus the enemy, remaining in possession of his works on Stewart's right, compelled Stewart by an enfilade fire to abandon the position he had carried. I have every reason to believe that our attack would have been successful had my order been executed. I am strengthened in this opinion by information since obtained through Brigadier-General Govan, some time a prisoner in the enemy's hands, touching the condition of the enemy at the time. The delay from 1 to 4 P. M. was unfortunate, but would not have proved irretrievable had the attack been vigorously made. Ascertaining that the attack had failed, I caused the troops to retire to their former positions.

The position and demonstration of McPherson's army on the right threatening my communications made it necessary to abandon Atlanta or check his movements. Unwilling to abandon, the following instructions were given on the morning of the 21st: The chief engineer was instructed to select a line of defense immediately about Atlanta, the works already constructed for the defense of the place being wholly useless from their position; Stewart's and Cheatham's corps to take position and construct works to defend the city, the former on the left, the latter on the right. The artillery, under the command of Brigadier-General Shoup, was massed on the extreme right. Hardee was ordered to move with his corps during the night of the 21st south on the McDonough Road, crossing Intrenchment Creek at Cobbs Mills, and to completely turn the left of McPherson's army. This he was to do, even should it be necessary to go to or beyond Decatur. Wheeler, with his cavalry, was ordered to move on Hardee's right, both to attack at daylight or as soon thereafter as possible. As soon as Hardee succeeded in forcing back the enemy's left, Cheatham was to take up the movement from his right and continue to force the whole from right to left down Peach Tree Creek; Stewart, in like manner to engage the enemy as soon as the movement became general. Hardee failed to entirely turn the enemy's left as directed, took position and attacked his flank. His troops fought with great spirit and determination, carrying several lines of intrenchments, Wheeler attacking on the right. Finding Hardee so hotly engaged, and fearing the enemy might concentrate upon him, I ordered Cheatham forward to create a diversion. Hardee held the ground he gained. Cheatham carried the enemy's intrenchments in his front, but had to abandon them in consequence of the enfilade fire brought to bear upon him. Cheatham captured five guns and five or six stand of colors, and Hardee eight guns and thirteen stand of colors. While the grand results desired were not accomplished, the movements of McPherson upon my communications were entirely defeated, and no further effort was made in that direction at any time. This engagement greatly inspired the troops and revived their confidence. Here, I regret to say, the brave and gallant Major-General W. H. T. Walker was killed. The enemy withdrew his left to the Georgia Railroad and strongly intrenched himself, and here properly began the siege of Atlanta. It became apparent almost immediately that he would attempt our left. He began to mass his forces in that quarter.

On the 28th, it became manifest that the enemy desired to place his left [right] on Utoy Creek. I desired to hold the Lick Skillet Road, and accordingly ordered Lieutenant-General Lee—who on the 25th [26th?] had relieved Major-General Cheatham from the command of the corps formerly commanded by myself—to move his forces so as to prevent the enemy from gaining that road. He was ordered to hold the enemy in check on a line nearly parallel with the Lick Skillet Road, running through to Ezra Church. General Lee, finding that the enemy had already gained that position, engaged him with the intention to recover that line. This brought on the engagement of the 28th. General Stewart was ordered to support General Lee. The engagement continued until dark, the road remaining in our possession.

On the 27th of July I received information that the enemy's cavalry was moving round our right with the design of interrupting our communication with Macon. The next day a large cavalry force also crossed the Chattahoochee River at Campbellton, moving round our left. Major-General Wheeler was ordered to move upon the force on the right, while Brigadier-General Jackson, with Harrison's and Ross' brigades, was sent to look after those moving on the left. I also dispatched Lewis' brigade of infantry down the Macon Railroad to a point about where they would probably strike the road. The force on the left succeeded in reaching the road, tearing up an inconsiderable part of the track. It was the design of the enemy to unite his forces at the railroad, but in this he was defeated. The movement was undertaken by the enemy on a grand scale, having carefully picked his men and horses. A Federal force, under General Stoneman, moved further south against Macon. He was defeated by our forces under Brigadier-General Iverson. General Wheeler, leaving General Kelly to hold the force on the right, moved against that already at the railroad. He succeeded in forcing them to give battle near Newnan on the 30th, and routed and captured or destroyed the whole force. Too much credit can not be given General Wheeler for the energy and skill displayed. He captured two pieces of artillery, nine hundred and fifty prisoners and

GENERAL JOHN B. HOOD, OF TEXAS.

BORN IN OWINGSVILLE, BATH COUNTY, KY., JUNE 1, 1831. DIED IN NEW ORLEANS, LA., AUGUST 30, 1879.

many horses, equipments, etc. Brigadier-General Iverson captured two pieces of artillery and five hundred prisoners. Believing the enemy's cavalry well broken, and feeling myself safe from any further serious operations of a like nature, I determined to dispatch a force of cavalry to the enemy's rear, with the hope of destroying his communications. I accordingly ordered Major-General Wheeler, with forty-five hundred cavalry, to effect this object. He succeeded in partially interrupting the enemy's communications by railroad. This still left sufficient cavalry to meet the necessities of the army. This is sufficiently shown by the fact that several determined cavalry movements were subsequently attempted and successfully met by our cavalry. From this time till the 26th of August there is nothing of any particular moment to mention. The enemy gradually extended his right, and I was compelled to follow his movement; our entire front was covered with a most excellent abatis and other obstructions. Too much credit can not be given the troops generally for the industry and endurance they displayed under the constant fire of the enemy.

On the 26th of August the enemy abandoned his works on the extreme right and took up a line, the left resting in front of our works on the Dalton Railroad and extending to the railroad crossing the river. Again he withdrew, on the night of the 27th, across the Utoy Creek, throwing one corps across the river to hold the railroad crossing and the intermediate points. His left then rested on the Chattahoochee River, strongly fortified and extending across the West Point Railroad. The corps defending the crossing of the Chattahoochee, his works on this side of the river and the obstacle formed by the Utoy and Camp creeks, rendered it impossible for me to attack him with any possibility of success between the river and railroad.

On the 30th, it became known that the enemy was moving on Jonesboro with two corps. I determined, upon consulting with the corps commanders, to move two corps to Jonesboro during the night and to attack and drive the enemy at that place across Flint River. This I hoped would draw the attention of the enemy in that direction, and that he would abandon his works on the left so that I could attack him in flank. I remained in person with Stewart's corps and the militia in Atlanta. Hardee's and Lee's corps moved accordingly, Hardee in command. It was impressed upon General Hardee that the fate of Atlanta depended upon his success. Six hours before I had any information of the result of his attack I ordered Lee to return in the direction of Atlanta, to be ready to commence the movement indicated in the event of success, and if unsuccessful to cover the evacuation of Atlanta, which would thus be compelled. As it turned out unsuccessful it allowed the enemy the opportunity either to strike us as we marched out of Atlanta or to concentrate on Hardee. Lee's corps constituted a guard against the former, and I did not fear the destruction of Hardee before Stewart and Lee could join him, as his position on a ridge between two rivers I thought strong in front, and want of time would prevent the enemy from attacking him in flank. The small loss in Hardee's corps, and the much greater loss of the enemy, show my views to have been correct. The attack at Jonesboro failed, though the number of men on our side considerably exceeded that of the enemy. The vigor of the attack may be in some sort imagined when only fourteen hundred were killed and wounded out of the two corps engaged. The failure necessitated the evacuation of Atlanta.

Thirty-four thousand prisoners at Andersonville, Ga., in my rear, compelled me to place the army between them and the enemy, thus preventing me at that time from moving on his communications and destroying his depots of supplies at Marietta. A raid of cavalry could easily have released those prisoners, and the Federal commander was prepared to furnish them arms. Such a body of men, an army of itself, could have overrun and devastated the country from West Georgia to Savannah. The subsequent removal of the prisoners, at my request, enabled me to make the movement on the enemy's communications at a later period.

On the night of the 1st of September, we withdrew from Atlanta. A train of ordnance stores and some railroad stock had to be destroyed in consequence of the gross neglect of the chief quartermaster to obey the specific instructions given him touching their removal. He had ample time and means, and nothing whatever ought to have been lost.

On the 1st of September, Hardee's corps was attacked in position at Jonesboro. The result was the loss of eight guns and some prisoners. Hardee then retired to Lovejoys Station, where he was joined by Stewart's and Lee's corps. The militia, numbering about three thousand, under Major-General G. W. Smith, was ordered to Griffin. It is proper to remark here that this force rendered excellent and gallant service during the siege of Atlanta. The enemy followed and took position in our front.

n the 6th of September, however, he abandoned his works and returned to Atlanta. Here properly ended the operations about Atlanta. Of the forces turned over to me nearly two months before, and since that day daily engaged in battle and skirmishes with a greatly superior enemy, there were remaining effective, as shown by the return of the 20th of September, infantry, 27,094; cavalry, 10,543; artillery, 2,766. There had been sent to Mobile one brigade of infantry, 800 strong, and to Macon three battalions of artillery, 800 strong. The militia had increased, as stated, but counting it at the same as originally turned over, we have, against the aggregate turned over, 48,750—present, 40,403; sent off, 3,100, making an aggregate of 43,503, thus giving a total loss of all arms of 5,247 men.

My operations are now fully stated. It may not be improper to close with a general resume of the salient points presented. I was placed in command under the most trying circumstances which can surround an officer when assigned to a new and most important command. The army was enfeebled in number and in spirit by long retreat and by severe and apparently fruitless losses. The Army of Tennessee between the 13th and 20th of May, two months before, numbered seventy thousand effective arms-bearing men, as the official reports show. It was at that time in most excellent condition and in full hope. It had dwindled day by day in partial engagements and skirmishes, without an action that could properly be called a battle, to forty-seven thousand two hundred and fifty, exclusive of fifteen hundred militia, which joined in the interim. What with this constant digging and retreating from Dalton to Atlanta, the spirit of the army was greatly impaired and hope had almost left it. With this army I immediately engaged the enemy, and the tone constantly improved and hope returned. I defended Atlanta, a place without natural advantages (or rather with all the advantages in favor of the enemy) for forty-three days. No point, of all passed over from Dalton down, was less susceptible of defense by nature. Every preparation was made for retreat. The army lay in bivouac a short distance from the town, without attempting to construct works of defense in front of the camps, ready to resume the line of march as soon as the enemy pressed forward. I venture the statement that there was neither soldier nor officer in that army who believed that in the open plain between Atlanta and the river a battle would be offered, which had so often been refused in strong positions on the mountains. My first care was to make an intrenched line, and the enemy, despairing of success in front, threw his army to the left and rear, a thing that he never could have done had it not been for the immense advantage the Chattahoochee River gave him. I arrived at Lovejoys Station, having fought four battles, and the official reports of the army on the 20th of September show an effective total of forty thousand four hundred and three present, giving a total loss in all this time of five thousand two hundred and forty-seven men.

J. B. HOOD, *General.*

BATTLE OF ATLANTA, GA., JULY 22, 1864.
[From an original painting.]

SOME people cry "Peace, peace," while there is no peace. Let us cry "War, war," while there is war. — *Louisville Journal.* While you are crying "War, war," George, your old brandy-scorched stomach is crying "*war*-ter!"—*Rebel.*

THE ATLANTA CAMPAIGN.

CAVALRY ENGAGEMENTS,

MAY 6 TO 31 AND JULY 17 TO OCTOBER 9, 1864.

BY

MAJOR-GENERAL JOSEPH WHEELER,
Commanding Cavalry Corps.

HEADQUARTERS CAVALRY CORPS,
June 1, 1864.

I HAVE the honor to submit the following memoranda of fights in which the cavalry under my command has been engaged since May 6th to date:

My command, consisting of Grigsby's, Allen's and Humes' brigades, and one regiment and one battalion under Colonel Hannon, was picketing the front and flank of our army, extending from Ships Gap on our left, to the Connesauga River on our right. For several days previous to the 6th of May strong demonstrations were made by the enemy driving in our pickets with a force varying from a brigade to a division of infantry, with cavalry and artillery. Howard's corps had marched from Cleveland and taken position in line of battle three miles from my headquarters at Tunnel Hill. A portion of Palmer's corps had moved through Ringgold Gap and formed upon Howard's right. Schofield's (Twenty-third) corps was moving from East Tennessee by way of Cleveland and Varnells Station to join General Howard. The enemy being in line but six miles from the proposed line of battle of our infantry, I devoted myself to obstructing the roads and passes to prevent a rapid advance upon our line.

May 6th the enemy advanced in force near Tunnel Hill; resisted by our skirmish line, supported by two regiments.

May 7th, at daylight, the enemy commenced a determined advance in line of battle not less than one mile in length, with a heavy skirmish line in front; stubbornly resisted by dismounted cavalry fighting behind our obstructions and breastworks thrown across the roads at various points north of Tunnel Hill. On reaching said place my artillery was brought to bear upon their line, driving them back from several positions. At about 11 o'clock we were forced to abandon the town, and by 3 o'clock were driven back to our fortifications, where our infantry line of battle was formed. At dark I sent a regiment of Grigsby's brigade to re-enforce the picket at Dug Gap.

May 8th, the remainder of Grigsby's brigade was sent to Dug Gap, and with the rest of my command I moved to the Cleveland Road, where I was joined by General Kelly, who had marched from Resaca the previous day. McCook's cavalry division advanced from Varnells Station, but after slight skirmishing retired before the command could be brought into position. We captured several prisoners. Grigsby's brigade was attacked about 4 P. M. at Dug Gap by Geary's division, of Hooker's corps. The enemy made several assaults upon the brigade, which repulsed them with great slaughter, killing and wounding nearly as many of the enemy as the effective total of Grigsby's brigade. The relative numbers engaged were about ten to one.

May 9th, McCook's division again advanced, supported by infantry. Dibrell's brigade and part of Allen's brigade were dismounted to check the enemy. They attempted to turn our right, which movement was checked by my escort. At this moment the dismounted men of Allen's and Dibrell's brigades charged the enemy on foot, and the Eighth Confederate and Eighth Texas regiments charged mounted, completely routing the enemy and capturing one colonel (La Grange, commanding brigade), and one hundred prisoners. We also captured one regimental stand of colors and a large number of small arms. The enemy's loss in killed and wounded was very heavy. The enemy's force was five thousand cavalry, supported by infantry. Our force engaged was less than nine hundred.

May 10th and 11th, skirmishing along our line. Allen's brigade sent to Resaca.

May 12th, attacked Stoneman's corps near Varnells Station and drove it to Rocky Face Ridge, killing, wounding and capturing fully one hundred and fifty of the enemy. The consternation of the enemy was so great that they fired a large number of wagons in order to prevent their capture. It was afterward ascertained from scouts and citizens that they burned four hundred wagons and a considerable amount of commissary stores; also developed the fact that all but two divisions of the enemy had turned our left flank, moving toward Resaca. This made it necessary for our army to take position on the Oostanaula.

May 13th, before daylight, my command had relieved all the infantry skirmishers in our breastworks. At daylight the enemy advanced in force, and after several severe engagements we gradually fell back toward Tilton, arriving there at 3 P. M. Here I was re-enforced by Brown's brigade of infantry. A considerable force of the enemy held my front while a division of the enemy's infantry turned my left flank and this necessitated my forming the command in a right angle. The enemy attacked both positions with infantry and cavalry, but were repulsed and held in check until 9 P. M. The resistance the enemy experienced can be appreciated when we consider the fact that during fifteen hours they pressed forward but ten miles.

BATTLE OF RESACA.

May 14th, early in the morning, pursuant to the commanding general's instructions, I moved out with Kelly's division to develop the enemy. After a severe fight the command was driven back near our works. We here formed, engaging the enemy warmly until 3 P. M. We then crossed the Connesauga and returned before night to cover our right flank.

May 15th, we were ordered to Calhoun, which point we reached about 3 P. M. There was considerable skirmishing along our lines. In obedience to orders from the general commanding I moved with Humes' division and Allen's brigade to a point near Resaca on the south side of the Oostanaula. Stoneman's command attacked General Hardee's hospitals. We charged Stoneman, defeating him, retaking the hospitals, and pursued the enemy two miles, capturing forty prisoners and two stand of colors.

May 16th, at about 4 A. M., the enemy having learned that our army had retreated from Resaca, shelled the woods in which Allen's brigade was encamping, without any injury. At early dawn my skirmishers near the river engaged the enemy's skirmishers, who were crossing the river. I found on the Calhoun Road a full battery of five rifled guns, with caissons, which had been left by our army. I immediately ordered sixty men to be dismounted from Allen's brigade and sent for these guns. They moved to the skirmish line, brought them out, and carried them safely to the rear. Allen's brigade continued skirmishing with enemy's line, which had been very much strengthened from the opposite side of the river, and was supported by their artillery from the opposite heights until about 12 M., when I ordered it to retire to my main line, which had been formed one mile to the rear of that position.

LIEUT.-GEN. JOSEPH WHEELER, OF GEORGIA.
[From a photograph taken in 1865.]

May 17th, with Kelly's and Harrison's divisions and Williams' brigade, I resisted the enemy, who were advancing on the Calhoun Road. They advanced with cavalry, infantry and artillery upon us, when we opened upon him with small arms from behind our temporary rail breastworks and from two pieces of artillery, causing him to deploy his lines. Hearing that the enemy's cavalry was moving on the Tanyard Ford Road to gain my rear, I sent Williams' brigade on that road to re-enforce that portion of General Martin's division on that road. By forming lines and fighting the enemy at every favorable position we had forced the enemy to advance in line all day. At about 3 o'clock I was obliged to retire to the position occupied by our infantry two miles south of Adairsville. The enemy moved around my left flank on the west side of the creek, which runs near and west of the Adairsville and Calhoun Road. General Kelly's division was sent to oppose this force and to prevent the enemy gaining our rear. Cheatham's division of infantry being formed in front of Adairsville, I formed Martin's division and Williams' brigade, dismounted, between Cheatham's division and General Kelly's command, and on a line with the infantry, with skirmishers deployed in front. Considerable skirmishing was kept up until after dark, when I withdrew the main portion of my command to near the town to feed and rest the horses.

On May 18th, I formed my line about one mile in rear of the town. The enemy advanced slowly, skirmishing. I held them in check until they deployed their line, when, the purpose being accomplished, I retired to another position. Allen's brigade, of Kelly's division, had been sent to assist General Jackson's command, on the left of our army. My forces were then disposed as follows: General Iverson's brigade, of Martin's division, and Humes' division on the Cassville and Adairsville Road; Dibrell's brigade, of Kelly's division, on the Copper Mine Road; the Fifty-third Alabama Regiment and Twenty-fourth Alabama Battalion on the ——— Road, and General Williams' brigade on the Tennessee Road. The enemy's skirmishers advanced upon those of General Martin at about 3 P. M., but were driven back. At about 7:30 P. M. my entire line was withdrawn to go into camp, feed and rest, leaving a line of skirmishers in front in a commanding position.

May 19th, at daylight, my line was formed about a mile in front of the infantry line. The enemy advanced a heavy line of skirmishers from a woods toward the field in our front. We opened two pieces of artillery upon them and drove them back. Dispatches had been sent by me, between 2 and 3 o'clock, to General Allen, supposed to be on the Kingston Road, by three different couriers, all of whom returned, stating that they had run into the enemy's pickets on that road about one mile from Cassville. I immediately informed Major-General Hindman, whose line was near me, taking one of the couriers to him with me. I sent a staff officer to Major-General Martin, on the Adairsville Road, with instructions for him to fall back at once, and sent a staff officer, who knew the country, with instructions to General Kelly for him to retire by a by-road with his command to the town. These orders were promptly delivered and executed. As the rear of General Kelly's command was near the town the enemy's cavalry charged his line of skirmishers, but were stampeded by the fire from a second line of his command, and were charged in return by his escort. I retired my command at about nightfall to the rear of the infantry lines and took position to guard the right flank of the army. General Allen's brigade had been ordered from the Kingston Road by the orders of some one unknown to me and without my knowledge.

May 20th, Allen's brigade, of Kelly's division, was sent to assist General Jackson, and with the remainder of my command I guarded all the roads to the right of the railroad leading to Cartersville. The enemy made no demonstration except upon the left of my line, and were easily held in check. The rear of my column retired across the Etowah River at about 5 P. M. The bridge was then burned.

May 21st and 22d, rested in camp near the Alabama Road.

May 23d, pursuant to orders from the general commanding, I crossed the Etowah River. At night I moved with one hundred men to near Cartersville, to ascertain the strength, location and movements of the enemy.

May 24th, my command rested all day on the north bank of the river. At midnight, pursuant to instructions from commanding general, I started on a reconnoissance with a portion of my command to strike the enemy's rear, near Cassville, and ascertain the dispositions of the enemy. I sent the First Georgia Regiment, under command of Colonel Davitte, accompanied by Major Messick, to attack the enemy at Cass Station, in order to attract their attention. I moved on to Cassville with my command and discovered a wagon train near Cass Station. Just at this moment the following dispatch was handed me:

SMITH'S HOUSE, May 24, 1864, 7 A. M.

Major-General Wheeler:

GENERAL: We are forced to retire. We drove in the enemy's advance two miles and a half, capturing two horses and one prisoner, causing the enemy to beat the long roll. It is Kentucky cavalry which we are fighting. They have been driven back on a heavy reserve. The prisoner states that there are three thousand cavalry and fifteen thousand infantry in Cass Station. We will return on your rear, coming up the Tennessee Road. We are still skirmishing and will continue to do so as long as they pursue. The cavalry is commanded by Stoneman.

O. M. MESSICK,
Major Eleventh Texas.

P. S. There is a large supply train at Cass Station. A citizen reports a large force of infantry and cavalry as having moved down on yesterday to Cartersville.

Not knowing the force guarding the train, and as the statements of citizens rather corroborated the information of Major Messick, I felt that it would not do to risk my entire command. I attacked with Kelly's division, using one regiment to guard its right flank on the Kingston Road. General Humes' division was formed in line of battle in rear of the town to be prepared to re-enforce General Kelly, if needed, or to cover his retreat if compelled to retire. The attack by charging was a complete success, driving the enemy from his wagons and capturing about eighty wagons, which were safely brought out, and burning the remainder of their train. While bringing the wagons from Cass Station to Cassville, the enemy pressed heavily upon Allen's brigade, which was now very weak on account of the heavy details required to bring out led mules, horses and prisoners. I placed the Eighth Texas and Second Tennessee regiments in position to re-enforce him while we were burning a number of wagons which could not be brought off. The enemy in their fright burned a considerable train below Cass Station, and also similarly destroyed a quantity of commissary stores recently brought to that point for transportation. Observing the rapid advance of a large force of the enemy's cavalry, I ordered the Eighth Texas and Second Tennessee to meet them at a fast trot when they (the enemy) reached a certain designated point, and as soon as the enemy wavered, to charge. This order was magnificently obeyed. The enemy came up in fine style and charged with great ferocity. They were met, however, as directed, and driven back in utter confusion. We continued our charge, killing and wounding large numbers of the enemy and capturing over one hundred prisoners. I had previously detached a regiment to cut the railroad, and having, from prisoners, citizens and personal observation, learned all regarding the enemy, I withdrew quietly toward the river, crossing with my prisoners, wagons, mules, horses, etc.

The results of this expedition, in addition to attaining the object for which we were sent, were the bringing out of the enemy's lines about seventy wagons and teams, one hundred and eighty-two prisoners, three hundred horses and saddles and mules, a large amount of stores, the destruction of the remainder of a large wagon train and stores at Cass Station.

May 26th, we moved from Acworth to join the main army, and took our position on its right on the Acworth and Dallas Road.

May 27th, General Cleburne's division of infantry having been formed upon the right of our infantry line, I placed portions of Hannon's and Allen's small cavalry brigade, of Kelly's division, upon General Cleburne's right flank. They were dismounted and intrenchments thrown up extending on the prolongation of General Cleburne's line for a distance of about eight hundred yards. The enemy having during the morning and preceding day made several attacks upon the pickets on the Burnt Hickory Road, I had placed General Martin's command in position to oppose the enemy, who were menacing that point, leaving a space of about two miles between General Martin's left and General Kelly's right, which was filled by a line of skirmishers from General Humes' command, which command was held in reserve to move to any point which might be attacked. About 3 o'clock this line of skirmishers was driven in by a force of the enemy's cavalry advancing up Pumpkin Vine Creek by Widow Pickett's house. I immediately galloped to this point and found a squadron moving, by General Humes' direction, to re-enforce the picket. On arriving at the creek I soon observed that a considerable force of infantry was before us, and I directed General Humes to bring one brigade (dismounted) to that point and to prolong his other brigade upon its right to fill the gap between said position and General Martin's left. These dispositions were made under a warm fire from the enemy. At this moment I received information that General Martin's line was being attacked, and at the same time that Granbury's brigade of infantry was moving up to relieve General Kelly, whom I ordered to move to the right and close upon General Humes. While making the movement, and before it was completed, the enemy moved a column up a ravine between Kelly's right and Humes' left. I ordered a regiment from Humes to oppose them, which was promptly placed in position, but finding it was warmly pressed General Humes re-enforced it with another regiment from his command. While this movement was going on Hazen's Federal infantry brigade charged our line but was repulsed by a countercharge of Humes' and Kelly's commands.

My command captured thirty-two prisoners, including one commissioned officer, whom they turned over to Lowrey's infantry brigade, which was just forming to their right to relieve General Humes' command. On the arrival of General Lowrey's brigade General Humes moved to the right in front of the temporary breastworks thrown up during the engagement. Quarles' brigade also reported to me during the fight, but too late to join in the action.

I will here state that I had but eight hundred and twenty-two men engaged, extending over ground to such length as to enable me to form little more than a line of skirmishers.

The enemy we fought proved to be Woods' division of Howard's corps, General Howard having moved to that position to turn our right flank. We successfully thwarted this movement, holding this large force of the enemy in check until we were relieved by a division of our infantry, to whom we gave up our temporary breastworks, and then moved to the right to guard their right flank. But one infantry brigade (Granbury's) got into position before the defeat of the enemy. The difficulty of maneuvering so thin a line in a thick woods under a heavy fire will be appreciated

May 28th, 29th, 30th and 31st, there was skirmishing along our entire line. Besides the capture and destruction of property at Cass Station and Tunnel Hill, we captured during this time over five hundred prisoners and five stands of colors. The prisoners were turned over to the proper authorities. We also captured no less than five hundred animals and successfully engaged superior forces of both the enemy's infantry and cavalry, inflicting upon them heavy losses.

J. WHEELER,
Major General.

A REDOUBT IN FRONT OF ATLANTA, GA.
[From a photograph taken in 1864.]

HEADQUARTERS CAVALRY CORPS,
October 9, 1864.

I submit the following brief report of the operations of my command from the date General Hood assumed command of the Army of Tennessee (July 17th) to the present time. My command consisted of two divisions of cavalry, under Generals Kelly and Iverson, and one small brigade under General Williams, in all. General Kelly, with his entire command, had been detached to guard the Augusta Railroad, and General Williams had also been detached and was reporting direct to Major-General Cheatham. With the remainder of my command, numbering about sixteen hundred men, re-enforced by Ferguson's brigade, I was engaged during the 17th and 18th of July opposing the advance of General Thomas, and during the 19th and 20th of July in opposing the advance of General McPherson's entire army, consisting of three army corps. During this time we fought behind successive lines of breastworks, inflicting heavy losses upon the enemy, and repulsing several assaults of his skirmish lines, which were almost dense enough to make them lines of battle, and were always supported by strong lines of battle.

On the 19th and 20th I was so heavily pressed as to be obliged to call for re-enforcements, but none could be sent me. About 4 o'clock the enemy charged my line with a heavy line of battle. General Ferguson, who was on the right, gave way, but on reaching his position I re-established his line on ground equally as favorable, and maintained the line thus established until night.

About daylight the following morning, General Cleburne, with his division of infantry, came, pursuant to General Hood's orders, to relieve me, while I was ordered to extend my line to the right. General Cleburne placed his troops so closely together that only a little more than half my line was occupied by General Cleburne's troops. While changing position, and before my troops had faced toward the enemy, a general attack was made on my own and General Cleburne's front. General Ferguson, who was on the right, reported a force turning his right flank, when, at the same moment, a general assault of several lines of battle was made by the enemy. Ferguson gave way in some confusion, which exposed the right of Allen's brigade, which, with the Georgia brigade, nevertheless, fought brilliantly, repulsing a desperate assault and killing the enemy in hand to hand conflicts. On the enemy's second assault both the Georgia and Alabama brigades, with the right brigade of Cleburne's division, were forced from their works by an overwhelming force. After falling back a short distance the Georgia and part of the Alabama brigades rallied, charged the enemy and retook the works, with two officers and twenty privates, besides a number of the enemy's dead and wounded, some of whom were killed in our rifle-pits. This was a most brilliant feat, and the Georgia brigade deserves great credit for its conduct upon that day.

Our loss in killed and wounded was not severe, and we did not lose any prisoners. The loss of the enemy was severe. I then established my line and maintained my position until relieved late in the day by Cheatham's division.

On the night of the 21st, pursuant to orders from General Hood, I moved around to the enemy's rear to attack him in conjunction with Lieutenant-General Hardee, who also moved upon their flank for the same purpose. My orders from General Hardee were to attack Decatur at 1 P. M., which was the enemy's extreme left, and, owing to the curvature of his line, was far in his rear. General Hardee supposed the place to be occupied only by cavalry, but on reconnoitering the position in person about 12 o'clock I found that a division of infantry, strongly intrenched, occupied the town. Having communicated this fact to General Hardee, I dismounted my command and moved upon the enemy at the appointed hour. Just as I was moving my line the enemy commenced to throw out two regiments of infantry to meet my approach. These were overthrown, a number of prisoners captured and the remainder driven in confusion into the enemy's works, from which we received a most galling fire from both infantry and artillery. Seeing the strength of the position in front, I threw a force upon his right flank and rear and formed my main line so as to bear obliquely upon the enemy's right, with the right of my line covering and engaging the enemy's front. From these positions simultaneous charges were made upon the enemy, the troops bearing upon the enemy's right being somewhat the most advanced. At first the galling fire made the most exposed portion of my line waver, but, quickly rallying, the onset was renewed, and with a triumphant shout the entire line of works was carried. Some two hundred and twenty-five prisoners, a large number of small arms, one 12-pounder gun, one forge, one battery wagon, one caisson and six wagons and teams, together with the captain of the battery and most of his men, were captured and brought off. We also captured his camp equipage, stores and hospitals. Just as I was pursuing the enemy beyond the town three of General Hardee's staff officers came to me in rapid succession, directing that I should re-enforce General Hardee as quickly as possible. The pursuit was stopped and all my available troops moved at a gallop to General Hardee's position. The forces under my command fought warmly until the pressure upon him had ceased, and night coming on we bivouacked for the night. Just before the troops were formed for the attack I reported to General Hardee that a large raiding force of the enemy had moved toward Covington, but he directed that it should not be followed, as he thought the attack about to be made would cause the raiders to return.

The following day, at 12 M., I was relieved from my position with a portion of my troops and ordered to pursue the enemy. My troops were in motion in ten minutes after I received the order, and by midnight I had traveled forty miles, only to find that the enemy's cavalry had returned to his main army before I had received orders to pursue. On returning I took my place on the right of the army, skirmishing with the enemy until the 27th. At daylight on that morning, pursuant to orders, I relieved General Hardee's entire line with my cavalry. While doing so I discovered that the enemy had abandoned their strong position in my front and fallen back to his position north of the railroad. At the same time I discovered that a large raiding party of the enemy, under Major-General Stoneman, had moved toward our line of communications. This was reported to the general commanding, and after being relieved I was ordered to pursue, but not to continue the pursuit in person unless it was absolutely necessary to take the greater portion of my command.

By daylight the following morning I had got ahead of the enemy and driven the advance of Garrard's division, which was marching for Jonesboro, across Flat Creek. He, finding himself so strongly opposed, retreated rapidly toward the left of the enemy's main army. We pursued a a few miles, capturing a few horses and arms, and caused him to abandon three wagons. About this time I discovered that General Stoneman, with twenty-two hundred men, had moved early that morning on toward Covington, with the intention, according to statements of prisoners, of continuing his march toward Macon. I felt unauthorized with my orders to pursue Stoneman's force of twenty-two hundred men in person, particularly as I had received a dispatch from General Shoup, chief of staff, that the left of the army was also threatened by a raid. I, therefore, ordered General Iverson, with his own, General Allen's and Colonel Breckinridge's brigades, to follow Stoneman rapidly and attack him wherever found. While this order was being executed I received additional dispatches from General Shoup stating that a large cavalry force, estimated at over three thousand, had crossed the Chattahoochee near Campbellton, and was making its way toward the Macon Railroad. General Shoup further stated that he feared Brigadier-General Jackson could not check its movements, and that General Hood desired me to move immediately to oppose this force with such troops as could be spared. I immediately ordered Ashby's brigade, under General Humes, which was then on the march to join me, to move rapidly to Jonesboro. I ordered General Kelly to remain and hold Garrard's division in check with Dibrell's brigade, and to send Anderson's brigade after me on the Jonesboro Road. By riding rapidly I arrived at 4 o'clock at Jonesboro with Ashby's brigade, five hundred strong, which I had overtaken on the march. I here learned that the enemy had struck the railroad some six miles south of that point. I arrived at that point about dark and found the enemy had moved off on the Fayetteville Road. A courier with a dispatch, and a staff officer whom I had sent to communicate with General Jackson, met me with a message from General Jackson to the effect that if I would press the enemy's rear he would gain their front and thus secure his capture. I immediately replied to General Jackson, agreeing to the proposition.

My scouts now reported that the enemy had taken the road crossing Flint River at —— bridge. Feeling confident the enemy would destroy the bridge, I sent a staff officer to ascertain, and also sent scouts to ascertain if any of the enemy went toward Griffin. Finding that the bridge had been destroyed and that all the enemy had moved toward Fayetteville, I changed my course and followed them rapidly. Upon the road I received the following dispatch from General Jackson:

TWO MILES AND A HALF FROM FAYETTEVILLE,
July 29, 1864, 10 P. M.

GENERAL: The latest reports represent the enemy moving toward Fayetteville. I am quite certain they are moving back to cross the Chattahoochee. I have Harrison's brigade in their front at Fayetteville, and am moving now with Ross' brigade to that place. Should enemy attempt to pass around the place I will gain their front or flank about Newnan. If you can follow and push them in rear it would be well.

Very respectfully,
W. H. JACKSON,
Brigadier-General.

Upon arriving at Fayetteville, about midnight, I learned that the enemy had passed through that place without meeting any opposition whatever, and was then not more than an hour in advance of me. I pressed on rapidly and overtook his rear at Tine Creek. The enemy had destroyed the bridge and were holding the opposite side with troops in strong barricades. With great difficulty the enemy was dislodged and driven from the bank. After an hour's hard labor a bridge was constructed and my command passed over. I had with me at this time but four hundred men, having traveled so rapidly that a number of my horses had been absolutely unable to keep up with the column, and General Anderson, whom I had ordered to follow me, had not, on account of the rapidity of my march, been heard from. After crossing the bridge I pressed on rapidly, in the extreme darkness encountering barricades every few hundred yards, the first intimation of the enemy being a volley from their small arms.

At daylight I received the following dispatch from General Jackson:

HEADQUARTERS CAVALRY DIVISION, THREE MILES AND A HALF FROM FAYETTEVILLE,
July 30, 1864, 3 A. M.

GENERAL: Since arrival of your courier I received notice from Colonel Harrison that he is opposite the enemy at Shakerag, three miles from here. The enemy has gone into camp there. I move at once with Ross' brigade. I forward Colonel James' [D. W. Jones'] report.

Very respectfully, your obedient servant,
W. H. JACKSON,
Brigadier-General.

Finding him so far in my rear I pushed on and in a few moments struck enemy's line of battle. I immediately attacked and drove him from his position, routing the entire line and capturing two hundred prisoners with their horses, equipments and arms. In this engagement and the running fight which ensued more than forty of the enemy were left dead on the field. My entire force, including my reserves, which were not engaged, did not exceed five hundred men. I pushed on, continually engaging the enemy's rear guard, until about 9 A. M., when they succeeded, by a rapid movement, in gaining some two miles upon my advance. Upon reaching a point two miles from Newnan I again overtook him, and captured twenty prisoners in the engagement which ensued. My command had, up to this time, traveled about seventy miles without having halted.

About this time Colonel Cook, with a portion of his regiment, and General Ross, with two small regiments, each about one hundred strong, reported to me, increasing my force to about seven hundred men. I here found that on the head of McCook's column approaching town he had observed Confederate troops in the town, and without engaging them turned off, leaving the town to the right. Feeling certain he would attempt to come into the LaGrange Road below the town, I ordered Colonel Ashby to move through Newnan and down the LaGrange Road to gain his front if possible. I then sent scouts and pickets out upon all roads by which the enemy could approach the town, and moved with the remainder of my command, now less than three hundred men, down between the railroad and the main LaGrange Road in the hope that I might strike the enemy's flank. After marching about three miles I discovered the enemy in a dense wood forming a line, the right flank of which was scarcely fifty yards in my front. Almost at the same moment I received a dispatch from Colonel Ashby informing me that he had struck the head of the enemy's column just as it was entering the main LaGrange Road, three miles and a half below Newnan, and that the enemy was forming a line of battle dismounted. Feeling that I was upon the flanks of the force to which he referred, I determined to attack immediately, notwithstanding the great disparity of numbers, the enemy having fully ten times my force. I immediately sent orders to Colonel Ashby to engage the enemy in front, while with the remainder of my troops I attacked with great vigor. I met with a strong resistance at first, but in a few moments the enemy gave way, when, with a shout and a gallant charge, the entire line was thrown into confusion and commenced a disorderly retreat. We pursued rapidly, captured a great number of prisoners and divided the enemy's forces.

While pursuing the enemy I heard firing in my rear, when I was surprised to learn that General Ross had left his horses where he had first dismounted. Feeling convinced that they were being attacked, I immediately recalled the line, returned and drove off the enemy, capturing a number of prisoners and horses, and recovering all of General Ross' horses. Immediately after this success, and before I had re-established my lines, the enemy made a most determined charge, driving back a portion of my line and throwing the whole of it into temporary confusion. In a moment my troops were rallied and the enemy repulsed. The fight had now lasted two hours. We had driven the enemy from every position and captured four hundred prisoners, including three brigade commanders, one of whom lay wounded upon the field. At this moment General Anderson came up with his brigade, four hundred strong, which was thrown into position. While doing so, General Anderson was wounded, and the brigade left under command of Colonel Bird.

CAPTURE OF A FEDERAL WAGON TRAIN NEAR CASSVILLE, GA., MAY 24, 1864.

Upon advancing my line I ascertained that the enemy had fallen back and taken a strong position in the edge of a wood, with a large field in front, and a deep ravine, only passable at certain points, intervening between my troops and the enemy's position. The enemy had thrown up strong barricades and was using his artillery freely. General Roddey, who had been in the town, and had not been engaged, came up with about six hundred men, and was placed in position on my left. He advised strongly against attacking the position. I immediately moved my troops to the right, and pressed down upon the enemy's left flank. Upon discovering this movement the enemy commenced retreating. I pressed rapidly down the road upon their flank, cutting off nearly two entire regiments, which surrendered in a body with all their artillery, wagons and ambulances. The entire column was thrown into disorder, and a number of prisoners, arms, horses and two stand of colors were captured in the pursuit which ensued. Some three hundred prisoners, mostly quartermasters, commissaries and other non-combatants, whom the enemy had captured the previous day, were also recaptured by our troops. General Roddey, on account of the fatigued condition of his men, had been authorized by me to retire to Newnan before this movement commenced. Afrer pursuing about four miles I found the enemy had become very much scattered through the woods and fields, and that the only party claiming organization had been served nearly equally. One column, estimated at about four hundred men, under General McCook in person, had moved at a gallop toward the mouth of New River; and the other party, under Colonel Brownlow, had moved on by-roads toward the Chattahoochee River. Near Franklin, I ordered Colonel Bird, commanding Anderson's brigade, to pursue the party with McCook vigorously. In anticipation that the enemy would take the direction pursued by the other party, I had some time previously sent Colonel McKenzie, with his own and the Third Arkansas Regiment, to gain the front of the enemy moving toward Franklin.

I omitted to state that a short time before dark General Jackson arrived, but his troops, numbering only about three hundred men, remained in rear, and did not come up to engage the enemy. After dark I ordered General Jackson to take his entire command to the battlefield and take charge of all the prisoners which had not been sent to the rear; to gather up the arms, wagons, horses, artillery, and all other public property, and take them to Newnan, and await my orders. The balance of my command left with me I ordered to search the woods and gather together the straggling parties of the enemy who had been cut off and were scattered over the country. Colonel McKenzie was very fortunate in his movements and succeeded in capturing between two and three hundred prisoners. Colonel Bird was not so successful. His instructions from me were to press on rapidly after the enemy, and to report by courier to me his progress and the force he found himself following. It was full daylight before I heard from him at all, and then I learned that he had fallen asleep and allowed the demoralized mass to escape to the river. On my arrival at that point in the morning I found that some four hundred of the enemy had succeeded in crossing, after abandoning some two hundred horses and equipments, throwing away most of their arms. These were still pursued on the other side of the river and a number captured, thus completing the entire destruction of the entire command. This proved to be a picked body of cavalry, and its destruction destroyed the flower of General Sherman's vast cavalry organization. General Iverson had been equally successful in his pursuit of General Stoneman, whom he met, defeated and captured, with five hundred of his command, some twenty miles from Macon. The remainder of Stoneman's command was much demoralized and scattered. Colonel Breckinridge pursued, and, in successive engagements, defeated and captured the only organized party which attempted escape.

Thus ended in most ignominious defeat and destruction the most stupendous cavalry operation of the war. As was acknowledged by the brigade commanders captured, their plan was to unite these columns on the railroad north of Macon, destroy the railroad, then move rapidly upon and release the thirty thousand prisoners of war we held at Andersonville. In this he was thoroughly thwarted at the cost of about five thousand men, with their horses, arms, equipments, colors, cannon, etc. The force which was sent on this expedition numbered as follows, all picked cavalry:

Garrard's division	4,000
McCook's division	3,200
Stoneman's division	2,200
Total	9,400

Garrard returned to the army without sustaining much damage except the morale of defeat. McCook, according to the enemy's own accounts, only succeeded in returning with five hundred men, most of whom were dismounted and unarmed; while none but a few stragglers from Stoneman's column ever returned—making their entire loss over five thousand men. Of these, I am informed, thirty-two hundred were lodged in prison and the remainder killed, wounded or scattered through the country. McCook's column was a picked body of men selected from his own division and a division a short time previously brought from Tennessee by Major-General Rousseau. All this was accomplished by a force of cavalry not exceeding an aggregate of thirty-eight hundred men.

On my return to the army I was ordered by General Hood to move upon the enemy's line of communications, destroy them at various points between Marietta and Chattanooga, then cross the Tennessee River, break the line of communication on the two roads running from Nashville to the army; to there leave twelve hundred men to continue their operations on those roads; to then return again, striking the railroad south of Chattanooga, and join the main army.

My command was much worn from the rapid marching and scarcity of forage for my horses. I nevertheless started promptly [August 10th] with a force of four thousand men; first tore up the railroad a few miles above Marietta, next near Cassville, and next near Calhoun. At Calhoun, Hannon's brigade captured seventeen hundred head of beef cattle, several wagons, a number of prisoners and several horses. These he brought safely to Ellijay, and pursuant to my orders returned with them to the army, where he arrived safely with the greater part of the captured property, although pursued by a superior body of the enemy's cavalry. For this service Colonel Hannon and his command deserve the highest commendation.

On August 14th, Humes' and Kelly's commands attacked and captured Dalton, with a large amount of stores and government property, their trains, two hundred horses and mules, and two hundred prisoners, the balance of the garrison on being driven from the town retreating to a small but strong fortification near the town. We also captured and destroyed a block-house and water-tank some two miles below the town. General Martin had been ordered by me to capture a small force of the enemy and destroy the railroad from Tilton up toward Dalton, while I was to meet him by working down from Dalton. Though I had ten miles further to travel than General Martin, he failed to comply with my orders and embarrassed me by placing his command where I could not hear from him, which caused me to fear he had met with disaster or been prevented from joining me by some force of the enemy interposing between him and myself, all of which gave me much uneasiness. Humes' and Allen's commands destroyed the railroad for several miles. The stores captured in the town were either appropriated or destroyed. Unfortunately we captured but little corn, and none could be obtained in the neighborhood.

FORTIFICATIONS AND ABATIS IN FRONT OF ATLANTA, GA.
[From a photograph taken in 1864.]

While moving out of the town the following day I was attacked by a large force of infantry and cavalry under Major-General Steedman. My loss was trifling, that of the enemy more severe, and including, according to their own accounts, one colonel killed and General Steedman slightly wounded. After leaving the town I found General Martin had been within seven miles of me, behind a bend in the river, but had not even informed me of his position, much less marched to my assistance in compliance with his orders. This and other circumstances convincing me I could not expect any help from him, I as soon as possible placed him in arrest and sent him back to the army.

Williams' brigade destroyed the road at various points between Tunnel Hill and Graysville, and by making demonstrations at various other points the enemy were prevented from any attempt to repair the railroad until after the 20th, when we left its immediate vicinity with the main body of my command to carry out the rest of my orders. This work was accomplished under the most disadvantageous circumstances, the heavy rains having so completely saturated the ties and all other wood as to make it almost impossible to burn them. Before leaving I detached two hundred selected men, with orders to strike the railroad every night at some five or six designated points. These parties were very successful in their efforts, succeeding in running off some twenty trains during my absence in Tennessee. The interruption of railroad communication by the destruction of the road was for fourteen days, commencing on the 9th, the day the road was first struck near Marietta. This does not include interruptions caused by the detachments of two hundred men sent back by me upon leaving Dalton. My horses were in a suffering condition, having during the march subsisted upon an insufficient supply of green corn, scarcely more than half matured and so soft as to be easily crushed by a slight pressure of the hand. This alone made it impossible for me to remain on the railroad any longer and compelled me to seek the rich soil on the Ocoee and Hiawassee to save my command from becoming dismounted.

I had intended to cross the Tennessee River at Cotton Port, but the continuous rains which had fallen since I left the army had raised the Tennessee River some ten feet, making it impossible to ford any point below Kingston. After maturely considering the matter I concluded to move above said point, and by crossing Little Tennessee and Clinch to accomplish the desired object. I here learned that the enemy had made extensive arrangements to procure forage for their army from the country along the line of railroad from Cleveland to Loudon. Feeling that it was important to stop this source of supply, I made a demonstration upon Cleveland, and with hard labor destroyed the railroad from Cleveland to Charleston. I then crossed the Hiawassee and captured Athens, with a large quantity of valuable supplies, and destroyed the railroad almost completely from Charleston to Loudon, during which we were almost continuously menaced by the enemy's cavalry, who were, however, repulsed in every attack. This was accomplished with hard labor on the part of our troops.

At Stewarts Landing we attacked and captured a garrison of about one hundred men, and captured some thirty wagons and between two and three hundred horses and mules, besides stores of the troops

We crossed Little Tennessee River with but little difficulty, when, to our disappointment, we found the Holston River had risen too high to be crossed, which compelled me to move still further up and cross it and the French Broad above Knoxville. The crossings of the Holston were guarded by the enemy, which caused us some embarrassment, but we succeeded in crossing and captured or drove off the enemy. While crossing we were warmly attacked by a column of cavalry from Knoxville. The attack was quickly repulsed. We then charged the enemy and drove them back at full speed to the city with a loss of over one hundred in killed, wounded and prisoners, all of whom fell into our hands.

Before crossing the river General Williams urgently requested permission to be allowed to take two brigades, including his own, and half of my artillery, with which he promised to capture the garrison and destroy the bridge at Strawberry Plains. I at first objected to the movement upon the ground that it might cause delay, while rapidity of movement was of the greatest importance. Upon his further urging the matter, and promising to overtake me that night by traveling by moonlight, I consented. General Williams failed to take the garrison or to touch the bridge. I then ordered General Williams to follow on rapidly and join me as soon as possible. This he failed to do, and left me with the balance of my command to carry out the principal part of the expedition with the embarrassment of making numerous delays in endeavoring to bring the troops under General Williams to my assistance.

After crossing the river and mountain I destroyed the railroad at various points between Chattanooga and Nashville, captured two trains of cars and a number of small depots of stores, including McMinnville, and caused the abandonment of several posts, all the public property connected therewith being destroyed. We captured several stockades in block-houses, and destroyed bridges and the railroad to such an extent as to completely stop communication for fifteen days. When near Nashville I was attacked by General Rousseau with a superior force of infantry and cavalry. The attack was repulsed. Harrison's brigade charged the enemy and drove him rapidly for two miles, capturing three stand of colors, a number of prisoners, arms, etc. Near this place we also captured some thirty wagons and teams and a number of prisoners.

After spending ten days upon the Chattanooga Railroad, I moved over to the Nashville & Decatur Road, which I most thoroughly destroyed at various points for several miles from Nashville to Decatur. This road was never completely repaired by the enemy. We also destroyed several loaded trains. During these movements Major-Generals Rousseau and Steedman and Brigadier-Generals Croxton and Granger had concentrated their forces and had attacked me at Franklin, Lynnville, Campbellville and other points. In every instance they were repulsed, although their troops outnumbered mine fourfold.

On reaching the Alabama border, and having determined to await General Williams' arrival (I having sent him several peremptory orders to march on and join me), I sent a dispatch to Corinth, and from there I telegraphed the commanding general the progress of my operations, at the same time recommending that the work be continued upon the railroad. To my disappointment I learned that General Williams had returned to East Tennessee and carried with him three large regiments, which I had sent on detached service, and which by chance met him.

In reply to my telegram to the commanding general, I was ordered to return to the Army of Tennessee again, striking the railroad south of Chattanooga.

General Forrest having arrived, to move into Tennessee, I ordered the twelve hundred men (now increased by recruits to sixteen hundred) whom I had left in Tennessee, pursuant to General Hood's orders, to report to him, and moved with the balance of my command to the railroad near Dalton, captured and destroyed a train of cars, and destroyed the railroad to such an extent that, with the additional effect of a heavy rain, no train passed over the road for a period of thirteen days. I here received an order to return immediately to the army, which I joined near Cedartown.

My entire loss on the entire expedition was about one hundred and fifty men, killed, wounded and missing, while I brought out more than two thousand recruits for my own and other commands, and brought out at least eight hundred absentees from the army, who were returned to their proper commands. During the expedition I was behind the enemy's lines, compelled continually to engage superior forces of the enemy. In all of this work my troops acted well, fought well and worked well.

I desire particularly to thank Generals Humes and Allen for their gallantry and good conduct throughout the entire expedition. I am satisfied these officers and their commands did all that brave and devoted men could do.

I brought off all my wounded who could bear transportation, and also brought out nearly one hundred wagons, which had been captured on the expedition.

All expeditions to the rear of an enemy are attended with great difficulties. This was particularly so. The jaded condition of my horses was one cause of embarassment, which was increased by the great scarcity and unwholesome character of the forage which we were compelled to subsist upon the first ten days. The heavy rains which fell during the same time caused small rivers to swell beyond fording and made the roads almost impassable for artillery. The results of the expedition were as follows:

First. Causing the enemy to send to their rear to re-enforce their garrisons, troops several times as strong as my force.

Second. The destruction of the enemy's line of communication for a longer period than any cavalry expedition, however large, has done.

Third. The capture, destruction or appropriation of stores.

Fourth. Breaking up depots and fortified posts in Tennessee and Georgia.

Fifth. Capture of 1,000 horses and mules, 200 wagons, 600 prisoners and 1,700 head of beef cattle.

Sixth. Capture and destruction of over twenty trains of cars loaded with supplies.

Seventh. Bringing into the service of the Confederate States over three thousand recruits.

All this was accomplished behind the enemy's lines, with a loss of but one hundred and fifty men killed, wounded and missing. In every engagement with the enemy's cavalry we were in all respects victorious, capturing prisoners, colors and arms.

During the time embraced in this report my command has averaged twenty-five miles a day in direct marching, either swam or forded twenty-seven rivers, and has captured, killed or wounded three times the greatest effective strength it has ever been able to carry into action. Besides this it has captured and turned over to the government an amount of property of more value than the entire expense my command has been to the Confederate States.

This report is necessarily brief and imperfect. The capture and destruction of property on the raid in Tennessee, and the great success and large captures in the victories during the enemy's [raid] in the latter part of July, reflect the highest credit upon my officers and men. I can not commend them too highly.

I desire to return my special thanks to Generals Humes, Allen, Dibrell, Robertson and Anderson, and to Colonels Breckinridge, McLemore, Wheeler, Harrison, Crews, Hagan and Hobson, all of whom were brave and faithful. General Anderson was wounded in our brilliant victory at Newnan and has since been absent. Colonel Hobson was also badly wounded at Franklin, Tenn.

To my brave division commander, General Kelly, who gave up his life at Franklin, Tenn., while gallantly fighting at the head of his division, I ask his country to award its gratitude. No honors bestowed to his memory could more than repay his devotion.

Lieutenants Warren, Staples and Lowery, of my staff, were killed while gallantly discharging their appropriate duties. Their gallantry and devotion were highly appreciated by me.

To Lieutenant Hudson, my aid-de-camp, [and] Major Wailes, my assistant adjutant-general, who were wounded by my side, and Lieutenant Bellinger, signal officer, also severely wounded, I desire to express my appreciation of their gallantry and devotion.

JOS. WHEELER, *Major-General.*

BATTLE OF RESACA, GA.,

MAY 13 TO 15, 1864.

BY

BRIG.-GEN. EDWARD C. WALTHALL,

Commanding Brigade of Operations.

HEADQUARTERS WALTHALL'S BRIGADE, HINDMAN'S DIVISION, HOOD'S CORPS, ARMY OF TENNESSEE, IN LINE OF BATTLE NEAR NEW HOPE CHURCH, GEORGIA. June 2, 1864.

DURING the morning of the 7th of May I was directed by the major-general commanding to move my command from its camp near Dalton through Alts Gap and take position in the trenches north of the gap, on the left of Manigault's and right of Tucker's brigade, facing to the east.

About noon on the 8th, under his orders, I moved my command, following Tucker's brigade in the direction of

MAJ.-GEN. E. C. WALTHALL, OF MISSISSIPPI.
[From a photograph taken in 1863.]

Rocky Face Ridge, but was halted when I had gone about half a mile, and in two hours or so was ordered back to my position in the trenches, and remained there till 2:30 o'clock on the morning of the 10th. I then moved through Dalton to a point on the Resaca Road nearly opposite Tilton. After I had been there about two hours I was directed to move rapidly back on the Dalton Road to the railroad crossing, about three miles distant, and to carry my command by a train of cars then in waiting back to the trenches near Alts Gap, there to be under the orders of Lieutenant-General Hardee. During the night I received orders from that officer to relieve Govan's brigade at 4 o'clock on the morning of the 11th. This I did at the hour appointed, and remained in Govan's position till the afternoon, when, by instructions from headquarters of the army, I reported to the major-general commanding, and with my command rejoined my proper division in the neighborhood of Dalton.

Early on the morning of the 12th, I was directed to move with the division to the neighborhood of Varnells Station, and by 12 M. we reached the point indicated, and formed line of battle on the left of the Cleveland Railroad. Two hours later I was directed to move back, left in front, through Dalton on the Resaca Road. About an hour after dark I was halted, and after resting several hours resumed the march in time to reach a point six miles north of Resaca, where my command had been on the 10th, about an hour before daylight. I remained here till about the middle of the day on the 13th, when I moved about two miles further in the direction of Resaca, and formed line of battle facing northwest at a point indicated by the major-general commanding on the left of the road. At 6:30 o'clock in the evening I was directed by him to move to the left, and spent the night at a point where I was halted about dark by an order which he delivered to me in person.

Early on the morning of the 14th, as directed by him, I moved about a mile further to the left and occupied a position from which a brigade of Major-General Bate's division had just withdrawn. As soon as my line was formed, and I had thrown forward a skirmish line connecting with that on the right and left already established, I employed all the tools at my disposal in strengthening the earthworks left by the troops which had preceded me, and in cutting out the undergrowth in front. The Thirty-fourth Mississippi Regiment, Colonel Samuel Benton, occupied the right of my line, connecting with the left of Deas' brigade; the Twenty-fourth and Twenty-seventh Mississippi regiments (consolidated), Colonel R. P. McKelvaine, the center, and the Twenty-ninth and Thirtieth Mississippi regiments (consolidated), Colonel W. F. Brantly, the left. Captain G. W. Reynolds, with three companies of sharpshooters, previously selected from the several regiments of my command, and organized and drilled specially for such service, covered my front. Tucker's brigade was posted in my rear as support. My command was the left brigade of Lieutenant-General Hood's corps, and on my left was Lewis' brigade, the right of Lieutenant-General Hardee's. Between Brigadier-General Lewis' right and the left of my intrenched line was Hotchkiss' battalion of artillery, behind which, under cover of the hill it was posted on, Colonel Brantly's consolidated regiment was put in position, except the three right companies, which were put in the trenches, the major-general commanding having notified me that on my command the protection of this artillery would devolve. It was posted on a bare knob, the highest to be seen on the ridge along which the army line extended, and from it the line in either wing was slightly refused, conforming in its general direction to the course of the ridge, and forming an obtuse angle, of which it was the point. Immediately in front of this elevation is an open field in a valley, about three hundred yards in width, extending from the base of the ridge we occupied to that of a wooded hill beyond, and through it runs a small creek nearly parallel to the course of our trenches. This field extends some distance to the left of the high point the artillery was on, and on the right and opposite the position of my center and right regiments it is six or eight hundred yards wide, but between it and the position of those regiments there is a skirt of woods some two or three hundred yards in width, very uneven and thickly covered with undergrowth and timber. Beyond the field and running nearly parallel with that part of the battle line occupied by Bate's division, and about half a mile from it, is a thickly-timbered ridge, as high as the point on which our batteries were posted.

About 11 A. M. the enemy's skirmish line encountered my own, but the latter held its ground, as directed, till forced back by a line of battle which advanced about 12. The artillery poured upon it a rapid and well-directed fire from the time it came in view, but it moved steadily forward till within three hundred yards of my line, when, from both small arms and artillery, it was subjected to a fire so deadly and destructive that it soon wavered and then gave way in confusion. In half an hour another line appeared and advanced under a similar fire, nearer than before, and until that part of it confronting the batteries was sheltered by means of a depression in the hillside, within one hundred and fifty yards of the guns. It was promptly dislodged by Colonel Brantly, who moved upon it with that part of his command not in the trenches, and at the same time the remainder of the line, which was in the woods opposite my right and center, yielded to the constant and steady fire of the troops occupying those positions and the whole line fell back. It crossed the field in the wildest disorder, under a damaging fire from the artillery, which was admirably served. As soon as the flying troops reached the woods beyond, a third line moved on us, but it was checked before advancing as far as either of the others had done, and fled before some parts of my command were able to discharge even a single volley. The enemy's sharpshooters, however, in large numbers secured themselves in the woods opposite my right and center, and so irregular and thickly wooded is the ground that it was found impossible to dislodge them. From these, and others posted in woods beyond the field in front of my left, a constant fire was kept up on my own line, as well as the batteries. The number of these sharpshooters in the woods nearest us was gradually increased by small bodies passing at irregular intervals rapidly across the open field to the cover of the woods. Many of them were enabled to shelter themselves behind some slight earthworks which had been constructed in front of the main intrenched line, before I occupied it, for skirmishers. By reason of the unevenness of the ground, these were without the range of our artillery. Others found cover in a small ravine, and by sundown the force in the woods was almost as strong as a line of battle and very well protected. When the enemy made his first advance he employed his artillery, posted directly in our front, but with little effect; but soon after his third repulse, he opened a furious fire from the ridge opposite Bate's division, which furnished him very fine positions for his guns, opposite my left, and about three-quarters of a mile distant. The fire of both small arms and artillery was kept up till 8:30 in the evening. During the afternoon a battery from Martin's battalion was sent to my line. After the firing ceased most of the night was spent in strengthening the works

BATTLE OF RESACA, GA., MAY 15, 1864.

General Hindman Repulsing an Attack on his Position by a Portion of the Army of the Cumberland.

all along the line, for they had been materially damaged during the day.

About 5 o'clock on the morning of the 15th the firing was resumed and was kept up incessantly during the entire day. In the night artillery had been concentrated on the point I occupied, and besides the small arms, which were used without intermission, not less than thirty guns were vigorously employed against us, and with considerable effect. The guns on my left enfiladed the greater portion of my line of works, and the position would scarcely have been tenable but for the fact that its extreme left was its highest point, and in consequence furnished a partial protection for the remainder. The firing ceased about 8 P. M.

My loss in killed was disproportionate to the number wounded, because most of the casualties were caused by

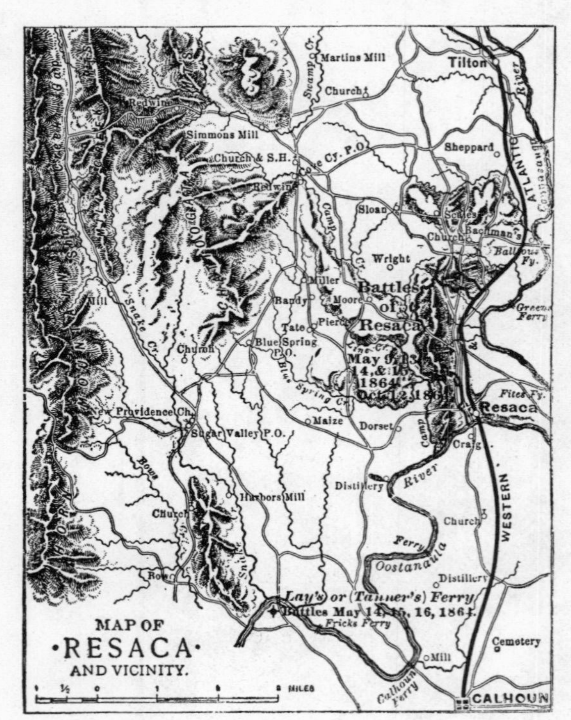

artillery, and those men struck by balls from small arms were in most cases shot in the head or upper part of the body while in the act of firing over the breastworks. When the engagement opened I had in line 1,158 men. Of this number 48 were killed and 116 wounded, and 5 of them mortally.

I think the loss of the enemy in my front was very heavy. None who have looked upon the field estimate it at less than one thousand in killed and wounded during both days.

Except Lieutenant Wiygle, Twenty-fourth Mississippi Regiment, who, when six men of his company were killed and five wounded by a single shell, abandoned his command and fled from the field, every member of my command did his whole duty during the entire engagement. My regimental commanders and the members of my staff gave me the full benefit of their efficient support and cordial co-operation, for which I here desire to acknowledge my indebtedness. Troops were never more severely tested than mine were in this battle, and none could have endured with more steadiness than they the furious and continuous fire to which they were subjected. To discriminate would be invidious when all did their duty so well. I regret to name among the killed, Lieutenant-Colonel A. J. Jones, Twenty-seventh Mississippi Regiment, who fell while discharging the duties of his position with that gallantry for which he had been distinguished on other fields. The fine brigade which was posted in my rear for support, though it had the shelter of the ridge, sustained considerable loss, mainly from the enemy's artillery. Its commander, Brigadier-General W. F. Tucker, was severely wounded while observing the enemy's movements from my position during the first day's engagement, and was succeeded in command by Colonel Jacob H. Sharp, of Blythe's (Mississippi) regiment. To both these efficient officers I am indebted for valuable suggestions and repeated offers of assistance, for which their command was kept in a constant state of readiness.

About 10 o'clock the night of the 15th, pursuant to orders from [the] major-general commanding, I withdrew my command from the intrenched line we had occupied for two days and crossed the Oostanaula River on the railroad bridge at Resaca. By way of Calhoun and Adairsville we moved to Cassville, reaching there on the 18th. The next day we took up a line east of Cassville, on a ridge, when we were fired upon heavily by the enemy's artillery and anticipated an engagement, a battle order having been read to the troops from army headquarters.

Pursuant to orders received that night we moved at an early hour the following morning toward Cartersville and crossed the Etowah River in the afternoon of the 20th.

All the marches referred to in this report were orderly. There was no straggling and no loss of property in any department.

E. C. WALTHALL,
Brigadier-General Commanding.

BATTLE OF ALLATOONA, GA.,

OCTOBER 5, 1864.

BY

MAJ.-GEN. SAMUEL G. FRENCH.

HEADQUARTERS FRENCH'S DIVISION,
TUSCUMBIA, ALA., November 5, 1864.

ABOUT noon on the 4th of October, when at Big Shanty, the following order was handed to me by Lieutenant-General Stewart, it being a copy of one to him:

HEADQUARTERS ARMY OF TENNESSEE,
October 4, 1864, 7:30 A. M.

Lieutenant-General A. P. Stewart, Commanding Corps.

GENERAL: General Hood directs that later in the evening you move Stevenson back to Davis Crossroads, and that you bring two of your divisions back to Adams and between Adams and Davis Crossroads, placing them in such a way as to cover the position at Adams now occupied by Stevenson, and that your third division (say French's) shall move up the railroad and fill up the deep cut at Allatoona with logs, brush, rails, dirt, etc. To-morrow morning at daylight he desires Stevenson to be moved to Lieutenant-General Lee's actual left, and that two of your divisions, at that time at Adams, to draw back, with your left in the neighborhood of Davis Crossroads and your right in the neighborhood of Lost Mountain, and the division that will have gone to Allatoona to march thence to New Hope Church and on the position occupied by your other troops—that is, that the division shall rejoin your command by making this march out from the railroad and via New Hope. General Hood thinks that it is probable that the guard at the railroad bridge on Etowah is small, and when General French goes to Allatoona, if he can get such information as would justify him, if possible move to that bridge and destroy it. General Hood considers that its destruction would be of great advantage to the army and the country. Should he be able to destroy the bridge, in coming out he could move, as has been heretofore indicated, via New Hope. Yours respectfully,

A. P. MASON,
Assistant Adjutant-General.

Soon after, an order, of which the following is a copy, was sent me:

HEADQUARTERS ARMY OF TENNESSEE,
OFFICE OF CHIEF OF STAFF,
October 4, 1864, 11:30 A. M.

Lieutenant-General Stewart, Commanding.

GENERAL: General Hood directs me to say that it is of the greatest importance to destroy the Etowah Railroad Bridge if such a thing is possible. From the best information we have now he thinks the enemy can not disturb us before to-morrow, and by that time your main body will be near the remainder of our army. He suggests that if it is considered practicable to destroy the bridge when the division goes there and the artillery is placed in position, the commanding officer call for volunteers to go to the bridge with light wood and other combustible material that can be obtained and set fire to it.

Yours respectfully,
A. P. MASON,
Major and Assistant Adjutant-General.

General Stewart's corps had struck the railroad at Big Shanty on the evening of the 3d, and all three of his divisions had worked all night in destroying the railroad from near Kennesaw up to Acworth Station. As we had been informed at Big Shanty that the Allatoona Pass or cut was fortified, and that the enemy had there a garrison of three regiments and had accumulated a considerable amount of provisions, it was considered a matter of importance that the place should be captured, and after the orders were handed me General Stewart sent me with Major Myrick, with twelve pieces of artillery. It would appear, however, from these orders that the general-in-chief was not aware that the pass was fortified and garrisoned that I was sent to have filled up. Under these orders I left Big Shanty about 3:30 P. M., and marched to Acworth, a distance of six miles, arriving there before sunset. There I was detained awaiting the arrival of rations until 11 o'clock at night. As I knew nothing of the roads, the enemy's works or position, it was important to procure a guide, and at last a young man, or rather a boy, was found who knew the roads and had seen the position of the fortifications at Allatoona, he being a member of a cavalry company. At Acworth, Captain Taylor, of Pinson's regiment of cavalry, with twenty-five men, reported to me for duty. He was immediately directed to send fifteen men under a trusty officer to strike the railroad as near the Etowah Railroad Bridge as possible, and to take up rails and hide them, so as to prevent trains from reaching Allatoona with re-enforcements, as well as to prevent any trains that might be there from escaping.

From an eminence near Acworth the enemy could be seen communicating messages by their night signals from Allatoona with the station on Kennesaw, and to the east of us were the fires of a large encampment of the Federals, and apparently opposite Moons Station. Citizens residing here informed me that there was a block-house with a garrison of about one hundred men at the Allatoona Bridge; that at Allatoona there were two small redoubts with out-works, defended with four pieces of artillery and garrisoned with three and a half regiments of infantry.

About 11 P. M. the march was resumed. The night was very dark and the road bad. After crossing Allatoona Creek, Colonel Adaire, with the Fourth Regiment Mississippi Volunteers and one piece of artillery, was left near the block-house, with instructions to surround it, capture the garrison and destroy the bridge over the creek. Continuing the march, the division arrived before Allatoona about 3 A. M. Nothing could be seen but one or two twinkling lights on the opposite heights, and nothing was heard except the occasional interchange of shots between our advanced guards and the pickets of the garrison in the valley below. All was darkness. I had no knowledge of the place, and it was important to attack at break of day. Taking the guide and lights I placed the artillery in position on the hills south and east of the railroad, and the Thirty-ninth North Carolina Regiment, under Colonel Coleman, and the Thirty-second Texas were left as a supporting force, both under command of Colonel J. A. Andrews commanding the latter regiment. This being done, I proceeded with the guide to gain the heights or ridge crowned by works of the enemy. Without roads or paths, the head of the line reached the railroad, crossed it and began the ascending and descending of the high, steep and densely-timbered spurs of the mountains, and after about an hour's march it was found we were directly in front of the works and not on the main ridge. The guide made a second effort to gain the ridge and failed, so dark was it in the woods. I therefore determined to rest where we were and await daylight.

With dawn the march was resumed and finally, by 7:30 o'clock in the morning, the head of the column was on the ridge, and about six hundred yards west of the fortifications, and between those he occupied and an abandoned redoubt on our left. Here the fortifications for the first time were seen, and instead of two redoubts there were disclosed to us three redoubts on the west of the railroad cut and a star fort on the east, with outer works, and the approaches defended to a great distance by abatis and, nearer the works, by stockades and other obstructions. The railroad emerges from the Allatoona Mountains by crossing this ridge through a cut sixty-five feet deep.

Dispositions for the assault were now made by sending General Sears' brigade to the north side or rear of the works, General F. M. Cockrell's (Missouri) brigade to rest with center on the ridge, while General W. H. Young, with the four Texas regiments, was formed in rear of General Cockrell. Major Myrick had opened on the works with his artillery, and was ordered to continue his fire until the attacking force should interfere, or until he heard the volleys of musketry. General Sears was to

MAJ.-GEN. S. G. FRENCH, OF MISSISSIPPI.

commence the assault on the rear, and when musketry was heard General Cockrell was to move down the ridge, supported by General Young, and carry the works by (as it were) a flank attack. So rugged and abrupt were the hills that the troops could not be got into position until about 9 A. M., when I sent in a summons to surrender. The flag was met by a Federal staff officer, and he was allowed seventeen minutes to return with an answer. The time expired without any answer being received, whereupon Major D. W. Sanders, impatient at the delay, as bearer of the summons broke off the interview and returned. No reply being sent me, the order was given for the assault by directing the advance of Cockrell's brigade. Emerging from the woods and passing over a

BATTLE OF ALLATOONA (ALLATOONA PASS), GA., OCTOBER 5, 1864.

THE MESSAGE, "HOLD THE FORT, FOR I AM COMING!" SIGNALED FROM KENNESAW MOUNTAIN TO THESE HEIGHTS, GAVE RISE TO THE FAMOUS GOSPEL HYMN.

long distance of abatis formed of felled timber, and under a severe fire of musketry and artillery, nobly did it press forward, followed by the gallant Texans. The enemy's outer line and one redoubt soon fell. Resting to gather strength and survey the work before them, again they rushed forward in column, and in murderous hand-to-hand conflict, that left the ditches filled with the dead, did they become masters of the second redoubt.

The third and main redoubt, now filled by those driven from the captured works on the west side of the railroad, was further crowded by those that were driven out of the fort on the east side of the road by the attack made by General Sears. They had to cross the deep cut through which our artillery poured a steady and deadly fire. The Federal forces were now confined to one redoubt, and we occupied the ditch and almost entirely silenced their fire, and were preparing for the final attack. Pending the progress of these events I had received a note from General F. C. Armstrong, dated 7 A. M., asking me at what time I would move toward New Hope and pass Acworth, informing me also that the enemy had moved up east of the railroad above Kennesaw and encamped there last night. I had observed this movement when at Acworth, but at 12 M. I received another dispatch from him, written at 9 A. M., saying:

"My scouts report enemy's infantry advancing up the railroad. They are now entering Big Shanty. They have a cavalry force east of the railroad."

On receipt of this second note from General Armstrong I took my guide aside and particularly asked him if, after the capture of the place, I could move to New Hope Church by any other route than the one by the block-house at Allatoona Creek, and thence by the Sandtown Road to the Acworth and Dallas Road, and he said I could not. Here, then, was General Sherman's whole army close behind me and the advance of his infantry moving on Acworth, which changed the whole condition of affairs. Ammunition had to be carried from the wagons, a mile distant at the base of the hills, by men, and I was satisfied it would take two hours to get it up and distribute it under fire before the final assault. I had learned from prisoners that before daylight the place had been re-enforced by a brigade under General Corse. I knew the enemy was in Big Shanty at 9 A. M. By noon he could reach Acworth and be within two miles of the road on which I was to reach New Hope Church. I knew General Stewart had been ordered to near Lost Mountain. My men had marched all day on the 3d; worked all the night of the 3rd, destroying the railroad; they had worked and marched all day on the 4th; marched to Allatoona on the night of the 4th; had fought up to the afternoon of the 5th, and could they pass the third day and night without rest or sleep if we remained to assault the remaining work? I did not doubt that the enemy would endeavor to get in my rear to intercept my return. He was in the morning but three hours' distant and had been signaled to repeatedly during the battle. Under these circumstances I determined to withdraw, however depressing the idea of not capturing the place after so many had fallen, and when in all probability we could force a surrender before night; yet, however desirous I was for remaining before the last work and forcing a capitulation, or of carrying the work by assault, I deemed it of more importance not to permit the enemy to cut my division off from the army. After deliberately surveying matters as they presented themselves to me, I sent word to General Sears to withdraw his men at once, moving by the route he went in, and directed General Cockrell to withdraw at 1:30 P. M.

Before the action commenced it was foreseen that it would be impossible to carry any wounded on litters to the road, where the ambulances were placed, owing to the steepness of the hills, the ravines and the dense woods. Accordingly, the wounded were brought to the springs near the ridge. All that could be moved without the use of litters were taken to the ambulances. The others were left in charge of surgeons detailed to remain with them.

The troops reformed on the original ground west of the works and marched back to the south side near the artillery, and at 3:30 P. M. commenced the move toward New Hope. After the troops engaged in the assault had left, I rode on down to Colonel Andrews' position, in front of the works, and directed him to remain until 5 P. M., and then withdraw and move on in our rear. Before I had determined to withdraw the infantry from the captured works (but after the guide said I would have to return by the way I came) I sent orders to Major Myrick to send two of his batteries and his caissons to a point beyond the block-house on the Sandtown Road, to act in concert with the troops left there. Having been informed by Colonel Adaire that the block-house at the Allatoona Bridge had not been captured, I directed Captain Kolb, with his battery, that had remained with Colonel Andrews, to move on and report to General Cockrell for the purpose of taking the block-house. Shortly after 4 P. M., and when not a person could be seen in or around the forts, I left the command of Colonel Andrews and overtook the division near the block-house. Colonel Adaire had burnt the railroad bridge over the Allatoona Creek (over two hundred feet long) and the duplicate of the bridge, already framed to replace the older structure. Under an increased artillery fire the garrison of the block-house surrendered.

We captured two hundred and five prisoners, one United States flag, and the colors of the Ninety-third Illinois Regiment, a number of horses, arms, etc., and killed and wounded seven hundred and fifty of the enemy;

ALLATOONA, GA. SCENE OF THE BATTLE ON OCTOBER 5, 1864.

being, with the garrison of the block-house, over one thousand.

History will record the battle of Allatoona one of the most sanguinary conflicts of the war; and when it is remembered that the enemy fought from within their strong redoubts, the desperate deeds of daring performed by our troops in overcoming so many of the foe, a meed of praise is due to their heroic valor.

The artillery opened about 7 o'clock in the morning, and, except when the flag of truce was sent in, continued till 2 P. M. The assault, commencing about 10, continued unremittingly till 1:30 P. M., and the rattle of musketry did not cease entirely till near 3 P. M., when it died away and a silence like the pall of death rested over the scene, contrasting strangely with the previous din of battle.

I can not do justice to the gallantry of the troops. No one faltered in his duty, and all withdrew from the place with the regret that General Sherman's movements—closing up behind us—forbade our remaining longer to force a surrender of the last work. After leaving out the three regiments that formed no part of the assaulting force, I had but a little over two thousand men.

My entire loss in killed, wounded and missing was seven hundred and ninety-nine, as follows:

	Killed.	Woun'd	Missing	Capt'rd.
Cockrell's brigade	42	182	22	. . . .
Sears' brigade	37	114	200	. . . .
Ector's brigade	43	147	11	. . . .
Staff	. . . .	. . . .	. . . .	1
Total	122	443	233	1

AN UNKNOWN HERO'S GRAVE ON THE WESTERN & ATLANTIC RAILROAD, IN ALLATOONA PASS, GA.

Among the killed from Sears' brigade is Colonel W. H. Clark, Forty-sixth Mississippi. He fell in the advance near the enemy's works with the battle-flag in his hands. He was an excellent and gallant officer. Also were killed Captain B. Davidson and Lieutenants G. C. Edwards, J. R. Henry and G. D. Davis.

Colonel W. S. Barry, Thirty-fifth Mississippi, and Major Parton, Thirty-sixth Mississippi, were wounded, together with Captains R. G. Yates and A. J. Farmer; and Lieutenants J. N. McCoy, G. H. Bannerman, J. M. Chadwick, J. Coopwood, R. E. Jones, E. W. Brown, G. H. Moore; and Ensigns G. W. Cannon and A. Scarborough.

Texas will mourn for the death of some of her bravest and best men. Captain Somerville, Thirty-second Texas, was killed after vainly endeavoring to enter the last work, where his conspicuous gallantry had carried him and his little band. Captains Gibson, Tenth Texas; Bates, Ninth Texas; Conley, Twenty-ninth North Carolina; and Adjutant Griffin, Ninth Texas; Lieutenants Alexander, Twenty-ninth North Carolina, and Dixon E. Wetzel, Ninth Texas, were killed gallantly leading their men.

Brigadier-General W. H. Young, commanding brigade, was wounded. Most gallantly he bore his part in action.

Colonel Camp, commanding Fourteenth Texas, one of the best officers in the service, was seriously wounded; also Majors McReynolds, Ninth Texas, and Purdy, Fourteenth Texas.

Of captains wounded were Wright, Lyles, Russell, Vannoy and Ridley; and lieutenants, Tunnell, Haynes, Gibbons, Agee, Morris, O'Brien, Irwin, Reeves and Robertson.

In the Missouri brigade were killed or mortally wounded, Majors W. F. Carter and O. A. Waddell; Captains A. J. Byrne, A. C. Patton and John S. Holland; Lieutenants Thomas R. Shelly, Joel F. Yancey, G. R. Elliott, R. J. Lamb, G. T. Duvall and W. H. Dunnica; and Ensign H. W. DeJarnett—men who had behaved well and nobly during the whole campaign.

Among the wounded are Major R. J. Williams, Captains Thomas Alvord, G. McChristian, G. W. Covell and A. F. Burns, Lieutenants Joseph Boyce, Silas H. F. Hornback, J. L. Mitchell, A. H. Todd and H. Y. Anderson, and Ensign William A. Byrd.

I have named the killed and wounded officers in this report. The names of the private soldiers who fell or were wounded will also be filed with this as soon as they are received. It is due to the dead, it is just to the living, that they who have no hopes of being heralded by fame, and who have but little incentive except the love of country and the consciousness of a just cause to impel them to deeds of daring, and who have shed their blood for a just cause, should have this little tribute paid them by me.

For the noble dead the army mourns, a nation mourns. For the living, honor and respect will await them wherever they shall be known as faithful soldiers, who have for their dearest rights so often gone through the fires of battle and the baptism of blood. It would, perhaps, be an invidious distinction to name individual officers or men for marked or special services or distinguished gallantry where all behaved so well, for earth never yielded to the tread of nobler soldiers.

To Colonel Earp, on whom the command of the gallant Texans devolved, and to Colonel Andrews, who commanded on the south side, and Major Myrick, commanding the artillery, I return my thanks for services.

Major D. W. Sanders, Assistant Adjutant-General; Lieutenant Wiley Abercrombie, Aid; Captain W. H. Cain, Volunteer Aid; Captain Porter and Lieutenant Mosby, Engineers, were zealous in the performance of their duties, and E. T. Freeman, Assistant Inspector-General, was conspicuous for his gallant conduct. I commend the last named to the government for promotion.

Colonel E. Gates, First and Third Missouri; Major E. H. Hampton, Twenty-ninth North Carolina, and Adjutant W. J. Sparks, Tenth Texas, and Lieutenant Cahal, of General Stewart's staff, are named for gallant services.

Lieutenant M. W. Armstrong, Tenth Texas, seized the United States standard from the Federals, and, after a struggle, brought it and the bearer of it off in triumph.

The cavalry officer who was sent to cut the railroad and failed to perform that duty, is, in my opinion, much to blame. Had he taken up the rails—and there was nothing to prevent it—re-enforcements could not have been thrown in the works and the result would have been different. After-events showed that a cavalry force of the enemy arrived at Allatoona as we were withdrawing.

S. G. FRENCH,

Major-General Commanding.

ATLANTA CAMPAIGN.

Approximate Statement of Ordnance Stores Destroyed in the Evacuation of Atlanta, September 1, 1864.

	Quantity.
32-pounder gun shells	100
24-pounder gun shells	16
24-pounder gun canister	57
20-pounder Parrott shells	1,050
12-pounder gun shells	2,268
12-pounder gun shot	1,544
12-pounder gun canister	818
12-pounder howitzer shells	637
12-pounder howitzer canister	782
12-pounder mountain howitzer shells	60
12-pounder mountain howitzer, spherical case	384
10-pounder Parrott shells	3,181
6-pounder gun shot	448
6-pounder gun, spherical case	110
6-pounder gun canister	368
3-inch rifle canister	154
3-inch rifle shells	339
2½-inch rifle shells	20
12-pounder howitzers, bronze	3
6-pounder rifles, bronze	2
12-pounder Napoleon caissons and limbers (no chests), damaged	10
12-pounder Napoleon caissons, damaged	2
12-pounder howitzer caissons and limbers, damaged	4
3-inch rifle caissons and limbers, damaged	7
12-pounder Napoleon ammunition chests, damaged	9
6-pounder Napoleon ammunition chests, damaged	1
Battery forges and limbers, damaged	3
Spare wheels, damaged	7
3-inch Hotchkiss shells, damaged	173
10-pounder Parrott shells, damaged	320
12-pounder solid shot, damaged	327
12-pounder shells, damaged	324
12-pounder canister, damaged	18
20-pounder Parrott shells, damaged	181
6-pounder smooth-bores, iron	4
3-inch rifle	1
6-pounder gun carriages and limbers	4
6-pounder gun carriages and limbers, damaged	2
12-pounder howitzer carriages and limbers	2
12-pounder howitzer carriage	1
12-pounder Napoleon carriage, damaged	1
12-pounder Napoleon caissons and limbers	7
12-pounder Napoleon caissons and limbers (no chests)	2
12-pounder Napoleon caissons and limbers, damaged	7
20-pounder Parrott shot, damaged	9
10-pounder Parrott shells, damaged	49
24-pounder shells, damaged	24
30-pounder shells, damaged	31
32-pounder shells, damaged	22
42-pounder shells, damaged	1
Hotchkiss shells, damaged	211
3-inch shot, damaged	17
6-pounder shot, damaged	58
6-pounder spherical cases, damaged	67
6-pounder shells, damaged	35
6-pounder canister, damaged	81
6-pounder James shells, damaged	21
3-inch rifle shells, damaged	109
Boxes of ammunition, damaged	43
Ammunition chests, damaged	33
Artillery saddles, damaged	12
Breeching, damaged	20
Breast-straps, damaged	24
Lead traces, damaged	97
Wheel traces, damaged	18
Pairs hames, damaged	142
Hip-straps, damaged	36
Valise saddles, damaged	32
Collars, damaged	48
Single sets lead harness, damaged	25
Single sets wheel harness, damaged	1
Prolonges, damaged	3
Leg-guards, damaged	11

GRIFFIN, GA., September 16, 1864.

W. D. HUMPHRIES,
Captain and Depot Ordnance Officer Army of Tennessee.

Abstract from Return of the First District of Texas, Commanded by Brigadier-General P. O. Hebert, for October —, 1862, Headquarters San Antonio, Tex.

Commanding Officers.	Troops.	Present for Duty.		Aggregate Present.	Aggregate Present and Absent.	Horses.		Pieces of Artillery.	
		Officers.	Men.			Serviceable.	Unserviceable.	Heavy.	Mountain.
Brigadier-General H. P. Bee	Sub-District of the Rio Grande	136	2,288	2,801	3,902	1,189	5	5	1
Colonel X. B. Debray	Sub-District of Houston	196	3,042	4,020	5,403	1,365	...	13	...
General J. R. Baylor	Northern Frontier	...	...	...	...	...	...	...	...
Grand total		332	5,330	6,821	9,305	2,554	5	18	1

NOTE FROM ORIGINAL RETURN.

Aggregate present and absent	9,338
Colonel P. N. Luckett	480
Lieutenant-Colonel R. R. Brown	927
Captain L. C. Rountree	102
Total	10,847

Statement of Forces in the Sub-Military District of the Rio Grande, November 1, 1862.

Rank.	Number of Companies and Corps.	Station.	Force.
Colonel P. N. Luckett	Ten companies Third Regiment Texas Infantry	Rio Grande	648
Colonel P. C. Woods	Ten companies Thirty-sixth Regiment Cavalry	Lavaca River and Fort Clark	823
Colonel C. L. Pyron	Ten companies Second Regiment Texas Mounted Rifles	Columbus	752
Major D. D. Shea	Two companies artillery	Lavaca	204
Major A. M. Hobby	Four companies infantry	Corpus Christi	303
Major W. O. Yager	Four companies cavalry	Fort Brown	404
Major Joseph Taylor	Five companies cavalry	San Antonio	407
Captain James Duff	Two companies Partisan Rangers	San Antonio	142
Captain E. Crenzbaur	One company heavy artillery	Rio Grande	62
Captain R. B. Maclin	One company light battery	Rio Grande	52
Captain S. Benavides	One company Texas Mounted Rifles (unattached)	Rio Grande	76
Captain R. Benavides	One company Texas Mounted Rifles (unattached)	Rio Grande	79
Captain J. M. Penaloza	One company infantry (unattached)	San Antonio	104
Captain R. Willke	One company light battery	Corpus Christi	87
Captain B. F. Neal	One company heavy artillery (unattached)	Corpus Christi	91
Captain J. A. Ware	One company Texas Mounted Rifles (unattached)	Corpus Christi	83
Captain John Ireland	One company infantry (unattached)	Corpus Christi	120
Captain J. T. Brackenridge	One company Texas Mounted Rifles (unattached)	Lavaca	79
Captain A. Navarro	One company Texas Mounted Rifles (unattached)	Atascosa	80
Total			4,596

Many of the companies are still recruiting, and the force may safely be considered five hundred stronger than the returns for October show, especially as many conscripts have been sent to the commands which are not accounted for on the returns for October.

November 1, 1862.

E. F. GRAY, *Major and Acting Assistant Adjutant-General.*

A Night Scene at the Rendezvous of Colonel Mosby and his Men in the Pass of the Blue Ridge Mountain, Shenandoah Valley, Virginia.

MOSBY'S OPERATIONS,

MARCH 1 TO SEPT. 11, 1864.

BY

COLONEL JOHN S. MOSBY.

HEADQUARTERS FORTY-THIRD VIRGINIA
PARTISAN RANGER BATTALION,
September 11, 1864.

I HAVE the honor to submit, for the information of the commanding general, the following brief description of the operations of this command since the 1st day of March last:

On August 9th, with a detachment of thirty-seven men, I defeated a body of one hundred cavalry at Fairfax Station, killing the captain commanding and six men, and capturing twenty-one prisoners and thirty-four horses. Two detachments sent out at the same time in Fairfax brought in six more prisoners and horses; another detachment of five sent to Duffields Depot brought in ten prisoners with their horses, etc.

On the morning of August 13th I attacked, near Berryville, the enemy's supply train, which was guarded by some seven or eight hundred infantry and cavalry, under command of Brigadier-General Kenly. Completely routed the guard with a loss of over two hundred prisoners, including three lieutenants, besides several killed and wounded. Captured and destroyed seventy-five loaded wagons, and secured over two hundred head of beef-cattle, between five and six hundred horses and mules, and many valuable stores. My loss, two killed and three wounded. My force numbered something over three hundred men, with two mountain howitzers. One howitzer became disabled before being brought into action, by breaking of a wheel; the other, after firing a few rounds, was rendered useless also by breaking of the carriage.

Too much praise can not be awarded to Captains Richard and William Chapman, commanding their respective squadrons, for the bravery with which they scattered largely superior forces of the enemy. The gallant Captain Sam Chapman, commanding Company E, although burning for the strife, was prudently held in reserve.

A few days after this, Lieutenant Glasscock, with fourteen men, captured twenty-nine prisoners, including several officers, with their horses, arms, etc., near Kearnstown. At the same time Captain Richard, with a small squad, killed a captain and captured seven or eight men and horses near Charlestown.

About August 20th, I crossed with my command at Snickers Gap, the enemy being near Berryville, sending the larger portion, under Captain William Chapman, to operate around Berryville and restrain the enemy from devastating the country. With a small detachment I went to their rear, near Charlestown, and captured twelve prisoners and ten horses. Captain Chapman, coming upon a portion of the enemy's cavalry which was engaged in burning houses, attacked and routed them. Such was the indignation of our men at witnessing some of the finest residences in that portion of the State enveloped in flames that no quarter was shown, and about twenty-five of them were shot to death for their villainy. About thirty horses were brought off, but no prisoners.

On Friday, September 5th, I sent Captain Sam Chapman, in command of Companies C and E, to harass the enemy around Berryville, while I made a detour to gain their rear, near Charlestown. Arriving at the river, I left the two companies that were with me (A and B), under Lieutenant Nelson, on the east bank of the river, while with six men I went on a reconnoissance across, previous to carrying my whole force over. Some time after, a force of the enemy's cavalry crossed the mountain in their rear, surprised and stampeded them, killing one, wounding three and capturing three. One of the enemy's cavalry was killed and five wounded. With the six men with me I succeeded in capturing and bringing out safely about twenty-five prisoners, two ambulances and eighteen horses. Captain Chapman routed a largely superior force near Berryville, killing and wounding some fifteen or twenty, besides securing over thirty prisoners, including a captain and lieutenant, with their horses, arms, etc.

On September 8th, with about thirty men, having gained a position in the enemy's rear near Charlestown, I divided the command for greater safety. One portion, under Captain Richard, captured a captain and twelve men, with their horses, etc. With mine I captured a lieutenant and five men, with their horses, etc.

I have made no attempt—for it would be impossible—to embrace in this report a full recital of the innumerable affairs with the enemy in which the heroism of both men and officers of this command has been illustrated; yet the fame of their deeds will still live in the grateful remembrance of those whose homes and whose firesides their valor has defended.

JNO. S. MOSBY,
Lieutenant-Colonel Commanding.

COLONEL JOHN S. MOSBY AND HIS MEN.

Hoverson. Parrott. Gooden. Palmer. —— Senatt. Punyear. Manson. Booker. Mosby. Babcock. Newell. Butler. Randolph. Rahn. Quarles Gentry.

OPERATIONS

ON THE

SOUTH SIDE OF THE JAMES,

INCLUDING

DREWRYS BLUFF, BERMUDA HUNDRED, PETERSBURG, ETC.,

MAY 4 TO JUNE 2, 1864.

BY

GENERAL G. T. BEAUREGARD.

HEADQUARTERS IN THE FIELD,
SWIFT CREEK, VA., June 10, 1864.

WHILE we were hurriedly assembling by fragments an army weak in numbers, and wanting the cohesive force of previous organization and association, the enemy, operating from his fortified base at Bermuda Hundred Neck, had destroyed much of the Richmond & Petersburg Railroad, and occupied the main lines of communication from the capital southward, and menaced its river gate (Drewrys Bluff) and south-side land defenses with a formidable army and fleet. In these conditions the possession of our line of communication southward became the main point of contest. To wrest it from the enemy I selected a course which promised the most fertile results, that of capturing or destroying his army in its actual position, after cutting him off from his base of operations; or, failing in this, of robbing him of future power to control or obstruct our communications by driving him before our front and locking him up in his fortified camp at Bermuda Hundred Neck.

Our army was organized into three divisions (right, left and reserve), under Major-Generals Hoke and Ransom and Brigadier-General Colquitt. The general direction of the roads and adjacent river was north and south, the general alignment of both armies east and west. Our left wing (Ransom) lay behind the trenches on Kingsland Creek, which runs an easterly course, not far in front of Drewrys Bluff. Our right wing (Hoke) occupied the intermediate line of fortifications from Fort Stevens, crossing the turnpike to the railroad. Colquitt's reserve, in rear of Hoke, centered at the turnpike. The cavalry were posted on our flanks and in reserve, and the artillery distributed among the divisions.

A column from Petersburg, under Major-General Whiting, had been directed to proceed to Swift Creek, on the turnpike, over three miles from Petersburg and nine

GENERAL G. T. BEAUREGARD.

BORN NEAR NEW ORLEANS, LA., MAY 28, 1818. DIED AT NEW ORLEANS, LA., FEBRUARY 20, 1893.

[From a crayon portrait.]

from my lines, and was under orders to advance at daybreak to Port Walthall Junction, three miles nearer. The line of the enemy's forces, under Butler, comprising the corps of Gillmore and W. F. Smith (Tenth and Eighteenth), was generally parallel to our intermediate line of works, somewhat curved, concentric and exterior to our own. They held our own outer line of works, crossing the turnpike half a mile in our front. Their line of breastworks and intrenchments increased in strength with its progress westward and northward; its right and weakest point was in the edge of William Gregory's woods, about half a mile west of James River. The line of hostile breastworks from their right flank continued westwardly, intersecting the turnpike near our outer line of fortifications. Near this point of intersection at Charles Friend's farm was advantageously posted a force of the enemy throughout the day's struggle, and here are said to have been the headquarters of Generals Butler and Smith. Butler's lines thence following partly the course of our outer works, crossed them and ran westwardly through fields and woods until after crossing the railroad, when his extreme left inclined to the north.

With the foregoing data I determined upon the following plan: That our left wing, turning and hurled upon Butler's weak right, should with crushing force double it back on its center, thus interposing an easterly barrier between Butler and his base; that our right wing should, simultaneously with its skirmishers, and afterward in force, as soon as the left became fully engaged, advance and occupy the enemy to prevent his re-enforcing his right and thus form his northern barrier, without, however, prematurely seeking to force him far back before our left could completely outflank him and our Petersburg column close up on his rear; and, finally, that the Petersburg column, marching to the sound of heaviest firing, should interpose a southern barrier to his retreat. Butler, thus environed by three walls of fire, with his defeated troops, could have no resource against substantial capture or destruction, except in an attempt at partial and hazardous escape westward, away from his base, trains or supplies. Two difficulties alone might impede or defeat the success of this plan. One was a possible stubborn and effective resistance by the enemy, in virtue of his superior numbers. Another (probably a graver one) existed as to the efficient, rapid handling of a fragmentary army like ours, so hastily assembled and organized—half the brigades without general officers, some of the troops unacquainted with their commanders and neighbors, staff officers unknown to each other, etc. The moral force which tells so significantly of the unity which springs from old association was entirely wanting, and from these causes, generally so productive of confusion and entanglement, great inconvenience arose. On the other hand, I reckoned on the advantages of being all in readiness at daybreak, with short distances over which to operate, a long day before me to maneuver in, plan, direct routes, and simplicity in the movements to be executed.

Accordingly, at 10:45 A. M. on May 15th, preparatory information and orders were forwarded to Major-General Whiting, then at Petersburg, twelve miles from me, with instructions to move his force to Swift Creek, three miles nearer, during the night, and at daybreak next morning to proceed to Port Walthall Junction, about three miles still nearer. These instructions were duly received by that officer, and were as follows:

"I shall attack enemy in front to-morrow at daybreak by River Road, to cut him off from his Bermuda base. You will take up your position to-night at Swift Creek with Wise's, Martin's, Dearing's [brigades], and two regiments of Colquitt's brigade, with about twenty field-pieces, under Colonel Jones.

"At daybreak you will march to Port Walthall Junction, and when you hear an engagement in your front you will advance boldly and rapidly by the shortest road in the direction of heaviest firing to attack enemy in rear or flank. You will protect your advance and flanks with Dearing's cavalry, taking necessary precautions to distinguish friends from foes. Please communicate this to General Hill. This revokes all former orders of movements.

"G. T. BEAUREGARD, *General Commanding*.

"P. S.—I have just received a telegram from General Bragg, informing me that he has sent you orders to join me at this place. You need not do so, but follow to the letter the above instructions."

DREWRYS BLUFF ON THE JAMES RIVER, NEAR RICHMOND, VA.

In the early afternoon I delivered in person to the other division commanders assembled the following circular instructions of battle, with additional oral instructions to Major-General Ransom that while driving the enemy he should promptly occupy with a brigade the crossing of Proctors Creek by the River Road, which was the enemy's shortest line of retreat to Bermuda Hundred Neck:

[*Circular*.]

HEADQUARTERS DEPARTMENT OF NORTH CAROLINA AND SOUTHERN VIRGINIA,
DREWRY'S FARM, May 15, 1864.

GENERAL: The following instructions for battle to-morrow are communicated for your information and action:

The purpose of the movement is to cut off the enemy from his base of operations at Bermuda Hundred and capture or destroy him in his present position. To this end we shall attack and turn by the River Road his right flank, now resting on James River, while his center and left flank are kept engaged to prevent him from re-enforcing his right flank. Major-General Ransom's division will to-night take position, the most favorable for attack, on the enemy's right flank, to be made by him at daybreak to-morrow morning. His skirmishers will drive back vigorously those of the enemy in his front, and will be followed closely by his line of battle, which will, at the proper time, pivot on its right flank, so as to take the enemy in flank and rear. He will form in two lines of battle and will use his battalion of artillery to the best advantage. Colonel Dunovant's regiment of cavalry will move with this division under the direction of General Ransom. Major-General Hoke's division, now in the trenches on the right of the position herein assigned to General Ransom, will, at daylight, engage the enemy with a heavy line of skirmishers and will hold the rest of his forces in hand ready to attack with vigor the enemy's line in his front as soon as he shall find it wavering before his skirmishers, or so soon as Ransom's line of battle shall have become fairly engaged with the enemy. General Hoke will form in two lines of battle, four hundred yards apart, in front of his trenches at the proper time, and in such manner as not to delay his forward movement. He will use his battalion of artillery to the best advantage. Colonel Baker's regiment of cavalry will move in conjunction with Hoke's division, so as to protect his right flank. He will receive more definite instructions from Major-General Hoke. Colonel Shingler's regiment of cavalry will move with the reserve division.

The division commanded by Brigadier-General Colquitt will constitute the reserve, and will to-night form in column by brigades in rear of Hoke's present position, the center of each brigade resting on the turnpike. The division will be massed under cover of the hills now occupied by Hoke's troops, so as to be sheltered at the outset from the enemy's fire in front. During the movement the head of the reserve column will be kept at a distance of about five hundred yards from Hoke's second line of battle. As soon as practicable, the intervals between the brigades of the reserve division will be maintained at from two hundred or three hundred yards. The reserve artillery, under General Colquitt, will follow along the turnpike about three hundred yards in rear of the last brigade. He will use it to the best advantage. Simultaneously with these movements, Major-General Whiting will move with his division from Petersburg along the Petersburg and Richmond Turnpike, and attack the enemy's flank and rear.

The movements above indicated must be made with all possible vigor and celerity.

The generals commanding divisions and Colonels Baker and Shingle, commanding cavalry, will report at these headquarters at 6 P. M. to-day. In the meantime, they will give all necessary instructions for providing their respective commands with sixty rounds of ammunition issued to each man, and at least twenty rounds for each in reserve. They will cause their commands to be supplied with two days' cooked rations.

G. T. BEAUREGARD, *General Commanding*.

TO DIVISION COMMANDERS.

Ransom moved at 4:45 A. M., being somewhat delayed by a dense fog, which lasted several hours after dawn and occasioned some embarrassment. His division consisted of the following brigades, in the order mentioned, commencing from the left: Gracie's, Kemper's (commanded by Colonel Terry), Barton's (under Colonel Fry), and Colonel Lewis' (Hoke's old brigade).

He was soon engaged, carrying, at 6 A. M., with some loss, the enemy's line of breastworks in his front, his troops moving splendidly forward to the assault and capturing five stand of colors and some five hundred prisoners. The brigades most heavily engaged were Gracie's and Kemper's, opposed to the enemy's right, the former turning his flank. He then halted to form, reported his loss heavy and troops scattered by the fog, his ammunition short, and asked for a brigade from the reserve. Colquitt's brigade was sent him at 6:30 A. M., with orders for its return when it ceased to be indispensable. Before either ammunition or the reserve brigade had arrived, he reported the enemy driving Hoke's left and sent the right regiment of Lewis' brigade forward at double-quick toward the point of supposed danger. This held the enemy long enough for the reserve brigade to arrive, charge and drive him back from the front of our left center, where the affair occurred, over and along the works to the turnpike.

It will be seen in a subsequent part of this report that one of Hagood's advance regiments had unexpectedly come in contact with the enemy and been ordered back, it not being contemplated to press at this point until Ransom should swing around his left, as directed in the battle order. This possibly originated Ransom's impression as to the situation of Hoke's left, which had, in fact, steadily maintained its proper position. At 7:15 A. M. Colquitt's brigade, of the reserve, was recalled from Ransom, and a slight modification of the original movement was made to relieve Hoke, on whose front the enemy had been allowed to mass his forces by the inaction of the left. Ransom was ordered to flank the enemy's right by changing the front of his right brigade to support it by another in echelon, to advance a third toward Proctors Creek, and to hold a fourth in reserve. This modification was intended to be temporary and the original plan was to be fully carried out on the seizure of the River Road and Proctors Creek crossing. In proceeding to execute this order Ransom found the reserve brigade engaged and his own troops moving by the right flank toward the firing at the center. He, therefore, sent Barton's brigade back instead of Colquitt's and reported a necessity to straighten and reform his lines in the old position near the lines he had stormed. Here his infantry rested during the greater part of the day, Dunovant's cavalry, dismounted, being thrown forward as skirmishers toward a small force which occupied a ridge in the edge of George Gregory's woods, north of Proctors Creek. This force, with an insignificant body of cavalry, believed to be negroes, and a report of threatening gunboats, which came some hours earlier, as since ascertained, were the only menace to our left. At 10 A. M. I withheld an order for Ransom to move until further arrangements should be made, for the following reasons:

The right was heavily engaged; all of the reserve had been detached right and left at different times; the silence of Whiting's guns, which had been heard a short time about 8 A. M., gave reasonable hope that he had met no resistance and would soon be on. A dispatch had been sent to Whiting at 9 A. M., which was repeated at 9:30 A. M., to "Press on and press over everything in your front, and the day will be complete;" and Ransom not only reported the enemy in strong force in his front, but expressed the opinion that the safety of his command would be compromised by an advance.

On the right, Hoke had early advanced his skirmishers and opened with his artillery. The fog and other causes temporarily delayed the advance of his line of battle. When he finally moved forward he soon became hotly engaged and handled his command with judgment and energy. Hagood and Johnson were thrown forward with a section of Eshleman's Washington Artillery, and found a heavy force of the enemy, with six or eight pieces of artillery, occupying the salient of the outer line of works on the turnpike and his own defensive lines. Our artillery engaged at very short range, disabling some of the enemy's guns and blowing up two limbers. Another section of the same command opened from the right of the turnpike. They both held their positions, though with heavy loss, until their ammunition was spent, when they were relieved by an equal number of pieces from the reserve artillery, under Major Owen. Hagood, with great vigor and dash, drove the enemy from the outer lines in his front, capturing a number of prisoners, and, in conjunction with Johnson, five pieces of artillery—three 20-pounder Parrotts and two fine Napoleons. He then took position in the works, his left regiment being thrown forward by Hoke to connect with Ransom's right. In advancing, this regiment encountered the enemy behind a second line of works in the woods, with abatis interlaced with wire. Attack at that point not being contemplated, it was ordered back to the line of battle, but not before its intrepid advance had brought on it considerable loss. This circumstance has been referred to before as the occasion of a mistake by Ransom. Johnson, meanwhile, had been heavily engaged. The line of the enemy bent around his right flank, subjecting his brigade for a time to fire in flank and front. With admirable firmness he repulsed frequent assaults of the enemy moving in masses against his right and rear. Leader, officers and men alike displayed their fitness for the trial to which they were subjected. Among many instances of heroism I can not forbear to mention that Lieutenant Waggoner, of the Seventeenth Tennessee Regiment, went alone through a storm of fire and pulled down a white flag which a small isolated body of our men had raised, receiving a wound in the act.

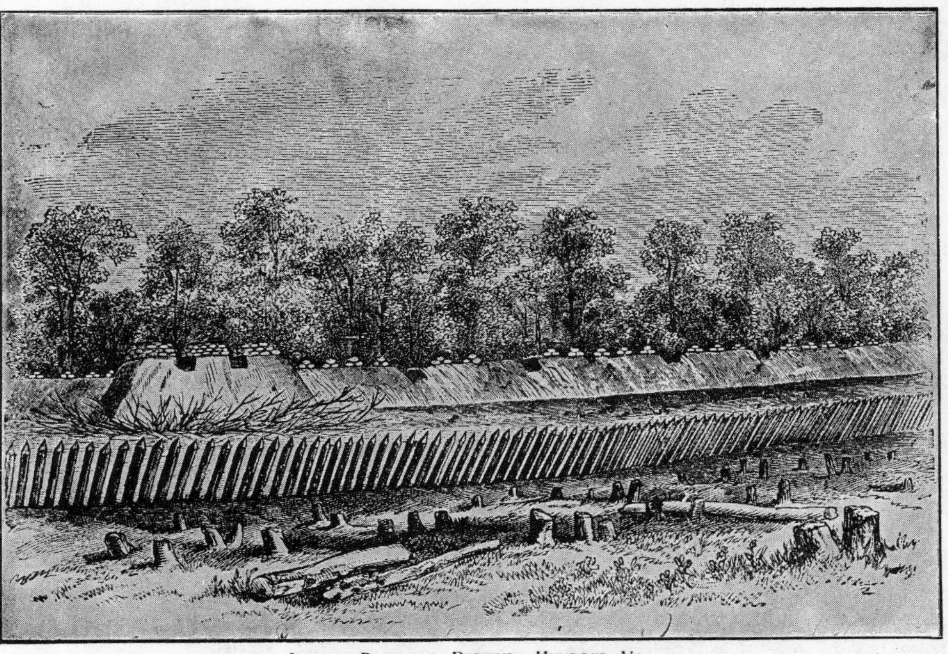

LINE OF DEFENSES, BERMUDA HUNDRED, VA.

The brigade, holding its ground nobly, lost more than a fourth of its entire number. Four regiments of the reserve were sent up to its support, but were less effective than they should have been through a mistake of the officer posting them. Hoke also sent two regiments from Clingman to protect Johnson's flank. These partially partook of the same mistake, being posted in the woods where the moral and material effect of their presence was lost. I now ordered Hoke to press forward his right for the relief of his right center, and he advanced Clingman with his remaining two regiments and Corse with his brigade. They drove the enemy with spirit, suffering some loss, but the gap between Clingman and the troops on his left induced him to retire his command to prevent being flanked and reform it in the intermediate lines. Thus Corse became isolated, and learning from his officers that masses were forming against his right flank, he withdrew some distance back, but not quite so far as his original position. These two brigades were not afterward engaged, though they went to the front—Corse about one hour after he fell back, and Clingman at about 2:15 P. M. The enemy did not reoccupy the ground from which they drove him before they retired.

In front of Hagood and Johnson the fighting was stubborn and prolonged. The enemy, slowly retiring from Johnson's right, took strong position on the ridge in front of Proctors Creek, massing near the turnpike, and occupying advantageous ground at the house and grove of Charles Friend. At length Johnson, having brushed the enemy from his right flank in the woods with some assistance from the Washington Artillery, and cleared his front, rested his troops in the shelter of the outer works. One of the captured pieces having opened on the enemy's masses, he finally fell back behind the woods and ridge at Proctors Creek, though his skirmish line continued the engagement some hours longer.

Further movements were here suspended to wait communication from Whiting or the sound of his approach and to reorganize the troops which had become more or less disorganized. Brief firing at about 1:45 P. M. gave some hope of his proximity. I waited in vain. The firing heard was probably an encounter between Dearing and the enemy's rear guard. Dearing had been ordered by Whiting to communicate with me, but, unsupported as he was by infantry or artillery, he was unable to do so, except by sending a detachment by a circuitous route, which reached me after the work of the day was closed. At 4 P. M. all hope of Whiting's approach was gone, and I reluctantly abandoned so much of my plan as contemplated more than a vigorous pursuit of Butler and driving him to his fortified base. To effect this I resumed my original formation, and directed General Hoke to send two brigades forward along the Courthouse Road, to take the enemy in flank, and establish enfilading batteries in front of the heights west of the railroad. The formation of our line was checked by a heavy and prolonged storm of rain. Meanwhile the enemy opened a severe fire, which was soon silenced by our artillery. Before we were ready to advance, darkness approached, and, upon consultation with several of my subordinate commanders, it was deemed imprudent to attack, considering the probability of serious obstacles and the proximity of Butler's intrenched camp. I, therefore, put the army in position for the night and sent instructions to Whiting to join our right at the railroad in the morning.

During the night the enemy retired to the fortified line of his present camp, leaving in our hands some fourteen hundred prisoners, five pieces of artillery and five stand of colors. He now rests there hemmed by our lines, which have since, from time to time, been advanced with every skirmish, and now completely cover the southern communications of the capital, thus securing one of the principal objects of the attack. The more glorious results anticipated were lost by the hesitation of the left wing and the premature halt of the Petersburg column before obstacles in neither case sufficient to have deterred from the execution of the movements prescribed.

Too much praise can not be bestowed on the officers and men who fought the battle of Drewrys Bluff, for the order and intrepidity displayed by them whenever called upon to meet the foe, regardless of his advantage in numbers and position. I shall take pleasure in presenting the names of those who most distinguished themselves as soon as the detailed reports of subordinate commanders shall have been received at these headquarters. The same opportunity will be taken to mention the names and services of those members of my personal and general staff who were present during the battle, and of those officers who, belonging to other commands, kindly volunteered their services on that occasion. The intelligent zeal and activity of all these officers in transmitting orders and conveying information from one portion of the field to the other, contributed largely to the success of the day.

G. T. BEAUREGARD, *General.*

CAMPAIGN

FROM THE

RAPIDAN TO SPOTTSYLVANIA C. H.,

MAY 4 TO 27, 1864.

BY

LIEUTENANT-GENERAL R. S. EWELL.

RICHMOND, VA., March 20, 1865.

WHEN General Grant crossed the Rapidan, R. D. Johnston's North Carolina brigade, of Rodes' division, was at Hanover Junction; the Twenty-first Georgia, of Doles' brigade, same division, and Hoke's brigade, of Early's division, were in North Carolina. About thirteen thousand five hundred effective infantry and two thousand artillery were present. By order of General Lee, his corps and division commanders met him on Monday, 2d of May, 1864, at the Signal Station on Clarks Mountain. He then gave it as his opinion that the enemy would cross by some of the fords below us, as Germania or Elys. They began to do so next day.

About noon of the 4th we moved from our camps on the Rapidan toward Locust Grove, on the old turnpike from Orange Courthouse to Fredericksburg. Johnson's division and Nelson's battalion of artillery bivouacked two miles south of Locust Grove; Rodes just behind them, and Early at Locust Grove. The artillery was close behind Early. Ramseur's brigade, of Rodes' division, with three regiments from each of the other divisions, was left on picket. Next morning, I moved down the pike, sending the First North Carolina Cavalry, which I found in my front, on a road that turned to the left toward Germania Ford. About 8 A. M., I sent Major Campbell Brown, of my staff, to General Lee to report my position. In reply, he instructed me to regulate my march by General A. P. Hill, whose progress down the Plank Road I could tell by the firing at the head of his column, and informed me that he preferred not to bring on a general engagement before General Longstreet came up.

Advancing slowly with J. M. Jones' brigade, of Johnson's division, in advance, prepared for action, I came, about 11 A. M., in sight of a column of the enemy crossing the pike from Germania Ford toward the Plank Road. The "Stonewall" (Walker's) brigade had been sent down a left-hand road, driving in the enemy's pickets within a mile and a half of Germania Ford. Being a good deal ahead of General Hill, I halted and again reported through Lieutenant-Colonel A. S. Pendleton, of my staff, receiving substantially the same instructions as before. Just after they came the enemy demonstrated against Jones' brigade, and I placed Battle's, of Rodes' division, to support it, with Doles on Battle's right. They were instructed not to allow themselves to become involved, but to fall back slowly, if pressed. Some artillery posted near the pike, on Jones' front, was withdrawn. Soon afterward the enemy fell suddenly upon Jones' right flank and front, broke his brigade and drove it back upon Battle's, which it disordered. Daniel's brigade, of Rodes' division, and Gordon's, of Early's, were soon brought up and regained the lost ground, the latter capturing, by a dashing charge, several hundred prisoners, and relieving Doles, who, though hard pressed, had held his ground. General J. M. Jones and his aid-de-camp, Captain Robert Early, fell in a desperate effort to rally their brigade. I placed it in reserve to reorganize—Battle's brigade, which had rallied in time to do good service, taking its place in the line, which was now formed on the ground first occupied. The brigades were as follows from right to left of my line: Daniel, Doles, Battle (Rodes' division), G. H. Steuart's, "Stonewall" (Walker's), Stafford's (Johnson's division), Pegram, Hays, Gordon (Early's division); Battle's left and Steuart's right rested on the pike. Slight works were at once thrown up, and several partial attacks of the enemy repulsed. In a counter attack by Steuart's and Battle's brigades, two 24-pounder howitzers, brought up the pike within eight hundred yards of our works, were captured. The troops were brought back to the works after posting skirmishers to hold the captured pieces till dark, when they were brought off.

General Stafford was mortally wounded in a similar attack by his own and the "Stonewall" brigades late in the afternoon. The fighting closed at dusk with the repulse of a fierce attack on Pegram's brigade. General Pegram was severely wounded, and Colonel Hoffman (Thirty-first Virginia) succeeded to the command. This evening General Ramseur came up with the picket regiments, which rejoined their brigades. Ramseur went to the extreme right of my line next morning.

The 6th of May was occupied in partial assaults on my line, now greatly strengthened, and in efforts to find my flank, which were promptly checked. About 9 A. M. I got word from General Gordon, through General Early in person, that his scouts reported the enemy's right exposed, and he urged turning it; but his views were opposed by General Early, who thought the attempt unsafe. This necessitated a personal examination, which was made as soon as other duties permitted; but in consequence of this delay and other unavoidable causes, the movement was not begun until nearly sunset. After the examination, I ordered the attack and placed Robert D. Johnston's brigade, of Rodes' division, that morning arrived from Hanover Junction, to support Gordon. Each brigade, as its front was cleared, was to unite in the attack. Hays was partly moved out of his works to connect with Gordon. The latter attacked vehemently, and when checked by the darkness had captured, with slight loss, a mile of the works held by the Sixth Corps, six hundred prisoners and two brigadier-generals (Seymour and Shaler). Of the force encountered not an organized regiment remained, and nearly all had thrown away their arms. They made no attempt to recover the lost ground, but drew back their line so as to give up Germania Ford entirely. Major Daniel, of General Early's staff, joined in Gordon's attack and was desperately wounded and maimed for life while gallantly assisting in this brilliant movement.

On the 7th of May no fighting took place except that in extending to join General Hill's left, General Ramseur came upon a division of the Ninth Corps intrenching. This he put to flight by a sudden attack of his skirmishers, capturing several hundred knapsacks and occupying the ground. On the night of the 7th the general commanding sent me word to extend to the right in conformity to the movements of the troops there and if, at daylight, I found no large force in my front, to follow General Anderson toward Spottsylvania Courthouse. This was done. On the march, orders were received placing General Early in command of Hill's corps, transferring Hays' brigade to Johnson's division, and consolidating both Louisiana brigades under General Hays, and assigning R. D. Johnston's brigade to Early's division, of which General Gordon came in command. After a very distressing march through intense heat and thick dust and smoke from burning woods, my troops reached Spottsylvania Courthouse about 5 P. M., just in time for Rodes to repel an attempt to turn Anderson's right, which rested on the road. Rodes advanced nearly half a mile, when his left, coming upon strong works, was checked and he was forced to halt. Johnson's division formed on his right; Gordon remained in reserve.

On the 9th, the lines were defined and intrenched. There were two salients, one at Rodes' right brigade (Doles'), the other at Johnson's center, where I occupied a high open point, which if held by the enemy would enable their artillery to command our line. Johnson's right was connected by skirmishers with Hill's (Early's) left. A second line from Rodes' left center to Hill's left, cutting off the salients, was laid out by the chief engineer and built and occupied by Gordon's division. Heavy skirmishing took place. General Hays was severely wounded.

TUESDAY, MAY 10th.—The enemy's batteries getting an enfilade and reverse fire on Gordon's line, he was withdrawn and placed in rear of Rodes' left and Anderson's right (Kershaw's division), where an attack was expected. About 4 P. M., I learned that General Doles' skirmishers were driven into his works. He was ordered to regain his skirmish-line at any cost, but while preparing to do so his lines were attacked and broken, he losing three hundred prisoners. The right of Daniel's brigade was exposed and fell back to the second line already mentioned. Battle's brigade and Gordon's division were rapidly brought up and the former thrown across the head of the enemy's column, while the leading brigade (R. D. Johnston's) of the latter, with the remnants of Doles' and the right of Daniel's brigades, struck on one flank, and the "Stonewall" (Walker's), of Johnson's division, on the other. In a short time the enemy were driven from our works, leaving a hundred dead within them, and a large number in front. Our loss as near as I can tell was six hundred and fifty, of whom three hundred and fifty were prisoners. Captain Thomas T. Turner, my aid-de-camp, was very efficient in rallying the fugitives, and was severely wounded while assisting in recapturing several pieces of artillery which the enemy had got temporary possession of.

WEDNESDAY, MAY 11th.—It rained hard all day, and no fighting took place. Toward night the enemy were reported withdrawing from Anderson's front, and were heard moving to our right; scouts stated them to be retiring to Fredericksburg. I received orders to withdraw the artillery, which was done along Johnson's front.

THURSDAY, MAY 12th.—Soon after midnight Major-General Johnson reported the enemy massing before him, and General Long was directed to return the artillery to the intrenchments, and General Gordon ordered to be prepared to support Johnson. Different artillery was sent back and, owing to the darkness and ignorance of the location, it only reached the lines in time to be taken. The enemy attacked in heavy force at earliest dawn and, though gallantly resisted, their numbers and the want of artillery enabled them to break through our lines, capturing Major-General Ed. Johnson, Brigadier-General G. H. Steuart, about two thousand eight hundred men and twenty pieces of artillery. The smoke of the guns and the mist kept the air dark until comparatively a late hour, thereby assisting the enemy, as he was enabled to mass his troops as he chose. They poured through our lines in immense numbers, taking possession to the right and left of the salient, and keeping up a constant fire of artillery and musketry for twenty-four hours. General Gordon was heavily engaged, one brigade broken and its commander, General R. D. Johnston, wounded; but he held his ground, drove out the enemy in his immediate front by a strong effort, and regained a portion of our works to the right of the salient. Their main effort was evidently against Rodes' position to the left of the angle, and here the fighting was of the most desperate character. General Rodes moved Daniel's brigade from its works to meet the enemy. General Kershaw extended so as to allow Ramseur to be withdrawn, and as Daniel's right was unprotected Ramseur was sent in there. He retook the works to Daniel's right along his whole brigade front by a charge of unsurpassed gallantry. But the salient was still held by the enemy, and a most deadly fire poured on his right flank. Accordingly, Harris' Mississippi brigade, which came to my assistance about 9 A. M., was sent to Ramseur's right; but as it still failed to fill the trenches, McGowan's South Carolina brigade, which arrived an hour later, was ordered to the same point. Only part of this brigade succeeded in reaching the trenches and joining Harris' brigade. Spite of the terrible flank fire to which they were yet exposed, the brave troops of these three brigades held their ground till 3 A. M. the 13th of May, when ordered back to the new line. General Daniel was killed and General Ramseur severely wounded early in the day, but the latter refused to leave the field. The nature of the struggle will be apparent from the fact that after the loss of Johnson's division (before sunrise) my force barely numbered eight thousand — the re-enforcements about fifteen hundred more. General Ed. Johnson estimated the enemy's force at this part of the field at over forty thousand, and I have every reason to believe this a moderate calculation. The engagement was spoken of in Northern papers as a general attack by their army. It was met only by my corps and three brigades sent to my aid, and after lasting with unintermitted vigor from 4:30 A. M. till 4 P. M. of the 12th of May, ceased by degrees, leaving us in possession of two-thirds of the works first taken from us, and of four of the captured guns which the enemy had been unable to haul off. These guns were withdrawn by hand to the McCoull house, and General Long was directed to send after them at night. Major Page, whom he instructed to get them, left the duty to an orderly sergeant, who failed to find them, and they were again allowed to fall into the enemy's hands. As it was unadvisable to continue efforts to retake the salient with the force at my command, a new line was laid out during the day by General Lee's chief engineer, some eight hundred yards in rear of the first, and constructed at night. After midnight my forces were quietly withdrawn to it and artillery placed in position. But his efforts and losses on the 12th seemed to have exhausted the enemy, and all was quiet till the 18th of May, when a strong force advanced past the McCoull house toward our new line. When well within range General Long opened upon them with thirty pieces of artillery, which, with the fire of our skirmishers, broke and drove them back with severe loss. We afterward learned that they were two fresh divisions, nearly ten thousand strong, just come up from the rear.

On the 19th of May, General Lee directed me to demonstrate against the enemy in my front, as he believed they were moving to his right, and wished to ascertain. As they were strongly intrenched in front, I obtained leave to move around their right. After a detour of several miles through roads impassable for my artillery, I came on the enemy prepared to receive me. My force was about six

OUTPOSTS OF THE CONFEDERATE AND FEDERAL ARMIES ON THE JAMES RIVER.

thousand, his much larger. His position being developed and my object attained, I was about to retire when he attacked me. Part of my line was shaken, but Pegram's brigade, of Early's division (Colonel Hoffman commanding), and Ramseur's, of Rodes', held their ground so firmly that I maintained my position till nightfall; then withdrew unmolested. My loss was about nine hundred, killed, wounded and missing. Next day General Early returned to his division, and General Gordon was put in command of one composed of his own brigade and the remnants of Johnson's division. Hoke's brigade (Colonel Lewis commanding) returned to Early's division, and the Twenty-first Georgia Regiment to Doles' brigade. We moved to Hanover Junction, where my corps took the right of the line. After some days' skirmishing we marched toward the Totopotomoy. When we removed, I reported to the general commanding that, in consequence of a severe attack of diarrhœa, I would leave General Early in command while the troops were on the march, and on Friday I rode in an ambulance to Mechanicsville, remaining in my tent Saturday and Sunday, the 28th and 29th of May. On Sunday I reported that I would be on

My staff during this campaign consisted of Lieutenant-Colonel A. S. Pendleton and Major Campbell Brown, Acting Adjutant-Generals; Colonel A. Smead (Colonel of Artillery), Acting Inspector-General; Major B. H. Greene, Engineer; Lieutenant Thomas T. Turner, Aid-de-camp; Lieutenant-Colonel William Allan, Chief of Ordnance; Surgeon Hunter McGuire, Medical Director; Majors John Rogers and A. S. Garber, Quartermasters (Major Harman having been transferred just before the campaign opened); Major W. J. Hawks and Captain J. J. Locke, Commissaries of Subsistence. All except Majors Brown, Greene and Rogers, and Lieutenant T. T. Turner, had been of the staff of Lieutenant-General Jackson. That officer should be held hardly more remarkable for his brilliant campaigns than for the judgment he almost invariably showed in his selections of men. It would be difficult, without personal knowledge, to appreciate Colonel Pendleton's great gallantry, his coolness and clearness of judgment under every trial, his soldier-like and cheerful performance of every duty. On one occasion I expressed a wish to recommend him to a vacant brigade, but he declined, thinking his services more valuable on the staff.

enemy; the third and largest made no report. When we moved, probably one-third or more were still unburied of those who were in reach of our lines. At Spottsylvania, though the enemy held the ground for a week, we found on regaining it many of their dead still unburied, while the numerous graves showed their loss to have been immense; it must have exceeded ours in the proportion of at least six to one, taking all the engagements together.

R. S. EWELL, *Lieutenant-General.*

IT is related that a gentleman from some Northern city entered Mr. Lincoln's private office in the spring of 1862 and earnestly requested a pass to Richmond. "A pass to Richmond!" exclaimed the President. "Why, my dear sir, if I should give you one it would do you no good. You may think it very strange, but there's a lot of fellows between here and Richmond who either can't read or are prejudiced against every man who totes a pass from me. I have given McClellan and more than two hundred thousand others passes to Richmond, and nor a darned one of 'em has yet gotten there."

WINTER QUARTERS (1863-64) OF THE LEFT WING OF THE ARMY OF NORTHERN VIRGINIA ON THE RAPIDAN.

duty in two days more, and sent a certificate of Staff-Surgeon McGuire to the same effect. The commanding general relieved me on Sunday, placing General Early in temporary command of my corps. I reported for duty on Tuesday, four days after my attack, and remained over a week with the army, wishing to place the question of health beyond a doubt; but the change of commanders was made permanent, and on the 14th of June I was placed in command of the defenses of Richmond.

The losses of my corps from the 4th to the 27th of May were, it will be seen, very heavy and, including prisoners, amounted to over one-half. Of the fourteen generals who began the campaign under me, Generals J. M. Jones, L. A. Stafford and Junius Daniel were killed; Generals John Pegram, Harry T. Hays, James A. Walker and Robert D. Johnston, wounded; Generals Ed. Johnson and G. H. Steuart taken prisoners, and General Early most of the time detached. General Jones had been twice wounded—at Gettysburg and Mine Run. I considered his loss an irreparable one to his brigade. General Ed. Johnson once said of General Stafford that "he was the bravest man he ever saw." Such a compliment from one himself brave almost to a fault and habitually sparing of praise, needs no remark. General Daniel's services at Gettysburg, as well as on the bloody field where he fell, were of the most distinguished character. General Walker was wounded in the attempt to stem the attack on his division early on the 12th of May.

Major Hawks deserves the highest praise I can give him for his ability and zeal in the performance of his duties, so impressing me that I have often wished he could have a command in the line, if it were possible to fill his place on the staff.

It is but simple justice to say that the quiet and efficient manner in which Surgeon McGuire performed the duties of his important department left nothing to be desired, while Colonel Allan's abilities were recognized at headquarters by both compliments and promotion.

Major Brown had been with me from the first battle of Manassas, and on nearly every field had been intrusted with important duties. On no occasion did I have reason to regret my confidence in his coolness, judgment and discretion. I also wished to recommend him for promotion to a Tennessee brigade, but he declined.

Probably no officer had more distinguished himself by repeated acts of personal bravery and dash than Lieutenant T. T. Turner, or with so slight personal advancement. Up to the time when he was wounded at Spottsylvania Courthouse he had constantly been foremost wherever opportunities presented themselves.

Lieutenant Harper Carroll and Lieutenant John Taliaferro, Acting Aids-de-camp, had horses shot under them, on the 12th of May, and displayed much personal gallantry.

My total loss at the Wilderness was twelve hundred and fifty killed and wounded. The burial parties from two divisions reported interring over eleven hundred of the

THE FATAL VOLLEY.

BY I. W. CANADY.

All day the struggle had progressed between opposing foes,
And oft the brazen bugle's blast above the din arose.
In valiant charge and countercharge across the smoking plain
They grappled in a fierce embrace, regardless of the slain,
Till Night her friendly mantle drew above the shattered lines,
And her refreshing breezes blew among the fragrant pines.

But not content to wait the dawn in perfecting his plans,
Our tireless chieftain's eager eye the foe's position scans.
With but a slender body-guard out to the front he passed,
To find a salient where his troops in silence could be massed.
From his completed task he turns his charger to the rear,
To gain the shelter of his camp, nor dreams of danger near.

Mistaken in the deep'ning gloom for an advancing foe,
A bullet from his own command laid the great leader low.
A thousand soldiers of his corps would thankfully have shared
Their foemen's graves if in their stead their idol's life was spared.
Ah! when that fatal volley rang out on the evening air,
Mars placed a wreath on Jackson's brow, and Clio leaves it there!

THE MAN OF THE TWELFTH OF MAY.*

BY ROBERT FALLIGANT, SAVANNAH, GA.

When history tells her story
Of the noble hero band
Who have made the green fields gory
For the life of their native land,
How grand will be the picture
Of Georgia's proud array,
As they drove the boasting foeman back
On that glorious twelfth of May, boys,
That glorious twelfth of May!

Chorus—Then hurrah! while we rally around
The hero of that day,
And a nation's grateful praises crown
The man of the twelfth of May, boys,
The man of the twelfth of May.

Whose mien is ever proudest,
When we hold the foe at bay?
Whose war cry cheers us loudest
As we rush to the bloody fray?
'Tis Gordon's! Our reliance!
Fearless as on the day
When he hurled his grand defiance
In that charge of the twelfth of May, boys,
In the charge of the twelfth of May.

Who can be a coward,
What freeman fears to die,
When Gordon orders "Forward!"
And the red cross floats on high?
Follow his tones inspiring!
On, on to the field away!
And we'll see the foe retiring,
As they did on the twelfth of May, boys,
As they did on the twelfth of May.

This is no time for sighing!
Whate'er our fate may be,
'Tis sweet to think that, dying,
We will leave our country free.
When the storms of battle pelt her
She'll defy the tyrant's sway,
And our breasts shall be her shelter,
As they were on the twelfth of May, boys,
As they were on the twelfth of May.

*In commemoration of General J. B. Gordon's charge against Hancock's corps at Spottsylvania Courthouse, May 12, 1864.

CAMPAIGN
FROM THE
RAPIDAN TO JAMES RIVER,
MAY 4 TO JUNE 12, 1864,
INCLUDING BATTLES OF
SPOTTSYLVANIA, WILDERNESS AND COLD HARBOR.
BY
BRIG.-GEN. WILLIAM N. PENDLETON,
Chief of Artillery.

THE campaign opened with active movements on May 4th. The artillery force of the army as then distributed will be seen in the following tables:

ARTILLERY SERVING WITH THE FIRST CORPS, BRIGADIER-GENERAL E. P. ALEXANDER, CHIEF COMMANDING.

HUGER'S BATTALION.*
Lieutenant-Colonel Huger; Major Jordan.

	GUNS.
Smith's battery	4
Moody's battery	5
Woolfolk's battery	4
Parker's battery	4
Taylor's battery	4
Fickling's battery	4
Total	25

HASKELL'S BATTERY.†
Major John C. Haskell.

	GUNS.
Garden's battery	4
Flanner's battery	4
Ramsay's battery	6
Lamkin's battery ‡	—
Total	14

CABELL'S BATTALION. §
Colonel Cabell; Major Hamilton; Major Gibbes.

	GUNS.
Manly's battery	4
McCarthy's battery	4
Callaway's battery	3
Carlton's battery ‖	4
Total	15

* This battalion had recently arrived with Longstreet's corps from East Tennessee, and was recruiting near Cobhams Depot, Albemarle County, when it received orders to march on May 4th, via Orange Courthouse, to Richards shop, southeast of the Wilderness.

† This battalion was still near Cobhams Depot, where it had wintered, when it received orders to march as above.

‡ This battalion was equipped and armed with small guns.

§ This battalion had wintered near Mortons Ford, on the Rapidan, on picket duty. Ordered to march to Richards shop; also to join its command.

‖ This battery accompanied Daniel's brigade to Germanna Ford on 4th; rejoined its battalion on 5th.

This artillery* rendezvoused and bivouacked at Richards shop on the night of the 5th, and at 3 A. M. on the 6th marched for Parkers store, on the Plank Road, in rear of the battlefield of the Wilderness, where it was obliged to halt, there being no suitable ground for more artillery on the front. Cabell's and Huger's battalions proceeded that evening under orders to New Hope Church, still further to the right, where they remained until the morning of the 8th. Haskell's battalion remained in rear of the battlefield for service, if required, till the morning of the 8th.

HARDAWAY'S BATTALION.†
Lieutenant-Colonel Hardaway; Major Watson.

	GUNS.
Dance's battery	4
Smith's battery	4
Griffin's battery	4
Graham's battery	4
Jones' battery	4
Total	20

NELSON'S BATTALION.†
Lieutenant-Colonel William Nelson.

Kirkpatrick's battery	5
Milledge's battery	4
Massie's battery	4
Total	13

BRAXTON'S BATTALION.†
Lieutenant-Colonel Braxton; Major Moorman.

Cooper's battery	4
Carpenter's battery	4
Hardwicke's battery	4
Total	12

MAJ.-GEN. STEPHEN RAMSEUR, OF NORTH CAROLINA.

CUTSHAW'S BATTALION.
Major Cutshaw; Major Stribling.

	GUNS.
Carrington's battery	4
Garber's battery	4
Tanner's battery	4
Total	12

PAGE'S BATTALION.
Major R. C. M. Page.

Fry's battery	4
Carter's battery	4
Reese's battery	4
Page's battery	4
Total	16

This artillery, which had wintered near Fredericks Hall, on the Virginia Central Railroad, and subsequently, as the spring opened, distributed in grazing camps near Liberty Mills, Orange County, received orders to march on May 4th, and was early on the 5th all concentrated at Locust Grove, on the old turnpike between Orange Courthouse and Fredericksburg, near the infantry of the Second Corps. Nelson's battalion was pushed forward with General Edward Johnson's infantry division, which was then deployed across the turnpike, the enemy, who had crossed at Germanna Ford, being in front. Milledge's battery was posted on the right of the road in front of Jones' brigade, but as the movement of the enemy required the brigade to change position, the battery was withdrawn. The enemy being repulsed with loss in an attack then made, General Ewell established his line without further difficulty. The dense growth of the Wilderness left few openings for the use of artillery. Some of Nelson's guns were, however, posted on the right on a commanding ridge, with a small field in front, about a mile from the Lacy house. Two of his guns were also placed on the road leading to the Germanna Plank Road, to operate with the troops of the left wing of the corps. The artillery thus posted was used several times during the day with good effect in repelling partial attacks of the enemy. While these dispositions were in progress the Third Corps was also put in motion, and its artillery distributed as below:

* Artillery serving with Second Corps, Brigadier-General A. L. Long, chief commanding.

† These three battalions were, by General Long, assigned to the special direction of Colonel J. T. Brown.

POAGUE'S BATTALION.
Lieutenant-Colonel Poague; Major Ward.

	GUNS.
Richard's battery	4
Williams' battery	4
Wyatt's battery	2
Utterback's battery	2
Total	12

McINTOSH'S BATTALION.
Lieutenant-Colonel McIntosh; Major Johnson.

Donald's battery	1
Hurt's battery	2
Price's battery	4
Clutter's battery	4
Total	11

PEGRAM'S BATTALION.*
Lieutenant-Colonel Pegram; Major McGraw.

Marye's battery	4
Ellett's battery	2
Brander's battery	3
Zimmerman's battery	3
Cayce's battery	4
Total	16

CUTT'S BATTALION.*
Colonel Cutt; Major Lane.

Ross' battery	5
Patterson's battery	4
Wingfield's battery	4
Total	13

RICHARDSON'S BATTALION.*
Lieutenant-Colonel Richardson; Major Miller.

Penick's battery	3
Landry's battery	4
Grandy's battery	3
Moore's battery	4
Total	14

Early on the morning of May 5th this command was put in motion, attending Heth's and Wilcox's divisions of the Third Corps, down the Plank Road toward the Wilderness, Poague's battalion in front, Heth's division in the advance having encountered a portion of the enemy's cavalry, Richard's battery was pushed forward and assisted in driving it back upon the main body. The head of column on the Plank Road having about midday reached an opening to the left, about two miles from the crossing of the branch road, was halted, and observation from that opening, which was on an elevated ridge, having exhibited the enemy in force near the intersection of the Germanna Road and Old Turnpike, dispositions were made for an encounter. The opening mentioned being the only place near the front where the artillery could be used, the general chief of artillery, with approval of the commanding general, directed Poague's guns, as a precautionary measure, to be placed in position. One gun of this battalion was also advanced down the Plank Road a few hundred yards to Heth's line of battle, and was effectively used in the bloody repulse given by Heth and Wilcox that afternoon to a very heavy assault of the enemy.

While the artillery thus operating with the three infantry corps was being adjusted and arranged, that serving with the cavalry was performing its part. Its composition was as follows:

HORSE ARTILLERY SERVING WITH ARMY OF NORTHERN VIRGINIA, MAJOR R. P. CHEW COMMANDING.

BREATHED'S BATTALION.
Major Breathed.

	GUNS.
Thomson's battery †	4
Johnston's battery †	4
Shoemaker's battery †	4
McGregor's battery ‡	4
Hort's battery §	4
Total	20

Most of the Horse Artillery was thus operating with the cavalry on the right flank of our army, and there holding back the enemy as our heavier guns engaged his masses.

On the morning of May 6th, the battle of the Wilderness, which had begun the previous afternoon, was renewed with great vigor, and Poague's guns, placed near the Plank Road as already described, were soon brought into requisition and proved to have been most advantageously placed. Opening upon the enemy, as with immense masses he pressed back the weary divisions of Heth and Wilcox, they at once checked his advance and enabled Longstreet's troops, just arriving on the field, to seize the favorable moment and compel him to recede with heavy loss. McIntosh's battalion was now placed in position some distance to the left of Poague's, and three of his guns (two Napoleons and a

* These battalions, which had wintered near Cobhams and Lindsays depots, Central Railroad, Albemarle County, Va., received orders to march on May 4th, and bivouacked that night near Verdierville, on the Plank Road, between Orange Courthouse and Fredericksburg, except Cutt's battalion, which had wintered near Rapidan Station, on the Orange & Albemarle Railroad, on picket duty, and was directed to remain with Anderson's division, of the Third Corps, serving as a rear guard to the army.

† These three batteries marched from near Gordonsville on the 4th and engaged the enemy on Catharpin road, with Rosser, under General Stuart, on the 5th.

‡ This battery left with General W. H. F. Lee near Orange Courthouse.

§ This, with General Fitzhugh Lee, engaged the enemy at Todd's Tavern.

From an original painting copyrighted by Kurz & Allison, Chicago, Ill.

BATTLE OF THE WILDERNESS, MAY 6, 1864.

24-pounder howitzer of Price's battery) were advanced on the Plank Road to co-operate with General Longstreet in his attack upon the enemy. They were well served and with good effect. Pegram's battalion was also placed in position about half a mile to the left of McIntosh's, and assisted materially in driving back the enemy attempting to penetrate between our right wing on the Plank Road and Ewell's corps, constituting the left wing, on the Old Turnpike. Cutt's battalion was at a later hour also placed on the line near Pegram's. Richardson's guns meanwhile guarded the roads which centered upon our rear at Parkers Store, on the Plank Road, and on the evening of the 6th relieved Poague's, which had been engaged for two days on the lines.

Simultaneously with these events on our right, the artillery with the Second Corps, on the left, was participating in the battle on that front as the nature of the country admitted. Colonel Carter, under direction of General Long, massed a number of his guns on the extreme left to protect that flank, which the enemy was beginning to threaten, and those guns effectively aided Gordon's brigade, there posted, in repelling the attack which the enemy were not slow to make. Cutshaw's battalion was placed in position on the right of the Turnpike, relieving some of Nelson's guns, and a portion of Hardaway's, on the left, relieving others. Braxton's occupied the central space between the troops on the Turnpike and those on the Plank Road. These guns also did well such work as ordered, aiding in successfully driving back the enemy whenever and wherever he attempted to advance.

At an early hour of this memorable day Colonel J. T. Brown, second in command of the artillery of the Second Corps, fell, instantly killed by the bullet of a sharpshooter, as he was seeking an advanced and favorable position for some of his guns. While the main armies were thus engaged from left to right, on the 6th, the Horse Artillery was sharing the action with the cavalry on our right flank, Johnston's battery remaining in position near Shady Grove, Thomson's and Shoemaker's being engaged most of the day near Rowe's farm, and Hort's not far from Todd's Tavern.

On the 7th, the enemy, apparently despairing of forcing our line, remained mainly passive and not many shots were fired. The general chief of artillery, under instructions from the commanding general, reconnoitered positions on the right and caused a road to be opened by portions of the artillery to facilitate a rapid movement in that direction. At the same time, on the extreme left, a reconnoissance was made by the chief of artillery, Second Corps, under orders from General Ewell, with Jones' infantry brigade, attended by Carter's battery. Striking the Germanna Road near Beale's house, this force encountered there, about a mile from the ford, several regiments of the enemy's cavalry. These received but a few cannon shots, when they dispersed, a few retreating toward the ford, the major number going toward the main body of the enemy. The ford and Germanna Road being thus found virtually abandoned, it became obvious that the enemy was contemplating another movement and leaving our immediate front. The battle of the Wilderness was over. The enemy, wholly repulsed and foiled, was leaving his dead and some of his wounded within the range of our guns. About dark of the 7th, the general chief of artillery [was] directed by the commanding general to send to General Anderson, who had, on General Longstreet being wounded, succeeded to the command of the First Corps, a staff officer who could guide that general along the new road cut out that day. The general chief of artillery went himself to General Anderson, described the route and left an officer as guide. Here a circumstance occurred which should be specially noticed. General Anderson stated that his orders were to march by 3 next morning. He was preparing to start at 11 that night. Those four hours anticipated proved of incalculable value next day. The artillery of the First Corps, which, as already mentioned, had not been able to find opportunity in the battle of the Wilderness, received orders to march, on the night of the 7th, and from its several positions struck into the column en route for Spottsylvania Courthouse.

About 9 A. M. of the 8th, the head of the column came in sight of the Courthouse and found the enemy just getting into view on the Fredericksburg Road, driving back a small cavalry force which there opposed them. At the same time a strong infantry column assailed another cavalry force which disputed their entrance on Todd's Tavern Road. General Alexander, accompanying General Anderson with his advanced column, immediately sent Major Haskell with two batteries to the assistance of our cavalry. On the Todd's Tavern Road two infantry brigades also went in support. These batteries were stubbornly engaged for two hours. Their ammunition being then exhausted and considerable loss experienced, they were withdrawn. During a part of the action they had suffered under a flank reverse fire from a battery belonging to that force of the enemy which had reached the Courthouse by the other route. In the engagement Captain Potts, a most deserving, gallant and efficient officer, was mortally wounded. Field's division meanwhile drove the enemy from the Courthouse, and Huger's battalion was posted on the front. Upon the Todd's Tavern Road, the enemy still pressing in force, more of our infantry had to be there concentrated, and five of Cabell's guns were sent, under Major Hamilton, to that line and assisted materially in repelling the enemy's assaults. Subsequently, a front line having been selected by the general chief of artillery, under advice of General Stuart, crossing the Todd's Tavern Road, on a piny knoll, with an opening in front, five of Huger's batteries were placed in position on that line in very close proximity to the enemy, his guns being not more than four hundred yards off, his sharpshooters scarcely over one hundred yards. The same afternoon (8th) Ewell's corps (Second), which had left the Wilderness at dawn, arrived and bivouacked on the line which it was to occupy on the right of the Todd's Tavern Road and beyond that wing of the First Corps. A few of its guns were put in position on the Courthouse front, the rest parked for the night. The Third Corps, temporarily commanded by General Early (General Hill being unwell), remaining with its artillery as rear guard of the army, did not leave position at the Wilderness till late in the day of the 8th, and did not that night proceed beyond Shady Grove. One section of McIntosh's battalion was, in the evening, engaged with the rear guard of the enemy.

On the 9th, our line being established, most of the artillery was posted along its entire course and protected by slight earthworks; Cabell's battalion on the left flank, four Napoleons, under Major Gibbes, occupying the left of the line of battle, the remaining guns being on an interior or second line upon higher ground, so as to cover and assist the front line. Haskell's battalion and Woolfolk's battery, of Huger's battalion, on the second line, to Cabell's right, and Huger's five batteries close up to the enemy on the front line, crossing the Todd's Tavern Road. Further to the right, Page's and Braxton's guns were in position, with the infantry (Second Corps) on the intrenched line of battle. On this part of the line, as at the Wilderness, dense woods prevented the effective use of much artillery. A portion of Hardaway's and Nelson's guns occupied the line much further to the right on the left of the Courthouse opening, Cutshaw's being in reserve. As the artillery of the Third Corps arrived in the course of this day it was posted on the line still further to the right—Poague's guns on the left of the front to be occupied by this corps, Pegram's next, crossing the Fredericksburg Road a few hundred yards from the Courthouse, and Cutt's on the extreme right, in advance of the road to Massaponax Church. Lieutenant-Colonel Pegram advanced with a section of Ellett's battery and operated with the cavalry in pressing back the enemy until our line was established. McIntosh's battalion remained with Mahone's division near the crossing of the Po River by the Shady Grove Road, to guard the left flank of our army, and Richardson's battalion was held in reserve. Along the left wing and left center there was, on this day, continual skirmishing. Our artillery, however, fired but little and almost entirely at the enemy's infantry.

The 10th was a day of more vigorous battle. The enemy made incessant attacks on Anderson's (First Corps) front, but were continually repulsed with great slaughter. The guns on the front line, and two others from Manly's battery brought forward about noon, again and again during the day mowed down the enemy's columns with canister at short range.

Skirmishing also occurred during the forenoon on the left of Ewell's (Second Corps) front, occupied by Rodes' division, with Hardaway's guns, which had relieved Page's, but did not extend to its right, held by Johnson's division, where Nelson's guns had relieved Braxton's. Early on this day Richardson's battalion accompanied Heth's division in a flank movement con-

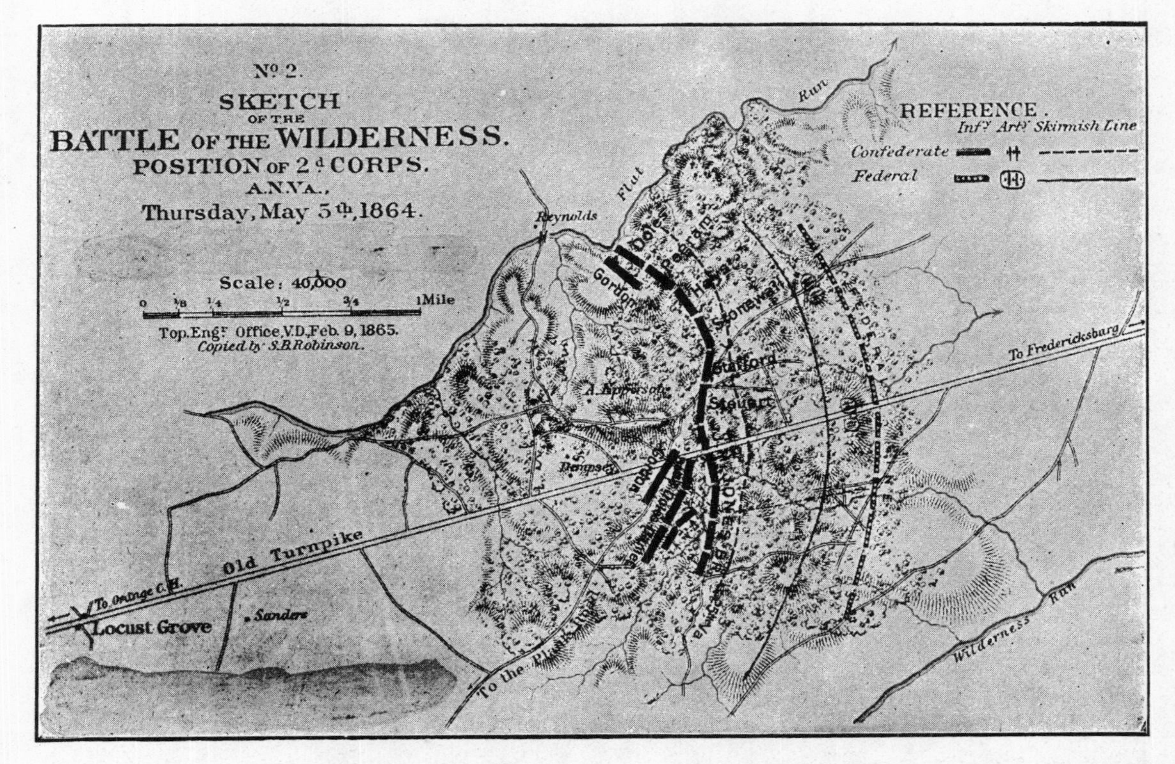

ducted by General Early around our left upon the enemy's right, and was severely engaged. A section of Ellett's battery, Pegram's battalion, accompanied Richardson's battalion in this expedition and did good service.

As our troops in this movement came upon the enemy's flank they were met by a galling fire from a number of batteries he had there posted; and Cabell's guns from their elevated position on our left, were directed by the general chief of artillery to open upon those batteries, so as to draw their fire and aid Early's advance. The effect was as anticipated. Soon after, McIntosh's guns from the east bank of the Po poured into the ranks of the enemy, retreating before General Early, a destructive fire; and some of the guns of this battalion advancing with a portion of Mahone's division as soon as the bridge was cleared, contributed still further to the good effect of the movement on that flank.

On this day the enemy made also a demonstration against our right immediately at Spottsylvania Courthouse, advancing several lines of infantry. Pegram's and Cutt's guns, however, opened upon them with vigor and speedily drove them back to the cover of their trenches. In the afternoon the enemy, having massed a large force in front of Second Corps' left center, under cover of a pine thicket, made a sudden attack upon Doles' brigade, which, having no skirmishers out in consequence of the close proximity of the lines, was taken entirely by surprise.

The brigade gave way for a season, and the enemy entered our works and captured Smith's battery, of Hardaway's battalion. Our infantry, being soon rallied and re-enforced, repulsed the enemy with considerable loss and recovered the guns. The captain had fought his battery until he was actualy seized by soldiers from the enemy's ranks, and some of his men were carried off by the retreating foe and not recovered.

On this occasion Hardaway's guns alone were engaged and were extremely well served. Two of Cutshaw's batteries were hastened up for the crisis and put in position to command the broken line. The men from one of these batteries (Graham's) being called for to work the guns on the line left weak-handed by the capture of Smith's cannoneers, sprang forward under their captain and served two of those guns with fine spirit.

Major David Watson, second in command of Hardaway's battalion, an accomplished gentleman, faithful patriot and gallant soldier, fell at his post during this attack mortally wounded. Lieutenant-Colonel Hardaway was also wounded—only slightly, however, though his clothes were riddled with bullets. He did not leave the field.

The enemy, thus punished along the entire line on the 10th, made no serious attack on the 11th. Heavy skirmishing, however, occurred from left to right, in which the artillery occasionally took part. Late in the afternoon of this day the commanding general, having reason to believe the enemy withdrawing, and intending to leave him no time to gain distance upon us, directed the general chief of artillery to have brought back from the front line before it should be entirely dark, all guns so situated as to be difficult to withdraw at night, so that everything might be ready to march at any hour. Under this order General Alexander had his ammunition chests in the trenches mounted on the caissons, and gun carriages taken to the vicinity of their guns, but retained the latter in position as the safest course.

General Long having a more difficult route for his artillery on Johnson's front—by a narrow and intricate road through a wood—preferred executing the order literally, especially as the night promised to be very dark. Nelson's and Page's battalions were accordingly withdrawn. This left unprotected an extensive salient of about a quarter of a mile across and nearly a mile around, which constituted the left of Johnson's line. A section of Page's battalion was sent, with a proper infantry guard, to escort a wagon train to Guineys Depot, on the Richmond & Fredericksburg Railroad.

At 3 A. M. of the 12th, Page's battalion was hastily summoned back to the line, it having been found that the enemy was preparing to make there a heavy attack. It was prepared and moved up with extraordinary speed and arrived at the proper point, but not in time to arrest disaster. Before the guns could be brought into action, or even more than one or two unlimbered, the enemy's masses had overpowered Johnson's division and taken possession of the salient.

All of Page's guns were enveloped and captured except two, which succeeded in getting off. At the same time two of Cutshaw's batteries which had the previous evening been posted on the left bank of the salient to enfilade Doles' front, were also captured. The enemy could thus boast of getting twenty guns—twelve from Page and eight from Cutshaw.

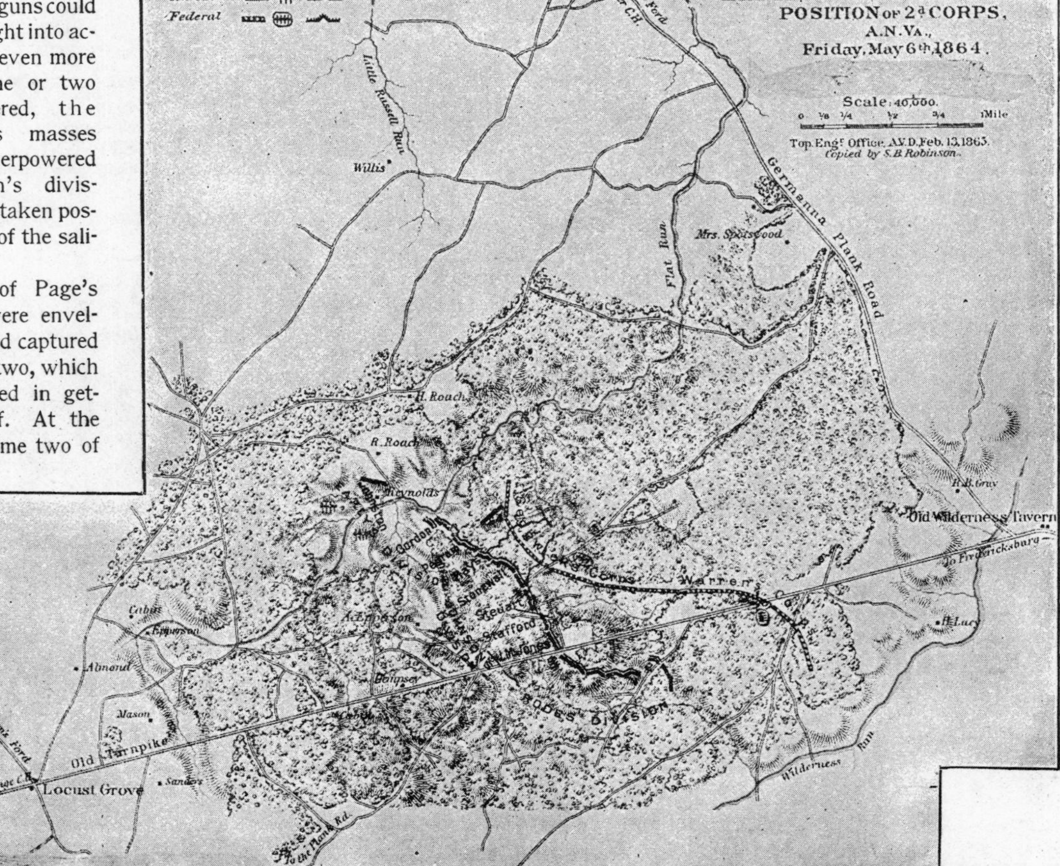

In addition to the unfortunate withdrawal of our guns, the enemy was favored in his movement and we were obstructed in counteracting it by the extreme darkness of a very dense fog. Arrangements were made as soon as possible to check the enemy and prevent any additional damage. Braxton's and Nelson's and a portion of Hardaway's battalions were posted by Colonel Carter on a second line about the prolongation leftwise of that held by the guns near the Courthouse. Other guns were also taken to the front near the gorge of the salient. Major Cutshaw and Captain Garber, with their men that had escaped capture, reached some of the guns which the enemy could not carry off, and, turning them, used them with good effect. Captain Montgomery ylied effectively also a single gun at short range, and with such constancy as to exhaust three caissons of ammunition.

The enemy could not advance, but the pressure of his enormous force rendered it necessary to increase our own efforts. Hardaway's battalion was, therefore, moved forward and posted to command the rear of the salient, Captain Dance in command, Lieutenant-Colonel Hardaway having been wounded in the act of advancing to the front. Colonel Cabell also came from the left with four of his guns and took position on the left of Dance's. These guns were brought up and used with admirable steadiness under a severe fire. McIntosh's battalion was in like manner brought to the support of this point. Only one section of it was, however, actively engaged. By these and other vigorous measures the enemy was prevented from profiting by the advantage he had gained. Repelled from the most of the salient and kept at bay in its apex, he could not during the day carry off the guns he had captured.

While this contest was raging battle was also joined with great fury along the entire line. On the left, from early dawn, column after column of the enemy as it came up to assault was shivered by the tremendous destructiveness of missiles hurled upon them at close range from our guns. Batteries here posted on our second line participated in the action by firing upon the enemy's batteries, so as to draw their fire away from our line of battle. That fire from the enemy was at times most furious. One or two of our guns in the front line were struck and disabled, and First Lieutenant Dent Burroughs, a gallant young officer commanding Moody's battery, was killed by a shot which passed through the parapet. On the right center another salient of our line attacked by the masses of Burnside's corps was effectively swept by Nelson's, Poague's and Pegram's guns. The enemy was here driven back in confusion, those guns contributing largely to the result. To the right our batteries engaged those of the enemy, so as to prevent their fire being concentrated on our center. Thus passed and closed this eventful day. At all points except at the prominent salient the enemy had been repulsed with immense loss. There he had gained a lodgment and captured a number of guns and prisoners, but he had been effectually prevented from profiting by it, and had himself suffered severely. Our interior line was there well established and protected during the night with guns in position, so that by next morning the enemy was as far from his object as ever.

The enemy now for some days remained quiet, and the time was improved on our part in strengthening our lines and reorganizing commands that had been seriously shattered. Major Cutshaw was assigned to the command of Hardaway's battalion and Major Page put in command of the combined remnants of his own and Cutshaw's battalions.

While the artillery with the main army was thus engaged in this great conflict, that with the cavalry was actively operating—one portion with General W. H. F. Lee on our right flank, another with General Hampton on our left, and the remainder (Johnston's battery, Baltimore Light Artillery and a section of Hort's battery, under Major Breathed), with General Stuart and Fitzhugh Lee in their pursuit of Sheridan attempting to raid into Richmond. In the severe conflict which ensued at the Yellow Tavern all these guns were used, though Hort's section and the Baltimore Light Artillery bore the brunt of the fight. The latter suffered most severely and lost a number of men and horses captured by the enemy.

On the 14th, the enemy were found to have withdrawn from Anderson's front (our left), leaving his thickly strewn dead unburied, and among them many who had fallen wounded between the lines and had lain there perishing for days. His demonstration then appearing on our right, Anderson's corps was, on the night of the 15th, transferred to that flank, extending our lines in that direction to the Po. Huger's and Haskell's battalions were here placed in position and Cabell's held in reserve.

On the morning of the 18th the enemy again attempted to carry the line still held by the Second Corps near the scene of the former conflict. This time, however, he met guns in position to receive him. His heavy force was allowed to get within good range of our breastworks. There the guns under Colonel Carter (Hardaway's battalion and Page's reorganized) opened upon him a murderous fire of spherical case and canister which at once arrested his advance, threw his columns into confusion and forced him to retreat in disorder. Heavily as he suffered on this occasion, our loss was nothing, and this was accomplished against a force of twelve thousand picked infantry by twenty-nine pieces of artillery alone, but well handled. In the afternoon, General Ewell having determined to make a flank movement, Lieutenant-Colonel Braxton was directed to accompany him with six guns of select caliber. The roads, however, were found impracticable for artillery, and Colonel Braxton was ordered to return to his position on the line. Simultaneously with his attack on Ewell's front, on this day the enemy assailed, but in a different manner, our line near the Courthouse. Having gotten a number of guns into a position to enfilade a part of our line, he attempted, under cover of their fire, to advance his front batteries. Pegram's and Cutt's guns promptly opened in reply. A furious cannonade ensued for about an hour. By that time the enemy's batteries in front were silenced and all further attempt to advance there was abandoned. In this cannonade Major McGraw, second in command of Pegram's battalion, was severely wounded, as were several other officers. Richardson's battalion on this day occupied the line to the right of Cutt's guns, those of First Corps being still further to the right. The enemy, apparently satisfied with his fruitless efforts near Spottsylvania Courthouse, made there no further attempt, and being found on the 21st shifting his position and moving beyond our right, our army was also on that day put in motion in the same direction. The Second Corps (Ewell's), then our left, having no enemy remaining on its front, moved with its artillery early in the day, passing the other corps, to the Telegraph Road south of the Po, and then by that road toward Hanover Junction. Later in the day the Third Corps (Hill's) marched, accompanied by a portion of its artillery, toward the same point on a road nearly parallel to and not far to the west of the Telegraph Road; and in the afternoon the First Corps (Anderson's) took up the line of march toward and on the Telegraph Road, attended by Huger's and Haskell's battalions, Cabell's battalion, with others from the Third Corps, having previously marched by other roads a little to the west, so as to avoid crowding. By the afternoon of the 22d our whole army had reached the south bank of the North Anna River near Hanover Junction, the First Corps occupying localities in the center near the Telegraph Road Bridge, the Second extending on its right down the river, and the Third on its left up the stream. General Breckinridge's division, which had just arrived from the Valley with two battalions of artillery, remained in reserve at Hanover Junction.

An Incident of the Battle of Spottsylvania, Va. A Dead Soldier found Sitting on a Broken Hospital Stretcher the Day after the Battle.
[Sketched on the spot by a Confederate soldier.]

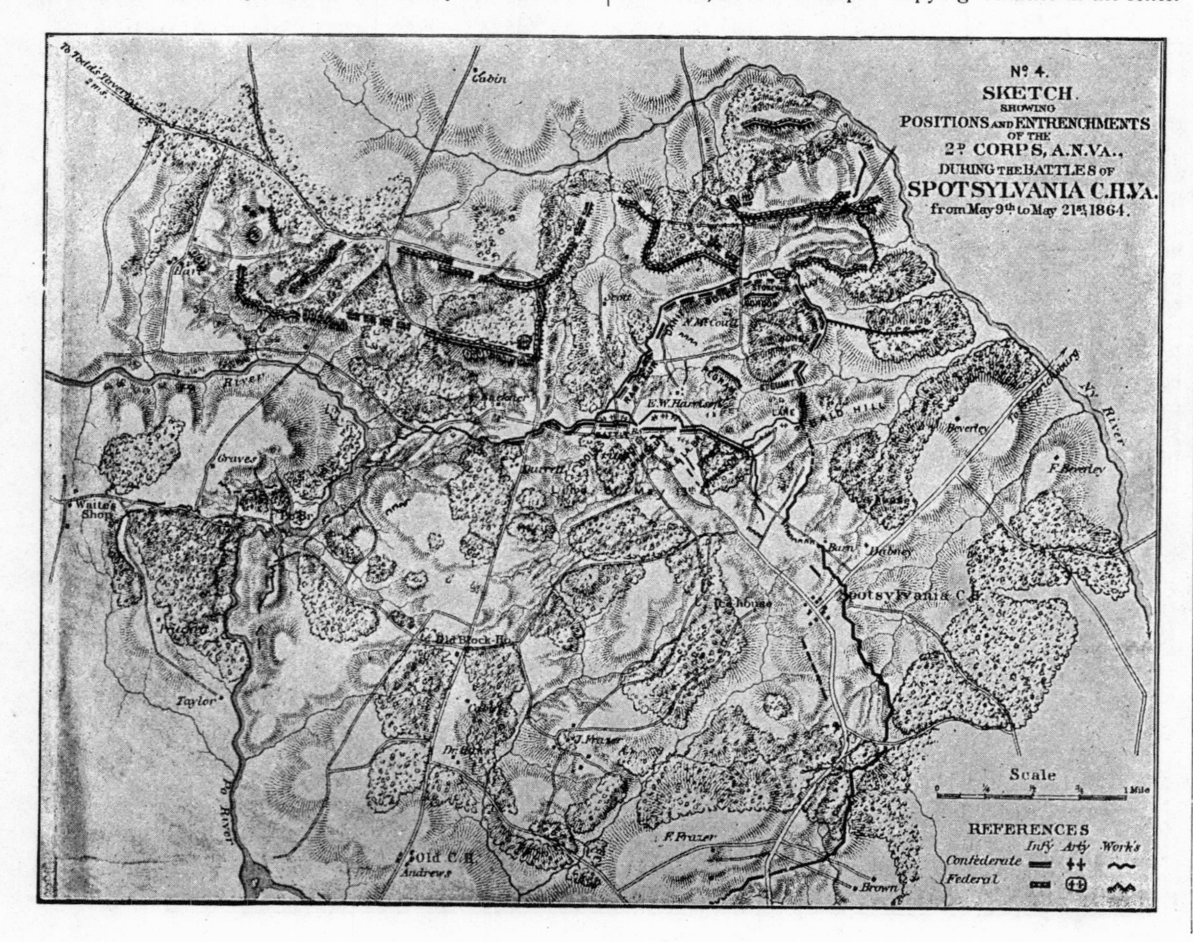

On the morning of the 23d, eight guns of Huger's battalion, eight of Haskell's and four of Cabell's were placed in position near the river to defend the Telegraph Road and railroad bridges. Reconnoissances were also made for other positions above and below. That afternoon the enemy appeared in heavy force and engaged those batteries. One small body of infantry—one or two regiments left on the north side to defend that extremity of the Telegraph Road Bridge—had to retire before the enemy's superior numbers, but our guns kept the enemy himself from then attempting the bridge. While this occurred in the center, fords on the right were guarded by guns of the Second Corps, Braxton's battalion especially being posted advantageously for the purpose near the Dosnell house. The enemy at the same time made a demonstration in force on our left, higher up the river, at Jericho Ford, and forces of the Third Corps occupying that flank were sent to meet him, Poague's battalion accompanying Heth's division, and Pegram's co-operating with Wilcox. Most of the artillery was arranged on the right and rather in the rear of the infantry, under cover of some rising ground. Simultaneously with the attack of our infantry the batteries were rapidly advanced to the crest of the hill and opened fire on the enemy's reserve line immediately at the ford. This fire was continued with vigor until the enemy's line gave way and disappeared. His batteries were soon after brought up and a sharp cannonade ensued, but without material results. Major Ward, second in command of Poague's battalion (a devout Christian, gallant soldier and efficient officer), was here killed by a cannon shot. McIntosh's battalion was about the same time placed in position to cover Andersons Ford, and was on this day partially engaged with the enemy's guns, having a limber blown up in Clutter's battery, and Lieutenant Pearce, commanding the battery, mortally wounded. Still further to the right and nearer our center, Major Lane, of Cutt's battalion, was assigned position, with six rifles, on a bluff back of the Montgomery house, which commanded both the Telegraph Road Bridge, below, and Andersons Ford, above.

On the night of the 23d a new line of battle for our center and right was selected further back from the river and on more advantageous ground, and on that line the guns of the First and Second Corps were posted, from center to right, as before. Portions of the enemy, having crossed the river, appeared in view of this line at several points, on the 24th, and occasional skirmishing and cannon shots ensued, but no attack was made. On this day, also, the enemy continued demonstrating on our left so as to require there on our part a considerable accumulation of force. Poague's battalion, occupying position on the extreme left to Little River, Pegram's, McIntosh's and Lane's guns retaining their places of the previous day, Richardson's, accompanying Mahone's division, holding a second line near the Anderson house, and Braxton's, of the Second Corps, from the right wing, coming with Gordon's division as a support to the same point, their place on the right being supplied by Breckinridge's troops and guns. Lane's guns were used with good effect all this day, annoying and damaging the enemy as his troops would approach and cross the Telegraph Road Bridge. A severe fire from the enemy's batteries was brought to bear upon him, killing and wounding several men and shattering an ammunition chest, but not otherwise interfering with his work.

Captain Wingfield and Private E. Hennington, with an intrepidity deserving of honorable mention, extinguished the burning tow of the ammunition chests, and thus saved the ammunition for use, and probably preserved valuable lives. Another instance of good conduct and skill in a part of Major Lane's command was brought to notice on this day in the safe arrival of Lieutenant L. G. Rees with four guns which had been assigned to his charge in attendance upon McGowan's brigade as a rear guard to the Third Corps in its march from Spottsylvania Courthouse. A body of the enemy having crossed North Anna River at a point below their own crossing and taken possession of their road, unexpectedly appeared before them. Lieutenant Rees, however, although closely pressed, rescued his command with the loss of only one man mortally wounded, and by a circuit to the south of Little River, joined his battalion on the 24th. Skirmishing continued on portions of this entire line at Hanover Junction until the 27th, when the enemy withdrew for another flank movement beyond our right.

Early on the 27th, our army marched by the Telegraph Road, and such others parallel thereto as were available, toward Ashland, and thence toward Atlees Station, on the Virginia Central Railroad, bivouacking after an exhausting day's march near Hughes shop.

On the next day (28th), our cavalry, with the horse artillery, being heavily engaged near Haws shop, on the road between Hanovertown (where the enemy had crossed the Pamunkey) and Atlees Station, our army took position on the southwest bank of Totopotomoy Creek, General Breckinridge with his division and McLaughlin's battalion of artillery occupying the left, and crossing the Hanovertown Road, the First Corps, under General Anderson, with artillery in suitable position on his right, and the Second Corps, now under General Early, with a sufficient number of guns, still further to the right, near and beyond Pole Green Church, the Third Corps, with its artillery, encamping in reserve to support Breckinridge.

On the 29th, McIntosh's battalion was posted on the left of the Hanovertown Road in aid of General Breckinridge's line, before which the enemy had appeared and was threatening in force, and the following day some of Major Lane's guns were placed on the same line between McIntosh's command and those of General Breckinridge's command. Most of the guns on this line were repeatedly engaged, successfully repelling the heavy demonstrations of the enemy upon General Breckinridge on the 30th and 31st. Portions of Cabell's and Huger's battalions on Breckinridge's right, and so arranged as to enfilade his front, were all hotly engaged with the enemy's sharpshooters and artillery on those two days, and did much execution in the ranks of his infantry apparently attempting to advance upon that line. While such engagements were going on upon Breckinridge's front, active movements also occurred upon our right, where the command of the artillery of the Second Corps had devolved upon Colonel Carter in consequence of General Long being unwell. Nelson's battalion, on the evening of the 30th, accompanied Rodes' division on the Old Church Road and aided in an attack made by that division on the enemy's left flank and driving it from Johnson's farm to Bethesda Church. In the sharp engagement which occurred at the latter point, First-Lieutenant Ancell, of Massie's battery, a meritorious officer, was killed. This force having returned the same night to our selected line, Nelson's guns were placed in position, Hardaway's (whose commander had returned to duty on the 21st), being also posted on his left, Braxton's and Cutshaw's being in reserve.

On the night of the 31st, the First Corps (Anderson's) with its artillery marched to the vicinity of Cold Harbor to co-operate with General Hoke in an attack upon the enemy's left, which it was expected to turn. For this attack Cabell's battalion was ordered to report to General Kershaw, Huger's to General Pickett and Haskell's to General Field. Read's battalion had accompanied General Hoke from the south side of James River. Hoke's advance, supported by Kershaw, discovered the enemy strongly intrenched and in large force, obviously intending an attempt to turn our flank. His position was, after careful reconnoissance, deemed too strong to attack, and our troops began to fortify the line of battle, in which they happened to be formed. This had been but very partially done when, about 4 P. M., June 1st, the enemy made a furious assault upon Hoke's line and the right of Kershaw's separated from Hoke's by a narrow strip of swampy ground. Pushing a considerable force through this interval, he compelled Kershaw's right brigade and Hoke's left to break their line and face the interval. This arrested his advance; he could make no further progress. Dense wood prevented artillery being used in this conflict. During the night a Napoleon gun from Cabell's battalion, under Lieutenant Falligant, was advanced to the angle where Kershaw's line broke back to the rear, a position much exposed, the enemy's sharpshooters being within fifty yards, but enfilading and very badly annoying him. Others of Cabell's guns were also put in position in Kershaw's line, as were Huger's and Haskell's on those of Pickett's and Field's extending to the left. On the next day (June 2d), heavy skirmishing was kept up along Kershaw's front, and Lieutenant Falligant's gun constantly engaged the enemy, who repeatedly attempted its capture. It, howevever, successfully repelled their advances, expending upon them a large amount of ammunition. During these operations on our right, fighting also occurred, June 1st, further to the left. The enemy assailing the line defended by Hardaway's guns near the Manor house, was handsomely repulsed. Under cover of a skirt of woods, his first line of battle came within fifty yards of our works. It was, however, driven back in confusion by an effective fire of canister. These batteries being on Heth's front (Third Corps), were that night relieved by Poague's battalion. General Long, on this day, resumed command of artillery Second Corps.

LIEUTENANT-GENERAL JOHN B. GORDON, OF GEORGIA.

The next day (June 2d), the Second Corps, with Heth's division, advanced against the right flank of the enemy, making a wheel, the pivot of which was at the Johnson house. Cutshaw's battalion moved out in front of our works. The brigade supporting Stafford, of Gordon's division, being driven back and retreating through Garber's battery, stationed on and to the right of the Old Church Road, Garber's guns opened with canister and sent the enemy retreating in terror. During this attack by the Second Corps and a portion of the Third, Haskell's battalion, on Field's front, was severely engaged, co-operating with it by a vigorous fire upon the flank of the opposing line. That night, Cutshaw's battalion was relieved by Hardaway's. Kershaw's line was also, during the night, slightly changed and four additional guns of Cabell's battalion arranged in position. Falligant's gun was noiselessly removed by hand to a new location—the angle of the new line. During the operations of the main army, the horse artillery was with the several cavalry divisions, no less actively engaged. McGregor's battery which, after being sharply engaged at Stanards Mill, on the Po, from May 16th to the 19th, accompanied General W. H. F. Lee's division as rear guard to the army marching to Hanover Junction, moved with the same division to Hanover Courthouse on the 31st, and there encountering the enemy in force rendered efficient service. Lieutenant Ford, who, with conspicuous gallantry, commanded his section, was instantly killed by a minie-ball. Hort's battery participated in a slight engagement at Ashland on the 1st, and on the same day Shoemaker's and Johnston's, under Major Breathed, were warmly engaged at Bottoms Bridge and Cold Harbor.

At dawn, on the 3d, a very heavy attack was made by the enemy upon Hoke, Kershaw and our forces on the left. Read's guns, on Hoke's line, and Cabell's on Kershaw's, though exposed to a fierce fire of infantry and artillery, were used with great energy and success. Lieutenant Callaway, commanding one of Cabell's batteries, is especially commended for gallantry on this occasion. Huger opened to assist Kershaw on his right, and also to disturb the enemy in front, and as a demonstration, which was followed by an advance of Pickett's skirmishers. Haskell also opened to aid the troops on his left and drew down upon himself a very serious fire. Hardaway's guns, beyond Haskell's, co-operated effectively by an oblique fire on the enemy's line, and Cutshaw's, some distance still further to the left and advanced on a new line, delivered a telling enfilade fire on the enemy's line in front of Rodes' division. On

BATTLE OF SPOTTSYLVANIA COURTHOUSE, VA., MAY 10, 1864. THE FIGHT ON THE LEFT OF THE LINE.
[From an original sketch, owned by Mrs. Frank Leslie, New York.]

the extreme left of our advanced line Poague's battalion operated with Heth's division. The division commander directed Lieutenant-Colonel Poague to post two batteries (Wyatt's and Richard's) on his left flank. Colonel Poague, having made a rapid reconnoissance of the position and discovered a heavy line of the enemy's skirmishers near at hand, reported to the division commander the disadvantages of the situation and indicated a better position. The former order was, however, reiterated, and in the attempt to obey it extremely heavy loss was suffered. The two batteries were, in fact, almost entirely crippled and many valuable lives lost to very little purpose. Wyatt's unprotected detachments were so rapidly cut up by the fire upon them, at only two hundred and fifty yards, that they could only fire a few rounds. Richard's pieces were with much difficulty gotten to the works occupied by the infantry. They were there, however, used with some effect, as the enemy attempted to advance, the cannoneers being to some extent protected. On this occasion Lieutenant-Colonel Poague narrowly escaped death from a cannon shot, receiving a disabling contusion, and Captain Wyatt and Lieutenant Rives were killed. A number of men were also killed and wounded and many horses disabled.

The enemy was, in this contest of June 3d, bloodily repulsed along the entire line. While the portions of our forces mentioned were engaged in that good work, as described, Breckinridge's command and the Third Corps, except Heth's division and Poague's battalion, moved to the right and took position on or near Gaines' farm, with right flank resting on the Chickahominy, Pegram's battalion occupying Turkey Ridge, McIntosh's on Pegram's left (Dement's and Chew's batteries having been here added to this battalion), Richardson's battalion on McIntosh's left, Lane's on Richardson's left. A 24-pounder howitzer of McIntosh's battalion was adjusted a little in rear of the line and served as a mortar. It did good service in annoying the enemy's working parties. All the guns of this line were engaged in the battle of the 3d and materially assisted in checking the enemy's advance. Lieutenant Hunton, of Price's battery, was instantly killed by a sharpshooter. Poague's two batteries, disabled in their severe service on the left, were subsequently withdrawn and steps taken for their restoration. His other two batteries held in reserve. On this day and the succeeding (June 3d and 4th), by direction of the commanding general, the fords of the Chickahominy below the right of our line were examined by the general chief of artillery, and the batteries of the Louisiana Washington Artillery Battalion, which had arrived from the south side of James River, were posted to guard them as far down as the York River Railroad Bridge. Those guns of the horse artillery attending General Fitzhugh Lee's cavalry, were placed in position, as were those of the Richmond Defense Battalion, under Lieutenant-Colonel Pemberton, at Bottoms Bridge. At all these points the enemy appeared and made demonstrations as if with a view to crossing, but the fire which they received seemed to deter them from any heavy attack, though skirmishing was for some days continued at certain points.

On the 7th, the enemy having withdrawn from Field's front, Haskell's battalion was transferred to the south bank of the Chickahominy and posted to command the Grape Vine and Federal bridges. Meanwhile, and to the 13th, the enemy remained in force upon our front from Pickett's line to the extreme right, and fighting was incessant at very short range, the opposing lines being at some points not a stone's throw apart. Our guns were often used with excellent effect, especially a number of howitzers adjusted as mortars on some parts of the line. This mode of using guns became the more important from the fact that they were screened from the sharpshooting, which was ceaseless and frequently fatal, owing to the extraordinary proximity of the lines. Guns on our lines had to be covered from sight, and many valuable men were lost at them, particularly in Cabell's battalion. Among these was Captain McCarthy, First Richmond Howitzers, a veteran officer, whose gallantry had been conspicuous on nearly every field fought by this army since its organization. He was, on June 4th, instantly killed by a minie-ball through the head. While the armies were thus engaged near Cold Harbor and Gaines' farm, Sheridan's cavalry attempted, against Lynchburg via Gordonsville, another raid in co-operation with Hunter's movement down the Valley, and on the 8th, Hort's, Thomson's, Johnston's and Shoemaker's batteries, under charge of Majors Chew and Breathed, moved with our cavalry force to intercept this raiding expedition. In a series of severe engagements, which occurred near Trevilian Depot, Virginia Central Railroad, these batteries materially aided in frustrating the enemy and compelling the abandonment of his enterprise.

On the 10th General Breckinridge's division, with McLaughlin's battalion of artillery, having marched for the Valley, and Lieutenant-Colonel King, being relieved from his own battalion to accompany the expedition, Major Gibbes, who had been serving with Cabell's battalion, was assigned to the command of King's battalion, known as Thirteenth Virginia Battalion. On the evening of the 13th, it being discovered that the enemy had during the night left our front, our army was again put in motion, the Second Corps, under General Early, with Nelson's and Braxton's battalions, proceeding toward the Valley to meet the enemy advancing there under Hunter, and the remainder of the army marching by the right beyond White Oak Swamp to Riddles Shop. Our cavalry there, holding the enemy in check, was relieved by Wilcox's division, and the enemy pressed a considerable distance, one of Pegram's batteries assisting in the operation. Line of battle being formed near the intersection of roads at this point, Pegram's and McIntosh's battalions were placed in position, but the enemy attempted no further advance. On this day (June 13th) Read's battalion, accompanying Hoke's division, marched from Cold Harbor directly toward Petersburg, then threatened by the enemy, and arriving there on the afternoon of the 15th, was immediately, in part, put in position, not far from Hare's house, to co-operate with other guns on the east of the city.

During the 14th and 15th the First and Third Corps remained observing the operations of the enemy toward Malvern Hill, and on the morning of the 16th, General Grant's movement to the south side of James River being sufficiently developed, our forces were also put in motion in that direction. Huger's, Haskell's and Gibbes' battalions crossed James River on the pontoon bridge near Drewrys Bluff, accompanying Pickett's and Field's divisions, and marched toward Bermuda Hundred. Skirmishing with the enemy ensued near Port Walthall Junction. The enemy was driven back, and on the next (17th) the line previously held by General Beauregard and evacuated by him because of the demand for all of his force in the immediate defense of Petersburg, was recovered and part of the artillery placed on it in position.

W. N. PENDLETON.

BATTLE OF DREWRYS BLUFF,

MAY 16, 1864.

BY

MAJOR-GENERAL R. F. HOKE.

HEADQUARTERS HOKE'S DIVISION,
May 25, 1864.

ON Sunday, the 15th instant, the intention to attack the enemy on the morning of the 16th at early light was made known to me by the commanding general, while occupying the intermediate line of intrenchments around Drewry's Bluff, and confronting the enemy,

MAJ.-GEN. ROBERT F. HOKE, OF NORTH CAROLINA.

who occupied the outer line of said intrenchments, extending his right through the woods in the direction of James River, while his left rested upon an elevated position across the railroad, with his masses immediately in front of our right and resting upon the railroad.

The commanding general, seeing the right was the weak point of the enemy, determined upon this as the point of attack. The brigades of Colquitt and Ransom were ordered relieved by an extension of my line to the right, which placed my division in line of battle, commencing at Fort Stephens, with Hagood's brigade on the left, Johnson's on his right, then Clingman, with Corse upon his right. These two brigades, under the command of General Colquitt, were held in reserve immediately in rear of Hagood's brigade. The division commanded by Major-General Ransom, being in the field on our extreme left, was to turn the right of the enemy and pivot upon his right and connect with my left, while I was to engage the enemy in front with strong lines of skirmishers, and also open upon them with my artillery. At the earliest dawn I ordered my entire artillery to open and advanced the skirmishers of my whole front, and awaited the movement on my left for one hour before advancing my line of battle, thinking it would require this length of time to make the move, and knowing I must lose heavily by an advance upon the front, which it was the desire of the commanding general to avoid by the flank move. Owing to the dense fog I could see nothing of the movement of Major-General Ransom, and supposing by this time the right of the enemy had been turned, I ordered forward the brigades of Hagood and Johnson, with one section of Lieutenant-Colonel Eshleman's artillery, and found the enemy still occupying our entire line of intrenchments in heavy force, supported by eight pieces of artillery, with a second line of intrenchments along the line of woods immediately in front of our outer line of works.

After commencing the move I could not recede, and ordered an attack by these two brigades, which was handsomely and gallantly done, which resulted in the capture of five pieces of artillery by Hagood's brigade and a number of prisoners, besides killing and wounding many, and also in occupying the works. One regiment on the left of Hagood's brigade extended across the outer line of works in the direction of James River, which was ordered forward to connect with the right of General Ransom's division, but to my amazement found the enemy in strong force behind intrenchments. It was not intended that this regiment should attack the enemy in this position, as the movement was to be made by the troops on the left; but they, in their eagerness to enter the engagement, did so and, I am sorry to say, suffered most heavily. When it was seen that the enemy still occupied my front, this regiment was ordered back to the line of intrenchments to await the further development of the flank movement. In the meantime the enemy made two charges upon the front of Hagood and Johnson to retake the lost works and artillery, but were most handsomely repulsed, and were followed on the left of Hagood's brigade and driven from the woods in their front, and with the assistance of our artillery the "pike" was cleared of the enemy before the flanking column reached that point. During this time the masses of the enemy between our intermediate and outer line of works had moved upon the right flank and rear of General Johnson, which was some distance on the right of the pike and in the outer line of works, and made his position quite critical; but the stubbornness of the general made it all right. He was repeatedly attacked in this position, but repulsed every effort of the enemy.

It was at this time I was anxious to get a brigade to throw down the outer line of works, which would have completely placed that portion of the enemy in the woods between our outer and intermediate lines at our mercy; but owing to a misunderstanding of the officer who conducted these forces they were placed in position improperly, and were of no avail during these repeated attacks upon the right of General Johnson. I became alarmed for him, as he had several times sent to me for assistance, and ordered two regiments of Clingman's brigade to report to him, which I did with great reluctance, as I felt it would defeat my plans on my right; but necessity compelled me. In order, also, to relieve the position of General Johnson, which was our key, I ordered forward Corse with his brigade and Clingman with his two regiments. They went forward in good style and drove the enemy from their front, but owing to the superior numbers and strong intrenchments they were not able to drive them entirely from their positions.

The commanding general will recollect that I before stated that the strength of the enemy was in front of these two brigades, both in position and forces, and therefore great credit should be given them for their actions. They were both small commands, but did their duty well. At the time the attack was made the enemy felt as if our forces were coming on them from all sides, and commenced retreating hastily. The losses of these commands were necessarily heavy, owing to a front attack.

I can not refrain from calling the attention of the general commanding to the fact that his desire to relieve my command of a front attack by the flank move was in no portion of the line accomplished, in consequence of which my losses were very heavy.

My brigade commanders entered into the move with spirit, and rendered every co-operation, for which I am under many obligations. A report of casualties has been furnished. I respectfully call attention to the names who are spoken of for gallantry mentioned in the inclosed reports of the brigade commanders.

R. F. HOKE, *Major-General.*

ONE day opposing pickets on the Rappahannock agreed not to fire. A brisk conversation arose between a Texan and an Irishman on the Federal side. "What are *you* doing in the Yankee army?" said the Texan. "What are you fightin' for, anyhow?" "I'm fitin' for thirteen dollars a month. I belave ye're fitin' for eleven."

Capt. Hugh McGuire. Capt. Hatcher. Col. E. V. White. Maj. P. B. Winston. Maj. Holmes Conrad. Gen'l Rosser. Col. Nash. Gen'l R. A. Alger.

CAVALRY BATTLE AT TREVILIAN STATION, JUNE 12, 1864.

[From an original painting owned by General Thomas L. Rosser.]

BATTLE OF
TREVILIAN STATION, VA.,

JUNE 11 AND 12, 1864.

BY

BRIG.-GEN. THOMAS L. ROSSER,
Commanding Brigade.

JUNE 30, 1864.

AFTER I had dismounted my brigade about two miles west of Trevilian Station and was waiting to hear from scouts which I had sent out around the right flank of the enemy to ascertain if he were moving toward Gordonsville, a trooper from Young's brigade came galloping up from the rear with a saber cut

MAJ.-GEN. THOMAS L. ROSSER, OF VIRGINIA.
[From a photograph taken in 1863.]

across his face, and reported that the enemy had gotten in the rear of Young's and Butler's brigades, which were fighting on foot, and had captured the division wagon train and the horses of the dismounted men of these two brigades. I ordered a company to mount and go back and see if this report were true, but before it started off, several more men from the same command came running at full speed, yelling "Yankees! Yankees!" I then mounted the brigade at once, and riding at the head of it went back at a brisk trot in the direction whence these men had come.

Scrub oaks, almost a "chaparral," covered the ground on each side of the narrow road, and as the road was very crooked, I could not see a stone's throw ahead of me, and, expecting to find the enemy at or near the station, I was as much surprised as he appeared to be, when, turning a sharp curve in the road, I came immediately on him. It was Custer's brigade, which had passed around Butler's right and between him and Fitzhugh Lee, had gotten in the rear of the former and captured the wagon train and the horses of the two brigades then fighting on foot. Not expecting trouble from the direction from which I came, Custer had not taken the precaution of putting pickets on that road, and thinking when he saw the head of my column that it was only a scouting party, he wheeled so as to meet the charge which I sounded on the sight of him; but I was too quick and too strong for him, and as I went crashing into him, breaking up and scattering his squadrons, he made a gallant and manly effort to resist me. Sitting on his horse in the midst of his advanced platoons, and near enough to be easily recognized by me, he encouraged and inspired his men by appeal as well as by example. His color-sergeant was shot down at his side, by Major Holmes Conrad, of my staff, when Custer grabbed the staff to save his flag, but the death-grip of the sergeant would not release it, so, with a quick jerk, Custer tore the flag from its staff and in triumph carried it off. Closely pursuing, I recaptured our men, horses and wagons, as well as many prisoners from the enemy, and drove Custer back, with heavy loss, into Sheridan's lines.

* * * * * * *

THOMAS L. ROSSER,
Brigadier-General.

A CERTAIN officer of Company C, Ninth Virginia Cavalry, was noted for his neatness, and consequently was chaffed by the boys a great deal. He had occasion, in the fall of '63, to pass through the camp of General Barringer's North Carolina brigade. He sat as straight as an arrow, and with great dignity rode along amidst such bantering as, "Good morning, general;" "Come out of that hat," and "Where did you get those boots?" etc. On arriving near the general's tent he was stopped by the Tarheel guard, who observed to him, with great sympathy: "Don't you mind them boys, mister. They are always hollering at some fool going along by here."

TUPELO, MISS., EXPEDITION
FROM
LAGRANGE, TENN.,
INCLUDING
BATTLE OF HARRISBURG, MISS.,

JULY 14, 1864.

BY

BRIG.-GEN. ABRAHAM BUFORD,
Commanding Second Division.

HEADQUARTERS SECOND DIVISION,
FORREST'S CAVALRY,
EGYPT, MISS., July 22, 1864.

MY division, during the late engagement in and around Tupelo, was composed of Lyon's brigade, comprising the Third, Seventh, Eighth and Faulkner's Kentucky regiments, nine hundred strong; Bell's brigade, comprising the Second, Fifteenth and Sixteenth and Newsom's Tennessee regiments, thirteen hundred strong, and Mabry's brigade, temporarily attached to the division, comprising the Sixth and Thirty-eighth Mississippi, Fourth Mississippi and Fourteenth Confederate regiments, one thousand strong; in all thirty-two hundred effective men.

On the 7th of July, I was ordered to send Bell's brigade to Ellistown. He accordingly moved at 5 o'clock, the morning of the 8th, for that point, and guarded the approach from Ripley via Ellistown to Tupelo.

On the morning of the 9th, by order of Major-General Forrest, I moved from Tupelo to Ellistown with the Kentucky brigade, Brigadier-General Lyon commanding. At this point I was joined by Colonel H. P. Mabry with his brigade of Mississippians, who had moved from Saltillo. Learning from scouts that the enemy were not advancing on the Ripley and Ellistown Road, but on the road from Ripley via New Albany to Pontotoc, I moved my division to the latter place, marching all night, halting about daylight two miles from Pontotoc. I received during the day several orders directing me to develop the enemy's strength, not to bring on a general engagement, but keep in the enemy's front and on his flanks and gradually fall back to Okolona. I accordingly made dispositions to carry out these orders. I sent a regiment of Mabry's brigade, Colonel Isham Harrison commanding, accompanied by a staff officer, toward Plentytude, on the Plentytude and Chesterville Road. I ordered Colonel Bell to send the Second Tennessee, Colonel Barteau commanding, in the direction of New Albany. I had hardly made these dispositions, and was preparing to make others, when, at 7:30 A. M. on the 10th of July, I received an order from Major-General Forrest to get on the Chesterville Road, if I could, and join the command at Okolona, and to send a squadron of one hundred good men in rear of the enemy to cut off his communications, etc. I immediately detached one hundred picked men, under Captain Tyler, Company A, Faulkner's (Kentucky) regiment, to proceed to rear of the enemy and carry out the instructions I had received. For the operations of this squadron I refer to the report of Captain Tyler, herewith forwarded. About 9 A. M., I was joined at Pontotoc by McCulloch's brigade, of Chalmers' division. I left Pontotoc about 1 A. M. Sunday, 10th of July, and marched to a strong position on a creek five or six miles from town, leaving McCulloch's brigade at Pontotoc and Barteau's regiment (Second Tennessee) on the Pontotoc and New Albany Road to skirmish with the enemy and gradually fall back. During the day I received orders to report to Brigadier-General Chalmers, who had been fully instructed by the major-general commanding, and to co-operate with him. I did so.

The enemy made his appearance Monday morning, 11th instant, in Pontotoc. His force consisted of thirteen thousand infantry (including one brigade of negroes), twenty-five hundred cavalry and twenty-four pieces of artillery, under command of Major-General A. J. Smith. This force was admirably equipped, commanded by an officer of experience and skill, and moved with great caution, always prepared. Colonel McCulloch's brigade and Colonel Barteau's regiment were gradually driven, and fell back three miles on the Pontotoc and Okolona Road. Dispositions were made to hold the enemy in check.

On Tuesday morning the enemy advanced and Lyon's brigade met them. The enemy dismounted and moved against the position taken in the road by this brigade, but were handsomely repulsed. Tuesday night, Generals Lee and Forrest arrived on the field, bringing with them the entire force of infantry and dismounted cavalry. I reported to them all the information in my knowledge, and the fact that up to that time I had discovered no evidence of the demoralized condition of the enemy, but had found him ever ready for action.

On Wednesday it was discovered that the enemy had left Pontotoc that morning and was marching on Tupelo. I was immediately ordered to move on his flank on the Pontotoc and Carmargo Ferry Road, known as the Chanappa Valley Road, leading via Dr. Calhoun's house to Verona. I did so, moving on his right flank, Colonel Bell's brigade in advance. General Lyon was relieved from his brigade and ordered to take command of the division of infantry. The command of the Kentucky brigade then devolved upon Colonel Crossland, Seventh Kentucky Regiment. General Forrest, with Mabry's brigade, followed immediately in rear of the enemy. About 5 o'clock Wednesday evening (13th), under the order of Lieutenant-General Lee, with Bell's brigade and a section of artillery from Martin's battery, I attacked the enemy on his right flank during the march. At no time had I found the enemy unprepared. He marched with his column well closed up, his wagon train well protected, and his flanks covered in an admirable manner, evincing at all times a readiness to meet any attack, and showing careful generalship. After fighting him about an hour, suffering considerable loss, the enemy was heavily re-enforced, and I was compelled to withdraw the brigade from action. They fell back and reformed across a creek. The Kentucky brigade having by this time arrived at the scene of action, I formed the two brigades to repel any attack that might be made, but the enemy, being pushed in the rear, moved on to Harrisburg. I followed him to within two miles of that place, when I joined General Forrest at the intersection of the Harrisburg and Verona and the Pontotoc and Tupelo roads. The enemy formed his line at Harrisburg, where he had a strong natural position, and during the night threw up a line of fortifications and awaited an attack from us. I camped for the night, throwing the Kentucky brigade forward on picket.

During the night I received orders to bring up my division to the crossroads by daylight next morning, about a mile and a half from Harrisburg. The troops were there formed for the attack—Mabry's brigade on the left of the road from Pontotoc to Tupelo, the Kentucky brigade on the right, and Bell's brigade immediately in rear of Mabry's brigade as a support. Brigadier-General Roddey's division was formed on the right of the Kentucky brigade. Chalmers' division of cavalry and Lyon's division of infantry were held as reserves. About 7 P. M., I was ordered to move forward to the attack, when I modestly expressed the opinion that the attack should not be a direct one, but the majority of the forces should be thrown on the Verona and Tupelo Road, and a vigorous assault made on his left flank; that a direct charge was what the enemy most desired, and for which he was strongly posted both by nature and art. The ground moved over was open timber intersected by hills and ravines. In moving forward, the Kentucky brigade obliqued to the left. Observing these intervals I reported the fact to General Lee, who immediately ordered Colonel Bell to move forward and form between Mabry's and Crossland's brigades.

BRIGADIER-GENERAL A. BUFORD, OF KENTUCKY.
[From a photograph taken in 1864.]

Immediately in front of the enemy's position, which was on elevated ground, commanding the entire approach, the country was open, there being no timber in front for a distance of one or two hundred yards at different points of his line. The enemy's skirmishers were driven in. When the Kentucky brigade arrived at the edge of the timber, discovering the enemy's position, raising a shout, they charged his line of works. The enemy reserved his fire until our men were in close range, and poured upon them a galling fire. They continued, however, to advance. The enemy's artillery was fired with great rapidity, charged with canister, upon our advancing columns. Perceiving that the force on our extreme right

(Roddey's) did not advance, the enemy turned the fire of his batteries, posted on an elevation in Roddey's front, on the advancing Kentuckians, and they, under a galling fire of musketry and artillery, both in front and obliquely from the enemy in Roddey's front, were compelled to fall back. They had advanced, however, to the enemy's intrenchments. Some fell and were taken prisoners within his line, and several within thirty steps of his breastworks. Colonel Faulkner's horse was killed, within sixty steps, under him. The loss was very severe in this charge; and it was only under a fire which dealt death on every side, and decimated their ranks fully one-third, that they were forced to fall back. Mabry's and Bell's brigades advanced to within close musket-range and engaged the enemy. Approaching gradually, they poured a very destructive fire upon his line. Arriving at the open space, and having to cross a cornfield, they slowly advanced, but so deadly was the concentrated fire that, after penetrating some fifty steps, they retired to the cover of timber, where they kept up a heavy and continual fire upon the enemy for three hours, dealing destruction in his ranks. General Chalmers' division was ordered forward to relieve my command, and I was directed to fall back and hold my command immediately in rear of the position where the first line of battle was formed. During the night I was ordered to mount Bell's brigade and station it at Dr. Calhoun's house, to be in readiness to oppose the enemy if an advance was made toward Verona, and the Kentucky brigade to be thrown between the enemy and Dr. Calhoun's house. I was further ordered to send a mounted regiment from Mabry's brigade through Harrisburg to ascertain what the enemy was doing, while the remainder of that brigade was left in its original position. I made the dispositions required by these orders, and the next morning (Friday, the 15th of July,) I was ordered to attack the enemy on his left flank, on the Verona Road. I moved against him with Bell's and Crossland's brigades, and drove him back about one mile to the cover of timber upon his main line. I then halted, threw out a line of skirmishers to hold the enemy in check, and rested my division, who were exhausted from hard fighting, the excessive heat and want of water. I had eighty men carried off the field that morning perfectly exhausted, most of whom were insensible. About 2 P. M. I received orders to move up, as the enemy were evidently retreating on the road to Ellistown, and to pursue him vigorously. I marched on the Harrisburg and Ellistown Road, Bell's brigade in the advance, and commenced the pursuit. Rice's battery was also ordered to report to me.

I overtook the enemy's rear at Old Town Creek, five miles from Tupelo. I ordered Rice's battery immediately in position on elevated ground, which commanded the bottom and the crossing of the creek, and opened on the retiring enemy. I formed Bell's and Crossland's brigades on either side of the road and moved forward. From casualties of action, from exhaustion, and from broken-down horses, my division, now composed of those two brigades (Mabry's having been sent on another road), was reduced to less than a thousand. I drove the enemy's rear before me to the creek bottom with considerable loss. Rice's battery did good execution. The enemy, finding himself pushed in the rear, immediately re-enforced his rear-guard with two brigades of infantry, whom I fought for thirty minutes. The support I was expecting not arriving, and the force of the enemy being so much superior to my own, I was forced to withdraw. Colonel McCulloch came up soon afterward with his brigade, engaged the enemy, and was driven back. The division was then, by order, withdrawn from the pursuit, and returned to camp near Harrisburg.

BATTLE AT HARRISBURG, MISS., JULY 14, 1864.

Words are inadequate to express the daring action, the imperturbable bravery, the indomitable endurance, exhibited by both officers and men. The country has rarely witnessed such boldness of execution as was performed by the troops of the division. They attacked with precision and earnestness, determined not to give up the struggle until the enemy was driven from the field.

The long list of dead and wounded echo the history of their actions. To Colonel Harrison, Lieutenant-Colonels Cage and Nelson, and Major McCoy, of Mabry's brigade of Mississippians, who fell in the foremost rank, every meed of praise for bravery, coolness and gallant bearing on the march, and especially in action, is due. They fill a soldier's grave, deeply lamented, but are a monument of themselves, the reflection of whose lives will add to the determination of their surviving comrades to fight on until the blessings of peace and independence crown our efforts.

The brave and lamented Sherrill, Lieutenant-Colonel Seventh Kentucky, deserves the most commendable notice for his actions. A modest, retiring officer, he was yet ever found in the thickest of the fight, cheering forward his men until the missile of death laid him low.

The long list of field and line officers and men wounded shows the deadly nature of the conflict and their daring and devotion to duty. I take the highest pleasure in mentioning as worthy of the notice of their superiors and of the Government, the following-named officers: Brigadier-General T. H. Bell, commanding brigade; Colonel Ed Crossland, commanding brigade, who was severely wounded; Colonel H. P. Mabry, commanding brigade (the coolness with which these officers maneuvered their commands under a most galling fire, their ready appreciation of positions and full obedience to all orders were specially noted); Colonels W. W. Faulkner, Faulkner's (Kentucky) regiment; R. M. Russell, Fifteenth Tennessee; A. N. Wilson, Sixteenth Tennessee; C.R. Barteau, Second Tennessee; J. F. Newsom, Newsom's (Tennessee) regiment (all wounded); G. A. C. Holt, Third Kentucky; Lieutenant-Colonels Stockdale, Fourth Confederate [Fourth Mississippi Cavalry] (wounded); A. R. Shacklett, Eighth Kentucky; Wisdom, Newsom's (Tennessee) regiment (wounded); J. A. Forrest, Sixteenth Tennessee; and Majors Hale, Seventh Kentucky (severely wounded), Parham, Sixteenth Tennessee (wounded), and T. S. Tate, Faulkner's (Kentucky) regiment, all displayed evidences of soldierly qualities, both in action and in the manner of handling their troops, that merit approbation from all superiors. Captain Rice, Rice's battery, should not be forgotten; his battery did fine execution. The gallant list of line officers who fully performed all duties required of them should not be forgotten by their generals. To the privates no flattering words can add to their deeds. If we desire to look for deeds of noble daring and worthy of imitation we must go to the ranks.

For particular mention of officers and men I refer to accompanying reports of brigade and regimental commanders.

The loss sustained by my division, including Mabry's brigade, was: Officers—killed, 22; wounded, 104; total, 126. Enlisted men—killed, 131; wounded, 694; total, 825. Grand total, 951. That sustained by the enemy was much heavier, and does not fall short of 2,000. The missing amount to 48, including 3 officers.

In conclusion, I would call attention to the meritorious actions of my staff. They cheerfully, promptly and with bravery carried every order and performed every duty required of them. I am especially indebted to Chief Surgeon Thomas F. Clardy, who, in addition to his professional duties, materially aided me as aid-de-camp. I am also indebted to Lieutenant D. A. Given, aid-de-camp, and Acting Assistant Adjutant-General in the absence of Captain Crowder; Captain F. G. Terry, Eighth Kentucky, Acting Assistant Inspector-General, and to Major Matthews and Captain James, volunteer aids, for their devotion. I was deprived by sickness of the aid of Captain Thomas M. Crowder, Assistant Adjutant-General; Major H. Nicholson, Acting Assistant Adjutant-General, and Lieutenant D. E. Myers, aid, who were at hospital.

I would call attention to the energy and promptness displayed by Lieutenant John D. Gardner, ordnance officer of the division, who, being the only officer who had his train of ordnance on the field, distributed to the whole army. This officer has always been on the ground, diligent in the discharge of his duties, ready at all times, and merits promotion.

I would mention as performing their whole duty faithfully and fearlessly Captain William Campbell and eighty men of Morgan's command, who, having escaped through the lines in this direction, volunteered for the fight. Their loss was 5 killed, 19 wounded and 2 missing.

My escort (Captain J. Clay Horne, Company M, Third Kentucky Regiment) were ever ready to obey all orders required of them, and gave valuable information of movements and disposition of enemy.

The record of this action shows that the second division performed with alacrity and spirit every duty required of them, whether in attacking the enemy in front, on the flank, or in the pursuit, and few troops have ever borne themselves on a field with more distinguished courage, with more patient endurance or with the loss of so many field officers, there being seven regiments which were deprived of every field officer by the casualties of action.

My command was supplied with forage and provisions through the exertions of my chief quartermaster, Captain J. L. Lea, and my acting commissary, Major J. R. Finch.

A. BUFORD,
Brigadier-General Commanding Division.

PRICE'S MISSOURI EXPEDITION,

AUGUST 28 TO DECEMBER 2, 1864.

BY

MAJOR-GENERAL STERLING PRICE.

WASHINGTON, ARK., December 28, 1864.

I HAVE the honor to make the following report of my operations in the late expedition into Missouri. I regret to state that the report is meager and incomplete in many of its details, for the reason that Major-General Marmaduke and Brigadier-General Cabell, who bore so honorable and conspicuous a part in the greater part of the expedition, were captured before its close and are now prisoners in the hands of the enemy, while Major-General Fagan, who commanded the Arkansas troops, who composed so large a portion of the forces engaged in it, has as yet been unable to make any report; neither have any been received from his subordinate commanders.

MAJ.-GEN. JOHN S. MARMADUKE, OF MISSOURI.

In conformity with the letter of instructions of General E. Kirby Smith, of the 11th of August, 1864, I made immediate arrangements for a movement into Missouri, as concluded upon in my interview and conference with him upon that subject, with the cavalry forces in the District of Arkansas which was then under my command, being promised, in addition, the brigade of Louisiana cavalry commanded by Colonel Harrison, estimated at fifteen hundred strong. At the same time information in full detail of the proposed movement, of the routes intended to be pursued, and probable time when it would be made, was without delay sent by me to Brigadier-General Shelby, who then commanded in Northeastern Arkansas, with instructions to make an attack when, in his judgment, he should deem it advisable, upon Devalls Bluff and the railroad between Little Rock and the White River, in possession of the enemy, and by diverting their attention from my own movements enable me to cross the Lower Arkansas—the route proposed—and unite our forces without danger of failure. These instructions were carried out in full by General Shelby, and resulted in his attack upon the railroad, terminating in the most complete success, over four hundred Federals being captured, three hundred killed and wounded, six forts taken and destroyed, ten miles of railroad destroyed, as well as vast quantities of forage. This exploit was one of the most brilliant of the war and cast additional luster upon the well-earned fame of that gallant general and the men and officers under his command.

It was part of the plan concluded upon that I should cross the Arkansas River about the 20th of August, with the troops under my immediate command, but from delay in receiving the necessary ordnance stores I was unable to do so. Finally the required complement was received on the 27th, and on the 28th of August I was relieved from the command of the District of Arkansas, crossed the Ouachita River, and on the 29th arrived at Princeton, where the divisions of Fagan and Marmaduke were, and assumed command of all the cavalry in the District of Arkansas, according to the instructions of General E. Kirby Smith above referred to. In the meantime, owing to the delay in starting, I was of the opinion that the enemy had become informed of my intended line of march, and I concluded that I would cross the Arkansas River at the most feasible point north of Little Rock and south of Fort Smith, taking into consideration the probable means of obtaining forage and subsistence.

On the 30th, I accordingly took up my line of March in the direction of Little Rock and arrived that afternoon at Tulip, a distance of nine miles. Colonel Harrison's brigade had not yet arrived, but as I could no longer delay I left instructions at Princeton, directing him, if he should arrive there within three days, to follow on and form a junction with me, giving him information of the route I should travel; but in case he did not reach that place within that time that he should then report to the commanding-general of the District of Arkansas. Colonel Harrison did not take part in the expedition.

On the morning of the 31st, I resumed my line of march in the same direction as on the previous day, and continued on the same until I arrived within seven miles of Benton, when I diverged to the left, taking a northwest direction, sending Major-General Fagan across the Saline River to make a demonstration toward Little Rock, and at the same time protect my right flank.

On the 5th of September he rejoined me, bringing up the rear. I reached Dardaneille on the 6th day of September. The country through which I had passed was hilly and in some parts mountainous, sparsely settled, but plenty of forage and subsistence had been obtained.

The Arkansas River being fordable at this point, on the 7th I crossed it with the command and train and marched to Dover, a distance of fourteen miles. Major-General Marmaduke, with his division and a portion of his train, had already crossed it before my arrival, thus covering the crossing of the remaining portion of the army. At Princeton, verbal and written communications had been sent to Brigadier-General Shelby, apprising him of the change of route and directing him to form a junction with me at Batesville, but up to this time had received no information from him of his movements or position. I resumed my line of march in the direction of the last-mentioned place, Major-General Fagan, with his command, marching along the Springfield road, and Major-General Marmaduke's headquarters and train on the Clinton road, marching by separate roads on account of the scarcity of forage and for the purpose of ridding that section of the country of

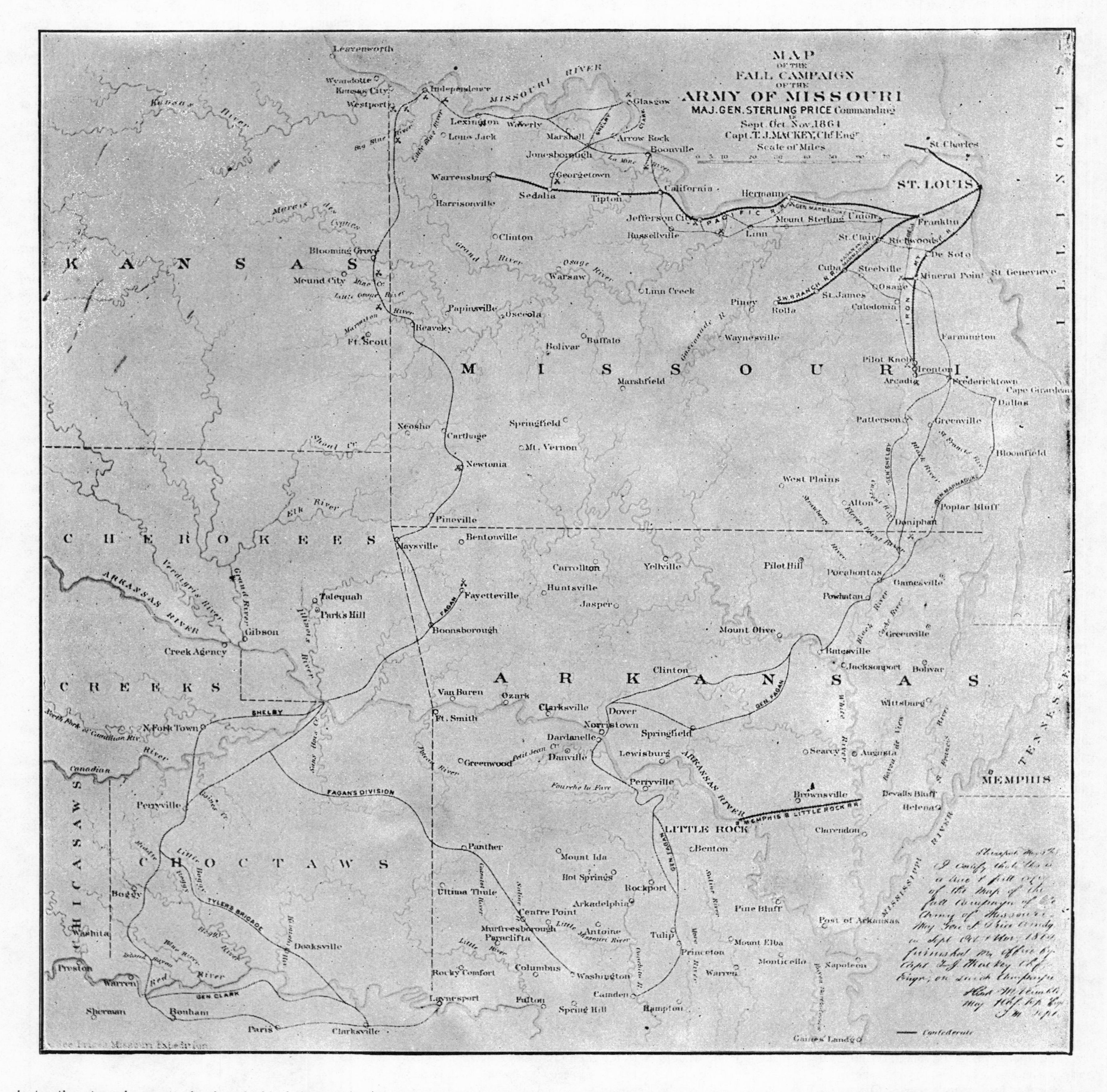

deserters and Federal Jayhawkers, as they are termed — *i. e.*, robbers and murderers — with which that country is infested. These bands, however, dispersed and took refuge in the mountains at the approach of the army, although several of them were killed and a small number taken prisoners.

On arriving at Little Red River on the 10th, still without information of the position or movements of General Shelby, I dispatched an officer of known skill and daring to communicate with him, directing that he should unite himself with the rest of the command at once.

On the 12th, I arrived at a point on White River, eighteen miles above Batesville, and having received information that Brigadier-General Shelby, with his command, was at Powhatan, about sixty-four miles northeast of Batesville, and on the selected route to Missouri, I adopted the town of Pocahontas as the point of rendezvous, and directed Major-General Marmaduke, with his own command, his train, and that of headquarters, to march to that point direct, while I proceeded with my staff to Batesville, and from thence to Powhatan, while Major-General Fagan, with his division, who had arrived at Batesville, marched to Powhatan on the left.

FORT SMITH, ARK.

I arrived on the 13th of September and found Brigadier-General Shelby there with a portion of his command. The next day I reached Pocahontas, a distance of three hundred and fifty-six miles from Camden, and there the remaining portion of Shelby's command reported, including the brigades of Jackman, McCray and Dobbin. In fine, the whole army was concentrated. The country over which I had passed was rugged and mountainous in the extreme, and had damaged the transportation to some extent; but it had already been or was on the point of being repaired, and on the other hand, by adopting the routes marched over, sufficient forage and subsistence had been obtained. The towns and villages through which I had passed had been robbed, pillaged, burned or otherwise destroyed by the enemy, and were nearly deserted by the former inhabitants; in fact, the whole country presented but a scene of devastation. Upon arriving at Pocahontas, I immediately proceeded to organize the army, which was completed on the 18th, as follows: Fagan's division, commanded by Major-General J. F. Fagan, was composed of Brigadier-General W. L. Cabell's brigade, Colonel Slemon's brigade, Colonel McCray's brigade, Colonel Dobbin's brigade, Colonels Lyles' and Rogan's commands and Captain Anderson's battalion. Marmaduke's division, commanded by Major-General J. S. Marmaduke, was composed of Brigadier-General John B. Clark, Jr.'s brigade, Colonel Freeman's brigade, Colonel Kitchen's regiment and Lieutenant-Colonel R. C. Wood's battalion. Shelby's division, commanded by Brigadier-General J. O. Shelby, consisted of Colonel Shank's brigade, Colonel Jackman's brigade and Colonel Coleman's command.

Having determined to invade Missouri in three columns, Major-General Fagan, with his division, was ordered to march to Fredericktown, Mo., by the way of Martinsburg, Reeves Station and Greenville. Major-General Marmaduke, with his division, was ordered to march to the vicinity of Fredericktown, to the right of the route to be followed by Fagan's division, as above designated, varying from it from ten to thirty miles, or as nearly within these limits as might be practicable on account of roads and forage. Brigadier-General Shelby, with his command, was to march to the vicinity of Fredericktown by a route to the left of General Fagan's, varying from it from ten to twenty miles, as nearly as practicable, on account of roads and forage. The headquarters to march with the center column. At Fredericktown the three divisions were ordered to form a junction. A map of the route to be followed was furnished each of the division commanders. The most stringent orders were issued against straggling and pillaging under the severest penalties, and the division commanders earnestly enjoined to use their utmost endeavors to have the orders carried into effect in every particular and without delay.

On the 19th of September the army marched in the order above designated, and on that day I entered Missouri with nearly twelve thousand men, of whom eight thousand were armed, and fourteen pieces of artillery, and on the 24th day of September reached Fredericktown, Mo., with the center column. Brigadier-General Shelby, with his division, was in advance, passing in his route through Doniphan and Patterson, while Major-General Marmaduke, whose route was by Poplar Bluff, Castorville and Dallas, had not yet come up. On the 19th, before Brigadier-General Shelby reached Doniphan, news of the arrival of the army having been received, a force of the enemy, composed of the Twelfth Missouri (Federal) Cavalry,* then occupying the place, withdrew and retreated to Ponders Mill, burning the houses of citizens as they passed along, where they were overtaken the next day by scouting parties sent in pursuit and were routed with a loss of a lieutenant and three men killed, four wounded and six prisoners, besides several horses and small arms captured. Our loss, two killed and five wounded.

* It was the Third Missouri State Militia Cavalry.

On the 22d, Brigadier-General Shelby attacked the town of Patterson, but the garrison having received information of the approach, hastily evacuated the place with a loss of twenty-eight killed and several wounded; also telegraph battery and operator captured. No loss on our part.

On the 25th, I remained at Fredericktown awaiting the arrival of Marmaduke's division, which came up that evening within eight miles of the place. Major-General Marmaduke, on his route, had a few skirmishes with the Federal militia, killing and wounding four and capturing eleven.

Colonel Jeffers, of Marmaduke's division, had, before the arrival of the army at Pocahontas, been sent with his regiment to Bloomfield, Mo., which the enemy evacuated at his approach, whereupon he attacked their rear, killing a number and capturing arms and six wagon-loads of army stores. He rejoined his brigade (Clark's) on the 24th; detached again on the 25th, he attacked and, by a gallant charge, drove the enemy out of the town of Old Jackson.

I received at Fredericktown satisfactory information that the strength of the enemy at Ironton was about fifteen hundred and that the Federal general, A. J. Smith, was encamped about ten miles from St. Louis with his corps, composed of about eight thousand infantry, on the St. Louis & Iron Mountain Railroad. I immediately issued orders to Brigadier-General Shelby to proceed at once with his division by the way of Farmington to a point on the St. Louis & Iron Mountain Railroad, where there were three fine bridges in close proximity to each other, and to destroy the railroad there and the bridges; after effecting that object to fall back in the direction of Ironton and Pilot Knob, which would effectually prevent General A. J. Smith from re-enforcing the garrison at those places, while I would attack and take them with the divisions of Major-Generals Fagan and Marmaduke. General Shelby proceeded to the point indicated and performed the duty assigned him in the most complete and effective manner, destroying the splendid bridge at Irondale as well as the three bridges mentioned, tearing up miles upon miles of the track, burning the ties, rails, etc.

On the morning of the 26th, being rejoined by Major-General Marmaduke's division, I proceeded at an early hour with Fagan's and Marmaduke's divisions, in the direction of Ironton and Pilot Knob, at the same time sending forward a portion of Fagan's division to take and hold a difficult pass in that direction, between two mountains, within three or four miles of Ironton. This was effected rapidly and with success. That evening I sent forward the remainder of his division, leaving his train at St. Francis Creek, six miles from Ironton, where forage could be obtained for the animals and where I encamped for the night with the rest of the command. That evening Major-General Fagan drove in the Federal pickets at Arcadia and took position before the town for the night. The next morning he drove the enemy from Arcadia, where they abandoned a very strong position, through Ironton, where he also took a strong fort in the most gallant and brilliant manner. The enemy took refuge behind their

SOLDIERS PICKING BLACKBERRIES DURING A HALT OF THE ARMY.

fortifications at Pilot Knob. Having received such information as appeared to be perfectly reliable concerning the character and strength of the fortifications as induced me to believe the place could be taken without great loss, I accordingly directed Major-General Marmaduke to take possession of Shepherd's Mountain, which was west of the fortifications and completely commanded them. This was most satisfactorily accomplished and his artillery placed in position on the mountain. Major-General Fagan formed on the south and east. Skirmishing took place all the day and heavy firing of artillery from the enemy until about 2 P. M., when a charge was ordered and made in the most gallant manner, officers and men of both divisions vying with each other in unsurpassed bravery, charging up nearly to the muzzle of the enemy's cannon.

Where all acted as heroes, it seems almost invidious to make any exceptions, but I must be allowed to call attention to the courage and gallantry of Brigadier-General Cabell in leading his men to the assault, having his horse killed under him within forty yards of the fort.

But the information I had received in regard to the strength of the fortifications proved totally incorrect. Our troops were repulsed, and it being too late to renew the assault, they were withdrawn beyond the reach of the enemy's guns and preparations were made for a renewal of the assault on the next day. I had dispatched a courier on the morning of the 27th to Brigadier-General Shelby, informing him of the proposed operations and directing him to rejoin the main army to assist in the attack, and on the evening of the 27th another courier was dispatched to him, informing him of the capture of Arcadia and Ironton, and of the repulse at Pilot Knob, and of my design to renew the attack on the following morning; and hoping that the courier would meet him on the way, instructed him to join me, as also the route to pursue. Neither of these communications, as it appears, was received by Brigadier-General Shelby, who, having heard that there was a force of the enemy at Potosi, had left the railroad and marched to attack them at that place, which was captured by him with its garrison of one hundred and fifty Federals, arms, ammunition, etc. The depot of the railroad at that place, with seven fine cars, was also destroyed.

The enemy at Pilot Knob, on the night following the first attack, evacuated the fort, blowing up the magazine and leaving in my possession sixteen pieces of artillery, a large number of small arms, a large amount of army stores, consisting of bales of blankets, hundreds of barrels of flour, many tierces of bacon, a great quantity of coffee, etc. After destroying the artillery, which I could not take with me, and distributing such of the stores as were needed among the troops, I moved my command twelve miles on the road the retreating army had gone, sending Marmaduke forward in pursuit in command of his own and Shelby's division, which had rejoined the command. Untiring pursuit was made night and day, but it was not until the evening of the following day (the 27th [29th]) that he was overtaken, owing to the natural difficulties presented by the country over which the enemy retreated. Major-General Marmaduke, who was in advance, fought him until an hour before sunset, when Shelby was thrown in front, and the fight was continued until darkness put an end to the combat. The enemy having thrown up fortifications during the night, it was deemed advisable not to renew the attack and the forces were withdrawn. My loss in this report I can not give, as I have no report from Fagan's division, but the loss in Marmaduke's division was fourteen officers and eighty men killed and wounded, and the loss in Fagan's was doubtless greater.

While at Ironton, receiving information that the Federal force in St. Louis far exceeded my own, two to one, and knowing the city to be strongly fortified, I determined to move as fast as possible on Jefferson City, destroying the railroad as I went, with a hope to be able to capture that city, with its troops and munitions of war. I arrived at Richmond on the 30th, having passed through Potosi. Lieutenant Christian, whom I had previously sent to the Mississippi River before I left Camden, for the purpose of obtaining gun-caps, joined me at this place, bringing me one hundred and fifty thousand. Lieutenant Christian is a most energetic and efficient officer, and deserves especial notice.

Major-General Fagan sent three hundred men to DeSoto to destroy the depot at that place, which was effected, and the militia, who had gathered there in some numbers at the same time, scattered. At the same time General Cabell was sent, with his brigade, to cut the Pacific Railroad east of Franklin, which he did effectually, at the same time burning the depot in that town.

On the 29th Colonel Burbridge and Lieutenant-Colonel Wood were detached from his command by Major-General Marmaduke, and sent to Cuba to destroy the railroad depot at that place, which they succeeded in doing. The divisions of Marmaduke and Shelby tore up several miles of the southwest branch of the Pacific Railroad. Lieutenant-Colonel Wood, of Marmaduke's division, destroyed the important bridge over the Moselle. These two divisions were sent forward, in the direction of Union, which was attacked and captured by Brigadier-General Clark, killing thirty-two and wounding seventy of the Federal garrison.

BATTLE OF FREDERICKTOWN, MO.

On the 2d of October Clark's bridage, of Marmaduke's division, took possession of the town of Washington without opposition, and destroyed the Pacific Railroad about two miles from that place.

On the 3d a train was captured at Millers Station, with a large amount of clothing and four hundred Sharps rifles, and on the same evening the town of Hermann was taken possession of, after a slight opposition, by Clark's brigade.

On the 4th of October Major-General Marmaduke sent a force of four hundred men, with one gun, under the command of Lieutenant-Colonel Wood, for the purpose of destroying the Pacific Railroad Bridge over the Gasconade River, which he effected. Linn was captured with about one hundred prisoners and as many arms, by a portion of Shelby's division.

On the 6th Brigadier-General Shelby sent a force, under Colonel Shanks, to destroy the bridge over the Osage, on the Pacific Railroad, which was successfully accomplished. A passage was then forced by him across the Osage, six miles below Castle Rock. The enemy disputed the passage warmly, but in vain. In this action the gallant Colonel Shanks received a severe, if not a mortal, wound, and, left in the hands of friends to be cared for, he afterward fell into the possession of the enemy, and is reported to have since died, a loss to be greatly deplored. Ever foremost in the battle and last in the retreat, his death would be regretted by all who mourn the loss of the good and the brave. At the same time that Colonel Shanks forced the passage of the Osage, as stated, Colonel Gordon, of the same division, forced its passage at Castle Rock, and the division bivouacked that night seven miles from Jefferson City.

On the next morning Major-General Fagan was thrown in advance with his division, and on the march came upon the enemy about five miles from Jefferson City in large force. A hotly contested battle ensued, but the enemy were gradually driven back to the Moreau Creek, where, being re-enforced, they again made an obstinate resistance, but were finally routed and forced to seek shelter in their intrenchments, Fagan occupying the heights in full view of the city. On this occasion Major-General Fagan handled his troops with marked skill and ability under my immediate observation. Night approaching, I determined to move my forces two miles south of the city to a point where water and forage were abundant, and I accordingly did so and encamped for the night. I had received positive information that the enemy were twelve thousand strong in the city, and that three thousand more had arrived on the opposite bank of the river by the North Missouri Railroad before I withdrew my troops to the encampment selected, whereupon I gave immediate instructions to Brigadier-General Shelby to send a sufficient force to burn the bridges and destroy the railroad on the west of Jefferson City in the direction of California, the county-seat of Moniteau County, and, after consultation with my general officers, I determined not to attack the enemy's intrenchments, as they outnumbered me nearly two to one and were strongly fortified, but to move my command in the direction of Kansas, as instructed in my original orders, hoping to be able to capture a sufficient number of arms to arm my unarmed men, at Boonville, Sedalia, Lexington and Independence, places which I intended to occupy with my troops en route. The next day I accordingly took up my line of march in the direction of Kansas, and upon leaving Jefferson City was followed by General McNeil, who made an attack upon my rear-guard (Fagan's division), but was easily repulsed. Brigadier-General Shelby, who with his division constituted my advance, reached California on the 8th, having sent a portion of his command on before him to destroy the Pacific Railroad at that place, which he did, destroying track and bridges, etc. Pushing rapidly on to Boonville, he, by a rapid charge, drove in their pickets, and the garrison taking refuge in their defenses, Brigadier-General Shelby, disposing such of his forces as he had with him in a manner to prevent the arrival of any re-enforcements, waited until his artillery could come up. In the meantime propositions for the surrender of the town were made to him, which were accepted, and accordingly the place, with its garrison, stores, etc., was delivered into his hands.

I followed on with the divisions of Major-Generals Fagan and Marmaduke, and encamped on the night of the 8th fourteen miles from Jefferson City, and on the 9th marched through and beyond California, making twenty-six miles.

On the 10th I arrived at Boonville with the rest of the command. My reception was enthusiastic in the extreme. Old and young, men, women and children, vied in their salutations and in ministering to the wants and comforts of my wearied and war-worn soldiers. About three hundred prisoners were captured at Boonville, with arms, ammunition and many stores, which were distributed among the soldiers.

On the 11th, hearing of the approach of the Federal General McNeil, with a cavalry force estimated at twenty-five hundred men, for the purpose of attacking Boonville by the Tipton Road, I selected my position about half a mile from the river and placed the divisions of Major-Generals Fagan and Marmaduke in line of battle to receive him. The enemy attacked them, but was easily driven back with considerable loss, and was afterward pursued by a portion of Fagan's division and Jackman's brigade a distance of twenty-one miles from Boonville with heavy loss, in spite of obstinate resistance and the ruggedness of the country over which the pursuit was made.

Captain Anderson, who reported to me that day with a company of about one hundred men, was immediately

BRIG.-GEN. J. O. SHELBY, OF MISSOURI.
[From an old photograph.]

sent to destroy the North Missouri Railroad. At the same time Quantrill was sent with the men under his command to destroy the Hannibal & St. Joseph Railroad, to prevent the enemy, if possible, from throwing their forces in my front from St. Louis. These officers, I was afterward informed, did effect some damage to the roads, but none of any material advantage, and totally failed in the main object proposed, which was to destroy the large railroad bridge that was in the end of St. Charles County.

I moved that evening from Boonville to Chouteau Springs on my proposed route, a distance of eleven miles, having recruited at Boonville between twelve and fifteen hundred men, mostly unarmed. That night, receiving information that there was a large number of arms (amounting to five thousand) stored in the city hall at Glasgow, I sent Brigadier-General Clark, of Marmaduke's division, with his own brigade and five hundred of Jackman's brigade, with orders to cross the river at Arrow Rock and attack the place the next morning at daylight and capture it, at the same time sending Brigadier-General Shelby with a small portion of his division and a section of his artillery to attack the town from the west side of the river at the same hour, to divert the attention of the enemy and protect their advance under the cover of the fire of his artillery. Owing to unforeseen difficulties in crossing the river, Brigadier-General Clark was unable to commence the attack for one hour after Brigadier-General Shelby had engaged them. The place was surrendered, but not until after the city hall was destroyed and the arms consumed by fire. By the capture of this place, however, we obtained between eight and nine hundred prisoners, about twelve hundred small arms, about the same number of overcoats, one hundred and fifty horses, one steamboat and large amounts of underclothing. This enterprise was a great success, effected with but comparatively small loss on our side, and reflects great honor on all the parties concerned in it. The captured prisoners were paroled, such of the ordnance and other stores captured as could not be carried were distributed, and the remaining portion, together with the steamboat, burned.

On the night of the 13th I encamped at Mr. Marshall's, marching fourteen miles, and on the next day marched to Jonesboro—a distance of eight miles—where I was joined by Major-General Fagan, who had been left behind at the La Mine. I there ordered Brigadier-General M. Jeff. Thompson, then commanding Shelby's old brigade, to take with him a force of not less than eight hundred or a thousand men and one section of artillery, by Longwood, and from thence to Sedalia, to attack the Federal force at that place if he should deem it advisable and prudent. This order was promptly and completely carried out by Brigadier-General Thompson. The place, though strongly fortified and well garrisoned, was carried by a bold and daring assault and fell into our hands with over two hundred prisoners, who were paroled, several stand of arms, many pistols, and several wagon-loads of goods suitable to soldiers.

On the 15th I reached Keiser's, having passed through Marshall, marching seventeen miles, where I remained two days awaiting the arrival of Brigadier-General Clark, for whose safety I began to entertain fears, inasmuch as information had been received that the enemy were on my left flank and in my rear in large force. Previous to the attack on Sedalia, the large and magnificent bridge on the La Mine River on the Pacific Railroad had been destroyed by Lieutenant James Wood, of Elliott's battalion, who had been sent there by Brigadier-General Shelby for that purpose.

On the 17th I received information that the enemy (Kansas troops) had entered Lexington on the 16th.

On the 17th I received news of the capture of Sedalia by Brigadier-General Thompson.

On the 18th, having been joined by Brigadier-General Shelby's division, and Clark's brigade, of Marmaduke's division, I marched to Waverly, a distance of twenty-two miles.

On leaving Pocahontas I had sent an agent into St. Louis, of great intelligence and tact, to ascertain the strength of the enemy at that city, with directions to report to me, if possible, at Potosi. He was, however, so closely watched that he could not join me until after I had passed that city. Upon overtaking me, he informed me that I would be pursued by twenty-four thousand men from St. Louis, fifteen thousand from Jefferson City, which, with the forces in my front from Kansas, he believed to be the entire force with which I would have to contend. I then abandoned my former determination to issue an address to the people calling upon them to rally to me, as they were already pouring in on me so rapidly that I knew I would not be able to protect and feed them, and as it would require that my army should be kept together to protect them on a rapid and dangerous retreat from the State.

At daybreak on the morning of the 19th I moved from Waverly in the direction of Lexington, Brigadier-General Shelby's division in the advance, and having received information that Generals Blunt, Lane and Jennison, with between three and four thousand Federals (Colorado, Kansas and Missouri Federal troops), were at Lexington, and fearing that they might make a junction with McNeil and A. J. Smith, who were at Sedalia and Salt Fork, I made a flank movement to the left after crossing the Tabo, so as to intercept their line of march. The advance, under Shelby, met them about 2 P. M., and a battle immediately ensued. For a time the Federals fought well and resisted strenuously, but, finally giving way, they were pressed by our troops, driven well past Lexington, and pursued on the road to Independence until night put an end to the combat. That night the enemy evacuated Lexington in great haste and confusion. Shelby's old brigade, under General M. Jeff. Thompson, bivouacked that night in the suburbs of the town. I encamped at General Shield's farm, three miles south of Lexington, marching that day twenty-six miles.

On the morning of the 20th I moved west in the same direction as before to Fire Creek Prairie, a distance of twenty-two miles, where I encamped. Information reached me that the enemy had fallen back to the Little Blue.

On the 21st I resumed my line of march to the Little Blue, on the Independence Road, Major-General Marmaduke's division in the front, whose advance soon came upon the enemy's pickets, who, being driven across the Blue, destroyed the bridge as they crossed. A ford half a mile below the bridge was seized by our troops and Marmaduke's division crossed it. His advance (Colonel Lawther's regiment) soon came upon the enemy, who were strongly posted behind a stone fence in superior numbers. Lawther's regiment was driven back and was hotly pursued by the foe, when they were re-enforced by Colonel Greene, with about one hundred and fifty men. A fierce engagement ensued, with varying success, Colonel Greene stubbornly contesting every inch of ground, when Wood's battalion arrived and the enemy gave way, but, being re-enforced, again renewed the attack, when, as the ammunition of our troops engaged (who still manfully resisted with success the far superior numbers of the enemy) was about to become exhausted, Colonel Kitchen's regiment arrived to their relief. The enemy again fell back to their former strong position. Hearing of the critical condition of Major-General Marmaduke's division, I had sent orders to Brigadier-General Shelby to march rapidly to his relief, who accordingly hastened to the scene of action with his division and arrived there at the time when the enemy had taken refuge in their first position. An immediate attack was made upon them and a furious battle ensued, but the enemy were finally forced from their position and they retreated. Brigadier-General Shelby now taking the lead, drove them in a stubborn running fight on foot (his men having been dismounted) for seven miles and beyond Independence.

In this action Major-General Marmaduke acted with distinguished gallantry, having not less than two horses shot under him. Brigadier-General Clark, of his division, also exhibited great bravery and skill, while Colonel Greene, by the manner in which he handled his regiment against vastly superior forces flushed with previous success, beating them back with his handful of men and stubbornly contesting every inch of ground until assistance came to his relief, as well as the personal courage exhibited by him, justly excited the admiration of his superior officers. Fagan's division, under my orders, supported Shelby, but were not immediately engaged.

I encamped that night in Independence, having marched twenty-six miles, the troops being engaged with the enemy most of the time and driving them before them.

On the evening of the 21st Captain Williams, of Brigadier-General Shelby's division, who had been sent on recruiting service by him, rejoined his command with about six hundred men, capturing on his route the town of Carrollton, with three hundred prisoners, and armed his entire command.

On the morning of the 22d I left Independence. The enemy had fallen back to Big Blue, on the Kansas City Road, to a position strong by nature and strengthened by fortifications, upon which all their art had been exhausted, and where they had been joined by General Curtis and his forces, thus increasing Blunt's army to between six and eight thousand men. Receiving this information, I determined to advance on the Santa Fe Road, which had been obstructed by felling trees, and did so, Brigadier-General Shelby's division in front, who advanced, detaching Jackman and sending him on the Kansas City Road to engage the enemy, there skirmishing with the pickets. Brigadier-General Shelby crossed the Big Blue with the remainder of his division, meeting some opposition from the enemy, which was soon overcome. After crossing the Big Blue he engaged the enemy to cover the crossing and the passage of the train.

Brigadier-General Thompson with his brigade, except Gordon's regiment, pressed the enemy too near the town of Westport, where he was ordered to fall back to the Blue. Colonel Gordon, with his regiment, who had been retained to guard the left, soon became engaged and was sorely pressed by overpowering numbers, when he was rejoined by Jackman, and, gallantly charging, they repulsed the enemy, capturing a 24-pounder howitzer, and pursued them some distance, inflicting upon the enemy heavy loss. A large force of the enemy came out from Westport and a severe fight ensued, the enemy obstinately endeavoring to regain the gun which they had lost; but they were sternly resisted and, finally, the arrival of Brigadier-General Thompson and night put an end to the conflict.

Two flags were also captured, which were presented me on the battlefield by Captains McCoy and Wood, of Gordon's regiment, who had taken them from the enemy with their own hands. In the meantime other forces had engaged me in the rear. Having received information that other bodies of the enemy were pursuing me, I had directed pickets to be placed at the Little Blue to give notice of their approach. This had been done by Major-General Fagan and, being advised on the morning of the 22d that the enemy had attacked and driven in his pickets, he dispatched Brigadier-General Cabell to drive back the enemy,

BRIG.-GEN. WILLIAM L. CABELL, OF VIRGINIA.

which he succeeded in doing, but on his return, on coming out of Independence, the enemy struck Cabell a blow in the flank, cutting off three or four hundred men, and capturing two pieces of artillery. Major-General Marmaduke's division, which formed the rear of the army, became engaged with the same enemy about half an hour before sundown. The division was then about two miles from Independence. The advance of the enemy was checked by our troops, who then fell back about half a mile and took a new position, which the enemy attacked with increased fierceness, driving our troops steadily back until a late hour of the night, and in almost impenetrable darkness. I encamped that night on the battlefield near Westport, in line of battle, having marched twelve miles, the troops almost constantly engaging the enemy the whole distance.

On the morning of the 23d I took up my line of march, and in a short time discovered the enemy in position on the prairie. The train had been sent forward on the Fort Scott Road. I had instructed Major-General Marmaduke to resist the advance of the enemy, who was in his rear, if possible, as he was on the same road as the train. Brigadier-General Shelby immediately attacked the enemy, assisted by Major-General Fagan, with two brigades of Arkansas troops, and though they resisted most stubbornly, and contested every point of the approach, drove them six or seven miles, into Westport. In the meantime, Major-General Marmaduke, who was to my right and rear, being attacked with great fierceness by an overwhelming force of the enemy, after a most strenuous resistance, his ammunition being exhausted, had to fall back before the foe.

Being at that time near Westport, and in full view of Generals Fagan and Shelby and their commands, I received information that my train, which was in front and on the right of the Fort Scott Road, was threatened by the enemy, some two thousand or twenty-five hundred strong, who were moving on a line parallel to the Fort Scott Road. I immediately sent the information to Major-General Fagan and Brigadier-General Shelby, and directed them to fall back to the train as soon as they could do so with safety, which I would attempt to defend until they arrived. I immediately pushed forward to the front of the train with my escort and there formed in line of battle the unarmed men, which were present to the number of several thousand, throwing my escort and the whole number of armed men of Tyler's brigade forward as skirmishers (the whole not exceeding more than two hundred), to the front of the enemy, and directing Brigadier-General Cabell, who arrived soon after, to hold the crossing of the creek on my left, sending forward at the same time for a portion of Colonel McCray's brigade, which was in advance of the train, and on his approach forming him in line of battle on the left flank of the enemy, which caused the enemy to fall back a considerable distance on the prairie. In the meantime, the rear and flank of the commands of Major-General Fagan and Brigadier-General Shelby, by the falling back of Major-General Marmaduke, were uncovered, and the former, in attempting to rejoin me, was attacked by a large force of the enemy, but with the aid of Colonel Jackman and his brigade, who came to his assistance, and who acted so heroically and skillfully as to receive the thanks of Major-General Fagan on the field, the enemy were repulsed, while Brigadier-General Shelby, in attempting to obey my instructions, was attacked in the flank and his command thrown into some confusion, but rallied, repulsed the enemy and rejoined me that evening, as did also Major-General Fagan. I encamped that night on the Middle Fork of Grand River, having marched twenty-four miles and the troops having been engaged with the enemy nearly all day. The number of the enemy's troops engaged that day exceeded twenty thousand well-armed men, while I did not have eight thousand armed men.

On the morning of the 24th I moved with the command on the Fort Scott Road to the Marais des Cygnes, where I encamped, having marched thirty-three miles, no enemy appearing. During the night I received information from Major-General Marmaduke, who was placed in charge of the approaches in front, that the enemy were threatening his pickets, and upon consultation with the General we were both of the opinion that the enemy were marching upon our right by Mound City on a road parallel to the one on which we were. We were strengthened in that belief by a dispatch which had been captured from the commanding Federal officer at that place to his scouts, stationed near our then encampment, stating that he would be largely re-enforced that night, and that he wanted a sharp lookout [kept] for my army, and to give him the earliest information of the route on which I would travel and the direction. I also received at a late hour at night information, from some new recruits who joined me and who had traveled fifteen miles on the route I had traveled, that there was no enemy in my rear.

On the morning of the 25th I resumed my march in the same direction as before, and I considered from the information I had received the night before that if I should encounter the enemy it would be in my front or on my right flank. Brigadier-General Shelby's division composed the advance, Major-Generals Fagan's and Marmaduke's divisions composed the rear-guard, Colonel Tyler's brigade to the right of the center of the train four hundred yards, Brigadier-General Shelby's old brigade to the right of the front four hundred yards, and Colonel Jackman's brigade to the immediate front.

On reaching Little Osage River I sent forward a direction to Brigadier-General Shelby to fall back to my position in rear of Jackman's brigade for the purpose of attacking and capturing Fort Scott, where I learned there were one thousand negroes under arms. At the moment of his reaching me I received a dispatch from Major-General Marmaduke, in the rear, informing me that the enemy, three thousand strong, were in sight of his rear, with lines still extending; and on the note Major-General Fagan had indorsed that he would sustain Major-General Marmaduke. I immediately ordered Brigadier-General Shelby to take his old brigade, which was on my immediate right, and return to the rear as rapidly as possible to support Major-Generals Fagan and Marmaduke. I immediately mounted my horse and rode back at a gallop, and after passing the rear of the train I met the divisions of Major-Generals Fagan and Marmaduke retreating in utter and indescribable confusion, many of them having thrown away their arms. They were deaf to all entreaties or commands, and in vain were all efforts to rally them. From them I received the information that Major-General Marmaduke, Brigadier-General Cabell, and Colonel Slemons, commanding brigade, had been captured, with three or four hundred of their men and all their artillery (five pieces).

PILOT KNOB, MO. FORTIFICATIONS AND INTRENCHMENTS CAPTURED BY THE CONFEDERATES.

Major-General Fagan and several of his officers, who had there joined me, assisted me in trying to rally the armed men, without success. I then ordered Brigadier-General Shelby to hold the enemy (who were pressing their success hotly and fiercely) in check if possible at the crossing of the Osage until the train could be placed in safety, which he succeeded in doing for several hours. I again formed the unarmed men, numbering several thousand, in line of battle on the prairie beyond the river. Major-General Fagan, in the meantime, had succeeded in rallying a portion of his forces and assisted Brigadier-General Shelby in again holding the enemy in check upon the prairie and in front of the immense lines of unarmed men until nightfall, when I withdrew. The train having reached the Marmiton, a distance of ten miles, I there overtook it, having marched a distance of twenty-eight miles.

On the next morning, after destroying many wagons with broken-down teams that could not be replaced, I took up my line of march at 2 o'clock, there being but little forage in the neighborhood of my encampment. We marched over beautiful prairie roads, a distance of fifty-six miles, and encamped at Carthage, on Spring River, the nearest point that forage could be procured, as I was informed by Major-General Fagan and Brigadier-General Shelby, who earnestly desired me to reach Spring River, as no forage could be procured short of it. The Federal prisoners I had with me became so much exhausted by fatigue that, out of humanity, I paroled them.

On the next morning, at 9 o'clock, after giving the men and animals time to rest and feed, I resumed my line of march and encamped on Shoal Creek, a distance of twenty-two miles. During the march a number of desertions took place among the Arkansas troops and new recruits. No enemy having appeared, the morale of the troops had considerably improved.

On the morning of the 28th I resumed my line of march in the direction of Newtonia, Brigadier-General Shelby in advance, Major-Generals Fagan's and Marmaduke's divisions (the latter now commanded by Brigadier-General Clark), in the rear. On approaching Newtonia the advance of our forces was discovered by the Federal garrison, who commenced a retreat. On seeing this, Shelby's advance endeavored to intercept them. The distance they had gained, however, was too great for this to be effected. They succeeded in killing the Federal Captain Christian, a notorious bushwhacker, as it is termed—that is, robber and murderer—noted for his deeds of violence and blood. After passing over the prairie about four miles beyond Newtonia, Brigadier-General Shelby halted his command at the edge of the prairie in a skirt of timber and there encamped for the night. The other divisions of the army passed on beyond him and encamped in the proper positions they were to assume in the line of march the following day. Ere long our scouts brought the information the enemy were crossing the prairie in pursuit of us. Preparations were immediately made to receive him, and about 3 o'clock General Blunt, with three thousand Federal cavalry, moved rapidly across the prairie in pursuit of us and made a furious onslaught upon our lines. He was engaged by Shelby, supported by a portion of Fagan's command. A short but obstinate combat ensued, when Blunt was repulsed and driven across the prairie three miles with heavy loss. This was the last we saw of the enemy. The army marched that day twenty-six miles and encamped.

On the 29th we marched twenty-six miles; encamped on Sugar Creek, five miles south of Pineville, passing through the town. No information was received in regard to the enemy.

On the 30th and 31st we reached Maysville, near the Arkansas line; marched forty-three miles, and on the 1st of November I reached Boonsboro, on Cane Hill, as it is called, marching seventeen miles. There information was received by Major-General Fagan, from Colonel Brooks, that he had the town of Fayetteville, Arkansas, closely invested, and the Federal garrison forced to seek shelter within their inner fortifications, and asking for a sufficient number of men to enable him to capture the place and garrison. As this was a place of considerable importance to the Federals, and its capture would be of great advantage to the cause, upon Major-General Fagan's earnest solicitation I ordered a detail of five hundred men and two guns to be made for that purpose, which were furnished by General Shelby, under Colonel Elliott, the two guns being furnished by Collins' battery. The expedition started to Fayetteville, formed a junction with Colonel Brooks, but before the place could be taken the approach of General Blunt, with a large force of Federal cavalry, caused the siege to be raised, and Colonel Elliott rejoined his command. Our march from Illinois River to Cane Hill was over a bad road, very rough and hilly, and rendered much worse than usual by the constant rains, consequently much of the stock became worn out and was abandoned on the route.

On the 3d I remained in camp. The weather was very bad, both snowing and raining during the day. I there received information that the Federal army at Little Rock had been greatly re-enforced by a portion of General Canby's command, and as it was necessary that I should here adopt the line of march I should pursue on my return to Arkansas, at district headquarters or elsewhere, as I should be directed, I determined not to risk the crossing of the Arkansas between Fort Smith and Little Rock, on which route I could not procure subsistence, forage or grass in anything like sufficient quantity, but I decided to cross through the Indian country, where beef, at least, could be obtained, which would at least subsist my men for the few days it would require them to march until they would meet supplies, even if no salt or breadstuffs could be procured, while some grass could be obtained for the animals. In addition, the route across the Arkansas River below Fort Smith would be over a rough, hilly and, in many parts, mountainous country that the stock, in its then condition, would be unable to travel over, while the route through the Indian country would be over a level and beautiful prairie country, traversed by good roads. Again, by the route below Fort Smith I would expose my whole army to be destroyed by a joint attack from Federal forces detached from the heavy garrison there and acting conjointly with large forces from Little Rock, which could easily be spared for the purpose, and which would in every probability take place, as information of my adopting that line of route would certainly reach them, and the slowness with which I would necessarily have to travel would give them ample time to make all necessary preparations.

I was, furthermore, induced to come to this conclusion from the fact that it coincided with my instructions, in the propriety and reasonableness of which my own judgment fully concurred. Colonels Freeman, Dobbin and McCray were ordered to return such of their men as still remained with their colors to the places where they had raised their commands, in order to collect the absentees together and bring them within our lines during the month of December, if possible, and on the 4th day of November I took up my line of march with the balance of my command through the Indian Territory, in the direction of Boggy Depot.

On the 13th I arrived at Perryville, in the Indian Nation, a distance of one hundred and nineteen [miles], where I met with three wagons with supplies, and encamped, remaining over one day to rest and recruit my men. I had marched carefully and slowly, stopping to graze my stock whenever an opportunity offered.

On the 14th General Shelby, at his own request, was left behind on the Canadian to recruit.

On the 10th Cabell's brigade was furloughed, as also the brigade formerly commanded by Colonel Slemons, who was captured.

On the 21st of November I arrived at Clarksville, where I received an order from Major-General Magruder to march to Laynesport and there establish my headquarters. I arrived there on the 2d of December, 1864, having marched fourteen hundred and thirty-four miles.

The march through the Indian country was necessarily a severe one, especially upon the stock, many of which died or became worn out and were consequently abandoned. The men in some instances hungered for food, but never approached starvation, nor did they suffer to anything like the extent that other of our soldiers have cheerfully endured without complaint for a much longer time during this war. At all events, I arrived in the country where forage and subsistence could be obtained in abundance, bringing with me in safety all the sick and wounded and all my command with which I entered the Indian country, without a single exception, except those who voluntarily straggled off and deserted their colors.

Federal Breastworks in Front of Jefferson City, Mo., Captured by the Confederates.

To enumerate specially the names of the officers who distinguished themselves for their skill and courage would swell this report beyond all reasonable limits; therefore, as to all but general officers and those who acted in that capacity, I would simply refer to the accompanying reports, heartily concurring in the meed of praise awarded to such officers as are therein enumerated by their immediate commanding officers. Major-General J. F. Fagan, commanding the division of Arkansas troops, bore himself throughout the whole expedition with unabated gallantry and ardor and commanded his division with great ability. Major-General J. S. Marmaduke, commanding division, proved himself worthy of his past reputation as a valiant and skillful officer, and rendered with his division great service. His capture was a great loss to the army. Brigadier-General J. O. Shelby, commanding division, added new luster to his past fame as a brilliant and heroic officer, and without disparagement to the officers, I must be permitted to say that I consider him the best cavalry officer I ever saw. The services rendered by him and his division in this expedition are beyond all praise. Brigadier-General Cabell bore himslf as a bold, undaunted, skillful officer. Impetuous, yet wary, he commanded his brigade in such a manner as to win praise from all. I regret that, for the want of reports from their several commanding officers, I am not able to do justice to this as well as other brigades of Arkansas troops. Brigadier-General Cabell's capture was a great misfortune, and his place will be difficult to fill. Brigadier-General Clark, true to his past fame, bore himself with undaunted courage and bravery, as well as skill and prudence. His brigade was most skillfully handled. Colonels Slemons, Dobbin and McCray (the former of whom was captured) acted throughout as brave, daring, yet prudent officers, and are each entitled to great praise. Colonel Freeman proved himself to be a brave and energetic officer, but as his men were mostly unarmed they were not able to render the same brilliant services as other brigades that were armed. Colonel Tyler, who was placed in command of a brigade of new recruits, for the most part unarmed, deserves great praise for the success with which he kept them together and brought them within our lines, and deserves especial mention for the cool gallantry he displayed in charging the enemy with them at an important juncture, thereby greatly aiding in saving the train of the army from destruction.

My thanks are due to my staff officers for their untiring energy and unremitting attention to their duties during the entire campaign. Their zeal and devotion can not be too highly commended by me. In conclusion, permit me to add that in my opinion the results flowing from my operations in Missouri are of the most gratifying character. I marched fourteen hundred and thirty-four miles, fought forty-three battles and skirmishes, captured and paroled over three thousand Federal officers and men, captured eighteen pieces of artillery, three thousand stand of small arms, sixteen stand of colors that were brought out by me (besides many others that were captured and afterward destroyed by our troops who took them), at least three thousand overcoats, large quantities of blankets, shoes and ready-made clothing for soldiers, a great many wagons and teams, large number of horses, great quantities of subsistence and ordnance stores. I destroyed miles upon miles of railroad, burning the depots and bridges, and, taking this into calculation, I do not think I go beyond the truth when I state that I destroyed in the late expedition to Missouri property to the amount of ten million dollars in value. On the other hand, I lost ten pieces of artillery, two stand of colors, one thousand small arms, while I do not think I lost one thousand prisoners, including the wounded left in their hands and others than recruits on their way to join me, some of whom may have been captured by the enemy.

I brought with me at least five thousand new recruits, and they are still arriving in large numbers daily within our lines, who bring the cheering intelligence that there are more on their way to the army. After I passed the German settlements in Missouri my march was an ovation. The people thronged around us and welcomed us with open hearts and hands. Recruits flocked to our flag in such numbers as to threaten to become a burden instead of a benefit, as they were mostly unarmed. In some counties the question was not, who should go to the army, but who should stay at home. I am satisfied that could I have remained in Missouri this winter the army would have been increased fifty thousand men. My thanks are due to Lieutenant-Colonel Bull, my provost-marshal, for the able, energetic and efficient discharge of his duties.

STERLING PRICE,
Major-General Commanding.

ITINERARY OF PRICE'S ARMY,*

AUGUST 28 TO DECEMBER 3, 1864.

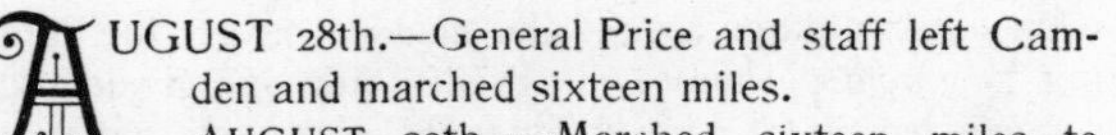

AUGUST 28th.—General Price and staff left Camden and marched sixteen miles.

AUGUST 29th.—Marched sixteen miles to Princeton. Fagan and Marmaduke reported. General Price assumed command of cavalry and announced staff.

AUGUST 30th.—Marched nine miles to Tulip. Raining all day. Wood's battalion reported to Marmaduke. Orders left at Princeton for Colonel Harrison.

AUGUST 31st (Camp No. 4).—Near Claridy's, on Benton Road. Sent back two iron guns of Hughey's battery, not having suitable horses. Heard of Shelby cutting railroad twice and capturing twenty-five hundred men and eight companies of the Fifty-fourth Illinois; twenty-five miles.

SEPTEMBER 1st (Camp No. 5).—On Middle Fork of Saline River. Fagan on right flank toward Benton; eighteen miles.

SEPTEMBER 2d (Camp No. 6).—Road rough; passed Goose Pond Mountain; nineteen miles.

SEPTEMBER 3d (Camp No. 7).—Road rocky and hilly; fifteen miles.

SEPTEMBER 4th (Camp No. 8).—Marched fifteen miles to Dr. Hill's.

SEPTEMBER 5th (Camp No. 9).—Cabell's brigade going over the mountains. Heard that Brooks and Stinman had passed from Danville to Dardanelle on the 3d. Weather warm and sultry. Joined by Fagan from the rear; eighteen miles.

SEPTEMBER 6th (Camp No. 10).—At Dardanelle. Scouting parties of Federals on the north side of river this morning. Sent letter No. 11 to Colonel S. S. Anderson. Marmaduke's brigade, and most of the train, crossed the Arkansas River; fourteen miles.

SEPTEMBER 7th (Camp No. 11).—At Dover, having forded the Arkansas. A Federal scout at Morristown this morning captured six horses from our pickets; fourteen miles.

SEPTEMBER 8th (Camp No. 12).—On Clinton Road. Fagan moving on Springfield Road; thirteen miles.

SEPTEMBER 9th (Camp No. 13).—Road rough and rocky; forage scarce; eighteen miles.

SEPTEMBER 10th (Camp No. 14).—On Little Red River, eight miles southeast from Clinton. Companies of Federal jayhawkers disbanded on approach of army; a few taken prisoners. Burbridge's regiment went by Clinton. Letter sent to General Shelby by Captain Norman; twenty miles.

SEPTEMBER 11th (Camp No. 15).—Road through Big Bottom of Little Red River. Whole country around infested with deserters from Confederate army, two of whom were killed; one of ours wounded. Fagan within eight miles, ahead; fourteen miles.

SEPTEMBER 12th (Camp No. 16).—After marching twelve miles on direct road to Batesville, diverged to the left, over a road so mountainous as to be almost impracticable; struck the river at a point eighteen miles above Batesville; considerable damage to train; total distance traveled, thirty miles.

SEPTEMBER 13th (Camp No. 17).—At Batesville. Forded the river one mile above camp of yesterday; crossing good; marched along left bank of the river; town completely deserted and destroyed. General Marmaduke and command, with ordnance train, marched by Powhatan direct, marching up the left; traveled eighteen miles.

SEPTEMBER 14th (Camp No. 18).—On Strawberry Creek. Returns and reports received from General Shelby; thirty-two miles.

SEPTEMBER 15th (Camp No. 19).—At Powhatan,

*Kept by Lieutenant-Colonel Lauchlan A. Maclean, Assistant Adjutant-General.

another deserted village. General Shelby with headquarters of his command at this point. Traveled fourteen miles.

SEPTEMBER 16th (Camp No. 20).—At Pocahontas, another deserted village and ruined community. Jackman, McCray and others reported. Army organized, as per orders, No. 8, on the 18th. Traveled eighteen miles.

SEPTEMBER 19th (Camp No. 21).—At Indian Ford, on Current River. To-day the army marched in three columns, Marmaduke on the right, Shelby on left, with Fagan and the headquarters in the center. A scout of Federals at 10 A. M. to-day burnt up Doniphan and retired; two scouting parties sent in pursuit. Marched twenty-two miles and entered Missouri.

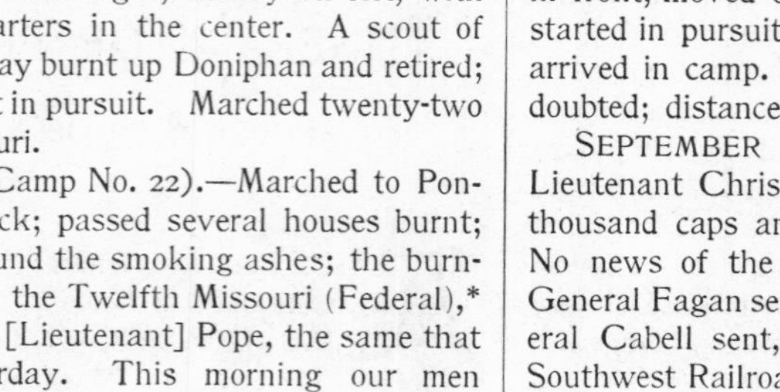

SEPTEMBER 20th (Camp No. 22).—Marched to Ponders Mill, on Little Black; passed several houses burnt; women and children around the smoking ashes; the burning done by a portion of the Twelfth Missouri (Federal),* commanded by Captain [Lieutenant] Pope, the same that burnt Doniphan yesterday. This morning our men attacked them at this point; killed a lieutenant and three men, wounded four and took six prisoners. Our loss: Two killed and five wounded.

We captured several horses and small arms; distance, twenty miles.

SEPTEMBER 21st (Camp No. 23).—Marched to Cane Creek; forage abundant; heard from Marmaduke; forty-two miles on march last night; found a Federal who had crawled from the fight of yesterday to a house on roadside; distance, twelve miles.

SEPTEMBER 22d (Camp No. 24).—Marched to Greenville, county-seat of Wayne County; deserted; only two families in the place. Two companies of Federals passed through toward Ironton to-day. Shelby took Patterson, killing fourteen and wounding several; took telegraph apparatus also; distance, twenty-two miles.

SEPTEMBER 23d (Camp No. 25).—Marched to Cedar Creek; roads rough; distance, eighteen miles.

SEPTEMBER 24th (Camp No. 26).—Reached Fredericktown; Shelby ahead of us, Marmaduke behind; more killed by fourteen than at first reported by Shelby. Citizens generally Southern in sentiment; many coming to greet us; recruiting; distance, twenty miles.

SEPTEMBER 25th.—Still at Camp No. 26, waiting for Marmaduke to come up. He encamped eight miles off.

SEPTEMBER 26th (Camp No. 27).—On Saint Francis. Shelby went by Farmington with a view of cutting the railroad. Fagan drove in the Federal pickets at Arcadia and took position before the town for the night; distance, twelve miles.

SEPTEMBER 27th (Camp No. 28).—At Arcadia. This morning Fagan drove the Federals from Arcadia, where they abandoned a very strong position. He also drove them through Ironton. They fell back on Fort Davidson, in Pilot Knob. Fagan formed on the south and east. Marmaduke took possession of Shepherds Mountain. Heavy skirmishing all day and continued artillery firing by the enemy. About 2 P. M., charge made on the fort, but the men were repulsed, but reformed by brigade commanders, but too late to renew the charge that night. Men placed in position and ammunition replenished; distance, eight miles.

SEPTEMBER 28th (Camp No. 29).—Enemy evacuated Pilot Knob last night; found many stores of government goods. Twelve miles.

SEPTEMBER 29th (Camp No. 30).—Passed through Caledonia and Potosi. At the latter place General Shelby fought and captured —— Federals. The enemy who left Pilot Knob under General Ewing, hearing of Shelby being in front, moved off to the west; Marmaduke and Shelby started in pursuit last night. General M. Jeff Thompson arrived in camp. Rumors of Steele leaving Little Rock doubted; distance, twenty-two miles.

SEPTEMBER 30th (Camp No. 31).—At Richwoods. Lieutenant Christian arrived with one hundred and fifty thousand caps and dispatches from General Magruder. No news of the enemy. Flag captured at this place. General Fagan sent three hundred men to De Soto. General Cabell sent, with his brigade, to cut the Pacific & Southwest Railroad east of Franklin; ten miles.

PICKETS ON THE LITTLE OSAGE RIVER, MO.

OCTOBER 1st (Camp No. 32).—Near St. Clair. Met Marmaduke and Shelby; returned from unsuccessful pursuit of enemy; many prisoners brought in found straggling. Report from De Soto: Militia scattered and depot burned. Marmaduke and Shelby destroyed the Southwestern Railroad for several miles. Marmaduke and Shelby went on to Union to-night; distance traveled, nineteen miles.

OCTOBER 2d (Camp No. 33).—Joined Marmaduke and Shelby early in the morning; found Cabell; returned, burned a bridge east of Franklin, and in the dawn burned the depot and destroyed the railroad. Lieutenant-Colonel Wood also returned from burning the bridge on the southwest branch over the Moselle. General Clark went to Washington, on Missouri River; Federals retreated across the river. Marmaduke ordered to Hermann with his division. Fagan and Shelby encamped on road to Mount Sterling, eight miles from Union, making in all fifteen miles.

OCTOBER 3d (Camp No. 34).—Distance, fourteen miles.

OCTOBER 4th (Camp No. 35).—Marched to Mount Sterling. One division crossed the Gasconade; horrible road bottom, and bottomless mud on west side; raining all day. Report from Marmaduke of his taking Millers Bend and Hermann; distance, seventeen miles.

OCTOBER 5th (Camp No. 36).—Marched to a point beyond Linn. General Marmaduke returned, having destroyed Osage (Gasconade) Bridge, having taken Hermann and Millers Landing the day before. Shelby sent a force under Colonel Shanks to destroy the Moreau Bridge; distance, fourteen miles.

OCTOBER 6th (Camp No. 37).—Marched to the Moreau. Crossing forced after some resistance by the enemy. Shelby in front. Colonel Shanks mortally wounded.

OCTOBER 7th (Camp No. 38).—Near Jefferson City. Fagan in front and the only division engaged. Enemy in strong position, but driven from one position to another until, about 3 P. M., they retired to their fortifications in and around the city, when we formed in line to west and south of Jefferson. Cut the Pacific Railroad. Loss very slight; ten [miles].

OCTOBER 8th (Camp No. 39).—At Russellville. Finding the enemy to be strongly fortified and in heavy force (twelve thousand) in town, supported by three thousand on north bank of river, drew off in the morning. Fagan protecting the rear and skirmishing all day; distance fourteen [miles].

OCTOBER 9th (Camp No. 40).—On the Moniteau. Marmaduke in the rear. Several skirmishes with the enemy's cavalry, who followed as far as California. Shelby, with Thompson's brigade, went on to Boonville. Railroad destroyed from Lookout west beyond California; distance, twenty-six miles.

OCTOBER 10th (Camp No. 41).—At Boonville. All the people turned out to greet us. Crossed a portion of command to north side, but recalled them. About three hundred surrendered; distance, sixteen miles.

OCTOBER 11th.—Enemy approached on Tipton Road; was met and repulsed by Fagan's command.

OCTOBER 12th.—Engaged slightly with the enemy; recruiting; distributing goods. Left Boonville at 10 P. M. and marched to Chouteau Springs (Camp No. 42); eleven miles.

OCTOBER 13th (Camp No. 43).—At Marshalls. Clark went across by Arrow Rock to attack Glasgow; fourteen miles.

OCTOBER 14th (Camp No. 44).—At Jonesboro. Fagan came up, having been left at the La Mine. Shelby left with a section to attack Glasgow from this side. Thompson went to Sedalia; eight miles.

OCTOBER 15th (Camp No. 45).—At Keisers, on Salt Fork; passed through Marshall; rumors of the enemy on our left; seventeen miles.

OCTOBER 16th.—Remained in camp; news of surrender of Glasgow. Thompson reports the enemy in force on road from Georgetown to Lexington.

OCTOBER 17th.—News of the capture of Sedalia by Thompson; recruits coming in; Federals enter Lexington on 16th.

OCTOBER 18th (Camp No. 46).—At Waverly; twenty-two miles.

OCTOBER 19th (Camp No. 47).—At General Shield's, three miles south of Lexington. Left Waverly at daybreak. Knowing that Generals Blunt, Lane and Jennison. with between three and four thousand Federals, were at Lexington (Colorado, Kansas and Missouri troops), fearing they might make a junction with McNeil and A. J.

* It was the Third Missouri State Militia Cavalry.

BATTLE OF BOONVILLE, MO. CHARGE OF GENERAL MARMADUKE'S CAVALRY.
[From a sketch by Corporal W. Blome.]

Smith, who were on Salt Fork and at Sedalia, made a flank movement to the left after crossing Tabo, so as to intercept their line of march. Met the enemy about four miles from Lexington, on Salt Pond Road; Shelby in front. Fought him back to the old Independence Road, when night closed the fight. Federals evacuated by the River Road; loss very slight; went home that night; distance, twenty-six miles.

OCTOBER 20th (Camp No. 48). — To Fire Creek Prairie. Scouts report enemy falling back to the Blue; recruits from Chariton; twenty-two miles.

OCTOBER 21st (Camp No. 49).—At Independence. At [Little] Blue met the enemy, who had burned the bridge; Marmaduke, in front, fought and drove them back through Independence; Shelby sustained Marmaduke on his left; loss, between forty and fifty; twenty-six miles.

OCTOBER 22d (Camp No. 50).— Left Independence; Shelby in front; drove the enemy toward Kansas City, then struck a column on the left in open ground; charged

BRIG.-GEN. JEFF. THOMPSON, OF MISSOURI.
[From a photograph of an oil portrait.]

and took a 24-pounder howitzer. In coming out of town in column enemy struck Cabell on the flank and took two guns and cut off some three or four hundred men. Marmaduke, who was behind in town, fearing he might be taken prisoner, led Cabell's men and cut his way to the command.

OCTOBER 23d (Camp No. 51).—Enemy in position on prairie; attacked by Shelby, assisted by Fagan with two brigades; drove the enemy five or six miles, into Westport. The column in rear, under McNeil, pushed Marmaduke and Clark until Shelby and Fagan had to withdraw. Enemy threatened left flank of train; driven off by drawing up the unarmed men in line. Encamped on Middle Fork of Grand River; twenty-four miles.

OCTOBER 24th (Camp No. 52).—At Potosi. Skirmishing with the enemy, who are following in rear; thirty-three miles.

OCTOBER 25th (Camp No. 53).—On Marmiton. When near the Little Osage, Shelby in front and Marmaduke in rear, a dispatch received from Marmaduke stating that the enemy were in sight, about three thousand strong, with the line still extending. A brigade was ordered back from the front. Fagan stated on the note that he would sustain Marmaduke, but before we could go back a mile we met the command coming on in the most demoralized condition. The details can only be given from the reports of those present. Marmaduke, Cabell and Slemons taken prisoners, five pieces of artillery captured and the morale of the army ruined. Everything hurried on, a mass of confusion, from which it took every exertion to redeem it; but, after crossing the Osage, the enemy again appeared in sight, but General Shelby was in the rear, and, after an action of two hours, they were held in check until after dark, when the troops were withdrawn; twenty-eight miles.

OCTOBER 26th (Camp No. 54). — At Carthage. No enemy; left everything behind; distance, fifty-six miles.

OCTOBER 27th (Camp No. 55).—Encamped on Shoal Creek; enemy still far behind; morale of the troops improving, but many desertions among Arkansas troops; twenty-two miles.

OCTOBER 28th (Camp No. 56). — Marched through Granby and Newtonia; a small detachment at the latter place left night before; one cavalry company remained; charged and routed; the Captain (Christian, a noted bushwhacker) killed; encamped about four miles below Newtonia, when Blunt, with about three thousand men, came upon us. He was met and signally repulsed by Shelby, sustained by Fagan with cavalry, and driven for over three miles. Our train was moved forward seventeen miles.

OCTOBER 29th (Camp No. 57). — On Sugar Creek, five miles south of Pineville, through which we passed. Nothing known of any advance on the part of the enemy; twenty-six miles.

OCTOBER 30th (Camp No. 58). — At Maysville on line; headquarters in Indian lands; seventeen miles.

OCTOBER 31st (Camp No. 59). — Marched to Illinois River, near line of Arkansas; twenty-six miles.

NOVEMBER 1st (Camp No. 60). — Marched to Boonsboro; raining all day; roads bad and hilly; stock worn out; much of it abandoned. Reports from Colonel Brooks, who was investing Fayetteville; asks aid; seventeen miles.

NOVEMBER 2d.—In camp all day. General Fagan, with re-enforcements, went to Fayetteville. Colonel Freeman, with his command, started for Northern Arkansas. Colonel McCray ordered to go on the 3d, and Colonel Dobbin on the 4th, to report south of Arkansas River on December 15th, 20th and 25th; raining hard.

NOVEMBER 3d. — In camp; rain and snow. Letter from Rosecrans.

NOVEMBER 4th (Camp No. 61).—Marched to Indian Territory; roads good; fourteen miles.

NOVEMBER 5th (Camp No. 62).—Marched along Sallisaw River; eighteen miles.

NOVEMBER 6th (Camp No. 63).—Marched to Arkansas River; twenty miles.

NOVEMBER 7th (Camp No. 64).—Crossed Arkansas River at Pheasant Ford; good crossing; four miles.

NOVEMBER 8th (Camp No. 65).—Raining; ten miles.

NOVEMBER 9th (Camp No. 66).—Raining; nine miles.

NOVEMBER 10th (Camp No. 67).—Order for Cabell's and Slemons' brigades approved. Slemons' command, commanded by Colonel Crawford, furloughed to December 10th, to rendezvous at Millers Bluff. Cabell's brigade, commanded by Lieutenant-Colonel Reiff, to rendezvous on December 10th at Spring Hill, Ark.; twelve miles.

NOVEMBER 11th (Camp No. 68).—Shelby left behind on Canadian to recruit. Tyler and Wood gone ahead. Wrote to General Maxey; fourteen miles.

NOVEMBER 12th (Camp No. 69).—Marched for good grazing at Gaines Creek; two miles.

NOVEMBER 13th (Camp No. 70).—Passed through Perryville. Three wagons of supplies received; sixteen miles.

NOVEMBER 14th.—Lay over in camp one day.

NOVEMBER 15th (Camp No. 71).—General Fagan ordered to establish his headquarters at Washington, Ark.; seventeen miles.

NOVEMBER 16th (Camp No. 72).—Seven miles.

NOVEMBER 17th (Camp No. 73).—At a point two miles south of Stand Watie's headquarters; fourteen miles.

NOVEMBER 18th (Camp No. 74).—Raining. Colonel Tyler started to Clarksville; ten miles.

NOVEMBER 19th (Camp No. 75).—Nine miles.

NOVEMBER 20th (Camp No. 76).—Nine miles.

NOVEMBER 21st (Camp No. 77).—Thirteen miles.

NOVEMBER 22d (Camp No. 78). — Crossed Red River. Clark went on to Clarksville; Shelby caught up; sixteen miles.

NOVEMBER 23d (Camp No. 79).—Marched to Bonham; twelve miles.

NOVEMBER 24th (Camp No. 80).—Fourteen miles.

NOVEMBER 25th (Camp No. 81).—Ten miles.

NOVEMBER 26th (Camp No. 82).—Reached Paris.

NOVEMBER 27th (Camp No. 83).—Sixteen miles.

NOVEMBER 28th (Camp No. 84).—At Clarksville; fourteen miles.

NOVEMBER 29th.—Remained at Clarksville. Thompson's command came up. Leave granted to Shelby and other officers.

NOVEMBER 30th.—Still at Clarksville. Order from Magruder received to march to Laynesport.

DECEMBER 1st (Camp No. 85).—Clark's command on the march. Thompson to move to-morrow; eighteen miles.

DECEMBER 2d (Camp No. 86). — At Laynesport; crossed river; nineteen miles.

DECEMBER 3d.—Clark arrived and sent courier to Washington.

Whole distance marched, fourteen hundred and thirty-four miles.

A SHORT time before the battle of Fredericksburg, Jackson had his headquarters near the family mansion of the Corbins. This was very fortunate for Dick Corbin, who was a member of Jackson's corps, and who was camped near home. It also enabled him to play the host occasionally to a man he almost adored. One day Jackson said to Dick that he would like to get his permission to cut one of the lawn trees down, saying that it was already nearly dead. "Cut a tree down!" said the indignant soldier. "Why, general, you can cut them all down if they are in your way. Move the house, too, if you wish it. In fact, sir, I shall feel honored if you will act just as though the place belonged to you."

ORGANIZATION OF PRICE'S ARMY IN THE MISSOURI EXPEDITION,

MAJOR-GENERAL STERLING PRICE, Commanding.

FAGAN'S DIVISION.

Major-General James F. Fagan.

CABELL'S BRIGADE.

Brigadier-General William F. Cabell; Lieutenant-Colonel A. V. Reiff.

Monroe's (Ark.) Cavalry—Colonel J. C. C. Monroe.
Gordon's (Ark.) Cavalry—Colonel Anderson Gordon.
Morgan's (Ark.) Cavalry—Colonel T. J. Morgan.
Hill's (Ark.) Cavalry—Colonel J. F. Hill.
Gunter's (Ark.) Cavalry Battalion—Lieutenant-Colonel Thomas M. Gunter.
Harrell's (Ark.) Cavalry Battalion—Lieutenant-Colonel John M. Harrell.
Witherspoon's (Ark.) Cavalry Battalion—Major J. L. Witherspoon.
Hughey's (Ark.) Battery—Captain W. M. Hughey.

SLEMONS' BRIGADE.

Colonel W. F. Slemons; Colonel William A. Crawford.

Second Arkansas Cavalry—Colonel W. F. Slemons.
Crawford's (Ark.) Cavalry—Colonel William A. Crawford.
Carlton's (Ark.) Cavalry—Colonel Charles H. Carlton.
Wright's (Ark.) Cavalry—Colonel John C. Wright.

DOBBIN'S BRIGADE.

Colonel Archibald S. Dobbin.

Dobbin's (Ark.) Cavalry—Colonel Archibald S. Dobbin.
McGhee's (Ark.) Cavalry—Colonel James McGhee.
Witt's (Ark.) Cavalry—Colonel A. R. Witt.
Blocher's (Ark.) Battery (one section)—Lieutenant J. V. Zimmerman.

M'CRAY'S BRIGADE.

Colonel Thomas H. McCray.

Forty-fifth Arkansas (mounted)—Colonel Milton I. Baber.
Forty-seventh Arkansas (mounted)—Colonel Lee Crandall.
Fifteenth Missouri Cavalry—Colonel Timothy Reves.

UNATTACHED.

Lyles' (Ark.) Cavalry—Colonel Oliver P. Lyles.
Rogan's (Ark.) Cavalry—Colonel James W. Rogan.
Anderson's (Ark.) Cavalry Battalion—Captain Wm. L. Anderson.

MAJ.-GEN. J. F. FAGAN, OF ARKANSAS.
[From a photograph taken in 1864.]

MARMADUKE'S DIVISION.

Major-General John S. Marmaduke; Brigadier-General John B. Clark, Jr.

ESCORT.

Company D, Fifth Missouri Cavalry—Captain D. R. Stallard.

MARMADUKE'S BRIGADE.

Brigadier-General John B. Clark, Jr.; Colonel Colton Greene.

Third Missouri Cavalry—Colonel Colton Greene.
Fourth Missouri Cavalry—Colonel John Q. Burbridge.

MARMADUKE'S BRIGADE—Continued.

Seventh Missouri Cavalry	Colonel S. G. Kitchen.
Davies' (Mo.) Battalion Cavalry	Lieutenant-Colonel J. F. Davies.

Eighth Missouri Cavalry—Colonel Wm. L. Jeffers.
Tenth Missouri Cavalry—Colonel Robert R. Lawther.
Fourteenth Missouri Cavalry (Battalion)—Lieutenant-Colonel Robert C. Wood.
Hynson's (Tex.) Battery—Captain H. C. Hynson.
Harris' (Mo.) Battery—Captain S. S. Harris.
Engineer Company—Captain James T. Hogane.

FREEMAN'S BRIGADE.
Colonel Thomas R. Freeman.

Freeman's (Mo.) Cavalry—Colonel Thomas R. Freeman.
Fristoe's (Mo.) Cavalry—Colonel Edward T. Fristoe.
Ford's (Ark.) Cavalry Battalion—Lieutenant-Colonel Barney Ford.

SHELBY'S DIVISION.
Brigadier-General Joseph O. Shelby.

SHELBY'S BRIGADE.
Colonel David Shanks; Colonel Moses W. Smith; Brigadier-General M. Jeff. Thompson.

Fifth Missouri Cavalry—Colonel B. Frank Gordon.
Eleventh Missouri Cavalry—Colonel Moses W. Smith.
Twelfth Missouri Cavalry—Colonel David Shanks.
Elliott's (Mo.) Cavalry—Colonel Benjamin Elliott.
Slayback's (Mo.) Cavalry Battalion—Lieutenant-Colonel Alonzo W. Slayback.
Collins' (Mo.) Battery—Captain Richard A. Collins.

JACKMAN'S BRIGADE.
Colonel Sidney D. Jackman.

Jackman's (Mo.) Cavalry—Lieutenant-Colonel C. H. Nichols.
Hunter's (Mo.) Cavalry—Colonel De Witt C. Hunter.
Williams' (Mo.) Cavalry Battalion—Lieutenant-Colonel D. A. Williams.
Schnable's (Mo.) Cavalry Battalion—Lieutenant-Colonel John A. Schnable.
Collins' (Mo.) Battery (one section)—Lieutenant Jacob D. Conner.

UNATTACHED.

Forty-sixth Arkansas (mounted)—Colonel W. O. Coleman.

TYLER'S BRIGADE.
Colonel Charles H. Tyler.

Perkins' (Mo.) Cavalry—Colonel Caleb Perkins.
Coffee's (Mo.) Cavalry*—Colonel John T. Coffee.
Searcy's (Mo.) Cavalry—Colonel James J. Searcy.

* Transferred from Jackman's brigade.

ORGANIZATION OF TROOPS
IN THE DEPARTMENT OF
SOUTH CAROLINA, GEORGIA AND FLORIDA,
LIEUT.-GEN. WILLIAM J. HARDEE,
Commanding.

NOVEMBER 20, 1864.

MCLAWS' DIVISION.
Major-General Lafayette McLaws.

First Georgia Regulars—Colonel Richard A. Wayne.
Barnwell's (Ga.) Light Artillery—Colonel Richard A. Wayne.
Twenty-Second Georgia Battalion (six companies)—Major Thomas D. Bertody.
Twenty-seventh Georgia Battalion, Company D—Lieutenant W. R. McLaws.
Twenty-ninth Georgia Battalion Cavalry (six companies)—Captain J. T. Wimberly.
Third South Carolina Cavalry (eight companies)—Captain A. M. Lowry.
Symon's Reserves (ten companies)—Major John Cunningham.
Beaufort (S. C.) Artillery—Lieutenant John J. Rhodes.
Bonaud's (Ga.) Battalion (two companies)—Captain Malcolm T. McGregor.
Terrell's (Ga.) Light Artillery—Captain John W. Brooks.
Clinch's (Ga.) Light Artillery (two companies)—Major Alfred L. Hartridge.

Daniell's (Ga.) Light Battery, Guerard's (Ga.) Light Battery, Maxwell's (Ga.) Light Battery,	Captain J. A. Maxwell.

German (S. C.) Artillery, Company A—Captain F. W. Wagener.
German (S. C.) Artillery—Captain William K. Bachman.
Hanleiter's (Ga.) Battery—Captain Cornelius R. Hanleiter.
South Carolina Horse Artillery (section)—Lieutenant Richard Johnson.
Lafayette (S. C.) Artillery—Captain J. T. Kanapaux.
Mercer (Ga.) Artillery—Lieutenant-Colonel William R. Pritchard.
Second Engineer Troops, Company D—Captain James W. McAlpine.

MAJ.-GEN. WILLIAM B. TALIAFERRO, OF VIRGINIA.

RIPLEY'S BRIGADE.
Brigadier-General Roswell S. Ripley.

Thirty-second Georgia Volunteers (seven companies and detachments)—Captain S. J. Heath.
First South Carolina Regulars (ten companies)—Colonel William Butler.
First South Carolina Cavalry, Company K—Captain Angus P. Brown.
Keitt's (S. C.) Mounted Rifles—Captain Ellison S. Keitt.
Ripley (S. C.) Rangers—Lieutenant C. P. Bolton.
First South Carolina Artillery (seven companies)—Major Ormsby Blanding.
Gist Guards (S. C.) Artillery—Lieutenant Theodore G. Brag.

TRAPIER'S BRIGADE.
Brigadier-General James H. Trapier.

Kirk's Squadron (S. C.) Cavalry (two companies)—Captain M. J. Kirk.
Steele's Company (S. C.) Cavalry—Captain J. J. Steele.
German (S. C.) Artillery, Company B—Captain F. Melchers.
Santee (S. C.) Light Artillery—Captain Christopher Gaillard.
Waccamaw (S. C.) Light Artillery—Captain Mayham Ward.

ROBERTSON'S BRIGADE.
Brigadier-General Beverly H. Robertson.

Third South Carolina Cavalry, Company B—Captain Archibald L. Campbell.
Stono (S. C.) Scouts—Captain John B. L. Walpole.

BRIG.-GEN. B. H. ROBERTSON, OF VIRGINIA.
[From an old portrait.]

Second South Carolina Artillery (ten companies)—Captain Medicus Rickenbaker.
Marion (S. C.) Artillery—Captain Edward L. Parker.
Palmetto Battery Light Artillery (three companies)—Captain Charles E. Kanapaux.
Washington (S. C.) Artillery—Captain George H. Walter.
Mathewes' (S. C.) Heavy Artillery—Captain J. Raven Mathewes.
South Carolina Siege Train, Company A—Captain Benjamin C. Webb.

TALIAFERRO'S BRIGADE.
Brigadier-General William B. Taliaferro.

Forty-seventh Georgia (six companies)—Colonel Aaron C. Edwards.

First South Carolina Cavalry (nine companies), Palmetto Light Artillery, Company E, South Carolina Siege Train, (two companies),	Lieutenant-Colonel Wm. H. Campbell.
First South Carolina Artillery (three companies), Bonaud's Battalion Georgia Volunteers	Lieutenant-Colonel Joseph A. Yates.

Second South Carolina Artillery (eight companies)—Colonel A. D. Frederick.
Lucas' (S. C.) Battalion (three companies)—Major J. Jonathan Lucas.
Chatham (Ga.) Artillery—Lieutenant Samuel B. Palmer.
Orleans Guard Battery—Captain G. Le Gardeur, Jr.

MILLER'S BRIGADE.
Brigadier-General William Miller.

Battalion Florida Reserves—Captain Isaac B. Nichols.
Second Florida Cavalry (ten companies)—Lieutenant-Colonel Abner H. McCormick.
Fifth Florida Battalion (three companies)—Captain W. H. Milton.
Twenty-ninth Georgia Battalion (two companies)—Captain F. L. Pepper.
Independent (Fla.) Cavalry Company—Captain —— Chisolm.
Florida Reserves (seven companies)—Captain —— Gilchrist.
Abell's (Fla.) Artillery—Captain Henry F. Abell.
Kilcrease (Fla.) Light Artillery—Captain F. L. Villepigue.
Campbell's (Ga.) Siege Artillery—Captain Charles G. Campbell.

POST OF FLORENCE, S. C.
Colonel George P. Harrison, Jr.

First South Carolina Cavalry—Captain J. S. Wilson.
Third Battalion South Carolina Reserves—Major William P. Gill.
Fourth Battalion South Carolina Reserves—Lieutenant-Colonel James H. Williams.
Fifth Battalion South Carolina Reserves—Lieutenant-Colonel Thomas R. Brown.
Sixth Battalion South Carolina Reserves—Major Robt. Meriwether.
Seventh Battalion South Carolina Reserves—Major J. W. Ward.

POST OF COLUMBIA, S. C.
Lieutenant-Colonel Robert S. Means.

South Carolina State Reserves (five companies)—Captain Edward Powell.
Williams' Battalion (S. C.) State Reserves (ten companies)—Lieutenant John McCarley.
Detachment of Artillery—Lieutenant —— Holyland.
Post Guard—Captain Rufus D. Senn.
Provost Guard—Captain D. H. Hamilton, Jr.

WHILE in Virginia I witnessed a scene between two officers of my regiment—one the lieutenant-colonel, the other the adjutant—which, if rather disgraceful for "officers and gentlemen," was redeemed somewhat by a little witty passage or two which occurred. Both were slightly "elevated," the adjutant being, in fact, in that state to which a stronger term would have been applied had he been a simple private; for "what in the captain's but a choleric word in the soldier is rank blasphemy." The colonel had mounted his horse, and the adjutant made a scrambling effort to get up alongside of him. "Hold on," says the colonel, "don't you see that mark?" pointing to the "C. S." brand on his horse. "Yes," says the adjutant. "What mark is that, anyhow? What's them letters stand for, kurnel? 'Cut with saber?'" "No," replied the colonel, "that means 'Carry single.'" Somebody assisted the adjutant to his own steed, which, when he had mounted, became very restive, and shied about, owing to the rider's unsteady management. "Say, kurnel, see that mark on my horse too? Know what that means? That means 'Caper sideways.'"

VIEWS OF PETERSBURG AND ITS SUBURBS FROM GENERAL LEE'S HEADQUARTERS.

IN FRONT OF PETERSBURG, VA.

DIARY OF THE

FIRST CORPS ARMY OF NORTHERN VIRGINIA,

FROM JUNE 16 TO JULY 31, 1864.

JUNE 16th.—Pickett and Field move at 3 and 5 A. M., cross James River at Drewrys Bluff and move down the turnpike toward Petersburg to occupy the line abandoned by General Beauregard. We found a picket of the enemy on the turnpike near Chester and the line occupied by the enemy reconnoitering, and an effort to get him out, we get the left, including Howlett's.

JUNE 17th.—During the day we possess ourselves of the line by an advance of Pickett and Field. On the night of this day there is heavy fighting at Petersburg, and urgent calls are made by General Beauregard for aid. Kershaw arrives near Perdue's.

JUNE 18th.—At 3 A. M. Kershaw moves for Petersburg, followed by Field, Pickett, occupying the whole line. We arrive at Petersburg and Kershaw relieves Bushrod Johnson's division, Field taking position on Kershaw's right. A feeble attack is made in the afternoon on Elliott's brigade, of Johnson's division.

PETERSBURG, VA. EARTHWORKS ON THE LEFT OF THE CONFEDERATE LINE.

JUNE 19th.—Sharp skirmishing during the day and a sort of advance on Kershaw's right and Field's left during the night.

JUNE 20th and 21st.—Affairs unchanged.

JUNE 22d.—A. P. Hill goes out with Mahone and Wilcox, B. R. Johnson supporting, and drives the enemy from our right. It is a handsome affair, two thousand prisoners, four pieces of artillery, seven colors being among the captures.

JUNE 23d.—Preparations made for the contemplated attack to-morrow. Field at night withdraws from the trenches, Bushrod Johnson relieving him and moves to the left in support of and co-operation with Hoke. Field did not get out clear until dawn next morning.

JUNE 24th.—At 7:05 A. M. our artillery opens, followed in a half hour by an advance of Hagood's brigade. The affair is a farce and is not continued. Field leaves a brigade in Hoke's trenches and returns with the balance of his division, to be in reserve.

JUNE 25th.—Usual skirmishing. At night two of Kershaw's brigades (Humphreys' and Kershaw's) are relieved by B. R. Johnson.

JUNE 26th.—The enemy shows some disposition to dig up to us. Anderson's brigade, of Field's division, still with Hoke.

JUNE 27th.—Some mortar firing.

JUNE 28th.—Orders given to Field to go on the line to the left of the Rives house, the disposition being thus: Hoke on extreme left, Johnson on his right, and Field on right of Johnson. The change takes place on the night of the 28th, and Field does not get on the line until near morning. Until G. T. Anderson can be brought from the left of Hoke, Wofford occupies that portion of the line near the Rives house. Field's brigades are posted as follows: From left to right, Bratton, Benning, Gregg and Law.

JUNE 29th.—Kershaw in reserve. Wofford taken out of Field's line and G. T. Anderson is retained in reserve for Field. At 12 M., orders are sent to Kershaw to move with three brigades to Reams Station to aid Mahone and the cavalry operating against the raiders. He returned about 11 P. M.

JUNE 30th.—Unchanged.

JULY 1st.—At 2 A. M., Kershaw moves to the intersection of the Weldon Railroad with the line of breastworks to support Hill, who is to attack the enemy's force at Reams Station (Sheridan and the Sixth Corps). That force, however, has disappeared in the night, and our troops returned to their positions.

JULY 2d.—Field still on the line, preferring not to be relieved.

JULY 3d to 7th.—All pass without change or incident.

JULY 8th.—We make in the afternoon something of a Chinese demonstration in the way of shooting and artillery firing to ascertain the enemy's strength.

JULY 9th.—No change.

JULY 10th.—Kershaw moves out on the railroad at night to cover the movement of some railroad trains laden with corn.

JULY 11th to 16th.—Are passed without change or incident.

JULY 17th.—General Anderson makes a personal reconnoissance for an assault. At night two men desert from Law's brigade.

JULY 18th.—Further reconnoissance and preparation, in the course of which the desertions of the previous night are learned. The contemplated attack is in consequence abandoned.

JULY 19th to 22d.—No change. Usual shelling and picket-firing.

JULY 23d.—Kershaw moves at 6:30 A. M. for Chaffins Bluff.

JULY 24th to 26th.—Affairs unchanged.

JULY 27th.—At 1:30 P. M. we received orders to move our headquarters to the north side of James River. Heth's division moved over. We arrived at Chaffins at 8:30 P. M. Before our arrival four guns of the Rockbridge Artillery, on the left of Kershaw, had been captured by the enemy.

JULY 28th.—In the morning we moved with four brigades—Conner's, Lane's, Kershaw's and Wofford's—to dislodge the enemy from the Long Bridge Road. The first three became engaged near Whitlock's and Darby's house, capturing one piece of artillery and about seventy-five prisoners, but without gaining the Long Bridge Road. Our loss is about two hundred and fifty in killed, wounded and missing. At night the troops are returned to their positions about Fussells Mill. W. H. F. Lee's cavalry arrived at night on the north side of the James.

JULY 29th.—Nothing done in the morning. In the afternoon, Kershaw and Conner moved down to Darby's to occupy with skirmishers the junction of the Long Bridge and Darbytown roads. Field's division is sent to us from the south side, and arrives at Fussells Mill about sundown. He came to Rices Turnout by rail. Fitz Lee's division of cavalry is also sent to the north side.

JULY 30th.—In the morning the enemy is discovered to have abandoned the Long Bridge Road and retired to the other side of the river, leaving a force at Deep Bottom, on the right of our line. Heth's division is sent back to Rices Turnout. His trenches are occupied by Field. In the evening Kershaw recrosses to the south side by Chaffins Bluff, to halt for the night near the Clay house.

JULY 31st.—Affairs unchanged.

IN the old First in 1861 two of the boys, whom we will call A and B, had left sweethearts in Richmond. One of them soon forgot the soldier boy who had left her behind, and married a gentleman named Point. At this time B was much pleased and joked A terribly. All day long he would ask him "If he could see the Point?" etc. Soon after this B's sweetheart, whose name was Hurt, forgot the vows she made, and got married also. This was A's sweet revenge, and he gave B no peace by constantly asking him "What Hurt him?" "Where was he Hurt?" etc. It was a case of diamond cut diamond.

ASSAULTS ON THE PETERSBURG LINES

JUNE 16 TO JULY 30, 1864.

BY

BRIG.-GEN. WILLIAM N. PENDLETON,

Chief of Artillery, Army of Northern Virginia.

HEADQUARTERS ARTILLERY CORPS,
ARMY OF NORTHERN VIRGINIA,
February 28, 1865.

ON the 17th [June], Kershaw's division, First Corps, with Cabell's battalion, and the Third Corps, with its artillery, which had encamped the previous day near Chaffins Bluff, crossed James River on the pontoon bridge near Drewrys and proceeded toward Petersburg.

On June 18th, while Pickett's division, with Huger's battalion, was left to hold the line fronting Bermuda Hundred from Howlett's, on James River, to the confluence of Swift Creek with the Appomattox—a line which, with Cabell's battalion, assigned there a day or two later, they have since held in almost unbroken quiet, notwithstanding the close proximity of the enemy in large force—the other troops were placed on the lines for the defense of Petersburg, on the east and south of that city, where the enemy was pressing heavily.

General Beauregard having, with his limited force, on the 17th, engaged the enemy in very large numbers on the east of Petersburg and maintained the same contest, unequal as it was, so successfully as to preserve the city, found himself, however, unable to hold the extended outer line of works on that side, and, therefore, during the night, fell back to an interior line, extending from the Appomattox, in a direction between the Hare house and Blandford Cemetery, to the Rives house. This new line, selected mainly by the lamented Colonel D. B. Harris, of the engineers, amid all the difficulties attendant upon the conflict of the day, and afterward fortified under his skillful direction, was seized and held against the enemy's most vigorous pressure by the divisions of Generals Bushrod Johnson and Hoke, aided by the artillery under Colonel Jones, consisting of Read's, Moseley's, Coit's and Boggs' battalions. This artillery force, now merged in this army, is exhibited in the following table:

Artillery Originally of General Beauregard's Command (Department of Southern Virginia and North Carolina) and now of Anderson's Corps, Army of Northern Virginia, Colonel H. P. Jones, Commanding.

READ'S BATTALION.*
Major Read.

	GUNS.
Marshall battery	4
Macon's battery	5
Sullivan's battery	4
Dickerson's battery	4
Total	17

MOSELEY'S BATTALION.†
Lieutenant-Colonel Moseley.

Young's battery	4
Miller's battery	4
Slaten's battery	4
Cummings' battery	3
Total	15

* This battalion (formerly Dearing's, of Army of Northern Virginia), served in North Carolina on Plymouth Expedition; acted under General Beauregard in repelling Butler on Bermuda Hundred line between May 15th and 21st, and accompanied Hoke's division to Cold Harbor and engaged there June 1st, 2d, 3d; fought at Petersburg on June 17th, and thereafter engaged almost daily.

† This battalion, organized about the time of Butler's advance, also helped in repelling him at Drewrys Bluff and on the Bermuda Hundred line, and shared the fights at Petersburg on June 16th, 17th and 18th. It has been more or less engaged on this line ever since.

COIT'S BATTALION.*
Major Coit.

	GUNS.
Wright's battery	5
Pegram's battery	4
Kelly's battery	3
Bradford's battery	3
Total	15

BOGGS' BATTALION.†
Major Boggs.

Sturdivant's battery	2
Martin's battery	4
Total	6

Of this artillery a portion of Coit's battalion, Bradford's three guns (20-pounder Parrotts), and Wright's battery were, on the morning of June 18th, placed in position on the north side of the Appomattox to sweep with an enfilade fire the left of General Beauregard's new line on the south of, and resting on, the river. The other guns were posted on that line and at commanding points in its rear to aid in the defense. They were nearly all effectively engaged on that day (18th) in repelling the attempts of the enemy on their front, reaching from the river to near the Baxter Road.

mattox affording an enfilade fire upon the lines of the enemy, a number of guns, principally rifles, were assigned to that service. They consisted of the rifles of Lane's battalion, with Penick's battery, of Richardson's battalion, fortified on a commanding eminence at the Archer house; Chew's and Clutter's rifles, of McIntosh's battalion, under Major Johnson, on a lower point, half a mile higher up the river, and Poague's battalion, under Captain Utterback, on the line still higher up, already held by Bradford's and Wright's guns.

On the morning of the 20th these guns opened upon the enemy with such power—from their number and from the direction in which they struck flank and reverse—as to produce much confusion in his ranks and compel him to effect a sudden change of position. Additional guns, among them several 30-pounder Parrotts and 12-pounder Whitworths, were subsequently posted near the Archer house to enable the armament there to hold its ground against the tremendous efforts of the enemy to silence it. These guns were opened upon the enemy whenever his infantry appeared and when his shells were thrown into the city. Batteries erected in every available position on

teristic zeal, undertaken by General Alexander. They were so placed as most effectually to protect the exposed points of our lines, and, at the same, annoy that of the enemy. Their number and weight were gradually increased until the defense of this part of our works included twenty-seven mortars (12-pounder and 24-pounder and 8-inch) on General Beauregard's front, and thirteen of like caliber on that beyond the River Salient. A few heavier guns were also added to the armament on their fronts, and an interior line arranged to cover exposed points. The horse artillery had, during this interval, continued active with the cavalry.

On the 20th, Thomson's, Harts, Shoemaker's and Johnston's batteries were engaged the entire day at the White House, although the enemy brought to bear both gunboats and field batteries. McGregor's battery participated in General W. H. F. Lee's engagement with Wilson, at the Davis house, on the Weldon Railroad, on the 21st [22d], and in his subsequent pursuit of that raider.

On June 22d, Mahone's division, Third Corps, having moved out of the works to attack the enemy's left, Lieutenant-Colonel McIntosh accompanied him with Dement's battery, under Lieutenant Gale. The batteries on the line

A Night Scene in the Trenches in Front of Petersburg, Va.
[From an original sketch, owned by Mrs. Frank Leslie, New York.]

On the right of General Beauregard's forces those of the First Corps, Army of Northern Virginia, took position as they arrived, and on the night of the 18th, Gibbes' battalion and a portion of Haskell's were placed on the line from near the Baxter Road to the Rives house, under a severe fire of sharpshooters, Haskell's other guns being adjusted at commanding points on a second line in rear. The guns of the Third Corps were assigned position on the line to the right of those of the First Corps, Richardson's battalion occupying the salient at the junction of the new line with the old works, known as the River Salient, and the others, including the Louisiana Washington Artillery Battalion, were ordered to co-operate with Third Corps, being arranged further round to the south and west, extending to and covering the Weldon Railroad.

The following day (June 19th), the general chief of artillery having, under instructions from the commanding general, after special reconnoissances with General Beauregard, selected positions on the north side of the Appo-

the opposite side and armed with their most formidable guns and mortars were plied with fierceness and constancy against this armament—a sufficient proof of the efficiency with which it disturbed the enemy's operations and frustrated his plans.

Colonel Cutts, who here commanded, subordinate commanders who co-operated with him, and the men who toiled at the substantial works rendered necessary by the extraordinary force of artillery hurled against them, and worked their guns, notwithstanding, to such good purpose, deserve honorable mention for their services at this point. Lieutenant L. G. Rees, of Ross' battery, a gallant and meritorious officer, fell here; Lieutenant James, of the same battery, was severely wounded; some men were also killed or disabled. The guns to the right of these, and on the same side of the river, co-operated with them to excellent effect in annoying the enemy and protecting our main line. Along that line, on General Beauregard's entire front, and on most of that held by the First Corps, sharpshooting and cannonading were ceaseless and severe, and on several salient points the enemy, who had pressed up his skirmish line very near our breastworks, brought to bear an annoying mortar practice. To counteract this, and otherwise damage our assailants, recourse was also had to mortars on our side. Of these, consisting chiefly of 24-pounder Coehorns, the supervision was, with charac-

were directed to co-operate by a combined fire upon the enemy's batteries and on his troops in the woods. At the proper time Dement's battery moved rapidly forward, took position near the enemy's works and opened, when the infantry, under cover of this fire and of that from the batteries on our line, rushed forward and carried the enemy's intrenchments, capturing a number of prisoners and four pieces of artillery, which were broken off. A section of Clutter's battery, under Lieutenant Wilkes, was subsequently brought up and participated with distinguished spirit in the continuance of this successful affair.

On the 24th our guns opened by order along the entire line, those on the north of the Appomattox especially exerting their whole power with a view to a vigorous attack on the enemy's right. Circumstances prevented the full execution of the design, but the development of our artillery strength apparently exerted a wholesome influence upon the enemy.

On the 28th Lieutenant-Colonel Pegram accompanied Mahone's division to Reams Station, on the Weldon Railroad, with Brander's and Cayce's batteries, and during the day following used them effectively against Wilson's cavalry.

On June 30th General Alexander was interrupted in his valuable services by a wound from a minie-ball, received under the sharp and continuous skirmishing on

* This battalion served in North Carolina in the early spring; acted with the others in repelling Butler on Swift Creek and at Drewrys Bluff, and participated in the defense of Petersburg June 16th and 17th. It has also since been engaged constantly.

† This battalion formed only June 17th. Its batteries separately engaged in operating near Petersburg from Butler's advance May 5th, Captain Sturdivant captured in works carried by the enemy June 15th, with two pieces.

his line. Happily, though disabling, it was not dangerous. During his absence, which continued until August 18th, Lieutenant-Colonel Huger was assigned to the command of the guns and mortars on that part of the line.

Throughout the month of July sharp skirmishing, day and night, and desultory cannonading were continued, but nothing material was developed till near the close of the month.

During the night of the 26th the enemy crossed to the north side of the James River, near Deep Bottom, a large force of infantry and artillery, making in that direction a formidable demonstration. Colonel Carter commanded, on that side of James River, Hardaway's and Cutshaw's battalions of artillery, belonging to the Second Corps, which had remained behind when the rest of their corps moved westward. With this artillery Colonel Carter had efficiently patrolled that bank of the river against the enemy's gunboats since the transfer of the army to Petersburg. He now met the enemy's advance, supported by Kershaw's division. A portion of the latter giving way too easily left the four 20-pounder Parrotts, of Graham's (Rockbridge) battery, to be captured, although they were served with admirable steadiness for a considerable time after the infantry had retired. The enemy, however, did not venture far. No considerable conflict there appeared to be his intention. The event proved his movement to be a feint to draw our troops from Petersburg. In this, however, he succeeded only very partially. Lieutenant-Colonel Poague's battalion, with Penick's battery in addition, was, on the night of the 28th, detached from position north of the Appomattox and sent to Colonel Carter. The withdrawal did not materially weaken our lines, and when, on the night of the 29th, the enemy recrossed from the north to south side of James River, Colonel Poague was directed, instead of returning to his former location, to take position on the left of General Pickett's line and guard that flank against approach from Dutch Gap. There he has remained ever since, doing admirable service with guns and mortars, annoying working parties on Butler's canal and otherwise frustrating the enemy's plans.

July 30th the significance of the enemy's movements for the day or two previous was revealed.

About dawn of July 30th a mine was sprung by the enemy under the salient occupied by Pegram's battery, Coit's battalion, near the right of General Beauregard's line. Two of the guns were thrown to a great distance outside the works and a considerable breach effected. The enemy profiting by our surprise and his own elaborate preparations, presssed forward his assaulting column and, entering the chasm, seized a portion of our lines on its right and left. At the same time he opened a furious cannonade from perhaps over one hundred guns on the adjacent parts of our line and the approaches to them; but his advance was speedily arrested and his achievements rendered in the end eminently disastrous to himself by the vigor with which his troops were met, and the deadly fire poured into his ranks by Wright's battery, on the left, and by Haskell's guns and mortars, previously arranged to bear directly upon this salient. The enemy, unable either to advance or retreat, and, by the co-operating fire of all our artillery on this front, crouching into the crater to escape this deadly fire, were literally crushed and torn asunder by mortar shells.

Major Haskell, with conspicuous gallantry taking personal charge of two 12-pounder mortars, moved them forward to the trenches within fifty yards of the crater, so as to render their fire peculiarly accurate and destructive. Such of the enemy as survived this treatment, hopeless of support from their friends under the fire directed against the latter by all our guns, gladly surrendered on the last charge of our infantry. The enemy had gained nothing save a wholesome lesson, and that he had purchased at immense cost of life and labor. Major Gibbes, commanding the guns on the right of the crater, as soon as possible caused all of them that bore on the enemy's approaches to be opened. His left gun alone had effective command, and it was culpably left for a time unserved, through the misbehavior of Lieutenant James C. Otey who, owing to a combination of circumstances, was the only officer at the time present with the company. This was remedied by Major Gibbes himself repairing to that gun and having it worked with excellent effect until he received a severe and dangerous wound and was borne from the field. The guns thus again silent for a season were reopened by the timely arrival of Lieutenant-Colonel Huger who, with the assistance of Captains Winthrop and Haskell, of General Alexander's staff, and of Private L. T. Covington, of Pegram's blown-up battery, worked the guns again under a concentrated fire until another officer of the battery arrived from the rear and continued its service with cannoneers obtained from other guns. Our guns on the north of the Appomattox, meanwhile, put forth their strength, as did those all along General Beauregard's line and those further off to the right, to occupy the enemy elsewhere and prevent his too great concentration at his point of attack. The result was signally satisfactory. A subsequent attempt of the enemy to reach Gracie's salient, further to the left, by a sap, was with comparative ease frustrated by the fire of our mortars.

Respectfully, your obedient servant,

W. N. PENDLETON,

Brigadier-General and Chief of Artillery, Army of Northern Virginia.

ASSAULTS ON THE PETERSBURG LINES,

JUNE 16 TO JULY 30, 1864.

REPORTS OF GENERAL ROBERT E. LEE.

HEADQUARTERS CLAY'S HOUSE,
June 17, 1864, 10:30 A. M.

AT 11 o'clock last night took breastworks at Howlett's house. Other portions of same line were retaken. Pickett's division now occupies trenches from Howlett's to front of Clay's. Field's division is on the right, but I believe whole of front line not occupied. Battery at Howlett's is being re-established. Saw five vessels sunk by enemy in Trents Reach. Behind lie the monitors; counted ten steamers within the Reach. Enemy made two attacks last night on Beauregard, but were repulsed, with loss—four hundred prisoners, including eleven commissioned officers, captured. He has not entirely recovered his original position. Some fighting has occurred there this morning without results. Have ordered railroad at Port Walthall, destroyed by enemy yesterday, to be repaired and reopened.

R. E. LEE, *General.*

HIS EXCELLENCY, JEFFERSON DAVIS.

INTERIOR OF FORT MAHONE, CALLED FORT DAMNATION.
[From a photograph taken the morning after the Assault on Petersburg.]

CLAY'S HOUSE, June 17, 1864, 5 P. M.

At 4 P. M. assaulted that portion of our front line held by enemy and drove him from it. We again have the entire line from Howlett's to Dunns Hill.

R. E. LEE, *General.*

HIS EXCELLENCY, JEFFERSON DAVIS.

HEADQUARTERS ARMY OF NORTHERN VIRGINIA,
June 22, 1864.

Since Friday last there has been skirmishing along the lines in front of Bermuda Hundred and around Petersburg. The Federal army appears to be concentrated at these two places, and is strongly intrenched. Yesterday a movement of infantry, cavalry and artillery was made toward the right of our forces at Petersburg, in the direction of the Weldon Railroad. The enemy was driven back, and his infantry is reported to have halted. His cavalry have continued to advance upon the road by a route further removed from our position. The enemy's infantry was attacked this afternoon, on the west side of the Jerusalem Plank Road, and driven from his first line of works to his second on that road, by General Mahone with a part of his division. About sixteen hundred prisoners, four pieces of artillery, eight stand of colors and a large number of small arms were captured.

Very respectfully, your obedient servant,

R. E. LEE, *General.*

HON. JAMES A. SEDDON, *Secretary of War.*

HEADQUARTERS ARMY OF NORTHERN VIRGINIA,
June 24, 1864, 9 P. M.

Yesterday the enemy made a demonstration with infantry upon the Weldon Railroad, but before he had done much damage was driven back by General Mahone with a portion of his command. About six hundred prisoners and twenty-eight commissioned officers were taken, most of whom were captured by Perry's (Florida) brigade. This morning the enemy was felt on both flanks, and a part of one of General Hoke's brigades entered his works. Not being supported, they were unable to hold the position and retired with few casualties, but losing the advance line, which had succeeded in entering the enemy's intrenchments. A small number of prisoners was taken, but the enemy's loss is supposed to have been slight.

Very respectfully, your obedient servant,

R. E. LEE, *General.*

HON. SECRETARY OF WAR.

HEADQUARTERS ARMY OF NORTHERN VIRGINIA,
June 25, 1864, 9 P. M.

Our entire loss yesterday morning was ninety-seven killed and wounded and two hundred and nine missing. Nothing of moment has occurred to-day on the lines in front of Bermuda Hundred and around Petersburg. General Hampton reports that the enemy's cavalry advanced yesterday to Nances Shop and intrenched themselves there. He attacked them and drove them from their works, pursuing them until 9 P. M., to within two miles of Charles City Courthouse. They left their dead and wounded on the field and along the route. Great credit is due to General Hampton and his command for their handsome success.

Very respectfully, your obedient servant,

R. E. LEE, *General.*

HON. SECRETARY OF WAR.

HEADQUARTERS ARMY OF NORTHERN VIRGINIA,
June 25, 1864.

General W. H. F. Lee pursued the enemy's cavalry, which advanced along the South Side Railroad. He had a skirmish on the 22d, near Dinwiddie Courthouse, and the next day struck their column in flank near Blacks and Whites, cutting in two and getting possession of the road by which they were moving toward Nottoway Courthouse. The road was held after an engagement which continued from 12 M. until dark, the enemy making repeated attempts to break through and regain his advance. He withdrew from General Lee's front at daylight on the 24th, leaving his dead and wounded on the field, taking the road to Hungarytown and Keysville. General Lee is still following them. Very respectfully, your obedient servant,

R. E. LEE, *General.*

HON. SECRETARY OF WAR.

DUNNS HILL, NEAR PETERSBURG,
June 29, 1864, 8:30 P. M.

General Hampton reports that he attacked the enemy's cavalry yesterday afternoon, on their return from Staunton River Bridge, this side of Sappony Church, and drove them beyond that point. The fight continued during the night, and at daylight this morning he turned their left and routed them. When they reached Reams Station they were confronted by a portion of Mahone's division, who attacked them in front, while their left flank was turned by General Fitzhugh Lee's cavalry. The enemy was completely routed and several pieces of artillery, with a number of prisoners, wagons, ambulances, etc., captured. The cavalry are in pursuit.

R. E. LEE, *General.*

HON. JAMES A. SEDDON, *Secretary of War.*

DUNNS HILL, July 30, 1864, 3:25 P. M.

At 5 A. M. the enemy sprung a mine under one of the salients on General B. R. Johnson's front and opened his batteries upon our lines and the city of Petersburg. In the confusion caused by the explosion of the mine he got possession of the salient. We have retaken the salient and driven the enemy back to his lines with loss.

R. E. LEE.

HON. JAMES A. SEDDON, *Secretary of War.*

HEADQUARTERS, NEAR PETERSBURG,
July 30, 1864, 6:30 P. M.

General A. P. Hill reports that General Mahone, in retaking the salient possessed by the enemy this morning, recovered the four guns with which it was armed, captured twelve stand of colors, seventy-four officers, including Brigadier-General Bartlett and staff, and eight hundred and fifty-five enlisted men. Upward of five hundred of the enemy's dead are lying unburied in the trenches. His loss slight.

R. E. LEE.

HON. JAMES A. SEDDON, *Secretary of War.*

HEADQUARTERS, NEAR PETERSBURG,
August 1, 1864.

There was a cessation of hostilities this morning from 6 to 10 A. M., at the request of the enemy, for the purpose of caring for the dead and wounded. Seven hundred of the enemy's dead were buried or turned over to him for burial; twenty stand of colors instead of twelve, as reported, were captured on the 30th.

R. E. LEE.

HON. J. A. SEDDON, *Secretary of War.*

HEADQUARTERS ARMY OF NORTHERN VIRGINIA,
August 13, 1864.

I have the honor to forward three stand of colors captured by a part of General B. R. Johnson's division in the attack of the enemy upon our works around Petersburg on the 30th of July.

With great respect, your obedient servant,

R. E. LEE, *General.*

HON. SECRETARY OF WAR.

[*Indorsement.*]
August 14, 1864.

Adjutant-General:

Receive and let suitable acknowledgment be made. Let me see it.

J. A. SEDDON, *Secretary.*

HEADQUARTERS ARMY OF NORTHERN VIRGINIA,
August 13, 1864.

I have the honor to forward by the hands of Acting Assistant Adjutant-General B. H. Nash, of Mahone's brigade, seventeen stand of colors and two guidons captured by a portion of General Mahone's division in the attack of the enemy upon the works around Petersburg on the 30th of July. The accompanying report of Major-General Mahone contains the names of the captors, to which the attention of the Department is respectfully invited.

Very respectfully, your obedient servant,

R. E. LEE, *General.*

HON. SECRETARY OF WAR.

[*Indorsement.*]
August 20, 1864.

Adjutant-General:

Let appropriate acknowledgment be made to the gallant general and his brave troops. Let the names of the captors be noted on the roll of honor and published.

J. A. SEDDON.

[INCLOSURE.]

LIST OF COLORS CAPTURED BY MAHONE'S, SANDERS' AND WRIGHT'S BRIGADES AT PETERSBURG, VA., JULY 30, 1864.

DESCRIPTION.	CAPTORS.		
	NAME.	RANK AND REGIMENT.	BRIGADE.
Eleventh New Hampshire Volunteers	W. B. Wellons	Private, Company H, Sixth Virginia	Mahone's.
Stars and Stripes	R. O. Whitehead	Lieutenant-Colonel, Sixteenth Virginia	Mahone's.
One Hundredth Regiment (Blank)	L. R. Kilby	Captain, Company B, Sixteenth Virginia	Mahone's.
Stars and Stripes	Joseph R. Goodwin	Lieutenant, Company F, Sixteenth Virginia	Mahone's.
Twenty-eighth United States (Colored)	Solomon V. Butler	Corporal, Company D, Sixteenth Virginia	Mahone's.
Stars and Stripes	David Barnes	Private, Company G, Sixteenth Virginia	Mahone's.
Fifty-eighth Massachusetts Regiment (State Flag)	A. J. Sadler	Private, Company F, Sixteenth Virginia	Mahone's.
Stars and Stripes	W. F. Lane	Private, Company G, Sixteenth Virginia	Mahone's.
Guidon (marked 2)	John W. Miles	Private, Company D, Forty-first Virginia	Mahone's.
Portion of staff and flag	Lemuel Tucker	Private, Company B, Forty-first Virginia	Mahone's.
Fifty-seventh Massachusetts Regiment	St. Julien Wilson	Lieutenant, Company C, Sixty-first Virginia	Mahone's.
Stars and Stripes	J. J. Bilisoby	Lieutenant, Company D, Sixty-first Virginia	Mahone's.
—— Regiment Infantry	Peter F. Howell	Sergeant, Company G, Sixty-first Virginia	Mahone's.
Thirty-first Regiment Infantry	Wm. H. Harrison	Corporal, Company A, Sixty-first Virginia	Mahone's.
Portion of staff and fringe	John E. Foreman	Company E, Sixty-first Virginia	Mahone's.
Second Michigan Regiment	John H. Deaton	Sergeant, Company E, Eighth Alabama	Sanders'.
Twentieth Michigan Regiment	John M. Critcher	Company K, Ninth Alabama	Sanders'.
Guidon (Stars and Stripes)	James N. Keeton	Company G, Eleventh Alabama	Sanders'.
Fifty-eighth Massachusetts regimental flag	F. J. Herndon	Corporal, Company F, Third Georgia	Wright's.

SUMMARY.

MAHONE'S BRIGADE.	
Sixth Virginia Regiment	1
Sixteenth Virginia Regiment	7
Forty-first Virginia Regiment	2
Sixty-first Virginia Regiment	5
SANDERS' BRIGADE.	
Eighth Alabama Regiment	1
Ninth Alabama Regiment	1
Eleventh Alabama Regiment	1
WRIGHT'S BRIGADE.	
Third Georgia Regiment	1
Entire number	19

WM. MAHONE, *Major-General, etc.*

ASSAULT ON THE CRATER AND EXPLOSION OF THE MINE,

PETERSBURG, VA., JULY 30, 1864.

BY

MAJOR-GENERAL B. R. JOHNSON.

HEADQUARTERS JOHNSON'S DIVISION,
August 20, 1864.

FOR a proper understanding of the condition of my command on the occasion of the action of Saturday, the 30th of July, 1864, it is necessary to state that on the night of the 28th of July every man in reserve in this division was placed in the trenches. Colquitt's brigade, of Hoke's division, was temporarily transferred to my command, in exchange for Gracie's brigade, and placed on my right. For the purpose of relieving Field's division from the trenches my line was extended to an attenuation that was deemed barely secure against an ordinary assault. From the left to the right the brigades were stationed in the trenches in the following order, viz.: Ransom's, Elliott's, Wise's and Colquitt's brigades.

About 4:55 o'clock on the morning of the 30th of July the enemy sprung a large mine under that portion of my line about two hundred yards north of the Baxter Road,

MAJ.-GEN. BUSHROD R. JOHNSON, OF TENNESSEE.
[From a tintype taken in 1864.]

known as Pegram's salient. In this salient there were four guns of Captain Pegram's battery, and the Eighteenth and Twenty-second South Carolina regiments, of Elliott's brigade, occupied the parapets in the battery and adjacent to it. The Twenty-second South Carolina Regiment extended from a point some seventy yards to the right of the right gun to a point beyond, but near to, the left gun of the battery. The Eighteenth was posted on the left of the Twenty-second South Carolina Regiment. The regiments of Elliott's brigade were distributed along the parapet from left to right as follows, viz.: The Twenty-sixth, Seventeenth, Eighteenth, Twenty-second and Twenty-third South Carolina regiments. To strengthen Pegram's salient a second line on trench cavalier had been thrown up in its rear, commanding our front line and the enemy's works at a distance of from one hundred and fifty to two hundred yards. Owing to the extension of our line, already explained, our troops occupied only the front line of our works. The mine, as has been since ascertained, was laid along two wings, extending to the right and left of the main gallery, nearly parallel to the interior crest of our work and beneath the foot of the slope of the banquette, or perhaps further back, and completely destroyed a portion of the front or main line of our fortification and the right of the trench cavalier. The crater measures 135 feet in length, 97 feet in breadth and 30 feet deep. The two right guns of Pegram's battery were not disturbed by the explosion. The two left guns were thrown out in front of our works, and only eight men out of twenty-eight men and two officers with the battery escaped alive and unhurt. The battery was occupied by five companies of the Twenty-second South Carolina Regiment, which were blown up. The Eighteenth South Carolina Regiment, on the left of the battery, had four companies blown up or destroyed by the falling earth.

From the facts furnished by Colonel F. W. McMaster, commanding Elliott's brigade since Brigadier-General S. Elliott was wounded, it appears that the losses sustained by the explosion of the mine are as follows:

	Killed.	Woun'd	Total.
Twenty-second South Carolina Regiment—Officers and men	. . .	. . . .	170
Eighteenth South Carolina Regiment—Officers	4	5	9
Men	39	38	77
Pegram's battery—Officers and men	. . .	. . . .	22
Aggregate losses known to have occurred from explosion	. . . .	. . . .	278

Of four officers and seventy-two men missing from the Eighteenth South Carolina Regiment, over and above the the foregoing estimate, a part may have been blown up or killed by the falling earth, but most of them are supposed to have been captured.

The astonishing effect of the explosion, bursting like a volcano at the feet of the men, and the upheaving of an immense column of more than one hundred thousand cubic feet of earth to fall around in heavy masses, wounding, crushing or burying everything within its reach, prevented our men from moving promptly to the mouth of the crater and occupying that part of the trench cavalier which was not destroyed, and over which the debris was scattered. Each brigade of this division had, however, been previously instructed as to the course to be pursued and the stubborn resistance to be offered on each flank in case a breach was made in our line, and the troops of Elliott's brigade not blown up or injured, maintained their ground with remarkable steadiness. When the torrents of dust had subsided, the enemy was found in the breach. Some four flags were counted, and a continuous column of white and black troops came pouring on from the enemy's lines to support those in the advance, while their artillery, mortars and cannon opened all along their lines, concentrating on our works and grounds adjacent to the crater one of the heaviest artillery fires known to our oldest officers in the field. Their heaviest fire was from batteries in the vicinity of the Baxter Road, where they had, since the 16th of June, seemed to concentrate their greatest strength, worked with greatest industry, built the strongest works and fought with unwearied energy.

On the advancing column the Twenty-third and a part of the Twenty-second South Carolina regiments, on the right, and the Seventeenth and part of the Eighteenth South Carolina regiments on the left, opened from our parapets a most destructive fire. The flanking arrangements of our works, on both sides of the breach, afforded peculiar advantages. Soon the fire along the line of the division, extending far out on each flank, wherever the enemy's columns could be reached, swept the ground in front of the crater. To the men of Wise's brigade, occupying the eminence south of the Baxter Road, about two hundred yards from the crater, the enemy's masses moving on the open ground up to the breach, presented a most inviting and accessible target, upon which their fire took unerring effect. Wright's battery of four guns, admirably located, and intrenched on the left of Elliott's brigade and in rear of our lines, poured its whole column of fire in the right flank of the enemy's masses. The position of this excellent battery was, perhaps, unknown to the enemy, and the superior manner in which it was served, the rapidity of the fire, and the terrible effect on the enemy's forces, no doubt greatly astonished and demoralized them.

One gun of Davidson's battery, commanded by Lieutenant Otey, occupying a position on our main line, on the right of the Baxter Road—admirably adapted to throw canister shot into the enemy's left flank, and with Wright's battery to sweep the ground in front of the breach with a destructive cross-fire—opened with a few rounds, and, for some reason not explained to me, became silent, and was deserted by the officers and men. This battery was connected with my command on the night of the 28th of July, by the extension of my line to the right, and did not comprise a part of the artillery properly serving with this division. This battery was, however, subsequently manned and officered by Wise's brigade, under instructions from Colonel Goode, and did excellent service.

Major Haskell's mortar batteries, in charge of Captain Lamkin, consisting of four Coehorns, on the Jerusalem Plank Road, one Coehorn and two 12-pounder mortars in the ravine, some two hundred yards to the left and in rear of the breach, and two mortars to the left of Wright's battery, were all opened promptly upon the enemy's columns. The practice of the four mortars on the Plank Road was admirable. Its shells were dropped with remarkable precision upon the enemy's masses, clustering in disorder in front of and in the crater. Some three mortars on the right of the Baxter Road, commanded by Lieutenant Langhorne, also opened early in the engagement, and continued to fire at intervals with good effect until its close.

As soon as I was aware that the enemy had sprung the mine and broken my line near the center, I immediately communicated with the brigades in both wings of the division, and directed them to extend their intervals and re-enforce the wings of Elliott's brigade, so as to give as great strength as possible to the forces on which the weight of the enemy's columns must first fall. At the same time I dispatched staff officers to the two divisions on my flanks for re-enforcements. From the left I received, through Captain Saunders, aid-de-camp, the response that no re-enforcements could be furnished, as the line was already too weak. Captain Smith, acting aid-de-camp, who went to the right, promptly reported that General Mahone unsuccessful assault by a very inferior force without any support.

The new line to the left and rear of the salient was scarcely formed when the enemy attempted, with a force thrown out to the rear of our works, with those in our trenches, and with a line in front of our trenches, to charge to our left along our breastworks and in rear and front. The Twenty-fourth and Forty-ninth North Carolina regiments, Ransom's brigade, had promptly closed in on the part of the Seventeenth South Carolina Regiment remaining in the trenches when the intermediate regiments were drawn out to form the rear line, and now met and repulsed the charge in front, while the line under Colonel Smith, of the Twenty-sixth South Carolina Regiment, was equally successful in rear. Two companies of the Forty-ninth North Carolina Regiment, posted in the covered way near the main line, poured a heavy volley on the flank of the enemy in rear, and our men of the Seventeenth South Carolina and Forty-ninth North Carolina regiments, under cover of angles, boyaux, etc., drove back the charge along the trenches. After this the enemy continued to fight along the parapet, keeping under cover; but, though our forces on the left failed in several attempts to throw up barricades in the trenches, the former made but slow progress in this movement.

In the meantime, the Twenty-third South Carolina Regiment, under Captain White, and a few remaining men of the Twenty-second South Carolina Regiment, Ninth and parts of two other army corps, was directed upon the breach at Pegram's salient, and was held in check by little more than three regiments of Elliott's, two regiments of Ransom's and two regiments of Wise's brigades, with the efficient aid of artillery, especially of Wright's battery and the four mortars, under Captain Lamkin, on the Jerusalem Plank Road. The enemy also made considerable demonstration in front of Wise's brigade, and appeared in front of their works on south side of Baxter Road. On the left of the crater a large force was advanced to threaten the works occupied by Ransom's brigade. It came forward in irregular order and took shelter at the foot of a steep hill. This force was engaged without any important results by Ransom's brigade and the right howitzer of Slaten's battery. Our whole line, from the right of Colquitt's to the left of Gracie's brigade, suffered from artillery fire.

The Sixty-first North Carolina Regiment, of Hoke's division, sent to re-enforce the troops engaged at the breach, arrived at the same time with Mahone's division and proceeded to form in the ravine in rear of Pegram's salient, for the purpose of charging the enemy in the breach. General Mahone had placed one brigade in position, and was waiting for the second to come up, when the enemy advanced upon his line of battle. He met their advance by a charge, in which the Twenty-fifth and Forty-ninth North Carolina and the Twenty-sixth and part of the Seventeenth South Carolina regiments, all under

BATTLE OF PETERSBURG, VA., JULY 30, 1864. EXPLOSION OF THE MINE IN FRONT OF THE CONFEDERATE WORKS.
[From a sketch by Andrew McCallum, owned by Mrs. Frank Leslie, New York.]

was moving up to our support, with two brigades. As soon as the enemy occupied the breach they attempted to advance along our trenches upon the flanks of our broken line; but our men, sheltering themselves behind the angles and flanks of our works, in the boyaux running perpendicular to the rear of our trenches, and behind the piles of earth above their bomb-proofs, opened a fatal fire on every point where the foe exposed themselves. Thus their advance was stayed. and they commenced the work of intrenching, while they still tried, by more cautious means, to press back our faithful and gallant men.

Brigadier-General S. Elliott, the gallant commander of the brigade which occupied the salient, was making prompt disposition of his forces to assault the enemy and reoccupy the remaining portion of the trench cavalier when he was dangerously wounded. He had given the necessary orders for the Twenty-sixth and the left wing of the Seventeenth South Carolina regiments to be withdrawn from the trenches, and had preceded them to the open ground to the left and in rear of the cavalier when he was struck by a rifle-ball. The command of this brigade now devolved upon Colonel F. W. McMaster, of the Seventeenth South Carolina Regiment. This officer (having received the re-enforcement of one regiment, sent to him by Colonel McAfee, commanding Ransom's brigade), directed Colonel Smith, of the Twenty-sixth South Carolina Regiment, to form in a ravine on the left and rear of the breach, a rear line consisting of the Twenty-fifth North Carolina, Twenty-sixth South Carolina and three companies of the Seventeenth South Carolina regiments, arranged from left to right in the order named. Some fourteen Federal flags were now counted on our works, and it became evident that it would be better to endeavor to hold the enemy in check until larger re-enforcements arrived, than risk the disaster that might follow from an under Captain Shedd, aided by the Twenty-sixth and part of the Forty-sixth Virginia regiments, gallantly defended the trenches on the right of the breach.

The South Carolina troops on that side succeeded in placing a barricade in the trenches on the side of the hill, and, planting themselves behind it and in the boyaux running to the rear, maintained their position within thirty yards of the crater for about five hours, during which the enemy never drove them a foot to the right, though they made several assaults, and attempted several times to form a line in rear of our works, so as to move on the flank and rear of this gallant little band. In the events of the 30th of July there will perhaps be found nothing more heroic or worthy of higher admiration than this conduct of the Twenty-second and Twenty-third South Carolina regiments

Colonel Goode, commanding Wise's brigade, caused the Fifty-ninth Virginia Regiment, under Captain Wood, to be formed in a ditch running perpendicular to the rear of the main work, and when the enemy attempted some five times to form in rear of the breach for the purpose of charging to the right, and after they had planted four colors on the line, by which the movement designated was to be made, this regiment, under Captain Wood, and the Twenty-sixth Virginia Regiment, under Captain Steele, with the Twenty-second and Twenty-third South Carolina regiments and two guns of ——— battery near the junction of the Baxter and Jerusalem Plank roads, opened with a fire that drove them precipitately back to the crater. In this way the conflict was maintained from 5 till nearly 10 A. M. with coolness and steadiness by determined men and officers on both flanks of the breach, and with a success worthy of much praise and with great damage to the enemy.

The assailing force of the enemy, consisting of the Colonel Smith, of Elliott's brigade, gallantly joined, moving upon the left of General Mahone's line. The enemy was driven from three-quarters of the trench cavalier and most of the works on the left of the crater, with moderate loss to our forces and heavy losses to the enemy, especially in prisoners. During this charge a large number of the enemy's troops, black and white, abandoned the breach and fled precipitately to their rear. Upon this fleeing mass, in full view from our works on the right of the Baxter Road, the left regiments of Wise's brigade poured a raking fire at the distance of from one hundred and fifty to five hundred yards, while the left gun of Davidson's battery (which Colonel Goode had manned with a company of the Thirty-fourth Virginia Regiment, under Captain Samuel D. Preston), discharged upon them several rounds of canister.

It is proper here to state that Captain Preston was wounded, and Edward Bagby, aid-de-camp to Colonel Goode, commanding brigade, was killed while serving this gun, and that Captain A. F. Bagby, with Company K, Thirty-fourth Virginia Regiment, then took charge of it, and served it with fine effect, until near the close of the action. The first charge having failed in completely dislodging the enemy, I ordered all of my available forces to press steadily on both flanks with a view to their final expulsion.

Between 11 and 12 A. M., a second unsuccessful charge having been made by Wright's brigade, of Mahone's division, I proceeded to concert a combined movement on both flanks of the crater, to which most of the enemy's troops were now drawn. By arrangement a third charge was made a little before 2 P. M., which gave us entire possession of the crater and the adjacent lines. This charge was made on the left and rear of the crater by Sanders' brigade, of Mahone's division, by the Sixty-first

North Carolina, of Hoke's division, and Seventeenth South Carolina Regiment, of this division. The last two regiments under Major Culp, of the Seventeenth South Carolina Regiment, Elliott's brigade, advanced on the right of Sanders' brigade. These movements on the left were all placed under the direct supervision of General Mahone, while I proceeded to the right to collect what troops I could from the thin line on that flank to co-operate in the charge, and divide the force of the enemy's resistance. The time allotted only permitted me to draw out the Twenty-third and the fragments of the Twenty-second South Carolina regiments, under Captain Shedd. They moved gallantly forward as soon as the main line was

DEAD CONFEDERATE SOLDIER IN THE TRENCHES IN FRONT OF PETERSBURG, VA.

seen advancing on the left, and entered the crater with the troops of that line, capturing three stand of colors and about one hundred and thirty prisoners. Previous to this charge the incessant firing kept up by our troops on both flanks and in rear had caused many of the enemy to run the gauntlet of our cross-fires, in front of the breach, but a large number still remained, unable to advance, and perhaps afraid to retreat. The final charge was, therefore, made with little difficulty, and resulted in the complete re-establishment of our lines and the capture of many additional prisoners.

To Major-General Hoke I am indebted for some sixty men of the Twenty-first South Carolina Regiment, who occupied, about 1 P. M., a portion of the works on right of Baxter Road, from which my troops were moved to the left; and also for Colonel Radcliffe's Sixty-first North Carolina Regiment, which re-enforced my command in the morning and joined the charge, as already stated.

To the able commander and gallant officers and men of Mahone's division, to whom we are mainly indebted for the restoration of our lines, I offer my acknowledgments for their great service. It is not, however, my privilege to make any further report of the operations of that division than is necessary for a proper understanding of those of my own command.

To the officers and men of my command, whose steadiness, determination and courage held in check for five hours a greatly superior force elated with success, and aided to inflict on them a chastisement so memorable, my admiration and gratitude are due. It is believed for each buried companion they have taken a ten-fold vengeance on the enemy, and have taught them a lesson that will be remembered as long as the history of our wrongs and this great revolution endures.

The troops of this division I would invite to a lesson yet more profitable, in view of what may lie before them. They have learned in practice that which has been taught them by theory and historical example — that the coolness and steadiness of a few resolute and determined officers and men will prove the salvation of a command, whether in an unavoidable surprise or against the disordered lines of a charging column.

To the prompt and energetic co-operation of Colonel Jones, chief of artillery, and Major Haskell, commanding the mortar battery, and to their officers and men, my acknowledgments are due.

The gallantry of Private Patrick Sweeney, Company A, Fifty-ninth Virginia Regiment, has been justly reported by his brigade commander. He voluntarily joined in the last charge and captured two colors of the Twentieth Michigan Regiment, and, though wounded through the body, he persisted in bringing them off, with a Sharps rifle.

In the last charge Sergeant J. W. Connelly, Company F, Twenty-second South Carolina Regiment, captured the colors of the First Michigan Sharpshooters, which he delivered to General Beauregard in person.

The zeal and activity of my aids, Captains E. R. Smith, John E. Saunders and T. H. Skinner, were arduously tasked on the lines and fully merit the compliment of this official notice. Captain Skinner, who had joined me within the previous twenty-four hours as a volunteer aid from a foreign soil, besides doing much arduous duty during the day, gallantly joined the troops on the right in the final charge, by which the enemy was utterly repulsed.

The following is the state of casualties of the division:

COMMAND.	KILLED.		WOUN'D.		MISSING.		TOTAL.		Aggregate . . .
	Officers . .	Men . . .	Officers . .	Men . . .	Officers . .	Men . .	Officers . .	Men . . .	
Elliott's brigade . .	15	110	18	204	14	337	47	651	698
Wise's brigade .	1	24	5	81	. .	. .	6	105	111
Ransom's brigade .	3	11	7	53	. .	8	10	72	82
Colquitt's brigade .	. .	4	3	24	. .	. . .	3	28	31
Total	19	149	33	362	14	345	66	856	922

For the purpose of preserving the records of this division, the following casualties of Gracie's brigade are added, though that brigade was detached from my command on this occasion. It, however, occupied its usual position in the trenches on my left: Killed, one commissioned officer and nine enlisted men; wounded, one commissioned officer and forty-five enlisted men; total, two commissioned officers and fifty-four enlisted men.

The losses of the enemy have been pretty well ascertained, and are between five and six thousand, including prisoners.

B. R. JOHNSON, *Major-General.*

MISSOURI.

WORDS AND MUSIC BY HARRY MACARTHY.

Missouri! Missouri! bright land of the West,
Where the way-worn emigrant always found rest,
Who gave to the farmer reward for the toil
Expended in breaking and turning the soil,
Awake to the notes of the bugle and drum!
Awake from your peace, for the tyrant hath come;
And swear by your honor that your chains shall be riven,
And add your bright Star to our Flag of Eleven.

They'd force you to join in their unholy fight
With fire and with sword, with power and with might,
'Gainst fathers and brothers and kindred near,
'Gainst women and children and all you hold dear;
They've o'errun your soil, insulted your press,
Murdered your citizens, shown no redress;
So swear by your honor that your chains shall be riven,
And add your bright Star to our Flag of Eleven.

Missouri! Missouri! where is thy proud fame?
Free land of the West, thy once-cherished name?
Trod in the dust by a tyrant's command,
Proclaiming there's martial law in the land.
Men of Missouri! strike without fear!
McCulloch, Jackson and brave men are near;
Swear by your honor that your chains shall be riven,
And add your bright Star to our Flag of Eleven.

THE RICHMOND CAMPAIGN,

AUGUST 10 TO DECEMBER 31, 1864.

BY

BRIG.-GEN. WILLIAM N. PENDLETON,

Chief of Artillery, Army of Northern Virginia.

HEADQUARTERS ARMY CORPS, ARMY OF NORTHERN VIRGINIA,
February 28, 1865.

ABOUT August 10th General Fitzhugh Lee's division of cavalry having received orders to join General Early in the Valley, Johnston's and Shoemaker's batteries marched with the division, Captain Johnston in command, Major Breathed having been wounded in a skirmish on June 29th. This force reached Front Royal on August 14th, and thenceforward participated in General Early's campaign.

Nothing material occurred on the Petersburg line until August 18th. On that day Brander's battery, Pegram's battalion, accompanied Heth's division and was warmly engaged in an attack upon the enemy at the Davis house, on the Weldon Railroad. The next day Lieutenant-Colonel Pegram was sent with three of his batteries to co-operate with Generals Heth and Mahone in another attack at the same point. His battalion again participated on the 21st in an attack at Poplar Spring Church. Again, on the 24th, Colonel Pegram was directed, with Brander's and Cayce's batteries, of his own battalion, Ross', of Lane's, and sections of Hurt's and Clutter's, of McIntosh's, to accompany the column sent to attack the enemy at Reams Station, on the Weldon Railroad. Success was marked on this occasion, and due, in no small degree, to the efficiency of Colonel Pegram and the good conduct of his officers and men.

BRIGADIER-GENERAL E. PORTER ALEXANDER, OF GEORGIA, Commanding Artillery, Army of Northern Virginia.
[From a photograph taken in 1863.]

From September 14th to 30th, Hart's and McGregor's batteries, and Graham's, previously connected with General Beauregard's command, participated in several spirited affairs of the cavalry in our right flank, under command of General Hampton. Desultory skirmishing continued along the lines during this month and the following, with no further movement of importance till September 29th. On that day the enemy commenced more vigorous operations on the north side of James River, and succeeded in carrying, chiefly by surprise, a commanding salient of our works, known as Fort Harrison, not far from Chaffins Bluff. To meet this advance of the enemy forces were promptly moved from Petersburg. Major Johnson, of McIntosh's battalion, marched the same evening in command of Clutter's battery, of his own battalion, and

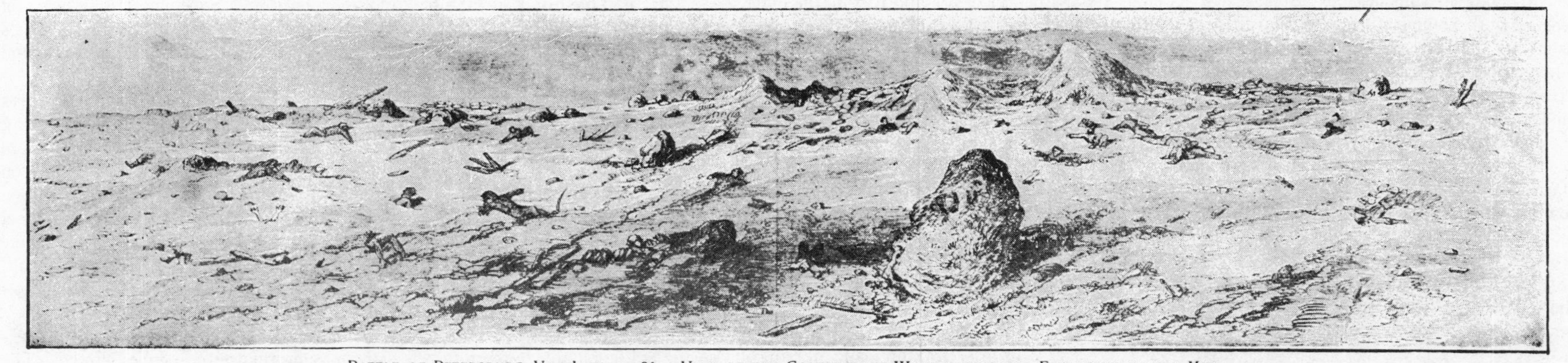

BATTLE OF PETERSBURG, VA., JULY 30, 1864. VIEW OF THE CONFEDERATE WORKS AFTER THE EXPLOSION OF THE MINE.
[From a sketch by E. F. Mullen, owned by Mrs. Frank Leslie, New York.]

the Fredericksburg Artillery, of Pegram's battalion, and the next morning Haskell's battalion moved also to co-operate with the troops north of the James. General Alexander accompanied the expedition to command the artillery. Lieutenant-Colonel Hardaway, commanding his own battalion, and Major Stark, previously of Lieutenant-Colonel Pemberton's command, reported at once to General Alexander. The field artillery on that line had been left in his charge, when Colonel Carter repaired under orders on September 2d to General Early's army in the Valley, as his chief of artillery in place of General Long, disabled by sickness. These battalions (Hardaway's and Stark's, Haskell's and Johnson's) constituted an effective artillery force for operations in that front. Hardaway's and Stark's battalions co-operated as far as practicable, though, from the nature of the ground and the course of the lines and the position of the enemy, they could accomplish but little in the unsuccessful attempt to secure Fort Harrison on the 30th, and in the attack, resumed for the same purpose, on October 1st, Haskell's guns were added to them and posted as favorably as possible, Lamkin's company, experienced in mortar practice at Petersburg, having charge of a number of mortars. The attack being abandoned and defensive measures resumed, Johnson's and Haskell's guns were posted for use as occasion might arise. Lamkin's mortars remained, as they have done ever since, in position bearing on Fort Harrison. While these occurrences transpired on the lines below Richmond, active movements were also going on upon the right of our line below Petersburg. Lieutenant-Colonel Pegram, with Brander's and Ellett's batteries, participated in an attack made by Heth upon the enemy's left.

On the following day (October 1st), with Brander's and Cayce's batteries, he again took part in the combined attack of Heth and Wilcox. Colonel Pegram warmly commends Captain Brander and Lieutenant Hollis, commanding these batteries, for their gallantry and efficiency on this occasion.

On the day succeeding (2d) the enemy attacking Heth's line, was effectually repulsed by the vigorous co-operation of Ellett's battery with the infantry, Cayce's and Gregg's batteries also assisting from their respective positions.

On October 8th [7th] Haskell's and Johnson's battalions, north of James River, shared in the repulse of the enemy by our troops on the Darbytown and New Market roads, and performed their part with accustomed energy and success. On this occasion Major Haskell, narrowly escaping with his life, received a grazing wound on the head from a minie-ball, and Lieutenant McQueen, of one of his batteries (Gardner's), was severely wounded.

Haskell's battalion, under Captain Gardner, was again slightly engaged on the 12th [13th] in repelling feeble attacks of the enemy. Corporal Fulsher, of Flanner's battery, performed on this occasion a service deserving of special mention to his honor. Explosion having occurred among some ammunition improperly exposed, wounding six men, this soldier, though himself wounded, caught up several shells with hissing fuses and extinguished them in a pool of water near by, and this when other shells were bursting around him.

On October 27th, the enemy made a simultaneous attack on our lines below Richmond, and on our right flank beyond Petersburg. His advance below Richmond was general and in considerable force. It was, however, repelled with comparative ease, the artillery rendering, as usual, its share of service. Haskell's and Johnson's battalions operated against the enemy's flanking on our extreme left as far as Williamsburg, and even the Nine-mile wood, and thence across to Charles City Road. Hardaway's and Stark's battalions met the direct attacks on their front between the Darbytown Road and Fort Harrison. On this occasion Lieutenant C. H. Wilkes, commanding Clutter's battery, while gallantly discharging his duty, fell at his post, mortally wounded. No further attempt has since been made by the enemy on the line north of James River, and the field artillery has remained there, with supporting troops, quietly awaiting such further service as future operations of the enemy may render necessary.

The enemy, on October 27th, experienced on the extreme right, below Petersburg, as serious reverse as on the left below Richmond. Early in the day, when accompanied by the cavalry alone, his numbers proved of avail to advance, gradually pressing back our horsemen to and across the Boydton Plank Road. Hart's battery, resolutely served, rendered valuable service in checking that advance. Its faithful commander, Captain Hart, received in this engagement a severe wound. Subsequently McGregor's and Graham's batteries effectually co-operated in the combined attack which drove back the enemy in confusion and with heavy loss, Two of Lieutenant-Colonel Pegram's batteries (Ellett's, under Lieutenant Hollis, and Gregg's) also participated in the sharp conflict on this wing, that afternoon, Gregg's battery being partially and Ellett's sharply engaged and contributing to the success of the day. After this signal reverse, the enemy for some time attempted no movement of consequence, though skirmishing and shelling were continuously practiced on considerable portions of the lines, and, at times, with much severity.

On December 7th, an extensive raid by a large force of the enemy being in progress along the Weldon Railroad, toward Belfield and beyond, our cavalry hastened to arrest the operation, attended by Hart's, McGregor's and Graham's batteries. Their guns were effectual in repelling the enemy at Hicksford and admonishing him speedily to retrace his steps. Our infantry column, which followed in pursuit of this raiding force, was accompanied by four batteries, under Lieutenant-Colonel Pegram and Major Owen. They were not able to obtain a fair opportunity at the enemy, or more than a slight skirmish, owing to his prompt retreat, and after a tour of seven days' extremely hard service, in severe weather and through roads scarcely passable, returned to camp. This effort closed the campaign. Nothing significant has since transpired.

PASSAGE OF THE SHENANDOAH RIVER AT FRONT ROYAL, VA., BY THE DIVISIONS OF GENERALS KERSHAW AND FITZHUGH LEE.
[From a sketch made by an artist representing the *London News*.]

While the campaign around Richmond and Petersburg had thus progressed to its close, that portion of our army detached under General Early on June 18th, and operating mainly in the Valley of Virginia, had been engaged in a series of movements and conflicts of very great importance, the artillery performing throughout a conspicuous part. Nelson's and Braxton's battalions (Second Corps), which accompanied the expedition to Lynchburg to meet Hunter, though marching with great effort, could not reach that place in time to deal a decisive blow to that atrocious dispenser of fire and fury to the defenseless. He had hastily retreated before General Early and was making as rapidly as possible toward the Ohio. On June 22d, these two battalions joined the artillery of General Breckinridge's command, and all the other troops under General Early, near Salem, in Roanoke County. Thence the Army of the Valley moved by the direct route to Staunton. Here, in the delay of two days which occurred, some judicious adjustments in his command were made by General Long, chief of artillery, Second Corps. Leaving Major Leyden, of the Department of Southwestern Virginia, in charge of a reserve camp of batteries least efficient, he fitted out with the best guns McLaughlin's battalion and a force of horse artillery. The army thus moved from Staunton, for the lower Valley, with three efficient battalions of artillery—Wilson's, Braxton's and McLaughlin's—under Lieutenant-Colonel King, having forty reliable guns well equipped, and ten additional, also well provided, to serve with the cavalry.

Encountering little resistance on any part of the route, General Early's forces crossed the Potomac into Maryland, at Shepherdstown, on July 5th and 6th.

On the morning of the 9th, they advanced upon Fredericktown. The enemy had evacuated that place, but was found in force on the line of the Monocacy, a mile or two to the east, the railroad bridge and ford below, on the Georgetown Road, being the principal points of demonstration. Here a number of our guns were judiciously posted to bear upon the opposite side and operated with great effect, when McCausland's cavalry and Gordon's infantry, having crossed the stream, attacked the enemy and were met by him in line of battle at right angles to the river. Taken in flank and reverse by our artillery, the enemy's line immediately gave way, and was soon routed and driven from the ford and bridge. The victory was complete.

Officers and men of the artillery behaved on this occasion with accustomed fidelity. Lieutenant-Colonels Nelson, Braxton and King and Major McLaughlin were engaged throughout the day in maneuvering and fighting their commands. With the exception of Lieutenant Hobson, of Kirkpatrick's battery (an officer beloved for his worth and admired for his gallantry), who was killed by a musket ball near the close of the action, and Lieutenant Southall, Acting Assistant Adjutant-General, painfully wounded, the loss in the artillery on this occasion was slight.

The artillery subsequently accompanied the army in its demonstration against Washington City; then with it recrossed the Potomac at Whites Ford on the 14th and encamped for a few days at Leesburg; thence it proceeded across the Blue Ridge at Snickers Gap, encamped near Berryville, and held the adjacent fords of the Shenandoah. King's battalion was here engaged in repelling an attempt of the enemy to cross at Castlemans Ferry. From this position the army retired before the enemy's forces, the main body moving by White Post to Newtown. Lieutenant-Colonel Nelson, however, with his two battalions, accompanied Ramseur's division to Winchester. Ramseur attacked the enemy but was unsuccessful, and Kirkpatrick's battery was lost. The guns had been advanced so close to the enemy that it was impossible to withdraw them when the infantry gave way. Colonel Nelson and his command elicited warm commendations for their gallantry in this affair.

General Early, after retiring to Strasburg and allowing the enemy to occupy Winchester and push his advance to Newtown, turned upon him a few days later and drove him in great haste through Winchester toward Martinsburg. His retreat was so rapid that little punishment could be inflicted on him. General Early subsequently pursued him across the Potomac at Williamsport, but soon returned into Virginia, and, after some time, resumed position at Strasburg. During these movements the artillery could do little more than march and counter-march.

Sheridan now commanded the enemy in the Valley. General Early moved back before his large force to Fishers Hill and took position. Meanwhile re-enforcements arrived for General Early. Cutshaw's battalion of artillery, accompanying General Anderson with Kershaw's division of infantry, and Johnson's and Shoemaker's batteries of horse artillery, accompanying General Fitzhugh Lee's division of cavalry, reached Front Royal on the 14th, and were engaged in driving off the enemy on the 15th. The enemy, after demonstrating a few days in front of Fishers Hill, retired. General Early again pursued, and driving out of Winchester the force there remaining, once more occupied the town. The artillery was but little used on this advance. General Long, being now taken ill, turned over the command of the artillery to Lieutenant-Colonel Nelson on August 19th, and Captain Kirkpatrick came into command of Nelson's battalion. The enemy still, with occasional skirmishes, in which our artillery took part, retired and reached Harpers Ferry on the 21st.

Our troops remained in the neighborhood of Charlestown till the 25th, moving thence to Shepherdstown. The army afterward encamped at Bunker Hill, and on the 31st

Milledge's and Massie's batteries accompanied Rodes' division to Martinsburg, and Massie's was engaged with the enemy's cavalry and artillery. Kirkpatrick's battery received guns in place of those lost July 20th. The army then moved to and encamped near Stephensons Depot.

September 9th Colonel Carter, having been detached from his immediate command below Richmond, arrived and took command of the artillery with General Early's army, in place of General Long, disabled by sickness. From this date to the 19th several movements occurred, with considerable skirmishing, on the line toward Martinsburg.

On the 19th was fought a sanguinary battle near Winchester. Ramseur's division, aided by Colonel Nelson's artillery, first received Sheridan's attack on the Berryville Turnpike, and well held their ground. Braxton's battalion artillery, with Rodes' and Gordon's divisions, was then hurried up and posted on Ramseur's left, and received the concentrated assault hurled against that point. The artillery did noble service. Nelson's guns held back the enemy on the right and enabled Ramseur's infantry to rally after being much broken; and Braxton's pieces, in the center, were equally effective, sweeping from the field the enemy's masses as they rushed on, pursuing Gordon's yielding line, and enabling a portion of Rodes' division to dash in and drive back their shattered column a considerable distance. Unhappily the accomplished division commander, General Rodes, here fell when his practiced skill was greatly needed. Meanwhile Breckinridge's division, with King's artillery battalion, which had held the Martinsburg Turnpike, was removed toward the right, and Generals Fitzhugh Lee and Lomax left to withstand the enemy's large force of cavalry. This, however, becoming impracticable, one of Breckinridge's brigades was detached to aid General Lee in keeping back the enemy's cavalry. At the same time the enemy's main force was moved nearer to their cavalry and advanced on Gordon's left. This necessarily gave ground to the rear, and our whole left wing swung back nearly at right angles to the original front, Braxton's guns at the salient still maintaining their hold and doing noble service. King's battalion held a hill in rear of Breckinridge's line, fronting to the left, and Breathed's guns, of the horse artillery, were operating with good effect from point to point as occasion offered. Late in the day the right was still steady, but the left was becoming more and more critical. The enemy's cavalry, in driving back Fitzhugh Lee's small force, dashed through the infantry brigade sent to his support and captured many of its men. Our left still receding, the center became more and more salient and had also to be gradually drawn back. The retrograde movement was, of course, each time more difficult and the infantry was becoming unmanageable.

"Fortunately," says Colonel Carter, "the artillery was under perfect control to the last, and maneuvered and fought with untiring courage. The guns retired from point to point, halting, unlimbering and firing, while efforts were made by general officers to rally the infantry."

Near the close of the day Colonel Carter received a painful wound from a fragment of shell, which compelled him to turn over the command of the artillery to Lieutenant-Colonel Nelson. Happily, it did not permanently disable him. For a fuller account of the battle I refer to Colonel Carter's intelligent and interesting report. It is, however, just that one or two more of his important statements be here quoted:

"The whole army will testify to the stout resistance made by the artillery in this long and exhaustive struggle. . . . It may be safely said that had the other arms of the service done their duty as faithfully as did the artillery, the army might have rested afterward on the Potomac. . . . Our loss of the day was mainly due to the enemy's immense excess in cavalry. This, by enveloping our left, forced it steadily back and ultimately compelled the abandonment of the field. For a strictly defensive battle, as this soon became, I had not artillery enough. Another artillery battalion to have held the Martinsburg Turnpike and the heights northwest of Winchester, would have prevented the fatal progress of the enemy's cavalry."

Three guns were lost on this occasion—two lent by Lieutenant-Colonel King to the cavalry, and another from the same battalion late in the evening on the retreat. Cutshaw's battalion was all the time absent with Kershaw's division on an expedition resisting a force of the enemy east of the Blue Ridge in Fauquier and Culpeper counties.

After this serious reverse of September 19th, the army retired during the night, and reaching Fishers Hill, beyond Strasburg, formed line of battle early on the 20th, King's guns on the right, Braxton's next and Nelson's still further to the left.

Owing to some misapprehension or oversight, certain precautions recommended by the acting chief of artillery in adjusting the line on the left, where the enemy's movements indicated his chief attack was to be made, were neglected and the result proved again disastrous.

On the evening of the 22d the enemy made a dash upon our extreme left, occupied by General Lomax's cavalry. It soon gave way, and the enemy swept down the line, capturing four of Nelson's, two guns from Lomax's Horse Artillery, seven of Braxton's and one of King's—fourteen in all. Yet the artillery was not in fault. Colonel Nelson affirms that they did their duty fully and efficiently, as testified by all officers and men who had opportunity to observe. All was brought off which could possibly be secured, and while retiring halted, unlimbered and checked the enemy from point to point, that the trains might be gotten safely to the rear.

MAJOR-GENERAL KERSHAW'S AND FITZHUGH LEE'S DIVISIONS MARCHING UP THE SHENANDOAH VALLEY OF VIRGINIA.
[From a sketch made by an artist representing the *London News*.]

The army still moved back on the 24th beyond New Market, retiring in line of battle, and portions of each artillery battalion, from time to time, taking position and operating effectually in keeping the enemy in check. While assisting in keeping the enemy at bay, about seven miles from New Market, Captain John L. Massie, of Nelson's battalion—a gentleman of fine character, superior powers and high culture, a soldier of tried merit and a battery commander unsurpassed in this service—received a mortal wound. Lieutenant N. B. Cooke, a promising young officer of Braxton's battalion, was also wounded.

The army then deflected toward Port Republic, and arriving at Browns Gap on the 25th encamped.

Here it was joined on the 26th by Kershaw's division and Cutshaw's artillery battalion. On the same day Colonel Carter again reported for duty and resumed command of the artillery. Carpenter's and Hardwick's batteries were engaged in skirmishes near Port Republic on the 26th and 27th.

On the 28th, the army was again put in motion, and marched by Waynesboro to Mount Sidney, and thence slowly down the Valley, the advance reaching Hupps Hill, below Strasburg, on October 13th. Here an affair occurred between a force of the enemy and Gardner's division, with Conner's brigade, of Kershaw's division, attended by Fry's battery. In this affair the enemy was repulsed with considerable loss. Lieutenant S. S. France, acting adjutant to Colonel Carter, was on this occasion severely wounded.

Meanwhile the cavalry marched by the back road, and on the morning of the 8th encountered the enemy. Thomson's and Johnston's guns were used with good effect to the last. Their supports giving way at a critical moment the six guns were lost. As on other occasions the artillery officers and men faithfully did their duty.

On the next day (October 9th) Shoemaker's battery and a section of Thomsons,' accompanying Lomax's cavalry as a guard to the wagon train on the Valley Turnpike near Woodstock, were greatly exposed by the irresolution of the cavalry, but were all, except one of Thomson's guns, saved by the extraordinary gallantry of artillery officers and men. On this occasion, Captain Carpenter, of Braxton's battalion, was particularly distinguished. Observing the hazard occasioned by the failure of the cavalry, he pressed forward as a volunteer, and by judicious intrepidity succeeded in rallying a few of the fugitives, so as again and again to keep the enemy at bay. He thus contributed materially toward rescuing the guns and saving the trains. I regret to add that, in this gallant service, he received a painful wound, resulting in the loss of an arm.

On October 19th, at a very early hour, the artillery was moved forward with the main body of the army to attack the enemy beyond Cedar Creek, and by 10 A. M. remarkable results had been achieved. Two corps of the enemy had been surprised and routed, their camps captured, and they driven from the field. The Sixth Corps had been dislodged from its strong position near Middletown chiefly by the fire of our artillery, and the whole hostile army driven three or four miles. Twenty-four pieces of artillery, by the enemy's admission (seventeen are known to us), had been captured, and some fifteen hundred prisoners. There was a lull from 10 to 3:30 P. M., our line of battle ranging across the turnpike at right angles north of Middletown, Wofford's brigade on the right; then Wharton; then Pegram, crossing the turnpike; then Ramseur, considerably in advance; then Kershaw; then Gordon; then an interval of about a mile; and then Rosser's cavalry, which, with Thomson's battery, had joined General Early in his last advance after October 1st.

About 3 P. M. six of Cutshaw's pieces and two of Jones' were posted to guard the interval between Gordon and Rosser. On the enemy's attack at 3:30, Gordon's line gave way, and the guns were retired by order of General Gordon. The guns operating with the other divisions held their positions until the left gave way. They were then posted on commanding ground, one to two hundred yards in rear, and, aided by a small infantry force, held the enemy in check for more than an hour and until ammunition failed. Other guns were posted on the heights south of Cedar Creek, to cover the withdrawal of the infantry and artillery from the field.

An important victory had thus been strangely reversed, but everything was brought safely across Cedar Creek. Night had come and no further danger was apprehended. But a more serious disaster now occurred. The artillery being on the march in column toward Hupps Hill, a small body of the enemy's cavalry charged the train on the right flank, and by their bugle blasts, cheers, horses' feet clattering and pistol shots in the darkness, occasioned an incurable panic in the infantry, already seriously disorganized. The artillery officers and men appealed in vain for muskets, with which they would have stoutly and effectually defended their guns. They could not secure them, and the result was a large capture by the enemy, as elating to them as it was disgraceful to us. All the guns taken from the enemy in the morning and twenty-three of our own fell into their hands. "One hundred men in an organized state, with muskets," Colonel Carter thinks, "could have saved the train." As it was, the loss would not have been so great but for a very narrow passage south of Strasburg, between the river on one side and the bluff on the other, and had not the road been blocked with ordnance wagons, ambulances and fourteen hundred prisoners, and the difficulty of proceeding been increased by the breaking of the bridge near Strasburg. This instance suggests the desirableness of having a certain proportion of artillery men ever armed with carbine, at least, when serving in campaigns like this of the Valley.

It is due to these admirable soldiers to state that on this occasion, as previously, they behaved with exemplary fidelity. Officers and men did their whole duty, and throughout remained uninfluenced by the general panic. After this misfortune the army retreated to New Market, in the neighborhood of which it remained with occasional advances and skirmishes with the enemy, in which the artillery slightly participated, until the last of November, when it withdrew to the neighborhood of Harrisonburg, and active operations having ceased for the season, the artillery subsequently went into winter quarters, not far from Staunton.

In the whole eventful campaign of 1864 the artillery of the Army of Northern Virginia bore, it will be perceived, a distinguished part, and in every portion of the widely extended field of operation rendered signal service. In common with other arms, in so great a contest against vastly preponderating numbers, it again and again suffered severely, having many valuable officers and men killed and wounded and horses destroyed, and in two or three unfortunate affairs an unusual number of guns captured, making our loss in guns considerable on the whole, though in several instances valuable captures were made from the enemy. But it has everywhere, and at all times, proved reliable, how great soever the emergency. In the wildest fury of battle, under ceaseless harassment and exposure from sharpshooters and shelling on the lines; on the toilsome march, amid all the hardships of the trenches, through summer, fall and winter, and when steadily breasting the tide of reverse against friends unnerved or overpowered, and foes flushed with triumph, the brave officers and men of this branch of our army have, almost without exception, exemplified the very highest virtues of Christian soldiers battling for their faith, their honor and their homes.

EARTHWORKS AND ABATIS IN FRONT OF RICHMOND, VA.

To mention all who have thus admirably done their duty would be well nigh to repeat the rolls of our battalions and companies. I can only designate those chief commanders whose position has necessarily rendered their services most conspicuous, and refer to their reports and those of their sub-commanders for fuller details. General Long, until disabled by sickness, managed his command (artillery, Second Corps) with characteristic judgment and vigor; and Colonel Carter, who then succeeded him, earned, as usual, high encomiums for the care, sagacity and skill, as well as boldness, with which he handled the command, as also did Lieutenant-Colonel Nelson during the brief but important intervals in which the command devolved upon him. General Alexander, ever active, full of resources, energetic and enterprising, conducted his command (artillery, First Corps) at all times with skill and success, and in the interval of his absence from a disabling wound, his place was well supplied on one part of his line by Colonel Cabell, on another by Lieutenant-Colonel Huger. Colonel Walker, zealous, bold and vigorous, directed his force (artillery, Third Corps) with efficiency throughout the campaign, and was aided in his responsible charge by the judicious co-operation of Colonel Cutts; and Colonel Jones, first as chief of artillery of General Beauregard's command, and subsequently of General Anderson's corps, earned high commendation by diligent, intelligent and successful attention to his arduous trust on a portion of the line most exposed and harassed during all the latter months of the campaign.

The officers speak in high terms of their subordinates and of the men in their respective commands, and describe instances more than a few of extraordinary good conduct and admirable achievements. Their reports and those of battalion commanders are herewith submitted.

Of the several members of my own staff—Captain Dudley D. Pendleton, assistant adjutant-general; Lieutenant George W. Peterkin and Acting Lieutenant Charles Hatcher, aids-de-camp; Captain John Esten Cooke and Lieutenant E. P. Dandridge, assistant inspectors-general; Major John G. Barnwell, ordnance officer; Dr. John Graham, surgeon, and Major John Page, quartermaster—it is just I should say that they have uniformly discharged their duties with faithful alacrity and to my entire satisfaction.

In conclusion, I am enabled to report that our artillery remains, at the close of this arduous campaign, in a condition of most encouraging efficiency, and that with reasonable effort toward supplying it with a few guns to replace some lost in unfortunate affairs that have been described, and with horses to re-establish a number of teams disabled in action or worn down by hard service, it will be in full strength for the campaign of the ensuing spring. It may be confidently relied upon to accomplish, by the Divine blessing, during the next season, as it has so well done throughout the last, its entire share in the defense of our country.

W. N. PENDLETON,

Brigadier-General and Chief of Artillery, Army of Northern Virginia.

A COLUMN of infantry was one day marching along a dusty road under a broiling sun. Close by, under some trees, was discovered a cluster of sleek commissaries seated at dinner. A tall, raw-boned and dust-begrimed North Carolinian went up to the fence and, putting his chin upon it, stared long and earnestly at the tempting table. At last, bursting with envy, he yelled out: "I say, misters, did any of ye ever hearn tell of the battle of Chancellorsville."

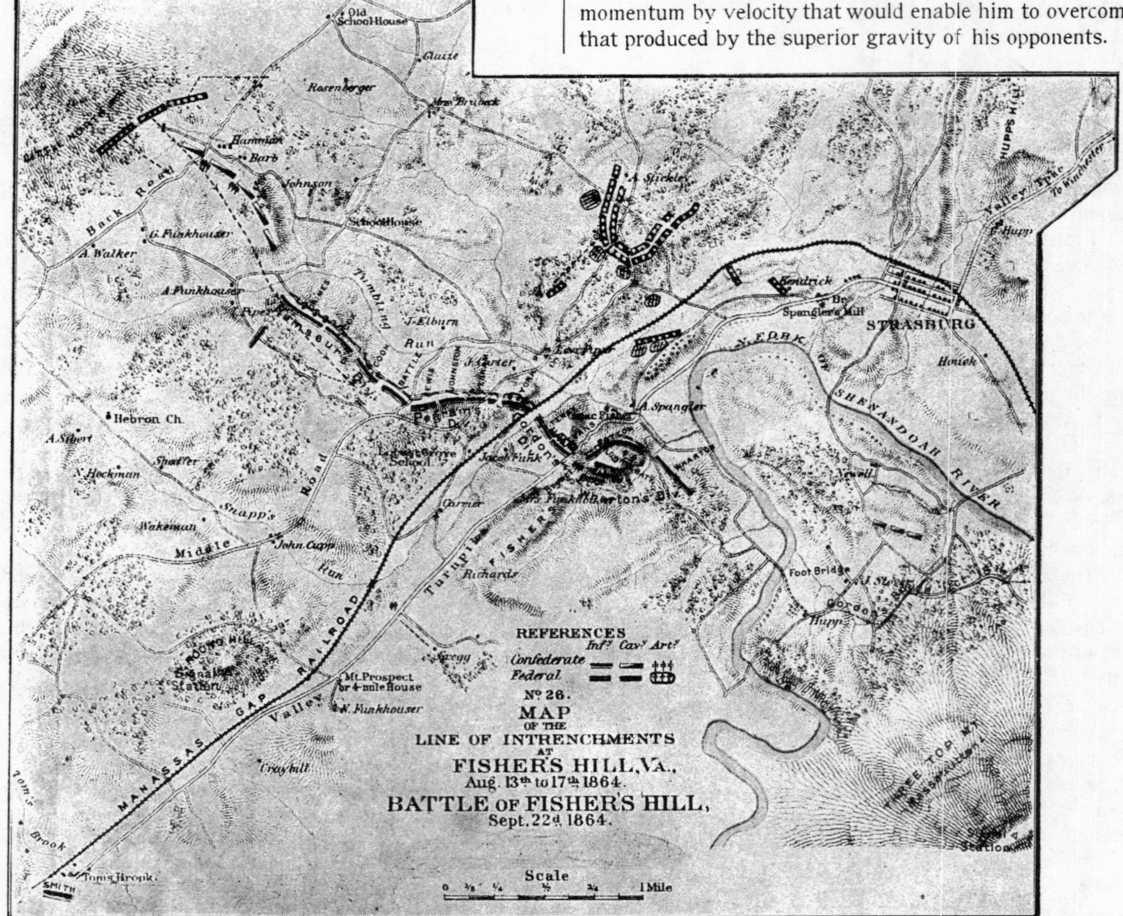

EARLY'S VALLEY CAMPAIGN,

JUNE 13 TO OCTOBER 30, 1864.

BY

BRIG.-GEN. A. L. LONG,
Chief of Artillery, Second Corps, Army of Northern Virginia.

IN compliance with his instructions, General Early, on the 13th of June withdrew his corps, consisting of about eight thousand infantry and twenty-four pieces of artillery, from the Army of Northern Virginia, and proceeded toward Staunton. The artillery was subsequently increased to forty guns, and his forces were further augmented by the addition of about fifteen hundred cavalry and two thousand infantry. At Charlottesville Early received intelligence of the rapid advance of Hunter upon Lynchburg with a force of twenty thousand men.

Promptly shifting his objective point, and availing himself of the Orange & Alexandria Railroad, he moved with such rapidity that he reached Lynchburg in time to rescue it. At that time the only force at hand for the defense of Lynchburg was the division of Breckinridge, less than two thousand strong, and a few hundred home-guards, composed of old men and boys, whose age exempted them from active service. Hunter, finding himself unexpectedly confronted by Early, relinquished his intended attack upon the city and sought safety in a rapid night retreat.

The next day Early instituted a vigorous pursuit, which continued with uninterrupted pertinacity until Hunter was overtaken in the neighborhood of Salem, a small town on the Virginia & Tennessee Railroad, where he was defeated and forced to a hazardous and disorganizing retreat through the mountains to the Ohio River.

Having at a single blow liberated the Valley, Early determined upon an immediate invasion of Maryland and a bold advance on Washington City. As his instructions were discretionary, he was at liberty to adopt that course, which, at the time, was, both in a political and military point of view, the best plan of action that could have been assumed.

The defense of Richmond being the settled policy of the Confederate Government, General Lee had on two occasions assumed the offensive in order to relieve that place from the paralyzing influence of the Federals.

The invasion of Maryland in 1862 and the campaign into Pennsylvania the following year had relieved Richmond of the presence of the enemy for more than a year, but the tide of war had again returned, and that celebrated city was gradually yielding to the powerful embrace of her besiegers, which could only be loosened by a strong diversion in her favor.

This, Early undertook with the force at his command, after the disposal of Hunter's army. By uniting with his own corps the division of Breckinridge and Ransom's cavalry, Early found himself at the head of about twelve thousand men. Though he knew this force to be inadequate to the magnitude of the work in hand, nevertheless he determined to overcome his want of numbers by the rapidity of his movements, thus hoping to acquire a momentum by velocity that would enable him to overcome that produced by the superior gravity of his opponents.

After the dispersion of Hunter's forces, one day in preparation sufficed Early for the commencement of his advance upon Maryland. His route through the Valley extended over a distance of two hundred miles or more, but the road was good, and although the country had been laid waste a short time before by Hunter, the genial season and fertile soil had already reproduced abundant subsistence for the horses and mules of the expedition; but the greater part of the supplies for the troops were necessarily drawn from Lynchburg and Richmond. To prevent delay, therefore, orders were sent to these places directing supplies to be forwarded to convenient points along the line of march. Staunton was reached on the 27th of June. This was the most suitable point at which to supply the army, and there Early made a short halt to make the necessary arrangements to insure the uninterrupted continuance of his march. In this he was ably assisted by Colonel Allan, Majors Harman, Rogers, Hawks and other members of his staff. The beautiful Valley of Virginia everywhere gave evidence of the ravages of war. Throughout the march down the Valley the unsparing hand of Hunter was proclaimed by the charred ruins of the once beautiful and happy homes. At Lexington the cracked and tottering walls of the Virginia Military Institute, the pride of Virginia and the *Alma Mater* of many of the distinguished sons of the South, were seen, and near them appeared the blackened remains of the private residence of Governor Letcher.

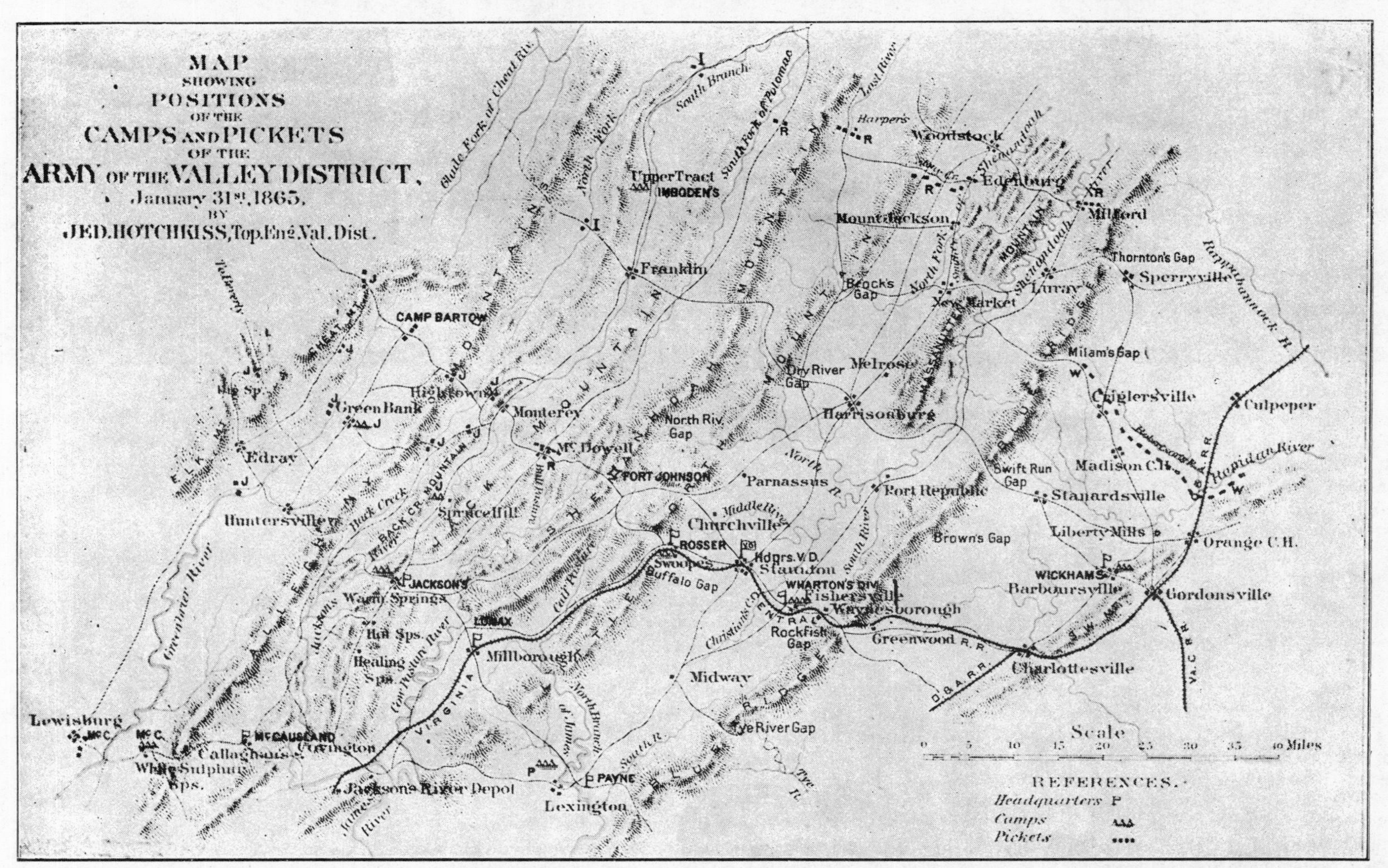

When Early reached Winchester he learned that there was a Federal force at Harpers Ferry and another at Martinsburg, which it was necessary to dislodge before attempting the passage of the Potomac; and this was effected by the 4th of July without much opposition, the Federals having withdrawn without waiting an attack. The way being now clear, the passage of the Potomac was made on the 5th at Shepherdstown, and the army advanced to Sharpsburg.

Since the defeat of Hunter the advance of Early had been so rapid that his design to invade Maryland had not reached the Federal authorities in time to oppose his passage of the Potomac. But his entrance into Maryland being now known, it had produced great consternation as far as Baltimore and Washington. The boldness of this movement caused Early's forces to be greatly exaggerated, and rumor soon magnified it to four or five times its real strength.

The invasion was considered of such magnitude that the cities of Washington and Baltimore were thought to be in such imminent danger, that the greatest alacrity was instituted in every direction to collect troops for the defense of those places.

The object of General Early being simply a diversion in favor of the operations about Richmond, he remained a day or two at Sharpsburg, in order that the impression created by his invasion might have time to produce its full effect before he exposed his weakness by a further advance. At this time all the troops in the vicinity of Washington had been collected, besides which a large number of quartermaster's employes had been improvised as soldiers, thus making the force at hand exceed twenty thousand men, while two corps from the army besieging Richmond and a part of another corps from North Carolina, intended to re-enforce that army, had been detached and put in rapid motion for the defense of the Capital.

In the face or these odds Early continued his advance into Maryland. At Frederick he found General Wallace, with about ten thousand men, in position to oppose the passage of the Monocacy. Immediate preparations were made to dislodge Wallace and effect a crossing of that stream. Rodes was thrown forward on the Baltimore, and Ramseur on the Washington City Road, while Gordon and Breckinridge, with a portion of Ransom's cavalry inclining to the right, moved to the fords a mile or two below the Railroad Bridge. At the same time the heights contiguous to the river were crowned by Long's artillery (consisting of the guns of Nelson, Braxton, King and McLaughlin), to cover the movement of the other troops.

When the troops had gained their position, the crossing at the lower fords was promptly accomplished, and Breckinridge and Gordon, quickly forming their line of battle, advanced rapidly up the stream toward the Federal position and, after a short but spirited conflict, defeated Wallace, whose army soon fell into a panic and fled in wild confusion, spreading dismay for miles in every direction by the terrible accounts they gave of the tremendous force Early was leading through the country. The route being now open, Early proceeded by rapid marches to within cannon-shot of the walls of Washington. Since his entrance into Maryland his force had been exaggerated by the inhabitants and the soldiery he had met, until in their terrified imagination it was magnified to thirty or forty thousand men.

On his arrival before the Federal Capital, the exaggerated rumor of his strength having preceded him, its occupants were variously affected. The Federal authorities and all of their adherents were in a state of consternation, while the Southern sympathizers were full of exultation—for at the time it was thought by many he would take the city. Had he had twenty or thirty thousand men he would have done so, with a prospect of holding it, and giving a new turn to subsequent military operations. But Early was too prudent and sagacious to attempt an enterprise with a force of eight thousand men which, if successful, could only be of temporary benefit. He was therefore content to remain in observation long enough to give his movement full time to produce its greatest effect, and then withdrew in the face of a large army and recrossed the Potomac without molestation.

This campaign is remarkable for having accomplished more in proportion to the force employed, and for having given less public satisfaction, than any other campaign of the war. The want of appreciation of it is entirely due to the erroneous opinion that the city of Washington should have been taken; but this may be passed over as one of the absurdities of public criticism on the conduct of the war.

By glancing at the operations of Early from the 13th of June to the last of July, it will be seen that in less than two months he had marched more than four hundred miles, and, with a force not exceeding twelve thousand men, had not only defeated but entirely dispersed two Federal armies of an aggregate strength of more than double his own; had invaded Maryland, and, by his bold and rapid movement upon Washington, had created an important diversion in favor of General Lee in the defense of Richmond, and had re-entered Virginia with a loss of less than three thousand men. After remaining a short time in the neighborhood of Leesburg he returned to the Valley by way of Snickers Gap, and about the 17th of July occupied the neighborhood of Berryville.

Early had no sooner established himself at Berryville than a considerable force of the enemy appeared on the Shenandoah, near Castlemans Ferry, and partially effected a crossing, but were promptly driven back with heavy loss, after which they retired to the neighborhood of Harpers Ferry.

About the same time a large force, under General Averill, was reported to be advancing from Martinsburg to Winchester. Being unwilling to receive an attack in an unfavorable position, Early sent Ramseur, with a division and two batteries of artillery, to Winchester, to retard Averill, while he withdrew with the main body of the army and supply trains, by way of White Post and Newtown, to Strasburg.

Ramseur, having encountered the enemy a few miles east of Winchester, was defeated, with a loss of four pieces of artillery, and forced to retire to Newtown, where he rejoined Early.

Averill, being arrested in his pursuit of Ramseur near Newtown, fell back to Kernstown, where he was soon joined by General Crook with the forces from Harpers Ferry.

From Newtown, Early continued his march to Strasburg without interruption. On the 23d he was informed of the junction of Crook and Averill, and of their occupation of Kernstown; thereupon it was determined to attack them without delay. The security of the trains having been properly provided for, the army was put in motion early on the morning of the 24th toward the enemy.

About noon a position was gained from which it was observed that the enemy was in possession of the identical ground which had been occupied by Shields when encountered by Stonewall Jackson in March, 1862. The memory of that battle evidently did much to inspire the troops to deeds of valor in the approaching conflict.

Early quickly made his disposition for battle. The divisions of Breckinridge and Rodes were thrown to the right of the turnpike, and those of Ramseur and Gordon were deployed to its left, the artillery being disposed of so as to cover the advance of the infantry, while the cavalry received instructions to close behind the enemy as soon as defeated.

Perceiving that the left flank of the enemy was exposed, Breckinridge, under cover of a wooded hill, gained a position from which he bore down upon it, and in gallant style doubled it upon the center. This success was so vigorously followed up by the other troops, that the Federals gave way at all points, and were soon in rapid retreat, which was accelerated by a vigorous pursuit. In this battle the losses on the part of the Confederates were insignificant, while those of the Federals in killed, wounded and prisoners were considerable. While on the retreat a large number of their wagons and a considerable quantity of their stores were destroyed to prevent capture.

Finding that the enemy had again sought safety behind his defenses, Early determined to re-enter Maryland, for the double purpose of covering a retaliatory expedition into Pennsylvania, and to keep alive the diversion which had already been made in favor of the defense of Richmond. Therefore, about the 6th of August, he crossed the Potomac in two columns—the one at Williamsport and the other at Shepherdstown—and took a position between Sharpsburg and Hagerstown.

BATTLE OF FISHERS HILL, VA., SEPTEMBER 23, 1864. THE CHARGE OF THE CAVALRY.

This occupation of Maryland was destined to be of short duration, for since Early's audacity had caused his strength to be so greatly magnified, and the importance of his operations so exaggerated, Grant had considered it necessary to largely increase the Army of the Shenandoah, and to supersede Hunter, whose incapacity had long been obvious, by Phil. Sheridan, one of the most energetic of his lieutenants. Being aware of the great increase of force prepared to be brought against him, Early recrossed the Potomac and returned up the Valley, being slowly followed by Sheridan, who had now taken command of the Middle Department.

On reaching Fishers Hill, a position three miles west of Strasburg, Early halted and offered battle, which Sheridan made a show of accepting until the morning of the 17th, when he was discovered to be retreating toward Winchester. He was immediately pursued by Early, and being overtaken near Kernstown a spirited skirmish ensued while he continued to retire. Night coming on, the combatants separated, Early bivouacking in the neighborhood of Winchester, while Sheridan crossed the Opequon.

About this time Lieutenant-General Anderson joined Early with one division of infantry and a division of cavalry, thus increasing his force to about twelve thousand men, while that of Sheridan exceeded forty thousand. Notwithstanding the great disparity of numbers, the campaign was characterized by a series of skillful movements and brilliant skirmishes, which resulted, on the 19th of September, in the battle of Winchester, which had doubtless been hastened to a conclusion by the departure of Anderson from the Valley, on the 15th, with Kershaw's division for Richmond. Anderson had no sooner turned his back on the mountains, than Sheridan threw his whole force against Early at Winchester and defeated him, not so much by force of numbers as by one of those chances of war which sometimes beset the ablest commander; for, after having gallantly contested the field and firmly maintained their position until near the close of the day, a portion of his troops was seized with a panic, which rapidly spread until the greater part of the infantry and cavalry fell into confusion, and troops who had never before turned their backs upon the enemy retired in disorder from the field. The artillery alone remained firm, and covered with distinguished gallantry the retreat of the other troops, until a place of safety was gained and order restored, and then retired fighting, step by step, until it extricated itself from overwhelming numbers, leaving heaps of dead to testify to its matchless conduct and power. Sheridan's forces were so shattered that he could not immediately avail himself of the success he had gained, and Early was permitted an uninterrupted retreat to Fishers Hill.

Notwithstanding his force had been considerably weakened by its late disaster, Early determined to maintain his position on Fishers Hill. He could not realize that every man was not as stout-hearted as himself, nor that the troops he had so often led to victory were not invincible; and, besides his reluctance to abandon the rich and beautiful Valley, there were other and stronger reasons for his decision. It was evident that, if left unopposed in the Valley, Sheridan would immediately concert a plan of co-operation with Grant, either by advancing directly upon Richmond or by operating on its lines of communication with a powerful cavalry until a junction was formed with him below Petersburg; in which case the important diversion in favor of Lee would have come to naught. Therefore the object of detaining Sheridan with his formidable force in the Valley sufficiently warranted Early, on the soundest military principles, in his determination to oppose him at all hazard.

The defiant attitude assumed by him was the most effective he could have adopted for accomplishing his object, and it created a deception as to his strength that made his opponent cautious, but which was quickly dissipated by a collision. His force at this time was less than seven thousand men, while that of Sheridan was greater by at least four to one.

Sheridan's forces, having sufficiently recovered from the effect of the battle, pursued Early, and on the 22d attacked him in his position on Fishers Hill. The thin Confederate ranks could offer but feeble resistance to the overwhelming force brought against them, and the conflict was consequently of short duration; and, owing to the extent and difficulty of the position, the Confederates sustained considerable loss before they could extricate themselves.

Early then retired up the Valley to a position above Harrisonburg, while Sheridan pursued as far as New Market. Both armies then remained inactive for some days, in order to rest and reorganize their forces.

About the first of October, Sheridan retraced his steps down the Valley to the neighborhood of Middletown, where he took up a position on an elevated plateau behind Cedar Creek. Early, perceiving that his adversary had retired, pursued him to the neighborhood of Strasburg, where he took up a position from which he might be able to attack with advantage. Sheridan had unwittingly assumed a

BRIGADIER-GENERAL A. L. LONG, OF VIRGINIA.
[From a tintype taken in 1864.]

position that gave his adversary admirable advantages and opportunity to execute a surprise.

Early intrusted a considerable force to General Gordon for that purpose. Having made himself familiar with the work in hand, Gordon, on the night of October 18th, proceeded to its execution. Crossing Cedar Creek sufficiently below the Federal pickets to avoid observation, he cautiously proceeded in the direction of the Federal encampments without accident or discovery. A favorable point for the accomplishment of his plans was gained just before daybreak on the 19th. The camp was reached, and in the midst of quiet sleep and peaceful dreams the war-cry and the ringing peals of musketry arose to wake the slumbering warriors and call them, affrighted, to their arms. The drums and bugles loudly summoned the soldier to his colors, but alas! there was no ear for those familiar sounds! The crack of the rifle and the shouts of battle were upon the breeze, and no other sounds were heeded by the flying multitude.

Gordon's surprise had been complete, and when the dawn appeared long lines of fugitives were seen rushing madly toward Winchester. Such a rout had not been seen since the famous battle of Bull Run.

The Federals left artillery, baggage, small arms, camp equipage, clothing, knapsacks, haversacks, canteens, in fact everything, in their panic. The whole camp was filled with valuable booty, which in the end proved a dangerous temptation to the Confederates—many of whom, instead of following up their brilliant success, left their ranks for plunder.

If an apology for such conduct were ever admissible, it was so on this occasion—the troops having been so long unaccustomed to the commonest comfort while making long and fatiguing marches and battling against large odds, and being now broken down, ragged and hungry, they would have been superhuman had they resisted the tempting stores that lay scattered on every hand. Our censure of this conduct must be mingled with compassion, when we remember that instances arise when the demand of nature is irresistible.

The Federals, finding that they were not pursued when they reached the neighborhood of Middletown, their spirits began to revive, and the habit of discipline and order assumed its sway, and the shapeless mass of the morning regained the appearance of an army.

Sheridan, having been absent, met his fugitive army a little below Newtown. Order having been restored, he reformed his troops, and, facing them about, returned to the scene of their late disaster. The Confederates being unprepared for an attack, were quickly defeated and forced to retire to Fishers Hill; from there to New Market, where Early maintained a bold front for several weeks. By this return of fortune Sheridan not only recovered all that had been lost in the morning, but acquired considerable captures from the Confederates.

The Confederates then retired to the neighborhood of Staunton, and further operations were suspended on account of the inclemency of the season.

Sheridan then occupied the lower Valley, where he employed himself in completing the work of destruction so bravely begun by Hunter, in which he seemed to vie with Alaric. His work of devastation was so complete that he exultingly reported to his superior that a "crow in traversing the Valley would be obliged to carry his rations." Before the spring was open, Sheridan was in motion with a cavalry, or rather mounted infantry force, nine thousand strong, his objective point being Staunton. The force of Early having been greatly reduced, was entirely inadequate for an effective resistance. Staunton was, therefore, evacuated, and Early retired to Waynesboro. His entire force now only consisted of Wharton's division of infantry, six pieces of artillery and a small body of cavalry, making in all about eighteen hundred men. With this force he took a position to protect an important railroad bridge over the south branch of the Shenandoah, and, at the same time, to cover Rockfish Gap, a pass connecting the Valley with Eastern Virginia. This pass was doubly important, as it gave a passage both to the Charlottesville Turnpike and Central Railroad.

As Sheridan was without artillery, and the ground being unfit for the operation of cavalry, Early could have easily maintained his position with reliable troops; but, contrary to his belief, there was considerable disaffection in Wharton's division. Therefore, without his knowledge his little army harbored the elements of defeat, for at the first show of an attack the malcontents threw down their arms, and, almost without opposition, Sheridan carried the position, compelling Early, with his faithful few, to seek safety in retreat. A number of these, however, were captured before they could make their escape.

Sheridan, having now removed all opposition, passed through Rockfish Gap into Eastern Virginia, traversed the interior of the State, and formed a junction with Grant almost without interruption.

On reaching Gordonsville, Early collected a handful of men and threw himself upon the flank and rear of Sheridan, but his force was too small to make any impression. He was only induced to make this effort by his extreme reluctance to witness an unopposed march of an enemy through his country.

It has been said that Early, at the head of his faithful band, hovering like an eagle about the columns of Sheridan, displayed more heroic valor than when at the head of his victorious army in Maryland.

Among some of those whom superior rank has not brought into special notice are Colonels Carter (acting chief of artillery), Nelson, King and Braxton; Majors Kirkpatrick and McLaughlin, of the artillery, distinguished at Winchester; Captains Massie, killed, and Carpenter, wounded; Colonel Pendleton, adjutant-general of Early's corps, killed at Fishers Hill while gallantly rallying the fugitives; Colonel Samuel Moore, inspector-general of Early's corps; Colonel Green Peyton, adjutant-general Rodes' division; Captain Lewis Randolph, of Rodes' staff; Colonel R. W. Hunter, adjutant-general Gordon's division; Colonel Carr, inspector-general Breckinridge's division, captured near Cross Keys, Valley of Virginia; Major Breathed, artillery; Major S. V. Southall, adjutant-general of artillery, wounded at Monocacy; Captain Percy, inspector of artillery; Major Moorman, of artillery; Lieutenant Long, engineer corps, killed at Cedar Creek while rallying fugitives; Lieutenant Hobson, of artillery, killed at Monocacy; Dr. McGuire, medical director of Early's corps; Dr. Strath, chief surgeon of artillery; Major Turner, chief quartermaster of artillery; Major Armstrong, chief commissary of artillery. Besides these, there are many others, whose names are not in my possession, worthy of the highest distinction.

In operations of the character above described, long lists of casualties may naturally be expected, in which the names of the bravest, noblest and truest are sure to be found. While it is impossible for me to make separate mention of these, memory dictates the names of Rodes and Ramseur. From Richmond to the memorable campaign of the Wilderness they bore a conspicuous part, and their names rose high on the roll of fame. Rodes fell in the battle of Winchester, at the head of his splendid division, and Ramseur was mortally wounded at Cedar Creek in his heroic attempt to retrieve the fortune of the day. Their fall was a noble sacrifice to the cause for which they fought, and their memory will ever remain green in the hearts of their countrymen.

* * * * * * *

A. L. LONG.

BATTLE OF CEDAR CREEK, VA.,

OCTOBER 19, 1864.

BY

LIEUT.-GEN. JUBAL A. EARLY.

NEW MARKET, October 21, 1864.

HAVING received information that the enemy was continuing to repair the Manassas Road, and that he had moved back from Fishers Hill, I moved on the 12th toward Strasburg, for the purpose of endeavoring to thwart his purposes if he should contemplate moving across the bridge or sending troops to Grant.

On the 13th, I made a reconnoissance in force beyond Strasburg, and found the enemy on the north bank of Cedar Creek and on both sides of the pike. This was too strong a position to attack in front. I therefore encamped my force at Fishers Hill and waited to see whether the enemy would move; but he commenced fortifying.

On the night of the 16th, Rosser, with two brigades of cavalry and a brigade of infantry mounted behind his men, was sent around the left to surprise what was reported by his scouts to be the camp of a division of cavalry. He found, however, that the camp had been moved, and he only found a picket, which he captured. As I could not remain at Fishers Hill for want of forage, I then determined to try and get around one of the enemy's flanks and surprise him in camp. After ascertaining the location of the enemy's camps from observations from a signal station on Massanutten Mountain, I determined to move around the left flank of the enemy. I selected this flank from information furnished by General Gordon and Captain Hotchkiss, who had gone to the signal station, and because the greater part of the enemy's cavalry was on his right, and Rosser's attempt had caused that flank to be closely picketed. To get around the enemy's left was a very difficult undertaking, however, as the river had to be crossed twice, and between the mountain and river, where the troops had to pass to the lower ford, there was only a rugged pathway. I thought, however, the chances of success would be greater from the fact that the enemy would not expect a move in that direction on account of the difficulties attending it and the great strength of their position on that flank. The movement was accordingly begun on the night of the 18th, just after dark, Gordon's, Ramseur's and Pegram's divisions being sent across the river and around the foot of the mountain, all under the command of General Gordon, and late at night I moved with Kershaw's division through Strasburg toward a ford on Cedar Creek just above its mouth, and Wharton was moved on the pike toward the enemy's front, in which road the artillery was also moved. The arrangement was for Sixth Corps, which was on the enemy's extreme right of his infantry, was not surprised in camp, because Rosser had commenced the attack on that flank about the same time as the attack on the other, and the firing on the left gave that corps sufficient time to form and move out of camp and it was found posted on a ridge on the west of the pike and parallel to it, and this corps offered considerable resistance. The artillery was brought up and opened on it, when it fell back to the north of Middletown and made a stand on a commanding ridge running across the pike.

LIEUT.-GEN. JUBAL A. EARLY, OF VIRGINIA.

In the meantime the enemy's cavalry was threatening our right flank and rear, and the country being perfectly open, and having on that flank only Lomax's old brigade, numbering about three hundred men, it became necessary to make dispositions to prevent a cavalry charge, and a portion of the troops were moved to the right for that purpose, and word was sent to Gordon, who had got on the left with his division, and Kershaw, who was there also, to swing round and advance with their divisions, but they stated in reply that a heavy force of cavalry had got in their front, and that their ranks were so depleted by the number of men who had stopped in the camps to plunder that they could not advance them.

Rosser also sent word that when he attacked the cavalry he encountered a part of the Sixth Corps supporting it; that a very heavy force of cavalry had massed in his front, and that it was too strong for him, and that he would have to fall back. I sent word to him to get some position that he could hold, and the cavalry in front of Kershaw and

BATTLE OF WINCHESTER (OPEQUON), VA., SEPTEMBER 19, 1864.

ONE day during the war while General McLaws was riding down his picket line, on a tour of observation, he encountered a genuine son of the Old Pine Tree State on duty, who had taken his gun apart with the intention of giving it a thorough cleaning. The general halted in front of him, when the following conversation ensued: "Look here, my man, are you not a sentinel on duty?" "Well, y-a-a-s, a bit of a one!" "Don't you know it is wrong to take your gun apart while on duty?" "Well, now, who the d—l are you?" The general saw his chance, and, with a sly twinkle of the eye, replied: "I'm a bit of a general." "Well, gineral, you must excuse me. You see, thar is so many d—n fools ridin' 'round here, a feller can't tell who's gineral and who ain't. If you will jist wait till I git Betsy Jane fixed I will give you a bit of a s'lute." The general smiled and rode on, firmly convinced that the sentinel would prove equal to any emergency.

Gordon to come around in the rear, for Kershaw to attack the left flank, and for Gordon [Wharton?] to advance in front, supporting the artillery, which was to open on the enemy when he should turn on Gordon or Kershaw, and the attack was to begin at 5 A. M., on the 19th. Rosser was sent to the left to occupy the enemy's cavalry; and Lomax, who had been sent down the Luray Valley, was ordered to pass Front Royal, cross the river and move across toward the Valley Pike.

Punctually at 5, Kershaw reached the enemy's left work, attacked and carried it without the least difficulty; and very shortly afterward Gordon attacked in the rear, and they swept everything before them, routing the Eighth and Nineteenth corps completely, getting possession of their camp and capturing eighteen pieces of artillery and about thirteen hundred prisoners. They moved across the pike toward the camp of the Sixth Corps, and Wharton was crossed over, the artillery following him; but the Gordon having moved toward Rosser, they were moved forward, and a line was formed north of Middletown facing the enemy. The cavalry on the right made several efforts to charge that flank, but was driven back.

So many of our men had stopped in the camp to plunder (in which I am sorry to say that officers participated), the country was so open, and the enemy's cavalry so strong, that I did not deem it prudent to press further, especially as Lomax had not come up. I determined, therefore, to content myself with trying to hold the advantages I had gained until all my troops had come up and the captured property was secured. If I had had but one division of fresh troops I could have made the victory complete and beyond all danger of a reverse. We continued to hold our position until late in the afternoon, when the enemy commenced advancing, and was driven back on the right center by Ramseur, but Gordon's division, on the left, subsequently gave way, and Kershaw's and Ramseur's did so also, when they found Gordon's giving way, not because there was any pressure on them, but from an insane idea of being flanked. Some of them, however, were rallied, and with the help of the artillery the army was checked for some time, but a great number of the men could not be stopped, but continued to go to the rear. The enemy again made a demonstration, and General Ramseur, who was acting with great gallantry, was wounded, and the left again gave way, and then the whole command, falling back in such a panic that I had to order Pegram's and Wharton's commands, which were very small and on the right, to fall back, and most of them took the panic also. I found it impossible to rally the troops. They would not listen to entreaties, threats, or appeals of any kind. A terror of the enemy's cavalry had seized them, and there was no holding them. They left the field in the greatest confusion. All the captured artillery had been carried across Cedar Creek, and a large number of captured wagons and ambulances, and we succeeded in crossing our own artillery over, and everything would have been saved if we could have rallied five hundred men, but the panic was so great that nothing could be done. A small body of the enemy's cavalry dashed across Cedar Creek above the bridge, and got into the train and artillery running back on the pike, and passed through our men to this side of Strasburg, tore up a bridge, and then succeeded in capturing the greater part of the artillery and a number of ordnance and medical wagons and ambulances. The men scattered on the sides; and the rout was as thorough and disgraceful as ever happened to our army.

After the utter failure of all my attempts to rally the men, I went to Fishers Hill with the hope of rallying the troops there and forming them in the trenches, but when they reached that position the only organized body of men left was the prisoners, thirteen hundred in number, and the provost guard in charge of them, and I believe that the appearance of these prisoners moving back in a body alone arrested the progress of the enemy's cavalry, as it was too dark for them to discover what they were. Many of the men stopped at Fishers Hill and went to their old camps, but no organization of them could be effected, and nothing saved us but the inability of the enemy to follow with his infantry and his expectation that we would make a stand there. The state of things was distressing and mortifying beyond measure. We had within our grasp a glorious victory, and lost it by the uncontrollable propensity of our men for plunder, in the first place, and the subsequent panic among those who had kept their places, which was without sufficient cause, for I believe that the enemy had only made the movement against us as a demonstration, hoping to protect his stores, etc., at Winchester, and that the rout of our troops was a surprise to him. I had endeavored to guard against the dangers of stopping to plunder in the camps by cautioning the division commanders and ordering them to caution their subordinates and take the most rigid measures to prevent it, and I endeavored to arrest the evil while in progress without avail. The truth is, we have very few field or company officers worth anything, almost all our good officers of that kind having been killed, wounded or captured, and it is impossible to preserve discipline without good field and company officers.

I send you a map of the battlefield with the surrounding country. You will see marked out on it the different routes of the several columns. The plan was a bold one and was vigorously pursued by the division commanders, and it was successful, but the victory, already gained, was lost by the subsequent bad conduct of the troops. The artillery throughout, from first to last, in this as well as in all the actions I have had, behaved nobly, both officers and men, and not a piece of artillery has been lost by any fault of theirs. I attribute this good conduct on their part to the vast superiority of the officers. Colonel Carter and all his battalion commanders richly deserve promotion. They not only fought their guns gallantly and efficiently, but they made the most strenuous efforts to rally the infantry.

It is mortifying to me, General, to have to make these explanations of my reverses. They are due to no want of effort on my part, though it may be that I have not the capacity or judgment to prevent them. I have labored faithfully to gain success, and I have not failed to expose my person and to set an example to my men. I know that I shall have to endure censure from those who do not understand my position and difficulties, but I am still willing to make renewed efforts. If you think, however, that the interests of the service would be promoted by a change of commanders, I beg you will have no hesitation in making the change. The interests of the service are far beyond any mere personal considerations, and if they require it I am willing to surrender my command into other hands. Though this affair has resulted so disastrously to my command, yet I think it is not entirely without compensating benefits. The Sixth Corps had already begun to move off to Grant and my movement brought it back, and Sheridan's forces are now so shattered that he will not be able to send Grant any efficient aid for some time. I think he will be afraid to trust the Eighth and Nineteenth corps.

The enemy's loss in killed and wounded was very heavy, and we took thirteen hundred prisoners, making, with some taken by Rosser, and others taken on the day of reconnoissance, over fifteen hundred. My loss in killed and wounded was not more than seven or eight hundred, and I think very few prisoners were lost. A number of my men are still out, but they are coming in. Except for the loss of my artillery, the enemy has far the worst of it. We secured some of the captured artillery, and our net loss is twenty-three pieces. I still have twenty pieces besides the horse artillery. The enemy is not pursuing, and I will remain here and organize my troops.

J. A. EARLY.

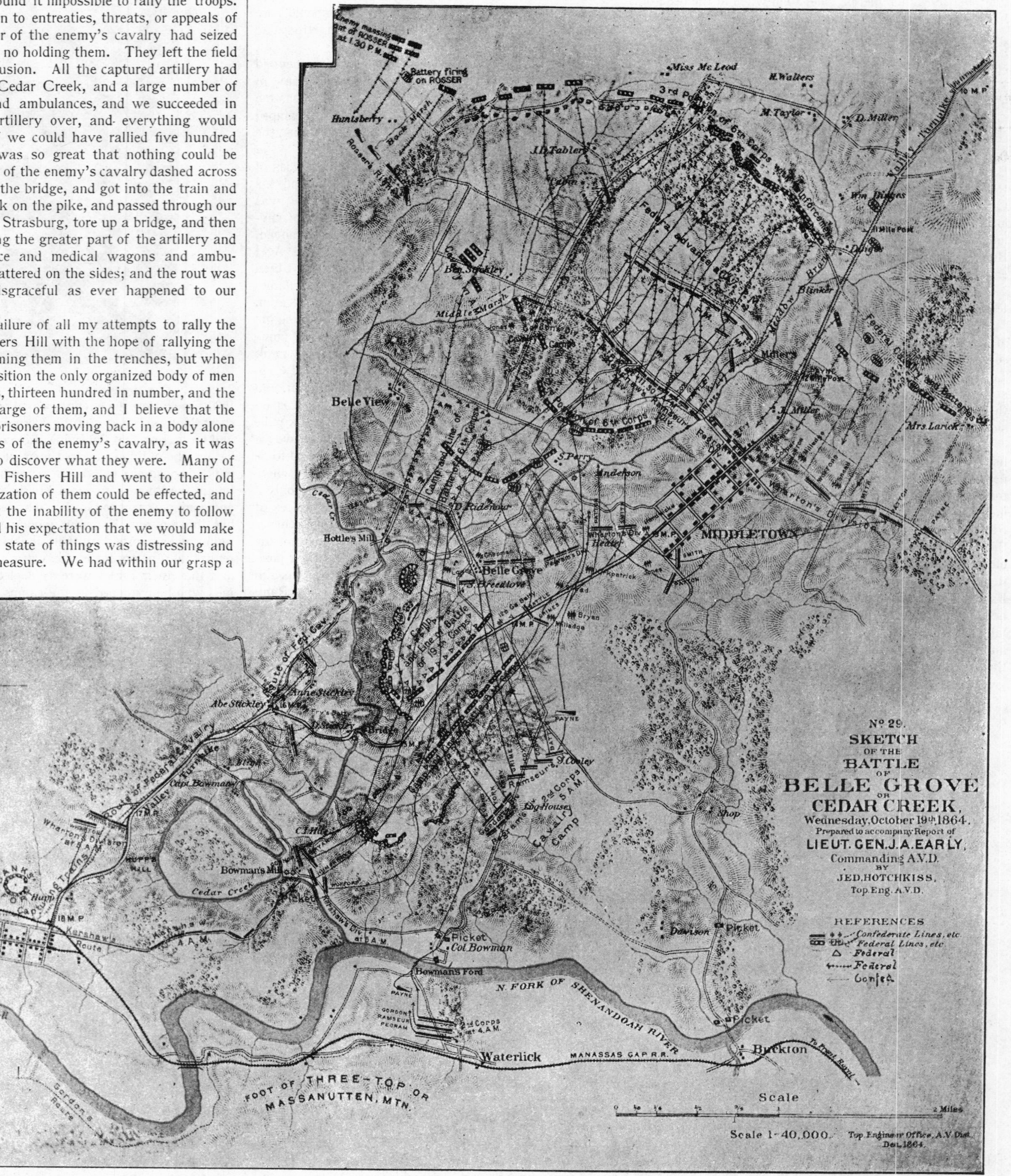

ARMY OF THE SHENANDOAH,

(VALLEY DISTRICT)

SEPTEMBER 30, 1864.

LIEUT.-GEN. JUBAL A. EARLY,
Commanding.

RODES' DIVISION.

Major-General S. D. Ramseur.

GRIMES' BRIGADE.
Brigadier-General Bryan Grimes.

Thirty-second North Carolina—Colonel D.G. Cowand.
Forty-third North Carolina—Colonel J. R. Winston.
Forty-fifth North Carolina—Colonel J. R. Winston.
Fifty-third North Carolina—Colonel D. G. Cowand.
Second North Carolina Battalion—Colonel D. G. Cowand.

COX'S BRIGADE.
Brigadier-General W. R. Cox.

First North Carolina—Captain W. H. Thompson.
Second North Carolina—Captain T. B. Beall.
Third North Carolina—Captain W. H. Thompson.
Fourth North Carolina—Colonel Ed. A. Osborn.
Fourteenth North Carolina—Captain Joseph Jones.
Thirtieth North Carolina—Captain J. C. McMillan.

COOK'S BRIGADE.
Brigadier-General Phil. Cook.

Fourth Georgia—Lieutenant-Colonel W. H. Willis.
Twelfth Georgia—Captain James Everett.
Twenty-first Georgia—Captain H. J. Battle.
Forty-fourth Georgia—Lieutenant-Colonel J. W. Beck.

BATTLE'S BRIGADE.
Brigadier-General C. A. Battle.

Third Alabama—Colonel Charles Forsyth.
Fifth Alabama—Lieutenant-Colonel E. L. Hobson.
Sixth Alabama—Captain J. Green.
Twelfth Alabama—Captain P. D. Rose.
Sixty-first Alabama—Major W. E. Pinckard.

GORDON'S DIVISION.

Major-General John B. Gordon.

HAYS' BRIGADE.
Colonel William Monaghan.

Fifth Louisiana—Major A. Hart.
Sixth Louisiana—Lieutenant-Colonel J. Hanlon.
Seventh Louisiana—Lieutenant-Colonel T. M. Terry.
Eighth Louisiana—Captain L. Prados.
Ninth Louisiana—Colonel William R. Peck.

STAFFORD'S BRIGADE.
Colonel Eugene Waggaman.

First Louisiana—Captain Joseph Taylor.
Second Louisiana—Lieutenant-Colonel M. A. Grogan.
Tenth Louisiana—Lieutenant-Colonel H. D. Monier.
Fourteenth Louisiana—Lieutenant-Colonel David Zable.
Fifteenth Louisiana—Captain H. J. Egan.

EVANS' BRIGADE.
Colonel E. N. Atkinson. (October 30th, Brigadier-General C. A. Evans.)

Thirteenth Georgia—Colonel John H. Baker.
Twenty-sixth Georgia—Lieutenant-Colonel James S. Blain.
Thirty-first Georgia—Colonel John H. Lowe.
Thirty-eighth Georgia—Major Thomas H. Bomar.
Sixtieth Georgia—Captain Milton Russell.
Sixty-first Georgia—Captain E. F. Sharpe.
Twelfth Georgia Battalion—Captain J. W. Anderson.

TERRY'S BRIGADE.*
Brigadier-General William Terry.

Second Virginia; Fourth Virginia; Fifth Virginia; Twenty-seventh Virginia and Thirty-third Virginia (Stonewall Brigade), Colonel J. H. S. Funk; October 30th, Colonel A. Spangler.

Twenty-first Virginia; Twenty-fifth Virginia; Forty-second Virginia; Forty-fourth Virginia; Forty-eighth Virginia and Fiftieth Virginia (J. M. Jones' brigade), Colonel R. H. Dugan; October 30th, Colonel W. A. Witcher.

Tenth Virginia; Twenty-third Virginia and Thirty-seventh Virginia (G. H. Steuart's brigade), Lieutenant-Colonel S. H. Saunders; October 30th, Lieutenant-Colonel Martz.

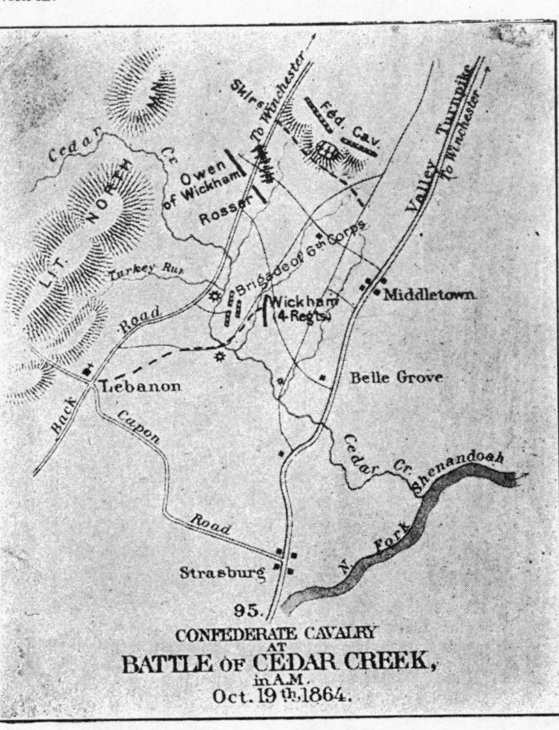

CONFEDERATE CAVALRY AT BATTLE OF CEDAR CREEK, in A.M. Oct. 19th, 1864.

EARLY'S DIVISION. †

Brigadier-General John Pegram.

PEGRAM'S BRIGADE.
Colonel John S. Hoffman.

Thirteenth Virginia—Captain Felix Heiskell.
Thirty-First Virginia—Lieutenant-Colonel J. S. K. McCutchen.
Forty-ninth Virginia—Captain John G. Lobban.
Fifty-second Virginia—Captain J. M. Humphreys.
Fifty-eighth Virginia—Captain L. C. James.

JOHNSTON'S BRIGADE.
Brigadier-General Robert D. Johnston.

Fifth North Carolina—Colonel John W. Lea. ‡
Twelfth North Carolina—Colonel Henry E. Coleman. ‡
Twentieth North Carolina—Colonel T. F. Toon.
Twenty-third North Carolina—Colonel C. C. Blacknall. ‡

* Composed of the "fragmentary remains of fourteen of the regiments of Johnson's division, most of which was captured by the enemy, May 12, 1864." The inspection report of August 21st says that the fusing of Hays' and Stafford's brigades into one, under York, and the consolidation of the three brigades, "the remains of fourteen regiments," into one, under Terry, produced a bad discipline on the troops, who lost their chance of perpetuating their brigade history; and that Evans' brigade had lost by casualty so many valuable officers as to interfere seriously with its good management.

† Commanded by Ramseur, until he took Rodes' division, after the battle of the Opequon.

‡ These officers absent and actual commanders not indicated. October 31st, after the Battle of Cedar Creek, the officers in place of Lea, Coleman and Blacknall, respectively, were Captains E. M. Duguid, Kemp Plummer and Abner D. Peace.

GOODWIN'S BRIGADE.
Lieutenant-Colonel W. T. Davis.

Sixth North Carolina—Lieutenant-Colonel S. McD. Tate.
Twenty-first North Carolina—Major W. J. Pfohl.
Fifty-fourth North Carolina—Captain A. H. Martin.
Fifty-seventh North Carolina—Captain M. H. Hunter.
First North Carolina—Captain R. E. Wil.

WHARTON'S DIVISION.

Brigadier-General G. C. Wharton.

ECHOLS' BRIGADE.
Captain Edmund S. Read.

Twenty-second Virginia—Captain Henry S. Dickerson.
Twenty-third Virginia—Captain John M. Pratt.
Twenty-sixth Virginia—Captain Frank S. Burdett.

WHARTON'S BRIGADE.
Captain R. H. Logan.

Forty-fifth Virginia—Major Alex. M. Davis.
Fifty-first Virginia—Colonel August Fosberg. *
Thirtieth Virginia Battalion—Lieutenant-Colonel J. Lyle Clarke. *

SMITH'S BRIGADE.
Colonel Thomas Smith.

Thirty-sixth Virginia—Lieutenant Jackson Vin.
Sixtieth Virginia—Captain A. G. P. George.
Forty-fifth Virginia Battalion—Captain W. B. Hensly.
Thomas Legion—Lieutenant-Colonel R. J. Love.

KERSHAW'S DIVISION.

Major-General J. B. Kershaw.

WOFFORD'S BRIGADE.
Colonel C. C. Sanders.

Sixteenth Georgia—Major J. S. Gholston.
Eighteenth Georgia—Colonel Joseph Armstrong.
Twenty-fourth Georgia—Colonel C. C. Sanders.
Third Georgia Battalion—Lieutenant Colonel N. L. Hutchins.
Cobb's Legion—Lieutenant-Colonel L. J. Glenn.
Phillips' Legion—Lieutenant-Colonel J. Hamilton.

HUMPHREYS' BRIGADE.
Brigadier-General B. G. Humphreys.

Thirteenth Mississippi—Lieutenant-Colonel A. G. O'Brien.
Seventeenth Mississippi—Captain J. C. Cochran.
Eighteenth Mississippi—Colonel T. M. Griffin.
Twenty-first Mississippi—Colonel D. N. Moody.

KERSHAW'S BRIGADE.
Brigadier-General —— Conner.

Second South Carolina—Colonel J. D. Kennedy.
Third South Carolina—Colonel W. D. Rutherford.
Seventh South Carolina—Captain E. J. Goggans.
Eighth South Carolina—Colonel J. W. Henagan.
Fifteenth South Carolina—Colonel J. B. Davis.
Twentieth South Carolina—Colonel S. M. Boykin.
Third South Carolina Battalion—Lieutenant-[Colonel] W. G. Rice.

BRYAN'S BRIGADE.
Brigadier-General Goode Bryan.

Tenth Georgia—Colonel W. C. Holt.
Fiftieth Georgia—Colonel P. McGloshan. †
Fifty-first Georgia—Colonel E. Ball. †
Fifty-third Georgia—Colonel J. P. Simms.

* These officers absent and actual commanders not indicated. The Fifteenth Virginia, Vandeventer's, is ascribed to this brigade in a roster of October 31st.

† Absent, wounded, and actual commanders of these regiments not stated. The foregoing organization is for August, when Kershaw arrived in the Valley.

BATTLE OF CEDAR CREEK, OR BELLE GROVE, VA., OCTOBER 19, 1864.

ARTILLERY DIVISION.

Colonel T. H. Carter.

BRAXTON'S BATTALION.

Lieutenant-Colonel C. M. Braxton.

Alleghany Artillery (Va.)—Captain J. C. Carpenter.
Stafford Artillery (Va.)—Captain W. P. Cooper.
Lee Battery (Va.)—Lieutenant W. W. Hardwick.

M'LAUGHLIN'S BATTALION.

Major William McLaughlin.

Bryan's Virginia Battery; Chapman's Virginia Battery; Lowry's Virginia Battery.

CUTSHAW'S BATTALION.*

Major W. E. Cutshaw.

Orange Artillery (Va.)—Captain C. W. Fry.
Staunton Artillery (Va.)—Captain A. W. Garber.
Courtney Battery (Va.)— —— L. F. Jones.

NELSON'S BATTALION.

Lieutenant-Colonel William Nelson.

Amherst Artillery (Va.)—Captain T. J. Kirkpatrick.
Fluvanna Artillery (Va.)—Captain J. L. Massie.
Milledge's Artillery (Ga.)—Captain John Milledge.

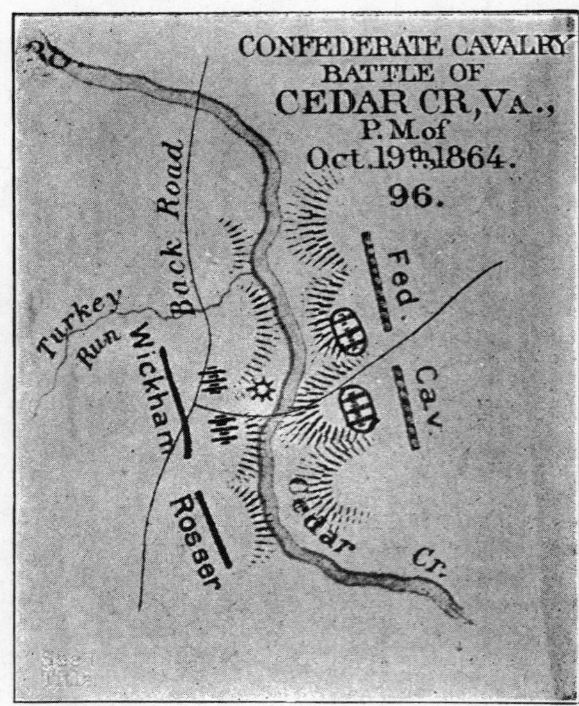

CAVALRY FORCES.†

LOMAX'S DIVISION.

Major-General J. J. Lomax.

M'CAUSLAND'S BRIGADE.

Brigadier-General J. McCausland.

Fourteenth Virginia; Sixteenth Virginia; Seventeenth Virginia; Twenty-fifth Virginia; Thirty-seventh Virginia Battalion.

JOHNSON'S BRIGADE.

Brigadier-General B. T. Johnson.

Eighth Virginia; Twenty-first Virginia; Twenty-second Virginia; Thirty-fourth Virginia Battery; Thirty-sixth Virginia Battery.

JACKSON'S BRIGADE.

Brigadier-General H. B. Davidson.

First Maryland; Nineteenth Virginia; Twentieth Virginia; Forty-sixth Virginia Battalion; Forty-seventh Virginia Battalion.

IMBODEN'S BRIGADE.

Colonel George H. Smith.

Eighteenth Virginia; Twenty-third Virginia; Sixty-second Virginia Mounted Infantry.

LEE'S DIVISION.

Major-General Fitzhugh Lee.

WICKHAM'S BRIGADE.

Brigadier-General W. C. Wickham.

First Virginia—Colonel —— Carter.
Second Virginia—Colonel —— Munford.
Third Virginia—Colonel —— Owen.
Fourth Virginia—Colonel —— Payne.

LOMAX'S BRIGADE.

Brigadier-General L. L. Lomax.

Fifth Virginia—Colonel H. Clay Pate.
Sixth Virginia—Colonel Julien Harrison.
Fifteenth Virginia—Colonel C. R. Collins.

ROSSER'S BRIGADE.

Brigadier-General Thomas L. Rosser.

Seventh Virginia—Colonel R. H. Dulany.
Eleventh Virginia—Colonel O. R. Funsten.
Twelfth Virginia—Colonel A. W. Harman.
Thirty-fifth Virginia Battalion—Lieutenant-Colonel E. V. White.

* In an earlier roster Fry's Orange Battery is ascribed to Carter's Battalion, and in its place appears the Charlottesville Artillery, Captain J. M. Carrington.

† These forces are, for convenience, here grouped together, although the reader of the text will observe that they were not all present September 30th in this exact form. Rosser's Brigade, for example, was at that time only on its way to the Valley; and when it arrived Rosser received command of the division. The organization of Lomax's Cavalry is from the roster of October 30th, after the battle of Cedar Creek.

THE TENNESSEE CAMPAIGN,

BEGINNING SEPTEMBER 29, 1864.

BY

LIEUT.-GEN. S. D. LEE.

COLUMBUS, MISS., January 30, 1865.

I HAVE the honor to offer the following as my official report of the operations of my corps during the offensive movement commencing at Palmetto Station, Ga., September 29, 1864. It is impracticable now, in consequence of the movement of troops and my temporary absence from the army, to obtain detailed reports from my division commanders.

As a corps commander, I regarded the morale of the army greatly impaired after the fall of Atlanta, and in fact before its fall the troops were not by any means in good spirits. It was my observation and belief that the majority of the officers and men were so impressed with the idea of their inability to carry even temporary breastworks, that when orders were given for attack, and there was a probability of encountering works, they regarded it as recklessness in the extreme. Being impressed with these convictions, they did not generally move to the attack with that spirit which nearly always insures success. Whenever the enemy changed his position, temporary works could be improvised in less than two hours, and he could never be caught without them. In making these observations, it is due to many gallant officers and commands to state that there were noticeable exceptions, but the feeling was so general that anything like a general attack was paralyzed by it. The army having constantly yielded to the flank movements of the enemy, which he could make with but little difficulty, by reason of his vastly superior numbers, and having failed in the offensive movements prior to the fall of Atlanta, its efficiency for further retarding the progress of the enemy was much impaired; and besides, the advantages in the topography of the country south of Atlanta were much more favorable to the enemy for the movements of his superior numbers than the rough and mountainous country already yielded to him. In view of these facts, it was my opinion that the army should take up the offensive, with the hope that favorable opportunities would be offered for striking the enemy successfully, thus insuring the efficiency of the army for future operations. These opinions were freely expressed to the commanding general.

My corps crossed the Chattahoochee River on September 29th, and on October 3d took position near Lost Mountain, to cover the movement of Stewart's corps, on the railroad, at Big Shanty and Allatoona. On October 6th I left my position near Lost Mountain, marching via Dallas and Cedartown, crossing the Coosa River at Coosaville, October 10th, and moved on Resaca, partially investing the place by 4 P. M. on October 12th. The surrender of the place was demanded in a written communication, which was in my possession, signed by General Hood. The commanding officer refused to surrender, as he could have easily escaped from the forts with his forces and crossed the Oostanaula River. I did not deem it prudent to assault the works, which were strong and well manned, believing that our loss would have been severe. The main object of appearing before Resaca being accomplished, and finding that Sherman's main army was moving from the direction of Rome and Adairsville toward Resaca, I withdrew from before the place to Snake Creek Gap about midday on the 13th. The enemy made his appearance at the gap on the 14th in large force, and on the 15th it was evident that his force amounted to several corps. Several severe skirmishes took place on the 15th, in which Deas' and Brantly's brigades, of Johnson's division, were principally engaged. This gap was held by my command till the balance of the army had passed through Matex's Gap, when I followed with the corps through the latter. The army moved to Gadsden, where my corps arrived on October 21st. At this point clothing was issued to the troops, and the army commenced its march toward Tennessee. My corps reached the vicinity of Leighton, in the Tennessee Valley, October 29th. Stewart's and Cheatham's corps were then in front of Decatur. On the night of the 29th I received orders to cross the Tennessee River at Florence, Ala. By means of the pontoon boats two brigades of Johnson's division were thrown across the river two and a half miles above South Florence, and Gibson's brigade, of Clayton's division, was crossed at South Florence. The enemy occupied Florence with about one thousand cavalry, and had a strong picket at the Railroad Bridge. The crossing at this point was handsomely executed and with much spirit by Gibson, under the direction of General Clayton, under cover of several batteries of artillery. The distance across the river was about one thousand yards. The troops landed and, after forming, charged the enemy and drove him from Florence. The crossing was spirited, and reflected much credit on all engaged in it. Major-General Edward Johnson experienced considerable difficulty in crossing his two brigades, because of the extreme difficulty of managing the boats in the shoals. He moved from the north bank of the river late in the evening with one brigade, Sharp's Mississippi, and encountered the enemy on the Florence and Huntsville Road about dark. A spirited affair took place, in which the enemy were defeated with a loss of about forty killed, wounded and prisoners. The enemy retreated during the night to Shoal Creek, about nine miles distant. The remainder of Johnson's and Clayton's divisions were crossed on the night of the 30th and on the morning of the 31st. Stevenson's division was crossed on November 2d. My corps remained in Florence till November 20th, when the army commenced moving for Tennessee, my command leading the advance and marching in the direction of Columbia via Henryville and Mount Pleasant. I arrived in front of Columbia on the 26th, relieving Forrest's cavalry then in position there, which had followed the enemy from Pulaski.

The force of the enemy occupying Columbia was two corps. They confined themselves to the main works around the city, and their outposts and skirmishers were readily driven in. On the night of the 27th the enemy evacuated Columbia and crossed Duck River. Stevenson's division of my corps entered the town before daylight. After crossing, the enemy took a strong position on the opposite side of the river and intrenched, his skirmishers occupying rifle pits two hundred and fifty yards from the river. There was considerable skirmishing across the river during the day, and some artillery firing, resulting in nothing of importance.

On the morning of the 29th Johnson's division of my corps was detached and ordered to report to the general commanding. I was directed to occupy and engage the enemy near Columbia, while the other two corps and Johnson's division would be crossed above and moved to the rear of the enemy in the direction of Spring Hill. The entire force of the enemy was in front of Columbia till about midday on the 29th, when one corps commenced moving off — the other remaining in position as long as they could be seen by us, or till dark. I had several batteries of artillery put in position, to drive the skirmishers of the enemy from the vicinity of the river bank, and made a display of pontoons—running several of them down to the river, under a heavy artillery and musketry fire. Having succeeded in putting a boat in the river, Pettus' brigade of Stevenson's division was thrown across, under the immediate direction of Major-General Stevenson, and made a most gallant charge on the rifle-pits of the enemy, driving a much superior force and capturing the pits. The bridge was at once laid down and the crossing commenced. During the affair around Columbia, the gallant and accomplished soldier, Colonel R. F. Beckham, commanding the artillery regiment of my corps, was mortally wounded while industriously and fearlessly directing the artillery firing against the enemy. He was one of the truest and best officers in the service.

LIEUT.-GEN. S. D. LEE, OF SOUTH CAROLINA.
[From a photograph of an oil portrait.]

The enemy left my front about 2:30 A. M. on the morning of the 30th, and the pursuit was made as rapidly as was prudent in the night time. The advance of Clayton's division arrived at Spring Hill about 9 A. M., when it was discovered that the enemy had made his escape, passing around that portion of the army in that vicinity. My corps, including Johnson's division, followed immediately after Cheatham's corps toward Franklin. I arrived near Franklin about 4 P. M. The commanding general was just about attacking the enemy with Stewart's and Cheatham's corps, and he directed me to place Johnson's, and afterward Clayton's, division in position to support the attack. Johnson moved in rear of Cheatham's corps. Finding that the battle was stubborn, General Hood directed me to move forward in person, to communicate with General Cheatham, and, if necessary, to put Johnson's division in the fight. I met General Cheatham about dark, and was informed by him that assistance was needed at once. Johnson was immediately moved forward to the attack, but, owing to the darkness and want of information as to the locality, his attack was not felt by the enemy till about one hour after dark. This division moved against the enemy's breastworks under a heavy fire of artillery and musketry, gallantly driving the enemy from portions of his line. The brigades of Sharp and Brantly (Mississippians), and of Deas (Alabamians), particularly, distinguished themselves. Their dead were mostly in the trenches and in the works of the enemy, where they fell in a desperate hand-to-hand conflict. Sharp captured three stand of colors. Brantly was exposed to a severe enfilade fire. These noble brigades never faltered in this terrible night struggle. Brigadier-General Manigault, commanding a brigade of Alabamians and South Carolinians, was severely wounded in this engagement while gallantly leading his troops to the fight; and his two successors in command, Colonel Shaw was killed and Colonel Davis wounded. I have never seen greater evidence of gallantry than was displayed by this division, under command of that admirable and gallant soldier, Major-General Ed. Johnson. The enemy fought gallantly and obstinately at Franklin, and the position he held was, for infantry defense, one of the best I had ever seen. The enemy evacuated Franklin hastily during the night of the 30th. My corps commenced the pursuit about 1 P. M. on December 1st, and arrived near Nashville about 2 P. M. December 2d. The enemy had occupied the works around the city. My command was the center of the army in front of Nashville, Cheatham's corps being on my right and Stewart's on my left. Nothing of importance occurred till the 15th. The army was engaged in intrenching and strengthening its position.

On the 15th the enemy moved out on our left, and a severe engagement was soon commenced. In my immediate front the enemy still kept up his skirmish line, though it was evident that his main force had moved. My line was much extended, the greater part of my command being in single rank. About 12 M. I was instructed to assist Lieutenant-General Stewart, and I commenced withdrawing troops from my line to send to his support. I sent him Johnson's entire division, each brigade starting as it was disengaged from the works. A short time before sunset the enemy succeeded in turning General Stewart's position, and a part of my line was necessarily changed to conform to his new line. During the night Cheatham's corps was withdrawn from my right and moved to the extreme left of the army. The army then took position about one mile in rear of its original line. My corps being on the extreme right, I was instructed by the commanding general to cover and hold the Franklin pike. Clayton's division occupied my right, Stevenson's my center and Johnson's my left. It was evident, soon after daylight, that a large force of the enemy was being concentrated in my front on the Franklin Pike. About 9 A. M. on the 16th the enemy, having placed a large number of guns in position, opened a terrible artillery fire on my line, principally on the Franklin Pike. This lasted about two hours, when the enemy moved to the assault. They came up in several lines of battle.

View of a Section of the Fortifications in Front of Franklin, Tenn., after an Assault made by the Confederate Troops.

My men reserved their fire till they were within easy range and then delivered it with terrible effect. The assault was easily repulsed. It was renewed, however, with spirit several times, but only to meet each time with a like result. They approached to within thirty yards of our line, and their loss was very severe. Their last assault was made about 3:30 P. M., when they were driven back in great disorder. The assaults were made principally in front of Holtzclaw's Alabama, Gibson's Louisiana and Stovall's Georgia brigades, of Clayton's division, and Pettus' Alabama brigade, of Stevenson's division; and too much credit can not be awarded Major-General Clayton and these gallant troops for their conspicuous and soldierly conduct.

The enemy made a considerable display of force on my extreme right during the day, evidently with the intention of attempting to turn our right flank. He made, however, but one feeble effort to use this force, when it was readily repulsed by Stovall's Georgia and Brantly's Mississippi brigades, which latter two had been moved to the right. Smith's division, of Cheatham's corps, reported to me about 2 P. M., to meet any attempt of the enemy to turn our right flank; it was put in position, but was not needed, and, by order of the commanding general, it started to Brentwood about 3:30 P. M. The artillery fire of the enemy during the entire day was heavy, and right nobly did the artillery of my corps, under Lieutenant-Colonel Hoxton, perform their duty.

Courtney's battalion, under Captain Douglas, was in Johnson's front, Johnson's battalion was in Stevenson's front, and Eldridge's battalion, under Captain Fenner, was in Clayton's front. The officers and men of the artillery behaved admirably, and too much praise can not be bestowed upon this efficient arm of the service in the Army of Tennessee. The troops of my entire line were in fine spirits, and confident of success (so much so that the men could scarcely be prevented from leaving their trenches to follow the enemy on and near the Franklin Pike). But, suddenly, all eyes were turned to the center of our line of battle near the Gracey White Pike, where it was evident the enemy had made an entrance, although but little firing had been heard in that direction. Our men were flying to the rear in the wildest confusion and the enemy following with enthusiastic cheers. The enemy at once closed toward the gap in our line and commenced charging on the left division—Johnson's—of my corps, but were handsomely driven back. The enemy soon gained our rear and were moving on my left flank when our line gradually gave way.

My troops left their lines in some disorder, but were soon rallied and presented a good front to the enemy. It was a fortunate circumstance that the enemy was too much crippled to pursue us on the Franklin Pike. The only pursuit made at that time was by a small force coming from the Gracey White Pike. Having been informed by an aid of the general commanding that the enemy were near Brentwood, and that it was necessary to get beyond that point at once, everything was hastened to the rear. When Brentwood was passed, the enemy was only half a mile from the Franklin Pike, where Chalmers' cavalry was fighting them. Being charged with covering the retreat of the army, I remained in rear with Clayton's and part of Stevenson's divisions, and halted the rear-guard about seven miles north of Franklin about 10 P. M., on the 16th.

Early on the morning of the 17th our cavalry was driven in in confusion by the enemy, who at once commenced a most vigorous pursuit, his cavalry charging at every opportunity and in the most daring manner. It was apparent that they were determined to make the retreat a rout if possible. Their boldness was soon checked by many of them being killed and captured by Pettus' Alabama and Stovall's Georgia brigades and Bledsoe's battery, under Major-General Clayton. Several guidons were captured in one of their charges.

I was soon compelled to withdraw rapidly toward Franklin, as the enemy was throwing a force in my rear from both the right and left of the pike on roads coming

View of one of the Fortifications in Front of Nashville, Tenn.

into the pike near Franklin and five miles in my rear. This force was checked by Brigadier-General Gibson, with his brigade and a regiment of Buford's cavalry under Colonel Shacklett. The resistance which the enemy had met with early in the morning, and which materially checked his movements, enabled us to reach Franklin with but little difficulty. Here the enemy appeared in considerable force and exhibited great boldness, but he was repulsed and the crossing of the Harpeth River effected.

I found that there was in the town of Franklin a large number of our own and of the enemy's wounded, and not wishing to subject them and the town to the fire of the enemy's artillery, the town was yielded with but little resistance. Some four or five hours were gained by checking the enemy about one and a half miles south of Franklin, and by the destruction of the trestle bridge over the Harpeth, which was effected by Captain Coleman, the engineer officer on my staff and a party of pioneers, under a heavy fire of the enemy's sharpshooters. About 4 P. M., the enemy, having crossed a considerable force, commenced a bold and vigorous attack, charging with his cavalry on our flanks and pushing forward his lines in the front. A more persistent effort was never made to rout the rearguard of a retiring column.

This desperate attack was kept up till long after dark, but gallantly did the rear-guard, consisting of Pettus' Alabama and Cummings' Georgia brigades (the latter commanded by Colonel Watkins), of Stevenson's division, and under that gallant and meritorious officer, Major-General C. L. Stevenson, repulse every attack. Brigadier-General Chalmers, with his division of cavalry, covered our flanks. The cavalry of the enemy succeeded in getting in Stevenson's rear, and attacked Major-General Clayton's division about dark, but they were handsomely repulsed, Gibson's and Stovall's brigades being principally engaged. Some four or five guidons were captured from the enemy during the evening.

About 1 P. M. I was wounded while with the rear-guard, but did not relinquish the command of my corps till dark. Most of the details in conducting the retreat from that time were arranged and executed by Major-General Stevenson, to whom the army is much indebted for his skill and gallant conduct during the day. I can not close this report without alluding particularly to the artillery of my corps. On the 16th sixteen guns were lost on the lines — the greater portion of them were without horses — they having been disabled during the day; many of the carriages were disabled also. The noble gunners, reluctant to leave their guns, fought the enemy, in many instances, till they were almost within reach of the guns. Major-General Ed. Johnson was captured on the 16th; being on foot, he was unable to make his escape from the enemy in consequence of an old wound. He held his line as long as it was practicable to do so. The Army of Tennessee has sustained no greater loss than that of this gallant and accomplished soldier. To all my division commanders, Stevenson, Johnson and Clayton, I am indebted for the most valuable services; they were always zealous in the discharge of their duties.

To the officers of my personal staff and also of the corps staff, I am indebted for valuable services; they were always at their posts and ready to respond to the call of duty.

S. D. LEE, *Lieutenant-General.*

CARRY ME TO THE REAR!—It was at the second battle of Bull Run that a cannon ball carried off a poor soldier's leg. "Carry me to the rear!" he cried, to a tall companion who had been fighting by his side. "My leg is shot off!" The comrade caught the wounded soldier up and, as he was about to put him across his shoulders, another cannon ball carried away the poor fellow's head. His friend, however, in the confusion, did not notice this, but proceeded with his burden to the rear. "What are you carrying that thing for?" cried an officer. "Thing!" said he. "It's a man with his leg shot off!" "Why, he hasn't any head!" cried the officer. The soldier looked at his load and, for the first time, saw that what the officer said was true. Throwing down the body, he thundered out: "Confound him! he told me it was his leg."

CAMPAIGN IN NORTH ALABAMA AND MIDDLE TENNESSEE,

NOVEMBER 14, 1864, TO JANUARY 23, 1865,

INCLUDING BATTLES OF

FRANKLIN AND NASHVILLE.

BY

GENERAL JOHN B. HOOD.

FORREST'S cavalry joined me on the 21st of November and the movement began, Major-General Cheatham's corps taking the road toward Waynesboro, and the other two corps moving on roads somewhat parallel with this, but more to the eastward, with their cavalry under General Forrest in the advance and upon their right flank. The enemy's forces at this time were concentrated at Pulaski, with some force also at Lawrenceburg. I hoped to be able to place the army between these forces of the enemy and Nashville; but he evacuated Pulaski upon the 23d, hearing of our advance (our cavalry having furiously driven off their forces at Lawrenceburg), and moved rapidly by the turnpike and railroad to Columbia.

GENERAL JOHN B. HOOD, OF TEXAS.

The want of a good map of the country, and the deep mud through which the army marched, prevented our overtaking the enemy before he reached Columbia, but on the evening of the 27th of November our army was placed in position in front of his works at that place. During the night, however, he evacuated the town, taking position on the opposite side of the river about a mile and a half from the town, which was considered quite strong in front.

Late in the evening of the 28th of November General Forrest, with most of his command, crossed Duck River, a few miles above Columbia, and I followed early in the morning of the 29th, with Stewart's and Cheatham's corps, and Johnson's division of Lee's corps, leaving the other divisions of Lee's corps in the enemy's front at Columbia. The troops moved in light marching order, with only a battery to the corps, my object being to turn the enemy's flank, by marching rapidly on roads parallel to the Columbia and Franklin Pike, at or near Spring Hill, and to cut off that portion of the enemy at or near Columbia. When I had gotten well on his flank the enemy discovered my intention and began to retreat on the pike toward Spring Hill. The cavalry became engaged near that place about midday, but his trains were so strongly guarded that they were unable to break through them.

About 4 P. M. our infantry forces, Major-General Cheatham in the advance, commenced to come in contact with the enemy about two miles from Spring Hill, through which place the Columbia and Franklin Pike runs. The enemy was at this time moving rapidly along the pike, with some of his troops formed on the flank of his column to protect it. Major-General Cheatham was ordered to attack the enemy at once vigorously and get possession of this pike, and, although these orders were frequently and earnestly repeated, he made but a feeble and partial attack, failing to reach the point indicated.

Had my instructions been carried out there is no doubt that we should have possessed ourselves of this road. Stewart's corps and Johnson's division were arriving upon the field to support the attack. Though the golden opportunity had passed with daylight, I did not at dark abandon the hope of dealing the enemy a heavy blow. Accordingly, Lieutenant-General Stewart was furnished a guide and ordered to move his corps beyond Cheatham's and place it across the road beyond Spring Hill. Shortly after this General Cheatham came to my headquarters, and when I informed him of Stewart's movement, he said that Stewart ought to form on his right. I asked if that would throw Stewart across the pike. He replied that it would, and a mile beyond. Accordingly, one of Cheatham's staff officers was sent to show Stewart where his (Cheatham's) right rested. In the dark and confusion he did not succeed in getting the position desired, but about 11 P. M. went into bivouac.

About 12 P. M., ascertaining that the enemy was moving in great confusion, artillery, wagons and troops intermixed, I sent instructions to General Cheatham to advance a heavy line of skirmishers against him and still further impede and confuse his march. This was not accomplished. The enemy continued to move along the road in hurry and confusion, within hearing nearly all the night. Thus was lost a great opportunity of striking the enemy, for which we had labored so long — the greatest this campaign had offered and one of the greatest during the war.

Lieutenant-General Lee, left in front of the enemy at Columbia, was instructed to press the enemy the moment he abandoned his position at that point. The enemy did not abandon his works at that place till dark, showing that his trains obstructed the road for fifteen miles during the day and a great part of the night.

At daylight we followed as fast as possible toward Franklin, Lieutenant-General Stewart in the advance, Major-General Cheatham following, and General Lee, with the trains, moving from Columbia, on the same road. We pursued the enemy rapidly and compelled him to burn a number of his wagons. He made a feint as if to give battle on the hills, about four miles south of Franklin, but as soon as our forces began to deploy for the attack and to flank him on his left, he retired slowly to Franklin.

I learned, from dispatches captured at Spring Hill, from Thomas to Schofield, that the latter was instructed to hold that place till the position at Franklin could be made secure, indicating the intention of Thomas to hold Franklin and his strong works at Murfreesboro. Thus I knew that it was all important to attack Schofield before he could make himself strong, and, if he should escape at Franklin, he would gain his works about Nashville. The nature of the position was such as to render it inexpedient to attempt any further flank movement, and I, therefore, determined to attack him in front, and without delay.

On the 30th of November Stewart's corps was placed in position on the right, Cheatham's on the left, and the cavalry on either flank, the main body of the cavalry on the right, under Forrest. Johnson's division of Lee's corps also became engaged on the left during the engagement. The line advanced at 4 P. M., with orders to drive the enemy into or across the Big Harpeth River, while General Forrest, if successful, was to cross the river and attack and destroy his trains and broken columns. The troops moved forward most gallantly to the attack. We carried the enemy's first line of hastily constructed works handsomely. We then advanced against his interior line and succeeded in carrying it also in some places. Here the engagement was of the fiercest possible character. Our men possessed themselves of the exterior of the works, while the enemy held the interior. Many of our men were killed entirely inside the works. The brave men captured were taken inside his works in the edge of the town. The struggle lasted till near midnight, when the enemy abandoned his works and crossed the river, leaving his dead and wounded in our possession. Never did troops fight more gallantly. The works of the enemy were so hastily constructed, that while he had a slight abatis in front of a part of his line, there was none on his extreme right. During the day I was restrained from using my artillery on account of the women and children remaining in the town. At night it was massed ready to continue the action in the morning, but the enemy retired.

We captured about one thousand prisoners and several stand of colors. Our loss in killed, wounded and prisoners was four thousand five hundred. Among the killed was Major-General P. R. Cleburne, Brigadier-Generals Gist, John Adams, Strahl and Granbury. Major-General Brown, Brigadier-Generals Carter, Manigault, Quarles, Cockrell and Scott were wounded and Brigadier-General Gordon captured.

The number of dead left by the enemy on the field indicated that his loss was equal or near our own. The next morning at daylight, the wounded being cared for and the dead buried, we moved forward toward Nashville, Forrest, with his cavalry, pursuing the enemy vigorously.

On the 2d of December the army took position in front of Nashville, about two miles from the city. Lieutenant-General Lee's corps constituted our center, resting upon the Franklin Pike, with Cheatham's corps upon the right and Stewart's on the left, and the cavalry on either flank, extending to the river. I was causing strong detached works to be built to cover our flanks, intending to make them inclosed works, so as to defeat any attempt of the enemy should he undertake offensive movements against our flank and rear.

The enemy still held Murfreesboro with about six thousand men, strongly fortified; he also held small forces at Chattanooga and Knoxville. It was apparent that he would soon have to take the offensive to relieve his garrison at those points or cause them to be evacuated, in which case I hoped to capture the forces at Murfreesboro, and should then be able to open communication with Georgia and Virginia. Should he attack me in position I felt that I could defeat him, and thus gain possession of Nashville, with abundant supplies for the army. This would give me possession of Tennessee. Necessary steps were taken to furnish the army with supplies, which the people were ready and willing to furnish. Shoe shops were in operation in each brigade. We had captured sufficient railroad stock to use the road to Pulaski, and it was already in successful operation. Having possession of the State, we should have gained largely in recruits, and could, at an early day, have moved forward to the Ohio, which would have frustrated the plans of the enemy, as developed in his campaign toward the Atlantic Coast.

Brig.-Gen. S. R. Gist, of South Carolina.
Killed at the battle of Franklin, Tenn., November 30, 1864.
[From a photograph taken in 1864.]

I had sent Major-General Forrest, with the greatest part of his cavalry and Bate's division of infantry, to Murfreesboro, to ascertain if it was possible to take the place. After a careful examination and reconnoissance in force, in which, I am sorry to say, the infantry behaved badly, it was determined that nothing could be accomplished by assault. Bate's division was withdrawn, leaving Forrest with Jackson's and Buford's divisions of cavalry, in observation. Mercer's and Palmer's brigades of infantry were sent to replace Bate's division. Shortly afterward Buford's division was withdrawn and ordered to the right of the army, on the Cumberland River.

Nothing of importance occurred until the morning of the 15th of December, when the enemy, having received heavy re-enforcements, attacked simultaneously both our flanks. On our right he was handsomely repulsed, with heavy loss, but on our left, toward evening, he carried some partially completed redoubts of those before mentioned.

Train with Re-enforcements for General Johnston's Army Running off the Track in the Forests of Mississippi.
[From a sketch made by an artist representing the *London News*.]

During the night of the 15th our whole line was shortened and strengthened; our left was also thrown back; dispositions were made to meet any renewed attack. The corps of Major-General Cheatham was transferred from our right to our left, leaving Lieutenant-General Lee on our right—who had been previously in the center—and placing Lieutenant-General Stewart's corps in the center, which had been previously the left.

Early on the 16th of December the enemy made a general attack on our lines, accompanied by a heavy fire of artillery. All his assaults were repulsed with heavy loss till 3:30 P. M., when a portion of our line to the left of the center, occupied by Bate's division, suddenly gave way. Up to this time no battle ever progressed more favorably; the troops in excellent spirits, waving their colors and bidding defiance to the enemy. The position gained by the enemy being such as to enfilade our line, caused, in a few moments, our entire line to give way and our troops to retreat rapidly down the pike in the direction of Franklin, most of them, I regret to say, in great confusion, all efforts to reform them being fruitless. Our loss in artillery was heavy—fifty-four guns. Thinking it impossible for the enemy to break our line, the horses were sent to the rear for safety, and the giving way of the line was so sudden that it was not possible to bring forward the horses to move the guns which had been placed in position. Our loss in killed and wounded was small. At Brentwood, some four miles from our line of battle, the troops were somewhat collected, and Lieutenant-General Lee took command of the rear-guard, encamping for the night in the vicinity. On leaving the field I sent a staff officer to inform General Forrest of our defeat, and to direct him to rejoin the army with as little delay as possible to protect its rear, but owing to the swollen condition of the creeks, caused by the heavy rain then falling, he was unable to join us until we reached Columbia, with the exception of a portion of his command which reached us while the enemy was moving from Franklin to Spring Hill.

On the 17th we continued the retreat toward Columbia, encamping for the night at Spring Hill. During this day's march the enemy's cavalry pressed with great boldness and activity, charging our infantry repeatedly with the saber, and at times penetrating our lines. The country being open was favorable to their operations. I regret to say that also on this day Lieutenant-General Lee, commanding the covering force, was severely wounded in the foot. We continued our retreat across Duck River to Columbia, the corps alternating as rear-guards to the army. Lieutenant-General Lee and the corps commanded by him deserve great credit.

After the fight at Nashville, I at first hoped to be able to remain in Tennessee, on the line of Duck River; but after arriving at Columbia I became convinced that the condition of the army made it necessary to recross the Tennessee without delay; and on the 21st the army resumed its march for Pulaski, leaving Major-General Walthall, with Ector's, Strahl's, Maney's, Granbury's and Palmer's infantry brigades, at Columbia as a rear-guard, under General Forrest. From Pulaski I moved by the most direct road to the Bainbridge crossing on the Tennessee River, which was reached on the 25th, where the army crossed without interruption, completing the crossing on the 27th, including our rear-guard, which the enemy followed with all his cavalry and three corps of infantry to Pulaski, and with cavalry between Pulaski and the Tennessee River. After crossing the river the army moved by easy marches to Tupelo, Miss. Our pontoon and supply train, were ordered at once to the vicinity of Columbus, Miss., by the most direct route, that the animals might be more easily foraged, and while on the march there were pursued by a small body of the enemy's cavalry, and owing to the neglect of Brigadier-General Roddey's cavalry were overtaken, and the pontoon train and a small portion of the supply train destroyed. Here, finding so much dissatisfaction throughout the country as in my judgment to greatly impair, if not destroy, my usefulness and counteract my exertions, and with no desire but to serve my country, I asked to be relieved, with the hope that another might be assigned to the command who might do more than I could hope to accomplish. Accordingly, I was so relieved on the 23d of January by authority of the President.

My reasons for undertaking the movement into Tennessee have, I think, been sufficiently stated already. Had I not made the movement I am fully persuaded that Sherman would have been upon General Lee's communication in October, instead of at this time.

From Palmetto to Spring Hill the campaign was all that I could have desired. At Nashville, had it not have been for an unfortunate event which could not justly have been anticipated, I think we would have gained a complete victory. At any time it was in the power of the army to retire from Tennessee in the event of failure, as is established by the leisurely retreat which was made under the most difficult and embarrassing circumstances. It is my firm conviction, that, notwithstanding that disaster, I left the army in better spirits and with more confidence in itself than it had at the opening of the campaign. The official records will show that my losses, including prisoners, during the entire campaign do not exceed ten thousand men. Were I again placed in such circumstances I should

Brig.-Gen. Oscar F. Strahl, of Tennessee.
Killed at the battle of Franklin, Tenn., November 30, 1864.
[From a tintype taken in 1864.]

make the same marches and fight the same battles, trusting that the same unforeseen and unavoidable accident could not again occur to change into disaster a victory which had been already won.

In support of the statement touching the strength and losses of the army, I respectfully tender the official records of the assistant adjutant-general (Major Kinloch Falconer), alike on duty with General Johnston and myself. Those who have seen much service in the field during this war will at once understand why it was that desertion, which had been so frequent on the retreat from Dalton to Atlanta, almost entirely ceased as soon as the army assumed the offensive and took a step forward. I did not know of a desertion on the march from Palmetto to Dalton, or from Dalton to Florence. I am informed that the provost-marshal general of the Army of Tennessee reports less than three hundred desertions during the whole Tennessee campaign. The Tennessee troops entered the State with high hopes as they approached their homes. When the fortunes of war were against us, the same faithful soldiers remained true to their flag, and, with exceptions, followed it in retreat as they had borne it in advance.

But few of the subordinate reports have reached me. I am consequently unable, without risk of injustice, to describe the instances of individual skill and gallantry.

J. B. HOOD, *General.*

CAMPAIGN

IN

NORTH ALABAMA AND MIDDLE TENNESSEE,

NOVEMBER 29, 1864, TO JANUARY 20, 1865,

INCLUDING BATTLES OF

FRANKLIN AND NASHVILLE.

BY

LIEUT.-GEN. ALEX. P. STEWART,
Commanding Army Corps.

HEADQUARTERS STEWART'S CORPS,
ARMY OF TENNESSEE,
NEAR TUPELO, MISS., January 20, 1865.

THE following brief outline of the operations of this corps from September 29, 1864, to the close of the campaign is respectfully submitted. It is necessarily an imperfect report, being made at the request of the commanding general, without the aid of the reports of subordinate commanders.

On Tuesday, November 29th, following Cheatham's corps, we crossed Duck River above Columbia, and arrived near sunset at Rutherfords Creek. Crossing it I moved to the right of Cheatham's corps, then in line near the pike from Columbia to Franklin, and about 11 P. M. bivouacked in rear of his right.

The next morning (30th) we moved at daylight, taking the advance in pursuit of the retreating enemy. About midday we came in sight of his line, formed on a commanding ridge some two miles from Franklin. In compliance with the instructions of the commanding general, I moved to the right toward Harpeth River, and formed to attack the enemy, who fell back to an intrenched line around the town. Loring's division was on the right, Walthall's in the center, French's on the left. Ector's brigade of the last named division marched from Florence as guard to the pontoon train, and had not rejoined. Buford's division of cavalry covered the space between Loring's right and the river, while another was thrown across to the other bank. In the meantime Cheatham's corps was also formed for attack, and the two corps were to move forward simultaneously. I had one battery only, the pieces of which were distributed to the three divisions. About 4 P. M. a staff officer from the commanding general brought me the order to advance, and the word forward was given. A body of the enemy's cavalry in front of Loring and the division on his right was soon routed, and the cavalry division (Buford's) ceased to operate with us. The line moved forward in fine order, the men in high spirits, drove the enemy from his outer line and fiercely assailed the second. The ground over which Loring's division advanced was obstructed by a deep railroad cut and an abatis and hedge of osage orange. With these exceptions the space in front of the enemy's position on our side was perfectly open and swept by a terrible and destructive cross-fire of artillery from the works and from the opposite bank of the narrow stream—the Harpeth. The men, however, pressed forward again and again, with dauntless courage, to the ditch around the inner line of works, which they failed to carry, but where many of them remained, separated from the enemy only by the parapet, until the Federal army withdrew.

A return of casualties has heretofore been made, the number reported amounting to something over two thousand in killed, wounded and missing; among them were many of our best officers and bravest men. Brigadier-General John Adams was killed, his horse being found lying across the inner line of the enemy's works. Brigadier-General Scott was paralyzed by the explosion near him of a shell. Brigadier-Generals Quarles and Crockett were wounded severely, the former subsequently becoming a prisoner. Major-General Walthall had two horses killed, and was himself severely bruised. Many field and staff and company officers were either killed or severely wounded. They deserve special mention, but not having yet received reports from divisions, brigades and regiments, it is not in my power to give all their names or to do justice to their heroic conduct.

On Friday, December 2d, we moved to the vicinity of Nashville, finally taking a position on the left of the army, extending across the Granny White (or Middle Franklin) Pike to a hill near the Hillsboro Pike. This line was intrenched, was just a mile in length, and occupied by Loring's division alone. To protect our left flank, works were commenced on four other hills lying along, near to and on either side of the Hillsboro Pike, the one furthest in rear being some mile and a half distant from the left of the front line. This latter line, to the left of the Hillsboro Pike, was prolonged toward Cumberland River by the cavalry, though toward the last of our stay there Ector's brigade, under Colonel Coleman, was placed on picket on the Hardin Pike, having Chalmers' cavalry on his right and left.

On the morning of December 15th information was received that the enemy were advancing west of the Hillsboro Pike. General Walthall, whose troops were in bivouac, excepting the working parties engaged on the flank redoubts, was directed to place his men under arms and man the redoubts. General French having received leave of absence, his division, which was small, was attached to General Walthall's. Finding the enemy were advancing in force, and that Ector's brigade and the cavalry were forced to retire, all of Walthall's command not required for the redoubts was placed behind the stone fence along the Hillsboro Pike, between two redoubts. The map exhibits the position of Loring's division in the front line of the five hills crowned with unfinished works, and of Walthall's command, including his own and French's divisions. Each redoubt contained a section or battery of artillery and from one hundred to one hundred and fifty infantry. The enemy appeared in force along the entire line, extending around redoubts One, Two and Three, and as far as or beyond Four and Five. My own line was stretched to its utmost tension, but could not reach far enough toward Four and Five without leaving the way open to the enemy between Loring's left and Walthall's right. The commanding general, who was notified as soon as practicable of the approach of the enemy, sent me as re-enforcements, first, Manigault's, and soon after Deas' brigades, of Johnson's division, Lee's corps, and later the two remaining brigades of that division, and I was informed that one or more divisions from Cheatham's corps (the extreme right) had been ordered to the left. As the object of the enemy seemed to be to turn our left flank by carrying the redoubts Four and

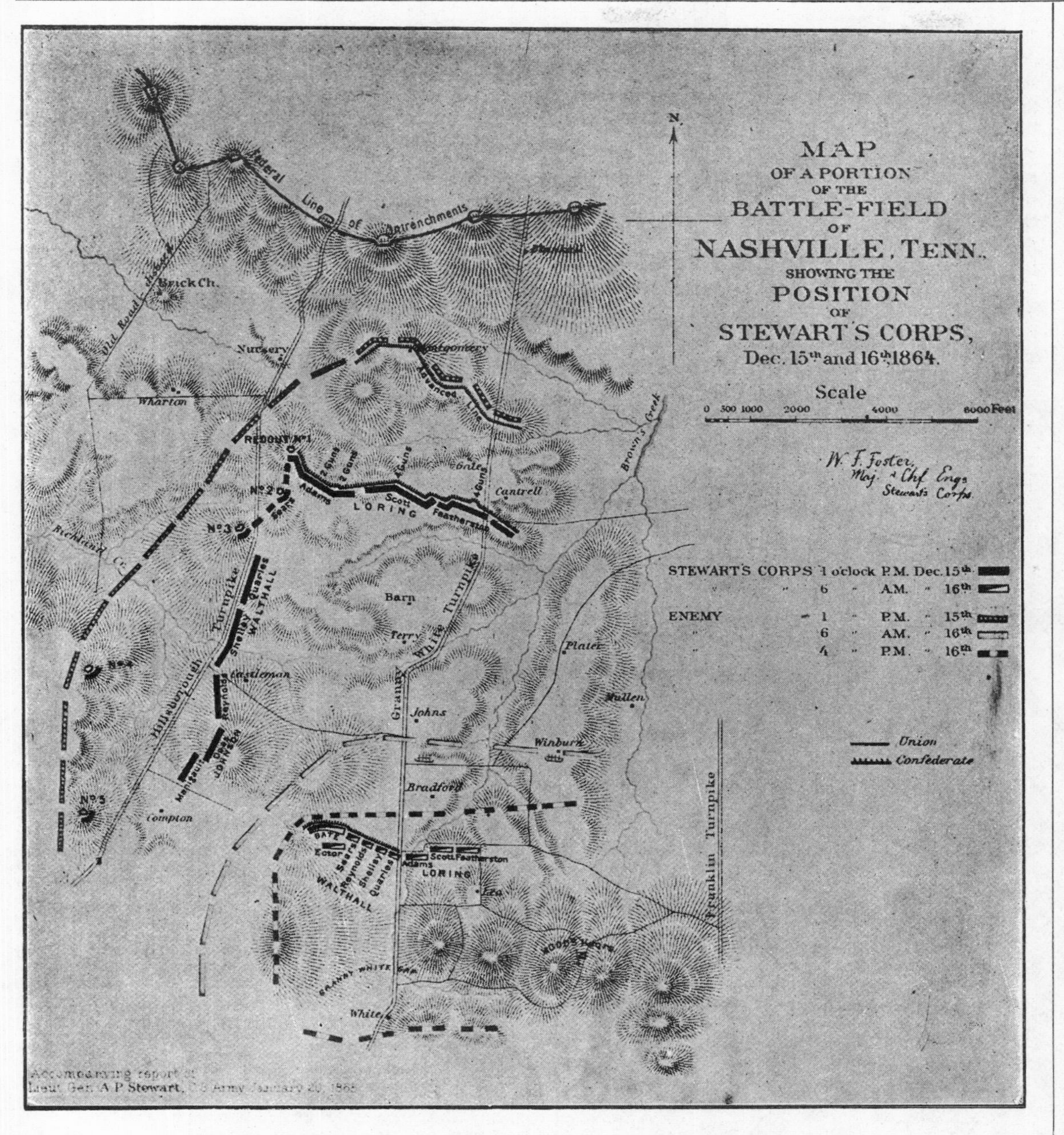

Five, Manigault's brigade, on coming up, was moved in line about parallel to the Hillsboro Pike and opposite redoubt Four. Major-General Johnson arriving soon afterward was directed to place Deas' brigade on Manigault's right, so as to connect with Walthall's line. By this time the enemy had carried redoubts Four and Five, capturing many of the men and all the artillery in them, besides killing and wounding many, and were making for the pike. The two brigades named, making but feeble resistance, fled, and the enemy crossed the pike, passing Walthall's left. Loring's line not being yet pressed, a battery had been ordered from it, which, arriving just at this moment, was placed on a commanding hill, and these same brigades rallied to its support. These again fled, however, on the approach of the enemy, abandoning the battery, which was captured. By this time the other brigades of Johnson's division had come up, but were unable to check the progress of the enemy, who had passed the Hillsboro Pike a full half mile, completely turning our flank and gaining the rear of both Walthall and Loring, whose situation was becoming perilous in the extreme. Their positions were maintained to the last possible moment, in the hope that the expected succor would arrive and restore the fight on the left. Deeming it absolutely necessary for them to fall back, orders were dispatched to that effect, when it was found that Walthall had already ordered his line to retire, not a moment too soon, and this of itself made it necessary for Loring to withdraw. The latter was directed also to form along the Granny White Pike (which would place him nearly at right angles to his former position), to check the anticipated rush of the enemy from his and Walthall's fronts. This was gallantly and successfully done by this fine division, the corps retiring to a position between the Granny White and Franklin pikes, when night put an end to the conflict.

Brigadier-General Sears late in the day lost a leg, and subsequently fell into the enemy's hands. All the artillery in the redoubts, the battery above mentioned, and another on Loring's line, the horses of which were killed or wounded, were captured by the enemy.

In the meantime, one or two divisions from Cheatham's corps had come up on the left, where the commanding general was in person, but, being separated from that part of the field, I am unable to state what occurred. Also Ector's brigade, commanded by Colonel Coleman, in falling back from its position on the Hardin Pike, was thrown over on the left and beyond my personal observation. Colonel Coleman's operations were meritorious. They were characterized by the usual intrepidity of his small but firm and reliable body of men.

During the night of the 15th the army was placed in position to receive the attack expected at an early hour next morning. The map shows the position of this corps, it being in the center, Lee's corps on the right, Cheatham's on the left, extending from the hill occupied by Bate's division, Cheatham's corps, along the range of hills on the west side of the Granny White Pike. The line of this corps extended from the side of the hill occupied by Bate across the pike, along a stone fence on east side of the pike. In rear of the line and some half mile or more distant, a high ridge lies in a general east and west direction, through the gaps of which run the Franklin, Granny White and other pikes.

It was the order of the commanding general that in case of disaster Lee's corps should hold the Franklin Pike, this corps retiring by that pike and taking up position at or beyond Brentwood, so as to permit Lee to withdraw, while Cheatham was to move out on the Granny White Pike. Instructions accordingly were given to subordinate commanders.

At an early hour in the morning the enemy approached, placing artillery in position and opening a heavy fire, which continued almost incessantly through the day. They confronted us everywhere with a force double or treble our own. Occasional attacks were made on various parts of our lines and repulsed, though their chief efforts seemed to be directed against our flanks, for the purpose of gaining the roads in our rear. Every attack made on the lines occupied by this corps to the last was repulsed with severe loss to the enemy.

In the course of the morning, the commanding general calling on me for a brigade to go to the right flank, Ector's being in reserve, was dispatched. It was finally sent to the hills in our rear and on the east side of the Granny White Pike to drive back the enemy, who had passed our left, crossed to the east side of the pike, and held this portion of the ridge. Later in the day, Reynolds' (Arkansas) brigade was withdrawn from Walthall's line and sent to the assistance of Ector's. They were strong enough to check the enemy, but not sufficiently so to drive him back and regain the pass by which this pike crosses the ridge, so that retreat was cut off in that direction, and greatly endangered even by the Franklin Pike, the only route now left open for the whole army. At one time the enemy gained the spurs on the west side of the Granny White Pike occupied by Cheatham's men, some of whom, falling back, formed parallel to Bate's line on the south side of the hill occupied by his division, but a few hundred yards from his line and fronting in the opposite direction.

The situation then, briefly, was this: The left flank completely turned, the enemy crossing to east side of Granny White Pike in our rear, and holding the ridge on that side and the pass through which this road runs. The ridge was high and steep, and extended beyond the Frank-

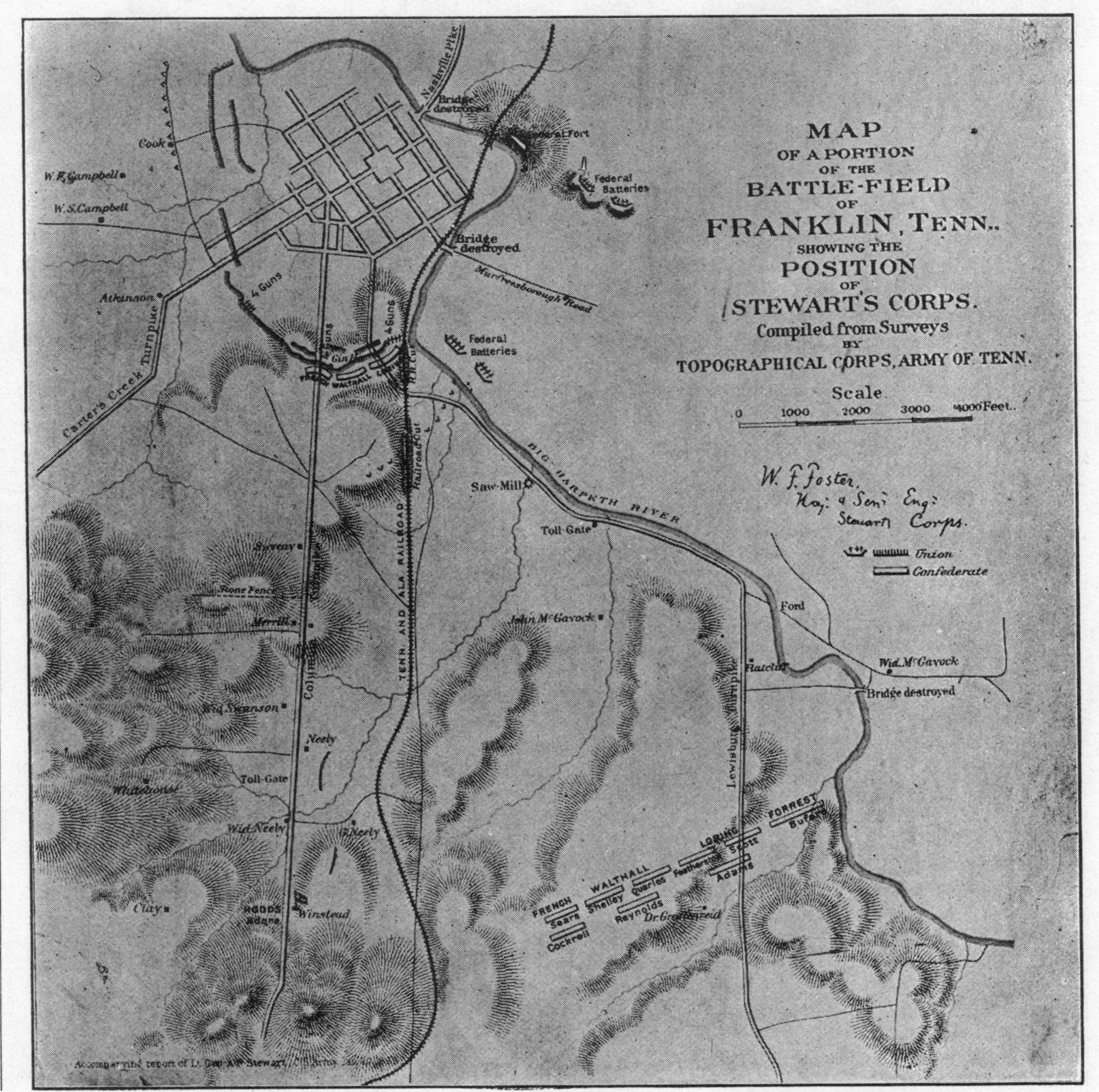

lin Pike to the east, and was but a short distance in rear of our line. It seemed as though, in case of disaster, escape was impossible. There was no reserve force that could be brought up to restore any break that might occur.

About 2 or 3 o'clock in the afternoon the commanding general sent for me, and while in conversation with him, an officer of his staff announced that the line had given way. Not being present at the moment this took place, at least where I could witness it, and not yet being in possession of the official reports of subordinate commanders, I do not deem it proper to attempt to decide where the line first yielded. It would seem, however, that when once broken it very soon gave way everywhere, and the whole army made for the Franklin Pike. In accordance with the orders of the commanding general before attended to, I had dispatched Major Foster, of the engineers, to find a suitable position beyond Brentwood for holding this road.

On reaching Brentwood, however, about dark, I received orders to move on to Franklin, and next morning to move toward Spring Hill and Columbia. Arriving at the latter place on the morning of the 18th, this corps took position on the north bank of Duck River, covering the passage of the entire army, and crossing about daylight of the 20th; so the following week at Tennessee River, Bainbridge, this corps covered the operations and was the last to cross, which it did on the morning of December 28th. At Columbia, a rear-guard, composed of several brigades from this and the other corps, was organized and placed under the command of Major-General Walthall. This force, in connection with the cavalry, covered the retreat from Columbia to the Tennessee River.

It is due to the officers and men of this corps that I should bear testimony to their patient endurance of fatigue and privations, their cheerfulness and alacrity in obeying orders, and, above all, their heroic valor, as displayed on many occasions since I have had the honor to command them, but pre-eminently at Franklin. My thanks are due to Major-Generals Loring, Walthall and French for their cordial co-operation and skillful management of their respective divisions, and to the several members of my staff, who have uniformly shown themselves competent, faithful and zealous in the discharge of their duties.

I have omitted to state in its proper place that a short time after our advance to the vicinity of Nashville, Cockrell's brigade of Missourians, French's division, was ordered by the commanding general to the mouth of Duck River. It rejoined at Bainbridge, where we recrossed the Tennessee River. Accompanying this report are maps of the fields at Franklin and Nashville, as accurate as it is possible to make them.

I deem it proper to say that after the fall of Atlanta the condition of the army and other considerations rendered it necessary, in my judgment, that an offensive campaign should be made in the enemy's rear and on his line of communications. It is not my purpose, nor does it pertain to me, to explain the reasons which prompted the campaign, but simply to express my concurrence in the views which determined the operations of the army.

There were many conspicuous acts of gallantry exhibited by general, field and company officers, and by different commands. The officers were always zealous in the discharge of their duties.

To the officers of my personal staff, and also of the corps staff, I am indebted. They were always at their posts and ready to respond to the call of duty.

* * * * * * *

ALEX. P. STEWART,
Lieutenant-General.

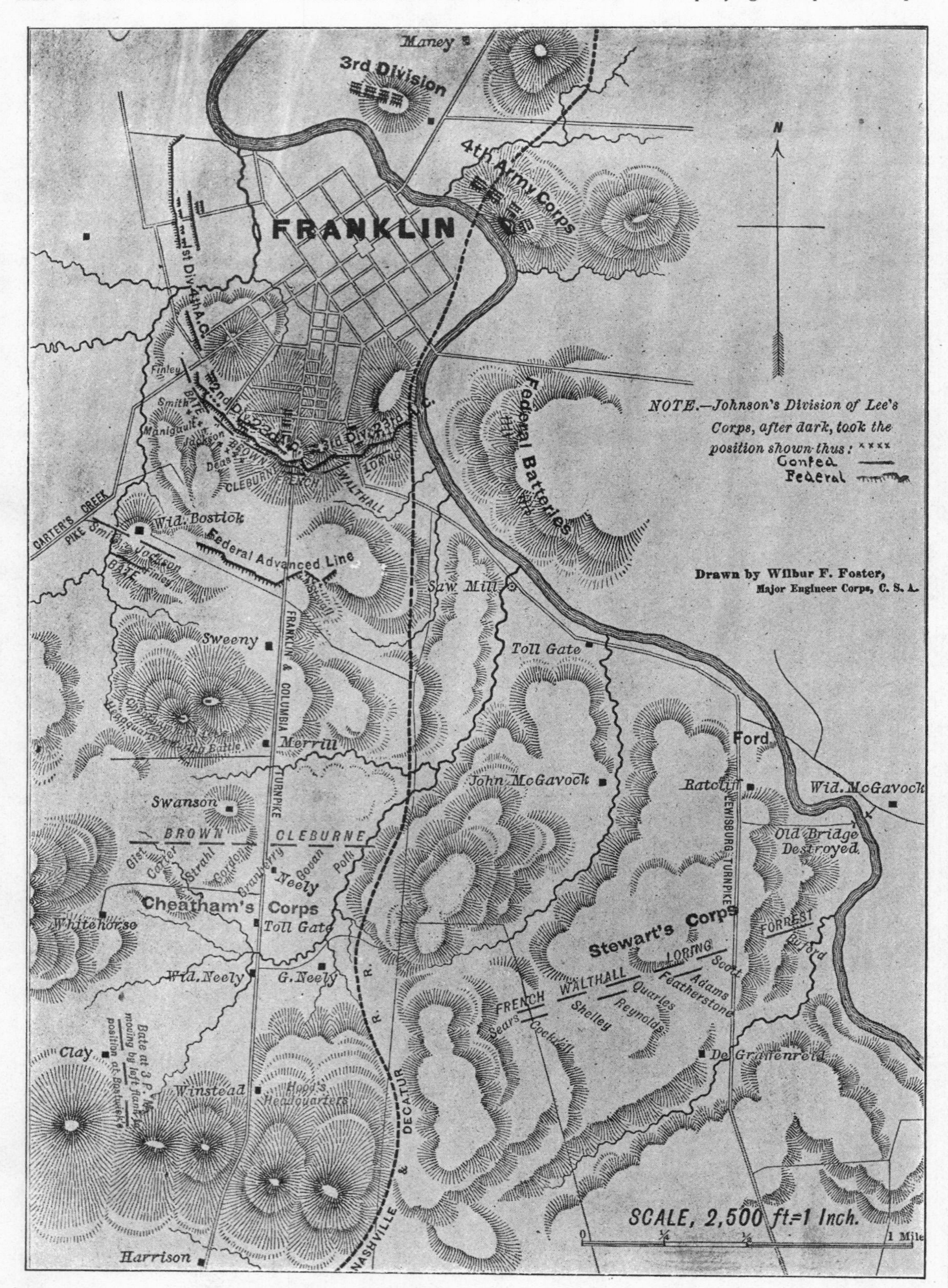

HEADQUARTERS ARMY OF TENNESSEE, NEAR SMITHFIELD DEPOT, N. C.,
April 3, 1865.

In my report of the operations of my corps during the campaign made by General Hood into Tennessee I omitted the details of what transpired near Spring Hill during the afternoon and night of the 29th of November, 1864. I respectfully submit the following statement and ask that it be filed as a part of my report:

LIEUT.-GEN. A. P. STEWART, OF TENNESSEE.

On the morning of November 29th General Hood moved with Cheatham's corps and mine and Johnson's division, of Lee's corps (the latter reporting to me), Cheatham's corps in advance. We made a forced march to get in rear of the enemy. In the course of the afternoon, about 3 or 4 o'clock, I reached Rutherfords Creek as Cheatham's rear division was crossing. I received orders to halt and form on the south side of the creek, my right to rest on or near the creek, so as to move down the creek if necessary. Subsequently I received an order to send a division across the creek, and finally, between sunset and dark, an order was received to cross the creek, leaving a division on the south side. Johnson's division, being in rear, was designated to remain.

Riding in advance of the column, about dusk, I found General Hood some half mile from the creek and about as far west of the road on which we were marching and which led to Spring Hill. The commanding general gave me a young man of the neighborhood as a guide, and told me to move on and place my right across the pike beyond Spring Hill, "your left," he added, "extending down this way." This would have placed my line in rear of Cheatham's, except that my right would have extended beyond his. The guide informed me that at a certain point the road made a sudden turn to the left going into Spring Hill; that from this bend there used to be a road leading across to the pike, meeting it at the toll-gate some mile and a half beyond Spring Hill, toward Franklin. I told him if he could find it, that was the right road. Arriving at the bend of the road we passed through a large gateway, taking what appeared in the darkness to be an indistinct path.

MAJ.-GEN. PATRICK R. CLEBURNE, OF ARKANSAS.
Killed at the Battle of Franklin, Tenn., November 30, 1864.

Within a short distance I found General Forrest's headquarters and stopped to ascertain the position of his pickets covering Cheatham's right and of the enemy. He informed me that his scouts reported the enemy leaving the direct pike—leading from Spring Hill to Franklin and Nashville—and taking the one down Carters Creek.

While in conversation with him I was informed that a

staff officer from General Hood had come up and halted the column. It turned out to be a staff (engineer) officer of General Cheatham's, who informed me that General Hood had sent him to place me in position. It striking me as strange the commanding general should send an officer not of his own staff on this errand, or indeed any one, as he had given directions to me in person, I inquired of the officer if he had seen General Hood since I had. He replied that he had just come from General Hood, and that the reason why he was sent was that I was to go into position on General Brown's right (the right of Cheatham's corps), and he and General Brown had been over the ground by daylight.

Thinking it possible the commanding general had changed his mind as to what he wished me to do, I concluded it was proper to be governed by the directions of this staff officer, and therefore returned to the road and moved on toward Spring Hill. Arriving near the line of Brown's division, General Brown explained his position, which was oblique to the pike, his right being further from it than his left. It was evident that if my command were marched up and formed on his right, it being now a late hour, it would require all night to accomplish it, and the line, instead of extending across the pike, would bear away from it. Feeling satisfied there was a mistake, I directed the troops to be bivouacked, while I rode back to find the commanding general to explain my situation and get further instructions. On arriving at his headquarters I inquired of him if he had sent this officer of General Cheatham's staff to place me in position. He replied that he had. I next inquired if he had changed his mind as to what he wished me to do. He replied that he had not. "But," said he, "the fact is, General Cheatham has been here and represented that there ought to be somebody on Brown's right." I explained to him that in the uncertainty I was in, I had directed the troops, who had been marching rapidly since daylight, and it was now 11 P. M., to be placed in bivouac, and had come to report. He remarked, in substance, that it was not material to let the men rest, and directed me to move before daylight in the morning, taking the advance toward Franklin. Subsequently General Hood made to me the statement:

"I want you and your people to understand that I attach no blame to you for the failure at Spring Hill. On the contrary, I know if I had had you with your corps there the attack would have been made. I feel, and have felt, that Tennessee to-day would have been in our possession."

* * * * * *

ALEX. P. STEWART,
Lieutenant-General.

LIST OF DIVISION,* BRIGADE AND REGIMENTAL COMMANDERS KILLED, WOUNDED, MISSING AND CAPTURED IN THE BATTLE OF FRANKLIN, NOVEMBER 30, 1864.

LEE'S CORPS.

JOHNSON'S DIVISION.

DEAS' BRIGADE.

Major E. H. Armistead, Twenty-second Alabama, wounded.

SHARP'S BRIGADE.

Colonel W. H. Bishop, Seventh and Ninth Mississippi, killed.

Lieutenant-Colonel W. H. Sims, Tenth and Forty-fourth Mississippi, wounded.

Captain J. M. Hicks, Forty-first Mississippi, wounded.

MANIGAULT'S BRIGADE.

Brigadier-General A. M. Manigault, wounded.

Colonel N. N. Davis, Twenty-fourth Alabama, wounded.

Colonel T. P. Shaw, Nineteenth South Carolina, wounded.

BRANTLY'S BRIGADE.

Lieutenant-Colonel J. M. Johnson, Thirtieth Mississippi, wounded.

Major G. W. Reynolds, Twenty-ninth Mississippi, killed.

Major J. K. Allen, Thirtieth Mississippi, missing.

STEWART'S CORPS.

LORING'S DIVISION.

ADAMS' BRIGADE.

Brigadier-General John Adams, killed.

Colonel M. Farrel, Fifteenth Mississippi, wounded.

Colonel W. N. Brown, Twentieth Mississippi, wounded.

SCOTT'S BRIGADE.

Brigadier-General T. M. Scott, wounded.

Colonel S. S. Ives, Twenty-seventh, Thirty-fifth and Forty-ninth Alabama (consolidated), wounded.

Colonel C. J. L. Cunningham, Fifty-seventh Alabama, wounded.

Colonel N. L. Nelson, Twelfth Louisiana, killed.

FEATHERSTON'S BRIGADE.

Colonel M. D. L. Stephens, Thirty-first Mississippi, wounded.

Lieutenant Colonel S. M. Dyer, Third Mississippi, wounded.

FRENCH'S DIVISION.

COCKRELL'S BRIGADE.

Brigadier-General F. M. Cockrell, wounded.

Colonel H. A. Garland, First and Fourth Missouri, killed.

Colonel E. Gates, First and Third Missouri, wounded.

Lieutenant-Colonel W. F. Carter, Second and Sixth Missouri, wounded.

Captain P. Canniff, Third and Fifth Missouri, killed.

SEARS' BRIGADE.

Colonel W. W. Witherspoon, Thirty-sixth Mississippi, killed.

Colonel T. N. Adaire, Fourth Mississippi, wounded.

Major T. D. Magee, Forty-sixth Mississippi, wounded.

WALTHALL'S DIVISION.

QUARLES' BRIGADE.

Brigadier-General W. A. Quarles, wounded.

Colonel Isaac N. Hulme, Forty-second Tennessee, wounded.

Lieutenant-Colonel T. M. Atkins, Forty-ninth Tennessee, wounded and captured.

Major S. C. Cooper, Forty-sixth Tennessee, wounded and captured.

Major S. L. Knox, First Alabama, wounded and captured.

Major J. E. McDonald, Fifty-fifth Tennessee, killed.

Captain James J. Rittenbury, Fifty-third Tennessee, wounded and captured.

CANTEY'S BRIGADE.

Colonel V. S. Murphey, Seventeenth Alabama, missing.

Lieutenant-Colonel J. S. Garvin, Twenty-sixth Alabama, wounded.

Captain A. V. Gardner, Twenty-ninth Alabama, wounded.

REYNOLDS' BRIGADE.

Major J. C. Bratton, Ninth Arkansas, wounded.

* No casualties in Stevenson's and Clayton's divisions.

NASHVILLE, TENN., FROM THE SOUTHEAST, SHOWING THE STATE CAPITOL.

CHEATHAM'S CORPS.

CLEBURNE'S DIVISION.

Major-General P. R. Cleburne, killed.

GRANBURY'S BRIGADE.

Brigadier-General H. B. Granbury, killed.

Lieutenant-Colonel R. B. Young, Tenth Texas, killed.

Major W. A. Taylor, Twenty-fourth and Twenty-fifth Texas Cavalry, missing.

Captain J. W. Brown, Seventh Texas, missing.

Captain R. Fisher, Sixth and Fifteenth Texas, missing.

Captain A. A. Cox, Fifth Confederate, missing.

LOWREY'S BRIGADE.

Colonel W. H. H. Tison, Thirty-second Mississippi, wounded.

Colonel John Weir, Fifth Mississippi, wounded.

Colonel F. A. Ashford, Sixteenth Alabama, killed.

Colonel R. F. Crittenden, Thirty-third Alabama, missing.

Lieutenant-Colonel R. H. Abercrombie, Forty-fifth Alabama, wounded.

GOVAN'S BRIGADE.

Major A. T. Meek, Second and Twenty-fourth Arkansas, killed.

Captain M. P. Garrett, First and Fifteenth Arkansas, killed.

Captain M. H. Dixon, Third Confederate, missing.

BROWN'S DIVISION.

Major-General John C. Brown, wounded.

GIST'S BRIGADE.

Brigadier-General S. R. Gist, killed.

Colonel E. Capers, Twenty-fourth South Carolina, wounded.

Major S. J. C. Dunlap, Forty-sixth Georgia, wounded.

MANEY'S BRIGADE.

Brigadier-General J. C. Carter, wounded.

STRAHL'S BRIGADE.

Brigadier-General O. F. Strahl, killed.

Colonel J. A. Wilson, Twenty-fourth Tennessee, wounded.

Colonel M. Magevney, Jr., Fifteenth Tennessee, wounded.

Lieutenant-Colonel F. E. P. Stafford, Thirty-first Tennessee, killed.

VAUGHAN'S BRIGADE.

Brigadier-General G. W. Gordon, captured.

BATE'S DIVISION.

JACKSON'S BRIGADE.

Colonel George A. Smith, First Confederate, Georgia, killed.

Lieutenant-Colonel A. S. Hamilton, Sixty-sixth Georgia, wounded.

FINLEY'S BRIGADE.

Lieutenant-Colonel E. Badger, First Florida Cavalry and Fourth Florida Infantry, wounded.

SUMMARY.

RANK OF OFFICER.	Killed.	Woun'd	Missing	Captr'd.
Major-General	1	1	....	....
Brigadier-General	4	5	....	1
Colonel	6	15	2	....
Lieutenant-Colonel	2	9	....	....
Major	3	5	2	....
Captain	2	3	4	...
Total	18	38	8	1

THE SAVANNAH CAMPAIGN,

NOVEMBER 19 TO 30, 1864.

BY

MAJ.-GEN. JOSEPH WHEELER,

Commanding Cavalry Corps.

NEAR SAVANNAH, GA., December 24, 1864.

I SUBMIT the following report of the operations of my command from November 19, 1864, the date General Hardee assumed command.

For several days previous to that date I had been resisting the enemy's advance from Atlanta toward Macon, reporting daily to Generals Bragg, Hood, Hardee and Taylor, and also to Governor Brown, almost the exact movements and intentions of the enemy. Anderson's brigade had been ordered to report to Major-General Howell Cobb, at Macon, in order that he might place him in position to observe the enemy approaching Macon on the east side of the Ocmulgee River. This brigade was placed in position by General Cobb on the Clinton Road.

CUMBERLAND GAP.

On the 19th I sent Crews' (Georgia) brigade with orders also to report to General Cobb. This brigade, Colonel Crews reports, was placed in position on the Milledgeville Road, with instructions, as I afterward learned, to follow and engage any raiding party of the enemy which might move toward the railroad. Toward evening on the 19th I ascertained from my scouts that the main forces of the enemy had crossed the Ocmulgee River above the mouth of the Towaligo, which induced me to move to Macon in person, directing all my command, except Ferguson's and Breckinridge's brigades, to follow me.

On arriving at Macon, about 11 P. M., I found Lieutenant-General Hardee, who had assumed command of the department. He directed me to move at daylight, with all my available force, except Crews' brigade, out on the Clinton Road and ascertain the enemy's force and location. In obeying this order, and before marching toward Clinton, both my flanks were menaced by small parties of the enemy, which I was obliged to drive off, causing some delay. I then moved on rapidly with my advance guard to Clinton, and found Osterhaus' corps moving through the town. This was not observed until very near the column, owing to a dense fog. Six men dashed into the town and captured General Osterhaus' servant (an enlisted man) within twenty feet of General Osterhaus' headquarters. A regiment of the enemy's cavalry charged us, making the retreat of my small escort necessary. A squad of the enemy's cavalry had pressed in upon my line of retreat between my position and the body of my command. These, however, were soon cleared away by the approach of two of my regiments, which came up rapidly to my assistance. I immediately charged the advancing column of the enemy and drove it back upon their infantry. They then rallied and charged me again. We met this charge, checked and returned it with success, driving them back toward Clinton. I now learned from my scouts that the enemy in considerable force were pressing down the road toward Griswoldville. I started promptly with a portion of my command in that direction, and soon met a courier from Colonel Crews, with a note from him stating that the enemy's cavalry had moved toward the railroad, and that, pursuant to General Hardee's orders, he was going in pursuit. This left the Milledgeville Road open, and, fearing some difficulty, I moved rapidly to that point. On arriving I found our artillery engaging the enemy's advance, and our infantry in the redoubts ready to receive an attack. The enemy had already charged up the road, and four of them had attempted to capture a gun, but had been driven back, leaving an officer (whose horse was killed) in the hands of our infantry. Finding large, unprotected intervals between redoubts, I placed Harrison's and Hagan's brigades in line, making the connection complete. After slight skirmishing the enemy retreated a short distance. Pursuant to orders from General Hardee, I moved out during the night, and the next day drove the enemy from Griswoldville, capturing a few prisoners. The next morning I again attacked and drove the enemy for some distance, capturing sixty prisoners, besides killing and wounding a large number.

It now being evident that the enemy were not intending to make any further demonstration upon Macon, I moved on toward the Oconee, which river I reached on November 24th and completed crossing the next day by swimming. A brigade under Lieutenant-Colonel Gaines was immediately sent to hold in check a portion of the enemy who were menacing the river near Balls Ferry, and with the remainder of my command I moved during the night to Station No. 13, on the Central Railroad. Scouts and pickets were sent upon all roads by which the enemy could reach the railroad or march in an easterly direction. The following day, pursuant to General Hardee's orders, I moved to Sandersville.

The Fourteenth and Twentieth Corps of the enemy had marched from Milledgeville, crossed Buffalo Creek, and were marching upon the town, preceded by cavalry, which had dispersed the local troops who had attempted to oppose them. I moved out on the lower road and sent a force out on the upper road. After moving three miles we were charged by the enemy, whom we met and checked, and then in turn charged and drove them back for a mile, capturing, killing and wounding about thirty of the enemy, besides capturing several horses, mules and one loaded wagon. I immediately sent word to the citizens of Sandersville that the enemy would enter the town next morning, and I advised them to send off all movable property of value. At dark we established our pickets close to the enemy, and next morning were slowly driven back toward and finally through the town.

At evening I was informed by my pickets near Ogeechee Shoals that General Kilpatrick, with a large force of cavalry, had crossed the river on his way to Augusta. Leaving General Iverson to observe the enemy, I started immediately with my command, overtaking him about midnight. I immediately attacked and captured his picket and pushed on to his camp, and drove him back from the main Augusta Road and out of his camps, capturing one stand of colors, some prisoners, some fifty horses, clothing, blankets, camp-equipage, etc., in considerable quantities. The enemy immediately started toward Augusta on the lower Augusta Road.

On reaching the house where General Kilpatrick had staid I learned that he and his officers had been overheard talking a great deal in private about Augusta. It was the opinion of citizens that this move was intended as a raid upon that place. Being mindful of the great damage that could be done by the enemy's burning the valuable mills and property which were not protected by fortifications, including the factories in the vicinity, the large portion of the city outside of the fortifications, the arsenal and sand hills, I hoped by pressing him hard he might be turned from his purpose. I also learned that the night previous he had sent a party of some five hundred men to Waynesboro to destroy the railroad bridge, which convinced me

BRIG.-GEN. ROBERT H. ANDERSON, OF GEORGIA.

that Augusta and not Waynesboro was Kilpatrick's destination, as had the latter place been the point he designed striking, he would not have sent a small party there on the preceding day. Notwithstanding the jaded condition of my command, I therefore pushed on rapidly, engaging and defeating his rear-guards, whom I found fortified at every favorable point, frequently separated by but two or three hundred yards. Horses, arms and prisoners were captured in nearly every engagement.

On reaching Brier Creek Swamp we pressed the enemy so warmly that he turned off toward Waynesboro. During the chase the enemy set fire to all corncribs, cotton gins and a large number of barns and houses. We succeeded in driving him off in nearly half the instances in time to extinguish the flames, and frequently pressed him so rapidly as to prevent his firing a number of houses, thus saving a large amount of property.

I entered the town of Waynesboro with my staff just after dark and just as the enemy were leaving it. The town was in flames, but with the assistance of my staff and escort we succeeded in staying the flames and extinguishing the fire in all but one dwelling, which was so far burned that it was impossible to save it. I immediately moved on and attacked the enemy, who were engaged in tearing up the railroad. The attack had the effect to stop their work upon the railroad and to keep them in line of battle all night.

About 3 A. M. I sent Humes' division to gain the enemy's rear by turning his left flank, and sent a regiment to gain his rear by moving around his right. Unfortunately the commands failed to get into position. At daylight the enemy withdrew for a short distance unobserved, in consequence of a dense fog. As we advanced upon them they charged our line, which charge we met and easily repulsed. I charged the enemy's flank with Humes' and Anderson's commands, and attacked the front with the balance of my command, driving the enemy from his fortified position, capturing a number of prisoners, arms and horses, and killing a great many who refused to surrender, and who were shot in the pursuit which ensued. The rout was complete, and General Kilpatrick was himself very nearly captured. We continued the charge until reaching a swamp where the enemy had so constructed barricades as to make a very strong resistance.

The enemy was soon driven from this position by a flank movement, after which I again charged and routed their entire force, capturing, killing and wounding nearly two hundred, and completely stampeding the whole force. His destruction was only prevented by an intervening swamp at Buck Head Creek, which made it almost impossible to approach, and by the failure of the Fourth Tennessee Regiment to gain the enemy's rear, for which purpose it had been detached some two hours previous. The bridge over Buck Head Creek had been carefully prepared for burning by Kilpatrick's advance guard, and on our reaching it the torch had been applied and the bridge was in flames, while a terrific fire from the enemy on the other side prevented me from immediately extinguishing the flames. I dismounted the advance brigade and advanced it through the creek bottom to the bank, and finally drove the enemy sufficiently far from the opposite bank to enable a few brave men to work their way across and drive the enemy beyond range.

By great energy and hard labor on the part of my men the fire was soon extinguished, and in little more than an hour the bridge was reconstructed and our troops passing over. The passage, however, was very slow, on account of the rude and frail construction of the bridge. After advancing a mile I discovered the enemy's position, and ordered General Dibrell's to turn their right flank by moving through a wood which screened the movement.

As night was fast approaching it became imp rtant to strike the enemy immediately, although only about twelve hundred of my command had crossed the creek. I moved upon the enemy and drove in his pickets. On discovering his line I observed that General Dibrell, in attempting to turn his flank (although he had moved nearly a mile to our left) had, nevertheless, encountered the enemy's line of battle, which extended still beyond his position. Having parts of Harrison's and Ashby's brigades with me, the former being in advance, I placed the Third Arkansas Regiment in line, and the Eighth and Eleventh Texas Regiments in column and charged the enemy's position. Nothing could have exceeded the gallantry with which these troops responded to the bugle's call and hurled themselves upon the enemy, driving his cavalry in confusion and finally encountering the breastworks. This so terrified the enemy as to cause him to flee in uncontrollable confusion. Unfortunately the open ground did not continue, and we finally encountered a line so positioned that it could not be approached by cavalry. I ordered Ashby's brigade to turn the enemy's left flank and take possession of the Louisville Road, upon which the enemy was retreating. Owing to approaching dusk, Colonel Ashby, by accident, got on a road to the left of the one indicated by my order and notified me that he held possession of the Louisville Road. This error enabled the enemy to move off by scattering through fields and woods without order or organization.

During the night Kilpatrick sought the protection of his infantry, which he did not venture to forsake again during the campaign, no doubt being too much demoralized to again meet our cavalry. Fearing the enemy might make another attempt to raid or march upon Augusta, I placed pickets at all the crossings of Brier Creek and located my main force at Rocky Springs Church.

On the morning of December 2d the Fourteenth Army Corps and Kilpatrick's cavalry marched upon Waynesboro by the Louisville Road. I met and checked them at Rocky Creek. After a warm engagement they moved off to my left and crossed a short distance below on a temporarily constructed bridge, and, by moving through the fields, turned off toward Thomas Station. This necessitated my falling back.

The following day I moved down and attacked the enemy, driving in their pickets and stopping their destruction of the railroad. Perceiving after nightfall that they had recommenced their work, I again attacked them about midnight, shelling their camp with good effect. At daylight the enemy in strong force marched upon Waynesboro. Most of my command had necessarily been sent some three miles after forage. We quickly concentrated and hastily threw up barricades, while a single regiment held the entire column in check. This rough screen was hardly completed when a general charge was made upon our lines, which was repulsed with considerable loss to the enemy. A second, third and fourth charge were made by the enemy, each of which was repulsed or met and driven back by counter-charges. Finally their long lines of infantry advanced, and, after warm fighting, their cavalry having turned our flanks, we were compelled to fall back, which was done by taking successive positions till we reached the town of Waynesboro. Here we were so warmly pressed that it was with difficulty we succeeded in withdrawing from our position. The moment our lines left our works I directed the Eighth Texas (Colonel Cook) and the Ninth Tennessee [Battalion] (Captain Bromley) to charge the enemy, which was gallantly done, meeting and driving back a charge of the enemy and so staggering him that no further demonstration was made upon us until we were prepared to receive the enemy at our new position north of the town. During all the enemy's charges the loss of men and horses must have been severe. According to his own account his loss in men numbered fifty killed and one hundred and forty-seven wounded. The enemy remained in town about three hours and then moved down the Savannah Road. During all the engagements the enemy's cavalry were at least double my own numbers, and were, besides, re-enforced by one or more divisions of infantry.

Having been notified by the lieutenant-general commanding that the roads toward Savannah had been blockaded by his order, and having sent Lewis' brigade

SAVANNAH, GA., AND FORTIFICATIONS, FROM FORT BLOGGS, LOOKING UP THE SAVANNAH RIVER.

FEDERAL FORCES DESTROYING THE RAILROAD AT WAYNESBORO, GA.

(re-enforced by the Fourth Tennessee Regiment) to fall back before the enemy, I, with the remainder of my command, remained to protect Augusta and to strike his flanks and rear.

On the first day I attacked his rear several times, driving him from his several positions, killing and wounding a great number and capturing about one hundred prisoners. During his movement toward Savannah so warmly was he pressed that he blockaded the roads in his rear, frequently building fortifications two or three miles in length and destroyed all bridges on his line of march. He occasionally attacked us by charging with his cavalry, which was invariably met by counter-charges and driven back in confusion with heavy loss. In every fight we captured horses, arms and prisoners.

On the night of December 8th we shelled the camp of the Fourteenth Corps with good effect, throwing the corps into confusion and causing it to leave camp at midnight, abandoning clothing, arms, etc. By breaking up the camp during the extreme darkness a great many negroes were left in our hands, whom we sent back to their owners. We also captured three wagons and teams and caused the enemy to burn several more wagons. The whole number of negroes captured from the enemy during the movement was nearly two thousand.

On the 8th we captured a dispatch from General Slocum to General Davis, giving the proposed location of Sherman's army before Savannah, which afterward proved to be correct. This paper was forwarded to General Hardee. On reaching a point within ten miles of the city, and finding it impossible to do any further harm to the enemy in that position, I moved back and crossed the Savannah River, leaving General Iverson's command to watch the enemy should he move in the direction of Augusta or Western Georgia. On reaching the South Carolina side, I moved down, and was placed by Lieutenant-General Hardee in command of the defenses of New River and adjacent landings and charged with the duty of holding the line of communication from Hugers Landing to Hardeeville. This we succeeded in doing, although the enemy held the South Carolina side of the river with a division of infantry. After the evacuation of the city, December 20th, I removed all the guns and ammunition from Tunbridge and Morgans Landings and New River Bridge; also the heavy guns, weighing nine thousand pounds each, from Red Bluff, together with the ammunition.

I ommitted to state that during the entire movement of the enemy through Georgia I kept all my superiors fully informed of the strength and of all the movements of the enemy. At the same time I kept my cavalry in his front, rear and on both flanks, preventing his cavalry from spreading over the country, retarding the enemy by fighting him on all sides and felling trees in his advance. This duty was fully done, and I thank my officers and men for their devotion, gallantry and self-sacrificing spirit they have ever exhibited. Every engagement was a success, and the utter defeat and discomfiture of the enemy's cavalry was most signal and complete, notwithstanding his force of cavalry was always superior to mine.

My force never exceeded thirty-five hundred men, and was so distributed in front, rear and on both flanks that I seldom had more than two thousand under my immediate command, which two thousand frequently charged and routed more than double their numbers. The enemy had been falsely informed by their officers that we took no prisoners, which caused him to fight with desperation, and to run very dangerous gauntlets to escape capture, which frequently accounts for the large proportion of killed. In every rout of their cavalry, and in the many fights which ensued, they continued to flee, refusing to surrender, notwithstanding the demands of my men in close pursuit, consequently no alternative was left but to shoot or saber them to prevent escape.

View of Macon, Ga., from College Hill, October, 1863.

During the trip I had parties to move a day or more in advance of the enemy, informing citizens where to run their negroes and stock in order to insure the safety of their property, offering them every assistance in so doing; but generally the citizens were so frightened as to be perfectly helpless. On the enemy's approach, pursuant to orders, I drove off such horses and mules as were exposed to the enemy's view, and have since taken every pains to restore said stock to its owners, generally with success. My command captured about five hundred horses, many of which had been taken from citizens by the enemy, and have been returned to their owners when it was possible to do so.

I desire to tender my thanks for the devoted gallantry of my division and brigade commanders. Those whose conduct came especially under my notice were Generals Allen, Humes, Anderson and Dibrell, and Colonels Ashby, Hagan, Crews, and Lieutenant-Colonel Anderson. General Allen was slightly wounded and had two horses shot under him at Waynesboro; Generals Humes and Dibrell also had their horses shot while gallantly engaging the enemy.

I also tender my thanks to General Robertson, who, while acting as my chief of staff in the temporary absence of his command, was severely wounded while gallantly charging the enemy.

Captain S. W. Steele and Lieutenant M. G. Hudson aids-de-camp of my staff, were highly distinguished for gallantry and zeal. Lieutenants R. B. Ryan, J. M. Stewart and Henry Chapman, acting upon my staff, were gallant and efficient.

In closing this report I will state that during the last five months my command has been without wagons or cooking utensils, with order to subsist upon the country. Its food has been limited to bread baked upon boards and stones and meat broiled upon sticks. It has not been paid in twelve months, and has not had the regular issues of clothing which have been made to the infantry. During this time it has averaged in direct marching sixteen miles a day, and, being without wagons, has been obliged to pack all the forage and rations to camp on horseback, which, together with scouting and other duties, would make the average traveling of each soldier at least twenty miles each day. During these five months my troops have been continuously in the immediate presence of the enemy, fighting nearly every day, and with valiant success, except in a few instances, when small detachments sent off from my command met vastly superior forces.

During these five months my command has captured, killed and wounded more than its own effective strength. It has captured from the enemy in action and carried off the field 4 pieces of artillery, with caissons and battery wagons, 1,200 mules, over 200 wagons, 2,000 head of beef cattle, 3,000 cavalry horses, with equipments, and over 4,000 stand of arms. It has also captured a great number of the enemy's posts, with large amounts of stores, and has destroyed more railroad used by the enemy—stopping his communication for a longer time and with less loss—than any other cavalry command, although expeditions double its strength have been sent out on that duty. It has also captured and destroyed over a dozen trains of cars, generally loaded with supplies.

As we were continually fighting the enemy, our camps could not be designated before nightfall. Details had then to be sent out to procure forage and rations, frequently making it midnight before supper could be prepared for my men, and then they were often compelled to be in the saddle before daylight. No men in the Confederate States have marched more, fought more, suffered more, or had so little opportunities for discipline; yet they are to-day as orderly and as well disciplined as any cavalry in the Confederate service.

In our line of march officers and men were met, who, in their anxiety to increase their commands, used every exertion to induce my men to desert, frequently offering them promotion and furloughs as a reward for dishonor. Notwithstanding this, my command is to-day stronger and more efficient than it was at the beginning of a continuous campaign of eight months' hard, constant and successful fighting.

I must particularly commend my Tennessee and Kentucky troops, whom, though they saw their homes thrown open by the advance of General Hood's army, I brought from the Coosa River to Savannah without a single desertion. Afterward I had the mortification to see a body desert who had been informed they were to be punished without trial for crimes they had never committed.

J. WHEELER, *Major-General.*

BRANTLY'S BRIGADE.
Brigadier-General W. F. Brantly.

Twenty-fourth Mississippi, Thirty-fourth Mississippi, } Captain C. Dancy.
Twenty-seventh Mississippi—Captain S. M. Pegg.
Twenty-ninth Mississippi, Thirtieth Mississippi, } Captain R. W. Williamson.
Dismounted Cavalry—Captain D. W. Alexander.

STEVENSON'S DIVISION.
Major-General C. L. Stevenson.

CUMMING'S BRIGADE.
Colonel E. P. Watkins.

Thirty-fourth Georgia—Captain R. A. Jones.
Thirty-sixth Georgia—Colonel Charles E. Broyles.

STEWART'S ARMY CORPS.
Lieutenant-General A. P. Stewart, commanding.

LORING'S DIVISION.
Major-General W. W. Loring.

FEATHERSTON'S BRIGADE.
Brigadier-General W. S. Featherston.

First Mississippi—Captain O. D. Hughes.
Third Mississippi—Captain O. H. Johnston.
Twenty-second Mississippi—Major M. A. Oatis.
Thirty-first Mississippi—Captain R. A. Collins.
Thirty-third Mississippi—Captain T. L. Cooper.
Fortieth Mississippi—Colonel W. B. Colbert.
First Mississippi Battalion—Major J. M. Stigler.

CONFEDERATE TROOPS CROSSING THE SAVANNAH RIVER ON PONTOON BRIDGE ON THE EVACUATION OF THE CITY OF SAVANNAH.
[From an original sketch, owned by Mrs. Frank Leslie, New York.]

ARMY OF TENNESSEE,
FOR THE PERIOD ENDING
DECEMBER 10, 1864.*

GENERAL JOHN B. HOOD,
Commanding.

LEE'S ARMY CORPS.
Lieutenant-General Stephen D. Lee, commanding.

JOHNSON'S DIVISION.
Major-General Edward Johnson.

DEAS' BRIGADE.
Brigadier-General Zach. C. Deas.

Nineteenth Alabama—Lieutenant-Colonel George R. Kimbrough.
Twenty-second Alabama—Captain H. W. Henry.
Twenty-fifth Alabama—Captain N. B. Rouse.
Thirty-ninth Alabama—Lieutenant-Colonel W. C. Clifton.
Fiftieth Alabama—Colonel J. G. Coltart.

BRIG.-GEN. ZACH. C. DEAS, OF ALABAMA.
(From a tintype taken in 1863.)

MANIGAULT'S BRIGADE.
Lieutenant-Colonel W. L. Butler.

Twenty-fourth Alabama—Captain T. J. Kimbell.
Twenty-eighth Alabama—Captain W. M. Nabors.
Thirty-fourth Alabama—Lieutenant-Colonel J. C. Carter.
Tenth South Carolina—Lieutenant-Colonel C. Irvin Walker.
Nineteenth South Carolina—Captain T. W. Getzen.

SHARP'S BRIGADE.
Brigadier-General J. H. Sharp.

Seventh Mississippi, Ninth Mississippi, } Major H. Pope.
Tenth Mississippi, Forty-fourth Mississippi, Ninth Battalion Mississippi Sharpshooters, } Captain R. A. Bell.
Forty-first Mississippi—Captain J. M. Hicks.

* Composition of the cavalry not given on original return.

Thirty-ninth Georgia—Captain W. P. Milton.
Fifty-sixth Georgia—Captain B. T. Spearman.

PETTUS' BRIGADE.
Brigadier-General E. W. Pettus.

Twentieth Alabama—Colonel J. N. Dedman.
Twenty-third Alabama—Lieutenant-Colonel J. B. Bibb.
Thirtieth Alabama—Lieutenant-Colonel J. R. Elliott.
Thirty-first Alabama—Lieutenant-Colonel T. M. Arrington.
Forty-sixth Alabama—Captain G. E. Brewer.

BROWN'S AND REYNOLDS' BRIGADES.*
Colonel Joseph B. Palmer.

Sixtieth North Carolina—Major J. T. Huff.
Third Tennessee, Eighteenth Tennessee, } Lieutenant-Colonel W. R. Butler.
Twenty-third Tennessee, Twenty-sixth Tennessee, Forty-fifth Tennessee, } Colonel A. Searcy.
Thirty-second Tennessee—Colonel J. B. McGuire.
Fifty-fourth Virginia—Captain W. G. Anderson.
Sixty-third Virginia—Lieutenant-Colonel C. H. Lynch.

CLAYTON'S DIVISION.
Major-General H. D. Clayton.

STOVALL'S BRIGADE.
Brigadier-General M. A. Stovall.

Fortieth Georgia—Colonel A. Johnson.
Forty-first Georgia—Captain J. E. Stallings.
Forty-second Georgia—Colonel R. J. Henderson.
Forty-third Georgia—Colonel H. C. Kellogg.
Fifty-second Georgia—Captain R. R. Asbury.

GIBSON'S BRIGADE.
Brigadier-General R. L. Gibson.

First Louisiana—Captain J. C. Stafford.
Fourth Louisiana—Colonel S. E. Hunter.
Thirteenth Louisiana—Lieutenant-Colonel F. L. Campbell.
Sixteenth Louisiana—Lieutenant-Colonel R. H. Lindsay.
Nineteenth Louisiana—Major C. Flournoy.
Twentieth Louisiana—Captain A. Dresel.
Twenty-fifth Louisiana—Colonel F. C. Zacharie.
Thirtieth Louisiana—Major A. Picolet.
Fourth Louisiana Battalion—Captain T. A. Bisland.
Fourteenth Louisiana Battalion Sharpshooters—Lieutenant A. T. Martin.

HOLTZCLAW'S BRIGADE.
Brigadier-General J. T. Holtzclaw.

Eighteenth Alabama—Lieutenant-Colonel P. F. Hunley.
Thirty-second and Fifty-eighth Alabama—Colonel Bush. Jones.
Thirty-sixth Alabama—Captain N. M. Carpenter.
Thirty-eighth Alabama—Captain C. E. Bussey.

* Reported on detached service.

ADAMS' BRIGADE.
Colonel R. Lowry.

Sixth Mississippi—Lieutenant-Colonel Thomas J. Borden.
Fourteenth Mississippi—Colonel W. L. Doss.
Fifteenth Mississippi—Lieutenant-Colonel J. R. Binford.
Twentieth Mississippi—Major Thomas B. Graham.
Twenty-third Mississippi—Major G. W. B. Garrett.
Forty-third Mississippi—Colonel Richard Harrison.

MAJ.-GEN. H. D. CLAYTON, OF ALABAMA.

SCOTT'S BRIGADE.
Colonel John Snodgrass.

Fifty-fifth Alabama—Major J. B. Dickey.
Fifty-seventh Alabama—Major J. M. Wyley.
Twenty-seventh, Thirty-fifth and Forty-ninth Alabama (consolidated)—Lieutenant-Colonel J. D. Weeden.
Twelfth Louisiana—Captain J. T. Davis.

FRENCH'S DIVISION.*
Major-General S. G. French.

ECTOR'S BRIGADE.
Colonel D. Coleman.

Twenty-ninth North Carolina—Major E. H. Hampton.
Thirty-ninth North Carolina—Captain J. G. Crawford.
Ninth Texas—Major J. H. McReynolds.

* Sears' brigade not given in the original. It and Cockrell's reported as on detached service. Actual commanders given as reported December 9, 1864. These are not indicated on original of above return.

ECTOR'S BRIGADE—Continued.

Tenth Texas Cavalry*—Colonel C. R. Earp.
Fourteenth Texas Cavalry*—Captain R. H. Harkey.
Thirty-second Texas Cavalry*—Major W. E. Estes.

COCKRELL'S BRIGADE.
Colonel P. C. Flournoy.

First and Fourth Missouri—Captain J. H. Wickersham.
Second and Sixth Missouri—Lieutenant-Colonel S. Cooper.
Third and Fifth Missouri—Captain B. E. Guthrie.
First and Third Missouri Cavalry—Lieutenant-Colonel C. B. Cleveland.

WALTHALL'S DIVISION.
Major-General E. C. Walthall.

QUARLES' BRIGADE.
Brigadier-General George D. Johnston.

First Alabama—Lieutenant C. M. McRae.
Forty-second, Forty-sixth, Forty-ninth, Fifty-third and Fifty-fifth Tennessee—Captain A. M. Duncan.
Forty-eighth Tennessee—Colonel W. M. Voorhies.

CANTEY'S BRIGADE.
Brigadier-General C. M. Shelley.

Seventeenth Alabama—Captain John Bolling.
Twenty-sixth Alabama—Captain D. M. Gideon.
Twenty-ninth Alabama—Captain S. Abernathy.
Thirty-seventh Mississippi—Major S. H. Terral.

REYNOLDS' BRIGADE.
Brigadier-General D. H. Reynolds.

First Arkansas Mounted Rifles*—Captain R. P. Parks.
Second Arkansas Mounted Rifles*—Major J. P. Eagle.
Fourth Arkansas—Major J. A. Ross.
Ninth Arkansas—Captain W. L. Phifer.
Twenty-fifth Arkansas—Lieutenant T. J. Edwards.

CHEATHAM'S ARMY CORPS.
Major-General B. F. Cheatham, commanding.

CHEATHAM'S DIVISION.†

GIST'S BRIGADE.
Lieutenant-Colonel Z. L. Waters.

Forty-sixth Georgia—Captain Malcom Gillis.
Sixty-fifth Georgia and Eighth Georgia Battalion—Captain W. W. Grant.
Second Georgia Battalion Sharpshooters—Captain William H. Brown.
Sixteenth South Carolina—Captain J. W. Boling.
Twenty-fourth South Carolina—Captain W. C. Griffith.

BRIG.-GEN. M. P. LOWREY, OF MISSISSIPPI.
[From an old tintype.]

STRAHL'S BRIGADE.
Colonel A. J. Kellar.

Fourth, Fifth, Thirty-first, Thirty-third and Thirty-eighth Tennessee—Lieutenant-Colonel L. W. Finlay.
Nineteenth, Twenty-fourth and Forty-first Tennessee—Captain D. A. Kennedy.

MANEY'S BRIGADE.
Colonel H. R. Feild.

Fourth Confederate, Sixth, Ninth and Fiftieth Tennessee—Lieutenant-Colonel G. W. Pease.
First and Twenty-seventh Tennessee—Lieutenant-Colonel J. L. House.
Eighth, Sixteenth and Twenty-eighth Tennessee—Colonel J. H. Anderson.

* Dismounted.
† Actual commander not indicated on original return.

VAUGHAN'S BRIGADE.
Colonel W. M. Watkins.

Eleventh and Twenty-ninth Tennessee—Major J. E. Burns.
Twelfth and Forty-seventh Tennessee—Captain C. N. Wade.
Thirteenth, Fifty-first, Fifty-second, and One Hundred and Fifty-fourth Tennessee—Major J. F. Williamson.

CLEBURNE'S DIVISION.
Brigadier-General J. A. Smith.

SMITH'S BRIGADE.*
Colonel C. H. Olmstead.

First Georgia Volunteers—Major M. J. Ford.
Fifty-fourth Georgia—Captain George W. Moody.
Fifty-seventh Georgia Captain L. C. Bryan.
Sixty-third Georgia—Captain E. J. Craven.

GOVAN'S BRIGADE.
Brigadier-General D. C. Govan.

First, Second, Fifth, Thirteenth, Fifteenth and Twenty-fourth Arkansas—Colonel Peter V. Green.
Sixth and Seventh Arkansas—Lieutenant-Colonel P. Snyder.
Eighth and Nineteenth Arkansas—Major D. H. Hamiter.

LOWREY'S BRIGADE.
Brigadier-General M. P. Lowrey.

Sixteenth, Thirty-third and Forty-fifth Alabama—Lieutenant-Colonel R. H. Abercrombie.
Fifth Mississippi and Third Mississippi Battalion—Captain F. M. Woodward.
Eighth and Thirty-second Mississippi—Major A. E. Moody.

GRANBURY'S BRIGADE.
Captain E. T. Broughton.

Fifth Confederate—Lieutenant W. E. Smith.
Thirty-fifth Tennessee—Colonel B. J. Hill.†
Sixth and Fifteenth Texas—Captain B. R. Tyus.
Seventh Texas—Captain O. P. Forrest.
Tenth Texas—Captain R. D. Kennedy.
Seventeenth and Eighteenth Texas Cavalry‡—Captain F. L. McKnight.
Twenty-fourth and Twenty-fifth Texas Cavalry‡—Captain J. F. Matthews.
Nutt's (Louisiana) Cavalry Company—Captain L. M. Nutt.

BATE'S DIVISION.

TYLER'S BRIGADE.§
Brigadier-General T. B. Smith.

Thirty-seventh Georgia—Captain J. A. Sanders.
Fourth Georgia Battalion Sharpshooters—Major T. D. Caswell.
Second, Tenth, Twentieth and Thirty-seventh Tennessee—Lieutenant-Colonel W. M. Shy

FINLEY'S BRIGADE.
Major Jacob A. Lash.

First Florida, Third Florida, } Captain M. H. Strain.
Sixth Florida—Captain A. M. Williams.
Seventh Florida—Captain R. B. Smith.
First Florida Cavalry,‡ Fourth Florida Infantry, } Captain G. R. Langford.

JACKSON'S BRIGADE.
Brigadier-General H. R. Jackson.

First [Georgia] Confederate, Sixty-sixth Georgia, } Lieutenant-Colonel J. C. Gordon.
Twenty-fifth Georgia—Captain J. E. Fulton.
Twenty-ninth Georgia, Thirtieth Georgia, } Colonel W. D. Mitchell.
First Georgia Battalion Sharpshooters—Lieutenant R. C. King.

ARTILLERY.

LEE'S CORPS.
Major J. W. Johnston.

COURTNEY'S BATTALION.
Captain J. P. Douglas.

Dent's (Ala.) battery—Captain S. H. Dent.
Douglas' (Tex.) battery—Lieutenant Ben Hardin.
Garrity's (Ala.) battery—Lieutenant H. Ferrell.

ELDRIDGE'S BATTALION.
Captain C. E. Fenner.

Eufaula (Ala.) battery—Captain W. J. McKenzie.
Fenner's (La.) battery—Lieutenant W. T. Cluveruis.
Stanford's (Miss.) battery—Lieutenant J. S. McCall.

* Reported as on detached service.
† So in original, though a captain is reported as commanding the brigade.
‡ Dismounted.
§ The Thirtieth Tennessee reported as in this brigade Dec. 13, 1864.

JOHNSTON'S BATTALION.
Captain J. B. Rowan.

Corput's (Ga.) battery—Lieutenant W. S. Hoge.
Marshall's (Tenn.) battery—Captain L. G. Marshall.
Stephens' (Ga.) Light Artillery*—Lieutenant W. L. Ritter.

STEWART'S CORPS.
Lieutenant-Colonel S. C. Williams.

TRUEHART'S BATTALION.†

Lumsden's (Ala.) battery; Selden's (Ala.) battery; Tarrant's (Ala.) battery.

MYRICK'S BATTALION.†

Bouanchaud's (La.) battery; Cowan's (Miss.) battery; Darden's (Miss.) battery.

STORRS' BATTALION.

Guibor's (Mo.) battery; Hoskins' (Miss.) battery; Kolb's (Ala.) battery.

BRIG.-GEN. E. W. PETTUS, OF ALABAMA.
[From a photograph taken in 1864.]

CHEATHAM'S CORPS.
Colonel M. Smith.

HOXTON'S BATTALION.†

Perry's (Fla.) battery; Phelan's (Ala.) battery; Turner's (Miss.) battery.

HOTCHKISS' BATTALION.†

Bledsoe's (Mo.) battery; Goldthwaite's (Ala.) battery; Key's (Ark.) battery.

COBB'S BATTALION.†

Ferguson's (S. C.) battery; Phillips' [Mebane's] (Tenn.) battery; Slocomb's (La.) battery.

* Prior to November, 1863, known as Third Maryland Battery.
† Actual commanders not indicated on original return.

THE BIVOUAC OF THE DEAD.

BY CAPTAIN THEODORE O'HARA.

The muffled drum's sad roll has beat
The soldier's last tattoo;
No more on life's parade shall meet
That brave and fallen few.
On Fame's eternal camping ground
Their silent tents are spread,
And glory guards with solemn round
The bivouac of the dead.

No rumor of the foe's advance
Now sweeps upon the wind.
No troubled thoughts at midnight haunt
Of loved ones left behind;
No vision of the morrow's strife
The warrior's dream alarms;
Nor braying horn nor screaming fife
At dawn shall call to arms.

Their shivered swords are red with rust,
Their plumed heads are bowed.
Their haughty banner, trailed in dust,
Is now their martial shroud.
And plenteous funeral tears have washed
The red stains from each brow;
And the proud forms, by battle gashed,
Are freed from anguish now.

The neighing troop, the flashing blade,
The bugle's stirring blast,
The charge, the dreadful cannonade,
The din and shout are past.
Nor war's wild note, nor glory's peal,
Shall thrill with fierce delight
Those breasts that never more may feel
The rapture of the fight.

Operations Against Fort Fisher,

December 7 to 27, 1864.

by

COLONEL WILLIAM LAMB,
Colonel Commanding.

Fort Fisher, N. C.,
December 24, 1864.

I HAVE the honor to report, by telegraph, that the enemy's fleet, consisting of over fifty vessels, including two monitors, several armored vessels, and a large proportion of heavily armed frigates and sloops of war, commenced a furious bombardment of Fort Fisher at 12:40 P. M., which they kept up until 5:30 P. M., when they withdrew. They took position from opposite Howards Hill to opposite the mound, thus enfilading our land face and our camp. They destroyed about one-half our quarters, including headquarters. They damaged, more or less, some of our parapets and traverses, but no part of the work was greatly injured, except in front of Blakely gun, on right of the northeast salient. They disabled one 10-inch carriage, one 8-inch carriage, and two 32-pounder carriages. The 10-inch in the pulpit and the 8-inch in the left of the northeast salient were dismounted by recoil; they will be mounted to-night.

The casualties were as follows: Wounded, 1 mortally, 3 severely, and 19 slightly; total 23, viz., 2 commissioned officers (Lieutenant Matthew Washington Pridgen, Company H, Thirty-sixth Regiment, and Passed Midshipman Clarence Cary, Confederate States Navy), both slightly; 3 non-commissioned officers, 16 privates, 2 seamen.

The garrison flag was shot away and the staff cut down. Battle-flags were raised as soon as possible on the mound and on the left flank.

The officers, soldiers and seamen all did their whole duty, and are entitled to the thanks of their countrymen.

As the enemy attempted no passage of the bar, and staid out at long range with the exception of their ironclads, I fired very slowly and deliberately. I am unable to know what damage was done them, but I am certain the injury inflicted upon them far exceeds the injury their bombardment did us. Our Heavenly Father has protected my garrison this day, and I feel that He will sustain us in defending our homes from the invader.

Tuesday morning, December 20th, a Federal fleet commenced gathering off New Inlet. Rough weather prevailed until Saturday, December 24th, when the weather was beautiful and the sea as calm as a lake. At noon the fleet weighed anchor and advanced in one line toward the fort. The Ironsides opened and the other ships followed as they took their positions on left, front and right of the fort, enfilading both land and sea faces. About fifty vessels of the fleet, including one double-turreted and two single-turreted monitors, joined in the engagement, and kept up an incessant fire until dark (5.30 P. M.). The enemy directed the warmest fire at the flag-staff at headquarters until they had cut the flag and staff down and knocked headquarters into a mass of ruins. They fired projectiles of every description, from a 3-inch rifle shell to a 15-inch round shell. They destroyed about one half of the quarters, disabled three gun carriages, tore up large quantities of the earthworks, splintered some of the revetments, but did not injure a single bomb-proof or endanger any magazine. The greatest penetration noticed was not over five feet perpendicularly.

Our casualties were: Wounded, mortally, 1; seriously, 3; slightly, 19; total, 23. Commissioned officers: Lieutenant Matthew Washington Pridgen, Company H, Thirty-sixth North Carolina Regiment, and Passed Midshipman Clarence Cary, Confederate States' Navy, both slightly.

As no attempt was made by the enemy to cross the bar, the fort fired slowly and deliberately, expending only six hundred and seventy-two projectiles. The day was so calm that the smoke hung around our batteries and the enemy's ships, and prevented our gunners generally from seeing the effects of their shots, but enough were seen to strike the enemy to know that their casualties must very far exceed ours. A number of vessels were withdrawn and some were seen being towed off. The frigate Wabash, apparently bearing the admiral's pennant, was driven from her position late in the afternoon, and withdrew, stern foremost, as if afraid to expose her broadsides. At dark the enemy withdrew, Fort Fisher firing the last gun. Everything remained quiet during the night. At about 10 A. M., next morning, December 25th (Christmas, the anniversary of the Prince of Peace), the fleet advanced again in single line toward the fort, led by the Ironsides. At 10:30 A. M. the fleet, with the addition of another monitor (single-turreted), and some wooden steamers, recommenced an incessant bombardment, if possible more noisy and furious than that of the preceding day, which they kept up until after dark (nearly 6 P. M.). During the day a few more quarters were burnt, more of the earthworks were displaced, but none seriously damaged, and five guns were disabled by the enemy.

About 2 P. M. the flag-ship and other frigates came closer to the bar and lowered boats, which approached to sound the bar. The Brooke gun battery opened upon them with other guns and drove them out. The Armstrong gun, which had been held in reserve during the fight, was pointed late in the afternoon on the flag-ship lying off the bar and one steel shot amidships caused the admiral's pennant again to withdraw. At 3:30 P. M. twelve of the enemy's barges came on the Carolina Shoals, about one mile to the right of the mound, apparently to sound a passage for barges. It was a bold act, but the enemy paid for their temerity. A few shots from Battery Buchanan, the naval command under Lieutenant Chapman, first cut the flag from a barge and then cut the barge in two, causing the whole to retreat rapidly. The enemy made no attempt to pass the bar, and the firing was even slower and more deliberate than on the previous day, only six hundred shots being expended. Occasionally the fire of the land or sea face was directed on a single ship, and it never failed to drive her out, at least for a while. One frigate, more stubborn than the rest, received six large Blakely rifle shells in her sides before she would move. During the day the enemy landed a large force at Battery Anderson, a one-gun battery three miles up the beach. At 4:30 P. M. sharpshooters were seen on our left flank, and they fired upon our gunners from the quarters across the causeway. A few discharges of canister quieted them. At 5:30 P. M., after a most furious enfilading fire from the fleet down our palisade line, a heavy line of skirmishers were seen advancing on our works. A fire of grape was opened along the line, the palisades manned by the infantry and the advance repelled. Two battalions of Junior Reserves joined the Regulars in defending this line. Two prisoners from the One Hundred and Forty-second New York Regiment were taken, and next morning a number of new graves were seen on the beach, and an officer's sword and some small-arms and accouterments found scattered in front. Firing occurred along this line at night as skirmishers would show themselves, but no advance in force was made. At about 3 A. M. a boat party was reported as advancing on the mound. The preparations made for the reception of such an advance were found amply sufficient to repel it if it were seriously made, the boats seen disappearing very quickly. During the night the rain fell in torrents, wetting the troops and their arms, but it did not dampen their spirits nor interfere with their efficiency.

The following is the list of casualties for the day: Killed, 3; wounded, mortally, 2; severely, 7; slightly, 26; total wounded, 35. Total casualties, 38. Commissioned officers, Captain W. C. Strong, aid-de-camp, and Lieutenant Brown, adjutant Junior Reserves, both slightly wounded. Lieutenant T. L. Dornin, Confederate States Navy, wounded in foot. One of the three killed fell from the shot of a sharpshooter on our left flank. For the two days (24th and 25th): Killed, 3; wounded, 61.

The enemy were seen in heavy force on our land face, Monday morning, but made no demonstration against us.

This (Tuesday) morning, December 27th, the foiled and frightened enemy left our shores. I can not speak too highly of the coolness and gallantry of my command. In the fierce bombardment of twelve hours by the heaviest armed fleet that ever floated on the seas, not one gun detachment was driven from their piece. The last gun on both days was fired by Fort Fisher. The battalion of the Thirty-sixth North Carolina Regiment that had helped to erect the works fought with a determination never to allow the enemy to take them, and the gallant officers and men representing the other artillery organizations of the Old North State, Tenth North Carolina Regiment, First, Third and Thirteenth battalions North Carolina Artillery—equaled in bravery and heroism their comrades of the Thirty-sixth. Adams' light battery not only skillfully handled their Napoleons under the fire of sharpshooters in the evening, but in the day did effective service at the heavy guns.

Major James Reilly, Tenth North Carolina Regiment, and Captain Daniel Munn, Thirty-sixth Regiment, my field officer, discharged their whole duty. To the coolness and experience of Major Reilly we are indebted for the defense of the land face, and to Captain Munn we owe our thanks for keeping our battle-flag always floating defiance to our foe.

Fort Fisher, Commanding the Entrance to Cape Fear River, North Carolina.
The British Steamer Hansa Running the Blockade under the Protection of the Guns of the Fort.
[From a sketch by a special artist representing the *Illustrated London News*.]

My adjutant, Lieutenant George D. Parker, left his bed to repair to his post, but, unable to attend to the arduous duties of adjutant, of which he was relieved by Lieutenant John N. Kelly, he went to the batteries and fought gallantly through the whole bombardment.

The excellent order in which the attack found the ammunition and armament of this fort is due mainly to the practical experience and untiring energy of my ordnance men, at whose head is Ordnance Sergeant Montgomery Long, of Thirty-sixth North Carolina Regiment. I would be pleased to have his services rewarded by a commission.

The staff on the mound being unprovided with halyards, the battle-flag had not been raised when the garrison flag was shot away. The order was immediately given to raise the flag, when Private Christopher C. Bland, Company K, Thirty-sixth North Carolina Regiment, volunteered, and, climbing the staff under a heavy fire, fastened the flag to its top. At once a terrific fire was poured on the mound, and, one end of the flag requiring to be fastened, Bland repeated the heroic deed, and, unscathed by the fearful ordeal, fastened the flag firmly to the staff, where it now floats, although torn and rent by fragments of shell.

During the bombardment on Sunday a burning shell fell into a gun chamber, when it was coolly extinguished and thrown out by Privates John Turner and J. H. Brisson, Company H, Thirty-sixth North Carolina Regiment.

Lieutenant W. H. Williford, Company F, Thirty-sixth North Carolina Regiment, and his gallant detachment never flinched from the Blakely in the redan, although the parapet in front was torn away and the gun and carriage splintered by shells.

I could mention numberless cases of daring equally deserving commendation, but I must leave this for the roll of honor. In the management of my long line of works it was impossible for me to see everything, and those acts observed among my own men attracted me most, as I know the individual actors from our long association. I would make mention, however, of the detachment of officers, sailors and marines for the navy, under Lieutenant Roby, who came as volunteers from Battery Buchanan to join us. Besides the severe bombardment of the enemy from which this detachment suffered their full share, they had another ordeal to try them.

In the afternoon of Sunday both of their 7-inch Brooke rifles burst—one at 2:30 P. M. and one at 4 P. M.—wounding quite a number, but, undaunted, they asked for other guns to continue the skillful firing which they had so gallantly done during the whole bombardment.

The skillful and efficient manner in which our wounded and sick were cared for during this bombardment reflects the highest credit on Surgeon Singleton and his assistant surgeons.

I would mention the gallantry of my aid, Captain C. H. Blocker, in carrying my orders through the heaviest fire. I am indebted to Major W. J. Saunders, of General Hebert's staff, for most valuable assistance in his department during the engagement.

To the presence of Major-General Whiting and his staff, Colonel Tansill, Major Hill and Captain Strong, from the evening of the first day's bombardment to the retreat of the enemy, I owe much of the confidence I felt in my command, and much of the enthusiasm which inspired the men throughout the fight.

I feel that to God we owe this great victory. I appealed to Him during the hours of trial, and He protected my men and gave my garrison that bravery and unconquerable heroism which held Fort Fisher against a formidable attack by sea and land, and which saved our homes from the invader.

As soon as full reports of the officers are received I will furnish a list of those officers and men who were conspicuous for gallantry, to be forwarded to the adjutant and inspector-general to be inscribed on the roll of honor.

Forty-four heavy guns were brought into action, twenty on land face and twenty-four on sea front. The land face is 682 yards in length, the sea face 1,898⅓ yards. Total length of work, 2,580⅓ yards. Both faces bear on the sea.

On the 24th I had an effective total of 788 Regulars, 140 Junior Reserves; total, 928. On the 25th an effective force of 921 Regulars and about 450 Junior Reserves; total, 1,371. At night a re-enforcement came from Battery Buchanan, of about sixty sailors and marines, under Lieutenant Arledge and other officers.

WM. LAMB, *Colonel Commanding.*

[INCLOSURE.]

REPORT OF ORDNANCE DEPARTMENT OF FORT FISHER FOR DECEMBER 24 AND 25, 1864.

I respectfully submit the following as a report of the magazine-keepers at this fort of cartridges expended during the bombardment and land attack on the 24th and 25th of December:

MAGAZINE.	December 24th.	December 25th.
	Rounds.	Rounds.
No. 1	40	35
No. 2	34	62
No. 3	55	60
No. 4 (Armstrong gun)	. . .	4
No. 5	105	19
No. 6	106	18
No. 7	112	70
No. 8	25	84
No. 9	59	114
No. 10	6	70
No. 11	. . .	60
No. 14	130	122
Total	672	718

About one hundred and eighteen of the cartridges expended on the 25th were for grape, canister and shell fired at land forces and boats of the enemy.

Respectfully submitted,

M. LONG, *Ordnance Sergeant.*

COLONEL WM. LAMB, *Commanding.*

CAPTURE OF FORT FISHER, N. C.

OPERATIONS

JANUARY 13 TO 15, 1865.

BY

GENERAL BRAXTON BRAGG.

HEADQUARTERS DEPARTMENT OF NORTH CAROLINA, WILMINGTON, N. C.,
January 20, 1865.

ABOUT midnight on the 12th instant information reached me from Fort Fisher that the enemy's fleet was again assembling off New Inlet. The troops were promptly disposed to meet the movement, and orders and instructions were given to the several commanders for their guidance. Major-General Whiting repaired to Fort Fisher, and called to the assistance of that garrison, now twelve hundred strong, about six hundred men from the adjacent forts. Major-General Hoke, with all the movable force, about six thousand effectives, including reserves and cavalry, took position on the peninsula north of Fort Fisher to watch the enemy and confront his land force should they disembark in that region.

The bombardment of Fort Fisher was renewed by a portion of the fleet on the morning of the 13th, while the transports, under cover of another portion, proceeded to a point some six miles north and commenced to disembark troops on the sand-spit between the sea and Masonboro Sound. Owing to the intervening swamp and sound, it was impossible for us to attack the enemy at their landing point, even if the heavy metal of the fleet had not securely covered them. Nothing was left but to post our troops to watch their movements, which was judiciously done by Major-General Hoke. A detachment of cavalry was thrown to his right and front, some three miles toward Fort Fisher, by a military causeway leading through the swamp to Battery Anderson, the nearest point accessible to the sea-beach. This swamp, which skirts along the sound to its head, near Battery Anderson, there turns nearly due west across the peninsula and terminates in a small stream which conveys its waters into the river through a narrow neck of high land about three miles from the fort. Along this narrow ridge runs the only practicable route to the fort west of the sea-beach. Works had been ordered, and were under construction, to enable a small force to hold the passage along the sea-beach to the fort from the secure landing above, but they had not sufficiently progressed to render them useful. Nor is it believed any ordinary work could have been long held against the enormous weight of metal which could be concentrated on it at short range, the water from this point north being deep close in shore.

On the afternoon of the 13th I joined Major-General Hoke's command at his headquarters near Sugar Loaf, and, after a free conference, fully approved his disposition. The command could not have been divided with any safety, and to have placed it between the enemy and Fort Fisher would have enabled them to seize our intrenched camp, and securely confine our entire force on the southern end of the peninsula, exposed without cover to the fire of the whole fleet, which reached from the sea to the river throughout the whole distance. The troops were ordered to lie upon their arms, and to move promptly and attack, should the enemy attempt to extend his lines toward the fort.

In making a reconnoissance early next morning, the 14th, toward our right, while I was on the left, Major-General Hoke was fired upon by the enemy before reaching the line assigned his cavalry. Upon due investigation, he found a heavy force occupying an intrenched line between us and the fort, entirely across the peninsula from Battery Anderson on the sea to the river. Putting his command in motion, and promptly reporting what had occurred, he was ordered to move upon the enemy and to dislodge him if practicable. The movement had been made by the enemy under cover of darkness, and the cavalry stationed on our flank, for the purpose, had failed to give any notice. Passing to the front with the troops, I united in another examination of the enemy's lines, and, concurring in the opinion already expressed to me, I suspended the order for the attack. The enemy largely exceeded us in numbers, and was well intrenched from sea to river, a distance not exceeding one mile. I do not believe this change of position by the enemy could have been prevented with the enormous fleet to cover his movements, though he might have been retarded, if timely information had been received. But its successful accomplishment was not considered as placing the fort in much danger, if boldly defended by a vigilant garrison, as our communication with it by water at night could not be interrupted, unless the fleet forced a passage into the river.

From different sources I had learned with certainty that the enemy had landed neither horses nor artillery, intending to confine himself to the naval bombardment and infantry assault. Telegraphic reports from Major-General Whiting, received at 1:30 P. M. on the 14th instant, during this examination, represented the garrison of the fort in fine condition and spirits. He asked for fresh troops, on account of the exhaustion produced by the necessity for great vigilance at night to prevent surprise. Eleven hundred veteran infantry, under an approved commander, were immediately put in motion for the fort, and the general informed. From an accident to the transportation, the steamer grounding, only five hundred of these reached their destination during the night of the 14th. The remainder were, however, close at hand, with orders to land as soon as the enemy's fire would allow. But, as the garrison had been under fire for two days and on duty but one night, not the slightest apprehension was felt. The land front, on which the assault must be made, was just four hundred and fifty yards in extent, and the garrison now fully twenty-three hundred arms-bearing men, or four to the yard, after manning all the artillery. My only apprehension was in regard to a surprise, and, therefore, as a matter of precaution, instructions were given to keep out pickets to the front, and to look well to the flanks of the work, they being the only points considered at all vulnerable. Its commander was further informed that the troops in the fort would be regularly relieved by fresh details as their physical condition might require.

The work on the land front consisted of a parapet fifteen or twenty feet high, with a broad ditch more or less flooded, according to tide, and in front of this a line of sharpened palisades ten or twelve feet high, extending from sea to river, and loop-holed for infantry. To have assaulted the enemy behind his intrenchments, covered by his fleet, with inferior numbers, would have exhausted our means to aid the fort, and thereby not only have insured its ultimate fall, but have opened the country behind it. To make him the assaulting party, considering our means for attack and defense, seemed to me the only policy, and it promised his early and complete discomfiture, as the first change of weather would drive off the fleet and leave him unsupported and cut off from supplies.

In this condition matters continued until the afternoon of the 15th, the naval bombardment being kept up by day.

At 1:30 P. M. it was reported that the entire loss up to that time had been three killed and thirty-two wounded. No report had been received of any damage to the fort or its armament. About one hour later a dispatch announced the enemy forming for a land assault, and that most of the guns on the land front were disabled. General Hoke's command was immediately formed for attack, and he moved forward in person, with his skirmish line, through the thick undergrowth, close to the enemy's intrenchments, receiving two balls through his coat.

INTERIOR VIEW OF FORT FISHER.

A heavy line of battle was formed along their whole front in rear of the intrenchments, which were well manned. About this time the fire of the fleet slackened, and a feeble, desultory fire of musketry was heard for a few minutes at the fort. Soon the fire from the fleet was resumed with great vigor. Knowing we had retained a very large portion of the enemy's land force, and relying on the strength of our works and the large force to defend them, confidence was felt that the assault was successfully repulsed. Some unpleasant rumors and reports from the west of the river were heard about 4:30 P. M., but, with the certainty of being able to re-enforce the garrison that night, all apprehension was dispelled by the following dispatches, received respectively at 7:30 and 10 P. M.:

FORT FISHER, January 15, 1865.

General Braxton Bragg:

The enemy are assaulting us by land and sea. Their infantry outnumbers us. Can't you help us? I am slightly wounded.

WHITING, *General.*

FORT FISHER, January 15, 1865.

Colonel Anderson:

We still hold the fort, but are sorely pressed. Can't you assist us from the outside?

HILL, *Major.*

Brigadier-General Colquitt had been ordered to proceed to the fort and enter upon the immediate command, with special instructions. He reached Battery Buchanan in time only to witness the capture of such portions of the garrison as had retreated to that point. The written statements made by him and his staff officers as to what they saw are herewith inclosed, together with reports which I called for from Lieutenant-Colonel Gordon and Major Saunders, two officers of General Whiting's staff, sent out

INTERIOR OF FORT FISHER, NEAR WILMINGTON, DURING THE SECOND BOMBARDMENT.

by him at the last moment, and a topographical map of the country.

From all the information to be obtained it would seem that the enemy's assault on the sea-beach by his naval forces was handsomely repulsed with great loss to them, but that while most of the garrison on duty was thus engaged, his army column, preceded by a single regiment, approached along the river and entered the work on that flank almost unopposed; that they were met, after a secure lodgment had been made, by Major-General Whiting and Colonel Lamb with such force as they could collect, and most gallantly, even desperately, resisted, until the superior numbers of the enemy prevailed.

In this severe conflict, in which we were frequently the attacking party, all accounts agree that the courage and devotion of Major-General Whiting and Colonel Lamb were most conspicuous; they both fell pierced by severe wounds, at the head of their men; but the moment the enemy secured the sally-port his superior numbers gave him every advantage.

Without better information than is now possessed no opinion should be hazarded as to how this misfortune was brought about. During the short and sharp struggle which ensued after the enemy entered the fort our loss is represented to have been about five hundred killed and wounded. The garrison consisted of about one hundred and ten commissioned officers and twenty-four or twenty-five hundred men.

The enemy's fleet consisted of some seventy vessels, five of which were iron-clads of the heaviest class, and in all carried at least six hundred guns.

Upon ascertaining with certainty the fall of Fort Fisher, I directed the evacuation of the forts below it on the other side of the river, which had now become useless. The withdrawal of the garrison on Smiths Island was barely accomplished before the enemy's gunboats entered the Cape Fear, through New Inlet, and the force at the other works, having been so weakened in re-enforcing Fort Fisher as, under the altered circumstances, to be at the mercy of a few regiments which the enemy might land above Smithville, necessarily retired to Fort Anderson during the 16th and 17th. With the means of transportation by land at command it was impossible to bring off any part of the armament of the forts, and accordingly the guns were disabled as far as practicable and the magazines blown up.

* * * * * * *

BRAXTON BRAGG,
General Commanding.

A CAPTAIN of the Twelfth Georgia Infantry refused to surrender his company with his regiment when ordered so to do, and fought his way out. He justified his action on the ground that the women had given him his company flag, and he promised to take it back to them.

CAPTURE OF FORT FISHER, N. C.,

JANUARY 15, 1865.

BY

MAJ.-GEN. WILLIAM H. C. WHITING.

FORT FISHER, January 18, 1865.

I AM sorry to have to inform you, as a prisoner of war, of the taking of Fort Fisher on the night of the 15th instant, after an assault of unprecedented fury, both by sea and land, lasting from Friday morning until Sunday night.

On Thursday night the enemy's fleet was reported off the fort. On Friday morning the fleet opened very heavily. On Friday and Saturday, during the furious bombardment on the fort, the enemy were allowed to land without molestation and to throw up a light line of field works from Battery Ramseur to the river, thus securing his position from molestation and making the fate of Fort Fisher, under the circumstances, but a question of time.

On Sunday the fire of the fleet reached a pitch of fury to which no language can do justice. It was concentrated on the land front and fort. In a short time nearly every gun was dismounted or disabled, and the garrison suffered severely from the fire. At 3 o'clock the enemy's land force, which had been gradually and slowly advancing, formed into two columns for assault.

The garrison during the fierce bombardment was not able to stand to the parapets, and many of the re-enforcements were obliged to be kept at a great distance from the fort. As the enemy here slackened his fire to allow the assault to take place, the men hastily manned the ramparts and gallantly repulsed the right column of assault. A portion of the troops on the left had also repelled the first rush to the left of the work. The greater portion of the garrison being, however, engaged on the right, and not being [able] to man the entire work, the enemy succeeded in making a lodgment on the left flank, planting two of his regimental flags in the traverses. From this point we could not dislodge him, though we forced him to take down his flag from the fire from our most distant gun, our own traverses protecting him from such fire. From this [time] it was a succession of fighting from traverse to traverse, and from line to line until 9 o'clock at night, when we were overpowered and all resistance ceased.

The fall both of the general and the colonel commanding the fort, one about 4 and the other about 4:30 P. M., had a perceptible effect upon the men, and no doubt hastened greatly the result; but we were overpowered, and no skill or gallantry could have saved the place after he effected a lodgment, except attack in the rear.

The enemy's loss was very heavy, and so, also, our own. Of the latter, as a prisoner, I have not been able to ascertain.

At 9 P. M. the gallant Major Reilly, who had fought the fort after the fall of his superiors, reported the enemy in possession of the sally-port. The brave Captain Benthuysen, of the marines, though himself badly wounded, with a squad of his men, picked up the general and colonel and endeavored to make their way to Battery Buchanan, followed by Reilly with the remnant of the force. On reaching there it was found to be evacuated; by whose order or what authority I know not. No boats were there. The garrison of Fort Fisher had been coolly abandoned to its fate. Nothing was left but to await the approach of the enemy, who took us about 10 P. M. Thus fell Fort Fisher after three days' battle, unparalleled in the history of the war. The fleet surpassed its tremendous effort upon the previous attack.

The fort has fallen in precisely the manner indicated so often by myself, and to which your attention has been so frequently called, and in the presence of the ample force provided by you to meet the contingency. The fleet never attempted to enter until after the land force had done its work, and, of course, unless the supporting force played its part, Fort Fisher must have fallen. Making every allowance for the extraordinary vigor and force of the enemy's assault, and the terrific effect of the fire of the fleet upon the garrison and the continual and incessant enfilading of the whole point from Battery Buchanan to the fort, thereby preventing, to a great extent, the movement of my troops, I think that the result might have been avoided and Fort Fisher still held if the commanding general had done his duty. I charge him with this loss; with neglect of duty in this, that he either refused or neglected to carry out every suggestion made to him in official communications by me for the disposition of the troops, and especially that he, failing to appreciate the lesson to be derived from previous attempt of Butler, instead of keeping his troops in the position to attack the enemy on his appearance, he moved them twenty miles from the point of landing, in spite of repeated warnings. He might have learned from his failure to interrupt either the landing or the embarking of Butler for two days with his troops, though disgraceful enough, would indicate to the enemy that he would have the same security for any future expedition. The previous failure was due to Fort Fisher alone, and not to any of the supporting troops. I charge him further, with making no effort whatever to create a diversion in favor of the beleaguered garrison during the three days' battle, by attacking the enemy, though that was to be expected, since his delay and false disposition allowed the enemy to secure his rear by works, but works of no strength.

I desire that a full investigation be had of this matter and these charges which I make; they will be fully borne out by the official records. I have only to add that the commanding general, on learning the approach of the enemy, would give me no orders whatever, and persistently refused from the beginning to allow me to have anything to do with the troops from General Lee's army. I

THE MOUND BATTERY, FORT FISHER.
[From an old sketch.]

consequently repaired to Fort Fisher as the place where my own sense of duty called me.

W. H. C. WHITING,
Major-General (prisoner of war).

HOSPITAL, FORT COLUMBUS, GOVERNOR'S ISLAND, NEW YORK HARBOR,
February 19, 1865.

The above is an exact copy of the dispatch dictated to Major Hill in the hospital at Fort Fisher (and preserved in his note-book) on the 18th of January, 1865, and which I intended to have endeavored to forward at that time by flag of truce, and accordingly made a request of General Terry. On his reply that it would be necessary to refer it to Lieutenant-General Grant, I concluded to postpone the report. I wish to add a few remarks upon the difference between the two attacks, and also give some information which I have acquired. Had the enemy assaulted the work on the first attack he would have been beaten off with great slaughter. The fire of the fleet on that occasion, though very severe and formidable, was very diffuse and scattered, seemingly more designed to render a naval entrance secure than a land attack, consequently our defense was but slightly damaged. We had nineteen guns bearing on the assault, and, above all, the palisade was almost as good as new. Moreover, the fleet, during the first bombardment, hauled off at night, leaving the garrison time for rest, cooking and refreshment. It is remarkable that during the first bombardment no gun's crew was ever driven from its guns; but on the 13th and 14th of January the fleet stationed itself with the definite object of destroying the land defense by direct and enfilade fire—the latter a *feu d'enfilement* to knock down the traverses, destroying all guns, and pound the northeast salient into a practicable slope for the assaulting column. By 12 M. Sunday not a gun remained on the land front. The palisade was entirely idly looking on, only three miles off, which could see the columns on the beach, to have made an attack upon the rear of the assaulting columns; at any rate to have tried to save Fort Fisher, while the garrison had hurled one assaulting column, crippled, back, and were engaged for six hours with five thousand men vigorously assaulting it.

General Bragg was held in check by two brigades of United States colored troops, along a line of no impediment whatever. Once at this line by the river bank with his three batteries of artillery, and his whole force steadily advancing, the enemy's fleet could not have fired again without hurting their own men. The enemy had not a single piece of artillery; altogether about seven or eight thousand men. Pushing our batteries to Camp Wyatt and Colonel Lamb's headquarters, and opening heavily on Shepherd's battery, with an advance of our troops, and such of the enemy as could not have escaped in boats must have fallen into our hands; but it was not to be. I went into the fort with the conviction that it was to be sacrificed, for the last I heard General Bragg say was to point out a line to fall back on if Fort Fisher fell. In all his career of failure and defeat, from Pensacola out, there has been no such chance missed, and no such stupendous disaster.

Wounded, in the hospital, with mortification at the shameful haste, I heard the blowing up of Fort Caswell before the enemy had dared to enter the harbor.

I demand, in justice to the country, to the army, and to myself, that the course of this officer be investigated. Take his notorious congratulatory order No. 14 [17], with its numerous errors, and compare his language with the result. I do not know what he was sent to Wilmington for. I had hoped that I was considered competent. I acquiesced with feelings of great mortification. My proper place was in command of the troops you sent to support the defense; then I should not now be a prisoner, and an effort at least would have been made to save a harbor on which I had

HEAVY GUNS IN POSITION AT FORT FISHER AT CAPTURE.

No.	Kind.	Condition of Gun.	Condition of Carriage.
		LAND FRONT.	
1	10 -inch columbiad	Unserviceable .	Unserviceable.
2	6⅜-inch rifle (old 32) . . .	Unserviceable .	Serviceable.
3	8 -inch smooth, of 1841 . .	Serviceable . .	Unserviceable.
4	— -inch smooth	Unserviceable .	Unserviceable.
5	8 -inch columbiad	Serviceable .	Serviceable.
6	4½-inch rifled Parrott . . .	Serviceable . .	Serviceable.
7	6⅜-inch smooth-bore (32) .	Unserviceable .	Serviceable.
8	5⅞-inch smooth-bore (24) .	Unserviceable .	Unserviceable.
9	6⅜-inch smooth-bore (32) .	Unserviceable .	Unserviceable.
10	5½-inch Coehorn mortar . .	Serviceable . .	Serviceable.
11	6⅜-inch smooth (32) .	Unserviceable .	Unserviceable.
12	5½-inch Coehorn mortar . .	Serviceable . .	Serviceable.
13	6½-inch smooth (32) . . .	Serviceable . .	Serviceable.
14	8 -inch smooth (32) . . .	Serviceable .	Unserviceable.
15	6⅜-inch smooth (32) . .	Serviceable . .	Serviceable.
16	— -inch smooth	Serviceable . .	Unserviceable.
17	— -inch smooth	Unserviceable .	Unserviceable.
18	6⅜-inch rifle (32)	Serviceable . .	Unserviceable.
19	7 -inch rifle, Brooke . .	Serviceable . .	Serviceable.
20	6⅜-inch rifle (32)	Serviceable . .	Unserviceable.
21	— -inch rifle	Unserviceable .	Unserviceable.
22	10 -inch columbiad	Unserviceable .	Unserviceable.
23	8 -inch mortar	Serviceable . .	Serviceable.
24	8 -inch smooth-bore . . .	Serviceable . .	Serviceable.
		SEA FRONT.	
25	8⅓-inch rifle, Blakely . . .	Serviceable . .	Serviceable.
26	10 -inch columbiad	Serviceable . .	Unserviceable.
27	6⅜-inch rifle (32)	Serviceable . .	Unserviceable.
28	10 -inch columbiad	Serviceable . .	Unserviceable.
30	— -inch columbiad	Serviceable . .	Serviceable.
31	8 -inch columbiad	Serviceable . .	Serviceable.
32	— -inch columbiad	Serviceable . .	Serviceable.
33	— -inch columbiad	Serviceable . .	Unserviceable.
34	— -inch columbiad . . .	Serviceable .	Serviceable.
35	7 -inch rifle, Brooke . . .	Unserviceable .	Unserviceable.
36	8 -inch columbiad	Serviceable . .	Serviceable.
37	6⅜-inch rifle (32)	Serviceable . .	Serviceable.
38	— -inch rifle	Serviceable . .	Serviceable.
39	8 -in. rifle (150), Armstrong,	Serviceable . .	Serviceable.
40	10 -inch columbiad	Serviceable . .	Serviceable.
41	— -inch columbiad	Serviceable . .	Serviceable.
42	7 -inch rifle, Brooke . . .	Serviceable . .	Serviceable.
43	6⅜-inch rifle (32)	Serviceable . .	Serviceable.
44	10 -inch columbiad	Serviceable . .	Serviceable.
45	— -inch columbiad	Serviceable .	Serviceable.
46	— -inch columbiad, mound,	Serviceable . .	Unserviceable.
47	6⅜-inch rifle (32), mound .	Serviceable . .	Serviceable.

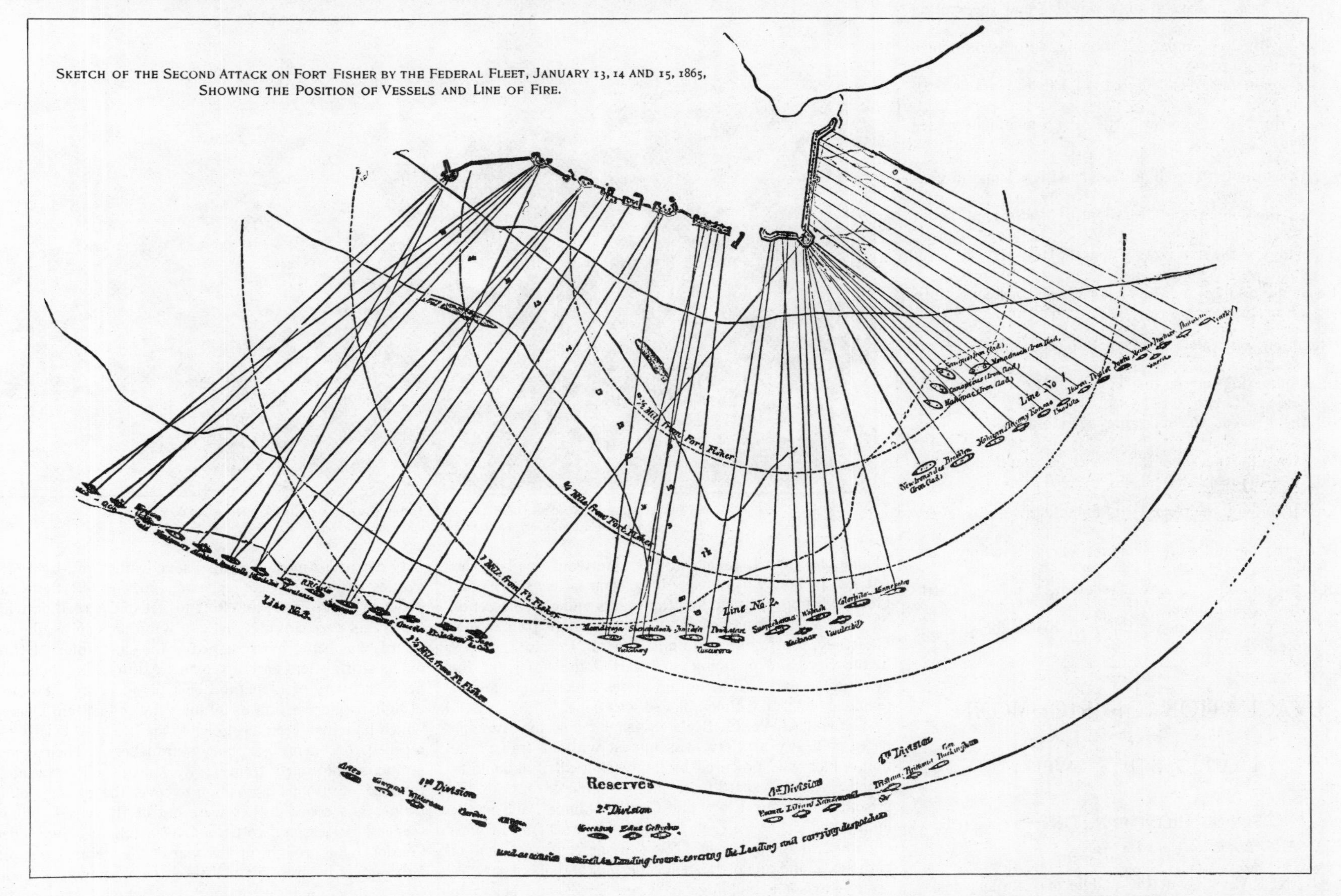

SKETCH OF THE SECOND ATTACK ON FORT FISHER BY THE FEDERAL FLEET, JANUARY 13, 14 AND 15, 1865, SHOWING THE POSITION OF VESSELS AND LINE OF FIRE.

swept away, the mines in advance, so deeply did the enemy's shot plow, were isolated from the wires and could not be used. Not a man could show his head in that infernal storm, and I could only keep a lookout in the safest position to inform me of the movements of the enemy. Contrary to previous practice, the fleet kept up the fire all night. Cooking was impracticable. The men, in great part, in Fisher at the second attack were not those of the first, and were much more demoralized. The casualties were greater, with but one ration for three days. Such was the condition when the parapets were manned on the enemy's ceasing firing for assault.

As soon as a lodgment was made at Shepherd's battery on the left, the engineers at once threw up a strong covering work in rear of Fisher, and no effort of ours against overwhelming numbers could dislodge them.

Then was the time for the supporting force, which was expended for two years all the labor and skill I had. I should not have had the mortification of seeing works which our very foes admire yielding after four days' attack, given up and abandoned without even an attempt to save them.

W. H. C. WHITING,
Major-General (prisoner of war).

IN the war between the States General Jackson (Stonewall) ordered one of his colonels to attack a certain strong position. The colonel hesitated, and at length went to General Jackson to expostulate. "General," said the colonel, "to attack that position is madness; my regiment will be exterminated." "Colonel," said the commander, "do your duty. I have made every arrangement to care for the wounded and to bury the dead."

ON the Peninsula the gallant and jolly General J. Bankhead Magruder had ordered a meal for himself and staff. A hungry Reb—and whoever saw one that was not hungry?—came up to the farmhouse, espied the nicely filled table, and, without leave or license, sat down and began to annihilate things. Just then the general and friends walked in, escorted by the host. All were surprised. "Hallo!" said the fiery Magruder, in terms more explicit than polite; "do you know whose table that is you are eating at?" "No, sir," said John Reb, with his mouth full; "whose is it?" "General Magruder's, sir, the commander of this department." "All right, general," with another big mouthful. "These war times I ain't particular where I eat or who I eat with; sit down and make yourself at home." The foraging private was unceremoniously fired out, but not before he had nearly gotten outside of a pretty square meal.

GENERAL LEE AT THE BATTLE OF THE WILDERNESS.

There he stood, the grand old hero, great Virginia's god-like son,
Second unto none in glory—equal of her Washington;
Gazing on his line of battle, as it wavered to and fro;
'Neath the front and flank advances of the almost conquering foe;
Calm as was that clear May morning, ere the furious death-roar broke
From the iron-throated war lions crouching, 'neath the cloudy smoke;

Cool, as tho' the battle raging was but mimicry of fight,
Each brigade an ivory castle, and each regiment a knight;
Chafing in reserve beside him, two brigades of Texans lay,
All impatient for their portion in the fortunes of the day.

Shot and shell are 'mong them falling, yet unmov'd they silent stand,
Longing, eager for the battle, but awaiting his command.
Suddenly he rode before them, as the forward line gave way,
Raised his hat with courtly gesture, "Follow me and save the day!"

But as tho' by terror stricken, still and silent stood that troop,
Who were wont to rush to battle with a fierce avenging whoop.
It was but a single moment, then a murmur thro' them ran,
Heard above the cannon's roaring, as it passed from man to man.

"You go back and we'll go forward!" now the waiting leader hears,
Mixed with deep, impatient sobbing, as of strong men moved to tears;
Once again he gives the order, "I'll lead you on the foe!"
Then, thro' all the line of battle rang a loud, determined "No!"

Quick as thought a gallant major, with a firm and vise-like grasp,
Seized the general's bridle, shouting, "Forward, boys! I'll hold him fast!"
Then again the hat was lifted, "Sir, I am the older man;
Loose my bridle, I will lead them!" in a measured tone and calm.

Trembling with suppressed emotion, with intense excitement hot,
In a quivering voice, the Texan, "No, by God, sir, you shall not!"
By them swept the charging squadron, with a loud, exultant cheer,
"We'll retake the salient, General, if you'll watch us from the rear!"

And they kept their word right nobly, sweeping every foe away,
With that grand gray head uncovered, watching how they saved the day—
But the god-like calm was shaken, which no battle shock could move,
By this true, spontaneous token of his soldiers' child-like love!

EVACUATION OF RICHMOND.

BY

LIEUT.-GEN. R. S. EWELL.

SPRING HILL, TENN., December 20, 1865.

General R. E. Lee, Lexington, Va.

GENERAL: About the middle of February last I received a communication from you, inclosing a law which I was directed to carry out. This law required preparations to be made for destroying the cotton, tobacco, etc., which the owners could not remove, in places exposed to capture by the enemy. I immediately sent Major Brown, of my staff, to Mayor Mayo with the document, and requested him to call a meeting of the Common Council to give their opinion as to the measures proper to be taken. After a free discussion with some of the Council and by their advice, I issued a circular to the "Merchants and Owners of Cotton and Tobacco," embodying the substance of your order and the law that accompanied it. This I intrusted to those gentlemen and to Major Isaac N. Carrington, Provost-Marshal, for distribution. Being informed a few hours later that it was misunderstood as to take effect at once, I substituted another, stating expressly that the "necessity had not yet arisen." Together with Mr. Scott, a tobacco owner and councilman, I visited and inspected all the warehouses containing tobacco, and after consulting the keepers, we concluded they could be burned without danger of a general conflagration. I gave instructions to Major Carrington to make the necessary arrangements, and requested Mr. Scott and the other members of the Council to consult with him and give him their views. The Ordnance Department offered to furnish barrels of turpentine to mix with the tobacco so as to insure its burning; but this I declined, for fear of setting fire to the city. I sent for the Mayor and several of the most prominent citizens, earnestly urged upon them the danger of mob violence, should we be forced to evacuate and the entrance of Federal troops be delayed, and begged them to endeavor to organize a volunteer guard force for such an emergency, proffering the necessary arms. I regret to say but one man volunteered, and the rioters, as predicted, were unchecked. On the night of Saturday, April 1st, I received a dispatch from General Longstreet, telling me he was going to the south side with two divisions; that Kershaw would be left on the lines, directing me to move whatever troops I could collect down the Darbytown Road, and to ride by his headquarters for further instructions. I left my staff to see to the movements and collection of troops (of which only the cadets and three battalions of convalescents from the hospitals were in town), and rode down, but General Longstreet had gone before I reached his headquarters, and I received orders from his Acting Adjutant-General, Colonel Latrobe, to relieve and send forward two brigades left on picket, which was done soon after sunrise by Colonel Shipp, commanding the cadets and convalescents. At 10 A. M. of Sunday I received a message from Major Chestney, my Acting Adjutant-General, to return at once to the city, and on doing so received the order for the evacuation, and to destroy the stores which could not be removed. All that time allowed was done.

General G. W. C. Lee's division being mostly composed of heavy artillery, was almost without transportation, which was procured by impressing all that could be found. All the guard-forces were required to take the prisoners from the Libby and Castle Thunder, and as the militia had dispersed (being mostly foreigners), no troops remained in town except a few convalescents. A mob of both sexes and all colors soon collected, and about 3 A. M. set fire to some buildings on Cary Street, and began to plunder the city. The convalescents then stationed in the Square were ordered to repress the riot, but their commander shortly reported himself unable to do so, his force being inadequate. I then ordered all my staff and couriers who could be spared, to scour the streets, so as to intimidate the mob by a show of force, and sent word to General Kershaw, who was coming up from the lines, to hurry his leading regiment into town. By daylight the riot was subdued, but many buildings which I had carefully directed should be spared, had been fired by the mob. The Arsenal was thus destroyed, and a party of men went to burn the Tredegar Works, but were prevented by General Anderson's arming his operatives and declaring his intention to resist. The small bridge over the canal on Fourteenth Street was burned by incendiaries, who set a canal boat on fire and pushed it under the bridge. This was evidently done in hopes of embarrassing our retreat, and General Kershaw's division passed the bridge while on fire, at a "double quick." By 7 A. M. the last troops had reached the south side, and Mayos and the railroad bridges were set on fire.

From the hills above Manchester we watched for some time the progress of the flames, and all at once saw fire break out through the roof of one of the large mills on the side furthest from the burning warehouses, the flames from which scarcely reached half way up the sides of the mill. It was considered a fire-proof building, and extra precautions had been taken by the owners. I can not conceive how it could have caught in such a place, unless set on fire. I have been told that Mr. Crenshaw found his mill full of plunderers, whom he got out by agreeing to give them all the provisions in the mill and that they were in the act of building a fire on the upper story of the mill when discovered. I tried to find out if this was true, but no reply has come to the letters written for that purpose. If correct, it affords exact proof of what I am firmly convinced is the case, that the burning of Richmond was the work of incendiaries, and might have been prevented by the citizens.

General G. W. C. Lee's division crossed the river at Drewrys and united with Kershaw a few miles from Manchester. We marched very rapidly to join the main body, and though delayed by the swollen condition of the Appomattox, came up with it near Amelia Courthouse on the 5th of April. We were to march all that night, but, owing to the slow progress of the trains and troops in front, had only reached Amelia Springs, seven miles off, by 8 A. M. Parties of cavalry here appeared on our left flank, and about 11 A. M. made an effort to get to the road on which our trains were moving past us. Gordon's corps, the rear-guard, was being hard pushed at the same time. I threw out as skirmishers part of Colonel Atkinson's command of heavy artillery of General Lee's division, and a battery of light artillery acting as infantry under Captain Dement, which had just been assigned to me. These troops soon repelled the enemy's cavalry skirmishers. Their demonstrations continued from 11 A. M. till 2 P. M., and I retained my troops in position to cover the passage of the trains. As soon as they were out of the way I followed General Anderson's corps, and was followed by General Gordon, who brought up the rear of the trains, constantly fighting. On crossing a little stream known as Sailors Creek, I met General Fitzhugh Lee, who informed me that a large force of cavalry held the road just in front of General Anderson, and were so strongly posted that he had halted a short distance ahead. The trains were turned into a road nearer the river, while I hurried to General Anderson's aid. General Gordon's corps turned off after the trains. General Anderson informed me that at least two divisions of cavalry were in his front, and suggested two modes of escape, either to unite our forces and break through, or to move to the right through the woods and try to strike a road that ran toward Farmville. I recommended the latter alternative, but as he knew the ground and I did not, and had no one who did, I left the dispositions to him. Before any were made the enemy appeared in rear of my column in large force, preparing to attack. General Anderson informed me that he would make the attack in front, if I would hold in check those in the rear, which I did until his troops were broken and dispersed. I

CAMP OF FEDERAL PRISONERS ON BELLE ISLE, JAMES RIVER, IN FRONT OF RICHMOND, VA.
[From a sketch by a special artist representing the *Illustrated London News*.]

had no artillery, all being with the trains. My line ran across a little ravine which leads nearly at right angles toward Sailors Creek. General G. W. C. Lee was on the left, with the naval battalion, under Commodore Tucker, behind his right; Kershaw was on the right. All of Lee's and part of Kershaw's divisions were posted behind a rising ground that afforded some shelter from artillery. The creek was perhaps three hundred yards in their front, with brush pines between and a cleared field beyond it. In this the enemy's artillery took a commanding position, and finding we had none to reply, soon approached within eight hundred yards and opened a terrible fire. After nearly half an hour of this, their infantry advanced, crossing the creek above and below us at the same time. Just as it attacked, General Anderson made his assault, which was repulsed in five minutes. I had ridden up near his lines with him to see the result. When a staff officer, who had followed his troops in their charge, brought him word of its failure, General Anderson rode rapidly toward his command. I returned to mine to see if it were yet too late to try the other plan of escape. On riding past my left I came suddenly upon a strong line of the enemy's skirmishers advancing upon my left rear. This closed the only avenue of escape, as shells and even bullets were crossing each other from front and rear over my troops, and my right was completely enveloped. I surrendered myself and staff to a cavalry officer who came in by the same road General Anderson had gone out upon. At my request he sent a messenger to General G. W. C. Lee, who was nearest, with a note from me telling him "he was surrounded, General Anderson's attack had failed. I had surrendered, and he had better do so, too, to prevent useless loss of life;" though I gave no orders, being a prisoner. Before the messenger reached him, General Lee had been captured, as had been Kershaw and the whole of my command.

My two divisions numbered about three thousand each at the time of the evacuation. Twenty-eight hundred were taken prisoners, about one hundred and fifty killed and wounded. The difference of over three thousand was caused mainly by the fatigue of four days' and nights' almost constant marching, the last two days with nothing to eat. Before our capture I saw men eating raw fresh meat as they marched in ranks. The heavy artillery brigade of Lee's division was closely engaged for the first time on this occasion, and, spite of the fall of its commander, Colonel Crutchfield, displayed a coolness and gallantry that earned the praise of the veterans who fought alongside of it, and even of the enemy.

I was informed at General Wright's headquarters, where I was carried after my capture, that thirty thousand men were engaged with us when we surrendered, viz.: Two infantry corps and Custer's and Merritt's divisions of cavalry, the whole under command of General Sheridan.

I deem it proper to remark that the discipline preserved by General G. W. C. Lee in camp and on the march, and the manner in which he handled his troops in action, fully justified the request I had made for his promotion. General Kershaw, who had only been a few days under my command, behaved with his usual coolness and judgment.

* * * * * * *

R. S. EWELL,
Late Lieutenant-General, C. S. A.

RICHMOND, VA. RUINS OF THE ARSENAL.

EVACUATION OF RICHMOND, VA.

BY

MAJOR-GENERAL J. B. KERSHAW.

CAMDEN, S. C., October 9, 1865.

MAJOR: On the morning of Monday, the 3d of April last, I moved in obedience to the orders of Lieutenant-General Ewell, from my position on the lines near Fort Gilmer, through Richmond to Mayos Bridge, reporting in person to General Ewell. Under his orders I detached two battalions to suppress the mob then engaged in sacking the city. Arriving at the bridge I found it in flames, and rapidly passed my command over to Manchester, informing General Ewell of the facts. By the efforts of some boatmen the flames were arrested before they had rendered the bridge impassable. By the time the infantry had passed, the large mill above the Danville Depot, and too far distant from it to have been ignited by the burning of the latter, was observed to be on fire, the smoke being first seen to issue through the roof in all parts of it, and then the windows on all sides, indicating that it had been set on fire in the interior. As much of the conflagration which ensued was caused by the burning of this building, the circumstance has been deemed of sufficient importance to be stated here, in order to remove the erroneous imputation that the conflagration resulted from the action of the authorities.

A few miles from the river the command united with that of General Custis Lee, and moved in the direction of Amelia Courthouse. Learning that all the upper crossings of the Appomattox were impassable, on Tuesday the command moved to the railroad crossing, and by night had succeeded in passing the river with the entire train. The next day the rear of the Petersburg army was overtaken at Amelia Courthouse, and, marching all night, the command arrived at Amelia Springs a little after sunrise the next day. From this point Gordon's corps marched in rear. About 10 o'clock the command reached a point where the wagon train was moved to the right, upon a crossroad which intersected that upon which the troops moved at right angles. Here the column was posted to resist the cavalry of the enemy—Merritt's and Custer's divisions—which attacked at that point, and repulsed several charges upon different parts of the line. They were held at bay until the last of the train had passed the point attacked, when I was directed to follow the movement of General Custis Lee's division. Before my troops left the ground Gordon's advance appeared, while his rear was engaged with the enemy. I was not informed that Gordon would follow the wagon-train as he did, and was therefore surprised, on arriving at Sailors Creek, to find that my rear was menaced. As the troops in my front had halted, I detached Humphreys' brigade, commanded by Colonel Fitzgerald, and Gary's dismounted battalion, under Lieutenant-Colonel Barham, to take position near the house occupied as a hospital by Pickett's division, to cover my crossing of Sailors Creek.

Upon arriving at the top of the hill, on the south side of the creek, I was informed by General Ewell that the enemy had possession of the road in front of General Anderson, and that we were to hold the enemy in check while that officer attempted to open the way. My command then consisted of only three brigades Humphreys', Simms', Brigadier-General J. P. Simms commanding, and DuBose's brigade, Brigadier-General D. M. DuBose commanding, and the dismounted cavalry already mentioned. The whole at the time amounted to less than two thousand effective men. DuBose was placed in the edge of the wood, with his right resting on the road: Simms on the right of the road, a little in advance. General Lee's division was on the left of the road, his right occupying a line in front of DuBose, his left on the same line, or nearly so. In the meantime the enemy attacked and overpowered Humphreys and the dismounted cavalry, forcing them back to my position. They were formed at once on the left of the road, and Simms was moved further to the right. The enemy planted batteries near the hospital, and swept our position at short range, and under cover of the fire the Second and Sixth corps attacked us. Both in Lee's front and my own they were repulsed with loss on every advance, but pressed us constantly with fresh troops, extending all the while to our left. During the attack I received from General Anderson a message, through Captain S. D. Shannon, aid-de-camp, to the effect that he had commenced his movement, and hoped to be successful if I could hold out a few minutes longer. Sending him an encouraging reply, I continued to resist the enemy for some time, hoping to hear from General Anderson that the way was open. Unfortunately his attempt had failed, and the enemy made his appearance in rear of Simms' brigade, at the same time he was engaged in front and flank. That officer attempted to extricate his command, but found it impossible to do so without confusion, as he was attacked on all sides. This condition of things being discovered by the other troops, all fell back toward the rear and left. I kept up something of a skirmish as the command retreated; but after moving some four hundred yards I discovered that all who had preceded me had been taken by the Yankee cavalry, who were in line of battle across the road. I then directed the men about me and the members of my staff to make their escape in any way possible. I discovered afterward that but one had

RICHMOND, VA. RUINS OF THE ARMORY.

succeeded, as the enemy had completed the circle around our position when General Anderson's line was broken. My losses in killed and wounded must have been considerable, but I have no means of estimating the number. The conduct of the officers and men of the command under these trying circumstances is beyond all praise, and worthy the reputation of these veteran regiments. On no battle-field of the war have I felt a juster pride in the conduct of my command. I beg leave expressly to include in these just encomiums the little command of Lieutenant-Colonel Barham, and especially that officer.

J. B. KERSHAW,
Late Major-General C. S. A.

MAJOR CAMPBELL BROWN.

EVACUATION OF RICHMOND, VA.

EVENTS FROM APRIL 2 TO 6, 1865.

BY

MAJOR-GENERAL G. W. C. LEE.

RICHMOND, VA., April 25, 1865.

IN obedience to instructions, I have the honor to submit the following report of the operations of my command from the time of its leaving the lines at Chaffin's farm on Sunday night, April 2, 1865, to its capture on the afternoon of the following Thursday, April 6, 1865:

The order to withdraw from the intrenchments was received by me at Major-General Kershaw's quarters about 10 o'clock P. M. of the 2d of April, and was issued to the two brigades (Barton's and Crutchfield's) under my command at Chaffin's farm, about 11 o'clock P. M. of that night. The wagons which had been loaded up in obedience to the preparatory order received at Chaffin's on the afternoon of Sunday, April 2d, were at once sent off to cross James River at Richmond, and proceed to Amelia Courthouse via Buckingham Road and Meadville, as ordered. Not being able to cross the Appomattox River near Meadville, the wagon-train moved up to Clementtown, there made the passage of the river, and proceeded with safety until within about four miles of Amelia Courthouse, when it was destroyed by a detachment of the enemy's cavalry on the morning of Wednesday, April 5th, with the baggage of my division and twenty thousand good rations, as I have recently learned from the division commissary, who escaped. The troops (Barton's and Crutchfield's brigades) crossed the James River on the Wilton Bridge about 1 o'clock A. M. of Monday, April 3d. The picket line was withdrawn at 3 o'clock of that morning, and passed safely over the same bridge about daylight. My command then moved to Branch Church, and thence by Gregory's to the Genito Road, as directed, camping that night about half a mile beyond Tomahawk Church. In the absence of Lieutenant-General Ewell in a Northern prison, it may be proper for me to mention here that the detachments of troops in Richmond and Kershaw's division, followed by Gary's cavalry, or a portion of it, crossed the James River at Richmond and followed my division to Tomahawk Church. On the following morning, Tuesday, April 4th, it being positively ascertained that the Appomattox River could not be crossed at Genito Bridge, arrangements were made to prepare the railroad bridge at Mattoax Station for the passage of the wagons, artillery and troops, which was accomplished that night, and all went into camp on the hills beyond the river. Early on Wednesday, April 5th, the bridge having been destroyed, the column moved on to Amelia Courthouse, at which place the naval battalion, commanded by Commodore Tucker, and the command of Major Frank Smith, from Howlett's, were added to my division. From Amelia Courthouse General Ewell's column, following that of General Anderson, and followed by that of General Gordon, much impeded by the wagon-trains, moved toward Jetersville and Amelia Springs, marching slowly all night. During this night march, firing having commenced between our flankers and some of the enemy's scouts, as is supposed, Major Frank Smith was mortally wounded, Captain Nash, Acting Adjutant-General, Barton's brigade, lost a leg, and several others, whose names I have not been able to ascertain, were wounded. We passed Amelia Springs on the morning of Thursday, April 6th, and moved toward Rices Station. About midday, immediately after crossing a little stream, within about two miles of Sailors Creek, the enemy's cavalry made an attack upon a portion of General Anderson's column about a mile in advance of us, at the point where the wagon-train turned off to the right, causing some delay and confusion in the train. The cavalry were soon driven off, and my division, followed by General Kershaw's, closed upon General Anderson. About this time the enemy attacked our train at the stream we had shortly before crossed, and appeared in heavy force to the left of our line of march between this stream and Sailors Creek, which, measured on the road we traveled, are about two miles apart. Word was also received from General Gordon that the enemy was pressing him heavily. To cover the wagon-train and prevent General Gordon from being cut off, line of battle was formed along the road, and a strong line of skirmishers was thrown out, which drove back the enemy's skirmishers and held him in check until General Gordon came up in the rear of the wagons, which must have been from one to two hours after the skirmishing commenced. So soon as General Gordon closed up, my division, following General Anderson's rear, and followed by General Kershaw, moved on across Sailors Creek toward the point where General Pickett was understood to be engaged with the enemy's cavalry, which had cut the line of march in the interval between him and General Mahone. General Gordon having filed off to the right after the wagon-trains, the enemy's cavalry followed closely upon General Kershaw's rear, driving it across Sailors Creek, and soon afterward the enemy's infantry (said to be the Sixth Corps) massed rapidly in our rear. To meet this movement General Kershaw's division formed on the right and mine on the left of the road upon which we were moving, our line of battle being across the road, facing Sailors Creek, which we had not long passed. Before my troops got into position, the enemy opened a heavy fire of artillery upon our lines, which was continued up to the time of our capture. After shelling our lines and skirmishing for some time, an hour or more, the enemy's infantry advanced and were repulsed, and that portion which attacked the artillery brigade was charged by it and driven back across Sailors Creek. This brigade was then brought back to its original position in line of battle under a heavy fire of artillery. Finding that Kershaw's division, which was on my right, had been obliged to retire in consequence of the enemy having turned his right flank, and that my command was entirely surrounded, to prevent useless sacrifice of life the firing was stopped by some of my officers, aided by some of the enemy's, and the officers and men taken as prisoners of war. I can not too highly praise the conduct of my command, and hope to have an opportunity of doing it full justice when reports are received from the brigade commanders. Among a number of brave men killed or wounded, I regret to have to announce the name of Colonel Crutchfield, who commanded the artillery brigade. He was killed after gallantly leading a successful charge against the enemy. I have also to mourn the loss of Lieutenant Robert Goldsborough, my aid-de-camp, who was mortally wounded by a fragment of a shell while efficiently discharging his duty. In the absence of Generals Ewell and Kershaw in a Northern prison, I have endeavored to give the principal facts of the march and capture of the former's command, so far as I am acquainted with them, and although, for the want of reports, memoranda, or maps, I may be mistaken in some minor matters, I believe, in the main features this report will be found to be correct, so far as it goes. Very respectfully, your obedient servant,

G. W. C. LEE, *Major-General.*

RESIDENCE OF JEFFERSON DAVIS, AT RICHMOND, VA.

VIEW OF RICHMOND, VA., FROM THE JAMES RIVER, AFTER ITS EVACUATION BY THE CONFEDERATE GOVERNMENT, APRIL 3, 1865.

P. S.—I was told after my capture that the enemy had two corps of infantry and three divisions of cavalry opposed to us at Sailors Creek; and was informed by General Ewell that he had sent me an order to surrender, being convinced of the hopelessness of further resistance. The order was not received by me.

G. W. C. L.

MEMORANDUM.

On the morning of Thursday, April 6th, when the enemy attacked our wagon-train between Sandy and Sailors Creeks, General Anderson, in conjunction with General Ewell, formed the line of battle along the road between these two streams (as I have already stated in my report) to protect the wagon-train and prevent General Gordon, who was bringing up the rear of the wagon-train, from being cut off. General Anderson seemed anxious to push on, and said to me that he must move on to support General Pickett, who was engaged with the enemy further on toward Rices Station (and, as I suppose, beyond Sailors Creek). As soon as General Gordon closed up on General Ewell's rear (Kershaw), General Anderson moved forward toward Sailors Creek. My division followed, and while its head was halted on the hill beyond Sailors Creek to allow the rear to close up, General Ewell told me that the enemy had cut the road in advance of us, and that General Anderson wished us to unite with him to drive the enemy out of the way. To this end my division moved forward a few hundred yards, when the enemy's driving General Kershaw's rear across Sailors Creek, and his appearance in heavy force of infantry, cavalry and artillery in our rear, stopped the further movement. General Anderson told General Ewell that the latter would have as much as he could do to take care of the rear, and that he (General Anderson) would endeavor to drive the enemy out of the way in front. General Anderson did make the attack, but failed, losing Brigadier-Generals Hunton and Corse, and a number of his other officers and men as prisoners. No other general officers were captured, at that time, of General Anderson's command, as far as I know. General Ewell and all his general officers were taken prisoners.

But little of the above came under my personal observation; most of the statement was gathered from conversations with General Ewell and other officers after the capture.

Respectfully submitted,

G. W. C. LEE, *Major-General.*

THE APPOMATTOX CAMPAIGN.

OPERATIONS
OF THE
CAVALRY CORPS, ARMY OF NORTHERN VIRGINIA,
INCLUDING BATTLES OF
FIVE FORKS, DINWIDDIE COURTHOUSE AND AMELIA SPRINGS, VA.,

MARCH 28 TO APRIL 9, 1865.

BY

MAJOR-GENERAL FITZHUGH LEE.

RICHMOND, VA., April 22, 1865.

ON the 28th of March my division moved from its position on the extreme left of our lines in front of Richmond, on the north side of James River, marched to Petersburg and up the Southside Railroad, reaching Sutherland Station, nineteen miles from Petersburg, on the 29th. In compliance with verbal instructions received from you, I marched the next day (30th) toward Dinwiddie Courthouse, via Five Forks, to watch and counteract the operations threatened by the massing of the Federal cavalry at Dinwiddie Courthouse under Sheridan. After passing Five Forks a portion of the enemy's cavalry were encountered with success and driven back upon their large reserves near the Courthouse. Night put an end to further operations, and my division was encamped in the vicinity of Five Forks. My loss, though slight, included Brigadier-General W. H. Payne among the wounded; and the loss of the services of this bold, capable officer was severely felt in all subsequent movements. I was joined during the evening by the divisions of Major-Generals W. H. F. Lee and Rosser, and by order of the commanding general took command of the cavalry corps.

MAJ.-GEN. G. W. C. LEE, OF VIRGINIA.
[From a photograph taken in 1864.]

On the 31st of March, Pickett coming up with five small brigades of infantry, we attacked the very large force of the enemy's cavalry in our front at Five Forks, killed and wounded many, captured over one hundred prisoners, and drove them to within a half mile of Dinwiddie Courthouse. Munford, in command of my old division, held our lines in front of the enemy's position, while the remaining two divisions of cavalry, preceding the infantry, moved by a concealed wooded road to turn and attack their flank. A short stream, strongly defended at its crossing, presented an unexpected obstacle to the sudden attack contemplated. It was finally carried, however, with loss in W. H. F. Lee's and Rosser's divisions. Munford, attacking about the same time, also successfully carried the temporary works thrown up in his front, and by a gallant advance again united his command with the other division. Darkness put an end to our further advance. Among the wounded were numbered Major-General Rosser, slightly; Captain Dawson, my very efficient and gallant chief of ordnance, severely; and Lieutenant-Colonel Fields, Third Virginia Cavalry. Lieutenant Croxton, Fourth Virginia, was killed, and a number of others whose names I have not been able to obtain.

Our position in the vicinity of Dinwiddie Courthouse brought us in rear of the left of the infantry confronting the right of our line of battle at Burgess Mill, and ascertaining during the night that that force, consisting of the Fifth Corps, had about-faced and was marching to the support of Sheridan and his discomfited cavalry, which would have brought them directly upon our left flank, at daylight on the 1st we commenced moving back to our former position at Five Forks, where Pickett placed his infantry in line of battle. W. H. F. Lee was on his right, one regiment of Munford's command on his left, uniting with the pickets of General Roberts' command, who filled the gap between our position and the right of our main army, then at Burgess Mill. Rosser was placed just in rear of the center as a reserve, Hatchers Run intervening between him and our line.

Everything continued quiet until about 3 P. M., when reports reached me of a large body of infantry marching around and menacing our left flank. I ordered Munford to go in person, ascertain the exact condition of affairs, hold his command in readiness, and, if necessary, order it up at once. He soon sent for it, and it reached its position just in time to receive the attack. A division of two small brigades of cavalry was not able long to withstand the attack of a Federal corps of infantry, and that force soon crushed in Pickett's left flank, swept it away, and before Rosser could cross Hatchers Run, the position at the Fords was seized and held, and an advance toward the railroad made. It was repulsed by Rosser. Pickett was driven rapidly toward the prolongation of the right of his line of battle by the combined attack of this infantry corps and Sheridan's cavalry, making a total of over twenty-six thousand men, to which he was opposed with seven thousand men of all arms. Our forces were driven back some miles, the retreat degenerating into a rout, being followed up principally by the cavalry, while the infantry corps held the position our troops were first driven from, threatening an advance upon the railroad, and paralyzing the force of reserve cavalry by necessitating its being stationary in an interposing position to check or retard such an advance. The disastrous halt was made at Five Forks upon the day of our retrograde movement from Dinwiddie Courthouse, on account of the importance of the location as a point of observation to watch and develop movements then evidently in contemplation for an attack on our left flank or upon our line of railroad communication; the importance of preserving which, intact, could not be overestimated. It was thought Pickett's infantry and my cavalry could successfully contend against the superior numbers of the enemy's cavalry (and which the fighting the day before amply verified), and should their infantry be withdrawn from the position of their lines contiguous to our operations, a corresponding force of our own would have thus been made available, and could be used to restore the status; the distance from Burgess Mill, the terminus respectively of the right and left of the two lines of battle, being short from Five Forks, with a plain road joining the two.

I remained in position on Hatchers Run, near Five Forks, during the night, and was joined by the cavalry which was driven back the previous afternoon, and by Lieutenant-General Anderson with Wise's and Gracie's brigades, who, leaving the position at Burgess Mill, had marched by a circuitous route to our relief. Had he advanced up the direct road, it would have brought him on the flank and rear of the infantry forming the enemy's right, which attacked our left at Five Forks, and probably changed the result of the unequal contest. While Anderson was marching up, the Fifth Corps was marching back, and was enabled to participate in the attack upon our lines the next day. While the services of the three infantry brigades (which General Anderson re-enforced us by, too late for use), and the five with Pickett, by their absence, increased the disparity between the contending forces upon the next day for the possession of the lines circumvallating Petersburg.

On April 3d, General Anderson learning that the enemy had been successful in penetrating our lines, and that our army was withdrawing from the vicinity of Richmond and Petersburg, commenced moving back on the Namozine and Tabernacle Road toward Amelia Courthouse. I followed, protecting his rear, and skirmishing with the enemy's advance until Amelia Courthouse was reached on the 5th inst. At Deep Creek, en route, the command was placed in line of battle to take advantage of the defensive position offered, and to give a check to the enemy's rapid advance. Wise's and Hunton's brigades constituted a part of the rear-guard at that time. The attack was not made upon us until after dark, and was principally sustained by Munford's command, of my old division, with a steadiness reflecting high credit upon the valor and discipline of his men. Owing to the fact that General Heth's troops were expected to arrive by the road by which the enemy advanced, they were permitted to approach very close to our lines, and it was not until Lieutenant-Colonel Strother, Fourth Virginia Cavalry, was sent to reconnoiter, that it was ascertained who they were; he having walked into their line of skirmishers, which was so near to ours that the questions asked him were distinctly heard by our troops. At another of the temporary halts upon this march to check the enemy in the vicinity of Namozine Church, that very excellent North Carolina brigade of W. H. F. Lee's division suffered severely. The troops had been placed in motion again to resume the march. This brigade was the rear of the column, and I was obliged to retain it in position to prevent the enemy from attacking the remainder of the command. While getting in motion, their rapidly arriving forces soon augmented the troops it was so gallantly holding in check and produced a concentration impossible for it to resist. Its commander, Brigadier-General Barringer, was captured while in the steady discharge of his duties, and his loss was keenly felt by the command. I also had the great misfortune to be deprived of the services of my most efficient and untiring adjutant-general, Major J. Dugin Fergusson, who was captured about the same time, and whose assistance, always important, was especially desirable at this time.

Reporting to the commanding general at Amelia Courthouse on the 5th, I was ordered to move with my command on the Paineville Road to protect the wagon-train, a portion of which was reported to have been attacked by some of the enemy's cavalry. W. H. F. Lee was detached and sent in advance of Longstreet, who was moving from the Courthouse toward Jetersville. I found the enemy had attacked and burned a portion of the cavalry train, including my own headquarters wagons, and had retreated again toward Jetersville. I started at once in pursuit, and soon closed up on Gary with his brigade, who had been previously dispatched in that direction and was engaging their rear near Paineville. Re-enforcing him, the enemy were rapidly driven within a mile of Jetersville, where their infantry were formed in large force. (A dispatch captured that night showed General Grant to be there in person.) The pursuit was discontinued and the command placed in camp at Amelia Springs. In this encounter thirty of the enemy were killed, principally with the saber, and one hundred and fifty wounded and captured. The attack was made with Rosser's division mounted, supported by a portion of my old division dismounted. The gallantry of Brigadier-General Dearing in leading the charge of his command was here very conspicuous. Our loss was not very heavy, and I can only recall in the connection the mortally wounding of two of my bravest and best young officers—Captain Hugh McGuire, Eleventh Virginia Cavalry, and Captain James Rutherford, Assistant Inspector-General, General Dearing's staff. The portion of the enemy's cavalry engaged in this raid had preceded the column which had been marching on our left flank and had reached Jetersville, on the Danville Railroad, before Longstreet arrived in that vicinity. Their cavalry crossed the railroad and swept around on the north of our right marching flank, and hence came upon the wagon-train. During the night, at Amelia Springs, Longstreet's corps, deflected from its original line of march by the occupation of Jetersville and Burkesville by the enemy, passed by. The commanding general arrived also, and I received from him orders to march at daylight after General Longstreet. The main body of the enemy's cavalry had ceased to follow our rear after our approach to Amelia Courthouse, and was moving on a parallel route upon our left marching flank.

BRIG.-GEN. RUFUS BARRINGER, OF NORTH CAROLINA.

The next morning (6th of April) I started the main portion of my command under Rosser (the senior officer present), and remained, in compliance with instructions, to explain in person to the first infantry officer who came up the situation of things, and to urge the importance of his keeping a sharp watch upon his left flank, as it was feared by the commanding general the enemy might tap the marching column coming down from the Amelia Springs and Jetersville Road. I then rode on to rejoin the greater part of my command en route toward Rices Station, but was stopped after crossing Sailors Creek by the interposition of the enemy's cavalry, who, coming from their position on the railroad in the vicinity of Jetersville, had seized the road upon which we were marching, after the rear of Longstreet had passed along and previous to the arrival of the head of Ewell's command. I was detained there some time, hoping an attack would be made to reopen the way. The infantry were formed in line of battle at right angles to the road, and facing the direction in which they were marching. An attack commenced, but was stopped, though the enemy were being rapidly driven from our front. In the meantime the enemy made his appearance in the rear of Ewell's column, necessitating the formation of another line of battle on Sailors Creek, the direction from which they had marched. The line of battle thus originally formed faced in opposite directions, and remained quietly in position until the Federal infantry re-enforced their large force of cavalry, and with it had almost entirely surrounded them. Though portions of this force, particularly the command of General G. W. C. Lee, fought with a gallantry never surpassed, their defeat and surrender were inevitable, after the dispositions of the enemy to effect it. I am clearly of the opinion (and I only express it because I was a witness of all that happened until just previous to the surrender) that, had the troops been rapidly massed when their march was first interrupted, they could have cleared the way and been able to fall into line of battle on Longstreet's left, who was taking position at Rices Station, some few miles ahead. Or, had the heads of the column been turned obliquely off in a westerly direction, more toward the road Gordon and the wagons were moving upon, an echelon formation adopted, the nature of the ground, wooded and much broken, would have kept the cavalry from harassing them sufficiently to retard their progress until the arrival of their infantry. I rode out by that way with my staff and a few men just previous to Ewell's surrender, and found it so feasible that I immediately sent a staff officer back to Generals Ewell and Anderson to reiterate to them my convictions, previously expressed, and now so much strengthened by my own experience.

The halt, allowing time for the accumulation of the enemy's troops, proved fatal. General Rosser, in command of his own, and my old division, under Munford, proceeded to Rices Station, on the South Side Road, where, learning that a force had been detached from the Federal left, confronting Longstreet at that point, to open on his rear, moved at once to counteract their purpose. The enemy were overtaken and attacked on the road toward, and in the vicinity of, High Bridge. After a sharp encounter they were defeated, our forces capturing some seven hundred and eighty prisoners and killing and wounding a large number, including among the killed their commander, Brigadier-General Read, chief of staff to General Ord, commanding Army of the James, whose body fell into our hands. The enemy's force proved to be a picked body of infantry and a squadron of cavalry, which, placed under this staff officer, had for its object the destruction of the High Bridge over the Appomattox, in our rear. The success was, indeed, dearly bought, for the lives of Brigadier-General Dearing, of Rosser's division, Colonel Boston, Fifth Virginia Cavalry, commanding Payne's brigade of my old division, and Major James W. Thomson, Stuart's Horse Artillery, and Rosser's chief in that arm, were lost in attaining it. The splendid gallantry of these three officers had been tested on many fields, and their conspicuous valor was universally known. The genial and dashing Thomson was killed leading cavalry, his guns not being present.

BATTLE OF FIVE FORKS, VA. A SECTION SHOWING A CHARGE OF GENERAL FITZHUGH LEE'S CAVALRY DIVISION.

On the night of the 6th the position at Rices Station was abandoned, and I moved in rear of Longstreet, crossing the Appomattox a little above Farmville. Fighting took place between my rear and the enemy's advance in the vicinity and in the streets of Farmville, it being found necessary to retard their progress to give time for the passage of the river by our troops. On the 7th a portion of the enemy's cavalry, having crossed the river again, made an attack upon the wagon-train moving upon our line of march. They were met by Munford in front, while Rosser attacked their flank, and were driven back with considerable loss, including among the captured their commanding general, Irvin Gregg. Our position was held near this point of attack until 12 P. M., when the march was resumed toward Appomattox Courthouse. The cavalry followed in the rear of Longstreet's corps, and maintained that order of march throughout the 8th, followed by a portion of the Federal infantry. Their cavalry and the remainder of their infantry pursued the line of railroad from Farmville to Appomattox Station.

During the evening of the 8th I received orders to move the cavalry corps to the front, and to report in person to the commanding general. Upon arriving at his headquarters I found General Longstreet there, and we were soon after joined by General Gordon. The condition of our situation was explained by the commanding general to us as the commanders of his three corps, and the correspondence between General Grant and himself, as far as it had then progressed, was laid before us. It was decided that I should attack the enemy's cavalry at daylight, then reported as obstructing our further march. Gordon was to support me, and in case nothing but cavalry were discovered, we were to clear it from our route and open a way for our remaining troops; but in case they were supported by heavy bodies of infantry, the commanding general should be at once notified, in order that a flag of truce should be sent to accede to the only alternative left us. The enemy were enabled to take position across our line of march by moving up from Appomattox Station, which they reached earlier than our main advance, in consequence of our march being retarded by our wagon-trains. At daybreak on the 9th, Gordon's command, numbering about sixteen hundred muskets, was formed in line of battle half a mile west of Appomattox Courthouse, on the Lynchburg Road. The cavalry corps was formed on his right, W. H. F. Lee's division being nearest the infantry, Rosser's in the center, and Munford's on the extreme right, making a mounted force of about twenty-four hundred men. Our attack was made about sunrise, and the enemy's cavalry quickly driven out of the way with the loss of two guns and a number of prisoners. The arrival at this time of two corps of their infantry necessitated the retiring of our lines; during which, and knowing what would be the result, I withdrew the cavalry, W. H. F. Lee retiring toward our rear, and Rosser and Munford out toward Lynchburg, having cleared that road of the enemy.

Upon hearing that the Army of Northern Virginia had surrendered, the men were generally dispersed and rode off to their homes, subject to a reassembling for a continuation of the struggle. I rode out in person with a portion of W. H. F. Lee's division, the nearest to me at that time, and previous to the negotiations between the commanders of the two armies. It will be recalled that my action was in accordance with the views I had expressed in the council the night before, that if a surrender was compelled the next day I would try and extricate the cavalry, provided it could be done without compromising the action of the commanding general, but that I would not avail myself of a cessation of hostilities pending the existence of a flag of truce. I had an understanding with General Gordon that he should communicate to you the information of the presence of the enemy's infantry upon the road in our front. Apart from the fond, though forlorn, hope that future operations were still in store for the cavalry, I was desirous that they should not be included in the capitulations, because the ownership of their horses was vested in themselves, and I deemed it doubtful that terms would be offered allowing such ownership to continue. A few days convinced me of the impracticability of longer entertaining such hopes, and I rode into the Federal lines and accepted for myself the terms offered the officers of the Army of Northern Virginia; my cavalry are being paroled at the nearest places for such purposes in their counties.

The burning by the enemy of all my retained reports, records and data of every kind, near Paineville, in Amelia County, which were in one of the wagons destroyed, and my inability to get reports from my officers, is my apology for the rendition of a report incomplete in many, though I think minor, details. I particularly regret not being able to do justice, in this the only way I can, to the many acts of gallantry performed by officers and men upon the memorable retreat; but such conduct is usually derived from the reports of subordinate officers, the absence of which will explain it. I testify, however, to the general conduct of my officers and men as highly creditable to themselves upon every occasion which called forth its display. They fought every day from the 29th of March to the 9th of April, both inclusive, with a valor as steady as of yore, and whose brightness was not dimmed by the increasing clouds of adversity. I desire to call attention to the marked and excellent behavior of Generals W. H. F. Lee, Rosser and Munford, commanding divisions. The former was detached from the main command, being the senior division commander, whenever it became necessary for a force to operate separately, and I hope has made a report direct to the commanding general. He surrendered with the army at Appomattox Courthouse. The other two succeeded in getting out, and immediately made arrangements to continue the struggle until the capitulation of General Johnson's army brought the convincing proof that a further resistance was useless. The notice of the commanding general is also directed to Brigadier-Generals Henry A. Wise and Eppa Hunton, commanding infantry brigades, and who were more or less under my command until Amelia Courthouse was reached. The disheartening surrounding influences had no effect upon them; they kept their duty plainly in view, and they fully performed it. The past services of General Henry A. Wise, his antecedents in civil life, and his age, caused his bearing upon this most trying retreat to shine conspicuously forth. His unconquerable spirit was filled with as much earnestness and zeal in April, 1865, as when he first took up arms, four years ago; and the freedom with which he exposed a long life laden with honors proved he was willing to sacrifice it if it would conduce toward attaining the liberty of his country. Brigadier-General Munford, commanding my division, mentions most favorably Colonel W. A. Morgan, First Virginia Cavalry; Colonel W. B. Wooldridge, Fourth Virginia; Lieutenant-Colonel Cary Breckinridge, Second Virginia (a brother of the gallant Captain James Breckinridge, of the same regiment, who was killed at Five Forks, as was not previously mentioned); Lieutenant-Colonels Old, Fourth Virginia, and Irving, First Virginia, all of Munford's old brigade; Captain Henry Lee, assistant adjutant-general; Lieutenant Abraham Warwick, aid-de-camp; Lieutenant Mortimer Rogers, ordnance officer, and Sergeant-Major L. Griffin, Second Virginia Cavalry.

I can not close this, my last official report, without commending for their valuable services, the following officers of my staff not previously mentioned, and who at the last moment were found doing their duty on the fated field of Appomattox: Majors Mason and Treaner, assistant adjutant and inspector-generals; Major W. B. Warwick, chief commissary; Dr. A. C. Randolph, chief surgeon; Major Breathed, chief of artillery; Major G. M. Ryalls, formerly of General Stuart's staff; and Captain Lewellyn Saunderson who, having arrived from his native country, Ireland, joined me previous to the fall of Petersburg, and remained with me to the last. The proverbial intrepidity of the dashing Mason and reckless Breathed upon every battlefield of the war that the Army of Northern Virginia contended for is too well known for me to do more than refer to. Major Warwick, apart from his onerous duties, rendered services on many fields, his cool courage causing him often to be employed in duties not immediately pertaining to his office.

I deeply regret being obliged to mention the dangerous wounding of my aid-de-camp, Lieutenant Charles Minnigerode, Jr. One of the last minie-balls that whistled on its cruel errand over the field of Appomattox passed entirely through the upper part of his body. He fell at my side, where for three long years he had discharged his duties with an affectionate fidelity never exceeded, a courage never surpassed. Wonderfully passing unharmed through the many battles fought by the two principal armies in this State (for an impetuous spirit often carried him where the fire was hottest), he was left at last, writhing in his great pain, to the mercy of the victors upon the field of our last struggle. The rapidly-advancing lines of the enemy prevented his removal, and as we turned away the wet eyes and sorrowing hearts silently told that one was no longer in our midst. Lieutenant Minnegerode combined the qualities of an aid-de-camp to a general officer in a remarkable degree. His personal services to me will forever be prized and remembered, while his intelligence, amiability and brightness of disposition rendered him an object of endearment to all.

FITZHUGH LEE,
Major-General Commanding Cavalry.

McLEAN'S HOUSE, AT APPOMATTOX COURTHOUSE, VIRGINIA, WHERE GENERALS LEE AND GRANT MET TO ARRANGE TERMS OF SURRENDER.
[From a photograph taken in 1865.]

THE APPOMATTOX CAMPAIGN,

MARCH 29 TO APRIL 10, 1865,

INCLUDING

THE SURRENDER OF THE CONFEDERATE FORCES AT APPOMATTOX COURTHOUSE.

BY

GENERAL ROBERT E. LEE,

Commanding Army of Northern Virginia.

HEADQUARTERS, March 29, 1865.
(Via Petersburg. Received 1:45.)

ENEMY are reported to have crossed Hatchers Run at Monks Neck Bridge with infantry and cavalry coming toward Dinwiddie Courthouse.

R. E. LEE.

HON. J. C. BRECKINRIDGE, *Secretary of War.*

HEADQUARTERS ARMIES OF THE CONFEDERATE STATES,
March 29, 1865. (Received 11:15 P. M.)

The enemy crossed Hatchers Run this morning at Monks Neck Bridge with a large force of cavalry, infantry and artillery, and to-night his left extended to Dinwiddie Courthouse. Gregg's cavalry advanced a mile and a half on Fords Road toward the South Side Railroad. General Anderson moved out from his position and struck his column near the intersection of the Quaker Road and Boydton Plank Road, but did not succeed in driving him back.

R. E. LEE.

HON. SECRETARY OF WAR, RICHMOND.
(Copy sent to the President.)

HEADQUARTERS ARMY OF NORTHERN VIRGINIA,
April 1, 1865.

After my dispatch of last night I received a report from General Pickett, who, with three of his own brigades and two of General Johnson's, supported the cavalry under General Fitzhugh Lee near Five Forks on the road from Dinwiddie Courthouse to the South Side Road. After considerable difficulty, and meeting resistance from the enemy at all points, General Pickett forced his way to within less than a mile of Dinwiddie Courthouse. By this time it was too dark for further operations, and General Pickett resolved to return to Five Forks to protect his communication with the railroad. He inflicted considerable damage upon the enemy and took some prisoners. His own loss was severe, including a good many officers. General Terry had his horse killed by a shell and was disabled himself. General Fitzhugh Lee's and Rosser's divisions were heavily engaged, but their loss was slight. General W. H. F. Lee lost some valuable officers. General Pickett did not retire from the vicinity of Dinwiddie Courthouse until early this morning, when, his left flank being threatened by a heavy force, he withdrew to Five Forks, where he took position with General W. H. F. Lee on his right, Fitzhugh Lee and Rosser on his left, with Roberts' brigade on the White Oak Road connecting with General Anderson. The enemy attacked General Roberts with a large force of cavalry, and, after being once repulsed, finally drove him back across Hatchers Run.

A large force of infantry, believed to be the Fifth Corps, with other troops, turned General Pickett's left and drove him back on the White Oak Road, separating him from General Fitzhugh Lee, who was compelled to fall

APPOMATTOX, VA., COURTHOUSE.
[From a photograph taken in 1865.]

back across Hatchers Run. General Pickett's present position is not known. General Fitzhugh Lee reports that the enemy is massing his infantry heavily behind the cavalry in his front. The infantry that engaged General Anderson yesterday has moved from his front toward our right, and is supposed to participate in the operations above described. Prisoners have been taken to-day from the Twenty-fourth Corps, and it is believed that most of that corps is now south of the James. Our loss to-day is not known. A report from Staunton represents that the Eighth Corps passed over the Baltimore & Ohio Railroad from the 20th to the 25th ultimo. General Hancock is at Harpers Ferry with two thousand men. One division of the Nineteenth Corps is at Winchester with about one thousand cavalry. The infantry at Winchester have marching orders, and all these troops are said to be destined for General Grant's army. The enemy is also reported to have withdrawn all his troops from Wolf Run Shoals and Fairfax Station, and to be concentrating them at Winchester.

Very respectfully, your obedient servant,

R. E. LEE,
General.

HON. SECRETARY OF WAR, RICHMOND.

HEADQUARTERS,
April 2, 1865.
(Via Petersburg. Received 10:40 o'clock.)

I see no prospect of doing more than holding our position here till night. I am not certain that I can do that. If I can I shall withdraw to-night north of the Appomattox, and, if possible, it will be better to withdraw the whole line to-night from James River. The brigades on Hatchers Run are cut off from us; enemy have broken through our lines and intercepted between us and them, and there is no bridge over which they can cross the Appomattox this side of Goodes or Beavers, which are not very far from the Danville Railroad. Our only chance, then, of concentrating our forces is to do so near Danville Railroad, which I shall endeavor to do at once. I advise that all preparation be made for leaving Richmond to-night. I will advise you later, according to circumstances.

R. E. LEE.

GENERAL J. C. BRECKINRIDGE.

HEADQUARTERS,
April 2, 1865.
(Received 4:55 o'clock.)

I think the Danville road will be safe until to-morrow.

R. E. LEE.

GENERAL J. C. BRECKINRIDGE, *Secretary of War.*

PETERSBURG, April 2, 1865.
(Received 7 o'clock.)

It is absolutely necessary that we should abandon our position to-night or run the risk of being cut off in the morning. I have given all the orders to officers on both sides of the river, and have taken every precaution that I can to make the movement successful. It will be a difficult operation, but I hope not impracticable. Please give all orders that you find necessary in and about Richmond. The troops will all be directed to Amelia Courthouse.

R. E. LEE.

GENERAL J. C. BRECKINRIDGE, *Secretary of War.*

NEAR APPOMATTOX COURTHOUSE, VA.,
April 12, 1865.

It is with pain that I announce to Your Excellency the surrender of the Army of Northern Virginia. The operations which preceded this result will be reported in full. I will, therefore, only now state that upon arriving at Amelia Courthouse on the morning of the 4th with the advance of the army on the retreat from the lines in front of Richmond and Petersburg, and not finding the supplies ordered to be placed there, nearly twenty-four hours were lost in endeavoring to collect in the country subsistence for men and horses. This delay was fatal and could not be retrieved. The troops, wearied by continual fighting and marching for several days and nights, obtained neither rest nor refreshments, and on moving, on the 5th, on the Richmond & Danville Railroad, I found at Jetersville the enemy's cavalry and learned the approach of his infantry and the general advance of his army toward Burkesville. This deprived us of the use of the railroad, and rendered it impracticable to procure from Danville the supplies ordered to meet us at points of our march. Nothing could be obtained from the adjacent country. Our route to the Roanoke was, therefore, changed, and the march directed upon Farmville, where supplies were ordered from Lynchburg. The change of route threw the troops over the roads pursued by the artillery and wagon-trains west of the railroad, which impeded our advance and embarrassed our movements.

On the morning of the 6th General Longstreet's Corps reached Rices Station, on the Lynchburg Railroad. It was followed by the commands of Generals R. H. Anderson, Ewell and Gordon, with orders to close upon it as fast as the progress of the trains would permit, or as they could be directed on roads further west. General Anderson, commanding Pickett's and B. R. Johnson's divisions, became disconnected with Mahone's division, forming the rear of Longstreet. The enemy's cavalry penetrated the lines of march through the interval thus left and attacked the wagon-train moving toward Farmville. This caused serious delay in the march of the center and rear of the column, and enabled the enemy to mass upon their flank. After successive attacks Anderson's and Ewell's Corps were captured or driven from their position. The latter general, with both of his division commanders, Kershaw and Custis Lee, and his brigadiers were taken prisoners. Gordon, who all the morning, aided by General W. H. F. Lee's cavalry, had checked the advance of the enemy on the road from Amelia Springs and protected the trains, became exposed to his combined assaults, which he bravely resisted and twice repulsed, but the cavalry having been withdrawn to another part of the line of march, and the enemy massing heavily on his front and both flanks, renewed the attack about 6 P. M., and drove him from the field in much confusion.

GENERAL ROBERT E. LEE.

[From a pen-and-ink portrait made in 1863, from a photograph taken by Minnis & Cowell, Richmond, Va.]

The army continued its march during the night, and every effort was made to reorganize the divisions which had been shattered by the day's operations, but the men being depressed by fatigue and hunger many threw away their arms, while others followed the wagon-trains and embarrassed their progress.

On the morning of the 7th rations were issued to the troops as they passed Farmville, but the safety of the trains requiring their removal upon the approach of the enemy, all could not be supplied. The army, reduced to two corps, under Longstreet and Gordon, moved steadily on the road to Appomattox Courthouse; thence its march was ordered by Campbell Courthouse, through Pittsylvania, toward Danville. The roads were wretched and the progress slow. By great efforts the head of the column reached Appomattox Courthouse on the evening of the 8th, and the troops were halted for rest. The march was ordered to be resumed at 1 A. M. on the 9th. Fitzhugh Lee, with the cavalry, supported by Gordon, was ordered to drive the enemy from his front, wheel to the left and cover the passage of the trains; while Longstreet, who, from Rices Station, had formed the rear-guard, should close up and hold the position. Two battalions of artillery and the ammunition wagons were directed to accompany the army, the rest of the artillery and wagons to move toward Lynchburg. In the early part of the night the enemy attacked Walker's artillery train near Appomattox Station, on the Lynchburg Railroad, and were repelled. Shortly afterward their cavalry dashed toward the Courthouse, till halted by our line. During the night there were indications of a large force massing on our left and front. Fitzhugh Lee was directed to ascertain its strength and to suspend his advance till daylight, if necessary. About 5 A. M. on the 9th, with Gordon on his left, he moved forward and opened the way. A heavy force of the enemy was discovered opposite Gordon's right, which, moving in the direction of Appomattox Courthouse, drove back the left of the cavalry and threatened to cut off Gordon from Longstreet, his cavalry at the same time threatening to envelop his left flank. Gordon withdrew across the Appomattox River, and the cavalry advanced on the Lynchburg Road and became separated from the army.

Learning the condition of affairs on the lines, where I had gone under the expectation of meeting General Grant, to learn definitely the terms he proposed in a communication received from him on the 8th, in the event of the surrender of the army, I requested a suspension of hostilities until these terms could be arranged. In the interview which occurred with General Grant in compliance with my request, terms having been agreed on, I surrendered that portion of the Army of Northern Virginia which was on the field, with its arms, artillery and wagon-trains, the officers and men to be paroled, retaining their side-arms and private effects. I deemed this course the best under all the circumstances by which we were surrounded.

On the morning of the 9th, according to the reports of the ordnance officers, there were seven thousand eight hundred and ninety-two organized infantry, with arms, with an average of seventy-five rounds of ammunition per man. The artillery, though reduced to sixty-three pieces, with ninety-three rounds of ammunition, was sufficient. These comprised all the supplies of ordnance that could be relied on in the State of Virginia. I have no accurate report of the cavalry, but believe it did not exceed twenty-one hundred effective men. The enemy were more than five times our numbers. If we could have forced our way one day longer it would have been at a great sacrifice of life, and at its end I did not see how a surrender could have been avoided. We had no subsistence for man or horse, and it could not be gathered in the country. The supplies ordered to Pamplins Station from Lynchburg could not reach us, and the men, deprived of food and sleep for many days, were worn out and exhausted.

With great respect, your obedient servant,

R. E. LEE, *General.*

HIS EXCELLENCY, JEFFERSON DAVIS.

FAREWELL ADDRESS OF GENERAL ROBERT E. LEE TO THE ARMY OF NORTHERN VIRGINIA.

HEADQUARTERS ARMY OF NORTHERN VIRGINIA,
April 10, 1865.
[General Order No. 9.]

After four years of arduous service marked by unsurpassed courage and fortitude, the Army of Northern Virginia has been compelled to yield to overwhelming numbers and resources. I need not tell the brave survivors of so many hard-fought battles, who have remained steadfast to the last, that I have consented to the result from no distrust of them. But, feeling that valor and devotion could accomplish nothing that could compensate for the loss that must have attended the continuance of the contest, I determined to avoid the useless sacrifice of those whose past services have endeared them to their countrymen. By the terms of the agreement officers and men can return to their homes, and remain until exchanged. You will take with you the satisfaction that proceeds from the consciousness of duty faithfully performed; and I earnestly pray that a merciful God will extend to you his blessing and protection.

With an increasing admiration of your constancy and devotion to your country, and a grateful remembrance of your kind and generous considerations for myself, I bid you all an affectionate farewell.

R. E. LEE, *General.*

ARTICLES OF SURRENDER OF THE ARMY OF NORTHERN VIRGINIA AT APPOMATTOX COURTHOUSE, VA.

APPOMATTOX COURTHOUSE, VA.,
April 10, 1865.

Agreement entered into this day in regard to the surrender of the Army of Northern Virginia to the United States authorities:

First. The troops shall march by brigades and detachments to a designated point, stack their arms, deposit their flags, sabers, pistols, etc., and from thence march to their homes under charge of their officers, superintended by their respective division and corps commanders, officers retaining their side-arms and the authorized number of private horses.

Second. All public horses and public property of all kinds to be turned over to staff-officers, designated by the United States authorities.

Third. Such transportation as may be agreed upon as necessary for the transportation of the private baggage of officers, will be allowed to accompany the officers, to be turned over at the end of the trip to the nearest United States quartermaster, receipts being taken for the same.

Fourth. Couriers and mounted men of the artillery and cavalry, whose horses are their own private property, will be allowed to retain them.

Fifth. The surrender of the Army of Northern Virginia shall be construed to include all the forces operating with that army on the 8th instant, the date of the commencement of negotiations for surrender, except such bodies of cavalry as actually made their escape previous to the surrender; and except, also, such pieces of artillery as were more than twenty miles from Appomattox Courthouse at the time of the surrender on the 9th instant.

J. LONGSTREET,
Lieutenant-General.
J. B. GORDON,
Major-General.
W. N. PENDLETON,
Brigadier-General and Chief of Artillery.

JOHN GIBBON,
Major-General Volunteers.
CHARLES GRIFFIN,
Brevet Major-General United States Volunteers.
W. MERRITT,
Brevet Major-General.

A "CONFED" who was in the battle of Shiloh happened to be inordinately fond of card playing. During the fight he had three of his fingers shot off. Holding up his mangled member, he gazed at it with a look of ineffable sorrow, and exclaimed, as a big tear stole in the corner of his eye, "I shall never be able to hold a full hand again!" Poor fellow!

PETERSBURG, VA. THE LAST BOMBARDMENT ON THE NIGHT OF MARCH 31, 1865.
[From an original sketch, owned by Mrs. Frank Leslie, New York.]

ON the evening of May 6, 1864, at Spottsylvania, General J. E. B. Stuart, finding it necessary near nightfall to ascertain if the line of Federal earthworks in his front had been abandoned, sent an orderly to the Eleventh Virginia Cavalry, near by, with the request that the officer in command would send him a good man for the performance of a hazardous duty. Private Jim O'Meara, of Company F, was selected, and reported to the general. General Stuart, replying to his salutation, said: "You see that line of earthworks? I want to know if it is manned. Ride down within seventy-five or a hundred yards of it, and then turn to the left and gallop parallel with it. If the Yanks are there, you go fast, and they'll shoot behind you." "All right, gineral. I know it," said Jim, with an appreciative wink. He rode within seventy-five yards of the line, started in the twilight on his run parallel with the line, which, being well manned, was immediately illumined. The fusillade did not cause Jim to swerve. When he had gone nearly half the length of the line his horse received a bullet through his nose, midway between the nostril and eye. Jim deliberately stopped, unslung his carbine, took as careful an aim as he would have done at a squirrel, fired, and resuming his parallel course, completed his run the entire length of the line, and slowly riding to where the general stood at the head of his command, touched his hat and reported, "They're thar yit, gineral."

THE NINTH OF APRIL, 1865.

BY PERCY GREG.

It is a Nation's death-cry—yes, the agony is past,
The stoutest race that ever fought to-day has fought its last;
Aye! start and shudder, well thou may'st, well veil thy weeping eyes;
England! may God forgive thy part—man can not but despise.

Aye! shudder at that cry that speaks the South's supreme despair—
Thou that could save and saved'st not—that would, yet did not dare;
Thou that hadst might to aid the right and heart to brook the wrong,
Weak words of comfort for the weak, and strong hands to help the strong.

That land, the garden of thy wealth, one haggard waste appears—
The ashes of her sunny homes are slaked in patriot tears:
Tears for the slain who died in vain for freedom on the field;
Tears, tears of bitter anguish still for those who live to yield.

The cannon of *his country* pealed Stuart's funeral knell;
His soldier's cheers rang in his ears as Stonewall Jackson fell;
Onward o'er gallant Ashby's grave swept war's successful tide,
And Southern hopes were living yet when Polk and Morgan died.

But he, the leader, on whose words the captains loved to wait,
The noblest, bravest, best of all, hath found a harder fate;
Unscathed by shot and steel he passed o'er many a desperate field,
Oh, God! that he hath lived so long, and only lived to yield!

Along the war-worn, wasted ranks that loved him to the last,
With saddened face and weary pace the vanquished chieftain passed,
Their own hard lot the men forgot, they felt what *his* must be,
What thought in that dark hour must wring the heart of General Lee.

The manly cheek with tears was wet—the stately head was bow'd,
As, breaking from their shatter'd ranks, around his steed they crowd:
"I did my best for you"—'twas all those trembling lips could say.
Ah! happy those whom death hath spared the anguish of to-day.

Weep on, Virginia! weep these lives given to thy cause in vain—
The sons who live to wear once more the Union's galling chain;
The homes whose light is quench'd for aye—the graves without a stone—
The folded flag—the broken sword—the hope forever flown.

Yet raise thy head, fair land, thy dead died bravely for the right—
The folded flag is stainless still—the broken sword is bright;
No blot is on thy record found, *no treason soils thy fame!*
Weep thou thy dead—with cover'd head we mourn our England's shame.

DORSET HALL, SURREY, 1865.

CONFEDERATE FORCES AT APPOMATTOX COURTHOUSE,

APRIL 10, 1865.

COMMANDED BY

GENERAL ROBERT E. LEE.

(Compiled from Reports of Operations and Parole Lists.)

PROVOST GUARD.

First Virginia Battalion, —— ——
Forty-fourth Virginia Battalion, Company B, ——

ESCORT.

Thirty-ninth Virginia Battalion—Captain Samuel B. Brown.

ENGINEER TROOPS.

Colonel Thomas M. R. Talcott.

First Regiment, —— ——
Second Regiment, —— ——

FIRST ARMY CORPS.

Lieutenant-General James Longstreet.

PICKETT'S DIVISION.

Major-General George E. Pickett.

STEUART'S BRIGADE.

Brigadier-General George H. Steuart.

Ninth Virginia—Captain John P. Wilson, Jr.
Fourteenth Virginia—Major William D. Shelton.
Thirty-eighth Virginia—Colonel George K. Griggs.
Fifty-third Virginia—Captain Henry Edmunds.
Fifty-seventh Virginia—Lieutenant-Colonel William H. Ramsey.

FALLS CHURCH, VA.

CORSE'S BRIGADE.

Brigadier-General Montgomery D. Corse;* Colonel Arthur Herbert.

Fifteenth Virginia—Major Charles H. Clarke.
Seventeenth Virginia—Colonel Arthur Herbert.
Twenty-ninth Virginia—Lieutenant John A. Coulson.
Thirtieth Virginia—Colonel Robert S. Chew.
Thirty-second Virginia—Captain Samuel W. Armistead.

HUNTON'S BRIGADE.

Brigadier-General Eppa Hunton;* Major Michael P. Spessard.

Eighth Virginia —— ——
Eighteenth Virginia—Lieutenant Charles H. Wilkinson.
Nineteenth Virginia —— ——
Twenty-eighth Virginia—Major Michael P. Spessard.
Fifty-sixth Virginia—Captain John W. Jones.

TERRY'S BRIGADE.

Brigadier-General William R. Terry;† Major William W. Bentley.

First Virginia, —— ——
Third Virginia, —— ——
Seventh Virginia, —— ——
Eleventh Virginia, —— ——
Twenty-fourth Virginia—Major William W. Bentley.

BOLLINBROOK STREET THEATER, PETERSBURG, VA.

FIELD'S DIVISION.

Major-General Charles W. Field.

PERRY'S (LATE LAWS') BRIGADE.

Brigadier-General William F. Perry.

Fourth Alabama—Lieutenant-Colonel Lawrence H. Scruggs.
Fifteenth Alabama—Colonel Alexander A. Lowther.
Forty-fourth Alabama—Lieutenant-Colonel John A. Jones.
Forty-seventh Alabama—Captain Eli D. Clower.
Forty-eighth Alabama—Major John W. Wigginton.

* Captured April 6th.
† Disabled March 31st.

ANDERSON'S BRIGADE.

Brigadier-General George T. Anderson.

Seventh Georgia—Colonel George H. Carmical.
Eighth Georgia—Colonel John R. Towers.
Ninth Georgia—Major John W. Arnold.
Eleventh Georgia—Captain William H. Ramsey.
Fifty-ninth Georgia—Colonel Jack Brown.

BENNING'S BRIGADE.

Brigadier-General Henry L. Benning.

Second Georgia—Captain Thomas Chaffin, Jr.
Fifteenth Georgia—Major Peter J. Shannon.
Seventeenth Georgia—Major James B. Moore.
Twentieth Georgia, —— ——

GREGG'S BRIGADE.

Colonel Robert M. Powell.

Third Arkansas—Lieutenant-Colonel Robert S. Taylor.
First Texas—Colonel Frederick S. Bass.
Fourth Texas—Lieutenant-Colonel Clinton M. Winkler.
Fifth Texas—Captain W. T. Hill.

BRATTON'S BRIGADE.

Brigadier-General John Bratton.

First South Carolina—Colonel James R. Hagood.
Fifth South Carolina—Colonel A. Coward.
Sixth South Carolina—Colonel John M. Steedman.
Second South Carolina (Rifles)—Colonel Robert E. Bowen.
Palmetto (S. C.) Sharpshooters—Captain Alfred H. Foster.

KERSHAW'S DIVISION.*

Major-General Joseph B. Kershaw.†

DU BOSE'S BRIGADE.

Brigadier-General Dudley M. Du Bose;† Captain J. F. Espy.

Sixteenth Georgia—Lieutenant William M. Montgomery.
Eighteenth Georgia { Captain J. F. Espy. / Lieutenant Gideon J. Lasseter.
Twenty-fourth Georgia—Captain J. A. Jarrard.
Third Georgia—Battalion Sharpshooters, —— ——
Cobb's (Ga.) Legion—Lieutenant W. G. Steed.
Phillips' (Ga.) Legion—Lieutenant A. J. Reese.

HUMPHREYS' BRIGADE.

Colonel William H. Fitz Gerald; Captain Gwin R. Cherry.

Thirteenth Mississippi—Lieutenant W. H. Davis.
Seventeenth Mississippi—Captain Gwin R. Cherry.
Eighteenth Mississippi—Lieutenant John W. Gower.
Twenty-first Mississippi—Lieutenant Benjamin George.

SIMMS' BRIGADE.

Brigadier-General James P. Simms; Captain George W. Waldron.

Tenth Georgia—Lieutenant, John B. Evans.
Fiftieth Georgia { Captain George W. Waldron. / Lieutenant Hillary W. Cason.
Fifty-first Georgia—Captain H. R. Thomas.
Fifty-third Georgia—Captain R. H. Woods.

ARTILLERY.‡

Brigadier-General Edward P. Alexander.

HASKELL'S BATTALION.

Lieutenant-Colonel John C. Haskell.

North Carolina battery—Captain Henry G. Flanner.
North Carolina battery (Ramsay's)—Lieutenant Jesse F. Woodard.
South Carolina battery—Captain Hugh R. Garden.
Virginia battery (Lamkin's)—Lieutenant Fletcher T. Massie.

HUGER'S BATTALION.

Major Tyler C. Jordan.

Louisiana battery (Moody's)—Lieutenant George Poindexter.
South Carolina battery (Fickling's)—Lieutenant E. L. Purse.
Virginia battery (Parker's)—Lieutenant Edwin S. Wooldridge.
Virginia battery—Captain John Donnell Smith.
Virginia battery (Taylor's)—Lieutenant John H. Waddell.
Virginia battery—Lieutenant James Woolfolk.

SECOND ARMY CORPS.

Major-General John B. Gordon.

GRIMES' (LATE RODES') DIVISION.

Major-General Bryan Grimes.

* During the retreat, Kershaw's and G. W. C. Lee's divisions, with other troops from the defenses of Richmond, were commanded by Lieutenant-General Richard S. Ewell.
† Captured April 6th.
‡ The artillery of the army was commanded by Brigadier-General William N. Pendleton.

BATTLE'S BRIGADE.

Colonel Edwin L. Hobson.

Third Alabama—Captain Cornelius Robinson, Jr.
Fifth Alabama—Colonel Edwin L. Hobson; Captain Thomas M. Riley.
Sixth Alabama—Major Isaac F. Culver.
Twelfth Alabama—Captain Poleman D. Ross.
Sixty-first Alabama—Captain Augustus B. Fannin, Jr.

GRIMES' BRIGADE.

Colonel David G. Cowand.

Thirty-second North Carolina—Captain P. C. Shuford.
Forty-third North Carolina—Captain Wiley J. Cobb.
Forty-fifth North Carolina—Colonel John R. Winston.
Fifty-third North Carolina—Captain Thomas E. Ashcroft.
Second North Carolina Battalion, ——— ——

COX'S BRIGADE.

Brigadier-General William R. Cox.

First North Carolina—Major Lewis C. Latham.
Second North Carolina—Major James T. Scales.
Third North Carolina—Major William T. Ennett.
Fourth North Carolina—Captain John B. Forcum.
Fourteenth North Carolina—Lieutenant-Colonel William A. Johnston.
Thirtieth North Carolina—Captain David C. Allen.

COOK'S BRIGADE.

Colonel Edwin A. Nash.

Fourth Georgia { Colonel Edwin A. Nash. / Captain John M. Shiver.
Twelfth Georgia—Captain Josiah N. Beall.
Twenty-first Georgia—Captain Edward Smith.
Forty-fourth Georgia—Captain John A. Tucker.
Georgia battery (Patterson's), —— ———

ARCHER'S BATTALION.*

Lieutenant-Colonel Fletcher H. Archer.

Third Battalion Virginia Reserves—Captain Joseph A. Rogers.
Forty-fourth Virginia Battalion—Captain A. B. Morrison.

EARLY'S DIVISION.

Brigadier-General James A. Walker.

JOHNSTON'S BRIGADE.

Colonel John W. Lea.

Fifth North Carolina { Colonel John W. Lea. / Captain James M. Taylor.
Twelfth North Carolina—Captain P. Durham.
Twentieth North Carolina—Lieutenant Archibald F. Lawhon.
Twenty-third North Carolina—Captain Abner D. Peace.
First North Carolina Battalion, Sharpshooters—Lieutenant R. W. Woodruff.

FRONT OF THE DUNLOP HOUSE, PETERSBURG, VA., AFTER THE BOMBARDMENT.

LEWIS' BRIGADE.

Captain John Beard.

Sixth North Carolina—Captain Joseph H. Dickey.
Twenty-first North Carolina—Captain John H. Miller.
Fifty-fourth North Carolina, —— ———
Fifty-seventh North Carolina—Captain John Beard.

WALKER'S (late Pegram's) BRIGADE.

Major Henry Kid Douglas.

Thirteenth Virginia—Captain George Cullen.
Thirty-first Virginia—Major William P. Cooper.
Forty-ninth Virginia—Captain William D. Moffett.
Fifty-second Virginia—Captain Samuel W. Paxton.
Fifty-eighth Virginia—Lieutenant Robert L. Walrond.

* Temporarily attached during the retreat.

GORDON'S DIVISION.

Brigadier-General Clement A. Evans.

EVANS' BRIGADE.

Colonel John H. Lowe.

Thirteenth Georgia—Lieutenant-Colonel Richard Maltbie.
Twenty-sixth Georgia—Captain James Knox.
Thirty-first Georgia—Captain Edward C. Perry.
Thirty-eighth Georgia—Lieutenant-Colonel Philip E. Devant.
Sixtieth Georgia / Sixty-first Georgia } Colonel Waters B. Jones.
Ninth Georgia Battalion Artillery—Sergeant Horace L. Crawford.
Twelfth Georgia Battalion Artillery—Captain Samuel H. Crump.
Eighteenth Georgia Battalion Infantry—Captain G. W. Stiles.

TERRY'S BRIGADE.

Colonel Titus V. Williams.

Second Virginia—Captain Joseph J. Jenkins.
Fourth Virginia—Captain Hamilton D. Wade.
Fifth Virginia—Captain Peter E. Wilson.
Tenth Virginia—Lieutenant-Colonel D. H. Lee Martz.
Twenty-first Virginia—Colonel William A. Witcher.
Twenty-third Virginia—Lieutenant-Colonel John P. Fitzgerald.
Twenty-fifth Virginia—Major Wilson Harper.
Twenty-seventh Virginia—Captain Franklin C. Wilson.
Thirty-third Virginia—Captain Henry A. Herrell.
Thirty-seventh Virginia—Captain John A. Preston.
Forty-second Virginia—Lieutenant James L. Tompkins.
Forty-fourth Virginia—Major David W. Anderson.
Forty-eighth Virginia—Colonel Robert H. Dungan.

YORK'S BRIGADE.

Colonel Eugene Waggaman.

First Louisiana, —— ———
Second Louisiana—Captain A. S. Blythe.
Fifth Louisiana—Lieutenant Hiram Baxter.
Sixth Louisiana—Major William H. Manning.
Seventh Louisiana, —— ———
Eighth Louisiana—Captain Louis Prados.
Ninth Louisiana, —— ———
Tenth Louisiana, —— ———
Fourteenth Louisiana, —— ———
Fifteenth Louisiana—Colonel Edmund Pendleton.

ARTILLERY.

Brigadier-General Armistead L. Long.

BRAXTON'S BATTALION.

Lieutenant-Colonel Carter M. Braxton.

Virginia battery (Carpenter's), —— ———
Virginia battery (Cooper's), —— ———
Virginia battery—Captain William W. Hardwicke.

CUTSHAW'S BATTALION.

Captain C. W. Fry.

Alabama battery (Reece's), —— ———
Virginia battery (Carter's)—Lieutenant Lucian D. Robinson.
Virginia battery (Montgomery's), —— ———
Virginia battery (Fry's)—Lieutenant William A. Deas.
Virginia battery—Captain Asher W. Garber.
Virginia battery—Captain Lorraine F. Jones.

HARDAWAY'S BATTALION.

Lieutenant-Colonel Robert A. Hardaway.

Virginia battery (Dance's)—Lieutenant John R. Bagby.
Virginia battery—Captain Archibald Graham.
Virginia battery—Captain Charles B. Griffin.
Virginia battery—Captain Benjamin H. Smith, Jr.

JOHNSON'S BATTALION.

Lieutenant-Colonel Marmaduke Johnson.

Virginia battery (Clutter's)—Lieutenant Lucas McIntosh.
Virginia battery—Captain John G. Pollock.

LIGHTFOOT'S BATTALION.

Virginia battery (Caroline Artillery), —— ———
Virginia battery (Nelson Artillery), —— ———
Virginia battery (Surry Artillery), —— ———

STARK'S BATTALION.

Lieutenant-Colonel Alexander W. Stark.

Louisiana battery (Green's), —— ———
Virginia battery—Captain David A. French.
Virginia battery—Captain Andrew D. Armistead.

THIRD ARMY CORPS.*

Lieutenant-General Ambrose P. Hill.†

PROVOST GUARD.

Fifth Alabama Battalion—Captain Wade Ritter.

* Attached to First Corps April 2d, after the death of General Hill.
† Killed April 2d.

HETH'S DIVISION.

Major-General Henry Heth.

DAVIS' BRIGADE.

Brigadier-General Joseph R. Davis.

First Confederate Battalion—Captain Anthony B. Bartlett.
Second Mississippi, —— ———
Eleventh Mississippi, —— ———
Twenty-sixth Mississippi, —— ———
Forty-second Mississippi, —— ———

COOKE'S BRIGADE.

Brigadier-General John R. Cooke.

Fifteenth North Carolina—Colonel William H. Yarborough.
Twenty-seventh North Carolina—Lieutenant-Colonel Joseph C. Webb.
Forty-sixth North Carolina—Colonel William L. Saunders.
Forty-eighth North Carolina—Colonel Samuel H. Walkup.
Fifty-fifth North Carolina—Captain Walter A. Whitted.

VIEW SHOWING EFFECTS OF SHELL IN THE EAST PARLOR OF THE DUNLOP HOUSE, PETERSBURG, VA.

M'RAE'S BRIGADE.

Brigadier-General William McRae.

Eleventh North Carolina—Colonel William J. Martin.
Twenty-sixth North Carolina—Lieutenant-Colonel James T. Adams.
Forty-fourth North Carolina—Major Charles M. Stedman.
Forty-seventh North Carolina, —— ———
Fifty-second North Carolina—Lieutenant-Colonel Eric Erson.

McCOMB'S BRIGADE.

Brigadier-General William McComb.

Second Maryland Battalion—Captain John W. Lorsch.
First Tennessee (Provisional Army)—Major Felix G. Buchanan.
Seventh Tennessee—Lieutenant-Colonel Samuel G. Shepard.
Fourteenth Tennessee—Major James H. Johnson.
Seventeenth Tennessee / Twenty-third Tennessee } Colonel Horace Ready.
Twenty-fifth Tennessee / Forty-fourth Tennessee } —— ———
Sixty-third Tennessee, —— ———

WILCOX'S DIVISION.

Major-General Cadmus M. Wilcox.

THOMAS' BRIGADE.

Brigadier-General Edward L. Thomas.

Fourteenth Georgia—Colonel Richard P. Lester.
Thirty-fifth Georgia—Colonel Bolling H. Bolt.
Forty-fifth Georgia—Colonel Thomas J. Simmons.
Forty-ninth Georgia—Major James B. Duggan.

LANE'S BRIGADE.

Brigadier-General James H. Lane.

Eighteenth North Carolina—Major Thomas J. Wooten.
Twenty-eighth North Carolina—Captain T. James Lineborger.
Thirty-third North Carolina—Colonel Robert V. Cowan.
Thirty-seventh North Carolina—Major Jackson L. Bost.

M'GOWAN'S BRIGADE.

Brigadier-General Samuel McGowan.

First South Carolina (Provisional Army)—Lieutenant-Colonel Andrew P. Butler.

Twelfth South Carolina—Captain J. C. Bell.

Thirteenth South Carolina—Colonel Isaac F. Hunt.

Fourteenth South Carolina—Lieutenant-Colonel Edward Croft.

Orr's (S. C.) Rifles—Lieutenant-Colonel James T. Robertson.

SCALES' BRIGADE.

Colonel Joseph H. Hyman.

Thirteenth North Carolina—Lieutenant-Colonel E. Benton Withers.

Sixteenth North Carolina—Colonel William A. Stowe.

Twenty-second North Carolina—Colonel Thomas S. Gallaway, Jr.

Thirty-fourth North Carolina—Lieutenant-Colonel George M. Norment.

Thirty-eighth North Carolina, { Colonel John Ashford. Lieutenant-Colonel George W. Flowers.

MAHONE'S DIVISION.

Major-General William Mahone.

FORNEY'S BRIGADE.

Brigadier-General William H. Forney.

Eighth Alabama—Lieutenant-Colonel John P. Emrich.

Ninth Alabama—Major James M. Crow.

Tenth Alabama—Major Lewis W. Johnson.

Eleventh Alabama—Captain Martin L. Stewart.

Thirteenth Alabama—Captain Samuel Sellers.

Fourteenth Alabama—Captain John A. Terrell.

WEISIGER'S BRIGADE.

Brigadier-General David A. Weisiger.

Sixth Virginia—Colonel George T. Rogers.

Twelfth Virginia—Major Richard W. Jones.

Sixteenth Virginia—Lieutenant-Colonel Richard O. Whitehead.

Forty-first Virginia—Lieutenant-Colonel Joseph P. Minetree.

Sixty-first Virginia—Colonel Virginius D. Groner.

HARRIS' BRIGADE.

Brigadier-General Nathaniel H. Harris.

Twelfth Mississippi—Captain A. K. Jones.

Sixteenth Mississippi—Lieutenant-Colonel James H. Duncan.

Nineteenth Mississippi—Colonel Richard W. Phipps.

Forty-eighth Mississippi—Colonel Joseph M. Jayne.

SORREL'S BRIGADE.

Colonel George E. Taylor.

Third Georgia—Lieutenant-Colonel Claiborne Snead.

Twenty-second Georgia—Captain Geo. W. Thomas.

Forty-eighth Georgia—Captain Alexander C. Flanders.

Sixty-fourth Georgia—Captain James G. Brown.

Second Georgia Battalion—Major Charles J. Moffett.

Tenth Georgia Battalion—Captain Caleb F. Hill.

FINEGAN'S BRIGADE.

Colonel David Lang.

Second Florida—Colonel Walter R. Moore.

Fifth Florida, ——— ———

Eighth Florida—Major Thomas E. Clarke.

Ninth Florida, ——— ———

Tenth Florida—Colonel Charles F. Hopkins.

Eleventh Florida, ——— ———

ARTILLERY.

Brigadier-General R. Lindsay Walker.

M'INTOSH'S BATTALION.

Lieutenant-Colonel William M. Owen.

Alabama battery (Hurt's)—Lieutenant George A. Ferrell.

Louisiana battery—Captain Edward Owen.

Maryland battery (Chew's), ——— ———

Virginia battery (Chamberlayne's), ——— ———

Virginia battery—Captain Berryman Z. Price.

Virginia battery (Donald's)—Lieutenant W. T. Wilson.

POAGUE'S BATTALION.

Lieutenant-Colonel William T. Poague.

Mississippi battery (Richards')—Lieutenant W. Yeargain.

North Carolina battery—Captain Arthur B. Williams.

Virginia battery—Captain Charles F. Johnston.

Virginia battery—Captain Addison W. Utterback.

Virginia battery—Captain Nathan Penick.

THIRTEENTH VIRGINIA BATTERY.

Otey battery—Captain David N. Walker.

Ringgold battery—Captain Crispin Dickenson.

RICHARDSON'S BATTALION.

Lieutenant-Colonel Charles Richardson.

Louisiana battery—Captain R. Prosper Landry.

Virginia battery (Moore's), ——— ———

Virginia battery (Grandy's), ——— ———

PEGRAM'S BATTALION.

Colonel William J. Pegram; Lieutenant-Colonel Joseph McGraw.

South Carolina battery—Captain Thomas E. Gregg.

Virginia battery—Captain George M. Cayce.

Virginia battery—Captain Thomas Ellett.

Virginia battery (Brander's)—Lieutenant James E. Tyler.

ANDERSON'S CORPS.

Lieutenant-General Richard H. Anderson.

JOHNSON'S DIVISION.

Major-General Bushrod R. Johnson; Brigadier-General William H. Wallace.*

WISE'S BRIGADE.

Brigadier-General Henry A. Wise.

Twenty-sixth Virginia—Major William K. Perrin.

Thirty-fourth Virginia—Colonel John Thomas Goode.

Forty-sixth Virginia, ——— ———

Fifty-ninth Virginia—Colonel William B. Tabb.

WALLACE'S BRIGADE.

Brigadier-General William H. Wallace.

Seventeenth South Carolina—Captain E. A. Crawford.

Eighteenth South Carolina—Lieutenant-Colonel W. B. Allison.

Twenty-second South Carolina—Colonel William G. Burt.

Twenty-third South Carolina—Lieutenant-Colonel John M. Kinlock.

Twenty-sixth South Carolina—Major Ceth. S. Land.

Holcombe (S. C.) Legion, ——— ———

VIEW OF HOUSE IN BOLLINBROOK STREET, PETERSBURG, VA., AFTER THE BOMBARDMENT.

MOODY'S BRIGADE.

Brigadier-General Young M. Moody.

Forty-first Alabama—Colonel Martin L. Stansel.

Forty-third Alabama—Major William J. Mims.

Fifty-ninth Alabama—Major Lewis H. Crumpler.

Sixtieth Alabama—Colonel John W. A. Sanford.

Twenty-third Alabama Battalion—Major Nicholas Stallworth.

RANSOM'S BRIGADE.

Brigadier-General Matthew W. Ransom.

Twenty-fourth North Carolina, ——— ———

Twenty-fifth North Carolina—Colonel Henry M. Rutledge.

Thirty-fifth North Carolina—Major Robert E. Petty.

Forty-ninth North Carolina—Major Charles Q. Petty.

Fifty-sixth North Carolina—Colonel Paul F. Faison.

ARTILLERY.

Colonel Hilary P. Jones.

BLOUNT'S BATTALION.

Georgia battery—Captain C. W. Slaten.

North Carolina battery (Cumming's)—Lieutenant Alexander D. Brown.

North Carolina battery (Miller's), ——— ———

Virginia battery (Young's), ——— ———

STRIBLING'S BATTALION.

Virginia battery (Dickerson's), ——— ———

Virginia battery (Marshall's)—Lieutenant T. Marshall Archer.

Virginia battery (Macon's), ——— ———

Virginia battery (Sullivan's)—Lieutenant William S. Archer.

SMITH'S BATTALION.

Captain William F. Dement.

First Maryland battery—Lieutenant John Gale.

Virginia battery (Johnston's)—Lieutenant Thomas R. Adams.

Virginia battery (Neblett)—Lieutenant Robert J. Braswell.

Virginia battery—Captain John W. Drewry.

Virginia battery—Captain Thomas Kevill.

* In command April 9th.

COIT'S BATTALION.

Mississippi battery (Bradford's), ——— ———

Virginia battery (Richard G. Pegram's), ——— ———

Virginia battery (Wright's), ——— ———

CAVALRY CORPS.

Major-General Fitzhugh Lee.

FITZHUGH LEE'S DIVISION.

Brigadier-General Thomas T. Munford.

PAYNE'S BRIGADE.

Brigadier-General William H. Payne;* Colonel Reuben B. Boston.†

Fifth Virginia—Colonel Reuben B. Boston.

Sixth Virginia, ——— ———

Eighth Virginia, ——— ———

Thirty-sixth Virginia Battalion, ——— ———

MUNFORD'S BRIGADE.

First Virginia—Colonel William A. Morgan.

Second Virginia—Lieutenant-Colonel Cary Breckinridge.

Third Virginia, ——— ———

Fourth Virginia—Colonel William B. Wooldridge.

GARY'S BRIGADE.

Brigadier-General Martin W. Gary.

Seventh Georgia—Captain William H. Burroughs.

Seventh South Carolina—Colonel Alexander C. Haskell.

Hampton (S. C.) Legion—Lieutenant-Colonel Robert B. Arnold.

Twenty-fourth Virginia—Colonel William T. Robins.

W. H. F. LEE'S DIVISION.

Major-General William H. F. Lee.

BARRINGER'S BRIGADE.

Brigadier-General Rufus Barringer.‡

First North Carolina, ——— ———

Second North Carolina, ——— ———

Third North Carolina, ——— ———

Fourth North Carolina, ——— ———

BEALE'S BRIGADE.

Captain Samuel H. Burt.

Ninth Virginia, ——— ———

Tenth Virginia, ——— ———

Thirteenth Virginia, ——— ———

Fourteenth Virginia, ——— ———

ROBERTS' BRIGADE.

Brigadier-General William P. Roberts.

Fourth North Carolina, ——— ———

Sixteenth North Carolina Battalion, ——— ———

ROSSER'S DIVISION.

Major-General Thomas L. Rosser.

DEARING'S BRIGADE.

Brigadier-General James Dearing;† Colonel Asher W. Harman.

Seventh Virginia, ——— ———

Eleventh Virginia, ——— ———

Twelfth Virginia—Colonel Asher W. Harman.

Thirty-fifth Virginia Battalion, ——— ———

M'CAUSLAND'S BRIGADE.

Sixteenth Virginia, ——— ———

Seventeenth Virginia, ——— ———

Twenty-first Virginia, ——— ———

Twenty-second Virginia, ——— ———

ARTILLERY.

Lieutenant-Colonel R. Preston Chew.

BREATHED'S BATTALION.

Major James Breathed.

Virginia battery (P. P. Johnston's), ——— ———

Virginia battery (Shoemaker's), ——— ———

Virginia battery (Thomson's), ——— ———

CHEW'S BATTALION.

Virginia battery (Graham's), ——— ———

Virginia battery (McGregor's), ——— ———

G. W. C. LEE'S DIVISION.

Major-General G. W. Custis Lee.§

BARTON'S BRIGADE.

CRUTCHFIELD'S BRIGADE.

Colonel Stapleton Crutchfield.†

TUCKER'S NAVAL BATTALION.‖

EWELL'S RESERVE CORPS.

Lieutenant-General Richard S. Ewell;§ Lieutenant-Colonel Thomas J. Spencer.

NOTE.—The following battalions of artillery, borne on the return of the Army of Northern Virginia for January 31, 1865, are not enumerated in the Appomattox parole lists, viz.: Cabell's, of the First Corps; Nelson's of the Second Corps; Lane's and Eshleman's, of the Third Corps, and Sturdivant's, of Anderson's Corps.

* Wounded March 30th. † Killed April 6th. ‡ Captured April 3d. § Captured April 6th. ‖ Attached.

STRENGTH OF THE ARMY OF NORTHERN VIRGINIA, COMMANDED BY GENERAL ROBERT E. LEE, CONFEDERATE STATES ARMY.

FROM RETURNS (BEFORE SURRENDER AT APPOMATTOX), JANUARY 10, 1865.

COMMAND.	Present for Duty.		Aggregate Present.	Aggregate Present and Absent.
	Officers.	Men.		
FIRST ARMY CORPS (Longstreet)—				
Staff	11	....	11	18
Pickett's Division	308	4,704	6,308	9,294
Field's Division	433	4,569	6,090	11,661
Kershaw's Division *	295	3,140	4,352	9,277
Total, First Army Corps	1,047	12,413	16,761	30,250
SECOND ARMY CORPS (Gordon)—				
Rodes' Division	240	3,077	4,371	12,447
Early's Division	163	2,411	3,181	8,194
Gordon's Division	195	2,684	3,532	13,602
Total, Second Army Corps	598	8,172	11,084	34,243
THIRD ARMY CORPS (A. P. Hill)—				
Staff	18	...	18	20
Mahone's Division	354	4,536	6,003	12,676
Heth's Division	386	4,827	6,111	12,704
Wilcox's Division	402	5,827	7,293	11,855
Total, Third Army Corps	1,160	15,190	19,425	37,255
ANDERSON'S CORPS—Johnson's Division †	461	6,608	8,042	12,981
CAVALRY CORPS (Hampton)—				
Staff	12	....	12	16
Butler's Division ‡	147	2,183	3,066	7,761
W. H. F. Lee's Division §	161	3,190	4,016	6,618
Horse Artillery ‖	3	104	114	145
Total, Cavalry Corps ¶	323	5,477	7,208	14,540
EARLY'S COMMAND (Early)—				
Staff	16	....	16	20
Wharton's Division **	132	1,914	2,461	6,771
Long's Artillery	54	950	1,214	2,447
Total, Early's command	202	2,864	3,691	9,238
ARTILLERY RESERVE, ETC. (Pendleton)—				
Staff	8	9	17	17
First Corps Artillery	92	2,165	2,493	3,271
Third Corps Artillery	114	2,003	2,389	3,377
Anderson's Corps Artillery	68	943	1,170	1,665
Total, Artillery Reserve, etc	282	5,120	6,069	8,330
RICHMOND & DANVILLE RAILROAD DEFENSES (WALKER)	118	1,472	1,822	3,331
PROVOST GUARD (Bridgford)	22	219	306	386
Grand Total	4,213	57,535	74,408	150,554

* Conner's brigade transferred to South Carolina.
† Hoke's division transferred to North Carolina.
‡ 955 dismounted men.
§ 762 dismounted men.
‖ 42 dismounted men.
¶ 1,759 dismounted men.
** Cavalry of Valley District not reported.

JANUARY 26–31, 1865.
[From Inspection Reports.]

COMMAND.	Present for Duty.		Aggregate Present.	Aggregate Present and Absent.	Present Effective for the Field.	
	Officers.	Men.			Officers.	Men.
FIRST ARMY CORPS—						
Staff	14	....	14	19	..	....
Pickett's Division *	316	4,572	6,199	9,239	284	4,572
Field's Division †	370	4,403	5,692	11,504	322	4,247
Kershaw's Division ‡	288	3,106	4,201	9,232	283	3,267
Total First Army Corps	988	12,081	16,106	29,994	889	12,086
SECOND ARMY CORPS—						
Staff	8		8	9	7	....
Early's Division *	152	2,304	3,154	8,092	130	2,223
Rodes' Division *	217	2,946	4,343	12,291	185	2,911
Gordon's Division *	200	2,525	3,455	13,426	216	2,479
Total Second Army Corps	577	7,775	10,960	33,818	538	7,613
THIRD ARMY CORPS—						
Headquarters §	17	107	145	248	8	107
Heth's Division ‖	369	4,347	5,553	11,868	331	4,345
Mahone's Division ¶	...	....	....	...	....	....
Wilcox's Division **	377	5,613	6,946	10,994	350	5,517
Total Third Army Corps	763	10,067	11,644	23,110	689	9,969
JOHNSON'S DIVISION—Anderson's Corps ††	468	6,226	7,562	12,230	455	6,356
W. H. F. LEE'S CAVALRY DIVISION ‡‡	226	3,933	5,088	8,885	204	3,029
VALLEY DISTRICT ††	147	1,843	2,524	10,714	139	1,775
Grand Total §§	3,169	41,925	54,884	118,751	2,914	40,828

* Inspected January 28–30; only 4,330 guns reported in Pickett's division.
† Inspected January 27–31; includes Corse's brigade attached; only 3,080 guns reported in the division.
‡ Inspected January 27–29.
§ Inspected January 31.
‖ Inspected January 27–30.
¶ No report.
** Inspected January 26–30.
†† Inspected January 26–31.
‡‡ Inspected January 28–31.
§§ The Artillery and Fitzhugh Lee's cavalry not accounted for.

JANUARY 31, 1865.

COMMAND.	Present for Duty.		Aggregate Present.	Aggregate Present and Absent.	Present Effective for the Field.	
	Officers.	Men.			Officers.	Men.
FIRST ARMY CORPS (Longstreet)—						
Staff	14	....	....	14	19	....
Pickett's Division	328	4,684	4,684	6,365	9,519	....
Field's Division	367	4,418	4,418	5,721	11,600	....
Kershaw's Division	286	3,066	3,066	4,175	9,221	....
Total First Army Corps	995	12,168	12,168	16,275	30,359	....

JANUARY 31, 1865—Continued.

COMMAND.	Present for Duty.		Aggregate Present.	Aggregate Present and Absent.	Present Effective for the Field.	
	Officers.	Men.			Officers.	Men.
Brought forward	995	12,168	12,168	16,275	30,359	....
SECOND ARMY CORPS (Gordon)—						
Rodes' Division	209	2,914	2,914	4,344	12,289	....
Early's Division	153	2,319	2,319	3,177	8,090	....
Gordon's Division	197	2,529	2,529	3,470	13,570	....
Total Second Army Corps	559	7,762	7,762	10,991	33,949	....
THIRD ARMY CORPS (A. P. Hill)—						
Staff	18	....	....	18	20	....
Heth's Division	339	4,309	4,319	5,470	11,254	....
Wilcox's Division	410	5,840	5,840	7,264	11,931	....
Mahone's Division	386	4,654	4,646	6,141	12,800	....
Total Third Army Corps	1,153	14,803	14,805	18,893	36,005	....
ANDERSON'S CORPS—Johnson's Division *	467	6,248	6,248	7,643	12,824	...
CAVALRY CORPS—W. H. F. Lee's Division	234	4,057	4,057	5,256	9,199	....
VALLEY DISTRICT (Early)—						
Staff	18	....	....	18	22	....
Wharton's Division	84	1,112	1,112	1,581	4,686	...
Artillery	53	775	775	1,012	2,576	32
Total Valley District †	155	1,887	1,887	2,611	7,284	32
ARTILLERY RESERVE, ETC. (Pendleton)—						
Staff	8	8	8	16	16	....
First Corps Artillery	81	2,104	2,104	2,413	3,254	....
Third Corps Artillery	100	1,873	1,873	2,245	3,346	....
Anderson's Artillery	56	896	896	1,128	1,637	....
Total Artillery Reserve, etc.	245	4,881	4,881	5,802	8,253	....
DEFENSES RICHMOND & DANVILLE R. R. (Walker)	115	1,438	1,438	1,886	3,366	....
PROVOST GUARD (Bridgford)	21	199	199	302	374	....
Grand Total	3,944	53,443	53,445	69,659	141,613	32

* Hoke's Division in North Carolina.
† Cavalry not reported.

FEBRUARY 10, 1865.

COMMAND.	Present for Duty.		Aggregate Present.	Aggregate Present and Absent.	Aggregate Present Last Return.	In Hands of Enemy.	
	Officers.	Men.				Officers.	Enlisted Men.
FIRST ARMY CORPS (Longstreet)—							
Staff	14	....	14	18	14	...	...
Pickett's Division	336	4,773	6,520	9,487	6,365	115	666
Field's Division	367	4,453	5,797	11,563	5,721	73	1,312
Kershaw's Division	258	3,083	4,178	9,211	4,175	100	1,635
Gary's Cavalry Brigade	60	1,112	1,584	3,595	1,754	20	335
Total, First Army Corps	1,035	13,421	18,093	33,874	18,029	308	3,948
SECOND ARMY CORPS (Gordon)—							
Rodes' Division	208	2,929	4,445	12,232	4,344	181	3,642
Gordon's Division	179	2,281	3,372	13,513	3,470	357	4,137
Early's Division	140	2,151	2,991	8,027	3,177	166	2,282
Total, Second Army Corps	527	7,361	10,808	33,772	10,991	704	10,061
THIRD ARMY CORPS (A. P. Hill)—							
Staff	18	...	18	20	18	...	..
Mahone's Division	317	3,890	5,489	12,431	5,913	117	1,867
Heth's Division	331	4,190	5,543	11,966	5,647	204	2,352
Wilcox's Division	350	5,445	6,822	11,550	6,860	93	1 774
Total, Third Army Corps	1,016	13,525	17,872	35,967	18,438	414	5,993
EARLY'S COMMAND—							
Staff	18	...	18	20	18	2	....
Wharton's Division	82	1,076	1,528	6,924	1,581	104	1,549
Long's Artillery	27	390	469	940	492	3	99
Total, Early's Command	127	1,466	2,015	7,884	2,091	109	1,648
ANDERSON'S CORPS—Johnson's Division	466	6,527	7,874	12,778	....	..	1,149
DEFENSES RICHMOND & DANVILLE R. R. (Walker)	109	1,417	1,775	3,355	....	...	....
W. H. F. LEE'S CAVALRY DIVISION	156	2,664	3,508	6,579	3,782	37	439
INDEPENDENT SIGNAL CORPS (Milligan)	7	153	165	240	238	...	12
PROVOST GUARD (Bridgford)	20	188	301	378	303	...	....
Grand Total	3,463	46,722	62,411	134,827	53,872	1,572	23,250

FEBRUARY 20, 1865.

COMMAND.	Present for Duty.		Aggregate Present.	Aggregate Present and Absent.
	Officers.	Men.		
GENERAL HEADQUARTERS	12	.....	12	12
FIRST ARMY CORPS (Longstreet)—				
Staff	14	.....	14	18
Pickett's Division	335	4,761	6,557	9,442
Field's Division	374	4,436	5,732	11,508
Kershaw's Division	240	2,967	4,121	9,179
Total, First Army Corps	963	12,164	16,424	30,147
SECOND ARMY CORPS (Gordon)—				
Gordon's Division	175	2,309	3,334	13,520
Rodes' Division	211	3,022	4,596	12,176
Early's Division	152	2,292	3,196	8,010
Total, Second Army Corps	538	7,623	11,126	33,706
THIRD ARMY CORPS (A. P. Hill)—				
Staff	20	...	20	20
Mahone's Division	296	3,880	5,538	12,854
Heth's Division	334	4,324	5,562	11,852
Wilcox's Division	343	5,383	6,769	11,411
Total, Third Army Corps	993	13,587	17,889	36,137
ANDERSON'S CORPS—Johnson's Division	475	6,505	7,846	12,642
Carried forward	2,981	39,879	53,297	112,644

FEBRUARY 20, 1865—Continued.

COMMAND.	Present for Duty. Officers	Present for Duty. Men	Aggregate Present	Aggregate Present and Absent
Brought forward	2,981	39,879	53,297	112,644
EARLY'S COMMAND—				
Staff	16	....	16	20
Wharton's Division	84	1,112	1,584	6,735
Lomax's Cavalry Division	174	1,383	1,790	7,150
Long's Artillery	32	368	457	1,432
Total, Early's Command	306	2,863	3,847	15,337
CAVALRY CORPS—				
W. H. F. Lee's Division	210	3,935	5,148	9,299
Fitzhugh Lee's Division	120	1,825	2,499	9,446
Total, Cavalry	330	5,760	7,647	18,745
ARTILLERY (Pendleton)—				
Staff	8	8	16	16
First Corps	83	2,089	2,398	3,262
Third Corps	110	1,862	2,237	3,344
Anderson's Corps	72	1,196	1,462	2,752
Total, Artillery	273	5,155	6,113	9,374
DEFENSES RICHMOND & DANVILLE RAILROAD (Walker)	114	1,414	1,749	3,269
UNATTACHED COMMANDS	42	504	696	1,042
Grand Total	4,046	55,575	73,349	160,411

FEBRUARY 24—MARCH 1, 1865.
[From Inspection Reports.]

COMMAND.	Present for Duty. Officers	Present for Duty. Men	Aggregate Present	Aggregate Present and Absent	Present Effective for the Field. Officers	Present Effective for the Field. Men
FIRST ARMY CORPS.						
STAFF *	13	....	13	16	...	....
PICKETT'S DIVISION *	424	5,967	8,073	11,745	388	6,151
FIELD'S DIVISION—						
Staff †	12	....	12	16	...	....
Anderson's Brigade ‡	77	1,019	1,242	2,617	69	1,003
Benning's Brigade ‡	61	709	849	1,787	61	642
Bratton's Brigade ‡	99	1,435	1,762	2,873	99	1,435
Laws' Brigade ‡	70	788	1,052	2,539	73	782
Texas Brigade ‡	49	480	733	1,594	39	435
Total, Field's Division	368	4,431	5,650	11,426	341	4,297
KERSHAW'S DIVISION—						
Staff *	13	....	13	17	...	....
Bryan's Brigade *	50	605	824	2,047	39	579
Humphreys' Brigade †	33	416	598	1,690	39	463
Wofford's Brigade †	59	746	1,012	3,017	59	746
Total, Kershaw's Division	155	1,767	2,447	6,771	137	1,788
Grand Total, First Army Corps	960	12,165	16,183	29,958	866	12,236
SECOND ARMY CORPS.						
EARLY'S DIVISION—						
Staff *	10	1	11	14	10	1
Johnston's Brigade *	47	652	945	2,499	55	859
Lewis' Brigade *	45	860	1,156	3,028	45	860
Pegram's Brigade §	46	665	889	2,332	47	665
Total, Early's Division	148	2,178	3,001	7,873	157	2,385
GORDON'S DIVISION—						
Staff †	16	....	16	17	...	....
Evans' Brigade †	61	1,007	1,328	3,882	56	1,013
Terry's Brigade †	79	894	1,293	6,297	79	894
York's Brigade †	19	382	566	3,032	19	382
Total, Gordon's Division	175	2,283	3,203	13,228	154	2,289
RODES' DIVISION—						
Staff *	9	2	11	19	...	....
Battle's Brigade ‖	49	822	1,056	2,964	48	777
Cook's Brigade §	47	500	702	2,200	40	500
Cox's Brigade §	50	715	1,135	3,681	45	715
Grimes' Brigade §	54	1,008	1,366	3,260	71	1,294
Total, Rodes' Division	209	3,047	4,270	12,124	204	3,286
Grand Total, Second Army Corps	532	7,508	10,474	23,225	515	7,960
THIRD ARMY CORPS.						
HETH'S DIVISION—						
Staff *	10	....	10	17	...	....
Cooke's Brigade §	108	1,448	1,806	3,017	104	1,448
Davis' Brigade †	67	562	735	2,005	67	661
McComb's Brigade *	103	865	1,185	2,822	87	860
MacRae's Brigade †	58	1,209	1,509	3,531	55	1,119
Total, Heth's Division	346	4,084	5,245	11,392	313	4,088
MAHONE'S DIVISION—						
Finegan's Brigade §	57	517	1,039	2,775	49	517
Forney's Brigade †	59	995	1,239	2,911	58	1,039
Harris' Brigade *	40	501	801	1,766	38	507
Sorrel's Brigade *	60	989	1,329	2,786	60	989
Weisiger's Brigade *	68	771	1,005	2,473	60	757
Total, Mahone's Division	284	3,773	5,413	12,711	265	3,809
WILCOX'S DIVISION—						
Staff *	13	2	15	20	...	....
Lane's Brigade *	68	1,094	1,384	3,407	70	1,092
McGowan's Brigade *	92	1,398	1,764	2,930	91	1,313
Scales' Brigade *	89	1,430	1,785	2,810	87	1,573
Thomas' Brigade ¶	78	958	1,159	2,062	75	943
Total, Wilcox's Division	340	4,882	6,107	11,229	323	4,921
Grand Total, Third Army Corps	970	12,739	16,765	35,332	901	12,818
JOHNSON'S DIVISION (Anderson's Corps)—						
Staff *	12	....	12	14	...	....
Elliott's (Wallace's) Brigade †	129	1,840	2,139	3,666	123	1,891
Gracie's Brigade *	107	1,096	1,431	2,521	103	1,105
Ransom's Brigade *	143	2,113	2,405	3,573	143	1,853
Wise's Brigade ‖	104	1,269	1,605	2,368	116	1,428
Total, Johnson's Division	495	6,318	7,592	12,142	485	6,277
Grand Total of Infantry	2,957	38,730	51,014	100,657	2,767	39,291
Carried forward	2,957	38,730	51,014	100,657	2,767	39,291

FEBRUARY 24—MARCH 1, 1865—Continued.

COMMAND.	Present for Duty. Officers	Present for Duty. Men	Aggregate Present	Aggregate Present and Absent	Present Effective for the Field. Officers	Present Effective for the Field. Men
Brought forward	2,957	38,730	51,014	100,657	2,767	39,291
CAVALRY.						
LEE'S (FITZHUGH) DIVISION—						
Staff ¶	6	....	6	9	...	....
Gary's Brigade †	63	1,021	1,539	3,580	54	1,037
Payne's Brigade *	31	472	582	2,147	25	472
Wickham's Brigade †	33	394	497	3,564	33	394
Total, Lee's (Fitzhugh) Division	133	1,887	2,624	9,300	112	1,903
LEE'S (W. H. F.) DIVISION—						
Staff *	7	....	7	12	...	....
Barringer's Brigade *	85	1,703	2,062	3,657	78	1,298
Dearing's Brigade *	58	838	1,188	2,522	48	560
Total, Lee's (W. H. F.) Division	150	2,541	3,257	6,191	126	1,858
Grand Total of Cavalry	283	4,428	5,881	15,491	238	3,761
Grand Total Army of Northern Virginia **	3,240	43,158	56,895	116,148	3,005	43,052

* Inspected February 28th.
† Inspected February 27th.
‡ Inspected February 24th.
§ Inspected February 25th.
‖ Inspected February 26th.
¶ Inspected March 1st.
** The artillery not accounted for.

TABULAR STATEMENT OF OFFICERS AND MEN OF THE CONFEDERATE ARMY PAROLED AT APPOMATTOX COURTHOUSE.

[Compiled from Parole List.]

COMMAND.	Officers	Enlisted Men	Aggregate
GENERAL HEADQUARTERS.			
GENERAL LEE'S STAFF AND ESCORT	11	87	98
STAFF CORPS	58	125	183
Total	69	212	281
INFANTRY—FIRST CORPS.			
LIEUTENANT-GENERAL LONGSTREET AND STAFF	16	....	16
PICKETT'S DIVISION—			
Major-General Pickett and Staff	14	....	14
Corse's Brigade—Colonel A. Herbert	32	262	294
Hunton's Brigade—Major M. P. Spessard	17	149	166
Steuart's Brigade—Brigadier-General Steuart	46	358	404
Terry's Brigade—Major W. W. Bentley	11	142	153
Total, Pickett's Division	120	911	1,031
FIELD'S DIVISION—			
Major-General Charles W. Field and Staff	9	....	9
Anderson's Brigade—Brigadier-General Anderson	92	895	987
Benning's Brigade—Brigadier-General Benning	76	733	809
Bratton's Brigade—Brigadier-General Bratton	130	1,418	1,548
Perry's (late Law's) Brigade—Brigadier-General Perry	91	892	983
Texas Brigade—Colonel R. M. Powell	64	553	617
Total, Field's Division	462	4,491	4,953
KERSHAW'S DIVISION—			
——— ——— and Staff	4	13	17
DuBose's Brigade—Captain J. F. Espy	22	325	347
Humphreys' Brigade—Captain G. R. Cherry	20	231	251
Simms' Brigade—Captain G. W. Waldron	12	178	190
Total, Kershaw's Division	58	747	805
Total, First Corps	656	6,149	6,805
SECOND CORPS.			
MAJOR-GENERAL GORDON, STAFF, ETC. *	28	115	143
GRIMES' (LATE RODES') DIVISION—			
Major-General Grimes and Staff	13	5	18
Battle's Brigade—Colonel E. L. Hobson	33	331	364
Cook's Brigade—Colonel E. A. Nash	28	322	350
Cox's Brigade—Brigadier-General Cox	51	521	572
Grimes' Brigade—Colonel D. G. Coward	34	496	530
Archer's Battalion	13	52	65
Total, Grimes' Division	172	1,727	1,899
EARLY'S DIVISION—			
Brigadier-General Walker and Staff	11	1	12
Johnston's (R. D.) Brigade—Colonel J. W. Lee	30	433	463
Lewis' Brigade—Captain John Beard	26	421	447
Walker's (late Pegram's) Brigade—Major H. K. Douglas	42	262	304
Total, Early's Division	109	1,117	1,226
GORDON'S DIVISION—			
Brigadier-General Evans and Staff	10	....	10
Evans' Brigade—Colonel J. H. Lowe	51	790	841
Terry's Brigade—Colonel T. V. Williams	67	477	544
York's Brigade—Colonel E. Waggaman	28	345	373
Total, Gordon's Division	156	1,612	1,768
Total Second Corps	465	4,571	5,036
THIRD CORPS. †			
STAFF AND PROVOST GUARD	28	119	147
HETH'S DIVISION—			
Major-General H. Heth and Staff	15	....	15
Cooke's Brigade—Brigadier-General Cooke	70	490	560
Davis' Brigade—Brigadier-General Davis	21	54	75
MacRae's Brigade—Brigadier-General MacRae	42	400	442
McComb's Brigade—Brigadier-General McComb	54	426	480
Total, Heth's Division	202	1,370	1,572
MAHONE'S DIVISION—			
Major-General Mahone and Staff	13	1	14
Finegan's Brigade—Colonel D. Lang	64	441	505
Forney's Brigade—Brigadier-General W. H. Forney	72	880	952
Harris' Brigade—Brigadier-General N. H. Harris	33	339	372
Sorrel's Brigade—Colonel G. E. Taylor	71	962	1,033
Weisiger's Brigade—Brigadier-General Weisiger	78	583	661
Total, Mahone's Division	331	3,206	3,537
Carried forward	1,121	10,720	11,841

* Provost guard, couriers, escort and hospital attendants included.
† Attached to First Corps after death of A. P. Hill.

CONFEDERATE ARMY PAROLED AT APPOMATTOX COURTHOUSE.—Continued.

COMMAND.	Officers	Enlisted Men	Aggregate
Brought forward	1,121	10,720	11,841
THIRD CORPS—Continued.			
WILCOX'S DIVISION—			
Major-General Wilcox and Staff	12	. . . . .	12
Lane's Brigade—Brigadier-General Lane	56	514	570
McGowan's Brigade—Brigadier-General McGowan	69	798	867
Scales' Brigade—Colonel Joseph H. Hyman	92	627	719
Thomas' Brigade—Brigadier-General E. L. Thomas	57	456	513
Total, Wilcox's Division	286	2,395	2,681
Total, Third Army Corps	847	7,090	7,937
ANDERSON'S CORPS.			
——— ——— AND STAFF	. . . .	24	24
JOHNSON'S DIVISION—			
Major-General B. R. Johnson and Staff	10	. . . . .	10
Elliott's Brigade—Brigadier-General Wallace	62	568	630
Moody's Brigade—Brigadier-General Moody	63	515	578
Ransom's Brigade—Brigadier General Ransom	41	394	435
Wise's Brigade—Brigadier-General Wise	72	528	600
Total, Anderson's Corps	248	2,029	2,277
EWELL'S COMMAND—Lieutenant-Colonel Thomas J. Spencer	19	275	294
Total Infantry	2,235	20,114	22,349
CAVALRY.			
MAJOR-GENERAL FITZHUGH LEE AND STAFF	6	1	7
FITZHUGH LEE'S DIVISION—			
Gary's Brigade—Colonel A. C. Haskell	61	772	833
Payne's Brigade	6	82	88
Wickham's Brigade	10	177	187
Total, Fitzhugh Lee's Division	77	1,031	1,108
W. H. F. LEE'S DIVISION—			
Major-General W. H. F. Lee and Staff	7	1	8
Barringer's Brigade	2	21	23
Beale's Brigade—Captain S. H. Burt	22	152	174
Roberts' Brigade—Brigadier-General W. P. Roberts	5	88	93
Total, W. H. F. Lee's Division	36	262	298
LOMAX'S DIVISION—			
Jackson's Brigade	. . . . .	9	9
Total, Lomax's Division	. . . .	9	9
ROSSER'S DIVISION—			
Major-General Rosser and Staff	* 8	1	9
Dearing's Brigade—Colonel A. W. Harman	6	95	101
McCausland's Brigade	1	26	27
Total, Rosser's Division	15	122	137
Total Cavalry	134	1,425	1,559

* Officers whose paroles are signed by Rosser included.

CONFEDERATE ARMY PAROLED AT APPOMATTOX COURTHOUSE.—Continued.

COMMAND.	Officers	Enlisted Men	Aggregate
ARTILLERY.			
GENERAL HEADQUARTERS.			
BRIGADIER-GENERAL PENDLETON AND STAFF	12	13	25
FIRST ARMY CORPS.			
BRIGADIER-GENERAL E. P. ALEXANDER AND STAFF	11	36	47
Haskell's Battalion—Lieutenant-Colonel John C. Haskell	15	139	154
Huger's Battalion—Major T. C. Jordan	21	307	328
McIntosh's Battalion—Lieutenant-Colonel W. M. Owen	14	268	282
Poague's Battalion—Lieutenant-Colonel W. T. Poague	17	279	296
Thirteenth Virginia Battalion—Captain D. N. Walker	2	10	12
Richardson's Battalion—Captain R. Prosper Landry	4	77	81
Total, First Army Corps	84	1,116	1,200
SECOND ARMY CORPS.			
BRIGADIER-GENERAL A. L. LONG AND STAFF	8	22	30
Carter's Command—Colonel T. H. Carter	2	4	6
Braxton's Battalion—Lieutenant-Colonel Carter M. Braxton	7	19	26
Cutshaw's Battalion—Captain C. W. Fry	12	199	211
Hardaway's Battalion—Lieutenant-Colonel R. A. Hardaway	19	382	401
Johnson's Battalion—Lieutenant-Colonel M. Johnson	8	135	143
Lightfoot's Battalion—Assistant Surgeon J. B. Coakley	1	29	30
Stark's Battalion—Lieutenant-Colonel A. W. Stark	11	154	165
Total, Second Army Corps	68	944	1,012
ANDERSON'S CORPS.			
COLONEL H. P. JONES	2	1	3
Blount's Battalion	3	21	24
Coit's Battalion	. . . . .	37	37
Stribling's Battalion	2	8	10
Total, Anderson's Corps	7	67	74
MISCELLANEOUS.			
SMITH'S BATTALION—Captain W. F. Dement	13	252	265
Total Artillery *	184	2,392	2,576
MISCELLANEOUS TROOPS †	159	1,307	1,466

RECAPITULATION.

	Officers	Enlisted Men	Aggregate
General Headquarters	69	212	281
Infantry	2,235	20,114	22,349
Cavalry	134	1,425	1,559
Artillery	184	2,392	2,576
Miscellaneous Troops	159	1,307	1,466
Grand Total	2,781	25,450	28,231

* Cabell's, King's, Lane's, Nelson's, Pegrams' and Sturdivant's battalions borne on return for January 31, 1865, are not accounted for by the paroles.

† Composed of detachments of engineers, invalids, naval brigade, provost guards, etc.

NIGHT AMUSEMENTS AROUND THE CONFEDERATE CAMP FIRE.
"We'll Sing To-night and Fight To-morrow, Bully-boys, Oh!"

THE LAST CONFEDERATE SURRENDER.

BY

LIEUT.-GEN. RICHARD TAYLOR.

To write an impartial and unprejudiced account of exciting contemporary events has always been a difficult task. More especially is this true of civil strife, which, like all "family jars," evolves a peculiar flavor of bitterness. But slight sketches of minor incidents, by actors and eye-witnesses, may prove of service to the future writer who undertakes the more ambitious and severe duty of historian. The following *memoir pour servir* has this object.

In the summer of 1864, after the close of the Red River Campaign, I was ordered to cross the Mississippi and report my arrival on the east bank by telegraph to Richmond. All the fortified posts on the river were held by the Federals, and the intermediate portions of the stream closely guarded by gunboats to impede and, as far as possible, prevent passage. This delayed the transmission of the order above mentioned until August, when I crossed at a point just above the mouth of the Red River. On a dark night, in a small canoe, with horses swimming alongside, I got over without attracting the attention of a gunboat anchored a short distance below. Woodville, Wilkinson County, Mississippi, was the nearest place in telegraphic communication with Richmond. Here, in reply to a dispatch to Richmond, I was directed to assume command of the Department of Alabama, Mississippi, etc., with headquarters at Meridian, Mississippi, and informed that President Davis would, at an early day, meet me at Montgomery, Alabama. The military situation was as follows: Sherman occupied Atlanta, Hood lying some distance to the southwest; Farragut had forced the defenses of Mobile Bay, capturing Fort Morgan, etc., and the Federals held Pensacola, but had made no movement into the interior.

THE CLOSING SCENES.

Major-General Maury commanded the Confederate forces garrisoning Mobile and adjacent works, with Commodore Farrand, Confederate Navy, in charge of several armed vessels. Small bodies of troops were stationed at different points through the department, and Major-General Forrest, with his division of cavalry, was in northeast Mississippi. Directing this latter officer to move his command across the Tennessee River, and use every effort to interrupt Sherman's communications south of Nashville, I proceeded to Mobile to inspect the fortifications; thence to Montgomery, to meet President Davis. The interview extended over many hours, and the military situation was freely discussed. Our next meeting was at Fortress Monroe, where, during his confinement, I obtained permission to visit him. The closing scenes of the great drama succeeded each other with startling rapidity. Sherman marched unopposed to the sea. Hood was driven from Nashville across the Tennessee, and asked to be relieved. Assigned to this duty I met him near Tupelo, North Mississippi, and witnessed the melancholy spectacle presented by a retreating army. Guns, small arms and accouterments lost, men without shoes or blankets, and this in a winter of unusual severity for that latitude. Making every effort to re-equip this force, I suggested to General Lee, then commanding all the armies of the Confederacy, that it should be moved to the Carolinas, to interpose between Sherman's advance and his (Lee's) lines of supply, and, in the last necessity, of retreat. The suggestion was adopted, and this force so moved. General Wilson, with a well-appointed and ably-led command of Federal cavalry, moved rapidly through North Alabama, seized Selma, and, turning east to Montgomery, continued into Georgia.

General Canby, commanding the Union armies in the Southwest, advanced up the Eastern shore of Mobile Bay and invested Spanish Fort and Blakely, important Confederate works in that quarter. After repulsing an assault, General Maury, in accordance with instructions, withdrew his garrisons in the night to Mobile, and then evacuated the city, falling back to Meridian, on the line of the Mobile & Ohio Railway. General Forrest was drawn in to the same point, and the little army, less than eight thousand of all arms, held in readiness to discharge such duties as the waning fortunes of the "cause" and the honor of its arms might demand.

SOLDIERLY COURTESY.

Intelligence of Lee's surrender reached us. Staff officers from Johnston and Sherman came across the country to inform Canby and myself of their "convention." Whereupon, an interview was arranged between us to determine a course of action, and a place selected ten miles north of Mobile, near the railway. Accompanied by a staff officer, Colonel William M. Levy (now a member of Congress from Louisiana), and making use of a "hand-car," I reached the appointed spot, and found General Canby with a large escort and many staff and other officers. Among these I recognized some old friends, notably General Canby himself and Admiral James Palmer. All extended cordial greetings. A few moments of private conversation with Canby led to the establishment of a truce, to await further intelligence from the North. Forty-eight hours' notice was to be given by the party desiring to terminate the truce. We then joined the throng of officers, and although every one present felt a deep conviction that the last hour of the sad struggle approached, no allusion was made to it. Subjects awakening memories of the past, when all were sons of a loved, united country, were, as by the natural selection of good breeding, chosen. A bountiful luncheon was soon spread, and I was invited to partake of patis, champagne-frappe, and other "delights," which to me had long been as lost arts. As we took our seats at table a military band in attendance commenced playing "Hail Columbia." Excusing himself, General Canby walked to the door. The music ceased for a moment, and then the strain of "Dixie" was heard. Old Froissart records no gentler act of "courtesie." Warmly thanking General Canby for his delicate consideration, I asked for "Hail Columbia," and proposed we should unite in the hope that our Columbia would soon be, once more, a happy land. This and other kindred sentiments were duly honored in "frappe," and, after much pleasant intercourse, the party separated.

THE SURRENDER.

The succeeding hours were filled with a grave responsibility, which could not be evaded or shared. Circumstances had appointed me to watch the dying agonies of a cause that had fixed the attention of the world. To my camp, as the last refuge in the storm, came many members of the Confederate Congress. These gentlemen were urged to go at once to their respective homes and, by precept and example, teach the people to submit to the inevitable, obey the laws and resume the peaceful occupations on which society depends. This advice was followed, and with excellent effect on public tranquillity.

LIEUT.-GEN. RICHARD TAYLOR, OF LOUISIANA.

General Canby dispatched that his government disavowed the Johnston-Sherman convention, and it would be his duty to resume hostilities. Almost at the same instant came the news of Johnston's surrender. There was no room for hesitancy. Folly and madness combined would not have justified an attempt to prolong a hopeless contest.

General Canby was informed that I desired to meet him for the purpose of negotiating a *surrender* of my forces, and that Commodore Farrand, commanding the armed vessels in the Alabama River, desired to meet Rear Admiral Thatcher for a similar purpose. Citronville, some forty miles north of Mobile, was the appointed place, and there in the early days of May, 1865, the great war virtually ended.

After this, no hostile gun was fired, and the authority of the United States was supreme in the land. Conditions of surrender were speedily determined, and of a character to soothe the pride of the vanquished; officers to retain side-arms, troops to turn in arms and equipments to their own ordnance officers, so of the quartermaster and commissary stores; the Confederate Cotton Agent for Alabama and Mississippi to settle his accounts with the Treasury Agent of the United States; muster rolls to be prepared, etc.; transportation to be provided for the men. All this under my control and supervision. Here a curious incident may be mentioned: At an early period of the war, when Colonel Sidney Johnston retired to the south of Tennessee River, Isham G. Harris, Governor of Tennessee, accompanied him, taking, at the same time, the coin from the vaults of the State Bank of Tennessee, at Nashville. This coin, in the immediate charge of a bonded officer of the bank, had occasioned much solicitude to the governor in his many wanderings. He appealed to me to assist in the restoration of the coin to the bank. At my request, General Canby detailed an officer and escort, and the money reached the bank intact.

AFTER THE WAR

The condition of the people of Alabama and Mississippi was at this time deplorable. The waste of war had stripped large areas of the necessaries of life. In view of this, I suggested to General Canby that his troops sent to the interior should be limited to the number required for the preservation of order, and be stationed at points where supplies were more abundant; that trade would soon be established between soldiers and people—furnishing the latter with currency, of which they were destitute—and friendly relations promoted. These suggestions were adopted, and a day or two thereafter, at Meridian, a note was received from General Canby, inclosing copies of orders to Generals Granger and Steele, commanding army corps, by which it appeared these officers were directed to call on me for and conform to advice relative to movements of their troops. Strange, indeed, must such confidence appear to statesmen of the "bloody-shirt" persuasion. In due time, Federal staff-officers reached my camp. The men were paroled and sent home. Public property was turned over and receipted for, and this as orderly and quietly as in time of peace between officers of the same service.

DEPARTURE OF PRESIDENT DAVIS AND CABINET FROM RICHMOND, VA.,

AND

THE LAST DAYS OF THE CONFEDERATE TREASURY AND WHAT BECAME OF ITS SPECIE.

BY

CAPTAIN M. H. CLARK,

The Last Acting Treasurer of the Confederacy.

CLARKSVILLE, TENN., January 10, 1882.

I WILL state briefly as possible my connection with the Confederate Treasury, and run hastily over the route from Richmond, Va., to Washington, Ga.

I left Richmond, Va., the night of the evacuation, with all the papers of the Executive office, on the special train containing the President, his staff, his Cabinet (except the Secretary of War, General John C. Breckinridge), and many other government officials, being at the time the chief and confidential clerk of the Executive office. The party reached Danville, Va., next day (General Breckinridge arriving a few days afterward), where the government offices were partially reorganized and opened, remaining there until the 10th of April, when the news of General R. E. Lee's surrender was received. The next move was to Greensboro, N. C., the headquarters of General G. T. Beauregard's little army. A stay of some days was made there, during which General J. E. Johnston reported for a conference as to the general situation. When the President's party prepared to leave, as the railroads were cut at several points south of us by the Federal cavalry under General Stoneman, who were still raiding to the southwest of our line of travel, by orders of Colonels William Preston Johnston and John Taylor Wood (of the President's staff) I applied to General Beauregard for the necessary facilities for the journey, who directed Colonel A. R. Chisolm, of his staff, to give me *carte blanche* orders upon his Chief Quartermaster, Major Chisman, and his Commissary Department for what I needed, from which departments I made up a full train of wagons and ambulances for my papers, the baggage of the party and the provisions necessary for our large following, for many had attached themselves to the party, and I had brought out from Richmond, Va., the "President's Guard"—disabled soldiers, commanded by three one-armed officers, Captain Coe and Lieutenants Brown and Dickinson. General Beauregard sent as escort a small cavalry division, under command of that gallant Tennesseean, General George G. Dibrell, comprising Williams' brigade, under command of Colonel W. C. P. Breckinridge; Dibrell's brigade, under Colonel W. S. McLemore, and Hewitt's battery, under Lieutenant Roberts, and perhaps a few detached small regiments. Captain Given Campbell (an active, efficient officer) and his company from the Ninth Kentucky Cavalry were detailed for special service with the President, his men being used as scouts, guides and couriers, the cavalry force not traveling, as a rule, upon the same road as the party.

The party proceeded to Charlotte, N. C., where, after a stay of a week (where we heard of the assassination of President Lincoln), the route was taken to Abbeville, S. C. At Charlotte a large accession was made to the cavalry force—General Basil W. Duke with his brigade, General

Vaughn and some other detachments from Southwest Virginia, and General Ferguson, and scattering battalions, making quite a full force, which was taken charge of by General John C. Breckinridge in his position as major-general.

General Duke had just before won the most complete victory of his career, attacking and driving away from Marion, Va., a large force of General Stoneman's mounted infantry, who left dead and wounded on the ground, man for man, as many as Duke had under his command in the battle—a brilliant sunset in the closing career of this Kentucky soldier.

Of General Breckinridge I saw a good deal, as we occupied the same room at Mr. Heilbrun's, his son, Captain Cabell Breckinridge, being with him. At Charlotte, N. C., I replenished my stores under an order from Hon. S. R. Mallory, Secretary of the Navy, upon the Naval Storekeeper, and an incident occurred which, perhaps, caused the escape of Colonel Wood when the President's party was captured in Southern Georgia. Finding a lot of good blue navy shirts among the stores, he suggested taking a few to secure change of raiment to such as might need it. He had on one of these shirts the morning of the capture, and in the dim light was enabled to pass through the blue-coated Federal cavalry, mistaken for one of their own men. Leaving Charlotte, N. C., the cavalry force also took the route south under command of General John C. Breckinridge.

We arrived at Abbeville, S. C., the morning of the 2d of May. Mr. Haldeman, of the *Courier-Journal*, was there, according to recollection, and saw the party come in. While there, the President made his headquarters at Colonel Armistead Burt's, Colonel William Preston Johnston at Colonel Henry J. Leovy's, with that patriotic family, the Monroes, of Kentucky. At Abbeville, S. C., the Treasury officers reported the train at the depot, having been a part of the time under escort of Admiral Raphael Semmes' little naval force to protect it from the Federal cavalry, who were raiding on a parallel line with our route, between us and the mountains. Mr. J. A. Trenholm, the Secretary of the Treasury, having been left quite ill near the Catawba River, the President appointed the Postmaster-General, Hon. John H. Reagan, Acting Secretary of the Treasury, who took charge of that department and placed the train under charge of the cavalry to convoy it to Washington, Ga. The party, except General John C. Breckinridge, left for Washington that night, crossing the Savannah River on a pontoon bridge, stopping for breakfast and to feed horses a few miles from Washington. Colonel Burton N. Harrison had previously left the party to join Mrs. Davis and her family. At our breakfast halt, when the road was taken, Mr. Benjamin came to me and said "good-bye," as he did not intend to go further with the party, and turned off south from that point. I never saw him again, though traveling on his track over four hundred miles. Mr. Mallory left the party at Washington, Ga., going to a friend's in the neighborhood.

President Davis' headquarters were at Dr. Robertson's, whose charming family were profuse in their hospitalities, as were many others, General A. R. Lawton's (the Quartermaster-General) and General E. P. Alexander's among the rest.

Next morning Colonel William Preston Johnston informed me that Mr. Reagan had applied for me to act as Treasurer, to take charge of the Treasury matters, and I was ordered to report to him, and doing so was handed my commission, which is now before me and reads as follows, viz.:

WASHINGTON, GA., May 4, 1865.

M. H. Clark, Esq., is hereby appointed Acting Treasurer of the Confederate States, and is authorized to act as such during the absence of the Treasurer.

JEFFERSON DAVIS.*

Returning to my train to get some necessary articles, President Davis rode up with his party, when what I supposed were farewell words passed between us, and my train, under charge of its quartermaster, moved out. The Treasury train arrived shortly after President Davis' party left, and being reported at General Basil W. Duke's camp, about a mile from town, I went there with the proper authority and he turned the whole of it over to me. Selecting the shade of a large elm tree as the "Treasury Department," I commenced my duties as "Acting Treasurer C. S."

Now for the specie assets of the Treasury.

It must be remembered that a month or more before the evacuation of Richmond, Va., for the relief of the people, to furnish them a currency to buy supplies outside of our lines, and also to call in currency to pay off the troops, and for other purposes, the Treasury Department had opened its depositories and had been selling silver coin, the rate being fixed at $60 for $1 in coin. While at Danville, Va., the Treasury Department resumed these sales, the rate there being $70 for $1.

About $40,000 in silver, generally reported (and no doubt correctly) at $39,000, was left at Greensboro, N. C., as a military chest for the forces there, under charge of the Treasurer, Mr. John C. Hendren; all of the balance was turned into my hands, which amounted, in gold and silver coin, gold and silver bullion, to $288,022.90. Adding the $39,000 left at Greensboro, N. C., the Treasury contained in coin and bullion when it left Danville, Va., $327,022.90.

If the Treasury at Richmond had contained $2,500,000 in coin, certainly the brave men of our armies would never have suffered so severely from want of sufficient food and clothing as they did during the winter of 1864–65, for it had been demonstrated that gold could draw food and raiment from without the lines. With the train at Washington, Ga., however, was the specie belonging to the Virginia banks, which some time before had been ordered to be turned over to their officers, who had accompanied it out from Richmond, and, devoted to their duties, had never left it; but the proper officer had not been present to make the transfer. It had never been mixed with the Treasury funds, but kept apart and distinct, and when Acting Secretary Reagan ordered the transfer to be made, no handling of specie or counting was necessary, but merely permission for the cashiers and tellers to take control of their own matters. I knew them all personally, having been a Richmond boy myself. The papers of this transaction are not before me, and my recollection is not positively clear as to the amount, but my impression is that it was about $230,000. As a history of the Virginia banks' specie would make a chapter of itself, and as it was not a part of the Confederate Treasury assets, I drop further mention of it.

While at Washington, Ga., communications were received from General John C. Breckinridge that payments had been promised to the cavalry from the train by him at a halt on the road the night of the 3d. The action of General Breckinridge in the premises was ratified, and President Davis gave some other directions before he left. General Breckinridge arrived in Washington, Ga., an hour or so after President Davis left, and my recollection of his statement was in brief as follows: That during the night of the 3d, en route from Abbeville, S. C., to Washington, Ga., he found the cavalry and train at a halt, resting. Stopping, he learned from the officers that the men were dissatisfied at the position of affairs; that they were guarding a train which could not be carried safely much further; the Federal cavalry were known to be in

PRESIDENT JEFFERSON DAVIS, HIS MINISTERS AND ESCORT PASSING OVER THE GEORGIA RIDGE, FIVE DAYS BEFORE THEIR CAPTURE BY THE FEDERAL FORCES, MAY 5, 1865.
[From a sketch by a special artist representing the *Illustrated London News*.]

* This was the last official signature President Davis affixed to any paper.

full force not a great distance off; the destination and disposition of their own force was an uncertain one; their paper money was worthless for their needs; that they might never reach Washington, Ga., with it, etc. A crowd gathered around, when General Breckinridge made a little speech, appealing to their honor as Confederate soldiers not to violate the trust reposed in them, but to remain Southern soldiers and gentlemen; and that when they reached Washington with the train fair payments should be made to them from it.

The men responded frankly and openly, saying they proposed to violate no trust; they were there to guard the train from all, and would guard it, but expressed as above what they considered due them in the matter, and, as they would be paid some money in Washington, Ga., and no one could tell what would happen before they reached there, they could give no good reason for delay.

General Breckinridge replied that, if they wished an instant compliance with his promise, he would redeem it at once, and ordered up the train to the house at which he had stopped, and had the wagons unloaded; the quartermasters being ordered to make out their pay-rolls, when a certain amount was counted out and turned over to the proper officers. The wagons were then reloaded, and, after the rest, the route was taken up, reaching Washington, Ga., next morning, where the quartermasters paid off from their rolls. The boys told me they got about $26 apiece; enough, they hoped, to take them through.

It is this transaction which has produced so many contradictory statements from men and officers, many seeing nothing more, and regarding it as the final disbursing of the Confederate specie. Proper receipts were given and taken at the time, and I rated it as it disbursed by myself, and covered it into the Treasury accounts by the paper, of which below is a copy:

CONFEDERATE STATES OF AMERICA,
WASHINGTON, GA., May 4, 1865.

Hon. J. C. Breckinridge, Secretary of War:

There is required for payment of troops now on the march through Georgia, the sum of one hundred and eight thousand three hundred and twenty-two dollars and ninety cents ($108,322.90), to be placed to the credit of Major E. C. White, Quartermaster.

A. R. LAWTON,
Quartermaster-General.

[*Indorsed.*]

The Secretary of the Treasury will please issue as requested.

JOHN C. BRECKINRIDGE,
Secretary of War.

[*Indorsed.*]

M. H. Clark, Acting Treasurer, will turn over to Major E. C. White the amount named within, preserving the necessary vouchers, warrant hereafter to be drawn when settlement can be regularly made.

JOHN H. REAGAN,
Acting Secretary Treasury.

[*Indorsed.*]

WASHINGTON, GA., May 4, 1865.

Received of M. H. Clark, Acting Treasurer, C. S., the sum of one hundred and eight thousand three hundred and twenty-two dollars and ninety cents ($108,322.90) in specie, the amount called for by within paper.

My own transportation having gone forward, General Breckinridge kindly gave me his own ambulance, team and driver, which I used in driving back and forth from town to Duke's camp as my duties called me. I obtained permission from General Breckinridge and Mr. Reagan to burn a mass of currency and bonds, and burnt millions in their presence.

After the cavalry were paid there was a general order that all unattached officers and men should receive a month's pay, and below are copies of some of the receipts; but some receipts quoted are in different form; comment on these will be made later on:

"Estimate of funds required for the service of the Quartermaster's Department at Washington, Ga., by Captain John M. Garnett, A. Q. M.: Specie, $5,000.

[*Indorsed.*]

Respectfully submitted to the Secretary of War.
Approved: A. R. LAWTON, *Q. M. Gen.*

Secretary of the Treasury is requested to furnish within funds.

JOHN C. BRECKINRIDGE,
Secretary of War.

M. H. Clark, Acting Treasurer, will turn over to Captain Garnett the amount within named, taking the proper vouchers, a warrant to be drawn when settlement can be regularly made.

JOHN H. REAGAN,
Secretary of Treasury.

WASHINGTON, GA., May 4, 1865.

Received of M. H. Clark, Acting Treasurer, the amount of within estimate, five thousand dollars, in specie.

JOHN M. GARNETT,
Capt. and A. Q. M.

WASHINGTON, GA., May 4, 1865.

I require for the payment of the officers and men of the President's Guard fourteen hundred and fifty-four dollars ($1,454) in specie.

C. H. C. BROWN,
Lieutenant Commanding.

Approved: WM. PRESTON JOHNSTON,
Col. and A. D. C.

A. R. LAWTON,
Q. M. G.

M. H. Clark, Acting Treasurer, will pay the within fourteen hundred and fifty-four dollars in silver, retaining this paper and the proper receipt subject to future regular settlement.

JOHN H. REAGAN,
Acting Secretary Treasury.

M. H. Clark will pay, in addition to the within requisition, eighteen dollars, one month's pay, for E. H. Burns.

JOHN H. REAGAN,
Acting Secretary Treasury.

Received of M. H. Clark, Acting Treasurer, C. S., fourteen hundred and seventy-two dollars ($1,472) in full of within requisition.

C. H. C. BROWN,
Lieutenant Commanding President's Guard.

WASHINGTON, GA., May 4, 1865.

M. H. Clark, Acting Treasurer:

Pay to A. G. Cantley, a clerk in the Post-office Department, fifty dollars in specie, and preserve necessary vouchers until warrant can be drawn and settlement regularly made.

JOHN H. REAGAN,
Acting Secretary of the Treasury.

Received the within fifty dollars in specie from M. H. Clark, Acting Treasurer, C. S. A.

A. G. CANTLEY.

WASHINGTON, GA., May 4, 1865.

The Secretary of the Treasury is requested to turn over four thousand dollars to Major J. Foster, C. S., to be used for the support of the troops now under my command.

JOHN C. BRECKINRIDGE,
Secretary of War.

M. H. Clark, Acting Treasurer:

Turn over the above-named amount of money as requested, keeping necessary vouchers, warrant to be drawn when regular settlement can be made.

JOHN H. REAGAN,
Acting Secretary of Treasury.

WASHINGTON, GA., May 4, 1865.

Received of M. H. Clark, Acting Treasurer, C. S., four thousand dollars ($4,000) in gold, on within requisition.

J. M. FOSTER, *Major, C. S.*

ABBEVILLE, S. C., May 3, 1865.

Assistant Paymaster J. F. Wheless, C. S. N.:

SIR: You will proceed to Washington, Ga., and there present to the Hon. Judge Reagan, Acting Secretary of the Treasury, estimates of the amount required to pay off the officers of the Naval School for one or more months, as he may specify.

Respectfully, your obedient servant,

WM. H. PARKER,
Lieutenant-Colonel Commanding.

M. H. Clark, Acting Treasurer, will pay over to J. F. Wheless the sum of $1,500 in silver, to be by him paid out pro rata, according to rank, to the officers of the navy and midshipmen who were employed in guarding the specie from Richmond to Abbeville, as shown by the accompanying petitions and list of names, and take his receipt and retain these papers.

JOHN H. REAGAN,
Acting Secretary Treasury.

$1,500. Received of M. H. Clark, Acting Treasurer, C. S., $1,500 in gold, in full of within requisition.

J. F. WHELESS,
Assistant Paymaster.

WASHINGTON, GA., May 4, 1865.

M. H. Clark, Acting Treasurer:

Pay over to Assistant Paymaster Wheless, in addition to the sum of $1,500 called for to pay naval officers, etc., three hundred dollars in silver to be paid to First Lieutenant Bradford, of the Marine Corps, taking receipt and retaining this.

JOHN H. REAGAN,
Acting Secretary Treasury.

Received, at Washington, Ga., May 4, 1865, of M. H. Clark, Acting Treasurer, C. S., three hundred dollars in gold, to be turned over to Lieutenant Bradford, of the C. S. Marine Corps.

J. F. WHELESS,
Assistant Paymaster.

WASHINGTON, GA., May 4, 1865.

M. H. Clark, Acting Treasurer, will pay over to General Braxton Bragg two thousand dollars in coin for transmission to the Trans-Mississippi Department, and warrant for the same to be drawn when settlement can be regularly made, taking his receipt therefor.

JOHN H. REAGAN,
Acting Secretary Treasury.

WASHINGTON, GA., May 4, 1865.

Received of M. H. Clark, Acting Treasurer, two thousand dollars ($2,000) in coin, called for by within paper.

BRAXTON BRAGG,
General, C. S. A.

WASHINGTON, GA., May 4, 1865.

. . . . Received of A. R. Lawton, Quartermaster-General, C. S. A., the following pay funds in specie: $806 for payment of five commissioned officers and twenty-six men belonging to Brigadier-General L. York's Louisiana Brigade.

LEIGH WATKINS,
Acting Assistant Quartermaster.

Approved: D. GATLEY, *Lieutenant-Colonel.*

Respectfully referred to the Secretary of War.

Approved: A. R. LAWTON, *Quartermaster-General.*

Secretary of Treasury, please issue.

JOHN C. BRECKINRIDGE,
Secretary of War.

THE BURT MANSION, ABBEVILLE, S. C., WHERE THE LAST MEETING OF THE CONFEDERATE CABINET WAS HELD.

M. H. Clark, Acting Treasurer, will please pay over to Captain Watkins for payment to the troops specified, taking proper vouchers. Warrant to be drawn when settlement can be regularly made.

JOHN H. REAGAN,
Acting Secretary Treasury.

WASHINGTON, GA., May 4, 1865.

Received of M. H. Clark, Acting Treasurer, eight hundred and six dollars ($806), in full of within requisition.

LEIGH WATKINS,
Captain and Acting A. Q. M.

Estimate of funds required for the service of the Quartermaster's Department at —— by Captain Joseph M. Brown. . . . . Specie, $3,000.

Respectfully submitted to the Secretary of War, approved for the sum of five hundred and twenty dollars ($520).

A. R. LAWTON,
Quartermaster-General.

MAY 4, 1865.

Secretary of Treasury:
Please issue.

JOHN C. BRECKINRIDGE,
Secretary of War.

M. H. Clark, Acting Treasurer, will turn over to Captain Brown the amount specified within, preserving the necessary vouchers. Warrant to be drawn when a regular settlement can be made.

JOHN H. REAGAN,
Acting Secretary of Treasury.

containing coin and bullion, and a little iron safe in my ambulance, he giving me an escort of twenty or thirty men, whose silver dollars were jingling in their saddle-bags. Before reaching town I was halted by Major R. J. Moses to turn over to him an amount of specie which President Davis, before he left, had ordered to be placed at the disposal of the Commissary Department to feed the paroled soldiers and stragglers who were passing through, to prevent their being a burden to a section already well stripped of supplies. I went through the wagons, removing to my ambulance the gold coin and gold bullion, and turned over to Major Moses the wagons and silver bullion, and all of the escort except about ten men. The amounts stated on the boxes footed up $40,000, but Major Moses claimed that possibly some of their contents might have been disturbed. I opened the most of them, finding the contents intact, but as a compromise wrote the following receipt:

WASHINGTON, GA., May 4, 1865.

Received of M. H. Clark, Acting Treasurer, C. S., twenty (20) boxes of silver bullion, supposed to be worth in coin from thirty-five to forty thousand dollars, upon requisitions of the Quartermaster-General and the Commissary-General of Subsistence.

To this Major Moses added:

The same having been delivered in Washington, Ga., uncounted, to be counted and weighed before two officers and certified to, a copy of certificate to be forwarded to Judge Reagan.

R. J. MOSES,
Major and Chief Commissary.

evening a few miles south of Sandersville, Ga. There the President heard disturbing reports from Mrs. Davis' party, they fearing attempts to steal their horses by stragglers, and decided next morning to take his staff and join her party for a few days. As everything on wheels was to be abandoned by him, and as it was decided that I was to remain with my train, the chances of the capture of which were steadily increasing, the Federal General Wilson having spread his large cavalry force out like a fan from Macon, I called the staff together, and inquiring as to their funds, found that they had only a small amount of paper currency each, except, perhaps, Colonel F. R. Lubbock, A. D. C., who had, I believe, a little specie of his private funds. Colonel William Preston Johnston told me that the President's purse contained paper money only. I represented to them the chances of capture of my slower-moving train, which would be compelled mainly to keep the roads in case of danger—that they would need money for their supplies en route and to buy boats in Florida, etc., and that I wished to pay over to them funds to be used for those purposes, and they consenting, I paid, with the concurrence of Hon. John H. Reagan, the acting Secretary of the Treasury, $1,500 in gold each to Colonel John Taylor Wood, A. D. C.; Colonel Wm. Preston Johnston, A. D. C.; Colonel F. R. Lubbock, A. D. C.; and Colonel C. E. Thorburn (a naval purchasing agent who was with the party), taking a receipt from each one, but as they were all of the same verbiage I merely give one, as follows:

SANDERSVILLE, GA., May 6, 1865.

$1,500. Received of M. H. Clark, Acting Treasurer, C. S., fifteen hundred ($1,500) in gold coin, the property of the

VIEW OF RICHMOND, VA., 1861, FROM THE OPPOSITE BANK OF THE JAMES RIVER.

WASHINGTON, GA., May 4, 1865.

Received of M. H. Clark, Acting Treasurer, C. S., five hundred and twenty dollars ($520) in gold on within requisition.

JOSEPH M. BROWN,
Captain and A. Q. M.

We the undersigned, are officers in the First Auditor's office, and desire to draw one hundred dollars in gold for our services to this date, May 4, 1865.

S. BRITTAIN.

M. H. Clark, Acting Treasurer:

Pay fifty dollars to each, keeping vouchers until warrants can be drawn.

JOHN H. REAGAN,
Acting Secretary of Treasury.

WASHINGTON, GA., May 4, 1865.

We, the undersigned, have received fifty dollars each in gold on within order.

S. BRITTAIN,
JAS. MILLER,
J. B. MACMURDO.

WASHINGTON, GA., May 4, 1865.

M. H. Clark, Acting Treasurer:

Turn over to John C. Breckinridge, Secretary of War, one thousand dollars for transmission to the Trans-Mississippi Department, taking his receipt therefor. Warrant to be drawn when regular settlement can be made.

JOHN H. REAGAN,
Acting Secretary Treasury.

MAY 4, 1865.

Received the within sum from M. H. Clark, Acting Treasurer.

JOHN C. BRECKINRIDGE,
Secretary of War.

The above are examples of the receipts taken. About sunset I took leave of General Duke, with two wagons

It was after dark when I reached Washington, and, failing to find General A. R. Lawton, Quartermaster-General, and General I. M. St. John, Commissary General, I made the following indorsement on the receipt:

This property was turned over to Major R. J. Moses by verbal order of Hon. John H. Reagan, Acting Secretary of the Treasury, and in his presence the proper requisitions were promised to be furnished by Generals Lawton and St. John, which promise was not fulfilled.

M. H. CLARK,
Acting Treasurer, C. S.

WASHINGTON, GA., May 4, 1865.

In my statement of the specie assets of the Treasury being $288,022.90, I counted the payment to Major Moses as being $40,000.

My last payment in Washington, Ga., was of eighty-six thousand dollars ($86,000) in gold coin and gold bullion, to a trusted officer of the navy, taking his receipt for its transmission out of the Confederacy, to be held for the Treasury Department.

Judge Reagan and myself left Washington, Ga., about 11 o'clock P. M., taking with us a few of Duke's men as guides, whom we dismissed with thanks a few hours afterward, and joined President Davis' party next morning, as they came out of their bivouac about sunrise.

After greetings, I found the party consisting of the President and staff and a few others, Captain Given Campbell and twelve of his men, my train and its quartermaster and party. (After Duke's command had been paid off, the men learning that full freedom was given to their action, some sixty formed themselves into a company, among them my fellow-townsmen, Messrs. W. R. Bringhurst and Clay Stacker, and rode to town and offered themselves to President Davis as an escort just as he was leaving; but it seems that he declined their courtesy, and they afterward left town with General J. C. Breckinridge.) We traveled together that day and went into camp that

Confederate States, for transmission abroad, of the safe arrival of which due notice to be given the Secretary of the Treasury.

I also paid to each $10 in silver for small uses, from a little executive office fund, which I had obtained in Danville, Va., by converting my paper when the Treasurer was selling silver there. For this I took no receipt, charging it in my office accounts. I also called up Captain Given Campbell and paid him for himself and men $300 in gold, taking the following receipt:

Received of M. H. Clark, Acting Treasurer, C. S., three hundred dollars ($300) in gold, upon requisition of Colonel John Taylor Wood, A. D. C.

GIVEN CAMPBELL,
Captain Company B, Second Kentucky Cavalry, Williams' Brigade.

I then went to Judge Reagan with a bag containing thirty-five hundred dollars ($3,500) in gold, and asked him to take it in his saddle-bags as an additional fund in case of accidents or separation. He resisted, saying that he was already weighted by some $2,000 of his own personal funds, which he had brought out from Richmond, Va., in a belt around his person; but after some argument on my part he allowed me to put it in his saddle-bags. The party then were already on horse, and "Good-bye" was said.

The President's party was captured a few days afterward, and upon their release from prison several of the party told me that every one was robbed of all they had, except Colonel F. R. Lubbock, who, after stout resistance and great risk, retained his money, upon which the party subsisted during their long imprisonment at Fort Delaware. No gold was found on President Davis when captured, for he had none. He could only have received it through me, and I paid him none. Mr. Trenholm was left sick in South Carolina. Attorney-General Davis was left at Charlotte, N. C. Mr. Benjamin left us before reaching Washington, Ga., and Mr. Mallory at Washington. I paid the members of the Cabinet nothing, except to General Breckinridge, and his receipt quoted shows the character of that payment. The only money Judge Reagan received was the money mentioned above, near Sandersville—which was a deposit, not a payment. The Treasury train was never with President Davis' party. They found it at Abbeville, S. C., rode away and left it there, and rode away from Washington, Ga, shortly after its arrival there, while it was being turned over to me. It will have been noted that the receipts quoted are of two classes—payments to troops and clerks for their own services; but to officers of higher rank, like Generals Bragg and Breckinridge, or to members of the President's military family, they were for transmission to a distance, to be afterward accounted for to the Treasury Department. In my narrative of events I have given full names of persons, most of whom are still living, witnesses of the occurrences at Washington, Ga. Colonel James Wilson, of General Breckinridge's staff, was, perhaps, cognizant of much that I have related. A few concluding remarks may make clearer the condition of affairs which arose at Washington, Ga., on that 4th of May, 1865.

The last Cabinet meeting which could be called such, was held at Abbeville on the 2d of May, at which it seems to have been decided that the attempt was hopeless to carry the organized force to the Trans-Mississippi Department, it being too small to cope with the enemy it would have to encounter, and it was left free to the soldiers to decide their own action—the move was to be a voluntary one. The soldiers before this had intuitively grasped the situation. The roads were full of men—paroled soldiers from Lee's and Johnston's armies; escaped men from both, having evaded surrender; men who had been exchanged and had started to join their commands—and north of Abbeville and all the way to Florida, I met men who, being still free to fight, were wending their way to the Mississippi River. I met them on my return from Florida in June, plodding their weary way back to their homes. These belong to the Atlantic States. I traveled with some all the way to Virginia; those belonging to the States west of Georgia were already home again. These men and officers were some of the pick and flower of the Confederate States armies; men who, in the four years' desperate struggle, having to fight every nationality under the sun, except the "heathen Chinee," were still volunteers. Who dare say, if twenty thousand such men had re-enforced the troops of the Trans-Mississippi Department, what the result might have been?

Both sections were traveling in the same financial rut; but the Southern money traveled downward the faster.

The soldiers jingling their silver dollars on every road told the tale of the disbursement of the little Treasury, and I found on my return the wildest rumors through the country as to the amount it had contained. Five million dollars was the smallest amount mentioned.

Federal detectives were swarming along the route we had traveled, hunting papers, the Treasury and "the last man who had it in charge," "for an immense amount must have been secreted somewhere; $5,000,000 to $15,000,000 could not vanish in the air in a day."

But the undersigned wasn't eager to make new acquaintances, and wasn't then signing himself "Acting Treasurer, Confederate States." An impression has prevailed with some that on that last day great demoralization, confusion and panic existed. Such was not so. The soldiers were orderly, and though the town was filled with men under no command, there was no rioting or violence, though the citizens feared something of the kind. In the hearts of the educated and the thinking there was a hush of deep emotion, and it seemed to me as if a gloomy pall hung in the atmosphere repressing active expression. As it was realized that a government which had been strong and loved, the exponent of all their hopes and wishes, was, perhaps, dying the death before their eyes, that whatever might be accomplished "over the river," all east of it for a possibly long future was to be abandoned to the conqueror, with all the unnumbered woes which that implied—an agony too great for words, with the bitterness of an almost despair filling all hearts—I rode out into the darkness that night as if from a death-bed.

You have before you a plain, unvarnished statement of the last days. The personal pronoun has been used more than I could have wished, but it was unavoidable. The sketch might have been studded with incidents of the "retreat from Richmond," interesting, perhaps, to those who followed the "Starry Cross" to that bitter end, but this article is already too long.

The old Confederates brought nothing out of the war, save honor; for God's sake, and the precious memory of the dead, let us preserve that untarnished, and defend it from slanderous insinuations. To do my part, I have spoken.

M. H. CLARK,
Ex-Captain P. A. C. S., and ex-Acting Treasurer, C. S. A.

WHEN General Gordon was about to lead an attack at Petersburg he and General Heth and some others went into a little schoolroom on the lines to pray. Sol Heth, the general's brother and adjutant-general, who was always on the lookout for a drink, was standing a little way off, and Henry Peyton, one of General Lee's staff, beckoned him to come to the house and join them. Sol did not understand the object, but totally misconstruing it, held up his canteen, and shaking it, said: "No, I thank you; I have just got hold of some."

LAST LETTERS AND TELEGRAMS OF THE CONFEDERACY.

CORRESPONDENCE OF GENERAL JOHN C. BRECKINRIDGE.

WE are indebted to Hon. C. R. Breckinridge for allowing us to copy the following letters and telegrams, which were among the last in the official correspondence of his distinguished father, the last Secretary of War of the Confederacy:

GREENSBORO, 25th.

Hon. J. C. Breckinridge:

The officers named shall be sent.

J. E. JOHNSTON, *General.*

This paper is indorsed as follows in General Breckinridge's handwriting:

"Mill. Papers, April. 1865." "They did not come."

GREENSBORO, 26th, 7 A. M.

General J. C. Breckinridge, Secretary War:

I am going to meet General Sherman at the same place.

J. E. JOHNSTON, *General.*

GREENSBORO, April 24th.

Hon. Jno. C. Breckinridge, Secretary War:

I telegraphed you yesterday that General Sherman informed me he expected his messenger to return from Washington to-day. Please answer.

J. E. JOHNSTON, *General.*

GREENSBORO, April 24th.

Hon. J. C. Breckinridge:

General Johnston directs me to remain in this office to ascertain if you can decipher the telegram. You will please notify me, that I may report to him.

D. S. RYAN,
Opr. for General J.

GREENSBORO, April 25th, 11:30 A. M.

Hon. J. C. Breckinridge, Secretary of War:

I have proposed to General Sherman military negotiations in regard to this army.

J. E. JOHNSTON, *General.*

GREENSBORO, April 25th, 10 A. M.

Hon. J. C. Breckinridge, Secretary War:

Your dispatch received. We have to save the people, save the blood of the army, and save the high civil func-

VIEW OF THE BENNETT HOUSE, FOUR MILES WEST OF DURHAM, N. C.
THE HOUSE IN WHICH GENERAL JOSEPH E. JOHNSTON SURRENDERED TO GENERAL W. T. SHERMAN, APRIL 26, 1865.

tionaries. Your plan, I think, can only do the last. We ought to prevent invasion, make terms for our troops and give an escort of our best cavalry to the President, who ought to move without loss of a moment. Commanders believe the troops will not fight again. We think your plan impracticable. Major-General Wilson, U. S. A., has captured Macon, with Major-Generals Cobb and G. W. Smith, Brigadiers Mackall, Mercer and the garrison. Federal papers announce capture of Mobile with three thousand prisoners.

J. E. JOHNSTON, *General.*

[*Cipher.*]

CHARLOTTE, N. C., April 24, 1865, 11 P. M.

General J. E. Johnston, Greensboro, N. C.

Does not your suggestion about disbanding refer to the infantry and most of the artillery? If it be necessary to disband these, they might still save their small arms and find their away to some appointed rendezvous. Can you not bring off the cavalry and all the men you can mount from the transportation and other animals, with some light field-pieces? Such a force could march away from Sherman and be strong enough to encounter anything between us and the Southwest. If this course is possible, carry it out and telegraph your intended route.

JOHN C. BRECKINRIDGE,
Secretary of War.

HALF MILE WEST OF SAVANNAH BRIDGE,
May 3, 1865, 8 P. M.

DEAR SIR: I have not heard from you in answer to my note of this day, and the condition of things here, together with great fatigue, have prevented my going forward.

Nothing can be done with the bulk of this command. It has been with difficulty that anything has been kept in shape. I am having the silver paid to the troops, and will in any event save the gold and have it brought forward in the morning, when I hope Judge Reagan will take it.

Many of the men have thrown away their arms. Most of them have resolved to remain here under Vaughn and Dibrell, and will make terms. A few hundred men will move on and may be depended on for the object we spoke of yesterday. I would respectfully and earnestly repeat the suggestions I then made. Let me know if you desire me to adopt any other course than that proposed. If you are at Washington, or this side, I can ride forward in the morning to see you.

Yours very truly,
JOHN C. BRECKINRIDGE,
Secretary of War.

TO PRESIDENT DAVIS.
Official: WM. J. DAVIS, *A. A. G.*

BRIG.-GEN. JOHN ECHOLS, OF VIRGINIA.
[From a photograph taken in 1865.]

P. S.—9 P. M.: Your note of 3:15 P. M., this date, just received. What I have written above explains condition of affairs. The specie train could not have been moved on but for the course adopted. Out of nearly four thousand men present but a few hundred could be relied on, and they were intermixed with the mass. Threats have just reached me to seize the whole amount, but I hope the guard at hand will be sufficient.

(Signed) J. C. B.

CONFEDERATE STATES OF AMERICA,
WAR DEPARTMENT, ONE AND A HALF MILES
WEST OF SAVANNAH BRIDGE, GA.,
May 3, 1865.

[*Extract Special Order No.* ——.]

Major E. C. White, senior quartermaster, will take charge of silver (in specie and bullion) belonging to the Government, and estimated at one hundred and eight thousand, three hundred and twenty-two $\frac{90}{100}$ dollars ($108,322.90).

He will distribute the specie, proportionately, to the troops present upon certified returns of the strength of their commands by the several brigade commanders. He will correctly estimate the value of the bullion in coin; and pay in gold, placed in his hands for the purpose, as above required for the distribution of the silver in specie.

By command of the Secretary of War.

(Signed) W. J. DAVIS, *A. A. G.*
For MAJOR WHITE, *Quartermaster.*

General J. C. Breckinridge: GREENSBORO, April 23d.

General Sherman writes that he expects the return of his officer from Washington to-morrow.

J. E. JOHNSTON.

CHARLOTTE, N. C., April 23, 1865.

To His Excellency, the President:

SIR: In obedience to your request, I have the honor to submit my advice on the course you should take upon the memorandum or basis of agreement made on the 18th inst., by and between General J. E. Johnston, of the Confederate States Army, and General W. T. Sherman, of the United States Army, provided that paper should receive the approval of the Government of the United States

The principal army of the Confederacy was recently lost in Virginia. Considerable bodies of troops not attached to that army have either dispersed or marched toward their homes, accompanied by many of their officers. Five days ago the effective force in infantry and artillery of General Johnston's army was but fourteen thousand seven hundred and seventy men, and it continues to diminish. That officer thinks it wholly impossible for him to make any head against the overwhelming forces of the enemy. Our ports are closed and the sources of foreign supply lost to us. The enemy occupy all or the greater part of Missouri, Kentucky, Tennessee, Virginia and North Carolina, and move almost at will through the other States to the east of the Mississippi. They have recently taken Selma, Montgomery, Columbus, Macon and other important towns, depriving us of large depots of supplies and of munitions of war. Of the small force still at command many are unarmed, and the ordnance department can not furnish five thousand stand of small arms. I do not think it would be possible to assemble, equip and maintain an army of thirty thousand men at any point east of the Mississippi. The contest, if continued after this paper is rejected, will be likely to lose entirely the dignity of regular warfare. Many of the States will make such terms as they may; in others, separate and ineffective hostilities may be prosecuted, while war, wherever waged, will probably degenerate into that irregular and secondary stage out of which greater evils will flow to the South than to the enemy.

For these, and for other reasons which need not now be stated, I think we can no longer contend with a reasonable hope of success. It seems to me the time has arrived when, in a large and clear view of the situation, prompt steps should be taken to put a stop to the war. The terms proposed are not wholly unsuited to the altered condition of affairs. The States are preserved, certain essential rights secured, and the army rescued from degradation.

It may be said that the agreement of the 18th instant contains certain stipulations which you can not perform. This is true, and it was well understood by General Sherman that only a part could be executed by the Confederate authorities. In any case, grave responsibilities must be met and assumed. If the necessity for peace be conceded, corresponding action must be taken. The modes of negotiation which we deem regular, and would prefer, are impracticable. The situation is anomalous and can not be solved upon principles of theoretical exactitude. In my opinion you are the only person who can meet the present necessities.

I respectfully advise—

First. That you execute, so far as you can, the second article of the agreement of the 18th instant.

Second. That you recommend to the several States the acceptance of those parts of the agreement upon which they alone can act.

Third. Having maintained, with faithful and intrepid purpose, the cause of the Confederate States while the means of organized resistance remained, that you return to the States and the people the trust which you are no longer able to defend.

Whatever course you pursue, opinions will be divided. Permit me to give mine. Should these or similar views accord with your own, I think the better judgment will be that you can have no higher title to the gratitude of your countrymen and the respect of mankind than will spring from the wisdom to see the path of duty at this time, and the courage to follow it, regardless alike of praise or blame.

Respectfully and truly your friend,
JOHN C. BRECKINRIDGE,
Secretary of War.

HEADQUARTERS FIRST BRIGADE
EAST TENNESSEE CAVALRY DIVISION,
LINCOLNTON, N. C., April 23, 1865.

GENERAL: I have the honor to acknowledge receipt by flag of truce from you of two communications addressed to Major-General Stoneman, one from Major-General Sherman and one from General J. E. Johnston.

These communications were immediately forwarded to General Stoneman through the headquarters of this cavalry division, and I have no doubt that a reply will be sent by flag of truce within a few days.

I am, General, your obedient servant,
WM. J. PALMER,
Brevet Brigadier General Commanding Brigade.

MAJOR-GENERAL J. C. BRECKINRIDGE,
Secretary of War, Charlotte, N. C.

LIEUT.-GEN. WADE HAMPTON, OF SOUTH CAROLINA.

GREENSBORO, April 27th.

Brigadier-General Z. York:

Your dispatch received. Will communicate with you. Forward following to General Breckinridge immediately.

WADE HAMPTON, *Lieutenant-General.*

GREENSBORO, 27th, 11 P. M.

General J. C. Breckinridge:

You gave me orders on 25th to move on my return on 26th. I found military convention. I think I am free from its terms by your previous order. Have notified General Johnston that I will abide by your decision. Am ready to move as ordered. Answer here or Lexington.

WADE HAMPTON, *Lieutenant-General.*

CATAWBA BRIDGE, April 28, 1865.

Hon. John C. Breckinridge, Secretary of War:

MY DEAR SIR—I send you a dispatch just received from General Hampton, by my A. A. G.

Have the kindness to send me two mounted couriers.

I sent you early this morning by my only courier two dispatches.

Yours truly,
Z. YORK, *Brigadier-General.*

This is from General Hoke, as follows:

HEADQUARTERS, CHARLOTTE, April 27, 1865.

General John C. Breckinridge, Secretary of War:

DEAR SIR—I send copy of telegram received at 11 o'clock to-day:

GEEENSBORO, 27th April.

Brigadier-General Echols:

A military convention has been made by General Sherman and myself terminating hostilities between our commands. Send intelligence to Secretary of War, if you can, and give information to Major-General Stoneman.

(Signed) J. E. JOHNSTON.

I have sent a flag of truce, with a letter of General Cooper to General Stoneman. Yours, respectfully,

WILLIAM J. HOKE, *Colonel Com. Post.*

CATAWBA BRIDGE, 28th April, 1865.

Hon. John C. Breckinridge, Secretary of War:

MY DEAR SIR—I send you a dispatch just received, with instructions to deliver it without delay. I have heard nothing from General Wade Hampton except what is mentioned in the inclosed dispatch.

I have answered him at every point along the line, informing that the ferry at this point was in good order and that you had ordered me to hold it till he (General

Hampton) came, which I shall do, regardless of consequences, unless relieved by your order.

Yours, respectfully,

Z. YORK, *Brigadier-General.*

GREENSBORO, April 24th, 6:30 P. M.

Hon. J. C. Breckinridge, Secretary of War:

I have just received dispatches from General Sherman informing me that instructions from Washington direct him to limit his negotiations to my command, demanding its surrender on the terms granted to General Lee, and notifying me of the termination of the truce in forty-eight hours from noon to-day. Have your instructions. We had better disband this small force to prevent devastation of country.

J. E. JOHNSTON, *General.*

HEADQUARTERS, GILBERT'S HOUSE, May 2, 1865.

Major-General J. C. Breckinridge, Secretary of War:

SIR—For the purpose of executing the orders received from you this evening, it is necessary that I be supplied with public funds, the amount turned over to my disbursing officers having been exhausted. I respectfully request that a portion of the funds be furnished in specie, if practicable.

I have the honor to be, General, very respectfully your obedient servant,

BRAXTON BRAGG, *General.*

"My own money all in Confed. paper, and very limited.

"B. B."

CHESTER, 27th April.

General York:

Forward following dispatch by courier to General Breckinridge.

(Sig.) WM. PRESTON JOHNSTON.

Hon. J. C. Breckinridge, Company Shops:

Some time ago I notified General Johnston not to include me in any surrender. You gave me orders to move on (25th). In return I find army surrendered. Think I am free. What is your decision? Answer here and Greensboro.

WADE HAMPTON, *Lieutenant-General.*

LOVES FORD, BROAD RIVER, April 28, 1865.

Lieutenant-General Wade Hampton, Greensboro, Lexington, Salisbury, or any other point on line:

Your dispatches of 27th received. The verbal directions to you contemplated your meeting General Johnston, and his action before any convention with enemy. If my letter to him of 25th, which you carried, was not received before completion of terms, the Government, with its imperfect knowledge of the facts, can not interfere as to the body of the troops; but, in regard to yourself, if not present nor consenting, it is the opinion of the Government that you, and others in like condition, are free to come out.

JOHN C. BRECKINRIDGE, *Secretary of War.*

ORDNANCE DEPARTMENT OF THE CONFEDERATE GOVERNMENT.

BY

BRIGADIER-GENERAL JOSIAH GORGAS,
Chief of Ordnance of the Confederate States.

AT the formation of the Government, or, at the beginning of the war, the arms at command were distributed as follows, as nearly as I can recollect:

SMALL ARMS.

	RIFLES.	MUSKETS.
At Richmond, Va. (about)	4,000	. . .
Fayetteville Arsenal, North Carolina (about)	2,000	25,000
Charleston Arsenal, South Carolina (about)	2,000	20,000
Augusta Arsenal, Georgia (about)	3,000	28,000
Mount Vernon Arsenal, Alabama	2,000	20,000
Baton Rouge Arsenal, Louisiana	2,000	27,000
	15,000	120,000

There were at Richmond about sixty thousand old, worthless flint muskets, and at Baton Rouge about ten thousand old Hall's rifles and carbines.

Besides the foregoing, there were at Little Rock, Ark., a few thousand stands, and some few at the Texas arsenals, increasing the aggregate of serviceable arms to, say, one hundred and forty-three thousand. To these must be added the arms owned by the several States and by military organizations throughout the country, giving, say, one hundred and fifty thousand in all for the use of the armies of the Confederacy. The rifles were of the caliber fifty-four, known as Mississippi rifles, except those at Richmond, taken from Harpers Ferry, which were caliber fifty-eight; the muskets were the old flint-lock, caliber sixty-nine, altered to percussion. Of sabers there were a few boxes at each arsenal, and some short artillery swords. A few hundred holster pistols were scattered here and there. There were no revolvers.

AMMUNITION, POWDER AND LEAD.

There was little ammunition of any kind, or powder, at the arsenals in the South, and that little relics of the Mexican war, stored principally at Baton Rouge and Mount Vernon arsenals. I doubt whether there were a million rounds of small-arm cartridges in the Confederacy. Lead there was none in store. Of powder the chief supply was that captured at Norfolk, though there was a small quantity at each of the Southern arsenals, say sixty thousand pounds in all, chiefly old cannon powder. The stock of percussion caps could not have exceeded one-quarter of a million.

ARTILLERY.

There were no batteries of serviceable field artillery at any of the Southern arsenals. A few old iron guns, mounted on Gribeaural carriages, fabricated about the time of the war of 1812, composed nearly the entire park which the Confederate States fell heir to. There were some serviceable batteries belonging to the States, and some which belonged to volunteer companies. There were neither harness, saddles, bridles, blankets, nor other artillery or cavalry equipments.

Thus to furnish one hundred and fifty thousand men on both sides of the Mississippi, on, say, the 1st of May, 1861, there were on hand no infantry accouterments, no cavalry arms or equipments, no artillery, and, above all, no ammunition; nothing save small arms, and these almost wholly smooth-bore, altered from flint to percussion. Let us see what means we had for producing these supplies.

BRIG.-GEN. JOSIAH GORGAS, OF ALABAMA,
Chief of Ordnance.

ARSENALS, WORKSHOPS, FOUNDRIES, ETC.

Within the limits of the Confederate States there were no arsenals at which any of the material of war was constructed. No arsenal, except that at Fayetteville, N. C., had a single machine above a foot-lathe. Such arsenals as there were had been used only as depots. All the work of preparation of material had been carried on at the North; not an arm, not a gun, not a gun-carriage, and, except during the Mexican war, scarcely a round of ammunition had for fifty years been prepared in the Confederate States. There were, consequently, no workmen, or very few of them, skilled in these arts. No powder, save, perhaps, for blasting, had been made at the South; and there was no saltpeter in store at any point; it was stored wholly at the North. There was no lead, nor any mines of it, except on the northern limit of the Confederacy, in Virginia, and the situation of that made its product precarious. Only one cannon foundry existed—at Richmond. Copper, so necessary for field artillery and for percussion caps, was just being produced in East Tennessee. There was no rolling mill for bar iron south of Richmond, and but few blast furnaces, and these small and, with trifling exceptions, in the border States of Virginia and Tennessee.

Such were the supplies and such the situation when I took charge of the Ordnance Department on the 8th of April, 1861.

The first thing to be attended to was the supply of powder. Large orders had been sent to the North, both by the Confederate Government and some of the States, and these were being rapidly filled at the date of the attack on Fort Sumter. The entire product of one large Northern mill was being received at a Southern port. Of course, all the ports were soon sealed to such importations from the North. Attention was at once turned to the production of niter in North Alabama and in Tennessee—in the latter State under the energetic supervision of its Ordnance Department. An adequate supply of sulphur was found in New Orleans, where large quantities were in store to be used in sugar-refining. The entire stock was secured, amounting to some four or five hundred tons.

The erection of a large powder-mill was early pressed by President Davis, and about the middle of June, 1861, he directed me to detail an officer to select a site and begin the work. The day after this order was given Colonel G. W. Rains, a graduate of West Point, in every way qualified for this service, arrived in Richmond, through the blockade, and at once set out, under written instructions from me, to carry out the President's wishes. He, however, went first to East Tennessee to supervise and systematize the operations of two small private mills, which were then at work for the State of Tennessee.

Thus, in respect to powder and our means of making it, we had, perhaps, at this time (June 1, 1861), two hundred and fifty thousand pounds, chiefly cannon, at Norfolk and in Georgia, and as much more niter (mainly imported by the State of Georgia). We had no powder-mills, except the two rude ones just referred to, and no experience in making powder or in getting niter. All had to be learned.

As to a further supply of arms, steps had been taken by the President to import these and other ordnance stores from Europe; and Major Caleb Huse, a graduate of West Point, and at that moment professor in the University of Alabama, was selected to go abroad and secure them. He left Montgomery, under instructions, early in April, with a credit of ten thousand pounds (!) from Mr. Memminger. The appointment proved a happy one, for he succeeded, with a very little money, in buying a good supply, and in running the Ordnance Department into debt for nearly a half million sterling—the very best proof of his fitness for his place, and of a financial ability which supplemented the narrowness of Mr. Memminger's purse.

Before this, and immediately upon the formation of the Confederate Government, Admiral Semmes had been sent to the North by President Davis as purchasing agent of arms and other ordnance stores, and succeeded in making contracts for, and purchases of, powder, percussion caps, cap machinery (never delivered), revolvers, etc. He also procured drawings for a bullet-pressing machine, and other valuable information.

The sets of machinery for making the rifle with sword bayonet, and the rifle-musket model of 1855, had been seized at Harpers Ferry by the State of Virginia. That for the rifle-musket was being transferred by the State to her ancient armory at Richmond under the direction of Lieutenant-Colonel Burton, an officer in the service of Virginia, whose experience in the armories of the United States and in the erection of the works at Enfield, near London, qualified him above all for the work. The other set of machines was sent to Fayetteville, N. C., by consent of the State of Virginia, to be there re-erected, as there was at that point an arsenal with steam power and some good buildings, which had heretofore never been put to any use. These two sets of machinery—capable, if worked with but one set of hands to each, of producing two thousand to two thousand five hundred stands per month in all—were the only prospective resources at home. With additional workmen and some extension of the machinery, much larger results could be obtained. But the workmen were not to be had. As it was, it would take many months to put it in working order. Parts were missing and some injury done in the hasty transfer (partly under fire*) from Harpers Ferry. There were no private armories at the South; nor was there any inducement, prior to the war, to turn capital in that direction. Thus, the class of skilled operatives needed were unknown to this region. In New Orleans the Brothers Cook were embarking in the business of making small arms, assisted by the purses and encouraged by the sympathy of patriotic citizens.

In field artillery the production was confined almost entirely to the Tredegar Works in Richmond. Some castings were made in New Orleans, and foundries were rapidly acquiring the necessary experience to produce good bronze castings. The Ordnance Department of Tennessee was also turning its attention to the manufacture of field and siege artillery at Nashville. At Rome, Ga., a foundry —Noble & Son—was induced to undertake the casting of three-inch rifles after drawings furnished at Montgomery, but the progress made was necessarily slow. The State of Virginia possessed a number of old four-pounder iron guns, which were reamed out to get a good bore, and were rifled with three grooves, after the manner of Parrott. The army in observation at Harpers Ferry and that at Manas-

*The saving of this machinery from the flames was due to the heroic conduct of the operatives themselves, headed by Mr. Ball, the master armorer, who clung to his machinery, and by the greatest efforts, continued often under fire, saved almost the entire "plant." The names of Mr. Copeland and Major W. S. Downer are also mentioned in this connection. The older brother, Frederick, was a most competent mechanic and a man of decided administrative ability. He was almost the only one who succeeded in producing a good service arm. He was finally killed in the trenches at Savannah, fighting with a command composed of his own operatives.

sas were supplied with old batteries of six-pounder guns and twelve-pounder howitzers. A few Parrott guns, purchased by the State of Virginia, were with Magruder at Big Bethel.

For the ammunition and equipments required for the infantry and artillery a good laboratory and shops had been established at Richmond by the State, but none of the Southern arsenals were yet in a condition to do much work. The arsenal at Augusta, Ga., was directed to organize for the preparation of ammunition and the making of knapsacks, of which there were none wherewith to equip the troops now daily taking the field. The arsenal at Charleston and the depot at Savannah were occupied chiefly with local work. The arsenal at Baton Rouge was rapidly getting under way, and that at Mt. Vernon, Ala., was also being prepared for work. None of them had had facilities for the work usually done at an ranges of our artillery and small arms—unavoidably so, of course. We were only too glad to take any sort of powder; and we bought some brought into Florida, the best range of which scarcely exceeded one hundred and sixty yards with the *eprouvette*.

Contracts were made abroad for the delivery of niter through the blockade, and for producing it at home from caves. The amount of the latter delivered by contracts was considerable—chiefly in Tennessee.

The consumption of lead was in part met by the Virginia Lead Mines (Wytheville), the yield from which was from one hundred thousand to one hundred and fifty thousand pounds per month. A laboratory for the smelting of other ores from the Silver Hill Mines, North Carolina, and Jonesboro, East Tennessee, was put up at Petersburg, under the direction of Dr. Piggott, of Baltimore. It was very well constructed; was capable of smelting a good

FORTS AND BREASTWORKS ON FREDERICKSBURG HEIGHTS, VA.

arsenal. Fayetteville, N. C., was in the hands of that State, and was occupied chiefly in repairing some arms and in making up a small amount of small arm ammunition. Little artillery ammunition was being made up, except for local purposes, save at Richmond.

Such was the general condition of supplies when the Government, quitting Montgomery, established itself at Richmond.

PROGRESS OF MANUFACTURE.

Colonel Rains, in the course of the summer of 1861, established a refinery of saltpeter at or near Nashville, and to this point chiefly were sent the niter obtained from the State of Georgia, and that derived from caves in East and Middle Tennessee. He supplied the two powder mills in that State with niter properly refined, and good powder was thus produced. A small portion of the Georgia niter was sent to two small mills in South Carolina—at Pendleton and Walhalla—and a powder produced, inferior at first but afterward improved. The State of North Carolina established a mill near Raleigh, under contract with certain parties to whom the State was to furnish the niter, of which a great part was derived from caves in Georgia. A stamping mill was also put up near New Orleans, and powder produced before the fall of the city. Small quantities of powder were also received through the blockade from Wilmington to Galveston, some of it of very inferior quality. The great quantity of artillery placed in position from the Potomac to the Rio Grande required a vast supply of powder (there was no immediate want of prejectiles) to furnish even the scant allowance of fifty rounds to each gun. I think we may safely estimate that on the 1st of January, 1862, there were fifteen hundred sea coast guns of various calibers in position from Evansport on the Potomac to Fort Brown on the Rio Grande. If we average their caliber at thirty-two pounders, and the charge at five pounds, it will, at forty rounds per gun, give us six hundred thousand pounds of powder for these. The field artillery, say three hundred guns, with two hundred rounds to the piece, would require, say one hundred and twenty-five thousand pounds, and the small-arm cartridges, ten million, would consume one hundred and twenty-five thousand pounds more—making in all eight hundred and fifty thousand pounds. If we deduct two hundred and fifty thousand pounds, supposed to be on hand in various shapes at the beginning of the war, we have an increment of six hundred thousand pounds. Of this perhaps two hundred thousand pounds had been made at the Tennessee and other mills, leaving four hundred thousand to have been supplied through the blockade and before the commencement of actual hostilities.

The site of the Government Powder-Mills was fixed at Augusta, Ga., on the report of Colonel Rains, and progress was made on the work in this year. There were two large buildings, in the Norman (castellated) style of architecture; one contained the refinery and store-rooms — the other being the mills, twelve in number. They were arranged in the best way on the canal which supplied water-power to Augusta. This canal served as the means of transport for the material from point to point of its manufacture, though the mills were driven by steam. All the machinery, including the very heavy rollers, was made in the Confederate States. The various qualities of powder purchased, captured and produced were sources of irregularity in the

many thousand pounds per day, and was in operation before midsummer of 1862. Mines were opened on account of Government in East Tennessee, near the State Line of Virginia. They were never valuable, and were soon abandoned. Lead was collected in considerable quantities throughout the country by the laborious exertions of agents employed for this purpose. The battle-field of Bull Run was fully gleaned and much lead collected.

By the close of 1861 the following arsenals and depots were at work, having been supplied with some machinery and facilities, and were producing the various munitions and equipments required: Augusta, Ga.; Charleston, S. C.; Fayetteville, N. C.; Richmond, Va.; Savannah, Ga.; Nashville, Tenn.; Memphis, Tenn.; Mount Vernon, Ala.; Baton Rouge, La.; Montgomery, Ala.; Little Rock, Ark., and San Antonio, Texas—altogether eight arsenals and four depots. It would, of course, have been better, had it been practicable, to have condensed our work and to have had fewer places of manufacture; but the country was deficient in the transportation which would have been required to place the raw material at a few arsenals. In this way only could we avail ourselves of local resources, both of labor and material. Thus, by the close of 1861, a good deal had been done in the way of organization to produce the material of war needed by an army, as far as our means permitted. But our troops were still very poorly armed and equipped. The old smooth-bore musket was still the principal weapon of the infantry; the artillery had the 6-pounder gun and 12-pounder howitzer chiefly; and the cavalry were armed with anything they could get — sabers, horse-pistols, revolvers, Sharp's carbines, musketoons, short Enfield rifles, Hale's carbines (a wretched apology), muskets cut off, etc. Equipments were, in many cases, made of stout domestic, stitched in triple folds and covered with paint or rubber, varnished.

But poor as were our arms, we had not enough of these to equip the troops which were pressing to the front in July and August, 1861. In the winter of 1861–'62, while McClellan was preparing his great army near Alexandria, we resorted to the making of pikes for the infantry and lances for the cavalry; many thousands of the former were made at the various arsenals, but were little used. No access of enthusiasm could induce our people to rush to the field armed with pikes. I remember a formidable weapon, which was invented at this time, in the shape of a stout wooden sheath containing a two-edged straight sword some two feet long. The sheath or truncheon could be leveled, and the sword, liberated from the compression of a strong spring by touching a trigger, leaped out with sufficient force to transfix an opponent.

About December, 1861, arms began to come in through the purchases of Major Huse, and we had a good many Enfield rifles in the hands of our troops at Shiloh, which were received in time for use there through the blockade. Major Huse had found the market pretty well cleaned of arms by the late war in Europe, but he had succeeded in making contracts with private manufacturers, of which these arms were the result.

I will not attempt to trace the development of our work in its order, as I at first intended, but will note simply what I can recollect, paying some attention to the succession of events.

The winter of 1861–'2 was the darkest period of my department. Powder was called for on every hand—Bragg, at Pensacola, for his big 10-inch columbiads; Lovell, at New Orleans, for his extended defenses, and especially for his inadequate artillery at Forts Jackson and St. Phillips; Polk, at Columbus, Ky.; Johnston, for his numerous batteries on the Potomac; Magruder, at Yorktown. All these were deemed most important points. Then came Wilmington, Georgetown, Port Royal and Fernandina. Not a few of these places sent representatives to press their claims—Mr. Yulee, from Fernandina, and Colonel Gonzales, from Charleston. Heavy guns, too, were called for in all directions—the largest guns for the smallest places.

The abandonment of the line of the Potomac and of the upper Mississippi, from Columbus to Memphis; the evacuation of the works below Pensacola and of Yorktown somewhat relieved us from the pressure for heavy artillery; and after the powder mills at Augusta went into operation in the fall of 1862, we had little trouble in supplying ammunition.

To obtain the iron needed for cannon and projectiles, it became necessary to stimulate its production in Virginia, North Carolina, Tennessee, Georgia and Alabama. To this end, contracts were made with ironmasters in these States on liberal terms and advances of money made to them, to be refunded in products. These contracts were difficult to arrange, as so much had to be done for the contractor. He must have details from the army and the privilege of transport of provisions and other supplies over the railroads. And then the question of the currency was a continually recurring problem. Mr. Benjamin, who succeeded Mr. Walker in the War Department, gave me great assistance in the matter of making contracts, and seemed quite at home in arranging these details. His power of work was amazing to me, and he appeared as fresh at 12 o'clock at night, after a hard day's work, as he had been at 9 o'clock in the morning.

About May, 1862, finding that the production of niter and of iron must be systematically pursued, and to this end thoroughly organized, I sought for the right person to place in charge of this vital duty. My choice fell on Colonel I. M. St. John (afterward Commissary-General of Subsistence), and was eminently fortunate. He had the gift of organization, and I placed him in charge of the whole subject of producing niter from caves and from other sources, and of the formation of niter beds, which had already been begun in Richmond. Under his supervision beds were instituted at Columbia, S. C., Charleston, Savannah, Augusta, Mobile, Selma and various other points. We never extracted niter from these beds, except for trial; but they were carefully attended to, enriched and extended, and were becoming quite valuable. At the close of 1864 we had, according to General St. John, 2,800,000 cubic feet of earth collected and in various stages of nitrification, of which a large proportion was prepared to yield one and a half pounds of niter per foot of earth, including all the niter beds from Richmond to Florida.

Through Colonel St. John, the whole niter-bearing area of country was laid off into districts; each district in

WHERE A BATTERY FOUGHT.

charge of an officer, who made his monthly reports to the office at Richmond. These officers procured details of workmen, generally from those subject to military duty in the mountain regions where disaffection existed, and carried on extended works in their several districts. In this way we brought up the niter production, in the course of a year, to something like half our total consumption of niter. It was a rude, wild sort of service; and the officers in charge of these districts, especially in East Tennessee, North Carolina and North Alabama, had to show much firmness in their dealings with the turbulent people among whom and by whose aid they worked. It is a curious fact that the district on which we could rely for the most constant yield of niter, having its headquarters at Greensboro, N. C., had no niter caves in it. The niter was produced by the lixiviation of nitrous earth dug from under old houses, barns, etc.

The niter production thus organized, there was added to the Niter Bureau the duty of supervising the production of iron, lead, copper, and, in fine, all the minerals which needed development, including the making of sulphuric and nitric acids; which latter we had to manufacture to insure a supply of fulminate of mercury for our percussion caps. To give an idea of the extent of the duty thus performed: Colonel Morton, Chief of the Niter and Mining Bureau, after the transfer of General St. John, writes: "We were aiding and managing some twenty to thirty furnaces, with an annual yield of fifty thousand tons or more of pig metal. We had erected lead and copper smelting furnaces [at Petersburg, before referred to] with a capacity sufficient for all our wants, and had succeeded in smelting zinc of good quality at the same place." The

A Battery of Flying Artillery.
The cannoneers being mounted, this arm of the service was enabled to move with great rapidity, and was usually detailed to operate with the cavalry.

chemical works were placed at Charlotte, N. C., where a pretty large leaden chamber for sulphuric acid was put up. Our chief supply of chemicals continued to come however from abroad, through the blockade, and these works, as well as our nitraries, were as much preparation against the day when the blockade might seal all foreign supply, as for present use. These constituted our reserves for final conflict.

We had not omitted to have a pretty thorough though general exploration of the mountain regions from Virginia to Alabama, with the hope of finding new deposits of lead. One of the earliest of these searches was made by Dr. Maupin, of the University of Virginia. No favorable results came from it. I remember an anecdote he told touching one of his researches. An old settler showed the doctor a small lump of lead which he had extracted from ore like some he had in his possession. There was the lead and here was the ore, but it was not an ore of lead. The doctor cross-examined: "Did he smelt it himself?" "Yes." "What in?" "An iron ladle," such as is used for running lead balls. "Was there nothing in the ladle but this sort of ore?" "No, nothing." "Nothing at all? No addition—no flux?" "No, nothing but a little handful of common shot, thrown in to make it melt more easily!"

Much of the niter region was close to the lines of the enemy, and here and there along its great extent became debatable ground. Not seldom the whole working force had to be suddenly withdrawn on the approach of the enemy, the "plant" hurried off, to be again returned and work resumed when the enemy had retired. Much of the work, too, lay in "Union" districts, where our cause was unpopular and where obstacles of all kinds had to be encountered and overcome. It was no holiday duty, this niter digging, although the service was a good deal decried by such as knew nothing of its nature.

MANUFACTURE OF INFANTRY, ARTILLERY AND CAVALRY EQUIPMENTS.

In equipping the armies first sent into the field the supply of these accessories was amazingly scant; and these deficiencies were felt more keenly, perhaps, than the more important want of arms. We had arms, such as they were, for over one hundred thousand men; but we had no accouterments nor equipments; and these had to be extemporized in a great measure. In time, knapsacks were little thought of by the troops, and we at last contented ourselves with supplying haversacks, which the women (Heaven reward their labors) could make, and for which we could get cotton cloth. But cartridge boxes we *must* have; and as leather was also needed for artillery harness and cavalry saddles, we had to divide the stock of leather the country could produce among these much-needed articles. But soldiers' shoes were even more needed than some of these; so that as all could not be fully provided, a scale of preference was established. Shoes and cartridge boxes were most needed, and then saddles and bridles. The President, whose practical sagacity was rarely at fault, early reduced these interests to logical sequence. He said, "For the infantry, men must first be fed, next armed, and even clothing must follow these; for if they are fed and have arms and ammunition they can fight." Thus the Subsistence Department had, in a general way, a preference for its requisitions on the Treasury; my department came next, and the Quartermaster's followed. Of course the Medical Department had in some things the lead of all, for its duties referred to the men themselves, and it was necessary first of all to keep the hospitals empty and the ranks full.

To economize leather, the cartridge-boxes and waist-belts were made of prepared cotton cloth, stitched in three or four thicknesses. Bridle-reins were also so made, and even cartridge-boxes covered with it, except the flap. Saddle skirts, too, were sometimes made in this way, heavily stitched. An ardent admirer of the South came over from Washington to offer his patent for making sholdiers' shoes with no leather except the soles. The shoes were approved by all except those who wore them. The soldiers exchanged them with the first prostrate enemy who no longer needed his leathern articles. To get leather each department bargained for its own hides—made contracts with the tanner—procured hands for him by exemption from the army—got transportation over the railroads for the hides and for supplies, and, finally, assisted the tanner to procure food for his hands and other supplies for his tannery. One can readily see from this instance how the labors of the heads of the departments became extended. Nothing but thorough organization could accomplish these multiplied and varied duties. We even established a fishery on the Cape Fear River to get oil for mechanical purposes, getting from the sturgeon *beef* at the same time for our workmen.

In cavalry equipments the main thing was to get a good saddle—one that did not ruin the back of the horse; for that, and not the rider's seat, is the point to be achieved. The rider soon accommodates himself to the seat provided for him. Not so the animal's back, which suffers from a bad saddle. We adopted Jenifer's tree, which did very well while the horses were in good condition, and was praised by that prince of cavalrymen, General J. E. B. Stuart; but it came down on the horse's backbone and withers as soon as the cushion of fat and muscle dwindled. The McClellan tree did better on the whole, and we finally succeeded in making a pretty good saddle of that kind—comfortable enough, but not as durable as the Federal article. In this branch of the service, one of the most difficult wants to supply was the horseshoe for cavalry and artillery. The want of iron and labor both were felt. Of course such a thing as a horseshoe machine, to turn out thousands an hour, was not to be dreamed of; besides, we would have had little store of iron wherewith to feed it. Nor could we set up such machinery without much provision; for to concentrate all work on one machine required the transportation of the iron to one point, and the distribution of the shoes from it to all the armies. But the railroads were greatly overtasked, and we were compelled to consider this point. Thus we were led to employ every wayside blacksmith shop accessible, especially those in and near the theater of operations. These, again, had to be looked after, supplied with material, and exempted from service.

BUREAU OF FOREIGN SUPPLIES.

It soon became obvious that in the Ordnance Department we must rely greatly on the introduction of articles of prime necessity through the blockade ports. As before stated, President Davis early saw this, and had an officer detailed to go abroad as the agent of the department. To systematize the introduction of the purchases, it was soon found advisable to own and run our own steamers. Major Huse made the suggestion also from that side of the water. Accordingly, he purchased and sent in the Robert E. Lee at a cost of £30,000, a vessel capable of stowing six hundred and fifty bales of cotton. This vessel was kept running between Bermuda and Wilmington, and made some fifteen to eighteen successive trips before she was finally captured—the first twelve with the regularity of a packet. She was commanded first by Captain Wilkinson, of the navy. Soon the Cornubia, named the Lady Davis, was added, and ran as successfully as the R. E. Lee. She had a capacity of about four hundred and fifty bales, and was, during the latter part of her career, commanded also by a former naval officer, Captain R. H. Gayle. These vessels were long, low and rather narrow, built for swiftness, and with their lights out and with fuel that made little smoke they contrived to slip in and out of Wilmington at pleasure, in spite of a cordon of Federal cruisers eager for the spoils of a blockade runner. Other vessels—the Eugenia, a beautiful ship, the Stag and several others—were added, all devoted to carrying ordnance supplies, and finally general supplies. To supervise shipments at Bermuda, to which point they were brought by neutrals, either by steam or sail, Major Norman Walker was sent there by Mr. Secretary Randolph, about midsummer, 1862. Later, an army officer, Lieutenant-Colonel Smith Stansbury, was detached to take charge of the stores accumulated there. Depots were likewise made at Nassau and Havana. Thus much of the foreign organization.

But the organization of the business outside of our own soil was much the simplest part of the service. The home administration involved a variety of work so foreign to my other duties that I soon looked about for the proper person to discharge them in the most effective manner by exclusive devotion to them; and I had Lieutenant-Colonel Bayne detailed to my office for this duty. He had been wounded at Shiloh, and on his recovery joined me about September, 1862.

It was soon found necessary, in order that the vessels coming in through the blockade might have their lading promptly on their arrival, that the bureau should undertake the procuring and shipment of cotton to Wilmington, Charleston and other points, for we had vessels arriving at half a dozen ports from Wilmington to Galveston. This necessitated the establishment of a steam compress at Wilmington, and, affiliated with it, agents to procure the cotton in the interior and see it to its destination; for the railroads were now so overtasked that it was only by placing positive orders from the Secretary of War in the hands of a selected agent that the cotton could be certainly forwarded over the various roads. The steam press was kept fully at work, in charge of Captain James M. Seixas (Washington Artillery). The necessity for transportation over the railroads brought us in contact with them, and

Horrors of War.
[From a photograph taken in the "Wheatfield" at Gettysburg, July 4, 1863.]

gave them claim on us for assistance in the matter of supplies, such as steel, iron, copper, etc., and especially for work at the various foundries and machine-shops, in which precedence was, of course, claimed for army work, and which were, therefore, in great part controlled by the Ordnance Department. The foreign supplies were not all conveyed through steamers. Contracts were out for supplies through Texas from Mexico.

Finding that the other departments of the Government would naturally claim a share in this avenue for supplies, which had been opened chiefly through my bureau, it was detached at my own instance, but remained in charge of Colonel Bayne, with a good staff of officers and agents, as a separate bureau.

Thus the Ordnance Department consisted of a Bureau proper of Ordnance, having its officers in the field and at the arsenals and depots; of the Niter and Mining Bureau, and of the Bureau of Foreign Supplies.

GROUP OF FEDERAL DEAD AT GETTYSBURG, PA.
These soldiers were killed by a single discharge of canister-shot and were photographed soon after the battle, just as they fell.

DEVELOPMENT OF THE ARSENALS, ARMORIES AND OTHER PLACES OF MANUFACTURE OF ORDNANCE STORES.

The arsenal at Richmond soon grew into very large dimensions, and produced all the ordnance stores that an army may require, except cannon and small arms in quantities sufficient to supply the forces in that part of the field. I have, by accident, preserved a copy of the last number of the Richmond *Enquirer*, published under Confederate rule. It is dated April 1, 1865, and contains the following "Statement of the principal issues from the Richmond arsenal from July 1, 1861, to January 1, 1865":

"Three hundred and forty-one columbiads and siege guns (these were made at the Tredegar works, but issued from the arsenal); 1,306 field-pieces, made chiefly at Tredegar works or captured; 1,375 gun carriages; 875 caissons; 152 forges; 6,852 sets of artillery-harness; 921,441 rounds field, siege and sea-coast ammunition; 1,456,190 friction primer; 1,110,966 fuses; 17,423 port-fires; 3,985 rockets; 323,231 infantry arms (most of these were turned in from the army, from battlefields and from the Richmond armory); 34,067 cavalry arms (same remark); 44,877 swords and sabers (from army, battlefield and contractors); 375,510 sets of infantry and cavalry accouterments; 180,181 knapsacks; 328,977 canteens and straps; 72,413,854 small-arm cartridges; 115,087 gun and carbine slings; 146,901,250 percussion caps; 69,418 cavalry-saddles; 85,139 cavalry-bridles; 75,611 cavalry-halters; 35,464 saddle-blankets; 59,624 pairs spurs; 42,285 horse-brushes; 56,903 curry-combs."

This "statement" appears as an editorial, but the items were furnished from the office of the arsenal, and may be relied on. Its commandant at this time was Lieutenant-Colonel LeRoy Broun, of Virginia. In the items of cavalry-saddles, bridles, harness, infantry accouterments, canteens and other articles of this character much assistance was received from contractors. A small part of the percussion caps also came from other arsenals. When we reflect that the arsenal grew to these great dimensions in a little over two years, it must be confessed that good use was made of the time. The laboratory attached to the arsenal was well conducted and did much work. It covered the island known as Green Island, which was connected with the shore by a bridge built by the Engineer Department especially for the service of this laboratory.

Besides the cap machinery, which was a very large and improved plant, machinery for pressing balls, for driving time fuses, for drawing friction primers and metallic cartridges and other labor-saving machines were invented, made and used with effect. In all respects the establishment, though extemporized and lodged in a cluster of tobacco warehouses, was equal to the first-class arsenals of the United States in extent and facilities.

The arsenal of Augusta, Ga., was in great part organized in the city, where suitable buildings were obtained, and did much the same class of work done at Richmond, though on a smaller scale. It was very serviceable to the armies serving in the South and West, and turned out a good deal of field artillery complete, the castings being excellent. Colonel George W. Rains, in charge of arsenal and powder works, found that the fusion of a small per cent of iron with the copper and tin improved the strength of the bronze castings very much.

The powder mills at Augusta, Ga., which I have already mentioned as the direct result of the order of President Davis, were wonderfully successful and never met with serious accident—a safe indication of the goodness of its arrangements. It showed, too, that, under able direction, the resources of Southern workshops and the skill of its artisans had already become equal to the execution of great enterprises involving high mechanical skill.

The arsenal and workshops at Charleston were also enlarged, steam introduced, and good work done in various departments.

The arsenal at Mount Vernon, now furnished with steam power and having a good deal of machinery, was considered out of position after the fall of New Orleans, and was moved to Selma, Ala., where it grew into a large, well-ordered arsenal of the best class, under the charge of Lieutenant-Colonel White. It was relied on to a great extent for the equipment of the troops and fortifications in the southern part of the Confederacy.

Attracted by the deposits of fine ore immediately north of Selma, made accessible by the Selma, Rome & Dalton Railroad, the War Department accepted the proposition of Mr. Colin McRae to undertake the erection at Selma of a large foundry for the casting of cannon of the heaviest caliber. A large contract was made with him and advances of money made from time to time as the work progressed. After a time Mr. McRae was called on by President Davis to go abroad in connection with Confederate finances. He made it a condition that he should be relieved of his works and contract at Selma without pecuniary loss to himself. The works were thereupon assumed by the War and Navy Departments jointly, and placed at first under the charge of Colonel Rains as general superintendent, while an officer of less rank took immediate charge. Subsequently it was agreed by the War Department that the Navy should take sole charge, and use the works for its own purposes. It was here that Commander Brooke made many of his formidable banded and rifled guns.

The foundry and rolling-mills then grew into large proportions, supplied by the iron and coal of that region. Had the Confederacy survived, Selma bid fair to become the Pittsburg of the South. The iron obtained from the brown hæmatite at the furnaces in Bibb County (Brierfield), and from the Shelby Works, was admirable, the former being of unusual strength.

Mount Vernon Arsenal was still continued, after being in a great measure dismantled, and was utilized to get lumber and timber for use elsewhere, and to gather and prepare moss for making saddle-blankets.

At Montgomery shops were kept up for the repair of small arms, and for the manufacture of articles of leather, of which some supplies were obtained in that region.

There were many other small establishments and depots, some of them connected immediately with the army, as at Dublin, Southwest Va.; Knoxville, Tenn.; and Jackson, Miss. Some shops at Lynchburg, Va., were moved to Danville, near the south line of Virginia, and it grew into a place of some value for repairs, etc.

The Ordnance shops at Nashville had been hurriedly transferred to Atlanta, Ga., on the fall of Fort Donelson; and when Atlanta was seriously threatened by the operations of Sherman, the arsenal there, which had become very important, was moved to Columbus, Ga., where there was the nucleus of an Ordnance establishment. Colonel M. H. Wright soon made this nearly as valuable as his arsenal at Atlanta had been.

ARMORIES AND SMALL ARMS.

Besides the arsenals, a brief account of which has just been given, we had the armories at Richmond and Fayetteville, N. C.; and arms were also made at other points.

The State of Virginia claimed all the machinery captured at Harpers Ferry, and was bringing it all to Richmond. It was agreed, however, with the State of North Carolina that that part of the machinery which was specially adapted to make the Mississippi rifle (caliber 54) should go to Fayetteville, where there was an arsenal with good steam-power, the machinery to be returned at the close of the war to the State of Virginia. Colonel Burton, an admirably-educated machinist, superintended the re-erection of the works at Richmond. He was subsequently made Superintendent of Armories, and given full charge of the entire subject of manufacture of arms in the Confederacy. The machinery of the rifle-musket (caliber 58), retained at Richmond, got to work as early as September, 1861. If we had possessed the necessary number of workmen this "plant" could have been so filled in as to have easily produced 5,000 stands per month, working night and day. As it was, I don't think it ever turned out more than 1,500 in any one month. Fayetteville did not get to work until the spring of 1862, and did not average 400 per month, for want of hands.

To supplement this scarcity of operatives, Colonel Huse was authorized to engage for us a number of skilled workmen, used to work on small arms, and to pay their passage over. They came in through the blockade at Wilmington without difficulty, but we could do nothing with

CONFEDERATE DEAD IN FRONT OF THE DUNKER CHURCH, ANTIETAM.
A battery of light artillery was posted in front of the church. This view shows where one gun of the battery stood. The dead artillerymen and horses, and the shell-holes through the little church, show how terrible a fire was rained on the spot by Federal batteries.

them. They had been engaged to be paid in gold, which meantime had risen to such a price as to make their pay enormous, and would have produced utter disintegration among our own operatives. I offered to pay one-half of the wages promised them in gold, to their families in England, if they would take the remainder in Confederate money, which would support them here. I brought the British Consul to confer with them. But they stood upon their bond; and foreseeing that their presence would do more harm than good, I simply, with their consent, reshipped them by the next steamer, and paid their passage back. The experiment cost us something like £2,000

UNBURIED DEAD ON THE BATTLEFIELD
Sometimes the exigencies of war made it impossible for either army to bury its dead.

in gold, and made us shy of foreign workmen, especially English. I think the Treasury Department did succeed in getting engravers and printers for their purposes at Columbia, S. C., to some extent by importation; but my impression is they were not English. Of all obstinate animals I have ever come in contact with, these English workmen were the most unreasonable.

The Cook Brothers had, as heretofore stated, undertaken the making of rifle-muskets in New Orleans at the very commencement of the war. On the fall of New Orleans their machinery was hurriedly taken off by boats up the Mississippi They finally selected Athens, Georgia, as their point of manufacture, and under a contract with me, and assisted with funds under that contract, proceeded to reorganize and extend their "plant." They were reasonably successful.

The want of cavalry arms caused me to make a contract with parties in Richmond to make the Sharp's carbine—at that time the best cavalry arm we had. A set of machinery capable of turning out one hundred arms a day was driven to completion in less than a year, nearly all the machinery being built up "from the stumps." The arms were never perfect, chiefly for want of nice workmanship about the "cut-off." It was not gas-tight. We soon bought out the establishment, and converted it into a manufactory of rifle-carbines, caliber fifty-eight, as the best arm our skill would enable us to supply to the cavalry.

Recognizing the necessity of some great central establishment for the production of small arms, plans of buildings and estimates of machinery were made for such a one, to be built at Macon, Ga.,—a point of easy access and near to a fertile corn region, out of the way of the enemy. Colonel Burton went to England and easily negotiated for the machinery, which was to have been of sufficient capacity to turn out about ten thousand arms per month. Buildings were immediately obtained for some machinery for pistols, which was transferred there; and Colonel Burton had made good progress in erecting ample buildings for the new machinery, part of which had arrived at Bermuda and Nassau when the Confederacy fell. But about six months before the close of the war, finding that the blockade had become so stringent that the introduction of machinery would be very difficult, and reflecting, too, that as long as the war continued this extended machinery would be of but little use to us, for want of workmen, I got the authority of the Secretary of War to set it up at some point abroad and bring in the arms, which would be less difficult than to bring in the machinery and train the workmen. Colonel Burton was abroad on this duty when the war closed. Had the war been prolonged, we should in twelve months have been making our own arms in a foreign land, under the sanction of a private name. After the war it was proposed to transfer the entire "plant" to the buildings which were in course of construction for it at Macon. Peace would have then found us in possession of a great armory, which I much desired.

One of the earliest difficulties forced upon us in the manufacture of arms was to find an iron fit for the barrels. The "skelps" found at Harpers Ferry served for awhile, and when these were exhausted Colonel Burton selected an iron produced at a forge in Patrick County, Va., and by placing a skilled workman over the rolling process at the Tredegar Works he soon produced "skelps" with which he was satisfied. We found that almost any of the good brown hæmatite ores produced an iron of ample strength for the purpose, and the even grain and toughness could be attained by careful rerolling.

Besides the larger armories at Richmond and Fayetteville, smaller establishments grew up at Asheville, N. C., and at Tallassee, Ala. The former was the development of a private enterprise undertaken to repair and fit up old arms, by a citizen (Mr. Pullem) resident there, and afterward as a matter of necessity assumed by the Confederate Government. Most of the machinery was moved before the close of the war to Columbia, S. C., whither, as a place of safety, other arms-manufacturing machinery was moved from other points. Tallassee was selected as a good manufacturing point, a large building having been offered to us by the proprietors of the cotton mills there, and some machinery for making pistols moved thither from Columbus, Ga.

A great part of the work of our armories consisted in repairing arms brought in from the battlefield or sent in from the armies in too damaged a condition to be effectually repaired at the arsenals. In this way only could we utilize all the gleanings of the battlefields. My recollection is that we saved nearly ten thousand stands of arms from the field of Bull Run, and that the battlefields about Richmond in 1862 gave us about twenty-five thousand excellent arms through the labors of the armory at Richmond.

The original stock of arms, it will be remembered, consisted almost wholly of smooth-bore muskets,

WOUNDED BEING CARRIED FROM THE HOSPITAL, TO BE TRANSPORTED SOUTH.

altered from flint to percussion, using ounce balls (caliber 69). There were some 15,000 to 20,000 Mississippi rifles; and then some irregular arms, like Hall's rifles and carbines—some short carbines smooth-bore; and there were even some of the old flint-lock muskets. All this original stock disappeared almost wholly from our armies in the first two years of the war, and were replaced by a better class of arms, rifled and percussioned. It is pretty safe to assume that we had altogether, east and west of the Mississippi, 300,000 infantry, pretty well armed, by the middle of 1863. We must therefore have procured at least that number for our troops. But we must also have supplied the inevitable waste of two years of active warfare. Placing the good arms thus lost at the moderate estimate of 100,000, we must have received from various sources 400,000 stands of infantry arms in the two years of fighting ending July 1, 1863. I can only estimate from memory the several sources from which this supply was derived, as follows:

Good rifled arms on hand at the beginning of the war (this includes the arms in the hands of volunteer companies)	25,000
New arms manufactured in the Confederacy and in private establishments	40,000
Arms received from the battlefields and put in good order (this includes the great number of arms picked up by the soldiers)	150,000
Imported from January 1, 1862, to July 1, 1863	185,000
Total	400,000

This estimate does not include pistols and sabers, of which a small supply was imported.

To account for the very large number obtained from the enemy (rather an under than an over estimate), it must be remembered that in some fights, where our troops were not finally successful, they were so at first, and swept over the camps and positions of the enemy. Whenever a Confederate soldier saw a weapon better than his own he took it and left his inferior arm; and although he may have been finally driven back, he kept his improved musket. So, too, on every field there were partial successes, which in the early part of the war resulted in improved weapons; and although on another part of the field there may have been a reverse, the enemy had not the same advantage; the Confederate arms being generally inferior to those of their adversaries. The difference of arms was not so marked at a later day, except in cavalry arms, in which we were always at a disadvantage, the celebrated Spencer carbine being generally in the hands of the enemy's cavalry during the last two years of the war.

A CENTRAL LABORATORY.

The unavoidable variation in the ammunition made at the different arsenals, pointed out, early in the war, that there should be a general superintendent of all the laboratories, invested with authority to inspect and supervise their manipulations and materials. To this end Lieutenant-Colonel Mallet, a chemist and scientist of distinction, who had for some years been professor in the University of Alabama, was selected and placed in charge of this delicate and important duty. I attribute much of the improvement in our ammunition to this happy selection. A more earnest and capable officer I can not imagine. What a set of men we would have had after the war out of which to form an ordnance department had we been successful! Rains, St. John, Mallet, Burton, Wright, White, Baldwin, Rhett, Ellicott, Andrews, Childs, DeLagnel, Hutter and others, who would have remained in the service. Then there were some no less admirable, like LeRoy Broun, Allan, Wiley Browne, Morton, Colston, Bayne, Cuyler, E. B. Smith, etc., who would doubtless have returned to their civil avocations.

Among the obvious necessities of a well-regulated service was one large central laboratory, where all ammunition should be made—thus securing absolute uniformity where uniformity was vital. The policy of dissemination so necessary to husband our transportation and to utilize the labor of non-combatants must here yield to the greater necessity of obtaining our ammunition uniform in quality and in dimensions. Authority was, therefore, obtained from the War Department to concentrate this species of work at some central laboratory. Macon, Ga., was selected, and Colonel Mallet placed in charge of the central laboratory, as Burton was later placed in charge of a national armory. Plans of the buildings and of the machinery required were submitted to the Secretary of War, approved, and the work begun with energy. This pile of buildings had a facade of 600 feet, was designed with taste, and comprehended every possible appliance for good and well-organized work. The buildings were nearly ready for occupation at the close of the war, and some of the machinery had arrived at Bermuda. In point of time, this project preceded that of the national armory, and was much nearer completion. These, with our admirable powder mills at Augusta, would have completed a set of works for the Ordnance Department; and in them we would have

LAID OUT FOR BURIAL.
The above is from a photograph of Confederate dead in front of Atlanta, Ga., awaiting identification and burial.

been in condition to supply arms and munitions to three hundred thousand men. To these would have been added a foundry for heavy guns at Selma or Brierfield, Ala., at which latter place the strongest cast-iron in the country was produced, and where we had already purchased and were carrying on a furnace for the production of cold-blast charcoal pig for this special purpose. All these establishments were in the heart of the country not readily reached by the enemy, and were, in fact, never reached by them until just at the close of the war. Being in or near an excellent agricultural region, they would have had the advantage of cheap living for operatives; and they had all sufficient facilities for transportation, being situated on main lines of railroad.

SUMMARY.

I have thus, from memory, faintly traced the development of the means and resources by which our large armies were supplied with arms and ammunition. This involved manufacturing, mining and importation. The last two were confided in time to sub-bureaus created *ex necessitate*, which were subsequently detached. The first was carried on by the armories, arsenals, laboratories and depots above mentioned. We began in April, 1861, without an arsenal, laboratory or powder mill of any capacity, and with no foundry or rolling mill, except at Richmond, and before the close of 1863, in little over two years, we had built up, during all the harassments of war, holding our own in the field defiantly and successfully against a powerful and determined enemy. Crippled as we were by a depreciated currency; throttled with a blockade that deprived us of nearly all means of getting material or workmen; obliged to send almost every able-bodied man to the field; unable to use the slave labor with which we were abundantly supplied, except in the most unskilled departments of production; hampered by want of transportation even of the commonest supplies of food; with no stock on hand even of the articles, such as steel, copper, lead, iron, leather, which we must have to build up our establishments; and in spite of these deficiencies we persevered at home as determinedly as did our troops in the field against a more tangible opposition, and in a little over two years created, almost literally out of the ground, foundries and rolling mills (at Selma, Richmond, Atlanta and Macon); smelting works (at Petersburg), chemical works (at Charlotte, N. C.), a powder mill far superior to any in the United States and unsurpassed by any across the ocean, and a chain of arsenals, armories and laboratories equal in their capacity and their improved appointments to the best of those in the United States, stretching link by link from Virginia to Alabama. Our people are justly proud of the valor and constancy of the troops which bore their banners bravely in the front of the enemy; but they will also reflect that these creations of skill and labor were the monuments which represented the patience, industry and perseverance of the devoted and patriotic citizens; for of the success which attended the operations of any department of the Confederate Government the larger moiety was due to the co-operation of the body of the people—a co-operation founded in their hearty sympathy with and their entire faith in the cause which that government represented.

ORGANIZATION.

The Ordnance Bureau, as finally organized, consisted of one brigadier-general, one colonel, and of such additional number of field-officers, captains and first lieutenants as the service required. They were artillery officers on ordnance duty.

Appointments to these positions were at first made by selection, on nomination by the Ordnance Bureau, but about October, 1862, Congress created fifty officers of artillery especially for ordnance duty, to which two hundred more were subsequently added. As selection for these offices involved much political contrivance, I obtained the order of the Secretary of War to hold examinations for appointment to the grade of captain and first lieutenant. This plan succeeded entirely and relieved us from a thousand personal solicitations. The first examination was held at Richmond. Of some five hundred applications found on file for ordnance officers, less than one hundred came to the examination, and of these only some forty or fifty passed. The examination for captain involved a fair knowledge of a college course of mathematics, and none, I believe, passed this, except the M. A.'s of the University of Virginia. That for first lieutenant embraced only an ordinary English education, with a full examination on the Ordnance Manual. This gave us an excellent set of officers—educated men; and although a few of them were, as was said, "Virginia school-masters," and can not be said to have distinguished themselves professionally, yet they were all respectable on account of their education, and I am sure there never were in any army a better class of such officers.

Scene in the Trenches at Petersburg, Va.

These examinations were extended, and were held at the heaquarters of each army in the field by a commission, of which Lieutenant-Colonel Le Roy Broun and Lieutenant-Colonel S. Stansbury, Colonel T. A. Rhett and Major J. Wilcox Browne were the chief members. These, or one of them, went to an army and associated with themselves one or more officers detailed by the general at headquarters. In order to provide for that class of valuable officers, distinguished for excellent qualities developed by service on the field but not prepared for a somewhat technical examination, each general of an army designated one or two of this class, who were appointed on his recommendation alone.

Officers in the field were distributed as follows: To each army a "chief ordnance officer," with the rank of lieutenant-colonel; to each army corps, an ordnance officer with the rank of major; to each division, a captain, and to each brigade a first lieutenant; all these attached to the staff of their respective generals, but reporting also directly, if necessary, to the ordnance officer, through his superior in the field, and receiving instructions as to special duties through the same channel. Every regiment had an ordnance sergeant in charge of ordnance wagon, containing the spare arms and the ammunition of each regiment.

In the Trenches—After a Charge.

Mutilated Confederate Soldier.

The officers in command of the greater ordnance establishments—such as Richmond and Augusta, etc.—had the grade of lieutenant-colonel, like the "chief ordnance officers" of armies in the field, while at the lesser establishments the officers had rank according to the gravity of the duties devolving on them.

The Superintendent of Armories, Lieutenant-Colonel Burton, and the Superintendent of Laboratories, Lieutenant-Colonel Mallet, had also the grade of the higher officers on duty in the field.

The labors and reponsibilities of my department closed practically at Charlotte, N. C., on the 26th of April, when the President left that place with an escort for the Trans-Mississippi. My last stated official duty, that I can recall, was to examine a cadet in the Confederate service for promotion to commissioned officer.

On the afternoon of the 25th of April I received due formal notice from the Adjutant-General's office that General Lawton, Quartermaster-General, General Gilmer, Chief Engineer, and I were constituted a Board of Examiners on Cadet —— We met a little before sundown, in the ample upper story of a warehouse in Charlotte, N. C., and by the waning light of the last day of the Confederate Government, we went through all the stages of an examination of an expectant lieutenant of the Confederate armies. Lawton, I think, took him on geography and history, Gilmer on the mathematics, while I probably tested his English grammar. He passed the ordeal in triumph and got his commission, which I dare say he prizes very highly, as he ought to do, considering the august body that signed the certificate which pronounced him qualified for it.

DETACHED OBSERVATIONS.

Consumption of Small-Arm Cartridges.

It appears that the Richmond laboratory made 72,000,000 cartridges in three and a half years, say one thousand working days. As this laboratory made nearly as much as all the others combined, we may safely place the entire production at 150,000,000, or 150,000 per day. As our reserves remained nearly the same, being but slightly increased toward the latter part of the war, there must have been only a little less than this consumption in the field, say half a cartridge per man per day for the average force of 300,000 men, to cover all the accidents and expenditures of service in the field. An average, then, of half a cartridge per day per man would be a safe assumption for protracted warfare.

In examining the returns of ordnance officers after heavy actions, I found that the reduction of ammunition amounted to from about nineteen to twenty-six rounds per man. At Gettysburg the reports of a few days before the battle and a short time after showed a difference of twenty-five or twenty-six rounds on the average. This was the heaviest consumption to which my attention was called. When our troops first took the field commanders were very nervous because they had only fifty to seventy rounds per man instead of the two hundred rounds prescribed by the Ordnance Manual. Later we raised it to about eighty or ninety rounds. The results of battles show that with proper dispositions for transfer from one corps to another there need be no scarcity with sixty rounds on hand, or even fifty.

Our soldiers were, however, in the habit of supplying themselves with ammunition by throwing away their empty cartridge-boxes and taking any well-supplied one that they might espy with the proper cartridges. What splendid fellows they were, taking even better care of their powder and lead than of themselves or of their rations. They were in downright earnest.

Consumption and Supply of Lead.

Allowing for waste, 150,000,000 of cartridges would require 10,000,000 pounds of lead for these alone, to say nothing of other needs. Where did all this lead come from? I make the following rough calculation:

	POUNDS.
From Trans-Mississippi mines (early in the war)	400,000
From the mines in Virginia (60,000 lbs. per month)	2,160,000
On hand at arsenals, etc.	140,000
Imported (not over)	2,000,000
Picked up through the country and on battlefields	5,300,000
Total	10,000,000

This leads to the surprising conclusion that we must have picked up throughout the country over 5,300,000 pounds of lead during the four years of the war. I remember that the window-weights and loose lead about houses yielded 200,000 pounds in Charleston alone; while the disused lead water-pipes in Mobile supplied, if I am not mistaken, as much more. So that these two items alone supplied one-thirteenth of this vast gleaning of the country.

TRANSFER OF ARMS TO THE SOUTH.

It was a charge often repeated against Governor Floyd that, as Secretary of War, he had, with traitorous intent, abused his office by sending arms to the South just before the secession of the States. The transactions which gave rise to this accusation were in the ordinary course of an economical administration of the War Department. After it had been determined to change the old flint-lock musket, which the United States possessed, to percussion, it was deemed cheaper to bring all the flint-lock arms in store at Southern arsenals to the Northern arsenals and armories for alteration, rather than to send the necessary machinery and workmen to the South. Consequently, the Southern arsenals were stripped of their deposits, which were sent to Springfield, Watervelet, Pittsburg, St. Louis, Frankford, Pa., and other points. After the conversion had been completed the denuded Southern arsenals were again supplied with about the same numbers, perhaps slightly augmented, that had formerly been stored there. The quota deposited at the Charleston arsenal, where I was stationed in 1860, arrived there full a year before the opening of the war.

THE NAPOLEON FIELD-GUN.

I think I will be sustained by the artillery in saying that, on the whole, this gun became the favorite for field service, perhaps because our rifle-shells with percussion fuses were, as stated by General Alexander, less successful than those of the enemy. When copper became scarce we fabricated an iron Napoleon with a wrought-iron jacket, weighing in all, twelve hundred and fifty pounds, which was entirely satisfactory, and was cheerfully accorded by the artillery companionship with their bronze favorites. The simplicity and certainty of the ammunition of this smooth-bore, its capacity for grape and canister, its good range, and its moderate draught, as it was not too heavy for four horses, were certainly strong reasons in its favor. At the distance at which the serious work of the artillery was done, it was an over-match for rifled artillery.

HEAVY GUNS.

It was, of course a matter of keen regret to me that we could not rapidly produce guns of heavy caliber for points, the defense of which, against men-of-war, was of vital importance. But the 10-inch columbiad could only be cast at the Tredegar Works, and although this establishment was in able hands and responded nobly to the calls made upon it, yet tasked, as it was, to produce artillery of all calibers—especially field artillery—we could but slowly answer the appeals made with equal vehemence from Pensacola, Yorktown, Charleston and New Orleans.

About the close of 1863, Maj. Huse sent in two Blakely rifles of about 13-inch caliber, splendid looking, superbly mounted, and of fearful cost!—£10,000 for the two in England, with fifty rounds each. Charleston claimed them on their arrival at Wilmington, and I was glad to strengthen General Beauregard's hands. Unfortunately one of them cracked in some trial firing, with comparatively weak charges. The full charge, which was never reached, was fifty pounds of powder, and a solid rifle-shell of say four hundred and fifty pounds. These guns were built up of a wrought-iron cylinder, closed at the breech with a brass-screw plug, some thirty inches long, and chambered to seven inches. This cylinder had three successive jackets, each shorter than its predecessor, so that from muzzle to breech the thickness of the gun increased by steps of about three and a half inches. The object of the seven-inch chamber in the brass plug was to afford an air or gas space which would diminish the strain on the gun. Such was the theory. General Ripley, however, cut down the big cartridge bags of ten or eleven inches in diameter, so as to introduce the charge into the brass chamber. This not being over three inches thick, cracked, and the crack, I believe, extended into the cylinder. On a report of the facts direct from Charleston to Captain Blakely, he attributed the bursting to the high elevation given, though the highest, I think, had been only about one hundred and fifty; an impotent conclusion for a scientific artillerist to reach. The fact of the introduction of the charge into the air space may have been omitted in the narrative to him, and thus he may have been drawn into this helpless conclusion. I never saw the drawings of the gun until after the report of the accident. Captain Brooke, Chief of Ordnance of the Navy, with me then looked over the drawings and evolved the design of the air-chamber. After this the gun was fired, and with moderate elevations attained fair, but not remarkable ranges, as I was advised. The cracked gun was skillfully repaired at Charleston, and restored to a reliable condition.

Just before the war closed, the Tredegar Works had cast its first 12-inch gun, after the method of Rodman—cast on a hollow core, with water kept flowing in and out of it to cool the castings from the inside. This method of cooling has been found to give a marked increase of strength, and greater hardness and consequent smoothness to the finished bore.

JOSIAH GORGAS,
Late Brigadier-General and Chief of Ordnance.

GENERAL E. KIRBY SMITH, OF FLORIDA.
BORN IN ST. AUGUSTINE, FLA., MAY 16, 1824. DIED IN SEWANEE, TENN., MARCH 28, 1893.

RED RIVER CAMPAIGN,

MARCH 10 TO MAY 22, 1864.

BY

GENERAL E. KIRBY SMITH.

HEADQUARTERS
TRANS-MISSISSIPPI DEPARTMENT,
SHREVEPORT, June 11, 1864.

SOON after my arrival in this department I became convinced that the Valley of Red River was the only practicable line of operations by which the enemy could penetrate the country. This fact was well understood and appreciated by their generals.

In the latter part of August I received information that a formidable expedition was preparing under the auspices of Generals Grant and Banks. The main advance would be up Red River Valley, with subordinate columns moving from Helena and Berwick Bay. The defeat of Rosecrans at Chickamauga frustrated this plan. General Grant, with the larger portion of his command, was drawn to Tennessee. The columns from Helena and Berwick Bay moved, with what success has already been reported to the department.

Feeling assured that the Red River expedition, so suddenly interrupted, would be renewed at some future day, I addressed myself to the task of meeting it with the slender means at my disposal. Fortifications were directed on the Lower Red River. Shreveport and Camden were fortified and works were ordered on the Sabine and the crossings of Upper Red River. Depots were established on the shortest lines of communication between the Red River Valley and the troops serving in Arkansas and Texas. Those commands were directed to be held ready to move with little delay, and every preparation was made in advance for accelerating a concentration, at all times difficult over long distances and through a country destitute of supplies and with limited means of transportation.

In February, 1864, the enemy were preparing in New Orleans, Vicksburg and Little Rock for offensive operations. Though twenty-five thousand men were reported on the Texas Coast, and though repeatedly urged to send troops to that district, my information convinced me that the Valley of Red River would be the principal theater of operations and that Shreveport would be the objective point of the columns moving from Arkansas and Louisiana. I continued steadily preparing for that event.

On February 21st General Magruder was ordered to hold Green's division of cavalry in readiness to move at a moment's notice.

On March 5th he was telegraphed. About that time the enemy commenced massing his forces at Berwick Bay.

On the 15th I received information of the enemy's landing at Simsport.

On March 18th the infantry of General Price's command was, by telegraph, ordered to Shreveport.

The enemy were operating with a force of full fifty thousand effective men. With the utmost powers of concentration not twenty-five thousand men could be brought to meet their movements. Shreveport was made the point of concentration. With its fortifications covering the depots, arsenals and shops at Jefferson, Marshall and above, it was a strategic point of vital importance. All the infantry not with Taylor opposed to Banks was directed to Shreveport. General Price, with his cavalry command, was instructed to delay the march of Steele's column while the concentration was effected. Occupying a central position at Shreveport, with the enemy's columns approaching from opposite directions, I proposed drawing them to within striking distance, when, by concentrating upon and striking them in detail, both columns might be crippled or destroyed.

On April 4th Churchill's and Parson's divisions were ordered to Keachie, within supporting distance of General Taylor, at Mansfield.

On the morning of April 5th I repaired to General Taylor's headquarters at Mansfield, and on the afternoon of the same day returned to Shreveport, from which point the operations of Generals Price's and Taylor's commands could best be directed.

In my interview with General Taylor, at Mansfield, on April 5th, my plan of operations was distinctly explained. He agreed with me, and expressed his belief that General

Steele, being the bolder and more active, would advance sooner and more rapidly than Banks, and was the column first to be attacked.

General Taylor reported the advance of the enemy's cavalry to Pleasant Hill. His headquarters was between four and five hours by courier from Shreveport. The action was unexpectedly brought on by Mouton engaging the enemy at 5 o'clock in the evening of April 8th.

I received General Taylor's dispatch announcing the engagement, at 4 o'clock on the morning of April 9th, and rode sixty-five miles that day to Pleasant Hill, but did not reach there in time for the battle, which opened at 4 o'clock in the afternoon.

On April 10th, General Taylor returned with me to Mansfield, where the further operations of the campaign were discussed and determined upon by us. Banks was in full retreat, with the cavalry in pursuit. Our infantry was withdrawn by General Taylor to Mansfield for supplies. The country below Natchitoches had been completely desolated and stripped of supplies. The navigation of the river was obstructed, and even had our whole force been available for pursuit it could not have been subsisted below Natchitoches. General Steele was advancing, and nineteen miles from Minden, on April 20th, 21st and 22d. The fortifications at Camden were too strong to be taken by assault. A few days' delay in operations awaiting the arrival of the pontoon train was necessary. Minden, from its strategic position, was the point for detaining Walker during this delay.

On April 17th I made my headquarters near Calhoun, in telegraphic communication with Shreveport, and a few hours' distance from General Price by courier. He here submitted to me his proposed attack upon the enemy's train, which, on April 18th, resulted in the battle of Poison Springs, under General Maxey.

On April 19th I found that General Price had not crossed any cavalry to the north side of the Arkansas River as directed, and that the day previous the enemy had received from Pine Bluff a commissary train of two hundred wagons, guarded by an escort of fifty cavalry. I immediately organized an expedition of four thousand picked cavalry, under General Fagan, who were ordered across the Ouachita and White rivers.

The destruction of the enemy's entire supply train and the capture of its escort at Marks Mills by General Fagan precipitated General Steele's retreat from Camden. He and Walker were marched by the most direct route to Louisiana, with orders to report to General Taylor. After the enemy left Grand Ecore, General Taylor attacked his rear at Cloutierville, while a detachment under Bee held the Federal advance in check at Monettes Ferry. General Taylor's force was, however, too weak to warrant the hope that he could seriously impede the march of Banks' column. After the latter reached Alexandria, General Taylor transferred a part of his command to the river below Alexandria, and with unparalleled audacity and great ability and success operated on the enemy's gunboats and transports. The construction of the dam, aided by a temporary rise in Red River, enabled Admiral Porter to get his fleet over the falls. Had he delayed but one week longer our whole infantry force would have been united against him.

Banks evacuated Alexandria on the 12th and 13th of May, the fleet quitted the Red River, and the campaign ended with the occupation of all the country we had held at its beginning, as well as of the lower Teche.

* * * * * * *

E. KIRBY SMITH, *General.*

VIEW OF THE LEVEE AT ALEXANDRIA, LA., 1864. STEAMERS LOADING WITH COTTON.

to have pushed our whole force in pursuit of a fleeing enemy, while Steele's column was in position to march upon our base and destroy our depots and shops, would have been sacrificing the advantages of our central position and abandoning the plan of campaign at the very time we were in position to have insured its success.

General Taylor agreed with me that the main body of our infantry should be pushed against Steele, and requested that he might accompany the column moving to Arkansas. He selected the troops that were to remain, placed General Polignac in command and gave him his instructions for pushing the retreating army of General Banks.

On the morning of April 11th I returned to Shreveport and made preparations for the prosecution of the campaign in Arkansas.

On April 14th I received information that Steele had turned the head of his column and was moving toward Camden. General Price was instructed that the infantry were moving to his support. He was ordered to throw his force within the fortifications at Camden if he believed himself strong enough to hold them against General Steele. If too weak, he was directed to throw a division of cavalry across the Ouachita and intercept all communication with and cut of all supplies going into Camden.

General Taylor arrived at Shreveport on the morning of April 16th. I informed him that the change of Steele's column and his march toward Camden had determined me in leaving him to conduct the operations on Red River, while in person I marched with the column moving to Arkansas; that should Steele retreat across the Ouachita, the infantry column under my command would be turned at Minden and take the direct route to Campti, and thus be in time to operate against Banks' retreating column.

In the meantime, orders were given to remove the obstructions in Red River and to float the pontoon bridge down to Campti. Banks was reported fortifying at Grand Ecore; Steele about occupying our fortifications at Camden. His dislodgment was an absolute necessity. He threatened any movement down Red River against Banks. He held a strong base from which he could either unite with Banks at Grand Ecore, or, by a short line of march, occupy Shreveport and destroy our shops, depots and supplies while the army was operating on Red River below.

The infantry passed through Shreveport on April 16th. I moved in person to the neighborhood of General Price's headquarters. General Walker was halted at his camp, evacuated the place on the morning of April 27th. By a forced march of forty-two miles we overtook him at Saline Bottom on the morning of April 30th. Our troops marched through mud and rain the previous night and attacked under great disadvantages—tired, exhausted, with mud and water up to their knees and waists. Marmaduke's brigade of cavalry, dismounted, as skirmishers, opened the fight, and were hotly engaged through the morning. The battle closed at 1 o'clock, a complete victory, the enemy leaving his dead, wounded, wagons, etc., on the field. The rise of the river, which flooded the bottom for some miles, and the exhausted condition of our men, prevented pursuit. Marmaduke's was the only cavalry with me.

On the evacuation of Camden, General Maxey, with his command, had been ordered back to the Indian country, where the movements of the enemy imperatively demanded his presence. Had General Fagan, with his command, thrown himself on the enemy's front, on his march from Camden, Steele would have been brought to battle and his command utterly destroyed long before he reached the Saline. I do not mean to censure General Fagan. That gallant officer taking the road to Arkadelphia after the battle of Marks Mills was one of those accidents which are liable to befall the best of officers. After the battle of Jenkins Ferry the infantry divisions of Churchill, Parsons

CONFEDERATE COMMISSIONERS TO FOREIGN COUNTRIES.

Hon. James M. Mason, Virginia, Commissioner to Europe, especially to the Court of England; delegate from Virginia to the Provisional Congress.

Hon. John Slidell, Louisiana, Commissioner to Europe, especially to the Court of France.

Hon. William L. Yancey, Alabama, Commissioner to Great Britain; Confederate Senator from Alabama, etc.

Hon. A. Dudley Mann, Virginia, Commissioner to Belgium.

Hon. P. A. Rost, Louisiana, Commissioner to Spain.

Hon. L. Q. C. Lamar, Mississippi, Commissioner to Russia.

Major-General William Preston, Kentucky, Commissioner to Mexico; brigadier-general and major-general in the Confederate Army.

Colonel John T. Pickett, Kentucky, Commissioner to Mexico; colonel in the Confederate Army.

Bishop P. N. Lynch, D. D., South Carolina, Commissioner to the States of the Church.

Hon. John Forsyth, Alabama, Commissioner to the United States of America.

Hon. Martin J. Crawford, Georgia, Commissioner to the United States of America; delegate to the Provisional Congress.

Hon. A. B. Roman, Louisiana, Commissioner to the United States of America.

CONSULAR, CONFIDENTIAL AND OTHER FOREIGN AGENTS.

Hon. Clement C. Clay, Jr., Alabama, Special Agent to Canada; formerly Confederate Senator from Alabama.

Hon. Jacob Thompson, Tennessee, Special Agent to Canada.

Hon. James P. Holcombe, Virginia, Special Agent to Canada; formerly member of Confederate Congress.

Hon. Edwin De Leon, South Carolina, Special Agent to Paris.

Hon. Charles J. Helm, Kentucky, Special Agent to Havana.

L. Heylinger, ——, Special Agent to Nassau.

Hon. Colin J. McRae, Mississippi, Special Agent to London and Paris; formerly deputy from Alabama to the Confederate Congress at Montgomery.

Hon. George N. Saunders, ——, Special Agent to London.

Hon. Beverly Tucker, Virginia, Special Agent to London.

J. L. O'Sullivan, ——, Special Agent to London.

Emile Erlanger & Co., France, Financial Agents at Paris.

RED RIVER DAM. GUNBOATS PASSING THROUGH THE RAPIDS AT DAWN.

BATTLE OF SHILOH, OR PITTSBURG LANDING, APRIL 6 AND 7, 1862.

(For Description, See Pages 76 to 84.)

ARMIES, CORPS AND GEOGRAPHICAL COMMANDS

IN THE

CONFEDERATE STATES, 1861-1865.

ALPHABETICALLY ARRANGED.

ABINGDON, DISTRICT OF.

(Established May 2, 1862.)

Brigadier-General Humphrey Marshall, May 2, 1862; relieved May 9, 1863.

Brigadier-General William Preston, assigned May 9, 1863; relieved January 7, 1864.

Embraced the counties of Lee, Wise, Buchanan, McDowell and Wyoming.

Comprising, April 26, 1863, that portion of Southwestern Virginia embraced in the counties of Washington, Russell, Buchanan, Wise, Scott and Lee.

Merged into Department of Southwestern Virginia, May 8, 1862.

ALABAMA, DISTRICT OF.

(Department of Alabama, Mississippi and East Louisiana.)

(Established March 11, 1865.)

Brigadier-General D. W. Adams, assigned March 11, 1865.

Embraced all that portion of State of Alabama not included in the District of the Gulf.

ALABAMA, DISTRICT OF.

(Department of Alabama and West Florida.)

(Established October 14, 1861.)

Brigadier-General J. M. Withers,* assigned October 14, 1861.

Embraced the State of Alabama and that portion of Mississippi east of the Pascagoula River.

Extended December 20, 1861, westward to include Pascagoula Bay and that portion of Mississippi east of Pascagoula River.

Denominated Army of Mobile, January 27, 1862.

ALABAMA, MISSISSIPPI AND EAST LOUISIANA,† DEPARTMENT OF.

(Established January 28, 1864.)

Lieutenant-General Leonidas Polk, January 28, 1864; relieved May 4, 1864.

Major-General S. D. Lee, assigned May 4, 1864; assumed May 9, 1864.

Lieutenant-General R. Taylor, assigned August 15, 1864; assumed September 23, 1864; reassumed December 12, 1864; relieved January 23, 1865.

Major-General D. H. Maury assumed temporarily November 22, 1864.

To embrace the States of Alabama, Mississippi and that part of Louisiana east of the Mississippi River.

Boundaries defined May 8, 1864: Beginning at the confluence of Tennessee and Ohio Rivers; thence along the Tennessee to Gunter's Landing; thence in a direct line to Gadsden, on Coosa River; thence down that river to its junction with Tallapoosa River; thence in a direct line to intersection of northern boundary of Florida with the Choctawhatchee River, and down that river and bay to the gulf; south by the Gulf of Mexico and west by the Mississippi River to mouth of Ohio; thence up the Ohio to mouth of Tennessee River.

Merged into the Military Division of the West (under Beauregard), October 3, 1864.

ALABAMA, RESERVE FORCES OF.

Major-General Jones M. Withers, assigned April 30, 1864; ordered to take immediate command July 27, 1864.

ALABAMA AND WEST FLORIDA, DEPARTMENT OF.

(Established October 14, 1861.)

Major-General Braxton Bragg, October 14, 1861; relinquished February 28, 1862.

Brigadier-General Samuel Jones, assigned February 27, 1862; assumed March 3, 1862; relieved March 24, 1862; reassumed April 2, 1862.

Colonel W. L. Powell, assigned temporarily March 24, 1862.

Brigadier-General J. H. Forney, assigned temporarily April 28, 1862.

Embraced Pensacola, Florida, and the coast and State of Alabama.

Extended December 12, 1861, west to include Pascagoula Bay and that portion of Mississippi east of Pascagoula River.

Discontinued June 27, 1862.

* Former command consisted of the State of Alabama and that portion of Mississippi east of the Pascagoula River.

† Brigadier-General Wirt Adams commanded a district lying north of the country south of a line running due east from Natchez to Pearl River ———, 1864. August 22, 1864, Brigadier-General B. Hodge relieved Brigadier-General Wirt Adams of his command.

ALBEMARLE,* DISTRICT OF THE.

(Department of Norfolk.)

(Established December 21, 1861.)

Brigadier-General H. A. Wise, assigned December 21, 1861; assumed January 11, 1862.

Embraced that part of North Carolina east of the Chowan River, together with the counties of Washington and Tyrrel.

Extended January 22, 1862, to embrace Roanoke Island.

ALEXANDRIA,† DEPARTMENT OF.

(Established April 24, 1861.)

Brigadier-General P. St. George Cocke, assigned April 24, 1861.

Brigadier-General M. L. Bonham, assigned May 21, 1861.

Brigadier-General G. T. Beauregard,‡ assigned May 31, 1861; assumed June 2, 1861.

Embracing Alexandria and troops in vicinity.

Extended June 10, 1861, to embrace forces in Prince William, Fairfax and Loudoun counties, Va.

Denominated Army of the Potomac June 20, 1861. (See Army of the Potomac.)

ALEXANDRIA LINE.

(See Department of Alexandria.)

AQUIA DISTRICT.

(Department of Northern Virginia.)

(Established October 22, 1861.)

Brigadier-General T. H. Holmes, October 22, 1861; relieved March 23, 1862; assigned to duty temporarily with General R. E. Lee.

Colonel R. M. Cary, assigned temporarily July 18, 1861.

Brigadier-General G. W. Smith,§ assigned and assumed March 23, 1862.

Embraced the section of country between Powell's River and the mouth of the Potomac, including the Northern Neck, and embracing the counties on either side of the Rappahannock from its mouth to Fredericksburg.

AQUIA, DISTRICT OF.

(Department of Fredericksburg.)

(Established July 18, 1861.)

Colonel R. M. Cary, assigned July 18, 1861, until relieved by Colonel Daniel Ruggles.

ARIZONA.

Lieutenant-Colonel John R. Baylor in command October, 1861; assigned to immediate command of northern and Indian portion of Texas November 8, 1862.

Brigadier-General H. H. Sibley, assigned to command troops in, December 14, 1861.

Merged into Trans-Mississippi Department May 26, 1862.

ARKANSAS, DISTRICT OF.

(Established June 25, 1861.)

Brigadier-General W. J. Hardee, assigned June 25, 1861; assumed July 22, 1861.

Embraced that portion of Arkansas lying west of the White and Black Rivers and north of the Arkansas River to the Missouri line.

Merged into the Trans-Mississippi Department May 26, 1862.

* Command also called Fourth Brigade, which was turned over to Brigadier-General Mahone by General Wise, February 23, 1862.

† Sometimes called Potomac Department, formerly Alexandria line.

‡ Previously in command of the troops in and near Charleston Harbor, S. C.

§ Assigned to command south of line of operations of General Lee, including the Department of North Carolina, September —, 1862.

ARKANSAS,* DISTRICT OF.

(Trans-Mississippi Department.)

(Established August 20, 1862.)

Major-General T. C. Hindman, August 20, 1862; relieved September 28, 1862.

Lieutenant-General T. H. Holmes, assigned March 18, 1863; relinquished temporarily July 24, 1863; resumed September 25, 1863; relieved March 11, 1864; relinquished March 16, 1864.

Major-General Sterling Price, assigned temporarily (during illness of General Holmes) July 24, 1863; relieved September 25, 1863; reassigned March 11, 1864; assumed March 16, 1864.

Brigadier-General T. J. Churchill, August —, 1864; relieved August 4, 1864.

Major-General J. B. Magruder, assigned August 4, 1864; relinquished temporarily January 29, 1865; resumed February 1, 1865; relinquished temporarily February 15, 1865; relieved March 31, 1865.

Brigadier-General M. M. Parsons, January 29, 1865; assigned temporarily February 15, 1865.

Embraced the States of Arkansas and Missouri, and Indian country west thereof.

Extended March 18, 1863, to embrace the Indian Territory and Missouri.

Consolidated with the District of West Louisiana April 19, 1865, to be known as the District of Arkansas and West Louisiana.

ARKANSAS AND WEST LOUISIANA, DISTRICT OF.

(Trans-Mississippi Department.)

(Established April 19, 1865.)

Lieutenant-General S. B. Buckner; assigned April 19, 1865.

Embraced the Districts of Arkansas and West Louisiana.

BUREAUS, HEADS OF.

CONSCRIPT BUREAU.

Rains, G. J., Brigadier-General, assigned as superintendent of, December 30, 1862.

Field, C. W., Brigadier-General, assigned as superintendent of, March 25, 1863.

ENGINEER BUREAU.

Gilmer, J. F., Colonel, assigned as chief of, October 4, 1862.

Smith, M. L., Major-General, assigned temporarily as chief of, March 9, 1864.

Gilmer, J. F., Major-General, ordered to resume as chief of, April 2, 1864.

ORDNANCE BUREAU.

Gorgas, Josiah, Major, assigned to duty as chief of, April 8, 1861.

PRISONERS, COMMISSARY-GENERAL OF.

Winder, John H., Brigadier-General, assigned as, November 21, 1864.

Ruggles, Daniel, Brigadier-General, assigned as, March 24, 1865.

QUARTERMASTER-GENERAL.

Myers, A. C., Lieutenant-Colonel, announced as acting, March 25, 1861.

Lawton, A. R., Brigadier-General, assigned as, August 7, 1863, to take effect the 10th instant.

SUBSISTENCE, COMMISSARY-GENERAL OF.

Northrop, Lucius B., Lieutenant-Colonel, assigned to duty as acting, March 27, 1861.

SURGEON-GENERAL.

Gibbs, R. W., Surgeon, April 12, 1861.

TORPEDO SERVICE.

Rains, G. J., Brigadier-General, assigned superintendent of, June 17, 1864.

CAPE FEAR, DISTRICT OF.

(Department of North Carolina.)

(Established September 29, 1861.)

Brigadier-General J. R. Anderson,† October 5, 1861; relieved about March 20, 1862.

* Also called District of Upper Arkansas.

† September 24, 1861, in command of coast defenses of North Carolina.

Brigadier-General S. G. French, assigned March 15, 1862; assumed about March 20, 1862.

Brigadier-General W. H. C. Whiting, commanding December, 1862, and January and February, 1863.

Embraced Wilmington and its defenses, etc.

Extended March 5, 1862, to embrace the counties of Robeson, Cumberland, Bladen, Columbus and Sampson.

Made separate command September 26, 1863, under Major-General W. H. C. Whiting.

United April 18, 1864, with Department of North Carolina, and placed under command of General Beauregard.

CAVALRY CORPS (ARMY OF NORTHERN VIRGINIA).

Major-General J. E. B. Stuart, commanding January 31, 1864.

CAVALRY CORPS (ARMY OF TENNESSEE).

Major-General Joseph Wheeler, commanding August 15, 1863.

CENTRAL ALABAMA, DISTRICT OF.

(Department of Alabama, Mississippi and East Louisiana.)

(Established September 24, 1864.)

Brigadier-General D. W. Adams, assigned September 24, 1864.

Formed of part of District of North Alabama.

CENTRAL KENTUCKY, ARMY CORPS OF.

(See Central Army of Kentucky.)

CHARLESTON, SOUTH CAROLINA.

(Confederate States Army at.)

Brigadier-General G. T. Beauregard, commanding from March 3 to May 27, 1861.

Colonel R. H. Anderson, assigned May 27, 1861.

EAST FLORIDA, DISTRICT OF.

(Department of South Carolina, Georgia and Florida.)

(Established November 4, 1862.)

Brigadier-General Joseph Finegan, assigned November 4, 1862.

Embraced all that portion of Florida east of the Suwannee River.

Consolidated February 23, 1864, with District of Middle Florida and denominated District of Florida.

EAST AND MIDDLE FLORIDA, DEPARTMENT OF.

(See Department of Middle and Eastern Florida.)

EAST TENNESSEE, ARMY OF.

(See Department of East Tennessee.)

Denominated Army of Kentucky August 25, 1862, Major-General E. K. Smith commanding.

EAST TENNESSEE, DEPARTMENT OF.

(Established March —, 1862.)

Major-General E. K. Smith, March —, 1862; resumed December 23, 1862.

Major-General J. P. McCown, assigned temporarily August 24, 1862; assumed September 1, 1862; relieved September 19, 1862; reassigned September 27, 1862.

Major-General Samuel Jones, assumed September 23, 1862.

Brigadier-General H. Heth, commanding December 19, 1862.

Brigadier-General Daniel S. Donelson, assigned January 17, 1863.

Brigadier-General W. G. M. Davis, spring of 1863.

Major-General Dabney H. Maury, assigned April 15, 1863; assumed April 25, 1863; relieved May 12, 1863.

Major-General S. B. Buckner, assigned April 27, 1863; assumed May 12, 1863; in command July 20, 1863; reassumed April 12, 1864; relinquished May 2, 1864.

Brigadier-General William Preston, assigned temporarily June 26, 1863; assumed July 4, 1863.

Lieutenant-General James Longstreet, December 5, 1863; relieved April 12, 1864.

Brigadier-General W. E. Jones, assigned May 1, 1864; assumed May 2, 1864; May 23, 1864, commanding Trans-Alleghany, or Western Department of Virginia, in addition.

Colonel G. B. Crittenden, commanding temporarily May 31, 1864; relieved June 22, 1864. Commanded Trans-Alleghany, or Western Department of Virginia, in addition.

Brigadier-General John H. Morgan, assumed temporarily June 22, 1864; relieved August 30, 1864. Commanded Trans-Alleghany, or Western Department of Virginia, in addition.

Brigadier-General John C. Breckinridge, September 27, 1864. Commanded Trans-Alleghany, or Western Department of Virginia, in addition.

Lieutenant-General J. A. Early, commanding March 25, 1865. Commanded Trans-Alleghany, or Western Department of Virginia, in addition.

Extended March 21, 1862, to embrace Chattanooga and troops in the vicinity.

Defined more particularly March 27, 1862: Extends west of Chattanooga on a line north of that place.

Extended June 3, 1862, to embrace that part of North Carolina west of the Blue Ridge Mountains, and adjoining East Tennessee.

Extended July 18, 1862, to embrace that part of Georgia which is north of the railroad leading from Augusta via Atlanta to West Point, and so much of North Carolina as is west of the Blue Ridge Mountains in that State.

Defined more particularly September 12, 1862: The district west of the Hiawassee belongs to General Bragg; this side of the river to Department of East Tennessee.

Extended January 17, 1863, to embrace the counties of Washington, Russell, Buchanan, Wise, Scott and Lee, Va., including General Marshall's command.

Western limits defined June 8, 1863: Following Little Tennessee and Tennessee Rivers to Kingston; thence up Clinch River to mouth of Emery's Creek; up said creek to Cumberland Mountains and following said mountains to Cumberland Gap. All the country in Tennessee west of this line will be added to General Bragg's command.

Merged* into Department of Tennessee July 25, 1863, General Bragg commanding.

Extended August 4, 1863, to embrace the counties of Franklin, Lawrence, Morgan, Blount, St. Clair, Calhoun, Cherokee, De Kalb and Marshall, Ala.

Extended February 1, 1864, on the east to include the counties of Russell, Buchanan, Wise, Scott, Lee and Washington, Va., and that part of North Carolina west of the Blue Ridge Mountains; on the south the country north of the Little Tennessee River; on the west the country east of Tennessee and Clinch Rivers and Emery's Creek.

EAST TENNESSEE, DISTRICT OF.

(Established July 26, 1861.)

Brigadier-General F. Zollicoffer, assigned July 26, 1861; commanding October 8, 1861.

Major-General G. B. Crittenden, assigned November 11, 1861; assumed December 8, 1861.

Major-General E. K. Smith, assigned February 25, 1862; assumed March 8, 1862.

Denominated Department of East Tennessee March —, 1862.

FIFTH MILITARY DISTRICT.

(Department of Mississippi and Eastern Louisiana.)

(Established —, ——.)

Brigadier-General J. R. Chalmers, commanding in April, 1863.

FIFTH MILITARY DISTRICT OF SOUTH CAROLINA.†

(Department of South Carolina, Georgia and Florida.)

(Established December 10, 1861.)

Brigadier-General T. F. Drayton, assigned December 10, 1861.

Colonel W. S. Walker, assigned May 6, 1862 (also of the Fourth Military District).

Colonel ——— Rhett, assigned October 22, 1863.

Embraced the country between the boundary of Fourth Military District and Savannah River.

Discontinued in May, 1862.

Re-established October 22, 1863, to embrace the city, including the lines on the Neck, Fort Ripley and Castle Pinkney.

Extended October 28, 1863, to include Fort Sumter.

FIRST CORPS,‡ ARMY OF THE MISSISSIPPI.

(Department No. 2.)

Major-General Leonidas Polk, assigned March 29, 1862; relieved § July 2, 1862.

FIRST CORPS,‖ ARMY OF MISSISSIPPI.

(Department of Mississippi and Eastern Louisiana.)

Major-General Earl Van Dorn, December -, 1862; resumed December 7, 1862.

Major-General W. W. Loring, assigned, temporarily, December 15, 1862.

FIRST CORPS, ARMY OF THE POTOMAC.

Brigadier-General G. T. Beauregard, July 21, 1861; relieved October 22, 1861.

FIRST CORPS, ARMY OF NORTHERN VIRGINIA.

Lieutenant-General James Longstreet, commanding August 13, 1862, and August 15, 1863.

Major-General R. H. Anderson, assigned May 7, 1864.

FIRST CORPS (POLK'S), ARMY OF TENNESSEE.

(Department No. 2.)

Lieutenant-General L. Polk, November 26, 1862; relieved June 23, 1864.

Lieutenant-General A. P. Stewart, assigned June 23, 1864.

* August 28, 1863, continued in its former limits as far as the administrative duties were concerned, in strategic operations subordinate to, and part of, the Department of Tennessee; August 6, 1863, troops in, constituted the Third Army Corps.

† Probably extended and called Military District of Georgia.

‡ The First, Second, Third and Reserve Corps reorganized into Right and Left Wings, Army of the Mississippi, August 15, 1862.

§ According to organization, on page 6, volume 7, commanded Right Wing and First Corps, Army of the Mississippi, August 18, 1862.

‖ Called by General Van Dorn, Army of the West.

FIRST CORPS,* ARMY TRANS-MISSISSIPPI.†

Major-General T. C. Hindman, assigned September 28, 1862; relieved January 30, 1863, and ordered to Vicksburg to await orders.

FIRST DISTRICT.

(Department of South Mississippi and East Louisiana.)

(Established June 26, 1862.)

Brigadier-General Daniel Ruggles, assigned, temporarily, June 26, 1862.

Embraced that part of Louisiana east of Mississippi River and the counties of Mississippi lying on the Gulf.

FIRST DISTRICT OF TEXAS.

(Trans-Mississippi Department.)

(Established ——, 1862.)

Major-General P. O. Hebert commanding, October 15, 1862.

FIRST GEOGRAPHICAL DIVISION.

(Department No. 2.)

(Established ——, 1861.)

Major-General Leonidas Polk commanding, September 2, 1861; resumed December 4, 1861.

Embraced the country beginning at the point on the State line crossed by the Memphis & Louisville Railroad, and running along the Henderson & Nashville & Central Alabama, excluding the city of Nashville; thence west along said boundary and the northern boundary of Mississippi to the Mississippi River; thence northwardly along the western bank of the river, on the north side. It will extend so far into the State of Kentucky, west of the Cumberland River, as the major-general may find it advisable to cover by his army. The commander of this division is charged with the defenses of the Mississippi from the southern line of his division northward as far as his troops occupy.

FIRST MILITARY DISTRICT.

(Department of North Carolina and Southern Virginia.)

(Established ——, ——.)

Colonel —— Butler, assigned ——.

Brigadier-General H. A. Wise, assigned June 1, 1864.

Extended May 12, 1864, to embrace that section of country from Appomattox River running north to Swift Creek.

Extended June 2, 1864, to embrace all that portion of the Department between the James and Roanoke Rivers, including the defenses immediately around Richmond on south side of James River.

FIRST MILITARY DISTRICT.

(Department of Mississippi and East Louisiana.)

(Established October 21, 1862.)

Brigadier-General Daniel Ruggles, assigned October 21, 1862; commanding in April, 1863.

Embraced that part of Mississippi east of the Mississippi & Tennessee Railroad and the New Orleans & Jackson Railroad, excluding counties of Mississippi bordering on the Gulf of Mexico.

Abolished September 2, 1863.

FIRST MILITARY DISTRICT OF SOUTH CAROLINA.

(Department of South Carolina, Georgia and Florida.)

(Established December 10, 1861.)

Colonel A. M. Manigault, assigned December 10, 1861.

Brigadier-General H. W. Mercer, assigned May 28, 1862.

Brigadier-General W. D. Smith, assigned July 8, 1862. (Deceased.)

Brigadier-General S. R. Gist, temporarily in command from October 4 to 16, 1862.

Brigadier-General R. S. Ripley, assigned October 16, 1862; assumed 17, 1862; commanding, October 22, 1863.

Brigadier-General N. G. Evans, assigned ——, 1864; assumed March 21, 1864.

Resubdivided, December 28, 1862.

Rearranged, October 22, 1863, to embrace Fort Sumter, Sullivan's and Long Islands, and the parishes of Christ Church and St. Thomas.

October 28, 1863, Fort Sumter detached, and attached to Fifth Military District.

Extended from Little River inlet to South Santee River.

Denominated Sub-district No. 2, October 17, 1864.

FOURTH MILITARY DISTRICT.

(Department of Mississippi and East Louisiana.)

(Established ——, ——.)

Brigadier-General John Adams, commanding in April, 1863.

FOURTH MILITARY DISTRICT OF SOUTH CAROLINA.

(Department of South Carolina, Georgia and Florida.)

(Established December 10, 1861.)

Brigadier-General J. C. Pemberton, assigned December 10, 1861.

Brigadier-General Maxcy Gregg, April 11, 1862.

* Composed of troops in northwestern Arkansas, southwestern Missouri and the Indian Territory.

† Also called Army of the West.

LIEUTENANT-GENERAL JAMES LONGSTREET.

BORN IN EDGEFIELD DISTRICT, SOUTH CAROLINA, JANUARY 8, 1821.

Colonel W. S. Walker, assigned May 6, 1862. (Also of the Fifth Military District.)

Brigadier-General Thomas F. Drayton, assigned May 28, 1862.

Brigadier-General J. H. Trapier,* assigned November 6, 1862; reassigned June 16, 1863.

Extending from the Ashepoo River to the Port Royal entrance; thence through the Colleton River and Ocetee Creek to Ferebeeville.

Extended, April 11, 1862, as far west as Coosawhatchee River, including the station at Coosawhatchee; from and below Coosawhatchee station bounded by the east bank of Coosawhatchee River.

Resubdivided December 28, 1862.

Re-established November 6, 1862, to embrace the territory east and north of the Santee and South Santee Rivers.

Re-established June 16, 1863, to embrace the troops then in the parishes of St. James and St. Stephens about Georgetown, and to the North Carolina line, Brigadier-General J. H. Trapier commanding.

Denominated Sub-district No. 1, October 17, 1864.

FLORIDA, DEPARTMENT OF.

(See Department of Middle and Eastern Florida.)

FLORIDA, DISTRICT OF.

(Department of South Carolina, Georgia and Florida.)

(Established February 23, 1864.)

Major-General J. Patton Anderson, assigned February 23, 1864; assumed March 4, 1864.

Brigadier-General J. K. Jackson, assigned August —, 1864; relieved September 29, 1864.

Brigadier-General William Miller, assigned September 29, 1864.

Major-General Samuel Jones, assigned December 31, 1864; assumed February 2, 1865, to the end, about May 10, 1865.

Embraced the Districts of Middle and Eastern Florida.

FLORIDA, RESERVE FORCES OF.

Major-General J. Patton Anderson, assigned April 30, 1864 (in addition to his present duties).

Brigadier-General William Miller, assigned September 8, 1864.

FREDERICKSBURG,† DEPARTMENT OF.

(Afterward Aquia District.)

(Established April 22, 1861.)

Brigadier-General D. Ruggles, assumed April 22, 1861.

Brigadier-General T. H. Holmes, assumed June 5, 1861.

Major-General D. H. Hill, assigned July 17, 1862; relieved July —, 1862.

Merged into Department of Northern Virginia October 22, 1861.

GALVESTON, MILITARY DISTRICT OF.

(Department of Texas.)

(Established October 2, 1861.)

Colonel J. C. Moore, assigned October 2, 1861; relieved December 7, 1861.

Colonel E. B. Nichols, assigned December 7, 1861; commanding December 10, 1861.

Embraced Galveston Island, Virginia Point, adjacent bay coast, and the Peninsular of Bolivar.

Denominated Military Sub-district of Galveston February 25, 1862.

GALVESTON,‡ MILITARY SUB-DISTRICT OF.

(Department of Texas.)

(Established February 25, 1862.)

Colonel E. B. Nichols, February 25, 1862.

GALVESTON, TEXAS, AND ISLAND, DEFENSES OF.

Captain J. C. Moore, assigned June 25, 1861; October 2, 1861, assigned immediate command of Galveston Island and its defenses, Virginia Point, and the troops stationed on Bolivar Point and Peninsula.

GEORGIA, DEPARTMENT OF.

(Established October 26, 1861.)

Brigadier-General A. R. Lawton, October 26, 1861.

Merged into the Department of South Carolina, Georgia and Florida November 5, 1861.

GEORGIA, DISTRICT OF.

(Department of South Carolina, Georgia and Florida.)

(Established May 28, 1862.)

Brigadier-General A. R. Lawton, assigned May 28, 1862.

Brigadier-General W. H. Mercer, December 28, 1862; re-assigned November 11, 1863.

Major-General D. H. Hill, assigned January 21, 1865.

Extended December 28, 1862, to embrace the State of Georgia, excluding the defenses of the Apalachicola River and its main affluents.

* Assigned to the command of Sub-district No. 2, First Military District, March 14, 1863.

† Not recognized as a department until May 26, 1861.

‡ Formerly called District of Galveston.

Comprised January 21, 1865, that portion of Georgia (see extension January 6, 1865, of Department of South Carolina, Georgia and Florida).

GEORGIA, DISTRICT OF.

(Department of Tennessee and Georgia.)

(Established September 28, 1864.)

Major-General Howell Cobb, assigned September 28, 1864; relieved March 27, 1865.

Embraced all that portion of the State of Georgia included within the limits of the Department of Tennessee and Georgia, excepting that portion lying in the immediate vicinity of the Army of Tennessee.

GEORGIA, RESERVE FORCES OF.

Brigadier-General Howell Cobb,* assigned March 30, 1864.

GULF, DEPARTMENT OF THE.

(See District of the Gulf.)

GULF,† DISTRICT OF THE.

(Department No. 2.)

(Established July 2, 1862.)

Brigadier-General John H. Forney, assigned July 2, 1862; relieved December 8, 1862.

Brigadier-General W. W. Mackall, assigned temporarily December 8, 1862; relieved December 14, 1862.

Brigadier-General S. B. Buckner, assigned December 14, 1862; relieved April 27, 1863.

Major-General Frank Gardner,‡ temporarily in command, April 27, 1863.

Major-General D. H. Maury, commanding May —, 1863.

Embraced all the country east of Pearl River to the Apalachicola, and as far north as the thirty-second parallel of latitude.

Extended November 3, 1862, to the thirty-third parallel.

Boundaries defined February 7, 1864: Beginning on the west at the mouth of Pearl River, and running north with said river to the thirty-second parallel of latitude; thence along that parallel eastward to its intersection with the Georgia State line; thence southward, with the eastern boundary line of the Department of Alabama, Mississippi and East Louisiana, to the Gulf.

Extended May 8, 1864: Beginning on the west at the mouth of Pearl River, and running north with said river to the thirty-second parallel of latitude; thence along said parallel, eastward to its intersection with a line drawn from the junction of the Coosa and Tallapoosa Rivers, to the intersection of the northern boundary of Florida with the Choctawhatchee River; thence along said line to said intersection; thence along Choctawhatchee River and bay, to the Gulf.

HARPERS FERRY.

Major-General Kenton Harper, of the Virginia Militia, April 27, 1861.

Colonel T. J. Jackson, assigned April 27, 1861; assumed April 28, 1861.

Brigadier-General J. E. Johnston,§ assigned May 15, 1861; assumed May 24, 1861.

Evacuated June 15, 1861.

HARPERS FERRY DISTRICT.

(See Harpers Ferry and Army of the Shenandoah.)

HENRICO, DEPARTMENT OF.

(Established October 21, 1861.)

Brigadier-General J. H. Winder, October 21, 1861.

Embraced the County of Henrico.

Extended March 26, 1862, to include Petersburg and ten miles of surrounding country.

Merged into the Department of Richmond May 5, 1864.

HOUSTON, MILITARY DISTRICT OF.

(Department of Texas.)

(Established January 3, 1862.)

Colonel J. C. Moore, assigned January 3, 1862.

Embraced Houston, Harrisburg and Lewis' Bayou.

Denominated Military Sub-district of Houston, February 25, 1862.

HOUSTON,|| MILITARY SUB-DISTRICT OF.

(Department of Texas.)

Colonel J. C. Moore, February 25, 1862.

Colonel Thomas S. Flournoy, June 3, 1862.

Colonel X. B. Debray, assumed July 8, 1862; commanding September 25, 1862.

Extended June 3, 1862, to embrace the counties of Austin, Harris, Galveston, Liberty, Chambers and Jefferson.

* September 8, 1863, organizing the Georgia Militia at Atlanta, etc., for Confederate service.

† In 1864 in the Department of Alabama, Mississippi and East Louisiana.

‡ October 4, 1864, assigned to district composed of East Louisiana and all that portion of Mississippi not included in the District of the Gulf, in Department of Alabama, Mississippi and East Louisiana.

§ Command denominated Harpers Ferry District and the Army of the Shenandoah.

|| Formerly called District of Houston.

INDIAN DEPARTMENT.

(See Indian Territory.)

INDIAN TERRITORY.*

Brigadier-General Benjamin McCulloch, assigned May 13, 1861; command embraced the Indian Territory west of Arkansas and south of Kansas.

Brigadier-General Albert Pike, commanding November 22, 1861.

Brigadier-General D. H. Cooper, commanding January 20, 1862.

Brigadier-General William Steele, commanding October 3, 1863.

Brigadier-General S. B. Maxey, assigned December 11, 1863.

Merged into the Trans-Mississippi District and Trans-Mississippi Department May 26, 1862.

INDIAN TERRITORY, DISTRICT OF.

(Trans-Mississippi Department.)

(Established July 21, 1864.)

Brigadier-General D. H. Cooper,† assigned July 21, 1864; reassigned February 21, 1865.

Brigadier-General S. B. Maxey, assigned —— —, 1865; relieved February 21, 1865.

Embraced the Indian Territory west of Arkansas.

KANAWHA, ARMY OF THE.

(Organized August 12, 1861.)

Brigadier-General John B. Floyd, assumed August 12, 1861; commanding September 19, 1861.

Merged (probably) into the Department of Northern Virginia October 22, 1861.

KANAWHA VALLEY, TROOPS IN.

(See Army of the Kanawha.)

Colonel C. Q. Tompkins, assigned May 3, 1861.

Brigadier-General H. A. Wise, assigned June 6, 1861; relieved August 12, 1861.

KENTUCKY,‡ ARMY OF.

(Organized August 25, 1862.)

Major-General E. K. Smith, commanding August to October, 1862.

Composed of McCown's, C. L. Stevenson's and Heth's divisions.

Merged into Army of Tennessee November 20, 1862, and called "Smith's Corps."

KENTUCKY,§ CENTRAL ARMY OF.

(Department No. 2.)

(Organized October —, 1861.)

General A. S. Johnston, assumed immediate command October 28, 1861; resumed immediate command December 18, 1861; reassumed February 23, 1862.

Major-General W. J. Hardee, assigned December 4, 1861; assumed December 5, 1861; relieved February 23, 1862.

United with Army of the Mississippi March 29, 1862, under immediate command of General A. S. Johnston.

Reorganized February 23, 1862.

KENTUCKY, CENTRAL (GEOGRAPHICAL) DIVISION OF.

(Department No. 2.)

(Established —— —, 1861.)

Brigadier-General S. B. Buckner, assumed September 18, 1861; relieved ——, 1862.

LEWISBURG, DISTRICT OF.

(Established January 28, 1862.)

Brigadier-General Henry Heth, assigned January 28, 1862.

Embraced all the troops in and around Lewisburg.

Merged into Department of Southwestern Virginia May 8, 1862.

LOUISIANA,|| ARMY OF.

(Organized February 22, 1861.)

Major-General Braxton Bragg, February 22, 1861.

Colonel P. O. Hebert, assumed April 16, 1861.

LOUISIANA, DISTRICT OF.

(Trans-Mississippi Department.)

(See District of West Louisiana.)

LOUISIANA, MILITARY DISTRICT OF.

(Established April 17, 1861.)

Major-General David E. Twiggs, assigned April 17, 1861.

Embraced the city of New Orleans and its defenses.

Merged into Department No. 1 May 27, 1861.

MIDDLE AND EASTERN FLORIDA,¶ DEPARTMENT OF.

(Established August 21, 1861.)

Brigadier-General John B. Grayson, August 21, 1861; relieved October 10, 1861.

* Separated from District of Arkansas October 3, 1863.

† Assigned Superintendent of Indian Affairs, in District of Indian Territory, February 14, 1865.

‡ Formerly Army of East Tennessee.

§ Formerly called Army Corps of Central Kentucky.

|| Also called Department of Louisiana.

¶ Also called Department of Florida.

Brigadier-General E. K. Smith, assigned October 10, 1861; countermanded October 22, 1861.
Brigadier-General James H. Trapier, assigned October 22, 1861; reassigned March 14, 1862; relieved by order March 19, 1862.
Colonel W. C. Dilworth, assigned temporarily March 19, 1862; assumed April 1, 1862.
Brigadier-General Joseph Finegan, assigned April 8, 1862; assumed April 18, 1862.

Embraced Middle and Eastern Florida.

Extended October 26, 1861, west to Choctawhatchee River.

Under the Department of South Carolina, Georgia and Florida April 7, 1862.

Re-established April 9, 1862.

Constituted a district to form a part of General Beauregard's command, October 7, 1862.

Divided into two districts November 4, 1862, to be known as Districts of East and Middle Florida, and merged into Department of South Carolina, Georgia and Florida.

MIDDLE FLORIDA, DISTRICT OF.

(Department of South Carolina, Georgia and Florida.)

(Established November 4, 1862.)

Brigadier-General Howell Cobb, assigned November 11, 1862.
Brigadier-General Joseph Finegan, assumed temporarily August 7, 1863.
Brigadier-General W. M. Gardner, assigned October 6, 1863; assumed November 11, 1863.

Embraced, December 28, 1862, that part of Florida between the Suwannee and Choctawhatchee Rivers, and will include all works for the defense of the Apalachicola and its main affluents.

Consolidated with District of East Florida, and denominated, February 23, 1864, District of Florida.

MIDDLE TENNESSEE, ARMY OF.

(Department No. 2.)

(Organized October 28, 1862.)

Major-General John C. Breckinridge, October 28, 1862.
General J. E. Johnston, ordered to assume direct charge May 9, 1863.

Embraced all troops in Middle Tennessee.

MIDDLE TENNESSEE, DISTRICT OF.

(Department No. 2.)

(Established September 27, 1862.)

Major-General Samuel Jones, assigned September 27, 1862; relieved November 4, 1862.

Includes the State of Alabama north of the Tennessee River.

MISSISSIPPI, ARMY OF.

(Department of Mississippi and East Louisiana.)

(Organized ——, 1862.)

Major-General Earl Van Dorn, assigned temporarily December 9, 1862, during absence of General J. C. Pemberton.

Denominated, December 17, 1862, Army Department of Mississippi and East Louisiana, to consist of First and Second Corps, under Generals Van Dorn and Price, respectively.

Reorganized January 2, 1862.

MISSISSIPPI,* ARMY OF THE.

(Department No. 2.)

(Organized March —, 1862.)

Major-General Braxton Bragg, assigned March 6, 1862; reassigned May 6, 1862; reassumed May 7, 1862; relinquished July 5, 1862; resumed August 15, 1862; relinquished temporarily September 28, 1862; resumed November 7, 1862.
General G. T. Beauregard, assigned March 17, 1862; relieved June 27, 1862.
Major-General W. J. Hardee, assumed July 5, 1862; relieved August 15, 1862.
Major-General L. Polk, assigned temporarily September 28, 1862; relieved November 7, 1862.

Central Army of Kentucky united with Army of the Mississippi, March 29, 1862, under immediate command of General A. S. Johnston.

Denominated by General Bragg, Army of Tennessee, November 20, 1862.

MISSISSIPPI,† DISTRICT OF THE.

(Department No. 2.)

(Established July 2, 1862.)

Brigadier-General Earl Van Dorn, assigned July 2, 1862; commanding October 3, 1862.
Brigadier-General D. Ruggles, assumed temporarily September 5, 1862.

Embraced all that country west of Pearl River, from its mouth to Jackson, Miss., and the line of Mississippi Central Railroad to Grand Junction.

Denominated Department of Mississippi and East Louisiana October 1, 1862.

* August 15, 1862, reorganized into Right and Left Wings, under command of Major-Generals L. Polk and W. J. Hardee, respectively; November 7, 1862, reorganized into First and Second Corps, with the same commanders.

† Formerly Department of Southern Mississippi and East Louisiana.

MISSISSIPPI AND EAST LOUISIANA, ARMY DEPARTMENT OF.

(See Army of Mississippi, Department of Mississippi and East Louisiana.)

MISSISSIPPI AND EAST LOUISIANA, DEPARTMENT OF.

(Established October 1, 1862.)

Major-General J. C. Pemberton, assigned October 1, 1862; assumed October 14 or 17, 1862; commanding in April, 1863.
Lieutenant-General L. Polk, assigned December 22, 1863; assumed December 23, 1863.

Embraced the State of Mississippi and that part of Louisiana east of Mississippi River, and included the forces intended to operate in Southern Tennessee.

Divided into three military districts October 21, 1862, to be known as the First, Second and Third.

Merged into Department of Alabama, Mississippi and East Louisiana January 28, 1864.

MISSISSIPPI AND EAST LOUISIANA, DISTRICT OF.

(Department of Alabama, Mississippi and East Louisiana.)

(Established —— —, 1864.)

Major-General Frank Gardner, commanding in September, 1864.
Brigadier-General W.T. Martin, assumed January 16, 1865.
Brigadier-General N. B. Forrest, assigned January 27, 1865.

Subdivided February 3, 1865, as follows: District of North Mississippi and West Tennessee, and District of Southern Mississippi and East Louisiana.

MISSISSIPPI, RESERVE FORCES OF.

(See Reserve Corps State of Mississippi.)

MISSISSIPPI, CENTRAL, SUB-DISTRICT OF.*

(Department of Alabama, Mississippi and East Louisiana.)

(Established —— —, 1864.)

Colonel R. C. Wood, Jr., commanding in 1864.

MISSISSIPPI, NORTHERN, SUB-DISTRICT OF.*

(Department of Alabama, Mississippi and East Louisiana.)

(Established —— —, 1864.)

Brigadier-General Wirt Adams, commanding in 1864.

MISSOURI,† ARMY OF.

(Organized September 8, 1864.)

Major-General Sterling Price, assigned September 8, 1864.
Brigadier-General J. B. Clarke, Jr., assigned temporarily December 18, 1864.

Composed of Fagan's, Marmaduke's and Shelby's divisions.

MISSOURI,‡ CONFEDERATE FORCES IN.

Brigadier-General Benjamin McCulloch, July 30, 1861; in command November 10, 1861.
Brigadier-General W. J. Hardee, August 3, 1861.

MISSOURI, STATE GUARD.

(Organized July 30, 1861.)

Under Brigadier-Generals Sterling Price § and M. M. Parsons from October 29, 1861, to April 8, 1862.

Merged into the Army of the West, March 17, 1862.

MOBILE, ARMY OF.

(Department of Alabama and West Florida.)

(Organized January 27, 1862.)

Brigadier-General Jones M. Withers, January 27, 1862.
Colonel J. B. Villepigue, assigned temporarily February 28, 1862.
Brigadier-General Samuel Jones, assigned February 27, 1862; assumed March 15, 1862.

Comprising all troops in and about Mobile and south of it.

Discontinued June 27, 1862.

NEW MEXICO,|| ARMY OF.

(Organized December 14, 1861.)

Brigadier-General H. H. Sibley, assigned December 14, 1861; relieved December 1, 1862.

Embraced all the forces on the Rio Grande at and above Fort Quitman, and all in the Territories of New Mexico and Arizona.

DEPARTMENT NO. 1.

(Established May 27, 1861.)

Major-General David E. Twiggs, assigned May 27, 1861; assumed May 31, 1861; relieved October 7, 1861.
Major-General Mansfield Lovell, assigned October 7, 1861; commanding April 16, 1862.

* Under District of Mississippi and East Louisiana.

† Variously called Price's Division, Army in the Field, and Price's Army.

‡ Divided into nine military districts.

§ Assigned to command of First Division, Army of the West, March 17, and assumed March 22, 1862.

|| Formerly known as Sibley's Brigade.

Embraced the State of Louisiana and southern portions of Mississippi and Alabama, including Fort Morgan.

Extended May 26, 1862, to embrace the State of Mississippi south of the thirty-third parallel, and west of the Pascagoula and Chickasawha Rivers, and Louisiana east of the Mississippi.

Merged into Department No. 2 June 25, 1862.

DEPARTMENT NO. 2, OR WESTERN DEPARTMENT.

(Established June 25, 1861.)

Major-General Leonidas Polk, assigned June 25, 1861; assumed July 13, 1861; temporarily assigned October 24, 1862.
General Albert S. Johnston, assigned September 10, 1861; assumed September 15, 1861; killed at battle of Shiloh, April 6, 1862.
General G. T. Beauregard, assumed April 6, 1862; relinquished June 17, 1862.
General Braxton Bragg, assumed temporary command June 17, 1862; assigned to permanent command June 27, 1862; assumed July 2, 1862; relinquished temporarily October 24, 1862; resumed November 3, 1862.

Embraces that portion of North Alabama north of the Tennessee River, beginning at Waterloo and running thence east with the river to Decatur, and also that portion of North Alabama lying north of the Memphis & Charleston Railroad from Decatur to Stevenson; that portion of Tennessee west and south of the Tennessee River; the river counties of Arkansas and Mississippi, including Corinth, Mississippi, and the country adjacent thereto, and extending to Eastport, on Tennessee River; the river parishes of Louisiana north of Red River, and that portion of Arkansas, besides the river counties, therein lying north and east of White and Black rivers.

Extended September 2, 1861, to embrace State of Arkansas and all military operations in Missouri.

Extended September 10, 1861, to embrace the States of Tennessee and Arkansas and that part of the State of Mississippi west of the New Orleans, Jackson & Great Northern & Central Railroad, and also the military operations in Kentucky, Missouri and Kansas, and Indian Territory immediately west of Missouri and Arkansas.

Extended May 26, 1862, south to the thirty-third parallel, east of Mississippi River, and extending on that parallel to eastern boundary of Alabama.

Extended June 25, 1862, to embrace that portion of its former limits which is east of Mississippi River, and in addition thereto shall comprise Department No. 1, and have its eastern boundary extended to the line of railroad from Chattanooga via Atlanta and West Point on the Chattahoochee River, and thence down the Chattahoochee and Apalachicola rivers to the Gulf of Mexico.

Extended July 2, 1862, to embrace all of Alabama.

Extended July 18, 1862, to embrace Mississippi, Alabama and East Louisiana, and that part of Florida which is west of the Chattahoochee and Apalachicola Rivers.

Extended January 30, 1863, to embrace the line of railroad from Atlanta to West Point, Georgia, with the towns, villages and stations on it, including the post of Atlanta, and as much adjacent territory as may be necessary for military purposes.

Extended July 25, 1863, to embrace the Department of East Tennessee.

Denominated Department of Tennessee July 25, 1863.

NO. 2 SUB-DISTRICT.

(First Military District of South Carolina, Department of South Carolina, Georgia and Florida.)

(Established ——, 1863.)

Brigadier-General J. H. Trapier, assumed March 14, 1863.

NO. 2* SUB-DISTRICT.

(Department of South Carolina, Georgia and Florida.)

(Established October 17, 1864.)

Major-General R. Ransom, assigned November 5, 1864; assumed November 22, 1864.

NORFOLK, DEPARTMENT OF.

(Established May 26, 1861.)

Major-General Benjamin Huger, May 26, 1861; commanding April 5, 1862.

Extended† December 21, 1861, to embrace that part of North Carolina east of Chowan River, and the counties of Washington and Tyrrell.

Extended February 5, 1862, to embrace the counties of Martin, Bertie, Halifax, Northampton and Hertford, North Carolina.

Merged into Department and Army of Northern Virginia, April 12, 1862.

NORFOLK, STATE FORCES IN AND ABOUT.

Major-General Walter Gwynn, commanding from April 26 to May 23, 1861, turning over command temporarily to Colonel Withers, May 24, 1861.
Major-General Benjamin Huger, assigned May 23, 1861. (See Department of Norfolk.)

* Formerly First Military District of South Carolina.

† Extension constituted District of the Albemarle, under Brigadier-General H. A. Wise.

North Alabama, District of.

(Department of Alabama, Mississippi and East Louisiana.)

(Established in fall of 1864.)

Brigadier-General D. W. Adams, —, 1864; relieved September 24, 1864.

Brigadier-General P. D. Roddy, assigned September 24, 1864.

To comprise that portion of the State of Alabama, lying north of the railroad running through Columbus, Georgia, Opelika, Montgomery, Selma and Demopolis (four latter towns and post of Cahawba in the district).

Divided September 24, 1864, into two districts, to be known as "North Alabama" and "Central Alabama."

North Alabama, District of.

(Department of Alabama and West Florida.)

(Established ——, 1862.)

Brigadier-General D. Ruggles, assigned February 22, 1862; assumed February 23, 1862.

Abolished* March 11, 1865.

North Carolina, Defenses of.

Colonel T. H. Holmes, assigned April 22, 1861. (See Department of North Carolina.)

Brigadier-General J. R. Anderson, assigned September 3, 1861.

North Carolina, Department of.

(Established ——, 1861.)

Brigadier-General R. C. Gatlin, assigned August 19, 1861; assumed August 20, 1861; relieved March 19, 1862.

Brigadier-General J. R. Anderson, assigned March 15, 1862; assumed March 19, 1862.

Major-General T. H. Holmes, assigned March 24, 1862; assumed March 25, 1862.

Major-General D. H. Hill, assigned July 17, 1862; relieved July 1, 1863.

Major-General S. G. French, second in command under General Hill.

Major-General W. H. C. Whiting, assigned July 14, 1863; relieved September 26, 1863, and assigned to separate command of the Cape Fear District and charged with the defense of Wilmington, N. C.

Major-General George E. Pickett,† assigned September 23, 1863.

General Braxton Bragg, commanding November 27, 1864.

Extended November 26, 1861, to embrace Roanoke Island, N. C.

Extended June 21, 1862, to the south bank of James River, including Drewry's Bluff.

Discontinued September 19, 1862.

Re-established April 1, 1863, to embrace the State of North Carolina.

Extended May 28, 1863, to include Department of Southern Virginia as far north as to embrace the city of Petersburg and its environs, and the Appomattox River.

Under department of North Carolina and Southern Virginia May 19, 1864.

North Carolina, District of.

(Department of North Carolina.)

(Established August 18, 1862.)

Brigadier-General J. G. Martin, assigned August 18, 1862.

Embraced the country from the right bank of the Roanoke River to the South Carolina line.

North Carolina, Reserve Forces of.

Lieutenant-General T. H. Holmes, relieved from duty in Trans-Mississippi Department and assigned April 18, 1864.

North Carolina and Southern Virginia,‡ Department of.

(Established September 19, 1862.)

Major-General G. W. Smith, assigned September 19, 1862; resigned February 17, 1863.

Brigadier-General James Longstreet, assigned February 25, 1863; assumed February 26, 1863.

Major-General S. G. French, in temporary command from February 17 to 25, 1863.

Embraced the defenses of Richmond and extending south to include the State of North Carolina, the whole under the supervision of General R. E. Lee.

Extended May 14, 1864, to embrace all that portion of Virginia south of James River, including Drewry's Bluff and its defenses.

Excluded May 19, 1864, line of defenses around Richmond on south side of James River.

Divided April 1, 1863, into three departments—Richmond, Southern Virginia and North Carolina.

* At this date in Department of Alabama, Mississippi and East Louisiana.

† Ordered to Goldsborough, N. C., to take immediate command of forces within this department.

‡ Also called Department of Virginia and North Carolina.

North Carolina, Western District of.

(Department of Tennessee.)

(Established September 16, 1863.)

Brigadier-General Robert B. Vance, assigned September 16, 1863; relieved November 18, 1863.

Colonel J. B. Palmer, assumed November 18, 1863; relieved by Brigadier-General R. B. Vance December 4, 1863.

Embraced all that portion of North Carolina west of Blue Ridge Mountains.

Northern Alabama, District of.

(Department of Alabama, Mississippi and East Louisiana.)

(Established February 6, 1864.)

Major-General J. M. Withers,* February 6, 1864; relieved July 27, 1864.

To embrace that portion of Department of Alabama, Mississippi and East Louisiana lying within the State of Alabama and north of thirty-second parallel of latitude.

Northern Mississippi, District of.

(Department of Alabama, Mississippi and East Louisiana.)

(Established ——, 1864.)

Brigadier-General Wirt Adams, assigned November 6, 1864.

Northern Virginia, Army of.

(Organized March 14, 1862. See Department of Northern Virginia.)

Northern Virginia,† Department of.

(Established October 22, 1861.)

General Joseph E. Johnston, October 22, 1861; relieved (wounded) May 31, 1862.

Major-General G. W. Smith, commanding temporarily May 31 to June 1, 1862.

General Robert E. Lee, assumed June 1, 1862.

Comprising Aquia District, Potomac District and Valley District.

Extended April 12, 1862, to embrace the Departments of Norfolk and Peninsula in its operations.

Extended June 1, 1862, to embrace the armies in Eastern Virginia and in North Carolina.

Extended April 2, 1863, to embrace the post of Staunton, Va.

North Mississippi and West Tennessee, District of.

(Department of Alabama, Mississippi and East Louisiana.)

(Established February 3, 1865.)

Brigadier-General Marcus J. Wright, assigned February 3, 1865.

To embrace the District of West Tennessee and all that portion of Mississippi north of the counties of Noxubee, Winston, Attala, Holmes and Washington.

Northwest,‡ Army of the.

(Organized June 8, 1861.)

Brigadier-General R. S. Garnett, assigned June 8, 1861; killed July 13, 1861.

Brigadier-General H. R. Jackson, assumed July 14, 1861.

Brigadier-General W. W. Loring, assigned July 20, 1861.

General R. E. Lee, commanding August 3, 1861.

Brigadier-General Edward Johnson, commanding May 17, 1862, when it was immediately under Lieutenant-General Jackson.

Merged into Department and Army of Northern Virginia, November —, 1861.

Northwestern Army.

(See Army of the Northwest.)

Northwestern Virginia, Department of.

(See Army of the Northwest.)

Pamlico, District of.

(Department of North Carolina.)

(Established September 29, 1861.)

Brigadier-General D. H. Hill, assigned September 29, 1861; assumed about October 4, 1861.

Brigadier-General L. O'B. Branch, assigned November 16, 1861.

Brigadier-General S. G. French, assigned March 17, 1862; assumed March 18, 1862.

Brigadier-General R. Ransom, assigned March 20, 1862.

Embraced that portion of the State lying between Albemarle Sound and the Neuse River and Pamlico Sound, including those waters.

Extended November 26, 1861, to embrace Roanoke Island.

Extended December 21, 1861, to embrace that part of the coast of North Carolina between the military district under General Wise and Bogue Inlet.

Embraced, March 17, 1862, the counties of Edgecombe, Wilson, Pitt, Greene, Lenoir, Duplin, Jones, Carteret, Craven, Beaufort and Hyde.

* July 27, 1864, assigned to command of reserve forces of State of Alabama.

† For boundaries see Aquia, Potomac and Valley Districts.

‡ Also called Northwestern Army.

Pass Cavallo, Etc., Texas, Defenses of.

Major John W. Glenn, assigned October 26, 1861.

Peninsula, Army of the.

(See Department of the Peninsula.)

Peninsula,* Department of the.

(Established May 21, 1861.)

Colonel John B. Magruder, assigned May 21, 1861; commanding February 1, 1862.

Colonel D. H. Hill, assumed temporarily May 31, 1861.

Embraced the troops and military operations on the line to Hampton.

Extended June 14, 1861, to embrace the troops at Gloucester Point, Va.

Extended June 28, 1861, to embrace the military positions of West Point and Jamestown Island.

Extended August 26, 1861, to embrace the counties of Gloucester, Matthews and Middlesex.

Embraced within the limits of the operations of the Army of Northern Virginia April 12, 1862.

Pensacola, Army of.

(Department of Alabama and West Florida.)

(Organized October 29, 1861.)

General Braxton Bragg, commanding October 29, 1861.

Brigadier-General A. H. Gladden, assigned temporarily December 22, 1861.

Brigadier-General Samuel Jones, assigned January 27, 1862.

Composed of forces at and near Pensacola, Fla.

Discontinued March 13, 1862.

Pensacola,† Florida, Troops in and Near.

Brigadier-General Braxton Bragg,‡ assigned March 7, 1861; assumed March 11, 1861.

Potomac,§ Army of the.

(Organized June 20, 1861.)

Brigadier-General G. T. Beauregard, commanding June 20, 1861.

General Joseph E. Johnston supersedes, July 20, 1861.

Merged into the Department of Northern Virginia October 22, 1861.

Potomac, Army of the.

(Department of Northern Virginia.)

(Organized October 22, 1861.)

Organized into four divisions February 5, 1862. For commanders see Department of Northern Virginia.

Denominated Army of Northern Virginia, March 14, 1862.

Potomac Department.

(See Department of Alexandria.)

Potomac District.

(Department of Northern Virginia.)

(Established October 22, 1861.)

Brigadier-General G. T. Beauregard, assigned October 22, 1861; relieved January 29, 1862; assigned to command at Columbus, Kentucky.

Embraced the section of country between the Blue Ridge Mountains and left bank of Powell's River.

Richmond, Defenses of.

(See Department of North Carolina and Southern Virginia.)

Richmond, Department of

(Established April 1, 1863.)

Major-General A. Elzey, assigned April 1, 1863; relieved March 23, 1864.

Major-General R. Ransom, Jr., assigned April 25, 1864; relieved June 13, 1864.

Lieutenant-General R. S. Ewell, June —, 1864.

Embraced all that part of Virginia north of the James River.

Extended April 23, 1863, to embrace the defenses of Drewry's Bluff and Manchester.

Extended May 5, 1864, to embrace the Department of Henrico.

Rio Grande, Military Sub-District of the.

(Department of Texas.)

(Established February 25, 1862.)

Colonel H. E. McCulloch, assigned February 25, 1862.

Brigadier-General H. P. Bee, assumed April 24, 1862; commanding December 31, 1862.

Embraced the military posts north, west and south of San Antonio, including those at Victoria, Indianola and Saluria.

Denominated (probably) Western Sub-district, ——, 1863.

* Called District of Yorktown, also Army of the Peninsula.

† Designated Army of Pensacola December 22, 1861.

‡ Command extended October 7, 1861, to include the coast and State of Alabama, and denominated by General Bragg Department of Alabama and West Florida October 14, 1861.

§ Formerly known as Department of Alexandria.

LIEUTENANT-GENERAL AMBROSE P. HILL.

BORN IN CULPEPER COUNTY, VA., NOVEMBER 9, 1825. KILLED NEAR PETERSBURG, VA., APRIL 2, 1865.

Reserve Corps, Army of the Mississippi.
(Department No. 2.)

Major-General G. B. Crittenden, assigned March 29, 1862.
Brigadier-General J. C. Breckinridge, commanding April 6 and August 18, 1862.
Brigadier-General J. M. Withers, commanding June 30, 1862.

Reserve Corps, State of Mississippi.

Brigadier-General W. M. Brandon, assumed July 23, 1864.
Divided into two departments (Eastern and Western) July 23, 1864.

Reserve Corps, Trans-Mississippi Department.
(Organized September 10, 1864.)

Brigadier-General J. B. Robertson, assigned September 10, 1864; relieved March 27, 1865.
Brigadier-General T. P. Dockery, assigned September 12, 1864.
Brigadier-General E. Greer, assigned March 27, 1865.

Roanoke Island, Forces at.

Colonel H. M. Shaw, commanding February 9, 1862.

Savannah, Ga., Defenses of.

Major-General J. F. Gilmer, assigned August 31, 1863.
Major-General Samuel Jones, assigned April 2, 1864, relieving General Gilmer.
Major-General L. McLaws, assigned May 18, 1864.

Savannah, Military District of.
(Established April 13, 1861.)

Brigadier-General A. R. Lawton, assigned April 13, 1861; assumed April 17, 1861.
Embraced Fort Pulaski and Savannah, Ga., and the surrounding country.
Extended May 4, 1861, to the whole sea coast of the State of Georgia.
Merged into the Department of Georgia October 26, 1861.

Second Corps, Army of the Mississippi.
(Department No. 2.)

Major-General Braxton Bragg,* assigned March 29, 1862.
Major-General Samuel Jones, commanding June 30, 1862.

Second Corps,† Army of Mississippi.
(Department of Mississippi and East Louisiana.)

Major-General Sterling Price,‡ December 17, 1862.
Composed, in December, 1862, of Brown's and Maury's divisions.

Second Corps, Army of the Potomac.

Major-General G. W. Smith, assigned September 25, 1861.

Second Corps, Army of Northern Virginia.

Major-General G. W. Smith, assigned March 14, 1862; relieved March 23, 1862.
Lieutenant-General T. J. Jackson, commanding from March, 1862, to May, 1863.
Lieutenant-General R. S. Ewell, assigned May 10, 1863; commanding January 31, 1864.
Major-General J. A. Early, assigned temporarily May 29, 1864.

Second Corps (Hardee's), Army of Tennessee.
(Department No. 2.)

Lieutenant-General W. J. Hardee, November 26, 1862; relieved July 14, 1863.
Lieutenant-General Daniel H. Hill, assigned July 19, 1863; assumed July 24, 1863; relieved November 8, 1863.
Major-General J. C. Breckinridge, assigned temporarily November 8, 1863; relieved December 15, 1863.
Major-General T. C. Hindman, assigned December 15, 1863; relieved February 25, 1864.
Lieutenant-General J. B. Hood, assigned February 9, 1864; assumed February 25, 1864; relieved July 18, 1864.
Major-General C. L. Stevenson, assumed July 18, 1864; relieved July 27, 1864.
Lieutenant-General S. D. Lee, assumed July 27, 1864.

Second District.
(Department of South Mississippi and East Louisiana.)
(Established June 26, 1862.)

Brigadier-General W. N. R. Beall, assigned June 26, 1862.
Embraced all the counties of Mississippi below and touching the thirty-second parallel of latitude, except at those Gulf counties.

* Commanding Army of the Mississippi, and Second Corps, same army, August 18, 1862.
† Called by General Price Army of West Tennessee.
‡ January 22, 1863, assumed command of Second Division; February 27, 1862, ordered to report for duty in Trans-Mississippi Department.

Second Military District.
(Department of Mississippi and East Louisiana.)
(Established October 21, 1862.)

Brigadier-General M. L. Smith, assigned October 21, 1862.
Embraced that portion of Mississippi included between the Mississippi & Tennessee Railroad, the Mississippi River and the Big Black River.
Abolished September 2, 1863.

Second Military District.
(Department of North Carolina and Southern Virginia.)
(Established ——, ——.)

Brigadier-General John H. Winder, assigned May 25, 1864; relieved ——, 1864.
Brigadier-General L. S. Baker, assigned June 9, 1864.

Second Military District of South Carolina.
(Department of South Carolina, Georgia and Florida.)
(Established December 10, 1861.)

Brigadier-General R. S. Ripley, assigned December 10, 1861; relieved May 28, 1862.
Brigadier-General H. W. Mercer, assigned May 26, 1862; assumed May 28, 1862.
Brigadier-General N. G. Evans, assigned May 28, 1862; relieved June 15, 1862.
Brigadier-General B. H. Robertson, December 2, 1863.
Brigadier-General J. Hagood, December 28, 1863.
Brigadier-General J. H. Trapier, assigned May 10, 1863.
Embraced that section of country beginning at the South Santee and extending to the Stono River and up Rantowles Creek.
Re-subdivided December 28, 1862.
Extended December 2, 1863, to embrace all the country between the western limits of the Sixth Military District and the Combahee and the Little Salkehatchie rivers and the southern boundary of Barnwell District to the Edisto River.
Consolidated with the Sixth Military District October 17, 1864, and denominated Sub-district No. 4.

Seventh Military District of South Carolina.
(Department of South Carolina, Georgia and Florida.)
(Established October 22, 1863.)

Brigadier-General W. B. Taliaferro, assigned October 22, 1863.
Embraced James Island.
Denominated Sub-district No. 3 October 17, 1864.

Shenandoah, Army of the.
(Organized July 4, 1861.)

General J. E. Johnston, July 4, 1861.
United with the Army of the Potomac (afterward known as the Army of Northern Virginia) July 20, 1861.

Sibley's Brigade.
(See Army of New Mexico.)

Sixth Military District of South Carolina.
(Department of South Carolina, Georgia and Florida.)
(Established October 22, 1863.)

Brigadier-General H. A. Wise, assigned October 22, 1863.
Embraced all that part of St. Andrew's Parish south of the Ashley River and west of Wappoo Cut, and to include the *tete-de-ponts* at Rantowles Station and the work at Church Flats.
Extended December 2, 1863, to embrace all the country to the east bank of the North Edisto from the mouth to Giohams Ferry.
Consolidated with Second Military District October 17, 1864, and denominated Sub-district No. 4.

Smith's Corps, Army of Tennessee.
(See Army of Kentucky.)

South Carolina, Department of.
(Established August 21, 1861.)

Brigadier-General R. S. Ripley, assigned August 21, 1861.
Embraced coast defenses of South Carolina.
Merged into the Department of South Carolina, Georgia and Florida November 5, 1861.

South Carolina, District of.
(Department of South Carolina, Georgia and Florida.)
(Established October 17, 1864.)

No commander designated; probably Samuel Jones.
To embrace the State of South Carolina, except that portion of it comprised in the Third Military District of South Carolina.

South Carolina and Georgia, Department of.
(See Department of South Carolina, Georgia and Florida.)

South Carolina, Georgia and East Florida, Department of.
(See Department of South Carolina, Georgia and Florida.)

South Carolina, Georgia and Florida,* Department of.
(Established November 5, 1861.)

General R. E. Lee,† assigned November 5, 1861; assumed November 8, 1861.
Major-General J. C. Pemberton, assigned temporarily March 3, 1862; assumed March 4, 1862; assigned permanently March 14, 1862; assumed March 19, 1862; relieved September 24, 1862.
Brigadier-General G. T. Beauregard,‡ assigned August 29, 1862; assumed September 24, 1862; relieved temporarily April 20, 1864.
Major-General J. F. Gilmer, announced as second in command August 31, 1863.
Major-General Samuel Jones, assigned temporarily April 20, 1864.
Lieutenant-General W. J. Hardee, assigned September 28, 1864; assumed October 5, 1864 (official order issued October 28, 1864); relieved February 16, 1865, and ordered to report to Headquarters Military Division of the West.
Embraced the coasts of South Carolina, Georgia and East Florida.
Extended April 7, 1862, to include Eastern and Middle Florida as far west as the Choctawhatchee River; East Florida formerly in this department.
Extended October 7, 1862, to embrace the States of South Carolina and Georgia, and that part of Florida east of Apalachicola River.
Extended November 4, 1862, to embrace the Districts of East and Middle Florida.
Extended November 17, 1864, to embrace all that part of Georgia south of the Chattahoochee River.
Limits changed January 4, 1865, to west of Augusta and Millen, embracing approaches.
Extended January 6, 1865, to embrace that part of Georgia commencing at Augusta, and running along the Georgia Railroad to Warrenton; thence via Sparta and Milledgeville, following the line of railroad to Ocmulgee River, but not including Macon; down the Ocmulgee to Coffee County, following the western boundary of that county to Allapaha River, and down that river and the Suwannee to the Gulf.

South Carolina, Reserve Forces of.

Brigadier-General James Chestnut, assigned April 30, 1864; ordered to take immediate command June 20, 1864.

Southern Mississippi and East Louisiana,§ Department of.
(Established —— —, 1862.)

Major-General Earl Van Dorn, assigned June 20, 1862.
Denominated by General Bragg District of the Mississippi July 2, 1862.

Southern Mississippi and East Louisiana, District of.
(Department of Alabama, Mississippi and East Louisiana.)
(Established —— —, 1864.)

Colonel Edward Dillon, March 5, 1864.
Brigadier-General T. H. Taylor, assigned March 5, 1864.
Colonel John S. Scott, assigned April 5, 1864.

South Mississippi and East Louisiana,‖ District of.
(Department of Alabama, Mississippi and East Louisiana.)
(Established February 3, 1865.)

Brigadier-General Wirt Adams, assigned February 3, 1865.
Brigadier-General G. B. Hodge, assigned March 14, 1865.
To embrace the Sub-district of Southwest Mississippi and East Louisiana, and all that portion of State of Mississippi not included in District of North Mississippi and West Tennessee or the District of the Gulf.

Southern Virginia, Department of.
(Established April 1, 1863.)

Major-General S. G. French,¶ assigned April 1, 1863; relieved May 28, 1863.
Embraced all that part of Virginia south of the James River and east of Powhatan County.
Merged into Department of North Carolina May 28, 1863.

Southern Virginia and North Carolina, Department of.
(See Department of North Carolina and Southern Virginia.)

* Called Department of South Carolina, Georgia and East Florida; also Department of South Carolina and Georgia.
† Previously in command of Virginia forces.
‡ February 16, 1865, assumed command of all the troops operating in the State of South Carolina.
§ Called by General Van Dorn District of the Mississippi August 17, 1862.
‖ Under the District of Mississippi and East Louisiana.
¶ Ordered to report to General Johnston in Mississippi, May 28, 1863.

SOUTHWESTERN ARMY.

(Organized January 14, 1863.)

Lieutenant-General E. K. Smith,* assigned January 14, 1863.

Extended, February 9, 1863, to embrace Trans-Mississippi Department.

SOUTHWESTERN KENTUCKY, DEPARTMENT OF.

(See Department of Western Kentucky.)

SOUTHWESTERN VIRGINIA,† DEPARTMENT OF.

(Established May 8, 1862.)

Major-General W. W. Loring, assigned May 8, 1862; relieved October 16, 1862.

Brigadier-General John Echols, assigned October 15, 1862; relieved November 19, 1862.

Brigadier-General S. Williams, assigned November 10, 1862; assumed November 19, 1862.

Embraced the districts of Lewisburg and Abingdon.

Denominated Trans-Allegheny or Western Department of Virginia, November 25, 1862.

SOUTHWEST MISSISSIPPI AND EAST LOUISIANA, DISTRICT OF.

(Department of Alabama, Mississippi and East Louisiana.)

(Established ——, 1864.)

Brigadier-General St. John R. Liddell, August 2, 1864; relieved August 4, 1864.

Brigadier-General G. B. Hodge, assigned August 4, 1864; assumed about August 25, 1864.

Comprising the country south of a line running due east from Natchez to Pearl River.

Constituted part of District of South Mississippi and East Louisiana, February 3, 1865.

SOUTHWEST MISSISSIPPI AND EAST LOUISIANA,‡ SUB-DISTRICT OF.

(Department of Alabama, Mississippi and East Louisiana.)

(Established ——, 1865.)

Brigadier-General Wirt Adams ——; relieved February 3, 1865.

Merged into the District of South Mississippi and East Louisiana, February 3, 1865.

TENNESSEE,§ ARMY‖ OF.

(Department No. 2.)

(Organized November 20, 1862.)

Composed of Smith's, Polk's and Hardee's¶ Corps, November 20, 1862.

TENNESSEE,** DEPARTMENT OF.

(Established July 25, 1863.)

General Braxton Bragg, assumed August 6, 1863; relinquished December 2, 1863.

Lieutenant-General W. J. Hardee, assigned temporarily December 2, 1863; relieved December 22, 1863.

Lieutenant-General L. Polk in command temporarily August —, 1863, and December 23 to 27, 1863.

General J. E. Johnston, assigned December 18, 1863; assumed December 27, 1863; relieved July 18, 1864; reassumed February 25, 1865.

General J. B. Hood, assigned July 18, 1864.

General G. T. Beauregard, announced as second in command March 16, 1865.

Extended, July 25, 1863, to embrace the country now included in the Department of East Tennessee and west of the Blue Ridge Mountains, in North Carolina, and a line running south to the Georgia Railroad; thence along the line of railroad, via Atlanta, to West Point; from that place north to Tennessee River, and down that stream to its mouth.

Extended, February 13, 1864: Bounded on the north and east by the country east of the Tennessee and Clinch rivers and Emery's Creek and a line south of source of Little Tennessee River to Greensborough, Georgia; on the south and west by the Georgia Railroad from that place to Atlanta, Georgia, and the Montgomery & West Point Railroad to West Point, Georgia; the country west of the Chattahoochee and Apalachicola Rivers, and of the Alabama and Georgia State line until it strikes the southeastern corner of Calhoun County, Alabama; thence along the southern line of Calhoun, St. Clair, Blount, Morgan, Lawrence and Franklin counties, Alabama; thence along the Alabama and Mississippi State line to the Tennessee River; along that river to its confluence with Ohio River. All the country north of the counties named above come within the limit of General Bragg's Department.

* Embraced the District of West Louisiana and Texas, and separate and distinct from the command of the Trans-Mississippi Department.

† Also called Department of Western Virginia.

‡ Under the District of Mississippi and East Louisiana.

§ Formerly Army of the Mississippi.

‖ For commanders, see Department of Tennessee.

¶ Lieutenant-General W. J. Hardee relieved from duty September 28, 1864, and assigned to the command of Department of South Carolina, Georgia and Florida.

** Formerly Department No. 2.

More particularly defined March 25, 1864: From Gunter's Landing, on Tennessee River, in a direct line to Gadsden, on Coosa River; thence down that river to its junction with the Tallapoosa River; thence in a direct line to the intersection of the northern boundary of Florida with the Chattahoochee River, and down that river and bay to the Gulf. All west of said line will be considered in the Department of Alabama, Mississippi and East Louisiana; and east of that line, from the northern boundary of Florida at its intersection by the Chattahoochee River, in the Department of Tennessee.

Extended August 15, 1864, to include all the State of Georgia north and west of following line: Commencing at Augusta and running along the Augusta & Savannah Railroad to Millen; thence along the western boundary lines to the counties of Bullock and Tatnall; thence along the south bank of the Ocmulgee River to the northeast corner of Irwin County; thence south to the Florida line; thence along the Florida line to the Apalachicola River.

Denominated as Department of Tennessee and Georgia August 15, 1864.

TENNESSEE, DISTRICT OF THE.

(Department No. 2.)

(Established July 21, 1862.)

Major-General S. Price, commanding July 21, 1862.

Embraced, July 21, 1862, Northwestern Alabama and all that portion of the State of Mississippi which is north of the thirty-second parallel of latitude and east of Pearl River, and of the Mississippi Central Railroad from Jackson to Grand Junction.

TENNESSEE AND GEORGIA,* DEPARTMENT OF.

(Established August 15, 1864.)

General J. B. Hood, August 15, 1864; relieved at own request January 23, 1865.

Lieutenant-General R. Taylor, assumed January 23, 1865.

General J. E. Johnston, assigned to the two military departments known as the Department of Tennessee and Georgia and the Department of South Carolina, Georgia and Florida, and the troops therein, etc., February 22, 1865; assumed February 25, 1865.

Major-General Howell Cobb, assigned March 27, 1865.

More particularly defined October 1, 1864: Commencing at the southwestern boundary between Georgia and Florida on the Apalachicola River; thence along the Chattahoochee River north, and following the boundary line between Georgia and Alabama to Tennessee River. All west of said line will be considered in the Department of Alabama, Mississippi and East Louisiana, and east of the line, from the northern boundary of Florida at its intersection by the Chattahoochee River, in the Department of Tennessee [and Georgia].

TEXAS, DEPARTMENT OF.

(Established April 21, 1861.)

Colonel Earl Van Dorn, assumed April 21, 1861.

Brigadier-General P. O. Hebert, assigned August 14, 1861; assumed September 18, 1861.

Colonel H. E. McCulloch, commanding temporarily from September 4 to 18, 1861.

Embraced the State of Texas.

Divided into two districts February 10, 1862, called the Eastern and Western.

Merged into the Trans-Mississippi Department May 26, 1862.

TEXAS,† DISTRICT OF.

(Trans-Mississippi Department.)

(Established August 20, 1862.)

Brigadier-General P. O. Hebert, assigned August 20, 1862; relieved ——— —, 1862.

Major-General J. B. Magruder, assigned October 10, 1862.

Denominated District of Texas, New Mexico and Arizona December —, 1862.

TEXAS, EASTERN DISTRICT OF.

(Department of Texas.)

(Established February 10, 1862.)

Embraced the country between the northern and eastern boundaries of the State and the eastern shore of Galveston Bay, and the left bank of Trinity River to the intersection of the Cross-Timbers at Alton; thence following Cross-Timbers to Red River.

TEXAS, EASTERN SUB-DISTRICT OF.

(Trans-Mississippi Department.)

(Established —— —, 1863.)

Colonel X. B. Debray, assigned ——— —, 1863; relieved February 13, 1863; reassigned temporarily June 10, 1863; relieved July 1, 1863.

Brigadier-General W. R. Scurry, assigned and assumed February 13, 1863; relieved permanently September 17, 1863.

Brigadier-General P. N. Luckett assigned temporarily July 1, 1863.

* For geographical boundary see Department of Tennessee.

† Also called District of Texas and Territory of Arizona.

Brigadier-General H. E. McCulloch, assigned temporarily August 15, 1863.

Embraced that part of the State included between the Sabine River on the east and a line commencing at Watsons Ferry, on the Sabine, and running along the southern boundary of Panola, Rusk, Cherokee, Anderson, Freestone and Limestone counties, to Marlin, Falls County, on the Brazos; thence up the Brazos, to McLennan; thence along the western boundary to Falls, Bell, Williamson, Travis, Bastrop, Fayette, Colorado, Wharton and Madagorda counties, to Passa-Cavallo, but excluding said place.

Extended, temporarily, March 4, 1863, to embrace Lavaca and Victoria.

TEXAS, NEW MEXICO AND ARIZONA, DISTRICT OF.

(Trans-Mississippi Department.)

(Established December —, 1862.)

Major-General J. B. Magruder, commanding February 28, 1863; reassigned August 11, 1864, and March 31, 1865.

Major-General J. G. Walker, assigned August 4, 1864; relieved March 31, 1865.

TEXAS,* NORTHERN SUB-DISTRICT OF.

(Trans-Mississippi Department.)

(Established June 5, 1863.)

Lieutenant-Colonel S. P. Bankhead, assumed July 9, 1863.

Brigadier-General H. E. McCulloch, assigned August 29, 1863.

Embraced the following: Commencing at Hattens Ferry, on the Sabine River, and running along the southern boundary of the counties of Sabine, San Augustine, Angelina, Houston, Limestone, and the eastern part of Falls County, to Marlin, on the Brazos River; thence up said river to Fort Belknap; thence due north to Red River, inclusive.

TEXAS,† RESERVE FORCES OF.

Brigadier-General J. B. Robertson, assigned June 24, 1864.

TEXAS AND TERRITORY OF ARIZONA, DISTRICT OF.

(See District of Texas.)

TEXAS, WESTERN DISTRICT OF.

(Department of Texas.)

(Established February 10, 1862.)

Embraced all of Texas not included in the Eastern District.

TEXAS,‡ WESTERN SUB-DISTRICT OF.

(Trans-Mississippi Department.)

(Established ——, 1863.)

Brigadier-General H. P. Bee, June 23, 1863.

Brigadier-General J. E. Slaughter, commanding October 25, 1864.

Embraced that part of the State bounded on the east by the Eastern Sub-district; up the southern boundary of McLennan County, on the Brazos; thence by the Brazos River to Fort Belknap; thence by line drawn due south to Red River; thence to the extreme limits of the State, nclusive.

THIRD CORPS, ARMY OF THE MISSISSIPPI.

(Department No. 2.)

Major-General W. J. Hardee, assigned March 29, 1862.

THIRD CORPS, ARMY OF NORTHERN VIRGINIA.

Lieutenant-General A. P. Hill, July 19, 1863; relieved May 8, 1864.

Major-General J. A. Early, assigned temporarily May 8, 1864.

THIRD DISTRICT.

(Department of South Mississippi and East Louisiana.)

(Established June 26, 1862.)

Brigadier-General M. L. Smith, assigned June 26, 1862.

Embraced all the counties of Mississippi lying between the thirty-second and thirty-third parallels of latitude.

THIRD MILITARY DISTRICT.

(Department of Mississippi and East Louisiana.)

(Established October 21, 1862.)

Brigadier-General W. N. R. Beall, assigned October 21, 1862; relieved December 27, 1862; reassigned May 6, 1863; relieved May 11, 1863.

Major-General Frank Gardner, assigned December 27, 1862; assumed December 28, 1862; relinquished May 6, 1863; reassumed May 11, 1863.

Embraced that portion of Mississippi included between the Big Black and Mississippi rivers and the New Orleans & Jackson Railroad; also that portion of Louisiana east of Mississippi River, together with such counties in Mississippi as border on the Gulf of Mexico.

Abolished September 2, 1863.

* Formerly known as Third Military Sub-district.

† Afterward known as Reserve Corps Trans-Mississippi Department.

‡ Formerly known (probably) as Sub-District of the Rio Grande under General Bee.

THIRD MILITARY DISTRICT.

(Department of North Carolina and Southern Virginia.)

(Established —— —, ——.)

Major-General W. H. C. Whiting, commanding in June, 1864.

THIRD MILITARY DISTRICT OF SOUTH CAROLINA.*

(Department of South Carolina, Georgia and Florida.)

(Established December 10, 1861.)

Brigadier-General N. G. Evans, assigned December 18, 1861.

Colonel W. S. Walker, assigned May 28, 1862; commanding December 2, 1863.

Embraced the country between the Stono and the Ashepoo rivers.

Re-subdivided December 28, 1862.

Extended December 2, 1863, to embrace all the country between the western limits of the Second Military District and the Savannah River.

Denominated Sub-district No. 5 October 17, 1864.

THIRD MILITARY SUB-DISTRICT.

District of Texas (Trans-Mississippi Department).

(Established —— —, 1863.)

Colonel S. P. Bankhead, assigned May 30, 1863.

Denominated Northern Sub-district June 5, 1863.

TRANS-ALLEGHANY OR WESTERN DEPARTMENT OF VIRGINIA.†

(Established November 25, 1862.)

Brigadier-General John S. Williams, November 25 to December 10, 1862.

Major-General Sam Jones, assigned November 25, 1862; assumed December 10, 1862; relieved February 25, 1864.

Brigadier-General J. C. Breckinridge, assigned February 25, 1864; assumed March 5, 1864; relieved temporarily May 25, 1864; ordered to resume September 17, 1864, and ordered to take immediate command of reserve forces of East Tennessee in addition September 27, 1864. Commanded Department of East Tennessee in addition.

Brigadier-General W. E. Jones, assigned temporarily May 23, 1864; assumed May 25, 1864, and commanding Department of East Tennessee in addition; relieved May 31, 1864.

Colonel George B. Crittenden, commanding temporarily May 31, 1864; relieved June 22, 1864. Commanded Department of East Tennessee in addition.

Brigadier-General John H. Morgan, assumed temporarily June 22, 1864; relieved August 30, 1864. Commanded Department of East Tennessee in addition.

Lieutenant-General J. A. Early, commanding March 25, 1865; relieved March 29, 1865. Commanded Department of East Tennessee in addition.

Brigadier-General John Echols, commanding March 29, 1865.

Extended November 25, 1862, west to the eastern boundary of Kentucky, and as far west of that boundary as may be necessary.

Extended September 5, 1863, to embrace that part of Southwestern Virginia which belongs to the Department of East Tennessee, and all the forces east of Knoxville.

Brigadier-General John S. Williams, commanding temporarily.

Extended March 19, 1864, to embrace Saltville, Va.

TRANS-MISSISSIPPI DEPARTMENT.

(Established May 26, 1862.)

Brigadier-General P. O. Hebert, temporarily in command.

Major-General T. H. Holmes, assigned July 16, 1862; assumed July 30, 1862; relieved March 18, 1863.

Lieutenant-General E. K. Smith, assigned February 9, 1863; assumed March 7, 1863; relinquished temporarily April 19, 1865; resumed April 22, 1865.

Lieutenant-General S. B. Buckner, assigned temporarily April 19, 1865.

Embraced the States of Missouri and Arkansas, including the Indian Territory, the State of Louisiana west of Mississippi River, and the State of Texas.

TRANS-MISSISSIPPI DISTRICT, DEPARTMENT NO. 2.

(Established January 9, 1862.)

Major-General Earl Van Dorn, assigned January 9, 1862; assumed January 29, 1862.

Major-General T. C. Hindman, assigned May 26, 1862; assumed May 31, 1862.

Embraced that part of Louisiana north of the Red River, and Indian Territory west of Arkansas, and Arkansas and Missouri, excepting the tract of country east of the St. Francis bordering on the Mississippi River from mouth of the St. Francis to Scott County, Missouri, which tract will remain in the district of Major-General Polk.

Merged into Trans-Mississippi Department May 26, 1862.

* Attached to the Second Military District temporarily December 10, 1861.

† Formerly called Department of Southwestern Virginia.

UPPER ARKANSAS, DISTRICT OF.

(See District of Arkansas, Trans-Mississippi Department.)

VALLEY DISTRICT, DEPARTMENT OF NORTH VIRGINIA.

(Established October 22, 1861.)

Major-General T. J. Jackson, assigned October 22 and 28, 1861; assumed November —, 1861; relieved September 29, 1862; reassumed —— —, 1863; died May 10, 1863.

Major-General D. H. Hill, commanding temporarily September 6, 1862.

Brigadier-General W. E. Jones, assigned temporarily December 29, 1862; commanding January 7, 1863.

Major-General J. A. Early,* assigned temporarily June 15, 1863.

Brigadier-General J. D. Imboden, assigned July 28, 1863.

Brigadier-General L. L. Lomax, assigned March 29, 1865.

Embraced the section of country between the Blue Ridge and Alleghany mountains.

VIRGINIA FORCES,† ARMY AND NAVY.‡

Major-General Robert E. Lee,§ assumed April 23, 1861.

VIRGINIA AND NORTH CAROLINA, DEPARTMENT OF.

(See Department of North Carolina and Southern Virginia.)

VIRGINIA, RESERVE FORCES OF.

Brigadier-General J. L. Kemper, assigned April 30, 1864.

WEST,‖ ARMY OF THE.

(Department No. 2.)

(Organized March 4, 1862.)

Major-General Earl Van Dorn, assumed March 4, 1862; relieved June 20, 1862.

Major-General J. P. McCown, assumed June 20, 1862; relinquished June 27, 1862.

Brigadier-General D. H. Maury, assumed, temporarily, June 27, 1862.

Major-General S. Price, assumed July 3, 1862; commanding September 26, 1862.

Composed of the divisions of Price and McCulloch.

Reorganized October 19, 1862, with Brigadier-Generals Bowen and Maury commanding divisions.

United with the Army of Tennessee at battle of Corinth.

WEST,¶ DEPARTMENT OF THE.

(Established November 24, 1862.)

General J. E. Johnston,** assigned November 24, 1862; assumed December 4, 1862.

Embraced the following: Commencing with the Blue Ridge range of mountains running through the western part of North Carolina, and following the line of said mountains through the northern part of Georgia to the railroad south from Chattanooga; thence by that road to West Point, and down the west or right bank of Chattahoochee River to the boundary of Alabama and Florida; following that boundary west to Choctawhatchee River, and down that river to Choctawhatchee Bay (including the waters of that bay) to the Gulf of Mexico, including all that portion of country west of said line to Mississippi River.

Extended November 29, 1862, to embrace the city of Atlanta, Georgia.

Embraced, July 31, 1863, the country west of the line between Georgia and Alabama, and running south to the Gulf as before General Bragg's Department was formed. Its western limit is the Mississippi River, and its northern boundary the Tennessee River and Kentucky line.

Limits more particularly defined August 12, 1863; embraced the country west of the Apalachicola and Chattahoochee rivers, and of the Alabama and Georgia State line until it strikes the southeastern corner of Calhoun County, Alabama; thence along the southern line to the following tier of counties in Alabama: Calhoun, St. Clair, Blount, Morgan, Lawrence and Franklin; thence along the Alabama and Mississippi State line to Tennessee River, and along that river to its confluence with the Ohio River. The counties named above, and all that country north of them, to come within the limits of General Bragg's Department.

* "Department of Winchester," comprising all the Valley south and as far as Woodstock, and north as far as the lines of the army.

† A district created April 26, 1861, to include all the State forces in and about Richmond; Major-General Joseph E. Johnston assigned to command. Discontinued November 5, 1861.

‡ Military and Naval Forces of Virginia transferred to the Confederate States June 8, 1861.

§ Ordered to assume command of all forces from other States tendering their services to Virginia May 7, 1861; assumed control of Confederate States May 10, 1861.

‖ Called by Price, District of the Tennessee, August 1 to September 4, 1862; Second Army Corps (Department of Mississippi and East Louisiana), December 9, 1862, to March 6, 1863; Price's Division April 3 to December 8, 1863; proper designation of Van Dorn's and Price's commands should be first and second corps.

¶ Known as General J. E. Johnston's Geographical command.

** July 22, 1863, relieved of command of Department of Tennessee, which was united to that of East Tennessee to extend Bragg's command over that of Buckner's.

WESTERN DEPARTMENT.

(See Department No. 2.)

WESTERN KENTUCKY,* DEPARTMENT OF.

(Established September 6, 1864.)

Brigadier-General A. R. Johnson, assigned September 6, 1864.

Brigadier-General H. B. Lyon, assigned September 26, 1864.

Embraced the following: Commencing at the mouth of Salt River, Kentucky, and extending through Elizabethtown, Glasgow and Tompkinsville, Kentucky, to Carthage, Tennessee; thence along Cumberland River to Nashville; thence with the line of the Northwestern Railroad to Tennessee River; thence west to Hickman, Kentucky; thence along Mississippi River to mouth of Ohio River; thence along Ohio River to the beginning of the line.

WESTERN MILITARY DISTRICT.

(Department of Texas.)

(See Military Sub-District of the Rio Grande.)

WESTERN VIRGINIA, DEPARTMENT OF.

(See Departments of Southwestern Virginia and Trans-Alleghany or Western Department of Virginia.)

WEST LOUISIANA,† DISTRICT OF.

(Trans-Mississippi Department.)

(Established August 20, 1862.)

Major-General R. Taylor,‡ assigned August 20, 1862; relieved June 10, 1864.

Major-General J. G. Walker, assigned June 10, 1864.

Major-General S. B. Buckner, assigned August 4, 1864.

Embraced the State of Louisiana west of Mississippi River.

Re-established ——, 1863.

Consolidated with District of Arkansas April 19, 1865, to be known as the District of Arkansas and West Louisiana.

WEST LOUISIANA AND TEXAS, DISTRICT OF.

(Trans-Mississippi Department.)

(Established May 28, 1862.)

Brigadier-General P. O. Hebert, assigned May 28, 1862; assumed June 18, 1862.

Embraced the State of Texas and all that part of Louisiana west of the Mississippi River and south of Red River, and all posts, camps and troops within the limits thereof.

Merged into the Trans-Mississippi Department February 9, 1863.

WEST, MILITARY DIVISION OF THE.

(Established October 3, 1864.)

General G. T. Beauregard, assigned October 3, 1864; assumed October 17, 1864.

Composed of the Department of Tennessee and Georgia, and of Alabama, Mississippi and East Louisiana.

WEST TENNESSEE,§ ARMY OF.

(See District of the Mississippi, Department No. 2.)

WEST VIRGINIA AND EAST TENNESSEE, DEPARTMENT OF.

(See Department of East Tennessee and Trans-Alleghany or Western Department of Virginia.)

WEST TENNESSEE, DISTRICT OF.

(Department of Alabama, Mississippi and East Louisiana.)

(Established ——, ——.)

YORKTOWN, DEPARTMENT OF.

(See Department of the Peninsula.)

YORKTOWN, DISTRICT OF.

(See Department of the Peninsula.)

* Also called Department of Southwestern Kentucky.

† Also called District of Louisiana.

‡ Relieved from duty in Trans-Mississippi Department August 15, 1864, and assigned to command of Department of Alabama, Mississippi and East Louisiana.

§ Also called Army of Tennessee.

ANECDOTE OF "STONEWALL" JACKSON.—During "Stonewall's" brilliant campaign in the Shenandoah Valley it became necessary that a bridge over a small creek should be built in great haste. One evening Jackson sent for his old pioneer captain, Myers by name, and pointed out to him the urgency of the occasion, saying that he would send him the plan of his colonel of engineers as soon as it was done. Next morning Jackson rode down to Captain Myers' quarters, and saluting the veteran, said: "Captain, did you get the plan of the bridge from Colonel ——?" "Well," said the captain, "the bridge, general, is built, but I don't know whether the *picture* is done or not!"

ROSTER OF THE

GENERAL OFFICERS OF THE CONFEDERATE ARMY AND THEIR COMMANDS, 1861-1865.

COMPILED FROM THE ORIGINAL MANUSCRIPT COPY, FOUND AMONG THE ARCHIVES OF THE LATE CONFEDERACY.
ALL OFFICERS TO WHOSE NAMES THIS MARK [*] IS PREFIXED, WERE GRADUATES OF THE UNITED STATES MILITARY ACADEMY AT WEST POINT.

COMMANDER-IN-CHIEF.

*LEE, ROBERT E., VIRGINIA.

Major-General commanding Virginia State forces, April 23, 1861, and charged with organization of State forces.
Brigadier-General, C. S. A., May 14, 1861.
General, C. S. A., June 14, 1861.
General-in-Chief, January 31, 1865.
Died at Lexington, Va., October 12, 1870.

COMMANDS.

In command of operations in the Trans-Alleghany region of Virginia, August 3, 1861.

November 5, 1861, in charge of the defenses on the coast of South Carolina, Georgia and Florida.

Commanding the Army of Northern Virginia, June —, 1862.

March 13, 1862, assigned to duty at Richmond, and charged with the conduct of all military operations of the Confederate States Army, under the direction of the President.

In command of the Army of Northern Virginia, from June 1, 1862, to the surrender of his army at Appomattox Courthouse, Va., to General U. S. Grant, United States Army, on April 9, 1865.

February 6, 1865, assigned command of all the armies of the Confederate States.

GENERAL ROBERT E. LEE, OF VIRGINIA.
[From a photograph taken in 1865.]

GENERALS.

(7.)

ARRANGED IN ORDER OF RANK.

1. COOPER, SAMUEL, VIRGINIA.

General, C. S. A., May 16, 1861.
Adjutant and Inspector-General, C. S. A., from May 16, 1861, until the close of the war.
Died at Cameron, Alexandria County, Va., December 3, 1876.

2. *JOHNSTON, ALBERT SIDNEY, TEXAS.

General, C. S. A., May 30, 1861.

COMMANDS.

September 10, 1861, assigned to the command of Department No. 2, embracing the territory of the States of Tennessee and Arkansas, all that part of the State of Mississippi west of the New Orleans, Jackson and Great Northern Railroad and the Great Northern and Central Railroad, and the military operations in the States of Kentucky, Missouri and Kansas, and the Indian Territory west of Missouri and Arkansas.

Commanding the Army of the Mississippi at the battle of Shiloh, Tenn., on the 6th of April, 1862, where he was killed.

3. *BEAUREGARD, G. T., LOUISIANA.

Brigadier-General, C. S. A., March 1, 1861.
General, C. S. A., July 21, 1861.
Died at New Orleans, February 20, 1893.

COMMANDS.

Assigned to command at Charleston, S. C., March 1, 1861.

June 2, 1861, assigned command of Department of Alexandria, Va.

On June 20, commanding Army of Potomac.

In command at Manassas, Va., July 19-21, 1861.

In command of District of the Potomac, by General Orders No. 15, Adjutant and Inspector General's Office, Richmond, October 22, 1861.

Ordered to command at Columbus, Ky., by Secretary of War, January 29, 1862.

On March 5, 1862, in command of the Army of the Mississippi.

In command of the Department of South Carolina and Georgia, August 29, 1863; Florida added to the department in 1863.

In command of the Department of North Carolina and Southern Virginia, April 23, 1864.

In command of the troops in Southeastern Virginia, including Petersburg and Drewrys Bluff, May 14, 1864.

Commanding October 17, 1864, Military Division of the West, east of the Mississippi River, comprising the Department of Tennessee and Georgia, commanded by General J. B. Hood, and the Department of Alabama, Mississippi and East Louisiana, commanded by Lieutenant-General Richard Taylor.

February 16, 1865, in command of all troops operating in South Carolina.

February 25, 1865, announced as second in command of Army of Tennessee to General Joseph E. Johnston.

4. *JOHNSTON, JOS. E., VIRGINIA.

Major-General, Virginia State forces, April 26, 1861.
Brigadier-General, C. S. A., May 14, 1861.
General, C. S. A., August 13, 1861 (under act of Confederate Congress, approved May 16, 1861), and to rank from July 4, 1861.
Died March 29, 1891.

COMMANDS.

Assigned to command of Virginia State forces in and about Richmond, April 26, 1861.

Assigned to command at Harpers Ferry, May 15, 1861, and assumed command May 24, 1861.

Assumed command at Manassas, Va., July 20, 1861.

Department of Northern Virginia organized October 22, 1861.

April 15, 1862, command extended to include Norfolk and the Peninsula, and in command of the troops on Peninsula.

November 24, 1862, commanding Department of the West, including the commands of Generals Bragg, Kirby Smith and Pemberton.

March 9, 1863, ordered to the command of General Bragg's army.

May 9, 1863, commanding Department of Mississippi.

December 18, 1863, assigned to the command of the Army of Tennessee.

Removed from that command July 17, 1864.

Assigned to command of the Army of Tennessee, February 23, 1865, in North Carolina, and of all troops in the Department of South Carolina, Georgia and Florida.

Surrendered his army to Major-General W. T. Sherman, United States Army, by military convention entered into and signed April 26, 1865.

5. * SMITH, E. KIRBY, FLORIDA.

Lieutenant-Colonel, Corps of Cavalry, C. S. A., March 16, 1861.
Brigadier-General, P. A. C. S., June 17, 1861.
Major-General, P. A. C. S., October 11, 1861.
Lieutenant-General, P. A. C. S., February 19, 1862.
Died at Sewanee, Tenn., March 28, 1893.

COMMANDS.

Chief of staff to General Joseph E. Johnston, commanding Army of the Potomac, June to July, 1861.

Commanding Reserve Division, Army of the Potomac, July 2, 1861, consisting of the brigades of Trimble, Taylor and Elzey, brigade composed of the Ninth, Tenth and Eleventh Alabama, Fourteenth Mississippi, and Thirty-eighth Virginia regiments infantry, Army of the Potomac.

Commanding Department of East Tennessee and Kentucky, North Georgia and Western North Carolina, and the infantry divisions of Stevenson, McCown and Heth, and cavalry brigades of Forrest, Morgan, Scott and Ashby, March 21 to October —, ——.

Assigned February 9, 1863, to the command of the Trans-Mississippi Department, with subdivisions as follows: The District of Louisiana, first occupied by Major-General R. Taylor's (afterward Major-General Buckner's) corps, consisting of Walker's and Polignac's divisions of infantry and Green's cavalry brigade; the District of Texas, occupied by Magruder's corps, consisting of Forney's, McCulloch's and Wharton's divisions; the District of Arkansas, occupied by Price's corps, consisting of the divisions of Price and Churchill and the unattached brigades of Fagan, Shelby and Marmaduke; also the District of the Indian Territory, under command of Major-General Maxey.

6. * BRAGG, BRAXTON, LOUISIANA.

Brigadier-General, P. A. C. S., March 7, 1861.
Major-General, P. A. C. S., September 12, 1861.
General, C. S. A., April 12, 1862.
Died at Galveston, Texas, September 27, 1876.

COMMANDS.

Commanding Department and Army of Louisiana, February 22, 1861.

Commanding troops and defenses at Pensacola, October 29, 1861, including the brigades of Colonels Chalmers, Clayton and Gladden, and the command of Major Bradford.

Commanding Department of Alabama and West Florida, 1861–2.

General Samuel Cooper, of Virginia.
Adjutant and Inspector General, Confederate States Army.
[From a photograph taken in 1861.]

Commanding Right Wing Army of the Mississippi, under General A. S. Johnston, at Shiloh, April 6–7, 1862.

Commanding Second Corps, Army of the Mississippi; the Army of Tennessee, and Department of the West.

Commanding Army of the Mississippi, March 6, 1862, to November 3, 1862.

Commanding Department of Tennessee (formerly Department No. 2), August 6, 1863, to December 22, 1863.

Assigned to duty at Richmond, under direction of the President, charged with the conduct of military operations in the armies of the Confederate States, by General Orders, No. 23, A. and I. G. O., February 24, 1864.

Commanding Department of North Carolina, November 27, 1864.

January 13, 1865, charged with command and defense of Wilmington, N. C.

7. * HOOD, JOHN B., TEXAS.

Captain, Corps of Cavalry, C. S. A., March 16, 1861.
Colonel Fourth Texas Infantry, September 30, 1861.
Brigadier-General, P. A. C. S., March 3, 1862.
Major-General, P. A. C. S., October 10, 1862.
Lieutenant-General, P. A. C. S., September 20, 1863.
General (with temporary rank), July 18, 1864.
Died in New Orleans, August 30, 1879.

COMMANDS.

Brigade composed of the First, Fourth and Fifth Texas and Eighteenth Georgia regiments infantry, and Hampton's Legion, Longstreet's division, Army of Northern Virginia.

Division composed of the brigades of Robertson, Law, Benning and Jenkins. At the battle of Fredericksburg, December 15 and 16, 1862, division composed of the brigades of Law, Toombs, Robertson and Anderson, Army of Northern Virginia.

Army corps, composed of the divisions of Hindman, Stevenson and Stewart.

Commanding Army of Tennessee, July 18, 1864.

August 15, 1864, commanding Department of Tennessee and Georgia.

January 23, 1865, at his own request, relieved of command of Army of Tennessee, and ordered to Richmond, Va.

LIEUTENANT-GENERALS.

(19.)

ARRANGED IN ORDER OF RANK.

1. * LONGSTREET, JAMES, ALABAMA.

Lieutenant-Colonel, Infantry, C. S. A., March 16, 1861.
Brigadier-General, P. A. C. S., June 17, 1861.
Major-General, P. A. C. S., October 7, 1861.
Lieutenant-General, P. A. C. S., October 9, 1862.

COMMANDS.

Brigade composed of the First, Seventh, Eleventh and Seventeenth Virginia regiments infantry, being the Fourth Brigade, First Corps, Army of the Potomac.

Division composed of the brigades of Kemper, Pickett, Wilcox, Anderson, Pryor and Featherston, Army of Northern Virginia.

Commanding First Corps, Army of Northern Virginia, from August 13, 1862, to August 15, 1863.

At battle of Fredericksburg, November —, 1862, corps composed of the divisions of Anderson, Pickett, Ransom, Hood and McLaws, and the artillery battalions of Colonels Alexander and Walton.

In October, 1863, commanding corps in the Army of Tennessee, composed of the divisions of McLaws, Preston, Walker, Hood and Bushrod R. Johnson, and the artillery battalions of Alexander, Williams, Leyden and Robertson. Pickett's division also constituted a part of this corps.

Commanding, from December 5, 1863, until April 12, 1864, the Department of East Tennessee.

Commanding First Corps, Army of Northern Virginia, January 31, 1865.

2. * POLK, LEONIDAS, LOUISIANA.

Major-General, P. A. C. S., June 25, 1861.
Lieutenant-General, P. A. C. S., October 10, 1862.
Killed on Pine Mountain, near Marietta, Ga., June 14, 1864.

COMMANDS.

Assigned, June 25, 1861, to the command of Department No. 2, comprising the defenses of the Mississippi River.

March 29, 1862, commanding the First Corps, Army of the Mississippi, composed, first, of the divisions of Cheatham and Clark, and the detached brigade of Maxey; subsequently of the divisions of Cheatham and Withers.

Commanding Army of the Mississippi, September and October, 1862.

Commanding, October and November, 1862, the Armies of Kentucky and Mississippi.

Commanding, in ——, 1863, corps in the Army of Tennessee composed of the divisions of Cheatham, Withers, and McCown.

Commanding, August 31, 1863, the Army of Tennessee (temporarily).

In Chickamauga campaign, commanding the Right Wing of the Army of Tennessee.

January 28, 1864, commanding the Department of Alabama, Mississippi and East Louisiana.

In May and June 1864, commanding army in Mississippi co-operating with the army of General Joseph E. Johnston in Northern Georgia.

3. * JACKSON, THOMAS J. (STONEWALL), VIRGINIA.

Major, Corps of Artillery, C. S. A., ——, 1861.
Brigadier-General, P. A. C. S., June 17, 1861.
Major-General, P. A. C. S., October 7, 1861.
Lieutenant-General, P. A. C. S., October 10, 1862.
Died, from wounds received at Chancellorsville, May 10, 1863.

COMMANDS.

Commanding at Harpers Ferry, Va., April 27, 1861.

Commanding, July 21, 1861, First Brigade of the Army of the Shenandoah, composed of the Second, Fourth, Fifth,

General John B. Hood, of Texas.
[From a photograph taken in 1862.]

Twenty-seventh and Thirty-third Virginia regiments infantry and Pendleton's light battery.

Commanding Army of the Monongahela, commonly called the Army of the Valley, October 22, 1861.

Commanding Army Corps, consisting of the divisions of Jackson (T. J.), A. P. Hill, Ewell and Rodes, Army of Northern Virginia.

Commanding Second Corps, Army of Northern Virginia, composed of the divisions of Early and the Stonewall Division, Taliaferro and Colston (afterward Johnson's division), A. P. Hill, D. H. Hill, and two battalions of artillery, from June 1, 1862, to May 10, 1863.

4. * HARDEE, WILLIAM J., GEORGIA.

Colonel, Corps Cavalry, C. S. A., March 16, 1861.
Brigadier-General, P. A. C. S., June 17, 1861.
Major-General, P. A. C. S., October 7, 1861.
Lieutenant-General, P. A. C. S., October 10, 1862.
Died at Wytheville, Va., November 6, 1873.

COMMANDS.

Brigade, ——, 1861, composed of First, Second, Fifth, Sixth, Seventh and Eighth Arkansas regiments of infantry.

Commanding Fort Morgan, Mobile Bay, March, 1861.

Commanding division under General A. S. Johnston, in Kentucky and Tennessee, 1861–2.

Commanding Third Corps, Army of the Mississippi, composed of Hindman's, Wood's and Cleburne's divisions, April 6 and 7, 1862, at Shiloh.

June to August, 1862, commanding the Army of the Mississippi, afterward called the Army of Tennessee.

August to October, 1862, commanding left wing of General Bragg's army in the Kentucky campaign, composed of Buckner's and Patton Anderson's divisions and Wheeler's cavalry.

Commanding, December 31, 1862, at Murfreesboro, Tenn., corps consisting of Breckinridge's and Cleburne's divisions; also in command at this battle of McCown's division.

Commanding, at Missionary Ridge, November 25, 1863, the right wing of the army, consisting of Cheatham's, Stevenson's, Walker's and Cleburne's divisions.

Commanding, in December, 1863, the Army of Tennessee.

Commanding, May to September, 1864, in the Dalton-Atlanta campaign, a corps composed of Cheatham's, Cleburne's, Walker's and Bate's divisions.

October —, 1864, commanding the Department of South Carolina, Georgia and Florida.

Commanding troops of his department, and some troops of the Army of Tennessee, at Bentonville, in March, 1865.

5. *HOLMES, T. H., NORTH CAROLINA.

Colonel, Corps of Infantry, C. S. A., March 16, 1861.
Brigadier-General, P. A. C. S., June 5, 1861.
Major-General, P. A. C. S., October 7, 1861.
Lieutenant-General, P. A. C. S., October 10, 1862.
Died at Fayetteville, N. C., June 20, 1880.

COMMANDS.

Commanding defenses of North Carolina, April 22, 1861.

Commanding Department of Fredericksburg, June 5, 1861.

Commanding brigade, Army of the Potomac, July 21, 1861.

LIEUT.-GEN. THEOPHILUS H. HOLMES, OF NORTH CAROLINA.

Commanding Acquia District, Department of Northern Virginia, October 22, 1861, to March 23, 1862.

Division composed of the brigades of Daniel, Walker and Wise, Army of Northern Virginia.

Commanding Department of North Carolina, March 24, 1862.

Commanding Trans-Mississippi Department, July 16, 1862, to March 18, 1863.

Commanding District of Arkansas, March 18, 1863, to March 11, 1864.

Commanding reserve forces of North Carolina, April 18, 1864.

Commanding paroled prisoners of Mississippi, Arkansas, Missouri, Texas and Louisiana, which formed the garrisons of Vicksburg and Port Hudson.

Commanding district in Department of North Carolina, ——, 1865.

6. *PEMBERTON, JOHN C., VIRGINIA.

Lieutenant-Colonel, Corps of Artillery, C. S. A., March 16, 1861.
Brigadier-General, P. A. C. S., June 17, 1861.
Major-General P. A. C. S., January 14, 1862.
Lieutenant-General, P. A. C. S., October 10, 1862.
Died at Penllyn, Penn., July 13, 1881.

COMMANDS.

As brigadier-general, commanded Confederate forces north of the Nansemond, on the east bank of James River, Va., April 29 to November 28, 1861.

Brigade composed of the Third Virginia, Thirteenth and Fourteenth North Carolina regiments, Wilson's Virginia battalion and Manley's North Carolina battery of light artillery.

In 1861–2, as brigadier-general, commanded the Eighth Military District of South Carolina; command then composed of Donelson's and Gregg's brigades and other unattached troops.

As major-general, commanded the same military district and troops in 1862.

In 1862, commanding the Department of South Carolina, Georgia and East and Middle Florida, temporarily, in the absence of General R. E. Lee.

In March, 1862, assigned to the command of the Department of South Carolina, Georgia and East and Middle Florida.

Assigned, October 4, 1862, to the command of the Department of Mississippi and East Louisiana.

Assigned, October 10, 1862, to the same command, and, in addition, to the command of the Army of Tennessee, relieving Major-General Earl Van Dorn.

May 7 to July 4, 1863, commanding army in and around Vicksburg, Miss.

May 18, 1864, resigned commission as lieutenant-general, ordered to report to General Robert Ransom for assignment to command of artillery defenses of Richmond; served the remainder as lieutenant-colonel commanding artillery defenses of Richmond, Va.

7. *EWELL, RICHARD S., VIRGINIA.

Lieutenant-Colonel, Corps of Cavalry, March 16, 1861.
Brigadier-General, P. A. C. S., June 17, 1861.
Major-General, P. A. C. S., January 24, 1862.
Lieutenant-General, P. A. C. S., May 23, 1863.
Died at Spring Hill, Tenn., January 25, 1872.

COMMANDS.

Brigade composed of the Fifth, Sixth and Twelfth Alabama and the Twelfth Mississippi regiments, being the Second Brigade, First Corps, Army of the Potomac, July 18, 1861.

Brigade afterward composed of the First, Seventh, Eleventh and Seventeenth regiments Virginia infantry, Army of Northern Virginia.

Division composed of the brigades of Brigadier-Generals Elzey, Trimble and Taylor, Army of Northern Virginia.

Commanding Second Corps, Army of Northern Virginia, May 10, 1863, to January 31, 1864.

Commanding the Department of Richmond, June 27, 1864, to end of war.

8. *HILL, AMBROSE P., VIRGINIA.

Colonel Thirteenth Virginia Infantry, ——, 1861.
Brigadier-General, P. A. C. S., February 26, 1862.
Major-General, P. A. C. S., May 26, 1862.
Lieutenant-General, P. A. C. S., May 24, 1863.
Killed at Petersburg, Va., April 2, 1865.

COMMANDS.

Brigade composed of the First, Seventh, Eleventh and Seventeenth regiments, Virginia infantry and Rogers' light battery of artillery, Army of Northern Virginia.

Division composed of the brigades of Pender, Heth, Archer, Lane, Thomas and McGowan, Army of Northern Virginia.

Commanding Third Corps, Army of Northern Virginia, composed of the divisions of Anderson, Heth and Pender, July 19, 1863, to April 2, 1864.

9. *HILL, DANIEL H., NORTH CAROLINA.

Colonel First North Carolina Regiment Infantry, May 10, 1861.
Brigadier-General, P. A. C. S., July 10, 1861.
Major-General, P. A. C. S., March 26, 1862.
Lieutenant-General, P. A. C. S., July 11, 1863.
Died at Charlotte, N. C., September 25, 1889.

COMMANDS.

Organized and in command of Camp of Instruction at Raleigh, N. C., May 1, 1861.

Brigade composed of Thirteenth, Seventeenth, Eighteenth and Twenty-first Mississippi regiments, Army of Northern Virginia.

Commanding Department of North Carolina, September 25, 1861.

August 13, 1862, to July 12, 1863, in command of Department of Southern Virginia and North Carolina.

Division composed of the brigades of Brigadier-Generals Rains, Rodes, Garland and G. B. Anderson, Jackson's Corps, Army of Northern Virginia, 1862–3; also brigades of Generals Doles, Iverson, Rodes and Colquitt, in Jackson's Corps, Army of Northern Virginia; also brigades of Brigadier-Generals Deas, Manigault, Sharp and Brantly, Army of Tennessee.

August 31, 1863, commanding corps in Army of Tennessee composed of the divisions of Cleburne and Breckinridge.

At battle of Bentonville, N. C., March 19, 1865, in command of S. D. Lee's corps.

10. TAYLOR, RICHARD, LOUISIANA.

Brigadier-General, P. A. C. S., October 21, 1861.
Major-General, P. A. C. S., July 28, 1862.
Lieutenant-General, P. A. C. S., April 8, 1864.
Died in New York City, April 12, 1879.

COMMANDS.

Brigade composed of the Sixth, Seventh, Eighth and Ninth regiments Louisiana infantry, Wheat's Louisiana battalion and a Virginia battery of light artillery, Army of Northern Virginia.

Commanding district of West Louisiana, called also District of Louisiana, August 20, 1862, to June 10, 1864.

Commanding Department of Alabama, Mississippi and East Louisiana, September 23, 1864, to January 23, 1865.

11. *EARLY, JUBAL A., VIRGINIA.

Colonel, Twenty-fourth Virginia Regiment Infantry, May 2, 1861.
Brigadier-General, P. A. C. S., July 21, 1861.
Major-General, P. A. C. S., January 17, 1863.
Lieutenant-General, P. A. C. S., May 31, 1864.

COMMANDS.

As colonel, commanded a brigade, composed of the Seventh Louisiana and Seventh and Twenty-first Virginia regiments infantry. Was at Blackburn's Ford on July 18th, and Manassas, July 21, 1861.

Afterward appointed brigadier-general; brigade composed of (at first) the Fifth and Twenty-third North Carolina and Twenty-fourth Virginia regiments, the Twenty-third North Carolina being then designated as the Thirteenth North Carolina Volunteers. In the fall of 1861, the Twentieth Georgia Regiment was added, and in May, 1862, the latter-named regiment was exchanged for the Thirty-eighth Virginia. At the battles of Malvern Hill, Cedar Run and Slaughter Mountain, brigade composed of the Twelfth Georgia and the Thirteenth, Twenty-fifth, Thirty-first, Forty-fourth and Fifty-eighth Virginia regiments. In the campaign against General Pope and battles of Sharpsburg and Fredericksburg, the brigade was composed of the Thirteenth, Twenty-fifth, Thirty-first, Forty-fourth, Forty-ninth, Fifty-second and Fifty-eighth Virginia regiments; but at Fredericksburg, as senior brigadier-general, was in command of division.

Division (formerly Ewell's) composed of Hays' (formerly Taylor's), Gordon's (formerly Lawton's), Smith's (formerly Early's) and Hoke's (formerly Trimble's), at Fredericksburg (confronting Sedgwick), at time of the battle of Chancellorsville, and at Gettysburg, in the campaign of 1864. Pegram succeeded to command of Smith's brigade in fall of 1863. Corps (formerly Ewell's) was composed of Rodes', Gordon's and Ramseur's (formerly Early's) divisions, and five battalions of artillery under command of Brigadier-General A. L. Long.

In command of operations in Maryland and Shenandoah Valley in 1864.

January 31, 1865, commanding a division, Second Corps, Army of Northern Virginia.

March 29, 1865, relieved from command of Departments of Trans-Alleghany, or Western Virginia, and East Tennessee, and ordered to Lynchburg, Va., to await orders.

12. *LEE, STEPHEN D., SOUTH CAROLINA.

Captain, Corps of Artillery, C. S. A., March 16, 1861.
Major, Corps of Artillery, P. A. C. S., November—, 1861.
Lieutenant-Colonel, Corps of Artillery, P. A. C. S., November —, 1862.
Colonel, Corps of Artillery, P. A. C. S., December —, 1862.
Brigadier-General, P. A. C. S., November 6, 1862.
Major-General, P. A. C. S., August 31, 1863.
Lieutenant-General, P. A. C. S., June 23, 1864.

LIEUT.-GEN. AMBROSE P. HILL, OF VIRGINIA.
Killed in front of Petersburg, April 2, 1865.

COMMANDS.

Assigned as Captain, C. S. A., to command of company of Washington Artillery, ——, 1861.,

April, 1863, commanding brigade composed of Seventeenth, Nineteenth, Twenty-second and Twenty-seventh Louisiana regiments, and Second and Forty-sixth Mississippi regiments, the First Louisiana Heavy Artillery, First Tennessee Heavy Artillery; the last two regiments garrisoning the fixed batteries at Vicksburg.

Assigned August 16, 1863, to command of all the cavalry in the Department of Alabama, Mississippi, East Louisiana and West Tennessee.

Assigned May 4, 1864, to the command of the Department of Alabama, Mississippi, East Louisiana and West Tennessee.

Assigned July 27, 1864, to the command of Hood's Corps, composed of the divisions of D. H. Hill, Stevenson and Clayton, Army of Tennessee.

13. *ANDERSON, RICHARD H., SOUTH CAROLINA.

Major, Corps of Cavalry, C. S. A., March 19, 1861.
Major, Assistant Adjutant-General, P. A. C. S., September 4, 1861.
Colonel Fifth Georgia Cavalry, ——, 1861.
Brigadier-General, P. A. C. S., July 19, 1861.
Major-General, P. A. C. S., July 14, 1862.
Lieutenant-General, P. A. C. S., May, 31, 1864.
Died in Beaufort, S. C., June 26, 1879.

COMMANDS.

Brigade composed of First Louisiana Regiment, Colonel Gladden; First Florida Regiment, Colonel J. Patton Anderson; Fifth Georgia Regiment, Colonel Jackson; Seventh and Eighth Mississippi regiments; and Tyler's battalion of marines.

Subsequently, brigade composed of the Fourth, Fifth and Sixth South Carolina Volunteer regiments and the Second South Carolina Rifles, Longstreet's Corps, Army of Northern Virginia.

Division composed of Mahone's, A. R. Wright's, Armistead's and Martin's brigades (Posey's, Wilcox's and Pryor's brigades also subsequently formed a part of the division), Army of Northern Virginia.

At Fredericksburg, December 13 to 15, 1862, division composed of the brigades of Perry, Featherston, A. R. Wright, Wilcox and Mahone.

Commanding divisions of Hoke and Bushrod R. Johnson and Hilary Jones' artillery. Subsequently, his corps was composed of the divisions of Pickett and B. R. Johnson and Jones' artillery.

Commanding corps in Army of Northern Virginia, January 31, 1865.

14. *STEWART, ALEXANDER P., TENNESSEE.

Major of Artillery, Provisional Army of Tennessee, May 17, 1861.
Brigadier-General, P. A. C. S., November 8, 1861.
Major-General, P. A. C. S., June 2, 1863.
Lieutenant-General, P. A. C. S., June 23, 1864.

COMMANDS.

Brigade composed of the Fourth, Fifth, Twenty-ninth, Thirty-first and Thirty-third Tennessee regiments infantry, being Second Brigade of Western Department, Clark's division of Major-General Polk's command.

March 31, 1862, commanding brigade in Cheatham's division, Polk's corps, Army of Tennessee, composed of the Fourth, Fifth, Nineteenth, Twenty-fourth, Thirty-first and Thirty-third Tennessee regiments infantry and Captain Stanford's battery of artillery.

Division composed of the brigades of John C. Brown,

LIEUT.-GEN. NATHAN BEDFORD FORREST, OF TENNESSEE.

B. R. Johnson, O. F. Strahl and H. D. Clayton, June 6, 1863, in Army of Tennessee.

August 31, 1863, commanding division composed of the brigades of Brown, Bate, Clayton and Stovall, Army of Tennessee.

In autumn of 1863, division composed of the brigades of Stovall, Clayton, Gibson and Baker, Army of the West.

June 23, 1864, army corps composed of the divisions of French, Loring and Walthall, Army of Tennessee.

March 16, 1865, assigned command of infantry and artillery of Army of Tennessee.

15. *BUCKNER, SIMON B., KENTUCKY.

Brigadier-General, P. A. C. S., September 14, 1861.
Major-General, P. A. C. S., August 16, 1862.
Lieutenant-General, P. A. C. S., September 20, 1864.

COMMANDS.

Commanding Central Division of Kentucky, Department No. 2, September 15, 1861.

Commanding division at Bowling Green, Ky., and subsequently at Fort Donelson, Tenn.

Commanding corps composed of the division of Major-General A. P. Stewart, the brigades of Brigadier-Generals B. R. Johnson, John C. Brown, W. B. Bate, H. D. Clayton, and the division of Brigadier-General William Preston, consisting of the brigades of Brigadier-Generals Gracie, Trigg and Kelly, and three battalions of artillery.

Commanding Department of East Tennessee, July 20, 1863, to April 12, 1864.

Commanding District of West Louisiana, Trans-Mississippi Department, August 4, 1864.

Commanding District of Arkansas and West Louisiana, Trans-Mississippi Department, April 19, 1865.

May 9th, announced as chief of staff to General E. K. Smith, in addition.

16. HAMPTON, WADE, SOUTH CAROLINA.

Colonel Hampton's South Carolina Legion, July 12, 1861.
Brigadier-General, P. A. C. S., May 23, 1862.
Major-General, P. A. C. S., August 3, 1863.
Lieutenant-General, P. A. C. S., February 14, 1865.

COMMANDS.

Brigade composed of Hampton's South Carolina Legion, the Fourteenth and Nineteenth Georgia, and Sixteenth North Carolina regiments infantry.

July 28, 1862, assigned to cavalry brigade; brigade composed of First and Second regiments South Carolina Cavalry, First Regiment North Carolina Cavalry, Jeff Davis' Legion, Cobb's Georgia Legion and Phillips' Georgia Legion, Tenth Virginia Cavalry, Army of Northern Virginia.

Division composed of the cavalry brigades of Young, Butler, Rosser and Gordon, Army of Northern Virginia.

Commanding Corps of Cavalry, Army Northern Virginia.

Commanding cavalry of General J. E. Johnston's army and Butler's division of cavalry, Army of Northern Virginia, from February 16, 1865, during march of General Sherman through the Carolinas.

17. FORREST, NATHAN BEDFORD, TENNESSEE.

Captain Company Tennessee Cavalry, May —, 1861.
Colonel —— Regiment Tennessee Cavalry (known as Forrest's Regiment), 1861–2.
Brigadier-General, P. A. C. S., July 21, 1862.
Major-General, P. A. C. S., December 4, 1863.
Lieutenant-General, P. A. C. S., February 28, 1865.
Died at Memphis, Tenn., October 29, 1877.

COMMANDS.

Brigade composed of the Fourth, Eighth and Ninth Tennessee regiments cavalry, Russell's Fourth Alabama Cavalry and Freeman's battery of artillery.

Assigned to the command of all the cavalry in West Tennessee and North Mississippi, consisting of his own brigade and the brigades of Chalmers, McCulloch, Richardson, Bell, Jeffrey, Forrest, and subsequently Lyon's Brigade, the whole organized into two divisions, commanded by Chalmers and Buford, respectively.

As lieutenant-general, commanding the cavalry divisions of Chalmers, Jackson and Buford, McCulloch's Regiment Second Missouri Cavalry, and the Mississippi Militia forces.

Commanding District of Mississippi and East Louisiana, January —, 1865.

18. *WHEELER, JOSEPH, GEORGIA.

First Lieutenant, Corps of Artillery, C. S. A., April 3, 1861.
Colonel Nineteenth Regiment Alabama Volunteers, September 4, 1861.
Brigadier-General, P. A. C. S., October 30, 1862.
Major-General, P. A. C. S., January 20, 1863.
Lieutenant-General, P. A. C. S., February 28, 1865.

COMMANDS.

Brigade composed of Seventeenth, Eighteenth and Nineteenth Alabama regiments, and Second Texas Regiment, from April 6, 1862.

Assigned to cavalry, July 18, 1862.

Brigade composed of First and Second Mississippi regiments, First and Third Alabama regiments, Second Arkansas Regiment, and Eighth Confederate Regiment, from July 20 to August 16, 1862.

Brigade composed of the First and Third Alabama regiments until September 16th, when it was re-enforced by First Kentucky, First Confederate and Third Georgia regiments.

October 1st, command of cavalry in Kentucky.

October 13th, chief of cavalry of department; command composed of brigades of Colonels John H. Morgan, John A. Wharton, and the old Wheeler brigade, commanded by Colonel W. W. Allen.

November 20th, chief of cavalry, Army of Tennessee; command composed of old brigade commanded by Colonel James Hagen and brigade of Brigadier-General John A. Wharton, and, after December 20th, of brigade of Brigadier-General John Pegram.

January 20th, in command of cavalry, Army of Tennessee, composed of brigades of Brigadier Generals Forrest, John A. Wharton, Martin and Morgan.

March 15, 1863, command of army corps of cavalry, composed of divisions of Brigadier-Generals John H. Mor-

MAJ.-GEN. DAVID E. TWIGGS, OF GEORGIA.

gan, W. T. Martin and John A. Wharton, each division being composed of two brigades. June 20th, Morgan's division was detached.

September 28th, in command of cavalry, Army of Tennessee, composed of divisions of Brigadier-Generals William T. Martin, John A. Wharton and H. B. Davidson.

November 20th, corps composed of divisions of Major-Generals John A. Wharton, William T. Martin, John H. Kelly and Frank Armstrong, each division having two brigades. November 27th, Martin's and Armstrong's divisions were detached.

November 30, 1863, command composed of General Kelly's division, composed of Allen's and Grigsby's brigades; and Davidson's division, composed of Humes' and Ashby's brigades.

May 10, 1864, command composed of Major-General Martin's division, comprising Brigadier-Generals Iverson's and John T. Morgan's brigades; Brigadier-General Humes' division, comprising brigades of Harrison and McKenzie; Brigadier-General Kelly's division, comprising brigades of Ashby and Allen, afterward Anderson's; also the brigade of Brigadier-General John S. Williams, formerly Grigsby's brigade; Brigadier-General William H. Jackson's division, comprising brigades of Ferguson, Armstrong and Ross, was directed to report directly to General Johnston, but was often under General Wheeler's command and orders.

August 10, 1864, command composed of divisions of Generals W. W. Allen (formerly Martin's), W. Y. C. Humes and J. H. Kelly, and brigade of Brigadier-General J. S. Williams.

August 22d, Kelly's division and Williams' brigade and Dibrell's brigade, of Humes' division, detached, remaining absent in West Virginia until November 30th.

November 30th, command composed of divisions as follows: Brigadier-General W. W. Allen's division, comprising brigades of Colonels C. C. Crews and James Hagen; Brigadier-General W. Y. C. Humes' division, comprising brigades of General Thomas Harrison and Colonel Ashby; Brigadier-General Alfred Iverson's division, composed of brigades of Brigadier-Generals S. W. Ferguson and Joseph H. Lewis.

19. GORDON, JOHN B., GEORGIA.

Lieutenant-Colonel Sixth Alabama Infantry, December 26, 1861.
Colonel Sixth Alabama Infantry, April 28, 1862.
Brigadier-General, P. A. C. S., November 1, 1862.

* * * * * * *

Brigadier-General, P. A. C. S., May 7, 1863.
Major-General, P. A. C. S., May 14, 1864.
Lieutenant-General, P. A. C. S., ——, 1865.

COMMANDS.

Brigade composed of the Thirteenth, Twenty-sixth, Thirty-first, Thirty-eighth, Sixtieth and Sixty-first Georgia regiments infantry (originally Lawton's brigade), and the Sixth and Twelfth battalions Georgia infantry, Early's division, Army of Northern Virginia.

August 31, 1864, commanding a division in Second Corps, Army Northern Virginia.

Division composed of the brigades of Evans, Terry and York, Army of Northern Virginia.

October 31, 1864, commanding a division in Army of Valley District.

Commanding Second Corps, Army of Northern Virginia, January 31, 1865.

Commanding Left Wing Army of Northern Virginia, May ——, at the surrender of General Lee at Appomattox.

MAJ.-GEN. GUSTAVUS W. SMITH, OF KENTUCKY.

MAJOR-GENERALS.

(81.)

ARRANGED IN ORDER OF RANK.

1. *TWIGGS, DAVID E., GEORGIA.

Major-General, P. A. C. S., May 22, 1861.
Died July 15, 1862.

COMMANDS.

Commanding Military District of Louisiana, April 17, 1861.

May 27, 1861, assigned to command Department No. 1.

October 7, 1861, relieved of command.

2. *VAN DORN, EARL, MISSISSIPPI.

Colonel Corps Cavalry, C. S. A., March 16, 1861.
Brigadier-General, P. A. C. S., June 5, 1861.
Major-General, P. A. C. S., September 19, 1861.
Killed at Spring Hill, Tenn., May 8, 1863.

COMMANDS.

Commanding Forts Jackson and St. Phillip, March 15, 1861.

Commanding Department of Texas, April 11, 1861.

Ordered to report to General J. E. Johnston, at Manassas, September 30, 1861.

Commanding First Division, Army of the Potomac, October and November, 1861.

Assigned, January 9, 1862, to command of Trans-Mississippi District, in Department No. 2.

March 4, 1862, commanding Army of the West.

June 20, 1862, commanding District of Southern Mississippi and East Louisiana.

June 28, 1862, commanding defenses at Vicksburg, Miss.

July 2, 1862, commanding District of Mississippi and Army of West Tennessee.

October 12, 1862, commanding all troops in State of Mississippi.

December 7, 1862, commanding First Corps, Army of the Mississippi.

December 9, 1862. commanding Army of the Mississippi.

December 17, 1862, commanding First Corps Army, Department of Mississippi and East Louisiana.

3. SMITH, GUSTAVUS W., KENTUCKY.

* * * * * * *

Major-General, P. A. C. S., September 19, 1861.
Resigned, February 11, 1863.

COMMANDS.

Commanding, September 25, 1861, Second Corps, Army of the Potomac.

October 22, commanding Second Division, in Army of Northern Virginia, under General Joseph E. Johnston.

Relieved General T. H. Holmes of command at Yorktown, Va.

Division composed of the brigades of Whiting, Hood, Hampton, Pettigrew and Hatton.

Acting Secretary of War, from November 17 to November 20, 1862.

June 1, 1864, assigned command of Georgia militia at and near Atlanta, Ga.

September 15, 1864, relieved General Wagner at Macon, Ga.

4. *HUGER, BENJAMIN, SOUTH CAROLINA.

Colonel Corps of Artillery, C. S. A., March 16, 1861.
Brigadier-General, P. A. C. S., June 17, 1861.
Major-General, P. A. C. S., October 7, 1861.
Died in Charleston, S. C., December 7, 1877.

COMMANDS.

Commanding State forces at Norfolk, Va., May 23, 1861.

Commanding troops and defenses, Department of Norfolk, Va., May 26, 1861.

Division composed of the brigades of Mahone, A. R. Wright, Blanchard and Armistead.

June 25, 1862, commanding a division in Army of Northern Virginia.

July 14, 1862, assigned Inspector of Artillery Ordnance in Armies of the Confederate States.

July 27, 1863, announced as Chief of Bureau of Ordnance of Trans-Mississippi Department.

5. *MAGRUDER, JOHN B., VIRGINIA.

Colonel Corps of Infantry, C. S. A., March 16, 1861.
Brigadier-General, P. A. C. S., June 17, 1861.
Major-General, P. A. C. S., October 7, 1861.
Died in Houston, Tex., February 19, 1871.

COMMANDS.

April 29, 1861, assigned command of artillery in and about Richmond.

May 8, 1861, assigned command of Virginia State forces in and about Richmond.

Commanding District of Yorktown, Department of the Peninsula, May 21, 1861, to February 1, 1862.

April 18, 1862, assigned to command Right Wing, Army of Northern Virginia.

Commanding District of Texas, Trans-Mississippi Department, October 10, 1862.

Commanding District of New Mexico and Arizona, Trans-Mississippi Department, August 11, 1864, to March 31, 1865.

6. *LOVELL, MANSFIELD, MARYLAND.

Brigadier-General, P. A. C. S., ——.
Major-General, P. A. C. S., October 7, 1861.
Died in New York City, June 1, 1884.

COMMANDS.

Commanding Department No. 1, headquarters at New Orleans, from May 31, 1861, to October 7, 1861.

Commanding First Division, Army of the District of Mississippi, composed of the brigades of Rust, Villepigue and Bowen.

April 7, 1865, assigned a command in the State of South Carolina.

MAJ.-GEN. GEORGE B. CRITTENDEN, OF KENTUCKY.

7. *CRITTENDEN, GEORGE B., KENTUCKY.

Colonel, Corps of Infantry, C. S. A., March 16, 1861.
Brigadier-General, P. A. C. S., August 15, 1861.
Major-General, P. A. C. S., November 9, 1861.
Resigned October 23, 1862.
Died in Danville, Ky., November 27, 1880.

COMMANDS.

Brigade composed of the Sixteenth Mississippi, Twenty-first Georgia, Twenty-first North Carolina and Fifteenth Alabama regiments infantry, and Captain Courtney's battery of artillery, Longstreet's corps, Army of Northern Virginia.

Commanding Trans-Alleghany Department.

Assumed command of District of East Tennessee and military operations in East Tennessee and Kentucky, December 8, 1861.

Commanding Confederate forces at battle of Fishers Creek, or Mill Springs, Ky., January 19, 1862.

October 23, 1862, resigned.

May 31, 1864, commanding as colonel, temporarily, the Departments of Western Virginia and Tennessee.

September 5, 1864, relieved of command of troops in East Tennessee, commanding as colonel.

8. *LORING, W. W., FLORIDA.

Colonel, Corps of Infantry, C. S. A., March 16, 1861.
Brigadier-General, P. A. C. S., May 20, 1861.
Major-General, P. A. C. S., February 15, 1862.
Died in New York City, December 31, 1886.

MAJ.-GEN. SAMUEL JONES, OF VIRGINIA.
[From a photograph taken in 1862.]

COMMANDS.

* * * * * * *

Commanding Army of the Northwest, July 20, 1861.

* * * * * * *

Commanding, from May 8, 1862, to October 16, 1862, Department of Southwestern Virginia, or Western Virginia.

Commanding First Corps, Army of the Mississippi, December 15, 1862.

January 26, 1863, commanding forces about Grenada, Miss.

Commanding division in Department of Alabama, Mississippi and East Louisiana.

9. PRICE, STERLING, MISSOURI.

Major-General, commanding Missouri State Guard, July 30, 1861.

* * * * * * *

Major-General, P. A. C. S., March 6, 1862.
Died at St. Louis, Mo., September 29, 1867.

COMMANDS.

Commanding Missouri State Guard, July 30, 1861, to March 16, 1862.

Commanding District of Arkansas, July 24 to September 18, 1863, and from March 11 to March 16, 1864.

Commanding First Division, Army of the West, March 17, 1862.

Commanding, July 3, 1862, the Army of the West.

July 24 to September 26, 1863 commanding District of Arkansas.

Commanding, in 1864, division composed of the brigades of Drayton, Churchill, Tappan and Parsons.

Commanding, in 1864, army corps, composed of the divisions of Fagan, Marmaduke and Shelby.

Commanding Army of Missouri, September 8, 1864.

10. CHEATHAM, BENJAMIN F., TENNESSEE.

Major-General Provisional Army of Tennessee, May 9, 1861.

Brigadier-General, P. A. C. S., July 9, 1861.
Major-General, P. A. C. S., March 10, 1862.
Died at Nashville, Tenn., September 4, 1886.

COMMANDS.

Brigade composed of One Hundred and Fifty-fourth Tennessee Senior Regiment and the Sixth and Ninth Tennessee regiments infantry, and Blythe's Mississippi battalion infantry.

Commanding Second Division of the Western Department, at Columbus, Ky., consisting of the brigades of Colonels Preston Smith and William H. Stevens.

Division composed of the brigades of Brigadier-Generals George Maney, Preston Smith, Marcus J. Wright and O. F. Strahl, ——, 1862–3.

In 1864, in command of Hardee's Corps, consisting of the divisions of Cheatham, Cleburne and Bate.

Division at one time composed of the brigades of Brigadier-Generals George Maney, Marcus J. Wright, O. F. Strahl and A. J. Vaughan (to which, subsequently, John K. Jackson's brigade was added), Army of Tennessee.

11. * JONES, SAMUEL, VIRGINIA.

Major, Corps of Artillery, C. S. A., May —, 1861.
Lieutenant-Colonel and A. A. G., military forces of Virginia, May —, 1861.
Chief of Artillery and Ordnance, Army of Northern Virginia, May — to July 22, 1861.
Colonel, P. A. C. S., June —, 1861.
Brigadier-General, P. A. C. S., July 21, 1861.
Major-General, P. A. C. S., May 10, 1862.
Died at Washington, D. C., October, 1892.

COMMANDS.

Brigade, ——, 1861, composed of the Seventh, Eighth, Ninth and Eleventh Georgia and First Kentucky regiments infantry and Alburti's battery of Virginia Light Artillery.

Assigned to the command of the Army of Pensacola, Fla., January 27, 1862.

Commanding Department of Alabama and West Florida, 1862.

April 29, 1862, commanding division, Army of the West.

June 2, 1862, commanding Second Division, Army of the Mississippi.

Commanding base of operations of General Bragg's army, August — to September 22, 1862.

Assigned to command of Department of East Tennessee, September 23, 1862.

In command of the Trans-Alleghany or Western Department of Virginia, from December 4, 1862, to March 4, 1864.

In command of the Department of South Carolina, Georgia and Florida, from April 16 to October —, 1864.

Commanding District of South Carolina, from October —, 1864, to January —, 1865.

Commanding Department of Florida and South Georgia, from January 12 to May 10, 1865.

12. MCCOWN, JOHN P., TENNESSEE.

Lieutenant-Colonel, Corps of Artillery, C. S. A., March 16, 1861.
Colonel, commanding Corps of Artillery, Provisional Army of Tennessee, May —, 1861.
Brigadier-General, P. A. C. S., October 12, 1861.
Major-General, P. A. C. S., March 10, 1862.

MAJ.-GEN. JOHN P. MCCOWN, OF TENNESSEE.

COMMANDS.

Commanding, October 24, 1861, the Third Division of the Western Department, embracing the brigades of Colonels Neely and Marks.

Division composed of brigades of Cabell and Churchill, Army of the West.

Division also composed of the brigades of Ector, Rains and McNair.

Commanding Army of the West, composed of the divisions of McCown, Little and Maury, in June, 1862.

Commanding, September 1, 1862, Department of East Tennessee.

Commanding division in Army of Kentucky, under General E. Kirby Smith, November —, 1862.

13. WITHERS, JONES M., ALABAMA.

Brigadier-General, P. A. C. S., July 10, 1861.
Major-General, P. A. C. S., April 6, 1862.
Resigned July 13, 1863.
Reappointed major-general July 21, 1863.

COMMANDS.

Commanding District of Alabama, in Department of Alabama and West Florida, October 14, 1861.

Commanding Reserve Corps of the Army of the Mississippi, composed of the brigades of Gardner, Chalmers, Jackson and Manigault, June 30, 1862.

Commanding Army of Mobile, Department of Alabama and West Florida, January 27, 1862.

Commanding division in Polk's corps, Army of Tennessee, composed of the brigades of Deas, Chalmers, Manigault and Patton Anderson.

Commanding, April 30, 1864, the reserve forces of Alabama.

Commanding, February 6 to July 27, 1864, the District of North Alabama, in Department of Alabama, Mississippi and East Louisiana.

14. HINDMAN, THOMAS C., ARKANSAS.

Colonel, Second Arkansas Infantry, June 21, 1861.
Brigadier-General, P. A. C. S., September 28, 1861.
Major-General, P. A. C. S., April 14, 1862.
Died at Helena, Ark., September 28, 1889.

COMMANDS.

Brigade composed of the First, Second, Fifth, Sixth, Seventh and Eighth Arkansas regiments infantry, Army of the West.

Division composed of the brigades of Deas, Walthall, Manigault and Anderson, Polk's corps, Army of Tennessee.

Subsequently division composed of the brigades of Tucker, Deas, Manigault and Walthall, Army of Tennessee.

MAJ.-GEN. JONES M. WITHERS, OF ALABAMA.

Commanding the Trans-Mississippi District, Department No. 2, May 26, 1862.

Commanding army corps composed of divisions of Hindman, Breckinridge and Stewart, Army of Tennessee.

Commanding District of Arkansas, August and September, 1862.

Commanding Second Corps, Army of Tennessee, December 15, 1863, to February 25, 1864.

15. BRECKINRIDGE, JOHN C., KENTUCKY.

Brigadier-General, P. A. C. S., November 2, 1861.
Major-General, P. A. C. S., April 14, 1862.
Acting Secretary of War, February 6, 1865.
Died May 17, 1875.

COMMANDS.

Commanding First Brigade of Kentucky Infantry.

Commanding division composed of the brigades of Brigadier-Generals Daniel W. Adams, Helm and Stovall.

Commanding Reserve Corps, Army of the Mississippi, April 6 to August 18, 1862.

Commanding, September 8, 1862, division under Major-General Van Dorn.

October 28, 1862, commanding Army of Middle Tennessee.

In December, 1862, commanding division in Polk's corps, Army of Tennessee, composed of the brigades of Hanson, Palmer and Walker.

Commanding, August 20, 1863, division composed of the brigades of Helm, Preston, Brown and Adams.

Commanding, November 8, 1863, to December 15, 1863, Second Corps (Hardee's), Army of Tennessee.

Commanding, September 27, 1864, Department of East Tennessee and Trans-Alleghany Department.

16. * MCLAWS, LAFAYETTE, GEORGIA.

Major, Corps of Infantry, C. S. A., March 10, 1861.
Colonel Tenth Georgia Volunteer Infantry, June 17, 1861.
Brigadier-General, P. A. C. S., September 25, 1861.
Major-General, P. A. C. S., May 23, 1862.

COMMANDS.

Brigade, in October, 1861, composed of the Fifteenth and Thirty-second Virginia, the Fifth and Tenth Louisiana and the Tenth, Fiftieth, Fifty-third and Fifty-seventh Georgia regiments infantry and Manley's light battery of artillery.

Division, in June, 1862, composed of the brigades of Kershaw, Wofford, Humphreys and Bryan.

MAJ.-GEN. THOMAS C. HINDMAN, OF ARKANSAS

At battle of Chancellorsville, May 3, 1863, division composed of brigades of Wofford, Kershaw, Barksdale and Semmes.

In 1864, commanding District of Georgia, extending to Salkehatchie, S. C.

December —, 1864, commanding division under General Hardee.

In 1865, command'ng division under General Hardee, in General J. E. Johnston's Army.

17. * STUART, J. E. B., VIRGINIA.

Captain, Corps of Cavalry, C. S. A., March 16, 1861.
* * * * * * *
Brigadier-General, P. A. C. S., September 24, 1861.
Major-General, P. A. C. S., July 25, 1862.
Died of wounds received at Yellow Tavern, Va., May 12, 1864.

COMMANDS.

Chief of Cavalry, Army of Northern Virginia, January 31, 1864.

Division composed of the brigades of Hampton, Fitzhugh Lee and W. H. F. Lee, commanding Second Corps, Army of Northern Virginia (General A. P. Hill's) at battle of Chancellorsville.

18. * FRENCH, S. G., MISSISSIPPI.

Lieutenant-Colonel, Chief of Ordnance, Army of State of Mississippi, February 12, 1861.
Major, Corps of Artillery, C. S. A., April 2, 1861.
Brigadier-General, P. A. C. S., October 23, 1861.
Major-General, P. A. C. S., August 31, 1862.

COMMANDS.

From November 14, 1861, to March 8, 1862, commanding at Evansport, Va., blockading Potomac River.

Brigade composed of Colonel Judge's Alabama regiment, Colonel Bate's Second Tennessee Regiment, Colonel Pettigrew's Twenty-second North Carolina Regiment, Colonel Thomas' Georgia regiment, Colonel Brockenbrough's Fortieth Virginia Regiment, Colonel Fagan's Arkansas regiment, Colonel Walker's Arkansas regiment, Major Bronaugh's Arkansas battalion, Captains Walker's and Swann's companies of Florida cavalry, and light batteries of Captains Chatard and McCorkle; Lieutenants Simms and Wood, Confederate States Navy, co-operating.

March 14, 1862, relieved General L. O'B. Branch in command at Newberne, N. C.

March 17, 1862, assumed command of forces at Kinston, N. C.

March 20, 1862, assumed command at Wilmington, N. C.

July 17, 1862, ordered to the command of the Department of Southern Virginia and North Carolina, headquarters at Petersburg, Va.

In command of line of defense from the Appomattox and James rivers.

July 31, 1862, moved to Coggins Point with infantry and artillery.

May 28, 1863, ordered to report to General J. E. Johnston, at Jackson, Miss.

Command, at various times in 1862, composed of brigades of Pettigrew, Ransom, Martin, Clingman, Daniels, Jenkins, Davis, Stone, Pryor, Evans, Cook and Colston.

Division, in 1863, at Jackson, Miss., composed of the brigades of Maxey, McNair and Evans.

In ——, 1864, division composed of the brigades of Cockrell, Ector and Sears.

MAJ.-GEN. DAVID R. JONES, OF GEORGIA.

19. *STEVENSON, CARTER L., VIRGINIA.

Lieutenant-Colonel, Corps of Infantry, C. S. A., March 16, 1861.

Colonel, Fifty-third Virginia Infantry, ——

Brigadier-General, P. A. C. S., February 27, 1862.

Major-General, P. A. C. S., October 10, 1862.

COMMANDS.

Commanding garrison at Cumberland Gap.

June 22, 1862, to July, 1864, commanding a division in Army of Tennessee.

Division composed of the brigades of Brown, Cumming, Pettus and Reynolds, and the light batteries of Anderson, Rowan, Corput and Carne, Army of Tennessee.

Division composed of the brigades of Pettus, Palmer, and Cumming, Army of Tennessee.

July 18, 1864, assumed command of Hood's Corps (2d), Army of Tennessee.

20. *PICKETT, GEORGE E., VIRGINIA.

Major, Corps of Artillery, C. S. A., March 16, 1861.

* * * * * *

Brigadier-General, P. A. C. S., January 14, 1862.

Major-General, P. A. C. S., October 10, 1862.

Died at Norfolk, Va., July, 1875.

COMMANDS.

July 23, 1862, commanding Third Brigade, Longstreet's division, Army of Northern Virginia.

Brigade composed of the Eighth, Eighteenth, Nineteenth, Twenty-eighth and Fifty-sixth Virginia regiments of infantry, Army of Northern Virginia.

August 13, 1862, commanding division in Longstreet's corps, Army of Northern Virginia, composed of the brigades of Garnett, Armistead, Kemper and Jenkins. Corse's brigade was afterward added.

Commanding Department of North Carolina, September 23, 1863.

August 31, 1864, Commanding a division in First Corps, Army Northern Virginia.

21. *JONES, DAVID R., GEORGIA.

* * * * * *

Brigadier-General, P. A. C. S., June 17, 1861.

Major-General, P. A. C. S., October 11, 1862.

Died at Richmond, Va., January 19, 1863.

COMMANDS.

Brigade composed of the Fourth, Fifth, Sixth and Ninth South Carolina regiments infantry, being the Third Brigade, First Corps, Army of the Potomac; brigade afterward composed of the Seventeenth and Eighteenth Mississippi and Fifth South Carolina regiments infantry, Army of Northern Virginia.

August 13, 1862, division composed of the brigades of Toombs, Anderson, Drayton, Kemper, Garnett and Jenkins, Longstreet's corps, Army of Northern Virginia.

22. *FORNEY, JOHN H., ALABAMA.

Captain, Corps of Artillery, C. S. A., March 16, 1861.

Colonel, Tenth Alabama Regiment Infantry, June 4, 1861.

Brigadier-General, P. A. C. S., March 10, 1862.

Major-General, P. A. C. S., October 27, 1862.

COMMANDS.

Brigade composed of the Ninth, Tenth and Eleventh Alabama, the Nineteenth Mississippi and Thirty-eighth Virginia regiments of infantry, Army of Northern Virginia.

Commanding Department of Alabama and West Florida, April 28, 1862.

Division composed of the brigades of Hebert and Moore, and subsequently of the brigades of King, Waterhouse, Waul and McLain; afterward of the brigades of Cockrell and Green.

Commanding District of the Gulf, July 2 to December 8, 1862.

23. *MAURY, DABNEY H., VIRGINIA.

Captain, Corps of Cavalry, C. S. A., March 16, 1861.

Brigadier-General, P. A. C. S., March 12, 1862.

Major-General, P. A. C. S., November 4, 1862.

COMMANDS.

* * * * * *

Commanding division composed of the brigades of Moore, Ross and Cabell.

Commanding division, in 1862, composed of the brigades of Dockery, Moore and Phifer, being Third Brigade, Army of the West.

Commanding Army of the West, June 27, 1862.

Commanding Department of East Tennessee, from April 15 to May 12, 1863.

Commanding District of the Gulf, May —, 1863.

Commanding, November 22, 1864, Department of Alabama, Mississippi and East Louisiana.

MAJ.-GEN. DABNEY H. MAURY, OF VIRGINIA.

24. *SMITH, M. L., FLORIDA.

Major, Corps of Engineers, C. S. A., March 16, 1861.

* * * * * *

Brigadier-General, P. A. C. S., April 11, 1862.

Major-General, P. A. C. S., November 4, 1862.

Died, July 29, 1866.

COMMANDS.

Commanding Third District, Department of South Mississippi and East Louisiana, June 26, 1862.

Commanding Second Military District, Department of Mississippi and East Louisiana, October 21, 1862.

April 16, 1862, assigned as Chief Engineer, Army of Northern Virginia.

January 4, 1865, relieved from duty at Mobile, Ala., and ordered to resume as Chief Engineer, Military Division of the West.

25. *WALKER, JOHN G., MISSOURI.

Major, Corps of Cavalry, C. S. A., March 16, 1861.

Lieutenant-Colonel, Eighth Texas Cavalry, ——, 1861.

Brigadier-General, P. A. C. S., January 9, 1862.

Major-General, P. A. C. S., November 8, 1862.

Died at Washington, D. C., July 20, 1893.

COMMANDS.

Brigade composed of the Thirtieth and Fortieth Virginia, the First, Second and Third North Carolina and Third Arkansas regiments infantry, and the light batteries of artillery of Captains Walker and Cooke.

Division composed of the brigades of Hawes, McCulloch and Randall.

1864–5, in command in the Trans-Mississippi Department.

26. *ELZEY, ARNOLD, MARYLAND.

Lieutenant-Colonel, Corps of Infantry, C. S. A., March 16, 1861.

Colonel, First Maryland Regiment, June 17, 1861.

Brigadier-General, P. A. C. S., July 21, 1861.

Major-General, P. A. C. S., December 4, 1862.

Died, February 21, 1871.

COMMANDS.

Brigade composed of the Twelfth Georgia and the Thirteenth, Twenty-fifth, Thirty-first, Forty-fourth, Fifty-second and Fifty-eighth Virginia regiments, Ewell's division, Jackson's corps, Army of Northern Virginia.

First Brigade, composed of the First Maryland, Tenth and Thirteenth Virginia and Second Tennessee regiments.

Commanding Department of Richmond, Va., April 1, 1863, to March 23, 1864.

September 25, 1864, assigned Chief of Artillery of Army of Tennessee.

27. *GARDNER, FRANKLIN, LOUISIANA.

Lieutenant-Colonel, Corps of Infantry, C. S. A., March 16, 1861.

Brigadier-General, P. A. C. S., April 11, 1862.

Major-General, P. A. C. S., December 13, 1862.

Died in Louisiana, April 29, 1873.

COMMANDS.

Commanding the First Brigade, Reserve (Withers') Division, Army of the Mississippi, composed of the Nineteenth, Twenty-second, Twenty-fifth, Twenty-sixth and Twenty-ninth Alabama regiments infantry and Robertson's battery of artillery.

Commanding Third Military District, Department of Mississippi and Eastern Louisiana, from December 28, 1862, to May —, 1863.

Commanding District of Mobile.

Commanding Port Hudson, Louisiana.

Commanding District of Mississippi and East Louisiana, October 4, 1864.

28. CLEBURNE, PATRICK R., ARKANSAS.

Colonel, First Regiment Arkansas Infantry, ——, 1861.

Brigadier-General, P. A. C. S., March 4, 1862.

Major-General, P. A. C. S., December 13, 1862.

Killed at the battle of Franklin, Tenn., November 30, 1864.

COMMANDS.

Brigade composed of the Second, Fifth, Twenty-fourth and Forty-eighth Tennessee and Fifteenth Arkansas regiments infantry, and Calvert's battery of artillery, being Second Brigade, Third Corps, Army of the Mississippi.

Division composed of the brigades of Brigadier-Generals Lucius E. Polk, S. A. M. Wood and James Deshler, and the batteries of artillery of Calvert, Semple and Douglass.

Division subsequently composed of the brigades of Brigadier-Generals L. E. Polk, Lowry, Govan and Granbury, and, subsequently, of the brigades of Brigadier-Generals Wood, Johnson, Liddell and Polk, Hardee's corps, Army of Tennessee.

MAJ.-GEN. JOHN G. WALKER, OF MISSOURI.

29. *TRIMBLE, ISAAC R., MARYLAND.

Brigadier-General, P. A. C. S., August 9, 1861.

Major-General, P. A. C. S., January 17, 1863.

Died at Baltimore, Md., January 2, 1888.

COMMANDS.

Commanding brigade at Evansport, on Potomac River, November 13, 1861.

Afterward commanding brigade composed of the Twenty-first Georgia, Twenty-first North Carolina and Sixteenth Mississippi regiments infantry, and Courtney's Virginia battery of light artillery, Longstreet's corps, Army of Northern Virginia.

At battle of Fredericksburg, commanding brigade composed of the Twelfth and Twenty-first Georgia, the Fifteenth Alabama and Twenty-first North Carolina regiments infantry, Ewell's division, Jackson's corps, Army of Northern Virginia.

Commanding T. J. Jackson's old division, Second Corps, Army of Northern Virginia.

At battle of Chancellorsville, division composed of the brigades of Colston, Paxton, Nichols and Jones.

30. DONELSON, DANIEL S., TENNESSEE.

Brigadier-General, Provisional Army of Tennessee, March 9, 1861, as A. A. G.

Brigadier-General, P. A. C. S., July 9, 1861.

Major-General, P. A. C. S., January 17, 1863.

Died, April 17, 1863, at Knoxville, Tenn.

COMMANDS

Brigade composed of the Eighth, Sixteenth, Twenty-eighth, Thirty-eighth, Fifty-first and Fifty-second Tennessee regiments infantry, and Carnes' Tennessee battery of artillery; known as the First Brigade, Second Division, First Corps, Army of the Mississippi.

Commanding First Division of the Right Wing of the Army of the Mississippi, composed of the brigades of Brigadier-Generals Maney and Stewart, and Donelson's brigade, commanded by Colonel John H. Savage.

Commanding the Department of East Tennessee, January 17, 1863.

31. *WHITING, W. H. C., MISSISSIPPI.

Major, Corps of Engineers, C. S. A., March 16, 1861.

Brigadier-General, P. A. C. S., July 21, 1861.

Major-General, P. A. C. S., February 28, 1863.

Died at Governors Island, N. Y., March 10, 1865.

COMMANDS.

Brigade composed of the Second and Eleventh Mississippi, the Fourth Alabama and the Sixth North Carolina regiments of infantry, Army of the Potomac.

Commanding Third Brigade of the Army of the Shenandoah.

Division composed of the brigades of Hood and Law, and the light batteries of artillery of Reilly and Balthis.

Commanding District of Cape Fear, Department of North Carolina, November 8, 1862, to July 13, 1863.

The District of Cape Fear made a separate command, September 26, 1863, and General Whiting assigned to it.

MAJ.-GEN. FRANKLIN GARDNER, OF LOUISIANA.

32. *JOHNSON, EDWARD, VIRGINIA.

Lieutenant-Colonel, Corps of Infantry, C. S. A., March 16, 1861.

Brigadier-General, P. A. C. S., December 13, 1861.

Major-General, P. A. C. S., February 28, 1863.

Died, February 22, 1873.

COMMANDS.

May 17, 1862, commanding Army of the Northwest.

* * * * * * *

Commanding division in Ewell's corps, Army of Northern Virginia, composed of the brigades of Walker, Stewart and J. M. Jones.

September 1, 1864, assigned command of Anderson's division, Lee's corps (Second), Army of Tennessee.

33. RODES, R. E., ALABAMA.

* * * * * * *

Brigadier-General, P. A. C. S., October 21, 1861.

Major-General, P. A. C. S., May 2, 1863.

Killed at Winchester, Va., September 19, 1864.

COMMANDS.

Brigade composed of the Third, Fifth, Sixth, Twelfth, Twenty-sixth and Sixty-first Alabama regiments infantry, D. H. Hill's division, Jackson's corps, Army of Northern Virginia.

Division composed of the brigades of Doles, Daniel and Ramseur.

34. *WALKER, W. H. T., GEORGIA.

Major-General, Georgia Volunteers, ——, 1861.

Brigadier-General, P. A. C. S., May 25, 1861.

Resigned October 29, 1861.

Brigadier-General, P. A. C. S., February 9, 1863.

Major-General, P. A. C. S., May 23, 1863.

Killed near Atlanta, Ga., July 22, 1864.

COMMANDS.

June 30, 1862, commanding brigade Second Corps, Army of the Mississippi.

* * * * * *

August 31, 1863, commanding a division in D. H. Hill's corps, Army of Tennessee.

Division composed of the brigades of Liddell, Walthall, Ector and Wilson. Afterward composed of the brigades of Mercer, Jackson, Gist and Stevens.

In October, 1863, division composed of the brigades of Gregg, Gist and Wilson.

MAJ.-GEN. DANIEL S. DONELSON, OF TENNESSEE.

35. *HETH, HENRY, VIRGINIA.

Major, Corps of Infantry, C. S. A., March 16, 1861.

Colonel, Forty-fifth Virginia Infantry, June 17, 1861.

Brigadier-General, P. A. C. S., January 6, 1862.

Major-General, P. A. C. S., May 24, 1863.

COMMANDS.

Brigade, in ——, 1862, composed of the Fortieth, Forty-seventh and Fifty-fifth Virginia regiments of infantry, and Twenty-second Virginia battalion infantry, A. P. Hill's division, Army of Northern Virginia.

Division composed of Pettigrew's, Archer's, Davis', Cook's and Brockenbrough's brigades, Third Corps, Army of Northern Virginia, 1863-5.

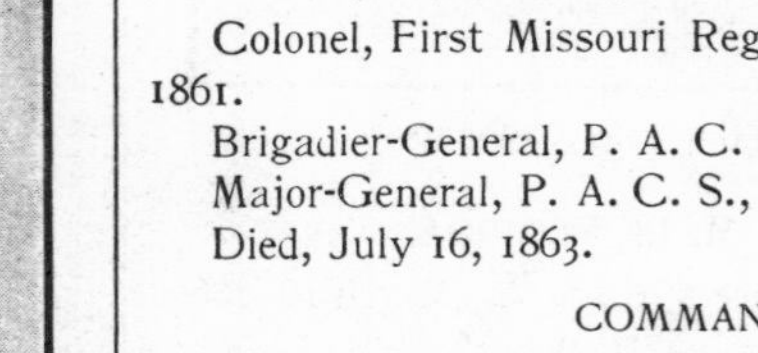

36. BOWEN, JOHN S., MISSOURI.

Colonel, First Missouri Regiment Infantry, June 11, 1861.

Brigadier-General, P. A. C. S., March 14, 1862.

Major-General, P. A. C. S., May 25, 1863.

Died, July 16, 1863.

COMMANDS.

Brigade composed of Fourteenth, Sixteenth, Seventeenth and Eighteenth Arkansas regiments infantry, Adams' Arkansas infantry regiment and Jones' Arkansas infantry battalion.

Commanding the Fourth Division, Western Department; embracing the brigades of Martin and Bonham.

Commanding Third brigade, First Division, Army of the Mississippi.

MAJ.-GEN. EDWARD JOHNSON, OF VIRGINIA.

37. *RANSOM, JR., ROBERT, NORTH CAROLINA.

Captain, Corps of Cavalry, C. S. A., March 16, 1861.

* * * * * *

Brigadier-General, P. A. C. S., March —, 1862.

Major-General, P. A. C. S., May 26, 1863.

COMMANDS.

Commanding brigade, near Kinston, N. C., March 20, 1862.

Commanding Department of Richmond, April 25, 1864.

Division, at battle of Fredericksburg, composed of the brigades of Ransom and Cook.

Commanding Department of Richmond, April 25 to June 13, 1864.

Commanding Subdistrict No. 2, Department South Carolina, Georgia and Florida, November 5, 1864.

38. *PENDER, W. D., NORTH CAROLINA.

Colonel, Sixth North Carolina Regiment, May 27, 1861.

Brigadier-General, P. A. C. S., June 3, 1861.

Major-General, P. A. C. S., May 27, 1863.

Died from wounds at Gettysburg, July 18, 1863.

COMMANDS.

Brigade composed of the Thirteenth, Sixteenth, Twenty-second, Thirty-fourth and Thirty-eighth North Carolina regiments infantry, Anderson's division, A. P. Hill's corps, Army of Northern Virginia.

Division composed of the brigades of Pender, McGowan, Lane and Thomas, Army of Northern Virginia.

39. *WILCOX, CADMUS M., TENNESSEE.

Captain, Corps of Artillery, C. S. A., March 16, 1861.

Colonel, Ninth Regiment Alabama Infantry, July 9, 1861.

Brigadier-General, P. A. C. S., October 21, 1861.

Major-General, P. A. C. S., August 3, 1863.

COMMANDS.

Brigade composed of the Eighth, Ninth, Tenth, Eleventh and Fourteenth Alabama, the Nineteenth Mississippi, and Thirty-eighth Virginia regiments infantry, Anderson's division, A. P. Hill's corps, Army of Northern Virginia.

Division composed of the brigades of Lane, Scales, McGowan and Thomas.

MAJ.-GEN. R. E. RODES, OF ALABAMA.
Killed at Opequon (Winchester), Va., September 19, 1864.

40. *GILMER, J. F., SOUTH CAROLINA.

Lieutenant-Colonel, Corps Engineers, C. S. A., —— 1861.

Brigadier General, P. A. C. S., ——, 1862.

Major-General, P. A. C. S., ——, 1863.

COMMANDS.

* * * * * * *

Chief Engineer, Department No. 2, January 29, 1862.

Chief Engineer, Department Northern Virginia, August 4, 1862.

Chief of Engineer Bureau, October 4, 1862.

Second in command in Department of South Carolina, Georgia and Florida, August 31, 1863.

February 23, 1864, on special duty in Department of the Gulf.

April 2, 1864, resumed duties as Chief of Engineer Bureau.

41. *LEE, FITZHUGH, VIRGINIA.

First Lieutenant, Corps of Cavalry, C. S. A., March 16, 1861.

Lieutenant-Colonel, First Virginia Cavalry, August —, 1861.

Colonel, First Virginia Cavalry, March —, 1862.

Brigadier-General, P. A. C. S., July 24, 1862.

Major-General, P. A. C. S., August 3, 1863.

COMMANDS.

Brigade, in August, 1862, composed of the First, Second, Third, Fourth, Fifth and Ninth Virginia regiments of cavalry, and Breathed's battery of six-gun horse artillery, Army of Northern Virginia.

Division, in August, 1863, composed of the cavalry brigades of W. H. F. Lee, Lomax and Wickham.

Subsequently assigned to the command of the cavalry corps, Army of Northern Virginia, composed of the divisions of W. H. F. Lee, Rosser and Munford.

42. SMITH, WILLIAM, VIRGINIA.

Colonel, Forty-ninth Virginia Infantry, ——, 1861.
Brigadier-General, P. A. C. S., January 31, 1863.
Major-General, P. A. C. S., August 30, 1863.
Resigned, December 31, 1863, having been elected Governor of Virginia.
Died at Warrenton, Va., May 18, 1889.

COMMANDS.

Brigade composed of the Fifty-eighth Virginia Regiment, Colonel Board; Fifty-second Virginia Regiment, Colonel Harman; Thirteenth Virginia Regiment, Colonel Terrell; Thirty-first Virginia Regiment, Colonel Hoffman, and Forty-ninth Virginia Regiment, Colonel Gibson, January —, 1863.

May 3, 1863, brigade composed of the Thirteenth, Forty-ninth, Fifty-second, Fifty-eighth and Thirty-first Virginia regiments, Early's division, Army of Northern Virginia.

43. COBB, HOWELL, GEORGIA.

Colonel, Sixteenth Georgia Regiment Infantry, July 15, 1861.
Brigadier-General, P. A. C. S., February 13, 1862.
Major-General, P. A. C. S., September 9, 1863.
Died in New York City, ——, 1867.

MAJ.-GEN. HENRY HETH, OF VIRGINIA.

COMMANDS.

Brigade composed of the Fifteenth North Carolina, the Second Louisiana and the Sixteenth and Twenty-fourth Georgia regiments infantry, and Cobb's Georgia Legion, Army of Northern Virginia.

Commanding reserve forces of the State of Georgia.

44. WHARTON, JOHN A., TEXAS.

Colonel, Eighth Texas Cavalry, June 13, 1862.
Brigadier-General, P. A. C. S., November 18, 1862.
Major-General, P. A. C. S., November 10, 1863.

COMMANDS.

Brigade composed of Eighth Texas, Second and Third Georgia, Fourth Tennessee and First and Second Confederate regiments of cavalry, a battalion of Tennessee cavalry, and Gibbons' battery of artillery, Wheeler's cavalry corps, Army of Tennessee.

Commanding division in Wheeler's cavalry corps, Army of Tennessee.

45. * MARTIN, WILL. T., MISSISSIPPI.

Captain, Adams' Troop, First Virginia Cavalry, July 8, 1861.
Major, "Jeff Davis Legion," November 14, 1861.
Lieutenant-Colonel, "Jeff Davis Legion," February 13, 1862.
Brigadier-General, P. A. C. S., December 2, 1862.
Major-General, P. A. C. S., November 10, 1863.

COMMANDS.

Commanding division composed of the cavalry brigades of Roddey and Crosby, subsequently composed of Colonels Hagan's and Russell's brigades.

Commanding cavalry corps in East Tennessee, under General Longstreet, November —, 1863, to February —, 1864; subsequently commanding a division in Wheeler's cavalry corps, composed of the brigades of Brigadier-Generals John T. Morgan and Alfred Iverson.

46. * FIELD, CHARLES W., KENTUCKY.

Captain, Corps of Cavalry, C. S. A., March 11, 1861.
Major, Sixth Virginia Cavalry, June —, 1861.
Lieutenant-Colonel, Sixth Virginia Cavalry, July — 1861.
Colonel, Sixth Virginia Cavalry, August —, 1861.
Brigadier-General, P. A. C. S., March 9, 1862.
Major-General, P. A. C. S., February 12, 1864.
Died at Washington, D. C., April, 1892.

COMMANDS.

Brigade composed of the Fortieth, Forty-seventh, Fifty-fifth and Sixtieth Virginia regiments infantry, the Twenty-second Virginia Battalion of Infantry, and Captain

MAJ.-GEN. JOHN. S. BOWEN, OF MISSOURI.
Died July 16, 1863.

Pegram's battery of light artillery, A. P. Hill's division, Jackson's corps, Army of Northern Virginia.

Division composed of the brigades of Brigadier-Generals Jenkins, Law, Benning, Anderson and Gregg, Longstreet's corps, Army of Northern Virginia.

47. ANDERSON, J. PATTON, FLORIDA.

Colonel, First Florida Regiment Infantry, April 19, 1861.
Brigadier-General, P. A. C. S., February 10, 1862.
Major-General, P. A. C. S., February 17, 1864.
Died in Memphis, Tenn., ——, 1873.

COMMANDS.

Brigade composed of the First Florida, Seventeenth Alabama and Fifth and Eighth Mississippi regiments infantry.

Commanding division formerly commanded by Major-General Hindman, Polk's corps, Army of Tennessee.

Commanding District of Florida, ——, 1864.

48. BATE, WILLIAM B., TENNESSEE.

Colonel, Second Tennessee Regiment Infantry, April 27, 1861.
Brigadier-General, P. A. C. S., October 3, 1862.
Major-General, P. A. C. S., February 23, 1864.

MAJ.-GEN. CHARLES W. FIELD, OF KENTUCKY.
[From a photograph taken in 1865.]

COMMANDS.

Brigade composed of the Second, Tenth, Fifteenth, Twentieth, Thirtieth and Thirty-seventh regiments Tennessee infantry; Thirty-seventh Georgia Regiment Infantry, Fourth Battalion Georgia Sharpshooters and the Eufaula Light Battery of Artillery in Hardee's corps, A. P. Stewart's division, Army of Tennessee. In September, 1863 (after battle of Chickamauga), in General Breckinridge's command, until February 23, 1864, when it became a part of Bate's division, on Brigadier-General Bate's promotion.

Division composed of the brigades of Tyler, Lewis and Finley, and the light batteries of Slocomb, Cobb and Mebane, Army of Tennessee. In August, 1864, H. R. Jackson's brigade replaced Lewis', which was transferred to the cavalry.

49. MAXEY, SAMUEL BELL, TEXAS.

Colonel, Ninth Texas Infantry, September —, 1861.
Brigadier-General, P. A. C. S., March 4, 1862.
Major-General, P. A. C. S., April 18, 1864.

COMMANDS.

From December 27, 1861, to March —, 1862, Superintendent of Indian Affairs in Indian Territory, and commanding District of the Indian Territory.

In ——, 1862, commanding brigade in Army of the Mississippi, composed of the Forty-first Georgia, Twenty-fourth Mississippi and Ninth Texas regiments, and Eldridge's Tennessee battery of light artillery, Cheatham's division, Polk's corps.

In winter and spring of 1862–3, commanding brigade at Port Hudson, La., and commanding brigade composed of the Fourth and Thirtieth Louisiana regiments, the Forty-sixth, Forty-eighth, Forty-ninth and Fifty-fifth Tennessee regiments, a Texas battalion of sharpshooters and Fenner's Louisiana battery of artillery.

December 27, 1863, in command of District of the Indian Territory and Superintendent of Indian Affairs.

Commanding forces at battle of Poison Springs, Ark., April 18, 1864.

February 21, 1865, commanding division of Texas cavalry.

50. * HOKE, ROBERT F., NORTH CAROLINA.

* * * * * * *

Brigadier-General, P. A. C. S., January 17, 1863.
Major-General, P. A. C. S., April 20, 1864.

MAJ.-GEN. CADMUS WILCOX, OF TENNESSEE.

COMMANDS.

Brigade composed of the Sixth, Twenty-first, Fifty-fourth and Fifty-seventh North Carolina regiments, and First North Carolina Battalion Infantry, Early's division, Jackson's (afterward Ewell's) corps, Army of Northern Virginia.

Commanding District of North Carolina.

Division composed of the brigades of Martin, Hagood, Clingman and Colquitt, Army of Northern Virginia.

51. * LEE, W. H. F., VIRGINIA.

Captain, Corps of Cavalry, C. S. A., May 6, 1861.
Major, Corps of Cavalry, C. S. A., May —, 1861.
Lieutenant-Colonel Ninth Virginia Cavalry, December —, 1861.
Colonel Ninth Virginia Cavalry, March —, 1862.
Brigadier-General, P. A. C. S., September 15, 1862.
Major-General, P. A. C. S., April 23, 1864.

COMMANDS.

Brigade, in ——, 1862, composed of the Ninth and Thirteenth regiments Virginia cavalry, the Second Regiment of North Carolina Cavalry, and McGregor's battery of horse artillery, Fitzhugh Lee's division, Army of Northern Virginia.

Division, in June, 1864, composed of the cavalry brigades of Chambliss, Barringer and Roberts, and two batteries of horse artillery under command of Captain McGregor, Army of Northern Virginia.

52. * JOHNSON, BUSHROD E., TENNESSEE.

Colonel, Regiment Engineers, Provisional Army of Tennessee, June 28, 1861.
Brigadier-General, P. A. C. S., January 24, 1862.
Major-General, P. A. C. S., May 21, 1864.
Died at Miles Station, Ill., September 10, 1880.

COMMANDS.

Brigade composed of the Seventeenth, Twenty-third, Twenty-fifth, Thirty-seventh and Forty-fourth Tennessee regiments infantry, and Captain Darden's battery of light artillery, Army of Tennessee.

Commanding, in ——, 1862, the Third Brigade, Third Division, Army of the Mississippi.

Division composed of Johnson's (commanded by Colonel Fulton), Wise's, Elliott's and Gracie's brigades, and Sixty-fourth Georgia Regiment, Army of Northern Virginia.

MAJ.-GEN. L. L. LOMAX, OF VIRGINIA.
[From a photograph taken in 1864.]

53. KERSHAW, J. B., SOUTH CAROLINA.

Colonel, Second South Carolina Volunteer Infantry, May 22, 1861.
Brigadier-General, P. A. C. S., February 13, 1862.
Major-General, P. A. C. S., May 18, 1864.
Died at Camden, S. C., April 13, 1894.

COMMANDS.

Brigade composed of the Second, Third, Seventh, Eighth, Fifteenth and Twentieth South Carolina regiments infantry, McLaws' division, Longstreet's corps, Army of Northern Virginia.

Division composed of the brigades of Conner, Wofford, Humphreys and Bryan, Army of Tennessee.

54. POLIGNAC, DE, CAMILLE J., FRANCE.

Lieutenant-Colonel, Corps of Infantry, C. S. A., July 6, 1861.
Brigadier-General, P. A. C. S., January 10, 1863.
Major-General, P. A. C. S., April 8, 1864.

COMMANDS.

On staff of General G. T. Beauregard, in Virginia, and, subsequently, in Mississippi.

Commanding, as lieutenant-colonel, Confederate States Army, the Fifth Tennessee Regiment Infantry, at battle of Richmond, Ky.

Brigade composed of Seventeenth Texas (consolidated), Hanope's Texas regiment, Alexander's Texas regiment and the Texas battalions of Speight, Stevenson and Stone.

Division composed of Moulton's brigade and unattached Texas troops.

MAJ.-GEN. J. L. KEMPER, OF VIRGINIA.
[From a tintype taken in 1864.]

55. FAGAN, JAMES F., ARKANSAS.

Colonel First Regiment Arkansas Infantry, ——, 1862.
Brigadier-General, P. A. C. S., September 12, 1862.
Major-General, P. A. C. S., April 24, 1864.

COMMANDS.

* * * * * * *

Commanding District of Arkansas.

56. GORDON, JAMES B., NORTH CAROLINA.

Major Ninth North Carolina Volunteers (cavalry), May 8, 1861.
Lieutenant-Colonel Ninth North Carolina Cavalry, March 1, 1862.
Colonel, ——, 1862.
Brigadier-General, P. A. C. S., September 5, 1863.
Major-General, P. A. C. S. (temporary rank), May 14, 1864.
Killed at Yellow Tavern, Va., ——, 1864.

COMMANDS.

Brigade composed of the First, Second, Third, Fourth and Fifth North Carolina regiments cavalry, Army of Northern Virginia.

57. MAHONE, WILLIAM, VIRGINIA.

Colonel Sixth Virginia Regiment Infantry, ——, 1861.
Brigadier-General, P. A. C. S., November 16, 1861.
Major-General, P. A. C. S. (temporary rank), June 1, 1864; declined.
Major-General, P. A. C. S., July 30, 1864.

COMMANDS.

Brigade composed of the Third Alabama, the Sixth, Twelfth, Sixteenth and Forty-first Virginia, and Second (afterward the Twelfth) North Carolina regiments infantry, Anderson's division, A. P. Hill's corps, Army of Northern Virginia.

Division composed of Wright's Georgia, Weisiger's Virginia, Saunders' Alabama, Harris' Mississippi and Finegan's Florida brigades.

58. *RAMSEUR, STEPHEN D., NORTH CAROLINA.

Major Tenth North Carolina Artillery (State troops), August 20, 1861.
Colonel Forty-ninth North Carolina Infantry, April 12, 1862.
Brigadier-General, P. A. C. S., November 1, 1862.

MAJ.-GEN J. F. GILMER, OF NORTH CAROLINA.
Chief of the Engineer Bureau

Major-General, P. A. C. S. (temporary rank), June 1, 1864.
Killed at the Battle of Cedar Creek, Va., October 19, 1864.

COMMANDS.

Brigade composed of the Second, Fourth, Fourteenth and Thirtieth North Carolina regiments infantry, D. H. Hill's division, Army of Northern Virginia.

Division composed of the brigades of Pegram, Johnston and Godwin, Army of Northern Virginia.

59. WALTHALL, ED. C., MISSISSIPPI.

Colonel Twenty-ninth Mississippi Infantry, April 11, 1862.
Brigadier-General, P. A. C. S., December 13, 1862.
Major-General, P. A. C. S., June 6, 1864.

COMMANDS.

Brigade composed of the Twenty-fourth, Twenty-seventh, Twenty-ninth, Thirtieth and Thirty-fourth Mississippi regiments infantry, Withers' division, Polk's corps, Army of Tennessee.

Division composed of the brigades of Cantey (afterward Shelley's) and Quarles and Reynolds, Stewart's corps, Army of Tennessee.

60. CLAYTON, H. D., ALABAMA.

Colonel First Alabama Regiment Infantry, March 28, 1861.
Brigadier-General, P. A. C. S., April 22, 1863.
Major-General, P. A. C. S., July 7, 1864.
Died at Tuscaloosa, Ala., October 13, 1889.

COMMANDS.

Commanding, at Pensacola, Fla., ——, 1861, brigade composed of the First Alabama and First Georgia regiments infantry, and the Second Alabama Battalion Infantry.

Commanding brigade composed of the Eighteenth, Thirty-second, Thirty-sixth, Thirty-eighth and Fifty-eighth Alabama regiments infantry.

Division composed of the brigades of Stovall, Baker and Henry R. Jackson; subsequently, of the brigades of Brigadier-Generals M. A. Stovall, R. L. Gibson, A. Baker and J. T. Holtzclaw, Army of Tennessee.

MAJ.-GEN. A. R. WRIGHT, OF GEORGIA.
[From a photograph taken in 1862.]

61. BROWN, JOHN C., TENNESSEE.

Colonel, Third Regiment Tennessee Infantry, Provisional Army of Tennessee, May 16, 1861.
Brigadier-General, P. A. C. S., August 30, 1862.
Major-General, P. A. C. S., August 4, 1864.

COMMANDS.

Brigade composed of the Eighteenth, Twenty-sixth, Thirty-second and Forty-fifth regiments Tennessee infantry and Newman's battalion of Tennessee infantry, Stewart's division, Polk's corps, Army of Tennessee. The Third Regiment Tennessee Infantry was subsequently added to the brigade.

Division composed of the brigades of Generals Govan and J. A. Smith, Army of Tennessee.

62. *LOMAX, L. L., VIRGINIA.

Colonel, Eleventh Virginia Cavalry, February 8, 1863.
Brigadier-General, P. A. C. S., July 23, 1863.
Major-General, P. A. C. S., August 10, 1864.

COMMANDS.

Brigade composed of the Fifth, Sixth and Fifteenth Virginia regiments cavalry and First Regiment Maryland Cavalry, Army of Northern Virginia.

Division composed of the cavalry brigades of Johnston, Jackson, Davidson, Imboden and McCausland, Army of Northern Virginia.

MAJ.-GEN BRYAN GRIMES, OF NORTH CAROLINA.
[From a tintype taken in 1865.]

63. ALLEN, HENRY W., LOUISIANA.

Lieutenant-Colonel, Fourth Louisiana Infantry, May 20, 1861.
Brigadier-General, P. A. C. S., August 19, 1863.
Major-General, P. A. C. S., ——, 1864.
Resigned, January 10, 1864, having been elected Governor of Louisiana.
Died in the City of Mexico, April 22, 1866.

COMMANDS.

August 5, 1862, commanding Second Brigade, Ruggles' division, Breckinridge's command.

1864, commanding division Trans-Mississippi Department.

64. *KEMPER, JAMES L., VIRGINIA.

Colonel Seventh Virginia Infantry, May 2, 1861.
Brigadier-General, P. A. C. S., June 3, 1862.
Major-General, P. A. C. S., September 19, 1864.

COMMANDS.

Brigade composed of the First, Seventh, Eleventh, Seventeenth and Twenty-fourth Virginia regiments infantry. Subsequently the Seventeenth Virginia Regiment was transferred to Corse's brigade, and the Third Virginia was substituted for it.

As major-general, commanding the reserve forces of Virginia.

65. *MARMADUKE, JOHN S., MISSOURI.

First Lieutenant, Corps of Cavalry, C. S. A., March 16, 1861.
Colonel Third Confederate Regiment, January 1, 1862.
Brigadier-General, P. A. C. S., November 15, 1862.
Major-General, P. A. C. S., March 17, 1865.
Died, December 28, 1887.

COMMANDS.

Brigade composed of the Third Confederate, the Twenty-fifth, Twenty-ninth and Thirty-seventh Tennessee regiments, and Snell's light battery of artillery, constituting the Fourth Brigade, Third Corps, Army of the Mississippi.

Commanding all the cavalry forces in Northern Arkansas.

Commanding division composed of the brigades of Clarke and Harrison.

MAJ.-GEN. C. J. DE POLIGNAC, OF FRANCE.
[From an old tintype.]

66. WRIGHT, A. R., GEORGIA.

Colonel Third Regiment Georgia Infantry, May 8, 1861.
Colonel Thirty-eighth Regiment Georgia Infantry, October 15, 1861.
Resigned, April 23, 1862.
Brigadier-General, P. A. C. S., June 3, 1862.
Major-General, P. A. C. S., November 26, 1864.

COMMANDS.

Brigade composed of the Third, Twenty-second, Forty-sixth and Forty-eighth regiments Georgia infantry, and Second Georgia Battalion, Anderson's division, A. P. Hill's corps, Army of Northern Virginia.

Division composed of the brigades of Mercer and John K. Jackson.

67. *PEGRAM, JOHN, VIRGINIA.

Captain, Corps of Cavalry, March 16, 1861.
* * * * * *
Brigadier-General, P. A. C. S., November 7, 1862.
Major-General, P. A. C. S., ——.
Killed at Hatchers Run, Va., February 5, 1865.

COMMANDS.

Brigade composed of the Thirteenth, Thirty-first, Forty-ninth, Fifty-second and Fifty-eighth regiments Virginia infantry, Army of Northern Virginia.

Commanding Early's division, Army of Northern Virginia.

68. *YOUNG, P. M. B., GEORGIA.

Second Lieutenant, Corps of Artillery, C. S. A., April —, 1861.
First Lieutenant, Corps of Artillery, C. S. A., June —, 1861, and Aid-de-camp to General W. H. T. Walker.
First Lieutenant and Adjutant, Cobb's Georgia Legion, July 24, 1861.
Major, P. A. C. S., September 5, 1861, and assigned to Cobb's Legion.
Lieutenant-Colonel, P. A. C. S., November 15, 1862, and assigned to Cobb's Georgia Legion.
Colonel, Cobb's Legion, December —, 1862.
Brigadier-General, P. A. C. S., September 28, 1863.
Major-General, P. A. C. S., December 30, 1864.

MAJ.-GEN. JOHN C. BROWN, OF TENNESSEE.

COMMANDS.

Brigade composed of the Cobb Legion, the Jeff. Davis Legion, Phillips' Legion and the Seventh Georgia (all cavalry), Hampton's division, Army of Northern Virginia. In November, 1864, the Tenth Regiment Georgia Cavalry was substituted for the Seventh Georgia Cavalry, withdrawn, and Miller's battalion of Georgia cavalry was added to the command.

Division composed of the brigades of Lewis, Ferguson and Harrison.

69. BUTLER, M. C., SOUTH CAROLINA.

Captain, Hampton (S. C.) Legion, June 12, 1861.
Major, Hampton Legion, July 21, 1861.
Colonel Second South Carolina Cavalry, August 22, 1862.
Brigadier-General, P. A. C. S., September 1, 1863.
Major-General, P. A. C. S., September 19, 1864.

MAJ.-GEN. WM. MAHONE, OF VIRGINIA.

COMMANDS.

In May, 1864, commanding brigade composed of the Fourth, Fifth and Sixth regiments South Carolina cavalry, and Keitt's squadron was afterward added. The First and Second South Carolina regiments, formerly of this brigade, were sent to South Carolina to recruit, and were substituted by the Fourth, Fifth and Sixth regiments.

Division composed originally of the cavalry brigades of Rosser, Young, Butler and Dearing.

Original brigade composed of First and Second South Carolina cavalry, Cobb's Legion of cavalry, Jeff. Davis' Legion of cavalry, Phillips' Legion of cavalry and the First Regiment North Carolina Cavalry.

70. *ROSSER, THOMAS L., TEXAS.

Colonel Fifth Virginia Cavalry, June 24, 1862.
Brigadier-General, P. A. C. S., September 28, 1863.
Major-General, P. A. C. S., November 1, 1864.

COMMANDS.

Brigade composed of the Seventh, Eleventh and Twelfth regiments Virginia cavalry, and Twenty-fifth Battalion Virginia Cavalry, Army of Northern Virginia.

Division composed of the cavalry brigades of McCausland and Dearing, subsequently of the brigades of Payne and Munford, Army of Northern Virginia.

71. *LEE, G. W. C., VIRGINIA.

Captain, Corps of Engineers, C. S. A., July 1, 1861.
Colonel and Aid-de-camp to the President, August 31, 1861.
Brigadier-General, P. A. C. S., June 25, 1863.
Major-General, P. A. C. S., October 20, 1864.

COMMANDS.

Commanding brigade of local troops for the defense of Richmond, consisting of Confederate States employes in Richmond and some unattached companies.

As major-general, commanding troops for local defense of Richmond, consisting of Barton's brigade, the brigade of Confederate States employes and several battalions of heavy artillery manning the batteries at Chafins Bluff.

MAJ.-GEN. JOHN PEGRAM, OF VIRGINIA.
[Killed at Hatchers Run, Va., February 5, 1865.]

72. *PRESTON, WILLIAM, KENTUCKY.

* * * * * *
Brigadier-General, P. A. C. S., April 14, 1862.
Major-General, P. A. C. S., January 1, 1865.
Died at Lexington, Ky., September 21, 1887.

COMMANDS.

Commanding Third Brigade, in Breckinridge's division, Army of Tennessee, composed of the Twentieth Tennessee, Sixtieth North Carolina and the First, Second and Third Florida regiments infantry, and Mebane's light battery of artillery.

Commanding division formerly commanded by Major-General Polignac.

In October, 1863, commanding division composed of the brigades of Gracie, Trigg and Kelly, in Longstreet's corps, Army of Tennessee.

73. TALIAFERRO, WILLIAM B., VIRGINIA.

Colonel, Provisional Army of Virginia, May 1, 1861.
Brigadier-General, P. A. C. S., March 4, 1862.
Major-General, P. A. C. S., January 1, 1865.

COMMANDS.

May 1, 1861, commanding post and troops at Gloucester Point, Va.

June 1, 1861, commanding Twenty-third Virginia Regiment Infantry, and commanding troops in engagement at Carricks Ford, July 13, 1861.

August —, 1861, as colonel, commanding brigade composed of Twenty-third, Thirty-seventh and Forty-fourth Virginia regiments infantry and Rogers' battery of artillery.

December —, 1861, as colonel, commanding brigade composed of Twenty-third and Thirty-seventh Virginia, Third Arkansas and First Georgia regiments.

March —, 1862, as brigadier-general, commanding brigade composed of Tenth, Twenty-third and Thirty-seventh Virginia regiments, Army of the Valley, under Major-General T. J. Jackson.

August —, 1862, brigade composed of the Tenth, Twenty-third and Thirty-seventh Virginia and Forty-seventh and Forty-eighth Alabama regiments.

August 9, 1862, to January —, 1863, commanding division composed of the "Stonewall Brigade" and the brigades of Campbell and Stark.

March —, 1863, commanding District of Savannah, Ga.

July —, 1863, commanding defenses and troops on Morris Island, S. C.

August —, 1863, in command, on James Island, S. C., of forces consisting of Colquitt's Georgia, Anderson's Georgia and Hagood's South Carolina brigades and unattached troops.

February —, 1864, commanding division in Florida composed of Finegan's, Colquitt's, Wise's and Page's brigades.

May —, 1864, commanding Seventh Military District, South Carolina.

December —, 1864, commanding District of South Carolina.

January —, 1865, commanding division composed of Elliott's, Rhett's and Anderson's brigades.

MAJ.-GEN. T. J. CHURCHILL, OF ARKANSAS.
[From a photograph of a crayon portrait.]

74. GRIMES, BRYAN, NORTH CAROLINA.

Major Fourth North Carolina Infantry (State troops), May 16, 1861.
Lieutenant-Colonel, May 19, 1861.
Colonel Fourth North Carolina Infantry, May 19, 1862.
Brigadier-General, P. A. C. S., May 19, 1864.
Major-General, P. A. C. S., February 15, 1865.
Died, August 14, 1880.

COMMANDS.

Brigade composed of the Thirty-second, Forty-third, Forty-fifth and Fifty-third North Carolina regiments infantry, and the Second North Carolina Battalion Infantry, formerly Brigadier-General Daniels' brigade, May —, 1864.

Division composed of his own brigade and the brigades of Battle, Cook and Cox, Army of Northern Virginia, from September 19, 1864, to April 9, 1865.

75. ALLEN, W. W., ALABAMA.

Major First Alabama Cavalry, March 18, 1862.
Colonel First Alabama Cavalry, —— —, 1862.
Brigadier-General, P. A. C. S., February 26, 1864.
Major-General; P. A. C. S., —— —, 1865.

COMMANDS.

Brigade composed of the First, Third, Eighth and Tenth Confederate regiments.

Afterward of the First, Third, Fourth, Ninth, Twelfth and Fifty-first regiments Alabama cavalry, Wheeler's corps, Army of the West.

Commanding cavalry division in Wheeler's corps.

76. CHURCHILL, T. J., ARKANSAS.

Colonel First Arkansas Cavalry, June 9, 1861.
Brigadier-General, P. A. C. S., March 4, 1862.
Major-General, P. A. C. S., March 17, 1865.

COMMANDS.

Commanding Second Brigade in Major-General Van Dorn's division, —— —, 1862.

Commanding in ——, 1862, Second Brigade, Second Division, Army of the West, composed of the Fourth

MAJ.-GEN. P. M. B. YOUNG, OF GEORGIA.
[From a photograph taken in 1864.]

Arkansas Infantry, First and Second dismounted Arkansas riflemen, Fourth Arkansas battalion of infantry, Turnbull's Arkansas battalion of infantry reserves, Missouri Scouts and Humphries' light battery of artillery.

Division composed of McNair's Arkansas brigade and McCrary's Texas brigade, August 30, 1862.

Transferred to Trans-Mississippi Department in December, 1863, commanding Arkansas Post, where he surrendered and was made a prisoner of war, January 9–11, 1863. After exchange, reported to General Bragg, at Chattanooga.

In ——, 1864, transferred to Trans-Mississippi Department.

MAJ.-GEN. JOHN H. MORGAN, OF KENTUCKY.

Commanded corps at battle of Pleasant Hill, La., composed of Arkansas and Missouri troops.

Commanded Churchill's division Arkansas troops at the battle of Jenkins Ferry, Ark.

77. HUMES, W. Y. C., TENNESSEE.

Captain, Artillery, Provisional Army of Tennessee, June —, 1861.
Brigadier-General, P. A. C. S., November 16, 1863.
Major-General, P. A. C. S., March, 1865.
Died at Huntsville, Ala., September 12, 1883.

MAJ.-GEN. W. W. ALLEN, OF ALABAMA.
[From a photograph taken in 1865.]

COMMANDS.

Commanding brigade of cavalry in Wheeler's cavalry corps, ——, 1863.

Commanding division in Wheeler's cavalry corps consisting of the brigades of Ashby, Harrison and Williams.

78. HAYS, HARRY T., LOUISIANA.

Colonel Sixth Louisiana Infantry, ——, 1861.
Brigadier-General, P. A. C. S., July 25, 1862.
Major-General, P. A. C. S., April —, 1865.
Died at New Orleans, August 21, 1876.

COMMANDS.

Brigade composed of the Fifth, Sixth, Seventh, Eighth and Ninth Louisiana regiments infantry. Early's division, Jackson's corps, Army of Northern Virginia.

79. LAW, E. M., ALABAMA.

Lieutenant-Colonel Fourth Alabama Regiment Infantry, May 2, 1861.
Colonel Fourth Alabama Regiment Infantry, October 28, 1861.
Brigadier-General, P. A. C. S., October 3, 1862.
Major-General P. A. C. S., April 9, 1865.

COMMANDS.

Brigade composed of the Fourth, Fifteenth, Forty-fourth, Forty-seventh and Forty-eighth Alabama regiments infantry, Hood's division, Longstreet's corps, Army of Northern Virginia.

Brigade, at battle of Fredericksburg, December 13, 1862, composed of the Sixth, Fifty-fourth and Fifty-seventh North Carolina and Fourth and Forty-fourth Alabama regiments. Brigade subsequently composed of the Fourth Alabama, Sixth North Carolina and Second and Eleventh Mississippi regiments.

As major-general, commanding division formerly commanded by Major-General Wade Hampton, composed of Young's Georgia brigade, commanded by Colonel Wright, and Logan's South Carolina brigade.

80. GARY, M. W., SOUTH CAROLINA.

Colonel, Hampton Legion, August 25, 1862.
Brigadier-General, P. A. C. S., May 19, 1864.
Major-General, P. A. C. S., ——, 1865.
Died, April —, 1881.

MAJ.-GEN. WILLIAM PRESTON, OF KENTUCKY.
[From a photograph taken in 1864.]

COMMANDS.

Brigade composed of the Hampton Legion, the Seventh South Carolina Cavalry, the Seventh Georgia Cavalry, the Twenty-fourth Virginia Cavalry, and Captain Harkerson's Virginia battery artillery, Army of Northern Virginia.

As major-general, division assigned, but never concentrated, consisting of his old brigade and Roberts' brigade of North Carolina cavalry.

81. RANSOM, MATT. W., NORTH CAROLINA.

Lieutenant-Colonel First North Carolina Infantry, ——.
Colonel Thirty-fifth North Carolina Infantry, ——.
Brigadier-General, P. A. C. S., June 13, 1863.
Major-General, ——, 1865.

COMMANDS.

Brigade composed of the Twenty-fourth, Twenty-fifth, Thirty-fifth, Forty-ninth and Fifty-sixth North Carolina regiments infantry, Longstreet's corps, Army of Northern Virginia.

BRIGADIER-GENERALS.

(362.)

ALPHABETICALLY ARRANGED. QUESTIONS OF RANK OF MANY OFFICERS HAD TO AWAIT OFFICIAL CONFIRMATION.

ADAMS, DANIEL W., LOUISIANA.

Second Lieutenant, Second Regiment Mississippi State Troops, ——, 1861.
Colonel, First Regiment Louisiana Infantry, October 30, 1861.
Brigadier-General, P. A. C. S., May 23, 1862.
Died in New Orleans, La., June 14, 1872.

COMMANDS.

Brigade composed of the Thirteenth, Sixteenth, Nineteenth, Twentieth and Twenty-fifth Louisiana and Thirty-second Alabama regiments, Austin's Louisiana battalion of sharpshooters, and Slocumb's battery of light artillery, Breckinridge's division, Army of Tennessee.

BRIG.-GEN. JOHN ADAMS, OF TENNESSEE.
Killed at the Battle of Franklin, Tenn., November 30, 1864.

* ADAMS, JOHN, TENNESSEE.

Captain, Corps of Cavalry, C. S. A., March 16, 1861.
Colonel, P. A. C. S., ——, 1862.
Brigadier-General, P. A. C. S., December 29, 1862.
Killed at the battle of Franklin, Tenn., November 30, 1864.

COMMANDS.

Commanding Post of Memphis, Tenn., 1861-2.
Commanding brigade composed of the Sixth, Fourteenth, Fifteenth, Twentieth, Twenty-third and Forty-third Mississippi regiments infantry, Loring's division, Stewart's corps, Army of Tennessee.

ADAMS, WIRT, MISSISSIPPI.

Colonel, First Mississippi Cavalry (called Adams' Regiment), October 15, 1861.
Brigadier-General, P. A. C. S., September 28, 1863.

COMMANDS.

Brigade composed of First Mississippi Cavalry, Colonel Woods; the Eleventh and Seventeenth Arkansas cavalry, consolidated; the Fourteenth Confederate Regiment Cavalry; the Ninth Tennessee Battalion of Cavalry, and King's battery of light artillery.

ALCORN, J. L., MISSISSIPPI.

* * * * * *

Commanding a brigade of Mississippi State troops at Columbus, Ky.

* ALEXANDER, E. P., GEORGIA.

Captain, Corps of Engineers, C. S. A., April 2, 1861.
On staff of General G. T. Beauregard, as Engineer and Chief of Signal Service, July 1, 1861, to August —, 1861.
Chief of Ordnance, Army of Northern Virginia, August —, 1861, to November 8, 1862.
Lieutenant-Colonel of Artillery, December 31, 1861.
Colonel of Artillery, December 5, 1862,
Commanding Alexander's battalion of artillery, November 8, 1862, to February 26, 1864.
Acting Chief of Artillery, Longstreet's corps, September 25, 1863, to February 26, 1864.
Brigadier-General of Artillery, P. A. C. S., February 26, 1864.
Chief of Artillery, Longstreet's corps, Army of Northern Virginia, to surrender at Appomattox Courthouse.

ANDERSON, C. D., GEORGIA.

Brigadier-General, P. A. C. S., May, 1864.
Held commission in Georgia State forces.

COMMANDS.

Commanding the Third Georgia Brigade, composed of the Seventh, Eighth and Ninth regiments.

* ANDERSON, GEORGE B., NORTH CAROLINA.

Colonel Fourth North Carolina Infantry (State troops), July 16, 1861.
Brigadier-General, P. A. C. S., June 9, 1862.
Died, October 16, 1862, from wounds received at the battle of Sharpsburg.

COMMANDS.

Brigade composed of the Second, Fourth, Fourteenth and Thirtieth Carolina regiments infantry, D. H. Hill's division, Jackson's corps, Army Northern Virginia.

ANDERSON, GEORGE T., GEORGIA.

* * * * * *

Brigadier-General, P. A. C. S., November 1, 1862.

COMMANDS.

Brigades composed of the Seventh, Eighth, Ninth and Eleventh Georgia regiments and the First Kentucky Regiment, whose term of service had expired, all of the Army of Northern Virginia.

ANDERSON, JOSEPH R., VIRGINIA.

* * * * *

Brigadier-General, P. A. C. S., September 3, 1861.
Resigned, July 19, 1862.
Died at Isle of Shoals, N. H., September 7, 1892.

COMMANDS.

Brigade composed of the Fourteenth, Thirty-fifth, Forty-fifth and Forty-ninth Georgia regiments infantry, and the Third Louisiana Battalion Infantry, Army of Northern Virginia.

ANDERSON, ROBERT H., GEORGIA.

First Lieutenant, Corps of Artillery, C. S. A., March 16, 1861.
Major, A. A. General, P. A. C. S., September —, 1861.
Major First Battalion Georgia Sharpshooters, June 20, 1862.
Colonel Fifth Georgia Cavalry (temporary rank), ——, 1862.
Colonel Fifth Georgia Cavalry, January 20, 1863.
Brigadier-General, P. A. C. S., July 26, 1864.
Died, February 8, 1888.

COMMANDS.

Brigade composed of the Fifth Georgia and the First, Third, Eighth and Tenth Confederate regiments of cavalry, Kelly's division, Army of Tennessee.

ANDERSON, SAMUEL R., TENNESSEE.

Major-General, Provisional Army of Tennessee, May 9, 1861.
Brigadier-General, P. A. C. S., July 9, 1861.
Resigned, May 8, 1862.
Brigadier-General, P. A. C. S., November 7, 1864.

COMMANDS.

Brigade composed of the First, Seventh and Fourteenth Tennessee regiments infantry, and one company of Tennessee cavalry.

* ARCHER, JAMES J., MARYLAND.

Captain, Corps of Infantry, C. S. A., March 16, 1861.
Colonel ——— Regiment, October 2, 1861.
Brigadier-General, P. A. C. S., June 3, 1862.
Died, October 24, 1864.

COMMANDS.

Brigade composed of the First, Seventh and Fourteenth Tennessee regiments, the Thirteenth Alabama Regiment and the Fifth Alabama Battalion Infantry, Heth's division, A. P. Hill's corps, Army of Northern Virginia.

*ARMISTEAD, LOUIS A., VIRGINIA.

Major, Corps of Infantry, C. S. A., March 16, 1861.
Colonel Fifty-seventh Virginia Infantry, ——, 1861.
Brigadier-General, P. A. C. S., April 1, 1862.
Killed at Gettysburg, July 2, 1863.

COMMANDS.

Brigade composed of the Ninth, Fourteenth, Thirty-eighth, Fifty-third and Fifty-seventh Virginia regiments infantry, Army of Northern Virginia.

* ARMSTRONG, FRANK C., TENNESSEE.

Second Lieutenant, Corps of Cavalry, C. S. A., March 16, 1861. (Declined the commission.)
Assistant Adjutant-General to General Ben. McCulloch to March 6, 1862.
Colonel Third Louisiana Infantry, May 14, 1862.
Brigadier-General, P. A. C. S., January 30, 1863.

COMMANDS.

Commanding brigade in Forrest's division, Van Dorn's cavalry, 1863, consisting of Tennessee, Kentucky and Arkansas troops.
Afterward commanding division, consisting of Dibrell's Tennessee and Harrison's Texas brigades, under General Longstreet, in East Tennessee.
Afterward commanding cavalry brigade in Chalmer's division, under General Richard Taylor.

ASHBY, TURNER, VIRGINIA.

Lieutenant-Colonel Seventh Virginia Cavalry, July 17, 1861.
Brigadier-General, P. A. C. S., May 23, 1862.
Killed near Harrisonburg, Va., June 6, 1862.

COMMANDS.

Original command of twenty-six companies of cavalry, which were subsequently organized into the Sixth, Seventh and Eleventh Virginia regiments, and Colonel Funsten's Sixteenth Battalion Virginia Cavalry, Army of Northern Virginia.

* BAGBY, A. P., TEXAS.

Major Seventh Texas Infantry, ——, 1861.
Colonel Seventh Texas Cavalry, ——, 1862.
Brigadier-General, P. A. C. S., ——, 1863.

COMMANDS.

Brigade composed of First, Seventh and Thirty-seventh Texas regiments of cavalry.
In 1864, commanded a division composed of DeBray's, Terrell's and Brent's brigades.

BAKER, ALPHEUS, ALABAMA.

Colonel First Alabama and Mississippi Regiment, December 23, 1861.
Captured at Island No. 10, April 8, 1862.
Colonel Fifty-fourth Alabama Regiment, October 9, 1862.
Brigadier-General, P. A. C. S., March 5, 1864.

COMMANDS.

Brigade composed of Thirty-seventh, Fortieth, Forty-second and Fifty-fourth Alabama regiments.

* BAKER, LAWRENCE S., NORTH CAROLINA.

Captain, Corps of Cavalry, C. S. A., March 16, 1861.
Lieutenant-Colonel Ninth North Carolina Regiment, May 8, 1861.
Colonel Ninth North Carolina (First Cavalry), March 1, 1862.
Brigadier-General, P. A. C. S., July 23, 1863.

COMMANDS.

Commanding Second Military District, Department North Carolina and Southern Virginia.

BALDWIN, WILLIAM E., MISSISSIPPI.

Colonel Fourteenth Mississippi Infantry, ——, 1861.
Brigadier-General, P. A. C. S., September 19, 1862.
Died, February 19, 1864.

COMMANDS.

Brigade composed of Twentieth and Twenty-sixth Mississippi and Twenty-sixth Tennessee regiments infantry.
Commanding brigade in District of Mobile, Ala.

BRIG.-GEN. GEORGE T. ANDERSON, OF GEORGIA.
[From a photograph taken in 1864.]

BARKSDALE, WILLIAM, MISSISSIPPI.

* * * * * *

Brigadier-General, P. A. C. S., August, 1862.
Killed at Gettysburg, July 1, 1863.

COMMANDS.

Brigade composed of the Thirteenth, Seventeenth, Eighteenth and Twenty-first Mississippi regiments infantry, McLaws' division, Longstreet's corps, Army of Northern Virginia.

BARRINGER, RUFUS, NORTH CAROLINA.

Captain Company F, First North Carolina Cavalry, April 19, 1861.
Major First North Carolina Cavalry, ——, 1862.
Lieutenant-Colonel First North Carolina Cavalry. October 17, 1863.
Brigadier-General, P. A. C. S., June 1, 1864.

COMMANDS.

Brigade composed of the First, Second, Third and Fifth North Carolina regiments of cavalry, Major-General W. H. F. Lee's division, Army of Northern Virginia.

BARRY, JOHN D., NORTH CAROLINA.

Major Eighteenth Regiment North Carolina Infantry, ——.

Colonel Eighteenth North Carolina Regiment, May 3, 1863.

Brigadier-General, P. A. C. S. (temporary rank), August 3, 1864.

BARRY, WILLIAM S., MISSISSIPPI.

Colonel Thirty-fifth Mississippi Infantry.

Brigadier-General, ——, 1865.

Commanded a brigade in the Army of the Mississippi.

*BARTON, SETH M., VIRGINIA.

Captain, Corps of Infantry, C. S. A., March 16, 1861.

* * * * * * *

Brigadier-General, P. A. C. S., March 11, 1862.

COMMANDS.

Brigade composed of the Ninth, Fourteenth, Thirty-eighth, Fifty-third and Fifty-seventh Virginia regiments infantry, Army of Northern Virginia.

BARTOW, FRANCIS S., GEORGIA.

Colonel Eighth Georgia Infantry.

Brigadier-General, July —, 1861.

Killed at the battle of First Manassas, July 21, 1861.

COMMANDS.

Brigade composed of the Seventh and Eighth Georgia regiments, Army of the Potomac.

BATTLE, CULLEN A., ALABAMA.

Colonel Third Alabama Infantry, May 31, 1862.

Brigadier-General, P. A. C. S., August 20, 1863.

COMMANDS.

Brigade (formerly commanded by Brigadier-General Rodes) composed of the Third, Fifth, Sixth, Twelfth, Twenty-sixth and Sixty-first Alabama regiments infantry, Army of Northern Virginia.

BAYLOR, JOHN R., TEXAS.

Lieutenant-Colonel Second Texas Cavalry.

Brigadier-General, ——.

COMMANDS.

Commanding brigade Trans-Mississippi Department; also in command of Confederate forces in Arizona.

BEALE, RICHARD L. T., VIRGINIA.

Colonel Ninth Virginia Cavalry, October 18, 1862.

Brigadier-General, P. A. C. S., February 6, 1865.

COMMANDS.

Commanding brigade in Major-General W. H. F. Lee's cavalry division, Army of Northern Virginia, composed of the Ninth, Tenth and Thirteenth regiments of Virginia cavalry. The Fourteenth Regiment Virginia Cavalry was added to the brigade in March, 1865.

BRIG.-GEN. JOSEPH R. ANDERSON, OF VIRGINIA.
[From a photograph taken in 1862.]

*BEALL, W. N. R., ARKANSAS.

Captain, Corps of Cavalry, C. S. A., March 16, 1861.

* * * * * * *

Brigadier-General, P. A. C. S., April 11, 1862.

Died at McMinnville, Tenn., July 26, 1883.

COMMANDS.

Commanding Third Military District, Department of Mississippi and East Louisiana, October 21, 1862, to May 11, 1863.

*BEE, BARNARD E., SOUTH CAROLINA.

Major, Corps Infantry, C. S. A., ——, 1861.

Brigadier-General, P. A. C. S., June 17, 1861.

Killed at the battle of Manassas, July 21, 1861.

COMMANDS.

Brigade composed of the Second and Eleventh Mississippi, the Sixth North Carolina and Fourth Alabama regiments, Army of the Potomac.

BEE, HAMILTON P., TEXAS.

Brigadier-General, Provisional Army of Texas, commanding State troops on coast of Texas in ——, 1861.

Brigadier-General, P. A. C. S., March 4, 1862.

COMMANDS.

Brigade composed of De Bray's, Buchell's, Wood's, Terrell's, Gould's and Likens' Texas regiments.

Commanded the Military Subdistrict of the Rio Grande (Department of Texas).

BELL, TYREE H., TENNESSEE.

Captain Twelfth Regiment Tennessee Infantry, June 4, 1861.

Lieutenant-Colonel Twelfth Regiment Tennessee Infantry, June 5, 1861.

Colonel Twelfth Regiment Tennessee Infantry, July —, 1862.

Brigadier-General, P. A. C. S., November —, 1864.

COMMANDS.

As colonel, commanded, in 1864, brigade composed of the regiments of Colonels Russell, Greer, Wilson and Newman, and Lieutenant-Colonels Wisdom and Barteau.

As brigadier-general, commanded brigade in Jackson's division, Forrest's cavalry.

BENNING, H. L., GEORGIA.

Colonel Seventeenth Georgia Infantry.

Brigadier-General, P. A. C. S., January 17, 1863.

COMMANDS.

Brigade composed of the Second, Fifteenth, Seventeenth and Twentieth Georgia regiments infantry, Hood's division, Longstreet's corps, Army of Northern Virginia.

BENTON, SAMUEL, MISSISSIPPI.

Colonel Thirty-fourth Mississippi Regiment Infantry, April 9, 1862.

Brigadier-General, P. A. C. S., July 26, 1864.

Died of wounds received at Atlanta, Ga., July 28, 1864.

COMMANDS.

Brigade composed of the Twenty-seventh, Twenty-ninth, Thirtieth and Thirty-fourth Mississippi regiments.

BLANCHARD, A. G., LOUISIANA.

Colonel First Louisiana Infantry, ——.

Brigadier-General, P. A. C. S., September 1, 1861.

Died at New Orleans, July 25, 1891.

COMMANDS.

Brigade composed of Third, Fourth and Twenty-second Georgia regiments infantry, the Third Alabama Regiment Infantry, Third Louisiana Battalion Infantry, and Colonel Williams' North Carolina battalion infantry, Girardey's Louisiana Guard artillery, Grimes' Portsmouth artillery and the Sussex cavalry, Army of Northern Virginia.

*BOGGS, W. R., GEORGIA.

Captain, Corps of Engineers, C. S. A., May —, 1861.

Resigned, December 21, 1861.

* * * * * * *

Brigadier-General, P. A. C. S., November 4, 1862.

COMMANDS.

Chief of staff to General E. Kirby Smith, commanding Trans-Mississippi Department.

*BONHAM, M. L., SOUTH CAROLINA.

Major-General, Provisional Army of South Carolina, March —, 1861.

Brigadier-General, P. A. C. S., April 23, 1861.

Commission expired, July 14, 1861.

Reappointed brigadier-general, October 21, 1861.

Died, August 27, 1890.

COMMANDS.

Brigade at first (July —, 1861) composed of the Second, Third, Seventh and Eighth South Carolina regiments infantry, being First Brigade, First Corps, Army of the Potomac.

Afterward, October —, 1861, brigade composed of the First, Second and Third regiments South Carolina cavalry, and Lieutenant-Colonel Trenholm's battalion of South Carolina cavalry.

May 21, 1861, commanding Department of Alexandria.

Resigned, January 27, 1862.

Reappointed, February 20, 1865, and brigade composed of First, Second and Thirtieth regiments South Carolina cavalry, and Lieutenant-Colonel Trenholm's battalion of South Carolina cavalry.

BOWLES, PINCKNEY D., ALABAMA.

Major Fourth Alabama Infantry, August 22, 1862.

Lieutenant-Colonel Fourth Alabama Infantry, September 30, 1862.

Colonel Fourth Alabama Infantry, October 3, 1862.

Brigadier-General, P. A. C. S., April 2, 1865.

COMMANDS.

Brigade composed of Twenty-first Virginia Battalion, Second and Sixth Virginia reserves, First and Second Confederate regiments, Walker's division, Army of Northern Virginia.

As colonel, commanded Third Alabama Brigade, Field's division, Longstreet's corps, Army of Northern Virginia.

*BRANCH, L. O'B., NORTH CAROLINA.

Colonel Thirty-third North Carolina Regiment, September —, 1861.

Brigadier-General, P. A. C. S , November 16, 1861.

Killed at the battle of Sharpsburg, September 17, 1862.

BRIG.-GEN. TURNER ASHBY, OF VIRGINIA
Killed near Harrisonburg, Va., June 6, 1862.

COMMANDS.

Brigade composed of the Seventh, Eighteenth, Twenty-eighth, Thirty-third and Thirty-seventh North Carolina regiments infantry.

Major-General, A. P. Hill's division, Jackson's corps, Army of Northern Virginia.

BRANDON, W. L., MISSISSIPPI.

Lieutenant-Colonel Twenty-first Mississippi Regiment, ——, 1861.

Colonel Twenty-first Mississippi Regiment, ——, 1862.

Brigadier-General, P. A. C. S., June 18, 1864.

COMMANDS.

Commanded a brigade of cavalry in Mississippi.

BRANTLY, W. F., MISSISSIPPI.

Colonel Twenty-ninth Mississippi Infantry, December 13, 1862.

Brigadier-General, P. A. C. S., with temporary rank, July 26, 1864.

COMMANDS.

Brigade composed of the Twenty-fourth, Twenty-seventh, Twenty-ninth, Thirtieth and Thirty-fourth Mississippi regiments infantry, Walthall's division, Army of Tennessee.

BRATTON, JOHN, SOUTH CAROLINA.

Second Lieutenant Sixth South Carolina Volunteers, June 25, 1861.

Lieutenant-Colonel Sixth South Carolina Volunteers, April 12, 1862.

Colonel Sixth South Carolina Volunteers, May 1, 1862.

Brigadier-General, P. A. C. S., May 6, 1864.

COMMANDS.

Brigade composed of First South Carolina (Hagood's), Second South Carolina Rifles, the Fifth and Sixth South Carolina volunteers, and Palmetto Sharpshooters, Longstreet's corps, Army of Northern Virginia.

BRENT, JOSEPH L., LOUISIANA.

* * * * * * *

Brigadier-General, P. A. C. S., October —, 1864.

COMMANDS.

Brigade composed of the Second, Fifth, Seventh and Eighth regiments Louisiana cavalry, Bagby's division, Army of West Louisiana.

BREVARD, THEODORE W., FLORIDA.

Colonel Eleventh Florida Regiment Infantry, June 11, 1864.

Brigadier-General, P. A. C. S., March 22, 1865.

BROWNE, WM. M., GEORGIA.

A. D. C. to President Davis, ——, 1861-2, with rank of Colonel of Cavalry.

Brigadier-General, P. A. C. S., December —, 1864.

Died at Macon, Ga., ——, 1884.

COMMANDS.

Commanding brigade under General H. W. Mercer at the siege of Savannah, Ga., in December, 1864.

BRYAN, GOODE, GEORGIA.

Colonel Sixteenth Georgia Infantry, February 15, 1862.

Brigadier-General, P. A. C. S., August 29, 1863.

Resigned, September 20, 1864.

BRIG.-GEN. FRANCIS S. BARTOW, OF GEORGIA.
Killed at the Battle of First Manassas (Bull Run), July 21, 1861.

COMMANDS.

Brigade composed of the Tenth, Fiftieth, Fifty-third and Fifty-fifth Georgia regiments infantry, McLaws' division, Longstreet's corps, Army of Northern Virginia.

* BUFORD, A., KENTUCKY.

* * * * *

Brigadier-General, P. A. C. S., September 2, 1862.

Died, June 9, 1884.

COMMANDS.

Commanding Second Division of Forrest's cavalry, composed of the brigades of Colonels Thompson and Bell, to which subsequently Lyon's brigade was added.

Commanding, in ——, 1865, division composed of the brigades of Roddey, Clanton and Armistead.

BULLOCK, ROBERT, FLORIDA.

Lieutenant-Colonel Seventh Florida Infantry, ——, 1862.

Colonel Seventh Florida Infantry, June 2, 1863.

Brigadier-General, P. A. C. S., with temporary rank, November 24, 1864.

* CABELL, W. L., VIRGINIA.

Major (Quartermaster-General's Department), C. S. A., March 16, 1861.

Brigadier-General, P. A. C. S., January 20, 1863.

COMMANDS.

Brigade composed of four regiments Arkansas cavalry and one battery of light artillery. At one time in command of the Eighteenth, Nineteenth, Twentieth and Twenty-first regiments Arkansas infantry. In 1862, commanding First Brigade, Second Division, Army of the West.

CAMPBELL, ALEXANDER W., TENNESSEE.

Colonel Thirty-third Tennessee Infantry, ——, 1861-2.

Colonel, Inspector-General on the staff of Major-General L. Polk, ——, 1862-3.

Brigadier-General, P. A. C. S., March 15, 1864.

COMMANDS.

Commanding brigade in Jackson's division, Forrest's cavalry.

CANTEY, JAMES, ALABAMA.

Colonel Fifteenth Alabama Infantry, April —, 1862.

Brigadier-General, P. A. C. S., January 8, 1863.

COMMANDS.

Commanding garrison and District of Mobile. Command composed of the Seventeenth, Twenty-first and Twenty-ninth Alabama regiments infantry, Fourth and Nineteenth regiments Louisiana infantry, Thirtieth Louisiana battalion of infantry and artillery.

CAPERS, ELLISON, SOUTH CAROLINA.

Major First Regiment South Carolina Rifles (State troops), ——, 1861.

Lieutenant-Colonel Twenty-fourth South Carolina Infantry, April 1, 1862.

Colonel Twenty-fourth South Carolina Infantry, January 20, 1864.

Brigadier-General, P. A. C. S., November 30, 1864.

COMMANDS.

Succeeded to command of Gist's brigade, November 30, 1864, composed of the Sixteenth and Twenty-fourth South Carolina and the Forty-sixth Georgia regiments infantry, the Eighth Georgia Battalion Infantry, and the First Battalion of Georgia Sharpshooters.

Wounded at Jackson, Mississippi, May 14, 1863; at Chickamauga, Georgia, September 20, 1863; and at Franklin, Tennessee, November 30, 1864.

CARROLL, WM. H., TENNESSEE.

Brigadier-General Provisional Army of Tennessee,——, 1861.

Brigadier-General, P. A. C. S., October 21, 1861.

Resigned, February 1, 1863.

COMMANDS.

Commanding a brigade in District of East Tennessee and forces therein.

Also commanded a brigade at the battle of Fishing Creek, Ky.

CARTER, JOHN C., TENNESSEE.

Captain Thirty-eighth Tennessee Infantry, ——, 1861.

Major Thirty-eighth Tennessee Infantry, ——, 1862.

Colonel Thirty-eighth Tennessee Infantry, ——, 1863.

Brigadier-General, P. A. C. S., with temporary rank, July 7, 1864.

Killed at the battle of Franklin, Tenn., November 30, 1864.

COMMANDS.

Commanding Brigadier-General Marcus J. Wright's brigade, composed of the Eighth, Sixteenth, Twenty-eighth, Thirty-eighth, Fifty-first and Fifty-second regiments Tennessee infantry, Murray's battalion of Tennessee infantry, and Captain W. W. Carne's battery of artillery, Cheatham's division; afterward Brown's division, Cheatham commanding Polk's corps.

CHALMERS, JAMES R., MISSISSIPPI.

Colonel Ninth Mississippi Regiment Infantry, ——, 1861.

Brigadier-General, P. A. C. S., February 13, 1862.

COMMANDS.

Commanding at Pensacola, ——, 1861.

Brigade composed of the First and Second Mississippi regiments infantry, the Quitman artillery, the Vicksburg artillery and the Judson artillery.

Commanding, April 6, 1862, the Second Brigade of Withers' reserve corps, Army of the Mississippi, composed of the Fifth, Seventh, Ninth, Tenth and Twenty-ninth regiments Mississippi infantry, Blythe's Mississippi battalion infantry and Ketchum's battery.

April —, 1863, assigned to command the Fifth Military District (Department of Mississippi and East Louisiana).

Assigned, January —, 1864, to the command of the cavalry brigades of Forrest and McCulloch, being the First Division of Forrest's cavalry; subsequently Rucker's brigade was added to the division.

CHAMBLISS, JR., J. R., VIRGINIA.

Colonel Thirteenth Regiment Virginia Cavalry, July 13, 1861.

Brigadier-General, P. A. C. S., December 19, 1863.

Killed in action below Richmond, August 16, 1864.

COMMANDS.

Commanding brigade of cavalry in Major-General W. H. F. Lee's division, Army of Northern Virginia.

CHESTNUT, JAMES SOUTH CAROLINA.

Colonel, and A. D. C. to the President, ——, 1861.

Brigadier-General, P. A. C. S., April 23, 1864.

COMMANDS.

April 30, 1864, commanding brigade on the coast of South Carolina.

*CHILTON, R. H., VIRGINIA.

Lieutenant-Colonel, Adjutant-General's Department, C. S. A., March 16, 1861.

Colonel, Adjutant-General's Department, October 13, 1862.

Brigadier-General, P. A. C. S., October 20, 1862 (not confirmed by the Senate).

Brigadier-General, P. A. C. S., December 21, 1863.

Resigned, April 1, 1864.

COMMANDS.

May 19, 1861, assumed command of camp of instruction at Ashland, Va.

Chief of staff, Army of Northern Virginia.

CLANTON, JAMES H., ALABAMA.

Colonel First Regiment Alabama Cavalry, December 3, 1861.

Brigadier-General, P. A. C. S., November 16, 1863.

Died at Knoxville, Tenn., September 27, 1871.

COMMANDS.

Commanding brigade of cavalry under General Maury in the Department of Alabama, Mississippi and East Louisiana.

CLARK, CHARLES, MISSISSIPPI.

Brigadier-General, P. A. C. S., May 22, 1861.

Resigned, October 3, 1863.

COMMANDS.

July 25, 1861, in command of troops at Corinth, Miss.

August 1, 1861, assigned to command of troops in Trenton and Jackson, Tenn.

November 1, 1861, assigned to command of a Mississippi brigade, relieving Brigadier-General Tilghman.

August 5, 1862, assigned to command First Division, Breckinridge's command.

CLARKE, JR., JOHN B., MISSOURI.

Captain Sixth Missouri Infantry, ——, 1861.

Colonel Ninth Missouri Infantry, June 28, 1862.

Brigadier-General, P. A. C. S., March 8, 1864.

COMMANDS.

Commanding Third District Missouri State Guard.

Commanding brigade of cavalry in Marmaduke's division, and commanded temporarily Generals Marmaduke's and Shelby's divisions, Price's army.

CLINGMAN, THOMAS L., NORTH CAROLINA.

Colonel Twenty-fifth North Carolina Regiment, August —, 1861.

Brigadier-General, P. A. C. S., May 17, 1862.

COMMANDS.

Brigade composed of the Eighth, Thirty-first, Fifty-first and Sixty-first North Carolina regiments infantry, Army of Northern Virginia.

December 17, 1862, commanding a brigade in Department of North Carolina.

In December, 1862, and part of 1863, commanding at Wilmington, N. C.

In ——, 1863, at Sullivans Island, S. C.

COBB, THOMAS R. R., GEORGIA.

Colonel, Cobb's Georgia Legion, August 28, 1861.

Brigadier General, P. A. C. S., November 1, 1862.

Killed at Fredericksburg, December —, 1862.

BRIG.-GEN. ALPHEUS BAKER, OF ALABAMA.
[From a photograph taken in 1863.]

COMMANDS.

Brigade composed of the Eighteenth, Twenty-fourth and Sixteenth Georgia regiments infantry, the Georgia legions of Cobb and Phillips, the Third Battalion Georgia Sharpshooters, McLaws' division, Longstreet's corps, Army of Northern Virginia.

COCKE, PHILIP ST. GEORGE, VIRGINIA.

* * * * * * *

Brigadier-General, P. A. C. S., October 21, 1861.

Died, December 26, 1864.

COMMANDS.

Brigade composed of the Eighteenth, Nineteenth, Twenty-eighth and Forty-ninth regiments Virginia infantry, being the Fifth Brigade of the First Corps, Army of the Potomac. Subsequently, the brigade was composed of the Eleventh, Eighteenth, Nineteenth and Twenty-eighth regiments Virginia infantry.

COCKRELL, FRANCIS M., MISSOURI.

Colonel, Second (Burbridge's, also called First), Missouri Infantry.

Brigadier-General, P. A. C. S., July 18, 1863.

COMMANDS.

Brigade composed of the First, Second, Third, Fourth, Fifth and Sixth regiments Missouri infantry and the First Regiment and the Third Battalion Missouri Cavalry, dismounted, Bowen's division, Army of the West.

* COLQUITT, A. H., GEORGIA.

Colonel Sixth Regiment Georgia Infantry, May 27, 1861.

Brigadier-General, P. A. C. S., September 1, 1862.

COMMANDS.

Brigade composed of the Sixth, Nineteenth, Twenty-third, Twenty-seventh and Twenty-eighth Georgia regiments infantry, D. H. Hill's division, Jackson's corps, Army of Northern Virginia.

COLSTON, R. E., VIRGINIA.

Colonel Sixteenth Regiment Virginia Infantry, May 2, 1861.

Brigadier-General, P. A. C. S., December 24, 1861.

COMMANDS.

Commanding the First Brigade, in Department of Norfolk, 1861, composed of the Third Virginia and the Thirteenth and Fourteenth North Carolina regiments of infantry, with unattached companies of artillery and cavalry.

Commanding, in 1862, brigade composed of the Thirteenth and Fourteenth North Carolina infantry regiments and Manley's light battery of artillery.

At the battle of Chancellorsville, brigade composed of the Tenth, Twenty-third and Thirty-seventh regiments Virginia infantry, and the First and Third North Carolina regiments infantry, Trimble's division, Army of Northern Virginia.

CONNER, JAMES, SOUTH CAROLINA.

Captain Company A, Hampton's Legion, May —, 1861.

Major, Hampton's Legion, July —, 1861.

Colonel Twenty-second North Carolina Regiment, July 25, 1861.

Pender's brigade, A. P. Hill's division. Wounded and disabled.

Resigned, May 23, 1863.

Appointed judge of military court of Ewell's corps, January —, 1864, with the rank of colonel of cavalry.

Brigadier-General, P. A. C. S., June 1, 1864.

Died, June 26, 1883.

COMMANDS.

Assigned to command of McGowan's brigade, South Carolina troops, A. P. Hill's corps, Wilcox's division, June —, 1864.

Commanding on north side of James River, July —, 1864.

McGowan's brigade South Carolina troops, Lane's North Carolina brigade, Bushrod Johnson's Tennessee brigade, Gary's South Carolina brigade of cavalry, and Colonel Thomas H. Carter's regiment of artillery.

Commanding, September 1, 1864, brigade (formerly Kershaw's) composed of the Second, Third, Seventh, Eighth, Fifteenth and Twentieth South Carolina regiments and James' battalion.

Wounded, October —, 1864, at Strasburg, Virginia, and not again on active duty.

COOK, PHILIP, GEORGIA.

Colonel Fourth Georgia Regiment Infantry, November 1, 1862.

Brigadier-General, P. A. C. S., August 5, 1864.

COMMANDS.

Succeeded Brigadier-General Doles in command of his brigade, composed of the Fourth, Twelfth, Twenty-first and Forty-fourth Georgia regiments infantry, Rodes' division, Jackson's corps, Army of Northern Virginia.

* COOKE, JOHN R., NORTH CAROLINA.

First Lieutenant, Corps of Infantry, C. S. A., March 16, 1861.

Colonel Twenty-seventh North Carolina Infantry, ——, 1862.

Brigadier-General, P. A. C. S., November 1, 1862.

Died, April 9, 1891.

COMMANDS.

Brigade composed of the Fifteenth, Twenty-seventh, Forty-sixth and Forty-eighth North Carolina regiments infantry, Heth's division, A. P. Hill's corps, Army of Northern Virginia.

COOPER, DOUGLAS H., MISSISSIPPI.

Colonel of the First Choctaw and Chickasaw regiments, mounted riflemen, ——, 1861.

Brigadier-General, P. A. C. S., May 2, 1863.

Died, in the Indian Territory, ——, 1867.

COMMANDS.

Commanding Indian brigade, composed of the First Choctaw and Chickasaw Regiment, the Second Choctaw Regiment, the First and Second Cherokee regiments, the First and Second Creek regiments, a Choctaw, Seminole and Creek battalion, each, and Howell's Texas battery of artillery.

Subsequently, assigned to the command of the District of the Indian Territory.

BRIG.-GEN. JOHN D. BARRY, OF NORTH CAROLINA.
[From a tintype taken in 1861.]

CORSE, M. D., VIRGINIA.

* * * * * *

Brigadier-General, P. A. C. S., November 1, 1862.

COMMANDS.

Brigade composed of the Fifteenth, Seventeenth, Twenty-ninth, Thirtieth and Thirty-second Virginia regiments infantry, Longstreet's corps, Army of Northern Virginia.

* COSBY, GEORGE B., KENTUCKY.

Captain, Corps of Cavalry, C. S. A., March 16, 1861.

* * * * * *

Brigadier-General, P. A. C. S., January 20, 1863.

COMMANDS.

Commanding cavalry brigade in Major-General Stephen D. Lee's division, Department of Alabama, Mississippi and East Louisiana.

BRIG.-GEN. WM. S. BARRY, OF MISSISSIPPI.
[From an old portrait made in 1860.]

COX, WILLIAM R., NORTH CAROLINA.

Lieutenant-Colonel Second Regiment North Carolina Infantry, ——, 1861.

Colonel Second Regiment North Carolina Infantry, March 20, 1863.

Brigadier-General, P. A. C. S., May 31, 1864.

COMMANDS.

Brigade composed of the Second, Fourth, Fourteenth and Thirtieth North Carolina regiments infantry, and portions of the First and Third North Carolina regiments of infantry, Rodes' division, Ewell's corps, Army of Northern Virginia.

COX, JOHN Z., VIRGINIA.

Colonel commanding First (also called Twelfth) Confederate Cavalry, Acting Brigadier-General.

CREWS, C. C., GEORGIA.

Colonel Second Regiment Georgia Cavalry, ——, 1861.

* * * * * *

Brigadier-General, P. A. C. S., ——, 1865.

COMMANDS.

Commanding brigade under Major-General Joseph Wheeler, composed of the First, Second, Third, Fourth and Sixth regiments of Georgia cavalry, Army of Tennessee.

* CUMMING, ALFRED, GEORGIA.

Major, Corps of Infantry, C. S. A., March 16, 1861.

Lieutenant-Colonel Tenth Georgia Regiment Infantry, June —, 1861.

Colonel Tenth Georgia Regiment Infantry, September 25, 1863.

Brigadier-General, P. A. C. S., October 29, 1862.

COMMANDS.

Brigade composed of the Thirty-fourth, Thirty-sixth, Thirty-ninth and Fifty-sixth Georgia regiments infantry, Stevenson's division, Army of the West.

DAHLGREN, CHAS. G., MISSISSIPPI.

* * * * * *

Brigadier-General State forces, Mississippi; never mustered into the Confederate service, except temporarily.

DANIEL, JUNIUS, NORTH CAROLINA.

Colonel Fourteeth (formerly Fourth) North Carolina Infantry, also colonel Forty-fifth North Carolina Infantry.

Brigadier-General, P. A. C. S., September 1, 1862.

Killed in action, May 12, 1864.

COMMANDS.

Brigade composed of the Thirty-second, Forty-third, Forty-fifth and Fifty-third North Carolina regiments infantry, and the Second North Carolina Battalion, Army of Northern Virginia.

DAVIDSON, H. B., TENNESSEE.

* * * * * *

Brigadier-General, P. A. C. S., August 18, 1863.

COMMANDS.

Commanding cavalry brigade, Wheeler's corps, Army of the West.

DAVIS, JOSEPH R., MISSISSIPPI.

Lieutenant-Colonel Tenth Regiment Mississippi Infantry, April 12, 1861.

Aid-de-camp to the President, with rank of colonel of cavalry, August 31, 1861.

Brigadier-General, P. A. C. S., September 15, 1862.

COMMANDS.

Brigade composed of the Second, Eleventh, Twenty-sixth and Forty-second regiments Mississippi infantry, the Fifty-fifth North Carolina Regiment Infantry, the First Confederate Battalion Infantry, and the Madison Light Artillery, Army of Northern Virginia.

DAVIS, REUBEN, MISSISSIPPI.

Brigadier-General, P. A. C. S., ——.

COMMANDS.

In command of sixty-day troops from Mississippi, at Bowling Green, Ky.

DAVIS, W. G. M., FLORIDA.

Colonel First Florida Regiment Cavalry, January 1, 1862.

Brigadier-General, P. A. C. S., November 4, 1862.

Resigned, May 6, 1863.

COMMANDS.

Brigade composed of the First Regiment Florida Cavalry, the Sixth and Seventh regiments Florida infantry, and Martin's (afterward McCant's) light battery.

In ——, 1863, commanding the Department of East Tennessee.

DEARING, JAMES, VIRGINIA.

Colonel, Dearing's Confederate Cavalry (also called the Eighth).

Brigadier-General, ——, 1864.

Killed at High Bridge, Va., April 6, 1865.

COMMANDS.

In command of a cavalry brigade, W. H. F. Lee's division, Army of Northern Virginia.

DEAS, ZACH. C., ALABAMA.

Colonel Twenty-second Regiment Alabama Infantry, October 25, 1861.

Brigadier-General, P. A. C. S., December 13, 1862.

Died in New York City, March —, 1882.

COMMANDS.

Brigade composed of the Nineteenth, Twenty-second, Twenty-fifth, Twenty-sixth, Thirty-ninth and Fiftieth Alabama regiments infantry and Dent's battery of artillery, Withers' division, Polk's corps, Army of Tennessee.

DEBRAY, X. B., TEXAS.

Major Second Regiment Texas Infantry, September —, 1861.

Lieutenant-Colonel, DeBray's battalion cavalry, December —, 1861.

Colonel Twenty-sixth Regiment Texas Cavalry, ——, 1862.

* * * * * *

Brigadier-General, P. A. C. S., April 13, 1864.

COMMANDS.

Brigade composed of the Twenty-third, Twenty-sixth and Thirty-second regiments Texas cavalry, ——, 1864.

Commanding, July 3, 1862, Subdistrict in Department of Texas.

January 1 to July 25, 1863, commanding at Galveston Island.

March 14, 1864, transferred to District of Louisiana (General R. Taylor commanding).

DESHLER, JAMES, GEORGIA.

* * * * * *

Brigadier-General, P. A. C. S., July 28, 1863.

Killed at Chickamauga, September 20, 1863.

COMMANDS.

Brigade composed of the Texas regiments of Colonels Wilkes and Mills, the Arkansas regiment of Lieutenant-Colonel Hutchinson, and Douglas' Texas light battery; brigade at one time composed of the Seventeenth, Eighteenth, Twenty-fourth and Twenty-fifth Texas regiments consolidated; the Sixth, Tenth and Fifteenth Texas regiments, and the Nineteenth and Twenty-fourth Arkansas.

DIBRELL, GEORGE G., TENNESSEE.

Lieutenant-Colonel Twenty-fifth Regiment Tennessee Infantry, August 10, 1861.

Colonel regiment partisan rangers, September —, 1861.

Brigadier-General, P. A. C. S., July 26, 1864.

Died, May 9, 1888.

COMMANDS.

Brigade composed of Fourth Alabama and Eighth and Ninth Tennessee regiments cavalry and the Tennessee cavalry battalions of Cox and Napier, Shaw's Tennessee battalion and the Kentucky light battery of Woodward, ——, 1862–3.

In ——, 1863, commanding Armstrong's brigade.

Commanding, July 1, 1863, Forrest's brigade (succeeding Colonel Starnes).

In ——, 1865, commanding Dibrell's two and General John S. Williams' cavalry brigades, the latter composed of the First, Second and Ninth Kentucky cavalry, Colonel W. C. P. Breckinridge commanding.

On April 12, 1865, ordered from Raleigh, N. C., to Greensboro, with command, to escort President Davis to Washington, Ga.

Original brigade composed of Fourth, Eighth, Ninth, Tenth and Eleventh regiments Tennessee cavalry, and Shaw's battalion.

DICKISON, J. J., FLORIDA.

* * * * * *

Acting Brigadier-General, P. A. C. S., ——

COMMANDS.

In command of East and South Florida.

DOBBINS, ARCH. J., ARKANSAS.

Colonel, Dobbins' regiment Arkansas cavalry.

COMMANDS.

Commanding brigade in Fagan's division, Price's Army of Missouri.

DOCKERY, T. P., ARKANSAS.

Colonel Nineteenth Smead's and Dockery's Arkansas Infantry.

Brigadier-General, August 10, 1863.

COMMANDS.

Commanding Middle Subdistrict of Arkansas in 1862, in command of the First Brigade, Third Division, Army of the West, composed of the Eighteenth, Nineteenth and Twentieth Arkansas regiments and the Arkansas battalions of McCairns and Jones.

DOLES, GEORGE, GEORGIA.

Colonel Fourth Regiment Georgia Infantry, May 8, 1861.

Brigadier-General, P. A. C. S., November 1, 1862.

Killed in action at Bethesda Church, Va., June 2, 1864.

COMMANDS.

Brigade composed of the Fourth, Twelfth, Twenty-first and Forty-fourth Georgia regiments infantry, D. H. Hill's division, Army of Northern Virginia; also commanded a brigade in Rodes' division, Second Corps, Army of Northern Virginia.

* DRAYTON, THOMAS F., SOUTH CAROLINA.

Brigadier-General, P. A. C. S., September 25, 1861.

Died, February 26, 1891.

COMMANDS.

Commanding Fifth Military District of South Carolina, December 10, 1861.

Commanding Fourth Military District in South Carolina, May 28, 1862; subsequently transferred to the Trans-Mississippi Department.

Brigade composed of the Eighth and Ninth regiments Missouri infantry and Ruffner's battery of artillery.

BRIG.-GEN. SAMUEL BENTON, OF MISSISSIPPI.
Died of wounds received at Atlanta, Ga., July 28, 1864.
[From a photograph taken in 1862.]

DUBOSE, DUDLEY M., GEORGIA.

Colonel Fifteenth Georgia Regiment Infantry, January —, 1863.

Brigadier-General, P. A. C. S., November 16, 1864.

Died in Georgia, ——, 1883.

COMMANDS.

Brigade composed of the Eighteenth, Twenty-fourth and Sixteenth Georgia regiments of infantry, Cobb's and Phillips' Georgia legions and the Third Battalion of Georgia Sharpshooters, Kershaw's division, Longstreet's corps, Army of Northern Virginia.

DUKE, BASIL W., KENTUCKY.

Lieutenant-Colonel Second Regiment Kentucky Cavalry, July —, 1861.

Colonel Second Regiment Kentucky Cavalry, December—, 1861.

Brigadier-General, P. A. C. S., September 15, 1864.

BRIG.-GEN. A. G. BLANCHARD, OF LOUISIANA.
[From a photograph taken in 1862.]

COMMANDS.

Succeeded General John H. Morgan in command of cavalry forces, composed of parts of the First, Second, Third, Fifth, Sixth, Seventh, Eighth and Eleventh regiments of Kentucky cavalry and Ninth Tennessee Cavalry, Wheeler's cavalry corps, Army of Tennessee.

DUNCAN, JOHNSON K., LOUISIANA.

* * * * * *

Brigadier-General, P. A. C. S., January 7, 1862.

Chief of Staff to General Bragg, November 23, 1862.

Died at Knoxville, Tennessee, December 18, 1862.

COMMANDS.

Commanding river defenses below New Orleans, ——, 1862.

DUNOVANT, JOHN, SOUTH CAROLINA.

Colonel First South Carolina Volunteer Infantry, July 22, 1861.

Colonel Fifth Regiment South Carolina Cavalry, ——, 1862.

Brigadier-General, P. A. C. S., temporary rank, August 22, 1864.

Killed at Vaughn Road, October 1, 1864.

COMMANDS.

Commanding a brigade in Butler's division, cavalry corps, Army of Northern Virginia.

* ECHOLS, JOHN, VIRGINIA.

Colonel Twenty-seventh Virginia Infantry, ——, 1862.

Brigadier-General, P. A. C. S., April 16, 1862.

COMMANDS.

Brigade composed of the Twenty-seventh, Fiftieth, Sixtieth and Sixty-third regiments Virginia infantry and Edgar's and Derrick's Virginia battalions infantry, Heth's division, Army of Northern Virginia.

Commanding, October 15, 1862, to November 19, 1862, Department of Southwestern Virginia.

Commanding Trans-Alleghany Department, May 29, 1865.

ECTOR, M. D., TEXAS.

Colonel Fourteenth Texas Cavalry, September —, 1862.

Brigadier-General, P. A. C. S., August 23, 1862.

COMMANDS.

Brigade composed of the Tenth, Eleventh, Fourteenth and Thirty-second Texas regiments of dismounted cavalry.

Afterward in command of brigade in McCown's division, Polk's corps, Army of Tennessee.

ELLIOTT, JR., STEPHEN, SOUTH CAROLINA.

Captain, Beaufort Artillery, ——, 1861.

Colonel, Holcombe's Legion, April 20, 1864.

Brigadier-General, P. A. C. S., May 24, 1864.

Died of wounds received in front of Petersburg, Va., ——, 1864.

COMMANDS.

Brigade composed of the Seventeenth, Eighteenth, Twenty-second, Twenty-third and Twenty-sixth regiments South Carolina volunteers and the Holcombe South Carolina Legion.

EVANS, C. A., GEORGIA.

Major Thirty-first Georgia Infantry, November 19, 1861.

Colonel Thirty-first Georgia Infantry, May 13, 1862.

Brigadier-General, P. A. C. S., May 19, 1864.

COMMANDS.

Brigade composed of the Thirteenth, Twenty-sixth, Thirty-first, Thirty-eighth, Sixtieth and Sixty-first Georgia regiments infantry (and subsequently the Twelfth Georgia Regiment was added), Army of Northern Virginia.

* EVANS, N. G., SOUTH CAROLINA.

Captain, Corps of Cavalry, C. S. A., March 16, 1861.

Brigadier-General, P. A. C. S., October 21, 1861.

COMMANDS.

Commanding Third Military District of South Carolina, in Department of South Carolina, Georgia and Florida, December 18, 1861.

Brigade composed of the Thirteenth, Seventeenth and Eighteenth Mississippi regiments infantry, being the Seventh Brigade, First Corps, Army of the Potomac.

At battle of Leesburg, Va., September 2, 1862, brigade composed of the Thirteenth, Seventeenth and Eighteenth Mississippi regiments infantry, and Eighth Virginia Regiment Infantry.

Brigade subsequently composed of the Seventeenth, Eighteenth, Twenty-second, Twenty-third and Twenty-sixth regiments South Carolina volunteer infantry, and the Holcombe Legion.

In June, 1862, in command on James Island, S. C., and commanding Second Military District, Department of North Carolina and Southern Virginia.

Commanding, March —, 1864, First Military District of South Carolina.

FAUNTLEROY, T. T., VIRGINIA.

Major Fifty-fifth Virginia Infantry.

Brigadier-General, May 18, 1861; rank conferred by the State of Virginia.

Resigned, October 8, 1861.

COMMANDS.

May 19, 1861, assigned command of artillery in and about Richmond.

Relieved of command, August 30, 1861.

FEATHERSTON, W. S., MISSISSIPPI.

Colonel Seventeenth Mississippi Regiment Infantry, May ——, 1861.
Brigadier-General, P. A. C. S., March 4, 1862.
Died, May 28, 1891.

COMMANDS.

Brigade composed of the Twelfth, Sixteenth, Nineteenth and Forty-eighth Mississippi regiments, and Smith's battery of light artillery, Army of Northern Virginia.
In February, 1863, transferred to Vicksburg, Miss., and was placed in command of a division by General Pemberton.

BRIG.-GEN. WILLIAM R. BOGGS, OF GEORGIA.

*FERGUSON, S. W., MISSISSIPPI.

First-Lieutenant, Corps of Cavalry, C. S. A., March 16, 1861.
Colonel Fifth South Carolina Cavalry, January 18, 1863.
Colonel of Cavalry, temporary rank, May 7, 1863.
Brigadier-General, P. A. C. S., July 23, 1863.

COMMANDS.

Brigade composed of the Second Regiment Tennessee Cavalry, the Second and Fifty-sixth regiments Alabama cavalry, Seventeenth Battalion Tennessee Cavalry, the Twelfth Battalion Mississippi Cavalry and Waite's South Carolina battery of light artillery.

FINEGAN, JOSEPH, FLORIDA.

* * * * * *

Brigadier-General, P. A. C. S., April 5, 1862.
Died at Sanford, Fla., October 29, 1885.

COMMANDS.

Commanding Department Middle and Eastern Florida from April 8, 1862.
January 31, 1865, commanding a brigade in Mahone's division, Third Army Corps, Army of Northern Virginia.
Brigade composed of the Second, Fifth, Ninth, Tenth and Eleventh regiments Florida infantry.

FINLEY, J. J., FLORIDA.

Colonel Sixth Florida Regiment Infantry, April 14, 1862.
Brigadier-General, P. A. C. S., November 16, 1863.

COMMANDS.

Brigade composed of the First, Third, Fourth, Sixth and Seventh regiments Florida infantry, and the First Regiment Florida Cavalry, dismounted.

FIZER, JOHN C., MISSISSIPPI.

Colonel Seventeenth Mississippi Infantry.
Brigadier-General, P. A. C. S., ——, 1865.

COMMANDS.

Commanding mixed brigade in Lieutenant-General Hardee's corps on the retreat through the Carolinas.

FLOYD, JOHN B., VIRGINIA.

Brigadier-General, P. A. C. S., May 23, 1861.
Died, August 26, 1863.

COMMANDS.

Commanding forces in Kanawha Valley, August 12 to September 19, 1861.
Brigade, in ——, 1862, composed of the Twentieth Mississippi and the Thirty-sixth, Fiftieth and Fifty-first regiments Virginia infantry.
Commanding division at Fort Donelson, February 13, 1862.
Commanding Virginia State Line, November 13, 1862.

FORNEY, WM. H., ALABAMA.

Captain Tenth Alabama Infantry, June 4, 1861.
Major Tenth Alabama Infantry, December 21, 1861.
Lieutenant-Colonel Tenth Alabama Infantry, March 14, 1862.
Colonel Tenth Alabama Infantry, June 27, 1862.
Brigadier-General, P. A. C. S., November 9, 1864.

COMMANDS.

Brigade composed of the Eighth, Ninth, Tenth, Eleventh, Thirteenth and Fourteenth Alabama regiments infantry, Mahone's division, A. P. Hill's corps, Army of Northern Virginia.

*FRAZER, J. W., ALABAMA.

Captain, Corps of Infantry, C. S. A., March 16, 1861.

* * * * * *

Brigadier-General, P. A. C. S., May 19, 1863.

COMMANDS.

Brigade composed of the Fifty-fifth Georgia, the Sixty-second and Sixty-fourth North Carolina regiments infantry and Rain's battery of artillery.
Commanding garrison at Cumberland Gap to September 9, 1863.

FROST, DANIEL M., MISSOURI.

Brigadier-General, P. A. C. S., March 3, 1862.
Dropped, December 9, 1863.

COMMANDS.

Commanded the Third Brigade Missouri State Guard.

FRY, B. D., ALABAMA.

Colonel Thirteenth Alabama Infantry, July 19, 1861.
Brigadier-General, P. A. C. S., May 24, 1864.

COMMANDS.

Commanded, in spring and summer of 1864, brigade formerly commanded by General H. H. Walker, consisting of Twenty-second Virginia Battalion and the Fortieth, Forty-seventh and Fifty-fifth Virginia regiments infantry, Heth's division, Hill's corps, Army of Northern Virginia.
Commanded brigade formerly commanded by Brigadier-General Archer, consisting of Second Alabama Battalion, Thirteenth Alabama Regiment and Fourteenth and Fifteenth Tennessee regiments, Heth's division, Hill's corps, Army of Northern Virginia.
Commanding, in winter of 1864-5, the District of Augusta, Ga.

GANO, RICHARD M., TEXAS.

Colonel Seventh Kentucky Cavalry, September 1, 1862.
Brigadier-General, P. A. C. S., March 17, 1865.

COMMANDS.

Commanding Second Brigade of Morgan's cavalry command.
Commanding brigade of Texas cavalry, operating in Arkansas and the Indian Territory, composed of the regiments of Colonels DeMorse, Martin, Gurley, Duff and Hardeman, and Lieutenant-Colonel Showalter's battalion, Captain Welch's company and the light batteries of Captains Howell and Krumbhar.

GANTT, E. W., ARKANSAS.

Colonel Twelfth Arkansas Regiment Infantry, ——, 1861.
Brigadier-General, P. A. C. S., ——, 1862.

COMMANDS.

Commanding troops and defenses, Fort Thompson, Mo.
Commanding Third Brigade, First Division, Army of the Mississippi.

GARDNER, WILLIAM M., GEORGIA.

Major, Corps of Infantry, C. S. A., March 16, 1861.
Colonel Eighth Regiment Georgia Infantry, July 21, 1861.
Brigadier-General, P. A. C. S., November 14, 1861.

COMMANDS.

Commanding District of Middle Florida, October 6 to November 11, 1863.
July 26, 1864, assigned command of military prisons in States east of Mississippi River, excluding Georgia and Alabama.
November 28th, commanding at Salisbury, N. C.
Commanding Post of Richmond, Va., from January, 1865.

GARLAND, JR., SAMUEL, VIRGINIA.

Brigadier-General, P. A. C. S., May 23, 1862.
Killed at South Mountain, September 14, 1862.

COMMANDS.

Brigade composed of the Fifth, Twelfth, Thirteenth Twentieth and Twenty-third regiments of North Carolina infantry, Army of Northern Virginia.

GARNETT, RICHARD B., VIRGINIA.

Third Lieutenant Fourteenth Virginia Infantry, ——, 1861.
Major, Corps of Artillery, C. S. A., March 16, 1861.

* * * * * *

Brigadier-General, P. A. C. S., November 14, 1861.
Killed at Gettysburg, July 2, 1863.

COMMANDS.

Commanding brigade formerly commanded by Brigadier-General T. J. Jackson, known as the "Stonewall Brigade," and composed of the Second, Fourth, Fifth, Twenty-seventh and Thirty-third Virginia regiments infantry.
Commanding brigade composed of the Eighth, Eighteenth, Nineteenth, Twenty-eighth and Fifty-sixth regiments Virginia infantry, D. R. Jones' division, Army of Northern Virginia.

*GARNETT, ROBERT S., VIRGINIA.

Lieutenant-Colonel, Corps of Infantry, C. S. A., March 16, 1861.
Brigadier-General, P. A. C. S., June 6, 1861.
Killed at Rich Mountain or Craddocks Ford, July 13, 1861.

GARROTT, ISHAM W., ALABAMA.

Colonel Twentieth Regiment Alabama Infantry, October 8, 1861.
Brigadier-General, P. A. C. S., May 28, 1863.
Killed at Vicksburg, June 17, 1863.

COMMANDS.

Commanding Tracy's brigade.
Commanding Twentieth Alabama Regiment at time of his death, before his commission as brigadier-general, P. A. C. S., had reached him.

GARTRELL, LUCIUS J., GEORGIA.

Colonel Seventh Georgia Infantry, May 31, 1861.
Resigned, December —, 1862, having been elected to Confederate Congress.
Brigadier-General, P. A. C. S., August 22, 1864.

COMMANDS.

Second Brigade of Georgia Reserves, composed of the First, Second, Third and Fourth regiments.

*GATLIN, RICHARD C., NORTH CAROLINA.

Adjutant-General of North Carolina, with rank of Major-General, ——, 1861.
Colonel, Corps of Infantry, C. S. A., March 16, 1861.
Brigadier-General, P. A. C. S., July 8, 1862.
Resigned, September 8, 1862.

BRIG.-GEN. M. L. BONHAM, OF SOUTH CAROLINA.
[From a portrait made in 1861.]

COMMANDS.

Commanding Southern Department of Coast Defense of North Carolina.

GHOLSON, S. J., MISSISSIPPI.

Colonel commanding Mississippi State forces, ——, 1861.
Brigadier-General commanding Mississippi State forces, ——, 1861.
Brigadier-General, P. A. C. S., May 6, 1864.

COMMANDS.

Commanding brigade of cavalry in Department of Alabama, Mississippi and East Louisiana.

GIBBS, GEORGE C., NORTH CAROLINA.

Acting Brigadier-General, ——, 1864.
Commanding Post, etc., at Macon, Ga.

GIBSON, RANDALL LEE, LOUISIANA.

Captain First Louisiana Artillery, ——, 1861.
Colonel Thirteenth Louisiana Infantry, ——, 1861.
Brigadier-General, P. A. C. S., January 11, 1864.

COMMANDS.

Brigade composed of the First, Fourth, Eleventh, Thirteenth, Sixteenth, Nineteenth, Twentieth, Twenty-fifth and Thirtieth Louisiana regiments infantry and Austin's Louisiana Battalion of Sharpshooters, Breckinridge's division, Hardee's corps, Army of Tennessee.

In April, 1865, commanded division at Spanish Fort, near Mobile, consisting of the brigades of Campbell, Holtzclaw and Ector, and Thomas' and Patton's regiments of artillery.

GIRARDEY, VICTOR J. B., GEORGIA.

* * * * * *

Brigadier-General, P. A. C. S. (temporary rank), July 30, 1864.
Killed at Petersburg, Va., August —, 1864.

COMMANDS.

Commanding Brigadier-General A. R. Wright's brigade, composed of the Third, Twenty-second, Forty-sixth and Forty-eighth Georgia regiments of infantry, and Second Georgia Battalion Infantry, Anderson's division, A. P. Hill's corps, Army of Northern Virginia.

GIST, S. R., SOUTH CAROLINA.

Inspector-General of South Carolina, June 6, 1861.
Brigadier-General, P. A. C. S., March 20, 1862.
Killed at the battle of Franklin, Tenn., November 30, 1864.

COMMANDS.

Brigade composed of the Sixteenth and Twenty-fourth South Carolina, the Forty-sixth and Sixty-fifth Georgia regiments infantry, the Eighth Georgia Infantry Battalion and First Battalion Georgia Sharpshooters.

Commanding First Military District of South Carolina, October 4, 1862.

GLADDEN, A. H., LOUISIANA.

Brigadier-General, P. A. C. S., September 30, 1861.
Killed at the battle of Shiloh, Tenn., April 6, 1862.

COMMANDS.

Brigade at Pensacola, Fla., composed of Lieutenant-Colonel Adams' Louisiana battalion, Lieutenant-Colonel Coppen's battalion Louisiana Zouaves, a Georgia battalion, Colonel Patton Anderson's First Florida Regiment, and the artillery company of Captain Lee.

Commanding, temporarily, December 22, 1861, Army of Pensacola.

BRIG.-GEN. PINCKNEY D. BOWLES, OF ALABAMA.
[From an oil portrait.]

GODWIN, A. C., NORTH CAROLINA.

First Lieutenant, Corps of Infantry, C. S. A., October 18, 1861.
Colonel Fifty-seventh North Carolina Regiment Infantry, July 16, 1862.
Brigadier-General, P. A. C. S., August 5, 1864.
Killed at Opequon (Winchester), Va., September 19, 1864.

COMMANDS.

Provost-Marshal of Richmond, ——, 1861.

Commanding brigade formerly commanded by General Hoke, composed of the Sixth, Twenty-first, Fifty-fourth and Fifty-seventh North Carolina regiments infantry, Early's division, Army of Northern Virginia.

GORDON, G. W., TENNESSEE.

Colonel Eleventh Tennessee Regiment Infantry, December —, 1862.
Brigadier-General, P. A. C. S., August 15, 1864.

COMMANDS.

Brigade composed of the Eleventh, Twelfth, Thirteenth, Twenty-ninth, Forty-seventh and One Hundred and Fifty-fourth Senior Tennessee regiments, Army of Tennessee.

*GORGAS, JOSIAH, ALABAMA.

Colonel, Chief of Ordnance, C. S. A., ——, 1861.
Brigadier-General, Chief of Ordnance, November 10, 1864.
Died at Tuscaloosa, Ala., May 15, 1883.

GOVAN, D. C., ARKANSAS.

Colonel, Second Arkansas Infantry.
Brigadier-General, P. A. C. S., December 29, 1863.

COMMANDS.

Brigade composed of the First, Second, Fifth, Sixth, Seventh and Eighth Arkansas regiments, commanded in turn by Generals Hardee, Hindman and Liddell.

GRACIE, JR., ARCHIBALD, ALABAMA.

Major Eleventh Alabama Infantry, July 12, 1861.
Colonel Forty-third Alabama Infantry, November —, 1862.
Brigadier-General, P. A. C. S., November 4, 1862.
Killed at Petersburg, Va., December 2, 1864.

COMMANDS.

Brigade composed of the Sixty-third Tennessee and Forty-third Alabama regiments infantry, and the First, Second, Third and Fourth battalions of the Alabama Legion, Longstreet's corps, Army of Northern Virginia.

GRANBURY, H. B., TEXAS.

Colonel Seventh Texas Infantry, August 29, 1861.
Brigadier-General, P. A. C. S., February 29, 1864.
Killed at Franklin, Tenn., November 30, 1864.

COMMANDS.

Brigade composed of the Sixth, Seventh, Tenth, Fifteenth, Seventeenth, Nineteenth, Twenty-fourth and Twenty-fifth Texas regiments.

*GRAYSON, JOHN B., LOUISIANA.

Brigadier-General, P. A. C. S., August 15, 1861.
Died at Tallahassee, Florida, October 21, 1861.

COMMANDS.

Commanding Department of Middle and Eastern Florida, August 21 to October 10, 1861.

GRAY, HENRY, LOUISIANA.

Colonel Twenty-eighth Louisiana Infantry, May 17, 1862.
Brigadier-General, P. A. C. S., March 17, 1865.

GREGG, JOHN, TEXAS.

Brigadier-General, P. A. C. S., August 29, 1862.
Killed at Petersburg, June 17, 1864.

COMMANDS.

Brigade composed of the First, Fourth and Fifth Texas regiments, and Third Arkansas Regiment, Longstreet's corps, Army of Northern Virginia; subsequently composed of the Seventh Texas, the Third, Tenth, Thirtieth, Forty-first and Fiftieth Tennessee regiments infantry, and Bledsoe's light battery.

*GREGG, MAXCY, SOUTH CAROLINA.

Colonel First Regiment South Carolina Infantry, July 25, 1861.
Brigadier-General, P. A. C. S., December 14, 1861.
Killed at Fredericksburg, Va., December 13, 1862.

COMMANDS.

Brigade composed of the First, Twelfth, Thirteenth and Fourteenth regiments South Carolina infantry and Orr's First South Carolina Rifles, A. P. Hill's division, Jackson's corps, Army of Northern Virginia.

GREEN, MARTIN E., MISSOURI.

Brigadier-General, P. A. C. S., July 21, 1862.
Killed during siege of Vicksburg, June 27, 1863.

COMMANDS.

Commanding Third Brigade, First Division, Army of the West, composed of the Fourth Missouri Regiment Infantry, a Missouri battalion of infantry, a battalion of Missouri cavalry (dismounted), the Confederate Rangers and King's light battery of artillery.

During the siege of Vicksburg commanding brigade in Major-General Bowen's division, composed of the remnants of the Second and Sixth Missouri regiments infantry, the First and Third Missouri regiments cavalry (dismounted), and the light batteries of Landis and King.

GREEN, THOMAS, TEXAS.

Colonel Fifth Texas Mounted Rifles, August 20, 1861.
Brigadier-General, P. A. C. S., May 20, 1863.
Killed in action at Bayou Pierre, April 12, 1864.

COMMANDS.

Commanding brigade of Texas cavalry, in Trans-Mississippi Department.

In June, 1863, commanding brigade composed of the Fourth, Fifth and Seventh regiments of Texas cavalry and the Texas regiments of Phillips and Stone.

Commanding cavalry of Trans-Mississippi Department, ——, 1864.

GREENE, COLTON, MISSOURI.

Colonel Third Missouri Cavalry, ——.
Brigadier-General Missouri State Guards, ——.

COMMANDS.

Commanding cavalry brigade, Marmaduke's division, Trans-Mississippi Department.

BRIG.-GEN. JOHN R. CHAMBLISS, JR., OF VIRGINIA.
Killed at Deep Bottom, Va., August 16, 1864.
[From an old portrait.]

GREER, ELKANAH, TEXAS.

Colonel Third Regiment Texas Cavalry, July 1, 1861.
Resigned, June 1, 1862.
Brigadier-General, P. A. C. S., October 8, 1862.
Died at Duvalls Bluff, Arkansas, March 25, 1877.

COMMANDS.

Chief of Bureau of Conscription, Trans-Mississippi Department.

Commanding reserve corps, Trans-Mississippi Department, March 27, 1865.

GRIFFITH, RICHARD, MISSISSIPPI.

Brigadier-General, P. A. C. S., November 2, 1861.
Killed at Savage Station, June 29, 1862.

COMMANDS.

Brigade composed of the Thirteenth, Seventeenth, Eighteenth and Twenty-first Mississippi regiments infantry, Army of Northern Virginia.

GRIGSBY, J. WARREN, KENTUCKY.

Colonel Sixth Kentucky Cavalry, ——.
Brigadier-General, P. A. C. S., ——.

COMMANDS.

Commanding cavalry brigade, Army of Tennessee.

HAGAN, JAMES, ALABAMA.

Colonel Third Alabama Cavalry, ——.
Brigadier-General, P. A. C. S., February —, 1865.

COMMANDS.

Brigade composed of the First, Third, Fourth, Twelfth and Fifty-first Alabama cavalry regiments, Wheeler's cavalry corps, Army of the West.

HAGOOD, JOHNSON, SOUTH CAROLINA.

Colonel First South Carolina Volunteer Infantry, January 27, 1861.
Brigadier-General, P. A. C. S., July 21, 1862.

COMMANDS.

Brigade composed of the Eleventh, Twenty-first, Twenty-fifth and Twenty-seventh South Carolina regiments and Seventh South Carolina Battalion Infantry.

On duty, ——, 1864, in Department of South Carolina, Georgia and Florida.

In May, 1864, assigned to the command of Hoke's division, then in General Beauregard's command, but subsequently in Anderson's corps, Army of Northern Virginia.

HANNON, M. W., ALABAMA.

Colonel Fifty-third Alabama Partisan Rangers.
Brigadier-General, P. A. C. S., ——, 1865.

COMMANDS.

Commanding brigade in Wheeler's cavalry corps, Martin's division, composed of the Fifty-third Alabama and the Twenty-fourth Alabama Battalion.

HANSON, ROGER W., KENTUCKY.

Colonel Second Kentucky Infantry Regiment, September 2, 1861.
Brigadier-General, P. A. C. S., December 13, 1862.
Killed at Murfreesboro, Tenn., December 31, 1862.

COMMANDS.

Brigade composed of the Second, Fourth, Sixth and Ninth Kentucky regiments and Forty-first Alabama Regiment Infantry, Breckinridge's division, Polk's corps, Army of Tennessee.

HARDEMAN, W. P., TEXAS.

* * * * * *

Brigadier-General, P. A. C. S., March 17, 1865.

COMMANDS.

Commanding brigade in the District of Texas, under Major-General John B. Magruder.

HARRIS, D. B., VIRGINIA.

* * * * * *

Brigadier-General, P. A. C. S., ——, 1863.

COMMANDS.

Chief Engineer in charge of Confederate defenses during the siege of Charleston, etc.

HARRIS, N. H., MISSISSIPPI.

Captain Nineteenth Mississippi Infantry, April —, 1861.
Major Nineteenth Mississippi Infantry, May 5, 1862.
Lieutenant-Colonel Nineteenth Mississippi Infantry, November 24, 1862.
Colonel Nineteenth Mississippi Infantry, April 2, 1863.
Brigadier-General, P. A. C. S., January 20, 1864.

COMMANDS.

Brigade composed of the Twelfth, Sixteenth, Nineteenth and Forty-eighth regiments Mississippi infantry, Mahone's division, A. P. Hill's corps, Army of Northern Virginia.

HARRIS, THOS. A., MISSOURI.

Brigadier-General Missouri State Guard. Commissioned June 10, 1861.
Resigned in September, 1861, to occupy a seat in the Confederate Congress.

HARRISON, GEORGE P., JR., GEORGIA.

Colonel, Thirty-second Georgia Infantry, ——.
Brigadier-General, P. A. C. S., February —, 1865.

COMMANDS.

Brigade composed of the First Georgia Regulars, the Thirty-second and Forty-seventh and the Fifth Regiment Georgia Volunteers, and the Fifth Regiment Georgia Reserves.

HARRISON, J. E., TEXAS.

* * * * * *

Brigadier-General, P. A. C. S., December 22, 1864.

COMMANDS.

Brigade composed of the Fifteenth, Seventeenth and Thirty-first Texas regiments and Stevens' Texas Regiment, in Major-General C. J. Polignac's division, Trans-Mississippi Department.

HARRISON, RICHARD, TEXAS.

Colonel, Terry's Texas Cavalry Regiment, ——.
Brigadier-General, P. A. C. S., ——, 1865.

COMMANDS.

Succeeded General J. A. Wharton in command of his brigade of Texas cavalry; afterward in command of brigade in Steuart's corps.

HARRISON, THOMAS, TEXAS.

Colonel Eighth Texas Cavalry, November 8, 1862.
Brigadier-General, P. A. C. S., with temporary rank, January 14, 1865.
Died at Waco, Texas, July 14, 1891.

COMMANDS.

Brigade composed of the Eighth and Eleventh Texas, the Fourth Tennessee, the Third Arkansas and First Kentucky regiments cavalry, Major-General Wharton's division, Army of Tennessee.

HATTON, ROBERT, TENNESSEE.

Colonel Seventh Regiment Tennessee Infantry, ——, 1861.

* * * * * *

Brigadier-General, P. A. C. S., May 23, 1862.
Killed at Seven Pines, May 31, 1862.

* HAWES, J. M., KENTUCKY.

Major, ——, C. S. A., June 16, 1861.
Colonel Second Kentucky Infantry, June 26, 1861.
Resigned, September 3, 1861.
Brigadier-General, P. A. C. S., March 5, 1862.

COMMANDS.

On duty with General A. S. Johnston to April —, 1862, commanding advance of army on Green River.
Assigned to command of cavalry of General A. S. Johnston's army, April 3, 1862, and declined.
Commanding Louisiana brigade, April —, 1862.
Commanding brigade, in ——, 1862, composed of two

BRIG.-GEN. PHILIP ST. GEORGE COCKE, OF VIRGINIA.
[From an oil portrait.]

Kentucky, one Mississippi and one Confederate regiment in Breckinridge's division, Army of Tennessee.
In October, 1862, commanding brigade of cavalry under General T. H. Holmes.
In January, 1863, assigned to command of infantry brigade, Major-General J. G. Walker's division, Trans-Mississippi Department.
In March, 1864, commanding troops and fortifications at Galveston Island, Texas.

HAWTHORN, A. T., ARKANSAS.

Lieutenant-Colonel Sixth Arkansas Infantry, ——, 1861.
Colonel Sixth Arkansas Infantry, ——, 1862.

* * * * * *

Brigadier-General, P. A. C. S., February 18, 1864.

BRIG.-GEN. R. E. COLSTON, OF VIRGINIA.
[From a tintype taken in 1863.]

COMMANDS.

Brigade composed of the Seventeenth, Twenty-first and Twenty-third Tennessee and Thirty-third Alabama regiments infantry, and Austin's light battery of artillery, Third Corps, Army of the Mississippi.

HEBERT, LOUIS, LOUISIANA.

Colonel Third Louisiana Infantry, May 17, 1861.
Brigadier-General, P. A. C. S., May 26, 1862.

COMMANDS.

Commanding Second Brigade, First Division, Army of the West, composed of the Third Louisiana and Fourteenth and Seventeenth Arkansas regiments infantry, Whitfield's Texas Legion, Greer's regiment dismounted Texas cavalry and McDonald's light battery of artillery.
Commanding brigade in Maury's division, Army of the West.
Chief Engineer Department of North Carolina.

HEBERT, PAUL O., LOUISIANA.

* * * * * *

Brigadier-General, P. A. C. S., August 17, 1861.
Died at New Orleans, La., August 30, 1880.

COMMANDS.

In 1861, commanded Army of Louisiana, and in special command of defenses of New Orleans.
Commanding District of Texas, Trans-Mississippi Department, August 20, 1862.
August 11, 1864, assumed command of District of Texas and Territory of Arizona.

HELM, B. H., KENTUCKY.

First Lieutenant, Corps of Cavalry, C. S. A., October 19, 1861.
Colonel First Kentucky Cavalry, October —, 1861.
Brigadier-General, P. A. C. S., March 14, 1862.
Killed at Chickamauga, September 19, 1863.

COMMANDS.

Brigade composed of the Second, Fourth, Sixth and Ninth Kentucky regiments infantry, the Forty-first Alabama Regiment Infantry, and Cobb's light battery of artillery, Breckinridge's division, Army of Tennessee.

HIGGINS, EDWARD, LOUISIANA.

Lieutenant-Colonel Twenty-first Louisiana Infantry, February 13, 1862.
Colonel Twenty-first Louisiana Infantry, April 11, 1862.
Brigadier-General, P. A. C. S., October 29, 1863.

COMMANDS.

Commanding forts and batteries around Mobile, Ala.

HILL, BENJAMIN J., TENNESSEE.

Colonel Thirty-fifth Regiment Tennessee Infantry, September 6, 1861.
Brigadier-General, P. A. C. S., November 30, 1864.
Died at McMinnville, Tenn., January 5, 1880.

COMMANDS.

Provost-Marshal-General, Army of Tennessee, ——, 1862–3.
Commanding brigade in Cheatham's division, Army of Tennessee.

HODGE, GEORGE B., KENTUCKY.

Captain, A. A. G., ——, 1861.
Major, A. A. G., May —, 1862.
Colonel, A. A. G., May 6, 1863, and May 17, 1864.
Brigadier-General, P. A. C. S., August 2, 1864.

COMMANDS.

Brigade composed of, in 1863, the First, Second and Third battalions of Kentucky cavalry, the Twenty-seventh Virginia Partisan Rangers, and Logan's section of light artillery.
Commanded, in August, 1864, the District of South Mississippi and East Louisiana, and until the end of the war.

HOGG, JOSEPH L., TEXAS.

* * * * * *

Brigadier-General, P. A. C. S., February 14, 1862.
Died, May 16, 1862.

COMMANDS.

Brigade composed of the Tenth, Eleventh and Lieutenant-Colonel Crump's First Battalion Texas Dismounted Cavalry, Major McCray's battalion Arkansas infantry and Captain Goode's battery of light artillery, Army of the West.

HOKE, W. I., NORTH CAROLINA.

Colonel Thirty-eighth North Carolina Infantry, ——.
Acting Brigadier-General, ——.

COMMANDS.

In command of Post at Charlotte, N. C.

HOLTZCLAW, J. T., ALABAMA.

Major Eighteenth Alabama Infantry, ——, 1861.
Lieutenant-Colonel Eighteenth Alabama Infantry, July 1, 1862.
Colonel Eighteenth Alabama Infantry, May 10, 1863.
Brigadier-General, P. A. C. S., July 7, 1864 (temporary rank).
Died, July 25, 1893.

COMMANDS.

Brigade composed of the Eighteenth, Twenty-first, Thirty-sixth and Thirty-eighth Alabama regiments infantry, and the Thirty-second and Fifty-eighth Alabama regiments infantry, consolidated, and Williams' Alabama battalion infantry.

BRIG.-GEN. THOMAS M. SCOTT,
OF LOUISIANA.
[From a photograph taken in 1864.]

BRIG.-GEN. L. S. ROSS,
OF TEXAS.
[From a photograph taken in 1864.]

BRIG.-GEN. JOHNSON HAGOOD,
OF SOUTH CAROLINA.
[From a photograph taken in 1862.]

BRIG.-GEN. WILLIAM R. COX,
OF NORTH CAROLINA.
[From a photograph taken in 1864.]

BRIG.-GEN. THOMAS GREEN,
OF TEXAS.
Killed at Battle of Pleasant Hill, La., April 9, 1864.
[From a photograph taken in 1863.]

BRIG.-GEN. JOHN S. PRESTON,
OF SOUTH CAROLINA,
In charge of the Bureau of Conscription.
[From a photograph taken in 1865.]

BRIG.-GEN. J. H. WINDER,
OF MARYLAND.
Commanding Prison Camps at Andersonville, Millen, Etc.
[From a photograph taken in 1861.]

BRIG.-GEN. STEPHEN ELLIOTT, JR.,
OF SOUTH CAROLINA.
Mortally wounded in front of Petersburg, 1864.

BRIG.-GEN. GOODE BRYAN,
OF GEORGIA.
[From a photograph taken in 1863.]

BRIG.-GEN. ELLISON CAPERS,
OF SOUTH CAROLINA.
[From a photograph taken in 1862.]

BRIG.-GEN. WM. R. PECK,
OF LOUISIANA.
[From a photograph taken in 1865.]

BRIG.-GEN. B. M. THOMAS,
OF ALABAMA.
[From a photograph taken in 1864.]

HUMPHREYS, BENJAMIN G., MISSISSIPPI.

Captain Twenty-first Mississippi Regiment, May 18, 1861.

Colonel commanding Sixth and Twenty-first Mississippi regiments, September 11, 1861.

Brigadier-General, P. A. C. S., August 12, 1863, succeeding General William Barksdale (killed).

Died in Leflore County, Miss., December 22, 1882.

COMMANDS.

Brigade composed of the Thirteenth, Seventeenth, Eighteenth and Twenty-first Mississippi regiments infantry, McLaws' division, Longstreet's corps, Army of Northern Virginia.

HUNTON, EPPA, VIRGINIA.

Colonel Eighth Virginia Infantry, May 8, 1861.

Brigadier-General, P. A. C. S., August 9, 1863.

COMMANDS.

Brigade composed of the Eighth, Eighteenth, Nineteenth, Twenty-eighth and Fifty-sixth regiments Virginia infantry, Pickett's division, Longstreet's corps, Army of Northern Virginia.

IMBODEN, J. D., VIRGINIA.

Colonel Eighth Virginia Cavalry, ——, 1861.

Brigadier-General, P. A. C. S., January 28, 1863.

COMMANDS.

Commanding Valley District, Department of Northern Virginia, July 28, 1863.

Brigade composed of the Eighteenth, Twenty-third and Twenty-fifth regiments Virginia cavalry, the Sixty-second Virginia Infantry (mounted), and McClanahan's battery of horse artillery.

*IVERSON, JR., ALFRED, GEORGIA.

Captain, Corps of Infantry, C. S. A., March 16, 1861.

Colonel Twentieth North Carolina Infantry, August 20, 1861.

Brigadier-General, P. A. C. S., November 1, 1862.

COMMANDS.

Brigade composed of the Fifth, Twelfth, Twentieth and Twenty-third North Carolina regiments infantry, D. H. Hill's division, Jackson's corps, Army of Northern Virginia.

In ——, 1864, brigade composed of the First, Second, Third, Fourth and Sixth regiments of Georgia cavalry, Martin's division, Wheeler's corps, Army of Tennessee.

JACKMAN, SIDNEY D., MISSOURI.

Colonel of the Seventh (afterward the Sixteenth) Missouri Infantry.

Brigadier-General, P. A. C. S., February 9, 1865.

COMMANDS.

Brigade composed of the Seventh (afterward the Sixteenth) Missouri, Second and Williams' regiments Missouri State Guards.

JACKSON, ALFRED E., TENNESSEE.

* * * * * * *

Brigadier-General, P. A. C. S., April 22, 1863.

COMMANDS.

Assigned to the command of the Fourth Military District of East Tennessee.

JACKSON, HENRY R., GEORGIA.

* * * * * * *

Brigadier-General, P. A. C. S., June 4, 1861.

COMMANDS.

Brigade composed of the First Confederate, the Sixty-sixth, Twenty-ninth, Thirtieth and Twenty-fifth Georgia regiments and Major Shaaf's battalion; brigade, in May, 1862, composed of the Third Arkansas, Thirty-first Virginia and First and Twelfth Georgia regiments and Hansborough's battalion.

JACKSON, JOHN K., GEORGIA.

Colonel Fifth Georgia Infantry, ——.

Brigadier-General, February 13, 1862.

COMMANDS.

Brigade composed of the Fifth and Eighth Mississippi and the Fifth Georgia regiments, the First Confederate Regiment, Second Georgia Battalion of Sharpshooters and Scroggins' light battery.

In 1862, in command of the Reserve Corps, Army of the Mississippi, composed of the Seventeenth, Eighteenth, Twenty-first and Twenty-fourth Alabama and the Fifth Georgia regiments and Bartwell's light battery.

JACKSON, WILLIAM H., TENNESSEE.

Colonel First Tennessee Cavalry, ——.

Brigadier-General, P. A. C. S., December 29, 1862.

COMMANDS.

Commanding cavalry brigade, Forrest's command; subsequently commanded cavalry division, Department of Alabama, Mississippi and East Louisiana.

JACKSON, WILLIAM L., VIRGINIA.

Colonel of the Thirty-first Virginia Infantry, afterward colonel of the Nineteenth Virginia Cavalry.

Brigadier-General, P. A. C. S., September —, 1864.

COMMANDS.

Brigade composed of the Nineteenth, Twentieth and Forty-sixth regiments Virginia cavalry, the Thirty-seventh Battalion Virginia Cavalry and the First Maryland Cavalry.

JENKINS, ALBERT G., VIRGINIA.

Lieutenant-Colonel Eighth Virginia Cavalry.

Brigadier-General, P. A. C. S., August 5, 1862.

COMMANDS.

Commanding cavalry brigade, Army of Northern Virginia.

BRIG.-GEN. T. P. DOCKERY, OF ARKANSAS.
[From a photograph taken in 1863.]

JENKINS, MICAH, SOUTH CAROLINA.

Colonel Fifth Infantry; afterward of the South Carolina Palmetto Sharpshooters.

Brigadier-General, P. A. C. S., July 22, 1862.

Killed at the Battle of the Wilderness, May 6, 1864.

COMMANDS.

Brigade composed of the First, Fourth, Fifth and Sixth regiments South Carolina volunteers, the Second Regiment South Carolina Rifles and the Palmetto Sharpshooters, Hood's division, Longstreet's corps.

BRIG.-GEN. GEORGE DOLES, OF GEORGIA.

JOHNSON, A. R., TEXAS.

Colonel of the Tenth (Johnson's) Kentucky Partisan Rangers.

Brigadier-General, P. A. C. S., August 4, 1864.

COMMANDS.

Commanding Second Brigade General Morgan's cavalry, subsequently in command in Tennessee and Kentucky.

JOHNSON, BRADLEY T., MARYLAND.

Captain Company A, First Maryland Regiment, May 21, 1861.

Major First Maryland Regiment, June 17, 1861.

Lieutenant-Colonel First Maryland Regiment Infantry, July 21, 1861.

Colonel First Maryland Regiment Infantry, March 18, 1862.

Colonel First Maryland Regiment Infantry, of the Maryland Line, June 22, 1863.

Colonel, commanding the Maryland Line, February —, 1864.

Brigadier-General, P. A. C. S., June 28, 1864.

COMMANDS.

Commanding First Maryland Regiment Infantry, Maryland Line, Army of Northern Virginia, composed of First Maryland Infantry, First Maryland Cavalry, Second Maryland Artillery, ——, 1862.

Commanding Second Brigade, Jackson's division, 1862–3.

Commanding Johnson's cavalry brigade in Valley campaign, June to December, 1864.

Commanding Maryland Line, composed of Second Maryland Infantry, First Maryland Cavalry, and First, Second and Fourth Maryland artillery, from December 19, 1863, to May —, 1864.

In 1865, commanded a division in Anderson's corps, Army of Northern Virginia.

JOHNSTON, GEORGE D., ALABAMA.

Second Lieutenant, Fourth Alabama Infantry, April 6, 1861.

Major Twenty-fifth Alabama Infantry, January 28, 1862.

Lieutenant-Colonel Twenty-fifth Alabama Infantry, April 6, 1862. Assigned to duty by order of General B. Bragg, commanding Army of Tennessee.

Colonel Twenty-fifth Alabama Infantry, October 27, 1863.

Brigadier-General, P. A. C. S., July 26, 1864.

COMMANDS.

Brigade composed of the Nineteenth, Twenty-second, Twenty-fifth, Thirty-ninth and Fiftieth Alabama regiments, Brown's division, Cheatham's corps, Army of Tennessee.

JOHNSTON, ROBERT D., NORTH CAROLINA.

Second Lieutenant, Beatties Ford Rifles, State Troops, May 9, 1861.

Captain Company K, Twenty-third North Carolina Regiment Infantry, July 15, 1861.

Lieutenant-Colonel Twenty-third North Carolina Regiment Infantry, May 21, 1862.

Brigadier-General, P. A. C. S., September 1, 1863.

COMMANDS.

Brigade composed of the Fifth, Twelfth, Twentieth and Twenty-third North Carolina regiments infantry, and Second North Carolina Battalion Infantry, Army of Northern Virginia.

JONES, JOHN M., VIRGINIA.

Lieutenant-Colonel, Corps of Artillery, C. S. A., March 16, 1861.

Lieutenant-Colonel (Assistant Adjutant-General), September 4, 1861.

Brigadier-General, P. A. C. S., May 15, 1863.

Killed at battle of the Wilderness, May 5, 1864.

COMMANDS.

Commanding brigade in Johnston's division, Ewell's corps, Army of Northern Virginia.

JONES, JOHN R., VIRGINIA.

Captain Thirty-third Regiment Virginia Infantry, ——, 1861.

Lieutenant-Colonel Thirty-third Regiment Virginia Infantry, ——.

Brigadier-General, P. A. C. S., June 23, 1862.

COMMANDS.

Brigade composed of the Twenty-first, Twenty-fifth, Forty-second, Forty-fourth and Fiftieth regiments Virginia infantry, and First Battalion Virginia Regulars, Trimble's division, Army of Northern Virginia.

October 31, 1864, commanding a brigade in J. B. Gordon's division, Army of the Valley.

JONES, WILLIAM E., VIRGINIA.

Captain First Regiment Virginia Cavalry, ——, 1861.

Colonel Eleventh Virginia Cavalry, June 20, 1862.

Brigadier-General, P. A. C. S., September 19, 1862.

Killed in action, June 5, 1864.

COMMANDS.

Commanding cavalry brigade, Army of Northern Virginia.

Commanding Valley District, Department of Northern Virginia, December 29, 1862, to January 7, 1863.

May 23, 1864, commanding the Trans-Alleghany or Western Department of Virginia.

*JORDAN, THOMAS, VIRGINIA.

Captain, Corps of Infantry, C. S. A., March 16, 1861.

* * * * * * *

Brigadier-General, P. A. C. S., April 14, 1862.

COMMANDS.

Chief of staff to General Beauregard.

KELLY, J. H., ALABAMA.

Captain (Assistant Adjutant-General), October 5, 1862.
Brigadier-General, P. A. C. S., November 16, 1863.
Killed near Franklin, Tenn., September 2, 1864.

COMMANDS.

Commanding brigade in Wheeler's cavalry, composed of the Sixty-third Virginia, the Fifty-eighth North Carolina, the Fifth Kentucky and the Sixty-fifth Georgia regiments; subsequently commanding division in Wheeler's cavalry corps, composed of the brigades of Allen, Dibrell and Hannon.

KENNEDY, JOHN D., SOUTH CAROLINA.

Colonel Second South Carolina Cavalry, ——, 1861.
Colonel Second South Carolina Volunteers, May 13, 1862.
Brigadier-General, P. A. C. S. (temporary rank), December 22, 1864.

COMMANDS.

Brigade composed of the Second, Third, Seventh, Eighth, Fifteenth and Twentieth South Carolina regiments infantry, and James' Third South Carolina Battalion Infantry, Longstreet's corps, Army of Northern Virginia.

KING, WM. H., TEXAS.

Colonel Eighteenth Texas Infantry, ——.
Brigadier-General, P. A. C. S., April 8, 1864.

COMMANDS.

Assigned to the command of "Walker's division of infantry," Trans-Mississippi Department; afterward in command of a Texas brigade in General Polignac's division.

KIRKLAND, W. W., NORTH CAROLINA.

Colonel Twenty-first North Carolina Infantry Regiment, April 21, 1863.
Brigadier-General, P. A. C. S., August 29, 1863.

COMMANDS.

Brigade composed of the Eleventh, Twenty-sixth, Forty-fourth, Forty-seventh and Fifty-second regiments North Carolina infantry, and subsequently of the Seventeenth, Forty-second, Fiftieth and Sixty-sixth regiments North Carolina infantry, Army of Northern Virginia.

LAGNEL, JULIUS A. DE, VIRGINIA.

Captain, Corps of Artillery, C. S. A., March 16, 1861.
Major Twentieth Battalion Virginia Artillery, July 3, 1862.
Brigadier-General, P. A. C. S., April 15, 1862. Declined the appointment.
On duty in the Ordnance Bureau at Richmond, Va.

LANE, JAMES H., NORTH CAROLINA.

Adjutant North Carolina Camp of Instruction, ——, 1861.
Major First North Carolina Volunteers, May 11, 1861.
Lieutenant-Colonel First North Carolina Volunteers, September 1, 1861.
Colonel Twenty-eighth North Carolina Troops, September 21, 1861.
Colonel Twenty-eighth North Carolina Troops, ——, 1861–2.
Brigadier-General, P. A. C. S., November 1, 1862.

COMMANDS.

Commanding brigade, as colonel, September 20, 1862.
Brigade, November 1, 1862, composed of the Seventh, Eighteenth, Twenty-eighth, Thirty-third and Thirty-seventh North Carolina regiments infantry, A. P. Hill's division, Jackson's corps, Army of Northern Virginia.
Brigade afterward in Pender's division, A. P. Hill's corps.

LANE, WALTER P., TEXAS.

Colonel Third Texas Cavalry, ——, 1861.
Brigadier-General, P. A. C. S., March 17, 1865.

COMMANDS.

Commanding brigade composed of Lane's, Baylor's, Chisholm's, Madison's, Walker's and Carter's regiments of Texas cavalry, in Major-General John A. Wharton's division, Trans-Mississippi Department.

*LAWTON, A. R., GEORGIA.

* * * * * * *

Brigadier-General, P. A. C. S., April 13, 1861.
Quartermaster-General, P. A. C. S., February 17, 1864.

COMMANDS.

Brigade composed of the Thirteenth, Twenty-sixth, Thirty-first, Thirty-eighth, Sixtieth and Sixty-first regiments Georgia infantry, Ewell's division, Jackson's corps, Army of Northern Virginia.
Commanding Ewell's division.
Commanding Department of Georgia, October 26, 1861.
Commanding District of Georgia, in Department of South Carolina, Georgia and Florida, May 28, 1862.

LEADBETTER, DANVILLE, ALABAMA.

Major, Corps of Engineers, C. S. A., March 16, 1861.
Brigadier-General, P. A. C. S., February 27, 1861.

COMMANDS.

Commanding in Knoxville, Tenn., in February, 1862.
Brigade composed of the Twentieth and Twenty-third Alabama and Colonel John C. Vaughn's Tennessee regiments infantry.

LEE, EDWIN G., VIRGINIA.

* * * * * * *

Colonel Thirty-third Virginia Infantry, ——.
Brigadier-General, P. A. C. S., September 20, 1864.

COMMANDS.

Commanding at Staunton, Va., ——.
Subsequently assigned to special service.

BRIG.-GEN. N. G. EVANS, OF SOUTH CAROLINA.
[From a photograph taken in 1863.]

LEVENTHORPE, C., NORTH CAROLINA.

Colonel Eleventh North Carolina Regiment of Infantry, October 26, 1861.
Brigadier-General, P. A. C. S., February 3, 1865.
Died, December 1, 1889.

COMMANDS.

Commanding at Fort Fisher, N. C., ——.

LEWIS, JOSEPH H., KENTUCKY.

Colonel Sixth Kentucky Regiment Infantry, November 1, 1861.
Brigadier-General, P. A. C. S., September 30, 1863.

COMMANDS.

Brigade composed of the Second, Fourth, Fifth, Sixth and Ninth Kentucky and Forty-first Alabama regiments infantry, Breckinridge's division, Army of Tennessee.
Succeeded General Helm in command of this brigade.
Subsequently commanded a brigade of cavalry.

BRIG.-GEN. JOSEPH FINEGAN, OF FLORIDA.

*LEWIS, WILLIAM G., NORTH CAROLINA.

Third Lieutenant Company A, First North Carolina Regiment Infantry, April 21, 1861.
Major Thirty-third North Carolina troops, January 17, 1862.
Lieutenant-Colonel Forty-third North Carolina Regiment, April 25, 1862.
Brigadier-General, P. A. C. S., May 31, 1864.

COMMANDS.

Brigade composed of the Sixth, Twenty-first, Fifty-fourth and Fifty-seventh North Carolina regiments, in Ramseur's (afterward Pegram's and, subsequently, Walker's) division, Second Corps, Army of Northern Virginia.

LIDDELL, ST. JOHN R., LOUISIANA.

* * * * * * *

Brigadier-General, P. A. C. S., July 12, 1862.

COMMANDS.

Brigade composed of the Second and Fifteenth, Fifth and Thirteenth, the Sixth, Seventh and Eighth Arkansas regiments, a company of pioneers and Roberts' battery of light artillery, being First Brigade, Third Corps, Army of the Mississippi.

LILLEY, R. D., VIRGINIA.

Captain "Augusta Lee Rifles," Company D, Twenty-fifth Virginia Regiment, May 21, 1861.
Major Twenty-fifth Virginia Regiment Infantry, January 28, 1863.
Lieutenant-Colonel Twenty-fifth Virginia Regiment Infantry, August 27, 1863.
Brigadier-General, P. A. C. S., May 31, 1864.
Died, November 12, 1886.

COMMANDS.

Brigade composed of the Thirteenth, Twenty-fifth, Forty-ninth, Fifty-second and Fifty-eighth Virginia regiments (formerly Pegram's brigade), in Ramseur's division, Early's corps, Army of Northern Virginia.

*LITTLE, HENRY, MISSOURI.

Major, Corps of Infantry, C. S. A., March 16, 1861.

* * * * * * *

Brigadier-General, P. A. C. S., April 16, 1862.
Killed at battle of Iuka, Miss., September 19, 1862.

COMMANDS.

Commanding First Division, Army of the West, composed of the brigades of Gates, Hebert and Green.

LOGAN, T. M., SOUTH CAROLINA.

Lieutenant-Colonel, Hampton's South Carolina Legion, ——, 1861.
Colonel, Hampton's Legion, May 19, 1864.
Brigadier-General, P. A. C. S., February 15, 1865.

COMMANDS.

Brigade composed of the First, Fourth, Fifth and Sixth regiments South Carolina cavalry and Keitt's South Carolina squadron and the First Regiment (Colonel Black) South Carolina Cavalry, Army of Northern Virginia.

*LONG, A. L., VIRGINIA.

Captain, Corps of Artillery, C. S. A., March 16, 1861.
Military Secretary (rank of colonel of cavalry), April 21, 1862.
Brigadier-General, P. A. C. S., September 21, 1863.
Died, April 29, 1891.

COMMANDS.

Brigadier-General, commanding artillery; chief of artillery Ewell's corps, Army of Northern Virginia.

LOWREY, M. P., MISSISSIPPI.

Colonel Thirty-Second Mississippi Infantry, April 3, 1862.
Brigadier-General, P. A. C. S., October 6, 1863.

COMMANDS.

Brigade composed of the Thirty-second and Forty-fifth Mississippi regiments, the Sixteenth, Thirty-third and Forty-fifth Alabama regiments, the Eighteenth Alabama Battalion of Infantry and Semple's battery of light artillery, Cleburne's division, Army of Tennessee. The Fifth and Eighth Mississippi regiments were subsequently added to the brigade.

LOWRY, ROBERT, MISSISSIPPI.

Colonel Sixth Regiment Mississippi Infantry, May 23, 1862.
Brigadier-General, P. A. C. S., February 4, 1865.

COMMANDS.

Brigade composed of the Sixth, Fourteenth, Fifteenth, Twentieth, Twenty-third and Forty-third Mississippi regiments of infantry, to which the Fifth and Eighth Mississippi regiments infantry were subsequently added.

*LYON, H. B., KENTUCKY.

First Lieutenant, Corps of Artillery, C. S. A., October 4, 1862.
Colonel Eighth Kentucky Regiment Infantry, February 3, 1862.
Brigadier-General, P. A. C. S., June 14, 1864.

COMMANDS.

Brigade composed of the Third, Seventh, Eighth and Twelfth regiments Kentucky cavalry, Forrest's division, Army of Tennessee.

MABREY, H. P., TEXAS.

Colonel Third Regiment Texas Cavalry, April —, 1862.
Brigadier-General, P. A. C. S., March —, 1862.

COMMANDS.

Brigade composed of the Fourth and Sixth regiments Mississippi cavalry, Thirtieth-eighth Regiment Mississippi Mounted Infantry, Fourteenth Regiment Confederate Cavalry, and the Fourteenth and Seventeenth regiments of Arkansas cavalry, consolidated, and —— battery of artillery.

* MACKALL, W. W., MARYLAND.

Lieutenant-Colonel, Corps of Infantry, C. S. A., March 16, 1861.
Brigadier-General, P. A. C. S., February 28, 1862.
Died, August 19, 1891.

BRIG.-GEN. WM. M. GARDNER, OF GEORGIA.
[From a photograph taken in 1861.]

COMMANDS.

Assigned assistant adjutant-general, staff of General A. S. Johnston, February 12, 1862.
Assigned chief of staff to General Braxton Bragg, April 11, 1862.
Chief of staff to General J. E. Johnston, October 17, 1863, to July 24, 1864.
Commanding troops and defenses of Island No. 10, Mississippi River, February 25 to April 8, 1862, when the garrison was surrendered.

MACRAE, WILLIAM, NORTH CAROLINA.

Colonel Fifteenth North Carolina Infantry, February 27, 1863.
Brigadier-General, P. A. C. S. (temporary rank), June 22, 1864.
Brigadier-General, P. A. C. S., November 4, 1864.

COMMANDS.

Brigade composed of the Eleventh, Twenty-sixth, Forty-second, Forty-seventh and Fifty-second North Carolina regiments infantry, Army of Northern Virginia.

* MAJOR, J. P., LOUISIANA.

* * * * * *

Brigadier-General, P. A. C. S., July 21, 1863.

COMMANDS.

Commanding Second Cavalry Brigade, District of Western Louisiana.

MANEY, GEORGE, TENNESSEE.

Colonel First Tennessee Regiment Infantry, May 8, 1861.
Brigadier-General, P. A. C. S., April 16, 1862.

COMMANDS.

Brigade composed of the First, Fourth, Sixth, Ninth and Twenty-seventh Tennessee regiments infantry, Major Maney's battalion of Tennessee infantry and Captain Melancthon Smith's battery of light artillery, being Second Brigade, Second Division, First Corps, Army of the Mississippi. The Forty-first and Fiftieth regiments Tennessee infantry were subsequently added to the brigade in Army of Tennessee.

MANIGAULT, A. M., SOUTH CAROLINA.

Colonel Tenth South Carolina Infantry, May 31, 1861.
Brigadier-General, P. A. C. S., April 26, 1863.

COMMANDS.

Brigade composed of the Tenth and Nineteenth South Carolina, the Twenty-fourth, Twenty-eighth and Thirty-fourth regiments Alabama infantry and Water's light battery.

MARSHALL, HUMPHREY, KENTUCKY.

Brigadier-General, P. A. C. S., October 30, 1861.
Resigned, June 16, 1862.
Reappointed, June 20, 1862, with rank from October 30, 1861.
Resigned, June 17, 1863.
Died, March 28, 1872.

COMMANDS.

At Princeton, Va., May —, 1862, command composed of the Twenty-ninth and Fifty-fourth Virginia and Fifth Kentucky regiments infantry, Dunn's battalion, Bradley's mounted Kentucky rifles and Jeffree's light battery.
Commanding District of Abingdon, Va., from May 2, 1862, to June —, 1863.

* MARTIN, JAMES G., NORTH CAROLINA.

Captain, Corps of Cavalry, C. S. A., March 16, 1861.

* * * * * *

Brigadier-General, P. A. C. S., May 15, 1862.
Resigned, July 25, 1862.
Reappointed, September 30, 1862.

COMMANDS.

Brigade composed of the Seventeenth, Forty-second, Fiftieth and Sixtieth North Carolina regiments infantry.

MCCAUSLAND, JOHN, VIRGINIA.

Colonel Thirty-sixth Virginia Infantry, July 16, 1861.
Brigadier-General, P. A. C. S., May 18, 1864.

COMMANDS.

Brigade composed of the Fourteenth, Sixteenth, Seventeenth, Twenty-first and Twenty-second regiments Virginia cavalry and Jackson's battery of artillery.

MCCOMB, W., TENNESSEE.

Colonel Fourteenth Regiment Tennessee Infantry, September 2, 1862.
Brigadier-General, P. A. C. S., January 20, 1865.

COMMANDS.

Commanding brigade in Heth's division, Third Corps, Army of Northern Virginia.

MCCRAY, T. H., ARKANSAS.

Colonel Thirty-first Arkansas Infantry, ——.
Brigadier-General, P. A. C. S., ——.

COMMANDS.

Commanding Third Brigade, McCown's division, Army of Tennessee.

* MCCULLOCH, BEN, TEXAS.

Colonel, commanding Texas State troops operating against San Antonio and adjacent forts, February —, 1861.
Brigadier-General, P. A. C. S., May 14, 1861.
Killed at the Battle of Elkhorn, March 7, 1862.

COMMANDS.

Commanding Texas State troops, February —, 1861.
August —, 1861, brigade composed of McNair's regiment Arkansas infantry, Churchill's regiment Arkansas mounted infantry, McIntosh's regiment Arkansas mounted infantry, McRae's battalion Arkansas infantry, Green's regiment Sixth Texas (mounted), Hebert's Third Louisiana Regiment Infantry and Arkansas State troops, consisting of regiments of Dockery, Gratiot, Carroll, Reif's company, and batteries of Woodruff and Reid; the Arkansas State troops being under command of General N. B. Pearce, commissioned by State of Arkansas.
March 6-8, 1861, commanding division under Major-General Earl Van Dorn, consisting of Third Louisiana Regiment Infantry, Colonel Hebert; Colonels Frank Rector's, Hill's, Mitchell's and McNair's regiments Arkansas infantry, and Lieutenant-Colonel McRae's Arkansas battalion infantry; the mounted Arkansas regiments of Colonels Churchill and McIntosh and King's Arkansas infantry; also, Major Brooks' battalion Arkansas mounted men, Captain H. S. Bennett's company of Texas cavalry, Colonel B. Warren Stone's Sixth Regiment Texas Cavalry, Colonel U. S. Young's Eleventh Texas Cavalry, Colonel Simms' —— Texas Cavalry, Colonel Elkanah Greer's Third Texas Cavalry, Major John W. Whitfield's battalion dismounted Texas cavalry and Captain John J. Good's First Texas Battery, Captain Province's Arkansas battery and Captain McDonald's Arkansas battery.

MCCULLOCH, HENRY E., TEXAS.

Colonel First Regiment Texas Mounted Volunteers, March —, 1861.
Brigadier-General, P. A. C. S., March 14, 1861.

COMMANDS.

Commanding Department of Texas, April 15, 1861.
Commanding District Northwestern Texas, May —, 1861.
Commanding Department of Texas, September 4, 1861.
Commanding Western District of Texas, December 3, 1861.
Commanding Northeastern District of Texas, June 12, 1862.
Commanding Texas and Arkansas troops, near Little Rock, Ark., August 4, 1862, consisting of eighteen regiments of Texas and six regiments of Arkansas troops.
Commanding Walker's division, Texas infantry, December 3, 1861.
Commanding brigade, December 20, 1861, composed of the Eighteenth Texas, Colonel Waterhouse; Colonel George Flournoy's Texas regiment; Sixteenth Texas, Colonel Fitzhugh; and Colonel Allen's Texas regiment.
August 5, 1863, commanding the Northern Subdistrict of Texas.

MCGOWAN, SAMUEL, SOUTH CAROLINA.

Lieutenant-Colonel Fourteenth Regiment South Carolina Volunteers, September 9, 1861.
Colonel Fourteenth Regiment South Carolina Volunteers, August 11, 1862.
Brigadier-General, P. A. C. S., January 17, 1863.

COMMANDS.

Brigade composed of the First, Twelfth, Thirteenth and Fourteenth 'South Carolina regiments, and Orr's Rifles (formerly Maxcy Gregg's brigade), Pender's division, A. P. Hill's corps, Army of Northern Virginia.

* MCINTOSH, JAMES, FLORIDA.

Captain, Corps of Cavalry, C. S. A., March 16, 1861.
Colonel Second Mounted Arkansas Infantry, May 1, 1861.
Brigadier-General, P. A. C. S., January 24, 1862.
Killed at Pea Ridge, May 7, 1862.

COMMANDS.

Commanding Missouri brigade, in General Price's division of General Van Dorn's army.

MCMURRY, J. A., TENNESSEE.

Colonel Thirty-fourth Tennessee Infantry, ——.
Brigadier-General, P. A. C. S., ——.

COMMANDS.

Commanding Maney's brigade, Second Division, First Corps, Army of Mississippi.

MCNAIR, EVANDER, ARKANSAS.

Colonel Fourth Arkansas Infantry, August 17, 1861.
Brigadier-General, P. A. C. S., November 4, 1862.

COMMANDS.

Brigade composed of the First, Second, Fourth, Twenty-fifth and Thirty-first Arkansas and the Thirty-ninth North Carolina regiments of infantry and Culpepper's light battery of artillery, Army of Tennessee.

BRIG.-GEN. RANDALL L. GIBSON, OF LOUISIANA.

MCRAE, DANDRIDGE, ARKANSAS.

Colonel Twenty-first Regiment Arkansas Infantry, ——, 1861.
Brigadier-General, P. A. C. S., November 5, 1862.

COMMANDS.

Commanding Third Brigade of Trans-Mississippi Department (Arkansas infantry), composed of the regiments of Colonels Glenn, Gause, Morgan and Hart and Marshall's battery of light artillery.

*MERCER, HUGH W., GEORGIA.

* * * * * *

Colonel First Georgia Volunteers, ——.
Brigadier-General, P. A. C. S., October 29, 1861.

COMMANDS.

* * * * * *

Brigade composed of the First, Fifty-fourth, Fifty-seventh and Sixty-third Georgia regiments infantry, Army of Tennessee.
Commanding at Savannah, Ga., ——.

MILES, W. R., MISSISSIPPI.

Colonel, Miles' Louisiana Legion.
Brigadier-General, P. A. C. S., ——, 1864.

COMMANDS.

Assigned to the command of Northeast Mississippi; afterward with Major-General D. H. Maury.

MILLER, WILLIAM, FLORIDA.

Colonel First Florida Regiment Infantry, ——, 1861.
Brigadier-General, P. A. C. S., August 2, 1864.

COMMANDS.

Commanding Reserve Forces of Florida, September 8, 1864.
Commanding District of Florida, September 29, 1864.

MOODY, YOUNG M., ALABAMA.

Colonel Forty-third Regiment Alabama Infantry, November 4, 1862.
Brigadier-General, P. A. C. S., March 4, 1865.

COMMANDS.

Assigned to the command of the District of Florida.

MOORE, J. C., TEXAS.

Colonel Second Texas Regiment Infantry, September 2, 1861.
Brigadier-General, P. A. C. S., May 26, 1862.
Resigned, February 3, 1864.

COMMANDS.

Brigade composed of the Second Texas, the Thirty-fifth Mississippi and the Thirty-seventh, Fortieth and Forty-second Alabama regiments infantry.
In ——, 1862, commanding Second Brigade, Third Division, Army of the West.

MOORE, P. T., VIRGINIA.

* * * * * * *

Brigadier-General, P. A. C. S., September 20, 1864.

COMMANDS.

Assigned to organization and command of reserve forces in and around Richmond, ——, 1864.

MORGAN, JOHN T., ALABAMA.

* * * * * * *

Colonel Fifty-first Alabama Regiment Cavalry, September 2, 1862.
Brigadier-General, P. A. C. S., June 6, 1863. Declined the appointment.
Brigadier-General, P. A. C. S., November 16, 1863.

COMMANDS.

Commanding cavalry brigade composed of the First, Third, Fourth, Seventh and Fifty-first Alabama regiments, Martin's division, Wheeler's corps, Army of Tennessee.

BRIG.-GEN. A. C. GODWIN, OF NORTH CAROLINA.

MOUTON, ALFRED, LOUISIANA.

Colonel Eighteenth Louisiana Regiment Infantry, October 5, 1861.
Brigadier-General, P. A. C. S., April 16, 1862.
Killed at Battle of Mansfield, La., April 9, 1864.

COMMANDS.

Brigade composed of the Eighteenth and Twenty-eighth Louisiana regiments, the Crescent Louisiana Regiment and Eighth Louisiana Battalion Infantry.

MUNFORD, THOMAS T., VIRGINIA.

Colonel Second Regiment Virginia Cavalry, April 25, 1862.

* * * * * * *

Brigadier-General, P. A. C. S., November —, 1864.

COMMANDS.

Brigade composed of the First, Second, Third, Fourth and Fifth regiments of Virginia cavalry, Army of Northern Virginia.

* * * * * * *

Commanding, August —, 1862, Brigadier-General B. H. Robertson's brigade of cavalry, in Stuart's division, Army of Northern Virginia.

NELSON, ALLISON, TEXAS.

Colonel Tenth Texas Regiment Infantry, ——, 1861.
Brigadier-General, P. A. C. S., September 12, 1862.

COMMANDS.

Brigade composed of the Tenth Texas Regiment Infantry and the Fifteenth, Seventeenth and Eighteenth regiments Texas cavalry.

NICHOLLS, FRANCIS T., LOUISIANA.

Lieutenant-Colonel Eighth Regiment Louisiana Infantry, June 9, 1861.
Colonel Fifteenth Louisiana Regiment Infantry, June 24, 1862.
Brigadier-General, P. A. C. S., October 14, 1862.

COMMANDS.

Commanding District of Lynchburg, Va.

* * * * * * *

Brigade at the battle of Chancellorsville, composed of the First, Second, Tenth, Fourteenth and Fifteenth Louisiana regiments infantry, Trimble's division, Army of Northern Virginia.

O'NEALL, E. A., ALABAMA.

Major Ninth Alabama Infantry, June 26, 1861.
Lieutenant-Colonel Ninth Alabama Infantry, October 21, 1861.
Colonel Twenty-sixth Alabama Infantry, April 2, 1862.
Brigadier-General, P. A. C. S., June 6, 1863.
Died, November 5, 1890.

COMMANDS.

Brigade (formerly commanded by Brigadier-General R. E. Rodes), 1862-3, composed of the Third, Fifth, Sixth, Twelfth and Twentieth Alabama regiments of infantry, in D. H. Hill's division, Army of Northern Virginia; afterward in Rodes' division.

PAGE, RICHARD L., VIRGINIA.

* * * * * * *

Brigadier-General, P. A. C. S., March 1, 1864.

COMMANDS.

Brigade composed of the Twenty-first Regiment Alabama Infantry, First Battalion Alabama Artillery, First Battalion Tennessee Heavy Artillery, four companies of the Seventh Regiment Alabama Cavalry, and a portion of the First Alabama Confederate Regiment.
Assigned to command of Fort Morgan and outer defenses of Mobile Bay.

PALMER, JOSEPH B., TENNESSEE.

Colonel Eighteenth Tennessee Regiment Infantry, ——, 1862.
Brigadier-General, P. A. C. S. (temporary rank), November 15, 1864.
Died, November 4, 1890.

COMMANDS.

Commanding, in 1862, as colonel, brigade in Breckinridge's division, Polk's corps, Army of Tennessee.
Brigade composed of the Third, Eighteenth, Twenty-sixth, Thirty-second and Forty-fifth regiments Tennessee infantry, the Twenty-third Battalion Tennessee Infantry, the Fifty-eighth and Sixtieth North Carolina regiments infantry.

PARSONS, MOSBY MUNROE, MISSOURI.

* * * * * * *

Brigadier-General, P. A. C. S., November 5, 1862.
Died, August 7, 1865.

COMMANDS.

Brigade composed of the regiments of Colonels Pickett, Hunter, Poulter and Caldwell, and Lieutenant-Colonel Pindall's battalion, and Captain Tilden's battery of light artillery.
Commanding Fourth Brigade, Price's division.

PARSONS, W. H., TEXAS.

Acting Brigadier-General in command of a brigade composed of the Twelfth, Nineteenth and Twenty-first Texas cavalry, Major Morgan's battalion of Texas cavalry and Pratt's battery of light artillery.

PAYNE, WILLIAM H., VIRGINIA.

Captain Black Horse Troop ——, 1861.
Major Fourth Virginia Cavalry, September 12, 1861.
Lieutenant-Colonel Fourth Virginia Cavalry, June 9, 1862.
Colonel Fourth Virginia Cavalry, September 3, 1863.
Brigadier-General, P. A. C. S., November 1, 1864.

COMMANDS.

Brigade composed of the Fifth, Sixth, Eighth and Fifteenth regiments of Virginia cavalry and Thirty-sixth Battalion Virginia Cavalry in Major-General Fitzhugh Lee's division, Army of Northern Virginia.

PAXTON, E. F., VIRGINIA.

Major, Adjutant-General's Department, August 15, 1862.
Brigadier-General, P. A. C. S., November 1, 1862.
Killed at Chancellorsville, May 3, 1863.

COMMANDS.

Brigade composed of the Second, Fourth, Fifth, Twenty-seventh and Thirty-third regiments Virginia infantry, Trimble's division, Jackson's corps, Army of Northern Virginia.

BRIG.-GEN. GEORGE W. GORDON, OF TENNESSEE.
[From a photograph taken in 1865.]

PEARCE, N. B., ARKANSAS.

Commissioned Brigadier-General, May —, 1861, by the secession convention of Arkansas.

COMMANDS.

Command composed of Carroll's cavalry regiment, the Third and Fifth regiments Arkansas infantry, Woodruff's infantry battalion and Reid's light battery.

PENDLETON, W. N., VIRGINIA.

Captain, Corps of Artillery, C. S. A., July 19, 1861.
Colonel and Chief of Artillery of Army of Northern Virginia, July 21, 1861, to surrender at Appomattox, 1865.
Brigadier-General, P. A. C. S., March 26, 1862.
Died at Lexington, Va., January 15, 1883.

PERRIN, ABNER, SOUTH CAROLINA.

* * * * * * *

Colonel Fourteenth South Carolina Regiment Infantry, February 20, 1863.
Brigadier-General, P. A. C. S., September 10, 1863.
Killed at Spottsylvania, Va., May 12, 1864.

COMMANDS.

Commanding brigade formerly commanded by Brigadier-General C. M. Wilcox.

PERRY, E. A., FLORIDA.

Colonel Second Florida Regiment, May —, 1862.
Brigadier-General, P. A. C. S., August 28, 1862.
Died at Knoxville, Tenn., October 15, 1889.

COMMANDS.

Brigade composed of the Second, Fifth and Eighth regiments Florida infantry, Anderson's division, A. P. Hill's corps, Army of Northern Virginia.

PERRY, W. F., ALABAMA.

Major Forty-fourth Alabama Infantry, ——, 1861.
Lieutenant-Colonel Forty-fourth Alabama Infantry September 1, 1862.
Colonel Forty-fourth Alabama Infantry, September 17 1862.
Brigadier-General, P. A. C. S., February 26, 1865.

COMMANDS.

Brigade composed of the Fifteenth, Forty-fourth, Forty-seventh and Forty-eighth Alabama regiments infantry, Longstreet's corps, Army of Northern Virginia.

PETTIGREW, J. JOHNSTON, NORTH CAROLINA.

Colonel Twenty-second North Carolina Regiment Infantry, July —, 1861.
Brigadier-General, P. A. C. S., February 26, 1862.
Died, July 18, 1863, of wounds received at Falling Waters, July 14, 1863.

BRIG.-GEN. JAMES CHESTNUT, JR., OF SOUTH CAROLINA.
[From a photograph taken in 1861.]

BRIG.-GEN. T. M. LOGAN, OF SOUTH CAROLINA.
[From a photograph taken in 1864.]

BRIG.-GEN. DUDLEY M. DUBOSE, OF GEORGIA.
[From a photograph taken in 1865.]

BRIG.-GEN. ARCH. J. DOBBINS, OF ARKANSAS.
[From a photograph taken in 1864.]

BRIG.-GEN. JUNIUS DANIEL, OF NORTH CAROLINA.
Killed at Spottsylvania, May 12, 1864.
[From a photograph taken in 1862.]

BRIG.-GEN. JOHN R. COOKE, OF NORTH CAROLINA.
[From a photograph taken in 1862.]

BRIG.-GEN. JOSEPH H. LEWIS, OF KENTUCKY.
[From a photograph taken in 1864.]

BRIG.-GEN. X. B. DEBRAY, OF TEXAS.

BRIG.-GEN. GEORGE B. COSBY, OF KENTUCKY.
[From a photograph taken in 1865.]

COMMANDS.

Brigade composed of the Eleventh, Seventeenth, Twenty-sixth, Forty-second, Forty-fourth, Forty-seventh and Fifty-second North Carolina regiments infantry, Heth's division, A. P. Hill's corps, Army of Northern Virginia.

PETTUS, E. W., ALABAMA.

Major Twentieth Alabama Regiment Infantry, September 9, 1861.
Lieutenant-Colonel Twentieth Alabama Regiment, October 8, 1861.
Colonel Twentieth Alabama Regiment, May 28, 1863.
Brigadier-General, P. A. C. S., September 18, 1863.

BRIG.-GEN TYREE H. BELL, OF TENNESSEE.
[From a tintype taken in 1863.]

BRIG.-GEN. DOUGLAS H. COOPER, OF MISSISSIPPI.
[From a tintype taken in 1863.]

BRIG.-GEN. HUGH W. MERCER, OF GEORGIA.
[From a tintype taken in 1861.]

COMMANDS.

Brigade composed of the Twentieth, Twenty-third, Thirtieth, Thirty-first and Forty-sixth Alabama regiments, Stevenson's division, Army of Tennessee.

PHIFER, CHARLES W., TEXAS.

* * * * * *

Brigadier-General, P. A. C. S., May 25, 1862.

COMMANDS.

June 30, 1862, commanding Third Brigade, Third Division, Army of the West.
Brigade composed of the Sixth and Ninth Texas Cavalry, the Third Arkansas Cavalry, and the battalions of Stevenson and Bridges.

PIKE, ALBERT, ARKANSAS.

Brigadier-General, P. A. C. S., August 15, 1861.
Resigned, November 11, 1862.

COMMANDS.

In command of the forces and Department of the Indian Territory, 1861-2.

PILLOW, GIDEON J., TENNESSEE.

Major-General Provisional Army of Tennessee, May 9, 1861.
Brigadier-General, P. A. C. S., July 9, 1861.
Died, September —, 1878.

COMMANDS.

July 30, 1861, commanding at New Madrid, Mo.
Commanding, October 24, 1861, First Division of the Western Department.
Commanding cavalry brigade, Army of Tennessee, -
Commanded Third Division, Central Army of Kentucky, ——.
In charge of conscripts in Western Department, ——.

POLK, LUCIUS E., ARKANSAS.

First Lieutenant Company B, Fifteenth Arkansas Regiment, March 4, 1861.
Colonel Fifteenth Arkansas Regiment Infantry, April 11, 1862.
Brigadier-General, P. A. C. S., December 13, 1862.
Died, December 3, 1892.

COMMANDS.

Brigade composed of the First and Fifteenth Arkansas regiments, the Third and Fifth Tennessee regiments (consolidated and known as Fifth Confederate), the Second, Fifth and Forty-eighth Tennessee regiments and Calvert's battery of light artillery, Cleburne's division, Hardee's Corps, Army of Tennessee.

POSEY, CARNOT, MISSISSIPPI.

Colonel Sixteenth Regiment Mississippi Infantry, June 4, 1861.
Brigadier-General, P. A. C. S., November 1, 1862.
Died of wounds received at Bristol Station, on October 14, 1863.

COMMANDS.

Brigade composed of the Twelfth, Sixteenth, Nineteenth and Forty-fifth regiments Mississippi infantry, Anderson's division, A. P. Hill's corps, Army of Northern Virginia.

PRESTON, JOHN S., SOUTH CAROLINA.

* * * * * * *

Brigadier-General, P. A. C. S., June 10, 1864.

COMMANDS.

In charge of the Bureau of Conscription.

PRYOR, ROGER A., VIRGINIA.

Colonel Third Virginia Infantry, ——, 1861.
Brigadier-General, P. A. C. S., April 16, 1862.
Resigned, August 18, 1863.

COMMANDS.

Brigade composed of the Fourteenth Louisiana, the Fourteenth Alabama, the Second Florida and the Third Virginia regiments of Infantry and Coppen's battery of light artillery; subsequently composed of the Third Virginia, Fourteenth Alabama and the Second, Fifth and Eighth Florida regiments infantry, Army of Northern Virginia.

QUARLES, WILLIAM A., TENNESSEE.

Colonel Forty-second Tennessee Regiment Infantry, ——, 1861.
Brigadier-General, P. A. C. S., August 25, 1863.
Died, December 28, 1893.

COMMANDS.

Brigade composed of the Forty-second, Forty-sixth, Forty-eighth and Fifty-fifth regiments Tennessee infantry, consolidated, the Forty-ninth and Fifty-third Tennessee regiments infantry and the First Alabama and Fourth and Thirtieth regiments Louisiana infantry, Walthall's Division, Stewart's corps, Army of Tennessee, and Fifty-third and Fifty-fifth Tennessee, Fourth and Thirtieth Louisiana and Fenner's Louisiana battery.

*RAINS, GABRIEL J., NORTH CAROLINA.

Colonel, Corps of Infantry, C. S. A., March 16, 1861.
Brigadier-General, P. A. C. S., September 23, 1861.

COMMANDS.

In charge of Bureau of Conscription, December —, 1862.
Chief of Torpedo Service, June 17, 1864.

RAINS, JAMES E., TENNESSEE.

Colonel Eleventh Tennessee Regiment Infantry, May 10, 1861.
Brigadier-General, P. A. C. S., November 4, 1862.
Killed at Murfreesboro, Tenn., December 31, 1862.

COMMANDS.

Brigade composed of the Eleventh Tennessee, Twentieth North Carolina and Forty-first Georgia regiments infantry, the Third Georgia Battalion Infantry and Captain McTyere's battery of light artillery, Army of Tennessee.

RANDALL, HORACE, ——.

Colonel Twenty-eighth Texas Cavalry, ——.
Commanded a brigade in Walker's division, Army of Tennessee.
Killed at Jenkins Ferry, April 30, 1864.

RANDOLPH, GEORGE W., VIRGINIA.

* * * * * * *

Brigadier-General, P. A. C. S., February 13, 1862.
Secretary of War, March 17 to December 18, 1862.

REID, JOHN C., ALABAMA.

Colonel Twenty-eighth Alabama Infantry, ——.
Acting as Brigadier-General in recruiting and mustering into service and brigading cavalry, Northern Alabama.

REYNOLDS, A. E., MISSISSIPPI.

Colonel Twenty-sixth Mississippi Infantry.
Brigadier-General, P. A. C. S., March —, 1865.

COMMANDS.

Colonel, commanding Tilghman's brigade after he was killed at battle of Bakers Creek; afterward senior colonel commanding brigade of General Jos. R. Davis during his absence; brigade composed of the Twenty-sixth, Second, Eleventh and Forty-second Mississippi regiments, the First Alabama Regiment and the Fifty-fifth North Carolina Regiment.

*REYNOLDS, A. W., VIRGINIA.

Captain, Corps of Infantry, C. S. A., March 16, 1861.
Colonel Fiftieth Regiment Virginia Infantry, July 10, 1861.
Brigadier-General, P. A. C. S., September 14, 1863.
Died, May 26, 1876.

COMMANDS.

Brigade composed of the Fifty-fourth and Sixty-third regiments Virginia Infantry, and the Fifty-eighth and Sixtieth North Carolina regiments infantry, Stevenson's division, Army of Tennessee.

REYNOLDS, D. H., ARKANSAS.

Captain First Arkansas Cavalry, June 14, 1861.
Major First Arkansas Cavalry, April 14, 1862.
Lieutenant-Colonel First Arkansas Cavalry, May 1, 1862.
Colonel First Arkansas Cavalry, September 20, 1863.
Brigadier-General, P. A. C. S., March 5, 1864.

COMMANDS.

Brigade composed of the First and Second regiments of Arkansas cavalry (dismounted), the Fourth, Twenty-third and Thirty-first regiments Arkansas infantry, the Fourth Arkansas Battalion of Infantry, and the Thirty-ninth Regiment North Carolina Infantry, which was subsequently exchanged for the Ninth Arkansas Infantry.

RICHARDSON, R. V., TENNESSEE.

Colonel Twelfth Regiment Tennessee Cavalry, February 14, 1863.
Brigadier-General, P. A. C. S., December 11, 1863. Nomination not confirmed by the Confederate States Senate.

COMMANDS.

Brigade composed of the Seventh, Twelfth, Fourteenth and Fifteenth regiments Tennessee cavalry, and McDonald's Tennessee Battalion Cavalry.

RIPLEY, ROSWELL S., SOUTH CAROLINA.

Brigadier-General, P. A. C. S., August 15, 1861.
Died, March 29, 1887.

COMMANDS.

Commanding Department of South Carolina, August 21, 1861.
Commanding Second Military District of South Carolina, from December 10, 1861, to May 28, 1862.
Commanding First Military district of South Carolina, October 16, 1862, to October 22, 1863.
Brigade at the battle of Fredericksburg, Va., December —, 1862, composed of the Fourth and Forty-fourth Georgia and First and Third North Carolina regiments infantry, D. H. Hill's division, Jackson's corps, Army of Northern Virginia.

BRIG.-GEN. GEORGE B. HODGE, OF KENTUCKY.
[From a photograph taken in 1862.]

ROANE, JOHN SELDON, ARKANSAS.

Brigadier-General, P. A. C. S., March 20, 1862.
Died, April 7, 1867.

COMMANDS.

Commanding at Little Rock, Arkansas, ——.
Commanding brigade, attached to Major-General Sam Jones' division, Army of the West.

ROBERTS, W. P., NORTH CAROLINA.

Third Lieutenant Nineteenth Regiment North Carolina Infantry, August 30, 1861.

First Lieutenant Nineteenth Regiment North Carolina Infantry, September 13, 1862.

Captain Nineteenth Regiment North Carolina Infantry, November 19, 1863.

Colonel Nineteenth Regiment North Carolina Infantry, July 19, 1864.

Brigadier-General, P. A. C. S., February 21, 1865.

COMMANDS.

Commanding, in ——, 1865, brigade composed of the Second Regiment North Carolina Cavalry, Twelfth Battalion North Carolina Cavalry, Sixteenth Battalion North Carolina Cavalry, and — Battalion of Georgia Cavalry, formerly commanded by Brigadier-General Deas, in Major-General W. H. F. Lee's division, Army of Northern Virginia.

BRIG.-GEN. SAMUEL W. FERGUSON, OF MISSISSIPPI.
[From a photograph taken in 1863.]

* ROBERTSON, BEVERLY H., VIRGINIA.

Colonel of Virginia Volunteer Cavalry, August 21, 1861.

Captain, Corps of Artillery, C. S. A., September 14, 1861.

Captain, A. A. G., P. A. C. S., December 24, 1861.

Brigadier-General, P. A. C. S., June 9, 1862.

COMMANDS.

Brigade composed of the Second, Sixth, Seventh and Eleventh Virginia regiments, and Lieutenant-Colonel Funsten's Sixteenth Virginia Battalion.

In December, 1862, commanding cavalry and infantry forces under General G. W. Smith, near Goldsborough, North Carolina.

December 16, 1862, commanding forces at battle of White Hall, on the Neuse River.

In March, 1863, assigned to the command of a division composed of his own and W. E. Jones' brigade.

In autumn of 1863 assigned to the command of the forces operating between Charleston and Savannah.

In command of cavalry forces covering retreat of General Hardee from Charleston to Raleigh, North Carolina.

June 9, 1864, commanding forces which attacked John's Island, South Carolina.

Commanding cavalry forces in engagement at Honey Hill, ——, 1865.

ROBERTSON, E. S. C., TEXAS.

Brigadier-General of Texas State forces, commanding the Twenty-seventh Brigade; on staff duty with General McCulloch.

ROBERTSON, FELIX H., TEXAS.

Second Lieutenant, Corps of Artillery, C. S. A., March 9, 1861.

Captain and A. A. G., on staff of Brigadier-General A. H. Gladden, October —, 1861.

Captain, commanding Robertson's battery of artillery, January 1, 1862.

Major of artillery, commanding reserve artillery, Army of Tennessee, July 1, 1863.

Lieutenant-Colonel of artillery, commanding the artillery of Wheeler's cavalry corps, Army of Tennessee, January —, 1864.

Brigadier-General, P. A. C. S., July 26, 1864.

COMMANDS.

Brigade composed of the Eighth and Tenth Texas and Fourth Tennessee regiments of cavalry, Wheeler's corps, Army of Tennessee.

ROBERTSON, JEROME B., TEXAS.

Captain Fifth Texas Regiment Infantry, ——, 1861.

Lieutenant-Colonel Fifth Texas Regiment Infantry, November —, 1861.

Colonel Fifth Texas Infantry, June 3, 1862.

Brigadier-General, P. A. C. S., November 1, 1862.

COMMANDS.

Brigade composed of the First, Fourth and Fifth Texas and Third Arkansas regiments infantry, Hood's division, Longstreet's corps, Army of Northern Virginia.

The Eighteenth Georgia Regiment of Infantry and Hampton's Legion formed a part of the brigade at one time.

September 10, 1864, assigned command of reserve corps of Texas.

In 1865, commanding brigade in General Maxwell's division, District of Arkansas.

RODDEY, P. D., ALABAMA.

Captain, Alabama company cavalry, ——, 1861.

Colonel, Alabama regiment cavalry, ——, 1862.

Brigadier-General, P. A. C. S., August 31, 1863.

COMMANDS.

In 1863, commanding brigade in Wheeler's corps, Army of Tennessee.

ROSS, L. S., TEXAS.

Colonel Sixth Texas Regiment Cavalry, May 24, 1862.

Brigadier-General, P. A. C. S., December 21, 1863.

COMMANDS.

Commanding brigade cavalry formerly commanded by Brigadier-General W. Y. C. Humes, in Wheeler's cavalry corps.

ROSS, REUBEN R., ——.

Acting Brigadier-General, commanding Humes' cavalry brigade, Wheeler's corps.

RUCKER, E. W., ——.

Acting Brigadier-General commanding brigade in General Forrest's cavalry, composed of the Seventh, Twelfth, Fourteenth and Fifteenth Tennessee regiments, Forrest's old regiment and the Seventh Alabama and Fifth Mississippi.

* RUGGLES, DANIEL, VIRGINIA.

Lieutenant-Colonel Virginia Volunteers, April 22, 1861.

Brigadier-General of Virginia Volunteers, April 23, 1861, and, as such, assigned to the command of the Department of Fredericksburg.

Brigadier-General, P. A. C. S., August 9, 1861.

COMMANDS.

Command (while brigadier-general of Virginia volunteers, in command of Department of Fredericksburg) composed of Captain Lindsay Walker's battery of artillery, Captain C. S. Braxton's battery of artillery, the Ninth Virginia Cavalry, the Thirtieth, Fortieth, Forty-second and Forty-seventh Virginia infantry, the Second Tennessee Regiment Infantry, Captain Wise's company "Richmond Blues," and the First Arkansas Infantry.

August 25, 1861, ordered to Pensacola, Fla., and assigned to the command of brigade composed of the Ninth and Tenth Mississippi and First and Seventh Alabama regiments infantry and Villepigue's battalion of Georgia infantry, the Quitman battery of artillery (Captain F. Kerr commanding), and the Vicksburg battery of artillery (Captain Isaac N. Edwards).

October —, 1861, commanding troops and defenses under Major-General Mansfield Lovell at New Orleans.

February 17, 1862, commanding brigade at Corinth, Miss., composed of Sixteenth, Seventeenth, Eighteenth, Nineteenth and Twentieth Louisiana regiments infantry, Company A, Miles' artillery (Captain Gibson), and Captain Higgins' battery of artillery.

February 20, 1862, assigned to the command of all troops near the line of the Memphis & Charleston Railroad.

March 29, 1862, commanding division consisting of Gibson's, Patton's, Anderson's and Colonel Pond's brigades.

May 18, 1862, assigned to the command of Special Department of East Louisiana and Southern Mississippi.

July 29, 1862, assigned to the command of the Second Division of Breckinridge's command.

January 10, 1863, assigned to the command of the First District of Department of Mississippi.

March 25, 1865, assigned to duty as commissary-general of prisoners of war.

RUST, ALBERT, ARKANSAS.

Colonel Third Arkansas Regiment Infantry, July 5, 1861.

Brigadier-General, P. A. C. S., March 4, 1862.

COMMANDS.

Brigade composed of the Arkansas infantry regiments of Colonels Carroll, King and Snead, the Arkansas infantry battalions of Lieutenant-Colonels McCarver, Lemoyne and Jones, and a light battery attached to Major-General Samuel Jones' division, Army of the West.

SAUNDERS, J. C. C., ALABAMA.

Colonel Eleventh Regiment Alabama Infantry, June 11, 1861.

Brigadier-General, P. A. C. S. (temporary rank), May 31, 1864.

Killed near Petersburg, Va., August 21, 1864.

COMMANDS.

Brigade composed of the Eighth, Ninth, Tenth, Eleventh and Fourteenth regiments Alabama infantry, Army of Northern Virginia.

SCALES, ALFRED M., NORTH CAROLINA.

Colonel Thirteenth North Carolina Infantry, October —, 1861.

Brigadier-General, P. A. C. S., June 13, 1863.

COMMANDS.

Brigade composed of the Thirteenth, Twenty-second, Thirty-second and Thirty-eighth regiments North Carolina infantry (formerly Pender's brigade), Wilcox's division, A. P. Hill's corps, Army of Northern Virginia.

SCOTT, THOMAS M., LOUISIANA.

Colonel Twelfth Louisiana Infantry, August 9, 1861.

Brigadier-General, P. A. C. S., May 10, 1864.

COMMANDS.

Brigade composed of the Twelfth Louisiana, the Twenty-seventh, Thirty-fifth, Forty-ninth, Fifty-fifth and Fifty-seventh Alabama regiments infantry, and the Third, Seventh and Eighth Kentucky regiments, which afterward were detached.

SCURRY, W. R., TEXAS.

Lieutenant-Colonel Fourth Texas Mounted Infantry, August 23, 1861.

* * * * * *

Brigadier-General, P. A. C. S., September 12, 1862.

Killed at Jenkins Ferry, April 30, 1864.

COMMANDS.

February 2, 1862, commanding Fourth Texas Mounted Volunteers, Army of New Mexico.

December 20, 1862, assigned command of Sibley's brigade.

February 13, 1863, assigned command of Eastern Sub-district of Texas (Trans-Mississippi Department).

September 17th, assigned command of Walker's division, District of West Louisiana.

SEARS, C. W., MISSISSIPPI.

Colonel Forty-sixth Mississippi Regiment Infantry, December 11, 1862.

Brigadier-General, P. A. C. S., March 1, 1864.

COMMANDS.

Brigade composed of the Fourth, Thirty-fifth, Thirty-sixth, Thirty-ninth and Forty-sixth regiments Mississippi infantry and Seventh Battalion Mississippi Infantry.

BRIG.-GEN. D. H. REYNOLDS, OF ARKANSAS.
[From a tintype taken in 1863.]

BRIG.-GEN. ALFRED M. SCALES, OF NORTH CAROLINA.
[From a tintype taken in 1863.]

BRIG.-GEN. F. A. SHOUP, OF FLORIDA.
[From a tintype taken in 1863.]

SEMMES, PAUL J., GEORGIA.

Colonel Second Regiment Georgia Infantry, May 7, 1861.

Brigadier-General, P. A. C. S., March 11, 1862.

Died, July 10, 1863, of wounds received at Gettysburg, Pa.

COMMANDS.

Brigade composed of the Tenth, Fiftieth, Fifty-first and Fifty-third regiments Georgia infantry, McLaws' division, Longstreet's corps, Army of Northern Virginia.

BRIG.-GEN. JOHN BRATTON, OF SOUTH CAROLINA.
[From a tintype taken in 1864.]

SHARP, JACOB H., MISSISSIPPI.

Colonel Forty-fourth Regiment Mississippi Infantry, ——, 1863.

Brigadier-General, P. A. C. S. (temporary rank), July 26, 1864.

COMMANDS.

Brigade composed of the First Mississippi Battalion Sharpshooters and the Seventh, Ninth, Tenth, Forty-first and Forty-fourth regiments Mississippi infantry, Hindman's division, Polk's corps, Army of Tennessee.

SHELBY, JOSEPH O., MISSOURI.

Colonel Fifth Missouri Cavalry, ——.

Brigadier-General, P. A. C. S., December 15, 1863.

COMMANDS.

Commanding brigade in General Price's army, ——.

Commanding division in Price's army, Trans-Mississippi Department, September 8, 1864.

SHELLEY, CHARLES M., ALABAMA.

Colonel Thirtieth Regiment Alabama Infantry, March 22, 1862.

* * * * * *

Brigadier-General, P. A. C. S. (temporary rank), September 17, 1864. Made permanent, December —, 1864.

BRIG.-GEN. MICAH JENKINS, OF SOUTH CAROLINA.
Killed at Battle of the Wilderness, May 6, 1864.
[From a photograph taken in 1863.]

COMMANDS.

Brigade composed of the Seventeenth, Twenty-sixth and Twenty-ninth regiments Alabama infantry and Thirty-seventh Mississippi Regiment Infantry, Walthall's division, Stewart's corps, Army of Tennessee.

SHINGLER, WM. P., SOUTH CAROLINA.

Colonel Seventh South Carolina Cavalry, ——.

Acting Brigadier-General, ——.

* SHOUP, FRANCIS A., FLORIDA.

Major of Artillery, C. S. A., October —, 1861.

Brigadier-General, P. A. C. S., September 12, 1862.

COMMANDS.

Brigade composed of the Seventh, Ninth, Tenth, Forty-first and Forty-fourth regiments and Ninth Mississippi Battalion Infantry.

Commanding brigade at Vicksburg, composed of the Twenty-Sixth, Twenty-seventh and Twenty-eighth Louisiana regiments.

Commanding artillery at Mobile, winter of 1863-4.

Commanding division, December 7, 1862, composed of Fagan's and McRae's Arkansas brigades, at Prairie Grove, Arkansas.

In command of Fort Morgan, and lower defenses of Mobile Bay, April —, 1863.

Chief of Artillery of the Army of Tennessee, under General Joseph E. Johnston, during the Dalton-Atlanta campaign, and constructed the defensive works at the Chattahoochee River, Georgia.

Chief of Staff to General J. B. Hood, July 25, 1864.

* SIBLEY, H. H., LOUISIANA.

Lieutenant-Colonel of infantry, C. S. A., March 16, 1861.

Brigadier-General, P. A. C. S., June 17, 1861.

COMMANDS.

Commanding, in 1861-2, the District and forces in New Mexico and Arizona.

In 1862-3 commanding District and forces in Louisiana south of Red River.

Brigade composed of Fourth Texas Regiment of Cavalry, Colonel Tom Green; Fifth Regiment Texas Cavalry, Colonel Riley; Sixth Regiment Texas Cavalry, Colonel Steele; Pyson's Texas battalion cavalry; and Herbert's battalion of Arizona cavalry.

BRIG.-GEN. A. J. VAUGHAN, OF TENNESSEE.
[From a tintype taken in 1864.]

SIMMS, JAMES P., GEORGIA.

Major Fifth Georgia Regiment Infantry, ——.

Colonel Fifty-third Georgia Regiment Infantry, ——.

Brigadier-General, P. A. C. S., December 8, 1865.

COMMANDS.

Brigade composed of the Tenth, Fiftieth, Fifty-first and Fifty-second regiments Georgia infantry, Kershaw's division, Longstreet's corps, Army of Northern Virginia.

SLACK, W. Y., MISSOURI.

* * * * * *

Brigadier-General, P. A. C. S., ——, 1862.

Killed at Pea Ridge, March 6, 1862.

COMMANDS.

Commanding brigade in Price's division, Army of the West.

* SLAUGHTER, J. E., VIRGINIA.

Captain, Corps of Artillery, C. S. A., March 16, 1861.

* * * * * *

Brigadier-General, P. A. C. S., March 8, 1862.

COMMANDS.

Inspector-General of Department No. 2, Army of the Mississippi and Army of Tennessee.

SMITH, GEORGE A., GEORGIA.

Colonel First Confederate Infantry.

Acting Brigadier-General in command of Fort Gaines, etc., in Mobile Bay.

SMITH, JAMES ARGYLE, MISSISSIPPI.

Captain, Corps of Infantry, C. S. A., March 16, 1861.

Colonel Ninth Confederate regiment, ——.

Brigadier-General, P. A. C. S., September 30, 1863.

COMMANDS.

Commanding Brigade in Cleburne's division, Hardee's corps, Army of Tennessee.

SMITH, PRESTON, TENNESSEE.

Colonel One Hundred and Fifty-fourth Senior Tennessee Regiment Infantry, May —, 1861.

Brigadier-General, P. A. C. S., October 27, 1862.

Killed at Chickamauga, September 20, 1863.

COMMANDS.

Brigade composed of the Eleventh, Twelfth, Thirteenth, Twenty-ninth, Forty-seventh and One Hundred and Fifty-fourth Senior Tennessee regiments infantry, a battalion of sharpshooters, and Captain W. L. Scott's battery of light artillery, Cheatham's division, Polk's corps, Army of Tennessee.

SMITH, THOMAS BENTON, TENNESSEE.

Colonel Twentieth Tennessee Regiment Infantry, ——.

Brigadier-General, P. A. C. S. (temporary rank), July 29, 1864.

BRIG.-GEN. JOHN C. CARTER, OF TENNESSEE.
Killed at Battle of Franklin, Tenn., November 30, 1864.
[From a tintype taken in 1863.]

COMMANDS.

Brigade composed of the Second, Tenth and Twentieth Tennessee, the Thirty-seventh Georgia, the Fifteenth, Thirtieth and Thirty-seventh Tennessee (consolidated) regiments infantry and a Georgia battalion of sharpshooters, Army of Tennessee.

* SMITH, WILLIAM D., GEORGIA.

Captain, Corps of Cavalry, C. S. A., March 16, 1861.

Colonel Twentieth Regiment Georgia Infantry, July 14, 1861.

Brigadier-General, P. A. C. S., March 7, 1862.

Died at Charleston, S. C., October 4, 1862.

COMMANDS.

Commanding First Military District of South Carolina, in the Department of South Carolina, Georgia and Florida, July 8, 1862.

SORREL, G. M., GEORGIA.

Captain, A. A. G., Longstreet's brigade, September 1, 1861.

Major, A. A. G., Longstreet's division, July 24, 1862.

Lieutenant-Colonel, A. A. G., Longstreet's corps, June 23, 1863.

Brigadier-General, P. A. C. S., October 31, 1864.

COMMANDS.

Brigade composed of the Second, Twenty-second, Forty-eighth and Sixty-fourth regiments Georgia infantry and the Second and Tenth battalions Georgia infantry, Mahone's division, A. P. Hill's corps, Army of Northern Virginia.

BRIG.-GEN. J. J. PETTIGREW, OF NORTH CAROLINA.
Killed at Battle of "Falling Waters," Md., July 14, 1863.
[From a photograph taken in 1862.]

STAFFORD, LEROY A., LOUISIANA.

Colonel Ninth Regiment Louisiana Infantry, April 24, 1862.

Brigadier-General, P. A. C. S., October 8, 1863.

Died from wounds received at battle of the Wilderness, May 10, 1864.

COMMANDS.

Brigade composed of the First, Second. Ninth, Tenth and Fifteenth Louisiana regiments infantry and Coppen's Louisiana battalion, Jackson's division, Army of Northern Virginia.

STARKE, PETER B., MISSISSIPPI.

Colonel Twenty-eighth Regiment Mississippi Infantry, February 24, 1862.

Brigadier-General, P. A. C. S., November 4, 1864.

COMMANDS.

Commanding cavalry brigade in Chalmers' division, Forrest's cavalry corps.

STARKE, WILLIAM E., LOUISIANA.

Colonel Sixtieth Virginia Regiment Infantry, October 12, 1861.

Brigadier-General, P. A. C. S., August 6, 1862.

Killed at Sharpsburg, September 17, 1863.

BRIG.-GEN. JAMES H. LANE, OF NORTH CAROLINA.
[From a photograph taken in 1862.]

COMMANDS.

Brigade composed of the Second, Fifth, Ninth, Tenth, Fourteenth and Fifteenth Louisiana regiments infantry, Jackson's division, Army of Northern Virginia.

*STEELE, WILLIAM, TEXAS.

Colonel Seventh Texas Cavalry, October 29, 1861.

Brigadier-General, P. A. C. S., September 12, 1862.

COMMANDS.

Commanding district in Western Arkansas and Indian Territory, January —, 1863, and forces therein, consisting of Indian brigade and DeMorse's Twenty-ninth Texas Regiment of Infantry and Cabell's and Speight's command.

In December —, 1863, commanding at Galveston, Tex.

January —, 1864, commanding, at Shreveport, brigade composed of Twelfth Texas, Colonel Parsons; Nineteenth Texas, Colonel Watson; and the Twenty-first Texas, Colonel Carter.

Commanding division composed of his own and a Louisiana brigade.

STEEN, A. E., MISSOURI.

Colonel Tenth (also called Twelfth) Missouri Infantry.

Brigadier-General, P. A. C. S., April —, 1862.

COMMANDS.

Brigade composed of the battalions of Colonels Winston and Cearnal, and the companies of Rives and Bennett, and the light battery of Kennealy, constituting Third Brigade of the First Division, Army of the West.

*STEUART, GEORGE H., MARYLAND.

Captain, Corps of Cavalry, C. S. A., March 16, 1861.

Colonel, First Maryland Regiment Infantry, July 21, 1861.

Brigadier-General, P. A. C. S., March 6, 1862.

COMMANDS.

Commanding Maryland Line, ——.

Brigade composed of the Twenty-fifth, Forty-fourth and Fifty-eighth Virginia regiments infantry and First Maryland Regiment, Army of Northern Virginia.

STEVENS, C. H., SOUTH CAROLINA.

* * * * * * *

Colonel Twenty-fourth South Carolina Infantry, April 1, 1862.

Brigadier-General, P. A. C. S., January 20, 1864.

Killed at Atlanta, Ga., July 27, 1864.

COMMANDS.

Brigade composed of the First Georgia Confederate, the Twenty-fifth, Twenty-ninth, Thirtieth, and Sixty-sixth Georgia regiments infantry, and the First Battalion Georgia Sharpshooters, Army of Tennessee.

*STEVENS, WALTER H., VIRGINIA.

Major, Corps of Engineers, C. S. A., March 16, 1861.

Colonel, Corps of Engineers, C. S. A., ——, 1862.

Brigadier-General, P. A. C. S., August 28, 1864.

Died at Vera Cruz, Mexico, November 12, 1867.

COMMANDS.

In charge of defensive works around Richmond from autumn of 1862 to autumn of 1863.

Commanding troops and defenses of Richmond, ——, 1863, to August —, 1864.

Chief Engineer Army of Northern Virginia, August —, 1864, to end of the war.

ST. JOHN, ISAAC M., GEORGIA.

Captain, Corps of Engineers, C. S. A., February 15, 1862.

Major of artillery and Superintendent of Niter and Mining Corps, April 18, 1862.

Lieutenant-Colonel Niter and Mining Corps, May 28, 1863.

Brigadier-General and Commissary-General, February 16, 1865.

Died, April 7, 1880.

STOVALL, MARCELLUS A., GEORGIA.

Lieutenant-Colonel Third Georgia Battalion, October 8, 1861.

* * * * * * *

Brigadier-General, P. A. C. S., January 20, 1863.

COMMANDS.

Brigade composed of the Fortieth, Forty-first, Forty-second, Forty-third and Fifty-second regiments Georgia infantry, and First Regiment Georgia State Line, Stewart's division, Hood's corps, Army of Tennessee.

Former command composed of the First, Third and Fourth Florida, Sixth North Carolina and Forty-seventh Georgia regiments, Breckinridge's division.

STRAHL, O. F., TENNESSEE.

Captain, commanding company in Fourth Tennessee Regiment Infantry, May —, 1861.

Lieutenant-Colonel Fourth Tennessee Regiment Infantry, ——, 1862.

Colonel Fourth Tennessee Infantry, ——, 1863.

Brigadier-General, P. A. C. S., July 28, 1863.

Killed at battle of Franklin, Tenn., November 30, 1864.

COMMANDS.

Brigade composed of the Fourth, Fifth, Nineteenth, Twenty-fourth, Thirty-first and Thirty-third Tennessee regiments infantry, and Stanford's light battery of artillery, Cheatham's division, Polk's corps, Army of Tennessee.

TAPPAN, J. C., ARKANSAS.

Colonel Thirteenth Regiment Arkansas Infantry, May —, 1861.

Brigadier-General, P. A. C. S., November 5, 1862.

BRIG.-GEN. GABRIEL J. RAINES, OF NORTH CAROLINA.
Chief of Bureau of Conscription; afterward Chief of Torpedo and Shell Department.
[From a photograph taken in 1861.]

COMMANDS.

Brigade composed of the Arkansas infantry regiments of Colonels Thaler, Grinstead, Shaver and Dawson and Captain Etter's Arkansas battery of artillery, Churchill's division, Trans-Mississippi Department.

TAYLOR, THOMAS H., KENTUCKY.

Colonel First Kentucky Infantry, ——.

Brigadier-General, P. A. C. S., November 5, 1862.

COMMANDS.

April —, 1863, commanding Third Brigade, Stevenson's division, Army of Tennessee.

March 5, 1864, assigned command of District of Southern Mississippi and East Louisiana (Department of Alabama, Mississippi and East Louisiana), relieving Colonel Edward Dillon.

TERRILL, JAMES B., VIRGINIA.

* * * * * * *

Brigadier-General, P. A. C. S. (temporary rank), May 31, 1864.

Killed at the battle of the Wilderness, May 7, 1864.

COMMANDS.

Brigade composed of the Thirteenth, Thirty-first, Forty-ninth, Fifty-second and Fifty-eighth Virginia regiments infantry (Pegram's old brigade), Army of Northern Virginia.

BRIG.-GEN. M. A. STOVAL, OF GEORGIA.
[From a photograph taken in 1863.]

TERRY, WILLIAM, VIRGINIA.

Captain Fourth Regiment Virginia Infantry, ——, 1861.

Major Fourth Regiment Virginia Infantry, ——, 1862.

Colonel Fourth Regiment Virginia Infantry, September 11, 1863.

Brigadier-General, P. A. C. S., May 19, 1864.

Died, September 12, 1888.

COMMANDS.

Brigade composed of the Second, Fourth, Fifth, Tenth, Twenty-first, Twenty-third, Twenty-fifth, Twenty-seventh, Thirty-third, Thirty-seventh, Forty-second, Forty-fourth, Forty-eighth and Fiftieth regiments Virginia infantry, being parts of the brigades formerly commanded by Generals T. J. Jackson, D. R. Jones and Stuart, Army of Northern Virginia.

TERRY, WILLIAM R., VIRGINIA.

Second Lieutenant Fifty-first Virginia Regiment Infantry, ——, 1861.

Colonel Twenty-fourth Virginia Infantry, September 21, 1861.

Brigadier-General, P. A. C. S. (temporary rank), May 31, 1864.

COMMANDS.

Brigade composed of the First, Third, Seventh, Eleventh and Twenty-fourth regiments Virginia infantry, Army of Northern Virginia.

THOMAS, ALLEN, LOUISIANA.

Colonel Twenty-ninth Regiment Louisiana Infantry, May 3, 1862.

Brigadier-General, P. A. C. S., February 4, 1864.

COMMANDS.

Brigade composed of the Seventeenth, Twenty-sixth, Twenty-seventh, Twenty-eighth and Thirty-first Louisiana regiments infantry and Weatherby's battalion sharpshooters, Army of Northern Virginia.

THOMAS, B. M., ALABAMA.

* * * * * * *

Brigadier-General, P. A. C. S., August 4, 1864.

COMMANDS.

Assigned to command of a brigade composed of the First, Second and Third regiments Alabama reserves, afterward known as the Sixty-first, Sixty-second and Sixty-third Alabama regiments.

THOMAS, EDWARD L., GEORGIA.

Colonel Thirty-fifth Regiment Georgia Infantry, October 15, 1861.

Brigadier-General, P. A. C. S., November 1, 1862.

Brig.-Gen. Ben. G. Humphreys, of Mississippi.
[From a portrait made in 1863.]

Brig.-Gen. Daniel Leadbetter, of Alabama.

Brig.-Gen. George Maney, of Tennessee.
[From a photograph taken in 1862.]

Brig.-Gen. T. J. Moody, of Alabama.

Brig.-Gen. John McCausland, of Virginia.
[From a portrait made in 1864.]

Brig.-Gen. Samuel McGowan, of South Carolina.

Brig.-Gen. H. B. Lyon, of Kentucky.

Brig.-Gen. W. R. Scurry, of Texas.
Killed at Jenkins Ferry, Ark., April 30, 1864.
[From an old portrait.]

Brig.-Gen. P. D. Roddy, of Alabama.
[From an old photograph.]

COMMANDS.

Brigade composed of the Fourteenth, Thirty-fifth, Forty-fifth and Forty-ninth Georgia regiments infantry, the Third Louisiana Battalion Infantry and Captain Davidson's light battery, Pender's division, A. P. Hill's corps, Army of Northern Virginia.

THOMPSON, M. JEFF., MISSOURI.

Brigadier-General, Missouri State Guards, July 30, 1861.
Brigadier-General, P. A. C. S., ——, 186—.
Died in 1876.

COMMANDS.

Commanding First Military District of Missouri, State Guards.

* * * * * * *

Commanding Shelby's brigade, February 26—March 3, 1862.

BRIG.-GEN. JOHN DUNOVANT, OF SOUTH CAROLINA.
Killed at the Battle of Vaughan Road, Virginia, October 1, 1864.
[From a photograph taken in 1864.]

TILGHMAN, LLOYD, KENTUCKY.

Colonel Third Kentucky Infantry, July 19, 1861.
Brigadier-General, P. A. C. S., October 18, 1861.
Killed at the battle of Bakers Creek, Miss., May, 16, 1863.

COMMANDS.

October 23, 1861, assigned command of troops at Hopkinsville, Ky.
November 28, 1861, commanding Forts Donelson and Henry.
In 1862, commanding defenses of Tennessee and Cumberland Rivers. Also camps of rendezvous and instruction, etc., for exchanged prisoners.
Commanding First Division, First Corps, Army of Tennessee, October 29, 1862.
Commanding brigade under General Loring, April, 1863.

TOOMBS, ROBERT, GEORGIA.

Brigadier-General, P. A. C. S., July 19, 1861.
Resigned, March 4, 1863.
Died, December 15, 1885.

COMMANDS.

Brigade composed of the Second, Fifteenth, Seventeenth and Twentieth Georgia regiments infantry and First Regiment Georgia Regulars, Longstreet's corps, Army of Northern Virginia.

TOON, THOMAS F., NORTH CAROLINA.

Colonel Twenty-sixth Regiment North Carolina Infantry, February 26, 1863.
Brigadier-General, P. A. C. S. (temporary rank), May 3, 1864.

COMMANDS.

Brigade composed of the Fifth, Twelfth, Twentieth and Twenty-third North Carolina regiments infantry and Wilson's battalion, Army of Northern Virginia.

TRACEY, EDWARD D., ALABAMA.

Major Twelfth Regiment Alabama Infantry, July 17, 1861.
Lieutenant-Colonel Nineteenth Alabama Regiment Infantry, October 12, 1861.
Brigadier-General, P. A. C. S., August 16, 1862.
Killed near Port Gibson, Mississippi, May 1, 1863.

COMMANDS.

Brigade composed of the Twentieth, Twenty-third, Thirtieth, Thirty-first and Forty-sixth Alabama regiments infantry, Stevenson's division, Army of Tennessee.

TRAPIER, JAMES H., SOUTH CAROLINA.

Major Quartermaster's Department, June 19, 1861.
Brigadier-General, P. A. C. S., October 21, 1861.

COMMANDS.

Commanding at Georgetown, South Carolina, ——.
Commanding at Fort Moultrie and Sullivans Island, South Carolina, April 7, 1863.

TRUDEAU, J., LOUISIANA.

Never mustered into Confederate service; commanded Louisiana State troops.
In charge of water batteries at Columbus, Ky.

TUCKER, W. F., MISSISSIPPI.

Captain Company H, Eleventh Mississippi Regiment, May 13, 1861.
Colonel Forty-first Mississippi Regiment Infantry, May 8, 1862.
Brigadier-General, P. A. C. S., March 1, 1864.
Killed by an assassin at Okolona, Miss., September 15, 1881.

COMMANDS.

Brigade composed of the Seventh, Ninth, Tenth, Forty-first and Forty-fourth regiments Mississippi infantry and Ninth Mississippi Battalion Sharpshooters, Hindman's division, Hood's corps, Army of Tennessee.

TYLER, R. C., TENNESSEE.

Captain (assistant quartermaster), April —, 1861.
Major (assistant quartermaster), ——, 1861.
Colonel Fifteenth Regiment Tennessee Infantry, ——, 1863.
Brigadier-General, P. A. C. S., February 23, 1864.
Killed at Fort Tyler, near West Point, Ga., April 16, 1865.

COMMANDS.

Brigade composed of the Thirty-seventh Georgia, the Tenth, Fifteenth, Twentieth, Thirtieth and Thirty-seventh Tennessee regiments infantry and Fourth Battalion Georgia Sharpshooters.
Commanding military post, West Point, Ga.

VANCE, ROBERT B., NORTH CAROLINA.

Colonel Twenty-ninth North Carolina Infantry, ——, 1861.
Brigadier-General, P. A. C. S., March 4, 1863.

COMMANDS.

Commanding Second Brigade, McCown's division, Polk's corps, Army of Tennessee, composed of the Twenty-ninth and Thirty-ninth regiments of North Carolina infantry, the Third and Ninth battalions Georgia infantry and McDuffie's battery of light artillery, January to May, 1863.

VAUGHAN, A. J., TENNESSEE.

Lieutenant-Colonel Thirteenth Regiment Tennessee Infantry, June 7, 1861.
Colonel Thirteenth Regiment Tennessee Infantry, ——, 1862.
Brigadier-General, P. A. C. S., November 18, 1863.

COMMANDS.

Brigade (formerly Preston Smith's) composed of the Eleventh, Twelfth, Thirteenth, Twenty-ninth, Forty-seventh and One Hundred and Fifty-fourth Senior Tennessee regiments infantry, a battalion of sharpshooters and Captain W. L. Scott's battery of light artillery, Cheatham's division, Polk's corps, Army of Tennessee.

VAUGHN, JOHN C., TENNESSEE.

Colonel Third Tennessee Regiment Infantry, May 3, 1861.
Brigadier-General, P. A. C. S., September 29, 1862.
Died, September 10, 1875.

COMMANDS.

Commanding Second Brigade, M. L. Smith's division, Department of Mississippi and East Louisiana; brigade composed of seven regiments and two battalions (all mounted) from East Tennessee and one battalion Georgia cavalry.

* VILLEPIGUE, J. B., SOUTH CAROLINA.

Colonel Thirty-sixth Regiment Georgia Infantry, October 21, 1861.
Brigadier-General, P. A. C. S., March 13, 1862.
Died, November 9, 1862.

COMMANDS.

Commanding Second Brigade, First Division, Army of the District of Mississippi.
Commanding Subdistrict in Mississippi.

WADE, WM. B., MISSISSIPPI.

Colonel Eighth Confederate Cavalry, ——.
Brigadier-General, P. A. C. S., ——.

COMMANDS.

Commanding First Cavalry Brigade, First Division, Forrest's cavalry command.

* WALKER, HENRY H., VIRGINIA.

Captain, Corps of Infantry, C. S. A., March 16, 1861.

* * * * * * *

Brigadier-General, P. A. C. S., July 1, 1863.

COMMANDS.

Brigade composed of the Fortieth, Forty-seventh and Fifty-fifth regiments Virginia infantry and Twenty-second Virginia Battalion.
Commanding Archer's brigade, Army of Northern Virginia, ——.

WALKER, JAMES A., VIRGINIA.

* * * * * * *

Brigadier-General, P. A. C. S., January 15, 1863.

COMMANDS.

Brigade composed of the Thirteenth, Twenty-fifth, Thirty-first, Forty-fourth, Fifty-second and Fifty-eighth regiments Virginia infantry, and the Twelfth Georgia Regiment Infantry, Army of Northern Virginia.
Commanding the "Stonewall Brigade,"——.
Commanding Pegram's division, ——, 1865.

* WALKER, L. M., TENNESSEE.

Colonel Fortieth Tennessee Regiment Infantry, November 11, 1861.
Brigadier-General, P. A. C. S., March 11, 1862.
Killed in duel in 1863.

COMMANDS.

Commanding brigade of cavalry in Army of the West, ——.

WALKER, LEROY POPE, ALABAMA.

Brigadier-General, P. A. C. S., September 17, 1861.
Resigned, March 31, 1862.
Secretary of War, from February 21 to September —, 1861.

WALKER, R. LINDSAY, VIRGINIA.

Captain, Nelson's battery Virginia artillery, ——.
Colonel ——, March 14, 1863.
Brigadier-General, P. A. C. S., February 18, 1865.
Died, June 7, 1890.

COMMANDS.

Commanding artillery of General A. P. Hill's corps, of Northern Virginia.

* WALKER, W. S., FLORIDA.

Captain, Corps of Infantry, C. S. A., March 16, 1861.

* * * * * * *

Brigadier-General, P. A. C. S., October 30, 1862.

COMMANDS.

Commanding Third Military District of South Carolina, ——.

* * * * * * *

Brigade composed of the Seventeenth, Eighteenth, Twenty-second and Twenty-sixth South Carolina regiments infantry and Holcombe's Legion.

BRIG.-GEN. ISHAM W. GARROTT, OF ALABAMA.
Killed at Vicksburg, Miss., June 17, 1863.
[From a photograph taken in 1863.]

WALLACE, W. H., SOUTH CAROLINA.

Lieutenant-Colonel Eighteenth Regiment South Carolina Infantry, May 5, 1862.
Colonel Eighteenth Regiment South Carolina Infantry, August 30, 1862.
Brigadier-General, P. A. C. S., September 20, 1864.

COMMANDS.

Brigade composed of the Seventeenth, Eighteenth, Twenty-second, Twenty-third and Twenty-sixth regiments of South Carolina Volunteer Infantry, and the Holcombe Legion, Army of Northern Virginia.

WATERHOUSE, R., TEXAS.

Colonel Nineteenth Texas Regiment Infantry, May 13, 1862.
Brigadier-General, P. A. C. S., March 17, 1865.

COMMANDS.

Brigade composed of the Third, Sixteenth, Seventeenth and Nineteenth regiments Texas infantry and the Sixteenth Regiment Texas Cavalry, dismounted.

WAITIE, STAND, INDIAN TERRITORY.

Colonel First Cherokee Regiment Infantry, October —, 1861.

Brigadier-General, P. A. C. S., May 10, 1864.

Died, August ——, 1876.

COMMANDS.

Chief of the Cherokee Nation from October —, 1862, to September —, 1865.

Brigade composed of the First and Second Cherokee regiments of infantry, the First and Second Creek regiments of infantry, a Cherokee battalion of infantry, a Seminole battalion of infantry and a battalion of Osage Indians, recruited from different States.

WAUL, T. N., TEXAS.

Colonel Waul's Texas Legion, May 17, 1862.

Brigadier-General, P. A. C. S., September 18, 1863.

*WAYNE, HENRY C., GEORGIA.

Adjutant and Inspector-General of State of Georgia, with rank of colonel, November 12, 1860.

Adjutant and Inspector-General of State of Georgia, with rank of major-general, November 30, 1861.

Brigadier-General, P. A. C. S., December 16, 1861. Declined the appointment.

WEISIGER, D. A., VIRGINIA.

Colonel Twelfth Regiment Virginia Infantry, July 1, 1861.

Brigadier-General, P. A. C. S. (temporary rank), May 31, 1864.

Brigadier-General, P. A. C. S., July 30, 1864.

COMMANDS.

Brigade composed of the Sixth, Twelfth, Sixteenth, Forty-first and Sixty-first regiments Virginia infantry (formerly Mahone's brigade), Army of Northern Virginia.

WHARTON, G. C., VIRGINIA.

Major Forty-fifth Regiment Virginia Infantry, June 17, 1861.

Colonel Fifty-first Regiment Virginia Infantry, July 17, 1861.

Brigadier-General, P. A. C. S., July 8, 1863.

COMMANDS.

Brigade composed of the Fiftieth, Fifty-first and Sixty-third regiments Virginia infantry and Thirtieth Virginia Battalion, Army of Northern Virginia.

WHITFIELD, JOHN W., TEXAS.

Colonel Twenty-seventh Regiment Texas Cavalry, ——.

Brigadier-General, P. A. C. S., May 9, 1863.

COMMANDS.

Brigade composed of Whitfield's Texas legion and the Third, Sixth and Ninth Texas cavalry.

BRIG.-GEN. PAUL O. HEBERT, OF LOUISIANA.
[From a photograph taken in 1861.]

WICKHAM, WILLIAM C., VIRGINIA.

Captain Hanover Dragoons, Fourth Virginia Cavalry, May —, 1861.

Lieutenant-Colonel Fourth Virginia Cavalry, September —, 1861.

Colonel Fourth Virginia Cavalry, June 9, 1862.

Brigadier-General, P. A. C. S., September 1, 1863.

Resigned, November 9, 1864.

Died, July 23, 1888.

COMMANDS.

Brigade composed of the First, Second, Third and Fourth regiments Virginia cavalry, Major-General Fitzhugh Lee's division, Army of Northern Virginia.

WIGFALL, LOUIS T., TEXAS.

Colonel Second Regiment Texas Infantry, August 28, 1861.

Brigadier-General, P. A. C. S., October 21, 1861.

Resigned, February 20, 1862.

Died, February 18, 1874.

COMMANDS.

Brigade composed of the First, Fourth and Fifth Texas and First Georgia regiments infantry, Army of the Potomac.

WILLIAMS, JOHN S., KENTUCKY.

Colonel Fifth Kentucky Regiment Infantry, November 16, 1861.

Brigadier-General, P. A. C. S., April 16, 1862.

COMMANDS.

Brigade composed of the Twenty-second, Thirty-sixth and Forty-fifth regiments Virginia infantry, the Eighth Regiment Virginia Cavalry, Bailey's and Edgar's battalions, and the light batteries of artillery of Captains Otey and Lowry.

Brigade subsequently composed of the First, Second and Ninth Kentucky regiments cavalry, the Second Kentucky Battalion, Allison's squadron, and Hamilton's battalion.

WILSON, CLAUDIUS C., GEORGIA.

Colonel Twenty-fifth Regiment Georgia Infantry, September 2, 1861.

Brigadier-General, P. A. C. S., November 16, 1863.

Died, November 24, 1863.

COMMANDS.

Brigade composed of the Thirteenth, Twenty-fifth, Twenty-ninth and Thirtieth regiments Georgia infantry, the First Battalion Georgia Sharpshooters, and the Fourth Louisiana Battalion, Army of Tennessee.

WILLIS, EDWARD, GEORGIA.

Colonel Twelfth Regiment Georgia Infantry, January 22, 1863.

Brigadier-General, P. A. C. S.,——.

* * * * * *

Killed, ——, before his commission reached him.

*WINDER, CHARLES S., MARYLAND.

Major, Corps of Artillery, C. S. A., March 16, 1861.

Colonel Sixth Regiment South Carolina Infantry, July 8, 1861.

Brigadier-General, P. A. C. S., March 1, 1862.

Killed at the battle of Cedar Run, August 9, 1862.

COMMANDS.

Brigade composed of the Second, Fourth, Fifth, Twenty-seventh and Thirty-third Virginia regiments infantry, Jackson's division, Army of Northern Virginia.

*WINDER, JOHN H., MARYLAND.

Colonel, Corps of Infantry, C. S. A., March 16, 1861.

Brigadier-General, P. A. C. S., June 21, 1861.

Died at Florence, South Carolina, February 7, 1865.

COMMANDS.

Commanding prison camps.

WISE, HENRY A., VIRGINIA.

Brigadier-General, P. A. C. S., June 5, 1861.

Died at Richmond, Virginia, September 10, 1876.

COMMANDS.

Brigade composed of the Twenty-sixth, Thirty-fourth, Forty-sixth and Fifty-ninth regiments Virginia infantry, and the light batteries of artillery of Captains McComas and Armistead, Army of Northern Virginia.

WOOD, S. A. M., ALABAMA.

Colonel Seventh Alabama Infantry, ——.

Brigadier-General, P. A. C. S., January 7, 1862.

Resigned, October 17, 1863.

COMMANDS.

Brigade composed of the Seventh Alabama, the Fifth, Seventh and Eighth Arkansas and Forty-fourth Tennessee regiments infantry, the infantry battalions of Majors Hardcastle and Kelley, and a Mississippi battery of light artillery.

At the battle of Chickamauga, September 19-20, 1863, brigade composed of the Thirty-second and Forty-fifth Mississippi, the Sixteenth, Thirty-third and Forty-fifth Alabama regiments infantry, Major Hawkins' infantry battalion and Semple's battery of light artillery.

WOFFORD, W. T., GEORGIA.

Colonel Eighteenth Georgia Infantry, ——, 1862.

Brigadier-General, P. A. C. S., January 17, 1863.

COMMANDS.

Brigade composed of the Sixteenth, Eighteenth and Twenty-fourth Georgia regiments, Cobb's Georgia Legion, Phillips' Georgia Legion and the Third Battalion Georgia Sharpshooters, McLaws' division, Longstreet's corps, Army of Northern Virginia.

WRIGHT, G. J., GEORGIA.

Acting Brigadier-General in command of P. M. B. Young's brigade.

WRIGHT, M. H., GEORGIA.

Acting Brigadier-General; at one time on ordnance duty at Atlanta, Ga.

WRIGHT, MARCUS J., TENNESSEE.

Lieutenant-Colonel One Hundred and Fifty-fourth Senior Tennessee Regiment Infantry, Provisional Army of Tennessee, April 4, 1861.

Lieutenant-Colonel, A. A. G., June 10 to September —, 1862.

Brigadier-General, P. A. C. S., December 13, 1862.

BRIG.-GEN. BRADLEY T. JOHNSON, OF MARYLAND.

COMMANDS

April 29, 1861, commanding battalion One Hundred and Fifty-fourth Senior Tennessee Regiment and Steuben artillery and defenses at Fort Wright (Randolph, Tenn., Mississippi River), April — to May —, 1861.

Military Governor of Columbus, Ky., from February 3 to March —, 1862.

Commanding conscript camp at McMinnville, Tenn., September — to December 6, 1863.

Assigned to command of Hanson's Kentucky brigade, January 10, 1863, which he relinquished February 1st to assume command of Donelson's Tennessee brigade, to which he was assigned.

Commanding Post and District of Atlanta, Ga., ——, 1863-4.

Commanding Post, Macon, Ga., ——, 1864.

Brigade composed of the Eighth, Sixteenth, Twenty-eighth, Thirty-eighth, Fifty-first and Fifty-second regiments Tennessee infantry, Murray's Tennessee battalion of infantry and Captain W. W. Carne's Tennessee battery of artillery, Cheatham's division, Polk's corps, Army of Tennessee.

Commanding District of North Mississippi and West Tennessee, from February 3, 1865, until the end of the war.

YORK, ZEBULON, LOUISIANA.

Colonel Thirteenth Regiment Louisiana Infantry, August 15, 1862.

Brigadier-General, P. A. C. S. (temporary rank), May 31, 1864.

COMMANDS.

Brigade composed of the First, Second, Third, Fifth, Sixth, Seventh, Eighth, Ninth, Tenth, Fourteenth and Fifteenth regiments Louisiana infantry.

YOUNG, W. H., TEXAS.

Colonel Ninth Regiment Texas Infantry, ——, 1862.

Brigadier-General, P. A. C. S., August 15, 1864.

COMMANDS.

Brigade composed of the Ninth Regiment Texas Infantry, the Tenth, Fourteenth and Thirty-second Texas dismounted cavalry and the Twenty-ninth and Thirty-ninth North Carolina regiments of infantry, Army of Tennessee.

ZOLLICOFFER, FELIX K., TENNESSEE.

Major-General, Provisional Army of Tennessee, May 9, 1861.

Brigadier-General, P. A. C. S., July 9, 1861.

Killed at battle of Mill Spring or Fishing Creek, Kentucky, January 19, 1862.

COMMANDS.

Commanding Camp of Instruction at Camp Trousdale, Tennessee, June —, 1861.

Commanding District of East Tennessee, July 26 to October 8, 1861.

CASUALTIES IN THE CONFEDERATE SERVICE.

THE following tables only give a few of the many instances of heavy percentages of loss. They represent only the few cases in which the official reports happen to mention the number of men taken into action, and which, again, happened to appear before the order was issued, forbidding any further mention in official reports of the number of men in action, etc.

There are no muster-out rolls of the Confederate regiments. There are partial sets of muster rolls and monthly returns in the War Records Office, Washington, D. C., but they are defective and incomplete. There is no way of determining accurately the mortality loss of each regiment during the entire service.

The following order, the one referred to above, was issued by General Lee, which has an important bearing on the subject of casualties in Confederate regiments:

HEADQUARTERS, ARMY OF NORTHERN VIRGINIA,
May 14, 1863.

[General Orders, No. 63.]

The practice which prevails in the army of including in the list of casualties those cases of slight injuries which do not incapacitate the recipients for duty, is calculated to mislead our friends, and encourage our enemies, by giving false impressions as to the extent of our losses. The loss sustained by a brigade or regiment is by no means an indication of the service performed or perils encountered, as experience shows that those who attack most rapidly, vigorously and effectually generally suffer the least. It is, therefore, ordered that in future the reports of the wounded shall only include those whose injuries, in the opinion of the medical officers, render them unfit for duty. It has also been observed that the published reports of casualties are in some instances accompanied by the number of men taken into action. The commanding general deems it unnecessary to do more than direct the attention of the officers to the impropriety of thus furnishing the enemy with the means of computing our strength, in order to insure immediate suppression of the pernicious and useless custom.

W. H. TAYLOR, *Assistant Adjutant-General.*

BY COMMAND OF GENERAL LEE.

It is evident that all subsequent casualty lists are of little value for statistical purposes, if the above order was observed, and, if enforced, that many a gallant regiment has been deprived of the laurels to which its heroic record would entitle it.

GREATEST PERCENTAGES OF LOSS IN CONFEDERATE REGIMENTS AT PARTICULAR ENGAGEMENTS.

From a Compilation (from Official Reports) of "Regimental Losses in the Civil War," by Colonel William F. Fox, Albany, N. Y.

BATTLE.	REGIMENT.	DIVISION.	Present.	Killed.*	Wounded.	Missing.	Total Loss.	Per Cent.
Antietam	First Texas	Hood's	226	45	141	..	186	82.3
Manassas	Twenty-first Georgia	Ewell's	242	38	146	..	184	76.0
Gettysburg	Twenty-sixth North Carolina	Heth's	820	86	502	†	588	71.7
Shiloh	Sixth Mississippi	Hardee's	425	61	239	..	300	70.5
Stones River	Eighth Tennessee	Cheatham's	444	41	265	..	306	68.2
Chickamauga	Tenth Tennessee	Johnson's	328	44	180	..	224	68.0
Glendale	Palmetto Sharpshooters	Longstreet's	375	39	215	..	254	67.7
Manassas	Seventeenth South Carolina	Evans'	284	25	164	1	190	66.9
Manassas	Twenty-third South Carolina	Evans'	225	27	122	..	149	66.2
Mechanicsville	Forty-fourth Georgia	D. H. Hill's	514	71	264	..	335	65.1
Chickamauga	First Alabama Battalion	Preston's	260	24	144	..	168	64.6
Gettysburg	Second North Carolina Battalion	Rodes'	240	‡29	124	..	153	63.7
Antietam	Sixteenth Mississippi	Anderson's	228	27	117	..	144	63.1
Antietam	Twenty-seventh North Carolina	Walker's	325	31	168	..	199	61.2
Chickamauga	Fifth Georgia	Cheatham's	317	27	165	2	194	61.1
Chickamauga	Second Tennessee	Cleburne's	264	13	145	1	159	60.2
Chickamauga	Fifteenth and Thirty-seventh Tenn.	Stewart's	202	15	102	4	121	59.9
Seven Pines	Sixth Alabama	D. H. Hill's	632	91	277	5	373	59.0
Chickamauga	Sixteenth Alabama	Cleburne's	414	25	218	..	243	58.6
Antietam	Fifteenth Virginia	McLaws'	128	11	64	..	75	58.5
Chickamauga	Sixth and Ninth Tennessee	Cheatham's	335	26	168	..	194	57.9
Antietam	Eighteenth Georgia	Hood's	176	13	72	16	101	57.3
Gaines Mill	First South Carolina Rifles	A. P. Hill's	537	81	225	..	306	56.9
Antietam	Tenth Georgia	McLaws'	148	15	69	..	84	56.7
Seven Days	Eighteenth North Carolina	A. P. Hill's	396	45	179	..	224	56.5
Malvern Hill	Third Alabama	D. H. Hill's	354	37	163	..	200	56.4
Chickamauga	Eighteenth Alabama	Stewart's	527	41	256	..	297	56.3
Antietam	Seventeenth Virginia	Pickett's	55	7	24	..	31	56.3
Seven Days	Seventh North Carolina	A. P. Hill's	450	35	218	..	253	56.2
Stones River	Twelfth Tennessee	Cheatham's	292	18	137	9	164	56.1
Chickamauga	Twenty-second Alabama	Hindman's	371	44	161	..	205	55.2
Gettysburg	Ninth Georgia	Hood's	340	27	162	..	189	55.0
Stones River	Sixteenth Tennessee	Cheatham's	377	36	155	16	207	54.9
Seven Pines	Fourth North Carolina	D. H. Hill's	678	77	286	6	369	54.4
Shiloh	Twenty-seventh Tennessee	Hardee's	350	27	115	48	190	54.2
Chickamauga	Twenty-third Tennessee	Buckner's	181	8	77	13	98	54.1
Manassas	Twelfth South Carolina	A. P. Hill's	270	23	121	2	146	54.0
Manassas	Fourth Virginia	Jackson's	180	18	79	..	97	53.8
Antietam	Fourth Texas	Hood's	200	10	97	..	107	53.5
Chaplin Hills	Twenty-seventh Tennessee	Cleburne's	210	16	84	12	112	53.3
Manassas §	First South Carolina	A. P. Hill's	283	25	126	..	151	53.3
Fair Oaks	Forty-ninth Virginia	D. H. Hill's	424	32	170	22	224	52.8
Chickamauga	Twenty-ninth Mississippi	Liddell's	368	38	156	..	194	52.7
Fair Oaks	Twelfth Alabama	D. H. Hill's	408	59	156	..	215	52.6
Antietam	Seventh South Carolina	McLaws'	268	23	117	..	140	52.2
Chickamauga	Fifty-eighth Alabama	Stewart's	288	25	124	..	149	51.7
Raymond	Seventh Texas	John Gregg's	306	22	136	..	158	51.6
Fair Oaks	Sixth South Carolina	D. H. Hill's	521	88	181	..	269	51.6
Gettysburg	Fifteenth Georgia	Hood's	335	19	152	..	171	51.0
Glendale	Eleventh Alabama	Longstreet's	357	49	121	11	181	50.7
Manassas	Seventeenth Georgia	Hood's	200	10	91	..	101	50.5
Chickamauga	Thirty-seventh Georgia	Stewart's	391	19	168	7	194	50.1
Gettysburg	Third North Carolina	Johnson's	312	29	127	‖	156	50.0
Chickamauga	Sixty-third Tennessee	Preston's	402	16	184	..	200	49.7
Chickamauga	Forty-first Alabama	Breckinridge's	325	27	120	11	158	48.6
Chancellorsville	Fourth Virginia	Trimble's	355	14	155	3	172	48.4
Chickamauga	Thirty-second Tennessee	Stewart's	341	9	156	..	165	48.3
Chickamauga	Twentieth Tennessee	Stewart's	183	8	80	..	88	48.0
Gettysburg	First Maryland	Johnson's	400	52	¶140	..	192	48.0
Stones River	Eighth Mississippi	Breckinridge's	282	20	113	..	133	47.1
Malvern Hill	Forty-fourth Georgia	D. H. Hill's	142	9	40	16	65	45.7
Antietam	Thirty-second Virginia	McLaws'	158	15	57	..	72	45.5
Chickamauga	First Arkansas	Cleburne's	430	13	180	1	194	45.1
Antietam	Eighteenth Mississippi	McLaws'	186	10	73	..	83	44.6
Chickamauga	Ninth Kentucky	Breckinridge's	230	11	89	2	102	44.3
Gaines Mill	Fourteenth South Carolina	A. P. Hill's	500	18	197	..	215	43.0
Chancellorsville	Thirty-third North Carolina	A. P. Hill's	480	32	167	..	199	41.4
Malvern Hill	Fifth Alabama	D. H. Hill's	225	26	66	..	92	40.8
Fair Oaks	Hampton Legion	Hood's	350	21	120	..	141	40.2
Malvern Hill	Twenty-sixth Alabama	D. H. Hill's	218	10	76	..	86	40.0

*Including the mortally wounded.

† In addition to the five hundred and eighty-eight killed and wounded, this regiment lost one hundred and twenty missing, many of whom were killed.

‡ General Ewell, in his official report, states that the Second North Carolina Battalion lost two hundred killed and wounded out of two hundred and forty present.

§ Including Ox Hill (Chantilly).

‖ There were fifty-one missing, also, who are not included, most of whom were killed or wounded.

¶ From inscription on monument at Gettysburg; but Surgeon-General Guild (C. S. A.) reported their loss, officially, at the time as sixty-five killed and one hundred and nineteen wounded.

BRIGADE LOSSES IN PARTICULAR ENGAGEMENTS.

BATTLE.	BRIGADE.	DIVISION.	Present.	Killed.	Wounded.	Missing.	Total Loss.	Per Cent.
Gettysburg	Garnett's (Va.)	Pickett's	1,427	78	324	*539	941	65.9
Gettysburg	Perry's (Fla.)	Anderson's	700	33	217	205	455	65.0
Antietam	Wofford's (Texas)	Hood's	854	69	417	62	548	64.1
†Seven Days	Anderson's (S. C.)	Longstreet's	1,250	136	638	13	787	62.9
†Seven Days	Pryor's	Longstreet's	1,400	170	681	11	862	61.5
Franklin	Cockrell's (Mo.)	French's	696	98	229	92	419	60.2
†Seven Days	Wilcox's (Ala.)	Longstreet's	1,850	229	806	20	1,055	57.0
Chickamauga	Benning's (Ga.)	Hood's	900	88	412	10	510	56.6
Chickamauga	Bate's	Stewart's	1,187	66	541	...	607	51.1
Chancellorsville	Ramseur's (N. C.)	D. H. Hill's	1,509	154	526	108	788	52.2
†Seven Days	Featherston's (Miss.)	Longstreet's	1,350	115	542	9	666	49.3
Gettysburg	Lane's (N. C.)	Pender's	1,355	41	348	271	660	48.7
Stones River	Donelson's (Tenn.)	Cheatham's	‡1,529	108	575	17	700	45.7
Chickamauga	Gregg's	B. R. Johnson's	1,352	109	474	18	601	44.4
Chickamauga	Clayton's (Ala.)	Stewart's	1,446	86	535	13	634	44.4
Antietam	Semmes'	McLaws'	709	53	255	6	314	44.2
Gettysburg	Daniel's (N. C.)	Rodes'	2,100	165	635	116	916	43.6
Malvern Hill	Rodes' (Ala.)	D. H. Hill's	1,027	81	344	...	425	41.3

* The official report for Garnett's brigade says: "It is feared from the information received that the majority of those reported missing are either killed or wounded."

† This loss occurred in the two actions at Gaines Mills and Glendale.

‡ General Donelson stated the number in his official report, "about fourteen hundred men."

CONFEDERATE REGIMENTS WHICH SUSTAINED THE GREATEST LOSS IN PARTICULAR BATTLES.

From a Compilation of "Regimental Losses in the Civil War," by Colonel Wm. F. Fox, Albany, N. Y.

[In the following table is only given the leading regiments, in point of loss, in various battles. The list is incomplete, as there are very few Confederate official reports for the latter part of the war.]

REGIMENT.	BRIGADE.	DIVISION.	Killed.	Wounded.*	Missing.	Total.
FIRST BULL RUN, VA.—July 21, 1862.						
Eighth Georgia	Bartow's	Johnston's	41	159	...	200
Fourth Alabama	Bee's	Johnston's	40	157	...	197
Seventh Georgia	Bartow's	Johnston's	19	134	...	153
Thirty-third Virginia	Jackson's	Johnston's	45	101	...	146
Twenty-seventh Virginia	Jackson's	Johnston's	19	122	...	141
Fourth Virginia	Jackson's	Johnston's	31	100	...	131
Hampton Legion	....	Beauregard's	19	100	2	121
WILSONS CREEK, MO.—August 10, 1861.						
Third Arkansas	....	Pearce's	25	84	1	110
Third Missouri State Guards	Graves'	Rains'	22	49	3	74
BALLS BLUFF, VA.—October 21, 1861.						
Eighteenth Mississippi	Evans'	....	22	63	...	85
BELMONT, MO.—November 7, 1861.						
Thirteenth Tennessee	....	Pillow's	27	73	49	149
CAMP ALLEGHANY, VA.—December 13, 1861.						
Twelfth Georgia	E. Johnson's	....	6	37	4	47
DRANESVILLE, VA.—December 20, 1861.						
Tenth Alabama	Stuart's	....	15	45	6	66
Sixth South Carolina	Stuart's	....	18	45	...	63
MILL SPRINGS, KY.—January 1, 1862,						
Fifteenth Mississippi	Zollicoffer's	Crittenden's	44	153	29	226
Twentieth Tennessee	Zollicoffer's	Crittenden's	33	59	18	110
Twenty-fifth Tennessee	Zollicoffer's	Crittenden's	10	28	17	55
FORT DONELSON, TENN.—February 15, 1862.						
Eighth Kentucky	Simonton's	Pillow's	27	72	...	99
Twenty-sixth Tennessee	Baldwin's	Buckner's	11	85	...	96
Third Tennessee	Brown's	Buckner's	12	76	...	88
Twenty-sixth Mississippi	Baldwin's	Buckner's	12	69	...	81
NEW BERNE, N. C.—March 14, 1862.						
Thirty-third North Carolina	Branch's	....	32	28	144	204
Twenty-sixth North Carolina	Branch's	....	5	10	72	87
KERNSTOWN, VA.—March 23, 1862.						
Thirty-seventh Virginia	Fulkerson's	Jackson's	12	*62	39	113
Forty-second Virginia	Burke's	Jackson's	11	50	9	70
Thirty-third Virginia	Garnett's	Jackson's	18	27	14	59
Fifth Virginia	Garnett's	Jackson's	9	48	4	61
SHILOH, TENN.—April 6 and 7, 1862.						
Fourth Tennessee	Stewart's	Clark's	36	*183	...	219
Fourth Kentucky	Trabue's	Breckinridge's	30	183	...	213
Fourth Louisiana	Gibson's	Ruggles'	24	163	22	209
One Hundred and Fifty-fourth Tennessee	B. R. Johnson's	Cheatham's	25	163	11	199
Twenty-seventh Tennessee	Wood's	Hardee's	27	105	48	180
Thirty-third Tennessee	Stewart's	Clark's	20	103	17	140
Ninth Arkansas	Bowen's	Breckinridge's	17	115	...	132
Crescent Regiment (Louisiana)	Pond's	Ruggles'	23	84	20	127
Eighteenth Alabama	J. K. Jackson's	Withers'	20	80	20	120
Thirteenth Arkansas	Stewart's	Clark's	25	72	3	100
WILLIAMSBURG, VA.—May 5, 1862.						
Twenty-fourth Virginia	Early's	D. H. Hill's	30	93	66	189
Eleventh Virginia	A. P. Hill's	Longstreet's	26	105	3	134
Nineteenth Mississippi	Wilcox's	Longstreet's	15	85	...	100
Seventh Virginia	A. P. Hill's	Longstreet's	13	64	...	77
Ninth Alabama	Wilcox's	Longstreet's	10	45	6	61
MCDOWELL, VA.—May 8, 1862.						
Twelfth Georgia	....	E. Johnson's	35	140	...	175
Twenty-fifth Virginia	....	E. Johnson's	7	65	...	72
Fifty-eighth Virginia	....	E. Johnson's	11	39	...	50
FRONT ROYAL, VA.—May 23-25, 1862.						
Twenty-first North Carolina	Trimble's	Ewell's	21	59	...	80
Sixth Louisiana	Taylor's	Ewell's	5	42	3	50
FAIR OAKS, VA.—May 31—June 1, 1862.						
Sixth Alabama	Rodes'	D. H. Hill's	91	*277	5	373
Fourth North Carolina	G. B. Anderson's	D. H. Hill's	77	286	6	369
Sixth South Carolina	Jenkins'	D. H. Hill's	88	164	17	269
Forty-ninth Virginia	G. B. Anderson's	D. H. Hill's	32	170	22	224
Twelfth Alabama	Rodes'	D. H. Hill's	59	149	...	208
Fifth Alabama	Rodes'	D. H. Hill's	29	181	...	210
Second Florida	Garland's	D. H. Hill's	37	152	9	198
Twelfth Mississippi	Rodes'	D. H. Hill's	41	152	...	193
Twenty-third North Carolina	Garland's	D. H. Hill's	18	145	6	169
Twenty-seventh Georgia	G. B. Anderson's	D. H. Hill's	16	129	9	154
Thirty-eighth Virginia	Garland's	D. H. Hill's	16	117	14	147
Hampton Legion	Whiting's	Smith's	21	120		141
Twenty-eighth Georgia	G. B. Anderson's	D. H. Hill's	24	95	...	119
Twenty-fourth Virginia	Garland's	D. H. Hill's	12	86	9	107
HARRISONBURG, VA.—June 6, 1862.						
Fifty-eighth Virginia	Stewart's	Ewell's	11	39	3	53
CROSS KEYS, VA.—June 8, 1862.						
Fifteenth Alabama	Trimble's	Ewell's	9	37	5	51
Sixteenth Mississippi	Trimble's	Ewell's	6	28	...	34

* Includes the mortally wounded.

CONFEDERATE REGIMENTS WHICH SUSTAINED THE GREATEST LOSS IN PARTICULAR BATTLES.—Continued.

Regiment.	Brigade.	Division.	Killed	Wounded*	Missing	Total
PORT REPUBLIC, VA.—June 9, 1862.						
Seventh Louisiana	Taylor's	Ewell's	8	115	...	123
Fifth Virginia	Winder's	Jackson's	4	89	20	113
Thirty-first Virginia	Elzey's	Ewell's	15	79	4	98
Fifty-second Virginia	Stewart's	Ewell's	12	65	...	77
Sixth Louisiana	Taylor's	Ewell's	11	55	...	66
Forty-fourth Virginia	Stewart's	Ewell's	14	35	...	49
SECESSIONVILLE, S. C.—June 16, 1862.						
First South Carolina Artillery	Evans'		15	39	1	55
First South Carolina Battalion †	Evans'		10	30	2	42
OAK GROVE, VA.—June 25, 1862.						
First Louisiana	Wright's	Huger's	22	109	4	135
Twenty-second Georgia	Wright's	Huger's	10	77	2	89
Forty-eighth North Carolina	Ransom's	Holmes'	18	70	...	88
MECHANICSVILLE, VA.—June 26, 1862.						
Forty-fourth Georgia	Ripley's	D. H. Hill's	71	264	...	335
First North Carolina	Ripley's	D. H. Hill's	36	105	1	142
GAINES MILL, VA.—June 27, 1862.						
First South Carolina Rifles	Gregg's	A. P. Hill's	81	234	4	319
Twentieth North Carolina	Garland's	D. H. Hill's	70	202	...	272
Fourth Texas	Hood's	Whiting's	44	208	1	253
Fourteenth South Carolina	Gregg's	A. P. Hill's	18	190	...	208
Thirty-eighth Georgia	Lawton's	Jackson's	54	118	...	172
Thirty-first Georgia	Lawton's	Jackson's	29	141	...	170
Eighth Alabama	Wilcox's	Longstreet's	31	132	...	163
Eleventh Mississippi	Law's	Whiting's	18	142	3	163
Eleventh Alabama	Wilcox's	Longstreet's	27	130	...	157
Sixth Georgia	Colquitt's	D. H. Hill's	22	131	3	156
First South Carolina	Gregg's	A. P. Hill's	20	125	...	145
Eighteenth Georgia	Hood's	Whiting's	14	128	3	145
Ninth Alabama	Wilcox's	Longstreet's	34	96	4	134
Fourth Alabama	Law's	Whiting's	22	108	2	132
Tenth Alabama	Wilcox's	Longstreet's	24	105	...	129
Eighteenth Virginia	Pickett's	Longstreet's	14	99	5	118
Thirteenth Virginia	Elzey's	Ewell's	27	84	...	111
GARNETT'S AND GOLDING'S FARMS, VA.—June 27–28, 1862.						
Second Georgia	Toombs'	Jones'	14	106	...	120
Eighth Georgia	Anderson's	Jones'	24	57	11	92
Seventh Georgia	Anderson's	Jones'	12	66	..	78
SAVAGE STATION, VA.—June 29, 1862.						
Third South Carolina	Kershaw's	McLaws'	23	108	4	135
Seventh South Carolina	Kershaw's	McLaws'	13	64	5	82
Tenth Georgia	Semmes'	McLaws'	10	47	...	57
GLENDALE, VA.—June 30, 1862.						
Palmetto Sharpshooters	Anderson's	Longstreet's	39	215	...	254
Eleventh Alabama	Wilcox's	Longstreet's	49	121	11	181
Ninth Alabama	Wilcox's	Longstreet's	31	95	4	130
Seventeenth Virginia	Kemper's	Longstreet's	17	23	73	113
Seventh Virginia	Kemper's	Longstreet's	14	66	31	111
Fourteenth Alabama ‡	Pryor's	Longstreet's	71	253	11	335
Nineteenth Mississippi ‡	Featherston's	Longstreet's	58	264	3	325
Fourteenth Louisiana ‡	Pryor's	Longstreet's	51	192	...	243
Twelfth Mississippi ‡	Featherston's	Longstreet's	34	186	5	225
MALVERN HILL, VA.—July 1, 1862.						
Third Alabama	Rodes'	D. H. Hill's	37	163	..	200
Second Louisiana	Cobb's	Magruder's	30	152	...	182
Third Georgia	Wright's	Huger's	25	110	22	157
Twenty-first Mississippi	Barksdale's	Magruder's	32	119	...	151
Fifteenth Alabama ‡	Trimble's	Ewell's	35	115	...	150
Thirteenth Mississippi	Barksdale's	Magruder's	28	107	...	135
Eighteenth Mississippi	Barksdale's	Magruder's	16	116	...	132
Fifteenth North Carolina	Cobb's	Magruder's	21	110	...	131
Twenty-fifth North Carolina	Ransom's	Holmes'	22	106	5	133
Thirty-fifth North Carolina	Ransom's	Holmes'	18	91	18	127
Forty-ninth North Carolina	Ransom's	Holmes'	14	75	16	105
Fifty-seventh Virginia	Armistead's	Huger's	13	83	17	113
SEVEN DAYS, VA.—June 25—July 1, 1862.						
Seventh North Carolina	Branch's	A. P. Hill's	35	218	...	253
Eighteenth North Carolina	Branch's	A. P. Hill's	45	179	...	224
Twelfth North Carolina	Garland's	D. H Hill's	51	160	1	212
Sixtieth Virginia	Field's	A. P. Hill's	31	173	...	204
Fortieth Virginia	Field's	A. P. Hill's	30	150	...	180
Second South Carolina Rifles	Anderson's	Longstreet's	33	108	8	149
Twenty-eighth North Carolina	Branch's	A. P. Hill's	19	130	...	149
Thirty-seventh North Carolina	Branch's	A. P. Hill's	27	111	...	138
Second Florida	Pryor's	Longstreet's	23	114	...	137
CEDAR MOUNTAIN, VA.—August 9, 1862.						
Twenty-first Virginia	Jones'	Jackson's	37	85	...	122
Forty-second Virginia	Jones'	Jackson's	36	71	...	107
Thirty-seventh Virginia	Taliaferro's	Jackson's	12	76	...	88
Forty-seventh Virginia	Taliaferro's	Jackson's	12	76	...	88
Forty-eighth Alabama	Taliaferro's	Jackson's	12	61	...	73
MANASSAS, VA.—August 28—September 1, 1862.						
Fifth Texas	Wofford's	Hood's	15	224	1	240
Eleventh Georgia	Anderson's	Jones'	20	178	...	198
Seventeenth South Carolina	Evans'	Anderson's	25	163	1	189
Twenty-first Georgia	Trimble's	Ewell's	38	146	...	184
Thirteenth South Carolina	Gregg's	A. P. Hill's	31	142	...	173
Twelfth South Carolina	Gregg's	A. P. Hill's	25	131	...	156
Holcombe Legion	Evans'	Anderson's	24	131	...	155
First South Carolina	Gregg's	A. P. Hill's	25	126	...	151
Eighteenth Georgia	Wofford's	Hood's	19	133	...	152
Twenty-third South Carolina	Evans'	Anderson's	27	122	...	149
First South Carolina Rifles	Gregg's	A. P. Hill's	24	122	...	146
Twentieth Georgia	Toombs'	Jones'	19	113	...	132
Ninth Georgia	Anderson's	Jones'	12	116	...	128
Twenty-sixth Georgia	Lawton's	Ewell's	37	87	...	124
Sixtieth Georgia	Lawton's	Ewell's	22	101	...	123
Sixth Georgia	Jenkins'	Pickett's	13	102	...	115
Fifteenth Alabama	Trimble's	Ewell's	21	91	...	112
Second Louisiana	Starke's	Jackson's	25	86	...	111
RICHMOND, KY.—August 30, 1862.						
Second Tennessee	B. J. Hill's	Cleburne's	17	95	...	112
Thirteenth Tennessee	Preston Smith's	Cleburne's	12	35	1	48
MARYLAND HEIGHTS, MD.—September 13, 1862.						
Seventh South Carolina	Kershaw's	McLaws'	13	100	...	113
CRAMPTONS GAP, MD.—September 14, 1862.						
Sixteenth Georgia	Cobbs'	McLaws'	24	56	107	187
Twenty-fourth Georgia	Cobb's	McLaws'	12	59	55	126
Fifteenth North Carolina	Cobb's	McLaws'	11	48	124	183
ANTIETAM, MD.—September 17, 1862.						
Third North Carolina	Garland's	D. H. Hill's	46	207	...	§ 253
Thirteenth Georgia	Lawton's	Ewell's	48	169	2	219
Forty-eighth North Carolina	Walker's	Walker's	31	186	...	217
Twenty-seventh North Carolina	Walker's	Walker's	31	168	...	199
Thirteenth North Carolina	G. B. Anderson's	D. H. Hill's	41	149	...	§ 190
First Texas	Wofford's	Hood's	45	141	...	186
Third Arkansas	Walker's	Walker's	27	155	..	182
Thirtieth Virginia	Walker's	Walker's	39	121	..	160
First North Carolina	Garland's	D. H. Hill's	18	142	...	§ 160
Fifteenth North Carolina	Cobb's	McLaws'	16	143	...	‖ 159
Twenty-fourth Georgia	Cobb's	McLaws'	13	145	...	‖ 158
Second Mississippi	Law's	Hood's	27	127	...	154

* Includes the mortally wounded.
† Charleston Battalion.
‡ Includes loss at Gaines Mill.
§ Includes loss at South Mountain on the 14th.
‖ Includes loss at Cramptons Gap on the 14th.

CONFEDERATE REGIMENTS WHICH SUSTAINED THE GREATEST LOSS IN PARTICULAR BATTLES.—Continued.

Regiment.	Brigade.	Division.	Killed	Wounded*	Missing	Total
ANTIETAM, MD.—September 17, 1862—Continued.						
Fourth Georgia	Ripley's	D. H. Hill's	22	119	...	† 141
Seventh South Carolina	Kershaw's	McLaws'	23	117	..	140
Sixteenth Mississippi	Featherston's	Anderson's	27	100	...	127
Fiftieth Georgia	Drayton's	Jones'	29	97	...	126
Sixth North Carolina	Law's	Hood's	10	115	...	125
Fifteenth South Carolina	Drayton's	Jones'	26	84	...	110
Sixty-first Georgia	Lawton's	Ewell's	16	91	7	114
Fourth Texas	Wofford's	Hood's	10	97	...	107
Twenty-seventh Georgia	Colquitt's	D. H. Hill's	15	89	...	† 104
Eighth Louisiana	Hays'	Ewell's	10	93	...	103
Second South Carolina	Kershaw's	McLaws'	17	77	..	94
Seventeenth Mississippi	Barksdale's	McLaws'	9	77	2	88
Tenth Georgia	Semmes'	McLaws'	16	67	...	83
Eighteenth Mississippi	Barksdale's	McLaws'	11	69	...	80
Nineteenth Georgia	Colquitt's	D. H. Hill's	13	76	...	† 89
Ninth Louisiana	Starke's	Jackson's	25	57	...	82
Forty-ninth North Carolina	Ransom's	Walker's	16	61	...	77
MUNFORDVILLE, KY.—September 14–17, 1862.						
Tenth Mississippi	Chalmers'	Withers'	13	95	...	108
IUKA, MISS.—September 19, 1862.						
Third Texas, dismounted (Cavalry)	Hebert's	Little's	22	74	...	96
First Texas Legion	Hebert's	Little's	18	80	1	99
Fortieth Mississippi	Hebert's	Little's	10	39	21	70
SHEPHERDSTOWN, VA.—September 20, 1862.						
Fourteenth South Carolina	Gregg's	A. P. Hill's	10	45	...	45
CORINTH, MISS.‡—October 3–5, 1862.						
Sixth Texas	Phifer's	Maury's	55	63	30	148
Thirty-fifth Mississippi	Moore's	Maury's	32	110	347	489
Sixth Missouri	Green's	Hebert's	31	130	53	214
Second Missouri	Gates'	Hebert's	19	122	21	162
Forty-third Mississippi	Green's	Hebert's	13	56	156	225
Twenty-first Arkansas	Cabell's	Maury's	27	41	58	126
Jones' Arkansas Battalion	Cabell's	Maury's	36	43	11	90
Thirty-seventh Mississippi		Hebert's	19	62	...	81
CHAPLIN HILLS, KY.—October 8, 1862.						
Sixteenth Tennessee	Donelson's	Cheatham's	41	151	7	199
First Tennessee	Maney's	Cheatham's	49	129	1	179
Ninth Tennessee	Maney's	Cheatham's	32	114	8	154
Forty-first Georgia	Maney's	Cheatham's	23	125	3	151
Twenty-seventh Tennessee	Maney's	Cheatham's	16	81	11	108
Thirty-first Tennessee	Stewart's	Cheatham's	17	78	5	100
Sixth Tennessee	Maney's	Cheatham's	16	64	11	91
Fifth Tennessee	Stewart's	Cheatham's	14	64	12	90
POCOTALIGO, S. C.—October 22, 1862.						
Seventh South Carolina Battalion	Walker's		3	22	..	25
Eleventh South Carolina	Walker's		4	15	2	21
Nelson's Battalion	Walker's		4	17	...	21
FREDERICKSBURG, VA.—December 13, 1862.						
Fifty-seventh North Carolina	Law's	Hood's	32	192	...	224
Forty-eighth North Carolina	Cooke's	Ransom's	17	161	...	178
First South Carolina Rifles	Gregg's	A. P. Hill's	21	149	...	170
Fourteenth Georgia	Thomas'	A. P. Hill's	22	110	...	132
Third South Carolina	Kershaw's	McLaws'	15	104	...	119
Fifteenth North Carolina	Cooke's	Ransom's	10	93	...	103
Sixty-first Georgia	Lawton's	Ewell's	17	83	...	100
Thirty-eighth Georgia	Lawton's	Ewell's	10	91	...	101
Thirty-seventh North Carolina	Lane's	A. P. Hill's	17	76	...	93
Eighteenth North Carolina	Lane's	A. P. Hill's	13	77	...	90
Thirty-fifth Georgia	Thomas'	A. P. Hill's	10	79	...	89
Twenty-fifth North Carolina	Ransom's	Ransom's	13	75	...	88
Seventh North Carolina	Lane's	A. P. Hill's	5	81	...	86
Thirty-first Georgia	Lawton's	Ewell's	15	63	...	78
Phillips' Legion	Cobb's	McLaws'	13	56	...	69
Twenty-eighth North Carolina	Lane's	A. P. Hill's	16	49	...	65
Nineteenth Georgia	Archer's	A. P. Hill's	15	39	...	54
Sixteenth North Carolina	Pender's	A. P. Hill's	6	48	...	54
CHICKASAW BLUFFS, MISS.—December 26–29, 1862.						
Forty-second Georgia	Barton's	Stevenson's	10	18	..	28
Twenty-eighth Louisiana		Lee's	9	29	9	43
Thirty-first Georgia		Lee's	9	16	...	25
STONES RIVER, TENN.—December 31, 1862—January 1, 1863.						
Eighth Tennessee	Donelson's	Cheatham's	41	265	...	306
Twenty-ninth Mississippi	Walthall's	Withers'	34	202	...	236
Thirtieth Mississippi	Walthall's	Withers'	63	146	...	209
Thirteenth Louisiana, Twentieth Louisiana	Adams'	Breckinridge's	46	168	102	316
Sixteenth Louisiana, Twenty-fifth Louisiana	Adams'	Breckinridge's	41	176	21	238
Sixth Arkansas, Seventh Arkansas	Liddell's	Cleburne's	29	140	8	177
Fourth Florida	Preston's	Breckinridge's	34	129	31	194
Seventeenth Tennessee	Johnson's	Cleburne's	17	164	26	207
Sixteenth Alabama	Wood's	Cleburne's	24	142	..	166
Forty-first Mississippi	Chalmers'	Withers'	25	123	8	156
Eighth Arkansas	Liddell's	Cleburne's	29	124	..	153
Twelfth Tennessee	Smith's	Cheatham's	18	137	9	164
Forty-fourth Tennessee	Johnson's	Cleburne's	14	136	2	152
Fifth Arkansas	Liddell's	Cleburne's	12	135	1	148
Eighteenth Tennessee	Pillow's	Breckinridge's	17	120	8	145
Eighth Mississippi	Jackson's		20	113	..	133
Nineteenth Tennessee	Stewart's	Cheatham's	16	111	...	127
Ninth Texas	Smith's	Cheatham's	18	102	2	122
Twenty-fourth Alabama	Anderson's	Withers'	20	95	3	118
Forty-first Alabama	Hanson's	Breckinridge's	16	94	38	148
Twenty-ninth Tennessee	Smith's	Cheatham's	27	82	.	109
Thirty-second Alabama	Adams'	Breckinridge's	21	86	21	128
Second Arkansas	Liddell's	Cleburne's	15	94	9	118
Second Arkansas Rifles	McNair's	McCown's	10	99	11	120
Tenth South Carolina	Anderson's	Withers'	16	91	2	109
Tenth Texas Cavalry, dismounted	Ector's	McCown's	10	93	15	118
ARKANSAS POST, ARK.—January 11, 1863.						
Twenty-fourth Texas			12	17	25	54
Sixth Texas			8	24	21	53
THOMPSONS STATION, TENN.—March 5, 1863.						
First Texas Legion,			11	59	7	77
Fourth Mississippi			9	37	...	46
CHANCELLORSVILLE, VA.—May 1–3, 1863.						
Thirty-seventh North Carolina	Lane's	A. P. Hill's	34	193	...	227
Second North Carolina	Ramseur's	D. H. Hill's	47	167	...	214
Thirteenth North Carolina	Pender's	A. P. Hill's	31	178	7	216
Third North Carolina	Colston's	Trimble's	38	141	17	196
Twenty-second North Carolina	Pender's	A. P. Hill's	30	139	15	184
Seventeenth North Carolina	Lane's	A. P. Hill's	37	127	...	164
Fourth North Carolina	Ramseur's	D. H. Hill's	45	110	58	213
Fifth Alabama	Rodes'	D. H. Hill's	24	130	121	275
Fiftieth Georgia	Semmes'	McLaws'	17	153	...	170
Fourth Georgia	Dole's	D. H. Hill's	29	121	11	161
Fourth Virginia	Paxton's	Trimble's	14	149	3	166
Fifty-first Georgia	Semmes'	McLaws'	30	119	26	175
Cobb's Legion	Wofford's	McLaws'	22	135	...	157
Thirty-third North Carolina	Lane's	A. P. Hill's	32	101	66	199
Twenty-third North Carolina	Iverson's	D. H. Hill's	32	113	35	180
Sixth Alabama	Rodes'	D. H. Hill's	24	125	14	163
Thirteenth Alabama	Archer's	A. P. Hill's	13	127	8	148
Third Alabama	Rodes'	D. H. Hill's	17	121	16	154

* Includes the mortally wounded.
† Includes loss at South Mountain on the 14th.
‡ Includes loss at Hatchie Bridge, October 5th.

Brig.-Gen. Francis T. Nichols, of Louisiana.

Brig.-Gen. John S. Williams, of Kentucky.

Brig.-Gen. George H. Stuart, of Maryland.

Brig.-Gen. James E. B. Terrill, of Virginia.
Killed at the Battle of the Wilderness, Va., May 7, 1864.

Brig.-Gen. John M. Jones, of Virginia.
Killed at the Battle of the Wilderness, Va., May 5, 1864.
[From a photograph taken early in 1864.]

Brig.-Gen. J. B. Villepigue, of South Carolina.
Died, November 9, 1862.

Brig.-Gen. Thomas F. Toon, of North Carolina.

Brig.-Gen. Mosby M. Parsons, of Arkansas.
[From an old portrait made in 1862.]

Brig.-Gen. John C. Vaughn, of Tennessee.

CONFEDERATE REGIMENTS WHICH SUSTAINED THE GREATEST LOSS IN PARTICULAR BATTLES.—Continued.

REGIMENT.	BRIGADE.	DIVISION.	Killed	Wounded *	Missing	Total
CHANCELLORSVILLE, VA.—May 1-3, 1863—Continued.						
Sixteenth Georgia	Wofford's	McLaws'	18	115	. . .	133
Forty-second Virginia	J. R. Jones'	Trimble's	15	120	. . .	135
First North Carolina	Colston's	Trimble's	34	83	27	144
Eighteenth North Carolina	Lane's	A. P. Hill's	30	96	. . .	126
Thirty-fourth North Carolina	Pender's	A. P. Hill's	18	110	20	148
Fourteenth North Carolina	Ramseur's	D. H. Hill's	15	116	. . .	131
Tenth Virginia	Colston's	Trimble's	23	101	25	149
Tenth Georgia	Semmes'	McLaws'	23	105	. . .	128
Thirtieth North Carolina	Ramseur's	D. H. Hill's	25	98	1	124
Fifty-third Georgia	Semmes'	McLaws'	15	105	. . .	120
RAYMOND, MISS.—May 12, 1863.						
Third Tennessee	Gregg's	. . .	27	90	70	187
Seventh Texas	Gregg's	. . .	22	73	63	158
Tenth Tennessee	Gregg's	. . .	8	37	7	52
JACKSON, MISS.—June 14, 1863.						
Twenty-fourth South Carolina	Walker's	. . .	11	38	56	105
CHAMPIONS HILL, MISS.—May 16, 1863.						
First Missouri	Cockrell's	Bowen's	29	94	52	175
Third Missouri	Cockrell's	Bowen's	13	63	44	120
MILLIKENS BEND, LA.—June 6-8, 1863.						
Seventeenth Texas	. . .	Walker's	21	68	3	92
Sixteenth Texas, Dismounted Cavalry	. . .	Walker's	19	47	1	67
HOOVERS GAP, TENN.—June 24, 1863.						
Twentieth Tennessee	Bates'	Stewart's	9	24	. . .	33
Thirty-seventh Georgia	Bates'	Stewart's	3	45	. . .	48
LIBERTY GAP, TENN.—June 25, 1863.						
Second Arkansas	Liddell's	Cleburne's	14	35	10	59
Fifth Arkansas	Liddell's	Cleburne's	5	10	7	22
VICKSBURG, MISS.—May 18—July 4, 1863.						
Third Louisiana	Hebert's	Forney's	49	119	7	175
Sixth Missouri	Cockrell's	Bowen's	33	133	. . .	166
Twenty-seventh Louisiana	Shoup's	Smith's	58	96	. . .	154
Second Texas	Moore's	Forney's	39	65	. . .	104
Thirty-sixth Mississippi	Hebert's	Forney's	28	72	1	101
Thirty-fifth Mississippi	Moore's	Forney's	20	82	. . .	102
Second Missouri	Cockrell's	Bowen's	17	89	. . .	106
Third Missouri	Cockrell's	Bowen's	18	83	. . .	101
Thirty-eighth Mississippi	Hebert's	Forney's	35	37	. . .	72
Twenty-sixth Louisiana	Shoup's	Smith's	28	44	. . .	72
HELENA, ARK.—July 4, 1863.						
Seventh Missouri	Parson's	Price's	16	124	53	193
Thirty-sixth Arkansas	McRae's	Price's	21	70	68	158
GETTYSBURG, PA.—July 1-3, 1863.						
Twenty-sixth North Carolina	Pettigrew's	Heth's	86	502	§120	708
Forty-second Mississippi	Davis'	Heth's	60	205	. . .	265
Second Mississippi	Davis'	Heth's	49	183	. . .	232
Eleventh North Carolina	Pettigrew's	Heth's	50	159	. . .	209
Forty-fifth North Carolina	Daniel's	Rodes'	46	173	. . .	219
Seventeenth Mississippi	Barksdale's	McLaws'	40	160	. . .	200
Fourteenth South Carolina	Gregg's	Pender's	26	220	6	252
Eleventh Mississippi	Davis'	Heth's	32	170	. . .	202
Fifty-fifth North Carolina	Davis'	Heth's	39	159	. . .	198
Eleventh Georgia	G. T. Anderson's	Hood's	32	162	. . .	194
Thirty-eighth Virginia	Armistead's	Pickett's	23	147	. . .	170
Sixth North Carolina	Hoke's	Early's	20	131	21	172
Thirteenth Mississippi	Barksdale's	McLaws'	28	137	. . .	165
Eighth Alabama	Wilcox's	Anderson's	22	139	. . .	161
Forty-seventh North Carolina	Pettigrew's	Heth's	21	140	. . .	161
Third North Carolina	Stewart's	Johnson's	29	127	. . .	156
Second North Carolina Battalion	Daniel's	Rodes'	29	124	. . .	153
Second South Carolina	Kershaw's	McLaws'	27	125	2	154
Fifty-second North Carolina	Pettigrew's	Heth's	33	114	. . .	147
Fifth North Carolina	Iverson's	Rodes'	31	112	. . .	143
Thirty-second North Carolina	Daniel's	Rodes'	26	116	. . .	142
Forty-third North Carolina	Daniel's	Rodes'	21	126	. . .	147
Ninth Georgia	G. T. Anderson's	Hood's	28	115	. . .	143
First Maryland Battalion	Stewart's	Johnson's	25	119	. . .	144
Third Arkansas	Robertson's	Hood's	26	116	. . .	142
Fifty-seventh Virginia	Armistead's	Pickett's	35	105	4	144
Twenty-third North Carolina	Iverson's	Rodes'	41	93	. . .	134
CHARLESTON HARBOR, S. C.—July 10—September 6, 1863.						
Twenty-first South Carolina †	Graham's	Ripley's	14	112	56	182
Twenty-fifth South Carolina	Colquitt's	Ripley's	16	124	3	143
First South Carolina Artillery	Hagood's	Ripley's	18	50	52	120
—— Charleston Battalion ‡	Hagood's	Ripley's	13	70	2	85
Fifty-first North Carolina ‡	Taliaferro's	Ripley's	17	60	. . .	77
First South Carolina (Third Artillery) ‡	Taliaferro's	Ripley's	10	32	22	64
Thirty-first North Carolina	Clingman's	Ripley's	13	32	. . .	45
CHICKAMAUGA, GA.—September 19-20, 1863,						
Eighteenth Alabama	Clayton's	Stewart's	41	256	. .	297
Twenty-second Alabama	Deas'	Hindman's	44	161	. .	205
Sixteenth Alabama	Wood's	Cleburne's	25	218	. . .	243
Nineteenth Alabama	Deas'	Hindman's	34	158	12	204
Thirty-eighth Alabama	Clayton's	Stewart's	37	151	5	193
Fifth Georgia	Jackson's	Cheatham's	27	165	2	194
Sixty-third Tennessee	Gracie's	Preston's	16	184	. . .	200
First Arkansas	Polk's	Cleburne's	13	180	1	194
Thirty-seventh Georgia	Bate's	Stewart's	19	168	7	194
Thirty-third Alabama	Wood's	Cleburne's	19	166	. . .	185
Sixth Florida	Trigg's	Preston's	35	130	. . .	165
Second Tennessee	Polk's	Cleburne's	13	145	1	159
Forty-first Alabama	Helm's	Breckinridge's	27	120	11	158
Nineteenth Louisiana	Adams'	Breckinridge's	28	114	11	153
Eighteenth Tennessee	Brown's	Stewart's	20	114	1	135
Twenty-fourth Mississippi	Walthall's	Liddell's	10	103	19	132
BRISTOE STATION, VA.—October 14, 1863.						
Twenty-seventh North Carolina	Cooke's	Heth's	30	174	. . .	204
Forty-eighth North Carolina	Cooke's	Heth's	8	115	. .	123
Fifteenth North Carolina	Cooke's	Heth's	14	87	. . .	101
Twenty-sixth North Carolina	Kirkland's	Heth's	16	83	. . .	99
WAUHATCHIE, TENN.—October 27, 1863.						
Fifth South Carolina	Bratton's	Jenkins'	9	84	9	102
—— Hampton Legion	Bratton's	Jenkins'	8	65	12	85
MINE RUN, VA.—November 27, 1863.						
Third North Carolina	Steuart's	Johnson's	7	65	. . .	72
Fourth Virginia	Walker's	Johnson's	7	48	4	59
OLUSTEE, FLA.—February 20, 1864.						
Thirty-second Georgia	Harrison's	Finegan's	15	149	. . .	164
Sixty-fourth Georgia	Harrison's	Finegan's	17	88	2	107
Second Florida Battalion	Harrison's	Finegan's	12	95	2	109

* Includes the mortally wounded.

† Morris Island, July 10th.

‡ Fort Wagner, July 18th.

§ These missing ones were lost in Pickett's charge.

CONFEDERATE LOSSES IN KILLED, WOUNDED AND MISSING IN PARTICULAR BATTLES, ALSO TOTAL FEDERAL LOSS IN THE SAME BATTLES.

NOTE.—The losses are from the official reports made by the generals or other officers in command. Many battles are not quoted, for the reason that no casualty reports were made. There are no casualty official reports for the latter part of the war. Estimates might be quoted, but they would not be reliable.

NAME OF BATTLE.	STATE.	DATE.	Killed	Wounded	Captured or Missing	Total Confederate Loss	Total Federal Loss
1861.							
Balls Bluff	Virginia	October 21	36	117	2	155	921
Belmont	Missouri	November 7	105	419	117	641	501
Camp Alleghany	West Virginia	December 13	20	96	28	144	137
Dranesville	Virginia	December 20	43	143	8	194	68
Greenbrier River	West Virginia	October 3	6	33	13	52	43
Lexington	Missouri	September 12-20	25	72	. . .	97	2,800
Manassas or Bull Run	Virginia	July 21	387	1,582	13	1,982	3,334
Wilsons Creek	Missouri	August 10	265	800	30	1,095	1,235
1862.							
Antietam	Virginia	September 16-17	See	Maryl	and Ca	mpaign.	12,410
Baton Rouge	Louisiana	August 5	84	313	56	453	383
Bull Run (Second)	Virginia	. . .	See	Second	Manas	sas.	14,462
Camden	North Carolina	April 19	6	19	3	28	127
Cedar Mountain	Virginia	August 9	223	1,060	31	1,314	2,381
Chantilly	Virginia	September 1	See	Second	Manass	as or Bu	ll Run.
Chaplin Hills (Perryville)	Kentucky	October 8	510	2,635	251	3,369	4,211
Charles City Cross Roads	Virginia	June 30	SeeSe	ven Day	s Bat'ls.	3,615	. . .
Chickasaw Bluffs	Mississippi	December 26-29	57	120	10	187	1,776
Coffeeville	Mississippi	December 5	7	43	10	60	114
Corinth and Hatchie River	Mississippi	October 3-5	505	2,150	2,183	4,838	2,520
Cramptons Gap	Maryland	September 14	See	Maryl	and Ca	mpaign.	533
Cross Keys	Virginia	June 8	56	392	47	495	625
Fayetteville	West Virginia	September 10	16	32	. . .	48	310
Fair Oaks	Virginia	May 31	980	4,749	405	6,134	5,031
Fort Donelson	Tennessee	February 14-16	466	1,534	13,829	15,829	2,832
Fredericksburg	Virginia	December 13	596	4,068	651	5,315	12,653
Front Royal (Winchester)	Virginia	May 23-25	39	172.	3	214	1,808
Gainesville	Virginia	August 28	See	Manas	sas.	. . .	. . .
Gaines Mill	Virginia	June 27	SeeSe	ven Day	s Bat'ls.	8,751	6,837
Garnett's or Golding Farm	Virginia	June 28	SeeSe	ven Day	s Bat'ls.	461	368
Hanover Courthouse	Virginia	May 27	73	192	. . .	265	355
Harrisonburg	Virginia	June 6	17	50	3	70	. . .
Harpers Ferry	Maryland	September 12-15	See	Maryl	and Ca	mpaign.	12,737
Hartsville	Tennessee	December 7	21	104	14	139	2,096
Hatchie River	Mississippi	October 5	See	Corinth,	Miss.	. . .	570
Iuka	Mississippi	September 19	86	408	199	693	790
Kernstown	Virginia	March 23	80	375	263	718	590
Kinston (Whitehall)	North Carolina	December 12-17	71	268	400	739	591
Malvern Hill	Virginia	July 1	SeeSe	ven Day	s Bat'ls.	5,355	3,214
Manassas or Bull Run *	Virginia	August 21-Septem'r 2	1,481	7,627	89	9,197	14,462
Maryland Campaign †	Maryland	September 12-20	1,886	9,348	1,367	12,601	27,856
Mechanicsville	Virginia	June 26	SeeSe	ven Day	s Bat'ls.	1,365	361
McDowell	Virginia	May 8	75	423	. . .	498	256
Mill Springs	Kentucky	January 19	125	309	95	529	246
Munfordville	Kentucky	September 14-17	40	211	. . .	251	4,148
New Berne	North Carolina	March 14	64	101	413	578	471
Oak Grove	Virginia	June 25	SeeSe	ven Day	s Bat'ls.	441	626
Peach Orchard and Savage Station	Virginia	June 29	SeeSe	ven Day	s Bat'ls.	626	1,590
Perryville	Kentucky	October 8	510	2,635	251	3,396	4,211
Pocotaligo	South Carolina	October 22	21	124	18	163	340
Port Republic	Virginia	June 9	78	533	4	615	1,018
Prairie Grove	Arkansas	December 7	164	817	. . .	981	1,251
Rappahannock	Virginia	August 20-23	See	Manas	sas (Sec	ond).	. . .
Richmond	Kentucky	August 30	78	372	1	451	5,353
Roanoke Island	North Carolina	February 8	23	58	2,527	2,608	264
Savage Station	Virginia	June 29	SeeSe	ven Day	s Bat'ls.	626	1,590
Secessionville	South Carolina	June 16	52	144	8	204	683
Seven Days Battles ‡	Virginia	June 25—July 1	3,478	16,261	875	20,614	15,849
Shepherdstown	West Virginia	October 1	See	Maryl	and Ca	mpaign.	363
Shiloh	Tennessee	April 6-7	1,723	8,012	959	10,694	13,047
South Mountain	Maryland	September 14	See	Maryl	and Ca	mpaign.	1,813
Stones River	Tennessee	December 31	1,294	7,945	1,029	10,266	13,249
West Point	Virginia	May 7	8	40	. . .	48	186
White Oak Swamp	Virginia	June 30	SeeSe	ven Day	s Bat'ls.	3,615	2,853
Williamsburg	Virginia	May 5	288	975	297	1,560	2,239
Winchester	Virginia	May 23-25	See	Front	Royal.	214	1,808
1863.							
Beverly Ford	Virginia	June 9	59	280	184	§523	866
Boonesboro	Maryland	July 7-9-12	See	Funksto	wn, Md.	216	80
Bristoe Station	Virginia	October 14	136	797	445	1,378	546
Champions Hill	Mississippi	May 16	380	1,018	2,441	3,839	2,441
Chancellorsville	Virginia	May 1-4	1,665	9,081	2,018	12,764	17,287
Charleston Harbor	South Carolina	July 19—Septemb'r 6	75	404	27	506	2,212
Chattanooga	Tennessee	November 23-25	See M	issionar	y Ridge.	6,667	5,382
Chickamauga	Georgia	September 19-20	2,402	14,877	1,498	18,770	16,179
Deserted House	Virginia	January 30	8	31	. . .	39	143
Droop Mountain	Virginia	November 6	. . .	. . .	. . .	275	119
Fort Sanders ‖	Tennessee	November 29	129	458	226	813	687
Fort Wagner	South Carolina	July 11	6	6	. . .	12	339
Fort Wagner	South Carolina	July 18	36	140	5	181	1,515
Funkstown or Boonesboro	Maryland	July 12	26	130	60	216	80
Gettysburg ¶	Pennsylvania	July 1-3	2,701	39	7,528	22,968	23,001
Hanover	Pennsylvania	June 30	9	50	58	117	215
Hagerstown or Williamsport	Maryland	July 6-11	8	65	181	254	383
Hartville	Missouri	January 11	See	Springfi	eld, Mo.	262	73
Helena	Arkansas	July 4	173	645	772	1,590	239
Jackson	Mississippi	July 9-16	71	504	765	1,340	1,122
Kellys Ford	Virginia	March 17	11	88	34	133	78
Kellys Ford	Virginia	November 7	. .	. . .	. . .	359	45
Knoxville (including Fort Sanders)	Tennessee	November 14-30	198	850	248	1,296	687
Lookout Mountain	Tennessee	November 24	See	Mission	ary Rid	ge.	. . .
Magnolia Hills	Mississippi	May 1	68	380	384	832	875
Middleburg and Upperville	Virginia	June 19-21	65	279	166	510	299
Millikens Bend	Louisiana	June 6	101	285	266	652	428
Mine Run Campaign	Virginia	November 26-30	110	570	65	745	1,653
Missionary Ridge, Lookout Mountain and Chattanooga	Tennessee	November 25	361	2,160	4,146	6,667	5,382
Morris Island	South Carolina	July 10	40	124	127	291	. . .
Plains Store	Louisiana	May 21	12	36	. . .	48	100
Port Hudson	Louisiana	May 25—July 9	176	447	. . .	623	4,362
Rappahannock Station	Virginia	November 7	. . .	. . .	. . .	1,674	417
Raymond	Mississippi	May 12	73	251	190	514	442
Rocky Gap—White Sulphur Springs	Virginia	August 26-27	20	129	13	162	218
Springfield	Missouri	January 2-11	32	201	29	262	165
Thompsons Station	Tennessee	March 5	56	289	12	357	1,446
Upperville	Virginia	June 21	See	M ddle	burg, Va	. . .	. . .
Wauhatchie	Tennessee	October 27	33	306	58	397	. . .
Williamsport	Maryland	July 6	See	Hagerst	own, Md	254	383
Winchester	Virginia	June 13	47	219	3	269	4,443
1864.							
Atlanta Campaign **	Georgia	May 5 to September 1	3,117	19,293	12,983	35,393	31,687
Allatoona Pass	Georgia	October 5	127	456	290	873	706
Brices Cross Roads	Mississippi	June 10-11	96	396	. . .	492	2,240
Cavalry Engagements	Georgia	May 6-31	73	341	††	414	. . .
Cedar Creek	Virginia	October 19	320	,1540	1,050	2,910	5,665
Dallas	Georgia	May 20 to June 5	See N	ew Hope	Church.	2,230	2,800
Deaveaux Neck	South Carolina	December 6-9	. . .	. . .	. . .	400	629
Fishers Hill	Virginia	September 22	30	210	995	1,235	528
Hatchers Run	Virginia	October 27	. . .	. . .	. . .	1,000	1,902

* Compiled from official reports of Longstreet, Jackson and Stuart.

† Includes Antietam, South Mountain, Harpers Ferry, Cramptons Gap and Shepherdstown.

‡ See Oak Grove, Mechanicsville, Gaines Mill, Garnett's and Golding Farm, Savage Station and Peach Orchard, White Oak Swamp and Glendale or Charles City Road and Malvern Hill.

§ Includes losses in White's Battalion.

‖ Included in Knoxville losses,

¶ From official reports of Longstreet, Ewell, Hill and Stuart.

** Includes Rocky Face Ridge, Resaca, New Hope Church, Dallas, Kennesaw Mountain, Peach Tree Creek Atlanta, Utoy Creek, Jonesboro, and cavalry engagements.

†† See Atlanta Campaign.

CONFEDERATE LOSSES IN KILLED, WOUNDED AND MISSING IN PARTICULAR BATTLES, ALSO TOTAL FEDERAL LOSS IN THE SAME BATTLES.—Continued.

NAME OF BATTLE.	STATE.	DATE.	Killed	Wounded	Captured or Missing	Total Confederate Loss	Total Federal Loss
1864.—Continued.							
James Island, Johns Island	South Carolina	July 1–11	33	92	...	125	110
Jenkins Ferry	Arkansas	April 30	86	356	1	443	528
Jonesboro	Georgia	...	See	Utoy	Creek.	3,705	3,237
Kennesaw Mountain	Georgia	June 10 to July 4	468	3,480	*	3,948	4,200
Marks Mills	Arkansas	April 25	41	108	144	293	450
New Hope Church, Dallas	Georgia	May 20 to June 5	309	1,921	*	2,230	2,800
New Market	Virginia	May 15	34	484	13	581	831
Olustee	Florida	February 20	93	847	6	946	1,861
Opequon	Virginia	September 19	226	1,567	1,818	3,611	5,018
Peach Tree Creek, Atlanta	Georgia	July 4–31	1,341	7,500	*	8,841	9,719
Petersburg Mine Explosion	Virginia	July 30	...	...	...	4,008	1,200
Rocky Face Ridge, Resaca	Georgia	May 7–20	444	2,828	*	3,272	3,900
Tupelo	Mississippi	July 13–15	210	1,049	49	1,308	528
Utoy Creek, Jonesboro	Georgia	July 31 to Septemb'r 1	482	3,223	*	3,705	3,237
1865.							
Averasboro	North Carolina	March 16	108	540	217	865	678
Bentonville	North Carolina	March 19	239	1,694	673	2,606	1,646
Boydton or White Oaks Road	Virginia	March 31	...	...	...	1,235	1,867
Dabneys Mill, Hatchers Run	Virginia	February 5–7	...	...	...	1,200	1,480
Fall of Petersburg	Virginia	April 2	...	...	...	3,361	3,200
Fort Fisher	North Carolina	June 13–15	...	...	...	2,483	955
Petersburg	Virginia	March 25	...	...	...	834	1,176
Spanish Fort	Alabama	March 26 to April 8	...	...	...	552	795

* See Atlanta Campaign.

DEATHS IN CONFEDERATE ARMIES.*

STATE.	KILLED.			DIED OF WOUNDS.			DIED OF DISEASE.			Deaths—Grand Total
	Officers.	Enlisted Men	Total	Officers.	Enlisted Men	Total	Officers.	Enlisted Men	Total	
Alabama	14	538	552	9	181	190	8	716	724	1,466
Arkansas	104	2,061	2,165	27	888	915	74	3,708	3,782	6,862
Florida	47	746	793	16	490	506	17	1,030	1,047	2,346
Georgia	172	5,381	5,553	140	1,579	1,719	107	3,595	3,702	10,974
Louisiana	70	2,548	2,618	42	826	868	32	3,027	3,059	6,545
Mississippi	122	5,685	5,807	75	2,576	2,651	103	6,704	6,807	15,265
North Carolina	677	13,845	14,522	330	4,821	5,151	541	20,061	20,602	40,275
South Carolina	360	8,827	9,187	257	3,478	3,735	79	4,681	4,760	17,682
Tennessee	99	2,016	2,115	49	825	874	72	3,353	3,425	6,414
Texas	28	1,320	1,348	13	1,228	1,241	10	1,250	1,260	3,849
Virginia	266	5,062	5,328	200	2,319	2,519	168	6,779	6,947	14,794
Regular C. S. Army	35	972	1,007	27	441	468	25	1,015	1,040	2,515
Border States	92	1,867	1,959	61	672	733	58	2,084	2,142	4,834
Total	2,086	50,868	52,954	1,246	20,324	21,570	1,294	58,003	59,297	133,821

* The above abstracts are made from General James B. Fry's tabulation of Confederate losses from the muster rolls on file in the bureau of Confederate archives. The returns are incomplete. North Carolina makes the best showing. Nearly all the Alabama rolls are missing, still the figures are worth noting, as they show that at least 74,524 were killed or died of wounds, and that 59,297 died of disease.

ORGANIZATIONS IN THE SERVICE OF THE CONFEDERATE STATES FROM EACH SOUTHERN STATE.

	CAVALRY.				INFANTRY.		ARTILLERY.			TOTAL.			
	Regiments	Battalions	Regiments Partisan Rangers	Battalions Partisan Rangers	Regiments	Battalions	Regiments	Batteries (Light)	Battalions (Heavy)	Regiments	Battalions.	Regiments Artillery	Batteries
Alabama	5	...	3	...	55	11	...	16	...	63	11	..	16
Arkansas	6	2	...	...	35	12	...	15	...	41	14	...	15
Florida	2	1	...	...	10	2	...	6	...	12	3	...	6
Georgia	11	2	1	1	68	17	...	28	2	80	22	...	28
Louisiana	2	1	1	...	34	10	2	26	...	36	11	2	26
Mississippi	7	4	2	...	49	6	...	20	...	58	10	...	20
North Carolina	1	5	...	...	69	4	..	9	2	70	11	..	9
South Carolina	7	1	...	...	33	2	1	28	1	40	4	1	28
Tennessee	21	11	...	...	61	2	1	32	1	82	14	1	32
Texas	28	4	...	...	22	5	..	16	...	50	9	..	16
Virginia	22	11	1	...	65	10	1	53	...	89	21	1	53
Border States	9	5	...	...	21	4	...	11	...	30	9	...	11
C. S. Regulars	6	...	...	...	7	...	...	1	...	13	..	...	1
Grand Total	127	47	8	1	529	85	5	261	6	664	139	5	261

AGGREGATE.—529 regiments and 85 battalions of infantry; 127 regiments and 47 battalions of cavalry; 8 regiments and 1 battalion of Partisan Rangers; 5 regiments and 6 battalions heavy artillery, and 261 batteries light artillery. In all, equivalent to 764 regiments, of 10 companies each.

These were all troops of the line, and they served during the whole or the greater part or the war. The number does not include regiments which served a short time only; neither does it include disbanded or consolidated regiments, nor State militia, Junior Reserves, Senior Reserves, Home Guards, Local Defense Regiments and separate companies, and yet these miscellaneous organizations rendered effective service at times and took the place of regular troops.

The Petersburg intrenchments on June 15, 1864, were held successfuly by militiamen during the first assault until the arrival of Lee's army. Partisan bands, like Mosby's and John Morgan's, kept eight or ten times their number of Union cavalry employed in protecting the territory in which they operated, or in watching their movements.

The next question arises is as to the average enrollment of the Confederate regiments. That known, the strength of the army could be soon computed.

The rolls of the North Carolina regiments have been printed, and with the eight regiments of Junior and Senior Reserves, not included in the foregoing list, show a total enrollment of one hundred and twenty-five thousand men. These rolls, incomplete as they necessarily are, show that twenty-two of the North Carolina regiments numbered over fifteen hundred men each, and some of them over eighteen hundred. The Confederacy organized but few new regiments after 1862; the recruits and conscripts were assigned to the old regiments to keep them up to an effective strength.

Gettysburg was the greatest battle of the war; Antietam the bloodiest. The largest army was assembled by the Confederates at the Seven Days' battles—the Unionists at the Wilderness.

A CORPS OF THE CONFEDERATE ARMY UNDER GENERAL HOOD MARCHING BY NIGHT THROUGH A BURNING WOODS IN GEORGIA.

BRIG.-GEN. ZEBULON YORK, OF LOUISIANA.
[From an old photograph.]

BRIG.-GEN. CARNOT POSEY, OF MISSISSIPPI.
Died of wounds received at Battle of Bristoe Station.
[From an old daguerreotype.]

BRIG.-GEN. WILLIAM R. TERRY, OF VIRGINIA.
[From an old photograph.]

BRIG.-GEN. WILLIAM B. WADE, OF MISSISSIPPI.
[From an old tintype.]

BRIG.-GEN. J. B. PALMER, OF TENNESSEE.
[From an old photograph.]

BRIG.-GEN. WILLIAM A. QUARLES, OF TENNESSEE.
[From a photograph taken in 1864.]

BRIG.-GEN. FELIX K. ZOLLICOFFER, OF TENNESSEE.
Killed at the Battle of Mill Springs, or Fishing Creek, Ky., January 19, 1862.
[From a photograph of an old portrait.]

BRIG.-GEN. HUMPHREY MARSHALL, OF KENTUCKY.

BRIG.-GEN. EDWARD HIGGINS, OF LOUISIANA.
[From a tintype taken in 1861.]

ORGANIZATION OF TROOPS

IN THE

THIRD MILITARY DISTRICT,

DEPARTMENT OF MISSISSIPPI AND EAST LOUISIANA,

COMMANDED BY

MAJ.-GEN. FRANK GARDNER,

APRIL 30, 1865.

MAXEY'S BRIGADE.

Brigadier-General S. B. Maxey, Commanding.

Tenth Arkansas—Colonel A. R. Witt.
Fourth Louisiana—Lieutenant-Colonel W. F. Pennington.
Thirtieth Louisiana—Major Charles J. Bell.
Forty-second Tennessee—Lieutenant-Colonel Isaac N. Hulme.
Forty-sixth Tennessee *—Colonel A. J. Brown.
Forty-eighth Tennessee—Colonel A. S. Godwin.
Forty-ninth Tennessee—Major D. A. Lynn.
Fifty-third Tennessee—Captain H. H. Aymett.
Fifty-fifth Tennessee *—Colonel A. J. Brown.
Texas Battalion Sharpshooters—Major James Burnett.
Fenner's Louisiana battery—Captain C. E. Fenner.
Roberts' (Miss.) battery—Lieutenant F. W. Coleman.
Watson (La.) battery—Lieutenant E. A. Toledano.

BEALL'S BRIGADE.

Brigadier-General W. N. R. Beall, Commanding.

Forty-ninth Alabama—Colonel Jeptha Edwards.
First Arkansas Battalion—Lieutenant-Colonel Bart Jones.
Eleventh Arkansas †—Colonel John L. Logan.
Seventeenth Arkansas †—John Griffith.
Twelfth Arkansas—Colonel T. J. Reid.
Fourteenth Arkansas ‡—Colonel F. P. Powers.
Eighteenth Arkansas ‡—Colonel R. H. Crockett.
Twenty-third Arkansas ‡—Colonel O. P. Lyles.
Fifteenth Arkansas §—Colonel B. W. Johnson.
Sixteenth Arkansas §—Colonel David Provence.
First Mississippi—Colonel J. M. Simonton.
Thirty-ninth Mississippi—Colonel W. B. Shelby.
Company B, First Mississippi Light Artillery—Captain A. J. Herod.
Company F, First Mississippi Light Artillery—Captain J. L. Bradford.
Company K, First Mississippi Light Artillery—Captain George F. Abbay.

GREGG'S BRIGADE.

Brigadier-General John Gregg, Commmanding.

Ninth Louisiana Battalion; Third Tennessee; Tenth Tennessee; Thirtieth Tennessee; Forty-first Tennessee; Fiftieth Tennessee; First Tennessee Battalion; Seventh Texas; First Missouri Light Battery, Brookham Light Battery.

PONCHATOULA.

Colonel J. M. Simonton, Commanding.

McLannin's battalion; Cochran's command; Herren's company; Lester's company.

CAVALRY COMMAND.

Lieutenant-Colonel George Grant, Commanding.

Ninth Tennessee Battalion—Major James H. Aikin.
Garland's battalion—Major W. H. Garland.
Hughes' battalion—Lieutenant-Colonel Wilbourn.
Bryan's company—Captain Bryan.
Cage's company—Captain Cage.
Gonzales' (Daigre's) company—Captain Gonzales.
Norman's company—Captain Norman.
Stockdale's company—Captain Stockdale.
Terrell's company—Captain Terrell.

UNATTACHED.

Ninth Louisiana Battalion Partisan Rangers—Major J. DeBaur.
Rhodes' company—Captain T. C. Rhodes.

HEAVY ARTILLERY.

Lieutenant-Colonel M. J. Smith, Commanding.

First Alabama—Lieutenant-Colonel M. B. Locke.
Twelfth Louisiana Battalion, Lieutenant-Colonel P. F. De Gournay.
First Tennessee Battalion, ——.
Provost Guard (unattached companies).
Lewis' company light infantry, Lieutenant C. L. Barrot.
English's (Miss.) artillery, Lieutenant W. W. Wilkins.

*Consolidated.
†Consolidated under Logan's command.
‡Consolidated under Lyles' command.
§Consolidated under Johnson's command.

HEADQUARTERS DEPARTMENT TRANS-MISS.,
SHREVEPORT, LA., April 30, 1863.

[General Orders, No. 9.]

The following officers are announced upon the staff of the commanding general:

Major George Williamson, Assistant Adjutant-General.
Major T. G. Rhett, Chief of Artillery.

By command of
LIEUTENANT-GENERAL E. KIRBY SMITH.

H. P. PRATT,
Assistant Adjutant-General.

Abstract from report of troops in the District of the Gulf, commanded by Major-General John H. Forney, October 31, 1862 (headquarters, Mobile, Ala.).

TROOPS.	Present for Duty.		Effective Total . .	Aggregate Present.	Aggregate Present and Absent . .
	Officers . .	Men . . .			
Army of Mobile	254	3,475	3,700	4,888	5,605
Detachment of observation .	130	1,949	2,104	2,462	2,818
Forts Morgan and Gaines . .	64	1,162	1,295	1,484	1,629
Choctaw and Owen Bluffs .	20	217	246	295	338
Grand total	468	6,803	7,345	9,129	10,390

ORGANIZATION OF TROOPS

IN THE

DISTRICT OF THE GULF,

COMMANDED BY

MAJ.-GEN. JOHN H. FORNEY,

OCTOBER 31, 1862.

ARMY OF MOBILE.

Brigadier-General J. E. Slaughter, Commanding.

Seventeenth Alabama; Eighteenth Alabama; Thirty-sixth Alabama; Thirty-eighth Alabama; Fortieth Alabama; Cavalry (company); Marianna Dragoons; Mobile Dragoons; Partisan Rangers (battalion); Partisan Rangers (company); Second Battalion Alabama Artillery, Company A; Second Battalion Alabama Artillery, Company E; Gid. Nelson Artillery.

CHOCTAW AND OWEN BLUFFS.

Colonel C. D. Anderson, Commanding.

Twenty-first Alabama Infantry, First Battalion.

DETACHMENT OF OBSERVATION.

Colonel J. R. F. Tatnall, Commanding.

Twenty-ninth Alabama; Nineteenth Louisiana; Second Alabama Cavalry; Florida cavalry (battalion); Fowler's battery.

FORTS MORGAN AND GAINES.

Colonel W. L. Powell, Commanding.

Twenty-first Alabama, Second Battalion; First Confederate Regiment Georgia Troops; Arrington's company cavalry; Barlow's company cavalry; Alabama Artillery, First Battalion.

Abstract from report of the troops in the Department of the Gulf, Major-General S. B. Buckner, commanding, May 1, 1863 (headquarters, Mobile, Ala.).

COMMAND.	Present.			Aggregate Present and Absent . .	Aggregate last Report . . .
	Effective Total	Total . . .	Aggregate . .		
Department staff *	. . . . .	. . . . .	15	15	15
EASTERN DIVISION.					
Staff *	. . . . .	. . . . .	7	7	7
Infantry	756	864	903	949	950
Artillery	132	141	145	151	152
Cavalry	320	368	384	456	453
WESTERN DIVISION.					
Staff *	. . . . .	. . . . .	23	25	31
Artillery †	2,622	2,847	3,010	3,431	4,444
Cavalry	706	750	784	1,025	1,022
Total infantry	756	864	903	949	950
Total artillery	2,754	2,988	3,155	3,582	4,596
Total cavalry	1,026	1,118	1,168	1,481	1,475
Grand total *	4,536	4,970	5,271	6,059	7,074

* Including department and division staff.
† Two battalions transferred to Tennessee.

STATEMENT OF TROOPS

IN THE

DEPARTMENT OF THE GULF,

COMMANDED BY

MAJ.-GEN. S. B. BUCKNER,

APRIL, 1863.

EASTERN DIVISION. *

Brigadier-General James Cantey.

Second Alabama Cavalry—Lieutenant-Colonel James Cunningham.
Twenty-ninth Alabama Infantry—Colonel John F. Conoley.
—— Florida Cavalry Battalion—Captain T. J. Myers.
Nineteenth Louisiana Infantry—Colonel W. P. Winans.
Amos' cavalry—Captain Amos.
Barry's (Tenn.) battery—Captain Robert L. Barry.
Pegues' command—Captain Pegues.

WESTERN DIVISION.

Brigadier-General William W. Mackall.

FIRST BRIGADE.

Brigadier-General James E. Slaughter.

Ninth Alabama Battalion—Lieutenant-Colonel Bushrod Jones.
Seventeenth Alabama Infantry †—Colonel V. S. Murphey.
Twenty-first Alabama Infantry ‡ (First Battalion)—Colonel C. D. Anderson.
Charpentier's (Ala.) battery †—Captain S. Charpentier.
Gid Nelson (Ala.) Artillery—Captain Joseph Selden.
Humes' (Tenn.) battery †—Captain W. Y. C. Humes.
Apalachee Battery—Major E. L. Winder.
Belmont Battery †—Captain John James Word.
Mobile, Ala.—Lieutenant-Colonel N. Wickliffe.
Pinto Battery §—Captain C. E. Sadler.
Selma, Ala.—Major N. R. Chamblin.
Spanish River Battery §—Captain J. H. Hutchisson.

SECOND BRIGADE. ‖

Brigadier-General A. Cumming.

Eighteenth Alabama Infantry—Colonel J. T. Holtzclaw.
Thirty-sixth Alabama Infantry—Colonel R. H. Smith.
Thirty-eighth Alabama Infantry—Colonel Charles T. Ketchum.
—— Alabama Battalion Partisan Rangers—Major William Boyles.
First Confederate Infantry (First Battalion)—Lieutenant-Colonel J. W. Aderhold.
Fowler's (Ala.) battery—Captain W. H. Fowler.
Dorrance Rangers—Captain John W. Murrell.

THIRD BRIGADE.

Colonel William L. Powell.

First Alabama Artillery Battalion ¶—Lieutenant-Colonel R. C. Forsyth.
Twenty-first Alabama Infantry ¶ (Second Battalion)—Lieutenant-Colonel C. S. Stewart.
First Confederate Infantry ** (Second Battalion)—Lieutenant-Colonel George A. Smith.
Baldwin Rangers ††—Captain T. C. Barlow.
Cary's (Ala.) battery ‡‡—Captain J. M. Cary.
City Troop ††—Captain E. T. Arrington.

* Troops at and near Pollard.
† Bay Shore, Near Mobile, Colonel Murphey commanding. Detachment of Seventeenth Alabama manning Apalachee Battery.
‡ Choctaw and Owen Bluff, as heavy artillery.
§ Pinto Island and mouth of Spanish River, Major Quattlebaum commanding.
‖ About Mobile.
¶ Fort Morgan.
** Fort Gaines.
†† Perdido River.
‡‡ Grants Pass.

A BRAVE MAN.—One of the Alabama regiments was fiercely attacked by a whole brigade in one of the battles around Richmond. The Alabamians, unable to withstand such great odds, were compelled to fall back about thirty or forty yards, losing, to the utter mortification of the officers and men, their flag, which remained in the hands of the enemy. Suddenly a tall Alabamian, a private in the color company, rushed from the ranks across the vacant ground, attacked a squad of Yankees who had possession of the flag with his musket, felled several to the ground, snatched the flag from them, and returned safely back to his regiment. The bold fellow was of course immediately surrounded by his jubilant comrades and greatly praised for his gallantry. His captain appointed him to a sergeantcy on the spot, but the hero cut everything short by the reply: "Oh, never mind, captain! Say no more about it. I dropped my whisky flask among the Yankees and fetched that back, and I thought I might just as well bring the flag along!"

DEFENSE AND FALL OF THE SPANISH FORT,

MARCH 26 TO APRIL 8, 1865.

BY

BRIGADIER-GENERAL R. L. GIBSON.

MERIDIAN, MISS., April 16, 1865.

ON the 23d of March I was ordered by Major-General Maury, commanding District of the Gulf, to report with my brigade to Brigadier-General St. John Liddell, at Blakely, and by him directed to move toward Deer Park, near Fish River, and with two regiments of Holtzclaw's brigade, Colonel Bush. Jones commanding, and Colonel P. B. Spence's cavalry, to hold the enemy in observation. The following day I disposed these troops for this purpose, and early the next morning the enemy moved in force on the Durant Road, toward Sibleys Mills, about two miles to the east, beyond Spanish Fort, in the direction of Blakely. I had selected a line of battle on the north side of D'Olive Creek, intending to dispute its passage and develop him, having already thrown my small cavalry force upon his flanks, with orders to harass him. At this point the major-general commanding District of the Gulf came up to offer battle with his whole force; but in consequence of the rapid movement of the enemy to our left and rear, as above indicated, the larger portion of the troops were ordered to Blakely under Brigadier-General Liddell, and my instructions were to assume immediate command of the defenses of Spanish Fort. Set apart for this purpose were Brigadier-General Bryan M. Thomas' brigade of Alabama Reserves, about nine hundred and fifty muskets strong; Colonel I. W. Patton's artillery, three hundred and sixty effectives; and my own brigade of five hundred rifles, Colonel F. L. Campbell commanding. Batteries Huger and Tracy likewise constituted a part of this general command; and the garrisons in them, under Major Wash. Marks, Twenty-second Louisiana Artillery, formed Patton's artillery, but are not included in the above estimate; for though they rendered valuable services, they only furnished occasional re-enforcements in defense of the field-works near the water battery, called Spanish Fort.

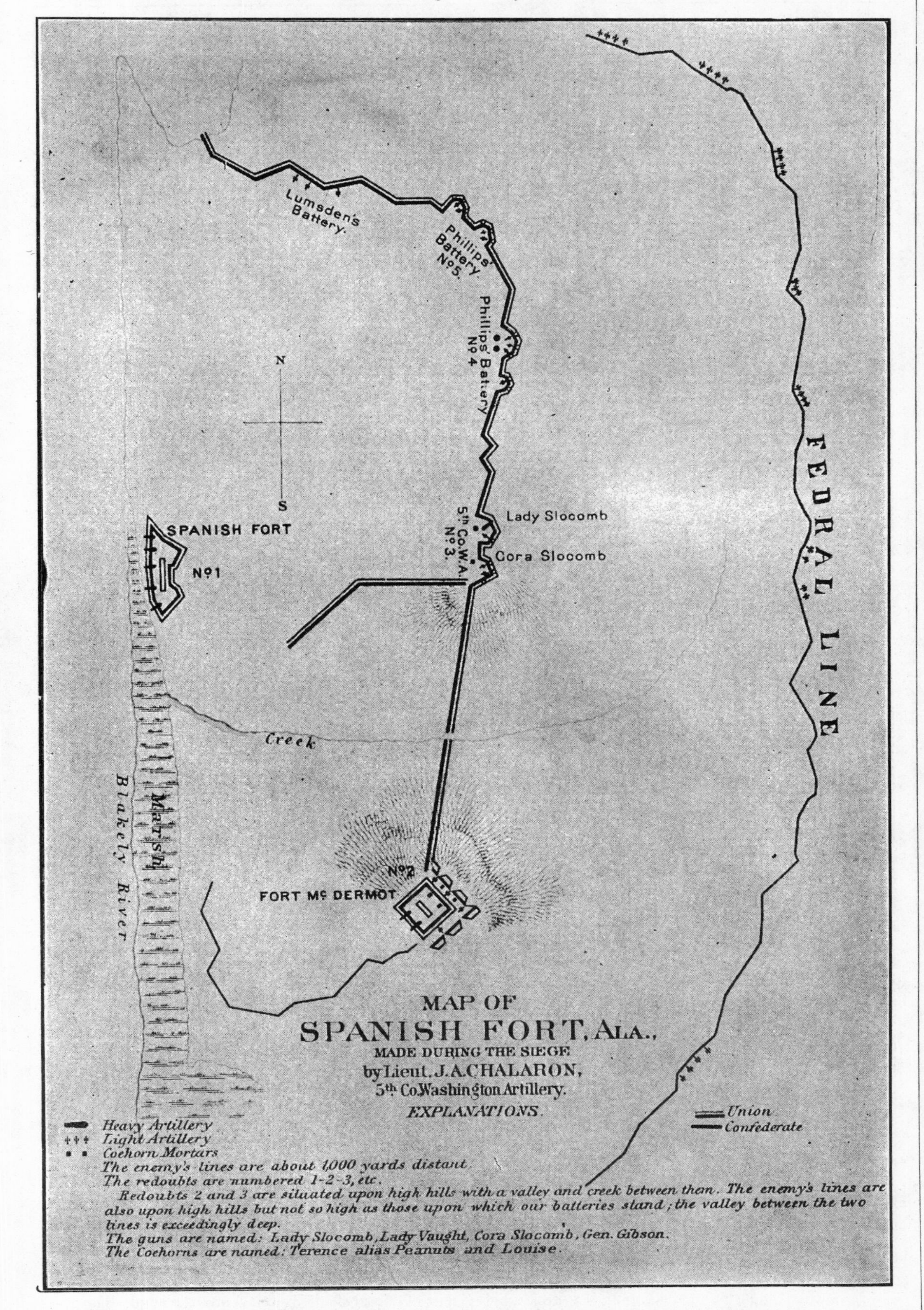

Upon examination I discovered the line of defense to be about three thousand five hundred yards long, inclosing a battery of four heavy guns in Spanish Fort, overlooking the bay, and strengthened by three redoubts so located that they commanded very well the right and center of the position.

The whole artillery consisted of six heavy guns, fourteen field-pieces and twelve Coehorn mortars. Several additional guns were received during the operations. Of this line there were four hundred yards on the extreme right, in front of which the forest had been cut down, but no defensive works constructed; about three hundred and fifty yards in the center, across a deep ravine, in front of which there was only a slight curtain partially complete; and about six hundred yards on the extreme left, with no works of any kind, and the dense forest covering that flank untouched.

The three redoubts gave no mutual support with the exception of two guns in redoubts 2 and 3, and no cross-fire could be obtained. The main line from redoubt 3 was retired without any deviation, and the left flank was thrown back and fell off into such low ground that artillery could not be used to any extent along its front, as in a regularly laid out *cremaillere*. The works from redoubt 3 were placed so far back on the retreating slope that the infantry could only command its crest, but not the ravine beyond; and, generally, from the center to the extreme left flank, the enemy's was upon the highest ground.

Such was the extent and incomplete condition of the defenses at Spanish Fort when, on assuming command, I carefully inspected them.

It was apparent that an immense work with the spade, pick and axe was before us, and that some decisive measure must be adopted to prevent the large army already upon our front from coming upon us vigorously or by an onset. At once the main body was disposed along the rifle-pits and set hard at work, though there was quite a deficiency of tools.

Special parties were detailed to lay off a long line of battle as far in advance of the position as they could go, and to make camp fires along its whole length; and other devices were employed to create an exaggerated impression of our numbers and to conceal the exact locality of our positions. To gain time, and by a show of confidence and boldness, to make the enemy cautious, I resolved to attack him before daylight the next morning. Lieutenant-Colonel R. L. Lyndsay, with five hundred and fifty men, in gallant style charged his lines, surprised and drove in his skirmishers, capturing a few prisoners and a large number of arms and accouterments, and was only recalled after the enemy was revealed in a heavy and extended order of battle.

Our object seemed to be accomplished, for it was not until late in the evening that he advanced, feeling his way cautiously, and, making no assault, invested our defenses.

My scouts had reported two *corps d'armee* in front of us (the Thirteenth and Sixteenth), Major-General Canby commanding. From information derived from the prisoners, and from drawings and maps captured with one of the engineers of the Sixteenth Corps, I estimated the force to be not less than twenty thousand muskets strong—perhaps much larger.

On his first advance he succeeded at some points in pushing his skirmishers to within two hundred yards; on the center and right he was driven back. Our artillery fire was reserved until his light batteries came well up, when it was suddenly opened, and it appeared to be with decided effect. On the left the ground was more favorable to the enemy, and to this fact and the want of works may be ascribed the nearness with which he was enabled to establish himself. On the right and center he was held at bay to the very close of the operations, nor did he at any time gain any decided advantages without severe contests and heavy losses. He sat down before us and developed rapidly a system of regular approaches by parallels. He gradually converted his advanced lines into heavy works, and after the first week displayed an exceedingly large armament of artillery. The absolute necessity of first completing our lines, and the smallness of my force, prevented the attempt to meet his approaches by any system of advance. There was a great deficiency of tools. Spades, axes and every available instrument that could be of service in any way were kept busy night and day from the commencement to the close. In the first days of the investment (the third I believe) Thomas' brigade of Alabama Reserves was relieved by Holtzclaw's and Ector's brigades, both together exceeding Thomas' by about one hundred muskets. Large detachments from these commands did not rejoin them. While the transfer was being made my force was greatly swollen, but the troops were for the most part out of position awaiting transportation. Sickness and constant heavy details diminished the number of muskets.

For the first ten days my artillery, aided by well-trained sharpshooters, was able to cope with that of the enemy; sometimes silenced his guns and often broke up his working parties in handsome style; but after this time it was evident, from his overwhelming resources in men and guns, that it would be impossible with the means at my disposal to arrest his gradual advance. While he was steadily digging up to our front and flanks, his fleet kept up a well-directed and heavy fire in our rear, and mortars dropped over the entire surface shells of the largest size; his batteries in rear of his right flank bombarded batteries Huger and Tracy, exposing our communication and sweeping the woody flat upon the left flank, enfiladed for several hundred yards that part of the line, and took in reverse—the center and right—the batteries and rifle-pits. So his batteries in front of redoubt McDermott, No. 2, looked down upon our whole right, and took in reverse the left center and left.

Our works were shaped a good deal like a horseshoe pressed open, and those batteries at the toe and heels could command every part of the line, and these batteries were of the weightiest metal. An expedition between us and Blakely, in Bay Minette, was daily growing more formidable, and it became necessary to guard our water flanks by picket-boats, and to dispose a considerable force to protect our rear and the telegraph lines and the headway against his fleet and barges.

Several attempts were made by concentrated bombardment from day to day to demoralize the troops, with the intention to take advantage of any accident, and likewise repeated efforts to advance his lines without digging; but in each instance he was repulsed with a loss proportioned to the vigor of the attack.

At one time he established himself very close to redoubt 2, and it became necessary, in order to hold this battery and use it effectively, to dislodge him. It was designed to make a general attack on his part of the line to the extreme right, and Captain Clement S. Watson, my inspector-general, led the sortie in front of the battery and was completely successful. This party captured three times their own number of the enemy under cover of our artillery; and the moral effect was still more important, for it inspired our troops with a bolder spirit and the enemy with increased caution. After this the enemy guarded carefully against sudden dashes; and though frequent combats at particular points took place, and a few more sorties were contemplated, none could be undertaken with a reasonable prospect of success.

I found by the 8th of April that all my artillery was about silenced; that the enemy had largely increased his; that his working parties, greatly re-enforced at every point and carefully protected against sorties, were pushing forward at a rate that would bring them up to our main works; that the pressure upon my flanks, especially the left, was so heavy that it would take my whole force to resist it successfully; that his preparations of launches in the Bay of Minette had assumed formidable proportions; and, finally, that there was unusual activity and movement in his lines.

I determined to develop the situation; to discover as accurately as possible his strength and intentions, and to measure our ability for further defense. It was apparent from his superiority in heavy guns and numbers, and the nearness of his approach at several points, that unless extraordinary re-enforcements could be had, the moment had at length arrived when I could no longer hold the position without imminent risk of losing the garrison.

Not an officer or man had taken any unbroken rest except such as they could snatch while on duty in the main works. When there was no fighting there was digging, cutting, moving ammunition, taking down and putting up heavy guns and repairing damages and extending the main lines.

Two weeks of constant work, night and day, with the musket and spade, failed to discourage, but could not fail to fatigue and jade, the troops.

Just at sunset, therefore, all the batteries were ordered to open, and the skirmishers and parts even of the main line to keep up a brisk fire, and all officers to observe the enemy closely and to hold themselves in readiness for any contingency.

My artillery was soon disabled and silenced, and the fire from his advanced lines showed them to be filled with men—strong lines of battle.

Shortly after dark, while the firing was very heavy from all points, and especially upon the flanks, the enemy broke through the line on the extreme left, completely turned the flank of the main works and captured some of the men in them. He was enabled to do this, for the ground here was covered with water, a marshy and densely-wooded flat, and it had been impossible to get earth to throw up works or to make any covering for our men. A battery from an elevated point on the enemy's line, just in front of this flat, swept through it and rendered it almost untenable.

He was at once attacked with the force disposed in advance for this very contingency, and the moment General Holtzclaw gave the information re-enforcements were hastened to him with orders to drive back the enemy by a front and flank attack.

The general reported his force not sufficient for this purpose, and there was some confusion among the troops on the extreme left; that in the dark woods and fallen timber the necessary disposition could not be made, and that the enemy was certainly in overwhelming strength. My staff officers and scouts brought similar intelligence. Colonel F. L. Campbell, commanding Gibson's brigade, was at once withdrawn from the right and directed to dispose a part of his command in skirmish order around the enemy, and to post the rest as a rear-guard at the headway, so as to hold and secure the retreat. They at once drove back the advancing line of the enemy, and so strong and vigorous were these attacks that they soon compelled his overwhelming and constantly swelling forces to assume the defensive. He set to work to intrench. Our left might have been thrown back and re-established, but the labor for such an undertaking was altogether beyond our ability.

Moreover, he had advanced several hundred yards in rear of our works, and the probability arose almost to a certainty that as soon as he discovered where he really was a general assault would be ordered, and he surely would ascertain this fact either during the night or, beyond all question, at daylight. His lodgment, too, when developed, would have enabled him to cut off retreat. I determined, therefore, to withdraw my troops.

My standing orders from Major-General D. H. Maury, commanding District of the Gulf, had been not to hold Spanish Fort for a moment after the garrison was in danger of capture—not to risk in the defense of an outpost forces intended to occupy and defend the stronghold and the works around Mobile.

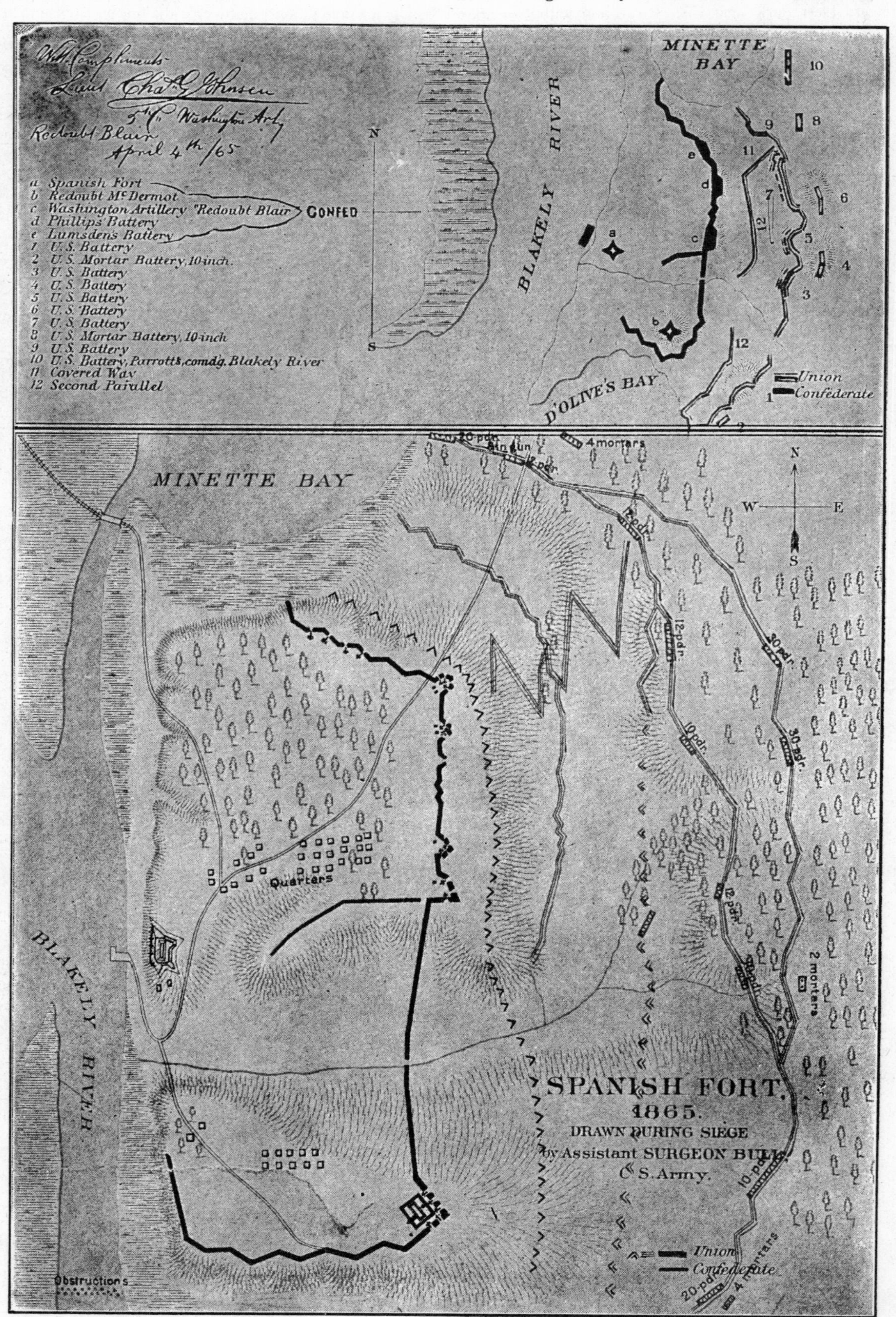

It was always a difficult and delicate task to decide, but I thought the moment had at length arrived, contemplated by my instructions, when, however painful to the devoted defenders, the position had to be given up.

The guns were ordered to be spiked, and time was allowed for this purpose; the few remaining stores were issued; the sick and wounded were carefully removed—the infirmary corps and several hundred negroes who arrived that evening to be employed in the defense; and finally, in good order, the whole garrison was withdrawn. The retreat was along a narrow treadway, about eighteen inches wide, which ran from a small peninsula from the left flank across the river, and over a broad marsh to a deep channel opposite Battery Huger. It was about twelve hundred yards long and was commanded throughout by the enemy's heavy batteries in front of our left flank.

It was concealed by the high grass and covered with moss, and the troops pulled off their shoes and thus, in a noiseless manner, succeeded in retiring without attracting the attention of the enemy. The night was rather dark and the movement could not be hurried. From the end of the treadway they were conveyed in light boats to Battery Huger, and thence to Blakely in steamers, except a few under Colonel Bush. Jones, who were directed to go up the marsh to Blakely. My scouts had already moved along this route with a view of ascertaining whether it was practicable. This was necessary in order to enable all the troops to get beyond range of the enemy's batteries before daylight. From Blakely they were ordered to Mobile by the major-general commanding District of the Gulf. I regret to report that some of the skirmishers, in spite of the precautions taken and the ample time given, and the pointed inquiries made on the occasion, and the vigilance of brigade commanders and staff officers, which I did not fail to observe, were left upon the lines. The officers in command reported all their men called in and safe. It is to be hoped and presumed that these accidents will be satisfactorily explained. I deeply deplore the capture of even a part of these brave men.

I desire to express in the strongest terms my admiration of the steady valor and cheerful endurance of the officers and members of Ector's, Holtzclaw's and Gibson's brigades, as well as of Patton's artillery. I thank them for their zealous co-operation and soldierly bearing: Brigadier-General J. F. Holtzclaw, commanding the left wing; Colonel J. A. Andrews, commanding Ector's brigade; Colonel Bush. Jones, commanding Holtzclaw's brigade; Colonel F. L. Campbell, commanding Gibson's brigade;

From an original crayon lithograph published by Kurz & Allison, Chicago, Ill.

LIEUTENANT-GENERAL NATHAN BEDFORD FORREST.

BORN IN BEDFORD COUNTY, TENN., JULY 13, 1821. DIED AT MEMPHIS, TENN., OCTOBER 29, 1877.

Colonel Frank Zacharie, Colonel I. W. Patton, commanding the artillery, and also Brigadier-General Bryan M. Thomas and Colonel D. E. Huger, of the Alabama Reserves.

The artillery, under the command of Patton, assisted by Marks, Slocomb, Barnes, Theard, Massenburg, Wells, Phillips, Chaleson, Leverich, Garrity, Hawkins and their associated officers, was handled with skill and courage, and rendered valuable services not only on land but against the fleet. Three vessels were believed to be sunk during the operations.

I desire to make my special acknowledgment to the major-general commanding District of the Gulf, and to his staff officers, particularly to Major D. W. Flowerree, assistant adjutant-general, and Colonels Lockett and Elmore, of the engineers. I may be pardoned for commending the intelligence and efficiency of my own staff officers: Captain C. S. Watson, inspector-general; Captain George Norton, adjutant-general; Lieutenants Cartwright Eustis and S. L. Ware, my aids-de-camp; Major W. V. Crouch, commissary; Major J. H. Henshaw, quartermaster; and Captain W. P. Richardson, ordnance officer, were energetic and untiring. The medical department, in charge of Surgeon J. S. Holt and J. F. Fryar, was conducted in a manner highly creditable to them and to their confreres.

The Rev. Father Turgis shared our dangers and hardships, and gave the consolations of religion whenever occasion offered along the trenches and in the hospital.

I must refer you to the reports of my subordinate officers for the details of their operations. The losses reported up to the evacuation were 73 killed, 350 wounded, and about 6 missing. I have not been able to get the exact number of casualties on the evening of the evacuation. I estimate our loss to have been about 20 killed and 45 wounded and 250 captured, making a total loss of 93 killed, 395 wounded, and 250 missing—out of a force of less than 2,000 men, contending for two weeks against two *corps d'armee* and a large fleet with over 75 cannon on land and nearly as many on water. We had no means of estimating the exact loss or strength of the enemy, but from every indication he largely exceeded 20,000 muskets, and his loss must have reached 2,500.

Among the killed were Colonel Burnett, chief of artillery of the District of the Gulf, who fell while examining the enemy's lines. His loss was greatly lamented by all of us, who knew and admired him as a skillful soldier and accomplished gentleman. Lieutenant A. G. Clark, of my staff, commandant of the post, was killed while charging at the head of the garrison guard to dislodge the enemy when he had turned the left flank. Louisiana has not lost during the war a truer man or a more thorough-going soldier.

The list might be prolonged; for, with the position, we left behind, filling soldier's graves, many of the bravest and best; and if any credit shall attach to the defense of Spanish Fort, it belongs to the heroes whose sleep shall no more be disturbed by the cannon's roar.

* * * * * * *

R. L. GIBSON,
Brigadier-General Commanding

FAREWELL ADDRESS OF BRIGADIER-GENERAL R. L. GIBSON TO THE LOUISIANA BRIGADE.

HEADQUARTERS GIBSON'S BRIGADE,
NEAR MERIDIAN, MISS.,
May 8, 1865.

FELLOW SOLDIERS—For more than four years we have shared together the fortunes of war. Throughout all the scenes of this eventful revolution you have been fully tried, and now retire with the consciousness of having achieved a character for discipline, for valor and for unselfish patriotism, of which you may be justly proud.

There is nothing in your career to look back upon with regret. You have always been in front of the enemy; you have never feasted in soft places at the rear, nor fought your battles at comfortable firesides. Your banners are garlanded with the emblems of every soldierly virtue; more than twenty battle-fields have seen them unfurled, they were never lowered save over the bier of a comrade.

Forget not the good and true men who have fallen. No sculptured marble may perpetuate the memory of their services; but you will wear their names ever green in your hearts, and they will be enshrined forever in the affections of the Southern people, in whose cause they fell.

Comrades, henceforth other duties will devolve upon you. Adversities can only strengthen the ties that bind you to your country and increase the obligations you owe to her interests and her honor. As soldiers, you have been among the bravest and most steadfast; and, as citizens, be law-abiding, peaceable and industrious.

You have not surrendered, and will never surrender, your self-respect and love of country.

You separate not as friends, but brethren, whom common hopes, mutual trials, and equal disasters have made kinsmen.

Hereafter you shall recount to your children with conscious pride the story of these rugged days, and you will always greet a comrade of the old brigade with open arms.

Having commanded a company and regiment in the brigade, I have known many of you from the very beginning of the struggle; have been with you through all its varied fortunes, and offer to each one of you a grateful and affectionate farewell.

May God bless you. R. L. GIBSON,
Brigadier-General Commanding.

GENERAL FORREST'S OPERATIONS,

DECEMBER, 1863.

BY

LIEUT-GEN. N. B. FORREST.

HEADQUARTERS, DEPARTMENT OF WEST TENNESSEE.
HOLLY SPRINGS, December 29, 1863.

I ARRIVED with the greater portion of my troops in this vicinity this morning, regretting very much that I had to leave West Tennessee so early. The concentration of a heavy force compelled me to move on the 24th from Jackson.

The Corinth force of the enemy reached Jacks Creek, within twenty-five miles of Jackson, on the 23d. I sent out a force to meet and develop their strength and retard their progress. They were found to consist of three regiments of cavalry, a brigade of infantry and four pieces of artillery.

We drove the cavalry back to the infantry, and then retired. I moved my force to Estnaula, on the Hatchie, crossing it by the night of the 25th. Met a cavalry regiment and routed them. Fought the enemy again on the 26th at Somerville, killing and wounding eight or ten and capturing about thirty-five prisoners.

I then moved a part of my force, under Colonel Faulkner, to Raleigh, and with the balance moved square to the left to Lafayette Bridge, on Wolfe River. On the morning of the 27th my advance reached the bridge and attacked the bridge-guard; drove them back and put to flight the force at Lafayette Station, killing several and capturing four or five prisoners. Cavalry advanced on me from Collierville, which we met and drove back. The enemy also sent re-enforcements by train from Moscow, which we held in check until all my wagon-train was safely across the river and on the road in the rear of my advance on Collierville.

We closed the fight at Collierville about 8 o'clock at night, driving the enemy into their fortifications. Not being able to hear anything of General Chalmers, and my men being worn out, I felt it to be prudent to retire, which I did, and my command is camped about seven miles west of this place. Another difficulty in the matter was that all my men armed with Austrian rifles were out of ammunition, having had the misfortune to lose my Austrian ammunition by the upsetting of a wagon at Forked Deer River.

I have brought out about twenty-five hundred men. Colonel Faulkner, who is to cross at Raleigh, has with him about eight hundred men. I hope to hear that they have gotten out safely by to-morrow. If I could have stayed there ten days longer, I could have almost doubled that number. I brought out my wagon-train and artillery safely, although I have never experienced such weather and roads. My stock, however, is much jaded and requires rest.

I have a lot of prisoners, and General Tuttle has signified his willingness to exchange man for man. Would I be justified in doing so?

I think of moving my headquarters to Oxford, and will encamp my command in Panola, in order to organize it and arm and equip it. The locality is a good one for forage, unless my command can be supplied with forage from the railroad. If so, I would prefer to be south of the Tallahatchie to organize.

N. B. FORREST,
Major-General Commanding.

AN amusing thing occurred in the Twelfth Tennessee. On one occasion a soldier, in passing to the lower part of the encampment, saw two others from his company making a rude coffin. He inquired who it was for. "Johnny Bunce," said the others. "Why," replied he, "John is not dead yet. It is too bad to make a man's coffin when you don't know if he's going to die or not." "Don't trouble yourself," replied the others. "Dr. Coe told us to make his coffin, *and I guess he knows what he gave him.*"

FORREST'S OPERATIONS AGAINST SMITH AND GRIERSON.

BY

LIEUTENANT-GENERAL N. B. FORREST.

HEADQUARTERS, STARKVILLE, MISS.,
February 26, 1864.

WE met the enemy's forces under Generals Smith and Grierson on Sunday morning last at Ellis Bridge, or Succartouchee Creek, three miles south of West Point, in front of which Colonel Forrest's brigade was posted to prevent the enemy from crossing. After a brisk engagement of an hour and a half the enemy retired toward West Point. It was not my intention to attack them, or bring on a general engagement, but to develop their strength, position and movements.

I moved forward with my escort and a portion of Faulkner's Kentucky regiment and found the enemy had begun a systematic retreat, and, being unwilling they should leave the country without a fight, ordered the advance of my column.

Will forward a detailed official report as soon as reports from brigade commanders are received. It is sufficient for me to say here that with twenty-five hundred men the enemy, numbering from six to seven thousand strong, were driven from West Point to within ten miles of Pontotoc in two days; all his efforts to check our advance failed, and his forces at last flying utterly defeated and demoralized, leaving six pieces of artillery, one hundred killed, and one hundred prisoners, and wounded estimated at three hundred or over. The seriously wounded, about fifty in number, fell into our hands. They took in their retreat every carriage, buggy, cart and wagon along the road to move their killed and wounded officers, and all their slightly wounded—according to report of citizens—were moved in front with their pack train.

Our loss is about twenty-five killed, seventy-five wounded, and probably eight or ten captured. Among the killed are my brother, Colonel Jeff E. Forrest, commanding brigade; Lieutenant-Colonel Barksdale, commanding George's regiment, and several other officers, whose names are not now remembered.

It affords me pleasure to mention the fortitude and gallantry displayed by the troops engaged, especially the new troops from West Tennessee, who, considering their want of drill, discipline and experience, behaved handsomely, and the moral effect of their victory over the best cavalry in the Federal service will tell in their future operations against the enemy—inspiring them with courage and confidence in their ability to whip them again. Considering the disparity in numbers, discipline and drill, I consider it one of the most complete victories that has occurred since the war began.

After the enemy succeeded in reaching the hills between Okolona and Pontotoc, the resistance of the enemy was obstinate, compelling me frequently to dismount my advance to drive them from favorable positions defended by the broken condition of the country. About three hundred men of the Second Tennessee Cavalry, under Colonel Barteau, and the Seventh Tennessee Cavalry, Colonel Duckworth, received the repeated charges of seven regiments of the enemy in open ground; drove them back time after time, finally driving them from the field, capturing three stand of colors, and another piece of their artillery. A great deal of the fighting was almost hand to hand, and the only way I can account for our small loss, is the fact that we kept so close to them that the enemy overshot our men. Owing to the broken down and exhausted condition of men and horses, and being almost out of ammunition, I was compelled to stop pursuit.

Major-General Gholson arrived during Monday night, and his command, being comparatively fresh, continued the pursuit, and when last heard from was still driving the enemy, capturing horses and prisoners. The enemy had crossed the Tallahatchie River on the night of the 23d, burning the bridge behind them at New Albany, and retreating rapidly toward Memphis, with Gholson still in pursuit.

N. B. FORREST,
Major-General.

ASKING FOR PARDON.—Many amusing incidents might be reported of pardon-seekers at the White House. Mr. Hilliard, of Georgia, former Minister to Belgium, rushed up to President Lincoln, seized his hand, and hoped his pardon would not be delayed. The President quietly remarked to the ex-reverend gentleman that "hope was the reward of the righteous," and vouchsafed no other reply. On another occasion a Confederate of some notoriety raised quite a laugh by saying: "I thank you, Mr. President, for my pardon; I am now a good Union man—am emphatically one of you; but didn't Stonewall Jackson give us h—l in the Valley?"

COMPREHENSIVE HISTORY OF CONFEDERATE STATES NAVY

FROM ITS

FIRST ORGANIZATION TO THE END OF THE WAR.

[NOTE.— This sketch is intended only as a summary of the operations of the Confederate States Navy. Details and descriptions of some of the operations of Fleets, Squadrons and particular vessels engaged will follow, described by the commanding officers.]

THE annals of warfare furnish no more brilliant or determined contest than that waged by the Confederate States Navy against the great and powerfully equipped Navy of the United States. The opening of the war found the South unprepared for the struggle, as it was not believed that the Federal Government would resort to coercion in order to retain the seceding States in the Union. Had the true situation been comprehended the Southern States would have been better prepared for the mighty struggle which ensued. The beginning of hostilities found the South without a single war ship, piece of ordnance, shipyard, machine shop or rolling mill with capacity for turning out armor plate or naval machinery, or any of the various kinds of manufactories necessary for the preparation of war material. The timber needed for the building of naval ships still stood in the forests, and the iron for armor plates rested in the bosom of the Alleghanies. On the other hand the North was strong and rich in all these essentials which the South needed for the creation and maintenance of armies and navies. Being extensively engaged in manufacturing of all kinds, that section was well prepared for the struggle by reason of the possession of extensive foundries and machinery plants that were readily convertible to the work of supplying army and navy equipments. The South was strictly an agricultural section, selling her products to the world and taking in exchange for them manufactured articles. She was illy prepared for the unexpected and extraordinary demands made upon her, but with a vigor and patriotism that halted at no discouragement she set about her great task.

HON. STEPHEN RUSSELL MALLORY,
Secretary of the Navy.

In addition to these discouragements, there was only a very moderate supply of specie in the South, which was soon expended in the purchase of war material. After this was exhausted the only remaining reliance was the exchange of cotton for war material in European ports, and the issue of an unredeemable currency, supported by the faith and confidence of the people.

And out of this poverty of resources was evolved that splendidly commanded and efficient navy which astonished the world by its active movements and effective services, against a powerfully equipped opponent with unlimited resources.

The great navy of the United States, augmented by numerous vessels and thousands of sailors who had been educated in the whaling service and merchant marine, enabled the Federal Government to promptly close the ports of the South and cut off their commerce, except such as might elude the vigilance of the enemy's blockading vessels in entering or leaving port. The North possessed an ample plant with which to meet the emergency. With numerous foundries, rolling-mills and manufactories, there was no delay in the production of such supplies and armaments as were needed by her army and navy. She also possessed vast resources in money and men, with the world to draw from in case of necessity. The South made a brave and determined effort to place herself in a position for effective defense. Every available shop and mill was equipped as rapidly as possible, and what could not be produced at home was drawn from abroad by the aid of swift-sailing blockade-runners. Much of these supplies from abroad was captured in transmission, but what escaped, when added to the home products, enabled the South to carry on the gallant struggle with credit to herself, her army and her navy.

The Southern officers who resigned from the United States Navy because they believed that allegiance was due primarily to their States, carried no ships with them to the Confederacy. These had to be provided. But the people were equal to the demands made upon their patriotism and energy, and how well they executed their vast undertaking history reveals in the brilliant achievements of the Virginia (Merrimac), Sumter, Florida, Albemarle, Shenandoah and other gallant ships that sailed under the Stars and Bars.

South Carolina seceded on December 20, 1860, being rapidly followed by the other Southern States. Then followed the evacuation of Fort Moultrie by Major Anderson, and the transfer of his command to Fort Sumter, on December 25th. On January 1st, Governor Pickens forbade the removal of lighthouse vessels, and three tenders in Charleston harbor were seized by the State authorities. The United States cutter Wm. Aiken was lying in the harbor. She was a first-class boat of ninety tons, and armed with a 42-pounder pivot gun. She was also seized, and, together with the steam cutter Gray, purchased by the State, constituted the first ships of what was afterward known as the Confederate States Navy.

As the various States seceded, other vessels were seized. These were the McClellan, five guns; Lewis Cass, Washington, Dodge, James Gray, Bonita, Nina, Everglade, one gun each; Fulton, United States war steamer, three guns. Total number of vessels, ten; number of guns, fifteen. The heaviest of these guns was a 68-pounder, carried by the Lewis Cass. Three others were 42-pounders, and the balance of smaller caliber. These vessels, seized by the respective States in whose waters they were found, remained in possession of the same until the adoption of a constitution for the Confederate States at Montgomery, on March 11, 1861, which empowered Congress "to provide and maintain a navy," and constituted the President "commander-in-chief of the army and navy." Congress also passed a resolution authorizing the committee on naval affairs to "procure the attendance at Montgomery, of all such persons versed in naval affairs as they may deem advisable to consult with." The chairman telegraphed a number of United States naval officers who were known to be in sympathy with the South, requesting their attendance at Montgomery. Among this number was Commander Raphael Semmes, then on duty at Washington, on the Lighthouse Board, who promptly tendered his resignation, arriving at Montgomery on the 18th, where he found a number of other officers. Among these were Captains Rousseau, Tatnall, Hollins, Ingraham and Randolph, and Commanders Brent, Farrand and Hartstene. Then followed a joint session of the military and naval committees, and on the 20th Congress passed an act to "provide munitions of war" by purchase and manufacture.

CAPTAIN JAMES D BULLOCK.
Confederate States Navy Agent in England.

COMMANDER JOHN K MITCHELL,
Confederate States Navy.

On the 21st of February Jefferson Davis, who had been inaugurated president on the 18th, dispatched Caleb Huse to Europe to purchase arms and munitions, and Commander Semmes to the North for the same purpose. On the same day Congress passed an "act to establish the navy department." President Davis at once tendered the position of Secretary to Hon. Stephen Russell Mallory, of Florida, who accepted it and proceeded vigorously to the work of organizing a navy department. The Secretary assigned Captain Franklin Buchanan to the Bureau of Orders and Detail; Commander Geo. Minor, to that of Ordnance and Hydrography; Jas. A Semple, paymaster, to that of Provisions and Clothing, and W. A. W. Spotswood, surgeon, to that of Medicine and Surgery. Commander Semmes, after his return from the North, was made a member of the Lighthouse Board, and Edward M. Tidball was selected as chief clerk of the navy department.

With his department thus organized, Mr. Mallory found himself in possession of a few small cutters and one three-gun ship, all carrying an armament of but fifteen guns. During his visit to the North, Commander Semmes succeeded in purchasing a large quantity of war supplies of various kinds, some light batteries and a plant for rifling cannon. He failed, however, as directed, to secure two steamers of strength and light draft. Commander Semmes returned to Montgomery on April 4, 1861, and the herculean task of adding better ships to the navy was pushed with great energy. From February, 1861, to August, 1862, the sum of $14,605,777 was spent in the building and equipment of a navy. By June 3, 1861, about one-fifth of the officers in the United States Navy had resigned and tendered their services to the Confederate Government. Of the Southern-born officers in the old navy, 321 left it and 350 remained. But there were few ships to command and many officers, a number of whom were assigned to shore batteries, to procuring ordnance supplies and devising means of defense.

Numerous contracts were made for the construction of gunboats and cruisers, both in Atlantic ship-yards and on the lower Mississippi.

The State of South Carolina, previous to the formation of the Confederate Government, had assigned Captain Hartstene, former commander of the United States gunboat Pawnee, to the command of the naval forces in Charleston Harbor, and on January 8th the first gun of the war was fired at the Star of the West, during her attempt to re-enforce Fort Sumter. After the formation of the Confederate Government, General Beauregard assumed command of the defenses of Charleston.

The plan of iron-plating war vessels was early discussed and decided upon, and efforts were made to secure such armor. A naval school was established at Richmond, with Lieutenant William H. Parker as superintendent. In 1861, the United States Navy consisted of ninety vessels, sixty-nine of which were serviceable. Secretary Wells purchased, altered and put in commission one hundred and thirty-six more, mounting five hundred and eighteen guns, and fifty-two more were ordered to be

CONFEDERATE BATTERY AT COCKPIT POINT, POTOMAC RIVER.
[From a sketch by A. Lumley, 1862.]

built, carrying two hundred and fifty-six guns. By December, 1861, the Federal Navy numbered 264 vessels, carrying 2,557 guns, and manned by 22,000 seamen. In addition, there was constructed for service on the Western rivers a large fleet of rams, tinclads, ironclads and mortar boats. From 1861 to 1865 there were built 126 wooden vessels, carrying 1,307 guns, and 74 ironclads, carrying 213 guns, a total of 200 vessels and 1,520 guns. Against this vast fleet was pitted the Confederate States Navy, consisting of a few vessels commanded by a band of gallant and accomplished officers who had seen service in the old navy.

In May, 1861, Mr. Mallory recommended the construction of an iron-armored ship, and a law to that effect was passed. Accordingly the sunken United States frigate Merrimac was raised, plated with three-inch iron, armed with heavy guns, christened the Virginia and dispatched against the United States fleet in Hampton Roads. Lieutenant James H. North was sent to Europe to purchase ironclad ships, but being unsuccessful, returned home and commenced their construction in Southern waters.

Mr. Mallory, Secretary of the Navy, used the utmost exertion to secure all the ironclad vessels possible for the Confederate States Navy. The work of constructing these and other war ships went on as rapidly as possible in a country poorly supplied with material and ship-building facilities. As fast as sea-going cruisers were finished, or secured by purchase abroad, they were armed and sent upon the high seas to prey on the enemy's commerce. Of these the Sumter and McRea were converted at New Orleans, but the latter was delayed in her departure and remained to become a part of Flag-Officer Hollins' Mississippi River fleet.

In April, 1861, the United States Government converted three staunch river boats into the gunboats Conestoga, Tyler and Lexington. Shortly after, eight ironclad gunboats were built. In September Admiral A. H. Foote took command of this formidable fleet which carried 157 large guns, and was put afloat in less than four months.

Commander Rousseau and Captains Hollins and Ingraham were greatly hampered by the want of skilled workmen. At New Orleans and Memphis work proceeded with all possible vigor. At the latter place the construction of the Tennessee and Arkansas was begun. It was not long until the Confederates had converted, and put in commission the McRea (flagship), General Polk, Ivy, Manassas, Jackson, floating battery, Pontchartrain, Livingston, Maurepas and Calhoun.

When the year 1862 opened the Federal fleet had been increased by the ironclad gunboats Essex and St. Louis, of ten guns each. Nine of this fleet of twelve vessels were ironclad. Against these were opposed five Confederate vessels, the McRea, Polk, Livingston, Maurepas and Ivy, all converted river craft. Being relieved of command at New Orleans by Commander W. C. Whittle, Flag-Officer Hollins ascended the Mississippi with this little fleet, in February, 1862, and, carrying but twenty guns, prepared to oppose the Federal flotilla.

The fall of Forts Henry and Donelson compelled the evacuation of Columbus, and the formation of a new line resting on Island No. 10. This position was defended by seventy guns in battery on the island and river banks. On the night of April 4th, Commander Walke, of the United States gunboat Carondelet, ran the blockade, being followed two nights after, by Commander Thompson, with the Pittsburg. This movement compelled the evacuation of the island and opened the river to the enemy down to Fort Pillow. Captain Whittle, in command at New Orleans, dispatched Flag-Officer Hollins, that the enemy's fleet under Farragut had appeared in great force off the mouth of the Mississippi, and requested that he come to the assistance of that city and its defenses. Captain Hollins wired Secretary Mallory for permission to take his fleet down, at the same time going down himself in the Ivy. Mr. Mallory refused the request, so far as the withdrawal of the Confederate vessels from Fort Pillow was concerned, and directed that the senior officer, Commander Pinkney, should use all the means in his power to retard the descent of the river by the enemy's fleet. He also directed that the Louisiana, then nearing completion, join the squadron as soon as possible. By Commander Pinkney's order, the McRea followed Captain Hollins to New Orleans, and when Fort Pillow was evacuated, the Maurepas and Pontchartrain ran up White River, and the Polk

On March 15th Congress authorized the construction or purchase of ten steam gunboats for coast defense. The States turned over to the Confederate Government the vessels, forts, arsenals, navy-yards and dock-yards seized or captured by them, and other property formerly belonging to the United States. The work of organizing the naval stations, in order to make them effective, was pushed with great vigor. To New Orleans, Commanders Rousseau and Farrand and Lieutenant Robert Chapman were dispatched to purchase or contract for the construction of cruisers and gunboats, and under this commission was constructed and sent to sea on April 18, 1861, the Sumter, the first Confederate cruiser.

On July 31st Commander Rousseau was relieved by Captain George N. Hollins. Captain D. N. Ingraham was assigned to the duty of procuring armor-plates for delivery at New Orleans. He found great difficulty in carrying out his instructions, owing to the fact that there were no mills of sufficient capacity to roll heavy armor-plates. Such mills had to be built. In the following November Captain Ingraham was transferred to duty in Charleston Harbor, under orders of Flag-Officer Tatnall. Captain Victor M. Randolph was ordered to the command of the navy-yard at Pensacola. Commander Tatnall, upon his resignation from the United States Navy, was, by the Confederate Government, made a captain and assigned to the command of the naval defenses in Georgia and South Carolina waters, with directions to improvise a squadron of light steamers. Commodore French Forrest, after his resignation from the United States Navy, was assigned by the State of Virginia to duty as flag-officer at Norfolk navy-yard, after its evacuation by the United States forces.

In spite of the discouragements surrounding its efforts, the Navy Department had afloat in November, 1861, the Sumter, Dixie, Jeff. Davis, Gordon, Virginia (Merrimac), Petrel, Everglade, Savannah (captured), Webb, McClelland, McRea, Yorktown, Patrick Henry, Resolute, Sallie Bonita, James Gray, Calhoun, Ivy, Dodge, Lady Davis, Lewis Cass, Washington, Nina, Jackson, Tuscarora, Pickens, Bradford, Nelms, Coffee, Nashville, Manassas, George Page, Judith (destroyed), and several other ships, all sea-going vessels.

By an amendatory act, passed on April 21, 1862, the official personnel of the navy was made to consist of four admirals, ten captains, thirty-one commanders, one hundred first lieutenants, twenty-five second lieutenants, twenty masters, twelve paymasters, forty assistant paymasters, twenty-two surgeons, fifteen past-assistant surgeons, thirty assistant surgeons, one engineer-in-chief and twelve engineers.

FORT DRAYTON. A CONFEDERATE FORTIFICATION ON OTTER ISLAND, S. C.

and Livingston up the Yazoo, where they were burned. The defense of the river now devolved upon the Montgomery flotilla, composed of fourteen river craft, officered by river captains, and manned by river men. A million and a half dollars were appropriated for this nondescript fleet, which had for its primary object the destruction of the Federal fleet at Cairo, but the evacuation of Columbus rendered that object futile. On May 10, 1862, a spirited engagement took place just above Fort Pillow between the Federal fleet, under Flag-Officer Davis, and that of Captain Montgomery, in which the Federal gunboats Cincinnati and Mound City were rammed and sunk. On June 6th a second engagement between these fleets took place at Memphis. This struggle was a desperate one, ending with the destruction of the Confederate fleet and the opening of the river to the enemy down to Vicksburg. The Federal Government now bent all its energies to the purpose of opening the Lower Mississippi. On April 16th Admiral Farragut crossed the bar and appeared below Forts Jackson and St. Phillip, with a combined fleet of 46 war ships, carrying 348 guns and 21 mortars. On the morning of the 18th he opened the bombardment. In order to hold what Farragut might secure, an army of 15,000 men followed, under command of General B. F. Butler. The forts, commanded by General Johnson K. Duncan, mounted 75 and 53 guns respectively. They were manned by 700 men. The Confederate naval squadron co-operating consisted of the Louisiana, 16 guns; ram Manassas, 1 32-pounder; McRea, 7 guns; Jackson, 2 guns; two launches, Nos. 3 and 6, one howitzer, the whole commanded by Commodore John K. Mitchell. Assisting the fleet also, were two State gunboats, the Governor Moore, two 32-pounder rifled guns, and the General Quitman These were supplemented by what was left of the river defense fleet, mounting from one to two guns each, and commanded by Captain John A. Stephenson.

On the morning of the 24th the enemy advanced up the river, a division of eight gunboats leading. The second division of the Federal fleet, under Admiral Farragut, followed and also passed the forts. The battle waged fiercely on both side, but the more powerful foe triumphed in the end. The Confederate ships were defeated after a brilliant and heroic struggle. Farragut sailed on up the river and captured New Orleans. General Duncan surrendered the forts and the enemy thus had the Mississippi cleared from its mouth to New Orleans. The victory of Farragut's fleet sent a thrill of joy throughout the North, and a feeling of gloom into the hearts of the brave people of the South. The Federal fleet was now devoted to attacks upon Confederate works on the Tallahatchie and Yazoo, at Haines Bluff, and other points. When the Federal gunboats, under Commander Walke, approached Yazoo City on May 21st, Commander Isaac N. Brown, Confederate States Navy, burned the Mobile and Republic and another large ship in course of construction. In July Commander Brown planted a torpedo in the Yazoo which sunk the gunboat Baron De Kalb. In an expedition up Red River the Queen of the West was disabled by the fire of Fort Taylor, and captured. She was repaired and put into the Confederate service, under command of Captain James McClosky, and added to a squadron under Major J. L. Brent, consisting of the gunboats Webb, Dr. Beaty and Grand Era. These gunboats, going in pursuit of the Federal gunboat Indianola, overhauled her at New Carthage, and, after a spirited engagement, captured her. The Indianola was afterward blown up to prevent her capture by the Federals. The Queen of the West, now a Confederate vessel, commanded by Captain Fuller, encountered a Federal squadron at Grand Lake, and in the engagement which followed she was destroyed. Numerous other desperate encounters between the Federal gunboats and the few remaining vessels of the Confederates took place, with varying success, until the triumph of the enemy in the capture of Vicksburg and Baton Rouge. In all of these the Confederate Navy and soldiers conducted themselves with conspicuous gallantry.

The sounds along the coast of North Carolina early became the theater of active naval operations. On August 29, 1861, Forts Clark and Hatteras, at Hatteras Inlet, commanded by Flag-Officer Samuel Barron, Confederate States Navy, were attacked by a Federal fleet under Commodore Stringham, supported by a land force under General B. F. Butler, and after an ineffectual resistance of three days duration they surrendered. This gave the enemy's fleet entrance to the sounds and rivers of North Carolina. Captain Wm. F. Lynch succeeded Flag-Officer Barron in command of the naval defenses. On October 1st this enterprising officer, with his little squadron, captured the Federal gunboat Fanny, loaded with a valuable supply of arms and ammunition.

It was some months after the fall of the forts at Hatteras Inlet before the Federal fleets again attempted hostile operations in the North Carolina sounds. But in January, 1862, the Federal Government fitted out an expedition for the purpose of attempting the capture of the rest of those inland seas and arresting the building of Confederate ironclads. Rear-Admiral Goldsborough commanded the Federal fleet, and General A. E. Burnside the army co-operating with him. The fleet consisted of seventeen vessels, and the army numbered seventeen thousand. This combined force arrived off Hatteras on January 12, 1862, and on February 8th appeared before Roanoke Island. General Henry A. Wise commanded the Confederate forces. Commodore Lynch's little squadron was composed of nine vessels. Two of these were side-wheel vessels, and the other seven tugboats built for canals, with the exception of the Black Warrior, a schooner. The forts and the squadron made a gallant resistance, the enemy retiring at dark. The Federals having succeeded in landing a force of about fifteen thousand men, infantry and artillery, outflanked the small Confederate force of less than a thousand men, and forced the evacuation of Forts Bartow and Blanchard. This result compelled Commodore Lynch to withdraw his squadron to Elizabeth City. The Federal fleet followed and, steaming up Pasquotauk River to Fort Cobb, another engagement was fought, resulting in the destruction of Commodore Lynch's squadron. This victory gave the enemy complete control of the sounds and rivers and command of the seaboard from Oregon Inlet to Cape Henry. Newberne surrendered after the fall of Fort Hatteras.

The Federal fleet then captured Edenton and destroyed a vessel in course of construction. A long period of inactivity on the part of the enemy again ensued, which was at last broken by the expedition of Commander John Taylor Wood, with a small force of picked men, in January, 1864. In this brilliant affair the Federal gunboat Underwriter was boarded, captured and burned. Another exceedingly brilliant affair was that of April 19, 1864, in which the ironclad Albemarle, Commander J. W. Cooke, sunk the Federal gunboat Southfield. Soon afterward the Albemarle again engaged the enemy, defeating six vessels. The Albemarle was destroyed in the following November by a Federal torpedo boat.

In this year took place the combined attack of the enemy's fleet and army upon Fort Fisher. The Federal fleet was composed of one hundred and fifty vessels and was commanded by Rear-Admiral David D. Porter. The attack was made late in December, and after a bombardment the enemy retired. He returned in a couple of weeks, the troops on the transports being commanded by General

CONFEDERATE FORTIFICATIONS ON CRANEY ISLAND, DEFENDING THE APPROACH TO NORFOLK, VA.

CONFEDERATE FORTIFICATIONS AT SEWALLS POINT, DEFENDING THE APPROACH TO NORFOLK, VA.

CONFEDERATE FORTIFICATIONS ON TANNERS CREEK, DEFENDING THE APPROACH TO NORFOLK, VA.

Terry, instead of by General Butler, as in the first attack. After a gallant resistance, in which the guns of Fort Fisher were worked effectually by officers and sailors of the Confederate States Navy, the fort fell, and Wilmington was soon afterward evacuated.

After the capture of New Orleans the Confederate Government rightly concluded that Mobile would be the next point of attack on the Gulf, and Admiral Buchanan was assigned to command of naval defenses. This enterprising officer had ready for service by June, 1863, the ironclad ram Baltic, the gunboats Morgan, Gaines and Selma, and the tender, Crescent. But the year ended without incident in Mobile Bay, On February 23, 1864, the long-looked-for attack of Farragut, with a powerful fleet, began. The entrance to the bay was commanded by Forts Morgan, Gaines and Powell, the first mounting 30 guns, the second 27, the third 6. The water battalions, in addition, had an armament of 29 guns, and the channel was obstructed by a row of piles and numerous torpedoes. Farragut sent a squadron of mortar boats and light draft vessels up the sound from the Mississippi, attacking first Fort Powell, at Grant's Pass. The bombardment continued for three days and nights, doing little damage. Meanwhile Admiral Buchanan's little fleet remained out of the contest.

General Dabney H. Maury commanded the military defenses of Mobile. He and Admiral Buchanan bent all their energies and resources to the task of resisting the enemy. Unfortunately for them, the Nashville and several other powerful vessels were lying unfinished at Mobile and Selma, and Admiral Buchanan felt sorely the necessity of their aid in the pending action.

Another season of delay ensued by reason of the non-arrival of co-operating troops and ironclads expected by Farragut. A Federal force of two thousand men, under General Gordon Granger, landed on August 3d, on Dauphine Island, under cover of a squadron of gunboats, and invested Fort Gaines.

Farragut, having completed all his preparations, on the morning of August 5th advanced to the attack. Admiral Buchanan prepared to receive the enemy with his little fleet, and the action soon became general. Farragut, on the Hartford, pushed through the torpedo line, followed by his other ships. Within an hour Fort Morgan was passed and the fleets were engaged at closer quarters. But the odds were too great, and all of the Confederate ships but the Tennessee were forced up the bay. A terrific contest then ensued between the Tennessee and Farragut's monitors, in which the gallant Confederate ship sustained the combined assaults of the enemy's numerous wooden ships and monitors, being frequently rammed. Admiral Buchanan was wounded and carried below, and, further resistance being madness, Commander Johnston surrendered his ship.

The enemy next turned his attention to Fort Powell, and, after pounding it for some time with his heavy guns, its commander, Lieutenant-Colonel J. M. Williams, withdrew his forces during the night. The guns were spiked and the magazine blown up.

The next day Farragut opened on Fort Gaines, which, on the morning of the 7th, was surrendered by Colonel Anderson. All efforts were now directed by the enemy to the capture of the remaining stronghold, Fort Morgan. General Granger invested it on the land side, with ten thousand troops and numerous heavy guns.

On the 8th its commmander, General Paige, refused a demand for surrender. After elaborate preparation the enemy commenced a fierce bombardment on the 22d of August, and during the day three thousand shells were thrown into the fort. After a tremendous contest, in which the Confederate garrison greatly distinguished themselves, General Paige surrendered on the morning of the 23d, his fort being almost battered down and many of his guns dismounted. And thus ended one of the fiercest and most stubbornly fought naval battles of modern times.

The last Confederate stronghold in the Gulf was now in the hands of the enemy. The remaining defenses of Mobile Bay, Spanish Fort, Fort Blakely, and batteries Tracy, Huger, McIntosh, Gladiator and Alexis and the Tower battery yet remained to dispute the enemy's advance upon the city.

The military defense of Mobile was transferred to Major-General Frank Gardner, and the naval command to Commodore Ebenezer Farrand. The ships left were the Baltic, Nashville, Morgan, Tuscaloosa and Huntsville. With the exception of a reconnoissance made by several of Farragut's light vessels and monitors at the mouth of Mobile River, on August 15th, and an expedition up Fish River about the middle of September, operations around Mobile were suspended until the following spring. Charleston and Fort Fisher had fallen, and large numbers of Federal troops were available for the final assault on Mobile. General R. S. Canby was given an army of fifty thousand men for operation on land, and Rear-Admiral Henry K. Thatcher succeeded Farragut in command of the United States fleet, which had several strong warships added to it. The attack began on March 21, 1865, Spanish Fort sustaining the first assault. After a heavy bombardment until April 8th, the starved-out garrison evacuated it. About thirty thousand Federal troops were engaged in its siege. With twelve thousand more troops added, the enemy laid siege to Fort Blakely, which was abandoned on April 11th. In these contests the Confederate fleet were able to take but a desultory part. Eight of the Federal lighter ships and monitors were destroyed by torpedoes. Since the first investment of Mobile the torpedo service had destroyed nine of the Federal vessels. On the same day that Fort Blakely was evacuated, April 11th, batteries Tracy and Huger were abandoned. The next day Admiral Thatcher conveyed eight thousand troops under General Granger to the front of Mobile, and demanded a surrender of the city. Mayor Slough replied that the military forces had evacuated the city, and asked protection for the citizens in the name of humanity. Commodore Farrand sunk the uncompleted ironclads Tuscaloosa and Huntsville in the channel of Mobile river, and with the balance of his ships and several blockade runners retired up the Alabama River in an effort to reach Selma. But the latter place and its naval station surrendered on April 27th to a Federal army under Major-General Frank Steele and a squadron under Lieutenant-Commander Harmony. Being blockaded in Tombigbee River, and seeing further resistance to be useless, Commodore Farrand, on May 4th, made a proposition to Admiral Thatcher to surrender. This proposition was accepted, and the two commanders met and ratified it. In addition to the five vessels of Commodore Farrand, four blockade runners and sixteen river craft fell into the enemy's hands.

Naval operations in Florida waters commenced early in January, 1861, with the surrender, without a shot, of Pensacola navy-yard to a force of State troops under Major Wm. H. Chase. The Federal commander was Commodore James Armstrong. The defenses of Pensacola Bay were Forts Barancos, Pickens and McRea. On the morning of January 10th, Lieutenant A. J. Slemmer, commander of the harbor defenses, abandoned Forts McRea and Barancos, after destroying a large quantity of ammunition and stores, transferring his men to Fort Pickens. The Florida troops took possession, and the abandoned forts were rapidly put into a more defensible condition. General Braxton Bragg was ordered to command of the Confederate troops at Pensacola, and proceeded to invest Fort Pickens. Lieutenant Slemmer, on January 24th, refused a demand for surrender. An artillery force on board the Brooklyn was en route to Fort Pickens, but by an agreement between Confederate and Federal officers this force was retained on board the Brooklyn until Mr. Lincoln came into the Presidency. The provisions, however, were allowed to be landed. The Federal Government, through Lieutenant John L. Worden, ordered the landing of the artillerymen under Captain Vogdes, and on the night of April 12th they re-enforced Fort Pickens. The Federal squadron was commanded by Captain H. A. Adams. General Bragg intended to begin the attack on the night of the 13th, but this new accession of troops to Lieutenant Slemmer's force delayed him. A number of Federal war vessels gathered in front of Pensacola, and on May 6th a blockade of the port was proclaimed. On June 8th Flag-Officer Wm. Mervine, at Key West, proclaimed a blockade of that port, pursuant to instructions from Washington. Preparations for the capture of Fort Pickens went on rapidly. Tampa Bay was blockaded on July 12th. During the summer the Confederates constructed nineteen batteries between Pensacola and Fort McRea. Defensive operations also proceeded rapidly at Fernandina and other points. On November 22d the bombardment of Fort McRea was commenced by United States naval vessels, and Barancos and the navy-yard by Fort Pickens. Fort McRea was badly damaged, the village of Warrington destroyed and the navy-yard set on fire three times. Fort Pickens was also badly breached. During the night of May 9, 1862, the navy-yard, forts and public buildings were set on fire and the city evacuated by the Confederate forces. The next day Commodore D. D. Porter appeared before the city, and a large Federal force landed from the fleet and took possession of Pensacola. The Wabash, flagship of Commodore C. P. R. Rodgers, appeared, March 11th, at St. Augustine. The city surrendered, and the next day Jacksonville was peaceably taken possession of by the United States gunboat Ottawa.

Georgia passed the ordnance of secession on January 19, 1861. Anticipating an early beginning of hostilities, the State troops, by order of Governer Brown, took possession, on January 7th, of Fort Pulaski, at the mouth of Savannah River, and in less than a month all the United States military posts in the State were occupied by Confederate troops without resistance.

On February 28th Commodore Josiah Tatnall, who had resigned from the United States Navy, tendered his services to Governor Brown, and they were accepted. He

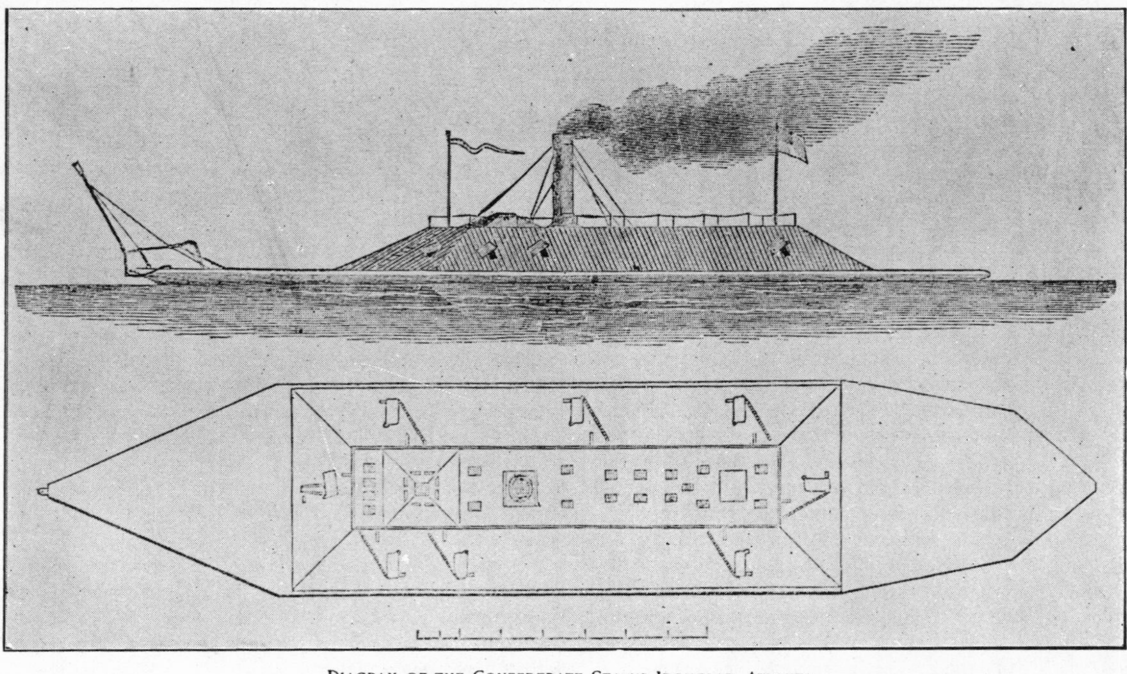

Diagram of the Confederate States Ironclad, Atlanta.

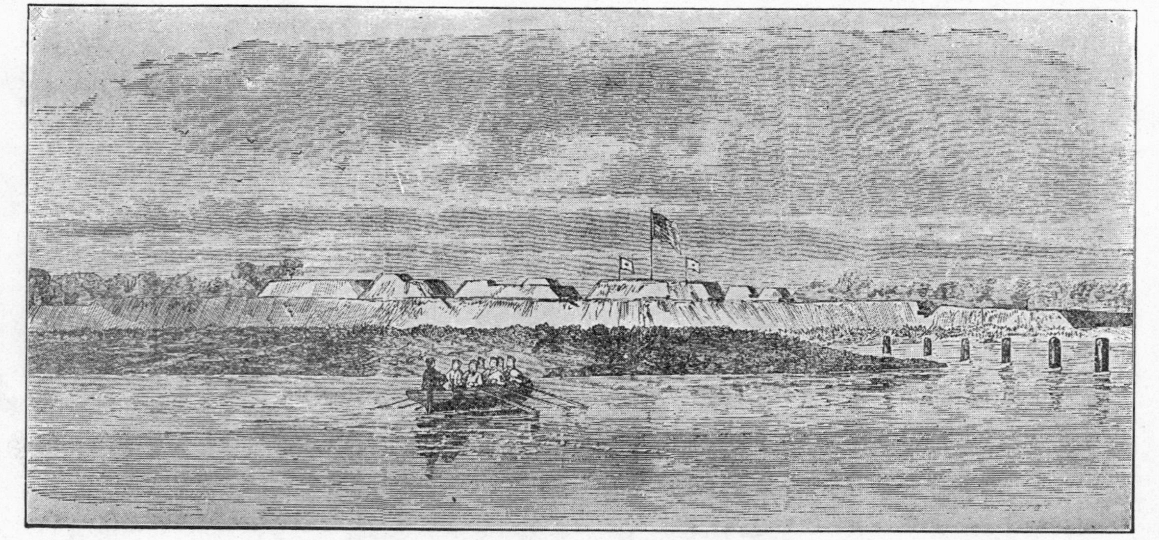

View of Fort McAllister on the Ogeechee River, Georgia.

was appointed senior flag-officer for Georgia and ordered to the command of naval affairs at Savannah. In March, he was appointed a commander in the Provisional Confederate Navy, and his command extended to include South Carolina waters. Besides Fort Pulaski, there were two other defenses of Savannah River, Forts Jackson and Causton. On November 24th Commodore John Rodgers, with a United States squadron, occupied Tybee Island. The enemy soon gained control of all the sounds on the South Carolina and Georgia coasts, as far down as Florida, the Confederates being unable to place proper armaments on the hastily constructed defenses. Savannah alone still held out. On the 26th Commodore Tatnall, with four vessels, dropped down and engaged the Federal gunboats without damage to either side. The Federals bombarded Fort Pulaski at long range for several days, and then, evacuating Tybee Island, sailed away. On December 26th Commodore Tatnall's squadron of five vessels steamed down the river and engaged the enemy's blockading vessels. The latter stood to sea, and after a short pursuit the Confederate squadron returned. The Federals sunk about twenty whaling vessels loaded with stone, in order to close navigation of the river. These accomplished the purpose for a time, but they were finally cleared out by the action of the tides. Battery Cheves was erected opposite Fort Jackson to help guard the rear defenses. It was placed in charge of the navy.

On January 26, 1862, Commodore Rodgers and Fleet-Captain C. H. Davis, with six gunboats and several armed launches, aided by transports with a force under General H. G. Wright, entered Tybee Roads. Ammunition and provisions being short in Fort Pulaski, Commodore Tatnall convoyed a supply down to it, passing between the squadrons of Davis and Rodgers, who did not attack him, hoping to get in his rear before doing so. The Federals had thirteen ships, and as Tatnall returned with two ships they made a fierce attack upon him. But Tatnall's vessels came through unhurt. As the Sampson returned she was also assailed by the Federal squadrons, and escaped serious injury, although penetrated by several shots. On April 10, 1862, General David Hunter, the Federal commander, summoned Colonel Charles Olmstead to surrender Fort Pulaski, which was refused. Then followed a fierce bombardment for two days, at the end of which time the fort capitulated. On March 25th Commodore Tatnall was ordered to Norfolk to take command of the Virginia, Commodore Buchanan having been wounded in the battle between that ship and the Monitor. Tatnall was succeeded in command at Savannah by Captain Richard L. Page. In July, 1862, the cruiser Nashville ran into Savannah with a cargo of arms, and was blockaded. Some months after, in February, 1863, she was destroyed during the attack of the enemy's ironclad fleet upon Fort McAllister, on Ogeechee River. This attack upon the fort, as well as several succeeding ones, proved futile. In the harbor of Savannah, the Scotch ship Fingal, that had run the blockade with a large consignment of arms, was cut down and converted into the ironclad Atlanta. The ironclad Georgia was also built, but her machinery proved defective. March 3d the Federals again bombarded Fort McAllister. In July, 1862, Commodore Tatnall was sent back to the command of Savannah. In January, 1863, he planned an attack upon the blockading fleet, but was delayed by obstructions in the river, which it was necessary to remove before the Atlanta could engage the enemy. This was not accomplished until February, and the Confederate Government, impatient at the delay, relieved Commodore Tatnall of his command. The Federal ironclads had now gathered for an assault upon Fort McAllister. Lieutenant Wm. A. Webb was put in command of the Atlanta, and steaming into Warsaw Sound engaged the Weehawken and Nahant, two of the most powerful of Admiral Dupont's monitors. In the battle which ensued the Atlanta ran fast aground, in which position she was almost helpless, and was pounded almost in pieces by the powerful guns of the Weehawken. After a contest of fifteen minutes, in which she failed to damage the Federal monitor, she was surrendered by Lieutenant Webb. The Savannah, another ironclad, was built, and the Milledgeville, a similar ship, was nearly completed when the city was evacuated. The blockade of the port remained unbroken. Fort McAllister was captured on December 13th by General Sherman, after several assaults, in which the Federals suffered severely. General Hardee, under cover of a vigorous fire from the ironclad Savannah, on the 20th, evacuated the city and fell back into South Carolina, and General Sherman entered the city next day. On the night of the 20th Commodore Tatnall ordered the destruction of the Georgia, Milledgeville and Water Witch, and large quantities of ship timber were also burned. Commodore W. W. Hunter, by direction of General Hardee, ascended the river with the Sampson and Macon and burned the Charleston & Savannah Railroad bridge, in order to impede Sherman's advance into South Carolina. Returning to Savannah the Sampson and Macon became hotly engaged with numerous batteries along the shores, and drawing out of the conflict retreated up the river, reaching Augusta, where they finally fell into the enemy's hands at the surrender. The Federals captured Fort Jackson on December 21st. The Savannah opened fire on the fort, shelling it for several hours. That night her commander, Captain Brent, proceeded to the South Carolina shore, where she was blown up. The Federals captured at Savannah one hundred and fifty heavy cannon and large quantities of cotton, rice and naval stores.

The State of South Carolina was the first of the Southern States to take action toward the creation of a navy by the seizure of the Aiken and other small United States vessels in Charleston Harbor, on January 1, 1861. The ironclad battery that rendered effective service in the reduction of Fort Sumter was a new departure in naval warfare. In April, Captain W. J. Hartstene assumed charge of the naval defenses of Charleston, with the rank of commander, his squadron being composed of the Gordon (flagship), Lady Davis and General Clinch. To these, other vessels were shortly added. When Captain Fox arrived before Charleston, on April 12th, with a United States squadron composed of the gunboats Hornet Lance, Pocahontas and Pawnee, he found the bombardment of Sumter in progress, but made no effort to help Major Anderson. The Confederate squadron did not take part in the engagement, but some of their officers rendered efficient services at the batteries. Sumter surrendered on the 13th, and the work of naval construction was pushed with great vigor. Other vessels were added to the State's navy, and the governor issued a number of naval commissions. Charleston Harbor was blockaded by a United States squadron early in May, and blockade-running at once began. The first prize captured by the enemy was the General Parkhill, on May 15th, by the frigate Niagara. Some of the blockade-runners were commissioned as privateers and armed. Great excitement was created both in this country and England by the act of Captain Chas. Wilkes, of the United States frigate San Jacinto, on November 8, 1861, when he overhauled the British ship Trent and took forcible possession of two of her passengers, the Confederate commissioners, Messrs. Mason and Slidell. These gentlemen had left Charleston on the Theodora and gone

Road to Evansport. Rough Earthworks. Fort Embrasured for Four Guns. Ship Point, Quantico Creek.

CONFEDERATE BATTERIES AND ENCAMPMENTS ON THE POTOMAC, NEAR AND AT THE MOUTH OF QUANTICO CREEK, VA.

Battery on the Hill. Steamer George Page and captured schooners, Fairfax and Mary Virginia, in Quantico Creek.

THE POTOMAC RIVER NEAR AND AT THE MOUTH OF QUANTICO CREEK.

to Havana and reshipped on the Trent. The participation of England in the war was only averted by the surrender of the commissioners.

On December 20th a fleet of whale-boats loaded with stone was sunk by the Federals in the channels of Charleston Harbor. These were soon washed out or settled in the sands by the tides. Late in October a fleet under Commodore S. F. Dupont, accompanied by a military force of twelve thousand men under General Thos. W. Sherman, sailed from Hampton Roads to Port Royal, arriving there, after a stormy passage, on November 5th to 7th. The Confederate defenses consisted of Forts Beauregard and Walker, commanded by General Thos. F. Drayton with two thousand men, among whom there were but a few good artillerists. Commodore Tatnall, with the Savannah (flagship), Resolute, Sampson and Lady Davis, went to the assistance of Port Royal, moving up the sounds from Savannah. Tatnall's little fleet gallantly engaged the enemy on the 7th as he attacked the forts. After a fierce bombardment, the command of General Drayton evacuated the forts and Tatnall's squadron returned to Savannah. This success gave the Federals command of the sounds from Charleston down to Savannah. Various minor engagements along the sounds and in the rivers took place between the Federal gunboats and the Confederates, during the balance of the year. Great efforts were made during the year 1862 to construct ironclad vessels. The Palmetto State, Chicora and Charleston were launched and the Columbia was under construction when Charleston fell. The blockade of Charleston Harbor was broken on January 31, 1863, by the two first-named vessels, under Commodore Ingraham, the enemy's ships being scattered like chaff. This exploit of the Palmetto State and Chicora astounded the North and delighted the people of the South, and the blockade was declared raised in Charleston Harbor.

On April 7th Dupont, with a fleet composed of the New Ironsides and eight powerful monitors, with five other ships in reserve, attacked the forts, and after an engagement of three hours was repulsed, the ships of Ingraham taking no part in the fight. In March Flag-Officer Ingraham was relieved from command of vessels afloat by Commodore Tucker, but retained command of the Station. On July 6th Dupont was relieved by Dahlgren of command of the blockading fleet, the ironclads returning on the 10th. Then ensued a long and desperate siege, which ended only with the approach of Sherman in February, 1865. On the night of the 18th Fort Moultrie and the other defenses of Sullivans Island were evacuated. This siege was marked by many stirring scenes, and exhibitions of distinguished valor on the part of the little Confederate fleet. The vast fleets of the enemy appalled them not, and they fought with a valor and devotion that will illumine the pages of history and be contemplated with pride as long as heroic and unselfish patriotism is honored by mankind. But valor and patriotism were compelled to succumb at last to numbers and unlimited resources, and in Charleston Harbor, where the sun of the Southern Confederacy rose in splendor, in April, 1861, it set in gloom in February, 1865.

The operations of the Confederate Navy in Virginia waters, after the battle in Hampton Roads between the Monitor and Virginia, were conducted with all the enterprise and skill possible in the face of vast armies and navies. Other powerful ironclads were built, and under their gallant officers and crews added fresh laurels to the Confederate Navy. In numerous encounters with the Federal ships they made a record of imperishable renown. For the greater part of the year 1863 naval operations in Virginia waters were not very active. But during the ensuing year they were of a more exciting character, continuing so until the last sad scene in the great drama was enacted at Appomattox.

No less brilliant and enduring are the records made by the Confederate cruisers built by the government or purchased abroad. The principal ones were the Florida, Alabama, Shenandoah and Rappahannock. The latter and the ram Stonewall never made a cruise. Eleven cruisers figured in the "Alabama Claims" settlement, but England only admitted three first named. The Sumter was the first cruiser put afloat, departing from New Orleans under Captain Semmes. After she was blockaded and sold at Gibraltar, Captain Semmes took command of the Alabama. After a brilliant and destructive cruise, she appeared off Galveston, decoyed one of the blockading vessels, the Hatteras, out to sea, where she engaged and sunk her after a short action. No less brilliant was the cruise of the Shenandoah under Captain James I. Waddell. After an exciting career among the enemy's commerce, she was the last vessel to lower the Confederate flag, learning of the surrender from a passing ship in the Pacific. Her flag was furled, and she stood away for England, where she was surrendered to the British Navy.

THE largest army assembled by Confederates was at the Seven Days' Battles. It numbered 80,762 men. By Federals, at the Wilderness, numbering 118,769 men.

DEFENSE OF ROANOKE ISLAND AND ELIZABETH CITY.

BY

COMMODORE W. F. LYNCH,
Flag-Officer.

FLAGSHIP SEABIRD,
OFF ROANOKE ISLAND,
February 7, 1862.

THE enemy at 10 A. M. to-day with twenty-two heavy steamers and one tug, made an attack upon the Confederate squadron and the battery at Park Point.

As his numerical force was overwhelming, we commenced the action at long range, but as our shell fell short, while his burst over and around us (owing, I think, to the superior quality of his powder), we were eventually compelled to shorten the distance.

The fight lasted continuously from 10 A. M. to 5:30 P. M., throughout which the soldiers in the battery sustained their position with a gallantry which won our warmest approbation. The fire was terrific, and at times the battery would be enveloped in the sand and dust thrown up by shot and shell.

And yet their casualties was only one man killed and three wounded. The earthwork, however, was very much cut up. I mention the battery because, in all probability, communication will reach you before intelligence will be received from appropriate official source. The enemy approached in two divisions, the rear one having the schooner transports in tow.

The advance, which was the attacking division, again subdivided, and one portion assailed us and the other the battery. Repeatedly, in the course of the day, I feared that our little squadron of seven vessels would be utterly demolished, but a gracious Providence preserved us.

Master-Commanding Moall, of the Forrest, received a wound in the head, which is pronounced serious if not mortal. I yet trust that this promising young officer, who so bravely fought his ship, will be spared to the service. Midshipman Camm, of the Ellis, and ——, of the Curlew, each lost an arm, which, with three others slightly wounded, constitute the sum of our personal casualties.

I am sorry to say that the Curlew, our largest steamer, was sunk, and the Forrest, one of the propellers, disabled. We have received other injuries, from the shot and shell,

Mainland North Carolina. Channel into Albemarle Sound. Fort Bartow.

ATTACK ON THE CONFEDERATE BATTERIES AT ROANOKE ISLAND BY THE FEDERAL GUNBOATS, FEBRUARY 8, 1862.

VIEW OF FORT BARTOW, ROANOKE ISLAND, AFTER THE BOMBARDMENT, FEBRUARY 8, 1862.

but comparatively of light character, and could, with the exception of the Forrest, be prepared to renew the action to-morrow if we only had ammunition. I have not a pound of powder nor a loaded shell remaining, and few of the other vessels are better off. During the latter part of the engagement, when the ammunition was nearly exhausted, I sent to the upper battery for a supply, but ten charges were all that could be spared, and these were expended at dark, as the enemy was withdrawing from the contest.

In all probability the contest will be renewed to-morrow, for the enemy having landed a force below the battery will doubtless endeavor to divert its fire. I have decided, after receiving the guns from the wreck of the Curlew, to proceed direct with the squadron to Elizabeth City, and send express to Norfolk for ammunition. Should it arrive in time we will return to aid in the defense; if not, will there make a final stand and blow up the vessels rather than they shall fall into the hands of the enemy.

There are reasons for retiring upon Norfolk, but it would be unseemly thus to desert this section of country. If I have erred in judgment, by a speedy notification the error will be corrected.

Commander Hunter, Lieutenant-Commanders Cooke, Parker and Alexander and Masters-Commanding McCarrick, Taylor and Hoole bravely sustained the credit of the service, and every officer and man performed his duty with alacrity. Lieutenant-Commanding Simms, although absent on detailed service, exhibited such an eagerness to participate in the conflict as to give full assurance that, if gratified, he would have upheld his high reputation.

W. F. LYNCH, *Flag-Officer*.

BATTLE BETWEEN THE VIRGINIA (MERRIMAC,) AND MONITOR, AND THE OPERATIONS OF THE JAMES RIVER SQUADRON,

MARCH 8 AND 9, 1862.

BY

CAPT. FRANKLIN BUCHANAN, C. S. N.,
Commander of the Virginia and Flag-Officer of James River Squadron.

NAVAL HOSPITAL,
NORFOLK, VA., March 27, 1862.

HAVING been confined to my bed in this building since the 9th instant, in consequence of a wound received in the action of the previous day, I have not had it in my power at an earlier date to prepare an account of the proceedings on the 8th and 9th instant of the James River squadron under my command, composed of the following-named vessels: Steamer Virginia, flagship, ten guns; steamer Patrick Henry, Commander John R. Tucker, twelve guns; steamer Jamestown, Lieutenant-Commanding J. N. Barney, two guns; and gunboats Teaser, Lieutenant-Commanding W. A. Webb, Beaufort, Lieutenant-Commanding W. H. Parker, and Raleigh, Lieutenant-Commanding J. W. Alexander, each one gun. Total, twenty-seven guns.

On the 8th instant, at 11 A. M., the Virginia left the navy-yard (Norfolk), accompanied by the Raleigh and Beaufort, and proceeded to Newport News, to eng ge the enemy's frigates Cumberland and Congress, gunboats and shore batteries. When within less than a mile of the Cumberland, the Virginia commenced the engagement with that ship with her bow gun, and the action soon became general, the Cumberland and Congress, gunboats and shore batteries concentrating upon us their heavy fire, which was returned with great spirit and determination. The Virginia stood rapidly on toward the Cumberland, which ship I had determined to sink with our prow, if possible.

THE VIRGINIA RAMMING AND SINKING THE UNITED STATES FRIGATE, CUMBERLAND.

In about fifteen minutes after the action commenced we ran into her on her starboard bow. The crash below the water was distinctly heard, and she commenced sinking, gallantly fighting her guns as long as they were above water. She went down with her colors flying.

During this time the shore batteries, Congress and gunboats kept up their heavy concentrated fire upon us, doing us some injury. Our guns, however, were not idle; their fire was very destructive to the shore batteries and vessels, and we were gallantly sustained by the rest of the squadron.

Just after the Cumberland sunk, that gallant officer, Commander John R. Tucker, was seen standing down James River, under full steam, accompanied by the Jamestown and Teaser. They all came nobly into action, and were soon exposed to the heavy fire of shore batteries. Their escape was miraculous, as they were under a galling fire of solid shot, shell, grape and canister, a number of which passed through the vessels without doing any serious injury, except to the Patrick Henry, through whose boiler a shot passed, scalding to death four persons and wounding others. Lieutenant-Commanding Barney promptly obeyed a signal to tow her out of the action. As soon as damages were repaired the Patrick Henry returned to her station, and continued to perform good service during the remainder of that day and the following.

Having sunk the Cumberland, I turned our attention to the Congress.

We were some time in getting our proper position, in consequence of the shoaliness of the water and the great difficulty of managing the ship when in or near the mud. To succeed in my object I was obliged to run the ship a short distance above the batteries on James River in order to wind her. During all the time her keel was in the mud; of course, she moved but slowly. Thus we were subjected twice to the heavy guns of all the batteries in passing up and down the river, but it could not be avoided. We silenced several of the batteries and did much injury on shore.

A large transport steamer alongside the wharf was blown up, one schooner sunk, and another captured and sent to Norfolk. The loss of life on shore we have no means of ascertaining.

While the Virginia was thus engaged in getting her position for attacking the Congress the prisoners state it was believed on board that ship that we had hauled off. The men left their guns and gave three cheers. They were soon sadly undeceived, for, a few minutes after, we opened upon her again, she having run on shore in shoal water. The carnage, havoc and dismay caused by our fire compelled them to haul down their colors and to hoist a white flag at their gaff and half-mast, and another at the main. The crew instantly took to their boats.

Our fire immediately ceased, and a signal was made for the Beaufort to come within hail. I then ordered Lieutenant-Commanding Parker to take possession of the Congress, secure the officers as prisoners, allow the crew to land, and burn the ship.

He ran alongside, receiving her flag and surrender from Commander William Smith and Lieutenant Pendergrast, with the side-arms of those officers. They delivered themselves as prisoners of war on board the Beaufort, and afterward were permitted, at their own request, to return to the Congress to assist in removing the wounded to the Beaufort. They never returned, and I submit to the decision of the department whether they are not our prisoners. While the Beaufort and Raleigh were alongside the Congress, and the surrender of that vessel had been received from the commander, she having two white flags flying,

FORTRESS MONROE, VIRGINIA, AS SEEN FROM THE JAMES RIVER, 1861.

hoisted by their own people, a heavy fire was opened upon them from the shore and from the Congress, killing some valuable officers and men. Under this fire the steamers left the Congress, but as I was not informed that any injury had been sustained by those vessels at that time, Lieutenant-Commanding Parker having failed to report to me, I took it for granted that my order to him to burn her had been executed, and waited some minutes to see the smoke ascending from her hatches.

During this delay we were still subject to the heavy fire from the batteries, which was always promptly returned.

The steam frigates Minnesota and Roanoke, and the sailing frigate St. Lawrence, had previously been reported as coming from Old Point, but as I was determined that the Congress should not again fall into the hands of the enemy, I remarked to that gallant young officer, Flag-Lieutenant Minor, "That ship must be burned." Lieutenant Minor promptly volunteered to take a boat and burn her, and the Teaser, Lieutenant-Commanding Webb, was ordered to cover the boat. Lieutenant Minor had scarcely reached within fifty yards of the Congress, when a deadly fire was opened upon him, wounding him severely and several of his men. On witnessing this vile treachery, I instantly recalled the boat, and ordered the Congress destroyed by hot shot and incendiary shell. About this period I was disabled, and transferred the command of the ship to that gallant, intelligent officer, Lieutenant Catesby Jones, with orders to fight her as long as the men could stand to their guns.

The ships from Old Point opened their fire upon us. The Minnesota grounded in the north channel, where, unfortunately, the shoaliness of the channel prevented our near approach. We continued, however, to fire upon her, until the pilots declared it was no longer safe to remain in that position, and we accordingly returned by the south channel (the middle ground being necessarily between the Virginia and Minnesota, and the St. Lawrence and the Roanoke having retreated under the guns of Old Point), and again had an opportunity of opening upon the Minnesota, receiving her heavy fire in return, and shortly afterward upon the St. Lawrence, from which vessel were received several broadsides. It had by this time become dark, and we soon after anchored off Sewalls Point. The rest of the squadron followed our movements, with the exception of the Beaufort, Lieutenant-Commanding W. H. Parker, who proceeded to Norfolk with the wounded and prisoners as soon as he had left the Congress, without reporting to me. The Congress having been set on fire by our hot shot and incendiary shell, continued to burn, her loaded guns being successively discharged as the flames reached them, until a few minutes past midnight, when her magazine exploded with a tremendous report.

The facts above stated as having occurred after I had placed the ship in charge of Lieutenant Jones were reported to me by that officer.

At an early hour next morning (the 9th), upon the urgent solicitations of the surgeons, Lieutenant Minor and myself were very reluctantly taken on shore. The accommodations for the proper treatment of wounded persons on board the Virginia are exceedingly limited, Lieutenant Minor and myself occupying the only space that could be used for that purpose, which was in my cabin. I therefore consented to our being landed on Sewalls Point, thinking that the room on board vacated by us could be used for those who might be wounded in the renewal of the action.

In the course of the day Lieutenant Minor and myself were sent in a steamer to the hospital at Norfolk.

The following is an extract from the report of Lieutenant Jones of the proceedings of the Virginia on the 9th:

"At daylight on the 9th we saw that the Minnesota was still ashore, and that there was an iron battery near her. At eight o'clock we ran down to engage them (having previously sent the killed and wounded out of the ship), firing at the Minnesota, and occasionally at the iron battery. The pilots did not place us as near as they expected. The great length and draught of the ship rendered it exceedingly difficult to work her. We ran ashore about a mile from the frigate, and were backing fifteen minutes before we got off. We continued to fire at the Minnesota, and blew up a steamer alongside of her, and we also engaged the Monitor, and sometimes at very close quarters. We once succeeded in running into her, and twice silenced her fire.

"The pilots declaring that we could get no nearer the Minnesota, and believing her to be entirely disabled, and the Monitor having run into shoal water, which prevented our doing her any further injury, we ceased firing at twelve o'clock, and proceeded to Norfolk. Our loss is two killed and nineteen wounded.

"The stem is twisted and the ship leaks. We have lost the prow, starboard anchor and all the boats. The armor is somewhat damaged; the steam-pipe and smoke-stack are both riddled; the muzzles of two of the guns, shot away. It was not easy to keep a flag flying. The flagstaffs were repeatedly shot away. The colors were hoisted to the smoke-stack and several times cut down from it.

"The bearing of the men was all that could be desired; the enthusiasm could scarcely be restrained. During the action they cheered again and again. Their coolness and skill were the more remarkable from the fact that the great majority of them were under fire for the first time. They were strangers to each other and to the officers, and had but a few days' instruction in the management of the great guns.

"To the skill and example of the officers is this result in no small degree attributable."

Having thus given a full report of the actions on the 8th and 9th, I feel it due to the gallant officers who so nobly sustained the honor of the flag and country on those days to express my appreciation of their conduct.

To that brave and intelligent officer, Lieutenant Catesby Jones, the executive and ordnance officer of the Virginia, I am greatly indebted for the success achieved. His constant attention to his duties in the equipment of the ship; his intelligence in the instruction of ordnance to the crew, as proved by the accuracy and effect of their fire, some of the guns having been personally directed by him; his tact and management in the government of raw recruits; his general knowledge of the executive duties of a man-of-war, together with his high-toned bearing, were all eminently conspicuous, and had their fruits in the admirable efficiency of the Virginia.

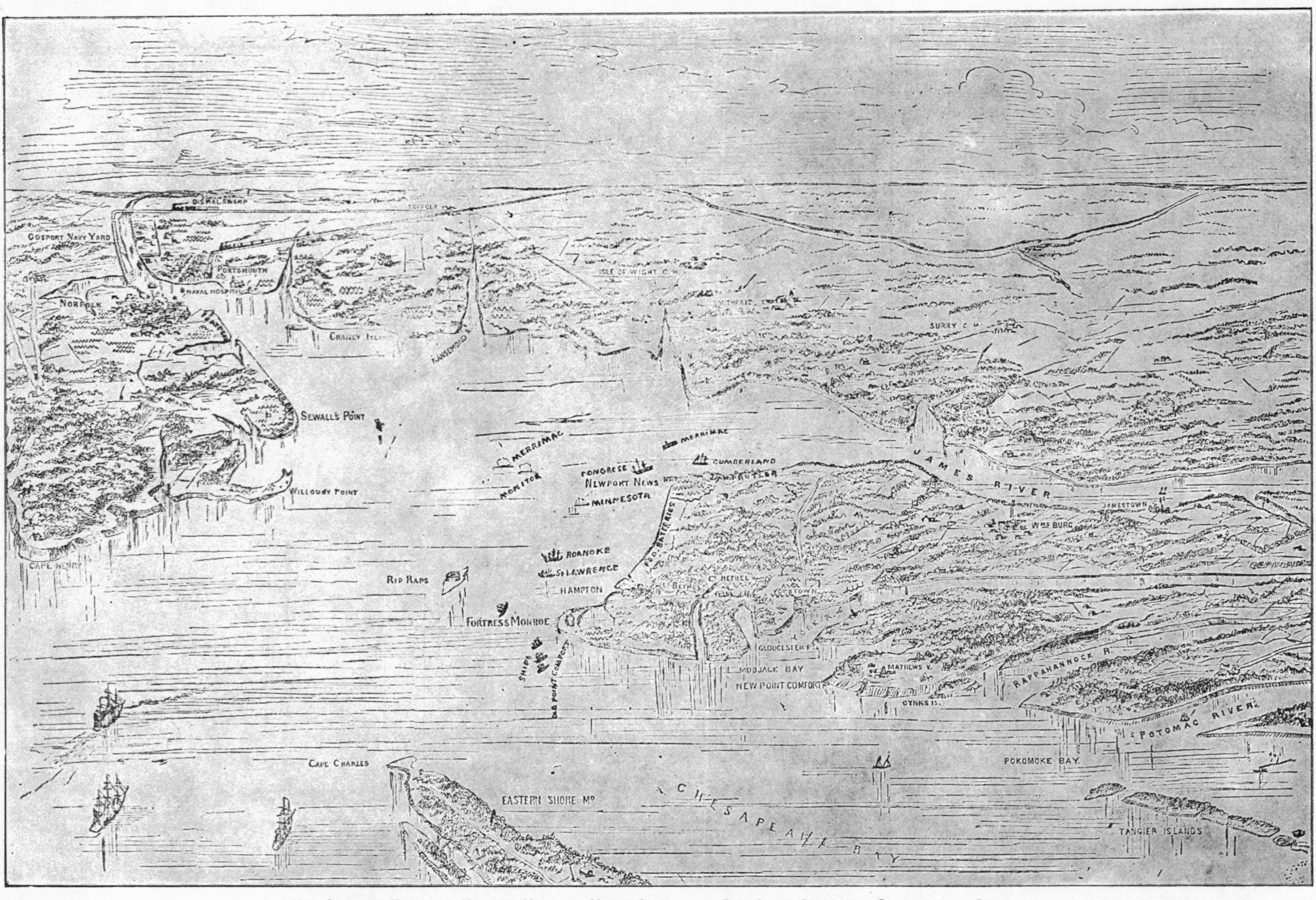

Map Showing Fortress Monroe, Newport News, Chesapeake Bay, James River and Surrounding Country.

If conduct such as his (and I do not know that I have used adequate language in describing it) entitles an officer to promotion, I see in the case of Lieutenant Jones one in all respects worthy of it. As flag-officer I am entitled to some one to perform the duties of flag-captain, and I should be proud to have Lieutenant Jones ordered to the Virginia as lieutenant commandant, if it be not the intention of the department to bestow upon him a higher rank.

Lieutenant Sims fully sustained his well-earned reputation. He fired the first gun, and when the command devolved upon Lieutenant Jones, in consequence of my disability, he was ordered to perform the duties of executive officer. Lieutenant Jones has expressed to me his satisfaction in having had the services of so experienced, energetic and zealous an officer.

Lieutenant Davidson fought his guns with great precision. The muzzle of one of them was shot away. He continued, however, to fire it, though the wood-work around the port became ignited at each discharge. His buoyant and cheerful bearing and voice were contagious and inspiring.

Lieutenant Wood handled his pivot gun admirably, and the executive officer testifies to his valuable suggestions during the action. His zeal and industry in drilling the crew contributed materially to our success.

Lieutenant Eggleston served his hot shot and shell with judgment and effect, and his bearing was deliberate and exerted a happy influence on his division.

From an original painting, owned and copyrighted by Kurz & Allison, Chicago, Ill.

ENGAGEMENT BETWEEN THE VIRGINIA AND MONITOR AT HAMPTON ROADS, CHESAPEAKE BAY, MARCH 9, 1862, AS SEEN FROM THE FEDERAL FORTIFICATIONS.

Lieutenant Butt fought his gun with activity, and during the action was gay and smiling.

The Marine Corps was well represented by Captain Thom, whose tranquil mien gave evidence that the hottest fire was no novelty to him. One of his guns was served effectively and creditably by a detachment of the United Artillery of Norfolk, under the command of Captain Kevill.

The muzzle of their gun was struck by a shell from the enemy, which broke off a piece of the gun, but they continued to fire as if it was uninjured.

Midshipmen Foute, Marmaduke, Littlepage, Craig and Long rendered valuable services. Their conduct would have been creditable to older heads, and gave great promise of future usefulness. Midshipman Marmaduke, though receiving several painful wounds early in the action, manfully fought his gun until the close. He is now at the hospital.

Paymaster Semple volunteered for any service, and was assigned to the command of the powder division, an important and complicated duty, which could not have been better performed.

Surgeon Phillips and Assistant Surgeon Garnett were prompt and attentive in the discharge of their duties. Their kind and considerate care of the wounded, and the skill and ability displayed in the treatment, won for them the esteem and gratitude of all who came under their charge, and justly entitled them to the confidence of officers and crew.

I beg leave to recall the attention of the department to the case of Dr. Garnett. He stands deservedly high in his profession, is at the head of the list of assistant surgeons, and there being a vacancy, in consequence of the recent death of Surgeon Blacknall, I should be much gratified if Dr. Garnett could be promoted to it.

The engines and machinery, upon which so much depended, performed better than was expected. This is due to the intelligence and experience of Acting Chief Engineer Ramsey. His efforts were ably seconded by his assistants, Tynan, Campbell, Herring, Jack and White.

Admiral Franklin Buchanan, of Maryland.

As Mr. Ramsey is only acting chief engineer, I respectfully recommend his promotion to the rank of chief; and would also ask that Second Assistant Engineer Campbell may be promoted to first assistant, he having performed the duties of that grade during the engagement.

The forward officers—Boatswain Hasker, Gunner Oliver and Carpenter Lindsey—discharged well all the duties required of them. The boatswain had charge of a gun and fought it well. The gunner was indefatigable in his efforts. His experience and exertions as a gunner have contributed very materially to the efficacy of the battery.

Acting Master Parrish was assisted in piloting the ship by Pilots Wright, Williams, Clark and Cunningham. They were necessarily much exposed.

It is now due that I should mention my personal staff. To that gallant young officer, Flag-Lieutenant Minor, I am much indebted for his promptness in the execution of signals; for renewing the flagstaffs when shot away, being thereby greatly exposed; for his watchfulness in keeping the Confederate flag up; his alacrity in conveying my orders to the different divisions, and for his general cool and gallant bearing.

My aid, Acting Midshipman Roots, of the navy, Lieutenant Forrest, of the army, who served as a volunteer aid, and my clerk, Mr. Arthur Sinclair, Jr., are entitled to my thanks for the activity with which my orders were conveyed to the different parts of the ship. During the hottest of the fight they were always at their posts, giving evidence of their coolness.

Having referred to the good conduct of the officers in the flagship immediately under my notice, I come now to a no less pleasing task when I attempt to mark my approbation of the bearing of those serving in the other vessels of the squadron.

Commander John R. Tucker, of the Patrick Henry, and Lieutenants-Commanding J. N. Barney, of the Jamestown, and W. A. Webb, of the Teaser, deserve great praise for their gallant conduct throughout the engagement. Their judgment in selecting their positions for attacking the enemy was good; their constant fire was destructive, and contributed much to the success of the day. The general order under which the squadron went into action required that, in the absence of all signals, each commanding officer was to exercise his own judgment and discretion in doing all the damage he could to the enemy, and to sink before surrendering. From the bearing of those officers on the 8th I am fully satisfied that that order would have been carried out.

Fortress Monroe, 1861.

Commander Tucker speaks highly of all under him, and desires particularly to notice that Lieutenant-Colonel Cadwalader St. George Noland, commanding the post at Mulberry Island, on hearing of the deficiency in the complement of the Patrick Henry, promptly offered the services of ten of his men as volunteers for the occasion, one of whom, George E. Webb, of the Greenville Guards, Commander Tucker regrets to say, was killed.

Lieutenant-Commanding Barney reports every officer and man on board of the ship performed his whole duty, evincing a courage and fearlessness worthy of the cause for which we are fighting.

Lieutenant-Commanding Webb specially notices the coolness displayed by Acting Master Face and Third Assistant Engineer Quinn when facing the heavy fire of artillery and musketry from the shore while the Teaser was standing in to cover the boat in which, as previously stated, Lieutenant Minor had gone to burn the Congress. Several of his men were badly wounded.

The Raleigh, early in the action, had her gun carriage disabled, which compelled her to withdraw. As soon as he had repaired damages as well as he could Lieutenant-Commanding Alexander resumed his position in the line. He sustained himself gallantly during the remainder of the day, and speaks highly of all under his command. That evening he was ordered to Norfolk for repairs.

The Beaufort, Lieutenant-Commanding Parker, was in close contact with the enemy frequently during the day, and all on board behaved gallantly. Lieutenant-Commanding Parker expresses his warmest thanks to his officers and men for their coolness. Acting Midshipman Foreman, who accompanied him as volunteer aid, Midshipmen Mallory and Newton, Captain's Clerk Bain and Mr. Gray, pilot, are all specially mentioned by him.

On the 21st instant I forwarded to the department correct lists of the casualties on board all the vessels of the squadron on the 8th. None, it appears, occurred on the 9th.

While in the act of closing this report I received the communication of the department, dated 22d inst., relieving me temporarily of the command of the squadron for the naval defense of James River. I feel honored in being relieved by the gallant Flag-Officer Tatnall.

I much regret that I am not now in a condition to resume my command, but trust that I shall soon be restored to health, when I shall be ready for any duty that may be assigned me.

FRANKLIN BUCHANAN,
Flag-Officer.

THE SERVICES OF THE VIRGINIA. (MERRIMAC.)

BY

CAPTAIN CATESBY AP R. JONES,
Confederate States Navy.

When, on April 21, 1861, the Virginians took possession of the abandoned navy-yard at Norfolk, they found that the Merrimac had been burned and sunk. She was raised, and on June 23d following the Hon. S. R. Mallory, Confederate Secretary of the Navy, ordered that she should be converted into an ironclad, on the plan proposed by Lieutenant John M. Brooke, Confederate States Navy. The hull was two hundred and seventy-five feet long. About one hundred and sixty feet of the central portion was covered by a roof of wood and iron, inclining about thirty-six degrees. The wood was two feet thick; it consisted of oak plank four inches by twelve inches, laid up and down next the iron, and two courses of pine; one longitudinal of eight inches thickness, the other twelve inches thick.

The intervening space on top was closed by permanent gratings of two inch square iron two and one-half inches apart, leaving openings for four hatches, one near each end, and one forward and one abaft the smoke-stack. The roof did not project beyond the hull. There was no knuckle, as in the Atlanta, the Tennessee and other ironclads of later and improved construction. The ends of the shield were rounded.

The armor was four inches thick. It was fastened to its wooden backing by one and three-eighths inch bolts, countersunk and secured by iron nuts and washers. The plates were eight inches wide. Those first made were one inch thick, which was as thick as we could then punch cold iron. We succeeded soon in punching two inches, and the remaining plates, more than two-thirds, were two inches thick. They were rolled and punched at the Tredegar Works, Richmond. The outside course was up and down, the next longitudinal. Joints were broken where there were more than two courses

Commander Catesby Ap R. Jones,
Executive and Ordnance Officer of the Virginia.

The hull, extending two feet below the roof, was plated with one-inch iron; it was intended that it should have had three inches.

The prow was of cast iron, wedge shape, and weighed fifteen hundred pounds. It was about two feet under water and projected two feet from the stem; it was not well fastened. The rudder and propeller were unprotected.

The battery consisted of ten guns, four single-banded Brooke rifles and six 9-inch Dahlgren shell guns. Two of the rifles, bow and stern pivots, were 7-inch, of fourteen thousand five hundred pounds; the other two were 6.4-inch (thirty-two pounds caliber), of nine thousand pounds, one on each broadside. The 9-inch gun on each side, nearest the furnaces, was fitted for firing hot shot. A few 9-inch shot, with extra windage, were cast for hot shot. No other solid shot were on board during the fight.

The engines were the same the vessel had while in the United States Navy. They were radically defective, and had been condemned by the United States Government. Some changes had been made, notwithstanding which the engineers reported that they were unreliable. They performed very well during the fight, but afterward failed several times, once while under fire.

There were many vexatious delays attending the fitting and equipment of the ship. Most of them arose from the want of skilled labor and lack of proper tools and appliances. Transporting the iron from Richmond also caused much delay; the railroads were taxed to supply the army.

The crew, three hundred and twenty in number, were obtained with great difficulty. With few exceptions they were volunteers from the army; most of them were landsmen. Their deficiencies were as much as possible overcome by the zeal and intelligence of the officers. A list of these is appended. In the fight one of the 9-inch guns was manned by a detachment of the Norfolk United Artillery.

The vessel was, by the Confederates, called the Virginia. She was put in commission during the last week of February, but continued crowded with mechanics until the eve of the fight. She was badly ventilated, very uncomfortable and very unhealthy. There was an average of fifty or sixty at the hospital, in addition to the sick list on board.

The flag-officer, Franklin Buchanan, was detained in Richmond in charge of an important bureau, from which he was only relieved a few days before the fight. There was no captain; the ship was commissioned and equipped by the executive and ordnance officer, who had reported for duty in November. He had, by special order, selected her battery and was also made responsible for its efficiency.

A trial was determined upon, although the vessel was in an incomplete condition. The lower part of the shield forward was only immersed a few inches, instead of two feet, as was intended; and there was but one inch of iron on the hull. The port shutters, etc., were unfinished.

The Virginia was unseaworthy, her engines were unreliable, and her draught, over twenty-two feet, prevented her from going to Washington. Her field of operation was therefore restricted to the bay and its immediate vicinity; there was no regular concerted movement with the army.*

The frigates Congress and Cumberland temptingly invited an attack. It was fixed for Thursday night, March 6, 1862, the pilots—of whom there were five—having been previously consulted. The sides were slushed, supposing that it would increase the tendency of the projectiles to glance. All preparations were made, including lights at obstructions. After dark the pilots declared that they could not pilot the ship during the night. They had a high sense of their responsibility. In justice to them it should be stated that it was not easy to pilot a vessel of our great draught under favorable circumstances, and that the difficulties were much increased by the absence of lights, buoys, etc., to which they had been accustomed.

The attack was postponed to Saturday, March 8th. The weather was favorable. We left the navy-yard at 11 A. M., against the last half of the flood tide, steamed down the river past our batteries, through the obstructions, across Hampton Roads, to the mouth of the James River, where, off Newport News, lay at anchor the frigates Cumberland and Congress, protected by strong batteries and gunboats. The action commenced about 3 P. M. by our firing the bow gun* at the Cumberland, less than a mile distant. A powerful fire was immediately concentrated upon us from all the batteries afloat and ashore. The frigates Minnesota, Roanoke and St. Lawrence, with other vessels, were seen coming from Old Point. We fired at the Congress on passing, but continued to head directly for the Cumberland, which vessel we had determined to run into, and in less than fifteen minutes from the firing of the first gun we rammed her, just forward of the starboard fore chains. There were heavy spars about her bows, probably to ward off torpedoes, through which we had to break before reaching the side of the ship. The noise of the crashing timbers was distinctly heard above the din of battle. There was no sign of the hole above water. It must have been large, as the ship soon commenced to careen. The shock to us on striking was slight. We immediately backed the engines. The blow was not repeated. We here lost the prow, and had the stem slightly twisted. The Cumberland † fought her guns gallantly as long as they were above water. She went down bravely, with her colors flying. One of her shells struck the still of the bow port, and exploded; the fragments killed two and wounded a number. Our after nine-inch gun was loaded and ready for firing, when its muzzle was struck by a shell, which broke it off and fired the gun. Another gun also had its muzzle shot off; it was broken off so short that at each subsequent discharge its port was set on fire. The damage to the armor was slight. Their fire appeared to have been aimed at our ports. Had it been concentrated at the water line we would have been seriously hurt, if not sunk. Owing to the ebb tide and our great draught we could not close with the Congress without first going up stream and then returning, which was a tedious operation, besides subjecting us twice to the full fire of the batteries, some of which we silenced.

We were accompanied from the yard by the gunboats Beaufort, Lieutenant-Commander W. H. Parker, and Raleigh, Lieutenant-Commander J. W. Alexander. As soon as the firing was heard up James River the Patrick Henry, Commander John R. Tucker; Jamestown, Lieutenant-Commander J. N. Barney, and the gunboat Teaser, Lieutenant-Commander W. A. Webb, under command of Captain John R. Tucker, stood down the river, joining us about 4 o'clock. All these vessels were gallantly fought and handled, and rendered valuable and effective service.

The prisoners from the Congress stated that when on board that ship it was seen that we were standing up the river three cheers were given, under the impression that we had quit the fight. They were soon undeceived. When they saw us heading downstream, fearing the fate of the Cumberland, they slipped their cables, made sail and ran ashore bows on. We took a position off her quarter, about two cables' length distant, and opened a deliberate fire. Very few of her guns bore on us, and they were soon disabled. The other batteries continued to play on us, as did the Minnesota, then aground about one and one-half miles off. The St. Lawrence also opened on us shortly after. There was great havoc on board the Congress. She was several times on fire. Her gallant commander, Lieutenant Joseph B. Smith,* was struck in the breast by the fragment of a shell and instantly killed, The carnage was fearful. Nothing remained but to strike their colors, which they did. They hoisted the white flag, half-masted, at the main and at the spanker gaff. The Beaufort and Raleigh were ordered to burn her. They went alongside and secured several of her officers and some twenty of her men as prisoners. The officers urgently asked permission to assist their wounded out of the ship. It was granted. They did not return. A sharp fire of musketry from the shore killed some of the prisoners and forced the tugs to leave. A boat was sent from the Virginia to burn her, covered by the Teaser. A fire was opened on them from the shore, and also from the Congress, with both of her white flags flying, wounding Lieutenant Minor and others. We replied to this outrage

BURNING OF THE NORFOLK NAVY-YARD AND THE FRIGATE MERRIMAC BY THE UNITED STATES AUTHORITIES, APRIL 21, 1861.

* There was, however, an informal understanding between General Magruder, who commanded the Confederate forces on the Peninsula, and the executive officer, to the effect that General Magruder should be kept advised by us, in order that his command might be concentrated near Hampton when our attack should be made. The movement was prevented in consequence of a large portion of the command having been detached just before the fight.

* It killed and wounded ten men at the after pivot gun of the Cumberland. The second shot from the same gun killed and wounded twelve men at her forward pivot gun. Lieutenant Charles C. Simms pointed and fired the gun.

† She was a sailing frigate of 1,726 tons, mounting two 10-inch pivots and twenty-two 9-inch guns. Her crew numbered 376; her loss in killed and wounded was 121.

* His sword was sent by flag of truce to his father, Admiral Joseph Smith.

upon the usages of civilized warfare by reopening on the Congress with hot shot and incendiary shell. Her crew escaped by boats, as did that of the Cumberland. Canister and grape would have prevented it; but in neither case was any attempt made to stop them, though it had been otherwise stated, possibly from our firing on the shore or at the Congress.

We remained near the Congress to prevent her recapture. Had she been retaken it might have been said that the flag-officer permitted it, knowing that his brother* was an officer of that vessel.

A distant and unsatisfactory fire was at times had at the Minnesota. The gunboats also engaged her. We fired canister and grape occasionally in reply to musketry from the shore, which had become annoying.

About this time the flag-officer was badly wounded by a rifle ball, and had to be carried below. His bold daring and intrepid conduct won the admiration of all on board. The executive and ordnance officer, Lieutenant Catesby Ap R. Jones, succeeded to the command.

The action continued until dusk, when we were forced to seek an anchorage. The Congress was riddled and on fire. A transport steamer was blown up. A schooner was sunk and another captured. We had to leave without making a serious attack on the Minnesota, though we fired at her as we passed on the other side of the middle ground, and also at the St. Lawrence.† The latter frigate fired at us by broadsides—not a bad plan for small calibers against ironclads, if concentrated. It was too dark to aim well. We anchored off our batteries at Sewalls Point. The squadron followed.

The Congress‡ continued to burn; "she illuminated the heavens and varied the scene by the firing of her own guns and the flight of her balls through the air," until shortly after midnight, "when her magazine exploded, and a column of burning matter appeared high in the air, to be followed by the stillness of death." [Extract from report of General Mansfield, United States Army.] One of the pilots chanced, about 11 P. M., to be looking in the direction of the Congress, when there passed a strange-looking craft, brought out in bold relief by the brilliant light of the burning ship, which he at once proclaimed to be the Monitor. We were therefore not surprised in the morning to see the Monitor at anchor near the Minnesota. The latter ship was still aground. Some delay occurred from sending our wounded out of the ship; we had but

THE UNITED STATES FRIGATE MERRIMAC BEFORE CONVERSION INTO THE IRONCLAD VIRGINIA.

one serviceable boat left. Admiral Buchanan was landed at Sewalls Point.

At 8 A. M. we got under way, as did the Patrick Henry, Jamestown and Teaser. We stood toward the Minnesota and opened fire on her. The pilots were to have placed us half a mile from her, but we were not at any time nearer than a mile. The Monitor§ commenced firing when about a third of a mile distant. We soon approached, and were often within a ship's length; once while passing we fired a broadside at her only a few yards distant. She and her turret appeared to be under perfect control. Her light draught enabled her to move about us at pleasure. She once took position for a short time where we could not bring a gun to bear on her. Another of her movements caused us great anxiety; she made for our rudder and propeller, both of which could have been easily disabled. We could only see her guns when they were discharged; immediately after the turret revolved rapidly, and the guns were not again seen until they were again fired. We wondered how proper aim could be taken in the very short time the guns were in sight. The Virginia, however, was a large target, and generally so near that the Monitor's shot did not often miss. It did not appear to us that our shell had any effect upon the Monitor. We had no solid shot. Musketry was fired at the lookout holes. In spite of all the care of our pilots we ran ashore, where we remained over fifteen minutes. The Patrick Henry and Jamestown, with great risk to themselves, started to our assistance. The Monitor and Minnesota were in full play on us. A small rifle gun on board the Minnesota, or on the steamer alongside of her, was fired with remarkable precision.

When we saw that our fire made no impression on the Monitor we determined to run into her if possible. We found it a very difficult feat to do. Our great length and draught, in a comparatively narrow channel, with but little water to spare, made us sluggish in our movements and hard to steer and turn. When the opportunity

THE MERRIMAC AFTER CONVERSION INTO THE IRONCLAD VIRGINIA.

presented all steam was put on; there was not, however, sufficient time to gather full headway before striking. The blow was given with the broad wooden stem, the iron prow having been lost the day before. The Monitor received the blow in such a manner as to weaken its effect, and the damage was to her trifling. Shortly after an alarming leak in the bows was reported. It, however, did not long continue.

While contending with the Monitor we received the fire of the Minnesota,* which we never failed to return whenever our guns could be brought to bear. We set her on fire and did her serious injury, though much less than we then supposed. Generally the distance was too great for effective firing. We blew up a steamer alongside of her.

The fight had continued over three hours. To us the Monitor appeared unharmed. We were, therefore, surprised to see her run off into shoal water, where our great draught would not permit us to follow, and where our shell could not reach her. The loss of our prow and anchor and consumption of coal, water, etc., had lightened us so that the lower part of the forward end of the shield was awash.

We for some time awaited the return of the Monitor to the roads. After consultation it was decided that we should proceed to the navy-yard, in order that the vessel should be brought down in the water and completed. The pilots said if we did not then leave that we could not pass the bar until noon the next day. We, therefore, at 12 M., quit the roads and stood for Norfolk. Had there been any sign of the Monitor's willingness to renew the contest, we would have remained to fight her. We left her in the shoal water, to which she had withdrawn, and which she did not leave until after we had crossed the bar on our way to Norfolk.

The official report says: "Our loss is two killed and nineteen wounded. The stem is twisted and the ship leaks; we have lost the prow, starboard anchor and all the boats; the armor is somewhat damaged, the steam-pipe and smoke-stack both riddled, the muzzles of the two guns shot away; the colors were hoisted to the smoke-stack and several times cut down from it." None were killed or wounded in the fight with the Monitor. The only damage she did was to the armor. She fired forty-one shots. We were enabled to receive most of them obliquely. The effect of a shot striking obliquely on the shield was to break all the iron, and sometimes to displace several feet of the outside course; the wooden backing would not be broken through. When a shot struck directly at right angles, the wood would also be broken through, but not displaced. Generally the shot were much scattered; in three instances two or more struck near the same place, in each case causing more of the iron to be displaced and the wood to bulge inside. A few struck near the water line. The shield was never pierced, though it was evident that two shots striking in the same place would have made a large hole through everything.

The ship was docked, a prow of steel and wrought iron put on, and a course of two-inch iron on the hull below the roof, extending in length one hundred and eighty feet. Want of time and material prevented its completion. The damage to the armor was repaired; wrought iron port-shutters were fitted, etc. The rifle-guns were supplied with bolts of wrought and chilled iron. The ship was brought a foot deeper in the water, making her draught twenty-three feet.

Commodore Josiah Tatnall relieved Admiral Buchanan in command. On the 11th of April he took the Virginia down to Hampton Roads, expecting to have a desperate encounter with the Monitor. Greatly to our surprise the Monitor refused to fight us. She closely hugged the shore under the guns of the fort, with her steam up. Hoping to provoke her to come out, the Jamestown* was sent in and captured several prizes, but the Monitor would not budge. It was proposed to take the vessel to York River, but it was decided in Richmond that she should remain near Norfolk for its protection.

Commodore Tatnall commanded the Virginia forty-five days, of which time there were only thirteen days that she was not in dock or in the hands of the navy-yard. Yet he

A. Prow of Steel. B. Wooden Bulwark. H. Pilot House. DD. Iron under water. C. Propeller.

THE VIRGINIA (MERRIMAC). FROM A SKETCH MADE THE DAY BEFORE THE FIGHT.

succeeded in impressing the enemy that we were ready for active service. It was evident that the enemy very much overrated† our power and efficiency. The South also had the same exaggerated idea of the vessel.

On the 8th of May a squadron, including the Monitor, bombarded our batteries at Sewalls Point. We immediately left the yard for the roads. As we drew near, the Monitor and her consorts ceased bombarding and retreated under the guns of the forts, keeping beyond the range of our guns.

Men-of-war from below the forts and vessels expressly fitted for running us down joined the other vessels between the forts. It looked as if the fleet was about to make a fierce onslaught on us. But we were again to be disappointed. The Monitor and other vessels did not venture to meet us, although we advanced until projectiles from the Ripraps fell more than half a mile beyond us. Our

* One of the sad attendants of civil war, divided families, was here illustrated. The flag-officer's brother was paymaster of the Congress. The first and second lieutenants had each a brother in the United States Army. The father of the fourth lieutenant was also in the United States Army. The father of one of the midshipmen was in the United States Navy.

† A sailing frigate of 50 guns and 1,726 tons.

‡ A sailing frigate of 1,867 tons, mounting 50 guns. She had a crew of 434, of whom there were 120 killed and missing.

§ She was 173 feet long and 41 feet wide. She had a revolving circular iron turret 8 inches thick, 9 feet high and 20 feet inside diameter, in which were two 11-inch guns. Her draught was 10 feet.

* She was a screw steam frigate of 3,200 tons, mounting 43 guns, of 8, 9 and 10-inch caliber. She fired 145 10-inch, 349 9-inch and 34 8-inch shot and shell, and 5,567 pounds of powder. Her draught was about the same as the Virginia.

* French and English men-of-war present. The latter cheered our gunboat as she passed with the prizes.

† Some of the Northern papers estimated her to be equivalent to an army corps.

THE BATTLE OF THE IRONCLADS.

object, however, was accomplished; we had put an end to the bombardment, and we returned to our buoy.

Norfolk was evacuated on the 10th of May. In order that the ship might be carried up the James River we commenced to lighten her, but ceased on the pilots saying they could not take her up. Her shield was then out of water; we were not in fighting condition. We therefore ran her ashore in the bight of Craney Island, landed the crew and set the vessel on fire. The magazine exploded about 4:30 on the morning of the 11th of May, 1862. The crew arrived at Drewrys Bluff the next day, and assisted in defeating the Monitor, Galena and other vessels on the 15th of May.

Commodore Tatnall was tried by court-martial for destroying the Virginia, and was "honorably acquitted" of all the charges. The court stated the facts, and their motives for acquitting him. Some of them are as follows: "That after the evacuation of Norfolk, Westover on James River became the most suitable position for her to occupy; . . . That when lightened she was made vulnerable to the attacks of the enemy. . . The only alternative, in the opinion of the court, was to abandon and burn the ship then and there, which, in the judgment of the court, was deliberately and wisely done."

NOTE.—The above deeply interesting narrative of the gallant and accomplished executive officer of the Virginia was prepared for the Southern Historical Society, Richmond, Va., not long before his lamented death.

THE VIRGINIA AND MONITOR AT CLOSE QUARTERS.

LIST OF OFFICERS OF THE CONFEDERATE STATES IRONCLAD VIRGINIA, MARCH 8, 1862.

Flag-Officer — Franklin Buchanan. Lieutenants — Catesby Ap R. Jones, Executive and Ordnance Officer; Charles C. Sims, R. D. Minor (flag), Hunter Davidson, J. Taylor Wood, J. R. Eggleston and Walter Butt. Midshipmen—Foute, Marmaduke, Littlepage, Craig, Long and Roots. Paymaster—James Semple. Surgeon—Dinwiddie Phillips. Assistant Surgeon—Algernon S. Garnett. Captain of Marines—Reuben Thom. Engineers—H. A. Ramsey, Acting Chief; Assistants—Tynan, Campbell, Herring, Jack and White. Boatswain—Hasker. Gunner—Oliver. Carpenter—Lindsey. Clerk—Arthur Sinclair, Jr. Volunteer Aid—Lieutenant Douglass Forrest, Confederate States Army. Captain Kevill, commanding detachment of Norfolk United Artillery. Signal Corps—Sergeant Tabb.

ACCOMPLISHMENTS OF THE CONFEDERATE FLEET.

On the 8th and 9th of March, 1862, the Confederate States fleet had successfully encountered, defied and beaten a force equal to 2,890 men and 230 guns, as follows:

	MEN.	GUNS.
Congress (burned)	480	50
Cumberland (sunk)	360	22
Minnesota (riddled)	550	40
Roanoke (scared off)	550	40
St. Lawrence (peppered)	480	50
Gunboats (two or three disabled)	120	6
Forts (silenced)	200	20
Ericsson (Monitor)	150	2
Total	2,890	230

DESTRUCTION OF THE VIRGINIA.

(MERRIMAC.)

BY

CAPTAIN JOSIAH TATNALL.

RICHMOND, May 14, 1862.

IN detailing the circumstances which caused the destruction of the Confederate States steamer Virginia, and her movements a few days previous to that event, I received telegraphic dispatches, on the 4th and 5th inst., from the Secretary of the Navy, directing me to take such a position in the James River as would entirely prevent the enemy's ascending it.

General Huger, commanding at Norfolk, on learning that I had received this order, called on me and declared that its execution would oblige him to abandon immediately his forts on Craney Island and Sewalls Point, and their guns, to the enemy. I informed him that as the order was imperative I must execute it, but suggested that he should telegraph the Secretary of the Navy and state the consequences. He did so, and on the 5th inst. the secretary telegraphed me to endeavor to afford protection to Norfolk as well as the James River, which replaced me in my original position. I then arranged with the general that he should notify me when his preparations for the evacuation of Norfolk were sufficiently advanced to enable him to act independently.

On the 7th inst. Commodore Hollins reached Norfolk with orders from the Secretary of the Navy to consult with me and such officers as I might select in regard to the best disposition to be made of the Virginia under the present aspect of things.

We had arranged the conference for the next day, the 8th; but on that day, before the hour appointed, the enemy attacked the Sewalls Point battery, and I left immediately with the Virginia to defend it.

We found six of the enemy's vessels, including the ironclad steamers Monitor and Naugatuck, shelling the battery. We passed the battery, and stood directly for the enemy for the purpose of engaging him, and I thought an action certain, particularly as the Minnesota and Vanderbilt, which were anchored below Fortress Monroe, got under way, and stood up to that point, apparently with the intention of joining their squadron in the roads. Before, however, we got within gunshot, the enemy ceased firing and retired with all speed, under the protection of the guns of the fortress, followed by the Virginia until the shells from the Ripraps passed over her.

The Virginia was then placed at her moorings near Sewalls Point, and I returned to Norfolk to hold the conference referred to.

It was held on the 9th, and the officers present were Colonel Anderson and Captain ——, of the army, selected by General Huger, who was too unwell to attend himself; and of the navy, myself, Commodore Hollins and Captains Sterrett and Lee, Commander Richard L. Jones and Lieutenants Catesby Ap R. Jones and J. Pembroke Jones.

The opinion was unanimous that the Virginia was then employed to the best advantage, and that she should continue for the present to protect Norfolk and thus afford time to remove the public property.

On the next day, at 10 A. M., we observed from the Virginia that the flag was not flying on the Sewalls Point battery, and that it appeared to have been abandoned. I dispatched Lieutenant J. P. Jones, the flag-lieutenant, to Craney Island, where the Confederate flag was still flying, and he there learned that a large force of the enemy had landed on the bay shore and were rapidly marching on Norfolk, that the Sewalls Point battery was abandoned and our troops were retreating. I then dispatched the same officer to Norfolk, to confer with General Huger and Captain Lee. He found the navy-yard in flames, and that all the officers had left by railroad. On reaching Norfolk he found that General Huger and all the officers of the army had also left; that the enemy were within half a mile of the city, and that the mayor was treating for its surrender.

On returning to the ship he found that Craney Island and all the other batteries on the river had been abandoned.

It was now 7 o'clock in the evening, and this unexpected confirmation rendered prompt measures necessary for the safety of the Virginia.

The pilots had assured me that they could take the ship, with a draught of eighteen feet, to within forty miles of Richmond.

This, the chief pilot, Mr. Parrish, and his chief assistant, Mr. Wright, had asserted again and again; and on the afternoon of the 7th, in my cabin, in the presence of Commodore Hollins and Captain Sterrett, in reply to a question of mine, they both emphatically declared their ability to do so.

COMMODORE JOSIAH TATNALL, OF GEORGIA.

Confiding in these assurances, and after consulting with the first and flag-lieutenants, and learning that officers generally thought it the most judicious course, I determined to lighten the ship at once and run up the river for the protection of Richmond.

All hands having been called on deck, I stated to them the condition of things, and my hope that by getting up the river before the enemy could be made aware of our designs we might capture his vessels which had ascended it and render efficient aid in the defense of Richmond, but that to effect this would require all their energy in lightening the ship. They replied with three cheers, and went to work at once. The pilots were on deck and heard this address to the crew.

Being quite unwell I had retired to bed. Between 1 and 2 o'clock in the morning the first lieutenant reported to me that, after the crew had worked for five or six hours and lifted the ship so as to render her unfit for action, the pilots had declared their inability to carry eighteen feet above the Jamestown flats, up to which point the shore on each side was occupied by the enemy.

On demanding from the chief pilot, Mr. Parrish, an explanation of this palpable deception, he replied that

Virginia. Jamestown. Yorktown. Monitor. Congress. Cumberland Minnesota. Newport News.

ACTION BETWEEN THE VIRGINIA AND THE MONITOR.

eighteen feet could be carried after the prevalence of easterly winds, and that the winds for the last two days had been westerly.

I had no time to lose. The ship was not in a condition for battle even with an enemy of equal force, and their force was overwhelming. I therefore determined, with the concurrence of the first and flag-lieutenants, to save the crew for future service by landing them at Craney Island, the only road for retreat open to us, and to destroy the ship to prevent her falling into the hands of the enemy. I may add that, although not formally consulted, the course was approved by every commissioned officer in the ship. There was no dissenting opinion. The ship was accordingly put on shore, as near the mainland in the vicinity of Craney Island as possible, and the crew landed. She was then fired, and after burning fiercely fore and aft for upward of an hour, blew up a little before 5 on the morning of the 11th.

We marched for Suffolk, twenty-two miles, and reached it in the evening, and from thence came by railroad to this city.

It will be asked what motives the pilots could have had to deceive me. The only imaginable one is that they wished to avoid going into battle.

Had the ship not been lifted so as to render her unfit for action, a desperate contest must have ensued, with a force against us too great to justify much hope of success, and, as battle is not their occupation, they adopted this deceitful course to avoid it. I can not imagine another motive, for I had seen no reason to mistrust their good faith to the Confederacy.

My acknowledgments are due to First Lieutenant Catesby Ap R. Jones for his untiring exertions and for the aid he rendered me in all things. The details for firing the ship and landing the crew were left to him, and everything was conducted in the most perfect order.

To the other officers of the ship, generally, I am thankful for the great zeal they displayed throughout.

The Virginia no longer exists, but three hundred brave and skillful officers and seamen are saved to the Confederacy.

I presume that a court of inquiry will be ordered to examine into all the circumstances I have narrated, and I earnestly solicit it. Public opinion will never be put right without it.

JOSIAH TATNALL,
Flag-Officer Commanding.

A SOLDIER, being on picket reserve, went to a farmhouse, as he said, to borrow a frying pan, but for what none could imagine, as there was nothing to fry. However, he went to the house, and knocked at the door, which was opened by a lady who asked what he wished. "Madam, could you lend me a frying pan? I belong to the picket down here." "Yes, sir;" and forthwith came the pan. He took it, looked in it, turned it over again and looked into it very hard, as if not certain 't was clean. "Well, sir," said the lady, "can I do anything more for you?" "Could—could—could you lend me a piece of meat to fry in it, ma'am?" and he laughed in spite of himself. He got it.

BATTLE ON THE MISSISSIPPI, NEAR FORT PILLOW,

BETWEEN THE

CONFEDERATE AND FEDERAL GUNBOATS,

MAY 10, 1862.

BY

CAPTAIN J. E. MONTGOMERY,
Commanding River Defense Service.

FLAGBOAT LITTLE REBEL,
FORT PILLOW, TENN., MAY 11, 1862.

HAVING previously arranged with my officers the order of attack on the Federal gunboats, our boats left their moorings at 6 A. M., and, proceeding up the river, passed around a sharp point, which brought us in full view of the enemy's fleet, numbering eight gunboats and twelve mortar boats.

The Federal gunboat Carondelet [should be the Cincinnati] was lying nearest us, guarding a mortar boat that was shelling the fort. The General Bragg, Captain Leonard, dashed at her, she firing her heavy guns and retreating toward a bar, where the depth of water would not be sufficient for our boats to follow. The Bragg continued boldly on under fire of nearly the whole fleet, and struck her a violent blow that stopped her further flight, then rounded down the river under a broadside fire, and drifted until her tiller-rope, that had got out of order, could be readjusted. A few moments after the Bragg struck her blow, the General Sterling Price, Flag-Officer Thos. E. Henthorn, ran into the same boat, a little aft of her starboard midship, carrying away her rudder, stern-post and a large piece of her stern. This threw the Carondelet's [Cincinnati's] stern to the Sumter, Captain W. W. Lamb, who struck her, running at the utmost speed of his boat.

The General Van Dorn, Captain Isaac D. Fulkerson, running according to orders, in rear of the Price and Sumter, directed his attention to the Mound City, at the time pouring broadsides into the Price and Sumter. As the Van Dorn proceeded, by skillful shots from her thirty-two pounder, W. G. Kendall, gunner, silenced a mortar boat that was filling the air with its terrible missiles. The Van Dorn still holding on the Mound City's midship, in the act of striking, the Mound City sheered, and the Van Dorn struck her a glancing blow, making a hole four feet deep in her starboard forward quarter, evidenced by splinters left on the iron bow of the Van Dorn. At this juncture the Van Dorn was above four of the enemy's boats.

As our remaining boats, the Jefferson Thompson, Captain J. H. Burke, the Colonel Lovell, Captain J. C. Delancy, and the General Beauregard, Captain J. H. Hart, were entering boldly into the contest in their prescribed order, I perceived from the flagboat that the enemy's boats were taking position where the water was too shallow for our boats to follow them, and as our cannon were far inferior to theirs, both in number and size, I signalled our boats to fall back, which was accomplished with a coolness that deserves the highest commendation.

I am happy to inform you, while exposed at close quarters to a most terrific fire for thirty minutes, our boats, although struck repeatedly, sustained no serious injury.

Our casualties were two killed and one wounded—arm broken.

General M. Jeff. Thompson was on board the General Bragg; his officers and men were divided among the boats. They were all at their posts, ready to do good service, should an occasion offer.

To my officers and men I am highly indebted for their courage and promptness in executing all orders.

On the 11th instant I went, on the Little Rebel, in full view of the enemy's fleet. Saw the Carondelet [the Cincinnati] sunk near the shore, and the Mound City sunk on the bar.

J. E. MONTGOMERY,
Senior Captain, Commanding River Defense Service.

A JOKE IN THE THICK OF THE BATTLE.—An old Tarheel, who was "thar," says that at the battle of Chancellorsville, while the fight was raging, General Rodes rode up to General Ramseur and asked him what time it was. Ramseur, pulling out his old timepiece slowly, said: "General, in such an emergency as this my old watch never runs." Rodes "took" right off, and returned to where the bullets were "ticking" the seconds. —*Waynesboro Times.*

Benton (Federal). Van Dorn (Confederate). Price and Little Rebel (Confederate). Cincinnati (Federal). Carondelet (Federal).

BATTLE NEAR FORT PILLOW, MISSISSIPPI RIVER, BETWEEN THE CONFEDERATE AND FEDERAL GUNBOATS.

CRUISE OF THE STEAMER PRICE

UP THE

MISSISSIPPI RIVER FROM NEW ORLEANS TO MEMPHIS,

INCLUDING THE

BATTLE ABOVE FORT PILLOW.

FROM THE STEAMER'S "LOG" BOOK.

WRITTEN BY PURSER L. F. DELISDIMIER.

MARCH 25, 1862.—Left New Orleans at 9 P. M., with the following officers: J. H. Townsend, captain; Thos. E. Henthorn, first officer; L. F. Delisdimier, purser; George L. Richardson, second officer; William Branden, chief engineer; J. H. Frobees, assistant engineer.

MARCH 28th.—Laid up last night on account of fog; left Red River at 10 A. M.; passed the General Bragg to-day.

MARCH 29th.—Arrived at Vicksburg at 4 P. M., and found the Bragg had stopped here; left at 5:30 P. M.; found no iron there. Weather pleasant.

MARCH 31st.—Arrived at Eunice at 8 P. M. Informed the railroad agent that we wanted some iron. He said he had none. Our captain then told him he would have to tear up his track, and set the men at it, and soon had some three miles torn up and ready to carry on board.

APRIL 3d.—Left Eunice yesterday afternoon, after getting on board all the iron that we wanted to finish the Price and Van Dorn. Arrived at Memphis at 3 P. M., found the Bragg had arrived yesterday afternoon. At 4 P. M. the Van Dorn came up. Captain Townsend, being senior captain, set all available men at work to finish the boats as soon as possible.

APRIL 11th.—Weather rainy. Received order to leave Fort Pillow. Got two pilots to-day, viz., W. W. Hayden and Oscar Postall. Left Memphis at 6:30 P. M.

APRIL 12th.—Arrived at the fort, and reported to the general at 6:30 A. M., and then dropped down to coal. Orders were sent down for us to escort the transport Lockland up the river on a foraging expedition. We started at 5 P. M., left orders for the Van Dorn to follow us. Those of Hollins' fleet went up ahead of us; passed them at 11 P. M. at anchor near Island No. 25. As soon as we rounded the bend saw a United States transport and gave her chase. She either heard us or saw our smoke, and started up the river. We chased her about eight miles, when she met the Federal fleet at the mouth of the Obion River.

APRIL 13th, 1 A. M.—Sent a note to Captain Huger, flag-officer on the McRea, notifying him of the presence of the enemy. At 5 A. M. received his answer that he would be along after daylight. At 8:30 the lookouts report the fleet coming up; dropped out into the stream and formed in line of battle, and stood up to meet the enemy; and when within three miles of us, the United States gunboat Benton opened on us; her shot fell short. The Confederate States gunboat Maurepas replied to her from a 9-inch Dahlgren, also falling short. The Federals now showed their whole fleet, consisting of eleven gunboats and eight mortars. So Captain Huger, knowing it to be folly to contend with them, left us alone with them. We then rounded to and waited until the enemy came within two miles, and let them have the contents of our stern guns, and then we went after the balance of the fleet. The Yankees followed us and kept up a running fire, but without any damage. We arrived at the fort at 11:30, and reported the fleet coming down. The guns were immediately manned, and all waited for the appearance of the fleet. At 2:30 they made their appearance, but only exchanged a few shots, rounded to and went up the river about six miles.

APRIL 14th.—This morning the Federals opened fire on the fort, and every fifteen minutes they gave three shells. The bombardment was kept up till 9 P. M. A scouting party from our boat and the Van Dorn, under command of First-Officer T. E. Henthorn, went out this morning on the Arkansas shore, and went within six hundred yards of the Federal fleet, and report their forming in line of battle and dropping down stream, stern foremost. 10 P. M.—No demonstration made by fleet as yet.

APRIL 15th.—First-Officer T. E. Henthorn, with a party of thirteen men and officers from the River Defense fleet, has gone out again this morning. The bombardment was renewed at an early hour this morning, and has been kept up at regular intervals of ten minutes. They have three mortar boats in position, at the distance of three and a half miles, and lay around a point opposite the forts. 10 P. M.—The firing ceased at 8 P. M. The scouting party have just returned; report three men captured at Mr. Lamie's, by Federal mounted infantry; were chased by a party, but made their escape.

APRIL 16th.—Went down to Mr. Lamie's, and moved him and family on board of steamer transport Charm, and sent them below, under convoy of the Bragg. A party of fifty "Feds" came down last night to capture one of our boats but, not finding us, they returned at daylight. This morning a party of United States soldiers appearing in sight, gave them a few rounds of grape. Scouts report fifteen men killed and wounded; burned ninety bales unginned cotton.

APRIL 17th.—Went down and moved Mr. Morgan to a place of safety.

MAY 8th.—The bombardment has been kept up day by day, but no damage done; loss, two killed. This morning the Sumter, Bragg and Van Dorn were ordered to go up and cut out the mortar floats. Arrived at the field where they had been posted, but found they had been moved up the fleet. The Sumter remained there until 9 A. M., the Federals firing a few shots at her, but did not come down, and commenced a furious bombardment, throwing over two hundred and fifty shells, but most of them fell short.

MAY 10th.—Agreeably to the decision of the council of war, held yesterday, the fleet left their moorings at 7 A. M. and the several positions in line of battle, as follows: The Bragg, Sumter, Sterling Price, Van Dorn, Jeff. Thompson, General Lovell, Beauregard and Little Rebel. On rounding the point, the Federal fleet was plainly visible in Bulletin Bar, with the exception of the Cincinnati, who had come down as a protection to the mortar, but made (as soon as we appeared) for the balance of the fleet. According to orders, the Bragg immediately gave her chase, and soon overtook her, striking her a violent blow on the larboard bow, dismounting one of her forward guns and slewing her round. The Cincinnati fired a broadside into the Bragg, one shot going through her, killing a cook. The Price next in turn started for her, and at the same time delivering an effective fire at the mortar, silencing it. The Cincinnati kept a running fire as the Price kept away from her, soon overtaking her, and struck her aft a little starboard of midships, carrying away her rudder and sternpost, disabling her; the Sumter came soon after, and also struck her, and she then lifted on the bar and sank. The Van Dorn in the meantime had come up. Those of the Federal fleet came down to the assistance of the Cincinnati, and surrounded the Van Dorn, who made a sudden dash at the Mound City, striking her amidships, driving in her hull about six feet, causing her to leak badly; but as the Federal gunboats are all built in water-tight compartments, it was some time before she sunk; she was able to make the bank. The United States gunboat Pittsburg was disabled by getting between the fires of the two fleets. The firing between both fleets was rapid and heavy, and our boats were struck several times, doing some damage to the cabins, but only one was damaged in the hull, and that was the General Price, who received a shell (one hundred and twenty-eight pounds) between wind and water, cutting off the supply pipes and causing her to leak. As the "Feds" had drawn off into shoal water, where we could not reach them, Commodore J. E. Montgomery signaled the fleet to retire, which was done in good order, all dropping down stream below the guns of the fort. The total loss was two killed; but several firemen were wounded with splinters, and one man had his arm broken. The only damage was to the upper works of the Van Dorn and Price, with the exception of the damage done the Price as reported. As soon as we arrived at Fulton, commenced to repair damages.

MAY 11th.—All damages on our boats repaired, and all ready for another engagement with the enemy. At 4 P. M. scouts came in from Osceola; report the loss of the enemy to be three boats sunk, and several killed and wounded. The enemy are hard at work raising their boats. The Little Rebel went up on a reconnoissance to-day. On her appearance the Yankees took their mortar floats and started up the river.

JUNE 3d.—The bombardment has been kept up, but no damage done to the fort. Second Officer John C. Rawson and a party of seven men went after ice, and were captured. At 3:30 P. M. two gunboats and three rams came down to cut out the Jeff. Thompson, but the fort opened on them and they retired. The Confederate States fleet then went up to the fort and were actively employed in taking on shot and shell and commissary stores, as the fort is to be evacuated.

JUNE 4th.—The fort being completely demolished, the fleet started down the river. At Randolph the Van Dorn got aground and had to send men in the woods to cut spars and spar her off.

JUNE 5th.—Arrived at Memphis at 1 P. M.; 9 P. M. all were aroused by the report of a cannon, and a rush was made to find out the cause, and found the General Lovell out in the stream, dropping down. All then dropped out in the stream, in line of battle, but the "Feds" not making their appearance returned to our anchorage. The tug Gordon Grant was sent up as a picket boat, but grounded, and had to be burned.

Mound City (Federal). Carondelet, Mortar (Federal). Cincinnati (Federal) General Price. Van Dorn Bragg. Sumter. Little Rebel.

BATTLE OF FORT PILLOW. FIRST POSITION

ENGAGEMENT AT ST. CHARLES, ARKANSAS,

BETWEEN THE

CONFEDERATE FORCES AND THE FEDERAL GUNBOATS.

BY

LIEUTENANT JOHN W. DUNNINGTON,
Confederate States Navy.

C. S. GUNBOAT PONTCHARTRAIN,
LITTLE ROCK, ARK., June 21, 1862.

I REACHED St. Charles on Monday evening, 16th instant, about 6 P. M., with the men I carried with me to work the two rifled 32-pounder cannon, which I had previously placed there in battery. I found our forces there under arms. The smoke of the enemy's gunboats was plainly seen from the bluff, and the pickets who had come in reported two gunboats, one tug and two transports below advancing. Owing to the unexpected approach of the enemy, Captain Fry had not time to land his guns, but immediately placed his vessel across the river above my battery of rifled guns, and intended to resist their progress. Finding the enemy did not advance,

Lovell. Thompson. Beauregard. Bragg. Sumter Carondelet. Cincinnati. Little Rebel. Van Dorn Mound City. Benton. St Louis. Tug. Cairo. Pittsburg.

BATTLE OF FORT PILLOW. SECOND POSITION.

after dark it was determined to sink the gunboat Maurepas, the transports Eliza G. and Mary Patterson in a line across the river. The sinking of the transports was intrusted to Captain Leary. Captain Fry, with his own crew, sunk the Maurepas, remaining on deck till the gun-deck was submerged. The blockading of the river was necessarily so hastily done that no ballast or weight could be placed in the transports. About daybreak the last vessel was sunk, and the river blockaded temporarily. Supposing the enemy would make the attack at early daylight, one rifled Parrott gun and ammunition, in command of Midshipman [F. M.] Roby, were moved some four hundred yards below the rifled battery and placed in position. The sailors who manned the different batteries were ordered to sleep within a few feet of their guns. Shortly after daylight two rifled Parrott 8-pounder guns, that had been sent to the rear for want of ammunition, were brought up and placed in position near the guns commanded by Midshipman Roby. These three guns were manned by the crew from the Maurepas, and Captain Fry in person superintended the fighting of them. One 12-pounder howitzer from the Maurepas, manned also by the crew, was sent down the river to assist Captain Williams in checking the enemy's advance by land.

At 7 A. M. on the morning of the 17th, the pickets reported the enemy getting up steam. At 8:30 they had advanced up the river to our lines, and two gunboats commenced throwing shell, grape and canister among our troops on the right bank of the river. They advanced very slowly, attempting to find our heavy guns. When they arrived abreast of Captain Fry's rifled guns they opened on his battery very rapidly for three-quarters of an hour, endeavoring to silence his guns. Failing to do so, they slowly moved up the river until they came within point-blank range of one of the rifled 32-pounders. The leading gunboat stopped to fight that gun; but finding the gun still further up was firing at her, she moved up the river to get its position, and, in doing so, placed herself between the two guns, and in point-blank range. The other gunboat, in obedience to signal I suppose, came abreast of the lower battery and opened a brisk fire upon us. About this stage of the action, 10 A. M., Captain Fry sent me word the enemy were landing a large force below. All the available men that could be found were immediately sent to Captain Williams' assistance. At 10:30 a shot from the rifled 32-pounder furthest up the river penetrated the leading gunboat, and either passed through the boilers, steam chest or pipes, filling the entire vessel with steam, and causing all that were not killed or scalded with steam to jump into the river. The vessel was completely deserted and drifted across the stream into the bank, near Captain Fry's battery. He immediately hailed, and directed their flag hauled down. They failing to do so, although the order was given by some of their own officers in hearing of our own people, our own men were directed to shoot those in the water attempting escape. The two rifled guns were immediately directed to fire upon the lower gunboat, which was still engaging us. She was struck several times and soon ceased firing, slowly dropping down the river, I think, materially damaged, as she made no effort to assist the boat we had blown up or save their friends in the river. Near 11:30, Captains Fry and Williams came to my battery and told me the enemy had completely surrounded us; the battery of small rifled guns had been spiked and our people were in retreat. I trained one of the rifled guns to take a last shot at the enemy, and as we fired, their infantry appeared over the brow of the hill, about fifty yards distant, and opened on us with musketry. Captain Fry then proposed to make a stand with the sailors, and attemped to hold the guns, but they were only armed with single-barreled pistols which they had fired at the enemy in the water. Nothing was now left but to save all the men we could, and as the enemy had us under a cross-fire, the men were ordered to retreat, the officers bringing up the rear, until scattered in the woods. I had confined in single irons, at my battery, six prisoners, captured by Captain Fry at Little Red River. Deeming it inexpedient to bring them away, and as Captain Fry told me he had no positive proof against them, I left them for the enemy. The gallantry of Captains Fry and Williams was so conspicuous as to cause general notice and remark.

To my own men and several of Captain Fry's who served with me, I am particularly indebted. Mr. William Smith (acting master), Mr. William Barclay (engineer), Midshipman Roby, who commanded one of the guns, Mr. W. L. Campbell and Dr. Addison, of the Maurepas, acted with great gallantry, and displayed a coolness and courage unsurpassed by any one in the engagement. To Colonel Belknap, one of the citizens of St. Charles, we are all indebted for the untiring energy and zeal with which he assisted before and during the action. He was always where he was needed, encouraging the men and assisting the officers. I am unable to furnish a list of killed and wounded, but do not think the numbers exceed three up to the time of the retreat.

J. W. DUNNINGTON,
Commanding Gunboat Pontchartrain.

HOSPITAL SORE EYES.—A tall, fine-looking fellow, the picture of health, went to the doctor for an excuse for the day. When his turn came the surgeon looked at him in surprise and said, "Well, sir, what's the matter with you?" "Well, doctor," said he, putting on a most woebegone look and rubbing his eyes, "my eyes are sore, and it hurts me to dress to the right!" He didn't get his excuse that day.

CONFEDERATE STATES GUNBOAT GENERAL PRICE.

ENGAGEMENT BETWEEN THE CONFEDERATE STATES STEAMER COTTON AND THE FEDERAL GUNBOATS IN BERWICKS BAY, LA.,

NOVEMBER 1 TO 6, 1862.

GUNBOAT COTTON, November 12, 1862.

I EMBRACE the opportunity of giving an account of the affair between the Cotton, under my command, and the squadron of Federal gunboats that occupied Berwicks Bay.

On Saturday evening, November 1st, the smoke from the enemy's boats warned me of their near approach in such force that resistance at the bay was considered by me to be rashness. Acting upon your order, received but a few minutes previously, I immediately gave the necessary orders for leaving the bay. The steamers Hart and Segur were there at the time, also Launch No. 1, under command of J. M. Rogers, whom I had temporarily appointed to the position of acting master. My order to the officers of these boats was to get immediately under way; the Hart, under command of Lieutenant E. Montaigne, to proceed up to the Teche with a barge loaded with government sugar in tow. This was safely done according to orders, with one exception. Lieutenant Montaigne at one time dropped his barge and returned, like a gallant soldier, to aid the Cotton in an unequal conflict. As soon as I could communicate to him my wishes, he resumed his tow, and proceeded safely to his destination.

Launch No. 1 also obeyed the order given to her commander, and conveyed the launch up the lake to a place near Indian Bend, from where he has since safely reported, and is now in position to render valuable service.

The Segur, under the command of Acting Master J. C. Coons, disobeyed the orders I gave of proceeding up the lake. I turned up the Atchafalaya, and was ignobly abandoned to the enemy at a time when the Cotton was between the enemy and the Segur. The commanding officer has not since reported. I have been informed that he abandoned his men and proceeded as fast as possible to St. Martinsville. Up to the present time the only reliable fact I have about the Segur is that it is in the hands of the enemy, prowling about Grand Lake and bayous in the vicinity; of the crew, nothing.

CONFEDERATE STATES GUNBOAT LITTLE REBEL

The enemy came into Berwicks Bay on Saturday evening, just at dark, as the Cotton was in range, having had to wait to get the other boats off. They immediately opened fire upon us and gave chase up the bay with three boats, continuing the fire, which I did not return until rounding into the Atchafalaya, when one of our guns was brought to bear and we fired one shot, which sped straight to its mark, striking one of the Federal boats in her bows, breaking many timbers, and, I have since been informed, killing three and wounding five men. The Federals continued to fire shot and shell at us from eighteen guns for about thirty minutes, when they gave up the chase.

The Cotton came up to the Teche, turned bows down and backed into it, keeping our teeth to the enemy. We backed up to the Fuselier plantation, where we stopped for the night. On Sunday morning, the 2d instant, I received orders to move the Cotton above Cornay Bridge, which I did as soon as possible. The bayou had some obstructions thrown across at that point which I was ordered to defend until it got too hot for me and then to fall back, turn my boat across the bayou at the second bridge and, if pursued, sink her.

On Monday, at 2 o'clock P. M., the four Federal boats, mounting twenty-seven guns, came up and opened fire upon us. They came up in full confidence of overpowering numbers, giving us broadside after broadside, frequently the whole four delivering their fire at once. The shot and shell literally rained on and about our boat, several striking us, but without doing serious damage. We returned their fire, my brave boys cheering frequently when a well directed shot struck the Federal boats. One of them retired from the contest in about fifteen minutes, her place being taken by another. One boat for several minutes had her colors down. Whether accidentally down or that they hauled them down to indicate a surrender, we had no means of learning. However, they hoisted them again after a delay of about twenty minutes. One, more venturesome than the rest, steadily steamed up the bayou. When in about two hundred yards of the obstructions, we gave her a plunging shot from each of our guns, which all struck near the water on the starboard quarter; the boat immediately ran her head up on shore, and was listed down so as to throw her guns out of use, and ceased her fire, except occasionally from one gun on the bow. At this time, when but one of the enemy's boats fired with any vigor, when victory seemed to be within our reach, it was announced that we had no more cartridges, having fired the last one. Retreat was all that remained for us; but as we slowly backed up, we had some sacks made, and by cutting off the legs from the pantaloons of some of our men, which we filled up, and returned fire with one as often as we could, in that manner, obtain a cartridge; this we

RUINS OF THE NAVY YARD, MEMPHIS, TENN.

continued until out of range, and the enemy had ceased their fire.

We had to mourn the loss of one brave soldier killed by an accidental discharge of his gun, which severely wounded another. Another was accidentally wounded at another gun by recoil of the carriage, and has since died. One man was wounded by a piece of the enemy's shell. These are all the casualties that occurred. The boat sustained no perceptible damage.

On Tuesday morning we resumed our original position near the obstructions, the enemy having previously retired. We worked hard to improve the condition of our boat, and got up some iron to shield the engines. Nothing occurred worthy of note during the day.

On Wednesday, the 5th inst., the enemy again opened fire upon us with four boats at about 10:30 o'clock. They fired from behind a point out of our range for about twenty minutes, when two of them steamed up into sight. We then immediately returned their fire, and with such effect that the enemy retired and abandoned the contest in fifty-five minutes from firing their first shot. The two boats that came into sight were badly damaged and their loss heavy; ours nothing, the only damage being a trifling break in the cabin roof. This day's victory was clearly ours; the enemy retired from the action badly discouraged, with severe loss. We were unhurt.

On Thursday the enemy came up and opened fire upon us, but took care not to come into sight. I did not return their fire. They threw shells at us for half an hour, and retired without doing us any damage. Since that time up to the present date they have not assailed us.

I can not close this report without returning thanks to officers and men. When all did their duty gallantly, it may seem invidious to mention particular names, yet I must particularly mention the good conduct of O. S. Burdett, pilot, who for two hours and a half, during the full contest on the 3d inst., maneuvered the boat with the utmost coolness; also the same gallant conduct on the 5th inst. Each of my lieutenants did their duty nobly and ably. Also F. G. Burbank, gunner, and privates F. D. Wilkinson and Henry Dorning, deserve particular mention for their gallant conduct; but all did their duty well, and are again ready to meet the enemy should they come up and try us again.

E. W. FULLER,
Captain, Commanding Gunboat Cotton.

IT will be remembered that a curious habit prevailed among the soldiers, in the latter part of the war, of designating their respective companies and battalions by the queer names of "outfit" and "layout," while they would call a brigade a "shebang." The story goes that General Polignac, the noble Frenchman who so generously espoused the cause of the South and served her with distinguished bravery to the last, was once accosted by a bright-eyed Creole boy, who announced to the general that he had just returned from a furlough, and wished to know where he could find Colonel Censir's "layout." "Colonel Censir's what?" shouted the general, his eyes bulging with astonishment. "Colonel Censir's 'layout,'" repeated the lad; "it belongs to your 'shebang.'" "Well, I hope to land in h—" ejaculated Polignac, who, when excited, sometimes became profane, "if I know what ze little diable mean! I have been educate all my life in ze armee. I have hear of ze compagnie, ze battalion, ze brigade and ze division, but I agree to be hanged if I ever hear of ze 'layout' or ze 'shebang' before."

THE BATTLE OF MEMPHIS, TENN.,

JUNE 6, 1862.

BY

CAPTAIN J. HENRY HART,

Commanding Confederate States Steamer Beauregard.

OUR gunboat flotilla arrived at Memphis on the evening of the 5th of June, 1862, to await the arrival of the Federal fleet, which came down about 9 o'clock the same evening, and laid on "Paddy's hen and chickens" in sight of Memphis. On being informed of this, our commodore sent up a small tug, in charge of Captain Bennett, as a picket. By some mismanagement she got aground on the foot of the island, and she could not be got off with her own power; consequently, the torch was applied, and she was left to her fate in flames. Nothing more of importance happened during the night, but the general understanding with all the fleet was that we would not make a stand.

Queen. Monarch. Little Rebel. Jeff. Thompson. Bragg. Sumter. Louisville. Cairo. St. Louis. Beauregard. Benton. Carondelet. Lovell.

BATTLE OF MEMPHIS.

After daylight on the morning of the 6th, we could see by the movements of the enemy that they were making preparations to come down, for the heavens were one solid cloud of black smoke. In the meantime, we were not idle in making preparations to back out in the stream, which we did, one after another, until our whole fleet, eight in number, were drawn in line of battle. It was here we received the first intelligence that we were going to make a stand. The enemy was now in full view, coming down in line of battle. The following boats were sent up to draw the Federal gunboats off the bar: General M. Jeff. Thompson, Sumter, General Beauregard and Colonel Lovell, from the fact that they had sixty-four pound guns mounted on their bows. The fire was opened by the Thompson, but not until she had fired three rounds did the enemy make any reply. The fire on the Federal side was opened by the flagship Benton. The fight now became general. Brisk firing from both sides was the order of the day. It was while the battle was raging with intense fury between our rams and the Federal gunboats that their rams made their appearance. First came the Queen of the West, which made a bee-line for the Colonel Lovell, which tried to back out of the way, but in so doing got in such a position as to show her opponent a broadside, when she ran into her and sunk her immediately in water to her hurricane deck in the channel of the river. Life-boats were immediately dispatched from the Little Rebel to assist her crew in getting ashore. Before the Queen of the West could regain her position the Confederate ram Sumter struck her in midship, sending her ashore during the balance of the engagement. Next came the Switzerland, bearing down on the Sumter. The Beauregard, next in turn, singled out the Switzerland for her antagonist. The Federal ram, seeing her intention, drew off from the Sumter and headed down on the Beauregard. They struck head-on, but glanced, placing the Switzerland *hors de combat*, knocking down her bridge-tree, when she had to go ashore, where she threw out her sharpshooters as pickets. Next came the Federal ram Monarch in chase of the Jeff. Thompson, she at the same time rounding to, head up stream, followed by the Monarch. Here the General Price was put under a heavy head of steam to overtake the Monarch, which she did, striking her a heavy blow in the starboard quarter, driving in her hull and rounding her to, after which she stopped to back around and give her another blow, but, unfortunately, the Beauregard had made a dash at the Monarch, and missed her object, and striking the Price on the port-side, completely disabling her. During this, with only one wheel left, she managed to get ashore, but too late for the crew to make their escape. Disabled as she was, the enemy kept up a constant fire into her, and for humanity's sake the "stars and bars" were hauled down. It was about this time the Beauregard got headed up again to meet another of her adversaries, when a shell was shot into her hull, and burst, damaging her boilers and hull, killing one engineer, wounding three others, and scalding three firemen. She was unfit for duty, floated down the river about one-fourth of a mile, and sunk in twenty feet of water, face to the enemy and colors flying. It was about this time the Little Rebel made a dash at one of the rams; but before she could reach her received a shot in her boilers, when she kept her course into the shore, where all but three made their escape. In the meantime the Sumter had been run ashore, and crew all escaped; also the Thompson was run ashore, and burned to the water's edge. The General Bragg stood off and looked at the fight, likewise the General Earl Van Dorn; neither offering any assistance. The Bragg, in attempting to round to, to make good her retreat, was run into by one of the Federal rams, which drove in her side. The crew of the Bragg nearly all made their escape in yawls and life-boats. The Van Dorn, handling much better than the Bragg, was fortunate in making good her escape. Thus ended one of the hottest naval engagements ever fought in the Mississippi.

The following is a list of the principal officers, as far as could be ascertained:

EARL VAN DORN—Captain, Isaac Fulkerson; Purser, Charles Reynolds; First Officer, John W. Jordan; Second Officer, John Mardis; Chief Engineer, William Hurst; First Assistant Engineers, John Swift, William Camon and William Molloy.

GENERAL STERLING PRICE—Captain, Thomas E. Henthorn; Purser, L. F. Delisdimier; First Officer, N. J. Henthorn; Second Officer, George L. Richardson; Chief Engineer, William Brauden; First Assistant Engineers, William Orin, W. W. Hayden and Oscar Postall.

Jeff Thompson Exploding.

AFTER THE BATTLE OF MEMPHIS.

GENERAL BEAUREGARD—Captain, J. Henry Hart; Purser, J. C. Haynes; First Officer, R. D. Court; Second Officer, John Rawson; Chief Engineer, Joseph Swift; First Assistant, Edward Connolly; Pilot, J. Pope Altram.

GENERAL BRAGG—Captain, W. H. H. Leonard; Purser, William Riply; First and Second Officers, names unknown; Chief Engineer, John Porter; First Assistant Engineer, Henry Sisson; Pilot, James Russell.

SUMTER—Captain, Wallace W. Lamb; Purser, John Wilbanks; First Officer, Lemuel Murray; Second Officer, name unknown; Chief Engineer, Robert T. Patterson; First Assistant Engineer, John Ramsey; Pilots, Thad Siederburg and Moses Gray.

LITTLE REBEL—Captain, J White Fowler; Purser, Charles Smedley; First Officer, James Wall; Second Officer, name unknown; Chief Engineer, Gus Mann; First Assistant Engineer, William Reeder; Pilots, Newton Pue and John Bernard.

GENERAL M. JEFF. THOMPSON—Captain, John Burk; Purser, James Bissell; First Officer, Louis Camfield; Second Officer, Henry Moore; Chief Engineer, Thomas Mitchell; Pilots, Barney Arnold and Daniel Thomas.

GENERAL LOVELL—Captain, James C. Dellaney; Purser, Hardy; First Officer, Thomas Johnson; Pilot, William Cable.

COMMODORE OF THE FLEET—J. E. Montgomery.

The Federal fleet consisted of sixteen mortar boats, six rams and eight gunboats, besides any number of tugs and transports.

* * * * *

J. HENRY HART,
Commanding C. S. Steamer Beauregard.

EXPLOITS OF THE RAM ARKANSAS.

BY

LIEUTENANT GEORGE W. GIFT.

THE 15th day of July, 1862, was a warm day, literally and figuratively, for some two hundred persons cooped up in the famous Confederate steamer Arkansas.

Our good ship had been gotten up under the peculiar circumstances of haste. What she was designed for no man probably knows. I imagine that she was intended for a powerful ironclad gunboat, with an iron beak for poking and several heavy guns for shooting. But, before she had arrived at anything like a state of completion, the plan was altered. Instead of finishing the ship with an ordinary rail and bulwark all around, her sides were "built on" amidships for fifty or sixty feet in length, so as to give an apology for protection to three guns in each broadside. The sides, it must be understood, were perpendicular. The ends of this "castle," or "gun-box," as Captain Brown dubbed it, were sloping or inclined, from which were thrust four more guns, two at each end. This gave us a battery of ten guns, which, by the way, were of all sizes and descriptions, to-wit: Two 8-inch columbiads; one 8-inch shell gun; two 9-inch shell guns; one smooth bore, 32-pounder (sixty-three hundredweight), and four rifle guns, formerly 32-pounders, but now altered, three banded and one unbanded. Four of the carriages were mounted on railroad iron *chassis;* the six broadside guns were on carriages constructed at Canton, Miss., by parties who never saw or heard of such things before. The timber had not left the stump ten days when we received the carriages on board. The ship was built at Fort Pickering, a short distance below Memphis, by Captain John T. Shirley, as contractor, and Prime Emmerson, constructor. Her engines were built at a foundry on Adams Street, and the timber of which she was composed grew in our vicinity. The Confederate Congress appropriated $125,000 to build two rams to defend the upper Mississippi. The Arkansas was the first constructed under the act, and was towed up the Yazoo after the fall of New Orleans. It is sufficient that we had the craft, incomplete and rough as she was, with railroad bars on her hull and sides and ends of the "gun-box." We have a crew and an officer for every gun, and on the aforesaid morning we are steaming down the Yazoo River, bound to Mobile. Our orders were to pass Vicksburg shortly after dawn; proceed from thence down the river, destroying any stray vessels of the enemy in the road; coal ship at New Orleans; pass Forts Jackson and St. Phillip at night, and proceed to Mobile Bay and raise the blockade—a programme easy of accomplishment had not the pilot miscalculated his distance, and sunrise found us in the Yazoo River, with more than twenty ships barring our way to the goal of our hopes and ambition. However, we were in for one of the most desperate fights any one ship ever sustained since ships were first made.

Queen of the West. Taylor. Arkansas Carondelet.
BATTLE BETWEEN THE ARKANSAS AND CARONDELET.

Some time after midnight we lifted our anchor from in front of Haines Bluff, on the Yazoo, and steamed down the river. Just before daylight we stopped the ship and sent a boat on shore to obtain information from a plantation. Getting no satisfaction, we proceeded, and when the sun rose we were still in the Yazoo.

Many of the men had stripped off their shirts and were bare to the waists, with handkerchiefs bound round their heads, and some of the officers had removed their coats and stood in their undershirts. The decks had been thoroughly sanded to prevent slipping after the blood should become plentiful. Tourniquets were served out to division officers by the surgeons, with directions for use. The division tubs were filled with water to drink; fire buckets were in place; cutlasses and pistols strapped on; rifles loaded and bayonets fixed; spare breechings for the guns, and other implements made ready. The magazines and shell-rooms forward and aft were open, and the men inspected in their places. Before getting under way, coffee (or an apology therefor) had been served to the crew, and daylight found us a grim, determined set of fellows, grouped about our guns, anxiously waiting to get sight of the enemy.

Shortly after sunrise the smoke from several steamers was discovered by Captain Brown, who, with the first lieutenant, Henry K. Stevens, stood on a platform entirely exposed to the enemy's fire. This was the signal for fresh girding up, last inspections and final arrangements for battle. Lieutenant John Grimball and myself divided the honor of commanding the 8-inch columbiads. He fought the starboard, and I the port gun Midshipman Dabney M. Scales was his lieutenant, and a youngster named John Wilson, of Baltimore, was mine. Lieutenant A. D. Wharton, of Nashville, came next on the starboard broadside, with Midshipman R. H. Bacot for his assistant. Lieutenant Charles W. Read, of Mississippi, had the two stern chasers, both rifles, to himself, and the remaining two guns on the port side were under command of Lieutenant Alphonse Barbot. Each lieutenant had two guns. Grimball and myself had each a bow-chaser and a broadside gun. The two masters, John L. Phillips and Samuel Milliken, were in charge of the two powder divisions. Stevens busied himself passing about the ship, cool and smiling, giving advice here and encouragement there. Our commander, Lieutenant Isaac Newton Brown, passed around the ship, and after making one of his sharp, pithy speeches, returned to his post with glass in hand to get the first sight of the approaching enemy. In a few moments we see three gunboats round a point in full view, steaming toward us gallantly and saucily, with colors streaming in the wind. The ironclad Carondelet, of twelve guns, commanded by Commander Walke, was on the right. The Tyler, the vessel which annoyed our troops at Shiloh, commanded by Lieutenant Gwin, was in the center, and the unlucky river-ram, Queen of the West, commanded by an army "mustang" named Hunter, was on the left.

Owing to the fact that our bow-ports were quite small, we could train our guns latterly very little; and as our head was looking to the right of the enemy's line, we were compelled to allow them to begin the action, as we had leveled all our guns with a spirit-level the day before, marked the trunnions, and agreed that we would not fire until we were sure of hitting an enemy direct, without elevation. The gunnery of the enemy was excellent, and his rifle bolts soon began to ring on our iron front, digging into and warping up the bars, but not penetrating. Twice he struck near my port, and still we could not "see" him. The first blood was drawn from my division. An Irishman, with more curiosity than prudence, stuck his head out the broadside port, and was killed by a heavy rifle bolt which had missed the ship. Stevens was with me at the time; and, fearing that the sight of the mangled corpse and blood might demoralize the gun's crew, sprang forward to throw the body out of the port, and called upon the man nearest him to assist. "Oh, I can't do it, sir," the poor fellow replied, "it's my brother." The body was thrown overboard. As soon as we could point straight for the enemy, with safety from grounding, the pilot steered direct for the Tyler, and I got the first shot, with an 8-inch shell with 5-second fuse. It struck her fair and square, killing a pilot in its flight and bursting in

Sumter. Bragg. Lancaster. Farragut's Fleet. Arkansas. Transports, U. S.
Admiral Davis' Fleet. Vicksburg.
CONFEDERATE RAM ARKANSAS RUNNING THE GAUNTLET.

the engine-room. She reported seventeen killed and fourteen wounded.

The broadside guns thus far were not engaged; but they were not to remain entirely idle. The Queen of the West, summoning courage, shot up as though she would poke us gently in our starboard ribs. Captain Brown divined her intent and gave notice in time. The starboard battery was trained sharp forward, and as the Queen ranged up, Scales gave her the first shell, followed quick by Wharton and Bacot. This settled the account on that side. This left us with the Tyler and the Carondelet to deal with.

The fight had been an advance on our part; we had never slowed the engines, but stood forward as though we held such small fry in contempt. Gwin handled and fought the Tyler with skill as long as there was any hope; but he finally took to his heels, badly crippled, and went after the Queen of the West. The Carondelet was right ahead of us, distant about one hundred yards, and paddling down stream. Her armor had been pierced four times, and we were running after her to use our ram, having the advantage of speed.

We are now using 15-pound charges of powder and solid shot, which latter were hastily made in Canton, and had very little windage, so that I think we bored the fellow through and through from end to end. It was an exceedingly good thing we had. If her stern guns were not dismounted the crews had deserted them, for they were not used after my gun came into action the second time. I think I had hit four times, and our beak was nearly up to her, when Brady discovered that she was taking to shoal water with the hope of our grounding—we drew four feet more water than she. Therefore, we sheered off, and passed so close that it would have been easy to have jumped on board. Stevens passed rapidly along the port broadside, and saw the guns depressed to their utmost, and bade us wait for a good chance and fire down through her bottom. As we lapped up alongside, and almost touching, we poured in our broadside, which went crashing and plunging through her timbers. Although her four broadside guns—one more than we had—were run out and ready, she did not fire them. We were running near the left or Vicksburg side of the river (we are now in what is called Old River), and as soon as passed, we headed for the middle of the stream, which gave Read his first opportunity—and right well did he use it. His rifles "spoke" to the purpose, for the enemy hauled down his colors. In an instant Captain Brown announced the fact from the deck, and ordered the firing to cease; but the ship still swinging, gave Wharton and the others a chance at her with the starboard guns before it was known that she had surrendered. White flags now appeared at her ports, and the news of our victory was known all over the ship in a moment.

We now had no time to stop to secure our prize, as the enemy would be apprised of our coming and swarm in the river like bees, if we did not hurry. These fellows we had beaten were but skirmishers of a main army. Consequently we pushed down the river, and the Carondelet sunk on a sand bar on the right side.

We pursued the Tyler and Queen of the West. Both were swifter vessels than the Arkansas, and in our efforts to overtake them we worked off steam too rapidly, and the result was that when we entered the Mississippi River they had gained sufficiently on us to notify the fleets of Farragut and Davis of our approach, and that before we had come in sight around the point. The result was instant and rapid preparation by the squadrons for our reception. Stean. was hurried up on all the river vessels, and they weighed or slipped, and took up such positions as would enable them to hit us and at the same time keep away from our powerful beak, if possible. On coming in sight of them the scene was one of intense interest. A dozen or more war vessels were steaming about in an uneasy, uncertain way, somewhat after the manner of a brood of chickens on the approach of a hawk. Tugs, transports and hospital vessels were smoking up or trying to hide. The heavy sloops-of-war and gunboats of Farragut's squadron were anchored in the middle of the stream, with fires out, but with batteries manned and ready for battle. On the banks batteries of field artillery were run up, and several thousands of soldiers prepared to shoot minie balls into our ports. The "mustang" rams were under way also. I think I do not overestimate the force of the enemy when I say he had twenty pennants flying: and we were about to attack him in an unfinished and untried vessel, with engines totally and entirely unreliable. As we stood down to them there was a decided and painful pause. We were in range, but preferred to save our strength and ammunition for a close grapple. The first vessel which stood out to engage us was "No. 6" (Kineo), against which we had a particular grudge, inspired by Read, who desired us all to handle roughly any sea-going vessel we should see with "No. 6" on her smoke-stack, as that vessel was engaging the McRea, above Forts Jackson and St. Phillip, when Lieutenant-Commander Huger was killed. Read, who was first lieutenant under Captain Huger, and devotedly attached to him, saw the "No. 6" by the flashes of the guns,* and had ever since treasured the hope of getting alongside the fellow some day. This "No. 6" came out like a game cock, steamed to the front to take the fire of a great monster, from which "mustangs" and river ironclads were hiding and fleeing. I sent my powder boy to Read with a message to come forward, as his friend was in sight. He came leisurely and carelessly, swinging a primer lanyard, and I think I have never looked at a person displaying such remarkable coolness and self-possession. On observing the numbers ahead, his eye was as bright and his smile as genuine as if he had been about to join a company of friends instead of enemies. We were now getting close aboard "No. 6," and she sheered with her port helm and unmuzzled her eleven-inch pivot gun, charged with grape. It was hastily pointed, and the charge fell too low to enter our ports, for which it was intended. This broke the terrible quiet which hung over us like a spell. Every man's nerves were strung up again, and we were ready for the second battle. With a sharp touch of the starboard helm Brady showed me "No. 6" straight ahead, and I gave her a shell through and through, and as we passed she got the port broadside. She did not follow us up. These two shots opened the engagement. Soon we were a target for a hundred or more guns, which poured in an unceasing and terrible fire. Generals Breckinridge, Van Dorn and others viewed the engagement from the top of the courthouse in Vicksburg, and were appalled at the apparent rashness of attempting the passage. The fire of the enemy was almost unceasing, nor were we idle, by any means. Every gun was fully manned, and wherever we looked, in every direction, we saw gunboats. It was only necessary to load the guns and fire, and we hit. The rams were taking up a position to come out and strike us as we passed. One of them, the Lancaster, was slowly moving across our path, and I heard Brady ask Captain Brown if he should cut that boat in two. The captain returned an affirmative answer, and the game pilot steadied our ship for the ram. I had in a five-second shell, which I wished to get rid of before we got to the iron-clads, and so set it in motion. It struck his mud-drum, emptying the hot steam and water into the small barricaded engine-room, where the crew and a company of sharpshooters were seeking protection. A very large number were killed. The poor fellows came pouring up the scuttles, tearing off their shirts and leaping overboard as soon as they reached the air. But that gave us no rest. The shot struck upon our sides as fast as sledgehammer blows. Captain Brown was twice knocked off the platform, stunned, his marine glass was broken in his hand, and he received a wound on his temple; but recovering himself, he gallantly—no, heroically—resumed his place, and continued to direct the movements of his ship from a position entirely exposed to the fire of not only great guns, but thousands of sharpshooters, who were pattering the balls all around and about him. The man of steel never flinched, but carried us straight and clear through.

The Arkansas Fighting Her Way Through the Federal Fleet.

Some one called out that the colors had been shot away. It reached the ear of Midshipman Dabney M. Scales, and in an instant the glorious fellow scrambled up the ladder past Captain Brown, and fearlessly treading the terrible path of death, which was being swept by a hurricane of shot and shell, deliberately bent on the colors again, knotted the halyards and hoisted them up; and when they were again knocked away would have replaced them had not he been forbidden by the captain. Midshipman Clarence Tyler, aid to the captain, was wounded at his post alongside the captain. We were passing one of the large sloops-of-war when a heavy shot struck the side abreast of my bow-gun, the concussion knocking over a man who was engaged in taking a shot from the rack. He rubbed his hip, which had been hurt, and said they would "hardly strike twice in a place." He was mistaken, poor fellow, for immediately a shell entered the breach made by the shot, and bedding itself in the cotton-bale lining on the inside of the bulwark proper, exploded with terrible effect. I found myself standing in a dense, suffocating smoke, with my cap gone and hair and beard singed. The smoke soon cleared away, and I found but one man (Quartermaster Curtis) left. Sixteen were killed and wounded by that shell, and the ship set on fire. Ste-

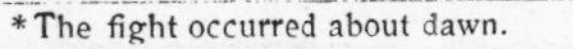

*The fight occurred about dawn.

The Arkansas in a Storm on the Mississippi River.

vens, ever cool and thoughtful, ran to the engine-room hatch, seized the hose and dragged it to the aperture. In a few moments the fire was extinguished, without an alarm having been created.

The columbiad was fired but once after its crew was disabled. By the aid of an army captain belonging to a Missouri battery, Curtis and myself succeeded in getting a shot down the gun, with which we struck the Benton. The ill luck which befell the crew of the bow-gun was soon to be followed by a similar misfortune to the crew of my broadside gun. An eleven-inch shot broke through immediately above the port, bringing with it a shower of iron and wooden splinters, which struck down every man at the gun. My master's mate, Mr. Wilson, was painfully wounded in the nose, and I had my left arm smashed. Curtis was the only sound man in the division when we mustered the crew at quarters, at Vicksburg. Nor did the mischief of the last shot end with my poor gun's crew. It passed across the deck, through the smoke-stack and killed eight and wounded seven men at Scales' gun. Fortunately, he was untouched himself, and afterward did excellent service at Grimball's columbiad. Stationed on the ladder leading to the berth-deck was a quartermaster named Eaton. He was assigned the duty of passing shells from the forward shell-room, and also had a kind of superintendence over the boys who came for powder. Eaton was a character. He had thick, rough, red hair, an immense muscular frame, and a will and courage rarely encountered. Nothing daunted him, and the hotter the fight, the fiercer grew Eaton. From his one eye he glared furiously on all who seemed inclined to shirk, and his voice grew louder and more distinct as the shot rattled and crashed upon our mail.

At one instant you would hear him pass the word down the hatch: "Nine-inch shell, five-second fuse—here you are, my lad, with your rifle shell, take it and go back quick—what's the matter that you can't get that gun out?" and, like a cat, he would spring from his place and throw his weight on the side tackle, and the gun was sure to go out. "What are you doing here, wounded? Where are you hurt? Go back to your gun or I'll murder you on the spot—here's your nine-inch shell—mind, shipmate (to a wounded man), the ladder is bloody; don't slip; let me help you."

I have thrown in this slight sketch to show that our men were beginning to straggle, so badly were we cut up. But still the ship was not disabled; seven guns were yet hammering away, and the engines were intact. But steam was down to a terribly low ebb. The party who fitted up the boilers had neglected to line the fire-front with non-conducting materials; the consequence was, that when a heavy fire of coal was put in the whole mass of iron about the boilers became red-hot, and nearly roasted the firemen, who had also got a tub of ice-water, of which they drank freely. The result was that we had to hoist them all out of the fire-room during the action, and Grimball headed a party to supply their place. But I will not detain the reader. We got through, hammered and battered though. Our smoke-stack resembled an immense nutmeg-grater, so often had it been struck, and the sides of the ship were spotted as if it had been peppered. A shot had broken our cast iron ram. Another had demolished a hawse-pipe. Our boats were shot away and dragging. But all this was to be expected, and could be repaired. Not so on the inside. A great heap of mangled and ghastly slain lay on the gun-deck, with rivulets of blood running away from them. There was a poor fellow torn asunder, another mashed flat, while in the "slaughter-house" brains, hair and blood were all about. Down below, fifty or sixty wounded were groaning and complaining, or courageously bearing their ills without a murmur.

We eventually reached Vicksburg and were hailed with delight by the army. The officers came on board to see the marks of the struggle, while squads of eager privates collected on the bank to get a near view of the wonderful craft which had just stood so much hammering. This attracted a band of daring sharpshooters to the other bank, and we were forced to open with our heavy guns to disperse them, which was easily accomplished by half a dozen discharges. The enemy below showed decided signs of demoralization. A mortar boat, which had been allowed to get aground, was hastily set on fire and blown up. A sea-going vessel (commanded by Craven), left to guard the transports, sprung her broadside athwart the stream to be ready for an attack. Everything got up steam and Porter's flag-boat opened with a 100-pounder Parrott gun in a spiteful, angry fashion, throwing her shot over and beyond us. If we had had a smoke-stack, and proper boiler fronts, and good engines, and a new crew, and many other things, how we would have made a smash of those fellows! But as our smoke-stack was so riddled, the draught was destroyed, and as our engines were troublesome, faulty affairs, and our crew were nearly all killed, wounded or used up, we had to bide where we were and see this chance slip away from us. Read cast many longing glances down the river, and I think would have been perfectly willing to undertake the task, broken down as we were. But there is a limit to human endurance; we could do no more, and we rested. During the day the telegraph informed Captain Brown that he had been promoted to the rank of commodore, and we were thanked from Richmond for our brilliant achievement. Our dead were removed on shore for burial and our wounded were taken to an army hospital. As soon as we arrived at Vicksburg the detachment of soldiers left us to rejoin their command, which reduced our force to a very low ebb. As well as we could, we put the ship to rights, and the day wore away. As soon as dark began to set in it was evident that the enemy meant mischief.

Confederate Gunboats.

Night Scene at Randolph, on the Mississippi River

Everything was under way, and soon the guns from the upper battery opened quick and sharp, to be replied to by the broadsides of the heavy ships coming down—the Richmond (Alden) leading. Our plucky men were again at their quarters, and steam was ready, should we be compelled to cast off and take our chances in the stream against both fleets. About that time things looked pretty blue. It is true we were under the batteries of Vicksburg, but practically we had as well have been a hundred miles from there. The guns were perched on the high hills; they were not provided with sights, and if ever they hit anything it was an accident or the work of one of Brooke's rifles. This we well knew, and stripped this time for what we supposed would be a death struggle. The sea-going fleet of Farragut was to pass down, drag out and literally mob us; while the ironclad squadron of Davis was to keep the batteries engaged. Down they came, steaming slowly and steadily, and seemed to be on the lookout for us. But they had miscalculated their time. The darkness which partially shrouded them from the view of the army gunners completely shut us out from their sight, inasmuch as our sides were the color of rust and we lay under a red bank; consequently, the first notice they had of our whereabouts came from our guns as they crossed our line of fire, and then it was too late to attempt to check up and undertake to grapple with us. They came by singly, each to get punished, as our men were again feeling in excellent spirits. The Hartford stood close in to the bank, and as we spit out our broadside at her she thundered back with an immense salvo. Our bad luck had not left us. An 11-inch shot pierced our side a few inches above the water-line and passed through the engine-room, killing two men outright (cutting them both in two) and wounding six or eight others. The medicines of the ship were dashed into the engine-room, and the debris from the bulkheads and splinters from the side enveloped the machinery. The shot bedded itself so far in the opposite side that its position could be told by the bulging protuberance outside. On account of my disabled arm I had turned over my division to Scales, and remained with Captain Brown on the platform. To be a spectator of such a scene was intensely interesting and exciting. The great ships with their towering spars came sweeping by, pouring out broadside after broadside, while the batteries from the hills, the mortars from above and below, and the ironclads, kept the air alive with hurtling missiles and the darkness lighted up by burning fuses and bursting shells. On our gun-deck every man and officer worked as though the fate of the nation hung on his individual efforts. Scales was very near, and I could hear his clear voice continually. He coaxed and bullied alternately, and finally, when he saw his object in line, his voice rose as clear as a bell, and his "ready! fire!" rang out like a bugle note. The last vessel which passed us was that commanded by Nichols, and she got one of our shots in her out-board delivery. He pivoted his 10-inch gun to starboard, heeled his vessel to keep the leak above water, and drifted past the batteries without further damage.

We had more dead and wounded; another hole through our armor, and heaps of splinters and rubbish. Three separate battles had been fought, and we retired to anything but easy repose. One of our messmates in the ward-room (a pilot) had asserted at supper that he would not again pass through the ordeal of the morning for the whole world. His mangled body, collected in pieces, was now on the gun-deck; another had been sent away to the

Scene on Board of the Arkansas.

hospital with a mortal hurt. The steerage mess was short four or five members, while on the berth-deck many poor fellows would never again range themselves about the mess-cloth.

The enemy now had a fleet above and below us, and, though foiled and angry, he made no immediate active effort to do us more harm, other than to shell us incessantly by day, and once by night, with mortar shells. Half a dozen or more 13-inch mortars kept missiles continually in the air, directed at us. We were twice struck by fragments—otherwise the business was very harmless.

We were dealing with a bold and confident enemy, determined to take some desperate chances to compass our destruction. As the reader already knows, our crew was fearfully used up on the 15th. Daily we sent more men to the hospital, suffering with malarious diseases, until we had not in a week more than thirty seamen, ordinary seamen and landsmen, and, I think, but four or five firemen. Many of the younger officers had also succumbed; those of us who were left were used up also. We slept below, with our clothes on, in an atmosphere so heated by the steam of the engines as to keep one in a constant perspiration. No more men were to be had. It was disheartening enough to see a ship which but a week before was the pride of the country now almost deserted.

On the morning of the 22d of July, a week after our arrival, we were awakened early in the morning by the drum calling us to quarters. Great commotion was observed in the fleet above. Everything seemed under way again, and it was evident that we were soon to have another brush. On our decks were not men enough to man two guns, and not firemen enough to keep steam up if we were forced into the stream! Rather a doleful outlook! We were moored to the bank, head up the river, as a matter of course. The fires under the boilers were hastened and every possible preparation made for resistance. In a few minutes we observed the ironclad steamer Essex steaming around the point and steering for us. The upper battery at once opened, but she did not reply. Grimball then unloosed his columbiad, but she did not stop. I followed, hitting her fair, but still she persevered in sullen silence. Her plan was to run into and shove us aground, when her consort, the Queen of the West, was to follow and butt a hole in us; and thus the dreaded ram was to be made away with. On she came like a mad bull; nothing daunted or overawed. As soon as Captain Brown got a fair view of her, followed at a distance by the Queen, he divined her intent, and seeing that she was as square across the bow as a flatboat or scow, and we as sharp as a wedge, he determined at once to foil her tactics. Slacking off the hawser which held our head to the bank, he went ahead on the starboard screw, and thus our sharp prow was turned directly for her to hit against. This disconcerted the enemy and destroyed his plan. A collision would surely cut her down and leave us uninjured. All

Isaac N. Brown, of Mississippi.
Commander of the ram Arkansas.

this time we had not been idle spectators. The two columbiads had been ringing on her front and piercing her at every shot, to which she did not reply until she found that the shoving off game was out of the question. Then, and when not more than fifty yards distant, she triced up her three bow port-shutters and poured out her fire. A 9-inch shot struck our armor a few inches forward of the unlucky forward port, and crawling along the side, entered. Seven men were killed outright and six wounded. Splinters flew in all directions. In an instant the enemy was alongside, and her momentum was so great that she ran aground a short distance astern of us. As she passed we poured out our port broadside, and as soon as the stern rifles could be cleared of the splinters and broken stanchions and woodwork, which had been driven the whole length of the gun-box, we went ahead on our port screw and turned our stern guns on her, and every man—we had but seventeen left—and officer went to them. As she passed she did not fire, nor did she while we were riddling her close aboard. Her only effort was to get away from us. She backed hard on her engines and finally got off; but getting a shot in her machinery just as she got afloat, she was compelled to float down stream and join the lower fleet, which she accomplished without damage from the batteries on the hills. She fired only the three shots mentioned, but our troubles were not over. We had scarcely shook this fellow off before we were called to the other

Confederate Gunboats. Iron Bluffs. Federal Fleet. Chalk Bluffs.
Scene on the Mississippi. A Reconnoiter.

end of the ship—we ran from one gun to another to get ready for a second attack. The Queen was now close to us, evidently determined to ram us. The guns had been fired and were now empty and inboard. Somehow we got them loaded and run out, and by the time she had commenced to round to. I am not sure, but I think we struck her with the columbiads as she came down, but at all events the broadside was ready. Captain Brown adopted the plan of turning his head to her also, and thus received her blow glancing. She came into us going at an enormous speed, probably fifteen miles an hour, and I felt pretty sure that our hour had struck. I had hoped to blow her up with the 32-pounder as she passed, but the gun being an old one, with an enlarged vent, the primer drew out without igniting the charge. One of the men—we had no regular gun crews then, every man was expected to do ten men's duty—replaced it and struck it with a compressor lever; but too late; her boilers were past, and the shot went through her cylinder tinders without disabling her. Her blow, though glancing, was a heavy one. Her prow, or beak, made a hole through our side and caused the ship to careen and roll heavily; but we all knew in an instant that no serious damage had been done, and we redoubled our efforts to cripple her so that she could not again attempt the experiment. As did the Essex, so she ran into the bank astern of us, and got the contents of the stern battery; but being more nimble than she, was sooner off into deep water. Returning up stream she got our broadside guns again, and we saw that she had no disposition to engage us further. As she passed the line of fire of the bow-guns she got it again, and I distinctly recollect the handsomest shot I ever made was the last at her. She was nearly a mile away, and I bowled at her with the gun lying level. It ricochetted four or five times before it dropped into her stern. But it dropped there. As I have before said, the Essex was drifting down stream unmanageable, and now would have been our time to have ended her in sight of both squadrons, but we had but seventeen men, and they well-nigh exhausted. Beating off these two vessels, under the circumstances, was the best achievement of the Arkansas. That we were under the batteries of Vicksburg did not amount to anything. I do not believe that either vessel was injured by an army gun that day. We were left to our fate, and if we had been lost it would have been no unusual or unexpected thing. The Essex did not return the fire as she lay alongside us; did not attempt to board, although she had a picked crew for that purpose, and fired but three guns in the fight, and thereafter kept her ports closed. Brown, no longer able to play the lion, assumed the role of the fox with consummate skill.

Shortly after the enemy left the shore opposite Vicksburg an expedition was planned against Baton Rouge, General John C. Breckinridge to command. After the army had arrived at Tangipahoa it was determined to ask for the assistance of the Arkansas. Captain Brown was sick at Grenada, and telegraphed Stevens not to go down, as the machinery was not reliable. Application was made by General Van Dorn to Commodore Lynch, who gave the order to proceed down the river as soon as possible. The vessel was hurriedly coaled and provisioned, and men and officers hastened to join her. Captain Brown left his bed to regain his ship, but arrived too late. He subsequently followed down by rail and assumed command of the crew shortly after the destruction of the vessel. We left Vicksburg thirty hours before General Breckinridge had arranged to make his attacks. The short time allowed to arrive at the rendezvous made it imperative that the vessel should be driven up to her best speed. This resulted in the frequent disarrangements of the machinery and consequent stoppages to key up and make repairs. Every delay required more speed thereafter in order to meet our appoinment. Another matter operated against us. We had been compelled to leave behind, in the hospital, our chief engineer, George W. City, who was worn out and broken down by excessive watching and anxiety. His care and nursing had kept the machinery in order up to the time of leaving. We soon began to feel his loss. The engineer in charge, a volunteer from the army, had recently joined us, and though a young man of pluck and gallantry, and possessed of great will and determination to make the engines work, yet he was unequal to the task. He had never had anything to do with a screw vessel or short-stroke engines, and, being zealous for the good repute of his department, drove the machinery beyond its powers of endurance.

At or near the mouth of Red River, the engines had grown so contrary and required to be hammered so much that Stevens deemed it his duty to call a council of war to determine whether it was proper to proceed or return. The engineer was summoned and gave it as his opinion that the machinery would hold out, and upon that statement we determined to go ahead. A few miles below Port Hudson he demanded a stoppage to key up and make all things secure before going into action. We landed at the right bank of the river, and I was dispatched with Bacot to a house near by to get information. After a deal of trouble we gained admittance and learned that the naval force of the enemy at Baton Rouge consisted of our particular enemy, the Essex, and one or two small sea-going wooden gunboats. This was very satisfactory. We learned, also, that General Breckinridge was to attack at daylight. At daylight we heard our gallant troops commence the engagement. The long rattle of the volleys of musketry, mixed with the deep notes of artillery, informed us that we were behind, and soon came the unmistakable boom of heavy navy guns, which plainly told us that we were wanted—that our iron sides should be receiving those missiles which were mowing down our ranks of infantry. In feverish haste our lines were cast off and hauled aboard, and once more the good ship was driving toward the enemy. Like a war-horse she seemed to scent the battle from afar, and in point of speed outdid anything we had ever before witnessed. There was a fatal error. Had she been nursed then by our young and over-zealous engineer she would have again made her mark in the day's fight. We were in sight of Baton Rouge. The battle had ceased; our troops had driven the enemy to the edge of the water, captured his camps and his positions, and had in turn retired before the heavy broadsides of the Essex, which lay moored abreast of the arsenal. Our officers and crew went to quarters in high spirits, for once there was a chance to make the army and country appreciate us. Baton Rouge is situated on a "reach" or long, straight stretch of river, which extends three or four miles above the town. We were nearly to the turn and about to enter the "reach," the crew had been mustered at quarters, divisions reported, and all the minute preparations for battle which have before been detailed, when Stevens came on deck with Brady, the pilot, to take a final look and determine upon what plan to adopt in his attack on the Essex. It was my watch and we three stood together. Brady proposed that we ram the Essex and sink her where she lay, then back out and put ourselves below the transports and wooden gunboats as soon as possible to cut off their retreat. Stevens assented to the proposal and had just remarked that we had better go to our stations, for we were within a hundred yards of the turn, when the starboard engine stopped suddenly, and before the man at the wheel could meet her with the helm, the ship ran hard and fast aground, jamming herself on to some old cypress stumps that were submerged. We were in full view from the position General Breckinridge had taken up to await our attack. All day long he remained in line of battle prepared to move forward again, but in vain. On investigation it was found that the engine was so badly out of order that several hours must be consumed before we could again expect to move. There lay the enemy in plain view, and we as helpless as a shear-hulk. Hundreds of people had assembled to witness the fight. In fact, many ladies in carriages had come to see our triumph. They waved us on with smiles and prayers, but we couldn't go. But Stevens was not the man to give up. A quantity of railroad iron, which had been laid on deck loose, was thrown overboard, and in a few hours we were afloat, The engineers had pulled the engine to pieces and with files and chisels were as busy as bees, though they had been up constantly then for the greater parts of the two preceding nights. At dark it was reported to the commanding officer that the vessel could be moved. In the meantime some coal had been secured (our supply was getting short), and it was determined to run up stream a few hundred yards and take it in during the night, and be ready for hot work in the morning. Therefore we started to move, but had not gone a hundred yards before the same engine broke down again; the crank pin (called a "wrist" by Western engineers) of the rock-shaft broke in two. Fortunately one of the engineers was a blacksmith, so the forge was set up and another pin forged. But this with our improvised facilities used up the whole night. Meantime the enemy became aware of our crippled condition, and at daylight moved up to the attack. The Essex led, and came up very slowly, at a rate not to exceed two miles an hour. She had opened on us before the last touch had been given to the pin, but it was finished and the parts thrown together. As the ship again started ahead Stevens remarked that we were brought to bay by a superior force, and that he should fight it out as long as we would swim. The battle for the supremacy of the river was upon us, and we must meet the grave responsibility as men and patriots. His plan was to go up the river a few hundred yards and then turn on and dispatch the Essex, then give his attention to the numerous force of wooden vessels which had been assembled since the morning before. The pleasant sensation of again being afloat and in possession of the power of locomotion, was hardly experienced before our last and final disaster came. The port engine this time gave way, broke down and would not move. The engineer was now in despair, he could do nothing, and so reported. The Essex was coming up astern and firing upon us. We had run ashore and were a hopeless, immovable mass. Read was returning the fire, but the two ships were scarcely near enough for the shots to tell. We were not struck by the Essex, nor do I think we struck her. An army force was reported by a mounted "home guard" to be coming up the river to cut off our retreat. Stevens did not call a council of war, but himself assumed the responsibility of burning the ship. I recollect the look of anguish he gave me, and the scalding tears were running down his cheeks when he announced his determination. Read kept firing at the Essex until Stevens had set fire to the ward-room and cabin, then all jumped on shore, and in a few moments the flames burst up the hatches. Loaded shells had been placed at all the guns, which commenced exploding as soon as the fire reached the gun-deck. This was the last of the Arkansas.

The following is a complete list of the officers who served in the Arkansas during her four great battles. Some others were attached to her, but were not present at the time indicated:

I. N. Brown, Mississippi, Commander. Lieutenants—Henry K. Stevens, South Carolina; John Grimball, South Carolina; A. D. Wharton, Tennessee; Charles W. Read, Mississippi; Alphonse Barbot, Louisiana, and George W. Gift, Tennessee. Masters — Samuel Milliken, Kentucky, and John L. Phillips, Louisiana. Midshipmen — Dabney M. Scales, Mississippi; Richard H. Bacot, South Carolina, and Clarence W. Tyler, Virginia. Master's Mate—John A. Wilson, Maryland. Surgeon—H. W. M. Washington, Virginia. Assistant Surgeon — C. M. Morfit, Maryland. First Assistant (Acting Chief) Engineer — George W. City, Virginia. Second Assistant Engineer — E. Covert, Louisiana. Third Assistant Engineers — W. H. Jackson, Maryland; J. T. Dolan, Virginia; C. H. Browne, Virginia; John S. Dupuy and James Gettis, Louisiana. Gunner—T. B. Travers, Virginia. Pilots—John Hodges, James Brady, William Gilmore and J. H. Shacklett.

RECAPTURE OF GALVESTON, TEX.,

AND THE CAPTURE OF THE

STEAMER HARRIET LANE,

JANUARY 1, 1863.

BY

MAJ.-GEN. J. BANKHEAD MAGRUDER,

Commanding the District of Texas, New Mexico and Arizona.

GALVESTON, February 26, 1863.

ON my arrival in Texas I found the harbors of this coast in the possession of the enemy, from the Sabine River to Corpus Christi, the line of the Rio Grande virtually abandoned, most of the guns having been removed from that frontier to San Antonio, only about three or four hundred men remaining at Brownsville. I resolved to regain the harbor, if possible, and to occupy the valley of the Rio Grande in force. The latter would be a very serious undertaking, on account of the scarcity of supplies in Mexico and the difficulty of transporting them across the desert from Eastern Texas. Having announced this determination as soon as I arrived on the Sabine, Captain A. R. Wier, of Cook's regiment of artillery, commanding a fort on that river, stepped forward and volunteered with his company to man a steamboat on the Sabine, and to clear the Pass. This officer and this company had the honor to be the first volunteers for the desperate enterprise of expelling the enemy's fleets from our waters.

I remained a day or two in Houston, and then proceeding to Virginia Point, on the mainland, opposite to Galveston Island, I took with me a party of eighty men, supported by three hundred more, and, passing through the city of Galveston at night, I inspected the forts abandoned by our troops when the city was given up. I found the forts open in the rear, and taken in reverse by every one of the enemy's ships in the harbor. They were, therefore utterly useless for my purposes. The railway track had been permitted to remain from Virginia Point to Galveston, and by its means I purposed to transport to a position near to the enemy's fleet the heavy gun hereinafter mentioned, and by assembling all the movable artillery that could be collected together in the neighborhood I hoped to acquire sufficient force to be able to expel the enemy's vessels from the harbor.

Meeting here Captain Leon Smith, whom, from my acquaintance with him in California, I knew to be of great experience in steamboat management, I employed him in the quartermaster's department, placing him as a volunteer aid on my staff. I intrusted to his charge all the steamers on the Sabine River and in the bayous emptying into Galveston Bay, and at the same time directed that those on the Sabine should be fitted out forthwith. Learning subsequently that the enemy had landed at Galveston a considerable force (strength unknown), I directed Captain Leon Smith, without delaying preparations on the Sabine, to fit up as gunboats the steamers Bayou City and Neptune, and to employ two others as tenders, for the purpose of supplying the larger vessels with wood. At the same time I received information that other Federal troops were on the way to Galveston. I therefore directed that the work on the last-mentioned steamers should be carried on night and day, and that captains and crews should be forthwith provided for them.

Fearing that the enemy might land troops at Galveston and fortify himself there, I determined to make the first attack at that point, with the object of destroying in detail his land forces as fast as they might arrive. Captain Wier, who had first volunteered, was therefore, with his company, ordered from the Sabine on board of the Bayou City. Captain Martin, commanding a company of cavalry, having arrived from New Iberia, La., volunteered his services, and was likewise assigned to duty on board the same steamer. When the boats designed for the Galveston expedition were nearly ready I called for volunteers from Sibley's brigade, then stationed in the neighborhood, under orders for Monroe, La. It is proper to state that I had previously ascertained that the services of these troops at Galveston would not delay a moment their departure for Louisiana, they being unable, for want of transportation, to move in that direction. This call was for three hundred men. It was promptly responded to, Colonels Green and Bagby volunteering to lead the men of their respective regiments. After these officers had volunteered, Colonel James Reily, commanding the brigade, also offered to lead the troops from his command, but his services in that capacity were declined, as he was then the brigade commander. About sixty men of Reily's regiment likewise volunteered, but they did not accompany the expedition, having been ordered back to their regiment by Colonel Reily after having once reported to Colonel Green, who commanded the land forces on the steamers. In addition to these troops, Lieutenant Harby, late captain in the revenue service of the United States, with a company of infantry, acting as artillery, was ordered on board the Neptune. The men destined for the naval expedition were armed with Enfield rifles, which I had brought with me from Richmond, and with double-barrel shot-guns.

CAPTURE OF THE FEDERAL STEAMER HARRIET LANE BY THE CONFEDERATES, JANUARY 1, 1863.

The enemy's fleet, then lying in the waters of Galveston, consisted of the Harriet Lane, carrying four heavy guns and two 24-pounder howitzers, commanded by Captain Wainwright, United States Navy; the Westfield, flagship of Commodore Renshaw, a large propeller, mounting eight heavy guns; the Onasco, a similar ship to the Westfield, mounting eight heavy guns; the Clifton, a steam propeller, four heavy guns; the Sachem, a steam propeller, four heavy guns; two armed transports, two large barks and an armed schooner. The enemy's land forces were stationed at the end of a long wharf, and were crowded into large buildings immediately under the guns of the steamships. The approaches landward to this position were impeded by two lines of strong barricades, and communication with the shore was destroyed by the removal of portions of the wharf in front of the barricades. It thus became necessary for our storming parties to advance by wading through the water; and to enable them to mount on the end of the wharf fifty scaling ladders were constructed. As there were no breastworks or other protection for our artillery making the attack on the enemy's ships and land forces, my object was to bear as heavy a fire of artillery as possible after reaching the wharves and

Captain J. R. Tucker, of District of Columbia,
Confederate States Navy.

Captain Duncan N. Ingraham, of South Carolina,
Confederate States Navy.

Commander James W. Cooke, of North Carolina,
Confederate States Navy.

Lieutenant-Commander William H. Parker, of Virginia.
Confederate States Navy

Captain Frederick Chatard, of Maryland.
Confederate States Navy

Captain William C. Whittle, of Virginia.
Confederate States Navy.

Captain John C. Brain,
Confederate States Navy.
[From a photograph taken in 1865.]

Commander James H. Rochelle, of Virginia,
Confederate States Navy.

Lieutenant Thomas B. Huger, of South Carolina,
Confederate States Navy,

other points selected for the purpose under cover of the night. I knew that the co-operation of the cotton boats with the land forces would be extremely difficult to attain, the distance the former had to run being thirty miles. I therefore had not calculated with confidence on a success greater than that of the expulsion of the enemy's fleet from the harbor. If the desired co-operation should be secured the result would be immediately accomplished, and would be attended probably with the capture or destruction of some of the enemy's ships. If the co-operation should fail, I nevertheless felt satisfied that by throwing up intrenchments at the ends of the streets leading to the water I could gradually expel the fleet from the harbor. For this purpose intrenching tools in large quantities were prepared.

To attain the object in view, I had at my disposal six siege pieces, the heaviest weighing five thousand four hundred pounds. I also caused to be constructed a railroad ram, armed with an 8-inch Dahlgren and mounted on a railway flat. This flat and gun were carried by railway to a point within a few hundred yards of the Harriet Lane. A large quantity of cotton was transported in the same way, with the view of using it in making a breastwork for this gun should we not succeed in our object before daylight. In addition, I had fourteen field-pieces, some of them rifled and some smooth bore. Three of the heaviest of the siege guns had to be transported nine miles, the others seven miles, between sunset and 12 o'clock, under cover of the darkness and over very difficult roads.

A system of rapid communication with our gunboats by telegraph and otherwise having been established, it was arranged that the attack should take place at 12, midnight, the fire of our land batteries constituting the signal for the naval attack. Nevertheless, I informed Commodore Smith, in command of the naval expedition, that I would attack the enemy's fleet whether gunboats made their appearance or not. The key of the whole position was Fort Point, at the mouth of the harbor, two miles below the mouth of the town [?]. The fort was entirely open in the rear, thus affording no protection for our artillery against the enemy's vessels inside of the harbor.

The attack from this point was intrusted to Captain [S. T.] Fontaine, of Cook's regiment artillery, supported by six companies of Pyron's regiment, dismounted dragoons, under command of the gallant Colonel Pyron.

Wilson's battery of six pieces was to attack the enemy from the center wharf; the railroad ram was sent to the upper wharf. The remainder of the artillery was manned from Cook's regiment and posted in eligible positions. Colonel [J. J.] Cook himself was intrusted with the command of the storming party of about five hundred men, composed of details from Pyron's and Elmore's regiments and Griffin's battalion, and furnished with ladders to scale the wharf on which the enemy's land forces were barricaded. Brigadier-General W. R. Scurry was placed in command of Pyron's regiment and of the remainder of Sibley's brigade, and Elmore men, commanded by Lieutenant-Colonel [L. A.] Abercrombie, the latter acting as a support for the whole. Lieutenant-Colonel J. H. Manly, of Cook's regiment, was ordered to Virginia Point to defend that work, which was our base of operations, and which was connected with Galveston Island by a railroad bridge two miles in length, open to the attack of the enemy.

Leading the center assault in person, I approached within two squares of the wharves, at which point I directed the horses of the field-pieces to be removed from them and placed behind some brick buildings for shelter from the anticipated discharges of grape and canister. After allowing the lapse of what turned out to be ample time for Captain Fontaine to reach and occupy his more distant position, the guns were placed along a line of about two and one-half miles, principally within the limits of the city. It having been agreed that the fire of the center gun should furnish signal for a general attack, I proceeded to carry out this portion of the plan by discharging the piece myself. The signal was promptly responded to by an almost simultaneous and very effective discharge along the whole line. The moon had by that time gone down, but still the light of the stars enabled us to see the Federal ships. The enemy did not hesitate long in replying to our attack. He soon opened on us from his fleet with a tremendous discharge of shell which was followed with grape and canister. Our men, however, worked steadily at their guns under cover of the darkness. Colonel Cook now advanced with his storming party to the assault; his men, wading through the water and bearing with them their scaling ladders, endeavored to reach the end of the wharf on which the enemy was stationed. Colonel Cook was supported by Griffin's battalion, and by sharpshooters deployed on the right and left, in order to distract the enemy's attention. A severe conflict took place at this point, our men being exposed to a fire of grape and canister and shell from the ships as well as of musketry from the land forces. The water was deep, the wharf proving higher than was anticipated, and the scaling ladders, as was reported to me by Colonel Cook, were found to be too short to enable the men to accomplish their object. After an obstinate contest the infantry were directed to cover themselves, and fire from the buildings nearest this wharf, which was accordingly done.

THE EXPLOSION OF THE UNITED STATES GUNBOAT WESTFIELD, AT GALVESTON, TEX.

The enemy's fire was deadly. The ships being not more than three hundred yards from our batteries, it was extremely difficult to maintain the positions we had assumed, and some of the artillery-men were driven from their pieces. As daylight, which was now approaching, would expose these men still more to the enemy's fire, and as our gunboats had not yet made their appearance, I ordered the artillery to be withdrawn to positions which afforded more protection, but from which the fire could be continued on the adversary with greater advantage to us. Knowing Captain Fontaine to be in a position the most exposed of all, I at the same time dispatched a staff-officer with instructions to have his pieces likewise withdrawn. This order reaching Captain Fontaine's men before it was received by their captain, and the concentrated fire from the enemy's ships, but a few hundred yards distant, having increased in intensity, they were compelled to leave their pieces. They were, however, soon formed by Captain Fontaine in a position of greater security.

The delicate duty of withdrawing the pieces in the city from the close vicinity of the enemy was intrusted to Brigadier-General Scurry, who performed it with skill and gallantry. Preparations were then ordered for the immediate fortification and permanent occupation of the city. But at this moment, our fire still continuing, our gunboats came dashing down the harbor and engaged the Harriet Lane, which was the nearest of the enemy's ships, in the most gallant style, running into her, one on each side, and pouring on her deck a deadly fire from rifles and shot-guns. The gallant Captain Wainwright fought his ship admirably. He succeeded in disabling the Neptune and attempted to run down the Bayou City, but he was met by an antagonist of even superior skill, coolness and heroism. Leon Smith, ably seconded by Captain [Henry S.] Lubbock, the immediate commander of the Bayou City, and by her pilot, Captain McCormick, adroitly evaded the deadly stroke, although as the vessels passed each other he lost his larboard wheelhouse in the shock. Again the Bayou City, while receiving several broadsides almost at the cannon's mouth, poured into the Harriet Lane a destructive fire of small arms. Turning once more she drove her prow into the iron wheel of the Harriet Lane, thus locking the two vessels together. Followed by the officers and men of the heroic volunteer corps, Commodore Leon Smith leaped to the deck of the hostile ship, and after a moment of feeble resistance she was ours. The surviving officers of the Harriet Lane presented their swords to Commodore Leon Smith on the quarter-deck of the captured vessel. After the surrender the Onasco passed alongside, pouring into the Harriet Lane a broadside at close quarters, but she was soon forced to back out by the effect of our musketry.

Commodore Smith then sent a flag to Commodore Renshaw, whose ship had in the meantime been run aground, demanding the surrender of the whole fleet, and giving three hours' time to consider. These propositions were accepted by the commanding officer, and all the enemy's vessels were immediately brought to anchor, with white flags flying. Most of this time was occupied in attempting to get the Harriet Lane to the wharf, in order to remove the wounded to a place of safety. The ships and boats were so much damaged that this was found to be impossible with the means at hand. Proceeding myself to the wharf I met one of my most distinguished and scientific staff officers, Major A. M. Lea, who informed me that on board the Harriet Lane he had found his son, the second in command, mortally wounded. He represented to me that there were other officers badly wounded, and urged me to delay, if possible, their removal. It now being within an hour of the expiration of the period of truce, I sent another flag to Commodore Renshaw, whose ship was among the most distant, claiming all his vessels immediately under our guns as prizes, and giving him further time to consider the demand for the surrender of the whole fleet. This message was borne by Colonel Green and Captain Lubbock. While these gentlemen were on their way in a boat to fulfill their mission, Commodore Renshaw blew up his ship, and was himself accidentally blown up with it. They boarded the ship of the next command, which dropped down the bay, still having them on board, and carried them some distance toward the bar, while still flying the white flag at the mast-head.

In the meantime General Scurry sent to know if he should fire at the ships immediately in his front at the expiration of the period of truce. To this I replied in the negative. As another demand under a flag of truce expired, the enemy's ships under our guns, regardless of the white flags still flying at their mast-heads, gradually crept off. As soon as this was seen I sent a swift express on horseback to General Scurry, directing him to open fire on them. This was done with so much effect that one of them was reported to have sunk near the bar, and the Onasco was seriously damaged. I forward a correspondence on this subject between Commodore Bell and myself. In this correspondence Commodore Bell states that the truce was violated by the firing of cannon and small arms by our men on shore, as he had been informed. This is an error; not a gun or small arm was discharged during the stipulated period, or until the enemy's vessels were discovered to be creeping off out of the harbor. Commodore Leon Smith fired a heavy stern gun at the retiring ships with effect from the Harriet Lane. Jumping on board the steamer Carr, he proceeded to Bolivar Channel, and captured and brought in, in the immediate presence of the enemy's armed vessels, the two barks and schooner before spoken of. As soon as it was light enough to see the land force surrendered to General Scurry.

THE STEAMER HARRIET LANE, CAPTURED BY THE CONFEDERATES, JANUARY 1, 1863.

We thus captured one fine steamship, two barks and one schooner. We ran ashore the flagship of the commodore, drove off two war steamers and sunk another, as reported, all of the United States Navy, and the armed transports, and took three or four hundred prisoners. The number of guns captured was fifteen, and, being found on Pelican Spit, a large quantity of stores, coal and other material also was taken. The Neptune Camp, her officers and crew, with the exception of those killed in battle, were saved, as were also her guns.

The loss on our side was twenty-six killed and one hundred and seventeen wounded. Among the former was the gallant Captain Wier, the first volunteer for the expedition. The alacrity with which officers and men, all of them totally unacquainted with this novel kind of service, some of whom had never seen a ship before, volunteered for an enterprise so extraordinarily and apparently desperate in its character, and the bold and dashing manner in which the plan was executed, are certainly deserving of the highest praise.

Although it may appear invidious to make distinctions, I nevertheless regard it as a duty to say that too much credit can not be bestowed on Commodore Leon Smith, whose professional ability, energy and perseverance, amid many discouraging influences, were so conspicuously displayed in the preparation for the attack, while in its execution his heroism was sublime. In the battle he was most ably and gallantly seconded by Colonel Green, commanding the land forces serving on board of our fleet; by withdraw the pieces. While in the act of consummating this design he was badly wounded by a fragment of shell striking him in the left eye, which unfortunately has lost its sight; Captain E. P. Turner, assistant adjutant-general, likewise behaved with conspicuous gallantry. Lieutenants George A. Magruder, and H. M. Stanard, my aids-de-camp, executed my orders with remarkable gallantry, promptness and intelligence. These two officers have thus been distinguished in the battles of Bethel, Yorktown, Savage Station and Malvern Hill. It is only just that I should commend them to the special consideration of the Government. Lieutenant Magruder volunteered for the service, and brought off in the most gallant manner some pieces which the men had been compelled to retire from. Lieutenant Stanard behaved with equal gallantry in the execution of orders, exposing himself to the enemy's fire. Lieutenant-Colonel McNeill, of Sibley's brigade, adjutant and inspector-general, rendered distinguished service in carrying out my orders, as also did Lieutenant Carrington, of the same regiment, acting on my staff. Mr. Dennis Brashear, who has been in every battle in which I have been engaged, except that of Bethel, and served with great gallantry everywhere without pay or reward of any kind for more than a year, rendered important and most gallant services on this occasion. I am also under obligations to Lieutenant-Colonel Nichols, volunteer aid, whose ability and local knowledge were of great service in arranging the details of the attack. I likewise thankfully acknowledge the services of Judge P.

CONFEDERATE CITIZENS QUITTING BROWNSVILLE, TEX., ON LEARNING OF THE APPROACH OF FEDERAL TRANSPORTS.

Captain Lubbock, commanding the Bayou City; by her pilot, Captain McCormick; Captain Wier, commanding the artillery; Captain Martin, commanding dismounted dragoons, and by the officers and men on board of that boat. Though in the case of the Neptune the result was not so favorable, her attack on the Harriet Lane was equally bold and dashing and had its weight in the capture. Colonel Bagby, commanding the land troops on board the Neptune; Captain Sangster; her pilots, Captains Swift and McGovern; Captain Harby, and the officers and crew of the ship, likewise deserve, as they have received, my thanks for their participation in this brilliant battle. The engineers, among them Captain Seymour, of the Bayou City, and Captain Conner, of the Neptune, were distinguished by remarkable coolness, skill and devotion in the discharge of their important duties.

In the land attack especially commendations are due to Brigadier-General W. R. Scurry, Colonel X. B. Debray, Major Von Harten, Cook's regiment of artillery; Captain Fontaine, Cook's regiment; Major J. Kellersberg, of the Engineer Corps; also to Colonels Cook, Pyron, Lieutenant-Colonel Abercrombie, commanding Elmore's men; Major Griffin, Major Wilson, of the artillery; Captain Mason, Captain McMahan, and to the accomplished and devoted Lieutenant Sherman, who fell at his piece, mortally wounded, and to Privates Brown and Shoppman, of Daly's company of cavalry, the latter of whom kept up the fire of one piece almost without assistance under the enemy's grape and canister. The officers of my staff exhibited on this, as on previous occasions, conspicuous ability and gallantry. When some of the men were compelled to leave their pieces at one of the wharves nearest the enemy, Major Dickinson, assistant adjutant-general, calling for volunteers, dashed down the street in order to W. Gray and the Hon. J. A. Wilcox, members of Congress from Texas, who, as volunteer aids, accompanied me to the front when the battle opened, and remained with me during its continuance. The assistance of General [Thomas B.] Howard, of the militia, and his adjutant-general, Major Tucker, residents of Galveston, was of great value, as was also that of Mr. E. W. Cave, volunteer aid, from Houston. Hon. M. M. Potter, of Galveston, was likewise conspicuous during the engagement for his activity and devotion.

I take this occasion to recommend to the special consideration of the President the conduct of Governor J. R. Baylor, of Arizona, who, though not in command of any troops nor attached to any staff, was conspicuous for his gallant conduct as a private, serving the guns during the hottest of the fire, and with his coat off working to place them in position during the night.

Lieutenant-Colonel Manly sustained the operations from Virginia Point with great ability and activity. Captain [W. J.] Pendleton, acting aid-de-camp, who accompanied the troops, proved himself to be an officer of very remarkable ability, energy and devotion. Captain Stoy, assistant quartermaster, is also deserving of high commendation. Major J. B. Eustis, acting ordnance officer on my staff, assisted by Lieutenant M. Hughes, of the artillery, performed admirably his difficult and important duties in the preparation for the attack. The former, by my order, remained in charge of his depot at Virginia Point, while the latter discharged gallantly his duties on the field. I likewise take pleasure in recognizing the efficient and gallant services of Major [O. M.] Watkins, in charge of conscript business, on my staff; of Col. [C. G.] Forshey, of the engineer corps; of Captain H. Pendleton, assistant quartermaster, who accompanied me to the front; and of Major [E. B.] Pendleton, chief commissary, on my staff, who discharged his important duties with gallant ability. Lieutenants Stringfellow, Jones and Hill, of the artillery, behaved with remarkable gallantry during the engagement, each of them volunteering to take charge of guns and personally directing the fire after the officers originally in charge of them had been wounded.

It would be improper to close this report without directing the particular attention of the Government to invaluable services rendered by Major B. Bloomfield, quartermaster, of my staff, and by Captain [E. C.] Wharton, assistant quartermaster at Houston. These officers, by their intelligence, energy and activity, proved themselves fully adequate to all the demands made upon them in the preparation of the means appropriate to their department, and contributed materially to the successful result of the expedition. Nor should I here omit to mention Captain [W. S.] Good, in command of ordnance. I commend him especially to the chief of ordnance, and to the consideration of His Excellency, the President.

Besides the names mentioned above, I would call attention to the names of the officers and men reported by their respective commanding officers to have distinguished themselves by gallant and meritorious services. As it would have been imprudent to give full warning to the inhabitants of Galveston of my intention to attack the Federal fleet, lest information of the design might reach the enemy, as soon as the head of our column entered the suburbs of the town I directed the ambulances, in charge of one of my staff officers, to proceed to the convent of Ursuline nuns near that point, and place the conveyances at their disposal for their immediate removal to the houses provided for them. I also in like manner informed the foreign consuls and the mayor of the contemplated attack, and gave them time to move their families and the citizens most exposed to a place of safety. The noble women of the convent, while recognizing the courtesy extended to them, expressed a preference to remain and nurse the wounded, offering their building as a hospital. Many of the inhabitants left the houses most exposed to the enemy's fire, and I am happy to state that, although many edifices were much injured and the town riddled by balls, no casualty occurred among the citizens. The wounded of the enemy were conducted to the same hospital, and the same attentions were bestowed on them as if they had been our own men. Captain Wainwright and Lieutenant Lea, of the Federal Navy, were buried with marine and military honors, in the same grave, Major Lea, of the Confederate Army, father of Lieutenant Lea; performing the funeral services. Having buried the dead, taken care of the wounded, and secured the captured property, my exertions were directed to getting the Harriet Lane to sea. The enemy's ships fled to New Orleans, to which place one of their steam transports was dispatched during the action. I knew that a large naval force might be expected to return in a few days. I therefore ordered the employment at high wages of all the available mechanics to repair the Harriet Lane, her main shaft having been dislocated and her iron wheel greatly disabled, so that the engine could not work. The United States flags were ordered to remain flying on the customhouse and at the mast-heads of the ships, so as to attract into the harbor any of the enemy's vessels which might be bound for the port of Galveston. A line of iron buoys, which he had established for the guidance of his ships in the harbor, were displaced and so arranged as to insure their getting aground.

On the 3d of January, I being then on board of the Harriet Lane, a yawl-boat, containing several men, in command of a person named Thomas Smith, recently a citizen of Galveston, and who had deserted from our army, was reported alongside. He informed me that he was sent from the United States transport steamship Cambria, then off the bar, for a pilot, and that they had no idea of the occupation of the city by us. I forthwith ordered a pilot-boat, under command of Captain Johnson, to bring in this ship, but, through a most extraordinary combination of circumstances, the vessel, which contained E. J. Davis and many other apostate Texans, besides several hundred troops and twenty-five hundred saddles for the use of native sympathizers, succeeded in making her escape. The man Smith, who had, it is said, several times set fire to the city of Galveston before he deserted, had been known as Nicaragua Smith, and was dreaded by every one. He returned to Galveston in order to act as Federal provost-marshal. His arrival produced much excitement, during which some one, without orders, sent a sail-boat to Pelican Spit, now occupied by our troops, to direct the commanding officer there not to fire on our pilot-boat, although she was under Yankee colors. The sail-boat thus sent was at once supposed to be destined for the Yankee transport. The pilot-boat gave chase to her, and the guns from the shore opened on her within hearing of the ship.

Night coming on, I thought it surer, as the alarm might be taken, to capture her at sea before morning, but the Harriet Lane could not move, and our cotton gunboats could not live on the rough sea on the bar. Therefore one of the barks, the Royal Yacht, a schooner of ours, the pilot-boat, and the leader, a schooner loaded with cotton, which I had ordered to be sent to a foreign port, with a proclamation of the raising of the blockade at Galveston, were directed to be prepared and armed with light artillery. This was done by 2 o'clock the same night, our little fleet being manned by volunteers, under the command of Captain Mason, of Cook's regiment of artillery. Unfortunately the wind lulled and none but the pilot-boat could reach the enemy's ship. The pilot-boat went out under the command of a gallant sailor, Captain Payne, of Galveston. The enemy's ship proved to be a splendid iron steamer, built in the Clyde. I had ascertained from her men taken ashore that she had only two guns, and they were packed on deck under a large quantity of hay, and I anticipated an easy conquest and one of great political importance, as this ship contained almost all the Texans out of the State who had proved recreant to their duty to the Confederacy and to Texas. The pilot-boat was allowed to get close to the ship when the boat was hailed and the pilot ordered to come on board. Captain Payne answered that he thought there were rather too many men to trust himself to; whereupon he was directed to come on board or he would be fired into. He went on board as ordered, and soon after the steamer sailed in all haste seaward, leaving the pilot-boat and hands to return to us.

I am thus particular in this narration, as the friends of Captain Payne fear that he may meet with foul play from the enemy. I shall ascertain, through Commodore Bell, his fate, and act accordingly. Smith, the deserter, was tried regularly the next day before a general court-martial, and, being convicted of deserting to the enemy, was publicly shot in Galveston in accordance with his sentence. The proceedings, which were formal in all respects, legal and regular, are forwarded.

At the time of these occurrences I received, through Colonel [W. G.] Webb, reliable imformation of an insurrection among the Germans in Colorado, Fayette and Austin counties, eight hundred being reported in arms to resist the conscript law and the State draft. I immediately ordered the Arizona brigade, with a section of artillery, to the disaffected region, declared martial law in these three counties, and had the ringleaders arrested and lodged in jail. The rest yielded, and tranquillity and obedience to the laws are now prevalent.

Major Webb contributed much by his personal activity and influence to produce these results, and I earnestly recommend him to the President for the appointment of assistant adjutant-general, with the rank of lieutenant-colonel, to be stationed in the disaffected regions, and to take charge of the business growing out of these affairs and those of the militia. He was an officer of the old army and colonel under General Taylor in the Mexican War.

The German ringleaders, above mentioned, have been turned over to the civil authorities for trial.

The whole coast and islands are now in our possession and the Rio Grande is strongly occupied.

J. BANKHEAD MAGRUDER,
Major-General Commanding.

ON one occasion a man from Georgia had been persistent in personal application to General Lee for a furlough. One morning the general asked his tormentor if he understood the position of a soldier. The latter said he did. He was ordered to assume it. General Lee then gave the command, "Right about face; forward, march." As he never gave the command to "halt," the Georgian kept on marching until he got tired; but this little hint cured him, and his next application was through the usual channels.

ATTACK ON THE BLOCKADING SQUADRON OFF CHARLESTON, S. C., BY THE CONFEDERATE GUNBOATS PALMETTO STATE AND CHICORA. THE RAMMING OF THE FEDERAL GUNBOAT MERCEDITA, JANUARY 30, 1863.

ATTACK ON THE BLOCKADING SQUADRON IN CHARLESTON HARBOR,

JANUARY 30, 1863.

BY

FLAG-OFFICER DUNCAN N. INGRAHAM.

CHARLESTON, S. C., February 2, 1863.

ON the night of the 30th ultimo, I left the wharf at this place in company with the steam-ram Chicora, Commander John R. Tucker, at 11:15 o'clock, and steamed slowly down to the bar, as from our draught we could not cross until high water. At 4:30 o'clock we crossed the bar with about a foot and a half to spare, and soon after made a steamer at anchor; made for her and directed Lieutenant-Commander [John] Rutledge to strike her with our prow. When quite near we were hailed: "What steamer is that? Drop your anchor, or you will be into us." He was informed that it was the Confederate steamer Palmetto State. At this moment we struck her and fired the seven-inch gun into her as he gave an order to fire. I then inquired if he surrendered, and was answered in the affirmative. I then directed him to send a boat on board, which was done. After some delay Lieutenant Abbott, commanding, came on board and informed me that the vessel was the United States steamer Mercedita, Commander Stillwagen, and that she was in a sinking condition, and had a crew of one hundred and fifty-eight, all told, and wished to be relieved; that all his boats were lowered without the plugs being in, and were full of water.

At this time the Chicora was engaged with the enemy and the alarm was given. I knew our only opportunity was to take the enemy unawares, as the moment he was under way, from his superior speed we could not close with him. I then directed Lieutenant Rutledge, commanding, to require from Lieutenant-Commander Abbott his word of honor for his commander, officers and crew, that they would not serve against the Confederate States until regularly exchanged, when he was directed to return with his boat to his vessel to render what assistance he could. I then stood to the northward and eastward, and soon after made another steamer getting under way. We stood for her and fired several shots at her, but as we had to fight the vessel in a circle to bring the different guns to bear, she was soon out of our range. In this way we engaged several vessels, they keeping at long range and steering to the southward. Just as the day broke we made a large steamer (supposed to be the Powhatan) on starboard bow, with another steamer in company, which had just got under way. They stood to the southward under full steam and opened their batteries upon the Chicora, which was some distance astern of us. I then turned and stood to the southward to support the Chicora, if necessary, but the enemy kept on his course to the southward. I then made signal to Commander Tucker to come to anchor, and led the way to the entrance of Beach Channel, where we anchored at 8:45 A. M., and had to remain seven hours for the tide, as the vessels can not cross the bar except at high water. The sea was perfectly smooth, as much so as in the harbor. Everything was most favorable for us and gave us no opportunity to test the sea qualities of the boats. The engines worked well and we obtained a greater speed than they had ever before attained.

I can not speak in too high terms of the conduct of Commander Tucker and Lieutenant-Commander Rutledge. The former handled his vessel in a beautiful manner, and did the enemy much damage. Lieutenant-

Commander Rutledge also fought the Palmetto State in a manner highly gratifying to me.

Every officer and man did his duty nobly and deserves well of his country.

We had but little opportunity of trying our vessels, as the enemy did not close, and not a single shot struck either vessel.

I am highly indebted to Commander [H. J.] Hartstene, who gallantly volunteered to take charge of three steamers, with fifty men on board, who accompanied us in case we should need their services, but they could not get over the bar, but joined us after daylight at the North Channel and rendered us their assistance in getting through the channel, which is very narrow.

Of the conduct of Mr. —— Gladden, the pilot of the Palmetto State, I can not speak in too high terms. He was perfectly cool under the great responsibility he had in taking the vessels over at night with so great a draught, and during the action rendered me great assistance in pointing out the vessels as we approached them in the uncertain light.

D. N. INGRAHAM,
Flag-Officer Commanding

CAPTURE OF THE FEDERAL GUNBOAT MERCEDITA BY THE CONFEDERATE RAM PALMETTO STATE, OFF CHARLESTON HARBOR, JANUARY 30, 1863.

ATTACK ON THE BLOCKADING SQUADRON IN CHARLESTON HARBOR,

JANUARY 30, 1863.

BY

COMMANDER JOHN R. TUCKER,
Commanding Steamer Chicora.

January 31, 1863.

IN obedience to the orders of Flag-Officer Ingraham, I got under way at 11:30 P. M. yesterday and stood down the harbor in company with the Confederate States steamer Palmetto State, bearing your flag. We crossed the bar at 4:40 A. M., and commenced the action at 5:20 A. M. by firing into a schooner-rigged propeller, which we set on fire, and have reason to believe sunk, as she was nowhere to be seen at daylight. We then engaged a large side-wheel steamer twice our length from us, on the port bow, firing three shots into her with telling effect, when she made a run for it. This vessel was supposed to be the Quaker City. We then engaged a schooner-rigged propeller and a large side-wheel steamer, partially crippling both and setting on fire the latter, causing her to strike her flag. At this time the latter vessel, supposed to be the Keystone State, was completely at my mercy, having a raking position astern, distance some two hundred yards. I at once gave the order to cease firing, and directed Lieutenant Bier, first lieutenant of the Chicora, to man a boat and take charge of the prize; if possible, to save her; if that was not possible, to rescue the crew. While the boat was in the act of being manned I discovered that she was endeavoring to make her escape by working her starboard wheel, the other being disabled. Her colors being down I at once started in pursuit and renewed the engagement. Owing to her superior steaming qualities she soon widened the distance to some two thousand yards. She then hoisted her flag and commenced firing her rifled gun, her commander, by this faithless act, placing himself beyond the pale of civilized and honorable warfare. We next engaged two schooners—one brig and one bark-rigged propeller—but, not having the requisite speed, were unable to bring them to close quarters. We pursued them six or seven miles seaward. During the engagement (near its termination) I was engaged at long range with a large bark-rigged steam sloop of war, but in spite of all our efforts was unable to bring her to close quarters, owing to her superior steaming qualities.

At 7:30 A. M., in obedience to your orders, we stood ashore, leaving the partially-crippled and fleeing enemy about seven miles clear of the bar, standing to the southward and eastward. At 8 A. M., in obedience to signal, we anchored in four-fathom water of the Beach Channel.

It gives me pleasure to testify to the good conduct and efficiency of the officers and crew of the Chicora. I am particularly indebted to the pilots, Messrs. Payne and Aldert, for the skillful pilotage of the vessels.

It gives me pleasure to state that I have no injuries or casualties.

J. R. TUCKER,
Commander, C. S. Navy.

[INCLOSURE.]

We, the undersigned, certify that a steamer (side-wheel) supposed to be the Keystone State, not only struck her flag on the morning of January 31st, but that we saw a number of her men rush upon the after part of her deck and extend their arms toward us in an imploring manner, she being at that time completely at our mercy, distant from us some two hundred yards.

G. H. BIER,
First Lieutenant and Executive Officer Chicora.
W. T. GLASSELL,
Lieutenant.
BENJ. F. SHELBY,
Squadron Quartermaster.

IMMEDIATELY after the ordinances of secession had been passed, and it became apparent that there would be war, the attention of the Southern youth was directed almost exclusively to Hardee's Tactics, and especially the Drill of the Company. Military organizations sprang up thick as hops all over the country, and the rivalry between them, as well as the interest elicited from their civilian friends and admirers, was immense. There was a very fine company organized at Memphis, which acquired a wide reputation for excellence in all the evolutions. It was commanded by a Mexican veteran who was a master of tactics and a martinet in drill. Every afternoon a throng of people would resort to the large vacant lot where this company was receiving instruction to witness and applaud its performance. On one occasion, when an unusually large and appreciative crowd was collected and many ladies present, the captain became so enthused that, after exhausting every recognized movement, he began to extemporize, and shouted out the command: "Company, right and left oblique, march." The men gallantly essayed to obey the order, and diverging from either flank, scattered widely. The captain racked his brain for a proper command to bring them together again, but the tactics provided no formula for such a dilemma. At length, when the boys had become strung out like a flock of wild pigeons and seemed about to separate forever, he yelled in desperation: "*Huddle, gol darn ye!*"

THE EXPLOITS OF THE CONFEDERATE CRUISER SUMTER.

BY

CAPTAIN RAPHAEL SEMMES,
Commander.

November 9, 1861—January 3, and June 20, 1862.

AFTER many vexatious delays in the city of New Orleans, incident to fitting out a ship of war there for the first time, much of the work required being new to the mechanics and many articles being difficult to be procured, we were enabled to drop down the river to Forts St. Philip and Jackson, on the evening of the 18th of June. I anchored here to put my ship in something like order, my crew being composed, with two or three exceptions, of men taken entirely from the merchant service, and ignorant, therefore, of all the military duties required of them on board a ship of war. In the few days that we lay at this anchorage we readjusted the stowage of the ship, set up our rigging, rove running gear, stationed and quartered the men, and exercised them frequently at the great guns and with small arms. Major Duncan, the commanding officer of the forts, was kind enough to loan me a 24-pounder howitzer, with a supply of ammunition, for use on my upper deck against any expedition of boats that the enemy might be disposed to send against us when we should drop down in his vicinity. Major Duncan also kindly kept me advised of the movements of the enemy's ships off the mouths of the river, by means of the telegraph which he had under his control. On the 20th of June, Governor Moore, of Louisiana, Hon. John Slidell, and other distinguished gentlemen having visited the forts, they were invited on board and visited this ship.

Just at nightfall of the 21st I received the following dispatch from Major Duncan's adjutant:

"*Captain:* I am desired by the commanding officer to state that the Ivy reports that the Powhatan has left in pursuit of two ships, and that he has received a telegraphic dispatch from Pass a l'Outre to the effect that a boat from the Brooklyn had put into the river and was making for the telegraphic station, where she was expected to arrive in a few minutes."

Upon receipt of this intelligence I ordered steam gotten up and in half an hour afterward I was steaming down to the head of the passes, where I anchored at about 10:30 P. M. I immediately dispatched a lieutenant on shore, both to the lighthouse at the head of the passes and to the telegraph station, to endeavor to procure a pilot, hoping to run out during the night and before the Powhatan should return to her station. But there was no pilot to be had and I learned the next day that the Powhatan had returned to her station after an absence of only a few hours. On the next morning I could plainly reconnoiter the blockading vessels at both passes with my glass. The Brooklyn and Powhatan, both of them assisted occasionally by other vessels, kept watch and ward faithfully, the former at Pass a l'Outre and the latter at the Southwest Pass. The Powhatan, in particular, was anchored close under the bar, and scarcely ever stirred from her position. To my astonishment I learned here that the lights at Pass a l'Outre and South Pass had both been kept burning; of course this could only be for the convenience of the enemy. I therefore ordered them to be extinguished. At the former station I was obliged to destroy the oil, as the light was under the guns of the Brooklyn, and I was compelled to operate in a small boat. I found the pilots, too, in a quasi state of rebellion, owing to their fears. I was obliged to send an officer and arrest several of them and bring them on board; or rather they came on board peaceably with the officer without the necessity of an arrest, upon learning his object. I required them to keep one of their number always on board of me, which they did, relieving each other every few days. I remained at my anchors at the head of the passes, occasionally shifting my berth, for the space of nine days, patiently watching the enemy and seeking an opportunity of running the blockade. But this time was by no means lost, as I needed all of it for drilling and disciplining my very green crew. The men were exercised at the guns every day, and as the nights grew dark, for the want of the moon, I caused guard or scout boats to be sent out, one in each of the passes, to prevent being surprised by the boats of the enemy. Although we were now in the latter end of June, and had gathered our crew so recently from the streets of New Orleans, the health of the ship continued good.

Finally, on Sunday morning, the 30th of June, it having been reported to me that the Brooklyn was absent from her station, I caused steam to be gotten up, got under way and ran down toward the Pass. As we approached the mouth of the river we discovered the Brooklyn, with our glasses, standing back under steam and sail to regain her station, and it was for some time a little doubtful whether we could pass the bar before she came up. To add to my perplexity, the pilot protested that he knew only the bar of the Southwest Pass, and could not undertake to run me out of Pass a l'Outre. I continued on, however, hoisting a signal for a pilot at the fore. As luck would have it, a pilot happened to be present at the pilot's station a little above the lighthouse, and as we ran by it the gallant fellow pushed aboard in his boat, and in fifteen minutes afterward he had us outside the bar. We discharged him in great haste and made all sail and steam, the Brooklyn being in pursuit about four miles distant.

The next four hours were, of course, very anxious ones for me, as the Brooklyn had the reputation of great speed, and our relative powers were to be tested. Owing to the frothing of our boilers the enemy at one time gained on us, but this having subsided we soon began to drop him gradually under the joint influence of sail and steam, and by 3:30 Commander Poor gave up the chase. As he bore up, I sent my men into the rigging, and we gave three hearty cheers for the flag of the Confederate States, thus for the first time thrown to the breeze on the high seas by a ship of war. The evening was beautiful and calm and we made rapid way over the water, experiencing a sensation of great relief after our long confinement in the river.

Captain Raphael Semmes,
Commander of the Steamer Sumter.

On the morning of the 3d, before daylight, we made the light on Cape [San] Antonio, west end of Cuba. Late in the afternoon of this day, near the Isle of Pines, we fell in with and captured our first prize, the ship Golden Rocket, of Bangor, Me., of six hundred and ninety tons burden. The register of this ship showed that she belonged to citizens of the United States, and as she had no cargo on board I burned her a few hours after her capture, having first removed on board this ship a few provisions, sails, etc. You may imagine that, as the flames which consumed this first holocaust laid upon the altar of our country upon the high seas leaped into the air and shed their lurid glare upon the waters around, we were much affected by so gratifying and at the same time so melancholy a spectacle.

The next day, which was the 4th of July, we captured the brigantines Cuba and Machias, both of the State of Maine and the property of citizens of the United States. As both these vessels had cargoes on board that were documented as neutral property, I could not destroy them, but sent them into the port of Cienfuegos, whence they had sailed and where the cargoes were said to belong. I gave a tow to one of these vessels, and as I approached the light of Cienfuegos, on the evening of the 5th, we descried two other sail in the southeast, distant some eight or nine miles. I cast off my tow and gave chase, and soon came up with the brigs Ben Dunning and Albert Adams, both of which, being property of citizens of the United States, I captured. These vessels, like the two former, had recently come out of Cienfuegos, and their cargoes being in the same category, I made the same disposition of them.

I lay off and on the light during the night, intending to enter the port with my prizes as soon after daylight the next morning as I could procure a pilot. A little after sunrise the next morning, and while I was still waiting off the port with a signal for a pilot flying, the barks West Wind and Louisa Kilham, and the brigantine Naiad came out of the port, in full view of me, and stood out to sea. I made no movement toward these until the one which remained the nearest to the land was distant from it some five miles. I then put my ship under steam (the pilot having boarded me in the meantime) and captured them all. My other prizes (except the Cuba) having come up to me about 1 o'clock P. M., I sent all these vessels into the port and followed them myself. As I passed the fort, situated a short distance within the harbor, a couple of muskets were fired therefrom, and I was hailed and directed to anchor, which I did. I sent a lieutenant on shore to demand an explanation of the commandant, and was informed that he, the commandant, never having seen our flag before, did not know what flag it was, and that he had orders to stop all vessels of war or otherwise, until their flags could be distinguished. The commandant called on board himself in the evening to say that he had the governor's orders to permit me to proceed to the town, if I desired to do so. I was treated with hospitality during the short time I remained in the port, and was permitted to refresh my crew, and coal and water ship. On the evening of the 7th I again got under way and passed out of the port.

Finding that I could not make Barbadoes, as I intended, I bore up on the fifth day out for Curacao, uncoupling the propeller and putting the ship under sail for a part of the way to economize fuel. I arrived off St. Anne's [Santa Ana], Curacao, on the 16th of July, after nightfall, and, having fired a gun, was soon after boarded by the pilot, who is at the same time harbor-master. Having been informed of the character of the vessel and of my desire to enter the port, the pilot promised to return at daylight next next morning and take me in. I accordingly stood in, as by appointment, at daylight, and was astonished to receive from the pilot, who soon afterward came on board, a message from the governor to the effect that he, the governor, was very sorry, but that he could not permit me to enter the port, he having instructions to this effect from the home government. Feeling sure either that some misrepresentation had been made to the governor of our character or that he had blundered, I dispatched a lieutenant to him with a communication, and in the meantime lay off and on until I could receive his answer. This was delayed some two or three hours to enable his Excellency to convoke and take the opinion of his council; but at length the lieutenant returned with the verbal permission of the governor for me to enter, and bringing with him the pilot.

During the run from Cuba to Curacao we saw but two sails. The first one we chased, and, coming up with her, she proved to be a Spaniard. The second we did not chase, as she was seen at a long distance, and it was blowing half a gale of wind, with a very heavy sea on. We remained in Curacao seven days, refitting and coaling and watering ship. I steamed out of the harbor on the evening of the 24th of July, and the next morning, about thirty miles to the northeast of La Guayra, on the coast of Venezuela, I chased and captured the schooner Abby Bradford, from New York to La Guayra, with a cargo documented as belonging to citizens of Puerto Cabello. I took her in tow and ran down to Puerto Cabello with her, where I arrived next morning. Having anchored in the port, I dispatched a lieutenant to call on the governor with a communication. I left Puerto Cabello with my prize, as requested by the governor, in twenty-four hours after having anchored, and as I was going out of the port we descried a sail running down the coast, some eight or nine miles to seaward. I gave chase, and in something less than an hour I came up with and captured the bark Joseph Maxwell, of Philadelphia, registered as property of citizens of the United States, with a small remnant of a cargo on board (the bulk of which she had landed at La Guayra), belonging, as it appeared, to a joint house of trade in Philadelphia and La Guayra. As one-half of this remnant of a cargo belonged to the partner in La Guayra (who had a correspondent in Puerto Cabello), I ran again into the port, leaving the prize outside, and dispatched the paymaster on shore with the master of the Maxwell to the house interested, with an offer to sell to it the ship and our half of the cargo, or, if this did not suit, to permit it to unlade the portion of the cargo which belonged to it, for which purpose I would either permit the ship to come in, or it (the house) might send out a lighter, as it preferred. Neither of these proposals was accepted; on the contrary, the governor, or military commandant (having around him all the parties interested), made the extraordinary assertion that the prize had been captured within a marine league of the land, and that, as the capture was invalid for this reason, he desired that I would not take the prize out of his waters. Of course, I paid no attention to this unfounded claim, and upon the return of the officers and the master of the captured vessel I steamed out of the port, and in a few hours afterward dispatched both prizes, in charge of prize crews, the Abby Bradford to New Orleans, and the Joseph Maxwell to Cienfuegos. I turned my head eastward, and ran the coast up to Trinidad, which island I entered on the 30th of July. Here I landed the prisoners taken from the Joseph Maxwell. Before setting them on shore I sent for the two mates of that vessel to come into my cabin, and told them I had brought them to this place to land them, because it was a mail station, at which I could receive late news from the United States, and that it had been my intention, had the Government of the United States dared to carry out its barbarous threat of treating the prisoners of the privateer Savannah, who had fallen into its hands, as pirates, to retaliate on them and their crew by hanging man for man, but that I was glad to inform them that this unpleasant duty had not, as appeared by late intelligence, been imposed upon me. The question of my being permitted to coal here was submitted to the law officers of the Crown, by the governor, who entertained some doubts on the subject, and decided in my favor, and I filled up with coal and watered ship, and replaced my main yard, which had been carried away, by a new one, and on the 5th of August I steamed out of the harbor. An English seaman, named John Smith, whom we had shipped at Curacao, ran away from us here.

In pursuance of the intention already expressed, of making my way to the coast of Brazil, I hoped to be able to run as far as Maranham, or at least Para, before coaling again, but I discovered, after being out five or six days, that this would be impossible, and on the 11th of August, being in latitude two degrees and thirty-eight minutes north and longitude forty-seven degrees and forty-eight minutes west, having only thirty hours of fuel left, I let the steam go down, put the ship under sail, and bore up for Cayenne, in French Guiana, distant some three hundred miles under our lee. I anchored in this port on the 15th, and on the 16th, finding that I could not procure coal, there being none in the market, I got under way again and ran further down the coast to Surinam, in Dutch Guiana, off the bar of which port I anchored on the afternoon

The Sumter and the United States Gunboats Kearsarge and Tuscarora at Gibraltar.

of the 18th, to await a pilot. Just at nightfall a steamer was descried in the west approaching the bar, but she was too far off to be made out distinctly. Not knowing but she might be an enemy, we cleared the ship for action and awaited her approach with the men at quarters. At a little after 10 P. M. she came up and anchored some five miles from us.

At early daylight next morning I caused steam to be got up, the stranger doing the same, got my anchor up, and we mutually stood toward each other. I showed French colors, and in a few minutes afterward the stranger showed the same colors. Soon becoming satisfied that the stranger was a French steamer of war, I hauled down the French colors and hoisted our own and ran down and spoke him. He proved to be H. M. S. Vulture, from Martinique to Cayenne, with French convicts on board, and being, like myself, bound into Surinam for coal, we went in together. I was detained twelve days in Surinam in coaling and watering the ship, and on the last day of my stay the cabin and wardroom stewards deserted—the former being my body servant and a slave, the only slave on board, and the latter being a Malay.

I sailed from Surinam on the 31st of August, and arrived at Maranham on the 6th of September, having we arrived and anchored at about 5 o'clock in the afternoon.

At Surinam there were only four small vessels of the enemy, at Cayenne one and at Maranham none. In turning my head eastward after leaving Cuba, it was my original intention to proceed off Cape St. Roque, the great fork road, as it were, of the commerce of the East and West, but upon my arrival at Maranham I abandoned this idea for the time, the season being unpropitious for operations off this cape. The southeast trade wind blows almost a constant gale in this parallel until the end of December or the first of January, when it relaxes its force and the rainy season sets in. Accompanying these fierce winds there is a current setting to the westward of from two and a half to four knots per hour. In such a wind and leeward current I could operate to very little purpose. Every chase would necessarily be a long one, unless by accident, and many of the fast sail ships would outrun me under a press of canvas before these gales. Chasing to leeward, too, would soon put an end to my cruise, as after every such chase I should be obliged to regain my station by the aid of steam, driving my ship against both wind and current. I therefore reluctantly abandoned this idea for the present, as before stated.

CONFEDERATE SLOOP OF WAR SUMTER CAPTURING TWO FEDERAL MERCHANTMEN OFF GIBRALTAR, JANUARY 18, 1862.

Another consideration with me, too, was that my funds were running short, for I had only brought $10,000 to sea with me. In the ten captures that I had made no more than the sum of $200 was found on board of them all. The masters, instead of being intrusted with money with which to defray their expenses, were uniformly authorized to draw on their consignees against their charter parties.

Coal is very high on the coast of Brazil. I paid $17.50 per ton for it in Maranham. It behooved me, therefore, to arrange my cruising so that I should not coal too often. I determined, on consideration of all these facts, to fill up with coal and run back to the equatorial calm belt, the southern edge of which at this season of the year was about in latitude five degrees north, and, placing myself in the track of returning ships from the Pacific, Rio, etc., cruise for awhile. Chasing would cost me but small expenditure of fuel here, because of the light winds and calms, and I might keep the sea six or eight weeks if need be, without the necessity of returning to port to renew my supplies. I was detained nine days in Maranham by the operations of coaling and watering ship. I made a small addition to my provisions here, also, and supplied myself with a new anchor in place of one I had lost on the coast. On the 14th of September, the day before sailing, I drew on the Secretary of the Navy in favor of Mr. J. Wetson, for the sum of $2,000, this gentleman having advanced me this sum. Mr. Wetson is a citizen of Texas, temporarily domiciled in Brazil in pursuit of his profession as an engineer, and has retained all his warm affection for his country, its institutions and its liberties, and volunteered his purse in aid of our cause.

Having completed all my arrangements, I steamed out of the port of Maranham on the 15th of September, and made the best of my way to my cruising ground. At meridian on the 17th, being in latitude two degrees and twenty minutes north, and longitude forty-one degrees and twenty-seven minutes west, I directed the fires to be banked, and put the ship under sail and cruised for the next twenty-six days between the parallels of two degrees and thirty minutes north, and nine degrees and thirty minutes north, and the meridians of forty-one degrees and thirty minutes west, and forty-seven degrees and thirty minutes west. By inspecting a chart of this portion of the Atlantic, it will be perceived that the northwest diagonal of the quadrilateral figure marked out by these parallels and meridians is the direct course between Cape St. Roque and New York, and it was near this diagonal that I kept my ship, sometimes to the eastward and sometimes to the westward of it.

On the 25th of September, at daylight, we descried and chased a sail to the northward and eastward, with which we came up about 10:30 A. M. She proved to be the brigantine Joseph Park, of Boston, from Pernambuco to Turks Island. The property of this vessel belonged to the citizens of Massachusetts. I captured her. She had no cargo on board, and had but a small sum of money (about $800)—part of her outward-earned freight—the remainder being in a bill on Turks Island. I put a prize crew on board this vessel and kept her in company with me for three days, as a lookout or scout ship. At the end of this time I set fire to and burned her. The number of prisoners removed from her was ten. Some water and provisions and a few spars, sails, etc., were obtained from her. Nothing was seen between this day and the 5th day of October, when "Sail, ho!" was again cried from aloft. The sail was far to windward of us, standing to the northwest, and it was blowing a very fresh northeast trade. We gave chase, and although the stranger was evidently very fast and had crowded on all the sail that would draw with the wind a little abaft his beam, we came up with him in three hours and a quarter. I showed him the United States colors, and was much disappointed, after the expenditure of so much steam and speed, to see him run up in return the English flag. I boarded him, nevertheless, found him what his colors represented him to be (the brig Spartan, of Halifax, from Rio de Janeiro to St. Thomas), seen but four sail since leaving Trinidad a month before, one near Trinidad, which I did not chase, as she was a long way off and in an opposite direction from our course, and which we could not have overhauled before night if we had chased; a Dutchman near Surinam; a brig off the Amazon, running before half a gale, and a Brazilian mail steamer near Maranham. After having run past the most difficult parts of the navigation, viz., the shoals off Itacolumi and the Do Meio Bank, I was suddenly brought up on a sand bank, in two fathoms of water, in a place represented as perfectly clear by the chart (one of the Blunt's compilation), and the ship hung for about half a minute. A rapid tide running out, however, soon swung her bow off the bank, the edge of which was up and down, and she slid off into deep water without receiving other damage than the loss of her false keel, a piece of scantling of about six inches in depth, which had been bolted on to the keel over her copper to guard her propeller and rudder against the effects of similar accidents. I had a leadsman in the chains, who had got a cast of his lead immediately preceding her striking, and found no bottom with eight or nine fathoms of line. Warned by this accident of the faithlessness of my chart, I came to, and seeing some fishermen on the neighboring beach, I dispatched a boat and brought one of them on board, who undertook to pilot me up to the town of Maranham, where and permitted him, without unnecessary detention, to proceed on his course. In reply to his question as to what we were doing in this latitude, my boarding officer stated that we were cruising in pursuit of the Sumter and Jeff Davis, and he no doubt so reported us at St. Thomas. No other sail having been seen between this date and the 13th, I came to the conclusion that the "beaten track" between Rio and New York had been abandoned, and I filled away and made sail to the northward and westward.

On the 27th of October we fell in with and captured the schooner D. Trowbridge, of New Haven, Conn., bound to Demerara with a cargo of provisions. I supplied myself from her with provisions for five months, took such sails and other articles as I needed from her, and burned her. As we approached the windward West India Islands (in pursuance of an intention to run into Martinique and replenish my water and fuel) we entered a new track of commerce, in which vessels became more abundant. Between the date of our capture of the Trowbridge and our arrival at Martinique on the 9th of November, a period of thirteen days, we overhauled and boarded fifteen sail, not one of which, however, proved to be an American. Indeed, from this striking fact, and other circumstances which have come to my knowledge, I have no doubt that almost the entire trade of the United States with the West Indies has been broken up.

On the 9th of November, being nearly out of water, and having but little fuel remaining, I ran into Fort de France, Martinique, and anchored, after an active cruise of fifty-five days at sea, having spoken in this time seventeen sail, only two of which proved to be American, and which two I burned, as already related. Three of the sixteen prisoners received from the burned vessels preferring to remain with me, I shipped them into the service; the remainder I put on parole and delivered to the United States consul. Finding no coal here in private hands, and the governor being unwilling to supply me from the public docks, I dispatched my paymaster to St. Pierre to ascertain if it could be procured there. In the meantime I had had an interview with the governor on the subject of supplies generally, and he had promised me that I might procure freely whatever I might need. My paymaster returned from St. Pierre in due course of steamer, and reported to me that, although coal in abundance could be had at that place, the collector of the customs had interposed and prohibited the merchants from selling or delivering it to me. Upon this being made known to the governor, the difficulty was then removed. Having remained no longer at Fort de France than was necessary to water ship and give my crew a short run on shore, I got under way on the 13th of November and proceeded to St. Pierre. I commenced coaling ship on the same evening. On the next day at about 3 P. M., the enemy's steam sloop, the Iroquois, of twice my size and force, made her appearance off the harbor, and, without coming to anchor, cruised to and fro across my bow in blockade for twenty-four hours. My ship was moored, head and stern, within one hundred yards of the shore for convenience of coaling; and the Iroquois sometimes approached me within a ship's length, especially during the night. I kept my crew constantly prepared for action, making them sleep at their guns, as from this offensive violation of the neutral waters in which I was lying I supposed that the enemy might possibly have the audacity to assault me. As soon as this conduct of the enemy was made known to the governor at Fort de France by his subordinates, he dispatched the French steamer of war Acheron, Captain Duchatel [Duchaxel], to St. Pierre to see that the neutral rights of France were properly respected. Soon after the arrival of the Acheron the Iroquois came to anchor, whereupon the captain of the Acheron went on board of her and demanded that she should either depart twenty hours before the Sumter, or permit the Sumter to depart twenty-four hours before her. Instead of acceding to this demand, however, Captain Palmer immediately got under way and stood to sea, placing himself about a league (though frequently coming witin a mile or a mile and a half under cover of night) from the shore. He continued to cruise in this manner until I made my escape.

On the night of the 23d of November, the moon having waned sufficiently to render the night partially obscure, at 8 P. M. I slipped my moorings and started under a full head of steam to the southward. Immediately, as I had predicted, blue lights were burned from the deck of a Yankee schooner in port, to signal to the Iroquois my departure and the direction I had taken, seeing which, in the course of about twenty minutes, I doubled, ran in under the shadow of the land, and stood in the opposite direction, to the northward. By this simple maneuver I not only deceived the enemy, but turned his signals to my own advantage. I steamed rapidly along the west side of Dominica after leaving Martinique, and the next morning the Iroquois and the Sumter were probably one hundred and fifty miles apart. The night, which was quite clear when I started, became squally and rainy soon afterward. But while the squalls were driving Captain Palmer with accelerated speed southward, in obedience to his signals, I had broken the force of them by taking shelter under the lee of Dominica, and was steaming with undiminished speed in the opposite direction. Some time previously to my arrival at Martinique I had resolved upon making the run to Europe, and, in accordance with this intention, I now shaped my course so as to get out of the trades as soon as possible, that I might use my sails, upon which I mainly depended. Judging from the experience of my last cruise, the enemy's West India trade seemed to be pretty well broken up, and I not only deemed the waters of Europe a better cruising ground for me, but it had become necessary to put my ship into dock for repairs. With this latter view, I directed my course to Cadiz, where I knew there were good docks, and to which port the distance was somewhat less than to England. I could make the passage, too, in parallels of latitude more favorable to good weather, which was important, as my upper works were too weak to encounter the heavy gales of the North Atlantic in midwinter. As it was, I suffered considerable damage on the passage in a very heavy gale, which I took some four hundred miles from the Azores.

THE SUMTER RUNNING THE BLOCKADE OF ST. PIERRE, MARTINIQUE, PASSING BY THE UNITED STATES GUNBOAT IROQUOIS, ON THE NIGHT OF NOVEMBER 23, 1861.

Between the 23d of November and the 8th of December I overhauled a number of foreign sail, bound principally to the West Indies.

On the 25th of November, in latitude eighteen degrees eleven minutes north and longitude fifty-eight degrees forty-eight minutes west, I brought to and boarded the ship Montmorency, of Bath, Me., from Newport in Wales to the Island of St. Thomas in the West Indies. This ship was laden with coal for the British Mail Steam Packet Company in St. Thomas, and as I could not burn her without destroying also neutral property, I was forced to liberate her, which I did, after putting the master and crew on parole and taking from the master, in behalf of the owners, a ransom bond in the sum of twenty thousand dollars.

This case illustrated in a forcible manner the hardship of the rule adopted by neutral nations, excluding prizes from their ports. Our own ports being blockaded, I could not send this ship to the Confederate States, and, as under the rule stated I could not send her to any neutral port, my only alternative was to destroy her, but this I could not do for the reason stated. The cargo of coal with which this ship was laden cost in Newport, Wales, about four thousand dollars, while the ship herself was worth, I suppose, ten times as much. Thus, to save four thousand dollars to British subjects, I was forced to abandon forty thousand dollars to the enemy.

On the next day, the 26th, I overhauled and burned the schooner Arcade, of Portland, Me., bound to the Island of Gaudeloupe, with a cargo of staves.

On the 3d of December, in latitude twenty-nine degrees ten minutes north and longitude fifty-seven degrees twenty-two minutes west, I overhauled and burned the fine ship Vigilant, of Bath, Me., bound in ballast from New York to the guano islands of Sombrero in the West Indies. We captured on board this vessel a rifled 9-pounder, which, with its ammunition, I took on board.

On the 8th of December I overhauled and burned the fine bark Eben Dodge, of New Bedford, Mass., twelve days out, and completely equipped for a whaling voyage in the Pacific. I had now forty-three prisoners on board, and as many as I could well take care of on the long passage which was before me, and I therefore made the best way across the Atlantic.

As I approached Madeira, and afterward the coast of Spain, however, I chased and overhauled a number of other sail, but they all proved to be foreign. I made the Cadiz light on the night of the 3d of January, and on the next morning entered the harbor. The first act of the authorities was to put me in quarantine for want of a bill of health, and after I had been put in port some twenty-four hours I was warned to depart. Upon the receipt of this warning I addressed to the military commandant a letter. The contents of this letter having been telegraphed to Madrid the central government overruled the proceed-

THE SUMTER RUNNING THE BLOCKADE OF PASS A L'OUTRE, PASSING BY THE U. S. SLOOP OF WAR BROOKLYN, JUNE 30, 1861.

Commander Charles F. McIntosh, of Virginia.
Confederate States Navy.

Commander John M. Brooke, of Florida.
Confederate States Navy.

Captain Matthew F. Maury, of Virginia.
Confederate States Navy.
[From a photograph taken in 1865.]

Captain French Forrest, of Virginia.
Confederate States Navy.

Colonel Lloyd I. Beall, of Maryland.
Confederate States Marine Corps.

Commander Joseph Fry, of Florida.
Confederate States Navy.

Colonel R. G. H. Kean,
Chief of War Bureau.
[From a photograph taken in 1863.]

Commodore George N. Hollins, of Maryland.
Confederate States Navy.

Colonel Thomas P. August, of Virginia.
Superintendent Bureau of Conscription.

ings of the local authorities and permitted me to land my prisoners and to remain in port for repairs. This decision was announced to me in a letter from the Civil Governor of Cadiz.

Having arrived at Cadiz without funds (there being only about six hundred dollars on board, the whole amount captured by me in the sixteen sail which I had seized being only about one thousand dollars), I telegraphed immediately to the Hon. W. L. Yancey to supply me.

On the 13th of January, my ship was admitted into one of the government docks for repairs.

I received a dispatch from Mr. Yancey on the 15th, informing me that my request for funds would be complied with. My ship came out of the dock, a part of one plank having been replaced under her bilge and the place recoppered and the propeller overhauled. We found a part of the false keel gone, but the authorities would not replace it, as not being necessary to the safety of the ship at sea. I anchored in the bay, calked my upper works, and repaired the boilers and condenser and pumps.

I left Cadiz on the evening of the 17th, and the next morning as I entered the Strait of Gibraltar, I descried a number of sail, two of which I chased and captured. They were the United States barks Investigator and Neapolitan. The former having an English cargo on board, I liberated her under a ransom bond; the latter, laden with brimstone (fifty tons) and fruit, I burned. The prisoners of both ships were paroled, and the crew of the burned ship was transferred to the one which was liberated. There were two grounds on which I condemned the cargo of the Neapolitan—one the spoliation of papers, the master not having produced any paper whatever in relation to his cargo; and the other, that the major part of the cargo being contraband and the hold cargo belonging to the same owners, according to the master's statement (the Baring Brothers, of London, though the ship was bound to Boston), the noxious articles infected the innocent and rendered the whole subject to condemnation. I have been received with much courtesy at Gibraltar, and have had the hospitality of the port freely extended to me for the purpose of repairing my ship, etc. I have had a conversation with the governor on the subject of neutral and belligerent rights, and I am happy to say there is no difference of opinion between us on this subject.

For some days after my arrival at Gibraltar I had hopes of being able to reach another English or a French port, where I might find the requisite facilities for repair. I patched my boilers and otherwise prepared my ship for departure. In consequence of a combination of the coal merchants against me, however, I was prevented from coaling; and, in the meantime, the enemy's steamers Tuscarora and Kearsarge and the sailing sloop Ino arrived and blockaded me. Notwithstanding the arrival of these vessels I should have made an effort to get to sea but for the timely discovery of further defects in my boilers, which took place under the following circumstances: An English steamer having arrived from Liverpool with an extra quantity of coal on board offered to supply me. I got steam up to go alongside of her for the purpose, when, with a very low pressure, my boilers gave way in so serious a manner as to extinguish the fires in one of the furnaces. I was obliged, of course, to "blow off," and, upon a re-examination of the boilers by a board of survey, it was ascertained that they had been destroyed to such an extent as to render them entirely untrustworthy. It was found, indeed, to be necessary either to supply the ship with new boilers or to lift the old ones out of her and renew entirely the arches and other important parts of them, which could only be done in a machine shop, and with facilities not to be found at Gibraltar.

In this state of things it became necessary, in my judgment, either to lay the ship up or to sell her. Of course, the remaining by her of myself, my officers and crew, in her disabled and useless condition, was not to be thought of. Still, I felt that the responsibility was a grave one, and deeming it more respectful to the department that it should be assumed by some one higher in authority than myself, I reported the facts to the Hon. James M. Mason, our commissioner in London, and requested him to assume the power. This he did very promptly, and in a few days afterward I discharged and paid off in full all the crew except ten men, and detached all the officers except Midshipman Armstrong and a master's mate. I placed Mr. Armstrong in charge of the ship, supplied him with money and provisions sufficient for him and his diminished crew for ten months, and departed myself for London, whither most of the officers also repaired on their way to the Confederate States.

[R. SEMMES,
Commander, C. S. Navy.]

NOTE.—Secretary of the Navy Mallory, in April, 1861, at the instance of Commander Raphael Semmes, then Chief of the Confederate States Lighthouse Bureau, directed the Naval Board at New Orleans to purchase the screw steamer Habana. The name was changed to the Sumter, and on the 18th of the month Commander Semmes was ordered to the command of the vessel, with the following officers: Lieutenants, John M. Kell, R. T. Chapman, John M. Stribling and William E. Evans; paymaster, Henry Myers; surgeon, Francis L. Galt; midshipmen, William A. Hicks, Richard F. Armstrong, Albert G. Hudgins, John F. Holden and Joseph D. Wilson. To these, before sailing, were added the following: First lieutenant of marines, B. K. Howell; engineers, Miles J. Freeman, William P. Brooks, Matthew O'Brien and Simon W. Cummings; boatswain, Benjamin P. McCaskey; gunner, T. C. Cuddy; sailmaker, W. P. Beaufort; carpenter, William Robinson; captain's clerk, W. Breedlove.

The Sumter was a ship of 437 tons register, 184 feet long, 30 feet beam, 12 feet depth of hold, barkentine rigged. Her speed was from nine to ten knots an hour. She could carry coal but for eight days' steaming, and was slow under sail alone on account of her propeller dragging. After Commander Semmes left the Sumter, she was sold by auction at Gibraltar, in December, 1862, and was bought by a Liverpool merchant for $19,500, battery and all, who changed her name to the Gibraltar. The commander of the Federal steamer Chippewa avowed his purpose to capture her if she ventured out of the harbor, but did not risk attempting such an outrage upon the British flag, which she now carried. In July, 1863, she ran the blockade into Wilmington, N. C., and returned to Liverpool in December with a cargo of cotton. After the war the United States Government entered suit in the Admiralty Court at London for the recovery of the ship as a prize, but the case was decided in favor of her owners, and she was eventually lost in a gale in the North Sea, not far from where the Alabama was sunk.

CONFEDERATE STATES CRUISER SUMTER.

WHILE the Confederate army occupied Bowling Green, the —— Kentucky Regiment was encamped some two miles below town at Ennis & Dishman's mills, and while there one M. W. was detailed to go to the regimental commissary to assist in bringing rations for the company, and among his stores was a camp kettle of nice potatoes, not down on the requisition. Upon being asked where he got them, he said, in his natural, peculiar way: "I went to the conersary to draw some visions, and seein' these taters, I consecated them." M. W. was, however, a good and gallant soldier, and could somehow manage to have a crosscut saw, maul and two wedges, and occasionally a frow, carried, which were very useful in camp. He also carried, mostly himself, a four-gallon jug, to fetch water to the ditches, during the long retreat from Dalton to Atlanta. Adjutant Buchanan used to say he carried a sledge hammer and anvil in his knapsack.

CAPTURE OF THE FEDERAL IRONCLAD INDIANOLA.

BY

MAJOR J. L. BRENT.

MAJ.-GEN. R. TAYLOR'S GUNBOAT EXPEDITION, C. S. WEBB, THIRTY MILES BELOW VICKSBURG, OFF PRIZE IRONCLAD INDIANOLA,

February 25, 1863.

THE Federal ironclad Indianola had forty-eight hours start of us at Acklins Landing; at Natchez she was less than twenty-five hours in advance. We left Natchez on the evening of the 23d instant; and I found that we could easily overhaul her on the evening of the 24th, but I determined not to do so, in order that I might bring the enemy to an engagement only at night, considering, for many reasons, that this time was most advantageous to us.

We reached Grand Gulf before sunset, and there learned that the enemy was only about four hours in advance of us. As we were running more than two miles to his one, the time required to overtake him could be easily calculated. and I determined to overtake and bring him to action early in the night.

We came up with the Indianola about 9:40 last night, just above New Carthage, near the foot of Palmyra Island, and I immediately signaled the Webb to prepare for action.

Our order of approach was as follows: The Queen of the West about five hundred yards in advance of the Webb, and the Batey, Lieutenant-Colonel Brand commanding (who I wrote you joined us with a force and steamer fitted out at Port Hudson), over two miles in the rear, and lashed to my tender, the Grand Era.

The moon was partially obscured by a veil of clouds, and gave and permitted just sufficient light for us to see where to strike with our rams, and just sufficient obscurity to render uncertain the aim of the formidable artillery of the enemy.

We first discovered him when about one thousand yards distant, hugging the western bank of the Mississippi, with his head quartering across and down the river.

Not an indication of life appeared as we dashed on toward him, his lights obscured and his machinery apparently without motion.

We had also covered our lights, and only the fires of the Era could be seen, two miles back, where she was towing the Batey. The distance between him and the Queen had diminished to about five hundred yards, when, for the first time, we could clearly distinguish the long black line of the two coal barges which protected his sides from forward of his bow to nearly abreast his wheels.

The impatient desire of our men to open fire could be scarcely restrained, but I would not allow it, as the vast importance of traversing the distance to be passed over without drawing the fire of his powerful guns was too apparent. At last, when within about one hundred yards, I authorized Captain McCloskey to open fire, which he accordingly did with his two Parrott guns and one Cross 12-pounder; but at the second round the 20-pounder Parrott was disabled by blowing out its vent-piece.

Our intention was to dash our bow near the enemy's wheel-house, just in rear of the coal barge, but when about fifty yards distant he backed and interposed the barge between us and him. Our bow went crushing clear through the barge, heavily loaded with coal, and was not arrested until it struck with a violent shock, and scattered some of his timbers amidship, deeply indenting the iron plating of his hull.

So tremendous had been the momentum of our attack, made under full pressure of steam, that for some minutes we could not disengage ourselves, but remained with our bows against the sides of the Indianola, held fast by the pressure of the coal and barge through which we had crushed. In this position our sharpshooters kept up fire, sweeping the deck of the enemy, who feebly answered.

After a brief interval one of the coal barges sunk, and the other drifted down the current; and the Queen, finding herself free, immediately rounded up stream, to add to her next charge the additional power obtainable from the descending current of the river. Just then the Webb came dashing by us, and plunged into the Indianola with great force just in rear, or on the turn of her bow.

Some of the iron plating was loosened, but this blow of the Webb produced no serious external injury, though prisoners since report that it disabled the left-hand engine.

As the Webb approached on this her first charge, the two 11-inch Dahlgren guns in the forward casemate of the enemy opened on her at seventy-five yards distant, but fortunately she was untouched.

The vigor of the Webb's onset forced the enemy around, and carrying her forward laid her across and in actual contact with these monitor guns, if run out in battery. Dashing safely around from this perilous position, the Webb swung across the bow and on to the starboard side of the enemy, getting between him and his remaining coal barge, breaking its fastenings and setting it adrift.

The result of our first onset was to strip the Indianola of the two coal barges which protected her sides, and to injure her to some extent in her wheel, which was apparent from the subsequent want of rapidity and precision in her movements.

As soon as the Webb swept away clear of the enemy the Queen swung around and again dashed upon him, who this time, with partial success, endeavored to break the force of the onset, by presenting his bow to our bow. But his movements were too torpid, and not entirely successful, which tends to confirm the belief that his machinery was injured by the first blow.

The Queen struck a little forward of midships, but, as he was turning, the force of the blow glanced his side and passed along his wheel-house.

Just as the Queen swung clear of his stern, he opened upon us with two 9-inch guns in his after iron casemate at so near a range that the flames of the guns almost touched us—their heat being felt.

One shot struck the Queen on her starboard shoulder, and knocked away ten or twelve bales of cotton, causing us to list over, and then a shell entered under our front port hole, on the port side, struck the chase of a brass 12-pounder gun and exploded, killing two men, wounding four, and disabling two pieces. This time the Queen swung around rapidly up stream, and in a very brief interval dashed on the enemy for the third time, striking a little to the rear of his starboard wheelhouse, crashing through and shattering his framework and loosening some of his iron plates. By this time the Webb had run up stream, making a wide circuit, had turned, and, for her second onset, came charging on with a full head of steam just as the Queen had rounded out after her third blow, and striking the enemy very nearly in the same place where the Queen had just before hit him.

Through and through his timbers, crushing and dashing aside his iron plates, the sharp bow of the Webb penetrated as if it were going to pass entirely through the ship. As the Webb backed clear, the Indianola, with all the speed she could raise, declined further fight and ran down the river toward the western bank, with the intention, as afterward appeared, of getting a line out on shore, in order that the officers and crew might land and abandon their steamer. In fact a line was got out on shore, but not fastened, and three of the crew effected their escape, but were captured to-day by the cavalry of Major Harrison.

After the Queen had struck the enemy for the third time, she was for some time almost unmanageable—she had listed so much over on the port side that one of her wheels was raised nearly out of the water. She was making water, and presented every appearance of sinking.

Captain McCloskey righted her a little by throwing over cotton from his upper decks.

He was able to bring her around very slowly; but still this gallant commander succeeded in weaning her with difficulty, and headed her for her fourth charge.

While the Webb had her bow knocked off to within fourteen inches of the water line, her splendid machinery was unhurt, and she quickly and gallantly bore up for her third charge. When bearing down and approaching the enemy, Captain Pierce reports that he was hailed from the enemy's deck, announcing his surrender, and begged to be towed ashore, as he was sinking. Captain Pierce further represents that he then placed a line on board and commenced towing the Indianola, when the line parted.

As the Queen of the West was running off from her last charge, making a circuit to obtain room and space to add increased momentum to her onset, we encountered the steamer Batey, Lieutenant-Colonel Brand commanding, who had cast off from the tender Grand Era, and was hovering around to enter the fight when an opportunity offered.

The Batey is a frail steamboat, with but little power, and incapable of being used as a ram. She was crowded with two hundred and fifty gallant volunteers from the forces at Port Hudson, who had embarked in the Batey with the resolution to fight the enemy by boarding him. We called out to them that the opportunity for boarding had arrived, as it was apparent the enemy was disabled and much demoralized.

Lieutenant-Colonel Brand with his command gallantly bore away, approached the enemy after the line from the Webb had parted, and gave, as I am informed by him, the command, "prepare to board," when he was greeted by a voice from the Indianola, announcing her surrender, and that she was in a sinking condition.

Lieutenant-Colonel Brand then boarded her upper deck, and received the sword of the Federal commander, Lieutenant Brown.

The result must have been very gratifying to Colonel Brand, as it was obtained without the loss or injury of a single man of his command.

Upon my reaching the deck of the Indianola, Lieutenant-Colonel Brand most handsomely acknowledged that the capture was entirely due to the Queen of the West and to the Webb, and he has so officially reported.

I have no doubt, if it had been necessary, that Colonel Brand and his gallant command would have again demonstrated that nothing can resist the desperation of troops who regard not their own lives, but victory.

Upon taking possession, I immediately appointed Lieutenant Thomas H Handy prize master.

WRECK OF THE INDIANOLA, CAPTURED BY THE CONFEDERATES.

We found our prize a formidable gunboat, mounting two 11-inch guns forward, and two 9-inch guns aft, all protected by thick iron casemates, utterly impenetrable to our artillery, even at the very shortest range. The motive power consisted of side wheels and two propellers. She was filled with a valuable cargo, embracing supplies, stores, etc. The officers and crew, amounting to over one hundred, fell into our hands as prisoners. Nothing shows more clearly how well she was protected than the fact that our artillery, though frequently fired at the range of twenty and thirty yards, utterly failed to injure her. Lieutenant Handy, of the Webb, fired an 80-pound shell from his rifled and banded 32-pound gun so close to the forward casemate of the enemy that it actually enveloped his portholes in flames, and yet no injury was sustained by the casemate.

Our sharpshooters deliberately and coolly fired at every onset.

Notwithstanding all these circumstances, the enemy lost but one man killed and none wounded. The Webb had one man wounded, and the Queen two killed and four wounded.

The fire of the enemy was terrific, and delivered at short range mostly. His huge shot and shell were directed a little wide of the mark, except the two shots that struck the Queen, and one shot that passed through the bulwarks of the Webb. This was remarkable, as he frequently fired at such close range that the flames of his enormous guns almost enveloped our bows.

The escape from destruction of the feeble crafts that were five times precipitated upon the iron sides of this powerful war steamer, mounting an armament of 9 and 11-inch guns, was providential.

On taking possession we found our prize rapidly making water, which we could not arrest. Seeing that she would sink, I did not wish that this should take place on the western side of the river, where the Federal forces could easily have retaken her, and therefore made fast to her with two of my steamers, and towed her over the river to the eastern side, where she sunk in the water up to her gun-deck, just as we reached the shallow water, thus losing us the enormous value of her capture, as well as the valuable stores that were in her hold.

I am much indebted for the success of the expedition to the skill and gallantry of my men. Captain James McCloskey, commanding the Queen, combined with the courage of the soldier, the skill and aptitude that characterizes the sailor of our Western waters. Lieutenant Thomas H. Handy, of the Crescent artillery, commanded the troops on the Webb. He exhibited skill and courage in handling his command, and in person assisted in manning the 32-pound rifled gun. Lieutenant Rice, of the Twenty-first Tennessee, was on the Webb with a detachment from his regiment, and bore himself well and gallantly. Lieutenant Prather, also on the Webb, served his two field-pieces entirely unprotected, with praiseworthy courage, and was well seconded by Mr. Charles Schuler, acting as chief of one of the guns.

Captain Charles Pierce, a civilian, commanded and controlled the movements of the Webb. It was he who selected the weak spots of the enemy, and with a steady hand and eye dashed the Webb against the Indianola.

Not only did the officers act well, but I have nothing but commendations for the private soldiers.

Captain Caines' and Lieutenant Rice's company, of the Twenty-first Tennessee, and the detachment of Lieutenant Doolan, adjutant of Major Burnett's battalion of Texans, and detachment from the Third Maryland artillery, were in the expedition, and acted with courage and discipline when under fire.

Captain J. W. Mangum, assistant adjutant-general of Brigadier-General Moore, accompanied the expedition as a volunteer and acted as my adjutant. He comported himself gallantly under fire, and throughout the expedition rendered me valuable services.

I herewith submit the report of Captain McCloskey, commanding the Queen. He mentions favorably Captain Caines and Lieutenant Miller, of the Twenty-first Tennessee; Lieutenant Doolan, adjutant of Major Burnett's battalion; Sergeant E. H. Langley, of the Third Maryland artillery, acting as lieutenant in charge of the two Parrott guns; and the volunteers, Captain J. H. White, slightly wounded, acting with efficiency as ordnance officer; Captain Tank and Lieutenants Fisk and Stanmeyer, both wounded, and Lieutenant R. R. Hyams, who as quartermaster and commissary exhibited much energy. As I was on board the Queen during the action, the conduct of the officers and men was under my own eye, and I cheerfully indorse the commendation of Captain McCloskey. He also speaks highly of the intrepid promptness and skill of his pilots and engineers, and of the conduct of Assistant Surgeon Blanchard, who manifested much care and coolness, coming on the gun-deck in the midst of the action and personally supervising the removal of the wounded.

Sergeant Magruder, of the signal corps, also deserves mention for having rendered very important services in the discharge of the responsible duties devolved upon him.

Captain Pierce, of the Webb, verbally reports to me that his pilots and engineers behaved themselves with coolness and bravery, and discharged their duties with promptness and energy.

I have no doubt that this is correct, from the skillful and efficient manner in which his boat was handled.

This is dated from the Webb, as I have dispatched the Queen, Captain McCloskey, to Warrenton, and, if possible, to Vicksburg.

* * * * * *

J. L. BRENT, *Major Commanding.*

UPON the re-occupation of Baton Rouge one of our "oldest and best" citizens, a noted practical joker, finding life among the bluecoats decidedly unpleasant, after much worry, succeeeded in getting a pass to remove to the country. When he arrived at the outpost he found a very weary picket, who obviously had been forgotten by the "relief." "Can you tell me the time of day?" he asked. "No, I can't," was the reply of our friend. "Haven't you got a watch?" "Yes." "Don't it keep time?" "Certainly." "Then why can't you tell me what o'clock it is?" "Look at that pass," was the reply, "and you will see that I am sworn to tell nothing to any one, in fact give information to nobody. Good morning;" and he rode on, leaving the bewildered Yankee scratching his head.

THE ALABAMA

AT

CAPE TOWN, SOUTH AFRICA.

[From *The Illustrated London News*, October 10, 1863.]

THE last mail from the Cape of Good Hope, South Africa, brought some news of the Confederate war steamer Alabama. She has been cruising, together with her consort, the Georgia, and her armed prize, the Conrad, now named the Tuscaloosa, in the neighborhood of the Cape of Good Hope. She had captured the Federal bark Sea Bride in the sight of thousands of spectators, while running into Table Bay. This capture was alleged by the Federal consul to have been made within British jurisdiction, which he considered to extend to the distance of "an Armstrong cannon-shot" from the shore, and he consequently protested. His protest was, however, disallowed by the governor, who likewise rejected his demand that the Tuscaloosa—which he maintained to be an uncondemned prize, and consequently excluded by the Queen's proclamation from British ports—should be delivered up to him for her owners. The Confederate vessels were allowed to make some repairs and take in supplies in the Cape harbors, and it was thought that they might probably cruise very successfully for Federal vessels bound to or from the East Indies and China.

A supplement to the *Cape Argus* of August 20th gives copious details of the excitement caused among the inhabitants of Cape Town by the presence of these two vessels in their bay. The *Argus* reporter gives the following list of the officers of the Alabama, some of whose portraits we have engraved: Captain Semmes, Lieutenants M'Intyre Kell, Armstrong, Wilson and Sinclair; Surgeon and Paymaster Galt; Master J. S. Bullock; Lieutenant Howell, Marines (brother-in-law of President Davis); Assistant Surgeon Llewellyn; Chief Engineer Freeman; Assistant Engineers Brooks, O'Brien, Pundt; Midshipmen E. A. Maffit (son of the commander of the Florida) and E. M. Anderson; Master's Assistants Fulham and Evans; Boatswain M'Caskie, Gunner Cuddy, Carpenter Robinson and Captain Semmes' secretary, Mr. Smith; a young officer, assistant engineer. Captain Semmes he describes as being about forty-eight years of age. He wears a mustache a la Napoleon, is rather gray, and has sharp, intelligent features. He wears a military frock coat of gray color, with very little ornament.

Captain Semmes read from his record book to the *Argus* reporter a list of his captures, as follows: "The Ocmulgee, a whaler of four hundred tons, thirty-two men on board, burned; the Starlight, of Boston, a schooner, burned off the Western Islands; the Ocean Rover, a whaler, bark, burned; the Alert, a whaler of seven hundred tons, burned; the whaling-schooner Weathergage, burned; the whaling-brig Altamaha, burned; the whaling-ship Benjamin Tucker, burned; the whaling-schooner Courser, burned; the whaling-bark Virginia, burned; the bark Elisha Dunbar, a whaler, burned; the ship Brilliant, with one thousand tons of grain on board, burned; the Emily Farnum, released as a cartel, and having so many prisoners we put some of them on board her and sent them off; the Wave Crest, with a general cargo on board for Europe, burned; the Dunkirk, brig, with a general cargo on board, burned; the ship Tonawanda, with a valuable freight on board, released, after taking a bond for a thousand dollars; the ship Manchester, with a cargo of grain, burned; the bark Lamplighter, with an assorted cargo, burned; the bark Lafayette, with an assorted cargo, burned; the schooner Crenshaw, with an assorted cargo on board bound for the West Indies, burned; the bark Lauretta, for Europe, with an assorted cargo on board, burned; the brig Baron de Castine, a bond taken and released; the whaling-ship Levi Starbuck, burned; the T. B. Wales, from Calcutta to Boston, with a valuable cargo on board, burned; the bark Martha, from Calcutta to the West Indies, with an assorted cargo, burned; the schooner Union had some English property on board, and was released on bond; the mail-steamer Ariel, running between New York and Aspinwall, released on bond; the United States gunboat Hatteras, who came out to fight us, had the same number of guns and crew—our guns were a little heavier than hers, but we equalized that by permitting her to fight us at three hundred yards—we sunk her in thirteen minutes by the watch; the bark Golden Rule, with an assorted cargo, burned; the brig Chastelaine, burned; the schooner Palmetto, burned; the bark Olive Jane, burned; the Golden Eagle, laden with guano, burned; the Washington from the Pacific, with guano, released on bond; the Bethia Thayer, from East India, with a valuable cargo on board, released on bond; the John A. Parker, with flour and lumber, from Boston to Buenos Ayres, burned; the Punjab, from East India, found to have some English cargo on board, released on bond; the ship Morning Star, released on bond; the whaling-schooner King Fisher, burned; the ship Nora, from Liverpool to the West Indies, with salt, burned; the Charles Hill, also from Liverpool, with coal, burned; the ship Louisa Hatch, from Cardiff to the West Indies, burned; the bark Lafayette, whaler, burned; the whaling-brig Kate Cory, burned; the whaling-bark Nye, burned; the ship Dorcas Price, with a general cargo, burned; the ship Lelah, with a general cargo for the East Indies, burned; the bark Union Jack, from Boston to Shanghai, burned; the ship Gildersleeve, from New York to the East Indies, burned; the bark Justiana, released on bond to take home prisoners; the ship Jabez Snow, from New York to the East Indies, burned; the bark Amazonian, from Boston to Buenos Ayres, burned; the ship Talisman, from New York to the East Indies, burned; the bark Conrad, fitted up as a Confederate cruiser, a tender to the Alabama. We call her the Tuscaloosa. After these came the Anna F. Schmidt, the Express and the Sea Bride you saw us take to-day. The estimated value of these captures is four million two hundred thousand dollars."

The Confederate cruiser Tuscaloosa, Lieutenant Low, commander, formerly the Conrad, of Philadelphia, captured by the Alabama, and converted by Captain Semmes into a tender to his ship, put into Simons Bay two days before the Alabama arrived there, for the purpose of refitting. She carries two guns and ten men before the mast.

About fourteen days before she fell in with the American ship Santee, bound from Rangoon to Falmouth, and captured her; but, as the vessel was laden with cargo belonging to British owners, she was allowed to proceed on giving a bond for $150,000. A few days afterward the Tuscaloosa fell in with the American China clippership Snow Squall, eight hundred tons, homeward bound. It was blowing hard at the time, and the Tuscaloosa, having fired at the Snow Squall without bringing her to, made chase; but the latter, being the fastest sailer, escaped.

On Sunday afternoon, August 16th, the Confederate steamer Georgia, Captain Maury, entered Simons Bay for coal and repairs. She appears (says the *Argus*) to be an ordinary iron-built packet-boat, certainly not intended for a fighting craft; but having a good crew, and being armed with two Whitworth rifled guns aft, one large 56-gun forward, and two 32's on her quarter-deck, and being a fast sailer, is well suited to capture merchant ships, and run from war vessels of superior armament, but inferior speed. We are indebted to one of her officers for a history of the vessel and her exploits. The Georgia was built by Messrs. Denny & Co., of Greenock. Her officers joined her off Ushant Island on the 9th of April, on which day she finished getting her armament on board, hauled down the English, and ran up the Confederate, flag. She then

CAPTAIN RAPHAEL SEMMES.
[From a photograph taken at Cape Town, South Africa, August 19, 1863.]

put to sea. On the 25th of April she captured the ship Dictator, of New York, bound to Shanghai with coal. After burning the Dictator, she proceeded to the Cape Verde Islands to land her prisoners. As she got into the entrance of the harbor of St. Vincent she discovered a man-of-war with the American colors flying, put about, and went to the north side of the island, where she lay until dark, and then stood out for sea. On the 13th of May she arrived in Bahia, where the Alabama was lying at the time. From Bahia she proceeded down the South American Coast. Off Cape Frio, in sight of land, she captured the George Griswold, which vessel had a British cargo on board, and was therefore bonded. The Georgia then proceeded to the island of Trinidad, on her way capturing the bark Good Hope, of Boston, bound to Agulhas, with a general cargo. Her captain had died some days before, and his body, being preserved in salt, Captain Maury had brought on board the Georgia, read the funeral service over it, and committed it to the deep. During the service the bark J. W. Seaver hove in sight, and was chased by the Georgia. She was from Boston, bound to the Amoor River with machinery for the Russian Government. The prisoners of the Good Hope were put on board and she was bonded. On June 18th the Georgia arrived at the island of Trinidad. On June 25th she captured the ship Constitution, of New York, laden with coal for Shanghai, made a prize of her, and took her into the island. On July 28th the Georgia captured the ship City of Bath, of Bath, from Callao to Antwerp; the cargo being neutral, she was bonded, and the prisoners of the Constitution were put on board her. On July 16th the Georgia captured the ship Prince of Wales, of Bath, from Valparaiso, bound to Antwerp with guano. The cargo being neutral, the ship was bonded.

The excitement in the bay is thus described by the *Argus* reporter:—"We went off in our boat in the midst of a vast fleet of dingies, cargo-boats, gigs and wherries, all as full as they could hold. Nearly all the city was at sea. The rowing clubs, in uniform, pulled off with favored members of their respective clubs on board. The

LIEUTENANT MCINTOSH KELL, EXECUTIVE OFFICER OF THE ALABAMA.
[From a photograph taken at Cape Town, South Africa, August 19, 1863.]

crews feathered their oars in double-quick time. We passed the Federal bark Urania at her anchorage, and that ship, regardful of the enemy, sported all her bunting with becoming pluck. The stars and stripes floated defiantly from her mizzen peak and her name from her main. On getting alongside the Alabama we found about a dozen boats before us; and we had not been on board five minutes before she was surrounded by nearly every boat in Table Bay, and as boat after boat arrived, three hearty cheers were given for Captain Semmes and the Alabama."

EXPLOITS OF THE ALABAMA,

INCLUDING A

DESCRIPTION OF HER FIGHT WITH THE KEARSARGE.

BY

ADMIRAL RAPHAEL SEMMES,
Commander of the Alabama.

CAPTAIN BULLOCK, agent of the Confederate Government, in June, 1861, opened communication with the Messrs. Laird, proprietors of extensive shipyards at Birkenhead, opposite Liverpool, for the building of a steam sloop. He paid them £47,500 for the vessel, which was known in the yards as "No. 290," and subsequently became the Alabama. On July 29, 1862, she steamed out of the Mersey a few hours before the British Foreign Office sent down orders to detain her, on the complaint of Minister Adams that she was a Confederate ship of war. Seven days later she arrived at Terceira, in the Azore Islands, where she was joined by the bark Agrippina, bringing her armament and stores, and the steamship Bahama, on which her officers and most of her crew had come out from England. On August 24th she was formally commissioned as the Confederate States cruiser Alabama, with the subjoined list of officers: Captain, Raphael Semmes; first lieutenant and executive officer, J. M. Kell; second lieutenant, Richard F. Armstrong; third lieutenant, Joseph D. Wilson; fourth lieutenant, Arthur Sinclair; fifth lieutenant, John Lowe; surgeon, Francis L. Galt; assistant surgeon, David H. Llewellyn; paymaster, Clarence R. Yonge; captain's clerk, William B. Smith; lieutenant of marines, Becker K. Howell; chief engineer, Miles J. Freeman; assistant engineers, William P. Brooks, S. W. Cummings, Matthew O'Brien, John W. Pundt; midshipmen, William H. Sinclair, Irvine S. Bullock, Eugene Maffit, Edwin M. Anderson; master's mates, George T. Fullam, James Evans; boatswain, Benjamin L. McCaskey; gunner, J. O. Cuddy; carpenter, William Robinson; sailmaker, Henry Alcott.

The Alabama was two hundred and twenty feet long, thirty-two feet breadth of beam, and ten hundred and forty tons burden. She was barkentine rigged, and her propeller was so constructed that it could be lifted out of the water, and when this was done she was to all intents and purposes a sailing ship. Under sail alone, with the wind abeam, she occasionally made ten knots an hour, and her best performance was eleven and a quarter knots under sail and steam combined. Her armament consisted of six 32-pounders in broadside, a 100-pounder Blakely rifle in the forecastle and a smooth bore 8-inch shell gun abaft the mainmast.

The cost of the Alabama was as follows:

Hulls, spars, sails, boats, anchors, cables and all equipment except armament	£47,500
Battery	2,500
Magazine tanks	616
Ordnance stores	500
Small arms	600
Total	£51,716

£51,716 @ $4.84 = $250,305.44.

She made her debut as a war ship by plunging in among the American whaling fleet that between the early spring and October finds employment around the Western Islands. On September 14, 1862, the Alabama was off Fayal, and before the equinoctial gales drove the whalers out of those waters she made prizes of a dozen of them. Captain Semmes selected for his next cruising ground the Newfoundland Banks, and the track of the American grain ships bound from the Eastern ports to Europe. He reached this station October 3, 1862, and began burning prizes, or ransoming, to carry away his prisoners, those containing cargoes documented as the indisputable property of neutrals. The first of the wheat ships taken was the Brilliant, and the second the Emily Farnham; and the latter returning to New York under bond, with the information that the Alabama was on the coast, a panic was created in shipping circles.

Between October 3d and 21st Semmes made sixteen captures, and then fell in with a number of ships whose cargoes were certified to be neutral property. A prize court was convened in the cabin of the Alabama, and upon its decision that the certificates were fraudulent the vessels and their ladings were burned. The Alabama ran down to within two hundred miles of New York, while the Federal men-of-war were looking for her up on the Grand Banks. About November 18th she put into Port de France, Martinique, when some of the men, who had smuggled liquor on board, created the first and only mutiny on the ship, which the commander promptly suppressed by no severer measure than drenching the guilty ones with cold water.

The United States frigate San Jacinto made her appearance off the port while the Alabama was there, but the latter's speed enabled her to go to sea past her slow and clumsy enemy. After coaling from a tender at Blanquilla, Venezuela, Semmes lay in wait between San Domingo and Hayti for one of the California treasure steamers bound from Colon to New York. On December 7, 1862, he captured a steamship, but she was outward bound from New York, with some five hundred women and children among her passengers, and as he could not take the prize into any port he was forced to release her on a ransom bond for $261,000, payable after the recognition of the independence of the Confederate States. He got nothing from the prize except $9,500 in money that her safe contained, while he might have captured a million if he had taken one of the steamers bound into New York.

The Alabama next went into the Gulf of Mexico, with a view of attacking the expedition known to be fitting out in the North under General N. P. Banks for a descent upon the Texas coast; but Banks had gone into New Orleans, and Semmes found off Galveston a Federal squadron bombarding that city. By concealing the identity of his ship and steaming slowly off he decoyed a vessel of the enemy twenty miles away, and then halted and cleared ship for action. To a hail he responded, first, "This is her Britannic Majesty's steamer Petrel," and then, "This is the Confederate States steamer Alabama." She fired the first broadside at 9 o'clock on the night of January 11, 1863; the other ship replied valiantly, and the engagement lasted just thirteen minute. Closing in with the foe, Semmes found that he had defeated the United States gunboat Hatteras, Lieutenant-Commander Homer C. Blake, and that she was in a sinking condition. Blake asked for assistance, which was so promptly rendered that, although the Hatteras went to the bottom within fifteen minutes after surrendering, every man on board, including the five

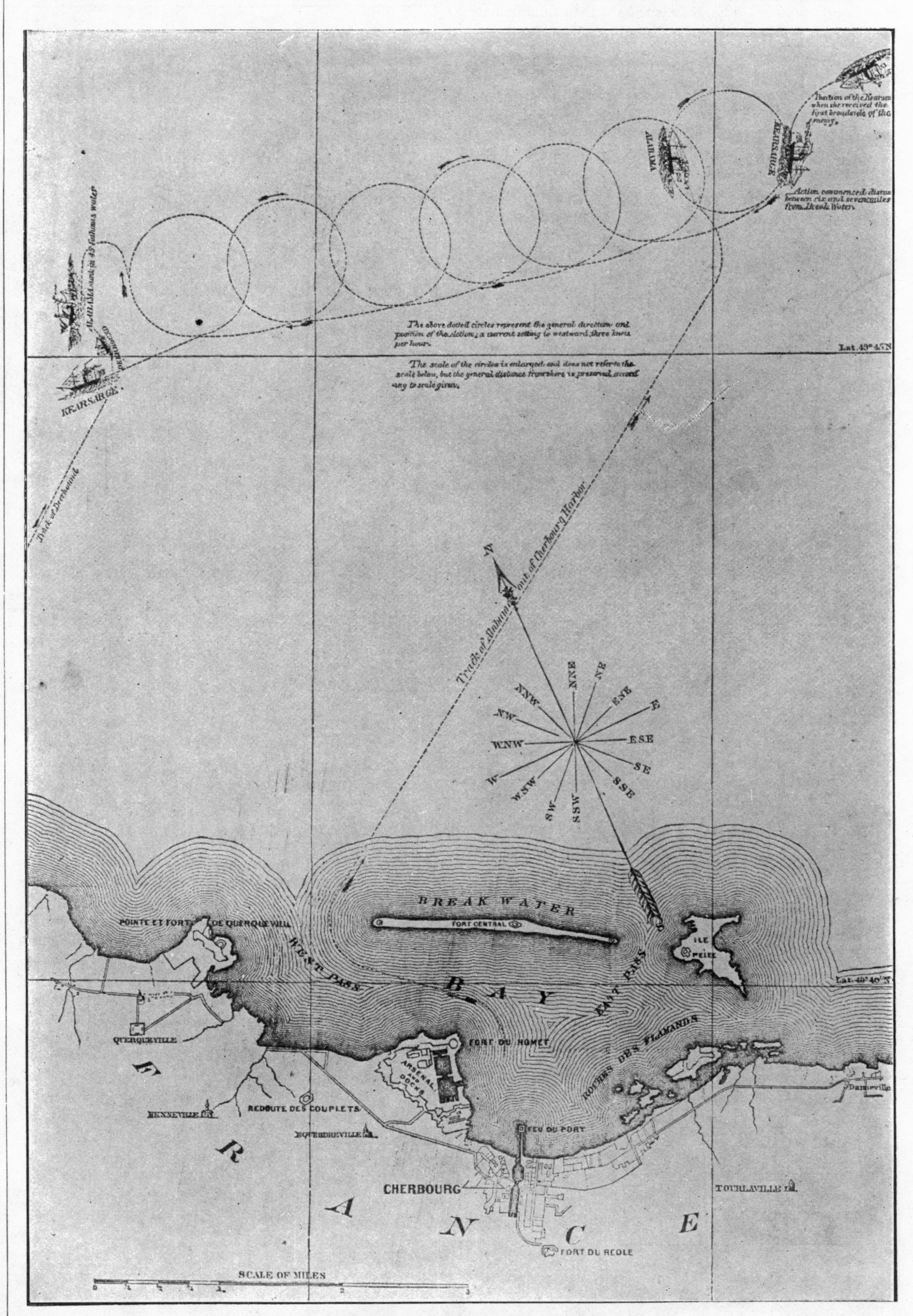

CHART OF THE ACTION BETWEEN THE ALABAMA AND KEARSARGE.

wounded, was transferred in safety to the Alabama. Two men were killed on the Hatteras and the Alabama had but one man wounded. The latter steamed for Jamaica, and on January 20th made the harbor of Port Royal, where Semmes expelled from the service his paymaster, Clarence R. Yonge, for debauchery.

On January 25th the Alabama left Kingston for a cruise down the Brazil coast, and thence to the Cape of Good Hope. At the forks of the marine roads, in the fairway of commerce, he captured twenty-four vessels, all of which were destroyed except the Conrad, which was converted into the Confederate States cruiser Tuscaloosa. Crossing the Atlantic to the southern point of Africa, two more prizes were taken, and on July 28, 1863, the Alabama put into Saldanha Bay. On this coast he captured only the bark Sea Bride, which vessel, with her cargo, Semmes sold to an English merchant, making the transfer at Angra Pequena, in the Hottentot country, to avoid any fracture of the British neutrality laws. For the remainder of the year he cruised in the Straits of Sunda, the China Sea and the Bay of Bengal, with moderate success. Beating up the waters of the Atlantic again, between Cape Town and the equatorial line on the Brazil coast, only two more captures were made. The ship Tycoon was taken on April 27, 1864, and she was the last of the long roll of the victims of the Alabama.

On June 11th the cruiser came to anchor in the port of Cherbourg, France, and three days later the United States corvette Kearsarge, Captain John A. Winslow, came across from Southampton. The vessels fought their famous battle on Sunday, June 19th. Thousands of people gathered on the southern heights overlooking the British Channel to witness the combat, and the French ironclad Couronne and the English yacht Deerhound, owned and sailed by Mr. John Lancaster, moved to and fro outside the line of fire.

The following, by Captain Semmes, gives all the needful particulars of the battle:

BATTLE BETWEEN ALABAMA AND KEARSARGE.

We entered Table Bay, Cape of Good Hope, on the 20th of March, 1864, after taking on board coal and provisions. In three days we were ready for sea again.

On the morning of the 25th we got up steam and moved out of the bay, amid lusty cheers and waving of handkerchiefs from the fleet of boats by which we were surrounded.

As we were going out, it so happened that a Yankee steamer was coming in. The Quang Tung, a fast steamer, recently built for the China trade, and now on her way to the Flowery Land, not dreaming that the Alabama was at the Cape, had made Table Mountain that morning, and now came steaming into the harbor. Both ships being within the marine league, we could not touch her, which was a sore trial, for the Quang Tung was a beauty and passed so close under our guns that the Confederate and United States flags nearly touched each other, the crews of the two ships looking on in silence. Reaching the offing, we permitted our fires to go down, and put the ship, as usual, under sail. My intention now was to make the best of my way to England or France, for the purpose of docking and thoroughly overhauling and repairing my ship, in accordance with my previously expressed design.

On the 2d of May we recrossed the equator into the northern hemisphere, took the northeast trade-wind, after the usual interval of calm and the usual amount of thunder, lightning and rain, and with it ran up to our old tollgate, at the crossing of the thirtieth parallel, where we halted, on our outward passage, and vised the passports of so many travelers. The poor old Alabama was not now what she had been then. She was like the wearied foxhound limping back after a long chase, foot-sore and longing for quiet and repose. Her commander, like herself, was well-nigh worn down. Vigils by night and by day, the storm and the drenching rain, the frequent and rapid change of climate, now freezing, now melting or broiling, and the constant excitement of the chase and capture, had laid, in the three years of war he had been afloat, a load of a dozen years on his shoulders. The shadows of a sorrowful future, too, began to rest upon his spirit. The last batch of newspapers captured were full of disasters. Might it not be that, after all our trials and sacrifices, the cause for which we were struggling would be lost? Might not our federal system of government be destroyed, and State independence become a phrase of the past; the glorious fabric of our American liberty sinking, as so many others had done before it, under a new invasion of Brennuses and Attilas? The thought was hard to bear.

We passed through our old cruising-ground, the Azores, sighting several of the islands, which called up reminiscences of the christening of our ship and of the sturdy blows she had struck at the enemy's whaling fleet, in the first days of her career. Thence we struck over to the coasts of Spain and Portugal, and thence to the British Channel, making the Lizard on the 10th of June, and being fortunate enough to get a channel pilot on board just as night was setting in, with a thick southwester brewing. By 11 P. M. we were up with the "start" light, and at 10 the next morning we made Cape La Hague, on the coast of France. We were now boarded by a French pilot, and at thirty minutes past noon we let go our anchor in the port of Cherbourg.

This was to be the Alabama's last port. She had run her career, her record had been made up, and in a few days more she would lay her bones beneath the waters of the British Channel, and be a thing of the past. I had brought back with me all my officers, except the paymaster, whom I had discharged at the island of Jamaica, as related in a former chapter, and the young engineer who had been accidentally killed at Saldanha Bay. Many changes had taken place, of course, among my crew, as is always the case with sailors, but still a large proportion of my old men had come back with me. These were faithful and true, and took more than an ordinary interest in their ship and their flag. There was harmony and mutual confidence between officers and men. Our discipline had been rigid, but mercy had always tempered justice, and the sailors understood and appeciated this. I had been successful with the health of my men beyond precedent. In my two ships, the Sumter and Alabama, I had had, first and last, say five hundred men under my command. The ships were small and crowded. As many as two thousand prisoners were confined, for longer or shorter periods, on board the two ships; and yet, out of the total of twenty-five hundred men, I had not lost a single man by disease. I had skillful and attentive surgeons. I gave them *carte blanche* with regard to medicine and diet, and my first lieutenant understood it to be an important part of his duty to husband the strength of his men. The means which were resorted to by all these officers, for preserving the health of the crew, have been detailed. The reader has seen, not only how their clothing was changed as we changed our latitude, but how it was changed every evening when we were in warm climates. He has seen how sedulously we guarded against intemperance, at the same time that we gave the sailor his regular allowance of grog. And last, though by no means least, he has seen how we endeavored to promote a cheerful and hilarious spirit among them, being present at and encouraging them in their diversions.

THE CONFEDERATE STEAMER ALABAMA, CAPTAIN RAPHAEL SEMMES.

Immediately upon anchoring, I sent an officer to call on the Port Admiral and ask leave to land my prisoners from the two last ships captured. This was readily granted, and the next day I went on shore to see him myself in relation to docking and repairing my ship. My arrival had, of course, been telegraphed to Paris, and, indeed, by this time had been spread all over Europe. The Admiral regretted that I had not gone into Havre, or some other commercial port, where I would have found private docks. Cherbourg being exclusively a naval station, the docks all belonged to the Government, and the Government would have preferred not to dock and repair a belligerent ship. No positive objection was made, however, and the matter was laid over until the Emperor could be communicated with. The Emperor was then at Biarritz, a small watering place on the south coast, and would not be back in Paris for several days. It was my intention, if I had been admitted promptly into dock, to give my crew a leave of absence for a couple of months. They would have been discharged and dispersed in the first twenty-four hours after my arrival but for this temporary absence of the Emperor. The combat, therefore, which ensued, may be said to be due to the Emperor's accidental absence from Paris.

When the Alabama arrived in Cherbourg, the enemy's steamer Kearsarge was lying at Flushing. On the 14th of June,

LIEUTENANT ARTHUR ST. CLAIR AND LIEUTENANT R. F. ARMSTRONG.
[From a photograph taken at Cape Town, South Africa, August 19, 1863.]

or three days after our arrival, she steamed into the harbor of Cherbourg, sent a boat on shore to communicate with the authorities, and, without anchoring, steamed out again and took her station off the breakwater. We had heard a day or two before of the expected arrival of this ship, and it was generally understood among my crew that I intended to engage her. Her appearance, therefore, produced no little excitement on board. The object which the Kearsarge had in view in communicating with the authorities, was to request that the prisoners I had sent on shore might be delivered up to her. To this I objected, on the ground that it would augment her crew, which she had no right to do in neutral waters, and especially in the face of her enemy. Captain Winslow's request was refused, and the prisoners were not permitted to go on board of her. I now addressed a note to Mr. Bonfils, our agent, requesting him to inform Captain Winslow, through the United States Consul, that if he would wait until I could receive some coal on board—my supply having been nearly exhausted by my late cruising—I would come out and give him battle. This message was duly conveyed, and the defiance was understood to have been accepted.

We commenced coaling ship immediately and making other preparations for battle—as sending down all useless yards and top-hamper, examining the gun equipments, and overhauling the magazine and shell-rooms. My crew seemed not only willing but anxious for the combat, and I had every confidence in their steadiness and drill; but they labored under one serious disadvantage—they had had but very limited opportunities of actual practice at target-firing with shot and shell. The reason is obvious: I had no means of replenishing either shot or shell, and was obliged, therefore, to husband the store I had on hand for actual conflict.

The stories that ran the round of the Federal papers at the time—that my crew was composed mainly of trained gunners from the British practice-ship Excellent—were entirely without foundation. I had on board some half dozen British seamen, who had served in ships of war in former years, but they were in no respect superior to the rest of the crew. As for the two ships, though the enemy was superior to me, both in size, stanchness of construction and armament, they were of force so nearly equal that I can not be charged with rashness in having offered battle. The Kearsarge mounted seven guns—two 11-inch Dahlgrens, four 32-pounders and a rifled 28-pounder. The Alabama carried one gun more than her antagonist, though the latter was enabled to throw more metal at a broadside, there being a difference of three inches in the bore of the shell guns of the two ships. Still the disparity was not so great but that I might hope to beat my enemy in a fair fight. But he did not show me a fair fight, for, as it afterward turned out, his ship was iron-clad. It was the same thing as if two men were to go out to fight a duel, and one of them, unknown to the other, were to put a shirt of mail under his outer garment. The days of chivalry being past, perhaps it would be unfair to charge Captain Winslow with deceit in withholding from me the fact that he meant to wear armor in the fight. He may have reasoned that it was my duty to find it out for myself. Besides, if he had disclosed this fact to me, and so prevented the engagement, the Federal Secretary of the Navy would have cut his head off to a certainty.

In the way of crew, the Kearsarge had one hundred and sixty-two, all told; the Alabama, one hundred and forty-nine. I had communicated my intention to fight this battle to Flag-Officer Barron, my senior officer in Paris, a few days before, and that officer had generously left the matter to my own discretion. I completed my preparations on Saturday evening, the 18th of June, and notified the Port Admiral of my intention to go out on the following morning. The next day dawned beautiful and bright. The cloudy, murky weather of some days past had cleared off, and a bright sun, a gentle breeze, and a smooth sea, were to be the concomitants of the battle. While I was still in my cot, the Admiral sent an officer off to say to me that the ironclad frigate Couronne would accompany me a part of the way out, to see that the neutrality of French waters was not violated. My crew had turned in early and gotten a good night's rest, and I permitted them to get their breakfasts comfortably—not turning them to until 9 o'clock—before any movement was made toward getting under way beyond lighting the fires in the furnaces.

I ought to mention that Midshipman Sinclair, son of Captain Terry Sinclair, of the Confederate Navy, whom I had sent with Low, as his first lieutenant in the Tuscaloosa, being in Paris when we arrived, had come down on the eve of the engagement, accompanied by his father, and endeavored to rejoin me, but was prevented by the French authorities. It is opportune, also, to state that, in view of possible contingencies, I had directed Galt, my acting paymaster, to send on shore, for safe keeping, the funds of the ship and complete pay-rolls of the crew, showing the state of the account of each officer and man.

The day being Sunday and the weather fine, a large concourse of people — many having come all the way from Paris — collected on the heights above the town, in the upper stories of such of the houses as commanded a view of the sea and on the walls and fortifications of the harbor. Several French luggers employed as pilot-boats went out, and also an English steam yacht called the Deerhound. Everything being in readiness between 9 and 10 o'clock we got under way and proceeded to sea, through the western entrance of the harbor; the Couronne following us. As we emerged from behind the mole, we discovered the Kearsarge at a distance of between six and seven miles from the land. She had been apprised of our intention of coming out that morning, and was awaiting us. The Couronne anchored a short distance outside of the harbor.

We were three-quarters of an hour in running out to the Kearsarge, during which time we had gotten our people to quarters, cast loose the battery and made all the other necessary preparations for battle. The yards had been previously slung in chains, stoppers prepared for the rigging, and preventer braces rove. It only remained to open the magazine and shell-rooms, sand down the decks, and fill the requisite number of tubs with water. The crew had been particularly neat in their dress on that morning and the officers were all in the uniforms appropriate to their rank. As we were approaching the enemy's ship, I caused the crew to be sent aft, within convenient reach of my voice, and, mounting a gun-carriage, delivered them the following brief address. I had not spoken to them in this formal way since I had addressed them on the memorable occasion of commissioning the ship:

THE CONFEDERATE CRUISER ALABAMA LEAVING THE MERCHANT SHIP BRILLIANT, OCTOBER 3, 1862, AFTER PLACING HER UNDER BOND.

Officers and seamen of the Alabama! You have, at length, another opportunity of meeting the enemy, the first that has been presented to you since you sunk the Hatteras! In the meantime you have been all over the world, and it is not too much to say that you have destroyed and driven for protection under neutral flags one-half of the enemy's commerce, which, at the beginning of the war, covered every sea. This is an achievement of which you may well be proud, and a grateful country will not be unmindful of it. The name of your ship has become a household word wherever civilization extends. Shall that name be tarnished by defeat? The thing is impossible! Remember that you are in the English Channel, the theater of so much of the naval glory of our race, and that the eyes of all Europe are at this moment upon you. The flag that floats over you is that of a young republic, who bids defiance to her enemies whenever and wherever found. Show the world that you know how to uphold it! Go to your quarters.

The utmost silence prevailed during the delivery of this address, broken only once in an enthusiastic outburst of Never! Never! when I asked my sailors if they would permit the name of their ship to be tarnished by defeat.

My official report of the engagement, addressed to Flag-Officer Barron, in Paris, will describe what now took place. It was written in Southampton, England, two days after the battle:

SOUTHAMPTON, June 21, 1864.

Sir: I have the honor to inform you that, in accordance with my intention as previously announced to you, I steamed out of the harbor of Cherbourg between 9 and 10 o'clock on the morning of the 19th of June, for the purpose of engaging the enemy's steamer Kearsarge, which had been lying off and in the port for several days previously. After clearing the harbor we descried the enemy with his head off shore, at the distance of about seven miles. We were three-quarters of an hour in coming up with him. I had previously pivoted my guns to starboard, and made all preparations for engaging the enemy on that side. When within about a mile and a quarter of the enemy he suddenly wheeled, and bringing his head inshore, presented his starboard battery to me. By this time we were distant about one mile from each other, when I opened on him with solid shot, to which he replied in a few minutes, and the action became active on both sides. The enemy now pressed his ship under a full head of steam, and to prevent our passing each other too speedily and to keep our respective broadsides bearing, it became necessary to fight in a circle, the two ships steaming around in a common center and preserving a distance from each other of from three-quarters to half a mile. When we got within good shell range we opened upon him with shell. Some ten or fifteen minutes after the commencement of the action our spanker gaff was shot away and our ensign came down by the run. This was immediately replaced by another at the mizzen mast-head. The firing now became very hot, and the enemy's shot and shell soon began to tell upon our hull, knocking down, killing and disabling a number of men at the same time in different parts of the ship. Perceiving that our shell, though apparently exploding against the enemy's sides, were doing him but little damage, I returned to solid-shot firing, and from this time onward alternated with shot and shell.

THE ALABAMA ENCOUNTERING A SEVERE STORM OFF THE STRAITS OF MAGELLAN.

After the lapse of about one hour and ten minutes our ship was ascertained to be in a sinking condition, the enemy's shell having exploded in our side and between decks, opening large apertures through which the water rushed with great rapidity. For some few minutes I had hopes of being able to reach the French coast, for which purpose I gave the ship all steam and set such of the fore and aft sails as were available. The ship filled so rapidly, however, that before we had made much progress the fires were extinguished in the furnaces and we were evidently on the point of sinking. I now hauled down my colors, to prevent the further destruction of life, and dispatched a boat to inform the enemy of our condition. Although we were now but four hundred yards from each other, the enemy fired upon me five times after my colors had been struck. It is charitable to suppose that a ship of war of a Christian nation could not have done this intentionally.

We now directed all our exertions toward saving the wounded and such of the boys of the ship as were unable to swim. These were dispatched in my quarter boats, the only boats remaining to me, the waist boats having been torn to pieces. Some twenty minutes after my furnace fires had been extinguished and when the ship was on the point of settling, every man, in obedience to a previous order which had been given the crew, jumped overboard and endeavored to save himself. There was no appearance of any boat coming to me from the enemy until after my ship went down. Fortunately, however, the steam yacht Deerhound, owned by a gentleman of Lancashire, England—Mr. John Lancaster —who was himself on board, steamed up in the midst of my drowning men and rescued a number of both officers and men from the water. I was fortunate enough myself thus to escape to the shelter of the neutral flag, together with about forty others all told. About this time the Kearsarge sent one, and then, tardily, another boat.

Accompanying, you will find lists of the killed and wounded and of those who were picked up by the enemy and by a couple of French pilot-boats, which were also fortunately near the scene of action. At the end of the engagement it was discovered by those of our officers who went alongside of the enemy's ship with the wounded that her midship section on both sides was thoroughly ironcoated, this having been done with chains constructed for the purpose, placed perpendicularly from the rail to the water's edge, the whole covered over by a thin outer planking, which gave no indication of the armor beneath. This planking had been ripped off in every direction by our shot and shell, the chain broken and indented in many places and forced partly into the ship's side. She was effectually guarded in this section from penetration.

My officers and men behaved steadily and gallantly, and though they have lost their ship they have not lost honor. Where all behaved so well it would be invidious to particularize, but I can not deny myself the pleasure of saying that Mr. Kell, my first lieutenant, deserves great credit for the fine condition in which the ship went into action with regard to her battery, magazine and shell-rooms, and that he rendered me great assistance by his coolness and judgment as the fight proceeded.

The enemy was heavier than myself, both in ship, battery and crew; but I did not know until the action was over that she was also ironclad. Our total loss in killed and wounded is 30, to-wit: 9 killed and 21 wounded.

With the greatest respect, I am your obedient servant,

RAPHAEL SEMMES.

It was afterward ascertained that as many as ten were drowned. As stated in the above dispatch, I had the satisfaction of saving all my wounded men. Every one of them was passed carefully into a boat and sent off to the enemy's ship, before the final plunge into the sea was made by the unhurt portion of the crew. Here is the proper place to drop a tear over the fate of a brave officer. My surgeon, D. H. Llewellyn, of Wiltshire, England, a grandson of Lord Herbert, lost his life by drowning. It was his privilege to accompany the wounded men in the boats, to the Kearsarge, but he did not do so. He remained and took his chance of escape, with the rest of his brethren in arms, and perished almost in sight of his home, after an absence of two years from the dear ones who were to mourn his loss.

PAY TABLE OF THE CONFEDERATE STATES CRUISER ALABAMA.

CREW.	Pay per Month.
Master-at-Arms	$29 04
Yeoman	29 04
Ship's Steward	29 04
Ship's Corporal	26 62
Armorer	29 04
Ship's Cook	26 62
Chief Boatswain's Mate	29 04
Second Boatswain's Mate	26 62
Gunner's Mate	29 04
Carpenter's Mate	29 04
Sailmaker's Mate	26 62
Quartermasters	26 62
Quarter Gunners	26 62
Cockswains	26 62
Captain of Forecastle	26 62
Captains of Tops	24 20
Captains of Afterguard	24 20
Captains of Hold	24 20
Cabin Steward	24 20
Wardroom Steward	24 20
Seamen	21 78
Ordinary Seamen	19 36
Landsmen	14 94
Boys	9 68
Firemen	33 88
Trimmers	24 20

THE FIGHT AT CLOSE RANGE BETWEEN THE ALABAMA AND KEARSARGE.

CAPTURE OF THE U. S. GUNBOAT WATERWITCH.

BY

LIEUTENANT JOSEPH PRICE.

AT 8 o'clock P. M., June 2, 1864, the expedition got under way, and formed two columns—boats Nos. 1, 3, 5 and 7 composing the port column; Nos. 2, 4 and 6 the starboard column. Lieutenant Thomas P. Pelot, commanding, with Second Assistant Engineer Caldwell, Confederate States Navy, and Moses Dallas (colored) pilot, led in boat No. 1; Lieutenant Price, with Master's Mate Gray and Second Assistant Engineer Fabins, in No. 2; Midshipman Minor, with Master's Mate Freeman, in boat No. 3; Midshipman Trimble in boat No. 4; Boatswain Seymour, with Master's Mate Baccalay, in boat No 5; Master's Mate H. Golder, with Assistant Surgeon Thomas, in boat No. 6; Master's Mate Rostler, with Assistant Surgeon Jones, in boat No. 7; and proceeded with muffled oars to the spot where we supposed the enemy's vessel to be. On arriving we found that she had either shifted her anchorage or that we had been mistaken as to her position. After searching in vain until nearly daylight, Lieutenant Pelot ordered Boatswain Seymour, with one man, to remain on Racoon Keys as scouts, and the expedition to return to camp at Beaulair battery.

On the next day (June 3d) at 9 o'clock P. M., we got under way and proceeded to Racoon Keys, where we took on board our scouts, who reported that one of the enemy's vessels was lying at Ossabow Sound, about three miles from where we then were. After waiting there until midnight, we were ordered to get under way and pull cautiously. The night being dark and rainy, we got close aboard of her without being discovered. On being hailed, Lieutenant Pelot answered we were "rebels," and gave the order to "board" her. The vessel having steam up at the time, as soon as the alarm was given commenced turning her wheels backward and forward rapidly, thus thwarting the earnest efforts of Boatswain Seymour and Master's Mate Rostler to get on board with the entire boat's crew.

The port column, led by Lieutenant Pelot, boarded on the port side; starboard column, led by Lieutenant Price, boarded on the starboard side. In coming alongside, the enemy's fire with small arms was quite severe; in fact it was during that time, and while the boarding netting, which was triced up, was being cut through, that the most of our loss in killed and wounded was sustained. After a sharp hand-to-hand fight of some ten minutes, the ship was taken. Lieutenant Pelot was the first to gain the deck, and while bravely fighting was shot and instantly killed. In his death the country has lost a brave and gallant officer, and society one of her highest ornaments.

The command then devolved upon me, and I proceeded forthwith to extricate the vessel from the position she was then in to avoid recapture by the enemy. Our pilot having been killed before the boats reached the side of the ship, I sought for the enemy's pilot and found that he was too badly wounded to assist me, but finally procured one of the quartermasters, whom I compelled to pilot me to the upper end of the Racoon Key, where, at the top of high water, the ship grounded. I then found it necessary to lighten her, which I did by throwing overboard some barrels of beef and pork, a few coils of hemp rigging, the remainder of the chain, which I had slipped as soon as we took the vessel, and lowering two of the guns into the boats. On getting ashore I immediately landed the killed, wounded and prisoners at Beaulair battery. At 4 o'clock P. M., having in the meantime obtained a pilot from the shore, I succeeded in getting off, and anchored her at 7 o'clock P. M. under the guns of Beaulair battery, above the obstructions, when Lieutenant W. W. Carnes, Confederate States Navy, arrived on board and assumed command.

In the darkness and confusion on board it was impossible for me to observe each and every man; but I will state with pride, every one, officers and men, did their duty most gallantly. I would state, however, that I owe my life to E. D. Davis, ordinary seaman, of the Confederate States steamer Savannah, he having cut down every opponent when I was sorely pressed by them.

Boatswain's Mate J. Perry, of the steamer Savannah, and Boatswain's Mate W. S. Johnston, of the steamer Sampson, rendered me most valuable assistance in lightening the vessel and in general duties on board. The former, although severely wounded, remained on deck as long as he could.

* * * * * *

JOSEPH PRICE,
Lieutenant C. S. Navy.

BATTLE OF MOBILE BAY,

AUGUST 5, 1864.

BY

ADMIRAL FRANKLIN BUCHANAN.

U. S. NAVAL HOSPITAL,
PENSACOLA, August 26, 1864.

THE enemy's fleet, under Admiral Farragut, consisting of fourteen steamers and four monitors, passed Fort Morgan on the 5th instant, about 6:30 A. M., in following order, and stood into Mobile Bay: The four monitors—Tecumseh and Manhattan, each carrying two 15-inch guns; the Winnebago and Chickasaw, each carrying four 11-inch guns—in a single line ahead, about half a mile from the fort; the fourteen steamers—Brooklyn, of 26; Octorara, 10; Hartford, 28; Metacomet, 10; Richmond, 24; Port Royal, 8; Lackawanna, 14; Seminole, 9; Monongahela, 12; Kennebec, 5; Ossipee, 13; Itasca, 4; Oneida, 10; and Galena, 14 guns—in a double line ahead, each two lashed together, the side-wheel steamers off shore, all about one-quarter of a mile from the monitors, carrying in all 199 guns and 2,700 men. When they were discovered standing into the channel, signal was made to the Mobile squadron, under my command, consisting of the wooden gunboats Morgan and Gaines, each carrying 6 guns, and Selma, 4, to "follow my motions" in the ram Tennessee, of 6 guns; in all 22 guns and 470 men. All were soon under way and stood toward the enemy in a line abreast. As the Tennessee approached the fleet, when opposite the fort, we opened our battery at short range upon the leading ship, the admiral's flag-ship Hartford, and made the attempt to run into her, but owing to her superior speed, our attempt was frustrated. We then stood toward the next heavy ship, the Brooklyn, with the same view; she also avoided us by her superior speed. During this time the gunboats were also closely engaged with the enemy. All our guns were used to the greatest advantage, and we succeeded in seriously damaging many of the enemy's vessels. The Selma and Gaines, under Lieutenant-Commanders P. U. Murphy and J.W. Bennett, fought gallantly, and I was satisfied to hear from officers of the enemy's fleet that their fire was very destructive.

ADMIRAL FRANKLIN BUCHANAN, OF MARYLAND.

SINKING OF THE ALABAMA. THE ENGLISH YACHT DEERHOUND RESCUING A PORTION OF THE CREW.

The Gaines was fought until she was found to be in a sinking condition, when she was run on shore near Fort Morgan. Lieutenant-Commander Murphy was closely engaged with the Metacomet, assisted by the Morgan, Commander G. W. Harrison, when, upon the approach of another steamer, the Selma surrendered. Lieutenant-Commander Murphy lost two promising young officers, Lieutenant Comstock and Master's Mate Murphy, and a number of his men were killed and wounded, and he was also wounded severely in the wrist. Soon after the gunboats were dispersed by the overwhelming superiority of force, and the enemy's fleet had anchored about four miles above Fort Morgan, we stood for them again in the Tennessee and renewed the attack with the hope of sinking some of them with our prow; again we were foiled by their superior speed in avoiding us. The engagement with the whole fleet soon became general at very close quarters, and lasted about one hour; and notwithstanding the serious injury inflicted upon many of their vessels by our guns, we could not sink them.

Frequently, during the contest, we were surrounded by the enemy, and all our guns were in action almost at the same moment. Four of the heaviest vessels ran into us, under full steam, with the view of sinking us; one vessel, the Monongahela, had been prepared as a ram, and was very formidable. She struck us with great force, injuring us but little. Her prow and stern were knocked off and the vessel so much injured as to make it necessary to dock her. Several of the other vessels of the fleet were found to require extensive repairs.

After I was carried below, unfortunately wounded, I had to be governed by the reports of that valuable officer, Commander J. D. Johnston, as to the condition of the ship and the necessity and time of her surrender, and when he represented to me her utterly hopeless condition to continue the fight with injury to the enemy and suggested her surrender, I directed him to do the best he could, and when he could no longer damage the enemy, to do so. It affords me much pleasure to state that the officers and men cheerfully fought their guns to the best of their abilities, and gave strong evidence, by their promptness in executing orders, of their willingness to continue the contest as long as they could stand to their guns, notwithstanding the fatigue they had undergone for several hours, and it was only because the circumstances were as represented by Captain Johnston, that she was surrendered to the fleet about 10 A. M., painful as it was to do so. I seriously felt the want of experienced officers during the action; all were young and inexperienced, and many had but little familiarity with naval duties, having been appointed from civil life within the year.

Fleet Surgeon D. B. Conrad accompanied the wounded

of the Tennessee and Selma to this hospital, assisted by Assistant Surgeons Booth and Bowles, of the Selma and Tennessee, all under the charge of Fleet Surgeon Palmer, of the United States Navy, from whom we have received all the attention and consideration we could desire or expect. The crews and many officers of the Tennessee and Selma were sent to New Orleans. Commander J. D. Johnston, Lieutenant-Commandant P. U. Murphy, Lieutenants W. L. Bradford and A. D. Wharton, Second Assistant Engineer J. C. O'Connell and myself are to be sent North; Master's Mates W. S. Forrest and R. M. Carter, who are with me, acting as my aids, not having any midshipmen, are permitted to accompany me. They are valuable young officers, zealous in their duties, and both have served in the army, where they received honorable wounds; their services are important to me.

September 17, 1864.

Since writing the above I have seen the report of Admiral Farragut, a portion of which is incorrect. Captain Johnston did not deliver my sword on board the Hartford. After the surrender of the Tennessee, Captain Girand, the officer who was sent on board to take charge of her, said to me that he was directed by Admiral Farragut to ask for my sword, which was brought from the cabin and delivered to him by one of my aids.

F. BUCHANAN,
Admiral, Commanding.

OPERATIONS IN MOBILE BAY,

AUGUST 2 TO 23, 1864.

BY

BRIGADIER-GENERAL R. L. PAGE,
Commanding Fort Morgan and the Outer Defenses of Mobile Bay.

FORT MORGAN, August 6, 1864.

I HAVE the honor to report that at 6 o'clock yesterday morning the enemy's fleet, consisting of twenty-three men-of-war, of which four were monitors, moved up in line to pass this fort, the monitors leading, the wooden vessels lashed together in two's, following, the sloops of war and larger craft on the inshore side protecting their consorts, which could convoy them in should they be seriously damaged. The first monitor, Tecumseh, single-turreted, was sunk under our guns immediately abreast the fort. She went down rapidly; only a few, who were picked up by a boat from the enemy, and four who swam ashore and are now in our hands, were saved from her crew. The wooden gunboat, Philippi, was sunk by the second shot and after being run ashore was deserted by her crew, and afterward burned by a boat from the Confederate States gunboat Morgan. One man was found in her whose legs had been so shattered that he died while the officer was on board. He was thrown overboard.

The spirit displayed by the garrison was fine, the guns admirably served, and all did their duty nobly; and though subjected to a fire which for a time was probably as severe as any known in the annals of war, our casualties were slight.

Four of the fleet, when discovering what a fire they would have to encounter in passing, turned back and assisted other vessels in an enfilading fire from the gulf side during the action. As to the damage inflicted on those which succeeded in passing, I can not speak definitely. Shot after shot was distinctly seen to enter the wooden ships, but, as was evident, their machinery being protected by chains, no vital blow could be given them there. Their loss in men, I am assured, was vey great.

Four hundred and ninety-one projectiles were delivered from this fort during the passage of the fleet. Our naval forces, under Admiral Buchanan, fought most gallantly against odds before unknown to history.

Yesterday morning at daylight Colonel Anderson communicated with enemy by flag of truce without my sanction. I immediately asked him, by signal, the purpose of it. He made no acknowledgment, though I fired signal guns to gain his attention, and telegraphed repeatedly in case he was on lookout, but unable to make signal, "Hold on to your fort." I went there last night and was greatly surprised to find Colonel Anderson absent in the fleet making terms for surrender. I gave peremptory orders on his return if the enemy did not return with him all terms were annulled and he was relieved from command. This morning fired signal guns and telegraphed same effect. No reply. At 9:30 o'clock enemy's flag hoisted on Fort Gaines. Colonel Anderson's conduct inexplicable and disgraceful. On the 4th I visited Gaines, encouraged the garrison and found good feeling. All my orders have been for protracted resistance.

HEADQUARTERS THIRD BRIGADE,
DISTRICT OF THE GULF,
FORT MORGAN, August 8, 1864.

After the entrance of the enemy's fleet into the bay when this outer line was taken in the rear, Colonel Anderson commanding the western part of the line, Gaines, Powell and Cedar Point, signaled me as to the holding the last position, and was ordered to do so as long as it was tenable. In the afternoon Colonel Williams, commanding Fort Powell, after a bombardment from monitors in the rear of that work, telegraphed to this effect: "My rear not defensible. I must evacuate to-night or surrender in forty-eight hours;" and was replied to: "When no longer tenable save your garrison. Hold on as long as you can." During the night a fire and explosion occurred there, and my conjecture was that he had evacuated, which was confirmed by the occupation of it by the enemy on the next morning.

On the 4th instant I visited Gaines, encouraged the garrison, and had the assurance from Colonel Anderson of a protracted and determined resistance. On the morning of the 5th, Colonel Anderson's dispatch was to this effect: "The enemy are planting batteries in the sand-hills within easy range. If the fleet opens upon me from the other direction I can not cover more than half of my men, but will do the best I can. My situation is critical." To which my reply said: "Do your best and keep the men in good cheer. . . . ." Later he telegraphed: " . . . . We will emulate our glorious old admiral and do our very best;" and on the next day (the 6th) that "the enemy are planting mortar batteries in the sand-hills," and that "all his heavy guns save one were disabled" (these were, however, afterward got in working order), "and they (the enemy) are pushing up their batteries and intrenchments vigorously." Colonel Anderson, that afternoon, having received something of an attack from two monitors, though without serious injury to his works or loss of men, thought his position precarious, and inquired of me could I do anything in his behalf, and requested that an officer be sent to consult with him some time in the night. This was complied with, and the officers sent were ordered to urge Colonel Anderson to make a determined resistance and keep his hold on his fort to the last extremity. They were of the impression that such was his design on their return.

Early on the morning of the 7th I was astonished to receive report from my lookout that a flag of truce had proceeded from Fort Gaines to the enemy's fleet. I could hardly believe that Colonel Anderson would do so without my sanction. I immediately signaled him, "What is flag of truce boat for? Answer at once;" and when I received no reply in acknowledgment, after firing a gun to get his attention, this, "Hold on to your fort." After a short time, receiving no response, another signal gun was fired and the dispatch repeated.

At sundown a flag of truce was reported from the enemy's fleet to Gaines, and there remained some time. Immediately after I took a small boat and crossed over, and can convey no conception of my utter astonishment at

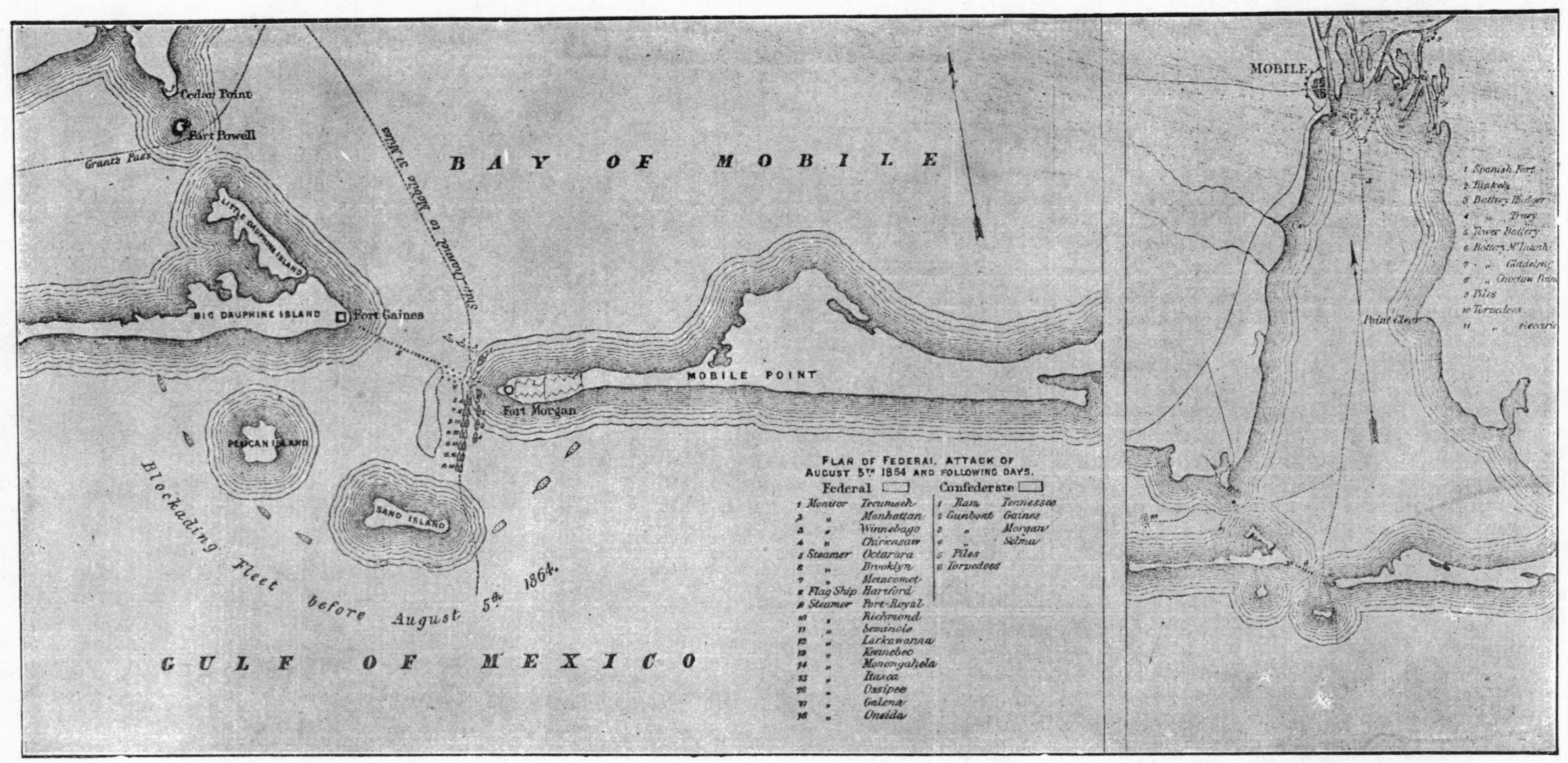

CHART SHOWING POSITION OF CONFEDERATE FORTS AND VESSELS, AND OF THE FEDERAL FLEET PASSING FORT MORGAN. ALSO CHART OF MOBILE BAY UP TO THE CITY OF MOBILE, SHOWING FORTS AND OBSTRUCTIONS.

KILLED AND WOUNDED OF CONFEDERATE FLEET IN ACTION OF AUGUST 5, 1864, MOBILE BAY.

Tennessee, flagship: Killed—John Silk, first-class fireman; William Marrs, seaman—2. Wounded—Admiral F. Buchanan, fracture right leg; A. T. Post, pilot, slightly in head; J. C. O'Connell, second assistant engineer, slightly in head and shoulder; James Kelly, boatswain's mate, slightly in knee; Andrew Racmison, quartermaster, slightly in head, William Daly, seaman, in head, Robert Barry, marine, gunshot wound of ear and head; James McKunn, marine, contusion of shoulder—9.

Selma, P. U. Murphy, lieutenant commanding: Killed—J. H. Comstock, lieutenant and executive officer; J. R. Murray, acting master's mate; William Hall, gunner's mate; James Rooney, seaman; James Montgomery, seaman; Bernard Riley, ordinary seaman; J. R. Frisly, landsman; Christopher Shepherd, landsman—8. Wounded—P. U. Murphy, lieutenant commanding, slightly in wrist; John Villa, seaman, badly, leg and arm; Henry Fratee, landsman, badly in hand; Daniel Linnehan, seaman, slightly in arm; John Shick, seaman, slightly in face; John Davis, fireman, slightly; John Gilliland, seaman, slightly—7. Total killed, 10; wounded, 16.

D. B. CONRAD,
Fleet Surgeon, C. S. Navy.

A DAY or so after the old First reached Manassas Junction, in August, 1861, one of the men, who did not clearly comprehend his position, had the impudence to ask General Beauregard where certain big guns that had just arrived from Richmond would be placed. The general replied: "Young man, if the coat on my back knew the secrets of my heart I would cut it in pieces."

finding that the flag of truce of the morning was to ask for terms of surrender from the enemy; that Colonel Anderson had ordered his signal corps [not] to reply to nor acknowledge any of my dispatches (such being, as he strangely conceived, a breach of honor of the flag of the morning, as I learned from his adjutant); that he was absent in the enemy's fleet making terms of surrender, and what is still more unaccountable, that he had so far proceeded, though my dispatches of the morning asking the purpose of his flag and ordering him to hold on to his fort had been received and reported to him by his signal corps, when I had given orders to Major Johnston, the next in command, that on the return of Colonel Anderson, if the disgraceful proceeding had not been completed and the

Commander Richard L. Page, of Virginia, C. S. N.
Also Brigadier-General, C. S. A.

capitulation made in binding form, all terms were annulled, all communications with the enemy were to cease, and he would relieve Colonel Anderson of command and order him to Fort Morgan. After I had given these instructions, on the approach of the return of the enemy's flag, fearing from what I had learned that Colonel Anderson would probably bring with him some of the enemy to receive the surrender, I returned to Fort Morgan, hoping that he should soon follow me and Major Johnston be left in command. This morning our flag flying at Gaines, and Colonel Anderson not having reported during the night, I dispatched him, after a signal gun: "Stop communicating with the enemy; all terms or stipulations made by you are annulled;" and when he made no reply, after another signal gun, to Major Johnston: "Colonel Anderson is relieved from command. You assume it and stop communicating with the enemy. All terms annulled." Both these dispatches, the officer who had the transmission of them, feels confident were received. The signal men were at their usual station on the lookout. At 9:30 o'clock the enemy's flag was hoisted over Gaines, the evidence and the emblem of the consummation of the deed of dishonor and disgrace to its commander and garrison.

Very respectfully your obedient servant,

R. L. Page,
Brigadier-General Commanding.

Major-General D. H. Maury,
Commanding, etc., Mobile.

Fort Morgan, August 23, 1864, 12 M.

I held the fort as long as it was tenable. The parallels of the enemy had reached the glacis, the walls were breached, all the guns save two were disabled. The woodwork of the citadel being repeatedly fired by the shells of the enemy endangered the magazines. All my powder was destroyed, every gun effectually spiked and otherwise damaged and, indeed, the whole fort (everything that could prove of value to the enemy) is now a mass of debris. I turn this over to their forces at 2 o'clock to-day. The garrison behaved gallantly and gained honor for themselves and country. Respectfully, etc.,

R. L. Page,
Brigadier-General.

New Orleans, August 30, 1864.

Report of the evacuation of Fort Powell and the surrender of Fort Gaines, I had the honor of addressing you from Fort Morgan on the 8th instant. It embraced the military operations to that date. After the reduction of Gaines I felt confident that the whole naval and land force of the enemy would be brought against Morgan, and was assiduous in preparing my fort for as good a defense as possible. For the state of the works I beg leave to refer you to Chief Engineer Sheliha's letter to headquarters department, of July 9th, from which time no material change or addition was made, and further to state that it had been demonstrated by the fire from the enemy that the enceinte of the fort (in which was its main strength) protected the scarp of the main wall only about one-half its height from curveted shots; that it was now in the power of the enemy to open fire from every point of the compass, and consequently none of the casemates without heavy traverses in their front would be safe; that it was manifest by this concentration of fire my heavy guns could soon be dismounted, and my making a protracted resistance depended on my ability to protect my men from the heavy fire and hold the fort from the flank casemates against an assault. With these views I employed my men day and night, most of the time under fire, in erecting traverses to protect my guns on the main wall as long as possible, to render the casemate selected for the sick and wounded secure, and provide safe quarters for themselves in their rest from the arduous duties they would have to endure. It was necessary also to put a large traverse at the sally-port which was entirely exposed. Thus, absolutely to prevent the probability of Fort Morgan's being reduced at the first test and onset by the heavy batteries of the enemy, it was necessary for my limited garrison (of some four hundred effective) to labor to perform a work equal almost in extent to building a new fort.

On the early morning of the 9th the enemy proceeded with monitors and transports and disembarked troops at Navy Cove, commencing at once their first work of investment by land. The new redoubt (2,700 yards from the fort) from which the guns had been withdrawn, and the work formerly known as Battery Bragg, were destroyed as far as possible by burning the woodwork; the buildings around the fort (hospitals, quarters, stables, etc.), were also this morning fired and cleared away as much as possible. Two monitors, three sloops of war, and several gunboats engaged the fort for two or three hours (the wooden vessels at rather long range) with no material damage apparent to either side. Soon thereafter a flag of truce was reported from the fleet and communicated to this effect:

Brigadier-General R. L. Page, Commanding Fort Morgan:

Sir: To prevent the unnecessary sacrifice of human life, which must follow the opening of our batteries, we demand the unconditional surrender of Fort Morgan and its dependencies.

We are, very respectfully, your obedient servants,

D. G. Farragut,
Rear-Admiral.
Gordon Granger,
Major-General.

To which my reply said:

Sirs: I am prepared to sacrifice life, and will only surrender when I have no means of defense. I do not understand that while being communicated with under flag of truce the Tennessee should be towed within range of my guns. Respectfully, etc.,

R. L. Page,
Brigadier-General, C. S. Army.

From this time to the fifteenth day and night, we were engaged by the fleet, sometimes in a brisk fight of several hours' duration, at others in a desultory firing, without any very effective damage being done to our fort save a demonstration of the fact that our brick walls were easily penetrable to the heavy missiles of the enemy and that a systematic, concentrated fire would soon breach them. On the 15th, three of the 15-inch shells striking the right-flank face of bastion No. 4, breached the wall and disabled the flank howitzers therein. During this time a pretty continuous fire was kept up on the fort from the Parrott guns in several batteries erected by the enemy. In the intervals of serving the guns my men were engaged in the work, before mentioned, for their protection in the anticipation of a vigorous bombardment. The sharpshooters in our front had become very numerous and active, and with these encircling us on the land and the fire delivered from the fleet on the flanks, our guns had to be served with much care and under great difficulty.

The land forces of the enemy completed their first approach on the 9th and 10th across the peninsula; the second, through 11th and 12th; the third (a bayou near and parallel to gulf shore), 13th and 14th; their first parallel, five hundred and seven hundred yards distant, 15th, night, 16th, 17th, 18th, 19th; approaches on 20th, 21st, night, to within two hundred yards of our glacis. Such guns as I could use on this force I annoyed them with, especially at night, and to the extent possible retarded their work, though nothing very effective could be accomplished in this way as their working parties were well concealed in the sand hills, and when our fire was concentrated on any one point they would merely, unseen, remove to some other.

To the morning of the 22d, our efforts were with the heavy guns that bore on them to interfere with the investing approaches of the enemy. The topography of our front, however, was to their advantage, and they made a steady advance, covering it somewhat with an irregular fire from the batteries already in position, and lining their works already completed with sharpshooters to pick off our gunners. At daylight the fleet was reported moving up to encircle us, and shortly its batteries, in conjunction with those on land, which numbered thirty-six guns and mortars, opened a furious fire, which came from almost every point of the compass, and continued unabated throughout the day, culminating in increased force at sundown, after which the heavy calibers and mortars kept it up during the night. This fire disabled all the heavy guns save two, which did not bear on the land approach, partially breached the walls in several places and cut up the fort to such extent as to make the whole work a mere mass of debris. Their mortar practice was accurate. Apprehensive, from the great effect already had on the walls, that my magazines, containing now eighty thousand pounds, were in danger in continuation of the bombardment in the night, with great care and under continuous fire I had the powder brought out and flooded. The guns in the water and lunette batteries, now unserviceable and in jeopardy from the enemy, I ordered spiked and otherwise effectually damaged. All the guns on the main rampart dismounted by the fire from the enemy were to-night likewise destroyed as of no further avail in defense. Early in the night the woodwork of the citadel was fired by the mortar shells and burned furiously for some hours, the enemy, during the conflagration, pouring in his missiles with increased vigor. With great efforts the fire was arrested and prevented extending around near the magazines, which would have been in imminent danger of explosion. In the gallant endeavor to prevent this disaster, I would especially mention privates Murphy, Bumbaugh and Stevens, First Tennessee, for great courage and daring displayed.

At daylight on 23d (all my powder had then been destroyed) the citadel was again set on fire in several places by shells and burned until it was consumed. The report now made to me was that the casemates, which had been rendered as safe as possible for the men, some had been breached, others partially (Captains Johnston, Fisher and Hughes informed me that another shot on them would bring down the walls of their company quarters), so that a resumption of the severe fire from the

Fort Morgan, Commanding the Entrance to Mobile Bay.

enemy would in all likelihood inflict great loss of life, there being no bomb-proof in the fort. The enemy's approach was very near the glacis. My guns and powder had all been destroyed; my means of defense gone; the citadel, nearly the entire quartermaster's store and a portion of the commissariat burned by the enemy's shells. It was now evident the fort could hold out but a few hours longer under a renewed bombardment. The only question was, Hold it for this time, gain the eclat, and sustain the loss of life from the falling of the walls, or save the life and capitulate. I capitulated to the enemy at 2 P. M., and though they refused to insert it in the terms, there was a full understanding, and I was assured, that my sick and wounded should be sent at once to Mobile by a flag of truce. This was not done. Considering the great exposure to which the men were subjected, and the fact that shells frequently burst among them when in the casemates, the casualties were unusually small.

The garrison in this severe test behaved well, and I would make little distinction. Captain J. Gallimard, engineer in charge, performed his duties to my satisfaction. To the officers of the First Alabama Battalion of Artillery, Major J. T. Gee, commanding, and of Captain Cothran's company, Twenty-first Alabama, I give my thanks for their promptness and alacrity in every duty, and to Colonel Jackson, commanding First Tennessee, and Captains Johnston and Fisher, and their brave companies of that regiment, for very efficient service. To Captain C. H. Smith, assistant adjutant-general, and Captain R. T. Thorn, assistant inspector-general, for prompt performance of all their duties, I am under obligations, and to my aid-de-camp, J. C. Taylor, I owe much for his promptness and energy and for his active and gallant assistance throughout the operations.

* * * * * * *

R. L. PAGE, *Brigadier-General.*

BATTLE OF MOBILE BAY,

AUGUST 5, 1864.

BY

LIEUT.-COM. PATRICK U. MURPHY,

Commanding Gunboat Selma.

PENSACOLA HOSPITAL,
August 5, 1864.

BETWEEN 5 and 6 of the morning of the 5th it was reported to me a move was made by the fleet outside. I gave the order at once to get up steam, to weigh the anchor, and to lash it securely, then to go to breakfast, and, if we had time, for the crew to dress themselves in their best clothes. The Selma was lying to the south and east of the flagship, and much nearer the shore. After the anchor was weighed, the steamer drifted up with the tide to the northward and eastward. While the crew were at breakfast the engagement commenced, and many shots were fired by both sides before I went to quarters; but as soon as the crew were through with their breakfast and the decks were cleared up, I went to quarters and stood to northward and westward, and as soon as I passed the stern of the Tennessee I opened fire on the enemy with all my guns, and continued to fire all of them for some time. When I perceived the Metacomet was towing the leading vessel (the Hartford) I gave the order to give her all the steam they could, that I might get ahead and on the port side of her. My intention was perceived, and before I could get into the position I wanted the Metacomet cast off and gave chase. A constant fire had been kept up all the time, first at one vessel, then at another, as the opportunity offered. Before the Metacomet cast off, my best gunner had been killed by a piece of shell from the Hartford, I think; but several vessels were firing at me at the same time, and in a short time my next best met the same fate. The fight was then with the Metacomet, carrying ten guns, eight 9-inch and two 100-pounder Parrotts, one of the fastest vessels of their squadron. She tried hard to rake me, but was prevented by good steering. The Metacomet being so much faster, came quite near, and one of her 9-inch shells killed and wounded seven at the same gun and disabled the gun. I had only been able to use two guns for some time, and the crew of No. 1 gun had just been sent off to assist in working those two. My first lieutenant, Mr. Comstock, and Master's Mate Murray, were both killed by the same shell, and myself wounded in the arm. After firing one or two shots more, I perceived the Metacomet was about to rake me with grape and shrapnel, and the Port Royal, a steamer of the same class, was about to open fire on me, when I gave the order to haul down the colors, as I did not believe I was justified in sacrificing more of my crew in such an unequal contest. My wound was bleeding fast. I knew if I left the deck for one moment the vessel might be sunk. My deck was a perfect slaughter-pen when I surrendered.

I can not speak too highly of the officers and crew under my command. Not the least confusion occurred during the action. The wounded were taken below and the men returned instantly to their quarters. The powder division, under the charge of Paymaster Richardson, was beautifully attended to; every charge and every shell was sent to the different guns without a single mistake.

P. U. MURPHY,
Lieutenant Commander, C. S. Navy.

OLD HUNTER was deaf as a post, and through his deafness and his shrewdness he managed to hide his sympathy for either Federal or Confederate. On one occasion a party drinking in his store to test the old man's deafness proposed the following toast: "Here's to old Hunter, the two-sided old villain; may he be kicked to death by mules and his body sunk in the sea a hundred fathoms deep. May no prayer be said over him, and his blind soul wander rayless through all eternity." The toast was drunk in great glee, in which the old man joined. "The same to yourselves, gentlemen," said he—"the same to yourselves." Of course he had not heard a word that was said.

BATTLE OF MOBILE BAY,

AUGUST 5, 1864.

BY

LIEUTENANT JOHN W. BENNETT,

Commanding Steamer Gaines.

MOBILE, ALA., August 8, 1864.

I HAVE the honor to submit a report of the part taken by the Gaines, under my command, in the action of the 5th inst. off Fort Morgan, and the circumstances which led to the beaching and abandonment of the ship.

The Gaines was cleared for action about 6:20 A. M., and in obedience to signal from the admiral to "follow his motions," waited for him to open upon the advancing enemy, advancing with four monitors in line ahead and fourteen wooden vessels by two's, each large ship having a smaller one lashed to her port side, the whole forming one compact line of battle. As soon as the Tennessee delivered fire, the Gaines, having placed herself next the admiral, commenced at about two thousand yards distance with her pivot-guns upon the leading wooden ships, supposed to be the Hartford and her consort, at about 6:50, as nearly as I can determine, and continued to deliver a raking fire upon the leading wooden ships until their passage past the fort. She then made one circle to prevent too close action, as she

BATTLE OF MOBILE BAY BETWEEN THE CONFEDERATE FLEET, FORT MORGAN AND THE FEDERAL FLEET OF GUNBOATS AND MONITORS.

was lying nearly in the track of the advancing fleet, and afterward steered in nearly parallel lines with the enemy at distance gradually diminishing until she was within at least seven hundred yards and engaging with her port guns. The enemy being now clear of the fort was enabled to direct attention exclusively to our little squadron. Early in the action a shell exploded near the steering wheel, wounding the two men stationed at it and cutting the wheel rope. The ship was then steered with the relieving tackles until the after wheel ropes could be repaired. Shortly after this it was reported that the forward magazine was filled with smoke and thought to be on fire. This on examination, luckily, proved a mistake. An 11-inch shot had entered the starboard bow, striking the deck above the magazine, had broken it in and made so much dust that the gunner's mate, serving powder in that magazine, thought it smoke, and believed, from the shock and dust, a shell had exploded and fired that part of the ship. He reported accordingly. This occasioned a short delay in the serving of powder to the forward division. The firemen of this division, with hose and buckets, went promptly to the spot, under the executive officer, and soon discovered the mistake. About this time the ship was subjected to a very heavy concentrated fire from the Hartford, Richmond, and others at short range as the enemy passed me. Nearly their whole fire seemed for a time to be directed at the Gaines. The after magazine was now discovered filling with water. I went below to examine it and found much water had accumulated in it and was rapidly increasing. Not being aware of any shot having entered near the water that part of the ship, and being unable to see any danger, upon inspection from the side, which could have caused such a leak, I directed the executive officer, with the carpenter's mate, to get into a boat and make examination of the counter. He found a shot had broken in the outer planking under the port quarter, about the water line, and which from marks seemed to have glanced below in the direction of the stern-post. This could not be stopped, by reason of the impossibility of getting to it, because of the flare of the counter. As this breach could not have caused all the water which flowed into the ship, I am of opinion that it was a shell which caused the break, and had probably exploded below water under the counter, and had started the timbers near the stern-post. The ship had received a shock during the engagement which shook her from stem to stern, being much more violent than that of shots passing through. The bilge pumps were immediately worked, but there was no water in the engine-room. Finding the magazine rapidly filling, also the after hold and shell-room, with no water in the engine-room, I caused the after bulkhead of the engine-room to be knocked down, so as to allow the flow of water to the bilge pumps. By this time the stern had settled some and the steering became difficult. Under these circumstances I determined to withdraw from action. The enemy's fleet had now passed. Finding the ship would sink in a short time, and thinking I might be able to reach the shore, now about two or three miles distant, I withdrew from the action and made the best of my way toward the fort, steering the ship principally with the side-wheel, which position I reached without embarrassment from the enemy (thanks to an opportune rain squall, which shut me from view) and placed her bow upon the beach within five hundred yards of Fort Morgan at about 9:30. I am happy to state there was no confusion nor panic under the circumstances of our position, but that every work was done with deliberation and without undue excitement. The ship delivered fire to the enemy at the moment of striking the shore.

ENGAGEMENT BETWEEN FORT MORGAN AND THE FEDERAL FLEET.

At the time of beaching the magazine was nearly filled. I had caused all the powder to be removed to the cabin. The shells were removed as rapidly as possible, but not before many of them had become submerged. The usefulness of the ship having been destroyed by the enemy, I devoted myself and crew to the preservation of all valuable material, and landed all the powder, shell, shot, gun equipment, etc., which I gave to the general commanding at Fort Morgan, to whom I thought they might be useful in the expected siege. The crew were then landed with their bags and blankets, muskets, cutlasses, small arms and ammunition, and the ship abandoned at 12 o'clock with her battle-flags flying and her stern settled as far as it could, about two fathoms. I did not spike the guns, because they could be secured by the fort and could not be taken by the enemy. Having then left my command, it became necessary to devise a retreat for my crew. They were not necessary to the fort, as I was informed when I offered their services. Already I had secured two boats belonging to the Tennessee, left by her at anchor, and with four boats of the Gaines, one having been destroyed by shot, I left the fort at 8 P. M., and reached Mobile at 7 A. M. on the 6th, with one hundred and twenty-nine officers and men, small arms, etc., and six boats, passed the enemy's fleet without observation, and reported myself and crew to the senior officer for further service.

Not a man was lost by straggling, and I brought up the wounded. The dead were buried on the afternoon of the 5th in the fort's burial ground. We had only two killed and three wounded.

While running the gauntlet up the bay I became apprehensive of capture or of being forced to land and make a march to Mobile. The Morgan was being chased by the enemy, as I knew it was her intention to pass near the eastern shore and could see her approach us. I feared she might lead the enemy upon the boats. Under these circumstances I deemed it prudent to drop the signal boat into the sea. I did so. The officers and crew of the Gaines, for about ten or fifteen minutes, were subjected to a very heavy fire from the enemy at short distance, and, I am proud to say, stood it with great gallantry. There were two or three exceptional cases only.

Without casting censure upon any by silence, I can not withhold the expression of my thanks to Lieutenant Payne, Passed Assistant Surgeon Iglehart, Second Assistant Engineer Deboise, Gunner Offutt and Paymaster's Clerk Wilson (in charge of the supply of shells to after division), for their examples of coolness and gallantry under the trying circumstances of this combat against an overwhelming force and the influence it must have had among the crew, most of whom had never before been in action. Frequent interviews with these officers caused me to regard them with admiration.

The ship received seventeen shots in her hull and smoke-stack. Of these, only two can be said to have caused her any distress—that which caused the leak and the cutting of the wheel ropes.

J. W. BENNETT, *Lieutenant Commanding.*

DURING the retreat of the Confederates through South Carolina, at the time of Sherman's advance, Sergeant McD——, of Western North Carolina, was sent on detail to the town of M——, where a regiment of home guards was stationed. These valorous heroes, seeing a soldier from the front, gathered around him, eagerly inquiring the news. "News?" says Mac, solemnly. "I believe there is none.—Yes, there is a little, too, but it's not of much importance. Old Hardee burned up a regiment of home guards at Florence the other day, to keep them from falling into the enemy's hands." No more questions were asked.

BATTLE OF MOBILE BAY,

AUGUST 5, 1864.

BY

COMMANDER JAMES D. JOHNSTON,
Commanding Ram Tennessee.

UNITED STATES HOSPITAL,
NAVY YARD, PENSACOLA,
August 13, 1864.

I HAVE the honor to submit the following report of the circumstances under which the Confederate States ram Tennessee, recently under my command, surrendered to United States fleet, commanded by Rear-Admiral Farragut, in Mobile Bay. At 6 A. M. on the 5th instant the enemy's fleet, consisting of four iron-clad monitors and fourteen wooden vessels, were discovered to be steaming up the channel into the bay—the former in a single line nearest to Fort Morgan, and the latter in a double line, each two vessels lashed together. When they approached sufficiently near to draw the fire from Fort Morgan, signal was made to the squadron to follow your motions, and the Tennessee was moved down to the middle of the channel, just outside the line of torpedoes stretching across it, from whence she immediately opened her battery upon the advancing fleet. Every effort was made at the same time to ram each of the leading vessels as they entered the bay; but their superior speed enabled them to avoid this mode of attack, the first, with the admiral's flag, passing ahead and the remainder astern before the ship could be turned to encounter them. As she followed them into the bay, the leading monitor, the Tecumseh, was discovered to be sinking, and in a few minutes she disappeared, taking down nearly all on board, consisting, as since learned, of one hundred souls.

The Tennessee's battery was used to the greatest advantage as long as the fleet were within range, and when they reached a point about four miles from Fort Morgan, and were in the act of anchoring, she steamed alone up toward them (the other vessels of your squadron having been dispersed) and attacked them as soon as she was near enough to render her fire effective. The whole fleet was again put in motion to receive her, and she received four tremendous shocks by the heaviest vessels running into her at full speed, soon after which I received an order from you in person to stand for Fort Morgan, as it had been reported by the acting chief engineer that the ship was leaking rapidly. At this time it was reported to me that the wheel chain had been carried away, and, ordering the relieving tackles to be used, I made a personal examination of the broken chain, to ascertain if it could be repaired. This was found to be impossible, without sending men outside of the shield to expose themselves several minutes to the fire of the enemy's vessels, by which the after deck, over which the chains lead, was closely watched and constantly swept until the close of the action. Returning to the pilot-house for the purpose of observing more closely the movements of the enemy, I soon received a report that you had been wounded, when I went aft to see you, and while there learned that the after port cover had been struck by a shot, which instantly killed a man engaged in removing the pivot bolt upon which it revolved, and wounded yourself and one of the gun's crew, the latter mortally. I then learned that the two quarter-port covers had been so jammed by the fire of the enemy as to render it impracticable to remove them, and the relieving tackles had been shot away and the tiller unshipped from the rudder-head. The smoke-pipe, having been completely riddled by shot, was knocked down

THE CONFEDERATE RAM TENNESSEE FIGHTING THE FEDERAL FLEET.

close to the top of the shield by the concussion of vessels running into the ship. At the same time the three monitors were using their 11 and 15-inch solid shot against the after end of the shield, while the largest of the wooden vessels were pouring in separate broadsides at the distance of only a few feet; and I regret to say that many favorable opportunities of sinking these vessels were unavoidably lost by the failure of our gun-primers.

The bow port cover was struck by a heavy shot, as also the cover of the forward port on the port side; and two of the broadside port covers were entirely unshipped by the enemy's shot. The enemy was not long in perceiving that our steering gear had been entirely disabled, and his monitors and heaviest vessels at once took position at each quarter and astern, from whence they poured in their fire without intermission for a period of nearly half an hour, while we were unable to bring a single gun to bear, as it was impossible to change the position of the vessel, and the steam was rapidly going down as a natural consequence of the loss of the smoke-pipe. Feeling it my duty to inform you of the condition of the vessel, I went to the berth-deck for this purpose, and, after making my report, asked if you did not think we had better surrender, to which you replied, "Do the best you can, and when all is done, surrender," or words to that effect. Upon my return to the gun-deck, I observed one of the heaviest vessels of the enemy in the act of running into us on the port quarter, while the shot were fairly raining upon the after end of the shield, which was now so thoroughly shattered that in a few moments it would have fallen and exposed the gun-deck to a raking fire of shell and grape. Realizing our helpless condition at a glance, and conceiving that the ship was now nothing more than a target for the heavy guns of the enemy, I concluded that no good object could be accomplished by sacrificing the lives of the officers and men in such a one-sided contest, and therefore proceeded to the top of the shield and took down the ensign, which had been seized onto the handle of a gun-scraper and stuck up through the grating. While in the act several shots passed close to me, and

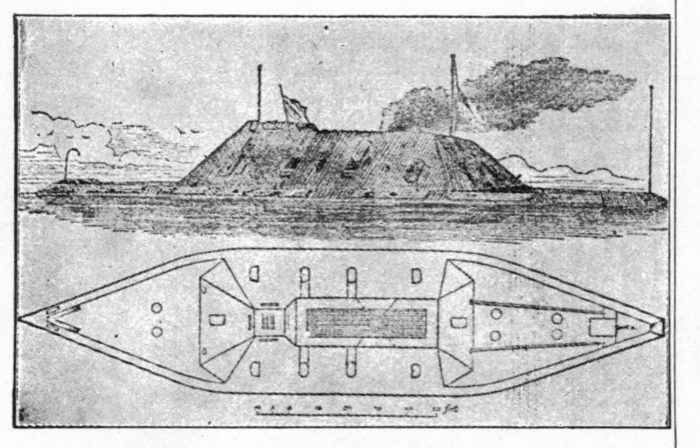

CONFEDERATE RAM TENNESSEE AFTER HER SURRENDER TO THE FEDERAL FLEET.

when I went below to order the engines to be stopped, the fire of the enemy was continued. I then decided, though with an almost bursting heart, to hoist the white flag; and returning again to the shield placed it in the spot where but a few moments before had floated the proud flag for whose honor I would so cheerfully have sacrificed my own life, if I could possibly have become the only victim, but at that time it would have been impossible to destroy the ship without the certain loss of many valuable lives, your own among the number.

It is with the most heart-felt satisfaction that I bear testimony to the undaunted gallantry and cheerful alacrity with which the officers and men under my immediate command discharged all their duties; and to the executive officer, Lieutenant Bradford, it is due that I should commend the regular and rapid manner in which the battery was served in every particular. While a prisoner on board the Ossipee and since coming into the hospital, I have learned from personal observation and from other reliable sources of information that the battery of the Tennessee inflicted more damage upon the enemy than that of Fort Morgan, although she was opposed by one hundred and eighty-seven guns of the heaviest caliber, in addition to the twelve 11 and 15-inch guns on board the monitors. The entire loss of the enemy, most of which is ascribed to the Tennessee, amounts to quite three hundred in killed and wounded, exclusive of the one hundred lost on the Tecumseh, making a number almost as large as the entire force under your command in this unequal conflict. Fifty-three shot marks were found on the Tennessee, thirty-three of which had penetrated so far as to cause splinters to fly inboard, and the washers over the ends of the bolts wounded several men.

J. D. JOHNSTON,
Commander, Provisional Navy, C. S., late of the Tennessee.

TO ADMIRAL FRANKLIN BUCHANAN,
Late Commanding Naval Defenses of Alabama.

ATTACK UPON THE FEDERAL GUNBOAT UNDERWRITER BY A SMALL FORCE OF PICKED MEN UNDER COMMANDER JOHN TAYLOR WOOD.

TURRET SHIP BUILT BY LAIRD BROTHERS, ENGLAND, FOR THE CONFEDERATE GOVERNMENT. NEVER IN SERVICE.

CONFEDERATE IRONCLAD STONEWALL.

UNITED STATES VESSELS DESTROYED BY CONFEDERATE CRUISERS.

BY THE NASHVILLE.

Name of Vessel.	Character.	When Destroyed.	Property Destroyed.	Value.
Harvey Birch	Ship	Nov. 19, 1861	Vessel, etc.	$66,000 00
Robert Gilfillan	Schooner	Feb. 26, 1862	Personal property	

BY THE OLUSTEE.

Name of Vessel.	Character.	When Destroyed.	Property Destroyed	Value.
A. J. Bird	Schooner	Nov. 3, 1864	Vessel, etc.	$24,869 00
Arcole	Ship	Nov. 3, 1864	Cargo	18,000 00
E. F. Lewis	Schooner	Nov. 3, 1864	Vessel, etc.	
Empress Theresa	Bark	Nov. 1, 1864	Vessel, etc.	30,000 00
T. D. Wagner	Brig	Nov. 3, 1864	Vessel, etc.	
Vapor	Schooner	Nov. 3, 1864	Cargo	

BY THE ALABAMA.

Name of Vessel.	Character.	When Destroyed.	Property Destroyed.	Value
Alert	Ship	Sept. 9, 1862	Vessel and outfits	$ 52,000 00
Altamaha	Brig	Sept. 13, 1862	Brig, outfits, etc.	6,000 00
Amanda	Bark	Nov. 6, 1863	Vessel and freight	104,442 00
Amazonian	Bark	June 2, 1863	Bark and charter	97,655 00
Anna F. Schmidt	Ship	July 2, 1863	Dif. val. and ins.	350,000 00
Ariel (bonded)	Steamer	Dec. 7, 1862	United States Treasury notes	261,000 00
Baron de Castine	Brig	Oct. 29, 1862	Bonded	6,000 00
Benjamin Tucker	Ship	Sept. 14, 1862	Vessel, outfit, etc.	70,200 00
Bethia Thayer	Ship	Mar. 1, 1863	Bonded	40,000 00
Brilliant	Ship	Oct. 3, 1862	Bonded	164,000 00
Charles Hill	Ship	Mar. 25, 1863	Bonded	28,450 00
Chastelaine	Brig	Jan. 27, 1863	Vessel and cargo	10,000 00
Clara L. Sparks	Schooner	Nov. 21, 1862	Vessel and cargo	
Conrad	Bark	June 19, 1863	Vessel and cargo	69,000 00
Contest	Ship	Nov. 11, 1863	Vessel and cargo	122,815 00
Courser	Schooner	Sept. 16, 1862	Vessel and cargo	7,000 00
Crenshaw	Schooner	Oct. 26, 1862	Vessel and cargo	33,869 00
Dorcas Prince	Ship	April 26, 1863	Vessel and cargo	44,108 00
Dunkirk	Brig	Oct. 7, 1862	Vessel and cargo	25,000 00
Elisha Dunbar	Bark	Sept. 18, 1862	Vessel and cargo	27,000 00
Emily Farnum	Ship	Oct. 3, 1862	Released	
Emma Jane	Ship	Jan. 14, 1864	Vessel and charter	40,000 00
Express	Ship	July 6, 1863	Vessel and freight	121,300 00
Golden Eagle	Ship	Feb. 21, 1863	Vessel and freight	61,000 00
Golden Rule	Bark	Jan. 26, 1863	Vessel and freight	112,000 00
Harriet Spalding	Bark	Nov. 18, 1863		
Hatteras	Gunboat	Jan. 11, 1863		160,000 00
Highlander	Ship	Dec. 26, 1863	Vessel and freight	75,965 00
Jabez Snow	Ship	May 29, 1863	Vessel and freight	72,881 00
John A. Parks	Ship	Mar. 2, 1863	Vessel and freight	70,000 00
Justina	Bark	May 25, 1863		7,000 00
Kate Cory	Brig	April 15, 1863	Vessel, etc.	28,268 25
Kingfisher	Schooner	Mar. 26, 1863	Vessel, etc.	24,000 00
Lafayette (1)	Ship	Oct. 23, 1862	Vessel, etc.	110,337 00
Lafayette (2)	Bark		Vessel, etc.	36,025 50
Lamplighter	Bark	Oct. 15, 1862	Vessel, etc.	117,600 00
Lauretta	Bark	Oct. 28, 1862	Vessel, etc.	32,800 00
Levi Starbuck	Ship	Nov. 2, 1862	Vessel, etc.	203,962 50
Louisa Hatch	Ship	April 4, 1863	Vessel, etc.	82,250 00
Manchester		Oct. 11, 1862	Vessel, etc.	164,000 00
Martha Wenzell	Bark	Aug. 9, 1863	Released	
Martaban	Ship	Dec. 24, 1863	Vessel, etc.	97,628 00
Morning Star	Ship	Mar. 23, 1863	Bonded	61,750 00
Nina	Schooner	Dec. 5, 1862	Bonded	
Nora	Ship	Mar. 25, 1863	Vessel, etc.	80,000 00
Nye	Bark	April 24, 1862	Vessel, etc.	31,127 00
Ocean Rover	Bark	Sept. 8, 1862	Vessel, etc.	98,820 00
Ocmulgee	Ship	Sept. 5, 1862	Vessel, etc.	131,712 00
Olive Jane	Bark	Feb. 21, 1863	Merchandise	43,208 00
Palmetto	Schooner	Feb. 3, 1863	Merchandise	18,434 00
Parker Cook	Bark	Nov. 30, 1862	Vessel, etc.	25,399 86
Punjab	Ship	Mar. 15, 1863	Bonded	52,000 00
Rockingham	Ship	April 23, 1864	Vessel, etc.	105,000 00
Sea Bride	Bark	Aug. 5, 1863	Vessel, etc.	100,000 00
Sea Lark	Ship	May 3, 1863	Vessel, etc.	550,000 00
S. Gildersleeve	Ship	May 25, 1863	Vessel, etc.	62,783 00
Sonora	Ship	Dec. 26, 1863	Vessel, etc.	46,545 00
Starlight	Schooner	Sept. 7, 1862	Vessel, etc.	4,000 00
Talisman	Ship	June 5, 1863	Vessel, etc.	139,135 00
Thomas B. Wales	Ship	Nov. 8, 1862	Vessel, etc.	245,625 00
Tonawanda	Ship	Oct. 9, 1862	Bonded	80,000 00
Tycoon	Bark	April 27, 1864	Vessel, etc.	88,559 78
Union	Schooner	Dec. 5, 1862	Bonded	1,500 00
Union Jack	Bark	May 3, 1863	Vessel, etc.	77,000 00
Virginia	Ship	Sept. 17, 1862	Vessel, etc.	30,074 00
Washington	Ship	Feb. 27, 1863	Bonded	50,000 00
Wave Crest	Bark	Oct. 7, 1862	Vessel, etc.	44,000 00
Weather Gage	Schooner	Sept. 9, 1862		10,000 00
Winged Racer	Ship	Nov. 10, 1863	Vessel, etc.	150,000 00

BY THE SHENANDOAH.

Name of Vessel.	Character.	When Destroyed.	Property Destroyed.	Value.
Abigail	Bark	May 27, 1865	Vessel, etc.	$ 74,659 00
Adelaide	Bark		Bonded	24,000 00
Alina	Bark	Dec. 4, 1864	Vessel, etc.	95,000 00
Brunswick	Ship	Oct. 30, ——	Vessel, etc.	16,272 00
Catharine	Bark	June 26, 1865	Vessel, etc.	26,174 00
Charter Oak	Schooner	Nov. 5, 1864	Vessel, etc.	15,000 00
Congress	Schooner	June 28, 1865	Vessel, etc.	90,827 00
Covington	Bark	June 28, 1865	Vessel, etc.	43,764 00
Delphine	Bark	Dec. 29, 1864	Vessel, etc.	76,000 00
D. Godfrey	Bark	Nov. 8, 1864	Vessel, etc.	36,000 00
Edward	Bark	Dec. 4, 1864	Vessel, etc.	20,000 00
Edward Casey	Ship	April 1, 1865	Vessel, etc.	109,582 70
Euphrates	Ship	June 21, 1865	Vessel, etc.	168,688 50
Favorite	Bark	June 28, 1865	Vessel, etc.	130,000 00
General Pike	Bark	June 26, 1865	Ransomed	
Gipsey	Bark	June 26, 1865	Vessel, etc.	80,000 00
Harvest	Bark	April 1, 1865	Vessel, etc.	34,759 00
Hector	Ship	April 1, 1865	Vessel, etc.	75,000 00
Fillmore	Ship	June 28, 1865	Vessel, etc.	71,451 75
Isaac Howland	Ship	June 28, 1865	Vessel, etc.	115,000 00
Isabella	Bark	June 26, 1865	Vessel, etc.	87,765 00
James Maury	Bark	June 28, 1865	Ransomed	
Jireh Swift	Bark	June 24, 1865	Vessel, etc.	61,960 00
Kate Prince	Ship	Nov. 12, 1864	Bonded	
Lizzie M. Stacey	Schooner	Nov. 13, 1864	Vessel, etc.	30,000 00
Martha	Bark	June 28, 1865	Vessel, etc.	65,000 00
Nassau	Ship	June 28, 1865	Vessel, etc.	89,424 50
Nile	Bark	June 28, 1865	Bonded	25,500 00
Nimrod	Bark	June 26, 1865	Vessel, etc.	29,260 00
Pearl	Bark	April 1, 1865		10,000 00
Sophia Thornton	Ship	June 24, 1865	Vessel, etc.	70,000 00
Susan	Bark	Nov. 10, 1865	Vessel, etc.	5,436 00
Susan and Abigail	Brig	June 25, 1865	Vessel, etc.	225,848 37
Waverly	Bark	June 28, 1865	Vessel, etc.	84,655 00
William Thompson	Ship	June 22, 1865	Vessel, etc.	105,093 75
William C. Nye	Bark	June 26, 1865	Vessel, etc.	62,087 50

BY THE WINSLOW (FITTED OUT AT WILMINGTON IN 1861).

Name of Vessel.	Character.	When Destroyed.	Property Destroyed.	Value.
Herbert	Schooner	July 18, 1861		
Itasca	Brig	Aug. 4, 1861		
Mary Alice	Schooner	July —, 1861		
Priscilla	Schooner	July —, 1861		
Transit	Schooner	July 15, 1861		

UNITED STATES VESSELS DESTROYED BY CONFEDERATE CRUISERS.—Continued.

BY THE FLORIDA.

Name of Vessel.	Character.	When Destroyed.	Property Destroyed.	Value.
Aldebaran	Schooner	Mar. 13, 1863	Vessel, etc.	$ 22,998 00
Anglo Saxon	Ship	Aug. 20, 1863	Vessel, etc.	
Arabella	Brig	Jan. 12, 1863		
Avon	Ship	Mar. 29, 1864	Vessel, etc.	
B. F. Hoxie	Ship		Vessel, etc.	70,000 00
Clarence	Brig	May 6, 1863		
Commonwealth	Ship	April 17, 1863	Vessel, etc.	352,000 00
Corris Ann	Brig	Jan. 22, 1863	Cargo	
Crown Point	Ship	May 13, 1863	Personal property, etc.	
David Lapsley	Bark			
Electric Spark	Steamer	July 10, 1864	Cargo, etc.	166,000 00
Estelle	Brig	Jan. 19, 1863	Vessel, etc.	12,000 00
Francis B. Cutting	Ship	Aug. 6, 1863		
George Latimer	Schooner	May 18, 1864	Bonded	
General Berry	Bark	July 10, 1863		
Golconda	Bark	July 8, 1864	Vessel, etc.	
Greenland	Bark		Personal property, etc.	
Harriet Stevens	Bark	July 1, 1864	Vessel, etc.	10,500 00
Henrietta	Bark	April 23, 1863	Vessel, etc.	57,049 60
Jacob Bell	Ship	Feb. 12, 1863	Vessel, etc.	1,500,000 00
Kate Dye	Ship	June 17, 1863		
Lapwing	Bark	Mar. 9, 1863	Vessel and cargo	77,000 00
Margaret Y. Davis	Schooner	July 9, 1864		
M. J. Colcord	Bark	Mar 13, 1863	Vessel and cargo	
Mondamin	Bark	Sept. 26, 1864	Vessel and cargo	
Oneida	Ship	April 24, 1863	Vessel and cargo	760,000 00
Red Gauntlet	Ship		Vessel and cargo	
Rienzi	Schooner	July 8, 1863	Vessel and cargo	
Southern Cross	Ship	June 6, 1863	Vessel and cargo	
Southern Rights	Ship	Aug. 22, 1863	Bonded	
Star of Peace	Ship	Mar. 6, 1863	Vessel, etc.	
Sunrise	Ship	July 7, 1863	Bonded	60,000 00
Varnum H. Hill	Schooner	June 26, 1863	Bonded	70,000 00
William B. Nash	Brig	July 8, 1863	Vessel and cargo	
Windward	Brig	Jan. 22, 1863	Vessel and cargo	
William C. Clark	Brig	June 17, 1864		
Zelinda	Bark	June 10, 1864		

BY THE TALLAHASSEE.

Name of Vessel,	Character.	When Destroyed.	Property Destroyed.	Value.
Adriatic	Ship	Aug. 12, 1864	Vessel, etc.	
A. Richards	Brig	Aug. 11, 1864		
Atlantic	Schooner			
Bay State	Bark	Aug. 11, 1864		
Billow	Brig	Aug. 10, 1864		
Carrie Estelle	Brig	Aug. 11, 1864		
Castine	Ship			
Coral Wreath	Brig	Aug. 11, 1864		
Etta Caroline	Steamer	Aug. 10, 1864		
Floral Wreath	Schooner	Aug. 15, 1864	Vessel, etc.	
Glenavon	Bark		Vessel, etc.	
Goodspeed	Schooner	Aug. 12, 1864		
Howard	Bark	Aug. 12; 1864		
James Funk	Pilot-boat	Aug. 11, 1864		$24,000 00
James Littlefield	Ship	Aug. 14, 1864		
J. H. Howen	Schooner	Aug. 14, 1864		
Josiah Achorne	Schooner	Aug. 17, 1864		8,000 00
Lamont Dupont	Schooner	Aug. 13, 1864		
Magnolia	Schooner	Aug. 15, 1864		
Mercy A. Howes	Schooner	Aug. 15, 1864		
North America	Schooner	Aug. 17, 1864	Vessel, etc.	
P. C. Alexander	Bark			
Pearl	Schooner	Aug. 16, 1864		
Restless	Schooner	Aug. 23, 1864		
Rowan	Schooner	Aug. 20, 1864		
Sarah A. Boyce	Schooner	Aug. 11, 1864		
Sarah Louisa	Schooner			
Spokane	Schooner	Aug. 12, 1864		
William Bell	Pilot-boat	Aug. 11, 1864		24,000 00

BY THE SUMTER.

Name of Vessel.	Character.	When Destroyed.	Property Destroyed.	Value.
Abbie Bradford	Schooner	July 25, 1861	Recaptured	
Albert Adams	Brig	July 5, 1861	Released	
Arcade	Schooner	Nov. 26, 1861	Burned	
Ben Danning	Brig	July 5, 1861	Released	
Cuba	Brig	July 4, 1861	Released	
Daniel Trowbridge	Schooner	Oct. 27, 1861	Burned	
Ebenezer Dodge	Bark	Dec. 8, 1861	Burned	
Golden Rocket	Ship	July 3, 1861	Burned	$40,000 00
Investigator		Jan. 18, 1862	Bonded	15,000 00
Joseph Maxwell	Bark	July 27, 1861	Released	
Joseph Parkes	Brig	Sept. 25, 1861	Burned	
Louis Kilham	Bark	July 6, 1861	Released	
Machias	Brig	July 4, 1861	Released	
Montmorency		Nov. 25, 1861	Bonded	20,000 00
Naiad	Brig	July 6, 1861	Released	
Neapolitan	Bark	Jan. 18, 1862	Burned	
Vigilance	Ship	Dec. 3, 1861	Burned	40,000 00
West Wind		July 6, 1861	Released	

BY THE TACONY (A TENDER OF THE FLORIDA).

Name of Vessel.	Character.	When Destroyed.	Property Destroyed.	Value.
Ada	Schooner	June 23, 1863		
Arabella	Brig	June 12, 1863	Bonded	
Archer	Schooner	June 24, 1863	Recaptured	
Byzantium	Ship	June 16, 1863	Cargo	
Elizabeth Ann	Schooner	June 22, 1863		
Florence	Schooner	June 22, 1863	Bonded	
Goodspeed	Bark	June 23, 1863		
Isaac Webb	Ship	June 20, 1863	Bonded	
L. A. Macomber	Schooner	June 20, 1863		
Marengo	Schooner	June 22, 1863		
Ripple	Schooner	June 22, 1863		
Rufus Choate	Schooner	June 22, 1863		
Shattemuc	Ship	June 24, 1863	Bonded	
Umpire	Brig	June 14, 1863	Vessel, etc.	
Wanderer	Schooner	June 22, 1863		

BY THE GEORGIA.

Name of Vessel.	Character.	When Destroyed.	Property Destroyed.	Value.
Bold Hunter	Ship	Oct. 9, 1863	Vessel, etc.	
City of Bath	Ship	June 28, 1863		
Constitution	Ship	June 25, 1863	Vessel, etc.	
Dictator	Ship	April 25, 1863	Vessel, etc.	
George Griswold	Ship	June 8, 1863	Bonded	
Good Hope	Bark	June 13, 1863	Vessel, etc.	
John Watt	Ship	Oct. —, 1863	Bonded	
J. W. Seaver	Bark	June 22, 1863	Bonded	
Prince of Wales	Ship	July 16, 1863	Bonded	

BY THE CHICKAMAUGA.

Name of Vessel.	Character.	When Destroyed.	Property Destroyed.	Value.
Albion Lincoln	Bark	Oct. 29, 1864		
Emma L. Hall	Bark	Oct. 31, 1864	Vessel, etc.	
M. L. Potter	Bark	Oct. 30, 1864	Merchandise	
Shooting Star	Bark		Vessel, etc.	

UNITED STATES VESSELS DESTROYED BY CONFEDERATE CRUISERS.—Continued.

BY THE CLARENCE (A TENDER OF THE FLORIDA).

Name of Vessel.	Character.	When Destroyed.	Property Destroyed.	Value.
Alfred H. Partridge	Schooner	June 7, 1863	Bonded	
Caleb Cushing	Cutter	June 24, 1863		
Kate Stewart	Schooner	June 12, 1863		
Mary Alvina	Brig	June 9, 1863	Vessel, etc.	$11,304 00
Mary Schindler	Schooner	June 12, 1863		
Tacony	Bark	June 12, 1863		
Whistling Wind	Bark	June 6, 1863		
Conrad (s. Tuscaloosa)				

BY THE RETRIBUTION (A SCHOONER FITTED OUT IN CAPE FEAR RIVER).

Name of Vessel.	Character.	When Destroyed.	Property Destroyed.	Value.
Emily Fisher	Brig	Feb. 19, 1863	Cargo	$ 9,352 26
Hanover	Schooner	Jan. 31, 1863	Vessel, etc.	11,630 00
J. P. Ellicott	Brig	Jan. 10, 1863		

BY THE TUSCALOOSA (A TENDER OF THE ALABAMA).

Name of Vessel.	Character.	When Destroyed.	Property Destroyed.	Value.
Living Age	Ship	Sept. 13, 1863		
Santee	Ship	July 31, 1863	Bonded	$150,000 00

BY THE YORK.

Name of Vessel.	Character.	When Destroyed.	Property Destroyed.	Value.
George V. Baker	Schooner	Aug. 9, 1861	Recaptured	

UNITED STATES VESSELS DESTROYED BY CONFEDERATE CRUISERS.—Continued.

BY THE JEFF DAVIS (FITTED OUT AT CHARLESTON, JUNE 28, 1861).

Name of Vessel.	Character.	When Destroyed.	Property Destroyed.	Value.
D. C. Pierce	Bark	June —, 1861		
Ella	Schooner	—— —, 1861		
Enchantress	Schooner	July 16, 1861		
John Crawford	Ship	Aug. —, 1861		
John Welsh	Brig	July 16, 1861		
Rowena	Bark	June —, 1861		
S. J. Waring	Schooner	July 16, 1861	Recaptured	
W. McGilvery	Brig	July —, 1861		

BY THE CALHOUN (A STEAMER FITTED OUT AT NEW ORLEANS).

Name of Vessel.	Character.	When Destroyed.	Property Destroyed.	Value.
John Adams	Schooner	May —, 1861		
Mermaid	Schooner	May —, 1861		
Panama	Brig	May 29, 1861		

BY THE BOSTON (A STEAMER CAPTURED IN JUNE, 1863).

Name of Vessel.	Character.	When Destroyed.	Property Destroyed.	Value.
Lennox	Bark	June 12, 1863		
Texana	Bark	June 12, 1863	Cargo	

BY THE ECHO.

Name of Vessel.	Character.	When Destroyed.	Property Destroyed.	Value.
Mary E. Thompson	Brig	July 9, 1862		
Mary Goodell	Schooner	July 9, 1862		

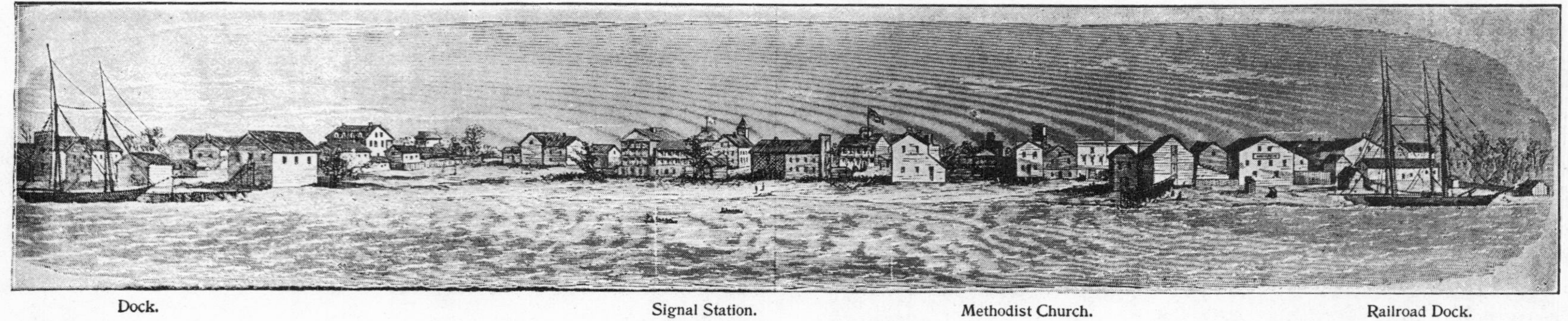

VIEW OF FERNANDINA, FLA., FROM ST. MARY'S RIVER.
[From a sketch made in 1861 by Mr. Such.]

LIST OF PRIVATEERS COMMISSIONED BY THE CONFEDERATE GOVERNMENT TOGETHER WITH A LIST OF THEIR PRIZES.

NOTE.—No reports of the operations of the Confederate privateers having been found, this list is compiled only from such official documents as the office of "Naval War Records" has been able to obtain. It is believed, however, that other privateers were fitted out and other prizes captured by the below-mentioned vessels, but having no official documents from which to gather data, their names have been omitted.

NAME OF PRIVATEER.	Ports From Which Fitted Out.	Class.	Master.	When Commissioned.	Tonnage.	Guns.	Men.	Date of Capture of Prize.	REMARKS.
A. C. Gunnison	Mobile, Ala.	Steam Tug	Peter G. Cook	May 25, 1861	52	Two 6-pounders	15		
Beauregard	Charleston, S. C.	Schooner	Gilbert Hay	October 14, 1861	101	One	40		Captured November 12, 1861, by the bark Wm. G. Anderson.
Calhoun	New Orleans, La.	Steamer	John Wilson	May 15, 1861	500	One 18-pounder; Two 12-pounders; Two 6-pounders	150		
Prizes—John Adams		Schooner	C. B. Averall					May, 1861	
Mermaid		Schooner	—— Soper					May, 1861	
Panama		Brig	—— Powell					May 29, 1861	
Dixie	Charleston, S. C.	Schooner	Thos. J. Moore	July, 1861	150		30		
Prizes—Glenn		Bark						July 31, 1861	
Rowena		Bark						July —, 1861	
May Alice		Schooner						July 25, 1861	
Gibraltar	Mobile, Ala.	Schooner	W. G. Ford	February 5, 1864	60	Two	30		
Gordon	Charleston, S. C.	Steamer	Thos. J. Lockwood	July 15, 1861	518	Three	50		
Prizes—Protector		Schooner	T. J. Linnekin					July 28, 1861	
Wm. McGilvery		Brig	—— Harriman					July —, 1861	
Governor A. Mouton	New Orleans, La.	Steamboat	Sam'l E. Parker	June 10, 1861	125	19-pounder; 16-pounder	25		
Isabella	New Orleans, La.	Steam Propeller	James I. Bond	June 4, 1861	800	Ten	225		
Jefferson Davis	Charleston, S. C.	Brig	Louis M. Oxetter	June 18, 1861	187	Five	75		Formerly the slaver, Echo.
Prizes—John Welsh		Brig	—— Fifield					July 6, 1861	
Enchantress		Schooner	—— Devereaux					July 6, 1861	
S. J. Waring		Schooner	—— Smith					July 7, 1861	
Alvarado		Bark						July 21, 1861	
Santa Clara		Brig						August 5, 1861	
John Carver		Ship	—— Edge					August —, 1861	
Mary E. Thompson		Brig	—— Havener					July 9, 1861	
Mary Goodell		Schooner	—— McGilvery					July 9, 1861	
J. O. Nixon	New Orleans, La.	Schooner	John Wilson	July 3, 1861	95	One 18-pounder; Two Carronades	40		
Lorton	Baltimore, Md.	Schooner	W. T. Kendall	June 11, 1861	95	One	25		
Manassas	New Orleans, La.	Steam Propeller	John A. Stevenson	September 12, 1861	387	One	36		
Mariner	Wilmington, N. C.	Steam Propeller	B. W. Berry	July 14, 1861	135	One 6-pounder; Two 12-pounders	30		
Prize—Nathaniel Chase		Schooner	Daniel Doane					July 25, 1861	
Matilda	New Orleans, La.	Bark	F. Belcher	June 8, 1861	400	Four to Six	150		
Music	New Orleans, La.	Steamer	Thos. McLellan	May 15, 1861	273	Two 6-pounders	100		
Petrel	Charleston, S. C.	Schooner	Wm. Perry	July 10, 1861	82	Two	35		Formerly revenue cutter Aiken, sunk by United States frigate St. Lawrence, July 28, 1861.
Pioneer	New Orleans, La.	Submarine Propeller	John K. Scott	March 31, 1862	4	Mag'zne of Explos'vs			
Rattlesnake	Charleston, S. C.	Steamship	T. Harrison Baker	November 5, 1862	1204	Six	130		Formerly Nashville, destroyed February 28, 1863, by United States monitor Montauk.
Retribution	Galveston, Texas	Schooner	Thos. B. Power	October 27, 1862	150	Three	30		
Prizes—Emily Fisher		Brig	—— Staples					February 19, 1863	
Hanover		Schooner	Washington Case					January 31, 1863	
J. P. Ellicott		Brig	—— Deveraux					January 10, 1863	
Sallie	Charleston, S. C.	Schooner	Henry S. Lebby	September 28, 1861	171	One	46		Formerly the Virginia.
Prizes—B. K. Eaton		Brig						October 30, 1861	
Betsey Ames		Brig	Richard C. Bartlett					October 17, 1861	
Elsmore		Brig							
Granada		Brig	A. C. Pettengill					October 12, 1861	
Savannah	Charleston, S. C.	Schooner	T. Harrison Baker	May 18, 1861	53	One	30		
Prize—Joseph		Brig	—— Myers					June 3, 1861.	
Sealine	Baltimore, Md.	Brig	W. T. Kendall	June 11, 1861	179	One	35		
V. H. Ivy	New Orleans, La.	Steamer	N. B. Baker	May 16, 1861	454	One 15-pounder	60		
Wm. H. Webb	New Orleans, La.	Steamer	Joseph Leach	May 18, 1861	656	Four 12-pounders	100		
York	Norfolk, Va.	Schooner	John Geoffroy	July 9, 1861	68	One 6-pounder	30		Driven ashore and destroyed by the United States steamer Union, August 9, 1861.
Prizes—B. T. Martin		Brig							
Geo. G. Baker		Schooner							Recaptured.

CONFEDERATE STATES CRUISERS.

THE NASHVILLE.

BY

LIEUTENANT W. C. WHITTLE.

IN 1861 the Nashville, then used as a freight and passenger steamer, was seized in the port of Charleston, S. C., by the Confederate authorities and soon fitted out for the purpose of taking Messrs. Mason and Slidell to Europe. She was a side-wheel, brig-rigged steamer, of about twelve or fourteen hundred tons, and was therefore deemed by them too large a vessel to run the blockade. That purpose was accordingly abandoned.

Fort Macon. Nashville. Beaufort. State of Georgia.

CONFEDERATE STEAMER NASHVILLE RUNNING THE BLOCKADE AT BEAUFORT, N. C.

Captain R. B. Pegram, then in command of the Nashville, fitted her with two small guns and made her ready for sea, with a full crew of officers and men. The following is a list of her officers: Captain, R. B. Pegram; First Lieutenant, Charles M. Fauntleroy; Second Lieutenant, John W. Bennett; Third Lieutenant, William C Whittle; Master, John H. Ingram; Surgeon, Jno. L. Ancrum; Paymaster, Richard Taylor; Chief Engineer, James Hood; Assistant Murray and two others, and the following midshipmen: W. R. Dalton, William H. Sinclair, Clarence Cary, J. W. Pegram, W. P. Hamilton, —— Thomas and —— McClintock.

On the night of October 21, 1861, she ran out of Charleston, touched at Bermuda. After stopping there a few days for coal, she headed across the Atlantic, and on November 19th captured in the entrance of the British Channel, the ship Harvey Birch, an American merchantman in command of Captain Nelson; she was boarded by an officer and boat's crew who carried away all that was valuable and burned the ship. On the 21st she arrived at Southampton, England.

The Nashville enjoyed the distinction of being the first war vessel to fly the flag of the Confederate States in the waters of England. Here we remained until the latter part of January, 1862. About the 1st of February, 1862, we sailed for the Confederacy, evading the United States steamer Tuscarora, which had for some time been watching an opportunity to capture the Nashville, having been sent for that purpose. The manner of our escape is worthy of mention. The Queen's proclamation of neutrality required that neither belligerent should leave port until twenty-four hours after the hour set for the sailing of the other. The Tuscarora immediately got under way and lay off the port to avoid the restriction, awaiting our departure, but one evening came to anchor near the Isle of Wight, within the limit of British jurisdiction. Captain Pegram, learning this, at once notified the Government that he would set sail at a certain hour the next day, and the Tuscarora was notified that she must remain until the expiration of the twenty-four hours thereafter. A British vessel was sent down to see that this order was not violated and the Nashville, with flying colors, steamed proudly by the Tuscarora and passed out to sea, leaving her commander and crew to meditate on the delightful uncertainties of the law of nations.

The run to Bermuda was without incident, save that we encountered a gale of wind which did us considerable damage. After repairing and coaling ship we took on board the master and crew of a North Carolina schooner, which had been wrecked by the gale at Bermuda. The master agreed to pilot us into the harbor of Beaufort, N. C., and we made for that port. On the passage the schooner Gilfillan was captured and destroyed. Arriving off Beaufort we found one United States blockade steamer and determined to pass in by a *ruse de guerre*. A steamer very much like the Nashville was then employed by the United States Navy in carrying the mails and communicating with the blockading squadron. Personating this steamer and flying the United States flag, we ran confidently up to the blockader and made signal to her to come and get her mails. The Nashville was hove to under gentle pressure of steam and the blockader lowered a boat. While pulling toward us we changed our course and ran for port. Before their mistake was discovered the Nashville was out of reach of the enemy's guns, which, however, fired shot after shot in impotent rage, all falling short as we widened the distance under full steam, making safe harbor at Morehead City on the 28th day of February, 1862.

Captain Pegram, after visiting Richmond and reporting to the Navy Department for instructions, returned to the ship, bringing information that the Nashville had been sold to private parties in Charleston. The order to remove all Confederate States property, including armament, charts and instruments, from the vessel, was promptly executed, and the ship was left under my command with two midshipmen, Messrs. Sinclair and Hamilton, Boatswain Sawyer, Chief Engineer Hood, three sailors, four firemen, cook and steward, to be kept in order until taken possession of by the agent of the purchasers.

General Burnside's movement upon Newbern, N. C., was then being executed, and Captain Pegram, with the officers and crew of the Nashville, went through on one of the last trains that could escape, after which all communication inland was completely cut off. Burnside's expedition was moving upon Morehead City, and the capture of the Nashville seemed inevitable. The blockading fleet had been increased to two steamers and one sailing vessel, and the Federal troops were on the march to seize the vessel as she lay tied up at the wharf.

Without a crew or means of defense, without even a chart or chronometer, short of coal and provisions, the idea of saving the ship was simply vain. There seemed a single chance, however, and I determined to take that chance. The fall of Fort Macon was only a question of time, and a very short time at that; the blockade must, therefore, be broken. Quietly and secretly we set to work, and being assured by my chief engineer (Hood) that with his small force and the assistance of the deck hands he could keep the vessel under steam, we made ready to run through the blockading fleet. I was fortunate in securing the services of Captain Gooding, an excellent coast pilot, who was then in command of a sailing ship blockaded in the harbor. He brought with him a chart, chronometer and sextant, and such instruments as were deemed absolutely necessary for navigation, with the promise that if his efforts were successful the ultimate command of the ship would be given him by the purchasers.

Having made all my preparations to destroy the ship, if necessary, to prevent her capture in passing out, I dropped down under the guns of Fort Macon. Colonel White, in command of the fort, came on board and told me of the efforts that were being made for my capture. He suggested that, as I had no means of defense, I should, on the approach of the expedition, destroy my vessel and come into his fort as a re-enforcement to him. I then divulged to Colonel White my plan of escape, and notified him of my intention to run out that evening, requesting him to see that I was not fired upon by his command. He was delighted with the plan, and wished me God-speed. On the evening of March 17, 1862, between sunset and moonrise, the moon being nearly full, I tripped my anchor and ran out. As soon as I was under way a rocket was sent up from the lower side of Bogue Island, below Fort Macon, by an enemy's boat, sent ashore from the blockaders for the purpose of watching me, giving me the assurance that my movement had been detected.

Steaming toward the entrance at the bar, I found the three vessels congregated close together under way and covering the narrow channel. Just before reaching the bar I slipped my anchor, which in hoisting had caught under the forefoot, in order to prevent its knocking a hole in the ship's bottom, as I knew we would strike in going over the bar. We were going at full speed, say fourteen knots per hour. I was in the pilot-house with Gooding, and two others were at the wheel. The blockaders, under way and broadside to me, were across my path. I ran for the one furthest to the northward and eastward, with the determination to go through or sink both ships. As I approached rapidly I was given the right of way and passed through and out under a heavy fire from the three vessels. They had commenced firing as soon as I got within range, and continued until I passed out, firing in all, as well as we could determine, about twenty guns. The moon rose clear and full a short time afterward and found us well out to sea, no attempt being made to pursue us that we could discover.

We ran on out to the inner edge of the Gulf Stream, where we remained until the next day, and in the afternoon of the 18th of March shaped our course for Charleston. Arriving in the midst of the blockading fleet there before dawn of the 19th, we discovered their position by the great number of rockets which they were sending up to signal the fact that our presence was known. This, together with the fact that the stone fleet had been sunk in the channel, leaving only the Maffitts Channel open, and not knowing how far even that was obstructed, made me conclude not to attempt to run in. With an exhausted crew and short of coal, I put back and ran clear of the blockaders. At daylight on the 19th, made Cape Roman, steaming close in to land, and tracked up the beach, intending to try to enter Georgetown, S. C.; but seeing

CONFEDERATE STEAMER NASHVILLE DESTROYING A FEDERAL VESSEL.

the smoke of two steamers to the northward, I stopped the engines and made ready to destroy the vessel on their approach, as we were in a condition too exhausted to run successfully.

Fortunately, the smoke of the blockaders disappeared on the horizon, and we steamed on up to the entrance of Georgetown, but on going in got aground on the bar. Sending out a boat to take soundings, I observed a boat pulling around a point of land inside, filled with armed men. At the same moment a body of horsemen came down on the beach. Not knowing but that this port also had fallen into the hands of the enemy, I called my boat alongside and made such preparations for defense as I could devise. When close enough, the boat hailed us to know what ship it was. I answered by asking whether they were Federals or Confederates. Their reply was: "We are South Carolinians," and I answered: "This is the Confederate States steamer Nashville," which at first they seemed to discredit. Finally they approached, and I was told by the officer in command that Colonel Manigault, who was commanding ashore, had directed that if I was a Confederate vessel I should hoist another flag under the one already up. I told him I had no other except the United States flag, and this might mislead him. I then told him I needed a pilot. He readily and very quickly pulled ashore, and returned with one, bringing me a message from Colonel Manigault that I could place implicit confidence in him, to let him take the ship up to Georgetown, and requested me to come ashore and confer with him. In the meantime the Nashville, having been gotten afloat by me, was placed in charge of this pilot and steamed up to Georgetown.

I went ashore and was received by Colonel Manigault, of the South Carolina forces, with a hearty welcome and cheers from his troops. Colonel Manigault inquired whether I had seen the blockaders off Georgetown. I replied that I had seen their smoke going off up the coast, whereupon he informed me that this was the first day for many weeks that they had absented themselves from their post in front of the harbor. I proceeded at once to Richmond and reported to S. R. Mallory, Secretary of the Navy, who directed me to return to Charleston and confer with Messrs. Fraser, Trenholm & Co., the purchasers of the vessel, and to take all necessary steps to effect her transfer to them as speedily as possible. I went to Charleston and in concert with them or their agents the business was closed, they giving the command of the ship, at my request, to Captain Gooding. Being unable to carry out any cargo on account of the bar, she sailed in ballast, having taken in coal and such crew as could be secured for her. She left Georgetown in the broad light of day, flying the Confederate flag, before the blockaders returned to port.

After this she made several successful trips through the blockade and later was transferred to other parties, and subsequently she was attacked by the enemy and destroyed at the mouth of the Ogeechee River. I am persuaded that the Federals did not know that the Nashville went into

REMAINS OF THE CONFEDERATE CRUISER NASHVILLE IN THE OGEECHEE RIVER NEAR FORT MCALLISTER, GA.

Georgetown until it was revealed to them by my capture below New Orleans in April, 1862. I had then among my private papers the rough draft of my report to Secretary Mallory, in which I had announced to him the escape of the vessel from Morehead City and her entrance into Georgetown. The Federal officer who read this rough report seemed to have the impression that the Nashville had sailed direct to Nassau, and so expressed himself to me. On my telling him that I had taken her into Georgetown he was greatly surprised, and the circumstances of her escape were thus, for the first time, communicated to the Federal Government.

W. C. WHITTLE.
Lieutenant, C. S. N.

A STRAGGLING Yankee soldier was in a squad that was captured and passed before General Paul Jones Semmes. One of the men remarked that this prisoner was hungry. "Feed him," said General Semmes. "Shoot 'em in the line, but feed 'em on this side of it."

THE FLORIDA.

WM. C. MILLER & SONS, of Liverpool, under contract with Captain J. D. Bullock, naval agent of the Confederate States, built a steam cruiser. She bore the dock-yard name of the Oreto. She was the first Confederate cruiser built in England. On March 22, 1862, she sailed from Liverpool, having on board as a passenger, Master John Lowe, Confederate States Navy, who was instructed to deliver the vessel at Nassau to Captain J. N. Maffitt. The Oreto arrived at Nassau April 28th. During the interval between April 28th and

COMMANDER JOHN NEWLAND MAFFITT, OF NORTH CAROLINA.
[From a photograph taken in 1863.]

August 1st was twice seized by the British governor, on the complaint of the United States consul that she was intended for the Confederate service. The admiralty, from the evidence submitted, found that she was properly documented as British property, and ordered her release. At Nassau her armament was placed on a schooner which the Oreto met, about August 10th, at Green Cay, sixty miles distant. There it was transferred to the steamer, which was regularly commissioned as a ship of war and the name changed to Florida. Her battery embraced two 7-inch and four 6-inch Blakely rifled guns. The yellow fever broke out among the crew and in five days the working force was reduced to one fireman and four deck hands. The ship was run into Cardenas, Cuba, in a desperate plight, and there Captain Maffitt was stricken with the disease. Before he recovered the Florida was summoned to Havana by the captain general. She was still far from being fully equipped or manned, and because of the stringency of the Spanish regulations Maffitt determined to run into Mobile. On September 4, 1862, she was off the bar, and, hoisting the British colors, stood toward the three blockading vessels. Deceived by her ensign, they allowed her to come up to them before ordering her to stop. The only response was the substitution of the Confederate for the British flag. The Florida received the broadside of the Federal sloop of war Oneida within pistol range, and for two hours the little ship was pelted by the enemy until she found shelter under the guns of Fort Morgan. Two shells had passed through her and her rigging was badly cut up; one man was killed and seven wounded. Maffitt came out of his berth to handle the ship, and during the whole war there was no incident in which bravery and energy were more brilliantly displayed.

At Mobile the Florida was fully fitted out and manned, and on the night of January 15, 1863, made her escape to sea, although the blockading fleet had been strengthened with a view to her capture, and she was vainly pursued by one fast gunboat, the R. R. Cuyler. Under steam and sail (her screw could be lifted clear out of water when it was intended that she should go under sail alone) she outran the enemy. She was now officered as follows: Lieutenant Commanding, John Newland Maffitt; Lieutenants, S. W. Averill, Thomas K. Porter, J. L. Hoole, C. W. Read and S. G. Stone; Midshipmen, R. S. Floyd, G. D. Bryan, J. H. Dyke, G. T. Sinclair and W. B. Sinclair; Chief Engineer, A. M. Spidell; Assistants, Charles W. Quinn, Thomas A. Jackson and E. H. Brown; Surgeon, Frederick Garrettson; Paymaster, ——— Lynch.

The Florida in a few days made the west end of Cuba and captured her first prize, a small brig, which was burned. Putting into Havana, she remained forty-eight hours, taking in coal; and on January 25th arrived at Nassau, having taken two more prizes in the meantime. Cruising to the southward, a halt was made at Green Cay, to paint the ship, and upon the day after leaving that island the United States gunboat Sonoma was sighted. All hands were called to quarters, but although the Florida was slowed down, the enemy kept at a distance, and at the approach of night the Florida went on her course. Off the Windward Islands she had a long chase after the clipper ship Jacob Bell, from Foo Chow, China, for New York, which she caught and burned. The vessel and her cargo of tea, silks, etc., was valued at $1,500,000, the most valuable single prize taken by any Confederate cruiser.

The Florida cruised along the meeting of the great routes of commerce along the Brazilian coast, taking many prizes. Near there a tender was made of the prize brig Clarence, and then worked her way back to St. Georges, Bermuda, where she arrived July 16, 1863. Up to this date she had destroyed fourteen prizes and bonded three.

The Florida sailed from Bermuda July 25th, and after capturing the ships F. B. Cutting (bonded) and the Avon (burned), arrived at Brest, France, where she remained six months in a government dock refitting and recruiting. Captain Maffitt's health was broken and he was relieved of command by Commander Joseph N. Barney, who was also seized with illness, and on January 4, 1864, Lieutenant Charles M. Morris was ordered to the command of the cruiser. He got to sea from Brest, February 12th, and went to the West Indies, but finding no valuable quarry there, made a descent on the coast of the United States. On July 10th, thirty miles off the capes of the Delaware, he captured the United States mail steamer Electric Spark, from New York for New Orleans, which was scuttled after transferring her people and passengers to a passing English vessel. Other prizes taken in this dash were the Harriet Stevens, Golconda, Margaret Y. Davis and Mondamin. Morris crossed the ocean to Teneriffe, and cruised back leisurely toward Brazil, capturing the B. F. Hoxie, Cairaissanne, David Lapsley, Estelle, George Latimer, Southern Rights, Greenland, Windward, William C. Clark and Zelinda.

The Florida anchored at Bahia, Brazil, October 4th, and found in port the United States steam corvette Wachusett, Captain Napoleon Collins.

The annexed report of Lieutenant Thomas K. Porter embraces the particulars of the

CAPTURE OF THE CONFEDERATE STEAMER FLORIDA BY THE UNITED STATES STEAMER WACHUSETT.

LIVERPOOL, February 20, 1865.

I submit the following account of the capture of the Confederate States steamer Florida at Bahia, Brazil, on the 7th of October, 1864, by the United States steamer Wachusett, the treatment of the officers and crew while prisoners, and the manner of our release. But, before commencing, I beg to call your attention to the fact that before entering the harbor our shot were withdrawn from the guns; that after our being requested by the Brazilian naval commander to anchor inshore of his squadron we let our steam go down and hauled fires.

CAPTAIN CHARLES M. MORRIS,
Commander of the Florida.

At about 3 A. M., on the morning of the 7th of October, the officer of the deck, Acting Master T. T. Hunter, sent the quartermaster down to call me and tell me that the Wachusett was under way and standing toward us. I immediately jumped on deck, when I saw the Wachusett about twenty yards off, standing for our starboard quarter. A moment after, she struck us abreast the mizzenmast, broke it into three pieces, crushed in the bulwarks, knocked the quarter-boat in on deck, jammed the wheel, carried away the mainyard and started the beams for about thirty feet forward. At the same time she fired about two hundred shots from her small arms, and two from her great guns. She then backed off about one hundred yards and demanded our surrender. I replied to the demand, that I would let them know in a few moments.

The reply from the Wachusett was to surrender immediately, or they would blow us out of the water. As more than half our crew were ashore and those on board had just returned from liberty, I believed that she could run us down before we could get our guns loaded. But as I did not like to surrender the vessel without knowing what some of the other officers thought of it, I consulted Lieutenant Stone, the second officer in rank, and finding that he agreed with me that we could not contend against her with any hopes of success, I informed the commander of the Wachusett that, under the circumstances, I would surrender the vessel. I then went on board, and delivered to Commander Collins the ship's ensign and my sword. He immediately sent a prize crew on board the Florida, and towed her out of the harbor. During the day he transferred about two-thirds of those captured to the Wachusett. He then paroled the officers, and put the men in double irons. As there were so few men compared to the Wachusett's crew, and those divided between the two ships, I tried to get Captain Collins to allow the irons to be taken off of all or a part of them during the day, but he refused to do so. Beyond keeping the men in double irons for nearly two months, there were but two cases of severity toward them that were reported to me. Henry Norman (cox.) was ironed to a stanchion with his hands behind him for having the key of a pair of the Florida's irons in his pocket. He, as well as all the other men on the Wachusett, was ironed with the irons belonging to her (the Wachusett). John Brogan (fireman) was kept in the sweat box. Dr. Emory reported to me that he was sick and could not stand such treatment. I asked Captain Collins to tell me why he was so treated. His reply was that Brogan was seen talking, and that when his master-at-arms came up he stopped. He also said that Brogan had, the day the Florida was captured, cursed one of his engineers, who tried to get him to show him something about our engines. He said, though, that he had ordered his release two days before, and thought he had been taken out. This was about three weeks after our capture. Brogan informed me afterward that he had been confined there for several days and eighteen nights.

A few days before going into St. Thomas, I went to Captain Collins and told him that on a previous occasion he had informed me that he was going to put our men ashore at Pernambuco, and that as we would be in port a few days, I would like to know if he still intended to put them ashore, at the same time telling him that I thought the Florida would be given up by his Government, and that I thought any honorable man would try to return the ship and crew as nearly in the condition in which he found her as he could. His reply was, "I have not thought of it—I have not thought of it to-day." After further conversation I left him, believing that he would not try to break up the crew. But before leaving St. Thomas our men were informed that all of them who wished to go ashore could do so, and that Master George D. Bryan and one other officer would meet them to look out for them. They asked what was to become of their money which was taken from them, and were told that Mr. Bryan would take it ashore for them. A number of them thought this was a trick to get rid of them, and would not go, but eighteen were foolish enough to believe it, and had their irons taken off on the berth-deck, and were put in a boat from the bow port, and allowed to go ashore. The first Mr. Bryan heard of his part of the affair was when we left the Wachusett and had an opportunity of talking to the other men. After the men had time to get ashore, the commander of the Wachusett called away his boats, and sent an armed force after the boat in which our men had left. So anxious was he to get them ashore, that he sent them when the quarantine flag was flying at his fore in consequence of having the smallpox on board. The United States steamer Kearsarge left St. Thomas while we were there, and Dr. Charlton and the eighteen men on the Florida were transferred to her. When we arrived at Fortress Monroe, we were sent up to Point Lookout Prison, and there the officers were separated from the men, and sent to the Old Capitol Prison in Washington. But in three or four days we were sent back to the Wachusett at Fortress Monroe to go to Fort Warren, Boston. From Hampton Roads we were carried in the Wachusett to Boston. When we arrived at Fort Warren, the men were all put in one room, and the eleven officers were put into one with thirty-two other prisoners. These rooms were casemates, and were fifty feet long and about eighteen feet wide. At sunset we were locked up in these casemates, and released after sunrise and allowed to promenade the extent of five such rooms.

CONFEDERATE STATES CRUISER FLORIDA.

We were kept in close confinement until the 19th of January, when Lieutenant Woodman, of the United States Army, sent for me, and told me that he had an order from the Secretary of the Navy to release the officers and crew of the Florida from Fort Warren, and that as such was the case he would release all of us from close confinement. He showed me the order from the Secretary of the Navy, which was that we would be released on condition that we sign a parole to leave the United States within ten days.

After waiting a week and finding that the United States Government neither intended to pay our passage away, nor to give us our private money captured on the Florida, I sent Lieutenant Stone to Boston with directions to procure a passage in the British and North American steamer Canada, or, if he failed in that, to get us out of the United States in any manner possible. He succeeded in getting passage for all of us on the Canada, by my giving a draft to be paid at Liverpool. And on the 1st of February we signed the following parole: "We, the undersigned, officers and crew of the steamer Florida, in consideration of being released from confinement in Fort Warren, do jointly and severally pledge our sacred word of honor that we will leave the United States within ten days from date of release, and that while in the United States we will commit no hostile act," and I left the fort for the steamer Canada. It may be of importance to state that we were officially informed by Major Gibson, commanding the post part of the time we were there, that we could hold no communication with the Brazilian authorities.

THOMAS K. PORTER.
First Lieutenant, C. S. N.

NOTE.—On November 28, 1864, the Florida was sunk while lying in Hampton Roads, by being struck by an army transport.

CLARENCE, TACONY AND ARCHER.

THE brig Clarence, of Baltimore, Md., was captured off the Brazilian coast on May 6, 1863, by the Florida, and was converted into a Confederate cruiser. Lieutenant Charles W. Read was placed in command, and selected as his subordinate officers from the Florida's complement, Quartermaster Billups, Boatswain's Mate Matthewson and Quarter Gunner Pride, who were made master's mates. Engineer Brown was also taken on board, and sixteen men of the Florida's crew. The only armament was a 6-pounder boat howitzer, but with some spare spars Read constructed several Quaker guns, that frightened some of the American merchant skippers whom he overhauled. He dipped his colors to the Florida and squared away north and east.

Lieutenant Read captured his first prize off Cape Hatteras, the bark Whistling Wind, bound to New Orleans with army stores. The Whistling Wind and a few more prizes, the Kate Stewart, Mary Alvina and Mary Shindler, were burned, and the Alfred H. Partridge was bonded off the capes of the Delaware, to land the prisoners. The next prize was the fine bark Tacony, and as she was a much swifter vessel than the Clarence, the crew and battery were transferred to her, and the Clarence was burned. Read now proceeded along the coast of New England, capturing and burning with immense vigor. His prizes were the Ada, Arabella, Byzantium, Elizabeth Ann, Florence, Goodspeed, Isaac Webb, Z. A. Macomber, Marengo, Ripple, Rufus Choate, Shattemuc, Umpire and Wanderer. The schooner Archer was captured on June 25, 1863, and converted into a Confederate cruiser, taking the place of the Tacony. The latter was burned.

Lieutenant Read desired to capture a steamer. He learned from a fisherman that the armed revenue cutter Caleb Cushing, was at Portland, Me., and decided that she would be of service to him. On June 27th he sailed into Portland harbor in his peaceful-appearing schooner without molestation, and after dark he took the cutter by boarding, and securing her crew below deck. Going out of the harbor on the morning of the 28th, with the Archer and Cushing, the wind failed, and a Boston steamer passed in, having on board Captain Merriman, of the United States Revenue Marine, who had been ordered to Portland to take the cutter in search of the Tacony. The first known in Portland of the cutting out of the Cushing was Merriman's report that he had seen her going to sea and Major Andrews, commandant at Fort Preble, organized a recapturing expedition of troops and citizens in two steamers and three tugboats. At 11 o'clock in the morning they overtook the Cushing and Archer. Read opened fire on them from his guns, but, making wide detours, they hemmed him in and kept out of cannon range. He then took to his boats, after setting a slow match to the magazine of the cutter, which soon blew up. Surrounded by the enemy, he surrendered, and they towed the Archer into the harbor. The prisoners were charged with piracy, but were finally exchanged.

"Although the flag of the Confederate Navy went down in ultimate ruin and defeat, it will survive in history as the flag which waved over the first iron-clad."

THE CONFEDERATE STEAMER FLORIDA SUNK AT THE MOUTH OF THE JAMES RIVER, NEAR NEWPORT NEWS, VA., BY BEING RUN INTO BY THE UNITED STATES TRANSPORT ALLIANCE, NOVEMBER 28, 1864.

THE GEORGIA.

THE Japan, a new and powerful iron-screw steamer of six hundred tons burden, and two hundred horse-power engines, was bought in March, 1863, at Dumbarton, Scotland, by Captain M. F. Maury, Confederate States Naval Agent. She was converted into the Confederate cruiser Georgia.

April 1st she cleared from Greenock in ballast for the East Indies, her crew of fifty men, shipped at Liverpool, signing articles for a voyage to Singapore and intermediate ports. Although she left Greenock in the condition of an ordinary ship of commerce, her departure was accelerated by a suspicion that the British authorities had received knowledge of the uses for which she was designed, and orders to detain her reached Greenock the day after she had passed out of the Clyde.

On the French coast, off Ushant, she met by appointment the steamer Alar, from which she received her guns, ordnance stores and supplies. The Confederate flag was hoisted, the officers took charge, and the ship was formally put in commission as the Confederate States man-of-war Georgia. Her officers, who had come out in the Alar, were: Commander W. L. Maury, First Lieutenant Chapman, Second Lieutenant Evans, Third Lieutenant Smith, Fourth Lieutenant Ingraham, Passed Midshipman Walker, Midshipman Morgan, Paymaster Curtis, Surgeon Wheedon and Chief Engineer Pearson.

The Georgia was a swift and powerful ship of her class, her battery consisting of five Whitworth guns, two 100-pounders, two 24-pounders and one 32-pounder. Of the seamen who had come out from Greenock and signed for a trading voyage only thirteen consented to ship as man-of-war's men, and the remainder were sent back to England by the Alar, and the crew of the Georgia was filled up by men brought out in that vessel. The cruiser's field of operations was the Atlantic Ocean, but it had already been so well reaped of the enemy's commerce by other Confederate cruisers that only the gleanings were left to her, yet in her short career she made prizes aggregating in value $406,000. The first was the ship Dictator, taken on April 25th, and burned; then the Georgia ran across to Bahia, Brazil, where she coaled, and continued on to the Cape of Good Hope, capturing on the way the ships George Griswold and Constitution, and the barks Good Hope and J. W. Seaver. She arrived in St. Simons Bay on August 16th, and on the 29th set out for a return to Europe. During this run she made prizes of the ships City of Bath, Prince of Wales, John Watts and Bold Hunter. She put into Cherbourg, France, on October 28th, where Commander Maury was detached on account of ill health, and Lieutenant Evans was promoted to the command. Because of her insufficient sail power, which necessitated frequent coaling, it was not deemed worth while to continue her as a cruiser, and she was taken to Liverpool, where she arrived on May 2, 1864. There she was dismantled and offered for sale, Edward Bates, a Liverpool merchant, becoming her purchaser for the sum of £15,000. This was done against the protest of Mr. Adams, the United States Minister, who gave notice that his Government would not recognize the transfer, and notified Commander Craven, then in command of the United States frigate Niagara, lying in the port of Antwerp, that he must endeavor to intercept and capture the converted Confederate. Mr. Bates removed every vestige of war-fittings, effected a charter of the ship to the Portuguese Government, and on August 8, 1864, with a British register and under a British flag, she sailed from Liverpool for Lisbon. Off the mouth of the Tagus River, she was captured by the Niagara and sent to Boston with a prize crew, where she was condemned and sold as a lawful prize of the United States. Mr. Bates appealed to the British Foreign Office for redress, but was informed that the case of the Georgia must go before the prize court in the United States, and that he must be prepared to defend his interests therein. He was fortunate enough, however, to recover £6,000 insurance money in the British courts.

THE TALLAHASSEE, AFTERWARD THE OLUSTEE.

BY direction of Secretary Mallory the splendid twin-screw, 14-knot blockade-runner, built on the Thames, and known as the Atlanta, was purchased. She was commissioned as a Confederate States ship of war, under command of Captain J. Taylor Wood, and her name changed to the Tallahassee. The other officers were Lieutenants W. H. Ward, M. M. Benton, J. M. Gardner; Acting Master, Alex Curtis; Engineers—Chief, J. W. Tyman; Assistants, C. H. Leroy, E. G. Hall, J. F. Green, J. J. Lyell, H. H. Roberts, R. M. Ross; Assistant Paymaster, C. L. Jones; Assistant Surgeon, W. L. Sheppardson; Boatswain, J. Cassidy; Gunner, —— Stewart; Master's Mate, C. Russell; Lieutenant of Marines, —— Crenshaw; with a crew of about one hundred and ten men. The battery consisted of a 32-pounder rifle, a lighter rifle and a brass howitzer. On August 6, 1864, the Tallahassee went to sea from Wilmington under the fire of the blockading vessels whom the speedy ship soon left behind. She cruised along the Atlantic coast. On August 11th, when within one hundred miles of Sandy Hook, she took and scuttled her first prize, the schooner Sarah A. Boyce, of Egg Harbor, N. J. The pilot-boats James Funk and Wm. Bell, brig Carrie Estelle, and schooner Atlantic were captured. The Funk was converted into a tender under command of Acting Master Davis and captured the bark Bay State, brig A. Richards and schooner Carroll. All the vessels except the Carroll and tender were burned, and the Carroll was bonded and sent to New York, having on board the paroled prisoners. The captain of the Carroll landed on Fire Island, breaking his oath, and telegraphed information to the Federal authorities that a Confederate cruiser was within sixty miles of New York. Gunboats were sent in pursuit. Captain Wood's intention was to dash up the East River, burn the Brooklyn navy-yard and escape to sea by way of Hell Gate, but this scheme was abandoned and the Tallahassee ran to the eastward with the tender. Off the eastern end of Long Island on August 11th, the ship Adriatic was taken and destroyed, and the bark Suliate was ransomed to land the prisoners. The Tallahassee next captured the schooner Spokane, the brig Billow and the schooner Robert E. Packer, the Mercy A. Howes, Glenavon, Lamont Dupont, Howard, Floral Wreath, Restless, Sarah B. Harris, Etta Caroline, P. C. Alexander, Leopard, Pearl, Sarah Louisa and Magnolia. In taking these prizes Wood had made his way well up along the coast of Maine, and played havoc with the northeast fishing trade, and quite a number of gunboats were added to the fleet already in pursuit of him. When near Halifax, he captured the North America, Neva, Josiah Achorne, Ellis and Diadem. All were burned. The Tallahassee arrived at Halifax on August 18th and was ordered away, after getting only enough coal to take her back to Wilmington. She left Halifax on the 19th, and between there and the Cape Fear River captured the brig Rowan and was fruitlessly chased by Federal cruisers. On the 25th she boldly ran into that river, fighting the blockaders as she pushed through their midst until she dropped anchor under the guns of Fort Fisher. She had burned sixteen vessels, scuttled ten, bonded five and released two.

COMMANDER JOHN TAYLOR WOOD, OF LOUISIANA.
Lieutenant on the Virginia (Merrimac), afterward Commander of the Privateer Tallahassee.
[From a photograph taken in 1864.]

A SCENE ON THE BLOCKADE RUNNER LILIAN. RUNNING THE BLOCKADE INTO THE HARBOR OF WILMINGTON, N. C.

Captain Wood was detached, and was succeeded in command by Lieutenant Ward. Her name was changed to the Olustee, and on October 29, 1864, she ran through the blockading fleet to sea, but not without sustaining some damage from their shells. Off the Delaware capes she captured and destroyed the bark Empress Theresa, schooner A. J. Bird, schooner E. F. Lewis and schooner Goodspeed. Near Sandy Hook the ship Arcole, brig T. D. Wagner and schooner Vapor were made prizes and destroyed. The Olustee went southward again. On November 6th, off Cape Charles, she was sighted by the gunboat Sassacus, which chased her until she was lost in the darkness. The next day the Olustee arrived off Wilmington bar, and steam was allowed to go down for repairs to the engines. Three vessels, looking like blockade-runners, hove in sight. They were the captured blockade-runners Margaret and Jessie, the Lillian and the Banshee, converted into Federal cruisers, and were

COMMANDER JOHN WILKINSON, OF VIRGINIA.

soon joined by the gunboat Montgomery. All the vessels opened fire upon her, but the Montgomery was the only one close enough to be feared. She replied with her after gun; distanced her pursuers, and got into Wilmington unharmed. Her name was again changed to the Chameleon, and she became a blockade-runner. Under the command of Captain John Wilkinson, Confederate States Navy, on December 24th she ran the blockade of the Cape Fear River, while the Federal fleet was bombarding Fort Fisher, and started for Bermuda to procure a cargo of provisions for Lee's army. On the 30th she arrived at St. George's; was immediately seized by the British authorities on the demand of the United States consul, but she had been so thoroughly "sold" at Wilmington that she was, to all intents and purposes, a merchant ship. Laden with provisions on January 19, 1865, she departed from St. George's, but on arriving off New Inlet, Wilkinson found it closed by the fall of Fort Fisher, and put back to Nassau. The Chameleon left Nassau on January 30th for Charleston, but the blockaders being too thick off that port Wilkinson resolved to take the ship to England. On April 9th he arrived at Liverpool. Here she was seized by the British Government and sold, and her name changed to the Amelia. Before her new owners could make use of her the United States entered suit for possession. The court decided in favor of that government, and on April 26, 1866, she was handed over to the consul at Liverpool.

THE SHENANDOAH.

THE last Confederate cruiser and the one that inflicted the largest total of injury upon the commerce of the United States, with the exception of the Alabama, was the Shenandoah. She was purchased to take the place of the Alabama, sunk by the Kearsarge. She was known originally as the English merchant steamer Sea King, having a lifting screw so as to be used under sail alone and was fully rigged as a ship, and was very fast under either sail or steam. The ship was purchased for £45,000 through the medium of an English merchant captain named Corbett, who was to transfer her upon the high seas. The blockade-runner Laurel was purchased at same time and she was loaded at Liverpool with the guns, stores, etc., for the cruiser, and the Laurel also carried out to the rendezvous all the officers except Lieutenant Whittle, who went in the Sea King to make himself acquainted with her. She sailed from London and the Laurel from Liverpool on October 8, 1864. The Sea King was cleared for Bombay or any port in the East Indies, and the Laurel for Nassau. On the 18th they rendezvoused off Funchal, Madeira, and proceeded to Las Desertas, an uninhabited island near by, and in two days the armament and war material were transferred to the Sea King; Captain James I. Waddell hoisted her new colors and took command of her as the Confederate States man-of-war Shenandoah.

Commander James I. Waddell, of North Carolina.

The battery placed on board consisted of four 8-inch smooth bore guns, two Whitworth 32-pounder rifles and two 12-pounders.

The roster of officers was as follows:

Lieutenant-Commanding, James Iredell Waddell; First Lieutenants, W. C. Whittle, John Grimball, S. Smith Lee, Jr., Francis T. Chew; Second Lieutenant, Dabney M. Scales; Acting Master, J. S. Bullock; Acting Chief Engineer, Mat O'Brien; Passed Assistant Surgeon, C. E. Lining; Acting Assistant Paymaster, W. Breedlove Smith; Passed Midshipmen, Q. A. Browne, John T. Mason; Acting Assistant Surgeon, F. J. McNulty; Engineers—First Assistant, W. H. Codd; Second Assistant, John Hutchinson; Third Assistant, Ernest Muggaffeney; Acting Master's Mates, C. E. Hunt, J. T. Minor, Lodge Colton; Acting Boatswain, George Harwood; Acting Carpenter, J. O'Shea; Acting Gunner, J. L. Guy; Sailmaker, Henry Alcott; Second Carpenter, J. Lynch.

The Shenandoah steered for Australia, and on January 25, 1865, made prizes of the barks Alma, Godfrey, Edward and Delphine, schooners Charter Oak and Lizzy M. Stacey, and brig Susan; all were destroyed. The steamer Kate Prince was ransomed to take home the prisoners, and the bark Adelaide was bonded. At Melbourne, the Shenandoah was permitted to go into a private dock for repairs.

On February 8, 1865, the Shenandoah left Melbourne in excellent condition, and in three months passed from that latitude to the beginning of her destructive work among the whalers in the Okhotsk Sea, Bering Sea, and the Arctic Ocean. Between June 22d and the 28th she captured twenty-four ships. Twenty were destroyed, and four of them were released on bond, in order to get rid of the numerous prisoners. The names of the earliest prizes were the Edward Casey, Hector, Abigail, Euphrates, William Thompson, Sophia Thornton, Jireh Swift, Susan and Abigail, Nassau, Brunswick, Hillman, Waverly, Martha 2d, Congress 2d, Favorite, Covington, James Maury, Nile and the Milo. The three last-named were ransomed and they took the prisoners to San Francisco, and the others were burned. On one occasion eight prizes were taken in a lump, and when they were burned together the sea was lit up with a wondrous mass of fire. This occurred on June 28th, near the mouth of Bering Straits, and comprised the last war exploit of the Shenandoah. She captured in all thirty-eight ships, thirty-four of which were destroyed, and four ransomed; their total value was stated by the masters at $1,361,983. Waddell had faithfully executed his orders to obliterate the American whaling industry in those regions.

Many of his captures were effected after the close of the war, although unaware that the war was ended. The Shenandoah came out of the Straits on June 29th, and while running toward the California coast spoke, on August 2d, the British bark Baracouta, fourteen days out from San Francisco, from whose captain Waddell learned of the capture of President Davis, and the capitulation of the remaining military forces of the Confederacy. The Shenandoah's guns were at once dismounted, ports closed, funnels whitewashed, and the ship transformed, so far as external appearances went, into an ordinary merchantman. Waddell decided to give the ship up to the British authorities, and brought her into Liverpool on November 6th, not a vessel having been spoken during the long voyage from the North Pacific. He turned her over to Captain Paynter, commanding her Majesty's ship Donegal, who placed a prize-crew on board, and Waddell communicated with Lord Russell, British Secretary for Foreign Affairs. In this letter he stated his opinion that the vessel should revert, with other property of the Confederacy, to the United States Government, and that point was quickly settled; but Mr. Adams, the United States consul, raised the usual question of piracy against the officers and men of the ship, and there was also a liability to proceedings under the Foreign Enlistment Act, if British subjects could be found on board. Mr. Adams wanted the officers and crew held, he said, until he could procure evidence from San Francisco that Captain Waddell knew of the downfall of the Confederacy before his latest seizures of American vessels; but the law officers of the crown decided that there was no evidence to justify their detention. On November 8th Captain Paynter had the roll of the Shenandoah called upon her deck, and as not a member of the ship's company acknowledged to being a subject of Great Britain, they were discharged and allowed to depart. Captain Waddell and his officers were never molested. The Shenandoah was sold by the United States to the Sultan of Zanzibar, and in 1879 was lost in the Indian Ocean.

Confederate States Cruiser Shenandoah.

THREE CHEERS FOR BOLD BRAIN.

BY A SAILOR, C. S. N.

Three cheers for bold Brain and his gallant crew!
We will sail with bold Brain the world through and through.
Bold Brain's commission is to burn and destroy
All United States vessels that he can decoy.

Chorus—Huzza! huzza! for bold Brain so true,
We will sail with bold Brain the world through and through.

To Havana they went with a small crew of boys,
For to capture the Roanoke without making a noise.
On board they did go with cool looks, as you see,
And at nine that same night there was a bit of a spree.

They then shot the carpenter—I suppose you all know—
But to find out who shot him the chances are small.
On the bridge he did run with his hands on his head,
And swore to Bob Gage that he was going dead.

They sewed him in canvas and lowered him down
In the deepest blue water that could there be found.
The sharks, in their schools, were playing about,
They smelt that old "Chips" had gone up the spout.
There was then a great mess because he was dead,
But he was only a "Yank," and there's more to be bled.

They came to Bermuda, but coals could not get.
They set fire to and burned her. Says Brain, "Boys, don't fret."
On Sunday they landed on Bermudian shore,
And were soon introduced to the Station House door.

They washed and they dressed, and refreshment was had,
With a coat for a pillow and the floor for a bed.
The people in crowds stood gazing about
When they found that the Roanoke had gone up the spout.

Captain Brain was alarmed by the ring of a bell,
And was then introduced to "Boggs' Hotel."
For two or three days they were all drilled about,
But all they could say, "She has gone up the spout."

GENERAL STONEWALL JACKSON'S body servant was a negro boy who seemed to have a prescience of any forward movement; his camp utensils and his master's baggage were always ready packed in anticipation of the order to advance. This peculiarity excited remark among the general's staff, and one day several young officers called the black boy up and asked him how he guessed so accurately the intentions of the general. "Well, gemmen, whenever I sees Massa Stonewall get up in the night and go to kneeling and saying his prayers I know there's a fight on hand, sure, and I makes preparations accordin'."

TORPEDOES USED BY THE CONFEDERATE GOVERNMENT.

THE earliest instance of the use of torpedoes during the war was on July 7, 1861, when an attempt was made by the Confederates to destroy Federal vessels in the Potomac River at Aquia Creek by the aid of an infernal machine or barrel torpedo, in July of the same year. A barrel of powder was found adrift in Hampton Roads. This was so arranged with a floating line that if the anchor chains or the wheel of a ship fouled the line, a percussion cap placed on the powder would be fired.

In December, 1861, subterranean infernal machines and submarine torpedoes came into use on the Mississippi and Savannah Rivers. The Frame torpedo first made its appearance in the Neuse River in March, 1862.

In May, 1862, ordinary shells with sensitive primers were buried in the road leading to Williamsburg, by General S. J. Rains. A body of Federal cavalry, as they rode over them, suffered terribly from the effect of their explosion. Generals Joseph E. Johnston and Longstreet forbade the use of these implements of warfare, and the matter was referred to the Secretary of War, who decided that torpedoes must only be used in a parapet, or on a road to repel assaults or check the enemy, or in a river or harbor to drive off blockading or an attacking fleet. Electric torpedoes were first sunk in the James River in July, 1861, and in Lake Pontchartrain in August, 1861. On December 12, 1862, the United States ironclad gunboat Cairo was blown up, below Haines Bluff, on the Mississippi, by a torpedo fired with a friction primer, by a trigger line leading to torpedo pits on shore. This was the first vessel of war engaged in active warfare destroyed by a torpedo.

THE BARREL TORPEDO, OR INFERNAL MACHINE,

Consisted of two barrels connected by a rope fifty feet long. One of the barrels was attached to an iron cylinder. Running longitudinally along the middle of barrel was a plank, and on it was coiled a fuse fifty fathoms in length, of fine white thread inclosed in gutta percha, the whole well wrapped round with coarser thread. The inner thread was soaked in a chemical preparation that made it a slow match. The fuse ran through a gutta percha tube, passing out at the bottom of the barrel and into the iron cylinder, which was sixteen inches in diameter, over four feet long and weighed upward of six hundred pounds, and filled with an explosive compound. The barrels were intended to float down stream, one on each side of the bow of a vessel, with the fuses lighted. When the fuses burnt out, the machine would explode and blow up the vessel.

The Torpedo Bureau was established at Richmond, Va., in October, 1862, under the charge of Brigadier-General G. J. Rains. At the same time the Naval Submarine Battery Service was organized under the command of Captain M. F. Maury, who subsequently relinquished it to Lieutenant Hunter Davidson.

Torpedo stations were established at Mobile, Richmond, Charleston, Wilmington and Savannah, and substations at other points. The members of the Torpedo Corps were granted extraordinary privileges on account of the perilous nature of the service, and they were sworn to secrecy. Many of these courageous fellows were killed while engaged in laying torpedoes, through accidental explosions.

An act of Congress, April 21, 1862, provided that the inventor of a device by which a vessel of the enemy should be destroyed should receive fifty per cent of the value of the vessel and armament, and the general appropriation bill of May 1, 1863, embraced an item of $20,000 for this branch of the public service, to be expended under the direction of the Navy Department, which was the first appropriation of the kind. By act of February 17, 1864, $100,000 was appropriated for the construction of submarine batteries, and by the act of June 13, 1864, $250,000 was appropriated for the same purpose.

During the war there were one hundred and twenty-three torpedoes planted in Charleston Harbor and Stono River, which prevented the capture and burning of that city. There were one hundred and one torpedoes planted in Roanoke River, North Carolina, by which seven of the twelve Federal vessels sent with troops and means to capture Fort Branch were destroyed. One was sunk by the fire from the fort, and the rest by torpedoes. Of the vessels sent to take Mobile, Ala., twelve were destroyed by torpedoes, viz.: three ironclads, two tinclads, and seven transports. There were fifty-eight vessels sunk by torpedoes in the war, and some of them of no small celebrity, as Admiral Farragut's flagship the Harvest Moon, the Thorn, the Commodore Jones, the monitor Patapsco, ram Osage, monitor Milwaukee, Housatonic and others. (Cairo in Yazoo River.)

The following illustrations and descriptions are of the important torpedo inventions that played a most conspicuous part in this service of the Confederacy.

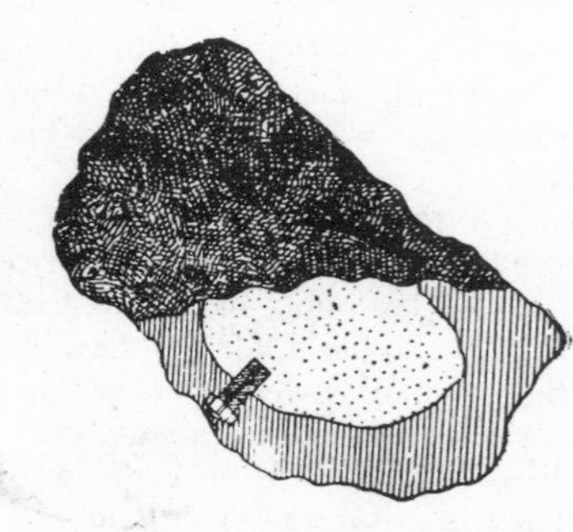

THE COAL TORPEDO

Looked like an innocent lump of coal, but, in reality, it was a block of cast iron with a core containing about ten pounds of powder. When covered with a mixture of tar and coal dust, it was impossible to detect its character. They could be placed in coal piles on barges from which Federal vessels took their supplies, and exploded with terrible effect in their boilers.

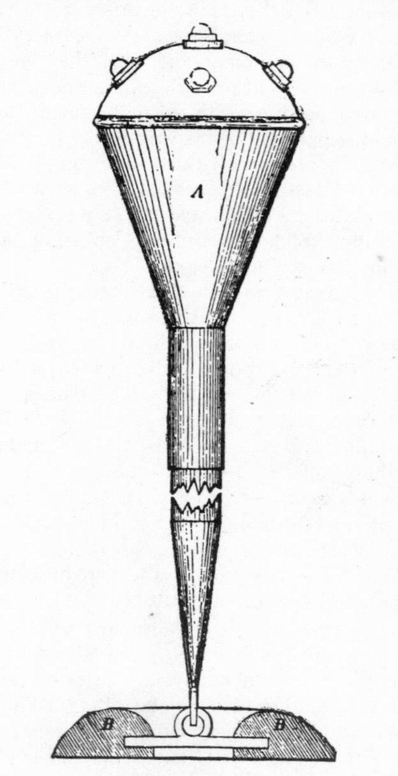

THE BUOYANT TORPEDO

Was a most dangerous one. It comprised a spar fastened by a universal joint to a fixed block at the bottom of the river, and bearing the torpedo at its summit. Swinging with the current and tide, this torpedo was always kept at a uniform depth below the surface, and was out of sight. The torpedo was studded with sensitive caps, and no matter where a ship touched it, would explode. They could not be grappled for, and it was only by good luck, care and ingenuity that the Federals got them out of the channels.

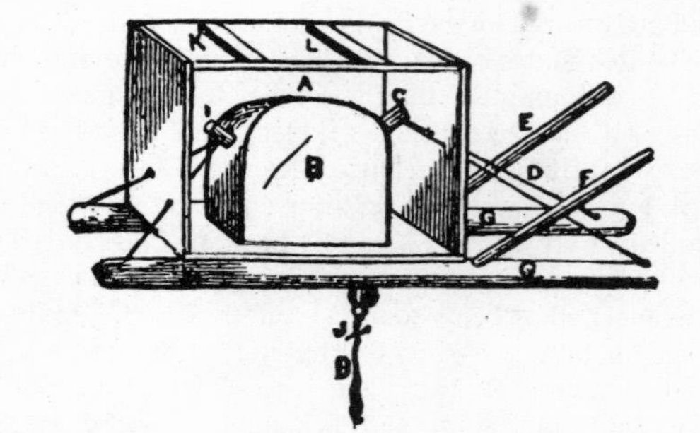

THE RAFT TORPEDO

Consisted of a raft, on which was a box five feet long, four and a half feet wide and four and three-fourths feet high, inclosing a powder tank, two and one-fourth feet square and three feet high.

A—The open top of the box. B—The iron tank. C—Brass tube. D—Iron rods connecting from tube to the end of the raft. E F—Parts of spars mortised to the runners of raft. G—The runners on which the box lay. H—The mooring. I—Tube with iron rods attached. J—The place where the warp was cut. K L—Braces across the top.

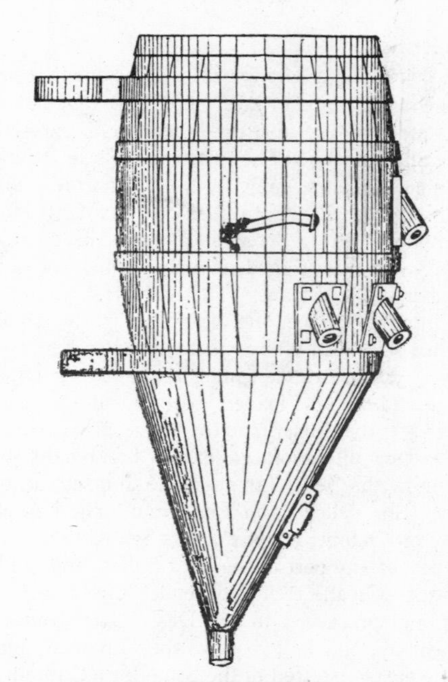

SPAR TORPEDO NO. 1.

This form of "ram torpedo" was taken from the ironclad Charleston, at Charleston, S. C. It was made from a strong wood cask, and had seven sensitive fuses. It contained about one hundred and fifty pounds of fine powder, and was fixed on the end of an iron spar about thirty feet long, attached to the bow near the water line.

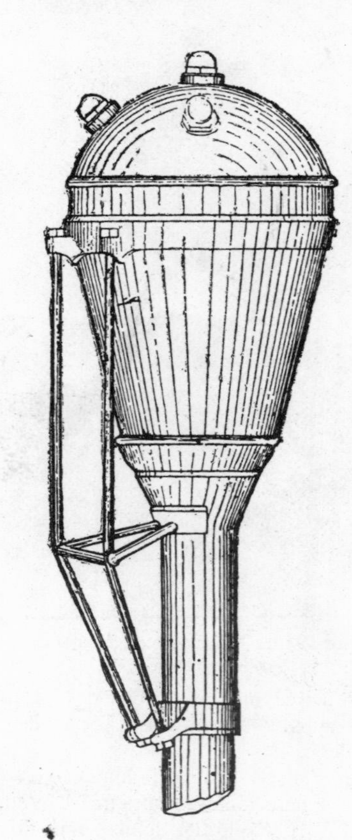

SPAR TORPEDO NO. 2.

This class of torpedo was generally used on all the Confederate gunboats. The braces were intended to support the weight of the torpedo, particularly when lifting out of water.

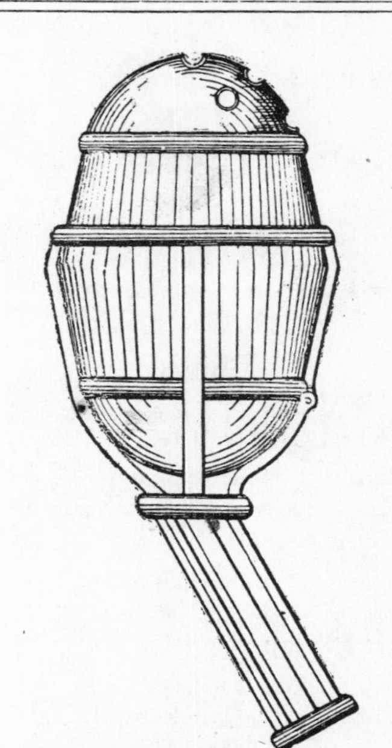

SPAR TORPEDO NO. 3.

This class of torpedo was among the first used. It was a soda water copper tank supported by iron straps, and had five chemical or sensitive fuses projecting from the upper half of the hemispherical surface.

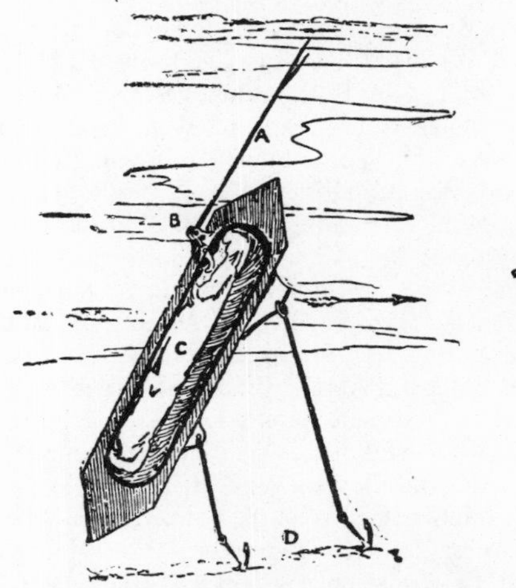

THE PRONGED TORPEDO

Consisted of a stout sheet iron cylinder, pointed at both ends, about five and a half feet long and one foot diameter. The iron lever was three and a half feet long, and armed with prongs to catch in the bottom of a boat. This lever was constructed to move the iron rod on inside of cylinder, thus acting upon the trigger of the lock to explode the cap and fire the powder. The machine was anchored, presenting the prongs in such a way that boats going down stream should slide over them, but those coming up should catch.

A—Iron rod armed with prongs to fasten upon bottom of boats going up stream and act upon. B—A lever connecting with trigger to explode a cap and ignite powder. C—Canvas bag containing seventy pounds of powder. D—Anchors to hold torpedo in place.

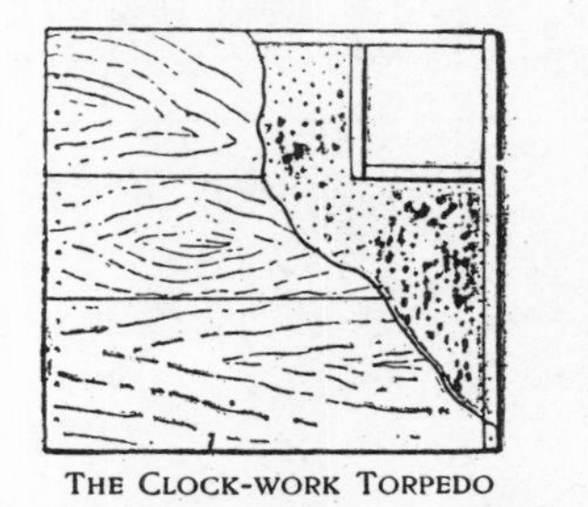

THE CLOCK-WORK TORPEDO

Consisted of a box containing a quantity of powder, and a clock arrangement set to fire a detonating cap at a given hour. This machine was the one that caused the great explosion at City Point, on the James River, August 9, 1864, destroying several vessels loaded with ordnance stores, and the warehouses on the wharf filled with army supplies, and killing and wounding some fifty men.

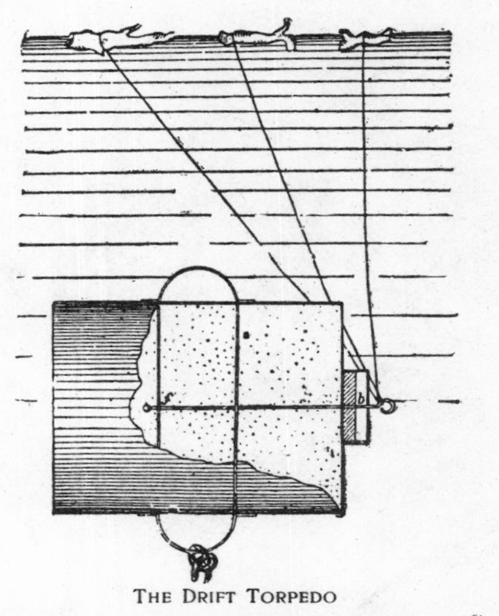

THE DRIFT TORPEDO

Was a tin case containing about seventy pounds of powder. A number of wires from the friction fuse led from the powder to small pieces of driftwood on the surface of the water. It was floated at a proper depth by a line fastened to a floating log, and was turned adrift with the view of fouling the trigger lines by the propellers of the enemy's vessels. In January, 1863, one of these torpedoes was picked up by the United States gunboat Essex in the Mississippi River.

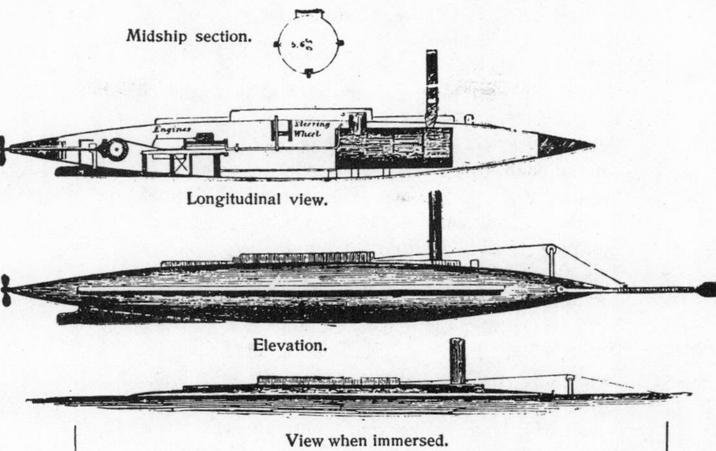

Midship section.

Longitudinal view.

Elevation.

View when immersed.

THE CONFEDERATE "DAVID"

Was a double-ended steam torpedo craft composed of wood and iron, twenty to sixty feet long, and about seven feet in diameter at the center. The boiler was forward, the engine aft, and between them was a cuddy-hole for the captain, engineer and whatever crew the boat might carry, and which was entered by a hatchway. The torpedo was carried on a spar that protruded from the bow, and which could be raised or lowered at will by a line passing back into the cuddy-hole. A two-bladed propeller drove the craft along. The torpedo was made of copper, with a mechanical fuse, and carried from fifty to seventy pounds of powder. When ready for action the boat was so well submerged that nothing was visible except her stunt smoke-stack, the hatch-coaming and the stanchion upon which the torpedo-line was brought aft.

THE KEG TORPEDO

Consisted of a lager beer barrel, calked and pitched, loaded with from forty to one hundred and twenty pounds of powder, capped with friction fuses, and when moored in a channel they proved of excellent defense, causing the loss of more vessels than any other kind used by the Confederates. Six vessels and a steam launch were blown up by them in Mobile Bay and tributaries between March 28th and April 18, 1865, and they also destroyed the Confederate steamers Ettiwan and Marion, in Charleston Harbor, they having drifted from their moorings.

THE FISH TORPEDO

Was a boat made of galvanized iron and shaped like a fish. It was twenty feet long and at the middle three and one-half feet wide by five feet deep, and was propelled by a screw worked from the inside by seven or eight men. It was so contrived that it could be submerged and worked under water for several hours, and to this end was provided with a fin on each side, worked also from the interior. By depressing the points of these fins the boat, when in motion, was made to descend; and by elevating them it was made to rise. This torpedo sunk the United States sloop of war Housatonic, on the night of February 17, 1864, but unhappily, from some unknown cause, the torpedo-boat was also sunk and all with it lost. Whether she was swamped by the water thrown up by the explosion, or was carried down by the sinking Housatonic, will never be known. After the war a diver examining the wreck of the Housatonic found the torpedo-boat lying alongside of its victim.

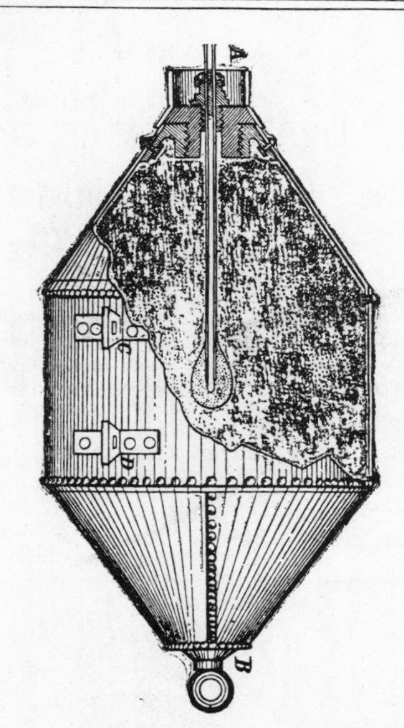

THE ELECTRIC TORPEDO

Was made of three-quarter-inch boiler-iron and filled with fine powder. Two wires connected it with the electric battery on shore, the conductor being covered with gutta percha, the submerged ends being additionally protected by a covering of tarred hemp and weighted with chain. The torpedo was anchored to bolts (C and D) and castings were bolted to the ends (A and B), the former to cover and protect the circuit wires.

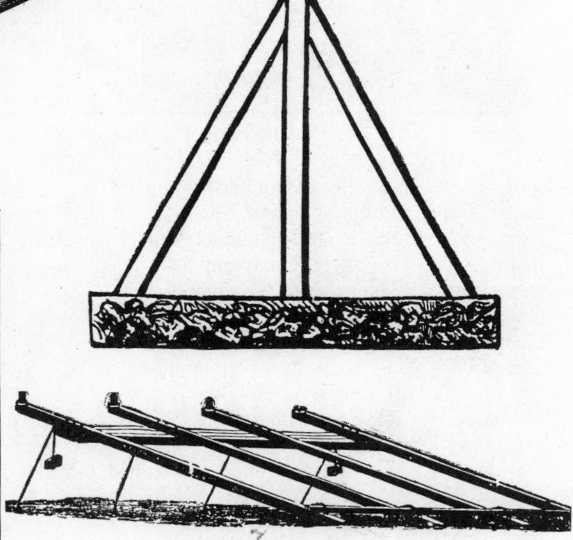

THE FRAME TORPEDO

Consisted of three heavy pieces of timber placed in position, at the bottom of which was placed a box filled with old iron, stones and other heavy materials. It was sunk in the river and then inclined forward at an angle of forty-five degrees by means of ropes and weights. This heavy frame was capped by a cylinder of iron about ten inches in diameter. Into this was fitted a shell, which was heavily loaded, resting on a set of springs so arranged that the least pressure on the cylinder would instantly discharge the shell by means of a percussion cap ingeniously placed.

UNITED STATES VESSELS DESTROYED OR INJURED BY CONFEDERATE TORPEDOES.

VESSEL.	PLACE.	DATE.	Tonnage.	Injury.
Cairo, ironclad	Yazoo River	December 12, 1862	512	Destroyed.
Montauk, monitor	Ogeechee River	February 28, 1863	844	Serious.
Baron DeKalb, ironclad	Yazoo River	July 22, 1863	512	Destroyed,
Commodore Barney, gunboat	James River	August 8, 1863	513	Disabled.
John Farron, transport	James River	September —, 1863	. .	Serious.
New Ironsides, ironclad	Off Charleston	October 5, 1863	. . . .	Serious.
Housatonic, sloop of war	Off Charleston	February 17, 1864	1,240	Destroyed.
Maple Leaf, transport	St. Johns River	April 1, 1864	508	Destroyed.
Minnesota, frigate	Newport News	April 9, 1864	3,307	Serious
General Hunter, transport	St. Johns River	April 15, 1864	350	Destroyed.
Eastport, ironclad	Red River	April 15, 1864	800	Destroyed.
Commodore Jones, gunboat	James River	May 6, 1864	542	Destroyed.
H. A. Weed, transport	St. Johns River	May 9, 1864	290	Destroyed.
Alice Price, transport	St. Johns River	June 19, 1864	320	Destroyed.
Tecumseh, monitor	Mobile Bay	August 5, 1864	1,034	Destroyed.
Several vessels	City Point, James River	August 9, 1864	. . . .	Destroyed.
Greyhound, transport	James River	November 27, 1864	900	Destroyed.
Narcissus, gunboat	Mobile Bay	December 7, 1864	101	Sunk.
Otsego, gunboat	Roanoke River	December 9, 1864	974	Destroyed.
Bazely, gunboat	Roanoke River	December 10, 1864	. . . .	Destroyed.
Launch No. 5	Roanoke River	December 10, 1864	. . . .	Destroyed.
Patapsco, monitor	Charleston, S. C.	January 15, 1864	844	Destroyed.
Osceola, gunboat	Cape Fear River	February 20, 1864	974	Slight.
Launch, Shawmut	Cape Fear River	February 20, 1864	. . . .	Destroyed.
Harvest Moon	Georgetown, S. C.	March 1, 1864	546	Destroyed.
Thorn, transport	Cape Fear River	March 4, 1864	403	Destroyed.
Althea, gunboat	Blakely River	March 12, 1864	. . . .	Destroyed.
Bibb, coast survey steamer	Charleston, S. C.	March 17, 1864	. . . .	Slight.
Massachusetts, gunboat	Charleston, S. C.	March 20, 1864	1,155	Slight.
Milwaukee, monitor	Blakely River	March 28, 1864	970	Destroyed.
Osage, monitor	Blakely River	March 29, 1864	523	Sunk.
Rudolph, gunboat	Blakely River	April 1, 1864	217	Destroyed.
Ida, tug	Blakely River	April 13, 1864	101	Destroyed.
Scioto, gunboat	Mobile Bay	April 14, 1864	507	Destroyed.
Cincinnati, tug	Blakely River	April 14, 1864	. . . .	Destroyed.
Itasca, gunboat	Mobile Bay	April 14, 1864	. . . .	Destroyed.
Rose, gunboat	Mobile Bay	April 14, 1864	. . . .	Destroyed.
St. Mary's, transport	Alabama River	April —, 1864	. . . .	Destroyed.
R. B. Hamilton, transport	Mobile Bay	April —, 1864	400	Destroyed.
Jonquil, gunboat	Ashley River	June 6, 1864	. . . .	Serious.

LIST OF VESSELS OF THE CONFEDERATE STATES NAVY AND THEIR COMMANDERS.

1861–1865.

This List is Correct as far as can be ascertained from Incomplete Records kept by the Confederate States Navy Department. These Vessels had other Commanders at different periods, but only those names that are found on the Records are given.

Alabama, Raphael Semmes, Commander.
Albemarle, James W. Cooke, Commander.
Arctic, —— ——, Commander.
Arkansas, Isaac N. Brown, Commander.
Roanoke, M. F. Clarke, Commander.
Resolute, J. Pembroke Jones, Commander; afterward, Wilburn B. Hall.
Savannah, John Kell, Commander; afterward, Wilburn B. Hall.
Selma, Peter U. Murphy, Commander.
Shenandoah, James Iredell Waddell, Commander.
Sumter, Raphael Semmes, Commander.
Stonewall Jackson, —— Phillips, Commander.
Sampson, Joel S. Kennard, Commander.
Tuscaloosa, Charles H. McBlair, Commander.
Tennessee, James D. Johnston, Commander.
Torpedo, Hunter Davidson, Commander.
Torch, Frank E. Sheppard, Commander.
Teaser, J. W. Alexander, Commander.
Uncle Ben, —— ——, Commander.
Van Dorn, Isaac Fulkerson, Commander.
Virginia, Robert B. Pegram, Commander.

The United States Gunboat Cairo Sunk by an Electric Spar Torpedo.

Atlanta, W. H. Webb, Commander.
Baltic, C. C. Simms, Commander.
Bragg, W. H. H. Leonard, Commander.
Beaufort, W. H. Parker, Commander.
Beauregard, J. Henry Hart, Commander.
Chattahoochie, John J. Guthrie, Commander.
Charleston, Isaac N. Brown, Commander.
Chicora, Thomas T. Hunter, Commander.
Drewry, C. H. Fauntleroy, Commander.
Defiance, —— McCoy, Commander.
Fredericksburg, T. R. Rootes, Commander.
Florida, J. N. Maffitt, Commander; when lost, Charles M. Morris.
Gaines, John W. Bennett, Commander.
Georgia, William L. Maury, Commander.
Governor Moore, Beverly Kennon, Commander.
General Quitman, —— Grant, Commander.
Georgia (ironclad), William Gwathmey, Commander; afterward, J. P. Jones; afterward, Oscar L. Johnson.
Hampton, John S. Maury, Commander.
Huntsville, Julian Myers, Commander.
Huntress, W. B. Hall, Commander; afterward, William G. Dozier; afterward, Charles M. Morris.
Harriet Lane, Nicholas Barney, Commander.
Isandiga, Joel S. Kennard, Commander.
Indian Chief, J. H. Ingraham, Commander.
Jackson, F. B. Renshaw, Commander.
John Bell, —— ——, Commander.
Judah, —— ——, Commander.
Juno, Philip Porcher, Commander.
Jeff Thompson, John Burk, Commander.
Jamestown, Thomas Jefferson Page, Commander.
Little Rebel, J. White Fowler, Commander.
Louisiana, Charles McIntosh, Commander.
Lovell, James C. Dellaney, Commander.
Manassas, A. F. Warley, Commander.
McRea, Thos. B. Huger, Commander.
Missouri, —— ——, Commander.
Morgan, George W. Harrison, Commander.
Mississippi (never was launched; destroyed by James I. Waddell), Arthur Sinclair, Commander.
Merrimac, Franklin Buchanan, Commander.
Nashville, Robert B. Pegram, Commander.
Neuse, William Sharp, Commander.
Nansemond, —— ——, Commander.
North Carolina, William S. Muse, Commander.
Price, Thomas Henthorn, Commander.
Palmetto State, John Rutledge, Commander.
Patrick Henry, John R. Tucker, Commander.
Raleigh, John Wilkinson, Commander; afterward, A. Armstrong.
Richmond, W. H. Parker, Commander.
Rappahannock, Charles M. Fauntleroy, Commander.
Water Witch, P. T. Pelot, Commander.
Webb, W. B. Hall, Commander; afterward, C. W. Reed.
Warrior, —— Stephenson, Commander.
Yadkin, W. A. Kerr, Commander.
Yorktown, Nicholas Barney, Commander.

WHEN General Mahone was wounded at second Manassas, some one, to comfort Mrs. Mahone, said: "Oh, don't be uneasy; it is only a flesh wound." Mrs. Mahone, through her tears, cried out: "Oh, I know that is impossible; there is not flesh enough on him for that." We don't know whether this is a joke on the general or the private.

OFFICERS OF THE CONFEDERATE STATES NAVY, FROM THE NAVY REGISTER, JUNE 1, 1864.

THE LAST ONE ISSUED.

ADMIRAL.

Franklin Buchanan.

CAPTAINS.

Samuel Barron, Raphael Semmes, W. W. Hunter, E. Farland, J. K. Mitchell, J. R. Tucker, T. J. Page, R. F. Pinckney, J. W. Cooke.

COMMANDERS.

T. R. Rootes, T. T. Hunter, I. N. Browne, R. B. Pegram, W. L. Maury, J. N. Maffitt, J. N. Barney, W. A. Webb, G. T. Sinclair, G. W. Harrison, J. D. Johnston, John Kell, W. T. Glassell, H. Davidson.

FIRST LIEUTENANTS.

Washington Gwathmey, John Rutledge, Joel S. Kennard, Charles M. Morris, John S. Maury, Charles W. Hays, Charles C. Simms, J. Myers, A. F. Warley, John W. Bennett, J. H. Carter, W. H. Parker, J. Pembroke Jones, Wm. H. Murdaugh, James H. Rochelle, Robert D. Minor, James I. Waddell, Joseph Fry, Charles P. McGary, Robert R. Carter, John B. Hamilton, Oscar F. Johnston, John R. Eggleston, R. T. Chapman, Wm. P. Campbell, B. P. Loyall Wm. H. Ward, John W. Dunnington, Francis E. Sheppard, Wm. G. Dozier, Wm. L. Bradford, Hamilton H. Dalton, Wm. E. Evans, George E. Shryock, Thomas K. Porter, Joseph W. Alexander, Charles J. Graves, Thos. B. Mills, Wm. C. Whittle, Jr., Wm. A. Kerr, John Grimball, Wm. K. Hall, Samuel W. Averett, H. B. Claiborne, George A. Borchert, Hilery Cenas, Walter A. Butt, Wm. Winder Pollock, A. D. Wharton, Thomas L. Dornin, Thomas L. Harrison, James L. Hoole, Francis L. Hoge, Edmund G. Reed, Charles W. Read, S. G. Stone, Alphonso Barbot, Robert J. Bowen, W. Gift, Thomas W. W. Davies, Patrick McCarrick, Wm. F. Carter, Wm. H. Wall, W. W. Carnes, John H. Ingraham, Wm. Van Comstock, Richard F. Armstrong, Albert G. Hudgins, Charles K. King, James H. Comstock, James D. Wilson, Julian M. Spencer, Sidney S. Lee, Samuel Barron, Jr., E. Canty Stockton, J. McCaleb Baker, John W. Murdaugh, Mortimer M. Benton, Charles L. Harralson, Sidney H. McAdam, Francis T. Chew, Alexander M. Mason, Thomas L. Moore, Ivey Foreman, Walter O'Crain, Joseph Price, Alexander Grant, Charles E. Yeatman, Charles B. Oliver, Charles W. Hasker, Francis Watlington, John L. Phillips, George H. Arledge, M. T. Clarke, John A. Payne, Henry W. Ray, Wm. E. Hudgins, John F. Ramsay, H. B. Littlepage, Lewis R. Hill, Edward J. Means, Henry Roberts, Richard H. Gale, Richard C. Foute, Francis M. Roby, Henry H.

Explosion of a Torpedo under the Commodore Barney, on the James River, August 4, 1863.

Marmaduke, John Lowe, Arthur Sinclair, Jr., Wm. W. Roberts, Edgar A. Lambert, Otey Bradford, Joseph M. Gardner, Matthew P. Goodwyn, Americus V. Wiatt, Thos. L. Skinner, Charles Borum, J. V. Johnson, C. L. Stanton.

SECOND LIEUTENANTS.

J. P. Claybrook, R. S. Floyd, W. P. Mason, W. F. Robinson, J. R. Price, D. A. Telfair, Daniel Trigg, I. C. Holcome, W. R. Dalton, A. S. Worth, R. A. Camm, D. M. Scales, J. T. Walker, S. S. Gregory, W. W. Read, R. H. Bacot, E. J. McDermott, R. B. Larmour, T. P. Bell, J. W. Billups.

SURGEONS.

J. W. B. Greenhow, W. D. Harrison, Wm. F. Carrington, Charles H. Williamson, Arthur M. Lynch, Daniel B. Conrad, F. L. Galt, W. M. Page, H. W. M. Washington, A. G. Garnett.

PASSED ASSISTANT SURGEONS.

Frederick Garretson, J. W. Sanford, T. J. Charlton, C. E. Lining, M. P. Christian, R. J. Freeman, B. W. Green, J. W. Herty, J. E. Lindsay, O. S. Iglehart.

ASSISTANT SURGEONS.

C. M. Morfitt, T. B. Ford, R. R. Gibbs, E. G. Booth, Thos. Emory, W. M. Turner, John DeBree, Marcellus Ford, W. W. Graves, W. J. Addison, N. C. Edwards, S. S. Herrick, N. M. Read, John Leyburn, R. C. Powell, R. C. Bowles, J. P. Lipscomb, W. C. Jones, W. Sheppardson, C. M. Parker, C. W. Thomas, H. B. Melvin, W. S. Stoakly, W. W. Griggs, J. F. Tipton, G. B. Weston, G. N. Halstead, J. V. Cook, J. O. Grant, Pike Brown, H. G. Land, G. W. Claiborne, J. M. Hicks, J. G. King, D. E. Ewart, Ed. Claire, J. V. Harris, L. R. Dickinson, J. B. Rutherford, G. A. Foote, N. K. Henderson, J. W. Beline, W. L. Warner, Robert Kuykendall, J. G. Thomas, W. E. Bondurant, J. E. Moyler, Fred. Peck, H. S. Paisy, J. E. Duffel, J. G. Bigley, K. Goldborough.

PAYMASTERS.

Felix Senac, James O. Moore, Richard Taylor, James E. Armour.

ASSISTANT PAYMASTERS.

D. F. Forrest, W. B. Micon, L. E. Brooks, J. S. Banks, J. J. McPherson, M. M. Seay, G. H. O'Neal, W. J. Richardson, P. M. DeLeon, Adam Tredwell, Edw. McKean, D. C. Seymour, L. B. Reardon, W. H. Chase, H. E. McDuffie, W. M. Ladd, S. S. Barksdale, S. S. Nicholas, Chas. W. Keim, W. E. Deacon, T. G. Ridgely, J. M. Pearl, L. M. Tucker, C. L. Jones, W. B. Cobb, J. F. Wheliss, M. L. Southron, Marsden Bellamy, B. M. Herriot, N. K. Adams, W. A. Hearne, C. G. Pearson.

MASTERS IN LINE OF PROMOTION.

S. P. Blanc, G. D. Bryan, Wyndam R. Mayo, D. D. Colcock, W. P. Hamilton, J. G. Long, H. L. Vaughan, J. M. Pearson, H. S. Cooke, C. W. Sparks, W. J. Craig.

MASTERS NOT IN LINE OF PROMOTION.

John Pearson, Lewis Parrish, A. Pacetty, Richard Evans, F. M. Harris, John C. Minor, C. W. Johnson, W. B. Whitehead, H. W. Perrin, B. W. Guthrie, Charles A. McEvoy, William D. Porter, James W. McCarrick, Lewis Musgrave, Peter W. Smith, G. Andrews, A. L. Myers, J. Y. Beall, D. W. Nash, Thomas L. Wragg, George M. Peek, Henry Wilkinson, Julian Fairfax, G. A. Peple, Levi G. White, Edward McGuire, John Maxwell, Bennett G. Burley, S. Milliken, Seth Foster, John L. Ahern, John Webb, B. J. Sage, Charles Beck, Lewis N. Huck, G. W. Armistead, B. J. Sherley, George W. Smith, John A. Curtis, William Collins, C. M. Hite, A. Robinson, C. Linn, John M. Gibbs, Henry Yeatman, C. E. Girardy, W. Frank Shippey, Louis Gonnart, James Cahoon, Charles E. Little, John E. Hogg, Joseph R. DeMahy, H. D. Edinborough, Wm. A. Hines, John C. Braine, W. B. Cox, Lemuel Langley.

MIDSHIPMEN—THIRD CLASS, SENIOR.

P. H. Gibbs, W. N. Shaw, F. C. Morehead, George A. Joiner, Roger Pinckney, C. Cary, R. J. Deas, B. Carter, C. F. Sevier, W. F. Clayton, W. K. Hale, F. M. Berrien, Thomas C. Pinckney, A. O. Wright, H. H. Scott, H. H. Tyson, F. B. Doonin, P. H. McCarrick, F. M. Thomas, F. S. Hunter, W. T. Carroll, D. M. Lee, J. B. Ratcliffe, C. Meyer, James R. Norris, W. D. Goode, L. M. Rootes, R. J. Crawford, L. D. Hamner, Thomas Wherritt, E. M. Jones, D. B. Talbott, R. E. Pinckney, H. J. Ellett, Raphael Semmes, Jr., A. M. Harrison, O. S. Manson, E. B. Prescott.

MIDSHIPMEN—THIRD CLASS, JUNIOR.

D. A. Dixon, John T. Lomax, John A. Lee, George B. Cloud, John H. Inglis, H. T. Minor, W. S. Hogue, J. D. Howell, John Johnson, Lewis Levy, J. G. Minnegerode, A. S. Doak, G. A. Wilkins, John D. Trimble, J. DeB. Northrop, Richard Slaughter, Eugene Phillips, H. J. Warren, John T. Scharf, W. A. Lee, A. T. Hunt, Preston B Moore.

MIDSHIPMEN—FOURTH CLASS.

Wm. M. Snead, W. J. Claiborne, W. S. Davidson, W. D. Haldman, J. C. Wright, M. J. McRae, W. H. Payne, B. S. Johnson, F. S. Kennett, F. L. Place, C. R. Breckenridge, C. G. Dandridge, T. D. Stone.

MIDSHIPMEN.

R. S. Floyd, R. J. Moses, W. W. Wilkinson, O. A. Brown, John T. Mason, Wm. B. Sinclair, James W. Pegram, J. H. Hamilton, J. H. Dyke, V. Newton, G. D. Bryan, G. T. Sinclair, W. H. Sinclair, I. D. Bulloch, Eugene Maffitt, E. M. Anderson, J. A. Wilson, J. M. Morgan.

CHIEF ENGINEERS.

Michael Quinn, Charles Schroeder, Henry X. Wright, James H. Toombs.

FIRST ASSISTANT ENGINEERS.

G. W. City, C. H. Levy, Loudon Campbell, G. D. Lining, W. J. Freeman, H. B. Willy, Hugh Clark, M. P. Jordan, J. H. Loper, W. T. Morrell, G. W. Tennant, Benj. Herring, J. T. Tucker, W. Ahern, J. R. Jordan, J. J. Darcy, W. Youngblood, C. W. Jordan, E. A. Jack, W. P. Brooks.

SECOND ASSISTANT ENGINEERS.

E. G. Hall, Isaac Bowman, J. F. Green, Junius Hanks, J. M. Freeman, Jr., C. H. Collier, N. O'Brien, W. M. Fauntleroy, Leslie King, J. L. Foster, R. J. Kilpatrick, W. B. Brockett, J. C. Johnson, D. H. Pritchard, J. C. O'Connell, E. H. Brown. J. H. Dent, John Langdon, L. A. McCarthy, J. S. West, J. J. Lyell, John Hayes, Jos. Cardy, G. W. Caldwell, Richard Finn, E. L. Dick, J. H. Baily.

THIRD ASSISTANT ENGINEERS.

J. T. Doland, R. J. Caswell, W. F. Harding, J. H. Parker, F. G. Miller, S. B. Jordan, J. K. Langhorne, J. W. Tomlinson, H. H. Roberts, E. F. Gill, R. J. Hackley, J. B. Brown, G. A. Bowe, A. De Blanc, C. C. Leavett, C. S. Peek, A. J. Schwarzman, M. P. Young, M. A. Newberry, B. F. Drago, Oscar Benson, J. C. Phillips, W. A. Luddington, Wm. Rogers, W. R. Doury, Peter Faithful, Donald McDonald, W. B. Patterson, E. P. Weaver, M. J. Cohen, J. T. Reams, R. S. Herring, J. W. McGrath, H. B. Goodrich, G. Wainwright, J. J. Kerrish, John Applegate, J. N. Ramsey, J. B. Weaver, R. E. Edwards, J. J. McGrath, Wm. C. Purse, T. O. McClosky, C. B. Thompson, R. J. O'Neal, J. F. Robinett, Achilles Lombard, J. P. Miller, W. C. Tilton, A. P. Wright, C. W. Ridle, W. H. Handy, G. H. Wellington, J. L. McDonald, S. K. Mooers, R. J. Smith, J. J. Lacklison, B. H. Bates, E. J. Dennigan, J. E. Viernelson, E. T. Homan, Holmes Ahern, Henry Discher, James Carlon, J. H. Haly.

Acquia Creek Batteries Resisting an Attack by the U. S Steamers Pawnee, Anacosta and Freeborn.

BOATSWAINS.

Lester Seymour, Thos. Ganley, A. J. Wilson, Andrew Blakie, J. C. Cronin, John Kavanaugh, Jas. Smith, W. J. Smith, H. J. Wilson, J. J. Ingraham, John McCredie, Robt. McCalla, Peter Taff, John Cassidy, John Brown.

GUNNERS.

John Owens, John A. Lovett, Wm. Cuddy, J. G. McCluskey, Z. A. Offutt, Wm. H. Haynes, T. B. Travers, W. A. Flemming, G. M. Thompson, E. R. Johnson, S. P. Schisano, E. G. Williams, B. F. Hughes, Wm. Shelly, T. Baker, W. F. Brittingham, C. Gormly, B. A. Barrow, W. J. Ballentyne, John Raabe, J. I. Mayberry, John Waters, Hugh McDonald, C. E. Porter, H. L. Smith, R. J. Webb, Ira W. Porter.

CARPENTERS.

R. M. Baine, J. T. Rustic, J. M. Burroughs, G. D. Fentress, Wm. R. Jarvis, R. J. Meads.

SAIL-MAKERS.

William Bennett, E. A. Mahoney, S. V. Turner, M. P. Beaufort, George Newton.

ACTING MASTERS' MATES.

J. L. Ahern, Wm. McBlair, J. T. Mayberry, J. A. Riley, T. T. Hunter, Jr., J. C. Young, W. G. Porter, T. B. Boville, T. L. Wragg, G. Waterman, W. W. Skinner, J. Y. Benson, J. T. Layton, T. J. Hudgins, W. Smith, R. Benthall, A. E. Alberton, T. E. Gibbs, S. S. Foster, C. Russell, T. M. Hazlehurst, B. M. Fogartie, J. C. Turner, C. B. Bohannon, G. Atchison, S. A. Brockenton, J. A. Rosier, E. M. Skinner, H. C. Barr, E. C. Parsons, J. A. Paschall, R. Battle, E. P. Winder, J. H. Turner, J. H. Hart, W. H. Fitzgerald, F. B. Green, C. N. Golder, L. S. Seymour, W. M. Snead, W. D. Oliveira, W. N. Brown, Edward W. Jordan, O. L. Jenkins, C. Hunter, C. M. Selden, C. E. Bragden, P. M. Baker, W. B. Littlepage, S. L. Simpson, L. L. Foster, R. N. Spraggins, E. T. Haynie, J. J. Bronson, E. C. Skinner, W. S. Forrest, W. R. Howle, C. R. McBlair, A. Campbell, E. W. C. Mayhin, A. G. Hall, J. R. Murray, W. R. Rowe, H. Gilliland, J.

Steamer Patrick Henry, Confederate Naval School Ship.

R. Chisman, C. Neil, W. A. Lamkin, R. M. Carter, A. McMillan, J. C. Graves, J. E. Ferral, R. Freeman, P. Power, A. G. Corran, J. C. Hill, W. E. Lester, T. S. Gray, M. J. Beebe, L. Pitts, J. J. Whitehead, W. A. Marschalk, R. Webb, T. Mason, G. C. Lyon, J. M. Hazlehurst, C. F. Curtis, A. W. Johnson, F. Marschalk, C. J. Yonge, P. G. Webb, H. Hermier, L. Bowdoin, E. Smith, W. A. Collier, C. Frazee, C. K. Floyd.

CONFEDERATE STATES BLOCKADE RUNNER ROBERT E. LEE.

The following names of regular officers in the Navy Register of January 1, 1864, are not among those of the Provisional Navy in the Register of June 1, 1864:

CAPTAINS.

Lawrence Rosseau, French Forrest, Josiah Tatnall, V. M. Randolph, Geo. N. Hollins, D. N. Ingraham, Wm. F. Lynch, Isaac S. Sterrett, S. S. Lee, Wm. C. Whittle.

NAVAL CONSTRUCTORS.

John L. Porter, chief; and J. Pearce, W. A. Graves, acting constructors.

MARINE CORPS.

The Confederate States Navy Register for January, 1864, gives the following roster of the Marine Corps:

COLONEL COMMANDANT.

L. J. Beall.

LIEUTENANT-COLONEL.

H. B. Tyler.

MAJOR.

G. H. Terrette.

PAYMASTER WITH RANK OF MAJOR.

R. T. Allison.

ADJUTANT WITH RANK OF MAJOR.

Israel Greene.

QUARTERMASTER WITH RANK OF MAJOR.

A. S. Taylor.

CAPTAINS.

J. D. Simms, J. R. F. Tatnall, A. J. Hayes, G. Holmes, R. T. Thom, A. C. Van Benthuysen, J. E. Meiere and T. S. Wilson.

FIRST LIEUTENANTS.

C. L. Sayre, B. K. Howell, R. H. Henderson, D. G. Raney, J. R. Y. Fendall, T. P. Gwynn, J. Thurston, F. H. Cameron, F. MacRee.

SECOND LIEUTENANTS.

D. Bradford, N. E. Venable, H. L. Graves, H. M. Doak, Albert S. Berry, E. F. Neuville, D. G. Brent, J. C. Murdoch, S. M. Roberts, John L. Rapier.

ENGAGEMENT ON THE MISSISSIPPI RIVER AT LUCAS BEND, BETWEEN THE CONFEDERATE GUNBOAT YANKEE AND THE UNITED STATES GUNBOATS LEXINGTON AND CONESTOGA.

COMMANDERS.

Robert D. Thorburn, Robt. G. Robb, Murray Mason, C. H. McBlair, A. B. Fairfax, Richard L. Page, Fred'k Chatard, Arthur Sinclair, C. H. Kennedy, Thos. W. Brent, Matthew F. Maury, Geo. Minor, H. J. Hartstene, J. L. Henderson, W. T. Muse, C. F. M. Spotswood, C. Ap R. Jones, J. Taylor Wood.

COMMANDERS FOR THE WAR.

Jas. D. Bulloch, James H. North, John M. Brooke.

FIRST LIEUTENANTS.

F. B. Renshaw, C. B. Poindexter, H. H. Lewis, P. W. Murphy, John J. Guthrie, Van R. Morgan, Edward L. Winder, John H. Parker, John Wilkinson, C. M. Fauntleroy, A. McLaughlin, A. M. De Bree, N. H. Van Zant, D. P. McCorkle, Wm. Sharp, Jos. D. Blake, Thos. P. Pelot, Philip Porcher.

LIEUTENANTS FOR THE WAR.

Joshua Humphreys, S. W. Corbin, Jas. L. Johnson, Thos. W. Benthall, John G. Blackwood, Wm. H. Odenheimer, Edward E. Stiles.

SURGEONS.

Jas. Cornick, Wm. F. Patton, W. A. W. Spotswood, Lewis W. Minor, W. F. McClenahan, John T. Mason, William B. Sinclair, Richard Jeffery, Jas. F. Harrison, D. D. Phillips, Chas. F. Fahs, Wm. E. Wysham.

PAYMASTERS.

John De Bree, Thos. R. Ware, Jas. A. Semple, John Johnston, W. W. J. Kelly, Jas. K. Harwood, Geo. H. Ritchie, Henry Myers, John W. Nixon.

MASTERS IN LINE OF PROMOTION.

Richard H. Bacot.

MASTERS NOT IN LINE OF PROMOTION.

Wm. H. Carlon.

PASSED MIDSHIPMAN.

A. P. Beirne.

ENGINEER-IN-CHIEF.

Wm. P. Williamson.

CHIEF ENGINEERS.

Jas. H. Warner, Thos. A. Jackson, Virginius Freeman, E. W. Manning, H. A. Ramsey, Wm. Frick, J. W. Tynan.

FIRST ASSISTANT ENGINEERS.

W. S. Thompson, W. P. Riddle.

LETTERS OF SAFEGUARD.

THE Confederate States of America to all their officers, civil and military, and to all other persons to whom these presents shall come:

The bearer of this is Bis-te-va-na, the principal chief of the Ya-pa-rih-ca band of the Ne-um, or Comanches of the Prairie, and those who accompany him are the head men of that band, all of whom have this day concluded and signed, in behalf of the whole Ya-pa-rih-ca band, articles of a convention of peace and friendship between that band and other bands of the Ne-um with us, and have thereby agreed to settle and live upon reserves in the country between the Red River and the Canadian, leased by us from the Choctaws and Chickasaws; and the said chief has also agreed to visit the other bands of the Ne-um, not parties to the same convention, and now on the Staked Plain, or elsewhere, and persuade them also to settle upon reserves in the same country.

We have accordingly taken the said chief and the said head men, and all other persons of both sexes and all ages, of the said Ya-pa-rih-ca band, from this day forward under our protection, until they shall for just cause forfeit the same, and that forfeiture be declared by us; and we have, therefore, granted, and do grant to them and to each of them, these our letters of safeguard for their protection, and to avail each and all of them as far as our authority and jurisdiction extends.

You are therefore hereby charged to respect these letters, and give all the said persons protection and safe-conduct; and any infraction by any of you of this safeguard will be visited by us with all the penalties due to those who violate the public faith and dishonor the Confederacy.

In testimony whereof, Albert Pike, Commissioner of the Confederate States to all the Indian nations and tribes west of those States, doth hereunto set his hand and affix the seal of his arms. [SEAL]

Done and granted at the agency of the Confederate States for the Comanches, Wichitas, and other bands of Indians near the False Wichita River, in the leased country aforesaid, this twelfth day of August, in the year of our Lord one thousand eight hundred and sixty-one.

ALBERT PIKE,

Commissioner of the Confederate States to the Indian nations and tribes west of Arkansas.

The following is a copy of John Ross' letter.

EXECUTIVE DEPARTMENT, PARK HILL,
CHEROKEE NATION, August 24, 1861.

To Major Clark, Assistant Quartermaster, C. S. A.:

SIR: I herewith forward to your care dispatches for General McCulloch, Confederate States Army, which I have the honor to request you will cause to be forwarded to him by the earliest express.

At a mass meeting of about four thousand Cherokees at Tahlegue, on the 21st instant, the Cherokees, with marked unanimity, declared their adherence to the Confederate States, and have given their authorities power to negotiate an alliance with them. In view of this action, a regiment of mounted men will be immediately raised and placed under the command of Colonel John Drew, to meet any exigency that may arise.

Having espoused the cause of the Confederate States, we hope to render efficient service in the protracted war which now threatens the country, and to be treated with a liberality and confidence becoming the Confederate States.

I have the honor to be sir, very respectfully, your humble servant,

JOHN ROSS,

Principal Chief of the Cherokee Nation.

FORT POWHATTAN, THE RIGHT OF THE FEDERAL LINES, AND CONFEDERATE VESSELS ON THE JAMES RIVER.
[From a sketch made in January, 1865.]

Monuments Erected to the Confederate Dead.

RICHMOND HOWITZER'S MONUMENT, RICHMOND, VA.

"LION OF LUCERNE ' ATLANTA, GA.

MONUMENT AT CHARLESTON, S. C.

JACKSON MONUMENT, RICHMOND, VA.

SOLDIERS' MONUMENT, LEXINGTON, KY.

LEE MONUMENT, RICHMOND, VA.

MONUMENT AT COLUMBIA, TENN.

MONUMENT AT LOUISVILLE, KY.

THE WICKHAM MONUMENT, RICHMOND, VA.

THE STUART MONUMENT, RICHMOND, VA.

MONUMENT AT KNOXVILLE, TENN.

THE PICKETT MONUMENT, RICHMOND, VA.

MONUMENT AT FREDERICKSBURG, VA.

MONUMENT AT MEMPHIS, TENN.

MONUMENT AT MARIANNA, FLA.

MONUMENT AT MONTGOMERY, ALA.

MONUMENT AT MACON, GA.

MONUMENT AT RICHMOND, VA.

MONUMENT AT ATLANTA, GA.

MEMORIAL MONUMENT AT NASHVILLE, TENN.

MONUMENT AT LEXINGTON, KY.

THE A P. HILL MONUMENT, RICHMOND, VA.

MONUMENT AT PENSACOLA, FLA

THE FORREST MONUMENT, MEMPHIS, TENN.
To be Erected.
[From a pen and ink design.]

ARMY OF NORTHERN VIRGINIA MONUMENT, NEW ORLEANS, LA.

WASHINGTON ARTILLERY MONUMENT, NEW ORLEANS, LA.

MONUMENT AT NEW ORLEANS, LA.

THE LEE MONUMENT, NEW ORLEANS, LA.

MONUMENT AT CHICAGO, ILL.

SOLDIERS AND SAILORS' MONUMENT, RICHMOND, VA.

MONUMENT AT ATLANTA, GA.

MONUMENT AT ST. AUGUSTINE, FLA.

MONUMENT AT SHEPHERDSTOWN, W. VA.

LAST MEETING OF GENERALS ROBERT E. LEE AND "STONEWALL" JACKSON AT THE BATTLE OF CHANCELLORSVILLE, VA.

[From the original and celebrated painting by Julio in the Arsenal of the Washington Artillery, New Orleans, La. Size 10 x 12 feet. Value, $5,000.]

FIRST BATTLE FLAG.

In 1861, after the first battle of Manassas, the flag with the St. Andrews Cross was adopted as the Battle Flag of the Confederate States Army, and the Misses Carev (Hettie and Constance) made three and presented them to Generals Johnston, Van Dorn and Beauregard. The latter's flag was sent by him to New Orleans, and upon the fall of the city, to Havana, then returned to New Orleans, and placed in custody of the Washington Artillery, where it is at present. The other two seem to have been lost.

DESCRIPTION.—Red ground, blue cross, gold stars and gold fringe.

CONFEDERATE TREASURY NOTES.

NOTE.—The Treasury notes presented on this and succeeding pages are exact photographic reproductions of the originals, without retouching or other alteration.

IT took money to carry on the war.

The Southern Confederacy started to oppose the invading foes with an empty Treasury. So a "promise to pay" had to be resorted to.

One of the first things to be done by the Treasury of the young nation was to issue legal tender of some kind.

The making of Confederate bonds and notes was a great task for the young Treasury; because, in the South, no engravers and nothing like good bank paper could be found. So arrangements were made to print some bonds in New York. The work was gone about very carefully, and every means used to avoid detection. But the bonds were seized, however, before they left New York. These bonds were printed by the American Bank Note Company, and when the Federal authorities found this out, through a telltale employe, the Southern Confederacy had to rely upon its own resources.

An engraver of cards and posters by the name of Hoyer, a German by nationality, lived in Richmond, and he, in connection with Mr. Ludwig, was employed to issue the first notes, which were eight one-hundred-dollar bills. One of these bills would bring considerable now as a relic.

A paper was smuggled through the lines from New York and given to Hoyer and Ludwig. They had only old and inferior stones for engraving purposes, and with them they made the first Confederate Treasury notes. The stones had previously been used to engrave placards. The notes were faulty and full of errors, and under any other circumstances would have been thrown away, but some kind of legal tender had to be secured at once, and they were accepted.

When the Secretary read the proofs he ordered them printed, indorsing on the margin of the proof the following: "When the money changers become familiar with these incoming bills it will be as difficult to pass a counterfeit as if they had been engraved on steel—perhaps more so."

The engravers used what was an old-fashioned press even in that day, and the bills were printed by hand, a very slow and tedious process.

These rude, uncouth bills found no buyers, but were accepted in good faith by loyal Southern hearts. They were pledges of a brave, fearless people, and by that people were accepted as such. They were not worth much upon their face, but thousands of men died to give them value, and three times as many died to make them worthless.

Soon the country was flooded with Confederate bills. The number circulated depended on how fast the Treasury could issue them. Bills of small denominations soon went out of style, and nothing under $100 left the Treasurer's hands, while $500 and $1,000 bills were as numerous as $5 bills are to-day. Of course the price of everything went up, and it was a mere bagatelle to pay $200 for a yard of flannel, or $300 for a pound of coffee, or $1,000 for a pair of boots, or $10,000 for a horse.

Worthless as were these "promises to pay," they cost more than any tender ever issued by a nation on earth. They were issued in integrity, defended in valor and bathed in priceless blood.

The following illustrations are of all the Treasury notes issued by the Confederate States Government:

1.—$1,000. Written date, April 26, 1861; Montgomery, Ala.; interest at ten cents per day; head of John C. Calhoun in lower left-hand corner; head of Andrew Jackson in lower right-hand corner; excessively rare; only five supposed to be in existence.

2.—$500. Written date, June 18, 1861; Montgomery, Ala.; interest at five cents per day; excessively rare; only three supposed to be in existence.

3.—$100. Written date, May 16, 1861; Montgomery, Ala.; interest at one cent per day.

4.—$50. Written date, May 29, 1861; Montgomery, Ala.; interest at one-half cent per day.

5.—$100. Written date, September 25, 1861; Richmond, Va.; interest at one cent per day.

6.—$50. Written date, September 14, 1861; Richmond, Va.; interest at one-half cent per day; head of Washington on right end.

7.—$100. July 25, 1861; Richmond, Va.; head of Washington in lower left corner.

8.—$50. July 25, 1861; Richmond, Va.; head of Washington in center.

9.—$10. July 25, 1861; Richmond, Va.

10.—$5. July 25, 1861; Richmond, Va.

11.—$5. Written date, July 25, 1861; Richmond, Va.; on back Confederate States of America, in blue; very rare; supposed to be worth its face value.

12.—$100. September 2, 1861; Richmond, Va.

13.—$50. September 2, 1861; Richmond, Va.

14.—$50. September 2, 1861; Richmond, Va.

15.—$50. September 2, 1861; Richmond, Va.; head of Jefferson Davis in center.

16.—$20. September 2, 1861; Richmond, Va.; head of Alexander H. Stephens in lower left-hand corner.

17.—$20. September 2, 1861; Richmond, Va.; Twenty and XX in green; head of Alexander H. Stephens in center.

18.—$20. September 2, 1861; Richmond, Va.; 20 and scroll in green.

19.—$20. September 2, 1861; Richmond, Va.

20.—$20. September 2, 1861; Richmond, Va.; 20's and band of 20's across the face in red.

21.—$10. September 2, 1861; Richmond, Va.

22.—$10. September 2, 1861; Richmond, Va.; camp scene—General Marion offering a breakfast of roast sweet potatoes to a British officer, in center; head of R. M. T. Hunter in lower left corner.

23.—$10. September 2, 1861; Richmond, Va.; head of R. M. T. Hunter in lower left corner; head and bust of Blanton Duncan's child in lower right corner; X's and Ten, with band of Ten Dollars across face in red.

24.—$10. September 2, 1861; Richmond, Va.; X's and Ten, with band of Ten's across face in red.

25.—$10. September 2, 1861; Richmond, Va.; X's and Ten's in red.

26.—$10. September 2, 1861; Richmond, Va.

27.—$10. September 2, 1861; Richmond, Va.; head of R. M. T. Hunter in lower left corner; head of C. G. Memminger in lower right corner.

28.—$10. Same as 27, with the addition of X's in red.

29.—$10. September 2, 1861; Richmond, Va.

30.—$5. September 2, 1861; Richmond, Va.; statue of Washington to the right; 5's and Five in red.

31.—$5. September 2, 1861; Richmond, Va.

32.—$5. September 2, 1861; Richmond, Va.; head of Memminger in lower left corner.

33.—$5. September 2, 1861; Richmond, Va.; head of Memminger in center.

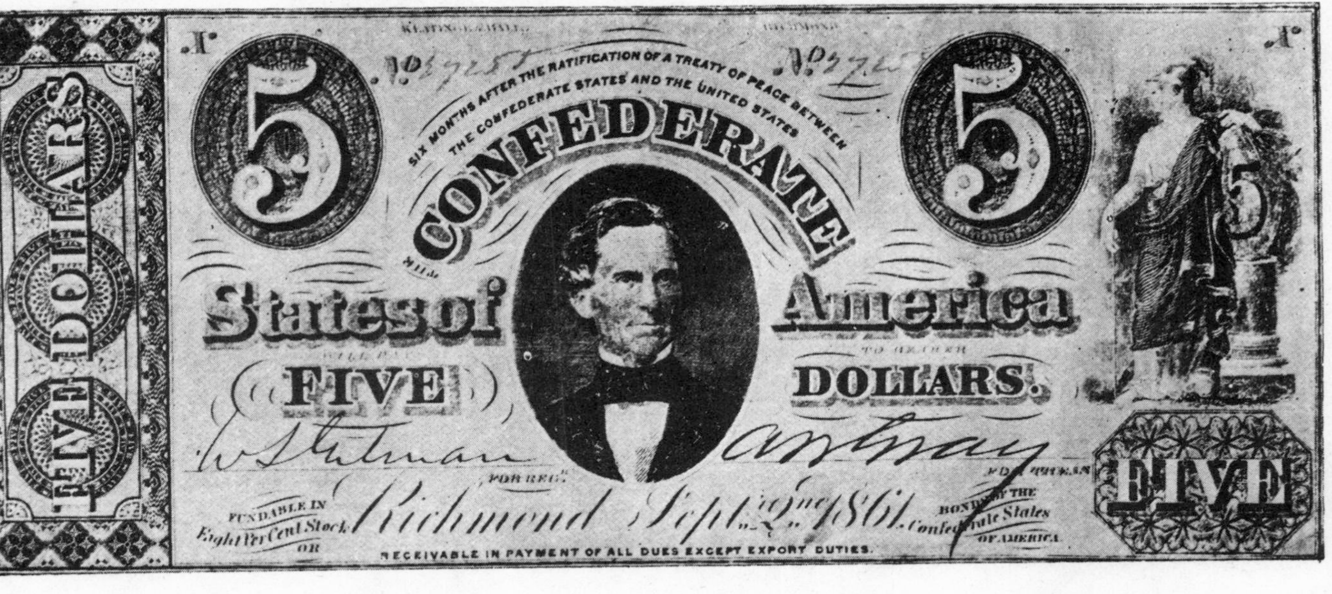

34.—$5. September 2, 1861; Richmond, Va.; head of Memminger in center; Five Dollars across left end, Five and 5's in green.

35.—$5. September 2, 1861; second series; Richmond, Va.

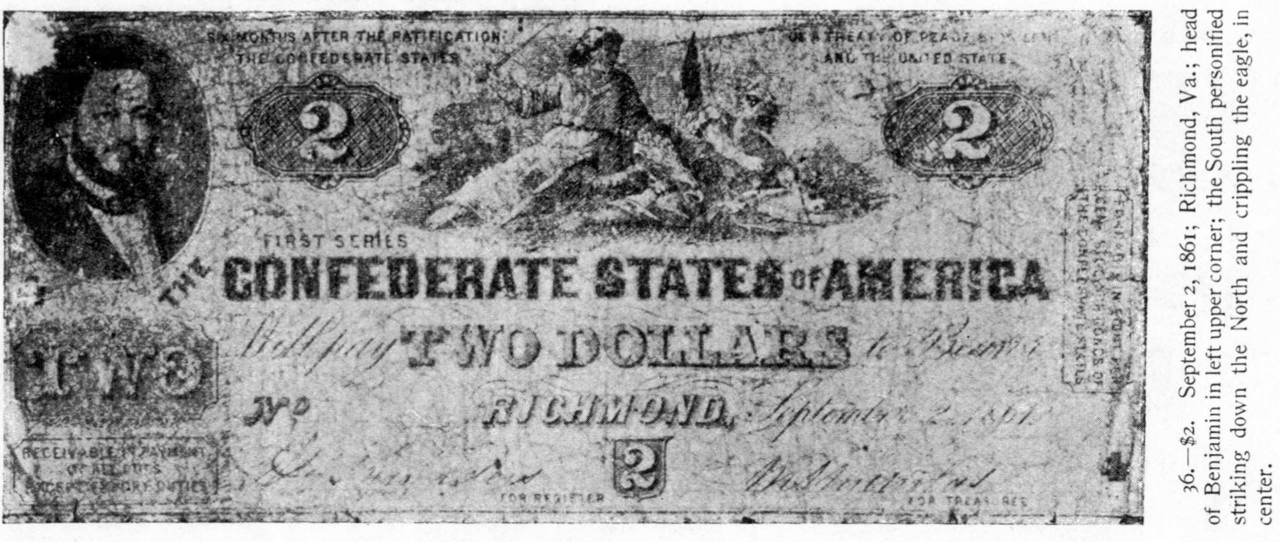

36.—$2. September 2, 1861; Richmond, Va.; head of Benjamin in left upper corner; the South personified striking down the North and crippling the eagle, in center.

37.—$100. Written date, January 6, 1862; Richmond, Va.; head of Calhoun in lower left corner; the word Hundred in red across lower face.

38.—$100. Written date, September 11, 1862; Richmond, Va.

39.—$100. Back of 38; green; rarest of all the notes; only two supposed to be in existence.

40.—$1. June 2, 1862; Richmond, Va.; head of Mrs. Governor Pickens in lower right corner.

41.—$10. September 2, 1862; Richmond, Va.; head of R. M. T. Hunter in lower right corner.

42.—$100. December 2, 1862; Richmond, Va.; head of Mrs. Davis in center; head of G. W. Randolph in lower right corner; green back.

43.—$20. December 2, 1862; Richmond, Va.; capitol at Nashville, Tenn., in center; head of Alexander H. Stephens in lower right corner; blue back; 20 XX 20 on back.

44.—$10. December 2, 1862; Richmond, Va.; capitol at Montgomery, Ala., in center; head of Hunter in lower right corner; pink paper; blue back with ten X's on it.

45.—$5. December 2, 1862: Richmond, Va.; head of Memminger in lower right corner; pink paper; blue back.

46.—$2. December 2, 1862; Richmond, Va.; head of Benjamin in right center; pink paper.

47.—$1. December 2, 1862; Richmond, Va.; head of C. C. Clay in center; pink paper.

48.—$100. April 6, 1863; Richmond, Va.; head of G. W. Randolph in lower right corner; green back.

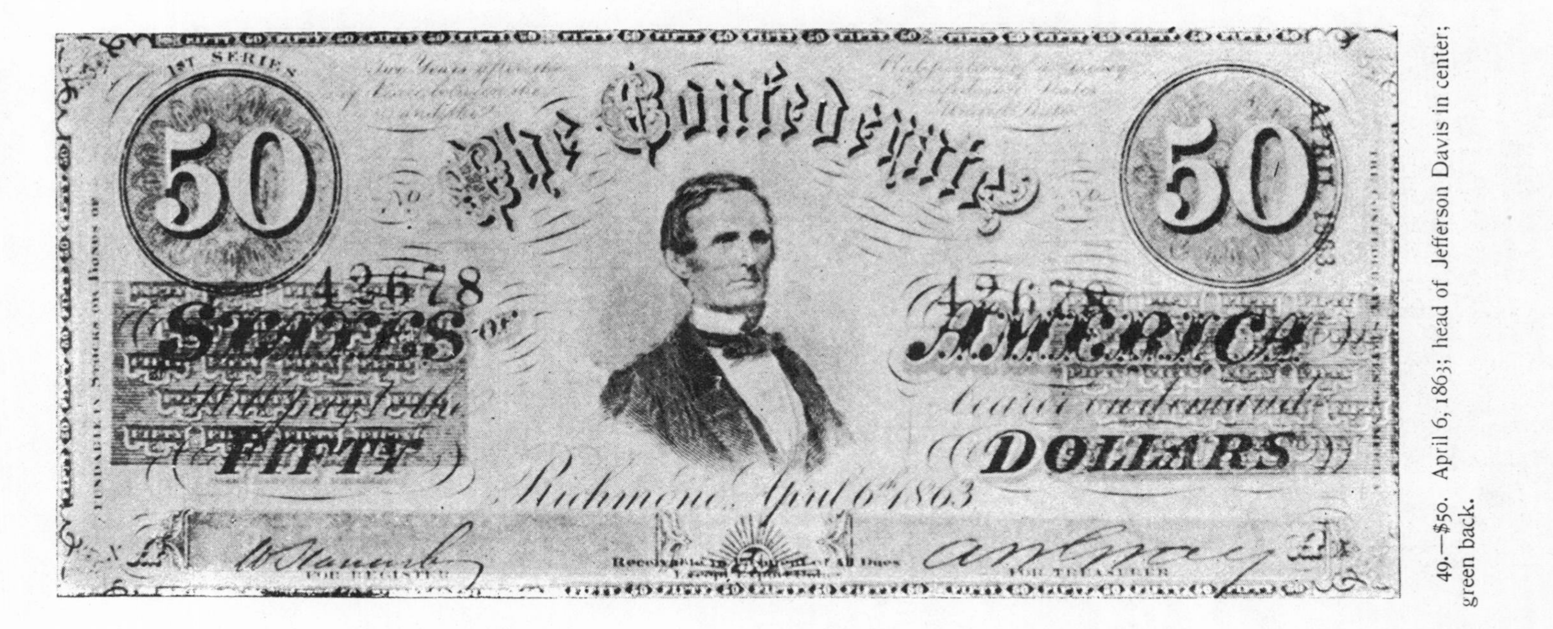

49.—$50. April 6, 1863; head of Jefferson Davis in center; green back.

50.—$20. April 6, 1863; Richmond, Va.; capitol at Nashville, Tenn., in center; head of Alexander H. Stephens in lower right corner; blue back, with ten X's on it.

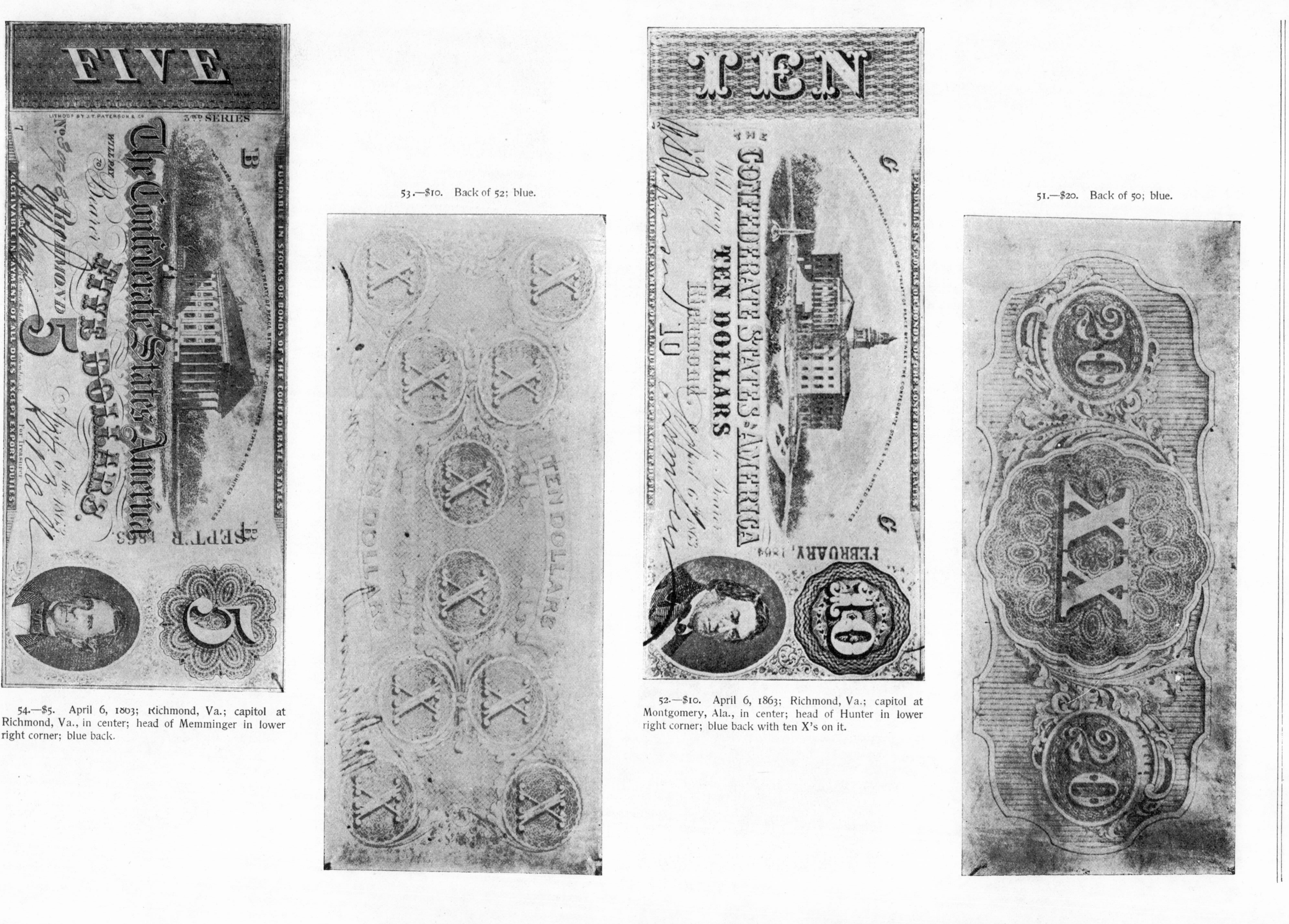

54.—$5. April 6, 1803; Richmond, Va.; capitol at Richmond, Va., in center; head of Memminger in lower right corner; blue back.

53.—$10. Back of 52; blue.

52.—$10. April 6, 1863; Richmond, Va.; capitol at Montgomery, Ala., in center; head of Hunter in lower right corner; blue back with ten X's on it.

51.—$20. Back of 50; blue.

55.—$5. Back of 54; blue.

56.—$2. April 6, 1863; Richmond, Va.; head of Benjamin on right center; pink paper.

57.—$1. April 6, 1863; Richmond, Va.; head of C. C. Clay in center; pink paper.

58.—50 cents. April 6, 1863; Richmond, Va.; vignette of Davis in center; pink paper.

59.—$500. February 17, 1864; Richmond, Va.; head of General T. J. Jackson in lower right corner; Confederate flag and seal of Confederacy at left.

60.—$100. February 17, 1864; Richmond, Va.; head of Mrs. Davis in center; head of G. W. Randolph in lower right corner; pink tinted net-work on face of note; blue back.

61.—$100. Back of 60.

62.—$50. February 17, 1864; Richmond, Va.; head of Jefferson Davis in center; pink tinted net-work on face of note; blue back.

63.—$20. February 17, 1864; Richmond, Va.; capitol at Nashville, Tenn., in center; head of Alexander H. Stephens in lower right corner; pink tinted network on face of note.

64.—$10. February 17, 1864; Richmond, Va.; head of R. M. T. Hunter in lower right corner; pink-tinted network across face of note; blue back.

65.—$5. February 17, 1864; Richmond, Va.; Capitol at Richmond; head of Memminger in lower right corner; pink tinted net-work across the face of note; blue back.

66.—$2. February 17, 1861. Richmond, Va.; head of Benjamin on right center; pink tinted net-work across the face of note; blue back.

Bird's-eye View of the City of Washington, showing the Capitol at the Outbreak of the War
[From a sketch made in January, 1861.]

Confederate Poems.

Martial Melodies Dear to Southern Hearts. Pathos and Patriotism, and the Songs Sung by the Lads in Gray.

THE CONQUERED BANNER.

BY FATHER ABRAM J. RYAN, THE POET PRIEST OF THE SOUTH.

Furl that banner! for 'tis weary,
Round its staff 'tis drooping dreary;
Furl it, fold it, it is best:
For there's not a man to wave it,
And there's not a sword to save it,
And there's not one left to lave it
In the blood which heroes gave it,
And its foes now scorn and brave it
Furl it, hide it, let it rest.

"Broken in its staff and shattered."

Take that banner down! 'tis tattered,
Broken is its staff and shattered,
And the valiant hosts are scattered
Over whom it floated high.
Oh! 'tis hard for us to fold it,
Hard to think there's none to hold it,
Hard that those who once unrolled it
Now must furl it with a sigh.

Furl that banner! furl it sadly—
Once ten thousands hailed it gladly,
And ten thousands wildly, madly,
Swore it should forever wave;
Swore that foeman's sword could never
Hearts like theirs entwined dissever,
Till that flag would float forever
O'er their freedom or their grave.

Furl it! for the hands that grasped it,
And the hearts that fondly clasped it,
Cold and dead are lying low:
And the banner, it is trailing,
While around it sounds the wailing
Of its people in their woe.
For, though conquered, they adore it,
Love the cold, dead hands that bore it,
Weep for those who fell before it,
Pardon those who trailed and tore it,
And—oh! wildly they deplore it—
Now to furl and fold it so.

Furl that banner! true 'tis gory,
Yet 'tis wreathed around with glory,
And 'twill live in song and story
Though its folds are in the dust;
For its fame on brightest pages,
Penned by poets and by sages,
Shall go sounding down the ages,
Furl its folds though now we must.
Furl that banner! softly, slowly,
Treat it gently—it is holy—
For it droops above the dead;
Touch it not, unfold it never,
Let it droop there, *furled* forever,
For its people's *hopes* are dead.

A REPLY TO THE CONQUERED BANNER.

BY SIR HENRY HOUGHTON, BART., ENGLAND.

Gallant nation, foiled by numbers!
Say not that your hopes are fled;
Keep that glorious flag which slumbers,
One day to avenge your dead.
Keep it, widowed, sonless mothers!
Keep it, sisters, mourning brothers!
Furl it with an iron will;
Furl it now, but keep it still—
Think not that its work is done.
Keep it till your children take it,
Once again to hail and make it
All their sires have bled and fought for;
All their noble hearts have sought for—
Bled and fought for all alone.
All alone! ay, shame the story!
Millions here deplore the stain;
Shame, alas! for England's glory,
Freedom called and called in vain!
Furl that banner sadly, slowly,
Treat it gently, for 'tis holy;
Till that day—yes, furl it sadly;
Then once more unfurl it gladly—
Conquered banner! keep it still!

ALL QUIET ALONG THE POTOMAC TO-NIGHT.

BY LAMAR FONTAINE, SECOND VIRGINIA CAVALRY.

"All quiet along the Potomac to-night,"
Except now and then a stray picket
Is shot, as he walks on his beat to and fro,
By a rifleman hid in the thicket.
'Tis nothing—a private or two now and then
Will not count in the news of the battle;
Not an officer lost—only one of the men—
Moaning out, all alone, the death-rattle.

"And thinks of the two on the low trundle-bed."

"All quiet along the Potomac to-night,"
Where the soldiers lie peacefully dreaming;
Their tents, in the rays of the clear autumn moon
Or the light of the watch-fires, are gleaming.
A tremulous sigh, as the gentle night wind
Through the forest leaves slowly is creeping,
While the stars up above, with their glittering eyes,
Keep guard—for the army is sleeping.

There is only the sound of the lone sentry's tread,
As he tramps from the rock to the fountain,
And thinks of the two on the low trundle-bed,
Far away in the cot on the mountain.
His musket falls slack—his face, dark and grim,
Grows gentle with memories tender,
As he mutters a prayer for his children asleep—
For their mother—may Heaven defend her!

The moon seems to shine as brightly as then,
That night when the love yet unspoken
Leaped up to his lips, and when low-murmured vows
Were pledged to be ever unbroken.
Then drawing his sleeve roughly over his eyes,
He dashes off tears that are welling,
And gathers his gun close up to its place,
As if to keep down the heart swelling.

He passes the fountain, the blasted pine tree,
The footstep is lagging and weary,
Yet onward he goes through the broad belt of light,
Toward the shades of the forest so dreary.
Hark! was it the night wind that rustled the leaves?
Was it moonlight so wondrously flashing?
It looked like a rifle—ha! Mary, good-by!
And his life-blood is ebbing and splashing!

"And his life-blood is ebbing and splashing"

"All quiet along the Potomac to-night,"
No sound save the rush of the river;
While soft falls the dew on the face of the dead—
The picket's off duty forever!

LITTLE GIFFIN.

BY DR. FRANCIS O. TICKNOR.

["A ballad of such unique and really transcendent merit, that in our judgment it ought to rank with the rarest gems of modern martial poetry." —P. H. Hayne.]

Out of the focal and foremost fire,
Out of the hospital walls as dire,
Smitten of grapeshot and gangrene
(Eighteenth battle, and he sixteen!),
Specter such as we seldom see,
Little Giffin of Tennessee!

"Take him and welcome!" the surgeon said;
"Much your doctor can help the dead!"
And so we took him and brought him where
The balm was sweet on the summer air;
And we laid him down on a wholesome bed—
Utter Lazarus, heel to head!

Weary War with the bated breath,
Skeleton boy against skeleton Death,
Months of torture, how many such!
Weary weeks of the stick and crutch!
Still a glint of the steel-blue eye
Spoke of the spirit that wouldn't die—

"Little Giffin was up and away."

And didn't!—nay, more! in death's despite,
The crippled skeleton learned to write!
"Dear Mother," at first, of course, and then,
"Dear Captain," inquiring about the "men."
Captain's answer: "Of eighty and five,
Giffin and I are left alive!"

"Johnston's pressed at the front, they say!"
Little Giffin was up and away;
A tear, his first, as he bade good-by,
Dimmed the glint of his steel-blue eye.
"I'll write, if spared." There was news of a fight,
But none of Giffin! he did not write!

I sometimes fancy that were I a king
Of the princely Knights of the Golden Ring,
With the song of the minstrel in mine ear,
And the tender legend that trembles here,
I'd give the best on his bended knee,
The whitest soul of chivalry,
For little Giffin of Tennessee.

READING THE LIST.

ANONYMOUS (SOUTHERN).

"Is there any news of the war?" she said.
"Only a list of the wounded and dead,"
Was the man's reply,
Without lifting his eye
To the face of the woman standing by.
"'Tis the very thing I want," she said;
"Read me a list of the wounded and dead."
He read the list; 'twas a sad array
Of the wounded and killed in the fatal fray.

In the very midst was a pause to tell
Of a gallant youth who fought so well
That his comrades asked: "Who is he, pray?"
"The only son of the Widow Gray,"
Was the proud reply
Of his captain nigh . . .
What ails the woman standing near?
Her face has the ashen hue of fear!
"Well, well, read on; is he wounded? Quick!
O God! but my heart is sorrow-sick!
Is he wounded?" "No; he fell, they say,
Killed outright on that fatal day!"
But see, the woman has swooned away!

"Read me a list of the wounded and dead."

Sadly she opened her eyes to the light;
Slowly recalled the events of the fight;
Faintly she murmured: "Killed outright!
It has cost me the life of my only son;
But the battle is fought, and the victory won,
The will of the Lord, let it be done!"

God pity the cheerless Widow Gray,
And send from the halls of eternal day
The light of His peace to illumine her way.

OH, NO! HE'LL NOT NEED THEM AGAIN.*

Oh, no! he'll not need them again—
No more will he wake to behold
The splendor and fame of his men,
The tale of his victories told!
No more will he wake from that sleep
Which he sleeps in his glory and fame,
While his comrades are left here to weep
Over Cleburne, his grave and his name.

Oh, no! he'll not need them again;
No more will his banner be spread
O'er the field of his gallantry's fame—
The soldier's proud spirit is fled!
The soldier who rose 'mid applause,
From the humblemost place in the van—
I sing not in praise of the cause,
But rather in praise of the man.

Oh, no! he'll not need them again;
He has fought his last battle without them,
For barefoot he, too, must go in,
While barefoot stood comrades about him;
And barefoot they proudly marched on,
With blood flowing fast from their feet;
They thought of the past victories won,
And the foes that they now were to meet.

Oh, no! he'll not need them again;
He is leading his men to the charge,
Unheeding the shells, or the slain,
Or the showers of the bullets at large.
On the right, on the left, on the flanks,
He dashingly pushes his way,
While with cheers, double quick and in ranks,
His soldiers all followed that day.

"I'm killed, boys, but fight it out."

Oh, no! he'll not need them again;
He falls from his horse to the ground!
Oh, anguish! oh, sorrow! oh, pain!
In the brave hearts that gathered around.
He breathes not of grief, nor a sigh
On the breast where he pillowed his head,
Ere he fix'd his last gaze upon high—
"I'm killed, boys, but fight it out," said.

Oh, no! he'll not need them again;
But treasure them up for his sake;
And oh! should you sing a refrain
Of the memories they still must awake,
Sing it soft as the summer-eve breeze,
Let it sound as refreshing and clear;
Tho' grief-born, there's that which can please
In thoughts that are gemmed with a tear.

*On the morning of the battle of Franklin, Tenn., Major-General Patrick Cleburne, while riding along the line encouraging his men, saw an old friend—a captain in his command—barefooted, and his feet bleeding. Alighting from his horse, he told the captain to "please" pull off his boots. Upon the captain doing so, the general told him to try them on, which he did. Whereupon the general mounted his horse, telling the captain he was tired wearing boots, and could do without them. He would hear of no remonstrance, and, bidding the captain good-by, rode away. In this condition he was killed.

THE PRIDE OF BATTERY B.

BY F. H. GASSAWAY.

South Mountain towering on our right,
Far off the river lay,
And over on the wooded height
We held their lines at bay.

At last the muttering guns were still,
The day died slow and wan;
At last the gunners' pipes did fill,
The sergeant's yarns began.

When, as the wind a moment blew
Aside the fragrant flood
Our brierwoods raised, within our view
A little maiden stood.

A tiny tot of six or seven,
From fireside fresh she seemed
(Of such a little one in heaven
One soldier often dreamed).

And as we stared, her little hand
Went to her curly head
In grave salute. "And who are you?"
At length the sergeant said.

"And where's your home?" he growled again.
She lisped out, "Who is me?
Why, don't you know? I'm little Jane,
The Pride of Battery B.

"My home? Why, that was burned away,
And pa and ma are dead,
And so I ride the guns all day,
Along with Sergeant Ned.

"And I've a drum that's not a toy,
A cap with feathers, too,
And I march beside the drummer boy
On Sundays at review.

"But now, our 'bacca's all give out,
The men can't have their smoke,
And so they're cross. Why, even Ned
Won't play with me and joke!

"And the big colonel said to-day—
I hate to hear him swear—
He'd give a leg for a good pipe
Like the Yank had over there.

"And so I thought, when beat the drum,
And the big guns were still,
I'd creep beneath the tent and come
Out here across the hill,

"And beg, good Mister Yankee men,
You give me some Lone Jack;
Please do; when we get some again
I'll surely bring it back.

"Indeed I will, for Ned, says he,
If I do what I say
I'll be a general yet, maybe,
And ride a prancing bay."

We brimmed her tiny apron o'er;
You should have heard her laugh
As each man from his scanty store
Shook out a generous half!

To kiss the little mouth, stooped down
A score of grimy men,
Until the sergeant's husky voice
Said, "'Tention, squad!" and then

We gave her escort, till good night
The pretty waif we bid,
And watched her toddle out of sight
Or else 'twas tears that hid

"Give me some Lone Jack!"

Her tiny form—nor turned about
A man, nor spoke a word,
Till after awhile a far, hoarse shout
Upon the wind we heard.

We sent it back, then cast sad eyes
Upon the scene around;
A baby's hand had touched the ties
That brothers once had bound.

That's all—save when the dawn awoke
Again the work of hell,
And through the sullen clouds of smoke
The screaming missiles fell,

Our general often rubbed his glass
And marveled much to see
Not a single shell that whole day fall
In the camp of Battery B.

THE COAT OF FADED GRAY.

BY G. W. HARRIS.

A low hut rests in Lookout's shade,
As rots its moss-grown roof away,
While sundown's glories softly fade,
Closing another weary day.
The battle's din is heard no more,
No more the hunted stand at bay,
The breezes through the lowly door
Swing mute a coat of faded gray,
A tattered relic of the fray,
A threadbare coat of faded gray.

'Tis hanging on the rough log wall,
Near to the foot of a widow's bed,

By a white plume and well-worn shawl—
His gift the happy morn they wed;
By the wee slip their dead child wore—
The one they gave the name of May;
By her rag doll and pinafore—
By right 'tis here, that coat of gray
A red-fleck'd relic of the fray,
An armless coat of faded gray.

" 'Tis hanging on the rough log wall."

Her all of life now drapes that wall;
But poor and patient, still she waits
On God's good time to gently call
Her, too, within the jewel'd gates;
And all she craves is here to die—
To part from these and pass away,
To join her love eternally
That wore the slip—the coat of gray,
The shell-torn relic of the fray,
Her soldier's coat of faded gray.

DEAR MOTHER, I'VE COME HOME TO DIE.

BY E. BOWERS. MUSIC BY HENRY TUCKER.

Dear mother, I remember well
The parting kiss you gave me,
When merry rang the village bell—
My heart was full of joy and glee:
I did not dream that one short year
Would crush the hopes that soared so high!
Oh, mother dear, draw near to me!
Dear mother, I've come home to die.

Chorus—Call sister, brother to my side,
And take your soldier's last good-by.
Oh, mother dear, draw near to me!
Dear mother, I've come home to die.

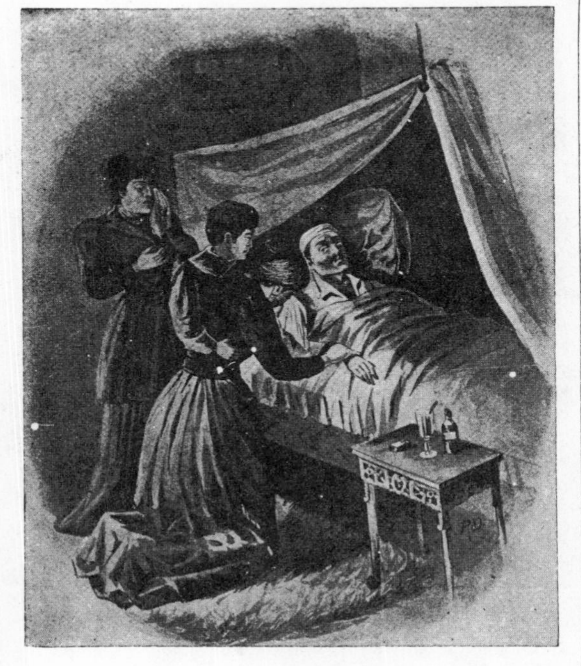

" Dear mother, I've come home to die."

Hark! mother, 'tis the village bell;
I can no longer with thee stay;
My country calls to arms! to arms!
The foe advance in fierce array!
The vision 's past—I feel that now
For country I can only sigh.
Oh, mother dear, draw near to me!
Dear mother, I've come home to die.

Dear mother, sister, brother, all,
One parting kiss—to all good-by:
Weep not, but clasp your hand in mine,
And let me like a soldier die!
I've met the foe upon the field,
Where hosts contending scorned to fly;
I fought for right—God bless you all!—
Dear mother, I've come home to die.

THE DYING SOLDIER BOY.

BY A. B. CUNNINGHAM, OF LOUISIANA.

Air—" Maid of Monterey."

Upon Manassas' bloody plain a soldier boy lay dying!
The gentle winds above his form in softest tones were sighing;
The god of day had slowly sunk beneath the verge of day,
And the silver moon was gliding above the Milky Way.

The stars were shining brightly, and the sky was calm and blue;
Oh, what a beautiful scene was this for human eyes to view!
The river rolled in splendor, and the wavelets danc'd around,
But the banks were strewed with dead men, and gory was the ground.

But the hero boy was dying, and his thoughts were very deep,
For the death wound in his young side was wafting him to sleep.
He thought of home and kindred away on a distant shore,
All of whom he must relinquish, and never see them more.

" But the hero boy was dying."

And as the night breeze passed by, in whispers o'er the dead,
Sweet memories of olden days came rushing to his head;
But his mind was weak and deaden'd, so he turned from where he lay,
As the Death Angel flitted by, and call'd his soul away!

LORENA.

[This was the great sentimental song of the war period.]

The years creep slowly by, Lorena;
The snow is on the grass again;
The sun's low down the sky, Lorena;
The frost gleams where the flowers have been.
But the heart throbs on as warmly now
As when the summer days were nigh;
Oh! the sun can never dip so low
Adown affection's cloudless sky.

A hundred months have passed, Lorena,
Since last I held that hand in mine,
And felt the pulse beat fast, Lorena,
Though mine beat faster far than thine.
A hundred months—'twas flowery May,
When up the hilly slope we climbed,
To watch the dying of the day
And hear the distant church bells chimed.

We loved each other then, Lorena,
More than we ever dared to tell;
And what we might have been, Lorena,
Had but our loving prospered well!
But then, 'tis past, the years have gone,
I'll not call up their shadowy forms;
I'll say to them, Lost years, sleep on,
Sleep on, nor heed life's pelting storms.

The story of the past, Lorena,
Alas! I care not to repeat;
The hopes that could not last, Lorena,
They lived, but only lived to cheat.
I would not cause e'en one regret
To rankle in your bosom now—
" For if we try we may forget,"
Were words of thine long years ago.

" A hundred months have passed, Lorena."

Yes, these were words of thine, Lorena—
They are within my memory yet—
They touched some tender chords, Lorena,
Which thrill and tremble with regret.
'Twas not thy woman's heart which spoke—
Thy heart was always true to me;
A duty stern and piercing broke
The tie which linked my soul with thee.

It matters little now, Lorena,
The past is in the eternal past;
Our hearts will soon lie low, Lorena,
Life's tide is ebbing out so fast.
There is a future, oh, thank God!
Of life this is so small a part—
'Tis dust to dust beneath the sod,
But there, up there, 'tis heart to heart.

ONLY A PRIVATE.

BY F. W. D.

Only a private! his jacket of gray
Is stained by the smoke and the dust;
As Bayard he's brave, as Rupert he's gay,
Reckless as Murat in heat of the fray,
But in God is his only trust!

" Only a private."

Only a private! to march and to fight,
To suffer and starve and be strong;

With knowledge enough to know that the might
Of justice and truth, and freedom and right
In the end must crush out the wrong!

Only a private! no ribbon or star
Shall gild with false glory his name!
No honors for him in braid or in bar,
His Legion of Honor is only a scar,
And his wounds are his roll of fame!

Only a private! one more hero slain
On the field lies silent and chill!
And in the far South a wife prays in vain—
One clasp of the hands she may ne'er clasp again,
One kiss from the lips that are still!

Only a private! there let him sleep,
He will need no tablet nor stone;
For the mosses and vines o'er his grave will creep,
And at night the stars through the clouds will peep,
And watch him who lies there alone!

Only a martyr! who fought and who fell,
Unknown and unmarked in the strife!
But still as he lies in his lonely cell,
Angel and seraph the legend shall tell—
Such a death is eternal life!

NOVEMBER 19, 1861.

'TWAS JUST LIKE JIM.

BY L. W. CANADY.

'Twas just like Jim, in his schoolboy days,
To protect the lad who threw
The paper wad at the big blackboard
On the wall, with aim so true;
'Twas just like Jim to say, "'Twas I,"
And the master's wrath defy—
To shift the blame from a weaker lad,
Jim faltered not at a lie.

"'Twas like Jim to march away."

'Twas just like Jim, when, in sixty-one,
There came the appeal to arms,
And the pleading voice of Peace was hushed
By War and his rude alarms;
'Twas just like Jim to march away—
Tap of drum and music gay—

Looking so handsome, so brave and true,
In his suit of homespun gray.

. . . . . .

'Twas just like Jim, that April day,*
When the broken and sullen lines of gray
Turned anon like a stag at bay,
Rallied and fought, then filed away:
'Twas just like Jim, I say:
To be the last
On guard at the bridge where his comrades passed.
Firm and motionless, gaunt and grim,
"*No surrender for me!*" said Jim.
Alone he stood, close by the bridge,
When Sheridan's troops rode over the ridge.
A "Yankee shout," a "Rebel yell"—
Three troopers from their saddles fell.
Fewer the living moments grew
For Jim, but his *aim* was never more true;
And when the foe the bridge had gained,
Not a ball in his cartridge box remained;
But never a saber that squadron drew—
They *rode him down, those lines of blue!*

. . . .

At Appomattox they called the roll,
But Jim answered not. His wayward soul
Had gone to God to be judged by *Him*.
No surrender! Ah! that was like *Jim*.

* The day before the surrender of Lee.

"No surrender."

THE BALTIMORE GRAYS.

BY BUTLER BRAYNE MINOR.

Ah, well I remember that long summer's day
When, round about Richmond our broken ranks lay.
Week in and week out we had been at the front,
And bore without flinching the battle's fierce brunt,
Till, shattered and weary, we needed repose
Ere we met in death struggle our numberless foes.
Our knapsacks were empty, our uniforms worn,
Our feet, from long marching, were naked and torn;
But not a man grumbled in the rank or the file,
We bore all our hardships with a joke and a smile,
For Jackson was with us, and, under his eye,
Each soldier determined to do or to die.

That evening old Jack had us out on review,
When a glance down the line showed us all something new—
Eighty-seven young boys from old Baltimore,
Who had run the blockade and that day joined our corps.
Their clothes were resplendent, all new, spick and span—
'Twas plain that a tailor had measured each man.
When we learned who they were what a shout we did raise!
How we cheered our new allies, the "Baltimore Grays"!
There were Lightfoots and Carters, and Howards and Kanes,

"Old Jack had us out on review."

The grandsons of Carroll, the nephews of Gaines,
And as the brave boys dressed up in a row,
You could see the pure blood of the proud Huguenot.

But we were old vets of Stonewall's brigade;
We'd been fighting so long that war seemed a trade,
And some of us laughed at the youngsters so gay
Who had come to the battle as if coming to play;
And all through the camp you could hear the rough wits
Cry, "Hullo, young roosters!" and "Dandified cits!"
But the boys took it bravely, and heartily laughed
At the hungry "Confeds" by whom they were chaffed,
Till one ragged soldier, more bold than the rest,
Fired off this rough joke, which we all thought the best:
"Boys, you'd better go home; 'tis getting quite late."
Then the girlish-faced captain spoke up, and said, "Wait!"

They didn't wait long, for the very next day
We were ordered right off to the thick of the fray;
For early that morning we'd heard the dull roar
Of the guns of our foemen on Rapidan's shore,
And all of us knew, with old Jack in command,
If fighting was near him, he'd at once take a hand.
And, sure enough, soon marching orders we got,
And we swung down the road in "foot-cavalry" trot
The boys were behind us. I fell to the rear,
To see how the youngsters on march would appear.
Their files were close up, their marching was true;
I reported to Stonewall, "Yes, general, they'll do."

In a few minutes more the action began.
We met the first shock, for we were the van;
But we stood to our ranks like oaks of the field,
For Stonewall's brigade never knew how to yield.
Upon us, however, a battery played,
And huge gaps in our ranks were now and then made,
Till Jackson commanded a charge up the hill.
We charged—in a moment the cannon were still.
Jackson said to the Grays, "Such valor you've shown,
You'll veterans be ere your beards are full grown;
In this, your first action, you've proved yourselves bold;
I'll station you here, these guns you must hold."

"Cried 'good-by' to the boys."

Then the girlish-faced captain, so straight and so tall,
Saluted, and said, "You'll here find us all,
For, wherever stationed, this company stays."
How we laughed, how we cheered the bold Baltimore Grays!
But the red tide of battle around us still flowed,
And we followed our leader, as onward he rode,
Cried "Good-by" to the boys; take care of the guns—
We'll relieve you as soon as the enemy runs."
Ah, yes, indeed! soon the brave boys were relieved,
But not in the manner we all had believed;
Alas, the sisters who weep and the mothers who pine
For the loved and the lost of the Maryland line!

By some fatal blunder our left was exposed,
And by thousands of Federals the boys were inclosed;
They asked for no quarter, their Maryland blood
Never dreamed of surrender—they fell where they stood.
We heard in the distance the firing and noise,
And double-quicked back to the help of the boys.
The guns were soon ours, but oh, what a sight!—
Every Baltimore boy had been killed in the fight,
Save the girlish-faced captain, and he scarce alive.
When he saw us around him he seemed to revive,
And smiled when we told him the field had been won,
And the Baltimore Grays had saved every gun.

Then Stonewall rode up and endeavored to speak,
But his utterance was choked, and down his bronzed cheek
The hot tears flowed, as he gazed on the dead.
"God pity their mothers and sisters!" he said.
Then, dismounting, he knelt on the blood-sodden sand,
And prayed while he held the dying boy's hand;
The gallant young hero said, "General, I knew
That the Grays to your orders would always be true;

You'll miss not a Gray from our final roll call;
Look around you, my general—you'll here find us all."
The blood gushed from his mouth, his head sunk on his breast
And the girlish-faced captain lay dead with the rest.

"You'll miss not a Gray."

THE CONTRABAND.

[*A Song of Mississippi Negroes in the Vicksburg Campaign.*]

Say, darkies, has you seed my massa,
Wid de mustache on his face?
He came along sometime dis morning
As dough he'd leave de place.
He seed de smoke way up de river,
Where de Lincum gunboats lay:
He took his hat and lef' bery sudden,
I speck he's runned away.

Chorus—Massa run, aha!
Darky stay, oho!
It must be now dat de kingdom's comin'
In de year of Jubilo.

He's six feet one way, four feet t'other,
And weighs three hundred pounds;
His coat's so big he can't pay de tailor,
And it won't go half around.
He drills so much dey call him cap'n;
And he am so very tan,
Speck he'll try to fool dem Yankees
And say he's contraban'.

Dis darky gets so very lonesome,
In de cabin on de lawn.
He moves his things to massa's parlor,
To keep 'em while he's gone.
There's wine and cider in de cellar,
And de darkies dey'll have some;
I speck it will be confiscated
When de Lincum soldiers come.

De overseer will give us trouble,
And run us round a spell;
We'll lock him up in de smokehouse cellar,
Wid de key thrown in de well.
De whip is lost and de handcuffs broken,
And massa'll lose his pay;
He's big enough and old enough
Dan to gone and runned away.

THE DEAD MAN THAT LAY AT MY DOOR.

BY A. I. MOORE.

[In June, 1863, the Kentucky Brigade was encamped at Jackson, Miss. While there the writer of the following lines was confined with fever in what was formerly the Dixon House, then temporarily converted into a hospital under the charge of the Sisters of Mercy. The place being destitute of the necessary equipments, those who died over night were left in the hallway to await the morning for burial.]

At last through the casement is streaming
The soft mellow glow of the dawn.
And night, with its visions and dreaming,
Thank Heaven! forever is flown.
Ah! fearful the night was to me,
As, noiseless, I crept o'er the floor,
With my eyes closed fast, lest I see
The dead man that lay at my door.

The wind o'er the chimney top sighing,
Wailed fitfully out on the night,
Like the wail of some lost spirit flying
Amid the dread regions of fright.
It seemed that all nature, in sorrow,
Did the fate of my comrade deplore,
And with howlings of pity awaited the morrow,
For the dead man that lay at my door.

The lamp on the mantel was burning,
And fitfully lighted the room;
The shadows were dancing and turning
Like specters that peopled the gloom.
In vain did I strive to forget me
In events that had passed long before,
But the demon of dread would not let me—
The dead man that lay at my door.

The rats, in the wainscot at work,
Their stores were moving about,
Whose rattling noise seemed the knock
Of some wandering spirit without.
It was in vain I strove to withstand
The dread impression it bore—
That it came from the cold, withered hand
Of the dead man that lay at my door.

Naught but the deep breathing around
Betrayed that the living was near,
And they in their slumbers profound,
Like the dead lay quietly there.
'Twas fruitless to try to awake them—
Their names did I call o'er and o'er:
As well might I strive to awaken
The dead man that lay at my door.

I can bear it no longer! To see
This sentinel grim at my door,
A feeling too potent for me
To withstand led me out on the floor,
And there, on his lone little bed,
So still, so calm and so hoar,
Lay the stark, frozen form of the dead—
This dead man that lay at my door.

A hand on my shoulder was laid.
A voice in my ear, low and kind,
In tones of sweet sympathy said:
"Come, get thee to bed, my poor friend!"
I pointed my finger, and she,
The direction her eyes glancing o'er,
Started and screamed, there to see
This dead man that lay at my door.

"The dead man that lay at my door."

On my couch again am I lain,
And in whispers they bade me forget
The visions so freighted with pain,
That my mind in its weakness beset.
But their voices were husky and drear,
And wild was the look that they wore;
They, too, felt a dread and a fear,
Of the dead man that lay at my door.

But the sun in my window shines warm,
And with night have my fears passed away,
And broken's the spell and alarm,
For none fear the dead during day.
I have heard them! They've nailed down the lid.
And slowly and sadly they bore
Away—oh! forever away—
The dead man that lay at my door.

THE SOLDIER'S AMEN.

As a couple of good soldiers were walking one day,
Said one to the other: "Let's kneel down and pray;
I'll pray for the war, and good of all men,
And whatever I pray for, do you say 'Amen!'

"We'll pray for the generals and all of their crew,
Likewise for the captains and lieutenants, too;
May good luck and good fortune them always attend,
And return safely home!" Said the soldier—"Amen!"

Said the soldier, "Amen."

"We'll pray for the privates, the noblest of all;
They do all the work and get no glory at all;
May good luck and good fortune them always attend,
And return crowned with laurels!" Said the soldier—"Amen!"

"We'll pray for the pretty boys who want themselves wives,
And have not the courage to strike for their lives;
May bad luck and bad fortune them always attend,
And go down to Old Harry!" Said the soldier—"Amen!"

"We'll pray for the pretty girls, who make us good wives,
And always look at a soldier with tears in their eyes;
May good luck and good fortune them always attend,
And brave gallants for sweethearts!" Said the soldier—"Amen!"

"We'll pray for the conscript, with frown on his brow,
To fight for his country he won't take the vow;
May bad luck and bad fortune him always attend,
And die with dishonor!" Said the soldier—"Amen!"

STONEWALL JACKSON'S WAY.

Found on the Body of a Sergeant of the Old Stonewall Brigade, Winchester, Va.

Come, stack arms, men! pile on the rails,
Stir up the camp-fire bright;
No matter if the canteen fails,
We'll make a roaring night;
Here Shenandoah brawls along.
There burly Blue Ridge echoes strong,
To swell the brigade's rousing song,
Of "Stonewall Jackson's way."

We see him now! the old slouched hat
Cocked o'er his eye askew—
The shrewd, dry smile, the speech so pat,
So calm, so blunt, so true.
The "Blue Light Elder" knows o'er well—
Says he: "That's Banks—he's fond of shell.
Lord, save his soul! we'll give him"—well,
That's "Stonewall Jackson's way."

Silence! ground arms! kneel all! caps off!
Old Blue Light 's going to pray;
Strangle the fool that dares to scoff!
Attention! 'tis his way!
Appealing from his native sod,
In forma pauperis to God—
"Lay bare thine arm, stretch forth thy rod;
Amen!" That's "Stonewall's way."

He's in the saddle now! Fall in!
Steady—the whole brigade!
Hill's at the ford, cut off! He'll win
His way out, ball and blade;
What matter if our shoes are worn!
What matter if our feet are torn!
"Quick step, we're with him before dawn!"
That's "Stonewall Jackson's way."

The sun's bright lances rout the mists
Of morning, and, by George,
There's Longstreet struggling in the lists,
Hemmed in an ugly gorge—
Pope and his Yankees whipped before—
"Bayonet and grape!" hear Stonewall roar,
Charge, Stuart! Pay off Ashby's score
In "Stonewall Jackson's way."

Ah, maiden! wait and watch and yearn
For news of Stonewall's band;
Ah, widow! read with eyes that burn
That ring upon thy hand;
Ah, wife! sew on, pray on, hope on,
Thy life shall not be all forlorn—
The foe had better ne'er been born,
Than get in "Stonewall's way."

POP GOES THE WEASEL.

King Abraham is very sick,
Old Scott has got the measles,
Manassas we have now at last—
Pop goes the weasel!

All around the cobbler's house
The monkey chased the people,
And after them in double haste
Pop goes the weasel!

When the night walks in, as black as a sheep,
And the hen on her eggs was fast asleep,
When into her nest with a serpent's creep
Pop goes the weasel!

Of all the dance that ever was planned
To galvanize the heel and the hand,
There's none that moves so gay and grand
As—pop goes the weasel!

MY WARRIOR BOY.

Thou hast gone forth, my darling one,
To battle with the brave,
To strike in Freedom's sacred cause,
Or win an early grave;
With vet'rans grim, and stalwart men,
Thy pathway lieth now,
Though fifteen summers scarce have shed
Their blossoms on thy brow.

My babe in years, my warrior boy!
Oh, if a mother's tears
Could call thee back to be my joy
And still these anxious fears,
I'd dash the traitor drops away,
That would unnerve thy hand,
Now raised to strike in Freedom's cause
For thy dear native land.

"If a mother's tears could call thee back."

God speed thee on thy course, my boy,
Where'er thy pathway lie,
And guard thee when the leaden hail
Shall thick around thee fly;
But when our sacred cause is won,
And peace again shall reign,
Come back to me, my darling son,
And light my life again.

THE ORIGINAL "DIXIE."

[The song of "Dixie" is indelibly connected with the South. We all know the air, but how few have seen the original song! There have been many versions, but we give here the original from which they all sprang.]

I wish I was in the land of cotton,
Old times dar am not forgotten;
Look away, look away, look away, Dixie Land.
In Dixie Land, whar I was born in,
Early on one frosty mornin',
Look away, look away, look away, Dixie Land.

Chorus—Den I wish I was in Dixie,
Hooray! hooray!
In Dixie Land I'll took my stand,
To lib and die in Dixie;
Away, away, away down South in Dixie;
Away, away, away down South in Dixie.

"Away down South in Dixie."

Old missus marry "Will de weaber."
William was a gay deceaber,
Look away, look away, look away, Dixie Land.
But when he put his arm around 'er,
He smiled as fierce as a forty-pounder,
Look away, look away, look away, Dixie Land.

His face was sharp as a butcher's cleaber,
But dat did not seem to greab 'er.
Look away, look away, look away, Dixie Land.
Old missus acted the foolish part,
And died for the man dat broke her heart,
Look away, look away, look away, Dixie Land.

Now here's a health to the next old missus,
And all the gals dat want to kiss us.
Look away, look away, look away, Dixie Land.
But if you want to drive away sorrow,
Come and hear dis nig to-morrow;
Look away, look away, look away, Dixie Land.

Dar buckwheat cakes and ingen batter
Makes you fat or a little fatter.
Look away, look away, look away, Dixie Land.
Den hoe it down and scratch your grabble,
To Dixie's Land I'm bound to trabble,
Look away, look away, look away, Dixie Land.

THE COUNTERSIGN.

Alas! the rolling hours pass slow—
The night is very dark and still—
And in the marshes far below
Is heard the lonely whippoorwill;
I scarce can see a foot ahead—
My ears are strained to catch each sound.
I feel the leaves beneath me spread
And the springs bubbling thro' the ground.

Along the beaten path I pace,
Where white rays mark my sentry's track;
In formless things I seem to trace
The foeman's form, with bended back.
I think I see him crouching low!
I stop and list—I stop and peer—
Until the neighboring hillocks grow
To groups of soldiers, far and near.

With ready piece I wait and watch
Until my eyes—familiar grown—
Detect each harmless earthern notch,
And turn "guerrillas" into stone;
And then amid the lonely gloom,
Beneath the tall magnolia trees,
My silent marches I resume
And think of other times than these.

"Halt! who goes there?" my challenge cry—
It rings along the watchful line—
"Relief!" I hear a voice reply.
"Advance and give the countersign!"
With bayonet at the charge I wait—
The corporal gives the mystic spell—
With "arms aport" I charge my mate
Then onward pass, and all is well!

But in my tent, that night awake,
I ask, "if in the fray I fall,
Can I the mystic answer make
When the angelic sentries call?"
And pray that heaven so ordain,
Where'er I go, what fate be mine,
Whether in pleasure or in pain
I still may have the "countersign!"

THE LITTLE SOLDIER.

BY J. L. MOLLOY.

"When I'm big I'll be a soldier—
That's what I will be;
Fight for father, fight for mother,
Over land and sea!"
And before him on the table
Stood in bright array
All his little wooden soldiers,
Ready for the fray.
Then he charged his little cannon,
Singing out in glee,
"When I'm big I'll be a soldier—
That's what I will be."

By the firelight sat the mother;
Tears were in her heart,
Thinking of the swift time coming
When they two must part.

* * * * *

"Then there came a dreadful battle"

Soon the shadow fell between them—
Soon the years flew by;
He has left his little mother—
Left her, perhaps to die.
All the laughter gone forever,
All the sunshine fled;
Only little mother praying
By his empty bed.

Then there came a dreadful battle,
And upon the plain
Crept the little mother, seeking
Some one 'mid the slain;
But she never found her darling
In the white moon gleam,
For the little cannon firing
Woke her from her dream.
All a dream! He stood beside her,
Singing out with glee,
"When I'm big I'll be a soldier—
That's what I will be!"

INDEX TO ILLUSTRATIONS.

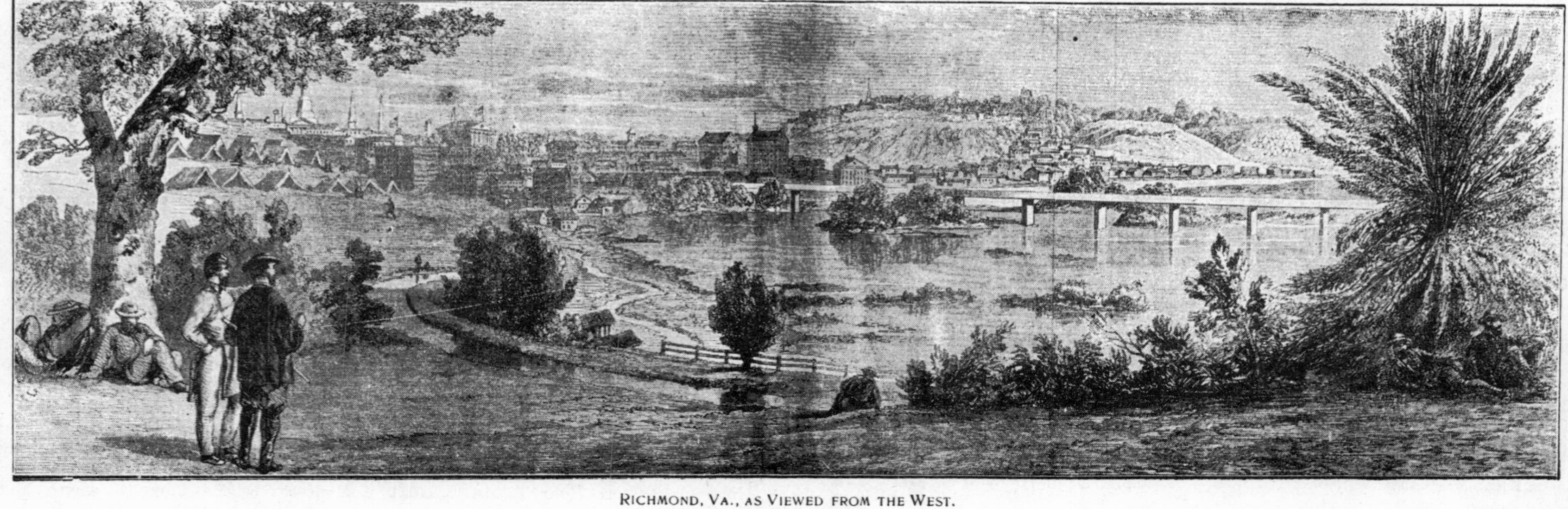

RICHMOND, VA., AS VIEWED FROM THE WEST.
[From a sketch made in 1862.]

General Index.

A

B

C

M

N

O

P

R

S